THE ENCYCLOPEDIA OF Record Producers

ERIC OLSEN

PAUL VERNA

ARLO WOLFF

AN INDISPENSABLE GUIDE
TO THE MOST IMPORTANT
RECORD PRODUCERS
IN MUSIC HISTORY

THE ENCYCLOPEDIA OF Record Producers

ERIC OLSEN

PAUL VERNA

CARLO WOLFF

BILLBOARD BOOKS
An imprint of Watson-Guptill Publications / New York

Senior editor: Bob Nirkind
Production manager: Ellen Greene
Book and cover design: Bob Fillie, Graphiti Design Inc.

Copyright © 1999 by Eric Olsen, Carlo Wolff, and Paul Verna
First published in 1999 by Watson-Guptill Publications
1515 Broadway, New York, NY 10036

Library of Congress Cataloging-in-Publication Data
The encyclopedia of record producers / [edited by] Eric Olsen,
    Paul Verna, Carlo Wolff.
            p.   cm.
        Includes index.
        ISBN 0-8230-7607-5
            1. Sound recording executives and producers Biography
    Dictionaries. 2. Popular music—History and criticism. 3. Popular
    music Discography. I. Olsen, Eric, 1961– . II. Verna, Paul.
    III. Wolff, Carlo.
        ML105.E53 1999
        781.64'092'2—dc21
        [B]   99-32191
                                                        CIP

Manufactured in the United States of America

First printing, 1999

Acknowledgments

The editors wish to thank the following:

The associate editors and contributors (see page v) for their diligent work beyond the call of duty and beyond the reach of pay.

The producers for their time, their thoughts, and the music that inspired this book.

The managers, publicists, assistants, et al. who set up the producer interviews and furnished us with biographies, photos, discographies, etc.: Paul Adams, Heidi Akin, Jeff Alderich, Louise Allen, Wally Amos, Mark Beaven, Bert Berman, Richard Bishop, Megan Brady, Evelyn Brechtlein, David Brinker, Gerry Bron, David Brown, Paul Brown, Coral Browning, Stephen Budd, Debbie Capponetta, Scott Carlson, Graham Carpenter, Melanie Ciccone, Holly Cislo, Cathy Cohen, Seth Cohen, Larry Cohn, Brian Coleman, Gail Colson, Mike Connelly, Tom Cording, Alan Cowderoy, Carol Crabtree, Sue Crawford, Carole Davis, Richard Davis, John Dee, Lisa Marie DeFranco, Jeffrey de Hart, Karen Devine, Marie Dixon, Michael Doneff, Paula Donner, David Dorn, Ben Edmonds, Karen Elliot, Clay Farmer, Tom Farrell, Bob Fead, Maria Ferrero, Len Fico, Gloria Gabriel, Debbi Gibbs, Suzanne Gilchrist, Dan Gilliam, Diane Gilmour, Susan Green, Eileen Gregory, John Guarnieri, Gorel Hanser, Kim Hardy, Lori Hehr, Marvin Heiman, Kent Henderson, Clinton Heylin, Terri Hinte, Amanda Hon, John Hornyak, Barney Hoskyns, Bones Howe, Bob Hyde, Bob Irwin, Safta Jaffery, Nancy Jeffreys, Dave Kaplan, Steve Karas, Bennett Kaufman, Chris Kettle, Jon Landau, Don Law Jr., Robert Leffelman, Mike Lembo, Gary Lemel, Lynn Lendway, Craig Leon, Bill Levenson, Arthur Levy, Steve Lewis, Michael Lippman, Leila Logan, Don Lucoff, Art Macnow, Michael Mahan, Cary Mansfield, Ruby Martin, Darcy Mayers, Dorothy McCormick, Tim McDaniel, Frank McDonough, Ben McLane, Mickey McLaurin, Jim Merlis, Mary Milner, LeAnn Moen, Joyce Moore, Ron Moss, David Nathan, Pat Nelson, Patty Nichols, John Oliver, Catherine Owens, Joe Nick Patoski, Tina Pelikan, Penton Media, Randy Poe, Nik Popa, Ron Pugh, Bob Raylove, John Reid, Jason Richardson, Bob Ringe, Ira Robbins, Sandy Roberton, Melani Rogers, David Sanjek, Nita Scott, Rick Scott, Nick Shaffran, Dylan Siegler, Harry Simmons, Winston Simone, Rani Singh, Don Snowden, Debbie Sommer, Greg Spotts, David Steinberg, Sunny Sumter, Jeff Tamarkin, Emily Taylor, Gill Taylor, Caroline Teeling, Bryan Thomas, Roy Trakin, Thom Trumbo, Joel Turtle, Jaan Uhelszki, Phil Walden, L. Jeff Walker, Cathy Wallis, Seven Webster, Lola Weidner, Jonathan Wexler, Chris Wheat, Meryl Wheeler, and Jill Zoeller. If we inadvertently left you out, we thank you too.

David Bates, Ed Cherney, Anthony DeCurtis, Martin Folkman, Susan Nunziata, Paul Sacksman, Bob Santelli, Ken Schlager, Chris Stone, and Timothy White for their encouragement and positive vibes.

Bob Nirkind at Billboard Books for buying the book and Martha Cameron and Sylvia Warren for helping to make it happen.

David Goggin and Ben Cromer for contributing excellent photographs from their personal collections.

Extra special thanks to our families: Ellen Dooley, Karen Sandstrom, Lylah Rose Sandstrom Wolff, Katy Nozar, Ramona, Oscar, Dawn Olsen, Kristen Olsen, Christopher Olsen, Ray Olsen, Barbara Olsen, Bruce Darling, and Leslie Darling.

—ERIC OLSEN, PAUL VERNA, AND CARLO WOLFF

Contents

About the Authors

Eric Olsen has written for numerous publications including *Playboy, Option,* Billboard's *Airplay Monitor,* and *Alternative Press,* and is co-author of *Networking in the Music Industry.* He lives in Aurora, Ohio, and is a well-known radio and TV personality in the Cleveland-Akron corridor.

Paul Verna, Pro Audio/Technology Editor and Reviews Editor at *Billboard* magazine in New York City, is also a freelance producer/engineer who operates a New York–based project/mobile recording studio, Vernacular Sound.

Clevelander **Carlo Wolff**'s prolific career as a music reviewer began in 1971 when he covered a concert by Edgar Winter's White Trash in Burlington, Vermont. Wolff, a regular contributor to *The Boston Globe,* the *Cleveland Plain Dealer, Goldmine, DISCoveries,* and *Jazziz,* is an associate editor at the hotel trade magazine *Lodging Hospitality.*

...ASSOCIATE EDITORS

Ben Cromer is president of Ben Cromer Communications, a U.S. consulting firm in the area of business communications services and telecommunications consulting, and is an Adjunct Assistant Professor of Music at Northern Virginia Community College.

Nashville resident **Deborah Evans Price** writes *Billboard*'s Higher Ground column focusing on the Christian music industry and also covers the country music beat.

David John Farinella is a California-based freelance writer who covers nearly every aspect of the art of music, from songwriting to players to studio techniques to producers. His work has appeared in *Billboard, Musician, Mix, Live!, Option, Request,* and the *San Francisco Chronicle.*

New Yorker **Larry Flick** is the talent editor at *Billboard.*

Chuck Foster writes the Reggae Update column for *Beat* magazine; hosts Reggae Central on KPFK in L.A.; and is author of *Roots Rock Reggae: An Oral History of Jamaican Music From Ska to Dancehall,* published by Billboard Books.

Daniel Levitin, Ph.D., is a lecturer in the Music Department at Stanford University and author of more than 250 articles on music technology, engineering, and production.

Los Angeles–based **Melinda Newman** is *Billboard* magazine's West Coast Bureau Chief.

Dawn Darling Olsen, avid music listener and professed computer geek, helped develop the format for this book, the discography database, and the www.mojavemusic.com Web site.

Anastasia Pantsios is a Cleveland-based writer and photographer whose work has appeared in dozens of periodicals and books over the last 25 years.

...AND CONTRIBUTORS

Jack Arky, a New York–based independent producer and engineer, is a contributor to *Billboard*'s Pro Audio section.

Bradley Bambarger is a senior writer and columnist with *Billboard.* His feature writing and criticism have also appeared in *Musician, EQ, Gramophone, Time Out New York,* and others.

Dennis Diken, a founding member and the drummer of the Smithereens, is also a record producer, composer, songwriter, author, disc jockey, and music historian.

Kevin Johnson is the pop music critic at the *St. Louis Post-Dispatch.*

Howard Massey, former technology editor for *Musician* magazine, is a musician, engineer, and producer who also works as a consultant and technical writer.

Scott Schinder is the author of several books about music and popular culture, including *Rolling Stone's Alt-Rock-A-Rama: An Outrageous Compendium of Facts, Fiction, Trivia, and Critiques on Alternative Rock,* and writes about music for *Entertainment Weekly, Pulse, Newsday,* and *Time Out New York.*

A Virgo born at the end of the Summer of Love, **Philip Smith** contraposits hypoxia and esoteric orrery exhibitions via research (Harry Smith and cognate improving topics), music (Lhasa Cement Plant and other grave Himalayan blunders), and the symptomatic gutter yoga of his age, when not eking out a living in the love-bead racket.

A Personal View

The only real misgiving—the constant bone-in-the-throat kind of irritation that I live with after making more than 100 albums in over 25 years—is that on my passport, alongside the word "occupation," it reads: "Record Producer." Don't misunderstand me—I have enjoyed the strongest passion for, and deepest reward from, the vocation itself. It's the title I resent.

No one outside the record business understands its meaning. Most people imagine that we are the music-biz equivalent of film producers. They assume that we finance projects and invest in up-and-coming artists. These perceptions seem to have one thing in common: the assumption that our sole motivation must surely be to make money—worse still, to make it out of other people's talents.

This is frustratingly misleading and, to me, somewhat degrading. Of course, producers have an inherent obligation to help an artist who has raised loans with record companies to be commercially successful. It would be dangerous to describe this necessity as a mere by-product. At the same time, such a necessity should never become confused with the inspiration for the work itself. Whenever (thankfully rarely) I have worked with artists who have been primarily motivated by a commercial and market-oriented outlook to music making, the end result has inevitably been empty.

Definition

But "record producer" does not accurately describe this most rewarding of occupations; "record director" would be a far more accurate term. While the producer's job did include both financial and directorial facets at one time, today most of us are, in fact, commissioned by the *real* producers—the record labels.

The very word "producer" implies a product, and herein lies the problem. As much as the shareholders of major labels may address the results of our efforts as "product"—like so many beans, ball bearings, or toasters—it is anathema (and downright insulting) to the creative heart to so reduce the output of the world's finest and most communicative abstract art. "Abstract?" you say. In essence, yes, as there is no definitive reference book of ingredients or methods for musical expression. One person's sequence of chords or melody portraying confusion or resignation is as likely to parallel another's as a person is likely to find an identical twin outside of the family. This is what makes it so futile to define a "production absolute" or a "perfect record." The number of variables—the sheer size of the sonic palette—ensures that musical communication is as complex as life itself.

The Producer's Function

In my view, the record director has three main functions: (1) to lead and direct, as in film director; (2) to observe and advise, as in consultant; and (3) to provoke and stimulate, as in catalyst. To understand these roles—and, even more important, to know when to switch from one to the other—becomes the record producer's primary goal in the studio. Some artists will require far more of one aspect than another, but the producer should always be ready to oscillate transparently between roles if the artist is to breathe creatively with the potential for innovation and the unexpected. There are even times when it is most appropriate to simply assist the artist with enthusiasm and grace.

The trick, I feel, is to be so taken by the possibilities of what might be achieved from the suggestions and substance in the artist's demos that what can be a tight-rope walk between giving enough creative space while creating focus becomes natural and effortless. For some, the notion that the producer can represent a provocative and catalytic role is an intriguing proposition; for others, a warmer, more sympathetic contribution will be more productive. Strictly speaking, the producer-as-catalyst is a process that needs to be renewed every time. After all, a challenge, by definition, cannot be repeated.

An Early Lesson

In the '60s, when I was an artist recording my first record, I learned a very significant lesson, and made a vow. The recording, which took place at Decca's famous studios in north London, featured a 26-piece orchestra; London's hottest session guitarist of the time, Jimmy

Page; and other eye-popping pressures for a 17-year-old.

During our debut three-hour recording session, the producer commanded—in a military tone—that I switch roles with my singing partner, David McIver, from lead vocal to harmony. Despite the obvious total breakdown of confidence that David and I were by then experiencing, and the utter inappropriateness of his idea, the producer remained insensitive and resolute. Here was a truly exceptional opportunity for me to start my life in music at the very highest level—and it was thrown away in an instant. I vowed then and there that if I ever glimpsed an opportunity to "do that job" (in effect, to do *his* job), I would grasp it with both hands. And I did.

Is a Producer Mandatory?

The notion of self-producing artists often provokes the question, Is a record producer really necessary? Not every artist wants a producer, and certainly, not every artist *needs* a producer. The blockbuster artist, for example, will always survive with a B-division engineer masquerading as producer, and will possibly retain more creative control, for better or worse. The instinctively experimental artist, with little to risk and everything to gain, may also make music that can take us somewhere new without the guidance of an experienced hand.

Here again we can draw the analogy to film. Self-directing actor/writers rarely achieve the typical film team's level of artistic success, but certain outstanding exceptions seem to prove my point about the new, young experimental artist. For instance, *Citizen Kane* could only have been achieved because Orson Welles was free to run with his untried ideas and instincts without supervision or guidance.

As a young artist, I was "produced" for the first of my 12 albums, but from my second album onward, I knew that I had to develop as a record maker myself. Even though my first priority was songwriting, I became so intoxicated with the arranging and producing skills of Brian Wilson and his *Pet Sounds* project that every one of my albums became a canvas that I alone could paint. Ask any painter what color or tint he'll use next, and he will probably shrug; at this level the process is intuitive, fluid, and ultimately inexplicable. After I was introduced to the many possibilities presented by the recording studio, I needed to take the reins myself and explore. Live performance paled into insignificance compared to the sound pictures it was possible to create in the studio.

The most common argument against self-production is an artist's inability to be truly objective, to develop a detached overview of his or her output. But as artist/producer Daryl Hall commented succinctly at a producer's convention some years ago, "Fuck objectivity. Just make the best subjective record you can make!"

There are definitely times when distance may not really be relevant. Both budding and experienced record makers may prefer to bounce their creativity off a project partner. There are also plenty of artists who live to express themselves in song, yet have no real desire to be a part of the record-making process. For those whose first love is the concert platform or gig, time spent in the studio is a necessity, not an interest—let alone a passion! For these artists, guidance and help in the studio is essential.

The Producer as Artist

It has been said that if a record producer is truly innovative and creative, sooner or later, he will have to find a way to become the artist. Having been both simultaneously all my adult life, I can safely say that the two occupations are wonderfully complementary and naturally cross-fertilizing. The opportunity to give myself wholly to the role of artist has always been there for me, and it is often my laboratory for musical and technical research and development. At the same time, the satisfaction of seeing the potential in someone else's raw ingredients realized in a fully blossomed work with the help of my direction or advice has been irreplaceable.

Most contemporary musical recordings can be divided, very broadly, into four categories:

- Recordings of communication—ideas, emotions, and narrative (art?)

- Recordings that may have nothing specific to communicate but are a celebration of any or all the aspects of writing, arranging, producing, and presentation (craft?)

- Recordings that appeal more to the body and feet than to the mind and heart (or when done best, to all four elements)

- Recordings that have no higher goal than to play the roulette wheel of chance with lowest-common-denominator ingredients of familiarity coupled to advertising agency–style hooks—insignificant moneymakers that keep the cash flow . . . umm . . . flowing (radio fodder?)

But there are producers who are turned on by innovation. Who want to find new ways of making fine music cut through mediocrity. Who know what music can achieve when that greater-than-the-sum-of-its-parts moment happens as music and words come together.

Who are in love with music as an abstract medium. Who are attracted to danger (the unknown) and risk (losing or not attracting funding by presenting the unexplored for global consumption). Some of the world's most outstanding records, both in artistic content and commercial success, have stemmed from these roots.

The Producer as Star

Over the last 35 years there have been times when a particular producer or production team has reached a more marketable level and higher public profile than the artists themselves. It's true, indeed, that a handful of the world's greatest pop singles have come from the star producer, while the artist becomes merely a face, a front end, to his talent and whim.

I am not personally interested in the hit-factory school of record making, yet I must confess that I have loved so many of the great Tamla-era singles, for example—undeniably a factory of extraordinary records throughout the '60s. Also in the '60s, "River Deep, Mountain High" from the highly stylized and idiosyncratic output of Phil Spector is there in my Top 10 singles of all time. Even Tina Turner acknowledges that her role on that record was minimal compared with her later output in the '80s and '90s (which I was fortunate to be able to contribute to, both as songwriter and producer). These were groundbreaking recordings—in my opinion, the exceptions that otherwise prove the rule.

The parallel with the film business holds here too: historically, the director has been hugely influential both in terms of raising money for a project and setting the tone, visual style, and objectives. Interestingly, the United States has become one of the few exceptions in this analogous comparison; in recent years, the blockbuster production–special effects syndrome has elevated visual bravado (prohibitively expensive for any other country outside the U.S.) above content and communication, preferring a widescreen graphic gang bang to intimate, sensual, and communicative lovemaking . . . if I may be so lurid!

There are certainly times when this attitude applies to the record industry too: the lust for making big artists even bigger (the star/superstar/megastar syndrome) taking precedence over support for developing musical expression through new artists. Of course, these tendencies mostly align themselves with the pendulum swing of generational reinvention. The record producer's importance oscillates with these same musical cycles. Somewhat unjustly, he is often connected more with the exploitation of a given trend than the invention or discovery of it.

Hot Tips

I am often asked if I have garnered any "hot tips" from recording and mixing over 100 projects. The questioner is usually seeking a response involving some kind of technical trick. For me, however, technical tips are relevant only to the moment. I have always discouraged this kind of production probe. Better to redirect the route of inquiry toward goals and objectives, and anyway, by the time today's hot tip has been used on another piece of music, it's probably lukewarm at best.

But I have learned that the most direct route to the soul of an artist or the center of an ensemble is often laughter. The finest takes of almost any emotion can come within seconds of the most openhearted buffoonery. Perhaps it is the same phenomenon that puts laughing and crying within a whisker of each other's presence. A more cultured meditation on the required mood can often result in a performance altogether too studied or theatrical to be a true reflection of the original intent.

Record making is no longer solely in the hands of record companies and expensive recording studios. Great contemporary music is being made in every imaginable location and environment: from the inexperienced enthusiast with a bedroom setup to the established artist in a lavish home studio with equipment that rivals the top commercial facilities. Terms that describe the harnessing of the wild stallion of contemporary music—"new wave," "postmodern," "alternative"— become outmoded almost overnight. But it seems sure that most groundbreaking releases into the next millennium will continue to be made under the umbrella of an independent adviser/consultant/therapist/arranger/writer/sound painter/assistant/friend known simply as the Record Producer.

P.S.: In over 25 years of record making I have never enjoyed making music as much as I do today. I have a funny feeling, though, that I say that every time!

—RUPERT HINE

Introduction

sk 500 record producers what they do for a living and you'll get 500 different answers. One might compare himself to a "creative obstetrician" who "delivers the brainchild of the artist." Another might say his job is "to do as little as possible." Another might quip that he engages in "a well-paid form of cowardice." Rupert Hine, in the essay that opens this book, writes that producers function simultaneously as directors, as consultants, and as catalysts. In our view, the producer's role is a magical one: they are the alchemists who transform recording artists' visions into the music we know and love. And, like the craft of the alchemist, the producer's craft is individual, private, and behind the scenes. What they do and how they do it are virtually unknown to the general public.

It is our main goal to bring these unsung heroes of the recording industry into the limelight, to introduce them to the public and let them tell their tales of glory and sorrow, accomplishment and failure. With a fair amount of variation, the entries in this book seek to give insight into how each producer came to do what he or she does (there are very few women producers in this book because there are still very few women producers—this situation seems to be slowly changing), how the producers perform and regard their work, and how that "work" measures up as music. We hope that by reading these first-hand accounts from the people at the heart of the process, you'll develop a new appreciation for the art and science of record making.

This project grew from a conversation the two of us had in 1996. We had separately but at about the same time come up with the concept of an encyclopedia of record producers, but had different ideas about how much ground to cover. One of us [Eric Olsen] wanted to keep the focus narrow, selecting the 100 most deserving record makers; the other [Paul Verna] had in mind a tome that would be as exhaustive as possible, with 1,000 or more entries.

Pushed by the natural forces of compromise and budgetary constraints, we met in the middle, agreeing to spotlight approximately 500 producers. We recruited longtime *Billboard* contributor Carlo Wolff to serve as co-editor and enlisted Dawn Darling to be our project coordinator.

Because there is no objective way to measure a producer's talent, the process of paring down our original list of more than 2,000 names to 500 was subjective. Our goal was to find the top 10 percent within each of several popular music genres—rock 'n' roll, jazz, country, pop, R&B, soul, hip-hop, reggae, contemporary Christian, alternative rock, punk, avant-garde, etc.

We began with a sampling of several large record collections and assembled a master list based on critical stature, chart success, industry influence, and overall popularity. We tried to balance artistic and commercial considerations, and we focused our efforts on the post–World War II era (our pre-'40s coverage is limited to a handful of the greats, including John Hammond, Milt Gabler, Norman Granz, Don Law, and Alfred Lion).

After we trimmed our original list to 1,000 names, we asked our contributing writers to help us cut it in half. In the end, we arrived at 463 entries, covering approximately 500 people who, in our estimation, represent the cream of the crop.

This final version is the work of more than 20 editors and writers over three years, and includes over 400 original interviews conducted expressly for this book. We cannot thank the producers enough for the time and effort they put into telling their life stories, and the editors cannot thank the writers enough for the care they have taken in relating these fascinating lives. As the editors assembled this collection and shined a spotlight on the real movers and shakers of popular recorded music history, we realized that, taken collectively, these lives and views present a new version of that history—one that is at least as valid as the history of performers.

No doubt some of you will disagree with our choices—an inevitable result of a subjective process. We urge you to provide us with feedback for future editions. In the meantime, please take this for what it is: a document full of entertaining, touching, and often humorous and surprising stories from inside the control room glass.

Finally, to all record producers—both those in the book and those who, for reasons of space, were left out: Thank you for the music!

—ERIC OLSEN AND PAUL VERNA,
April 1999

NOTES ON THE DISCOGRAPHIES

The Discography sections at the end of each essay can best be described as an ever-closer approximation of the truth. The very job of producer has mutated over the years, so one must try to find the titles that reflect what producers do today, which is, in the most basic sense, to run recording sessions. (But even within that simple job description, there is ambiguity. Engineers record sessions, but at what point does an engineer who also has musical input become an "assistant producer" or a "co-producer"?)

For the purpose of these discographies, we gave "producer" credit to any of the following titles: producer, co-producer, assistant producer. In cases in which no actual "producer" was present, we gave credit to "recorded by," engineer, supervisor, and A&R. We have typically avoided giving producer credit to executive producers or mixers. However, executive producers who made actual recording contributions are credited, as are a few remix specialists.

While the discographies in this book are, at minimum, representative of the work of the producer in question (and in many cases are virtually comprehensive), at a certain point we had to say, "Enough." In order to not burden these pages further with the weight of yet more discographic entries (there are already over 35,000 of them), we have established a web site at http://www.mojavemusic.com that includes more complete discographies for the producers from this book, as well as discographies on over 3,000 additional producers (which collectively includes most charting singles and albums). Please visit the site. It is updated regularly and is fully searchable, free of charge.

The information in the discographies reads as follows: For a given producer's discography the artists he or she produced are listed alphabetically by the first letter of a band's name (excluding "The"), or a single artist's last name. We do not mention co-producers. Albums are listed in italics, singles in quotations. An album in parentheses following a single indicates that the song can be found on that album. Following the title is the name of the record label. The date listed is the release date of the record. If there are two dates, the record in question has been reissued (very common since the advent of the CD). For a reissue, the name of the current label is listed. In some instances where there are two dates for jazz records, the earlier date represents when the music was recorded, not necessarily when it was first released. There are a few records for which we were unable to obtain a release date—if you can help us with this information, or provide corrections or additions, please contact me via e-mail. The address is ericolsen@compuserve.com.

—Eric Olsen

Producer Name List

Lou Adler	1	Thom Bell	48
Walter Afanasieff	2	Pete Bellotte	50
Brian Ahern	4	Joey Beltram	51
Ron and Howard Albert	5	John "Jellybean" Benitez	52
Steve Albini	6	Howard Benson	54
David Anderle	9	Tony Berg	55
Benny Andersson and Bjorn Ulvaeus	10	Steve Berlin	57
Aphex Twin (Richard D. James	358	Bert Berns	58
Rod Argent	11	Martin Birch	60
The Artist Formerly Known As Prince (Prince)	650	Martin Bisi	60
Art of Noise		Matt Black (Coldcut)	139
(Anne Dudley, J. J. Jeczalik, Gary Langan)	12	Chris Blackwell	62
Peter Asher	14	Robert "Bumps" Blackwell	64
Jon Astley	16	Tchad Blake	66
Chet Atkins	17	Archie Bleyer	67
Dallas Austin	20	Kurt Bloch	69
Babyface (Kenneth Edmonds)	21	Niko Bolas	70
Burt Bacharach	24	Bomb Squad (Carl Ryder, Hank Shocklee,	
Rodger Bain	25	Keith Shocklee, Eric "Vietnam" Sadler)	71
Arthur Baker	26	Bruce Botnick	73
Roy Thomas Baker	28	Jimmy Bowen	75
Glen Ballard	30	David Bowie	80
Michael Barbiero and Steve Thompson	31	Tommy Boyce and Bobby Hart	81
Steve Barri	33	Joe Boyd	82
Jeff Barry	34	John Boylan	84
Dave Bartholomew	36	Owen Bradley	87
Dave Bascombe	38	Daniel B. Bressanutti (Front 242)	242
Ralph Bass	40	David Briggs	89
Roger Bechirian	42	Gerry Bron	90
Walter Becker and Donald Fagen	43	Ian Broudie	91
Curt Bedeau (Full Force)	247	Steve Brown	93
Barry Beckett	45	Tony Brown	95
Michael Beinhorn	47	Cleveland Browne (Steely and Clevie)	748

Lou Adler

L ike many others in his field, Lou Adler can't read music and never played an instrument. These aren't limitations, however, because Adler knows how to run a session. And running a session, to him, is what counts.

"I think production changes through the years," says the former owner of Ode Records. "It's a lot different now than it was when I started, and it was a lot different before I came in, when there were basically A&R men. I was sort of in the first wave of independent producers."

Among the artists and groups Adler produced are the Mamas and the Papas, Johnny Rivers, Barry McGuire, Scott Mackenzie, Spirit, Cheech and Chong, the Everly Brothers, and Jan and Dean. Among the movies he produced are Cheech and Chong's debut, *Up in Smoke,* and the granddaddy of cult films, *The Rocky Horror Picture Show.*

For the past 20 years, he's largely been out of the music field. He focused on film, got involved in theater, and "made a bunch of kids," Adler says. "I've definitely filled the time."

Adler hasn't produced a full album, or worked "in a concentrated way with an artist," since the late '70s, though he recently produced the "Basketball Jones" cut for the *Space Jam* movie soundtrack.

"I did a lot of albums as opposed to just singles, and I haven't done that since the '70s," Adler says. "I can't say why, other than maybe I just haven't run across an artist—or an artist hasn't run across me—who interests me enough to go into the studio. And I don't recall ever consciously looking for artists."

Raised in the Boyle Heights section of Los Angeles, Adler is a high school dropout and Navy veteran who briefly attended Los Angeles City College as a journalism major. He dropped out to produce singles in a garage with a friend, Herb Alpert.

In 1959, he produced his first record, Jan and Dean's "Baby Talk," a Top 10 single. Five years later, he started Dunhill Records, which eventually became part of ABC Paramount. His first two projects there were Johnny Rivers' "Memphis" (a No. 2 single in 1964) and Barry McGuire's "Eve of Destruction," a protest song that reached No. 1 in 1965.

Adler gained even more success when he discovered the Mamas and the Papas and produced such classics as "Monday, Monday" and "California Dreamin' " (Nos. 4 and 1, respectively, in 1966) and Carole King's *Tapestry,*

an album that reached No. 1 in early 1971 and has sold more than 18 million copies.

Adler never confined himself to music, however. He also produced the *Monterey Pop* film commemorating an epochal 1967 event that led to the commercial and cultural breakthrough of Otis Redding, Janis Joplin, and Jimi Hendrix. As a film director, his debut (and production) was *Up in Smoke* (cost: $1.2 million; gross: $100 million-plus). Like his other projects, the Cheech and Chong movie focuses on Southern California pop culture.

When it comes to music, Adler thinks the artist determines how large a role the producer must play. "I think the role of the producer is determined by the type of artist you deal with," says Adler. "If it's Carole King, you develop the material; the songs are pretty much there before you get involved. If it's an artist who doesn't write, you have to bring the material to them." That was the case with Barry McGuire. ("Eve of Destruction" is by the elusive P. F. Sloan.)

"Johnny Rivers was a combination. When he started out, we were doing basically covers of old blues and rhythm 'n' blues records, then Motown records," Adler says. "Eventually, there were a few songs written."

Among his influences as a producer was pianist George Shearing, who taught him the power of keyboards. "I always, consciously or unconsciously, wanted something in the rhythm other than rhythm guitar, so I'd use a harpsichord or piano that would be playing lines," Adler says. "I think that came from growing up listening to Shearing records. "Listen to Carole King's 'It's Too Late' for an example," Adler suggests. "Piano runs through the song."

Adler considers King and chief Papa John Phillips the most talented musicians he ever produced. He also learned from working with "Bumps" Blackwell (see entry) and Sam Cooke at the Keen label in the late '50s. Cooke's first Keen single, "You Send Me," hit No. 1 in the fall of 1957.

Adler began in the business as a lyricist; his first professional work was writing with Cooke. "What I learned mostly from him was how to talk to musicians in a session without being a musician," he says. "There was always a clarity to my records, which sometimes were called slick," Adler says. "You could hear the instruments; they didn't meld that much together. I tried for definition to instruments as opposed to an overall sound." —CARLO WOLFF

Cheech and Chong: *Cheech and Chong,* Ode, 1971 • *Big Bambu,* Ode, 1972 • "Basketball Jones, Featuring Tyrone Shoelaces," Ode, 1973 • *Los Cochinos,* Ode, 1973 • "Earache My Eye, Featuring Alice Bowie," Ode, 1974 •

Wedding Album, Ode, 1974 • *Sleeping Beauty,* Ode, 1976 • *Up in Smoke,* Warner Bros., 1978.

City, The: *Now That Everything's Been Said,* Ode, 1968.

Clayton, Merry: *Gimme Shelter,* Ode, 1970.

Electric Flag: *Old Glory: The Best Of,* Legacy, 1995.

Elliot, Mama Cass: w/ the Mamas and the Papas, "Dream a Little Dream," Dunhill, 1968 • *Dream a Little Dream: The Cass Elliot Collection,* MCA, 1997.

Fabares, Shelley: *The Best Of,* Rhino, 1994.

Grass Roots: *Anthology, 1965–1975,* MCA, 1991.

Hendrix, Jimi: *Monterey Pop Festival,* Reprise, 1970 • *Kiss the Sky,* Polydor, 1984.

Jan and Dean: "Baby Talk," Dore, 1959 • "Dead Man's Curve," Liberty, 1964 • *Surf City,* EMI Legends, 1990 • *All the Hits—From Surf City to Drag City,* EMI America, 1996 • *Command Performance—Live in Person,* One Way, 1996.

Joplin, Janis: *Janis,* Legacy, 1993.

King, Carole: *Writer,* Ode, 1970 • "I Feel the Earth Move," Ode, 1971 • "It's Too Late," Ode, 1971 • *Music,* Ode, 1971 • "Smackwater Jack," Ode, 1971 • "So Far Away," Ode, 1971 • *Tapestry,* Ode, 1971 • "Been to Canaan," Ode, 1972 • *Rhymes and Reasons,* Ode, 1972 • "Sweet Seasons," Ode, 1972 • "Believe in Humanity," Ode, 1973 • "Corazon," Ode, 1973 • *Fantasy,* Ode, 1973 • "Jazzman," Ode, 1974 • *Wrap Around Joy,* Ode, 1974 • "Nightingale," Ode, 1975 • *Thoroughbred,* Ode, 1975 • "Only Love Is Real," Ode, 1976 • *Speeding Time,* Atlantic, 1983 • *A Natural Woman: The Ode Collection,* Legacy, 1994 • *The Carnegie Hall Concert,* Legacy, 1996.

L.A. Gospel Choir: *The Gospel According to Bob Dylan,* Ode, 1971.

London Symphony Orchestra: *Tommy,* Rhino, 1972, 1989.

Mamas and the Papas: "California Dreamin'," Dunhill, 1966 • "I Saw Her Again," Dunhill, 1966 • *If You Can Believe Your Eyes and Ears,* Dunhill, 1966 • "Look Through My Window," Dunhill, 1966 • "Monday, Monday," Dunhill, 1966 • *The Mamas and the Papas,* Dunhill, 1966 • "Words of Love," Dunhill, 1966 • "Creeque Alley," Dunhill, 1967 • "Dedicated to the One I Love," Dunhill, 1967 • *Deliver,* Dunhill, 1967 • "Twelve Thirty (Young Girls Are Coming to the Canyon)," Dunhill, 1967 • "Glad to Be Unhappy," Dunhill, 1968 • *The Papas and the Mamas,* Dunhill, 1968 • *16 Greatest Hits,* MCA, 1969, 1981 • *Monterey Pop Festival,* Dunhill, 1971 • *Creeque Alley,* MCA, 1991, 1995.

McGuire, Barry: "Eve of Destruction," ABC, 1965 • *Eve of Destruction,* ABC, 1965 • *Barry McGuire and the Doctor,* Ode, 1971.

McKenzie, Scott: "San Francisco (Wear Some Flowers in Your Hair)," Ode, 1967 • *The Voice of,* CBS, 1967.

Native: *No Boundaries,* Ode 2 Kids, 1989.

Phillips, John: *John, the Wolf King of L.A.,* Dunhill, 1970.

Redding, Otis: *Otis! The Definitive Otis Redding,* Rhino, 1993.

Rivers, Johnny: *At the Whisky A Go Go,* Imperial, 1964 • *Here We A-Go-Go Again,* Imperial, 1964 • "Maybelline," Imperial, 1964 • "Memphis," Imperial, 1964 • "Mountain of Love," Imperial, 1964 • *In Action,* Imperial, 1965 • *Meanwhile Back at the Whisky A Go Go,* Imperial, 1965 • "Midnight Special," Imperial, 1965 • *Rocks the Folk,* Imperial, 1965 • "Seventh Son," Imperial, 1965 • "Where Have All the Flowers Gone," Imperial, 1965 • *And I Know You Wanna Dance,* Imperial, 1966 • *Changes,* Imperial, 1966 • "(I Washed My Hands in) Muddy Water," Imperial, 1966 • "Poor Side of Town," Imperial, 1966 • "Secret Agent Man," Imperial, 1966 • "Under Your Spell Again," Imperial, 1966 • "Baby I Need Your Lovin'," Imperial, 1967 • *Rewind,* Imperial, 1967 • "The Tracks of My Tears," Imperial, 1967 • *Slim Slo Slide,* Imperial, 1970 • *The Johnny Rivers Anthology, 1964–1977,* Rhino, 1991.

Spirit: *Spirit,* Ode, 1968 • *The Family That Plays Together Stays Together,* Ode, 1968 • *Clear,* Ode, 1969 • *Best Of,* Epic, 1973 • *Time Circle,* Epic, 1991.

Tufano and Giammarese: *Tufano-Giammarese,* Ode, 1973.

COLLECTIONS

The Rocky Horror Picture Show soundtrack, Ode, 1974.
Beautiful Thing soundtrack, MCA, 1996.

Walter Afanasieff

Walter Afanasieff has been involved in some of the biggest-selling records of the '90s, including titles by Celine Dion, Michael Bolton, Kenny G, Luther Vandross, and the artist he is most closely associated with, Mariah Carey.

As a producer, he is deeply involved in all stages of the records he makes: he writes (or co-writes) the songs, creates the musical arrangements, and records all of the backing tracks before he brings the singer in. This style of working is far from the norm in the now-fractionated record business, and most closely emulates the work habits of Richard Carpenter, David Kahne, and Walter's own mentor, Narada Michael Walden (see entries).

"The way to make money in this business," Walden said in 1988, "is to find white artists and make them sound black." Afanasieff seems to have taken this advice to heart.

Born February 10, 1958, in São Paulo, Brazil, Afanasieff began as a keyboard player touring with Jean-Luc Ponty.

"I don't really like being on stage," he says. "It was

Photo by Ben Cromer, 1994

Afanasieff's "start-to-finish" production approach is ideal for the types of artists he works with, typically singers who are not themselves known for their writing. Afanasieff usually writes the song, sequences it using Apple Macintosh computers with Vision software, and brings in a stable of musicians to record the tracks. The singers overdub their vocal parts after all the tracking is done.

He is famous for his vocal sounds, with a rich, fat texture that cuts through the instrumental accompaniment; and for the layered keyboards and high-end "sparkle" on most of his tracks. —DANIEL J. LEVITIN

Allure, Featuring 112: "All Cried Out," Track Masters/Crave, 1997.

Belle, Regina: *Stay with Me,* Columbia, 1989 • *Passion,* Columbia, 1993.

Bolton, Michael: *Time, Love and Tenderness,* Columbia, 1991 • *Timeless,* Columbia, 1992 • *The One Thing,* Columbia, 1993 • *This Is the Time: The Christmas Album,* Columbia, 1996 • "Go the Distance," Columbia, 1997 • "The Best of Love," Columbia, 1997.

Bryson, Peabo: *Can You Stop the Rain* Columbia, 1991 • *Through the Fire,* Columbia, 1994.

Carey, Mariah: *Mariah Carey,* Columbia, 1990 • *Emotions,* Columbia, 1991 • *MTV Unplugged* (EP), Columbia, 1992 • "Hero," Columbia, 1993 • *Music Box,* Columbia, 1993 • *Merry Christmas,* Columbia, 1994 • *Daydream,* Columbia, 1995 • w/ Boyz II Men, "One Sweet Day," Columbia, 1995 • "Butterfly," Columbia, 1997.

Cherry, Ed: *Second Look,* RTE, 1997.

Cole, Natalie: "A Smile Like Yours," Elektra, 1997.

Dion, Celine: *Celine Dion,* Epic, 1992 • *The Color of My Love,* 550 Music, 1993 • "My Heart Will Go On" (love theme from *Titanic*), 550 Music/Epic, 1997 • w/ Barbra Streisand, "Tell Him," 550 Music/Epic/Columbia, 1997.

Johnson, Puff: *Miracle,* Columbia, 1996.

Kenny G.: *Breathless,* Arista, 1992 • *Moment,* Arista, 1996 • "Havana," Arista, 1997.

Lorenz, Trey: *Trey Lorenz,* Epic, 1992.

Murphy, Eddie: *So Happy,* CBS, 1989.

NKOTB: *Face the Music,* Columbia, 1994.

Streisand, Barbra: *Higher Ground,* Sony, 1997.

Vandross, Luther: *Songs,* Epic, 1994 • *One Night with You: The Best of Love,* Vol. 2, Sony, 1997.

COLLECTIONS

Aladdin soundtrack, Disney, 1992.

James Bond: Best of 30th Anniversary Collection, Capitol, 1992.

Hunchback of Notre Dame soundtrack, Disney, 1996.

Hercules, soundtrack, Disney, 1997.

A Smile Like Yours soundtrack, Elektra, 1997.

cool playing with Jean-Luc because of the intelligence of his music, but I'm so shy, I can't do that on-stage thing. When I got off the road, I was lucky enough to hook up with Narada, who hired me to do sessions for him. Before that I was just playing weddings on weekends, so that was a very lucky thing. Then one thing quickly led to another. I started playing with his fusion band, the Warriors—Mahavishnu Orchestra type of stuff." Afanasieff was writing tunes for The Warriors, and Walden suggested they co-write pop songs together.

Afanasieff began working as a staff producer, arranger, and session keyboardist in Narada Michael Walden's Marin County Tarpan Studios. This was the heady period when Walden was one of the country's most sought-after producers because of his successes with the debut album by Whitney Houston and Aretha Franklin's mid-'80s comeback album *Who's Zoomin' Who* (No. 13). Afanasieff's keyboard parts are heard on the Walden-produced records by these artists as well as by Lionel Ritchie, George Benson, and Barbra Streisand.

For several years, Walden tutored Afanasieff on all aspects of record production and the record business. Although they split bitterly over album credits after Carey's debut album, Afanasieff still feels indebted to Walden.

"I owe him everything," says Afanasieff. "If it wasn't for Narada Michael Walden moving to S.F., taking me under his wing, showing me everything about writing, the economics of music, and producing, I wouldn't be anywhere. And Narada has done some incredible stuff, produced and written some beautiful songs."

Brian Ahern

I f Brian Ahern had been a better guitar player, he might not have become a producer. And if he hadn't become a record producer, artists like Anne Murray and Emmylou Harris might have not enjoyed the kind of success they achieved under his direction.

"The reason I became a producer is I realized I could never play guitar as well as I wanted," says Ahern. "This way I got to work with the best guitar players in the world and yell at them in the studio," Ahern adds with a laugh.

Ahern says he was "intrigued at the impact that a producer could have on me through a speaker in an automobile. Decisions were being made beyond just the song and the singer that I thought were important. So I decided to look into that."

If Ahern wasn't the kind of musician he wanted to be, it wasn't for lack of trying. A native of Halifax, Nova Scotia, he began his career in his hometown performing simultaneously in four bands.

"Every band was totally different than the other," he says, "so, rarely did they play at the same time. One band played at late-night frat parties, and the band with the plaid jackets played totally other hours. So I kept everything in my car and worked until I flopped. If there was a conflict, I was the leader of all of them, so I could juggle it properly."

Performing in different bands helped Ahern develop an ear for hit potential. He heard it when he was working as music director for a television show in Halifax and saw a young woman named Anne Murray.

"I had a feeling something really good was going to happen," he says. "She was really talented and seemed to function well in a man's world, which is what I always look for in a female artist."

Ahern left Halifax for Toronto, where he began producing soundalike records. "I was working to maintain an apartment and to get to know Toronto," he says. "I brought [Murray] up from Nova Scotia. I used to write her a letter every 10 days to two weeks pleading with her to come to Toronto and make a record with this [small] company. I think our budget ran $2,000 to $2,500. I just wanted to get her in the studio to make this cheap record so I could take it over to a major company and get her the deal she deserved. So I did that and eventually took it into Capitol Records in Toronto, and she stayed with Capitol for years."

Restless to experience life outside of Toronto, Ahern moved on to new challenges in Los Angeles. In fact, his nomadic yearnings spawned one of the most interesting studios ever created: the Enactron truck.

"I was in Toronto when I realized I wasn't getting enough time in the studio when I got a project. I had a budget and that was it—I was out of there," Ahern recalls. "I wanted to experiment, plus I realized I probably wouldn't stay in Toronto. When you build a studio and then you leave town, you have to sell it, which is a big pain in the ass, and you lose money invariably. So I said, 'Why not put it on wheels so the whole world is my studio, put the control room on wheels with a small vocal room?' And no matter where I go, I won't have to sell my studio. I built it in Toronto and I got bored and went to L.A. to do two records and I stayed there 15 years."

Ahern and his mobile studio are currently based in Nashville. Since moving to Music City, he's worked with a variety of acts from newcomer Terry Radigan to former Country Music Association entertainer of the year Ricky Skaggs to the legendary George Jones, for whom Ahern produced *The Bradley's Barn Sessions*.

Ahern has always been known as something of a maverick and admits it's the element of surprise that makes his work intriguing. Mystery is what he feels his work is most known for. "I'm [known for] left-field stuff. I can take left-field stuff and lay it over the commonplace, traditional, normal things with skill. Almost every record I've made, if you stripped away one or two things, would sound pretty average. Another thing I do is present the singer sometimes with an unorthodox headphone mix and it makes them react to different things, and when you mix it normally they are back in the real world, but they had done a performance stimulated by odd stuff. It creates a kind of tension. If you listen to the old Emmylou vocals I did, you'll hear her do things she never does now."

Ahern, who was once married to Harris, is known for producing some of her best work. They recorded 11 albums together, including such critically acclaimed releases as *Roses in the Snow, Evangeline, Elite Hotel, Blue Kentucky Girl*, and *Pieces of the Sky*.

Ahern says the two most crucial aspects of producing are finding the right songs and having a good working relationship with an artist. "I think I respect the song more than anybody," he says. "In fact, I refuse to know who wrote the songs I'm listening to so I won't be biased. . . . I avoid the names of the author so I can look at the songs with the same cold eye."

Ahern has a secret tactic for getting bogged-down recording sessions back on track. "Once in a while, if an artist should fold up in trying to focus too hard and was intimidated by being the center of attention, I would have some kind of center-of-attention fit," he says.

"Something would happen where I would be the center of attention. So you create things like that once in a while to take the pressure off the artist."

Ahern fancies himself a detail-oriented producer, but admits sometimes the best results come from being sloppy. "Most of the George Jones record I did at Bradley's Barn, almost all of that was first or second takes," he says. "The concept there was to get all these luminaries all in one room and not give them time to learn the song and get really polished and start thinking about their snow tires, which a lot of them do, a lot of them play on automatic. I wanted to get their attention the first or second time through, so I guess that's an example of when sloppy is good."

Ahern has no regrets when it comes to his career. "I can't think of anything I would do different," he says. "At one point I regretted not learning to read music, but then I realized I made a lot of unorthodox decisions because of it that were good." —DEBORAH EVANS PRICE

Bromberg, David: *Midnight on the Water,* CBS, 1975 • *The Best of David Bromberg* (2 tracks), Columbia, 1977.
Brooks, Dianne: *Backstairs of My Life,* Warner Bros., 1979.
Campbell, Glen: *See* Murray, Anne.
Cash, Johnny: "Ghost Riders in the Sky," Columbia, 1979 • *Silver,* Columbia, 1979 • *Johnny 99,* Columbia, 1983 • *Biggest Hits,* Columbia, 1987 • *The Essential Johnny Cash, 1955–1983,* Legacy, 1992.
Crowell, Rodney: *Ain't Livin' Long Like This,* Warner Bros., 1977 • *The Rodney Crowell Collection,* Warner Bros., 1989.
Edwards, Jonathan: *Rockin' Chair,* Warner Bros., 1976 • *Sailboat,* Warner Bros., 1977.
Harris, Emmylou: *Pieces of the Sky,* Warner Bros., 1975 • "Too Far Gone," 550 Music/Epic, 1975, 1994 (*The Cowboy Way* soundtrack) • *Elite Hotel,* Warner Bros., 1976 • "Sweet Dreams," Reprise, 1976 • "Together Again," Reprise, 1976 • *Luxury Liner,* Warner Bros., 1977 • *Quarter Moon in a Ten Cent Town,* Warner Bros., 1978 • "Two More Bottles of Wine," Warner Bros., 1978 • *Blue Kentucky Girl,* Warner Bros., 1979 • *Light of the Stable,* Warner Bros., 1979 • "Beneath Still Waters," Warner Bros., 1980 • *Roses in the Snow,* Warner Bros., 1980 • *Cimarron,* Warner Bros., 1981 • *Evangeline,* Warner Bros., 1981 • "Mister Sandman," Warner Bros., 1981 • *Last Date,* Warner Bros., 1982 • "(Lost His Love) on Our Last Date," Warner Bros., 1983 • *White Shoes,* Warner Bros., 1983 • *Duets,* Reprise, 1990 • *Songs of the West,* Warner Bros., 1994 • *Portraits,* Warner Bros., 1996.
Jones, George: *The Bradley's Barn Sessions,* MCA, 1994.
Lee, Albert: *Hiding,* A&M, 1979.
Murray, Anne: "Snowbird," Capitol, 1970 • *Snowbird,* Capitol, 1970 • w/ Glen Campbell, *Anne Murray and Glen Campbell,* Capitol, 1972 • "A Love Song," Capitol, 1973 • "Danny's Song," Capitol, 1973 • *Danny's Song,* Capitol, 1973 • "He Thinks I Still Care," Capitol, 1974 • *Highly Prized Possession,* Capitol, 1974 • *Love Song,* Capitol, 1974 • "You Won't See Me," Capitol, 1974 • *The Best . . . So Far,* EMI, 1994.
Place, Mary Kay: *Tonite! At the Capri Lounge,* CBS, 1976 • *Aimin' to Please,* CBS, 1977.
Pringle, Peter: *Peter Pringle,* Warner Bros., 1976.
Robbins, Marty: *Biggest Hits,* CBS, 1984.
Ronstadt, Linda: *Get Closer,* Asylum, 1982.
Screamin' Sirens: "Maniac," Enigma, 1984, 1985 (*The Enigma Variations*).
Shaver, Billy Joe: *Gypsy Boy,* Capricorn, 1977 • *When I Get My Wings,* Capricorn, 1977 • *Honky Tonk Heroes,* Bear Family, 1994 • *Restless Wind: The Legendary Billy Joe Shaver, 1973–1987,* Razor & Tie, 1995.
Skaggs, Ricky: *My Father's Son,* Epic, 1991.
Williams, Don: *Lord I Hope This Day Is Good,* MCA, 1993.
Winchester, Jesse: *Nothin' but a Breeze,* Bearsville, 1977.

Ron and Howard Albert

Brothers Ron and Howard Albert have been in the recording industry for 30 years. Ron began his career as an assistant engineer at Miami's premier Criteria Recording Studios while still in high school. Howard played keyboard in various local bands and, after serving in Vietnam, returned to Miami to join his brother at Criteria.

Eventually, through time and skill (and a little luck) they worked themselves into being one of the most respected engineering-production teams of the '70s, producing acoustic-oriented rock artists such as Crosby, Stills and Nash; Firefall; Roger McGuinn; Clark and Hillman; Pure Prairie League; and John "Cougar" Mellencamp.

The engineering style for which they are known is clean, straightforward, and gimmick-free. Their typical rhythm section sound no doubt owes as much to the acoustics of Criteria as to any particular engineering decision: the drums often sound well-contained, and the bass guitar direct-injected with a warm, round resonance.

The Albert brothers' unobtrusiveness as producer-engineers allows the vocals to shine through the mix. Among their high points is 1977's *CSN* (No. 2) by Crosby, Stills and Nash, which featured the No. 7 hit "Just a Song Before I Go."

Graham Nash cites their "passion, humor, and an innate knowledge of what would work well on the radio" as the Albert brothers' strengths. "After I wrote 'Just a Song,' I played it for them and they immediately thought it would be a hit," he says. "Who the fuck knows what's going to be the hit? I don't think we've ever really known. But Ron and Howard knew. Also, they did a great 'good cop, bad cop' thing, and they could always figure out what to say to us so that we would accept it. They were very fast, and mostly I remember it being very fun. They were very involved musically as well, such as arrangements."

Nash adds that it wasn't easy working with *CSN*, "because we produced some pretty fine records ourselves. The problem was that we started to get in each other's way, so it was very nice to hand over that part of the process to someone else that we respected. They walked a tightrope between thrilling us and pissing us off. Ultimately, they love music and it shows in their body of work."

Today as partners with Steve Alaimo in Vision Records, Ron and Howard Albert continue to be a driving force in Miami music, and as captains of their boat the *Fintastic* they continue to be a driving force in the recreational fishing industry. —DANIEL J. LEVITIN

Black Oak Arkansas: *High on the Hog*, Atco, 1973.

Boyzz, The: *Too Wild to Tame*, Epic, 1978.

Chapin, Harry: *Sequel*, Boardwalk, 1981 • *The Gold Medal Collection*, Elektra, 1988.

Crosby, Stills and Nash: *CSN*, Atlantic, 1977 • "Just a Song Before I Go," Atlantic, 1977 • *Allies* (2 tracks), Atlantic, 1983.

Crosby, Stills, Nash and Young: *Crosby, Stills, Nash and Young*, Atlantic, 1991.

Curved Air: *Midnight Wire*, BTM, 1975.

DeSario, Terri: *Pleasure Train*, Casablanca, 1978.

Firefall: *Elan*, Atlantic, 1978 • *Undertow*, Atlantic, 1979 • *Break of Dawn*, Atlantic, 1982 • *Mirror of the World*, Atlantic, 1983 • *Greatest Hits*, Rhino, 1992.

Fotomaker: *Fotomaker*, Atlantic, 1978.

Gang of Four: *Hard*, EMI, 1983 • *A Brief History of the Twentieth Century*, Warner Bros., 1990.

Henry Paul Band: *Grey Ghost*, Atlantic, 1979.

Hillman, Chris: *Slippin' Away*, Asylum, 1976 • *Clear Sailin'*, Geffen, 1977.

James Gang: *Jesse Come Home*, Atco, 1976.

Law: *Breakin' It*, MCA, 1977.

McGuinn, Clark and Hillman: *McGuinn, Clark and Hillman*, Capitol, 1979 • *City*, Capitol, 1980 • *Return Flight*, Edsel, 1992.

Mellencamp, John "Cougar": *John Cougar*, Riva, 1979.

Mink De Ville: *Where Angels Fear to Tread*, Atlantic, 1983.

Pierce Arrow: *Pity the Rich* (2 tracks), CBS, 1978.

Procol Harum: *Something Magic*, Chrysalis, 1977 • *The Chrysalis Years, 1973–1977*, Chrysalis, 1989.

Pure Prairie League: *Can't Hold Back*, RCA, 1979.

Quatro, Michael: *Bottom Line*, Spector, 1981.

Rhodes, Chalmers, Rhodes: *Scandal*, Radio, 1980.

Shana: *I Want You*, Vision, 1989.

Sister Red: *Sister Red*, Vision, 1989.

Stills, Stephen: *Stills*, CBS, 1975 • *Thoroughfare Gap*, CBS, 1978 • *Stills Alone*, Vision, 1991.

Sutherland Brothers and Quiver: *Reach for the Sky*, Columbia, 1975 • *Slipstream*, Columbia, 1976.

Vitale, Joe: *Roller Coaster Weekend*, Atlantic, 1974.

White Witch: *Spirtual Greeting*, Capricorn, 1974.

Wilson, Tony: *Catch One*, Bearsville, 1978.

Wishbone Ash: *New England*, Atlantic, 1976 • *Time Was: The Wishbone Ash Collection*, MCA, 1993.

Wright, Betty: *Live*, TK/Alston, 1978.

Wylde, Zak: *Book of Shadows*, Geffen, 1996.

Steve Albini

Punk-rock provocateur or rigid dogmatist? Indie idealist or raging hypocrite? Opinions tend to polarize on the relative merits of Steve Albini, although few can deny that some of the most epochal albums of the alternative age benefited from the man's hand. From the Pixies to Nirvana, from PJ Harvey to the Jesus Lizard, Albini's blunt, take-no-prisoners approach helped throw into bold relief the virtues of a who's who of full-on rock bands.

As the leader of the seminal industrial-strength rage band Big Black and the meaner and less-than-seminal Rapeman, Albini was an acknowledged avatar of hard-ass post-punk values in the late '80s. As a burgeoning record maker, he became renowned not only for his aesthetic convictions and technical know-how but his suffer-no-fools attitude and unstinting protectiveness of bands' artistic and financial welfare. Not content to simply counsel against extramusical influence and corporate bias, he walked his talk by declining to take a percentage of an act's album sales and even disdaining the title of "producer," preferring a "recorded by" credit instead.

In 1987, Albini "recorded" the album that more than any other laid the template for mid-'90s modern rock: the Pixies' *Surfer Rosa*. True, the band's bent pop-punk genius was evident from its first EP and on several post–*Surfer Rosa* albums, but Albini captured the essence of the Pixies' appeal like no one else. And contrary to his subsequent rep as strictly a man's man, he guided one of the first big chick-rock albums, the Breeders' *Pod* from 1992 on. Less apparent but perhaps even more influential was Albini's work on a string of ferociously good EPs and albums by fellow Chicagoans the Jesus Lizard, culminating in the band's masterwork of hard-core noir, 1992's *Liar.*

Albini was at his peak in 1993, recording the two most powerful albums of the year: Nirvana's *In Utero* (No. 1) and PJ Harvey's *Rid of Me,* helping raise the emotional ante of each by emphasizing stark settings and intense dynamics. But even though that work has endured well (the austere force of *In Utero* sounds better today than the overripe sonics of the Butch Vig–produced *Nevermind;* see entry), it was controversial at the time—not only with the record companies and fans, but with the artists themselves.

No doubt under pressure from Geffen, Nirvana had Albini compress the audacious stereo spread of *In Utero* and gave R.E.M. producer Scott Litt (see entry) two tracks to rework ("All Apologies" and "Heart-Shaped Box"). So what should have been a crowning achievement for the meticulous, control-conscious, and avowed Nirvana admirer Albini ended up an infuriating and disillusioning episode. A milder affront came with Harvey's *Four-Track Demos;* although the EP included previously unissued songs, the ostensible reason for its release was to air Harvey's original vision of the *Rid of Me* material. Although the gulf between her demos and the final product isn't all that great, the EP versions don't hold a candle to the album's finely tuned fury.

After the exhilarating yet frustrating world of the big time, Albini welcomed the familiar realm of indie-rock underdogs for a while, as he guided records by Shadowy Men on a Shadowy Planet, Silkworm (his homies from Missoula, Montana), the Auteurs, the Palace Brothers, and his own band, Shellac, among many others, in the mid-'90s. Subsequently, he helped craft tracks by Guided By Voices as well as a dynamite Sub Pop single by power-pop legends Cheap Trick.

But going from the sublime to the ridiculous, Albini courted controversy once again in 1996 and 1997 by lowering his stated punk-rock standards to aid two commercially successful yet artistically questionable bands: platinum British grunge pretenders Bush and Chicago alt-pop cum arena-rock poseurs Veruca Salt. Yet Albini would reply to any criticism by saying that he recorded Bush's sophomore effort *Razorblade Suitcase* and Veruca Salt's EP *Blow It out Your Ass . . . It's Veruca Salt* in order to show moribund commercial alternative radio what a real rock record is supposed to sound like.

No matter who the band is, Albini considers the Hippocratic oath "Do no harm" his overriding credo when making records, and that extends from budgetary concerns to the actual processing of sounds.

"I have a lot of respect for rock bands as institutions," he says. "If a band is allowed to operate naturally, it will make as good a record as it's capable of. Facilitating a recording can be something really simple, like making sure band members are comfortable physically or not yelling at the band. Or, some people can only play like themselves on certain equipment or with certain idiosyncrasies. You have to respect the fact that the band does what it does for a reason, and those reasons can be intensely personal."

Record makers who don't have engineering backgrounds "are part of the problem," says Albini, who stresses that the role of a "producer" is one of ensuring technical solutions to artistic problems. "A lot of people making records don't have a grasp of the process. They do it thinking that it's some abstract art form that doesn't need to be comprehended on a technical or procedural level. In those cases, a band will end up with a record that isn't formally completed but that's finished when the bell rings."

For Albini, along with an appreciation for the cost-benefit ratio of different recording facilities comes a high regard for restraint in using their tools. The sound of his records has improved dramatically as he has grown to resist the "fiddling impulse," Albini says. "In quest of a distinctive sound, people endlessly process things. But because so many people use that method, those sounds have become quite commonplace. I've learned to leave things alone. Now when I set up a microphone and like the way it sounds, I consider the job done."

A self-described "microphone junkie," Albini is especially addicted to mikes made in Eastern Europe. He points out that because vacuum-tube electronics was the standard in the Eastern bloc long after the West graduated to solid-state technology, the audio community in those countries had the chance to perfect vintage mike styles. In particular, Albini has favored Neumann and Gefell microphones for their headroom and frequency response. "Modern equipment has far more flexibility, but the attention to sound quality isn't necessarily there," he says. "With vintage stuff, you usually get a stunning sound, though with much more limited application. It just depends on what you're after."

The biggest influence on Albini is "going to see live music," he says, adding that the hyperintensity of the early Jesus Lizard albums was captured live in the studio. "Those albums were made pretty much the way records were made in the beginning of recorded music—the whole band standing in front of microphones playing its songs. Those are albums I'm especially proud of having worked on. You're always trying to capture something like that, to make a record that's like the first time you see a band and its personality just leaps off the stage and grabs you. When you you're able to do that, it's really satisfying." —BRADLEY BAMBARGER

Auteurs, The: *After Murder Park*, Hut, 1996.

Bewitched: *Harshing My Mellow*, Number Six, 1992.

Big Black: *Lungs* (EP), Ruthless, 1983 • *Bulldozer* (EP), Ruthless/Fever, 1984 • *Racer-X* (EP), Homestead, 1984 • *Atomizer*, Touch & Go, 1985, 1992 • *The Hammer Party*, Homestead, 1986 • *Headache* (EP), Touch & Go, 1987 • *Songs About Fucking*, Touch & Go, 1987 • *The Rich Man's Eight-Track Tape*, Homestead, 1987 • *Pig Pile*, Touch & Go, 1992.

Big'n: *Discipline Through Sound*, Gasoline Boost, 1996.

Breadwinner: *Burner*, Merge, 1994.

Breeders, The: *Pod*, Elektra, 1990, 1992.

Bush: *Razorblade Suitcase*, Interscope, 1996.

Cheap Trick: "Baby Talk," Sub Pop, 1997.

Crain: *Heater*, Restless, 1994.

Craw: *Lost Nation Road*, Choke, 1994.

D.Q.E.: *But Me, I Fell Down*, Feel Good All Over, 1993.

Distorted Pony: *Instant Winner*, Trance Syndicate, 1994.

Don Caballero: *For Respect*, Touch & Go, 1993.

Fleshtones, The: *Laboratory of Sound*, Ichiban, 1995.

Flour: *LUV 713/Flour*, Touch & Go, 1989.

Fulks, Robbie: *Country Love Songs*, Bloodshot, 1996.

Glazed Baby: *Squeeze the Tail, Suck the Head* (EP), Allied, 1994.

Great Unraveling: *The Great Unraveling*, Kill Rock Stars, 1997.

Guided By Voices: *Under the Bushes Under the Stars* (2 tracks), Matador, 1996.

Helmet: *Meantime* (1 track), Interscope, 1992.

Jesus Lizard: *Pure*, Touch & Go, 1989 • *Head*, Touch & Go, 1990 • *Goat*, Touch & Go, 1991 • *Liar*, Touch & Go, 1992 • *Lash* (EP, 2 tracks), Touch & Go, 1993 • "Puss," Touch & Go, 1993 • *Down*, Touch & Go, 1994.

Johnboy: *Claim Dedication*, Trance Syndicate, 1994.

Les Thugs: *Strike*, Sub Pop, 1996.

Lizard Music: *Fashionably Lame*, World Domination, 1996.

Low: *Transmission* (EP), Vernon Yard, 1996.

Man or Astroman?: *Experiment Zero*, Touch & Go, 1996 • "Touch of Evil," Donna, 1996 (*Shots in the Dark*).

Melt-Banana: *Scratch or Stitch*, Skin Graft, 1996.

Mount Shasta: *Put the Creep On*, Skin Graft, 1994.

Murder, Inc.: "Mania/Murder Inc.," Invisible, 1992.

Nirvana: *In Utero*, DGC, 1993 • *Singles*, Alex, 1996.

Palace: *Arise Therefore*, Drag City, 1996.

Pigface: *Gub*, Invisible, 1990.

Pixies, The: *Surfer Rosa*, 4 A.D./Elektra, 1988, 1992 • "Born in Chicago," Elektra, 1990 (*Rubaiyat: Elektra's 40th Anniversary*) • "Where Is My Mind," Atlantic, 1991 (*A Matter of Degrees* soundtrack) • *Death to the Pixies, 1987–1991*, Elektra, 1997.

PJ Harvey: *Rid of Me*, Island, 1993.

Poster Children: *Daisychain Reaction*, Twin/Tone, 1991 • *Flowerpower* (4 tracks), Frontier, 1991.

Rapeman: *Budd* (EP), Touch & Go, 1988 • *Two Nuns and a Pack Mule*, Touch & Go, 1989.

Rodan: *Rusty*, Quarterstick, 1994.

Schneider, Fred: "Bulldozer," Reprise, 1996 • *Just Fred*, Reprise, 1996.

Scrawl: *Velvet Hammer*, Simple Machines, 1993 • *Travel on Rider*, Elektra, 1996.

Shadowy Men on a Shadowy Planet: *Sport Fishin': The Lure of the Bait, the Luck of the Hook*, Jetpac/Cargo, 1993.

Shellac: *Shellac at Action Park*, Touch & Go, 1994.

Shorty: *Fresh Breath*, Skin Graft, 1994.

Silkworm: *Libertine*, El Recordo, 1994 • *Firewater*, Matador, 1996 • *Developer*, Matador, 1997.

Silverfish: *Fat Axl*, Touch & Go, 1991.

Slint: *Tweez*, Touch & Go, 1988, 1993.

Smog: *Kicking a Couple Around* (EP), Drag City, 1996.

Space Streakings: *7-Toku*, Skin Graft, 1994.

Jon Spencer Blues Explosion: *The Jon Spencer Blues Explosion*, Caroline, 1992.

Superchunk: *Tossing Seeds*, Merge, 1992.

Tad: *Salt Lick*, Sub Pop, 1988.

Tar: *Handsome* (EP), Amphetamine Reptile, 1989.

Things That Fall Down: *Disbelief*, Sonic Noise, 1992.

Union Carbide Production: *Swing*, Puppet, 1992.

Urge Overkill: *Jesus Urge Overkill*, Touch & Go, 1986 • *Strange, I . . .* (EP), Ruthless, 1986.

Usherhouse: *Molting*, Cleopatra, 1993.

Veruca Salt: *Blow It out Your Ass . . . It's Veruca Salt*, Geffen, 1996.

Wedding Present: *Bizarro* (4 tracks), RCA, 1989 • *Seamonsters*, Planet 3, 1992, 1995.

Wreck: *Wreck* (EP), Play It Again Sam, 1989 • *Soul Train*, Play It Again Sam, 1990.

Zeni Geva: *Freedombondage*, Alternative Tentacles, 1995.

David Anderle

Although David Anderle's production résumé spans a "mere" 10 years and exactly 50 titles, his involvement and personal investment in the music business since 1964 transcends his discography.

Of all the artists he's introduced to the world and helped along the path, surely Van Dyke Parks, Frank Zappa (and the Mothers of Invention), the Doors, Bread, and Tim Buckley stand out as important additions to the rock 'n' roll lexicon.

Besides his work as an independent producer, Anderle has held positions as a talent director at MGM/Verve Records, co-founded the Beach Boys' Brother Records, headed up the A&R departments at Elektra and A&M Records, and assisted in the development of film soundtracks. With all that involvement, the natural question seems to be, Why are there just 50 albums on his production discography?

"I had always promised myself that if I ever got to a point where I got up in the morning and didn't want to spend the rest of the whole day and night in a control room, I would stop producing records," says Anderle. "That sort of happened right around the end of the '70s, when I made my 50th album, and I said, 'Well, it's providential, isn't it?' I didn't look at the 50 first, it just happened to be there."

Anderle says he's not sure how he found the creative impulses to bounce between genres, including albums with Kris Kristofferson, the Ozark Mountain Daredevils, Judy Collins, and the Circle Jerks.

"I don't know if it has to do with the fact that from a very early age I grew up in a house that was always filled with music," wonders Anderle. "At that time my mom and dad were always playing Nat "King" Cole records and big-band records, the old 78s. Then, when they would go out on an evening, the girl who would baby-sit for my sister and me was from an Oklahoma family that came in from the Dust Bowl, and as soon as my folks left she would put on country music. I loved that, too, and then growing up I loved jazz. I've always loved classical music and wished I would be a classical musician. I've loved all kinds of music."

Given his diverse background, variety came naturally to Anderle as a producer. "For me to have produced 12 or 13 Rita Coolidge albums and then have the Circle Jerks ask me to produce one of their records seemed logical to me," he says with a laugh. "Maybe not to many others, but I loved to have that kind of wide range of interests."

Through his experience in the studio, Anderle developed a consistent production philosophy. "I'm not a musician, so I would always have to work with artists who brought a lot to the table," he says. "In other words, I couldn't create tracks or write songs. I would always have to work with singer/songwriters or bands that had generated their own material."

Anderle says he learned from his first production client, Judy Collins, "that if you are working with an artist who does not write their own material, try to find them material that either sounds like they have written it themselves or was written specifically for them."

He also made sure that he hired the best musicians and engineers he could find. "Then I would just try to create a creative atmosphere for everybody to play in," he says. "It was a different time then—it was all live music and we tried to make cheap records, quick and fast."

But Anderle saw the technological changes on the horizon and knew it was either him or them. "That equipment was meaningless to me," he says of the MIDI revolution of the early '80s. "I couldn't do a drum machine. I couldn't get into synthesizers. I always like to say, 'As soon as the drummer stopped showing up, there's no reason for me to be here.' " —DAVID JOHN FARINELLA

Ackles, David: *David Ackles,* Elektra, 1968 • *Road to Cairo,* Elektra, 1968.

Benno, Marc: *Marc Benno,* A&M, 1970 • *Minnows,* A&M, 1971 • *Ambush,* A&M, 1972.

Bramlett, Bonnie: *Sweet Bonnie Bramlett,* CBS, 1973.

Circle Jerks: *Wild in the Streets,* Frontier, 1981.

Coast to Coast: *Coast to Coast,* Full Moon, 1977.

Collins, Judy: *Who Knows Where the Time Goes* Elektra, 1968 • *Forever: An Anthology,* Elektra, 1997 • *So Early in the Spring,* Asylum, 1977.

Color Me Gone: *Color Me Gone,* A&M, 1984.

Coolidge, Rita: *Nice Feeling,* A&M, 1971 • *Rita Coolidge,* A&M, 1971 • *Anytime Anywhere,* A&M, 1972 • *The Lady's Not for Sale,* A&M, 1972 • w/ Kris Kristofferson, *Full Moon,* A&M, 1973 • *Fall into Spring,* A&M, 1974 • *It's Only Love,* A&M, 1975 • *Love Me Again,* A&M, 1978 • w/ Kris Kristofferson, *Natural Act,* A&M, 1978 • *Satisfied,* A&M, 1979 • *Greatest Hits,* A&M, 1980 • *Never Let You Go,* A&M, 1983 • *Out of the Blues,* Beacon, 1996.

De Burgh, Chris: *Eastern Wind,* A&M, 1980.

Doc Holliday: *Rides Again,* A&M, 1981.

Grant, Amy: *Lead Me On,* A&M, 1989.

Hildebrand, Diane: *Early Morning Blues and Greens,* Elektra, 1965.

Jones, Booker T.: *Try and Love Again,* A&M, 1978 • *The Best of You,* A&M, 1980.

Kristofferson, Kris: *Spooky Lady's Sideshow*, One Way, 1974,
  1995 • *Who's to Bless and Who's to Blame*, Monument, 1975
  • *Surreal Thing*, Monument, 1976 • *Easter Island*,
  Monument, 1978 • *Shake Hands with the Devil*, Monument,
  1979 • *Singer/Songwriter*, Monument/Sony, 1991 • *See also*
  Coolidge, Rita.

Lamb, Annabel: *The Flame*, A&M, 1984.

Lambert and Nuttycombe: *At Home*, A&M, 1969.

McKenzie, Scott: *Stained Glass Morning*, A&M, 1970.

Mother Hen: *Mother Hen*, RCA, 1971.

Neville, Aaron: *Tattooed Heart*, A&M, 1995.

Ozark Mountain Daredevils: *It'll Shine When It Shines*, A&M,
  1974 • *The Ozark Mountain Daredevils*, A&M, 1974 •
  "Jackie Blue," A&M, 1975 • *The Car over the Lake Album*,
  A&M, 1975 • *Men from Earth*, A&M, 1976 • *The Best*,
  A&M, 1981.

Phoenix, Willie: *Willie Phoenix*, A&M, 1982.

Rhinceros: *Satin Chickens*, Elektra, 1969.

Roberts, Rick: *Windmills*, A&M, 1972.

Swimming Pool Q's: *Swimming Pool Q's*, A&M, 1984.

Wells, Cory: *Touch Me*, A&M, 1978.

COLLECTIONS

Good Morning, Vietnam, A&M, 1988.

Benny Andersson and Bjorn Ulvaeus

The Swedish pop group Abba was the world's most successful in the '70s—selling tens of millions of records by combining lush group vocals and gorgeous Euro-melodies with rock and disco rhythms. The group's lyrics ranged from silly to touching, many reflecting the real-life romantic complications within the group, à la Fleetwood Mac: songwriter/producer/guitarist Bjorn Ulvaeus was married to and divorced from singer Agnetha Faltskog, and songwriter/producer/keyboardist Benny Andersson was married to and divorced from singer Anni-Frid "Frida" Lyngstad during the life of the group.

Abba was dismissed by many (especially in America) as Swedish cheese, but the group's best songs ("Dancing Queen," No. 1; "Take a Chance on Me," No. 3; "Lay All Your Love on Me"; "SOS," No. 5) have aged well and stand alongside the Beach Boys and Phil Spector's girl groups at the pinnacle of pop rock.

Born December 16, 1946, in Stockholm, Benny came from an accordion-slinging family, and he picked up the squeeze box at age 6. Piano and Elvis followed soon thereafter, and by age 13, Benny was in a rock 'n' roll band, the Hep Stars, which by the early '60s was Sweden's most popular, playing the latest hits from America, sung in English.

The group grew weary of covers, and out of desperation Benny wrote "No Response," which rose to No. 2 and launched a songwriting career. Benny produced hits for the Fabulous Four and the DJs on the side.

"I always enjoyed being in the studio once I found out the possibilities," says Benny. "It's a nice environment to be in."

Bjorn, born April 25, 1945, in Gothenburg, played in a folk group, the Hootenanny Singers. Pop music circles being small in Sweden, Benny and Bjorn met and began writing and producing together by the late '60s. On one project, they enlisted their girlfriends, Agnetha and Frida, Swedish singing stars in their own right, to help out on background vocals on what turned out to be a hit single, "People Need Love."

Benny admits that "the girls sounded 600 percent better than we did," and the seed of Abba was planted. In 1974, the quartet (named "Bjorn, Benny, Anna and Frida" to capitalize on their individual popularity in Scandinavia) entered the Eurovision Song Contest with the rousing "Waterloo" (No. 6) and became the first Swedish group to win. Spurred by the show's massive television audience, the song became an instant international hit. Having hit through Eurovision also carried a stigma: it took the band about a year, and a name change, to be accepted as the real thing.

That acceptance came hardest in America. "We didn't do well in America, did we?" says Benny. "Not compared to people who actually go there and do their interview stuff and work their asses off. We've done OK, a couple of platinum albums, but only one No. 1 single, 'Dancing Queen.' " Success is relative, of course. Abba did score 10 Top 20 singles in America between 1974 and their breakup in 1982.

Benny took his production cues from America. "The biggest inspiration for me as a producer was definitely Brian Wilson [see entry] of the Beach Boys," he says. "There has always been a lot of vocals in American music. This is a tradition you had long before the Beach Boys. Wilson used vocals in a rhythmic way and added layer upon layer. Also Phil Spector. [see entry] He's another guy who makes as much sound as possible come out of the smallest speaker. We tried to do that with Abba. The human voice is the finest instrument."

Benny is most comfortable producing his own work.

"If one guy writes a tune and another guy comes in to produce it, it takes a long talk to correspond the feelings between them. It's a lot of responsibility, which is why I think it is nicer to stay with the song I write myself. I would never let anyone else produce what I write. It isn't necessarily the best way to do it, but at least it comes out the way I wanted to do it at the time."

Benny is proudest of "Dancing Queen" and "Knowing Me, Knowing You" (No. 14), which he says "are both good songs and well produced, although I have done plenty of corny things as well."

Benny has mixed feelings about the advance of technology in the studio. "I just bought a [Solid State Logic] 9000 console, and you touch a button and it does what you want. Now it's easy to work yourself step-by-step forward, and in that respect I think it's good. In the '60s and '70s, when you had to do a mixdown, there were three guys trying to concentrate on 50 different things. You'd always miss something."

Abba has lived on in recorded form through the '90s, with two collections charting in the U.S. and eight (including two No. 1s) charting in the U.K. Agnetha and Frida had several solo hits in the '80s, and Bjorn and Benny co-wrote the musical *Chess* with Tim Rice in 1984, which produced Murray Head's punchy electro-pop ditty "One Night in Bangkok" (No. 3). In 1992, Erasure released an EP of Abba songs, *Abba-Esque*, which shot to No. 1 in the U.K. In 1996, Bjorn and Benny wrote and produced the strong *Shapes* album for Swedish chanteuse Josefin Nilsson. —ERIC OLSEN AND DAWN DARLING

Abba: *Ring Ring,* Atlantic, 1973 • "Honey, Honey," Atlantic, 1974 • "Waterloo," Atlantic, 1974 • *Abba,* Atlantic, 1975 • "SOS," Atlantic, 1975 • "Fernando," Atlantic, 1976 • "I Do, I Do, I Do, I Do, I Do," Atlantic, 1976 • "Mamma Mia," Atlantic, 1976 • *Arrival,* Atlantic, 1977 • "Dancing Queen," Atlantic, 1977 • "Knowing Me, Knowing You," Atlantic, 1977 • "Take a Chance on Me," Atlantic, 1978 • *The Album,* Atlantic, 1978 • "The Name of the Game," Atlantic, 1978 • "Chiquita," Atlantic, 1979 • "Does Your Mother Know," Atlantic, 1979 • *Voulez-Vous,* Atlantic, 1979 • *Super Trouper,* Atlantic, 1980 • "The Winner Takes It All," Atlantic, 1980 • *The Visitors,* Atlantic, 1981 • "When All Is Said and Done," Atlantic, 1982 • *Live,* Polydor, 1986, 1995 • *Gold,* Polydor, 1992 • *Oro,* PolyGram Latino, 1993 • *Mas Oro,* PolyGram Latino, 1994 • *Thank You for the Music,* A&M, 1995 • *More Gold,* Polydor, 1996.
Head, Murray: "One Night in Bangkok," RCA, 1984.
Nilsson, Josefin: *Shapes,* Tristar, 1997.
Paige, Elaine: *Encore,* Atlantic Theater, 1996.
Rice, Tim: *Collection: Stage and Screen Classics,* Rhino, 1996.

COLLECTIONS
Chess soundtrack, Polydor, 1984.
Kristina Fran Duvemala (original cast), Mono, 1995.

Aphex Twin
See RICHARD D. JAMES

Rod Argent

Rod Argent, a highly acclaimed keyboardist, vocalist, songwriter, and producer, takes as much pride in his musicianship as he does in his studio work. For instance, his performances on Joshua Kadison's *Painted Desert Serenade,* Nanci Griffith's *Late Night Grande Hotel,* Tanita Tikaram's *Everybody's Angel,* and Jules Shear's *Healing Bones,* all co-produced with drummer Peter Van Hooke, are as special to him as the production credit itself.

Born June 14, 1945, in St. Albans, Hertfordshire, England, Argent co-founded the Zombies, a '60s band

Photo by Ben Cromer ©1994

that juxtaposed his jazz-tinged keyboards with Colin Blunstone's heartfelt vocals on such Top 10 U.S. hits as "She's Not There" (No. 2), "Tell Her No" (No. 6), and "Time of the Season" (No. 3), a track from the band's swan song, *Odessey and Oracle.*

"Chris [White] and I wanted to produce one last album ourselves, so we went to CBS, and they said, 'Here's $1,600. Go and make an album.' When it was finished they were sort of ho-hum about it. Then they said, 'Go and mix it in stereo.' We said, 'Well, we need some more money.' But they said, 'No, $1,600 is all you're getting.' So Chris and I had to pay $165 each just to do the stereo mixes."

Recorded in 1967 at EMI's Abbey Road Studios in London, *Odessey and Oracle* captured the whimsy of the summer of love with "Care of Cell 44," "Hung Up on a Dream," and "Time of the Season," a masterpiece featuring a breathless organ solo, a propulsive bass line, and a spooky lead vocal.

Argent and White then put together Argent, a band with singer/songwriter/guitarist Russ Ballard that fused hard rock with mainstream pop on "Liar," "It's Only Money," "God Gave Rock and Roll to You," and "Hold Your Head Up" (No. 5). Argent and White also supervised Blunstone's solo albums *One Year* and *Ennismore.*

In 1977, after Argent had run its course, Rod Argent decided to concentrate on session work. "I thought, 'I'm 30 years old, it's time to explore some different avenues.' " Argent played keyboards with The Who on *Who Are You;* with Roger Daltrey on *One of the Boys;* and with Andrew Lloyd Webber on *Variations, Cats,* and *Starlight Express,* the project where he met Van Hooke.

Argent, with Van Hooke as co-producer, scored the theme music for London Weekend Television's production of the 1986 World Cup and wrote incidental music for productions by the British Broadcasting Service. He also composed a musical, *Masquerade,* that was staged at the Young Vic Theatre in London.

Not surprisingly, Argent's musical instincts influence his approach to production. "The performance is everything," Argent says. "If you're recording a singer, then everything should stem from that. We try to get the master vocal at an early stage so that everything being played reacts to the vocal as in a live situation."

Yet, for all his achievements, Argent approaches each new project as if it were his first. "I honestly do think that I've only just got underway," he muses. "Maybe that's a state of mind." —BEN CROMER

Argent: *Argent,* Epic, 1969, 1970 • *All Together Now,* Epic, 1972 • "Hold Your Head Up," Epic, 1972, 1981 (*England Rocks 1*) • *In Deep,* Epic, 1973, 1995 • *Encore: Live in Concert,* Epic, 1974 • *Nexus,* Epic, 1974 • *Circus,* Epic, 1975 • *Counterpoints,* United Artists, 1975.

Blunstone, Colin: *Ennismore,* Epic, 1971 • *One Year,* Epic, 1971 • "I Don't Believe in Miracles," Epic, 1972, 1981 (*England Rocks 1*).

Doyle, Patrick: *Into the West* soundtrack, SBK, 1993.

Griffith, Nanci: *Late Night Grande Hotel,* MCA, 1991 • *MCA Years: A Retrospective,* MCA, 1993.

Kadison, Joshua: "Jessie," SBK, 1993 • *Painted Desert Serenade,* SBK, 1993, 1995.

Shear, Jules: *Jules Shear,* Polydor, 1993 • *Healing Bones,* Island, 1994 • *Sun Ain't Gonna Shine Anymore,* Island, 1994.

Siffre, Labi: *Man of Reason,* China, 1991.

Soraya: *En Esta Noche,* Polydor, 1996 • *On Nights Like This,* Island, 1996.

Stevens, Shakin': "Radio," Sony, 1992.

Tikaram, Tanita: *Ancient Heart,* Reprise, 1988 • "Loving You," NME, 1990 (*The Last Temptation of Elvis*) • *The Sweetkeeper,* Reprise, 1990 • *Everybody's Angel,* Reprise, 1991.

Zombies, The: *Odyssey and Oracle,* Rhino, 1968, 1987 • "Time of the Season," Date, 1969 • "Time of the Season," Epic, 1976, 1981 (*England Rocks 1*).

The Artist Formerly Known As Prince

See PRINCE

The Art of Noise

(ANNE DUDLEY, J. J. JECZALIK, GARY LANGAN)

The Art of Noise was assembled in London as the house band for Trevor Horn's (see entry) ZTT label, coming to prominence on ABC's *The Lexicon of Love* album in 1982.

Anne Dudley, J. J. Jeczalik, and Gary Langan—keyboard wizards all—made up the heart of the experimental sound collage, hip-hop ensemble. They were joined by Horn and Paul Morley, who created the song titles, and by 1984, the group had taken their samples and beats into the British Top 10 with "Close to the Edit."

Other hits followed, including a remake of "Peter Gunn" (No. 8 U.K.) with Duane Eddy; "Paranoimia" (No. 12 U.K.) with TV character Max Headroom; and their biggest hit, a stomping remake of Prince's (see entry) "Kiss" (No. 5 U.K.), with swinging Tom Jones on vocals.

Perhaps it's no surprise that sonic experimenters who could also craft hits would turn out to be producers of renown. Jeczalik, the Fairlight sampler master, has gone on to produce Pet Shop Boys (see entry), Nick Kamen, and Stephen "Tin Tin" Duffy. Langan, who engineered for Horn and A.O.N., has produced a variety of new wavers and modern rockers, including ABC, Big Country, and Public Image Limited (PIL). Anne Dudley has gone on to compose soundtracks for film and TV, including Phil Collins' *Buster, Say Anything,* and the Oscar-nominated *The Crying Game.* She won the 1997 Oscar for Original Musical or Comedy Score for *The Full Monty.* She also has a substantial career as an artist, working often with Killing Joke's Jaz Coleman.

Londoner Dudley played piano, recorder, and clarinet as a child, winning a piano competition at age 12. "I knew then that music was going to be my life," she relates in measured, refined tones.

In the Dudley household, music meant classical, so when she began to listen to pop music at around 14, she "found it to be incredibly glamorous." In particular, she loved the Beatles' *Sgt. Pepper's Lonely Hearts Club Band* album, "with its classical arrangements, beautiful counterpoint, and the drive of pop music."

At 16, she went wild and joined a dance band that played everything from waltzes to pop songs. She earned a bachelor's degree in piano and composition from London's Royal Academy of Music and a master's in musical analysis from London University, with her eye toward an academic career. But the siren call of pop was too strong, and as her freelance career heated up, Dudley found it "a bit more rewarding to be involved with something new rather than something centuries old."

Dudley met Horn when they worked in a dance band together. Meanwhile, she played piano for a BBC children's TV program, *Playschool,* and played in a pop rock band, Cindy and the Saffrons, with actress Joanne Whalley (Kilmer). As the '70s became the '80s, Horn turned his attention from his own band, the Buggles, to production, and Island set him up with his own label, ZTT Dudley, Langan, and Jeczalik joined him to work on albums for ABC, Malcolm McLaren, and Frankie Goes to Hollywood.

The Art of Noise arose from these sessions. As Dudley tells it, "We were just experimenting and having fun, and before we knew it we had a hit record. I was extremely surprised because I had never really thought about being an artist. It was quite fun while it lasted, and we made some seminal records."

How was the Art of Noise sound created? "We used the Fairlight to sample sounds like cars, doors, and machines," says Dudley. "We then adjusted the pitches of these samples and built the samples into patterns. Then, having done so, we put some nice jazzy chords and some beats underneath it all.

"I listened to 'Close to the Edit' recently and enjoyed it. It seems to be very confident, very humorous, with lots of changes in it. It isn't repetitive—that's the most irritating thing about a lot of dance music nowadays. I also like the eclectic influences we brought into the sound. A classical trumpet might appear, then a jazz saxophone, and then a bit of romantic poetry. Looking back on it, what was so experimental was bound to be commercial because of the joie de vivre."

The original Art of Noise split in the late '80s, but there are rumors of a Noise reunion with Dudley, Horn, Morley, and new member Lol Creme (10cc, Godley and Creme) bringing visuals into the mix. —ERIC OLSEN

Art of Noise: *The Art of Noise,* ZTT/Island, 1983 • *Into Battle With,* ZTT/Island, 1983 • "Close (to the Edit)," ZTT, 1984 • *Who's Afraid of the Art of Noise?,* Island, 1984, 1989 • "Legs," Chrysalis, 1985 • *In Visible Silence,* Off Beat, 1986, 1993 • "Paranoimia," China/Chrysalis, 1986 • *In No Sense? Nonsense!* China/Chrysalis, 1987 • *Best Of,* China/Polydor, 1988 • *Below the Waste,* Off Beat, 1989, 1994 • *The Ambient Collection,* China/Polydor, 1990 • "Yebo," China, 1995 • *Best Of,* Discovery, 1997.

Eddy, Duane: *Twang Thang: Anthology,* Rhino, 1993.

Jones, Tom: *Move Closer,* Jive, 1988.

Anne Dudley

Coleman, Jaz: *See* Dudley, Anne.

Collins, Phil: "A Groovy Kind of Love," Atlantic, 1988.

Deliverance: *Raise the Dragon,* IRS, 1984.

Dudley, Anne: w/ Jaz Coleman, *Songs from the Victorious City,* TVT, 1991 • w/ Jaz Coleman, "Ziggurats of Cinnamon/ Habebe," TVT, 1991 • *Knight Moves* soundtrack, Milan, 1993 • *Ancient and Modern,* Echo, 1995 • *Veni Emmanuel,* Echo, 1995 • *Kavanagh QC: Original Music from the ITV Series,* Virgin, 1997 • w/ Jaz Coleman, *Minarets and Memories,* TVT, 1997.

Harry, Debbie: *Debravation* (2 tracks), Sire/Reprise, 1993.

Moody Blues: *Greatest Hits,* Threshold/Polydor, 1989.

Sting (et al.): *Gentlemen Don't Eat Poets* soundtrack, Pangea, 1997.

COLLECTIONS

Buster soundtrack, Atlantic, 1988.

The World of Jeeves and Wooster, EMI, 1992.

Anne Dudley and J.J. Jeczalik

Mahlathini: *Paris: Soweto,* Polydor, 1989.

J.J. Jeczalik

Godley and Creme: *The History Mix,* Vol. 1, Polydor, 1985.
Kamen, Nick: *Us,* Sire, 1988.
Pet Shop Boys: *Disco,* EMI America, 1986 • "Opportunities,"
    EMI America, 1986 • *Please,* EMI America, 1986 •
    Discography: The Complete Singles Collection, EMI America,
    1991.
Tin Tin (Stephen Duffy): "Kiss Me," 10, 1984.

Gary Langan

ABC: *Beauty Stab,* Mercury, 1983 • *Absolutely ABC: The Best of
    ABC,* Mercury, 1990.
Big Country: *Eclectic,* Castle, 1996.
Divinyls: *What a Life,* Chrysalis, 1986.
Dream Academy: *The Dream Academy* (2 tracks), Warner
    Bros., 1985.
Hipsway: *Hipsway,* Columbia, 1986 • "The Honeythief,"
    Columbia, 1987.
Hothouse Flowers: *Home,* London, 1990.
Public Image Limited (PIL): "Body," Virgin, 1987 • *Happy?,*
    Virgin, 1987 • "Seattle," Virgin, 1987 • *Don't Ask Me* (EP),
    Virgin, 1990 • *Greatest Hits So Far,* Atlantic, 1990.
RPM: *Photogenic,* Warner Bros., 1984.
Spandau Ballet: *Through the Barricades,* Epic, 1986.
The The: *Infected,* Epic, 1986.
Then Jerico: *The Big Area,* MCA, 1989.
Voice of the Beehive: *Honey Lingers* (1 track), London, 1991.

Peter Asher

P eter Asher's productions are known for their clear
sonic quality and their enviable ability to yield hits
that don't compromise artistic integrity.

Born June 22, 1944, in London, Asher grew up in a
musical household, his mother having been an English
horn player with the London Symphony Orchestra. As
one half of the duo Peter and Gordon (with Gordon
Waller), Peter Asher had a taste of pop stardom when
his sister Jane's boyfriend, a certain Paul McCartney (see
entry), wrote the group its No. 1 "A World Without
Love" in 1964.

In all, Peter and Gordon had ten Top 40 hits, four of
them written by McCartney (nominally in collaboration

with John Lennon); the other three were "Nobody I
Know," "I Don't Want to See You Again," and
"Woman."

Had it been only for those hits, Asher might have
remained little more than an interesting footnote in pop
music history. But in 1969, while working as an A&R
man for the Beatles' Apple Records, Asher produced the
self-titled debut album for the then-unknown James
Taylor that was to set him on the road to production
superstardom. Although the record was not a huge hit,
it gave Asher the experience he needed for the work that
would soon follow.

The producer on more than 50 albums by artists as
diverse as Diana Ross, Randy Newman, Cher, and Tony
Joe White, Asher is best known for the string of hit
albums he produced for Taylor and Linda Ronstadt, two
artists he also represented through his management
company. The second Asher-produced Taylor album,
Sweet Baby James (No. 3), has worn well with time, and
has the same sort of home-grown charm of McCartney's solo debut album, with Taylor singing most of the
background vocals by himself, assisted by only a small
number of musicians. The album itself formed something of a blueprint for nearly all of Taylor's later
albums, combining ballads with straight-ahead rock
tunes, and a carefully chosen cover or two.

Besides propelling Taylor on a three-decade career
marked by spectacular commercial success and volumes
of critical acclaim, *Sweet Baby James* spawned the Amer-

ican singer/songwriter movement and inspired generations of like-minded artists, from Jackson Browne in the '70s to Tracy Chapman in the '80s to Shawn Colvin in the '90s.

Among Asher's most inspired works was Taylor's 1977 opus *JT* (No. 4), a gorgeous, lush production that featured multiple layers of instrumental and vocal harmonies and some of Taylor's best compositions. During this same period, Asher produced a series of albums that comprised Linda Ronstadt's commercial peak. *Heart Like a Wheel* (No. 1) featured the No. 1 single "You're No Good." Subsequent singles put the Asher-Ronstadt team on the map: "Poor Poor Pitiful Me," "Tumbling Dice," and "That'll Be the Day" (No. 11) proved that Asher could make as hard-driving a rock record as anyone, while "Blue Bayou" (No. 3) and "Ooh, Baby Baby" (No. 7) showed his depth and proved that his successes recording the deeper, more introspective side of Taylor were no accident.

After playing a prominent role in the music of the '60s and '70s, Asher proved himself ever capable of adapting to the times: he produced 10,000 Maniacs' *In My Tribe* and *Blind Man's Zoo* (No. 13), the first of which yielded the radio hits "What's the Matter Here?" and "Like the Weather." These albums combine the three elements that have become trademarks of Asher's style: careful craftsmanship, a relaxed atmosphere, and a compelling immediacy that draws the listener and the performers closer together.

Ronstadt says of their work together: "When I worked with Peter, I chose all the material, and I had a great deal to do with the arrangements. I think the producer's job is to listen to the sound in great detail and then make thoughtful adjustments. And sometimes that means you don't make any adjustments at all and sometimes you make a lot. For example, Burt Bacharach (see entry) would write the song, the arrangement, do all the background vocals—it was his picture and you colored it. With Peter it can be his picture and you're the crayon, or you can be the crayon and he holds it. . . . There was a project we started together and we eventually abandoned—the song 'Oh No Not My Baby.' Peter later did it with Cher, and I ended up recording it and producing it myself. If you listen to that song, you can hear what it was that Peter brought to our partnership: my version was done without him, and Cher's was done with him."

Ronstadt adds, "Peter is as good as they come. He has excellent ears. He can hear sound in greatly magnified detail. It is comparable to sitting around in the rain forest with a bunch of natives and all of a sudden they all get up and pick up their spears and run out and come back later with a pig, and you didn't hear anything at all. In any mix, there are lines and colors moving against the general soundscape and you become amazingly sensitive to detail. Like how the bass and drums fit together, or how the guitar tones have changed."

Besides producing her signature hits, Asher inspired Ronstadt's own production. "In terms of listening and how to layer on things and careful, practical, pragmatic considerations, Peter taught all of us—me, [collaborator] George Massenburg (see entry), [guitarist/songwriter] Andrew Gold, and [guitarist/producer] Waddy Wachtel. We all learned from his production and his careful organization. Now as a producer myself, I feel I benefited enormously from the Peter Asher school of record production."

Cher praises Asher for his even temperament. "He is so calm," she says. "He gives you the feeling that everything is fine and that if you make a mistake it's OK. He makes you feel really relaxed with him so that good things can come out. In the studio, you have this feeling that he is only doing your album, that there is nothing else going on in his life. Of course, you know that is not true, but he gives you that feeling."

Asked how he achieved intimacy in the artificial environment of the recording studio—particularly on Taylor's albums—Asher says, "I don't do anything deliberately to engender that intimacy. That's James' skill as a singer. I do try to make the artists feel at home in the studio so that they don't have to worry about other things such as, 'Are the musicians going to play the right parts?'"

Although he has made many "serious" albums in his career, Asher still has a predilection for pure pop. "I like serious albums, but I also really like catchy hit singles even if they are ephemeral," he says. "Sometimes as a business we're in danger of taking ourselves too seriously. It is just pop music. It's supposed to be ephemeral." —DANIEL J. LEVITIN

Arena, Tina: *Show Me Heaven,* Columbia, 1996.

Berlin, Irving: *The 100th Anniversary Collection,* MCA, 1988.

Blakeley, Peter: *Harry's Cafe De Wheels* (7 tracks), Echo Chamber/Capitol, 1989.

Broadway Cast: *The Pirates of Penzance,* Elektra, 1981.

Cetera, Peter: *You're the Inspiration: A Collection,* River North, 1997.

Cher: *Cher,* Geffen, 1987 • "Dangerous Times," Geffen, 1987 • w/ Peter Cetera, "After All," Geffen, 1989 • *Heart of Stone,* Geffen, 1989 • "Love on a Rooftop," Geffen, 1989 • "Baby I'm Yours," Geffen, 1990 (*Mermaids* soundtrack) • "Heart of Stone," Geffen, 1990 • "The Shoop Shoop Song (It's in His Kiss)," Geffen, 1990 (*Mermaids* soundtrack) • *Love*

Hurts (4 tracks), Geffen, 1990 • "Oh No Not My Baby," Geffen, 1992.

Diamond, Neil: *Lovescape* (2 tracks), Columbia, 1991 • *The Christmas Album*, Columbia, 1992 • *Up on the Roof—Songs from the Brill Building*, Columbia, 1993 • *The Christmas Album*, Vol. 2, Columbia, 1994 • *In My Lifetime*, Sony, 1996.

Fordham, Julia: "Love Moves in Mysterious Ways," Virgin, 1991 (*The Butcher's Wife* soundtrack) • *Swept*, Virgin, 1991.

Gold, Andrew: *What's Wrong with This Picture?*, Asylum, 1976 • "Lonely Boy," Asylum, 1977.

Ingram, James: *The Power of Great Music: The Best Of*, Qwest/WB, 1991.

Jo Mama: *Jo Mama*, Atlantic, 1970.

Joel, Billy: *Greatest Hits*, Vol. 3, Columbia, 1997 • "Hey Girl," Columbia, 1997 • "To Make You Feel My Love," Columbia, 1997.

Keith, Barbara: *Barbara Keith*, Verve, 1969.

Kosinec, Tony: *Bad Girl Songs*, Columbia, 1971.

Kreviazuk, Chantal: "Surrounded," Columbia, 1997 • *Under These Rocks and Stones*, Columbia, 1997.

Mary's Danish: *American Standard*, Morgan Creek, 1992.

McKee, Maria: "Show Me Heaven," Geffen, 1990 (*Days of Thunder* soundtrack).

Newman, Randy: *Randy Newman's Faust*, Reprise, 1995.

Newton-John, Olivia: *Olivia*, Festival, 1972, 1992 • *Back to Basics* (1 track), Geffen, 1992 • "I Want to Be Wanted," Geffen, 1992.

Raitt, Bonnie: *The Glow*, Warner Bros., 1979 • *The Bonnie Raitt Collection*, Warner Bros., 1990.

Ronin: *Ronin*, Mercury, 1980.

Ronstadt, Linda: *Heart Like a Wheel*, Capitol, 1975 • "Heat Wave/Love Is a Rose," Asylum, 1975 • *Prisoner in Disguise*, Asylum, 1975 • "When Will I Be Loved," Capitol, 1975 • "You're No Good," Capitol, 1975 • *Greatest Hits*, Vol. 1, Asylum, 1976 • *Hasten Down the Wind*, Asylum, 1976 • "That'll Be the Day," Asylum, 1976 • "The Tracks of My Tears," Asylum, 1976 • "Blue Bayou," Asylum, 1977 • "It's So Easy," Asylum, 1977 • *Simple Dreams*, Asylum, 1977 • "Someone to Lay Down Beside Me," Asylum, 1977 • "Back in the USA," Asylum, 1978 • *Living in the USA*, Asylum, 1978 • "Poor Poor Pitiful Me," Asylum, 1978 • "Tumbling Dice," Asylum, 1978 • "Ooh, Baby Baby," Asylum, 1979 • "How Do I Make You," Asylum, 1980 • "Hurt So Bad," Asylum, 1980 • "I Can't Let Go," Asylum, 1980 • *Mad Love*, Asylum, 1980 • "Get Closer," Asylum, 1982 • *Get Closer*, Asylum, 1982 • "I Knew You When," Asylum, 1983 • "What's New," Asylum, 1983 • *What's New* Asylum, 1983 • *For Sentimental Reasons*, Asylum, 1986 • "When You Wish upon a Star," Asylum, 1986 • *Canciones de Mi Padre*, Asylum, 1987 • w/ James Ingram, "Somewhere out There," MCA, 1987 (*American Tail* soundtrack) • *Cry Like a Rainstorm-Howl Like the Wind*,

Elektra, 1989 • w/ Aaron Neville, "Don't Know Much," Elektra, 1989 • w/ Aaron Neville, "All My Life," Elektra, 1990 • "The Blacksmith," Elektra, 1990 (*Rubaiyat: Elektra's 40th Anniversary*) • *Frenesi*, Elektra, 1992.

Ross, Diana: "If We Hold on Together," MCA, 1988 (*Land Before Time* soundtrack) • *Force Behind the Power* (6 tracks), Motown, 1991 • *Diana: The Ultimate Collection*, Motown, 1993.

Sanborn, David: *Love Songs*, Warner Bros., 1988.

Shrieve, Michael: *The Big Picture*, Atlantic, 1989.

Souther, John David: *Black Rose*, Asylum, 1976.

Starr, Ringo: *Time Takes Time* (3 tracks), Private, 1991.

Stewart, John: *Williard*, Capitol, 1970.

Taylor, James: *James Taylor*, Apple, 1969 • "Fire and Rain," Warner Bros., 1970 • *Sweet Baby James*, Warner Bros., 1970 • "You've Got a Friend," Warner Bros., 1970 • "Long Ago and Far Away," Warner Bros., 1971 • *Mud Slide Slim and the Blue Horizon*, Warner Bros., 1971 • *One Man Dog*, Warner Bros., 1972 • "Don't Let Me Be Lonely Tonight," Warner Bros., 1973 • *Greatest Hits*, Warner Bros., 1976, 1988 • "Handy Man," Columbia, 1977 • *JT*, Columbia, 1977 • "Your Smiling Face," Columbia, 1977 • *Flag*, Columbia, 1979 • "Up on the Roof," Columbia, 1979 • *Dad Loves His Work*, Columbia, 1981 • w/ J.D. Souther, "Her Town Too," Columbia, 1981 • *Live in Rio*, Columbia, 1991.

Taylor, Kate: *Sister Kate*, Cotillion, 1971.

10,000 Maniacs: *In My Tribe*, Elektra, 1987 • *Blind Man's Zoo*, Elektra, 1989 • *You Happy Puppet*, Elektra, 1989.

White, Tony Joe: *Tony Joe White*, Warner Bros., 1971 • *The Best Of*, Warner Bros., 1973.

Williams Brothers: *The Williams Brothers* (1 track), Warner Bros., 1991.

Zander, Robin: *Robin Zander*, Interscope, 1993, 1995.

Jon Astley

Jon Astley is one of the most successful producers of reissues and compilations. Yet, because he concentrates primarily on that market, he enjoys far less recognition than his exploits deserve.

Astley is largely responsible for the superbly crafted reissues of the Who's classic canon: from *The Who Sell Out* and *Live at Leeds* to *Who's Next* and *Who Are You*. Moreover, he produced *My Generation: The Very Best of The Who*, co-produced *The Best of Pete Townshend*, and was one of three producers who compiled *The Who: Thirty Years of Maximum R&B*.

The latter project, originally envisioned as a compilation of previously released material, was expanded to include unreleased studio and concert recordings. Consequently, the job involved sorting through years of tapes—a task that Astley, Townshend's brother-in-law, tackled with glee.

"He knew I was an old Who fan," Astley says of Townshend. "I also knew where the tapes were and what was on them. I said, 'Let's go back to the mults,'" referring to multitrack tapes.

Astley approaches each reissue as if he is restoring paintings by the great masters. Indeed, Astley's work is essentially transparent. "I want to recreate the same picture as the original: not just brighten up the sound but carefully transfer it to the digital domain."

An Englishman born January 22, 1951, Astley enjoyed his first taste of fame in the '70s as an engineer under the tutelage of Glyn Johns (see entry) before entering the production realm. "I was working with Glyn on Eric Clapton's *Slowhand* album when Glyn was offered the *Who Are You* project," recalls Astley. "He asked me, 'Do you want to do it?' So I said, 'I'd better ask Pete.'"

With Townshend's blessing, Astley co-produced that album with Johns, ultimately helping mold one of the Who's best-loved songs. "Pete came in with the backing track for 'Who Are You' that went on for 25 minutes," Astley explains. "Then Glyn said, 'Jon, sort that one out.' The next day I played them a 6-minute version of Pete's demo and that became the backing track."

Flushed with that success, Astley handled the production of Clapton's *Just One Night* (No. 2). In the '80s Astley hooked up with Phil Chapman, collaborating on Corey Hart's *Boy in the Box* (No. 20) with the hit "Never Surrender" (No. 3). Astley also launched a career as a performer, recording two albums that featured his Bowie-esque voice augmented by such guests as Clapton and Sad Cafe's Ian Wilson.

In the '90s Astley has emerged as a key confidant of Townshend's, coordinating the majority of Townshend's and the Who's back catalog. "He's taught me ever so much," Astley says of his mentor. Clapton, another old friend and fishing companion, has continued to rely on Astley's expertise. Astley, along with engineer and co-producer Andy MacPherson and PolyGram's Bill Levenson, was behind the Clapton boxed set *Crossroads II*.

Astley's production touches are subtle. For instance, for *My Generation: The Very Best of the Who* he used an alternate Townshend guitar track on "Let's See Action" and an additional flute on "Join Together." Another Astley trait that he often employs on the Who's compilations is tight song sequencing. As Astley puts it: "The Who always played that way on stage." —BEN CROMER

Astley, Jon: *The Compleat Angler,* Atlantic, 1988.
Astley, Virginia: *Promise Nothing,* Les Disques du Crepuscule, 1983, 1984 • *Hope in a Darkened Heart,* DGC, 1986.
Bethnal: *Crash Landing,* Vertigo, 1979.
Clapton, Eric: *The Rainbow Concert,* Polydor, 1973, 1995 • *Just One Night,* RSO, 1980 • *Crossroads,* Polydor, 1988 • *Crossroads 2: Live in the 70's,* Chronicles/Polydor, 1996.
Daltrey, Roger: *The Best Bits,* MCA, 1982 • *Parting Should Be Painless,* WEA, 1984.
Distractions: *Nobody's Perfect,* Island, 1980.
Gibbons, Steve: *Street Parade,* RCA, 1980.
Harry, Debbie: *Debravation* (2 tracks), Sire/Reprise, 1993.
Hart, Corey: *First Offense,* EMI America, 1983 • "Sunglasses at Night," EMI America, 1983 • "It Ain't Enough," EMI America, 1984 • *Boy in the Box,* EMI America, 1985 • *The Singles,* EMI America, 1992.
Haworth, Bryn: *Keep the Ball Rolling,* A&M, 1979.
Loz Netto: *Loz Netto,* Atlantic, 1982.
Mas, Carolyn: *Modern Dreamer,* Mercury, 1981.
McLelland, Sandy, and the Back Line: *Sandy McLelland and the Back Line,* Mercury, 1979.
Orphan: *Salute,* Portrait,1985.
Pretty Things: *Cross Talk,* Warner Bros., 1980.
Townshend, Pete:
Coolwalkingsmoothtalkingstraightsmokingfirestoking: *The Best Of,* Atlantic, 1996.
Who, The: *Who Sell Out,* Polydor, 1967, 1995 • *Live at Leeds,* MCA, 1970, 1995 • *Who's Next,* MCA, 1971, 1995 • *Quadrophenia,* Polydor, 1973, 1995 • *The Who by Numbers,* MCA, 1975, 1995 • "Who Are You," MCA, 1978 • *Who Are You,* Polydor, 1978 • *It's Hard,* MCA, 1982, 1995 • *Who's Better, Who's Best—This Is the Very Best of the Who,* MCA, 1988 • "Saturday Night's Alright (for Fighting)," Polydor, 1991 (*Two Rooms: Songs of Elton and Bernie Taupin*) • *The Who: Thirty Years of Maximum R&B,* Polydor, 1995 • *Live at the Isle of Wight 1970,* Columbia, 1996.

COLLECTIONS
Message to Love Wight Festival 1970, Columbia, 1996.

Chet Atkins

Chet Atkins has long been known as one of the world's greatest guitar players. That title has often eclipsed the fact that he's also a legendary producer credited with developing the "Nashville Sound." As head of RCA's Nashville division, Atkins' production skill shaped the careers of artists such as Jim Reeves, Don

Gibson, Jerry Reed, and Dolly Parton and helped the country genre gain deserved respect in the music world.

Born June 20, 1924, in Luttrell, Tennessee, Chester Burton Atkins developed a love for the guitar early. He watched his older brother play the instrument, and at 5, he started playing an old ukulele with strings made of screen door wire. A sickly child who battled asthma, Atkins went to live with his music teacher–evangelist father in Georgia when he was 10. At 17, he left home to pursue a music career and wound up working for local radio stations and with country artists such as Red Foley, Archie Campbell, Bill Carlisle, and Homer and Jethro.

He signed with RCA Victor in 1947 and moved to Nashville in 1950, the same year he began playing on the Grand Ole Opry as a soloist and guitarist for the Carter Sisters. It was during this period that singles like "Mainstreet Breakdown" and "Galloping Guitars" established Atkins as a major instrumentalist. In the mid-'50s he began working for RCA A&R man Steve Sholes. "I started out doing covers," he remembers. "My boss in New York would send a pop hit down and say 'Go in and record this with Johnny and Jack or Minnie Pearl and Grandpa Jones.' The first one I did was 'Papa Loves Mambo' with Minnie and Grandpa Jones. It was fun.

"Then Mr. Sholes, my boss, had bought Elvis's contract and became a big man in the company. He got promotions, so that gave me a chance to record all the artists. I took over and started recording all the country artists and eventually started recording some of the pop artists, too. We'd bring in Perry Como and people like that. It was fun making pop records. I did that and I finally realized I was working much too hard and putting too many hours in the day. . . . So I hired Jerry Bradley and he hired some more people and gradually I turned all the artists over to producers who worked within the company."

Before turning the reins over to other producers, Atkins carved a successful niche for himself at RCA and was known for adding his talents to a variety of important sessions. In 1956, he arranged the first Nashville sessions for Elvis Presley and played guitar on "Heartbreak Hotel" and "I Want You, I Need You, I Love You." His guitar prowess can also be heard on such Hank Williams hits as "Jambalaya," "Settin' the Woods on Fire," and "Your Cheatin' Heart." He was promoted to manager of operations for RCA in 1957, the year he moved his work to the legendary RCA Studio B. By 1968, he was named RCA's vice president of Nashville operations and continued to head the label until he resigned in 1981. A year later he signed as an artist to Columbia, for which he still records.

Atkins says he enjoyed his years in production. "It was one of my favorite roles because I was able to get with my friends in the studio and have a lot of fun producing records," he says. "We'd all gather around the piano and work out an arrangement and it was a good chore. I don't really know how they do it now. I think they do it different. I don't think they gang around the piano and everybody contributes like we used to."

Atkins' philosophy as a producer was simple. "I looked for good songs I thought fit the artist. I encouraged the artist to look for songs also, and I tried to find a hit along the line somewhere," he says. "I also watched for good musicians who came to town who would be able to add something different to the records I made. Floyd Cramer is an example of that. I talked him into coming in from Shreveport, Louisiana."

In addition to good musicians, Atkins was always on the lookout for good songs. When asked what he thought made a hit, he says, "It was my first impression, if I liked a tune when I first heard it. I realized that my senses were right. . . . I realized that I was kind of square and what I liked, the public would usually like also."

When it came to signing talent, Atkins says he looked for artists with a unique quality to their voice. "My boss told me years ago you have to find an artist with an edge to his voice," Atkins relates, "somebody who will sound good on the jukebox. On jukeboxes years ago, there were no highs; about all you could hear were the lows because of the way they were constructed. . . . So we selected artists who had an edge to their voices. Ernest Tubb and Charley Pride are good examples."

Asked whether being such a stellar guitar player gave him a different view as a producer, Atkins counters that his production skills were shaped more by his musical influences. "It was a combination of things," he says. "My dad was a classical teacher and I moved to Georgia when I was very young, and there was a lot of black blues down there and I got into that. And I got to listening to jazz a lot. I always loved jazz like they played in the '30s, '40s, and '50s. I had influence from a lot of different directions, including country. So when production was turned over to me, I had a lot of different things to draw from."

A key architect of the Nashville sound, Atkins pioneered a smoother, more pop-flavored style that took country to a wider audience. He won't take credit for that, however.

"I don't really remember," he says, when asked how the Nashville sound was born. "I was just trying to keep my job and keep from getting fired and I'm sure Owen [Bradley; see entry] was doing the same thing. I was working for Mr. Sholes in New York and Owen was working for Mr. Paul Cohen and we were just trying to survive, and the way you survive is by making hit records. I'd been fired many times in my life, in many time zones, so I was just trying to keep my job, and every once in a while I made some hit records. I made two smashes in one day, 'I Can't Stop Loving You' and 'Oh Lonesome Me' (for Don Gibson, No. 7 and No. 1 country, respectively). So after that I regained confidence and realized I knew a good song when I heard it and I realized I could go into the studio and make hit records, and I did that."

Atkins has won 9 Country Music Association Awards and 14 Grammy Awards. One of the entertainment industry's most lauded luminaries, Atkins has a street named after him in Nashville and has been inducted into the Georgia Music Hall of Fame. In 1992, the National Academy of Recording Arts and Sciences (NARAS) awarded him their Lifetime Achievement Award at the Grammy ceremony, and in 1997 he was honored with the Billboard Century Award. Atkins has recorded 75 albums and has collaborated with numerous artists, including Arthur Fiedler and the Boston Pops Orchestra, Mark Knopfler, Eric Johnson, Earl Klugh, Les Paul (see entry), Jerry Reed, Hank Snow, Merle Travis, Doc Watson, Paul McCartney (see entry), George Benson, Neil Diamond, Steve Wariner, Lenny Breau, and Tommy Emmanuel. Still active on Nashville's live music scene, Atkins could be found Monday nights performing to standing room only crowds at Nashville's Caffe Milano. In June 1997, Nashville held its first Chet Atkins Musician Days, a week-long festival celebrating Atkins' idea of honoring "the people who make the singers look good." —DEBORAH EVANS PRICE

Ann-Margret: *Let Me Entertain You,* RCA, 1996.

Arnold, Eddy: *Christmas with,* RCA, 1961 • *Have Guitar, Will Travel,* RCA, 1967 • "Then You Can Tell Me Goodbye," RCA, 1968 • *Last of the Love Song Singers: Then and Now,* RCA, 1995 • *Essential,* RCA, 1996.

Atkins, Chet: *Chet Atkins at Home,* RCA, 1958 • *Pickin' My Way,* RCA, 1959 • *Teensville,* RCA, 1960 • *Chet Atkin's Workshop,* RCA, 1961 • *Caribbean Guitar,* RCA, 1962 • *Down Home,* RCA, 1962 • *The Guitar Genius,* RCA, 1963 • *Chet Atkins Picks on the Beatles,* RCA, 1966, 1996 • *Chet,* RCA, 1967 • *Relaxin' with Chet,* RCA, 1969 • w/ Jerry Reed, *Me and Jerry,* RCA, 1970 • *In Hollywood,* RCA, 1971 • *Pick on the Hits,* RCA, 1972, 1989 • *Alone,* RCA, 1973 • w/ Les Paul, *Chester and Lester,* RCA, 1976 • w/ Les Paul, *Guitar Monsters,* RCA, 1978 • *Stay Tuned,* Columbia, 1985 • *Street Dreams,* Columbia, 1986 • *Sails,* Columbia, 1987 • *Chet Atkins, C.G.P.,* Columbia, 1988 • *Guitar for All Seasons,*

Pair, 1988 • *In Three Dimensions,* Longhorn, 1988 • *Country Gems,* Pair, 1990 • w/ Jerry Reed, *Sneakin' Around,* Columbia, 1992 • *Tennessee Guitar Man,* Pair, 1992. • *Read My Licks,* Columbia, 1994 • *Almost Alone,* Columbia, 1996 • *Music from Nashville, My Home Town,* RCA, 1996 • See also Reed, Jerry.

Bare, Bobby: "Detroit City," RCA, 1963 • "500 Miles Away from Home," RCA, 1963 • *Essential,* RCA, 1997.

Browns, The: "The Three Bells," RCA, 1959.

Brown, Jim Ed, and the Browns: *Essential,* RCA, 1996.

Burton, Gary: *Tennessee Firebird,* RCA, 1966.

Cline, Patsy: *Remembering,* MCA, 1976.

Como, Perry: *Legendary Performer,* RCA, 1976 • *Yesterday and Today: A Celebration in Song,* RCA, 1993.

Cramer, Floyd: *Best Of,* RCA, 1970 • *The Essential Series,* RCA, 1995.

Elledge, Jimmy: "Funny How Time Slips Away," RCA, 1961.

Endsley, Melvin: *I Like Your Kind of Love,* Bear Family, 1992.

Everly Brothers: *Pass the Chicken and Listen,* RCA, 1972 • *Heartaches and Harmonies,* Rhino, 1994.

Gibson, Don: *Collectors Series,* RCA, 1985 • *A Legend in His Time,* Bear Family, 1987 • *The Singer, the Songwriter,* Bear Family, 1991.

Hawkins, Hawkshaw: *Hawk, 1953–1961,* Bear Family, 1991.

Hirt, Al: *Sugar Lips,* RCA, 1964.

Homer and Jethro: *Playing It Straight,* RCA, 1962 • *America's Favorite Song Butchers,* Razor & Tie, 1997.

Jennings, Waylon: *Collectors Series,* RCA, 1968 • *Greatest Hits,* RCA, 1979 • *The Best of Waylon Jennings,* RCA, 1983 • *Only Daddy That'll Walk the Line: The RCA Years,* RCA, 1993 • *The Essential,* RCA, 1996.

Johnnie and Jack: *Johnnie and Jack and the Tennessee Mountain Boys,* Bear Family, 1992.

Little Richard: *Little Richard/Roy Orbison,* RCA, 1990.

Locklin, Hank: *Nashville Women,* RCA, 1967 • *Country Hall of Fame,* RCA, 1968 • *My Love Song for You,* RCA, 1968.

Martin, Janis: *Female Elvis: Complete Recordings, 1955–1960,* Bear Family, 1987.

Miller, Roger: *King of the Road,* Epic, 1992.

Orbison, Roy: *The RCA Days,* RCA, 1988 • *Little Richard/Roy Orbison,* RCA, 1990.

Paul, Les: See Atkins, Chet.

Piano Red: *The Doctor's In,* Bear Family, 1993.

Presley, Elvis: *Elvis,* RCA, 1956 • *Elvis Presley,* RCA, 1956 • "I Want You, I Need You, I Love You," RCA, 1956 • "A Big Hunk O' Love," RCA, 1959 • "Are You Lonesome Tonight," RCA, 1960 • *Elvis Is Back!* RCA, 1960 • "It's Now or Never," RCA, 1960 • "Can't Help Falling in Love," RCA, 1961 • "Good Luck Charm," RCA, 1962 • *The Lost Album,* RCA, 1991.

Pride, Charley: "All I Have to Offer You (Is Me)," RCA, 1969 • *Super Hits,* RCA, 1996 • *Essential,* RCA, 1997.

Reed, Jerry: "Amos Moses," RCA Victor, 1970 • "When You're Hot, You're Hot," RCA, 1971 • w/ Chet Atkins, *Me and Chet*, RCA, 1972 • "Lord, Mr. Ford," RCA, 1973 • *The Best of Jerry Reed*, RCA, 1992 • *Super Hits*, RCA, 1997 • *See also* Atkins, Chet.

Reeves, Jim: *He'll Have to Go and Other Hits*, RCA, 1960, 1992 • *12 Songs of Christmas*, RCA, 1963 • "I Guess I'm Crazy," RCA, 1964 • *Greatest Hits*, RCA, 1966 • *Am I That Easy to Forget* RCA, 1973 • *Four Walls: The Legend Begins*, RCA, 1991 • *Best Of*, RCA, 1992 • *The Essential Series: Jim Reeves*, RCA, 1995.

Rich, Charlie: "I Don't See Me in Your Eyes Anymore," RCA, 1974 • "She Called Me Baby," RCA, 1974 • *She Called Me Baby*, RCA, 1974 • "There Won't Be Anymore," RCA, 1974 • *There Won't Be Anymore*, RCA, 1974.

Robinson, Floyd: "Makin' Love," RCA, 1959.

Scott, Jack: *Scott on Groove*, Bear Family, 1984, 1989 • *Classic Scott*, Bear Family, 1994.

Snow, Hank: "Hello Love," RCA, 1974 • *Singing Ranger*, Vol. 2, Bear Family, 1990 • *Essential*, RCA, 1997.

West, Dottie: *Essential*, RCA, 1996.

Whittaker, Roger: *The Wind Beneath My Wings*, RCA, 1982 • *Classics Collection*, Vol. 2, Liberty, 1992 • *Annie's Song*, RCA, 1994 • *Greatest Hits*, RCA, 1994.

Dallas Austin

By the tender age of 26, Atlanta denizen Dallas Austin was already a veteran at writing, producing, and remixing hits for an impressive list of clients that includes Madonna, Boyz II Men, TLC, Michael Jackson, Janet Jackson, Joi, and Usher. Along with Antonio "L.A." Reid, Kenneth "Babyface" Edmonds, Jermaine Dupri (see entries), and the Organized Noize troop, Austin is synonymous with Atlanta's stature as one of the world's most vital sources of pop and R&B production talent.

Born in Columbus, Georgia, in 1972, Austin started playing guitar at age 6 and later switched to keyboards. He moved to Atlanta in 1986 and played keyboards in various funk bands. In 1989, he got his first taste of success as a producer when he worked with Joyce "Fenderella" Irby (formerly of Klymaxx) on "Mr. DJ," a No. 2 R&B hit that featured rapper Doug E. Fresh. Within two years, Austin's production talents would be heard on Troop's gold single "I Will Always Love You" and Another Badd Creation's "Iesha" and "Playground" (Nos. 9 and 10, respectively). Austin was on his way.

Although he had already amassed an enviable level of success by then, his breakthrough year was 1991, when he produced most of Boyz II Men's smash debut, *Cooleyhighharmony*, a nine-times platinum album that peaked at No. 3 on the Billboard 200. The following year, Austin produced and wrote material for TLC's quadruple-platinum debut album, *Ooooooohhh . . . on the TLC Tip* (No. 14), which spawned three Top 10 singles.

Besides his work as an independent producer, Austin operates a studio, Dallas Austin Recording Projects (DARP), whose clients have included Too Short, TLC, George Clinton, Nine Inch Nails, Madonna, and D.J. Jazzy Jeff & the Fresh Prince. Austin is also the proprietor of the Rowdy Records label, which had a short-lived association with Arista and later merged with Volcano Records to create the Freeworld imprint. —PAUL VERNA

A Few Good Men: "All My Love," LaFace, 1995 • "Let's Take a Dip," LaFace, 1995 • "Tonite," LaFace, 1995 • "Walk You Thru," LaFace, 1995.

Abdul, Paula: *Head over Heels* (1 track), Virgin, 1995.

After 7: "All About Love," Virgin, 1992 • "He Said, She Said," Virgin, 1992 • "Kickin' It," Virgin, 1992 • "No Better Love," Virgin, 1992 • *Takin' My Time*, Virgin, 1992.

Another Bad Creation: *Coolin' at the Playground Ya Know*, Motown, 1991 • "Iesha," Motown, 1991 • "Jealous Girl," Motown, 1991 • "Little Soldiers," Motown, 1991 • "My World," Motown, 1991 • "Parents," Motown, 1991 • "Playground" (remix), Tommy Boy, 1991, 1992 (*MTV Party to Go*, Vol. 2) • "That's My Girl," Motown, 1991.

Boyz II Men: *Cooleyhighharmony*, Motown, 1991 • "It's So Hard to Say Goodbye," Motown, 1991 • "Lonely Heart," Motown, 1991 • "Motownphilly," Tommy Boy, 1991, 1992 (*MTV Party to Go*, Vol. 2) • "Please Don't Go," Motown, 1991 • "Sympin'," Motown, 1991 • "This Is My Heart," Motown, 1991 • "Under Pressure," Motown, 1991 • *Cooleyhighharmony* (Spanish), Motown, 1993 • "Thank You," Motown, 1994 • *II* (1 track), Motown, 1994 • *The Remix Collection* (1 track), Motown, 1995 • *The Remix Collection* (2 tracks), Motown, 1995.

Brand New Heavies: "Dream on Dreamer" (remix), Delicious Vinyl, 1992.

Brown, Bobby: *Remixes in the Key of B*, MCA, 1993.

Clinton, George: *Hey Man . . . Smell My Finger*, Paisley Park, 1993.

Covington, Trisha: "Slow Down" (remix), Columbia, 1994.

Cox, Deborah: *Deborah Cox*, Arista, 1995 • "Just Be Good to Me," Arista, 1995 • "My Radio," Arista, 1995 • "Sentimental," Arista, 1995.

D.J. Jazzy Jeff & the Fresh Prince: *Code Red*, Jive, 1993 • "Scream," Jive, 1993.

Fishbone: *Chim Chim's Badass Revenge,* Rowdy, 1996.

Fled: *Fled,* Rowdy, 1996.

For Real: *Free,* Rowdy, 1996 • "Good Morning Sunshine," Rowdy, 1996 • "Hold Me," Rowdy, 1996 • "How Can I Get Close to You," Rowdy, 1996 • "Like I Do," Rowdy, 1996.

Franklin, Aretha: *Greatest Hits, 1980–1994,* Arista, 1994.

Funkadelic, Featuring George Clinton and Belita Woods: "Black People," PolyGram, 1995 (*Panther* soundtrack).

Hi-Five: "Faithful," Jive, 1993 • *Faithful,* Jive, 1993 • "Miss U Girl," Jive, 1993.

Highland Place Mobsters: "Let's Get Naked," LaFace, 1992 • *1746dcga30035,* LaFace, 1992.

Illegal: *The Illegal,* Rowdy, 1993 • *Untold Truth,* Rowdy, 1993.

Jackson, Michael: *History: Past, Present and Future Part 1,* Epic, 1995 • "This Time Around," Epic, 1995.

Joi: *Pendulum Vibe,* Capitol, 1994.

Jones, Grace: "7 Day Weekend," LaFace, 1992 (*Boomerang* soundtrack).

Lysette: "Young, Sad and Blue," Freeworld, 1997.

Madonna: *Bedtime Stories,* Maverick/Sire, 1994 • "Secret," Maverick/Sire, 1994.

Monica: "Don't Take It Personal," Rowdy/Arista, 1995 • "Like This and Like That," Rowdy, 1995 • *Miss Thang,* Rowdy, 1995 • w/ Naughty By Nature, "Ain't Nobody," Def Jam, 1996 (*The Nutty Professor* soundtrack).

QT: "My Baby Mama" (remix), Rowdy, 1996.

Questionmark Asylum: *Questionmark Asylum,* Kaper/BMG, 1995.

Shadz of Lingo: *A View to a Kill,* Limp, 1994.

TLC: "Ain't Too Proud 2 Beg," LaFace, 1992 • "Hat 2 Da Back," LaFace, 1992 • *Oooooohhh . . . on the TLC Tip,* LaFace, 1992 • "What About Your Friends," LaFace, 1992 • *Crazy Sexy Cool,* LaFace/Arista, 1995 • "Creep," LaFace/Arista, 1995.

Troop: *Attitude,* Atlantic, 1991.

Waters, Crystal: "Body Music," Mercury, 1997.

Babyface with L.A. Reid

Babyface

(KENNETH EDMONDS)

By 1997, Kenneth "Babyface" Edmonds had scored 116 Top 10 R&B and pop hits. Forty-six topped the R&B charts, 16 topped the pop charts. One of his productions, "End of the Road" by Boyz II Men, stayed at No. 1 for 13 weeks, breaking the record held by Elvis Presley's "Heartbreak Hotel."

Given his enviable track record, it is no surprise that Edmonds is one of the most sought-after writers, composers, and producers on the market. He has built a "Babyface" sound, resplendent in silky-smooth R&B flavor. While critics, peers, and fans heap him with praise, Edmonds doesn't believe he's that musically influential. He's quite content to point the finger at others, like L.A. Reid and Terry Riley (see entries).

"When L.A. and I were working together, we were trying to stay in the game," he says. "We weren't necessarily pioneers. Teddy Riley was a pioneer, he came up with new jack swing, with something different. It was hip and fresh. He created a movement there. We were following people, but because we played the way we played, it made it sound a little different. We had this slick L.A.-Babyface sound."

He feels he's got a way to go yet. "Hopefully, I'm just starting—there's a lot of things to come and some cool things in the future. I don't feel I've written my greatest song yet: the thing that is going to last forever. I think that goes hand in hand with producing as well."

Although he's best-known for production now, "Slow Jam," which Edmonds wrote for Midnight Star in the early '80s, launched him toward fame.

Before he was Babyface, a nickname bestowed upon

him by Parliament/Funkadelic bassist Bootsy Collins, Edmonds was a struggling songwriter in Michigan. While playing in a band called the Crowd Pleasers, he placed "Slow Jam" with Midnight Star. That band asked him to play guitar on the tune and possibly contribute background vocals. When he played his 4-track demo for Midnight Star in the studio, that band asked him to help the Deele, a group Star had signed to a production deal. Although Babyface had met Deele drummer Antonio "L.A." Reid in Indianapolis two years earlier, the Deele's album was the first time the two worked together, and they began to forge a natural chemistry.

"That's where the producing actually started," Edmonds recalls. "Before, I had just been doing demos on the 4-track machine." He went on to join the Deele and produced their second album. Production scared him at first. "The whole producing thing seemed a little intimidating," he says. "It seemed like the boards and all that stuff was too much to know. How do you know if you've got the right performance? How do you know when it feels good? It just seemed like a thing Quincy Jones [see entry] would know."

His songwriting prowess and less than fulfilling work with other producers helped his production style evolve, particularly after he and Reid ended their production team in 1994.

He records most of the song before the vocals, a practice he began with Reid. "What we did was we made it easy," Edmonds says. "We figured it out so all you had to do was come in and sing. The backgrounds were done, it was just the lead, so it was kind of quick-service production. That was one of the attractive things about working with us—we worked fast, but we still did it with quality."

Artists knew they wouldn't have to waste time trying out a bunch of different songs as the producers searched for the right material, Edmonds says. "We knew what we wanted. The other thing is, we brought the music. The songs were there and that was probably 70 percent of the reason why they were there—to get the songs. The production was, like, an add-on."

While work with the Deele and on his own was successful, he didn't feel he could legitimately call himself a producer until 1987, when his production of the Whispers' "Just Gets Better with Time" hit big. The L.A.-Face team went on to score hits galore in the late '80s, including Karyn White's self-titled debut album (No. 19), Bobby Brown's *Don't Be Cruel* (No. 1), and Babyface's own *Tender Lover* (No. 14), from 1989.

While Edmonds goes out of his way to give proper credit, he enjoys being a hot producer. "The best thing about it is you get a chance to work with artists that you

would never have been able to work with and people you grew up listening to and people you never listened to before. So, the future is always bright, there's always something else you can go to—it's endless."

The kind of collaboration he enjoys surfaced in his 1996 album, *The Day,* where his guest stars included Eric Clapton, Stevie Wonder, LL Cool J, Kenny G, and Mariah Carey. For Edmonds, the Clapton sessions were a return to when the two worked on Clapton's "Change the World," which Babyface produced.

"It was an honor to go in with Eric Clapton. It was a little scary, too," he admits. "I didn't know if he'd like anything I did. Being around good musicians only makes you a better musician. It makes you reach down and pull out things you haven't used in a long time, that you didn't know you still had in you. To go in with guys like Eric or Stevie Wonder is the coolest."

Despite his reputation, Babyface doesn't always score. "Everyone thinks I hit every time and I don't," he says. "But you get this type of reputation and it's not really about that. It's about trying to make good music and if we get hits, then that'll be great. But if not, at least we can say we got quality work." —DAVID JOHN FARINELLA

Abdul, Paula: *Forever Your Girl,* Virgin, 1988 • "Knocked Out," Virgin, 1988 • *Shut up and Dance: Dance Mixes,* Virgin, 1990.

After 7: *After 7,* Virgin, 1989 • "Can't Stop," Virgin, 1990 • "Ready or Not," Virgin, 1990 • *Reflections,* Virgin, 1995 • *Very Best Of,* Virgin, 1997.

Az Yet: *Az Yet,* LaFace, 1996 • "Last Night," LaFace, 1996 • featuring Peter Cetera, "Hard to Say I'm Sorry," LaFace, 1997.

Babyface: "It's No Crime," Solar, 1989 • *Lovers,* Columbia, 1989 • *Tender Lover,* Solar/Epic, 1989 • "Tender Love," Solar, 1990 • "Whip Appeal," Solar, 1990 • *A Closer Look,* Epic, 1991 • *For the Cool in You,* Epic, 1993 • "And Our Feelings," Epic, 1994 • "Never Keeping Secrets," Epic, 1994 • "When Can I See You," Epic, 1994 • *When Can I See You Again* (EP), Epic, 1995 • "Every Time I Close My Eyes," Epic, 1996 • *The Day,* Epic, 1996 • "This Is for the Lover in You," Epic, 1997.

Bell, Biv, Devoe: *Hootie Mack,* MCA, 1993.

Blige, Mary J.: "Not Gon' Cry," Arista, 1995 (*Waiting to Exhale* soundtrack) • *Share My World,* MCA, 1997.

Boys, The: "Dial My Heart," Motown, 1988 • *Messages from the Boys,* Motown, 1988 • "Lucky Charm," Motown, 1989.

Boyz II Men: "End of the Road," Biv 10, 1992 • "End of the Road," Tommy Boy, 1992, 1993 (*MTV Party to Go,* Vol. 3) • *Cooleyhighharmony* (Spanish), Motown, 1993 • "I'll Make Love to You," Motown, 1994 • *II* (2 tracks), Motown, 1994

• *The Remix Collection* (2 tracks), Motown, 1995 • "Water Runs Dry," 1995 • "A Song for Mama," Motown, 1997 • *Evolution,* Motown, 1997.

Brandy: "Sittin' up in My Room," Arista, 1995 (*Waiting to Exhale* soundtrack).

Braxton, Toni: "Another Sad Love Song," LaFace, 1993 • "Breathe Again," LaFace, 1994 • *Toni Braxton,* LaFace, 1994 • "You Mean the World to Me," LaFace, 1994 • "Let It Flow," Arista, 1995 (*Waiting to Exhale* soundtrack) • "You're Makin' Me High," LaFace, 1996 • "You're Makin' Me High" (remix), Arista, 1996 • *Secrets,* LaFace, 1996.

Brown, Bobby: "Don't Be Cruel," MCA, 1988 • *Don't Be Cruel,* MCA, 1989 • "Every Little Step," MCA, 1989 • "On Our Own," MCA, 1989 • "Rock Wit' Cha," MCA, 1989 • "Roni," MCA, 1989 • *Dance . . . Ya Know It!* Motown, 1990 • *Bobby* (3 tracks), MCA, 1992 • "Good Enough," MCA, 1992 • "Humpin' Around," MCA, 1992 • *Remixes in the Key of B,* MCA, 1993.

Campbell, Tevin: "Can We Talk," Qwest, 1993 • *I'm Ready,* Qwest, 1993 • "I'm Ready," Qwest, 1994.

Carey, Mariah: *Music Box,* Columbia, 1993.

Clapton, Eric: "Change the World," Reprise, 1996 (*Phenomenon* soundtrack).

Color Me Badd: *Now and Forever,* Warner Bros., 1996.

Cox, Deborah: *Deborah Cox,* Arista, 1995.

Dame, Damian: *Damian Dame,* LaFace, 1991.

Davis, Mary: *Separate Ways,* Tabu, 1989.

DeBarge, El: "Can't Get Enough," Reprise, 1994 • *Heart, Mind and Soul,* Reprise, 1994.

Deele, The: *Eyes of a Stranger,* Solar, 1988 • "Two Occasions," Solar, 1988.

Dru Hill: "We're Not Making Love No More," LaFace, 1997.

Easton, Sheena: *Lover in Me,* MCA, 1988 • "The Lover in Me," MCA, 1989.

En Vogue: *EV 3,* EastWest, 1997 • "Whatever," EastWest, 1997.

Evans, Faith: "Kissing You," Arista, 1995 (*Waiting to Exhale* soundtrack).

For Real: "Love Will Be Waiting at Home," Arista, 1995 (*Waiting to Exhale* soundtrack) • *Free,* Rowdy, 1996.

Franklin, Aretha: *Greatest Hits, 1980–1994,* Arista, 1994 • "Willing to Forgive," Arista, 1994 • "It Hurts Like Hell," Arista, 1995 (*Waiting to Exhale* soundtrack).

Gill, Johnny: *Johnny Gill,* Motown, 1990 • "My, My, My," Motown, 1990 • *Provocative,* Motown, 1993 • *Let's Get the Mood Right,* Motown, 1996.

Houston, Whitney: "I'm Your Baby Tonight," Arista, 1990 • *I'm Your Baby Tonight,* Arista, 1990 • "I'm Every Woman," Arista, 1992 (*The Bodyguard* soundtrack) • w/ CeCe Winans, "Count on Me," Arista, 1995 (*Waiting to Exhale* soundtrack) • "Exhale (Shoop Shoop)," Arista, 1995 (*Waiting to Exhale* soundtrack) • "Why Does It Hurt So Bad," Arista, 1995 (*Waiting to Exhale* soundtrack) • "My Heart Is Calling," Arista, 1997.

Jackson, Jermaine: *You Said,* LaFace, 1991.

Jacksons, The: *2300 Jackson Street,* Epic, 1989.

Jon B.: *Bonafide,* Yab Yum, 1995 • "Pretty Girl," Yab Yum/550/Epic, 1995 • "Someone to Love," Yab Yum, 1995.

Jones, Donnell: *My Heart,* LaFace, 1996.

Kenny G.: *Moment,* Arista, 1996.

Khan, Chaka: "My Funny Valentine," Arista, 1995 (*Waiting to Exhale* soundtrack).

LaBelle, Patti: "My Love, Sweet Love," Arista, 1995 (*Waiting to Exhale* soundtrack).

Mac Band, Featuring the McCampbell Brothers: "Roses Are Red," MCA, 1988 • "Stuck," MCA, 1988.

Madonna: *Bedtime Stories,* Maverick/Sire/WB, 1994 • "Take a Bow," Maverick/Sire/WB, 1995.

Marie, Sonja: "And I Gave My Love to You," Arista, 1995 (*Waiting to Exhale* soundtrack).

Milestone: "I Care 'Bout You," LaFace, 1997.

Moore, Chante: "Wey U," Arista, 1995 (*Waiting to Exhale* soundtrack).

Nadanuf, Featuring Kurtis Blow: "The Breaks," Reprise, 1997.

New Edition: *Solo Hits,* MCA, 1996.

Outkast: *ATLiens,* LaFace, 1996 • "Jazzy Belle," LaFace, 1997.

Pebbles: *Pebbles* (1 track), MCA, 1987 • "Girlfriend," MCA, 1988 • "Girlfriend" (remix), MCA, 1988 • *Always,* MCA, 1990 • "Giving You the Benefit," MCA, 1990.

Salter, Sam: "After 12, Before 6," LaFace, 1997 • *It's On Tonight,* LaFace, 1997.

Shanna: "How Could You Call Her Baby," Arista, 1995 (*Waiting to Exhale* soundtrack).

SWV: "All Night Long," Arista, 1995 (*Waiting to Exhale* soundtrack).

TLC: "Baby-Baby-Baby," LaFace, 1992 • *Ooooooohhh . . . on the TLC Tip,* LaFace, 1992 • *Crazy Sexy Cool,* LaFace/Arista, 1995 • "This Is How It Works," Arista, 1995 (*Waiting to Exhale* soundtrack).

Usher: *My Way,* LaFace, 1997.

Whispers, The: *Just Gets Better with Time,* Solar, 1987 • "Rock Steady," Solar, 1987.

White, Karyn: *Karyn White,* Warner Bros., 1988 • "The Way You Love Me," Warner Bros., 1988 • "Love Saw It," Warner Bros., 1989 • "Secret Rendezvous," Warner Bros., 1989 • "Superwoman," Warner Bros., 1989 • *Make Him Do Right,* Warner Bros., 1994.

Williams, Vanessa: *Sweetest Days,* Wing/Mercury, 1995.

COLLECTIONS

Waiting to Exhale soundtrack, Arista, 1995.

Burt Bacharach

Champion of an elegant but inviting pop sophistication, Burt Bacharach (winner of three Academy Awards and four Grammys) is among the best and most popular songwriters of this half-century. Ira Gershwin once signed a piece of sheet music to him: "For Burt, the 5th B in no particular order—Beethoven, Brahms, Berlin, Bach and Bacharach."

His outstanding productions of his own hit compositions for Dionne Warwick, B. J. Thomas, Neil Diamond, Roberta Flack, Patti LaBelle, and others—coupled with his track record as a recording artist, with five charting solo albums, including his 1971 eponymous album, which went to No. 18—make Bacharach an especially important and enduring figure.

Burt Bacharach was born in Kansas City in 1928. His father, a former professional football player, was a syndicated columnist whose work brought the family to Forest Hills, New York, when Burt was a child. A somewhat reluctant musical youth, Burt practiced piano, drums, and cello when he would rather have been playing football or chatting up girls.

"I didn't much like my lessons or what I was playing, but then I heard Ravel and I felt an excitement," he says. "I was also influenced when I was a kid by people like Dizzy Gillespie, Tadd Dameron, and Charlie Parker. I studied classical music with people like Henry Cowell and Darius Milhaud [at the New School for Social Research, the David Mannes School in New York, the Berkshire Music Center, Montreal's McGill University, and the Music Academy of the West in Santa Barbara, California]. I was influenced by a lot of Brazilian music. I guess that's why I don't much go for vanilla major chords. I much prefer a major or a minor seventh to a straight C."

The young hipster played piano in jazz bands while in high school in the '40s, and in the Army from 1950 to 1952. After the service, he played and arranged for Vic Damone, the Ames Brothers, Steve Lawrence, Paula Stewart (the first of his four wives—followed by actress Angie Dickinson, lyricist Carole Bayer Sager, and current wife Jane) and Marlene Dietrich, who doted on him. Bacharach's first big success as a writer was Marty Robbins' "The Story of My Life" (No. 15 U.S., No. 1 U.K.) in 1957, which was co-written by Bacharach's best-known collaborator, Hal David. The team followed in 1958 with Perry Como's "Magic Moments."

Arranging was next. "My first record as an arranger was Jerry Butler's 'Make It Easy on Yourself' [1962]. I wasn't the producer, Calvin Carter was, but they let me go in the studio with a big string section, and voices, and Jerry to make this record, and that started it. The most important thing was that I got the essence of what I heard when I was writing the song. When I write songs, I hear a pretty good outline of where the strings come in, where lines come, what the bass line is, what the percussion parts are, what the flow is. I hear it as a whole thing.

"I started producing the records out of self-defense, to protect the material. I just thought that my songs were getting changed from the way I heard them when I was writing them. There was a really good song that had a three-bar phrase, instead of the standard four-bar phrase, and the A&R man convinced me that it would be better with a four-bar phrase, making the song out of proportion and ruining it. I didn't want that to happen again."

In 1962 Bacharach wrote songs for the Drifters ("Mexican Divorce"), and at a Drifters session he met a young backup singer ("in pigtails and sneakers") named Dionne Warwick, who on the strength of Bacharach-David compositions and productions was to rival Aretha Franklin as the most important female singer of the '60s. The trio produced twenty Top 40 singles between 1962 and 1970, including seven Top 10s: "Anyone Who Had a Heart," "Walk on By," "Message to Michael," "I Say a Little Prayer," "Do You Know the Way to San Jose," "This Girl's in Love with You" and "I'll Never Fall in Love Again."

"If I had to pick a favorite singer, it would be Dionne," states Bacharach. "She was a dream vehicle for those years. She has such wide emotional range. She can be very understated and delicate, plus she is capable of going for the jugular. A marvelous voice. The only song I can think of where someone else approached Dionne's version is Aretha's 'Say a Little Prayer.' That's a great, great record."

Bacharach and Warwick waited until 1985 for their first No. 1 together, "That's What Friends Are For." "There are two records I have produced that thrill me. They're probably better records than songs. They're both with Carole [Bayer Sager]—'On My Own' [Patti LaBelle and Michael McDonald, No. 1] and 'Friends.' Those are both great-sounding records with a wide, broad spectrum."

Remarkably, Bacharach has been even more successful in the U.K. Frankie Vaughan, Cilla Black, Sandie Shaw, the Walker Brothers, Herb Alpert, and Burt himself all hit No. 1 there in the '60s with Bacharach-David tunes.

True "Kings of All Media," Bacharach and David

also wrote the film scores for *What's New, Pussycat?*, *Alfie*, *Casino Royale,* and *Butch Cassidy and the Sundance Kid,* which won Oscars for Best Original Score and Best Theme Song for "Raindrops Keep Fallin' on My Head" (No. 1 for B. J. Thomas) in 1969. They also wrote the musical *Promises, Promises,* which won a Tony and a Grammy (Best Score for an Original Cast album) in 1969 and ran for three years.

Sometimes, even the greats don't hear a song right. In 1970, the Carpenters' "(They Long to Be) Close to You" (arranged by Richard Carpenter; see entry) went to No. 1. "You can be awfully wrong, too. I made a record of 'Close to You' with Richard Chamberlain in the early '60s that was terrible in comparison to the Carpenters. They nailed it right on the head. I was a mile off base."

Bacharach has enjoyed a renaissance of late. In 1994 his picture appeared in homage on the cover of Oasis's huge *Definitely Maybe* album. Oasis's Noel Gallagher joined Bacharach onstage during a concert in 1996 for a duet on the enduring and endearing "This Guy's in Love with You." In 1996 Bacharach collaborated with Elvis Costello (see entry) on the soundtrack for the movie *Grace of My Heart.* The 1997 Julia Roberts film *My Best Friend's Wedding* features five Bacharach songs, including the film's centerpiece, where an entire wedding party, and fellow diners, belt out the classic "I Say a Little Prayer." Ever-suave Burt himself appears tinkling the ivories and crooning atop a Las Vegas limo in Mike Myers' 1997 spy-spoof *Austin Powers.* —ERIC OLSEN

Bacharach, Burt: *Reach Out,* A&M, 1967 • "I'll Never Fall in Love Again," A&M, 1969 • *Make It Easy on Yourself,* A&M, 1969 • *Burt Bacharach,* A&M, 1971 • *Living Together,* A&M, 1973 • *Greatest Hits,* A&M, 1974 • *Futures,* A&M, 1977 • *Burt Bacharach Plays the Burt Bacharach Hits,* MCA, 1997.
Bishop, Stephen: *On and On: Best Of,* MCA, 1994.
Bryson, Peabo: *Born to Love,* Capitol, 1983.
Cole, Natalie: *Everlasting,* Manhattan/Elektra, 1987, 1991.
DeBarge: *The Ultimate Collection,* Motown, 1997.
Diamond, Neil: "Heartlight," Columbia, 1982 • *Heartlight,* Columbia, 1982 • *Greatest Hits, 1966–1992,* Columbia, 1992 • *In My Lifetime,* Sony, 1996.
Flack, Roberta: "Making Love," Atlantic, 1982 • *Softly with These Songs: The Best Of,* Atlantic, 1993.
Franklin, Aretha: *What You See Is What You Sweat,* Arista, 1991.
Knight, Gladys: *I Feel a Song,* Buddah, 1974 • *All Our Love,* MCA, 1988.
LaBelle, Patti: w/ Michael McDonald, "On My Own," MCA, 1986 • *Be Yourself,* MCA, 1989 • *Greatest Hits,* MCA, 1996.
Pitney, Gene: "(The Man Who Shot) Liberty Valance," Musicor, 1962.

Sager, Carole Bayer: *Sometimes Late at Night,* Boardwalk, 1981.
Streisand, Barbra: *Till I Loved You,* Columbia, 1988.
Stylistics: *Love Talk,* Amherst, 1991.
Thomas, B.J.: "Raindrops Keep Falling on My Head," Scepter, 1969 • *Raindrops Keep Falling on My Head,* Scepter, 1969 • *Everybody's out of Town,* Scepter, 1970 • *Greatest Hits,* Rhino, 1990, 1991.
Warwick, Dionne: "Don't Make Me Over," Scepter, 1962 • "Anyone Who Had a Heart," Scepter, 1963 • "Reach Out for Me," Scepter, 1964 • "Walk On By," Scepter, 1964 • "You'll Never Get to Heaven (If You Break My Heart)," Scepter, 1964 • "Are You There (with Another Girl)," Scepter, 1966 • "I Just Don't Know What to Do with Myself," Scepter, 1966 • "Message to Michael," Scepter, 1966 • "Trains and Boats and Planes," Scepter, 1966 • "Alfie," Scepter, 1967 • *Golden Hits, Part One,* Scepter, 1967 • "I Say a Little Prayer," Scepter, 1967 • "The Windows of the World," Scepter, 1967 • "Do You Know the Way to San Jose," Scepter, 1968 • "Promises, Promises," Scepter, 1968 • "Who Is Gonna Love Me," Scepter, 1968 • "(Theme from) Valley of the Dolls," Sceptor, 1968 • "The April Fools," Scepter, 1969 • "This Girl's in Love with You," Scepter, 1969 • "I'll Never Fall in Love Again," Scepter, 1970 • "Let Me Go to Him," Scepter, 1970 • "Make It Easy on Yourself," Scepter, 1970 • and Friends, "That's What Friends Are For," Arista, 1985 • *Friends,* Arista, 1985 • *Reservations for Two,* Arista, 1986 • w/ Jeffrey Osborne, "Love Power," Arista, 1987 • *Greatest Hits, 1979–1990,* Arista, 1989 • *Friends Can Be Lovers,* Arista, 1993 • *Sings the Bacharach and David Songbook,* Music Collection Int., 1994.

COLLECTIONS

Together? soundtrack, RCA, 1979.
Lost Horizon soundtrack, Razor & Tie, 1997.

Rodger Bain

Rodger Bain's production career was relatively brief, covering only five or six years in the early '70s. However, if he had only produced the album that was apparently the first job of his career, he would still have had a hand in shaping rock history. That album was Black Sabbath's self-titled 1970 debut (No. 8 U.K.) on Britain's Vertigo label. According to discographies, and to Sabbath's bassist Geezer Butler, it was probably his first production credit.

"He was house producer at Vertigo, the label we were signed to," recalls Butler. "They didn't want to get an independent producer, but it was fine with us because we didn't even know you needed a producer. We were young and green. He was the only one that showed an interest."

Bain was sharing offices with Gus Dudgeon (see entry), who later became known for his role in creating the Elton John sound. (In fact, producer Neil Kernon—see entry—worked in that building for a music publisher and credits Bain and Dudgeon with steering him into a production career.) But Dudgeon was less taken with Sabbath than Bain was. Butler says, "We had a meeting with him and he said, come back when you can play your instruments and write songs. He said [our music] was the biggest load of crap he ever heard. But Rodger loved it and we got great feedback from him."

Indeed, Bain went on to produce Sabbath's next two albums, *Paranoid* (No. 12) and *Masters of Reality* (No. 8). The three albums he did were essential in establishing the Black Sabbath sound and image, and were the band's best-selling albums as well. The sound on those albums doesn't have the thickness of modern sound, but Butler explains the circumstances of the recording: "We had 16 hours to record over a two-day period with 4-track machines. The record company didn't want to spend any money. Nobody really understood what we were doing. He had us play live in the studio. Everything was first take—maybe three overdubs.

"I think he did an absolutely incredible job. I always remember when we heard it back—we had never heard ourselves and we were comparing it to the Beatles' big album production. We didn't realize how much he captured our raw sound until years later." Butler adds that Bain's simple production ("He didn't do anything that wasn't necessary") was essential to those albums' success. The bare production features Tony Iommi's isolated-sounding guitar up front in the mix, side-by-side with Ozzy Osbourne's shell-shocked yowl.

The fact that Bain encouraged a band whose take on the infant genre of metal was so extreme and so critically reviled at the time was likely crucial to their confidence. Today Sabbath's influence is heard in virtually every band making heavy music. Bain produced a series of other British bands, mostly in a heavy, dirty, blues-boogie vein, including Dirty Tricks, Barclay James Harvest, Wild Turkey, and the successful-in-England riff-rock trio Budgie. After Sabbath, the most significant credit in his portfolio was Judas Priest's 1974 debut, *Rocka Rolla*. Bain's production credits ceased after 1976. Butler says he thinks Bain may have become disillusioned with the business. "I think he got screwed on his royalties like we all did. The last time I saw him, he was with Huey Lewis—that was maybe 18, 19 years ago."
—ANASTASIA PANTSIOS

Alquin: *Nobody Can Wait Forever,* Polydor, 1975.
Barclay James Harvest: *Everyone Is Everybody Else,* Polydor, 1974 • *Live,* Polydor, 1974.
Black Sabbath: *Black Sabbath,* Vertigo/WB, 1970 • *Paranoid,* Vertigo/WB, 1970 • *Master of Reality,* Vertigo/WB, 1971 • *We Sold Our Souls for rock 'n' roll,* Warner Bros., 1976, 1988.
Brown, Arthur: *Dance,* Gull, 1974.
Budgie: *Budgie,* MCA, 1971 • *Squawk,* Roadrunner, 1971 • *In for the Kill,* MCA, 1974.
Dirty Tricks: *Dirty Tricks,* Polydor, 1974.
Freedom: *Through the Years,* Vertigo/Cotillion, 1971.
Judas Priest: *Rocka Rolla,* Gull/Visa, 1974 • *Hero Hero,* Transluxe, 1979, 1997.
Troggs, The: *Archeology, 1966–1976,* Fontana, 1992.
Wild Turkey: *Battle Hymn,* Chrysalis, 1971.

Arthur Baker

When Arthur Baker describes his production philosophy as being flexible, he knows what he's talking about. Whether he was acting as a producer, writer, or mixer, Baker has bounced among sessions with acts like Afrika Bambaataa, New Order, and Bob Dylan. Quite an array, and through it all Baker boils it down thus: "The philosophy is that with each project and each artist you need to lend a different ear. Some people do not need much, except you being there and telling them when it's finished or when it is as good as it could be; other people need a lot more."

For a guy who didn't want to be in a band, but wanted to make music, he seems to understand the personality dynamics behind the scenes. "When it's a band, [the producer] needs to play psychiatrist and get between them," he explains. "Working with New Order, a band like that, with four distinctive personalities, you have to really almost be a referee at times and inspire them and sort out problems and all that. Also, with New Order I would end up writing with them, where it was almost like becoming a member of the band. Working with Dylan or someone like that is a different thing altogether. It's just sort of cleaning up stuff that he would put on tape. He knew what he wanted, but you would have to make what he wanted work in the form of a record."

Photo by Pete Walsh

entry] on David Bowie [see entry] records and that was probably one of the first rock producers whose sound I noticed, along with George Martin and the Beatles."

Although he's been called upon purely to mix albums and songs, mixing is not his first choice. "The bad thing about mixing is you kind of lose contact with the band," he explains. "So, when you're just doing mixing and then you get put in a situation where you have to work with a band, you sort of forget how to do it in a way. I think I've done more mixing than production, and I think my production has been more of mixes in a way. When you're mixing and the band is away, then you can do what you want. You don't have to deal with the band, and mixing is much easier than record producing from that aspect. Some people just love to mix, like Tom Lord-Alge and Bob Clearmountain [see entry], because there's no one to bother you. You can get your head around the track and you just mix it. It's definitely a different mind set, and if you're in a really good position with a great band, it is really rewarding, but when it's one of those nightmare situations, it can go on forever."

In order to open his mind he's been spending time since he moved to London working with younger bands, such as the alt-popsters Ash. "I can learn a lot from them and their freshness. That is what keeps music exciting, working with new artists. I don't try to push my own sound, just add to it what it needs. I've worked on lots of different types of music and you can't really have a sound per se, if you do that. You really have to work with the artist."

Taking a glance at just three of Baker's credits (his own "Message Is Love" with Al Green, "Planet Rock" by Sonic Soul Force featuring Afrika Bambaataa, and the "Sun City" single and album), it's pretty clear that he's had an influence on the way music is performed.

Did he realize his music could have that power? "When I did "Planet Rock" I went home the night we finished the track and told my wife we had made music history," he says. "We did something different and I knew people would like it. When I recorded 'Message Is Love' [which he wrote as well] it was No. 6 in Germany when the Berlin Wall went down. When you do something great, you usually know it. I know there were times that I had that feeling, that I did something special, and people usually have felt the same."

Then again, he's had some "special" moments that perhaps people wouldn't find too satisfying. Remember Dylan's statement that he wanted to do an album like Madonna or Prince? Well, Baker didn't take him seriously until a mixing session one day, and with a laugh he describes the scene: "I was mixing his record and he was in front of the board playing his guitar," he recalls. "I

And some of those things were both producing and engineering nightmares, Baker recalls. "On *Empire Burlesque,* Dylan would have three background singers in the same mike as him, so let's say his vocal was good and the others' weren't." He pauses. "You have to work around his dislike of the studio."

While Dylan disliked the studio, Baker remembers that he was still attracted to its possibilities. "He would always say, 'I want to make a record like Madonna or Prince. I want to sell a lot of records.' I always told him he could do whatever he wanted. He always wanted things done really quickly to get out of the studio," Baker says. "I don't think he enjoyed being in the studio."

Which explains why Dylan depended on the engineers to clean up his work so much, and why Baker feels fortunate that he came by his technical knowledge honestly. After working as a DJ and in record stores, Baker spent time in some of Boston's better-known studios learning how to engineer. "I took an engineering course and the owner of a studio gave me some spec time to do dance music," he remembers. "That was my first experience working within a recording studio."

And yet he was aware of who was producing whom. "When I listened to records [when he was younger] I would always look at the back to see who wrote the song and who produced it," he remembers. "I was really into black music, which was really producer-oriented music. I also noticed names like Tony Visconti [see

turned the sound down and I hear him singing 'Like a Virgin.' " —DAVID JOHN FARINELLA

Artists United Against Apartheid: "Sun City," Manhattan, 1985.

Babes in Toyland: "We Are Family" (remix), Reprise, 1995.

Backbeat Disciples: "It's Your Time," Breakout/A&M, 1989 • *Merge*, Breakout/A&M, 1989 • "Talk It Over," Breakout/A&M, 1989 • w/ Al Green, "The Message Is Love," Breakout/A&M, 1989 • "Last Thing on My Mind," Breakout/A&M, 1990 • *Give in to the Rhythm*, RCA, 1991 • "Let There Be Love," Arista, 1991 • "Leave the Guns at Home," RCA, 1992.

Baker, Arthur, Featuring Nikeeta: "IOU," RCA, 1992.

Bambaataa, Afrika: w/ Soulsonic Force, "Looking for the Perfect Beat," Tommy Boy, 1982 • w/ Soulsonic Force, "Planet Rock," Tommy Boy, 1982 • w/ Soulsonic Force, *Planet Rock: The Album*, Tommy Boy, 1986 • *Don't Stop . . . Planet Rock* (remix EP), Tommy Boy, 1992.

Beck, Jeff: *Beckology*, Epic/Legacy, 1991, 1995 • *Flash*, Epic, 1985, 1995.

Big Audio: *Higher Power*, Columbia, 1994, 1995.

Black Uhuru: *Brutal*, RAS, 1986.

Bowie, David: "Fame 90," Rykodisc, 1990.

Brooklyn Funk Essentials: *Cool and Steady and Easy*, Dorado, 1994.

Campbell, Tevin: *T.E.V.I.N.*, Warner Bros., 1991.

Cherry, Neneh: "Buffalo Stance" (remix), Virgin, 1989.

Circuit II: *Can't Tempt Fate*, Elektra, 1985.

Clemons, Clarence: *Hero*, Columbia, 1985.

Criminal Element Orchestra: *Locked Up*, WTG, 1989.

Downing, Will: "A Love Supreme," 4th & B'Way, 1988.

Dylan, Bob: *Empire Burlesque*, Columbia, 1985.

Face to Face: *Face to Face*, Epic, 1984 • *Confrontation*, Epic, 1985, 1986.

General Public: "Never You Done That," IRS, 1984.

Harry, Debbie: *Def, Dumb and Blonde* (1 track), Sire/Reprise, 1989 • "Sweet and Low," Sire/Reprise, 1989 • *Debravation* (1 track), Sire/Reprise, 1993.

Hendryx, Nona: *The Heat*, RCA, 1985.

Holliday, Jennifer: *Best Of*, Geffen, 1996.

Hugh, Grayson: *Road to Freedom*, MCA, 1992.

Naked Eyes: *Fuel for the Fire*, EMI America, 1984 • "(What) in the Name of Love," EMI America, 1984.

New Edition: *Candy Girl*, Streetwise, 1983 • *Greatest Hits*, Vol. 1, MCA, 1991.

New Kids on the Block: *No More Games* (remix), Columbia, 1991.

New Order: "Touched By the Hand of God," Qwest, 1987 • *Substance*, Qwest, 1987 • "Confusion," Warner Bros., 1991 (*Volume One*) • "1963" (remix), London, 1995.

Pet Shop Boys: "In the Night" (remix), EMI America, 1986.

Planet Patrol: "I Didn't Know I Loved You ('til I Saw You Rock and Roll), Tommy Boy, 1983 • *Play at Your Own Risk*, Tommy Boy, 1983.

Rocca, John: *Best Of: I.O.U.*, Hot Productions, 1996.

Rockers Revenge: "Walking on Sunshine '89," FFRR, 1989 (*Silver on Black*).

Ross, Diana: *Greatest Hits: The RCA Years*, RCA, 1997.

Simon, Carly: *Spoiled Girl*, Epic, 1983.

Soulsonic Force: *See* Bambaataa, Afrika.

Springsteen, Bruce: "Dancing in the Dark" (remix), Columbia, 1984.

Tom Tom Club: "Call of the Wild," Reprise, 1989 (*Follow Our Tracks*, Vol. 2).

Roy Thomas Baker

B y producing the best albums of Queen and the Cars, the versatile Roy Thomas Baker played an essential role in ushering in two very different rock movements: pomp rock and new wave. Baker also produced pivotal albums by Be-Bop Deluxe, Dokken, Ozzy Osbourne, and Foreigner and brought the much-maligned corporate rock band Journey its first commercial success.

While Queen's albums are sonically and musically challenging epics, densely produced, the first four Cars albums are significantly sparer and more open-sounding, with an emphasis on high-gloss minimalism. What Baker's tracks share is his unfailing ear for taste, hooks, and musicality. Cutting-edge engineering plays an important role in the presentation of the songs, so in many cases the engineering and the songs become inseparable.

Baker's five Queen albums and the singles they spawned—including "You're My Best Friend" (No. 16), "Sheer Heart Attack," "Killer Queen" (No. 12), and "Bohemian Rhapsody" (No. 9)—are among the best-produced recordings in rock. The unique guitar tones on the solo for "Killer Queen," for example, (a sort of ultra harmonically distorted faux-violin tone) were utterly fresh at the time and have not been duplicated. The tongue-in-cheek "Bohemian Rhapsody" is an ambitious, boundary-stretching, meter-shifting opus that bathes the listener in dozens of Freddie Mercury vocal overdubs.

For *The Cars* (No. 18), Baker's instrumental layerings were more subtle, emphasizing the repetitive eighth-note rhythms that were to become a signature of the new wave sound. Their eponymous debut was recorded in London in just two weeks and produced three hit singles; the release of the follow-up had to be delayed until sales of *The Cars* subsided.

The high point of the Baker-Cars collaboration was their second album, the brilliant *Candy-O* (No. 3). This 1979 LP combined the urgency of the then-burgeoning punk movement with unabashedly pop arrangements and Beatles-like melodies, all delivered with quirky aloofness by frontman Ric Ocasek (see entry). Baker and the Cars repeated their success with two more platinum releases, *Panorama* (No. 5) and *Shake It Up* (No. 9).

The Cars notched their biggest sales with their fifth album (with producer Mutt Lange; see entry), the multiplatinum *Heartbeat City*. Yet *Heartbeat*, for all of its slick production and hit singles, failed to capture the brashness of the younger Cars, which Baker so deftly brought to vinyl. It is a testament to Baker's style that he was able to turn the minimalist arrangements of the Cars into records that sound so huge.

In both Queen and the Cars, Baker found brainy artists who appealed to college audiences and intellectuals. (All the members of Queen held Ph.D.s, while the Cars' often-cryptic lyrics provided hours of entertaining analysis for their legion of college fans.) As if to prove that he could simultaneously embrace the intelligentsia and the great unwashed, Baker spent part of 1978 and 1979 producing *Infinity* and *Evolution* (No. 20), the albums that established Journey's commercial viability. Had it not been for Baker, Journey might have disappeared into generic rock oblivion; sales of their first three albums had been disappointing, and their days at CBS were undoubtedly numbered. Baker brought the group two hit singles: "Lights" and "Wheel in the Sky." The two albums stayed on the Billboard charts for 123 weeks and 96 weeks, respectively, and each went triple-platinum.

Buoyed by such profits, CBS did what it is best at—it capitalized on its vaults. The patchwork *In the Beginning* was released while *Infinity* and *Evolution* were still on the charts, combining previously released tracks from the first three Journey albums.

Baker's ill-conceived Foreigner collaboration resulted in their third album (and its hit title track), 1979's *Head Games* (No. 5). Never known for production quality, Foreigner albums had a sort of garage quality that lent itself to such frat-rock songs as "Hot Blooded" and "Cold as Ice." But on *Head Games*, it sounded as though the garage band had moved into an even danker venue. What little clarity the instruments had had was now lost in dark, bleary engineering. The guitar tones are dull, the arrangements unimaginative. —DANIEL J. LEVITIN

Alice Cooper 80: *Flush the Fashion*, Warner Bros., 1980.

Anderson, Jon: *Three Ships*, Elektra, 1985.

Be-Bop Deluxe: *Futurama*, Harvest, 1975.

Calvert, Robert: *Captain Lockheed and the Starfighters*, UA/Passport, 1974.

Cars, The: "Just What I Needed," Elektra, 1978 • "My Best Friend's Girl," Elektra, 1978 • *The Cars*, Elektra, 1978 • *Candy-O*, Elektra, 1979 • "Let's Go," Elektra, 1979 • *Panorama*, Elektra, 1980 • "Touch and Go," Elektra, 1980 • "Shake It Up," Elektra, 1981 • *Shake It Up*, Elektra, 1981 • *Greatest Hits*, Elektra, 1985 • *Just What I Needed: The Cars Anthology*, Rhino, 1995.

Cheap Trick: *One on One*, Epic, 1982 • *Sex America Cheap Trick*, Epic, 1996.

Common Sense: "Never Give Up," Interscope, 1996 (*MOM: Music for Our Mother Ocean*) • *Psychedelic Surf Groove*, Surfdog, 1996.

Dangerous Toys: *Dangerous Toys*, Columbia, 1989 • *Hellacious Acres*, Columbia, 1991.

Devo: *Oh No It's Devo*, Warner Bros., 1982 • *Greatest Hits*, Warner Bros., 1990 • *Greatest Misses*, Warner Bros., 1990.

Dokken: *Tooth and Nail*, Elektra, 1984.

Espionage: *Espionage*, A&M, 1983.

Foreigner: "Dirty White Boy," Atlantic, 1979 • "Head Games," Atlantic, 1979 • *Head Games*, Atlantic, 1979 • *Records*, Atlantic, 1982 • *The Very Best . . . and Beyond*, Atlantic, 1992.

Furey, Lewis: *The Humours of Lewis Furey*, A&M, 1976.

Gasolin': *#3*, CBS, 1973 • *Stakkels Jim*, CBS, 1974 • *Gas 5*, CBS, 1975 • *What a Lemon*, CBS, 1976.

Hawkwind: "You'd Better Believe It," United Artists, 1974.

Hoey, Gary: *Bug Alley*, ULG, 1996 • w/ Donavon Frankenreiter, "Wipeout," Interscope, 1996 (*MOM: Music for Our Mother Ocean*).

Hunter, Ian: *Overnight Angels*, CBS, 1977.

Hustler: *Play Loud*, A&M, 1975.

Jet: *Jet*, CBS, 1975.

Journey: *Infinity*, Columbia, 1978 • *Evolution*, Columbia, 1979 • "Lovin', Touchin', Squeezin'," Columbia, 1979.

Knighton, Reggie: *The Reggie Knighton Band*, ARC/Columbia, 1978.

Lindisfarne: *Live*, Charisma, 1972 • *Roll on Ruby*, Charisma/Elektra, 1973.

Lone Star: *Lone Star*, Epic, 1976.

Man: *Winos, Rhinos and Lunatics*, United Artists, 1972.

Michael, George: See Queen.

Michaels, Hilly: *Calling All Girls*, Warner Bros., 1980.

Morales, Michael: *Michael Morales*, Wing, 1988.

Myhill, Richard: *The Richard Myhill Album*, EMI, 1973 • *21 Days in Soho*, EMI, 1974.

Nazareth: *Exercises*, Moon/WB, 1972.

Osbourne, Ozzy: *No Rest for the Wicked*, Epic, 1989.

Pilot: *Morin Heights,* EMI, 1976.

Queen: *Queen,* EMI/Elektra, 1973 • *Queen 2,* EMI/Elektra, 1974 • *Sheer Heart Attack,* EMI/Elektra, 1974 • *A Night at the Opera,* EMI/Elektra, 1975 • "Bohemian Rhapsody," Reprise, 1975, 1992 (*Wayne's World* soundtrack) • "Killer Queen," Elektra, 1975 • "Bohemian Rhapsody," Elektra, 1976 • "You're My Best Friend," Elektra, 1976 • *Jazz,* EMI/Elektra, 1978 • "Show Must Go On," Alex, 1991 • w/ George Michael, *Five Live* (EP), Hollywood, 1993.

Springfield, Dusty: *It Begins Again,* Mercury, 1978 • *Anthology,* PolyGram, 1997.

Sprung Monkey: *Swirl,* Surfdog, 1995 • "Good Times," Interscope, 1996 (*MOM: Music for Our Mother Ocean*).

Starcastle: *Citadel,* Epic, 1977 • *Fountains of Light,* Epic, 1977.

Straker, Pete: *This One's on Me,* EMI, 1977.

Stranglers, The: *Greatest Hits, 1977–1990,* Epic, 1990 • *10,* Epic, 1990.

T'Pau: "Heart and Soul," Virgin, 1987 • "Heart and Soul," EMI, 1987, 1993 (*Living in Oblivion: The 80s Greatest Hits,* Vol. 2) • *T'Pau,* Virgin, 1987.

Turner, Joe Lynn: *Rescue You,* Elektra, 1985.

Wood, Ron: *Gimme Some Neck,* CBS, 1979.

World, The: *Break the Silence,* Warner Bros., 1983.

Glen Ballard

A disciple of Quincy Jones (see entry) and a budding songwriter/arranger/producer in the late '70s and '80s, Glen Ballard made a big splash as a producer in 1988, when he collaborated with a Los Angeles Lakers cheerleader named Paula Abdul on her debut album, *Forever Your Girl,* which would reach seven-times platinum and occupy the No. 1 position on the Billboard 200 for 10 weeks.

Less than two years later, Ballard hit the jackpot again on the debut album by Wilson Phillips, a female trio made up of offspring of L.A. rock icons Brian Wilson (Carney and Wendy Wilson) and Michelle and John Phillips of the Mamas and the Papas (Chynna Phillips). The group's self-titled album sold 5 million copies in the U.S. and reached No. 2 on the Billboard 200.

If those two associations brought Ballard acclaim as a hit-making producer/arranger/songwriter, his next collaborator, Alanis Morissette, would catapult him to superstardom among pop music producers.

Not only did Ballard produce Morissette's No. 1 smash debut, *Jagged Little Pill,* he also co-wrote much of the material with the singer, arranged it, and performed

on the album. To date, *Jagged Little Pill* has sold in excess of 15 million copies in the U.S., nearly matching Boston's record for the top-selling debut album of all time.

Because most of *Jagged Little Pill* was recorded on Alesis Adat modular digital multitrack (MDM) recorders, Ballard became associated with the "MDM" revolution of the '90s. Because of their affordability, portability, and modular design, MDMs allow artists and producers to make high-quality recordings at home or in small, so-called project studios, thereby saving money on studio bookings and enjoying the freedom of working at a leisurely pace.

"I think it's great, and there's no stopping it," Ballard says of MDM recording. "There's a great depth and character to analog recording that won't be replaced by anything, but I'm always the first person to get something new. [Alesis] Adats have made my work so much easier. The Alanis record was 98 percent Adat, and I've done 10 or 12 other records that were 98 percent Adat. I'm not a purist in that if it's not analog it can't be good. I'm into capturing emotions. I try not to be too precious about it, because at the end of the day if what you're hearing in the studio is great and you put it on Adat, I don't think it's going to be any less great. As long as the technology isn't driving the boat, you're OK."

Asked if he considers himself primarily a producer, a songwriter, or an arranger, Ballard responds: "It's hard for me to delineate sometimes, because one bleeds into the other. As a record producer, I think of the song first, whether I'm the writer or not. It's all predicated on the song for me. That's no great secret, but oftentimes the way the marketplace is, there's an assumption that you can get by with a great track but not a great song. And you certainly *can* get by that way, but for a record to go all the way and have real resonance and quality, you better have the song. I always feel like if you get the great song, it's almost impossible to ruin the production."

Ballard defines the role of the record producer as "being a film director and a film producer, because you have the creative responsibilities and the financial responsibilities to make it happen."

He adds that people are often "mystified" by the title of record producer, and acknowledges that every producer regards his or her job differently. "For as many record producers it can mean as many things," he says. "For me it's a hands-on process that involves, long before you go into the studio, a preproduction process. That's where you make a hit record, in preproduction. So when you go in the studio, you've already got your genetic information to make something beautiful."

Following the release of *Jagged Little Pill,* Ballard worked on Aerosmith's *Nine Lives* album, but most of his tracks were scrapped at the band's discretion. Ballard also worked with Van Halen, and with Morissette on her follow-up album.

Born in Natchez, Mississippi, in 1953, Ballard grew up watching Jerry Lee Lewis perform. Ballard was also inspired by southern R&B singer Irma Thomas, Memphis-based soul singer Al Green, and all manner of New Orleans blues and jazz.

Ballard studied English, political science, and journalism at the University of Mississippi, where he graduated with honors in 1975. While at Ole Miss, Ballard recorded a self-titled solo album that sold respectably well locally but did not receive national recognition. Still determined to pursue a career as a songwriter and musician, Ballard turned down fellowships to attend law school and headed to Los Angeles.

He landed a job at Elton John's production company in L.A. and wound up playing piano for John's duet partner Kiki Dee. In 1978, Ballard got his first break as a songwriter when Dee covered his tune "One Step." Although the song was not a hit, it helped Ballard secure a publishing deal with MCA Music Publishing.

In the early '80s, Quincy Jones noticed the young songwriter and took him under his wing. As Jones' protégé, Ballard wrote hits for Michael Jackson, Philip Bailey, Aretha Franklin, Randy Crawford, Earth, Wind and Fire, Al Jarreau, James Ingram, Chaka Khan, George Strait, and Barbra Streisand, among others.

"First Quincy liked my songs, then he liked the arrangements, and in about 1984 he said, 'You're ready to produce a record,' " recalls Ballard. "Learning from him was the greatest gift I could ever have. I saw how creating an atmosphere of trust and confidence and sanctuary for an artist was always part of his process. I was staff producer for him for two years and I did everything from Patti Austin to Jack Wagner, Evelyn "Champagne" King, Teddy Pendergrass, and more. I did all styles of music."

Like many successful producers—particularly those who are also songwriters and proven talent scouts—Ballard recently established a record label, Java Records, under the auspices of Capitol Records. —PAUL VERNA

Abdul, Paula: *Shut Up and Dance,* Virgin, 1990 (remixes from *Forever Your Girl*).
Butcher, Jon: *Pictures from the Front,* Capitol, 1989.
Feelabeelia: *East to West,* Qwest, 1985.
King, Evelyn Champaigne: *Love Come Down: Best Of,* RCA, 1993.
Lorenz, Trey: *Trey Lorenz,* Epic, 1992.
Morissette, Alanis: "Hand in My Pocket," Maverick, 1995 •
"Ironic," Maverick, 1995 • *Jagged Little Pill,* Maverick, 1995

• "You Oughta Know," Maverick, 1995 • *Supposed Former Infatuation Junkie,* Maverick, 1998.
Oslin, K.T.: *Greatest Hits: Songs from an Aging Sex Bomb,* RCA, 1993.
Pendergrass, Teddy: *Workin' It Back,* Asylum, 1985.
Salonga, Lea: *Lea Salonga,* Atlantic, 1993.
Stigers, Curtis: *Time Was,* Arista, 1991, 1995.
Streisand, Barbra: *Till I Loved You,* Columbia, 1988.
Van Halen: *Best Of,* Vol. 1, Warner Bros., 1996.
Wagner, Jack: "All I Need," Qwest, 1984 • *All I Need,* Qwest, 1984 • *Alone in a Crowd,* RCA, 1993.
Wilson Phillips: "Hold On," SBK, 1990 • "Impulsive," SBK, 1990 • "Release Me," SBK, 1990 • *Wilson Phillips,* SBK, 1990 • "Daniel," Polydor, 1991 (*Two Rooms: Songs of Elton and Bernie Taupin*) • "The Dream Is Still Alive," SBK, 1991 • "You're in Love," SBK, 1991 • "Give It Up," SBK, 1992 • *Shadows and Light,* Gold Rush, 1992, 1996 • "You Won't See Me Cry," SBK, 1992.

Michael Barbiero and Steve Thompson

Michael Barbiero's favorite memory of his partnership with Steve Thompson is a Rolling Stone. "When we were working with Keith Richards [see entry], Steve walked out in the studio, looked at him and said, 'Keith, you're not slouching. This can't be the solo unless you're slouching. I need to see you get down like this . . .' He's playing air guitar down by his knees," Barbiero remembers with a laugh.

"Keith blew a solo then and it was incredible. He walked back into the control room and said, 'You know, you're the first motherfucker who's ever had the balls to tell me anything in the recording studio. I love that.' Steve is always pulling stuff like that, which I respect and admire." Then he pauses to add, "My role sometimes is to rein it all in when it gets out of hand."

Barbiero and Thompson's credits include a handful of mega-sellers, Grammy Awards, even timeless music. They met during disco, made some of the key rock albums of the '80s and quite a few favorite pop albums in the '90s.

Steve Thompson (born November 18, 1953) and

Michael Barbiero (born June 25, 1949) both grew up on Long Island. Thompson spent 16 years as a club disc jockey and Barbiero was a dance mix specialist. They knew each other professionally, so when disco died, Thompson started looking for an engineer who could help him with some production gigs. "Michael to me was the best at adapting to any type of musical style you could throw at him," Thompson says.

After their dance-disco work found success, early '80s bands solicited them. "We had the opportunity to do some producing because everything we were doing was ending up on the charts. Given the choice about what to produce, we looked at each other and said, 'Should we do dance records? Nah, let's do rock 'n' roll.'"

Their first rock project was for Geffen A&R executive Tom Zutaut: City Kid, the band that became Tesla. They also mixed Guns N' Roses' *Appetite for Destruction*. In 1988, the duo mixed Soundgarden's *Ultramega OK*, which Thompson calls "a breath of fresh air. If alternative hadn't hit in the '90s, I probably would have been out of the music industry, because I hated the music so much. When bands like Smashing Pumpkins and Mazzy Star came out, it was like I was 14 again, because that's the music I like."

Meanwhile, Barbiero was keeping his eye on Blues Traveler, and the duo threw their hat in the ring to mix their third album. "That gave us an entrée to produce their fourth album," Barbiero says. "That's the most successful album we've done." Thompson has also worked solo, producing the likes of Rollins Band, Butthole Surfers, and Life of Agony. Barbiero's solo production work includes Government Mule and Scarce.

Preproduction is key to Thompson. "In production you sit down with the band, go through the songs, find the strengths and work on the weaknesses. The best game plan for a successful production is not to burn out the songs. I want to get the song on either take one or take two. Mixing to me is probably the most fun of production," he adds. "You basically get to play the band on the console." —DAVID JOHN FARINELLA

Michael Barbiero

Jono Manson Band: "Big Daddy Blues," A&M, 1995 • "Miss Fabulous," A&M, 1996 (*Kingpin* soundtrack).
Marley, Ziggy: *People Get Ready*, Elektra, 1997.
Scarce: "All Sideways," A&M, 1996 • *Dead Sexy*, A&M, 1996.
Screamin' Cheetah Wheelies: *Magnolia*, Capricorn, 1996.
Scritti Politti: *Provision*, Warner Bros., 1988.
Sweet Vine: "Candy for Fools," Sony, 1997 • *Sweet Vine*, Sony, 1997.
Tesla: *Time's Makin' Changes: The Best Of*, Geffen, 1995.
Whitley, Chris: *Terra Incognita*, Sony, 1997.

COLLECTIONS

Serpico soundtrack, Paramount, 1973.

Michael Barbiero and Steve Thompson

Alarm, The: "Rain in the Summertime" (remix), IRS, 1987.
Alphaville: *Afternoons in Utopia* (2 tracks), Atlantic, 1986, 1989 • *First Harvest: The Best Of*, WEA, 1992.
Anthrax: *Live: The Island Years*, Island, 1994.
Bad Manners: *Mental Notes*, Portrait, 1985.
Blues Traveler: "But Anyway," A&M, 1994 (*Woodstock 94*) • *Four*, A&M, 1994 • "Get Out of Denver," A&M, 1995 (*Things to Do in Denver When You're Dead* soundtrack) • "The Mountains Win Again," A&M, 1995 • "Run-Around," A&M, 1996 (*The Truth About Cats and Dogs* soundtrack) • "Carolina Blues," A&M, 1997 • "Most Precarious," A&M, 1997 • *Straight on Till Morning*, A&M, 1997.
Butthole Surfers: "Who Was in My Room Last Night" (remix), Capitol, 1993.
Cocker, Joe: *Live!* Capitol, 1990.
Cutting Crew: *Broadcast*, Virgin, 1986 • *Been in Love Before*, Virgin, 1987 • "I've Been in Love Before," Virgin, 1987.
D.O. (Digital Orgasm): "Guilty of Love" (remix), Antler Subway/Whte Lbls, 1993.
Earth, Wind and Fire: "System of Survival" (remix), Columbia, 1987.
Expose: "I Wish the Phone Would Ring," Arista, 1992 • "I'll Never Get Over You Getting Over Me," Arista, 1992 • *Expose*, Arista, 1992 • "I Specialize in Love," Arista, 1995.
Hatters, The: *The Madcap Adventures of the Avocado Overlord*, Atlantic, 1994.
Houston, Whitney: "I Wanna Dance with Somebody (Who Loves Me)" (remix), Arista, 1987.
Icehouse: "Electric Blue" (remix), Chrysalis, 1988.
Jagger, Mick: "Let's Work" (remix), Columbia, 1987.
Jets, The: "Rocket 2 U" (remix), MCA, 1988.
Kaja: "Turn Your Back on Me" (remix), EMI America, 1985.
Madonna: "Over and Over" (remix), Sire, 1987 • "Who's That Girl" (remix), Sire, 1987.
Phantom, Rocker and Slick: *Phantom, Rocker and Slick*, EMI, 1985.
Psychedelic Furs: "Heartbreak Beat" (remix), Columbia, 1987.
Red Hot Chili Peppers: "Hollywood (Africa)" (remix), Enigma/EMI America, 1985.
Scritti Politti: "Boom! There She Was" (remix), Warner Bros., 1988.
Simply Red: "Money's Too Tight (to Mention)" (remix), Elektra, 1985.
Tesla: *Mechanical Resonance*, Geffen, 1987 • "Love Song," Geffen, 1989 • *The Great Radio Controversy*, Geffen, 1989 • *Psychotic Supper*, Geffen, 1991.
Toll, The: *The Price of Progression*, DGC, 1988.

Winwood, Steve: "Freedom Overspill" (remix), Island, 1986.

Steve Thompson

Butthole Surfers: "Pepper," Capitol, 1996 • *Electriclarryland* (6 tracks), Capitol, 1996.

Life of Agony: *Ugly*, Roadrunner, 1995.

Rollins Band: *Come In and Burn*, Dreamworks, 1997 • "Starve," Dreamworks, 1997.

Venom: *Welcome to Hell*, Combat, 1985.

World Bang: *Pedofiend* (EP), Critique, 1995 • *Alice D.*, Critique, 1996.

Steve Barri

Steve Barri was the King Midas of AM radio pop from 1968 to 1974, his string of hits often skirting the fragile line between pop and bubble gum. His discography reads like a Top 10 list from junior high school dances of that period: he produced all the hits by the Grass Roots (including "Midnight Confessions," No. 5; "Temptation Eyes," No. 15; "I'd Wait a Million Years," No. 15; "Don't Pull Your Love," No. 4, by Hamilton, Joe Frank and Reynolds; and "Billy Don't Be a Hero," No. 1, by Bo Donaldson and the Heywoods. All are textbook examples of formula pop, well-crafted and carefully assembled.

Born Steven Barry Lipkin, in Brooklyn, New York, on February 23, 1942, Barri found his finest vehicle in Tommy Roe. His best work came from his sometimes uncomfortable collaboration with Roe, which resulted in the singer's return to the charts and six hit singles. "Dizzy" featured a wild string arrangement by Jimmie Haskell and was a No. 1 record for four weeks in 1969. Further chart success followed with "Heather Honey," "Jam Up and Jelly Tight" (No. 8), and "Stagger Lee."

The Barri production team included Ben Benay on guitar (who has recorded with Steely Dan, the Beach Boys, and Joe Cocker), Don Randi on keyboards (Linda Ronstadt, the Righteous Brothers), Larry Knechtel on keyboards (Simon and Garfunkel, Duane Eddy, Bread, the Carpenters), Joe Osborne on bass (Simon and Garfunkel, the Carpenters, the Mamas and the Papas), and Hal Blaine on drums (see separate entry under session musicians).

During the '70s, Barri worked in A&R where he guided the careers of the Commodores and Lionel Richie. In 1989, after an absence from the charts of more than a decade, Barri formed a production team

with session guitarist Tony Peluso (the Carpenters, Paul Revere and the Raiders, Seals and Crofts) and produced the No. 9 hit "Room to Move," by techno-pop quintet Animotion. In 1991, the team produced the debut album by the Triplets, three Mexican sisters born seven seconds apart, yielding the No. 14 hit, "You Don't Have to Go Home Tonight." —DANIEL J. LEVITIN

Alaimo, Steve: *Anthology*, Hot Productions, 1997.

Animotion: "Room to Move," Polydor, 1989 • *Obsession: The Best Of*, Mercury, 1996.

Apollonia: *Apollonia*, Warner Bros., 1989.

Bland, Bobby "Blue": *California Album*, ABC/Dunhill, 1974 • *Dreamer*, ABC/Dunhill, 1974 • w/ B.B. King, *Together for the First Time Live!* MCA, 1974 • *Reflections in Blue*, ABC, 1977.

Brooks, Mel: *History of the World, Part 1*, Warner Bros., 1982.

Cashman and West: *A Song or Two*, ABC, 1972 • *Moondog Serenade*, ABC, 1973 • *Lifesong*, ABC, 1974 • *AM/FM Blues: Their Very Best*, Razor & Tie, 1993.

Chater, Kerri: *Love on a Shoestring*, Warner Bros., 1978 • *Part Time Love*, Warner Bros., 1978.

Cher: *I'd Rather Believe in You*, Warner Bros., 1976.

Cherokee: *Cherokee*, ABC, 1971.

Corbetta, Jerry: *Jerry Corbetta*, Warner Bros., 1978.

Cosby, Bill: *Himself*, Motown, 1982.

Couchois: *Couchois*, Warner Bros., 1979 • *Nasty Hardware*, Warner Bros., 1980.

Dion: *Streetheart*, Warner Bros., 1976.

Donaldson, Bo, and the Heywoods: "Billy, Don't Be a Hero," ABC, 1974 • *Bo Donaldson and the Heywoods*, ABC, 1974 • "Who Do You Think You Are," ABC, 1974.

Elliman, Yvonne: *Yvonne*, RSO, 1979 • *The Best Of*, Taragon, 1995 • *Best Of*, Polydor, 1997.

Elliot, Mama Cass: *Mama Cass*, Stateside, 1969 • *Dream a Little Dream: The Cass Elliot Collection*, MCA, 1997 • "Make Your Own Kind of Music," MCA, 1997.

Fabares, Shelley: *The Best Of*, Rhino, 1994.

Fantastic Baggies: *Tell 'Em I'm Surfin'*, Imperial, 1964.

Four Tops: "Keeper of the Castle," Dunhill, 1972 • "Are You Man Enough," Dunhill, 1973 • *Mainstreet People*, ABC, 1973 • *Meeting of the Minds*, Dunhill, 1974 • *Night Lights in Harmony*, ABC, 1974 • *Shaft in Africa* soundtrack, Probe, 1974 • *Ain't No Woman (Like the One I Got)*, MCA Special Products, 1987, 1994 • *Greatest Hits, 1972–1976*, MCA, 1982, 1987 • *Indestructable*, Arista, 1988 • *Keepers of the Castle: Their Best, 1972–1978*, MCA, 1997.

Fresh Start: *What America Needs*, Dunhill, 1974, 1975.

Friedman, Kinky: *Kinky Friedman*, ABC, 1974.

Grass Roots: "Let's Live for Today," Dunhill, 1967 • *Let's Live for Today*, Dunhill, 1967 • "Things I Should Have Said," Dunhill, 1967 • *Feelings*, Dunhill, 1968 • "Midnight

Confessions," Dunhill, 1968 • "Bella Linda," Dunhill, 1969 • "Heaven Knows," Dunhill, 1969 • "I'd Wait a Million Years," Dunhill, 1969 • *Leaving It All Behind,* Dunhill, 1969 • *Lovin' Things,* Dunhill, 1969 • "The River Is Wide," Dunhill, 1969 • "Baby Hold On," Dunhill, 1970 • *16 Greatest Hits,* MCA, 1971 • "Sooner or Later," Dunhill, 1971 • "Temptation Eyes," Dunhill, 1971 • "Two Divided By Love," Dunhill, 1971 • "Glory Bound," Dunhill, 1972 • *Move Along,* Dunhill, 1972 • "The Runway," Dunhill, 1972 • *A Lotta Mileage,* Dunhill, 1973 • *Greatest Hits,* Vols. 1–2, MCA, 1987 • *Anthology, 1965–1975,* MCA, 1991 • *All Time Greatest Hits,* MCA, 1996.

Hamilton, Joe Frank and Reynolds: "Don't Pull Your Love," Dunhill, 1971 • *Hamilton, Joe Frank and Reynolds,* Probe, 1971 • *Hallway Symphony,* Probe, 1972.

Henderson, Eric: *Faces,* JVC, 1997.

Kennedy, Mike: *Louisiana,* ABC, 1972.

Kidd Glove: *Kidd Glove,* Morocco, 1984.

King, B.B.: *See* Bland, Bobby "Blue."

King, Bobby: *Bobby King,* Warner Bros., 1981 • *Love in the Fire,* Motown, 1984.

Koz, Dave: *Dave Koz,* Capitol, 1990.

Kurtz, John Henry: *Reunion,* ABC, 1972.

Lambert, Dennis: *Bags and Things,* Dunhill, 1972.

Lawrence, Joey: *Joey Lawrence,* Impact, 1993.

Lovesmith, Michael: *I Can Make It Happen,* Motown, 1984.

Mamas and the Papas: *Creeque Alley,* MCA, 1991, 1995.

Manhattan Transfer: *Pastiche,* Rhino, 1977, 1995.

McGuire, Barry: "Eve of Destruction," Dunhill, 1965.

Mills, Stephanie: *Something Real,* MCA, 1992.

O'Day, Alan: *Appetizers,* Pacific, 1977 • "Undercover Angel," Pacific, 1977 • *Oh Johnny,* Pacific, 1979.

Pratt and McClain: *Pratt and McClain,* ABC, 1974 • "Happy Days" (from the Paramount TV series), Reprise/Warner, 1976 • *Happy Days,* Reprise, 1976.

Rejoice: *Rejoice,* Dunhill, 1969.

Rhythm Heritage: "Baretta Theme (Keep Your Eye on the Sparrow)," ABC, 1976 • "Theme from S.W.A.T.," ABC, 1976.

Rincon Surfside Band: *Surfing Songbook,* Dunhill, 1965.

Roe, Tommy: "Dizzy," ABC, 1969 • *Dizzy,* ABC, 1969 • "Heather Honey," ABC, 1969 • "Jam up Jelly Tight," ABC, 1969 • *Greatest Hits,* Stateside, 1970 • "Stagger Lee," ABC, 1971 • *We Can Make Music,* ABC, 1974.

Sebastian, John: "Welcome Back," Reprise, 1976 • *Welcome Back,* Reprise, 1976.

Shango: *Trampin',* Dunhill, 1970.

Shannon, Del: *Greatest Hits,* Rhino, 1990.

Smith: *A Group Called Smith,* Dunhill, 1969 • "Baby It's You," Dunhill, 1969.

Sober, Errol: *Day Dreamer,* Capitol, 1976.

Spencer, Tracie: *Make the Difference,* Capitol, 1990.

Springfield, Dusty: *Cameo,* Philips/ABC, 1973 • *Anthology,* PolyGram, 1997.

Temptations, The: *Surface Thrills,* Gordy, 1983.

Three's a Crowd: *Christopher's Movie Matinee,* Dunhill, 1967.

Triplets, The: *Thicker Than Water,* Mercury, 1991 • "You Don't Have to Go Home Tonight," Mercury, 1991.

Weaver, Patty: *Patty Weaver,* Warner Bros., 1982.

COLLECTIONS
Beautiful Thing soundtrack, MCA, 1996.

Jeff Barry

Jeff Barry has made a career out of writing and producing some of the greatest pop music ever recorded. With partner, and later wife, Ellie Greenwich, Barry wrote Phil Spector's (see entry) most luminous vehicles: the Ronettes' "Be My Baby" and "Baby I Love You," the Crystals' "Da Doo Ron Ron" and "Then He Kissed Me," Darlene Love's "Christmas (Baby Please Come Home)," and Ike and Tina Turner's "River Deep, Mountain High."

These songs perfectly balance anticipation and fulfillment, capturing the tender and tingling moment between childhood and adulthood. They gave Spector the ideal bones on which to flesh out his momentous, ornate creations.

Barry and Greenwich also wrote the No. 1 hits "Do Wah Diddy Diddy" for Manfred Mann and "Hanky Panky" for Tommy James and the Shondells.

As co-owners of Red Bird Records from 1964 to 1966 (with Jerry Leiber, Mike Stoller, and George Goldner—see entries), Barry and Greenwich helped define the girl group sound by writing and producing for the Dixie Cups ("Chapel of Love," No. 1; "People Say," No. 12; "Iko, Iko," No. 20); the Jelly Beans ("I Wanna Love Him So Bad," No. 9) and the Butterflys' ("Good Night Baby"). The pair took it a step further by writing, producing, and singing as the Raindrops ("The Kind of Boy You Can't Forget").

They also wrote and produced with Shadow Morton (see entry) for the Shangri-Las ("Leader of the Pack," No. 1; "Remember (Walkin' in the Sand)," No. 5). All but five of the first 20 Red Bird releases charted. The Barry-Greenwich team was elected to the Songwriters Hall of Fame in 1991.

Barry and Greenwich left Red Bird in 1966 to manage and produce Neil Diamond and ran up another string of hits ("Cherry, Cherry," No. 6; "Girl, You'll Be a Woman Soon," No. 10; "I Thank the Lord for the Night Time"). Barry also produced the Monkees ("I'm a Believer," No. 1; "A Little Bit Me, a Little Bit You," No. 2), wrote and produced for the Archies ("Sugar, Sugar," No. 1; "Jingle Jangle," No. 10), Bobby Bloom ("Montego Bay," No. 8 U.S./No. 3 U.K.) and co-wrote Olivia Newton-John's "I Honestly Love You" (No. 1, 1974).

Barry was born into a middle-class Brooklyn family in 1938. His parents split up when he was 7, the year he wrote his first song—tellingly, a happy little ditty about girls and horses.

Growing up in the '40s and '50s, Barry was expected to become a professional—as in doctor, lawyer, or engineer—not a songwriter. He dutifully entered college to study mechanical design and industrial engineering. "I wanted to design refrigerators and cars," he recalls. "At the same time, I was always cutting classes and singing with friends and bands. Someone in the family knew Arnold Shaw, a music publisher, and asked him to listen to me sing. The only songs I could play for him were songs I had written because I wasn't good enough to play other people's songs. I knew two chords: C and G."

Shaw thought Barry was a decent singer, but he was more interested in his songs. "He put me with some people who knew chords and I started to write," Barry continues. "My first record was a B-side of a Crests record. Things started happening and Shaw asked me if I'd consider working for him."

By spring 1960, the young man with two chords had his first hit, Ray Peterson's "Tell Laura I Love Her," produced by Hugo and Luigi (see entry). (Hugo and Luigi also produced a record by Barry himself, but it didn't go anywhere.)

Barry wrote hundreds of songs with various partners and began to feel his way around the studio.

"I was recording demos of my songs, and in 1961 my publisher came to me and said that they liked my demo so much, they wanted me to produce the record," he says. "Not knowing music very well, I got books and wrote out the parts for all the instruments meticulously by hand, including strings. Every dot was perfect. When I passed out the parts everybody started laughing. I thought, 'My God, it's all wrong signature-wise and everything.' But they said, 'Who's your copyist, a monk?' Then I got it. You didn't have to do all of this stuff by yourself. I had never heard the word 'copyist' before."

The experience also taught Barry that as a producer, "you just have to be the director," he says. "At the same time, I realized the value of a hit song."

Everything changed when Barry met Ellie Greenwich, a distant relative by marriage and another aspiring singer and songwriter. Soon they were working together and then married. Barry and Greenwich came into their own as producers at Red Bird.

The Dixie Cups' "Chapel of Love" is simple, sweeping joy. The song builds as the Cups' a capella voices are joined by finger snaps, then unobtrusive but swinging horns evocative of the girls' native New Orleans. Has there ever been a sunnier summation of marriage than the line, "We'll say I do / And we'll never be lonely anymore"?

"Iko, Iko" is even sparer, a lean, timeless gem: just the schoolyard chant and Barry and Greenwich clapping and percussing up a storm.

While Barry and Greenwich were producing and managing Neil Diamond, the Monkees called. "Don Kirshner asked if I would like to take a crack at the Monkees, and Neil Diamond's 'I'm a Believer' seemed like the right song," Barry recalls. "I made a basic track in New York and took it to L.A. to play for Kirshner and the Monkees. Mike Nesmith came with some 14-pound 16-year-old. They were slouching together on the couch, but everyone else was nice and polite. I played the track and everyone could hear that the song had some commercial appeal, at worst. Then Nesmith piped up, 'That ain't no hit.' Everyone was like, 'Woooo.' So to lighten things up, I made what I thought was an obvious joke: 'Mike, you've got to picture it with the strings and horns.'

"There was no way we were going to put strings and horns on a song like that, but his ego allowed him to say, 'Maybe with strings and horns.' And everybody broke up. That was the beginning of a rapidly degenerating relationship that ended with me chasing him out of the studio."

Though the Monkees were assembled for a TV show, they were real people. Barry took the next logical step toward pop abstraction when he wrote and produced for the Archies, an animated band.

"My assignment, if I cared to accept it, was to create music for a Saturday morning cartoon show, but I made it clear that I wanted to make pop records—music that would work for the 4-year-olds and fit the animation, but at the same time sound like something 16-year-old girls might buy. I made the RIAA [Record Industry Association of America] Record of the Year twice: 'I'm a Believer' and the Archies' 'Sugar, Sugar.' To be Record of the Year, everything has to fall in just right. The lyric and the melody fell at a certain tempo and groove, and it took me three hours to get it right—for the drummer to get that behind-the-beat feel. I played the organ because no one was playing laid back enough for me. It's a fantastic vocal, too. Ron Dante sounds like the Archie character looks."

Just after the Archies came Bobby Bloom's breezy, infectious "Montego Bay." "After we wrote it, we sat in my office and he played the guitar and I was banging on the desk and it just sounded great," Barry says. "I got the best band in New York, went in the studio, and hated it—no character." Another, younger band fared no better.

Eventually, they built on the original format. "We went into the studio, I hung a microphone up, played the key on the piano to get the pitch, and the two of us stood there and clapped our hands and sang the song," Barry says. "In essence, we made a click track of the record with the song being sung over it, we put on earphones and played every instrument, and did all the vocals. The last thing we did was erase the click track, put on a real vocal, real hand claps, and the record was done. It's handmade, but it has that certain something. It sounds like a Hawaiian shirt." —ERIC OLSEN

Archies, The: "Bang-Shang-A-Lang," Calendar, 1968 • *The Archies*, Calendar, 1968 • *Everything's Archie*, Calendar, 1969 • "Jingle Jangle," Kirshner, 1969 • *Jingle Jangle*, Kirshner, 1969 • "Sugar, Sugar," Calendar, 1969 • *Sunshine*, Kirshner, 1970 • *The Archies' Greatest Hits*, Kirshner, 1970 • "Who's Your Baby?," Kirshner, 1970.

Baby Sitters Club: *Songs for My Best Friends*, Warner Bros., 1992.

Bloom, Bobby: "Montego Bay," MGM/L&R, 1970 • *The Bobby Bloom Album*, L&R, 1970.

Butterflys, The: "Good Night Baby," Red Bird, 1964.

Chopper: *Chopper*, Ariola, 1979.

Dante, Ron: *Brings You Up*, Kirshner, 1970.

Davis, Paul: *A Little Bit of*, Bang, 1973.

Diamond, Neil: "Cherry, Cherry," Bang, 1966 • *Double Gold*, Bang, 1966, 1967 • "I Got the Feelin' (Oh No No)," Bang, 1966 • "Solitary Man," Bang, 1966, 1970 • *The Feel of Neil Diamond*, Bang, 1966 • "Girl, You'll Be a Woman Soon," Bang, 1967 • *Just for You*, Bang, 1967 • "Kentucky Woman," Bang, 1967 • "Thank the Lord for the Night Time," Bang, 1967 • "You Got to Me," Bang, 1967 • "Shilo," Bang, 1968, 1970 • "Do It," Bang, 1966, 1970 • *Greatest Hits, 1966–1992*, Columbia, 1992 • *In My Lifetime*, Sony, 1996.

Dixie Cups: "Chapel of Love," Red Bird, 1964 • *Chapel of Love*, Red Bird, 1964 • "People Say," Red Bird, 1964 • "You Should Have Seen the Way He Looked at Me," Red Bird, 1964 • "Iko Iko," Red Bird, 1965.

Drifters, The: *Rockin' and Driftin': The Box Set*, Rhino, 1996.

Francis, Connie: *Souvenirs*, PolyGram, 1996.

James, Tommy: *Midnight Rider*, Fantasy, 1976 • *The Solo Years, 1970–1981*, Rhino, 1991.

Jay and the Americans: *Try Some of This*, United Artists, 1967.

Jelly Beans: "I Wanna Love Him So Bad," Red Bird, 1964.

Kim, Andy: "How'd We Ever Get This Way," Steed, 1968 • "Shoot 'Em Up Baby," Steed, 1968 • "Baby, I Love You," Steed, 1969 • *Baby, I Love You*, Steed, 1969 • "So Good Together," Steed, 1969 • "Be My Baby," Steed, 1970 • *Greatest Hits*, Capitol, 1974.

King Harvest: *King Harvest*, A&M, 1975.

McNamara: "Lay a Little Lovin' on Me," Steed, 1970.

Monkees, The: "I'm a Believer," Colgems, 1966 • "A Little Bit Me, a Little Bit You," Colgems, 1967 • *More of the Monkees*, Colgems, 1967 • *The Monkees Greatest Hits*, Colgems, 1969 • *Changes*, Rhino, 1970, 1995 • *Listen to the Band*, Rhino, 1991.

N Motion: *N Motion*, Warner Bros., 1991.

Persuasions: *More Than Before*, A&M, 1974.

Raindrops, The: "The Kind of Boy You Can't Forget," Jubilee, 1963.

Ronettes, The: "I Can Hear Music," Philles, 1966.

Sha Na Na: *The Night Is Still Young*, Kama Sutra, 1972.

Shangri-Las, The: "Leader of the Pack," Red Bird, 1964 • "Remember (Walkin' in the Sand)," Red Bird, 1964.

Springfield, Dusty: *Anthology*, PolyGram, 1997.

Travolta, John: "All Strung Out on You," Midland International, 1977 • *Can't Let You Go*, Midland International, 1977 • *Sings*, Varese Vintage, 1996.

COLLECTIONS

The Idolmaker soundtrack, A&M, 1980.

The Brill Building Sound: Singers and Songwriters Who Rocked the 60's, Era, 1993.

Dave Bartholomew

Dave Bartholomew would merit a hallowed spot in the ranks of immortal producers if he had only produced Fats Domino. That he also produced Smiley Lewis, Roy Brown, and Jewel King only solidifies the claim that Bartholomew, perhaps more than any of the artists he served, brought the New Orleans sound mainstream. He has been enshrined at the Rock and Roll Hall of Fame in Cleveland as a key influence on rock 'n' roll.

"I'm known for rock 'n' roll, but I really came from jazz," says Bartholomew. "I worked on a riverboat, and with lots of bands in New Orleans. By the time I was 16, I was playing in all the top bands in the city. I came up reading, always did read. We were playing jazz, and we were playing commercial music, like dance tunes, up the Mississippi River to St. Louis and up the Illinois to Peoria."

Born December 24, 1920, in Edgard, Louisiana, 30 miles upriver from New Orleans, Bartholomew grew up in the Crescent City. His father was a barber who also played tuba in Dixieland bands. As a teenager, Bartholomew began playing trumpet under the instruction of Peter Davis, who taught Louis Armstrong.

He began playing in high school and worked in parade bands, soon graduating to stints with the big bands of Toots Johnson, Papa Celestin, and Clairborne Williams. He gained his riverboat experience in Fats Pichon's band between 1938 and 1941.

According to Jeff Hannusch's highly informative notes to *Antoine "Fats" Domino: The Legendary Imperial Recordings*, Bartholomew took over Pichon's band when the latter went to work in the French Quarter.

"We were playing jazz and things like that," Bartholomew says, noting that he sat in with the Jimmie Lunceford Band. "I was considered one of the best trumpet players in New Orleans."

When World War II broke out, Bartholomew was drafted into the 196th Air Ground Forces (AGF) Band, where he learned arrangement as well as the rudiments of production. "I started writing in the service," he recalls. "I came out of the service, started my own band in 1948. And in 1949, I was discovered by Lew Chudd."

Life was a little more complicated than that, according to Hannusch's notes for the 1991 EMI Domino box. Before he went to work for Chudd as Imperial Records' staff producer, Bartholomew's band became the most popular in the city. Not only did it play all over town, the band began to broadcast live from the J&M Record Shop, on Dr. Daddy-O's show on WJMR.

DeLuxe Records, a New Jersey label that recorded Bartholomew's chief competitors, Roy Brown and Mac Gayten, recorded Bartholomew, too. Bartholomew also recorded for King and Imperial, but never made more than a regional mark as a solo artist.

His "Country Boy," on DeLuxe, became a regional hit in 1949, selling about 100,000 copies. "Country Boy" sold so well, Bartholomew's band was booked into a Houston club (owned by Duke/Peacock label magnate Don Robey) for several weeks. One night, Imperial Records founder Chudd, always on the prowl for a new commercial sound, walked in.

The band trumpeter Bartholomew led—guitarist Ernest McLean; tenor saxmen Herbert Hardesty,

Clarence Hall, and Alvin "Red" Tyler; alto saxman Joe Harris; pianist Salvador Doucette; and the prodigious, oft-recorded Earl Palmer on drums—became the foundation of the New Orleans, or Domino, sound. Marked by a big beat, stirring vocals, and proud arrangements with an odd sort of Dixieland swagger at their core, it would bring Imperial sales of hundreds of millions of 45s, EPs, and albums in the '50s and early '60s.

West Coast entrepreneur Chudd launched Imperial Records in 1947 and began recording all kinds of American vernacular music: jump blues, jazz, country. But two years on, Imperial hadn't notched any hits. That would change when Bartholomew signed on with the label in late 1949.

That fall, Chudd and Bartholomew checked out local New Orleans talent in the form of Fats Domino; Chudd signed Domino, cutting eight tracks at Cosimo Matassa's 1-track studio in December 1949. The tunes on the double session, featuring Domino over Bartholomew's band, were recorded on just one track directly to lacquer acetate disc; Matassa used four microphones. The first single was "Detroit City/The Fat Man." The B-side clicked in March 1950, launching a string of massive rhythm 'n' blues hits, as well as the crossover smashes "Blueberry Hill" (No. 2), "Ain't It a Shame" (No. 10; later bleached and renamed "Ain't That a Shame" by Pat Boone), and "I Hear You Knockin' " (initially produced on Smiley Lewis by Bartholomew and eventually covered by British revivalist Dave Edmunds; see entry). The string lasted until 1963, when Chudd sold Imperial to Liberty Records and returned to his native California.

"I could never actually get a big record off on my own," Bartholomew says, "but I found out I could be most successful as a writer and a composer. I would say my trademark was the New Orleans sound," based on marching bands, even bands playing commercials on trucks during the early days of radio.

"I remember when I was playing in one of my first bands," Bartholomew recalled to Hannusch, "there was an older musician who used to say, 'I don't know why they don't make the bass drum stand out more when they arrange music. That's the biggest instrument in the band, but they forget to play it.' What he said always stuck in my mind."

"Everything was mono," Bartholomew says today. "We didn't have all the tracks that guys got to work with now. We would switch instruments around, in a small studio, and put the drums wherever we could to get a better sound. We had no separation; everything leaked into the other. But we worked hard at it, and it was always real hard. Sometimes, we were in the studio 10,

12 hours. It was hard working to get the sound that you wanted."

Ironically, Bartholomew never did like "Blueberry Hill," which sold 3 million copies. He did like Smiley Lewis's "One Night of Sin" (Elvis Presley covered it as "One Night") and Lewis's "I Hear You Knockin.' "

What makes a rock 'n' roll hit? "You can have everything," says the lifelong New Orleans resident. "You can have a good story, but the public decides what's a hit. Sometimes, a record is too perfect. You can put everything together, get a good piece of material, a good story, the sound is good, and it's a piece of shit. I really don't know."

Although he's officially retired, Bartholomew occasionally works with two of his three sons, Ron and Don, at the family's Broadmoor studios. Ron and Don record rap and some rhythm 'n' blues.

He also has 30 to 40 tunes, including big-band music, ready "to go to press," he says. "But I don't have a distributor. I'd rather sit on it until I can get somebody who can do me some good.

"I'm still playing, but I'm semi-retired," Bartholomew says. "I'm not ripping and running, but every now and then, I do some things. Sometimes, I put together bands, play rhythm 'n' blues hits and turn them into jazz."

Not that he needs the work. With BMI since 1942, Bartholomew has amassed a catalog of over 400 tunes. "Not all were hits," he avers, "but some were. We're very lucky. You can have the greatest record in the world, but if you're not exposed, nothing's going to happen." —CARLO WOLFF

Bartholomew, Dave: *Fats Domino Presents Dave Bartholomew*, Imperial, 1961 • *New Orleans House Party*, Imperial, 1963 • *Jump Children*, Pathe, 1984 • *Monkey*, Pathe, 1985 • *In the Alley*, Charly, 1991 • *The Spirit of New Orleans: The Genius of Dave Bartholomew*, Capitol, 1993 • *Dave Bartholomew and Maryland Jazz Band*, GHB, 1995.

Booker, James: "Doing the Hambone/Thinkin' About My Baby," Imperial, 1953.

Brown, Roy: *The Complete Imperial Recordings of*, Capitol Blues, 1995.

Domino, Fats: "Ain't It a Shame," Imperial, 1955 • "Blueberry Hill," Imperial, 1956 • "Bo Weevil," Imperial, 1956 • "I'm in Love Again," Imperial, 1956 • "My Blue Heaven," Imperial, 1956 • "When My Dreamboat Comes Around," Imperial, 1956 • "Blue Monday," Imperial, 1957 • "I Want You to Know," Imperial, 1957 • "I'm Walkin'," Imperial, 1957 • "It's You I Love," Imperial, 1957 • "The Big Beat," Imperial, 1957 • "Valley of Tears," Imperial, 1957 • "Wait and See," Imperial, 1957 • "When I See You," Imperial, 1957 • "Sick and Tired," Imperial, 1958 • "Whole Lotta Loving," Imperial, 1958 • "Be My Guest," Imperial, 1959 • "I Want to Walk You Home," Imperial, 1959 • "I'm Gonna Be a Wheel Some Day," Imperial, 1959 • "I'm Ready," Imperial, 1959 • "I've Been Around," Imperial, 1959 • "Country Boy," Imperial, 1960 • "Don't Come Knockin'," Imperial, 1960 • "My Girl Josephine," Imperial, 1960 • "Natural Born Lover," Imperial, 1960 • "Three Days a Week," Imperial, 1960 • "Walking to New Orleans," Imperial, 1960 • "Ain't That Just Like a Woman," Imperial, 1961 • "Fell in Love on Monday," Imperial, 1961 • "It Keeps Raining," Imperial, 1961 • "Jambalaya (on the Bayou)," Imperial, 1961 • "Let the Four Winds Blow," Imperial, 1961 • "Shu Rah," Imperial, 1961 • "What a Party," Imperial, 1961 • "What a Price," Imperial, 1961 • "You Win Again," Imperial, 1962 • "Red Sails in the Sunset," ABC/Paramount, 1963 • *My Blue Heaven: The Best Of*, EMI America, 1990 • *They Call Me the Fat Man*, EMI, 1991 • *Out of New Orleans*, Bear Family, 1993 • *Fat Man: 25 Classic Performances*, Capitol, 1996.

Lewis, Smiley: *I Hear You Knocking*, Collectables, 1992, 1995.

Mitchell, Bobby: *I'm Gonna Be a Wheel Someday*, Bear Family, 1997.

Shirley and Lee: *Legendary Masters*, EMI America, 1974, 1990.

Turner, Big Joe: *Jumpin' with Joe: The Complete Aladdin and Imperial Recordings*, EMI, 1995.

Dave Bascombe

In addition to being a prolific modern rock producer, Dave Bascombe is one of the most sought-after mixers and engineers in the business.

Bascombe has engineered standards for Echo and the Bunnymen (*Porcupine*), Peter Gabriel (*So*), and Tears For Fears (*Songs from the Big Chair*). He has mixed for James ("Sit Down"), Del Amitri ("Always the Last to Know"), Human League (*Octopus*), Erasure (*Chorus*, *Erasure*), the Verve ("History"), and a plethora of others.

This is not to minimize Bascombe's production abilities. In the '90s, he has produced or co-produced the Lightning Seeds, Erasure (*Abba-esque* EP, No. 1 U.K.), Gavin Friday, Tim Finn, and ABC. In one remarkable year, 1987, Bascombe produced or co-produced Danny Wilson's *Meet Danny Wilson* ("Mary's Song"), Depeche Mode's *Music for the Masses* (No. 10 U.K.), the Silencers' *A Letter from St. Paul*, and Tom Verlaine's *Flash Light*. And we don't want to leave out Tears For Fears' *The Seeds of Love* (No. 1 U.K., No. 8 U.S.) from 1989.

David Bascombe was born in the northern England town of Chester and moved to London with his family when he was 7. As a boy he listened intently to records and the radio and played a bit of piano. In school, he played in a few bands, but after he left school to pursue music seriously, a year of unemployment led to a job at a studio as an errand boy. He never looked back.

Bascombe's hands-on work began when he weaseled studio time for friends' bands during weekend downtimes. He produced and engineered their demos because no one else was around. Though no deals developed, by 1978 he had picked up valuable studio experience and some freelance engineering jobs by word of mouth, including work with metal monsters Iron Maiden. He then moved on to London studio Maison Rouge, where he assisted for a few years, eventually engineering Echo and the Bunnymen in 1983. He went freelance for good soon thereafter, cementing his reputation by engineering *Songs from the Big Chair* in 1985.

Of late, Bascombe has been concentrating primarily on mixing, enjoying the short, intense bursts of activity. "There are two kinds of jobs in mixing," he says. "In the first, I am asked to come in and mix an album from scratch. An example is Suede's last album, *Coming Up* [1997]. It was a question of listening to it in the rough and getting an idea of what the songs were all about. My role was to get the basic tracks kicking in the first place, and then we spent a long time working on the various aspects of the overdubs.

"The second general role is to come in and remix something, when somebody hasn't got it right in the first place, and perhaps [do] additional production as well—maybe cleaning up the vocals, adding some guitar or whatever, and editing the track. I really enjoy that because I'm mostly there as a special pair of ears to give another. A lot of times it's hard to mix your own stuff if you've lived with it for a long time and you've pushed the fader up every day, over and over again, and you've balanced so many times that you can't be fresh with the track anymore."

Elaborating on the process, Bascombe says, "The drum sound is absolutely crucial. If it's not right you can end up messing around and EQ-ing a lot of stuff that doesn't really need it. It's not a question of getting the greatest drum sound in the world—it's a question of getting a sound all the other instruments will work with. Then you can throw everything else up fast and get a vibe with it."

Bascombe says there are two main approaches to production. The first involves new bands. The first step is to show them how the studio works so they can see what can be done.

"That gets them excited and you'll get the best out of them. I might have a suggestion for a melody that may be crap, but it might spark something. It's also a question of getting a vibe going in the studio. It should be fun.

"I may also help choose the songs. Sometimes a song might be overlooked by the band because it was written as a throwaway, but often that's the one that will do the business."

Bascombe works differently with veteran bands, citing Depeche Mode's classic *Music for the Masses*. "We were really trying to push the limits of what you can do in the studio with sound. That album was the first they used guitars on. I really enjoyed getting some rockier sounds that they hadn't used before. We also spent a lot of time collecting eclectic sounds. With them, atmosphere is really important, so it's a question of trying to find weird and interesting ambiences for their tracks."

Though he is a master mixer, Bascombe is no slave to technology. "Technology can get in the way so easily. I find that too much messing around with a mouse on a computer screen holds me back. I still prefer the old tape-based method of recording where you can actually cut the tape. I get into technology when I need it, like if you want to get the drums fed in time for whatever reason, you get the ProTools in with a programmer and let him do it.

"But I am more interested in old technology than anything else. And making great records." —Eric Olsen and Dawn Darling

ABC: "Say It," MCA, 1991 • *Abracadabra,* MCA, 1991.

Adams, Oleta: *Circle of One,* Fontana, 1990.

Danny Wilson: "Mary's Prayer," Virgin, 1987 • *Meet Danny Wilson* (4 tracks), Virgin, 1987.

Depeche Mode: "Behind the Wheel," Mute, 1987 • *Music for the Masses,* Sire, 1987 • "Never Let Me Down Again," Sire, 1987 • "Route 66," Mute, 1987 • "Little 15," Sire, 1988, 1991 • "Nothing," Sire, 1988 • "Strangelove," Sire, 1988.

Erasure: "Breath of Life," Sire/Reprise, 1992 • "Breath of Life" (remix), Sire/Reprise, 1992 • *Abba-esque,* Mute, 1992 • *Pop! the First 20 Hits,* Sire, 1992.

Finn, Tim: *Before and After,* Capitol, 1993.

Friday, Gavin: *Adam and Eve,* Island, 1992.

Happy Mondays: "Sunshine and Love," Elektra, 1992.

It's Immaterial: *Life's Hard and Then You Die,* Siren/Virgin/A&M, 1986.

Lightning Seeds: *Jollification,* Trauma, 1994 • *Dizzy Heights,* Epic, 1996.

Silencers, The: *A Letter from St. Paul,* RCA, 1987 • "Painted Moon," RCA, 1987.

Tears For Fears: *Flip,* Fontana, n.d. • "Sowing the Seeds of

39

Love," Fontana, 1989 • *The Seeds of Love*, Fontana, 1989 • "Woman in Chains," Fontana, 1989 • "Advice for the Young at Heart," Fontana, 1990 • *Tears Roll Down: Greatest Hits, 1982–1992*, Fontana, 1992.

Verlaine, Tom: *Flash Light* (1 track), IRS, 1987.

Ralph Bass

A prolific and successful producer, Ralph Bass was an integral part of the most important sociocultural change in postwar America: the infiltration of black music into the body and soul of white America.

Born Ralph Basso in 1911 into an Irish/German/ Jewish neighborhood in the Bronx, New York, the future producer of James Brown and Etta James didn't meet a black person until high school. But he became interested in black music as a young violin player in society bands during the Prohibition era. As he told Michael Lydon in *Boogie Lightning*, "We'd stop up in Harlem . . . and get some bathtub gin, and then we'd hear Duke playing the Cotton Club. . . . I would just sit there and watch the bodies sway. It was sensuous to me, the music itself, very emotional. It was an earthy kind of thing."

Bass, who was half-Jewish, felt a melodic affinity for black music as well. "When the cantor would sing the chants in synagogue in minor keys, it was like the bluesmen singing in minor keys, so the blues was a familiar sound in my ears."

During the Depression, Bass worked at the usual grab bag of odd jobs, from a brokerage house on Wall Street to serving bottled water in California. After he settled in Los Angeles in 1944, Bass recorded a series of jazz greats, among them Charlie Parker, Dizzy Gillespie, Slim Gaillard, Erroll Garner, and Dexter Gordon, for various independent labels, including his own, Portrait and Bop. This was in the day of 16-inch lacquer master discs—1-track, mono, and positively no overdubbing.

Jazz was his thing until suddenly, Bass had an epiphany. "One day I sat in Birdland, I forget who was playing . . . and I thought, 'I don't think there is one cat here who understands what he is playing.' Then I realized the cat was playing for himself. . . . I didn't understand what he was feeling. . . . It was selfish music, man, great but selfish. . . . If you're entertaining, play for me, baby, let me understand what you're doing." So Bass turned to R&B and the blues.

Bass produced T-Bone Walker for the Black and White label in 1946–1947, including the classic "Call It

Stormy Monday." Bass's first pop and R&B hit was "Open the Door, Richard" (No. 3), a novelty track by Jack McVea based on a bawdy old vaudeville routine. Bass moved to Savoy Records in 1948 to work with R&B bandleader Johnny Otis, who led a group featuring the teenage Little Esther (Phillips), Mel Walker and the Robins. Otis and company had 14 R&B hits in the late '40s and early '50s, including "Barrel House Stomp," "Double Crossing Blues," "Mistrustin' Blues," "Rockin' Blues," and Little Esther's "Cupid's Boogie."

Bass switched labels in 1951 when King Records owner Syd Nathan created the subsidiary label Federal expressly for Bass (who told writer Norbert Hess, "When you're hot, everybody licks your butt; but when you're cold, everybody kicks your butt. And I was hot!"). Little Esther went with him to Federal and continued to hit with "Ring-a-Ding-Doo," but Bass found his biggest success to date with Billy Ward and the Dominoes.

The 1951 hit "Sixty Minute Man" (No. 17) swings with an irresistible groove and sly lyrics ("I rock-um, roll-um, all night long") that made it a million-seller and the first R&B vocal group crossover hit. Although the Dominoes featured Clyde McPhatter (and later Jackie Wilson) on lead vocals, Bill Brown's cheerfully lascivious bass vocal steals the song. The production is remarkably bright and modern-sounding, with lively guitar and chiming harmonies, and the song deserved its 17 weeks atop the Billboard R&B chart. Another Dominoes hit was "The Bells," with McPhatter weeping his way through his own funeral, but Bass hit even bigger with Hank Ballard and the Midnighters and the notorious Annie series: "Work with Me, Annie," "Annie Had a Baby" (as a result of the work), and "Annie's Aunt Fannie."

As talent scout and producer, Bass combed the highways, byways, and back alleys of 1950s black America, especially the South, for fresh talent. "I had to go out there and look and beat the bushes . . . you'd get a tip on somebody and go down to listen. . . . We were in the ghetto. There were no rich kids who were singing. . . . And I was fortunate to be able to recognize what was good and what was wrong."

Bass discovered Little Willie Littlefield (who sang the original version of "Kansas City," "K. C. Lovin'"), Guitar Lewis, Big Jay McNeely, Johnny "Guitar" Watson, and the Platters (Bass recorded the original version of "Only You"). But his greatest discovery for Federal was James Brown.

Bass told Lydon, "I was in Atlanta . . . and I heard a dub, . . . it was so different that it knocked me out. A disc jockey and I drove to Macon in a pouring rainstorm. James was out on parole to his manager, a Macon promoter and club owner named Clint Brandly. I was told to meet Brandly by parking my car in front of a barbershop, which was across the street from a railroad station, and when the venetian blinds went up and down, to come in."

All of this intrigue was to avoid the potential unpleasantries of a white-black meeting in the Jim Crow Macon of 1956. There was an even greater sense of urgency than normal because Leonard Chess was on his way, but Leonard had to fly from Chicago. "They had no radar and all that jive they have today, and so he was grounded. . . . I gave the cat $200, and that was that."

Bass produced Brown's first hit, "Please, Please, Please." "This was a very young James Brown," recalls Bass. "He was so browbeaten with that shit down there . . . he used to call me Mister Ralph. . . . I says, Well man, don't call me no Mister Ralph. Either call me Mister Bass or call me Ralph."

By recording great black artists, Bass helped create momentous social change, but he also saw that change firsthand. "In many areas, the blacks would let the [white] kids come in, they had a thing with the promoter. In these towns the promoter was the connecting link between the white establishment and the black community. He was usually the richest man, he had property and the political thing that went on. . . . Then they got white spectator tickets . . . and by the early '50s they'd . . . put a rope across the middle of the floor. The blacks on one side, whites on the other, digging how the blacks were dancing and copying them. Then, hell, the rope would come down, and they'd all be dancing together. And you know, it was a revolution. Music did it," Bass confided to Lydon.

Bass moved to Chess in 1960 and stayed there until 1976, working with Etta James, Muddy Waters, Howlin' Wolf, Sonny Boy Williamson, gospel greats Clara Ward and the Soul Stirrers, as well as comedians Moms Mabley and Pigmeat Markham.

In 1977, Bass was hired to produce a series of Chicago blues artists for the T.K. label. Bass wanted to experiment with the sessions, insisting on virtually no preparation time and four-hour-maximum recording sessions. The project was shelved in the U.S. until Delmark began issuing discs of the sessions in 1993. Artists in the series include Carey Bell, Lonnie Brooks, Eddie Clearwater, and Lacy Gibson.

Bass was inducted into the Rock and Roll Hall of Fame in 1991. He died of a heart attack in 1997 while on board a flight to Nassau, the Bahamas, to visit his wife, Shirley Hall-Bass, who operates the Sammy Dyer School of Dance and Theatre there. —Eric Olsen

Ballard, Hank, and the Midnighters: "Annie Had a Baby," Federal, 1954 • "Annie's Aunt Fannie," Federal, 1954 • "Work with Me Annie," Federal, 1954.

Bell, Carey: *Heartaches and Pain,* Delmark, 1977, 1994.

Brooks, Lonnie: *Let's Talk It Over,* Delmark, 1977, 1993.

Brown, James: "Please Please Please," Federal, 1956 • *Please Please Please,* Federal, 1959 • *Star Time,* Polydor, 1991.

Clearwater, Eddie: *Boogie My Blues Away,* Delmark, 1977, 1995.

Eckstine, Billy: *Billy Eckstine, Big Joe Turner, Johnny Otis,* Savoy, 1951.

5 Royales, The: "Dedicated to the One I Love," King, 1958.

Garner, Erroll: *Yesterdays,* Savoy, 1949.

Gibson, Lacy: *Crying for My Baby,* Delmark, 1977, 1996.

Hooker, John Lee: *The Real Folk Blues,* Chess/MCA, 1966 • *More Real Folk Blues: The Missing Album,* Chess/MCA, 1991 • *The Best of John Lee Hooker, 1965–1974,* MCA, 1992 • *His Best Chess Sides,* MCA, 1997.

Howlin' Wolf: *Live and Cookin' at Alice's Revisited,* Chess, 1972 • *The Back Door Wolf,* Chess, 1973, 1995.

James, Etta: *Rocks the House,* Cadet, 1963 • *Essential,* Chess, 1993 • *Her Best,* Chess/MCA, 1997.

Mabley, Moms: *Moms Sings Mabley,* Chess, 1969.

Memphis Slim: *The Real Folk Blues,* Chess/MCA, 1966.

Otis, Johnny: "Barrel House Stomp," Savoy, 1949 • "Double Crossing Blues," Savoy, 1950 • "Mistrustin' Blues," Savoy, 1950 • "Rockin' Blues," Savoy, 1950 • *The Original Johnny Otis Show,* Savoy Jazz, 1994 • *See also* Eckstine, Billy.

Phillips, Little Esther: "Cupid's Boogie," Savoy, 1950 • "Ring-a-Ding-Doo," Federal, 1952.

Ramsey Lewis Trio: *Sound of Christmas,* Cadet, 1961.

Sunnyland Slim: *I Don't Give a Damn If Whites Bought It,* Red Lightnin, 1977, 1985.

Turner, Big Joe: *See* Eckstine, Billy.

Walker, T-Bone: "Call It Stormy Monday," Black and White, 1947.

Ward, Billy, and the Dominoes: "Sixty Minute Man," Federal, 1951 • "The Bells," Federal, 1953.

Waters, Muddy: *Folk Singer,* Chess/MCA, 1964, 1987 • *Muddy Brass and the Blues,* Chess/MCA, 1967 • *Live (at Mr. Kelly's),* Chess/MCA, 1971, 1977 • *They Call Me Muddy Waters,* Chess/MCA, 1971 • *Can't Get No Grindin',* Chess/MCA, 1973 • *The Chess Box,* Chess, 1989 • *One More Mile,* Chess/MCA, 1994.

COLLECTIONS

Modern Jazz Piano, Savoy, 1946, 1956.

Black California, Savoy, 1952.

Chess Blues Classics: 1957–1967, Chess/MCA, 1997.

Roger Bechirian

Roger Bechirian was a vital cog in the transition from English pub rock to the new wave of Elvis Costello, Nick Lowe, Dave Edmunds (see entries), Graham Parker, and Lene Lovich in the '70s and early '80s.

Bechirian engineered a number of Nick Lowe's most important productions, including Parker's *Stick to Me,* Edmunds' *Trax on Wax 4* and *Repeat When Necessary,* Lowe's own *Labor of Lust* with "Cruel to Be Kind," and most importantly, Costello's *My Aim Is True, This Year's Model, Armed Forces, Get Happy,* and *Taking Liberties.*

Bechirian then co-produced (with Lowe) Costello's *Trust* (No. 9 U.K.), Lowe's *The Abominable Showman,* and (with Costello) Squeeze's *East Side Story* (No. 19 U.K.) with the great "Tempted." Bechirian has also produced the seminal Irish pop-punk band the Undertones in addition to Wang (Huang) Chung, the Flamin' Groovies, the latter-day Monkees, Shakin' Pyramids, and the Trashcan Sinatras.

Roger A. Bechirian was born in 1954 in Calcutta, India, and moved with his family to England when he was 10. Bechirian began piano lessons at age 5 and has continued to play, recording as a soloist and with the band Blanket of Secrecy. "I was always very interested in harmony structures and bass end. It's the bass that's always interested me. I think you'll probably notice from my mixes that I am quite bass mad, I am always trying to keep the bass caught up with the vocal."

Bechirian's interest in music was augmented with a love of the technical. "My father had an old Philips stereo tape recorder quite early on, and he was a film buff, so he would show me how to edit tape. I was recording theme tunes on television, cutting them up with speech, writing my own tunes, and chopping it onto the tape. It was an amazing magical medium. Later, my friends and I would look at records, and they would check out who played what—who was the guitarist, who was the singer—but I used to check out where it was recorded and who engineered it. I was really interested in how the sound was made.

"Eventually, I was at college studying for an electronics degree and I dropped out. I just found it very, very tedious. I finally got an interview with Eden Studios, which was a 4-track studio at the time. They needed someone to train as a disc-cutting engineer, so that's how I finally got into studio work in about 1972."

Bechirian had keys to the studio and friends in bands. The combination was too much to resist. "We used to sneak in at night when all the sessions were finished and record. Everything was recorded in mono and you'd bounce down to stereo and then back again, build up another few tracks and keep going backwards and forwards."

When Eden moved to Chiswick, Bechirian was involved with the design and construction of the new 24-track studio. "We had this electronic wizard who basically used Neve circuit designs, improvised here and there, improved things, and built this marvelous board. A lot of records I worked on were recorded there: the first two Undertones, most of the Costello stuff.

"I was a tea boy for quite a while. They wouldn't let me loose with important clients, but finally they let me do small sessions, demo work. I guess I had a really big mouth, I couldn't resist suggesting an idea. I met Dave Robinson and Jake Riviera, the co-founders of Stiff records, around 1974 and they signed lots of people like Wreckless Eric, Lene Lovich, Nick Lowe, Elvis Costello. They sent me tapes to mix, and they liked what I was doing with some of the material, so I started working with them.

"In the meantime, I had been working as an engineer for Nick Lowe's productions. I learned a lot from him: the importance of a very good arrangement, strong vocal delivery, and how to get the best out of people. Everyone has a feeling of what their limitations are, and I really enjoy pushing down those barriers and getting more from them than they imagined—hitting a high note they never thought they could ever hit, playing a solo they never dreamed, that kind of thing."

Bechirian reveals that he often achieves his desired result in the studio by pushing musicians to their utmost limit. "I have a terrible thing I do now," he says. "I've found that you get the best results from people when they are really really pissed off about something—unless it's one of those days when everybody has got a permanent grin and things just work, but that just doesn't happen very often. People get really angry when the take isn't down yet, and they think they've played pretty well a hundred times. I'll say, 'Well, no. It's still not there, there's something missing. It sounds great, but it's not really great yet.' I've found that's how to push people."

Another important Bechirian production is Squeeze's melodic ode to infidelity, "Tempted," a modern rock radio favorite for almost two decades. It almost didn't happen at all.

"We tried 'Tempted' about five different ways—a country version, a rock version, all these crazy versions with Glenn Tilbrook singing, and none of them worked. We finally put the song in the form it is now, said 'Ah, this is fine,' and went home. We turned up the next morning, and Paul Carrack, who had just joined the band, said, 'I have an idea. Do you mind if I sing it?' I threw a mike up, and he went up and sang against it, and it was this magical transformation. It's like the song just came alive." —ERIC OLSEN AND DAWN DARLING

Attractions, The: *Mad About the Wrong Boy,* F-Beat, 1980.

Barracudas, The: *Endeavor to Persevere,* Mau Mau, 1984, 1995.

Bechirian, Roger: *The Art of Roger Bechirian,* Vol. 1, RivGlob, 1982.

Blanket of Secrecy: *Ears Have Walls,* Warner Bros., 1982.

Blues Band: *Itchy Feet,* Arista, 1981.

Byrne, Simon: *Dream Crazy,* Epic, 1986.

Carrack, Paul: *The Carrack Collection,* Chrysalis, 1988.

Carter, Carlene: *Blue Nun,* F-Beat/WB, 1977, 1981 • *C'est C Bon,* Epic, 1983 • *Best Of,* Columbia, 1985 • *See also* the Attractions.

Costello, Elvis, and the Attractions: *Trust,* F-Beat/CBS, 1981 • *Girls, Girls, Girls,* Columbia, 1989.

dB's, The: *Stands for Decibels,* IRS, 1981.

Flamin' Groovies: *Jumpin' in the Night,* Sire, 1979.

Koklin, Tony: *Time Chaser,* Chiswick, 1981.

Lovich, Lene: *Stateless,* Stiff, 1977 • *Flex,* Stiff/Epic, 1979 • *Stateless . . . Plus,* Rhino, 1979, 1995.

Lowe, Nick: *The Abominable Showman,* Columbia, 1983 • *Basher: The Best Of,* Columbia, 1989 • *Boxed,* Demon, 1994.

Monkees, The: *Pool It!* Rhino, 1986 • *Listen to the Band,* Rhino, 1991.

Orrall, Robert Ellis: *Special Pain* (EP), RCA, 1983 • *Contain Yourself,* RCA, 1984.

Photos: *The Photos,* Epic, 1980.

Rumour, The: *Frogs, Sprouts, Clogs and Krauts,* Stiff, 1978.

Shakin' Pyramids: *Celts and Cobras* (10 tracks), Virgin, 1982 • *rock 'n' roll Records,* Epic, 1982.

Siouxsie & the Banshees: "New Skin," Virgin, 1996 (*Striptease* soundtrack).

Squeeze: *East Side Story,* A&M, 1981 • *Singles 45 and Under,* A&M, 1982.

Trash Can Sinatras: *Cake,* Go!, 1990.

Undertones, The: *The Undertones,* Sire, 1979 • *Hypnotised,* Sire, 1980 • *The Positive Touch,* Rykodisc, 1981, 1994 • *The Sin of Pride,* Ardeck, 1983 • *Best Of,* Rykodisc, 1994.

Huang Chung: *Huang Chung* (3 tracks), Arista, 1982.

Walter Becker and Donald Fagen

Walter Becker (born February 20, 1950, in Queens) and Donald Fagen (born January 10, 1948, in Passaic, New Jersey) were the brains behind Steely Dan, whose discs are among the most high-fidelity recordings ever. Although Gary Katz (see entry) received sole production credit for their seven albums, engineers who worked with them say Becker and Fagen were very hands-on producers throughout their Steely Dan careers.

Becker and Fagen met at Bard College in upstate New York and played in a variety of bands, including Chameleon Church, which sported Chevy Chase on drums, and the popular Boston band Ultimate Spinach. A&R executive Katz found jobs for the duo as staff songwriters at ABC/Dunhill, where they wrote songs for and toured with Jay and the Americans.

After a period in which they'd placed only one song (the long-forgotten "I Mean to Shine," with Barbra Streisand), Katz suggested they form their own band. The original Steely Dan lineup included Jim Hodder (drums), Denny Dias and Jeff Baxter (guitars), David Palmer (keyboards and vocals), Becker (bass), and Fagen (keyboards and vocals).

"I was a reluctant vocalist at first," Fagen explains, "but we never found anyone who could do the tunes. My mother sang pop standards with a band; she actually used to work up at the Catskills. Her stage name was Ellen Ross. She quit singing when she was 18, but sang every summer during the Depression to make money. She used to sing around the house all the time, so I grew up knowing all the standards."

Fagen's voice has an unusual timbre, but his expressiveness, phrasing, and sense of pitch are exceptional; he credits his mother for all those qualities.

While Fagen was a vocal constant, it soon became apparent that a fixed lineup wouldn't serve the songwriters' musical ideas. Gradually, Steely Dan became the working name for a constantly changing group of studio musicians, brought in for their ability to accommodate individual songs.

The group hired the best guitarists in the world: from early members Baxter and Dias to Mark Knopfler (*Gaucho;* see entry), Rick Derringer (*Countdown to Ecstasy*), Lee Ritenour (*Aja*), Elliot Randall (many tracks, including the solo in "Reelin' in the Years," which Jimmy Page (see entry) once called his favorite), Larry Carlton, Dean Parks, Steve Khan, Hugh McCracken, and Ben Benay.

A tour of the Steely Dan repertoire also features the greatest drummers of the day, including Jeff Porcaro, Hal Blaine, Steve Gadd, Rick Marotta, Bernard Purdie, Ed Greene, Jim Keltner, and Jim Gordon.

Fagen's vocals were typically double-tracked to obtain the distinctive Steely Dan vocal sound. Rather than split-panning the unison double, as the Beatles often did, or panning them together in the stereo field at identical volume levels, Fagen's unison-dubbed vocals were most often mixed so that the second part was at roughly 75 percent of the volume of the first. This gave the vocal the thickness of a unison double without the in-your-face obviousness of one.

The sonic clarity of Steely Dan records was made possible by Becker and Fagen's attention to detail and the enlistment of Roger Nichols, a former nuclear engineer turned recording engineer.

The group's first two releases, Can't Buy a Thrill and Countdown to Ecstasy, were experiments in equalization, or more accurately, in the lack thereof.

"Roger didn't use any EQ on those albums," recalls Jeff "Skunk" Baxter. "He believed that the records would sound more natural if we just concentrated on good mike placement."

Audiophile Becker pushed the recording team to greater and greater clarity. From the opening jangle of glass chimes on Can't Buy a Thrill to the last chord of Gaucho, listeners knew they were in for a hell of a sonic ride, each album sounding better than the last.

Their fourth release, Katy Lied, was an unprecedented sonic masterpiece. At the beginning of one session, Nichols reportedly walked into the studio to find the assistant engineer recording test tones to calibrate the machines for that day's recordings. Nichols asked the assistant where he got the tape for setting up the tones. "From over there," the assistant said, pointing to a corner of the room.

The story goes that Nichols' face turned ashen as he recognized that the assistant had just recorded over—and erased—one of the 24-track master tapes. A further disaster befell the project when the DBX noise reduction unit malfunctioned. Yet, when it was finally released, Katy Lied still sounded better than any other record on the market.

Each of the two best-sounding albums, Aja and Gaucho, won much-deserved Grammys for best recording, in 1977 and 1980, respectively.

After Becker and Fagen decided to break up "the band," Fagen recorded a solo album in 1983, The Night-

fly, which Katz nominally produced. It remains a standard by which audiophiles evaluate the performance and clarity of high-end equipment.

Fagen's 1993 release, Kamakiriad, was reportedly 10 years in the making. According to Nichols, two of those years were spent programming the drum machines and trying to get "just the right feel" to satisfy Fagen's increasingly exacting standards.

Becker and Fagen continued to produce outside projects throughout the '80s and '90s, both together and separately. Becker produced Rickie Lee Jones, China Crisis, and jazz artists Bob Sheppard and John Beasley. Fagen produced David Sanborn and a live Steely Dan reunion album, Made in America. —DANIEL J. LEVITIN

Walter Becker

Beal, Jeff: *Objects in the Mirror,* Triloka, 1991.
Beasley, John: *Cauldron,* Windham Hill, 1992 • *A Change of Heart,* Windham Hill, 1993.
China Crisis: "Black Man Ray," Virgin/EMI, 1985 (*Now That's What I Call Music 5*) • *Flaunt the Imperfection,* Virgin/WB, 1985 • "Wake up (King in a Catholic Style)," Virgin/WB, 1985 • *Diary of a Hollow Horse,* Virgin/A&M, 1989 • *Collection,* Virgin, 1990.
Fagen, Donald: *Kamakiriad,* Reprise, 1993.
Franks, Michael: *Blue Pacific,* Reprise, 1990.
Jones, Rickie Lee: *Flying Cowboys,* Geffen, 1989.
Kikoski, Dave: *Persistent Dreams,* Triloka, 1992.
LaVerne, Andy: *Pleasure Seekers,* Triloka, 1991 • *Double Standard,* Triloka, 1993.
Sheppard, Bob: *Tell Tale Signs,* Windham Hill, 1991.
Steig, Jeremy: *Jigsaw,* Triloka, 1992.

Walter Becker and Donald Fagen

Becker, Walter: *11 Tracks of Whack,* Giant, 1994.
Christlieb, Pete, and Warne Marsh: *Quintet,* Warner Bros., 1978.

Donald Fagen

New York Rock and Soul Revue: *Live at the Beacon,* Giant, 1991.
Sanborn, David: "The Finer Things," Warner Bros., 1983 (*The King of Comedy* soundtrack).
Steely Dan: *Alive in America,* Giant, 1995.

Curt Bedeau
See FULL FORCE

Barry Beckett

Barry Beckett belongs to that elite group of producers who have been behind the board on more than 100 albums, but praise him on the honor and in his laconic, humble way, he only replies, "Well, I guess according to my age, it's possible, but I sure don't remember each and every one."

Among his most notable projects are Bob Dylan's *Slow Train Coming* (No. 3) and *Saved* (No. 24), Dire Straits' *Communiqué* (No. 11), and Bob Seger's *Beautiful Loser, Stranger in Town* (No. 4), and *Against the Wind* (No. 1). Beckett has produced or co-produced a staggering range of artists including Phish, the Waterboys, Paul Simon, Etta James, Hank Williams Jr., and Tammy Wynette.

As part of the famed Muscle Shoals Rhythm Section, Beckett played keyboards on some classic tunes, including the Staple Singers' "I'll Take You There" and Simon's "Kodachrome." That period was instrumental in his growth as a producer.

"It helped me to think [with] all the artists that I produce to strive to get everything sounding as a band," he says in his slow, Southern drawl. "Even when we're doing single acts, I always try to have the musicians appear as a band, not as something that was a sterile or conceived thing to put behind a single act or piece of music."

That desire to go against the grain made it tough going for Beckett when he relocated to Nashville from Alabama in 1985, even though he'd produced a number of pop hits, including his first chart topper: Mary MacGregor's "Torn Between Two Lovers."

"Nashville was a different animal back then; it was a very conservative environment," Beckett recalls. "There were only a few people in town who even dared to try to take the more left or more liberal approach to country music. I moved up here because I was beginning to hear it. There were people like Tony Brown, Harold Shedd, and James Stroud [see entries], who I could say thought pretty much the way I do about bands."

Beckett took a job as an A&R executive at Warner Bros., which was "very hard for me because I had to think very conservative back then," but it led him to one of his most successful and long-term collaborations, co-producing Hank Williams Jr.

"He understands rock 'n' roll and that's what he wanted to do," says Beckett of Williams. "And me, I like more blues and I like rock 'n' roll, and he understands blues too, that's what he's all about. We just clicked basically." Although Beckett left Warner Bros. in 1987, he

and Williams continued to work together, ultimately winning the Country Music Association's award for vocal event of the year for "There's a Tear in My Beer" (No. 7 country). Beckett delved back into pop production in the late '80s, working again with Seger and James, as well as Jason and the Scorchers and Delbert McClinton, among others. In the mid-'90s, he's concentrated more on country, having tremendous success with acts like Wynette, Kenny Chesney, Confederate Railroad, and Neal McCoy. Beckett says he loves straddling the line between musical genres. "It's fun!" he enthuses. "It wakes me up!"

Through the years, Beckett has had the chance to work with many of his favorites. He thinks Seger is the best singer he's ever worked with ("definitely the most passionate"), followed closely by newcomer William Topley; Knopfler is the best musician ("he's just awesome"). Not surprisingly, he was most humbled by working with Dylan, with whom he hooked up via his mentor, legendary Atlantic Records producer Jerry Wexler (see entry). Of Wexler, Beckett simply says, "I owe everything to him."

"Wexler called me and asked me if I wanted to work with Dylan, and I said, 'Sure, that will be great, but it's important that we get away from the sound that he's doing presently and we come up with a new sound,' and he agreed," Beckett recalls. "About two more weeks went by and Wexler calls me back and says, 'Barry, we're screwed.' And I said, 'Why? What's wrong?' and he says, 'Dylan's going Christian!' And I said, 'So, that's hip nowadays, it's the thing to do. Have you watched TV lately man? Jeez!'"

Beckett went to hear some of Dylan's material for what ultimately became *Slow Train Coming,* and "was just blown away. I thought, 'My God, this is what it's all about, right here. All these other people are just fakes.' " Wexler heard the tunes with Beckett and Dylan shortly thereafter, "and Wexler sat there and listened to the songs and he looked at me and winked. Anytime you can get a wink out of Wexler, you got it made."

It took some time for Beckett to figure out what that new sound with Dylan should be on *Slow Train Coming.* "I was trying to figure out something different than just the piano or just the organ, and [so] I went to No. 2 standby, which is a Wurlitzer piano. We put a harmonizer on it and for Dylan it was a new sound, so it worked."

Naturally, because of his background, Beckett says he pays special attention to keyboards. "It's a very transparent instrument," he says. "It's very easy to come up with a mood on a track." In fact, Beckett still dabbles with the instrument, playing on a number of albums, including a recent Kirk Whalum project produced by Beckett's buddy Steve Buckingham (see entry).

While Beckett has had more than his share of successes, he's the first to admit that he's produced a number of albums that he wishes had fared better. "Oh yeah, there are plenty that got away," he says. "I thought the Waterboys [*Room to Roam*] should have been a little bit bigger. I think Feargal Sharkey [*Songs from the Mardi Gras*] should have been bigger; he's a great singer. T. Graham Brown probably should have been bigger, but I think I probably screwed that up myself [by not making Brown sound more country]. It's a bad feeling because you decide to go with the artist there, but then again, it is my job to work for the artist."

Despite working with scads of superstars, Beckett says he loves producing baby acts. "I love starting new artists, I love starting them out because usually they've had a hard time. . . . It's just more exciting to break a new act."

However, Beckett has found that sometimes new artists can be intimidated by his fame and that the first few days can be tense until they understand each other. "I've had it where the artist starts crying because they can't understand where I'm coming from and it takes a while just to put them at ease and settle them down. I mean, it's fine being famous as a producer sometimes. It's all fine and good, you work for that end, but sometimes you intimidate people, and I have to watch out for that," says Beckett, "but then again, some of the artists because of their youth aren't intimidated because they don't know that much about you. The less intimidation the better for me because I don't scare them."

What scares Beckett is the increasing amount of interference in the recording process by inexperienced label executives who rule by committee. "The committee aspect will drive producers crazy if you're dealing with an A&R staff that don't know what they're doing. A lot of the A&R staffs are put together because they don't have anyone else to do it, and they're grabbing young people out of college to put together these staffs. You can't deal with that; you just have to float through it and hope they make the right decisions."

Despite the label influence, Beckett says he's having more fun as a producer than he ever has, but he admits he misses something from those Muscle Shoals days. "The equipment back then was better equipment than they make now because it was tube equipment. Now they're making stuff that's transistorized and all that stuff. A lot of people are trying to find tube equipment right now, but it's hard to find." —MELINDA NEWMAN

Adams, Greg: *Runaway Dreams*, Attic, 1979.

Alabama: "If I Had You," RCA, 1989 • *Southern Star*, RCA, 1989.

Asleep at the Wheel: *Keepin' Me Up Nights*, Arista, 1990.

Baez, Joan: *Honest Lullaby*, Portrait, 1979 • *Rare, Live and Classic*, Vanguard, 1993.

Bassett, Steve: *Bassett, Steve*, CBS, 1984.

Blackfoot: *Flyin'*, Atco, 1975.

Brown, T. Graham: *Bumper to Bumper*, Capitol, 1990.

Buffalo Club: *If She Don't Love You*, Rising Tide, 1996 • *Buffalo Club*, Rising Tide, 1997 • "Heart Hold On," Rising Tide, 1997 • "If She Don't Love You," Rising Tide, 1997 • "Nothin' Less Than Love," Rising Tide, 1997.

Burnette, Billy: *Gimme You*, CBS, 1981.

Canned Heat: *One More River to Cross*, Atlantic, 1974.

Carnes, Kim: *Sailin'*, A&M, 1976.

Cartwright, Lionel: *Chasin' the Sun*, MCA, 1991.

Chesney, Kenny: *In My Wildest Dreams*, Capricorn, 1994 • *All I Need to Know*, BNA, 1995 • *Me and You*, BNA, 1996 • "When I Close My Eyes," BNA, 1997.

Confederate Railroad: *Confederate Railroad*, Atlantic Nashville, 1992 • *Notorious*, Atlantic Nashville, 1994 • *When and Where*, Atlantic, 1995 • *Greatest Hits*, Atlantic, 1996.

Crewe, Bob: *Motivation*, Elektra, 1977.

Cryner, Bobbie: *Girl of Your Dreams*, MCA Nashville, 1996.

Daniels, Charlie: *Same Ol' Me*, Capitol, 1995.

Dire Straits: *Communique*, Warner Bros., 1979 • *Money for Nothing (Greatest Hits)*, Warner Bros., 1988.

Dylan, Bob: *Dylan*, Columbia, 1973 • *Slow Train Coming*, Columbia, 1979 • *Saved*, Columbia, 1980 • *Bootleg Series*, Columbia, 1991 • *Greatest Hits*, Vol. 3, Columbia, 1995.

Edwards and Ralph: *Edwards and Ralph*, Ariola, 1978.

Emilio: *Life Is Good*, Capitol Nashville, 1995 • "I'd Love You to Love Me," Capitol, 1997 • *It's on the House*, Capitol, 1997 • "She Gives," Capitol, 1997.

Feliciano, Jose: *Sweet Soul Music*, Private Stock, 1976.

Forester Sisters: "You Again," Warner Bros., 1987 • *Greatest Hits*, Warner Bros., 1989.

Frey, Glenn: "Sexy Girl," MCA, 1984 • *The Allnighter*, MCA, 1984 • *Soul Searchin'*, MCA, 1986.

Garfunkel, Art: *Watermark*, Columbia, 1978.

Gill, Vince: *I Never Knew Lonely*, RCA, 1992.

Graham, Tammy: *Tammy Graham*, Career, 1996 • "Cool Water," Career, 1997.

Haggard, Noel: *One Lifetime*, Atlantic Nashville, 1997 • "Tell Me Something Bad About Tulsa," Atlantic, 1997.

Helm, Levon: *Levon Helm*, Capitol, 1982.

Hinton, Eddie: *Very Extremely Dangerous*, Capricorn, 1978.

James, Etta: *Seven Year Itch*, Island, 1989 • *Stickin' to My Guns*, Island, 1990 • *How Strong Is a Woman: The Island Sessions*, 4th & B'Way, 1993 • *Life's Been Rough on Me*, Private Music, 1997.

Jason and the Scorchers: *Thunder and Fire*, A&M, 1989.

John, Elton: *Duets,* MCA, 1993.

LeBlanc, Lenny: *Breakthrough,* Capitol, 1981.

Lee, Woody: *Get Over It,* Atlantic, 1995.

Linhart, Buzzy: *Pussycats Can Go Far,* Atco, 1974.

Lynyrd Skynyrd: *The Last Rebel,* Atlantic, 1993 • *Endangered Species,* Capricorn, 1994.

MacGregor, Mary: "Torn Between Two Lovers," Ariola America, 1977 • *Torn Between Two Lovers,* Ariola, 1978.

McClinton, Delbert: "Giving It Up for Your Love," MMS/Capitol, 1980 • *The Jealous Kind,* Capitol, 1980 • *Plain from the Heart,* Capitol, 1981 • *I'm with You,* Curb, 1990 • *Delbert McClinton,* Curb/Capitol, 1993.

McCoy, Neal: "No Doubt About It," Atlantic, 1994 • *No Doubt About It,* Atlantic, 1994 • "Wink," Atlantic, 1994 • *You Gotta Love That!* Atlantic, 1994 • *Neal McCoy,* Atlantic, 1996 • *Greatest Hits,* Atlantic Nashville, 1997.

McGuinn Hillman: *McGuinn Hillman,* Capitol, 1980.

McGuinn, Clark and Hillman: *Return Flight,* Edsel, 1992.

Mel and Tim: "Starting All Over Again," Stax, 1972 • *Starting All Over Again,* Stax, 1972.

Miller, Frankie: *Standing on the Edge,* Capitol, 1982.

Moore, Ian: *Ian Moore,* Capricorn, 1993.

Morgan, Lorrie: *Leave the Light On,* RCA, 1989 • *Trainwreck of Emotion,* BNA, 1993.

Muscle Shoals Horns: *Born to Get Down,* Bang, 1976 • *Doin' It to the Bone,* Ariola America, 1977.

Orlando, Tony: *Tony Orlando,* Elektra, 1978.

Orleans: *Orleans,* ABC, 1973 • *Before the Dance,* ABC, 1977.

Oslin, K.T.: *Love in a Small Town,* RCA, 1990 • *New Way Home,* RCA, 1993.

Parnell, Lee Roy: *Lee Roy Parnell,* Arista, 1989, 1990 • *Love Without Mercy,* Arista, 1992.

Phish: *Rift,* Elektra, 1993.

Prine, John: *Storm Windows,* Asylum, 1980 • *Great Days: The John Prine Anthology,* Rhino, 1993.

Proclaimers, The: "Gentle on My Mind/Waiting for a Train," Chrysalis, 1994.

Raven, Eddy: "I'm Gonna Get You," RCA, 1988 • "Joe Knows How to Live," RCA, 1988 • "Bayou Boys," Universal, 1989 • "In a Letter to You," Universal, 1989.

Sanford Townsend Band: *Sanford Townsend Band,* Warner Bros., 1976 • "Smoke from a Distant Fire," Warner Bros., 1977.

Santana: *Havana Moon,* Columbia, 1983.

Seger, Bob: *Beautiful Loser,* Capitol, 1975 • *Night Moves,* Capitol, 1976 • *Stranger in Town* (5 tracks), Capitol, 1978 • "We've Got Tonight," Capitol, 1978 • *Against the Wind,* Capitol, 1980 • "Fire Lake," Capitol, 1980 • *The Fire Inside,* Capitol, 1991.

Sharkey, Feargal: *Songs Fron the Mardi Gras,* Virgin, 1991.

Simon, Paul: "Kodachrome," Columbia, 1973 • "Loves Me Like a Rock," Columbia, 1973 • *There Goes Rhymin' Simon,* Columbia, 1973 • "Kodachrome," Warner Bros., 1993 (*Coneheads* soundtrack).

Smith, Russell: *Russell Smith,* Capitol, 1982.

Snow, Phoebe: *Against the Grain,* Columbia, 1978 • *The Best Of,* Columbia, 1982.

Southside Johnny and the Asbury Jukes: *All I Want Is Everything: The Best Of, 1979–1991,* Rhino, 1993 • *The Jukes,* Mercury, 1979.

Staple Singers: *Unlock Your Mind,* Warner Bros., 1978.

Staples, Mavis: *Oh, What a Feeling,* Warner Bros., 1979.

Starland Vocal Band: *4x4,* Windsong, 1980.

Taylor, Kate: *It's in There,* Columbia, 1979.

Tillis, Pam: *Pam Tillis Collection,* Warner Bros., 1994.

Topley, William: *Black River,* Mercury Nashville, 1997.

Walker, Jerry Jeff: *Reunion,* SouthCoast, 1981.

Waterboys, The: *Room to Roam,* Ensign/Chrysalis, 1990.

Williams, Hank Jr.: "Mind Your Own Business," Warner Bros., 1986 • *Live,* Curb/WB, 1986 • *Montana Cafe,* Curb/WB, 1986 • "Born to Boogie," Warner Bros., 1987 • *Born to Boogie,* Warner Bros., 1987 • *Wild Streak,* Warner Bros., 1988 • *Greatest Hits,* Vol. 3, Curb/WB, 1989 • "There's a Tear in My Beer," Curb/WB, 1989 • *America (The Way I See It),* Curb/WB, 1990 • *Lone Wolf,* Curb/WB, 1990 • *Pure Hank,* Warner Bros., 1990 • *Maverick,* Capricorn, 1991 • *The Bocephus Box: Hank Williams Jr. Collection, '79–'92,* Capricorn, 1992 • *Out of Left Field,* Capricorn, 1993.

Womack, Bobby: *Communication,* United Artists, 1971 • *Understanding,* United Artists, 1972 • *Looking for a Love,* United Artists, 1974.

Wright, Chely: *Woman in the Moon,* Polydor Nashville, 1994.

Wynette, Tammy: *Without Walls,* Epic, 1994.

Yarrow, Peter: *Hard Times,* Warner Bros., 1975.

COLLECTIONS

Skynyrd Friends, MCA, 1995.

Michael Beinhorn

A meticulous producer whose talent has helped such rock acts as Soul Asylum and Soundgarden realize their creative and commercial peaks, Michael Beinhorn started his career at age 20 as a keyboardist in Bill Laswell's (see entry) groundbreaking ensemble Material. Despite a string of critically acclaimed records as a member of that unit starting in the late '70s, Beinhorn realized early that his days as a musician were numbered.

"I knew I wanted to be a producer after I'd done it a

few times, and it became a lot easier than trying to play in a band," says Beinhorn. "I never felt I was cut out to master an instrument; I felt my role was better in trying to initiate great ideas and help people develop what they were trying to do."

During his first fruitful years with Material, Beinhorn worked on the *Temporary Music, Memory Serves,* and *One Down* albums. His first big break came when he branched out with Laswell to produce and co-write Herbie Hancock's breakthrough album, *Future Shock.* That gig scored Beinhorn a Grammy and earned him a place in an exclusive group of adventurous new writer/producers in the early '80s.

In the '90s, Beinhorn has established himself as a hard-rock specialist thanks to his raw and immediate productions for the likes of the Red Hot Chili Peppers, Violent Femmes, Soul Asylum, Soundgarden, Aerosmith, and Ozzy Osbourne.

In his quest for the ultimate rock sound, Beinhorn co-developed the Ultra Analog format, an 8-track, 2-inch tape recorder that runs at 7.5 ips. Because of its wide track width and slow speed, Ultra Analog "enhances the low end like you wouldn't believe," says Beinhorn. "It gives you a strange tonal effect on the drums—a punch that didn't seem to exist before. Plus, you can get an hour's worth of music on a reel, and it winds faster than a digital machine."

Beinhorn used Ultra Analog on Ozzy Osbourne's 1995 release *Ozzmosis* (No. 4) and Social Distortion's 1996 album *White Light, White Heat, White Trash,* cutting drum and bass tracks on the 8-track and synchronizing it to other multitrack machines. Although he's a big fan of the Ultra Analog sound, Beinhorn admits that it's sometimes impractical to use the medium because of its delicacy and high degree of maintenance. For instance, when he began working with Hole on the band's follow-up to its breakthrough album, *Live Through This,* Beinhorn said he would forgo the 2-inch 8-track.

"At this stage I'd like to keep things as simple as possible," he says. "I don't want to drive everyone else crazy with my experiments."

As hard as he works on the sonic aspects of his records, Beinhorn values musicality above all, and regards his role as coaxing artists to produce their best possible performances. "I wish for the musical information to come purely from the artists, and the only way it'll do that is if they're adequately stimulated," he says.

Another of Beinhorn's distinctions is his position as a staff producer and A&R representative for Epic Records—a relationship that has put him together with Living Colour, Osbourne, and Nicky Holland. —PAUL VERNA

Aerosmith: *Big Ones,* Geffen, 1994.

Buck Pets: *Mercurotones,* Island, 1990.

Cavedogs: *Soul Martini,* Capitol, 1992.

Hammerbox: *Numb,* A&M, 1993.

Hancock, Herbie: *Future Shock,* Columbia, 1983 • "Hardrock," Columbia, 1984 • *Sound-System,* Columbia, 1984 • *Perfect Machine,* Columbia, 1988.

Hawke, Ethan: "I'm Nuthin'," RCA, 1994 (*Reality Bites* soundtrack).

Holland, Nicky: "Nobody's Girl," Epic, 1997 • *Sense and Sensuality,* Epic, 1997.

Idle Eyes: *Love's Imperfection,* Atco, 1986.

Liquid Jesus: *Pour in the Sky,* MCA, 1991.

Living Colour: "Sunshine of Your Love," Epic, 1994.

Love Battery: *Far Gone,* Sub Pop, 1993.

Osbourne, Ozzy: *Ozzmosis,* Epic, 1995.

Parachute Club: *At the Feet of the Moon,* RCA, 1984.

Raw Youth: "Tame Yourself," RNA, 1991 (*Tame Yourself*).

Red Hot Chili Peppers: "Behind the Sun," EMI, 1987 • "Fight Like a Brave," EMI, 1987 • "Fight Like a Brave" (remix), EMI, 1987 • "Fire," EMI, 1987 • *The Abbey Road EP,* EMI, 1987 • *The Uplift Mofo Party Plan,* EMI, 1987 • *Mother's Milk,* EMI, 1989 • *Positive Mental Octopus,* EMI, 1990 • "Higher Ground," EMI, 1992.

Social Distortion: *White Light, White Heat, White Trash,* 550 Music/Epic, 1996.

Soul Asylum: *Grave Dancers Union,* Columbia, 1992 • "Black Gold," Columbia, 1993 • "Runaway Train," Columbia, 1993.

Soundgarden: "Black Hole Sun," A&M, 1994 • "Fell on Black Days," A&M, 1994 • "Spoonman," A&M, 1994 • *Superunknown,* A&M, 1994 • *Alive in the Superunknown,* A&M, 1995 • "My Wave," Interscope, 1996 (*MOM: Music for Our Mother Ocean*).

Violent Femmes: "American Music," Slash/Reprise, 1991 • *Why Do Birds Sing?,* Slash/Reprise, 1991 • *Add It Up, 1981–1993,* Slash, 1993.

Thom Bell

Arranger, producer, keyboardist, and brilliant melodist, Thom Bell created a signature rhythm-and-strings sound, the elegant soul of the "Philly sound" (associated with Gamble and Huff; see entry) of the '70s. Bell wrote (with Linda Creed and others) and produced a stellar string of hits for the Delfonics, the Stylistics, Spinners, Johnny Mathis, Elton John, Deniece Williams, James Ingram, Phyllis Hyman, and a host of others. Bell was the recipient of the first Grammy for Producer of the Year in 1974.

Thom Bell was born into a musical family in Kingston, Jamaica, in 1943. His father is an accountant and plays pedal steel and accordion. His mother is a classical pianist. The family moved to Philadelphia when Bell was very young. All of the children in the family were required to master piano first, under the theory that they could then learn additional instruments more easily. By age 9, Bell could read music and play piano, percussion, and trumpet (he now plays 18 instruments). Together with his parents and various siblings, he performed at teas, recitals, service club functions, and church.

He and his twin sister Barbara went to school with Kenny Gamble, and the musical lads began writing some songs together in their midteens. When Bell was 16, producer Luther Dixon (the Shirelles, Chuck Jackson) saw him perform a Gamble-Bell composition at a Philadelphia club on electric piano, the first Dixon had seen. Dixon asked Bell if he would like to do some recording in New York, and would he also "bring along that electric piano." Bell had been renting the piano from the head of the local musician's union for weekend gigs, because, as Bell recalls with a chuckle, "all these places had old, hard, junky pianos that were out of tune."

Bell became a regular on New York sessions run by King Curtis, but he grew weary of the grind and the low pay, and following his aspirations to become a conductor and orchestrator, he headed for Broadway in 1960. He passed a conductor's test on musical theory with flying colors, but management regretfully informed him that they really couldn't use a "colored" conductor, adding that he would fit very well at the Apollo Theater in Harlem.

Bell stayed at the Apollo for a couple of years, but the low pay and seven-shows-a-day schedule eventually led him back to Philadelphia where he took a similar job at the Uptown Theater, playing piano behind top R&B acts like Marvin Gaye, the Supremes, Sam Cooke, and Brenda Holloway. The pay was still bad, however, and the ambitious young man grew tired of "banging away on the piano, breaking my fingernails night after night." In a big band of 15, the piano was the only unamplified instrument.

One day, Bell saw an ad in the paper for rhythm section auditions at Philadelphia's Cameo/Parkway records, the home of Chubby Checker and Dee Dee Sharp. Again, Bell passed the audition, but the label wasn't looking for a "colored" rhythm section.

"I was young, could write music and play anything they put in front of me, so they gave me a job as a lead sheet writer. I had to listen to the demos that came in, decipher the words, and write out the words and music."

Bell did that for about a year; then, Chubby Checker tapped him to tour with him as musical director and keyboardist. Also at that time, "Motown was kicking Cameo's behind, so they decided it would be okay to have a 'colored' rhythm section," Bell recalls.

Bell played and recorded with the "colored" acts on the label through the mid-'60s, and "then five guys came in to audition and asked if I would like to produce them. The only problem was they didn't sing very well, or have any songs," chuckles Bell. Only the guitar player could sing, so Bell made him the lead singer, ruffling some feathers. Next they needed songs, but when Bell went to the big publishers, all they would send him was hopelessly dated material. So, "necessity being the mother of invention," Bell started writing songs for the group himself. With the group's name mutating almost daily, they released two singles that "did okay." Then Cameo went out of business, the group was down to three, there was "no money, no distributor, and time was running out." Somehow the money was scraped together for a third single. That was "La-La Means I Love You," and the group was the Delfonics. The song, a classic soul ballad boasting a beautiful Bell melody, was picked up by Bell (no relation) Records owner Larry Utall, distributed under the Philly Groove label, and climbed the pop charts all the way to No. 4. in early 1968. Thom Bell was 25 and on his way.

The Delfonics hit again in 1970 with "Didn't I (Blow Your Mind This Time)" (No. 10), another delicate but firm gem. "Didn't I" won the 1970 Grammy for R&B Record of the Year, but Bell, who "wrote the melody, arranged, produced, and played the song," wasn't called to the podium to collect the award, Utall was, and with "no money and no Grammy," Bell decided to take his services elsewhere.

Bell wanted to sharpen his arranging skills so he made a deal with Gamble and Huff as an independent arranger, and worked with the Intruders, the O'Jays, and others. He returned to writing and production in 1971, churning out a remarkable series of velvety ballads with the Stylistics and more rhythmic, R&B-inclined smashes with the Spinners. The Stylistics' hits employ a harmonic sophistication equal to that of Burt Bacharach (see entry), with Russell Thompkins and Airrion Love's silky falsettos carrying classic melodies, especially on "You Make Me Feel Brand New" (No. 2), "Betcha By Golly, Wow" (No. 3) and "I'm Stone in Love with You" (No. 10).

To use a Motown analogy, the Spinners were Bell's Temptations and the Stylistics were his Miracles. The

1973 self-titled album yielded four grooving classics: "I'll Be Around" (No. 3) and "Could It Be I'm Falling in Love" (No. 4), driven by punchy strings, Phillippe Wynne's lead vocal, and Bell's own percussion; "One of a Kind (Love Affair)" (No. 11); and "Ghetto Child," which displays a gentle but persistent social conscience—a nice metaphor for Bell's life and music.

Prolific in life as in art, Bell, the father of eight, now lives in Maui, Hawaii. —ERIC OLSEN

Delfonics, The: "La-La Means I Love You," Philly Groove, 1968 • *La-La Means I Love You,* Philly Groove, 1968 • "Didn't I (Blow Your Mind This Time)," Philly Groove, 1970.

Dyson, Ronnie: *One Man Band,* Columbia, 1973.

Hyman, Phyllis: *Living All Alone,* Philadelphia International, 1987 • *Under Her Spell: Phyllis Hyman's Greatest Hits,* Arista, 1989 • *The Legacy of,* Arista, 1996.

Ingram, James: "Aren't You Tired," Warner Bros., 1989 • "I Don't Have the Heart," Warner Bros., 1989 • *It's Real,* Warner Bros., 1989 • *The Power of Great Music: The Best Of,* Qwest/WB, 1991 • *Always You,* Warner Bros., 1993.

John, Elton: "Mama Can't Buy You Love," MCA, 1979 • *Greatest Hits, 1979–1987,* MCA, 1987 • *The Complete Thom Bell Sessions* (EP), MCA, 1989 • *Greatest Hits, 1976–1986,* MCA, 1992.

Little Anthony and the Imperials: *The Best Of,* EMI, 1996.

Mangione, Chuck: *Eyes of the Veiled Temptress,* Columbia, 1988.

Mathis, Johnny: *I'm Coming Home,* Columbia, 1973 • *Mathis Is . . . ,* Columbia, 1977 • *Love Songs,* Columbia, 1988 • *Better Together: Duet,* Columbia, 1991 • *Music of Johnny Mathis: A Personal Collection,* Legacy/Columbia, 1995.

New York City: "I'm Doing Fine Now," Chelsea, 1973 • *I'm Doing Fine Now,* Chelsea, 1973.

O'Jays, The: *Back Stabbers,* Philadelphia International, 1972, 1996 • *Ship Ahoy,* Philadelphia International, 1973 • *So Full of Love,* The Right Stuff, 1978, 1993.

Spinners, The: "Could It Be I'm Falling in Love," Atlantic, 1973 • "I'll Be Around," Atlantic, 1973 • "One of a Kind (Love Affair)," Atlantic, 1973 • *Spinners,* Atlantic, 1973 • "Ghetto Child," Atlantic, 1974 • "I'm Coming Home," Atlantic, 1974 • "Love Don't Love Nobody," Atlantic, 1974 • "Mighty Love-Pt. 1," Atlantic, 1974 • w/ Dionne Warwick, "Then Came You," Atlantic, 1974 • "Living a Little, Laughing a Little," Atlantic, 1975 • *Mighty Love,* Rhino, 1975, 1995 • *Pick of the Litter,* Rhino, 1975, 1995 • "They Just Can't Stop It (The Games People Play)," Atlantic, 1975 • *Happiness Is Being with the Spinners,* Atlantic, 1976 • "Love or Leave," Atlantic, 1976 • "The Rubberband Man," Atlantic, 1976 • *Best Of,* Atlantic, 1978 • *From Here to Eternity,* Atlantic, 1979 • *One of a Kind Love Affair,* Rhino, 1991.

Stylistics, The: "Stop, Look, Listen (to Your Heart)," Avco Embassy, 1971 • *The Stylistics,* Avco, 1971 • "Betcha By Golly Wow," Avco, 1972 • "I'm Stone in Love with You," Avco, 1972 • "People Make the World Go Round," Avco, 1972 • *Round 2,* Avco, 1972 • "You Are Everything," Avco, 1972 • "Break up to Make Up," Avco, 1973 • "Rockin' Roll Baby," Avco, 1973 • "You'll Never Go to heaven (If You Break My Heart)," Avco, 1973 • "You Make Me Feel Brand New," Avco, 1974 • *The Best Of,* Avco, 1975 • *Best Of, Vol. 2,* Amherst, 1976, 1985.

Temptations, The: *Hear to Tempt You,* Atlantic, 1978.

Warwick, Dionne: *See* the Spinners.

Williams, Deniece: *My Melody,* ARC, 1981 • "It's Gonna Take a Miracle," ARC, 1982 • *Niecy,* ARC, 1982.

COLLECTIONS

City Slickers soundtrack, Varese Sarabande, 1991.

Pete Bellotte

Mention the name of British producer/songwriter Pete Bellotte to music fans with fond memories of the disco '70s and more often than not a smile will cross their faces as melodies from classic Donna Summer songs begin infiltrating their minds. Known the world over for his award-winning, chart-topping music, Bellotte, working with Giorgio Moroder (see entry), was responsible for the production of all of Summer's recordings between 1976 and 1980. Such albums as *A Love Trilogy, Once upon a Time, Live and More* (No. 1), *Bad Girls* (No. 1), and *The Wanderer* (No. 13) all bear Bellotte's distinct sound—coined Eurodisco—which majestically combined the robotic, trancelike riffs of such songs as "I Feel Love" (No. 6) and "Sunset People" with the glorious orchestrated backdrops of "I Love You," "MacArthur Park" (No. 1), and "Heaven Knows" (No. 4).

Teaming up with Moroder in the mid-'70s, Bellotte initially entered the spotlight with Summer's epic, 17-minute "Love to Love You Baby" (No. 2) which was the title track of her 1975 debut album. While Summer, Moroder, and Bellotte collaborated on the music and lyrics, Bellotte was the sole operator in the producer's seat. Little did he know that this sexy, breathy orgasm of a song would be credited with setting the disco movement in motion.

Unbeknown to the three individuals involved in the making of the song, they had created something totally new and refreshing, completely obliterating tried and true disco formulas that had come before. Within one year, Bellotte and Moroder had become names to watch. Within two years, they had become the two most important producers of disco music. Working alongside the duo's syncopated Eurodisco beats were lead guitar lines that sounded as if they might have been intended for an Aerosmith track. Magically, this blurring of musical borderlines worked, sending the album to the top of the pop charts. Disco-rock fusion was born. Unfortunately, the style did not work on *Victim of Love*, an album Bellotte produced for Elton John in 1979. And while Bellotte has kept a somewhat low profile over the years, he did produce songs for the film *Flashdance* in the early '80s. —LARRY FLICK

Fleming, Joy: *The Final Thing,* Atlantic, 1979.

Giorgio and Chris: *Love's in You/Love's in Me,* Casablanca, 1978.

Gonzalez: *Move It to the Music,* Side/Capitol, 1979.

John, Elton: *Victim of Love,* Rocket/MCA, 1979.

Kelly, Roberta: *Trouble Maker,* Oasis, 1974 • *Zodiac Lady,* Oasis/Casablanca, 1977 • *Gettin' in the Spirit,* Casablanca, 1978.

Moore, Melba: *Burn,* Epic, 1979.

Schloss: *Schloss,* Casablanca, 1975.

Summer, Donna: *A Love Trilogy,* GTO/Oasis, 1975 • "Love to Love You Baby," Oasis, 1975 • *Love to Love You Baby,* GTO/Oasis, 1975 • *Four Seasons of Love,* GTO/Casablanca, 1976 • *Love Trilogy,* Casablanca, 1976 • "I Feel Love," Casablanca, 1977 • *I Remember Yesterday,* GTO/Casablanca, 1977 • *Once upon a Time,* Casablanca, 1977 • "I Love You," Casablanca, 1978 • "Last Dance," Casablanca, 1978, 1979 (*A Night at Studio 54*) • *Live and More,* Casablanca, 1978 • *Bad Girls,* Casablanca, 1979 • *On the Radio: Greatest Hits 1 & 2,* Casablanca, 1979 • "Cold Love," Geffen, 1980 • "On the Radio," Casablanca, 1980 • "The Wanderer," Geffen, 1980 • *The Wanderer,* Geffen, 1980 • "Walk Away," Casablanca, 1980 • *The Summer Collection,* Mercury, 1985 • *The Dance Collection,* Casablanca, 1987 • *Anthology,* Casablanca/Mercury, 1993 • *I'm a Rainbow,* Casablanca/Mercury, 1996.

Trax: *Watch Out!* Polydor, 1977.

Joey Beltram

B orn and raised in Queens, New York, DJ/remixer/producer Joey Beltram has always been way ahead of his time. Widely acknowledged for making and keeping techno music an integral part of the dance floor experience, Beltram's hard-hitting beats and jagged synth lines were heard years before the electronica explosion of the '90s that spawned such acts as the Chemical Brothers (see entry) and Prodigy. An absolute innovator, Beltram was establishing and developing a musical movement that, while not called electronica, certainly did lay down the foundation for it.

Honing his DJ skills since the age of 12, and recording his first single at 17, Beltram has showcased his turntable skills around the world, playing at hugely popular dance events in England, Germany, Holland, Sweden, Japan, Australia, and the more cutting-edge cosmopolitan centers of the United States. Not your typical techno DJ who plays track after track, event after event, Beltram is an artist who nurtures the music he plays, the end result being a sound that is constantly favored and imitated by DJs, producers, and remixers worldwide.

Although widely known for his Belgian style of techno, Beltram derived most of his musical inspiration from Detroit and Chicago house music. It was the raw, electro-driven beats and kinetic energy of such '80s house artists as Chip E and Adonis that initially sparked an interest to begin producing his own tracks. By the late '80s, Beltram was recording for a variety of New York independent dance music labels, most notably Nu Groove, Atmosphere, and Easy Street. Relentless in their energy, his productions, many of which remain as fine examples of classic post-Detroit European dance music, set the tone for pre-breakbeat hardcore techno.

A trip to Belgium in 1989 proved to be a major turning point in Beltram's career. Not only did he launch and solidify his future as an American DJ in Europe, but he unknowingly added a new chapter in the ever-expanding musical history books. That is, he wrote and produced the now-legendary track "Energy Flash." Originally released on Detroit label Transmat, the track was later licensed to Belgium label R&S, which further enhanced his presence in that important techno territory.

"Energy Flash" ushered in a new era in dance music with its bass-fueled foundation and infamous sampling of voices exclaiming, "Ecstasy, ecstasy." He followed with "Mentasm," a sonic blast that featured the noise from a vacuum cleaner riding atop heart-pounding beats. Embraced by the techno community at large, "Mentasm" was the first in a (thankfully) short line of what became known as "Hoover"-style techno.

In 1994, Beltram may have confused his core contingent with his debut album *Aonox*, which had the technomeister experimenting with both house and ambient styles. A year later, he returned to typical form with the highly acclaimed *Places*, an album that the trend-setting British music magazine *Muzik* referred to as "one of the best albums of the year" due to its minimalist simplicity and originality. And in 1997, *Joey Beltram Live* combined the highlights of his tenacious career with Beltram beat-mixing his favorite tracks from the archives of techno music. —LARRY FLICK

Altern 8: "Move My Body" (remix), Network, 1992.

Beltram, Joey: *Energy Flash* (EP), R&S, 1991 • "Time Warp," Low Price Music, 1993, 1995 (*Best of Trance*) • *Aonox*, Visible, 1994 • *Caliber* (EP), Warp, 1994 • *The Caliber EP*, Warp, 1994 • *Fuzz Tracks* (EP), X-Sight, 1995 • *Odyssey Nine*, Visible, 1995 • "Instant/Game Form," Logic, 1996 • *Classics*, R&S, 1996 • as JB3, *Close Grind*, Nova Mute, 1996 • *Places*, Logic, 1996 • *Joey Beltram Live*, Logic, 1997 • "Start It Up," Trax, 1997.

BG, the Prince of Rap: "Take Control of the Party" (remix), Columbia, 1991.

Digitized: *Digitized*, Logic, 1996.

EMF: "The Light That Burns Twice As Bright" (remix), EMI, 1992 • "They're Here" (remix), EMI, 1992.

Erasure: "Breath of Life" (remix), Sire/Reprise, 1992.

House of Venus: "Dish and Tell" (remix), Radikal, 1992.

Human Resource: "Dominator" (remix), FFRR, 1992 (*Only for the Headstrong*).

Information Society: "Peace and Love, Inc." (remix), Tommy Boy, 1992 • *Peace and Love, Inc.*, Tommy Boy, 1992.

JDS: "Reclone," C&S, 1993 (*Trance Odyssey*).

Lords of Acid: "Rough Sex" (remix), Antler Subway/Caroline, 1991 (*Techno Mancer*) • "Crab Louse" (remix), American, 1994.

Nerve Control: "In Tracey," Faze 2, 1993 (*Faze 2*, EP).

Orbital: "Chime" (remix), FFRR, 1992 • "Oolala" (remix), FFRR, 1992.

Prodigy: "Charly" (remix), XL/Elektra, 1992.

Program 2: "The Omen," R&S, 1991.

Project, The: "Here We Go," R&S, 1991 (*Order to Dance*).

Second Phase: "Mentasm," R&S, 1993 • "Mentasm" (remix), R&S, 1993 • "Vortex," R&S, 1993 • "Vortex" (remix), R&S, 1993.

Space Opera: "Electrowave" (remix), R&S, 1991 (*Order to Dance*).

Therapy?: "Trigger Inside" (remix), A&M, 1994.

TRF: "Open Your Mind" (remix), Faze 2, 1993 (*Faze 2*, EP).

TZO: "Rush to the Rhythm," Radikal, 1993.

John "Jellybean" Benitez

John "Jellybean" Benitez is a true rarity in the entertainment business. With a history etched in platinum and gold, he has more than simply survived the constant evolution of trends; he has thrived and earned permanent residency among dance music's scant enduring elite.

The durability and vitality of Jellybean's 20-year career can be attributed to his appetite for perpetual growth and experimentation, which has resulted in impressive forays into music, film, and television. He has produced and remixed more than thirty No. 1 hits, more than 90 Top 10 singles, and is deservedly credited as one of the architects of Madonna's rise to pop stardom. Along the way, such superstars as Whitney Houston, Michael Jackson, Paul McCartney, and Barbra Streisand have enlisted Jellybean's unique production expertise and savvy rhythm sensibility in concocting smash hits.

An interest in the field of music publishing led to the establishment of a company that sparkles with familiar and budding tunesmiths. All the while, his musical tastes have shaped the soundtracks to a string of films that include *2 Days in the Valley, Species,* and *Carlito's Way.*

Jellybean has also enjoyed success as a recording artist and composer in his own right. A revered pioneer of dance music as a DJ, he continues to be one of its staunchest and most respected activists, viewed by many within the industry as playing an integral role in the genre's continued and growing visibility within the highly contentious pop arena. At the same time his role as a mixer on the nation's No. 1–rated WKTU radio keeps him immersed in the club game.

But these are only the preliminary chapters in an ever-broadening career ripe with exciting ventures that promise to elevate Jellybean to astonishing new heights. First, there is his eponymous Jellybean Recordings, an independent outlet focused on discovering and nurturing the next generation of dance music producers and artists. Then there is H.O.L.A. Records, a company targeting the powerful but sorely untapped Latin market.

To properly comprehend Jellybean's incredible ascent to fame and success, one must meet the man himself. Despite the affluent framework of his current lifestyle, he retains the soul of that wide-eyed and energetic kid from the Bronx who first started collecting records in 1975. "The key for me has always been that I allow myself the freedom to follow my instincts and explore whatever interests me," he says. "I take great pride in the fact that I become very driven once I focus on something that inspires me. By continually getting involved in projects that I find exciting, I don't have time to sit back and get caught up in weird attitudes or anything like that."

Jellybean's roots go back to a boyhood spent on Burnside Avenue in the Bronx during the musical period when the rich Philly soul of Harold Melvin and the Blue Notes and the lush disco-funk of Thelma Houston saturated radio airwaves and Billboard's Hot 100. He fondly recalls commandeering control of the turntable, entertaining family and friends by spinning the hits of the day. "I always really enjoyed guiding the sequence of events," he says. "After a while, I learned that you could get a lot of different moods based on the song you played, which was very intriguing to me."

The direction of his life changed forever the night he walked into a Manhattan nightclub called Sanctuary. "To me, a DJ was a person on the radio," he says. "This was an entirely new experience."

Jellybean was further intrigued by the concept of the DJ simultaneously operating two turntables and blending music together. In fact, he was intrigued enough to take a crack at doing it himself. He went on to developing his own special way of combining grooves and song hooks that every club owner coveted. It was under the blazing strobe lights of the legendary Funhouse that he enjoyed his greatest turntable fame, juggling an on-air gig at the first incarnation of WKTU radio. It was also during this time that he laid the foundation for an eventual transition into the recording studio as a producer and remixer. His first effort was "The Bubble Bunch" by Jimmy Spicer, with "Walking on Sunshine" by Rockers Revenge and the Afrika Bambaataa chestnut "Planet Rock" quickly following. It was on the fuel of these records that he rode into prominence as a remixer during the '80s.

"Back then, you were not allowed to do any overdubs," he says. "All you could do was take the existing tracks and create DJ-friendly intros and breakdowns. There were live drum tracks then, so remixing could be a nightmare without patience. There was a lot more editing involved."

Jellybean's first attempt at producing a record from scratch was with an ambitious ingenue from Detroit named Madonna. They teamed up for what would become her early signature recordings: "Burning Up," "Borderline" (No. 10), "Lucky Star" (No. 4), and "Holiday" (No. 16). "I was petrified, but thrilled at the same time," he says of assembling these tracks. "I called a lot of musicians that I had worked with and hummed out the arrangements to them. It was unforgettable."

From there, there was no other more logical step than turning his natural charisma into a spree as a recording artist. His EMI debut, *Wotupski!?!* spawned two No. 1 dance hits in "The Mexican" and "Sidewalk Talk." Later alliances with Chrysalis and Atlantic led to several more albums, including the million-selling *Just Visiting the Planet* on Chrysalis.

With his reputation as a club and radio tastemaker firm, it made sense that Hollywood would beckon. First came the opportunity to compose television themes for shows like *The Ricki Lake Show*, John Leguizamo's *House of Buggin'*, and *The Charles Perez Show*. Then came such motion pictures as Brian DePalma's *Carlito's Way*, Alison Sander's *Mi Vida Loca*, and *The Perez Family* by Mira Nair.

The trappings of Hollywood could not, however, quell Jellybean's thirst to stay deeply involved with his first love—making music. "It's everywhere around me," he says. "I can't even walk down the street without hearing a rhythm or a chorus in my head. The fact that music is constantly changing at a rapid pace is enticing to me. It keeps you on your toes like nothing else."
—LARRY FLICK

Brown, Peter: "They Only Come Out at Night," Columbia, 1984.

Easton, Sheena: *The Lover in Me,* MCA, 1988.

Fiorillo, Elisa: "You Don't Know," Chrysalis, 1987.

General Public: "Tenderness" (remix), IRS, 1984, 1991 (*IRS Greatest Hits,* Vol. 4, *The Remixes*).

Gibson, Debbie: *Anything Is Possible,* Atlantic, 1990 • *Smart Pack,* Atlantic, 1990.

Harry, Debbie: "Feel the Spin," Chrysalis, 1988 • *Once More into the Bleach,* Chrysalis, 1989.

Hot Streak: "Body Work," Polydor, 1984 (*Breakin'* soundtrack).

Houston, Whitney: "How Will I Know," (remix), Arista, 1986 • *Whitney,* Arista, 1987 • "Love Will Save the Day," Arista, 1988.

Jellybean: "The Mexican," EMI America, 1984 • *Wotupski!?!* EMI America, 1984 • "Sidewalk Talk," EMI America, 1985 • *Just Visiting the Planet,* Chrysalis, 1987 • w/ Elisa Fiorillo, "Who Found Who," Chrysalis, 1987 • *Jellybean Rocks the House,* Chrysalis, 1988 • *Spillin' the Beans,* Atlantic, 1991 •

"Twilight Dome/Toot Toot," Relief, 1995 • *Toot Toot,* Relief, 1995.

Kennedy, Joyce: "Activate My Love," A&M, 1985 • "Let Me Know (If Love's on Your Mind)," A&M, 1985 • "Never Let a Night Go By," A&M, 1985.

Lattisaw, Stacy: "Nail It to the Wall," Motown, 1986.

Madonna: "Holiday," Sire, 1983 • "Borderline," Sire, 1984 • "Dress You Up" (remix), Sire, 1984 • "Lucky Star," Sire, 1984 • *Madonna,* Sire, 1984 • "Crazy for You," Geffen, 1985 • "Spotlight" (remix), Sire, 1987 • *You Can Dance,* Sire, 1987 • *Royal Box,* Sire, 1990 • *The Immaculate Collection,* Sire, 1990.

Mandel, Howie: "I Do the Watusi," Warner Bros., 1986.

Martika: "More Than You Know" (remix), Columbia, 1988.

Rozalla: "I Love Music," Epic, 1993 • *Look No Further,* Epic, 1995.

Rush, Jennifer: *Passion,* Epic, 1986.

Tosh, Peter: "Johnny B. Goode" (remix), EMI, 1983.

Veronica: "Rise," H.O.L.A., 1997 • *Rise,* Hola, 1997.

Voices of Theory: "Somehow," H.O.L.A., 1997.

Howard Benson

Although Howard Benson's career took off in the late '80s, thanks to his extensive work with the pop-metal groups known as "hairspray" bands, experience and interests beyond that genre allowed him to flourish as a producer.

Benson was exposed to music by his pianist mother, who taught music in Philadelphia public schools. After hearing "Light My Fire" on the radio, he persuaded his father to buy him a little combination organ. He taught himself material by Deep Purple, Emerson, Lake and Palmer, and Steppenwolf, as well as various Hammond B3 tunes.

A degree in aerospace engineering led to a job in Los Angeles, where he played in bar bands at night. "Eventually the careers became mutually exclusive," he says. "I did demos for one of my bands and when we were shopping them around, A&R guys were telling me how good they sounded. I liked being in the studio; I got tired of carrying the organ around."

Benson's first break was doing demos and an unreleased album for Jack Mack and the Heart Attack. He soon acquired a manager who also handled seminal punkers TSOL. He helmed their Enigma album, *Hit and Run,* which led to more work with the label. Then he produced the Wild Seeds' 1987 album *Mud, Lies and Shame.* "That was the record where I felt I hit my stride," he says. "The musicianship and songwriting were so good, but they needed my arrangements. That's probably the record I look back to the most."

Commercial metal was hot, and Benson found himself working with bands like Tuff, Southgang, Child's Play, Bang Tango, Sweet F.A., and the genre's nadir, Pretty Boy Floyd. "They couldn't play," he acknowledges. "It was a science project. You'd have to punch in guitar parts. I got hired to do a couple of records because A&R people heard it after they saw the band and they sucked."

Then things changed. "I was producing a band called Little Caesar when Nirvana came out. I remember where I was, in this parking lot. A friend of mine at Geffen brought the tape over. It hit me: we're fucked. There's nothing we can do to make Little Caesar sound like Nirvana. Once it was coming, nothing could stop it."

Benson always had his eye on the future. Bands like the bluesy Bang Tango and funky Kingofthehill bridged the gap between '80s and modern heavy music, and the production Benson did for them sounds less inflated than other hard rock efforts of the time. Benson says of his 1991 production for groove-rockers Kingofthehill, "I mixed them to sound like an alternative band. The label brought in another mixer to make them sound like a hairspray band with big drums, big everything. I was really upset." Still, Benson's productions, while beefy and forceful, tended to be less glossy than those of other pop-metal producers.

Former Giant Records head Irving Azoff trusted Benson's ear enough to hire him to do A&R in 1994. He continued to produce, returning to full-time production in 1996. In the next year, he produced Cellophane, Blue Meanies, Body Count, and Motorhead. The latter two demonstrate his knack for getting a metal sound that's full, but raw and nasty, without the glossy earmarks of '80s pop-metal. "I did the last three Motorhead albums. I'm kind of Lemmy's staff producer," he observes. "All we do is argue for three months. It's his way of honing his music. He said he likes working with me because I'm the best arguer."

He compares producing to coaching a football team. "Some coaches are people coaches, some only care about the end result and don't care who gets hurt," he says. "I'm a music person. I get hired to do arrangement work. There's a lot of preproduction. You have to take stuff out, strip it down to the essence of what the band is. The most important things are a great song and a great performance. If you don't have that, you've got nothing. It doesn't matter how good your guitar sound is." Benson prefers to concentrate on music and hire engineers.

His attitude about technology is utilitarian. "You need to know the whole breadth of technology. I own technology 50 years old and stuff so new it isn't on the market yet. You can have an old tube mike plugged into a digital console. You can buy processors with effects upon effects upon effects, but I like to keep things simple. I worry about things like great separation, having the leaks between instruments helping you rather than hurting you, the positioning of the mikes. That's more experience than technology."

Looking back on his "hair band" days, Benson says, "One thing that bugs me about the hairspray thing is that people deny they were there. Hey, I was there. It was great. There was a lot of good in hairspray music. The musicianship wasn't always that good. Now bands like Cellophane or Blue Meanies have incredible musicianship. You're dealing with, What can we do to make this great stuff sound greater? A lot of producers who worked with hair bands can't get work right now. It is incredibly important to keep doing demos. Developing new bands keeps you current as a producer.

"It's a great time now," he continues. "There's lots of different music. There's roots-oriented music and Marilyn Manson and something like the Cardigans. I'm fond of working with artists who are passionate about their music. To me, humanity moves forward because artists say things that are controversial and that people do not want to hear." —Anastasia Pantsios

Bang Tango: *Live Injection,* Important, 1989 • *Psycho Cafe,* Mechanic, 1989.

Blue Meanies: *Pave the World,* Beach, 1996.

Body Count: *Violent Demise: Last Days,* Virgin, 1997.

Cadillac Tramps: *It's Allright,* Doctor Dream, 1994.

Caulfield, Tom: *Long Distance Calling,* Paradox, 1987.

Cellophane: *Cellophane,* Virgin, 1997.

Child's Play: *Rat Race,* Chrysalis, 1990.

Kilgore Smudge: *Blue Collar Solitude,* Unsound, 1995.

Kingofthehill: *Kingofthehill,* SBK, 1991.

Little Caesar: *Influence,* DGC, 1992.

Motorhead: *Bastards,* ZYX, 1993 • w/ Ice-T and Whitfield Crane, "Born to Raise Hell," Fox, 1994 • *Sacrifice,* CMC Int., 1995 • *Overnight Sensation,* CMC Int., 1996.

Pretty Boy Floyd: *Leather Boyz with Electric Toyz,* MCA, 1990.

Sanctuary: *Into the Mirror Black,* Epic, 1990.

Seed: *Ling,* Giant, 1994.

Slammin' Watusis: *King of Noise,* Epic, 1989.

Smith, Greg: *No Baggage,* Intima, 1987.

Southgang: *Tainted Angel,* Charisma, 1991 • *Group Therapy,* Charisma, 1992.

Sweet F.A.: *Stick to Your Guns,* MCA, 1989 • *Temptation,* Charisma, 1991.

TSOL: *Revenge,* Enigma, 1986 • "All Along the Watchtower," Geffen, 1987 (*Scream: The Compilation*) • *Hit and Run,* Enigma, 1987 • *Hell and Back Together, 1984–1990,* Restless, 1992.

Tuff: *What Comes . . . ,* Atlantic, 1991.

Wakeland: *Magnetic,* Giant, 1995.

Wild Seeds: *Mud, Lies and Shame,* Passport, 1988.

Tony Berg

Producer and A&R veteran Tony Berg displays an honest affection and deep respect for the artists he has worked with that often translates into a personal approach to production. For example, take the case of the vocal tracking for Michael Penn's albums *March* and *Free-For-All,* recorded at Berg's 48-track facility adjacent to his Los Angeles home.

"Michael likes to experiment with his vocals," Berg explains. "But he was very intimidated to have me there in the studio with him while he worked out his ideas." So Berg would set the artist up with a few tracks to record on, give him the keys to the studio, and head up to bed. "Michael ended up tracking most of his vocals alone in my backyard between midnight and 6 A.M."

The artists and bands with whom Berg has worked include Squeeze, X, Edie Brickell, Johnny Lydon, Aimee Mann, Stewart Copeland, Stanley Clarke–led Animal

Logic, Charlie Sexton, Michelle Shocked, and legendary Venice Beach boardwalk performer Ted Hawkins.

"The word 'producer' is such a nebulous term," Berg observes. "For some people it means sitting on the phone for 10 hours a day. For me it means becoming a partner with the artist but maintaining the focus on them. I'm not a big fan of the record that bears the imprint of the producer."

At the onset of a project, Berg will sit down with the artist and hash through the songs on acoustic guitar, responding specifically to lyrics, chords, and song structure. "You want to figure out what the record wants to be about sonically—what you want to evoke with the record. Because an environment is created when you make an album, and it has a subliminal effect upon the listener."

Berg enjoys being at the console, guitar in hand, engaging the artist. "Being a musician and writer, I can collaborate with them if the artist gets stuck." Then there are those times when the producer needs to know when to back off, as Berg had to do with Glenn Tilbrook of Squeeze.

"He wouldn't play his guitar in front of me," Berg explains. "I'm not sure why, I guess because I'm a guitarist too. He just felt more comfortable recording his solos alone."

An avid collector of antique musical instruments, Berg's studio walls are adorned with rare finds from around the world. Many of the instruments have wound up on his productions. A trite guitar riff on folk-pop duo Wendy and Lisa's *Eroica* was transformed when Wendy performed it on an oud. Strains of hurdy-gurdy have made it from Berg's collection into several productions.

Berg's interest in world music has carried through to his work with the Terem Quartet, a Russian folk group of conservatory-trained musicians who perform on balalaika, accordion, and contrabass and record for Peter Gabriel's Real World label.

Born in Los Angeles in 1954, Berg began his career in 1972 as the musical director for L.A.'s Mark Taper Forum. Then only 18 years old, he arranged six musical productions there before becoming a guitarist in the pit band for the Roxy Theater's production of *The Rocky Horror Picture Show*. Other band members included David Foster (see entry) on keyboards, Frank Zappa, drummer Ralph Humphrey, Don Mensa on sax, and Doors bassist Ray Neopolitan.

Berg worked for the next 15 years as a session guitarist for film, television, and album projects (often with producer, composer, and mentor Jack Nitzsche; see entry) and also served one-year stints as musical director

for Bette Midler in 1978 and for *The Tracy Ullman Show* in the mid-'80s. He scored several feature films and episodic television, including Robert Altman's *Perfect Couple* and the CBS miniseries *Space,* based on the James Michener novel.

In the late '80s, following completion of his home facility, he signed a management deal with newly organized Steve Moyer management. "For the next seven years, I worked every single day," Berg claims. In 1993 he signed on to the A&R team at Geffen Records. As both a producer and A&R man, Berg acknowledges that he navigates dangerous waters. He is mindful of avoiding the production end of a project when he is handling A&R but admits that sometimes a conflict is inevitable. In a few instances he has felt compelled to re-produce portions of albums.

Berg's respect and admiration for artists is evident when he recounts stories of working with the late Hawkins, who made few recordings and was not used to the atmosphere of the studio. "I realized that putting Ted in a room with a band would be an intimidating experience for him," Berg recalls.

A familiar sight on the Venice Beach boardwalk, Hawkins was accustomed to playing his guitar atop a milk crate, tapping out time on an old wooden board. Berg had Hawkins record that way and then over-dubbed a band behind him.

But when it came to recording a remake of John Fogerty's (see entry) "Long As I Can See the Light," Hawkins demonstrated that he could already hear the band before they put down their parts. "Ted had a special tuning worked out that allowed him to play only major chords on his guitar," Berg explains. Being that the Fogerty tune contained a number of minor chords, Hawkins took a stab at singing the tune a cappella. "With perfect pitch and rhythm, Ted recorded the song a cappella, including a 16-bar solo where all he did was tap his foot!" marvels Berg. "It's amazing!" Tragically, Hawkins died of a stroke just months after completing *The Next Hundred Years,* an album that was on many critics' Top 10 lists in 1994.

"I count many of the artists I've worked with among my closest friends," says Berg. "One of the greatest things I've been able to do is have them at my home for months. My kids grew up with all these people in the backyard with them." Berg adds with a chuckle, "The image I have of Johnny Lydon swimming with my kids is something I'll carry always." —JACK ARKY

Animal Logic: *Animal Logic II*, IRS, 1991 • *Rose Colored Glasses* (EP), Capitol, 1991.

Attaway, Murray: *In Thrall*, DGC, 1993.

Brickell, Edie and the New Bohemians: "Black and Blue," Geffen, 1990 • *Ghost of a Dog,* Geffen, 1990.

Broken Homes: *Straight Line Through Time,* MCA, 1987.

Hawkins, Ted: *The Next Hundred Years,* DGC, 1994.

Holland, Deborah: "It Only Comes Once a Year," IRS, 1990 (*Just in Time for Christmas*).

Mann, Aimee: *Whatever* (1 track), Imago, 1993.

Noa: *Calling,* Geffen, 1996.

Penn, Michael: *March,* RCA, 1989 • "No Myth," RCA, 1990 • *Free-For-All,* RCA, 1992.

Public Image Limited (PIL): *Don't Ask Me* (EP), Virgin, 1990 • *Greatest Hits So Far,* Atlantic, 1990.

Replacements, The: *All for Nothing/Nothing for All,* Warner Bros., 1997.

Sexton, Charlie: *Charlie Sexton,* MCA, 1989.

Shocked, Michelle: *Kind Hearted Woman,* Private, 1994, 1996.

Squeeze: *Play,* Reprise, 1991.

Terem Quartet: *Terem,* Virgin, 1992.

Uma: *Fare Well,* MCA, 1997.

Wendy and Lisa: *Eroica,* Virgin, 1990.

Wild Colonials: *This Can't Be Life,* DGC, 1996.

X: "Country at War," Big Life/Mercury, 1993 • *Hey Zeus!* Big Life/Mercury, 1993.

Steve Berlin

Steve Berlin, a producer who leads a double life as a member of Los Lobos, specializes in crafting sounds for "acoustic astronauts." He's too modest.

"The funny thing about my so-called career is that this is just the sort of stuff that came to me," says Berlin, who was born in 1956. The "sort of stuff" Berlin specializes in spans everything from Leo Kottke to Faith No More. A former member of the Blasters, the Plugz (who, briefly, became the Cruzados), and the Flesheaters, Berlin plays all manner of wind instruments, keyboards, and percussion.

"I don't have a catalog of sounds or samples," says Berlin, a full-time member of Los Lobos for more than 16 years. "I don't bring anything but, hopefully, an open mind and willing heart to what I do. What I hope would be the case is that no two records of mine sound close enough to be identifiably mine."

Those records include Dave Alvin's *Romeo's Escape,* Leo Kottke's *Great Big Boy,* and, in conjunction with T Bone Burnett (see entry), Los Lobos' *How Will the Wolf Survive?* Oh, yes, Berlin co-produced EIEIO's *Land of Opportunity,* a wonderful slice of rootsy Americana.

The Kottke disc has special appeal to Berlin. "He came to me and said, 'I've always felt crowded by other musicians, never felt I could do what I wanted to do.' Leo really plays like '20s blues guys like Leadbelly and Blind Willie McTell. He has his own personal style and chord vocabulary. Try to figure out what he's doing chordally and it's almost pointless."

Berlin celebrates his versatility, noting he produced "full-on country" in a Prairie Oyster album that won a Juno in that group's native Canada, as well as a "pretty hard record": Faith No More's *Introduce Yourself,* which he co-produced with Matt Wallace (see entry).

Berlin also recently produced an album for Seattle band Citizens Utilities, who record for Mute. "There's not a lot of people I think that highly of, which sounds really pompous," says Berlin. "There are people I'd love to work with, but I'm not under any misconception as to where I am in the grand pecking order of producers. It's hard, as a member of a band that works pretty much nonstop, to maintain the identity producers need. I've never had that kind of time.

"I love being part of my band, but to get to another echelon, I'd have to have put out more records than I have and to keep at it, to stay in the arena."

Any "lost" productions? "I've had a lot of ones that got away," says Berlin. "The one I think hurts me still is an album with David Baerwald, who is very notable for his contribution to the first Sheryl Crow record." Baerwald was part of David and David, responsible for the fine album *Bedtime Stories.*

"I loved the David and David record, and never thought in a million years I'd ever get to work with a guy like that," Berlin recalls. "We met, I think we really got along well together, we started working in his garage studio with a 12-track Akai—this is the early days of multitracking. It was one of those things where it was very inspired; it was with Matt Wallace. We were all coming up with really, really good ideas."

The tracks were a testament to "the power of low-fi" before people's ears were open to that virtue. "We did the record once, and we did it again, and I didn't realize until after the fact that Mr. Baerwald had fallen in love with the process. There were days when he'd just kind of change personality, and as the project came to an end, he became more and more unhappy over things that were finished."

Baerwald ultimately fired Berlin, then Wallace; eventually, a Baerwald record—a third try—came out under the production aegis of Larry Klein.

Berlin says he learned the diplomacy of record production by having to balance his ideas and desires with those of his band mates, and by observing such masters of the craft as Mitchell Froom (see entry).

"If you're smart about it, everybody feels connected to it and nobody feels steamrollered," he says of record production. "That's something I learned really well from Mitchell Froom. He's a master ombudsman. Nobody feels like he's getting steamrollered, but Froom's agenda gets realized because he's very masterful in how he goes about his work, and very opaque, in that he lets people feel like they're contributing the best they have. At the same time, he's cajoled them into doing what he wants or what's best for the record. And the experience is always pleasurable.

"I've done stuff all over the world," says the Seattle resident. "Basically, you're a mobile intelligence unit, and people are hiring you for that, for the sort of stuff that's kind of floating around between your ears."
—CARLO WOLFF

Alvin, Dave: *Every Night About This Time*, Demon, 1987 • *Romeo's Escape*, Razor & Tie, 1987, 1995.
Beat Farmers: *Tales of the New West*, Rhino, 1985.
Bounce the Ocean: *Bounce the Ocean*, Private, 1991.
Buckwheat Zydeco: *Five Card Stud*, Island, 1994.
Citizens' Utilities: *No More Medicine*, Mute, 1997.
Crash Test Dummies: *The Ghosts That Haunt Me*, Arista, 1991.
EIEIO: *Land of Opportunity*, Frontier, 1986.
Faith No More: *Introduce Yourself*, Slash, 1987.
Fearing, Stephen: *The Assassin's Apprentice*, Cooking Vinyl, 1996.
Harding, John Wesley: *Pett Levels: The Summer EP* (2 tracks), Sire/Reprise, 1993.
Hinojosa, Tish: *Homeland*, A&M, 1989.
Kottke, Leo: *Great Big Boy*, Private, 1991.
Los Lobos: *And Time to Dance*, Slash, 1983 • "We're Gonna Rock," Rhino, 1983 (*The Best of L.A. Rockabilly*) • *How Will the Wolf Survive?*, Slash/WB, 1984 • "Will the Wolf Survive?," Slash/WB, 1984 • "Charlena," Slash/WB, 1987 (*La Bamba* soundtrack) • "Come On, Let's Go," Slash/WB, 1987 (*La Bamba* soundtrack) • "Donna," Slash/WB, 1987 (*La Bamba* soundtrack) • "Framed," Slash/WB, 1987 (*La Bamba* soundtrack) • "Goodnight My Love," Slash/WB, 1987 (*La Bamba* soundtrack) • "Ooh! My Head," Slash/WB, 1987 (*La Bamba* soundtrack) • "We Belong Together," Slash/WB, 1987 (*La Bamba* soundtrack) • *Just Another Band from East L.A.*, Slash/WB, 1993.
Paladins, The: *The Paladins*, Big Beat, 1986 • *Years Since Yesterday*, Alligator, 1988 • "I Don't Believe," Alligator, 1989 (*Genuine Houserockin' Music*, Vol. 4) • *Let's Buzz*, Alligator, 1990.
Picketts, The: *Euphonium*, Rounder, 1996.

Spedding, Chris: *Cafe Days*, Mobile Fidelity Sound Lab, 1991, 1992.
Tail Gators: *Tore Up*, Wrestler, 1989.

Bert Berns

Bert Berns was an extravagantly talented songwriter and producer who brought Latin rhythms to soul music and soul to rock 'n' roll. Before Berns' amazing seven-year run was cut short (at age 38 by a fatal heart attack) in 1967, he produced "Brown-Eyed Girl" (No. 10) by Van Morrison; "Under the Boardwalk" (No. 4) by the Drifters; "Baby, I'm Yours" and "Make Me Your Baby" (both No. 11) by Barbara Lewis; "Cry Baby" (No. 4) by Garnet Mimms; "Cry to Me" by Betty Harris; "Everybody Needs Somebody to Love," "Goodbye Baby (Baby Goodbye)," "Got to Get You Off My Mind," and "If You Need Me" by Solomon Burke; "Killer Joe" (No. 16) by the Rocky Fellers; "A Little Bit of Soap" (No. 12) by the Jarmels; and "Here Comes the Night" by Them.

In addition, he wrote or co-wrote "Twist and Shout" (Isley Brothers, the Beatles), "Hang On Sloopy" (the McCoys), "Piece of My Heart" (Aretha Franklin's sister Erma Franklin, Janis Joplin), "Tell Him" (the Exciters), and "I Want Candy" (the Strangeloves, Bow Wow Wow), among many others. Berns (aka Bert Russell) was also a partner in the Atlantic offshoot labels Bang and Shout.

Bert Berns was born in the Bronx in 1929. Berns' Russian immigrant parents were so intent on ensuring the success of their dress shop that they put Bert and his sister in an orphanage rather than raise them. Berns studied classical piano as a child and worked as a record salesman, music copyist, and session pianist in his teens and twenties. Envisioning himself a player, Berns spent time in pre-Castro Cuba working in nightclubs, absorbing Latin-American rhythms, and hobnobbing with shady characters. Berns' Latin influence can be heard on "Twist and Shout," "A Little Bit of Soap," "Hang On Sloopy," and especially his work with the Drifters ("Under the Boardwalk," "I've Got Sand in My Shoes").

Berns returned to New York, and in 1960 went to work for Robert Mellin Music, writing and plugging songs. He drifted to Atlantic in 1961 where he wrote and produced Solomon Burke, Ben E. King, Wilson Pickett, and the Drifters, creating some of the greatest uptown soul on record. Like all of the greats, Berns had an ability to bring out the best in the singers he worked with. Berns' style may have been a bit goofy (loud clothes, defiant hairpiece, dangling cigarette), but his passion was unassailable.

Solomon Burke has spoken disparagingly of Berns (calling him a "paddy motherfucker," according to Jerry Wexler; see entry), but Berns produced Burke's best work. "Everybody Needs Somebody to Love" swings at midtempo with a gospel intensity. Burke's spoken sermon intro simultaneously rouses the tent and winks at his own background as a lay preacher. When the horns enter, Burke responds with gut-rattling force. "Goodbye Baby (Baby Goodbye)" is soul. Ben E. King's "Let the Water Run Down" jams to the Bo Diddley beat with charging guitar and piano. King's impassioned vocal emphasizes both the pain and the relief of tears.

Even better is Berns' work with the Drifters. "Under the Boardwalk" is one of the great productions of all time, wherein Berns balances a bewildering array of Latin-esque percussion (including castanets, a ratchet, and a triangle), strings, a loping bass line, and Johnny Moore's career-topping vocal. Besides the amazing arrangement, Berns was also able to capture an emotional moment. Lead singer Rudy Lewis had been found dead of a drug overdose in his hotel room the night before, and it was too late to cancel the session. There wasn't even time to transpose the song into a more suitable key for Moore, but Berns was able to channel Moore's emotion from shock and grief into blissful relief: from the punishing heat of the summer sun to the subterranean cool under the boardwalk.

In 1965 Berns went into partnership with Jerry Wexler and the Erteguns (see entries) to form the Bang (for Bert, Ahmet, Neshui, Gerald) and Shout labels. The Strangeloves, the McCoys, Neil Diamond, and Van Morrison were all big winners on Bang. Berns had worked with Them (with Morrison on lead vocals) in London in 1964 (and had discovered a session guitarist named "Little" Jimmy Page; see entry). When Them broke up, Berns signed Morrison to Bang.

On "Brown-Eyed Girl," Berns removes the perpetual cloud over Van Morrison's head and the result is transcendent. You can literally hear Morrison smile as he breezes through sweet memories of a summer love gone by. After a great bass and guitar intro, Morrison's wistful reflection has real meat—we can see and feel the scenes of verdant hollows, misty mornings, waterfalls, and the greenest of grass behind the stadium. Berns' little touches are everything: a comforting organ enters for the second verse, hand claps bolster the third, and the bridge turns the bass and guitar intro inside out to neatly convey the passage of time. Most important, Van

has never again sounded so at home in his skin.

Then there was some trouble at Bang. Berns wanted more control of the publishing. Wexler alleges that Berns' affinity with an unsavory element was increasing. Berns sued the partners for breach of contract and went his separate way. Shortly after that he died, taking his talent and his secrets with him. —Eric Olsen

Burke, Solomon: "Cry to Me," Atlantic, 1961 • "Just out of Reach (of My Two Open Arms)," Atlantic, 1961 • *Greatest Hits,* Atlantic, 1962 • "If You Need Me," Atlantic, 1963 • "Everybody Needs Somebody to Love," Atlantic, 1964 • "Goodbye Baby (Baby Goodbye)," Atlantic, 1964 • "Got to Get You off My Mind," Atlantic, 1965 • "Tonight's the Night," Atlantic, 1965 • *Home in Your Heart: Best of Solomon Burke,* Rhino, 1992.

Drifters, The: "I've Got Sand in My Shoes," Atlantic, 1964 • "Saturday Night at the Movies," Atlantic, 1964 • "Under the Boardwalk," Atlantic, 1964 • *Take You Where the Music's Playing,* Atlantic, 1965 • *The Drifters' Golden Hits,* Atlantic, 1966 • *Rockin' and Driftin': The Box Set,* Rhino, 1996.

Franklin, Erma: "Piece of My Heart," Shout, 1967.

Harris, Betty: "Cry to Me," Jubilee, 1963.

Isley Brothers: *Twist and Shout!* Sundazed, 1962, 1993 • *Rockin' Soul,* Vol. 1, Rhino, 1991 • *The Isley Brothers Story,* Vol. 1, Rhino, 1991.

Jarmels, The: "A Little Bit of Soap," Laurie, 1961.

Johnson, Marv: *You Got What It Takes,* EMI Legends, 1992.

King, Ben E.: "Let the Water Run Down," Atco, 1964 • *Anthology,* Atlantic, 1993.

LaBelle, Patti: *Greatest Hits,* MCA, 1996.

Lewis, Barbara: "Hello Stranger," Atlantic, 1963 • "Baby, I'm Yours," Atlantic, 1965 • "Make Me Your Baby," Atlantic, 1965.

Lulu: *Something to Shout About,* Decca, 1965.

Lynn, Tamiya: *Love Is Here and Now You're Gone,* Cotillion, 1972.

Mimms, Garnet: w/ the Enchanters, "Cry Baby," United Artists, 1963 • *The Cry Baby: The Best Of,* EMI, 1993.

Morrison, Van: *Blowin' Your Mind,* Bang, 1967 • "Brown Eyed Girl," Bang, 1967 • *T.B. Sheets,* Bang, 1973 • *The Best of Van Morrison,* Mercury, 1990 • *Bang Masters,* Legacy/Epic, 1991.

Phillips, Esther: *The Best Of, 1962–1970,* Rhino, 1997.

Pickett, Wilson: "Everybody Needs Somebody to Love," Atlantic, 1967.

Rocky Fellers: "Killer Joe," Scepter, 1963.

Scott, Freddie: "Are You Lonely for Me?," Shout, 1967 • *Are You Lonely for Me?,* Joy/Bang, 1967.

Them: "Here Comes the Night," Parrot, 1965 • *Them, Featuring Van Morrison,* Parrot, 1972.

Martin Birch

Producer Martin Birch started working in England in the early '70s. He produced a couple of pre-Buckingham-and-Nicks Fleetwood Mac records, *Mystery to Me* and *Penguin*, among other things. But his career took off toward the middle of that decade when he became associated with some of the biggest names in the nascent genre of grandiose arena metal, including Deep Purple, Rainbow, and Whitesnake. With such albums as Rainbow's self-titled 1975 debut and 1976 follow-up, *Rising* (both No. 11 U.K.), the two David Coverdale–era Deep Purple albums, Jon Lord's 1976 solo disc *Sarabande*, and Whitesnake's first seven albums (1978–1984), he was implicated in the "densifying" of metal, away from its original Led Zeppelin–Black Sabbath streamlined trio format, to the huge, often bloated, style that inspired *This Is Spinal Tap* and '80s "melodic hard rock" (aka "hair metal"), with glistening keyboards, thundering bass and drums, multiple layers of guitar, and heavily processed sound . . . no space allowed!

In the early '80s, he moved on to working with some '70s metal monsters trying to survive and modernize in the '80s: Black Sabbath and Blue Oyster Cult. But his real rescue from David Coverdale ignominy came from his long association with Iron Maiden, with whom he did eight albums, starting with their second album, *Killers* (No. 12 U.K.), in 1981. One of the leaders of the so-called New Wave Of British Heavy Metal that arose in opposition to punk, Iron Maiden was also one of the first and most successful thrash metal bands, whose lack of mainstream commercial radio airplay was a key selling point with their fan base. With their long, complex songs and blistering guitar playing, and the operatic yet natural vocals of Bruce Dickinson, who avoided David Coverdale–style posturing, Maiden retained their "underground" credibility even as they sold out arenas. They made increasingly glossy albums with Birch that meticulously assembled the multiple pieces of their music into a powerful whole that never sank to the level of the overblown shininess reached by latter-day Whitesnake or its progeny, such as Europe and Def Leppard.

Birch's last known production was Iron Maiden's 1992 *Fear of the Dark* (No. 12), after which he dropped completely out of sight. He is reputedly enjoying retirement, living off his royalties and playing golf in a tropical paradise somewhere. —ANASTASIA PANTSIOS

Black Sabbath: *Heaven and Hell*, Vertigo/WB, 1980 • *Mob Rules*, Vertigo/WB, 1981.

Blue Oyster Cult: *Cultosaurus Erectus*, Columbia, 1980 • *Fire of Unknown Origin*, Columbia, 1981 • *Workshop of the Telescopes* (3 tracks), Legacy, 1995.

Cortinas: *True Romances*, CBS, 1978.

County, Wayne: *Storm the Gates of Heaven*, Safari, 1978.

Deep Purple: *Machine Head*, Warner Bros., 1972 • *Stormbringer*, Purple/WB, 1974 • *Come Taste the Band*, Purple/WB, 1975 • *Made in Europe*, Purple/WB, 1976.

Electric Chairs: *Electric Chairs*, Safari, 1978.

Fleetwood Mac: *Then Play On*, Reprise, 1969 • *Mystery to Me*, Warner Bros., 1973 • *Penguin*, Warner Bros., 1973.

Glover, Roger: *Elements*, Polydor, 1978.

Iron Maiden: *Killers*, EMI/Harvest, 1981 • *The Number of the Beast*, Castle, 1982, 1995 • *Piece of Mind*, EMI/Harvest, 1983 • *Powerslave*, Castle, 1984, 1995 • *Live After Death*, Castle, 1985, 1995 • *Somewhere in Time*, Castle, 1986, 1995 • *Seventh Son of a Seventh Son*, Castle, 1988, 1995 • *No Prayer for the Dying*, Castle, 1990, 1995 • *Running Free Run to the Hills*, EMI, 1990 • *The Clairvoyant*, EMI, 1990 • *Fear of the Dark*, Castle, 1992, 1995.

Lord, Jon: *Sarabande*, Purple, 1976.

Mainland: *Exposure*, Christy, 1978.

Marsden, Bernie: *And About Time Too*, EMI, 1979.

Moore, Gary: *Grinding Stone*, CBS, 1973.

Powell, Cozy: *Over the Top*, Ariola/PolyGram, 1979.

Rainbow: *Rainbow*, Oyster/PolyGram, 1975 • *Rising*, Polydor, 1976 • *On Stage*, Polydor, 1977 • *Long Live Rock and Roll*, Polydor, 1978.

Michael Schenker Group: *Assault Attack*, Chrysalis, 1982 • *Essential*, Chrysalis, 1992.

Silverhead: *Silverhead*, MCA, 1972.

Stray: *Saturday Morning Pictures*, Track/Mercury, 1971.

Whitesnake: *Snakebite*, United Artists, 1978 • *Trouble*, United Artists, 1978 • *Love Hunter*, United Artists, 1979 • *Live . . . in the Heart of the City*, UA/Mirage, 1980 • *Ready and Willing*, UA/Mirage, 1980 • *Come and Get It*, UA/Mirage, 1981 • *Saints and Sinners*, Liberty, 1982 • *Slide It In*, Liberty/Geffen, 1984 • *Greatest Hits*, DGC, 1994.

Martin Bisi

Situated in an industrial no-man's-land in Brooklyn's Red Hook district, Martin Bisi's B.C. Studios is as much a part of his production and engineering arsenal as all the skills he has acquired over the past two decades making records with artists as varied as Bill

Laswell, Brian Eno (see entries), Live Skull, and Sonic Youth. In his labyrinthine warehouse, Bisi makes use of hidden corridors and stairwells to process sounds. His clients, too, take full advantage of Bisi's city-within-a-city for both creature comforts and musical inspiration.

It was at B.C. that Sonic Youth camped out to make its *Evol* album, still considered one of the New York noisemakers' finest works. It was also at B.C. that Motherhead Bug cut its kaleidoscopic *Zambodia*, Cop Shoot Cop recorded its underrated opus *Ask Questions Later*, and Unsane committed *Total Destruction* to tape. White Zombie, Helmet, Alice Donut, Foetus, Railroad Jerk, Live Skull, and Lubricated Goat used B.C. to maximum effect on their recordings.

Before Bisi's space became known as a haven for New York's cutting-edge rockers, it was a space shared by a bunch of young guys—a combination rehearsal studio, hangout, and sleeping quarters. "My dad died when I was 17, so I blew off college and got this space," recalls Bisi. "It was just a place to eat. It had two floors, and friends of mine could rehearse downstairs. I was playing drums at the time and hanging out with the guys from Material—Bill Laswell, Michael Beinhorn, Fred Maher [see entries]. It became a little den of future producers."

According to Bisi, it was Laswell's idea to install recording equipment in the space. "It just seemed like a good idea," says Bisi. "It was something to do. I hardly thought I would become anything like a professional. I certainly didn't think I'd produce records. It was never a conscious decision."

Like many young, enthusiastic musician/producers, Bisi got in over his head financially and nearly had to dismantle the facility in the early '80s. However, a felicitous intervention by Eno not only ensured the survival of the studio space but also catapulted Bisi into a career in production, engineering, and studio ownership. "Eno started coming around to the Material shows," recalls Bisi. "I was the sound man, and Eno liked the way I did sound. He was looking to take a couple of different collaborators and do an ambient record. This would turn out to be *On Land*."

The project netted Bisi an engineering credit and money to revitalize and upgrade the studio. In 1983, Bisi engineered Herbie Hancock's *Future Shock* album, which yielded the Grammy-winning single "Rockit." Following the success of *Future Shock*, Laswell expressed his desire to move the studio to Manhattan, and Bisi rebelled, reasoning that the operation would get away from him. The dispute led to a bitter split, with Laswell establishing his own successful operation and Bisi remaining as the proprietor and steward of B.C. He and Laswell eventually reunited when the latter cut basic tracks for a White Zombie album at B.C.

Bisi regards himself as an unobtrusive but sensitive producer who goes to great lengths to help his clients realize their musical ideas. Neither a sonic purist nor a gratuitous knob twiddler, Bisi likes each sound to have its own personality. He occasionally mixes radically to achieve that goal, but when things sound good immediately, he likes to leave them alone.

"I try to get a little bit of all worlds," he says. "These days I don't subscribe to either the corporate stuff or the purist kind of indie, Steve Albini-esque [see entry] sort of thing—you know, mixing without automation and taking the approach that, 'Hey it's the band, don't touch anything!' I'm into looking a little further into it."

Bisi says he often baffles his underground clients by referring to commercially successful music in the course of his productions. "At a very early stage—this was definitely a curiosity to a lot of the people I was working with a long time ago, like Sonic Youth—I actually paid attention to real commercial recordings, and would refer to them and listen to them. They thought that was a completely incompatible realm. They thought it was weird that what they were doing in a mix would stack up to something that might be on Top 40 radio." —Paul Verna

Alice Donut: "Nadine," Alternative Tentacles, 1994 • *Pure Acid Park*, Alternative Tentacles, 1995.

Bisi, Martin: *Creole Mass*, New Alliance, 1991 • *All Will Be Won*, New Alliance, 1992 • w/ Cochinas, *See Ya in Tia Juana*, New Alliance, 1995 • w/ Cochinas, *Dear Popi, I'm in Jail*, New Alliance, 1996.

Blind Idiot God: *Blind Idiot God*, SST, 1987, 1991.

Chain Gang: *Perfumed*, Matador, 1993.

Christmas: *Vortex*, Matador, 1993.

Cochinas, The: See Bisi, Martin.

Cop Shoot Cop: *Consumer Revolt* (9 tracks), Big Cat, 1992 • *Suck City* (EP), Interscope, 1992 • *Ask Questions Later*, Interscope, 1993.

Die Haut: *Head On*, Triple X, 1993.

Dystopia One: *Attempted Mustache*, Rawkus, 1996.

Golden Palominos: *A History, 1982–1985*, Restless, 1992 • *A History, 1986–1989*, Restless, 1993.

Live Skull: *Dusted*, Homestead, 1987 • *Positraction*, Caroline, 1989.

Material: *Memory Serves*, Celluloid/Elektra Musician, 1982.

Motorhead Bug: *Zambodia*, Pow Wow, 1993.

Ordinaires, The: *The Ordinaires*, Bar None, 1985 • *One*, Bar None, 1989 • "Kashmir," Safe House, 1993 (*The Song Retains the Name*, Vol. II)

Railroad Jerk: *Raise the Plow*, Matador, 1992 • *We Understand* (EP), Matador, 1993.

Season to Risk: *In a Perfect World,* Columbia, 1995.

Sleepyhead: *Communist Love Songs,* Homestead, 1996.

Sonic Youth: *Evol,* SST, 1986.

Surgery: "Little Debbie," Amphetamine Reptile, 1992 • *Trim, 9th Ward High Roller* (EP), Amphetamine Reptile, 1993.

Swans, The: *Love of Life,* Young Gods/Sky, 1992.

Tirez Tirez: *Against All Flags,* IRS, 1988.

Ultra Bide: *God Is God . . . Puke Is Puke,* Alternative Tentacles, 1995 • *Ultra Bide* (EP), Alternative Tentacles, 1995.

Undernation: *Something on the TV,* Bot, 1991 • *Anger,* Brake Out, 1993.

Unsane: *Total Destruction,* Matador, 1994.

Matt Black

See COLDCUT

Chris Blackwell

Every so often, when he was producing Bob Marley, Chris Blackwell would tell the natural mystic not to worry about it when he made a mistake singing. The gaffe would give Marley's vocal extra soul, Blackwell felt.

Born in Jamaica on June 22, 1937, Blackwell grew up as part of the island aristocracy; his family belonged to Jamaica's elite, successful in such indigenous industries as cattle, rum, coconuts, and sugar. His father was Irish and his mother was a descendant of Sephardic Jews who had fled Portugal in the 18th century and settled in the Caribbean. He attended school in England and held a variety of odd jobs before he plunged into music seriously at the dawn of the '60s.

Blackwell crossed reggae over to pop in the '60s and '70s. A diversified entrepreneur who runs a record company, oversees MTV competitor the Box, and owns a chain of boutique hotels, he maintains residences in Jamaica, Miami, the Bahamas, and London—at least. He enjoys the spontaneous more than the designed, he suggests.

"I think some of the real magic comes from a mistake or something that happens which sounds wrong at the time but sounds interesting," says the tousle-haired founder of Island Records. "It can be lots of things. Suddenly, somebody plays something on guitar, there's feedback, something weird happens. At times, one would wipe that track and record it again. I would be inclined to leave it for a bit and decide whether to use it."

Blackwell founded Island in 1962 and began producing in 1964, when he notched a worldwide hit with "My Boy Lollipop" (No. 2), an enticing bit of ska fluff rendered by Millie Small. He has since gone on to produce the likes of Traffic, Bob Marley, the B-52's, and Grace Jones and, as head of Island, has signed such megastars as U2, Melissa Etheridge, and the Cranberries.

He hasn't produced a record in 15 years, he says, save for one stillborn Grace Jones project, shelved "because I wasn't able to get it to sound as good as I wanted it to sound." Meanwhile, Jones' *Warm Leatherette* and *Nightclubbing* albums, respectively released in 1980 and 1981, still do Blackwell proud. Those are discs he approached with a particular sound in mind. But most of the time, Blackwell suggests, his role is to be a reflector and massager.

"The producer's role is to make the very best record of the material he's given," he says. "It's got to bring out the best in the song and the best in the performance of the artist and the musicians. I think there are two different jobs: a producer has one, an engineer another. Sometimes they work together; in fact, recently, they work together a lot. But producers who are engineer-oriented will in most cases not be as strong in the song sense as in the sound and impact of a record. But it's very important to also have a good song sense, know how to bring out the most dynamic in a song."

That's what he did with Millie Small's "Lollipop," a song he considers a perfect pop expression. "Your first hit is what moves you from being one of thousands to

Photo by Cookie Kinkead

being one of hundreds," he says. "What was special about 'My Boy Lollipop' was that it was a perfect choice of material matching to an artist, and I had in my head the type of sound, type of rhythm, and type of feel that I wanted to get. Often, you have those ideas in your head and they don't always get realized. In this case, it got realized pretty much exactly as I heard it in my head."

That mono production was also relatively straightforward, Blackwell says, suggesting technological advances may cut several ways. "The developments of technology have all been tools which have helped considerably," he says. "The problem is that, in general, technology allows you to delay your decisions. If you're making a record in mono, like 'My Boy Lollipop,' the record is cut with all the musicians and singers in the studio, it's finished, and there's no overdubbing. When you have 48 tracks to work with—with drums over 6 different tracks, the high hat on one, the bass drum on another—all that means is you're delaying the decision on how you want those drums to sound."

Blackwell didn't so much produce the likes of Marley and Traffic as facilitate them. "In the case of Bob Marley, there was only one track that I recorded from beginning to end: 'Redemption Song,' from *Uprising* [1980, Marley's last release in his lifetime]. Otherwise, he basically produced the music of all of his records and he'd give them to me to mix. In the case of Traffic—again, they knew what they wanted to do. I just acted as a sounding board. I just performed the role of trying to push them a little bit to do a little bit more. But I never directed them.

"Basically, the thing I really like is a groove," Blackwell says. "I love music that has a groove, that has a great rhythm feel to it. That's the primary importance to me."

After selling Island Records to PolyGram in 1989, Blackwell served on the PolyGram board of directors for eight years. In 1997, Blackwell departed PolyGram, and in April 1998 he announced plans to start a new music and film company, Palm Pictures, with offices in London and New York. —Carlo Wolff

B-52's, The: *B-52's,* Warner Bros., 1979 • "Rock Lobster," Warner Bros., 1979 • *Party Mix!* Warner Bros., 1981.

Baah, Reebop Kwaku: *Reebop,* Island, 1972.

Badarou, Wally: "Guidance," Mango/Island, 1982 (*Countryman* soundtrack) • *Echoes,* Island, 1983, 1985.

Blue in Heaven: *Explicit Material,* Island, 1985.

Capaldi, Jim: *Oh How We Danced,* Island, 1972 • *Short Cut Draw Blood,* Island, 1975.

Cocker, Joe: *Sheffield Steel,* Island, 1982.

Davis, Spencer: "Gimme Some Lovin'," United Artists, 1966, 1970 (*Progressive Heavies*) • "I'm a Man," United Artists, 1967, 1970 (*Progressive Heavies*).

Derek and Clive: *Derek and Clive Live,* Island, 1976.

Free: *Free,* Island, 1977 • *Molten Gold: The Anthology,* Island, 1995.

Hammill, Claire: *One House Left Standing,* Island, 1971.

Harrison, Mike: *Smokestack Lightning,* Island, 1972.

Inner Circle: *The Best of Inner Circle, Featuring Jacob Miller,* Mango, 1992.

Jones, Grace: *Warm Leatherette,* Island, 1980 • *Nightclubbing,* Island, 1981 • *Living My Life,* Island, 1983 • *Island Life,* Island, 1985.

Kossoff, Paul: *Koss,* DJM, 1977.

Marley, Bob, and the Wailers: "Stir It Up," Island, 1973 • *Natty Dread,* Island, 1974 • *Live,* Island, 1975 • "No Woman, No Cry," Island, 1975 • *Babylon By Bus,* Island, 1978 • "Could You Be Loved," Island, 1980 • "Redemption Song," Island, 1980 • "Pass It On," Mango/Island, 1982 (*Countryman* soundtrack) • "Rastaman Chant," Mango/Island, 1982 (*Countryman* soundtrack) • "Small Axe," Mango/Island, 1982 (*Countryman* soundtrack) • "Three O'Clock Roadblock," Mango/Island, 1982 (*Countryman* soundtrack) • *Talkin' Blues,* Tuff Gong, 1991 • See also The Wailers.

Martyn, John: *One World,* Island, 1977.

Nirvana: *The Story of Simon Simopath,* Island, 1967.

Plastics: *Come Back,* Initiation, 1981.

Roden, Jess: *Jess Roden,* Island, 1974.

Small, Millie: "My Boy Lollipop," Smash, 1964.

Spencer Davis Group: *First Album,* Fontana, 1965 • *Autumn '66,* Fontana, 1966 • "Gimme Some Lovin'," United Artists, 1966 • *Second Album,* Fontana, 1966 • *Gimme Some Lovin',* CEMA, 1967, 1992 • *Best of the Spencer Davis Group,* Gold Rush, 1996.

Spooky Tooth: *The Last Puff,* Island, 1970.

Third World: *Journey to Addis,* Island, 1978 • *Prisoner in the Street,* Island, 1980 • *Reggae Ambassadors: 20th Anniversary Collection,* Mercury, 1993.

Toots and the Maytals: *Funky Kingston,* Mango, 1973 • *Reggae Got Soul,* Mango, 1976 • *Just Like That,* Island, 1980 • "Bam Bam," Mango/Island, 1982 (*Countryman* soundtrack) • *Reggae Greats,* Mango, 1984.

Traffic: *John Barleycorn Must Die,* Island/United Artists, 1970 • *Welcome to the Canteen,* Island/United Artists, 1971 • *On the Road,* Island, 1973 • *When the Eagle Flies,* Island/Asylum, 1974.

Wailers, The: *Burnin',* Island, 1973 • *Catch a Fire,* Island, 1973 • "Get Up Stand Up," Island, 1973 • "I Shot the Sheriff," Island, 1973.

Winwood, Steve: *Steve Winwood,* Island, 1977 • *Chronicles,* Island, 1987 • *Finer Things,* Island, 1995.

Zap Pow: "This Is Reggae Music/Break Down the Barriers," Mango, 1973.

COLLECTIONS

Countryman soundtrack, Island, 1982.
They Called It an Accident soundtrack, Island, 1983.

Robert "Bumps" Blackwell

Bumps Blackwell was, along with Dave Bartholomew and Henry Glover (see entries), among the first great black producers, and through his pioneering work with Little Richard and Sam Cooke he helped create rock 'n' roll and soul.

Robert "Bumps" Blackwell was born in 1918 and brought up in Seattle, where he became a pianist and sometime bandleader of a group that at times featured a young Ray Charles and a little-known trumpet player named Quincy Jones (see entry). After service in the Army and a stay in Canada, Blackwell returned to Seattle in 1949 and set up a series of businesses, including a barbershop, a meat market, and a music school. He visited Los Angeles in 1953 and was smitten. As he told writer Rob Finnis, "The sun was shining, everything was happening, and I got to meet some musicians."

Blackwell was a self-styled college man (one class at the University of Washington and some piano classes from a conservatory), and at 37, he saw himself as a man of the world. Blackwell hit the streets of L.A., going from label to label trying to sell the jazz masters he had recorded. In the spring of 1955, he was hired as an A&R trainee by owner Art Rupe of the R&B and gospel label Specialty. Rupe liked Blackwell's arranging skills, his ambition and his savoir faire. A few weeks after he was hired, Blackwell and Rupe listened to a demo tape by Little Richard and the Upsetters, and both thought they heard a something in the young singer's voice.

Richard was playing in New Orleans and signed to the Peacock label when a demo arrived at Specialty "wrapped in a piece of paper looking as though someone had eaten off it," according to Blackwell in Charles White's *The Life and Times of Little Richard.* Rupe allowed Blackwell to buy Richard out of his Peacock contract for $600 and sign him to Specialty. As is typical

with the passage of time, there is some dispute as to the relative contributions of Rupe and Blackwell in the creation of Richard's records. It is clear, however, that Blackwell was the man calling the shots in the studio, but with an ear toward pleasing Rupe, who would then sort through the takes and either accept a recording or send Blackwell and the artist back to the studio. Today we would call Blackwell the producer and Rupe the executive producer.

In September 1955 Rupe sent Blackwell to New Orleans to produce Richard at Cosimo Matassa's primitive J&M studio with the rocking house band (Lee Allen on tenor sax, Red Tyler on baritone sax, Earl Palmer on drums, Edgar Blanchard or Justin Adams on guitar, Huey "Piano" Smith on piano, and Frank Fields on bass). This band, with some variations, had played on the records of Roy Brown, Fats Domino, Professor Longhair, Shirley and Lee, Lloyd Price, and many others. Neither the band nor Blackwell knew what to make of Little Richard when they first met in the studio. "When I walked in, there's this cat in this loud shirt, with hair waved up 6 inches above his head," recalls Blackwell. "He was talking wild, thinking up stuff just to be different."

Red Tyler recalls that Richard was, "You know, quite funny, and not funny ha ha."

After some uninspiring takes of blues numbers, Blackwell was worried. "If you look like Tarzan and sound like Mickey Mouse, it just doesn't work out. I didn't know what to do . . . because there was nothing there that I could put out."

So they took a break and went over to the Dew Drop Inn. Richard was much more at ease out of the studio and started joking around at the piano. The few patrons started egging him on, and all of sudden Richard broke into a crowd pleaser from his stage show, 'Awop-Bop-a-Loo-Mop A-Good Goddam / Tutti Frutti, Good Booty,' and the song scaled impressive scatological heights from there. The fire and life that had been missing in the studio was suddenly, explosively, there.

Chuck Berry was a sly wink. Little Richard was a poke in the eye. He was everything parents (including his own) worried about: a charismatic, narcissistic, ambisexual, dithyrambic black man. But by early 1956, both the black and the white teens were ready for such ecstatic rebellion. In an astonishing two-year period, Little Richard recorded all of his great hits for Specialty in New Orleans with the J&M house band, or in Los Angeles: "Tutti Frutti" (No. 17), "Long Tall Sally" (No. 6), "Slippin' and Slidin'," "Rip It Up" (No. 17), "Lucille," "Jenny, Jenny" (No. 10), "Keep a-Knockin" (No. 8), "Good Golly, Miss Molly" (No. 10), and "Girl Can't Help

It." With the piano pumping, the saxes wailing, and Richard tapping into some otherworldly energy flow, the rock 'n' roll revolution started by Bill Haley, Elvis Presley, and Chuck Berry was completed, and Little Richard was on top of the world.

Specialty also had great success with black gospel music in the '40s and '50s with such stars as Brother Joe May, Wynona Carr, the Pilgrim Travelers, and the Soul Stirrers with lead singer Sam Cooke.

Soon after joining Specialty, Blackwell attended a rousing gospel show at the Shrine starring Sam and the Soul Stirrers. "My initial impression was, this cat should be pop. . . . That was just too much voice to be in such a limited market," Bumps told author Daniel Wolff in his biography of Cooke. Blackwell met Cooke at a party that Rupe threw after the show and discussed a turn to pop. Cooke was afraid of losing his religious market. Bumps prodded Cooke along economic lines, and eventually he responded. "I wanted to do things for my family, and I wanted nice things for my own," Cooke reasoned. "Making a living was good enough, but what's wrong with doing better than that?"

Blackwell produced Cooke's first pop session (as Dale Cook) at J&M studio in New Orleans in December 1956, the same studio and players that Bumps had used for recording Little Richard, but the results were less felicitous and the resulting single died. Blackwell knew what he wanted for Cooke. "We would like pop tunes with a blues chord structure that lend themselves to blues backgrounds. In writing the lyrics try to write white for the teenage purchaser rather than race lyrics," Blackwell advised. "It seems the white girls are buying records these days."

Blackwell intended to break Cooke directly into the mainstream pop market, instead of following the traditional route through R&B. He tried this approach at Cooke's next pop session in L.A. in 1957. "With Sam, being that his voice was so fluid and much different than the other singers—and he sang so far off the melody, which was like a jazz singer—I had to get the melody of the song back in. So, I had the Pied Pipers [a white vocal trio] on the melody. I used them like a string concept."

Rupe, who was suspicious of the move to pop, wanted things heavier and less white. Cooke threatened to quit. Rupe blamed his A&R man for Cooke's turn to pop, and it's always easier to fire the manager than the players, so Rupe fired Blackwell instead. Somehow the session continued and "You Send Me" was recorded. The simple, lilting melody, dreamy arrangement, and Cooke's buttery, soulful vocals made "You Send Me" an instant classic. Bumps admitted that the song sounded kind of dumb to him at the time.

The argument resumed a week later as the men negotiated Blackwell's departure from the label. As the discussion turned ugly, they accused each other of not having ears for a hit. Rupe made Bumps an offer. "Just forget what you got coming in royalties with Little Richard, and you take Sam. And you can have the masters." Bumps figured it was a $50,000 gamble. The divorce was signed June 17. Bumps had been negotiating with a brand new label, Keen, since May. Along with Sam Cooke, whom he also managed, Bumps brought the gospel group Pilgrim Travelers and their young lead singer Lou Rawls with him to Keen.

Keen released "Summertime/You Send Me" in September 1957. "You Send Me" was an immediate hit at Dolphins Record Shop, the R&B record shop in L.A. Next, sales took off in Chicago, Cooke's hometown. Casey Kasem helped break the song in Detroit. It rose to No. 3 in two weeks, hit No. 1, and eventually sold 1.7 million copies.

Blackwell then got carried away with Cooke's crossover potential. He had the singer record a collection of insipid ballads for his first album and perform in tails for a disastrous Copacabana appearance with a full orchestra. After that, and an appearance at the first integrated show at the Southeastern Fairgrounds in Atlanta, Cooke made a decision.

"When the whites are through with Sammy Davis Jr., he won't have anywhere to play. I'll always be able to go back to my people 'cause I'm never gonna stop singing to them," Wolff quotes Cooke.

Cooke stopped straightening his hair and returned to the black nightclub circuit. Ironically, as his social consciousness became more black, Cooke became convinced that the only way for him to make it to the next level was to have a white manager. He had been stewing since the Copa affair, and in the fall of 1959, Cooke and Blackwell went to a restaurant in Santa Barbara, where Cooke broke the news. They shook hands like gentlemen and parted.

Cooke went on to work with Hugo and Luigi (see entry) before his untimely death in 1965, and Blackwell went on to produce Art Neville and Bob Dylan, as well as manage Little Richard when he returned to showbiz in the '60s. Bumps Blackwell died in 1985. —Eric Olsen

Bradford, Prof. Alex: *Too Close,* Specialty, 1958.

Carr, Wynona: *Jump Jack Jump!* Specialty, 1993.

Cooke, Sam: "You Send Me," Keen, 1957 • "Lonely Island," Keen, 1958 • "Love You Most of All," Keen, 1958 • *Sam Cooke,* Keen, 1958 • "You Were Made for Me," Keen, 1958 • w/ the Soul Stirrers, *Sam Cooke with the Soul Stirrers,* Specialty, 1991.

Dylan, Bob: *Shot of Love,* Columbia, 1981.

Five Blind Boys of Alabama: *The Original/Sermon,* Specialty, 1993.

Guitar Slim: *Sufferin' Mind,* Specialty, 1991.

Little Richard: "Long Tall Sally," Specialty, 1956 • "Rip It Up," Specialty, 1956 • "Slippin' and Slidin'," Specialty, 1956 • "Tutti Frutti," Specialty, 1956 • *Here's Little Richard,* Specialty, 1957 • "Jenny Jenny," Specialty, 1957 • "Keep a-Knockin'," Specialty, 1957 • "Lucille," Specialty, 1957 • "Send Me Some Lovin'," Specialty, 1957 • "Good Golly, Miss Molly," Specialty, 1958 • *Little Richard,* Specialty, 1958 • *The Fabulous Little Richard,* Specialty, 1959 • *The Specialty Sessions,* Specialty, 1989 • *The Georgia Peach,* Specialty, 1991 • *Shag On Down by the Union Hall,* Specialty, 1996.

Neville, Art: *His Specialty Recordings,* Specialty, 1993.

Neville Brothers: *Treacherous Too! A History of the Neville Brothers, Vol. 2, 1955–1987,* Rhino, 1991.

Soul Stirrers, The: *See* Cooke, Sam.

Turner, Ike and Tina: *Finger Poppin',* JCI, 1988.

Williams, Larry: "Bony Maronie," Specialty, 1957 • "High School Dance," Specialty, 1957 • "Short Fat Fanny," Specialty, 1957 • *Larry Williams,* Specialty, 1959.

COLLECTIONS

Women of Gospel's Golden Age, Vol. 1, Specialty, 1994.

Tchad Blake

Tchad Blake has visited Africa five times. "I really got into African music when I was about 15," says Blake. "I always wanted to go to Africa." Blake's real first name is Chad, but whenever he identified himself during his first African trip, at 19, the T was added. So the spelling stuck. It's also the name of an African country. Blake's fascination with Africa yielded his own label, Document, which Peter Gabriel created for him.

Born February 16, 1955, in Baytown, Texas, southeast of Houston, Blake is best-known as a recordist and engineer. "I might be getting into documenting," he says, "but not really. I like music and I like the emotions in music and how it makes your body want to move. I'm also very much into the visual arts. I love photography and painting. I also weld. I'm a pretty bad welder."

Blake, who has lived in Los Angeles since he was 3, has produced all kinds of people, from the Wild Colonials to the Latin Playboys to Los Lobos, many with mentor Mitchell Froom (see entry). Blake and Froom met in the mid-'80s at the Sound Factory in Los Angeles. When Blake told Froom his favorite record was the soundtrack to *Barbarella,* they hit it off; Blake gave Froom a copy of *Barbarella* and Froom countered with the soundtrack he'd written for a porn film called *Cafe Flesh,* released on the influential early alternative label Slash. Eventually, Blake ended up engineering a Crowded House album Froom produced. "I got along with the band and Neil Finn and I didn't get fired," he says.

"For me, the difference between producing and engineering isn't so great. I'm not an arranger or a composer or a songcrafter, which is what Mitchell does. I get atmospheres, and I'm a good arranger at mix stage. I'm pretty good at mute buttons and creating environments."

He got into the record business in 1980 as a janitor at Wally Heider's studio in Los Angeles. "They went out of business and I lost my job, but I made a lot of friends who let me come in late at night and watch sessions," he recalls. One of the earliest sessions he attended—as a janitor, mind you—was the Rolling Stones' *Some Girls.*

Blake also learned a great deal about engineering from Heider staffer Sherman Keene, "a maintenance engineer who was trying to teach us things in sort of an organized fashion. He was really good," Blake says. "Mainly he taught about studio etiquette, which nobody teaches. He stressed being sensitive to the studio situation, like being quiet and knowing when to speak, knowing when to give suggestions and to whom."

As a producer, Blake likes "things to come together with the least amount of pain, to keep things moving on a bit," he says. "It's about creating an atmosphere where people want to work and have a good time working with each other."

As befits an admirer of field-recordist extraordinaire Alan Lomax, Blake favors ambience. "I like a mixture of good sounds and really low-fi sounds, pretty distorted and gritty," he says. "I rarely use reverb, so just about every record I do is pretty dry; very few effects go on in the mix."

A self-described desert rat, Blake is "fascinated with people who do a lot with very little, and there are lots of cultures like that. Unfortunately, they happen to be kind of poor," he says. "That's fascinating to me."

Blake's latest sonic endeavor is binaural recording, a two-channel technique that attempts to recreate a soundscape more naturally than stereo. "I'm putting microphones in my ears," says Blake. "Humans hear binaurally. You don't hear stereo. It has to do with your head being part of a mechanism. You head is like some sort of audio matrix. Instead of putting up two mikes with nothing in between, I take two little mikes and stick them in my ears and record exactly what's going into them, or as closely as I can approximate it."

Several cuts on the Latin Playboys were recorded binaurally, including "Mira!" Listening to that "is like walking down the street in India and there are wedding bands playing, about five of them at once," Blake says. "There's a lot of ambient sounds on there, like cars in the distance, city noise. I use that kind of stuff a lot. I like it. It just seems strange to me when you hear a car rumbling through the music. High contrast, that's what I like." —CARLO WOLFF

Cibo Matto: "Know Your Chicken," Warner Bros., 1996 • *Viva! La Woman,* Warner Bros., 1996 • *Super Relax* (1 track, EP), Warner Bros., 1997.

Crowded House: *Instinct,* Capitol, 1996 • *Recurring Dream: The Very Best Of,* Capitol, 1996.

Deiana, Gesuino: *Solo in Sardinia,* Womad, 1997.

Finn Brothers: "Angel's Heap," Parlophone, 1995 • "Suffer Never," Parlophone, 1995 • *Finn Brothers,* Discovery, 1996.

Los Lobos: *Colossal Head,* Warner Bros., 1996.

Rogie, S.E.: *Dead Men Don't Smoke Marijuana,* Realworld/Caroline, 1994.

Sexsmith, Ron: *Other Songs,* Interscope, 1997.

Soul Coughing: *Ruby Vroom,* Slash/WB, 1994 • "Screenwriter's Blues," Slash/WB, 1994 • "Down to This," Slash/WB, 1995 • "Sugar Free Jazz," Slash/WB, 1995.

Thompson, Richard: *You? Me? Us?,* Capitol, 1996.

Wild Colonials: "Evil," A&M, 1994 (*Fast Track to Nowhere: Songs from Rebel Highway*) • *Fruit of Life,* DGC, 1994 • "Spark," DGC, 1994.

Archie Bleyer

Archie Bleyer was a bandleader, a pioneer television music director, record producer, and owner of one of the most successful indie labels of the rock 'n' roll era. Bleyer also brought some class to a business that was notorious for shady characters and unscrupulous operators.

Archie Bleyer was born into an established New York family in 1909 and began playing piano by age 7. A musical lad, Bleyer also sang in his church choir. He enrolled at Columbia University in 1927 as an electrical engineering student (an interest that aided him later in the studio), but switched to music by his sophomore year, and left school in his junior year to be a musical arranger. By 1934, Bleyer had his own big band that played regularly in the New York area. The band record-ed for Brunswick in the mid-'30s and featured Johnny Mercer (who later founded Capitol Records) on vocals.

Bleyer gravitated to Hollywood in 1938, but returned to New York in 1940 to conduct for Broadway shows. CBS radio called shortly thereafter, and in the late '40s Bleyer became musical director of *Arthur Godfrey and Friends* on radio and then on television. Godfrey became the first to host two different shows on television at the same time when his show *Talent Scouts* came on the air in 1948, and Bleyer joined him on the second show as well.

Bleyer milked the Godfrey connection for all it was worth when he founded Cadence Records in 1952 in order to record Godfrey mainstay Julius LaRosa, the Chordettes, and other talent from the shows. LaRosa recorded the first eight singles for Cadence and hit right away with "Anywhere I Wander," which reached No. 4 on the Billboard pop chart in early 1953. LaRosa was a traditional pop singer. The vocal-over-orchestra arrangement of "Wander" and the jaunty faux-Italian feel of "Eh, Cumpari!" (No. 2) from the same year are firmly in the entertainer/show biz tradition commensurate with Bleyer's background.

Having judiciously plucked talent from the shows, Bleyer left Godfrey in 1953 to concentrate on his label. Bleyer's own orchestra had two big hits in 1954, "Hernando's Hideaway" (No. 2) from the movie *The Pajama Game,* and "The Naughty Lady of Shady Lane" (No. 17). On those hits and on the Chordettes' (a female harmony quartet featuring Bleyer's future wife Janet Ertel) "Mr. Sandman" (No. 1), Bleyer's talents as a producer began to come to the fore.

"Hideaway" is driven by Maria Alba's exuberant castanets and humorous sound effects (door knocks, match striking). The inherent self-importance of the tango is exaggerated by conspiratorial male unison vocals revealing a sense of self-aware irony that is almost postmodern. "Mr. Sandman" could have been a standard Andrews Sisters–type vehicle, but Bleyer's use of syncopated hand claps, vocal arpeggios, and bells create a sonic dreamscape that is a direct precursor of Buddy Holly's "Everyday" and the Velvet Underground's "Sunday Morning."

Bleyer brought an engineer's precision and a musician's feel to his productions. Besides the importance of his own work, Bleyer's influence has been felt through the efforts of his most important follower—Phil Spector (see entry). Spector held Cadence as a model for his own Philles label and followed Bleyer's credo of quality, not quantity.

Cadence never had a large roster of artists, and it put out records judiciously so that each could be worked to achieve its full potential. Bleyer spent as long as it took to find the right material for his artists, and even then would not hesitate to dump a session that didn't meet his standards. He even took out ads in the trades chastising his industry brethren for their recording profligacy.

In 1957, Bleyer decided that he needed a country act to balance out his pop roster, so he went a-courtin' in Nashville. Bleyer met with Wesley Rose of publishing giant Acuff-Rose in an effort to recruit talent and came away with Anita Carter, Gordon Terry, and the Everly Brothers.

Don and Phil Everly were at least third-generation folk and country singers from central Kentucky. Father Ike was a guitar picker of some renown and friends with Chet Atkins (see entry). After traveling about performing live and on radio with their parents, the Everlys ended up in Nashville. A deal with Columbia resulted in less than zero, but eventually the duo ended up signed to Acuff-Rose as songwriters. Although Bleyer had turned down an Everly demo several months before, when he made his trip to Nashville in the spring of 1957, he signed the Everly Brothers at the strong urging of Rose.

Much to everyone's surprise, "Bye, Bye Love," the Everlys' first release on Cadence, became a huge crossover hit that reached No. 2 on the pop chart and No. 1 on the country chart. The song was written by veteran Acuff-Rose songwriters Boudleaux and Felice Bryant. The Bryants had shown the song to 30 different artists and had been rejected by them all. The boys heard something though, and by grafting on the intro from a song Don had written called "Give Me a Future," a smash was created and a career began that established the Everlys as the most important duo in rock history.

There are obvious reasons why siblings or other close blood relatives (Andrews Sisters, Beach Boys, Judds, Rank and File) would achieve a remarkable harmonic blend: similar genes, similar environment, growing up singing together. The Everlys and Cadence brought this phenomenon to its artistic apex by creating a crack creative and production team that included the Bryants' songs, guitarist Atkins, and pianists Floyd Cramer and David Briggs backing the Everlys' acoustic guitars and vocals. Bleyer supervised.

The team achieved a lightness and brightness that wove in and around the Everlys' angelic tenors. "All I Have to Do Is Dream" (No. 1) is perhaps the most wistful song ever recorded—with a love divine just out of the Everlys' reach, tantalizing and forever perfect. The beauty and intimacy of the Everlys' best ballads, "Love of My Life," "Let It Be Me" (No. 7), "Dream," render potentially mawkish sentiments into undeniable Truth.

The uptempo "Bye, Bye, Love," "Wake Up Little Susie" (No. 1) and "Problems" (No. 2) proved that the acoustic guitar is a rock 'n' roll instrument, and paved the way for the power strumming of the '60s. Artists as far flung as Bob Dylan, the Who, the Beatles, the Byrds, CSNY, and the Eagles are in debt to the Everlys.

In 1958, Cadence contributed further to rock 'n' roll history by issuing guitarist Link Wray's instrumental hit "Rumble" (No. 16), his only record with Cadence, and by far the hardest rock song that the label ever released. Before consulting with his stepdaughter, Bleyer, ever the perfectionist, nearly passed on "Rumble" because the bass was out of tune.

Earle Doud, a comedy writer and agent for young Greenwich Village comedian Vaughn Meader, approached Bleyer in mid-1962 with sample sketches for a comedy album based upon the Kennedy clan. Although Meader did a mean JFK, the industry didn't get it and the idea had already been rejected by every major label in New York. One astute A&R man had told Doud that he wouldn't touch the project with a 10-foot pole. For Christmas, Doud sent the man a 10-foot pole because by then *The First Family* (No. 1) had sold more than 4 million copies for Cadence and had broken all sales records. How to follow up such a sensation? Neither Meader nor Bleyer ever did.

By 1964, with most of his talent signed to major-label deals, the 55-year-old Bleyer felt out of touch with the lurching changes of the record industry and decided to call it a career. He died from Parkinson's disease in 1979. —ERIC OLSEN

Bleyer, Archie: "Hernando's Hideaway," Cadence, 1954 • "The Naughty Lady of Shady Lane," Cadence, 1954 • *Golden Classics,* Collectables, 1997.

Chamber Jazz Sextet: *The Chamber Jazz Sextet Plays Pal Joey,* Candid, 1958.

Chordettes, The: "Born to Be with You," Cadence, 1956 • "Eddie My Love," Cadence, 1956 • "Lay Down Your Arms," Cadence, 1956 • "Just Between You and Me," Cadence, 1957 • "Lollipop," Cadence, 1958 • "Zorro," Cadence, 1958 • "No Other Arms, No Other Lips," Cadence, 1959 • "Never on Sunday," Cadence, 1961.

Everly Brothers: "Bye Bye Love," Cadence, 1957 • "Wake Up Little Susie," Cadence, 1957 • "All I Have to Do Is Dream," Cadence, 1958 • "Bird Dog," Cadence, 1958 • *The Everly Brothers,* Cadence, 1958 • "('Til) I Kissed You," Cadence, 1959 • *The Fabulous Style of the Everly Brothers,* Cadence, 1960 • *Songs Our Daddy Taught Us,* Rhino, 1964, 1988 • *Cadence Classics: Their 20 Greatest Hits,* Rhino, 1985 • *All They Had to Do Was Dream,* Rhino, 1988 • *Classic,* Bear Family, 1992 • *Heartaches and Harmonies,* Rhino, 1994.

Hayes, Bill: "The Ballad of Davy Crockett," Cadence, 1955.

Hodges, Eddie: "I'm Gonna Knock on Your Door," Cadence, 1961 • "(Girls, Girls, Girls) Made to Love," Cadence, 1962.

LaRosa, Julius: "Anywhere I Wander," Cadence, 1953 • "Eh, Cumpari," Cadence, 1953 • "Domani," Cadence, 1955 • "Suddenly There's a Valley," Cadence, 1955.

Marlowe, Marion: "The Man in the Raincoat," Cadence, 1955.

Tillotson, Johnny: "Poetry in Motion," Cadence, 1960 • "Jimmy's Girl," Cadence, 1961 • "Without You," Cadence, 1961 • "Dreamy Eyes," Cadence, 1962 • "It Keeps Right on a-Hurtin'," Cadence, 1962 • *It Keeps Right on a-Hurtin',* Cadence, 1962 • *Johnny Tillotson's Best,* Cadence, 1962 • "Out of My Mind," Cadence, 1962 • "Send Me the Pillow You Dream On," Cadence, 1962 • "You Can Never Stop Me Loving You," Cadence, 1963 • *Poetry in Motion: The Best Of,* Varese Sarabande, 1995.

Welch, Lenny: "Since I Fell for You," Cadence, 1963 • *Since I Fell for You,* Cadence, 1963.

Williams, Andy: "Baby Doll," Cadence, 1956 • "Canadian Sunset," Cadence, 1956 • "Butterfly," Cadence, 1957 • "I Like Your Kind of Love," Cadence, 1957 • "Lips of Wine," Cadence, 1957 • "Are You Sincere," Cadence, 1958 • "Promise Me, Love," Cadence, 1958 • "Lonely Street," Cadence, 1959 • *Lonely Street,* Cadence, 1959 • "The Bilbao Song," Cadence, 1959 • "The Hawaiian Wedding Song," Cadence, 1959 • "The Village of St. Bernadette," Cadence, 1959 • *Andy Williams' Best,* Cadence, 1962 • *Million Seller Songs,* Cadence, 1962 • *I Like Your Kind of Love: The Best of the Cadence Years,* Varese Sarabande, 1996.

COLLECTIONS

The History of Cadence Records, Vols. 1–2, Varese Sarabande, 1996.

Kurt Bloch

K urt Bloch sees his job as producer to "make the best of what you have to work with." His ripping guitar, songwriting, and production are associated with two very good rock bands, the Fastbacks and the Young Fresh Fellows.

The musically minded Bloch has a flair for the technical. He says, "Most rock bands in my world do not have a lot of extra money to throw around, so if they could get one person to be the main engineer and production person, that makes for a little extra studio time or a little higher quality beer in the refrigerator." Bloch is perfectly happy to do either job—or both.

His interest in recording dates from age 8. A thrift-store quarter-inch reel-to-reel gave him a way to experiment while "making funny tapes" and to learn splicing. *The Partridge Family* sicked the "band bug" on him, and the household piano and ukulele—combined with violin lessons—gave young Bloch some formal musical direction.

He played guitar and worked at the radio station in junior high school. When his first band, the Cheaters (formed in 1978), recorded a 45, Bloch's ears and eyes opened to the unlimited possibilities offered by a real studio. In 1980, the Fastbacks began; his fine power-pop–punk unit thrives to this day.

Solid hands-on learning was his, recording his band on a Teac 3340 4-track, a quarter-inch machine popular with home recordists of the '70s and '80s. Paying attention while recording with the Fastbacks and the Young Fresh Fellows at Seattle's Egg Studio, with Conrad Uno (see entry) manning the console, furthered Bloch's knowledge and confidence. He produced the Fastbacks' records and folks liked what they heard. The phone began to ring. His calendar gradually filled up with production gigs.

Bloch's production style is characterized by up-front, compressed sounds. His records are immediate, often downright explosive. This sometimes entails more work than might initially meet the ear.

"In order to recreate the excitement of a live rock band, it takes more than just plugging in a microphone

and turning on a tape recorder," he says. "When you record records, you have to set up a work scene, or, in some ways, an artistic vibe. Some people might misunderstand it, but sometimes it might be appropriate to have incense and candles burning and the lights down. Sometimes it works better to have all the lights on and have everybody going 'yeahhrrgghh' and drink a lot of coffee and be screaming at each other and all revved up so they rip through their songs, or whatever. Everybody is different."

Although he appreciates the innovations of the '60s, Bloch thinks today is the best time for recording because "there is so much technology available. You have more choices and more ways to do things than ever today. Ten to 30 years ago nobody had the option of having a digital 8-track recorder at their house. Now you can buy reissues of vintage gear, so you can have the best of both worlds. But you have to let the music dictate what you do, and not let all the new technology dictate the music. All the technology in the world is secondary to great music."

Bloch likens capturing a magical musical moment to a "snapshot, frozen in time." It's not the same as a great live show, but a record lasts. The magic "almost always starts with the song," Bloch says. "If there's a genius piece of songwriting and there's something special about the way the singer is singing it, the song is the dynamite, the singer is the fuse, and the band and the recording situation are the match." —DENNIS DIKEN

Bum: *Wanna Smash Sensation,* Pop Llama, 1993.

Crackerbash: *Tin Toy,* Empty, 1993.

Fastbacks: *Very, Very Powerful Motor,* Pop Llama, 1990 • *Gone to the Moon,* Sub Pop, 1993 • *Zucker,* Sub Pop, 1993 • *Answer the Phone, Dummy,* Sub Pop, 1994 • *Here They Are Live at Crocodile Shop,* Lance Rock, 1996 • *New Mansions in Sound,* Sub Pop, 1996.

Flop: *World of Today,* Frontier, 1995.

Gas Huffer: *The Inhuman Ordeal of Special Agent,* Epitaph, 1996.

Les Thugs: *As Happy As Possible,* Sub Pop, 1993.

Meices, The: *Tastes Like Chicken,* External/London, 1994.

Mudhoney: *Five Dollar Bob's Mock Cooter Stew,* Reprise, 1993.

Overwhelming Colorfast: *Two Words,* Relativity, 1994.

Sicko: *You Can Feel the Love in This Room,* Empty, 1994 • *Laugh While You Can, Monkey Boy,* Empty, 1995.

Supersnazz: *Superstupid!* Sub Pop, 1993.

Tad: *Salem,* Sub Pop, 1992.

Uncle Joe's Big Ol' Driver: *Chick Rock,* Headhunter, 1995.

Niko Bolas

T he publicity-shy Niko Bolas (born June 10, 1957, in Los Angeles) is known for bringing out unparalleled raw power and energy in a series of excellent recordings.

An expert in vocal production, he owes part of his technique to the artful use of tube compressors to tightly package and position the voice so it won't be swamped by a guitar army barrage.

Among Bolas's standout productions are Neil Young's *This Note's for You* and *Freedom* and the puissant 1987 Warren Zevon album *Sentimental Hygiene,* which featured otherworldly drum sounds and backing tracks by Bill Berry, Mike Mills, and Peter Buck of R.E.M. The Zevon-R.E.M. collective was later formalized under the moniker Hindu Love Gods, which recorded a highly acclaimed album with Bolas in 1990.

Bolas, who can make everything seem extra-loud and intense, has been called the "Viscount of Volume," a nickname justified by his productions of New Model Army and the Circle Jerks. —DANIEL J. LEVITIN

Circle Jerks: *Oddities, Abnormalities and Curiosities,* Mercury, 1995.

Crosby, Stills, Nash and Young: *American Dream,* Atlantic, 1988.

Etheridge, Melissa: *Melissa Etheridge,* Island, 1988 • *Brave and Crazy,* Island, 1989.

Goops, The: *Lucky,* Kinetic/Reprise, 1996 • "Vulgar Appetites," Kinetic/Reprise, 1996.

Hindu Love Gods: *Hindu Love Gods,* Giant, 1990.

Mary's Danish: *American Standard,* Morgan Creek, 1992.

New Model Army: *The Love of Hopeless Causes,* Epic, 1993.

Salem, Kevin: "Lighthouse Keeper," Roadrunner, 1994 • *Soma City,* Roadrunner, 1994 • *Glimmer,* Roadrunner, 1996.

Scott, Mike: *Bring 'Em All In,* Chrysalis, 1995 • *Thirst Through the Wire,* Iguana, 1996.

Thorogood, George: "Sonny Rides Again," 550 Music/Epic, 1994 (*The Cowboy Way* soundtrack).

Young, Neil: *This Note's For You,* Reprise, 1987 • *Freedom,* Reprise, 1989 • "Rockin' In the Free World," Reprise, 1989 • *Lucky Thirteen,* Geffen, 1993.

Zevon, Warren: *Sentimental Hygiene,* Virgin, 1987 • *I'll Sleep When I'm Dead (An Anthology),* Rhino, 1996.

Bomb Squad

(CARL RYDER, HANK SHOCKLEE, KEITH SHOCKLEE, ERIC "VIETNAM" SADLER)

Hank Shocklee of Bomb Squad

Think of the one rap album that stands out as being the best of all time. What comes to mind? Run-D.M.C.'s self-titled debut? A Tribe Called Quest's *People's Instinctive Travels and the Paths of Rhythm*? N.W.A's *Straight Outta Compton*? Dr. Dre's *The Chronic*? Eric B. & Rakim's *Paid in Full*? Fugees' *The Score*? Ice Cube's *AmeriKKKa's Most Wanted*?

The list goes on and on, but one group that stands out is Public Enemy and its 1988 classic *It Takes a Nation of Millions to Hold Us Back*—almost a greatest-hits package within itself with cuts like "Don't Believe the Hype," "Bring the Noise," and "Black Steel in the Hour of Chaos."

For several years after *It Takes a Nation of Millions*, that album's title would prove true as the controversial Public Enemy seemed unstoppable.

Among the reasons for the group's success were the in-your-face, political raps of Chuck D. and his flow-with partner Flavor Flav, but behind the rappers and behind most of PE's work was the production outfit known as the Bomb Squad, who were single-handedly responsible for one of rap's most recognizable, popular, and hard-core sounds.

The Bomb Squad was, as its name implied, explosive. Core members Hank Shocklee, Keith Shocklee, Eric "Vietnam" Sadler, and Carl Ryder created unique, bombastic musical blasts often full of sirens, whistles, and other effects.

"We weren't looking for a sound, so to speak," says Hank Shocklee. "We were looking for sonics, and through sonics we shaped an image. We wanted the music we were doing to be as visual as possible. Like when you hear thunder you have thunder in your mind and what it is—what it represents—its intrinsic meaning. Thunder has the feeling of disaster about to happen, destruction," says Shocklee.

"Also, we wanted [the music] to have color. The color of thunder is black and dark gray. We approached it that way, looking for music with emotion and color."

True rap-heads will be surprised to learn that, in creating Public Enemy's music, the Bomb Squad was seeking a rock 'n' roll sound, not a rap or R&B edge. "We wanted the same effects of rock 'n' roll without using the instruments," explains Shocklee. "Groups like Metallica, Megadeth, and Guns N' Roses were using lots of glaring guitars, distortion, and frequencies hovering around the same area. We looked for things that gave you that emotion and feel without actually using them."

Shocklee, the Bomb Squad's core, first got into production during the mid-'80s when he was asked to work on a song for an unknown rap group that Chuck D. was part of. A dance producer was recruited to produce the song.

"He said he knew hip-hop," Shocklee says of the dance producer. "We were like, 'We don't want no fuckin' 115 or 120 beats per minute.' We didn't want none of that. We wanted to do something that was 83 beats per minute and that was funky and hot and would get play on the streets. That's the vibe we were looking for."

With that in mind, Shocklee figured he should take over the production, and he called in Sadler. "I wanted him to organize the samples, and then we kept working together." Though the record was a failure, entrepreneurs Russell Simmons and Rick Rubin (see entry) of Def Jam took notice and commissioned the group to do a 12-inch record; and with that money, Shocklee and crew stretched it out into several songs. Those tracks, which cost a mere $12,000, would become 1987's *Yo! Bum Rush the Show*, the first Public Enemy album.

The production crew, however, did not become known as the Bomb Squad until *It Takes a Nation of Millions*. "Before, we were together to fulfill a specific mission," says Shocklee. "Then we perfected that level. The beauty of what we were doing . . . we pushed the envelope, using techniques like filtering, the way we truncated samples, and we didn't sequence anything. Everything was played freehand. We wanted the feel of the nonexactness, so to speak."

A couple of things about *It Takes a Nation of Millions* make the album unique, says Shocklee. "We invented the [rap music] interlude on *Nation*, and now they're full-length skits," he says. Also, the album was marketed in a groundbreaking way. The track "Rebel Without a Pause," for example, was the B-side of one of the singles from *Yo! Bum Rush the Show*, while another popular song from *Nation*, "Bring the Noise," appeared on the soundtrack to *Less Than Zero*. The fact that these songs were underground hits prior to the release of *Nation* only increased the demand for the album.

More Public Enemy projects followed, like *Fear of a Black Planet* (No. 10) and the anthemic "Fight the Power," from the *Do the Right Thing* soundtrack. The Bomb Squad continually exploded into different genres with other groups, producing "Steppin' to the A.M." for Third Bass, "Don't Be Afraid (the Jazz You Up version)" by Aaron Hall, and a few songs for Bell Biv DeVoe, like "B.B.D. (I Thought It Was Me)" and "Let Me Know Something."

Though the Squad appeared to be as productive as ever, things weren't as they had once been behind the scenes. Bomb Squad players began shifting, with folks like Gary G. Wiz, Larry "Panic" Walford, and Kevin Young figuring in and out of the mix. Eventually, the original group disbanded.

"To be honest, after *Fear of a Black Planet*, I was keeping things together with smoke and mirrors," says Shocklee, who may continue to use the Bomb Squad moniker working with other people. "There were different agendas."

Shocklee, now senior vice president of black music at MCA Records, and the Bomb Squad reunited to produce Public Enemy's 1998 comeback album, *He Got Game*. —KEVIN JOHNSON

Bomb Squad

Bell Biv DeVoe: "B.B.D. (I Thought It Was Me)?," MCA, 1990 • *WBBD-Bootcity!* (remix), MCA, 1991.

Chilly Tee: "Get Off Mine," MCA, 1993 • *Get Off Mine*, MCA, 1993.

Gabriel, Peter: "Steam" (remix), Geffen, 1992.

Godfathers of Threatt: *See* Terminator X.

Ice Cube: "AmeriKKKa's Most Wanted," Priority, 1990 • *AmeriKKKa's Most Wanted*, Priority, 1990.

Jackson, Paul Jr.: *Out of the Shadows*, Atlantic, 1990.

K9 Posse: "It Gets No Deeper" (remix), Arista, 1989.

Khan, Chaka: *Life Is a Dance (The Remix Project)*, Warner Bros., 1989.

LL Cool J: *Walking with a Panther*, Def Jam, 1989.

Marley, Ziggy, and the Melody Makers: "Tumblin' Down" (remix), Virgin, 1988.

New Edition: *Solo Hits*, MCA, 1996.

O'Connor, Sinead: "Emperor's New Clothes" (remix), Atlantic, 1990.

Public Enemy: "Bring the Noise," Def Jam, 1987 (*Less Than Zero* soundtrack) • *Yo! Bum Rush the Show*, Def Jam, 1987 • *It Takes a Nation of Millions to Hold Us Back*, Def Jam, 1988 • "Fight the Power," Motown, 1989 • "Welcome to the Terrordome," Def Jam/Columbia, 1989 • "Anti-Nigger Machine," Def Jam, 1990 • "Brothers Gonna Work It Out," Def Jam, 1990 • *Fear of a Black Planet*, Def Jam, 1990 • "Power to the People," Def Jam, 1990 • *Apocalypse 91 . . . the Enemy Strikes Black*, Def Jam/Columbia, 1991 • *Greatest Misses*, Def Jam, 1992 • "Hazy Shade of Criminal," Def Jam/Chaos, 1992 • "Bedlam 13:13," Def Jam, 1994 • "Give It Up," Def Jam, 1994 • "Live and Undrugged pt. 2," Def Jam, 1994 • *Muse Sick-N-Hour Mess Age*, Def Jam, 1994 • *He Got Game*, Def Jam, 1998.

Run-D.M.C.: *Down with the King* (2 tracks), Profile, 1993.

Slick Rick: "Teenage Love," Def Jam, 1988 • *The Great Adventures of Slick Rick*, Def Jam, 1988 • "Treat Her Like a Prostitute," Def Jam, 1988.

Terminator X: "It All Comes Down to Money," Rush Asso./Chaos, 1994 • w/ the Godfathers of Threatt, *Super Bad*, Rush Asso./Chaos, 1994.

Third Bass: *Cactus Album*, Def Jam, 1989.

Watley, Jody: w/ Eric B. & Rakim, "Friends" (remix), MCA, 1989.

Williams, Alyson: *Raw*, CBS, 1989.

Williams, Vanessa: "The Right Stuff," Wing, 1988 • *The Right Stuff*, Wing, 1988.

Young Black Teenagers: *Young Black Teenagers*, MCA, 1991.

Eric "Vietnam" Sadler

Chuck D.: *The Autobiography of Mistachuck*, Mercury, 1996.

Subliminal NY: "Don't Make Me Wait Too Long," Sire, 1993 (*New Faces*) • "Loungin'," Sire, 1993 (*New Faces*) • "Twice As Cruel," Sire, 1993 (*New Faces*).

Hank Shocklee

GP WU: "Party People," MCA, 1997.

Hall, Aaron: *Truth*, Silas, 1993.

Kane, Big Daddy: *Looks Like a Job for Big Daddy*, Cold Chillin', 1993.

Kid Panic: *Don't Be Alarmed,* MCA, 1991.

Stop the Violence: "Self-Destruction," Jive, 1989.

Keith Shocklee

Young Black Teenagers: *Dead Enz Kidz Doin' Lifetime Bidz,* MCA, 1993.

Bruce Botnick

Bruce Botnick is one of the most important West Coast recording engineers of the last 40 years. In the '60s he worked with a who's who of rock 'n' roll: Johnny Burnette, the Ventures, Jan and Dean, Leon Russell, the Beach Boys, the Turtles, Buffalo Springfield, the Supremes, Marvin Gaye, and the Doors, and he has continued to engineer into the '90s, during which he recorded and mixed the great Disney soundtracks *Beauty and the Beast, Aladdin, The Hunchback of Notre Dame,* and *Hercules.*

In addition, the second-generation Los Angeleno has produced an assortment of rock and jazz standards, including Love's *Forever Changes,* with the timeless "Alone Again Or," the MC5's slammin' *Kick Out the Jams* (No. 30), and Eddie Money's first two albums. He also produced key albums by roots-jazz vocalist Ben Sidran, drummer Tony Williams, the Mark Almond Band, Kenny Loggins, and most significantly, the Doors' *L.A. Woman* (No. 9).

He has won a clutch of awards, including Best Spoken-Word Grammy for the Broadway production of *Lenny,* and has produced numerous original film soundtracks, including those by composers Jerry Goldsmith (*First Blood, Rambo, Hoosiers*) and John Williams (*E.T., Indiana Jones and the Temple of Doom*).

Botnick's father played viola and recorded with a number of popular jazz bands, including Paul Whiteman's, and Bruce (born in 1945) got an early feel for the excitement of the studio. Young Botnick played sax and clarinet but came to realize that he was more excited by the "control room side of the glass than the studio side." He began to record school concerts and musicals on a borrowed tape recorder, and after high school his father secured him an apprentice position at Liberty Records.

He was soon engineering and after moving to Sunset Sound in 1963, he recorded the Beach Boys' *Pet Sounds,* the first Love album, Tim Buckley, the Turtles' "Happy Together," Buffalo Springfield with Jack

Nitzsche (see entry) producing, and Motown work with the Supremes and Marvin Gaye. "We cut tracks here [in L.A.] and then they would overdub and mix them in Detroit. I almost didn't recognize the tracks when they were through with them," he says.

The producer was itching to supersede the engineer. "I would sit there in the chair and disagree in my head with what the producers were doing—saying 'You should be doing this, you should be doing that'—saying it to myself of course."

A studio veteran at 22, Botnick got his chance with Love's *Forever Changes* in 1967. "I was doing the Baja Marimba Band and the Tijuana Brass when I got a chance to do *Forever Changes,*" says Botnick. "I brought in this arranger from the Mexican brass stuff to work with this Sunset Strip–psychedelic band [Love], which is pretty wild when you listen to it now. But at the time it was a pretty popular thing to mix styles of music. . . . Nowadays, radio is all narrowcasting. In those days we had KFWB, KHJ, and Top 40 played everything from Frank Sinatra to the Doors, to Johnny Cash, to Aretha Franklin, to Blue Cheer, to Herb Alpert. It was wonderful because everybody listened to everything. Today a lot of kids grow up just listening to one style of music."

The Mexican horn, Spanish guitar arrangement of Love's "Alone Again Or" is brilliant as well as audacious: the pathos of the song is bolstered to Latin proportions (the Damned used the same arrangement for their version) without losing its L.A. rock foundation.

Botnick brought this kind of creativity to his greatest production—the Doors' *L.A. Woman.* Botnick had engineered all of the Doors' previous albums for producer Paul Rothchild (see entry). But by 1971 Rothchild had wearied of the psychodrama that was the Doors—in particular, their wildly erratic lead singer Jim Morrison. According to Botnick, Rothchild "went into the studio, didn't like what he was hearing, put his head down on the console, and said, 'I can't do this anymore. You do it.' We decided we could do it ourselves, went into the band's rehearsal room, set up some equipment, and made the record in about six days." It was the band's easiest and best album since their debut in 1967. "The feeling was that we had just got out of school and it was summer vacation. It was a great moment of freedom. We didn't have anyone telling us what to do. Jim was there all the time. He never got juiced, and we just had a great time. I think you can hear it on the record. It was a case where performance really comes through. I love the album."

The album's triumphs are the title track—the most incisive depiction of the beautiful whore that is Los Angeles on record—and "Riders on the Storm" (No.

14), the band's final hit single. "Riders" is an evocative cocoon of cool menace that opens with an undertow bass line slowed down from the surf classic "Pipeline," overlaid with sophisticated Fender Rhodes electric piano from Ray Manzarek. Robbie Krieger's reverbed surf guitar adds to the misty atmosphere and underpins the rhythm.

"The band came up with the arrangement," recalls Botnick, "and the more I heard it, the more I started to hear things in it. I heard the rainstorm, and then when I heard the rainstorm, I heard this sound in Jim's voice. I said to Jim, 'Why don't you whisper the lyrics behind your singing voice?' Don't ask me where it came from. That's what I love about what I do—I don't necessarily know where it comes from. When you least expect it things happen, and you have to be open to hear them and to recognize them because that's the magic, and the magic is everything."

Botnick's other magical moment came on the MC5's *Kick Out the Jams,* an album that sold remarkably well for a raw live album from a band of revolutionary anarchists. Botnick and Elektra Records owner Jac Holzman went to see the band live on their home turf of Detroit. "It was the loudest thing I had ever heard in my life. We recorded the show with a cassette and listened to it in the hotel after, and we were amazed to hear that there were actually songs being played. We recorded live for the record with Wally Heider's mobile, and captured some great moments, like the title track. Politically there were some problems. We had to drop the act because of government intervention, but I still love that album. That was the '60s." —ERIC OLSEN AND DAWN DARLING

Aerosmith: *Pandora's Box,* Columbia, 1991.
Beat, The: *The Beat,* Wagon Wheel, 1979, 1994 • *The Kids Are the Same,* Columbia, 1982.
Butts Band: *The Butts Band,* Blue Thumb, 1974 • *Complete Recordings,* One Way, 1996.
Cecilio and Kapono: *Night Music,* Columbia, 1986.
Collins, Paul: *Paul Collins Beat,* Columbia, 1979.
Crazy Horse: *Crazy Horse,* Reprise, 1971.
Doors, The: "Love Her Madly," Elektra, 1971 • *L.A. Woman,* Elektra, 1971 • *Other Voices,* Elektra, 1971 • "Riders on the Storm," Elektra, 1971 • *American Prayer,* Elektra, 1978, 1995 • *The Best Of,* Elektra, 1985, 1991 • *The Doors* soundtrack, Elektra, 1991 • *The Doors Box Set,* Elektra, 1997.
Dudek, Les: *Say No More,* Columbia, 1977 • *Ghost Town Parade,* Columbia, 1978.
Goldsmith, Jerry: *First Blood* soundtrack, Intrada, 1982, 1988 • *Rambo: First Blood Part 2* soundtrack, Varese Sarabande,

1985 • *Hoosiers* soundtrack, Polydor, 1986 • *Best Shot* soundtrack, That's Entertainment, 1995 • *Chain Reaction* soundtrack, Varese Sarabande, 1996.
Krieger, Robby: *No Habla,* IRS, 1989.
Laughing Dogs: *Laughing Dogs,* CBS, 1979.
Loggins, Kenny: *Alive,* Columbia, 1980 • "I'm Alright," Columbia, 1980 • "Heart to Heart," Columbia, 1982 • *High Adventure,* Columbia, 1982 • *Greatest Hits,* Columbia, 1997 • *Yesterday, Today and Tomorrow: The Greatest Hits,* Sony, 1997.
Love: *Forever Changes,* Elektra, 1967.
Manzarek, Ray: *The Golden Scarab,* Mercury, 1974.
Mark Almond Band: *Rising,* Columbia, 1972 • *The Best Of,* Rhino, 1991.
Mason, Dave: *Split Coconut,* Columbia, 1975.
MC5: "Kick Out the Jams," Elektra, 1969 • *Kick Out the Jams,* Elektra, 1969 • "Kick Out the Jams," Seeds and Stems, 1977 (*Michigan Rocks*).
Money, Eddie: *Eddie Money,* Columbia, 1977 • "Baby Hold On," Columbia, 1978 • *Life for the Taking,* Columbia, 1978 • *Greatest Hits: The Sound of Money,* Columbia, 1989 • *Super Hits,* Columbia, 1997.
Monroes, The: *The Monroes* (EP), Alfa, 1982.
original Broadway cast: *Lenny,* Blue Thumb, 1972 • *Beauty and the Beast,* Walt Disney, 1994 • *Beauty and the Beast: Australia,* Walt Disney, 1995 • *Beauty and the Beast: Japan,* Walt Disney, 1996 • *Beauty and the Beast: London,* Walt Disney, 1997.
original soundtrack: *King David,* Walt Disney, 1997 • *Star Trek: The Motion Picture,* Columbia, 1979.
Joe Perry Project: *I've Got the Rock and Rolls Again,* CBS, 1982.
Perry, Steve: "Foolish Heart," Columbia, 1984 • *Street Talk,* Columbia, 1984.
Raices: *Raices,* Nemperor, 1975.
Ross: *The Pit and the Pendulum,* RSO, 1974.
Schaffer, Janne: *Earmeal,* Columbia, 1979.
Sidran, Ben: *Feel Your Groove,* Capitol, 1971 • *I Lead a Life,* Blue Thumb, 1972 • *Puttin' in Time on Planet Earth,* Blue Thumb, 1973 • *Don't Let Go,* Blue Thumb, 1974.
Starwood: *Starwood,* Columbia, 1977.
Williams, John: *E.T.* soundtrack, MCA, 1982, 1996 • *Indiana Jones and the Temple of Doom* soundtrack, Polydor, 1984.
Williams, Tony: *The Best Of,* Capitol, 1996.
Williams, Tony, and Lifetime: *Believe It,* Columbia, 1975 • *Million Dollar Legs,* Columbia, 1976 • *The Collection,* Legacy, 1992.

COLLECTIONS
California Jam II, Columbia, 1978.
Caddyshack soundtrack, Columbia, 1980.
Twilight Zone soundtrack, Warner Bros., 1983.

Under Fire soundtrack, Warner Bros., 1983.

Movie Greats, MCA, 1990.

The Princess Collection, Walt Disney, 1995.

Jimmy Bowen

For someone who has produced such legendary artists as Frank Sinatra, Dean Martin, George Strait, and Reba McEntire, Jimmy Bowen has an interesting take on what it means to be a producer. "A producer's job is to do as little as possible," says the flamboyant New Mexico native. "The less you do, the more it's the artist's music, and that, therefore, makes the music different from all the other artists."

Not that it's a lesson Bowen knew himself when he began producing in the '60s. "When I was doing Sinatra, Dean Martin, and Sammy Davis, you could pretty well tell it was a record I'd produced because they were all pretty similar, but I learned from that. When I went to Nashville, it had to be George or Reba or Hank [Williams] Jr.'s music. You should not be able to tell who produced the records."

Bowen was one of the first A&R/producer executives, working at around a dozen labels in his career, including six in Nashville alone. His start in the music business came as a disc jockey on KDDD in Dumas, Texas, and as a member of the Orchids, a trio he formed in high school that eventually became the Rhythm Orchids. The group had some national success, but eventually ran out of steam, leaving Bowen to return to a short, ill-fated career as a disc jockey.

Bowen wended his way to Los Angeles, becoming a songwriter at American Music Publishing Company. Different twists and turns eventually led him to Reprise Records in 1963, the label founded by Frank Sinatra a few years earlier. As an A&R executive, Bowen produced a number of acts, but as he notes in his 1997 autobiography (*Rough Mix*), his big break came working with Dean Martin.

Bowen produced what was to become one of Martin's signature songs, "Everybody Loves Somebody" (No. 1), a tune, as it turns out, that Martin's keyboard player, Ken Lane, had written more than 20 years earlier. "What I didn't know was that Sinatra and Dinah Washington, all kinds of people had recorded this song, but no one had cut a single record with it. The night I found it, I said, 'Hey Dean, we need one more song that night to finish the album, and Ken said, 'Hey, what

about my song?' and he started playing it. I went, 'Oh shit, that's just great!' I went back into the control room after we got the arrangement worked out and said, 'Wow, what a great song that Ken just wrote,' and everybody started laughing at me because all the old characters in the studio knew it was an old song, but I had never heard it."

While Bowen considers Dean Martin the favorite artist he ever worked with "as a human being," he feels that Sinatra was "this incredible personality with probably the greatest instrument I ever worked with. Sinatra learned to sing watching trombone players; he phrased like a trombone. Dean Martin, on the other hand, was a stylist. He wasn't a great singer, he was a stylist, and there's a huge difference in the two, but as Dean used to tell Frank, 'I know you sing a lot better than me, pally, but I sell a lot more records.' "

Bowen remembers his time with Sinatra fondly, if for no other reason than because he was one of the few people who wasn't scared of Ol' Blue Eyes. "I think the reason we got along was when I worked with artists, I was never in awe," he says. "I don't know how you could work with someone if you were afraid of them. Maybe it was ignorance or good luck or just the way I was brought up, but I always looked Sinatra in the eye and looked at him as another man. He just happened to be an incredibly talented one. . . . Every powerful person has 'yes' people around them, but I think when it came to his music or anything important in his life, that's not what he wanted. He didn't want somebody to 'yes' him, he may not agree with you and he may not do what you want, but he wanted you to tell him what you really thought."

However, Bowen remembers one night in the studio, when he feared he may have stepped over the line. Sinatra was laying down vocals for "That's Life" (No. 4), and although the singer thought the take was fine, Bowen wasn't satisfied. And he had to tell the master that it just wasn't good enough. "I gotta tell you, those steely blue eyes did look clear through me for about 10 seconds, it felt like 20 minutes. I knew if it was done right, it was a hit, but the whole session got off crooked because the mike didn't work, everything was weird, and I just didn't want to let that go. I wanted it to be a hit record, so I guess that's what drove me to do it."

Bowen then got very lucky. He'd made Sinatra just mad enough that the singer changed his whole method. "He went back [into the studio] and he was pissed off and he bit the song instead of singing it smooth. He totally changed his approach to it. I told the rhythm section, 'Go out there and make this like [David Rose's 1962 hit] 'The Stripper.' Make this sucker cook, it's way too hip the way you're doing it.' When they started into it, combined with his being pissed, it just worked great, great."

After working at a number of other Los Angeles labels, Bowen headed for Nashville in 1976. He quickly sized up Music City as a place that could use his help. "When I first came there, I didn't even like country music necessarily, but I fell in love with it and it became a mission to make it sound as good as any other kind of music. The two things I set out to do in Nashville were to improve the overall quality of country albums," he says. "The second was to give control of the music back to the artists, where it belongs. [When I was in L.A.,] I was in my late twenties, working with guys in their mid-forties. When I got to Nashville, it was the other way around. I was the old fart helping these young artists learn how to make albums that would be distinctly theirs. One reason Nashville fell so far behind was because everything sounded alike."

One of Bowen's first mandates was to raise the budgets of country albums. "I left L.A. where we were spending $100,000 to $125,000 per album, and went to Nashville where they were spending $15,000. And I told them, you get what you pay for. You're asking people that will buy a pop album to come buy this album. They're not deaf, they can tell the difference."

Bowen is the first to admit that he felt he had to blaze his own often controversial path in Nashville, and because of that, he later went out of his way to develop new production talent. "When I got to Nashville, there were no James Strouds, no Tony Browns [two Bowen protégés; see entries]. Chet [Atkins] and Owen [Bradley] had retired [Bradley has since died; see entries]. Those guys didn't train, develop, or bring along any young producers, so there were no producers, so I found myself working with artists I normally wouldn't have worked with, especially in the first few years. A lot of those marriages really weren't ideal for me."

One marriage that was ideal for Bowen, however, was to Hank Williams Jr., with whom he made several records, including producing a number of tracks on the country classic *Family Tradition*. "Hank was properly crazy," Bowen says with extreme fondness. "He and I got along great. After I got *Family Tradition* from him, he came into the office [Bowen was at Elektra Records in Nashville], and I spent an hour or two telling him what he had to do to sell millions of records and be a superstar, and I said, 'One of them is you don't have to live in Nashville and you don't have to like it,' because he hated Nashville for all kinds of reasons. They wanted him to sound like his dad, and he'd get drunk and shoot trash cans up and down the street, properly crazy. I had that one meeting with him and he never varied

from what we agreed on in that hour for the five or six years we worked together."

Bowen also had great relationships with country superstars Strait and McEntire, both of whom he worked with when he ran MCA Nashville. He considers Strait "almost like the Sinatra of country. George could do Sinatra's songs if he wanted to. He doesn't want to, but he could. He is a singer. I think Reba's a country jazz singer. She can do anything she wants. She's a jazz singer who just happens to be country. It's like Willie Nelson is a jazz singer who happens to be country."

Despite making seminal records with both Strait and McEntire, Bowen says the day came with both artists where he knew they were ready for a change in the studio. However, he made both Strait and McEntire fire him. "They had to fire me. If they could fire a guy who was or had been the head of their label, who was their producer with great success, I knew then that they could make all the major decisions that they'd have to make in their careers," he says. "One of the first things I tell all my artists is you've got to be in charge of your life and your music, and when the time comes to change producers or anything else in your life, change it."

Bowen's last label stop in Nashville was running Capitol, which he renamed Liberty Records. His five-year tenure at the label, during which he produced such artists as Suzy Bogguss, Billy Dean, and Deana Carter (whose album came out after he left) came to an end when he retired after being diagnosed with throat cancer in 1994. Bowen got treatment, quit the business, and moved permanently to Hawaii, where he'd always spent a great deal of time. "One of the reasons it was easy for me to retire is I slowly lost the desire to do the music," he says. "I loved quitting the music, I had run my course being a producer. My life's been really well laid out. Whoever God put in charge of me, I really need to thank them when I cross over, which I hope is not for a good long while because I'm just learning to play golf again." —MELINDA NEWMAN

Anderson, John: *Blue Skies Again*, MCA, 1987 • *Too Tough to Tame*, Liberty, 1990, 1994.

Axelrod, David: *Seriously Deep*, Polydor, 1975.

Bellamy Brothers: "For All the Wrong Reasons," Elektra, 1982 • *Greatest Hits*, Warner Bros., 1982 • "Redneck Girl," Warner Bros., 1982 • *Strong Weakness*, Elektra/Curb, 1982 • "I Love Her Mind," Warner Bros., 1983 • "When I'm Away from You," Elektra, 1983 • *Howard and David*, Curb, 1985 • "Lie to You for Your Love," Curb, 1985 • "Old Hippie," Curb, 1985 • "Feelin' the Feelin'," Curb, 1986 • "Rebels Without a Clue," Curb, 1988 • "Big Love," Curb, 1989 • *Greatest Hits*, Vol. 3, MCA, 1989.

Berry, John: *John Berry,* Capitol, 1993 • "I Think About It All the Time," Patriot, 1995 • "Standing on the Edge of Goodbye," Patriot, 1995 • *Standing on the Edge,* Capitol, 1995.

Blue Diamond: *See* Bramlett, Delaney.

Bogguss, Suzy: *Moment of Truth,* Liberty, 1990 • "Someday Soon," Capitol, 1991 • *Aces,* Liberty, 1991 • "Aces," Liberty, 1992 • "Letting Go," Liberty, 1992 • "Outbound Plane," Capitol, 1992 • *Voices in the Wind,* Liberty, 1992 • "Drive South," Liberty, 1993 • "Just Like the Weather," Liberty, 1993 • *Something up My Sleeve,* Liberty, 1993 • *Greatest Hits,* Liberty, 1994 • "Hey Cinderella," Liberty, 1994.

Bowen, Jimmy: *Jimmy Bowen,* Roulette, 1957 • *The Best Of,* Collectables, 1991 • w/ Buddy Knox, *The Complete Roulette Recordings,* Sequel, 1996.

Bramlett, Delaney: w/ Blue Diamond, *Giving Birth to a Song,* MGM, 1975 • *Class Reunion,* Prodigal, 1977.

Bresh, Tom: "Home Made Love," ABC, 1976 • "Sad Country Love Song," ABC, 1976 • *Portrait,* ABC, 1978.

Brody, Lane: w/ Johnny Lee, "The Yellow Rose," Warner Bros., 1984.

Buffett, Jimmy: *Riddles in the Sand,* MCA, 1984 • "If the Phone Doesn't Ring, It's Me," MCA, 1985 • *Last Mango in Paris,* MCA, 1985.

Campbell, Glen: *Glen Travis Campbell,* Capitol, 1972 • *I Knew Jesus Before He Was a Star,* Capitol, 1973 • *I Remember Hank Williams,* Capitol, 1973 • *Reunion (The Songs of Jimmy Webb),* Capitol, 1974 • "Still Within the Sound of My Voice," MCA, 1987 • *Still Within the Sound of My Voice,* MCA, 1987 • w/ Steve Wariner, "The Hand That Rocks the Cradle," MCA, 1987 • "I Have You," MCA, 1988 • "She's Gone, Gone, Gone," Universal, 1989 • *Walkin' in the Sun,* Liberty, 1990 • *Essential,* Vol. 3, Capitol, 1995 • *Gentle on My Mind: The Collection, 1962–1989,* Razor & Tie, 1997.

Carnes, Kim: *View from the House,* MCA, 1988.

Carter, Deana: *Did I Shave My Legs for This?,* Capitol, 1996.

Cline, Patsy: w/ Loretta Lynn, *On Tour,* Vol. 2, MCA Special Products, 1996.

Crishan, Horea: *The Magic of the Pan Flute,* Polydor, 1984.

Dalton, Lacy J.: "The Heart," Universal, 1989 • *Survivor,* Universal, 1989 • "Black Coffee," Capitol, 1990 • *Best Of,* Liberty, 1993.

Daniels, Charlie: *America, I Believe in You,* Liberty, 1993.

Dave and Sugar: "Fool by Your Side," Elektra, 1981.

Davis, Sammy Jr.: *Greatest Hits,* Vol. 2, DCC, 1960 • "I've Gotta Be Me," Reprise, 1969 • *Greatest Hits,* Vol. 1, Garland, 1978.

Davis, Linda: *In a Different Light,* Liberty, 1991 • *Linda Davis,* Liberty, 1992.

Davis, Mac: "I Never Made Love (Till I Made Love with You)," MCA, 1985.

Dean, Billy: *Fire in the Dark,* SBK, 1993 • "Tryin' to Hide a Fire in the Dark," SBK, 1993 • "We Just Disagree," SBK, 1993 • *Greatest Hits,* Liberty, 1994 • *Men'll Be Boys,* Liberty, 1994.

Dresser, Lee: *El Camino Real,* Amos, 1968.

Evergreen Blueshoes: *The Ballad of Evergreen Blueshoes,* Amos/London, 1969.

Ewing, Skip: "Burnin' a Hole in My Heart," MCA, 1988 • "I Don't Have Far to Fall," MCA, 1988 • "Your Memory Wins Again," MCA, 1988 • "It's You Again," MCA, 1989 • "The Coast of Colorado," MCA, 1989 • "The Gospel According to Luke," MCA, 1989 • *Greatest Hits,* MCA, 1991.

First Edition: "But You Know I Love You," Reprise, 1969 • *See also* Rogers, Kenny.

Francis, Cleve: *Walkin',* Liberty, 1993.

Gayle, Crystal: "Baby, What About You," Elektra, 1983 • *Cage the Songbird,* Warner Bros., 1983 • " 'Til I Gain Control Again," Elektra, 1983 • "I Don't Want to Lose Your Love," Warner Bros., 1984 • "Me Against the Night," Warner Bros., 1984 • "The Sound of Goodbye," Warner Bros., 1984 • "Turning Away," Warner Bros., 1984.

Glaser, Tompall: *Outlaw,* Bear Family, 1977 • *The Wonder of It All,* ABC, 1978 • *Rogue,* Bear Family, 1992.

Tompall, Glaser, and the Glaser Brothers: "Just One Time," Elektra, 1981 • "Loving Her Was Easier (Than Anything I'll Ever Do Again)," Elektra, 1981 • *Loving Her Was Easier,* Elektra, 1981 • "It'll Be Her," Elektra, 1982.

Greenwood, Lee: "If There's Any Justice," MCA, 1987 • "Someone," MCA, 1987 • "I Still Believe," MCA, 1988 • "Touch and Go Crazy," MCA, 1988 • "You Can't Fall in Love When You're Cryin'," MCA, 1988 • *Greatest Hits,* Vol. 2, MCA, 1989 • "I'll Be Loving You," MCA, 1989.

Haggard, Merle: *Now Serving 190 Proof,* MCA, 1979 • *Back to the Barrooms,* MCA, 1980 • "I Think I'll Just Stay Here and Drink," MCA, 1981 • *Greatest Hits,* MCA, 1982 • *Merle Haggard's Greatest Hits,* MCA, 1982 • *His Greatest and His Best,* MCA, 1985 • *More of the Best,* Rhino, 1990 • *Down Every Road,* Capitol, 1996.

Hazlewood, Lee: *Poet, Fool or Bum,* Capitol, 1973.

Head, Roy: "Come to Me," ABC/Dot, 1977 • "Now You See 'Em, Now You Don't," ABC, 1978 • *Tonight's the Night,* ABC, 1978 • *In Our Room,* Elektra, 1979.

Jennings Waylon: *Man Called Hoss,* MCA, 1967 • w/ Hank Williams Jr., "The Conversation," RCA, 1983 • "The Devil's on the Loose," RCA, 1985 • "What'll You Do When I'm Gone," MCA, 1986 • "Will the Wolf Survive?," MCA, 1986 • *Will the Wolf Survive?,* MCA, 1986 • "Working Without a Net," MCA, 1986 • *A Man Called Hoss,* MCA, 1987 • "Fallin Out," MCA, 1987 • *Hangin' Tough,* MCA, 1987 • "My Rough and Rowdy Days," MCA, 1987 • "Rose in Paradise," MCA, 1987 • "If Old Hank

Could Only See Us Now (Chapter Five . . . Nashville)," MCA, 1988 • *My Rough and Rowdy Days,* MCA, 1990.

Kaempfert, Bert, and His Orchestra: *Fabulous Fifties and New Delights,* Capitol, 1973.

Kane, Kieran: "It's Who You Love," Elektra, 1981 • "You're the Best," Elektra, 1981.

Buddy Knox: *See* Bowen, Jimmy.

Laine, Frankie: *The Very Best of (ABC Years),* Taragon, 1996.

LeDoux, Chris: *Western Underground,* Liberty, 1991 • "Cadillac Ranch," Liberty, 1992 • *Whatcha Gonna Do with a Cowboy,* Liberty, 1992 • *Under This Old Hat,* Liberty, 1993 • *American Cowboy,* Liberty, 1994 • *Best Of,* Liberty, 1994.

Lee, Johnny: *Greatest Hits,* Full Moon, 1983, 1990 • "Hey Bartender," Full Moon, 1983 • *Hey Bartender,* Full Moon, 1983 • *'Til the Bars Burn Down,* Full Moon, 1984 • "You Could've Heard a Heart Break," Warner Bros., 1984 • *Workin' for a Livin',* Full Moon/WB, 1984 • "Rollin' Lonely," Warner Bros., 1985 • *See also* Brody, Lane.

Lynn, Loretta: "Heart Don't Do This to Me," MCA, 1985 • *Who Was That Stranger?,* MCA, 1988 • w/ Conrad Twitty, *Hey Good Lookin',* MCA Special Products, 1993 • *See also* Cline, Patsy.

Mandrell, Barbara: *No Nonsense,* Liberty, 1990 • *The Best Of,* Liberty, 1992.

Martin, Dean: "Everybody Loves Somebody," Reprise, 1964 • *Everybody Loves Somebody,* Reprise, 1964 • "The Door Is Still Open to My Heart," Reprise, 1964 • *The Door Is Still Open to My Heart,* Reprise, 1964 • *Dean Martin Hits Again,* Reprise, 1965 • "Houston," Reprise, 1965 • *Houston,* Reprise, 1965 • "I Will," Reprise, 1965 • "(Remember Me) I'm the One Who Loves You," Reprise, 1965 • *(Remember Me) I'm the One Who Loves You,* Reprise, 1965 • "Send Me the Pillow You Dream On," Reprise, 1965 • "You're Nobody Till Somebody Loves You," Reprise, 1965 • "Come Running Back," Reprise, 1966 • "Somewhere There's a Someone," Reprise, 1966 • *Somewhere There's a Someone,* Reprise, 1966 • *The Hit Sound of,* Reprise, 1966 • "In the Chapel in the Moonlight," Reprise, 1967 • "Little Ole Wine Drinker, Me," Reprise, 1967 • *Welcome to My World,* Reprise, 1967 • *For the Good Times,* Reprise, 1970 • *The Nashville Sessions,* Warner Bros., 1983.

McEntire, Reba: "Have I Got a Deal for You," MCA, 1985 • *Have I Got a Deal for You,* MCA, 1985 • "Only in My Mind," MCA, 1985 • "Little Rock," MCA, 1986 • "What Am I Gonna Do About You?," MCA, 1986 • *What Am I Gonna Do About You?,* MCA, 1986, 1989 • "Whoever's in New England," MCA, 1986 • *Whoever's in New England,* MCA, 1986 • *Greatest Hits,* MCA, 1987 • "Let the Music Lift You Up," MCA, 1987 • *Merry Christmas to You,* MCA, 1987 • "One Promise Too Late," MCA, 1987 • "The Last One to Know," MCA, 1987 • *The Last One to Know,* MCA, 1987 • "I Know How He Feels," MCA, 1988 • "Love Will Find Its

Way to You," MCA, 1988 • *Reba,* MCA, 1988 • "Sunday Kind of Love," MCA, 1988 • "Cathy's Clown," MCA, 1989 • "New Fool at an Old Game," MCA, 1989 • *Reba Live,* MCA, 1989 • "She's Got a Single Thing in Mind," MCA, 1989 • *Sweet Sixteen,* MCA, 1989 • "Till Love Comes Again," MCA, 1989 • "Little Girl," MCA, 1990 • "Walk On," MCA, 1990 • *Greatest Hits, Vol. 2,* MCA, 1993.

Morris, Gary: "The Wind Beneath My Wings," Warner Bros., 1983 • *Why Lady Why,* Warner Bros., 1983, 1987 • *Hits,* Warner Bros., 1987.

Nelson, Tracy: *Time Is on My Side,* MCA, 1976.

Nelson, Willie: *Healing Hands of Time,* Liberty, 1994.

Nitzsche, Jack: "The Lonely Surfer," Reprise, 1963 • *The Lonely Surfer,* Reprise, 1963, 1967.

Oak Ridge Boys: *The Oak Ridge Boys Have Arrived,* MCA, 1979 • "It Takes a Little Rain (to Make a Love Grow)," MCA, 1987 • "This Crazy Love," MCA, 1987 • *This Crazy Love,* MCA, 1987, 1992 • "Time In," MCA, 1987 • "Gonna Take a Lot of River," MCA, 1988 • *Monongahela,* MCA, 1988 • "True Heart," MCA, 1988 • "An American Family," MCA, 1989 • "Beyond These Years," MCA, 1989 • "Bridges and Walls," MCA, 1989 • *Greatest Hits, Vol. 3,* MCA, 1989 • "No Matter How High," MCA, 1989 • *The Collection,* MCA, 1992.

Pirates of the Mississippi: " 'Till I'm Holding You Again," Liberty, 1992 • *A Street Man Named Desire,* Liberty, 1992 • *Best Of,* Liberty, 1994.

Puckett, Gary: *The Gary Puckett Album,* Columbia, 1971 • *Looking Glass,* Legacy, 1992.

Rabbitt, Eddie: *#1's,* Warner Bros., 1985 • "She's Coming Back to Say Goodbye," Warner Bros., 1985 • "The Best Year of My Life," Warner Bros., 1985 • "Warning Sign," Warner Bros., 1985.

Raven, Eddy: *Desperate Dreams,* Elektra, 1981 • "I Should've Called," Elektra, 1981 • "Who Do You Know in California?," Elektra, 1981 • "A Little Bit Crazy," Elektra, 1982 • "She's Playing Hard to Forget," Elektra, 1982.

Revells, The: *The Go Sounds of the Slots!* Sundazed, 1965, 1995.

Rogers, Kenny: *Love Songs,* MCA, 1991.

Rogers, Kenny, and the First Edition: *First Edition '69,* Reprise, 1969 • "Ruby, Don't Take Your Love to Town," Reprise, 1969 • "Something's Burning," Reprise, 1970 • *Something's Burning,* Reprise, 1970 • "Tell It All Brother," Reprise, 1970 • *Tell It All Brother,* Reprise, 1971 • *Greatest Hits,* MCA, 1987.

Schneider, John: "I've Been Around Enough to Know," MCA, 1984 • *Too Good to Stop Now,* MCA, 1984 • "Country Girls," MCA, 1985 • "I'm Gonna Leave You Tomorrow," MCA, 1985 • "It's a Short Walk from Heaven to Hell," MCA, 1985 • "At the Sound of the Tone," MCA, 1986 • "What's a Memory Like You (Doing in a Love Like

This)," MCA, 1986 • "You're the Last Thing I Needed Tonight," MCA, 1986 • *A Memory Like You,* MCA, 1986 • "Love, You Ain't Seen the Last of Me," MCA, 1987 • "Take the Long Way Home," MCA, 1987 • *Greatest Hits,* MCA, 1987.

Sinatra, Frank: *Softly As I Leave You,* Reprise, 1964, 1989 • *Sinatra '65,* Reprise, 1965 • "Strangers in the Night," Reprise, 1966 • *Strangers in the Night,* Reprise, 1966 • "That's Life," Reprise, 1966 • *That's Life,* Reprise, 1966 • w/ Nancy, "Somethin' Stupid," Reprise, 1967 • *The World We Knew,* Reprise, 1967, 1991 • *Frank Sinatra and the World We Knew,* Reprise, 1967 • *Frank Sinatra and His Greatest Hits,* Reprise, 1968 • *Greatest Hits,* Vol. 1, Reprise, 1968 • *Some Nice Things I've Missed,* Reprise, 1974, 1991.

Strait, George: *Does Fort Worth Ever Cross Your Mind,* MCA, 1984 • "Does Fort Worth Ever Cross Your Mind," MCA, 1985 • *Greatest Hits,* MCA, 1985 • *Something Special,* MCA, 1985 • "The Chair," MCA, 1985 • "The Cowboy Rides Away," MCA, 1985 • "The Fireman," MCA, 1985 • "It Ain't Cool to Be Crazy About You," MCA, 1986 • *Merry Christmas Strait to You,* MCA, 1986, 1993 • "Nobody in His Right Mind Would've Left Her," MCA, 1986 • *Number 7,* MCA, 1986 • "You're Something Special to Me," MCA, 1986 • "All My Ex's Live in Texas," MCA, 1987 • "Am I Blue," MCA, 1987 • *Greatest Hits,* Vol. 2, MCA, 1987 • "Ocean Front Property," MCA, 1987 • *Ocean Front Property,* MCA, 1987 • "Baby Blue," MCA, 1988 • "Famous Last Words of a Fool," MCA, 1988 • "If You Ain't Lovin' (You Ain't Livin')," MCA, 1988 • *If You Ain't Lovin' You Ain't Livin',* MCA, 1988 • "Ace in the Hole," MCA, 1989 • "Baby's Gotten Good at Goodbye," MCA, 1989 • *Beyond the Blue Neon,* MCA, 1989 • "What's Going on in Your World," MCA, 1989 • "Drinking Champagne," MCA, 1990 • "I've Come to Expect It from You," MCA, 1990 • *Livin' It Up,* MCA, 1990 • "Love Without End, Amen," MCA, 1990 • "Overnight Success," MCA, 1990 • "If I Know Me," MCA, 1991 • *Ten Strait Hits,* MCA, 1991 • "The Chill of an Early Fall," MCA, 1991 • *The Chill of an Early Fall,* MCA, 1991 • "You Know Me Better Than That," MCA, 1991 • "Gone As a Girl Can Get," MCA, 1992 • *Holding My Own,* MCA, 1992 • "So Much Like My Dad," MCA, 1992 • *Strait out of the Box,* MCA, 1995.

Tillis, Mel: "Mental Revenge," MGM, 1976 • "Burning Memories," MCA, 1977 • "Heart Healer," MCA, 1977 • "I Got the Hoss," MCA, 1977 • "Ain't No California," MCA, 1978 • "I Believe in You," MCA, 1978 • "What Did I Promise Her Last Night?," MCA, 1978 • "Blind in Love," MCA, 1979 • "Coca Cola Cowboy," MCA, 1979 • *Are You Sincere,* MCA, 1979 • *Me and Pepper,* Elektra, 1979 • *M-M-M-Mel Live,* MCA, 1979 • *Mr. Entertainer,* MCA, 1979 • "Send Me Down to Tucson," MCA, 1979 • "Lying Time Again," Elektra, 1980 • *Southern Rain,* Elektra, 1980 •

"Steppin' Out," Elektra, 1980 • "Your Body Is an Outlaw," Elektra, 1980 • "A Million Old Goodbyes," Elektra, 1981 • "One Night Fever," Elektra, 1981 • "Southern Rains," Elektra, 1981 • *The Very Best Of,* MCA, 1981 • "Stay a Little Longer," Elektra, 1982.

Tillis, Pam: *Above and Beyond the Doll of Cutey,* Elektra, 1983.

Twitty, Conway: "Slow Hand," Elektra, 1982 • *Southern Comfort,* Elektra, 1982 • "The Clown," Elektra, 1982 • "We Did But Now You Don't," Elektra, 1982 • "Heartache Tonight," Warner Bros., 1983 • "Lost in the Feeling," Warner Bros., 1983 • "The Rose," Elektra, 1983 • "Ain't She Somethin' Else," Warner Bros., 1984 • "I Don't Know a Thing About Love (The Moon Song)," Warner Bros., 1984 • "Somebody's Needin' Somebody," Warner Bros., 1984 • "Three Times a Lady," Warner Bros., 1984 • *Borderline,* MCA, 1987 • "I Want to Know You Before We Make Love," MCA, 1987 • "Julia," MCA, 1987 • "That's My Job," MCA, 1987 • "Goodbye Time," MCA, 1988 • "I Wish I Was Still in Your Dreams," MCA, 1988 • *#1's: The Warner Bros. Years,* Warner Bros., 1988 • "Saturday Night Special," MCA, 1988 • *Still in Your Dreams,* MCA, 1988 • "House on Old Lonesome Road," MCA, 1989 • "She's Got a Single Thing in Mind," MCA, 1989 • "Crazy in Love," MCA, 1990 • *Crazy in Love,* MCA, 1990 • *Silver Anniversay Collection,* MCA, 1990 • "I Couldn't See You Leavin'," MCA, 1991 • *The Conway Twitty Collection,* MCA, 1994 • *See also* Lynn, Loretta.

Walker, Billy Joe Jr.: *Warm Front,* Liberty, 1993.

Wariner, Steve: "Heart Trouble," MCA, 1985 • "Some Fools Never Learn," MCA, 1985 • "What I Didn't Do," MCA, 1985 • "Life's Highway," MCA, 1986 • "Starting over Again," MCA, 1986 • "You Can Dream of Me," MCA, 1986 • *Greatest Hits,* MCA, 1987 • "Small Town Girl," MCA, 1987 • w/ Glen Campbell, "The Hand That Rocks the Cradle'," MCA, 1987 • "The Weekend," MCA, 1987 • "Baby I'm Yours," MCA, 1988 • "Hold on (A Little Longer)," MCA, 1988 • "I Should Be with You," MCA, 1988 • "I Got Dreams," MCA, 1989 • "Where Did I Go Wrong?," MCA, 1989 • "When I Come Home to You," MCA, 1990 • *Greatest Hits,* Vol. 2, MCA, 1991 • *Best Of,* RCA, 1994.

Weatherly, Jim: "The Need to Be," Buddah, 1974.

West Coast Pop Art Experimental Band: *Volume 3,* Reprise, 1976.

Whites, The: *Greatest Hits,* Curb/MCA, 1987.

Whittaker, Roger: *You Deserve the Best,* Capitol, 1990.

Williams, Andy: *Nashville,* Curb, 1991.

Williams, Hank Jr.: "Family Tradition," Elektra, 1979 • *Family Tradition* (3 tracks), Elektra, 1979 • "Whiskey Bent and Hell Bound," Elektra, 1979 • *Whiskey Bent and Hell Bound,* Elektra, 1979 • *Habits Old and New,* Elektra, 1980 • "Kaw Liga," Elektra, 1980 • "Old Habits," Elektra, 1980 •

"Women I've Never Had," Elektra, 1980 • "All My Rowdy Friends (Have Settled Down)," Elektra, 1981 • "Dixie on My Mind," Elektra, 1981 • *Rowdy*, Elektra, 1981 • "Texas Women," Elektra, 1981 • *The Pressure Is On*, Elektra, 1981 • "A Country Boy Can Survive," Elektra, 1982 • *Hank Williams Jr's Greatest Hits*, Curb/WB, 1982 • *High Notes*, Elektra, 1982 • "Honky Tonkin'," Elektra, 1982 • "If Heaven Ain't a Lot Like Dixie," Elektra, 1982 • "The American Dream," Elektra, 1982 • "Gonna Go Huntin' Tonight," Elektra, 1983 • "Leave Them Boys Alone," Curb/WB, 1983 • *Man of Steel*, Elektra, 1983 • "Queen of My Heart," Curb/WB, 1983 • *Strong Stuff*, Elektra, 1983 • w/ Waylon Jennings, "The Conversation," RCA, 1983 • "All My Rowdy Friends Are Coming over Tonight," Curb/WB, 1984 • "Attitude Adjustment," Curb/WB, 1984 • *Major Moves*, Elektra, 1984 • "Man of Steel," Curb/WB, 1984 • *Five-0-Five*, Curb/WB, 1985 • *Greatest Hits*, Vol. 2, Warner Bros., 1985, 1990 • "I'm for Love," Curb/WB, 1985 • "Major Moves," Curb/WB, 1985 • "This Ain't Dallas," Curb/WB, 1985 • "Ain't Misbehavin'," Warner Bros., 1986 • *Montana Cafe*, Curb/WB, 1986 • *Greatest Hits*, Vol. 3, Curb/WB, 1989 • *America (the Way I See It)*, Curb/WB, 1990 • *The Bocephus Box: Hank Williams Jr. Collection, '79–'92*, Capricorn, 1992.

Wilson, Dennis William: *One of Those People*, Elektra, 1979.

David Bowie

While David Bowie has spent the past 30 years collecting stage personae, platinum albums, and legions of fans, he has rarely lent his production touch to albums outside of his own catalog. Although Bowie has produced just eight albums by four different artists, his effect as an artist and as a producer is immense. Not only did he change the culture of rock by ushering in the era of decadence as Ziggy Stardust, he handed bands like Mott the Hoople hit singles and Iggy Pop a certain respectability. His work with Lou Reed yielded one of the most memorable rock songs ever, "Walk on the Wild Side" (No. 16), and his subsequent work on Reed's *Transformer* (No. 13 U.K., with Mick Ronson; see entry) pushed the former Velvet Underground icon into a new dimension of songwriting.

Bowie has stretched musical boundaries, blending rock and funk in his early days, pop and electronica in his later releases. Born David Robert Jones in Brixton, England, on January 8, 1947, Bowie began playing music when he was 15. Originally inspired by jazz, he first turned to the saxophone, an instrument he still plays on albums. After playing with and starting a number of bands, including the Kon-Rads, the King Bees, and the Mannish Boys, Jones became Bowie in 1966. His first success as a musician came in 1969, when he scored a Top 5 U.K. single with "Space Oddity." The 1971 album *The Man Who Sold the World* introduced him to American audiences. It was shortly after the birth of the Ziggy Stardust character that Bowie lent a hand to Mott the Hoople with their song "All the Young Dudes" (No. 3 U.K.).

After he finished producing that album in September 1972, Bowie jumped into the studio with Lou Reed, working up Reed's *Transformer* and "Walk on the Wild Side." All the while, Bowie was frantically writing and recording his own body of work, including some of his best-known and hardest-rocking songs. After Stardust perished in June 1973, Bowie debuted *Aladdin Sane* (No. 1 U.K., with Ken Scott; see entry) and the songs "Jean Genie" (No. 2 U.K.), "Cracked Actor," and "Panic in Detroit." Perhaps led by his personal research for his 1973 album *Pin Ups* (No. 1 U.K., with Ken Scott)—in which he covered his favorites from bands such as the Yardbirds, the Kinks, and the Who—he quickly produced two songs with British '60s pop icon Lulu, including his own "The Man Who Sold the World," which went to No. 3 in the U.K. He also produced Lulu's single "Watch That Man."

After 1974, Bowie concentrated on his performing career, contributing such albums as *Young Americans* (No. 9, with Harry Maslin and Tony Visconti; see entries), *Station to Station* (No. 3, with Maslin), and the first of three albums with former Roxy Music sound sculptor and brilliant producer Brian Eno (see entry). While he didn't hit big with that moody material, he was ready to resume the rock 'n' roll lifestyle in 1977.

Old friend Iggy Pop found Bowie in Germany, where he had been living for a couple of years. Bowie added his production touch to Pop's *The Idiot* (with Visconti) and joined him as pianist on its support tour. Pop's albums, *Lust for Life*, *TV Eye*, and *Blah Blah Blah*, also bear Bowie's production mark.

A major influence on Bowie, both as performer and producer, was Tony Visconti. The two met when Visconti was producing a T. Rex album and Bowie asked him to work on *Space Oddity*. Bowie learned how to make a song clear and simple from Visconti.

Bowie gave each of the four artists he worked with the tools he had learned from working on his own music: Mott's "All the Young Dudes" was influenced by Bowie's early '70s sound, and Reed benefited from Bowie's ability to polish a pop song, a quality clear on

Bowie's own *Hunky Dory* disc (with Scott).

Both as producer and artist, Bowie has been willing to experiment with electronics. Along with Eno, who has continued to contribute to Bowie's work (including his 1997 release *Earthling*) Bowie has blended synthesizers and "real" instruments to create every kind of sound. —DAVID JOHN FARINELLA AND ERIC OLSEN

Bowie, David: *Ziggy Stardust and the Spiders from Mars*, RCA, 1972 • *Pin Ups*, RCA, 1973 • *Diamond Dogs*, RCA, 1974 • "Fame," RCA, 1975 • "Young Americans," RCA, 1975 • *Young Americans*, RCA, 1975 • "Golden Years," RCA, 1976 • *Station to Station*, RCA, 1976 • *Heroes*, RCA, 1977 • *Low*, RCA, 1977 • *Stage*, RCA, 1978 • *Lodger*, RCA, 1979 • *Scary Monsters and Super Creeps*, RCA, 1980 • w/ Queen, "Under Pressure," Elektra, 1981 • *Bertolt Brecht's Baal*, RCA, 1982 • "Let's Dance/Cat People," EMI America, 1983 • *Let's Dance*, EMI America, 1983 • "Modern Love," EMI America, 1983 • *Ziggy Stardust Live*, RCA, 1983 • "Blue Jean," EMI America, 1984 • *Changesbowie*, Rykodisc, 1984, 1990 • "Tonight," EMI America, 1984 • *Tonight*, EMI America, 1984 • w/ Pat Metheny Group, "This Is Not America," EMI America, 1985 • w/ Pat Metheny Group, "This Is Not America," Virgin/EMI, 1985 (*Now That's What I Call Music 5*) • "Absolute Beginners," Virgin, 1986 • "Underground," EMI America, 1986 • "Day-In Day-Out," EMI America, 1987 • "Never Let Me Down," EMI America, 1987 • *Never Let Me Down*, EMI America, 1987 • "Fame 90," Rykodisc, 1990 • "Sound + Vision" (reissue), Tommy Boy, 1991 • *Black Tie White Noise*, Savage/BMG, 1993 • *Bowie: The Singles, 1969–1993*, Rykodisc, 1993 • "Jump They Say," Savage/BMG, 1993 • "Miracle Goodnight," Savage/BMG, 1993 • *Buddah of Suburbia*, Virgin, 1995 • *Outside*, Virgin, 1995 • "The Heart's Filthy Lesson," Virgin, 1995 • "Hallo Spaceboy," RCA, 1996 • *Earthling*, Virgin, 1997 • "I'm Afraid of Americans," Virgin, 1997 • "Little Wonder," Virgin, 1997.

Carmen: *Fandangos in Space*, Regal Zonophone/Dunhill, 1973.

Cherry, Ava, and the Astronettes: *People from Bad Homes*, Griffin, 1995.

Eno, Brian: *Eno Box 1*, Virgin, 1994.

Gillespie, Dana: *Weren't Born a Man* (2 tracks), RCA, 1973.

Lulu: "The Man Who Sold the World/Watch That Man," Chelsea, 1973 • *From Crayons to Perfume: The Best of Lulu*, Rhino, 1994.

Mott the Hoople: "All the Young Dudes," Columbia, 1972 • *All the Young Dudes*, Columbia, 1972 • "All the Young Dudes," Epic, 1972, 1981 (*England Rocks 3*).

Pop, Iggy: w/ the Stooges, *Raw Power*, CBS, 1973 • *Lust for Life*, RCA, 1977 • *The Idiot*, RCA, 1977 • *T.V. Eye-Live*, RCA, 1978 • *Blah Blah Blah*, A&M, 1986 • "Fall in Love with Me," Virgin America, 1989 (*Slaves of New York* soundtrack) • "Lust for Life," Capitol, 1990, 1996 (*Trainspotting* soundtrack).

Queen: w/ David Bowie, "Under Pressure," Elektra, 1981 • *Hot Space*, Elektra, 1982.

Reed, Lou: *Transformer*, RCA, 1972 • "Walk on the Wild Side," RSO, 1972, 1980 (*Times Square* soundtrack) • "Walk on the Wild Side," RCA, 1973 • *Walk on the Wild Side: The Best Of*, RCA, 1977 • *Between Thought and Expression: The Lou Reed Anthology*, RCA, 1992.

Stooges, The: *See* Pop, Iggy.

COLLECTIONS

Labyrinth soundtrack, Atlantic, 1986.
When the Wind Blows soundtrack, Virgin, 1987.

Tommy Boyce and Bobby Hart

Tommy Boyce, born September 29, 1939, in Charlottesville, Virginia, and Bobby Hart, born February 18, 1939, in Phoenix, Arizona, were songwriters who primarily produced their own recordings. They also had a successful performing career with their own recording of "I Wonder What She's Doing Tonight," which reached No. 8 in 1968. They wrote more than 300 songs and were responsible for sales of more than 42 million records.

Their first hit as songwriters came in 1964 with "Come a Little Bit Closer," recorded by Jay and the Americans (No. 3). Boyce and Hart were subsequently offered jobs as staff writers for Screen Gems, the future home of the "pre-fab four," the Monkees. Boyce and Hart wrote and produced four of the Monkees' hits: "(Theme from) the Monkees," "Last Train to Clarksville" (No. 1), "(I'm Not Your) Steppin' Stone" (No. 20), and "Valerie" (No. 3). While much of the Monkees' repertoire was mired in cloying mediocrity, these are well-crafted compositions. Under Boyce and Hart's direction, the four Monkees (and an assortment of top studio musicians) performed the tunes with the right balance of tongue-in-cheek enthusiasm and innocence.

Production tricks abound on Boyce and Hart records but miraculously never sound like gimmicks. The "(Theme from) the Monkees" begins with the tritest high-hat shuffle imaginable, but at just the right instant the song explodes into a frenzy of cheerful narcissism: "Hey hey, we're the Monkees / So come and watch us sing and play / We're the young generation / And we've got something to say." While it may have been too obvious and pandering for late teens, the 10- to 13-year-old crowd bought it in droves.

"Last Train to Clarksville" was a clear Beatles rip-off, its obbligato guitar hook straight from "Help" and background vocals that would have sounded completely at home on *Rubber Soul*. Among other production devices, the song featured one full stop (all instruments stop playing completely before coming in again after stark silence), several instrumental stops (the band stops playing, leaving the lead vocalist to sing expressively over silence), and a section where Mickey Dolenz performs a double-tracked scat over the chords. Throughout the song, guitars ring like the bells of Rhymney and the snare drum and guitar backbeat drive with solid urgency.

"(I'm Not Your) Steppin' Stone" (the writers apparently had a penchant for parentheses) had scornful lyrics (a nod in the direction of Dylan's "Like a Rolling Stone") and more hooks than hell's coatroom. The modified modal chord progression was unusual for rock in 1966, and the background harmonies simply hypnotic. The record was made with rich, springy reverbs and is so utterly distinctive that it sounds like no other record made before or since. "Valerie" was a tour de force of harmony and background vocal production. By its 1968 release, Monkeemania was subsiding and its album (the Monkees' fifth) was their first not to reach No. 1.

Boyce and Hart joined the group for tours in the 1970s, and in 1976 recorded an album with two of the Monkees as Dolenz, Jones, Boyce and Hart. Boyce produced records for British band Darts and worked with Meat Loaf, Iggy Pop, and Del Shannon. Hart co-wrote "Over You" (recorded by Lane Brody, nominated for an Academy Award in 1983), the 1985 New Edition single "My Secret," and Robbie Nevil's 1988 hit "Dominoes."

Boyce, after battling depression for many years, committed suicide in 1994 at his Nashville home.
—Daniel J. Levitin

Tommy Boyce

Darts: *The Darts*, Magnet, 1977 • *Everyone Plays Darts*, Magnet, 1978.
Late Show: *Snap*, Decca, 1979.
Pop, Iggy: *Party*, Arista, 1981.

Tommy Boyce and Bobby Hart

Boyce and Hart: "Out and About," A&M, 1967 • *Test Patterns*, A&M, 1967 • "Alice Long (You're Still My Favorite Girlfriend)," A&M, 1968 • "I Wonder What She's Doing Tonite," A&M, 1968 • *I Wonder What She's Doing Tonite*, A&M, 1968.

Dolenz, Jones, Boyce and Hart: *Dolenz, Jones, Boyce and Hart*, Capitol, 1975.

Monkees, The: "Last Train to Clarksville," Colgems, 1966 • *The Monkees*, Colgems, 1966 • "(Theme from) the Monkees," Colgems, 1966 • *More of the Monkees* (2 tracks), Colgems, 1967 • *Instant Replay*, Colgems, 1969 • *The Monkees Greatest Hits*, Colgems, 1969 • *The Monkees Present*, Colgems, 1969 • *Changes*, Rhino, 1970, 1995 • *Listen to the Band*, Rhino, 1991.

Shannon, Del: *The Liberty Years*, EMI Legends, 1991.
Shelton, Louie: *Touch Me*, Warner Bros., 1969.

Bobby Hart

Jackson, La Toya: *La Toya*, RCA, 1988.
Kyle: *Kyle*, ABC, 1974.
Neely, Sam: *Down Home*, A&M, 1974.
Roberts, Austin: "Something's Wrong with Me," Chelsea, 1972.
Rockville Junction: *Lord Protect Me from My Friends*, 20th Century, 1975.

Joe Boyd

Joe Boyd likes to emphasize the organic in records he produces. He's never worked with MIDI, deployed a sampler, or used a drum machine. He'll use computers in the studio to "remember the moves" and to mix, but his emphasis is on the natural and the vivid.

Boyd, who owns Hannibal Records—a Rykodisc-distributed label that specializes in the exotic and in world music—is known for his productions of Nick Drake, the Incredible String Band, Richard Thompson (with and without former wife and musical partner Linda), and Toumani Diabate, master of the kora, a multistringed, gourd-based African guitar. The intellectually restless Boyd has worked primarily as an independent producer, and that's the way he likes it. Records he produced for hire in the early '80s for such superstars-to-be as R.E.M. and 10,000 Maniacs aren't ones he views with particular favor.

Born August 5, 1942, in Boston, Boyd studied piano when he was a teenager; his grandmother, Mary Boxhall Boyd, was a concert pianist who had studied with Artur Schnabel and Theodor Leschetitzky, the legendary Galician keyboard master who taught Paderewski and Schnabel. Mary Boxhall Boyd's pianistic style—melodic, romantic, and emotional—was a 19th-century style that greatly affected Boyd. "I know that when I listen to music, even if it's pygmy music from Central Africa, I'm very influenced by the way she played," he says.

In Princeton, New Jersey, where Boyd grew up, he and his brother Warwick became friends with Geoff Muldaur, an early member of Jim Kweskin's Jug Band and eventual husband of folk chanteuse Maria Muldaur. It was the early '60s. The three teenagers would pore over old blues and jazz records, listening again and again to the phrases and licks of bluesman Blind Lemon Jefferson and Ellington clarinetist Johnny Dodds. Boyd also tuned into a Philadelphia AM station, grooving to the rock 'n' roll program of Dick Clark predecessor Bob Horn. Finally, when he was 17, he connected the dots, discovering the continuum of blues, jazz, and rock. The revelation came by way of a Fats Domino record.

"I realized they were all the same," Boyd says. "I understood the historical continuity; there weren't any books on it those days. I thought rock 'n' roll was stuff you danced to and tried to get your knee between a girl's legs with. Blues and jazz were serious; they're what you listened to with your male friends. Once I saw that the commercial and intellectual concepts of these great American musical forms were not inseparable, I realized I could apply my nerdlike obsession to the world of commerce, and it would be a very cool career."

He entered the field in 1961 during a semester off from Harvard University, when he worked for Contemporary/Good Time Jazz Records in Los Angeles. There, he assisted on sessions with Philly Joe Jones, Phineas Newborn, Teddy Edwards, Howard McGhee, and Shelley Manne. When Boyd returned to Harvard, he became Boston-area distributor for such folk and blues labels as Folk Lyric, Arhoolie, and Delmark. "My warehouse was under my dormitory bed," he says. Boyd also promoted concerts by Lightning Hopkins, Big Joe Williams, and Sleepy John Estes and began a company with Broadside owner Dave Wilson called Riverboat Enterprises; that, in turn, spawned Rounder Records.

In the summer of 1963, he was responsible for getting bluesman Jesse Fuller to a folk festival at Brandeis University that was also featuring Bob Dylan. The following spring, after graduating from Harvard as an English major, Boyd secured his first real job in the industry, working for Newport Festival producer George Wein. Boyd started by managing a European blues and gospel tour featuring Muddy Waters, Sister Rosetta Tharpe, Otis Spann, the Rev. Gary Davis, Brownie McGhee, and Sonny Terry. After touring

Europe again for Wein that autumn with Miles Davis, Roland Kirk, Sonny Stitt, and Dave Brubeck, Boyd returned to the U.S. and worked as production manager for the Newport folk and jazz festivals of the summer of 1965—the year Dylan went electric.

Boyd's reward for helping Elektra's Paul Rothschild (see entry) sign the Paul Butterfield Blues Band was a job running the Elektra London office. Boyd had met Rothschild in Cambridge a few years earlier when both frequented the legendary blues-and-folk hot spot Club 47. At Elektra, Boyd signed the Incredible String Band and produced its first album. When he and label owner Jac Holzman fell out over the latter's reluctance to sign Eric Clapton and Pink Floyd, Boyd left to start the UFO Club in London—the venue where future producer Tony Visconti (see entry) would discover Marc Bolan. In December 1965, he produced the first Pink Floyd single, "Arnold Layne" (No. 20 U.K.).

Not only was Boyd at the center of London's psychedelic movement, he also produced numerous albums in the late '60s and early '70s. Under the Witchseason Production banner, Boyd, primarily with engineer John Wood, nurtured such artists as Nick Drake, Fairport Convention, Fotheringay, John and Beverley Martyn, Chris McGregor's Brotherhood of Breath, and Geoff and Maria Muldaur. In 1971, Boyd sold Witchseason to Island Records and moved to Los Angeles to be director of music services for Warner Bros. Films. He supervised the soundtracks for *Deliverance* and *A Clockwork Orange* and produced a documentary on Jimi Hendrix.

Boyd returned to record producing in the mid-'70s, crafting Maria Muldaur's self-titled album (No. 3) and working with such other figures as Toots and the Maytals, Kate and Anna McGarrigle, and Julie Covington. Among his key productions of the '80s and '90s are records by Defunkt, crossover classical saxophonist John Harle, Toumani Diabate, Billy Bragg, and, in 1985, R.E.M.'s *Fables of the Reconstruction* and 10,000 Maniacs' *The Wishing Chair*.

In the past decade, Boyd's record production has taken a back seat to his administrative duties. "I run a label and try to get other people to produce records for me," he says, "but there are times it seems it's appropriate for me to do it, like going to Cuba. I really wanted to go to Cuba and make records."

Among his own productions, he can "still kick back and listen to" the first album by Kate and Anna McGarrigle, Nick Drake's *Bryter Later,* The Incredible String Band's *Hangman's Beautiful Daughter,* and Toots and the Maytals' *Reggae Got Soul.*

"Starting out as a tour manager and fussing over live sound, I suppose, was an influence in the sense that I

like the idea of records that feel like they're actually performed by a bunch of people in the same room at the same time," Boyd says. "I think it's possible to mix a record in a way that is more than just literal: you try and record it live, then mix it so it's hyper live. Give it three dimensions, give it a lot of care and time."
—CARLO WOLFF

Act, The: *Too Late at 20,* Hannibal, 1981.
Albion Band: *Rise up Like the Lark,* Harvest, 1978.
Alemany, Jesus: *Cubanismo,* Hannibal, 1996 • *Malembe,* Hannibal, 1997.
Ali Khan, Salamat and Nazakat: *Salamat and Nazakat Ali,* Hannibal, 1988.
Balkana: *The Music of Bulgaria,* Hannibal, 1995.
Blackgirls: *Procedure,* Mammoth, 1989 • *Happy,* Mammoth, 1991.
Booker, James: *Junco Partner,* Island, 1976.
Bragg, Billy: *Workers Playtime,* Elektra, 1988 • *The Internationale,* Elektra, 1990.
Brotherhood of Breath: *Brotherhood of Breath,* Neon, 1971.
Bunyan, Vashti: *Just Another Diamond Day,* Philips, 1968.
Covington, Julie: *Julie Covington,* Virgin, 1978.
Defunkt: *Thermonuclear Sweat,* Hannibal, 1982 • *Avoid the Funk: A Defunkt Anthology,* Hannibal, 1988.
Denny, Sandy: *Who Knows Where the Time Goes,* Hannibal, 1986, 1991 • *The Best Of,* Island, 1987.
Diabate, Toumani: *Kaira,* Hannibal, 1988 • *Djelika,* Hannibal, 1995.
Doctor Strangely Strange: *Kip of the Serenes,* Island, 1969.
Drake, Nick: *Five Leaves Left,* Island, 1969 • *Bryter Later,* Island, 1970 • *Nick Drake,* Island, 1971 • *Pink Moon,* Island, 1972 • *Fruit Tree,* Hannibal, 1986 • *Heaven in a Wildflower,* Island, 1986 • *Time of No Reply,* Hannibal, 1986 • *Way to Blue: An Introduction to Nick Drake,* Hannibal, 1994.
Duende: *Passion and Dazzling Virtuosity,* Ellipsis Arts, 1994.
Fairport Convention: *Fairport Convention,* Polydor, 1968 • *Liege and Lief,* Island, 1969 • *Unhalfbricking,* Island, 1969 • *What We Did on Our Holidays,* Island, 1969 • *Full House,* Island, 1970 • *Live at the L.A. Troubador,* Island, 1976 • *House Full,* Hannibal, 1986.
Fotheringay: *Fotheringay,* Island, 1970.
Harle, John: *Habanera,* Hannibal, 1987.
Hendrix, Jimi: *Jimi Hendrix* soundtrack, Reprise, 1973.
Heron, Mike: *Smiling Men with Bad Reputations,* Island, 1971.
Incredible String Band: *Incredible String Band,* Elektra, 1966 • *The 5000 Spirits of the Layers of the Onion,* Elektra, 1967 • *Big Tam and the Wee Huge,* Elektra, 1968 • *The Hangman's Beautiful Daughter,* Elektra, 1968 • *Changing Horses,* Elektra, 1969 • *Be Glad for the Song Has No Ending,* Island, 1970 • *I Looked Up,* Elektra, 1970 • *U,* Elektra, 1972.
Krause, Dagmar: *Supply & Demand: Songs by Brecht, Weill & Eisler,* Hannibal, 1988.
Martyn, John and Beverley: *Stormbringer,* Island, 1970 • *The Road to Ruin,* Island, 1970.
McGarrigle, Kate and Anna: *Kate and Anna McGarrigle,* Warner Bros., 1975 • *Dancer with Bruised Knees,* Warner Bros., 1977 • *French Record,* Hannibal, 1980, 1984 • *Metapedia,* Hannibal, 1996.
McGregor, Chris: *And the Brotherhood of Breath,* Neon, 1970.
Meurs, Ad Van: *The Watchman,* Hannibal, 1991.
Muldaur, Geoff and Maria: *Pottery Pie,* Reprise, 1970.
Muldaur, Geoff: *Geoff Muldaur Is Having a Wonderful Time,* Reprise, 1975.
Muldaur, Maria: "I'm a Woman," Reprise, 1974 • *Maria Muldaur,* Reprise, 1974 • "Midnight at the Oasis," Reprise, 1974 • *Waitress in a Donut Shop,* Reprise, 1974 • *Sweet Harmony,* Reprise, 1976.
Muleskinner: *Muleskinner,* Warner Bros., 1974 • *Potpourri of Bluegrass Jam,* Sierra, 1994.
Nico: *Desert Shore,* Reprise, 1971.
Nonenga, Poppie: *Poppie Nonenga,* Hannibal, 1984.
O'Connell, Maura: *Wandering Home,* Hannibal, 1997.
Orbestra: *Transdanubian Swineherd's Music,* Hannibal, 1992.
Papasov Orchestra, Ivo: *Orpheus Ascending,* Hannibal, 1989 • *Balkanology,* Hannibal, 1991.
Pink Floyd: *Relics,* Harvest, 1971 • *Works,* Capitol, 1983, 1987.
R.E.M.: *Fables of the Reconstruction,* IRS, 1985 • *Dead Letter Office,* IRS, 1987 • *Eponymous,* IRS, 1988.
Rodriguez, Alfredo: *Cuba Linda,* Hannibal, 1997.
Songhai: *Songhai,* Hannibal, 1988 • *Songhai 2,* Hannibal, 1995.
Tabor, June: *Some Other Time,* Hannibal, 1989.
10,000 Maniacs: *The Wishing Chair,* Elektra, 1985.
Thompson, Linda: *Shoot Out the Lights,* Hannibal, 1982.
Thompson, Richard: *Richard Thompson Live,* Island, 1977 • *Hand of Kindness,* Hannibal, 1983 • *Across a Crowded Room,* Polydor, 1985 • *Watching the Dark: The History of Richard Thompson,* Hannibal, 1993 • *See also* Thompson, Linda.
Toots and the Maytals: *Reggae Got Soul,* Mango, 1976.
Trio Bulgarka: *The Forest Is Crying,* Hannibal, 1995.
Watchman: *Watchman,* Hannibal, 1991.

John Boylan

John Boylan is an exemplar of the career producer. His life in the studio began making demo tapes for Tin Pan Alley publishers Charles Koppelman and Don Rubin in the mid-60's, and continues to this day.

Boylan has recorded, as an independent producer, artists across a wide pop/rock/country spectrum, including Rick Nelson, the Association, Linda Ronstadt, Pure Prairie League, Roger McGuinn, the Little River Band, Quarterflash, Carly Simon, and Bailie and the Boys.

He also guided Boston, Michael (Martin) Murphey, Mickey Gilley, Ozark Mountain Daredevils, and most enduringly, Charlie Daniels to success as a staff producer, and then vice president of A&R, for Epic in the '70s and '80s.

In the '90s Boylan has had great success with children's recordings of the Chipmunks, the Simpsons, the Muppets, and Sesame Street. And all the while he has produced music for film: *Goodbye Columbus, Urban Cowboy, Nightshift, Fast Times at Ridgemont High, Footloose, Born on the Fourth of July,* and *Crybaby,* to name a few.

As a producer or executive producer, Boylan has received 13 platinum and 21 gold record awards. John Boylan is the antithesis of the brash, selfish industry stereotype. He has chosen to share his experience and knowledge teaching record production at UCLA Extension since 1989, and by writing an instructional history of the profession, *Modern Record Production* (River Press, 1998). He sees the producer's role as that of a "creative obstetrician" who "delivers the brainchild of the artist."

Boylan was born in Buffalo, New York, in 1941. He watched R&B bands tear up clubs in Buffalo and listened to country on the radio. When rock 'n' roll hit, he listened to Buffalo's legendary DJ George "Hound Dog" Lorenz on WKBW. Boylan's education at Bard College was interrupted by two years in the Air Force Reserve, but he graduated in 1967 and went to work as a songwriter for Koppelman-Rubin, at 1650 Broadway, right around the corner from the Brill Building in New York. As a songwriter, Boylan was a good piano player. However, his employers noticed that he had some organizational abilities, so he was assigned to produce the demos used to pitch songs to artists and producers.

After a while, the powers noticed that the demos sounded pretty good, so they sent Boylan to L.A. in late 1967 to produce Rick Nelson. Boylan encouraged Nelson to begin writing, and though the albums they did together didn't do much, they led to Nelson's big comeback in the early '70s with "Garden Party."

On his own now, Boylan's next big move was to assemble a crack country rock band to back Linda Ronstadt for her second solo album in 1972. The band—featuring young players Don Henley, Glenn Frey, Randy Meisner, and Bernie Leadon—later came to be known as the Eagles.

One of Boylan's finest moments came on Ronstadt's next album, *Don't Cry Now.* "Love Has No Pride" features Ronstadt's aching vocals of abject longing, recorded live over Boylan's own piano. Boylan, among the handful of country rock's best producers (Peter Asher, Glyn Johns, Norbert Putnam, Bill Szymczyk; see entries), also recorded Pure Prairie League's swinging *Two Lane Highway.* Larry Goshorn's title track rolls with country harmonies and instrumentation (John David Call's pedal steel), but the rhythm and guitar make a beautiful rock alloy. "I'll Fix Your Flat Tire, Merle" and "Pickin' to Beat the Devil" are bluegrass rave-ups that sound like a cross between Bill Monroe and Kinky Friedman.

Boylan has worked with Charlie Daniels for almost 20 years, starting with "The Devil Went Down to Georgia" (No. 3) in 1979. Boylan relates, "I gave Charlie the title, and I was the first person at the company to think it was a single. 'It's got no hook. It's got no chorus. It's just some story about a kid and the devil.' I was so sure that it was going to be a single, that I asked him to do an alternative vocal, changing the 'I done told you once, you son-of-a-bitch' line, to 'son-of-a-gun.' I mixed that separately and stuck it at the end of the leader on the master. I went to Australia to do a Little River Band album, and a little later I got a panicky call from the head of A&R saying somehow the damn song was breaking as a single. It was kind of nice."

Boylan was the first American producer to work with a major Australian band and break them here. "I went to Australia and New Zealand in the mid-'70s to give some lectures, and I checked out some bands while I was there, including the Little River Band [from Melbourne], which at the time was called Mississippi. I liked three bands: Split Enz, Sherbet, and Mississippi."

The members of Mississippi turned out to be Boylan's most consistent hitmakers, with such quality pop tunes as "Reminiscing" (No. 3) and "Cool Change" (No. 10).

Boylan's biggest individual recording is the first Boston album (No. 3). "When I got the Boston tape, a lot of people had passed on it, including the people at Epic who eventually signed them. There were rumors that Tom Scholz had made the tape all by himself in his basement. Epic wanted a band that could tour. At the time, the 'band' was Scholz on guitar and organ, lead singer Brad Delp, and Barry Goudreau, also on guitar, who had taught Tom how to play. We got a drummer and a bass player, rented a rehearsal hall, and brought the company execs to see that we actually had some warm bodies.

"Scholz had very few shortcomings as a record maker. He's a graduate of MIT and a good technician. He didn't know how to record acoustic instruments and he wasn't great with vocals, but he was really good with anything electric: great bass, wonderful guitar. CBS had

a problem at that time with recording engineers, and if you lived within a certain distance from New York, you had to use a CBS engineer, and of course Scholz couldn't do that because he was recording in his basement after work every night. So we faked that. He recorded in his basement, and I paid out of my pocket to have a remote truck come up from Rhode Island, run a snake through his basement window, and then transfer the stuff from his 12-track to a 24-track on the remote truck, and those are the tapes we used. That album cost $28,000 to make and it has sold 16 million copies."
—ERIC OLSEN

Angelle: *Angelle,* Epic, 1977.

Appletree Theater: *Playback,* Verve, 1968.

Association, The: *Goodbye Columbus,* Warner Bros., 1969 • *The Association,* Warner Bros., 1969.

Baillie and the Boys: *The Best Of,* RCA, 1991.

Bear: *Greetings Children of Paradise,* MGM, 1968.

Boston: *Boston,* Epic, 1976 • "More Than a Feeling," Epic, 1976 • "Long Time," Epic, 1977 • "Peace of Mind," Epic, 1977.

Brewer and Shipley: *Brewer and Shipley,* Capitol, 1974.

Charlie Daniels Band: *Million Mile Reflections,* Epic, 1979 • "The Devil Went Down to Georgia," Epic, 1979 • *Full Moon,* Epic, 1980 • "In America," Epic, 1980 • *Volunteer Jam VI,* Epic, 1980 • *Windows,* Epic, 1982 • *A Decade of Hits,* Epic, 1983 • *Me and the Boys,* Epic, 1985 • *Powder Keg,* Epic, 1987.

Chipmumks, The: *Urban Chipmunks,* Epic, 1981 • *Chipmunks in Low Places,* Chipmunk/Epic, 1992.

Comanor, Jeffrey: *A Rumour in His Own Time,* Epic, 1976.

Commander Cody: *Commander Cody and His Lost Planet Airmen,* Warner Bros., 1975.

Daniels, Charlie: *Super Hits,* Columbia, 1994 • *Roots Remain,* Sony, 1996 • *See also* Charlie Daniels Band.

Denim: *Denim,* Epic, 1977.

Dillards, The: *Copperfields,* Elektra, 1976 • *There Is a Time, 1963–1970,* Vanguard, 1991.

Dinner, Michael: *The Great Pretender,* Fantasy, 1974.

Donohue, Dane: *Dane Donohue,* CBS, 1978.

Giguere, Russ: *Hexagram 16,* Warner Bros., 1971.

Gilley, Mickey: *Live at Gilley's,* Epic, 1978.

Goudreau, Barry: *Barry Goudreau,* CBS, 1980.

Great Buildings: *Great Buildings,* Columbia, 1981.

Hill, Dan: *Partial Surrender,* Epic, 1981.

KBC Band: *KBC Band,* Arista, 1986.

Kermit: *Kermit Unpigged,* Henson/BMG, 1995.

Lee, Johnny: "Lookin' for Love," Full Moon, 1980 • *Greatest Hits,* Full Moon, 1983, 1990.

Levy, Marcy: *Marcella,* Epic, 1982.

Little River Band: *Diamantina Cocktail,* EMI/Capitol, 1977 •

"Happy Anniversary," Capitol, 1977 • "Help Is on the Way," Capitol, 1977 • "Reminiscing," EMI/Capitol, 1978 • *Sleeper Catcher,* EMI/Capitol, 1978 • "Cool Change," Capitol, 1979 • *First Under the Wire,* Capitol, 1979 • "Lady," Capitol, 1979 • "Lonesome Loser," Capitol, 1979 • *Monsoon,* MCA, 1988 • *World Wide Love,* Curb, 1991 • *Reminiscing,* CEMA, 1992.

McGuinn, Roger: *Roger McGuinn and Band,* Columbia, 1975 • *Born to Rock and Roll,* Columbia, 1991.

Murphey, Michael: *Lone Wolf,* Epic, 1978 • *Peaks, Valleys, Honky Tonks and Alleys,* Epic, 1979.

Nelson: *Because They Can,* Geffen, 1995.

Nelson, Rick: *Perspective,* Decca, 1968 • *Another Side,* Decca, 1969 • "She Belongs to Me," Decca, 1970.

O'Keefe, Danny: *So Long Harry Truman,* Atlantic, 1975.

O'Neill, Sharon: *Foreign Affairs,* CBS, 1983.

Ozark Mountain Daredevils: *Ozark Mountain Daredevils,* CBS, 1980.

Party, The: *The Party,* Hollywood, 1990.

Pure Prairie League: *If the Shoe Fits,* RCA, 1975 • *Two Lane Highway,* RCA, 1975 • *Dance,* RCA, 1976.

Quarterflash: "Harden My Heart," Geffen, 1981 • *Quarterflash,* Geffen, 1981 • "Find Another Fool," Geffen, 1982 • "Take Me to Heart," Geffen, 1983 • *Take Another Picture,* Geffen, 1983.

REO Speedwagon: *You Can Tune a Piano But You Can't Tuna Fish,* Epic, 1978.

Ronstadt, Linda: *Linda Ronstadt,* Capitol, 1972 • *Don't Cry Now,* Asylum, 1973 • *Different Drum,* Capitol, 1974 • *Greatest Hits,* Vol. 1, Asylum, 1976.

Schmit, Timothy B.: *Tell the Truth,* MCA, 1983, 1990.

Shorrock, Glenn: *Victim of the Peace,* Capitol, 1983.

Simon, Carly: *Coming Around Again,* Arista, 1987.

Simpsons, The: *The Simpsons Sings the Blues,* Geffen, 1990.

Taylor, Livingston: *Man's Best Friend,* Epic, 1980.

Trillion: *Clear Approach,* Epic, 1980.

Uncle Jim's Music: *Uncle Jim's Music,* Kapp, 1971.

Unforgiven, The: *The Unforgiven,* Elektra, 1986.

COLLECTIONS

Urban Cowboy soundtrack, Asylum, 1980.

The Cowboys, Epic, 1981.

Fast Times at Ridgemont High soundtrack, Full Moon, 1982.

Footloose soundtrack, Columbia, 1984.

Back to the Beach soundtrack, Columbia, 1987.

Born on the Fourth of July soundtrack, MCA, 1989.

Owen Bradley

Owen Bradley is not only responsible for producing some of the most enduring records on Nashville's famed Music Row, he's also credited with planting the seeds from which Music Row grew to be the home of country music.

Known as a founding architect of the Nashville sound, Bradley is also credited with helping create the Music Row area with the development of the famed "Quonset Hut" studio, now a historic landmark.

The Westmoreland, Tennessee, native moved to Nashville in 1922. In the early '30s, he gained a foothold in the music industry as a piano player. His early experience was in pop and big-band music, and it wasn't until he returned from military service that he became involved in the country genre. While plying his trade as a musician, Bradley began working at WSM radio in 1935, at age 20. He stayed at the station, the home of the Grand Ole Opry, until 1958. He was promoted to music director there in 1947, the year he began his career at Decca Records assisting Paul Cohen, then chief of Decca's country division.

"I was like an understudy to Paul Cohen," recalled Bradley in an interview a few months before his death in January 1998. "When I first started working with Patsy [Cline], I was not a full-fledged producer. It wasn't until 1958 that I took full charge."

Bradley was named vice president and head of Decca Nashville when Cohen was promoted to another division in 1958. He remained chief of Decca Nashville until 1976 (during his tenure the label changed to MCA Records). At Decca, Bradley worked with the top stars of one of country music's most creative eras, including Patsy Cline, Ernest Tubb, Webb Pierce, Loretta Lynn, Brenda Lee, Conway Twitty, Kitty Wells, Red Foley, and Jack Greene.

Bradley was inducted into the Country Music Hall of Fame in 1974, and five of the acts he produced have also been inducted. His recordings with Cline have earned him a special place in history. He wished Cline was still here to see the impact her music continues to have.

"Actually, during Patsy's lifetime, only a few of her songs were really embraced that way," he said. " 'Sweet Dreams' was intended as an album cut. It was not one of her big songs. . . . It was done in the movie *Coal Miner's Daughter* and that made it even bigger. All those pieces weren't together while she was alive . . . and it's something that I'm just so sorry that she missed because

it's her singing they really liked, and we just kind of tagged along."

One thing that has distinguished Bradley's work from that of other producers of his era is how well the records have stood up over time because of the audio quality. Current producers and artists frequently comment that Bradley was "digital before there was digital" because his records sound so clean.

"We weren't digital, but we kept separation, kept the instruments from bleeding into each other," Bradley explained. "A lot of the records back in those days, you'd go into a room and just kind of jumble together. We learned how to separate the instruments, even before we had stereo. And after we got stereo, we got to be really fanatical about it."

Bradley said he always looked for the best song, not at who wrote what was being submitted. "We just tried to do the best song," he said. "I tried to find the best song I could find, then looked to see who wrote the song because you can twist your mind a little bit if you try to do somebody a favor."

Even after leaving Decca, Bradley continued as a force in recorded music. In 1988, k.d. lang enlisted him to produce her critically acclaimed *Shadowland* album. Up until his death at age 82, he still operated a studio, Bradley's Barn, that had been the site of numerous landmark albums, including George Jones' star-studded *The Bradley's Barn Sessions*. Among Bradley's last sessions were recordings with Brenda Lee and Jimmy Dean's wife, Donna Dean.

Bradley said he had enjoyed life as a producer. "I don't know how to do anything else," Bradley said. "I like the music business."

Asked what advice he'd give aspiring producers, Bradley said, "Just be lucky. Do whatever you can do to be lucky." —DEBORAH EVANS PRICE

Anderson, Bill: "My Life (Throw It Away If I Want To)," Decca, 1969 • "World of Make Believe," MCA, 1974 • w/ Mary Lou Turner, "Sometimes," MCA, 1976 • *Greatest Hits*, Varese Vintage, 1996.

Bradley, Owen: w/ Owen Bradley Quintet, "Blues Stay Away from Me," Coral, 1949 • *Christmas Time*, Coral, 1955 • *Strauss Waltzes*, Coral, 1955 • *Cherished Hymns*, Coral, 1956 • *Lazy River*, Coral, 1956 • *Singin' in the Rain*, Coral, 1956 • *Bandstand Hop*, Decca, 1958 • *Big Guitar*, Decca, 1959 • *Paradise Island*, Decca, 1960.

Burnette, Johnny: w/ the rock 'n' roll Trio, *Tear It Up* (14 tracks), Solid Smoke, 1956, 1978.

Cline, Patsy: "A Poor Man's Roses (Or a Rich Man's Gold)," Decca, 1957 • *Patsy Cline*, MCA, 1957 • "Walkin' After Midnight," Decca, 1957 • "Crazy," Decca, 1961 • "I Fall to

Pieces," Decca, 1961 • w/ the Jondanaires, *Showcase*, MCA, 1961 • "Imagine That," Decca, 1962 • "She's Got You," Decca, 1962 • *Sentimentally Yours*, MCA, 1962 • "So Wrong," Decca, 1962 • "When I Get Through with You (You'll Love Me Too)," Decca, 1962 • "Faded Love," Decca, 1963 • "Leavin' on Your Mind," Decca, 1963 • "Sweet Dreams (of You)," Decca, 1963 • *The Last Sessions*, MCA, 1963, 1988 • *The Patsy Cline Story*, MCA, 1963, 1989 • *A Portrait of Patsy Cline*, MCA, 1964 • "He Called Me Baby," Decca, 1964 • *Here's Patsy Cline*, MCA, 1965 • w/ Jim Reeves, *Remembering*, MCA, 1976, 1982 • *Always*, MCA, 1980 • *Songwriter's Tribute*, MCA, 1982 • *Last Sessions*, MCA, 1985 • *Sweet Dreams*, MCA, 1985 • *Greatest Hits*, MCA, 1988 • *Her First Recordings*, Vols. 1–3, Rhino, 1989 • *The Patsy Cline Collection*, MCA, 1991 • *Forever and Always*, Epic, 1992 • *Sings Songs of Love*, MCA, 1995 • w/ Loretta Lynn, *On Tour*, Vol. 2, MCA Special Products, 1996.

Cramer, Floyd: *Looking for Mr. Goodbar*, RCA, 1968.

Emmons, Buddy: *Amazing Steel Guitar: The Buddy Emmons Collection*, Razor & Tie, 1997.

Fountain, Pete: *Cheek to Cheek*, Ranwood, 1993.

Greene, Jack: "You Are My Treasure," Decca, 1968 • "Statue of a Fool," Decca, 1969 • "Until My Dreams Come True," Decca, 1969.

Helms, Bobby: "Jingle Bell Rock," MCA, 1957, 1986 (*Rockin' Little Christmas*).

Holly, Buddy: *Buddy Holly Collection*, MCA, 1993.

Johnnie and Jack: *Johnnie and Jack*, Bear Family, 1992.

Jondonaires, The: See Cline, Patsy.

Kalin Twins: *When*, Bear Family, 1984.

lang, k.d.: *Shadowland*, Sire, 1988.

Lee, Brenda: "I'm Gonna Lasso Santa Claus," MCA, 1956, 1986 (*Rockin' Little Christmas*) • "Rockin' Around the Christmas Tree," MCA, 1958, 1986 (*Rockin' Little Christmas*) • *Grandma, What Great Songs You Sang*, Decca, 1959 • *Brenda Lee*, Warner Bros., 1960, 1991 • "I'm Sorry," Decca, 1960 • "I Want to Be Wanted," Decca, 1960 • *This Is Brenda*, Decca, 1960 • *Merry Christmas from Brenda Lee*, MCA, 1964 • *Top Teen Hits*, Decca, 1965 • "Coming on Strong," Decca, 1966 • *Greatest Country Hits*, MCA, 1990 • *Anthology*, Vols. 1–2, MCA, 1991.

Locklin, Hank: *Send Me the Pillow You Dream On*, Bear Family, 1997.

Lynn, Loretta: "Fist City," Decca, 1968 • *Greatest Hits*, Decca, 1968 • "Woman of the World (Leave My World Alone)," Decca, 1969 • "Coal Miner's Daughter," Decca, 1970 • "One's on the Way," Decca, 1972 • "Love Is the Foundation," Decca, 1973 • "Rated 'X'," Decca, 1973 • "Trouble in Paradise," Decca, 1974 • "Somebody Somewhere (Don't Know What He's Missin' Tonight)," MCA, 1976 • "Out of My Head and Back in my Bed,"

MCA, 1978 • *Making Love from Memory*, MCA, 1982 • *Lyin', Cheatin', Woman Chasin', Honky Tonkin', Whiskey Drinkin' You*, MCA, 1983 • *Greatest Hits (MCA)*, MCA, 1987 • *Sings Patsy Cline's Favorites*, MCA Special Products, 1992 • *Hey Good Lookin'*, MCA Special Products, 1993.

Lynn, Loretta, and Conway Twitty: "After the Fire Is Gone," Decca, 1971 • *Coal Miner's Daughter*, Decca, 1971 • "Lead Me On," Decca, 1971 • *We Only Make Believe*, MCA, 1971 • *Lead Me On*, MCA, 1972 • "Louisiana Woman, Mississippi Man," Decca, 1973 • *Louisiana Woman, Mississippi Man*, MCA, 1973 • "As Soon As I Hang Up the Phone," MCA, 1974 • *Country Partners*, MCA, 1974 • "Feelins'," MCA, 1975 • *Feelins'*, MCA, 1975 • *United Talent*, MCA, 1976 • *Dynamic Duo*, MCA, 1977 • "She's Got You," MCA, 1977 • *Honky Tonk Heroes*, MCA, 1978 • *The Very Best Of*, MCA, 1979, 1988 • *Making Believe*, MCA, 1988 • *20 Greatest Hits*, MCA, 1988.

Martin, Jimmy: *Jimmy Martin and the Sunny Mountain Boys*, Bear Family, 1994.

Monroe, Bill: *Bluegrass, 1950–1958*, Bear Family, 1989 • *Bluegrass, 1959–1969*, Bear Family, 1991.

Montana Slim: *The Dynamite Trail: The Decca Years*, Decca, 1960.

Mullican, Moon: *Moon's Rock*, Bear Family, 1992.

Parton, Dolly: w/ Loretta Lynn and Tammy Wynette: *Honky Tonk Angels*, Columbia, 1994.

Pierce, Webb: *Sands of Gold/Sweet Memories*, MCA, 1985 • *Wondering Boy, 1951–1958*, Bear Family, 1990.

Reeves, Jim: *Greatest Hits*, RCA, 1966 • See also Cline, Patsy.

Riley, Billy Lee: *Classic Recordings, 1956–1960*, Bear Family, 1990.

Rock 'n' Roll Trio: "Train Kept A-Rollin'," Coral, 1956 • See also Burnette, Johnny.

Self, Ronnie: *Bop-a-Lena*, Bear Family, 1990.

Torok, Mitchell: *Mexican Joe in the Caribbean*, Bear Family, 1996.

Twitty, Conway: *A Night With*, MCA, 1981. • "Next in Line," Decca, 1968 • "I Love You More Today," Decca, 1969 • "To See My Angel Cry," Decca, 1969 • "Fifteen Years Ago," Decca, 1970 • "Hello Darlin'," Decca, 1970 • "How Much More Can She Stand," Decca, 1971 • *Greatest Hits*, Vol. 1, MCA, 1972, 1988 • "(Lost Her Love) on Our Last Date," Decca, 1972 • "I Can't Stop Loving You," Decca, 1972 • "She Needs Someone to Hold Her (When She Cries)," Decca, 1973 • "You've Never Been This Far Before," Decca, 1973 • "I See the Want in Your Eyes," MCA, 1974 • "There's a Honky Tonk Angel (Who'll Take Me Back In)," MCA, 1974 • "Linda on My Mind," MCA, 1975 • "This Time I've Hurt Her More Than She Loves Me," MCA, 1975 • "Touch the Hand," MCA, 1975 • "After All the Good Is Gone," MCA, 1976 • *Greatest Hits*, Vol. 2, MCA, 1976, 1987 • "I Can't Believe She Gives It All to

Me," MCA, 1976 • "The Games That Daddies play," MCA, 1976 • "I've Already Loved You in My Mind," MCA, 1977 • "Play, Guitar, Play," MCA, 1977 • *The Very Best of Conway Twitty*, MCA, 1978, 1987 • *Classic Conway*, MCA, 1983 • *Silver Anniversary Collection*, MCA, 1990 • *The Conway Twitty Collection*, MCA, 1994 • *See also* Lynn, Loretta, and Conrad Twitty.

Wynette, Tammy: *See* Parton, Dolly.

COLLECTIONS

Coal Miner's Daughter soundtrack, MCA, 1980.

Sweet Dreams soundtrack, MCA, 1985.

Rock Around the Clock: The Decca Rock and Roll Collection, Decca, 1994.

Stardust: The Classic Decca hits and Standards Collection, Decca, 1994.

The Nashville Sound: Owen Bradley, Decca Nashville, 1996.

David Briggs

D avid Briggs (born February 29, 1944, in Douglas, Wyoming) was a recurring presence in the music of Neil Young and Nils Lofgren. He arrived in Los Angeles on Christmas Day, 1960, and within a few years was a staff producer at Bill Cosby's Tetragrammaton label.

Young reportedly met Briggs while hitchhiking in Malibu in the late '60s, and the two struck up a lifelong friendship. Briggs co-produced 18 Young albums, both with and without Crazy Horse, beginning with Young's first solo LP, *Neil Young*, up through 1994's apocalyptic *Sleeps with Angels* (No. 9). Many songs considered definitive for Young were co-produced by Briggs: "Cinnamon Girl," "Like a Hurricane," "Only Love Can Break Your Heart," "Southern Man," "Out of the Blue and into the Black," and "Tonight's the Night." Briggs died November 26, 1995.

"David was more of an alchemist than anything," recalls Graham Nash. "David was into capturing the moment and fully knowing when that moment was and when that moment had passed. So he was perfect to work with Neil. Neil knows exactly what he's doing at all times and has a vision of what it should be, but I don't think he has been 'produced' no matter who he's had helping him. Neil just needs help to get it on tape—a sounding board, a friend, someone to allow him to be the artist. David was all those things. Neil really trusted David."

Commercial success has unfairly eluded the talented Lofgren, who makes consistently high-quality albums. It is hard to fault Briggs, who presented Lofgren's material and performances in the best way possible on six albums, first with Lofgren's band Grin and then as a solo artist.

Briggs' broad musical tastes also showed in his ability to work with artists ranging from Nick Cave and the Bad Seeds to Alice Cooper and Willie Nelson. In the 1990s, Briggs worked with artists such as Cave, 13 Engines, the Sidewinders, and Royal Trux and on a number of unreleased recordings by John Eddie, Blind Melon, and the Sweet and Low Orchestra.

A session keyboardist and producer from Nashville, also named David Briggs, should not be confused with this David Briggs. The Nashville Briggs produced Marty Haggard, Willie Nelson, Elvis Presley, Murray Roman, Tom Rush, Rob Ruzicka, and Troy Seals. —Daniel J. Levitin

Alice Cooper: *Easy Action*, Warner Bros., 1970.

Briggs, David: *Keyboard Sculpture*, Monument, 1969.

Cave, Nick and the Bad Seeds: *Henry's Dream*, Mute/Elektra, 1992.

Comeaux, Amie: *Moving Out*, Polydor, 1994.

Crazy Horse: *Crazy Moon*, RCA, 1978 • *See also* Young, Neil, and Crazy Horse.

Grin: *Grin*, Epic/Spin, 1971 • *1 + 1*, Epic/Spin, 1972 • *All Out*, Epic, 1972 • *Gone Crazy*, A&M, 1973 • *The Best of Grin, Featuring Nils Lofgren*, Epic, 1976.

Hopkins, Nicky: *The Tin Man Was a Dreamer*, CBS, 1973.

Lofgren, Nils: *Nils Lofgren*, A&M, 1975 • *Cry Tough* (4 tracks), A&M, 1976 • *Night After Night*, A&M, 1977 • *The Best Of*, A&M, 1985 • *See also* Grin.

Low and Sweet Orchestra: *Goodbye to All That*, Interscope, 1996.

McDonald, Kathi: *Insane Asylum*, Capitol, 1974.

Orbison, Roy: *King of Hearts*, Virgin, 1992.

Prine, John: *The Great Days: John Prine Anthology*, Rhino, 1993.

Quattrain: *Quattrain*, Tetragrammaton, 1969.

Royal Trux: *Thank You*, Virgin, 1995.

Sand Rubies: *Sand Rubies*, Atlas, 1993.

Spirit: *The Twelve Dreams of Dr. Sardonicus*, Epic, 1970 • *Feedback*, Epic, 1971 • *Best Of*, Epic, 1973 • *Time Circle*, Epic, 1991.

Stokes, Simon: *Simon Stokes and the Black Whip Thrill Band*, Spin, 1973.

Williams, Jerry: *Jerry Williams*, Spin, 1972.

Young, Neil: *Neil Young*, Reprise, 1968 • *After the Gold Rush*, Reprise, 1970 • "Southern Man," Reprise, 1970 • *On the Beach*, Reprise, 1974 • *Tonight's the Night*, Reprise, 1975 • *Zuma*, Reprise, 1975 • "Like a Hurricane," Reprise, 1976 •

American Stars 'n' Bars, Reprise, 1977 • *Comes a Time*, Reprise, 1979 • *Hawks and Doves*, Reprise, 1980 • *Re-Ac-Tor*, Reprise, 1981 • "Southern Pacific," Reprise, 1981 • *Trans*, Geffen, 1982 • *Old Ways*, Geffen, 1985 • *Lucky Thirteen*, Geffen, 1993 • *Unplugged*, Reprise, 1993.

Young, Neil, and Crazy Horse: "Cinnamon Girl," Reprise, 1969 • *Everybody Knows This Is Nowhere*, Reprise, 1969 • "Cowgirl in the Sand," Reprise, 1970 • "Down by the River," Reprise, 1970 • "Only Love Can Break Your Heart," Reprise, 1970 • *Live Rust*, Reprise, 1979 • *Rust Never Sleeps*, Reprise, 1979 • *Life*, Geffen, 1987 • "Mansion on the Hill," Reprise, 1990 • *Ragged Glory*, Reprise, 1990 • *Weld*, Reprise, 1991 • *Sleeps with Angels*, Reprise, 1994.

COLLECTIONS

Where the Buffalo Roam soundtrack, Backstreet, 1980.

Gerry Bron

Gerry Bron is a microcosm of the British recording industry of the last 40 years. Bron has been a sheet music printer, a clarinetist, a music publisher, an artist manager (Gene Pitney, Marianne Faithfull, Manfred Mann, Colosseum, Uriah Heep), a record producer (the aforementioned minus Faithfull, plus the Bonzo Dog Band, Osibisa, Juicy Lucy), a booking agent (all of the above), a record label owner (Bronze), a recording studio owner and manager (Roundhouse). Now, at an age when mere mortals are contemplating a leisurely retirement, the vigorous Bron has embarked upon a new career as a manager of record producers. Gerry Bron Management boasts an impressive roster of top producers and engineers, including Mike Howlett (see entry) and Stuart Epps.

Bron was born in 1933 in London. His father owned Bron's Orchestral Service, which was the largest supplier of sheet music in England. When Bron was 16, he was forced to leave school to learn the family business because his father wasn't well, "although I suspect I may have left school at 16 anyway," Bron confides.

The elder Bron recovered from his illness and gravitated toward publishing. One of his partners in publishing was Gene Pitney's manager, and the Brons ended up with the "doubtful pleasure of looking after Pitney's affairs." Pitney was huge in America starting in 1961, but not in England. He finally hit in England with "Twenty Four Hours from Tulsa" (co-written by Burt Bacharach; see entry) in 1963.

Bron came to handle Pitney's publishing for Europe, and they began discussing making records together. Bron made all of the demos for the publishing company, and they were good enough that people often mistook them for masters. This gave Bron the clue that he had "some ability in that area." Also important to Bron's development were the arrangers on staff at the publishing company, particularly Ron Goodwin, who scored many films and had a recording contract with EMI. His producer was George Martin (see entry).

Bron watched Martin produce Goodwin's orchestral music at Abbey Road, and thought, "I like what George is doing. That's really what I want to do." As Bron came to function as Pitney's European manager and occasional producer in the mid-'60s, he also began to manage Marianne Faithfull. Manfred Mann often appeared on the same TV shows as Pitney and Faithfull, and on their recommendation, Bron came to manage him as well. When Mann ran into difficulties with his producer, Bron also assumed those duties, producing the hit singles "Ha Ha Said the Clown" (No. 4 U.K.), "My Name Is Jack" (No. 8 U.K.) and "Fox on the Run" (No. 5 U.K.).

"I found myself producing pop records, and then found myself producing the heavier type of music, namely Colosseum and Uriah Heep," Bron recalls. Led by ex–John Mayall drummer Jon Hiseman, Colosseum was a pioneer of jazz-rock fusion in the U.K., and had three Top 20 albums there (*Those Who Are About to Die Salute You, Valentyne Suite, Live*). With the Nice and Yes, they helped usher in the progressive era in the late '60s.

Manfred Mann induced Bron to see the Bonzo Dog (Doo Dah) Band at a club in Manchester in 1968. "There was only one true musician (Neil Innes, later of the Rutles) in a band of seven. They were one of the greatest stage acts you'll ever see. They were so funny. I went into the studio with them to record some demos, and midway through a song, I noticed that the banjo of Vernon Dudley Bowhay-Nowell was painfully wrong. I asked him what he was playing in the chorus, and he said, 'I don't know.' I said, 'You've been playing that on stage for three months,' and he said, 'They won't tell me what the chords are.' They were trying to get rid of him. That's the way most things went with them. They really needed beating around the ears when it came to getting it right. On the other hand, if they got it too right, it was no longer funny. You had to steer a rather curious course between too good and too bad."

Bron discovered an embryonic band with heavy leanings called Spice in 1969. Their name soon changed to Uriah Heep. Bron and the Heep put out seven Top 40 albums in the U.K. and five in the U.S., and although the

Heep eventually ran out of ideas and went up in a flaming ball of bombast, *Demons and Wizards* (No. 20 U.K.) is a classic art-metal album, with "Easy Livin' " and "The Wizard" the highlights of a fine collection.

Bron started his own label, Bronze, in 1971. "I was a producer signed to Philips who had four acts on the label: Uriah Heep, Juicy Lucy, Colosseum, and Richard Barnes," he recalls. "They ran into severe distribution problems. I got them to release me in 1971 without any thought as to what the hell I was going to do. I phoned up Island, which had also had distribution problems with Philips, and asked if they would like to form a label, and that's how Bronze came to be.

"I probably should have continued as a record producer and let somebody else run the label for me," he adds. "Any good business person can run a label, but— not to sound conceited—there aren't that many people who can produce records."

Bron ran Roundhouse Studio for 10 years as part-owner and manager, until November 1995. Previously, he had owned the studio as headquarters for Bronze Records. Now he is a producer manager.

His background as a producer helps him relate to his charges. "One of the producers said to me, 'At last I'm being managed by someone who knows what I'm talking about.' When he tells me that he is going to do this, that, and the other thing, I know what he's talking about because I've done it myself. I can organize things easily. I can spot problems coming. They can have confidence in me because I'm not one of these A&R dummies who doesn't know a 2-inch tape from a half-inch tape."

Bron stopped producing in the late '80s, but you never know what may happen. "I can only produce when I love what the artist is doing," Bron says. "If you haven't got that enthusiasm, you won't get any results. I don't see that happening again, and I also don't want to stay up to 2 or 3 in the morning anymore. But never say never." —ERIC OLSEN

Bonzo Dog Band: *Gorilla,* Liberty, 1967 • *The Doughnut in Granny's Greenhouse,* Liberty, 1968.
Colosseum: *Those Who Are About to Die, We Salute You,* Fontana, 1969 • *Valentyne Suite,* Vertigo, 1969 • *Daughter of Time,* Fontana, 1970 • *Collector's Colosseum,* Bronze, 1971, 1977 • *Live,* Bronze, 1971.
Colosseum II: *Strange New Flesh,* Island, 1976.
Hensley, Ken: *Proud Words on a Dusty Shelf,* Bronze, 1973 • *Eager to Please,* Bronze, 1975.
Juicy Lucy: *Juicy Lucy,* Vertigo, 1970 • *Lie Back and Enjoy It,* Vertigo, 1970 • "Pretty Woman," Vertigo, 1970 • "Who Do You Love," Vertigo, 1970.

Mann, Manfred: "Ha Ha Said the Clown," Fontana, 1967 • "Fox on the Run," Fontana, 1968 • "My Name Is Jack," Fontana, 1968.
Osibisa: *Welcome Home,* Bronze, 1975 • *Ojah Awake,* Bronze, 1976 • *Live at the Royal Festival Hall,* Bronze, 1977.
Pitney, Gene: *Pitney '75* (2 tracks), Bronze, 1975.
U-Boat: *U-Boat,* Bronze, 1977.
Uriah Heep: *Salisbury,* Bronze/Mercury, 1970 • *Uriah Heep,* Bronze/Mercury, 1970 • *Very 'Eavy Very 'Umble,* Bronze/Mercury, 1970 • *Look at Yourself,* Bronze/Mercury, 1971 • *Demons and Wizards,* Bronze/Mercury, 1972 • "Easy Livin'," Bronze/Mercury, 1972 • *The Magician's Birthday,* Bronze/Mercury, 1972 • *Live,* Bronze/Mercury, 1973 • *Sweet Freedom,* Bronze/WB, 1973 • *Wonderworld,* Bronze/WB, 1974 • *Return to Fantasy,* Bronze/WB, 1975 • *The Best Of,* Bronze/Mercury, 1976 • *Firefly,* Bronze/WB, 1977 • *Fallen Angel,* Bronze/Chrysalis, 1978 • *Innocent Victim,* Bronze/WB, 1978 • *A Time of Revelation,* Castle, 1996.

Ian Broudie

Ian Broudie has quietly produced an exceptional body of intelligent, infectious pop rock for himself and numerous others (Echo and the Bunnymen, the Wild Swans, Frazier Chorus, Alison Moyet, Northside, the Fall, the Icicle Works, Sleeper) that is Beatlesque in the best sense of the word. Broudie's uncannily melodic ear yields music that is sweet but not cloying, effervescent but not lightweight, and spiced with surprising touches (often psychedelia) that taste good and are good for you. Broudie's own band, the Lightning Seeds, has produced four albums of taste and distinction. Two (*Cloudcuckooland* and *Sense*) stand with the best pop rock of the last 20 years.

Broudie was born in 1958 in Liverpool, England. He grew up under the influence of an older brother who gravitated toward the songy side of the '60s: the Beatles, Lovin' Spoonful, Bob Dylan. Following in the footsteps of many an intrepid young music man, Broudie would sneak into his brother's room and play records without permission.

Naturally, the first band he ever saw live was the Beatles when an uncle took him to see them in Liverpool. Seeing them is all he can really claim, since Beatlemania drove the girls in the audience into such a screaming frenzy he barely heard a note.

By 1976, punk was emerging in England, and the

young guitarist came under the sway of the Sex Pistols, the Stranglers, Buzzcocks, and the Clash. He also loved American bands like Television, Talking Heads, Patti Smith, and MC5. Broudie responded to the punk attitude, but still loved songs and a good beat. He got a job loading equipment at a club called Eric's on Matthew Street and watched the sound checks of the bands that came through the club.

"I realized that these people are human, not superhuman, and I thought, I can do that," he recalls. So he did. He got into his first band (Big in Japan) with another ambitious guitarist named Bill Drummond. Drummond ended up starting the record label Zoo (not the '90s label of the same name) and managing a couple of young Liverpudlian groups—Echo and the Bunnymen and the Teardrop Explodes. After Big in Japan, Broudie joined the Original Mirrors (with singer Steve Allen, ex–Deaf School), who recorded an album with Alan Winstanley (see entry). Though the album wasn't particularly successful, Broudie got a feel for the studio. Then, Drummond asked Broudie to help out Echo. "They were friends and I thought I could make their songs sound better. I started arranging songs, taking the band into the studio, and that ended up being part of their first LP (Crocodiles, No. 17 U.K.). Then I was a producer," Broudie recalls.

"It was weird, really. I never intended to be that and in some ways I don't know if it was the right thing to do, but I did. I stopped writing and started producing." He was 21.

"After I did another Echo and the Bunnymen album (Porcupine, No. 2 U.K.), "I think I was still resisting the idea of being a producer, but people asked me to do things. I think I approached it in a fairly haphazard way. I worked with a real assortment of bands in the '80s (Wall of Voodoo, the Fall, Icicle Works, Human Drama).

"I have always approached production as a songwriter—my philosophy is that the song is God—and I decided in 1989 that if I am ever going to write some songs I better get on with it. So I managed to get some time, and very cheaply we did a home recording, which ended up as Cloudcuckooland."

There is irony in the fact that as Broudie returned to writing and recording, he returned to production greatness as well. After his breakthrough work with Echo and the Bunnymen, which was somehow brooding but bright at the same time (especially the sensational singles "Do It Clean," "Back of Love," No. 19 U.K., and "The Cutter," No. 8 U.K.), the rest of the '80s were relatively fallow (notable exceptions include the Fall's "Hey! Luciani" and Icicle Works' "Understanding Jane").

But in 1989, as he wrote songs in preparation for his first album, Broudie produced and played guitar and organ on the criminally overlooked Space Flower album by the Wild Swans (essentially, singer/songwriter Paul Simpson and a backup band). A bubbly, neopsychedelic great, Flower is a bookend to Broudie's Cloudcuckooland. Broudie's wah-wah guitar is taffy for the ears as Simpson's lightly processed baritone irresistibly depicts his love-flavored "Melting Blue Delicious." Seldom have form and content melded so delectably. Other delights include "Butterfly Girl," "I'm a Lighthouse," and the epic "Sea of Tranquility," all with Broudie's tasty guitar, reminiscent of George Harrison at his Rickenbacker best. Throughout, Simpson sings like Morrissey sans the attitude.

In 1991, Broudie produced Chicken Rhythms (No. 19 U.K.) by Manchester's Northside. A fortuitous combination of Happy Mondays and Badfinger, the album's highlight is "Take 5," a power-pop classic driven by chiming guitar, percolating percussion, and a great melody. Dance floor revelers on both sides of the Atlantic gyrated ecstatically to Broudie's extended remix of the song all that summer.

Also from 1991 is Frazier Chorus's Ray. Singer/songwriter/keyboardist Tim Freeman's breathy vocals glide over slices of techno-pop ("Heaven," "We Love You," "Prefer You Dead") that ease into the brain and never leave. The electronics of Ray were a departure for Broudie.

"I had just recorded Cloudcuckooland and I did some programming on that for the first time," he says. "Frazier Chorus got in touch just after they heard it, and they were looking for that same sort of thing. I thought it turned out really well—Tim is a real talent. But I was sitting there with computers, and working on it was a little more head than heart sometimes."

In 1994, Broudie produced Alison Moyet's Essex, her best work since the breakup of Yaz in 1984. Highlights are the lush techno-pop of "Falling" and a near-operatic cover of Jules Shear's "Whispering Your Name" (No. 18 U.K.). Which leaves Broudie's own work with the Lightning Seeds.

Cloudcuckooland is a treasure. Working essentially alone, Broudie cobbled together a seamless collection that boasts no less than three great songs. The opener, "All I Want," begins with a synth swirl and another perfect Broudie guitar line. He sings with bright earnestness in a tenor reminiscent of the Zombies' Colin Blunstone—or Pet Shop Boy Neil Tennant (see entry) after a few testosterone treatments: "All I want to do / Is make you listen from now on / Stop what's going on / Stop what's going wrong," as he struggles to keep it all from slipping away. "Sweet Dreams" conveys the storm rush of passion and the spun-sugar cocoon of its aftermath in Broudie's most lilting voice.

"Pure" (No. 16 U.K.) was such a hit on American modern rock radio that it actually cracked the Top 40. Possibly the best pop-rock song of the last 10 years, the pure melody and chirping synth counterpoint are so compelling that the song doesn't even need a traditional chorus. The odd ABAB BBB structure is interrupted by a guitar break that gooses the song to even greater heights on the final two B iterations.

In an era of rasping grunge and punishing industrial music, Broudie's melodic purity has generated bemusement. "I try and do things in a positive, uplifting way," he says. "It can be taken as light and fluffy. In many ways that has been the criticism of it, but I think there is a depth to it. What it's all about is risk, taking self-expression and putting it in an area where it might be great, but close to something else [not great].

"I think that's the definition of pop music, but pop music can be dismissed as pap. I think there is quality pop music that transcends everything else and can be the music of the time." —ERIC OLSEN AND DAWN DARLING

Dodgy: *The Dodgy Album,* A&M, 1993.
Echo and the Bunnymen: *Crocodiles,* Korova/Sire, 1980 • "The Cutter," Korova/Sire, 1983 • *Porcupine,* Korova/Sire, 1983 • *Songs to Learn and Sing,* Korova/Sire, 1985, 1987.
Fall, The: *The Domesday Pay-Off,* Big Time, 1987 • *I Am Curious Oranj,* Beggars Banquet, 1988 • *458489 A Sides,* Beggars Banquet, 1990 • *458489 B Sides,* Beggars Banquet, 1990.
Frank and Walters: "After All," Go!, 1992.
Frazier Chorus: "Cloud 8," Charisma, 1990 • *Ray* (8 tracks), Charisma, 1991.
Hall, Terry: *The Collection: Terry Hall,* Chrysalis, 1993 • *Rainbows* (EP), Anxious, 1995 • *Rainbows Pt. 2* (EP), Anxious, 1995.
Hoovers, The: "Mr. Average," Produce, 1991.
Human Drama: *Hopes Prayers Dreams Heart Soul Mind Love Life Death,* RCA, 1989.
Icicle Works: *If You Want to Defeat Your Enemy Sing His Song,* Beggars Banquet, 1987.
Katydids: *Shangri-La* (2 tracks), Reprise, 1991.
Lightning Seeds: "All I Want," MCA, 1990 • *Cloudcuckooland,* MCA, 1990 • "Pure," MCA, 1990 • "Sweet Dreams," MCA, 1990 • "Lucky You," MCA, 1992 • "Sense," MCA, 1992 • *Sense,* MCA, 1992 • "The Life of Riley," MCA, 1992 • *Jollification,* Trauma, 1994 • "Change," Capitol, 1995 (*Clueless* soundtrack) • *Dizzy Heights,* Epic, 1996.
Moyet, Alison: "Whispering Your Name," Columbia, 1993 • *Essex* (8 tracks), Columbia, 1994.
Northside: "My Rising Star," Factory/London, 1990, 1997

(*Too Young to Know, Too Wild to Care: The Factory Story,* Part 1) • *Chicken Rhythms,* Factory/Geffen, 1991 • "Take 5," Factory/Geffen, 1991.
Popinjays: *Flying Down to Mono Valley,* Epic, 1992.
Primitives, The: *Galore,* Lazy/RCA, 1991.
Sleeper: *Smart,* Arista, 1995.
13 Engines: *A Blur to Me Now,* SBK, 1991.
Three O'Clock: *Even After,* IRS, 1986.
TV 21: *A Thin Red Line,* Deram, 1981.
Wall of Voodoo: *Seven Days in Sammytown,* IRS, 1985.
Wedding Present: *Hit Parade 1,* First Warning/RCA, 1992 • *Hit Parade 2,* First Warning, 1993.
Wendys, The: *Gobbledygook,* EastWest, 1991.
Wild Swans: *Space Flower,* Sire/Reprise, 1990.

Steve Brown

B eginning as a teen-age roadie for Elton John, Steve Brown has enjoyed, or perhaps survived, a roller-coaster career of big hits all over the British pop and rock spectrum as chief engineer at the Record Company and, later, as producer.

His production credits include the sophisticated neo-soul of ABC's "Tears Are Not Enough" (No. 19 U.K.), the classic techno-pop cascade of B-Movie's "Nowhere Girl," George Michael's teeny debut on Wham!'s *Fantastic* (No. 1 U.K.), Freddie Mercury's self-titled album (No. 4 U.K.), the militant Clashisms of the Manic Street Preachers' *Generation Terrorists* (No. 13 U.K.) and *The Holy Bible* (No. 6 U.K.).

His best production is the psychedelic stomp of the Cult's *Love* (No. 4 U.K.). But the line between pure pop pleasure and grated cheese is slim indeed, and Brown paid the price for some of his early pop success. He has thrown up a defiant wall of guitars against that, and the future looks bright again.

Brown was born in London in 1955. He was training to be an airline pilot when he was smitten by a young woman who took him to his first concert (Genesis) in the early '70s, and changed his career path. Brown dove into music and even managed a band at his school that included future production giant Steve Lillywhite (see entry) on bass.

While studying for his final exams to become a pilot, Brown worked at a gas station. Elton John came in to tank up and Brown chatted with the pop star about his love of music. After a few such encounters, John offered Brown a spot on his road crew. Brown contemplated the offer for a few days, chucked school, and headed off for the rock 'n' roll life. He was 17.

Brown roadied for 10 weeks, meeting producers Ken Scott and Gus Dudgeon (see entries), who took him to Trident Studios where they were rough-mixing *Don't Shoot Me, I'm Only the Piano Player*. He took one look inside the studio and said, "This is for me." Only it wasn't, yet.

When he approached Trident about a job, any job, they said he was too young. Determined, Brown hung out at Phonogram Studios in London and was finally hired as a tea boy in 1973. He worked his way up to engineer, and then to chief engineer. He moved to the Record Company, along the way engineering for the Sex Pistols, Graham Parker and the Rumour, and the Boomtown Rats. Brown's first production was an immediate hit: ABC's "Tears Are Not Enough." George Michael heard that recording and asked Brown to produce the first Wham! album.

Fantastic was pure teen soul pop that showed off Michael's voice and melodic gift. The sharp production was clean enough for the pop market and self-aware enough for the new wave market. For good or ill, Wham!'s success generated scads of similar business: B-Movie, Blue Rondo, Haysi Fantayzee. Suddenly, Brown realized that he had been typecast as a U.K.-based, white dance producer, and he was taken aback. He began ringing up people like the Damned and the Clash and the Stranglers, saying, "Hey, can I produce your record?" They said, "Well, you're not quite our cup of tea." So he took a two-year rest.

A revived Brown was visiting his friend John Giddings at the TBA agency when the Cult were there looking for representation. The Cult left their tape on Giddings' desk. Brown went in, pocketed the tape, and took it back to his flat. "It was a 90-minute demo, and about an hour into it, on the B-side, I found this track that turned out to be 'She Sells Sanctuary' [No. 15 U.K.]," he recalls. "I edited and transferred from one cassette machine to another, taking out all the bits I didn't want, and putting in all the bits I did want. I took that down to the band's rehearsal room and they listened to it.

"Billy Duffy and Ian Asbury looked at each other and said, 'Who the hell is this guy?' I told them I was Wham!'s producer. I asked them if they wanted to be on *Top of the Pops*, which I had learned was the first question to ask. They said, 'Yeah, we definitely want to be on *Top of the Pops*.' So we made 'She Sells Sanctuary' and we went on to make *Love*. That album was amazing."

Since then, Brown has done some production, most notably the Manic Street Preachers, but he hasn't regained the Wham!/Cult level of popular success.

After having children and resorting his priorities, Brown is ready to take on the world again.

"I am excited about working with new bands like the Gyres [from Scotland] again," he says. "With a new band, especially now that I am over 40, they look at you and ask, 'How does this compare to Neil Young?' or whoever. They trust me when I say, 'This is really good' or 'This is not good—it's cheesy and tacky and we won't go that way.'

"I say to the band, 'We need to appeal to a lot of people. It might not be the exact way you thought you were going to be, because you are listening to Neil Young and all that. But Neil Young had to start somewhere, and he probably hates the early stuff he did. We need to make an impact in the early days, we need to give you a career like the first Wham! album did for George Michael.'

"My aim is to establish 2.5 million fans around Europe. At that point you can pass wind through a microphone, put it on tape, and people will buy it. Once we've hooked people in, once we've done that, they will listen to anything you say." —ERIC OLSEN AND DAWN DARLING

ABC: "Tears Are Not Enough," London, 1981 • *Absolutely ABC: The Best of ABC*, Mercury, 1990.

Angels, The: *The Howling*, Telegraph, 1986.

Balaam and the Angel: *Live Free or Die*, Virgin, 1988 • *Days of Madness*, Virgin, 1989.

Blue Rondo: *Bees Knees and Chicken Elbows*, Virgin, 1984.

B-Movie: "Nowhere Girl," Some Bizarre/Sire, 1982.

Coast: *Big Jet Rising*, Sugar, 1996.

Cult, The: "Nirvana," Beggars Banquet, 1985 (*One Pound Ninety-Nine*) • "She Sells Sanctuary," Sire, 1985 • *Love*, Sire, 1985 • *Manor Sessions*, Beggars Banquet, 1988 • *Resurrection Joe* (EP), Alex, 1991 • *High Octane Cult*, Warner Bros., 1996.

Godfathers, The: *Unreal World*, Epic, 1991.

Haysi Fantayzee: *Battle Hymns for Children*, Regard, 1983.

High, The: *Hype*, London, 1992.

Manic Street Preachers: *Generation Terrorists*, Columbia, 1991 • *Stay Beautiful* (EP), Columbia, 1991 • *Holy Bible*, CBS U.K., 1994.

Mercury, Freddie: *The Freddie Mercury Album* (2 tracks), Maverick, 1992.

Moyet, Alison: "Love Letters," CBS U.K., 1987.

Nuclear Valdez: *I Am I*, Epic, 1990.

Nunn, Terri: *Moment of Truth*, Mercury, 1992.

Pogues, The: *Pogue Mahone*, Mesa/Bluemoon, 1996.

Ramone, Joey: w/ Holly Beth Vincent, "I Got You Babe," Virgin, 1982, 1991 (*Fun, Filth and Fury*).

Redwood: *Colourblind*, ALMO, 1997.

Then Jerico: "Muscle Deep," London, 1987.

Tony Brown

As the son of a traveling evangelist, Tony Brown was prohibited from listening to pop music during his youth. However, as his track record as one of Nashville's top producers shows, it clearly didn't hurt his musical development.

The way Brown sees it, his musical education just took a different course than most. "We'd play Baptist churches, which is basically a real simple music environment with a piano and a bad choir; black gospel, which has the bands; the Salvation Army, where they had brass and horns and we'd play on the sidewalk; and Pentecostals, where they threw babies in the air and spoke in tongues. So I was actually going through a lot of formats early in my life."

In some ways, he considers his lack of exposure to rock 'n' roll at an early age a blessing. "I can name some producers who grew up with rockabilly or the Beatles, and they are so into that that it always creeps into every song, even if it's a power-pop ballad. I don't have that."

Brown, who has been president of MCA Nashville since 1993, has produced many of Nashville's top acts, including George Strait, Reba McEntire, Wynonna, Vince Gill, Rodney Crowell (see entry), Lyle Lovett, Marty Stuart, Patty Loveless, Steve Earle, Nanci Griffith, and Tracy Byrd. His has worked on more than a half-dozen Grammy Award–winning projects, and was nominated for producer of the year in 1994, making him the first country producer to be nominated since 1979.

In 1995, he won *Mix* magazine's Technical Excellence and Creativity Award for producer of the year. He easily has the highest profile of any of the current crop of country producers, regularly scoring features in such outlets as *GQ* and the *Los Angeles Times Magazine.* *Entertainment Weekly* has proclaimed him one of the 100 most powerful people in the entertainment industry.

Surprisingly, Brown (born 1947) credits much of his success as a producer to his grasp not exceeding his reach. "I think some people that are musicians or writers or artists think there are no limits, and really, there *are* limits. I learned what mine were and accepted them, not as a liability, but maybe that my gift was more my taste and ability to work with musicians, rather than to be a musician."

Given his gospel background, it was natural for the Greensboro, North Carolina, native to go on to play keyboards with the Oak Ridge Boys, a country-gospel outfit, in the early '70s. He then moved to the Sweet Inspirations before joining Elvis Presley's band for two years, until the death of the King in 1977. He next signed on with Emmylou Harris's band, eventually playing with Harris's bandmate Rodney Crowell and Rosanne Cash from 1980 until 1983.

It was during his time with Harris that he finally received a traditional pop education. "Emmy really is a musicologist," he says. "When we were on the bus or in the car, she'd be listening to country music and she played a lot of tapes—Rodney, Gram Parsons, Merle Haggard, Buck Owens, Hank Williams—so I kind of got turned onto country music through her and actually learned how country rock got started. And between [band members] Hank DeVito, Emory Gordy Jr., and Rodney, I sort of learned about Elvis and the Beatles."

Such a statement is staggering given the fact that Brown played with Presley. (The only jewelry he wears is a ring Presley gave him.) However, he explains that during his tenure with Elvis, he saw Presley more as a pop icon than a musical pioneer. "When I played with Elvis, I was coming out of gospel music. Elvis was a celebrity to me, and once I got around people [like Emmy, Rodney, and Emory] who were really into music, it turned me onto music for music's sake."

While still working as a keyboardist, Brown began his association with RCA, first in L.A. doing A&R for an affiliated pop label, and then in Nashville. "When I got into the record business from being a musician, my intentions were to get into the secular record business. I'd never produced a record, and I wanted to produce, but I couldn't get anyone at RCA to let me produce anything because I didn't have a track record. And I kept wondering, How do you get a track record if you don't get an opportunity?"

Opportunity came in the form of black gospel music titan Shirley Caesar in 1983. A friend of Brown's had signed Caesar to Word Records and asked him to help produce. "I'd never worked in black gospel music, but I just sort of went with the moment because it was Shirley Caesar—she's like Mahalia Jackson," says Brown. "It was just a matter of jumping into that moment and hanging on and I learned that's sort of basically what you do, you help when you have to and otherwise you just shut up and keep the creative process happening."

His work with Caesar gained him his entrance into country production, starting with Steve Wariner and Razzy Bailey. He made the move to MCA in 1984 when the legendary Jimmy Bowen (see entry), who was heading the label, came calling. In his 1997 autobiography, *Rough Mix,* Bowen calls Brown "as fine a protégé as I could have had at MCA."

Under Bowen's watchful (and sometimes skeptical) eye, Brown helped pioneer the progressive country movement when he signed Nanci Griffith, Steve Earle, and Lyle Lovett to MCA in the mid-'80s. Brown says Lovett's "vision was just as strong the day he walked into my office as it is now. He was just as fully formed, the hair, the clothes."

"Those projects are probably the [albums] that shaped my career and shaped my whole look at the way you cut records," he says. He declares that Earle's 1986 MCA debut *Guitar Town* is his favorite record that he ever made. "That's the one I go back to," he says, "I love it better now. It was one of those things we—me and [co-producer] Emory Gordy Jr. and [session guitarist] Richard Bennett—were really trying to make our mark. We finished it and nobody liked it but the press, and the press turned our company and Nashville back on to it."

It was also during that time that Brown reunited with his former bandmate Crowell to create country music history when they co-produced Crowell's seminal 1988 album *Diamonds & Dirt,* the first country album to spawn five No. 1 singles. Brown then moved into a more commercial period, taking over production duties for MCA artists Strait and McEntire after Bowen moved to Capitol Nashville. McEntire has recently begun to produce herself along with her engineer, but Strait and Brown remain a tight twosome. The pair have their routine down: they express-mail songs back and forth, ultimately spending two days selecting the songs that have passed muster with both of them. Then, unbelievably, Strait commits only four days to recording his vocals per album, making the trip to Nashville from his Texas home.

"We cut Monday through Thursday, and I'll go, 'Why don't you give me Friday this time, just in case we don't get a vocal?' " says Brown. "And he says, 'Have I ever let you down?' " While it might be easy to criticize their speed, the proof of Strait's success is his dominance as one of the top country male artists for almost 20 years. Plus, Brown plans far in advance. "I book every musician that's going to play on the record, except for if I use strings or some other instrument. They're there for all the sessions. Those guys play better for an artist they really respect who's got his or her act together. You want to be your best when George is singing that song, and George comes in prepared, trust me."

While Strait is exceptionally speedy, country albums are generally cut much quicker than their pop counterparts. Brown defends the short studio stays: "With country music, the arrangements are so simple. In fact, the thing to be really aware of is not to overarrange," he says. "It's all about the singer and the songs and it's not about the production value. It's not demanding production value, meaning any elaborate arrangement like on a Celine Dion, or, hell, even a Smashing Pumpkins record. . . . I would say 50 percent of my No. 1 records were cut in the first take. Sometimes I'll even cut it for another hour even if I know I have it, just because I think everybody will be thinking I'm moving [too fast]."

No one thought Brown was moving too fast during production of Wynonna's 1996 release, *Revelations* (No. 9), which took a year and a half to record, a virtual lifetime in country music. "It cost like a pop record and it was the least successful one we did," says Brown, shaking his head. "There was a lot of indecisiveness about the material," Brown says, his frustration showing. "She was going through a lot of personal things, like getting married and having babies, and she couldn't sing, and we just recut and recut and remixed."

Brown has no future plans to work with Wynonna. "I feel like Wynonna and I did those three records [platinum *Revelations,* quintuple-platinum *Wynonna,* No. 4, and platinum *Tell Me Why* No. 5], we've done it and we'll never recapture that again."

However, there have been other times when Brown hasn't been so involved in the decision to stop working with an act. "Steve Earle and I were on a panel at Belmont College and were talking about the records and someone asked him about the next record [after *Copperhead Road*] and he said, 'Well, Tony doesn't know it, but he's not doing the next record.' That's how I officially found out."

Fear not, Brown is in no danger of having open spaces on his dance card; he gets requests to work on albums by artists of all different musical stripes. For the most part, he's not interested in noncountry productions. "I don't want to get myself in a position of doing things that I'm not really qualified to do." However, he does send out an invitation to one rock 'n' roller. "The only kind of pop record I could produce would be if Bruce Springsteen wanted to cut an acoustic record in Nashville. I'm such a big fan of his, and I've actually drawn from his music. It he came to Nashville and said, 'Do you want to do it?' I'd say, 'Absolutely!' " —MELINDA NEWMAN

Bellamy Brothers: *Greatest Hits,* Vol. 3, MCA, 1989.
Brown, Marty: *High and Dry,* MCA, 1991 • *Wild Kentucky Skies,* MCA, 1993.

Buffett, Jimmy: *Riddles in the Sand,* MCA, 1984 • *Last Mango in Paris,* MCA, 1985 • *Boats, Beaches, Bars and Ballads,* MCA, 1992.

Byrd, Tracy: *Tracy Byrd,* MCA, 1993 • *Love Lessons,* MCA, 1995 • *Big Love,* MCA Nashville, 1996 • "Don't Love Make a Diamond Shine," MCA, 1997 • "Don't Take Her She's All I Got," MCA, 1997 • "Good Ol' Fashioned Love," MCA Nashville, 1997.

Caesar, Shirley: *Jesus, I Love Calling Your Name,* Word/Epic, 1983, 1992.

Campbell, Glen: w/ Steve Wariner, "The Hand That Rocks the Cradle," MCA, 1987

Cartwright, Lionel: *Lionel Cartwright,* MCA, 1989 • *I Watched It on the Radio,* MCA, 1990 • *Chasin' the Sun,* MCA, 1991.

Chesnutt, Mark: "Trouble," Decca Nashville, 1995 • *Wings,* Decca Nashville, 1995 • *Greatest Hits,* Decca Nashville, 1996 • "It's a Little Too Late," Decca, 1997 • "Let It Rain," Decca, 1997.

Collie, Mark: *Hardin County Line,* MCA, 1990 • *Born and Raised in Black and White,* MCA, 1991.

Crowell, Rodney: *Diamonds and Dirt,* Columbia, 1987, 1988 • "I Couldn't Leave You if I Tried," Columbia, 1988 • w/ Rosanne Cash, "It's Such a Small World," Columbia, 1988 • "Above and Beyond," Columbia, 1989 • "After All This Time," Columbia, 1989 • "She's Crazy for Leavin'," Columbia, 1989 • *Keys to the Highway,* Columbia, 1990 • *Let the Picture Paint Itself,* MCA, 1994 • *Jewel of the South,* MCA, 1995.

Cryner, Bobbie: *Girl of Your Dreams,* MCA Nashville, 1996.

Dean, Billy: *Greatest Hits,* Liberty, 1994.

Desert Rose Band: *True Love,* Curb, 1991.

Earle, Steve: *Guitar Town,* MCA, 1986 • *Exit O,* MCA, 1987 • *Copperhead Road,* Uni, 1988 • *Essential Steve Earle,* MCA, 1993 • *Ain't Ever Satisfied: The Steve Earle Collection,* HIPP, 1996.

Ely, Joe: *Love and Danger,* MCA, 1992.

Gill, Vince: "Never Knew Lonely," MCA, 1989 • *When I Call Your Name,* MCA, 1989 • "When I Call Your Name," MCA, 1990 • *Pocket Full of Gold,* MCA, 1990 • "That's All Right," Epic Soundtrax, 1992 (*Honeymoon in Vegas* soundtrack) • *I Still Believe in You,* MCA, 1992 • *Let There Be Peace on Earth,* MCA, 1993 • "Tryin' to Get over You," MCA, 1994 • *When Love Finds You,* MCA, 1994 • *Souvenirs,* MCA, 1995 • *High Lonesome Sound,* MCA Nashville, 1996 • "A Little More Love," MCA, 1997 • "Pretty Little Andriana," MCA, 1997 • "You and You Alone," MCA, 1997.

Griffith, Nanci: *Lone Star State of Mind,* MCA, 1987 • *Little Love Affairs,* MCA, 1988 • *One Fair Summer Evening,* MCA, 1988 • *The MCA Years: A Retrospective,* MCA, 1993 • w/ the Crickets, "Well . . . All Right," Decca, 1996 [*Not Fade Away (Remembering Buddy Holly)*].

House, James: *Hard Times for an Honest Man,* MCA, 1990.

Joel, Billy: "Light As the Breeze," A&M, 1995 (*Tower of Song: The Songs of Leonard Cohen*).

Jones, George, and Tammy Wynette: *One,* MCA, 1995.

Krekel, Tim: *Crazy Me,* Capricorn, 1979.

Larson, Nicolette: *Say When,* MCA, 1985.

Loveless, Patty: *Patty Loveless,* MCA, 1987 • *Honky Tonk Angel,* MCA, 1988 • *If My Heart Had Windows,* MCA, 1988 • "Timber I'm Falling in Love," MCA, 1989 • *On Down the Line,* MCA, 1990 • *Up Against My Heart,* MCA, 1991 • *Greatest Hits,* MCA, 1993.

Lovett, Lyle: *Lyle Lovett,* Curb/MCA, 1986 • *Pontiac,* Curb/MCA, 1987 • *Lyle Lovett and His Large Band,* Curb/MCA, 1989 • "Stand By Your Man," SBK/EMI, 1993 (*The Crying Game* soundtrack).

McAnally, Mac: *Live and Learn,* MCA, 1992 • *Knots,* MCA, 1994.

McBride and the Ride: *Burnin' Up the Road,* MCA, 1990 • *Sacred Ground,* MCA, 1992 • *Hurry Sundown,* MCA, 1993.

McEntire, Reba: *Merry Christmas to You,* MCA, 1987 • *Reba,* MCA, 1988 • *Rumor Has It,* MCA, 1990 • *For My Broken Heart,* MCA, 1991 • *It's Your Call,* MCA, 1992 • *Read My Mind,* MCA, 1994 • "The Heart Is a Lonely Hunter," MCA, 1995 • *Starting Over,* MCA Nashville, 1995.

Murphy, David Lee: *Out with a Bang,* MCA, 1994 • "Dust on the Bottle," MCA, 1995 • *Gettin' the Good Stuff,* MCA Nashville, 1996 • "All Lit Up in Love," MCA, 1997 • "Breakfast in Birmingham," MCA, 1997 • "Just Don't Wait Around Til She's Leavin," MCA Nashville, 1997.

Raybon Brothers: "Butterfly Kisses," MCA, 1997 • w/ Olivia Newton-John, "Falling," MCA, 1997 • *Raybon Brothers,* MCA, 1997 • "The Way She's Looking," MCA, 1997.

Snider, Todd: *Songs for the Daily Planet,* Margaritaville, 1994.

Strait, George: *Pure Country* soundtrack, MCA, 1992 • *Easy Come, Easy Go,* MCA, 1993 • *Lead On,* MCA, 1994 • "The Big One," MCA, 1994 • "Check Yes or No," MCA, 1995 • *Strait out of the Box,* MCA, 1995 • "Blue Clear Sky," MCA, 1996 • *Blue Clear Sky,* MCA, 1996 • "Carried Away," MCA, 1996 • "Carrying Your Love with Me," MCA, 1997 • "One Night at a Time," MCA, 1997 • "Today My World Slipped Away," MCA Nashville, 1997.

Stuart, Marty: *Hillbilly Rock,* MCA, 1989 • *Tempted,* MCA, 1991 • *This One's Gonna Hurt You,* MCA, 1992 • *Love and Luck,* MCA, 1994 • *Marty Party Hit Pack,* MCA, 1995 • *Honky Tonkin'' What I Do Best,* MCA Nashville, 1996 • "Sweet Love," MCA, 1997.

Tyler, Kris: "What a Woman Knows," Rising Tide, 1997 • *Keeping Your Kisses,* Rising Tide, 1997.

Wariner, Steve: "Some Fools Never Learn," MCA, 1985 • "Life's Highway," MCA, 1986 • "Starting over Again," MCA, 1986 • "You Can Dream of Me," MCA, 1986 • *Greatest Hits,* MCA, 1987 • "Lynda," MCA, 1987 • "Small

Town Girl," MCA, 1987 • w/ Glen Campbell, • "The Weekend," MCA, 1987 • *Laredo,* MCA, 1990 • *Greatest Hits,* Vol. 2, MCA, 1991 • *Best Of,* RCA, 1994.

Willis, Kelly: *Well-Travelled Love,* MCA, 1990 • *Bang Bang,* MCA, 1991 • *Kelly Willis,* MCA, 1993.

Wright, Chely: "Just Another Heartache," MCA, 1997.

Wynette, Tammy: *See* Jones, George.

Wynonna: *Wynonna,* MCA, 1992 • *Tell Me Why,* MCA, 1993 • *Revelations,* MCA, 1996 • "To Be Loved by You," Curb, 1996 • *Collection,* Curb, 1997.

Yearwood, Trisha: "Coming Back to You," A&M, 1995 (*Tower of Song: The Songs of Leonard Cohen*) • "How Do I Live?," MCA, 1997 • *Songbook: A Collection of Hits,* MCA Nashville, 1997.

COLLECTIONS

Skynyrd Friends, MCA, 1995.

Cleveland Browne

See STEELY AND CLEVIE

Daniel Bressanutti

See FRONT 242

Lindsey Buckingham

Fleetwood Mac became one of the largest-selling groups in the world in 1975, the year they hired Lindsey Buckingham as a guitarist, singer, and songwriter. It is no accident.

Although he has generously shared production credit with colleagues Richard Dashut and Keith Olsen (see entries), the group themselves and other industry insiders, including Lenny Waronker (see entry), cite Buckingham (born October 3, 1947, in Palo Alto, California)

as the production force behind five studio albums: *Fleetwood Mac Live, Rumours, Tusk* (No. 4), *Mirage* (No. 1), and *Tango in the Night* (No. 7).

Buckingham is regarded as one of the finest and most intuitive arrangers in pop music, alongside Brian Wilson (an early inspiration) and Richard Carpenter (see entries). In particular, Buckingham's genius lies in his ability to take skeletal outlines of songs—often little more than amorphous ideas—and turn them into artfully arranged pop classics.

"If I were to pick one thing as my main contribution to the group," Buckingham states, "it wouldn't be as a guitar player, a singer, or a songwriter. It would be as someone who can take raw material and forge it into something complete—I guess to some degree with more success than I can do with my own material.

"If you heard the way some of their [Christine McVie's and Stevie Nicks's] songs sounded in their raw state, and tried to make sense out of them . . . my contribution was to give them form, and balance these things with what the players would all have to offer the song, and make hit records out of them."

Buckingham learned his craft as a teenager in the San Francisco Bay area experimenting with a 4-track tape machine: learning how to stack parts "and to make them fit, like pieces of a jigsaw puzzle." Buckingham's production style emphasizes this "jigsaw" puzzle metaphor for carefully arranged parts. On the tracks he produced for Dream Academy, Walter Egan, and Semi Twang, his personal stamp is clearly heard in contrast to the other producers' contributions to these albums.

Buckingham's brilliant solo album, *Out of the Cradle,* contains some of the best material and production of his career, including the standout tracks "Countdown," "Don't Look Down," and "Soul Drifter." He pays homage to an early influence on his version of the Kingston Trio's "All My Sorrows," massively overdubbing his own four-part harmonies. —DANIEL J. LEVITIN

Buckingham, Lindsey: "It Was I," Asylum, 1981 • *Law and Order,* Asylum, 1981 • "Trouble," Asylum, 1981 • "Go Insane," Elektra, 1984 • *Go Insane,* Elektra, 1984 • "Trouble," Elektra, 1984 • *Out of the Cradle,* Reprise, 1992 • w/ Stevie Nicks, "Twisted," Warner Bros., 1996 (*Twister* soundtrack).

Dream Academy: *Remembrance Days,* Reprise, 1987.

Egan, Walter: *Fundamental Roll,* Columbia, 1977 • "Magnet and Steel," Columbia, 1978 • *Not Shy,* Columbia, 1978.

Fleetwood Mac: *Fleetwood Mac Live,* Warner Bros., 1979 • "Sara," Warner Bros., 1979 • "Tusk," Warner Bros., 1979 • *Tusk,* Warner Bros., 1979 • "Gypsy," Warner Bros., 1982 • "Hold Me," Warner Bros., 1982 • *Mirage,* Warner Bros.,

1982 • "Big Love," Warner Bros., 1987 • "Everywhere," Warner Bros., 1987 • "Little Lies," Warner Bros., 1987 • "Seven Wonders," Warner Bros., 1987 • *Tango in the Night,* Warner Bros., 1987 • *Greatest Hits,* Reprise, 1988 • "Silver Springs," Reprise, 1997 • *The Dance,* Reprise, 1997.

Welch, Bob: "Sentimental Lady," Capitol, 1977 • *French Kiss,* Capitol, 1977 • *Best Of,* Rhino, 1991.

Steve Buckingham

To pigeonhole two-time Grammy winner Steve Buckingham as only a country producer would be to deny all the work he's done in virtually every other genre of music, including pop, R&B, jazz, Latin, contemporary Christian, and even disco. All told, he's produced at least 27 No. 1 hits. It was under the twinkle of a glittering, spinning disco ball that Buckingham had his first success, as producer of Alicia Bridges' 1978 smash "I Love the Nightlife" (No. 5). As part of the late '70s Atlanta scene, where he was also a noted session guitarist, Buckingham unwittingly jumped on the hot dance scene.

"Alicia was bizarre by today's standards, not to mention 20 years ago," he recalls with a laugh. "People just didn't know how to take her. She was a really ballsy chick with a blonde crew cut. The first thing we cut on her was a song called 'Disco Round.' None of us knew anything about disco, all I was trying to do was make an Al Green record. 'Disco Round' became 'I Love the Nightlife.' It came out on PolyGram and the next thing you know, it became a monstrous disco record. None of us had even set foot in a disco!"

Buckingham's path to Atlanta started in Richmond, Virginia, where he grew up. As a guitar player, he played in a number of beach music and R&B bands, ending up in a group that signed to Columbia, although the outfit never had mainstream success. Buckingham eventually hooked up with publisher and studio owner Bill Lowery and moved to Atlanta, where acts like Atlanta Rhythm Section and Joe South were thriving.

After the international success with Bridges, Buckingham expected projects to beat their way to his door, "and nothing happened," he says with a laugh, so he started making calls, eventually hooking up with Arista head Clive Davis and producing a string of hits for artists like Melissa Manchester, Dionne Warwick, and other hitmakers.

"For a number of years there, it just seemed like,

'Wow, this is easy. You make records, other people call you, they all become hits, there's nothing to this.' After a few years, reality set in and by that time I'd moved to Nashville," Buckingham recalls. "It wasn't necessarily to do country music, but I didn't want to have to be on the road all the time to go to other cities to use studios, and I wanted a farm, I wanted land."

Buckingham worked on noncountry projects, like the Grammy-winning *Follow That Bird* soundtrack. However, eventually he turned to country music when Rick Blackburn, who was then the head of CBS in Nashville, asked him to produce Tammy Wynette. That led to Buckingham's being hired as head of A&R at CBS, where he produced acts like Sweethearts of the Rodeo, Ricky Van Shelton, and Ricky Skaggs. "I'd produce two or three acts and then we'd get [outside] producers to produce other things," Buckingham says. "Now it seems like the trend is if you're given an A&R position, everything's almost always done in-house. And I question the vision of that."

Although most active in country, Buckingham has by no means been limited by the genre. Through the years, he's continued to produce albums by artists in a variety of genres, such as jazz saxophonist Kirk Whalum and gospel greats the Winans, with whom he won his second Grammy Award.

He also stretched the boundaries of country when he began working with Mary Chapin Carpenter, whom he produced with John Jennings. By the time they began work on *Come On, Come On* in 1992, he was beginning to chafe at the confines he felt Sony put on him and some of its more creative artists. "She turned in that album and it was very very dark and it was rejected by the company," he says. "I thought it was very artful in creative ways, but the company thought there was nothing they could do. Roy Wunsch [then head of Sony Nashville] takes her to dinner. She goes to dinner thinking she's done the best piece of work in her life and leaves with the realization that this album has been turned down. It was the worst."

Buckingham went into the studio with Carpenter and Jennings and recut "I Feel Lucky" (No. 4 country), which turned into one of the biggest hits of her career, and added a few songs, including the snappy "The Bug" (No. 16 country), written by Mark Knopfler (see entry). The album that was initially rejected turned into a 3 million seller.

But the artist with whom Buckingham formed his greatest alliance at Sony is Dolly Parton. Their association began when he worked with her as an A&R exec in Sony Nashville, which led to his producing her albums for the last six years. Eventually, he left Sony to form a record label with Parton, Blue Eye Records, which is distributed through Rising Tide/Universal.

They first met in 1989 when Ricky Skaggs was producing an album for Parton. For her next project, she came to Buckingham and asked him to let her produce herself, as well as use her own band in the studio. "She said to me, 'The powers that be say I can't do this,' and I said, 'For better or worse, I'm one of the powers that be.' If I can't trust Dolly Parton's instincts about making a country record, my God, who can I trust?"

Unfortunately, Parton's instincts weren't completely on the mark. "I got to the studio the first day, " recalls Buckingham, "and I listened for about an hour and thought, 'This is not going to work,' just because the guys didn't have the experience to put a record together.' It had nothing to do with their musical abilities. It's a complicated animal to put a record together."

Buckingham ended up serving as a de facto co-producer on the project, "molding things a bit and being there every day." The album, *Eagle When She Flies*, ended up going to No. 1 (country) and started a comeback for Parton.

Although a bona fide superstar, Parton's resurgence at country radio, where she is now virtually ignored, was relatively short-lived. Such treatment infuriates Buckingham. "It's upsetting to see how anyone of immense talent is mistreated or pretty much dismissed," he says. "Particularly when I see someone who's at the top of their game. It would be one thing if she lost her chops, but she still tears it up in the studio."

Following a stint as head of Parton's Blue Eye Records, Buckingham is now senior vice president of Santa Monica–based Vanguard Records. "In a perfect world," he dreams, "I would do maybe one country record a year, a couple of jazz albums a year, and a soundtrack, and I'd be a happy camper." —MELINDA NEWMAN

Ball, David: *Starlite Lounge,* Warner Bros., 1996.

Boone, Larry: *One Way to Go,* Columbia, 1991.

Bridges, Alicia: *Alicia Bridges,* Polydor, 1978 • "I Love the Night Life (Disco 'Round)," Polydor, 1978 • "I Love the Night Life (Disco 'Round)," Casablanca, 1978, 1979 (*A Night at Studio 54*) • *Play It As It Lays,* Polydor, 1979.

Carpenter, Mary Chapin: *Hometown Girl,* Columbia, 1987 • *Come On, Come On,* Columbia, 1992 • ("I Feel Lucky," Columbia, 1992 • "The Bug," Columbia, 1993.

Fricke, Janie: *Saddle in the Wind,* Columbia, 1988.

Gray, Mark: *Magic,* CBS, 1984.

High Inergy: *High Inergy,* Motown, 1981.

Landis, Andy: *Stranger in a Strange Land,* Star Song, 1993.

LaVette, Bettye: "Right in the Middle (of Falling in Love),"

Motown, 1981 • *Tell Me a Lie,* Motown, 1981.

Manchester, Melissa: *For the Working Girl,* Arista, 1980 • *Greatest Hits,* Arista, 1983 • *Essence of,* Arista, 1997.

Morgan, Lorrie: *Something in Red,* RCA, 1990.

Parton, Dolly: *Slow Dancing with the Moon,* Columbia, 1993 • *Heartsongs: Live from Home,* Columbia, 1994 • w/ Loretta Lynn, and Tammy Wynette, *Honky Tonk Angels,* Columbia, 1994 • *Something Special,* Columbia, 1995 • *I Will Always Love You and Other Greatest Hits,* RCA, 1996 • "Peace Train," Flipit, 1996 • *Treasures,* Rising Tide, 1996 • See also Lynn, Loretta.

Reid, Mike: *Turning for Home,* Columbia, 1991.

Riders in the Sky: *Harmony Ranch,* Rounder/CBS, 1991 • *Merry Christmas from Harmony Ranch,* Columbia, 1992.

Sesame Street: *Follow That Bird* soundtrack, RCA, 1985.

Shelton, Ricky Van: *Wild-Eyed Dream,* Columbia, 1986 • *Wild-Eyed Dream/Loving Proof/RVS III,* Legacy, 1986, 1987, 1988, 1995 • *Loving Proof,* Columbia, 1987 • "Somebody Lied," Columbia, 1987 • "Don't We All Have the Right," Columbia, 1988 • "I'll Leave This World Loving You," Columbia, 1988 • "Life Turned Her That Way," Columbia, 1988 • *RVS III,* Columbia, 1988 • "From a Jack to a King," Columbia, 1989 • "Living Proof," Columbia, 1989 • *Sings Christmas,* Columbia, 1989 • *Backroads,* Columbia, 1991 • *Don't Overlook Salvation,* Columbia, 1992 • *Greatest Hits Plus,* Columbia, 1992 • "Wear My Ring Around Your Neck," Epic Soundtrax, 1992 (*Honeymoon in Vegas* soundtrack) • *A Bridge I Didn't Burn,* Columbia, 1993 • *Super Hits,* Columbia, 1995 • *Super Hits,* Vol. 2, Columbia, 1996 • "Our Love," RVS, 1997.

Skaggs, Ricky: *Kentucky Thunder,* Epic, 1989 • "Lovin' Only Me," Epic, 1989.

Sweethearts of the Rodeo: *Sweethearts of the Rodeo,* Columbia, 1986 • *One Time One Night,* Columbia, 1988 • *Buffalo Zone,* Columbia, 1990 • *Sisters,* Columbia, 1991.

Thomas, B.J.: *Night Life,* Columbia, 1989.

Tillis, Pam: *Pam Tillis Collection,* Warner Bros., 1994.

Trevino, Rick: *Dos Mundos,* Sony Discos, 1993 • *Rick Trevino,* Columbia, 1994 • *Looking for the Light,* Columbia, 1995 • *Learning As You Go,* Columbia, 1996 • *Mi Vida Eres Tu,* Sony International, 1996 • "I Only Get This Way with You," Columbia, 1997 • "Running out of Reasons to Run," Columbia, 1997 • "See Rock City," Columbia, 1997.

Warwick, Dionne: *No Night So Long,* Arista, 1980 • *Hot Live and Otherwise,* Arista, 1981 • *Greatest Hits, 1979–1990,* Arista, 1989.

Whalum, Kirk: *In This Life,* Columbia, 1995.

Winans, The: *All Out,* Qwest, 1993.

Wynette, Tammy: *Sometimes When We Touch,* Epic, 1985 • *Higher Ground,* Epic, 1987 • *Best Loved Hits,* Epic, 1990 • *Tears of Fire: The 25th Anniversary Collection,* Epic, 1992 • See also Parton, Dolly.

COLLECTIONS
Songs of Jimmie Rodgers: Tribute, Sony, 1997.

John Burgess

John Burgess was one of the most important producers in England from the late '50s through the British Invasion—at a time when "producer" meant finding the talent, signing them to a contract, finding songs, rehearsing and recording the act, all for no credit and no royalty. He scored hits with Adam Faith, Freddie and the Dreamers, Manfred Mann, Peter [Asher; see entry] and Gordon, and many others.

In 1965, Burgess helped change the face of the British recording industry when he founded—with George Martin (see entry), Ron Richards, and Peter Sullivan—Associated Independent Recordings (AIR) and became managing director of Air Studios. Air helped break the system under which producers were signed to exclusive (and disadvantageous) contracts with major labels, and initiated the era of independent producers who sold their work to the highest bidder, finally receiving credit and royalties for their labors. In 1974 Burgess founded Air Management to look after the careers of producers and engineers, including George Martin, Geoff Emerick (see entry), Jon Kelly, Steve Nye, and several others. In 1991, Air moved from Oxford Circus to Hampstead and was rebuilt under a new partnership with Pioneer. Burgess left Air after 1993 and continues to manage producers, including Martin.

John Burgess was born in 1932. He went to work for EMI in 1951, doing promotion and publicity and eventually rising to promotion manager for (EMI subdivision) Capitol Records. In 1958 he moved to A&R and began his production career. His mentor was songwriter/producer Norman Newell (Judy Garland, Johnny Ray, Shirley Bassey). From Newell he learned to "appear confident, even when not." Burgess developed his own conception—that the artist is paramount, a progressive notion indeed for the day.

Burgess produced a litany of hits for Adam Faith, none of which successfully crossed the Atlantic. He produced "I'm Telling You Now" by Freddie and the Dreamers, which survived the voyage to reach No. 1 in the U.S., as well as the Pipkins' (a Roger Greenaway–Tony Burrows vehicle) "Gimme Dat Ding" (No. 9 U.S.). But Burgess's most enduring work is with Peter and Gordon and Manfred Mann.

Peter and Gordon were England's answer to the early '60s folk-rock boom in the U.S.; their close harmonies, warm production, and Beatlesque tunes hold up better than most Invasion pop fare. "Lady Godiva" (No. 6) and "Knight in Rusty Armour" (No. 15) capture a pre-rock music hall amiability. Though burdened with opulent arrangements, "True Love Ways" (No. 14) and "To Know You Is to Love You" do justice to their American originals (Buddy Holly and Phil Spector's [see entry] Teddy Bears, respectively). "Woman" (No. 14) boasts a memorable melody and clever vocal interplay.

Burgess's productions with Peter and Gordon are memorable, but his work with Manfred Mann is classic. Ellie Greenwich and Jeff Barry's (see entry) "Do Wah Diddy Diddy" (No. 1 U.S. and U.K.) is one of the great pop-rock songs of the '60s.

Mann's charging organ fires up the energy and Mike Hugg's maracas and tympani rolls force a sideward twist to the forward motion. Best are Paul Jones' impassioned vocals, lending essentially goofy lyrics weight. To this day, who can doubt that she "Looked good (Looked good) / Looked fine (Looked fine) / And I nearly lost my mind"?

"5-4-3-2-1" (No. 5 U.K.) is a double-time blues-rock romp, á la Bluesbreakers, with Mann's organ and Jones' harmonica in the fore. "Sha-La-La" is more profound nonsense, and "Pretty Flamingo" (No. 1 U.K.; later covered by Rod Stewart) is sublime.

Jones' vigorously strummed acoustic guitar sets up his best vocal on a timeless, leaping melody. Charmingly local in a '60s pop world full of universals ("On our block / All of the guys / Call her flamingo"), the flamingo girl is exotic, unobtainable wildlife. Though daunted, Jones clings to a blissful vision: "Some sweet day / I'll make her mine / Pretty flamingo / And every guy will envy me / 'Cause paradise is where I'll be," and where we are as long as the song plays. —Eric Olsen

Barry, John: *EMI Years,* Vol. 2, *1961,* Scamp, 1993 • *EMI Years,*
    Vol. 3, *1962–1964,* Caroline, 1996.

Bennett, Cliff, and the Rebel Rousers: *Cliff Bennett and the*
    Rebel Rousers, Parlophone, 1964.

Bravo Brasso: *Bravo Brasso,* Columbia, 1969.

Burrows, Tony: *Voice of Tony Burrows,* Varese Sarabande,
    1996.

Cook, Roger: *Adam,* Parlophone, 1960 • *Minstrel in Flight,*
    Regal Zonophone, 1973.

English Congregation: *Jesahel,* Signpost, 1972 • *Softly*
    Whispering I Love You, Signpost, 1972 • *The Congregation,*
    Columbia, 1973.

Faith, Adam: *Beat Girl,* Columbia, 1961 • *Adam Faith,*
    Parlophone, 1962 • *For You,* Parlophone, 1963 • *From Adam*

with Love, Parlophone, 1963 • On the Move, Parlophone, 1964 • Faith Alive, Parlophone, 1965 • The Best of the EMI Years, EMI, 1994.

Freddie and the Dreamers: Freddie and the Dreamers, Columbia, 1963 • "I'm Telling You Now," Tower, 1963, 1965 • "You Were Made for Me," Tower, 1964, 1965 • You Were Made for Me, Columbia, 1964 • Do the Freddie, Mercury, 1965 • "I Understand (Just How You Feel)," Mercury, 1965 • Sing Along, Columbia, 1965 • In Disneyland, Columbia, 1966 • King Freddy and the Dreaming Knight, Columbia, 1967.

Goodhand-Tait, Philip: Oceans Away, Chrysalis, 1976.

Mann, Manfred: "5-4-3-2-1," HMV, 1964 • "Do Wah Diddy Diddy," Ascot, 1964 • "Hubble Bubble Toil and Trouble," HMV, 1964 • Mann Made, HMV/Ascot, 1964 • "Sha-La-La," Ascot, 1964 • The Five Faces of Manfred Mann, HMV/Ascot, 1964 • "Come Tomorrow," HMV, 1965 • "If You Gotta Go, Go Now," HMV, 1965 • "Oh No, Not My Baby," HMV, 1965 • "Pretty Flamingo," United Artists, 1966 • Soul of Mann, HMV/Cap, 1967 • The Best of Manfred Mann, Janus, 1974.

Peter and Gordon: In Touch, Columbia, 1964 • Peter and Gordon, Columbia, 1964 • "To Know You Is to Love You," Capitol, 1965 • "True Love Ways," Capitol, 1965 • Hurtin' n' Lovin', Columbia, 1965 • "Knight in Rusty Armour," Capitol, 1966 • "Lady Godiva," Capitol, 1966 • Somewhere, Columbia, 1966 • The Best of Peter and Gordon, Capitol, 1966 • "Woman," Capitol, 1966 • "Sunday for Tea," Capitol, 1967 • Meanwhile, Regal Z, 1972.

Pipkins: "Gimme Dat Ding," Capitol, 1970.

Malcolm Burn

In his late teens and early twenties, Malcolm Burn tried to figure out how members of certain groups "played all those instruments at the same time." Now, the producer of such acts as Chris Whitley, Iggy Pop, and the Neville Brothers has not only figured it out, he has his own production signature.

"When I'm working with an artist, whether it's Iggy Pop, Lisa Germano, or Chris Whitley, I tend to balance everything in the sound around that person," Burn says. "I don't like it when someone feels they're stuck on top of a track. I try to keep everything that's happening, while I'm recording, as integral as possible to what that person is doing, particularly if that person is playing an instrument while singing."

To Burn, a vocalist need not be great, only distinc-tive, like Whitley, Pop, and Emmylou Harris. The Neville Brothers, whom he also produced, are a strong vocal group. The greatest band of the current era, Burn says, is Nirvana, "and their vocals were always a feature."

"I like to manipulate sounds," Burn says. "I like the way sounds can mesh together to create new sounds. On Emmylou Harris's [Wrecking Ball], Dan [Lanois; see entry] and I play on most every song. For the most part, I played an old upright, tinkly sounding piano. Dan tended to play mandolin or electric guitar. You'll hear an interplay between those two instruments that almost creates other sounds, overtones that almost sound like other instruments."

While he uses modern technology—he recently produced an EP for Parlor James on ADAT 8-track machines—"I don't wear it on my sleeve," Burn says. "I use samplers and drum loops as much as anybody else. Chris Whitley's record is full of that, it's just not overt. If I'm going to use a drum loop, I like to screw up the sound so you think it's some other instrument. I'm always messing around with sounds until they take on their own character."

Born October 4, 1960, in Cornwall, Ontario, Burn lives in New Orleans, where he maintains a 16-track studio. He grew up in Deep River, a small town in northern Ontario, and began playing piano at age 5. Schooled in classical music, he became attracted to rock 'n' roll while in high school. "I wanted to be David Bowie [see entry] and Mott the Hoople. That was handy because it all led to Brian Eno [see entry], especially the Bowie phase. I bought a small stereo reel-to-reel tape machine and taught myself how to record music, in my bedroom, literally. From my teens to my early twenties, I did what everybody else does: try to survive in a variety of stupid jobs. But at night, at home, I would pursue this vision, to record music.

"I always liked records," he says. "I had to find out how they were made. I knew there was some trick to it, but I didn't know what it was."

He got a clue when he joined some friends in London, Ontario, studying production and engineering at Fanshaw College. Among them was Garth Richardson (see entry), who wound up producing Rage Against The Machine. Hanging out with these guys persuaded Burn to enroll, but the rock 'n' roll lifestyle beckoned first; he joined a glam-rock band in Toronto, one of several he worked in during the early '80s. One, Boys Brigade, did well enough in Canada to open for the Romantics, the Stray Cats, and Gang of Four. Burn met Lanois through Brigade, but that band didn't hire Lanois to produce its first album because, Burn laughs, "he wasn't big enough."

Burn quit Brigade in 1985 to pursue producing. He became reacquainted with Lanois through Lanois's sister, Jocelyne, a member of Martha and the Muffins, a talented Canadian band Lanois had produced. When Jocelyne quit the Muffins, she called Burn to suggest they make music. They did, they dated, and helped set up a studio in Hamilton for Lanois called the Lab; Burn became its manager. "It was sort of a benevolent move on Dan's part," says Burn.

Jocelyne, meanwhile, joined a group called Crash Vegas; at least half of its debut record, on Atlantic, was produced at the Lab by Burn. Guitarist Greg Keelor, who works full-time in Blue Rodeo, also is featured on Vegas; Burn went on to produce a Blue Rodeo album in the late '80s. By this time, Lanois—with Eno—had produced U2's *Unforgettable Fire* and had gone to New Orleans to record his first solo album, *Acadie*. He asked Burn to help, they wrote songs together and "traded inspiration," Burn says.

Burn's best production work is *Living with the Law,* Chris Whitley's stunning 1991 debut on Columbia. "His record's the one that's gotten me the most mileage," Burn says. "I think it's quite distinctive, because of the way his writing style and my production style work together to create a pretty interesting landscape. It's essentially blues, but not blues. It's not traditional in any way. His writing form is not traditional blues, either." Burn wanted to make the album "cinematic, not from any particular place." —CARLO WOLFF

Blue Rodeo: *Diamond Mine,* Atlantic, 1989.

Colvin, Shawn: "Sunny Came Home," Columbia, 1996.

Devlins, The: *Drift,* Capitol, 1993 • "Someone to Talk To," Capitol, 1994.

Doyle, Patrick: *Into the West* soundtrack, SBK, 1993.

Germano, Lisa: "You Make Me Want to Wear Dresses," Capitol, 1993 • *Geek the Girl,* 4 A.D., 1994 • *Happiness,* 4 A.D., 1994.

Harford, Chris: *Comet,* Black Shepherd, 1997.

Mellencamp, John "Cougar": *Human Wheels,* Mercury, 1993.

Midnight Oil: "Underwater," Work, 1996 • *Breathe,* Work, 1996 • *20,000 Watt R.S.L.: Greatest Hits,* Columbia, 1997.

Neville Brothers: "Mystery Train," A&M, 1990 • *Brother's Keeper,* A&M, 1990.

Parlor James: *Dreadful Sorry,* Discovery, 1996.

Pop, Iggy: *American Caesar,* Virgin, 1993 • "Wild America," Virgin, 1993.

Sexton, Charlie, and Sextet: "Dark," MCA, 1995 • *Under the Wishing Tree,* MCA, 1995.

Smith, Patti: *Gone Again,* Arista, 1996 • *Masters,* Arista, 1996.

Whitley, Chris: *Living with the Law,* Columbia, 1991 • *Din of Ecstacy,* Columbia, 1995.

T Bone Burnett

(JOHN HENRY BURNETT)

The man who helped create such masterpieces as Elvis Costello's *King of America,* Los Lobos' *How Will the Wolf Survive?* and Counting Crows' debut, *August and Everything After* (No. 4), got his start recording speed metal in Fort Worth.

"There was a place called Panther Hall where all the country and western acts would come through," recalls T Bone Burnett. "Frequently, on Saturday nights we'd go into the studio after the shows. They'd show up with a few fifths of whiskey and some amphetamines and we'd stay up till eight in the morning recording speed metal with a bunch of snuff queens hanging on, making really funny jokes. It was a funny time." No kidding.

While those Fort Worth speed-metal days were interesting, Burnett also recorded some noteworthy albums there, including one by Delbert (McClinton) and Glen (Clark) in 1972. A song from that album, "I Received a Letter," became a country hit for Waylon Jennings as well as a Hot 100 hit for Delbert and Glen.

Born John Henry Burnett on January 18, 1945, Burnett grew up in Fort Worth. He recorded his solo debut in 1972, toured with Delaney and Bonnie, and, in the mid-'70s, hooked up with the Rolling Thunder Revue, Bob Dylan's caravan of stars and legends. Burnett and fellow Thunder alumnus Steve Soles founded the Alpha Band in 1978, recording three albums for Arista.

Burnett recorded solo for Takoma in 1980 (*Truth Decay*), for Warner Bros. in 1983 (*Proof Through the Night*), and finally found his most commercial metier in producing the likes of Los Lobos, Marshall Crenshaw, Elvis Costello, and the BoDeans. He still releases solo albums occasionally; his latest was in 1992 for Columbia (*The Criminal Under My Own Hat*).

Married to Leslie (now Sam) Phillips, a Christian pop singer turned alterna-pop singer, whom he has also produced, Burnett is a soulful rock figure with a godly bent. He surrounds himself with the best—his guests have included Ry Cooder, Richard Thompson, and Pete Townshend—and has a reputation for writing and performing individualistic music. To Burnett, production and writing original material are equally rewarding. "One is more of a coach job or something or other—support, encouragement, watch the kids get out there and get after it," he says. "Making records is more debilitating. It's going mad with narcissism, which you try to keep other people from doing all the time when you're being a producer."

To Burnett, the word is God; he values lyrics highly. "There are 400,000 words in the English language and Shakespeare coined 10,000 of them," he says. "I think Elvis [Costello] has added several interesting phrases to the language. I remember he said when he started that he wanted to invent his own clichés. I thought, 'That's a terrific concept,' and I admire that. 'Pump It Up' is a tremendous cliché, and he invented it."

Whether he's working with an established artist or a new band, Burnett tries to be honest. "We are all so full of self-deceit, and it's a situation where you have to try to be really honest. I have different starting places with different people, but it always comes down to the song and what's being said and then working backward from there." —DAVID JOHN FARINELLA

Attractions, The: *See* Costello, Elvis.

Barton, Lou Ann: "Don't Slander Me," Sire/WB, 1990 (*Where the Pyramid Meets the Eye*).

BoDeans: "Fadeaway," Slash/WB, 1986 • *Love and Hope and Sex and Dreams*, Slash/WB, 1986 • *Go Slow Down*, Slash/Reprise, 1993.

Browne, Jackson: *The Next Voice You Hear: The Best of Jackson Browne*, Elektra/Asylum, 1997.

Burnett, T Bone: *Trap Door*, Warner Bros., 1984 • *The Talking Animals*, Columbia, 1988 • "God Rest Ye Merry Gentlemen," Columbia, 1990 (*Acoustic Christmas*) • "Nothing in Return," Sire/WB, 1990 (*Where the Pyramid Meets the Eye*) • "Humans from Earth," Warner Bros., 1991 (*Until the End of the World* soundtrack) • *The Criminal Under My Own Hat*, Columbia, 1992.

Case, Peter: *Peter Case*, Geffen, 1986.

Clark, Glen: *See* McClinton, Delbert.

Cockburn, Bruce: *Nothing But a Burning Light*, Columbia, 1991 • *Dart to the Heart*, Columbia, 1994.

Costello, Elvis: w/ the Attractions, *Girls, Girls, Girls*, Columbia, 1989 • *Out of Our Idiot*, Demon, 1987 • "Veronica," Warner Bros., 1989 • *Spike*, Warner Bros., 1989.

Costello, Elvis, and the Costello Show: "Don't Let Me Be Misunderstood," Columbia, 1986 • *King of America*, Columbia, 1986.

Counting Crows: *August and Everything After*, DGC, 1993 • "Mr. Jones," DGC, 1994.

Crenshaw, Marshall: *Downtown*, Warner Bros., 1985.

Croce, A.J.: *A.J. Croce*, Private, 1993.

Gilmore, Jimmy Dale: *Braver Newer World*, Elektra, 1996.

Henry, Joe: *Shuffletown*, A&M, 1990.

Keene, Tommy: *Run Now*, Geffen, 1986 • *Real Underground*, Alias, 1993.

Kottke, Leo: *Time Step*, Chrysalis, 1983 • *My Father's Face*,

Private/Atlantic, 1989 • *Essential*, Chrysalis, 1991.

Los Lobos: *And Time to Dance*, Slash, 1983 • *How Will the Wolf Survive?*, Slash/WB, 1984 • "Will the Wolf Survive?," Slash/WB, 1984 • *By the Light of the Moon*, Slash/WB, 1987 • *Just Another Band from East L.A.*, Slash/WB, 1993.

McClinton, Delbert, and Glen Clark: *Delbert and Glen*, Clean, 1972.

Nitty Gritty Dirt Band: *Live Two Five*, Liberty, 1991.

Orbison, Roy: "In Dreams," Virgin, 1987 • *Mystery Girl* (2 tracks), Virgin, 1989 • *Roy Orbison and Friends: A Black and White Night Live*, Virgin, 1989 • *King of Hearts*, Virgin, 1992 • *The Very Best Of*, Virgin, 1997.

Phillips, Leslie: *The Turning*, Myrrh, 1987.

Phillips, Sam: *The Indescribable Wow*, Virgin, 1988 • *Cruel Inventions*, Virgin America, 1991 • "Baby, I Can't Please You," Virgin America, 1994 • *Martinis and Bikinis* (1 track), Virgin America, 1994 • *Omnipop*, Virgin America, 1996.

Sexton, Charlie: "Race with the Devil," A&M, 1994 (*Fast Track to Nowhere: Songs from Rebel Highway*).

Spinal Tap: *Break Like the Wind*, MCA, 1992.

Tashian, Daniel: *Sweetie*, Elektra, 1996.

Tonio K.: *Romeo Unchained* (1 track), A&M, 1986.

Wallflowers, The: *Bringing Down the Horse*, Interscope, 1996 • "One Headlight," Interscope, 1997.

Welch, Gillian: *Revival*, ALMO, 1996.

Scott Burns

The very names of the bands comprising Scott Burns' discography could provide fodder for thousands of right-wing political campaign speeches: Obituary, Deicide, Napalm Death, Suffocation, Atheist, Cannibal Corpse, and of course, the almighty Death. Based in South Florida, Burns was associated with Morrisound Recording in Tampa for 10 years and helped make it the mecca for death metal in the late '80s and early '90s.

Burns was doing live sound for local Florida metal bands by age 18, and in 1985, at age 21, he started assistant engineering at Morrisound. Numerous Florida metal bands were getting signed to labels and, with bands like Death, Massacre, Obituary, Atheist and Deicide, the death-metal scene in particular was poised to explode.

"The studio was getting hired a lot by labels," Burns says. "I did some engineering for Dan Johnson, who was working a lot, and that got my name around. He produced Death's *Leprosy* and I was the engineer."

Burns' first production credit was Obituary's 1989 debut, *Slowly We Rot*. "I knew Obituary from doing live sound for them. [*Slowly We Rot*] was done on 8-track as a self-released album that Godly Records picked up and Roadrunner bought out. They were very inspired. I remember the first time I heard John Tardy sing, I thought, 'Holy fucking shit, this is the craziest thing I've ever heard.' That "crazy thing" was the unique garbled, raspy vocal sound that came to be death metal's hallmark: the "cookie monster" vocal.

Soon Burns was working on strings of albums for the genre's top bands, including Cannibal Corpse, Death, Obituary, and Deicide. Still a production novice, he recorded Sepultura's American debut, 1989's *Beneath the Remains*. "Roadrunner needed someone to go to Brazil to record an underground band named Sepultura. It was over Christmas and there was little money involved, so all the big-name producers turned it down. No one knew of me or them. Strange country, pure raw energy without label and media politics, unquestionable presence and focus."

The sound quality and the specific sounds of the bands varied quite a bit. Death, for instance, was more technical, featuring distinct lead guitar parts, while Cannibal Corpse, probably the most driving and extreme of the bands ("brutal" is the genre's favored adjective), was known for exceptionally guttural vocals placed deep in the mix and swamped in noisy guitars and drums. Budget and time constraints were probably a factor in the unevenness of the sound of Burns' output. While some albums (particularly early ones) sound thin and trebly, others, such as Obituary's *World Demise* (which Burns calls one of his favorites), have thundering, enveloping drums and bass that hits you in the gut. All Burns' death-metal albums feature dense clouds of jagged rhythm guitar, whose sounds resemble a massive swarm of particularly angry wasps. In fact, Burns describes the signature of his sound as "guitar, guitar, guitar, guitar . . . guitar that is so overly distorted that the people at Marshall just don't know what to think. Blues is not our world. We are about rhythm guitar and the heaviest, most over-the-top sound possible."

His recordings also feature "triggered double-bass drums for a loud, even sound, and the bass is recorded last so you know what it will sound like and can hear it over a wall of double-tracked guitars. The bass drum is just as important as the snare, which is unusual. Also vocals that are up front—similar to a pop record. The death-metal scene tapered off by '94, '95. It was a great scene, but now it has gotten hard for bands to be more extreme than they were," Burns says. "It will be a long time, I think, before there is a wave of music as extreme as the death-metal bands. There has been nothing ever recorded as brutal, as fast, as extreme, as over-the-top as death metal."

He's moved on to work with other types of bands, including Today Is The Day, the Hazies, Gravity Kills, and KMFDM. "Unfortunately," he says, "I have done so much work in a specific genre I have trouble getting work in other styles." —ANASTASIA PANTSIOS

Atheist: *Piece of Time*, Metal Blade, 1990.

Atrocity: *Hallucinations*, Roadrunner, 1991.

Cancer: *Death Will Rise*, Restless, 1992 • *To the Gory End*, Restless, 1992.

Cannibal Corpse: *Tomb of the Mutilated*, Metal Blade, 1993 • *Eaten Back to Life*, Metal Blade, 1990 • *Butchered at Birth*, Metal Blade, 1991, 1994 • *Hammer Smashed Face*, Metal Blade, 1993 • *The Bleeding*, Metal Blade, 1994 • *Vile*, Metal Blade, 1996.

Cynics: *Focus*, Roadrunner, 1993.

Death: *Spiritual Healing*, Combat, 1980 • *Human*, Relativity, 1991 • *Individual Thought Patterns*, Combat, 1993.

Deicide: *Deicide*, Roadrunner, 1990 • *Once upon the Cross*, Roadrunner, 1995.

Demolition Hammer: *Tortured Existence*, Century Media, 1991.

Devastation: *Idolatry*, Combat, 1991.

Exhorder: *Slaughter in the Vatican*, Roadrunner, 1990.

Gorguts: *Considered Dead*, Roadrunner, 1991.

Idolatry: *Devastation*, Relativity, 1991.

Malevolent Creation: *The Ten Commandments*, Roadrunner, 1991 • *Retribution*, Roadrunner, 1992 • *Joe Black*, Pavement, 1996.

Napalm Death: *Harmony Corruption*, Earache, 1990 • *Death By Manipulation*, Earache, 1991.

Obituary: *Slowly We Rot*, Roadrunner, 1989 • *Cause of Death*, Roadrunner, 1990 • *The End Complete*, Roadrunner, 1992 • *World Demise*, Roadrunner, 1994.

Sepultura: *Beneath the Remains*, Roadrunner, 1989 • *Arise*, Roadrunner, 1991 • *Dead Embrionic Cells* (EP), Roadrunner, 1991.

Skeletal Earth: *Eulogy for a Dying Fetus*, Pavement, 1991.

Suffocation: *Effigy of the Forgotten*, Roadrunner, 1991 • *Pierced from Within*, Roadrunner, 1995.

Phillip "Fatis" Burrell

It's interesting that Jamaica's Link 'n' Chain, one of the last groups produced by conscious roots man Jack Ruby (see entry), would turn to "Fatis" Burrell for its next album after Ruby's death. Though the man they call "the Exterminator" has produced dozens of Jamaican dancehall artists, some of his greatest success has been with the "return to roots" sound of singers like Luciano, Beres Hammond, and Cocoa Tea.

Born in Jamaica, Burrell spent time in England, where it's likely the very different take on reggae had some impact on the music he later produced. His first release was from Sugar Minott. This classic singer, himself an excellent producer, has exemplified roots in the dance from his earliest days to the present.

The year 1987 was one of reggae's pivot points. The sound of the '70s began to fade as the digital era dawned and raggamuffin dancehall took the stage. In that year Burrell formed the Vena label and began recording the new wave of artists as well as cutting records with established singers in the new style. Recording mainly at Music Works, then the hottest studio in Kingston, Fatis also cut at Black Scorpio, Aquarius, Mixing Lab, and Channel One. In 1988 he utilized dynamics and produced *The Summit* for Sly and Robbie (see entry); this was unusual at this point in their career as the duo are top reggae producers in their own right.

Vena quickly established itself as a crucial new label to check for. Burrell cut singers Sugar Minott, Johnny Osbourne, Frankie Paul, and Admiral Tibet as well as DJs Ricky Chaplain, General Trees, and Ninja Man. He changed the label name to Kings and Lions briefly, and then to Exterminator. After the film *Malcolm X* was released to movie theaters and baseball caps everywhere, he retooled the name again, eliminating the E and making Xterminator one of the most highly respected labels in Jamaica.

Among Burrell's best, and best-known, records are Cocoa Tea's *Good Life* and Beres Hammond's *Full Attention*. From the beginning Fatis kept his door open to new talent, often cutting artists' best early records before they make the rounds of other studios. Burrell is credited with being the first to record Thriller U, Pinchers, and Sanchez.

In all he produced three albums with Sanchez, including his first, using two of Bob Marley's I-Threes for backup vocals. He also recorded the first album for ragga rap–toaster Daddy Freddy (1989's *Cater Fi She*). Among other artists he helped to break were Lady Patra, Foxy Brown, Quench Aid, Tenor Fly, and Junior Demus. Old-time artists he's done good work with include Josey Wales, Gregory Isaacs, and Al Campbell.

Xterminator's sound is stripped to the bare essentials, with a mix of digital and "real" instruments provided in the main to this day by Sly and Robbie and the Fire House Crew. Horn and vocal arrangements are often by sax man Dean Fraser. Third World's Cat Coore plays lead guitar as well. The crew is tightly knit and it's said that a "family" atmosphere pervades the sessions.

Fatis has also issued several dubby instrumental albums for and with sax man Fraser as solo artist, including two in which he plays the songs of Bob Marley and one "theme" album with retitled tunes (like "Not Guilty" and "Rockingham Rocking") in reference to the end of the first Simpson trial (*The Verdict*). Burrell's mix of dancehall vibes and roots and culture has worked well with DJ Capleton, soul singer Beres Hammond (check the cool feel on Full Attention's "Six for a Nine"), and his in-house DJs and singers like Sizzla (Migel Collins) and Mikey General (whose autobiographical 7-inch "Miss Taylor Bwoy" is one of the rootsiest message singles of the '90s).

To date Burrell has produced four albums for Luciano, dreadlock heir apparent to the roots mantle of Bob Marley and the late Garnett Silk. Even Luciano's ballads have depth, and Burrell smoothes the sound on the later releases to deceive you into thinking you're listening to pop music while the singer engages your brain; the 1994 *One Way Ticket* is one of reggae's all-time top recordings. The teaming of these two created such a special sound and style that Burrell is also (in a style that harks back to some of the earliest Jamaican producers) Luciano's manager, even touring with him in the mid-'90s. Still and all, Burrell is a very humble and personal man and prefers to let his music speak for itself.
—CHUCK FOSTER

Brown, Foxy: *Whip Appeal,* Vena/VP, 1991.

Capleton: *Alms House,* RAS, 1993.

Cocoa Tea: *One Up,* VP, 1993 • *Good Life,* VP, 1994 • *Israel's King,* VP, 1996.

Fraser, Dean: *Taking Chances,* RAS, 1992 • *Dean Plays Bob,* RAS, 1994 • "Unforgettable," RAS, 1994 (*The Real Authentic Sampler 3*) • *Dean Plays Bob,* Vol 2, RAS, 1996 • *The Verdict,* RAS, 1996.

Hammond, Beres: *Full Attention,* VP, 1993.

Isaacs, Gregory: *Call Me Collect*, RAS, 1990 • *Come Again Dub,* ROIR, 1991, 1993.

Link 'N' Chain: *S.T.O.P.,* RAS, 1992.

Luciana: *Moving Up,* RAS, 1993.

Luciano: *One Way Ticket,* VP, 1994 • *Where There Is Life,* Island Jamaica, 1995 • *The Messenger,* Island Jamaica, 1997.

Ninja Man: *Artical Don,* VP, 1994 • *Out Pon Bail,* VP, 1990.

Paul, Frankie: *Best in Me,* VP, 1991 • *Freedom,* VP, 1996 • *Easy Mover,* Vena, 1988.

Pinchers (Delroy Thompson): *Mass Out,* RAS, 1987.

Ricks, Glen: *Ready for Love,* RAS, 1992.

Sanchez: *Sanchez,* Vena, 1987 • *Number One,* RAS, 1989 • *In Fine Style,* Exterminator, 1990.

Sizzla: *Burning Up,* RAS, 1995.

Sly and Robbie: *The Summit,* RAS, 1988.

Thriller U: *Young, Single and Fresh,* Vena, 1987.

Yellowman: *Yellow Like Cheese,* RAS, 1987.

COLLECTIONS

Exterminator, Vol. 2, World Enterprises, 1989.

Exterminator Presents Turn on the Heat One, Sir Coxone/Blacker Dread, 1989.

Reggae DJ Mash-Up, Positive Music, 1990.

Exterminator Presents, VP, 1990.

Best of the Best, Vol. 2, RAS, 1994.

Awakening, RAS, 1996.

Xterminator Dub, RAS, 1996.

The Butcher Brothers

See JOE AND PHIL NICOLO

Chris Butler

Chris Butler humbly sums up his role in the annals of pop musical endeavor as a "seminal new waver, blah, blah, and etc." He is equally blunt about the harsh realities of the record producer's position.

"Production is horrible, basically, because you're caught between a band and a record company. What a horrible place to be. I have gone full circle, where you spend days listening to the snare drum because 'that's what you're supposed to do' to now—throw the mikes up, bang bang bang, if it's reasonably great, fine, let's go, boom boom boom. The recording studio is a horrible environment and you should get out of there as fast as possible."

Pay no attention to the man's cragginess. Despite his biting words, he makes a beautiful noise and his talents are many. Butler is widely recognized as a former member of Tin Huey and for his role as the driving force behind the Waitresses (of "I Know What Boys Like" and "Christmas Rapping" fame). He has also been a musical director/bandleader/drummer for HBO/Comedy Central's *Two Drink Minimum* show and has done musical stage work. He really should be better known as the fine producer that he is. His production credits have encompassed an eclectic mix of good stuff, like Joan Osborne, the dB's, Freedy Johnston, and Scruffy the Cat.

Butler's musical life took wing at Kent State University, in Ohio, between 1967 and 1972. He is quick to interject, "Yes, I was there." He was on-site for what he describes as "the most 'devo' moment in the world."

"I was with Jeffrey Miller when he got shot and killed by the National Guard in the Kent State massacre. He was actually borrowing my drums at that time. It was an amazing, amazing little time. Kent State was a rum-dum, stupid college, but there was this incredible musical scene and all these wonderful, talented characters feeding off of each other. You had Devo, the James Gang with Joe Walsh, Phil Keaggy and the Glass Harp, Bob Kidney, Pere Ubu, Chrissie Hynde, Liam Sternberg, Ivy and Lux from the Cramps, and on and on and on. The main bars on the strip were JB's and the Cove. Out of that came this college-boy aesthetic, with improvisational music and a lot of blues."

He played drums, bass, guitar, "a million blues things," and the local "big good gig" called 15-60-75 (aka the Numbers Band). He started writing songs and joined Tin Huey, who inhabited a "band house" replete with a full-blown recording studio. Tapes flew back and forth between various other home setups in the Akron area, which collectively offered several miscalibrated 8-track machines and some Neumann microphones.

"Tin Huey were the most eclectic, creative, smartest bunch I ever played with," says Butler. "It was a really nutsy, cough syrup–driven, wacko, really wonderful band. We were in love with Captain Beefheart, Robert Wyatt, Soft Machine, anything with Tony Visconti (see entry) on it, Mott the Hoople." They released "one glorious flop" on Warner Bros. The album, originally untitled, became *Contents Dislodged During Shipment* when a mangled shipment of mastered acetates bore the post office label stating the condition of the cargo. Warner eventually bought the band out of its contract.

Butler grabbed his share of the buyout money and made his way to the musical hotbed that was New York City in 1979. Among a pile of his home recordings that he brought with him was an 8-track master of "I Know What Boys Like" and through the championing of DJ Mark Kamins at the prominent New York club Hurrah and various machinations, the song wound up on Polydor. They needed a B-side so Chris threw a band together with Dave Hofstra, Don Christensen, Pat Irwin (all from the Contortions), and Billy Ficca (from Televison), and with his last $50 sent a bus ticket to fetch Patty Donahue (now deceased) from Ohio. As Butler was trying to make it as a songwriter or score an A&R position to escape the burnout of playing in bands, he got jammed into maintaining a vehicle for his song instead. "I figured, 'Let's see how far we could take this joke.' " The band's recording and touring career spanned a five-year period from 1979 to 1983.

In conjunction with Kurt Munkacsi (see entry), Mike Frondelli, and Hugh Padgham (see entry), Butler produced The Waitresses' two albums and an EP. Butler was an enormous fan of the XTC records, so working with Padgham was a fantasy come true.

"I learned a lot about recording from him, especially the use of compression and ambient sound," says Butler. "He's from that British school of engineering where you have those wonderful wood and old shale stone studios, these incredible Neve and SSL consoles, a couple of good German mikes, and these amazing amplifiers."

Maybe producing ain't quite as bad as Chris Butler made it sound. "Producing is an awful job until two years later when you play back the thing you worked on and you realize that you couldn't see the forest for the trees. It actually does sound pretty damn good!"
—DENNIS DIKEN

dB's, The: *Like This*, Bearsville, 1984.
Johnston, Freedy: *The Trouble Tree*, Bar None/Restless, 1990.
Osborne, Joan: *Early Recordings*, PolyGram, 1996.
Scruffy the Cat: *Tiny Days*, Combat, 1987.
Waitresses, The: "I Know What Boys Like," Polydor, 1980 • "Wasn't Tomorrow Wonderful," Polydor, 1980 • *Wasn't Tomorrow Wonderful*, Polydor, 1980 • "Christmas Wrapping," Polydor, 1982 • "Square Pegs," Polydor, 1982 • *I Could Rule the World if I Could Only Get the Parts*, Polydor, 1982 • "Bruiseology," Polydor, 1983 • *Bruiseology*, Polydor, 1983 • *The Best of the Waitresses*, Polydor, 1990.

Albert Cabrera

See LATIN RASCALS

John Cale

Within John Cale lies the dichotomy at the heart of great rock 'n' roll: the contrast between exquisite beauty and naked power. Cale also embodies a temporal contradiction: that of a self-professed anachronism ("I'm a 19th-century personality with 20th-century demands, or urges") who has spent his artistic life ahead of his time. Cale's first band, the Velvet Underground (inducted into the Rock and Roll Hall of Fame in 1996), was decades ahead of its time, and Cale's subsequent solo work and productions have marched ahead of the pack as well. Cale has put his 19th-century sensibility to work on Nico's tragic romanticism, Siouxsie & the Banshees' melodic goth-rock (*The Rapture*), and many of his own songs. He has harnessed the raw energy under the hood of rock 'n' roll with the Stooges (self-titled debut), Modern Lovers (self-titled debut), Patti Smith (*Horses*), and many of his own songs.

Cale was born March 9, 1942, in Garnant, Wales. His father was a coal miner, his mother a music teacher. Cale began piano lessons with his mother at age 7 and pursued the viola at school. Within a few years he had composed and performed over the BBC. This success led him to believe he could make a career out of music—an ambition which so concerned his mother that she commanded him to stop playing when he was 11.

"That drove me nuts," relates Cale in his euphonious Welsh baritone. "I became a rebel and from that point on did nothing but play. I decided to prove to her that you could make a living in music."

Cale studied composition at London University's Goldsmith College from 1960 to 1963, and was drawn to contemporary experimental music. Rubbing elbows with the elite, Cale met Aaron Copland, who induced Leonard Bernstein to grant him a scholarship to study in the U.S. Cale soon came under the sway of John Cage and La Monte Young, pioneers in minimalism.

Cale played viola in Young's experimental combo (the Theater of Eternal Music, then the Dream Syndicate) from 1963 to 1965, concentrating on the sonic and metaphysical implications of the drone. Then he met a young songwriter/singer/guitarist named Lou Reed. After a brief period as the Primitives and a single called "The Ostrich," the pair formed the Velvet Underground, named after an S&M novel. Live, the Velvets were a bizarre amalgam of vigorous R&B, pretty pop songs, extended experimental noise jams (often grounded in Cale's drones), and the performance art of Andy Warhol's Exploding Plastic Inevitable. The original band lasted just two albums, *The Velvet Underground & Nico,* and *White Light/White Heat* (see Tom Wilson entry): temporary, yet timeless blendings of the centrifugal and centripetal.

"It seemed to work even when we were playing in the exact opposite corners of the musical spectrum on the same piece. We were capable of anything. The dichotomy was given as great a value as the ability to unify on something. That was something that Andy believed in as well. It just angers me that there wasn't more work done because we were so good at it," growls Cale.

Cale left the Velvets in 1968 and produced fellow Velvets refugee Nico on her second album, *The Marble Index.* Cale produced the haute-sensitive, doomed glamour queen throughout her sporadic career. "She had problems with the process of recording, which is often tedious and repetitive. Things get bogged down in the middle. But on every project, sure enough, I'd turn around to say something to her and she'd be sitting there in tears, and I'd say 'What's wrong, now?' And she'd say, 'It is so Beeeuuuteeful.' What can you do? One minute, this vicious onslaught. The next, a very tender moment."

Through Nico, Cale met Elektra owner Jac Holzman, who asked him to produce the first Stooges album. "Jac took me to Detroit to see the MC5 recording live (see Bruce Botnick entry). The opening band was the Stooges. . . . I fell in love with Iggy's character and personality as a performer. The challenge was to get that magic and impish behavior onto a record."

Cale succeeded. The Stooges' debut rocks with the psychedelic blues-rock fervor of a severely distempered Cream. The volatility of the Stooges' live act is implied rather than manifested, but such itchy odes to malaise as "1969" ("Another year for me and you / Another year with nothin' to do") helped set the tone and vocabulary (with the Velvets and the MC5) for punk rock and its permutations over the next 30 years.

In the early '70s, Cale climbed into the beast by accepting an A&R position with Warner Bros. Records. For his next major project, he moved to the opposite end of the misfit spectrum to produce Jonathan Richman and the Modern Lovers' first album (with future Talking Head and producer Jerry Harrison; see entry).

"They dropped off a tape of a song called 'Hospital' that sounded very lame at first hearing. What was magical about it was that they took this weakness, this lameness, and by the end of the song, it had become a strength. . . . There was an honesty there that you couldn't turn your back on. . . . We did a demo, and the demo turned out to be the best record. For some reason, best known to psychiatrists, when they were formally signed to the company, and formally introduced to management and a producer, the whole enterprise imploded. The closer they got to success, the more disorganized they became."

Cale's demo with the Lovers, released in 1975 as *Modern Lovers,* is a classic of simplicity, power and beauty that straddles the line between the cloying lameness that Richman eventually succumbed to and the jagged righteousness of rock 'n' roll. "Roadrunner" (about driving, the radio, nighttime, and jumping out of one's skin at the glory of it all) and "Pablo Picasso" ("He could walk down the street / Girls could not resist his stare/Pablo Picasso was not called an asshole") are two of the best rock songs ever written.

Cale completed a triptych of exemplary productions with Patti Smith's debut, *Horses,* also in 1975. "That was a case of recording a poet who was a mother hen over some inexperienced musicians, who had all the heart in the world. Once we were in the studio we discovered, 'My God, all of these instruments are warped!' We stopped, ordered in a whole slew of new instruments, and had them record that way. Just that act alone was enough to uproot some of the sensibilities there, and that created a whole new set of instabilities within the band and toward me. I was a little brusque with them. I'm sure I could have handled it a lot better. Everyone has their favorite instrument that they love and have gotten used to. You walk in there with muddy boots and somebody feels insulted: 'What, you don't like this gorgeous Fender with a bullet hole in it?' "

Muddy boots or not, the Patti Smith debut updated (in a '70s alterna-rock context) a distaff version of the poet cum naive musician archetype that stretches back in American music through Bob Dylan, Woody Guthrie, Robert Johnson, and Harry Smith's (see entry) *Anthology of American Folk Music.*

Smith's "Gloria" twists and extends the original into an odyssey. "Redondo Beach" is a tuneful faux-reggae tableau of a woman's body washing ashore. Smith's 10-minute, stream-of-consciousness opus, "Land: Horses," flashes by in a blur of piquant images. The inexperience of the band (led by Lenny Kaye on guitar; see entry) translates to raucous authority under Cale's direction.

Cale's best outside production since *Horses* is

Siouxsie & the Banshees' *The Rapture,* from 1995. The single "O Baby" somehow captures Siouxsie's 20 years of angular goth majesty and transports it into a luscious, buoyant three-minute pop shuffle.

Perhaps Cale carried some of that buoyancy over from the Eno-Cale (see Brian Eno entry) album *Wrong Way Up,* which blends the tuneful best of two avant-rock giants into a soulful, playful, jiggling joy. Catchy melodies, electronic Afro-Caribbean polyrhythms, and paired singing carry the album into a relaxed but grooving space where two men, who have literally seen it all, can muse charmingly upon the wild life ("Been There Done That"), transcendent universality ("One Word"), and an old-fashioned western tale ("Crime In the Desert").

The best introduction to Cale's large body of solo work is the *Seducing Down the Door* double-CD collection, highlighted by "Dixieland and Dixie," "Gun," "Heartbreak Hotel," "Pablo Picasso," "Hedda Gabler," "Dead or Alive," "Waiting for My Man," and the duet with Lou Reed, "Trouble with Classicists."

Unfortunately, Cale's best solo album, *Sabotage/Live,* is represented by only one song (an elastic "Walking the Dog"). *Sabotage* is symbolic of Cale's entire career: a live album replete with aching beauty ("Only Time Will Tell," Chorale") and punishing rock ("Mercenaries," "Baby You Know," "Sabotage"). Cale's purest vocal performance can be found on the Leonard Cohen tribute album *I'm Your Fan.* On "Hallelujah," accompanied only by his piano, Cale achieves an unhistrionic poignancy that brings a tear. —Eric Olsen

Cale, John: w/ Terry Riley, *Church of Anthrax,* CBS, 1971 • *Vintage Violence,* CBS, 1971 • *Helen of Troy,* Island, 1972 • *The Academy in Peril,* Reprise, 1972 • *Fear,* Island, 1974 • *Slow Dazzle,* Island, 1975 • "Animal Justice," Illegal, 1977 • *Guts* (6 tracks), Island, 1977 • "Memphis," IRS, 1977, 1981 (*IRS Greatest Hits,* Vols. 2–3) • *Sabotage-Live,* IRS, 1979 • *Music for a New Society,* Ze, 1982 • *Caribbean Sunset,* Ze, 1984 • *Comes Alive,* Mango, 1984 • *Artificial Intelligence,* Beggars Banquet, 1985 • "The Sleeper," Beggars Banquet, 1985 (*One Pound Ninety-Nine*) • *HN,* Mango, 1990 • *Even Cowgirls Get the Blues,* ROIR, 1991 • "Hallelujah," Atlantic, 1991 (*I'm Your Fan*) • *Fragments of a Rainy Season,* Hannibal, 1992 • *Paris S'Eveille,* Crepuscule, 1992 • *23 Solo Pieces for La Naissance de L'Amour,* Crepuscule, 1993 • w/ Bob Neuwirth, *Last Day on Earth,* MCA, 1994 • *Seducing Down the Door,* Rhino, 1995 • *Island Years,* Island, 1996 • *Walking on Locusts,* Hannibal, 1996 • *Eat/Kiss: Music for Films by Andy Warhol,* Hannibal, 1997.

Eno, Brian: *Eno Box II,* Virgin, 1993.

Eno and Cale: *Wrong Way Up,* Opal/WB, 1990.

Faction, The: *See* Nico.

Happy Mondays: *Squirrel and G-Man Twenty Four Hour Party People Plastic Face Carnt Smile,* White Out/Factory, 1987.

Kubinec, Dave: *Some Things Never Change,* A&M, 1978.

Maids of Gravity: *The First Second,* Vernon Yard, 1996.

Modern Lovers: *Modern Lovers,* Beserkley/Rhino, 1975.

Neuwirth, Bob: *See* Cale, John.

Nico: *The Marble Index,* Elektra, 1969 • *Desert Shore,* Reprise, 1971 • *The End,* Island, 1974 • w/ the Faction, *Camera Obscura,* Beggars Banquet, 1985, 1996 • "Win a Few," Beggars Banquet, 1985 (*One Pound Ninety-Nine*).

Reed, Lou and Cale, John: *Songs for 'Drella,* Sire, 1989.

Riley, Terry: *See* Cale, John.

Richman, Jonathan, and the Modern Lovers: *Beserkley Years,* Rhino, 1987.

Siouxsie & the Banshees: "O Baby," Geffen, 1994 • *The Rapture* (5 tracks), Geffen, 1995.

Smith, Patti: "Gloria," Arista, 1975, 1986 (*Rock at the Edge*) • *Horses,* Arista, 1975 • *Masters,* Arista, 1996.

Squeeze: "Backtrack," IRS, 1977, 1981 (*IRS Greatest Hits,* Vols. 2–3) • (*U.K.) Squeeze,* A&M, 1978.

Stooges, The: *The Stooges,* Elektra, 1969 • "1969," Seeds and Stems, 1977 (*Michigan Rocks*).

Warren (Warnes), Jennifer: *Jennifer,* Reprise, 1972.

COLLECTIONS

Chance Operation: The John Cage Tribute, Koch International, n.d.

Reggie Calloway

It took another producer's busy schedule to set off the production career of Cincinnati's Reggie Calloway. Leon Sylvers was hard at work producing an early Midnight Star album, the group Calloway founded, when Sylvers started getting overloaded with other productions.

"I was doing a lot of the work and he was doing other projects. He had to go to Africa with [R&B group] Dynasty, and while he was gone I took over the production role and mixed the album—not so much in credit but in the work," says Calloway. "It was a great learning experience. That experience gave me my roots."

During the '80s, Calloway racked up an impressive number of bright and bubbly R&B-pop hits, including the Grammy-winning "Love Overboard" (No. 13) for Gladys Knight and the Pips; Grammy-nominated songs like "Joy" by Teddy Pendergrass; "Casanova" (No. 5) by Levert (see entry); and "Jump Start" (No. 13) by Natalie

Cole; plus other notables like "Meeting in the Ladies Room" by Klymaxx; "Body Talk" by the Deele; and a number of Midnight Star songs like "No Parking on the Dance Floor," "Freak-a-Zoid," "Wet My Whistle," "Slow Jam," "Operator" (No. 18), and "Headlines."

And if all this weren't enough, he even scored as one-half of Calloway, a group he formed with his brother Cino-Vincent Calloway. (The duo was known for the No. 2 hit "I Wanna Be Rich.")

For Calloway, the task of the producer can be a number of things, or just one thing. "The producer oversees the quality of the record, everything from writing and arranging, to picking the musicians and picking the songs, to making sure the quality of the music is up to your standards and commercially accepted in the industry," says Calloway. "The job can be all of those things or just one thing. With me it tends to be a mixture. I had the pleasure of writing a lot of the hit songs I produced and to produce songs I didn't write. But I prefer to be the writer and producer," adds Calloway, who considers himself a songwriter first and a producer second, since he was writing tunes before he even knew what a producer was.

Once he started producing, he always tried to give the songs what they deserved, whatever that might be. "I produce a song in the style and position that the artist can best carry it off without making anything sound exactly the same, and forge ahead and do new things tailor-made to the artist," he says.

The early Midnight Star albums, he says, were a democracy, which isn't always a bad thing. "With nine group members, musicians, and vocalists, you can't discount what people say or feel. The producer can take all these great ideas and weed out what works best. The producer is not necessarily the dictator. It's like the president. You can listen to the cabinet and go out and make decisions." With Midnight Star, Calloway played trumpet, percussion, and keyboards and provided background vocals. He'd entertain the idea of another Midnight Star reunion. "If we could get everybody on the same stage, anything is possible," he says.

It is not surprising given Calloway's role in Midnight Star that the band's mid- to late '80s heyday was also Calloway's peak as a producer.

His favorite production of the period was Levert's "Casanova," because "it was the most stripped-down, honest song." He calls the group members "some of the most talented guys out there. Their youth connection at the time was something we really enjoyed, and I don't think anybody could have done a better job with 'Casanova.' "

Working with Pendergrass was another eye-opening experience for Calloway. "He has always been one of my idols," he says. "It was a treat to work with him after the main part of his career was over, trying to bring him back to the forefront."

Producing Cole was special as well, since the first Midnight Star concert years earlier was opening for the singer. "She's just a super classy lady with an awesome bloodline," says Calloway of Cole, who is the daughter of late pop legend Nat "King" Cole. "She's like the sister that everybody wants."

Calloway has equally fond memories of his namesake duo. "We had a great time," he recalls. "We're looking forward to doing a new studio album. We want to bring back a lot of the original Midnight Star sound—a dance aspect with a new feel."

Though Calloway has been absent from the music scene in recent years, he's not out. He has been doing lots of writing, and is preparing material for his solo album, in which he'll explore types of music he didn't get into too heavily during his heyday.

"My middle roots were in jazz," says Calloway, who has worked with jazz ensemble Pieces of a Dream. "On my solo album I want to do something totally different, something contemporary, romantic, and not overly produced. I always wanted to do lots of ballads and easy-listening music. I never had the chance to do that. As you get older, you get into a romantic mood." —KEVIN JOHNSON

Baka Boys: *Quick Mix,* Thump, 1995.

Calloway: *All the Way,* Solar, 1990 • "I Wanna Be Rich," Solar, 1990.

Cole, Natalie: *Everlasting,* Manhattan, 1987 • "Jump Start," EMI/Manhattan, 1987.

Deele, The: "Body Talk," Solar, 1983 • *Street Beat,* Solar, 1984.

Klymaxx: *Meeting in the Ladies Room* (2 tracks), MCA, 1984 • "Meeting in the Ladies Room," MCA, 1985.

Knight, Gladys: *All Our Love,* MCA, 1988 • w/ the Pips, "Love Overboard," MCA, 1988.

Levert: "Casanova," Atlantic, 1987 • "Casanova" (remix), Atlantic, 1987 • *The Big Throwdown,* Atlantic, 1987.

Midnight Star: "Freak-A-Zoid," Solar, 1983 • "No Parking (on the Dance Floor)," Solar, 1983 • *No Parking on the Dance Floor,* Solar, 1983 • "Wet My Whistle," Solar, 1983 • "Operator," Solar, 1984 • *Planetary Invasion,* Solar, 1984 • "Headlines," Solar, 1986 • *Headlines,* Solar, 1986 • "Midas Touch," Solar, 1986 • *Greatest Hits,* Solar/Atlantic, 1987.

Pendergrass, Teddy: "Joy," Asylum, 1988 • *A Little More Magic,* Elektrra, 1993.

Pieces of a Dream: *Goodbye Manhattan,* Blue Note, 1994.

Whispers, The: *So Good,* Solar, 1984.

Donnell Cameron

Donnell Cameron is one of the leading recorders of punk in the '90s. As an engineer, producer, and partner in L.A.'s Westbeach Recorders studio (with Brett Gurewitz; see entry), Cameron has been an integral part of punk standards by NoFX, Rancid, Sublime, Youth Brigade, Chemical People, and Rocket From The Crypt. Quiet, reserved (born in Victoria, British Columbia, in 1953), Cameron seems an unlikely candidate for punk avatar, yet his picaresque journey through life has taken many twists and turns.

Cameron played guitar and bass as a kid, and found himself in a band in Australia for a few years in the '60s. He also liked recording and owned one of the first cassette recorders, a Philips. Cameron drifted to the Caribbean in the '70s, where he owned a record store (specializing in Caribbean music like ska, reggae, soca, etc.) on the island of Montserrat from 1977 to 1982, and then a sailboat charter company until 1987. In the mid-'80s, Arrow built a new studio in Monserrat and Cameron assisted a friend, Pat Foley, on a few sessions for fun. Then in 1987, as Cameron tells it, "I got island fever and felt that I needed to do something more creative. I didn't feel like my life was over yet. Pat invited me to come to L.A. and work with him, so I moved to L.A. and went to audio engineering school. I helped Pat on some demos for bands at Brett Gurewitz's studio Westbeach Recorders and that's how it started. In the summer of '88 I was engineering for Brett. He rejoined Bad Religion and they went on tour over to Europe for six weeks. The sessions were booked, and he said, 'Here ya go, go for it.' And I did. Of course I never told the band it was my first session. A couple of years later I became a partner in the studio."

Though his introduction to the punk world was somewhat accidental, Cameron enjoys it. "I love the energy, the attitude, and the people are really nice. In punk music you don't look for perfection technically; I think it's more about capturing something in the studio, though I do try to maintain a certain standard sonically."

The punk recording ethos fits his own. "Here at West Beach we are fairly old school technology," he explains. "We have a lot of vintage equipment like an old spring reverb. I like to use tape delay instead of digital delay. I like to use tube mike pre-amps whenever possible. The less EQ and the less processing you do, I think, the better."

Cameron's best work includes the pre-hit Sublime and NoFX. Sublime's *Robbin' the Hood* captures a raw rasta/punk/hip-hop energy that was "professionalized" out of their later recording. NoFX's *White Trash, Two Heebs and a Bean*, besides having a hilarious politically incorrect title, is '90s punk at its best. The production is full, punchy, and clean. The band's amazing precision leaps out without losing power. Socially conscious without the portentiousness of Bad Religion, the band's humor shines throughout.

Standouts are the smoking "Soul Doubt" and "Stickin' in My Eye"; a jazzy and ironic version of Minor Threat's "Straight Edge"; a punchy and tuneful "Liza and Louise"; the Mexi-ska of "Johnny Appleseed"; and the neo–Rudy Vallee of "Buggley Eyes," a Cameron favorite.

"We rented a Gibson jazz bass guitar and made an imitation stand-up bass sound," says Cameron. "Al's Studio Rentals [film props] was next door to the studio, and they had this little gramophone in there, so we got that. My mom has some old 78s. We recorded the scratchy sound of the needle on the leading grooves just before the song starts, and used that as sort of a wash. That was really fun." —ERIC OLSEN AND DAWN DARLING

Big Drill Car: *"A Take Away,"* FS, 1990 (*The Big One*).
Chemical People: *Angels 'N Devils*, Cruz, 1990 • *Chemical People*, Cruz, 1992 • *Let It Go*, Cruz, 1992 • *Sound Tracks*, Cruz, 1992 • *Arpeggio Motorcade*, Cruz, 1997.
Distorted Pony: *"Jahr Null,"* FS, 1990 (*The Big One*).
Down By Law: *Blue*, Epitaph, 1992.
Drive Like Jehu: *Drive Like Jehu*, Headhunter, 1991.
Four One One: *This Isn't Me*, Workshed, 1991.
Guttermouth: *Musical Monkey*, NIT, 1997.
Heckle: *Complicated Futility of Ignorance*, Hopeless, 1997.
Hellhole: *Hellhole*, Justice, 1994.
Holy Love Snakes: *Blossom*, Headhunter/Cargo, 1991.
NoFX: *The Longest Line* (EP), Fat Wreck Chords, 1992 • *White Trash, Two Heebs and a Bean*, Epitaph, 1992.
No Use for a Name: *Incognito*, New Red Archives, 1990.
Rancid: *Rancid*, Epitaph, 1993.
Rhythm Collision: *Now/Pressure*, Dr. Strange, 1992.
Rich Kids on LSD: *Reactivate* (2 tracks), Epitaph, 1993.
Sublime: *Robbin' the Hood* (6 tracks), MCA, 1994.
Tommyknockers: *Perception Is Reality*, Skyclad, 1992.
Youth Brigade: *Happy Hour*, BYO, 1994.

Cecil Campbell

See PRINCE BUSTER

Ian Caple

L ondon-bred producer and engineer Ian Caple is a gentle confidant and collaborator with special artists in the beautiful, sometimes terrifying soundscapes they create: Tindersticks' classic pair of brooding, evocative, self-titled albums (1993, 1995); Sky Cries Mary's swirling and captivating *This Timeless Turning;* Shriekback's groundbreaking first three alterna-funk ambient albums; Tricky's space-age trip-hop masterpiece *Pre-Millennium Tension;* and the organic groove of the Mekons' *F.U.N. 90* EP.

The harsh structure of childhood classical violin lessons failed to drive out Caple's love of music, and at 13 he switched to the relative freedom of the guitar. Later, he worked in a music shop and met a variety of musicians, including a drummer who invited him to tag along to a studio, where he learned to set up drums and other preparatory tasks.

Caple's fascination with the studio grew and he soon gave up the guitar. At 17, he pounded the pavement looking for studio work, finally securing a gofer job at a little studio owned by EMI in the West End of London. In 1978, Caple was thrown into the lion's den of London's punk revolution, wrestling with younger bands that older studio hands didn't want to bother with. He quickly graduated from assistant to engineer, working with Adam and the Ants as they evolved from punks to New Romantics; he helped lay down the Ants' trademark tribal beat, though not without some innovation.

"The studio had been around since the '60s—the walls were padded, there was thick carpet on the floors, and it was acoustically dead," Caple recalls. "We were trying to get a big live drum sound, so I ended up pulling the lift up to the top floor, putting a microphone up there, and setting the drums up at the bottom of the shaft. It was a great time to experiment, break the rules, and change things."

Caple's big break came in 1982, when he was assigned to work with a new band, Shriekback, formed by keyboardist Barry Andrews (a founding member of XTC) and bassist David Allen (who had helped create punk funk in Gang of Four).

"We totally threw the rule book out the window. There was no real song structure and there was no real band as such," Caple says. "It was David, Barry, a guitarist, and a drum machine. I just recently listened to it again, and it sounds a lot like what guys are doing nowadays with drum loops and such. It reminds me a lot of

the Chemical Brothers [see entry]." "My Spine Is the Bassline" and "Lined Up" are dance floor masterworks of slithery funk and vocal strangeness.

With Shriekback, Caple helped develop the drumloop technique used extensively in house, techno, hiphop, and industrial music. "We'd record some drums on a piece of tape, make a loop out of it, and run it off the tape machine. Then, you'd just have a constant drum groove." The digital sampler now serves the same function with the touch of a key.

The Mekons' EP *F.U.N. 90* is among their best work: The band's version of Robbie Robertson's "Makes No Difference" catches the melodic midtempo groove of early Primal Scream and Happy Mondays. "Sheffield Park" is a carnival ride through eerie falsetto vocals and acid beats. "Having a Party" examines the pop-star life with a palpitating backbeat, and "One Horse Town" rides in on a Shriekback bass line and a drum sample from Eric B. & Rakim's "Paid in Full."

Tindersticks' emotionally devastating first album is one of the great discs of the '90s. Combining beauty and delicacy with stark emotional terror as well as any band since the Velvet Underground, Tindersticks unfolds through relaxed yet urgent pre-rock Euro melodies supported by sweet ringing guitar, chamber ensembles, Chet Baker–style trumpet, and bittersweet violin reminiscent of early Cockney Rebel. Singer Stuart Staples rumbles and mumbles through expressionistic vignettes of relationships forming and drifting apart in a river of "Blood," "Whiskey and Water," "Nectar," and "Jism." Leonard Cohen dances with Edith Piaf in a backroom littered with broken glass and flowers while raindrops fall on the roof.

Having set up the listener with a series of body blows, the final track, "The Not Knowing," delivers the knockout punch. Gone is Staples' mumbling as he sees and speaks with the diamond clarity that arrives just before the hangover.

Over woodwinds, Staples croons: "The not knowing is easy/And the suspecting, that's okay/Just don't tell me for certain /That our love is gone away." Self-deception vies with self-loathing for the singer's soul.

As Caple recalls the session, "They played it a few times and we couldn't quite work out the tempo. At some stages, it looked like it might be scrapped. It was a fairly tense atmosphere; then they recorded this one take and it was perfect. With a song like that, we were really nervous about changing anything, so we left it as it was." Perhaps a producer's most important talent is knowing when to leave perfection alone. —ERIC OLSEN AND DAWN DARLING

Compulsion: *Comforter,* One Little Indian, 1994.

Delicatessen: *Inviting Both Sisters out to Dinner* (EP), Big Life, 1994.

Elastic Purejoy: *The Elastic Purejoy,* World Domination, 1994.

Malacoda: *Cascade,* World Domination, 1997.

Mekons, The: *The Mekons Rock and Roll,* Twin/Tone/A&M, 1989 • *F.U.N. '90* (EP), Twin/Tone/A&M, 1990 • *The Curse of the Mekons,* Blast First, 1991 • "Born to Choose," Rykodisc, 1993 (*Born to Choose*).

Shreikback: *Tench* (EP), Y, 1982 • *Care,* Warner Bros., 1983 • "My Spine Is the Bassline," Warner Bros., 1983 • *Sacred City,* World Domination, 1992.

Sky Cries Mary: "Every Iceberg Is Afire," World Domination, 1994 • *This Timeless Turning,* World Domination, 1994.

Tindersticks: *Tindersticks,* Bar None, 1993 • *Tindersticks (Second Album),* London, 1995 • *Curtains,* PolyGram, 1997.

Tricky: *Pre-Millenium Tension,* Island, 1996.

Richard Carpenter

In the course of conducting interviews with other producers for this volume, artists and producers ranging from Paul Simon to Matt Wallace, Stevie Wonder, and Denny Diante (see entries) cited Richard Carpenter (born October 15, 1946, in New Haven, Connecticut) as one of the most brilliant producers of the '70s, and someone whose work they admire.

Richard's contributions to the Carpenters made them one of the top-selling American acts of all time,

with over 100 million albums sold. Although Jack Dougherty received credit for producing the first four Carpenters albums, it is widely known that the albums were produced by Carpenter, and that Dougherty's principal contribution was to book the studio time and pay the bills.

The skeptical reader need look no further than the several songs included on *From the Top* (the Carpenters' 4-CD boxed set) that were produced by Carpenter before he even met Dougherty. All of the elements of the Carpenters' sound are there: the lush, multitracked vocals, the meticulous arrangements, and the overall Carpenters gestalt.

Carpenter was nominated for a Best Arrangement Grammy five times. Artists as diverse as Sheryl Crow, Sonic Youth, Axl Rose, Redd Kross, and Chrissie Hynde have cited him as a major influence. "They are the best group ever," k.d. lang says. "Karen inspired me to become a singer, and Richard's production has influenced [co-producer] Ben Mink and me."

The rapid and vast commercial success of the Carpenters catapulted A&M from a small middle-of-the-road label to a major radio force, ushered in a new era of signings at A&M, and bankrolled a number of artists, including the Police, Joan Armatrading, and Supertramp.

"When Supertramp first went out on the road," Richard recalls, "the then head of marketing for A&M U.K. said to them, 'Whatever god you believe in, bow down to him before your shows and thank him for the Carpenters—because without them, you wouldn't be here.' "

Richard Carpenter's ability to predict hits is legendary. In 1969, Crocker Bank (since merged with Wells

114

Fargo Bank) featured a Paul Williams tune as part of a statewide advertising campaign emphasizing the bank's willingness to loan money to young couples. When Richard heard the ad one night on television, he knew instantly that it could be a commercial hit. "I recognized Paul Williams' voice on the song, and I assumed he had also written the song. I saw him soon afterward on the A&M lot and asked him if the song had other verses and a chorus. He assured me that it did, and so Karen and I recorded it."

Every A&R executive and musician in Los Angeles had heard "We've Only Just Begun" dozens, if not hundreds, of times; industry pundits had scoffed at the idea that a bank commercial could be turned into a rock single. The Carpenters' version of the song reached No. 2 in 1970 and stayed on the charts for three months.

Carpenter believes that the most important things to bring to a session are the song and the arrangement. "The arrangement is everything that makes a hit record," he explains. "You can have the best singer on the planet and the best song, but if you don't have the right arrangement for that song and singer, the singer's going nowhere and so is the song."

The best arrangements become inseparable from the song itself. Subsequent artists who cover such a tune find themselves keeping these arrangement ideas because performing the song without them is unimaginable. Artists who have covered Carpenters songs tend to stay very close to the original arrangements, as on the Carpenters tribute album *If I Were a Carpenter.*

One trademark of Richard's arrangement style is the use of "call-and-response" parts (where a horn, violin, or background vocal "answers" a line of the lead vocal). On "Superstar," for example, the violins echo Karen's line "Long ago . . ." with a parallel melody; on "Rainy Days and Mondays," the background vocals echo Karen's line "hangin' around," filling in the space in the melody.

Another Richard Carpenter arrangement device is the introduction of completely new music to the song. His piano intro to "Close to You" is an example of new music he added to a song, thereby creating one of the most instantly identifiable intros in all of pop music.

Carpenter has worked more or less continuously since Karen's death. In addition to reorchestrating, sequencing, and packaging a number of Carpenters compilation and greatest hits albums, he has released two solo albums: 1987's *Time,* and 1997's *Richard Carpenter: Pianist, Composer, Arranger, and Conductor.* Carpenter has also produced the MOR teenage singer Scott Grimes, Canadian popster Veronique, and Japanese pop star Akiko Kobayashi. —DANIEL J. LEVITIN

Carpenter, Richard: *Time,* A&M, 1987 • *Richard Carpenter: Pianist, Composer, Arranger, and Conductor,* PolyGram (Japan), 1997.

Carpenters, The: *Now and Then,* A&M, 1973 • "Sing," A&M, 1973 • "Top of the World," A&M, 1973 • "Yesterday Once More," A&M, 1973 • "I Won't Last a Day Without You," A&M, 1974 • *The Singles, 1969–1973,* A&M, 1974 • *Horizon,* A&M, 1975 • "Only Yesterday," A&M, 1975 • "Please Mr. Postman," A&M, 1975 • "Solitaire," A&M, 1975 • *A Kind of Hush,* A&M, 1976 • "There's a Kind of Hush (All Over the World)," A&M, 1976 • "Touch Me When We're Dancing," A&M, 1981 • *Lovelines,* A&M, 1989.

Grimes, Scott: *Scott Grimes,* A&M, 1989.

Kobayashi, Akiko: *City of Angels,* Funhouse (Japan), 1990.

Veronique: *Veronique,* A&M (Canada), 1989.

Rob Cavallo

Rob Cavallo is one of the young lions of the music industry as senior vice president of A&R at Reprise Records and as producer of the wildly successful pop-punk band Green Day, as well as the Muffs, Goo Goo Dolls, L7, Jawbreaker, and the Dance Hall Crashers. Green Day's *Dookie* (No. 2) is by far the best-selling punk album of all time, with sales topping the 14 million mark, and the band's follow-up, *Insomnia* (No. 2), is probably second, with sales over 4 million.

Cavallo was born in the Washington, D.C., area in 1963. His father is Bob Cavallo, who at the time owned the Shadows Club (later the Cellar Door) in D.C., and who went on to manage Little Feat, Weather Report, and Prince. The elder Cavallo was installed as chairman of the Walt Disney Music Group in early 1998, and still owns Atlas Third Rail Management (clients: Alanis Morissette, Green Day, Seal, Savage Garden, Weezer, the Goo Goo Dolls, and Earth, Wind and Fire).

Cavallo was literally baptized at the Shadows Club and raised on music. When he was around 10, the family moved to Los Angeles, and one of his first memories of L.A. is accompanying his father to a studio to watch Little Feat record. Lowell George (the late, great Feat guitarist) gave him his first guitar lesson.

Rob's father told him that music was a "kind of sucky" business, and didn't particularly encourage him to pursue it, but Rob spent untold hours in his room with his guitar and records (in succession: Beatles, Stones, Who, Motown, his father's clients, metal, and punk), learning songs by ear. By his midteens, Cavallo was playing in cover bands and was good enough that his father took notice and bought him a Teac A3340 4-track tape machine.

"I was interested in sounds from the beginning. I would get a new record and try to figure out how they made 'that sound,' " says Cavallo.

At 18, Cavallo went to work for George Massenburg's (see entry) G.M. Labs, laying cable, assembling circuit boards, and assisting on recordings by Linda Ronstadt, Jackson Browne, and Fleetwood Mac. He took some time off to complete a degree in English at USC, and then attended the Dick Grove School of Music, where he studied recording engineering, guitar, music theory, arrangement, and composition.

Full of youthful desire, Rob then decided it was time to produce. The elder Cavallo introduced Rob to Lenny Waronker (see entry) at Warner Bros./Reprise, who "grilled [him] for about two hours" on studio and musical matters, and pronounced him fit for A&R. At the label's request, Cavallo produced his first demo in 1988 for a band called Rhythm Corps, brought it in to (then) Reprise A&R head Michael Ostin, and was simultaneously dismayed and thrilled to find that he had "maxed out the potential of the band, exposed their weaknesses, and that therefore, the label was no longer interested in signing the band." However, the label was interested in the young Cavallo, and he went to work in the Reprise A&R department. Though studio-savvy, Cavallo had little knowledge of the inner workings of the music business, so for the next four years he assisted Michael Ostin, learning the ropes and observing such titans as Ted Templeman, Russ Titelman, and Tommy LiPuma (see entries).

In 1992, A&R compatriot David Katznelson found a band called the Muffs, a pop-punk, half male, half female four-piece, and offered to share A&R credit if Cavallo would co-produce the band with him. The result was *The Muffs*, a punchy, poppy workout (highlight: "Lucky Guy") that neatly presages Cavallo's work with Green Day.

Though veterans of two EPs and two albums on Lookout Records, the San Francisco East Bay's Green Day (Billy Joe Armstrong: guitar, vocals; Mike Pritchard: bass, vocals; Tre Cool: drums) were barely in their twenties when they came to Reprise seeking Cavallo for his work with the Muffs.

The band and the A&R/producer hit it off right away, and "the next thing I knew, I was in the studio with Green Day," recalls Cavallo. "I remember thinking, 'This record has a chance to be really good because the songs sound complete and the album is like a fun rock 'n' roll ride,' although I had no idea it would sell 14 mil-

lion records," he admits.

Cavallo created a crisp, dry sound for the band. "I was listening to Cheap Trick's *Black and White* and *In Color*, Black Sabbath's *Paranoid*, and the first Police record as sonic reference points," he says. "Most recent rock records had been huge, wet, and dark like Soundgarden. When I turned *Dookie* in to Reprise somebody said, 'Sounds like demos.' I said 'No, it sounds like demos to you because it sounds dry, but it has to be dry because the tempos are faster, and it actually sounds big enough.' I wanted to pump it up big enough to get it on the radio, but we had to be true to the band's past on Lookout. When [Lookout owner] Larry Livermore said it was okay, I knew we were cool."

Dookie succeeded wildly by being the right record at the right time. By 1994, Jane's Addiction, Nirvana, Pearl Jam, and Red Hot Chili Peppers had made rock radio safe for grunge and punk bands. *Dookie* retained touchstones of West Coast punk (strained, slightly out-of-tune vocals; blazing tempos; dry production), while offering memorable melodies ("Welcome to Paradise," "Basket Case," "She"), rhythmic variety ("Longview," "When I Come Around") and sharp, youthful humor.

Cavallo has continued to succeed with Green Day (*Insomnia, Nimrod*) and Goo Goo Dolls, and in early 1998, he recorded platinum angry-young-woman Alanis Morissette ("Uninvited") for the *City of Angels* soundtrack. —ERIC OLSEN

Dance Hall Crashers: "Enough," 510 Records, 1995 • "Enough," Reprise, 1995 (*Angus* soundtrack).
Goo Goo Dolls: *A Boy Named Goo,* Warner Bros., 1995.
Green Day: "Basket Case," Reprise, 1994 • "Longview," Reprise, 1994 • "When I Come Around," Warner Bros., 1994 • "When I Come Around" (live), A&M, 1994 (*Woodstock 94*) • *Dookie,* Reprise, 1994 • "Geek Stink Breath," Reprise, 1995 • *Insomniac,* Reprise, 1995 • "J.A.R.," Reprise, 1995 (*Angus* soundtrack) • *Live Tracks* (EP), Reprise, 1995 • *Nimrod,* Reprise, 1997 • "Time of Your Life (Good Riddance)," Reprise, 1997 • "Tired of Waiting for You," Warner Bros., 1997 (*Howard Stern's Private Parts*).
Jawbreaker: *Dear You,* DGC, 1995.
Kara's Flowers: *Fourth World,* Warner Bros., 1997.
L7: "Drama," Slash/Reprise, 1997 • "Off the Wagon," Slash/Reprise, 1997 • *The Beauty Process: Triple Platinum,* Slash/Reprise, 1997.
Love Spit Love: "Am I Wrong," Reprise, 1995 (*Angus* soundtrack).
Muffs, The: *The Muffs,* Warner Bros., 1993 • *Blonder and Blonder,* Reprise, 1995 • "Funny Face," Reprise, 1995

(*Angus* soundtrack) • "Kids in America," Capitol, 1995 (*Clueless* soundtrack).

Weezer: "You Gave Your Love to Me Softly," Reprise, 1995 (*Angus* soundtrack).

Ron Chancey

The skills that make someone a successful record producer can also apply to other areas of recorded music. Ron Chancey's career has not only encompassed hit records such as the Grammy-winning Oak Ridge Boys' "Elvira" (No. 1 country), but also some of America's best known commercial jingles, like the Chevy truck campaign that uses Bob Seger's "Like a Rock."

In the '90s, Chancey has continued to be an innovative producer, recording both successful jingles and hit records for such hot new country acts as Ricochet. Chancey is a rarity on Music Row: a native Nashvillean. He began his music career as an aspiring songwriter and got his first break when Buck Owens offered him a job running his Nashville-based publishing and production company, Bluebook Music.

"He wanted to open a company here in Nashville, so I gave up a really good job as a consultant for a textbook company," Chancey recalls. "I took a two-thirds cut in salary to get into the music business. Everybody thought I was nuts. I probably was."

Owens called Chancey one day and said he was sending Freddie Hart in for Chancey to produce. "I said, 'I don't know how to do that.' He said, 'Oh yeah, you can do it.' So I was nervous as a cat, but we went in and had a session and it did pretty good. That's how I got started."

After a couple of years, Owens pulled the plug on his Nashville operation. Chancey decided to start his own label and Cartwheel Records was born. "I think the first or second record we ever had was a hit," he recalls. "It was Billy 'Crash' Craddock's 'Knock Three Times' (No. 3 country). It got us started. We had a real good run. We had a bunch of hit records with Crash, David Frizzell, and Johnny Darrell. We did real well for two or three years. We won the Billboard New Country Label of the Year Award in 1972."

Chancey and his partners sold Cartwheel to ABC in 1973, and he stayed on with the company to work with Don Gant. "He did a whole lot for this town," Chancey says. "He signed [Jimmy] Buffett and the Amazing Rhythm Aces. . . . I was head of A&R and he was general manager. We shared an office for a year or two and we had a ball. That was back when the music business was a lot more fun than it is now. I think most people were in it back in those days because it was fun and the money you made was the secondary thing about it."

When MCA bought out ABC, Chancey became vice president of A&R. During his tenure with MCA, Chancey facilitated the Oak Ridge Boys' transition from popular gospel group to superstar country act. Their first country album, *Y'all Come Back Saloon,* quickly made the group one of country's most popular acts. He produced countless hits for the Oaks, including "Come On In" (No. 3 country), "Leavin' Louisiana in the Broad Daylight" (No. 1 country), "Bobby Sue" (No. 1 country), "American Made" (No. 1 country), "Make My Life with You" (No. 1 country), and "Thank God for Kids" (No. 3 country). He also produced R&B artist Bobby "Blue" Bland and such country talents as Conway Twitty, Brenda Lee, and Loretta Lynn.

Chancey says finding the right material is the most important responsibility a producer has. "The producer should know what songs are right for his artist," he says, "but these days it's kind of gone to a committee situation; most labels have three or four people out looking for songs, which is still good because the business has gotten so competitive that you have to get out and compete for the songs."

How does one match the song to the artist? "It's a gut instinct," Chancey says. "I think some people have a natural ability to do that. Some people are strong in the technical end, with all the new gear and stuff like that, but my [strength] is the back-to-basic thing where I've always believed the song is about 90 percent of it."

Chancey admits it's harder finding good songs right now because there are so many people recording. "There are so many new acts and we probably have three times as many people in the studio cutting. It just cuts down on the quality of songs," he says. "Sometimes I go for days listening to hundreds of tapes and don't find anything I like, and start thinking, 'Maybe I don't know it anymore.' And then all of a sudden, you'll hear one, and thank goodness."

Chancey had nearly retired from producing when he ran across the band Ricochet. "I had kind of lost my desire for it, I guess," he explains. "I had been in the commercial business doing jingles, and I've had a lot of success in that business. Then I went to a football game with one of my clients at the University of Missouri, and after the game, we went to this club and Ricochet was playing there. I got interested and we cut some demos."

Chancey's son Blake had just gotten a job at Columbia Records in A&R. According to the senior Chancey, "He said, 'Dad, I can't sign an act that you bring in first thing,' but I asked him to come over anyway and he liked them. Paul Worley came over and they gave them a development deal. So it was the first act that Blake signed and it all worked out. He helped me and I helped him."

With hits like "What Do I Know" (No. 5 country), "Daddy's Money" (No. 1 country), and "He Left a Lot to Be Desired," Ricochet has become one of country music's most popular new bands, reviving Chancey's career in record production in the process. He co-produced Ricochet with the technically oriented Ed Seay. Chancey feels Seay's technological savvy dovetails well with the fact that he is "a feel person." Chancey also co-manages Ricochet, a new role for him.

Chancey continues to work in the jingle industry and run his own publishing company, Chancey Tunes. "It isn't quite as much fun as doing records," he says of the jingles. "It's more of a business approach because you have so many guidelines to gear what you're doing by. But it's still fun when you come up with a really good commercial. And when you get down to it, more people have probably heard 'Like a Rock' than they've heard any record I ever did."

He's happy his son followed in his footsteps; Ron and Blake Chancey are co-producing newcomer Roger Hamilton. "Blake and I hope we can have a hit on it because I don't think anybody's ever done that before and it's really been a trip," he says. "If it works out, it would be pretty cool." —DEBORAH EVANS PRICE

Bland, Bobby "Blue": *Get On Down With,* ABC, 1975.
Brown, T. Graham: *Come As You Were,* Capitol, 1988 • "Darlene," Capitol, 1988.
Carver, Johnny: *The Best Of,* ABC, 1977.
Craddock, Billy "Crash": *Two Sides of Crash,* ABC, 1973 • "Rub It In," ABC, 1974 • "Ruby Baby," ABC, 1975 • *Crash,* ABC, 1976 • "Broken Down in Tiny Pieces," ABC/Dot, 1977.
Lee, Brenda: *Greatest Country Hits,* MCA, 1990 • *Anthology,* Vols. 1–2, MCA, 1991.
Lynn, Loretta: w/ Conway Twitty, *Two's a Party,* MCA, 1980 • *Lyin', Cheatin', Woman Chasin', Honky Tonkin', Whiskey Drinkin',* MCA, 1983 • w/ Conway Twitty, *20 Greatest Hits,* MCA, 1988.
Oak Ridge Boys: "Come On In," ABC, 1978 • "I'll Be True to You," ABC, 1978 • *Room Service,* ABC, 1978 • *The Oak Ridge Boys Have Arrived,* MCA, 1979 • *Greatest Hits,* Vol. 1, MCA, 1980 • "Leaving Louisiana in the Broad Daylight," MCA, 1980 • "Trying to Love Two Women," MCA, 1980

• "Elvira," MCA, 1981 • "Fancy Free," MCA, 1981 • *Fancy Free,* MCA, 1981 • "Bobbie Sue," MCA, 1982 • "Thank God for Kids," MCA, 1982 • "American Made," MCA, 1983 • *American Made,* MCA, 1983 • *I Guess It Never Hurts to Hurt Sometimes,* MCA, 1983 • "Love Song," MCA, 1983 • "Everyday," MCA, 1984 • *Greatest Hits,* Vol. 2, MCA, 1984 • "I Guess It Never Hurts to Hurt Sometimes," MCA, 1984 • "Little Things," MCA, 1985 • "Make My Life with You," MCA, 1985 • *Seasons,* MCA, 1985 • "Touch a Hand, Make a Friend," MCA, 1985 • *Step On Out,* MCA, 1987 • *Greatest Hits,* Vol. 3, MCA, 1989 • *The Collection,* MCA, 1992 • *You're the One,* MCA, 1992.
Ricochet: "Daddy's Money," Columbia, 1996 • "What Do I Know," Columbia, 1996 • *Ricochet,* Columbia, 1996 • "Blink of an Eye," Columbia, 1997 • "Ease My Troubled Mind," Columbia, 1997 • "He Left a Lot to Be Desired," Columbia, 1997 • *Blink of An Eye,* Columbia, 1997.
Sawyer Brown: *Somewhere in the Night,* Liberty, 1987 • *Wide Open,* Curb/Capitol, 1988.
Twitty, Conway: *A Night With,* MCA, 1981 • "Rest Your Love on Me/I Am the Dreamer (You Are the Dream)," MCA, 1981 • "Tight Fittin' Jeans," MCA, 1981 • "Red Neckin' Love Makin' Night," MCA, 1982 • *Classic Conway,* MCA, 1983 • *Silver Anniversay Collection,* MCA, 1990 • *The Conway Twitty Collection,* MCA, 1994 • *See also* Lynn, Loretta.

Chas Chandler

Chas Chandler will be forever linked to James Marshall Hendrix. Chandler spotted the talents of the brash guitarist, then called Jimmy James, and eventually managed him and produced the recordings that etched Jimi Hendrix into rock lore.

Chandler's production style was never grandiose: he always preferred the emotionally charged first take to the polished, freeze-dried relic left by a studio hack. That approach owed much to Chandler's pedigree as the bass guitarist of one of the supreme British acts of the '60s: the Animals. Indeed, Chandler's propulsive bass playing on such Animals classics as "It's My Life," "We Gotta Get Out of This Place," and "Inside, Looking Out," is the spiritual forerunner of Hendrix's elemental bursts of guitar on "Purple Haze" and "Foxy Lady."

Chandler supervised the first two Hendrix albums, *Are You Experienced?* (No. 5) and *Axis: Bold As Love* (No. 3), including essential tracks such as "The Wind Cries

Mary" (No. 5 U.K.) and "Little Wing." Moreover, Chandler helped put together the Jimi Hendrix Experience, arguably Hendrix's best band. As with any mentor, Chandler became redundant when Hendrix spread his wings to fly in new directions. In the '70s, Chandler took hold of Slade, managing the boisterous British glam band that, although a phenomenon at home, made little impact in the U.S. Chandler also took the production helm for the Animals' excellent 1977 reunion album, *Before We Were So Rudely Interrupted*. Subsequent Animals reunions were fleeting, leaving Chandler on his own once again.

A native of Heaton, a village near Newcastle-upon-Tyne in England's industrial northeast, Chandler died of a heart attack in 1996 at age 57. In addition to his musical exploits, Chandler helped establish the Newcastle Arena in his hometown. —BEN CROMER

Animals, The: *Before We Were So Rudely Interrupted*, Barn/Jet, 1977 • *Ark*, IRS, 1983.

Burdon, Eric: *Survivor*, Polydor, 1977.

Buzzards: *Jellied Eels to Record Deals*, Chrysalis, 1979.

Hendrix, Jimi: "Hey Joe," Polydor, 1967 • "Purple Haze," Reprise, 1967 • *War Heroes*, Reprise, 1973 • *The Essential*, Reprise, 1978 • *Kiss the Sky*, Polydor, 1984 • "Foxy Lady," Reprise, 1992 (*Wayne's World* soundtrack) • *Ultimate Experience*, MCA, 1993 • *South Saturn Delta*, MCA, 1997.

Jimi Hendrix Experience: *Are You Experienced?*, Reprise, 1967 • *Axis: Bold As Love*, Reprise, 1967.

Slade: *Play It Loud*, Polydor/Cottillion, 1970 • *Alive*, Polydor, 1972 • *Slayed*, Polydor, 1972 • *In Flame* soundtrack, Polydor/WB, 1974 • *Stomp Your Hands Clap Your Feet*, Warner Bros., 1974 • *Nobody's Fools*, Polydor/WB, 1976 • *Whatever Happened to Slade?*, Barn, 1977 • *Alive*, Vol. 2, Barn, 1978 • "Merry Xmas Everybody," Virgin/EMI, 1985 (*Now That's What I Call Music Xmas Album*).

Soft Machine: *Soft Machine*, One Way, 1968 • *Soft Machine*, Vols. 1–2, Big Beat, 1989.

Top Secret: *Another Crazy Day*, RCA, 1981.

Mike Chapman

A child singing sensation, songwriter, and producer, Australian-born Mike Chapman has been among the most successful and influential hitmakers of the last 30 years, specializing in a particularly tuneful and energetic brand of power pop. Chapman has written (with and without partner Nicky Chinn) or produced such U.S. No. 1 hits as "Kiss You All Over" (Exile), "Mickey" (Toni Basil), "My Sharona" (The Knack), "Hot Child in the City" (Nick Gilder), and "Heart of Glass," "The Tide Is High" and "Rapture" (Blondie).

His U.S. Top 10 hits include "Little Willy" and "Ballroom Blitz" (Sweet); "Heart and Soul" (Huey Lewis and the News); "Love Is a Battlefield" (Pat Benatar); "Love Touch" (Rod Stewart); "Stumblin' In" (Suzi Quatro and Chris Norman); as well as other smashes for Benatar, Divinyls, Lita Ford, Bow Wow Wow, Scandal, Material Issue, Smokie, Mud, and others.

Mike Chapman was born near Brisbane, Australia, in 1947, and from infancy on, he was glued to the radio; its invisible voices captured his ear and imagination. Recalls Chapman, "There was the rock 'n' roll of Buddy Holly, Elvis Presley, the Everly Brothers, and the Caribbean-inflected pop of the Hilltoppers and Harry Belafonte. I remember the feelings I had when I heard that music and it's never really left me. Right from that time I was plugged into these wonderful pop songs. I never got that out of my system, and I never had any doubts about what I was going to do with my life."

At 8, young Mike saved up his pennies and bought a guitar. At the time there were live radio shows in Brisbane with names like Rumpus Room that brought young talent on to perform. Soon the precocious tyke was performing Paul Anka's "Diana," "Wake Up Little Susie," and "All Shook Up" as a radio regular and local celebrity.

At 13, Chapman went to high school, where he formed a successful band with classmates and honed his "Elvis look and Buddy Holly sound." After graduating from high school and acting a bit, Chapman headed for England in 1966 to pursue his dreams of pop stardom. Chapman kicked about, glorying in the swinging London of the Beatles, flower power, and discotheques. He worked at one of London's bigger music stores with such future notables as Steve Marriott (Small Faces, Humble Pie) and Paul Kossoff (Free). Kossoff was "a lazy son of a bitch," remembers Chapman with a chuckle. "We'd always find him sitting in the corner with a guitar wailing away."

Chapman joined a few bands, ending up in Tangerine Peel—with whom he recorded (unsuccessfully) for RCA in 1969—giving him his first taste of the studio. While he was with Tangerine Peel, Chapman began writing songs. He augmented his meager "rock star" income by waitering at Tramps, a nightclub. Early one weeknight, Chapman was playing a demo of one of his songs over the club sound system when a customer asked about it. Chapman told the customer—Nicky Chinn, a fledgling lyricist—that he himself had written it, and by that weekend they were writing together. The third song they wrote was "Funny Funny," a takeoff on the Archies' "Sugar, Sugar" (see Jeff Barry entry), which they played for a producer acquaintance of Chinn's named Phil Wainman.

Wainman loved the song and brought it to Sweet, the band he was working with. The band had a bit of a problem with the song because, as Chapman tells it, "They thought they were Deep Purple, not the Archies." Despite the band's sneer, "Funny Funny" became the band and the writing team's first big hit, reaching No. 13 in the U.K. in 1971.

Chinnichap's (Chapman and Chinn's publishing company and nickname) relationship with Sweet continued through 1974. In that time, they kicked out a plethora of hits, including "Co-Co" (No. 2 U.K.), "Little Willy" (No. 3 U.S.), "Wig-Wam Bam" (No. 4 U.K.), "Blockbuster" (No. 1 U.K.), "Hell Raiser" (No. 2 U.K.), "Ballroom Blitz" (No. 5 U.S.) and "Teenage Rampage" (No. 2 U.K.). Though shamelessly commercial and frankly silly, the best of the Sweet hits ("Little Willy," "Ballroom Blitz") feature slamming guitar riffs, sharp tunes, vicious hooks, and orchestral group harmonies (later lifted whole by Queen).

When not writing international hits for Sweet, Chapman was spending time in the studio observing legendary producer Mickie Most (see entry). "Watching Mickie Most work was a real education for me. Number one is song. Number two is performance. Once you have a great song, a terrific performance can happen in a half-hour. So I learned to make records efficiently and cheaply, which is important."

Chapman's next big break came through Most, who discovered Suzi Quatro playing with her sisters in a band (Cradle) in Detroit. Most nixed the sisters and brought Suzi—a game singer, great bass player, and dynamite persona—to London and began working with her. Things weren't coming together, so Most brought in hitmakers Chinnichap to help out. Two weeks later Chapman and Chinn delivered "Can the Can," produced the song with Quatro and her tough three-piece band, and watched it shoot to No. 1 in the U.K.

The first Quatro album is a power-pop landmark, infusing pop into real rock 'n' roll, rather than the other way around. Besides boasting Chinnichap's hooky "Can," "48 Crash," and the pre–Adam Ant tribal beat of "Primitive Love," the album also features Quatro and guitarist Len Tuckey's "Official Suburban Superman," "Sticks and Stones," and best of all, "Skin Tight Skin," a spooky precursor to the electronic new wave of Gary Numan and Blondie: highlighted by Alastair McKenzie's atmospheric mellotron wash and jazzy electric piano.

Chinnichap did several albums with Quatro, generating a boatload of hits in the U.K. before finally hitting in the U.S. in 1979 with "Stumblin' In" (No. 4), her duet with Smokie lead singer Chris Norman. Quatro's tough-chick persona led to the role of Leather Tuscadero on TV's *Happy Days*. For Chapman, the hits just kept on coming.

"As a writer and producer in this business, there's nothing like success to feed success—you start snowballing," he says. "Once you start having hits, somehow you just can't do anything wrong for a period of time. It all comes to an end sooner or later, but you gotta ride that wave, and I rode it for a long time—from 1971 right to the end of that decade."

In the mid-'70s Chapman became enamored of the Eagles (Chinn had been a folk fan all along). He found a country rock band in England named Kindness, changed their name to Smokie, and, with Chinn, began writing Eagle-esque songs for them. Although Smokie sold more records worldwide than any Chapman artist other than Blondie, only one song ("Living Next Door to Alice," No. 25) cracked the U.S. Top 40. Though perhaps the fact that the U.S. had the real Eagles contributed to the problem, Chapman feels partner Chinn didn't help matters.

"'If You Think You Know How to Love Me' was Smokie's first big hit around the world," says Chapman. "Paul Drew was the programming guy at [Top 40 giant] KHJ in L.A., and for the whole RKO chain. Paul took it upon himself to break Smokie in America, and he played our song right out of the box. Unfortunately, my ex-partner told a friend of Paul's, 'Wow, look at that: I got our song played out of the box on KHJ.' And Paul said '*He* got it on? Okay I'll show him how we get it off,' and that was that."

Chapman finally broke away from Chinn and produced his most enduring work when he hooked up with Blondie. "I saw Blondie three nights in a row at the Whiskey in L.A. in 1977 and absolutely flipped out over them. The songs were incredible, and they weren't a particularly tight band, but their performance was spectacular. They sent me a little note and I was excited. About six months later Terry Ellis signed them to Chrysalis, came straight to me, and asked me to meet with them. Writer/guitarist Chris Stein, singer/writer Debbie Harry, and I got together in New York and decided to take a shot," says Chapman.

Parallel Lines (No. 6 U.S., No. 1 U.K.) was the first new wave album to trust its material enough to allow for broad stylistic diversity. "They were sort of punk, sort of funny, sort of pop, retro, futuristic, etc., and on *Parallel Lines* each track is different, but it's all glued together with the same sort of glue so it sounds like a terrific package," exclaims Chapman.

Terrific indeed. "Hanging on the Telephone" (No. 5 U.K.) and "One Way or Another" are great tough-girl rockers. "Pretty Baby" and "I'm Gonna Love You Too" are cool girl-group sing-alongs. "Sunday Girl" (No. 1 U.K.) is perfectly light and charming without being smarmy. "Heart of Glass" successfully united new wave techno-pop and disco for the first time, and rode that chariot to No. 1 the world over. Throughout, Chapman's production is hard and tight enough for new wave. Stein's and Frank Infante's guitars blaze and crunch while Clem Burke's drums thunder and shimmer, yet subtlety is never sacrificed as Jimmy Destri's keyboards range from '60s organ to space electronics, as needed. Hip, yet unabashedly pop, *Parallel Lines* is Chapman's best possible album, and it finally gave him an unqualified American success. —ERIC OLSEN AND DAWN DARLING

Altered Images: *Bite,* Portrait/Epic, 1983 • *I Could Be Happy: The Best Of,* Epic, 1997.

Atlantic Star: *Love Crazy,* Reprise, 1991.

Australian Crawl: *Sons of Beaches,* EMI America, 1982.

Baby Animals: *Baby Animals,* Imago, 1991.

Benatar, Pat: *In the Heat of the Night* (3 tracks), Chrysalis, 1979 • "Invincible (Theme from the Legend of Billie Jean)," Chrysalis, 1985 • *Best Shots,* Chrysalis, 1989 • *All Fired Up,* Chrysalis, 1995 • *16 Classic Performances,* EMI, 1996.

Blondie: *Parallel Lines,* Chrysalis, 1978 • *Eat to the Beat,* Chrysalis, 1979 • "Heart of Glass," Chrysalis, 1979 • *Autoamerican,* Chrysalis, 1980 • "The Tide Is High," Chrysalis, 1980 • *Best Of,* Chrysalis, 1981 • "Rapture," Chrysalis, 1981 • *The Hunter,* Chrysalis, 1982 • "Atomic" (remix), Brilliant/Chrysalis, 1995.

Blue Rondo á La Turk: *Chewing the Fat,* Virgin, 1982.

Bow Wow Wow: "Do You Wanna Hold Me," RCA, 1983 • *When the Going Gets Tough, the Tough Get Going,* One Way, 1983, 1997 • *The Best of Bow Wow Wow,* RCA, 1996.

Danceclass: *Danceclass,* A&M, 1982.

Derringer: *If I Weren't So Romantic, I'd Shoot You,* Blue Sky, 1978 • *Rock and Roll Hootchie Koo: The Best Of,* Sony, 1996.

Des Barres, Michael: *I'm Only Human,* Dreamland, 1980.

Device: "Hanging on a Heart Attack," Chrysalis, 1986 • *22B3,* Chrysalis, 1986.

Divinyls: "Pleasure and Pain," Chrysalis, 1985 • *What a Life,* Chrysalis, 1985 • *Temperamental,* Chrysalis, 1988.

Exile: "Kiss You All Over," Curb/WB, 1978 • "You Thrill Me," Curb/WB, 1978 • *Mixed Emotions,* Curb/WB, 1978 • *All There Is,* Curb/WB, 1979 • *Best Of,* Curb/MCA, 1985.

Faltskog, Agnetha: *Wrap Your Arms Around Me,* CBS, 1983.

Ford, Lita: "Kiss Me Deadly," RCA, 1988 • *Lita,* RCA, 1988 • w/ Ozzy Osborne, "Close My Eyes (Forever)," RCA, 1989 • *Stiletto,* RCA, 1990 • *Greatest Hits,* RCA, 1993.

4 Non Blondes: "I'm the One," Fox, 1994 (*Airheads* soundtrack).

Gilder, Nick: "Hot Child in the City," Chrysalis, 1978 • *City Nights* (3 tracks), Chrysalis, 1978.

Harry, Debbie: "The Tide Is High," Chrysalis, 1988 • *Def, Dumb and Blonde* (7 tracks), Sire/Reprise, 1989 • *Once More into the Bleach,* Chrysalis, 1989.

Knack, The: *Get the Knack,* Capitol, 1979 • "Good Girls Don't," Capitol, 1979 • "My Sharona," Capitol, 1979 • *But the Little Girls Understand,* Capitol, 1980 • *Retrospective: The Best of the Knack,* Capitol, 1992 • "My Sharona" (remix), RCA, 1994 (*Reality Bites* soundtrack).

Material Issue: *Freak City* soundtrack, Mercury, 1994.

Mud: *Mud Rock,* Rak, 1974 • *Greatest Hits,* Rak, 1975 • *Mud Rock 2,* Rak, 1975 • "Lonely This Christmas," Virgin/EMI, 1985 (*Now That's What I Call Music Xmas Album*).

Nervus Rex: *Nervus Rex,* Dreamland, 1980.

One of the Girls: *One of the Girls,* EastWest, 1993.

Penfield, Holly: *Full Grown Child,* Dreamland, 1980.

Quatro, Suzi: *Quatro,* Rak/Bell, 1974 • *Suzi Quatro,* Rak/Bell, 1974 • *Your Mama Won't Like Me,* Rak, 1975 • *If You Knew Suzi,* Rak/RSO, 1978 • w/ Chris Norman, "Stumblin' In," RSO, 1979 • *Suzi and Other Four Letter Words,* Rak, 1979 • "Rock Hard," RSO, 1980 (*Times Square* soundtrack) • *Rock Hard,* Dreamland, 1980.

Scandal: "The Warrior," Columbia, 1984 • *Warrior,* Columbia, 1984.

Shandi: *Shandi,* Dreamland, 1980.

Smokie: *Changing All the Time,* Rak, 1975 • *Pass It Around,* Rak, 1975 • *Midnight Cafe,* Rak/RSO, 1976 • *Bright Lights and Back Alleys,* Rak/RSO, 1977 • "Living Next Door to Alice," RSO, 1977 • *The Montreux Album,* Rak/RSO, 1978.

Spider: *Between the Lines,* Dreamland, 1981.

Squier, Billy: *Tell the Truth,* Capitol, 1993.

Stewart, Rod: "Love Touch," Warner Bros., 1986 • *Rod Stewart,* Warner Bros., 1986.

Sweet: *Desolation Boulevard,* Gold Rush, 1974, 1996.

TAMI Show: *The TAMI Show,* Chrysalis, 1985 • *Wanderlust,* RCA, 1991.

Thieves: *Yucatan,* Arista, 1980.

Tucker, Tanya: *Tear Me Apart,* MCA, 1979.

Gerry "Baby" Charles

See FULL FORCE

Chemical Brothers

(TOM ROWLANDS AND ED SIMONS)

The Chemical Brothers are alchemists who blend hip-hop rhythms, thumping bass lines, disjointed drum loops, groovy disco beats, and otherworldly samples into a head-trippy and soulful alloy. Ed Simons and Tom Rowlands, two unrelated Mancunians, are the Chemical Brothers and what they do is nothing less than science.

Tom Rowlands grew up within miles of Oxford University. Rowlands' father, a filmmaker (the legendary *Animals on Tour Behind the Iron Curtain,* assorted commercials), encouraged and financed his son's early efforts. At 12, Rowlands began writing songs on guitar with the aid of a drum machine, and this was the foundation of his musical future.

Rowlands, who gives his older brother credit for exposing him to the American urban music that would complete his musical architecture, played in a techno-funk band, Ariel, which recorded for the British dance label Deconstruction.

Photo by Richard Weedon

Ed Simons also had the benefit of a middle-class upbringing, living with his mother, a lawyer, in a suburb of London. Though he was financially well-off, Simons' happiness was not found in school or the 'burbs, but in the dance clubs of London on the weekends.

"I was one of those annoying kids you see in clubs now, looking all wrong and dancing badly to rare-groove records," he says. Now those annoying kids are hooked, lined, and sinkered into the groove the Chemical Brothers are serving up.

Rowlands and Simons, both born in 1970, met while studying history at Manchester University. They discovered they had mutual interests in hip-hop, techno, house, and rock 'n' roll. Their debut occurred spontaneously at a wedding when the hired DJ took a break and the lads took it upon themselves to wreak havoc on the turntables.

Realizing there was something special betwixt them, they dubbed themselves the "Dust Brothers" ("something to put on fliers") and started working as house DJs for the Manchester dance club, Naked Under Leather. After they put out remixes as the Dust Brothers, the existent L.A.-based production team of the same name (see entry) objected. Obliging the original Dust Brothers' requests, the Manchester duo rechristened themselves "The Chemical Brothers."

In 1994 they released "Song to the Siren" (from the EP *14th Century Sky*), generated by their displeasure with the stale house-rave music they heard in clubs. The single dismantled the accepted house and techno mixes of the time and revealed a harder-edged break-beat sound, soon to be their signature. The resultant excitement generated unprecedented major-label clambering—with Virgin winning world release rights, and Astralwerks/Caroline getting the U.S. The Chemical Brothers make extensive use of samples—as well as guitar work by Rowlands—to create their unique music. Rowlands states, "If I buy records, it serves two purposes: I can listen for enjoyment, and there might also be some creative spark there. To me, it's a beautiful combination."

Often, the Chemical Brothers' sampling is untraceable to the original. Simons explains, "Over the years, we've become so good at treating drums, twisting them up. On our first album we had these [virtual] 'supergroups' playing together—like a sort of trad English indie band playing with an old '70s funk band—which, for legal reasons, we can't get into."

The Chemical Brothers' fast and furious rise to fame has brought controversy to their genre and generated some snippiness from certain pundits: Is sampling creating music, or just scavenging the creative endeavors of others? The issue is too large to resolve here. Simons and Rowlands are happy to give credit where credit is due, and they make every effort to give appropriate recognition (and funds) to those they sample from. Rowlands claims that he and Simons went to great lengths to credit the holder of the recording rights after they appropriated a sample of rapper Keith Murray from a bootleg mix tape.

The Chemicals' musical input isn't limited to music from the past. Besides producing their own material, they have collaborated with, and produced remixes for, such artists as Noel Gallagher of Oasis, Charlatans UK, Prodigy, St. Etienne, and Manic Street Preachers.

"Leave Home," the first track on *Exit Planet Dust* (No. 9 U.K.), enters with a funky bass line so fat that it oozes out of the speakers, followed by the imperative "the brothers gonna work it out." Another track, "Alive Alone," features the haunting and beautiful vocals of British folk singer Beth Orton, who gives depth and dimension to the Chemicals' soothing synth rhythms, orchestral sounds, and childlike chiming. She sings, "And I'm Alive / And I'm Alone / And I never wanted to be either of those." Orton's voice sways back and forth before collapsing under the weight of the song.

The Chemicals' second LP, *Dig Your Own Hole*, continues in the groove. The first, and most radio-friendly track, "Block Rockin' Beats," is a derivative of Schooly D's "Gucci Again," featuring another funky-ass bass line. "Get Up on It Like This" delivers Beethoven on acid. Another collaboration with Orton, "Where Do I Begin?" is again exquisite, as layers of aural textures and vocals create a collage both hypnotizing and exhilarating.

The Chemical Brothers may owe the building blocks of their music to those they borrow from, but they craft those blocks into musical creations both artful and funky. Maybe the future belongs to those who can re-create with the past. —DAWN DARLING

Charlatans UK: "Toothache" (remix), Beggars Banquet/Atlantic, 1995.
Chemical Brothers: *Exit Planet Dust*, Astralwerks, 1995 • *Leave Home* (EP), Junior Boy's Own, 1995 • "Life Is Sweet," Astralwerks, 1995 • *Loops of Fury* (EP), Astralwerks, 1996 • "Setting Sun," Astralwerks, 1996 • "Block Rockin' Beats," Astralwerks, 1997 • *Dig Your Own Hole*, Astralwerks, 1997 • "Elektrobank," Astralwerks, 1997.
Primal Scream: "Jailbird" (remix), Creation, 1994.
Prodigy, The: "Voodoo People" (remix), XL, 1994.
Sandals: "Feet" (remix), Open Toe, 1994.
St. Etienne: "Like a Motorway" (remix), Creation, 1994 • *Casino Classics*, Heavenly, 1996.

Rick Chertoff

Grammy-nominated producer Rick Chertoff is responsible for such oft-spun hits as Joan Osborne's "One of Us" (No. 4), Cyndi Lauper's "Girls Just Want to Have Fun" (No. 2), Sophie B. Hawkins' "Damn, I Wish I Was Your Lover" (No. 5) and the Hooters' "All You Zombies." As president of his own Blue Gorilla Records, Chertoff has charted a course that combines bankable success with labor of love projects, maintaining a delicate balance between art and commerce and ensuring both his label's survival and artistic satisfaction.

A native of Great Neck, Long Island, Chertoff attended the University of Pennsylvania. It was there in Philadelphia in 1968 that he met long-time allies Rob Hyman and Eric Bazilian and formed a musical partnership that has lasted to this day. Hyman and Bazilian were the driving force behind the Hooters, whose records (*Nervous Night* (No. 12), *One Way Home,* and *Zig Zag*) Chertoff produced. An executive at Columbia Records for 12 years, Chertoff was serving as senior vice president of A&R when he left to form Blue Gorilla in 1994.

"Art and commerce travel in parallel lines and occasionally crash into each other," Chertoff explains. "My

daily tasks at Columbia were so broad. I was overseeing the careers of 180 artists. I got away from what I enjoyed doing."

At Blue Gorilla Chertoff is now allowed to concentrate on one project at a time, in depth. Right out of the starting block, Blue Gorilla performed well, exceeding expectations with Osborne's *Relish* (No. 9), a multiplatinum album and worldwide smash.

"Personally it's my most successful record to date," says Chertoff. "Here at my own label I was more able to make a record that I felt was right for me. I'm a huge blues fan. It made me happy to make a blues-friendly record."

Utilizing the indie ethic, *Relish* was recorded at an old hunting lodge on a reservoir in Katonah, New York. An experimental, uninhibited vibe was established where the band motto became "Dare to suck." Invigorated by the experience, Chertoff is currently looking for a barn in the same area in which to locate a production studio.

While Chertoff's major successes have come out of an alliance with three female vocalists, he maintains that there was no agenda at work in corralling that kind of talent, but rather it simply evolved. "At a certain point if someone like Joan sees that I've worked with Cyndi and Sophie, she probably is attracted to the fact that I welcome that point of view." Yet he cautions against making comparisons between the three. "These are three really different women, each with her own striking attitude."

While at Columbia, Chertoff had a tremendous pool of talent to draw on for songwriting. With a huge collection of songs waiting for the right singer, Chertoff found the talent to deliver them in Lauper. Her album *She's So Unusual* (No. 4) sold 8 million copies and yearly remains on radio playlists with the songs "Time After Time" (No. 1), "Girls Just Wanna Have Fun," "All Through the Night" (No. 5), "Money Changes Everything," and "She-Bop" (No. 3), which Chertoff co-wrote with Lauper.

Soft-spoken and matter-of-fact about his success, Chertoff paints a picture of a producer who follows his instincts and lets the marketplace do what it will. Of the enormous success of *She's So Unusual*, Chertoff asserts that there was no planned commercial attack. Admittedly certain the album would fare well, Chertoff says, "I was surprised by the amount [of sales]. You don't think that there are that many people out there that would buy a record."

Chertoff wistfully maintains that the album, in near Tao-like fashion, drifted into the arms of an eager marketplace. "I was moved and, without second-guessing the marketplace, I was lucky that it moved other people too."

A self-described analog dinosaur, Chertoff prefers to work on old Neve and API boards. He likes to keep things simple, hearing the room in the music, and feels that the most crucial part of his job takes place before any notes are laid down on tape.

Chertoff says he is a big fan of "first-take magic" but feels the best way to get that is through intense preparation. "It doesn't always work," he cautions, "but it's a great moment when the ether is in the room."

Whether by accident or design, Blue Gorilla, a PolyGram imprint, developed a strategy whereby the success of an album like Osborne's *Relish* has enabled the label to pursue the more esoteric projects for which a boutique imprint is often known. The most recent endeavor is a project based on the largo movement from Dvorak's *New World Symphony*. Entitled "Largo," the album includes Lauper, Osborne, the Chieftains, Rick Danko, Garth Hudson, Levon Helm, Carole King, Taj Mahal, songwriter David Forman, and old pals Hyman and Bazilian. Using Dvorak's theme as a stepping-off point, the tracks incorporate a variety of American idioms and sources. A self-described American music fan, Chertoff characterizes this labor of love as "a fantastic, spirited endeavor" and says, "We're all charged by how inspired we've been in the process."

Chertoff says that his career in production has provided him with invaluable insight. "I've learned a lot about myself," he says. "I've learned to trust my thought process. It sounds simple, but it's something that's always stuck with me. It teaches you who you are and to have faith in how you think."

To aspiring producers Chertoff says: "Do what you love to do, not what you think the market is calling for. It's a great tradition. There's still plenty of great music to be made." —JACK ARKY

A's, The: *The A's*, Arista, 1977 • *Woman's Got the Power*, Arista, 1981.

Air Supply: "Lost in Love," Arista, 1980 • *Lost in Love*, Arista, 1980.

Baby Grand: *Ancient Medicine*, Arista, 1978 • *Baby Grand*, Arista, 1978.

Band, The: *Jericho*, Pyramid, 1993.

Breakwater: *Splashdown*, Arista, 1980.

Conwell, Tommy and the Young Rumblers: *Rumble*, Columbia, 1988.

General Johnson: *General Johnson*, Arista, 1976.

Hawkins, Sophie B.: "Damn I Wish I Was Your Lover," Columbia, 1992 • *Tongues and Tails*, Columbia, 1992.

Hooters, The: "And We Danced," Columbia, 1985 • "Day by Day," Columbia, 1985 • *Nervous Night*, Columbia, 1985 • *One Way Home*, Columbia, 1987 • *Zig Zag*, Columbia, 1989

- *Hooterization: A Retrospective,* Columbia, 1996.

Lauper, Cyndi: "Girls Just Want to Have Fun," Portrait, 1983 • *She's So Unusual,* Portrait, 1983 • "All Through the Night," Portrait, 1984 • "Money Changes Everything," Portrait, 1984 • "She Bop," Portrait, 1984 • "Time After Time," Portrait, 1984.

Osborne, Joan: "One of Us," Blue Gorilla, 1995 • *Relish,* Blue Gorilla, 1995.

Outfield, The: *Play Deep,* Columbia, 1985.

Pee Shy: *Who Let All the Monkeys Out?,* Mercury, 1996.

Red Rockers: "Eve of Destruction," 415/Columbia, 1984 • "Just Like You," 415/Columbia, 1984 • *Schizophrenic Circus,* 415/Columbia, 1984.

Smith, Rex: *Everlasting Love,* CBS, 1981.

Smyth, Patty: *Never Enough,* Columbia, 1987.

Williams, John: "Theme from Close Encounters of the Third Kind," Arista, 1977.

Leonard and Phil Chess

The story of the Chess brothers and their label burrows into the heart of such charged issues as art versus commerce and exposure versus exploitation—all tangled up in the miasma of race relations.

Lazer and Philip Chez, aged 11 and 6, were herded through Ellis Island on Columbus Day, 1928, from their village near Pinsk, Poland, and transformed into Leonard and Phil Chess. They joined their father, who had been running a junkyard in a Jewish neighborhood near the South Side of Chicago. Their address, 1425 South Karlov Avenue, provided the catalog number for the first Chess Records release.

Phil served in the Army during World War II. Leonard's childhood polio left him with a limp, ineligible for military service. During the war, Leonard pursued various business interests, including liquor stores and bars of less than stellar repute. Eventually, he moved up to the Macomba Lounge, an upscale jazz and blues club at the heart of the South Side. The club featured major national acts, including Billy Eckstine, Ella Fitzgerald, Lionel Hampton, and Louis Armstrong. The predominantly black crowds were regular and enthusiastic, and as label talent scouts sniffed around the back door, Leonard realized he could sell records as well as drinks to his customers.

The Chess brothers bought into a local label called Aristocrat in 1947. Early releases were a hodgepodge of jazz, pop, and blues. Aristocrat generated controversy early on with the release of the single "Union Man Blues/Bilbo Is Dead" by Macomba house singer Andrew Tibbs. "Union Man" angered the Teamsters in the North, and "Bilbo Is Dead," an ironic lament about the passing of Mississippi segregationist Senator Theodore Bilbo, riled those who cared about such things in the South. Aristocrat Records first appeared in *Billboard* on August 30, 1947, with an ad for forthcoming releases by the Dozier Boys.

For his first Aristocrat session, "Johnson Machine Gun," veteran Chicago blues pianist Sunnyland Slim brought in a youthful guitarist, Muddy Waters, fresh from the Mississippi Delta. Waters recorded "I Can't Be Satisfied" in April 1948, and the first issue sold out in 12 hours. Reeking of the country funk of the Delta, Waters' single is a violent shout into the void that laid the foundation of the Chess sound—heavy on vicious electric slide guitar, thumping rhythm, and unadulterated blues wailing.

Leonard reportedly couldn't understand what Waters was singing in the studio, but he understood the sales and somehow knew the records sold because, not in spite, of the track's rawness. This insight is of such importance that *American Heritage* magazine (December 1994) selected the Chess brothers as among the 10 most important agents of change in America since 1950: "The Chess brothers made records that helped transport African-American culture, especially its language and music, to its central place in American culture. . . . The Chess brothers' story is one in which greed and inspiration swirled together in a characteristically American pot where the ingredients did not so much melt as alloy in a metallurgical sense: steel guitar, electricity, and vinyl transmuted into a wholly new cultural substance."

The 1948 session that produced Robert Nighthawk's "My Sweet Lovin' Woman," a jazzy piano blues, was particularly notable because it introduced bassist Willie Dixon (see entry) to the label. Dixon's talent as a producer, songwriter, and session player was integral to the label's success in the '50s and '60s.

Phil ran the nightclub and the label while Leonard primarily produced the records and dashed about the Midwest and South cheerfully handing out promotional 78s and payola (which he deducted from his income taxes as an expense) and tracking local talent. There is much debate regarding the Chesses as actual record producers, but little about their business acumen or their ear for talent. In his autobiography, Dixon tends to minimize Leonard's contributions as a producer, indicating that his main contribution was to rile up the musicians in the studio with a string of friendly curses and then leave them to take out their frustrations on the music. (Leonard was notoriously crude, answering the phone with a "Hello, Motherfucker.") However, an ability to bring out the best from musicians is one of the very definitions of producer. Also, it was in Dixon's interest to play down Leonard's input because Dixon was also a producer and writer with the company and felt unappreciated by the Chesses, especially financially.

Dixon's account of the first Chuck Berry session in 1955 leaves Leonard out of the picture entirely; Berry's account in his autobiography firmly places both Leonard and Phil on the scene as engineers and supervisors: "We struggled through the song, taking thirty-five tries before completing a track that proved satisfactory to Leonard," Berry wrote, observing that Leonard was clearly in charge of the session.

Perhaps inadvertently, the Chesses contributed to the perception that they were exploiters of black music by downplaying their personal interest in that music. They both claimed to be "just businessmen." Perhaps this attitude stemmed from some vestigial Old World notions of hierarchy, division of labor, or even the unseemliness of the music that they produced. Perhaps downplaying an affinity for the music helped the Chesses maintain emotional distance from their artists—many of whom they clearly took advantage of financially with recording, publishing, and personal appearance contracts that screamed of inequity but were standard for the time.

Another way to view them is as paternalistic: The Chesses "took care" of their most important artists. Muddy Waters worked with them for 20 years without a contract; they paid for the funeral of a destitute Little Walter; Howlin' Wolf grumbled but stuck around, and the like.

The Chesses explicitly thought of their company as a family, with Leonard the father and Phil the uncle. Inevitably, the artists were the children, and the fact that most of them were black further complicated matters. Many Chess artists expected and even needed a little paternalism: they were often difficult, erratic, and unscrupulous themselves; some worked under "exclusive contract" with more than one label at a time.

Despite their protestations, the Chesses, especially Leonard, had a feel for the blues, rock 'n' roll, and their permutations. Leonard's son Marshall (who became president of the company and now runs the Chess publishing company, ARC) put it this way to writer Peter Guralnick in his classic Feel Like Going Home: "My father

was a music lover in a very strange way. People used to talk, they'd think he was kind of a freak, because all he'd ever want to do was to go to these little funky clubs that no white person would ever dream of going to, to hear new acts, to buy new talent."

The late writer Robert Palmer feels that Leonard was a great blues producer, amplifying Little Walter's harmonica work with Muddy Waters from mere accompaniment into "forceful, big-toned lead work . . . combining the fluidity of a saxophone with the chordal richness of an organ."

Leonard, along with Sam Phillips (see entry), was among the first producers to use echo by placing a microphone and a speaker at opposite ends of a sewer pipe. He even played bass drum on Waters' "She Moves Me." Waters told Palmer: "My drummer . . . couldn't hold [the beat] to save his damn life. . . . So Leonard told him, 'Get the fuck out of the way. I'll do that.' " Marshall Chess believes his father's main contribution to the blues was to emphasize the beat by highlighting the drums in the mix.

In 1950, the Chess brothers bought out their partners in Aristocrat and launched Chess Records with Gene Ammons' dusky sax and piano instrumental "My Foolish Heart," quickly followed by Waters' "Rollin' Stone," the namesake for a rock band and a magazine.

Besides their own production work in Chicago, the Chesses also had the ears to license classics recorded by others: Sam Phillips sent them Memphis pianist Roscoe Gordon's smash "Booted" (1952), as well as masters by Rufus Thomas, Dr. Isaiah Ross, Joe Hill Louis, and Bobby Bland. Phillips's most important contribution to Chess was Chester Arthur Burnett—the force of nature called Howlin' Wolf—who subsequently moved to Chicago and, with Muddy Waters, Sonny Boy Williamson, and Little Walter, became the foundation of the Chess blues roster.

Other greats to work for the label include Bo Diddley, the Moonglows, the Flamingos, Buddy Guy, Elmore James, Little Milton, Etta James, Billy Stewart, Fontella Bass, and Chuck Berry. Waters, Wolf, Diddley, Berry, Dixon, James, and Leonard Chess himself are inductees of the Rock and Roll Hall of Fame and Museum.

As brilliant and lasting as the Chess blues work is, their work with Berry will stand the longest. Berry met his idol Muddy Waters on a road trip to Chicago from St. Louis, accepting Waters' advice to seek out Leonard Chess, whom Waters called the best in the business. Leonard has dismissed his acumen regarding Berry as riding a trend. But the master tapes show Leonard making decisions about takes and contributing ideas throughout. And when "Maybelline" began to look like a hit, Leonard took the record directly to Alan Freed in New York to push Berry with all the clout Chess could muster. Whether Leonard recognized Berry for the most important single figure in rock 'n' roll history is debatable, but he knew greatness when he heard it and was willing to back his judgments with money and muscle.

Berry is one of the greatest lyricists in rock, capturing the teenage experience with empathy and humor. He also was the architect of the riffing guitar sound at the base of the Beatles, the Rolling Stones, and every other guitar-based rock band on earth. "Johnny B. Goode" (No. 8), "Sweet Little Sixteen" (No. 2), "Rock and Roll Music" (No. 8), "Memphis," and "Brown Eyed Handsome Man" are but a few of the greats in the remarkable Berry canon.

As the '50s wound down, the Chesses turned their attention to running their label, their new radio station WVON, and publishing. Increasingly, they turned over the recording process to staff producers like Willie Dixon and Ralph Bass (see entry).

On October 16, 1969, Leonard Chess died of a heart attack at age 52, probably felled by his own type A personality. Earlier that year, he and Phil had sold the company to GRT for a reported $11 million. In 1975, GRT closed down the logo, selling it to All Platinum Records. Phil remains active at ARC, the Chess publishing company. The Chess catalog is now being aggressively reissued on CD by MCA (see Andy McKaie entry), giving another generation access to this timeless music. —ERIC OLSEN

Ammons, Gene: *Young Jug,* Chess, 1952, 1994.
Berry, Chuck: "Maybelline," Chess, 1955 • "Brown Eyed Handsome Man," Chess, 1956 • "Roll Over Beethoven," Chess, 1956 • *After School Session,* Chess, 1957 • "Oh Baby Doll," Chess, 1957 • "Rock and Roll Music," Chess, 1957 • "School Day," Chess, 1957 • "Beautiful Delilah," Chess, 1958 • "Carol," Chess, 1958 • "Jo Jo Gunne," Chess, 1958 • "Johnny B. Goode," Chess, 1958 • "Merry Christmas Baby," Chess, 1958 • "Merry Christmas Baby," MCA, 1958, 1986 (*Rockin' Little Christmas*) • *One Dozen Berrys,* Chess, 1958 • "Run Rudolph Run," Chess, 1958 • "Run Rudolph Run," MCA, 1958, 1986 (*Rockin' Little Christmas*) • "Sweet Little Rock and Roller," Chess, 1958 • "Sweet Little Sixteen," Chess, 1958 • "Almost Grown," Chess, 1959 • "Anthony Boy," Chess, 1959 • "Back in the U.S.A.," Chess, 1959 • *Chuck Berry Is on Top,* Chess, 1959 • "Little Queenie," Chess, 1959 • "Bye Bye Johnny," Chess, 1960 • "Let It Rock," Chess, 1960 • *Rockin' at the Hops,* Chess, 1960 • "Too Pooped to Pop," Chess, 1960 • *New Juke Box Hits,* Chess, 1961 • *Twist,* Chess, 1962 • *Chuck Berry on Stage,* Chess, 1963 • "Little Marie," Chess, 1964 •

"Nadine," Chess, 1964 • "No Particular Place to Go," Chess, 1964 • "Promised Land," Chess, 1964 • *St. Louis to Liverpool,* Chess, 1964 • "You Never Can Tell," Chess, 1964 • *Chuck Berry in London,* Chess, 1965 • "Dear Dad," Chess, 1965 • *Fresh Berrys,* Chess, 1966 • *The Great Twenty-Eight,* Chess, 1982 • *More Rock 'n' Roll Rarities,* Chess, 1986 • *Rock 'n' Roll Rarities,* Chess, 1986 • *The Chess Box,* Chess/MCA, 1988 • *Missing Berries: Rarities,* Vol. 3, Chess, 1990 • *His Best,* Vol. 1, Chess, 1997.
Diddley, Bo: "I'm a Man," Checker, 1955 • *Bo Diddley,* Chess, 1958 • "Dearest Darling," Checker, 1958 • *Go Bo Diddley,* Chess, 1959 • "Say Man," Checker, 1959 • "You Can't Judge a Book By Its Cover," Checker, 1962 • *The Chess Box,* Chess/MCA, 1990 • *His Best,* Chess/MCA, 1997.
Diddley, Bo and Chuck Berry: *Two Great Guitars,* Chess, 1964.
Flamingos, The: "The Vow," Checker, 1956 • *Complete Chess Masters Plus,* MCA, 1997.
Fulson, Lowell: *Hung Down Head,* Chess, 1954.
Guy, Buddy: *I Was Walkin' Through the Woods,* Chess/MCA, 1974, 1986 • *The Complete Chess Studio Sessions,* Chess/MCA, 1992 • *Buddy's Blues,* MCA, 1997.
Howlin' Wolf: *Change My Way,* Chess, 1975, 1977 • *Blues Master,* MCA Special Products, 1996.
Jamal, Ahmad: *At the Pershing/But Not for Me,* Chess, 1958, 1990.
James, Elmore: *Whose Muddy Shoes,* Chess/MCA, 1969, 1991.
Lenoir, J.B.: *Natural Man,* Chess, 1963, 1968.
Little Milton: *Greatest Hits,* MCA, 1997.
Little Walter: *Hate to See You Go,* Chess, 1968 • *Confessin' the Blues,* Chess/MCA, 1976, 1996 • *Essential,* MCA, 1993 • *His Best,* MCA, 1997.
Moonglows, The: *Blue Velvet: The Ultimate Collection,* Chess, 1993.
Rogers, Jimmy: *Chicago Bound,* Chess, 1976, 1990.
Waters, Muddy: "I Can't Be Satisfied," Chess, 1948 • "Rollin' Stone," Chess, 1950 • "I'm Your Hoochie Coochie Man," Chess, 1954 • "Mannish Boy," Chess, 1955 • *Sail On,* Chess, 1958 • *The Best Of,* Chess/MCA, 1958, 1987 • *The Chess Box,* Chess, 1989 • *Trouble No More (Singles, 1955–1959),* Chess/MCA, 1989 • *On More Mile: Chess Collectibles,* Vol. 1, Chess Collectibles, 1994 • *His Best, 1947–1955,* Chess/MCA, 1997.
Williamson, Sonny Boy: *One Way Out,* Chess, 1959, 1975 • *Bummer Road,* Chess, 1969 • *The Essential Sonny Boy Williamson,* Chess/MCA, 1993.

COLLECTIONS

Drop Down Mama, Chess, 1970.
Willie Dixon Box Set, Chess/MCA, 1989.
Chess Blues, Chess/MCA, 1992.
Chess Rhythm and Roll, Chess/MCA, 1994.

Aristocrat of the Blues: 50th Anniversary Collection, MCA, 1997.

Chess Blues Classics, 1947–1956, Chess/MCA, 1997.

Chess Blues Classics, 1957–1967, Chess/MCA, 1997.

Chess Blues Piano Greats, MCA, 1997.

Chess Blues-Rock Songbook, MCA, 1997.

Chess Soul: A Decade of Chicago's Finest, MCA, 1997.

Joe Chiccarelli

Since the late '70s, Joe Chiccarelli has been one of the top freelance engineers and mixers in the business: working with a panoramic array of artists from Frank Zappa (see entry) to Joan Baez, the Bee Gees, Etta James, Journey, Julio Iglesias, Poco, and Alison Moyet. Chiccarelli has also produced an idiosyncratic group of left-of-center artists (American Music Club, Oingo Boingo, Tori Amos, Stan Ridgway, the Verlaines, Steve Wynn), whose passion and individuality fly in the face of clichés about engineers-as-producers.

Chiccarelli was born in 1955, raised in the Boston area, and came alive when he first heard Jimi Hendrix. Throughout school he played bass and guitar in a series of bands, and though not a great player, the future engineer/producer looked after the big picture (the concept and direction of the band, the sound of the individual instruments, and the PA system).

A cousin owned small Fleetwood Studio in Boston, where Chiccarelli hung around and learned the basics of recording in the mid-'70s. Around 1977 Chiccarelli moved to Los Angeles and got a job as assistant engineer at Cherokee Studios. His big break came in 1978, when Frank Zappa booked the studio to record *Sheik Yerbouti*. As newcomer and low man on the assistant engineer totem pole, Chiccarelli was assigned to assist those who were "difficult, unpredictable, or who worked insane hours," which made Zappa three-for-three. Zappa's regular engineer was held up in London because of a visa snafu, so Joe was thrown into the breach.

Chiccarelli credits Zappa with changing his thinking about recording. "I went from the standard hi-fi model of getting everything to sound good to pushing the limits in search of the unique. Good sound quality wasn't enough for Zappa. He wanted his recordings to have character, to jump up and surprise you. He always had a vision of the way he wanted things, and he would go to any lengths musically, lyrically, or with recording techniques to achieve that vision. Zappa opened my eyes and twisted me," says Chiccarelli.

Chiccarelli learned to experiment on such Zappa discs as *Baby Snakes, Joe's Garage, Live in New York,* and *Shut Up and Play Your Guitar.*

Chiccarelli next engineered the Poco classic *Legend* (1978), a sonic and stylistic leap for the band, and then Juice Newton's *Juice*, her first big album. It is telling that Chiccarelli's first three engineering jobs all went platinum.

Like many an engineer, Chiccarelli sought to produce and got his chance when his old friend from Boston, Captain Beefheart drummer Robert Williams, got a deal with A&M. Though no commercial blockbuster, the Williams sessions went well enough that A&R vice president and producer David Anderle (see entry) took Chiccarelli under his wing and introduced him to Oingo Boingo. Anderle appreciated Chiccarelli's engineering skills, but in particular his musicality.

Oingo's *Nothing to Fear* was Chiccarelli's first major production and he aquitted himself well. Film composer Danny Elfman's quirky, choppy, alterna-horn band never translated that well to record, but *Fear* has some great moments, like "Grey Matter," "Private Life," and especially the charging ska-funk of "Insects." The sound is uncluttered: no mean feat for an eight-piece band rushing through stop-start arrangements, and Elfman's menace and humor shine through the mix.

In the '90s, Chiccarelli has produced three excellent and underappreciated artists: American Music Club, Steve Wynn, and the Verlaines. From San Francisco, the now-defunct A.M.C. was the outlet for singer/songwriter Mark Eitzel—as melancholy a romantic as stalks the earth. The band typically favored pre-rock styles to express Eitzel's angst and ennui, but on *San Francisco*, and in particular "Wish the World Away," they rocked out to great effect as Eitzel roused himself to shout the world away.

Chiccarelli also produced A.M.C.'s version of "Goodbye to Love" on the Carpenters tribute album. Where Karen's original focused on the tentative nature of her separation from love, Eitzel's sepulchral tone leaves no doubt as to the finality of his estrangement.

Steve Wynn has been an engaging singer/songwriter dating back to his paisley underground band, the Dream Syndicate, in the '80s. On "Kerosene Man," Wynn's reedy, lurching voice (reminiscent of Hoodoo Guru's David Faulkner) tells the tale of a world-class instigator over Robert Lloyd's rollicking piano and ripping slide guitar from Robert Mache. On the great *Dazzling Display* disc, Wynn and Chiccarelli achieve a lasting synthesis of energy and melody, especially on "Drag," "Tuesday," and the wistful "Halo."

The Verlaines are a tweaked, British Invasion–

inspired New Zealand quartet, led by college professor (and Mahler scholar) Graeme Downes. *Way Out Where* is a rousing dose of distorted power pop in the best tradition of the early Who, Shoes, the Records, and the Jam. —ERIC OLSEN

American Music Club: *"Goodbye to Love,"* A&M, 1994 (*If I Were a Carpenter*) • *San Francisco,* Reprise, 1994 • *Hello Amsterdam* (EP), Reprise, 1995.

Among Thieves: *Faith in Love,* EastWest, 1991.

Amos, Tori: *Y Kant Tori Read,* Atlantic, 1988.

Benatar, Pat: *Seven the Hard Way,* Chrysalis, 1985.

Bernhard, Sandra: *Without You I'm Nothing,* Enigma, 1989.

Black Watch: *Amphetamines,* Zero Hour, 1994.

Brown, Julie: *Trapped in the Body of a White Girl,* Sire, 1987 • *Time Slips Away,* Warner Bros., 1988.

Congo Norvell: *The Dope, the Lies, the Vaseline,* Basura!/Priority, 1996.

Ferron: *Phantom Center,* Chameleon, 1990.

Gem: *Hexed,* Restless, 1995.

Huffamoose: *"Tell 'Em Terry Sent Ya,"* Interscope, 1986.

LaMarca: *LaMarca,* Scotti Brothers, 1986.

Lone Justice: *Shelter,* Geffen, 1986.

Medley, Bill: *Best Of,* Curb, 1990.

Minami, Kosetsu: *Windharp,* CBS, 1988 • *Sampona,* CBS, 1989.

Oingo Boingo: *Nothing to Fear,* A&M, 1982 • *Skeletons in the Closet,* A&M, 1989.

Phoenix, Willie: *Willie Phoenix,* A&M, 1982.

Ridgway, Stan: *"The Big Heat,"* Illegal, 1985 • *The Big Heat,* IRS Vintage, 1986, 1993 • *Mosquitos,* Geffen, 1989 • *The Ridgway Compilation: Songs That Made This Country Great,* IRS, 1992.

Ritter, Julie: *Medicine Show,* New Alliance, 1995.

Sativa Luvbox: *Beloved Satellite,* Gasoline Alley, 1993.

Seven Day Diary: *Figure 6,* Warner Bros., 1994.

Slush: *North Hollywood,* Discovery, 1997.

Spirit of the West: *Go Figure,* EastWest, 1991.

Springhouse: *Postcards from the Arctic,* Caroline, 1993.

Stewart, Al: *Last Days of the Century,* Enigma, 1988 • *Famous Last Words,* Mesa, 1993.

Tailgators, The: *Rockin' in the 90's,* Enigma, 1989.

Tepper, Robert: *No Easy Way Out,* Scotti Brothers, 1986.

Tepper, Robert: *Modern Madness,* Scotti Brothers, 1988.

Throneberry: *Trot out the Encores,* Alias, 1996.

Truck Stop Love: *Truck Stop Love,* Scotti Brothers, 1993.

Verlaines, The: *"Heavy 33,"* Arista, 1993 (*No Alternative*) • *Way out Where,* Slash, 1993.

White Acre, Bill: *Billy's Not Bitter,* Touchwood, 1996.

Williams, Robert: *Buy My Record* (EP), A&M, 1981 • *Late One Night,* A&M, 1982.

Wynn, Steve: *Kerosene Man,* RNA, 1991 • *"A Dazzling Display,"* RNA, 1992 • *Dazzling Display,* RNA, 1992.

X-Tal: *Good Luck* (EP), Alias, 1993.

Junior "Shy Shy" Clark

See FULL FORCE

Augustus "Gussie" Clarke

Augustus Clarke was born in Kingston, Jamaica, and his early productions are solidly in the roots category, featuring classic '70s artists like Leroy Smart, Horace Andy, and Jacob Miller. His first record was "The Higher the Mountain," featuring DJ U Roy. He produced Big Youth's first LP, *Screaming Target,* and from its opening blood-curdling scream you know this is not going to be your average listening experience. That same year, 1973, he produced I Roy's debut, *Presenting I Roy,* as well. Both were issued in the U.K. by Trojan and helped usher in the first DJ era.

In the late '70s Clarke produced crucial tracks for singers Gregory Isaacs ("Never Be Ungrateful") and Dennis Brown ("To the Foundation"). He cut dubs and served as recording engineer for the two-volume *Dee-Jay Explosion* issued by Heartbeat in 1982. In the mid-'80s he began a long and fruitful association with the Mighty Diamonds that resulted in over a half-dozen excellent LPs and include their reworking of the Studio One rhythm "Full Up" with new lyrics, titled "Pass the Kouchie." It became a minor pop anthem when covered by U.K. kid group Musical Youth as "Pass the Dutchie" to eliminate a reference to herb.

Gussie's first Music Works studio opened in 1988 and soon a new sound ruled Jamaica. The kickoff record was "Rumors," a comeback for Gregory Isaacs. A combination 45 with Cocoa Tea, Shabba Ranks, and Home T. ("Stop Spreading Rumors") and J.C. Lodge's "Telephone Love" were all hits in England and Jamaica —and all on the same rhythm! By the late '80s the Music

Works sound was so hot almost every major reggae singer dropped by to cut a tune on one of Gussie's popular rhythms, including U.K. popsters Maxi Priest and Aswad.

Along with artists Deborahe Glasgow and Krystal, Clarke continued to record cultural singers like Sugar Minott and Admiral Tibet in a time when slackness and gun lyrics ruled the dance. Gussie had his own stable of dancehall DJs, though, including Johnny P., Papa San, Lady G., and early work from Shabba Ranks and Lady Patra. His '90s players generally include brothers Danny and Clevie Browne (see Steely and Clevie entry). Gussie returned with a bang in 1993 with Freddy McGregor and Snaggapuss' "Chatty Chatty Mouth," a new take on Justin Hines and the Dominoes "Carry Go Bring Come," issuing a whole album of cuts by various artists on that rhythm. Cocoa Tea's incendiary "Burn It Down" was one of the best Jamaican singles of 1994. Gussie issued a two-CD set of his own favorites from his 25-year career in 1996. —CHUCK FOSTER

Aswad: "Best of My Love," Island, 1990 • *The Wicked,* Island, 1990.

Big Youth: *Screaming Target,* Trojan, 1973 • *See also* Collections.

Brown, Dennis: *Unchallenged,* Music Works, 1985 • *See also* Gregory Isaacs; Collections.

Cocoa Tea: *Authorized,* Shanachie, 1992 • *Can't Live So,* Shanachie, 1994.

Eek-a-Mouse: *U-Neek* (2 tracks), Island, 1991.

Home T., Cocoa Tea and Shabba Ranks: *Holding On,* VP, 1990.

I Roy: *Presenting I Roy,* Gussie/Trojan, 1973.

Isaacs, Gregory: w/ Dennis Brown, *Two Bad Superstars!* Burning Sounds, 1978, 1984 • w/ Dennis Brown, *Judge Not,* Greensleeves, 1984 • *Private Beach Party,* RAS, 1985 • *Red Rose for Gregory,* RAS, 1988 • *I.O.U,* RAS, 1989 • w/ Dennis Brown, *No Contest,* Music Works, 1989 • *See also* Collections.

Lodge, J.C.: *I Believe in You,* VP, 1987 • *See also* Collections.

Maxi Priest: "Just a Little Bit Closer," Charisma, 1990.

Mighty Diamonds: *Changes,* Music Works, 1981 • *Backstage,* Music Works, c. 1982 • *Indestructable,* Alligator, 1982 • *The Roots Is There,* Shanachie, 1982 • *Kouchie Vibes,* Burning Sounds, 1984 • *The Real Enemy,* Rohit, 1987 • *Get Ready,* Rohit, 1988 • *See also* Collections.

Papa San: *The System,* Pow Wow, 1990.

Ranks, Shabba: *Rappin' with the Ladies,* VP, 1990 • *Shabba Ranks and the Music Works Crew: No Competition,* BMG, 1993 • *See also* Collections.

Smart, Leroy: "I Love Jah," JA, 1976, 1979 (*Best in the*

Business) • *Get Smart,* Gussie, c. 1978 • *Leroy Smart Disco Showcase,* Gussie, c. 1982.

Wilson, Delroy: "Come in Heaven," JA, 1976, 1979 (*Best in the Business*) • *Worth Your Weight in Gold,* Burning Sounds, 1984.

COLLECTIONS

Ram Dancehall, Mango, 1989.

Black Foundation, Burning Sounds, 1976.

Gussie Presenting: The Right Tracks, Creole, 1979: Andy Horace, "Delilah," "Love You Want Me" • Tommy McCook, "Schenectady's Shock," "The Right Track."

Music Works Showcase, Music Works, 1982: Johnny Clarke, "Gonna Love You More" • Cultural Roots, "Different Style" • Mighty Diamonds, "Declaration of Rights."

Music Works Showcase '88, VP, 1988: Josie Wales, "Everybody's Hustling" • Ken Boothe, "Choice."

Music Works Showcase '89, Pow Wow, 1989: Gregory Isaacs and Josie Wales, "Mind You Dis (Disrespect)" • Dean Fraser, "Pick of the Past" • J.C. Lodge, "Give a Little Love" • Mighty Diamonds, "Bad Boy Business" • Sugar Minott and Little Twitch, "Funking Song (Funk)" • Jackie Mittoo, "Space Flight" • Johnny Osbourne, "Struggle Ha Fi Gwan" • Shabba Ranks, "No Bother Dis (Sound Boy)" • Rebel Rockers, "Keep It Coming" • Nadine Sutherland, "Mr. Hard to Please."

Hardcore Ragga: The Music Works Dancehall Hits, Greensleeves, 1990: Gregory Isaacs, "Mind Yu Dis" • Lady G., "Nuff Respect" • J.C. Lodge and Shabba Ranks, "Hardcore Loving" • Shabba Ranks, "No Bother Dis (Sound Boy)."

Music Works Showcase '90, VP, 1990: Lady Patra, "Man Me Love" • Steely and Clevie, "Genie and the Dread," "Never Again" • Tiger, "Dancehall Vibes."

Music Works Twice My Age Showcase '91, Greensleeves, 1991.

Music Works Presents: Chatty Chatty Mouth Versions, Greensleeves, 1993.

Gussie Clarke Presents: Music Works, Vol. 1, *Roots and Culture,* Spy, 1996: Big Youth and U Roy, "The Higher the Mountain" • Dennis Brown and U Roy, "To the Fountain" • Mighty Diamonds, "Sinsemilla" • Augustus Pablo, "Born to Dub You" • Delroy Wilson, "Is It Because I'm Black."

Gussie Clarke Presents: Music Works, Vol. 2, *Lovers Dancehall,* Spy, 1996: Hortense Ellis, "Unexpected Places" • Larry Marshall, "I Admire You."

Bob Clearmountain

Ever since he mixed Bruce Springsteen's *Born in the U.S.A.* album and introduced the cannon-like snare drum that explodes throughout the song of the same name, Bob Clearmountain has been primarily known as one of the top mixing engineers in the world. Bands sometimes schedule his services a year or two in advance and plan release schedules around his availability. Although generally not known for their high fidelity, Clearmountain's mixes are always the epitome of musicality, and he seems to have a sixth sense for how to make a song sound good when played back over the radio. (To give his hi-fi its due, Clearmountain did mix Aimee Mann's *Whatever*, a truly outstanding hi-fi recording.)

Clearmountain was born January 15, 1953, in Greenwich, Connecticut, and came up as an engineer. What separates him from many engineers who make the transition into production is his very solid musical sense. An aspiring engineer who recognized him in a bar one night pestered the mix master with questions about equipment. Finally the engineer asked, "What do you listen for in [a certain kind of] wire?" Clearmountain answered, "I don't listen to wire. I listen to lyrics." Both in mixing and producing, Clearmountain's strength is that his decisions are always in the service of the song.

"To Bob," producer Jon Brion says, "the song is a puzzle, and everything is on tape for a reason. Bob likes putting it all together the best way possible—never forgetting that the vocal is the most important piece."

Clearmountain recalls, "After I finished mixing *Whatever*, I played it almost every day for six months—not because of me but just because I love the music so much."

"We had recorded all kinds of parts, all kinds of instruments," recalls Aimee Mann, "and Bob had a good sense of which ones to leave out; if a part wasn't working with the overall arrangement, he just wouldn't use it. He was very valuable that way."

"He's a super talent," says engineer Jeffrey Norman. "He's fast, he has a great sense of balance. As a producer he's very good at directing without being a megalomaniac. He was a drummer at one time and so in the sessions I worked on with him, he was able to give specific ideas to the players and make it work. He was also able to work within a very tight budget. Of course," Norman adds, "he is a good engineer and an excellent mixer."

How did Clearmountain make the transition from engineering to production?

"I was an engineer," Clearmountain recalls, "and worked at Media Sound in New York until the summer of 1977. When Tony Bongiovi [see entry] was putting together the Power Station studio he asked me to work for him, and I said I would if he'd let me help him design it. So I did, and I was chief engineer there. Now he had a production deal with Seymour Stein at Sire and I was a big punk fan. I was down at CBGBs and Max's Kansas City and Mud Club all the time, and Seymour had all these punk bands and Tony knew I was into that, so he asked me to co-produce some of those with him. We produced the Tuff Darts, Ramones, so I started getting into producing from that.

"It just went on from there. I had done a couple of things for David Kershenbaum [see entry] when he was in A&R at A&M, and he put Bryan Adams and me together. Plus I was remixing things: the Rolling Stones wanted a dance mix of "Miss You," and because I had done all these Chic records, the Stones asked me to do their mix. Mick liked what I was doing, so he asked me to mix *Tattoo You*. Then Roxy Music came in because they were also on Atlantic.

"When we did the Tuff Darts, one of those Sire punk bands," Clearmountain continues, "they were friends with Ian Hunter. He really liked the studio [Power Station] and so he did one of his solo albums there, *You're Never Alone with a Schizophrenic*. Ian hired the E Street band to play on it and the band just loved the studio, so they suggested to Bruce that he come over and try the studio. I had done some work on and off for Bruce—I mixed 'Hungry Heart,' for example—so that's how I came in to work on *Born in the U.S.A.* The single sort of mixed itself."

The snare drum sound didn't wash with everybody, it seems. It even felt a bit over-the-top to Clearmountain himself. "When I went to mix Robbie Robertson's first solo album, Daniel Lanois [see entry] had produced it, and Daniel apparently said to Robbie, 'Oh, you don't want him—he's just going to do that Born in the U.S.A. snare drum thing,' which is ridiculous because I don't have one sound I stick on every record, but that's all he knew about me.

"I think I have a sense of pop music—I'm aware of the pop song and what cuts through—what is memorable, what would make a record appealing to listen to by the general public. I like to feel that I am one of the general public, so I try to not let things get too obscure. Mixing is the same thing—I try to make the most out of what is the most fun to listen to." —DANIEL J. LEVITIN

Adams, Bryan: *You Want It, You Got It,* A&M, 1982 • "Cuts Like a Knife," A&M, 1983 • *Cuts Like a Knife,* A&M, 1983 • "Straight from the Heart," A&M, 1983 • "This Time," A&M, 1983 • "Run to You," A&M, 1984 • "Heaven," A&M, 1985 • w/ Tina Turner, "It's Only Love, A&M, 1985 • "One Night Love Affair," A&M, 1985 • *Reckless,* A&M, 1985 • "Somebody," A&M, 1985 • "Summer of '69," A&M, 1985 • "Hearts on Fire," A&M, 1987 • "Heat of the Night," A&M, 1987 • *Into the Fire,* A&M, 1987 • "Victim of Love," A&M, 1987 • *So Far, So Good,* A&M, 1993.

Aerosmith: "Draw the Line/F.I.N.E.," A&M, 1994 (*Woodstock 94*).

Blotto: *Collected Words,* One Way, 1994.

Blues Traveler: "But Anyway," A&M, 1994 (*Woodstock 94*).

Carroll, Jim: *Catholic Boy,* Atco, 1980, 1989.

Church, The: *The Church,* Carrere, 1981 • *The Blurred Crusade,* Carrere, 1982 • *Of Skins and Heart,* Arista, 1981, 1988.

Cocker, Joe: "Feelin' Alright," A&M, 1994 (*Woodstock 94*).

Collective Soul: "Shine," A&M, 1994 (*Woodstock 94*).

Cranberries, The: "Dreams," A&M, 1994 (*Woodstock 94*).

Crosby, Stills and Nash: "Deja Vu," A&M, 1994 (*Woodstock 94*).

Crow, Sheryl: "Run, Baby Run," A&M, 1994 (*Woodstock 94*).

Cure, The: "Just Like Heaven" (remix), Elektra, 1987.

Dylan, Bob: "Highway 61," A&M, 1994 (*Woodstock 94*).

Etheridge, Melissa: "I'm the Only One," A&M, 1994 (*Woodstock 94*).

Gabriel, Peter: "Biko," A&M, 1994 (*Woodstock 94*).

Hall, Daryl, and John Oates: "Adult Education," RCA, 1983 • "Say It Isn't So," RCA, 1983 • "Out of Touch," RCA, 1984 • *Big Bam Boom,* RCA, 1984 • *Live at the Apollo with David Ruffin and Eddie Kendrick,* RCA, 1985 • "Method of Modern Love," RCA, 1985 • "Possession Obsession," RCA, 1985 • "Some Things Are Better Left Unsaid," RCA, 1985 • "The Way You Do the Things You Do/My Girl," RCA, 1985.

Harris, Joey: *Joey Harris and the Speedsters,* MCA, 1983.

Jackyl: "Headed for Destruction," A&M, 1994 (*Woodstock 94*).

Jeffreys, Garland: *Escape Artist,* Epic, 1981 • "Jump Jump," Epic, 1981 (*Exposed*) • *Rock and Roll Adult,* Epic, 1981 • "True Confessions," Epic, 1981 (*Exposed*) • *Guts for Love,* Epic, 1982.

Johnny's Dance Band: *Love Wounds Flesh Wounds,* Windsong, 1978.

Keene, Tommy: *Run Now,* Geffen, 1986.

Laws, Hubert: *Romeo and Juliet,* Columbia, 1976.

McCartney, Paul: "Birthday," Capitol, 1990 • *Tripping the Live Fantastic,* Capitol, 1990.

Michael Stanley Band: "My Town," EMI America, 1983 • *You Can't Fight Fashion,* EMI America, 1983 • *Misery Loves Company: More of the Best, 1975–1983,* Razor & Tie, 1997.

Mi-Sex: "Castaway," Epic, 1984 • *Where Do They Go?,* Epic, 1984.

Morrissey: *Beethoven Was Deaf,* EMI, 1993.

Nine Inch Nails: "Happiness in Slavery," A&M, 1994 (*Woodstock 94*).

Public Image Limited (PIL): *Greatest Hits So Far,* Atlantic, 1990.

Pretenders, The: "Don't Get Me Wrong," Real/Sire, 1986 • *Get Close,* Real/Sire, 1986 • "My Baby," Real/Sire, 1986 • "Have Yourself a Merry Little Christmas," A&M, 1987 (*A Very Special Christmas*).

Rezillos, The: *Can't Stand the Rezillos,* Sire, 1978 • "Somebody's Gonna Get Their Head Kicked in Tonight," Sire/WB, 1992 (*Just Say Yesterday*) • *Can't Stand the Rezillos: The (Almost) Complete Rezillos,* Sire, 1993.

Rodgers, Paul: "The Hunter," A&M, 1994 (*Woodstock 94*).

Rolling Stones: "Miss You" (remix), Rolling Stones, 1978.

Santana, Jorge: *Jorge Santana,* Tomato, 1978.

Sexton, Charlie: *Charlie Sexton,* MCA, 1989.

Silencers, The: *Rock 'n' Roll Enforcers,* CBS, 1980.

Simple Minds: "Alive and Kicking," A&M/Virgin, 1985 • *Once upon a Time,* Virgin/A&M, 1985 • "All the Things She Said," Virgin/A&M, 1986 • "Sanctify Yourself," A&M/Virgin, 1986 • *Glittering Prize Simple Minds, 1981–1992,* A&M, 1993.

Smith, G.E.: *In the World,* Mirage, 1981.

Traffic: "Pearly Queen," A&M, 1994 (*Woodstock 94*).

Tuff Darts: *Tuff Darts,* Sire, 1978.

Turner, Tina: *Break Every Rule,* Capitol, 1986 • "Don't Turn Around," Capitol, 1986 • *Collected Recordings, Sixties to Nineties,* Capitol, 1994.

Verlaine, Tom: *Tom Verlaine,* Elektra, 1979.

Violent Femmes: "Dance, Motherfucker, Dance!/Kiss Off," A&M, 1994 (*Woodstock 94*).

Walden, Narada Michael: *The Dance of Life,* Atlantic, 1979 • *Victory,* Atlantic, 1980 • *Ecstasy's Dance: The Best Of,* Rhino, 1996.

Werner, David: *David Werner,* Epic, 1979 • *David Werner Live,* Epic, 1979.

Who, The: *Join Together,* MCA, 1990.

Jack Clement

You'd be hard-pressed to find a producer who has worked with a wider variety of acts than Jack "Cowboy" Clement. From the 20 albums he produced for Charley Pride to revisiting his days at Sun Records at the request of U2 when he recorded sessions for their *Rattle and Hum* album, Clement has lent his production prowess to some of the most noteworthy projects in popular music.

The Memphis native got his start in the business in the mid-'50s. "I first got involved with producing an artist named Billy Lee Riley," he recalls. "We went to a radio station in Memphis and produced these sides on Billy Lee and I took those tapes to Sam Phillips [see entry] to have them mastered. . . . Sam heard this stuff and really liked it and invited me to go to work for him." Riley is best known for the hit "Flying Saucers Rock 'n' Roll."

Clement started working for Sun in June 1956 and was an integral part of the label's heyday, producing and / or engineering classic hits such as Jerry Lee Lewis's "Whole Lot of Shakin' Going On." Clement's tenure with the label ended in spring 1959. "I got fired because Sam got drunk," Clement says. "It was some silly misunderstanding. I was ready to leave there anyway. I was about ready to go off on my own and do something. He fired me and Bill Justis at the same time. We were gone and then I started a record label for a year called Summer Records."

When that label faltered, Clement went to work for Chet Atkins (see entry) at RCA in 1960. After a year and a half, he left to move to Beaumont, Texas. "I built a studio down there," he recalls. "Within six months we cut 'Patches' (No. 6) with Dickey Lee and then we cut some more stuff. I was in Beaumont almost four years."

Clement returned to Nashville in 1965 and initially concentrated on songwriting and publishing. "Then Charley Pride came along," he says. "I guess that was sometime in 1966 that I cut that first master on him. We wound up getting him on RCA and I wound up producing about 20 albums with Chuck Pride."

Clement says he first heard about Pride when he was having drinks with his friend Jack Johnson. "He was telling me about this black guy he had a tape on and he played it for everybody in town, trying to get him signed up, but nobody would. So we wound up going over to his office at Cedarwood and listening to the tape. We had a few more cocktails and I said 'Hell, get him in here and I'll record him.' . . . It was quite an event. 'Cowboy's gonna produce this black dude.' I had a whole control room full of people. It was quite a festive thing, and Charley took right to that. He loved a crowd. I was never one to have a lot of people around when I was recording, but Charley liked it, so I would permit it. He fed off that."

Clement says Pride's career exceeded his expectations. "I didn't know he could be that big, but I thought he was good enough, and the thing with the racial thing seemed to be loosening up at the time," he says. "I

thought it was worth a shot. So I actually paid for the first session myself and ended up leasing it to RCA. It took off fairly quick."

Clement also became known as a hit songwriter and publisher. Among songs he penned are Johnny Cash's "Ballad of a Teenage Queen" and "I Guess Things Happen That Way," Bobby Bare's "Miller's Cave," and Pride's "I Know One." As a publisher, he nurtured such talented songwriters as Allen Reynolds (see entry), Dickey Lee, Sandy Mason, and Bob McDill, a talent pool responsible for such classic tunes as Lee's "She Thinks I Still Care," Mason's "When I Dream," and "Catfish John" by McDill and Reynolds.

But it was Clement's reputation as a producer that led to some of his most interesting gigs. "I produced an album with Louis Armstrong in the early '70s," he says. "That was one of the best experiences I ever had. I went to New York with a seven-piece band from here and hung out with Louis. It was sort of a country album. That's what they called it, although some of the songs weren't really country. He was a real joy to work with. He was just like he was in the movies."

Clement says he views his role as a producer as an "orchestrator." "I find a voice, and then I have to find out what works with that voice, what instrumentation and so on," he says. "Sometimes it's heavy with piano, sometimes it's heavy with guitars, and sometimes it's heavy with fiddles and steel guitars. Charley Pride worked real good with fiddle and steel guitar and a big heavy piano pounding rhythm. In the case of an artist who writes his own songs, it's sort of like harvesting a crop. You want to get them to record it right, so they can go home and write more."

Clement says U2 wanted him to produce them at Sun because of his history there. "They were huge at the time, but I didn't know who they were. This guy called one day and asked if I'd like to come to Memphis and help produce a rock 'n' roll group. . . . I said I didn't know if they had equipment in [the old Sun studios], and he said they had a 12-track. I said 'Well, I'm not sure if you can afford me if you are going to cut with that kind of equipment.' Then he said the group is U2. I had never heard of them, so I asked people around here if they'd heard of them, and they said 'Yeah, they are the biggest rock 'n' roll group in the world.'

"I had the time of my life with those characters," Clement recalls. "Then after they finished the album, Bono and Adam came and hung out with me here in Nashville all week. I took them to Tootsie's and the Bluebird, but mostly we hung out at my office."

Clement also has been known for owning some of the best studios in Nashville, among them Sound

Emporium and Jack's Tracks, which is currently owned by Allen Reynolds. "I had three of them at one point," he says. "Then I kind of got out of producing for a while and didn't need the studios. So I sold them."

Making music has always been what Cowboy has been all about. "It's just a matter of finding the right songs and getting the band together. Then try to forget the clock and the red light, and make music. "I never had a lot of philosophy about it," he says. —DEBORAH EVANS PRICE

Armstrong, Louis: *Louis "Country and Western" Armstrong,* RCA, 1971.

Bare, Bobby: *Essential,* RCA, 1997.

Bond, Eddie: *Walking Tall: The Legend of Buford Pusser,* Enterprise, 1973.

Burgess, Sonny: *Classic Recordings, 1956–1959,* Bear Family, 1989 • *We Wanna Boogie,* Rounder, 1990 • *Hittin' That Jug!: The Best of Sonny Burgess,* AVI, 1995.

Carter Sisters: *Wildwood Flower,* Mercury, 1988.

Cash, Johnny: *Up Through the Years, 1955–1957,* Bear Family, 1986 • *Water from the Wells of Home,* Mercury, 1988 • *The Sun Years,* Rhino, 1990 • *The Essential Johnny Cash, 1955–1983,* Legacy, 1992 • *Wanted Man,* Mercury, 1994.

Clement, Jack: *All I Want to Do in Life,* Elektra, 1978.

Colder, Ben: *Big Ben Strikes Again,* MGM, 1966 • *Wine, Women and Song,* MGM, 1967.

Hartford, John: *Gumtree Canoe,* Flying Fish, 1984 • *Annual Waltz,* MCA, 1988 • *Oh Me Oh My How the Time Does Fly,* Flying Fish, 1989.

Jennings, Waylon: *Collector's Series,* RCA, 1968 • *"Are You Sure Hank Done It This Way?/Bob Wills Is Still the King,"* RCA, 1975 • *Dreaming My Dreams,* RCA, 1975 • *Greatest Hits,* RCA, 1979 • *Are You Sure Hank Done It This Way?,* RCA, 1992 • *Only Daddy That'll Walk the Line: The RCA Years,* RCA, 1993 • *The Essential,* RCA, 1996.

Lewis, Jerry Lee: *Classic,* Bear Family, 1989 • *All Killer No Filler: The Anthology,* Rhino, 1993.

Pride, Charley: *"(I'm So) Afraid of Losing You,"* RCA, 1969 • *"All I Have to Offer You (Is Me),"* RCA, 1969 • *"I Can't Believe That You've Stopped Loving Me,"* RCA, 1970 • *"Is Anybody Goin' to San Antone?,"* RCA, 1970 • *"Wonder Could I Live There Anymore,"* RCA, 1970 • *"I'd Rather Love You,"* RCA, 1971 • *"I'm Just Me,"* RCA, 1971 • *"Kiss An Angel Good Mornin',"* RCA, 1971 • *"It's Gonna Take a Little Bit Longer,"* RCA, 1972 • *"She's Too Good to Be True,"* RCA, 1972 • *The Best of Charlie Pride,* Vol. 2, RCA, 1972, 1995 • *"A Shoulder to Cry On,"* RCA, 1973 • *"Amazing Love,"* RCA, 1973 • *"Don't Fight the Feelings of Love,"* RCA, 1973 • *Songs of Love by Charlie Pride,* RCA, 1973 • *Christmas in My Hometown,* RCA, 1990 • *My Six Latest and Six Greatest,* Honest, 1994 • *Greatest Hits,* Vol. 1,

Honest, 1995 • *Classics with Pride,* Honest, 1996 • *Super Hits,* RCA, 1996 • *Essential,* RCA, 1997.

Riley, Billy Lee: *Classic Recordings, 1956–1960,* Bear Family, 1990.

Smith, Warren: *The Classic Recordings, 1956–1959,* Bear Family, 1992.

Van Zandt, Townes: *Our Mother the Mountain,* Poppy, 1969 • *The Late Great Townes Van Zandt,* Poppy, 1973 • *Townes Van Zandt,* Tomato, 1978 • *At My Window,* Sugar Hill, 1987.

Watson, Doc: *Elementary Doctor Watson!* Poppy, 1972 • w/ Merle Watson, *Two Days in November,* Poppy, 1972 • w/ Merle Watson, *Then and Now/Two Days in November,* Sugar Hill, 1994.

Watson, Merle: *See* Watson, Doc.

Wheeler, Onie: *Onie's Bop,* Bear Family, 1991.

Williams, Hank Jr.: *Living Proof: The MGM Recordings, 1963–1975,* Mercury, 1992.

Mike Clink

Mike Clink is fortunate enough to have one of the landmark albums in his portfolio. With Guns N' Roses' 1987 album *Appetite for Destruction* (No. 1), he was offered the chance to work with music that altered the landscape, and he rose to the occasion.

Clink learned the ins and outs of the music business at Irving Azoff's booking agency in Champaign, Illinois. "I always knew I wanted to be a record producer," he says. "I used to spend all my money on records. I'd read the backs of album covers, listen to the music, and try to figure out how they were made."

Upon moving to Los Angeles after college he wangled an entry-level job at the legendary Record Plant, picking up engineering knowledge from the staff on his off time. "One day one of the second engineers quit," he recalls. "I was the only one around, so the engineer said, 'Get in there.'"

Clink spent several years working with panoramic Top 40 rock acts through his association with producer Ron Nevison (see entry), one of the acknowledged masters of that sound. Then, his first time out as head engineer, he struck gold with the theme song from *Rocky,* Survivor's No. 1 "Eye of the Tiger." In 1986 he stepped into production with Triumph's *The Sport of Kings.*

"People hired me because of the records I had engineered," he says. "I'd done a lot of pop-rock records like Starship, Eddie Money, and Heart. So when I moved into producing, it was mostly with rock bands that had a pop edge."

One of the projects Clink had engineered was UFO's *Strangers in the Night,* the album that caught the attention of Guns N' Roses. The notoriously temperamental GN'R had made several abortive attempts to work with other producers when the call came in to Clink. "I had a meeting with Tom Zutaut, Terry Lippman, Alan Niven, and Axl Rose over at Geffen," he says. "They pointed to the pop records I'd done and said, 'We don't want that.'"

"Guns N' Roses really wanted to capture the essence of timeless rock bands like Aerosmith or the Rolling Stones. To that end we developed their sound together—I started from the beginning with the drums and worked with each player to develop his sound and work it into the band. For example, we must have gone through something like 40 different amplifiers with Slash. We did use a couple of tiny keyboard things on the album, but we made a conscious effort not to go overboard. Consequently, *Appetite for Destruction* has a smooth roughness to it—it's a timeless record because of what we didn't do."

In fact, the over-15-times platinum record is one of the most energetic and alive albums to come out of '80s commercial metal. The bright, fanfare-like guitar sound and elastic, resonant drums and bass give it a distinctive sound that binds together with the chameleon-like vocals. Why was Clink successful with the band when others before him had failed?

"I knew when the band had peaked and I think other people had gone past it," he muses. "One of the things I excel at is in getting the best performance and knowing how far to push. When the band runs out of ideas, I step in and throw some down. In a way, I'm like a funnel—I take ideas from everybody involved. Then I sift through all these ideas and come to one concrete decision on the way to make the record."

Clink insists that on that first record with Guns N' Roses, personality conflicts didn't hamper the process because "everybody was so into making the perfect record—and arguments aren't as intense when you have a smaller budget. After the enormous success of the first album, it was the same personalities, but magnified."

Of *Use Your Illusion* (No. 1), GN'R's epic two-record sophomore effort, Clink says, "It was successful from the fact that we got it done! The band was committed to tour and went on the road before the record was completed. We were flying between cities almost daily; they'd come into a studio after a show and we'd record. It was a long process, and it's tough to keep up the momentum for that long. When you spend that much time working on a record some members tend to lose their enthusiasm."

Clink says his discography is limited by two factors: he's tended to work on projects that for various reasons take a long time, and he only works on projects that he really likes. He emphasizes the importance of picking the right projects. "The producers I listened to were George Martin, Peter Asher, Glyn Johns, Bill Szymczyk [see entries]. They didn't have all the tricks we have today, but they made wise choices in the bands that they worked with and they got great performances out of the bands. I think you have to wait until you have the right band. Some producers get involved with bands they can't make better; they're not suited to the style of music. Other producers pick bands just to keep working. But what you put down on tape you can't take away—it's all a testament to your work."

Clink stays flexible about where he chooses to work, although he often works at Record Plant because of his relationship with the staff. "There are so many great rooms in L.A.," he says. "I find it's the ambience of the room we choose to track or do overdubs in that's crucial—I like a natural sound, not too dead or too live. If a studio doesn't have the right gear you can always rent outboard, but you can't change the sound of the actual room.

"I love technology," he continues, "But I find it is also a crutch. A few years ago, if a member of the band had difficulty playing a part, I'd have to get another musician. Now, with technology, you can sample a note, fly it, and stretch it. I guess you keep the integrity of the band that way, but I find that you're taking a performance and making it great, rather than getting a great performance, and I miss the musicianship. That kind of technology enables people to not be as good as they used to be." —Anastasia Pantsios

Beth Hart Band: *Immortal,* Lava, 1996.

Boneclub: *Bellow,* Rocket Sound, 1993.

F Machine: *Here Comes the 21st Century,* Reprise, 1989.

Guns N' Roses: *Appetite for Destruction,* Geffen, 1988 • "Sweet Child O' Mine," Geffen, 1988 • "Welcome to the Jungle," Geffen, 1988 • "Paradise City," Geffen, 1989 • "Patience," Geffen, 1989 • *Use Your Illusion, I & II,* Geffen, 1991 • *The Spaghetti Incident,* Geffen, 1993.

Hagar, Sammy: *Unboxed,* Geffen, 1994 • "Little White Lie," Track Factory, 1997 • *Marching to Mars,* Track Factory, 1997.

Hurricane: *Over the Edge,* Enigma, 1988.

I Mother Earth: *Dig,* Capitol, 1993 • *I Mother Earth,* Capitol, 1993 • "Not Quite Sonic," Capitol, 1993 • "Rain Will Fall," Capitol, 1993.

Megadeth: *Rust in Peace,* Capitol, 1990.

Roxy Blue: *Want Some?,* Geffen, 1992.

Sea Hags: *Sea Hags,* Chrysalis, 1989.

Size 14: *Size 14,* Volcano, 1997.

Slash and Michael Monroe: "Magic Carpet Ride," Warner Bros., 1993 (*Coneheads* soundtrack).

Slash's Snakepit: *It's Five O'Clock Somewhere,* Geffen, 1995.

Triumph: *The Sport of Kings,* MCA, 1986 • *Classics,* MCA, 1989.

Whitesnake: "Fool for Your Loving," Geffen, 1989 • *Slip of the Tongue,* Geffen, 1989 • "The Deeper the Love," Geffen, 1989 • *Greatest Hits,* DGC, 1994.

XC-NN: *Lifted,* 550 Music, 1996.

George Clinton

It's easy to see why George Clinton has been known as the Godfather of Funk for over 20 years. And the Rock and Roll Hall of Fame inductee, born July 22, 1940, is still funkin' as he approaches his seventh decade.

Back in the mid-'60s, Clinton started producing his group, the Parliaments, and a few years later began producing Funkadelic, another group he created. Throughout the '70s, Clinton, with his Parliament-Funkadelic groups, found his hit-making stride, creating a long string of uncut funk classics that have made him a legend. An old-school funk party needs little more than a Clinton-derived hit.

Among his best are "One Nation Under a Groove," "Flash Light" (No. 16), "Aqua Boogie," "(Not Just) Knee Deep," "Mothership Connection (Star Child)," "Bop Gun (Endangered Species)," "Tear the Roof off the Sucker (Give Up the Funk)" (No. 15), "P. Funk (Wants to Get Funked Up)" and "Up for the Down Stroke." And, of course, there's the seminal "Atomic Dog," one of the most sampled songs in '80s and '90s rap and R&B. Clinton calls that production, perhaps his best-recognized, an accident.

"I wanted to do something strange. I wanted to do an electronic funk record because I saw that coming in style, so I said, 'Let me jump way ahead of that shit,' " says Clinton, who likes "Atomic Dog" more from a lyrical standpoint. "And I had no idea that would be a single."

But long before "Atomic Dog" topped the charts in 1983, there was the Parliaments, which Clinton formed in Newark, New Jersey, in 1955, though hits wouldn't come until several years later. In the meantime, Clinton honed his writing skills as a writer for Motown, where he was allowed to record some demos for the Parliaments.

"Motown to me was the epitome of productions," says Clinton, who believes Motown and its founder, Berry Gordy (see entry), set the standard for music production. Smokey Robinson (see entry) was his hero.

"You have to live up to Berry and the standards he set," says Clinton, who patterned some of his earliest songs after the Motown sound.

Walking around the halls of Motown back then was incredible, says Clinton, because no matter what room you entered, there was a producer hard at work, likely crafting a future classic. "You had to stay on your toes there."

Later in the '60s, after Clinton left Motown, moderate hits started surfacing for his Parliaments, who would later be rechristened Parliament after he lost the right to the group's original name (his group Funkadelic came about during this same period). Clinton and Parliament-Funkadelic ruled '70s funk with such must-have productions as "Flash Light."

"I had no idea that would be a single. To me it was an experiment. There was never a bass on a synthesizer like that before," says Clinton. "And I was looking for more of a 'Bop Gun.' "

Neither "Dog" nor "Gun" is Clinton's favorite production. That is "(Not Just) Knee Deep" (No. 13), which he refers to as an intricate production because of the way it was put together. "The beat was hard as hell to do," he says of "Knee Deep," originally a four-minute song he had to edit down.

Photo by Marcy Guiragossian

He's also a big fan of Parliament's *Mothership Connection* and *The Clones of Dr. Funkenstein* (No. 20), regarded by some as his best. He's big on these albums, "mainly because of the concepts . . . and all those characters. To this day, people want to know where Bootsy is and where the clones are," says Clinton.

There was a time when Clinton wanted to change "Free Your Mind and Your Ass Will Follow," until he found out that some rock groups felt it was his best work ever. "I put the kitchen sink in there. And we meant that: Free your ass and your mind will follow," says Clinton. "We did that in one day. I thought I wanted to change it. But once you've done something it represents the time when you did it. You should leave it there."

As a producer, Clinton says it's his job to collect all the ingredients to make a record. And he says that does not mean everything is left up to him. Instead, he believes in "finding people who are good at what they do, who can bring their personalities to it," like the writers, engineers, and singers. "I throw all the elements together." Otherwise, Clinton says, a producer is in danger of "personally wearing yourself out. You do your part and I do my part. I trust that. Let them do what they do naturally."

Although he consults with artists about their songs, he believes in giving them productions close to their conception and he'd rather artists write their own material. "I try to do something that nobody else has done," he says. "The industry wants you to copy the last hit record, but I want to be as far away from the last hit record as I can. As long as you can do the current dances to the beat, that's the only thing that matters."

A fan of sampling, he's one of the most-ever sampled artists, along with James Brown and the Isley Brothers (see entry). "Sampling really kept us alive," he says.

He's a particularly big fan of Dr. Dre (see entry), an artist big on sampling Clinton. "I respect Dre for what he's doing for hip-hop. He has no set boundaries and a respect for R&B," says Clinton. He also likes Cypress Hills' Muggs, Sean "Puff Daddy" Combs (see entry), and Wu-Tang Clan.

Though his hit-making days seem past, that hasn't stopped Clinton from putting out music. In 1997, for example, Clinton released various titles, including the double set *Live . . . and Kickin'*. In addition to renditions of "Mothership Connection," "One Nation Under a Groove," "Atomic Dog," and "Flash Light," the album also included new songs such as "Daddy's Little Angel," "Booty," and first single "Ain't Nuthin' But a Jam Y'all," which included backing from the Dazz Band.

Greatest Funkin' Hits, a collection of remixed Parliament, Funkadelic, and Clinton songs, with some of today's hot rappers on board, was released in 1996. It includes Coolio on "Atomic Dog"; Busta Rhymes, Q-Tip, and Ol' Dirty Bastard on "Flashlight"; Ice Cube on "Bop Gun"; and Digital Underground on "Knee Deep."
—KEVIN JOHNSON

Bootsy's Rubber Band: *Stretchin' Out,* Warner Bros., 1976 • *Aah . . . the Name Is Bootsy Baby,* Warner Bros., 1978 • "Bootzilla," Warner Bros., 1978 • *Player of the Year,* Warner Bros., 1978 • *This Boot Is Made for Fonkin',* Warner Bros., 1979 • *Ultra Wave,* Warner Bros., 1980.

Brides of Funkenstein: *Funk or Walk,* Atlantic, 1978 • *Never Buy Texas from a Cowboy,* Atlantic, 1979.

Clinton, George: *Computer Games,* Capitol, 1982 • "Atomic Dog," Capitol, 1983 • *You Shouldn't 'Nuff Bit Fish,* Capitol, 1984 • *Some of My Best Jokes Are Friends,* Capitol, 1985 • "Do Fries Go with That Shake?," Capitol, 1986 • *R&B Skeletons in the Closet,* Capitol, 1986 • *The Cinderella Theory,* Paisley Park, 1989 • *Hey Man . . . Smell My Finger,* Paisley Park, 1993 • *"P" Is the Funk,* AEM, 1993 • "Brainscan," Ruff House/Columbia, 1994 (*Brainscan* soundtrack) • *Greatest Funkin' Hits,* Capitol, 1996 • "If Anybody Gets Funked Up (It's Gonna Be You)," 550 Music/Epic, 1996 • *Testing Positive,* Castle, 1996 • *The Awesome Power of a Fully Operational Mothership,* 550 Music/Epic, 1996 • w/ P. Funk All-Stars, *Live and Kickin',* Intersound, 1997.

Collins, Bootsy: *Back in the Day: The Best of Bootsy,* Warner Bros., 1994 • *See also* Bootsy's Rubber Band.

Day, Otis: *Shout,* MCA, 1989.

Dells, The: *New Beginnings,* ABC, 1978 • *Passionate Breezes: The Best of the Dells, 1975–1991,* Mercury, 1995.

Ellis, T.C.: *True Confessions* (2 tracks), Paisley Park/WB, 1991.

Funkadelic: *Funkadelic,* Pye/Westbound, 1970 • *Free Your Mind and Your Ass Will Follow,* Pye/Westbound, 1971 • *Maggot Brain,* Westbound, 1971 • "You and Your Folks, Me and My Folks," Westbound, 1971 • *America Eats Its Young,* Westbound, 1973 • *Cosmic Slop,* Westbound, 1973 • *Standing on the Verge of Getting It On,* Westbound, 1974 • *Let's Take It to the Stage,* 20th Century/Westbound, 1975 • *Tales of Kidd Funkadelic,* Westbound, 1976 • "One Nation Under a Groove," Warner Bros., 1978 • *Hardcore Jollies,* Warner Bros., 1978 • *One Nation Under a Groove,* Warner Bros., 1978 • "(Not Just) Knee Deep," Warner Bros., 1979 • *Uncle Jam Wants You,* Warner Bros., 1979 • *The Electric Spanking of War Babies,* Warner Bros., 1981 • *Music for Your Mother,* Westbound, 1993.

Godmoma: *Godmoma Here,* Elektra, 1981.

Hazel, Eddie: *Games, Dames and Guitar Thangs,* Warner Bros., 1977.

JC 001 and D Zire: *Ride the Break,* Interscope, 1993.

Klymaxx: "Sexy," MCA, 1986.

Muruga U.F.M.: *Rock the Planet,* Musart, 1992.

Nitzer Ebb: "Fun to Be Had" (remix), Geffen, 1990.

Parlet: *The Pleasure Principle,* Casablanca, 1978 • *Invasion of the Body Snatchers,* Casablanca, 1979 • *Play Me or Trade Me,* Casablanca, 1980.

Parliaments: "(I Wanna) Testify," Revilot, 1967 • *Osmium,* Invictus, 1970 • *Up for the Down Stroke,* Casablanca, 1974 • *Chocolate City,* Casablanca, 1975 • *Mothership Connection,* Casablanca, 1975 • "Tear the Roof off the Sucker (Give Up the Funk)," Casablanca, 1976 • *The Clones of Dr. Funkenstein,* Casablanca, 1976 • *Funkentelechy,* Casablanca, 1977 • *Parliament Live—P. Funk Earth Tour,* Casablanca, 1977 • "Flash Light," Casablanca, 1978 • *Motor Booty Affair,* Casablanca, 1978 • "Aqua Boogie," Casablanca, 1979 • *Gloryhallastoopid,* Casablanca, 1979 • *Trombipulation,* Casablanca, 1980 • *Greatest Hits: The Bomb,* Casablanca, 1984.

P. Funk All-Stars: "Pumpin' It Up," CBS Associated, 1983 • *Urban Dancefloor Guerillas,* CBS Associated, 1983 • *Live at the Beverly Theater,* Westbound, 1990 • *See also* Clinton, George.

Powers, Johnny: *New Spark (for an Old Flame),* Schoolkids, 1994.

Primal Scream: "Funky Jam" (remix), Creation, 1994.

Red Hot Chili Peppers: *Freaky Styley,* Enigma/EMI America, 1985 • "Hollywood (Africa)," Enigma/EMI America, 1985 • *The Abbey Road EP,* EMI, 1987 • *Positive Mental Octopus,* EMI, 1990 • "If You Want Me to Stay," EMI, 1992.

Sweat Band: *The Sweat Band,* Uncle Jam, 1980.

Wesley, Fred: *A Blow for You a Toot for Me,* Atlantic, 1977 • *Say Blow by Blow Backwards,* Sequel, 1979, 1995.

Worrell, Bernie: *All the Woo in the World,* Arista, 1979.

Wynne, Philippe: *Wynne, Jamming,* Uncle Jam, 1980.

Robert Clivilles and David Cole

When the history of dance music is written, volumes will be needed to cover the impact of Robert Clivilles and David Cole. As a remix-production team, they cultivated an unusual sound that captured the raw energy of the club underground while dabbling in pure pop elements that rendered their work easy radio staples.

Clivilles and Cole (not to be confused with the rock producer of the same name) met in 1978 at the famed Better Days nightclub in New York. Clivilles had been building a solid reputation as a house DJ, while Cole was honing his skills as a musician and composer. After striking up a friendship, the two wound up behind the decks at Better Days, Cole playing improvised keyboard licks over the beats that Clivilles spun on the turntables.

"It was the perfect forum for us to reach our ultimate goal, which was to get into a recording studio and remixing," Clivilles says. "Record company executives always hung out at the club and were amazed at the sounds we were adding to their songs."

Their career hit stride when Larry Yasgar tapped them to record some tracks for his budding A&M subsidiary, Vendetta Records. The self-referential "A Cuban, A Black Man, & A Drum Machine" became an instant club smash in 1981, paving the way for Clivilles and Cole to focus on writing and producing for a wide range of dance acts that included Stacey Q. They forever rose above the club pack when they masterminded the three-girl group Seduction, which went on to score a string of pop hits, including "Two to Make It Right" (No. 2) and "Heartbeat" (No. 13).

From there, the bug to be a part of an act themselves bit hard. Thus, the formation of C+C Music Factory, an act that placed Clivilles and Cole behind the rapping skills of Freedom Williams and singers Zelma Davis and Martha Wash. Their Columbia debut disc, *Gonna Make You Sweat* (No. 2), became a Grammy-nominated, platinum-selling sensation.

"It was a wild time," Clivilles says. "We were riding high. We'd gone from spinning in clubs to performing in arenas."

Along the way, they maintained a high studio profile, helming hits like "Emotions" (No. 1) for Mariah Carey and remixing "I'm Every Woman" with Narada Michael Walden (see entry) for Whitney Houston. "It kept us in touch with the street, which was key to our survival," Clivilles says.

Unfortunately, this partnership ended tragically with David Cole's untimely death in 1994 of complications resulting from spinal meningitis. Within a few months, however, Clivilles found that he needed to continue, to create new music and carry on the spirit and tradition of C+C Music Factory. "When you work with someone that long, you already know what's going on," Clivilles says. "David could be in a room and know exactly what I didn't like in a song and change it without me going in there. And that's exactly what I would be doing when I'm sitting in a room today. I can sit back and think, 'What would he comment on?' you know. We were partners and best friends.

"The part that's really missing," Clivilles continues, "is getting to hear him say 'Yeah, that's great,' or 'Maybe we should change this.' That's the part that I really miss a lot. Of course, there's things missing, but I wouldn't say musically. When you hear new C+C material, it almost sounds like David and I did it. People are going to hear David's inspirations in it, because, damn it, we'd been together for 13 years! It's a style we created. Now that I have to do this by myself, I think you're always going to hear a piece of David in it. That's just the way it is." —LARRY FLICK

Robert Clivilles

Covergirls: "Because of You," Fever, 1987 • *Show Me,* Fever, 1994.

Robi-Rob's Clubworld: *Robi-Rob's Clubworld,* Sony, 1996 • "Shake That Body" (remix), Sony, 1996 • "Reach," Columbia, 1997.

Robert Clivilles and David Cole

Brown, James: *Universal James,* Scotti Brothers, 1992.

C & C Music Factory: "Gonna Make You Sweat (Everybody Dance Now)," Columbia, 1990 • *Gonna Make You Sweat,* Columbia, 1990 • "Here We Go," Columbia, 1991 • "Here We Go Let's Rock and Roll," Tommy Boy, 1991, 1992 (*MTV Party to Go,* Vol. 2) • "Things That Make You Go Hmmmmm . . . ," Columbia, 1991 • *Anything Goes,* Columbia, 1994 • "Do You Wanna Get Funky," Columbia, 1994 • *Ultimate,* Columbia, 1995 • *In the Groove,* Sony Special Products, 1996.

Carey, Mariah: "Emotions," Columbia, 1991 • *Emotions,* Columbia, 1991 • "Make It Happen," Columbia, 1991 • *Music Box,* Columbia, 1993.

Carrey, Jim: "Cuban Pete," Chaos, 1994.

Carroll, Dina: *So Close,* A&M, 1993.

Clivilles and Cole: *Greatest Remixes,* Vol. 1, Columbia, 1992.

Cole, Natalie: "Pink Cadillac" (remix), EMI/Manhattan, 1988.

Covergirls: "All That Glitters Isn't Gold," Capitol, 1990.

Dayne, Taylor: *Soul Dancing,* Arista, 1992 • *Send Me a Lover,* Arista, 1993 • "Can't Get Enough of Your Love," Arista, 1993.

E.U.: "Da' Butt" (remix), EMI/Manhattan, 1988.

Fox, Samantha: *Just One Night,* Jive, 1991.

Franklin, Aretha: "A Deeper Love," Arista, 1993 • *Greatest Hits, 1980–1994,* Arista, 1994..

Houston, Whitney: "I'm Every Woman" (remix), Arista, 1992.

Jones, Grace: *Bulletproof Heart* (3 tracks), Capitol, 1989.

Lisa Lisa and Cult Jam: *Straight Outta Hell's Kitchen,* Columbia, 1991 • *Super Hits,* Sony, 1997.

Khan, Chaka: *Life Is a Dance (The Remix Project),* Warner Bros., 1989.

Martika: *Martika's Kitchen,* Columbia, 1991.

New Kids on the Block: *No More Games/Remix Album,* Columbia, 1991.

S.O.U.L. S.Y.S.T.E.M.: "It's Gonna Be a Lovely Day," Arista, 1993.

Seduction: "Two to Make It Right," Vendetta, 1989 • "(You're My One and Only) True Love," Vendetta, 1989.

Stacey Q: *Nights Like This,* Atlantic, 1987.

David Cole

C-Bank: *Greatest Hits,* Next Plateau, 1997.

Yaz: "Situation" (remix), Mute, 1990.

Patrick Codenys

See FRONT 242

Coldcut

(JONATHAN MORE AND MATT BLACK)

Coldcut's first statement about itself also became the name under which it trades: "AheadOfOurTime." From their 1987 groundbreaking single "Say Kids, What Time Is It?" (one of the first sample-built records in the U.K.) to their exploration of the CD-plus format of their 1997 release, *Atomic Moog 2000,* Coldcut has challenged the rules of the music business. Former art teacher Jonathan More and computer programmer Matt Black have been a studio-and-turntable team since the golden age of acid house in the mid-'80s, when they hosted the famed *Solid Steel* show on KISS-FM radio in the U.K.

The release of "Say Kids" paved the way for acts like Bomb the Bass and MARRS and served as the launching pad into the realm of remixing for jams like "Paid In Full" by Eric B. & Rakim. It was on that record that they inserted the now-notorious sample of vocalist Ofra Haza. "We were just reaching for something that would freshen up the track," says More. "We weren't even sure the act would like it, much less people in the clubs and on radio. But it turned out to be the record that pushed us over the top with people outside of the clubs. It cre-ated acceptance for producers who didn't want to employ an orchestra of musicians, but rather build tracks from the ground up with just bits of tape. That has always been—and will always be—our style of production."

Coldcut's other mainstream claim to fame has been the role they played in launching the career of singer Lisa Stansfield, who provided the soulful lead vocal to the act's anthemic 1989 hit "People Hold On." It was that single and its subsequent album, *What's That Noise?* that earned Coldcut a nomination in the Producer of the Year category at the 1990 BPI Awards.

From that point, More and Black could have easily given into music industry pressure to remain a hit machine. But they are far too fascinated with the idea of perpetual experimentation to stick with any formula. It was while touring Japan that they made a discovery that forever changed their course as producers. "We found a book about cut-out-and-keep Ninjas," says More. "They build these amazing houses where they have special traps so they can disappear and reappear somewhere else. They were all about artifice and hidden identity."

This revelation gave the lads the inspiration needed to escape the confines of the music industry mainstream, and they formed their own label, Ninja Tune. In 1993, they issued their album, *Philosophy,* a quirky and adventurous foray into ambient-pop music that would set the tone for the label—not to mention contribute to the foundation of the U.K.'s burgeoning electronic club trend.

Since then, Coldcut has built a solid repertoire with its own albums, including the recent *More Beats & Pieces.* "We will always continue to mix ideas from as broad a life spectrum as possible," says Black. "The best thing we could ever have done for ourselves as producers was break out of the mold of our first hits. Since doing that, we've been able to see the full landscape of pop and dance music—and decide where we'd like to fit in."
—LARRY FLICK

Blondie: "The Tide Is High" (remix), Chrysalis, 1988.
Cibo Matto: *Super Relax* (1 track, EP), Warner Bros., 1997.
Coldcut: *Say Kids, What Time Is It?,* (EP), White Label, 1987 • *Out to Lunch with Ahead of Our Time,* AheadOfOurTime, 1988 • *Stop the Crazy Thing,* AheadOfOurTime, 1988 • featuring Lisa Stansfield, "People Hold On," Tommy Boy, 1989 • *What's That Noise?,* Tommy Boy/Reprise, 1989 • "Eine Kleine Hed Musick," 4th & B'Way, 1994, 1995 (*The Rebirth of Cool,* Vol. 3) • *Philosophy,* Arista, 1994 • "Autumn Leaves," Waveform, 1995 (*Two A.D.*) • *Journeys By DJ-70 Minutes of Madness,* Music Unites/Sony, 1996 • *Atomic Moog 2000,* Ninja Tune, 1997 • "Beats and Pieces," Ninja Tune, 1997 • *Boot the System* (EP), Ninja Tune, 1997 •

Coldcut and DJ Food Fight, Ninja Tune, 1997 • *Let Us Play,* Ninja Tune, 1997 • *More Beats & Pieces,* Ninja Tune, 1997.
DJ Food: *A Recipe for Disaster,* Shadow, 1995.
Eric B. & Rakim: "Paid in Full" (remix), 4th & B'Way, 1987.
Fall, The: *Extricate,* Cog Sinister/Fontana, 1990.
Hardkiss, Gavin: *Weekend,* Hardkiss, 1996.
Harry, Debbie: "The Tide Is High," Chrysalis, 1988.
Orb, The: *Little Fluffy Clouds* (EP), PolyGram, 1990.
Producers for Bob: *Bob's Media Ecology 2* (1 track), Time Again, 1992.
Reid, Junior: *Long Road,* Cohiba, 1991.
Stansfield, Lisa: *Affection,* Arista, 1989.
Yazz and the Plastic Population: "The Only Way Is Up," Big Life/Elektra, 1988.

David Cole

See ROBERT CLIVILLES AND DAVID COLE

Pat Collier

As the punk '70s became the new wave '80s, producer and ex-Vibrator Pat Collier hung up his bass and built the modest (4-track) Alaska Studio, and later the more elaborate (24-track) Greenhouse Studio in London. Greenhouse Studio was the midwife to some of the best guitar-driven modern rock of the '80s and '90s. Collier's production career began with the Cambridge group the Soft Boys; their breakup generated Collier's best-known future work: singer/songwriter Robyn Hitchcock went solo and later formed the Egyptians, and guitarist/songwriter Kimberley Rew put together Katrina and the Waves. In addition, Collier's love of youthful enthusiasm and spontaneity has attracted a steady stream of vibrant young English bands—the Wonder Stuff, Soup Dragons, Screaming Blue Messiahs, the Darling Buds, Candyskins, the Seers, and Adorable, to name a few.

Born in London in 1951, Collier happily recalls going to concerts in the '60s with his teenage mates. Most memorable was a Jimi Hendrix show. "It was devastatingly loud," he recalls. "I couldn't hear very well for about three days afterward. And it was also one of few times Hendrix set fire to his guitar!" Seemingly intent on ruining his hearing, Collier also played in bands. After college, he and three friends from high school formed the Vibrators and fell into the nascent London punk scene of the mid-'70s. Not particularly young or disaffected, and certainly not stellar musicians, the Vibes did have a flair for tuneful melodies and punky hooks. Collier's "Baby, Baby," a minor hit in 1977, sounds more like Mott the Hoople than the Sex Pistols, but they also rocked fast and hard, and the Vibrators' *Pure Mania* is a small classic of pop punk.

Pure Mania whetted Collier's taste for the studio, and he soon left the musician's life behind. He mapped out a route of the London studios and went door to door looking for work. His efforts landed him in a studio's MOR department, doing everything but rock and pop. Despite the chasm between the music and his personal taste, Collier found the experience rewarding. "It was a very old, institutionalized studio, and they made a big point of showing you stuff and telling you how it works. If you asked questions, someone would eventually give you the right answer. It was a brilliant education for me."

The leap from musician to producer wasn't traumatic for Collier. "I'm not really a natural musician," he says. "I would never have chosen to be in a band if it hadn't come up and hit me on the head. After a few years of playing in bands it dawned on me that I'm not one of the world's natural songwriters, so I was quite happy to have the 4-track and just work with people."

Collier's first recording work was with the Soft Boys and their effulgent, eccentric singer/songwriter Robyn Hitchcock. The Soft Boys concocted a bizarre array of pop songs with roots in the melodic psychedelia of Syd Barrett, Pink Floyd, the Byrds, and the Beatles.

Underwater Moonlight showcases Hitchcock's rollicking melodies, skewed vision, Syd Barrett-meets-Donovan vocals, and Rew's ringing neo–British Invasion guitar. Intrigued and intrepid, Collier enjoyed the simple complexities of Hitchcock and continued to work with him after the Soft Boys split up.

Fegmania!, the first Hitchcock and the Egyptians album (Andy Metcalfe on bass and keyboards; Morris Windsor on drums) opens emolliently with "Egyptian Cream," followed by the lovely harmonies of "Another Bubble." "My Wife and My Dead Wife" is both macabre and chirpy—a whimsical meditation on the relative merits of flesh and blood and "the smiling ghost." Snappy and full of tangy melodies, *Fegmania!* satisfies.

Collier cites the next Egyptians album, *Element of Light,* as a fave. Hitchcock and company rock like the Soft Boys on "If You Were a Priest," "The President," and "Bass." Collier marvels, "Robyn always strikes me as someone who has a respect for stuff that happened when he was young: the Beatles, Stones, Dylan. He has an innate idea of how rock and roll was in those days and a fantastic feel for what you can do in the simplest manner."

Collier would notch his biggest hit, "Walking on Sunshine" (No. 9), with another ex-Softy, guitarist Kimberley Rew and his band Katrina and the Waves. With boisterous horns, Alex Cooper's double-time backbeat drums, and Kansas native Katrina Leskanich's puissant vocals, Rew's "Walking" is one of the cheeriest and most infectious pop songs of the '80s. Another hit, "Do You Want Crying," and Rew's "Going Down to Liverpool" (covered by the Bangles) helped drive the band's eponymous debut to No. 25 on the U.S. album chart.

Collier's success with veterans like Hitchcock and Rew belies his preference for young, spirited talent. "A great thing about working with young bands is the excitement," he says. "Everyone is much more into it. I'd much rather bash through recordings and get some spontaneous excitement going, and then maybe go back at a later date and fine-tune stuff that missed the target by too much. Young bands are usually good at that, 'This is how we play, bang, bang, bang, and that's it.' If the vibe sounds young and exciting, then you're going in the right direction. I've done fourth or fifth albums with people, but by and large it all becomes very slow and ponderous—everyone thinks forever about the most minute detail."

Collier's Corollary explains what young bands have. "When you're a kid, you can tell what's cool and not cool because your peer group is essentially the market for pop music. When you're too close to the music business, or have been in it for too long, you lose the ability to have a gut reaction to something."

Collier's work with the Wonder Stuff illustrates these points aptly. *The Eight Legged Groove Machine* (No. 18 U.K.), the Stuffies' 1988 debut, is full of all the snarling punk bravado one could expect from a quartet of Birmingham youths. Collier captures the energy and flinty soul of the band (led by Miles Hunt's surly, savory vocals) with clean, immediate production. "Red Berry Joy Town" and "No, For the 13th Time" kick where it hurts. The cynical, jaded "It's Money I'm After, Baby" sounds like the Clash of *Give 'Em Enough Rope; Groove Machine* is an unambiguous classic.

The band's next, *Hup* (No. 5 U.K.), was still smoking, adding Martin Bell's fiddle and banjo and James Taylor's organ to diversify the sound. "Radio Ass Kiss" and "Don't Let Me Down, Gently" (No. 19 U.K.) are standouts. Though the group never even charted in the U.S., they were superstars in Britain by their third album, *Never Loved Elvis,* produced by Mick Glossop.

Collier returned for *Construction for the Modern Idiot* (No. 4 U.K.), but by 1993, the angry young punks had become listless pop stars and the bloom was way off the rose. The band broke up soon after, and Miles became a host for MTV Europe. —ERIC OLSEN AND DAWN DARLING

Adorable: *Against Perfection*, SBK, 1993 • "Sunshine Smile," Creation, 1993.

Angelic Upstarts: "Lust for Glory," Cherry Red, 1982, 1991 [*Burning Ambitions (A History of Punk)*].

Bandit Queen: *Hormone Hotel*, Playtime, 1995.

Candyskins: *Space I'm In*, DGC, 1991 • *Fun?*, DGC, 1993.

Darling Buds: *Pop Said*, Columbia, 1989 • *Crawdaddy* (1 track), Columbia, 1990.

Engine Alley: *Engine Alley*, Mother, 1994.

Falling Joys: *Psychohum*, IRS, 1992.

Hitchcock, Robyn: *Black Snake Diamond Role*, Armageddon, 1980 • *Invisible Hitchcock*, Rhino, 1986, 1995 • *Moss Elixer*, Warner Bros., 1996 • *Uncorrected Personality Traits: The Robyn Hitchcock Collection*, Rhino, 1997.

Hitchcock, Robyn, and the Egyptians: *Fegmania*, Slash, 1985 • *Element of Light*, Glass Fish/Relativity, 1986 • *Globe of Frogs*, A&M, 1988 • *Greatest Hits*, A&M, 1996.

Jack Rubies: *See the Money in My Smile*, TVT, 1988.

Katrina and the Waves: *Katrina and the Waves*, Capitol, 1985 • "Que Te Quiero," Capitol, 1985 • "Walking on Sunshine," EMI, 1985, 1993 (*Living in Oblivion: The 80s Greatest Hits*, Vol. 2) • "Walking on Sunshine," Virgin/EMI, 1985 (*Now That's What I Call Music 5*) • "Is That It?," Capitol, 1986 • *Waves*, Capitol, 1986.

Kingmaker: *Sleepwalking*, Chrysalis, 1993.

Men They Couldn't Hang: *The Domino Club*, Silvertone, 1990 • *Never Born to Follow*, Demon, 1996.

Modern English: "Life's Rich Tapestry," TVT, 1990 • *Pillow Lips*, Atlantic, 1990.

Motorcycle Boy: "Big Rock Candy Mountain," Rough Trade, 1987 • "The Road Goes On Forever," Nymphaea Pink, 1990.

New Model Army: *Impurity*, EMI, 1990.

Oyster Band: *The Shouting End of Life*, Cooking Vinyl, 1995.

Scorpio Rising: *Zodiac Killers*, Sire, 1992.

Screaming Blue Messiahs: *Gun-Shy*, Elektra, 1986.

Seers, The: *Psych Out*, Cherry Red/Relativity, 1990.

Soft Boys: *Underwater Moonlight*, Armageddon, 1980.

Sound, The: *Shock of Daylight*, Statik, 1984.

Soup Dragons: *Hang-Ten!* (3 tracks), Sire/WB, 1987.

Two Lost Sons: *Welcome to the World of Two Lost Sons*, Savage, 1992.

Vibrators, The: "Baby, Baby," Cherry Red, 1981 [*Burning Ambitions (A History of Punk)*] • *Guilty*, Anagram, 1983.

Voice of the Beehive: *Honey Lingers* (2 tracks), London, 1991.

Wonder Stuff, The: *The Eight Legged Groove Machine*, Polydor, 1988 • *Hup*, Polydor, 1989 • *Construction for the Modern Idiot*, Polydor, 1993.

Peter Collins

Peter Collins is most notable for two things: the extraordinary success of his productions and the almost inconceivable range of artists he has produced. Who else has produced both the Indigo Girls and Rush, Jewel and Suicidal Tendencies?

Collins was born January 15, 1951, in London and was given his first guitar at 13 by his uncle, Mel Collins, an artist manager (P.J. Proby, Colin Blunstone). Uncle Mel showed Peter around (including backstage at a live TV performance by the Who) and encouraged the youngster's interest in the music business. By the time he was 19, young Collins had written a body of contemporary folk songs under the sway of Dylan, Donovan, and the Incredible String Band. Mel persuaded Decca to sign Peter to a recording contract, and then produced Peter's self-titled album himself.

Recalls Collins, "It was an incredible experience—walking into a studio full of musicians waiting to play my music. But I quickly realized that my interest lay in being a producer—especially when my album didn't sell more than 6,000 copies."

Once again Uncle Mel came through; he helped the young ex-artist get a job as tea boy in the very same studio where he had recently recorded. "I went from being the big cheese to being an extremely little cheese," notes Collins. Mel also persuaded Peter's father that production was a good career and that the young man needn't go to university.

The early '70s were a transitional time for the British recording industry. The major labels (including Decca) all owned their own studios, which operated on a hierarchical apprentice system that began at the bottom with "tea boy" (entry-level factotum), rose through tape operator, then assistant engineer, on to engineer, and finally to house producer.

Collins entered the system in 1970 and aided such diverse acts as the Moody Blues, Tom Jones, Engelbert Humperdinck, and Keef Hartley. Alas, three years into Collins' apprenticeship, Decca encountered the slump that engulfed the entire recording industry, and the studio apprentice system was scrapped as inflexible and expensive.

Cast into the street, Collins took an entry-level job with a music publisher, learned the business, set up his own publishing company, and began writing commercial jingles under the tutelage of songwriter/producer Roger Greenaway (Fortunes, Foundations, White Plains), who had written the hugely successful "I'd Like to Teach the World to Sing" Coke jingle. Collins used the income from jingles to fund the recording of songs he had written, co-written, or obtained and published, then hawked these masters to record companies. He learned how to make records quickly and cheaply and got a further sense of the business.

Collins attended music conventions such as the *Marsh Internationale du Disque* (MIDEM) in Cannes, France, "with a whole bag of masters, and pulled in as many advances as possible to fund the next production," he says. This activity continued with marginal success through the late '70s, until the MIDEM of 1979, when a small London label, Magnet, bought a couple of his masters, liked the recordings better than the songs, and hired Collins as a producer. The second act Collins produced for Magnet was a neo-rockabilly group called Matchbox, and in November 1979, 10 years after he entered Decca Studios as an artist, Peter Collins had his first hit with "Rockabilly Rebel."

Eclectic (not to say schizophrenic) from the beginning, Collins' next project was a mod band, the Lambrettas (adversaries of "rockers" like Matchbox). He would "don a cowboy hat for the rockabilly sessions, then switch to RAF gear for the mod sessions. It helped to dress the part to get in the right mind set," recalls Collins with a laugh. Collins remembered from his Decca days that all successful producers possess two pieces of equipment: a hat and a cigar.

Collins credits his success with artists of every stripe to an absence of preconceived notions. "I dive in and let the music wash over me, then I react to it," he says. "I see myself as a catalyst to enable the artist to achieve the best performances of the best renditions of their work, on record. Having been an artist is a tremendous help. I know what it's like to try to feed yourself into machines." Also, since it took him 10 years to have his first hit, Collins is sensitive to "how hard it can be."

Though Collins spends a lot of time in preproduction, "pulling songs apart, pointing out where the lyrics or the melody could be better," he never writes for, or with, an artist. "It's their record, not mine," he says.

Collins worked with English bands in the early '80s and used a lot of technology. "I had an arsenal of equipment that was second only to Trevor Horn's [see entry] and I made the tightest of tight records possible [espe-

cially with Nik Kershaw]. There isn't a tradition of great playing in England—there's a tradition of great invention. So you don't have, generally speaking, the quality of players that you do in America. At least in the '80s, you had to use the technology to make competitive records in England. You had to do it with mirrors."

Regardless of technique, Collins made some great records in that time: the infectious pop reggae of Musical Youth's "Pass the Dutchie" (No. 10); the wistful techno-pop of Kershaw's "Wouldn't It Be Good"; the Belle Stars' Bananarama-like update of "Iko Iko" (No. 14); one of synth-pop's greatest hits, the wildly percussive "Don't Tell Me" (No. 2 U.K.) by Blancmange; Tracey Ullman's lavish girl-group sendup "They Don't Know" (No. 8); and the rousing horns of Roman Holliday's neo-jumpin' jive "Don't Try to Stop It."

Collins moved into harder sounds when guitarist Gary Moore introduced him to Rush in 1985, and he moved to America (Mississippi until 1994, then Nashville) a year later. Collins helped move Rush, then Queensryche, away from progressive noodling into more song-based structures, yielding monumental sounds and huge hits. He also made lasting friends.

"Rush was the first time I felt a real camaraderie with a band, and didn't feel like a hired gun," says Collins. "I hadn't had a sense of artist/producer loyalty to that point, either. As a producer, I always expected the artist to move on after working with me, and then move on again after that. With Rush, I realized you could get to a deeper level, which I now have with Queensryche and the Indigo Girls as well."

In the '90s, Collins has taken yet another left turn and ended up back where he started, stylistically at least. He has produced excellent acoustic-based music, including the alterna-folk duo Indigo Girls' biggest seller, *Swamp Ophelia* (No. 9), the autumnal melodic richness of October Project, and the Americana of Nanci Griffith. In addition, Collins has lent his golden ear to songstress Jewel, rearranging an album cut, "You Were Meant for Me," into a platinum single.

Through it all Collins keeps his perspective: "I love music and am very fortunate to be able to hop around telling artists what I think of their music, and make a living at it." —ERIC OLSEN

Air Supply: *Air Supply,* Arista, 1985. •
Alice Cooper: *Hey Stoopid,* Epic, 1991 • "Feed My Frankenstein," Reprise, 1992 (*Wayne's World* soundtrack) • *Classiks,* Epic, 1995.
Bailey, Philip: "Easy Lover," Kalimba/Columbia, 1984.
Belle Stars: *The Belle Stars,* Stiff/WB, 1982 • "Iko Iko," Stiff/WB, 1983.

Blancmange: "Don't Tell Me," Sire/WB, 1983, 1992 (*Just Say Yesterday*).

Bon Jovi: "Always," Mercury, 1994 • "Someday I'll Be Saturday Night," Mercury, 1995 • *These Days*, Mercury, 1995 • "This Ain't a Love Song," Mercury, 1995 • "Hey God/House of the Rising Sun/Living on a Prayer," Mercury, 1996.

Farmers Boys: *Get Out and Walk*, EMI, 1983.

Flip: *Flip*, Private, 1985.

Griffith, Nanci: *Flyer*, Elektra, 1994.

Indigo Girls: *Rites of Passage*, Epic, 1992 • "I Don't Wanna Talk About It," Epic, 1993 (*Philadelphia* soundtrack) • *Swamp Ophelia*, Epic, 1994.

Jewel: "Foolish Games," Atlantic, 1997 • "You Were Meant for Me," Atlantic, 1997.

Jones, Tom: *Move Closer*, Jive, 1988.

Kershaw, Nik: *Human Racing*, MCA, 1984 • *The Riddle*, MCA, 1984 • *Radio Musicola*, MCA, 1986 • *Anthology*, One Way, 1995.

Lambrettas, The: *Beat Boys in the Jet Age*, Rocket, 1980.

Letters to Cleo: *Go!* Revolution/Warner Bros., 1997.

Lynott, Phil: *Solo in Soho*, Warner Bros., 1980.

Matchbox: *Matchbox*, Magnet, 1979 • "Rockabilly Rebel," Magnet, 1979 • *Midnite Dynamos*, Magnet, 1980 • *Rockabilly Rebels*, Magnet/Sire, 1980 • *Flying Colors*, Magnet, 1981.

Moore, Gary: w/ Phil Lynott, "Out in the Fields," Virgin/EMI, 1985 (*Now That's What I Call Music 5*) • *Run for Cover*, 10, 1985 • *Wild Frontier*, Virgin, 1987 • *After the War*, Virgin, 1989.

Musical Youth: "Pass the Dutchie," MCA, 1982 • *The Youth of Today*, MCA, 1982 • *Different Style*, MCA, 1983.

October Project: *Falling Farther In*, Epic, 1995.

Pirhanas: *The Pirhanas*, Sire, 1980.

Queensryche: *Operation: Mindcrime*, Manhattan/EMI, 1988 • *Empire*, EMI, 1990 • "The Best I Can," EMI, 1990 • *Hear in the Now Frontier*, EMI America, 1997.

Roman Holliday: "Motor Mania," Jive, 1983 • *Cookin' on the Roof*, Jive, 1983 • *Roman Holliday* (EP), Jive, 1983.

Rush: *Power Windows*, Mercury, 1985 • *Hold Your Fire*, Mercury, 1987 • *Chronicles*, Mercury, 1990 • *Counterparts*, Atlantic Anthem, 1993 • *Test for Echo*, Atlantic, 1996.

Salty Dog: *Every Dog Has Its Day*, Geffen, 1990.

Save Ferris: "Goodbye," Epic, 1997 • *It Means Everything*, Epic, 1997.

Squier, Billy: *Reach for the Sky: The Anthology*, Capitol, 1996.

Stewart, Jermaine: "The Word Is Out," Arista, 1983 • *The Word Is Out*, Arista, 1983.

Suicidal Tendencies: *The Art of Rebellion*, Epic, 1992.

Tygers of Pan Tang: *The Cage*, MCA, 1982.

Ullman, Tracey: "Break-A-Way," Stiff/MCA, 1983 • *You Broke My Heart in Seventeen Places*, Stiff/MCA, 1983 • "They Don't Know," MCA, 1984 • *You Caught Me Out*, Stiff/MCA, 1984.

Voice of the Beehive: *Let It Bee* (7 tracks), London, 1988.

Wiedlin, Jane: *Very Best Of*, EMI, 1993.

Tom Collins

Knowing how to marry the right song to the right artist has made Tom Collins one of Nashville's most successful producers. Winner of seven Grammy awards and three-time winner of the Country Music Association's Producer of the Year accolade, Collins has worked with such luminaries as Ronnie Milsap, Barbara Mandrell, Steve Wariner, Sylvia, James Galway, and Marie Osmond.

"A producer, to me, is the person who helps create the marriage between the artist and the song," Collins says. "He can guide the artist and hear the song that's right. . . . He needs to know where the artist needs to go and therefore gets a certain piece of material that works."

A native of Lenoir City, Tennessee, Collins attended the University of Tennessee in Knoxville where he received a Bachelor of Science, majoring in psychology, zoology, and political science. However, music was his passion and in 1970 he moved to Nashville where he landed a job working for Charley Pride and Jack D. Johnson at Pi-Gem Music. In 1982, he left to form his own publishing company and that same year won BMI's Robert J. Burton Award for the most performed song of the year: the Sylvia hit "Nobody."

At the same time, Collins was carving out a reputation as one of Music Row's top producers. "I heard this guy in Memphis and took him into the studio, and started shopping him around town," he recalls of his first gig as a producer. "His name was Ronnie Milsap. The first three songs we did in the session went into the Top 10. That was a lot of fun."

Collins says he enjoyed his dual role as a producer and publisher. "I was into both aspects because I had watched what Wesley Rose had done at Acuff-Rose and what Buddy Killen had done at Tree, and it seemed to me like the publishers were helping to create the artists," he says. "If you have a song, you can find someone to sing it. That was my premise."

After launching Milsap, Collins moved on to another talent he believed in. "The next one was this little blonde girl named Barbara Mandrell, and that went on for about

14 years," he says. "Sylvia was there and Janie Fricke was there. [Both were receptionists at his publishing company and went on to be major stars.] It was a real fun time. We were so busy developing a lot of acts."

Collins says there was a different approach to recording in Nashville in the late '70s and early '80s. "I don't think the process was as time-consuming because the cost of the albums wasn't what it is today. So we went more on a groove and a feel. I know on a couple of big records, we may have overdubbed a couple of days on them, but it didn't take months to do. We could do an album in three weeks. . . . We are selling more records now and I think marketing has to be given large credit because they actually started promoting country product like pop and rock.

"It shouldn't take as much to cut these records as it does," he says. "That doesn't mean they aren't good, [but] to me, music is feeling instinctive emotions, and you cannot overdub a million times and have something that feels that good."

The session that yielded Sylvia's signature hit "Nobody" is one of Collins' favorite memories. "I think 'Nobody' was fun because we cut the rhythm track in 15 minutes," he recalls. "It was the last song on the session and there was another song on there that I thought was really going to do something and we spent an hour and a half on it. We then looked up and said we have 15 minutes left. We cut this track and it was about the second take of the vocal. We kept all the live vocal except for about three words. I realized what we had and I stayed in there for two days, overdubbing and to get synthesizers on there to get a certain attitude and groove I wanted, but the regular, raw rhythm track we cut in 15 minutes."

In addition to churning out No. 1 hits, Collins also knew how to have fun on Music Row, and his mischievous pranks are legendary. The time he dumped horse manure in front of RCA Records is a prime example. "There was a rumor going around that RCA was going to be sold," he says. "Jerry Bradley was head of RCA at that time and he detested that rumor. So a bunch of us at the publishing company got horse manure and dumped it out front of RCA and put a 'For Sale' sign out there. I was overdubbing a Steve Wariner record and Jerry drove by about 11 at night and saw it. He figured out what was going on. So he had me arrested and taken downtown by these setup police officers. They let me out and I was laughing. I got home and the next morning I got a call early that said 'You'd better come down here.' Someone had put horse manure in front of my office. Jerry Bradley hauled that horse manure, shoveled it, and took it to our office."

There was also the time producer Norro Wilson (see entry) had appeared in the local paper with a headline that read "I've Done It All." So Collins bought a burned-out bus for $300 and put it out front of RCA with a sign that said "Norro Wilson I've Done It All Tour." Stories about the good ol' days go on and on.

However, Collins is not one to live in the past. In 1991, he acquired Tom T. Hall's Hallnote Music and signed the veteran songwriter/artist. In 1996, he expanded into the pop and contemporary Christian markets by entering a co-venture with Gotee Records, the innovative independent label co-owned by dc Talk's Toby McKeehan, Todd Collins, and Joey Elwood. Not only is he grooming several acts, but he also intends to develop young producers. —DEBORAH EVANS PRICE

Brown, Jim Ed, and the Browns: *Essential,* RCA, 1996.
Galway, James: *Wayward Wind,* RCA, 1982.
Hall, Tom T.: *Songs from Sopchoppy,* Mercury Nashville, 1996.
Hunley, Con: *Don't It Break Your Heart,* Warner Bros., 1980.
Mandrell, Barbara: "Standing Room Only/Can't Help But Wonder," Dot/ABC, 1975 • "Love Is Thin Ice/Will We Ever Make Love Again?," Dot/ABC, 1976 • "Midnight Angel/I Count On You," Dot/ABC, 1976 • *Midnight Angel,* Dot, 1976 • "That's What Friends Are For/The Beginning of the End," Dot/ABC, 1976 • *This Is,* Dot, 1976 • "Hold Me/This Is Not Another Cheatin' Song," Dot, 1977 • *Lovers, Friends and Strangers,* ABC/Dot, 1977 • "Married, But Not to Each Other/Fool's Gold," Dot/ABC, 1977 • "Woman to Woman/Let the Rain Out," Dot, 1977 • *Love's Ups and Downs,* ABC/Dot, 1978 • *Moods,* ABC, 1978 • "Sleeping Single in a Double Bed," ABC, 1978 • "Tonight/If I Were a River," ABC, 1978 • "Fooled by a Feeling/Love Takes a Long Time to Die," MCA, 1979 • "(If Loving You Is Wrong) I Don't Want to Be Right," ABC, 1979 • *Just for the Record,* MCA, 1979 • "Crackers/Using Him to Get to You," MCA, 1980 • *Love Is Fair,* MCA, 1980 • "The Best of Strangers/Sometime, Somewhere, Somehow," MCA, 1980 • *The Best of (MCA),* MCA, 1980 • "Years," MCA, 1980 • *Barbara Mandrell Live,* MCA, 1981 • "I Was Country When Country Wasn't Cool," MCA, 1981 • "Love Is Fair," MCA, 1981 • "Wish You Were Here/She's out There Dancin' Alone," MCA, 1981 • *He Set My Life to Music,* Songbird/MCA, 1982 • *In Black and White,* MCA, 1982 • "Operator/Black and White," MCA, 1982 • " 'Til You're Gone," MCA, 1982 • "In Times Like These/Loveless," MCA, 1983 • "One of a Kind Pair of Fools," MCA, 1983 • *Spun Gold,* MCA, 1983 • *Christmas at Our House,* MCA, 1984 • *Clean Cut,* MCA, 1984 • "Crossword Puzzle/If It's Not One Thing It's Another," MCA, 1984 • "Happy Birthday, Dear Heartache/A Man's Not a Man (Till He's Loved By a Woman)," MCA, 1984 • "Only a Lonely Heart Knows/I

Wonder What the Rich Folks Are Doin' Tonight," MCA, 1984 • "Angel in Your Arms/Don't Look in My Eyes," MCA, 1985 • "Fast Lanes and Country Roads/You, Only You," MCA, 1985 • *Get to the Heart*, MCA, 1985 • *Greatest Hits*, MCA, 1985 • "It Should Have Been Love By Now/Can't Get Too Much of a Good Thing," MCA, 1985 • "There's No Love in Tennessee/Sincerely I'm Yours," MCA, 1985 • *Moments*, MCA, 1986 • "No One Mends a Broken Heart Like You/Love Is an Adventure in the Great Unknown," MCA, 1986 • w/ the Oak Ridge Boys, "When You Get to the Heart," MCA, 1986 • "Child Support/I'm Glad I Married You," Capitol/EMI America, 1987 • *Sure Feels Good*, Capitol/EMI America, 1987 • "I Wish That I Could Fall in Love Today/I'll Be Your Jukebox Tonight," Capitol, 1988 • *I'll Be Your Jukebox Tonight*, Capitol, 1988 • "My Train of Thought/Blanket of Love," Capitol, 1989 • *Precious Memories*, Quality, 1989 • *Morning Sun*, Capitol, 1990 • *The Best of (Liberty)*, Liberty, 1992 • See also Greenwood, Lee.

Mandrell, Barbara, and Lee Greenwood: "To Me," MCA, 1984 • *Meant for Each Other*, MCA, 1984.

Mandrell, Louise: *Me and My R.C.*, RCA, 1982.

Milsap, Ronnie: "I Hate You," RCA, 1973 • *Where My Heart Is*, RCA, 1973 • "Please Don't Tell Me How the Story Ends," RCA, 1974 • "Pure Love," RCA, 1974 • *Pure Love*, RCA, 1974 • *A Legend in My Time*, RCA, 1975 • "Daydreams About Night Things," RCA, 1975 • "(I'd Be) a Legend in My Time," RCA, 1975 • *Night Things*, RCA, 1975 • "(I'm a) Stand By My Woman Man," RCA, 1976 • *Live*, RCA, 1976 • *20/20 Vision*, RCA, 1976 • "What Goes On When the Sun Goes Down," RCA, 1976 • "It Was Almost Like a Song," RCA, 1977 • *It Was Almost Like a Song*, RCA, 1977 • "Let My Love Be Your Pillow," RCA, 1977 • "Let's Take the Long Way Around the World," RCA, 1978 • "Only One Love in My Life," RCA, 1978 • *Only One Love in My Life*, RCA, 1978 • "What a Difference You've Made in My Life," RCA, 1978 • *Images*, RCA, 1979 • "In No Time at All," RCA, 1979 • "Nobody Likes Sad Songs," RCA, 1979 • *Greatest Hits*, RCA, 1980 • *Milsap Magic*, RCA, 1980 • "Smoky Mountain Rain," RCA, 1980 • "Am I Losing You?," RCA, 1981 • "(There's) No Gettin' Over Me," RCA, 1981 • *There's No Gettin' Over Me*, RCA, 1981 • "Any Day Now," RCA, 1982 • "He Got You," RCA, 1982 • "I Wouldn't Have Missed It for the World," RCA, 1982 • *Inside Ronnie Milsap*, RCA, 1982 • *Ronnie Milsap Live*, RCA, 1982 • "Don't You Know How Much I Love You?," RCA, 1983 • "Inside/Carolina Dreams," RCA, 1983 • *Keyed Up*, RCA, 1983 • "Stranger in My House," RCA, 1983 • *One More Try for Love*, RCA, 1984 • "Show Her," RCA, 1984 • *Greatest Hits*, Vol. 2, RCA, 1985 • "Lost in the Fifties Tonight," RCA, 1985 • *Lost in the Fifties Tonight*, RCA, 1985 • "She Keeps the Home Fires Burning," RCA,

1985 • *Christmas with Ronnie Milsap*, RCA, 1986 • "Happy, Happy Birthday Baby," RCA, 1986 • "In Love," RCA, 1986 • *Heart and Soul*, RCA, 1987 • "How Do I Turn You On?," RCA, 1987 • "Snap Your Fingers," RCA, 1987 • "A Woman in Love," RCA, 1989 • "Don't You Ever Get Tired (of Hurting Me)," RCA, 1989 • "Houston Solution," RCA, 1989 • "Stranger Things Have Happened," RCA, 1990 • *Stranger Things Have Happened*, RCA, 1990 • "Are You Lovin' Me Like I'm Lovin' You?," RCA, 1991 • *Back to the Grindstone*, RCA, 1991 • *Greatest Hits*, Vol. 3, RCA, 1991 • *Essential*, RCA, 1996.

Newton, Wayne: *The Best of Wayne Newton Now*, Curb, 1985 • *Coming Home*, Curb, 1989.

Sylvia: "It Don't Hurt to Dream," RCA, 1980 • "Tumbleweed," RCA, 1980 • "Drifter," RCA, 1981 • *Drifter*, RCA, 1981 • "The Matador," RCA, 1981 • *Just Sylvia*, RCA, 1982 • "Like Nothing Ever Happened," RCA, 1982 • "Nobody," RCA, 1982 • "Sweet Yesterday," RCA, 1982 • "I Never Quite Got Back (from Loving You)," RCA, 1983 • "The Boy Gets Around," RCA, 1983 • "Snapshot," RCA, 1983 • *Snapshot*, RCA, 1983 • "Love over Old Times," RCA, 1984 • *Surprise*, RCA, 1984 • "Victims of Goodbye," RCA, 1984.

Wariner, Steve: "Your Memory," RCA, 1980 • "All Roads Lead to You," RCA, 1981 • "By Now," RCA, 1981 • "Kansas City Lights," RCA, 1982 • "Don't It Break Your Heart," RCA, 1983 • "Don't Plan on Sleepin' Tonight," RCA, 1983 • *Steve Wariner*, RCA, 1985.

Sean "Puffy" Combs

(PUFF DADDY)

"I call all the shots, rip all the spots. . . . / Ten years from now we'll still be on top / Yo, I thought I told you that we won't stop," Sean "Puffy" Combs (aka Puff Daddy) raps in "Mo Money, Mo Problems," from the Notorious B.I.G.'s posthumous 1997 album *Life after Death*. Named ASCAP's 1996 Songwriter of the Year, Combs has been responsible for over $100 million in total record sales.

Sean Combs was born in Harlem in 1970 and grew up with hip-hop. As he told writer Mikal Gilmore in *Rolling Stone* magazine: "From Run-D.M.C. to KRS-One to the Beastie Boys to LL Cool J. I was there. I seen that. I would be 12 years old, and sometimes I'd be out until 3, 4 in the morning, seeing the music. I had to sneak out to do it, but I was doing it."

An aspiring rapper, Combs was also a businessman with two paper routes in his teens. Combs attended Howard University in Washington, D.C., and while there, became an intern at Uptown Records. Within months he was an A&R executive and executive producer for Father MC's 1990 album *Father's Day,* which became a hit. Though he helped fire the careers of Mary J. Blige and Jodeci while at Uptown, he was eventually let go by then-Uptown president Andre Harrell. This served Combs well. He proved to be ambitious enough to be out there doing his own thing.

Within a short time, Combs could be found on Blige's *My Life* (No. 7), a contemporary classic, as well as on B.I.G.'s debut, *Ready to Die* (No. 15). After losing Blige to other producers, he molded a similar singer out of Faith Evans and gave her hits like "You Used to Love Me," "Ain't Nobody," and "Soon As I Get Home." His girl group Total brought on hits like "No One Else," "Can't You See" and "When Boy Meets Girl," while his boy group 112 scored with "Only You" and other songs. Now, the rapper/producer/label entrepreneur has become "The Man" for rap and R&B production, giving Kenneth "Babyface" Edmonds (see entry) a run for his money. While Babyface has had the lock on more mellow, pop-laced R&B for years, Combs has come up behind him, not only tapping into some of his market (it's Combs, not Babyface, on Mariah Carey's 1997 album *Butterfly*), but overtaking a market alien to Babyface: hip-hop.

Combs, a hit rapper and occasional video director, is CEO of his Arista-distributed Bad Boy Entertainment. (He once corrected a MTV reporter who called him the hardest-working man in hip-hop, referring to himself as the hardest-working man in show business.)

In 1997, Combs co-produced the No. 1 single "Hypnotize" by B.I.G. Before that song had a chance to get cold, Combs released "Can't Nobody Hold Me Down," the first single from his own No. 1 album *No Way Out.* And this chart-topping single was replaced at the top with the second *No Way Out* hit, "I'll Be Missing You," a tribute to B.I.G. set to the music of the Police hit "Every Breath You Take." Combs followed that single with his production of another B.I.G. blockbuster, "Mo Money, Mo Problems." Each of those tracks typifies Combs' productions—slick, bumpin', and dance-floor ready.

For all his success, Combs has his critics. Some say he has made hip-hop too flashy and promotes too much designer-label clothing in his songs. Some say he relies too heavily on sampling. Combs frequently digs into '70s and '80s music for inspiration, using generous samples to serve as foundation for his songs. He pumps the songs up with heavier bottoms, but he's still often criticized for this practice, as some consider him highly unoriginal.

Besides "Every Breath You Take," Combs draws heavily on other pop and R&B hits, like Herb Alpert's "Rise" (for "Hypnotize"), Grandmaster Flash & the Furious Five's "The Message" ("Can't Nobody Hold Me Down") and SWV's "Someone" ("Ten Crack Commandments"). Other notable Combs productions and the samples within: MC Lyte's "Cold Rock a Party" remix with Diana Ross's "Upside Down"; B.I.G.'s "Big Poppa" with the Isley Brothers' "Between the Sheets"; Mary J. Blige's "My Life" with Roy Ayers' "Sunshine"; and Total's "Can't You See?" with James Brown's "The Payback." Combs also helped set off the New Edition reunion with his production of "You Don't Have to Worry" and helped Lil' Kim get going with "No Time," on which he produced and rapped.

Surprisingly, Combs has not been foolproof. Few remember "You" by Pebbles, Tony Thompson's "I Know," Tevin Campbell's "I'll Be There," or Soul for Real's "Love You So." And his take on Prince's "If I Was Your Girlfriend" by TLC was sadly overlooked.

Combs has also helped launch the production careers of a number of other artists in his camp, either producing with them or letting them produce solo on Bad Boy's behalf. The latter group includes Chucky Thompson, Rodney Jerkins, and Stevie J. —KEVIN JOHNSON

Blige, Mary J.: "Real Love" (remix), Tommy Boy, 1992, 1993 (*MTV Party to Go*, Vol. 3) • *What's the 411?,* Uptown/MCA, 1992 • *What's the 411?* (remix), Uptown/MCA, 1993 • *My Life* (15 tracks), Uptown, 1994.

Boyz II Men: *Evolution,* Motown, 1997.

Brown, Horace: *Horace Brown,* Motown, 1996.

Campbell, Tevin: *Back to the World,* Warner Bros., 1996.

Carey, Mariah: "Fantasy" (R&B mix), Columbia, 1995 • *Butterfly,* Sony, 1997 • "Honey," Columbia, 1997.

Evans, Faith: "Soon As I Get Home," Bad Boy, 1996 • w/ Puff Daddy, "I'll Be Missing You," Bad Boy, 1997.

Father MC: *Father's Day,* Uptown/MCA, 1990.

Heavy D and the Boyz: *Blue Funk,* Uptown/MCA, 1992.

Jay-Z: *In My Lifetime,* Def Jam, 1997.

Jodeci: "Come and Talk to Me" (remix), Tommy Boy, 1991, 1993 (*MTV Party to Go*, Vol. 3) • *Jodeci,* MCA, 1991.

LL Cool J: "Phenomenon," Def Jam, 1997 • *Phenomenon,* Def Jam, 1997.

Lil' Kim: *Hard Core,* Undeas/Big Beat, 1996 • featuring Puff Daddy, "No Time," Undeas, 1997.

Mack, Craig: *Project: Funk Da World,* Bad Boy/Arista, 1994.

Mase: "Feel So Good," Bad Boy, 1997.

MC Lyte: "Cold Rock a Party," Eastwest, 1997.

McNight, Brian: featuring Mase, "You Should Be Mine (Don't Waste Your Time)," Mercury, 1997.

Mic Geronimo: *Mic Geronimo*, Blunt, 1997 • *Vendetta*, Blunt, 1997.

New Edition: *Home Again*, MCA, 1996 • "I'm Still in Love with You/You Don't Have to Worry," MCA, 1997.

Notorious B.I.G.: "Big Poppa/Warning," Bad Boy/Arista, 1995 • "One More Chance," Bad Boy/Arista, 1995 • "Hypnotize," Bad Boy, 1997 • "Can't You See," Tommy Boy, 1995 • *Ready to Die*, Bad Boy/Arista, 1995 • *Life After Death*, Bad Boy/Arista, 1997 • featuring Puff Daddy and Mase, "Mo Money, Mo Problems," Bad Boy, 1997.

112: *112*, Bad Boy, 1996.

Puff Daddy: featuring Mase, "Can't Nobody Hold Me Down," Bad Boy, 1997 • w/ Faith Evans, "I'll Be Missing You," Bad Boy, 1997 • *No Way Out*, Bad Boy, 1997 • w/ the Family, "It's All About the Benjamins," Bad Boy, 1997.

Ranks, Shabba: *A Mi Shabba*, Epic, 1995.

Soul for Real: "Love You So/Never Felt This Way," Uptown/Universal, 1996 • *For Life*, Uptown/Universal, 1996.

Sting and the Police: "Roxanne '97: Puff Daddy Remix," A&M, 1997.

SWV: featuring Puff Daddy, "Someone," RCA, 1997 • *Release Some Tension*, RCA, 1997.

Thompson, Gina: *Nobody Does It Better*, PolyGram, 1996.

Thompson, Tony: *Sexsational*, Giant, 1995.

Total: *Can't You See* (EP), Tommy Boy, 1995 • *Total*, Bad Boy/Arista, 1996.

Usher: *Usher* (4 tracks), LaFace, 1994.

Williams, Christopher: *Changes*, Uptown/MCA, 1992.

COLLECTIONS

Tribute to Notorious B.I.G., Bad Boy, 1997.

Don Cook

C ountry music producer Don Cook has an interesting theory about producing top vocalists: "Working with great singers is like working with racehorses; they're not workhorses, they don't pull wagons. They run real fast and they're real quirky and real finicky and you have to love working with them or they'll kill you."

The Texas native knows whereof he speaks. Among those he's produced are Raul Malo, lead singer of the Mavericks and possessor of the purest voice in country today; Ronnie Dunn, of country superstars Brooks & Dunn; and the late, velvet-voiced Conway Twitty.

For someone producing only since 1990, Cook has made a considerable mark, producing more than 20 No. 1 tunes, including Tracy Lawrence's "Time Marches On," "If Bubba Can Dance (I Can Too)" by Shenandoah, and over a dozen chart-toppers for Brooks & Dunn, among them "My Maria," "Boot Scootin' Boogie," and "She's Not the Cheatin' Kind."

Cook made his initial mark as a songwriter and publisher. His current title is senior vice president of Sony/ATV Publishing in Nashville, and he has his own Sony imprint, DKC Music.

Although he knew his way around a studio because of his demo work, his first time as producer was with then-new duo Brooks & Dunn, along with co-producer Scott Hendricks (see entry). Cook was tapped for his writing skills and relationship with the duo.

"I wasn't scared at all about producing," he says. "Strangely enough, what I was worried about was that it would be successful and I would have to do it more and then my life would change drastically, and all of those things have come true. I tried not to produce [the first Brooks & Dunn record]. I was really enjoying the life of being a songwriter at Tree Publishing. I had a new baby and was enjoying my life immensely and playing a lot of golf and fishing."

After the Brooks & Dunn debut sold 4 million, Cook called Arista Nashville president Tim DuBois, who had lured Cook into production, to say, " 'I don't know whether you helped me or cursed me. I thank you for

the opportunity, but my life is a lot different than it used to be and given the choice to go back, I'm not sure I wouldn't.' "

He hasn't. Cook's plate is crammed with production projects and he wouldn't have it any other way—at least most of the time. But his closeness with the artists he produces is accompanied by a feeling of responsibility for their musical welfare.

"That's the hardest part for me," he says. "As a producer, I take everybody's career so seriously. It gets to the point where you wonder how many nights you can lie awake worrying about each one of these acts."

Although Cook was skeptical about working with the Mavericks, he and the group have become a winning combination. "[MCA Records head] Tony Brown [see entry] asked me to meet with them and my answer was, 'I don't want to do it because they're on some artistic trip, and I'm just a flat-out mercenary,' " says Cook, a glint in his eye. "But I went and had lunch with them and we hit it off real well, found we have a lot more common ground. Although their music is very different, working with them is very similar to working with Brooks & Dunn. You're just working with huge talents and the problems inherent in putting together a record, choosing songs and doing really good recordings, and dealing with fragile egos sometimes—both mine and theirs, but mostly theirs."

Cook feels his success with the Mavericks has prompted the Nashville community to open its doors to more alternative country acts like BR5-49 and the Tractors. "The most important thing we've accomplished is getting record labels to take chances on people who aren't in the mainstream," he says.

Cook's top considerations in the studio are the song and the writer. "If I feel like I have to change something in a song, I would never do it without consulting the [songwriter] and doing what they felt appropriate," he says. "I'm a songwriter myself and would expect to be treated that way." He leaves the technical details to his engineer, Mike Bradley. "I wouldn't dare touch a knob," Cook says. "I make suggestions in the mixes from time to time, but he's so good I wouldn't tell him how to do what he does any more than he would tell me how to do what I do. And anyway, he's always right and I'm always wrong." —MELINDA NEWMAN

Alabama: *Dancin' on the Boulevard,* RCA, 1997 • "Dancin', Shaggin' on the Boulevard," RCA, 1997 • "Of Course I'm Right," RCA, 1997 • "Sad Lookin Moon," RCA, 1997.

Brooks & Dunn: "Boot Scootin' Boogie," Arista, 1991 • "Brand New Man," Arista, 1991 • *Brand New Man,* Arista, 1991 • "My Next Broken Heart," Arista, 1991 • *Hard*

Workin' Man, Arista, 1992 • "Neon Moon," Arista, 1992 • "Rock My World (Little Country Girl)," Arista, 1992 • "She Used to Be Mine," Arista, 1992 • "We'll Burn That Bridge," Arista, 1992 • w/ Johnny Cash, "Folsom Prison Blues," Mercury Nashville, 1994 (*Red Hot and Country*) • "She's Not the Cheatin' Kind," Arista, 1994 • "That Ain't No Way to Go," Arista, 1994 • *Waitin' on Sundown,* Arista, 1994 • "Little Miss Honky Tonk," Arista, 1995 • *Borderline,* Arista, 1996 • "My Maria," Arista, 1996 • "A Man This Lonely," Arista, 1997 • "He's Got You," Arista Nashville, 1997 • "Honky Tonk Truth," Arista, 1997 • "Why Would I Say Goodbye," Arista, 1997.

Collie, Mark: *Mark Collie,* MCA, 1993 • *Unleashed,* MCA, 1994.

Dallas County Line: *Dallas County Line,* Island, 1997.

Diamond, Neil: *Tennessee Moon,* Columbia, 1996.

Dunn, Holly: *Leave One Bridge Standing,* A&M, 1997.

Hayes, Wade: "I'm Still Dancin' with You," Columbia, 1995 • "Old Enough to Know Better," Columbia, 1995 • *Old Enough to Know Better,* Columbia, 1995 • *On a Good Night,* Columbia, 1996 • "The Day She Left Tulsa," Columbia, 1997 • "Wichita Lineman," Columbia, 1997.

Holland, Greg: *Exception to the Rule,* Asylum, 1997.

House, James: "Days Gone By," 550 Music/Epic, 1994 (*The Cowboy Way* soundtrack) • *Days Gone By,* Epic, 1995.

Jackson, Alan: *Honky Tonk Christmas,* Arista, 1993.

Lawrence, Tracy: "Time Marches On," Atlantic, 1996 • *Time Marches On,* Atlantic, 1996 • *Coast Is Clear,* Atlantic, 1997 • "How a Cowgirl Says Goodbye," Atlantic, 1997.

Lonestar: "Tequila Talking," BNA, 1995 • *Lonestar,* BNA, 1996 • "No News," BNA, 1996 • "Come Cryin' to Me," BNA, 1997 • *Crazy Nights,* BNA, 1997 • "Heartbroke Every Day," BNA, 1997 • "You Walked In," BNA, 1997.

Lynns, The: "Nights Like These," Reprise, 1997.

Mavericks, The: *What a Crying Shame,* MCA, 1994 • "All You Ever Do Is Bring Me Down," MCA, 1995 • *Music for All Occasions,* MCA, 1995.

Nelson, Nikki: "Too Little Too Much," Columbia, 1997.

Raybon Brothers: "Butterfly Kisses," MCA, 1997 • w/ Olivia Newton-John, "Falling," MCA, 1997 • *Raybon Brothers,* MCA, 1997 • "The Way She's Looking," MCA, 1997.

Shenandoah: "I Want to Be Loved Like That," RCA, 1993 • *Under the Kudzu,* RCA, 1993 • "If Bubba Can Dance (I Can Too)," RCA, 1994 • *In the Vicinity of the Heart,* Liberty, 1995 • *The Best Of,* RCA, 1995 • *Now and Then,* Capitol, 1996 • *Shenandoah Christmas,* Capitol Nashville, 1996.

Strait, George: "You Can't Make a Heart Love Somebody," MCA, 1995.

Stuart, Marty: *Marty Party Hit Pack,* MCA, 1995.

Twitty, Conway: *Final Touches,* MCA, 1993 • *The Conway Twitty Collection,* MCA, 1994.

COLLECTIONS

Skynyrd Friends, MCA, 1995.

Jessica Corcoran

Jessica Corcoran is a remarkably assured and accomplished young producer who has worked primarily with post-punk English guitar bands (Senseless Things, Mega City Four, Power of Dreams, Shed 7, Sussed, TC Hug). During her early twenties, Corcoran produced one of the great modern rock albums of the '90s—Ned's Atomic Dustbin's *God Fodder* (No. 4 U.K.)— a masterpiece of catchy hooks, painful insights, and thick, chunky guitar. She has branched out to work with power-pop bands such as Australia's Falling Joys and the Popinjays, in addition to producing Boy George's 1995 album *Cheapness and Beauty*.

Londoner Corcoran, born in 1969, became interested in studio work through her father, a bass player in a country band. A precocious interest in her father's instruments and musical equipment led to an overwhelming desire to find out what made the equipment work. In her midteens, Corcoran announced that she wanted to work in a studio. Somewhat to her surprise, her extremely supportive parents challenged her to pursue her dream.

After countless unanswered inquiries, she finally happened upon an instructional course that placed people in entry-level studio jobs, and eventually, she was offered a job working with producer and ex-Vibrator Pat Collier (see entry) at his Greenhouse studio. Corcoran worked with Collier for a few years, logged 80-hour workweeks, gained familiarity with equipment and procedures, and met many of the young guitar bands who frequented the studio.

In addition to learning technique, Corcoran trained her ears to listen for musical and sound quality. She was given her first solo experience at the tender age of 16 with an unnamed artist of particularly difficult repute— a fledgling producer's rite of passage. "I can remember trying to sync a drum machine to the tape without any codes," she recalls. "I really did not know what I was doing, but it was a good learning process."

While her friends bopped about footloose and fancy-free, Corcoran went for weeks without seeing the sun, but with the support of her family and her mentor Collier, she gained the confidence and experience she needed.

"The learning was very gradual and it never really stops, but it started to become fun at a point when I had learned a certain amount," she says. By age 21, she was ready for Ned's.

God Fodder announces itself from the fade-in of the opening song, "Kill Your Television." The dueling basses of Alex and Mat (band members are known by their first names) thrum frenetically and percussively, while Rat's guitar thrashes through a song of punklike speed and intensity, full of difficult stops and starts, which band and producer handle with panache and verve.

The bouncy single, "Grey Cells Green," almost obscures the rueful insight of singer Jonn Penney that when your desire has been found, it will be found to have come from within. A great loping melody is driven by the basses (used for melody, in the vein of Yes's Chris Squire or New Order's Peter Hook), guitar and masterfully pumping drums. Risking murk with a wall of fuzzy guitars, dueling basses, and stomping drums, Corcoran achieves a beautiful separation and balance that keeps Jonn's vocals at the heart of the powerful mix.

Despite the felicity of the outcome, there were some difficult moments. "I suggested that we put an acoustic guitar on a track, and the guitarist looked at me like, '*What!* Are you daft?' " Corcoran recalls. "We hired an acoustic in because [guitarist] Rat didn't even own one, but by the end of the session I think he was going to buy one. The acoustic can power up behind heavy guitar and really drive things along. It doesn't have to sound twiddle-dee. There are times when you have to very gently ease people into trying things."

Determined yet cheerful, Corcoran feels strongly about her role as a producer: "You are there to get down on record the best representation of what the band is doing. If you make a record and the bands turns around and loves it at the end of the day, you've done your job."
—ERIC OLSEN AND DAWN DARLING

Bedazzled: *Sugarfree*, Epic, 1992.

Boy George: *Cheapness and Beauty* (10 tracks), Virgin, 1995.

Drop: *Within and Beyond*, Chapter 22, 1991.

Falling Joys: *Psychohum*, IRS, 1992.

Kerosene: *My Friends* (EP), Sire, 1993.

Mega City Four: *Sebastopol Rd.,* Big Life, 1992 • *Stop* (EP), Big Life, 1992.

Ned's Atomic Dustbin: *Bite*, Chapter 22, 1991 • *God Fodder*, Columbia, 1991 • "Grey Cell Green," Columbia, 1991 • "Kill Your Television," Columbia, 1991.

Peach: *Burn* (EP), Mad Minute, 1993.

Popinjays: *Vote Elvis* (EP), Alpha, 1991 • *Flying Down to Mono Valley,* Epic, 1992.

Power of Dreams: *Second Son* (EP), Lemon, 1992 • *Positivity,* Lemon, 1993.

Reverse: "Stem the Slide/Filter," Damaged Goods, 1995.

Runway Picnic: "In the Middle of the Ocean," Redhead, 1995.

Senseless Things: "Everybody's Gone," Epic, 1991 • *The First of Too Many,* Epic, 1991 • "Got It at the Delmar," Epic, 1992.

Sensitize: "Falling Through/Maniac," Food, 1992.

Shed 7: "Mark/Casino Girl," Polydor, 1994 • "Speakeasy/Around Your House," Polydor, 1994 • *Change Giver,* Polydor, 1995.

Something Pretty Beautiful: *Something Pretty Beautiful,* Creation, 1990.

Sussed: "One in a Million," Dead Dead Good, 1996 • "Time's Up," Dead Dead Good, 1997.

TC Hug: "Day to Day," Playtime, 1996 • "I'm Doing Fine," Playtime, 1996 • *Pie Mondo,* Playtime, 1996.

Would Be's: *The Wonderful EP* (EP), Vinyl Solution, 1991.

Denny Cordell

D enny Cordell had a remarkable ability to bring out the best in the artists he worked with, and over a 30-year career he brought out the best in artists as varied as the Moody Blues, Procol Harum, the Move, Joe Cocker, Leon Russell, and Tom Petty. In addition, through astute A&R work with Island and his own Shelter label, he was instrumental in advancing the careers of Phoebe Snow, J.J. Cale, Dwight Twilley, Marianne Faithfull, Melissa Etheridge, the Grifters, the Cranberries, and producer Tony Visconti (see entry).

Dennis Cordell-Laverack was born in Buenos Aires in 1944, but attended public school in England. Cordell's initial interest in music was sparked by jazz. After he left school, Cordell went to Paris to track down Chet Baker, the cool trumpeter and vocalist from the West Coast school. Though still in his teens, Cordell managed the troubled troubadour for a time and even arranged and supervised a few recording sessions in the midst of Baker's heroin addiction.

Cordell joined Chris Blackwell (see entry) at Island Records to run the new sublabel Aladdin in 1965, but he left soon after to work with the Moody Blues. He convinced the band to cover an American soul track, "Go Now," by Bessie Banks. Sung by Denny Laine (who joined Paul McCartney's—see entry—Wings in 1971), it was a Top 10 hit, and for many, the band's defining moment.

Cordell set up the deal as an independent producer and made some large change—a pattern he continued when he set up his own production company, Straight Ahead. In 1967, Straight Ahead aligned with Decca's Deram label, for which Cordell produced the Move's first album. In September, Cordell moved to EMI's Regal Zonophone label to produce the soul classic "A Whiter Shade of Pale" by Procol Harum, which reached No. 1 in England and No. 5 in the U.S. Matthew Fisher's languid organ, derived from Bach's "Sleepers Awake" cantata, sets an atavistic tone for Gary Brooker's world-weary reading of Keith Reid's Chaucerian lyrics—a rare medieval blues.

Having set all of the elements in motion, Cordell was reportedly visiting the loo when the final take was recorded. This song began the art-rock movement while remaining incongruously soulful. Literary to a fault, Procol Harum's first album also included the Cervantes-inspired "Conquistador."

A young Tony Visconti met Cordell in New York just after "A Whiter Shade of Pale." Cordell was impressed by Visconti's production and arranging skills and tapped him to serve as his assistant in London. Cordell urged Visconti to explore the London club scene in search of talent. Visconti's first two finds were a pair of eccentric singer/songwriters named Marc Bolan and David Bowie (see entry). In an example of Cordell's 30 years of mentoring, he passed on T. Rex for himself, but invited Visconti to produce them under the auspices of Straight Ahead and funded the first recordings.

Having had success with blue-eyed soul, Cordell then moved to the next level with the production of Joe Cocker's first album. With his spastic motions and barbed wire bellow, Cocker is a ripe target for parody, but through sheer talent and passion he emerged as one of the great stylists in rock history, able to infuse every song with an intensity worthy of his idol, Ray Charles. Denny Cordell brought the right material and a savory, Memphis-style soul feel to Cocker's first four albums.

The title track of 1969's *With a Little Help from My Friends* dares to take on the Beatles and leaves poor Ringo gasping in the dust. Cocker's remake features a stirring guitar intro from Jimmy Page (see entry), then lies low before Cocker and his three female background singers call-and-respond á la the Raelettes, making the throwaway lyrics seem as serious as salvation.

Cordell and Leon Russell then put together an all-star band (Russell, Chris Stainton, Don Preston, Carl Radle, Jim Keltner, Jim Gordon, Bobby Keys, Rita Coolidge) to tour with Cocker, which led to one of the great live albums of all time: *Mad Dogs and Englishmen.*

Englishmen rocks with loose, wild renditions of "Cry

Me a River" (No. 11) and the Boxtops' "The Letter," highlighted by Cocker's wail, Russell's honky-tonk piano, and a smoking horn arrangement. Cordell and Russell were so inspired by the results that in 1970 they formed a record label together—Shelter—on Russell's home turf, Tulsa, Oklahoma.

Shelter had remarkable success. Cordell produced or co-produced Leon Russell's great early work, albums by Freddie and Albert King, and Tom Petty and the Heartbreakers' first two albums. In addition, Shelter released albums by J.J. Cale, Phoebe Snow, the Gap Band, and the first two Dwight Twilley albums.

Leon Russell, Leon Russell and the Shelter People—and the pseudonymous album of country covers, *Hank Wilson's Back Vol. 1* (No. 17)—are excellent, but 1972's *Carney* (No. 2) is the highlight of Russell's career. Cordell leads Russell into a highly personal and weird world of Roller Derby queens, expired junkie girlfriends, and the queasy thrills of the carnival. The jaunty hit "Tightrope" (No. 11) pushes Russell's vocals up front and neatly captures the vertigo inherent in relationships and similar balancing acts. On the album, Cordell and Russell peak on "This Masquerade" (later covered by George Benson), which opens with strange vibraphone and eerie electric guitar interplay that is beautiful, evocative, and fathoms deep. A simple strummed acoustic guitar and Russell's most natural singing blend with a light Latin beat into a flickering pool of intrigue and regret.

Cordell continued his amazing production streak with *Tom Petty and the Heartbreakers*, one of the great debuts of the '70s and Petty's most compelling album. Again, Cordell's production hits the mark. "Rockin' Around with You" kicks off the album with an insistent backbeat, Petty's patented mush-mouthed delivery and an almost new wave intensity. "Breakdown" was Petty's first radio hit; it comes alive with an insinuating guitar line from stalwart Mike Campbell and Petty's nuanced vocal over a great melody, buoyed by a loping beat. "American Girl" is the best song Petty has ever recorded: the kind of anthem that few southwest of Springsteen were recording in the '70s. "Girl" generates a level of excitement that belies a relatively tame arrangement. The chiming guitars, the syncopated drums, and Petty's vocals—both pleading and defiant—leave no doubt as to the archetypal nature of this "American Girl" or this American band.

Shelter also released Bob Marley's first U.S. single, "Duppy Conqueror," shortly before Cordell launched Mango Records in a joint venture with Blackwell in 1972. Cordell sold his interest in Mango in 1975, but not before releasing *The Harder They Come*, helping to acclimate American ears to reggae and paving the way for Marley's enormous success. In 1980, Cordell left the music business to concentrate on thoroughbred horses, and enjoyed moderate success in that field. He returned to the music business in 1991, again forming a partnership with Island's Blackwell. Cordell brought the Cranberries with him to the label from Ireland. The band's debut album, *Everybody Else Is Doing It So Why Can't We?* became the largest-selling Irish debut in history.

Prior to his death from lymphoma in 1995, Cordell had formed a new music-publishing company, Realization Music. A man who loved life and had not one, but two, successful careers in the music business, Cordell took a bottle of Irish whisky, a spliff, and his favorite Ellington record with him to the Great Beyond. —ERIC OLSEN

Cocker, Joe: *Joe Cocker*, A&M, 1969 • *With a Little Help from My Friends*, A&M, 1969 • "Cry Me a River," A&M, 1970 • *Mad Dogs and Englishmen*, A&M, 1970 • "The Letter," A&M, 1970 • *Something to Say*, Cube/A&M, 1972.

Fame, Georgie: *The Two Faces of Fame*, Columbia, 1967.

Gerber, Alan: *The Alan Gerber Album*, Shelter, 1972.

Horn, Jim: *Through the Eyes of a Horn*, Shelter, 1972.

Jesse, Wolf and Whings: *Jesse, Wolf and Whings*, Shelter, 1972.

King, Freddie: *Texas Cannonball*, Shelter, 1972 • *The Best Of,* Shelter/DCC, 1973, 1990.

McCreary, Mary: *Jezebel*, Shelter, 1974.

Moody Blues: "Go Now," Decca, 1965 • *Go Now*, London, 1965 • *The Magnificent Moodies*, Decca, 1965.

Move, The: *The Move*, Regal Z, 1966 • *Message from the Country*, One Way, 1971, 1989 • *The Best Of*, A&M, 1974 • *Movements: 30th Anniversary Anthology*, West Side, 1997.

Petty, Tom, and the Heartbreakers: *Tom Petty and the Heartbreakers*, Shelter, 1976 • *You're Gonna Get It*, Shelter, 1978 • *Greatest Hits*, MCA, 1993.

Procol Harum: "A Whiter Shade of Pale," Deram, 1967 • *A Whiter Shade of Pale*, Regal Z/Deram, 1967 • *Shine on Brightly*, Regal Z/A&M, 1969 • *Classics*, Vol. 17, A&M, 1987.

Ramsey, Willis Alan: *Willis Alan Ramsey*, Shelter/DCC, 1972, 1990.

Russell, Leon: *Leon Russell*, Shelter, 1970 • *Leon Russell and the Shelter People*, Shelter, 1971 • *Carney*, Shelter, 1972 • "Tight Rope," Shelter, 1972 • *Hank Wilson's Back*, Vol. 1, Shelter, 1973 • *Leon Live*, Shelter, 1973 • *Stop All That Jazz*, Shelter, 1974 • "Lady Blue," Shelter, 1975 • *Will O' the Wisp*, Shelter, 1975.

Seymour, Phil: *Precious to Me*, the Right Stuff, 1996.

Ritchie Cordell

Writer and producer Ritchie Cordell scored an impressive series of pop-rock hits (co-written and co-produced with Bo Gentry) with Tommy James and the Shondells in the mid-'60s, including "I Think We're Alone Now" (No. 4), "Mirage" (No. 10), "Gettin' Together" (No. 18) and "Mony Mony" (No. 3). Cordell and Gentry then moved to the Kasenetz-Katz stable, writing "Indian Giver" for the 1910 Fruitgum Co. and "Gimme Gimme Good Lovin' " for Crazy Elephant.

Cordell took time out to recuperate from the "pace and the drugs," and returned with a vengeance in the early '80s, co-producing (with Kenny Laguna; see entry) Joan Jett (*I Love Rock 'n' Roll*, No. 2; *Album*, No. 20), the Ramones (*Subterranean Jungle*), the Stompers, and Bow Wow Wow. He had a week to remember when, on November 21, 1987, Tiffany's "I Think We're Alone Now" was replaced by Billy Idol's "Mony Mony" at No. 1. Cordell was the first writer to accomplish this feat since the Beatles.

Ritchie Cordell was born in Great Neck, New York, in 1943. The first song that really turned him on was the Diamonds' "Little Darlin'." He soon became an "Elvis freak," strapping on his guitar and lip-synching in front of the mirror. He began to write songs and his mother got him in to see the manager of Tom and Jerry (later known as Simon and Garfunkel). Cordell wrote two minor hits with Paul Simon in the early '60s, "Tick Tock" and "Pied Piper." He co-wrote with several others before hooking up with Bo Gentry for his Tommy James success. His hits with James, especially "I Think We're Alone Now" and "Mony Mony," combine the best of pop (great melody, teen concerns) with the drive of rock 'n' roll.

Feeling that his services weren't properly appreciated, especially financially, by management at Roulette (James' label), Cordell moved on to the "bubble gum factory" of Kasenetz-Katz (1910 Fruitgum Co., Ohio Express, Crazy Elephant), which was "even worse." When Cordell returned to the business, he again struck the right balance between hooky pop tunes and rock guts with Jett, especially "I Love Rock 'n' Roll" (No. 1). Cordell and Laguna's production emphasizes the crunch of the guitar riff and the sing-along chorus, creating an instant classic for the '80s with its feet in the '60s. The Ramones appreciated this classic sound and tapped him to produce *Subterranean Jungle*, one of their

better efforts of the '80s. Cordell has recently hooked up again with Tommy James to write and produce, and with royalties from his classics pouring in, says he has "never been happier." —ERIC OLSEN

Bow Wow Wow: *I Want Candy* (1 track), RCA, 1982.
Bronz: *Taken by Storm*, Bronze, 1983.
James, Tommy: *In Touch*, Fantasy, 1976 • *The Solo Years, 1970–1981*, Rhino, 1991.
James, Tommy, and the Shondells: "It's Only Love," Roulette, 1966 • "Gettin' Together," Roulette, 1967 • *Getting Together*, Roulette, 1967 • "I Like the Way," Roulette, 1967 • "I Think We're Alone Now," Roulette, 1967 • *I Think We're Alone Now*, Roulette, 1967 • "Mirage," Roulette, 1967 • "Mony Mony," Roulette, 1968 • *Mony Mony*, Roulette, 1968 • *Something Special*, Roulette, 1968 • *Anthology*, Rhino, 1989.
Jett, Joan: *Flashback*, Blackheart, 1994.
Jett, Joan, and the Blackhearts: *Joan Jett*, Ariola, 1980 • "Bad Reputation," A&M, 1981 (*Urgh! A Music War*) • *Bad Reputation*, Boardwalk, 1981 • *I Love Rock 'n' Roll*, Boardwalk, 1981 • "Crimson and Clover," Boardwalk, 1982 • "Do You Wanna to Touch Me," Boardwalk, 1982 • "I Love Rock and Roll," Boardwalk, 1982 • *Album*, MCA, 1983 • *Glorious Results of a Misspent Youth*, Blackheart/MCA, 1984.
Ramones, The: *Subterranean Jungle*, Sire, 1983 • *Ramones Mania*, Sire, 1989.
Shrapnel: *Shrapnel*, Elektra, 1984.
Stompers, The: *One Heart for Sale*, Mercury, 1984.

The Corporation

(DEKE RICHARDS, FREDDIE PERREN, FONCE MIZELL, BERRY GORDY JR.)

The Corporation helped resurrect Motown in 1969 with three No. 1 hits for the Jackson 5, and for one magical year, it returned Berry Gordy Jr. (see entry) to the creative center of his organization. The Corporation also launched future disco great Perren ("I Will Survive," "Shake Your Groove Thing," "If I Can't Have You," and the Miracles' post-Smokey hits "Do It Baby" and "Love Machine") and talented groove instrumentalist/songwiter Fonce Mizell (Donald Byrd, Johnny Hammond Smith, "Boogie Oogie Oogie," "Love Ballad"). It also proved the premature peak of Deke Richards' career.

The Richards story could be a movie. Born in Los Angeles in 1944, Richards figured he would follow his screenwriter father into film until he heard "Heartbreak Hotel." The 12-year-old picked up a guitar and didn't put it down until he wrote his first song ("Bubblegum") at 14 and played it for family friend David Raksin (who wrote the theme to the film *Laura*). Raksin was so impressed that he transcribed the song for the self-taught songwriter and gave him the money to get it copyrighted.

As the '60s hit, Richards played in a hot R&B band, Deke and the Deacons (later the Four Sounds) on the Strip in clubs like the Galaxy. On Mondays, the band would take the freeway out to El Monte and fill in for Ike and Tina Turner. They toured as backup for many artists, including Dobie Gray, and ended up in Hawaii. The other guys wanted to add brass, Richards didn't, and the band split up in 1965.

Richards formed a new band that wound up backing singer Debbie Dean, one of the first white artists on Motown, in the early '60s. He wrote a song for Dean, and with $300 borrowed from 10 different people, cut the instrumental track for a reduced rate at Richard Podolor's (see entry) new American Recording studio. But Richards didn't have enough money to lay down the vocals.

Berry Gordy accompanied the Supremes when they came to town to play the Hollywood Palace in 1966. Debbie Dean gave Gordy a call at the Century Plaza Hotel, and he invited them to bring the track over. Dean sang live to the tape in the hotel room. Gordy offered Dean her second artist's contract with Motown, and Richards a producer/writer contract, on the spot.

Dean and Richards worked out of the L.A. office, putting out a few singles that didn't go anywhere over the following year. Then came the Holland-Dozier-Holland (see entry) crisis. The fabled writer/producers of dozens of Top 10 hits for the Supremes, the Four Tops, and many others left Motown over a royalty dispute—a serious breakdown in the Motown hit machine. Meanwhile, Richards and writer/producer Frank Wilson (the Temptations, the Supremes, the Four Tops) were languishing in Los Angeles. "In 1968, Detroit still viewed the West Coast office as shit," confides Richards. "The sound wasn't right on tracks cut in L.A. studios, the main talent was still in Detroit, and no one much cared."

Richards and Wilson wrote Gordy to that effect. In response to their letter (and the departure of Holland-Dozier-Holland), Gordy flew Richards and Wilson to Detroit to work with lyricists R. Dean Taylor and Pam Sawyer on a single for the Supremes and locked them all up in the Pontchartrain Hotel with instructions to come up with a hit.

Gordy was anxious and got personally involved. The team would come up with a chord structure and some lines, and Gordy would come over and fiddle around with it, tweak this, rearrange that. The result was "Love Child," a return to No. 1 for Diana Ross and the Supremes. Fresh from the H-D-H debacle, Gordy was leery of creating more "name" writer/producers, so he called the team the Clan. In the best Motown tradition, the follow-up was the similarly themed "I'm Living in Shame," which barely crept into the Top 10.

Dissension within the Clan over percentages unnerved Gordy. The Clan was dissolved and Richards returned to the West Coast, full of confidence and new-found knowledge. He worked out a deal with the Sound Factory to record Motown artists and added touches from the home office: direct boxes so that the guitars could be plugged into the mixing board and a drum stand just like Hitsville's.

Richards liked working in a group, but maybe the Clan was just the wrong group. He met a couple of young songwriters—college chums Freddie Perren and Fonce Mizell—liked their ideas and liked them even more. These were the right guys. Tired of internecine bickering, Gordy told Richards to take charge. The team picked Gladys Knight to work on because she hadn't had a hit for some time. They came up with a song called "I Want to Be Free," cut the instrumental track and took it to Gordy.

The Jackson 5 had been signed to Motown in March 1969. Richards saw them perform at a legendary private show in August at the Daisy Club in Beverly Hills and was astonished. When Gordy heard "Free," his mind began to race. "Give it the Frankie Lymon treatment, 'the little guy who lost his girl' kind of thing, and we'll use it with the kids," he told Richards.

As Richards, Perren, and Mizell worked on the song, Gordy grew more excited and made more suggestions. Finally, Richards said, "Berry, why don't you really get involved?" and the Corporation was born, ending up as four equal partners.

"I Want You Back," the Frankie Lymon version of "I Want to Be Free," cost more than $10,000 to make, when most Motown singles were running about $3,000. There were lots of overdubs and work on phonetics with the youngsters from Gary, Indiana. The Corporation wrote and produced three No. 1 hits in a row for the Jackson 5 in 1969 and 1970: "I Want You Back," "ABC" and "The Love You Save." These classic hits reinvigorated Motown and sent the Jacksons on their way to the Rock and Roll Hall of Fame.

The greatness of the songs lies in their tight musicianship (Perren on keyboards; David T. Walker, Louis Shelton, and Don Peake on guitar; Wilton Felder on bass; and Gene Pello on drums), technical precision (mix and dubs by Richards), and the incredible energy of Michael and his brothers. The Corporation had created a brilliant update of pre-soul music: carrying the vigorous doo-wop of Frankie Lymon—with its very unfunky downbeats—10 years forward with ringing, swinging guitars. Michael Jackson's leads possess a purity and intensity unclouded by the storms of adolescence, while his older, wiser siblings lend brotherly support.

Gordy was ecstatic because his era of Frankie Lymon, Jackie Wilson, and Marv Johnson had briefly returned through the lungs of an 11-year-old boy—and proved commercially viable.

Richards' next effort was Diana Ross's second solo album, *Everything Is Everything;* it produced a huge hit in England, "I'm Still Waiting," which never made it in the U.S. "It broke my heart," Richards says.

Richards ran the West Coast office, produced, wrote, and supervised, and time passed. By 1973, his contract was up with Motown. "The company was restructuring," he recalls. "I had to stop what I was doing to think about it. We went back and forth with offers and counteroffers, and it's amazing, but I walked. Maybe I just needed a break." He took 1974 off.

Then he met producer John Carter, who introduced him to Fleetwood Mac. As a singles expert, Richards helped the band pick "Over My Head" from the Fleetwood Mac album and remixed it for single release. "Everyone was pleased with the result, so much so that the band wanted me to do their next album," Richards says. "I was advised to stay low-key about things. I didn't push for credit [for the remix], and just got the $900 remix fee [as opposed to royalties]."

Richards prepared to work on the Mac's next album, *Rumours.* "At the last minute, they called to ask if I would take cash instead of royalties," he says. Richards said he would take $25,000 cash, but if the record went gold, he wanted royalties from record one. Richards signed the papers and sent them back, but the executed contract was not forthcoming.

"Then there was this big dinner for the band, and I picked up weird vibes," Richards says. "Management had talked the band out of using me, just to save money." A lawsuit ensued, and essentially, a career was ruined. After almost four years, Richards won, but received only enough money to pay his lawyers. Part of the settlement was a nondisclosure agreement.

After the suit, Richards did odd production work for Black Oak Arkansas, Ruby Starr, and Bonnie Bramlett

and had a successful run with Canadian star Jeanette Reno. But he has never returned to prominence and feels, perhaps, that the music business has passed him by. Returning to his first love, Richards is now a successful dealer in film posters and memorabilia out of his Washington state home. He thinks fondly of Berry Gordy.

"Berry gave me autonomy and let me make my dreams come true," Richards says. "If Berry ever said 'I need you,' I'd come in a minute." —ERIC OLSEN

The Corporation

Jackson 5: *Diana Ross Presents the Jackson 5,* Motown, 1969, 1989 • "I Want You Back," Motown, 1969 • "ABC," Motown, 1970 • *ABC,* Motown, 1970, 1989 • *Christmas Album,* Motown, 1970, 1989 • "The Love You Save / I Found That Girl," Motown, 1970 • *Third Album,* Motown, 1970, 1989 • "Mama's Pearl," Motown, 1971 • "Maybe Tomorrow," Motown, 1971 • *Maybe Tomorrow,* Motown, 1971, 1989 • "Sugar Daddy," Motown, 1971 • *Anthology,* Motown, 1976.

Jackson, Jackie: *Jackie Jackson,* Motown, 1973.

Jackson, Jermaine: "Daddy's Home," Motown, 1972 • *Greatest Hits and Rare Classics,* Motown, 1991.

Jackson, Michael: "Ben," Motown, 1972 • *Got to Be There,* Motown, 1972 • *Ben,* Motown, 1973 • *The Best Of,* Motown, 1975 • *Anthology,* Motown, 1976, 1989.

Jackson, Michael, and the Jackson 5: *Jackson 5 Christmas Album,* Motown, 1987 • "Up on the House Top," Motown, 1987.

Fonce Mizell

A Taste of Honey: "Boogie Oogie Oogie," Capitol, 1978 • *Beauty and the Boogie,* EMI America, 1997.

Brothers Johnson and L.T.D.: *Brothers 'n' Love,* A&M, 1996.

Byrd, Donald: *Places and Spaces,* Blue Note, 1975 • *Caricatures,* Blue Note, 1976.

Glenn, Roger: *Jazz Collective,* BGP, 1976, 1994.

Jackson, Michael: *One Day in Your Life,* Motown, 1981.

L.T.D.: "Love Ballad," A&M, 1976 • *Love to the World,* A&M, 1976, 1996.

Martha and the Vandellas: *Live Wire! The Singles, 1962–1972,* Motown, 1993.

Rance Allen Group: *Capitol Rare,* Blue Note, 1977, 1994.

Smith, Johnny "Hammond": *Gears,* Original Jazz Classics, 1996.

Starr, Edwin: *Motown Superstar Series,* Vol. 3, Motown, 1980.

Fonce Mizell and Freddie Perren

Jackson, Michael: "Farewell My Summer Love," Motown, 1974, 1984 • *Farewell My Summer Love,* Motown, 1974, 1984.

Starr, Edwin: *Hell up in Harlem,* Motown, 1974.

Freddie Perren

Elliman, Yvonne: "Love Me," RSO, 1976 • "If I Can't Have You," RSO, 1978 • *The Best Of,* Polydor, 1997 • "Hello Stranger," RSO, 1977.

Gaynor, Gloria: "I Will Survive," Polydor, 1979.

Mighty Clouds of Joy: *Sing and Shout,* Word/Epic, 1983, 1992 • *Memory Lane—Best Of: Recordings from, 1960–1993,* Word/Epic, 1993.

Miracles, The: "Do It Baby," Tamla, 1974 • *Do It Baby,* Tamla, 1974 • *City of Angels,* Tamla, 1975 • "Love Machine Pt. 1," Tamla, 1976.

Naughton, David: "Makin' It," RSO, 1979.

New Edition: "Earth Angel," MCA, 1986 • *Under the Blue Moon,* MCA, 1986.

Peaches and Herb: *2 Hot,* Polydor, 1978 • "Shake Your Groove Thing," Casablanca, 1978, 1979 (*A Night at Studio 54*) • "Reunited," Polydor, 1979 • "I Pledge My Love," Polydor/MVP, 1980 • *The Best Of,* Polydor, 1996.

Riperton, Minnie: *Stay in Love,* Epic, 1977.

Roussos, Demis: "L.O.V.E. Got a Hold of Me," Mercury, 1978.

Spinners: *Grand Slam,* Atlantic, 1982 • *One of a Kind Love Affair,* Rhino, 1991.

Sylvers, The: "Boogie Fever," Capitol, 1976 • "Hot Line," Capitol, 1976 • "High School Dance," Capitol, 1977.

Tavares: "Heaven Must Be Missing an Angel," Capitol, 1976 • "More Than a Woman," RSO, 1977 (*Saturday Night Fever* soundtrack) • *Sky High,* Capitol, 1977 • "Whodunit," Capitol, 1977 • *It Only Takes a Minute,* Capitol, 1997.

Deke Richards

Black Oak Arkansas: *Race with the Devil,* Capricorn, 1977 • *I'd Rather Be Sailing,* Capricorn, 1978 • *Hot and Nasty: The Best Of,* Rhino, 1993.

Jackson 5: "Corner of the Sky," Motown, 1972.

Lomax, Jackie: *Livin' for Lovin',* Capitol, 1976.

Ross, Diana: "I'm Still Waiting," Motown, 1970 • *Everything Is Everything,* Motown, 1970 • *I'm Still Waiting,* Motown, 1971 • *Touch Me in the Morning,* Motown, 1973 • *Diana's Duets,* Motown, 1982 • *Anthology,* Motown, 1986, 1995 • *Greatest Hits,* Motown, 1991.

Ross, Diana, and the Supremes: *Captured Live on Stage!* Motown, 1970 • *Anthology,* Motown, 1974, 1986 • *The Best Of,* Motown, 1995.

Supremes, The: "Love Child," Motown, 1968 • *Love Child,* Motown, 1968 • "I'm Livin' in Shame," Motown, 1969 • *Let the Sun Shine In,* Motown, 1969 • *Greatest Hits and Rare Classics,* Motown, 1991 • w/ the Temptations, "I'll Try Something New," Motown, 1969.

Taylor, Bobby, and the Vancouvers: *Bobby Taylor and the Vancouvers,* Motown, 1968, 1994.

Temptations, The: w/ the Supremes, "I'll Try Something New," Motown, 1969.

Wonder, Stevie: *My Cherie Amour,* Motown, 1969.

Duke and the Drivers: *Rollin' On,* ABC, 1976.

Don Costa

Primarily known as an arranger, orchestrator, and conductor, the late Don Costa (born June 10, 1925, in Boston; died 1983 in New York) was known as one of the premier arrangers of the pop era, alongside Billy May, Nelson Riddle, Jimmy Webb, Quincy Jones (see entry), and Jimmie Haskell.

Costa's orchestrations are lush without falling prey to the saccharinity that often characterizes string dates, showing that orchestras don't have to sound trite to fit into a contemporary pop format. In the late '50s, he produced two Paul Anka hits, "Diana" and "Lonely Boy" (both No. 1). A decade later, he produced one of Frank Sinatra's biggest hits, Anka's "My Way." Along with Mike Curb, Costa was responsible for some of Donny Osmond's biggest hits, including "Young Love" (No. 9) and "Puppy Love" (No. 3).

Costa's 1977 collaboration with Kenny Rankin, *The Kenny Rankin Album,* represented a peak for both artists. The album combines well-chosen standards ("When Sunny Gets Blue," "Here's That Rainy Day") with first-rate Rankin originals ("I Love You," "Through the Eye of the Eagle") in an atmosphere that shows off Rankin's formidable vocal skills.

The owner of one of the most liquid, velvety voices this side of Mel Tormé, Rankin is a poor judge of material. But that Costa-Rankin collaboration produced an album with no bad choices and soaringly beautiful performances. "Very simply, Costa was a genius," says producer Denny Diante (see entry). "He had great production ideas as well as being an incredible arranger. He had a tremendous commercial sense, and great song knowledge." —DANIEL J. LEVITIN

Anka, Paul: "Diana," ABC/Paramount, 1957 • "Lonely Boy," ABC/Paramount, 1959 • *Vintage Years, 1957–1961,* Sire, 1978.

Arnold, Eddy: *Best Of,* Curb, 1990.

Charlene: "I've Never Been to Me," Motown, 1982.

Clark, Petula: *Now,* MGM, 1972 • *Treasures,* Vol. 1, Scotti Brothers, 1992.

Como, Perry: *Yesterday and Today: A Celebration in Song,* RCA, 1993.

Costa, Don: *Instrumental Versions of Simon and Garfunkel,* Mercury, 1968 • *Soul of Nigger Charley* soundtrack, MGM, 1973.

Damone, Vic: *The Glory of Love,* RCA, 1992.

Darren, James: *The Best Of,* Rhino, 1994.

Davis, Sammy Jr.: *Greatest Hits,* Vol. 2, DCC, 1960 • "Candy Man," MGM, 1972 • *Greatest Hits,* Vol. 1, Garland, 1978 • *Greatest Songs,* Curb, 1990.

Goulet, Robert: *Best Of,* Curb, 1990.

Highwaymen, The: *Michael Row the Boat Ashore: The Best Of,* EMI America, 1992.

Ho, Don: *I Think About You,* Honey, 1995.

Johnson, Marv: *You Got What It Takes,* EMI Legends, 1992.

Lopez, Trini: "If I Had a Hammer," Reprise, 1963 • "Kansas City," Reprise, 1963 • *More Trini Lopez at PJ's,* Reprise, 1963 • *Trini Lopez at PJ's,* Reprise, 1963 • *Live at Basin Street East,* Reprise, 1964 • *On the Move,* Reprise, 1964 • *The Latin Album,* Reprise, 1964 • "Lemon Tree," Reprise, 1965 • *The Folk Album,* Reprise, 1965 • *The Love Album,* Reprise, 1965 • *The Rhythm and Blues Album,* Reprise, 1965 • *The Sing-Along World of,* Reprise, 1965 • *Greatest Hits,* Reprise, 1966 • "I'm Comin' Home, Cindy," Reprise, 1966 • *Trini,* Reprise, 1966.

Monte, Lou: *Very Best Of,* Taragon, 1997.

Osmond, Donny: "Lonely Boy," MGM/Kolob, 1972 • "Puppy Love," MGM, 1972 • "Too Young," MGM, 1972 • "Why," MGM/Kolob, 1972 • "A Million to One," MGM/Kolob, 1973 • "Are You Lonesome Tonight?" MGM/Kolob, 1973 • "The Twelfth of Never," MGM/Kolob, 1973 • "Young Love," MGM/Kolob, 1973 • w/ Marie Osmond, *Greatest Hits,* Curb, 1992 • w/ Marie Osmond, *25 Hits Special Collection,* Curb, 1995.

Osmond, Marie: See Osmond, Donny.

Osmonds, The: *Osmond Family Christmas,* Curb, 1991.

Price, Lloyd: "Stagger Lee," ABC/Paramount, 1958 • "(You've Got) Personality," ABC/Paramount, 1959

Rankin, Kenny: *The Kenny Rankin Album,* Little David/Atlantic, 1977 • *After the Roses,* Atlantic, 1980, 1990 • *Peaceful: The Best Of,* Rhino, 1996.

Sherman, Bobby: *The Very Best Of,* Restless, 1991.

Sinatra, Frank: "Cycles," Reprise, 1968 • *Cycles,* Reprise, 1968, 1991 • "My Way," Reprise, 1969 • *My Way,* Reprise, 1969, 1986 • *Sinatra and Company,* Reprise, 1971 • *Frank Sinatra's Greatest Hits,* Vol. 2, Reprise, 1972 • *Ol' Blue Eyes Is Back,* Reprise, 1973 • *The Main Event Live,* Reprise, 1974, 1987 • *Some Nice Things I've Missed,* Reprise, 1974, 1991 • "Theme from New York, New York," Reprise, 1980 • *She Shot Me Down,* Reprise, 1981, 1991.

Strunk, Jud: "Daisy a Day," MGM, 1973 • *Daisy a Day,* MGM, 1973.

Elvis Costello

Elvis Costello (b. Declan Patrick Aloysius McManus) hasn't produced many records, but the ones he has have been hits, influential, or both. In addition to important productions for the Specials, the Pogues, Mental As Anything, Squeeze, and Paul McCartney, Costello has co-produced most of his own records since 1981, when he felt confident enough to step out of the shadow of Nick Lowe (see entry), the "basher" who produced Costello's first five albums.

Costello says he effectively gave up production of other people in 1986, when he married former Pogues bass player Caitlin O'Riordan. But Declan Patrick Aloysius McManus also says he plans to return to record production in 2000, when he will produce a pop record by a classical female singer for Deutsche Gramophon. That's all the specifics this canny musician will give on that project.

Born August 25, 1954, into a musical family, Costello worked as a computer programmer until the mid-'70s, when he turned his attention to music. Although he first performed in public in 1969, it wasn't until 1976 that he released his debut album, *My Aim Is True,* one of the keystones of new wave. Since then, he has released more than a dozen albums and appeared on numerous others, from classical records to soundtracks. His solo albums are among the most influential in modern rock. Besides *My Aim,* they include *This Year's Model, Imperial Bedroom, Blood and Chocolate, Spike* (No. 5 U.K.), *The Juliet Letters* (No. 18 U.K.), and *Brutal Youth* (No. 2 U.K.).

His three main labels have been Stiff, Columbia, and Warner Bros. He released most of his early work on the first two, switching to Warner in 1989, when he released *Spike,* one of his best efforts. The single "Veronica," which Costello wrote with McCartney, became his first Top 20 U.S. hit. Costello says *Spike* was by far his biggest U.S. effort, selling 750,000 copies.

Costello signed a multilabel, PolyGram-based deal in early 1998 that will give him outlets in his various modes: classical, pop, and rock. He says he left Warner Bros. because its marketing department seemed "to have run out of ideas." Once this year's model, Costello is now an influence, which makes him hard to market.

"You have to use a little ingenuity to intrigue members of the public," he says. "I have a pretty good, faithful audience, but if the record company is not prepared to be ingenious in their way of presenting [the product] and to be tremendously enthusiastic and to spend some money, you will not connect with a larger audience, and that's basically what happened in the past two years.

"If you look at my production credits, they're mostly based on a very good live band, and most of the productions are reasonably unsophisticated," Costello says. "The exception would be Squeeze. Glenn Tilbrook is a very, very fluid musician."

In the case of the Specials and the Pogues, however, the players were of mixed ability. "My role with the Specials and the Pogues was, 'I better get in and record them before some other, slicker guy fucked them up,' " Costello says. "The Pogues had made one great raw record before, and the record with me was slightly more focused but pretty much still the way they sounded live." After that, the quality of the songs remained high, but there was slightly slicker production.

"For me, the Pogues lost something getting into veneer," Costello says. "It just loses some of that spontaneous edge. I'm saying that and I'm prepared to accept the same criticism for my own work; I obviously have adopted a more layered approach to my work, and I stand by the results."

He thinks a production can be both spontaneous and refined. "Just make sure you're not cutting your nose off to spite your face," Costello adds. "It really depends on whether it's faithful to the song. If the song is rubbish, you can't do anything."

Besides Lowe, Costello has enormous respect for Geoff Emerick (see entry), the legendary EMI Studios figure who co-produced and engineered Costello's *All This Useless Beauty*. "So much of what he did, in the modern day, would be regarded as production," Costello says, noting Emerick and other engineers associated with the Beatles and EMI's Abbey Road Studio are "responsible for sounds we take for granted today."

While George Martin (see entry) deserves crucial credit for producing the Beatles records, Emerick, as their engineer, should be better recognized, Costello believes. "He was responsible for making the most vivid use of things, like certain effects which we expect to find as basic equipment in any decent studio and a lot of the most interesting sounds that are decorating dance records now and a lot of records that use extreme distortion," he says. "Don't you think those sounds began in avant-garde music and electro-acoustic music?"

His most important production-related effort, though he didn't have control of it, was his collaboration with another Abbey Road disciple, McCartney. Costello speaks highly of the songs that issued from this pairing.

"It's wrong to say I was ever appointed the producer," he says of his relationship with the ex-Beatle. "The

way he works is, we were writing together and we wrote, from 1987 over the next five years, a dozen songs, most of which have surfaced on either his records or mine. The record we were actually writing for was *Flowers in the Dirt* (No. 1 U.K.). McCartney has the resources to run sessions endlessly if he wants to, so I never felt as if I'd been given the [production] job." Nevertheless, Costello is one of four producers credited on that McCartney record.

Costello is now writing songs with Burt Bacharach (see entry); their first collaboration, "Give Me Strength," was the centerpiece of the movie *Grace of My Heart*.

While Costello's focus remains the song, he has some advice for musicians when it comes to production. "I think it's good to have an attitude to start with," Costello says. "I have four half brothers who have a band; there are quite a few musicians in my family. They're just making their first record now, and they may get into a demo studio with somebody with a little bit of B or C equipment who thinks he can produce like Hugh Padgham (see entry) and thinks production involves putting a tambourine over drums.

"A lot of bands that are smart get a boom box with a condenser mike, which is a truer representation of their sound," he continues. "If you get a Dictaphone and turn it on and record and get something that sounds like the hint of excitement, you're probably doing something right. If you've got a crummy thing with a broken speaker and half-working microphone and you can get it to sound right, that is production. It's not rocket science. It's just recording music onto tape."

Think of the box, Costello counsels. "In 1967, the biggest box imaginable was Phil Spector (see entry), but play an Ella Fitzgerald produced in the '50s and then a Spector and tell me which has more dynamic range." It's the Fitzgerald. "Her voice sounds enormous because it takes up all available space." A Spector production is a "trick of the ear," Costello suggests. It's a "cathedral sound coming out of a matchbox."

While preproduction is critical, Costello, finally, opts for the natural. "An awful lot more good records have been produced by simply picking the right moment to turn on the tape recorder," he says. "I've only ever fired two engineers off a session, one because he looked at the meter and didn't tap his feet, and another who walked into the session wearing sunglasses and told me his future was so bright he had to wear shades."
—CARLO WOLFF

Attractions, The: *See* Costello, Elvis, and the Attractions.
Bluebells, The: *The Bluebells* (1 track), Sire, 1983.
Brodsky Quartet: *See* Costello, Elvis.

Carrack, Paul: *The Carrack Collection,* Chrysalis, 1988.

Costello, Elvis: *Taking Liberties,* Columbia, 1980 • *Out of Our Idiot,* Demon, 1987 • *Spike,* Warner Bros., 1989 • "Veronica," Warner Bros., 1989 • "Days," Warner Bros., 1991 (*Until the End of the World* soundtrack) • *Mighty Like a Rose,* Warner Bros., 1991 • w/ Richard Harvey, *Original Music from GBH,* Demon, 1991 • "Ship of Fools," Arista, 1991 (*Deadicated*) • w/ the Brodsky Quartet, *The Juliet Letters,* Warner Bros., 1993 • "Sulky Girl," Warner Bros., 1994 • *Brutal Youth,* Warner Bros., 1994 • *Kojak Variety,* Warner Bros., 1995 • w/ Brian Eno, "My Dark Life," Warner Bros., 1996 (*Songs in the Key of X*).

Costello, Elvis, and the Attractions: "Party Party," A&M, 1982 (*Party Party* soundtrack) • *Girls, Girls, Girls,* Columbia, 1989 • *All This Useless Beauty,* Warner Bros., 1996.

Costello, Elvis, and the Costello Show: "Don't Let Me Be Misunderstood," Columbia, 1986 • *King of America,* Columbia, 1986.

Hall, Terry: *The Collection: Terry Hall,* Chrysalis, 1993.

Harvey, Richard: *See* Costello, Elvis.

Langer, Clive: *Splash,* F-Beat, 1980.

Lowe, Nick: *Nick Lowe and His Cowboy Outfit,* Demon/Columbia, 1984.

McCartney, Paul: *Flowers in the Dirt,* Capitol, 1989.

Mental As Anything: *If You Leave Me Can I Come Too,* A&M, 1982.

Pogues, The: *Rum, Sodomy and the Lash,* Stiff/MCA, 1985 • *Poguetry in Motion* (EP), MCA, 1986.

Specials, The: *The Specials,* 2 Tone/Chrysalis, 1980 • "A Message to You Rudi," 2 Tone/Chrysalis, 1983 (*This Are Two Tone*).

Special AKA: "Free Nelson Mandela," Chrysalis, 1984.

Squeeze: *East Side Story,* A&M, 1981 • *Singles 45 and Under,* A&M, 1982 • *Sweets from a Stranger,* A&M, 1982.

Wyatt, Robert: *Compilation,* Gramavision, 1991.

Luigi Creatore

See HUGO AND LUIGI

Bob Crewe

Bob Crewe's genius for crafting million-selling masterpieces from the late '50s through the '70s was arguably as original and influential as that of Phil Spector's; but unlike his famous peer, Crewe's name is not as recognizable as those of the artists he has worked with: Freddie Cannon, the Four Seasons, Mitch Ryder and the Detroit Wheels, Lesley Gore, and Oliver, to name a few.

Crewe's productions stand as cinematic, impressionistic, aural pop snapshots. "When we would write and record those songs it was always very visual to me; whether it was 'Rag Doll' [No. 1] or 'Let's Hang On' [No. 3], there was always a movie going on in my head. I had to be able to see music," he confides.

Bob Crewe, born November 12, 1931, in Newark, New Jersey, and raised in neighboring Belleville, says his first creative love was drawing and painting, although as a restless kindergartner, he sang the popular songs of the day and danced around his sleeping classmates during naptime.

As a youth, Crewe was drawn to romantic composers (Chopin, Tchaikovsky, Sibelius, Shostakovich) and the big bands of Artie Shaw, Woody Herman, Tommy Dorsey, and Benny Goodman. In the early '50s, Crewe studied art and architecture at the Parsons School of Design in New York City and in museums and artists' studios throughout Europe (Andy Warhol would later champion Crewe's art). He also did some commercial modeling to pay the bills.

Crewe began writing songs with Frank Slay, but he wasn't particularly pleased with how they were recorded. He wanted to record them himself, but "in the early '50s, the phrase 'independent record producer' did not exist," he says. Crewe then heard of a singer, Portia Nelson, who had made a record with her own money and put it out.

"With this concept in mind, we approached Gene Goodman [Benny's brother] with four songs in 1957. He loved the whole package and he came up with $5,000, which was an enormous amount. . . . Out of that pile came 'Silhouettes' by the Rays [No. 3]," says Crewe. "My big mentor was always Jerry Wexler [see entry] up at Atlantic Records. He would sit with us, listen to our stuff, critique it, and encourage us," Crewe recalls. "He also impressed upon us that after you put the record on tape, you've got to get on the phone and promote it with the same verve that you put into making it."

As the vestiges of a bygone decade were fading, Crewe struck pay dirt with what was to become one of the hottest hitmaking institutions of the '60s. "I loved the Four Seasons. They were a joy and a godsend for everybody involved. We all kind of benefited one another," he enthuses. "One day, I was on the eleventh floor of 1650 Broadway in the office of Larry Utall. Bob Gaudio and Frankie Valli were dragging around a wonderful bunch of demos that they laid on me that day. I loved what I heard, and Bob Gaudio and I started collaborating as writers," he says. "I found Frankie's falsetto by a wonderful accident. He was goofing around one night between sets, doing an imitation of Rose Murphy singing 'I Can't Give You Anything But Love' with a bandanna on his head, and shaking two big maracas up under his shirt like two big, you know, boobs. He started singing in this funny little voice.

"I grabbed Bobby Gaudio after the set," Crewe continues, "and said, 'Bob, go home, write anything, but give him an octave jump where he goes from his normal voice to that Rose Murphy falsetto. Bob came up with 'Sherry.' The rest is history."

"Sherry" enjoyed an amazing Billboard Hot 100 run in 1962, reigning for five weeks during the end of summer into the early autumn of that year. The Four Seasons were on their way to becoming a mainstay on the charts. If the Beach Boys were the Seasons' West Coast rivals in chart-topping harmony—musically celebrating the promised land 'neath the warm California sunshine—the Four Seasons marched to the rhythms of a sooty existence walled by the steel, glass, and concrete of Manhattan and Newark.

Crewe fashioned a sleek, stylized production motif for the Seasons discs that signified a bridge spanning the stoop-step doo-wop world of the '50s to Camelot and the vistas of the "future" in the '60s. The "oldies" status that has etched the Seasons' hits into the American psyche sometimes overshadows the inventiveness and innovation of these productions. The rhythm section, featuring the late, great drummers Gary Chester and Buddy Saltzman, laid a tough, unshakable foundation, artfully punctuated by dynamic, startling fills and intros that were virtual hooks unto themselves. Cuts like "Big Girls Don't Cry" (No. 1) were categorized by the now-archaic term "chalypso," in the jargon of early '60s trade publications like Billboard and Cashbox. This phrase was an amalgam signifying grooves that married cha-cha and calypso rhythms. "Candy Girl" (No. 3), the haunting "Silence Is Golden," and their cover of Maurice Williams and the Zodiacs' "Stay" (No. 16) are marked by evocative, spacious eeriness brought about by unique (and sometimes intriguingly schmaltzy)

organ and keyboard sounds, exotic percussion, haunting guitar figures, and six-string bass guitar.

Crewe did not let his lack of formal musical or technical training hinder him in making great records. "I took a few piano lessons when I was very young and found it awfully difficult," he says. "It was as if my impatience just wouldn't let me go through the pedantic ritual of learning how to get my fingers on the board. I could hear the finished arrangements in my head. Why be bothered with playing this one little stupid line when I could hear a whole orchestra? So I had to find people with whom I could communicate and talk kind of a musical shorthand. When I worked with Bob Gaudio as a co-writer [and co-producer later on] it was genuinely a co-effort, as such. The bouncing off of one another that way was just incredible."

Crewe's visual inclination again came into play: "I would lean over to [arranger] Charlie Calello when he was writing some string line and I would quickly jot a bird or a waterfall, or he'd see my notations for a cloud. In other words, music always had a picture—had to be a picture. I had to be able to see music."

Crewe's association with the Four Seasons continued with chart-toppers into the late '60s. His work with Frankie Valli's solo career peaked in that decade with "Can't Take My Eyes off You," a No. 2 smash in July 1967, and was rekindled during the '70s with hits like "My Eyes Adored You" (No. 1) and "Swearin' to God" (No. 6).

Crewe's greatness is assured for his work with the Four Seasons alone, but there is more: most importantly, the scorching Mitch Ryder and the Detroit Wheels' records. "Devil with a Blue Dress/Good Golly Miss Molly" (No. 4), "Sock It to Me Baby" (No. 6), and "Shake a Tail Feather" are among the most electrifying, live-sounding rock 'n' roll moments captured in a recording studio in the '60s.

Crewe nailed a classic girl-group sound with Diane Renay's "Navy Blue" (No. 6) and Lesley Gore's "California Nights" (No. 16) and launched a hip, influential style of easy-listening music with the Bob Crewe Generation and "Music to Watch Girls By" (No. 15) in 1966. Crewe ended the decade in style with Oliver's "Good Morning Starshine" (from the musical Hair, topping off at No. 3) and "Jean" (No. 2) both from 1969. The '70s saw Crewe-produced chart action with "Get Dancin' " (No. 10) by Disco-Tex and the Sex-O-Lettes.

In more recent years, Crewe has turned his attention 100 percent to the visual form—his first love—and he continues to enjoy a creative and a rewarding life. He does not rule out a return to musical endeavors, and even considers returning to the studio with Gaudio or

Valli again. Whether or not this happens, the world is a richer place for having basked in the power, class, and art of Bob Crewe's musical productions. —DENNIS DIKEN

Billy and Lillie: "La Dee Dah," Swan, 1958 • "Lucky Ladybug," Swan, 1959.

Bryson, Peabo: *Born to Love,* Capitol, 1983.

Crewe, Bob: *Kicks,* Warwick, 1966 • *Crazy in the Heart,* Warwick, 1967 • "Music to Watch Girls By," Dynovoice, 1967 • *Music to Watch Girls Go By,* Dynovoice, 1967.

Darin, Bobby: *1936–1973,* Motown, 1975.

Dawson, Ronnie: *Rockin' Bones: The Legendary Masters,* Crystal Clear, 1996.

Disco-Tex and the Sex-O-Lettes: "Get Dancin'," Chelsea, 1974 • "I Wanna Dance Wit' Choo (Doo Dat Dance) Part 1," Chelsea, 1975.

Four Seasons: "Big Girls Don't Cry," Vee-Jay, 1962 • "Santa Claus Is Coming to Town," Vee-Jay, 1962 • "Sherry," Vee-Jay, 1962 • *Sherry and 11 Others,* Vee-Jay, 1962 • "Ain't That a Shame," Vee-Jay, 1963 • "Candy Girl," Vee-Jay, 1963 • *Golden Hits of the Four Seasons,* Vee-Jay, 1963 • "Marlena," Vee-Jay, 1963 • "New Mexican Rose," Vee-Jay, 1963 • "Walk Like a Man," Vee-Jay, 1963 • "Alone," Vee-Jay, 1964 • "Big Man in Town," Philips, 1964 • "Dawn," Philips, 1964 • *Dawn and 11 Other Great Songs,* Philips, 1964 • "Rag Doll," Philips, 1964 • *Rag Doll,* Philips, 1964 • "Ronnie," Philips, 1964 • "Save It for Me," Philips, 1964 • "Silence Is Golden," Philips, 1964 • "Stay," Vee-Jay, 1964 • "Bye, Bye, Baby (Baby Goodbye)," Philips, 1965 • as The Wonder Who? "Don't Think Twice," Philips, 1965 • "Girl Come Running," Philips, 1965 • *Golden Vault of Hits,* Philips, 1965 • "Let's Hang On," Philips, 1965 • *Big Hits by Burt Bacharach, Hal David, Bob Dylan,* Rhino, 1965, 1988 • *Christmas Album,* Philips, 1966 • "I've Got You Under My Skin," Philips, 1966 • "Opus 17 (Don't You Worry 'Bout Me)," Philips, 1966 • *Second Vault of Golden Hits,* Philips, 1966 • "Tell It to the Rain," Philips, 1966 • "Working My Way Back to You," Philips, 1966 • *Working My Way Back to You,* Rhino, 1966, 1988 • "Beggin'," Philips, 1967 • *Big Girls Don't Cry and 12 Others,* Vee-Jay, 1967 • "C'mon Marianne," Philips, 1967 • *New Gold Hits,* Philips, 1967 • "Watch the Flowers Grow," Philips, 1967 • *The Genuine Imitation Life Gazette,* Rhino, 1968, 1995 • "Will You Love Me Tomorrow," Philips, 1968 • w/ Frankie Valli, *Edizione d'Oro,* Philips, 1969 • *Story,* Private Stock, 1975 • *Anthology,* Rhino, 1988 • w/ Frankie Valli, *Greatest Hits,* Vols. 1–2, Rhino, 1991.

Gore, Lesley: *Golden Hits of Lesley Gore,* Mercury, 1965 • "California Nights," Mercury, 1967 • *It's My Party: The Mercury Years,* Mercury, 1996.

Oliver: "Good Morning Starshine," Jubilee, 1969 • *Good*

Morning Starshine, Crewe, 1969 • "Jean," Crewe, 1969 • "Sunday Mornin'," Crewe, 1969.

Rays, The: "Silhouettes," Cameo, 1957.

Renay, Diane: "Navy Blue," 20th Century, 1964.

Ryder, Mitch: "What Now My Love," Dynovoice, 1967 • *Sing the Hits,* New Voice, 1967 • *The Rockin' Hits,* Special Music, 1993.

Ryder, Mitch, and the Detroit Wheels: "Jenny Take a Ride," New Voice, 1965 • *Breakout!!* Sundazed, 1966, 1993 • "Devil with a Blue Dress On/Good Golly Miss Molly," New Voice, 1966 • "Little Latin Lupe Lu," New Voice, 1966 • *Take a Ride,* Sundazed, 1966, 1993 • "Sock It to Me-Baby," New Voice, 1967 • *Sock It to Me,* Sundazed, 1967, 1993 • "Too Many Fish in the Sea and Three Little Fishes," New Voice, 1967.

Streisand, Barbra: *Main Event,* Columbia, 1979.

Valli, Frankie: "(You're Gonna) Hurt Yourself," Smash, 1966 • "Can't Take My Eyes off You," Philips, 1967 • "I Make a Fool of Myself," Philips, 1967 • "To Give (the Reason I Live)," Philips, 1968 • "My Eyes Adored You," Private Stock, 1975 • "Swearin' to God," Private Stock, 1975 • *Close Up,* Private Stock, 1975 • *Inside You,* Motown, 1975 • *Heaven Above Me,* MCA, 1980 • *See also* The Four Seasons.

Steve Cropper

S teve Cropper doesn't like to deal directly with record labels, which isn't surprising considering how the guitar legend fared during the latter days of Stax.

"They're bottom-line, profit and loss guys, they're out of their league," Cropper says of record company executives. "They're lawyers and accountants and whatever. They seem to have sympathy for artists and want to show up at every showcase. They're always backstage. Then they'll turn around and hire some 21- or 22-year-old person, a lot of times female, and what do they know about rhythm 'n' blues from the '60s? Hell, they don't even know who the Beatles are.

"I'm sort of a dinosaur, I understand that," Cropper adds. "I'm not a frontline producer."

Maybe Cropper isn't today, though he recently produced a Verve record for guitarist Joe Louis Walker and worked on *Blues Brothers 2000,* the sequel to the original Dan Aykroyd–John Belushi movie. But Cropper certainly was frontline in the '60s and '70s, when he was one of the key people, both behind the board and onstage, at Stax. Not only was Cropper a member of Booker T. and the MGs, he produced sessions for that band, Eddie

Floyd, Darryl Banks, Eric Mercury, Jimmy Hughes, Mable John, the Staple Singers, Mavis Staples, and Rufus Thomas.

"I like to work in situations where my main function is to deal with the artist," says the Nashville resident. "I like to be one-on-one with the artist and music and do whatever it takes to pull the album off. My perfect situation is when the artist has a really good manager who handles all the business with the record company. Pay me, I do my job."

Born October 21, 1941, in Willow Springs, Missouri, Cropper studied engineering at Memphis State University. At the dawn of the '60s, he and Packy Axton, son of Estelle Axton, were leading the Royal Spades, the hottest white R&B band in Memphis. Cropper is said to have contributed to "Last Night," a Top 10 hit in the summer of 1961. The Mar-Keys, an outgrowth of the Royal Spades who also performed "Last Night," included saxophonists Packy Axton and Don Nix, trumpeter Wayne Jackson, bassist Donald "Duck" Dunn, drummer Terry Johnson, Jerry Lee "Smoochie" Smith on piano, and Cropper on guitar. According to accounts in Peter Guralnick's *Sweet Soul Music*, the Mar-Keys were heavily augmented by the black Memphis musicians on which they modeled themselves.

In 1961, Satellite Records, Jim Stewart and Estelle Axton's label, changed its name to Stax ("st" for Stewart and "ax" for Axton) following a lawsuit from a California label also called Satellite. And in 1961, Cropper went to work for Stax, lasting there for more than 10 years.

"I got hired just to be around at Stax in 1961," Cropper says. "I swept floors and filed tapes. I was working in the record shop up front and found myself spending more time in the studio."

Like fellow Stax employee David Porter (see entry), Cropper is ambivalent about his years at the fabled company. While he reveres the work he and his colleagues turned out, he, like Porter, suggests management kept the personalities at the label in check, perhaps to devalue them.

Cropper is particularly proud of work he did with Otis Redding and Wilson Pickett, "but if you want the real stuff, I was on the sessions on a lot of the Otis Redding material, and I worked with him, but I wasn't listed as producer," he reveals. "There was a period at Stax when the records either didn't have any producer listed or the label copy read 'produced by staff.' And there was a time when we struck a deal with the record company to get compensated for our production efforts over and above what we got paid for as musicians."

The pact signed with label owner Jim Stewart involved the cream of the Stax crop, a six-man produc-

tion team that shared in profits: drummer Al Jackson Jr., treasurer; keyboardist Booker T. Jones (see entry); bassist Donald "Duck" Dunn; Isaac Hayes (see entry); David Porter; and Cropper. The deal, intermittently renegotiated, held from 1963 to 1970, Cropper says. It meant that every quarter, the six-man team figured out the sales figures of the records it had helped produce, then split the lump sum six ways.

"We were a team," Cropper recalls. "Most of us played on the sessions; David Porter was either a writer or in the studio. We did have that production pool."

But Stax, under tremendous political and economic pressure—primarily from Atlantic, which used its New York power base to leverage Memphis and Georgia soul—began to capsize in 1970, finally shutting down in 1975.

"I always felt if Stax could have kept that production team going, it would have survived," Cropper says. "But that wasn't all of it. The big people wanted us to be a major album-producing company, but we weren't. We produced singles."

Among his Stax disappointments was "Marchin' Off to War," a tune he wrote with William Bell. He thought it was a hit, but "radio didn't want it." Another personal failure was "Raise Our Hand," produced as the follow-up to Eddie Floyd's 1966 hit "Knock on Wood." "He performs that song today worldwide, and the audience goes nuts," Cropper says of Floyd. "They get involved, they go crazy, and radio would not play it."

Besides producing *Jammed Together*, a 1969 Stax album featuring himself, Pops Staples, and Albert King, Cropper produced John Prine's 1975 album *Common Sense*, John "Cougar" Mellencamp's 1980 disc *Nothin' Matters and What If It Did*, and *Bump City*, a 1972 Tower of Power album for Warner Bros. that lists engineer Ron Capone as producer.

What Cropper brings to production depends on whom he's producing, he says. "In a situation where an artist has a self-contained band, you have to weed through that. Are they good enough to be on this record? If you find they're not, you have to handle that diplomatically. A lot of times, a musician may have some high school buddies who have been playing together, but they might have a weak link. Why would we suffer this when we have a roomful of musicians who do this for a living?"

Cropper feels he has "to inject reality" into the production situation, and to be a diplomat. "The bottom line to producing a good record is to pull the best performance out of an artist," Cropper says.

"I try to stay current," adds Cropper, who recently produced sessions by young country stars Neal McCoy and Bryan White. "I pride myself on the drum and bass sounds. I hate a muddy sound; I don't like that old distorted muddy sound."

While he leaves the technological tweaks to his engineers, he doesn't fight technology. Being able to mix digitally and work with DAT appeals to him because it's easy to upgrade a session using such tools. "There are a lot of producers whose thing is handling the business part for the artist, but that's not my forte," Cropper says. "Mine is music. A producer of a movie has totally different functions from a producer of music. The producer is the guy who puts the deal together in movies. They say you're 'producing' the music, but you're 'directing' the music. 'Producer' is a misnomer—we should be called 'musical directors.' " —CARLO WOLFF

Ambergris: *Ambergris,* Paramount, 1970.

Beck, Jeff: *The Jeff Beck Group,* Epic, 1972 • *Beckology,* Epic/Legacy, 1991, 1995.

Bell, William: *Little Something Extra,* Stax, 1992.

Booker T. and the MGs: *Universal Language,* Asylum, 1977 • *That's the Way It Should Be,* Columbia, 1994.

Cate Brothers: *Cate Brothers,* Asylum, 1975 • *In One Eye and out the Other,* Asylum, 1976.

Cold Blood: *Lydia,* Warner Bros., 1974.

Crimson Tide: *Reckless Love,* Capitol, 1979.

Cropper, Steve: *With a Little Help from My Friends,* Stax, 1971 • *Playing My Thing,* MCA, 1980 • *Night After Night,* MCA, 1982.

Doheny, Ned: *Hard Candy,* CBS, 1976 • *Prone,* CBS/Sony, 1979.

Dreams: *Imagine My Surprise,* Columbia, 1969.

Elliman, Yvonne: *Rising Sun,* RSO, 1975 • *The Best Of,* Polydor, 1997.

Feliciano, Jose: *Memphis Menu,* RCA, 1972 • *Compartments,* RCA, 1973 • *For My Love . . . and Other Music,* RCA, 1974.

Floyd, Eddie: "On a Saturday Night," Stax, 1967 • "Raise Your Hand," Stax, 1967 • "Bring It on Home to Me," Stax, 1968 • *Chronicle,* Stax, 1979 • *Rare Stamps,* Stax/Fantasy, 1993 • *California Girl/Down to Earth,* Stax, 1995.

Ford, Robben: *The Inside Story,* Elektra, 1979.

Head, Roy: *Dismal Prisoner,* TMI, 1972.

Iron City Houserockers: *Blood on the Bricks,* MCA, 1981.

King, Albert: w/ Steve Cropper and Pops Staples: *Pumping Iron and Sweating Steel: The Best Of,* Rhino, 1992.

Kolby, Diane: *Diane Kolby,* Columbia, 1973.

McCoo, Marilyn, and Billy Davis Jr.: *Marilyn and Billy,* CBS, 1978.

Mellencamp, John "Cougar": *Nothin' Matters and What If It Did,* Riva, 1980 • "Ain't Even Done with the Night," Riva, 1981.

Mercury, Eric: *Funky Sound Nurtured in the Fertile Soil of Memphis,* Enterprise, 1972.

Nilsson, Harry: *Flash Harry,* Mercury, 1980.

Pickett, Wilson: "Ninety-Nine and a Half Won't Do," Atlantic, 1966 • "634-5789 (Soulsville U.S.A.)," Atlantic, 1966 • *The Exciting Wilson Pickett,* Atlantic, 1966.

Poco: *From the Inside,* Epic, 1971 • *The Very Best Of,* Epic, 1975 • *The Forgotten Trail, 1969–1974,* Epic, 1990.

Prine, John: *Common Sense,* Atlantic, 1975 • *Great Days: The John Prine Anthology,* Rhino, 1993.

Redding, Otis: "I've Been Loving You Too Long," Stax, 1965 • "Respect," Volt, 1965 • "Fa-Fa-Fa-Fa-Fa (Sad Song)," Volt, 1966 • "I Can't Turn You Loose," Volt, 1966 • "Try a Little Tenderness," Volt, 1966 • "Glory of Love," Volt, 1967 • w/ Carla Thomas, "Knock on Wood," Stax, 1967 • w/ Carla Thomas, "Tramp," Stax, 1967 • *Dock of the Bay,* Atlantic, 1968 • "(Sittin' on) the Dock of the Bay," Volt, 1968 • "The Happy Song (Dum-Dum)," Volt, 1968 • "Love Man," Atco, 1969 • *Love Man,* Atco, 1969 • *Tell the Truth,* Atlantic, 1970 • *The Immortal Otis Redding,* Atlantic, 1972 • *Ultimate,* Warner Bros., 1986 • *Otis! The Definitive Otis Redding,* Rhino, 1993.

Ryder, Mitch: *The Detroit-Memphis Experiment,* Dot, 1970.

Sam and Dave: *Back at 'Cha,* United Artists, 1974 • *Very Best Of,* Rhino, 1995.

Skyking: *Secret Sauce,* CBS, 1975.

Staple Singers: *Soul Folk in Action,* Stax, 1991, 1968.

Staples, Mavis: *Mavis Staples,* Stax, 1969 • *Only for the Lonely,* Stax, 1970, 1993.

Stoots, Ronnie: *Ashes to Ashes,* TMI, 1972.

Stuff: *Stuff It,* Warner Bros., 1979 • *Right Stuff,* Warner Bros., 1996.

Thomas, Carla: *Hidden Gems,* Stax, 1992 • *Gee Whiz: The Best Of,* Rhino, 1994.

Thudpucker, Jimmy, and the Walden West Rhythm Section: *Jimmy Thudpucker and the Walden West Rhythm Section,* Windsong, 1977.

Tower of Power: *We Came to Play,* Columbia, 1978.

COLLECTIONS
Jammed Together, Stax, 1969, 1988.

Rodney Crowell

Few producers would be as candid as Rodney Crowell about their first production experience. "God looks after drunks and babies and I was a baby," he says of *Right or Wrong,* the 1979 work by ex-wife Rosanne Cash. "The stuff I did with Rosanne was really unconscious," Crowell says. "We were just young people living out our dreams. It was very romantic." More importantly, Crowell believes, "I was shown pretty soon, without any guile or anything, that I could do it. It was just my nature to be able to do that."

Few producers have as broad a range of entertainment experience as Crowell. A former member of Emmylou Harris's Hot Band, whose alumni also include Tony Brown (see entry), Emory Gordy Jr., Glen Hardin, and Hank DeVito, he is also a noted songwriter and solo performer whose 1988 album *Diamonds and Dirt* spawned five No. 1 country hits. He won a Grammy in 1990 for best country song for "After All This Time."

"For me, the main thing about being on the road with the Hot Band was something that I've cultivated since: the collaborative arranging effort," Crowell says. "Glen Hardin, Emory Gordy, Hank DeVito, myself, we were all arrangers of some sort. I was a songwriter first, which is sort of an arranging mindset, but the thing that really came to the fore for me from that experience was how to arrange, how to communicate arrangement."

Crowell says if an artist doesn't need his arrangement assistance, he might not be the right man for the job. "If somebody just wanted me to sit there and make sure they did it right, and they have their own arranging, I don't think I'd be interested in that. It wouldn't be any fun. It wouldn't be creative."

Of course, he remembers one member of a famous trio who didn't seem to need his arrangement skills—or any of his skills for that matter. One of the first records Crowell did was a live record with Carl Perkins, Johnny Cash, and Jerry Lee Lewis.

"It was my third record, maybe, and I was arrogant enough to not even be aware that there was a process to go through. I was just like, 'Damn the torpedoes,' " he recalls. "But Jerry Lee Lewis made it very clear to me that his part of that record was going to be on the first side and if it wasn't, I might be laying in a ditch somewhere. I said, 'Yes, sir! I'll do all I can.'

"So I spent a week making the audience sound like he came out on the fourth song instead of the thirteenth. Revisionist history for sure. Hey, I may have been an arrogant snot, but I was no match for Jerry Lee Lewis."

Crowell's productions don't rely on the same Nashville studio musicians other producers use. While he uses some session players, he tends to turn to musicians who perform outside of the studio as well.

"I like people who are performers," he says. "I think musicians who are still live performers just bring more sexuality to the music. Part of being in front of an audience is to entertain and to kind of use sexuality as part of the whole package. When a musician's been out on the road for a month and they come in, they got that thing, there's more sexuality at the surface, and I think music is very sexual."

As a producer, he picks each musician to play a special part. "I cast musicians in roles and situations based on what I know they'll bring to the table. I'll cast somebody who's one of those names on every record if they do what the song needs. I take a lot of pride and enjoyment in casting the situation. I'm a real student of film and sometimes it kind of overlays what I'm doing, because I also use film-making metaphors to describe what we're going for in making a record."

But the star is the artist, and as director, Crowell looks for a leading man or woman with a strong sense of self. "It's a nightmare to produce someone who doesn't know what they want," he says. "I don't want to be close to that. If someone comes in and they don't know who they are, you aren't going to get a good [album]. If someone comes in and doesn't know what they want and looks at you and whines, 'Tell me what to do, and I'll do it. I just want to be a star,' I'm not inspired—and I need to be inspired as much as they are."

Especially inspiring is a record Crowell finished in 1997 for Beth Nielsen Chapman, the touching *Sand and Water*. The album deals with her husband's death.

"With her husband getting cancer and dying, she went through this long process and wrote about it," Crowell notes. "Her husband was a friend of mine. I was involved with his death as a friend, and I started to hear the things that Beth was writing about, and it was extremely powerful stuff. I don't think anyone else could have made this record with Beth. I knew where she was all the time. She was grieving and making a record and it was a real process. It's the hardest record I've ever made. Beth was not a weak woman in her grief, but, [when] you're attempting to record songs that are so deeply personal about the loss of your mate, you can imagine what you have to go through to get to it."

Pain doesn't have to be part of the process. Crowell has found working with Little Texas ex-lead singer Brady Seals liberating because Seals' previous work only hinted at the depth Crowell has found. "I wasn't a Little Texas fan," he says. "To me, Little Texas was kind of bubblegummy and plastic, but the funny thing is, I met with Brady and he's not that way at all. He left the group to find a more creative part of himself and he's really a searcher. When all of this stuff starts to focus and come together for him, he's going to be a strong man."

While Crowell still performs—most recently in the Cicadas—producing becomes ever more satisfying for him. "As I've gotten older—and that may be the key—I find a lot of creative satisfaction in helping others," he says. He particularly enjoys refining the raw material in somebody's project and "watching it come to life."

The only artist he won't produce is Rodney Crowell. "I'm not a hard artist to produce for another producer, I think. I'm a real hard worker and I'm not precious in the studio and I'm not too vulnerable. I can take the hard knocks in the studio and respond to the truth. But producing myself is the hardest thing I've ever done," he says, "and probably the biggest mistakes I've ever made as a producer were producing myself. I think I've missed songs because I was wearing too many hats. I dressed them up in the wrong clothes. I've lived long enough to see the futility of that and the combination of fear and arrogance that I had.

"Hindsight ain't good sight, but it's my sight." — MELINDA NEWMAN

Bare, Bobby: *As Is,* CBS, 1981.
Cash, Johnny: w/ Jerry Lee Lewis and Marty Robbins, *Survivors,* Columbia, 1982.
Cash, Rosanne: "Baby, Better Start Turnin' Them Down," Epic, 1979, 1981 (*Exposed*) • *Right or Wrong,* Ariola, 1980 • "My Baby Thinks He's a Train," Columbia, 1981 • "Seven Year Ache," Columbia, 1981 • *Seven Year Ache,* Ariola/CBS, 1981 • "What Kinda Girl?," Epic, 1981 (*Exposed*) • "Blue Moon with Heartache," Columbia, 1982 • *Somewhere in the Stars,* Ariola, 1982 • "Never Be You," Columbia, 1986 • *King's Record Shop,* Columbia, 1987 • "The Way We Make a Broken Heart," Columbia, 1987 • "If You Change Your Mind," Columbia, 1988 • "Runaway Train," Columbia, 1988 • "Tennessee Flat Top Box," Columbia, 1988 • *Hits, 1979–1989,* Columbia, 1989 • "I Don't Want to Spoil the Party," Columbia, 1989 • "Real Woman," Columbia, 1990 • *Retrospective,* Columbia, 1995.
Chapman, Beth Nielsen: "Happy Girl," Reprise, 1997 • *Sand and Water,* Reprise, 1997.
Cicadas: *Cicadas,* Warner Bros., 1997.
Clark, Guy: *South Coast of Texas,* Warner Bros., 1981 • *Better Days,* Warner Bros., 1983.
Crowell, Rodney: *But What Will the Neighbors Think,* Warner Bros., 1980 • *Diamonds and Dirt,* Columbia, 1987, 1988 • *Rodney Crowell,* Warner Bros., 1981 • *Street Language,* Columbia, 1986 • "I Couldn't Leave You If I Tried," Columbia, 1988 • w/ Rosanne Cash, "It's Such a Small World," Columbia, 1988 • "Above and Beyond," Columbia, 1989 • "After All This Time," Columbia, 1989 • "She's Crazy for Leavin'," Columbia, 1989 • *The Rodney Crowell Collection,* Warner Bros., 1989 • *Keys to the Highway,* Columbia, 1990 • *Life Is Messy,* Columbia, 1992 • *Greatest Hits,* Columbia, 1993 • *Let the Picture Paint Itself,* MCA, 1994 • *Soul Searchin',* Sony Special Products, 1994 •

Jewel of the South, MCA, 1995.
Lauderdale, Jim: *Planet of Love,* Reprise, 1991.
Lee, Albert: *Albert Lee,* Polydor, 1982.
Lewis, Jerry Lee: *See* Cash, Johnny.
Robbins, Marty: *See* Cash, Johnny.
Seals, Brady: "Natural Born Lovers," Reprise, 1997 • "Still Standin Tall," Reprise, 1997 • *The Truth,* Reprise, 1997.
Spacek, Sissy: *Hangin' Up My Heart,* Warner Bros., 1983.
White, Lari: *Lead Me Not,* RCA, 1993 • *Best Of,* RCA, 1997.
Willoughby, Larry: *Building Bridges,* Atlantic, 1983.

COLLECTIONS

Time and Love: The Music of Laura Nyro, Astor Place, 1997.

Jerry Crutchfield

Like many Nashville producers, Jerry Crutchfield has often juggled many roles during his successful career, including publisher, songwriter, label executive, and, of course, producer. As a songwriter, he's had more than 160 songs recorded by artists in the country, pop, and R&B fields. As a publisher, he's been responsible for nurturing the talents of top songwriters like Dave Loggins, Don Schlitz, and Gary Burr. As a producer, he's worked with Anne Murray, Lee Greenwood,

Photo by Don Putnam © 1988

Glen Campbell, and Tracy Byrd and has had a lengthy association with Tanya Tucker, producing more than a dozen of her albums.

"I first actually got into the business as a recording artist," Crutchfield says. "I had a vocal group in school and we were originally called the Country Gentlemen, and later called the Escorts. We came to Nashville in the late '50s and recorded for RCA. We recorded for Chet [Atkins; see entry] for a couple of years and it was during that time that I started writing songs."

A native of Paducah, Kentucky, who attended college at Murray State, Crutchfield moved to Nashville in 1960. During the early '60s he and his brother recorded as a duo, Jan and Jerry, on MGM Records, but Crutchfield wound up trading the stage lights for a studio console as he settled into a job with Tree Publishing and began honing his skills as a writer and producer. "Back then Tree was three employees: Buddy Killen, myself, and a secretary," he recalls of the company that has become Nashville's most successful publishing operation. "Things have changed dramatically since then."

In 1965, Crutchfield opened MCA Music and began building that company into one of Music Row's most successful ventures. During that time he signed Don Schlitz, Gary Burr, and Dave Loggins. (He produced Loggins' classic "Please Come to Boston," No. 5.)

In addition to building the publishing operation, Crutchfield began gaining a reputation as a producer. "One of the first things I produced and really had any success with was an R&B record with a group called the Spidells," he says. "They did the original record on a song I wrote called 'Find Out What's Happening.' That song has since been recorded numerous times and later became a country hit with Bobby Bare. Tanya Tucker had it out as a single, and even Jeff Beck recorded it on one of his earlier rock groups over in London. It just keeps popping up."

During his tenure as head of MCA Nashville publishing, Crutchfield was also one of Music Row's most sought-after independent producers. "I see a producer as someone who really should be a multifaceted creative person," he says. "If I were making production assignments, I would look for people I really believe are good song people, who would recognize good songs and are creatively courageous enough to go in the studio and try something a little bit different. I'm not sure if there are as many people doing that today."

Crutchfield's reputation for finding hit artists and songs led to a gig for Capitol Records Nashville in 1989, leading to four years as the company's executive vice president and general manager. "Starting out with the label I didn't do as much production because I really

didn't intend to," Crutchfield says. "But over the last 18 months I was with Capitol, I was doing more producing than I ever had." Not only was he producing Tucker, he did the same for Campbell, Skip Ewing, and a band called Pearl River. He also signed and produced Lisa Brokop.

After his stint at Capitol, he returned to MCA Music for a few years before leaving in September 1996 to start his own company, Crutchfield Music.

"We have about eight writers and we'll probably grow to about ten or twelve writers, and that's as big as we want to be. . . . We have a writer who is doing extremely well, Mark Nesler, and I just recently signed Mark to Asylum Records." Crutchfield calls Nesler "one of the most completely talented people I've ever encountered. I'm really looking forward to getting in the studio with him to see what we can do."

One of his longest associations has been with Tucker, whom he started producing when she was in her teens. "I have a very close and special relationship with Tanya," he says. "I've always been, probably next to her dad, her biggest supporter."

Tracy Byrd is another of his favorite acts. "What I tried to do with Tracy was spend time with him to help him determine what it was he did best, and then try to find songs that were impact songs, songs that would get the job done. We had three Top 5 singles, and one No. 2 with 'Keeper of the Stars.' Tracy is really developing. A lot of singers have a way of reaching a plateau, but Tracy continues to get better all the time.

"There's something special about creating something that is real and has impact," Crutchfield says. "When I hear a song that's special and is produced well, I thoroughly enjoy it and can appreciate everything that went into it." —DEBORAH EVANS PRICE

Bogguss, Suzy: *Greatest Hits,* Liberty, 1994.

Bradshaw, Terry: *Terry and Jake,* Chordant, 1996.

Brokop, Lisa: *Every Little Girl's Dream,* Patriot, 1994 • *Lisa Brokop,* Capitol, 1996.

Byrd, Tracy: *No Ordinary Man,* MCA, 1994.

Campbell, Glen: *Unconditional Love,* Liberty, 1991 • *Somebody Like That,* Liberty, 1993.

Claypool, Philip: *A Circus Leaving Town,* Curb, 1995.

Crosby, Rob: *Starting Now,* River North, 1995 • "The Trouble with Love," River North, 1995.

Daniel, Dale: *Luck of Our Own,* BNA, 1993.

Ewing, Skip: *Homegrown Love,* Liberty, 1993.

Fairchild, Barbara: *Love Is a Gentle Thing,* Columbia, 1969 • *A Sweeter Love,* Columbia, 1972 • "Kid Stuff," Columbia, 1973 • *Kid Stuff,* Columbia, 1973 • "Teddy Bear Song," Columbia, 1973 • "Baby Doll," Columbia, 1974 •

"Standing in Your Line," Columbia, 1974 • *Greatest Hits,* Columbia, 1977.

Francis, Cleve: *Walkin',* Liberty, 1993.

Gatlin, Larry, and the Gatlin Brothers: "Houston (Means I'm One Day Closer to You)," Columbia, 1983 • *Sure Feels Like Love,* Columbia, 1983.

Gatlin Brothers: *Greatest Hits,* Vol. 2, Columbia, 1983 • *Best of the Gatlins: All the Gold in California,* Legacy/Columbia, 1996.

Greenwood, Lee: "Somebody's Gonna Love You," MCA, 1983 • *Somebody's Gonna Love You,* MCA, 1983 • "Going Going Gone," MCA, 1984 • "Dixie Road," MCA, 1985 • "I Don't Mind the Thorns (If You're the Roses)," MCA, 1985 • "Don't Underestimate My Love for You," MCA, 1986 • "Hearts Aren't Made to Break (They're Made to Love)," MCA, 1986 • "Mornin' Ride," MCA, 1987 • *Greatest Hits,* MCA, 1988, 1993 • *Greatest Hits,* Vol. 2, MCA, 1989 • *When You're in Love,* Capitol, 1991 • *American Patriot,* Liberty, 1992 • *Best Of,* Liberty, 1993 • *The Best of Lee Greenwood,* Liberty, 1993.

Jason Ringenberg: *One Foot in the Honky Tonk,* Liberty, 1992.

La Costa Tucker: *Lovin' Somebody,* Capitol, 1977.

LeDoux, Chris: *Western Underground,* Liberty, 1991 • "Cadillac Ranch," Liberty, 1992 • *Whatcha Gonna Do with a Cowboy,* Liberty, 1992 • *Under This Old Hat,* Liberty, 1993 • *American Cowboy,* Liberty, 1994 • *Best Of,* Liberty, 1994.

Lee, Brenda: "A Sweeter Love (I'll Never Know)," MCA, 1984.

LeFevre, Mylon: *Rustler,* Warner Bros., 1978.

Loggins, Dave: *Personal Belongings,* Vanguard, 1971, 1994 • "Please Come to Boston," Epic, 1974 • *Apprentice in a Musical Workshop,* Epic, 1974.

Mandrell, Barbara, and Lee Greenwood: *Meant for Each Other,* MCA, 1984.

McClinton, Delbert: *Delbert McClinton,* Curb/Capitol, 1993.

Medley, Bill: *I Still Do,* RCA, 1984 • *Still Hung up on You,* RCA, 1985.

Murray, Anne: *Greatest Hits,* Vol. 2, Liberty, 1989 • *You Will,* Liberty, 1990 • *Yes I Do,* Liberty, 1991.

Osmond, Marie: *Steppin' Stone,* Curb, 1989.

Overstreet, Paul: *Time,* Integrity, 1996.

Owens, Buck: *Act Naturally,* Liberty, 1989 • *Collection, 1959–1990,* Rhino, 1992.

Patton, Wayland: *Gulf Stream Dreamin',* Liberty, 1991.

Pearl River: *Find Out What's Happening,* Capitol, 1993.

Seals, Dan: *Fired Up,* Warner Bros., 1994.

Tucker, Tanya: "Here's Some Love," MCA, 1976 • *The Best Of,* MCA, 1982 • *Girls Like Me,* Capitol, 1986 • "Just Another Love," Capitol, 1986 • *Love Me Like You Used To,* Capitol, 1987 • w/ Paul Davis and Paul Overstreet, "I Won't Take Less Than Your Love," Capitol, 1988 • "If It Don't Come Easy," Capitol, 1988 • "Strong Enough to Bend," Capitol, 1988 • *Strong Enough to Bend,* Liberty, 1988 • *Greatest Hits Encore,* Liberty, 1990 • *Tennessee Woman,* Liberty, 1990 • *What Do I Do with Me,* Capitol, 1991 • *Can't Run from Yourself,* Liberty, 1992 • *Collection,* MCA, 1992 • *Greatest Hits, 1990–1992,* Liberty, 1993 • *Soon,* Liberty, 1993 • *Tanya Tucker,* Liberty, 1994 • *Fire to Fire,* Liberty, 1995 • *Love Songs,* Capitol Nashville, 1996.

West, Dottie: *Just Dottie,* Permian, 1984.

Wopat, Tom: *A Little Bit Closer,* EMI America, 1987 • *Don't Look Back,* Capitol, 1988.

Wynette, Tammy: *Tears of Fire: The 25th Anniversary Collection,* Epic, 1992.

Michael Cuscuna

Jazz producer Michael Cuscuna cut his teeth on folk and blues production, shifting to jazz in the mid-'70s when he became disillusioned with the direction pop was taking. Besides being in charge of reissues at Blue Note Records, Cuscuna is co-owner (with Charlie Lourie) of Mosaic Records, a jazz audiophile reissue company in Stamford, Connecticut.

Born September 20, 1948, Cuscuna grew up in Stamford listening to blues and R&B. He began collecting

Photo by Jimmy Katz © 1995

45s, fell in love with '50s R&B, and dabbled in drums. He launched his college career at the Wharton School at University of Pennsylvania, expecting to become a captain of the record industry. "They were preparing people to be CEO of General Motors," recalls Cuscuna. "I went there hoping to have a record company someday. Most of my college years were spent doing radio and promoting concerts and getting into records. The first record I did—with my own savings—was by a wonderful guitarist named George Freeman. I drove to Chicago and made a record on a shoestring budget; ultimately, it came out on the Delmark label in Chicago.

"I was always thinking of records to make, of different combinations," Cascuna adds. "I thought that in jazz and blues, a sameness was taking over, and I wanted records that were unique. When you get into the business, you realize you can't just think of records and make them happen. They involve other people's participation and desire."

In the late '60s, Cuscuna was working in radio and writing for *Down Beat, Rolling Stone,* and *Saturday Review* and got to know Chicago guitarist Buddy Guy through his radio show. Guy asked Cuscuna to produce his last date for Vanguard Records; Cuscuna happily agreed, forfeiting a Rolling Stones show to shepherd the session. But when it came time to mix the album, Vanguard wouldn't pay to fly Guy to New York, so Cuscuna called up Bob Krasnow at Blue Thumb, and together, they concocted a date for Guy with Junior Mance (piano) and Junior Wells (harmonica). The date, released on Blue Thumb as *Buddy and the Juniors,* was not only critically successful, it was coolly packaged in a foldout cover and the vinyl was marbleized.

Meanwhile, Cuscuna also got to know singer/songwriter Chris Smither, a New Orleans native and Boston resident who crafts remarkable cameos of personality and passion. He began shopping Smither around and secured a deal for him with Poppy Records; two albums came out on that long-defunct label (one remains unissued). Cuscuna also befriended Bonnie Raitt at that time; he wound up producing her second Warner Bros. album, the classic *Give It Up,* a 1972 release. At the time, Cuscuna also was an underground radio DJ at Philadelphia station WMMR-FM; when a similar slot opened up at WPLJ in New York, he happily jumped ship. But when FM began to become formatized with the advent of playlists, Cuscuna quit; fortunately, an old friend from Philly, another former DJ at WMMR, was working at Atlantic Records. So when Joel Dorn (see entry) asked Cuscuna if he wanted a job as staff producer at Atlantic, Cuscuna said, "No problem."

He worked at Atlantic in 1972 and 1973, dealing with such label stalwarts as pianist Richard Tee, guitarist Cornell Dupree, and drummer Bernard Purdie. He also produced albums by Garland Jeffries (a great one) and Eric Kaz (a bit of a snooze). In 1974, he struck out on his own, and he's been a freelance producer ever since.

"Around that time, I also shifted pretty much to jazz," Cuscuna says. "There were two reasons: The blues scene was pretty dead at that time—the coffin was about three feet down—and as far as the singer/songwriter syndrome, Peter Asher [see entry] was having tremendous success with Linda Ronstadt and James Taylor, and that whole sound, which was a lot more expansive and slicker than what I enjoyed doing, became the all-pervasive sound."

Cuscuna prefers intimate singer/songwriters like Smither, who works alone; Jeffries, who worked only with a second guitarist; and Raitt, who worked primarily with bassist Freebo (an alumnus of the Edison Electric Band). "So when it came time to make an album, you could work from scratch," Cuscuna says. "I didn't like being handed a working band. I liked to personalize every song, and a large part of arranging is whom you select as well as the approach you take."

Besides, jazz was always his first love. At Atlantic, he'd arranged jazz albums by the likes of Dave Brubeck and the Art Ensemble of Chicago. He'd caught the Ensemble bug at the Ann Arbor Blues and Jazz Festival in 1973, a great array including Sun Ra, Junior Walker, Raitt, and the Art Ensemble. (A subsequent album he recorded with the Ensemble in Montreux remains in the hands of the group; Atlantic never released it.)

In the late '70s, the record industry went into recession, leading to some lean years for Cuscuna. In the early '80s, he and Lourie approached Blue Note parent Capitol Records with a plan to revive the classic jazz label, but Capitol, which had been rebuilding itself genre by genre, wasn't ready then. So in 1982, Cuscuna and Lourie founded Mosaic Records, first as a vinyl effort and later as a full-service reissue operation.

"I had been working, on and off, for Blue Note over the years, and had researched everything in the vaults," Cuscuna says. "I came up with the idea of box sets because it was serendipitous: There were two and a half LPs of Monk material, some other material that had been on 10-inch LP, and another 32 minutes of unissued Monk that was exceptionally good. Normally, when you find such material, you try to put it out, but 32 minutes was too short. So I thought maybe I should take all the Monk stuff, rearrange it in chronological order, weave this unreleased stuff into it, and then it would be a really impressive document that would make up four LPs."

In July 1984, EMI, which owned Capitol, hired Bruce

Lundvall to start a jazz-pop label, Manhattan Records. As part of the deal, Capitol allowed Lundvall to resurrect Blue Note, so Lundvall "pulled me into it to do various little projects" as a consultant, Cuscuna says. Those "little projects," among them the development of Blue Note's limited-edition Connoisseur Series, became regular work, so Cuscuna now splits his time between Blue Note and Mosaic.

"Most of the fun of making records is in the details, whether it's horn obbligatos, a very tasteful slide guitar part, or a wonderful organ chord," Cuscuna says. "Those little things that can really finish off a song are the most fun. You can try a lot of things, and you can be wrong, but no one will know because you can throw them away. I always like to lay down three or four takes and then pick the best licks of each and lay them into a composite track, make the most perfect part you can. By perfect I don't mean pristine. Just soulful." —CARLO WOLFF

Allison, Luther: *The Motown Years, 1972–1976,* Motown, 1996.

Benny Green Trio: *That's Right,* Blue Note, 1993.

Blake, Ran: *Film Noir,* Arista, 1980.

Blakey, Art, and the Jazz Messengers: *The History of the Jazz Messengers,* Blue Note, 1992.

Braxton, Anthony: *New York (Fall 1974),* Arista, 1974 • *Seven Standards,* Magenta, 1985, 1991.

Brubeck, Dave: *All the Things We Are,* Rhino, 1973, 1987 • *Two Generations of Brubeck,* Atlantic, 1973 • *Brother, the Great Spirit Made Us All,* Atlantic, 1974 • *Time Signatures: A Career Retrospective,* Columbia, 1992.

Byrd, Donald: *Places and Spaces,* Blue Note, 1975.

Charles, Ray: *Genius and Soul: 50th Anniversary Collection,* Rhino, 1997.

Coltrane, John: *Stellar Regions,* Impulse!, 1967, 1995.

Coryell, Larry, and Eleventh House: *At Montreux,* Vanguard, 1978.

Davis, Eddie Lockjaw: *The Heavy Hitter,* Muse, 1979.

Dupree, Cornell: *Teasin',* Atlantic, 1979.

Gordon, Dexter: *The Complete Blue Note 60's Sessions,* Blue Note, 1965, 1996 • w/ Junior Mance, *At Montreux,* Prestige Records, 1970, 1985 • *Blue Dex: Dexter Gordon Plays the Blues,* Prestige, 1973, 1996 • *Homecoming,* Columbia, 1977 • *Sophisticated Giant,* Columbia, 1977 • *Manhattan Symphonie,* Columbia, 1978 • *Great Encounters,* Columbia, 1979 • *Gotham City,* CBS, 1981 • *Ballads,* Blue Note, 1991.

Guy, Buddy: w/ Junior Wells, *Play the Blues,* Atlantic, 1972 • w/ Junior Wells and Junior Mance, *Buddy and the Juniors,* MCA, 1992.

Henderson, Joe: *Best of the Blue Note Years,* Blue Note, 1991.

Hill, Andrew: *Spiral,* Freedom, 1975.

Hope, Elmo: *Trio and Quintet,* Blue Note, 1997.

Horace Silver Quintet: *Further Explorations,* Blue Note, 1959, 1997 • *See also* Silver, Horace.

Horne, Lena: *An Evening With: Live at the Supper Club,* Blue Note, 1995.

Hubbard, Freddie: *The Best Of,* Columbia, 1973, 1990 • *Best of Freddie Hubbard,* Blue Note, 1989 • *The Freddie Hubbard and Woody Shaw Sessions,* Blue Note, 1995.

Jefferson, Eddie: *The Live-liest,* Muse, 1979.

Jeffreys, Garland: *Garland Jeffreys,* Atlantic, 1973.

Johnson, J.J.: *J.J. Inc.,* Columbia, 1961, 1997.

Jordan, Stanley: *Cornucopia,* Blue Note, 1990.

Kaz, Eric: *Cul-De-Sac,* Atlantic, 1974 • *If You're Lonely,* Atlantic, 1972.

Lacy, Steve: *Raps,* Adelphi, 1975.

Mance, Junior: *See* Dexter, Gordon; Guy, Buddy.

Martino, Pat: *Consciousness,* Muse, 1975, 1989.

Newman, David "Fathead": *Still Hard Times,* Muse, 1982, 1990.

Pullen, Don: *New Beginnings,* Blue Note, 1989 • *Random Thoughts,* Blue Note, 1990 • *Kele Mou Bana,* Blue Note, 1992 • *Sacred Common Ground,* Blue Note, 1996.

Raitt, Bonnie: *Give It Up,* Warner Bros., 1972 • *The Bonnie Raitt Collection,* Warner Bros., 1990.

Rawls, Lou: *It's Supposed to Be Fun,* Blue Note, 1990 • *The Legendary Lou Rawls,* Blue Note, 1992.

Reeves, Diane: *I Remember,* Blue Note, 1991.

Rollins, Sonny: *There Will Never Be Another You,* Impulse!, 1978.

Rush, Chris: *The Cosmic Comedy of Chris Rush,* Atlantic, 1973.

Sanders, Pharoah and Norman Connors: *Beyond a Dream,* Novus, 1981.

Schmidt, Eric Von: *2nd Right, 3rd Row,* Poppy, 1972.

Shaw, Woody: *Little Red's Fantasy,* Muse, 1978 • *Stepping Stones,* CBS, 1978 • *Woody 3,* CBS, 1979 • *For Sure,* Columbia, 1980 • *The Moontrane,* Muse, 1993, 1995.

Shepp, Archie: *Montreux One,* Freedom, 1975, 1991 • *There's a Trumpet in My Soul,* Freedom, 1976, 1988.

Silver, Horace: *Sterling Silver,* United Artists, 1979.

Smither, Chris: *I'm a Stranger Too,* Poppy, 1973 • *I'm a Stranger Too,* Poppy, 1971 • *Don't It Drag On,* Poppy, 1972.

Taylor, Cecil: *Indent,* Freedom, 1973, 1989 • *Silent Tongues,* Freedom, 1974, 1987.

Teodross Avery Quartet: *In Other Words,* GRP, 1994.

Threadgill, Henry: *X-75 Volume 1,* Novus, 1979.

Tyner, McCoy: *Jazz Profile,* Blue Note, 1997.

Wells, Junior: *See* Guy, Buddy.

Williams, Tony: *Foreign Intrigue,* Blue Note, 1986 • *The Best Of,* Capitol, 1996.

COMPILATIONS

Adderley, Cannonball: *Jazz Profile,* Capitol, 1997.

Armstrong, Louis, and the All Stars: *The Complete Studio Recordings,* Mosaic, 1993.

Baker, Chet: *Pacific Jazz Years,* Pacific Jazz, 1952, 1995.

Blakey, Art, and the Jazz Messengers: *Jazz Profile,* Capitol, 1997.

Burrell, Kenny: *The Best Of,* Blue Note, 1957, 1995.

Cole, Nat "King": *The Best of the King Cole Trio,* Blue Note, 1949, 1992 • *Jazz Encounters,* Blue Note, 1950, 1992 • *Lush Life,* Blue Note, 1952, 1989 • *Big Band Cole,* Blue Note, 1961, 1991 • *The Billy May Sessions,* Capitol, 1961, 1989.

Davis, Miles: *The Best Of,* Blue Note, 1958, 1992 • *The Blue Note and Capitol Recordings,* Capitol, 1993 • w/ Gil Evans, *Best Of,* Legacy, 1997.

Donaldson, Lou: *The Best Of,* Vol. 1, *1957–1967,* Blue Note, 1993.

Dorham, Kenny: *The Best of Kenny Dorham: The Blue Note Years,* Blue Note, 1996.

Evans, Gil: *See* Davis, Miles.

Getz, Stan: *Stan Getz at Storyville,* Vols. 1–2, Roulette, 1951, 1990 • *Roost Years: The Best Of,* Roulette, 1952, 1991.

Guy, Buddy: *My Time After Awhile,* Vanguard, 1992.

Henderson, Joe: *Ballads and Blues,* Capitol, 1997.

Hubbard, Freddie: *Ballads,* Capitol, 1997.

Hutcherson, Bobby: *See* Tyner, McCoy.

McCoy Tyner Trio and Michael Brecker: *Infinity,* Impulse!, 1995.

Morgan, Lee: *Jazz Profile,* Capitol, 1997.

Powell, Bud: *Jazz Profile,* Vol. 8, Capitol, 1997.

Quebec, Ike: *Ballads,* Blue Note, 1997.

Shorter, Wayne: *Jazz Profile,* Blue Note, 1997.

Silver, Horace: *The Best Of,* Vol. 2, Blue Note, 1989.

Tatum, Art: *The Complete Capitol Recordings,* Vols. 1–2, Capitol, 1989.

Tyner, McCoy: *The Best of McCoy Tyner: The Blue Note Years,* Blue Note, 1996 • *Revelations,* Blue Note, 1989 • w/ Bobby Hutcherson, *McCoy Tyner and Bobby Hutcherson,* Blue Note, 1994.

Wilson, Nancy, and George Shearing: *The Swingin's Mutual,* Capitol, 1961, 1992.

REISSUES

Ammons, Albert, and Meade Lux Lewis: *The First Day,* Blue Note, 1939, 1992.

Baker, Chet: *Chet Baker Quartet,* Pacific Jazz, 1953, 1995 • *The Best of Chet Baker Plays,* Pacific Jazz, 1956, 1992.

Blakey, Art: w/ James Moody, *New Sounds,* Blue Note, 1947, 1991 • *A Night at Birdland,* Vols. 1–3, Blue Note, 1954, 1987 • *Moanin',* Blue Note, 1958, 1987 • *Buhaina's Delight,* Blue Note, 1962, 1992 • *Three Blind Mice,* Vol. 2, Blue Note, 1962 • *Freedom Rider,* Blue Note, 1963 • *Orgy in Rhythm,* Vols. 1–2, Capitol, 1997.

Brown, Clifford: *Memorial Album,* Blue Note, 1953, 1989 •

Complete Blue Note/Pacific Jazz, Pacific Jazz, 1954, 1995.

Byrd, Donald: *Byrd in Flight,* Blue Note, 1960 • *Donald Byrd at the Half Note Cafe,* Blue Note, 1960, 1997 • *Blackjack,* Blue Note, 1967.

Clark, Sonny: *Dial 'S' for Sonny,* Blue Note, 1959, 1997.

Coltrane, John: *Blue Train,* Blue Note, 1957, 1997 • *Newport '63,* Impulse!, 1963 • *Live at the Village Vanguard Again,* Impulse!, 1966 • *Retrospective: Impulse,* GRP, 1967 • *To the Beat of a Different Drummer,* Impulse!, 1981 • *See also* Monk, Thelonius.

Davis, Miles: *Miles Davis,* Vol. 2, Blue Note, 1953, 1989 • *Miles Davis,* Vol. 1, Blue Note, 1954, 1988.

Donaldson, Lou: *Sunny Side Up,* Blue Note, 1960, 1995 • *Gravy Train,* Blue Note, 1961.

Ellington, Duke: *Piano Reflections,* Capitol, 1953 • *Duke Ellington Live at the Blue Note,* Roulette, 1959, 1994.

Gerry Mulligan Quartet: *Best of with Chet Baker,* Pacific Jazz, 1957, 1991 • *Complete Pacific Jazz Recordings,* Pacific Jazz, 1957, 1991.

Gonzalez, Babs: *Weird Lullaby,* Blue Note, 1958, 1992.

Goodman, Benny: *Undercurrent Blues,* Blue Note, 1949.

Green, Bennie: *Soul Stirrin',* Blue Note, 1959.

Green, Grant: *Grant Stand,* Blue Note, 1961, 1987 • *Green Street,* Blue Note, 1961 • *Complete Quartets with Sonny Clark,* Blue Note, 1962, 1997 • *Feelin' the Spirit,* Blue Note, 1962, 1987 • *Idle Moments,* Blue Note, 1963, 1988 • *Matador,* Blue Note, 1965, 1990 • *Street of Dreams,* Blue Note, 1967.

Greene, Dodo: *My Hour of Need,* Blue Note, 1962.

Hancock, Herbie: *Takin' Off,* Blue Note, 1962, 1987 • *Best of the Blue Note Years,* Blue Note, 1988 • *Jazz Profile,* Capitol, 1997.

Hartman, Johnny: *The Voice That Is,* Impulse!, 1965.

Hawkins, Coleman: *Hollywood Stampede,* Capitol, 1945, 1990.

Hipp, Jutta: w/ Zoot Sims, *Jutta Hipp with Zoot Sims,* Blue Note, 1956.

Horace Silver Trio: *Spotlight on Drums,* Blue Note, 1952, 1989 • *See also* Silver, Horace.

Hubbard, Freddie: *Goin' Up,* Blue Note, 1960.

Hutcherson, Bobby: *Stick Up!* Blue Note, 1966.

Jackson, Milt: *Milt Jackson,* Blue Note, 1952, 1989 • *Statements,* Impulse!, 1964.

John Coltrane Quartet: *John Coltrane Quartet Plays Chim Cheree . . . ,* Impulse!, 1965, 1992.

Johnson, J.J.: *Proof Positive,* Impulse!, 1964.

Kelly, Wynton: *Piano Interpretations,* Blue Note, 1951, 1991.

Kenton, Stan: *City of Glass,* Blue Note, 1952, 1995.

Lambert, Hendricks and Ross: *Sing a Song of Basie,* GRP, 1958, 1972.

Lateef, Yusef: *Live at Pep's,* Impulse!, 1964.

Lewis, Meade Lux: *The First Day,* Blue Note, 1939, 1992.

Manne, Shelly: *2-3-4,* Impulse!, 1962, 1995.

McLean, Jackie: *Swing, Swang, Swung,* Blue Note, 1959, 1997 • *Destination Out,* Blue Note, 1964.

McRae, Carmen: *Sings Lover Man and Other Billie Holiday Classics,* Columbia/Legacy, 1997.

Mobley, Hank: *Peckin' Time,* Blue Note, 1958, 1988 • *A Slice of the Top,* Blue Note, 1966, 1979.

Moncur, Grachan, III: *Some Other Stuff,* Blue Note, 1964.

Monk, Thelonious: *Genius of Modern Music,* Vol. 1, Blue Note, 1947, 1989 • *Genius of Modern Music,* Vol. 2, Blue Note, 1952, 1989 • *Round Midnight,* TriStar, 1957, 1996 • *Best of the Blue Note Years,* Blue Note, 1991 • w/ John Coltrane, *Live at the Five Spot—Discovery!* Blue Note, 1993.

Moody, James: *See* Blakey, Art.

Morgan, Lee: *Candy,* Blue Note, 1959, 1987 • *Tom Cat,* Blue Note, 1964, 1990.

Nelson, Oliver: *More Blues and Abstract Truth,* Impulse!, 1964.

Oscar Pettiford Orchestra: *Deep Passion,* Impulse!, 1957.

Parlan, Horace: *Us Three,* Blue Note, 1960, 1997.

Powell, Bud: *The Amazing,* Vol. 2, Blue Note, 1953, 1989.

Quebec, Ike: *Blue and Sentimental,* Blue Note, 1961, 1995.

Red, Sonny: *Out of the Blue,* Blue Note, 1960.

Rollins, Sonny: *Alfie,* Impulse!, 1966, 1997.

Sanders, Pharoah: *Tauhid,* Impulse!, 1966.

Scott, Shirley: *Roll' Em,* Impulse!, 1966, 1995 • *See also* Turrentine, Stanley.

Shorter, Wayne: *JuJu,* Blue Note, 1964 • *Et Cetera,* Blue Note, 1965, 1981.

Silver, Horace: *Song for My Father,* Blue Note, 1964, 1989 • *Tokyo Blues,* Blue Note, 1962.

Sims, Zoot: *See* Hipp, Jutta.

Smith, Jimmy: *A New Star, a New Sound: Jimmy Smith at the Organ,* Vol. 1, Blue Note, 1956, 1997 • *Home Cookin',* Blue Note, 1959, 1984 • *Crazy Baby!* Blue Note, 1960, 1989 • *The Sermon,* Blue Note, 1960, 1987 • *I'm Movin' On,* Blue Note, 1967, 1995 • *The Best Of,* Blue Note, 1987.

Smith, Louis: *Here Comes Louis Smith,* Blue Note, 1957.

Taylor, Billy: *My Fair Lady Loves Jazz,* Paramount, 1957.

Three Sounds: *Black Orchid,* Blue Note, 1963.

Tristano, Lennie: *Intuition,* Capitol, 1956, 1996.

Turrentine, Stanley: *Z.T.'s Blues,* Blue Note, 1961, 1988 • w/ Shirley Scott, *Let It Go,* Impulse!, 1966, 1992 • *Spoiler,* Blue Note, 1966 • *Easy Walker,* Blue Note, 1969, 1997 • *The Best Of,* Blue Note, 1989.

Vaughan, Sarah: *Sarah Slightly Classical,* Roulette, 1963, 1991 • *Sassy Sings and Swings,* Blue Note/Cema, 1992.

Washington, Dinah: *Back to the Blues,* Capitol, 1997 • *Jazz Profile,* Vol. 5, Capitol, 1997.

Willette, Baby Face: *Face to Face,* Blue Note, 1961.

Lloyd "Matador" Daley

Like Jamaican producers Duke Reid, Coxsone Dodd, and Prince Buster (see entries), former Boy Scout troop leader Lloyd Daley ran a sound system (called Matador), initially playing American R&B records as well as dub plates he purchased from his rivals. They competed with each other at indoor and outdoor dances. Daley studied electronic engineering at Kingston Technical High, owned a repair shop, and built amplifiers before he began making records.

Using the studios and pressing facilities of Federal Records and (less often) Dynamic, he hired the cream of Jamaica's studio talent, including "Family Man" Barrett, Boris Gardner, and Jackie Jackson—and that's just on bass!

Records by ska soloists Roland Alphonso and Rico Rodriguez were among his earliest productions, cut first as exclusives for his sound system and later issued on blank-label 45s. They and fellow players might be the Skatalites for Coxsone one day, Duke Reid or Matador's All Stars the next. They also backed singers and groups.

In 1966 police destroyed Daley's sound system—a not uncommon practice at the time—and he stepped up his activities as a producer and label head, at times even going so far as to put a picture of a matador and bull on the labels, enhancing distribution somewhat.

Daley always seemed strangely ahead of his time. In the ska era he was recording the overtly rock-steady Overtakers, foreshadowing the rhythmically lilting style that would rule briefly between ska and reggae. But during the rock-steady era, Matador's productions were among the first to solidify the new surging rhythm of reggae and identify it with the downpressed.

Themes of sufferation and the lives of everyday people are prominent in Daley's productions. The baleful innocence of the Caribbeans' "Let Me Walk By," the serious bite of Audley Rollens' "Repatriation," and the haunting righteousness of Little Roy's "Hard Fighter" typify Matador's output. The latter seems to describe his own struggle: "No matter how they imitate / The things that I originate / Imitation can't last long / Origination will be strong." Daley also produced the classic "Bongo Nyah" for the same artist. Sensitive writers and singers like Little Roy and Lloyd Robinson were nurtured and gave Daley some of their best work.

The Matador also waved the red flag for vocal groups. The Viceroys, the Abyssinians, the Wailing Souls, and the Ethiopians all cut outstanding roots harmony records for him. His first major hit was "Uglyman" by the Scorchers. He produced and released important records with Owen Grey, Dennis Brown, and Alton Ellis ("Back to Africa," one of Daley's hardest singles). Daley's productions appeared on English labels like Pama, Gas, Bullet, Explosion, Crab, Camel, and others, and on 45 and anthology albums with the work of other producers, as well as on his own Matador label.

At the end of the '70s Daley left the record business (though not his thriving electronics store) for much the same reason he shut down his sound—only this time the destruction of the music business seemed to be coming from the inside out: Jamaica's antiquated copyright system, which allowed "the big dog feeding on the small," i.e., nonpayment of royalties.

Daley's output from the late '60s through the late '70s was issued in the heyday of the 7-inch single in Jamaica. All of his records (at present two Jamaican albums) and on reissue CD in the U.S. and Europe are anthologies. The most representative and readily available is Lloyd Daley's Matador Productions, 1968–1972, issued in 1992 by the Heartbeat label. —CHUCK FOSTER

COMPILATIONS

Lloyd Daley's Matador Productions, 1968–1972, Heartbeat, 1992: Abyssinians, "Y Mas Gan" • Blake Boy, "Deliver Us" • Dennis Brown, "Things in Life" • Caribbeans, "Let Me Walk By" • Lloyd Charmers, "Zylon" • Creators, "Bad Name" • Lloyd Daley, "Y Mas Gan Version" • Alton Ellis, "Back to Africa" • Ethiopians, "Owe Me No Pay Me" • 1. Jesters, "Cholera" • Little Roy, "Bongo Nyah" • Lloyd Robinson, "Death a Come" • Audley Rollens, "Repatriation" • Scorchers, "Uglyman" • U Roy, "Sound of the Wise" • Viceroys, "Take Yu Hand."

Scandal, Matador/JA, 1992: Dennis Brown, Little Roy, and Leroy Sibbles, "Righteous Man.

Way Back When, Matador/JA, 1992: Emotions, "Hallelujah" • Matador's All Stars, "Bridge View Shuffle," "Continental Shuffle" • Moore, Dizzy Johnny, "Big Big Boss."

From Matador's Arena, Vol. 1, *1968–1969,* Jamaica Gold, 1994: Count Ossie and the Lloyd All Stars, "I Dread Version" • Emotions, "Poor Man Story Long" • Mittoo, Jackie, "Dark of the Sun" • Paragons, "Equality and Justice," "You Mean the World to Me" • Scorchers, "Hold on Tight" • Uniques, "Secretly."

It's Shuffle 'n' Ska Time with Lloyd "The Matador" Daley, Jamaica Gold, 1994: Overtakers, "Beware," "Right Now," "Risk You a Run," "Unresistable You" • Raymond Harper, "Heart and Soul."

From Matador's Arena, Vol. 2, *1969–1970,* Jamaica Gold, 1995: Robinson, Lloyd, "The Worm" • U Roy, "Scandal" • Wailing Souls, "Gold Digger."

From Matador's Arena, Vol. 3, *1971–1979,* Jamaica Gold, 1995: Gladiators, "Freedom Train," "Rock a Soul Man" • I Roy, "Musical Drum Sound," "Problems of Life" • Little Roy, "Hard Fighter."

Marston Daley

See BUZZ McCOY AND GROOVIE MANN

Jack Dangers

(MEAT BEAT MANIFESTO)

As the driving force behind Meat Beat Manifesto, Jack Dangers has explored and mapped uncharted terrain between hip-hop, industrial, trance, jungle, and ambient music. Nimbly balancing art and the dance floor, Dangers is one of the few to have mastered studio technology as an organic instrument. In the process, he has created some stunning tracks: the Public Enemy-esque punch of "God O.D.," the loping groove of "Psyche-Out," the awesome headlong industrial funk of "Dogstar Man/Helter Skelter," the churning space jam

Photo by Jay Blakesberg

"Mindstream" and one of the finest electronic-based albums of all time, *Subliminal Sandwich*.

Dangers also has worked with political trip-hoppers Consolidated and Disposable Heroes of Hiphoprisy and is an important remixer.

He was born John Corrigan in 1965 in Swindon, England, a small town best known as the home of new wave–art rockers XTC. Dangers was interested in electronic music from an early age, reveling in the experimentalism of Kraftwerk, early Human League, and Cabaret Voltaire. "I liked the idea of experimenting and taking sounds to extremes; that has been completely ingrained in me," he says.

Never a trained musician, Dangers picked up the bass because, as he says, "I found I could play it. I am not from a musical family at all, but from a very working-class, normal background. I have no qualifications and I can't do anything else. I sold my soul to music when I was 15, decided that's what I would do and always knew that I would be able to do it, even if I couldn't play anything."

Dangers' defining moment came when he aided XTC (as a gofer) in rehearsal for a 1980 tour. Fascinated with music making, Dangers obtained one of the first home 4-track recorders and began experimenting with sound in earnest in the early '80s.

In 1986, he released his first record with the decidedly techno-poppish Perennial Divide. Longing for a more experimental avenue of expression, Dangers released beat-heavy singles "I Got the Fear" and "Strap Down" in 1987 as Meat Beat Manifesto. The next year, Dangers left Perennial Divide and began performing with a multimedia extravaganza of up to 13 members—replete with video, dancers, and elaborate costumes.

That same year, Meat Beat combined necessity with ideology when most of the material for their planned first album was destroyed in a fire. Instead of despairing, the industrious Dangers took four surviving songs and created two divergent mixes of each, "trying to take things to their logical conclusions" and creating one of the first known nonreggae remix albums in the process (collections of dub mixes of reggae songs date to the '70s).

Meat Beat's artistic breakthrough came with release of the "God O.D." single in late 1988. "God" kicks in with a defiant drumbeat worthy of Public Enemy, shifts into overdrive with Dangers' chant-sing vocals, and continues with kitchen-sink samples spicing the brew. Dance floor denizens the world over responded to the body-jacking beat, Dangers' percussive vocal delivery, and all the bells and whistles.

Though always funkier and more varied than traditional industrial groups Front 242 (see entry) and Skinny Puppy (see Dave Ogilvie entry), Meat Beat was identified with the industrial crowd through its affiliation with the Play It Again Sam label, and song titles like "Genocide," "Repulsion," and "Kick That Man" from their 1990 disc *Armed Audio Warfare*.

The quality groove has continued apace. *99%* is a superior collection highlighted by "Psyche-Out" ("This is what it's all about / Sex, drugs, and rock 'n' roll") and the 8 1/2 minutes of heaven and hell rammed together and chopped up as "Dogstar Man/Helter Skelter." The medley percolates on a fast hip-hop beat (now we call it jungle), underlined with Dangers' dancing bass line and drilled home with a penetrating keyboard riff. This time, Dangers' chant-sing is distorted into a dangerous buzz of warnings and incantations. Midway through, the beat is redoubled, the keyboard is sampled into a percussion line of its own, and the whole mess explodes in a hallucinatory orgasm of chopped beats and brain parts. No one had made music like this before.

Satyricon continues the excellence, but heads off in more melodic, techno- and trance-based directions, shedding the confinement of the "industrial" label. The double CD *Subliminal Sandwich* finds Dangers with assorted guests and confirms his position among the finest electronic musician/composers.

Sandwich leads the listener through a sonic tour of the ether on a radio ship picking up the most interesting sound tidbits floating about, bouncing around and intermingling with each other. These bits of raga, trance, ambient, trip hop, and jungle are invisibly sewn together in Dangers' magical, limpid mix. Seldom have 140 minutes gone by more quickly and soulfully, or registered more deeply.

Dangers wrote all of the music save for Keith Dobson's ghostly "Asbestos, Lead, Asbestos," and recorded the whole thing with a clarity and precision that lets us so deep into the mix that we fall in and become happily lost there, riding the groove, picking up signals. That all of this seems so alive and human attests to Dangers' artistry. "I think it's really important to mix technology with an organic aesthetic and not be controlled by the machines," explains Dangers.

Perhaps not surprisingly for a man who finds the organic in the soul of the machine, the favorite of his 15,000 records is the Beach Boys' *Pet Sounds*. Dangers is not an artist driven by pain. "I love what I do; it's the best job in the world, and I work hard to be able to do it well," says the San Francisco resident. "I got what I wanted and I am happy." —ERIC OLSEN AND DAWN DARLING

BiGod 20: "One" (remix), Sire/WB, 1994.

Bomb the Bass: *Earmuff,* Island, 1998.

Bowie, David: "Palais Athena" (remix), Savage, 1992 • "You've Been Around" (remix), Savage, 1992.

Bush: "Insect Kin" (remix), Trauma, 1997.

Byrne, David: "Forestry" (remix), Luaka Bop/WB, 1991 • "Back in the Box" (remix), Luaka Bop/Sire/WB, 1994.

Coil: "The Snow" (remix), Wax Trax!, 1991.

Consolidated: "Brutal Equation" (remix), Nettwerk, 1991 • *Friendly Fascism,* Nettwerk, 1991 • "The Sexual Politics of Meat," Nettwerk, 1991 (*Volume One*) • "This Is Fascism" (remix), Nettwerk, 1991 • "Unity of Oppression" (remix), Nettwerk, 1991 • *Play More Music,* Nettwerk, 1992 • "Tool and Die" (remix), Nettwerk, 1992 • *Business of Punishment,* London, 1994 • "Butyric Acid" (remix), London, 1994.

Depeche Mode: "Rush" (remix), Mute, 1993 • "Rush" (remix), Sire/Reprise, 1993.

Disposable Heroes of Hiphoprisy: "Language of Violence," Restless, 1991, 1993 (*In Defense of Animals Benefit Compilation*) • "Television, the Drug of the Nation," 4th & B'Way, 1991.

Emergency Broadcast Network: *Telecommunication Breakdown,* TVT, 1995.

Empirion: "Narcotic Influence" (remix), XL, 1996.

Fun Lovin' Criminals: "King of New York" (remix), EMI, 1997.

Laika: "Looking for the Jackalope" (remix), Red Hot/TVT, 1996.

Machines of Loving Grace: "Butterfly Wings" (remix), Mammoth, 1993.

MC 900 Ft. Jesus: "The Killer Inside Me" (remix), Nettwerk/IRS, 1991.

Meat Beat Manifesto: "I Got the Fear," Sweatbox, 1987 • *Suck Hard* (EP), Sweatbox, 1987 • "Strap Down," Sweatbox, 1988 • "Strap Down" (remix), Sweatbox, 1988 • "Dogstar Man," Wax Trax!, 1989 • "God O.D.," Wax Trax!, 1989 • "Mars Needs Women," Wax Trax!, 1989 • *Storm the Studio,* Wax Trax!, 1989 • *Armed Audio Warfare,* Mute, 1990, 1994 • "Helter Skelter," Wax Trax!, 1990 • "Psyche-Out," Mute, 1990 • "Psyche-Out" (remix), Mute, 1990 • *99%,* Mute, 1990 • "Love Mad," Play It Again Sam, 1991 (*Volume One*) • "Now," Mute, 1991 • "Now" (remix), Mute, 1991 • "Drop," Play It Again Sam, 1992 (*Volume Four*) • "Edge of No Control," Mute, 1992 • "Mindstream," Mute, 1992 • "Mindstream" (remix), Mute, 1992 • *Satyricon,* Mute, 1992 • "Untold Stories," Restless, 1992, 1993 (*In Defense of Animals Benefit Compilation*) • "Paradise Now" (remix), American, 1995 (*The Doom Generation* soundtrack) • "Asbestos Lead Asbestos," Play It Again Sam, 1996 • "I Control," Red Hot/TVT, 1996 (*Offbeat*) • *It's the Music* (EP), Play It Again Sam, 1996 • *Subliminal Sandwich,* Nothing/Interscope, 1996 •

"Transmission," Play It Again Sam, 1996 • "We Done It Again," Caroline, 1996 (*In Defense of Animals,* Vol. 2) • *Original Fire,* Nothing/Interscope, 1997 • *Actual Sounds + Voices,* Play It Again Sam/Interscope, 1998.

Meat Beat Manifesto Meets Skylab: "I Control" (remix), Red Hot/TVT, 1996.

Nine Inch Nails: "Closer" (remix), Nothing, 1995 • "The Perfect Drug" (remix), Nothing, 1997.

Orbital: "Oolaa" (remix), FFRR, 1991.

Papa Brittle: "Status Quo" (remix), Nettwerk, 1994.

Perennial Divide: "Burn Down," Sweatbox, 1986 • *Purge,* Sweatbox, 1986.

Public Enemy: "Go Cat Go," Def Jam, 1998.

Scorn: "Silver Rain Fell" (remix), Earache, 1994.

Shamen, The: "Hyperreal" (remix), Epic, 1991 • "Ebeneezer Goode" (remix), Epic, 1992.

Young Gods: "Kissing the Sun" (remix), Interscope, 1995.

Richard Dashut

Richard Dashut is best known for his production role in Fleetwood Mac's *Rumours,* one of the best-selling records of all time, with U.S. sales upward of 13 million, and widely acknowledged as one of the best-produced.

Dashut, born in 1951 in West Hollywood, California, began as a janitor in a Hollywood recording studio where, he recalls, he "wasn't even allowed in the control room except to vacuum and empty the ashtrays." He was saved from further custodial humiliation by friend Keith Olsen (see entry), who hired him as an assistant engineer at the Sound Factory, where Stevie Nicks and Lindsey Buckingham (see entry) were recording their album *Buckingham Nicks.* Although the album's sales were disappointing, it caught the attention of Mick Fleetwood, who invited the duo to join his band Fleetwood Mac, which had just lost its principal vocalist and songwriter, Bob Welch.

After the album *Fleetwood Mac* was released, the group went on tour to support it and Dashut was invited to engineer the monitor mixes. When the group returned from the road and began recording their follow-up, *Rumours,* at Sausalito's Plant Studio, Dashut was asked to produce, which he did with the assistance of his friend Ken Caillat.

The phenomenal success of *Rumours* is probably a result of solid songwriting and great performances, but it is tremendously well-produced and engineered as well.

The transparency of the recording was created by the producers' incredible attention to acoustic detail and their ability to find a unique place in the frequency spectrum for each instrument. Dashut's, Caillat's, and Buckingham's (uncredited) genius assures that the instruments somehow blend with each other musically while remaining separate sonically. The drums are recorded up close and dry, with nonpareil naturalness. The bass, round and deep, plays in near-perfect rhythmic synchrony with the kick drum, creating unanimity and cohesion in the pulse of such tracks as "Dreams" (No. 1).

Buckingham's guitar tones run the gamut of hot-summer-afternoon-on-the-porch acoustic to out-of-control, screaming, and distorted leads. The solo in "The Chain," played almost entirely on one note, is a powerful example of economy and force. On "Don't Stop" (No. 3), the producers equalized and compressed Buckingham's and Christine McVie's voices to make them so stunningly similar that many listeners are surprised to learn that there are actually two singers on the song.

Throughout the landmark album, parts swim in and out of consciousness effortlessly. While the Beatles were famous for the technique of bringing in instruments to play one crucial part and then disappear, Fleetwood Mac perfected it.

Rumours required so many overdubs that the 2-inch analog tape fell apart on several occasions as the adhesive backing gave out. Various reports have it that the massive overdubbing was either the result of the dogged perfectionism of the production team, the reduced musical efficiency resulting from the drug-fueled party atmosphere of southern Marin County in the '70s, or the inability of the band to decide on the arrangements.

The experimental *Tusk* (No. 4) though less commercially successful than *Rumours*, was musically just as rewarding, if less immediately accessible. *Mirage* (No. 1) has not worn well (save for Buckingham's wonderful Ricky Nelson tribute "Diane"). But 1987's *Tango in the Night* (No. 7) reached another production and musical peak for the team, with Buckingham playing an increasing role in arrangements and Nicks playing less of a role creatively.

Dashut also produced Buckingham's first two solo albums, yielding the catchy hits "Trouble" (No. 9) and "Go Insane." "Because he's not a musician," Buckingham notes, "Richard is great with the big picture. I can get lost in details sometimes, and he'll walk in and cut through that. Also, he can sit down with a guitar and come up with a great seed for a song. He just has a general, good sensibility about things. He's also my best friend, and that helps a lot."

Dashut also helmed two particularly fine releases by other artists. *Tongue Twister* by Shoes was easily their best-produced album, and the song "Girls of Today" has all the youthful, brash energy and infectious hookiness of Cheap Trick meets Brian Wilson (see entry). Matthew Sweet's *Altered Beast* brought the Lincoln, Nebraska, native into the studio with sometime Rolling Stones pianist Nicky Hopkins, Attractions drummer Pete Thomas, and Mick Fleetwood. —DANIEL J. LEVITIN

Buckingham, Lindsey: "It Was I," Asylum, 1981 • *Law and Order,* Asylum, 1981 • "Trouble," Asylum, 1981 • *Out of the Cradle,* Reprise, 1992.
Dream Academy: *Remembrance Days* (1 track), Reprise, 1987.
Egan, Walter: "Magnet and Steel," Columbia, 1978 • *Not Shy,* Columbia, 1978.
Fleetwood Mac: "Don't Stop," Warner Bros., 1977 • "Dreams," Warner Bros., 1977 • "Go Your Own Way," Warner Bros., 1977 • *Rumours,* Warner Bros., 1977 • "You Make Loving Fun," Warner Bros., 1977 • *Fleetwood Mac Live,* Warner Bros., 1979 • *Tusk,* Warner Bros., 1979 • "Sara," Warner Bros., 1979 • "Tusk," Warner Bros., 1979 • "Gypsy," Warner Bros., 1982 • "Hold Me," Warner Bros., 1982 • *Mirage,* Warner Bros., 1982 • "Big Love," Warner Bros., 1987 • "Everywhere," Warner Bros., 1987 • "Little Lies," Warner Bros., 1987 • "Seven Wonders," Warner Bros., 1987 • *Tango in the Night,* Warner Bros., 1987 • *Greatest Hits,* Reprise, 1988 • "Love Shines," Warner Bros., 1992 • "Paper Doll," Warner Bros., 1992 • *Time,* Warner Bros., 1995.
Fleetwood, Mick: *The Visitor,* RCA, 1981 • *I'm Not Me,* RCA, 1983.
Shoes: *Tongue Twister,* Elektra, 1981 • *Shoe's Best,* Black Vinyl, 1987.
Sweet, Matthew: "Superdeformed," Arista, 1992, 1993 (*No Alternative*) • *Altered Beast,* Zoo, 1993 • *Son of Altered Beast,* Zoo, 1994 • "This Moment," Thirsty Ear/Chaos/Columbia, 1993 (*Sweet Relief*).
Welch, Bob: *Three Hearts,* Capitol, 1980 • *Best Of,* Rhino, 1991.

Terry Date

Terry Date's star rose with the Seattle scene, but he was never associated with that scene to the same degree as fellow Seattle-ite Jack Endino (see entry). He was, however, responsible for some of the scene's high points and defining moments: Soundgarden's 1989 major-label debut, *Louder than Love,* and the group's artistic pinnacle, 1991's *Badmotorfinger;* Mother Love Bone's 1990 Mercury album; Screaming Trees' 1991 major-label debut, *Uncle Anesthesia;* and rapper Sir Mix-a-Lot's huge hit "Baby Got Back" (No. 1).

Date became known for working with some of the most creative and influential heavy post-metal bands of the '90s, including Pantera, White Zombie, and Prong.

The Cleveland native was a listener rather than a musician, absorbing music from late '60s, early '70s progressive rock radio stations WMMS and WNCR. When he moved to Idaho to go to college, he began borrowing the college station's tape recorders to record local bands. Since he wanted to hang out with bands and did not play an instrument, Date often found himself running live sound. In 1979, he moved to Seattle to further his recording career.

"I started to work with local bar bands to get to know the local scene," he recalls. "At that time, the studios in Seattle were not that sophisticated. They didn't have apprentice programs or second engineers. I learned on the small side of things. After a few years, I found a studio doing ads during the day and closing at night. I started doing bands at night. I did about five years as staff engineer and the producer thing came out of that. I remember hiring Kenny G for $25 to put sax on records I was engineering."

Date got his first break on Metal Church's first album, *Blessing in Disguise,* an indie effort that was sold to Elektra. That 1989 album pulls together a number of '80s metal threads, including thrash, power metal, and progressive metal, and features a massive, booming sound. The combination of density and power with clarity and separation became a hallmark of Date's sound.

"The first Metal Church album was probably the most important for me," he says. "It broke me out of being a Seattle engineer."

Date started to get calls from similar metal bands. "I was classified as a metal guy even though I tried hard not to get typecast," he says. Instead of moving away from heavy music, however, he picked acts like Soundgarden and Mother Love Bone, who put a different spin on it. That type of band selection also became a hallmark of his career.

"I was changing without going left field," he says. "I concentrated on heavy, dark music—what I called testosterone music. It's music you can turn up loud in your car and drive fast to. I lean towards things that try to challenge people, things that are at the front edge of a trend. My goal is to do something that people will listen to in 20 years. I'm careful who I work with. We're overwhelmed by the same thing over and over. It's hard to find something unique and passionate."

After producing *Badmotorfinger* (his last Seattle-based project) and losing out on Alice in Chains, Date turned his attention out of state, doing offbeat heavy projects like Fishbone, 24-7 Spyz, and Mindfunk. His most fruitful relationship was born when his old manager hooked him with a Texas band he was managing, Pantera. "We clicked musically and personally, which is why I've done four albums with them," he says.

Date has been extremely effective in capturing Pantera's chiseled grooves and Dimebag Darrell's distinctively tense, slashing guitar sound. "Pantera's musicianship is far beyond most of the bands I've worked with," Date says. "Their guitar player is the only person I've worked with where the guitar is like an appendage. It would be unnatural not to see a guitar in his hands. Those Pantera records tend to be a little more manufactured than the others. They like to hear razor-edge precision. It takes more punching in on guitar parts to make sure every note is where he wants it to be. I've tried to get them to do it differently, but anything sloppy eats at them. They have to give up some of their live energy."

While Pantera revolves around airtight guitar and rhythm grooves, the White Zombie and Prong projects demonstrated Date's proficiency at working with industrial-leaning metal projects that incorporate sampling. "The White Zombie recording is full of technology, but approached from a rock side. We tried to use computers as rock instruments rather than fitting rock onto a computer track," he says.

Neither the Prong nor the White Zombie recordings has the walloping feel of Date's more metal-oriented work; they're more angular and claustrophobic. But, Date asserts, "Technology is not as big a deal in what I do as in other styles of music. I'm way more into putting mike on source of sound and working that into something good. I'll use whatever's lying around. But I can do a record gladly with Shure SM57 mikes with a crappy board in a garage. That's how I did the last Pantera album [*The Great Southern Trendkill,* No. 4]. It's more about creating an environment for performance.

"A producer's main job is to stay out of the way," Date says. "I've seen too many bands ruined by producers who think they have a better idea. If I choose quality bands, the best thing I can do is not block what they have in their heads. My role is to make sure the people I pick are able to create without distractions, to keep four or five guys focused in one direction."

Date uses the same studios more and more often. In Los Angeles, he likes to record at NRG and mix at Larabee Sand. In Seattle, he uses Studio Litho or Bad Animals; he mixes at the latter and engineers all his records. Ulrich Wild spells him when he gets tired or wants a second opinion. —ANASTASIA PANTSIOS

Deftones: *Adrenaline,* Maverick/WB, 1995 • "Bored," Maverick/WB, 1995 • "7 Words," Maverick/WB, 1995 • *Around the Fur,* Maverick/WB, 1997.

Dream Theater: *When Dream and Day Unite,* One Way, 1989, 1996.

Fishbone: "Swim," Columbia, 1993 (*Last Action Hero* soundtrack) • *Give a Monkey a Brain and He'll Swear He's the Center of the Universe,* Columbia, 1993 • *Fishbone 101: Nuttasaurusmeg Fossil Fuelin',* Sony, 1996.

Handsome: *Handsome,* Epic, 1997.

Mantissa: *Mossy God,* Polydor, 1994.

Metal Church: *Metal Church,* Elektra, 1985 • *Blessing in Disguise,* Elektra, 1989.

Mindfunk: *Dropped,* Megaforce, 1993 • *Mindfunk,* Megaforce, 1993.

Mother Love Bone: *Mother Love Bone* (13 tracks), Stardog/Mercury, 1992.

Overkill: *The Years of Decay,* Megaforce, 1989 • *Horrorscope,* Megaforce, 1991.

Pantera: *Cowboys from Hell,* EastWest, 1990 • *Vulgar Display of Power,* Atco, 1992 • *Far Beyond Driven,* EastWest, 1994 • *The Great Southern Trendkill,* EastWest, 1996.

Prong: "Broken Peace," Epic, 1994 • "Inheritance," Fox, 1994 (*Airheads* soundtrack) • "Snap Your Fingers, Snap Your Neck," Epic, 1994 • "Snap Your Fingers, Snap Your Neck" (remix), Epic, 1994 • *Cleansing,* Epic, 1994 • *Rude Awakening,* Epic, 1996.

Screaming Trees: "Something About Today," Epic, 1991 • *Uncle Anesthesia,* Epic, 1991.

Sir Mix-A-Lot: "I'm a Trip," Nastymix, 1986 • "Square Dance Rap," Nastymix, 1986 • "Baby Got Back," Def American, 1992.

Soundgarden: "Get on the Snake," A&M, 1989 (*Lost Angels* soundtrack) • *Louder than Love,* A&M, 1989 • "Heretic," MCA, 1990 (*Pump Up the Volume* soundtrack) • *Badmotorfinger,* A&M, 1991 • "Rusty Cage," A&M, 1991 • "Birth Ritual," Epic Soundtrax, 1992 (*Singles* soundtrack) • "Jesus Christ Pose," A&M, 1994 (*S.F.W.* soundtrack).

White Zombie: *Astro-Creep: 2000,* Geffen, 1995 • "More Human Than Human," Geffen, 1995 • w/ Rob Zombie and Alice Cooper, "Hands of Death (Burn Baby Burn)," Warner Bros., 1996 (*Songs in the Key of X*) • "I'm Your Boogieman," Miramax/Hollywood, 1996 (*The Crow City of Angels* soundtrack) • "Ratfinks, Suicide Tanks and Cannibal Girls," Geffen, 1996 (*Beavis and Butt-head Do America* soundtrack) • *Supersexy Swingin' Sounds,* Geffen, 1996.

COLLECTIONS

Nativity in Black: Tribute to Black Sabbath, Sony, 1994.

David Z.

"I started with Gram Parsons and what was alternative country at that time, as a songwriter and player. I developed into R&B in the Minneapolis scene, then it went into what was progressive rock at that time—Fine Young Cannibals and Big Head Todd and the Monsters. Then I moved into blues, which I think is real cool. I kept trying to find things that were meaningful to me at the time. Not everybody can do that, it's pretty hard to find. You have to keep working on it. I look all the time."

And while he's now successfully worked a number of different genres and is happy to have done so, he didn't start out with the producer's job in mind. In fact, he started as a songwriter and guitarist and recorded many of his demos at A&M Studios in Los Angeles. During his time there he worked with such greats as Gram Parsons and Billy Preston, but after Parsons' death in 1973, Z. moved back to his Minneapolis home.

"I worked in a factory. To keep my chops up, I made a deal with a booking agent and took all these groups into the studio and half-assed supervised them. I didn't really know what I was doing." One day the owner and engineer told Z. that he was tired—it was Z.'s turn to step up to the knobs.

"It was completely foreign to me, I didn't have an electronics background. He locked me in there basically for a couple of years, and he wouldn't let me out. Along the way I studied Robert Hanson's book about recording techniques. I basically learned myself, so in that way I guess that I didn't learn the proper way to do a lot of things. I used the line trim on the board as distortion control," he remembers laughing. "I had no idea."

During the course of those recording sessions, Z. started working with a band called Grand Central. Don't recognize the band's name? On guitar was a youngster known as Prince Rogers Nelson (see entry), Morris Day sat behind the drum kit, and Andre Cymone was on the bass. Those three, both together and apart, were to the Minneapolis scene what Nirvana was to grunge. While they were an incredibly talented band together, it was after the band had broken up and during a recording session for Prince (as engineer/mixer/editor) that Z.'s eyes were truly opened.

"Basically the theory was to do anything that we needed to do to sound different," he remembers. "We even talked about putting guitars under water at one point, just to see what it would sound like. We just did all kinds of weird things—multiple source recordings—which I still do a lot of, especially with guitars. I take it from one amp and split it into another one—that way you can basically make sandwiches of sound.

"Or with extreme EQ on a small little effect pedal, you can change the character of a sound. [The Prince sessions] were where I got it from, out of necessity basically. That has always been my forte, spatial differences. I guess it works with the blues that I have been doing lately, putting a new twist on it since that is an art form that needed a change. One way that you can change it is in the drums and in the rhythm. That's where I am with that."

Z. has learned that in order to get into a different musical space, sometimes you have to change your physical space. "I believe that recording in different spaces—not your everyday, run-of-the-mill studio—is unique because you work a lot harder. There are a lot of records out there that sound the same because they are done in the same room. I like to stretch a little by using closets, bathrooms, and hallways, stuff like that," he explains.

As an example Z. points to a number of records he's recorded with Prince, the Family, and Vanity 6. "We did the *Purple Rain* record in a warehouse with no control room with only headphones," he comments. "We had to deaden a lot of things down and treat it as we saw it, because those rooms are definitely sonically screwed up, but sometimes that is great because it makes you work harder to adjust the parameters."

He's pulled that same vibe into his blues work with A&M's Jonny Lang. "We cut that record in a studio that was not a major studio and we went down and mixed it at the House of Blues in Memphis, and it was great. Where we cut it we had to go to the Salvation Army and buy millions of blankets and deaden the room completely. We had it looking like it was some sort of opium den from Pakistan, with blankets hanging everywhere. It isolated the sound in such a way that it reminded me of the old Muscle Shoals sound, where they had burlap on the walls. That's the thing I like to do: even if I go into a major studio I like to treat the walls with my own sort of things, like blankets and Chinese rugs and junk like that. I like to liven and deaden different areas in different degrees."

Playing with a variety of tones is a theme he carries over to his views on technology in the studio. "I have been using a combination of old and new. I cut my tracks analog and then when I get to the last overdub, vocal overdubs, and mixing, I bounce over to digital because I like to mix onto parallel digital tracks," he says, explaining then that it just makes editing and mak-ing changes simpler. "Also, I found that you can change the EQ and even use just an echo sound for the effect and actually make it 3-D a little bit.

"As far as everything else goes I like to mix old and new as well. Old guitar amps, old pedals, and new effects," he continues. "You can make cool older sounds now sound more brilliant by using that technology. I have a collection of old effects, old amps, old guitars and things, and depending on the project I bring either a semi truck or a suitcase," he finishes with a laugh.

And that, he thinks, sets one of the most important things for a session: vibe. "It's extremely important, because whoever is playing has to feel a certain way. They can't feel like it's a burden. I have been through that too, where you overanalyze every note and homogenize the record beyond belief," he says. "I have gone through that and gone back to whatever feels good is there. It has be a certain easygoing controlled professionalism, so that you still have the faucet open. You're not afraid you're going to have to stop every five minutes because something feels off," he says.

Then he adds, "Every situation with anybody is a different experience. That is what's cool about making music, because it's never the same, no matter what. You've got to suss out the situation and see how you can frame the artist. I have done a lot of first records, everybody from Prince to Big Head Todd, Jody Watley, Jonny Lang, and Kenny Wayne Shepherd.

"What I try to do is give them a sound and frame that sound so that when you hear the first four bars, then you know who it is. There is a personality to a recording, not just a service function. That is what I think a producer does: give it a personality. With some artists you can go outside and put their guitars underwater, and others like it plain and simple."

Now that he's gone through an alternative country phase, a R&B phase, a pop, a rock, and a blues phase, his next step is to almost return to his roots. "I am branching into what you would call insurgent country music with an act in Los Angeles called the Cousin Lovers. That is a purposeful taunt at country music," he explains. "They are the real thing, real bluegrass."

While he's kept his feet moving, he still looks back to an early session with Prince as his benchmark moment. "We used to laugh a lot in those sessions," he remembers. "There was a point where we did a lot of overanalytical punching in and everything had to be perfect, and then it evolved eventually where Prince would pick up a guitar and play the whole song down and bam, be done. If there was a little thing, not even a misnote, just something that could be perceived as a mistake, he would say that he meant to do that. That was a big influence, since that's the way it should be—let it run and have rough edges. It's a lot of fun.

"Then there was the time when I went in to edit 'Erotic City.' I was wearing a Hawaiian shirt because it was hot out and the machine I was working on was under the speakers. I was trying to make this edit and I said that I couldn't hear the bass on the edit. Prince looked at me and said, 'It's because your shirt is too loud.' " —DAVID JOHN FARINELLA

A-ha: *Memorial Beach,* Warner Bros., 1993.

Aswad: *Rise and Shine,* Mesa/Bluemoon, 1994.

Been, Michael: *On the Verge of a Nervous Breakthrough,* Qwest, 1994.

Big Head Todd and the Monsters: *Sister Sweetly,* Giant, 1993 • "Bittersweet," A&M, 1995 (*Things to Do in Denver When You're Dead* soundtrack).

Black, Paul: *King Dollar,* House of Blues, 1996.

Blakeley, Peter: "I've Been Lonely," Giant, 1993 • *The Pale Horse,* Giant, 1993.

BoDeans: *Black and White,* Slash/Reprise, 1991.

Cherry, Neneh: "I've Got You Under My Skin," Chrysalis, 1990 (*Red Hot and Blue*).

Doves, The: *Affinity,* Elektra, 1991.

Duarte, Chris: *Tailspin Headwhack,* Jive, 1997.

Family, The: "High Fashion," Paisley Park, 1985 • "Screams of Passion," Paisley Park, 1985 • *The Family,* Paisley Park, 1985.

Fine Young Cannibals: "She Drives Me Crazy," IRS, 1989 • "She Drives Me Crazy" (remix), IRS, 1989 • *The Raw and the Cooked* (2 tracks), IRS, 1989 • "I'm Not Satisfied," IRS, 1990 • *The Raw and the Remix,* IRS, 1990 • *Finest,* MCA, 1996.

Fiorillo, Elisa: "On the Way Up," Chrysalis, 1990.

Freddy Jones Band: *Lucid,* Capricorn, 1997.

Go-Go's, The: *Greatest,* IRS, 1990.

Guy, Buddy: *Heavy Love,* Silvertone, 1998.

Harris, Hugh: *Words for Our Years,* Capitol, 1989.

Jackson, Jermaine: *Jermaine Jackson,* Arista, 1984.

Jets, The: "The Same Love," MCA, 1989 • "You Better Dance," MCA, 1989 • *Best Of,* MCA, 1990.

Johnson, Syl: *Bridge to a Legacy,* Antone's, 1998.

Kidjo, Angelique: "Adouma," Mango, 1994 • *Aye,* Mango, 1994.

Kottke, Leo: *Standing in My Shoes,* Private, 1997.

Lang, Jonny: *Lie to Me,* A&M, 1997 • "Missing Your Love," A&M, 1997.

Mazarati: "!00 MPH," Paisley Park, 1986 • *Mazarati,* Paisley Park, 1986.

Nelson, Tyka: "L.O.V.E.," Cooltempo, 1988.

Nunn, Terri: *Moment of Truth,* Mercury, 1992.

Prince: *Girl 6* soundtrack, Warner Bros., 1996.

Sheila E.: "Hold Me," Paisley Park, 1987 • "Koo Koo," Paisley Park, 1987 • *Sheila E.,* Paisley Park, 1987.

Shepherd, Kenny Wayne: *Ledbetter Heights,* Giant, 1996.

Storyville: *A Piece of Your Soul,* Atlantic, 1996.

Surface: *Surface,* Columbia, 1987.

Vecindad, Malditay, y los Hijos del Quinto Patio: *Baile De Mas Caras,* RCA International, 1996.

Watley, Jody: *Jody Watley,* MCA, 1987 • "Looking for a New Love," MCA, 1987 • "Some Kind of Lover," MCA, 1987 • "Still a Thrill," MCA, 1987 • *You Wanna Dance with Me* (remix), MCA, 1990 • *Greatest Hits,* MCA, 1996.

COLLECTIONS

Goofy Movie soundtrack, Disney, 1995.

Rhett Davies

A world-class engineer (Dire Straits, Talking Heads), Rhett Davies also produced or co-produced some of the classiest new wave–art rock albums of the '70s and '80s: the raucous *Wild Planet* (No. 18), by the B-52's; the brilliant trilogy *Discipline, Beat,* and *Three of a Perfect Pair,* by King Crimson; *Another Green World, Before and After Science,* and *Music for Films,* by Brian Eno (see entry); *Boys and Girls* (No. 1 U.K.), by Bryan Ferry; and most important, the classic Roxy Music trio of *Flesh and Blood* (No. 1 U.K.), *Avalon* (No. 1 U.K.), and the live *Heart Still Beating,* which was recorded in 1982 and released in 1990. Davies has also produced fine work by Camel, Icehouse, 'Til Tuesday, Talk Talk, and Cock Robin.

Born in London in 1950 to one of Britain's top session trumpeters, Ray Davies (no relation to the Kink), Rhett was brought up to follow in his father's footsteps, studying trumpet from an early age. He loved the West Coast cool jazz records (Chet Baker, Gerry Mulligan) his father brought home but found classical trumpet study tedious.

In the mid-'60s, Davies dug the sophisticated pop of Burt Bacharach (see entry) as well as ska, soul, and the Beatles. He periodically accompanied his father to the studio and met his idol Bacharach in the control room at the *What's New, Pussycat?* sessions in 1965. "I thought, 'This is the place I want to be, not out on the floor, but up here in the booth with the knobs and gadgets,' " Davies relates.

At 17, Davies left college to "bum and hitch around Canada for about a year" with a couple of friends until they ran out of money and interest and returned to

England. Davies worked at—and later owned—a record store, but when his store went bust, he decided to pursue his interest in studio work.

He saw an ad in the paper for a tape operator trainee job at Island Studios, but when he rang, the receptionist informed him that, at 22, he was too old for the position. Unwilling to be thwarted by mere chronology, Davies waited a couple of hours, called back in a different voice, said he was 19, and got the interview. It took another four months of daily calls before Davies finally secured the position—only, the manager told him later, "so I would stop annoying the shit out of him."

In 1972, the studio system was still a fairly rigid hierarchy (see Peter Collins entry) and Davies had years of assisting ahead of him before he could expect to become an engineer, let alone a producer. However, talent will out, and after "some lucky breaks," Davies was engineering a mere six months into the job.

The lucky breaks involved Davies getting along well with the house engineers and sticking around for the regular post-midnight jam sessions with various Island artists, who then began requesting his presence at their daytime sessions. The first full album Davies engineered was Eno's *Taking Tiger Mountain by Strategy* in 1973. Though he was "shitting [his] pants" prior to the first session, Davies so impressed Eno that after the album was completed, the avant star called the young engineer and offered him a half-point royalty as a token of his appreciation. In essence, Davies became Eno's collaborator on that and subsequent albums.

Davies' inexperience—not knowing what he wasn't supposed to be able to do—meshed well with Eno's experimentalism in the studio, and the two ended up "playing the studio like an instrument," according to Davies. "We would do things like take distortion and redistort it to create new sounds. Eno would come in and say 'Roll the tape,' and he'd go in the studio and count from 1 to 100 onto the tape. Then he would plug in his Moog synthesizer and at 15 he would plug in a little instrumental passage. He'd say 'Roll on to 37,' and he would put in something else. We got seriously into tape loops and things I hadn't seen anyone else do before."

Another Green World features classic songs "I'll Come Running" (with Robert Fripp on "restrained lead" guitar) and "Golden Hours," along with quirky mood pieces like the title track and "Somber Reptiles." *Before and After Science* finds Eno and Davies incorporating the syncopated, Afro-Caribbean–based percussion that would come to dominate the Eno/David Byrne album *My Life in the Bush of Ghosts* (which Davies engineered) and the Talking Heads of *Remain in Light* and *Speaking in Tongues*. Greats songs on *Science* include "No One

Receiving," "Backwater," "King's Lead Hat," as well as the lovely moodies "Through Hollow Lands" and "Spider and I."

Roxy Music guitarist Phil Manzanera appeared on the Eno (himself a Roxy alumnus) albums, cementing the Roxy connection. Davies replaced his friend and mentor Phill Brown as engineer on the Roxy Music reunion album *Manifesto* in 1978, when Brown had to be hospitalized for a time.

Roxy had been recording in the band format: a song would be rehearsed, the band would set up in the studio, get appropriate levels, and then record the song live 5 or 30 times until they got it right. Then they would record vocals, solos, and other parts over that backing track.

Davies showed leader Ferry a new way: the "rhythm box" click-track method he had learned from Eno. "In the old-school method the drums are the most important part when you are cutting a backing track," Davies says. "Paul Thompson was a fantastic live drummer, but he was difficult to work with in the studio—there was a certain disinterest, and that frustrated Bryan as he was trying to get what he wanted out of him. But with the rhythm box you can lay down tracks and not worry about the drummer until later.

"When it came to making *Flesh and Blood,* we basically cut everything from the groove upward. Phil Manzanera had built a studio down at his house, so we laid all the backing tracks down there. Bryan really enjoyed that way of working and we had about four or five pieces down, but he was feeling a little bit uncomfortable that this was Phil's studio. Bryan didn't feel he was getting his stamp on the record, so he said, 'Look, can I just have a couple of days working with Rhett alone to try to write some songs and get some things down?'

"In those two days we wrote and cut 'My Only Love,' 'Over You' (No. 5 U.K.), 'Flesh and Blood' and 'Same Old Scene' (No. 12 U.K.). Bryan was just over the moon," recalls Davies.

And well he should have been, because those songs are the backbone of an album of indelible beauty, poignancy, and energy. *Flesh and Blood* is the nexus between the art-rock, jagged Roxy of the '70s and the smoothly romantic Roxy (and Bryan Ferry) of the '80s, bearing the best characteristics of each.

"Same Old Scene" grooves to Alan Spenner's thumping bass and Ferry's keyboard wash, as Ferry scrambles to staunch the flow of viscera from the "same old scene." In "Flesh and Blood," Ferry addresses his own penchant for dangerous beauty (he married models Jerry Hall and, later, Lucy Helmore) and their respective needs (his: "You'd nail her if you could"; hers:

"Love me for my mind") over his own monster guitar riff. "My Only Love" captures a suspended moment before love's loss becomes unbearable and features pungent solos from Manzanera and saxophonist Andy Mackay. "Over You" pours out after that moment is lost and then tries to look to a hopeful future when "Some day, yes it might come babe / When I'll be babe—over you." In that future lies a stunningly simple, elegant piano line from Ferry and an aching, soaring sax solo from Mackay.

Avalon followed Davies' "groove theory" even more closely. "I would get to the studio about 10 in the morning and I would set rhythms up—get interesting grooves going, weird things happening, and have the keyboard hooked in, ready to go," he explains. "Bryan would saunter through the door about 1 o'clock and this vibe would be happening already. Bryan would just come and sit down at the keyboard and work a chord progression, or whatever, to go with that. It was a fantastic way of working, and working down at Phil's studio was brilliant. They were paying for Phil's studio, but nowhere near top rates, so a looseness was there."

The perfect mate to *Flesh and Blood*, *Avalon* rides a mid-tempo groove through a world where love's death throes have given way to a languid acceptance of the inevitability of romantic failure. But the denizens of this *Avalon* (the isle of the heroic dead in Celtic legend) savor the temporary triumphs and meaning that romantic struggle brought to their lives and, as disembodied wraiths, twirl eternally together under a distant, shimmering pale moon.

In 1990, Davies left music to become partners in the most successful golf driving range in Europe, located in the heart of London. Five years later, he sold out and returned to music, albeit on a personal scale. Davies is now composing "picture rhythms," as he calls them, "happy to be creating" regardless of whether "anyone else ever hears them or not." —ERIC OLSEN AND DAWN DARLING

After the Fire: *Laser Love,* Epic, 1979.
B-52's, The: "Private Idaho," Warner Bros., 1980 • *Wild Planet,* Warner Bros., 1980 • *Party Mix!* Warner Bros., 1981.
Ballard, Russ: *Winning,* Epic, 1976.
Camel: *Moon Madness,* Decca, 1976 • *Rain Dances,* Janus, 1977 • *A Live Record,* Decca, 1978 • *Compact Compilation,* Rhino, 1986 • *Echoes: The Retrospective,* PolyGram, 1993.
Cock Robin: *First Love: Last Rites,* Columbia, 1990.
Eno, Brian: *Another Green World,* EG, 1975 • *Before and After Science,* EG, 1977 • *Music for Films,* EG/Antilles, 1978 • *Desert Island Selections,* Editions E.G., 1986 • *More Blank*

Than Frank, 1973–1978, Editions E.G., 1989 • *Eno Box II,* Virgin, 1993.
Ferry, Bryan: *Boys and Girls,* EG/WB, 1985 • "Don't Stop the Dance," EG/WB, 1985 • "Slave to Love," EG, 1985 • "Slave to Love," Virgin/EMI, 1985 (*Now That's What I Call Music 5*) • "Is Your Love Strong Enough," MCA, 1986 • "Is Your Love Strong Enough," Epic Soundtrax, 1994 (*Threesome* soundtrack) • *See also* Roxy Music.
Grand Hotel: *Do Not Disturb,* CBS, 1979.
Hitmen: *Torn Together,* CBS, 1981.
Huang Chung: *Huang Chung* (7 tracks), Arista, 1982.
Icehouse: "Cross the Border," Chrysalis, 1986 • *Measure for Measure,* Chrysalis, 1986 • "No Promises," Chrysalis, 1986.
King Crimson: *Discipline,* EG/Warner Bros., 1981 • *Beat,* EG, 1982 • *Three of a Perfect Pair,* EG, 1984.
Orchestral Manoeuvres in the Dark (OMD): *Dazzle Ships,* Virgin, 1983 • *Shame* (EP), Virgin, 1987.
Roxy Music: *Flesh and Blood,* Atco, 1980 • "Over You," Atco, 1980 • "Same Old Scene," RSO, 1980 (*Times Square* soundtrack) • *Avalon,* EG/WB, 1982 • "Always Unknowing," Warner Bros., 1983 (*Attack of the Killer B's*) • *The High Road,* EG/WB, 1983 • w/ Bryan Ferry, *Street Life: 20 Greatest Hits,* EG, 1986 • *Heart Still Beating,* Reprise, 1990.
Starjets: *Starjets,* Epic, 1979.
Talk Talk: *The Party's Over,* EMI America, 1982 • *The Very Best Of,* EMI, 1990.
Then Jerico: *The Big Area,* MCA, 1989.
'Til Tuesday: "What About Love," Epic, 1986 • *Welcome Home,* Epic, 1986 • *Everything's Different Now,* Epic, 1988 • *Coming Up Close: A Retrospective,* Sony, 1996.

COLLECTIONS
Legend soundtrack, MCA, 1986.

Jean-Luc De Meyer

See FRONT 242

Denny Diante

D enny Diante (born June 21, 1943, in New Kensington, Pennsylvania) has been involved with records for 30 years as an A&R man and producer. In that time he has worked with artists as diverse as Elton John, B.B. King, Johnny Mathis, Ike and Tina Turner, Paul Anka, Neil Diamond, Bill Withers, and Barbra Streisand. He engineers, produces, arranges, contracts the dates, and has worked in all genres: from R&B to pop, rock, adult contemporary, and soundtracks.

Diante began as a drummer and singer with surf bands the Cornells and the Sentinels. From 1965 to 1972, he worked in music publishing, gaining valuable training for A&R and production, which comes down to being able to recognize a good song under the most difficult conditions. In 1972, Diante was hired as vice president of pop A&R and staff producer at United Artists Records. During his tenure, he worked with War and produced a string of gold records for Paul Anka, including "One Man Woman/One Woman Man" (No. 7).

When Al Teller replaced Mike Stewart as president of UA, he and Diante began an association that would last for two decades. When Teller left UA to take over the presidency of RCA in 1978, he brought Diante with him. In 1980, Stewart brought Diante back into publishing, making him vice president and creative director of CBS Songs. One year later Diante was promoted to vice president of A&R for Columbia Records. When Teller, who briefly was president of Columbia, left to head MCA Records in 1989, he brought Diante with him as vice president of A&R. In 1996, Diante left MCA to start his own label, OutWest.

"Denny does a little bit of everything," says MCA A&R executive and archives specialist Andy McKaie (see entry). "He knows how to press the emotional buttons of the players to get the right performances. He brings enthusiasm and intelligence to anything he does."

While working in A&R, Diante earned the nickname "Dr. D." for his ability to salvage troubled projects. "Whenever a record was problematic," Diante explains, "Al Teller would just call me and say, 'Go fix it.' I never thought about what I do, I just did it. To me, 88 keys are still 88 keys. From my years in music publishing, I've got a good song sense. The best thing a producer can do is hire the right players and the right engineer. That's what I've always tried to do—that's what I'm doing on the new T.G. Shepard record—I've hired a bunch of good pickers, then I sit back and look busy.

"The most fun I've had in the studio was with B.B. King on the *Blues Summit* album. The Beebster has no ego. You ask him what to do, point him where to go, and he has no problem. It was a tremendous amount of work but it was an uplifting experience, like going to a singing church, with B.B. as the Rev." —DANIEL J. LEVITIN

Anka, Paul: *Anka*, United Artists, 1974 • w/ Odia Coates, "One Man Woman/One Woman Man," United Artists, 1974 • *Paul Anka Live*, Columbia, 1975 • *Times of Your Life*, United Artists, 1975 • *The Painter*, United Artists, 1976 • *Walk a Fine Line*, Columbia, 1983 • *Best of the United Artists Years, 1973–1977*, EMI, 1996.

Bayless, John: *The Movie Album: Classical Pictures*, Angel, 1996.

Bofill, Angela: *Teaser*, Arista, 1983.

Brown, Bobby: "She Ain't Worth It," MCA, 1990.

Diamond, Neil: *Primitive*, Columbia, 1984.

Easton, Sheena: *What Comes Naturally*, MCA, 1991 • *The World of: The Singles Collection*, Capitol, 1993 • *My Cherie*, MCA, 1995.

Goldsboro, Bobby: "A Butterfly for Bucky," United Artists, 1976.

Grateful Dead: *Blues for Allah*, Rounder/UA, 1975.

Hill, Z.Z.: "Keep On Lovin You," United Artists, 1975.

Jets, The: *Best Of*, MCA, 1990.

King, B.B.: *Blues Summit*, MCA, 1993 • *How Blue Can You Get? Classic Live Performances, 1964–1994*, MCA, 1996.

Kingfish: *Kingfish*, Grateful Dead, 1976.

Mancini, Henry: *See* Mathis, Johnny.

Mathis, Johnny: *A Special Part of Me*, Columbia, 1984 • w/ Deniece Williams, "Love Won't Let Me Wait," Columbia, 1984 • *Live from London Victoria Hall*, Columbia, 1985 • *Right from the Heart*, Columbia, 1985 • *Xmas Eve with Johnny Mathis*, Columbia, 1986 • w/ Henry Mancini, *The Hollywood Musicals*, Columbia, 1987 • *Love Songs*, Columbia, 1988 • *Better Together: Duet*, Columbia, 1991 • *Music of Johnny Mathis: A Personal Collection*, Legacy/Columbia, 1995.

Medeiros, Glenn: *Not Me*, MCA, 1988 • *Glenn Medeiros*, MCA, 1990 • "Me-U=Blue," MCA, 1990.

Nightingale, Maxine: *Nightlife*, United Artists, 1977 • "Lead Me On," Windsong, 1979 • *Lead Me On*, Windsong, 1979 • "Right Back Where We Started From," United Artists, 1979 • *Bittersweet*, RCA, 1981.

Rush, Merilee: *Save Me*, United Artists, 1977.

Stabilizers, The: *Tyranny*, Columbia, 1986.

Streisand, Barbra: *Till I Loved You*, Columbia, 1988.

Turner, Ike and Tina: *Proud Mary: The Best Of*, EMI America, 1975, 1991 • "Baby Get It On," Liberty, 1985 • *Get Back!* Liberty, 1985.

Turner, Tina: *Acid Queen*, United Artists, 1975.

Vartan, Sylvie: *I Don't Want the Night to End*, RCA, 1979.

Ventures, The: *Rocky Road*, United Artists, 1976.

Wagner, Jack: *Alone in a Crowd*, RCA, 1993.

Withers, Bill: *Lean on Me: The Best Of . . .* , Columbia, 1975 • *Watching Me, Watching You*, Columbia, 1985.

COLLECTIONS

George and Ira Gershwin: A Musical Celebration, MCA, 1994.

Jim Dickinson

S ince he's multiply visioned, Jim Dickinson has a different view of record production than most. "There's a field of energy that's present when you're making a record," says the Memphis legend, "and the producer manipulates that field of energy." Its elements? "There's sonic, of course, and there's psycho-dynamic. It can be as simple as how you put the musicians in the room."

Dickinson credits his training in set and stage design at Baylor University in Texas for his record production skills. He learned process at Baylor from department head Paul Baker.

Dickinson, who lives near Memphis in Hernando, Mississippi, took piano lessons when he was very young and began to develop as a folksinger in his teens. In 1963, a friend working with saxman and Sun Records arranger Bill Justis called Dickinson to Nashville to record a folk album.

"I had kind of a Bob Dylan act," Dickinson says. "When I went to Texas, I thought I'd quit music; then folk music came along and it was so damn easy, I had to do it. I was in school to get out of the Army. It was real simple back then."

Armed with his Martin D28, Dickinson did all right as a folk act. His trumpet-playing friend George Tidwell asked whether Dickinson wanted to cut a record for Justis with two other folksingers. Sure, Dickinson said.

"We get to the session, and there are three Anita Kerr Singers and the Jordanaires," Dickinson recalls. "I ended up being the star because Justis wanted a rough, reedy folk voice. It was called *Dixieland, Folk Style,* on Smash/Mercury. It sold a lot; it was by the Bill Justis Orchestra and Chorus. This was a concept party record. It's a purely wretched thing, but it was my first professional session."

When they were in the middle of cutting a track the second day, "this big fat redneck all dressed in black, in sunglasses, walks in," Dickinson says. "The session stopped cold. Obviously, this was somebody. He walks up to one of the Anita Kerr Singers and starts apologizing, says he bought two. We walk into the parking lot and see two new Jaguar XKEs, a hardtop and a convertible, both midnight blue. He has yet to stop talking."

Tidwell told Dickinson the motormouth was producer Shelby Singleton. Dickinson finally had a role model. "This is a job I could handle," Dickinson recalls thinking. "I was looking for something to do with my life."

In the past 30 years, bands and artists Dickinson has produced include Joe "King" Carrasco and the Crowns, Sid Selvidge, the Replacements, Brenda Patterson, Ry Cooder, the Knowbody Else, Panther Burns, Hal Newman, Jason and the Nashville Scorchers, Tommy Stinson, Green on Red, Mojo Nixon, Flat Duo Jets, Pigs in Space, Claw Hammer, Albert King, Rock City Angels, the True Believers, the Klitz. He has performed on records by the Rolling Stones (he played the piano intro on "Wild Horses" after Ian Stewart refused to play its minor chords) and Bob Dylan. He also leads a remarkable Memphis extraterrestrial funk aggregation, Mud Boy and the Neutrons.

"Bands come to me," says Dickinson. "It's really important that they come to me. They have to totally trust me, only for moments. What I specifically do as a producer is not for everybody. You've got to want it. It's going to change them. It is a subtle thing. True production is invisible."

Born November 21, 1941, in Little Rock, Arkansas, Dickinson grew up in Memphis, where he became a session player, primarily of piano. He worked many dates at Chips Moman's (see entry) American Recording Studios, everything from the Gentrys to Sandy Posey, "before Chips really hit it," Dickinson says. "That's when I went to work with Fry."

John Fry owns Ardent Records, home of influential power-pop act Big Star and Cargoe, a pop band that occasionally backed up singer/songwriter/producer Dan Penn (see entry).

In 1965, Dickinson played piano in the Chesters, a band produced by Sun Records owner Sam Phillips (see entry). That also was the year of Dickinson's first production, a garage band called Lawson and Four More. Terry Manning, who runs Compass Point Studios in Nassau for Chris Blackwell (see entry), was producer/engineer on the Lawson effort, an Ardent product. Dickinson was going to Memphis State, living in a prefab house. Fry was 19, a freshman in college, a "rich kid who had recording equipment," Dickinson recalls. Fry's partner, John King, "one of the only people in Memphis who understands the total record business to this day," taught Dickinson what a producer was, he says.

In 1966, Dickinson and Manning, both eager to be engineers, moved into Ardent Studios as assistants to Fry. "John was the best engineer I ever worked with, bar none, even better than Tom Dowd (see entry). Even as a teenager, he worked at a level nobody else in Memphis could touch. All of a sudden, we were making really professional sounding radio jingles, and the union in Memphis was so naive they didn't even know how to bill it out."

One night, Fry went home early, leaving production to his two charges. "Terry and I have an adversarial relationship to this day," says Dickinson. "I was older and a keyboard player, Terry was a young punk. To his eternal credit, Terry said, 'Let's do it together,' so we literally hit the red button at the same time, and two careers were born.

"Later on, in the '70s, I used to think, 'Man, I wish I could go to Los Angeles and work with some real producers.' Then I went to L.A., saw some, quote, real producers, and came back as fast as I could. The engineer's job is to record the sound as well as he possibly can. The producer's job is to finish."

Dickinson considers Cooder's *Into the Purple Valley*, Toots Hibberts's *Toots in Memphis* and *Sister Lovers* (aka *Big Star III*) his best productions. The Toots record, recorded at Ardent in 1988 for Island's reggae subsidiary Mango, is one of his favorite memories.

"We did it as fast as we could, with no budget," he says. "Cut it in three days. The uncredited hero is the A&R guy, Jerry Rappaport. He selected the songs, primarily, although we ended up doing whatever Toots could sing because he couldn't read.

"It was the first time I'd seen Eddie really screwed up," Dickinson says of Eddie Hinton, a legendary guitarist who played on numerous classic Southern rock sessions. "He'd always been a little weird, but together. I knew he had a reputation of going nuts on sessions, but he'd never done it to me."

When Hinton showed up for the Toots sessions, "he was big and fat and huge, like a zombie, and he had a keeper with him," Dickinson says. "A lesser man than Rappaport would have sent him home, but we did it,

and Eddie played—when he was playing that solo on 'Freedom Train,' I was in the control room weeping uncontrollably. Here's this guy, he must have weighed 300 pounds, he's completely fucking gone, he's playing like an angel on a borrowed guitar, capo on the fifth fret.

"In my career, whenever I would feel sorry for myself, I would think of Eddie, and of Teenie Hodges, the Hi rhythm guitarist who wrote 'Take Me to the River' and 'I Can't Stand the Rain,' going completely unrecognized. The persona of Al Green is Teenie; Al ripped him off for his personality.

"When I hear soul in a voice, there's usually a lot of pain in it, but the truly great ones, the best I've ever heard, slipped through the cracks," Dickinson says, citing Hinton, Jerry Sailor (a singer who used to be in the Mark Five, a Muscle Shoals band in which Dan Penn sang backup), and John Hurley, who wrote "Son of a Preacher Man," "Love of the Common People" and "Five O'Clock World." All three are dead.

"As a producer, what I'm looking for is soul," Dickinson says. "The cliché about the natives in the jungle is they won't let you take their pictures because you're capturing their soul. Capturing the soul of the moment, the spirit of the performance, is exactly what you're doing as a producer." —CARLO WOLFF

Big Star: *Sister Lovers,* Aura, 1978.

Caldwell, Toy: *Toy Caldwell,* Cabin Fever, 1992.

Carrasco, Joe "King": *Bandido Rock,* Rounder Records, 1987, 1997.

Chilton, Alex: *Like Flies on Sherbet,* Aura, 1980.

Chuck Prophet and the Creatures of Habit: *See* Dickinson, James Luther.

Cooder, Ry: *Boomer's Story,* Reprise, 1972 • *Into the Purple Valley,* Reprise, 1972 • *Long Riders,* Reprise, 1980 • *Slide Area,* Warner Bros., 1982, 1988 • *Alamo Bay* soundtrack, Slash, 1985 • *Blue City* soundtrack, Warner Bros., 1986.

Dash Rip Rock: *Not of This World,* Mammoth, 1990.

Dick Nixons, The: *Paint the White House Black,* Triple X, 1992.

Dickinson, James Luther: *Dixie Fried,* Atlantic, 1972 • w/ Chuck Prophet and the Creatures of Habit, *Thousand Footprints in the Sand,* Last Call/Sony, 1997.

Falco, Tav, and Panther Burns: *Deep in the Shadows,* Marilyn, 1994.

Flat Duo Jets: *Go Go Harlem Baby,* Sky, 1991.

God Street Wine: *$1.99 Romances,* Eleven, 1994.

Green on Red: *The Killer Inside Me,* Mercury, 1987 • *Here Come the Snakes,* Restless, 1989.

Gun Bunnies: *Paw Paw Patch,* Virgin, 1989.

Jason and the Scorchers: *Reckless Country Soul* (EP), Mammoth, 1982, 1996 • as the Nashville Scorchers, *Fervor* (EP), Praxis, 1983 • *Both Sides of the Line,* EMI, 1996.

Krist, Jan: *Curious,* Silent Planet, 1996.

Love, G. and Special Sauce: *Coast to Coast Motel,* Okeh/Epic, 1995 • "Kiss and Tell," Okeh/Epic, 1995 • "Outtasight," Okeh/Epic, 1995.

Nixon, Mojo and Skid Roper: *Root Hog or Die,* IRS, 1989, 1991 • *Otis,* Enigma, 1990.

Radiators, The: *Total Evaporation,* Epic, 1991.

Replacements, The: *Pleased to Meet Me,* Sire, 1987.

Russell, Calvin: *Soldier,* Last Call, 1997.

Chris Stamey Group: *Christmas Time,* Coyote, 1986.

Texas Tornados: *4 Aces,* Reprise, 1996 • "Little Bit Is Better Than Nada," Reprise, 1997.

Toots and the Maytals: *Toots in Memphis,* Mango, 1988.

True Believers: *True Believers,* EMI America, 1986 • *Hard Road,* Rykodisc, 1994.

Bobby "Digital" Dixon

(DIGITAL B)

Bobby Dixon had a background in electronics and worked sound systems in Kingston, Jamaica, before going to work for Prince Jammy (see entry), a former protégé of King Tubby. At Jammy's he ran the mixing board and eventually took over day-to-day production responsibilities before moving on to set up his own label. Both at Jammy's and on his own, he worked with rhythm builders Steely and Clevie (see entry).

All are major proponents of the '90s "digital" sound that eliminated the need for kit drums, bass and guitar amplifiers, and quarrelsome musicians. In the new digital age in Kingston, a producer needs only a keyboard, a computer, and a competent hand at the board to deal with details like talent and tone. On his late recordings Dixon also used Mafia and Fluxy, Dalton Brownie, and the Firehouse Crew (particularly Dean Fraser) for horn arrangements. The digital touch can be heard on many Jammy productions as surely as Jammy's can be found on later King Tubby material.

Digital's own Digital B Studio at 6 Ron's Road in Kingston, and the label of the same name he formed in 1988, cranked out singles (a still viable format in JA) and albums: the latter as well as CDs issued by the New York VP label. Two fine albums with underrated roots singer Admiral Tibet, and records with Johnny Osbourne,

Frankie Paul, Sanchez, and Leroy Smart helped build up Digital's stock. Other artists he's recorded include '90s icons Tony Rebel, Pinchers, Ninjaman, Cocoa Tea, Spanner Banner, Eccleton Jarrett, and Shaggy.

Dixon hit big with DJ Shabba Ranks. The single "Wicked in a Bed" was a massive sensation in Jamaica. Digital produced his album *Just Reality* and co-produced *As Raw As Ever,* which went on to win a Grammy. Shabba Ranks's success led to a stateside feeding frenzy as major labels gobbled up DJs and sat back waiting for their hits. Dixon expanded his horizons and produced albums for Tiger, Buju Banton, and the not-yet-Mad Cobra.

Jamaican hit singles include Gregory Isaacs's "Storm," Half Pint's "Substitute Lover," and "Cool" by Terror Fabulous. In 1992 Dixon recorded the debut album for young singer Garnett Silk, who showed great potential. Perhaps more than any other single factor, the tragic death of this gifted singer has helped turn the dance and music scene around once more in JA, and new young roots singers and DJs have returned to the conscious themes of the generation of Peter Tosh and Bob Marley and away from the slackness and gun lyrics that ruled the '80s. Some of Digital's most recent productions show him to be making records that return to the rhythms (albeit updated) and traditions of the music he helped to change forever. —CHUCK FOSTER

Campbell, Al: "Dress Black," VP, 1992 (*Moving Away*).

Cocoa Tea: *Love Me,* Digital, 1996.

Determine: *Rock the World,* VP, 1996.

Dirtsman: *Acid,* Supreme, 1988.

General Trees: *Ragga Ragga Raggamuffin,* Rohit, 1994.

Irie, Clement: "Bun and Cheese," VP, 1989 (*Digital B Selections*).

Jarrett, Eccleton: "Kill a Sound," VP, 1989 (*Digital B Selections*).

Johnny P: "Fi Real," VP, 1992 (*Things a Gwan*).

Ninjaman: "Things a Gwan," VP, 1992 (*Things a Gwan*).

Osbourne, Johnny: *Rougher Than Them,* VP, 1996.

Paul, Frankie: *I've Got the Vibes,* Digital B, 1995 • *Come Back Again,* VP, 1996.

Pinchers: *Hotter,* VP, 1992.

Prezident Brown: *Original Blue Print,* VP, 1996.

Rebel, Tony: "Defend My Own," VP, 1992 (*Things a Gwan*) • "Sweet Jamaica," Chaos, 1993 (*Cool Runnings* soundtrack).

Ricks, Glen: *Fall in Love,* VP, 1996.

Sanchez: "Give It a Chance," VP, 1992 (*Things a Gwan*) • *I Can't Wait,* VP, 1991.

Shabba Ranks: *Just Reality,* VP, 1990 • *As Raw As Ever* (7 tracks), Epic, 1991 • *X-Tra Naked* (4 tracks), Epic, 1992 • *A*

Mi Shabba, Epic, 1995 • "Think You Got It All,"
Scratchie/Roadrunner, 1996 (*Jam Down Vibrations*).

Shaggy: *Boombastic* (1 track), Virgin, 1995.

Shinehead: *Sidewalk University*, Elektra, 1992.

Silk, Garnett: *It's Growing*, VP, 1992 • "It's Growing," VP,
1992 (*Moving Away*).

Smart, Leroy: "Talk 'Bout Friends," VP, 1992 (*Moving Away*) •
Talk 'Bout Friends, VP, 1992.

Spanner Banner: "On My Honor," VP, 1990 (*Gal Yu Good*).

Spice, Mikey: *Born Again*, VP, 1996.

Terror Fabulous: *Terror Fabulous*, VP, 1994 • "Ghetto Youth
Rise," Scratchie/Roadrunner, 1996 (*Jam Down Vibrations*).

Thriller U: *See* Tibet, Admiral.

Tibet, Admiral: "Watch Watch," VP, 1992 (*Things a Gwan*) •
w/ Thriller U, *Two Good to Be True*, Digital B, 1989 •
Reality Time, VP, 1991 • *Separate Class*, VP, 1991.

Wailing Souls: "Shark Attack" (remix), Chaos, 1993.

Yellowman: *Blueberry Hill*, Rohit, 1993.

COLLECTIONS

Mix Up/Scandal, Cosmic Force, 1990.

Wicked Inna Bed, VP, 1989.

The World of Digital B, Mesa, 1995.

Vine Yard Record Sampler, Vine Yard, 1992.

Moving Away, VP, 1992.

Mad Dog, VP, 1993.

Strictly Dancehall, VP, 1993.

Top Ten, VP, 1993.

Operation D, Vols. 1–3, Digital B, 1996.

Pay Down Pon It, VP, 1996.

Don Dixon

Don Dixon is one of the pioneers of the organic,
guitar-based side of '80s new wave, working with
R.E.M., the Smithereens, Marshall Crenshaw, the
Connells, Richard Barone, Chris Stamey, his wife Marti
Jones, and on his own solo work.

Dixon's interest in sound and sound reproduction
dates to his childhood. "I come from the 'hanging
around the studio' side of production. As a child, I was
always interested in recording. This was before everyone had tape recorders," Dixon says. "I was also a musician, and out of those interests I started to play sessions
on bass at 15. I got interested in the technological side
as I was doing sessions and recording with a band [Arro-
gance]."

The first record Dixon produced in collaboration

was a minor R&B hit by Toby King in the early '70s
recorded at the studio he came to be identified with,
Reflection Sound, in Charlotte, North Carolina.

Dixon has listened to the masters. "A lot of that early
Stax/Volt stuff was influential to me, how to simplify
things," he says. "Jerry Wexler produced and Tom
Dowd engineered a lot of the stuff that I learned from.
Later on, Nick Lowe—a very compressed sound. His
early work with Elvis Costello sounds loud at low volume. That is very hard to achieve. Also George Martin.
[See entries.] I go back to the Beatles records to make
sure that I'm not getting too modern with my guitar
sounds, especially acoustic guitar. I also like their use of
dry vocals," Dixon says. "Dry is big again now, which is
good for me because now I can actually listen to some
of these new records that people make. I've always
hated that Phil Spector [see entry] wall of sound bullshit. That has nothing to do with real life."

Dixon likens the producer's job to that of the movie
director. "Your job is to set up the scene and help artists
play their roles correctly—help nudge them through the
script of the record and recognize when they have a
good performance. Sometimes it's hard for the artist to
know whether it's a good performance, and a lot of
what I do is reflective in that way. I try to find the things
that are working about the artist, and then show them
the good things and help them move in that direction. I
usually only work with bands that already have a strong
personality. I don't believe in going in there and telling
them 'Toss out your drummer and get a new guitar and
you'll be great.' That's the manager's job as far as I'm
concerned."

A reluctant production hero, Dixon sees producing as his "public service to rock 'n' roll. I'm more of the musician trying to save musicians from the kind of shit that producers put me through." Dixon believes that one of the producer's most important roles is that of ombudsman for the artist.

"One of the services I try to provide is to act as a buffer between the sometimes insensitive concerns of the record company and the artist. Often the tension between them is healthy and valuable in terms of making everyone work harder, but sometimes it can be destructive. As you get deeper and deeper into the marketing side, records become more and more like pantyhose. I try to keep that at bay as long as possible."

Dixon favors the artist's sense of career over the record label's more immediate concerns. "Sometimes, it's better for the long term if people develop on their own terms," he says. "Not everything can be measured in the short term. Often the records that nobody at the label paid any attention to are the ones that become the vanguard that everyone else tries to reproduce. If those people hadn't been left alone, then they would have been trying to copy whatever was successful at the time, and new wave would never have occurred. I think that's the reason college towns spawn so many bands that are influential—they're allowed to grow in their own petri dish without a lot of outside pressure from the industry."

Does Dixon have a sound? "I like to use guitars. I like the things that guitars do in that they're kind of out of tune and they have a real percussiveness," he says. "There's a real impact, a real human feel to a guitar. I like keyboards, but keyboards have a boxed-in quality to them that is less appealing to me than the floating tonality of something with strings that your hands actually touch."

While he acknowledges "amazing changes" in technology in the last 20 years, Dixon says "everything that is important about making a record was going on in 1963. I'm not thought of as a technically sophisticated producer, but I really am. We spend a lot of time on things like specific phase relationships within the room. We don't use the EQ as much as a lot of people, we use a lot of different microphones and old-style mikeing techniques rather than the EQ."

Surprisingly, Dixon says he is a "huge fan of digital recording. I have been using the Sony digital tape recorders for a long time. I find them extremely warm, and they have a real extended low end and a clarity in the upper bass that you have to fight for with analog. A lot of people like the tape compression that you get from hitting analog tape. It takes some of the peak off the instrument. I've always liked the sounds of the lim-iters coming through the console before it went to multitrack tape. I've always liked the sound of live to 2-track stuff. Digital allows me to achieve more of that in the final mix than analog."

Dixon's best work transcends genre and era and unassumingly takes its place in the history of rock 'n' roll. R.E.M.'s first album, *Murmur* (co-produced with Mitch Easter; see entry), is still the group's defining moment. Rated the eighth-best album of the '80s by *Rolling Stone*, the album emerges from an unexpected hole in the musical fabric awash in guitars, mind-clinging melodies, and mysterious lyrics about two-headed cows and moral kiosks. The subtle but astonishing production moves Michael Stipe's phlegmatic vocals in and out of the forefront of the mix ("Radio Free Europe," "Pilgrimage"), using echo and muffling effects to generate emotional movement independent of the intelligibility of the lyrics. The production encompasses murk and a contradictory brightness that intertwine with yin-yang totality.

Another highlight of Dixon's career is the Smithereens' classic first album, *Especially for You*, with "Behind the Wall of Sleep," "In a Lonely Place" and "Blood and Roses" cheek by jowl on side 2 of the vinyl release. "Sleep" rocks: Jim Babjak's guitar and Joe Kernich's piano bash out classic riffs in unison against Dennis Diken's huge backbeat and Pat DiNizio's wounded, smoky vocals confiding unrequited love for a female bass player with "hair like Jeanie Shrimpton," "legs that never end," and a stance "just like Bill Wyman." —ERIC OLSEN

Accelerators, The: *Leave My Heart*, Dolphin, 1983 • *The Accelerators*, Profile, 1988.

Arrogance: *Give Us a Break*, Sugarbush, 1972 • *Prolepsis*, Sugarbush, 1975 • *Lively*, Moonlight, 1981.

Barone, Richard: *Primal Dream*, Paradox/MCA, 1990.

Beat Rodeo: *Staying out Late with Beat Rodeo*, IRS, 1985.

Brock, Jim: *Tropic Affair*, Reference, 1989.

Carnes, Kim: *Gypsy Honeymoon: Best Of*, EMI, 1993.

Cash, Andrew: *Boomtown*, Island Canada, 1989.

Coastal Cohorts: *King Mackerel and the Blues Are Running*, Sugar Hill, 1996.

Cody, John: *Zelig Belmondo*, Duke Street/MCA,Canada, 1993.

Connells, The: *Darker Days*, TVT, 1987.

Crenshaw, Marshall: *Mary Jean and Nine Others*, Warner Bros., 1987.

DiNizio, Pat: *Songs and Sounds*, Velvel, 1997.

Dixon, Don: *Most of the Girls Like to Dance . . .* , Enigma, 1985 • *Romeo at Julliard*, Enigma, 1987 • *EEE*, Enigma, 1989 • *The Chi-Town Budget Show*, Enigma, 1989 • *If I'm a Ham, Well, You're a Sausage*, Restless, 1992 • *Romantic Depressive*, Sugar Hill, 1995.

Dumptruck: *Positively Dumptruck*, Big Life/RCA, 1986 •

"Alone," Big Time, 1987 (*Big Noise from Bigtime*).

Emmet Swimming: *Arlington to Boston*, Sony, 1996.

Fetchin' Bones: *Cabin Flounder*, DB, 1985 • *Bad Pumpkin*, DB/Capitol, 1986 • *Galaxie 500*, Capitol, 1987.

Guadalcanal Diary: *2x4*, Elektra, 1987 • *Walking in the Shadow of the Big Man*, Elektra, 1984, 1985.

InTuaNua: *The Long Acre*, Virgin UK, 1988.

Jones, Marti: *Unsophisticated Time*, A&M, 1985 • *Match Game*, A&M, 1986 • *Used Guitars*, A&M, 1988 • *Any Kind of Lie*, RCA, 1990 • *Live at Spirit Square*, Sugar Hill, 1996.

Keene, Tommy: *Back Again . . . Try*, Dolphin, 1984 • *Run Now*, Geffen, 1986 • *Real Underground*, Alias, 1993.

Lee, Kevin, and the Lonesome City Kings: *Restless*, MCA, 1993.

Let's Active: *Cypress/Afoot*, IRS, 1989.

McDermott, Michael: *From Chicago to Gethsemane*, SBK, 1993.

McMurtry, James: *Where'd You Hide the Body*, Columbia, 1995.

R.E.M.: *Murmur*, IRS, 1983 • *Reckoning*, IRS, 1984 • "Wind Out," IRS, 1984 (*Bachelor Party* soundtrack) • *Dead Letter Office*, IRS, 1987 • *Eponymous*, IRS, 1988.

Reivers, The: *Saturday*, DB/Capitol, 1987.

Shafer, Robert: *Hillbilly Fever*, Upstart, 1997.

Smithereens, The: *Especially for You*, Enigma/Capitol, 1986 • *Green Thoughts*, Enigma/Capitol, 1988 • "The Stroll," A&M, 1994 (*Fast Track to Nowhere: Songs from Rebel Highway*) • *A Date with the Smithereens*, RCA, 1994 • *Attack of*, Capitol, 1995

Spongetones, The: *Where-Ever-Land*, Triapore, 1987.

Stamey, Chris: *It's a Wonderful Life*, DB, 1983 • *Instant Excitement* (EP), Coyote/Twin Tone/A&M, 1984.

Surfaholics, The: *Tiki-A-Go-Go*, Pixler Discs, n.d.

Sweet, Matthew: as Buzz of Delight, *Sound Castles* (EP), DB, 1984 • *Inside*, Columbia, 1986.

Wednesday Week: *What We Had*, Enigma, 1987.

X-Teens: *Love and Politics*, Dolphin, 1984.

Willie Dixon

"I am the blues," said Willie Dixon. If Willie Dixon wasn't the literal embodiment of the blues—he lived too long and was too well fed to be the personification of deprivation and pain that, say, Robert Johnson was—then it is safe to say that the blues in its modern form wouldn't exist without Dixon's contributions.

Through his work as session bass player, arranger, producer, and composer for blues legends Muddy Waters, Little Walter, Howlin' Wolf, Sonny Boy Williamson, Koko Taylor, and dozens of others at the Chess and Cobra labels in the '50s and '60s, Dixon was the first bluesman to understand and use modern recording practices and techniques in the service of the blues. He also served as the link between the blues and rock 'n' roll communities through his work with Bo Diddley ("My Babe") and Chuck Berry at Chess, and through the covers of his songs by the Rolling Stones ("Little Red Rooster"), the Animals ("I Got to Find My Baby"), Jeff Beck and Rod Stewart ("I Ain't Superstitious"), Cream ("Spoonful"), Led Zeppelin ("Bring It On Home"), the Doors ("Back Door Man"), even Oingo Boingo ("Violent Love").

Dixon was born July 1, 1915, in Vicksburg, Mississippi, the seventh of 14 children. "The seventh Son is kind of a historical idea. The world has made a pattern out of this seven as a lucky number. Most people think the seventh child has the extra wisdom and knowledge to inflence other people," Dixon wrote in his autobiography, *I Am the Blues*.

Dixon's mother, Daisy, ran a restaurant and encouraged reading, especially the Bible. She had a knack for speaking in rhyme that Willie picked up at an early age. As a teen Dixon sang bass with the Union Jubilee Singers, a gospel quartet that had a weekly 15-minute radio broadcast.

Dixon, a large lad who grew to be an even larger man (at one point reaching 380 pounds), was also interested in boxing. He moved to Chicago in 1936, and in 1937 he was the novice Illinois State Golden Gloves heavyweight champion. He fought four professional fights and sparred with Joe Louis before his career ended with a scuffle in the boxing commissioner's office.

Dixon turned to music in earnest, playing bass with guitarist Leonard "Baby Doo" Caston and forming the Five Breezes. The group played around Chicago and recorded for Bluebird. In 1941 Dixon was arrested for refusing military service as a conscientious objector. "I explained to them in several court cases, 'Why should I go to work to fight to save somebody that's killing me and my people?' " Dixon was in prison on and off for about a year and then formed a new group, the Four Jumps of Jive.

When Caston returned from the service in 1945, he and Dixon formed the Big Three Trio with guitarist Bernardo Dennis, who was later replaced by Ollie Crawford. The trio featured an amalgam of harmony blues and pop with a slick stage show. The Big Three played and recorded until 1952.

To earn extra money and satisfy his yen for harder material, Dixon was also jamming with Muddy Waters and other bluesmen in the clubs of Chicago's South Side. One night late at the Macomba Lounge, Dixon met Phil and Leonard Chess (see entry), who had recently started the Aristocrat label (later Chess Records). Dixon played on Robert Nighthawk's "My Sweet Lovin' Woman" in 1948 and went to work at the label as studio bass player and general gofer.

Dixon's talents as something more than a glorified houseboy weren't really recognized by the Chesses until 1954 when Waters recorded Dixon's "Hoochie Coochie Man," Howlin' Wolf recorded "Evil," and Little Walter and His Jukes cut "Mellow Down Easy."

Dixon played bass on recordings by Waters, Chuck Berry, Bo Diddley, Little Walter, Jimmy Witherspoon, Wolf, and hundreds of others throughout the '50s.

Producing was a role that Dixon eased into over time as his arranging and writing talents came to the fore—although Leonard Chess's name appears as producer on virtually all Chess recordings made in the '50s.

The standard practice of designating as "producer" the A&R man at the major labels, or the owner of the label at the indies, confused the matter of production credits in general until at least the mid-'60s. The same people were also given often-spurious songwriting credits with the rationale that these recognizable "names" would help get the record played on the radio and in record stores. Much later Dixon, Waters, Berry, and others recovered copyright credit and royalties for songwriting, but as there were no producer royalties at the time (i.e., no money at stake), the veracity of these credits remain forever swirling in the ether. By way of compromise, the Chess Blues box set credits all Chicago productions to Leonard and Phil Chess and Willie Dixon.

Willie Dixon's income from Chess for all of these duties, including songwriting, was around $100 a week, leading to his growing dissatisfaction. Dixon went to work for local rival Cobra Records in 1957, and in the two years before the label's financial collapse, he recorded with Magic Sam, Otis Rush, and Buddy Guy, among others.

Dixon returned to Chess and stayed with the company throughout the '60s. As the electric bass sound became favored over his stand-up acoustic, Willie played little bass with Chess in the '60s. But he wrote and produced for Wolf, Waters, Albert King, Sonny Boy Williamson, Shakey Horton, and, most notably, Koko Taylor ("Wang Dang Doodle," the last Chess true blues hit).

A European concert promoter named Horst Lippmann began a series of shows called the American Folk-Blues Festival, under whose aegis he brought many of the top American blues players over to tour the continent. Dixon coordinated the musical side of these shows, performed and recorded at them with the Chicago Blues All-Stars throughout the '60s, and earned more money from this work than from Chess. This European connection helped foster interest in Dixon's songwriting, and the blues-rock bands of England began to cover his songs. The Stones even recorded their first American album at Chess to be near Willie and their other blues heroes like Muddy Waters and Howlin' Wolf.

Determined to consolidate his legacy, Dixon recorded an album of his best-known songs, I Am the Blues, for Columbia in 1970. Ironically, Dixon's best-known recording was produced not by himself, but by Abner Spector (no relation to Phil), who also produced the Jaynettes' hit "Sally Go 'Round the Roses."

A killer band—with Dixon belting out Howlin' Wolf–like vocals and thumping his bass, Shakey Horton on harmonica, Sunnyland Slim and Lafayette Leake on piano, Johnny Shines on guitar, and Clifton James on drums—makes Dixon's timeless tunes like "I Can't Quit You," "Seventh Son," "Spoonful," "I'm Your Hoochie Coochie Man," and "The Little Red Rooster" his own. Dixon's syncopated version of "Back Door Man" is definitive.

In the '70s Dixon came to realize that his deal with ARC, the publishing arm of Chess, was not yielding financial fruits commensurate with his songwriting success. ARC sued Led Zeppelin for copyright infringement over "Bring It on Home" on Led Zeppelin II, arguing that it was Dixon's song, and won a settlement that Dixon never saw any part of until his manager conducted an audit of ARC's accounts. Dixon also sued Led Zeppelin for copyright infringement over the resemblance between "Whole Lotta Love" and "You Need Love." The settlement of those two cases brought Dixon substantial sums of money.

Among other endeavors, Dixon got involved with film, scoring music for The Color of Money and producing Bo Diddley's version of "Who Do You Love?" for La Bamba.

In 1980 Dixon was inducted into the Blues Foundation Hall of Fame. Dixon formed the Blues Heaven Foundation, in part to help recover copyrights for blues songwriters who had been deprived of funds and credit for their songs in the bad old days.

Dixon's ill health forced him to perform only part-time with the Chicago Blues All-Stars by 1990, though he remained active with the Blues Heaven Foundation (now fittingly located in the old Chess building in Chicago). Willie Dixon died of a heart ailment in 1992 and was inducted into the Rock and Roll Hall of Fame in 1994—a man who helped the blues move from the Delta to Chicago to the world. —ERIC OLSEN

Chickasaw Mudd Puppies: *8 Track Stomp,* Mercury, 1991.

Diddley, Bo: *Bo Diddley,* Chess, 1958 • *Go Bo Diddley,* Chess, 1959 • "Who Do You Love?," Slash/WB, 1987 (*La Bamba* soundtrack) • *The Chess Box,* Chess/MCA, 1990.

Dixon, Willie: *I Feel Like Steppin' Out: Willie Dixon Live,* Dr. Horse, 1986 • *Collection,* Deja Vu, 1987 • *Hidden Charms,* Bug, 1988 • *Big Three Trio,* Columbia, 1990 • *Original Wang Dang Doodle,* Chess/MCA, 1995 • *Concert at Liberty Hall,* Collectables, 1996.

Guy, Buddy: *The Complete Chess Studio Sessions,* Chess/MCA, 1992 • *Southern Blues, 1957–1963,* Paula, 1994 • *Buddy's Blues,* MCA, 1997.

Howlin' Wolf: *Change My Way,* Chess, 1975, 1977 • *The Very Best of Howlin' Wolf,* Charly, 1995 • *Blues Master,* MCA Special Products, 1996.

James, Elmore: *Street Talkin',* Muse, 1973, 1988.

Little Walter: *Essential,* MCA, 1993 • *His Best,* MCA, 1997.

Littlejohn, Johnny: *Johnny Littlejohn and the Chicago Blues All Stars,* Arhoolie, 1968.

Magic Sam: *1957–1966,* Flyright, 1989.

Taylor, Koko: "Wang Dang Doodle," Checker, 1966 • *What It Takes: The Chess Years,* Chess, 1991.

Waters, Muddy: *The Best Of,* Chess/MCA, 1958, 1987 • *Folk Singer,* Chess/MCA, 1964, 1987 • *The Chess Box,* Chess, 1989 • *Trouble No More (Singles, 1955–1959),* Chess/MCA, 1989 • *His Best, 1947–1955,* Chess/MCA, 1997.

Wells, Junior: *Messin' with the Kid,* Vol. 1, Paula/Flyright, 1989.

Williamson, Sonny Boy: *Essential,* Chess/MCA, 1993.

COLLECTIONS

Willie Dixon Box Set, Chess/MCA, 1989.

Chess Blues, Chess/MCA, 1992.

Chess Blues Classics, 1947–1956, Chess/MCA, 1997.

Chess Blues Classics, 1957–1967, Chess/MCA, 1997.

Chess Blues Piano Greats, MCA, 1997.

Chess Blues-Rock Songbook, MCA, 1997.

DJ Premier and Guru

(CHRISTOPHER MARTIN AND KEITH ELAM)

Picky. That's the word DJ Premier, easily one of hip-hop's most in-demand beatmasters, uses to describe his approach to creation in the studio.

"I'm real picky about the vocals, the music, everything. If I hear one little tweak in anything, I'm on it like that. I want it that sharp and that tight. I ask myself if

it's worth it as I go back in, then I'll go back and fix it," says Brooklyn's Premier.

Premier's work with slain rapper Notorious B.I.G. on the song "Ten Crack Commandments" (from B.I.G.'s 1997 opus *Life After Death*) is a good example of how picky Premier can be. "The first time I did the song, Biggie called and said it needed more bottom, so I did another mix. I still like the first mix better, but I'm not gonna stress it," says Premier, who is also half of respected rap duo Gang Starr, which features rapper Guru (Keith Elam), a producer in his own right known for his Jazzamatazz hip-hop jazz albums.

Ever since the first Gang Starr album, *No More Mr. Nice Guy,* and throughout the course of several follow-ups like *Step in the Arena, Daily Operation,* and *Hard to Earn,* Premier has successfully and simultaneously managed to strike a serious chord within the hip-hop community; he has produced a number of outside projects all bearing his distinct stamp, mixing hip-hop with other genres like jazz, funk, and blues.

His tough, tight beats can be found on Nas' "I Gave You Power" and "New York State of Mind," B.I.G.'s "Kick In the Door" and "Unbelievable," Jeru the Damaja's *Wrath of the Math* album, several songs from Bahamadia's acclaimed *Kollage* album, and many others. He is also a top remixer.

Premier says it's his job as a producer to do more than create the music. "I feel the producer needs to have the final or main approval on how they lay down their vocals," he says. "Some people lay down a track and let anything happen. Then you just did a beat. I mix and coach vocalists. If I'm not hearing in it what I like, then I have to do them over. I analyze everything," he says.

Premier describes his style as original but consistent. "When I say my style is the same, it means I'm guaranteed to come with something good, but something different from the last joint. There's always some of me in there. The music is actually my vision," says Premier, "and I like to give the artist a track that fits them. When I'm working with Rakim, I give him a Rakim track."

The last point is especially important to Premier, who doesn't want people to think he's "sitting around the crib making beats all day. I get approached about a job, and if it's something I want to fuck with, I have the artist in mind when I create the track."

It usually works a little differently with Guru, however. "Guru always comes up with the title and tells me what it's about and I match the track to the title. With other artists I don't do that," he says, noting that he came up with the title to Gang Starr's *Hard to Earn.*

Premier and Guru met over the phone while they were in different groups. A record label executive put

Premier's demo in Guru's hands, and the rest is history. Premier calls the relationship odd, but very real, and not without some infighting. "We throw punches and throw stuff around. Anytime we got a problem we fight. Once we punch each other in the face, we're good to go. We're like little kids in elementary school. But somehow we still stay together. We have business to handle and make good records," says Premier.

His defining moments, he believes, are his cuts for B.I.G., Gang Starr's "Mass Appeal" and "Dwick," Nas' "New York State of Mind," and KRS-One's "Rappers Are in Danger." "Those are my main joints right there," he exclaims.

Premier believes rap production is getting better and better, though it's time to weed out the riffraff in favor of more original music and fewer remakes. "A lot of people are doing remakes and I'm not with that. I'm not mad, but you can't just do that. It's too easy. Let's create some shit," he says. —KEVIN JOHNSON

DJ Premier

Bahamadia: *Kollage,* Chrysalis, 1996.
Boogie Down Productions: " 'P' Is Still Free," Jive, 1993 (*Menace II Society* soundtrack).
Buckshot LeFonque: *Breakfast @ Denny's,* Columbia, 1994.
Cookie Crew: *Fade to Black,* London, 1991.
Da Youngsta's: *The Aftermath,* EastWest, 1993.
Dream Warriors: *Subliminal Stimulation,* EMI, 1995.
Guru: *Jazzamatazz,* Vol. 2, *The New Reality,* Cool Tempo/Chrysalis, 1995.
Heavy D and the Boyz: *Blue Funk,* Uptown/MCA, 1992.
Jay-Z: *Reasonable Doubt,* Freeze, 1996 • *Feelin' It,* Roc-a-fella/Priority, 1997.
Jeru the Damaja: *The Sun Rises in the East,* Payday, 1994 • *Wrath of the Math,* Payday, 1996 • "Me or the Papes," Payday, 1997.
Kane, Big Daddy: *Daddy's Home,* MCA, 1994.
KRS-One: *Return of the Boom Bap,* Jive, 1993 • *KRS-One,* Jive, 1995.
Lord Finesse and DJ Mike Smooth: *Funky Technician,* Wild Pitch, 1990.
M.O.P.: *Firing Squad,* Relativity, 1996.
Manilow, Barry: "I'd Really Love to See You Tonight" (remix), Arista, 1997.
Marsalis, Branford: *Music from Mo' Better Blues,* Columbia, 1990.
MC Solaar: *Qui Seme le Vent Récolte le Tempo,* PolyGram, 1991.
Mobb Deep: *Juvenile Hell,* 4th & B'Way, 1993.
Nas: *Illmatic,* Columbia, 1994 • *It Was Written,* Columbia, 1996.
Notorious B.I.G.: *Ready to Die,* Bad Boy/Arista, 1995 • *Life After Death,* Bad Boy/Arista, 1997.

O.C.: "Far from Yours," PolyGram, 1997 • *Jewelz,* PolyGram, 1997.
Rakim: *The 18th Letter: The Book of Life,* Uptown/Universal, 1997.
Shyheim: "On and On," Virgin, 1994.

DJ Premier and Guru

Gang Starr: *No More Mr. Nice Guy,* EMI America, 1989 • "Just to Get a Rep," Chrysalis, 1990 • "Who's Gonna Take the Weight?," Chrysalis, 1990 • *Step in the Arena,* Chrysalis, 1991 • *Daily Operation,* Chrysalis, 1992 • *Hard to Earn,* Chrysalis, 1994.
Marxman: *33 Revolutions per Minute* (1 track), A&M, 1993.

Guru

Coolbone: "Nothin' But Strife," Hollywood, 1997.
Cutthroats: "Stop Lookin' at Me," Jive, 1993 (*Menace II Society* soundtrack).
D*Note: "Now Is the Time" (remix), TVT, 1994.
Deee-Lite: "Picnic in the Summertime" (remix), Elektra, 1994.
Guru: *Jazzamatazz,* Chrysalis, 1993 • "Loungin'," Chrysalis, 1993 • Featuring Chaka Khan, "Watch What You Say," Cool Tempo/Chrysalis, 1995.
Lisa Lisa: *LL 77,* Pendulum, 1994.
Nefertiti: *L.I.F.E.: Living in the Fear of Extinction,* Mercury, 1994.

Clement Seymour "Coxsone" Dodd

If only one reggae producer were included in this book it would have to be C.S. "Coxsone" Dodd. Though not the earliest Jamaican producer, his work is certainly the most pervasive.

Coming up through the ranks from sound system to record producer in the ska era, his rock-steady and reggae productions are still the jumping-off point for the most popular reggae rhythms of today, and he was the producer of note for the early work of most of reggae's better-known acts: the Wailers, Toots and the Maytals, the Heptones, Dennis Brown, and hundreds of others.

"Downbeat," as he was originally called (most Jamaican producers and artists go through a series of names if their careers last long enough), started out building speaker boxes for some of the earliest sound systems in Jamaica. He went on to run his own sound and became chief rival to the island's then No. 1 sound, Duke Reid the Trojan (see entry).

Playing American R&B in the early days and scouting records in the U.S. in heated competition, they began recording their own homegrown music as good records got harder to find. One of his earliest productions, Theophilus Beckford's "Easy Snapping," helped usher in the era of ska, which celebrated Jamaica's independence both musically and as a nation.

Among his outstanding contributions to ska are "Guns Fever" by Baba Brooks; Don Drummond's "Man in the Streets," "Further East," and "Schooling the Duke"; Clancy Eccles' (see entry) "River Jordan"; several albums for Roland Alphonso; and the Skatalites. Tracks like Alphonso's "Ball of Fire" and the Skatalites' "Phoenix City" are what ska was all about—unbridled energy channeled through horn sections determined to stamp a Jamaican imprint on jazz, R&B, and the world.

Among hundreds of ska vocals, the Wailers' "Simmer Down" is perhaps the best example of how powerful an undercurrent this music could contain.

Recording mainly at Federal Records before building and opening his own Studio One on Brentford Road in Kingston, Dodd issued product on a series of sublabels like Supreme, Downbeat, Iron Side, Money Disc, Winro, Bongo Man, and others. Most of his product was released or later reissued under the Coxsone or Studio One imprint.

Because he never put dates on his records, the earliest pressings are sometimes the only way—besides the constantly evolving sound—to fasten down the time period of the original recordings. In the U.K. he issued product on Bamboo and Banana as well as Attack, Trojan, and others.

Dodd's Studio One was Jamaica's music school, and he employed a long line of bouncers who became engineers and arrangers and then went on to their own productions. Among them were some of the earliest, like Prince Buster, and best, like Lee "Scratch" Perry (see entry).

Sylvan Morris and Syd Bucknor both engineered for "Scorcher," another nickname Dodd used in the writer's credit of his singles. For musicians he employed the island's best. Like the singers whom they backed, they often cut their earliest and best records for Dodd for little remuneration. Having made their name with his productions, they moved on to Duke Reid, Buster, and others for later records.

"All these songs you're hearin' with us were just 2-track songs," says singer Ken Boothe of the early days at Studio One. "At first we have to record the same time, singers, musicians, everybody."

Among those who made great records at Studio One are Freddy McKay, an achingly talented singer who seems almost forgotten today; Horace Andy; and early duos like Jackie and Doreen, Owen and Millie, Larry and Alvin, and Alton and Eddie.

Coxsone recorded a diverse bag of music, from balladeer Lord Tanamo to Nyahbingi drummer Count Ossie, including calypso, soul, jazz, and gospel. Despite this and his groundwork in ska and rock steady, his name will always be associated with the early days of reggae.

Singer/songwriter Bob Andy began his career at Studio One, first as original lead singer for the Paragons (later replaced by John Holt). His major hits with Dodd include "I've Got to Go Back Home" (with backing vocals by Bob Marley and Peter Tosh) and "Too Experienced," a much-covered tune whose rhythm has become almost community property in Jamaica. He also penned hits like "Feel Like Jumping" for Marcia Griffiths when she recorded for Dodd.

Dodd went through an almost endless string of house bands: the Skatalites, Soul Brothers, Brentford All Stars, Soul Vendors, Soul Defenders, and Sound Dimension are a few. Among the musicians who contributed greatly to the sound were keyboardist Jackie Mittoo and bassist Leroy Sibbles (also lead singer of the Heptones), both of whom arranged and auditioned during their tenure, as well as guitarist Ernest Ranglin and keyman Pablove Black.

Incorporating talent was perhaps Dodd's greatest ability, and scores of well-known producers like Derrick Harriot, Lloyd Charmers, and Niney the Observer (see entry) began their careers working for Coxsone.

Among those whom Dodd was first to record is Winston Rodney, aka Burning Spear. His two Studio One albums sketched out the conscious roots sound he's modified but stayed with throughout his long and successful career.

The late Delroy Wilson was 14 when he cut some ripping ska sides for Coxsone, and his first two albums were done for Dodd as well. Freddie McGregor was all of 7 years old and had to stand on a crate to cut his earliest vocals for Dodd as a member of the Clarendonians. Others who scored early at Studio One include Slim Smith, Jackie Opel, and later singers as diverse as Clifton Gibbs and Sugar Minott.

Vocal groups were stock in trade at Studio One, from the pre–lovers rock style of Carlton and the Shoes to the early reggae sound of the Cables. The Gladiators, one of the first self-contained reggae bands, cut their first album for Dodd, including hits like "Hello Carol," that the group (and others) returned to over and over throughout their career.

Other groups that made their mark at Studio One include the early Clue J and his Blue Blasters, the Bassies, Gaylads, Westmorlites, Termites, the Wailing Souls, and the Heptones. Coxsone also recorded some of the best early reggae in the DJ style, including Dillinger, Prince Francis, and Dennis Alcapone. Later, the likes of Lone Ranger and (still later) Michigan and Smiley fired their opening salvos from Brentford Road.

King Stitt, who recorded mainly for producer Clancy Eccles, was originally a sound system DJ for Coxsone, and Prince Jazzbo, who later recorded for Lee Perry (then went on to become a producer in his own right), recorded for him as well.

Not only Coxsone's recordings but his original rhythms have stood the test of time as Jamaican producers have returned again and again to rework and "modernize" them. Dodd himself has revisited the original rhythms many times too, bringing new generations of singers like Johnny Osbourne or Earl Sixteen on to sing on tracks cut as much as two decades earlier. In the late '70s and early '80s he "updated" many of the rhythms by adding disco-era syndrums, though fortunately this tendency passed fairly quickly.

In that same time period Dodd moved his operations to New York, and though occasional new recordings were released, the bulk of his work from that point has been in reissues and licensing product for American and European release. A longstanding arrangement with Heartbeat has kept a large body of his work available in the U.S. The rest of the reggae industry never stopped nicking his rhythms (or artists), and Coxsone has remained the foundation for much of the best of reggae. After four decades in the business he is still issuing some of the best music ever recorded in Jamaica, and in the last year, for the first time, manufacturing and distributing his own compact discs.

—CHUCK FOSTER

Alcapone, Dennis: *Forever Version,* Heartbeat, 1971, 1991.

Alphonso, Roland: *Best Of,* Studio One, 1973 • *Ska Au Go Go,* Coxsone, c. 1966.

Andy, Bob: *Songbook,* Studio One, 1972, 1988.

Andy, Horace: *Best of (Skylarking),* Liberty, 1972 • *Skylarking,* Studio One, 1972 • *Best Of,* Studio One, 1974.

Black, Pablove: *Mr. Music,* Studio One, 1978.

Boothe, Ken: *More of Ken Boothe,* Studio One, 1968 • *Mr. Rock Steady,* Studio One, 1968 • *A Man and His Hits,* Studio One, 1970 • *Live Good,* United Artists, 1978.

Brooks, Cedric: *I'm Flash Forward,* Studio One, 1977.

Brown, Dennis: *If I Follow My Heart,* Studio One, 1971. • *No Man Is an Island,* Studio One, 1970 • "Impossible," Heartbeat, 1983 *(Best of Studio One).*

Burning Spear: *Burning Spear,* Studio One, 1973 • *Rocking Time,* Studio One, 1974.

Cables, The: *What Kind of World,* Heartbeat, 1970, 1991 • "Baby Why," Heartbeat, 1983 *(Best of Studio One).*

Carlton and the Shoes: *Love Me Forever,* Studio One, 1978.

Clarendonians, The: *Best Of,* Studio One, 1966 • "Rudie Bam Bam," Trojan, 1966, 1988 *(Dance Crasher: Ska to Rock Steady).*

Classics: "Mr. Fire Coal Man," Shelter, n.d.

Dillinger: *Ready Natty Dread,* Studio One, 1975.

Drummond, Don: *In Memory of Don Drummond,* Studio One, 1969 • *Best of Don Drummond,* Studio One, 1989.

Dub Specialist: (all Studio One) *Ital Dub,* c. 1974 • *Better Dub from Studio One,* c. 1975 • *Bionic Dub,* c. 1975 • *Dub Store Special,* 1975 • *Hi Fashion Dub Top Ten,* c. 1976 • *Roots Dub,* 1976 • *Sample Dub,* c. 1979 • *Juk's Incorporation,* c. 1978 • *African Rub 'A' Dub,* 1978 • *Juk's Incorporation, Part 2,* 1979 • *Mello Dub,* n.d.

Ellis, Alton: *The Best Of,* Studio One, 1988 • *Sings Rock and Soul,* Studio One, 1966 • *Showcase,* Studio One, 1980 • *Sunday Coming,* Heartbeat, 1980, 1995 • "Can I Change My Mind?," Heartbeat, 1983 *(Best of Studio One)* • w/ Hortense Ellis, *Alton and Hortense Ellis,* Heartbeat, 1990.

Ellis, Hortense: See Ellis, Alton.

Eskender, Judah Tarafi: "Rastafari Tell You," Heartbeat, 1983 *(Best of Studio One).*

Ethiopians, The: *Everything Crash,* Studio One, 1979 • "Owe Me No Pay Me," Trojan, 1966, 1988 *(Dance Crasher: Ska to Rock Steady).*

Gaylads, The: *Rock Steady with the Gaylads,* Coxsone, 1967 • *Sunshine Golden Folk and Calypso,* Studio One, 1967 • *Best of the Gaylads,* Studio One, 1992.

Gladiators, The: *Presenting the Gladiators,* Studio One, 1979 • "Roots Natty," Heartbeat, 1983 *(Best of Studio One).*

Gregory, Tony: *Tony Gregory Sings,* Coxsone, 1968.

Griffiths, Marcia: *Marcia Griffiths at Studio One,* Studio One, 1996 • "Melody Life," Heartbeat, 1983 *(Best of Studio One).*

Heptones, The: *Black Is Black,* Studio One, 1971 • *Freedom Train,* Studio One, 1970 • *Heptones,* Studio One, 1967 • *The Heptones on Top,* Studio One, 1968 • *Best Of,* Buddah, 1976 • *In Love with You,* United Artists, 1978 • "Party Time," Heartbeat, 1983 *(Best of Studio One).*

Hibbert, Lennie: *Creation,* Studio One, 1969.

Hiltonairs: *Best Of,* Coxsone, 1967 • *Kings of Calypso,* Coxsone, n.d.

Holt, John: "Holly Holy/Do You Want Me?," Shelter, 1970 • *Paragons and Friends,* Studio One, c. 1968 • *A Love I Can Feel,* Studio One, 1971 • *Best Of,* Studio One, 1990 • *Greatest Hits,* Studio One, 1972 • *Like a Bolt,* Studio One, c. 1972.

Lara, Jennifer: *Studio One Presents Jennifer Lara,* Studio One, 1978.

Lone Ranger: *Badda Dan Dem,* Studio One, 1982 • *On the Other Side of Dub,* Heartbeat, 1982, 1991.

Lord Creator: "Big Bamboo," Trojan, 1964, 1988 (*Dance Crasher: Ska to Rock Steady*).

Marley, Bob, and the Wailers: *Wailing Wailers at Studio One,* Heartbeat, 1965, 1994 • *Best Of,* Studio One, 1976 • *Early Music,* Calla, 1977 • *The Birth of a Legend,* Epic, 1977 • "Simmer Down," Columbia, 1984 (*Rhythm Come Forward*) • *One Love at Studio One,* Heartbeat, 1991 • *Simmer Down at Studio One,* Heartbeat, 1994.

Marshall, Larry: *Presenting Larry Marshall,* Heartbeat, 1973, 1992 • "Throw Me Corn," Heartbeat, 1983 (*Best of Studio One*).

Maytals, The: "Hallelujah," Trojan, 1963, 1988 (*Dance Crasher: Ska to Rock Steady*) • *Never Grow Old,* Studio One, 1966.

McGregor, Freddie: *Don't Want to Be Lonely,* Studio One, 1987 • *Bobby Bobylon,* Studio One, 1980 • *I Am Ready,* Studio One, 1982.

McKay, Freddie: "Sweet You Sour You," Shelter, n.d. • *Picture on the Wall,* Studio One, 1971.

Michigan and Smiley: "Rub a Dub Style," Heartbeat, 1983 (*Best of Studio One*) • *Rub a Dub Style,* Heartbeat, 1992.

Minott, Sugar: *More,* Studio One, 1982 • *Live Love,* Studio One, 1978 • *Showcase,* Heartbeat, 1979 • "Oh Mr. D.C.," Heartbeat, 1983 (*Best of Studio One*).

Mittoo, Jackie: *Keep On Dancing,* Coxsone, 1969. • *Now,* Studio One, 1970 • *Evening Time,* Studio One, 1967 • *In London,* Coxsone, 1967 • *Macka Fat,* Studio One, 1970 • *Jackie Mittoo,* UA/Liberty, 1978, 1985 • *Showcase,* Studio One, 1983 • *Tribute To,* Heartbeat, 1995.

Opel, Jackie: *Cry Me a River,* Studio One, 1969 • *The Best Of,* Studio One, 1970.

Osbourne, Johnny: *Truths and Rights,* Heartbeat, 1980 • "Jah Promise," Heartbeat, 1983 (*Best of Studio One*).

Perry, Lee "Scratch": w/ the Soulettes, "Doctor Dick," Trojan, 1966, 1988 (*Dance Crasher: Ska to Rock Steady*) • *Chicken Scratch,* Heartbeat, 1989 • *The Upsetter and the Beat,* Heartbeat, 1992.

Prince Jazzbo: *Choice of Version,* Studio One, 1990.

Ranglin, Ernest: *Surfin',* Studio One, c. 1968 • *Sounds and Power,* Studio One, 1997.

Russell, Devon: *Roots Music,* Studio One, 1982.

Sixteen, Earl: *Showcase,* Studio One, 1985.

Skatalites, The: "Ball O' Fire," Trojan, 1965, 1988 (*Dance Crasher: Ska to Rock Steady*) • "Beardman Ska," Trojan, 1965, 1988 (*Dance Crasher: Ska to Rock Steady*) • *Ska Authentic,* Studio One, 1967 • *Best Of,* Studio One, 1974 • *Celebration Time,* Studio One, 1988.

Smith, Slim: *Born to Love,* Heartbeat, 1979, 1991 • "Born to Love," Heartbeat, 1983 (*Best of Studio One*).

Soul Brothers: *Carib Soul,* Coxsone, 1966. • *Hot Shot Ska,* Coxsone, 1966.

Soul Defenders: *Soul Defenders at Studio One,* Heartbeat, 1991.

Soul Vendors: *On Tour,* Coxsone, 1967.

Sweeting, Harry: *From Jamaica with Love,* Coxsone, 1968.

Termites, The: "My Last Love," Heartbeat, 1983 (*Best of Studio One*) • *Do the Rock Steady,* Heartbeat, 1991.

Toots and the Maytals: *Life Could Be a Dream,* Studio One, 1992.

Tosh, Peter: w/ the Wailers, "Shame and Scandal," Trojan, 1965, 1988 (*Dance Crasher: Ska to Rock Steady*) • *The Toughest,* Heartbeat, 1996.

Viceroys, The: *The Viceroys at Studio One: Ya Ho,* Heartbeat, 1968.

Wailing Souls: *Studio One Presents Wailing Souls,* Studio One, 1976 • "Row Fisherman Row," Heartbeat, 1983 (*Best of Studio One*).

Williams, Willie: *Armagideon Time,* Heartbeat, 1982.

Wilson, Delroy: *I Shall Not Remove,* Studio One, 1966 • *The Best Of, Original Twelve,* Heartbeat, 1969, 1991 • *Good All Over,* Coxsone, 1969 • *Best Of,* UA/Liberty, 1978, 1985 • *Dancin' Mood,* Studio One, 1997.

COLLECTIONS

On the Attack label: *Big Bamboo,* 1974.

On the Bamboo label: *Freedom Sounds,* 1970.

On the Columbia label: *Rhythm Come Forward,* 1984.

On the Coxsone label: *All Star Top Hits,* 1961, 1991 • *Battle of the DJs: Dance Hall Style,* n.d. • *Blue Beat Special,* 1968 • *Jump Jamaica Way,* 1963 • *This Is Jamaica Ska,* 1965 • *Get Ready Rock Steady,* 1967 • *Rock Steady Coxsone Style,* 1968.

On the Heartbeat label: *Best of Studio One,* Vol. 1–3, 1985, 1988 • *Collector's Edition: Rare Reggae from the Vaults of Studio One,* 1989 • *Fire Down Below: Scorchers from Studio One,* 1990 • *Original Club Ska,* 1990 • *Ska Bonanza: The Studio One Ska Years,* 1991 • *Reggae Christmas from Studio One,* 1992 • *Solid Gold Coxsone Style,* 1992 • *Mojo Rock Steady,* 1994 • *Respect to Studio One,* 1994 • *Dub Specialist: 17 Dub Shots from Studio One,* 1995 • *Grooving at Studio One,* 1996.

On the Studio One label: *Christmas in Jamaica,* 1970 • *Christmas Stylee,* 1980 • *Dance Hall '63, Featuring King Stitt,* 1993 • *History of Ska: The Golden Years, 1960–1965,* 1968 • *History of Ska: The Golden Years, 1966–1969,* 1969 • *Jamaica All Stars,* Vol. 1, c. 1966 • *Jamaica All Stars,* Vol. 2, 1970 • *Jamaica Today: The Seventies,* 1971 • *Jazz Jamaica,* 1962 • *Natural Reggae,* 1970 • *Old Gold Soul: 14 Karat,* n.d. • *Oldies But Goodies,* Vols. 1–2, c. 1965 • *Party Time in Jamaica,* 1968 • *Pirates Choice,* 1981 • *Reggae in the Grass,* 1968 • *Reggaematic Sounds,* 1971 • *Reggae Time,* 1968 • *Ride Me Donkey: Solid Gold from Jamaica,* 1968 • *Rocking Steady,* 1993 • *Sales Conference,* 1975 • *A Scorcha from Studio One,* 1969 • *Ska Au Go Go,* c. 1965 • *Ska Strictly for You,* n.d. • *Soul Defenders at Studio One,* 1991 • *Sounds of Jamaica: Top Ten,* 1974 • *Sounds of Young Jamaica,* Vol. 1, n.d. • *Studio One*

Showcase, Vols. 1–2, 1972 • *Studio One Various Artists*, Vol. 3, 1973 • *Swing Easy*, 1968 • *Zodiac Dub*, n.d.

On the RAS label: *Dance Hall Session*, 1987 • *All on the Same Rhythm*, 1988.

On the Trojan label: *Musical Fever, 1967–1968*, 1989.

On the UA/Liberty/EMI label: *Old and New Sounds*, 1991.

Joel Dorn

Joel Dorn came down with mumps when he was 7, leaving him with only 40 percent of his hearing in his right ear. "I lost my hearing overnight," says Dorn, who has been producing records for close to 35 years. "I've never heard stereo. I don't give a shit about stereo."

What Dorn cares about is the artist. "I enjoy finding one-of-a-kind artists who are excellent at what they do, and I enjoy complementing what they do or putting them in a situation and capturing what they do," he says. "The ideal record, the zen record, would be to record the artist in a strictly documentary sense and have it be so pure and of itself that nothing other than the actual act of recording would be necessary."

Born April 7, 1942, Dorn grew up in Philadelphia always wanting to be a record producer. "I was fascinated by the visual part of records," says Dorn, who lives in New York City, where he owns and operates the 32 Records label. "I started listening to records when I was a year and a half old, during World War II. My mother used to play Al Jolson records all the time. When she played 'April Showers,' I used to get a picture of this hill with, like, a rainstorm and flowers growing, and it was wild. Anytime I heard a record, a visual part went along with it. It wasn't so much of people in a studio, it was more a picture the record made in my mind."

Some of Dorn's finest productions—Bette Midler's debut, *The Divine Miss M* (No. 9); Roberta Flack's *First Take* (No. 1); the Neville Brothers' *Fiyo on the Bayou;* and an amazing cult classic, David Forman's eponymous album—are vivid and pictorial.

Midler's album formalized the notion of pop nostalgia. Flack's legitimized what would come to be known as Quiet Storm. The Neville work brought the New Orleans second line into the mainstream. The Forman, suffused with soul and smoke, is one of the great unknown records by one of the greatest singer/songwriters of the singer/songwriter era, and is treasured by those lucky enough to have picked up on it way back

when. Recorded with just voice and piano, everything else on Forman's exceptional (and only) album was overdubbed later. Dorn used the same technique on albums he produced for mysterious faux-blues icon Dickran Gulbanian (better known as Leon Redbone).

Dorn hit his stride as a staff producer for Atlantic Records from the mid-'60s to the mid-'70s. "I really loved Ray Charles," he explains. "Not a minor obsession, I might add: I used to leave school when I was a kid and find out where Ray was playing. That's how I met Fathead and all those cats."

When Dorn was 14, he began to write Atlantic Records co-chairman Nesuhi Ertegun (see entry). "I used to give him ideas for records," Dorn recalls. "I knew somebody made the records. I didn't know how, exactly. Then when I became a disc jockey in Philly in 1961, on WHAT-FM, I became responsible for selling a lot of Atlantic jazz records in Philly, so our relationship accelerated. We met when I was 19, and I told him I wanted to work for Atlantic because it had my favorite music. After years of begging, he gave me a shot with a Hubert Laws record [*The Laws of Jazz*]. That turned out okay, led to some productions and, finally, a full-time gig."

Not only did Dorn wind up producing albums by saxophone mainstays David "Fathead" Newman and Hank Crawford, he helmed classic sessions by Yusef Lateef, Les McCann, Eddie Harris, Byard Lancaster, and

Photo by Ben Cromer, 1994

Don Braden. He has always managed to straddle folk and jazz; the common element is soulfulness.

Dorn left Atlantic in 1975 to become a freelancer. "The pace was changing. Also, I was pretty nuts in those years. Those were great, self-indulgent times and Atlantic was becoming more corporate. I joined Atlantic when it was the most incredible place that related to freewheeling artistry than ever before or since."

In the '70s, Dorn made a lot of money. But he burned out in the early '80s, when he couldn't get any work. "I wasn't in vogue, or what I was doing wasn't popular," he says. "I was making very abstract records in those years, what Thelonious Monk refers to as the 'un-years.' I blew the stash but I made it through."

Since 1986, he has focused on boxed sets, compilations, and reissues, most connected to Atlantic. Recently, he has resurrected much of the Muse catalog and issued a heretofore-unreleased collection of Ike and Tina Turner. His releases for Rhino/Atlantic include a remarkable John Coltrane compilation, *The Heavyweight Champion*, and lesser compilations by Lateef, Charles Mingus, Keith Jarrett, and Mose Allison.

"I'm a classically trained nothing," Dorn says. "I can't play a fucking kazoo. I don't know anything about technology, nor do I know anything about music, and I'm deaf. Nobody checks me out because I memorize the positions of the instruments on the wall—the left speaker, the right speaker, and the space in between. Many times I make mono records; the Leon Redbone records are half mono and half stereo, what I call 'expanded mono.' Mono records are much harder to make than stereo records because you create the sense of perspective in them by how you color and shade and place. A stereo record, a chimpanzee could make. That's why those Phil Spector (see entry) records are unbelievable. From time to time—I never mark them as mono—I make mono records. I don't talk about them, but they're there. They're hidden among the stereo records. I love to do that."

He never did produce Ray Charles. "Every time I went after him, it never worked out, and the time I would really have liked to produce him has been here and gone," Dorn says. "Ray Charles was great from the beginning up through a record called 'Have a Smile with Me' [on ABC Paramount]. It was the first time he failed at what he wanted to do, and he never sounded the same after that. He lost his fastball."

Catching that fastball at top speed is what Dorn strives for. "I can't bring anything to an artist," he says. "I can only capture what somebody already has. I don't make a record and put a person in at the end. They must be fully formed enough to get to where they want to be.

Given the choice, I like to work with great, original artists in the early stages of their careers. Before they lose the innocence."

Dorn has generated a musical family. One of Dorn's four sons, David, is head of media relations at Rhino; another, Adam, also a producer, studied bass with Marcus Miller (see entry); son Ryan produced the first Ugly Kid Joe record; and son Mike manages a chain of furniture stores in Philadelphia. —CARLO WOLFF

Adderley, Cannonball: *Radio Nights,* Night/Capitol, 1968, 1991.

Allen, Peter: *Continental American,* A&M, 1974 • *At His Best,* A&M, 1993.

Allison, Mose: *Western Man,* Atlantic, 1971 • *Best Of,* Sequel, 1995.

Allman Brothers Band: "Please Call Home," Polydor, 1969 • *Idlewild South,* Polydor, 1970.

Asleep at the Wheel: *Collision Course,* Capitol, 1978 • *Still Swingin',* Liberty, 1994.

Barron, Kenny: w/ Jimmy Owens, *You Had Better Listen,* Atlantic, 1968 • *Innocence,* Wolf, 1978.

Black Heat: *Black Heat,* Atlantic, 1972 • *No Time to Burn,* Atlantic, 1974.

Braden, Don: *Organic,* Epicure, 1995.

Brown, Oscar Jr.: *Movin' On,* Atlantic, 1972 • *Sin & Soul . . . and Then Some,* Columbia, 1996.

Bryant, Ray: *Alone at Montreux,* Atlantic, 1972.

Burton, Gary: *Gary Burton and Keith Jarrett/Throb,* Rhino, 1970, 1994 • *Alone at Last,* Atlantic, 1971.

Collins, Judy: *Fires of Eden,* CBS, 1990.

Crawford, Hank: *Heart and Soul,* Rhino, 1992.

Edison Electric Band: *Bless You Dr. Woodward,* Cotillion, 1970.

Flack, Roberta: *First Take,* Atlantic, 1969, 1995 • *Chapter Two,* Atlantic, 1970, 1992 • *Quiet Fire,* Atlantic, 1971, 1992 • "The First Time Ever I Saw Your Face," Atlantic, 1972 • "Jesse," Atlantic, 1973 • "Killing Me Softly," Atlantic, 1973 • *Killing Me Softly,* Atlantic, 1973 • *Softly with These Songs: The Best Of,* Atlantic, 1993.

Flack, Roberta, and Donny Hathaway: "You've Got a Friend," Atlantic, 1971 • *Roberta Flack and Donny Hathaway,* Atlantic, 1972, 1995 • "Where Is the Love?," Atlantic, 1972.

Forman, David: *Forman, David,* Arista, 1976.

Goodman, Steve: *Say It in Private,* Asylum, 1977 • *No Big Surprise: Anthology,* Red Pajamas, 1994.

Gordon, Dexter: w/ Junior Mance, *At Montreux,* Prestige, 1970, 1985 • *Blue Dex: Dexter Gordon Plays the Blues,* Prestige, 1973, 1996.

Harris, Eddie: *Silver Cycles,* Atlantic, 1968 • *Tale of Two Cities,* Night, 1983, 1991 • *The Electrifying Eddie Harris/Plug Me In,* Rhino, 1993 • *The Artist's Choice: The Eddie Harris Anthology,* Rhino, 1995.

Hathaway, Donny: *See* Flack, Roberta, and Donny Hathaway.

Hibbler, Al: *See* Kirk, Rahsaan Roland.

Hubbard, Freddie: *High Blues Pressure*, Atlantic, 1968 • *Echoes of Blue*, Atlantic, 1976.

Jarrett, Keith: *Foundations*, Rhino/Atlantic, 1968.

Jazz Passengers: *Individually Twisted*, 32 Records, 1997.

King Curtis and Champion Jack Dupree: *Blues at Montreux*, Atlantic, 1971.

Kirk, Rahsaan Roland: *The Inflated Tear*, Atlantic, 1967, 1991 • *Volunteered Slavery*, Atlantic, 1969 • *Rahsaan, Rahsaan*, Atlantic, 1970 • *Natural Black Inventions: Root Strata*, Atlantic, 1971 • w/ Al Hibbler, *A Meeting of the Times*, Atlantic, 1972 • *Blacknuss*, Atlantic, 1972 • *I, Eye, Aye*, Rhino, 1972, 1996 • *Bright Moments*, Rhino/Atlantic, 1973, 1993 • *Part of the Search*, Atlantic, 1973 • *Prepare Thyself to Deal with a Miracle*, Atlantic, 1973 • *The Art of*, Atlantic, 1973 • *The Case of the 3-Sided Dream in Audio Color*, Atlantic, 1975 • *Does Your House Have Lions? The Anthology*, Rhino, 1976, 1992 • *Other Folk's Music*, Atlantic, 1976 • *The Man Who Cried Fire*, Night, 1977, 1991 • *Boogie Woogie String Along*, Warner Bros., 1978 • *The Vibration Continues*, Atlantic, 1978 • *Simmer, Reduce, Garnish & Serve: The Warner*, Warner Archives, 1995.

Koloc, Bonnie: *Wild and Recluse*, Epic, 1978.

Lancaster, Byard: *It's Not up to Us*, Vortex, 1966.

Lateef, Yusef: *The Blue Yusef Lateef*, Rhino, 1968, 1992 • *The Gentle Giant*, Rhino, 1972, 1987 • *Part of the Search*, Rhino, 1974, 1994 • *10 Years Hence*, Atlantic, 1975 • *Every Vilage Has a Song*, Rhino, 1976, 1993 • *Anthology*, Rhino, 1994 • *The Diverse Yusef Lateef/Suite 16*, Rhino, 1994.

Laws, Hubert: *The Laws of Jazz/Flute By-Laws*, Rhino, 1966, 1994 • *Wild Flower*, Atlantic Jazz, 1972.

Mance, Junior: *See* Dexter, Gordon.

Mann, Herbie: *The Inspiration I Feel*, Atlantic, 1968 • *Evolution of Mann: The Herbie Mann Anthology*, Rhino, 1994.

McCann, Les: *Les Is More*, Atlantic, 1967 • *Much Les*, Atlantic, 1969 • *Swiss Movement*, Atlantic, 1969 • *Invitation to Openess*, Atlantic, 1971 • *Talk to the People*, Atlantic, 1972 • *Layers*, Rhino, 1973, 1993 • *Live at Montreux*, Atlantic, 1973.

McDaniels, Eugene: *Outlaw*, Atlantic, 1971.

McLean, Don: *Homeless Brother*, United Artists, 1974.

Micare, Franklin: *Franklin Micare*, Private Stock, 1978.

Midler, Bette: "*Do You Want to Dance?,*" Atlantic, 1972 • *The Divine Miss M*, Atlantic, 1972 • *Experience the Divine: Bette Midler's Greatest Hits*, Atlantic, 1993.

Mingus, Charles: *At Carnegie Hall*, Atlantic, 1974 • *Mingus at Carnegie Hall*, Rhino, 1975, 1996.

Modern Jazz Quartet: *Celebration*, Atlantic, 1994.

Neville, Aaron: *Orchid in the Storm*, Rhino, 1986.

Neville Brothers: *Fiyo on the Bayou*, A&M, 1981 • *Treacherous: A History of the Neville Brothers*, Rhino, 1988, 1995.

Newman, David "Fathead": *Bigger & Better/The Many Facets of David Newman*, Rhino, 1968, 1993 • *House of David Newman: Fathead Anthology*, Rhino, 1993.

Owens, Jimmy: *See* Barron, Kenny.

Parker, Leon: *Above and Below*, Epicure, 1994 • *Belief*, Columbia, 1996.

Previn, Dory: *We're the Children of Coincidence and Harpo Marx*, Warner Bros., 1976.

Rawls, Lou: *Shades of Blue*, Philadelphia International, 1981.

Redbone, Leon: *On the Track*, Warner Bros., 1975 • *Double Time*, Warner Bros., 1977 • *Champagne Charlie*, Warner Bros., 1978, 1988 • *From Branch to Branch*, Atlantic, 1981.

Roach, Max: *Lift Every Voice and Sing*, Atlantic, 1971.

Roden, Jess: *The Player Not the Game*, Island, 1977 • *Stonechaser*, Island, 1980.

Roomful of Blues: *The First Album*, 32 Records, 1979, 1996 • *Let's Have a Party*, Antilles, 1980.

Sanchez, David: *Street Scenes*, Columbia, 1996.

Sandoval, Arturo: *Flight to Freedom*, GRP, 1991.

Santamaria, Mongo: *Mongo '70*, Atlantic, 1970 • *Lost and Found*, Rhino, 1993.

Siegel, Janis: *Experiment in White*, Atlantic, 1982.

Silver, Horace: *Re-Entry*, Thirty-Two, 1996.

Simon, Lucy: *Lucy Simon*, RCA, 1975.

Tommy Dorsey Band: *Featuring Buddy Morrow*, MCA, 1981.

Vance 32: *Vance 32*, Atlantic, 1975.

Vance, Kenny, and the Planotones: *Looking for An Echo*, 32 Records, 1996.

Wheeler, Clarence: *And the Enforcers*, Atlantic, 1970.

Zawinul, Joe: *The Rise and Fall of The Third Stream/Money in the Pocket*, Rhino, 1967, 1994 • *Concerto Retitled*, Atlantic, 1970, 1976 • *Zawinul*, Rhino/Atlantic, 1970, 1995.

COLLECTIONS

Ertegun's New York, New York, Atlantic, 1987.

Singers, Atlantic Jazz, 1987.

Saxophones, Vol. 2, Atlantic Jazz/Rhino, 1988.

The History of Chess Jazz, Chess, 1996.

COMPILATIONS

Coltrane, John: *The Last Giant: John Coltrane*, Rhino, 1993 • *The Heavyweight Champion: The Complete Atlantic Recordings*, Rhino, 1995.

Criss, Sonny: *Out of Nowhere*, 32 Records, 1976, 1997.

Mingus, Charles: *Thirteen Pictures: The Charles Mingus Anthology*, Rhino, 1993.

REISSUES

Holiday, Billie: *The Complete Commodore Recordings*, GRP, 1997.

Jackson, Willis: *Bar Wars*, 32 Records, 1977, 1997.

Jack Douglas

Jack Douglas has had one of production's most colorful careers. A New Yorker who started playing folk music in the early '60s, he wrote campaign songs and performed at rallies for Robert Kennedy and Lyndon Johnson in 1964. Then the Beatles had a profound impact on him.

Just out of high school, he and pal Eddie Leonetti (who also became a producer before moving on to hairdressing) sailed to Liverpool on a tramp steamer carrying bananas (and tarantulas) from South America. "We arrived in England with our guitars and amps, no return ticket, no work permit," Douglas says. "We were held on a prison ship. I escaped and went to a newspaper office. I thought there was an angle there. They sent us back on the ship and hired girls to come and scream when we got off the ship. They said as long as we sent our guitars back to America, we could stay.

"That week, the Beatles were playing a homecoming concert in Liverpool. The Beatles should've had the front page to themselves, but it was split. We got into a band because we were celebrities. After a few months we got caught and got deported."

Back home, Douglas played in several bands with recording contracts and minor hits. On one project, he found himself in the control room, demonstrating what the group was aiming for. He was hooked: "I never wanted to go back to playing in a band."

He started at the Record Plant in 1969 as a janitor while attending the Institute of Audio Research as part of its first class. He worked up to assistant engineering on John Lennon's *Imagine* album under engineer Roy Cicala.

"After one session, I said to John, 'I've been to Liverpool.' He said, 'What the hell were you doing there?' I told him what happened. He said, 'I remember those two idiots.' He thought it was funny."

Among the producers Douglas was working with and learning from were Bill Szymczyk (see entry), Kit Lambert, and Bob Ezrin (see entry)—especially the latter. "He had everything. He was a brilliant arranger, a great musician, and had some technical knowledge," Douglas recalls. "He took charge in the studio, and he didn't get coked out of his mind. He was also honest, a difficult thing to be in the studio."

Douglas engineered the New York Dolls' 1973, Todd Rundgren–produced (see entry) debut, whose spontaneous, raw-edged sound foretold the sound of '70s punk.

Douglas says he also did some of the production work.

"Todd didn't want to involve himself once he got into the studio and found they couldn't play. It was done in a stupor, but it was a fun record. Todd came in and mixed it in one day, and that's what it needed."

Ezrin had a Canadian production company and brought Douglas there to hone his skills "out of town." He worked on Alice Cooper's *School's Out* and *Billion Dollar Babies* albums and produced a Crowbar album that went gold in Canada. Finally, Ezrin passed on Cooper's *Muscle of Love* (No. 10) album and gave it to Douglas to produce. "There was no looking back," says Douglas. He went on to produce Rick Derringer, Starz, Patti Smith, Cheap Trick, Graham Parker, and, most famously, Aerosmith.

Aerosmith was considering Ezrin for its second album, but again, Erzin found the music not to his taste and recommended Douglas. The connection led to a long relationship.

"I went to Boston to hear the band," Douglas recalls. "and I dug 'em. It was R&B-based and you really had to groove to it. They couldn't play that well at the time, but the energy was great. Our age and backgrounds were the same. We got along instantly."

Although the pairing produced some of Aerosmith's classic albums, including *Rocks* (No. 3) and *Toys in the Attic* (No. 11), they're sonically uneven, often surprisingly muddy and flat-sounding, with indistinct vocals. *Toys in the Attic* and *Rocks*, although they contain some classic material, suffer when compared to the crispness of Douglas's work on Starz' 1975 debut, which dramatically separates the instruments and outlines and emphasizes the wailing bluesiness of Michael Lee Smith's voice. Douglas hints at an explanation.

"Eventually, we got so fucked up we couldn't work anymore," he says. "Everybody was hitting the skids. I partied just as hard as they did. Drugs were first a cool thing, then they were a tool, then a disaster. In 1982, after *Rock in a Hard Place*, we severed our professional relationship."

By then, a revived relationship from the past had led to success followed by tragedy. In 1979, Douglas got a call from Lennon and was flown out to Lennon's estate on Long Island to become involved in clandestine plans for the ex-Beatle's return to music.

"He was going to make a record but it had to be a secret," says Douglas. "We had to write the charts, book the band and studio, rehearse, and no one was to know who it was for," Douglas says. "I was recording for a month before the press was onto it. He was insecure about whether he had the goods to make a record." The excitement surrounding *Double Fantasy* (No. 1),

Lennon's first new album in five years, turned dark when Lennon was murdered in December 1980, scant weeks after the album's release. Douglas was with him that night.

"I went into a spin," he recalls. "I was eating Valium. I did the Knack's third record [*Round Trip*] during that period and they still think I destroyed their career."

So Douglas called time out. "I didn't want to embarrass myself anymore," he says. "I didn't need the money so I took 10 years off and got to know my kids. Now my kids are in college and I decided a year and a half ago to go back to work. I had built a MIDI studio at my house, and put in ProTools and Performer. This dinosaur knows what he's doing."

He jumped in with Supertramp's 1996 *Some Things Never Change* and was soon booked solid with acts like Clutch, Core, and Black 47. Douglas loves the willingness of artists today to mix styles and sounds. "You can mix rap with an Irish jig. You can turn bluegrass into new grass and put it in a heavy metal record. You can make folk into alternative. You can do incredible things mixing analog and digital. I love playing with new things. I'm not one of those guys who, if an artist makes a crazy suggestion, says, 'You can't do that.' "

Calling himself a "musician and a song guy," Douglas says he's known "long preproduction periods, working on arrangements. I try to make a band record, not a Jack Douglas record. I'm thought of as a guy that's pretty easy to get along with in the studio. I tell artists upfront, 'If we're going to live together for a few months, let's have some fun. We're blessed individuals if this is what we're doing for a living.' It's a joyous celebration to make a record." —ANASTASIA PANTSIOS

Aerosmith: *Get Your Wings*, Columbia, 1974 • *Toys in the Attic*, Columbia, 1975 • "Walk This Way," Columbia, 1976 • *Rocks*, Columbia, 1976 • *Draw the Line*, Columbia, 1977 • "Come Together," Columbia, 1978 • *Live Bootleg*, Columbia, 1978 • *Greatest Hits*, Columbia, 1980 • *Rock in a Hard Place*, Columbia, 1982 • *Pandora's Box*, Columbia, 1991.

Alice Cooper: *Muscle of Love*, Warner Bros., 1973 • *Greatest Hits*, Warner Bros., 1974, 1988.

Artful Dodger: *Artful Dodger*, Columbia, 1975 • *Honor Among Thieves*, Columbia, 1976 • *Babes on Broadway*, Columbia, 1977.

Bux: *We Came to Play*, Capitol, 1976.

Cheap Trick: *Cheap Trick*, Epic, 1977 • "Ain't That a Shame," Epic, 1979 • "I Want You to Want Me," Epic, 1979 • *At the Budokan*, Epic, 1979 • *Found All the Parts* (EP), Epic, 1980 • *Standing on the Edge*, Epic, 1985 • *Sex America Cheap Trick*, Sony, 1996.

Crowbar: *Crowbar*, Epic, 1973.

Derringer, Rick: *Rock and Roll Hootchie Koo: The Best Of*, Sony, 1996.

Dufay, Rick: *Tender Loving Abuse*, Polydor, 1980.

Harlequin: *Love Crimes*, CBS, 1981 • *One False Move*, CBS, 1982 • *Harlequin*, Epic, 1985.

Knack, The: "Boys Go Crazy," Capitol, 1981 • "Pay the Devil (Ooo Baby Ooo)," Capitol, 1981 • *Round Trip*, Capitol, 1981 • *Retrospective: The Best of the Knack*, Capitol, 1992.

Lawrence, Karen: *Girls' Night Out*, RCA, 1981.

Lennon, John: w/ Yoko Ono, *Double Fantasy*, Geffen, 1980 • "(Just Like) Starting Over," Geffen, 1980 • "Woman," Geffen, 1980 • "Watching the Wheels," Geffen, 1981 • *The John Lennon Collection*, Capitol, 1990.

Miller, Frankie: *Double Trouble*, Chrysalis, 1976 • *The Very Best Of*, Chrysalis, 1993.

Montrose: *Jump on It*, Warner Bros., 1976.

Moxy: *Ridin' High*, Mercury, 1977.

Nineteen Ninety Four: *1994*, A&M, 1978 • *Please Stand By*, A&M, 1979.

Ono, Yoko: *See* Lennon, John.

Parker, Graham: *Another Grey Area*, RCA, 1982 • *Passion Is No Ordinary Word: The Graham Parker Anthology*, Rhino, 1993.

Joe Perry Project: *Let the Music Do the Talking*, Columbia, 1980.

Rockets, The: *Back Talk*, Elektra, 1981.

Schenker, Michael: *Assault Attack/Rock Will Never Die*, Beat Goes On, 1996.

Sha Na Na: *Hot Sox*, Kuma Sutra, 1974.

Smith, Patti: w/ Patti Smith Group, "Pissing in the River," RSO, 1976, 1980 (*Times Square* soundtrack) • *Radio Ethiopia*, Arista, 1976 • *Masters*, Arista, 1996.

Starz: *Starz*, Capitol, 1976 • "Cherry Baby," Capitol, 1977 • *Violation*, Capitol, 1977.

Zebra: *Zebra*, Atlantic, 1983 • *No Tellin' Lies*, Atlantic, 1984.

Tom Dowd

"I t's like going from a Piper Cub to landing on the moon," says legendary producer Tom Dowd of the technological changes he has seen since he entered the recording industry more than 50 years ago.

"The recording industry in 1947 was operating on used radio consoles because nobody was designing equipment for recording studios," Dowd explains, adding that he designed the first eight-channel console for Atlantic Records because no commercial counterpart was available.

After joining Atlantic in 1954, Dowd became involved in virtually every aspect of the recording process: from the original session to postproduction to disc mastering. During his tenure at Atlantic, he worked with such diverse acts as Aretha Franklin, Ornette Coleman, Joe Turner, Charles Mingus, the Drifters, and the Young Rascals. "Every session was an adventure," Dowd recalls. "You could be doing the Coasters at two in the afternoon and Mingus at two in the morning."

Dowd says that Atlantic Records, an independent in its early years, could challenge major labels such as Columbia, Victor, Decca, and EMI because it was developing artists "in a market that they didn't know existed, or if they knew existed didn't know how to cope with."

Dowd is understandably proud of Atlantic's storied past, particularly in light of the obstacles faced by what was then a struggling independent. "Victor, Columbia, and EMI were using cutting heads that cost $2,000 and $3,000 apiece and weighed 9 pounds," Dowd points out. "We were trying to compete with $150 and $200 cutter heads. We were going by the seat of our trousers."

Dowd made the transition from engineering to production by becoming a valuable technical resource in the studio. For instance, he constructed finished masters by using bits and pieces from various takes of a song, blurring the distinction between engineering and production.

"Here I am mixing down the first and third take up to point X, figuring out which one I want to use for the intro and which one for the chorus, then back to the other one until we get to the solo," Dowd explains. "All of a sudden I'm coming from a different place than they're accustomed to."

When he left Atlantic at the end of the '60s, Dowd quickly established himself as one of rock's preeminent producers, supervising such classics as *Live at Fillmore East* (No. 13) by the Allman Brothers Band and *Layla* (No. 16) by Derek and the Dominoes, an album Dowd considers one of his proudest moments. Yet, *Layla* was initially a commercial failure. "When I walked out of the studio after having done that album, I said, 'That's the best album I have made since *The Genius of Ray Charles,*'" Dowd recalls. "When it didn't sell I was talking to myself saying 'I'm wrong. There's something missing somewhere.' But Atlantic stuck to their guns, and a year later the thing was the rock 'n' roll national anthem of the world."

Dowd also collaborated with Eric Clapton on *461 Ocean Boulevard* (No. 1), *There's One in Every Crowd* (No. 21), and *EC Was Here* (No. 20), albums that included such songs as "I Shot the Sheriff" (No. 1), "Let It Grow," "Further On up the Road" and "Knocking on Heaven's Door."

Moreover, Dowd produced Rod Stewart's *Atlantic Crossing* (No. 9) and *A Night on the Town* (No. 2), featuring such tracks as "The First Cut Is the Deepest" (No. 21), "Sailing," "Tonight's the Night" (No. 1), and Stewart's first rendering of "This Old Heart of Mine." For *Atlantic Crossing*, Stewart's first American recording, Dowd suggested setting up shop in Muscle Shoals, Alabama, using such players as guitarist Steve Cropper (see entry) and the famed Muscle Shoals Rhythm Section. However, Stewart was shocked to discover that the band Dowd hired was not quite as he envisaged.

"We go into the studio [Muscle Shoals Sound] and here's Barry [Beckett; see entry], Jimmy [Johnson], David [Hood], and Roger [Hawkins]," Dowd remembers. "I introduce them to Rod and he gives me a nod like 'I want to see you outside.' Outside the studio door Rod says, 'You lied to me. That is not the band that you meant. They're all white.' All of a sudden, they start running down one of the songs and Rod stops in the middle of the conversation and slides over to the door, cracks it open, looks in and sees it's them playing, and says, 'I have never been so humiliated in my life. I swore they were all black.' "

Dowd's appointment book was perpetually full during the '70s and '80s, when he produced the likes of Eddie Money, Wet Willie, the James Gang, Lynyrd Skynyrd, Pablo Cruise, Firefall, and Wishbone Ash. Since much of Dowd's post-Atlantic recordings were produced at Criteria Studios in Miami, his adopted home, it is not surprising that he prefers staying close to southern Florida.

"With the cost of recording today, I'll go wherever the group is most comfortable, as long as the facility is professional," says Dowd. "When it comes to remixing I prefer working here in the warm climate, either at Criteria or [South Beach] Studios."

Even after a half-century in the industry, Dowd adapts to changing technology with a young man's ease. And while he loves digital technology, he hopes tape will eventually be eliminated as a recording medium. "Recording systems are still dragging an abrasive iron oxide tape across a head, wearing grooves in the head, and wearing the oxide off the tape," Dowd says. "We have to get rid of friction. I look forward to the day when we go to completely optic recording." —BEN CROMER

Allman Brothers Band: *Allman Brothers Band*, Atco, 1969 • *At Fillmore East*, Capricorn, 1969 • *Idlewild South*, Polydor, 1970 • *Eat a Peach*, Capricorn, 1971 • *Enlightened Rogues*, Capricorn, 1972 • *The Road Goes on Forever*, Polydor, 1975 •

Dreams, Polydor, 1989 • *Seven Turns,* Epic, 1990 • *Shades of Two Worlds,* Epic, 1991 • *An Evening with the Allman Brothers,* Epic, 1992 • "No One to Run With," 550 Music/Epic, 1994 (*The Cowboy Way* soundtrack) • *Where It All Begins,* Epic, 1994 • *2nd Set,* Epic, 1995.

Allman, Duane: *Anthology,* Capricorn, 1972 • *Anthology II,* Capricorn, 1974.

Bee Gees: *Tales from the Brothers Gibb,* Polydor, 1990.

Blackjack: *Blackjack,* Polydor, 1979.

Black Oak Arkansas: *Raunch 'n' Roll Live,* Atco, 1972 • *Street Party,* Atco, 1974 • *Best Of,* Atco, 1977 • *If An Angel Came to See You Would You Make Her Feel at Home,* Atco, 1979 • *Hot and Nasty: The Best Of,* Rhino, 1993.

Booker T. and the MGs: *Universal Language,* Asylum, 1977.

Burke, Solomon: *Home in Your Heart: Best of Solomon Burke* (7 tracks), Rhino, 1992.

Canned Heat: *The Ties That Bind,* Archive/Paradigm, 1997.

Cate Brothers: *Fire on the Tracks,* Atlantic, 1976.

Cher: *3614 Jackson Highway,* Atlantic, 1969.

Chicago: *XIV,* Columbia, 1980 • *If You Leave Me Now,* Columbia, 1982.

Chubby, Popa: *Booty and the Beast,* Okeh, 1995.

Clapton, Eric: *461 Ocean Blvd.,* RSO, 1974 • "I Shot the Sheriff," RSO, 1974 • *E.C. Was Here,* RSO, 1975 • "Knockin' on Heaven's Door," RSO, 1975 • *There's One in Every Crowd,* RSO, 1975 • *Another Ticket,* RSO, 1981 • "I Can't Stand It," RSO, 1981 • "I've Got a Rock and Roll Heart," Duck, 1983 • *Money and Cigarettes,* Duck, 1983 • *August,* Duck, 1986 • *Crossroads,* Polydor, 1988 • *Crossroads 2: Live in the 70's,* Chronicles/Polydor, 1996.

Conley, Arthur: "Funky Street," Atco, 1968.

Coolidge, Rita: *Inside the Fire,* A&M, 1984.

Copperhead: *Copperhead,* Mercury, 1992.

De Shannon, Jackie: *Jackie,* Atlantic, 1972.

Delaney and Bonnie: *To Delaney from Bonnie,* Atco, 1970 • *The Best Of,* Rhino, 1972, 1990.

Derek and the Dominoes: "Layla," Atco, 1970, 1972 • *Layla,* Atco, 1970.

Dickinson, James Luther: *Dixie Fried,* Atlantic, 1972.

Dr. John: *Remedies,* Atco, 1970 • *Mos' Scocious: The Dr. John Anthology,* Rhino, 1993.

Drifters, The: *Rockin' and Driftin': The Box Set,* Rhino, 1996.

Earl, Ronnie, and the Broadcasters: *The Color of Love,* Verve, 1997.

Ellis, Tinsley: *Fire It Up,* Alligator, 1996.

Firefall: "Strange Way," Atlantic, 1978 • *Elan,* Atlantic, 1978 • *Greatest Hits,* Rhino, 1992.

Franklin, Aretha: *Aretha Arrives,* Atlantic, 1967 • *I Never Loved a Man the Way I Love You,* Atlantic, 1967 • *Aretha Now,* Atlantic, 1968 • "Think," Atlantic, 1968 • "Eleanor Rigby," Atlantic, 1969 • "Share Your Love with Me," Atlantic, 1969 • *Soul '69,* Atlantic, 1969 • "The Weight," Atlantic, 1969 •

"Call Me," Atlantic, 1970 • "Don't Play That Song," Atlantic, 1970 • *Spirit in the Dark,* Atlantic, 1970 • *This Girl's in Love with You,* Atlantic, 1970 • "Bridge over Troubled Water," Atlantic, 1971 • "Rock Steady," Atlantic, 1971 • "Spanish Harlem," Atlantic, 1971 • "You're All I Need to Get By," Atlantic, 1971 • *Aretha's Jazz,* Atlantic, 1972, 1984 • "Day Dreaming," Atlantic, 1972 • *Young, Gifted and Black,* Atlantic, 1972 • *Let Me in Your Life,* Rhino/Atlantic, 1974, 1995 • *With Everything I Feel in Me,* Atlantic, 1974 • *Ten Years of Gold,* Atlantic, 1976 • *Love All the Hurt Away,* Arista, 1981 • *30 Greatest Hits,* Atlantic, 1986 • *Queen of Soul: The Atlantic Recordings,* Rhino, 1992 • *The Very Best Of,* Vols. 1–2, Rhino, 1994 • *Love Songs,* Atlantic, 1997.

Guy, Buddy: w/ Junior Wells, *Play the Blues,* Atlantic, 1972.

Hawkins, Ronnie: *Ronnie Hawkins,* Atlantic, 1970 • *The Hawk,* Atlantic, 1971.

Iron Butterfly: *Light and Heavy: The Best of Iron Butterfly,* Rhino, 1993.

James Gang: *Miami,* Atlantic, 1974 • *Newborn,* Atlantic, 1975.

James Montgomery Band: *High Roller,* Capricorn, 1974.

James, Colin: *Colin James,* Virgin, 1989.

Jo Mama: *J Is for Jump,* Atlantic, 1971.

King Curtis: *Instant Groove,* Edsel, 1968 • *Live at Small's Paradise,* Atlantic, 1966 • w/ the Kingpins, "Mempis Soul Stew," Atco, 1967.

King, Ben E.: *Anthology,* Atlantic, 1993.

King, Freddie: *Burglar,* PolyGram, 1974.

Lewis, John: *The Wonderful World of Jazz,* Atlantic Jazz, 1961, 1989.

Loggins, Kenny: *Keep the Fire,* Columbia, 1979 • "This Is It," Columbia, 1980 • *Yesterday, Today and Tomorrow: The Greatest Hits,* Sony, 1997.

Love and Money: *All You Need Is . . . ,* Mercury, 1986.

Lulu: *Melody Fair,* Atco, 1970 • "Oh Me Oh My(I'm a Fool for You Baby)," Atco, 1970 • *From Crayons to Pefume: The Best of Lulu,* Rhino, 1994.

Lynyrd Skynyrd: *Gimme Back My Bullets,* MCA, 1976 • *One More from the Road,* MCA, 1976 • *Street Survivors,* MCA, 1977 • *Best of the Rest,* MCA, 1982 • *Legend,* MCA, 1987 • *Skynyrd's Innyrds: Their Greatest Hits,* MCA, 1989 • *Their Greatest Hits,* MCA, 1989 • *Lynyrd Skynyrd,* MCA, 1991 • *Lynyrd Skynyrd, 1991,* Atlantic, 1991.

Mann, Herbie: *Best Of,* Atlantic, 1969 • *Memphis Underground,* MCA, 1969 • *Evolution of Mann: The Herbie Mann Anthology,* Rhino, 1994.

Mardin, Arif: *Glass Onion,* Atlantic, 1969.

Marshall Tucker Band: *Dedicated,* Atlantic, 1981.

Meat Loaf: *Midnight at the Lost and Found,* Epic, 1983.

Midler, Bette: *Live at Last,* Atlantic, 1977.

Money, Eddie: "Think I'm in Love," Columbia, 1982 • *No Control,* Columbia, 1982 • *Where's the Party,* Columbia,

1983 • *Greatest Hits: The Sound of Money*, Columbia, 1989 • *Super Hits*, Columbia, 1997.

Newman, David "Fathead": *House of David Newman: Fathead Anthology*, Rhino, 1993.

original soundtrack: *Family Thing*, Edeltone, 1996.

Pablo Cruise: *Reflector*, A&M, 1971 • "Cool Love," A&M, 1981.

Phillips, Esther: *The Best Of, 1962–1970*, Rhino, 1997.

Pickett, Wilson: *The Exciting Wilson Pickett*, Atlantic, 1966 • "I Found a True Love," Atlantic, 1967 • *I'm in Love*, Atlantic, 1967 • *The Sound of Wilson Pickett*, Atlantic, 1967 • "I'm a Midnight Mover," Atlantic, 1968 • "She's Looking Good," Atlantic, 1968 • "Sugar, Sugar," Atlantic, 1970 • *Man and a Half: The Best Of*, Atlantic, 1992.

Primal Scream: "Funky Jam," Creation, 1994 • *Give Out But Don't Give In*, Sire, 1994 • "Rocks," Creation, 1994.

Ramatam: *Ramatam*, Atlantic, 1972.

Rascals, The: "I Ain't Gonna Eat Out My Heart Anymore," Atlantic, 1965 • "I've Been Lonely Too Long, Atlantic, 1967 • *The Very Best Of*, Rhino, 1993.

Redding, Otis: *Live in Europe*, Atco, 1967.

Reid, Terry: *River*, Atlantic, 1973.

Roberts, Bruce: *Bruce Roberts*, Elektra, 1977.

Ross, Diana: *Endless Love*, Mercury, 1981 • *Greatest Hits: The RCA Years*, RCA, 1997.

Sam and Dave: *Sweat and Soul Anthology*, Vol. 2, Rhino, 1993.

Samudio, Sam "The Sham": *Hard and Heavy*, Atlantic, 1971.

Sloan, P.F.: *Measure of Pleasure*, Atco, 1968.

Souther Hillman Furay Band: *Trouble in Paradise*, Asylum, 1975.

Springfield, Dusty: *A Girl Called Dusty*, Fontana, 1964, 1970 • *Dusty in Memphis*, Atlantic, 1968 • "Son of a Preacher Man," Atlantic, 1969 • "Son of a Preacher Man," MCA, 1994 (*Pulp Fiction* soundtrack) • *Anthology*, PolyGram, 1997.

Stewart, Rod: *A Night on the Town*, Warner Bros., 1975 • *Atlantic Crossing*, Warner Bros., 1975 • "Tonight's the Night," Warner Bros., 1976 • *Footloose and Nancy Free*, Warner Bros., 1977 • "The First Cut Is the Deepest," Warner Bros., 1977 • *Blondes Have More Fun*, Warner Bros., 1978 • "You're in My Heart," Warner Bros., 1978 • "Ain't Love a Bitch," Warner Bros., 1979 • "Da Ya Think I'm Sexy?," Warner Bros., 1979 • *Foolish Behaviour* (1 track), Warner Bros., 1980 • "Baby Jane," Warner Bros., 1983 • *Body Wishes*, Warner Bros., 1983 • *Storyteller: The Complete Anthology*, Warner Bros., 1989 • *Downtown Train*, Warner Bros., 1990 • *If We Fall in Love Tonight*, Warner Bros., 1996.

Stills-Young Band: *Long May You Run*, Reprise, 1976.

Sullivan, Ira: *Horizons*, Discovery, 1983.

Sweet Inspirations: "Sweet Inspiration," Atlantic, 1968.

Tate, Eric Quincy: *Eric Quincy Tate*, Cotillion, 1971.

Taxxi: *Expose*, MCA, 1985.

Vera, Billy, and the Beaters: *Retro Nuevo*, Capitol, 1988.

Walden, Narada Michael: *Garden of Love Light*, Atlantic, 1976 • *Ecstasy's Dance: The Best Of*, Rhino, 1996.

Walker, Jerry Jeff: *Mr. Bojangles*, Atco, 1968 • *Bein' Free*, Atco, 1970.

Wells, Junior: *See* Guy, Buddy.

Wet Willie: "Keep on Smilin'," Capricorn, 1971 • *Dixie Rock*, Capricorn, 1974 • *Keep on Smilin*, Capricorn, 1974 • *Greatest Hits*, Capricorn, 1977.

White, Tony Joe: *Home Made Ice Cream*, Warner Bros., 1972 • *The Train I'm On*, Atlantic, 1972 • *The Best Of*, Warner Bros., 1973.

Wishbone Ash: *Locked In*, MCA, 1976.

Young Rascals: *Collections*, Atlantic, 1966 • "Good Lovin'," Atlantic, 1966 • *Young Rascals*, Atlantic, 1966.

Lamont Dozier

See HOLLAND-DOZIER-HOLLAND

Dr. Dre

Not many rap producers can lay claim to being behind two of the most acclaimed and popular rap albums in history. The production team of the Bomb Squad (see entry) can. So can the dynamo Dr. Dre, thanks to his 1992 album *The Chronic* (No. 3) and his work on Snoop Doggy Dogg's 1993 album, *Doggystyle* (No. 1).

The trip to the top of the rap industry by the Compton, California-bred Dre (born Andre Young, February 18, 1965) was unexpected, considering his musical beginnings: producing acts like the underrated Michel Le as well as the World Class Wreckin' Crew and Cli-N-Tel, as early as 1984. Dre didn't show his true capabilities until he played a part in N.W.A (Niggaz With Attitude) alongside Ice Cube (see entry) and the late Eazy-E. Dre was one of the last N.W.A members to leave. And when he did, there was no stopping him as a producer or rapper.

On *The Chronic*, the Dre production is a tour de force of up-to-the-minute G-funk that continues to age nicely. Dre, whose sinister, edgy style would carry over into later productions, liberally utilized old-school funk, such as "Mothership Connection" by Parliament, on "Let Me Ride." *The Chronic* was also significant in spotlighting Snoop Dogg on more than half the songs, including "Dre Day" (No. 8), "Nuthin' But a G Thang" (No. 2), "The Day the Niggaz Took Over" and "Rat-Tat-Tat-Tat." The album also put Death Row Records on the map.

Instead of following *The Chronic* with another Dr. Dre album, Dre put his efforts into Dogg's debut, *Doggystyle,* also on Death Row. The album was another G-funk keeper, spanning Curtis Mayfield (see entry) samples, a new performance by the Dramatics on "Doggy Dogg World," and instant classics in Dogg's "Lodi Dodi" cover, "Murder Was the Case," "Doggy Dogg World," and "Gin and Juice" (No. 8).

When Dogg released his 1996 follow-up, *Tha Doggfather,* a key criticism was that it wasn't the Snoop fans had grown to love on *Doggystyle.* It wasn't. Dre doesn't figure on *Doggfather.*

Dre, unlike some other hip-hop producers, hasn't spread his sound all over the industry. He produces sparingly; in the mid-'90s, he has confined his productions to such Death Row acts as Dogg, 2Pac ("California Love," No. 6), the Lady of Rage ("Afro Puffs") and Jewell ("Harvest for the World"). Only after Death Row began collapsing in 1996 with the fatal shooting of 2Pac Shakur and the arrest and imprisonment of Death Row CEO Suge Knight did Dre venture forth, notably on *Nas Is Coming* and a guest rap appearance on Blackstreet's "No Diggity."

After he quit Death Row, Dre resurfaced with his own company, Aftermath Entertainment, which released *Dr. Dre Presents . . . The Aftermath* in 1996. The album was a compilation of new acts, with production from Dre on "Shittin' on the World" by Mel-Man, "Blunt Time" by RBX, and RC's "Fame" and "Sexy Dance." Although the disc was an effective introduction to Aftermath Entertainment and a good blend of rap and R&B, it disappointed fans seeking an all-out Dre assault. Even the two songs featuring classic Dre— "Been There Done That" and Group Therapy's "East Coast/West Coast Killas"—didn't appease their appetites. The latter, which featured Dre rapping alongside Nas, Cypress Hill's B-Real, and KRS-One, was an attempt to show unity between East Coast and West Coast rap factions. In 1997, Aftermath Entertainment signed former En Vogue vocalist Dawn Robinson to a solo contract. —KEVIN JOHNSON

2Pac: *All Eyez on Me* (2 tracks), Death Row, 1996 • w/ KC and Jojo, "How Do You Want It/California Love," Death

Row/Interscope, 1996.

Above the Law: "Freedom of Speech," MCA, 1990 (*Pump Up the Volume* soundtrack) • *Livin' Like Hustlers,* Epic, 1990.

D.O.C., The: "It's Funky Enough," Atlantic, 1989 • "No One Can Do It Better," Atlantic, 1989 • "The D.O.C. and the Doctor," Atlantic, 1989 • *No One Can Do It Better,* Atlantic, 1989.

Decadent Dub Team: "Six Gun," Warner Bros., 1988 (*Colors* soundtrack).

Dre, Dr.: *The Chronic,* Priority/Interscope, 1992 • "Dre Day," Death Row, 1993 • "Let Me Ride," Death Row, 1993 • "Nuthin' But a G Thang," Death Row, 1993 • *Concrete Roots,* Triple X, 1994 • w/ Ice Cube, "Natural Born Killaz," Death Row, 1994 (*Murder Was the Case* soundtrack) • "Keep Their Heads Ringin'," Priority, 1995 • *Back in the Day,* Blue Dolphin, 1996 • *First Round Knockout,* Triple X, 1996.

Eazy-E: "The Boyz-N-The-Hood," Ruthless, 1987 • "We Want Eazy," Ruthless, 1989.

Firm, The: *The Firm,* Aftermath, 1997.

Ice Cube: *See* Dr. Dre

Jewell: "Harvest for the World," Death Row, 1994 (*Murder Was the Case* soundtrack).

Jimmy Z: *Muzical Madness,* Ruthless/Atco, 1991.

JJ Fad: "Way Out," Ruthless, 1988 • *Supersonic,* Ruthless, 1988.

Lady of Rage: "Afro Puffs," Death Row/Interscope, 1994 (*Above the Rim* soundtrack).

Michel'le: "Nicety," Ruthless, 1990 • "No More Lies," Ruthless, 1990 • "No More Lies" (remix), Ruthless, 1990 • "Something in My Heart," Ruthless, 1991.

N.W.A: "8-Ball," Ruthless, 1987 • "Dope Man," Ruthless, 1987 • "Panic Zone," Ruthless, 1987 • *Straight Outta Compton,* Ruthless/Priority, 1988 • "Express Yourself," Ruthless/Priority, 1989 • *Efil4Zaggin,* Ruthless, 1991 • *Niggaz4life,* Priority, 1991.

Nas: *It Was Written,* Columbia, 1996.

Party, The: *Free,* Hollywood, 1992.

Snoop Doggy Dogg: "What's My Name?," Death Row, 1993 • *Doggystyle,* Death Row/Interscope, 1993 • "Gin and Juice," Interscope, 1994 • "Murder Was the Case," Death Row, 1994 (*Murder Was the Case* soundtrack).

Tha Dogg Pound: *Dogg Food,* Death Row, 1995.

West Coast All-Stars: "We're All in the Same Gang," Warner Bros., 1990.

COMPILATIONS

Above the Rim soundtrack, Death Row/Interscope, 1994.

Dr. Dre Presents . . . The Aftermath, Aftermath/Interscope, 1996.

Death Row's Greatest Hits, Death Row, 1996.

Gus Dudgeon

In 1969, DJM Records hired producer Gus Dudgeon to oversee the second album by a struggling pianist and songwriter who did sessions to make ends meet: Elton John. Dudgeon says the timid John was not even sure he wanted to be a performer.

"He saw himself as a songwriter," Dudgeon recalls. "I was primarily commissioned to do the Elton John album as sort of a glamorous demo. We cut the album in a week, and I never stopped grinning from beginning to end because it all fell into place so brilliantly." With tracks such as "Your Song" (No. 8), "Take Me to the Pilot," and "Sixty Years On," the *Elton John* album (No. 4) was the start of a fruitful partnership that lasted throughout the '70s.

The John-Dudgeon collaboration resulted in a multitude of classic singles: "Rocket Man" (No. 6), "Daniel" (No. 2), "Saturday Night's Alright for Fighting" (No. 12), "Goodbye Yellow Brick Road" (No. 2), "Don't Let the Sun Go Down on Me" (No. 2), "Someone Saved My Life Tonight" (No. 4), and "Sorry Seems to Be the Hardest

Word" (No. 6). Dudgeon's role was to put the disparate pieces together from the sessions, guaranteeing the finished product as an accurate representation of the performances.

"Once Elton had done what he had to do, which was play the piano and sing, he left," Dudgeon explains, adding that John gave him complete freedom to craft the finished tracks. "Whatever you hear on the records that's over and above the essential construction of the song is down to myself and whoever else was working in the studio. I also used to dub things onto the record that he actually didn't hear until the record came out," adds Dudgeon mischievously. "It became a bit of a game. 'I Think I'm Gonna Kill Myself' wound up with a tap dancer on it," he says with a laugh.

Born September 30, 1942, in Surrey, England, Dudgeon began his career in the early '60s in London as a tea boy at the original Olympic Studios before landing at Decca Records' studios in West Hempstead. At Decca, Dudgeon engineered the Zombies' classic single "She's Not There," a task given to him when the first engineer was unable to complete the session.

"The producer [Ken Jones] just turned around and said, 'Right, it's time for you to take over.' I wound up continuing to do all their sessions after that. As an engineer, that was my first No. 1."

Dudgeon was also responsible for engineering one of the groundbreaking albums of the '60s: *John Mayall with Eric Clapton: Blues Breakers.* Dudgeon and Mike Vernon (see entry) collaborated on other blues recordings for Decca, including albums by Ten Years After and Savoy Brown. By then, Dudgeon had determined that production was the most satisfying function in the studio.

"I never really classified myself as a great engineer; I just loved music," Dudgeon insists. "I was interested in the construction of songs and the combination of sounds [of different instruments]."

Dudgeon's first production job was an album for EMI by Zoot Money's Big Roll Band, a group that included future Animals and Police guitarist Andy Summers. Dudgeon became an independent producer in 1968, working with such acts as Ralph McTell, the Strawbs and the Bonzo Dog Band, the legendary musical comedy troupe that included Neil Innes and Larry "Legs" Smith (see Gerry Bron entry). He also produced David Bowie's monumental single "Space Oddity" (No. 15) when Bowie's regular producer, Tony Visonti, declined to work on the track because he didn't like it.

In 1971, Dudgeon produced John's *Tumbleweed Connection* (No. 5) and *Madman Across the Water* (No. 8), demonstrating his uncanny ability to capture the drama in John's music on such tracks as "Burn Down the Mission," "Tiny Dancer," and "Madman Across the Water." By 1972, John was making so much money that he began to work offshore for tax purposes, so Dudgeon relocated the sessions to a studio in France, the Chateau, for *Honky Chateau, Don't Shoot Me, I'm Only the Piano Player,* and *Goodbye Yellow Brick Road* (all No. 1).

Dudgeon says that John was so prolific he needed only five days to write music for an album. "He would arrive five days before anyone else and write all the songs," Dudgeon marvels. Dudgeon also points out that *Goodbye Yellow Brick Road* was started in Jamaica but was moved to France because of an inadequate studio. In the meantime, John had written a second album's worth of material. "The only reason *Yellow Brick Road* became a double album was simply because of the disaster in Jamaica; otherwise, we'd have done a single album," Dudgeon muses.

When Dudgeon and John parted company in the late '70s, Dudgeon intended to work on a variety of projects, but first he had to convince potential clients he was not a one-dimensional producer. "We all get pigeonholed," he says. "When I quit working with Elton, all I got offered to work with were piano players."

Eventually, Dudgeon hit with "Fool If You Think It's Over" (No. 12) by Chris Rea and "Run for Home" by Lindisfarne. He also produced albums by Elkie Brooks, Audience, and XTC. In the '80s he built Sol Studios, now owned by Jimmy Page (see entry). Dudgeon's latest output includes a 1997 European release by veteran Danish pop-country singer Henning Staerk, *Somewhere Someone's Falling in Love,* featuring master guitarist Jerry Donahue. "It's five great musicians doing ten great songs," Dudgeon says proudly.

Dudgeon's success in finding good songs and fostering great performances has been his hallmark for 30 years, enabling him to move effortlessly from rock and pop to country and blues. "I love musicians and I love great songwriters," he says. "To me they are the lifeblood of the whole thing." —BEN CROMER

Armatrading, Joan: *Whatever's for Us,* Cube/A&M, 1972 • *Classics, Vol. 21,* A&M, 1989.

Audience: *The House on the Hill,* Charisma/Elektra, 1971 • *Lunch,* Elektra, 1972.

Bagatelle: *Bagatelle,* Polydor, 1981.

Beach Boys: "Crocodile Rock," Polydor, 1991 (*Two Rooms: Songs of Elton and Bernie Taupin*).

Bishop, Stephen: *Bowling in Paris,* Atlantic, 1989.

Blunstone, Colin: *Planes,* Epic/Rock, 1976.

Bonzo Dog Doo-Dah Band: *Gorilla,* Liberty, 1967 • *The Doughnut in Granny's Greenhouse,* Liberty, 1968 • *Tadpoles,* Liberty, 1969.

Bowie, David: *Space Oddity,* RCA, 1969 • "Space Oddity," RCA, 1973 • *Bowie: The Singles, 1969–1993,* Rykodisc, 1993.

Bristol, Johnny: *Free to Be Me,* Handshake, 1981.

Brooks, Elkie: *I've Got the Music in Me,* Rocket, 1976.

Chapman, Michael: *Rainmaker,* Harvest, 1969 • *Fully Qualified Survivor,* Harvest, 1970 • *Window,* Harvest, 1970.

Hill, Roy: *Roy Hill,* Arista, 1978.

Hornsby, Bruce: "Madman Across the Water," Polydor, 1991 (*Two Rooms: Songs of Elton and Bernie Taupin*).

John, Elton: *Elton John,* DJM/MCA, 1970 • *Tumbleweed Connection,* DJM/MCA, 1970 • "Your Song," Uni, 1970 • *11-17-1970,* DJM/MCA, 1971 • "Friends," Uni, 1971 • *Madman Across the Water,* DJM/MCA, 1971 • "Honky Cat," Uni, 1972 • "Levon," Uni, 1972 • "Rocket Man," Uni, 1972 • *Don't Shoot Me I'm Only the Piano Player,* DJM/MCA, 1972 • *Honky Chateau,* Uni, 1972 • "Crocodile Rock," MCA, 1973 • "Daniel," MCA, 1973 • "Goodbye Yellow Brick Road," MCA, 1973 • "Saturday Night's Alright for Fighting," MCA, 1973 • *Goodbye Yellow Brick Road,* DJM/MCA, 1973 • "Bennie and the Jets," MCA, 1974 • "Don't Let the Sun Go Down on Me," MCA, 1974 • *Caribou,* MCA, 1974 • *Greatest Hits,* MCA, 1974 • "Island Girl," MCA, 1975 • "Lucy in the Sky with Diamonds," MCA, 1975 • "Philadelphia Freedom," MCA, 1975 • "The Bitch Is Back," Decca, 1975 • *Captain Fantastic and the Brown Dirt Cowboy,* DJM/MCA, 1975 • *Rock of the Westies,* MCA, 1975 • "Don't Go Breaking My Heart," Rocket, 1976 • "Grow Some Funk of Your Own," MCA, 1976 • "I Feel Like a Bullet (in the Gun of Robert Ford)," MCA, 1976 • "Someone Saved My Life Tonight," MCA, 1976 • "Sorry Seems to Be the Hardest Word," Rocket/MCA, 1976 • *Blue Moves,* Rocket/MCA, 1976 • *Greatest Hits,* Vol. 2, MCA, 1976 • *Here and There,* DJM/MCA, 1976 • "Bite Your Lip (Get Up and Dance)," Rocket/MCA, 1977 • *Roy Hill,* Arista, 1978 • *Ice on Fire,* MCA, 1985, 1992 • "Step into Christmas," Virgin/EMI, 1985 (*Now That's What I Call Music Xmas Album*) • "Wrap Her Up," Geffen, 1985 • *Leather Jackets,* MCA, 1986, 1992 • "Nikita," Geffen/WB, 1986 • "Candle in the Wind," MCA, 1987 • *Greatest Hits,* Vol. 3, 1979–1987, MCA, 1987 • *Live in Australia with the Melbourne Symphony Orchestra,* MCA, 1987 • *Greatest Hits, 1976–1986,* MCA, 1992 • *Love Songs,* MCA, 1996.

Johnston, Davey: *Smiling Face,* Rocket, 1973.

Kiki Dee Band: "I've Got the Music in Me," MCA, 1974.

Kongos, John: "He's Gonna Step on You Again," Elektra, 1971 • *Kongos,* Elektra, 1971.

Lindisfarne: *Back and Fourth,* Mercury, 1978.

Locomotive, The: "Rudies in Love," EMI, 1969.

Magna Carta: *Songs from Wasties Orchard,* Vertigo, 1971.

McTell, Ralph: *Revisited,* Transatlantic, 1970 • *You Well-Meaning Brought Me Here,* Famous/ABC, 1971.

Miles, John: *Play On,* EMI, 1983.

O'Sullivan, Gilbert: *Off Centre,* Epic, 1980.

Rea, Chris: "Fool If You Think It's Over," Magnet, 1978 •
Deltics, Magnet/United Artists, 1979.

Rush, Jennifer: *Heart over Mind,* Epic, 1987.

Shooting Star: *Shooting Star,* Virgin, 1980 • *Touch Me Tonight:*
The Best Of, Enigma, 1989.

Sinceros: *Pet Rock,* CBS, 1981.

Steeleye Span: *Sails of Silver,* Chrysalis/Takoma, 1981.

Strawbs, The: *The Strawbs,* A&M, 1969.

Taupin, Bernie: *Bernie Taupin,* Elektra, 1971.

Ten Years After: *Ten Years After,* Deram, 1967.

Voyager: *Halfway Hotel,* Elektra, 1979 • *Act of Love,* RCA, 1980.

Werth, Howard, and the Moonbeams: *King Brilliant,*
Charisma, 1975.

XTC: *Nonsuch,* Geffen, 1992.

COLLECTIONS

For Our Children Too, Rhino, 1996.

Anne Dudley

See ART OF NOISE

Lowell Dunbar

See SLY AND ROBBIE

Jermaine Dupri

Back in the '80s when hip-hop producer Hurby "Luvbug" Azor was busy creating his own production camp with acts like Salt-N-Pepa and Kid 'n Play, Jermaine Dupri was busy taking notes.

"Production was always something I wanted to do and Hurby was my inspiration. I saw how he was taking groups and building a camp like he did. He was putting out groups every other month," says the Atlanta-based Dupri, who has followed the same path with acts like Da Brat, Xscape, and Kriss Kross and taken it to an even higher level.

"I can see why it didn't last for him," says Dupri, whose So So Def imprint is distributed by Columbia Records. "When you start building a camp it becomes a headache, an everyday, ongoing headache, because the artists don't continue to let you do what you did when you first started working with them. They think they know everything."

Thankfully for Dupri, this is changing. "I think it's getting back to how it used to be, but it got out of hand for a minute. People didn't know the definition of a producer and the records were suffering. Now they're noticing the role of the producer," concludes Dupri, whose father is longtime artist manager and Columbia executive Michael Mauldin.

"The producer is supposed to be able to tell the artist what to do and how to do it and decide if it does or doesn't sound right. Many artists can't respect people telling them what to do," says Dupri.

Dupri—who is a writer as well as a producer—dictates the formation of the song from beginning to end, including the writing and how the song is sung. "A lot of artists don't agree with the way I do it, but they gotta do what I say," he adds emphatically. Dupri won the 1997 ASCAP Rhythm and Soul Songwriter of the Year Award for "Always Be My Baby" (Mariah Carey; No. 1), "Keep On Keepin' On" (MC Lyte; No. 10) and "Tonite's Tha Night" (Kriss Kross; No. 12).

It's likely not too many artists are complaining too loudly since Dupri is among the handful of young producers whose name virtually guarantees a hit. "The producers got this thing locked down," says Dupri. "Me, Puff [Sean "Puffy" Combs], Babyface [see entries]—if you don't get one of us to do your record, you got problems. People are gonna listen to our records first."

He speaks the truth, judging from a sampling of some of Dupri's ace productions: "Understanding" and "Who Can I Run To?" (both No. 8) for Xscape; "Ghetto Love and "Give It 2 You" by Da Brat; "Jump" (No. 1) and "Tonite's Tha Night" (No. 12) for Kriss Kross; "I Got Your Back" by Aaliyah; and countless others for the Braxtons, Lil' Kim, Whodini, TLC, Usher; and Aretha Franklin.

"It was cool to see her going into the studio," he says of the legendary Franklin, "an artist who knows what she wants to do and knows she can sing. It was hard to mention if she hit a bad note or something."

One of Dupri's biggest hits is rapper MC Lyte's "Keep On Keepin' On," the success of which came as a real surprise to Dupri. "It was just something I said I was going to do. I said I was gonna put her back in the mix and sure enough, it happened. There was some magical shit going on there," he says. Another surprise, but not a good one as far as Dupri is concerned, was Xscape's second album, *Off the Hook.* By all accounts except Dupri's, the million-selling record was a success, but he sees it as a disappointment that the album didn't sell even more. "I wanted to sell a bunch of records, especially coming off of [hit single] 'Who Can I Run To?' It was strange not to go to 2 million," says Dupri, who attributes the disappointment to the fact that *Off the Hook* wasn't a straight-up pop record. "I made a real R&B record. It was a big black record, but it didn't cross over to the white community. But I'm a big R&B producer, so I can't be mad about it. I don't think I did anything wrong," states Dupri.

"I like my records to symbolize what's going on in the streets. I go out a lot. I try to be as fresh as possible—hit people with something they haven't heard," he says of his body of work.

Like Combs, his biggest competitor, Dupri is big on the use of samples, though Dupri says he doesn't use as many as people might think. Instead, he uses "replays," a device by which a producer or artist recreates the sound of a previous hit. Dupri used a replay of an SOS Band bit on Mariah Carey's "Always Be My Baby" and a replay of a Shalamar piece for Kriss Kross's "Tonite's Tha Night."

Given the chance, Dupri says there are many productions he'd go back and change "because every day I come out with a bunch of different ideas. If I had a longer time to make records, all of them would sound different. But I always go on my first instinct."

Though busy producing others, Dupri found time to put out his own album in 1998 featuring guest appearances from Da Brat, Usher, Snoop Doggy Dogg, and Nas. His dream gig is to produce Michael Jackson. "I wish he would let me do a song, let me try something. Michael is at the point in his life where he needs to come out with a track with a young arrangement. He needs to flip it and get his crowd back," says Dupri, who believes he could sell Jackson on the idea, given the chance. All he needs is for the singer to "feel my energy, see how I flow." —KEVIN JOHNSON

A Few Good Men: "Chillin' " (remix), LaFace, 1994.

Aaliyah: *One in a Million* (1 track), Blackground Enterprises, 1996.

Bell Biv DeVoe: "What'cha Wanna Do?," MCA, 1994.

Braxton, Toni: "Breathe Again" (remix), LaFace, 1993.

Braxtons, The: *So Many Ways,* Atlantic, 1996.

Brown, Bobby: "Humpin' Around" (remix), MCA, 1992.

Carey, Mariah: "Never Forget You" (remix), Columbia, 1994 • *Daydream,* Columbia, 1995 • "Always Be My Baby," Columbia, 1996.

Da Brat: "Funkdafied," So So Def/Chaos, 1994 • *Funkdafied,* So So Def/Chaos, 1994 • "Give It 2 You," Chaos, 1995 • *Anutha Tantrum,* So So Def/Columbia, 1996 • "Sittin' on Top of the World," So So Def/Columbia, 1996 • featuring T-Boz, "Ghetto Love," So So Def, 1997.

Da Bush Babees: "Get On Down," Warner Bros., 1993 • "Put It Down," Warner Bros., 1993 • *Ambushed,* Warner Bros., 1994.

Debarge, El: *Heart, Mind and Soul* (1 track), Warner Bros., 1995.

Delano: "Good Ol' Fashion Lovin'," Warner Bros., 1993 • "What I Like," Warner Bros., 1993.

Dupri, Jermaine: *Jermaine Dupri Presents: Life in 1472,* So So Def, 1998.

Gill, Johnny: *Let's Get the Mood Right,* Motown, 1996 • *See also* Levert, Gerald.

Immature: *On Our Worst Behavior,* Virgin, 1992.

Jagged Edge: featuring Da Brat and JD, "The Way You Talk," So So Def, 1997 • *A Jagged Era,* So So Def, 1997.

Johnson, Puff: *Miracle,* Columbia, 1996.

Jones, Donell: "Knocks Me Off My Feet" (remix), LaFace, 1996, 1997.

Kriss Kross: "Jump," Ruffhouse, 1992 • *The Best of Kriss Kross Remixed '92,* Ruff House, 1992, 1996 • *Totally Krossed Out,* Ruff House/Columbia, 1992 • "Alright," Ruffhouse, 1993 • *Da Bomb,* Ruff House/Columbia, 1993 • "Tonite's Tha Night," Ruffhouse, 1995 • *Young, Rich and Dangerous* (EP), Ruff House, 1996.

Levert, Gerald, Keith Sweat, and Johnny Gill: *Levert Sweat Gill,* Elektra, 1997.

Lil' Kim: *Hard Core,* Undeas/Big Beat, 1996.

Lorenz, Trey: "My Younger Days," So So Def/Columbia, 1996.

MC Lyte: "Everyday," EastWest, 1996 • "Keep On Keepin' On," EastWest, 1996 • *Bad As I Wanna B,* EastWest, 1996.

New Edition: *Home Again,* MCA, 1996.

Richie Rich: *Seasoned Veteran,* Def Jam, 1996.

Run-D.M.C.: *Down with the King* (1 track), Profile, 1993.

Shanice: "Ace Boon Coon," Motown, 1994 • *21 Ways to Grow,* Motown, 1994.

Silk Tymes Leather: *It Ain't Where Ya From . . . It's Where Ya At,* Geffen, 1990.

Sweat, Keith: *See* Levert, Gerald.

TLC: "Baby-Baby-Baby" (remix), LaFace, 1992 • "Hat 2 Da Back" (remix), LaFace, 1992 • *Oooooohhh . . . On the TLC Tip,* LaFace, 1992.

Tony! Toni! Toné!: "My Ex-Girlfriend" (remix), Wing, 1994.

Torres, Roberto: *Vallenatos a Mi Estilo,* Vol. 2, SAR, 1996.

Usher: *My Way,* LaFace, 1997 • "You Make Me Wanna," LaFace, 1997.

Watson, Kino: "Game Recognize Game," Columbia, 1996 • *True 2 the Game,* Columbia, 1996.

Whodini: *Six,* So So Def/Columbia, 1996.

Xscape: *Hummin' Comin' at 'Cha,* So So Def/Columbia, 1993 • "Love on My Mind," So So Def/Columbia, 1993 • "Understanding," So So Def/Columbia, 1994 • "Who's That Man?," Chaos, 1994 (*The Mask* soundtrack) • *Feels So Good* (EP), So So Def/Columbia, 1995 • *Off the Hook,* So So Def/Columbia, 1995 • "Who Can I Run To?," So So Def/Columbia, 1995 • "Let's Do It Again," LaFace, 1997.

COLLECTIONS
12 Soulful Nights of Christmas, Part 1, So So Def, 1996.

Dust Brothers

(JOHN KING AND MIKE SIMPSON)

Mike Simpson and John King (both born in 1964) are the Dust Brothers production team. Stumbling into production through a college radio show, the pair produced tracks for Tone-Loc's *Loc-Ed After Dark* (No. 1) and Young MC's *Stone Cold Rhymin'* (No. 9) in 1989. That experience led to co-writing and co-producing one of hip-hop's most organic albums, the Beastie Boys' *Paul's Boutique* (No. 14).

The team then survived primarily on remixes for seven years before resurfacing huge on Beck's *Odelay* (No. 16), co-writing and co-producing the Grammy-winning 1997 Male Rock Vocal "Where It's At," in addition to "Devil's Haircut," "The New Pollution," and "Jack-Ass."

As A&R man and staff producer for Dreamworks label, Simpson went solo to produce the Eels' glorious *Beautiful Freak* album. The Dust Brothers continued their roll in 1997 by producing tracks for the Rolling Stones' *Bridges to Babylon,* and by raising the infectious ghost of the Jackson 5 (Radio City Music Hall, 1973, Simpson's first concert) with Hanson's fabulously successful "MMM Bop" single. The Brothers have also become performers themselves, recording with Korn for the *Spawn* soundtrack and with Howard Stern for his *Private Parts* soundtrack. The pair also own Nickel Bag Records, which entered into a long-term joint-venture agreement with Disney's Mammoth Records in early 1998.

Growing up in New York, Simpson connected with the width and breadth of black music, from the fun-loving grooves of Kool and the Gang to the deepest funk of Parliament/Funkadelic to the sophisticated R&B of Gladys Knight and the Pips. In 1978 he was uprooted and repotted in the alien soil of Southern California. Missing the funk of home, he survived on tapes played over the phone by friends from New York. Second-hand living just wouldn't do, and in 1980 Simpson picked up two turntables and a microphone and began mixing, scratching, and rapping.

Mike pursued his education at Claremont College, east of Los Angeles, and started a mobile DJ business that introduced the white kids to the gritty sounds of hip-hop and rap at parties and over the airwaves from the college's radio station. Three years into the radio show, Simpson met kindred spirit King and they paired up for the show and the mobile business. The Dust Brothers were born.

Simpson was allowed to continue on the Claremont radio station after he graduated. He explains what happened next. "I was planning to go to law school. One day I'm sitting in the studio and this guy named Tone-Loc comes in and says 'Hey, what's goin' on. I'm getting ready to make a record and I heard you guys have this great radio show. I just wanted to check you out.' "

Loc hung out and freaked when he heard the music beds the pair had cut for public service announcements. He wanted to rap over them for his album. Continues Simpson, "The next day I find myself in Hollywood playing my PSA beds for some guys, and they say, 'Wow, we're starting a record company and it sounds like you really know what you're doing. We want your help. You can produce your own stuff and our stuff.' "

Those guys were Mike Ross and Matt Dike and the company was Delicious Vinyl. The Dust Brothers contributed to the multimillion selling *Loc-ed After Dark* and Young MC's *Stone Cold Rhymin',* among others. The Delicious crew were friends with the Beastie Boys, who were looking for help with their second album. The result: *Paul's Boutique* and the booty-bumping dance floor perennials "Hey Ladies" and "Shake Your Rump."

For *Paul's,* the Brothers wrote "95 percent of the music and the Beasties wrote 95 percent of the lyrics," according to Simpson. Whatever the breakdown of credits are, *Paul's Boutique* reclassified the Beasties from obnoxious metal-rap boneheads to avant-garde hip-hop groove merchants—a critical move for the band after their celebrated breakup with *License to Ill* Svengali producer Rick Rubin (see entry).

The Dust Brothers did not want to jeopardize the credibility they gained from the Beastie Boys' record by cashing in on weak projects, so they spent their royalties building a studio and honed their engineering skills while waiting for the next gem. Numerous remixes and a few productions paid the bills, and then in 1996 Beck came along and the excitement returned.

Odelay is a clutch of catchy melodies co-written by the Brothers and Beck, showcasing the urban folkster's knack for genre-munching. Every song on *Odelay* is good, but some are better. "Devil's Haircut" jams with an unstoppable guitar riff and oblique allusions. "Lord Only Knows" starts with a scream, then evolves into a country number complete with slide guitar, tambourines, and twang. "New Pollution" mashes together cheesy elevator music, break beats, bewildering samples, and a great refrain. "Derelict" captures the weird and unsettling Beck, with low distorted vocals and Middle Eastern percussion. "Where It's At," the big hit single, is a tongue-in-cheek ode to the DJs of the world. Amid kitchen-sink samples and a serious beat, Beck raps like a man who's down with his bad self—a funky and hilarious classic.

Happenstance struck again in 1996 when Simpson approached the newly formed Dreamworks label about signing a band he liked. Instead, they signed him to be A&R man and staff producer. There, Simpson produced modern rock great *Beautiful Freak* with Eels singer/songwriter/guitarist (and former solo artist) E, who alternates between his frayed lower register and a lilting, affecting falsetto to create a dialogue with himself on fables for self-absorbed suburban teens like "Your Lucky Day in Hell," "Susan's House," and "My Beloved Monster." The production is white-room clean yet intimate as traditional ringing guitar is spiced with Beck-like samples, loops, and exotic instruments like the theremin. On the startling, beautiful "Novocaine for the Soul," a light jazzy cymbal and bell intro is jolted by acute guitar and "I Am the Walrus" orchestration. Though heavy with ennui and solipsism, *Beautiful Freak* holds out the hope that life can be fixed, and is, like the huge-eyed figure of its cover, beautifully freaky. —ERIC OLSEN AND DAWN DARLING

Dust Brothers

Beastie Boys: *Love American Style* (EP), Capitol, 1989 • *Paul's Boutique*, Capitol, 1989.

Beck: *Odelay*, DGC, 1996 • "Jack-Ass," DGC, 1997 • "The New Pollution," Geffen, 1997.

Boden, Brigid: "Oh, How I Cry," A&M, 1996.

Boo Yaa T.R.I.B.E.: *New Funky Nation*, 4th & B'Way, 1990.

Buck Pets: *Mercurotones* (1 track), Island, 1990.

Charlatans UK: "Patrol" (remix), Beggars Banquet, 1994.

Chemical Brothers: "Elektrobank" (remix), Astralwerks, 1997.

Def Jef: *Just a Poet with Soul*, Delicious Vinyl, 1990.

Dust Brothers: w/ Korn, "Kick the P.A.," Sony, 1997 (*Spawn* soundtrack) • w/ Howard Stern, "Tortured Man," Warner Bros., 1997 (*Howard Stern's Private Parts*).

Hanson: *Middle of Nowhere*, Mercury, 1997 • "MMMBop," Mercury, 1997.

Harper, Ben: "Whipping Boy" (remix), Virgin America, 1994.

Jones, Kipper: *Ordinary Story*, Atlantic, 1990.

Korn: *See* Dust Brothers.

Nitzer Ebb: "Fun to Be Had" (remix), Geffen, 1990.

Rolling Stones: *Bridges to Babylon*, Virgin, 1997.

Stern, Howard: *See* Dust Brothers.

Sugartooth: *The Sounds of Solid*, Geffen, 1997.

Technotronic: *Trip on This*, Capitol, 1990 • *Trip on This (The Remixes)*, Capitol, 1990.

Tone-Loc: *Loc-ed After Dark*, Delicious Vinyl, 1989.

Willis, Wesley: *Feel the Power*, American, 1996.

Young MC: *Stone Cold Rhymin'*, Delicious Vinyl, 1989.

John King

Porno For Pyros: "Hard Charger," Warner Bros., 1997 (*Howard Stern's Private Parts*).

Michael Simpson

Eels: *Beautiful Freak*, Dreamworks, 1996.

Mitch Easter

Mitch Easter had a lot to do with the renaissance of guitars in the pop music scene during the '80s. Through his productions, he let it be known that it was okay to let a clean Rickenbacker jangle freely and drive a song during a period when popular music had become synthesizer-heavy. Nary a review of his productions for R.E.M. or his own band Let's Active, both critics' darlings in their day, ran without a reference to "jangly guitars."

Easter's records feature real, organic drum sounds and layers of guitars. His Drive-In Studio led the way during an era rife with the do-it-yourself spirit. Ask folks like Velvet Crush, Marshall Crenshaw, the Loud Family, and the Connells and they will tell you that he's one of the true "regular guys" making records today.

Mitch Easter was born in 1954 and grew up in Winston-Salem, North Carolina. He got the initial music jag with "Waltz of the Sugar Plum Fairies" from *The Nutcracker Suite* on an RCA Red Seal 45, but when he heard the guitar solo on Bill Justis's "Raunchy," he had found "the music of the spheres."

He became mobilized among the worldwide kid forces who were called to arms upon their first viewing of the Beatles on the silver screen in *A Hard Day's Night* in 1964.

"It played at the drive-in and every kid in town was there," he recalls. "Everybody was sitting on top of their cars, screaming and stuff. It was a transforming moment. My friend Doug Muir and I went down to my basement and tried to record something on my family's Sony mono tape recorder that same night! Of course, neither one of us could sing or play guitar at the time."

He got into the guitar in 1967 and started playing in bands. "It was almost all English fancy pants stuff. Anybody who wore velvet suits was likely to have my sound." He cites the likes of the Electric Prunes, the Idle Race, Kevin Ayres, the Soft Machine, Black Sabbath, and Led Zeppelin as favorites.

"I loved that sort of heavy pop thing like on the Move's *Shazam* album. That was the blueprint of the ultimate studio recording in my head for many years. My number one favorite drum thing in the world for a long time was Bev Bevan's double bass drum press roll things at the end of 'Hello Suzie.' He was so cool. It must kind of rankle him that he's only known for playing drum machine parts with ELO."

In 1970, Easter's band Sacred Irony held a session at Crescent City Sound studio in Greensboro, North Carolina, after untold hours of woodshedding on the mono Sony machine. Feeling "a notch closer to the mystic temple that was the recording studio," he spent the rest of high school "trying to get hold of some recording stuff." A few years later, he formed a band called Rittenhouse Square with Chris Stamey and Peter Holsapple. Together they began figuring out the mysteries of recording on a Teac 3340 4-track, 1/4-inch machine.

While Easter attended college, his parents bought him a "weird shacklike old house built by hippies," which he sold upon graduation in order to finance the purchase of some used gear. He found a 3M 2-inch 16-track machine (which he uses to this day), an old 2-track, a little Quantum console, and a couple of AKG 414 mikes. All of Easter's friends had moved to New York City, so he followed. After scuffling around in a few bands for a about a year, he went back and set up shop in his parents' garage in Winston-Salem. The scene there was about three years behind New York, so there were young bands aplenty seeking a cheap recording facility. He added some mikes and effects to his humble arsenal and the homegrown studio with the working garage door was christened Drive-In Studio in 1980.

When Easter met Don Dixon (see entry), Dixon was a college freshman, but he seemed like "an old session guy to me. He was the first guy I knew who really made records and really knew what he was doing. He gave me a lot of confidence and helped to bring in a lot of business to the studio," recalls Easter.

Bands Mitch knew from New York started to come down to record at Drive-In. "We were literally sawing a hole for a window when the dB's came to mix," he says. "It was so casual, so lame in a way. But it worked just because I didn't know any better and I had pretty good equipment. There weren't nearly as many alternatives as there are today."

The first release from a Drive-In session was a record on Twin-Tone by Easter's old New York band the Crackers. Easter upgraded pieces of gear and remodeled a bit. Within the first year of the opening the studio, R.E.M. cut the "Radio Free Europe" single at Drive-In and things got busier.

Easter waxes on R.E.M.: "R.E.M. were really fun, they were a very together bunch from the beginning. They seemed kind of original because they were playing with the clean guitar tones, and no one was really doing that in those years."

Let's Active kept Mitch from "jumping into the studio thing so hard that I never got around to playing anymore. I got Let's Active together in a very deliberate sort of way. All the Let's Active records sound incredibly strange to me now, but that's probably the best thing about them. Oddly, they're fondly remembered by a number of people to this day, so I guess they did what they had to do."

Easter still enjoys producing. "Amuse yourself while you're making a record and try to do something that is actually interesting," he says. "I don't always get to do it, but I'm a big fan of trying to make stuff that sounds kind of mysterious in some way." —DENNIS DIKEN

Barone, Richard: w/ James Mastro, *Nuts and Bolts,* Passport, 1983.

Connells, The: *Boylan Heights,* TVT, 1987.

Crenshaw, Marshall: *Downtown* (1 track), Warner Bros., 1985.

Dish: *Dish* (EP), Engine, 1994.

Drag: *Satellites Beaming Back at You,* Island, 1996.

Game Theory: *Real Nightmare,* Enigma, 1984 • *Big Shot Chronicles,* Rational/Enigma, 1985 • *Lolita Nation,* Enigma, 1987 • *Two Steps from the Middle Ages,* Rational/Enigma, 1988 • *Tinker to Evers to Chance,* Enigma, 1990.

Grover: *My Wild Life,* Zero Hour, 1996.

Helium: *The Magic City,* Matador, 1997.

Hummingbirds, The: *Love Buzz,* Roo Art, 1989 • "Alimony," Roo Art, 1990.

John and Mary: *Victory Gardens,* Rykodisc, 1991.

Kage, L.: *Brazilliant,* A&M, 1993 • "Freed By Your Love Cascade," A&M, 1993.

Lava Love: *Aphrodisia,* Sky, 1992.

Let's Active: *Big Plans for Everybody*, IRS, 1986 • *Every Dog Has His Day*, IRS, 1988.

Loud Family: *Plants and Birds and Rocks and Things*, Alias, 1993 • *Slouching Towards Liverpool* (EP), Alias, 1993 • *The Tape of Only Linda*, Alias, 1994.

Love Tractor: *Themes from Venus*, DB, 1989.

Mastro, James: *See* Barone, Richard.

Motocaster: *Acid Rock* (EP), Fistpuppet, 1994 • *Stay Loaded*, Interscope, 1994.

Pavement: *Brighten the Corners*, Matador, 1997.

R.E.M.: *Chronic Town* (EP), IRS, 1982 • *Murmur*, IRS, 1983 • *Reckoning*, IRS, 1984 • "Wind Out," IRS, 1984 (*Bachelor Party* soundtrack) • *Dead Letter Office*, IRS, 1987 • *Eponymous*, IRS, 1988.

Sneakers: *In the Red*, Carrere, 1978.

Stamey, Chris: *It's a Wonderful Life*, Albion, 1983.

Sutliff, Bobby: *Only Ghosts Remain*, Passport, 1987.

Velvet Crush: *Teenage Symphonies to God*, 550 Music/Epic, 1994.

Velvet Elvis: *Velvet Elvis*, Enigma, 1988.

Washington Squares: *From Greenwich Village: The Complete*, Razor & Tie, 1997.

Waxing Poetic: *Hermitage*, Emergo, 1987.

Windbreakers, The: *Run*, DB, 1986 • *At Home with Bobby and Tim*, DB, 1990 • *Electric Landlady*, DB, 1991.

Clancy Eccles

Clancy Eccles began his career as a singer, though he also made a living, like his father, as a tailor. It's said that Eccles made stage clothes for many a reggae act in Kingston, Jamaica. His first record as a vocalist was "Freedom" for C.S. Dodd (see entry), which was released in 1961.

He also recorded for Sonia Pottinger (see entry) and others before his first production, in 1967, "Say What You're Saying" by Monty Morris. Among his well-known productions are "No Good Girl" by the Beltones, "Foolish Fool" by Cynthia Richards, his own charming "Sweet Jamaica," and DJ King Stitt's "Fire Corner," a song about Eccles' shop on Orange Street across from Coxsone.

Clancy had a string of major hits with Stitt, also known as "The Ugly One," a longtime sound system chatter with a startling appearance and description-defying delivery. "Vigorton Two" and "Herbsman Shuffle" were a couple of their biggest hits, mixing snappy instrumentals with even snappier patter. The two together voiced "Dance Beat," a magnificent tour of the early world of dancehall inhabited by characters of mythological proportion both living and dead. As the two reminisce the early sound system scene comes alive for the listener.

He also had a hand in a couple of early records by friend Lee "Scratch" Perry (see entry). Like Stitt and Perry, Eccles had worked for Coxsone, and several of these records took a poke at him. They all seemed to get along with him fine when they weren't recording, though.

Most of Clancy's early productions were cut at West Indies Records before it burned down and reopened as Dynamic. Eccles also recorded at Federal, WIRL, and Treasure Isle. Musicians included Jackie Jackson on bass, guitarists Ernest Ranglin and Hux Brown, keyboardists Winston Wright and Gladstone Anderson, and drummers Hugh Malcolm and Winston Grennan.

When recording for Eccles, these musicians and others were collectively known as the Dynamites. They issued many instrumentals under that name as well as backing Eccles' artists. Seldom did the songs go over $3^1/_2$ minutes: many clock in at under $2^1/_2$. They are brilliant pop structures with rhythms drawing heavily on rock steady's bounce.

Eccles released his own records in England on the Clandisc and NuBeat labels from the late '60s through the mid-'70s. Some also came out on Trojan and Pama. Instrumentals by the Dynamites, vocals from Eccles and others, and hit after hit by King Stitt all sold well in the U.K..

Among his impressive works are early gems by Joe Higgs, a classic singer/songwriter influenced by jazz and influencing in turn the Wailers, Wailing Souls, and many other Jamaican singers whom he tutored in backyard sessions in Trenchtown.

Eccles also had a touch for nice arrangements of vocal groups like the Dingles (then called the Dingle Brothers) and the Coolers. He recorded several tracks with the late Exuma (an American) and cut, among others, "Kingston Town," later a U.K. hit for UB40, for the Trinidadian Lord Creator.

In the heated political elections of 1972, Eccles weighed his musical forces in on the side of socialist Michael Manley with a series of stinging singles like "Rod of Correction" and a "Bandwagon" stage show tour of Jamaica featuring big-name artists like Eccles and the Wailers as well as Manley's speeches. With songs like "Credit Squeeze," "Power for the People," and "Revolution" from Eccles, the powerful talent he assembled for these shows, and the credibility it (and a staff Manley said had been given to him by Haile Selassie) gave to Manley among the dissatisfied, it would be hard to underestimate Eccles' influence on the vote.

After Manley's election Eccles even briefly took a spot in the new government and continued his support with singles like "Hallelujah Free At Last" and "Stop the Criticism." However, politics did not suit him and he soon returned to the needle and thread and the pen that's mightier than the sword. But his involvement in politics pretty well capped his musical career. In the early '90s, Heartbeat issued two excellent anthologies of Eccles material on CD, and in recent years he's been licensing his productions for European release. —CHUCK FOSTER

Dynamites, The: *The Wild Reggae Bunch*, Jamaica Gold, 1996 • See also Stitt, King.

Eccles, Clancy: *Freedom*, Trojan, 1969 • *Top of the Ladder*, Top of the Ladder, 1973 • *Joshua's Rod of Correction*, Jamaica Gold, 1996.

Stitt, King: w/ the Dynamites, *Fire Corner*, Trojan, 1969 • *Reggae Fire Beat*, Jamaica Gold, 1996.

COLLECTIONS

Reggae Vintage Volume One, Clandisc, 1970: Busty Brown, "Let Us Be Lovers" • Eccles, "Two of a Kind" • Joe Higgs, "Mademoiselle" • Monty Morris, "Say What You're Saying" • Cynthia Richards, "Foolish Fool" • Stanger and Gladdy, "C.N. Express."

Herbman Reggae, Trojan, 1970.

Jamaica Reggae, 12 Golden Hits, Clandisc, 1972: Eccles, "Fatty, Fatty," "Sweet Jamaica" • Fabulous Flames, "Growing Up," "Holly Holy," • Lord Creator, "Kingston Town," "Passing Through," Monty Morris, "Say What You're Saying," "Tears in Your Eyes" • Cynthis Richards, "Conversation," "Foolish Fool" • King Stitt, "Fire Corner," "Vigorton 2."

Clancy Eccles and Friends: Fatty Fatty, 1967–1970, Trojan, 1988: Beltones, "No Good Girl," • Dynamites, "John Public," "Mr. Midnight," "Phantom" • Larry Marshall, "Please Stay" • Eccles, "Fatty Fat" • Eric Monty Morris, "Say What You're Saying," • "Simple Simon."

Clancy Eccles Presents His Reggae Review, Heartbeat, 1990: Val Bennett, "City Demonstration" • Coolers, "Witch Doctor" • Eccles, "Don't Brag, Don't Boast," "Stay Loose" • Alton Ellis, "Bye Bye Love," "Feeling Inside" • Higgs and Wilson, "Don't Mind Me" • King Stitt, "Dance Beat" • Hugh Malcolm, "Love Brother Love" • Larry Marshall, "Please Stay" • Hemsley Morris, "Stay Loose," "You Think I'm a Fool" • Morris Monty, "My Lonely Days" • Velma and Clancy, "Let Us Be Lovers" • Barry Wilson, "Live and Learn."

Kingston Town, Heartbeat, 1992: Eccles, "Sweet Jamaica" • King Stitt, "Vigorton Two" • Lord Creator, "Kingston Town," "Passing Through" • Perry, Lee, "I Was Meant for You" • Tito Simon, "I'll Be True."

Kenneth Edmonds

See BABYFACE

Dave Edmunds

There's no place like home, or so it seems to British musician/producer Dave Edmunds. Modern technology, says Edmunds, makes recording at home easier and faster, leaving commercial studios in the dust.

"When I book into a studio it drives me crazy; everything takes forever," Edmunds says. "Any little thing you want, it's 'Hang on, we have to patch that,' whereas everything in my studio is hard-wired. If I want something, I've got it in seconds."

Born April 15, 1944, in Cardiff, Wales, Edmunds' music is firmly rooted in the '50s and '60s. Edmunds, however, is no mere revivalist. Even when he records classics such as "Baby, Let's Play House" or "Singin' the Blues," he delivers a hard-edged authenticity to the performance that parallels the original. Moreover, he relies heavily on newer material by Elvis Costello, Nick Lowe (see entries), and Graham Parker, liberally sprinkling their songs with elements of roots rock. His other exploits include touring with Ringo Starr as part of the "All Starr Band" and taking part in projects with George Harrison and Jeff Lynne (see entry).

Edmunds logged his first hit in 1968 with "Sabre Dance" (No. 5 U.K.), a guitar-on-acid workout recorded with his band Love Sculpture. His classic 1971 album *Rockpile*, recorded at the legendary Rockfield Studios near Monmouth, Wales, yielded another hit, "I Hear You Knocking" (No. 4).

When Edmunds signed a deal with Swan Song Records, Led Zeppelin's label, he reached his zenith: *Get It, Tracks on Wax 4*, and *Repeat When Necessary* were delights, fueled largely by Rockpile, the band Edmunds founded with Nick Lowe.

Edmunds' lofty status as a performer also led to a production career. His portfolio includes albums by the Fabulous Thunderbirds, the Stray Cats, the Everly

Brothers, and k.d. lang. Yet, Edmunds says producing other artists isn't necessarily any easier than producing your own project.

"If everyone thinks that your ideas are good and you get that respect that's great," he says. "I always find that [in producing] I have to get over that hump with anyone I haven't worked with before. I need to contribute something artistic in a way so it's, 'He's okay—it's going to work out fine.'"

When recording and producing, Edmunds takes a measured approach to keep him from getting tunnel vision on any single track. "If I don't feel like putting the vocal on, I'll get the vocal all set up with the level, compression, track assignment, and lyrics ready to go," he explains. "Then I'll walk away from it. When I'm ready, all I've got to do is press go and record."

Because Edmunds designs his mixes from the outset, effects such as compression are recorded at the same time as the vocal track, avoiding "decision fatigue," as Edmunds puts it. "In the old days, if they had a slap effect on the vocal they didn't do it afterwards. It was done at the time, and then they compressed the whole lot. It brings it this lovely chunky sound, and you don't have to worry about what to do with the vocal in the mix."

Clearly, Edmunds relishes the life of a studio hermit, at least until the next tour or production job comes along. "It's heaven," Edmunds beams. "When it's going well and I get a few ideas I go into this little world. I've discovered it's the place to be." —BEN CROMER

Beck, Jeff: *Beckology,* Epic/Legacy, 1991, 1995.

Bogguss, Suzy: w/ Dave Edmunds, "It Doesn't Matter Anymore," Decca, 1996 [*Not Fade Away (Remembering Buddy Holly)*].

Brewers Droop: *The Booze Brothers,* Red Lightnin', 1989.

Brinsley Schwarz: *The New Favourites of Brinsley Schwarz,* United Artists, 1974 • *Surrender to the Rhythm,* EMI, 1991.

Dion: *Yo Frankie!* Arista, 1989.

Ducks Deluxe: *Taxi to the Terminal Zone,* RCA, 1975 • *Don't Mind Rockin' Tonight,* RCA, 1978.

Edmunds, Dave: "I Hear You Knocking," MAM, 1970 • *Rockpile,* EMI, 1971 • *Subtle As a Flying Mallet,* RCA, 1975 • *Get It,* Swan Song, 1977 • *Track on Wax 4,* Swan Song, 1978 • *Repeat When Necessary,* Swan Song, 1979 • *Twangin',* Swan Song, 1981 • "Run Rudolph Run," A&M, 1982 (*Party Party* soundtrack) • *DE 7,* Arista, 1982 • *Information,* Columbia, 1983, 1991 • *Riff Raff,* Columbia, 1984 • "The Wanderer," Columbia, 1986 • *I Hear You Rockin',* Columbia, 1987 • *Closer to the Flame,* Capitol, 1990 • *The Dave Edmunds Anthology, 1968–1990,* Rhino, 1993 • *Plugged In,* Pyramid, 1994.

Everly Brothers: *EB '84,* Mercury, 1984 • *Born Yesterday,* Mercury, 1986 • *The Mercury Years,* Mercury, 1993 • *Heartaches and Harmonies,* Rhino, 1994.

Fabulous Thunderbirds: "Tuff Enough," CBS Associated, 1986 • *Tuff Enough,* CBS Associated, 1986 • *Hot Number,* Epic Associated, 1987 • *Hot Stuff: The Greatest Hits,* Epic Associated, 1992.

Flamin' Groovies: *Shake Some Action,* Sire, 1976 • *Now,* Sire, 1978.

Foghat: *Foghat,* Rhino, 1972, 1990 • *Best Of,* Rhino, 1990 • *Best Of,* Vol. 2, Rhino, 1992.

King Kurt: *Ooh Wallah Wallah,* Stiff, 1983.

lang, k.d.: *Angel with a Lariat,* Sire, 1987.

Leonard, Deke: *Iceberg* (1 track), United Artists, 1973.

Love Sculpture: *Forms and Feelings,* EMI, 1969.

Lowe, Nick: *Basher: The Best Of,* Columbia, 1989 • *Party of One,* Reprise, 1990 • *Pinker and Prouder Than Previous,* Columbia, 1990 • *Boxed,* Demon, 1994.

Polecats: *Are Go,* Mercury, 1981 • *Make a Circuit with Me* (4 tracks), Mercury, 1983.

Ruffner, Mason: *Mason Ruffner,* Epic, 1979, 1985 • *Gypsy Blood,* Epic Associated, 1987.

Shannon, Del: *And the Music Plays On,* Sunset, 1978.

Stevens, Shakin': *A Legend,* EMI, 1970.

Sting: "Need Your Love So Bad," A&M, 1982 (*Party Party* soundtrack) • "Tutti Fruitti," A&M, 1982 (*Party Party* soundtrack).

Stray Cats: "Fishnet Stockings," EMI America, 1981, 1983 (*Spinning Pups*) • *Stray Cats,* Arista, 1981 • *Built for Speed,* EMI America, 1982 • "Rock This Town," EMI America, 1982 • "Stray Cat Strut," EMI America, 1982 • "I Won't Stand in Your Way," EMI America, 1983 • *Rant and Rave with the Stray Cats,* Arista, 1983 • "(She's) Sexy + Seventeen," EMI, 1983, 1993 (*Living in Oblivion: The 80s Greatest Hits,* Vol. 1) • *Blast Off,* EMI America, 1989 • *Choo Choo Hot Fish,* Pyramid, 1992, 1994 • *Runaway Boys: A Retrospective, 1981–1992,* Capitol, 1997.

Bernard Edwards

See NILE RODGERS AND BERNARD EDWARDS

Keith Elam

See DJ PREMIER AND GURU

Geoff Emerick

As one of the legendary craftsmen at EMI's Abbey Road Studios in London in the '60s, Geoff Emerick is justly renowned for his technical contributions to the Beatles' canon. In fact, Emerick was producer George Martin's (see entry) primary engineer during the Beatles' most creative period, the mid- to late '60s. He engineered *Revolver* and *Sgt. Pepper's Lonely Hearts Club Band* as well as the double-sided hit single "Penny Lane / Strawberry Fields Forever."

After the Beatles disbanded, Emerick entered the production realm with another EMI act, Badfinger. Emerick produced all but two tracks on *No Dice*, Badfinger's second album. That album included the classic Pete Ham–Tom Evans ballad "Without You," a worldwide hit for Harry Nilsson in 1972, and Ham's exquisite "We're for the Dark." Emerick also continued to engineer much of Paul McCartney's (see entry) post-Beatles works, including the albums *Band on the Run, Venus and Mars, Tug of War,* and *Pipes of Peace.* Moreover, he produced Robin Trower's *Victims of the Fury,* Echo and the Bunnymen's *Reverberation,* and Elvis Costello's underrated *Imperial Bedroom* (No. 6 U.K.) album, which includes the masterful "Beyond Belief."

In 1989, Emerick engineered McCartney's *Flowers in the Dirt,* resulting in the McCartney-Costello classic "My Brave Face." Emerick and Costello reunited on *All This Useless Beauty,* an album that amply displayed Emerick's ability to capture Costello's enigmatic personality on such tracks as "Shallow Graves," another Costello-McCartney composition.

Given his understanding of McCartney's music, it is not surprising that Emerick is one of McCartney's constant studio companions. In 1997, Emerick engineered McCartney's critically acclaimed *Flaming Pie,* including the single "The World Tonight." Clearly, Emerick's production skills have been overshadowed by his engineering abilities. In any event, Emerick's credentials as one of the Beatles' key technical advisors ensure his immortality in the pantheon of rock. —BEN CROMER

Badfinger: *No Dice,* Apple, 1970 • "No Matter What," Apple, 1970 • *Straight Up,* Apple, 1971 • *Best Of,* Capitol, 1995.

Costello, Elvis: *Best Of,* Columbia, 1985 • *Out of Our Idiot,* Demon, 1987.

Costello, Elvis, and the Attractions: *Imperial Bedroom,* Columbia, 1982 • *Girls, Girls, Girls,* Columbia, 1989 • *All This Useless Beauty,* Warner Bros., 1996.

Echo and the Bunnymen: *Reverberation,* Sire / WB, 1990.

Garfunkel, Art: w/ Amy Grant, *The Animals' Christmas,* Columbia, 1986 • *Lefty,* Columbia, 1988 • *Garfunkel: Best Of,* Columbia, 1990 • *Up 'Til Now,* Columbia, 1993.

Grant, Amy: *See* Garfunkel, Art.

Heyward, Nick: *North of a Miracle,* Arista, 1983.

Keene, Tommy: *Based on Happy Times,* Geffen, 1980 • *Songs from the Film,* Geffen, 1986.

McCartney, Paul: *Unplugged,* Capitol, 1991.

Split Enz: *Dizrhythmia,* Mushroom / Chrysalis, 1977 • *Enz of an Era,* Mushroom, 1983 • *Collection, 1973–1984,* Concept, 1986 • *Best Of,* Chrysalis, 1994.

Trower, Robin: *Long Misty Days,* Chrysalis, 1976, 1989 • *Victims of the Fury,* Chrysalis, 1980, 1989 • *Essential,* Chrysalis, 1991.

Vannelli, Gino: *The Gist of the Gemini,* A&M, 1976.

Jack Endino

When slick '80s producers complain about the "band-sound men" who put them out of business after the Nirvana revolution, they're probably thinking of Jack Endino. Endino is responsible for dozens of low-budget recordings of varied sound quality that ably captured some of the freshest and most incendiary music to come out of Seattle—or any other place.

"I was a musician in the scene," Endino says. "The musicians trusted me as one of their own." As a result, he produced early recordings by Nirvana, Mudhoney, Soundgarden, Screaming Trees, Green River, Blood Circus, and Tad—virtually every band that fed the Seattle grunge sound. After Nirvana broke out, the fact that he did much of the early Sub Pop output made him *the* cool indie producer.

Endino's career was mostly a self-taught affair, just like the punk bands he worked with. "I was an obsessed teenaged fan," he says. "I eventually wanted to do it myself. I learned to play drums and, later, guitar and bass, but I was also recording myself with a tape deck and one microphone. I recorded one instrument at a time with two tape decks, bouncing them back and forth. I always had the recording light on as I was playing."

Later, he acquired a 4-track machine, learned simple multitracking, and opened his basement for business. While recording the *Deep Six* compilation for Sub Pop, he met Chris Hensack. They opened 8-track studio Reciprocal Recording in July 1986.

"We were thriving from the moment we opened the door because we were cheap and we were good at what we did," Endino says. "You didn't need 24-track to do punk rock. Most of the early Sub Pop stuff was 8-track."

One of his first clients was Soundgarden; he recorded their debut, the *Screaming Life* EP, in 1987. In January 1988, he recorded Nirvana's first demos, some of which turned up on 1992's *Incesticide*. Nirvana's first album, 1989's *Bleach,* was one of the studio's last 8-track jobs before they went to 24-track. Though the recording sounds raw overall, all the instruments are distinct in the mix, especially the punchy bass that runs through the songs like a guideline. Kurt Cobain's vocals don't stand out as they would on a pop record; deep in the mix with the other instruments, they're more part of the overall sound than they were later.

Endino captured a heavy rock band making music together. "I didn't have a mentor," he says. "Sometimes I sort of wish I did. I would have learned things faster. Everyone here was inventing things as they went along. There was no money in Seattle to do anything else for a long time. Now I do only four or five records a year instead of twenty. I can stretch out and use what I've learned."

Endino worked at Reciprocal for five years before his partner bought him out and he went freelance. "It was the best thing for me. It forced me to be flexible," he says. "I learned to adapt. Now I can go anywhere in the world and get my sound."

That's pretty much what he's done. Although he has worked recently for some Seattle bands (Mudhoney, Tad), he found that familiarity breeds contempt, and most of the calls he gets are not only from out of town but out of the country. He has worked in Argentina, Brazil, Denmark, Mexico, Australia, England, Holland, Germany, and France.

"I haven't been around Seattle bands when they recorded for major labels," Endino says. "I think they took me for granted. I was Mr. 8-track; I wasn't a real producer. In other cities and other countries, people were asking me to make major-label records. Things aren't as hopping here as they were a few years ago. But there's always a kid with a guitar somewhere in the world. A band in France called me because of the Coffinbreak records I did a few years ago. A band in Australia called me because of a Rein Sanction album on Sub Pop. One thing begets another."

To Endino, simulating the feel of a band's live performance is the goal of recording. "You're trying to paint an idealized portrait of a song in sound," he says. "You can't actually get a live performance in the studio. What the microphones are hearing and what the audience perceives in a club are two different things. If you hang two mikes in the back of the room and listen to it later, it's going to sound bad. You have to find the emotion of the song and emphasize it. You give the band as conducive a situation as possible. You don't inhibit things by being nitpicky and anal. I abhor click tracks. I try to get the band playing together in the studio so you get some feeling of interaction, the feeling and sound of the band playing in real time. That may sound obvious but it's not. There are ways to record that are extremely analytical and broken-down."

The longest Endino spent on an album was four months; the artist was Bruce Dickinson. He says that as people become more successful, they become less efficient. "Any producer or engineer has to guard against the tendency—you have all these toys and you want to use them. That's one of the reasons I think spending a lot of time in the studio can be counterproductive," Endino says. "The most important thing is the emotional content of the music. If you bury a band under lots of fancy production techniques like reverb you're distracting the listener from the emotional content."

Alongside his production career, Endino has also maintained an active career as a musician, first with his longtime band Skin Yard, in the solo project Jack Endino's Earthworm, and in the trio Suitcase Nukes.

—Anastasia Pantsios

Accused: *Grinning Like an Undertaker,* Nastymix, 1990 • *Hymns for the Deranged* (EP), Empty, 1990 • *Straight Razor* (EP), Nastymix, 1991.

Afghan Whigs: *Up in It,* Sub Pop, 1990.

Ain't: *If It's Illegal to Rock and Roll, Then Throw My Ass in Jail,* Gluttony, 1997.

Alien Boys: *Doom Picnic* (EP), Gun Germany, 1992.

Babes in Toyland: *Spanking Machine,* Twin/Tone, 1990 • *Painkiller,* Warner Bros., 1993.

Blood Circus: *Primal Rock Therapy* (EP), Sub Pop, 1988.

Blue Cheer: *Highlights and Low Lives,* Nibelung/Semaphore, 1990.

Bluebottle Kiss: *Fear of Girls,* Murmur/Sony Australia, 1996.

Boghandle: *Step on It,* Rock Owl Denmark, 1992 • *Worth Dying For,* Sony Denmark, 1993.

Bucket: *Brother Fear,* Bucket, 1994.

Burning Heads: *Dive,* P.I.A.S. France, 1994.

Cat Butt: *Journey to the Center of EP,* Sub Pop, 1989.

Coffin Break: *Psychosis* (EP), C/Z, 1988 • *Rupture,* C/Z, 1990 • *Crawl,* Epitaph, 1991 • *No Sleep Til the Stardust Motel,* C/Z, 1991 • *Thirteen,* Epitaph, 1992.

Creed, Helios: *The Last Laugh,* Amphetamine Reptile, 1989.

Daddy Hate Box: *Sugar Plow* (EP), New Rage, 1990.

Dancing French Liberals of '48: *Dancing French Liberals of '48*

(EP), Broken Rekids, 1994.

Deadspot: *Built in Pain*, C/Z, 1990.

Derelicts: *Don't Wanna Live*, Sub Pop, 1991 • *Love Machine*, Penultimate, 1990 • *Going out of Style '86–'90*, Empty, 1994.

Dickinson, Bruce: *Skunkworks*, Castle/C.M.C, 1996.

Dirt Fishermen: *Vena Cava*, C/Z, 1993.

Don't Mean Maybe: *Real Good Life*, Dr. Dream, 1991.

Dwarves: *Blood, Guts and Pussy*, Sub Pop, 1990.

Endino, Jack: *Angle of Attack*, Bobok, 1990.

Endino's Earthworm: *Endino's Earthworm*, Cruz, 1992.

Fallouts: *Here I Come and Other Hits*, Estrus, 1993.

Fastbacks: *The Question Is No* (1 track), Sub Pop, 1992.

Fire Ants: *Stripped* (EP), Dekema, 1992.

Fitz of Depression: *Let's Give It a Twist*, K, 1994 • *Swing*, K, 1996.

Fluid, The: *Roadmouth*, Sub Pop, 1989.

Gas Huffer: *Janitors of Tomorrow*, Empty, 1991 • *Integrity Technology and Service*, Empty, 1992.

Green River: *Dry As a Bone*, Sub Pop, 1987.

Gruntruck: *Inside Yours*, Empty/Roadrunner, 1990 • *Push*, Roadrunner, 1993.

Guillotina: *Guillotina*, Warner Mexico, 1994 • *Rock Mata Pop*, Warner Mexico, 1996.

Hazel: *Toreador of Love*, Sub Pop, 1993.

Hole: "Beautiful Son," City Slang UK, 1993.

Hungry Crocodiles: *100,000,000 Watts*, Swamptown, 1992.

Icky Joey: *Pooh*, C/Z, 1991.

Johnson, Mike: *Where Am I?* Up, 1994.

Kerbdog: *Kerbdog*, Phonogram UK, 1994.

L7: *Smell the Magic* (4 tracks), Sub Pop, 1991 • "Shove," Elektra, 1995 (*Tank Girl* soundtrack).

Lanegan, Mark: *The Winding Sheet*, Sub Pop, 1990.

Love and Respect: *Love and Respect*, Penultimate, 1991.

Love Battery: *Between the Eyes*, Sub Pop, 1992.

Loveslug: *Beef Jerky*, Glitterhouse/Germany, 1990 • *Circus of Values*, Glitterhouse/Germany, 1993.

Mudhoney: "Touch Me I'm Sick," Sub Pop, 1987, 1991 • *Superfuzz Bigmuff*, Sub Pop, 1988 • *Mudhoney*, Sub Pop, 1989 • *My Brother the Cow*, Warner Bros., 1995.

Nirvana: "Love Buzz," Sub Pop, 1987 • *Bleach*, Sub Pop, 1989 • "Sliver," Sub Pop, 1989 • *Incesticide* (7 tracks), DGC, 1992.

Olivelawn: *Sap*, Cargo, 1990 • *Sophomore Jinx*, Cargo, 1991.

Pop Sickle: *Under the Influences*, C/Z, 1993.

Rein Sanction: *Mariposa*, Sub Pop, 1992.

Screaming Trees: *Buzz Factory*, SST, 1989 • "Change Has Come," Sub Pop, 1989 • *Change Has Come* (EP), Sub Pop, 1990.

Seaweed: *Despised* (EP), Sub Pop, 1991 • *Weak*, Sub Pop, 1992.

7 Year Bitch: *Viva Zapata*, C/Z, 1994.

SGM: *Aggression*, Restless, 1988.

Shark Chum: *Tres Homeboys*, Rats Ass, 1997.

silverchair: "Surfin' Bird," Interscope, 1996 (*MOM: Music for Our Mother Ocean*).

Skin Yard: *Skin Yard*, C/Z, 1987 • *Hallowed Ground*, Toxic Shock, 1988 • *Fist Sized Chunks*, Cruz, 1990 • *1000 Smiling Knuckles*, Cruz/SST, 1991 • *Inside the Eye*, Cruz/SST, 1993.

Solomon Grundy: *Solomon Grundy*, New Alliance, 1990.

Soundgarden: *Screaming Life*, Sub Pop, 1987 • "Come Together," A&M, 1989.

Spike: *Whelmed*, Y, 1995.

Supersuckers: *The Smoke of Hell*, Sub Pop, 1992.

Swallow: *Swallow*, Tupelo/Sub Pop, 1989 • *Sourpuss*, Glitterhouse Germany, 1990.

Tad: *God's Balls*, Sub Pop, 1989 • *Infrared Riding Hood*, EastWest, 1995.

Teen Angels: *Daddy*, Sub Pop, 1996.

Thrown-Ups: *Thrown-Ups*, Glitterhouse Germany, 1990 • *Seven Years Golden*, Amphetamine Reptile, 1997.

Titas: *Titanomaquia*, Warner Brazil, 1993 • *Domingo*, Warner Bros. Brazil, 1995.

Treepeople: *Time Whore* (EP), Silence, 1990.

Unearth: *Everything Was Beautiful*, New Rage, 1993.

Valentine Saloon: *Super Duper*, Pipeline, 1992.

Vexed: *Vexed*, C/Z, 1990 • *Cathexis*, C/Z, 1993.

Weather Theater: *Dusk*, Angry Fish Germany, 1991.

Willard: *Steel Mill*, Roadrunner, 1992.

Zip Gun: *Eight-Track Player*, Empty, 1992.

Maurice Engelen

See PRAGA KHAN AND THE LORDS OF ACID

Brian Eno

The scope of Brian Eno's influence spans beyond music into art, fashion, and the very fabric of our culture—and that was the goal all along.

"I suppose ideas are what I really think of as my job. My dream is to do for culture what Darwin did for the natural sciences. He established a frame in which it was possible to look at all life, ask serious questions about it and organize it in some way," he explained to an interviewer from *GQ* magazine's U.K. edition in 1996. "I've been wanting to do the same thing for culture for a long time."

Along the way he has produced groundbreaking albums for himself, David Bowie, Devo, Talking Heads, and, most famously, U2.

If ideas are his business, then Eno is a successful man. Born in the English village of Woodbridge, Suffolk, on May 15, 1948, he was educated by the De La Salle order. Then, disdaining conventional employment, Eno enrolled in a two-year course at the Ipswich Art School. He said: "I saw a job as a trap and something to avoid. In fact, that's a characteristic of my life: making moves not so much towards things as away from them, avoiding them."

While he was at Ipswich he began to experiment with tape machines, and by the time he left for the Winchester Art School in 1965, he had accumulated 30 recorders, although only two were in full working order. While his ear bowed toward avant-garde music, including the music he composed with his band, Merchant Taylor's Simultaneous Cabinet, Eno also had a budding taste for rock 'n' roll, spurred by the release of the Who's "My Generation."

"I thought, 'Oh-oh, rock music is going to do something' and realized that this area—which I'd previously imagined to be rather unserious—might actually turn out to be interesting after all," he said.

Soon thereafter Eno had a random encounter with a saxophone player whom he had met at an avant-garde concert in Reading. That player, Andy MacKay, had joined a band called Roxy Music. At the end of 1971 Eno received a phone call from the band, asking him if he would consider helping them out, mostly because he owned a Revox and they wanted to make a demo tape. Shortly thereafter he was introduced to the synthesizer, and a man with no formal musical training found himself in one of the most influential bands in the history of rock.

Eno contributed mightily to the first two classic Roxy albums *Roxy Music* and *For Your Pleasure*. Always more of a sound sculptor than a musician, Eno bent a weird band in even weirder directions by creating atmospheres with tape loops and his new toy, the synth. Eno's influence can be heard particularly on "Ladytron," "Virginia Plain," and "Sea Breezes" on the first album (1972); and "In Every Dream Home a Heartache," "The Bogus Man," and the awesome freakishness of the title track on *For Your Pleasure* (1973). Probably inevitably, Eno and singer/songwriter Bryan Ferry had a falling out over the direction of the band.

Eno left to concentrate on a solo career, which was launched with the 1974 release *Here Come the Warm Jets*. Ever since, Eno has been at the forefront of experimental music. He can claim ambient music as his own cre-

ation, just as he can take credit for finding the magic formula that has musicians creating some of their most accessible and successful songs while working with him.

In the *GQ* interview Eno explained the role of producer with what seemed to be classic understatement: "I always say that the first thing that you have to remember about producing is that it's a well-paid form of cowardice; you'll notice that producers never get blamed unless they make a total cock-up. . . . But producers can make a huge difference to the atmosphere in which a record is made."

Though Eno wasn't credited as producer, one of his early collaborators (after Robert Fripp) was David Bowie (see entry), who was attracted to Eno because of the sonic soundscapes he had created within his own music. The two collaborated on Bowie's 1977 release *Low* while Bowie was living in Berlin. Of the song "Sound and Vision," Eno has commented: "That's a beautiful song. I remember I had the idea of making the intro very long so that you wait and wait for the vocal to come in. That's me on synthesizer [playing the bit of percussion that goes tshhhhhhh]. The drum sound is interesting. Corgghh! Corgghh! Very boxy. The snare drum is being sent to a treatment that pitches it down, then fed back again, so it goes beuggh! beuggh! like it's talking. Boy. We used to make these records so fast. That's a couple of days' work."

For Bowie's second Berlin release, Eno worked on one of Bowie's most intimate and inspirational songs, "Heroes."

"Bowie has this ability to write songs that are full of yearning, and the music really echoes that. I remember we needed a guitarist, so we rang up Robert Fripp, who was in New York, and he got on a plane and came over the same night, I think, came straight from the airport to the studio, and started playing as soon as he heard the song. So you get this wonderful out-of-tune guitar circling round the melody, matching the yearning of the words, and then he finally gets there, and there's this great sense of relief," Eno has said.

Eno's work with Bowie gained him attention, and the offers started coming in, including the American new wave–art rockers Talking Heads. The band and producer collaborated on three albums, culminating in 1980's *Remain In Light* (No. 19), where Afro-Caribbean rhythms came to the fore. Of the song "Once in a Lifetime" (No. 14 U.K.), Eno remembers: "That's an interesting one. It's got a strange rhythm. I always heard it differently from the Talking Heads. I was hearing the 'one' on the first beat, which is empty. They were hearing it on the third beat, like a normal pop song. So there was this tension between my picture of the song and theirs. Impossible for classical people to understand."

Until that point Eno had worked with essentially quirky, culty-type artists. That all changed when he got a phone call from U2 drummer Larry Mullen. Although Eno wasn't convinced he was right for the band, they were convinced he was.

In a 1990 conversation with Robert Sandall from *Q* magazine, Eno remembered a long conversation with U2 lead singer Bono. "I said, 'Look, if I work with you, I will want to change lots of things you do, because I'm not interested in records as a document of a rock band playing on stage. I'm more interested in painting pictures. I want to create a landscape within which this music happens.' And so Bono said, 'Exactly, that's what we want too.' "

Unfortunately, U2's record label, Island, didn't see the pairing. Owner Chris Blackwell (see entry) was vehemently opposed. "He thought I was completely the wrong person for the job," recalled Eno. "He thought I'd turn it into art rock. And I thought this was a possible outcome myself. I took out the insurance policy of bringing Dan [Lanois—see entry—who had worked as Eno's engineer on some of his ambient albums] along. I thought that at least if he were there it would be a well-produced record with good performances, because Dan has a very good way of working with musicians. He's very encouraging and he can get people to do fantastic things. I was never very interested in musicians or musicianship until I met Dan."

Rather than mulling over song construction with the band day and night, Eno felt his role was to find songs the band had written which didn't seem typical. Such examples include "Promenade" and "Bullet the Blue Sky," as well as the song "Mothers of the Disappeared," which bears the Eno stamp. The song was created by slowing down the drum track from another song, dousing it with reverb, and then adding Bono's vocals. In short, classic Eno tape manipulation and studio trickery.

The result of all of this has been U2 standards *The Unforgettable Fire* (No. 12); 1987 Grammy winner for Album of the Year, *The Joshua Tree* (No. 1); *Achtung Baby* (No. 1); and *Zooropa* (No. 1).

A devout theorizer, of course Eno has a production philosophy: "I try to find out what isn't being done that ought to be done," he told *Q*. "Now sometimes that means somebody ought to make the tea. Sometimes it means somebody ought to re-write the whole bloody song. With Talking Heads I was a sort of tea boy/arranger. With U2 I championed the songs that didn't seem very U2-ish, or things that had strong beginnings but no clear destination."

Above all, Eno seeks to avoid "Hollywoodization," which, as he describes it, is "the process where things are evened out, rationalized, nicely lit from all sides, carefully balanced, studiously tested against all known formulas, referred to several committees, and finally made triumphantly noticeable. . . . It's where deficits of nerve, verve and imagination meet surfeits of glitz and gloss."

At least we know what the Eno catalog is not.
—DAVID JOHN FARINELLA AND ERIC OLSEN

Anderson, Laurie: *Strange Angels, Bright Red,* Warner Bros., 1994.

Bowie, David: "The Heart's Filthy Lesson," Virgin, 1995 • *Outside,* Virgin, 1995 • "Hallo Spaceboy," RCA, 1996.

Brook, Michael: w/ Brian Eno and Daniel Lanois, *Hybrid,* Editions E.G., 1990.

Budd, Harold: *Pavillion of Dreams,* Obscure, 1980 • *See also* Eno, Brian.

Byrne, David: *See* Eno, Brian.

Cale, John: *Guts* (2 tracks), Island, 1977 • *Words for the Dying,* Warner Bros., 1989.

Can: *Sacrilege: The Remixes,* Mute, 1997.

Costello, Elvis: w/ Brian Eno, "My Dark Life," Warner Bros., 1996 (*Songs in the Key of X*).

Depeche Mode: "I Feel You" (remix), Sire/Reprise, 1993 • "In Your Room" (remix), Sire/Reprise, 1993.

Devo: *Are We Not Men,* Warner Bros., 1980 • *Greatest Hits,* Warner Bros., 1990 • *Greatest Misses,* Warner Bros., 1990.

Edikanfo: *The Pace Setters,* EG Editions, 1981.

Eno, Brian: *Here Come the Warm Jets,* Island, 1973 • w/ Fripp, *No Pussyfooting,* EG, 1973 • *Taking Tiger Mountain by Strategy,* Island, 1974 • *Ambient 1-Music for Airports,* EG, 1975 • *Another Green World,* Editions E.G., 1975 • w/ Fripp, *Evening Star,* EG, 1975 • *Discreet Music,* Editions E.G., 1975, 1989 • *Before and After Science,* Editions E.G., 1977 • *Music for Films,* EG/Antilles, 1978 • w/ Moebius and Roedelius, *After the Heat,* Gyroscope, 1979, 1996 • w/ Harold Budd, *Ambient 2/Plateau of Mirrors,* Editions E.G., 1980, 1990 • w/ John Hassell, *Possible Musics,* EG, 1980 • w/ David Byrne, *My Life in the Bush of Ghosts,* Editions E.G., 1981 • *Ambient 4: On Land,* Editions E.G., 1982, 1989 • *Apollo: Atmospheres and Soundtracks,* EG, 1983, 1986 • w/ Harold Budd, *The Pearl,* Editions E.G., 1984, 1990 • *Thursday Afternoon,* Editions E.G., 1985, 1989 • *Desert Island Selections,* Editions E.G., 1986 • *Music for Film 3,* Opal/WB, 1988 • w/ John Cale, *Wrong Way Up,* Opal/WB, 1990 • *My Squelchy Life,* Opal, 1991 • *Nerve Net,* Opal/WB, 1992 • *The Shutov Assembly,* Opal, 1992 • "Under," Warner Bros., 1992 (*Cool World* soundtrack) • *Eno Box II,* Virgin, 1993 • *Neroli,* Gyroscope, 1993 • *Eno Box I,* Virgin, 1994 • "Force Marker," Warner Bros., 1995

(*Heat* soundtrack) • w/ Jah Wobble, *Spinner,* Gyroscope, 1995 • *The Drop,* Thirsty Ear, 1997.

Hassell, John: *Power Spot,* ECM, 1986, 1994 • w/ Farafina, *Flash of the Spirit,* Intuition, 1993 • *See also* Eno, Brian.

Fripp: *See* Eno, Brian.

Hobbs/Adams/Bryars: *Ensemble Pieces,* Obscure, 1975.

Jah Wobble: *See* Eno, Brian.

James: "Laid," Fontana, 1993 • *Laid,* Fontana, 1993 • *Wah Wah,* Mercury, 1994 • *Whiplash,* Fontana, 1997.

Laraaji: *Day of Radiance,* EG, 1980.

Moebius and Roedelius: *See* Eno, Brian.

Nusrat Fateh Ali Khan: *The Last Prophet,* Realworld/Caroline, 1994.

Oryema, Geoffrey: *Exile,* Realworld/Caroline, 1991.

Pacesetters: *Edikanfo,* EG, 1982.

Passengers: *Passengers: Original Soundtracks,* Island, 1995.

Portsmouth Sinfonia: *Hallelujah,* Transatlantic, 1979.

Siberry, Jane: "Temple," Reprise, 1993 • *When I Was a Boy,* Reprise, 1993.

Talking Heads: *More Songs About Buildings and Food,* Sire, 1978 • "Take Me to the River," Sire, 1978 • *Fear of Music,* Sire, 1979 • "Life During Wartime," Sire, 1979 • "Life During Wartime," RSO, 1979, 1980 (*Times Square* soundtrack) • *Remain in Light,* Sire, 1980 • *Popular Favorites: Sand in the Vasoline,* Sire, 1992.

Toop, David: *New and Rediscovered Musical Adventures,* Obscure, 1975.

Toto: *Dune* soundtrack, Pendulum, 1984, 1996.

U2: "Pride (in the Name of Love)," Island, 1984 • *The Unforgettable Fire,* Island, 1984 • "The Unforgettable Fire," Virgin/EMI, 1984, 1985 (*Now That's What I Call Music 5*) • "Three Sunrises," Island, 1985 • *Wide Awake in America,* Island, 1985 • "In God's Country," Island, 1987 • "I Still Haven't Found What I'm Looking For," Island, 1987 • "Sweetest Thing," Island, 1987 • *The Joshua Tree,* Island, 1987 • "Where the Streets Have No Name," Island, 1987 • "With or Without You," Island, 1987 • "With or Without You," 550 Music/Epic, 1987, 1994 (*Blown Away* soundtrack) • *Achtung Baby,* Island, 1991 • "Mysterious Ways," Island, 1991 • "Until the End of the World," Warner Bros., 1991 (*Until the End of the World* soundtrack) • "Even Better Than the Real Thing," Island, 1992 • "One," Island, 1992 • "Who's Gonna Ride Your Wild Horses?," Island, 1992 • "Lemon," Island, 1993 • "Stay (Faraway So Close)," Island, 1993 • *Zooropa,* Island, 1993.

Ultravox: *Ultravox!* Island, 1977.

Zvuki Mu: *Zvuki Mu,* Warner Bros., 1989.

COLLECTIONS

No New York, Antilles, 1978.

Angels in the Architecture, EG, 1987.

Dead Parrot Society: The Best of British Comedy, Rhino, 1993.

Ahmet and Nesuhi Ertegun

Like only a few other patriarchs of popular music, Ahmet M. Ertegun has produced records spanning the formats 78 rpm and compact disc. And, like such other primogenitors as Johnny Otis, Bob Johnston, and Ertegun's key ally, Jerry Wexler (see entries), he helped shape music more through taste than technology. Since he produced many key recordings on his label, Atlantic, from the late '40s to the early '60s, Ertegun can lay at least partial claim to the invention of rhythm 'n' blues.

Born July 31, 1923, in Istanbul, Ertegun is the son of the former Turkish ambassador to the United States. As a child, he lived in Switzerland, Paris, and London, following the diplomatic career of his father, M. Munir Ertegun. The family moved to Washington, D.C., when Ahmet was 12. Three or four years later, his mother gave him a birthday present: a machine that cut records.

"I didn't start listening to '20s music until the '30s," he says. "By the Depression, a lot of independent record companies had folded and the music changed a little bit," he says. "Jazz had evolved into a new phase, which

Ahmet Ertegun

eventually became swing. Those bands played until the Second World War, when most of the guys went into the Army, and there were a bunch of high school kids playing in them."

The big bands were basically done by 1950, except for Count Basie, Duke Ellington, and Stan Kenton's groups. The time was ripe for a new, compact format that would meld and streamline swing and blues.

"I started out trying to get a Southern sound in a Northern city with sophisticated artists who looked down on the primitive music called the blues," Ertegun says. "I wrote songs that forced them to make records we could sell to a black audience. Black audiences look for soul in music, and a certain kind of magic and beauty that they perceive. They like some pop records, but not the majority."

Ertegun founded Atlantic Records in 1947 with Herb Abramson, a New York jazz collector who happened to have founded the National and Jubilee labels. Ertegun dropped out of Georgetown University, where he had been working on a doctoral degree on Aristotle and St. Thomas, to enter the record business. He ran Atlantic as an independent until 1967, when it was absorbed into Warner Bros. Ertegun is now co-chairman and chief executive officer of the Atlantic Group, which comprises virtually every genre of music.

In its first two years, Atlantic issued several jazz and jump band releases that went nowhere, even though Ertegun and Abramson had hired a talented young engineer named Tom Dowd (see entry). In 1949, the label had its first hit, "Drinkin' Wine Spo Dee-O-Dee," a novelty blues by Sticks McGhee, Brownie McGhee's brother. That same year, the label signed Ruth Brown, who became known as "Miss Rhythm."

Among the artists Ertegun has produced or co-produced are the Bobbettes, LaVern Baker, the Cardinals, Ray Charles, Ivory Joe Hunter, the Drifters, the Honeydrippers, Ben E. King, Sylvia Syms, Joe Morris, Mabel Mercer, Joe Turner, and Manhattan Transfer. Among songs he has written or co-written (sometimes under the Nugetre appellation) are Joe Turner's "Chains of Love," Ray Charles' "Mess Around," Ruth Brown's "Wild Wild Young Man," and the Clovers' "Lovey Dovey."

Ertegun made his first recordings, in 1945, of the Boyd Raeburn Orchestra and of Little Miss Cornshucks. Raeburn was a bandleader known for his radical arrangements, a black counterpart to Kenton. Little Miss Cornshucks, who, according to Ertegun, "was maybe the best singer of that time," was a major influence on such singers as Dinah Washington, Ruth Brown, and LaVern Baker. "In those days, I was out

every night in clubs in Harlem looking for the next big star, and sometimes we'd come up with them," Ertegun says. "I was really a jazz fan and record collector, and once in a while, I wrote reviews for small magazines like *The Record Changer.*

"While I was still going to college [Ertegun graduated with a bachelor's degree in classical philosophy from St. John's College in Annapolis before attending Georgetown], I decided I wanted to start a record company and got a friend, my dentist in Washington, to invest $10,000. Then I got Herb."

The early Atlantic sessions were standard union dates: three-hour stints allowing a maximum of four songs recorded, paying $41.25 to band members, double that to bandleaders. "There was no remixing, because there was one track," Ertegun says, "so an engineer was much more important in those days than now because the engineer mixed while the record was being made.

"Very often, you had a very good performance in the studio but not a very good mix by the engineer, so we'd have to redo the track because, say, he'd forgotten to bring up the saxophone when the solo came up. There was no choice. You had controls over each microphone, but it all went into one pot, one track. Once it was recorded, that was the mix. That lasted until the early '50s."

At that time, tape began to supplant acetate, but recording was still 1-track. It wouldn't be until mid-decade that the first 8-track machine would surface. On the way to stereo, a 2-track machine was developed, "which gave you the possibility of making binaural records, as opposed to monaural," Ertegun says. These machines used two needles to play records, which, he says, "didn't work very well." Nevertheless, Atlantic cut a binaural record on Wilbur DeParis and his New Orleans Orchestra, selling 25,000 to 30,000 discs—even though only 5,000 binaural record players made it to market.

"They bought them because it was a new thing," Ertegun laughs. "We sold five times as many records as there were players."

In 1953, Atlantic co-founder Abramson was drafted; he sold his interest in the company a few years later. A year earlier, former *Billboard* writer Jerry Wexler joined Atlantic as executive vice president and partner to Ahmet and his brother, Nesuhi, who was in charge of Atlantic's robust and innovative jazz line (see below). In 1954, Atlantic cut its first multitrack recording, a Ray Charles project that signaled the first formalization of rhythm 'n' blues, an electrifying new genre designed to sanctify and simultaneously swing like hell. In 1957, Atlantic bought the second 8-track machine, an Ampex.

Ampex sold the first to Les Paul (see entry). The Navy got the third.

"Our first 8-track recording was about the time of the first Ray Charles sessions," Ertegun says. "Eight-track recording gave us a tremendous amount of possibility in remixing, but we were still recording singles mostly."

Ultimately, people put together two 8-tracks for 16 tracks, leading to development of the 16-track machine. Then two 24-track machines were yoked, leading to the development of the single 48-track machine. Such advances don't necessarily add up to progress, Ertegun says.

"Forty-eight tracks make the possibility of getting different productions of the same record infinite," he says. "You could take 15 years to work on one recording, doing it different ways. You can equalize each of the 48 tracks differently and get all sorts of different results from the same components. That's why it takes so long to make a record now: Mixing takes forever, because everybody has a different idea, especially when you have a group. You can have 10 tracks for each ego."

Production is a gradual process, he says. "When we had the 8-track, we wanted to leave some tracks open so if we had a vocal we thought the singer could do better, we wouldn't have to erase a track," he says. "That led us to try to combine two 8-tracks, which brought on the creation of the 16-track. With two 8-tracks, you record bass, guitar, drums, and piano on one track of the second 8-track, then balance the horns or strings and put them on the second track of your second 8-track. Now you have six tracks free for vocals. With two 8-tracks, you have infinite possibilities. In the several decades prior to multitrack inventions, when you made a record you were finished."

A principal founder and current chairman of the Rock and Roll Hall of Fame Foundation, Ertegun was inducted into the rock hall himself in 1987. Although his purview certainly includes rock 'n' roll, Ertegun's first love runs deeper. "There's what they used to call the Atlantic Sound," he says. "I guess that's the sound of our production: a much heavier backbeat than most other records had and a swinging groove on all the records. A very distinctive Motown sound came after us and really took over to become the dominant rhythm 'n' blues music. It was much more modern than what we were doing. But the sound that came from me, Herb Abramson, Jerry Wexler, and my brother Nesuhi—the sound we generated with Tommy Dowd as an engineer and Arif Mardin (see entry) as a producer—was the Atlantic Sound. I'm not sure what it is, but it changed a lot over the years."

Ertegun adores the music of the '20s because it "gave black people in America who were totally segregated a means of entertainment they couldn't get from the radio, which was all-white, or the movies, which were all white or portrayed blacks in demeaning situations. It was a great time of development of blues and jazz. Black American music has always been popular internationally, much more so than, say, Russian or Spanish music.

"You must admit, every country has beautiful music," he adds. "But you don't hear Greek music in Stockholm or German music in China. Black American music, from the very beginning, was international."

Nesuhi Ertegun was also integral to the Atlantic sound. Among the jazz artists Nesuhi produced for Atlantic after joining the label in 1956 are John Coltrane, Charles Mingus, Ornette Coleman, and the Modern Jazz Quartet. Nesuhi also became involved with the label's R&B and rock 'n' roll roster, producing several hits for Ray Charles, the Drifters, Bobby Darin, and Roberta Flack. Nesuhi died in 1989 and was inducted into the Rock and Roll Hall of Fame in 1991. —CARLO WOLFF

Ahmet Ertegun

Allyn, David: *See* Raeburn, Boyd.

Apache: *Apache,* Atco, 1981.

Baker, LaVern: "Jim Dandy Got Married," Atlantic, 1957 • "I Cried a Tear," Atlantic, 1958 • *Soul on Fire: The Best of LaVern Baker,* Rhino, 1991.

Barnaby Bye: *Room to Grow,* Atlantic, 1973.

Batdorf and Rodney: *Off the Shelf,* Atlantic, 1972.

Brown, Ruth: *Miss Rhythm (Greatest Hits and More),* Atlantic, 1959, 1990 • *Rockin' in Rhythm: The Best of Ruth,* Rhino, 1996.

Buffalo Springfield: *Buffalo Springfield* (1 track), Atco, 1973.

Casper: *Self Portrait,* Atlantic, 1983.

Cassello, Kathleen: w/ Kallen Esperian and Cynthia Lawrence, *The Three Sopranos,* Atlantic, 1996.

Charles, Ray: "I Believe to My Soul," Atlantic, 1959 • "(Night Time Is) the Right Time," Atlantic, 1959 • "What'd I Say," Atlantic, 1959 • *The Birth of Soul: The Complete Atlantic R&B,* Rhino, 1991 • *Blues and Jazz,* Rhino, 1994 • *The Best of Ray Charles: The Atlantic Years,* Rhino, 1994 • *Genius and Soul: 50th Anniversary Collection,* Rhino, 1997.

Clovers, The: "Blue Velvet," Atlantic, 1955 • *Down in the Alley: The Best of the Clovers,* Atlantic/Rhino, 1991.

Connor, Chris: *Sings the George Gershwin Almanac of Song,* Atlantic, 1957, 1989.

Corbett, Mike: w/ Jay Hirsh, *Mike Corbett and Jay Hirsh,* Atlantic, 1971.

Country: *Country, Featuring Tom Snow,* Clean/Atlantic, 1971.

Cream: *Live Cream,* Vol. 1, Polydor, 1970, 1983.

Darin, Bobby: *Bobby Darin,* Atlantic, 1958, 1994 • "Dream Lover," Atco, 1959 • *For Teenagers Only,* Atlantic, 1959 • "Mack the Knife," Atco, 1959 • *25th Day of December,* Atco, 1960, 1991 • *Ultimate Bobby Darin,* Warner Bros., 1988 • w/ Johnny Mercer, *Two of a Kind,* Atlantic, 1990 • *Splish Splash,* Atco, 1991 • *As Long As I'm Singing: The Bobby Darin Collection,* Rhino, 1995.

Devonsquare: *Bye Bye Route 66,* Atlantic, 1991.

Dixon, Floyd: *Marshall Texas Is My Home,* Specialty, 1958, 1991.

Domino, Fats: *Live at Montreux,* Atlantic, 1973.

Drifters, The: "Money Honey," Atlantic, 1953 • "White Christmas," Atlantic, 1955 • *Rockin' and Driftin': The Box Set,* Rhino, 1996.

Esperian, Kallen: *See* Cassello, Kathleen.

Flack, Roberta: *Blue Lights in the Basement,* Atlantic, 1978 • *Set the Night to Music,* Atlantic, 1991.

Greaves, R.B.: "Take a Letter Maria," Atco, 1969.

Guitar Slim: *Atco Sessions,* Atlantic, 1988.

Guy, Buddy: w/ Junior Wells, *Play the Blues,* Atlantic, 1972.

Hibbler, Al: *After the Lights Go Down Low,* Atlantic, 1956.

Hirsh, Jay: *See* Corbett, Mike.

J. Geils Band: *The J. Geils Band Anthology: Houseparty,* Rhino, 1993.

King, Ben E.: "Don't Play That Song (You Lied)," Atco, 1962 • *Anthology,* Atlantic, 1993.

Kowalczyk, Steve: *Moods and Grooves,* Atlantic, 1995.

Lampe, Nicholas: *It Happened a Long Time Ago,* Cotillion, 1970.

Lawrence, Cynthia: *See* Cassello, Kathleen

McPhatter, Clyde: *Deep Sea Ball: Best Of,* Atlantic, 1991.

McTell, Blind Willie: *Atlanta Twelve String,* Atlantic, 1949, 1992.

Manhattan Transfer: *The Manhattan Transfer,* Atlantic, 1975 • *Best of Manhattan Transfer,* Rhino, 1981 • *Anthology: Down in Birdland,* Rhino, 1992 • *The Very Best Of,* Rhino, 1994.

Mercer, Johnny: *See* Darin, Bobby.

Midler, Bette: "Friends," Atlantic, 1973 • *Experience the Divine: Bette Midler's Greatest Hits,* Atlantic, 1993.

Modern Jazz Quartet: *Celebration 40th Anniversary Box Set,* Atlantic, 1994.

Newman, David "Fathead": *House of David Newman: Fathead Anthology,* Rhino, 1993.

O'Keefe, Danny: *Danny O'Keefe,* Cotillion, 1970.

Professor Longhair: *New Orleans Piano,* Atlantic, 1972 • *'Fess: Anthology,* Rhino, 1993 • *Professor Longhair Anthology,* Rhino, 1993.

Raeburn, Boyd: w/ David Allyn, *Jewells,* Savoy Jazz, 1949, 1996.

Rockin' Dopsie and the Zydeco Twisters: *Louisiana Music,* Atlantic, 1991.

Short, Bobby: *Mad Twenties,* Atlantic, 1958, 1994.

Spencer, Jeremy: *Flee,* Atlantic, 1979.

Stitt, Sonny: *Stitt Plays Bird,* Atlantic, 1963.

Stone, Jesse: *Jesse Stone Alias Charles Calhoun,* Bear Family, 1996.

Tempo, Nino: w/ April Stevens, "Deep Purple," Atco, 1963 • *Tenor Saxophone,* Rhino, 1990 • *Nino,* Atlantic, 1993.

Turner, Big Joe: *Big Joe Turner's Greatest Hits,* Atlantic Jazz, 1958, 1989 • *Rhythm and Blues Years,* Atlantic, 1959 • *Big, Bad & Blue: The Big Joe Turner Box Set,* Rhino, 1994.

Twiggy and Tommy Tune: *My One and Only,* Atlantic, 1983.

Wells, Junior: *See* Guy, Buddy.

Yancey, Jimmy, and Mama: *Chicago Piano,* Vol. 1, Atlantic, 1972, 1988.

COLLECTIONS

Atlantic Hit Singles, 1980–1988, Atlantic, 1988.

Atlantic Honkers, Atlantic, 1986: Arnett Cobb, "Mr. Pogo," 1954, "Night," 1954, "Flying Home Mambo," 1955, "Light Like That," 1955 • Frank Culley, "Hop 'n' Twist," 1949, "Gone After Hours," 1950, "Culley Flower," 1951 • Tiny Grimes, "C.C. Rider," 1948, "Flyin' High," 1948, "Hot in Harlem," 1948, "Nightmare Blues," 1948 • Willis Jackson, "Harlem Nocturne," 1951, "Wine-O-Wine," 1951, "Gator's Groove," 1952, "Rock! Rock! Rock!," 1952 • Joe Morris, "Lowe Groovin'," 1947, "Weasel Walk," 1948, "Wow!," 1948 • Jesse Stone, "Barrel House," 1955, "Hey Tiger," 1955, "Night Life," 1955.

Atlantic Jazz: Kansas City, Rhino, 1987.

Atlantic Jazz: Soul, Rhino, 1987.

Atlantic Rhythm and Blues, 1952–1955, Atlantic, 1985: LaVern Baker, "Soul on Fire," 1953, "Tomorrow Night," 1954, "Tweedlee Dee," 1954, "Play It Fair," 1955 • Ruth Brown, "Mama He Treats Your Daughter Mean," 1953, "Wild Wild Young Men," 1953 • The Cardinals, "The Door Is Still Open," 1955 • Ray Charles, "Mess Around," 1953, "Greenbacks," 1954, "I Got a Woman," 1954, "A Fool for You," 1955, "This Little Girl of Mine," 1955 • The Chords, "Sh-Boom," 1954 • The Clovers, "One Mint Julep," 1952, "Good Lovin'," 1953, "Lovey Dovey," 1954 • The Diamonds, "A Beggar for Your Kisses," 1952 • Clyde McPhatter and the Drifters, "Money Honey," 1953, "Such a Night," 1953, "Honey Love," 1954, "White Christmas," 1954, "Watcha Gonna Do?," 1955 • Professor Longhair, "Tipitina," 1954 • Big Joe Turner, "Shake, Rattle and Roll," 1954, "Flip, Flop and Fly," 1955.

Atlantic Rhythm and Blues, 1955–1958, Atlantic, 1985: LaVern Baker, "Jim Dandy," 1956 • The Bobbettes, "Mr. Lee," 1957 • Ruth Brown, "Lucky Lips," 1956 • Ray Charles, "Drown in My Own Tears," 1956, "Hallelujah, I Love Her So," 1956, "Lonely Avenue," 1956 • The Clovers, "Devil or Angel," 1956, "Love, Love, Love," 1956 • The Cookies, "In

Paradise," 1956 • The Drifters, "Fools Fall in Love," 1956 • Ivory Joe Hunter, "Since I Met You Baby," 1956, "Empty Arms," 1957 • Clyde McPhatter, "Treasure of Love," 1956, "Without Love (There Is Nothing)," 1956, "A Lover's Question," 1958 • Big Joe Turner, "Corrine Corrina," 1956, "Midnight Special Train," 1956, "The Chicken and the Hawk," 1956 • Chuck Willis, "It's Too Late," 1956, "Betty and Dupree," 1957, "C.C. Rider," 1957, "Hang Up My Rock and Roll Shoes," 1958, "What Am I Livin' For?," 1958.

Atlantic Rock and Roll, Atlantic, 1991.

Ertegun's New York, New York, Atlantic, 1987.

Mainstream, Atlantic Jazz, 1987.

Singers, Atlantic Jazz, 1987.

The Golden Age of Black Music, 1977–1988, Atlantic, 1988.

Ahmet and Nesuhi Ertegun

Charles, Ray: *The Great,* Atlantic, 1956.

Darin, Bobby: *That's All,* Atco, 1959 • *Darin at the Copa,* Atlantic, 1960, 1994 • *This Is Darin,* Atlantic, 1960, 1994.

Davis, Eddie "Lockjaw": *That's All,* FD Music, 1986.

Mann, Herbie: *Best Of,* Atlantic, 1969.

Mercer, Mabel: *Sings Cole Porter,* Rhino, 1994.

Walker, T-Bone: *T-Bone Blues,* Atlantic Jazz, 1960, 1989.

Nesuhi Ertegun

Allison, Mose: *I Don't Worry About a Thing,* Rhino, 1962, 1993 • *Allison Wonderland,* Rhino, 1994 • *Best Of,* Sequel, 1995.

Almeida, Laurindo: See Modern Jazz Quartet.

American Jazz Orchestra: *Ellington Masterpieces,* Rhino, 1989.

Baker, LaVern: *Sings Bessie Smith,* Atco, 1958, 1988.

Blakey, Art: w/ Thelonius Monk, *Jazz Messengers with Thelonius Monk,* Atlantic Jazz, 1958.

Brubeck, Dave: *Last Set at Newport,* Atlantic, 1971.

Carter, Betty: *Round Midnight,* Atco, 1963, 1992.

Charles, Ray: *Ray Charles at Newport,* Atlantic, 1958 • *The Genius of,* Rhino, 1959, 1990 • *The Best Of,* Rhino, 1970, 1988 • "Come Rain or Come Shine," Warner Bros., 1983 (*The King of Comedy* soundtrack) • *Live,* Atlantic, 1987 • w/ Milt Jackson, *Soul Brothers/Soul Meeting,* Atlantic, 1989.

Cherry, Don, and John Coltrane: *The Avant Garde,* Rhino, 1967, 1990.

Coleman, Ornette: *The Shape of Jazz to Come,* Rhino, 1959 • *Change of the Century,* Atlantic, 1960, 1992 • *Ornette!* Atlantic, 1961 • *Ornette on Tenor,* Rhino, 1962, 1993 • *The Art of the Improvisers,* Rhino, 1970, 1988.

Coltrane, John: *The Art of John Coltrane: The Atlantic Years,* Rhino, 1958 • w/ Milt Jackson, *Bags and Trane,* Rhino, 1960, 1988 • *Coltrane Jazz,* Rhino, 1960 • *Coltrane Plays the Blues,* Rhino, 1960, 1989 • *Coltrane's Sound,* Rhino, 1960 • *Giant Steps,* Rhino, 1960 • *My Favorite Things,* Atlantic, 1960 • *Ole Coltrane,* Rhino/Atlantic, 1961, 1992 • *Best Of,* Rhino, 1970, 1990 • *Heavyweight Champion: The Complete Atlantic Recordings,* Rhino, 1995.

Connor, Chris, and Chris Craft: *A Jazz Date with,* Rhino, 1958, 1994.

Corea, Chick: *Chick Corea, with Herbie Hancock, Keith Jarrett, McCoy Tyner,* Rhino/Atlantic, 1981, 1988.

Crawford, Hank: *After Hours,* Atlantic, 1967, 1992 • *Heart and Soul,* Rhino, 1992.

Drifters, The: "Adorable," Atlantic, 1955, 1985 (*Atlantic Rhythm and Blues, 1952–1955*) • "Ruby Baby," Atlantic, 1956, 1985 (*Atlantic Rhythm and Blues, 1955–1958*) • "Your Promise to Be Mine," Atlantic, 1956.

Evans, Bill, and Herbie Mann: *Nirvana,* Rhino, n.d.

Gordon, Dexter: *Blue Dex: Dexter Gordon Plays the Blues,* Prestige, 1973, 1996.

Harris, Eddie: *In Sound/Mean Greens,* Rhino, 1966 • *The Artist's Choice: The Eddie Harris Anthology,* Rhino, 1995.

Herman, Woody: *Live at Monterey,* Atlantic Jazz, n.d.

Jackson, Milt: *Plenty, Plenty Soul,* Atlantic, 1957, 1992 • *Be Bop,* Rhino, 1988 • See also Charles, Ray; Coltrane, John.

King Curtis: "Castle Rock," Atlantic, 1958, 1986 (*Atlantic Honkers*) • "Jest Smoochin'," Atlantic, 1958, 1986 (*Atlantic Honkers*) • *Have Tenor Will Blow,* Atco, 1959 • "Honeydripper Part II," Atlantic, 1959, 1986 (*Atlantic Honkers*) • *Instant Groove,* Edsel, 1968.

Kirk, Rahsaan Roland: *Does Your House Have Lions? The Anthology,* Rhino, 1976, 1992.

Lawson, Yank: *Live,* Atlantic/Rhino, 1970, 1989.

Lewis, John: *The Wonderful World of Jazz,* Atlantic Jazz, 1961, 1989 • *The American Jazz Orchestra,* EastWest, 1989.

Mann, Herbie: *At the Village Gate,* Rhino, 1961 • *The Family of Mann,* Atlantic, 1961 • *The Inspiration I Feel,* Atlantic, 1968 • *Evolution of Mann: The Herbie Mann Anthology,* Rhino, 1994.

McCann, Les: *Swiss Movement,* Atlantic, 1969 • *Relationships: The Les McCann Anthology,* Rhino, 1993.

Mercer, Mabel, and Bobby Short: *At Town Hall,* Rhino, 1989.

Mingus, Charles: *Pithecanthropus Erectus,* Atlantic Jazz, 1956 • *Blues and Roots,* Rhino, 1960 • *Mingus at Antibes,* Rhino, 1960, 1994 • *The Clown,* Atlantic Jazz, 1961, 1989 • *Mingus Moves,* Rhino, 1974, 1993 • *Chair in the Sky,* Elektra, 1979 • *Thirteen Pictures: The Charles Mingus Anthology,* Rhino, 1993.

Mitchell, Red, and Harold Land: *Hear Ye!* Rhino, 1961, 1989.

Modern Jazz Quartet: *No Sun in Venice,* Atlantic, 1957, 1992 • *At the Music Inn with Sonny Rollins,* Vol. 2, Atlantic Jazz, 1958, 1989 • *Modern Jazz Quartet with Sonny Rollins,* Atlantic, 1958 • *European Concert,* Atlantic Jazz, 1960 • *Pyramid,* Atlantic Jazz, 1960 • *Comedy,* Atlantic, 1962, 1992 • *Lonely Woman,* Atlantic Jazz, 1962, 1987 • w/ Laurindo Almeida, *Collaboration with Almeida,* Atlantic, 1964 • *Blues on Bach,* Atlantic Jazz, 1973 • *Complete Last Concert,* Atlantic Jazz, 1974, 1989 • *Three Windows,* Atlantic, 1987 • *For Ellington,* EastWest, 1988.

Monk, Thelonious: See Blakey, Art.

Morrison, James, and Adam Macowicz: *Swiss Encounter,* EastWest, 1989.

Newborn, Phineas Jr.: *The Piano Artistry of,* Rhino, n.d.

Phillips, Esther: *Confessin' the Blues,* Rhino/Atlantic, 1976, 1991.

Piazzolla, Astor, and Gary Burton: *Suite for Vibraphone and New Tango Quintet,* Atlantic Jazz, 1987.

Redding, Otis: *In Person at the Whiskey A Go Go,* Rhino, 1968, 1992.

Rollins, Sonny: See Modern Jazz Quartet.

Scobey, Bob: *Frisco Band Favorites,* Good Time Jazz, 1986.

Short, Bobby: *Nobody Else But Me,* Atlantic, 1957 • *Bobby Short Is K-RA-ZY for Gershwin,* Atlantic, 1973, 1990.

Teddy Charles Tentet: *Teddy Charles Tentet,* Atlantic Jazz, 1988.

Torme, Mel: *Songs of New York,* Atlantic, 1963 • *The Mel Torme Collection,* Rhino, 1996.

Turner, Big Joe: *The Boss of the Blues,* Atlantic, 1956, 1981 • *Big Joe Rides Again,* Rhino, 1960, 1987.

Urbaniak, Michael: *Urban Express,* EastWest, 1989.

World's Greatest Jazz Band: *Live,* Rhino, 1988.

OLLECTIONS

Mainstream, Atlantic Jazz, 1987.

Saxophones, Vol. 2, Atlantic Jazz/Rhino, 1988.

Bob Ezrin

B ob Ezrin has produced some of the most brilliant and successful rock music of the last 30 years, including Alice Cooper's best work, Mitch Ryder's searing *Detroit,* Lou Reed's devastating *Berlin,* Peter Gabriel's first solo album, and Pink Floyd's magnum opus *The Wall* (No. 1). He has also delivered fine albums and big hits from Kiss, Tim Curry, Flo and Eddie, Hanoi Rocks, and recently, Catherine Wheel, Spain's Heroes del Silencio, and Kula Shaker. Ezrin is also co-founder and CEO of CD-ROM giant 7th Level and is active in charitable work (Communities in Schools, Mr. Holland's Opus Foundation).

Ezrin was born March 25, 1949, and "grew up in the confluence of American and English culture that is Toronto." From an early age radio was his "very best friend," he recalls. He reveled in the regional and stylistic variety of '50s radio, "DXing" (long-distance reception with a serious antenna) from the age of 8. Ezrin pulled in rock 'n' roll, R&B, pop, and country stations from Buffalo, Cleveland, Detroit, Boston, Wheeling, New Orleans, and elsewhere—his imagination riding the radio waves back to their point of origin. Ezrin played piano and guitar, and he and his siblings performed in commercials, plays, and shows. His uncle, Sid Ezrin, was an attorney who owned the first stereo system in Canada. An avowed "hi-fi nut," Uncle Sid collected audio equipment (including tape recorders) and over 15,000 albums.

He also lived right around the corner, and Bob "spent a lot of time in Sid's basement rummaging through his record collection and playing with his tape recorder. I had radio in my head and ferrous oxide in my veins," Ezrin chuckles. In his teens, Ezrin played guitar and sang in clubs and helped his friends' bands record at various low-end Toronto studios. "I was the guy who placed the mikes and told people where to stand and all. I guess I was producing already," he muses.

In 1968, Ezrin's arranging and organizational skills, demonstrated through a local rock musical production, led to a meeting with Jack Richardson (see entry), head of Nimbus 9 Productions and producer of the Guess Who. Nimbus hired Ezrin for "around $100 a week" to help bands with their material and arrangements before they went into the studio with Richardson. In addition to teaching him studio craft on the job, the company also sent Ezrin to the Eastman School of Music for a two-week summer course in record production, where his instructor was Phil Ramone (see entry).

In 1970, Shep Gordon, who managed Alice Cooper, was wandering the streets of Toronto, killing time as he awaited the arrival of funds to pay the band's hotel bill after the Strawberry Fields Festival. His wanderings led him to the door of Nimbus 9 and an epiphany: What Alice Cooper needed to break through to the big time was "the Guess Who sound."

Ezrin says, "Gordon plunked down the band's first two albums and pictures of these five 'things' of indeterminate gender and announced his intentions. Jack and his partners were these straight Canadians in their forties who surely wanted nothing to do with this 'Alice' person." However, Gordon was persistent, and finally Richardson foisted the whole thing onto "the kid," Ezrin. A decision was made to send Ezrin to see the band, and if he liked them, then Richardson would get involved. Soon, a trip was set up for Ezrin to go to New York to see a few acts, including Alice Cooper at Max's Kansas City. In the city, Ezrin "followed the searchlights to the club, and suddenly I was in this dark den of Spandex, spider eyes, and black fingernails. I had never seen anything like it in my life," he relates. A table was reserved for him in front of the stage.

"Suddenly," he continues, "a breeze blew past my cheek, then three loud 'whacks' on the stage followed by an orange light each time. Then Alice launched into 'Sun Arise' no further than two feet from my face. With his eyes wide open, and his lips widely parted, and his red red gums, and his white white teeth, and his black black mouth and eyes, I thought I was in hell. I watched the show with my jaw on the table. Then my friend said, 'What the fuck was that?' I said, 'I don't know, but I loved it.'"

Hyped on the show and the alien atmosphere, Ezrin bounded up the stairs to the dressing room, and with a big grin on his face, announced, "We'll do it!" Rather presumptuous, considering that Ezrin was a glorified coffee boy at the time. He continues, "The material was almost there, and my favorite song was 'I'm Edgy,' which Alice kindly told me was, in fact, 'I'm Eighteen.' 'Even better,' I said. The band was terrible but wonderful. It wasn't about 'being good,' it was about 'being.' It was the complete integration of the point of view and the personality into the presentation. They were—the songs, the antics, the theatricality—they were Alice Cooper. In a world of T-shirts, jeans, and beards, they were so refreshing and energizing."

Ezrin flew back to Toronto the next day, rehearsing his speech the whole way: "This isn't just about music, but a cultural movement. The whole building was full of people who looked like them and knew the words to the songs, which weren't even out on record yet."

After hours of discussion, ranging from the rational to abject pleading, Ezrin finally wore down Richardson, who said: "If you like them so damn much, you do it." Thus began, at 21, Ezrin's production career.

He produced Cooper's classic *Love It to Death* album, with the anthemic "I'm Eighteen" (No. 21)—a deeply perceptive look at the ambiguities of young adulthood ("I've got a baby's brain and an old man's heart")—and the rocking "Long Way to Go" and "Black Juju." Gordon never did get Alice "the Guess Who sound," and it's a damn good thing.

Ezrin and the original Alice Cooper band (Cooper, guitarists Michael Bruce and Glen Buxton, bassist Dennis Dunaway, and drummer Neal Smith) delivered two more stunners in a row: *Killer* (with "Under My Wheels") and *School's Out*, which soared to No. 2, with the great title track reaching No. 7. Those three albums conveyed danger and mystery. Who was this guy with a girl's name who chopped up babies, cuddled with his boa constrictor, and hanged himself onstage—yet delivered tuneful hard rock with a raw edge that appealed to all kinds of music fans, from the Stones, to Aerosmith, to the New York Dolls?

The band's greatness is evidenced by the influence it had on near-diametric opposites: the nascent punk movement and hair-metal bands. The original band was together for two more good, but not great, albums (*Billion Dollar Babies* (No. 1) and *Muscle of Love*), and then Alice left them for a "better" band (Lou Reed's Rock and Roll Animal band, with Steve Hunter on guitar). By then, it was no longer about "being," but about "being good," and the magic was lost.

Ezrin also produced the slamming *Mitch Ryder and the Detroit Wheels* album, featuring the finest version ever recorded of Lou Reed's "Rock and Roll," with Hunter drawing blood alongside Ryder's syncopated bellow. In 1973, Ezrin produced one of rock's most poignant and painfully beautiful albums, Reed's *Berlin*, a concept album about the deterioration of a beauty queen (much like Reed's bandmate in the Velvet Underground, Nico), full of jagged, telling moments and gorgeous melodies ("Caroline Says II," "Sad Song").

Recalls Ezrin, *"Berlin* was a turning point because it was the first album where I heard the record before recording it. Lou wrote brilliantly. The little lyrical moments tell it all. It's the best representation of synecdoche [where a small part represents the whole] on record. It was like making a movie—we went to hell and back."

Ezrin also presided over another concept album, Pink Floyd's multiplatinum *The Wall*, which he co-produced with an estranged Roger Waters and David Gilmour. "Initially the album was to be written by Roger alone, but there were holes," explains Ezrin. "I insisted that we go through Dave's repertoire. At that point, there was tension between them, and I had to be the glue," Ezrin says. "Dave played a bunch of demos, and after one—I don't even remember what the lyric was—I said, 'This must go on the album.' Roger resisted, but demurred, wrote the lyrics, and that song became 'Comfortably Numb.'"

The contoversy surrounding the song continued. Waters and Ezrin felt that the orchestra was integral to the song and Gilmour did not. They fought about it until the last three days of mixing. Imagine "Numb" without the orchestra and you will know how good Ezrin's ears are, as well as his powers of diplomacy.

Which brings to mind Ezrin's production philosophy: "The producer must wear the hat of the generalist, must have the eyes and ears of the specialist, have the personality of a humanist, and the good sense to know where you fall short in any of these areas (and when to bring in help)." Clearly, he has done so. —ERIC OLSEN

Air Supply: *Air Supply,* Arista, 1985 • "Just As I Am," Arista, 1985.

Alice Cooper: "Eighteen," Warner Bros., 1971 • *Killer,* Warner Bros., 1971 • *Love It to Death,* Warner Bros., 1971 • "School's Out," Warner Bros., 1972 • *School's Out,* Warner Bros., 1972 • "Billion Dollar Babies," Warner Bros., 1973 (*Appetizers*) • *Billion Dollar Babies,* Warner Bros., 1973 • *Greatest Hits,* Warner Bros., 1974, 1988 • "Only Women Bleed," Anchor/Atlantic, 1975 • *Welcome to My Nightmare,* Anchor/Atlantic, 1975 • *Goes to Hell,* Warner Bros., 1976 • "I Never Cry," Warner Bros., 1976 • *Lace and Whiskey,* Warner Bros., 1977 • *The Alice Cooper Show,* Warner Bros., 1977 • "You and Me," Warner Bros., 1977 • *Da-Da,* Warner Bros., 1983.

Babys, The: *The Babys,* Chrysalis, 1977 • *Anthology,* Gold Rush, 1981, 1996.

Berlin: *Count Three and Pray,* Geffen, 1986 • *Best Of, 1979–1988,* Geffen, 1988.

Bonham: *The Disregard of Timekeeping,* WTG, 1989.

Catherine Wheel: *Adam and Eve,* Mercury, 1997.

Curry, Tim: *Read My Lips,* A&M, 1978 • *Best Of,* A&M, 1989.

Daltrey, Roger: *A Celebration: The Music of the Who,* Continuum, 1994.

Dr. John: *Hollywood Be Thy Name,* United Artists, 1975 • *Mos' Scocious: The Dr. John Anthology,* Rhino, 1993.

Flo and Eddie: "Another Pop Star's Life," Warner Bros., 1973 (*Appetizers*) • *Flo and Eddie,* Warner Bros., 1973 • *Best Of,* Rhino, 1987.

Gabriel, Peter: "Solsbury Hill," Atco, 1977 • *Peter Gabriel (No. 1),* Atco, 1977 • *Shaking the Tree: 16 Golden Greats,* Geffen, 1990 • *Revisited,* Atlantic, 1992.

Gilmour, David: *About Face,* Columbia, 1984.

Hanoi Rocks: *Two Steps from the Move,* Epic, 1984.

Heroes del Silencio: *Avalancha,* IRS, 1995.

Hunter, Steve: *Swept Away,* Atco, 1977.

Hurricane: *Over the Edge,* Enigma, 1988.

Kansas: *In the Spirit of Things,* MCA, 1988.

Kings, The: *The Kings Are Here,* Elektra, 1980 • *Amazon Beach,* Elektra, 1981.

Kiss: "Beth," Casablanca, 1976 • *Destroyer,* Casablanca, 1976 • *The Elder,* Casablanca, 1976 • *Double Platinum,* Casablanca/Mercury, 1978 • *Music from the Elder,* Casablanca/Mercury, 1981, 1989 • *Smashes, Thrashes and Hits,* Mercury, 1988 • *Revenge,* Mercury, 1992.

Lennon, Julian: *Help Yourself,* Atlantic, 1991.

Lofgren, Nils: *Nils,* A&M, 1979 • *The Best Of,* A&M, 1985.

McLauchlan, Murray: *Storm Warning,* Asylum, 1981.

Pink Floyd: *The Wall,* Columbia, 1979 • "Another Brick in the Wall," Columbia, 1980 • *A Collection of Great Dance Songs, 1975–1981,* Columbia, 1981 • *A Momentary Lapse of Reason,* Columbia, 1987 • *The Division Bell,* Columbia, 1994.

Rabin, Trevor: *Can't Look Away,* Elektra, 1989.

Reed, Lou: *Berlin,* RCA, 1973 • *Walk on the Wild Side: The Best Of,* RCA, 1977 • *Between Thought and Expression: The Lou Reed Anthology,* RCA, 1992.

Ryder, Mitch, and the Detroit Wheels: *Greatest Hits,* Paramount, 1972 • "Rock and Roll," Seeds and Stems, 1977 (*Michigan Rocks*).

Stewart, Rod: *Rod Stewart,* Warner Bros., 1986.

Telephone: *Telephone,* Virgin, 1982.

Throbs, The: *The Language of Thieves and Vagabonds,* DGC, 1991.

Ursa Major: *Ursa Major,* RCA, 1972.

Wagner, Richard: *Wagner, Richard,* Atlantic, 1978.

Waite, John: *Essential,* Chrysalis, 1992.

Donald Fagen

See WALTER BECKER AND DONALD FAGEN

Bruce Fairbairn

Bruce Fairbairn—producer of huge guitar rock hits by AC/DC, Aerosmith, Bon Jovi, Loverboy, Poison, and Scorpions—seeks no "sound."

"I think my sound is the absence of a sound," he says. "I don't know whether it was because I wasn't visionary enough to have my own sound or because being in a band, I always felt that it was the band's sound that was most important. I try to fit myself into where the band is coming from, and find out what their vision is for their record. I probably could have had more big hits if I had done it the other way around," he laughs.

"Nobody's phoning me up and saying, 'Hey, we want the Bruce Fairbairn sound on our record.' At least I hope they never call me and say that, or they'll just get a trumpet record," he chuckles.

Fairbairn began his career as a trumpet player and arranger in the Canadian rock band Prism. The first time Fairbairn sat in the producer's chair was in 1978 for Prism's *See Forever Eyes*.

"We were an obscure Canadian band when we started and had some success in the United States," he says. "We couldn't afford a producer and I was sitting there, so I put the hat on. I didn't really know too much about

producing at that time, except you had to get everybody in the studio. It was a lot of fun, though, because it was my band's record, so I was doubly excited."

Looking back now, though, he can see it was the first Prism record that gave him an idea of how he wanted to work in the future: "I don't like doing records that aren't fun, so I tell everybody before we start, 'Fellas, ladies, if this is not going to be fun let's bail out now, before we torture ourselves.' "

He's taken that attitude into a number of different projects, and although they've all had their moments of fun, there are a couple that stick out in his mind.

"I'd have to say that Aerosmith's *Pump* (No. 5) was a big highlight in my career—with the combination of the sparks that were flying, and the great musical ideas that were being thrown out there, and the energy that was being put onto tape," he remembers. "I've been blessed with being able to work with a lot of really great bands," he comments, and then pauses. "Hearing AC/DC sit down in a studio and play is scary too."

His first steps down the music industry path came when he was called to work on the first solo album by Ian Lloyd, who had been the lead singer of Stories ("Brother Louie") in the early '70s. "It was a lot of fun, and remarkable in that Ian was very close to the guys in Foreigner," Fairbairn recalls. "So, showing up on the record was Mick Jones (see entry), Lou Graham, and

then Ric Ocasek (see entry) and Benjamin Orr [of the Cars] came down as well.

"For me—a little guy from Vancouver—I was recording in New York and all these great players were showing up. I was hanging on the skin of my teeth. The record was not a commercial success, but critically it was well-received and that really cut my teeth in the big-time recording thing."

Fairbairn's big-time commercial success would come soon enough though, when he went into the studio with fellow Canadians Loverboy to record their debut album (No. 13). "They were a great band that could actually play and deliver right off the floor of the studio, so my job there was to make sure that the tape kept rolling across the record heads," he says.

Then he busted out with such quintessential '80s tunes as Bon Jovi's "Bad Medicine" (No. 1), "Wanted Dead or Alive" (No. 7), and "You Give Love a Bad Name" (No. 1). When the '90s rolled around Fairbairn decided it was time to look elsewhere, including an album by the alternative band the Cranberries and the debut album from a London-based band called Never the Bride. As Fairbairn explains it, after successful albums in the '80s and '90s with bands like Aerosmith, Van Halen, AC/DC, and Bon Jovi, he worried about being pigeonholed.

"When you have a number of successful records [in a genre], you tend to get locked into that. For me, though, one of the most inspiring records I've done was the Chicago big-band jazz record. Those guys were heroes of mine for years. I don't know how many hours I spent in front of my stereo trying to cop their horn arrangements," he confides. "If you stay in one place you're dead. I'm not God's gift to music, and I think the interesting musicians, writers, and singers I work with all rub off a little, and it all helps make me a better producer. So, I like to throw my cards on the table in a different game every now and again."

In late May 1999, Bruce Fairbairn was found dead at his home in Vancouver. The cause of death was unknown. He was 49. —DAVID JOHN FARINELLA

AC/DC: "Moneytalks," Atco, 1990 • *The Razor's Edge*, Atco, 1990 • *Live*, Atco, 1991.

Aerosmith: "Dude (Looks Like a Lady)," Geffen, 1987 • *Permanent Vacation*, Geffen, 1987 • "Angel," Geffen, 1988 • "Rag Doll," Geffen, 1988 • "Janie's Got a Gun," Geffen, 1989 • "Love in an Elevator," Geffen, 1989 • *Pump*, Geffen, 1989 • "The Other Side," Geffen, 1990 • "What It Takes," Geffen, 1990 • "Cryin'," Geffen, 1993 • "Livin' on the Edge," Geffen, 1993 • *Get a Grip*, Geffen, 1993 • "Amazing," Geffen, 1994 • "Crazy," Geffen, 1994 •

"Deuces Are Wild," Geffen, 1994 • *Big Ones*, Geffen, 1994.

Black 'N Blue: *Without Love*, Geffen, 1985.

Blue Oyster Cult: *The Revolution by Night*, Columbia, 1983 • *Workshop of the Telescopes* (2 tracks), Legacy, 1995.

Bon Jovi: "Wanted Dead or Alive," Mercury, 1986 • *Slippery When Wet*, Mercury, 1986 • "You Give Love a Bad Name," Mercury/PolyGram, 1986 • "Livin' on a Prayer," Mercury, 1987 • "Bad Medicine," Mercury, 1988 • "Born to Be My Baby," Mercury, 1988 • "I'll Be There for You," Mercury, 1988 • "Lay Your Hands on Me," Mercury, 1988 • "Living in Sin," Mercury, 1988 • *New Jersey*, Mercury, 1988 • "Hey God/House of the Rising Sun/Living on a Prayer," Mercury, 1996.

Cheap Trick: *Woke Up with a Monster*, Warner Bros., 1994.

Chicago: *Night and Day (Big Band)*, Giant, 1995.

Cranberries, The: "Salvation," Island, 1996 • *To the Faithful Departed*, Island, 1996.

Gorky Park: *Gorky Park*, Mercury, 1989.

Honeymoon Suite: *The Big Prize*, Warner Bros., 1985.

INXS: *Elegantly Wasted*, Mercury, 1997.

Jackyl: *Push Comes to Shove*, Geffen, 1994.

Krokus: *The Blitz*, Arista, 1984 • *Stayed Awake All Night: The Best Of*, Arista, 1989.

Laine, Paul: *Stick It in Your Ear*, Elektra, 1990.

Lloyd, Ian: *Goose Bumps*, Atlantic/Scotti Brothers, 1979 • *Third Wave Civilization*, Scotti Brothers, 1980.

Loverboy: "Lady of the 80's," Columbia, 1980, 1981 (*Exposed*) • *Loverboy*, Columbia, 1980 • "The Kid Is Hot Tonite," Columbia, 1980, 1981 (*Exposed*) • *Get Lucky*, Columbia, 1981 • "Hot Girls in Love," Columbia, 1983 • *Keep It Up*, Columbia, 1983 • *Wildside*, Columbia, 1987 • *Big Ones*, Columbia, 1989.

Poison: *Flesh and Blood*, Capitol, 1990 • *Greatest Hits, 1986–1996*, Capitol, 1996.

Prism: *Prism*, Ariola, 1978 • *See Forever Eyes*, Ariola, 1978 • *Armageddon*, Capitol, 1979 • *Young and Restless*, Capitol, 1980.

Dan Reed Network: *Dan Reed Network*, Mercury, 1988 • *The Heat*, Mercury, 1991.

Rock and Hyde: *Under the Volcano*, Capitol, 1987.

Ronson, Mick: *Heaven and Hull*, Epic, 1994.

Scorpions: *Best of Rockers and Ballads*, Mercury, 1989 • *Face the Heat*, Mercury, 1993 • *Deadly Sting: The Mercury Years*, Mercury, 1997.

Shanghai: *Shanghai*, Chrysalis, 1982.

Strange Advance: *Worlds Away*, Capitol, 1983.

Sulton, Kasim: *Kasim*, EMI America, 1982.

Van Halen: *Balance*, Warner Bros., 1995 • *Best Of*, Vol. 1, Warner Bros., 1996 • "Humans Being," Warner Bros., 1996 (*Twister* soundtrack).

Anton Fier

Renowned for his art-pop amalgam the Golden Palominos, Anton Fier has made flux and mutability his bywords over the years, thriving on change and his ability to summon stirring performances from a shifting cast of characters.

"Despite whatever notions you have beforehand, a record inevitably takes on a life of its own—and that's when the magic happens," Fier says. "Imposing one's will or personality on a situation isn't the way to facilitate that. You have to be open to instinct, intuition, and improvisation—that's what great art has. And that's what I hope to capture, if even for a moment."

In the mid-'80s, Fier fashioned a series of riveting all-star albums with the Golden Palominos, in particular, *Visions of Excess* and *Blast of Silence*. Michael Stipe, Richard Thompson, Jack Bruce, John Lydon, Syd Straw, Bernie Worrell, Matthew Sweet, Bill Laswell (see entry), and drummer Fier all contributed writing and performances to the "band" in this period, with the music alternating between sinuous guitar rock and country-tinged laments.

Classic Golden Palomino collaborations midwifed by Fier included *Visions of Excess*'s "Boy Go," in which Stipe's vocals and Thompson's guitars intertwine like beautifully rusted barbed wire. And a highlight from *Blast of Silence* saw Bruce wailing like he hadn't since the glory days of Cream on "(Something Else Is) Working Harder," pushing the proceedings into hoodoo territory somewhere betwixt the backwoods and the big city.

The emotional immediacy and carefully crafted ensemble sound of these songs were constructed one performance at a time, with Fier working with an ad-hoc assortment of players in often intense situations—a complex mesh of talents facing time pressures and limited resources.

"In those instances, where someone is only going to be in town for a couple of days, I'm always breathing a sigh of relief when it's over," he says. "It's like, 'Whew, we got it.'"

The two albums immediately following *Blast of Silence* were blessed by lesser lights and were thus lesser affairs, but Fier found a new groove—literally—on the next pair, *This Is How It Feels* and *Pure* from 1993 and 1994. Pre-Portishead and Tricky, those were pioneering trip-hop albums, built on loose-limbed, bass-heavy rhythm beds and darkly evocative atmospheres. Adding considerably to the sexy creative tension of these albums was Fier's new collaborator, New York singer/ songwriter Lori Carson. On *Pure,* the better disc of the two, she delivers seriously sensual vocal performances and superior songs, particularly "Gun," "Little Suicides," and the title track.

In the late '80s, Fier helmed discs by singer/songwriters Victoria Williams and Joe Henry. But he revealed a particularly sensitive way with intimate chamber folk in his production of Carson's touching solo disc from 1995, *Where It Goes*—a record he says he's more proud of having worked on than any other. He also contributed to its follow-up, *Everything I Touch Runs Wild,* adding a *Pure*-like groove to the lead track, "Something's Got Me," and contributing a minor-key extended remix of the song that was not only dance floor hip but emotionally acute.

Fier has worked as a session drummer for the likes of Mick Jagger (see Glimmer Twins entry), Herbie Hancock, and, most notably, Bob Mould (see entry) on his solo albums *Workbook* and *Black Sheets of Rain,* and the accompanying tours. (Returning the favor, Mould contributed the terrifyingly beautiful "Dying from the Inside Out" to the otherwise desultory *Drunk with Passion,* the Golden Palominos effort from 1991.)

Fier remains a longtime co-conspirator of bassist/producer Laswell, crafting loops and textures with him for various dub and ambient projects. The most recent Golden Palominos album, *Dead Inside,* was a spoken-word project with musical underpinning.

"All the people I've worked with on Palominos records are true artists with strong individual styles and personalities," Fier says. "As a producer, what I do is foremost a collaboration. I try to develop a trust and understanding; I try to develop a relationship."

In meeting the technical challenge of record production, Fier says he considers all the available tools—"a computer is as much of a musical instrument as piano or drums; it just depends on how it's used"—as well as the example of great music.

"I'm a fan of records," he says. "I try to never be jaded about music." Fier was into English ambient-techno bands like Seefeel and New York nighttime artisans like DJ Soul Slinger long before they were known quantities, and for creative nourishment, he continues to look to the LPs that inspired him when he was growing up: Miles Davis's early '70s live electric recordings and Bob Dylan's *Blonde on Blonde,* for instance, as well as the example of master drummers like the late Tony Williams and John Bonham.

"I consider the making of records to be a spiritual endeavor," Fier says. "The art of making music is a magical thing. It's always amazed me, and I hope at some point to create something that approaches the magic of the recordings that have influenced my life." —BRADLEY BAMBARGER

Carson, Lori: *Where It Goes,* Restless, 1995 • *Everything I Touch Runs Wild,* Restless, 1997.
Drivin' N' Cryin': *Whisper Tames the Lion,* Island, 1988.
Face to Face: *One Big Day,* Mercury, 1988.
Fier, Anton: *Dreamspeed,* Avant, 1993.
Golden Palominos: *The Golden Palominos,* OAO/Celluloid, 1983 • *Visions of Excess,* Celluloid, 1985 • *Blast of Silence,* Celluloid, 1986 • *A Dead Horse,* Celluloid, 1989 • *The Best Of,* Oceana/Celluloid, 1990 • *Drunk with Passion,* Charisma, 1991 • *A History, 1982–1985,* Restless, 1992 • *A History, 1986–1989,* Restless, 1993 • "Prison of the Rhythm," Restless, 1993 • *This Is How It Feels,* Restless, 1993 • "Gun/Little Suicides," Restless, 1994 • "Heaven," Restless, 1994 • *Pure,* Restless, 1994.
Grapes of Wrath: *Now and Again,* Capitol, 1989.
Henry, Joe: *Murder of Crows,* Mammoth, 1989, 1994.
Williams, Victoria: *Happy Come Home,* Geffen, 1987.

COLLECTIONS
Altered Beats: Assassin Knowledges of the Remanipulated, Axiom, 1996.

Andre Fischer

Andre Fischer has melded the best of black and white music, moving effortlessly through genres (rock, R&B, Quiet Storm, traditional popular, and jazz) as a musician (Oscar Brown, Curtis Mayfield, American Breed, Rufus), producer and executive producer (Natalie Cole, Michael Franks, Brenda Russell, Tony Bennett, Immature, Nancy Wilson, Milt Jackson) and label executive (MCA, Dre Force). Along the way he has been involved with 13 gold and platinum records and received the 1993 Best Traditional Pop Vocal Grammy for Tony Bennett's *Perfectly Frank.*

Fischer was born in 1951 to a musical family with roots in Minnesota and Michigan. His mother had met his father, a trumpeter and band leader, when she sang for his band.

The oldest of three children, Andre moved with the family to Omaha, Nebraska, to be near the National Orchestra Service: the booking agency that placed his father with Stan Kenton, Woody Herman, and other bands. His father now has a master's degree in music and teaches at both College of the Canyons in Valencia, California, and Pasadena City College. Andre's uncle is Clare Fischer, a noted jazz arranger, composer, and pianist.

During breaks from school, Fischer traveled with his father as band boy, setting up the sheet music for the musicians and pretending to conduct the band. Fischer took up trumpet, trombone, and then drums, touring with jazz bands from the age of 15 on. He moved to San Francisco immediately after high school and played with Oscar Brown and Ahmad Jamal.

Around 1970, Fischer moved to Chicago and drummed with Curtis Mayfield, Jerry Butler, and Gene Chandler, as well as on commercial jingles. He studied under (and lived in the basement of) arranger Richard Evans, best known for his work with the popular Soulful Strings series.

Fischer drummed for the final iteration of the rock band American Breed ("Bend Me, Shape Me"), which then evolved into the funk-rock unit Ask Rufus. They met Chaka Khan, shortened the name to Rufus, and recorded their first album in 1973. Over a 10-year career, Rufus generated ten Top 40 singles, and five Top 20 albums.

The band, led by Fischer, took over production by their third album (*Rufusized*, No. 7), and Fischer's production career was under way. He produced Brenda Russell, Michael Franks, and Dusty Springfield before taking a break from music with a stay in Paris from 1986 to 1988. He returned to production after that and has been prolific and successful.

Fischer feels that being a drummer is excellent training for production because "you have to know everyone else's part," although he doesn't find producing as satisfying as playing.

"Producing is vicarious: it's like screwing by watching a video," he reasons. "I try to play as often I can [because] when you seclude yourself from all the elements that originally inspired you, then everything you are doing is only from memory, and that's not the same as a direct reaction against some kind of stimulus."

"I don't want to vicariously do anything," he continues, "I want to directly do it. I find that producers who started out as musicians, as they get older and more successful, hire subordinates to let them know what's really going on in the streets or in the studio."

Fischer tries to avoid that pitfall by playing as often as possible and by being a hands-on producer. "You can't fix it in the mix if you didn't record it properly, so I'm involved with the recording," he says. "I also do most of the mixes myself—in conjunction with the engineer—because I don't want anyone to reinterpret [what I've

done]. The hardest thing I have to do in life [other than be a father to five children] is to figure out the strengths and weaknesses of a vocalist. If they have shown me their vulnerability, and I spend the time to tailor a suit for them, I don't want the mixer to change it."

Fischer works with a combination of meticulous planning ("I hear the arrangements in my head and then write them out") and spontaneity. "I run a 'snoop tape' off the board so that I can catch anything that anyone does on the spur of the moment. Then I can play it back for them and say 'That's what I want.'

"With Rufus," he continues, "guitarist Tony Maiden would do little flourishes when he was sitting there talking with somebody. When I came out to ask him to do it again, he couldn't because he couldn't remember it. I would play the snoop tape for him and ask him to incorporate the flourish into the song; then I would ask the horns or a keyboard to do that same lick at a certain spot. I call it a little hook you can hang your hat on. All these little 'ear candies' throughout the tune keep you interested. It's like running a rope across a canyon," he says.

Fischer's best-known work is with then-wife Natalie Cole, especially her enormous 1991 No. 1 hit *Unforgettable with Love* (wherein Cole sings "duets" with her late father, Nat "King" Cole). Fischer feels the key to that project was understanding the priorities.

"I was selling the story," he explains. "My purpose for doing the record was to help a woman say 'goodbye' to her father by completing these songs, updating them sonically but with the essence of the original, so that when she heard them played back she would be complete inside—a catharsis would have taken place. She was only 15 and out of town when her pop passed.

"David [Foster] and Tommy [LiPuma; see entries], my co-producers on the project, didn't get it right away. Their whole thing was 'This is another project, this is kind of hip to do,' and my whole thing was 'This isn't just another project, and if you think like that then you will interact with other people feeling like that.' My whole goal was to empower everybody with the fact that we were doing something special here, helping someone say goodbye to her father."

Fischer accomplished that goal admirably. —Eric Olsen and Dawn Darling

Anderson, Carl: *Pieces of the Heart*, GRP, 1991 • *Fantasy Hotel*, GRP, 1992.

Bennett, Tony: *Perfectly Frank*, Columbia, 1992.

Boyz of Paradize: *BOP*, Dre Force, 1995.

Cole, Natalie: *Good to Be Back*, EMI, 1989 • "Wild Women Do," EMI, 1990 (*Pretty Woman* soundtrack) • *Unforgettable*

with Love, Elektra, 1991 • w/ Frank Sinatra, *Duets* (1 track), Capitol, 1993 • *Take a Look*, Elektra, 1993 • *Holly and Ivy*, Elektra, 1994.

Franks, Michael: *One Bad Habit*, Warner Bros., 1980.

Hathaway, Lalah: *Lalah Hathaway*, Virgin, 1990.

Immature: *Playtime Is Over*, MCA, 1994.

Jackson, Milt: *Reverence and Compassion*, Qwest, 1993.

Khan, Chaka: *See* Rufus.

Knight, Gladys: *Just for You*, MCA, 1995.

Nyro, Laura: "The Christmas Song," Columbia, 1990 (*Acoustic Christmas*).

Perry, Phil: *The Heart of the Man*, Capitol, 1991.

Rubin, Vanessa: "I Want to Spend the Night," RCA, 1997 • *New Horizons*, RCA, 1997.

Rufus: *Rufus*, ABC, 1973 • *Rags to Rufus*, ABC, 1974 • *Rufus, Featuring Chaka Khan*, ABC, 1975 • *Rufusized*, ABC, 1975 • *Ask Rufus*, ABC, 1977.

Russell, Brenda: *Brenda Russell*, Horizon, 1979 • *Get Here*, A&M, 1988 • featuring Joe Esposito, "Piano in the Dark," A&M, 1988 • *Greatest Hits* (1 track), A&M, 1992, 1994.

Schuur, Diane: *Pure Schuur*, GRP, 1991 • *In Tribute*, GRP, 1992.

Simone, Nina: *A Single Woman*, Asylum, 1993.

Sinatra, Frank: *See* Cole, Natalie.

Springfield, Dusty: *White Heat*, Casablanca, 1982.

Torres, Nester: *Talk to Me*, Sony Latin Jazz, 1996.

Tresvant, Ralph: *It's Goin' Down*, MCA, 1994.

Whalum, Kirk: *Cache*, Columbia, 1993 • "Fragile," Columbia, 1993.

Wilson, Nancy: *Love, Nancy*, Columbia, 1994.

COLLECTIONS

Garfield: Am I Cool or What, GRP, 1991.

Don Fleming

A singer/songwriter/guitarist and leader of noise-pop bands Velvet Monkeys, B.A.L.L., and Gumball, as well as a member of the *Backbeat* soundtrack band (with Greg Dulli, Dave Grohl, Mike Mills, Thurston Moore, and Dave Pirner), Don Fleming is also one of the top American alterna-rock producers of the '90s, scoring successes with tuneful guitar workouts, including Teenage Fanclub's *Bandwagonesque*, The Posies' *Frosting on the Beater*, Screaming Trees' *Sweet Oblivion*, and Hole's primal *Pretty on the Inside*.

A self-proclaimed "Air Force brat," Fleming was born September 25, 1957, in south Georgia, but spent his childhood hopping from Oklahoma to Florida to France. "Two years here, two years there—on the road already," he sighs.

A "total record-collecting freak" and desultory guitar player, the young Fleming chose the path less taken—eschewing the obvious Beatles and Stones fixations for Herman's Hermits—before succumbing to the inexorable pull of the Fab Four in the time of *Sgt. Pepper*.

Through the Beatles' Apple label connection, Fleming was drawn to Badfinger's *Straight Up* and the album's producer, Todd Rundgren (see entry). Fleming was attracted to the producer/musician stance of Rundgren's *Something/Anything?* "and all of that great analog sound."

In the mid-'70s Fleming threw himself into the punk revolution (Buzzcocks, Sex Pistols, Adverts), and recorded with the punkish Stroke Band out of Valdosta, Georgia, for the local Abacus label in 1979. Even then Fleming displayed studio awareness, keeping a wary eye on the mixing process. He next moved to Washington, D.C., and fronted the Velvet Monkeys, a prolific if ragged singles band. Fleming recorded the Monkeys' records "out of economic necessity and interest," and then began assisting friends' bands with their recordings for similar reasons.

Fleming gained engineering experience working at a D.C. studio that specialized in transferring old acetate discs to tape for the Smithsonian, Library of Congress, and other government agencies. There he learned to respect the sanctity of an original source: "You don't clean it up, you don't EQ it; maintain the integrity of the original."

Fleming moved to New York in the late '80s and joined B.A.L.L. with musician/producer Kramer (see entry). Fleming maintained his low-budget production schedule as well, producing friends and friends of friends for a six-pack and a smile.

Teenage Fanclub was his big breakthrough in 1991. He had produced the band's *God Knows It's True* EP in 1990, and then took the young Scots to Liverpool to record for their major-label debut. The result is a holy fusion of Big Star pop-rock sensibility; *Rust Never Sleeps*–era Neil Young guitar; and creamy Dream Academy vocals on chunky, mid-tempo rockers like "The Concept," "Pet Rock," and "Star Sign" and on dreamy numbers like "Guiding Star."

Fleming's next major projects were with two atypical Seattle bands: Screaming Trees and the Posies.

The Trees, led by beefy singer Mark Lanegan and the Connor brothers, Gary Lee and Van, packed the punch of the grunge bands but with much greater finesse and attention to songs. *Sweet Oblivion* features the insinuating radio hit "Nearly Lost You" with great wah-wah lead guitar from Gary Lee, the emotive acoustic number "Dollar Bill," and groovy rocker "Butterfly." Lanegan's husky vocals and Gary Lee's guitar shine throughout.

The Posies' *Frosting on the Beater* carries pop rock to its heaviest conclusion, with Jon Auer and Ken Stringfellow's ringing British Invasion harmonies chased by their own slashing guitars down a path both sweet and pungent on the sensational "Dream All Day" and the Badfinger-esque "Solar Sister" and "Flavor of the Month." The latter two, as well as many other Fleming productions, were at least partially recorded at Fleming's favorite studio, the "analog heaven" of New York's Sear Sound. Sear and Fleming neatly coincide: the best of the musical past filtered through a modern mentality, delicately balancing power and grace.

Fleming's best work as a musician is to be found on Gumball's *Revolution on Ice* (co-produced by John Agnello); Fleming's reedy vocal and guitar power the excellent title track and "Freegrazin'." A nice organ intro from Malcolm Riviera provides variety on "With a Little Rain." Fleming's tunes are memorable and his production, built from the drums up, never gets in the way—an apt summation of his fine career. —ERIC OLSEN

Alice Cooper: *The Last Temptation*, Epic, 1994 • *Classicks*, Epic, 1995.

Bracket: *4-Wheel Drive*, Caroline, 1995 • *4 Rare Vibes* (EP), Caroline, 1996.

Chopper One: *Now Playing*, Restless, 1997.

Dark Carnival: *Last Great Ride*, Sympathy for the Record Industry, 1997.

Fleming, Don: *Because Tomorrow Comes* (EP), Instant Mayhem, 1996.

Gravy: *After That It's All Gravy*, Fused Coil, 1996.

Grey, Rudolph: *Mask of Light*, New Alliance, 1991.

Gumball: *Special Kiss*, Primo Scree, 1991 • *Revolution on Ice*, Columbia, 1994.

Guv'ner: *The Hunt*, Merge, 1996.

Hole: *Pretty on the Inside*, Caroline, 1991 • "Teenage Whore," A&M, 1994 (*S.F.W.* soundtrack).

Hollyfaith: *Purrrr*, Epic, 1993.

Hunk: *Hunk*, Geffen, 1996.

Jack Off Jill: *Sexless Demons and Scars*, Risk, 1997.

Magnuson, Ann: *The Luv Show*, Geffen, 1995.

Posies, The: *Frosting on the Beater*, DGC, 1993.

Screaming Trees: "Nearly Lost You," Epic Soundtrax, 1992 (*Singles* soundtrack) • *Sweet Oblivion*, Epic, 1992.

Sleepington: *Sleepington*, Instant Mayhem, 1996.

Speaker: *Model Citizen* (EP), Capricorn, 1997.

Steel Miners: *All Hopped Up*, Instant Mayhem, 1996.

Swish: *Supermax* (EP), Instant Mayhem, 1996.

Teenage Fanclub: *Bandwagonesque*, DGC, 1991 • "What You

Do to Me," DGC, 1991 • *God Knows It's True* (EP), Matador, 1991 • "Like a Virgin," Epic Soundtrax, 1994 (*Threesome* soundtrack).

Tripl3fastaction: *Broadcaster*, Capitol, 1996.

John Fogerty

John Fogerty (born May 28, 1945, in Berkeley, California) is the Grandpappy of swamp rock, paving the way for bands such as Lynyrd Skynyrd, ZZ Top, and the Eagles by making country influences palatable to a mass audience in a way no one had done since Elvis Presley. As a band, Creedence Clearwater Revival was scarcely more than a convenient fiction, a marketing tool on which to hang Fogerty's prolific songwriting and production ideas.

With their swampy grooves, CCR's albums seem to be the epitome of laid-back front-porch casualness, but they are in fact impeccably produced and carefully orchestrated. Fogerty wrote every note that was played, and in many cases played most of those notes himself, alternating between guitar, dobro, saxophone, harmonica, and vocals. Fogerty's vocal scream is one of the most energizing, powerful, cutting, and sincere sounds in rock music.

Fogerty's production brilliance is his knack for finding the simplest statement of an idea—its pure essence—and then presenting it without any clutter. Fogerty's parts are simple enough for any bar band to play and sound good doing it, but his performances of them are subtle and intricate enough that no one has ever bettered them.

The first album, *Creedence Clearwater Revival*, carries the credit "Produced by Saul Zaentz"; the remaining albums carry the credit "produced and arranged by J.C. Fogerty." But there is such overwhelming consistency between the first and subsequent albums that it is difficult to imagine that Zaentz did anything more than sign the checks for the studio time.

Fogerty's production peak occurred on *Cosmo's Factory* (No. 1), in which he presented his guitar with a fuller sound than on previous records and layered even more instruments than usual to create more complex soundscapes, such as on "Who'll Stop the Rain" (No. 2) and the mind-splitting "Ramble Tamble."

Fogerty's ear for hits was infallible: during its first six albums, every single that CCR released charted in the Top 40. Although uncredited at the time, engineer Russ

Gary is responsible for getting all of the magic on tape.

Fogerty didn't just write, arrange, and perform the songs—he was also a savvy marketer. Inventing the image of Southern hillbillies, he spoke with a drawl in interviews and tended to wear the plaid shirts at the time associated with farm boys. Realizing early on that CCR's core audience was 10- to 14-year-olds, he made sure that the band appeared wholesome enough to draw regular coverage in *Teen* magazine and other fanzines.

After CCR disbanded, Fogerty released two solo albums: 1973's *Blue Ridge Rangers* and 1975's *John Fogerty*, on which he played all the instruments. The albums were disappointing.

Fogerty spent the next 10 years writing and rehearsing what was to be his comeback album, in 1985, *Centerfield* (No. 1). During this time, Fogerty taught himself to play drums, and he made countless demos of the record. By the time he set foot in Sausalito's Plant Studios with engineer Jeffrey Norman to record, Fogerty knew every note he was going to play, every amplifier and guitar pickup setting, and he recorded the album quickly and efficiently. The resulting album was a commercial and critical hit. For the follow-up release, *Eye of the Zombie,* Fogerty hired players to join him, but the album sounded disjointed and scattered, and sales were disappointing.

In 1997, Fogerty released *Blue Moon Swamp*, reportedly five years in the making. For *Swamp* Fogerty used backup musicians as he had on *Zombie,* but this time he got it right, with the band evoking the sound of the original CCR, Ricky Nelson, and Roy Orbison's bands all rolled into one.

Norman describes Fogerty's strength as a producer: "I always think of a producer as someone who goes in and helps interpret someone else's art. But as a self-producer I can't think of anyone who is any better at it except maybe Paul McCartney [see entry]. Fogerty really gets out of himself the best performances he can deliver. From the beginning he knows where every part is going to be—all the attention to detail and the scat lines and things. For example, in the 13th bar on the seventh 8th note he knows there's going to be a little 'yeah,' and it sounds completely spontaneous but it's all been planned."

Fogerty was heavily influenced by Orbison, the Ventures, and Duane Eddy. "The thing is," Fogerty explains, "as good as those guys are, there's not a lot of technique there, which is why they sound so good by garage bands. That's the same secret of Creedence. All the arrangements I did were for four people who were kind of mediocre or less on their instruments," he confides.

"I arranged everything, quite specifically, very much in the same way that Benny Goodman did with his swing band," Fogerty reports. "There are only a couple of right ways to play a song, and there are a whole lot of wrong ways. . . . I would know what parts were going to work long before we went into the studio. That was my *job* as the producer. I knew how to resolve those musical questions, and that's all arranging is: you're resolving those musical questions in a way that works so that you can go on." —DANIEL J. LEVITIN

Creedence Clearwater Revival: "Bad Moon Rising," Fantasy, 1969 • *Bayou Country,* Fantasy, 1969 • "Commotion," Fantasy, 1969 • "Down on the Corner," Fantasy, 1969 • "Fortunate Son," Fantasy, 1969 • "Green River," Fantasy, 1969 • *Green River,* Fantasy, 1969 • "Lodi," Fantasy, 1969 • "Proud Mary," Fantasy, 1969 • *Willy and the Poor Boys,* Fantasy, 1969 • *Cosmo's Factory,* Fantasy, 1970 • "Long As I Can See the Light," Fantasy, 1970 • "Lookin' out My Back Door," Fantasy, 1970 • *Pendulum,* Fantasy, 1970 • "Run Through the Jungle," Fantasy, 1970 • "Travelin' Band," Fantasy, 1970 • "Up Around the Bend," Fantasy, 1970 • "Who'll Stop the Rain," Fantasy, 1970 • "Have You Seen the Rain," Fantasy, 1971 • "Hey Tonight," Fantasy, 1971 • "Someday Never Comes," Fantasy, 1971 • "Sweet Hitchhiker," Fantasy, 1971 • *Mardi Gras,* Fantasy, 1972.

Blue Ridge Rangers: *Blue Ridge Rangers,* Fantasy, 1973 • "Hearts of Stone," Fantasy, 1973 • "Jambalaya (on the Bayou)," Fantasy, 1973.

Fogerty, John: *John Fogerty,* Fantasy/Asylum, 1975 • "Rockin' All over the World," Asylum, 1975 • *Centerfield,* Warner Bros., 1985 • "Rock and Roll Girls," Warner Bros., 1985 • "The Old Man Down the Road," Warner Bros., 1985 • *Eye of the Zombie,* Warner Bros., 1986 • *Blue Moon Swamp,* Warner Bros., 1997 • "Southern Streamline," Warner Bros., 1997.

Tumatoe, Duke, and Power Trio: *I Like My Job,* Warner Bros., 1989.

David Foster

D avid Foster's career is best exemplified by his massive chart success in the '90s. Winner of multiple Grammy Awards as well as *Billboard*'s Producer of the Year citation, Foster produced three of the decade's biggest pop hits, all No. 1 on the charts: "Because You Loved Me," by Celine Dion; "I Will Always Love You," by Whitney Houston; and "Un-Break My Heart," by

Toni Braxton. He also has produced hits by All-4-One, Chicago, Barbra Streisand, Neil Diamond, and Michael Bolton.

Foster, a master of the big ballad, crafts hits using a well-honed formula: Start with a voice able to deliver the knockout punch. Add a wash of keyboards, synthesizers, guitars, and drums. Season that concoction with a dash of strings. Then stir the mixture until done. The result is a veritable hit factory that shows no signs of abating.

A native of Victoria, British Columbia, Canada, Foster started his career in Los Angeles in 1971 as a musician, achieving his initial chart success as a member of Skylark, including the Top 10 single "Wildflower." After Skylark, Foster settled in as a session player, songwriter, and arranger for such acts as Boz Scaggs and Hall and Oates. By the end of the '70s, Foster had added production to his palette, working with Alice Cooper and Peter Allen, among others. In the '80s, Foster broke from the pack, scoring a string of hits that included "St. Elmo's Fire" (No. 1) by John Parr, "Hard Habit to Break" (No. 3) by Chicago, and "We've Got Tonight" (No. 6) by Kenny Rogers and Sheena Easton.

In addition to '90s hits by pop divas Dion, Houston, and Braxton, Foster produced "I Swear" (No. 1) by All-4-One and "To Love Somebody" (No. 11) by Michael Bolton. Foster, who owns and runs the Atlantic-affiliated 143 Records label, also has rekindled his performing career with several solo albums. —BEN CROMER

Adams, Bryan: *18 Till I Die,* A&M, 1996.

Airplay: *Airplay,* RCA, 1979 • "Stressed out (Close to the Edge)," Atlantic, 1985 (*St. Elmo's Fire* soundtrack).

Alice Cooper: *From the Inside,* Warner Bros., 1978 • "How You Gonna See Me Now," Warner Bros., 1978.

All-4-One: *All-4-One,* Blitzz, 1994 • "I Swear," Blitzz, 1994 • *And the Music Speaks* (1 track), Blitzz, 1995 • *My Brother's Keeper,* Blitzz, 1997.

Allen, Peter: *Bi-Coastal,* A&M, 1980 • *At His Best,* A&M, 1993.

Anderson, Jon: "This Time It Was Really Right," Atlantic, 1985 (*St. Elmo's Fire* soundtrack).

Anka, Paul: *Paul Anka y Amigos,* Sony International, 1996.

Average White Band: *Shine,* RCA/Arista, 1980 • *Volume 8,* Atlantic, 1980 • *Pickin' up the Pieces: Best Of, 1974–1980,* Rhino, 1992.

Barlow, Gary: "So Help Me Girl," Arista, 1997.

Bee Gees: *Still Waters,* Polydor, 1997.

Beth Hart Band: *Immortal,* Lava, 1996.

Bolton, Michael: *Timeless,* Columbia, 1992 • "To Love Somebody," Columbia, 1992 • *The One Thing,* Columbia, 1993 • *This Is the Time: The Christmas Album,* Columbia, 1996.

Braxton, Toni: *Secrets* (1 track), LaFace, 1996 • "Un-Break My Heart," LaFace/Arista, 1997.

Bryson, Peabo: *Through the Fire,* Columbia, 1994.

Carman: *Absolute Best,* Sparrow, 1993 • *The Standard,* Sparrow, 1993.

Cetera, Peter: *World Falling Down,* Warner Bros., 1992.

Champlin, Bill: *Single,* Full Moon, 1978 • *Runaway,* Elektra, 1981.

Chicago: *Chicago 16,* Full Moon/WB, 1982 • "Hard to Say I'm Sorry," Full Moon, 1982 • "Love Me Tomorrow," Full Moon, 1982 • *Chicago 17,* Full Moon/WB, 1984 • "Hard Habit to Break," Full Moon, 1984 • "Stay the Night," Full Moon, 1984 • "You're the Inspiration," Full Moon/WB, 1984 • "Along Comes a Woman," Full Moon, 1985 • *Chicago 18,* Warner Bros., 1986 • "If She Would Have Been Faithful . . . ," Warner Bros., 1987 • "Will You Still Love Me?," Warner Bros., 1987 • *Greatest Hits,* Vol. 2, *1982–1989,* Full Moon/Reprise, 1989.

Cole, Natalie: w/ Nat "King" Cole, "Unforgettable," Elektra, 1991 • *Unforgettable With Love,* Elektra, 1991 • *Stardust,* Elektra, 1996.

Cole, Samantha: *Samantha Cole,* Universal, 1997 • "Without You," Universal, 1997.

Color Me Badd: *Time and Chance,* Giant, 1993.

Corrs, The: *Forgiven, Not Forgotten,* Lava, 1995.

Crawford, Michael: *A Touch of Music in the Night,* Atlantic, 1993.

Diamond, Neil: *Best Years of Our Lives,* Columbia, 1988 • *In My Lifetime,* Sony, 1996.

Dion, Celine: *Unison,* Epic, 1990 • *The Color of My Love,* 550 Music, 1993 • w/ Clive Griffin, "When I Fall in Love," Epic Soundtrax, 1993 • "The Power of Love," Epic, 1994 • "Because You Loved Me," 550 Music, 1996 • *Falling into You,* 550 Music/Epic, 1996 • "All by Myself," 550 Music, 1997 • w/ Barbra Streisand, "Tell Him," 550 Music/Epic/Columbia, 1997.

Easton, Sheena: *The World of Sheena Easton: The Singles Collection,* EMI America, 1993.

Elefante: "Young and Innocent," Atlantic, 1985 (*St. Elmo's Fire* soundtrack).

En Vogue: "Too Gone, Too Long," EastWest, 1997 • *EV 3,* EastWest, 1997.

Foster, David: "Georgetown," Atlantic, 1985 (*St. Elmo's Fire* soundtrack) • "Love Theme from St. Elmo's Fire," Atlantic, 1985 (*St. Elmo's Fire* soundtrack) • *David Foster,* Atlantic, 1986 • w/ Marilyn Martin, "And When She Danced (Love Theme)," Atlantic, 1988 (*Stealing Home* soundtrack) • "Home Movies," Atlantic, 1988 (*Stealing Home* soundtrack) • "Katie's Theme," Atlantic, 1988 (*Stealing Home* soundtrack) • "Stealing Home," Atlantic, 1988 (*Stealing Home* soundtrack) • *Symphony Sessions,* Atlantic, 1988 • *River of Love,* Atlantic, 1990 • *Play It Again*

(Rechordings), Atlantic, 1991 • *The Christmas Album*, Interscope, 1993.

Griffin, Clive: *Clive Griffin*, 550 Music, 1993.

Hall, Daryl, and John Oates: *Along the Red Ledge*, RCA, 1978 • "It's a Laugh," RCA, 1978 • *X-Static*, RCA, 1979 • "Wait for Me," RCA, 1980.

Holliday, Jennifer: "And I Am Telling You I'm Not Going," Geffen, 1982 • *Best Of*, Geffen, 1996.

Houston, Whitney: "I Have Nothing," Arista, 1992, 1993 (*The Bodyguard* soundtrack) • "I Will Always Love You," Arista, 1992 (*The Bodyguard* soundtrack) • "Run to You," Arista, 1992 (*The Bodyguard* soundtrack) • "I Believe in You and Me," Arista, 1997.

Howard, Miki: *Femme Fatale*, Giant, 1992 • *Miki Sings Billie*, Giant, 1994.

Hyde, Paul, and the Payolas: *Here's the World for Ya*, A&M, 1985.

Iglesias, Julio: *Crazy*, Columbia, 1994.

Ingram, James: w/ Dolly Parton, *Beethoven's Second* soundtrack, Columbia, 1994.

Jackson, Michael: *History: Past, Present and Future, Part 1*, Epic, 1995.

Kennedy, Ray: *Ray Kennedy*, ARC, 1980.

Kenny G: *Breathless*, Arista, 1992 • w/ Peabo Bryson, "By the Time the Night Is Over," Arista, 1993.

LaBelle, Patti: "Does He Love You," MCA, 1997 • *Flame*, MCA, 1997.

Lightfoot, Gordon: *East of Midnight*, Warner Bros., 1987.

Loggins, Kenny: "Forever," Columbia, 1985 • *High Adventure*, Columbia, 1982 • "I'm Free (Heaven Helps the Man)," Columbia, 1984 • *Vox Humana*, Columbia, 1985 • *Greatest Hits*, Columbia, 1997.

Madonna: *Something to Remember*, Maverick, 1995 • "You'll See," Maverick, 1995.

Martin, Marilyn: *See* Foster, David.

Mathis, Johnny: *Music of Johnny Mathis: A Personal Collection*, Legacy/Columbia, 1995.

McCartney, Paul: *Flowers in the Dirt*, Capitol, 1989.

Monica: "For You I Will," Rowdy, 1997.

Moss, Vikki: "If I Turn You Away," Atlantic, 1985 (*St. Elmo's Fire* soundtrack).

Moten, Wendy: *The Pagemaster* soundtrack, Fox, 1994.

Murray, Anne: "Now and Forever (You and Me)," Capitol, 1986 • *Greatest Hits*, Vol. 2, Liberty, 1989 • *The Best . . . So Far*, EMI, 1994.

Newman, Randy: *The Natural* soundtrack, Atlantic, 1984.

Newton-John, Olivia: *Olivia*, Festival, 1972, 1992 • "Twist of Fate," MCA, 1984 • *Back to Basics: The Essential Collection, 1971–1992*, Geffen, 1992.

Night Ranger: *Big Life*, MCA, 1987 • *Greatest Hits*, Camel, 1989.

Nylons, The: "Poison Ivy," Atlantic, 1988 (*Stealing Home* soundtrack) • *Rockapella*, Windham Hill, 1989 • *The Best of the Nylons*, Windham Hill/Open Air, 1993 • *Perfect Fit*, Windham Hill, 1997.

Parr, John: "St. Elmo's Fire," Atlantic, 1985 (*St. Elmo's Fire* soundtrack).

Parton, Dolly: *See* Ingram, James; Rogers, Kenny.

Peck, Danny: *Heart and Soul*, Arista, 1977.

Richie, Lionel: *Can't Slow Down* (1 track), Motown, 1983 • *Louder Than Words*, PolyGram, 1996.

Ritenour, Lee: "Is It You," Elektra, 1981 • *Rit*, Elektra, 1981.

Roberts, Bruce: *Intimacy*, Atlantic, 1995.

Rogers, Kenny: *Greatest Hits*, EMI America, 1980 • w/ Sheena Easton, "We've Got Tonight," Liberty, 1983 • *We've Got Tonight*, Razor & Tie, 1983, 1994 • *20 Greatest Hits*, Liberty, 1983 • *Duets*, Capitol, 1984 • w/ Dolly Parton, *Once upon a Christmas*, RCA, 1984 • w/ Kim Carnes and James Ingram, "What About Me?," RCA, 1984 • "Crazy," RCA, 1985 • *What About Me?*, RCA, 1985 • *Timepiece*, Atlantic, 1994 • *Decade of Hits*, Warner Bros., 1997.

Scaggs, Boz: *Hits!* Columbia, 1980 • "Look What You've Done to Me," Columbia, 1980.

Shanice: "Saving Forever for You," Giant, 1993.

Sinatra, Frank: *Duets*, Capitol, 1993.

Squier, Billy: "Shake Down," Atlantic, 1985 (*St. Elmo's Fire* soundtrack).

Stewart, Rod: *If We Fall in Love Tonight*, Warner Bros., 1996.

Stigers, Curtis: *Time Was*, Arista, 1991, 1995.

Streisand, Barbra: *The Broadway Album*, Columbia, 1985 • *A Collection: Greatest Hits and More*, Columbia, 1989 • *Just for the Record*, Columbia, 1991 • *Back to Broadway*, Columbia, 1993 • *The Mirror Has Two Faces* soundtrack, Columbia, 1996 • *Higher Ground*, Sony, 1997 *See also* Dion, Celine.

Take 6: *Join the Band*, Reprise, 1994.

Tavares: *Supercharged*, Capitol, 1980.

Tubes, The: *Completion Backwards Principle*, Capitol, 1981 • "Talk to Ya Later," Capitol, 1981 • *Outside Inside*, Capitol, 1983 • "She's a Beauty," Capitol, 1983 • "The Monkey Time," Capitol, 1983.

Tyler, Bonnie: *Free Spirit*, Atlantic, 1996.

Universal Nubian Voices: *Universal Nubian Voices*, Maverick, 1995.

Voices That Care: "Voices That Care," Giant, 1991.

Warwick, Dionne: *Friends*, Arista, 1985.

Waybill, Fee: *Read My Lips*, Beat Goes On, 1984 • "Saved My Life," Atlantic, 1985 (*St. Elmo's Fire* soundtrack).

Williams, Deniece: *That's What Friends Are For*, Columbia, 1978 • *When Love Comes Calling*, Columbia, 1979.

Williams, Vanessa: *Star Bright*, Mercury, 1996.

Winans, Bebe, and Cece: *First Christmas*, Capitol, 1993 • *Relationships*, Capitol, 1995.

COLLECTIONS

Dreamgirls (original cast), Geffen, 1982.

For Our Children, Disney, 1991.

For Our Children Too, Rhino, 1996.

A Smile Like Yours soundtrack, Elektra, 1997.

Denzil Foster and Thomas McElroy

The Oakland-based Foster and McElroy have had huge successes with En Vogue, Tony! Toni! Toné!, Club Nouveau, and Timex Social Club. They are producers in the old-fashioned, classic, full-service sense: they write the songs, find artists to perform them, and then conduct the recording sessions.

Denzil Foster (born December 18, 1962) and Thomas McElroy (born June 28, 1964) first reached chart success as vocalists for Club Nouveau, a Sacramento-based dance group. "Lean on Me," a remake of the Bill Withers standard, reached No. 1 in 1987.

Their 1990 production of *The Revival* for Tony! Toni! Toné! went platinum and spawned five singles, including the Top 10 "Feels Good."

While still working with Tony! Toni! Toné!, Foster and McElroy envisioned an all-girl group that would combine modern R&B with hip-hop and new jack swing. They held open auditions and handpicked the members of En Vogue, wrote and arranged the material, and recorded them. "Hold On," from the group's debut *Born to Sing,* quickly reached platinum and No. 2 on the Billboard chart. The follow-up, *Funky Divas,* No. 8, went triple-platinum.

Foster and McElroy albums are characterized by solid musical arrangements and a special attention to vocal harmonies and catchy, infectious urban grooves. First-rate engineering and mixing are often provided by Ken Kessie, himself a producer and songwriter (e.g., Sylvester, Until December, Tower of Power, the Tubes).

"Denny and Tom have excellent grooves and unique arrangements," Kessie explains. "They often use untraditional instruments to cover traditional parts, or they'll have different instruments each doing fragments of parts and then bring them together. They do great background vocal stacks—they do that better than anybody today. And lyrically, they are a bit off-beat. Everything has a lyric twist. That's what makes them good pop tunes." —DANIEL J. LEVITIN

Asante: "All About You," Columbia, 1996 • *Asante Mode,* Columbia, 1996.

Channel 2: *Slammin' at 11,* Polydor, 1988.

Club Nouveau: "Jealousy," King Jay/WB, 1986 • "Lean on Me," King Jay/WB, 1986 • *Life, Love and Pain,* King Jay/WB, 1986 • "Why You Treat Me So Bad," Tommy Boy, 1986.

Cooper, Michael: *Life Is Such a Funny Game,* Reprise, 1987 • *Get Closer,* Reprise, 1992.

Ellis, Terry: *Southern Gal,* Elektra, 1995 • "What Did I Do to You?," Elektra, 1995 • "Where Ever You Are," Elektra, 1995.

En Vogue: *Born to Sing,* Atlantic, 1990 • "Hold On," Atlantic, 1990 • "Lies," Atlantic, 1990 • *Remix to Sing,* EastWest, 1991 • "Free Your Mind," EastWest, 1992 • *Funky Divas,* EastWest, 1992 • "Give It Up, Turn It Loose," EastWest, 1992 • "Giving Him Something He Can Feel," EastWest, 1992 • "My Lovin' (You're Never Gonna Get It)," EastWest, 1992 • "Love Don't Love You," EastWest, 1993 • *Runaway Love* (EP), EastWest, 1993 • "Free Your Mind," 550 Music/Epic, 1994 (*The Cowboy Way* soundtrack) • *EV 3,* EastWest, 1997.

FMob: *Once in a Blue Moon,* EastWest, 1994.

Nation of Funktasia: *In Search of the Last Trump of Funk,* EastWest, 1991.

O'Neal, Alexander: *My Gift to You,* Motown, 1988.

Samuelle: *Living in a Black Paradise,* Atlantic, 1990 • "So You Like What You See," Atlantic, 1990.

Timex Social Club: "Rumors," Jay, 1986.

To Be Continued: *Free to Be,* EastWest, 1993.

Tony! Toni! Toné!: "Born Not to Know," Wing, 1988 • "Little Walter," Wing, 1988 • *Who?,* Wing, 1988 • *Revival,* PolyGram, 1990.

Fred Foster

As founder, owner, and chief producer of Monument Records, Fred Foster is responsible for some great moments in pop, rock, country, light jazz, and folk from the '50s through the '80s, working with Roy Orbison, Willie Nelson, Boots Randolph, Dolly Parton, Kris Kristofferson, Ray Stevens, Larry Gatlin, Tony Joe White, Joe Simon, and Billy Swan.

Fred Foster was born in 1931 in Rutherfordton, North Carolina, and after high school he moved to

Washington, D.C., where his sister lived, to seek his fortune. He found employment as a carhop at a Marriott-owned restaurant, and in less than a year he was manager of the corporate kitchen.

Dizzy from his rapid rise, Foster took a month off from the kitchen and returned to the outdoors as a curb manager. One rush hour afternoon, an impressive Cadillac pulled into the lot with a young man and a beautiful young woman inside. The man asked for quick service and tipped accordingly, then returned daily with a different (beautiful) woman for weeks.

Finally, the man invited Foster to come watch him perform at the Club Famous. The man, Billy Strickland, was a sensational singer and guitarist, and "the best MC I have ever seen," marvels Foster.

One night at the club, Strickland, who had been drinking, introduced Foster as a famous songwriter (Foster had written some poems in high school), and challenged him to write a song on the spot. Foster, mortified, tried to leave, but was "surrounded by six or seven hundred people who wanted to see me write a song," he says. Foster thought a moment, wrote a poem, and sent it up to the stage.

Strickland read the lyrics, shouted out some chord progressions to the band, sang the song, and received a standing ovation. Paper money rained upon the stage and the song was repeated. Strickland raked in $1,300 (in 1950 dollars) that night and showed up the next day at the restaurant as usual.

Foster asked him to get out of the car, " 'because one of us has to have a whipping right now,' " Foster recalls saying. " 'Hell,' said Strickland, 'we wrote a good song together,' and pulled a guitar out of the back seat and sang the song on the spot," remembers Foster.

They began writing together. A publisher (Ben Adelman) came into the club one night, asked Strickland who had been writing his songs, commented that the lyrics were better than the music, offered to find Strickland a recording contract, and offered Foster a songwriting partnership. A few months later Strickland had a contract with King Records and a single on the charts with Adelman and Foster's "If This Is Sin."

One warm night Foster strolled into a D.C. club called the Covered Wagon and sat down to watch Jimmy Dean and the Texas Wildcats. Foster was impressed with Dean's songs and delivery and offered to help him find a recording contract. Foster helped Dean rearrange some songs and coached him on enunciation. Finally they cut a demo together and sent it to 4 Star Records, because "it seemed like the smallest label in the *Billboard* directory, and I wasn't overconfident, don't you know," laughs Foster.

To their amazement, 4 Star accepted the demo and sent Dean a contract with the caveat that the single had to be recorded by Foster in D.C. because there was no money for travel or an outside producer. So, in the summer of 1952 Dean and Foster entered the studio for a session of firsts: theirs, the musicians', and the engineer's.

"Bumming Around" was released in late summer to silence. But in January it charted first in Houston, then in Dallas, and by March it reached No. 5 on the national country chart. Foster was a hit producer at age 22. Foster then had to choose between Marriott—which wanted him to enter an executive-trainee program—and music. Music won, "because I had the bug," he sighs.

Foster, practical if bug-bitten, returned to the bottom and worked in retail at a record store for a year, then for a wholesale distributor in promotion and marketing. After stints with Mercury and ABC/Paramount (where he brought George Hamilton IV and Lloyd Price to the label), Foster wound up with J&F Distributors in Baltimore as head of their new pop line.

On March 11, 1958, the marketing director of London Records, J&F's largest client label, came to town for a sales meeting and criticized Foster for his promotion of the label's pop product. Rock 'n' roll had long since hit and London was still foisting the likes of Vera Lynn and Mantovani on an unresponsive youth market. Radio wouldn't touch the stuff and Foster's hands were tied.

When Foster told him this, the London man sniffed, "Do better, if you think you can." The next day Foster formed Monument Records and its publishing wing, Combine Music. Foster has done better, with dozens of commercial and critical successes to his name over Monument's 30-year life.

Foster's greatest gifts as a label owner and producer have been his ears. He heard the star potential of a young Dolly Parton and a struggling Willie Nelson in the mid-'60s; he heard the ragged realism in the voice of songwriting-great Kris Kristofferson in 1970; and he heard the pop potential of a shy rockabilly singer named Roy Orbison in late '59.

Foster took an Orbison song "Only the Lonely," removed its extended first verse, then lifted the background vocal figure from another Orbison song ("Come Back to Me, My Love") and grafted it onto "Lonely" (No. 2) to create a classic and launch Orbison's pop career in 1960.

Orbison's spectacular hits ("Lonely," "Running Scared," "Crying," "Dream Baby," "In Dreams," "Blue Bayou, " "Oh, Pretty Woman") combine Mexican mariachi melodies, rock rhythms, pop arrangements, and Orbison's near-operatic tenor voice into a unique, gorgeous body of work. Orbison's instrument conveys the fragility of love better than anyone's, yet his amazing delicacy is never precious or effete. His oceanic reserves of sadness are always life-affirming in the manner of great tragedy. Part of Orbison's power stems from the fact that he never resorted to falsetto to hit his high notes. Not that he didn't try, according to Foster.

"Running Scared" was Orbison's first No. 1, recorded in early '61. Recalls Foster, "The arrangement keeps building to where at the end you have 16 strings, 4 horns, 8 voices, and a full rhythm section just honking. When Roy went to falsetto for the high note, he just disappeared. This was before we had enough tracks to dedicate one to the voice, so I had to ask him to hit the note in full voice. He didn't think he could do it, but he did it beautifully, and that gave him so much confidence that from then on he just sailed through everything."

Therefore, while Foster loves the hi-fi aspects of modern recording technology, he believes that it can make people lazy. Orbison wouldn't have been forced to sing in full voice had he recorded today and his career might have taken on a different trajectory. Foster was reminded of this when he produced Willie Nelson's most recent No. 1 country hit ("Nothing I Can Do About It Now") in 1989 for Columbia.

"I was recording Willie on 32-track digital and his guitar part wasn't right. I said, 'It's okay, I'll fix it later.' Willie said, 'No, let's do it again. I've had 10,000 standing ovations and I've never overdubbed a damned one of them.' He was right—there is a spontaneity and a magic to a live performance that you don't get with all of this technology. Perfection doesn't equal greatness," states Foster.

And Foster knows greatness when he hears it—he has always trusted his golden ears. "I'm no freak. I figure if I like it, then there must be at least another million people who will like it," he says. In fact, his admonition to artists anticipates success: "I've always said, 'Let's not record anything you don't love, because if it hits, you'll have to sing it for the rest of your life."
—ERIC OLSEN

Bruce, Ed: *Shades of,* Monument, 1969.

Brush Arbor: *Page One,* Monument, 1976 • *Straight,* Monument, 1977.

Dean, Jimmy: "Bumming Around," 4 Star, 1953.

Gantry, Chris: *Introspection,* Monument, 1968.

Gatlin Brothers: *Love Is Just a Game,* Monument, 1977 • *Best of the Gatlins: All the Gold in California,* Legacy/Columbia, 1996 • *See also* Gatlin, Lary.

Gatlin, Larry: *Rain Rainbow,* Monument, 1974 • *Broken Lady,* Monument, 1976 • *High Time,* Monument, 1976 • w/ the Gatlin Brothers, "I Just Wish You Were Someone I Love," Monument, 1978 • *Oh Brother,* Monument, 1978 • w/ the Gatlin Brothers, *Greatest Hits,* Columbia, 1991.

Hawkins, Ronnie: *Rock and Roll Resurrection/Giant of Rock and Roll,* One Way, 1996.

Hirt, Al: *Raw Sugar, Sweet Sauce,* Monument, 1991.

Howard, Harlan: *All-Time Favorite Country Songwriter,* Koch, 1996.

Jones, Grandpa: *Everybody's Grandpa,* Bear Family, 1996.

Kristofferson, Kris: *Kristofferson,* Monument, 1970 • *Me and Bobby McGee,* Monument, 1971 • *The Silver-Tongued Devil and I,* Monument, 1971 • *Border Lord,* One Way, 1972, 1995 • *Jesus Was a Capricorn,* Monument, 1972 • "Why Me?," Sony Special Products, 1973, 1994 (*The Monument Story*) • *Breakaway,* Monument, 1974 • *Singer/Songwriter,* Monument/Sony, 1991 • *Live at the Philharmonic,* Monument, 1992 • "Loving Her Was Easier (Than Anything I'll Ever Do Again)," Sony Special Products, 1994 (*The Monument Story*).

McCoy, Charlie: *The World of,* Monument, 1968.

Nelson, Willie: *A Horse Called Music,* Columbia, 1989 • "Nothing I Can Do About It Now," Columbia, 1989 • *Born for Trouble,* Columbia, 1990 • *Super Hits,* Columbia, 1994 • *Super Hits,* Vol. 2, Columbia, 1995.

Orbison, Roy: "Only the Lonely," Monument, 1960 • "Crying," Monument, 1961 • *Lonely and Blue,* Monument, 1961 • "Running Scared," Monument, 1961 • "Blue Bayou," Monument, 1963 • "In Dreams," Monument, 1963 • "It's Over," Monument, 1964 • "Oh Pretty Woman," Monument, 1964 • *The All-Time Greatest Hits of Roy Orbison,* Monument, 1972 • *The All-Time Greatest Hits of Roy Orbison,* Vol. 2, CBS Special Products, 1972, 1982 • *Regeneration,* Monument, 1976 • *For the Lonely: A Roy Orbison Anthology,* Rhino, 1988 • *Our Love Song,* CBS Special Products, 1989 • *Super Hits,* Columbia, 1995.

Randolph, Boots: *Boots Randolph's Yakety Sax,* Monument, 1963 • *Boots Randolph Plays More Yakety Sax,* Monument, 1965 • *Boots with Strings,* Monument, 1966 • *Boots Randolph with the Knightsbridge Strings and Voices,* Monument, 1968 • *Sunday Sax,* Monument, 1968 • *The Sound of Boots,* Monument, 1968 • *Boots and Stockings,* Monument, 1969 • *With Love/The Seductive Sax of Boots Randolph,* Monument, 1969 • *Yakety Revisited,* Monument, 1969 • *Boots with Brass,* Monument, 1970 • *Hit Boots 1970,* Monument, 1970 • *Homer Louis Randolph III,* Monument, 1971 • *The World of Boots Randolph,* Monument, 1971 • *Boots Randolph Plays the Great Hits of Today,* Monument, 1972 • *Live,* Monument, 1992.

Roe, Tommy: *Full Bloom,* Monument, 1978.

Smith, Arthur: *Battling Banjoes,* Monument, 1973.

Smith, Clay: *Decoupage,* Monument, 1977.

Stevens, Ray: *Even Stevens,* Varese Sarabande, 1968, 1996 • "Gitarzan," Sony Special Products, 1969, 1994 (*The Monument Story*) • *Gitarzan,* Monument, 1969 • *Greatest Hits,* MCA, 1987 • *Collection,* MCA, 1993.

Paul Fox

Paul Fox was an exceptional studio keyboard and synthesizer player who has parlayed that experience into a career as a top producer. In a brief 10-year period Fox has produced excellent modern rock albums for XTC (*Oranges and Lemons*), 10,000 Maniacs (*Our Time in Eden* and *MTV Unplugged,* which reached No. 13 on the charts), Robyn Hitchcock and the Egyptians (*Perspex Island*), The Sugarcubes (*Stick Around for Joy*), Phish (*Hoist*), Edwin McCain (*Honor Among Thieves*), They Might Be Giants (*John Henry*), and Sky Cries Mary (*Moonbathing on Sleeping Leaves*).

Paul Fox was born in 1954 and was a thriving studio player by the late '70s. As the '80s gave rise to digital technology, Fox rose accordingly, programming keyboards and drum machines for other musicians as well as playing synthesizer. Gradually Fox became involved with arranging and songwriting, and by the mid-'80s, he was everything but a producer.

Fox's first production credit was an obscure single for George McCrae in 1987, but by early 1988, he had a hit single with Scarlett and Black ("You Don't Know," No. 20), and by 1989 he had produced XTC's killer *Oranges and Lemons.* Singer/songwriter/guitarist Andy Partridge's buoyant "The Mayor of Simpleton" leaps off the grooves with a snapping backbeat, a hummable tune, and endearing lyrics about a man so simple that his love can be trusted. Partridge's "Merely a Man" and "Pink Thing" and singer/songwriter/bassist Colin Moulding's "King for a Day" (strangely reminiscent of Tears For Fears' "Everybody Wants to Rule the World") also stand out.

Fox's big commercial breakthrough came with his work on 10,000 Maniacs' *Our Time in Eden* (with modern rock radio staples "These Are Days" and "Candy Everybody Wants") and *MTV Unplugged* (with "Because the Night," No. 11), which both went platinum. *Eden* was lead singer Natalie Merchant's last studio album with the band, and there were some special moments in the recording process.

Recalls Fox, "There were a few nights in particular where there was an incredible amount of joy in the studio—almost like when you go to a family celebration and everyone leaves unimportant differences off to the side. They got down to the core essence of why they became a band in the first place."

Fox has a knack for bringing out the melodic best in his charges, as he did in particular on Robyn Hitchcock's *Perspex Island. Perspex* is graced with Hitchcock's ebullient "So You Think You're in Love," a near-perfect British Invasion guitar-pop workout that was criminally ignored by the singles charts. Some of Hitchcock's most winning tunes and punchy riffs also bolster "Oceanside," "Ultra Unbelievable Love," and "Child of the Universe." With shimmering, but not glaring, production throughout, *Perspex Island* is Hitchcock's most consistent album.

Though Fox's productions are similarly tuneful and crisp, he approaches each record as something unique. "I try to convey each artist's vision, which becomes a collective vision as I come to understand it and we get into the record-making process. I always say that if everyone is trying to make the same record, you are probably going to have a successful venture."

Fox views the producer's role as "part film director, part musical collaborator, part team coach, and part family therapist. The producer helps to set the mood and create the environment for the performances to take place in the same way a director is going to light a certain scene or set a mood to ensure he gets the best performances out of his actors," he says.

"Musical collaboration ranges from preproduction work to songwriting, song-doctoring, and arranging," Fox continues. "The team coach is the person who is there trying to keep everything going by being encouraging or being critical as needed, and trying to find ways to have people rise to the occasion when they don't think they are able to perform something.

"As to the therapist role, I haven't met a band yet where everyone is on the same wavelength at all times. Like a family, everyone has their own personalities, likes, and dislikes. A good producer can somehow harness the tension in any given band to create something that is really a whole as opposed to each individual part." Fox concludes.

With equipment, Fox prefers a hybrid approach. "I prefer to record with older consoles, limiters, equalizers, and tube microphones. They have a sound that is fatter, warmer, and just classic. Then I like to mix records on modern equipment because I like the crack and the punch of some of the newer consoles, and the computer can really help facilitate the mixing process."

—ERIC OLSEN AND DAWN DARLING

Aleka's Attic: "Across the Way," RNA, 1991 (*Tame Yourself*).

Anubian Lights: *Eternal Sky*, Cleopatra, 1995.

Boy George: "Live My Life," Virgin, 1987.

Gene Loves Jezebel: *Kiss of Life*, Geffen, 1990 • *From the Mouths of Babes*, AV, 1995.

Grant Lee Buffalo: *Jubilee*, Warner Bros., 1998.

Hickman, Sara: *Necessary Angels*, Discovery, 1994 • *Misfits*, Shanachie, 1997.

Hitchcock, Robyn, and the Egyptians: "Dark Green Energy," A&M, 1991 • *Perspex Island*, A&M, 1991 • "So You Think You're in Love," A&M, 1991 • *Greatest Hits*, A&M, 1996.

Hookers: *Calico*, MCA, 1996.

McCain, Edwin: *Honor Among Thieves*, Lava, 1995.

Nields: *Gotta Get Over Greta*, Capitol, 1997.

Phish: "Down with Disease," Elektra, 1994 • *Hoist*, Elektra, 1994.

Rex Daisy: *Guys and Dolls*, Pravda, 1996.

Ruts DC/Mad Professor: *Rhythm Collision Dub*, Vol. 1, ROIR, 1982, 1993.

Scarlett and Black: *Scarlett and Black*, Virgin, 1987 • "You Don't Know," Virgin, 1988.

Semisonic: *Great Divide*, MCA, 1996.

Sky Cries Mary: "Moonbathing," World Domination/WB, 1997 • *Moonbathing on Sleeping Leaves*, World Domination/WB, 1997.

Straitjacket Fits: *Blow*, Arista, 1993 • "Brittle," Arista, 1993 (*No Alternative*).

Subject to Change: *Womb Amnesia*, Capitol, 1993.

Sugarcubes, The: *It's-It*, Elektra, 1992 • *Stick Around for Joy*, Elektra, 1992.

Sweet 75: *Sweet 75*, DGC, 1997.

10,000 Maniacs: *Our Time in Eden*, Elektra, 1992 • *Candy Everybody Wants* (EP), Elektra, 1993 • "Few and Far Between," Elektra, 1993 • *MTV Unplugged*, Elektra, 1993.

Texas: "Fade Away," Mercury, 1994 • *Ricks Road*, Mercury, 1994.

They Might Be Giants: *John Henry*, Elektra, 1994.

Tina and the B-Side Movement: *Salvation*, Sire, 1996.

Too Much Joy: *Cereal Killers*, Giant, 1991 • "Susquehanna Hat Company," Giant, 1991.

Turner, Nik: *Prophets of Time*, Cleopatra, 1994.

Wallflowers, The: *The Wallflowers*, Virgin, 1992.

Williams, Victoria: *Loose*, Mammoth/Atlantic/TAG, 1994 • "You R Loved," Mammoth/Atlantic/TAG, 1994.

XTC: *Oranges and Lemons*, Geffen, 1989.

COLLECTIONS

Fame L.A., Mercury, 1998.

Rob Fraboni

For 25 years Rob Fraboni has been a favored engineer and producer of some of the biggest names in the business: Bob Dylan, the Band, Eric Clapton, Bonnie Raitt, Joe Cocker, Pure Prairie League, Phoebe Snow, and recently, the Rolling Stones.

Rob Fraboni was born in 1951 and raised in an Italian neighborhood of Los Angeles. His musical career began in a back room of his family's home where various relatives gathered monthly to sing and play accordions, drums, saxophones, and sundry other instruments in an ever-evolving ensemble of musical mayhem.

Inspired by this friendly cacophony, Fraboni began "banging on the curb with little sticks" at a very young age. He recalls, "My mom took notice of this and when I was about 11 she got me a set of drums." He drummed in a band with friends until a fateful hand injury at 15 forced him into a year's hiatus.

Fraboni had been receiving informal electronics training from a neighbor who was an electrical engineer at a local aerospace lab; Fraboni used the year off to combine his interests in music and electronics. "The mother of the guitar player in our band had a dress factory, so we would go in there at night, set up our gear, and record," he says.

Fraboni found himself intrigued by the recording process, and he built a studio in another friend's parents' guest house—with the living room as the studio and the bedroom as the control room. "We would record on one track, bounce to the other track, then do an overdub, and go back and forth," he remembers.

Still not of driving age, Fraboni hitchhiked to Hollywood in pursuit of vague rumors about a Gold Star recording studio, which was reputed to have an unlocked door from a back alley. Fraboni found this gateway to nirvana, which led to a "funky lounge with a cigarette and a pop machine, a vinyl couch, and a sink," he recalls.

Fraboni hung out there for a month or two, looking nonchalant, until someone finally invited him into the control room of the studio. From there he raptly watched various recording sessions, including one for Sonny and Cher, and a session conducted by the great Phil Spector (see entry).

He used tips gleaned from studio-sitting to improve his own "studio," and at 16 Fraboni quit school to pursue his calling full time. He tried to get a job with various studios, including Gold Star, but no one would hire him because he was so young. At 17 he saw an article in *Rolling Stone* on the Institute of Audio Research in New York, packed up his belongings, and moved there.

After a brief stay at the YMCA, he found an apartment, got a job in a restaurant, and enrolled at the Institute. While he was studying there, Fraboni began calling New York studios out of the phone book in pursuit of work. First he called AAA, but they weren't interested; then he called Herb Abramson's A-1 Studio on the ground floor of a hotel at 72nd and Broadway, and got an interview. Abramson (who had founded Atlantic Records in 1947 with Ahmet Ertegun; see entry) hired Fraboni "based on some tall tales about multitrack experience, but at least I had seen the machines and knew what they did," he chuckles.

The day after the interview Fraboni had his first session. "I was working with Michael Brown from the Left Banke [and later Stories] and they wanted to do an insert on this song. I had never done an edit in my life, but I was a drummer and I was very serious. I washed my hands like I was doing surgery and I did the edit, but it turned out the band's tempo had been off. I was probably quivering from fear at that point, but I actually had to nerve to tell them their tempo was off. They said, 'Oh you're right,' and they went and redid the piece. I turned a big corner right there," he sighs.

Fraboni next worked at the legendary Record Plant—his dream studio because that was where Hendrix had just recorded *Electric Ladyland*—and there he met such future production powerhouses as Jimmy Iovine and Jack Douglas (see entries). Fraboni's tenure as second engineer there was cut short when he was "fingered on a mix-up."

"Jack Douglas was doing this project with a band called Chesapeake Jukebox something-or-other for Gulf and Western. There was a stool next to the multitrack where the second engineer would punch in [the tape], but the remote that shows the 'record' indicator was with the engineer at the console. So he put the track in record, I punched in, and we erased this choir thing. I didn't even know what had happened and I was made the fall guy."

While back in L.A. for Christmas of 1971, Fraboni saw an ad in *Billboard* for the Village Recorder in Westwood, and in that picture was an engineer he had watched at Gold Star. Fraboni went in for an interview, and two weeks later, when he was back in New York, he received a call from the Village Recorder and was hired. Fraboni moved back to L.A. and started working at Village as the chief of maintenance—the only opening at the time—but within three months he became the chief engineer.

Fraboni recorded the Beach Boys' *Holland* album in late 1972, the Rolling Stones came in to do some post-production for *Goat's Head Soup* in mid-'73, and then Bob Dylan and the Band came in to record *Planet Waves* in late '73. It was a dream come true for Fraboni. "The Band was my favorite band of all time. I was driving around L.A. in my VW and I heard 'Cripple Creek' on the radio. I thought to myself 'I would give anything to work with these guys,' but then I thought 'Never gonna happen: they're in New York, I'm in L.A.' Little did I know that some of *Big Pink* was done at Gold Star."

Planet Waves (No. 1) was recorded in four days. Fraboni became friends with the Band and during the Chrismas 1973 recording break, Robbie Robertson called to ask him to come check out Bill Graham's sound system at the Forum. Bob Dylan and the Band were doing a sound check and it sounded bad. Fraboni fiddled with the board for about five minutes and the sound came together. Dylan asked him on the spot to tour with them as "sound consultant."

In essence, that tour made Fraboni's career. He co-produced the Band's *Northern Lights—Southern Cross* album in '75—a step down from their glory days, but still peppered with great songs like "Ophelia" and "Acadian Driftwood." He also co-produced (with Robbie Robertson and John Simon; see entry) the Band's grand finale, *The Last Waltz*, where he met Eric Clapton and Emmylou Harris, both of whom he has subsequently produced.

From 1976 to 1985 Fraboni built and ran Bob Dylan and the Band's Shangri-La Studios in Malibu. From 1985 to 1990 he was a vice president at Island Records, where he remastered Bob Marley's entire catalog.

From 1991 to 1994 Fraboni owned two indie labels: Domino and Ardeo. In 1996 he returned to independent production, producing and mixing tracks for the Rolling Stones' *Bridges to Babylon*, and co-producing the Wingless Angels' album with Keith Richards (see entry).

—Eric Olsen and Dawn Darling

Band, The: *Northern Lights—Southern Cross*, Capitol, 1975 • *The Last Waltz*, Warner Bros., 1978.

Bellevue Cadillac: *Black and White*, Ardeo, 1995.

Bluerunners, The: *The Bluerunners*, Island, 1991.

Chaplin, Blondie: *Blondie Chaplin*, Asylum, 1977.

Clapton, Eric: *No Reason to Cry*, RSO, 1976 • *Crossroads*, Polydor, 1988.

Cocker, Joe: *Stingray*, A&M, 1976.

Comsat Angels: *Chasing Shadows*, Island, 1988.

Danko, Rick: *Rick Danko*, Arista, 1978.

Dylan, Bob: *Planet Waves*, Asylum, 1974.

Geyer, Renee: *Renee Geyer*, Portrait, 1982.

Gronenthal, Max: *Max*, Chrysalis, 1980.

Harris, Emmylou: *Duets*, Reprise, 1990.

Hughes/Thrall: *Hughes/Thrall*, Epic, 1982, 1991.

James, Etta: *Seven Year Itch*, Island, 1989 • *How Strong Is a Woman: The Island Sessions*, 4th & B'Way, 1993.

Kershaw, Rusty: *Now and Then*, Domino, 1991.

Killers: *Murder One*, Zoo, 1990.

Martyn, John: *Foundations*, Island, 1988.

McLagan, Ian: *Jump in the Night*, Mercury, 1981.

Mooney, John: *Testimony*, Domino, 1991 • *Against the Wall*, House of Blues, 1995.

Nascimento, Milton: *Milton*, A&M, 1976.

Neville, Ivan: w/ Nick Tremulis, *More Than Truth*, Island, 1988 • *Thanks*, Domino, 1993.

Nicholson, Gary: *The Sky Is Not the Limit*, Ardeo, 1994.

Place, Mary Kay: *Mary Kay Place*, Epic, 1978.

Pure Prairie League: *Something in the Night*, Casablanca, 1981.

Raitt, Bonnie: "Once in A Lifetime," Warner Bros., 1980 (*Coast to Coast* soundtrack) • *Green Light*, Warner Bros., 1982 • *Nine Lives*, Warner Bros., 1986 • *The Bonnie Raitt Collection*, Warner Bros., 1990.

Rolling Stones, The: *Bridges to Babylon*, Virgin, 1997.

Snow, Phoebe: *Something Real*, Elektra, 1989.

subdudes, the: *Lucky*, East/West, 1989.

Terenzi, Fiorella: *Music from the Galaxies*, Island, 1991.

Tonio K.: *Life on the Food Chain*, Full Moon, 1979.

Tremulis, Nick: *See* Neville, Ivan.

Trouble Funk: *Trouble over There*, Island, 1988.

Wall, Wendy: *Wendy Wall*, SBK, 1989.

Warnes, Jennifer: "I Know a Heartache When I See One," Arista, 1979 • *Shot Through the Heart*, Arista, 1979.

Wingless Angels: *Wingless Angels*, Mindless/Island, 1997.

Neil Fraser

See MAD PROFESSOR

Front Line Assembly

See BILL LEEB AND RHYS FULBER

Front 242

(DANIEL B. BRESSANUTTI, PATRICK CODENYS, JEAN-LUC DE MEYER, RICHARD K. 23 JONCKHEERE)

Formed in 1981, the Belgian industrial group Front 242 helped pioneer aggressive electronic "body" music throughout the 1980s with Skinny Puppy and Ministry. Front 242 produced two of the genre's most important albums (*Front by Front* and *Tyranny for You*) and, arguably, the genre's most important single, "Headhunter."

The machine-only Front 242 sound emerged out of necessity from a popular music vacuum in Belgium, according to founding member and co-producer Patrick Codenys. "Since there is no strong rock tradition in Belgium, there isn't a pool of musicians like there is in England or America. Since you don't have a drummer or bass player, many people in Belgium (and also Germany) began to work with machines. Everyone in the band was an entity working on his own. We met in the early '80s when we were living in Brussels and buying our stuff at the same shop."

Driven together, the intrepid little band jumped with both feet into a brave new world. "We were determined to create music with machines and create a new kind of aesthetic from those machines," says Codenys. "It was very exciting. We had art backgrounds and were very curious. There was a lot of 'sounds' research, things we weren't used to hearing. We had to fine-tune our machines [synthesizers] to try to find the right sound within the machine. It was difficult because the music was very stiff. In the '80s the technology was much less flexible. We had to fine-tune the sounds in preproduction by going very far into the process inside the machine before we entered the studio."

In developing an aesthetic, the band established some strictures. "There were no rules, so we created our own: Never, ever use the built-in factory sounds. Create sounds that no one has ever heard before, and then try to integrate them into the music. We developed the kind of abilities musicians develop on their instruments—a dexterity for going in there and pulling out the most incredible sounds. Eventually you become as good with knobs and cursors as with keys."

The band's self-discipline didn't preclude a relationship with their chosen "axes." "Any musician wants to 'possess' his instrument—to know it fully. It's not different for people working with machines, except that with normal instruments, there are rules and chords and notes. When I got my first synth, it took me a half-hour to get any sound out of the thing. It took me two years to know what a tuning was, because I was just doing noises, or sounds, or even notes, without knowing there was a tuning," he confides.

Like Depeche Mode in techno-pop, Front 242 faced stiff opposition. They used that opposition to toughen their music and their resolve, according to Codenys.

"The first three to five years we were doing music, we had no recognition. We were hated by a big chunk of the press and music business. It was very, very hard. Ours is not a kind of music that you can easily impose upon people. Most people would rather hear melodic music. The situation turned us into fighters because you have to stand behind something. The people inside the band are normal, though, thank God. We have a lot of humor. But when you present an art, or a concept, it's important to stand behind it and have a strong image."

The band's image and sonic vocabulary became dark, foreboding, and punishing by 1987's *Official Version*, with titles like "Slaughter" and "Aggressive Angst." Codenys feels that "happiness is something that can blind you. For some strange reason, it is when people are unhappy that they are the most creative. It's more complicated than that when you go to make lyrics. The tension between East and West was a good theme for us. Pictures on TV news gave us themes. When it comes to sound, we had a very strong anger inside ourselves."

The hard work and perseverance paid off in late 1988 with the release of the throbbing, pounding, menacing, yet somehow inviting single, "Headhunter," and the album *Front by Front*. The song struck a chord on the dance floor, where its seething groove melded perfectly with its story of a killer systematically stalking his victim, and in the process baring the psychology of dehumanization.

"Headhunter" opened many a dance floor to the bracing thrill of industrial music. "By then a lot of people had become used to hearing weird, noisy synthesizer sounds. There has been a double curve going both ways reflecting the popularity of our type of music: one curve goes up from the artists toward the audience as we have gotten better, and the other goes down from the audience toward the artists as their ears have adapted. It seemed to come together on 'Headhunter,' " Codenys avers.

Though not possessed of a standout track as galvanizing as "Headhunter," the band's next album, *Tyranny for You,* is its most consistent and carried the band's formula to its logical conclusion. Highlights are "Rhythm of Time" and "Tragedy for You." In the '90s the band experimented with screeching metallic guitar (*Up Evil*) and techno-trance (*Off*). After a hiatus to pursue solo projects, the band reunited in 1997 to tour and record new music—artistic spelunkers delving ever deeper into the machine.

Codenys worries that with the rise of technology, that exploration has become too easy. "The technology is so powerful, and there is such an abundance of factory-made sounds available, that it is easy to make 'music' within an hour. But behind the technology is an artist, and behind the artist is a man. I still believe that the start of everything is the quality of the man, who will develop the artist, who will make choices within the technology. I regret that the power of the technology can annihilate a person's ability to develop his human sensitivity and his 'man-power.' " —ERIC OLSEN

Front 242: *Take One* (EP), Wax Trax!, 1984 • "Masterhit," RRE, 1987 • *No Comment,* Epic, 1987, 1992 • *Tyranny for You,* Epic, 1991 • *Backcatalogue,* Epic, 1992 • *Front by Front,* Epic, 1989/1992 • *Geography,* Epic, 1992 • "Headhunter V3.0," Epic, 1992 • *Mixed by Fear,* RRE, 1992 • *Official Version,* Epic, 1992 • "Welcome to Paradise," Epic, 1992 • *05:22:09:12 Off,* Epic, 1993 • *06:21:03:11 Up Evil,* Epic, 1993 • "Religion," Epic, 1993 • *Angels vs. Animals,* RRE, 1994 • *Live Code,* RRE, 1994 • *Mutage.Mixage,* RRE, 1997.

Mitchell Froom

afe Flesh may be the one album credit you won't see on Mitchell Froom's discography, but Slash Records liked his soundtrack to the X-rated cult classic so much that the label released it as a solo album. "It wasn't really a solo album; it was very low-budget, done on an 8-track," Froom recalls. "They liked the way it sounded."

Slash liked it so much, it wanted to see how Froom might handle a band neither Slash nor Warner Bros. could deal with, the Del Fuegos. After several successful sessions, Slash and its parent gave Froom the go-ahead to produce a Del Fuegos album.

Froom grew up in the small town of Petaluma, about 50 miles north of San Francisco. He started taking piano lessons at 5, then classical organ lessons, eventually graduating from the University of California at Berkeley with a bachelor's degree in music.

He spent the requisite time in bad bands in Petaluma and San Francisco, eventually leaving for Los Angeles.

Photo by David Goggin © 1997

There, he began working as a session synthesizer player. He parlayed that then-rare talent into the *Cafe Flesh* gig, launching his career as a producer.

After Warner Bros. gave him the nod for the second Del Fuegos record, *Stand Up*, he was on to something. "All of a sudden, people thought I was some kind of genius, because I took this band that they didn't like at all and made a record that they liked," he says. "The next call I got after that was to work with Crowded House. It happened really quickly."

So did the success of Crowded House; its eponymous debut yielded the No. 2 hit, "Don't Dream It's Over" and the No. 7 follow-up, "Something So Strong." Froom began to dream of building a team. "I was having a hard time finding engineers whom I liked personally in Los Angeles," he says, explaining how he started a relationship with Tchad Blake (see entry).

"He was working at the Sound Factory as a second engineer and starting to do more first engineering," Froom recalls. "I had this opportunity to score a play, but only had two days to do it. There was no money, it was one of those things where I just said, 'Why don't we try this?' and we had fun doing it.

"Tchad is a really interesting guy with a lot of cool ideas, and he was also a guitar player. It seemed like if we started working together, we could get to where what we did together would be far superior to the work that we could do separately."

The collaboration jelled superbly on Los Lobos's great 1992 release, *Kiko*. "Right after that record I was getting calls as a producer and people would say, 'Oh, by the way, Tchad is doing it, right?' So, I saw more and more that it became something that people liked in combination."

Froom downplays a "Froom sound," suggesting Blake is at least as responsible for that sound as he is. To show how close they are, Blake produced Froom's 1998 solo disc.

One thing that distinguishes Froom from other producers is his range. Since 1985, his production work has spanned Crowded House's pop, Suzanne Vega's eclecticism, Los Lobos's multiethnic rock, even Sheryl Crow's folk-pop. "Many people have called because they feel we have a wide enough range that each record could be distinctive," he says. "That is the real goal, and the real struggle is to get on to that.

"The job of a producer is to supply what is needed, and sometimes what is needed is for you to get out of the way completely," he says. "At this point, I won't take a job unless I can hear a tape of someone's music and come forward with what I think are really compelling ideas that may be something different for the person that they haven't thought of.

"Usually, I spend a good amount of time working on the music with the person or the band before we go into the studio. The exception would be Los Lobos, where no preproduction is involved. They are a create-on-the-spot type of band." Froom calls Los Lobos sessions "free-flowing" and conversational. "The Los Lobos clock has no hand," a band member once said.

Froom greatly values his collaboration with Blake and doesn't care who gets producer credit. "I usually list us both as producers, and if the artist wants to be listed too, they can," he says. "It just doesn't matter that much." —DAVID JOHN FARINELLA

American Music Club: *Mercury*, Reprise, 1993.

Case, Peter: *Peter Case*, Geffen, 1986 • *Six-Pack of Love*, Geffen, 1992.

Cibo Matto: "Know Your Chicken," Warner Bros., 1996 • *Viva! La Woman*, Warner Bros., 1996 • *Super Relax* (1 track, EP), Warner Bros., 1997.

Costello, Elvis: *Mighty Like a Rose*, Warner Bros., 1991 • *Brutal Youth*, Warner Bros., 1994 • "Sulky Girl," Warner Bros., 1994.

Crow, Sheryl: *Sheryl Crow*, A&M, 1996 • "Tomorrow Never Dies," A&M, 1997 (*Tomorrow Never Dies* soundtrack).

Crowded House: *Crowded House,* Capitol, 1987 • "Don't Dream It's Over," Capitol, 1987 • "Something So Strong," Capitol, 1987 • "World Where You Live," Capitol, 1987 • *Temple of Low Men,* Capitol, 1988 • *Woodface,* Gold Rush, 1991, 1996 • *Instinct,* Capitol, 1996 • *Recurring Dream: The Very Best Of,* Capitol, 1996.

Del Fuegos: *The Longest Day,* Warner Bros., 1984 • *Boston, Mass.,* Slash/WB, 1985 • "Long Slide," Slash/WB, 1987 • *Stand Up,* Slash/WB, 1987.

Dobbyn, Dave: *Twist,* TriStar, 1995.

Finn, Tim: *Tim Finn,* Capitol, 1989.

LaFlamme, David: *Inside Out,* Amherst, 1978.

Latin Playboys: *Latin Playboys,* Slash/WB, 1994.

Los Lobos: "La Bamba," Slash/WB, 1987 (*La Bamba* soundtrack) • *The Neighborhood* (1 track), Slash/WB, 1990 • *Kiko,* Slash/WB, 1992 • *Just Another Band from East L.A.,* Slash/WB, 1993 • *Colossal Head,* Warner Bros., 1996.

McCartney, Paul: *Flowers in the Dirt,* Capitol, 1989.

McKee, Maria: *Maria McKee,* Geffen, 1989.

McLaughlin, Pat: *Pat McLaughlin,* Capitol, 1988 • *Get Out and Stay Out,* dos/Capitol, 1995.

Noel and the Red Wedge: *Peer Pressure,* Scotti Brothers, 1982.

Pretenders, The: "Hold a Candle to This," Sire, 1990 • "Never Do That," Sire, 1990 • *Packed!* Sire, 1990 • "Born for a Purpose," RNA, 1991 (*Tame Yourself*).

Ridgway, Stan: *The Big Heat,* IRS Vintage, 1986, 1993.

Scott, Jimmy: *Dream,* Blue Horizon/Sire/WB, 1994.

Scott, Tim: *The High Lonesome Sound,* DGC, 1987.

Semi-Twang: *Salty Tears,* Warner Bros., 1988.

Sexsmith, Ron: *Ron Sexsmith,* Interscope, 1995 • *Other Songs,* Interscope, 1997.

Thompson, Richard: *Daring Adventures,* Polydor, 1986 • *Amnesia,* Capitol, 1988 • "I Misunderstood," Capitol, 1991 • *Rumor and Sigh,* Capitol, 1991 • *Watching the Dark: The History of Richard Thompson,* Hannibal, 1993 • *Mirror Blue,* Capitol, 1994 • *You? Me? Us?,* Capitol, 1996.

Vega, Suzanne: *99.9 F,* A&M, 1992 • "99.9 F," A&M, 1992 • "When Heroes Go Down," A&M, 1992 • "In Liverpool," A&M, 1993 • "Story of Isaac," A&M, 1995 (*Tower of Song: The Songs of Leonard Cohen*) • "Caramel," A&M, 1996 (*The Truth About Cats and Dogs* soundtrack) • *Nine Objects of Desire,* A&M, 1996 • "No Cheap Thrill," A&M, 1996.

Zanes, Dan: *Cool Down Time,* Private, 1995.

COLLECTIONS

Time and Love: The Music of Laura Nyro, Astor Place, 1997.

John Fryer

English producer/engineer John Fryer's career began with a failed attempt to be the next Jimi Hendrix. Efforts to console himself led to soundman status with a friend's band, . . . which led to the studio, . . . which led to work as an assistant, . . . which led to engineering, . . . which led to production. Sort of the prototypical rise up the studio food chain, spiced with a dollop of luck and a splash of perseverance, resulting in a satisfying triumph of talent.

Fryer's work tends to cluster around two distant poles: the crash and burn of industrial music and the generally lilting sound of bands on the arty 4 A.D. label. His industrial credits include Nine Inch Nails' classic first album *Pretty Hate Machine;* Stabbing Westward's *Ungod* and *Wither Blister Burn and Peel;* Gravity Kill's self-titled first album and the *Manipulated* EP; Sister Machine Gun; and Die Krupps.

His 4 A.D. work includes the elegant and ethereal Cocteau Twins (*Head over Heels, Sunburst and Snowblind*); the ringing dual guitars and female leads of Lush (*Scar, Gala*); the Wolfgang Press; the Clan of Xymox; and Pale Saints. Fryer became so important to the label that he was asked to collaborate with owner/impresario Ivo Watts-Russell in the extremely influential studio group This Mortal Coil.

In addition, Fryer produced Love and Rockets' self-titled smash (No. 14, with "So Alive," which was No. 3) and their mid-'90s comeback *Sweet F.A.*

John Fryer was born in London in 1958. His musical education began with his older brother's record collection, which consisted of the Velvet Underground, Iron Butterfly, Lou Reed, and others heavy and underground in the late '60s and early '70s. After hearing Jimi Hendrix on the radio, Fryer, among legion contemporaries, aspired to similar string bending. He soon bowed to personal shortcomings vis-à-vis the guitar and began setting up and running the PA system for his friend's band at gigs.

When the band eventually recorded, John landed an assistant's job at Blackwing Studios in the late '70s. Blackwing began as an 8-track studio where the first Depeche Mode and Fad Gadget albums were recorded. Over Fryer's decade there, the studio evolved from one 8-track to two 24-track studios.

Fryer explains his transition from engineer to producer. "I suppose I am a creative engineer. I didn't keep my mouth shut when I probably should have. I was always trying to help people make a better record. So I started working with bands as an engineer, and if they liked working with me they would come back and we would co-produce."

The Scottish trio Cocteau Twins hit its stride with Fryer at the helm; singer Elizabeth Fraser dances sprite-like over Robin Guthrie's orchestral guitars, most impressively on the single "Sugar Hiccough." Fryer elaborates on the process. "It was drum machines that sound like drum machines—not trying to make them sound too real—and very lush processed guitars. Basically it's just a distortion pedal, long delays, long reverb, and you make the whole thing float."

By 1985, Fryer was ready for This Mortal Coil. Watts-Russell conceived of a mutating studio entity made up of members of Cocteau Twins, Dead Can Dance, the Wolfgang Press, and sundry others (Howard DeVoto, Kim Deal, Tanya Donelly), doing spacey arrangements of covers (Tim Buckley, Alex Chilton, Randy California, Rodney Crowell; see entry) and some originals—all linked by moody instrumentals (co-written by Watts-Russell and Fryer).

"Those records were great to work on. A lot of the process is making the music, putting the vocals on, and then fucking up the music so it doesn't sound anything like the original song. We start off with a proper drum track and proper chords on piano or guitar, but it sounds too straightforward, so then the whole thing is stuck through a processor, or six processors in a line, and we come up with a weird demented sound with a sweet vocal on top. The vocal is the most important thing and the music is backdrop for the vocal. It has to capture an atmosphere."

Atmosphere is often critical. "On the latest Stabbing Westward [*Wither Blister Burn and Peel*] we had to create an atmosphere because the studio we recorded at [Bearsville] is like a gigantic warehouse; so we set up the sound backboard to form a 5-foot-square box for the singer [Chris Hall]. He was sitting on the floor in the dark in this box, and we put a microphone in there and he did all his vocals. It had to be claustrophobic-sounding—like he was standing next to you talking or whispering into a girl's ear."

Fryer's best-known industrial work is Nine Inch Nail's *Pretty Hate Machine*, which he co-produced with creator Trent Reznor (see entry), and he remembers the experience fondly. "It was exciting. It was completely different from the stuff that was around. It's a pop record, really, 'pop-industrial' as I call it. Ministry and Skinny Puppy are industrial music, but Trent was different. It's like the Sex Pistols were pop-punk. *Never Mind the Bollocks* was pop songs with attitude. At the end of the day it's the songs that sell; it doesn't matter which way they are done." —Eric Olsen and Dawn Darling

Ash, Daniel: "Coming Down," RCA, 1990 • *Coming Down*, RCA, 1991.

Beautiful, The: *Storybook*, Giant, 1992.

Clan of Xymox: *Medusa*, 4 A.D., 1986.

Cocteau Twins: *Head over Heels*, 4 A.D./Capitol, 1983 • *Sunburst and Snowblind*, 4 A.D., 1983.

Colourbox: *Colourbox*, 4 A.D., 1985.

Course of Empire: *Telepathic Last Words*, TVT, 1998.

Cranes: "Clear" (remix), Dedicated/RCA, 1993.

Depeche Mode: "Pleasure Little Treasure" (remix), Mute, 1987.

Die Krupps: *One*, Rough Trade, 1992 • *A Tribute to Metallica*, Hollywood, 1993 • "Enter Sandman," Hollywood, 1993 • "One," Hollywood, 1993 • *Metalmorphosis 1981–92*, Cleopatra, 1996.

Dylans, The: "Godlike," Beggars Banquet, 1991 • "Lemon Afternoons," Beggars Banquet, 1991.

Easy: *Magic Seed*, Mute/Elektra, 1991.

Fad Gadget: *Incontinent*, Mute, 1981 • *Under the Flag*, Mute, 1982.

Gravity Kills: *Gravity Kills*, TVT, 1996 • "Guilty," TVT, 1996 • *Manipulated* (EP), TVT, 1997 • *Manipulated* (remixes), TVT, 1997.

He Said: *Hail*, Mute/Restless, 1985, 1989 • *Take Care*, Mute/Enigma, 1988, 1989.

His Name Is Alive: *Home Is in Your Head*, 4 A.D., 1991.

Love and Rockets: *Love and Rockets*, RCA, 1989 • "So Alive," Beggars Banquet/RCA, 1989 • *Sweet F.A.* (7 tracks), Beggars Banquet/American, 1996 • *The Glittering Darkness* (EP), Beggars Banquet, 1996.

Love in Reverse: *Words Become Worms*, Warner Bros., 1998.

Lush: *Scar*, 4 A.D., 1989 • *Gala* (6 tracks), 4 A.D./Reprise, 1990.

Marias, A.C.: *One of Our Girls (Has Gone Missing)*, Mute, 1996.

McLachlan, Sarah: "Into the Fire" (remix), Arista, 1992.

Moev: *Head Down*, Nettwerk/Atlantic, 1990.

Nine Inch Nails: *Pretty Hate Machine*, TVT, 1989 • "Sin," TVT, 1989.

Pale Saints: *The Comforts of Madness*, 4 A.D., 1990.

Play Dead: "Propaganda" (remix), Jungle, 1984 • *Resurrection*, CLA, 1992.

Radio Iodine: *Tiny Warnings*, Universal, 1997.

Sister Machine Gun: *Burn*, Wax Trax!/TVT, 1995 • *Metropolis*, TVT, 1997.

Stabbing Westward: "Lies," Columbia, 1994 • *Ungod*, Columbia, 1994 • "What Do I Have to Do?," Columbia, 1995 • "Falls Apart," Columbia, 1996 • "Shame," Columbia, 1996 • "Slipping Away," Columbia, 1996 • *Wither Blister Burn and Peel*, Columbia, 1996.

Swallow: *Blow,* 4 A.D., 1992 • "Lovesleep," 4 A.D., 1992 (*Volume Four*).

This Mortal Coil: *It'll End in Tears,* 4 A.D., 1984 • *Filigree and Shadow,* 4 A.D., 1986 • *Blood,* 4 A.D., 1991 • *1983–91 Box,* 4 A.D., 1993.

Tovey, Frank: *The Fad Gadget Singles,* Sire, 1987.

Wire: *It's Beginning to and Back Again,* Restless, 1989.

Wolfgang Press: *Standing Up Straight,* 4 A.D., 1986.

Xmal Deutschland: *Tocsin,* 4 A.D., 1984.

Rhys Fulber

See BILL LEEB AND RHYS FULBER

Full Force

(CURT BEDEAU, GERRY "BABY" CHARLES, JUNIOR "SHY SHY" CLARK, BRIAN "B-FINE" GEORGE, "BOWLEGGED" LOU GEORGE, PAUL ANTHONY GEORGE)

Full Force is a six-man recording/songwriting/production team (born between 1960 and 1967) that has scored an impressive series of hits since the mid-'80s, running the gamut of black music styles (with a rainbow coalition of artists) from buttery ballads to hard funk and hip-hop. Full Force has written and produced hits for themselves and others, including U.T.F.O. ("Roxanne, Roxanne"), Lisa Lisa and Cult Jam (*Spanish Fly,* No. 7; "All Cried Out," No. 8; "Head to Toe," No. 1; "Lost in Emotion," No. 1), Samantha Fox ("Naughty Girls Need Love Too," No. 3; "I Wanna Have Some Fun," No. 8), Cheryl Pepsii Riley ("Thanks for My Child"), and James Brown (*I'm Real*).

Recently, Full Force has written and produced a track on the multiplatinum Backstreet Boys album, and Allure and 112's remake of Force's "All Cried Out" was a platinum single in early 1998. Besides hits, Full Force's greatest contribution has been a highly danceable rhythm style that is a syncopated hybrid of Latin freestyle and hip-hop.

The seeds of Full Force were sown in the '70s when Brooklyn-bred brothers "Bowlegged" Lou, Paul Anthony, and Brian "B-Fine" George formed a vocal trio and performed Jackson 5, Isley Brothers (see entry), and Temptations songs in area talent shows, including numerous winning performances at the Apollo Theater in Harlem. Seeking to become a self-contained band, the trio added their three cousins Gerry "Baby" Charles, Junior "Shy Shy" Clark, and Curt Bedeau.

Full Force came to prominence in 1984 when they co-wrote and produced "Roxanne, Roxanne"—a spare, beat-driven rap about a smokin' but stuck-up young woman—for rappers U.T.F.O. The song inspired the "Roxanne" phenomena and led to over 100 answer records by the likes of Roxanne Shante and the Real Roxanne. B-Fine recalls, "We had produced these three kids from around the neighborhood, U.T.F.O., on a song called 'Beats and Rhymes' for Select Records. When we were ready to release another song ('Hanging Out'), I called [Select president] Fred Munao right before he was going to press it up, and I said, 'I had this thought that woke me up last night about the Police and Sting' (we were into that music). 'Why don't we do a rap song about a girl named Roxanne.' He said we had to hurry up if we wanted it on the B-side, and it just created history."

Full Force's next collaboration was their most enduring and successful: Lisa Lisa and Cult Jam. Says B-Fine: "We wanted to do something different. So we wrote songs for a young Hispanic woman because all the Latins in our community were listening to hip-hop and R&B and the only Hispanic artist on the charts was Menudo, which was definitely not R&B or hip-hop. So that's how we ended up working with Lisa Lisa."

Full Force's work with Lisa Lisa combined the "Full Force beat" with catchy melodies and good vocals. "On 'I Wonder If I Take You Home' the bass drum follows everything the bass is doing," says B-Fine, the group's drummer. "I came up with that beat the day I got fired from my day job. I came home and my cousin started laughing because he was already unemployed; I went downstairs and came up with that beat."

But the vocals are just as important. "We are very big on vocals; we always want to make sure that there is a vocal hook because a jam is good, but a song lives forever." "I Wonder If, "Can You Feel the Beat?," "Head to Toe," and "Lost in Emotion" (and their excellent remixes) are dance floor classics that were catchy enough for mainstream radio.

Force followed a similar rhythmic and melodic pattern with Samantha Fox, but had a new conceptual issue to deal with. "Samantha Fox was known all through the U.K. as a giant sex kitten. [Her label] Jive Records wanted the public to take her more seriously. We tried a few things but we didn't really feel good about them," says B-Fine. "We did our research and said 'No, why don't we just dive head-first into her image—it never hurt

Marilyn Monroe.' So we came up with a song called 'Naughty Girls Need Love Too.' It took off because it was a good song, but also because people related to her. Even with her naughty image, she's still a person, she needs love too."

Though a real drummer, B-Fine has kept up with technology. "When the 808 drum machine and then the DMX came out, I was so depressed being a drummer. I walked the streets in a fog; I was like, 'Who am I, where am I, what is my purpose?' So I forced myself to become a programmer."

B-Fine's most vivid memories are of working with James Brown. "When we did James Brown, people told us it's going to be rough: 'Mr. Brown likes things done a certain way.' We were like, 'Well he's the godfather of soul. If he wants it done a certain way, then we'll make it work.' Our thing was not to change things around, but just to bring James Brown back. Make James Brown now.

"It was mind-blowing to see him come in," he continues. "All true legends are visually as well as sonically caught in the time that made them a legend. Elvis Presley would have still been Elvis Presley today; Michael Jackson is still Michael Jackson; Prince is still Prince no matter how he changes; Little Richard is still Little Richard, and James Brown is still James Brown.

"He came in with his hair slicked all the way to the side, with his big huge fur coat, the rings, the shades, he walked in and [growled], 'Gentleman, gentleman, good to meetcha,' and I was like, 'Wow!' I remember when I would throw water on my face and act like him as a kid, pretending that I was sweating so much. When he felt our vibe and the respect we were giving him, he was fine," says B-Fine.

He continues, "We were in the booth recording him and he got real excited [out in the studio] and into what he was doing. Then he just disappeared—we couldn't see him anymore—but he was still singing his vocals. We looked and James Brown was on the floor; he did the splits and he was just jamming down there. We were just pointing and saying 'Wow, look at him go. That's James Brown.' " —ERIC OLSEN AND DAWN DARLING

Backstreet Boys: *Backstreet Boys* (1 track), Jive, 1997.
Barrio Boyzz: *How We Roll*, SBK, 1995.
Brown, James: *I'm Real*, Scotti Brothers, 1988.
Doctor Ice: *The Night Stalker*, Jive, 1989.
Ex-Girlfriend: *X Marks the Spot*, Reprise, 1991.
Force MD's: *Step to Me*, Tommy Boy, 1990.
Fox, Samantha: *Samantha Fox*, Jive, 1987 • *I Wanna Have Some Fun*, Jive, 1988 • "Naughty Girls (Need Love Too)," Jive, 1988 • "I Wanna Have Some Fun," Jive, 1989 (*In House,*

Volume 1) • *Just One Night*, Jive, 1991 • *Greatest Hits*, Jive, 1992.
Full Force: *Full Force*, Columbia, 1985 • *Full Force Get Busy 1 Time*, Columbia, 1986 • "Unfaithful So Much," Columbia, 1986 • *Guess Who's Comin' to the Crib?*, Columbia, 1987 • "Love Is for Suckers (Like Me and You)," Columbia, 1987 • *Smoove*, Columbia, 1989 • *Don't Sleep*, Capitol, 1992 • "Back Together Again," Caliber, 1997 • *Sugar on Top*, Caliber, 1997.
Guy, Jasmine: *Jasmine Guy*, Warner Bros., 1990.
Jackson, La Toya: *La Toya*, RCA, 1988.
LaBelle, Patti: *Be Yourself*, MCA, 1989.
Lisa Lisa and Cult Jam: "Head to Toe," Columbia, 1987 • "Head to Toe" (remix), Columbia, 1987 • "Lost in Emotion," Columbia, 1987 • "Lost in Emotion" (remix), Columbia, 1987 • *Spanish Fly*, Columbia, 1987 • "Little Jackie Wants to Be a Star," Columbia, 1989 • *Straight to the Sky*, Columbia, 1989 • "Let the Beat Hit 'Em," Columbia, 1991 • *Straight Outta Hell's Kitchen*, Columbia, 1991 • *Past, Present and Future*, Thump, 1996 • *Super Hits*, Sony, 1997.
Lisa Lisa and Cult Jam with Full Force: "I Wonder If I Take You Home," Columbia, 1984 • "Can You Feel the Beat," Columbia, 1985 • "Can You Feel the Beat" (remix), Columbia, 1985 • *Lisa Lisa and Cult Jam with Full Force*, Columbia, 1985 • "All Cried Out," Columbia, 1986.
Michele, Yvette: "DJ Keep Playin' (Get Your Music On)," Loud, 1997.
Real Roxanne: *The Real Roxanne*, Select, 1988.
Riley, Cheryl Pepsi: *Me, Myself and I*, Columbia, 1988 • "Thanks for My Child," Columbia, 1988 • *All That!* Reprise, 1993.
Selena: *Dreaming of You*, EMI Latin, 1995.
7669: *From a Bad Block*, Motown, 1993.
U.T.F.O.: "Hanging Out," Select, 1984 • "Roxanne, Roxanne," Select, 1984 • *Skeezer Pleezer*, Select, 1986 • *Lethal*, Select, 1987 • *Doin' It!* Select, 1989 • *Bag It and Bone It*, Jive, 1991.
Weather Girls: *The Weather Girls*, Columbia, 1989.
Whodini: *Greatest Hits*, Jive, 1990.

Garth Fundis

Country music producer Garth Fundis (born in 1949) came to the music business as a performer, playing in a number of blue-eyed soul bands in high school and college while growing up in Kansas. After moving to Nebraska, he joined a band called Smoke Ring, which was produced in 1970 by Dickey Lee, Knox Phillips, and Allen Reynolds (see entry), all of whom were living in

Memphis at the time. Fundis followed them to Nashville in 1971, where he got a job at Jack Clement's (see entry) studio as a gofer for $2.50 an hour.

"David Malloy (see entry) was there. He was glad [when I came] because he was no longer low man on the totem pole. I learned how to run the studio and became a second engineer, and then a staff engineer. I learned the recording process sitting on a chair behind the engineer and the producers, watching those fools make records," he says with a laugh.

He learned a great deal from Reynolds and singer Don Williams. He and Williams worked together in a number of capacities for 17 years, co-producing "Tulsa Time," which won the Academy of Country Music's Record of the Year in 1979, and *I Believe in You,* which was named the Country Music Association's (CMA) Album of the Year in 1981.

"Being an engineer for Allen Reynolds and working with Don taught me a lot about patience and how to deal with people—how to look at certain things in a very realistic way. It kind of grounded me in terms of my perspective."

From Clement, he learned, "you always need to have the red light on in the studio. Always have it in 'record' because you're trying to capture a moment in time and you don't know when it's going to happen."

Fundis has striven to work only with artists who capture his heart and imagination, like Keith Whitley. Although he only worked with the prodigious talent for about 18 months before Whitley died of alcohol poisoning, the artist had a profound effect on Fundis. "I met Keith and it was one of those things where I was intrigued by him immediately, but also realized that this guy is really frail. To be honest, I never really experienced [Keith's drinking problem]. He'd been through a lot by the time we met and was in a period where he was taking a chemical that made you sick if you drink alcohol.

"Keith and I had a musical relationship. I never talked to him about his drinking or anything and I think he respected me for that. The studio was a sanctuary for him. He was so at home on the stage; it was the other 23 hours a day that he had a problem." Fundis's work with Whitley produced five No. 1 songs, including "I'm No Stranger to the Rain," which won CMA single of the year in 1989.

Another artist who has captured Fundis's interest, and the one he is most identified with, is the spirited singer Trisha Yearwood. He and Yearwood have worked together for more than six years, and they have a rapport that defies description. "We talk to each other without talking—it kind of blows people's minds," he

says. "We can kind of look at each other and know what the other is thinking. We've just developed this innate sensibility with each other. She's a wonderful, wonderful artist."

Like most people Fundis has worked with, Whitley and Yearwood were both blessed with stellar voices. In fact, his resume is filled with some of the great voices in country music. "Trisha, Don [Williams], Collin [Raye], Keith, Randy Owen of Alabama, Lari White—just about everybody I've worked with has had something. Maybe because of that, I do think I put the vocal a little more up front than a lot of people."

However, Fundis is extremely proud to have worked with one act that is more noted for its musical prowess than singing style. He produced five albums with New Grass Revival, one of the finest musical collectives to ever pass through Nashville, featuring such instrumental luminaries as Bela Fleck and Sam Bush. "Working with New Grass Revival was one of the most exciting and frustrating experiences I've ever been through. I had not one gray hair before I worked with those guys," he laughs. "It was so exciting musically just to sit back and capture [them] on tape, but they were so frigging serious about what they were doing. I always wanted them to lighten up a little bit. They always felt like they were making history every measure—and they were. I learned a lot from those guys about searching for something beyond what you think you're capable of."

As if his life weren't hectic enough, Fundis also owns Sound Emporium, a Nashville studio he bought in '92. Additionally, like many producers in Nashville, Fundis also runs a label. He's head of Almo Sounds, owned by

Herb Alpert and Jerry Moss.

Prior to his current gig, he was head of A&R at RCA Records. "It's really difficult to shift gears [between label head and producer] because in the office you're scrambling to answer calls, to get paperwork done, everybody needs an answer to a question—and then you go into the studio and try to slow down and be creative," he says. "It's difficult to make the jump sometimes because you still think about all the crises you just left when you really are just trying to focus on how you're going to create something wonderful." —MELINDA NEWMAN

Alabama: *Super Hits,* RCA, 1996.

Bekka and Billy: *Bekka and Billy,* ALMO Sounds, 1997.

Conley, Earl Thomas: *The Essential,* RCA, 1996.

Davis, Mac: *Very Best and More,* PolyGram, 1984.

Dillon, Dean: *Hot, Single and Country,* Atlantic, 1993.

England, Ty: "Should've Asked Her Faster," RCA, 1995 • *Ty England,* RCA, 1995.

Fox, George: *Spice of Life,* Warner Bros., 1991.

Harris, Emmylou: *Cimarron,* Warner Bros., 1981 • *Duets,* Reprise, 1990 • *Portraits,* Warner Bros., 1996.

Jefferson, Paul: *Paul Jefferson,* ALMO Sounds, 1996.

New Grass Revival: *Fly Through the Country,* Flying Fish, 1975 • *When the Storm Is Over,* Flying Fish, 1977 • *On the Boulevard,* Sugar Hill, 1984 • *New Grass Revival,* EMI America, 1986 • *Hold to a Dream,* Capitol, 1987 • *Anthology,* Liberty, 1990 • *Best of New Grass Revival,* Liberty, 1994.

O'Hara, Jamie: *Rise Above It,* RCA, 1994.

Randall, Jon: *What You Don't Know,* RCA, 1995.

Raye, Collin: *In This Life,* Epic, 1992 • "In This Life," Epic, 1992.

Vincent, Rhonda: *Written in the Stars,* Giant, 1993.

Wariner, Steve: *Laredo,* MCA, 1990 • *Greatest Hits,* Vol. 2, MCA, 1991.

White, Lari: "Now I Know," RCA, 1994 • "That's My Baby," RCA, 1994 • *Wishes,* RCA, 1994 • *Best Of,* RCA, 1997.

Whitley, Keith: *Don't Close Your Eyes,* RCA, 1988 • "Don't Close Your Eyes," RCA, 1988 • "When You Say Nothing at All," RCA, 1988 • "I Wonder, Do You Think of Me," RCA, 1989 • *I Wonder, Do You Think of Me* RCA, 1989 • "I'm No Stranger to the Rain," RCA, 1989 • "It Ain't Nothin'," RCA, 1989 • *Keith Whitley,* RCA, 1990 • *The Best Of,* RCA, 1993 • *Essential,* RCA, 1996.

Williams, Don: *Till the Rivers All Run Dry,* MCA Special Products, n.d. • *Lovers and Best Friends,* MCA, 1975 • *Expressions,* ABC, 1978 • *Best Of,* Vol. 2, MCA, 1979 • "It Must Be Love," MCA, 1979 • "Tulsa Time," ABC, 1979 • "I Believe in You," MCA, 1980 • *I Believe in You,* MCA, 1980 • "Love Me Over Again," MCA, 1980 • *Prime Cuts,* Capitol Nashville, 1981, 1989 • "Lord, I Hope This Day Is Good," MCA, 1982 • "If Hollywood Don't Need You,"

MCA, 1983 • "Love Is on a Roll," MCA, 1983 • *Best Of,* Vol. 3, MCA, 1984 • "Stay Young," MCA, 1984 • "That's the Thing About Love," MCA, 1984 • *Greatest Hits,* MCA, 1985, 1992 • *Greatest Hits,* Vol. 4, MCA, 1985 • "Heartbeat in the Darkness," Capitol, 1986 • *One Good Well,* RCA, 1989 • *Lord, I Hope This Day Is Good,* MCA, 1993 • *The Best Of,* RCA, 1995.

Yates, Billy: *Billy Yates,* ALMO Sounds, 1997 • "Flowers," ALMO Sounds, 1997 • "When the Walls Come Tumblin' Down," ALMO Sounds, 1997.

Yearwood, Trisha: *Trisha Yearwood,* MCA, 1991 • "(You're the) Devil in Disguise," Epic Soundtrax, 1992 (*Honeymoon in Vegas* soundtrack) • *Hearts in Armor,* MCA, 1992 • w/ Don Henley, "Walkaway Joe," MCA, 1992 • "The Song Remembers When," MCA, 1993 • *The Song Remembers When,* MCA, 1993 • *The Sweetest Gift,* MCA, 1994 • "XXX's and OOO's (and American Girl)," MCA, 1994 • "Thinkin' About You," MCA, 1995 • *Thinkin' About You,* MCA, 1995 • "Everybody Knows," MCA, 1997 • *Everybody Knows,* MCA, 1996 • *Songbook: A Collection of Hits,* MCA Nashville, 1997.

Ron Furmanek

What do you want to be when you grow up? If your name happens to be Ron Furmanek, you take stock of the important sound recordings of the ages and darn well see to it that they are made available to the music fans of the world. In so doing, you make sure that the best existing source tapes are located and the greatest of care is employed in the preparation and presentation of this music.

"Back in the '50s, my dad had the first tape recorder on the block. He shot home movies of my brothers and me and synched up simultaneous sound recordings of us with the film. This was a big inspiration to me."

It was in Clifton, New Jersey, in 1962 that 6-year-old Furmanek received his first 45, a copy of "Return to Sender" by Elvis Presley. By 1980 he was rubbing elbows with Colonel Tom Parker, consulting on *This Is Elvis,* the first feature film documentary on the life of "The King."

Ron Furmanek is one of the pioneers of compact disc compilations and reissues, having produced over 200 CD titles since 1988. He gave birth to several celebrated CD compilation programs, most notably *Nipper's Greatest Hits* for RCA, The *Capitol Collectors Series,* and the EMI *Legendary Masters Series.* His *Les Paul—The*

Ron Furmanek and 19-month-old daughter Katherine.
Photo by Henry Diltz

Legend and the Legacy was nominated for a Grammy. *Frank Sinatra—The Capitol Years* is one of the most definitive and downright classy of all box sets to emerge from this golden age of reissues. He helped to initiate the relaunching of the Apple catalog after a 20-year interment.

When it comes to research, Furmanek will not take no for an answer. When tape librarians tell him that a certain master tape does not exist, that is when he gets out the miner's hat and starts to dig. "Sometimes, all it takes to strike gold is to put on some old work clothes and crawl through some wrecked, old, dusty tape vaults and not be afraid to get your hands a little dirty. I can't tell you how many times I've popped the tape off the end of a reel that hasn't been played in 35 years."

He has unearthed or created any number of full-dimensional gems, including first-time stereo versions of songs (Perry Como's "Catch a Falling Star" and the film version of Elvis's "Treat Me Nice") and unknown recordings by major artists.

The *Frank Sinatra—The Capitol Years* box (which went gold) offers one selection that not even the staunchest of Sinatra collectors recognized. "We went through literally thousands of reels of tape and we found a busting Billy May arrangement from 1958 called

'Here Goes.' It wasn't cataloged, it wasn't indexed. The writer and publisher are unknown."

Furmanek looks for a balance between fidelity to the original sound and sound fidelity. His main goal with regard to stereo remixing is to approximate the picture and punch of the original mono single. If it is possible to improve an existing stereo mix, he will do it.

Furmanek has been lucky with old magnetic analog tape in his quest for perfection. "Of all the tapes that I've worked with from studios all over the world, I've had trouble with maybe one tape and we had to resort to baking." "Baking" requires taking the tired analog source and exposing it to high temperatures to restructure the oxide onto the backing; usually only one or two successful playbacks are possible before further deterioration occurs.

"My work entails sources that date primarily from the late '40s through the '60s. If it was professionally recorded, chances are the tapes are going to sound great. There were a few times where I found tape that was completely warped and I had to hold cotton balls against the tape guides or rig up some cheap device in order to get it to play."

Working on the Les Paul (see entry) box presented Ron with some of his most rewarding moments of his career thus far. "We fired up Les's 8-track machine, the first one in existence, and put up some multitracks that hadn't been played in 40 years or more. We were mixing off the master tapes on the same machine and in the same room they were recorded in! Same console, same EQ. I did all the transfers at his house in Mahwah, New Jersey, and then mastered everything at Capitol in L.A. I sent him a DAT and he told me that he never heard his stuff sound so good"—a compliment not to be taken lightly, considering it came from the father of modern sound recording.

The *Capitol Collectors Series* and the EMI *Legendary Masters Series* have set sonic and packaging standards for the CD reissue world. "Back in '87 I went to Ron McCarrell at Capitol and proposed a series to replace the shoddy 10- or 15-track compilations they were issuing when compact discs were a new thing. The idea was to do definitive artist retrospectives with 20 or more tracks each, quality liner notes, layouts with ample archival visuals (including the use of correct period label designs printed on the face of the disc), and sell them at a bargain price."

Furmanek likes to keep his comps lively and fun. "I like to offer people something special on every CD I do, be it studio chatter, radio commercials, hidden tracks, interviews, unreleased songs, first-time stereo, count-offs, longer fades, instrumental tracks, label artwork. I don't rush these things out. I try to do them right."

Ron Furmanek has long been regarded as one of the foremost authorities on the Beatles' audio, film, and video history. His first "official" gig relating to the group dates back to research and consulting work for Capitol's vinyl-only releases, *The Beatles Rarities* of 1980 (an album that won in-print praise from John Lennon) and 1982's *Reel Music*. Recognizing the scope of Ron's insight, Apple called on him to restore the Beatles' film archive. Since 1987, he has color-corrected the visuals and remixed the audio (when applicable) on all the Fabs' promotional films: *The Beatles at Shea Stadium, Let It Be,* and *Magical Mystery Tour*.

The Beatles at Shea Stadium, the television special of a live concert filmed at the New York Mets' ballpark in August 1965, posed some challenges for Furmanek. "It took some searching, but ultimately we located the gentleman who worked for Bob Fine, the original on-site recording engineer for the concert. His assistant was the guy who left Shea with the tapes that night and took them home after the project was completed. They sat in his basement for 20 years. Fortunately for me, he lived in South Jersey!"

For some, hearing the actual session for a favorite record might help to dispel the youthful myth that their revered magical musical moments spontaneously combusted as the gods sprinkled fairy dust through the heavens to lowly mortals on this bitter earth. For Ron Furmanek, the revelation only heightens the enjoyment. "I'm honored to be working with this great stuff. Sometimes it's hard to believe that you're actually holding a tape in your hand and you can say 'I bought this record when it came out.'" —DENNIS DIKEN

COMPILATIONS

Andrews Sisters: *Capitol Collectors Series,* Capitol, 1991.

Anthony, Ray: *Capitol Collectors Series,* Capitol, 1991.

Bad Finger: *The Best of,* Apple/Capitol, 1995.

Bartholomew, Dave: *The Spirit of New Orleans: The Genius of Dave Bartholomew,* Capitol, 1993.

Burnette, Johnny: *The Best of: You're Sixteen,* EMI America, 1992.

Canned Heat: *Uncanned! The Best Of,* EMI America, 1994.

Carr, Vikki: *Que Sea El,* Sony, 1996.

Chad Mitchell Trio: *The Best of the Chad Mitchell Trio: The Mercury Years,* Chronicles/Mercury, 1998.

Cole, Nat "King": *Capitol Collectors Series,* Capitol, 1990.

Crew Cuts: *The Best of the Mercury Years,* Mercury, 1996.

Damone, Vic: *The Best of the Mercury Years,* Mercury, 1996.

Danleers, The: *The Best of the Mercury Years,* Mercury, 1996.

DeShannon, Jackie: *What the World Needs Now: The Definitive Collection,* EMI, 1994.

Diamonds, The: *The Best of: The Mercury Years,* Mercury, 1996.

Domino, Fats: *My Blue Heaven: The Best Of,* EMI America, 1990 • *Fat Man: 25 Classic Performances,* Capitol, 1996.

Ferrante and Teicher: *All-Time Great Movie Themes,* EMI, 1993.

Five Keys: *The Aladdin Years,* Collectables, 1991, 1995.

Fleetwoods, The: *Come Softly to Me: The Very Best Of,* EMI, 1993.

Four Freshmen: *Capitol Collectors Series,* Capitol, 1991.

Four Preps: *Capitol Collectors Series,* Capitol, 1989.

Freberg, Stan: *Capitol Colectors Series,* Capitol, 1990.

Gaylords, The: *The Best of the Mercury Years,* Mercury, 1996.

Goldsboro, Bobby: *The Best Of,* Collectables, 1996.

Highwaymen, The: *Michael, Row the Boat Ashore: The Best Of,* EMI, 1992.

Honeys, The: *Collectors Series,* Capitol, 1992.

Horne, Lena: *Merry from Lena,* EMI, 1990.

Howard, Eddy: *The Best of the Mercury Years,* Mercury, 1996.

Isley Brothers: *The Complete UA Sessions,* EMI America, 1991.

Laine, Frankie: *The Frankie Laine Collection: The Mercury Years,* Mercury, 1991.

Lee, Peggy: *Capitol Collectors Series,* Vol. 1, *The Early Years,* Capitol, 1990.

Lettermen, The: *Capitol Collectors Series,* Capitol, 1992.

Lewis, Gary: *Legendary Masters Series,* EMI America, 1990.

Lind, Bob: *The Best of Bob Lind: You Might Have Heard My Footsteps,* EMI, 1993.

Little Anthony and the Imperials: *The Best Of,* EMI, 1996.

Martin, Tony: *The Best of the Mercury Years,* Mercury, 1996.

Martino, Al: *Capitol Collectors Series,* Capitol, 1992.

Mercer, Johnny: *Capitol Collectors Series,* Capitol, 1989.

Milburn, Amos: *Down the Road Apiece: The Best Of,* EMI, 1995.

Mimms, Garnet: *The Cry Baby: The Best Of,* EMI, 1993.

Move, The: *Great Move! The Best Of,* EMI Legends, 1994.

Nelson, Rick: *The Best Of,* Vols. 1 and 2, Capitol, 1991.

Newton, Wayne: *Capitol Collectors Series,* Capitol, 1989.

Outsiders, The: *Collectors Series,* Collectables, 1996.

Page, Patti: *The Patti Page Collection,* Vols. 1–2, Mercury, 1991.

Paul, Les: *The Legend and the Legacy,* Capitol, 1992.

Penguins, The: *The Best of the Mercury Years,* Mercury, 1996.

Raspberries, The: *Capitol Collectors Series,* Capitol, 1991.

Sedaka, Neil: *All-Time Greatest Hits,* Vol. 2, RCA, 1991.

Seekers, The: *Capitol Collectors Series,* Capitol, 1992.

Serendipity Singers: *Don't Let the Rain Come Down: The Best Of,* Chronicles/Mercury, 1998.

Shirley and Lee: *Legendary Masters,* EMI, 1974, 1990.

Starr, Kay: *Capitol Collectors Series,* Capitol, 1991.

Sweet, The: *The Best Of,* Capitol, 1993.

Swinging Blue Jeans: *Hippy Hippy Shake: The Definitive Collection,* EMI, 1993.

Turner, Big Joe: *Jumpin' with Joe: The Complete Aladdin and Imperial Recordings,* EMI, 1995.

Ventures, The: *Walk, Don't Run: The Best Of,* EMI, 1990 • *Tele-Ventures: The Ventures Perform the Great TV Themes,* EMI, 1996.

Yardbirds, The: *Little Games Sessions and More,* Gold Rush, 1967, 1996.

Yuro, Timi: *The Best of: Hurt,* EMI America, 1992.

REISSUES

Brown, Charles: *Driftin' Blues: The Best Of,* Collectables, 1957, 1995.

Cher: *All I Really Wanna Do/The Sonny Side,* Capitol, 1965, 1992.

Cochran, Eddie: *Singing to My Baby/Never to Be Forgotten,* Gold Rush/Capitol, 1958, 1992.

Fitzgerald, Ella: *Ella Fitzgerald's Christmas,* Capitol, 1967, 1990.

Hourglass, The: *The Hourglass,* United Artists, 1968, 1973 • *Power of Love,* Liberty, 1968, 1992.

Jan and Dean: *The Little Old Lady from Pasadena,* EMI, 1964, 1992 • *Surf City,* EMI Legends, 1990 • *All the Hits—From Surf City to Drag City,* EMI, 1996.

Jay and the Americans: *Sands of Time/Wax Museum,* Capitol, 1969, 1993.

Lewis, Gary: *Everybody Loves a Clown/She's Just My Style,* EMI, 1965, 1992.

Lewis, Smiley: *I Hear You Knocking,* Collectables, 1961, 1995.

London, Julie: *Julie Is Her Name,* Vols. 1–2, EMI, 1956, 1992.

Vee, Bobby: *Merry Christmas from Bobby Vee,* EMI, 1962, 1990.

Ventures, The: *Play Telstar,* EMI, 1963, 1992 • *Ventures in Space,* EMI, 1964, 1992 • *The Ventures Christmas Album,* EMI, 1965, 1990.

COLLECTIONS (VARIOUS ARTISTS)

24 Greatest Hits of All Time, EMI America, 1991.

James Bond: Best of 30th Anniversary Collection, Capitol, 1992.

Legends of Christmas Past, A Rock 'n R&B Holiday Collection, EMI America, 1992.

Rock Is Dead But It Won't Lie Down, EMI, 1993.

The Minit Records Story, EMI, 1995.

That's Fats: A Tribute to Fats Domino, Capitol, 1996.

Milt Gabler

Milt Gabler's career in music dates back to the '20s, and runs like a river through the most important developments in pop and jazz history. Gabler ran the legendary Commodore Music Shop in New York (the first jazz record store anywhere), then Commodore Records (the first independent jazz label), then worked for 30 years as a producer and A&R man for Decca Records.

Along the way he became the first jazz impresario, promoted the first jazz jam sessions open to the public, and recorded Eddie Condon, Billie Holiday, Lester Young, Ella Fitzgerald, Brenda Lee, Peggy Lee, Louis Jordan, the Weavers, and Bill Haley and the Comets. His importance to the development and dissemination of American popular music in the 20th century is, arguably, second only to that of John Hammond (see entry), his friend and rival.

Milton Gabler was born in New York City in 1911. Gabler's father owned the Commodore Music Shop on 42nd Street, diagonally across from the Commodore Hotel: hence the name. When Milt started working at the shop as a Stuyvesant High School student in the mid-'20s, radio had burst onto the scene and replaced records as the primary source of musical entertainment.

The shop sold radios, and in order to draw customers in, Milt played the radio on loudspeakers outside the store. Customers began to ask for the recordings that they heard on the radio, so Milt was able to convince his reluctant father to start carrying records.

Milt loved jazz from the beginning, especially the "hot" swing of Eddie Condon, Pee Wee Russell, Jack Teagarden, Bud Freeman, and Bobby Hackett. The store soon became known for its selection of hard-to-find jazz. Musicians, writers (Ralph Gleason, Leonard Feather), and collectors hung out at the store to buy, chat, and listen to records in the free listening booths.

As Gabler told Ted Fox in *In the Groove,* "People would go in and stay for an hour or two until they picked out three records and it was a dollar sale! It was a cheap way to spend a lunch hour and not put nickels in the juke box. Jerry Wexler (see entry) courted his first wife in the booth."

By the early '30s Commodore was the center of the New York jazz world. "You could always find someone you could talk to about your hobby, including my salesmen, myself, my brothers or brothers-in-law [Jack Crystal, father of Billy Crystal is a brother-in-law and helped run the shop]. . . . Don't forget that jazz then, and even now, was a very small percentage of the record industry," noted Gabler.

The record business got so bad in the late '20s and early '30s (due to radio and the Depression) that companies discontinued making records. Through his inside sources, Gabler became aware that Columbia was closing its Okeh label, so he arranged to go through the company's inventory before it was sold in bulk, ending up with several thousand records.

Gabler continued to stock records any way he could—buying from dealer's stocks, the Salvation Army, customers—but this approach became wearisome, and by 1933 the young entrepreneur realized he had enough customers to start pressing his own records. Gabler's procedure was to lease a master from the original record company and then press a few hundred records on his own Commodore Music Shop label.

Always ahead of his time, Gabler saw the label primarily as advertising for the shop. "All the writers came in there . . . so I'd get the publicity—'The Commodore Music Shop just reissued a record'—[and] people would come to the store because I had that kind of merchandise in stock and no one else had it," he said.

When it became clear that there was a market for reissues, Columbia hired John Hammond to put out reissues for them. Because they already owned the masters, Columbia was able to put the records out for 50 cents; whereas Gabler's ran from 75 cents to $1.50.

Soon the other majors were doing the same and Gabler couldn't get masters. "I thought I better start making my own recordings because if I paid for a record date, and hired a studio, and did my own recording, I'd own it forever," he reasoned.

The first Commodore session was with Eddie Condon and the Chicago Rhythm Kings in 1938. The original band from the '20s had scattered into other groups; so Gabler had to wait until all of the individual bands happened to be in New York at the same time. The session was almost scrapped when Benny Goodman scheduled a last-minute session for the same day, precluding Gabler's use of pianist Jess Stacy. Gabler was able to persuade Goodman, an old friend from the shop, to take the day off, and the first Commodore session was on.

From the beginning, Gabler was a hands-on producer. "I told the engineer, 'They sound one way in the studio and another way through your monitor. You don't have the men balanced properly.' . . . I told the guys to play and then move around until I could hear all the instruments. Then I balanced the rhythm section because we only used two mikes in those years. . . . That's all there [was to it]."

Billie Holiday had opened a long engagement at Cafe Society downtown in late '38. By April 1939, she wanted to record a song that had become her stage finale, a bluesy ballad telling the stark—even shocking—tale of a lynching: "Strange Fruit." The "strange fruit" of the title was the body of a lynched man with "bulging eyes and twisted mouth" hanging from a poplar tree. Holiday's label at the time, Columbia, was afraid to put out the song for fear of alienating Southern customers, and Holiday came into Gabler's store unhappy about the situation.

Gabler expressed interest, and Columbia granted Holiday permission to record "Strange Fruit," "Yester-days," "I Got a Right" and "Fine and Mellow" with Gabler. "Fruit" got all of the attention, but "Fine and Mellow" became the hit.

The songs from the 1939 and 1944 sessions that Holiday did with Gabler appear in an excellent collection: *Billie Holiday: The Complete Commodore Recordings*. In the collection's liner notes, Holiday biographer Stuart Nicholson declares yet another first for Gabler. Nicholson believes that "Strange Fruit" was among the first popular songs "that became impossible to disentangle from a single, specific recording. . . . Singer and song are bonded in a way that exhausts the meaning of the material." This was at a time when success with a song did not convey ownership. Hit songs were recorded by many artists as a matter of course.

This concept is extremely important because prior to Holiday's recording of "Strange Fruit" (which no one covered until Cassandra Wilson's 1995 version), a song held primacy over any given recording of it. If a specific recording becomes "the" version of a song, that version achieves primacy over the song itself (just a collection of notes and words) or any given live performance of it. Under this process, a producer becomes a creator, not just a recordist. In keeping with this theory, then, Milt Gabler is the first true "producer."

Another first for Gabler was his Sunday jam sessions. In the mid-'30s Gabler got the idea to hold free jam sessions featuring top jazz musicians to publicize the music and the Commodore name. He got permission to use some of the studios around town for free because they were closed on Sundays. The musicians would play for booze.

Count Basie, Benny Goodman, Ella Fitzgerald, Eddie Condon, and many other luminaries participated. However, most musicians and guests smoked and ground out their cigarettes on the nice wooden floors, so Gabler's shows were soon banned from the studios. By 1940, Gabler had moved the jams to Jimmy Ryan's on 52nd Street, where they lasted for years.

By 1941, Gabler's reputation was established and Jack Kapp of Decca came knocking. Gabler negotiated a deal whereby he could do A&R and production work for Decca in the mornings, and his Commodore work in the afternoons.

Gabler worked for Decca until 1971 and produced Guy Lombardo, Jimmy Dorsey, Burl Ives, Bing Crosby, Louis Armstrong, the Four Aces, Ella Fitzgerald, Carmen McRae, Peggy Lee, Bert Kaempfert, the Weavers, Louis Jordan, and Bill Haley and His Comets, among untold others. Documentation is a problem because producers were rarely listed until the '50s, and then only sporadically.

Gabler's hits include Peggy Lee's "Lover," a smoky and smoking run-through of the Rodgers and Hart classic; the Weavers' folk standards "Goodnight Irene" and "On Top of Old Smokey"; Ella Fitzgerald's "Cryin' in the Chapel" and "My Happiness"; and R&B sax great Louis Jordan's "Choo Choo Choo Boogie," "Ain't Nobody Here But Us Chickens," "Let the Good Times Roll," and "Saturday Night Fish Fry."

Gabler's work with Jordan—among the most important precursors of rock 'n' roll—was pivotal. In Jerry Wexler's autobiography, *Rhythm and the Blues*, he states: "Louis was a true musician. His shuffle syncopations—those dotted eighth and sixteenth notes—became a foundation of commercial dance music. . . . His supertight sextet would be the model of mean-and-lean R&B bands for decades to come—Ray Charles, James Brown, the Muscle Shoals configurations, Tower of Power . . . and the Time." Jordan married "the harmonic sophistication of jazz with the folk wit of the blues," Wexler continues. "His humor and celebration of a black lifestyle . . . were picture-painting poetry."

He concludes, "Gabler . . . is one of my role models . . . because over the decades he truly understood the natural art of bending and blending genres," most particularly when he "infuse[d] Jordan's spirit into the work of Bill Haley and the Comets, one of the first seeds of black rhythm and blues to bloom into white rock and roll," and "Rock Around the Clock" became the first No. 1 hit of the rock 'n' roll era.

Gabler used recording techniques developed working with Jordan on Haley, who until then had been a semi-successful rockabilly performer. They recorded in the same place, the Pythian Temple, an old ballroom on West 70th, and Gabler used a lot of "tape reverb and reverb from the room," he told Ted Fox.

"On Jordan we used a perfectly balanced rhythm section from the swing era . . . but on rock and roll . . . he had the heavy back beat. At the Pythian, you could blow because there was this big high ceiling, we had drapes hanging from the balconies, and a live wooden floor.

"When they got it down by rote, that thing rocked! . . . I had three mikes on the drums. . . . We had the guy slap the bass . . . then I had . . . the steel player . . . hit what I called lightning flashes, where he'd take the steel bar and hit it across the strings of the steel guitar and make it arc. It'd make POW! POW! I'd say, 'Give me some of those lightning flashes, Billy!' " When "Rock Around the Clock" was added to the *Blackboard Jungle* soundtrack in 1955, all hell broke loose and the rock 'n' roll revolution began.

The Commodore Music Shop was closed in 1958, and Gabler was fired from Decca in 1971 for being too

old. Gabler has received numerous awards, including the NARAS President's Merit Award and the Grammy Trustees Award. In 1993 he was inducted into the Rock and Roll Hall of Fame. Gabler remains active today, helping reissue Commodore and Decca records he originally produced as much as 50 years ago. —ERIC OLSEN

Berry, Chu, and Lucky Thompson: *Giants of the Tenor Sax,* Commodore, 1988.

Brunis, George, and Wild Bill Davidson: *Jazz A-Plenty,* Commodore, 1989.

Byas, Don, and Ben Webster: *Giants of the Tenor Sax* series, Commodore, 1988.

Condon, Eddie: w/ His Windy City Seven and Bud Freeman and His Gang, *Jammin' at Commodore,* Commodore, 1988 • w/ His Band, *Ballin' the Jack,* Commodore, 1989 • w/ His All-Stars, *Dixieland All-Stars,* Decca Jazz, 1994.

Crosby, Bing: *Bing! His Legendary Years, 1931–1957,* MCA, 1989.

Davison, Wild Bill: *Commodore Master Takes,* GRP, 1997.

Davison, Wild Bill, and George Brunis: *Jazz A-Plenty,* Commodore, 1989.

Dorsey, Jimmy: *The Best Of,* MCA, 1975.

Fitzgerald, Ella: *Smooth Sailing,* Decca, 1955 • *Pure Ella,* Decca Jazz, 1994 • *The War Years (1941–1947),* Decca Jazz, 1994 • *Ella and Friends,* GRP, 1996 • *Priceless Jazz,* GRP, 1997.

Freeman, Bud, and His Gang: *See* Condon, Eddie.

Hackett, Bobby: *Jazz in New York,* Commodore, 1944.

Haley, Bill, and His Comets: "(We're Gonna) Rock Around the Clock," Decca, 1955 • *From the Original Master Tapes,* MCA, 1985.

Hampton, Lionel: *Midnight Sun,* Decca, 1947, 1993 • *Hamp: The Legendary Decca Recordings of,* Decca Jazz, 1996.

Hawkins, Coleman, and Frank Wess: *Giants of the Tenor Sax* series, Commodore, 1988 • *Body and Soul Revisited,* Decca Jazz, 1993.

Heywood, Eddie, and His Orchestra: *Jazz at the Cafe Society, NY in the 40's,* Commodore, 1989.

Holiday, Billie: *The Complete Decca Recordings,* Decca, 1950, 1991 • *Lady Day,* Commodore, 1988 • *Priceless Jazz,* GRP, 1997 • *The Complete Commodore Recordings,* Commodore, 1997.

Jordan, Louis: *Five Guys Named Moe,* Decca, 1946, 1992 • *Five Guys Named Moe: Original Decca Recordings* Vol. 2, Decca, 1952, 1992 • *The Best Of,* Decca Jazz, 1975, 1996 • *Louis Jordan and His Tympany Five,* Vols. 1–2, Decca, 1946, 1948 • *Just Say Moe-Mo' of the Best Of,* Rhino, 1992.

Kaempfert, Bert: *Strangers in the Night,* Decca, 1966 • *Best Of,* Mobile Fidelity Sound Lab, 1989 • *The Very Best Of,* TAR, 1995 • *Christmas Wonderland,* Taragon, 1996 • *That Happy Feeling,* Decca, 1996 • *That Latin Felling/Blue Midnight,* Taragon, 1997.

Kalin Twins: *When*, Bear Family, 1984.

Lee, Peggy: *The Best Of, 1952–1956*, Music Club, 1994.

McKuen, Rod: *Greatest Hits Collection*, Delta, 1996.

McRae, Carmen: *Here to Stay*, Decca Jazz, 1992 • *I'll Be Seeing You*, Decca Jazz, 1995.

Morgan, Russ: *The Best Of*, MCA, 1972.

Russell, Pee Wee: *Jazz Original*, GRP, 1997.

Stacy, Jess, and Friends: *Jess Stacy and Friends*, Commodore, 1989.

Thompson, Lucky: *See* Berry, Chu

Weavers, The: *The Best of the Decca Years*, MCA, 1996.

Webster, Ben: *See* Byas, Don

Wess, Frank: *See* Hawkins, Coleman

Young, Lester: *Kansas City Sessions*, GRP, 1997.

Young, Lester, and Friends: *Giants of the Tenor Sax* series, Commodore, 1988.

COLLECTIONS

Commodore Jazz Sampler: Classics in Swing, 1938–1944, Commodore, 1988.

Jazz in New York, Commodore, 1988.

Rock Around the Clock: The Decca Rock and Roll Collection, Decca, 1994.

Stardust: The Classic Decca Hits and Standards Collection, Decca, 1994.

The Commodore Story, Commodore, 1997.

COMPILATIONS

Armstrong, Louis: *Best of the Decca Years: The Singer*, MCA, 1989.

Fitzgerald, Ella: *75th Birthday Celebration*, Decca Jazz, 1993 • *The Best Of*, Decca Jazz, 1994.

Garland, Judy: *Best of the Decca Years*, Vol. 1, Decca/MCA, 1990.

Jim Gaines

Jim Gaines (born October 2, 1941) is a producer/engineer whose biggest successes have come from collaborations with a core group of northern California artists, including Huey Lewis and the News, Santana, Pablo Cruise, Tower of Power, John Lee Hooker, Paul Kantner, and Journey.

A familiar fixture at the Plant (formerly the Record Plant, Sausalito), Gaines' relaxed, Southern gentleman presence, sense of groove, and solid engineering have given his artists the freedom to be themselves on mike. Although his engineering and mixing are not known for being high-fidelity, they are very musical.

"Jim is the best tracking engineer I've ever worked with," says engineer Jeffrey Norman. "When he's producing, he can get laid-back with the artist and make them feel comfortable. And he's got the greatest sense of EQ of anyone I know. His tracks are a pleasure to mix."

Gaines' collaboration with Huey Lewis resulted in sales of more than 10 million albums, and covered the three most successful of the artist's career: *Picture This, Sports,* and *Fore*. Together, the three albums spawned 13 Top 40 singles. *Sports* and *Fore* each had an astonishing five Top 20 hits, and each reached No. 1 on the Billboard album chart (in 1983 and 1986, respectively, although *Sports* stayed on the chart for 158 weeks), making Lewis one of the most successful artists of the decade.

Gaines produced Tower of Power's only gold album, 1973's *Tower of Power,* and the group's only Top 20 hit, "So Very Hard to Go."

Gaines' Santana records coincided with a commercial dip in the band's career, but together they released a series of five excellent albums, including *Spirits Dancing in the Flesh,* featuring guest appearances by Vernon Reid (Living Colour lead guitarist) and Bobby Womack. In the '90s Gaines has focused on the blues, producing albums by such luminaries as Luther Allison, Lonnie Brooks, Albert Collins, the Eric Gales Band, and Jimmy Thackery and the Drivers. —DANIEL J. LEVITIN

Allison, Luther: *Soul Fixing Man*, Alligator, 1994 • *Blue Streak*, Alligator, 1995 • *Reckless*, Alligator, 1997.

Anderson, Chris: *Old Friend*, Relativity, 1995.

Blues Traveler: *Travelers and Thieves*, A&M, 1991.

Brooks, Lonnie: *Roadhouse Rules*, Alligator, 1996 • *Deluxe Edition*, Alligator, 1997.

Castro, Tommy: *Can't Keep a Good Man Down*, Blind Pig, 1997.

Collins, Albert: *Albert Collins*, Charisma, 1991 • *Iceman*, Charisma, 1991 • *The Best of Collins Mix*, Point Blank, 1993.

Connor, Joanna: *Fight*, Blind Pig, 1992.

Croce, A.J.: *Fit to Serve*, Ruf/A&M, 1998.

Davies, Debbie: *I Got That Feeling*, Blind Pig, 1997.

Dynatones, The: *Shameless*, Warner Bros., 1983.

El Tri: *Cuando Tu No Estas*, WEA Latina, 1997.

Eric Gales Band: *The Eric Gales Band*, Elektra, 1992 • *Picture of a Thousand Faces*, Elektra, 1993.

Every Mother's Nightmare: *Wake Up Screaming*, Arista, 1993.

FreeWorld: *You Are Here*, Real Beale, 1996.

Hole, Dave: *Steel on Steel*, Alligator, 1995.

Hooker, John Lee: *The Healer*, Chameleon, 1989.

James Solberg Band: *One of These Days*, Atomic Theory, 1996.

Jamison, Jim/Survivor: *Collection,* Scotti Brothers, 1993.

Journey: *Raised on Radio,* Columbia, 1986.

Kantner/Balin/Cassidy: *The KBC Band,* Arista, 1986.

Kinsey Report: *Crossing Bridges,* Point Blank, 1993.

Kubec, Smokin' Joe: *Take Your Best Shot,* Bullseye Blues, 1998.

Lewis, Huey, and the News: "Do You Believe in Love?," Chrysalis, 1982 • "Hope You Love Me Like You Say You Do," Chrysalis, 1982 • *Picture This,* Chrysalis, 1982 • "Workin' for a Livin'," Chrysalis, 1982.

Mark, Paul, and the Van Dorens: *Go Big or Go Home,* Continuum, 1991.

Montoya, Coco: *Ya Think I'd Know Better,* Blind Pig, 1996 • *Just Let Go,* Blind Pig, 1997.

Neville Brothers: *Uptown,* EMI America, 1987 • "Whatever It Takes," EMI America, 1987.

Santana: *Viva Santana,* Columbia, 1988 • *Spirits Dancing in the Flesh,* Columbia, 1990.

Studebaker John and the Hawks: *Tremoluxe,* Blind Pig, 1996.

Thackery, Jimmy, and the Drivers: *Trouble Man,* Blind Pig, 1994 • *Wild Night Out!* Blind Pig, 1995 • *Drive to Survive,* Blind Pig, 1996 • *Switching Gears,* Blind Pig, 1998.

Tower of Power: "So Very Hard to Go," Warner Bros., 1973 • *Tower of Power,* Warner Bros., 1973 • "What Is Hip?," Warner Bros., 1973.

Trout, Walter: *Walter Trout,* A&M, 1998.

Vaughn, Stevie Ray, and Double Trouble: *In Step,* Epic, 1989 • *The Sky Is Crying,* Epic, 1991.

Albhy Galuten

An apprentice of the fertile Ardent Studios in Memphis, Albhy Galuten was lucky enough to land a job as an assistant to legendary producer Tom Dowd (see entry) at Criteria Studio in Miami at a time when that historic facility was turning out some of the most momentous records in modern history, albums like the Allman Brothers Band's *Eat a Peach,* Derek and the Dominoes' *Layla,* the Eagles' *Hotel California.*

By the mid-'70s, the multitalented Galuten had worked with all of those artists—plus Kenny Loggins, Rod Stewart, Peter Tosh, and others—as a producer, engineer, assistant, musician (he plays guitar and keyboards), string arranger, and songwriter.

While many would be satisfied with such enviable laurels, Galuten's best days were still ahead of him. In 1976, he hooked up with engineer Karl Richardson and Barry Gibb to produce the Bee Gees' *Children of the World* (No. 8), which set the stage for their work on the

Saturday Night Fever soundtrack—an album that, on its way to becoming the best-selling soundtrack of all time at 25 million units worldwide, epitomized the disco craze of the late '70s.

The phenomenal success of *Saturday Night Fever*—which spent 24 weeks at No. 1—catapulted Galuten's career to such an extent that, in 1978, he aced out legendary producers Phil Ramone, Quincy Jones, Peter Asher, and Alan Parsons (see entries) for the coveted Best Producer of the Year Grammy Award.

Naturally, Galuten's association with the Bee Gees put him in contact with other top talent of the day, including Andy Gibb, Barbra Streisand, Kenny Rogers, Diana Ross, and Dionne Warwick. During those heady days when Galuten was on top of the world, he scored an unprecedented 11 consecutive No. 1 singles, and in one auspicious week produced each of the Top 3 hits.

As disco gave way to new wave and a horde of synthesizer-based bands, Galuten grew increasingly frustrated with the state of the industry and decided to return to his first love: rock 'n' roll. He produced albums that earned heaps of critical acclaim, if not commercial success, including Jellyfish's gorgeous debut, *Bellybutton,* and its follow-up, *Spilt Milk;* and Minneapolis all-female

Photo by David Goggin © 1995

rock trio ZuZu's Petals' debut. He was also involved with No Doubt's massive *Tragic Kingdom* album.

By 1994, Galuten had had enough of production. Excited by the budding enhanced-CD format, he decided to retire from the studio and devote all his energy to developing interactive entertainment. He worked at BMG-affiliated ION and later joined MCA as vice president of media services. —PAUL VERNA

Bee Gees: *Children of the World,* RSO, 1976 • "Love So Right," RSO, 1976 • "You Should Be Dancing," RSO, 1976 • "Boogie Child," RSO, 1977 • *Here at Last: Live,* RSO, 1977 • "How Deep Is Your Love?," RSO, 1977 • "More Than a Woman," RSO, 1977 (*Saturday Night Fever* soundtrack) • "Stayin' Alive," RSO, 1977 • "Night Fever," RSO, 1978 • "Love You Inside Out," RSO, 1979 • *Spirits Having Flown,* RSO, 1979 • "Too Much Heaven," RSO, 1979 • "Tragedy," RSO, 1979 • *Bee Gees Greatest,* RSO, 1980 • *Living Eyes,* RSO, 1981 • *Tales from the Brothers Gibb,* Polydor, 1990.

Cher: *Cher,* Geffen, 1987.

Clapton, Eric: *Crossroads,* Polydor, 1988.

Davis, Jesse Ed: *Ululu,* Atco, 1972.

De Sario, Terry: *Pleasure Train,* Casablanca, 1978.

Gibb, Andy: *Flowing Rivers,* RSO, 1977 • "I Just Want to Be Your Everything," RSO, 1977 • "(Love Is) Thicker Than Water," RSO, 1978 • "An Everlasting Love," RSO, 1978 • "Our Love, Don't Throw It All Away," RSO, 1978 • "Shadow Dancing," RSO, 1978 • *Shadow Dancing,* RSO, 1978 • *Andy Gibb's Greatest Hits,* RSO, 1980 • "Desire," RSO, 1980 • w/ Olivia Newton-John, "I Can't Help It," RSO, 1980 • "Time Is Time," RSO, 1980.

Gold, Frannie: *Frannie Gold,* Portrait, 1979.

James Montgomery Band: *High Roller,* Capricorn, 1974.

Jellyfish: *Bellybutton,* Charisma, 1990 • "I Wanna Stay Home," Charisma, 1990 • "Joining a Fan Club," Charisma, 1993 • *Spilt Milk,* Charisma, 1993 • "He's My Best Friend," Epic Soundtrax, 1994 (*Threesome* soundtrack).

Jo Mama: *J Is for Jump,* Atlantic, 1971.

Network: *Network,* Epic, 1977.

Parton, Dolly: *The RCA Years, 1967–1986,* RCA, 1993 • *See also* Rogers, Kenny.

Rogers, Kenny: *Greatest Hits,* EMI America, 1980 • *Eyes That See in the Dark,* RCA, 1983 • w/ Dolly Parton, "Islands in the Stream," RCA, 1983 • *Decade of Hits,* Warner Bros., 1997.

Ross, Diana: "Chain Reaction," RCA, 1985 • *Diana: The Ultimate Collection,* Motown, 1993 • *Diana Extended: The Remixes,* Motown, 1994 • *Greatest Hits: The RCA Years,* RCA, 1997.

Sang, Samantha: "Emotion," Private Stock, 1977 • *Emotion* (2 tracks), Private Stock, 1978.

Stone, Agnes: *Agnes Stone,* Qwest/Reprise, 1994.

Streisand, Barbra: "Guilty," Columbia, 1980 • *Guilty,* Columbia, 1980 • "Woman in Love," Columbia, 1980 • "What Kind of Fool," Columbia, 1981 • *Memories,* Columbia, 1982 • *Emotion* (2 tracks), Columbia, 1984 • *A Collection: Greatest Hits and More,* Columbia, 1989.

Titanic Love Affair: *Titanic Love Affair,* Charisma, 1991.

Valli, Frankie: "Grease," RSO, 1978 • *Greatest Hits* Vol. 2, Rhino, 1991.

Warwick, Dionne: "Heartbreaker," Arista, 1982 • *Heartbreaker,* Arista, 1982 • *Friends,* Arista, 1985 • "Whisper in the Dark," Arista, 1985 • *Greatest Hits, 1979–1990,* Arista, 1989.

Zuzu's Petals: *The Music of Your Life,* Twin/Tone, 1994.

COLLECTIONS
Stayin' Alive soundtrack, RSO, 1983.

Kenneth Gamble and Leon Huff

Songwriters, producers, entrepreneurs—Kenny Gamble and Leon Huff were the focal point (with Thom Bell; see entry) of the urbane soul of the Philly sound from the mid-'60s through the early '80s. Their Philadelphia International Records was to the '70s what Motown was to the '60s: the preeminent black-owned entertainment enterprise in America and the conveyance of the finest soul music to the world.

The pair's work with the Intruders, Archie Bell and the Drells, Jerry Butler, and Wilson Pickett is classic; but their innovations with the O'Jays, Harold Melvin and the Blue Notes, and their house band, MFSB, helped lay the foundations for both funk and disco and generated some of the most enduring music of the '70s.

Visionary lyricist Gamble and pianist/composer Huff gathered a street-tough rhythm section of Philadelphia road and studio veterans—Earl Young (also of the Trammps) on drums, Ronnie Baker on bass, Roland Chambers and Norman Harris on guitar, Vincent Montana Jr. (founder of the Salsoul Orchestra; see entry) on vibes, multi-instrumentalist Bunny Sigler, Huff on keyboards—and melded this rhythmic muscle with horns and strings from the Philadelphia Orchestra to create a fine-tuned machine that consumed and reconciled racial, sonic, and thematic contradictions to generate a transcendent, melodic groove.

Kenny Gamble was born August 11, 1943, in Philadelphia and grew up in the same neighborhood as Thom Bell, even dating Bell's twin sister Barbara. Gamble and Bell wrote songs together as teens and recorded a duet, "Someday," for the Heritage label in 1959. They also formed a band, the Romeos, which played around the area in the early to mid-'60s, backed up black acts on the local Cameo-Parkway label (Chubby Checker, the Orlons, Dee Dee Sharp—later Mrs. Kenny Gamble for a time), and toured with Chubby Checker and Little Anthony and the Imperials.

Leon Huff was born April 8, 1942, in Camden, New Jersey, and grew up in the Centerville section of town, where he played piano at home and drums in the school band. An eclectic music lover from the beginning, Huff listened to doo-wop, jazz, country, and classical on the radio, as well as his father's blues guitar and mother's gospel piano.

Huff perennially made the Camden All-City Orchestra on drums and accompanied many of the local street corner vocal groups on piano; after he graduated from high school in 1960, he started going into local recording studios. Huff's eclecticism and accompanying abilities led him to New York and the Brill Building, which housed, per Huff, "musical gods Burt Bacharach, Leiber and Stoller, Jeff Barry and Ellie Greenwich, and Phil Spector" (see entries).

Huff became a favored studio pianist for Spector in particular, playing on hits for the Ronettes, Darlene Love, and many others in the early '60s. Huff gravitated to the Shubert Building—Philadelphia's equivalent of the Brill Building—in 1964 and played on "The 81" for Candy and the Kisses, co-written by one Kenny Gamble.

One day in 1964 the pair shared the Shubert Building elevator; the outgoing Gamble asked the reticent piano-wiz Huff if he wrote songs. Recalls Huff, "I said 'Yeah, why don't you come over to my house.' I lived in the projects in Camden. That's when it really started. He came over to my house that night, and we sat down in my little music room and it sounded good from the beginning. We just started writing songs every day after that."

The first song they wrote together, "I'm Sorry Baby," was the B-side of the Sapphires hit "Who Do You Love?" for Swan in '64. Then Huff joined Gamble in the Romeos, hitting the road for Checker and Little Anthony tours.

Writing together in earnest and tired of the road, Gamble and Huff formed a writing and production company and had their first hit with Soul Survivors' "Expressway to Your Heart"—a confident, soul-rock workout of indeterminate racial origin (the band was white) that set the tone for things to come by hitting the

Top 5 on both the R&B and pop charts in 1967. The flawless production evokes the Rascals with a stomping bass and piano rhythm line, an organ interlude, sound effects, driving drum break, and clever lyrics that draw on the twin urban concerns of traffic and love.

At the same time Gamble and Huff began a 10-year association with Philly R&B group the Intruders, which was fronted by its engagingly pitch-challenged lead singer "Little Sonny" Brown. Brown's voice and a firm rhythm section (which evolved into MFSB) gave the group their edge, which the group's smooth harmonies and Bobby Martin's string-and-horn arrangements simultaneously mitigated and emphasized. Gamble and Huff and the Intruders had a minor hit with "(We'll Be) United" in mid-'66, and hit the big time in 1968 with "Cowboys to Girls" (No. 6 pop; No. 1 R&B), a sweet coming-of-age tale living precariously at the upper end of Brown's register.

Itinerant writers and producers still, Gamble and Huff whipped up hits for Archie Bell and the Drells (the infectious, choogling "I Can't Stop Dancing," No. 9) and Wilson Pickett (the rousing "Engine Number 9" and "Don't Let the Green Grass Fool You") for the Atlantic label, deep soul classics for Jerry Butler ("Never Give You Up," No. 20; "Hey, Western Union Man," No. 16; "Only the Strong Survive," No. 4) for Mercury, and more soul for Joe Simon ("Drowning in the Sea of Love," No. 11) for Spring.

By 1971, Gamble and Huff were tired of moving their tent from label to label and approached CBS president Clive Davis about a deal for an imprint of their own, to be distributed by CBS. Recalls Huff, "Clive was blown away by our talent, and it was a great move for us and them. Our company [Philadelphia International] really took off after we signed the O'Jays.

"I remember flying into Cleveland—a disc jockey had called to say 'Man, there's a group in Cleveland that's raising hell'—so we took a flight out to Cleveland and went to see them at a club. They had lines around the corner. Those guys were tearing that club up. We stayed in Cleveland until we signed them. We took them back to Philadelphia and recorded and recorded and recorded."

With the O'Jays, and Harold Melvin and the Blue Notes, the world of Gamble and Huff came together. In the '70s Gamble and Huff scored ten No. 1 R&B and nine Top 40 pop hits with the O'Jays; four No. 1 R&B and four Top 20 hits with Harold Melvin and the Blue Notes. But more importantly, all the disparate elements of the Gamble and Huff sound coalesced into something new: music with the aforementioned rhythmic muscle, melodic sophistication, and orchestral leavening, combined with a newfound social and interpersonal awareness, all funneled through the great pipes of the O'Jays' Eddie Levert and the Blue Notes' Teddy Pendergrass.

Recorded at Gamble and Huff's Sigma Sound with engineer Joe Tarsia, the roll began with the O'Jays' "Back Stabbers," a remarkable combination of shimmering strings, Latin percussion, postmodern paranoia, and a palpable sense of "This is it—there is nothing any of us could or should be doing other than making this music." In Motown, Norman Whitfield (see entry) was making parallel strides; elsewhere, Curtis Mayfield and Isaac Hayes (see entries) were independently exploring some of the same terrain. But Gamble and Huff weren't following anyone: they were leading.

In addition to making hits, Gamble and Huff allowed MFSB to stretch out in the grooves of the songs, laying a funky foundation for the extended disco remixes of the later '70s. Album cuts of such up-tempo masterworks as the Blue Notes' "Bad Luck" and "The Love I Lost"; MFSB's "TSOP" (The Soul Train theme song) and "Love Is the Message"; and the O'Jays' "992 Arguments," "I Love Music," and (best) "For the Love of Money" reached lengths of up to 10 minutes of dance floor ecstasy.

"Money" is Huff's all-time favorite "for the [anti-greed] message and for the song. I used to go the O'Jays' concerts and they would drive people insane when they would close the show with that song," he says.

Of course Gamble and Huff were also writing and producing great ballads for the Blue Notes ("If You Don't Know Me by Now," "I Miss You," "Yesterday I Had the Blues"), Billy Paul ("Me and Mrs. Jones," No. 1 R&B and pop), the Three Degrees ("When Will I See You Again?," No. 2), and many others.

The roll continued through the '70s and into the early '80s when hip-hop, hard funk, and electronic dance styles rendered soul and disco (temporarily) obsolete, and an industry-wide slump soured everyone's milk. When Teddy Pendergrass had his paralyzing car accident in 1982, Gamble and Huff decided to take a little break from making music.

Since then they have run their publishing empire and studios (recently revamped) and, after a 15-year hiatus, have returned to writing and producing with newcomer Damon Williams. The juices are flowing again and perhaps the world is ready for a new round of the sound of Philadelphia.

In the meantime, most of the songs mentioned herein are available on various collections in Legacy's *Rhythm and Soul* series, most notably, compilation producer Leo Sacks's (see entry) exceptional *The Philly Sound*: a three-CD extravaganza with photos, copious liner notes, and commentary from a small army of notables, putting Gamble and Huff's accomplishments in musical, political, and cultural perspective and arousing the envy of fellow compilers from Philadelphia to the Philippines. —ERIC OLSEN

Bell, Archie, and the Drells: "I Can't Stop Dancing," Atlantic, 1968 • "Girl You're Too Young," Atlantic, 1969 • "There's Gonna Be a Showdown," Atlantic, 1969 • *Strategy*, The Right Stuff, 1993 • *Tightening Up: The Best Of*, Rhino, 1994.

Butler, Jerry: "Are You Happy?," Mercury, 1968 • "Hey, Western Union Man," Mercury, 1968 • "Lost," Mercury, 1968 • "Never Give You Up," Mercury, 1968 • "Don't Let Love Hang You Up," Mercury, 1969 • *Ice on Ice*, Mercury, 1969 • "Moody Woman," Mercury, 1969 • "Only the Strong Survive," Mercury, 1969 • *The Ice Man Cometh*, Mercury, 1969 • *The Very Best Of*, PolyGram, 1969 • "What's the Use of Breaking Up," Mercury, 1969 • "I Could Write a Book," Mercury, 1970 • *Iceman: The Mercury Years*, PolyGram, 1992.

Carne, Jean: *Happy to Be with You*, The Right Stuff, 1979, 1994.

Dells, The: *I Salute You*, Volcano/Zoo, 1992.

Ebonys, The: "You're the Reason Why," Philadelphia International, 1971 • "It's Forever," Philadelphia International, 1973.

Gore, Lesley: *It's My Party: The Mercury Years*, Mercury, 1996.

Howard, Miki: *Femme Fatale*, Giant, 1992.

Huff, Leon: *Here to Create Music*, Philadelphia International, 1980.

Hyman, Phyllis: *Living All Alone*, Philadelphia International, 1987 • *Prime of My Life*, Volcano/Zoo, 1991 • *I Refuse to Be Lonely*, Volcano/Zoo, 1995 • *The Legacy of*, Arista, 1996.

Intruders, The: "(We'll Be) United," Gamble, 1966 • "Together," Gamble, 1967 • "(Love Is Like a) Baseball Game," Gamble, 1968 • "Cowboys to Girls," Gamble, 1968 • "Slow Drag," Gamble, 1968 • "Sad Girl," Gamble, 1969 • *The Intruders' Greatest Hits*, Gamble, 1969 • "When We Get Married," Gamble, 1970 • *When We Get Married*, Gamble, 1970 • "I Bet He Don't Love You (Like I Love You)," Gamble, 1971 • "I'm Girl Scouting," Gamble, 1971 • "(Win, Place or Show) She's a Winner," Gamble, 1972 • "I Wanna Know Your Name," Gamble, 1973 • "I'll Always Love My Mama," Gamble, 1973 • *Super Hits*, Philadelphia International, 1973 • *The Best of the Intruders: Cowboys to Girls*, Legacy/Sony, 1995.

Jacksons, The: "Enjoy Yourself," Epic, 1976 • *The Jacksons*, Epic, 1976, 1982 • *Going Places*, Epic, 1977 • "Show You the Way to Go," Epic, 1977.

Jones, Shirley: "Do You Get Enough Love?," Philadelphia International, 1986.

LaBelle, Patti: *The Spirit's in It,* The Right Stuff, 1981, 1993 • "If Only You Knew," Philadelphia International, 1984 • *I'm in Love Again,* The Right Stuff, 1984, 1993 • *This Christmas,* MCA, 1990 • *Greatest Hits,* MCA, 1996 • *See also* Nyro, Laura.

Mathis, Johnny: *Music of Johnny Mathis: A Personal Collection,* Legacy/Columbia, 1995.

Melvin, Harold, and the Blue Notes: "I Miss You," Philadelphia International, 1972 • "If You Don't Know Me by Now," Philadelphia International, 1972 • "The Love I Lost (Part 1)," Philadelphia International, 1972 • *Black and Blue,* Philadelphia International, 1973 • "Yesterday I Had the Blues," Philadelphia International, 1973 • "Satisfaction Guaranteed (or Take Your Love Back)," Philadelphia International, 1974 • "Where Are All My Friends?," Philadelphia International, 1974 • "Bad Luck, Part 1," Philadelphia International, 1975 • featuring Sharon Paige, "Hope That We Can Be Together Soon," Philadelphia International, 1975 • *To Be True,* Philadelphia International, 1975 • "Wake Up Everybody," Philadelphia International, 1975 • *Wake Up Everybody,* Philadelphia International, 1975 • *Greatest Hits—Collector's Item,* Philadelphia International, 1976 • *If You Don't Know Me by Now: The Best Of,* Legacy/Epic, 1995 • *Blue Notes and Ballads,* Legacy/Epic Associated, 1998.

MFSB: *Love Is the Message* (4 tracks), Philadelphia International, 1973 • w/ the Three Degrees, "TSOP," Philadelphia International, 1973 • "Sexy," Philadelphia International, 1975.

Nyro, Laura: *Gonna Take a Miracle,* Columbia, 1971 • w/ Labelle, "The Bells," Columbia, 1971 • *Stoned Soul Picnic: The Best Of,* Legacy, 1997.

O'Jays, The: *In Philadelphia,* Legacy, 1969, 1994 • "One Night Affair," Neptune, 1969 • "Deeper (in Love with You)," Neptune, 1970 • "Looky Looky (Look at Me Girl)," Neptune, 1970 • "992 Arguments," Philadelphia International, 1972 • "Back Stabbers," Philadelphia International, 1972 • *Back Stabbers,* Philadelphia International, 1972, 1996 • "Love Train," Philadelphia International, 1973 • *Ship Ahoy,* Philadelphia International, 1973 • "Time to Get Down," Philadelphia International, 1973 • "For the Love of Money," Philadelphia International, 1974 • "Put Your Hands Together," Philadelphia International, 1974 • "Sunshine," Philadelphia International, 1974 • *Family Reunion,* Philadelphia International, 1975 • "Give the People What They Want," Philadelphia International, 1975 • "I Love Music," Philadelphia International, 1975 • "Livin' for the Weekend," Philadelphia International, 1976 • "Message in Our Music," Philadelphia International, 1976 • *Message in the Music,* The Right Stuff, 1976, 1993 • "Darlin' Darlin' Baby (Sweet, Tender, Love)," Philadelphia International,

1977 • *Collector's Item,* Philadelphia International, 1978 • *So Full of Love,* The Right Stuff, 1978, 1993 • "Use Ta Be My Girl," Philadelphia International, 1978 • "Forever Mine," Philadelphia International, 1980 • *The Year 2000,* Philadelphia International, 1980 • "Lovin' You," Philadelphia International, 1987 • *Love Train: The Best Of,* Legacy, 1994 • *Give the People What They Want,* Legacy/Epic, 1995 • *Let Me Make Love to You,* Legacy, 1995 • *In Bed with the O'Jays,* Capitol, 1996 • *Super Hits,* Legacy/Epic, 1998.

Paige, Sharon: *See* Melvin, Harold, and the Blue Notes

Paul, Billy: *Going East,* Philadelphia International, 1971 • "Me and Mrs. Jones," Philadelphia International, 1972 • "Am I Black Enough for You?," Philadelphia International, 1973 • "Thanks for Saving My Life," Philadelphia International, 1974.

Peaches and Herb: *The Best of: Love Is Strange,* Legacy/Epic, 1996.

Pendergrass, Teddy: *Teddy Pendergrass,* The Right Stuff, 1977, 1993 • "I Don't Love You Anymore," Philadelphia International, 1977 • "Close the Door," Philadelphia International, 1978 • *Live! Coast to Coast Teddy,* The Right Stuff, 1979, 1994 • *Teddy,* The Right Stuff, 1979, 1993 • "Love T.K.O.," Philadelphia International, 1980 • *TP,* Philadelphia International, 1980 • *It's Time for Love,* Philadelphia International, 1981 • *A Little More Magic,* Elektra, 1993 • *The Best Of,* The Right Stuff, 1998.

People's Choice: "Do It Any Way You Wanna," TSOP, 1975 • *We Got the Rhythm,* TSOP, 1976 • *Golden Classics,* Collectables, 1996.

Pickett, Wilson: "Don't Let the Green Grass Fool You," Atlantic, 1970 • "Engine Number 9," Atlantic, 1970 • *Pickett in Philadelphia,* Atlantic/Atco Remasters, 1970, 1995.

Rawls, Lou: *All Things in Time,* The Right Stuff, 1976, 1993 • "You'll Never Find Another Love Like Mine," Philadelphia International, 1976 • *Unmistakably Lou,* Philadelphia International, 1977 • *When You Hear Lou, You've Heard it All,* Philadelphia International, 1977 • *Live,* Philadelphia International, 1978 • *Let Me Be Good to You,* The Right Stuff, 1979, 1993 • *The Best Of,* Capitol, 1990.

Scott, Freddie: *Cry to Me: The Best Of,* Sony, 1998.

Sigler, Bunny: *Best of Bunny Sigler: Sweeter Than the Berry,* Legacy, 1996.

Simon, Joe: "Drowning in a Sea of Love," Spring, 1971 • "Pool of Bad Luck," Spring, 1972.

Soul Survivors: "Expressway to Your Heart," Crimson, 1967.

Springfield, Dusty: "A Brand New Me," Atlantic, 1969.

Third World: *Hold On to Love,* Columbia, 1987 • *Serious Business* (3 tracks), Mercury, 1989.

Three Degrees: *The Three Degrees,* Philadelphia International, 1974 • "When Will I See You Again?," Philadelphia

International, 1974 • "I Didn't Know," Philadelphia International, 1975 • *When Will I See You Again? Best Of,* Legacy, 1996.

Whitehead, Kenny and Johnny: *The Whitehead Brothers,* Philadelphia International, 1986.

Williams, Johnny: "Slow Motion (Part 1)," Philadelphia International, 1972.

COLLECTIONS

Sex and Soul, Vols. 1–2, EMI, 1996.

Jackie Robinson Tribute: Stealing Home, Sony, 1997.

A Postcard from Philly (EP), Legacy, 1997.

The Philly Sound: Kenny Gamble, Leon Huff, and the Story of Brotherly Love, Legacy/Epic, 1997.

Val Garay

As musician, engineer, producer and label executive, Val Garay has dwelt at the top of the American record business for over 30 years. Garay engineered and mixed Linda Ronstadt and James Taylor's hits with Peter Asher (see entry) in the '70s, before building his own studio (Record One) and producing some of the greatest pop-rock moments of the '80s: Kim Carnes' *Mistaken Identity* (No. 1) with 1981 Record of the Year "Bette Davis Eyes" (No. 1); the Motels' *All Four One* (No. 16) with "Only the Lonely" (No. 9) and *Little Robbers* (No. 22) with "Suddenly Last Summer" (No. 9). He has also produced or co-produced successful albums for Randy Meisner, Joan Armatrading, Neil Diamond, Dramarama, the Nylons, Dolly Parton, Santana, and Dwight Twilley.

Val Garay was born in San Francisco in 1947 into showbiz royalty. His father was Joachin Garay—owner, operator, bandleader, singer, and MC of San Francisco's glamorous Copacabana nightclub. The elder Garay was born in Mexico, moved to San Francisco as an infant, and enjoyed a lengthy career on the stage, vaudeville, radio, and film (Disney's *The Three Caballeros*). In addition, Val's Aunt Margie was personal secretary to Cole Porter for 30 years. Garay believes that his greatest musical gift, his song sense, came to him by osmosis from this rarefied musical environment.

Despite his background Garay was on course to become a doctor, and was in his first year of medical school at Stanford when he fell for a cocktail waitress. Between playing guitar in clubs and hanging out with the waitress until 5 A.M., medical school seemed an unnecessary evil. Garay quit school, formed a Beatlesque band (the Giant Sunflower), moved to L.A., and recorded with Lou Adler (see entry). When the Sunflower didn't hit, Garay formed another band (Pan), recorded for CBS, didn't hit again, and became disillusioned with the artist's position: "dependent upon dozens of other people for my professional life," sighs Garay.

The producer's job seemed to afford greater self-determination, so Garay began the process as an engineer-in-training at Dave Hassinger's Sound Factory. Garay's first mix was a hit single, El Chicano's version of "Brown-Eyed Girl" in 1972, and by the time Asher brought in Ronstadt to record *Heart Like a Wheel* (No. 1 in 1974), Garay was an engineer. Garay's work with Asher came to encompass more than the traditional engineer's duties, so he coined the term "recorded by" and even received royalties on the Ronstadt albums (*Heart* through *Mad Love* in 1980); this was a first, to Garay's knowledge, for a nonproducer.

Garay stayed at the Sound Factory through most of the '70s, until he had a falling-out with Hassinger, at which point he left to become an independent producer. Used to working in a familiar environment, Garay found an investor who was willing to kick $3 million into a studio, which Garay built and named Record One.

Garay hit platinum early with Carnes' *Mistaken Identity* and the "Bette Davis Eyes" single in 1981. He knew he had something the minute "Eyes" was recorded. "It was recorded live with no overdubs. When I played it for Asher, he drooled," says Garay.

The Motels' *All Four One* is probably Garay's most consistent album as a producer. He faced the formidable task of moving a coolly dispassionate and quirky new wave band into the pop mainstream. He succeeded wildly but not without monumental effort.

All Four One was the Motels' third album, but most people thought it was their first because the previous two albums had flown well under the radar, especially outside of L.A., their hometown. When Garay came in, the band was led by singer/songwriter Martha Davis and her guitarist boyfriend Tim McGovern.

Garay recalls, "The basic problem was that the band couldn't play. Tim was the best player in the band, but he and Martha were severely into drugs and alcohol at the time and they would show up at the studio wrecked. I did a whole album with Tim telling me what to do. When we finished we gave it to Capitol. [Capitol president] Don Zimmerman called and said, 'I love this band, but I don't love this record. Would you be willing to do it over again?' I said, 'You'll have to talk to Martha because the band can't play and Tim is very controlling.'

"To cut a long story short," he continues, "they broke up. Martha threw Tim out of the house, and she wanted to do the record over again. So I took three people from [Kim Carnes'] band [Craig Krampf, drums; Craig Hull, guitar; Steve Goldstein, keyboards], put in some new songs, recut others, and redid 'Only the Lonely' three times until I thought it was right."

McGovern left to form Burning Sensations (which had one great song, "Belly of the Whale") and the Motels followed Garay into the Top 10. Davis's smoky voice rocks on "Mission of Mercy," dances through the clever "Take the L," and pauses a moment to reflect on it all in the brilliant semiballad "Only the Lonely." Garay's production is clean, deep, and dry without being parched.

Garay and the band followed up successfully with *Little Robbers*, but then "I told [Davis] to get rid of the band and go solo because she had had two platinum albums in a row," continues Garay. "She didn't like that idea at all, so she fired me as producer and manager."

Garay followed a similar pattern with punky '60s revivalists Dramarama: two successful albums (*Stuck in Wonderamaland* and *Live at the China Club*) and out. "They decided to work with someone else [Don Smith; see entry], and so they did, and they became history. It's funny, you know. It's amazing how self-destructive acts are in this business. That's why Peter [Asher] and Linda [Ronstadt], and Peter and James [Taylor] were so successful: If it didn't break, don't fix it."

Garay now runs the international music division of Warner Bros. He takes a movie with a hit soundtrack, like *The Bodyguard*, re-records the biggest song—usually the title track—with a local big-name artist, and adds the song to the CD as a bonus track, thereby selling many more copies of the soundtrack throughout the world. Clever guy. —ERIC OLSEN

Armatrading, Joan: *The Key*, A&M, 1983 • *Track Record*, A&M, 1983 • *Classics, Vol. 21*, A&M, 1989.

Balin, Marty: *Lucky*, EMI America, 1983.

Carmen, Eric: *Boats Against the Current*, Arista, 1977 • "She Did It," Arista, 1977.

Carnes, Kim: "Bette Davis Eyes," EMI America, 1981 • *Mistaken Identity*, EMI America, 1981 • *Voyeur*, EMI America, 1982 • *Gypsy Honeymoon: Best Of*, EMI, 1993.

Diamond, Neil: *Hot August Night 2*, Columbia, 1987 • *Lovescape*, Columbia, 1991 • *Greatest Hits, 1966–1992*, Columbia, 1992.

Dramarama: *Stuck in Wonderland*, Chameleon, 1989 • *Live at the China Club*, Chameleon, 1990 • *The Best of: 18 Big Ones*, Rhino, 1996.

E-Z-O: *E-Z-O*, Geffen, 1987.

Fuller, Craig, and Eric Kaz: *Craig Fuller/Eric Kaz*, Columbia, 1978.

Furay, Richie: *I Still Have Dreams*, Asylum, 1979.

Help: *Help*, Decca, 1971 • *Second Chance*, Decca, 1971.

Kane, Candye: *Knock Out*, Antone's, 1995, 1996.

Kostas: *XS in Moderation*, Liberty, 1994.

Kunkel, Leah: *Leah Kunkel*, CBS, 1979.

Lauber, Ken: *Ken Lauber*, MCA, 1971.

Meisner, Randy: *One More Song*, Epic, 1980 • "Hearts on Fire," Epic, 1981.

Motels, The: *All Four One*, Capitol, 1982 • "Only the Lonely," EMI, 1982, 1993 (*Living in Oblivion: The 80s Greatest Hits, Vol. 2*) • *Little Robbers*, Capitol, 1983 • "Remember the Nights," Capitol, 1983 • "Suddenly Last Summer," Capitol, 1983.

Mr. Big: *Photographic Smile* (7 tracks), Arista, 1976.

Nylons, The: *Seamless*, Windham Hill, 1984 • *Happy Together*, Windham Hill, 1987 • *The Best Of*, Windham Hill, 1993 • *Perfect Fit*, Windham Hill, 1997.

Pablo Cruise: *Lifeline*, A&M, 1978.

Pan: *Pan*, Columbia, 1973.

Parton, Dolly: *The Great Pretender*, RCA, 1984 • *Think About Love*, RCA, 1986.

Ronin: *Ronin*, Mercury, 1980.

Santana: *Beyond Appearances*, Columbia, 1985.

Twilley, Dwight: *Wild Dogs*, CBS Associated, 1986 • *XXI*, The Right Stuff, 1996.

Volunteers: *Volunteers* (3 tracks), Arista, 1976.

Wright, Michelle: *For Me It's You*, Arista, 1996.

Thomas "Snuff" Garrett

Snuff Garrett entered the music business from the radio door and became a multimillionaire by the time he was 30, having produced hits for Johnny Burnette ("You're Sixteen," No. 8), Bobby Vee ("Take Good Care of My Baby," No. 1), Gary Lewis and the Playboys ("This Diamond Ring," No. 1), and Gene McDaniels ("A Hundred Pounds of Clay," No. 3).

Then, after taking a year off to sleep, Garrett started all over again and scored another fistful of hits with Cher ("Gypsys, Tramps and Thieves," "Half-Breed," and "Dark Lady"—all No. 1), and a series of No. 1 country hits for Tanya Tucker ("Lizzy and the Rainman," "San

Antonio Stroll"), David Frizzell and Shelly West ("You're the Reason God Made Oklahoma"), Merle Haggard and Clint Eastwood ("Bar Room Buddies"), Ronnie Milsap ("Cowboys and Clowns"), and Eddie Rabbitt ("Every Which Way But Loose").

Thomas "Snuff" Garrett was born near Dallas, Texas, in 1938, and as a child saw his destiny on the movie screen. Garrett thought that "when Roy Rogers stepped out of the saddle, I'd step on Trigger and keep right on riding," he says with a laugh. Instead, as a young teen Garrett hung around Gordon McLendon's radio station, KLIF, in Dallas, where the DJs treated him as a younger brother. Garrett was around when McLendon and Todd Storz (owner of KOWH in Omaha) cooked up the idea of Top 40 radio.

The pair of moguls-to-be spent time at a bar near KLIF in the early '50s and noticed that although there were a hundred songs in the jukebox, a few were played over and over again; thus Top 40 was born.

At age 14, Garrett was hired by the station to be music librarian for the sum of $5 per week. At this time 45s were replacing 78s as the software of choice at radio stations, so Garrett was instructed to throw out all of the (thousands) of 78s on hand. Garrett was given permission to keep the records instead, and every night for weeks he carted home as many 78s as he could carry on the bus. Though it took him years, Garrett listened to both sides of every record—pop, blues, R&B, country—in that library, and he is convinced that the effort later enabled him to be a successful record producer.

At 15, Garrett took off for California with radio colleague Bill Jenkins and found work as a record packer for an independent record promoter for 50 cents an hour. Garrett turned 16 in Hollywood, and went back to Texas within the year, desperately homesick.

Garrett's radio friends found him a job as a DJ in Lubbock, where he met and befriended both Buddy Holly and Waylon Jennings. By the age of 20, Garrett had both a television show and a radio show, and commanded the princely sum of $350 per week. But Garrett wanted to be in the music business, not broadcasting, and through various connections he landed a job as a local promotion man (with a drastic pay cut) for Liberty Records in Los Angeles.

Garrett worked hard ("I didn't go to bed until I was 25 years old," he says) and held his tongue for about six months before asking to produce. His first production was a single for Johnny Burnette in 1959, and he had his first hit in 1960, with Burnette's "Dreamin' " (No. 11).

He next signed a young singer out of North Dakota whose tape reminded Garrett of Buddy Holly: Bobby Vee. Between Burnette, Vee, and Gene McDaniels, Gar-

rett had accumulated 16 Top 20 hits by early 1963, most arranged by Ernie Freeman. Several are pop classics, especially Burnette's teen anthem "You're Sixteen," Vee's "Take Good Care of My Baby" (Garrett's first No. 1), and McDaniels' "A Hundred Pounds of Clay."

Though he was neither a musician nor experienced in studio work, Garrett had ears gilded by thousands of 78s, and he learned quickly. Garrett stayed at Liberty until the mid-'60s, becoming head of A&R and learning to run a tight ship. "I ran a totalitarian dictatorship. It was my way or no way," he admits. "Our motto at Liberty was 'If you're not on the charts or headed up the charts, what the hell are you doing here?' I learned early on that there are 100 records on the charts every week, and if you're not one of them, it's nobody's fault but yours."

Workmanlike and practical, Garrett saw pop music as a fun way to make a good living. "I never thought of it as art. I thought of it as entertainment. My goal was to make entertainment in the form of 2- to 3-minute records that people would want to hear over and over again," he states.

For his style of production, the song was the key. "The most important thing was to find the song. I could hear how I wanted it in advance. Then it was finding the right mouth to sing the song and making sure that the record turned out the way I heard it in my head," he says.

Garrett produced a dozen albums and 20 singles a year while at Liberty. Then in 1965 he set up his own production and publishing company and scored a series of nine Top 20 hits with Gary Lewis and the Playboys in just two years. Most notable is the lost-love classic "This Diamond Ring." With his new company, Garrett employed a caricature that was drawn of him back in Lubbock (when he was out with Buddy Holly) as his now-famous logo. He still has the picture drawn of Holly the same day.

On the publishing side, Garrett bought and sold many a classic; he would buy up more songs as he made money from songs he already owned, like "Summertime Blues" or "My Special Angel." He still owns "Route 66."

In 1968 Garrett sold his production and publishing company to Warner Bros. for $2.5 million and retired to become a Dallas policeman because "I had something to prove to myself," he says. He signed up for the force, but when they didn't call him right away, Garrett spent the next year hunting and fishing.

Rested and bored, Garrett reentered the fray and hit again with Cher (who autographed a picture to him: "To Snuff, You bastard. What am I going to do with you? Love, Cher") and country music (in particular, songs affiliated with Clint Eastwood and Burt Reynolds movies).

In the early '80s Garrett bought a company that made silver saddles and experienced his first failure. Garrett's workaholic pace and the stress of the silver failure contributed to a stroke in 1983. Once again Garrett chucked it all; this time he moved to Arizona, where he has spent the last 15 years dabbling in American western art and film memorabilia. And though Garrett loved the music business, he doesn't miss it. —ERIC OLSEN

Allen, Rex Sr. and Rex Jr.: *Singing Cowboys,* Warner Western, 1995.

Boys in the Bunkhouse: *The Boys in the Bunkhouse,* United Artists, 1977.

Brennan, Walter: "Old Rivers," Liberty, 1962.

Burnette, Johnny: "Dreamin'," Liberty, 1960 • "You're Sixteen," Liberty, 1960 • "Little Boy Sad," Liberty, 1961 • *The Best of: You're Sixteen,* EMI America, 1992.

Campbell, Glen: *It's the World Gone Crazy,* Capitol, 1980.

Carr, Vikki: *Que Sea El,* Sony, 1996.

Chase, Carol: *Some Songs,* Casablanca, 1979.

Cher: *Cher,* Kapp, 1971 • "Gypsies, Tramps and Thieves," Kapp, 1971 • *Gypsies, Tramps and Thieves,* MCA, 1971, 1981 • *Foxy Lady,* Kapp, 1972 • "Living in a House Divided," Kapp, 1972 • "The Way of Love," Kapp, 1972 • "Half-Breed," MCA, 1973 • "Dark Lady," MCA, 1974 • *Greatest Hits,* MCA, 1974, 1990 • *Half-Breed,* MCA, 1974 • "Train of Thought," MCA, 1974.

Cochran, Eddie: *Singing to My Baby/Never to Be Forgotten,* Gold Rush/Capitol, 1960, 1992.

Crickets: *Rock Reflections,* United Artists, 1971.

Durrill, John: *Just for the Record,* United Artists, 1978.

Everly, Phil: *Living Alone,* Elektra, 1978.

Frizzell, David: "I'm Gonna Hire a Wino to Decorate Our Home," Warner Bros., 1982 • *On My Own Again,* Viva, 1983.

Frizzell, David, and Shelly West: "You're the Reason God Made Oklahoma," Warner Bros., 1981 • *Carrying on the Family Names,* Viva/WB, 1982 • *Our Best to You,* Viva/WB, 1983 • *In Session,* Viva, 1984 • *Greatest Hits —Alone and Together,* K-Tel, 1994.

Garrett, Thomas "Snuff": *Snuff Garrett's Texas Opera Company,* Rainwood, 1977.

Gringo: *Gringo,* Pravda, 1995.

Haggard, Merle, and Clint Eastwood: "Bar Room Buddies," Elektra, 1980.

Hyland, Brian: "The Joker Went Wild," Philips, 1966 • *The Joker Went Wild,* Philips, 1968 • *Brian Hyland's Greatest Hits,* MCA, 1994.

Inman, Jerry: *You Betchum,* Elektra, 1976.

Jan and Dean: *Surf City,* EMI Legends, 1990 • *All the Hits—From Surf City to Drag City,* EMI America, 1996 • *Command Performance—Live in Person,* One Way, 1996.

Lawrence, Vicki: "The Night the Lights Went Out in Georgia," Bell, 1973.

Lee, Brenda: *L.A. Sessions,* MCA, 1977.

Lewis, Gary, and the Playboys: *A Session with Gary Lewis and the Playboys,* Liberty, 1965 • "Count Me In," Liberty, 1965 • *Everybody Loves a Clown,* Liberty, 1965 • "Everybody Loves a Clown," Liberty, 1965 • "Save Your Heart for Me," Liberty, 1965 • "This Diamond Ring," Liberty, 1965 • *This Diamond Ring,* Liberty, 1965 • "My Heart's Symphony," Liberty, 1966 • "She's Just My Style," Liberty, 1966 • *She's Just My Style,* Liberty, 1966 • "Sure Gonna Miss Her," Liberty, 1966 • *You Don't Have to Paint Me a Picture,* Liberty, 1967 • "Sealed with a Kiss," Liberty, 1968 • *Gary Lewis and the Playboys,* EMI Legends, 1990 • *Gary Lewis and the Playboys,* Gold Rush, 1996.

London, Julie: *Time for Love: The Best Of,* Rhino, 1990.

Lopez, Trini: *Welcome to Trini Country,* Reprise, 1969 • *Best Of,* Royal, 1993.

Mahan, Larry: *King of the Rodeo,* Warner Bros., 1976.

Manhattan Transfer: *The Very Best Of,* Rhino, 1994.

McDaniels, Gene: "A Hundred Pounds of Clay," Liberty, 1961 • "Tower of Strength," Liberty, 1961 • "Chip Chip," Liberty, 1962 • *Best of Gene McDaniels: A Hundred Pounds of Clay,* Collectables, 1995.

Milsap, Ronnie "Cowboys and Clowns/Misery Loves Company," RCA, 1980.

Mouskouri, Nana: *Passport* (1 track), Mercury, 1976.

Nabors, Jim: *Town and Country,* Ranwood, n.d. • *Sincerely,* Ranwood, 1977.

Price, Ray: *Master of the Art,* Viva/WB, 1983.

Rabbitt, Eddie: "Every Which Way But Loose," Elektra, 1978 • *Eddie Rabbitt #1's,* Warner Bros., 1985.

Savalas, Telly: *Telly,* MCA, 1974.

Sandalwood: *Sandalwood,* Bell, 1973.

Shannon, Del: *Greatest Hits,* Rhino, 1990 • *The Liberty Years,* EMI Legends, 1991 • *This Is My Bag/Total Commitment,* Beat Goes On, 1996.

Sinnamon, Shandi: *Shandi Sinnamon,* Asylum, 1976.

Sonny and Cher: "All I Ever Need Is You," Kapp, 1971 • "A Cowboy's Work Is Never Done," Kapp, 1972 • *All I Ever Need Is You,* MCA, 1974.

Statler Brothers: *10th Anniversary,* Mercury, 1980.

Travel Agency: *The Travel Agency,* Dot, 1967.

Tucker, Tanya: "Lizzie and the Rainman," MCA, 1975 • "San Antonio Stroll," MCA, 1975 • *Tanya,* MCA, 1975 • *Greatest Hits,* MCA, 1978 • *Live,* MCA, 1982 • *The Best Of,* MCA, 1982 • *Collection,* MCA, 1992.

Vee, Bobby: "Devil or Angel," Liberty, 1960 • "Rubber Ball," Liberty, 1961 • "Run to Him," Liberty, 1961 • "Take Good Care of My Baby," Liberty, 1961 • *Meets the Crickets,* Liberty, 1962 • *Merry Christmas from Bobby Vee,* EMI

America, 1962, 1990 • "Sharing You," Liberty, 1962 • "Charms," Liberty, 1963 • "The Night Has a Thousand Eyes," Liberty, 1963 • *Tribute to Buddy Holly*, Liberty, 1963 • *EMI Legends of Rock and Roll*, EMI Legends, 1990 • w/ the Shadows, *Early Rockin Years*, Era, 1995.

Wagoner, Porter: *Viva Porter Wagoner*, Viva/WB, 1983.

West, Dottie: *New Horizons*, Liberty, 1983.

West, Shelly: "Jose Cuervo," Warner Bros., 1983 • *Red Hot*, Viva, 1983 • *West by West*, Viva/WB, 1983.

Williams, Roger: *The Artists Choice*, MCA, 1992 • *Greatest Movie Themes*, HIPP, 1996.

COLLECTIONS

Rhythm and Blues Christmas, United Artists, 1976.

Every Which Way But Loose soundtrack, Elektra, 1978.

Bronco Billy soundtrack, Elektra, 1980.

Smokey and the Bandit 2 soundtrack, MCA, 1980.

Any Which Way You Can soundtrack, Viva/WB, 1980.

Sharkey's Machine soundtrack, Warner Bros., 1981.

The Brill Building Sound: Singers and Songwriters Who Rocked the 60's, Era, 1993.

Don Gehman

D on Gehman achieves a live sound on his records by creating a live vibe. He knows that vibe as well as anyone because he broke into the music business as a live-sound engineer. Gehman has produced some of the biggest rootsy rock stars of the '80s and '90s, including John "Cougar" Mellencamp, R.E.M., Hootie and the Blowfish, Nanci Griffith, Better Than Ezra, Bruce Hornsby, and Tracy Chapman.

It was 1965 and a 15-year-old Gehman had to figure out how to get his new band's sound off the stage and into the crowd. He spent the next eight years working as a live engineer until he met Stephen Stills. The time was right because Gehman was running out of steam. "I was really burnt on this 300-one-nighters-a-year life," he says. "Stephen saw that my heart was really in the music and not in the travel thing, and he offered me an opportunity to help finish a record he was working on."

Stills was impressed and took Gehman to Criteria Studios in Miami, Florida, and set him up. "At the time it was Atlantic South," he says referring to the record label. "Tom Dowd was there, Jerry Wexler, Arif Mardin" (see entries).

Gehman worked on albums for artists as varied as the Bee Gees and the Eagles. "Criteria was a great place

to be for most of the '70s, and where I cut my teeth on how to produce records." He became staff engineer at Criteria, helped the Bee Gees build their own studio (where he worked on a Barbra Streisand album with Barry Gibb), and then met an artist by the name of John "Cougar" Mellencamp. After engineering Cougar's 1980 album *Nothing Matters and What If It Did*, Gehman was on the verge of becoming a producer.

When Mellencamp was ready to record again he approached Gehman and the two set out to record what would become *American Fool*. Before that album sold 5 million copies and scored the No. 1 hit "Jack and Diane," and a No. 2 with "Hurts So Good," Gehman had been fired and rehired, told by the label that the album wasn't strong enough, and battled the wolf at the door.

"The stakes were high because Miami had just about run through its musical success and I was having trouble finding good work," he remembers. "I was freelancing at the time and living on a $15,000 first-time producer advance."

Recording live is his preferred method and he does it as well as anyone. "Personality-wise I seem to do it well," he says. "It's still something that a lot of people come to me for, even in the land of loops and stuff." Gehman views his main task as setting up "the elements that create the magic that is a live performance." During those live tracking sessions he's looking to "create a chunk that you hang your whole record on. The core elements of a great record are a great groove, song, melody, and vocal performance. All of that can be got in one shot if you create the right moment. It's difficult to do because you have to balance a lot of personalities and make sure all your homework is done," he says.

Gehman travels with a "studio in a box." Included are a variety of tube microphones; Neve, Manley, and Fairchild tube recording equipment; his own monitoring system; his own lighting system; and a full complement of drums, organ, guitars, amps, and percussion instruments.

Gehman's preference for tube equipment derives from his engineering days. "I find that a lot of the character of recording is lost in 'modern' equipment. Somewhere along the line we decided that coloration is bad and that everything should be flat and neutral. Record production is painting and you need all of the colors you can get."

Gehman likes bands that can play. "I generally don't pick bands that are terrible musicians—I pick acts that can at least pull off the songs they've written. After all, you're looking for some kind of character that makes them unique and that doesn't mean bring in session guys to fix things."

He likes to work with a wide range of artists. "I always feel off balance, but it's good because I'm in that place of insecurity where you learn so much. I use a lot of the same recording techniques, but for the musical elements I look for a new set of tools for each record. That's made it harder because you fall down quite a bit; you find things that just don't work," he admits, "but that's part of the formula for keeping Don interested," he laughs.

While he may like to be kept off balance, he also likes to be prepared. Before he recorded Tracy Chapman's *New Beginnings,* Gehman studied techniques for recording acoustic guitars and African drums on digital equipment; he studied her songs and her voice as well.

Gehman is at peace, it seems, in part because of the Zen production philosophy he learned recording R.E.M.'s *Lifes Rich Pageant.* "Previous to that time I was used to the process being ordered: you've got a part, you put things together, and you come out over here. R.E.M. taught me how things don't have to be that focused. I taught them a lot about how to make records: the chorus has to come in and lift, doubling, making shifts in songs—all that Producer 101 stuff. But, they taught me about chaos," he says with a laugh. "You can let a lot of it go on and still come out with a viable commercial project. It will have a level of magic you would never have had any other way." —DAVID JOHN FARINELLA

Barnes, Jimmy: *Two Fires,* Atlantic, 1990.
Benatar, Pat: *Gravity's Rainbow,* Chrysalis, 1993 • *All Fired Up,* Chrysalis, 1995 • *16 Classic Performances,* EMI, 1996.
Better Than Ezra: *Friction, Baby,* Elektra, 1996.
Boom Crash Opera: *Boom Crash Opera,* Warner Bros., 1987.
Breathless: *Breathless,* EMI, 1979 • *Picture This: The Best Of,* Razor & Tie, 1993.
Carmen, Eric: *Eric Carmen,* Arista, 1976.
Chapman, Tracy: *New Beginnings,* Elektra, 1996.
Clarissa: *Silver,* Mammoth, 1996.
Cock Robin: *After Here Thru Midland,* Columbia, 1987.
Cutting Crew: "Everything But My Pride," Virgin, 1989 • *The Scattering,* Virgin, 1989.
Dambuilders, The: *Ruby Red,* EastWest, 1995.
Diesel: *Hep Fidelity,* Giant, 1993.
Dollshead: *Frozen Charlotte,* MCA, 1998.
Figgs, The: *Low-Fi at Society High,* Imago, 1994.
Griffith, Nanci: *Blue Roses from the Moons,* Elektra, 1997.
Havelinas, The: *Havelinas,* Elektra, 1990.
Hootie and the Blowfish: "Hold My Hand," Atlantic, 1994 • *Cracked Rear View,* Atlantic, 1995 • "Hey Hey What Can I Do," Atlantic, 1995 (*Encomium: A Tribute to Led Zeppelin*) • "I Go Blind," Reprise, 1995 (*Friends* soundtrack) • "Let

Her Cry," Atlantic, 1995 • "Only Wanna Be with You," Atlantic, 1995 • "Time," Atlantic, 1995 • *Fairweather Johnson,* Atlantic, 1996.
Hornsby, Bruce: *A Night on the Town,* RCA, 1990.
McDermott, Michael: *620 W. Surf,* Giant, 1991.
Mellencamp, John "Cougar": *American Fool,* Riva, 1982 • "Hand to Hold On To," Riva, 1982 • "Hurts So Good," Riva, 1982 • "Jack and Diane," Riva, 1982 • "Crumblin' Down," Riva, 1983 • "Pink Houses," Riva, 1983 • *Uh-huh,* Riva, 1983 • "The Authority Song," Riva, 1984 • "Lonely Ol' Night," Riva, 1985 • "R.O.C.K. in the U.S.A.," Riva, 1985 • *Scarecrow,* Riva, 1985 • "Small Town," Riva, 1985 • "Cherry Bomb," Mercury, 1987 • "I Saw Mommy Kissing Santa Claus," A&M, 1987 (*A Very Special Christmas*) • *Lonesome Jubilee,* Mercury, 1987 • "Paper in Fire," Mercury, 1987 • "Check It Out," Mercury, 1988 • "Do Re Mi," Columbia, 1988 (*Folkways: A Tribute to Woody Guthrie and Leadbelly*) • *The Best That I Could Do (1978–1988),* PolyGram, 1997.
Michael Stanley Band: *MSB,* EMI America, 1982 • *Misery Loves Company: More of the Best, 1975–1983,* Razor & Tie, 1997.
R.E.M.: *Lifes Rich Pageant,* IRS, 1986 • *Dead Letter Office,* IRS, 1987 • *Eponymous,* IRS, 1988.
Rain Dogs: *Border Drive-In Theater,* Atco, 1991.
River City People: *Say Something Good,* Capitol, 1990.
Rob Rule: *Rob Rule,* Mercury, 1994.
Satellite, Billy: *Billy Satellite,* Capitol, 1984.
Setzer, Brian: "Boulevard of Broken Dreams," EMI-America, 1986 • *Knife Feels Like Justice,* EMI America, 1986 • "Summertime Blues," Slash/WB, 1987 (*La Bamba* soundtrack).
Shaw/Blades: *Hallucination,* Warner Bros., 1995.
Stills, Stephen: *Illegal Stills,* Legacy, 1976, 1990.
Stills-Young Band: *Long May You Run,* Reprise, 1976.
subdudes, the: *the subdudes,* Atlantic, 1989.
Treat Her Right: *Tied to the Tracks,* RCA, 1989.
Ugly Americans: *Stereophonic Spanish Fly,* Capricorn, 1996.
Uma: *Fare Well,* MCA, 1997.

Brian "B-Fine" George

See FULL FORCE

"Bowlegged" Lou George

See FULL FORCE

Paul Anthony George

See FULL FORCE

Donovan Germain

For many die-hard roots fans the story of reggae ends in the late '70s. That's just when Donovan Germain was getting started. Germain Revolutionary Sounds was one of the few new labels of note to emerge in that time, and Germain's production style was already smooth without sounding soft. After a few interesting 7-inch releases he raised some eyebrows in the early '80s with "Mr. Boss Man" by Cultural Roots, following up with a vocal album and a limited-edition dub by the group. By the late '80s his Penthouse label defined the cutting-edge sound in Jamaica. The early '90s seemed for a while to belong to him alone.

His earliest records were cut at Channel One, Treasure Isle, and Joe Gibbs' (see entry) studios using the Revolutionaries for backing. His late '70s lovers cut of "Sentimental Reasons" with Joy White shows that hard-edged dub band (powered by Sly and Robbie; see entry) had a soft side too. Later he leapt full force into the digital age, even listing Korg Drums and Yamaha DX7 as "band" on one anthology. His later records were cut at Dynamic, then finally at his own Penthouse studio at 56 Slipe Road in Kingston.

Germain sessions might include digital masters Dalton and Danny Browne (pronounced Brown-ee), or Steely and Clevie (see entry) and old-school players like trombonist "Nambo" Robinson and trumpeter Chico Chin. Major Jamaican hits include Beres Hammond's "Emptiness Inside" and the late Tenor Saw's "No Work on Sunday," on the same rhythm as Audrey Hall's "One Dance Won't Do," a hit in the U.K. as well (and an answer record for a cut of Hammond's for another producer). Dave Kelly ran the board for him (and in some cases, as on Garnett Silk's "Lion Heart," was the sole musician) before moving on to his own Rude Boy productions.

The popularity of Penthouse was tied to the emergence of the first real reggae radio station in Jamaica, IRIE-FM. Jamaican radio had long been dominated by American music (you might be as likely to see a Jim Reeves or Simon and Garfunkel album in record shops there as local product), and IRIE-FM's jocks loved the clean Penthouse sound that "touched up" classic Studio One riddims for a sophisticated and mainstream feel. Even his raggamuffin DJ records crossed over because the tracks themselves were so musical.

Germain was also one of those who ushered in the age of the riddim. Heretofore a popular song might inspire a popular dub version and at least one DJ "toast." But by the early '90s Germain was issuing entire albums of riddims like *Fire Burning* and *What One Rhythm Can Do*, with singers, DJs, and instrumentalists all having a go. And many singles on these riddims have yet to make it to LP! The Penthouse label output became truly astonishing.

One of Germain's hottest DJs, Buju Banton, nearly derailed himself with a controversial 12-inch release cut for another producer, but came back with strong CDs for Germain, including *Voice of Jamaica,* and one of the best DJ albums ever cut, *'Til Shiloh.* The last two were co-produced with Lisa Cortes. Germain also produced Cobra before he became Mad Cobra and other top DJs, including Yellowman, Tiger, and Terry Ganzie.

Some of his best work was with artists who had already paid the rent for others. He had major hits reworking Bob Andy tunes, including the massive "Fire Burning" sung for Germain by Andy's former partner Marcia Griffiths. One artist who'd been around for years but didn't really hit big internationally until his work with Germain is the soulful Beres Hammond, who parlayed a string of Penthouse hits into an album with Atlantic. His "Preacherman" for Germain, though blackballed on Jamaican radio, is one of that fine singer's best records.

Though newer labels like Xterminator, Star Trail, and others may be calling the tunes in Jamaica today, Penthouse can still be counted on for innovative work, even if it's now as likely to appear on major American labels as on Germain's own local imprint. Recently he's begun to issue his own CDs as well, a move few JA labels are able to follow. With an impressive roster of talent Donovan Germain is still a force to be reckoned with in reggae today. —CHUCK FOSTER

Banton, Buju: *Mr. Mention,* Penthouse, 1991 • *Voice of Jamaica,* Mercury, 1993 • *'Til Shiloh,* Loose Cannon, 1995.

Cobra: *Bad Boy Talk,* Penthouse, 1991 • "Pon Pause," Penthouse, 1994 (*Penthouse Party Mix*).

Cultural Roots: *Drift Away from Evil,* Germain, 1982.

Cutty Ranks: "Half Idiot," Penthouse, 1994 (*Penthouse Party Mix*) • "Russia and America," Penthouse, 1994 (*Penthouse Party Mix*).

Ganzie, Terry: *Heavy Like Lead,* Profile, 1994.

Griffiths, Marcia: *Marcia,* RAS, 1988 • *Indomitable,* Penthouse, 1993.

Hall, Audrey: *Just You, Just Me,* Germain, 1987.

Hammond, Beres: *A Love Affair,* Penthouse, 1992.

Macka B: *Peace Cup* (1 track), RAS, 1991.

Marshall, Carla: "Class and Credential," Chaos, 1994.

Maxi Priest: *Man with the Fun,* Virgin, 1996.

Mighty Diamonds, The: *Heads of Government,* Germain, 1997.

Radics, Jack: *I'll Be Sweeter,* VP, 1993.

Rebel, Tony, and Macka B: "D.J. Unity," Penthouse, 1994 (*Penthouse Party Mix*).

White, Joy: *Sentimental Reasons,* Germain, 1979.

Wonder, Wayne, and Sanchez: *Penthouse Presents,* Penthouse, n.d.

COLLECTIONS

Die Hard, Part 1, VP, 1990.

Fire Burning, Penthouse, 1991.

Five Star General, Penthouse, 1994.

Penthouse Celebration, Part 3, Live Penthouse, 1992.

The Best of Penthouse, Tachyon, n.d.

Cultural Roots: Revolutionary Sounds Dub, Germain, c. 1982.

Dub Out Her Blouse and Skirt, Vol. 2, Germain, c. 1982.

Dub Out Her Blouse and Skirt, Germain, c. 1982.

Vintage Reggae, Vol. 1, Germain, c. 1983.

What One Rhythm Can Do, Penthouse, 1987.

Ninja Turtle, Parts 1–3, Penthouse, 1989.

Penthouse Presents: Reggae 1990, Penthouse, 1990.

Reggae Ambassadors, Vols. 1–2, Penthouse, 1990.

Reggae 1990, Penthouse, 1990.

Dance Hall Hits, Penthouse, 1993.

Lovers Rock, Penthouse, 1993.

Another Dimention: Nanny Goat Style, Penthouse, 1994.

Penthouse Party Mix, Penthouse, 1994.

Geza X

Geza X was an integral part of the explosive West Coast punk scene in the late '70s and early '80s: first as soundman at L.A.'s notorious Masque club, then as producer and co-producer of indispensable music by the Bags, Black Flag, Dead Kennedys, Germs, Redd Kross, and Weirdos. X spent the mid-'80s as a noted rock critic, writing for *Spin* and others, then returned to the studio in the late '80s, engineering for R&B-rap artists such as Club Nouveau, Ice-T, Sir Jinx, Uzi Brothers, and Keith Washington. In the early '90s X built his own 24-track recording studio, City Lab Sound Design, and returned to production, working with Butt Trumpet, 1000 Mona Lisas, Magnapop, and, most successfully, Meredith Brooks.

Geza X was born in L.A., the son of a real rocket scientist whose job it was to calculate the trajectory of orbiting vehicles, including the Pioneer and Voyager probes. Young Geza grew up on electronics and started to sing and play guitar at about 13; he was influenced musically by the Beatles, surf music, and later by psychedelia and the avant-weirdness of Frank Zappa (see entry) and Captain Beefheart. He played in high school

bands before being sucked into the vortex that was the '60s, hitchhiking and camping out around the country, communing with like-minded free spirits and malcontents. He returned to L.A. around 1975, where the scene was "death personified" for a musician. "There were coffee shops where you could play for free, and basically no amplified music at all," he says.

X put together a small PA system and some gear, running live sound for tiny clubs. He started a band called Band X (no relation to the later band X) with future Go-Go guitarist Charlotte Caffey and future Wall of Voodoo drummer Joe Nanini. The trio went to see the Ramones at the Whisky A-Go-Go in 1976, and were revivified by the blast of pure, loud noise.

X got a job at the now-defunct Artist's Recording Studio in Hollywood, sweeping the floors (which he also slept on) and learning to engineer on mariachi, disco, gospel, and funk sessions. By 1977 punk had swept into L.A. from New York and England, re-energizing a somnambulant music scene. Across the street from Artist's Recording Studio (in the basement of the Pussy Cat Theater), an Englishman named Brendan Mullen started the Masque—L.A.'s first punk-rock club, and a gathering place for the 200 or so charter members of L.A.'s punk-rock coterie.

X moved his sleeping bag from the recording studio to the Masque, and set about to build the club's first real sound system from scrap equipment. He also began recording live shows at the club (20 years later those recordings were released as *Live from the Masque, Vols. 1–3*) and continued to play in groups like the Bags and the Deadbeats.

While many British and East Coast punk–new wave bands were signed to major labels, or at least to established indies (like Seymour Stein's Sire Records; see Craig Leon entry), West Coast punkers drew no interest from the majors or the larger indies, so the bands did it themselves. Black Flag founder and guitarist Greg Ginn started SST in L.A.'s South Bay; Dead Kennedy founder and singer Jello Biafra started Alternative Tentacles in San Francisco. If you wanted to get it out, DIY was the way to go.

Now running sound for Masque, and with a fair amount of engineering expertise, X spread the word that he was available to produce for the fledgling scene. Darby Crash, singer of the Germs, was the first to bite: "You're a producer? So produce us," was his terse entreaty. What emerged was the first classic of the L.A. punk oeuvre, the "Lexicon Devil/No God" single, also the first release for fanzine-turned-record label, Slash.

Geza X must be credited with helping whip the Germs (including future Nirvana guitarist Pat Smear and bassist Lorna Doom) from hopelessly sloppy scenesters into an actual band. "Lexicon" rocks with the inspired force of a band suddenly gelling, while Crash (dead in 1980 at 22) spits out something recognizable as an actual tune. X delivered upon his professed production philosophy: "Capture the strident intensity of the music without compromise, yet with all of the production value of a commercial recording." Of course, there is no mistaking the Germs single for a major-label production.

X also began to learn valuable punk production techniques. "The most powerful sounds can only be achieved by almost damaging the equipment, pushing a track into the red so that the effect you hear on playback is a fuller, grittier, more physical sound than what the actual mic was capable of translating from the original equipment," he told *NY Rocker* magazine.

Geza produced singles for his own Deadbeats and Bags, and then a great single for Weirdos, "Message from the Underworld," which truly does boast major-label production values—none of the rickety lurching about and thin sound of most indie jobs (even his own Germs work).

X's career took a great leap forward when he combined the production quality of the Weirdos single with the energy and cultural impact of the Germs single, creating a radio-ready classic out of the Dead Kennedys' "Holiday in Cambodia" in 1980.

East Bay Ray's great surf-meets-Ramones guitar slinging (echoing to atmospheric effect in the intro and breaks), riding on top of a quick, efficient rhythm from drummer D.H. Peligro and bassist Klaus Flouride, are the perfect foils for Jello Biafra's jittery, almost-cartoonish vocals (laced equally with menace and glee) in a song about the smugness of American liberals. Biafra would like to ship the nonradical American left off to Cambodia for a taste of terror that would jolt it out of its complacency. As the percussive chant "Pol Pot" rises to an incantatory pitch, the chorus make a final return with the power and inevitability of monsoon season, before ending as abruptly as a decapitation. Another punk classic.

Geza X also did fine work with hard-core pioneers Black Flag (co-produced with Spot; see entry) and more psychedelically oriented Redd Kross, in addition to songs released under his own name, the Zappaesque "We Need More Power" (for the second *Rodney on the ROQ* album) and "Isotope Soap" (for the *Let Them Eat Jellybeans!* collection). He also led a band called the Mommymen.

After a writing stint in the mid-'80s, Geza X returned to studio life and engineered for Paramount Recording Studios, where he recorded mostly rap, including some great music from Ice-T. When grunge and neo-punk bands came to the fore around 1990, X decided it was time to give rock another chance. He has produced, engineered, and mixed a sizable number of punkish indie artists at the studio built into his house in the Hollywood Hills, but his most important '90s work has been with post-punk singer/songwriter Meredith Brooks (ex of the Graces) and her smash single, "Bitch" (No. 2), from 1997. Instead of making punk records with the quality of major-label releases, Geza X is now making major-label records with the energy and integrity of punk records. —ERIC OLSEN

1000 Mona Lisas: *New Disease,* RCA, 1996.

Aston, Michael: *Why Me Why This Why Now,* Triple X, 1995.

Bags, The: "Babylon Gorgon," Frontier, 1978, 1992 (*Dangerhouse,* Vol. 2: *Give Me a Little Pain!*) • "Survive," Frontier, 1978, 1991 (*Dangerhouse,* Vol. 1) • "We Don't Need the English/Babylon Gorgon," Dangerhouse, 1978.

Black Flag: *Everything Went Black,* SST, 1982 • *Six Pack,* SST, 1982, 1990 • *First Four Years,* SST, 1983 • "I've Heard It Before," SST, 1983 (*The Blasting Concept*).

Brooks, Meredith: "Bitch," Capitol, 1997 • *Blurring the Edges,* Capitol, 1997.

Butt Trumpet: *Primitive Enema,* Chrysalis , 1994.

Celebrity Skin: *Good Clean Fun,* Triple X, 1991.

Dead Kennedys: "Holiday in Cambodia," Alex, 1980, 1991 (*Burning Ambitions [A History of Punk]*) • "Too Drunk to Fuck," Alternative Tentacles, 1981 • *Plastic Surgery Disasters,* Alternative Tentacles, 1982 • *Give Me Convenience or Give Me Death,* Alternative Tentacles, 1987.

Deadbeats: "Kill the Hippies," Dangerhouse, 1978 • "Let's Shoot Maria," Frontier, 1978, 1991 (*Dangerhouse,* Vol. 1) • *Deadbeats on Parade,* Sympathy for the Record Industry, 1996.

Ethyl Meatplow: "Silly Dog/Abazab," Motive/Spasm, 1990.

Fender Buddies: "Furry Friend," Posh Boy, 1980, (*Rodney on the ROQ,* Vol. 1).

Germs: *(MIA) The Complete Anthology* (3 tracks), Slash, 1977, 1993 • "Lexicon Devil," Oglio, 1977, 1995 (*Punk University,* Vol. 2) • "Lexicon Devil/No God," Slash, 1977 • *Scam 101* (EP), Slash, 1978 • *Rock and Rule,* XES, 1985.

Geza X: "We Need More Power," Posh Boy, 1981 (*Rodney on the ROQ,* Vol. 2) • "Isotope Soap," Alternative Tentacles, 1982 (*Let Them Eat Jellybeans!*).

Magnapop: *Rubbing Doesn't Help,* Play It Again Sam, 1996.

Nuns, The: *The Nuns' Greatest Sins,* Posh Boy, 1994.

Outsideinside: *6.6,* Hell Yeah, 1994.

Redd Kross: "Citadel," Enigma, 1984, 1985 (*The Enigma Variations*) • *Teen Babies from Monsanto,* Gastanka/Enigma, 1984.

Rimitti: *Rimitti,* Absolute/Silences, 1995.

Roessler, Paul: *Abominable,* SST, 1988.

Saboteur: "Harder," Glass Note, 1997.

Weirdos: *Weird World, 1977–1981* (1 track), Frontier, 1991.

COLLECTIONS

Chunks, SST, 1981, 1988.

Live from the Masque, Vols. 1–3, ULG, 1996.

GGGarth

See GARTH RICHARDSON

Joe Gibbs

(JOEL GIBSON)

In the 1980 film *Rockers,* drummer Leroy "Horsemouth" Wallace, playing himself, attempts to cut a deal to distribute 45s with producer Joe Gibbs, also playing himself. Gibbs' portrayal shows just how hard he has worked to maintain his reputation as a cutthroat businessman. The opinion is shared by some artists, like Joseph Hill of Culture, who recorded for him. Allegations of exploitation aside (and they are not rare in Kingston, Jamaica), Gibbs was one of the most important producers in reggae from the rock-steady days through the so-called golden age of the '70s.

Joe Gibbs started selling records in his electronics store in Kingston in the days of ska, and his first foray into production resulted in what many consider to be rock steady's opening salvo, 1966's "Hold Them" by the "musical priest" Roy Shirley. Lyn Tait and the Jets' "El Casino Royale" and hilarious horse race tales from the Pioneers like "No Dope Me Pony" and "Long Shot Kick the Bucket" are among his hit rock-steady singles. The latter, like much of Gibbs' early work, was "engineered" by hired hand Lee Perry (see entry)—in the States we would say Perry produced and Gibbs was "executive producer." This arrangement resulted in many classic recordings from this group and others.

A falling-out between Perry and Gibbs included, in typical Jamaican fashion, dueling singles attacking each other. Perry had already recorded "The Upsetter" as vocalist for Gibbs, attacking his former employer Coxsone Dodd (see entry). He ripped Gibbs with the stinging single "People Funny Boy" arranged by mutual friend Clancy Eccles (see entry), and Gibbs fired back with what may be his only recorded vocal, "People Grudgeful."

Gibbs then hired Winston "Niney the Observer" Holness (see entry), another Coxsone alumni, to run the board—until he also broke away to become an independent producer. Gibbs' greatest successes were recorded with engineer Errol Thompson (often co-crediting production as by the "Mighty Two"). They cut hundreds of the hardest rhythms and produced some of the most outstanding records of reggae's "militant" rockers era.

Althea and Donna's "Uptown Top Ranking" was a massive hit for the duo in 1977, not only in Jamaica but in England as well, where it spent weeks at the top of the charts. It was even issued in the U.S. on the Sire label, a rare event for a Jamaican single. But it was albums like Culture's seminal Two Sevens Clash on Gibbs' U.K. Lightning label and 1980's Baldhead Bridge (on Lazer, another U.K. Gibbs imprint) that made anything he released essential listening. His other Jamaican labels included Pressure Beat, Crazy Joe, Heavy Duty, and Town & Country.

Singers Freddie McGregor, Jacob Miller, and Pat Kelly did important work for Gibbs. Dennis Brown recorded so much material there he seems to have lived in the studio for years. Their collaborations include 1981's U.S. crossover LP Love Has Found Its Way and the follow-up album Foul Play—the first co-produced by Brown and Willie Lindo and the latter with Clive Hunt—both for A&M. Gibbs made room at the mike for many aspiring DJs (Jamaica's rappers, though that's an odd thing to say since rap's roots lie in the Jamaican DJ style), including Prince Mohammed (who also recorded as singer George Nooks), Trinity (two of their best albums: Three Piece Suit and Bad Card), and the first album by "voice of authority" Prince Far I (the crucial Under Heavy Manners). Far I went on to a deal with Virgin and a huge cult following in England before being murdered in a robbery in Jamaica.

Junior Byles (with and without his early group the Versatiles), Sylford Walker (whose "Burn Babylon" attempts to do just that), the Mighty Diamonds, Gregory Isaacs, Peter Tosh (with "Arise Blackman"), Errol Dunkley, Stranger Cole, and the Heptones are among the many who recorded for Gibbs. He also issued an enormously popular series of dub discs titled African Dub. Though the mixes became increasingly gimmicky as the series progressed, the earliest are supreme dub masterpieces.

One of the more sought-after imports of the '70s was Joe Gibbs and the Professionals' instrumental album State of Emergency. At any given time the Professionals (his name for the revolving set of players who built the rhythms) might include Horsemouth Wallace or Sly Dunbar (see Sly and Robbie entry) on drums, Lloyd Parks or Robbie Shakespeare on bass, and guitarists BoPeep and the late Eric "Bingy Bunny" Lamont. As a result Gibbs' various artist compilations, like the two-volume United Dreadlocks, were among the few anthologies of that time worth taking a chance on. (Many of the English compilations available then were heavy on the "Lovers Rock" style not popular here.) Still, he wasn't above using the same lineup for a Byron Lee–styled "carnival" album now and then.

The Jamaican music industry remained incredibly creative partly because there was a great deal of "borrowing." With no international copyright agreements, singers and DJs were free to crib sections of melody or lyrics from someone else. Thousands of uncredited cover tunes were released. Instead of a credit, the label simply said "adapted" or, more often, "adopted." It was an "anything goes" musical anarchy that helped keep the creative juices flowing. Joe Gibbs wound up being one of the producers who paid for this when his Miami pressing plant was seized in the early '80s after one of his big Jamaican hits turned out to be an unpaid-for American cover.

In recent years Gibbs' son has begun a massive reissue campaign on a new label called Rocky One, making many of Gibbs' best and long unavailable productions available for the first time on CD. New anthologies of old material and old classics are again seeing the light of day. Two Heartbeat anthologies, Explosive Rock Steady: Joe Gibbs' Amalgamated Label, 1967–1973 and The Mighty Two: Joe Gibbs and Errol Thompson, are essential listening.
—CHUCK FOSTER

Aitken, Marcia: Reggae Impact, Joe Gibbs, 1981.
Althea and Donna: "Uptown Ranking/Mighty Two: Calico Suit," Sire, 1977.
Brown, Dennis: Best Of, Vols. 1–2, Joe Gibbs, 1980, 1982 • Visions of Dennis Brown, Joe Gibbs, 1976 • Words of Wisdom, Shanachie, 1979, 1990 • Spellbound, Joe Gibbs, 1980 • Foul Play, A&M, 1981 • "On the Rocks," A&M, 1981 • "Halfway Up, Halfway Down," A&M, 1982 • "Love Has Found Its Way," A&M, 1982 • Love Has Found Its Way, A&M, 1982 • Stage Coach, Joe Gibbs, 1982 • The Prophet Rides Again, A&M, 1983 • Visions, Shanachie, 1988 • Love and Hate: The Best of Dennis Brown (3 tracks), VP, 1996.
Campbell, Cornell: Boxing Around, Joe Gibbs, 1982.
Culture: Two Sevens Clash, Shanachie, 1976, 1988 • Baldhead Bridge, Disc Pressers, 1978 • Culture, Joe Gibbs, 1981 • At

Their Best—Stronger Than Ever, Rocky One, 1991.

Gibbs, Joe, and the Professionals: *Rocker's Carnival,* Joe Gibbs, n.d. • *State of Emergency,* Joe Gibbs, 1976 • *Ital Reggae Carnival,* Joe Gibbs, 1980.

Hammond, Beres: *Just a Man,* Joe Gibbs, 1976 • *From My Heart with Love,* Rocky One, 1994.

Heptones, The: *The Heptones and Friends,* Vols. 1–2, Trojan, 1995.

Kelly, Pat: *Wish It Would Rain,* Joe Gibbs, 1980.

McGregor, Freddie: *Love at First Sight,* Joe Gibbs, 1982.

Miller, Jacob: *I'm Just a Dread,* Rocky One, 1994.

Paul, Frankie: *Be My Lady,* Joe Gibbs, 1984.

Prince Far I: *Under Heavy Manners,* Joe Gibbs, 1977.

Prince Mohammed: *"? Inna Him Head,"* Joe Gibbs, 1980.

Sly and Robbie: *Syncopation,* Joe Gibbs, 1982.

Trinity: *Three Piece Suit,* Joe Gibbs, 1977 • *Bad Card,* Joe Gibbs, 1979.

COLLECTIONS

African Dub, Chapters 1–5, Joe Gibbs, c. 1977.

DJ Originators, **Vols. 1–2,** Rocky One, 1995.

Earthquake Dub, Joe Gibbs, c. 1975.

Explosive Rock Steady, Joe Gibbs, 1968.

Explosive Rock Steady: Joe Gibbs Amalgamated Label, 1967–1973, Heartbeat, 1992: Errol Dunkley, "Please Stop Your Lying" • The Inspirations, "Take Back Your Duck" • The Overtakers, "Girl You Ruff" • Lee Perry, "I Am the Upsetter" • Reggae Boys, "The Wicked" • Roy Shirley, "Be Good," "Hold Them" • The Versatiles, "Lulu Bell."

Good Old Days: Quadrille, Joe Gibbs, c. 1978.

Jackpot of Hits, Joe Gibbs, 1968.

Jackpot of Hits/Explosive Rock Steady, Trojan, 1997.

Joe Gibbs and Friends: Reggae Train, Trojan, 1988.

Joe Gibbs Revive 45's, Vols. 1–2, Rocky One, 1991.

Majestic Dub, Joe Gibbs, 1980.

Mighty Two: Joe Gibbs and Errol Thompson, Heartbeat, 1992: Black Uhuru, "Rent Man" • Dennis Brown, "Money in My Pocket" • Junior Byles, "Heart and Soul" • Culture, "Dem a Pyarka" • Joe Gibbs and the Professionals, "Rockers Dub" • Leo Graham, "A Win Them" • Prince Far I, "Heavy Manners" • Sylford Walker, "Burn Babylon" • Glen Washington, "Rockers."

Original DJ Classics, Rocky One, 1991.

Reggae Christmas, Joe Gibbs, 1982.

Rock Steady to Reggae: The Early Years, Vols. 1–3, Rocky One, n.d.

Spotlight on Reggae, Vols. 1–3, Rocky One, 1990.

Uncle Sam Goes Reggae, Joe Gibbs, 1980.

United Dreadlocks, Vols. 1–2, Joe Gibbs, 1980.

Wonderful World of Reggae, Joe Gibbs, 1980.

Lou Giordano

L ou Giordano has been on the battle lines with guitar-based alterna-rock bands for the last 15 years as a producer and engineer, working with Live, Sugar, Yo La Tengo, Zuzu's Petals, Fig Dish, Treblecharger, King Missile, Pere Ubu, Paul Westerberg, Lemonheads, and the Smithereens. From his live-sound duties with the grandpappy of melodic punk, Hüsker Dü, to his production of the double platinum *A Boy Named Goo* by the Goo Goo Dolls, Giordano has forged a career that began in the hard-core trenches of Boston's Kenmore Square and has evolved into a productive alliance with Fort Apache studios of Cambridge, Massachusetts.

Giordano's career evolved haphazardly. A native of Cresskill, New Jersey, he studied electrical engineering at MIT in the early '80s but spent most of his time either learning the rudiments of recording on MIT's 1-inch, 8-track machine or hanging out in the hard-core music clubs of Boston's Kenmore Square. Giordano made friends with many of the local bands and began mixing live sound for several of them, including SSD, with whom he first recorded.

Giordano's live-sound career went from local to global when Hüsker Dü came to town in '83. The band had no one to run their live sound so Giordano volunteered for the job and stayed with the Minneapolis trio for three years and two world tours. Giordano then returned to Boston with a desire to return to the recording studio.

Giordano began a partnership with the Fort Apache group that includes Gary Smith, Paul Kolderie, Sean Slade, and Tim O'Heir (see entries). The partnership was a natural for Giordano, who enjoyed the group's indie ethic. "I really admired what they were doing," Giordano says. "It was a real grass-roots thing. They got started out of the third floor of an apartment building and they had this teach-yourself kind of attitude. They were going out and grabbing every band in town and recording demo tapes for them. It seemed like that was my kind of place."

The indie scene may have thrived in Boston in the early '80s due to the inability of most local bands to hook up with a big label. "Nobody even thought all that much about record deals back then," Giordano explains. "There was a huge scene in Boston and most of the bands that had record deals were ruined by them."

Giordano modestly views his status as producer as a simple evolution from watchful engineer. Youthful and down-to-earth, Giordano gives off the impression of a sonic carpenter in the studio with pronouncements like, "With a little extra planning you can make a session more productive, more efficient and a lot more fun.

"You have to have a personal sensibility of what sounds good and what doesn't," he continues. "Consider yourself an auxiliary member of the band, offering constructive thoughts on song structure and lyrics," he adds. Finally, "You have to know how to present the musical performances. We all know the live performance has a lot of energy, but also a lot of rough edges. You have to decide which rough edges to keep and which to polish."

Giordano also places a lot of emphasis on the personal connection a producer needs to forge, in relatively short order, with the artists. "The band has to get to know you just enough to know if they are going to dig the decisions you're making or be horrified by them," he explains. "You may only have a couple of meetings with them before you start working—they're assessing you and you're sizing them up." Giordano cites as an example the band Fig Dish, who selected him to produce their first album for Atlas/A&M after one meeting, saying, "You've never made a record like we want to make, but we think you can do it."

When it comes to capturing a performance, Giordano is perfectly willing to sacrifice pristine audio in the service of an exciting performance. Working with the group Treblecharger, things became tense when a lackluster vocal track needed some help in the attitude department. Giordano turned off the lights in the control room, cranked the volume, handed the vocalist a mike, and told him to pretend it was a gig. "It really made for an exciting vocal," says Giordano. "Sure there was some leakage, but who cares?"

Giordano feels that a level head can serve you well in tense studio situations. "If you just have your wits about you and you can think your way through these things before somebody gets angry and puts a bottle through the control room window, you're going to be doing okay."

Giordano considers himself fortunate to have had a career without compromise. "I've been lucky enough to work only with bands that I like," he says. "I never had to say, 'Let's see if we can make it more commercially successful.' The commercial success met us." —JACK ARKY

Alloy: *Eliminate,* Bitzcore, 1996.

Bats, The: *Courage* (EP), Mammoth, 1993 • *Silverbeet,* Mammoth, 1993.

Belly: "It's Not Unusual," Sire/Reprise, 1993.

Big Dipper: *Boo Boo* (EP), Homestead, 1987 • *Craps,* Homestead, 1988.

Bim Skala Bim: *How's It Goin'?,* Unsigned, 1990 • *Bones,* Unsigned, 1991.

Blake Babies: *Innocence and Experience,* Mammoth, 1993.

Bleached Black: *Bleached Black,* Relativity, 1986.

Christmas: *In Excelsior Dayglo,* Big Time, 1986 • "Boy's Town Work Song," Big Time, 1987 (*Big Noise from Bigtime*) • "Stupid Kids," IRS, 1989 • *Ultra Prophets of Thee Psykick Revolution,* IRS, 1989.

Connells, The: *Ring,* TVT, 1993.

Dillon Fence: *Any Other Way* (EP), Mammoth, 1993 • *Outside In,* Mammoth, 1993.

Dogzilla: *There's Always Something Wrong,* Invisible, 1991.

Drumming on Glass: *Asparagus Tea,* Aurora, n.d. • *Here Comes Geezer,* Aurora, n.d.

Eidolon: *Sanctuary,* Jade Tree, 1992.

Embarrassment, The: *God Help Us,* Bar None, 1990, 1994.

Fig Dish: "Bury Me," Atlas, 1995 • "Seeds," Atlas/A&M, 1995 • *That's What Love Songs Often Do,* Atlas/A&M, 1995.

Goo Goo Dolls: *A Boy Named Goo,* Warner Bros., 1995 • "Ain't That Unusual," Reprise, 1995 (*Angus* soundtrack) • "Name," Metal Blade/WB, 1995 • "Long Way Down" (remix), Warner Bros., 1996 (*Twister* soundtrack).

Hatfield, Juliana: *I See You* (2 tracks, EP), Mammoth, 1992.

Hüsker Dü: *The Living End,* Warner Bros., 1994.

Hypnolovewheel: *Space Mountain,* Alias, 1991 • *Angel Food,* Alias, 1992 • *Altered States,* Alias, 1993.

Jerry's Kids: *Kill Kill Kill,* Taang!, 1989.

Jones, Very: *No More* (EP), Jade Tree, n.d. • *Words and Days,* Hawker, 1989.

King Missile: "My Heart Is a Flower," Atlantic, 1991 • *The Way to Salvation,* Atlantic, 1991.

Lustre: "Kalifornia," A&M, 1996 • *Lustre,* A&M, 1996.

Metal Flake Mother: *Beyond the Java Sea,* Moist, 1991.

Mission of Burma: *Forget,* Taang!, 1987 • *Mission of Burma (EP),* Taang!, 1987.

Moving Targets: *Burning in Water,* Taang!, 1986 • *Brave Noise,* Taang!, 1989 • *Fall,* Taang!, 1991.

Penny Dreadfuls: *Penny Dreadfuls,* Restless, 1996.

Proletariat, The: *Soma Holiday,* Homestead, 1983 • *Indifference,* Homestead, 1986.

Samiam: "Capsized," Atlantic, 1994 • *Clumsy,* Atlantic, 1994.

Serenes, The: *Back to Wonder,* BMG Holland, n.d.

Siege: *Drop Dead,* Relapse, 1994.

Small Ball Paul: *You in Flames,* Thirsty Ear, 1994.

Smithereens, The: *A Date with the Smithereens,* RCA, 1994 • "Miles from Nowhere," RCA, 1994.

SSD: *Decontrol,* XClaim!, n.d. • *Get It Away,* XClaim!, 1983 • *Break It Up,* Homestead, 1985 • *Power,* Taang!, 1991.

Sugar: *A Good Idea* (EP), Rykodisc, 1992 • "Changes," Rykodisc, 1992 • *Copper Blue,* Rykodisc, 1992 • *Helpless* (EP), Rykodisc, 1992 • "If I Can't Change Your Mind," Rykodisc, 1992 • *If I Can't Change Your Mind* (EP),

Rykodisc, 1992 • *Beaster*, Rykodisc, 1993 • "Running Out of Time," Rykodisc, 1993 (*Born to Choose*) • *Besides*, Rykodisc, 1995.

Titanics: *Titanics*, Taang!, 1991.

Treblecharger: *Maybe It's Me*, RCA, 1997.

Uzi: *Sleep Asylum*, Matador, 1986, 1993.

Westerberg, Paul: *Eventually*, Reprise, 1996.

Yo La Tengo: *Upside Down*, Alias, 1992.

Zuzu's Petals: *When No One's Looking*, Twin/Tone, 1992, 1993.

COLLECTIONS

This Is Fort Apache, Fort Apache/MCA, 1995.

Legacy: A Tribute to Fleetwood Mac's Rumours, Lava/Atlantic, 1998.

Glimmer Twins

(MICK JAGGER AND KEITH RICHARDS)

Mick Jagger and Keith Richards lead arguably the best rock 'n' roll band in the world: the Rolling Stones. Yet, for all the glory they receive as songwriters, musicians, and arrangers, they are largely unappreciated as producers.

Jagger (born July 26, 1943, in Dartford, England) and Richards (born December 18, 1943, also in Dartford), who produce together as the Glimmer Twins, have distilled the Stones' sound into a distinct trademark that is nearly impossible to replicate. In fact, the Stones' boozy, bar-band-at-midnight approach is successful because it has been honed to perfection by the Glimmer Twins.

Jagger and Richards officially took over the production reins from Jimmy Miller (see entry) on "It's Only Rock 'n' Roll (But I Like It)" (No. 16) in 1974. That song is indicative of how the Glimmer Twins work: The track was started at guitarist Ron Wood's demo studio in England, then reassembled at Musicland Studios in Munich, Germany. "We recut it later, but we kept the rhythm track from the original," Richards told interviewer Robert Sandall.

The Stones' next project, *Black and Blue* (No. 1), was a transition album with contributions from several guest guitarists who were auditioning for the role later filled by Wood. Highlights include the churning rocker "Hands of Fate," the road-weary ballad "Memory Motel," and Jagger's poignant "Fool to Cry" (No. 10).

In 1978 the Glimmer Twins began to demonstrate a modern rock ethos by mixing dance rhythms with the Stones' traditional bluesy swagger to create bold, irresistible tracks such as "Miss You" (No. 1) and "Beast of Burden" (No. 8) from the album *Some Girls* (No. 1); "Emotional Rescue" (No. 3) and "Dance (Pt. 1)" from the album *Emotional Rescue* (No. 1); and "If I Was a Dancer (Dance, Pt. 2)" and "Everything Is Turning to Gold" from the compilation album *Sucking In the '70s*.

Fittingly, the enigmatic Glimmer Twins remain coy about who does what in the studio. For instance, they left off the musician credits on the *Tattoo You* (No. 1) album in 1981, possibly to disguise the fact that the album was actually a hodgepodge of tracks culled from various sessions, some of which dated to the early '70s.

"Mick and Keith weren't talking to each other and we had to get an album together," recalls Chris Kimsey (see entry), the album's associate producer and engineer. "So I decided to go into the vaults." Kimsey points out that "Start Me Up" (No. 2) was originally recorded for *Some Girls*, while "Waiting on a Friend" (No. 13) was recorded during the *Goats Head Soup* period.

The friendship between Jagger and Richards began to show further signs of strain in the mid-'80s. Consequently, *Undercover* (No. 4) and *Dirty Work* (No. 4), with the exception of gems such as "Undercover of the Night" (No. 9) and "Harlem Shuffle" (No. 5) proved that the bonds that had held the Stones together were in danger of coming apart.

"There were a lot more overlays on ['Undercover of the Night'] because there was a lot more separation in the way we were recording at the time," Richards told Robert Sandall. "Mick and I were starting to come to loggerheads."

By 1989, however, the Stones' partnership was back on track with *Steel Wheels* (No. 3), a more cohesive work with such highlights as "Mixed Emotions" (No. 5), "Rock and a Hard Place," and "Almost Hear You Sigh."

The '90s have seen a further resurgence in the Stones' fortunes despite the retirement of bassist Bill Wyman. This rebirth is due in part to the input of coproducer Don Was (see entry) on the albums *Voodoo Lounge* (No. 2) and *Stripped* (No. 9). In addition to Was and Kimsey, the Glimmer Twins also worked with coproducer Steve Lillywhite (see entry) on the album *Dirty Work*. The Stones' 1997 album *Bridges to Babylon* was also well-received.

Working individually, Jagger is best known for his co-production of his solo albums—especially *She's the Boss* (No. 13, with Bill Laswell and Nile Rodgers; see entries)—and for his production of Living Colour's "Glamour Boys" track from their first album *Vivid* (No. 6). Richards is also known for the production of his solo albums, for his work with Chuck Berry on the *Hail!*

Hail! Rock and Roll film soundtrack, and for his co-production (with Rob Fraboni; see entry) of the Jamaican band Wingless Angels. —BEN CROMER

Glimmer Twins

Rolling Stones, The: *Their Satanic Majesties Request,* London, 1967 • "Ain't Too Proud to Beg," Rolling Stones, 1974 • "It's Only Rock and Roll (But I Like It)," Rolling Stones, 1974 • *It's Only Rock 'n' Roll,* Rolling Stones, 1974 • *Made in the Shade,* Columbia, 1975 • *Black and Blue,* Rolling Stones, 1976 • "Fool to Cry," Rolling Stones, 1976 • *Love You Live,* Rolling Stones, 1977 • "Beast of Burden," Rolling Stones, 1978 • "Faraway Eyes," Rolling Stones, 1978 • "Miss You," Rolling Stones, 1978 • *Some Girls,* Rolling Stones, 1978 • "Shattered," Rolling Stones, 1979 • "Emotional Rescue," Rolling Stones, 1980 • *Emotional Rescue,* Rolling Stones, 1980 • "She's So Cold," Rolling Stones, 1980 • "Start Me Up," Rolling Stones, 1981 • *Tattoo You,* Rolling Stones, 1981 • "Waiting on a Friend," Rolling Stones, 1981 • "Going to a Go-Go," Rolling Stones, 1982 • "Hang Fire," Rolling Stones, 1982 • *Still Life,* Rolling Stones, 1982 • *Undercover,* Rolling Stones, 1983 • "Undercover of the Night," Rolling Stones, 1983 • *Dirty Work,* Rolling Stones, 1986 • "Harlem Shuffle," Rolling Stones, 1986 • "One Hit (to the Body)," Rolling Stones, 1986 • "Mixed Emotions," Rolling Stones, 1989 • "Rock and a Hard Place," Rolling Stones, 1989 • *Steel Wheels,* Rolling Stones, 1989 • "Love Is Strong," Virgin, 1994 • "Out of Tears," Virgin, 1994 • *Voodoo Lounge,* Virgin, 1994 • *Stripped,* Virgin, 1995 • *Bridges to Babylon,* Virgin, 1997.

Mick Jagger

Arnold, P.P.: *The First Lady of Immediate* (3 tracks), Immediate, 1967.

Faithfull, Marianne: *Greatest Hits,* Abkco, 1969, 1987.

Farlowe, Chris: *The Art of Chris Farlowe,* Immediate, 1966 • *Paint It Farlowe,* Immediate, 1968.

Jagger, Chris: *Chris Jagger,* Asylum, 1973.

Jagger, Mick: "Just Another Night," Columbia, 1985 • *She's the Boss,* Columbia, 1985 • "Ruthless People," Epic, 1986 • "Let's Work," Columbia, 1987 • *Primitive Cool,* Columbia, 1987 • *Wandering Spirit,* Atlantic, 1992.

Living Colour: "Glamour Boys," Epic, 1988 • *Vivid* (1 track), Epic, 1988.

Keith Richards

Aranbee Symphony Orchestra: *Today's Pop Symphony,* Immediate, 1966, 1991.

Berry, Chuck: *Hail! Hail! Rock and Roll* soundtrack, MCA, 1987.

Faithfull, Marianne: *Faithfull: A Collection of Her Best Recordings,* Island, 1994.

Franklin, Aretha: *Aretha,* Arista, 1986 • "Jumpin' Jack Flash," Arista, 1986.

Johnson, Johnnie: *Johnnie B. Bad,* American Explorer, 1991.

Richards, Keith: *Talk Is Cheap,* Virgin, 1988 • *Live at the Hollywood Palladium,* Virgin, 1991 • *Main Offender,* Virgin, 1992.

Romeo, Max: *Holding Out My Love to You,* Shanachie, 1981.

Wingless Angels: *Wingless Angels,* Mindless/Island, 1997.

Henry Glover

Henry Glover was a trumpet player, arranger, and record company executive and, together with Dave Bartholomew and Bumps Blackwell (see entries), he was among the first great black producers. He worked with a genre-busting array of country, R&B, blues, jazz, and rock artists from the '40s through the '70s, including the Delmore Brothers, Bull Moose Jackson, Little Willie John, Moon Mullican, Wynonie Harris, Bill Doggett, Dinah Washington, Arthur Prysock, Sonny Rollins, Joey Dee and the Starliters, the Essex, Ronnie Hawkins and the Hawks, Tommy James and the Shondells, Paul Butterfield, and Muddy Waters. In addition, he was one of the finer songwriters of his era, penning such standards as "Drown in My Own Tears" (Lulu Reed, Sonny Thompson, Ray Charles), "Peppermint Twist" (Joey Dee and the Starliters), "Easier Said Than Done" (the Essex), "Peggy Sue Got Married" (Buddy Holly), and "California Sun" (the Rivieras, the Dictators, the Ramones).

Henry Glover was born in 1921 in the resort town of Hot Springs, Arkansas. He pursued a classical music education in cornet and singing and was exposed to a wide range of music—country, jazz, and gospel—through radio and recordings. As a resort town with many visitors from the North, Hot Springs was less segregated than most towns in the South at the time.

Glover matriculated to Alabama A&M in 1939 on a musical scholarship and played in the marching band, the concert band, the dance band, and various combos. He quickly became an adept performer and arranger and played with a formerly all-white dance band out of Hot Springs on breaks from school. Glover earned a B.A. from A&M in 1943, then entered a master's program in political science at Wayne University in Detroit. He played at a local club called Little Sam's where musicians who played with Duke Ellington, Lucky Millinder, Cab Calloway, and Buddy Johnson would often drop in to jam. When Glover was asked to join Johnson's band, he left school, as he said, "on account of illness. I got sick of education."

Glover performed, recorded, and arranged with the Johnson band and with Tiny Bradshaw, Willie Bryant, Skippy Williams, and Lucky Millinder through the mid-'40s, working out of New York. Glover wrote extensively for Millinder. When Millinder toured through Cincinnati, the owner of King Records, Syd Nathan, approached him about signing on with King; but Millinder was signed to another label at the time, so a contract was signed under the name of his sax player and lead singer, Bull Moose Jackson. Glover wrote Jackson's first hit, "I Love You, Yes I Do," in 1947 and subsequent hits, "All My Love Belongs to You" and "I Can't Go On Without You," in 1948. After these successes, Glover quit performing with the band to concentrate on songwriting and arranging.

King Records, founded in 1943, was one of the most successful independent record companies of the era, specializing in country in the '40s and then R&B in the '50s, as first Glover, then Ralph Bass (see entry) and other producers came on board. Nathan hired Glover to be staff producer in 1948 at the exalted rate of $250 per week, plus expenses.

Glover stayed in Cincinnati two years—much to his wife's chagrin—then returned to New York in 1950 to head King's New York office as a vice president. Glover then commuted between New York and Cincinnati to produce King acts. The working relationship between Nathan and Glover was similar to that of other owner-producer pairs such as Art Rupe and Bumps Blackwell at Specialty: the owner had final say on artists, material, and takes, but the producer did the arranging, conducted the sessions, and prepped the musicians. In addition, Glover helped balance Nathan's lack of musical training and his explosive personality. We would call this relationship "executive producer–producer" today. Nathan, but (criminally) not Glover, is an inductee of the Rock and Roll Hall of Fame.

Glover had a particular affinity for R&B, but he was comfortable with country to the point of telling historian John Rumble in the *Journal of Country Music*, "Moon [Mullican] had such a great soul, he was just like a black man to me, like he thought, felt, and expressed himself."

Glover did advanced country work, including the Delmore Brothers' "Blues Stay Away from Me" and Wayne Raney's "Why Don't You Haul Off and Love Me," both in 1949, and Moon Mullican's "Southern Hospitality" and "Well, Oh Well" in 1950. Mullican's "Rocket to the Moon," 1953, bridged the gap between country and R&B to become early rock 'n' roll. Glover

felt that if Mullican had not been old and bald, he could have been a rock star. Glover was also comfortable with more traditional country, working with Cowboy Copas, Grandpa Jones, Jimmy Osborne, and Hawkshaw Hawkins.

Little Willie John was one of the great R&B performers of the '50s and his "Fever" is perhaps Glover's finest R&B production. John's vocals bounce off a lurching mysterioso sax and finger-snapping instrumental backing that was copied whole by Peggy Lee. Both versions are classic, but the key to John's is a clean but febrile vocal that steams Lee's incongruously cool take. Glover's work on Bill Doggett's rollicking instrumental, "Honky Tonk," is also classic, with "Part 1" highlighting Billy Butler's tasty guitar and "Part 2" pushing Clifford Scott's bawdy sax to the fore (enthusiastically reproduced by a sax player named Bill Clinton on the *Arsenio Hall Show* years later). "Honky Tonk" reached No. 2 on the *Billboard* pop chart.

In 1960, Glover left King after being thrown to the wolves by Nathan in the payola investigations, and went to Old Town, producing most notably Billy Bland's only pop hit "Let the Little Girl Dance" (No. 7) and the Fiestas' "So Fine" (No. 11).

After briefly running his own Glover label, Henry moved to Roulette, where he wrote and produced his biggest rock hit, Joey Dee and the Starliters' sensational "Peppermint Twist," which camped out at No. 1 for three weeks in late 1961. Glover followed up with four other Top 40 hits with Dee in the next year, as well as the effervescent *Hey, Let's Twist* album. Glover's R&B background shines through the swinging backbeat, bouncing organ, and honking sax of "Peppermint" and utterly shreds Chubby Checker.

Glover owns another large chunk of rock history, producing the Ronnie Hawkins and the Hawks records of the early '60s. When Levon Helm, Robbie Robertson, Rick Danko, and Garth Hudson left Hawkins, they became the Canadian Squires, Levon and the Hawks, and then simply, the Band. Glover became a mentor to the young group, advising them not to sign a "life with no option" contract with an unscrupulous New York agent in the mid-'60s, per Helm's autobiography *This Wheel's on Fire*.

In the '70s Glover and Helm produced Muddy Waters' *Woodstock* album, which won a Grammy for best traditional recording, and worked together on the *Levon Helm and the RCO All-Stars* album, as well as the Band's epic *The Last Waltz*. In 1986, Henry Glover received the NARAS Honor Roll Award. He died of a heart attack in 1991. —Eric Olsen

Bennett, Boyd, and His Rockets: "Seventeen," King, 1955.

Bland, Billy: *Let the Little Girl Dance,* Ace, 1959, 1992 • "Let the Little Girl Dance," Old Town, 1960.

Butterfield, Paul: *Put It in Your Ear,* Bearsville, 1976.

Canadian Squires "Leave Me Alone," Ware, 1964 • "Uh Uh Uh," Ware, 1964.

Charms, The: "Hearts of Stone," DeLuxe, 1954.

Cortez, Dave "Baby": *In Orbit With,* Roulette, 1965.

Dee, Joey, and the Starliters: *Back at the Peppermint Lounge: Twistin',* Roulette, 1961 • "Peppermint Twist," Roulette, 1961 • "Hey, Let's Twist," Roulette, 1962 • *Hey, Let's Twist,* Roulette, 1962 • "Shout, Part 1," Roulette, 1962 • "What Kind of Love Is This?," Roulette, 1962 • "Hot Pastrami with Mashed Potatoes, Part 1," Roulette, 1963.

Delmore Brothers: "Blues Stay Away from Me," King, 1949 • *Freight Train Boogie,* Ace, 1993.

Doggett, Bill: "Honky Tonk, Parts 1 and 2," King, 1956 • "Slow Walk," King, 1956 • "Soft," King, 1957.

Essex, The: "Easier Said Than Done," Roulette, 1963 • *The Best Of,* Sequel, 1994.

Fiestas, The: "So Fine," Old Town, 1959.

Hawkins, Hawkshaw: "I'm Waiting Just for You," King, 1951 • "Slow Poke," King, 1952.

Hawkins, Ronnie, and the Hawks: *The Best Of,* Roulette, 1990.

Jackson, Bull Moose: "Why Don't You Haul Off and Love Me," King, 1949.

James, Tommy: *It's Only Love,* Roulette, 1967 • w/ the Shondells, *Anthology,* Rhino, 1989.

Little Willie John: "All Around the World," King, 1955 • "Need Your Love So Bad," King, 1956 • "Fever," King, 1958 • *Mister Little Willie John,* King, 1958 • "There Is Someone in This World for Me," King, 1958 • "Let Them Talk," King, 1960 • *Sure Things,* King, 1961 • *Fever: The Best Of,* Rhino, 1993.

Louisiana Red: *Back Porch Blues,* Vogue, 1963, 1984.

Millinder, Lucky: "I'm Waiting Just for You," King, 1951.

Mullican, Moon: "I'll Sail My Ship Alone," King, 1949 • "Southern Hospitality," King, 1950 • "Well, Oh Well," King, 1950 • "Cherokee Boogie," King, 1951 • "Rocket to the Moon," King, 1953 • *Sings His All-Time Hits,* King, 1958 • *Seven Nights to Rock: The King Years, 1946–1956,* Western, 1981.

Osborne, Jimmie: "The Death of Little Kathy Fiscus," King, 1949.

Raney, Wayne: "Why Don't You Haul Off and Love Me," King, 1949 • *Songs from the Hills,* King, 1987.

Vaughan, Sarah: *Sarah Slightly Classical,* Roulette, 1963, 1991.

Washington, Dinah: *In Love,* Roulette, 1962, 1991 • *Back to the Blues,* Capitol, 1997 • *Jazz Profile* Vol. 5, Capitol, 1997.

Waters, Muddy: *The Muddy Waters Woodstock Album,* Chess, 1975 • *The Chess Box,* Chess, 1989.

George Goldner

New York City in the '50s was the capital of the spanking new rock 'n' roll record business. The streets, subways, coffee shops, studios, and publishers' offices of musical Gotham were peopled with itinerant songwriters, song pluggers, street corner vocal groups, hungry jazzers, mooks, and wise guys—all hustling and dreaming up ways to make a buck off this new teenage phenomenon.

The major labels (RCA, Decca, Columbia, Capitol, and Mercury) ruled the musical world with show tunes and pop vocals and instrumentals, and with but a few exceptions (notably Elvis, Bill Haley and His Comets, and Gene Vincent), these labels had yet to embrace and bring home any real rock 'n' roll bacon during the Eisenhower years.

As a result, hundreds of small independent record companies sprang into being and often folded as quickly as they began. Even if a label was lucky enough to score a major hit, it was *de rigueur* for the distributors to hold out on the dough owed to a given firm unless they delivered a follow-up success. To survive in such a climate, a good independent-record man needed guts, acute street smarts, a good pair of ears, and healthy doses of luck. One such man was George Goldner.

Throughout a career spanning the 20-odd years from the late '40s to the dawn of the '70s, George Goldner (born 1928) owned or co-owned over a dozen different record labels, including Tico, Rama, Gee, Roulette, Gone, End, and Red Bird. On top of that, he recorded for or distributed more than 50 labels. He dealt regularly with early movers and shakers of the business—Alan Freed, Morris Levy, and Ahmet Ertegun (see entry) to name a few—and his efforts went a long way toward racially integrating the pop record charts and the music industry at large.

In 1948, Goldner founded Tico, a label that helped to successfully introduce Latin music into the pop mainstream by way of its strong artist roster (Tito Puente, Machito, Tito Rodriguez, et al.). When he heard neighborhood kids making noise about a burgeoning new music scene, he formed an offshoot label called Rama to record and release R&B platters. One of his first Rama releases—"Gee" by the Crows, issued in the summer of 1953—rose to such heights by the following spring that it became the first R&B record to make a splash with white audiences, just as the term "rock 'n' roll" was first becoming established in the American vernacular.

A sampling of the records either produced or released by Goldner in the '50s would virtually define the black R&B vocal group idiom: the Valentines' "Woo Woo Train"; Frankie Lymon and the Teenagers' "Why Do Fools Fall in Love?" (a 2 million seller that reached No. 1 on the R&B charts and crossed over to become a No. 7 pop hit in early 1956); the Cleftones' "Little Girl of Mine"; the Flamingos' incredibly atmospheric "I Only Have Eyes for You" (No. 11); Little Anthony and the Imperials' "Tears on My Pillow" (No. 4), and, perhaps of greatest import, the first successful girl-group record, the Chantels' "Maybe" (No. 15).

Independent record entrepreneurs of the '50s needed to wear any number of hats to get their records recorded, released, and played on the radio. The multitude of tasks required of these entrepreneurs included finding talent and material (and sometimes writing, co-writing, or, in some cases, simply cutting themselves into the credits for a given song), supervising the sessions, and dealing with distributors and DJs. The following story, excerpted from Michael Redmond and Steven West's essay found in Rhino Records' *The Best of the Cleftones* CD compilation, brings alive a slice of this colorful era:

"Flush with their high school success, the [Cleftones] traveled to 9th Avenue and 49th Street, headquarters of George Goldner's Tico/Rama operation. Upon arriving, the group encountered a rather brusque stock boy in rolled-up shirtsleeves, busy packing records. The group asked to see the owner and were told to wait upstairs while the stock boy located him. A few minutes later, the stock boy entered the room, wearing a sports jacket and puffing on a large cigar. It was the Cleftones' first meeting with George Goldner!"

In the studio, Goldner and his right-hand man Richard Barrett (who had recorded for Goldner as lead singer of the Valentines, and brought Frankie Lymon and the Teenagers, the Chantels, and Little Anthony and the Imperials, among others, to Goldner) had multifaceted jobs: find the right key and "groove" for a song; collaborate with the musicians to create a "head" arrangement; encourage *and* control the young, often inexperienced singers during their maiden visits to the recording studio; oversee the vocal balance by placing the singers at the proper distance from the microphones; keep an eagle eye on the clock (sessions were traditionally three hours in length, after which overtime kicked in); and, most importantly, recognize the magical "best take" that would ultimately click with the record-buying teenagers.

The early (pre-1956) songs were usually recorded with the band and singing group performing "live"

together. Though some examples of stereo emerged during the latter part of the '50s, the primary focus was on the monaural slab of plastic that would eventually come blasting out of tinny transistors and car radios. These records sported a punchy bottom and a fine balance of mids and highs (perhaps better heard on the 78 rpm discs of the era than on their 45 rpm counterparts).

Many of Goldner's sessions were held at Bell Sound, a state-of-the-art facility in midtown Manhattan. Instrumentation generally consisted of piano, upright bass, drums, electric guitar (used mainly for rhythm and melodic runs, riffs and accents), and tenor sax (usually played by wailing Jimmy Wright, who also served as bandleader). The musicians were often jazz players playing rock 'n' roll sessions to cover the rent, and as a result, Goldner's tracks swung like mad.

In those days, it was not unusual to record a new tune in one afternoon session, cut an acetate dub immediately thereafter, and have it aired on Alan Freed's highly influential radio show the following night. The actual commercial release of the disc would follow in a matter of days.

Here's how Goldner protégé Artie Ripp summed up his boss: "He was loving, caring, energetic, very self-assured, willing to take chances, an insane gambler, passionate, classy, and at the same time classless."

As with other great record entrepreneurs who flourished in the '50s, George Goldner's fortunes rose and fell numerous times, nearly always in association with his luck at the racetrack. He sold his interests in Tico, Rama, and Gee (not to mention Roulette, which he co-founded) to Morris Levy in 1957 and immediately started up two new labels, End and Gone, which he would also sell to Levy five years later.

It was on the latter label that he enjoyed success with Elvis soundalike Ral Donner, and recorded seminal sides by the Four Seasons, the Isley Brothers, and one John Ramistella, a young chap from Baton Rouge, Louisiana (by way of Brooklyn) whom Goldner renamed Johnny Rivers. Goldner, in association with humorists Bill Buchanan and Dickie Goodman, also produced the first "break-in" novelty recording ("The Flying Saucer"; No. 3) and later garnered another break-in hit with Goodman's "The Touchables" (on Mark-X, another Goldner label).

In the early '60s, Goldner produced records for his old partner Morris Levy at Roulette, and eventually joined forces with Leiber and Stoller (see entry) to co-found the highly successful Red Bird (and sister Blue Cat) label in 1964. These labels are largely associated with the creative work of Jeff Barry (see entry), Ellie Greenwich, and Shadow Morton (see entry) and with hits by the Shangri-Las, the Ad-Libs, and the Dixie Cups. Goldner remained active throughout the '60s, passing away in mid-April 1970, just as his newest label venture, Firebird Records, was about to launch its first releases. —DENNIS DIKEN

Buchanan and Goodman: "The Flying Saucer," Luniverse, 1956.

Chantels, The: "Maybe," End, 1957 • *The Best Of*, Rhino, 1990.

Christie, Lou: *Enlightnin'ment: The Best Of*, Rhino, 1991.

Cleftones, The: "Little Girl of Mine," Gee, 1956 • "Heart and Soul," Gee, 1961.

Colon, Johnny, and His Orchestra: *Boogaloo Blues*, Coutigue, 1992 • *Portrait of Johnny*, Coutigue, 1993.

Crows, The: "Gee," Rama, 1953.

Donner, Ral: "You Don't Know What You've Got (Until You Lose It)," Gone, 1961.

Dubs, The: "Don't Ask Me to Be Lonely," Gone, 1957 • "Could This Be Magic?," Gone, 1958.

Eddy, Duane: "Rebel Rouser," Jamie, 1958.

Flamingos, The: "I Only Have Eyes for You," End, 1959.

Gone All Stars: "7-11," Gone, 1958.

Goodman, Dickie: "The Touchables," Mark-X, 1960 • "On Campus," Cotique, 1966.

Harptones, The: "A Sunday Kind of Love," Bruce, 1953.

Heartbeats: "A Thousand Miles Away," Rama, 1956.

Lebron Brothers: *Lo Mejor*, Coutigue, 1992.

Little Anthony and the Imperials: "Tears on My Pillow," End, 1958 • "Shimmy Shimmy Ko Ko Bop," End, 1959.

Loco, Joe: "El Baion," Tico, 1953.

Lymon, Frankie, and the Teenagers: "I Promise to Remember," Gee, 1956 • "I'm Not a Juvenile Delinquent," Gee, 1956 • "The ABCs of Love," Gee, 1956 • "Why Do Fools Fall in Love," Gee, 1956 • *Why Do Fools Fall in Love?*, Gee, 1956 • *Teenagers*, Gee, 1958 • *Frankie Lymon and the Teenagers*, Bear Family, 1994.

Pastrano, Joey: *Let's Ball*, Coutigue, 1995.

Toad Hall: *Toad Hall*, Liberty, 1968.

Valentines, The: "Woo Woo Train," Rama, 1955.

Wrens, The: "Come Back My Love," Rama, 1955.

Jerry Goldstein

Jerry Goldstein, head of Avenue Records, began his career as a songwriter, arranger, and producer in New York in tandem with Bob Feldman and Richard Gottehrer (see entry). Goldstein and Gottehrer produced seminal '60s tracks, such as the Angels' "My Boyfriend's Back" (No. 1), the McCoys' "Hang on Sloopy" (No. 1), and the Strangeloves' "I Want Candy."

The production trio split off in the late '60s with Goldstein hooking up with an L.A. jazz-funk band, War, that had been backing ex-Animal kingpin Eric Burdon. That collaboration resulted in a 1970 hit, "Spill the Wine" (No. 3), from the album *Eric Burdon Declares War* (No. 18).

Burdon, however, got itchy feet, leaving Goldstein and War to plot their next move. "All Day Music," released in 1971, was a languid left-field hit, starting a roller-coaster that resulted in such War classics as "The Cisco Kid" (No. 2), "Why Can't We Be Friends?" (No. 6), and "The World Is a Ghetto" (No. 7).

Burdon and Goldstein reunited in 1974 for the album *Sun Secrets*, which failed to reach a mass audience, as did the follow-up, 1975's *Stop*. Goldstein also supervised War harmonica maestro Lee Oskar's superb 1976 album, *Lee Oskar*, which included a magnificent suite about Oskar's European roots, "I Remember Home."

Goldstein continued to produce War throughout the '80s, as well as projects for Blood, Sweat and Tears, the New Riders of the Purple Sage, and the Circle Jerks. In the early '90s Goldstein started Avenue Records as an outlet for reissues of the War catalog. —BEN CROMER

Aalon: *Cream City*, Arista, 1977.

Andersen, Eric: *Avalanche*, Warner Bros., 1970.

Angels, The: "My Boyfriend's Back," Smash, 1963.

Blood, Sweat and Tears: *Live*, Avenue, 1980, 1994 • *Nuclear Blues*, LAX, 1980.

Booty People: *Booty People*, ABC, 1977.

Buckley, Tim: *Greetings from L.A.*, Warner Bros., 1974.

Burdon, Eric, and War: *Eric Burdon Declares War*, Polydor, 1970 • "Spill the Wine," MGM, 1970 • *The Black Man's Burdon*, Liberty, 1970 • *Love Is All Around*, ABC, 1976 • See also Eric Burdon Band.

Circle Jerks: *Golden Shower of Hits*, Allegiance, 1983 • "Coup d'Etat," San Andreas, 1984 (*Repo Man* soundtrack).

Eric Burdon Band: *Sun Secrets*, Capitol, 1974 • *Stop*, Capitol, 1975.

Ford, Robben: *Discovering the Blues*, Rhino, 1997.

Glass, Dick: *Glass Derringer*, LAX, 1976.

McCoys, The: "Hang on Sloopy," Bang, 1965 • *Hang on Sloopy*, Bang, 1965.

New Riders of the Purple Sage: *Live*, Avenue/Rhino, 1982, 1995.

Oskar, Lee: *Lee Oskar*, MCA, 1976.

Pressure: *Pressure, Featuring Ronnie Laws*, Rhino, 1979, 1993.

Redbone: *Live*, Avenue/Rhino, 1977, 1994 • *Cycles*, RCA, 1978.

Strangeloves, The: "I Want Candy," Bang, 1965 • *I Want Candy,* Legacy, 1965, 1995 • "Night-Time," Bang, 1966.

Tucker, Tanya: *T.N.T.,* MCA, 1978 • *The Best Of,* MCA, 1982 • *Collection,* MCA, 1992.

War: "All Day Music," United Artists, 1971 • *All Day Music,* United Artists, 1971 • "Slippin' into Darkness," United Artists, 1971 • *War,* United Artists, 1971 • "The World Is a Ghetto," United Artists, 1972 • *Deliver the Word,* Island/United Artists, 1973 • "Gypsy Man," United Artists, 1973 • "Me and Baby Brother," United Artists, 1973 • "The Cisco Kid," United Artists, 1973 • *The World Is a Ghetto,* United Artists, 1973 • "Ballero," United Artists, 1974 • "Low Rider," United Artists, 1975 • "Why Can't We Be Friends," United Artists, 1975 • *Why Can't We Be Friends,* Island/United Artists, 1975 • "Summer," United Artists, 1976 • *Galaxy,* MCA, 1977 • *Platinum Funk,* Island/United Artists, 1977 • "Galaxy," United Artists, 1978 • *Youngblood* soundtrack, Avenue/Rhino, 1978, 1996 • *Music Band 2,* MCA, 1979 • *The Music Band,* MCA, 1979 • "Cinco De Mayo," RCA, 1982 • *Outlaw,* RCA, 1982 • *Life Is So Strange,* RCA, 1983 • "Don't Let No One Get You Down," Avenue/Rhino, 1992 (*Rap Declares War*) • *Anthology, 1970–1994,* Avenue/Rhino, 1994 • *Peace Sign,* Avenue/Rhino, 1994 • *See also* Burdon, Eric, and War.

Witherspoon, Jimmy: *Life Is a Five-Letter Word,* Capitol, 1975.

Kenny "Dope" Gonzalez

See MASTERS AT WORK

Berry Gordy Jr.

See also THE CORPORATION

The Berry Gordy Jr.–Motown story is an American legend. Gordy must be given his due as the meta-producer who assembled the vastly talented Motown creative team of Smokey Robinson, Holland-Dozier-Holland, Norman Whitfield (see entries), William Stevenson, Henry Cosby, Frank Wilson, Ashford and Simpson, and many others and created a com-petitive atmosphere that spurred the writer/producers to make the finest body of American music of the '60s, generating 79 Top 10 singles over that golden decade. Gordy was inducted to the Rock and Roll Hall of Fame in 1988.

Gordy was also a talented songwriter, arranger, and producer in his own right who recorded the Motown debuts of many of his brightest stars, including the Mir-acles, the Temptations, Stevie Wonder, and the Supremes. Gordy's finest production work probably came toward the end of his famous 10-year run as part of the Corporation (see entry), with his last great group, the Jackson 5.

Berry ("Pops") Gordy Sr. and his wife Bertha came to Detroit from the South in 1922. Once in Detroit, the dri-ven Pops first went into the plastering business, then opened a grocery store and a printing shop; he also pro-duced seven children, including Berry Jr., born in 1929. As his father had done before him, Pops instilled the twin tenets of hard work and family concord in his offspring.

Berry Jr. bought the dream but not the means, and in pursuit of big, quick cash, the adolescent turned to boxing. Pops encouraged this pursuit—he wanted his boys to be able to take care of themselves—and Berry rose to the challenge.

He trained hard—sometimes with Jackie Wilson, the local Golden Gloves winner—and had enough suc-cess as an amateur bantamweight (later featherweight) to quit school at 16 and turn professional. Berry finished his career after about 15 fights with a winning record. But purses weren't large for the little guys, opponents in his weight class were scarce, and he was tired of people beating on his face.

After a stint in the Army, Berry labored unenthusi-astically for his father during the day and frequented the hot jazz clubs of Detroit almost every night, making the scene and digging on Charlie Parker or Thelonious Monk. Gordy tried to turn his passion for jazz into a liv-ing when he opened the 3-D Record Mart in 1953, but the public was more interested in R&B and the blues, and the store closed two years later, a victim of public taste. Reluctantly, Gordy went to work at the Ford plant to support his young family, humming made-up tunes in his head as he fastened chrome strips to Lincolns, according to Nelson George in his excellent study of Motown, *Where Did Our Love Go?*

Meanwhile, two of Berry's older sisters, Anna and Gwen, snared the photography and cigarette conces-sion at the swinging Flame Show Bar. As Berry began to write his tunes down, the sisters started showing them to the musicians who played the club, including Jackie Wilson, who recorded Gordy's "Reet Petite" in 1957.

Overtly commercial, the bouncy "Reet" hit No. 11 on the R&B chart, followed by "Lonely Teardrops," which featured some future Motown emblems: lyrics with stories, a rocking backbeat with tambourine, a big sax break, and a family of supportive background singers. Marv Johnson's hits in 1959 and 1960 featured many of the same amenities as Gordy moved into production.

Gordy had met a 17-year-old Smokey Robinson at an open audition and had encouraged the youth's songwriting efforts. Gordy wrote and produced Smokey and the Miracles' first hit, "Got a Job" and licensed it to George Goldner's (see entry) End Records. The song hit No. 1 R&B, but Gordy's total royalty take was $3.19.

Despite his succession of hits, cash was short and Gordy was sick of it. His attitude can be found on his biggest pre-Motown hit, Barrett Strong's rock 'n' roll anthem "Money" (No. 23), written and produced by Gordy and released on his sister's Anna label with the immortal lines: "You're lovin' gives me a thrill, but you're lovin' won't pay my bills, I want money." It was time to combine love and commerce.

Gordy took the bull by the balls and, with help from Robinson and the Gordy family, he set up a recording studio (first with a single 3-track tape machine, then with a pair of Ampex 8-tracks with state-of-the-art equalizing capability by '65) with offices at 2648 West Grand Boulevard ("Hitsville, U.S.A.") and established the Motown/Tamla record group, Jobete Music Publishing, and International Talent Management.

Now he was in charge, and Motown was to become the most profitable black entertainment company in the country. Determined to hang on to the cash, Gordy set up restrictive accounting practices: performers were allowed to see the books only twice a year and outside agencies like the RIAA were prohibited from seeing them at all. Because of this practice, Motown did not receive any gold record certifications in its heyday.

Writers, producers, and artists were put on weekly salaries that were then deducted from their royalties. Studio musicians were on weekly retainer and 24-hour call, instead of being paid by the session. Motown succeeded where others failed because, in addition to his keen ear for talent, Gordy was able to achieve a family atmosphere (both figuratively and in reality—most of his brothers and sisters came to work for Motown); camaraderie and friendly competition brought out the best in talented artists, writers, and producers, while the company made most, but not all, of the money. Gordy also audaciously sought to capture both black and white audiences by emphasizing beat and soul in the vocals, but with a pop (i.e., non-blues-based) melody and relationship-based (i.e., non-race-specific) lyrics. (This formula changed in the late '60s when the Supremes and the Temptations tackled social themes.)

To ease his (black) artists' segue into the (white) world of television appearances and posh nightclubs, Gordy established the Artist Development Department, which included a vocal coach, choreographer Cholly Atkins, live-music director Maurice King, and an etiquette-and-style instructor. Some blossomed and some chafed under Gordy's paternalistic "I'll take care of you" eye. Mary Wells left after her first contract expired in 1964, while Smokey lasted until the '90s. Motown's most productive writer/producers—the team of Eddie and Brian Holland, and Lamont Dozier (see entry)—left after a royalty dispute in 1967, cutting off the flow of hits for the Four Tops and the Supremes. Only Gordy's personal devotion to the Supremes, and to Diana Ross in particular, kept them going for a few more years.

The family dream ended when Gordy picked up the company and moved to Los Angeles in 1971, where he expanded into film, producing *Lady Sings the Blues* (with Diana Ross as Billie Holiday) and *The Last Dragon,* among others. He sold Motown to MCA in the late '80s for around $60 million.

Motown's first big hit was the Miracles' "Shop Around" in 1961. Its evolution is telling of Gordy's skills. Smokey wrote the song and produced the first version. Gordy loved the song, but something was wrong with the arrangement. He sped up the beat and got drummer Benny Benjamin to play with brushes instead of sticks when they re-recorded the song at 3 A.M. When it shot to No. 1 R&B, Motown was on its way.

Gordy's assembly-line training expressed itself in the company's Quality Control Department, wherein creative staff (but not artists) reviewed the week's output—sometimes listening to as many as a dozen different takes of a given song—and then voted on the results. Gordy often brought in neighborhood teenagers to rate the songs, à la *American Bandstand.*

As Motown came to dominate the charts in the mid-'60s, there came to be something called a "Motown sound." This sound can be traced to the writers—Gordy, Robinson, Norman Whitfield, H-D-H; the artists; engineer Lawrence Horn; and the band—the fabled Funk Brothers—who backed up most of the artists recorded at Hitsville. The prototypical lineup was Benny Benjamin on drums, James Jamerson on bass, Earl Van Dyke on keyboards, James Giddons on percussion, and Robert White or Joe Messina on guitar.

In his history of record production, *Good Vibrations,* Mark Cunningham alleges that as early as 1963, white musicians from Phil Spector's (see entry) Wrecking

Crew, including Hal Blaine on drums, Carol Kaye on bass, and Tommy Tedesco on guitar were in fact contributing to the Motown sound from Los Angeles. If so, the real matter is that the West Coasters were forced to emulate the Funk Brothers. Confusion over results is a tribute to the power of the prototype and the skill of their imitators.

In addition to the classic rock 'n' roll of "Money," Gordy's best work as a producer includes the Contours' rocking "Do You Love Me?" (No. 3); Little Stevie Wonder's raucous debut on "Fingertips" (No. 1), a harmonica and call-and-response workout that captures the child genius at his most irrepressible; and Junior Walker's sax-plosion "Shot Gun" (No. 4), which captures a similar blast of adrenaline.

After several years in the mid- to late '60s concentrating on the business side, Gordy returned to production to help out his beloved Supremes after H-D-H left the company. He went to work with the writing and production team known as the Clan (Deke Richards, Frank Wilson, R. Dean Taylor, and Hank Cosby) to come up with the stinging single-mother commentary "Love Child" (No. 1), followed by the similar, but less so, "I'm Livin' in Shame" (No. 10). This was another Motown modus operandi: put out slight variations on a successful theme until the public cried uncle. The Clan evolved into the Corporation, which guided Motown's last great group, the Jackson 5. —ERIC OLSEN

Contours, The: "Do You Love Me?," Gordy, 1962 • *Do You Love Me?,* Motown, 1962, 1988 • "Shake Sherry," Gordy, 1963.

Darin, Bobby: *1936–1973,* Motown, 1975.

Gaye, Marvin: *How Sweet It Is,* Tamla, 1964 • "Try It Baby," Tamla, 1964 • *Anthology,* Motown, 1974 • *The Master (1961–1984),* Motown, 1995.

Holland, Eddie: "Jamie," Motown, 1962.

Holloway, Brenda: "You've Made Me So Very Happy," Motown, 1967.

Isley Brothers: *Greatest Hits and Rare Classics,* Motown, 1991.

Jackson 5: *Anthology,* Motown, 1976.

Jackson, Jermaine: "Let Me Tickle Your Fancy," Motown, 1982 • *Greatest Hits and Rare Classics,* Motown, 1991.

Jackson, Michael: *Got to Be There,* Motown, 1972 • *Ben,* Motown, 1973.

Johnson, Marv: "Come to Me," United Artists, 1959 • "(You've Got to) Move Two Mountains," United Artists, 1960 • "I Love the Way You Love," United Artists, 1960 • *You Got What It Takes,* EMI Legends, 1992.

Martha and the Vandellas: *Live Wire! The Singles, 1962–1972,* Motown, 1993.

Marvelettes, The: *The Marvelous Marvelettes,* Tamla, 1963.

Miracles, The: "Shop Around," Tamla, 1960 • *Hi! We're the Miracles,* Tamla, 1961 • *Cookin' with the Miracles,* Tamla, 1962 • "I'll Try Something New," Tamla, 1962 • *I'll Try Something New,* Tamla, 1962 • *Shop Around,* Tamla, 1962 • "Way Over There," Tamla, 1962 • "What's So Good About Good-Bye," Tamla, 1962 • *Doin' Mickey's Monkey,* Tamla, 1964 • *See also* Robinson, Smokey, and the Miracles.

Pointer, Bonnie: "Heaven Must Have Sent You," Motown, 1979.

Robinson, Smokey, and the Miracles: *Whatever Makes You Happy: More of the Best, 1961–1971,* Rhino, 1993 • *Thirty-Fifth Anniversary Box,* Motown, 1994.

Ross, Diana: *Lady Sings the Blues,* Motown, 1973 • w/ Marvin Gaye, "You're A Special Part of Me," Motown, 1973 • w/ the Supremes, *Anthology,* Motown, 1974, 1986 • *Anthology,* Motown, 1986, 1995 • w/ the Supremes, *The Best Of,* Motown, 1995.

Ruffin, David: *Feelin' Good,* Motown, 1969 • "I'm So Glad I Fell for You," Motown, 1969.

Strong, Barrett: "Money," Anna, 1960.

Supremes, The: *The Supremes at the Copa,* Motown, 1965 • "Let Me Go the Right Way," Motown, 1962 • *Meet the Supremes,* Motown, 1962 • *Love Child,* Motown, 1968 • "Love Child," Motown, 1968 • "I'm Livin' in Shame," Motown, 1969 • *Let the Sun Shine In,* Motown, 1969 • "No Matter What Sign You Are," Motown, 1969 • *Greatest Hits and Rare Classics,* Motown, 1991 • *See also* Ross, Diana.

Taylor, Bobby, and the Vancouvers: *Bobby Taylor and the Vancouvers,* Motown, 1968, 1994 • "Does Your Mama Know About Me," Gordy, 1968.

Temptations, The: "Dream Come True," Gordy, 1962 • *Meet the Temptations,* Motown, 1964, 1992 • *Anthology,* Motown, 1973 • "Happy People," Gordy, 1975 • "Shakey Ground," Gordy, 1975 • *Reunion,* Motown, 1982, 1994 • *All the Million Sellers,* Rhino, 1993 • *Emperors of Soul,* Motown, 1994 • *One by One: The Best of Their Solo Years,* Motown, 1996.

Walker, Junior, and the All Stars: "Shake and Fingerpop," Soul, 1965 • "Shotgun," Soul, 1965 • *Shotgun,* Soul, 1965 • *Home Cookin',* Soul/Motown, 1969, 1994.

Weston, Kim: *Greatest Hits and Rare Classics,* Motown, 1991.

Wonder, Stevie: "Fingertips, Part 2," Tamla, 1963 • *Little Stevie Wonder: The 12-Year-Old Genius,* Tamla, 1963.

Richard Gottehrer

Producer and label executive Richard Gottehrer has an uncanny ability to capture the innocence and energy of youth. Gottehrer's masterful production of the Go-Go's ("Our Lips Are Sealed," No. 20, and "We Got the Beat," No. 2), the Bongos ("Numbers with Wings," "Barbarella"), and Marshall Crenshaw ("Someday, Someway") resulted in '80s classics. Indeed, Gottehrer could be called the Dorian Gray of pop: an ageless producer who stays forever young by working with artists during the initial stage of their careers.

Born on June 12, 1940, in New York City, Gottehrer learned his craft in the early '60s by producing demos in mono and in 2-track, later graduating to singles done in 4-track. "All the Phil Spector (see entry) records were made on 4-track and those were monstrous-sounding," he says, pointing out that his apprenticeship occurred at a time when producers and songwriters wielded significant power. "It was all singles then. Albums were made only after you had a huge hit," he recalls. "The song was absolutely critical and the artist was, in many cases, an extension of the song, the producer, and the arranger."

Gottehrer's first significant hits, in tandem with Jerry Goldstein (see entry), were seminal tracks such as the Angels' "My Boyfriend's Back" and the McCoys' "Hang on Sloopy" (both No. 1) and the Strangeloves' "I Want Candy."

In the late '60s, Gottehrer and Seymour Stein started Sire Records, leaving Gottehrer little time for production work. He did, however, have chart success with Sire acts such as Focus and the Climax Blues Band.

Gottehrer returned to the studio full-time in the late '70s and early '80s. His keen pop sensibilities were the perfect match for the youthful energy of the Go-Go's, the retro-rock of Marshall Crenshaw, and the Bongos' edgy pop. Their aforementioned classics are prime examples of Gottehrer's ability to capture raw performances while adding stylistic touches such as cascading tambourines and jungle drums. "It took a long time to do those records," he explains. "I spent hours and hours trying to get the right touch on the tambourines on 'Numbers with Wings.' On 'We Got the Beat' we wanted to make the drums amazingly heavy, so I banged on the drums with Gina (Schock) and doubled her parts."

Gottehrer concedes that many of the musicians he produces are not virtuosos. Even so, he insists it is the producer's job to smooth out the rough edges and capture a performance. "I try to make each one of the elements be as good as they can possibly be," Gottehrer says. "A lot of guys would listen to some people play and say, 'No, we gotta get a [session] player in here.' I don't think that way: I'll figure a way of getting the most out of that person and make it work."

Gottehrer's explorations of new music continued in the late '80s and early '90s with his productions of critically acclaimed albums by the Judybats, ex-Bongos leader Richard Barone, and Jeffrey Gaines. In 1996, Gottehrer launched independent label Sol 3 Records to give him a platform to showcase young acts such as the Twistoffs and Scrub.

Ultimately, Gottehrer sees production in terms of "clarity of thought," emphasizing preproduction to ensure that sessions result in good songs and performances. "You can make a great record out of a great song; you cannot make a great record out of a lousy song," Gottehrer insists. "There's such a glut of material on the market and a lot of it is good. To stand out you really have to have good songs." —Ben Cromer

Aerosmith: *Pandora's Box*, Columbia, 1991.

All About Eve: "Every Angel," Mercury, 1988.

Angels, The: "My Boyfriend's Back," Smash, 1963.

Armatrading, Joan: *Me, Myself and I*, A&M, 1980 • *Track Record*, A&M, 1983 • *Classics, Vol. 21*, A&M, 1989.

Aum: *Bluesvibes*, Sire, 1969.

Barone, Richard: *Primal Dream*, Paradox/MCA, 1990.

Beat Rodeo: *Staying Out Late with Beat Rodeo*, IRS, 1985.

Blondie: "In the Sun," TVT, 1976, 1991 (*The Groups of Wrath*) • "X Offender," TVT, 1976, 1991 (*The Groups of Wrath*) • *Blondie*, Private Stock, 1976 • *Plastic Letters*, Chrysalis, 1977 • *Best Of*, Chrysalis, 1981.

Bogosian, Eric: *Sex Drugs and Rock on Roll*, SBK, 1990.

Bongos, The: *Numbers with Wings* (EP), RCA, 1983.

Brown, Julie: "Every Boy's Got One," Sire, 1987 • "Girl Fight Tonight!," Sire, 1987 • *Trapped in the Body of a White Girl*, Sire, 1987.

Broza, David: *Time of Trains*, November, 1993 • *David Broza*, Mesa, 1995.

Carrasco, Joe "King": *Party Weekend*, MCA, 1983.

Chiefs of Relief: *C.O.R.*, Sire, 1988.

Chilliwack: *Rockerbox*, Sire, 1975.

Climax Blues Band: *Rich Man*, Sire, 1972 • *FM Live*, Sire, 1973 • *Sense of Direction*, Polydor, 1974.

Colourfield: *Colourfield*, Chrysalis, 1986 • *Deception*, Chrysalis, 1987 • "Running Away," Chrysalis, 1987.

Crenshaw, Marshall: *Marshall Crenshaw*, Warner Bros., 1982.

Darling: *Put It Down to Experience*, Charisma, 1979.

Dirty Angels: *Kiss Tomorrow Goodbye*, Private Stock, 1977 • *Dirty Angels*, A&M, 1978.

Dr. Feelgood: *Private Practice*, United Artists, 1978.

Fleshtones, The: "American Beat '84," IRS, 1984 (*Bachelor Party* soundtrack) • *Speed Connection*, IRS, 1985.

Gaines, Jeffrey: *Jeffrey Gaines*, Chrysalis/EMI, 1992 • "I Like You," Chrysalis/ERG, 1994 • *Somewhat Slightly Dazed*, Chrysalis, 1994.

Geremia, Paul : *Paul Geremia*, Sire, 1970.

Godhead: *Power Tool Stigmata*, Sol 3, 1998.

Go-Go's, The: *Beauty and the Beat*, IRS, 1981 • "Our Lips Are Sealed," IRS, 1981 • "Vacation," IRS, 1982 • *Vacation*, IRS, 1982 • "We Got the Beat," IRS, 1982 • *Greatest*, IRS, 1990 • *Return to the Valley of the Go-Go's*, IRS, 1995.

Gordon, Robert: *Robert Gordon with Link Wray*, Private Stock, 1977 • w/ Link Wray, *Fresh Fish Special*, Private Stock, 1978 • *Rock Billy Boogie*, RCA, 1979 • *Bad Boy*, RCA, 1980 • *Too Fast to Live, Too Young to Die*, RCA, 1982 • *Robert Gordon Is Red Hot*, Bear Family, 1989.

Hall, Terry: *The Collection: Terry Hall*, Chrysalis, 1993.

Hell, Richard, and the Voidoids: "Blank Generation," Arista, 1977, 1986 (*Rock at the Edge*) • *Blank Generation*, Sire, 1977.

Holly and the Italians: "Tell That Girl to Shut Up," Virgin, 1979 • *The Right to Be Italian*, Virgin, 1981.

House of Schock: *House of Schock*, Capitol, 1988.

Judybats, The: "She Lives (in a Time of Her Own)," Sire/WB, 1990 (*Where the Pyramid Meets the Eye*) • *Native Son*, Sire/WB, 1991 • *Down in the Shacks Where the Satellite Dishes Grow*, Sire/WB, 1992.

Kelley, Peter: *Dealin' Blues*, Sire, 1971.

Lidon, Christine: *Avalanche*, Phonogram, 1989

Marta Marta: *Marta Marta*, IRS, 1996.

McCoys, The: "Hang on Sloopy," Bang, 1965 • *Hang on Sloopy*, Bang, 1965 • "Sorrow," Bang, 1965.

Medicine Men: *Keepers of the Sacred Fire*, Savage/MCA, 1992.

Mental As Anything: *Fundamental*, Columbia, 1986.

Moonpools and Caterpillars: *Lucky Dumpling*, EastWest, 1995.

Nuclear Valdez: *I Am I*, Epic, 1989.

Prissteens, The: *Scandal, Controversy and Romance*, ALMO, 1998.

Renaissance: *Turn of the Cards*, Sire, 1974 • *Tales of 1,000 Nights* Vol. 1, Sire, 1990.

Richards, Regina, and Red Hot : *Regina Richards and Red Hot*, A&M, 1981.

Roches, The: *Another World*, Warner Bros., 1985.

Royal Crescent Mob: *Spin the World*, Sire, 1989.

Scott, Tim: *Swear* (EP), Sire, 1983 • "Swear," Sire/WB, 1992 (*Just Say Yesterday*).

Scrub: *Wake Up*, Sol 3, 1996.

Smith, Darden: *Little Victories*, Chaos, 1993.

Strangeloves, The: "I Want Candy," Bang, 1965 • *I Want Candy*, Legacy, 1965, 1995 • "Night-Time," Bang, 1966.

Thomas, Allan: *Picture*, Sire, 1971.

Velez, Martha: *Matinee Weepers*, Sire, 1973.

Wilcox, David: *Big Horizon*, A&M, 1994.

Will and the Bushmen: *Will and the Bushmen*, SBK, 1989.

Won Ton Ton: *Home*, Mercury, 1987, 1989.

Wray, Link: *Bullshot*, Charisma/Instant, 1980 • *Live at El Paradiso*, Instant, 1980.

Yachts: *Yachts*, Radar, 1979.

Eddy Grant

Born March 5, 1948, in Guyana, Eddy Grant migrated to England, where he fronted the '60s rock group the Equals whose "Baby Come Back" spent nine weeks on the Billboard Top 100. The song was later covered by Player and Bonnie Raitt. The group cut three albums: *Baby Come Back* (which featured the song "Police on My Back," later covered by the Clash), *Unequaled Equals*, and *Equals Supreme*. When Grant left the band he purchased Coach House, Manfred Mann's former studio, upgrading it from 16 tracks to 24 tracks. He set up his own label, Ice, and later signed distribution deals with Mercury, Columbia, and RCA (which had released the first Equals album in America).

Though he produced an album for Jamaica's Pioneers (*Feel the Rhythm*, released on Mercury) and the hit "Jamaican Child" for his brother, a DJ who dubbed himself "The Mexicano" (he DJ'd in a hilarious fake Mexican accent—always popular in the Caribbean—releasing three albums on Ice), most of Grant's productions until the early '90s were of himself. His first solo LP in 1980, *Message Man*, was recorded in the grand tradition of Eddie Cochran, McCartney's (see entry) *McCartney*, and Stevie Wonder's (see entry) *Talking Book*, with Grant producing, playing most of the instruments, and singing lead vocals.

Relocating his studio to Barbados, he went on to release a dozen solo discs, scoring hits with singles "Boys in the Street," "Electric Avenue" (No. 2), and "Walking on Sunshine." Grant also realized the early potential of the video and became one of the few reggae artists (though he often resists that label in album titles like *File Under Rock*) to get videos in rotation on the early days of MTV. As a result the video for "Electric Avenue"—where Grant steps from his living room sofa to a floor that turns out to be underwater—is one of the memorable images for many reggae fans who watched those first fledgling videos.

Asked to contribute a song to the film *Romancing the Stone*, Grant wrote and recorded a cut that was promptly rejected. He released it anyway and got a hit single

(No. 26), though it was not included in the movie of the same title.

Grant's sound mixes elements of reggae, rock, and dance music—English, Caribbean, and American styles—and somehow manages to be commercial and uncompromising at the same time. In the early '90s Grant's Ice label became a major player in the soca field (a hybrid of soul and calypso), reissuing works by a number of prominent calypso artists like Roaring Lion (two separate discs collecting "sacred 78s"), Lord Melody, Mighty Spoiler, Lord Kitchener (in three volumes), and four from the Mighty Sparrow. The Ice catalog includes recordings from, in addition to Grant's own releases, Square One, Barnet "Preacher" Henry, KP's Sunshine Band, and the "soca trinity" of Gabby, Grynner, and Bert "Panta" Brown.

Grant's own music turned more in this direction with the release of 1993's *Soca Baptism*. He also produced soca albums for Calypso Rose, Black Stalin, and Superblue in 1994 and 1995. Ice has been on ice for the last couple of years with offices closed and phones disconnected, but Grant is a notorious survivor and it wouldn't be a surprise to see him back on the scene again soon. —CHUCK FOSTER

Black Stalin: *Rebellion,* Ice, 1994 • *Message to Sunder,* Ice, 1995.

Calypso Rose: *Soca Diva,* Ice, 1993.

Duke: *Mask,* Ice, 1994 • *Spirit of Calypso,* Ice, 1995.

Grant, Eddy: "Hello Africa," Ice, 1982 • *Message Man,* Ice, 1977 • *Walking on Sunshine: The Very Best of Eddy Grant,* Blue Wave/Parlophone, 1979, 1989 • *Love in Exile,* Ice, 1980 • *My Turn to Love You,* Epic, 1980 • *Can't Get Enough,* Ice, 1981 • *Live at Notting Hill,* Ice, 1981, 1984 • *Paintings of the Soul,* Ice, 1982 • "Electric Avenue," Portrait/Ice, 1983 • *Killer on the Rampage,* Portrait, 1983 • *All the Hits,* K-Tel, 1984 • "Boys in the Street," Ice, 1984 • *Going for Broke,* Ice/Portrait, 1984 • "Romancing the Stone," Portrait, 1984 • *Born Tuff,* Ice/Portrait, 1986 • *File Under Rock,* Blue Wave/Parlophone, 1988 • "Gimme Hope Jo'Anna," Enigma, 1988 • "Harmless Piece of Fun," Blue Wave/Parlor, 1988 • *Harmless Piece of Fun,* Blue Wave/Parlophone, 1988 • *Hits,* Starr/Polydor, 1988 • *Barefoot Soldier,* Ice/Enigma, 1990 • *Killer on the Rampage,* Ice, 1992 • *Soca Baptism,* Ice, 1993 • *Greatest Hits,* EMI, 1997 • *I Don't Wanna Dance,* Ariola Express, 1997.

Mexicano: *The Best Of,* Ice, 1979.

Pioneers, The: *Feel the Rhythm,* Mercury, 1976.

Superblue: *Bacchinal Time,* Ice, 1993 • *Flag Party,* Ice, 1994 • *Happy Carnival,* Ice, 1995.

Norman Granz

Norman Granz, a reclusive figure who lives in Montreux, Switzerland, is one of the major jazz impresarios and a noted producer in his own right. Born August 6, 1918, in Los Angeles, Granz is best known for his *Jazz at the Philharmonic* series and for founding the Verve Records label.

Granz popularized jazz, particularly bebop, beginning in the early '40s. In 1942, he began organizing jam sessions in the Beverly-Fairfax area of Los Angeles. In an interview for his official Verve Records biography, Granz said he approached Billy Berg, owner of Billy Berg's Capri Club, proposing to showcase jam sessions Sunday nights. "One condition I insisted on is that there be no color line at the door," said Granz, noting he "got into it more for sociological reasons" than musical. His full-time gig at the time was as a film editor at Metro-Goldwyn-Mayer.

In 1944, Granz began to expand, launching a series of concerts at Music Town, a hall in Los Angeles south. That July, Granz presented his first *Jazz at the Philharmonic* concert, effectively moving jazz from the exclusivity of clubs to the mass exposure of concert halls. That same year Granz decided to record concert performances of jazz, opening up a whole new market. The symbiosis of recordings and concerts was to be a hallmark of his career. And the recording of live concerts enabled listeners to experience long, spontaneous solos.

Although some have accused Granz of musical dilettantism, there's no doubting his racial probity. A newspaper clipping showcased in the booklet to *The Verve Story* recounts his preparation for the July 2, 1944, JATP debut, noting it was a benefit for the Sleepy Lagoon Defense Fund, the moniker applied to a group of Mexican boys jailed in the "zoot suit" riots of that spring.

"He was first and foremost an impresario and secondarily a producer," says jazz historian Mark Gridley. "The distinction wasn't there much for him because, essentially, he did in the studio what he had already refined in his concert promotion formula: the jam session with the most eminent musicians of the day."

Granz was conservative, Gridley says. "He never took any cutting-edge guys, but he took the most eminent guys who were already established and threw together these all-star jam sessions."

After two years of concerts along the West Coast, JATP moved east, delivering a concert at Carnegie Hall in New York. That year, 1946, also marked Granz's entry into record labels. His first recordings were issued by Disc, the small label owned by Moses Asch (who later founded Folkways Records). Then Granz founded Clef Records in 1947, distributed by Mercury Records until it went independent in 1953.

In 1949 Granz introduced Toronto pianist Oscar Peterson to a Carnegie Hall audience, launching a long-lasting relationship between the keyboard master and the impresario: Peterson frequently figured in Granz's many musical efforts.

Over the years, Granz essentially developed a stable of artists, both for recording and concerts. The key figures were trumpeters Roy Eldridge and Dizzy Gillespie; saxophonists Benny Carter, Lester Young, Charlie Parker, and Ben Webster; singers Billie Holiday and Ella Fitzgerald; and drummers Gene Krupa and Buddy Rich.

Granz was "a real big jazz buff and a very active political liberal," Gridley says. "He was very important in race relations, almost as important as John Hammond (see entry). They insisted that the hotels accommodate mixed bands and the stages present mixed bands, and they paid them top dollar. Granz paid Parker $1,000 a week. He gave people what they were worth."

The down side was Granz sought to control "spontaneous" sessions, Gridley says. "He liked to pick the guys and didn't want them to rehearse. He just wanted them to jam, and a lot of them had a sense of polish that made them feel bad if they couldn't at least work some stuff out."

By the late '40s, Granz was producing two national tours a year and expanding his jazz stable. He marketed his JATP concert recordings on Clef, traditional jazz artists on the Down Home Label, and modernists on Norgran. He didn't consolidate until 1956, when he not only became Ella Fitzgerald's manager but also established the Verve label.

In 1960, MGM bought Verve from Granz, but it continued to release new recordings, many produced by Creed Taylor (see entry). Polydor bought the label in 1967, but its catalog has continued to be released by affiliated firms; PolyGram has not only instituted a Verve reissue program; it is also releasing new Verve recordings. Granz, meanwhile, established the Pablo label, on which he issued key recordings by the likes of Art Tatum (Peterson's greatest influence), Joe Pass, and Fitzgerald.

Closely identified with Peterson, Granz is even more closely linked to Fitzgerald. Not only did her Duke Ellington and Irving Berlin songbook recordings win the first Grammys ever awarded a female jazz and pop vocalist; Granz also produced five other Fitzgerald Grammy winners.

Besides his jazz productions, Granz also pioneered spoken-word recordings by such comedians as Mort Sahl, Jonathan Winters, and Shelley Berman. "My talkers sold as well as Ella," Granz says in his Verve biography. Sahl, 1959 Grammy-winner Berman, and Winters "helped subsidize Webster and Tatum—not to mention Dorothy Parker, Linus Pauling, and Jack Kerouac."

In 1960, Granz moved to Europe, and a few years later, effectively retired from the record business. In 1972, following sporadic European jazz concert productions, Granz came out of retirement to produce a JATP-style concert in Santa Monica. *Jazz at the Santa Monica Civic '72* served as the launch pad for Pablo, his second major label. He sold the 350 album-plus Pablo catalog in 1986.

Asked what his goals were, Granz cited three: "First, to make money. Second, to help eliminate racial prejudice. And third, to put on jazz concerts and make records with the best jazz musicians in the world."
—CARLO WOLFF

Armstrong, Louis: *Compact Jazz,* Emarcy, 1957, 1992 • *Mack the Knife,* Pablo, 1957, 1990 • *Silver Collection,* Verve, 1957 • *Verve Jazz Masters 1,* Verve, 1994 • *See also* Fitzgerald, Ella; Peterson, Oscar.

Astaire, Fred: *The Astaire Story,* Verve, 1988 • *Steppin' Out: Astaire Sings,* Verve, 1994.

Baker, Chet: *See* Getz, Stan; Pace, Johnny.

Basie, Count: w/ Joe Williams, *Count Basie Swings—Joe Williams Sings,* Verve, 1955, 1993 • *Basie Jam,* Pablo, 1973, 1987 • w/ Joe Turner, *The Bosses,* Original Jazz Classics, 1974, 1994 • w/ Kansas City 3, *For the Second Time,* Original Jazz Classics, 1975, 1990 • *Jam Session at Montreux,* Pablo, 1975 • *The Basie Big Band,* Pablo, 1975 • w/ Zoot Sims, *Basie and Zoot,* Original Jazz Classics, 1976, 1994 • *Basie Jam 2,* Original Jazz Classics, 1976, 1991 • *Basie Jam 3,* Original Jazz Classics, 1976, 1991 • *Kansas City 5,* Original Jazz Classics, 1977, 1996 • w/ Dizzy Gillespie, *The Gifted Ones,* Original Jazz Classics, 1977, 1996 • w/ Kansas City 8, *Get Together,* Pablo, 1979, 1986 • *Kansas City 7,* Original Jazz Classics, 1980 • *Kansas City Shout,* Pablo, 1980, 1987 • *Kansas City 6,* Original Jazz Classics, 1981 • *Mostly Blues and Some Others,* Pablo, 1983, 1987 • *Basie and Friends,* Pablo, 1988 • w/ Roy Eldridge, *Loose Walk,* Pablo, 1988 • *Verve Jazz Masters 2,* Verve, 1994 • *See also* Basie, Count, and His Orchestra; Basie, Count, and Oscar Peterson; Count Basie Big Band; Count Basie Trio; Fitzgerald, Ella; Peterson, Oscar; Vaughan, Sarah.

Basie, Count, and His Orchestra: *Basie in London,* Verve, 1956, 1987 • *April in Paris,* Mobile Fidelity Sound Lab, 1956, 1995 • *I Told You So,* Original Jazz Classics, 1976, 1995 • *Prime Time,* Pablo, 1977, 1987 • *On the Road,* Original Jazz Classics, 1979, 1995 • *Fancy Pants,* Pablo, 1983, 1986 • *88 Basie Street,* Original Jazz Classics, 1983,

Gaillard, Slim: *Laughing in Rhythm: The Best of the Verve Years,* Verve, 1994.

Getz, Stan: *Stan Getz Plays,* Verve, 1952, 1988 • *At the Shrine,* Verve, 1954, 1992 • *Plays,* Verve, 1954 • w/ Lionel Hampton, *Hamp and Getz,* Verve, 1955 • w/ Gerry Mulligan, *Getz Meets Mulligan in Hi-Fi,* DCC Jazz, 1957, 1995 • w/ Chet Baker, *Stan Meets Chet,* Verve, 1958, 1996 • *Compact Jazz: Getz and Friends,* Verve, 1991 • *The Artistry of Stan Getz,* Vol. 1, Verve, 1991 • *The Artistry of Stan Getz,* Vol. 2, Verve, 1992 • *Verve Jazz Masters #8: Stan Getz,* Verve, 1994 • *East of the Sun: The West Coast Sessions,* Verve, 1996 • *Life in Jazz: A Musical Biography,* Verve, 1996 • *Best of the West Coast Sessions,* Verve, 1997.

Gillespie, Dizzy: w/ Sonny Rollins and Sonny Stitt, *Duets,* Verve, 1958, 1988 • w/ Stan Getz and Sonny Stitt, *For Musicians Only,* Verve, 1958, 1989 • w/ Sonny Rollins and Sonny Stitt, *Sonny Side Up,* Verve, 1958, 1986 • *Compact Jazz: Dizzy Gillespie,* Verve, 1964, 1992 • w/ Brown and Pass, *Dizzy's Big Four,* Original Jazz Classics, 1974, 1990 • *Dizzy's Party,* Original Jazz Classics, 1977, 1994 • w/ Freddie Hubbard and Clark Terry, *The Trumpet Summit Meets the Oscar Peterson Big 4,* Original Jazz Classics, 1980, 1990 • *Gillespiana/Carnegie Hall Concert,* Verve, 1993 • *Verve Jazz Masters 10,* Verve, 1994 • *Birks Works: The Verve Big-Band Sessions,* Verve, 1995 • *See also* Basie, Count; Carter, Benny; Eldridge, Roy; Peterson, Oscar; Turner, Big Joe.

Giuffre, Jimmy: *See* Konitz, Lee.

Grappelli, Stephane, and Stuff Smith: *Violins No End,* Original Jazz Classics, 1957, 1996.

Hampton, Lionel: *Compact Jazz,* Verve, 1955 • *See also* Getz, Stan; Tatum, Art.

Hawkins, Coleman: w/ Roy Eldridge, *At the Opera House,* Verve, 1957, 1994 • *Bean Stalkin',* Pablo, 1960, 1988 • *Sirius,* Original Jazz Classics, 1966, 1995.

Herman, Woody: *Compact Jazz,* Verve, 1963.

Hodges, Johnny: *Used to Be Duke,* Verve, 1956, 1991 • *At the Berlin Sportpalast,* Pablo, 1961, 1993 • *See also* Ellington, Duke.

Holiday, Billie: *The Billie Holiday Songbook,* Verve, 1952, 1986 • *Solitude,* Verve, 1952, 1993 • *Stormy Blues,* Verve, 1955, 1977 • *At Carnegie Hall,* Vol. 6, Verve, 1956, 1995 • *Songs for Distingue Lovers,* Verve, 1957 • *Compact Jazz,* Verve, 1987 • *Billie Holiday Story,* Vol. 3, *Recital by Billie,* Verve, 1994 • *Jazz at the Philharmonic,* Verve, 1994 • *Jazz 'Round Midnight,* Verve, 1994 • *Verve Jazz Masters 12,* Verve, 1994 • *All Or Nothing Al All,* Verve, 1995.

Hubbard, Freddie: w/ Oscar Peterson, *Face to Face,* Pablo, 1982, 1987 • *See also* Gillespie, Dizzy.

Jackson, Milt: w/ Milt Jackson Big 4, *At the Montreux Jazz Festival,* Original Jazz Classics, 1975, 1996 • *Night Mist,* Original Jazz Classics, 1981, 1995.

Jobim, Antonio Carlos: *Girl from Ipanema: The Antonio Carlos Jobim Songbook,* Verve, 1996.

Johnson, J.J.: *See* Pass, Joe.

Jones, Jo: *The Main Man,* Original Jazz Classics, 1977, 1995.

Kansas City 3: *See* Basie, Count.

Kansas City 8: *See* Basie, Count.

Konitz, Lee: w/ Jimmy Giuffre, *Lee Konitz Meets Jimmy Giuffre,* Verve, 1996.

Krupa, Gene: w/ Buddy Rich, *Krupa and Rich,* Verve, 1955, 1994 • *Drummer Man,* Verve, 1956, 1992.

Mann, Herbie: *Verve Masters 56,* Verve, 1996.

Modern Jazz Quartet: *Together Again! Live at Montreux Jazz Festival '82,* Pablo, 1982, 1987.

Mulligan, Gerry: w/ Paul Desmond, *Quartet,* Verve, 1957, 1993 • w/ Ben Webster, *Gerry Mulligan Meets Ben Webster,* Verve, 1959, 1963 • *The Silver Collection: Gerry Mulligan Meets the Saxophonists,* Verve, 1960 • *Legacy,* N2K, 1997 • *See also* Getz, Stan.

O'Day, Anita: *Pick Yourself Up,* Verve, 1956, 1992 • *Swings with Cole Porter and Billy May,* Verve, 1960, 1991 • *Compact Jazz,* Verve, 1993.

O'Farrill, Chico: *Cuban Blues: The Chico O'Farrill Sessions,* Verve, 1996.

Oscar Peterson Trio: *Jazz at the Philharmonic,* Verve, 1953 • *At the Stratford Shakespearean Festival,* Verve, 1956, 1993 • *Nigerian Marketplace,* Pablo, 1982 • *At the Concertgebouw,* Verve, 1994 • *Plays My Fair Lady/Music from Fiorello!* Verve, 1994 • *See also* Peterson, Oscar; Stitt, Sonny.

Pace, Johnny: *Chet Baker Introduces Johnny Pace,* Riverside, 1959, 1992.

Parker, Charlie: *1946 Jazz at the Philharmonic,* Verve, 1946, 1992 • *Jazz at the Philharmonic 1949,* Verve, 1949, 1993 • *Jam Session,* Verve, 1952, 1990 • *The Verve Years (1950–1951),* Verve, 1976 • *Compact Jazz,* Verve, 1987 • *The Cole Porter Songbook,* Verve, 1991 • *Verve Jazz Masters 15,* Verve, 1994 • *Charlie Parker with Strings: The Master Takes,* Verve, 1995 • *Confirmation: Best of the Verve Years,* Verve, 1995 • *South of the Border: The Verve Latin-Jazz Sessions,* Verve, 1995.

Pass, Joe: *Virtuoso,* Vol. 4, Pablo, 1973 • *Live at Akron University,* Pablo, 1974 • *Portraits of Duke Ellington,* Pablo, 1974 • w/ Herb Ellis, *Two for the Road,* Pablo, 1974 • *Virtuoso,* Pablo, 1974, 1987 • *Best Of,* Pablo, 1982, 1991 • *Ira, George and Joe,* Original Jazz Classics, 1982, 1995 • w/ J.J. Johnson, *We'll Be Together Again,* Pablo, 1996 • *Blues Dues (Live at Long Beach City College),* Original Jazz Classics, 1998 • *See also* Fitzgerald, Ella; Peterson, Oscar; Thielemans, Toots.

Peterson, Oscar: *Plays Count Basie,* Verve, 1956, 1993 • w/ Louis Armstrong, *Louis Armstrong Meets Oscar Peterson,* Verve, 1957, 1981 • *Cole Porter Songbook,* Verve, 1959 • *Jazz Portrait of Frank Sinatra,* Verve, 1959 • *Plays Porgy and Bess,*

Verve, 1959, 1993 • *Night Train,* Verve, 1962 • w/ Pass and Pedersen, *The Trio,* Pablo, 1973, 1987 • w/ Joe Pass and Ray Brown, *The Giants,* Original Jazz Classics, 1974, 1995 • w/ Dizzy Gillespie, *Oscar Peterson and Dizzy Gillespie,* Pablo, 1975, 1987 • w/ Joe Pass, *Porgy and Bess,* Original Jazz Classics, 1976, 1995 • *Jousts,* Original Jazz Classics, 1978, 1995 • *The Personal Touch,* Pablo, 1982, 1988 • w/ Oscar Peterson Four, *If You Could See Me Now,* Pablo, 1983 • w/ Milt Jackson, *Two of the Few,* Original Jazz Classics, 1983, 1992 • w/ Oscar Peterson Quartet, *A Tribute to My Friends,* Pablo, 1984, 1996 • w/ N.H. Pedersen, *Digital at Montreux,* Pablo, 1989 • *The History of An Artist,* Pablo, 1993 • *Verve Jazz Masters 16,* Verve, 1994 • *The Gershwin Songbooks,* Verve, 1996 • *The Song Is You: The Best of the Verve Songbooks,* Verve, 1996 • *Ultimate Oscar Peterson,* Verve, 1998 • *See also* Carter, Benny; DeFranco, Buddy; Fitzgerald, Ella; Hubbard, Freddie; Oscar Peterson Trio.

Phillips, Flip: *Flip Wails: The Best of the Verve Years,* Verve, 1994.

Powell, Bud: *Compact Jazz,* Verve, 1993 • *Ultimate Bud Powell,* Verve, 1998.

Ray Bryant Trio: *All Blues,* Original Jazz Classics, 1978, 1995.

Rich, Buddie: w/ His Orchestra, *This One's for Basie,* Verve, 1956 • *Compact Jazz,* Verve, 1961 • *See also* Krupa, Gene; Tatum, Art.

Riddle, Nelson: *See* Fitzgerald, Ella.

Sims, Zoot: *Soprano Sax,* Pablo, 1976, 1996 • *Hawthorne Nights,* Original Jazz Classics, 1977, 1995 • *For Lady Day,* Pablo, 1978, 1991 • w/ Zoot Sims Four, *The Innocent Years,* Original Jazz Classics, 1995 • *The Swinger,* Original Jazz Classics, 1995 • *See also* Basie, Count.

Stitt, Sonny: *Sits In with the Oscar Peterson Trio,* Verve, 1959, 1991.

Tatum, Art: w/ Lionel Hampton and Buddie Rich, *The Tatum Group Masterpieces,* Vols. 1–8, Pablo, 1954/1955/1956, 1990 • *Best Of,* Pablo, 1983 • *The Complete Pablo Solo Masterpieces,* Pablo, 1991.

Terry, Clark: *Memories of Duke,* Original Jazz Classics, 1980, 1990 • *Yes, the Blues,* Original Jazz Classics, 1981, 1995 • *See also* Eldridge, Roy; Gillespie, Dizzy.

Thielemans, Toots: w/ Joe Pass, *Live in the Netherlands,* Pablo, 1980.

Tormé, Mel: *Tormé,* Verve, 1958, 1992 • *Compact Jazz,* Verve, 1961 • *The Mel Tormé Collection,* Rhino, 1996.

Turner, Big Joe: *Life Ain't Easy,* Pablo, 1974 • *Everyday I Have the Blues,* Original Jazz Classics, 1975, 1991 • w/ Dizzy Gillespie, *The Trumpet Meets Joe Turner,* Original Jazz Classics, 1975, 1990 • *In the Evening,* Original Jazz Classics, 1976, 1995 • w/ Jimmy Witherspoon, *Patcha, Patcha All Night Long,* Original Jazz Classics, 1985, 1996 • *Stormy Monday,* Pablo, 1991 • *Big, Bad and Blue: The Big Joe Turner Anthology,* Rhino, 1994 • *See also* Basie, Count.

Vaughan, Sarah: *How Long Has This Been Going On?,* Pablo, 1978, 1987 • *Duke Ellington Songbook One,* Pablo, 1980, 1987 • *Duke Ellington Songbook Two,* Pablo, 1980, 1987 • w/ Count Basie, *Send in the Clowns,* Pablo, 1981 • *The Best Of,* Pablo, 1983, 1990.

Vinson, Eddie Cleanhead: *I Want a Little Girl,* Pablo, 1981, 1995.

Webster, Ben: *King of the Tenors,* Verve, 1954, 1993 • *Ben Webster and Associates,* Verve, 1959, 1988 • w/ Harry Carney, *Music for Loving: Ben Webster with Strings,* Verve, 1995 • *Music with Feeling,* Verve, 1995 • *The Soul of Ben Webster,* Verve, 1995 • *See also* Mulligan, Gerry.

Williams, Joe: *See* Basie, Count.

Wilson, Teddy: *See* Young, Lester.

Witherspoon, Jimmy: *See* Turner, Big Joe.

Young, Lester: *Complete Aladdin Sessions,* Blue Note, 1948 • w/ Harry Sweets Edison, *Pres and Sweets,* Verve, 1955, 1991 • *Jazz Giants '56,* Verve, 1956, 1992 • w/ Teddy Wilson, *Pres and Teddy,* Verve, 1956 • w/ Lester Young Trio, *Lester Young Trio,* Verve, 1994.

COLLECTIONS

Jazz at the Philharmonic: The First Concert, Verve, 1944, 1994.

The Jazz Scene, Verve, 1950, 1994.

Jazz at the Philharmonic: Hartford, 1953, Pablo, 1953.

Jazz at the Philharmonic: Stockholm '55, Pablo, 1955, 1990.

Jazz at the Philharmonic: The Greatest Jazz Concert in the World, Pablo, 1967, 1989.

Jazz at the Philharmonic: London, 1969, Pablo, 1969, 1989.

Jazz at the Philharmonic: At the Montreux Jazz Festival, Pablo, 1975, 1990.

The Jam Sessions: Montreux '77, Original Jazz Classics, 1977, 1989.

Jazz at the Philharmonic: Return to Happiness, Pablo, 1983.

Girl from Ipanema: The Jobim Songbook, Verve, 1996.

Wave: Jobim Songbook, Verve, 1996.

Blues in the Night: The Johnny Mercer Songbook, Verve, 1997.

James William Guercio

James William Guercio (born in 1945 in Chicago) is famous for his seminal work with the top horn-driven rock bands of the '60s: the Buckinghams; Blood, Sweat and Tears; and Chicago. In his dual role as Chicago's manager and producer of their first 11 albums,

Guercio launched the career of one of the most successful bands in history, yielding sales of 200 million.

Guercio began as a guitarist, and played with John Klemmer and Mitch Ryder as a teenager. He received classical training as a composition major in college and then moved to Los Angeles, where he worked with Dick Clark, played guitar with Chad and Jeremy (for whom he wrote the song "Distant Shores"), and was a session guitarist on numerous recordings.

"I played guitar with Frank Zappa [see entry] during that time," Guercio recalls, "and worked with him to put together the band that became the Mothers of Invention. Originally we had four guitarists including Frank and me, and the Mothers' Auxilliary, which was a horn section."

In the meantime, Guercio was producing the Buckinghams and scored a string of AM radio hits in 1967, including "Don't You Care," (No. 6), "Hey Baby (They're Playing Our Song)" (No. 12), and "Susan" (No. 11).

"Shortly after the Buckinghams," Guercio recalls, "I brought Chicago out to L.A., rented them a house, and gave them each $75 a week, all out of my Buckinghams money. I got them a job playing the Whiskey. I was living up in Topanga Canyon, where a lot of musicians and actors and artists were, and one night I was invited to a barbecue. The Firesign Theater was there. So were Janis Joplin and Jim Morrison, and they got into a huge fight. Morrison's girlfriend got pissed off and tried to leave but her car had a flat tire.

"So I'm sitting there changing Morrison's girlfriend's flat tire, and Bennett Glotzer, BS&T's manager, came out and asked me to produce Blood, Sweat and Tears' next album. I told him the next album I wanted to produce was for Chicago. Bennett said that if I would do BS&T, he would get me a deal for Chicago. I finally agreed.

"For three or four months, I commuted to New York where we recorded their second album, Blood, Sweat and Tears [No. 1]. They were difficult sessions, and I was very hard on that band. But most of those tracks were done in just one take. When I finished and delivered the album to CBS, they accused me of wasting their money. Nobody knew what it was; it wasn't jazz, it wasn't rock. CBS just about fired me.

"They canceled my studio time for Chicago. I said, 'There are three No. 1 records on this Chicago album I want to make, and none of your guys know what they are talking about.' So they let me go ahead with it. We recorded all of Chicago Transit Authority [No. 17] in 15 days: 10 days of recording, 5 days of mixing."

On the technical side, Guercio was a key player in sparking a revolution in recording. An engineer himself—he worked on Paul McCartney's (see entry) Ram—Guercio knew how to select from the best recording engineers of the day, collaborating first with Fred Catero and later with Wayne Tarnowsky and Phil Ramone (see entry).

Blood, Sweat and Tears and the first five Chicago albums were part of a movement in recording to render instruments in separable parts of the stereo soundscape, the goal being that a well-attuned listener could follow an individual horn part by locating it in a unique position of the stereo field. Previously, horns and drum kits tended to be recorded in a single, densely packed part of the stereo field (for example, James Brown and Stax/Volt). In 1969 and 1970, Guercio and Stevie Wonder (see entry) independently began to experiment with letting horns and drums occupy a much larger space in the mix, spreading them across the stereo field.

The result was an unprecedented clarity, and the beginnings of a hyperrealism that listeners take for granted today. In addition, Guercio and Wonder made multiple passes on tape for certain parts—unison overdubbing—to create a thicker texture. The combined result is that when the horns come in on a Guercio record, they sound enormous.

All too frequently, what makes a pop song enjoyable and compelling on the first listening makes it intolerable on the hundredth. One of the most difficult things a producer and arranger can do is generate hooks and melodic phrases that draw the listener in early on, yet resist becoming stale too quickly. When Guercio and his bands got it right, they were among the top in their field: the trumpet fanfares opening "Spinning Wheel" (No. 2), the locomotive guitar riff of "25 or 6 to 4" (No. 4), the horn obbligatos in "Make Me Smile" (No. 9) and "Does Anybody Really Know What Time It Is?" (No. 7) have all worn exceedingly well.

The first three Chicago albums blended uptempo rockers, jazz fusion, experimentalism, and ballads; later ones tended to lean on the ballads that had proved to be commercial successes for the band, emphasizing the exotic, smoky sensuality of Peter Cetera's voice over the gritty realism of Terry Kath's or the honesty and familiarity of Robert Lamm's.

Guercio managed the band as well as producing all their output until an uncomfortable split in 1977. With his personal share of Chicago's royalties (which exceeded the take of any individual member), Guercio built Caribou Studios in the Rocky Mountains. He owns, by his own reckoning, the largest cattle ranch in all of Colorado.

In the studio, Guercio was always very much in charge of the sessions, and toward the end of his Chicago days, the band members came in individually or in small groups to record at times the producer set. "After some point," Guercio explains, "I seldom had all of the guys in the studio at once because of the drugs. I don't do any drugs and never have—it really bothered me. When they started putting their dealers' names down as co-writers, that was the last straw."

Guercio concludes, "In retrospect, I was very rough on these kids. I wanted to be Stravinsky, I wanted to be Aaron Copland, and so I did it with them." —DANIEL J. LEVITIN

Beach Boys: *L.A. (Light Album)*, CBS, 1979 • *Good Vibrations: Thirty Years of the Beach Boys*, Capitol, 1993.

Blood, Sweat and Tears: *Blood, Sweat and Tears*, Columbia, 1968 • "And When I Die," Columbia, 1969 • "Spinning Wheel," Columbia, 1969 • "You've Made Me So Very Happy," Columbia, 1969 • *Greatest Hits*, Columbia, 1972.

Buckinghams, The: "Don't You Care," Columbia, 1967 • "Hey Baby (They're Playing Our Song)," Columbia, 1967 • "Mercy, Mercy, Mercy," Columbia, 1967 • "Susan," Columbia, 1967 • *Portraits*, CBS, 1968 • *Time and Changes*, CBS, 1970.

Chicago: *Chicago Transit Authority*, Columbia, 1968 • "25 or 6 to 4," Columbia, 1970 • *Chicago II*, Columbia, 1970 • "Does Anybody Really Know What Time It Is?," Columbia, 1970 • "Make Me Smile," Columbia, 1970 • "Beginnings," Columbia, 1971 • *Chicago at Carnegie Hall*, Columbia, 1971 • *Chicago III*, Columbia, 1971 • "Colour My World," Columbia, 1971 • "Free," Columbia, 1971 • "Lowdown," Columbia, 1971 • *Chicago V*, Columbia, 1972 • "Questions 67 and 68," Columbia, 1972 • "Saturday in the Park," Columbia, 1972 • *Chicago VI*, Columbia, 1973 • "Dialogue (Part I and II)," Columbia, 1973 • "Feelin' Stronger Every Day," Columbia, 1973 • "(I've Been) Searchin' So Long," Columbia, 1974 • "Call on Me," Columbia, 1974 • *Chicago VII*, Columbia, 1974 • "I've Been Searchin' So Long," Columbia, 1974 • "Just You 'n' Me," Columbia, 1974 • *Chicago VIII*, Columbia, 1975 • "Harry Truman," Columbia, 1975 • "Wishing You Were Here," Columbia, 1975 • "Another Rainy Day in New York City," Columbia, 1976 • *Chicago IX Chicago's Greatest Hits*, Columbia, 1976 • *Chicago X*, Columbia, 1976 • "If You Leave Me Now," Columbia, 1976 • "Old Days," Columbia, 1976 • "Baby, What a Big Surprise," Columbia, 1977 • *Chicago XI*, Columbia, 1977 • *Greatest Hits*, Vol. 2, Columbia, 1981 • *If You Leave Me Now*, Columbia, 1982.

Firesign Theater: *Shoes for Industry! The Best Of*, Legacy, 1993.

Gerard: *Gerard*, Caribou, 1976.

Illinois Speed Press: *The Illinois Speed Press*, CBS, 1968 • *Duet*, CBS, 1970.

Lake: *Ouch!* Caribou, 1981.

Mint Tattoo: *Mint Tattoo*, Dot, 1968.

Moondog: *Moondog*, CBS Masterworks, 1956, 1990.

Sailor: *Dressed for Drowning*, Caribou, 1980.

Wilson, Carl: *Carl Wilson*, Columbia, 1982.

COLLECTIONS

Electra Glide in Blue soundtrack, United Artists, 1973.

Brett Gurewitz

B rett Gurewitz caught the producing bug in the early '80s when he was recording with his punk band, Bad Religion. Besides Bad Religion, he has produced a number of punk standards by Dag Nasty, Down By Law, L7, NoFX, Pennywise, and Rancid, and owns Epitaph Records.

"I was captivated by recording and mixing," he says from the Los Angeles headquarters of Epitaph. "I have always dabbled in different fine arts, such as painting, music, and poetry. I was always attracted to creative pursuits, and producing just seemed like this magic thing. You get to paint with sound. It was perfect, it really clicked with me."

Although he played guitar with Bad Religion for years, Gurewitz says he never considered himself a musician. "I enjoyed songwriting," he says. "Being a songwriter and an intuitive musician helped me become a good producer. I tend to follow my instincts and they tend to lead me in the right direction."

He feels his intuition is his strongest asset. "My philosophy is that as a producer my job is to be a conduit," he says. "It is my job to help the group to realize their vision and capture on tape the essence of the way they perceive themselves. I don't believe that it is my job to put any of myself into their project."

One way Gurewitz made sure he could make bands comfortable in the studio was to master lo-fi technology. He considers himself a sounding board for technology and ideas. "Recording studios are intimidating and mysterious places," he says, noting that he also engineers. "I wouldn't know how to produce without engineering."

Creating the Epitaph label helped him as producer and engineer. "What it has done is given me a chance to spend time in a recording studio with other world-class engineers," he says, citing Andy Wallace (see entry) and Tom Lord-Alge.

"I feel technology needs to work for us," he says. "We cannot be in a position to work for it. I like a lot of the vintage Class A discrete electronics. I collect some vintage tube compressors, pre-amps, and microphones. The best-sounding records are not super technology; some are made with vintage gear, like *Sgt. Pepper's*. If one becomes too dependent on technology, one becomes less reliant on one's ears."

He would like to work with the Foo Fighters. He would like to produce George Harrison, even the Wallflowers. "I love pop music," Gurewitz says. "Punk rock is really pop music, it is certainly short, sweet, and to the point."

Gurewitz thinks he's gotten better as a producer. One reason for this is that he no longer does it full-time. "When you are doing it full-time," he says, "you don't have time to listen to records, and when that happens you are in trouble. You start to lose perspective and start forgetting what it is that you are doing. Now, I only make a few records a year and when I do, I have excellent perspective because throughout my day I listen to tons of records—ones I am making, ones that I'm buying for my leisure time, or ones that are in my collection.

"If you have been in the studio for a week straight, there's nothing as beneficial as grabbing the Rolling Stones' *Sticky Fingers* and popping it on," Gurewitz says. "All of a sudden, you say, 'Oh, yeah, this is what great rock and roll sounds like.' It puts you back into reality."
—DAVID JOHN FARINELLA

Bad Religion: *How Could Hell Be Any Worse?*, Epitaph, 1982 • *Into the Unknown*, Epitaph, 1983 • *Back to the Known* (EP), Epitaph, 1984 • *Suffer*, Epitaph, 1988 • *Control*, Epitaph, 1989 • *Against the Grain*, Epitaph, 1990 • "I Want Something More/Modern Man," Nemesis, 1990 • *Generator*, Epitaph, 1991 • *Recipe for Hate*, Epitaph, 1993.

Bators, Stiv: *L.A., L.A.*, Bomp, 1994.

Cacavas, Chris, and Junkyard Love: *Good Times*, Heyday, 1992.

Clawhammer: "Hey Old Lady and Bert's Song," FS, 1990 (*The Big One*) • *Ramwhale*, Sympathy for the Record Industry, 1992 • *Pablum*, Epitaph, 1993.

Dag Nasty: *Four on the Floor*, Epitaph, 1992.

Down By Law: *Down By Law*, Epitaph, 1991 • *Blue*, Epitaph, 1992.

Jughead's Revenge: *It's Lonely at the Bottom and Unstuck in Time*, B.Y.O., 1995.

L7: *L7*, Epitaph, 1987.

Little Kings: *Head First*, Epitaph, 1989.

NoFX: *Animal Liberation*, Epitaph, 1988 • *Ribbed*, Epitaph, 1990.

No Use for a Name: *Incognito*, New Red Archives, 1990.

Offspring, The: "Take It Like a Man," FS, 1990 (*The Big One*).

Pennywise: *About Time*, Epitaph, 1995.

Pietasters, The: *Willis*, Hellcat, 1997.

Pontiac Brothers: *Doll Hut/Fiesta en la Biblioteca*, Frontier, 1992.

Rancid: *Let's Go*, Epitaph, 1994.

Red Aunts: *#1 Chicken*, Epitaph, 1995.

Rich Kids on LSD: *Reactivate* (2 tracks), Epitaph, 1993.

Ruth Ruth: *Little Death*, Epitaph, 1996.

Tolman, Russ, and the Totem Polemen: *Goodbye Joe*, Skyclad, 1990.

Stephen Hague

At 16, Stephen Hague moved from his hometown of Portland, Maine, to Los Angeles to seek fame and fortune in the music business. After a year of painting cars, he hooked up with pop talent Walter Egan, for whom Hague played keyboards. After a marathon tour and an album (where he played on Egan's hit "Magnet and Steel") Hague and singer/songwriter Jules Shear put together Jules and the Polar Bears.

While they didn't sell many records, they made an impressive list of friends, and Hague started to collect home recording gear. One of his allies, Peter Gabriel, got Hague his first solo producing gig. In 1979, Hague decided to leave Los Angeles for Boston. Soon after he got a phone call from Gabriel's label, Charisma, asking him to produce the breakdance outfit Rock Steady Crew in New York. "I think it was because I was over here that they asked me to do it," he says. "It was a Top 5 hit in England and I had a hit as a producer."

Hague was then tapped to produce the World Famous Supreme Team and later worked with Malcolm McLaren on his "Madam Butterfly" release. His next call was from Orchestral Manoeuvres in the Dark; all of a sudden, Hague had five hits to his name.

His next project, the Pet Shop Boys, put him at the top of the charts in both England and the U.S. Hague had so much success in England that he moved there in 1985. In 1993, he bought a house in Woodstock, New York. He splits his time between the two countries.

Hague says taking on the producer's role was not his ultimate goal. "All through that musician time, I was making pretty good dough, buying Teac 4-tracks and assembling home gear. I certainly never wanted to be an engineer, although now I am by default. With the Polar Bears, it wasn't so much that we wanted to be producers, we just wanted to make our own records. Jules had the vision and I had a few technical chops, so we ended up making those records."

He feels fortunate he had time to grow before he became a successful producer. "It was kind of cool," he says, "because I started having hits relatively late. I still play and write and sing on records I produce, depending on what's needed, although my chops are practically nonexistent on all the instruments I used to play quite well."

Although he contributes to some of the albums he produces, Hague tries not to put his stamp on an album. "When I first started having successful records, I became a little self-aware," he says. "People were saying, 'Oh, you've got a little bit of a sound.' As I seasoned a bit and got used to the job, I realized that wasn't the issue. If the artist was happy, I was happy.

"One reason I might have gotten bagged a little bit in the mid-'80s is I was making records of a certain style. They tended to be quite programmed, with bits of live playing, and I was doing quite a bit of the programming, so I suppose that came through in the final version."

He doesn't feel he has to be Mr. Do It All in the studio anymore, however: "I think it was kind of an ego expression at the time, and I think it made for some good records."

Indeed. Hague almost single-handedly defined the mid-'80s and early '90s new wave synthesizer style. Albums by such bands as the Pet Shop Boys, Erasure, OMD, New Order, the Communards, and Siouxsie & the Banshees set trends. "When a producer goes through those periods—and you can see it happen to other people as they come up and establish themselves—the things you get sent for consideration for your next project tend to reflect what you just had a hit with on the radio," he reflects.

"I know a good song when I hear one," Hague says. "And because I didn't come up as an engineer but as a player, I think the sense of performance from players and singers in response to a good song is important."
—DAVID JOHN FARINELLA

Almond, Marc: *Treasure Box*, EMI, 1995.

Banderas: *Ripe*, London, 1991.

Blur: *Parklife*, SBK, 1994.

Bronski Beat: *Read My Lips*, London, 1990.

Chapterhouse: *Whirlpool* (1 track), Dedicated/RCA, 1991.

Communards, The: *Red*, London, 1987 • "Tomorrow," London, 1987.

Cracknell, Sarah: *Lipslide*, Gut, 1997.

DeLory, Donna: *Donna DeLory*, MCA, 1992, 1993.

Dubstar: *Goodbye*, Polydor, 1997.

Easton, Elliot: *Change No Change*, Elektra, 1985.

Electronic: "Feel Every Beat," Warner Bros., 1991 • "Disappointed," Warner Bros., 1992.

Erasure: "A Little Respect," Sire/Reprise, 1988 • "A Little Respect" (remix), Sire/Reprise, 1988 • "Chains of Love," Sire/Reprise, 1988 • "Ship of Fools," American Gramaphone, 1988 • *The Innocents*, Sire/Reprise, 1988 • *Pop! The First 20 Hits*, Sire, 1992.

Flesh for Lulu: "I Go Crazy," Capitol, 1987 • *Long Live the New Flesh*, Capitol, 1987.

Gleaming Spires: "Are You Ready for the Sex Girls," Posh Boy, 1981 (*Rodney on the ROQ*, Vol. 2) • *Songs of the Spires*, Posh Boy, 1982 • *Walk on Well-Lighted Streets*, PVC, 1983.

Gray, Gregory: *Euroflake in Silverlake*, EMI America, 1995.

Harket, Morten: "Can't Take My Eyes off You," Warner Bros., 1993 (*Coneheads* soundtrack).

Hollywood Beyond: *If*, Warner Bros., 1987.

House of Love: *House of Love*, Creation/Fontana, 1988.

James: *Whiplash*, Fontana, 1997.

Jules and the Polar Bears: *Got No Breeding*, Columbia, 1978 • *Fenetics*, Columbia, 1979 • *Bad for Business*, Columbia, 1980, 1996.

lang, k.d. w/ Andy Bell, "No More Tears (Enough Is Enough)," Warner Bros., 1993 (*Coneheads* soundtrack).

Manbreak: *Come and See*, ALMO, 1997 • "Kop Karma (Get Up)," ALMO, 1997.

Manic Street Preachers: *Everything Must Go*, Epic, 1996.

McLaren, Malcolm: "Madam Butterfly," Island, 1984 • *Opera House*, Island, 1984.

New Order: *Substance*, Qwest, 1987 • "True Faith," Qwest, 1987 • "Round and Round" (remix), Qwest, 1989 • "World in Motion," Qwest/WB, 1990 • *Republic*, Qwest/WB, 1993 • "Ruined in a Day," Qwest/WB, 1993 • "Spooky," Qwest/WB, 1993 • "World," Qwest/WB, 1993.

One Dove: *Morning Dove White*, FFRR, 1993.

Orchestral Manoeuvres in the Dark (OMD): *Crush*, Virgin, 1985 • "So in Love," Virgin/A&M, 1985 • "(Forever) Live and Die," Virgin, 1986 • *The Pacific Age*, Virgin, 1986 • *Shame* (EP), Virgin, 1987 • *Best Of*, A&M, 1988 • "Dreaming," Atlantic, 1988.

Other Two: "Selfish," Qwest/Reprise, 1994 • *The Other Two and You*, Qwest/Reprise, 1994.

Papa Wemba: *Emotion*, Real World/Caroline, 1995.

Pere Ubu: *Cloudland* (4 tracks), Fontana, 1989.

Pet Shop Boys: "West End Girls," EMI America, 1985 • *Disco*, EMI America, 1986 • "Love Comes Quickly," EMI America, 1986 • "Opportunities (Let's Make Lots of Money)," EMI America, 1986 • *Please*, EMI America, 1986 • *Actually* (2 tracks), Manhattan/EMI, 1987 • "It's a Sin" (remix), EMI America, 1987 • w/ Dusty Springfield, "What Have I Done to Deserve This?," EMI America, 1987 • *Discography: The Complete Singles Collection*, EMI America, 1991 • "DJ Culture," EMI, 1991 • "Go West" (remix), EMI, 1993 • *Relentless* (EP), Parlophone, 1993 • *Very*, EMI, 1993 • "Can You Forgive Her," EMI, 1994 • "I

Wouldn't Normally Do This Kind of Thing," EMI, 1994 • "Liberation," EMI, 1994 • *Disco 2,* EMI, 1995.

Public Image Limited (PIL): *9* (5 tracks), Virgin, 1989 • "Disappointed," Virgin, 1989 • "Warrior," Virgin America, 1989 (*Slaves of New York* soundtrack) • *Don't Ask Me* (EP), Virgin, 1990 • *Greatest Hits So Far,* Atlantic, 1990.

Robertson, Robbie: *Storyville,* DGC, 1991.

Rudi: "Crimson," Posh Boy, 1982 (*Rodney on the ROQ,* Vol. 3).

Shear, Jules: *Horse of a Different Color (1976–1989),* Razor & Tie, 1994.

Shelley, Pete: *Heaven and the Sea,* Mercury, 1986.

Signals: "Gotta Let Go," Posh Boy, 1982 (*Rodney on the ROQ,* Vol. 3).

Sigue Sigue Sputnik: *Dress for Excess,* Atlantic, 1988, 1989 • "Albinoni vs. Star Wars," Atlantic, 1989.

Siouxsie & the Banshees: "Fear (of the Unknown)," Geffen, 1991 • "Kiss Them for Me," Geffen, 1991 • *Superstition,* Geffen, 1991.

Slow Children: *Slow Children,* Ensign, 1981 • "Spring in Fialta," RCA, 1981 (*Blits*).

Somerville, Jimmy: *Read My Lips,* London, 1990 • *The Singles Collection, 1984–1990,* London, 1990.

Springfield, Dusty: *Anthology,* PolyGram, 1997.

Sweet, Matthew: *Inside,* Columbia, 1986.

Wiedlin, Jane: *Fur,* EMI/Manhattan, 1988 • "Rush Hour," EMI/Manhattan, 1988 • "Fur," RNA, 1991 (*Tame Yourself*) • *Very Best Of,* EMI, 1993.

Roy Halee

Roy Halee was a groundbreaker in blurring the lines between producer and engineer. After he joined Columbia Records in the early '60s, he spent his first two years editing classical music. Then he went into pop music, reducing multitrack tapes to 2-track masters.

Eventually, his contacts with artists led to more engineering and production. Artists would notice Halee's engineering and think, "This guy is contributing more than the producer and he should be producing these records," he says.

"I think I broke a lot of ground for engineers to be able to get into production," says Halee, who is best known for his work on Simon and Garfunkel records, engineering several classic Byrds discs and Bob Dylan sessions.

He says Clive Davis signed him to a production agreement in the '60s, "which was unheard of because

of union laws. So I really broke ground for a lot of guys who had the chops to get into that field."

Besides figuring heavily in the production of Simon and Garfunkel records, Halee says he also produced Peaches and Herb records for Epic that he never got production credit for. He also produced the Sparrow, the band John Kay headed before forming Steppenwolf. He didn't get production credit for that, either, "but that's sour grapes."

The engineer is "subservient to the producer," says Halee. "The producer calls the shots and wears many, many hats. An engineer's only function is sound. A lot of engineers get in trouble by crossing the line when they shouldn't. There is a line there, without a doubt. The producer's role is the sound, the artist, the arrangement, the songs. He's the captain of the ship, or should be.

"My first session was working with Bob Dylan on the 'Like A Rolling Stone' album," says Halee, referring to Dylan's *Highway 61 Revisited* disc of 1965. "That single and album were my first recording sessions just prior to meeting Paul Simon [see entry]. It was not fun working with Bob Dylan. It was not an enjoyable expe-

rience. Sloppy, you know, just sloppy. The standard of recording was low, and you had to be drunk—he drank a lot and he was not a nice person to be around."

Simon and Garfunkel, by contrast, "were always nice to be around," says Halee, who has been working with Simon for more than 35 years. Not only did he claim a "major engineering credit" for Simon's epochal *Graceland* album of 1986; Halee says he produced that, and its 1990 successor, *Rhythm of the Saints,* with Simon. On most of Simon's works, particularly since the '70s, Halee either is listed as having engineered them or as having supervised the recording. Halee also worked with Simon on *The Capeman,* a musical Simon wrote with Pulitzer Prize–winning poet Derek Walcott.

The connection to musicals is a natural for Halee, a New York native whose parents, Royal and Rebekah, were theatrical professionals. His mother starred with Al Jolson at the Winter Garden in the '20s. His father was the original singing voice of cartoon characters Mighty Mouse and those nattering magpies, Heckle and Jeckle, and was a legitimate tenor who also sang with Fred Waring and the Pennsylvanians.

Halee used to play trumpet, can read music but doesn't write it. "I wish I did." Besides his work for Columbia, he produced Cyndi Lauper's first effort, a record by Blue Angel. "Very bad band, great singer," says Halee. He also engineered the Lovin' Spoonful and worked with the Cyrkle (remember "Red Rubber Ball"?), who were managed by Brian Epstein. "I met Brian and thought I might have a shot at working with the Beatles," Halee says. "That never worked out. That was a bit frustrating."

Other artists he worked with include Blood, Sweat and Tears and Laura Nyro, who died of cancer on April 8, 1997. He calls Nyro "the great unsung female artist of all time." When he worked for ABC Records, he signed Stephen Bishop to the label, "and his first album was very successful. I also produced the Mark-Almond Band when I was there, and was involved with Rufus and Chaka Khan in a production capacity."

Halee, who says "classical music is where the legitimate recording's going on today," doesn't think much of current pop. "When somebody goes on stage to pick up a Grammy Award and brings 12 producers along with him, I don't think much of that," Halee says. "It's not about cultivating artists anymore, or about investing in talent. If one album doesn't make it, the second might, or the third, or the fourth—those days are gone forever."

Why? "Money," Halee says. "The Goddard Liebersons are no longer around. The Mitch Millers [see entry] of the world are gone. It's like comic books now. Let's put out a comic book and see how well it does."

When he was in the thick of the business 20, 30 years ago, "they would sign a young writer knowing full well they wouldn't have success for two or three years," Halee says. "But they knew they would have success because they believed in the talent of the people they were signing." —CARLO WOLFF

Big Wha-Koo: *The Big Wha-Koo,* ABC, 1977.

Blood, Sweat and Tears: *Blood, Sweat and Tears III,* Columbia, 1970 • "Hi-De-Ho," Columbia, 1970 • *Blood, Sweat and Tears IV,* Columbia, 1971 • *Greatest Hits,* Columbia, 1972 • *Brand New Day,* ABC, 1977.

Blue Angel: *Blue Angel,* Polydor, 1980.

Brickell, Edie: *Picture Perfect Morning,* Geffen, 1994.

Garfunkel, Art: "All I Know," Columbia, 1973 • *Angel Clare,* Columbia, 1973 • *Scissors Cut,* Columbia, 1981 • *Garfunkel: Best Of,* Columbia, 1990.

Hammond, Albert: *Albert Hammond,* Mums, 1974.

Hill, Dan: *If Dreams Had Wings,* Epic, 1980.

Journey: *Journey,* Columbia, 1977 • *In the Beginning,* Columbia, 1979.

Littlejohn: *Littlejohn,* Epic, 1971.

Mark-Almond Band: *To the Heart,* ABC, 1976 • *The Best Of,* Rhino, 1991.

Nile, Willie: *Willie Nile,* Arista, 1980.

Nyro, Laura: *New York Tendaberry,* Columbia, 1969 • *Stoned Soul Picnic: The Best Of,* Legacy, 1997.

Pomeranz, David: *The Truth of Us,* Pacific, 1980.

Roches, The: *Nurds,* Warner Bros., 1980.

Rufus: *Numbers,* ABC, 1979.

Rufus and Chaka Khan: *Street Player,* ABC, 1978 • *The Very Best of Rufus and Chaka Khan,* MCA, 1996.

Scaggs, Boz: *My Time,* Columbia, 1972 • *Hits!* Columbia, 1980.

Silverstein, Shel: *Freakin' at the Freaker's Ball,* CBS, 1969.

Simon and Garfunkel: *Bookends,* Columbia, 1968 • "Mrs. Robinson," Columbia, 1968 • "The Boxer," Columbia, 1969 • "Bridge over Troubled Water," Columbia, 1970 • *Bridge over Troubled Waters,* Columbia, 1970 • "Cecelia," Columbia, 1970 • "El Condor Pasa," Columbia, 1970 • *Collected Works,* Columbia, 1981, 1990 • *Reunion in Central Park,* Geffen, 1982 • *The Concert in Central Park,* Warner Bros., 1982, 1988.

Simon, Paul: "Mother and Child Reunion," Columbia, 1972 • *Paul Simon,* Columbia, 1972 • *There Goes Rhymin' Simon,* Columbia, 1973 • *Hearts and Bones,* Warner Bros., 1983 • *Negotiations and Love Songs (1971–1986),* Warner Bros., 1988 • *Paul Simon, 1964–1993,* Warner Bros., 1993 • *Songs from the Capeman,* Warner Bros., 1997.

Dave "Jam" Hall

Sometimes, a name says it all. That's certainly the case with R&B-pop music producer and songwriter Dave "Jam" Hall, who quietly rose to prominence during the early to mid-'90s with hits meshing soul and hip-hop sounds, including Madonna's "Human Nature," Mariah Carey's "Fantasy" (No. 1), Brownstone's "Grapevyne," Mary J. Blige's "You Remind Me" and "Reminisce," and Kenny Lattimore's "Never Too Busy."

Though Hall has formed his own company, the Sony-distributed Hall of Fame Records, he was an early associate of Sean "Puffy" Combs (see entry) and Combs's Bad Boy camp. While other producers were busy trying to draw from the drying well that was the new jack swing sound, folks like Hall and Combs were already moving on to something different. "I wasn't into the whole new jack swing thing and no one else was mixing the sounds I heard in my head, so I swung with what I felt was right for me," Hall has stated.

Hall's multilayered success was probably inevitable. At the age of 6, Hall started taking piano lessons from his father, and by high school he was sharing classes with the likes of Heavy D, Pete Rock, Al B. Sure, and Kyle West.

After graduating from SUNY Long Island with a degree in civil engineering, he saw himself heading toward the music business, knowing his big break would come. That break came in 1989, when Hall made one of his relatively few forays into straightforward rap with Brand Nubian's "Try to Do Me." Shortly afterward, he was on board with Eddie F. at Untouchables Entertainment, where a number of hits would follow.

Though Hall has worked with a number of established artists such as Madonna and Carey, his career is sprinkled with productions for budding talents he has helped foster. It was Hall, for example, who in 1992 helped put a then-unknown singer named Mary J. Blige on the map with early hits like "You Remind Me" (Blige's first hit), "Love No Limit," "My Love," and "Reminisce" (the latter co-produced with Combs). His productions for Blige helped her earn the title of "Queen of Hip-Hop Soul."

He also produced breakthrough hits for Intro ("Let Me Be the One," "So Many Reasons"), Jade ("If the Mood Is Right"), Usher ("The Many Ways"), and Horace Brown ("Taste Your Love"). Other new acts bearing his production include Michelle Valentine, Per-fect Blend, Assorted Phlavors, and Last Appeal.

"I love working with new talent because they are hungry for success, but I look for artists that I can nurture for the long haul. Gimmick groups aren't my thing," said Hall.

Hall has also excelled in remixes, including Michael Jackson's "Scream," LL Cool J's "Around the Way Girl," En Vogue's "Lies," and Taylor Dayne's "Can't Get Enough of Your Love."

His philosophy is a simple though concise one: "The music and the lyrics should stand on their own and come together to create a dope sound." But he believes the artists must give just as much. "When a consumer buys an artist's records, they are buying what that artist stands for musically. If you notice, artists who work with one to three producers per project are the ones who refine their sound and achieve long-lasting success. I ain't gonna try to make an artist come out of the box with something completely different. I prefer to keep improving on that artist's musical personality." —KEVIN JOHNSON

Assorted Phlavors: "Patience," Hall of Fame/Epic, 1996 • *Assorted Phlavors,* Hall of Fame/Epic, 1997.

Blige, Mary J.: *What's the 411?* (4 tracks), Uptown/MCA, 1992 • *What's the 411? The Remixes,* Uptown/MCA, 1993.

Brand Nubian: *One for All,* Elektra, 1990.

Brown, Horace: "Taste Your Love," Uptown, 1994 • *Horace Brown,* Motown, 1996.

Brownstone: *From the Bottom Up* (2 tracks), MJJ, 1995 • *Still Climbing,* Sony, 1997.

Carey, Mariah: *Music Box,* Columbia, 1993 • *Daydream,* Columbia, 1995 • "Fantasy," Columbia, 1995.

Changing Faces: *Changing Faces,* Spoiled Rotten/Big Beat, 1995.

Dayne, Taylor: "Can't Get Enough of Your Love" (remix), Arista, 1993.

En Vogue: "Lies" (remix), Atlantic, 1990 • *Remix to Sing,* EastWest, 1991.

Father MC: *Close to You,* Uptown/MCA, 1992.

Heavy D & the Boyz: *Peaceful Journey,* Uptown, 1991.

Hyman, Phyllis: *I Refuse to Be Lonely,* Volcano/Zoo, 1995.

Intro: *Intro,* Atlantic, 1993.

Jackson, Michael: "Scream" (remix), Epic, 1995.

Jade: *Mind, Body and Song,* Giant, 1995.

Joe: *Everything,* Mercury, 1993.

LL Cool J: "Around the Way Girl" (remix), Def Jam, 1991.

Lattimore, Kenny: *Kenny Lattimore,* Columbia, 1996 • "Never Too Busy," Columbia, 1996.

Madonna: *Bedtime Stories,* Maverick/Sire, 1994.

Mills, Stephanie: *Something Real,* MCA, 1992.

Peniston, CeCe: *Before I Lay (You Drive Me Crazy)* (EP), A&M,

1996 • *I'm Movin' On,* A&M, 1996 • "Movin' On," A&M, 1996.

Shinehead: *Sidewalk University,* Elektra, 1992.

Silk: "Now That I've Lost You," Elektra, 1995 • *Silk* (1 track), Elektra, 1995.

Terri and Monica: "Sexuality (If You Take Your Love)," Epic, 1996 • *Suga,* Epic, 1996.

Usher: "Final Goodbye," LaFace, 1994 • "The Many Ways," LaFace, 1994 • *Usher* (2 tracks), LaFace, 1994.

Veronica: *Rise,* Hola, 1997.

Rick Hall

Not the easiest person to get along with, Rick Hall admits to a lot of turnover at Fame Recording Studios, the legendary musical hothouse he built in Muscle Shoals, Alabama, in the early '60s. Hall has produced and engineered records by all kinds of musicians—many in R&B and now, increasingly, in country—including Otis Redding protégé Arthur Conley, Bettye Swann, Candi Staton, Clarence Carter (No. 4 hit "Patches" is a Hall favorite), fellow white soulman Dan Penn (see entry), Jimmy Hughes, Travis Wammack, Wilson Pickett, the Osmonds, T.G. Sheppard, Shenandoah, and Mac Davis.

Born January 31, 1932, in Tishimingo, Mississippi, about 40 miles from Muscle Shoals, Hall grew up poor, with whiskey makers, whiskey runners, and sawmillers.

Rick Hall (left) with Little Richard's manager and Little Richard

Hall's father, a singing teacher, pushed him toward a musical career. An uncle turned him on to an old-fashioned eight-string mandolin.

Hall and his sister joined their father shortly after the elder Hall moved to Cleveland in 1944 to work in a defense plant. It was Hall's first exposure to blacks; the Freedom Hills area in which he spent his early childhood was not exactly hospitable to them.

The family returned to Alabama at the end of the war, Hall's father remarried and went into sharecropping, and Hall quit school after his junior year. In 1951, he moved to Rockford, Illinois, to work in a tool-and-die plant. He also continued to play music. In 1952, he was drafted and became a conscientious objector. While home on leave, just prior to being shipped to Korea to be a front-line medic, he went to a dance, got drunk, turned his car over, and broke his back. Following his discharge, he played in an Army band with country star Faron Young and fiddler Gordon Terry. Hall returned to Alabama in 1955, got married, and went to work for the Muscle Shoals area's largest employer, Reynolds Aluminum.

In 1957, his wife died in a car accident and his father died when a tractor turned over on him. Hall moved to Nashville to crack the country music business; though George Jones, Brenda Lee, and Roy Orbison recorded his songs, he couldn't get anything going on his own there. By 1959, Hall was back in the Muscle Shoals area, hanging out above the City Drugstore in nearby Florence. The store was owned by Tom Stafford, whom many credit with launching the Muscle Shoals music industry.

Hall, Stafford, and Billy Sherrill (see entry) formed a partnership, Florence Alabama Music Enterprises (Fame), which dissolved in 1961 when Sherrill moved to Nashville (where he became a major force in commercial country). Coincidentally, Hall and Sherrill played in a band called the Fairlanes; its lead vocalist was Dan Penn.

In the winter of 1962, Hall recorded Arthur Alexander's "You Better Move On" (No. 24) in a converted tobacco warehouse, where he started to formulate what came to be known as the Muscle Shoals sound. The money he made on Alexander enabled him to build his own studio. He now runs two, Studio A and Studio B; each sports a 24-track machine and a Neve console.

"The black music as I know it, the southern R&B, has gone away," Hall says. He worked closely with Atlantic partner Jerry Wexler (see entry) on the production of such black stars as Aretha Franklin, including 1967 hits "I Never Loved a Man (the Way I Love You)" and "Do Right Woman, Do Right Man," and Wilson Pickett (Wexler and Hall co-produced "Land of 1,000 Dances" and "Mustang Sally" in 1966).

For better or worse, Hall's sound has been self-contained. "Because of the remote place I came from and where I've worked all my life," Hall says, "I've been isolated in the creative part. I do all my creating here; every bit of it's done in the studio. I used to fly to Los Angeles to use guys on strings, but the best horn players and R&B pickers are here in Muscle Shoals.

"We don't copy anybody," Hall says. "We make our own stuff." Hall doesn't pay well, either, which is why staff musicians have abandoned Muscle Shoals over the years for more lucrative gigs in Nashville, Los Angeles, and New York. The poor pay, combined with Hall's reputation for being overbearing, hasn't helped build loyalty.

By the end of the '60s, Fame had blown its R&B wad, Stax was on the ropes, and Atlantic was diversifying into pop and rock with such acts as Buffalo Springfield, Cream, and the Bee Gees. In 1969, Hall produced Bobbie Gentry's country hit, "Fancy." He soon ventured into pop, producing the Osmonds' 1971 hits "One Bad Apple" (No. 1) and "Yo-Yo" (No. 3). Hall's work earned him the *Billboard* Producer of the Year Award in 1971. Hall also produced "(You're) Having My Baby" (No. 1), a 1974 hit for Paul Anka, Mac Davis's 1972 smash "Baby Don't Get Hooked on Me" (No. 1), and, in the '80s, hits for Jerry Reed, the Gatlin Brothers, and T.G. Sheppard.

Hall keeps busy at Fame, producing records with his youngest son, Rod. Son Mark is a songwriter in Nashville, son G. Rick Hall is a lawyer in Tuscumbia.

"I'm looking for a song Rick Hall feels he can bring the best out of. My life has been tough. I grew up poverty-stricken without a mother. My father raised me; he was a sawmiller, a sharecropper, hard times have been my whole shtick. So I tend to be sort of a Tobacco Road–type record producer. Records with a lot of dirt and earth and soul and hardship are what I do best, and I try to paint pictures with my records, to set a stage so when you sit in front of the speakers, you are there. I'm a basics man," he continues. "I still believe in a great song with a great artist. Usually your first impression of a song is your best. It's instinctive." —CARLO WOLFF

Alexander, Arthur: "You Better Move On," Dot, 1962.

Allman Brothers Band: *Dreams,* Polydor, 1989.

Allman, Duane: *Anthology,* Capricorn, 1972 • *Anthology II,* Capricorn, 1974.

Anka, Paul: w/ Odia Coates, "(You're) Having My Baby," United Artists, 1974 • w/ Odia Coates, "I Believe There's Nothing Stronger Than Our Love," United Artists, 1975 • "I Don't Like to Sleep Alone," United Artists, 1975 • *Best of the United Artists Years, 1973–1977,* EMI, 1996.

Carter, Clarence: "Slip Away," Atlantic, 1968 • *The Dynamic Clarence Carter,* Atlantic, 1968 • *This Is Clarence Carter,* Atlantic, 1968 • "Making Love (at the Dark End of the Street)," Atlantic, 1969 • *Testifyin',* Atlantic, 1969 • "Patches," Atlantic, 1970 • *Patches,* Atlantic, 1970 • "Sixty Minute Man," Fame, 1973 • *60 Minutes With,* Fame, 1974 • *Snatching It Back: The Best Of,* Rhino, 1992.

Davis, Mac: "Baby Don't Get Hooked on Me," Columbia, 1972 • *Baby Don't Get Hooked on Me,* Columbia, 1972 • *Mac Davis,* Columbia, 1973 • "One Hell of a Woman," Columbia, 1974 • "Rock 'N Roll (I Gave You the Best Years of My Life)," Columbia, 1974 • *Stop and Smell the Roses,* Columbia, 1974 • *Greatest Hits,* Columbia, 1979 • *Very Best and More,* PolyGram, 1984.

Gatlin Brothers: *Biggest Hits,* Columbia, 1988 • *Best of the Gatlins: All the Gold in California,* Legacy/Columbia, 1996.

Gentry, Bobbie: "Fancy," Capitol, 1969.

Gibbs, Terri: *The Best Of,* Varese Sarabande, 1996.

Gosdin, Vern: *Nickels and Dimes and Love,* Columbia, 1993.

Gray, Dobie: *Midnight Diamond,* Infinity, 1978 • *Dobie Gray,* Infinity, 1979 • *Drift Away with Dobie Gray: His Best,* Razor & Tie, 1996.

James, Etta: "I'd Rather Go Blind," Cadet, 1967 • *Tell Mama,* Chess, 1968 • *The Sweetest Peaches, Part 2,* Chess/MCA, 1988 • *Essential,* Chess, 1993 • *Her Best,* Chess/MCA, 1997.

Lee, Laura: *That's How It Is: The Chess Years,* Chess, 1990.

Maurice and Mac: "You Left the Water Running," Checker, 1968.

Moore, Bobby, and the Rhythm Aces: "Searching for My Love," Checker, 1966.

Oak: *Set the Night on Fire,* Mercury, 1980.

Osmond, Donny: "Go Away Little Girl," MGM, 1971 • "Hey Girl/I Knew You When," MGM, 1971 • "Sweet and Innocent," MGM, 1971 • *25 Hits Special Collection,* Curb, 1995.

Osmonds, The: "Double Lovin'," MGM, 1971 • "One Bad Apple," MGM, 1971 • "Yo-Yo," MGM, 1971 • *21 Hits Special Collection,* Curb, 1995.

Pickett, Wilson: "Land of 1,000 Dances," Atlantic, 1966 • "Mustang Sally," Atlantic, 1966 • *The Exciting Wilson Pickett,* Atlantic, 1966 • "Hey Jude," Atlantic, 1968.

Rawls, Lou: *Love Is a Hurtin' Thing: The Silk and Soul of Lou Rawls,* EMI America, 1997.

Redding, Otis: *Otis! The Definitive Otis Redding,* Rhino, 1993.

Reed, Jerry: "She Got the Goldmine (I Got the Shaft)," RCA, 1982 • *Super Hits,* RCA, 1997.

Royal, Billy Joe: *Billy Joe Royal,* Atlantic Nashville, 1992.

Shenandoah: *Shenandoah,* Columbia, 1987 • "Sunday in the South," Columbia, 1989 • "The Church on Cumberland Road," Columbia, 1989 • *The Road Not Taken,* Columbia, 1989 • "Two Dozen Roses," Columbia, 1989 • *Extra Mile,* Columbia, 1990 • *Super Hits,* Columbia, 1994.

Sheppard, T.G.: "Strong Heart," Columbia, 1986.

Staton, Candi: *Young Hearts Run Free,* Warner Bros., 1976 • *Best Of,* Warner Archives, 1995.

Thomas, Irma: *Something Good: Muscle Shoals,* Chess, 1990.

Wammack, Travis: *Travis Wammack,* Fame, 1972 • *Not for Sale,* Capricorn, 1975.

Wopat, Tom: *Learning to Love,* Epic, 1992.

COLLECTIONS

Ertegun's New York, New York, Atlantic, 1987.

Chess Rhythm and Roll, MCA, 1994.

Chess Blues Classics: 1957–1967, Chess/MCA, 1997.

Chess Blues-Rock Songbook, MCA, 1997.

Chess Soul: A Decade of Chicago's Finest, MCA, 1997.

John Henry Hammond Jr.

John Hammond is the most important nonperformer in 20th-century popular music. The names of the artists he produced or championed attest to the remarkable reach of his long, long arm: Fletcher Henderson, Bessie Smith, Benny Goodman, Billie Holiday, Count Basie, Charlie Christian, Bob Dylan, Aretha Franklin, George Benson, Bruce Springsteen, Stevie Ray Vaughan. Perhaps Hammond's single greatest and most enduring achievement is the *From Spirituals to Swing* concert at Carnegie Hall in December 1938, which clarified the evolution of black music from Africa, through country blues and gospel, and on to jazz for a white urban audience. The importance of this concert can't be overstated from a musical, cultural, or political standpoint; in retrospect it was the moment of conception for the integration of blacks into the American mainstream. Though the process continues to this day, the differences between the America of the late '30s and the late '90s begin with Hammond and his musical emissaries.

John Henry Hammond Jr. was born December 15, 1910, the fifth child and first son of a prominent lawyer and the granddaughter of Cornelius Vanderbilt. The family lived in the lap of luxury on 91st Street in New York City in a six-story house with 15 servants, according to Hammond's autobiography (with Irving Townsend), *John Hammond on Record.*

His mother played classical piano and had a box at the New York Philharmonic; young John was exposed to the fine arts, attending concerts and taking piano lessons from the age of 4. He switched to violin at 8, played duets with his mother for social gatherings, and was the darling of her circle.

Meanwhile, this scion of wealth and privilege was joining the servants to listen to popular music on their Columbia Grafanola whenever he could sneak away. He began collecting records on his own at age 10. He loved the boogie-woogie piano of black players like James P. Johnson (who wrote the original "Charleston").

Hammond began reading *Variety* at 13 and went away to the Hotchkiss School in Connecticut at age 14. A religious young man who neither smoked nor drank, Hammond was granted the unprecedented liberty of traveling alone to New York every other weekend for violin lessons, and took the opportunity to explore Harlem and meet the musicians who made the music he loved.

In 1927, the formerly white Alhambra Theater "went black," and as Hammond walked by he read the sign: "This week in person the Empress of the Blues, Bessie Smith." Hammond went to the show that night and saw Smith at the peak of her career; he called it "the biggest thrill of my life." Hammond deemed Smith to be the "greatest vocalist to come out of the blues tradition," an opinion he held for the rest of his life.

The next year Hammond matriculated at Yale and switched from violin to viola because, as a matter of practicality, his fingers weren't as good as his ears, and as there was a scarcity of violists, he could play in string quartets with people who were much better than he was.

Hammond played with a cellist named Artie Bernstein who had worked his way through NYU law school playing bass with pop and jazz bands in the area. Bernstein knew most of the white musicians in the area, Hammond knew most of the black musicians, and together they knew them all. An enthusiastic evangelist, Hammond took Bernstein and other white friends to his favorite spot, an illegal Harlem speakeasy (Prohibition lasted from 1920 to 1933) called Small's Paradise that featured blues and jazz performers backed by Charlie Johnson's house band.

Hammond began writing about his enthusiasm for jazz, and Yale began to seem irrelevant. A bout with hepatitis the summer before his junior year helped him make up his mind and Hammond left school to pursue a life in music full time.

Recovered and writing for *Gramaphone,* Hammond went to England in late summer of 1931 because the English were more interested in jazz than white Americans, and because the bottom had fallen out of the American record market with the advent of the Depression. In England, Hammond met Spike Hughes, recording director for English Decca, who asked him to keep his eyes open for promising jazz musicians, including a white clarinetist named Benny Goodman. Hammond also came away from England as the U.S. correspondent for *Melody Maker*.

Full of confidence and ready to make a difference, Hammond saw a piano player named Garland Wilson and decided he should be recorded. Hammond went to Columbia's Frank Walker (because Walker had discovered Bessie Smith years before) and offered to fund and produce the Wilson session himself. Walker quoted Hammond the price of $125 for four 12-inch sides (12-inch 78s ran about five minutes a side and were recorded with one microphone, direct to acetate), and Hammond had to buy 150 of the finished records. "St. James Infirmary" backed with "When Your Lover Has Gone" sold several thousand copies and was a substantial hit for the day. At 20, John Hammond was a successful record producer.

On his 21st birthday Hammond moved to an apartment in Greenwich Village, where he felt at home among the artists, writers, and bohemian types. Though personally untouched by the Depression, Hammond was radicalized by it (he was a leftist but never a Marxist); and as an idealist and reformer, he was scandalized that segregation kept black jazz musicians from the more lucrative jobs on radio or in the white clubs.

To further spread the jazz word, Hammond became a DJ at radio station WEVD (named after Socialist leader Eugene V. Debs), owned by the *Jewish Daily Forward* newspaper. He instituted the first regular live jazz series anywhere, paying his favorite performers $10 each out of his own pocket to come in to the station to jam on Saturday nights. Unwilling to compromise his principles, Hammond took the series off the air after 10 weeks when the black musicians were asked to use the freight elevator.

As a jazz critic, Hammond's main theme was that white players couldn't match the "unbuttoned freedom and swing of a superb Negro rhythm section"—the foundation necessary for great improvisation—and for this stance he was called a "nigger lover," among juicier things. Undaunted, Hammond began to write on social issues as well as music for *The Nation*.

In 1932 he covered the Scottsboro case in Alabama: nine black youths falsely accused of raping two white women in a freight car. The case eventually went to four trials, twice before the Supreme Court, and scored a moral victory in that none of the defendants were executed (although some died in custody). Hammond helped finance the first appeal and second trial by staging a benefit concert with Benny Carter's Orchestra and

Duke Ellington playing solo in New York. Soon after, Hammond joined the board of the NAACP.

Later that year, Columbia recording director Ben Selvin asked Hammond if he knew of any jazz artists who should be recorded. Hammond's first choice was Fletcher Henderson, the "Father of Swing," whose arrangements were the first to allow room for his whole band to improvise. Henderson, always his own worst enemy, showed up late for the session, and only had time to record two songs—"Underneath the Harlem Moon" and "Honeysuckle Rose"—but the session remained one of Hammond's favorites.

In 1933 Hammond tracked down Bessie Smith, who hadn't recorded in some time, and recorded one of her best-known songs, "Do Your Duty." Hammond again financed the session himself and integrated it by including Benny Goodman.

Goodman was a tough guy from Chicago who Hammond called "one of the most important people in my life" in the PBS special *John Hammond: From Bessie Smith to Bruce Springsteen*. Hammond thought their close relationship was odd (Goodman later married Hammond's sister Alice) because Goodman "didn't have much of a social point of view and couldn't understand why I did, but he loved black music," said Hammond.

At the time Goodman, who was to become the greatest white musician in jazz history, made his living playing as a session man and fronted an all-white band. He told Hammond that if anyone knew he played with black musicians, he would be barred from work. New York was as segregated as Birmingham in 1933. Hammond's first two records with Goodman were with an all-white group, and were moderately successful. Hammond then took Goodman to see Billie Holiday, and they recorded together in late 1933. The color line was broken, at least in the studio.

Hammond then brought in black piano player Teddy Wilson from Chicago and he began to record with Goodman. Hammond encouraged the formation of a small jazz combo, and the Benny Goodman Trio with (great white drummer) Gene Krupa and Teddy Wilson was formed.

Throughout the '30s Hammond and Goodman broke barrier after barrier when first Wilson, then vibraphonist Lionel Hampton and electric guitar great Charlie Christian were added to the Goodman band, which became among the most popular in the land. Hammond brought in Fletcher Henderson to write arrangements for Goodman and the swing swung like never before.

Hammond's next major discovery was the Count Basie Band, whom he heard on the radio in his car in

Chicago, broadcast live from Kansas City one cold January night in 1936. The Basie band was one he "couldn't find any fault with." It included Hammond's favorite drummer Jo Jones (with "extraordinary wit in his playing"), Lester "Prez" Young on tenor sax, and Jimmy Rushing on vocals. According to Hammond, "Fletcher Henderson started the liberation of the soloist and Basie continued it," per the PBS special.

Hammond's other major discovery in the '30s was Billie Holiday. He first saw her at Monette Moore's club as a substitute singer in 1933. She was "17, chubby, quite beautiful. I had never heard anyone sing like that, as though she were the most inspired improviser in the world. She had an uncanny ear, an excellent memory for lyrics, and she sang with an exquisite sense of phrasing . . . she sang the way Louis Armstrong played horn," wrote Hammond. He followed her from speakeasy to speakeasy in Harlem that year and wrote about her in *Melody Maker*. He put her together with Teddy Wilson and small combos made up from members of Basie's band.

Hammond capped off his extraordinary decade of the '30s with the *Spirituals to Swing* concert in late '38. The concert began with recorded West African music; then boogie-woogie pianists Albert Ammons, Meade Lux Lewis, and Pete Johnson; blues shouter Big Joe Turner; gospel singer Sister Rosetta Tharpe; blues singer Ruby Smith; pure gospel from Mitchell's Christian Singers; blind harmonica player Sonny Terry; then the New Orleans Dixieland jazz of James P. Johnson, Tommy Ladnier, and Sidney Bechet; country blues singer Big Bill Broonzy; and finally, the elegant jazz of the Count Basie Band, with singers Jimmy Rushing and Helen Humes.

Hammond again put his money where his mouth was and invested in New York's first integrated nightclub, Cafe Society, which was a great success for many years and featured many of Hammond's favorite jazz and blues performers.

The '40s were a difficult time for Hammond: his second (of three) son Douglas died, he got divorced, and the onset of bebop alienated him from jazz. He mostly recorded classical music in Europe.

In the late '50s Goddard Lieberson, who had helped Hammond scout the South for talent for the *Spirituals to Swing* concert, was president of Columbia and invited Hammond back into the fold. On a songwriters demo tape, Hammond found an 18-year-old Aretha Franklin singing and immediately dubbed her the greatest singer since Billie Holiday. Hammond recorded her with jazz musicians, but Columbia wanted her to record pop and took her away from him. She came into her own on

JOHN PAUL HAMMOND

Sons of legends never have it easy. Life is difficult enough without the burden of matching nearly impossible achievements. Most either run screaming in another direction or coast in the slipstream of parental greatness. Perhaps hardest of all is the attempt to achieve independence within the same field. Such has been the noble pursuit and ultimate success of John Paul Hammond (JP), first son of John Henry Hammond Jr. (JH).

JP was born November 13, 1942, in Greenwich Village, New York. When he was 2, his father was drafted into the Army. JP was sent to the Little Red Schoolhouse, known as the "commie school" by the local Italian community. His parents divorced in 1948. At the Schoolhouse, JP had a black music teacher named Charity Bailey who got all of the children involved with playing some kind of instrument and singing songs like Leadbelly's "Jump Down, Turn Around, Pick a Bale of Cotton."

JP saw his father only on some weekends and for a few weeks in the summer, but in their time together JP attended recording sessions, met many of his father's musician friends like Count Basie and Jimmy Rushing, and became aware that music was a way of life for some people.

JP was more of a visual arts student and was encouraged in this direction. He loved R&B and early rock 'n' roll, but when his father took him to see Big Bill Broonzy, JP became hooked on the country blues. The "personal statement of the solo artist" deeply affected him.

He didn't get his first guitar until he was 17, but all he did was eat, sleep, and practice for the next two years; by 19 he was playing professionally, "much to the shock of everyone around me," he says. JH was "surprised and not pleased" when his first son left school to become a musician, informing him that it was a very difficult life and a hard way to make any money. However, within a year JP had a recording contract and his father's fears eased. When it became clear that his son wasn't going to change his mind or go back to school, JH became supportive, but they both tried to steer clear of the appearance or reality of the father's influence on the son's career.

JP was never dependent upon JH for "work or my own reality," he says. Father and son "connected deeply on the passion level" and even worked for the same company for a time when JP was signed to Columbia to do the *Little Big Man* soundtrack in 1970, but they never worked together.

JP has had an outstanding career as perhaps the most important white country blues player of the last 30 years, recording dozens of albums for Vanguard, Atlantic, Columbia, Capricorn, Rounder, and now Point Blank. Highlights include *Country Blues* (1964), *I Can Tell* (1967), *Live* (1983), and the recent *Trouble No More* (1993) and *Found True Love* (1995), where he proves his mettle with the electric guitar and as a bandleader. John Paul Hammond has quietly shined his own light. He has cleared a space within the monumental shadow of his father, and is deserving of respect and admiration for having done so. —ERIC OLSEN

Atlantic, where, as Jerry Wexler (see entry) told Hammond, "We put the church back in her."

According to the PBS special, "Hammond believed that music should be an engine of social change, and looked to the protest songs of the early '60s to counteract the sentimentality of the '50s." Pete Seeger had been blacklisted as a communist in the '50s, but Hammond brought him to Columbia in the early '60s. His "We Shall Overcome" became an American standard in 1963.

Hammond was an activist who wanted to change the world, and so did Bob Dylan. Hammond spotted Dylan for the talent he was among the folky rabble of the Village, signed him to Columbia, and recorded his first two albums plainly without overdubs or accompaniment other than Dylan's own guitar and harmonica. "Blowin' in the Wind" and "A Hard Rain's A-Gonna Fall" are about as pure as it gets. Dubbed "Hammond's folly" early on at the label, Dylan has gone on to be the most important songwriter of the last 40 years.

In the early '70s Hammond found the only "next Dylan" who ever amounted to much, Bruce Springsteen. When they met, Hammond asked Springsteen if he had ever written anything he wouldn't dare record. Springsteen replied with "If I Was the Priest," a scathing indictment from a lapsed Catholic. Hammond connected with Springsteen in the two-hour audition and signed him to Columbia, though he never produced the most important artist of the '70s.

In 1975 Hammond reached mandatory retirement age with Columbia, but he stayed on as an independent, found Stevie Ray Vaughan, and produced his first sessions. John Hammond died in 1987. He never accepted royalties from any of his productions, viewing them as the artist's due.

Hammond defined himself as he defined the role of the producer in his autobiography: "All [producers] have an ear for talent and tune, the courage and determination to hear performed what they hear in their lively imaginations, and the good fortune to be at the right place at the right time." In Hammond's case, being at the right place at the right time lasted over 50 years and changed the history of the United States and the world.
—ERIC OLSEN

Abyssinian Baptist Choir: *Shakin' the Rafters,* Legacy, 1960, 1991.

Addis and Crofut: *Eastern Ferris Wheel,* Columbia, 1968.

Albert Ammons Rhythm Kings: "Early Morning Blues/Mile or More Bird Rag," Decca, 1936 • "Nagasaki/Boogie Woogie Stomp," Decca, 1936.

Allman, Duane: *Anthology,* Capricorn, 1972.

Ammons, Albert: "Shout for Joy," Vocalion, 1938.

Bailey, Mildred: w/ the Mildred Bailey Swing Band, *Someday Sweetheart* (EP), Vocalion, 1935 • *Willow Tree* (EP), Parlophone England, 1935 • w/ Her Orchestra, *Sentimental Reasons* (EP), Parlophone England, 1936 • w/ the Mildred Bailey Orchestra, *If You Should Ever Leave* (EP), Vocalion, 1937 • *Ghost of a Chance* (EP), Vocalion, 1939 • w/ the Oxford Greys, *Gulf Coast Blues* (EP), Vocalion, 1939 • *Moon Love* (EP), Vocalion, 1939 • w/ John Kirby Sextet, *St. Louis Blues* (EP), Vocalion, 1939 • w/ the Ellis Larkins Cafe Society All Stars, *I'll Close My Eyes* (EP), Majestic, 1946.

Ballard, Kay: *Peanuts,* Columbia, 1962.

Barnes, Mae: *Mae Barnes,* DRG, 1958, 1991.

Basie, Count: w/ Kansas City, "Dickie's Dream/Lester Leaps In," Vocalion, 1939 • w/ Moms Mabley, George Kirby, etc., *A Night at the Apollo,* Vanguard, 1957 • *The Essential Count Basie* Vols. 1–3, Columbia, 1987, 1988 • *See also* Count Basie Orchestra.

Bell, Charles: *Contemporary Jazz Quartet,* Columbia, 1961.

Ben Ludlow Orchestra: *Dancing in High Society,* Vanguard, 1958.

Benny Carter Orchestra: *Devil's Holiday* (EP), Columbia England, 1933 • *Swing It* (EP), Okeh England, 1933.

Benny Goodman Modernists: *Stars Fell on Alabama* (EP), Banner, 1934.

Benny Goodman Music Hall Orchestra: *Cokey* (EP), Columbia, 1934.

Benny Goodman Orchestra: "Dr. Heckle and Mr. Jibe/Texas Tea Party," Columbia England, 1933 • "I Gotta Right to Sing the Blues/Ain't Cha Glad," Columbia England, 1933 • "Riffin' the Scotch," Columbia, 1933 • "Tappin' the Barrel/Keep on Doin'," Columbia, 1933 • "Your Mother's Son-In-Law," Columbia, 1933 • *Bugle Call Rag* (EP), Columbia, 1934 • *Junk Man* (EP), Columbia, 1934 • *Moonglow* (EP), Columbia, 1934 • *Always* (EP), Victor, 1935 • *Blue Skies* (EP), Victor, 1935 • *Hooray for Love* (EP), Victor, 1935 • *Original Dixieland Band* (EP), Columbia, 1935 • *Sometimes I'm Happy* (EP), Victor, 1935 • *When Buddha Smiles* (EP), Victor, 1935 • *Stealin' Apples* (EP), Columbia, 1939.

Benny Goodman Sextet: "Flying Home/Rose Room," Columbia, 1939 • *Soft Winds* (EP), Columbia, 1939 • "Till Tom Special/Gone with What Wind," Columbia, 1940 • *Featuring Charlie Christian,* Sony, 1989.

Benny Goodman Trio: *Body and Soul* (EP), Victor, 1935.

Benny Morton Orchestra: *Tailor Made* (EP), Columbia, 1934.

Benson, George: *The Essence of,* Columbia, 1993 • *See also* George Benson Quartet.

Bunny Berigan Orchestra: *I'm Comin' Virginia* (EP), Parlophone England, 1935.

Blake, Eubie: *Eighty-Six Years of,* Columbia, 1969.

Bloomfield, Mike: *Don't Say That I Ain't Your Man*, Legacy, 1994.

Braff and Larkins: *Two by Two*, Vanguard, 1956.

Bud Freeman Orchestra: *Buzzard* (EP), Parlophone England, 1935.

Burrell, Kenny: *Bluesin' Around*, Columbia, 1983.

Chandler, Len: *To Be a Man*, Columbia, 1966 • *The Lovin' People*, Columbia, 1968.

Chick Webb Orchestra: "If Dreams Come True/Get Together," Columbia, 1933 • "On the Sunny Side of the Street/Darktown Strutter's Ball," Columbia, 1933 • *Blue Minor* (EP), Okeh, 1934 • *Stompin' at the Savoy* (EP), Columbia, 1934.

Chocolate Dandies: "Blue Interlude/I Never Knew," Columbia England, 1933.

Christian, Charlie: *The Genius of the Electric Guitar*, Columbia, 1941, 1987.

Clara Fischer Orchestra: *Songs for Rainy Day Lovers*, Columbia, 1967.

Clayton, Buck: w/ the Clayton Buck All Stars, *Robbins Nest*, Columbia, 1956 • *The Essential Buck Clayton*, Vanguard, 1977, 1995.

Cohen, Leonard: *Leonard Cohen*, Columbia, 1967.

Coleman Hawkins Orchestra: *Day You Came Along* (EP), Parlophone England, 1933.

Count Basie Orchestra: *Bugle Blues* (EP), Columbia, 1937 • *How Long Blues* (EP), Vocalion, 1939 • "Miss Thing/12th Street Rag," Vocalion, 1939 • "Nobody Knows," Vocalion, 1939 • *Rockabye Basie* (EP), Vocalion, 1939 • *Lady Lady Blues* (EP), Columbia, 1946.

Cox, Ida, and the All-Star Band: *Four-Day Creep* (EP), Vocalion, 1939.

Crowell and Pokriss: *Original Cast*, Columbia, 1961 (*Earnest in Love*).

Davis, Miles: w/ Gil Evans, *The Complete Columbia Studio Recordings*, Columbia, 1996.

Davy, Dick: *You're a Long Way from Home, Whitey*, Columbia, 1966 • *Stronger Than Dirt*, Columbia, 1967.

Denny Zeitlin Trio: *Carnival*, Columbia, 1965 • *Shining Hour*, Columbia, 1966.

Dickenson, Vic: *The Essential Vic Dickenson*, Vanguard, 1977, 1995.

Douglas, Jack: *Live at the Bon Soir*, Columbia, 1961.

Dukes of Dixieland: *Breakin' It Up on Broadway*, Columbia, 1961 • *Now Hear This*, Columbia, 1962 • *At Disneyland*, Columbia, 1963 • *Hootenany*, Columbia, 1963 • w/ the Clara Ward Singers, *We Gotta Shout*, Columbia, 1963 • *Struttin' at the World's Fair*, Columbia, 1964.

Dylan, Bob: *Bob Dylan*, Columbia, 1962 • *The Freewheelin'*, Columbia, 1963 • *Bootleg Series*, Columbia, 1991.

Eldridge, Roy: *Little Jazz*, Columbia, 1940, 1991.

Ellington, Duke: *Hommage á Duke*, Tristar, 1996.

Elliott, Don, and Orchestra: *Love Is a Necessary Evil*, Columbia, 1962 • *Electric Bath*, Columbia, 1967 • *Shock Treatment*, Columbia, 1968.

Ellis, Herb w/ the Herb Ellis All Stars, *Midnight Roll*, Epic, 1963 • *Three Guitars in Bossa Nova Time*, Epic, 1963 • w/ Stuff Smith, *Together*, Epic, 1963.

Evans, Gil: *See* Davis, Miles.

Fitzgerald, Ella: *Newport Jazz Festival, Live*, Legacy, 1973, 1995.

Fletcher Henderson Orchestra: "Honeysuckle Rose/Underneath the Harlem Moon," Columbia, 1932 • "New King Porter Stomp," Okeh, 1932 • *Queer Notions* (EP), Columbia, 1933.

Franklin, Aretha: *Aretha*, Columbia, 1961 • *Sweet, Bitter Love*, Columbia, 1970, 1989 • *First 12 Sides*, Columbia, 1972 • *Aretha Sings the Blues (1961–1965)*, Columbia, 1985 • *Jazz to Soul*, Columbia, 1992 • "All Night Long," 550 Music/Epic, 1994 (*Blown Away* soundtrack).

Gene Krupa and the Chicagoans: *Blues of Israel* (EP), Parlophone England, 1935.

George Benson Quartet: *Cookbook*, Legacy, 1966, 1994 • *It's Uptown*, Columbia, 1966, 1991 • *The Most Exciting New Guitarist on the Jazz Scene*, Legacy, 1966, 1994.

Gieseking, Walter: *Debussy: Second Book of Preludes*, Columbia, 1939.

Ginsberg, Allen: *First Blues*, John Hammond Records, 1982.

Goodman, Benny, and Sid Catlett: *Roll 'Em Vol. 1*, Columbia, 1939 • *See also* under Benny Goodman.

Gulda, Friedrich: *Live at Birdland*, RCA Victor, 1956 • *From Vienna with Jazz*, Columbia, 1964 • *Ineffable*, Columbia, 1965.

Handy, John: *Live at Monterey*, Columbia, 1966 • w/ John Handy Orchestra, *New View*, Columbia, 1967 • *Projections*, Columbia, 1968.

Harry James Orchestra: *Jubilee* (EP), Brunswick, 1937 • "Texas Chatter/One O'Clock Jump," Brunswick, 1938 • "Song of the Wanderer/It's the Dreamer in Me," Brunswick, 1939.

Henderson, Bobby: *Call House Blues*, Vanguard, 1956 • *Handful of Keys*, Vanguard, 1957, 1992.

Hester, Carolyn: *This Life I'm Living*, Columbia, 1963.

Holiday, Billie: w/ Her Orchestra, "A Fine Romance/I Can't Pretend," Vocalion, 1936 • *Greatest Hits*, Vol 2, Columbia, 1987 • *Quintessential*, Vols. 1–7, 1933–1939, Columbia, 1987, 1991 • *Control Booth Series*, Vol. 1, 1940–1941, Jazz Unlimited, 1993 • *See also* Teddy Wilson–Billie Holiday Orchestra; Wilson, Teddy.

Horace Arnold Band: *Tribe*, Columbia, 1974.

Horace Henderson Orchestra: *Happy Feet* (EP), Parlophone England, 1933.

House, Son: *Father of Folk Blues*, Columbia, 1966.

Howard, Eddy, and the All Stars: *Old-Fashoined Love* (EP), Columbia, 1940.

Humes, Helen: *It's the Talk of the Town,* Columbia, 1975.

Hunter, Alberta: *Amtrak Blues,* Columbia, 1980 • *The Glory of Alberta Hunter,* Columbia, 1982 • *Look for the Silver Lining,* Columbia, 1983.

James, Harry, and Boogie Trio: *Boo Woo* (EP), Brunswick, 1939 • *See also* Harry James Orchestra.

Jeremy Steig Quartet: *Flute Fever,* Columbia, 1964.

Jerry Hahn Combo: *Brotherhood,* Columbia, 1972.

Jimmy Noone New Orleans Band: *He's a Different Type of Guy* (EP), Parlophone England, 1936.

Joe Sullivan Orchestra at Cafe Society: "I Cover the Waterfront/I Gotta Crush on You," Okeh, 1940 • "Low Down Dirty Shame/I Can't Give You Anything Bur Love," Vocalion, 1940.

Jones, Jo: *Jo Jones Plus Two,* Vanguard, 1958 • *The Essential Jo Jones,* Vanguard, 1977, 1995.

Jones-Smith, Inc.: *Shoe Shine Boy* (EP), Vocalion, 1936.

Jordan, Taft: *If the Moon Turns Green* (EP), Perfect, 1935.

Kirkpatrick, Ralph: *de Falla: Concerto for Harpsichord,* Mercury, 1947.

LaFarge, Peter: *Ira Hayes,* Columbia, 1962.

Lewis, Meade Lux: "Honky Tonk Train Blues," Parlophone England, 1935.

Lonnie Smith Combo: *Soul Organ,* Columbia, 1967.

Lundy, Pat: *Soul Ain't Nothin' But the Blues,* Columbia, 1968.

Makowicz, Adam: *Adam,* Columbia, 1977.

Marlowe Morris Quintet: *Play the Thing,* Columbia, 1962.

Masters, Joe: *Jazz Mass,* Columbia, 1966.

Mel Powell Trio: *Borderline,* Vanguard, 1955 • *Thingamajig,* Vanguard, 1955.

Metronome All-Star Band: "All-Star Strut," Columbia, 1940 • "KIng Porter Stomp," Columbia, 1940.

Miller, Mitch: *Cimarosa: Concerto for Oboe and Strings,* Mercury, 1947 • *V. Williams: Concerto for Oboe and Strings,* Mercury, 1947.

Newman, Alfred, and the Hollywood Symphony Orchestra: *Famous Ballet Themes,* Mercury, 1951 • *Gershwin: American in Paris,* Mercury, 1951.

Newton, Frankie, and the Cafe Society Orchestra: *Tab's Blues* (EP), Vocalion, 1939.

Norris, Bobbe: *The Beginning,* Columbia, 1966.

Nutty Squirrels: *Bird Watching,* Columbia, 1961.

Olatunji, Babatunde: *Drums of Passion,* Columbia, 1959 • *Flaming Drums,* Columbia, 1963 • *High Life,* Columbia, 1963.

Paul Winter Sextet: *Jazz Meets Bossa Nova,* Columbia, 1963 • *Jazz Premiere,* Columbia, 1963 • *New Jazz on Campus,* Columbia, 1963 • *Jazz Meets Folk Song,* Columbia, 1964.

Peck, Roberta: *Extraordinary,* Columbia, 1969.

Price, Nikki: *Nikki,* Epic, 1963.

Prima, Louis, and the New Orleans Gang: *Stardust* (EP), Brunswick, 1934.

Ray Bryant Combo: *Madison Time,* Columbia, 1960.

Ray Bryant Orchestra: *Hollywood Jazz Beat,* Columbia, 1963.

Ray Bryant Trio: *Little Susie,* Columbia, 1960 • *Con Alma,* Columbia, 1961.

Red Norvo Octet: "Old-Fashioned Love/I Surrender, Dear," Columbia, 1934 • "Tomboy/Night Is Blue," Columbia, 1934 • *Blues in E Flat* (EP), Columbia, 1935.

Redd Evans Orchestra: "Milenberg Joys," Okeh, 1939.

Reginald Foresythe Orchestra: *Dodging a Divorcee* (EP), Columbia England, 1934.

Reynolds, Melvina: *Sings the Truth,* Columbia, 1967.

Robeson, Paul: w/ the Count Basie Orchestra, "King Joe," Okeh, 1941.

Rolph Kuhn Quartet: *Streamline,* Vanguard, 1957.

Ronnell Bright Trio: *Bright Flight,* Vanguard, 1957.

Ruff, Willie: *Smooth Side of Ruff,* Columbia, 1968.

Rushing, Jimmy: *If This Ain't the Blues,* Vanguard, 1956 • *Listen to the Blues,* Vanguard, 1956 • *The Essential Jimmy Rushing,* Vanguard, 1989.

Schneider/Horszowski/Miller/Katims: *Brahms: Piano Quartets,* Mercury, 1947.

Seeger, Pete: *Story Songs,* Columbia, 1961 • *Bitter and the Sweet,* Columbia, 1963 • *Children's Town Hall Concert,* Columbia, 1963 • *We Shall Overcome,* Columbia, 1963 • *Strangers and Cousins,* Columbia, 1965 • *Dangerous Songs!?,* Columbia, 1966 • *God Bless the Grass,* Columbia, 1966 • *Waist Deep in the Big Muddy,* Columbia, 1967, 1993 • *Now,* Columbia, 1969 • *Young vs. Old,* Columbia, 1970 • *Rainbow Race,* Columbia, 1972 • *The World of Pete Seeger,* Columbia, 1973 • *Link in the Chain,* Sony, 1996.

Smith, Bessie: *Do Your Duty* (EP), Okeh, 1933 • *The Collection,* Columbia, 1989.

Spike Hughes Orchestra: *Arabesque* (EP), Decca England, 1933 • *Donegal Cradle Song* (EP), Decca England, 1933 • *Pastorale* (EP), Decca England, 1933.

Stravinsky, Igor: *Dumbarton Oaks Concerto,* Mercury, 1947.

Stridel, Gene: *This Is,* Columbia, 1964.

Stuyvesant String Quartet: *Bloch: String Quartet #2,* Columbia, 1939 • *Ravel: Introduction and Allegro,* Columbia, 1940.

Sullivan, Joe: *Honeysuckle Rose* (EP), Parlophone England, 1933 • *See also* Joe Sullivan Orchestra.

Szigeti, Joseph, and Orchestra: *Mozart: Divertimento #15 in B-flat Major,* Columbia, 1938 • *Bartok: Contrasts,* Columbia, 1940.

Teddy Wilson Orchestra: w/ Benny Goodman, *You Came to My Rescue* (EP), Brunswick, 1936 • *He Ain't Got Rhythm* (EP), Brunswick, 1937 • "Out of Nowhere," Columbia, 1941.

Teddy Wilson Quartet: *Just a Mood* (EP), Brunswick, 1937.

Teddy Wilson–Billie Holiday Orchestra: *I Wished on the Moon* (EP), Brunswick, 1935 • *If You Were Mine* (EP),

Brunswick, 1935 • *You Let Me Down* (EP), Brunswick, 1935 • "Life Begins When You're in Love," Brunswick, 1936 • *Sailin'* (EP), Brunswick, 1936 • "Who Loves You," Brunswick, 1936 • *Carelessly* (EP), Brunswick, 1937 • *Foolin' Myself*, Brunswick, 1937 • *Mood That I'm In* (EP), Brunswick, 1937 • *Yours and Mine* (EP), Brunswick, 1937.

Turner, Big Joe: *Big, Bad and Blue: The Big Joe Turner Anthology*, Rhino, 1994.

Vaughan, Stevie Ray: *Texas Flood*, Epic, 1983.

Venuti, Joe, and the Blue Six: *Jazz Me Blues* (EP), Columbia England, 1933.

Watrous, Bill: *Tiger of San Pedro*, Columbia, 1975 • w/ Bill Watrous Band, *Manhattan Wildlife Refuge*, Columbia, 1974.

Williams, Joe: *A Night at Count Basie's*, Vanguard, 1956.

Wilson, Garland: "Memories of You/Rockin' Chair," Okeh, 1932.

Wilson, Teddy: "I Found a Dream/Of Treasure Island," Brunswick, 1935 • *Liza* (EP), Brunswick, 1935 • w/ Ella Fitzgerald, *Christopher Columbus* (EP), Brunswick, 1936 • w/ Billie Holiday, *Easy to Love* (EP), Brunswick, 1936 • w/ Billie Holiday, *I Cried for You* (EP), Brunswick, 1936.

Winter, Paul: w/ Carlos Lyra, *Sound of Ipanema*, Columbia, 1964 • *Rio*, Columbia, 1965 • *See also* Paul Winter Sextet.

Young, Lester: *Evening of Basie-ite*, Columbia, 1980 • *Kansas City Sessions*, GRP, 1997.

Zeitlin, Denny: *Cathexis*, Columbia, 1964 • *Zeitgeist*, Columbia, 1968 • *See also* Denny Zeitlin Trio.

COLLECTIONS

The 1930's—The Singers, Columbia, 1938.
From Spirituals to Swing: 1938–1939, Vanguard, 1939, 1989.
The Real Kansas City, Legacy/Columbia, 1939, 1996.
Fifty Years of Jazz Guitar, Columbia, 1976.
Billie, Ella, Lena, Sarah! Legacy, 1980, 1994.
From Bessie Smith to Bruce Springsteen, Image/Sony, 1991.

Martin Hannett

Martin Hannett was a brilliant yet erratic producer whose work with the Buzzcocks, Joy Division, New Order, and Happy Mondays defined two generations of the Manchester sound. A staff producer in the late '70s and early '80s with Tony Wilson's legendary Factory label, Hannett also produced some of the most important English music of the punk and post-punk eras: very early U2, Psychedelic Furs, Magazine, and OMD (their finest single, the effervescent "Electricity").

Martin Hannett was born in 1948 and grew up in the Manchester suburb of Wythenshawe. By mid-'76, Hannett had produced an album by a band named the Belt and Braces Trucking Company and had taken it to the host of a local music television show, Tony Wilson, for a plug. Wilson passed, but did check out a punk show promoted by Hannett and his Music Force company, headlined by Slaughter and the Dogs, and came away a proselyte.

Perhaps in retaliation for the Belt and Braces turndown, the scruffy but enterprising Hannett, writing under a pseudonym, panned Wilson's TV program in a local publication. At the next Dogs show, an indignant Wilson stormed up to Hannett and screamed, "Did you write that review? . . . Well, fuck you!" Hannett stormed about in a garage behind the theater muttering dark threats and vile epithets after the show, but Wilson quietly slipped away, wishing no confrontations with "crazed Wythensharians," per Mick Middles in *From Joy Division to New Order: The Factory Story*.

In late December 1976, Hannett, under the nom de punk of "Martin Zero," produced the Buzzcocks' first and last recorded work with lead singer Howard Devoto (who left shortly thereafter to form Magazine), an EP called *Spiral Scratch*. Little more than a no-budget demo released on the band's own New Hormones label, the EP is pure and brilliant. "Boredom" is the highlight, with Devoto's spirited vocals belying the title and the band's angular, almost-mechanized rhythms foreshadowing Joy Division. Hannett also produced some of the Buzzcocks' great, cheerfully despondent pop punk of the early Pete Shelley–led period, including "Everybody's Happy Nowadays," "Lipstick," "Noise Annoys," "Oh Shit!" and the convulsive "Orgasm Addict."

Wilson decided to take his dream to the next level and opened a club called the Factory in 1978; it was but one logical step further to record the bands playing there. Their relationship mended, Wilson brought Hannett in as the producer/music director of the first Factory record, a sampler featuring Joy Division ("Digital," "Glass"), Durutti Column, Cabaret Voltaire, and comedian John Dowie. The 5,000 copies Wilson printed quickly sold out, generating a profit of £87 and the will to go on.

Joy Division had been formed in the fall of 1976 in response to the first Sex Pistols appearance in Manchester. Guitarist Bernard Dicken (later Albrecht, then Sumner) met bassist Peter Hook at the show and formed the Stiff Kittens, with Ian Curtis on vocals. Soon they were called Warsaw and made their live debut opening for the Buzzcocks the following May. After adding drummer Stephen Morris, they became Joy Division (the name of prostitution units in Nazi concentration camps taken from the novel *The House of Dolls*).

A planned first album was shelved when a studio technician added synthesizers to several tracks (later released as *Warsaw*). The band liked the sound Hannett got on the Factory sampler, so, spurning overtures from major labels, they went with Factory for their first album, *Unknown Pleasures*. Wilson zeroed out his trust fund to press 10,000 copies of the record, which was received ecstatically by the press, as was the follow-up, *Closer* (No. 6 U.K.). The epileptic, brooding Curtis hanged himself in 1980 at age 23, but Joy Division went on to release the double album *Still* (No. 5 U.K.) in 1981. Joy Division's influence runs the gamut of modern rock: from the Cure and Psychedelic Furs to Nine Inch Nails (see Trent Reznor entry) and Moby.

Great art grows in stature over time, and nearly 20 years after the band's demise, Joy Division has joined Curtis's heroes the Doors, along with Velvet Underground, the Stooges, and David Bowie (see entry) atop the moody wing of the rock pantheon. Hannett helped transform Joy Division from the screech and thrash of their early days to the mapping of dark emotional landscapes that characterized their greatest work. The white water rush and straining of Curtis's Bowie-esque upper register slowed and broadened into a majestic doomed baritone of stunning dark beauty.

The Joy Division sound employed Hook's melodic lead bass; Sumner's sweeping, twisting, ringing guitar; Morris's touchy, mechanistic drums; Hannett's synthesizer shadings, and Curtis traversing time and space seeking a hole in the fabric that would lead to peace—a peace he may or may not have found in death.

Hannett took particular interest in the drum sounds: obsessively requiring Morris to disassemble and reassemble his drum kit on the third day of the *Unknown Pleasures* sessions, making innovative use of echo and delay to create depth and resonance and helping to create the double snare rhythms that would propel a thousand modern rock dance tunes.

Wilson knew Hannett had a gift. He would "strip these sounds to their perfect, naked form, and then . . . start creating imaginary rooms for each sound. . . . He could see sound, shape it, rebuild it." This he did on the greatest Joy Division songs—the stately "Day of the Lords," with the ominous refrain, "Where will it end?"; the eerie familiarity of "New Dawn Fades" (covered reverentially by Moby on the *Heat* soundtrack); the robotic inexorability of "She's Lost Control"—all from *Unknown Pleasures*.

Closer contributed to the mystique, driven by the lonely, synth-based "Isolation," with Curtis's vocals appropriately remote and reverberant. Remarkably, *Still* contains even better music. "Transmission," with its joyless exhortation to "dance, dance, dance, dance, dance to the radio," reminds us that humans can be as thoughtlessly deterministic as radio waves. "Dead Souls" (NIN's cover on *The Crow* soundtrack makes the link between Joy Division and industrial music explicit) makes expert use of dynamics and is Curtis's finest moment as he rails against the voices from beyond the grave that beckon to him. "Love Will Tear Us Apart" (No. 13 U.K.) is one of the greatest singles of all time: a bright, percussive guitar strum gives way to a hypnotic synth line, and then Curtis is almost cheerful as he confides that even love is an agent of isolation.

After Curtis died, the remaining band members (plus Gillian Gilbert on guitar and keyboards) transformed into New Order and a more overtly electronic sound. Hannett produced their disappointing first album, *Movement,* then their first great single, "Everything's Gone Green," before parting ways with the group and Factory. In the late '80s Hannett returned to Factory and form, discovering Happy Mondays (named after New Order's "Blue Monday") in the hedonistic "Madchester" rave scene. He produced their classic *Bummed* album, a bizarre amalgam of pop rock, dance grooves, Shaun Ryder's unhinged vocals, and Hannett's huge sound, bouncing off walls and dancing into the druggy distance. Hannett himself danced to that same drummer and died of drug-related causes in 1991 at 42.
—Eric Olsen

A Certain Ratio: "All Night Party," Factory/London, 1979, 1997 (*Different Colours, Different Shades: The Factory Story, Part 2*) • "And Then Again," Factory/London, 1980, 1997 (*Too Young to Know, Too Wild to Care: The Factory Story, Part 1*) • *To Each . . .* , Factory, 1980 • *Sextet,* Factory, 1981.

Basement Five: *1965–1980,* Island, 1980 • *In Dub,* Island, 1980.

Buzzcocks, The: *Spiral Scratch,* New Hormones, 1977 • *Singles Going Steady,* IRS, 1979 • *The Buzzcocks* (4 tracks), IRS, 1980 • *Many Parts,* Restless Retro, 1988 • *Operator's Manual: The Buzzcocks Best,* IRS, 1991.

Clarke, John Cooper: *Disguise in Love,* Epic, 1978 • *Snap, Crackle, Bop,* Epic, 1980 • *Zip Style Method,* Epic, 1982.

Crispy Ambulance: "Live on a Hot August Night," Factory Benelux, 1981.

Durutti Column: *The Return of the Durutti Column,* Factory, 1979 • "For Belgian Friends," Factory/London, 1980, 1997 (*Too Young to Know, Too Wild to Care: The Factory Story, Part 1*).

ESG: *ESG,* 99 Records, 1981.

Happy Mondays: "Do It Better," A&M, 1988, 1989 (*Lost Angels* soundtrack) • *Bummed,* Elektra, 1989 • *Hallelujah,*

Elektra, 1989, 1990 • "WFL," Factory/London, 1989, 1997 (*Too Young to Know, Too Wild to Care: The Factory Story, Part 1*) • *Double Easy: The U.S. Singles* (6 tracks), Elektra, 1993.

Heart Throbs: *Cleopatra Grip*, Elektra, 1990.

Joy Division: "New Dawn Fades," Factory/London, 1979, 1997 (*Too Young to Know, Too Wild to Care: The Factory Story, Part 1*) • *Unknown Pleasures*, Factory, 1979 • *Closer*, Factory, 1980 • "Love Will Tear Us Apart," Factory, 1980 • "Decades," Factory/London, 1981, 1997 (*Different Colours, Different Shades: The Factory Story, Part 2*) • *Still*, Factory, 1981 • *Substance*, Qwest, 1988.

Magazine: *The Correct Use of Soap*, Virgin, 1980 • *Rays and Hail*, Virgin, 1987 • *Scree (Rarities, 1978–1981)*, Blue Plate, 1991.

Murray, Pauline, and the Invisible Girls: *Pauline Murray and the Invisible Girls*, RSO, 1980.

Names, The: "Night Shift," Factory/London, 1981, 1997 (*Different Colours, Different Shades: The Factory Story, Part 2*).

New Fast Automatic Daffodils: "Get Better," Mute, 1991.

New Order: "Ceremony," Factory, 1981 • "Everything's Gone Green," Factory/London, 1981, 1997 (*Different Colours, Different Shades: The Factory Story, Part 2*) • *Movement*, Factory, 1982 • *Substance*, Qwest, 1987.

Orchestral Manoeuvres in the Dark: *OMD* (2 tracks), Virgin/Epic, 1981.

Psychedelic Furs: *The Psychedelic Furs* (2 tracks), Columbia, 1980.

Section 25: *Always Now*, Factory, 1981.

Stone Roses: "So Young," Thin Line, 1985 • *Complete*, Silvertone, 1995.

U2: "11 O'Clock Tick Tock," Island, 1980.

COLLECTIONS

Martin: The Work of Record Producer Martin Hannett, Factory, 1991.

James Harris III

See JIMMY JAM AND TERRY LEWIS

Jerry Harrison

As Jerry Harrison sees it, his role as a producer is merely an extension of his life as a musician. "In many ways what I do as a producer is quite similar to what I did joining Talking Heads and Jonathan [Richman] in Modern Lovers: taking a songwriter who has a very distinct but in some ways inaccessible style, adding what I play, and helping him (or them) round out the sound or complete the picture," he says. He has helped such artists as Big Head Todd and the Monsters, Crash Test Dummies, BoDeans, Live, Poi Dog Pondering, Violent Femmes, and the Verve Pipe successfully complete their pictures.

Harrison (born February 21, 1949, in Milwaukee) has now spent more time working as a producer than as a musician, but he still has a musician's sensibilities when it comes to producing. "I always try to draw out from the artists what they can do," he says. "I'll sometimes suggest a player who I think can add something, who's a specialist; but even when there's a keyboard player, and I play keyboards, I'd rather work with [the band's keyboard player] on tones and sounds. I think maybe because I make my own records, my feeling is that this is their record and I want them to shine. I think the producer is the person who just tries to get whatever has to be done, done."

Harrison entered the production realm when the Talking Heads began to produce their own albums. "I really felt that since we had done all that work with [Brian] Eno [see entry] we had overcome the idea of the studio being sort of off-limits. I definitely saw it as a tool, the same way you'd think of an instrument as a tool."

And while he was part of the big puzzle at Heads sessions, when he went out on his own to produce a Nona Hendryx single, he remembers with a laugh that things were a bit different. "Having the engineer ask me all these questions like, 'What kind of tape do you want to use?' I said, 'I don't know—what tape do you usually use?' "

After the sessions with the Talking Heads and Hendryx, Harrison set off to work on his first solo album, *The Red and the Black*, and an album by his friend and co-producer on the Hendryx sessions, Busta Jones; he also assisted David Byrne on his *The Catherine Wheel* album.

While he had built a pretty extensive resume by then, it was during the recording of the Violent Femmes' *The Blind Leading the Naked* in 1986 that he felt at home in the producer's chair. "I think during that album I thought, 'This is going to be a part of my life.' "

And while he was getting more and more calls to produce, he was still committed to the Talking Heads. "I was really trying to juggle all of these careers that I had," he remembers. "I really liked producing and I really thought I was good at it." So, in between Heads albums and tours, he recorded with the Fine Young Cannibals, the BoDeans, and Poi Dog Pondering. "I think originally record companies saw that I had been in two bands that they would consider out on the fringes and they thought that I would be a good choice for bands they didn't know what to do with," he says.

Then he got a phone call from Gary Kurfirst, who was just about to sign a band out of Hershey, Pennsylvania, by the name of Live. "Gary said, 'I'm quite sure I want to sign them and I want you to produce them, I think you'd be perfect. Here's zero dollars, go make an album,' " he remembers. He met with the band and made Live's *Mental Jewelry* album; three years later they reconvened and made the wildly successful *Throwing Copper* (No. 1).

"When Live became successful I started to get more tapes from bands that were a little more mainstream. I think I got the reputation that I could develop someone and make a record that had potential to sell. Getting new bands to succeed is maybe the most difficult thing to do, to get their expression across," he says.

One of the keys to his success has been his dedication to finding a sound for each album. "I try to really come to terms with where I'm going to go with the record and feel comfortable with it," he explains. "There are times I hear good music, but I don't take the project because I don't have any idea what I want to do with it."

In fact, before working on Verve Pipe's *Villains* release, Harrison admits the he had turned down a couple of their previous independent releases merely because he couldn't find anything to add to their sound. But when he does take on a project, he wants to make sure that he's on the right track. "I discuss it with the band and make sure we're all on the same page, but things are always going to evolve in the studio. Sometimes I don't even have it quite in words, but I have a picture."

It's that philosophy he took into a session with Kenny Wayne Sheppard, which was a return to his blues beginnings. "I came up with a plan that I wanted to do. Everyone from Kenny Wayne Shepherd, to the record company, to the management thought it was good." That plan included adding Chris Layton and Tommy Shannon—the Double Trouble rhythm section—to Shepherd's early tracking dates. The trio recorded a version of Jimi Hen-

drix's "Voodoo Chile (Slight Return)" and "I Don't Live Today," which was a lifelong dream of Harrison's. "I was in [the studio) going, 'Wow, isn't this great?' "

Even after spending his entire life working around music, he says his production gigs are satisfying because he can immerse himself in any number of musical genres. "There's something wonderful about being a producer. It's like working in a genre where you know as a player you could never come up to the level they're at, but you can still think about it. So, as a producer you get to express yourself through the artist." —DAVID JOHN FARINELLA

Big Head Todd and the Monsters: *Beautiful World,* Revolution, 1997.

Black 47: *Home of the Brave,* SBK, 1994.

BoDeans: *Outside Looking In,* Slash, 1987.

Bogmen: *Life Begins at 40 Million,* Arista, 1995.

Bonzo Goes to Washington: "5 Minutes (C-C-C-Club Mix)," Sleeping Bag, 1984.

Crash Test Dummies: *God Shuffled His Feet,* Arista, 1993 • "Mmm Mmm Mmm Mmm," Arista, 1993 • "Afternoons and Coffeespoons," Arista, 1994.

Fatima Mansions: "The Loyaliser," Radioactive, 1994 • *Lost in the Former West,* Kitchenware, 1995.

Fine Young Cannibals: *The Raw and the Cooked* (1 track), IRS, 1989 • *Finest,* MCA, 1996.

General Public: *Rub It Better,* Epic, 1995.

Harrison, Jerry: *The Red and the Black,* Sire, 1981.

Harrison, Jerry, and Casual Gods: *Casual Gods,* Sire, 1988 • "Rev It Up," Sire, 1988 • *Walk on Water,* Fly/Sire/WB, 1990.

Heads: *No Talking Just Head,* MCA, 1996.

Hutton, Noella: *Noella Hutton,* MCA, 1998.

Kenny Wayne Shepherd Band: *Trouble Is . . . ,* Revolution, 1997.

Live: *Four Songs* (EP), Radioactive/MCA, 1991 • *Mental Jewelry,* Radioactive/MCA, 1991 • "Selling the Drama," Radioactive/MCA, 1994 • *Throwing Copper,* Radioactive/MCA, 1994 • "All Over You," Radioactive/MCA, 1995 • "I Alone," Radioactive/MCA, 1995 • "Lightning Crashes," Radioactive/MCA, 1995.

Murphy, Elliott: *Milwaukee* (2 tracks), EMIS, 1986 • *Going Through Something: The Best Of,* Dejadisc, 1996.

Neurotic Outsiders: *Neurotic Outsiders,* Maverick/WB, 1996.

Poi Dog Pondering: "Jack Ass Ginger," Columbia, 1992 • *Volo Volo* (4 tracks), Columbia, 1992.

Psychefunkapus: *Skin,* Atlantic, 1991.

Pure: *Purefunalia,* Reprise, 1992.

Rusted Root: *Remember,* Mercury, 1996.

Verve Pipe: *Villains,* RCA, 1996 • "The Freshmen," RCA, 1997.

Violent Femmes: "I Held Her in My Arms," Slash/WB, 1986, 1993 • *The Blind Leading the Naked,* Slash/WB, 1986 • "The Children of the Revolution," Slash/WB, 1986 • *Add It Up, 1981–1993,* Slash, 1993.

Harry J

(HARRY JOHNSON)

Harry Johnson, or "Harry J" as he's always been known, began producing right at the start of the reggae era and gained immediate Jamaican attention. "No More Heartaches" by the Beltones (1968) is slow reggae–rock steady with poignant harmonies that make you think maybe there are still a few heartaches left after all. "Cuss Cuss" by Lloyd Robinson is as universal a reaction to the woes of everyday living as has ever been put on vinyl. Both these tracks were cut by Harry J at Studio One with Coxsone Dodd's (see entry) house band. Both are reggae drenched in soul.

Another Harry J production, Tony Scott's innocently youthful "What Am I to Do?," was anthologized in England. Harry J then reworked the track as an instrumental with Winston Wright on soaring keyboards for a major U.K. chart smash called "The Liquidator" (by the Harry J All Stars). He followed up by pairing two Studio One veterans, sensitive singer/songwriter Bob Andy and pre-I-Threes vocalist Marcia Griffiths on a cover of "Young, Gifted and Black" that made it to No. 5 on the U.K. charts and was followed by an album of duets.

These hits enabled Harry J to make the next logical progression from record store owner/producer to his own 16-track studio and the Harry J label—with the added valence of getting his records released in England on his own imprint by Trojan as well. His house band in the early days included Wailers-to-be brothers Carlton and Aston Barrett on drum and bass, Glen Adams on keyboards, and Alva Lewis and Ranny "Bop" Williams (the original lead singer for the Beltones) on guitar. Coxsone alumni Syd Bucknor served briefly as engineer, as did Tony Robinson, who went on to successful productions of his own.

A few of Harry J's biggest hits include "Nice Nice Time" and the classic "This Is Reggae Music" by Zap Pow; reggae godfather Joe Higgs' turbulent but somehow reassuring "World Is Upside Down"; Heptones hits like "Fat Girl," the sublime "Book of Rules," and "Cool Rasta"; and Ras Midas's African roots chant "Kude a Bamba." Many who first broadened their view of reggae beyond Bob Marley and Peter Tosh instantly responded to cuts like these and Lorna Bennet's "Breakfast in Bed," as well as early DJ Scotty's gleeful answer-back "Skank in Bed." These and other Harry J productions were featured on volumes 1 and 2 of the Mango set *This Is Reggae Music.*

Because he funneled profits back into equipment, Harry J's studio was much in demand in the early '70s, and Bob Marley and the Wailers (in their first post-Perry recordings, which became their earliest Island releases—all of the *Burnin'* LP and some of *Catch a Fire*); Burning Spear (*Dry & Heavy* and parts of *Man In the Hills* and *Social Living*); and the Heptones (*Night Food*) all recorded major works there. Another wise move that kept the studio on top was hiring Sylvan Morris, former Coxsone engineer, to run the sessions. Since these records were all released on Island, Harry J's name was more well known in North America than many other Jamaican producers in the '70s.

In the late '70s his core studio band included Maxie Edwards on drums, Junior Dan on bass, and Leslie Butler on keyboards. This was the age of the vocal group in Jamaica and Harry J scored one of the finest albums by the Melodians, including big hits "Swing and Dine," "Rock It with I" (later covered in the States by David Lindley), and "Sweet Sensation." He racked up another major hit in 1980 with Sheila Hylton's cover of the Police's "The Bed's Too Big Without You." It was a natural to be picked for volume 5 of the *This Is Reggae Music* series (the last two volumes were issued many years after the first three), neatly nicking a pop group that borrowed much of its sound from reggae.

By 1982 Harry J's studio was being openly denigrated in Peter Simon & Stephen Davis's *Reggae International* as newer studios like Bob Marley's Tuff Gong moved to the fore. Still, Bunny Wailer, who left the Wailers after their first two Island LPs, continued to record there throughout the '80s, and even 1990's *Time Will Tell* was cut there, albeit self-produced. A Trojan compilation called *Return of the Liquidator,* issued in 1991, collects 18 vocal productions and 12 instrumentals for an excellent all-round Harry J sampler, available on CD.
—CHUCK FOSTER

Bennett, Lorna: "Breakfast in Bed," Island, 1974 (*This Is Reggae Music,* Vol. 1).

Bennett, Lorna and Scotty: "Breakfast in Bed," Mango, 1975 (*This Is Reggae Music,* Vol. 2).

Dawkins, Carl: *Carl Dawkins,* Harry J/JA, 1976.

Harry J All Stars: "Liquidator," A&M, 1973 (*Reggae Spectacular*).

Heptones, The: "Country Boy," Mango, 1975 (*This Is Reggae Music*, Vol. 2) • "Book of Rules," Island, 1976.

Higgs, Joe: "World Is Upside Down," MCA, 1971 • "The World Is Upside Down," Island, 1974 (*This Is Reggae Music*, Vol. 1).

Hylton, Sheila: "The Bed's Too Big Without You/Give Me Your Love," Mango, 1980.

I Roy: *Heart of a Lion*, Virgin, 1978 • *Crucial Cuts*, Virgin, 1983.

Melodians, The: *Sweet Sensation*, Harry J/JA, 1977.

Ras Midas: "Kude a Bamba/Congo Dub," Mango, 1976.

Zap Pow: "This Is Reggae Music/Break Down the Barriers," Mango, 1973 • *Revolution*, Trojan, 1976.

COLLECTIONS

What Am I to Do?, Harry J, 1970.

Cultural Dub, Harry J, 1978.

Reggae Gold, Gold Rush, c. 1982.

Return of the Liquidator: 30 Skinhead Classics, 1968–1970, Trojan, 1991.

Bobby Hart

See TOMMY BOYCE AND BOBBY HART

Dan Hartman

For more than two decades, Dan Hartman's music was propelled by feeling, his creative energy wrapping itself around more musical genres and projects than seem humanly possible.

Hartman was born December 8, 1950, in Harrisburg, Pennsylvania; his career dates to the early '70s, when, as singer/bassist for the Edgar Winter Group, he wrote and sang the classic, "Free Ride." That was followed by a string of disco-era hits for Columbia Records, including "Instant Replay," "Countdown/This Is It," and the extended play version of "Vertigo/Relight My Fire," featuring the vocals of Loleatta Holloway. He was contracted to Blue Sky, a subsidiary of Columbia's sister label, Epic.

While the *Instant Replay* album became a dance floor hit at the height of the disco boom, Hartman's foray into motion picture soundtracks provided some of his most notable successes. In 1983, Hartman befriended a struggling musician, Charlie Midnight, then meeting the rent as a proofreader.

Hartman arranged to meet Midnight at a Chock Full o'Nuts in midtown Manhattan and from that simple rendezvous emerged a songwriting partnership that would last a decade and produce a string of pop-dance-rock classics. The pair scored their first joint smash "Heart of the Beat" (topping 3 million sales) from the seminal hip-hop movie *Breakin'*. They followed with another breakdance anthem, "Can't Stop the Street," sung by Chaka Khan in the film *Krush Groove*.

Hartman, alone and with Charlie Midnight, contributed music to *Fletch*, *Down and Out in Beverly Hills*, *Ruthless People*, *Bull Durham*, *Innocent Man*, *Air America*, *Oliver & Company*, *Scrooged*, and the first two *Teenage Mutant Ninja Turtles* films.

"He was incredibly generous, inspirational, and very demanding," says Midnight. "He'd expect me to show up with 10 pages of lyrics, but he was very easy to work with. Working with Dan Hartman really spoiled me. I think he was a great blue-eyed soul singer; the quality of his voice and his passion was very striking. He had this ability to know what made a great song."

One such was the Hartman-Midnight composition "Living in America," which became James Brown's biggest hit (No. 4) in 15 years after Soul Brother #1 performed it in *Rocky IV*. The record also earned Brown a Grammy for Best R&B Male Vocal—and a Grammy nomination for Hartman.

One of the defining moments of Hartman's career occurred when he wrote and performed "I Can Dream About You" (No. 6), the worldwide hit from the 1984 film *Streets of Fire*. For reasons that make a lot less sense a decade after the fledgling era of MTV, Hartman elected to not appear in the video for "I Can Dream," thus relinquishing visual identification with the song. But for Hartman, the spirit of the music always came first. As long as he was in the studio discovering new sounds, finding that feeling and new ways to communicate it, he was happy.

In 1989, he recorded an instrumental album for Private Music, *New Green/Clear Blue*. It was not the radical departure from his dance-pop trademarks that it seemed at first. "This music is meant to be something that helps people connect with their own subconscious," he said. "It is intended to be played at very low levels in a rather tranquil environment. It's a platform for the imagination." He used this music in a counted breath and healing workshop he conducted weekly.

Hartman died on March 22, 1994, at home in Bridgeport, Connecticut, following a long battle with AIDS. He was 43. —LARRY FLICK

.38 Special: *.38 Special*, A&M, 1977 • *Special Delivery*, A&M, 1978.

3-V: "Heart of the Beat," Polydor, 1984 (*Breakin'* soundtrack).

Average White Band: *Cupid's in Fashion*, RCA, 1982.

Brown, James: *Gravity*, Scotti Brothers, 1986 • "Living in America," Scotti Brothers, 1986.

Foghat: *Night Shift*, Bearsville, 1976 • *Best Of*, Rhino, 1990 • *Best Of*, Vol. 2, Rhino, 1992.

Harrison, Jerry, and Casual Gods: *Walk on Water*, Fly / Sire / WB, 1990.

Hartman, Dan: *Images*, Blue Sky, 1976 • *Who Is Dan Hartman?*, Blue Sky, 1976 • "Countdown / This Is It," Blue Sky, 1978 • "Instant Replay," Blue Sky, 1978 • *Instant Replay*, Blue Sky, 1979 • *It Hurts to Be in Love*, Blue Sky, 1979 • *Relight My Fire*, Blue Sky, 1979 • "Vertigo," Blue Sky, 1979 • "I Can Dream About You," MCA, 1984 • *I Can Dream About You*, MCA, 1984 • "We Are the Young," MCA, 1984 • "Second Nature," MCA, 1985 • *We Are the Young*, MCA, 1987 • *New Green / Clear Blue*, Atlantic, 1989 • *Keep the Fire Burning*, Chaos, 1994.

Hendryx, Nona: *Female Trouble*, EMI America, 1987.

King, Paul: *Joy*, Epic, 1987.

Little Richard: "Great Gosh A' Mighty!," MCA, 1986.

Plasmatics: *Metal Priestess*, Stiff, 1981.

Sedaka, Neil: *Come See About Me*, MCA, 1984 • *Tuneweaver*, Varese Sarabande, 1995.

Turner, Tina: *Foreign Affair*, Capitol, 1989 • "The Best," Capitol, 1989 • *Collected Recordings, Sixties to Nineties*, Capitol, 1994.

Young, Paul: *From Time to Time: The Singles Collection*, Columbia, 1991.

COLLECTIONS

The Original Salsoul Classics: 20th Anniversary, Salsoul, 1992.

Isaac Hayes

Another man with Isaac Hayes' credentials—musician, singer, songwriter, producer, actor, humanitarian, radio personality—would be called a chameleon, but Hayes has always been resolutely, undeniably himself. As a sideman at Stax, then co-producer and co-writer (with David Porter; see entry) of the great Sam and Dave hits ("Hold On I'm Comin'," No. 21; "Soul Man," No. 2; "I Thank You," No. 9; "When Something Is Wrong with My Baby") and others for Otis Redding, Carla Thomas, Johnnie Taylor, William Bell, Judy Clay, and the Bar-Kays, Hayes helped define soul music in the '60s.

Then as a solo artist Hayes stretched the boundaries of soul, adding strings and social themes; with Sly Stone, Gamble and Huff, Curtis Mayfield, and Norman Whitfield (see entries), he helped move black music from a singles to an album format. On albums like *Hot Buttered Soul* (No. 8), *The Isaac Hayes Movement* (No. 8), *To Be Continued* (No. 11), *Black Moses* (No. 10), and especially the Oscar- and Grammy-winning *Shaft* (No.1), Hayes took his brand of elegant but funky soul to a huge new audience.

Isaac Hayes was born August 20, 1942, in Covington, Tennessee. He lived on a farm until he was 7, then moved to Memphis with his maternal grandparents (who raised him). The family was musical and active in the church, school, and community. Hayes' first public performance was a duet with his sister at church when he was 3. Already the musical perfectionist, Hayes halted his sister in mid-performance when she made a mistake.

In high school Hayes won a singing contest, noted the attention his performance generated, and said "Hmm, this is what I want to do." He took a year of band (tuba, then sax) and began singing with a variety of combos: rock 'n' roll, doo-wop, blues, gospel, jazz. "I loved it all—this adventure into music—I was sucking up everything like a sponge," he says.

"With the blues band we played the juke joints of Mississippi, Tennessee, Arkansas. We didn't make much money: it was all the corn liquor you could drink and enough money to get back home. If the owner didn't feel like paying you, he didn't pay you and you didn't argue because he had a .38 pistol on his hip," he laughs darkly. "With gospel it was all the food you could eat, and then maybe a collection was taken up for expenses."

Eventually he "learned enough piano to get along," and wound up on the staff at Memphis's Stax Records around 1963, having been turned down three times by the label as an artist. An old friend from his doo-wop days, David Porter, was already with the label and said to Hayes, "You play music and I write lyrics, let's team up and start writing and producing like Holland-Dozier-Holland [see entry] up at Motown."

"When we started writing," Hayes remembers, "guys around the city would tease us: 'Hey, hit men, how many hits did you write today?' But we kept our noses to the grindstone and we finally clicked with Carla Thomas's 'How Do You Quit?' in 1965. Then they chose David and me to write and produce for Sam and Dave, and after we had a big hit with them, more people around town wanted to write songs. We organized a writer's workshop and everything," recalls Hayes.

Their writing for Sam and Dave was typical of their

approach. "We would come up with a good subject or a good hook. For the meat of the song you have to ask yourselves some questions: If you want this girl, why do you want her? If you get her, what would you do? People have to able to get what you're trying to get across. As far as music is concerned, you've got to come up with a groove with changes and things that keep the emotional content in it.

"Usually our songs came from personal experiences," he continues. "For instance, with 'When Something Is Wrong with My Baby,' David and I were working and working and working, and we just couldn't come up with anything. So we gave up and each went home. After about 30 minutes, he called me: 'I got it, I got it, I got it.' I said, 'What do you mean?' He had just written it on toilet paper or something, and said, 'When something is wrong with my baby, something is wrong with me.'

"He came over and we started going over the lyrics. I sat down at the piano and started playing something slow. We got the changes and the melody and put it with the first verse, and the rest was easy. Sam and Dave were in town—we would usually work on their songs when they were around—sometimes we'd have them sitting there while we wrote to get a good feel for them.

" 'You Don't Know Like I Know' was originally a gospel song: 'You don't know like I know what the Lord has done for me.' Well, a woman can do some good things for you too. We just switched it around," Hayes says with a chuckle.

" 'Soul Man' came about during one of the riots. I was watching TV and they said something about businesses being bypassed when 'soul' was written on the door. That reminded me of Passover in the Bible. So I thought about this 'soul' thing: there's a lot of pride in it. I didn't look at the rioting as destroying. I looked at it as frustrated people taking out their frustrations on whatever got in their way. I told David about it and we started working on it. Everything just clicked."

Hayes recalls the Stax studio. "We only had a 1-track recorder at first. [Label owner] Jim Stewart was considered the king of 1-track. If anybody screwed up, we had to start all over again and [trumpet player] Wayne Jackson's lips would fall off. Eventually we got 2-track when Tom Dowd [see entry] came in and installed it for us.

"Regarding arrangements, we did them in our heads, whereas Motown may have had them written out. We went on feel. I continue to do that. Otis [Redding] would come in sometimes with just an idea. He would get behind the microphone and say, 'Work up a groove' and start doing lyrics spontaneously — [singing] 'I can't turn you loose.' "

Though deeply in the groove, Hayes was always a thinking man with a conscience as well. "I was active even in high school in marches and things. I was afraid but I thought it was the right thing to do. When Dr. King was killed [in 1968] I went through a period when I couldn't write, couldn't create. I just went blank. I was so hurt by that and I had so much bitterness and hatred for racist attitudes. Then one day after about a year I cognized: 'Hey man, the only way you can make a change is to do what you do.' So I got busy again."

Hayes had recorded a very casual album in 1967 that received a fair amount of critical praise and was given the opportunity to record again in 1969. This time he took the affair more seriously, but still felt no particular pressure to succeed as an artist. That album became *Hot Buttered Soul,* and it established the recording career of Isaac Hayes.

Hayes was shocked by his solo success. "I couldn't believe it because I had been behind the scenes so long. When David and I wrote together, we wrote for other people, so we had to match their personalities. I had a background in blues, jazz, pop, even classical, and I wanted to get it all out. I had a funky groove underneath, but those strings on top. I was happy with it for myself, but a few million other people got into it too," he laughs.

For *Shaft,* Hayes had the powerful image of a tough but vulnerable black screen detective to inspire him; he found his all-time resonant grooves for the title track and long instrumental passages that achieved a perfect balance between the funk and the sweet.

Hayes has released almost two dozen (mostly) successful albums since. He remains humble. "I never took myself too seriously. Each time I cut a hit record I would say 'Whew, I made it again.' I was honest with my music and said, 'If I hurt, I cry.' A lot of men liked it because it said what they wanted to say but didn't know how to. Women liked it because it showed sensitivity in a man, and that's what they were looking for."

Hayes could get away with sensitivity because of his tough, forbidding image. Some TV stations wouldn't let him on because they thought he was militant. "The image was my security blanket, especially the shades—tough on the outside, sensitive on the inside," he confides.

That image—shaved head, chains draped over muscles—led to an acting career. Hayes has appeared in over a dozen films and in recurring roles on TV. His favorite role so far is that of Gandolf Finch in James Garner's *Rockford Files* TV series from the '80s.

Hayes' most recent album is the notable *Raw and Refined* from 1995. He also did a *Shaft* parody for the

Beavis and Butt-head Do America soundtrack; and is the star of the *Isaac Hayes and Friends* radio show on KISS-FM (WRKS) in New York, playing "classic soul and today's R&B" weekday mornings. He is also the voice of "Chef" on the Comedy Central hit animated series *South Park*. But most of all, he is Isaac Hayes. —ERIC OLSEN

Bar-Kays: "Give Everybody Some," Volt, 1967 • "Soul Finger," Volt, 1967.

Bell, William: *Best Of*, Stax, 1991 • *Little Something Extra*, Stax, 1992.

Chuck D: *The Autobiography of Mistachuck*, Mercury, 1996.

Clay, Judy: *Private Numbers*, Stax, 1974.

Clifford, Linda: *I'm Yours*, RSO, 1980 • *Greatest Hits*, Curtom, 1991.

Eckstine, Billy: *Stormy*, Enterprise, 1970.

Emotions, The: *Chronicle: Greatest Hits*, Stax, 1991.

Hayes, Isaac: *Hot Buttered Soul*, Stax, 1969, 1978 • "Walk On By," Enterprise, 1969 • *The Isaac Hayes Movement*, Enterprise, 1970 • *To Be Continued*, Enterprise, 1970 • *Black Moses*, Enterprise, 1971 • "Never Can Say Goodbye," Enterprise, 1971 • *Shaft*, Enterprise, 1971 • "Theme from *Shaft*," Enterprise, 1971 • "Do Your Thing," Enterprise, 1972 • "Theme from *The Men*," Enterprise, 1972 • *Wonderful*, Stax, 1972, 1995 • *Joy*, Enterprise, 1973 • *Live at the Sahara Tahoe*, Enterprise, 1973 • *Double Feature*, Stax, 1974, 1993 • "Joy, Part 1," Enterprise, 1974 • *Tough Guys*, Enterprise, 1974 • *Truck Turner*, Enterprise, 1974 • *Chocolate Chip*, Enterprise, 1975 • *Disco Connection*, ABC, 1975 • *Groove-a-Thon*, ABC, 1976 • *Juicy Fruit*, ABC, 1976 • w/ Dionne Warwick, *A Man and a Woman*, ABC, 1977 • *New Horizon*, Polydor, 1977 • *For the Sake of Love*, Polydor, 1978 • "Don't Let Go," Polydor, 1979 • *And Once Again*, Polydor, 1980 • *Don't Let Go*, Polydor, 1980 • w/ Millie Jackson, *Royal Rappins*, Spring, 1980 • *Lifetime Thing*, Polydor, 1981 • *The Best Of*, Vols. 1–2, Stax, 1986 • *U-Turn*, Columbia, 1986 • *Love Attack*, Columbia, 1988 • *Greatest Hit Singles*, Stax, 1991 • *Greatest Hits*, RSP, 1992 • *Branded*, Point Blank, 1995 • "Fragile," Point Blank, 1995 • *Isaac's Moods: The Best Of*, Stax UK, 1995 • *Raw and Refined*, Point Blank, 1995 • *The Best of the Polydor Years*, Polydor, 1996 • "Two Cool Guys," Geffen, 1996 (*Beavis and Butt-head Do America* soundtrack).

Jackson, Chuck, and Maxine Brown: "Hold On, I'm Coming," Stax, 1967.

Jean and the Darlings: "How Can You Mistreat the One You Love," Stax, 1967.

John, Mable: *Stay Out of the Kitchen*, Stax, 1968, 1993 • "You're Good Thing Is About to End," Stax, 1966.

King, Albert, with Steve Cropper and Pop Staples: *Jammed Together*, Stax, 1969.

Lewis, Ramsey: "Soul Man," Stax, 1967.

Porter, David: *Gritty, Groovy and Gettin' It*, Enterprise, 1970.

Purify, James and Bobby: "I Take What I Want," Bell, 1967.

Redding, Otis: *Remember Me*, Stax, 1992 • *Otis! The Definitive Otis Redding*, Rhino, 1993.

Sam and Dave: *Double Dynamite*, Stax, 1966 • "Hold On, I'm Comin'," Stax, 1966 • *Hold On, I'm Coming*, Stax, 1966 • "Said I Wasn't Gonna Tell Nobody," Stax, 1966 • "You Don't Know Like I Know," Stax, 1966 • "You Got Me Hummin'," Stax, 1966 • "Soothe Me," Stax, 1967 • "Soul Man," Stax, 1967 • *Soul Men*, Stax, 1967 • "When Something Is Wrong with My Baby," Stax, 1967 • "I Thank You," Stax, 1968 • *I Thank You*, Stax, 1968 • "Wrap It Up," Stax, 1968 • *Sweat and Soul: Anthology*, Rhino, 1993 • *Sweat and Soul: Anthology*, Vol. 2, Rhino, 1993 • *Very Best Of*, Rhino, 1995.

Soul Children: *Soul Children*, Stax, 1969 • *Chronicle*, Stax, 1979 • *Hold On, I'm Coming*, Stax, 1997.

Taylor, Johnnie: "I Had a Dream," Stax, 1966 • "I've Got to Love Somebody's Baby," Stax, 1966.

Thomas, Carla: "How Do You Quit?," Stax, 1965 • "B-A-B-Y," Stax, 1966 • "Let Me Be Good to You," Stax, 1966 • *Hidden Gems*, Stax, 1992 • *Gee Whiz: The Best Of*, Rhino, 1994.

Vera, Billy, and Judy Clay: *Storybook Children/Greatest Love*, Soul Classics, 1995.

Mike Hedges

Mike Hedges has been one of the most important producers of English alterna-rock in the '80s and '90s, specializing in the moody goth and exotica of the Cure (*Three Imaginary Boys; Seventeen Seconds; Faith*, No. 14 U.K.), Siouxsie & the Banshees (*A Kiss in the Dreamhouse*, No. 11 U.K; *Hyaena*, No. 15 U.K., *Through the Looking Glass*, No. 15 U.K.), and Flesh for Lulu (*Long Live the New Flesh*), as well as a wide array of other wavey artists, including Mark Almond, The Beautiful South (*Welcome to the Beautiful South* and *Choke*, both No. 2 U.K), Everything But The Girl (*Baby the Stars Shine Bright*), Lush (*Split*), Texas (*White on Blonde*), and the Undertones (*The Sin of Pride*).

Shortly after Mike Hedges was born in Nottingham, England, in 1953, his family moved to Zambia, where he spent the first 16 years of his life. Music, any kind of music, was difficult to find and he could only get his hands on one album a month (Rolling Stones, Beatles, Motown), so he and his older brother pored over every detail of production, songwriting, and performance—excellent training for a producer-to-be.

After working as a musician and an inorganic chemist, Hedges got a phone call from a friend in 1976 who asked if he was interested in working as a tea boy in a local studio. Three months after Hedges walked into Morgan Studios in London he was asked to work as a tape operator. After he had spent six months pushing buttons and running tape, Chris Parry, who had just signed the Cure to his Fiction label, came looking for an engineer.

Hedges got the call because "I was really keen to work with them and I was cheap," he chuckles. His close relationship with the band continued through their next three albums, including their controversial single "Killing an Arab," the hypnotic and driving "Jumping Someone Else's Train," and one of Hedges' few recordings that he can still listen to: the mossy and dappled "A Forest."

Hedges explains: "After I finish with an act I don't go back and listen to the record because I have been so involved in [making] it. The things that bugged me in the studio still bug me listening back to it. It's not modesty, it's embarrassment. I'm never 100 percent happy with anything. I think it is one of my advantages as a producer. It's almost never excellent—good is great and good enough is common. Because of the time limit, that's just the way it is."

In 1981 Hedges opted to go freelance and opened his own studio, the Playground. It was there that he worked with such legendary bands as Siouxsie & the Banshees (and their offshoot, the Creatures), the Associates, Bauhaus, and the Beautiful South. "Most bands I work with tend to have some idea of what they want and it's my job to translate that onto tape as well as possible. It's also nice to have an album that the record company loves, so they can sell it," he explains practically. "A lot of the job is getting the band to perform the best they can. Sometimes it's by flattery; sometimes it is telling them to get some sleep."

In 1992 Hedges decided to retire to France. He began to go mad after about three weeks. "I just needed a break," he says with a laugh, "not to retire." He converted the Chateau Rouge Motte in Normandy to a residential studio, which he stocked with vintage equipment purchased from Apple Studios (where he worked for a time in the '80s) and some modern wonders like ProTools.

The key, he thinks, is to record live onto the vintage equipment and then figure out what needs to be fixed with technology. "A lot of people use too much Pro-Tools, so then we call it 'Slow Tools.' People sit in front of the screen for too long. You [should] listen to a take and if you hear something you think will take people's concentration off the performance—a tuning thing or a slip in timing—then that should be fixed. If it's something that doesn't throw you—a tuning thing that sounds great because of the performance, or a slight slip that shows that it was live and makes it more exciting because of it—then you just have to leave it." —ERIC OLSEN AND DAVID JOHN FARINELLA

A House: *I Want Too Much*, Sire/Reprise, 1990 • *No More Apologies*, Setanta, 1996.

Almond, Marc w/ the Willing Sinners, *Vermin in Ermine*, Some Bizarre, 1984 • "Love Letter," Virgin, 1985 • "Stories of Johnny," Virgin, 1985 • w/ the Willing Sinners, *Stories of Johnny*, Some Bizarre, 1985 • *The House Is Haunted By the Echo of Your Last Goodbye* (EP), Some Bizarre/Virgin, 1985 • *A Woman's Story*, Some Bizarre, 1986 • *Mother Fist . . . and Her Five Daughters*, Some Bizarre/Virgin, 1987.

Associates, The: *The Affectionate Punch*, Fiction, 1980, 1982 • *Fourth Drawer Down*, Situation Two, 1981 • *Sulk*, Sire, 1982 • *Popera: The Singles Collection*, Sire/WB, 1990.

Beautiful South: *Welcome to the Beautiful South*, Go!/Elektra, 1989 • *Choke*, Go!/Elektra, 1990 • *The Best of: Carry On Up the Charts*, Go!/Mercury, 1994, 1995.

Catchers, The: *Mute*, Discovery, 1995.

Creatures, The: *Feast*, Wonderland/Polydor, 1983 • *Boomerang*, Geffen, 1989.

Cure, The: *Three Imaginary Boys*, Fiction, 1979 • *Seventeen Seconds*, Elektra, 1980 • *Faith*, Elektra, 1981 • *Happily Ever After*, A&M, 1981 • *Standing on the Beach: The Singles*, Elektra, 1986.

English Beat: *Special Beat Service* (1 track), IRS, 1982 • *What Is Beat?*, IRS, 1982.

Everything But The Girl: *Baby, the Stars Shine Bright*, Sire, 1986, 1995.

Flesh for Lulu: *Long Live the New Flesh*, Capitol, 1987 • "Siamese Twist," Beggars Banquet, 1987.

Geneva: *Further*, Work, 1997.

Lush: "Lovelife," 4 A.D./Reprise, 1994 • *Split*, 4 A.D./Reprise, 1994 • "Undertow," 4 A.D./Reprise, 1994.

Manic Street Preachers: *Everything Must Go*, Epic, 1996.

McAlmont and Butler: *The Sound Of* (2 tracks), Gyroscope, 1996.

Sensation: "Beautiful Morning," 550 Music/Epic, 1994 • *Burger Habit*, 550 Music/Epic, 1994.

Shamen, The : *Drop*, Communion, 1987.

Siouxsie & the Banshees: *A Kiss in the Dreamhouse*, Geffen, 1982, 1992 • *Nocturne*, Geffen, 1983, 1992 • *Hyaena*, Geffen, 1984, 1989 • *Through the Looking Glass*, Geffen, 1987 • "Peek-A-Boo," Geffen, 1988 • *Peep Show*, Geffen, 1988 • "The Killing Jar," Geffen, 1988.

Southern Death Cult: *Southern Death Cult*, Beggars Banquet, 1983.

Texas: *White on Blonde*, Mercury, 1997.

Three O'Clock: *Arrive Without Travelling*, IRS, 1985.

Undertones, The: *The Sin of Pride*, Rykodisc, 1983, 1994.

Wah!: *A Word to the Wise Guy*, Eternal/Beggars Banquet, 1984.

Scott Hendricks

Every producer has a focal point when he's working in the studio, and for Scott Hendricks if the vocals aren't there, it doesn't matter how brilliant the rest of the track is. "Vocals are where I spend 90 percent of my time; they are definitely what I focus on the most," he says. "To me, once the song is there, the next most important thing is the vocal delivery. I'm convinced we could have recorded 'I Swear' with the ukulele, and if the vocal is there, we probably still would have had a hit with it."

John Michael Montgomery, who took "I Swear" to the top of the country charts, may disagree, but there's no arguing that Hendricks has brought the best out of some of Nashville's top artists: Brooks and Dunn (with co-producer Don Cook; see entry), Alan Jackson (with co-producer Keith Stegall; see entry), Faith Hill, Suzy Bogguss, Aaron Tippin, newcomer Trace Adkins, and many more. He has produced more than 30 songs that have gone to No. 1 on *Billboard*'s Hot Country Singles chart. He has been among the Top 5 in *Billboard*'s year-end list of top country producers since 1992. In 1992, Hendricks won an Emmy for producing and engineering ABC Sports' *Monday Night Football* theme, recorded by Hank Williams Jr.

Like many producers, Hendricks began his professional career as an engineer. He moved to Nashville after graduating from Oklahoma State University in the late '70s. Working at Glaser Brothers studio and Bullet Recording proved a strong training ground for him by the time he got ready to strike out as an independent producer in 1985.

Hendricks's first success as a producer came with Restless Heart, a group that included his college friend, Greg Jennings. He produced six No. 1 hits on the country charts for the band, including "I'll Still Be Loving You," which also became a Top 40 hit. He approached that work as he does any project. "I approach a record from the beginning trying to get what the artist wants; that is my goal," he says. "I want the artist to be proud of this record 10 years from now. I take it very seriously and am very intense in making sure that when it's done, it's done to the best of our collective ability."

In addition to his work with Alan Jackson, it was his work with Brooks and Dunn that helped catapult Hendricks to the ranks of Nashville's top producers. Not only has he co-produced the duo, he helped bring them together. Arista Records president Tim DuBois, whom Hendricks has known since they were at Oklahoma State together, was looking for a new duo for his label.

Songwriter/publisher Don Cook had introduced him to Kix Brooks, and Hendricks had known Ronnie Dunn since he had won a Marlboro talent contest. "Tim and I were making a trip to Knoxville to see a football game, and Tim was talking about his ideas for a duo," says Hendricks. "He played me four songs by Kix and then four from another guy who he thought might be the duet partner. I said, 'You know what, I don't hear it. I don't hear the blend.' And I happened to have a tape of Ronnie's in my bag, and I said, 'Here's who I think should be your partner.'" On that tape were three songs that ended up being No. 1 hits for Brooks and Dunn: "Boot Scootin' Boogie," "Neon Moon," and "She Used to Be Mine."

He also had great success with Faith Hill, producing her first two albums, both of which have gone double-platinum. "Initially she didn't want to record the biggest song of her career at all, 'It Matters to Me,'" he recalls. "She didn't think it was her. I convinced her to give it a try and we cut it. She still didn't want to record the vocals. I said, 'Please try.' She tried, and when she started doing it live and saw the reaction, she realized, 'This is me.'"

He also knew "I Swear" sounded good the minute Montgomery added the vocals, but he had no idea it would become one of the biggest hits of the '90s. Both he and Montgomery had heard the demo and wanted to record it. "We said we at least ought to cut it, just to see. Nobody knew for sure, but we gave it a chance, and only after we got the vocal on it and got it finished did we realize that we might have a big fish on the end of the line."

In 1995, Hendricks was named head of Capitol Nashville. At that point, he decided to stop producing acts other than those on his label. "I am a very focused person and I just didn't feel like it was fair for me if I'm going to give everything I've got to Capitol Records. I did have one exception in my contract and that was Faith, who was at the time my fiancée."

Among the acts he's broken at Capitol is Trace Adkins, a lanky 6-foot, 6-inch singer who captured the

Best New Male Vocalist Award from the Academy of Country Music for 1996. Another label had passed on Adkins, but for Hendricks, there was gold in that voice. "That was a no-brainer," he says of his decision to sign and produce Adkins. "I honestly wish every artist package that came to me was that clear to me. That guy has an incredible, unique, distinctive voice."

Although he started as an engineer, Hendricks jokes that "I'm only technical enough to be dangerous. For years I've had my own tape machine and I just drag it around with me everywhere. I've recently sold that and I'm in the process of deciding what to record on in the future."

One possibility is owning his own studio, but just an overdubbing studio, he notes. That way, when things aren't going as well as hoped in the studio, it would be easy to get away from it all. "It's a tough thing for a singer to come in and say, 'Okay, here's my window to sing this song and my whole career is riding on this.' That's a lot of pressure. With Trace Adkins, when we start to go downhill, I'll say 'Time out,' and we'll go get on four-wheelers and go ride or whatever, just to break away from it. That's one of the reasons I want to have my own studio in the country: so we can be closer to the four-wheelers, horses, and nature." —MELINDA NEWMAN

Adkins, Trace: *Dreamin' Out Loud*, Capitol Nashville, 1996 • "Every Light in the House," Capitol Nashville, 1996 • "There's a Girl in Texas," Capitol Nashville, 1996 • "(This Ain't) No Thinkin' Thing," Capitol Nashville, 1997 • *Big Time*, Capitol Nashville, 1997 • "I Left Something Turned On at Home," Capitol Nashville, 1997 • "The Rest of Mine," Capitol Nashville, 1997.

Asleep at the Wheel: *Keepin' Me Up Nights,* Arista, 1990.

Bogguss, Suzy: *Give Me Some Wheels,* Capitol, 1996 • "She Said, He Heard," Capitol, 1997.

Brooks and Dunn: "Boot Scootin' Boogie," Arista, 1991 • "Brand New Man," Arista, 1991 • *Brand New Man,* Arista, 1991 • "My Next Broken Heart," Arista, 1991 • *Hard Workin' Man,* Arista, 1992 • "Neon Moon," Arista, 1992 • "Rock My World (Little Country Girl)," Arista, 1992 • "She Used to Be Mine," Arista, 1992 • "We'll Burn That Bridge," Arista, 1992 • "Best of My Love," Giant, 1993 (*Common Thread: The Songs of the Eagles*) • w/ Johnny Cash, "Folsom Prison Blues," Mercury Nashville, 1994 (*Red Hot and Country*) • "She's Not the Cheatin' Kind," Arista, 1994 • "That Ain't No Way to Go," Arista, 1994 • *Waitin' on Sundown,* Arista, 1994 • "Little Miss Honky Tonk," Arista, 1995 • "You're Gonna Miss Me When I'm Gone," Arista, 1995 • *Greatest Hits,* Arista, 1997.

Crosby, Rob: *Solid Ground,* Arista, 1991 • *Another Time and Place,* Arista, 1992.

Hill, Faith: *Take Me As I Am,* Warner Bros., 1993 • "Wild One," Warner Bros., 1993 • "Piece of My Heart," Warner Bros., 1994 • "It Matters to Me," Warner Bros., 1995 • *It Matters to Me,* Warner Bros., 1995 • "I Can't Do That Anymore," Warner Bros., 1997.

Hutton, Sylvia: *Anthology,* Renaissance, 1997.

Jackson, Alan: *Here in the Real World,* Arista, 1990 • "Don't Rock the Jukebox," Arista, 1991 • *Don't Rock the Jukebox,* Arista, 1991 • "I'd Love You All Over Again," Arista, 1991 • "Someday," Arista, 1991 • *A Lot About Livin' (And a Little 'Bout Love),* Arista, 1992 • "Dallas," Arista, 1992 • "Love's Got a Hold on You," Arista, 1992 • *Honky Tonk Christmas,* Arista, 1993 • *Greatest Hits Collection,* Arista, 1995.

Mercer, Roy D.: *How Big a Boy Are Ya?,* Vol. 3, Capitol Nashville, 1997.

Montgomery, John Michael: "Be My Baby Tonight," Atlantic, 1994 • "I Swear," Atlantic, 1994 • "If You've Got Love," Atlantic, 1994 • *Kickin' It Up,* Atlantic, 1994 • "I Can Love You Like That," Atlantic, 1995 • *John Michael Montgomery,* Atlantic, 1995 • "Sold (The Grundy County Auction Incident)," Atlantic, 1995 • *Greatest Hits,* Atlantic, 1997.

Parnell, Lee Roy: *Love Without Mercy,* Arista, 1992 • *On the Road,* Arista, 1993 • *We All Get Lucky Sometimes,* Career, 1995.

Restless Heart: *Restless Heart,* RCA, 1985 • "That Rock Won't Roll," RCA, 1986 • *Wheels,* RCA, 1986 • "I'll Still Be Loving You," RCA, 1987 • "Why Does It Have to Be (Wrong or Right)?," RCA, 1987 • "A Tender Lie," RCA, 1988 • *Big Dreams in a Small Town,* RCA, 1988 • "Bluest Eyes in Texas," RCA, 1988 • "Wheels," RCA, 1988 • *Fast Movin' Train,* RCA, 1990 • *Best Of,* RCA, 1991.

River Road: "I Broke It, I'll Fix It," Capitol/Nashville, 1997 • *River Road,* Capitol/Nashville, 1997 • "Somebody Will," Capitol, 1997.

Stewart, Larry: *Down the Road,* RCA, 1993 • *Heart Like a Hurricane,* Columbia, 1994.

Tippin, Aaron: *Call of the Wild,* RCA, 1993 • *Greatest Hits and Then Some,* RCA, 1997.

Wariner, Steve: *I Am Ready,* Arista, 1991 • *Drive,* Arista, 1993.

Watson, Wayne: *Giants in the Land,* Dayspring, 1985 • *How Time Flies,* Word/Epic, 1992.

Dennis Herring

For Dennis Herring the role of producer is more about taking a band's music apart and building it back up than anything else. From the roots-rock stylings of Cracker, to the post-synth pop of the Ocean Blue, or even the eerie tones of the Innocence Mission, Herring has moved easily between genres and personalities.

Whether it's equipment—he had the Innocence Mission's drummer Steve Brown buy a brand new kit to capture the right vibe—or song perfection, Herring has worked all angles. "We pruned the arrangements and the structures down to the really essential," he explains of his Innocence Mission work. "Really down to a core about how statemental Don [Peris]'s guitar playing could be and then how pure and beautiful Karen [Peris]'s voice and songs are. Certainly we embellished beyond that, but I really tried to find a core that was a live statement the band could make and then I wanted to build off of that," he says from his Sweet Tea studio in Oxford, Mississippi.

Part of his assignment for the Innocence Mission sessions was to perfect the songs the band had written, but for Cracker's The Golden Age sessions the bulk of his work was picking the perfect songs for the album. "There were a lot of ways Cracker could go this time, and you kinda figure they'd all be good," he says. "I felt that if they were going to make a record that people would perceive as really great, it would be based on the songs more than any other single thing."

After receiving a ton of songs from the Cracker team of David Lowery and Johnny Hickman, he took only the songs that he felt matched a certain conversational quality that he finds attractive in Lowery. "He has a unique way of saying things directly to real people, so there were songs that didn't make it where I felt they were more lofty."

Perhaps it's a Southern thing, considering that Herring hails from Mississippi and Lowery is from Arkansas (although he's calling Virginia home for now). "I think we're both crackers, through and through," Herring jokes. "Growing up on a lot of Southern music like ZZ Top and the Allman Brothers is certainly not like growing up on the Mothers of Invention."

While the South flavors his music, it was his Los Angeles studio days that gave Herring a jump start in the music business. It was Herring's early '80s work as a session guitarist with Glen Ballard that led him to Phil Ramone (see entries). His work with Ramone took him all over the country, where he sat in on sessions with musicians like Julian Lennon and the folks who made up the Flashdance soundtrack. "To be 21 years old and doing that, it was really invaluable to me."

Though Herring made his living for years as a session guitar player, he doesn't automatically move toward the guitar to power an album. "I do get really attracted to counterpoint: I love the 'accompanying the singer' kind of quality. But my favorite instrument is bass; it does so much and it does nearly all of it without anybody noticing. Where bass leaves space, or pushes, or remains melodic, all those elements are subtle and yet effective. Drums have so much to do with modern music, but you know when they're doing it. Bass has got this nice mystery about it. It's a step closer to being a singer, because it's all about things that are inside your body and connected to your head."

Herring admits that although bands come to him for reinvention, it's not always an easy road to travel. For example, the Ocean Blue sessions: "I don't think they felt like they had made the records they'd wanted to yet, so they leapt off the diving board with me," he says of their sessions. "We definitely went up the creek, paddled hard, and they flinched sometimes. The Ocean Blue feel so ready to get to a vibrant place they feel in touch with—that resonates in today. That's their drive and why they called me up," although he admits they may not stick with his direction as a permanent career move. "Maybe I'll be one version of it—not that this will become their Bible and they should only adhere to the laws of Dennis."

Ironically, while bands like the Ocean Blue and Innocence Mission are coming to him for reinvention, during his first real gig as a producer he had to fight against it. "I can still remember working with Timbuk 3. They had been playing their songs for so long that they were really bored with all of it. Here I am, really knocked out with them. I can remember having a couple panic attacks wondering what I would do. . . . I'm just gonna make sure they eat, that's all they need," he says laughing.

"Fairly early in the recording process they came in and all the arrangements were different and they didn't want to do some of the songs I loved." So he pulled them aside and explained that while they were tired of it and 2,000 people had already heard the songs, this was not a time for change. He explained, "This is a time to take everything you've built up to now, take a picture of it, and show it to everybody. Then we can always go a lot of interesting places, but it seems that you should start from the start." —DAVID JOHN FARINELLA

American Girls: *American Girls,* IRS, 1986.

Beowulf: *Two Cents,* Restless, 1995.

Big Car: *Normal,* Giant/Reprise, 1992.

BWF: *Unsentimental,* Restless, 1993.

Camper Van Beethoven: *Our Beloved Revolutionary Sweetheart,* Virgin, 1988 • *Key Lime Pie,* Virgin, 1989 • *Virgin Years,* Virgin, 1994.

Caterwaul: "The Sheep's a Wolf" (remix), IRS, 1989, 1991 (*IRS Greatest Hips,* Vol. 4, *The Remixes*).

Chagall Guevara: "Tale o' the Twister," MCA, 1990 (*Pump Up the Volume* soundtrack).

Chris Duarte Group: *Texas Sugar Strat Magik,* Silvertone, 1994.

Concrete Blonde: "Everybody Knows," MCA, 1990 (*Pump Up the Volume* soundtrack) • *Recollection: The Best of Concrete Blonde,* IRS, 1996.

Cracker: "Euro-Trash Girl," Virgin, 1993 • *The Golden Age,* Virgin, 1996.

Critters Buggin: *Guest,* Loosegroove/Epic, 1994.

Dorff, Andrew: *Hint of Mess,* Work, 1997.

House of Freaks: *Cakewalk,* Giant, 1991.

Innocence Mission "Everything's Different Now," A&M, 1995 • *Glow,* A&M, 1995.

Ocean Blue: *See the Ocean Blue,* Mercury, 1996.

Penny Dreadfuls: *Penny Dreadfuls,* Restless, 1996.

Satchel: *Satchel* (5 tracks), Epic, 1994.

Sister Psychic: *Surrender, You Freak* (1 track), Restless, 1993 • "Velvet Dog," Restless, 1993 (*In Defense of Animals Benefit Compilation*).

Starr, Garrison: *Eighteen over Me,* Geffen, 1997.

Throwing Muses: "Red Shoes," 4 A.D., 1991 (*Volume One*) • *The Real Ramona,* Sire/WB, 1991.

Timbuk 3: "The Future's So Bright, I Gotta Wear Shades," IRS, 1986 • *Greetings from Timbuk 3,* IRS, 1987 • "Life Is Hard," IRS, 1987 • *Eden Alley,* IRS, 1988 • "All I Want for Christmas," IRS, 1990 (*Just in Time for Christmas*) • *Best Of,* IRS, 1992.

Truth, The: *Weapons of Love,* IRS, 1987.

Weapon of Choice: "Nutmeg Sez Bozo the Clown," Loosegroove/Epic, 1994 • *Nutmeg Phantasy,* Loosegroove, 1998.

Beau Hill

Beau Hill's career is virtually synonymous with high-gloss '80s pop metal. He worked with some of its best and biggest-selling bands and helped bring the sound to its fullest realization. He did four albums with Ratt, three with Warrant, and two with Winger, including the platinum debuts that launched their careers. He pulled Alice Cooper's career from the dumpster with 1986's *Constrictor* and was a founding partner of Interscope Records, where he was involved in A&R, artist development, and production from 1990 to 1993. With Hill more than anyone, it seems unfair that just because the music he produced wasn't fashionable he was an unfashionable producer. He did what he was supposed to do, and he did it brilliantly.

Hill began studying classical piano and composition at 6. By his early teens, he was playing guitar in bands in his native Colorado. After prep school, he worked his way up to head engineer at Applewood Recording Studios in Colorado and did some work at Caribou Ranch with James Guercio (see entry). He was part of the bands Airborn and Shanghai, which snagged major-label contracts but went nowhere. The latter precipitated his move to New York City in 1980.

In 1981, he did demos for a singer named Sandy Stewart, which landed her a deal with Stevie Nicks's label, Atlantic subsidiary Modern Records. In the process, Hill got to know Atlantic's Doug Morris, who asked him to produce the newly signed Ratt in 1983. The result was 1984's triple-platinum *Out of the Cellar* (No. 7).

"They weren't particularly happy having an unknown producer forced down their throat," Hill recalls. "They wanted Tom Allom. But we found common ground. I went on to do their next three records. I interpreted their songs, helping with the arrangements in a way that made them radio-friendly." In fact, when Hill stopped working with them, their sales slumped.

Hill gave their straightforward party-rock songs the grandiose sound that became hairspray metal's earmark: a huge, layered, sparkling sound in which everything sounds like it's being played in an arena. The drums thunder, and guitars and multitracked vocals form a swelling tidal mass. Hill cites producers George Martin, John Boylan, Keith Olsen, and Roy Thomas Baker (see entries) as influences. He took what he learned from them and created a sound that demanded attention, manipulating the listener's emotions in spite of himself.

Meanwhile, Hill was helping to put together a career for an old friend from Colorado, Kip Winger. Not only did he connect him with Alice Cooper's band (Winger played bass in the *Constrictor*-era Cooper band), but he introduced him to Pittsburgh guitarist Reb Beach. They formed the core of Winger, which Hill managed. Winger recorded two of the era's stellar albums, *Winger* and *In the Heart of the Young,* both platinum sellers. Winger displayed the versatility of Hill's production style. Unlike Ratt (and Hill's other hit group Warrant) Winger's players were excellent, and he simultaneously accented their abilities and packaged them in a pleasing sound: full and dramatic, but with strong dynamics that leave the songs and players breathing room. In fact, except for their unfortunate image, Winger was closer to the elegant, technical metal of Rainbow or Dio than Mötley Crüe or Poison.

Warrant's strength was their songwriting, and their debut album *Dirty Rotten Filthy Stinking Rich* (No. 10) is probably Hill's crown jewel. The sculpted sound, with its big drums, spiraling guitars, and declamatory vocals, helps the songs tell their stories. Every sound and emotion is heightened; it's a work of extreme joy and sentimentality. It was a perfect marriage of producer and band. Hill has continued to be involved with Warrant's career; he says that singer/songwriter Jani Lane has been sending him tapes and he hopes to be involved in Lane's solo project. He says, "I liked those guys because they didn't take themselves too seriously. There was always an element of humor in their music."

Hill has mixed feelings about the so-called hairspray era. He points to the exaggerated self-esteem of some of the artists. "They ended up with six- or seven-figure incomes overnight and they wigged out." And he says, "Labels expected you could sign any piece-of-shit band, and as long as they had pouty lips, it would go gold. The industry was ready for a hard-core enema. A lot of guys I knew took it on the chin. Basically, we were strangled by our own success. I never thought I'd be apologizing for selling 40 million albums in my career. It's a bizarre occurrence."

He adds, "I do think records got overly slick, overly reverbed. Bands came in the studio and they all wanted a big-arena record. It's easier making records now: people want a dryer, in-your-face sound. It's easier than trying to blend 80 layers. I'm not polarized one way or the other. If there's a compelling reason to use an effect, use it. If not, don't." He produced *Rise,* the 1993 comeback album of punk-funk-reggae-metal pioneers Bad Brains, in a meaty, but less slick, style.

In 1990, Hill became involved with Interscope, which took him out of the freelance market. In late 1993, he left the label, burned out by corporate politics. Hill cites his personal strengths as songwriting and arranging. "I can hear a song on a demo and go 'The chorus is brilliant but the verse needs work.' Then arm-in-arm with the band, we'll fix it. I'm a total preproduction freak." Hill has no favorite studio, although he's partial to Neve consoles. "It's what I learned on and that's what they used at Air Studios in London, which spilled out a ton of brilliant engineers."

Hill has recently done production for several young bands, including PolyGram's Hagfish, Crumb, and a Scottish band called Thrumm. He also hopes to launch his own label to expose new artists. —ANASTASIA PANTSIOS

Airrace: *Shaft on Light,* Atco, 1984.

Alice Cooper: *Constrictor,* MCA, 1986 • *Prince of Darkness,* MCA, 1989.

Bad Brains: *Rise,* Epic, 1993.

Daltrey, Roger: "Don't Let the Sun Go Down on Me," Atlantic, 1987 (*The Lost Boys* soundtrack).

Europe: *Prisoners in Paradise,* Epic, 1991 • *1982–1992,* Epic, 1993 • *Super Hits,* Legacy/Epic, 1998.

Fiona: *Beyond the Pale,* Atlantic, 1986 • *Heart Like a Gun,* Atlantic, 1989.

Hunger: *Cinematic Superthug,* Universal, 1998.

Kix: *Midnight Dynamite,* Atlantic, 1985.

Miles, John: *Transition,* Valentino, 1986.

Moore, Gary: *Run for Cover,* 10, 1985.

Ratt: *Out of the Cellar,* Atlantic, 1984 • "Round and Round," Atlantic, 1984 • *Invasion of Your Privacy,* Atlantic, 1985 • "Dance," Atlantic, 1986 • *Dancing Undercover,* Atlantic, 1986 • *Reach for the Sky,* Atlantic, 1988.

Roxx Gang: *Things You've Never Done Before,* Virgin, 1988.

Stevens, Steve: *Atomic Playboys,* Warner Bros., 1989.

Stewart, Sandy: *Catdancer,* Modern, 1984.

Streets: *Crimes in Mind,* Atlantic, 1985.

Twisted Sister: *Love Is for Suckers,* Atlantic, 1987.

Unruly Child: *Unruly Child,* Interscope, 1992.

Warrant: "Cold Sweat," Columbia, 1988 • *Dirty Rotten Filthy Stinking Rich,* Columbia, 1988 • "Down Boys," Columbia, 1988 • "Heaven," Columbia, 1989 • "In the Sticks," Columbia, 1989 • "Cherry Pie," Columbia, 1990 • *Cherry Pie,* Columbia, 1990 • "I Saw Red," Columbia, 1990 • *Ultraphobic,* CMC, 1995 • *Best Of,* Legacy, 1996.

Whitecross: *Best Of,* Star Song, 1993.

Winger: "Headed for a Heartbreak," Atlantic, 1989 • "Seventeen," Atlantic, 1989 • *Winger,* Atlantic, 1989 • *In the Heart of the Young,* Atlantic, 1990 • "Miles Away," Atlantic, 1990.

Zappa, Dweezil: *My Guitar Wants to Kill Your Mama,* Chrysalis, 1988.

Steve Hillage

S teve Hillage is a godfather of electronica, with deep roots in experimental and progressive rock. Hillage works with companion Miquette Giraudy, his collaborator of the past 20 years. Not only do Hillage and Giraudy create their own repertoire in the prescient, innovative group System 7; they also are involved in remixes, and Hillage, in particular, produces a wide variety of other artists. Among his latest production projects is an album by the Charlatans.

He produces albums by the French Algerian singer Rachid Taha (four and counting) because they are "a very interesting blend of modern dance techniques and traditional North African Arab music." Such blends have fascinated Hillage for years. "I was a young fan and saw people like Jimi Hendrix when I was 14," he recalls. "I grew up with a psychedelic view of things. The psychedelic culture has a very wide point of view, and I've carried it through into my professional life."

Born in London on August 2, 1951, Hillage attended the City of London School, where he formed Uriel with fellow pupils Dave Stewart (see entry) on organ and Mont Campbell on bass. The group turned professional in July 1968 under the name of Egg. When Hillage went to Kent University in Canterbury to study history and philosophy, he kept his hand in music by working with such local bands as Caravan. He returned to London to form Khan in April 1971.

For the next two years, Hillage and Stewart worked with Henry Cow, Egg, and other bands and performed in a series of concerts in the 16-piece Ottawa Company. Following the dissolution of Khan, Hillage contributed to Kevin Ayers' *Bananamour* and enlisted in Ayers' short-lived band Decadence.

Hillage joined Gong in January 1973 and played an important part in its rise to prominence. It was in Gong that he met his longtime partner Giraudy. He left Gong in 1975, when he released his first solo album *Fish Rising.* That same year, Hillage helped perform Mike Oldfield's *Tubular Bells* with the Royal Philharmonic and Scottish National orchestras.

In May 1976, Hillage went to the U.S. to record his second solo album, *L,* produced by Todd Rundgren (see entry) and accompanied by Rundgren's band, Utopia. After a Gong reunion concert in spring 1977, Hillage traveled to Los Angeles to record his third solo album, *Motivation Radio,* under the supervision of Malcolm Cecil, who had worked with Stevie Wonder and the

Isley Brothers (see entries). He then returned to England to tour with a band of American sessionmen (and synthesizer player/vocalist Giraudy).

The twilight of the '70s found Hillage touring and recording continuously. Not only did he co-produce his fourth solo album, *Green,* with Pink Floyd drummer Nick Mason, he produced Nik Turner's first solo album, performed with Sham 69, and assembled a live recording of his three bands.

At the end of the decade, however, he reconsidered his position and essentially quit being a guitar hero, instead focusing on studio work and production. Throughout the '80s, he produced such acts as Simple Minds, Murray Head, Robyn Hitchcock, Cock Robin, and many others. Among the favorite productions he has crafted for others are Simple Minds' 1981 album, *Sons and Fascination* (its single, the instrumental "Theme for Great Cities," was a big dance hit) and Cock Robin's eponymous 1984 album, which sold about 4 million in Europe alone.

In 1989, after meeting the Orb's Alex Patterson, who was playing, among other things, Hillage's *Rainbow Dome Musick* while DJing at the Land of Oz club, Hillage and Giraudy teamed up with a group of DJs, producers, and musicians to form System 7, named after a recent Apple computer operating system. Informal jams led to an album, and guesting with the Orb led to playing live for the first time in many years for Hillage. Hillage continues to make and produce records and perform at live dance events.

"I think I've remained true to the things that made me want to do music in the first place," Hillage says. "We've developed our own style of dance music, on which I play guitar in an unusual and techno way," Hillage says. "I do a lot of System 7 work and I play on some of the records I produce. I hear a guitar line, and I'll do it."

His view of production is not corporate. "I think the most important thing is if I hear that I can do a good job on somebody," he says. "It doesn't have to be that they're going to necessarily sell millions of records; I want to make a genuine contribution to their musical evolution. If I can hear in my mind's ear a result that will satisfy me and will say the right things about the artist, I'll be enthusiastic about doing the job."

Chemistry is important to Hillage. "You're becoming a temporary member of a team when you produce a band," he says. "I know all about the techniques of making records, but it's not just a question of technique. It's not my record; I'm not making a Steve Hillage record. I want the artist to make his record, and I want to be a fully involved co-conspirator with him."

Besides the psychological aspects, there are technological ones. "My main equipment at the moment is a Macintosh 9500 PCI PowerMac with Logic Audio and ProTools, a complete digital recording, editing and MIDI sequencing package," Hillage says. "A lot of technology goes into making rock records these days, which is kind of funny, considering how people criticize techno music for being about machines. Whatever works, that's what I say.

"I'm a very technologically literate producer," Hillage says. "I'm very hands-on. I'm very aware of mixing boards and automation. Gong was one of the first groups to use synthesizers, back in the early '70s, so I've kind of grown up with this stuff. I'm not just a guy with fancy machines and devices who can twiddle all the buttons and get all the clever sounds; that's first base. The most important thing is to get beyond all that and develop a creatively exciting relationship with the artist, so he gets the best performances and his songs are dealt with in the best way."

While Hillage spends most of his time producing others, he also enjoys DJing and performing at raves. "Where do I get the energy for them? I love the music, I like parties," he says. "Who doesn't like parties? Music journalists don't like parties." —CARLO WOLFF

Banks Statement: *Banks Statement*, Atlantic, 1989.
Blink: *A Map of the Universe*, Lime, 1995 • *Blink*, Lime, 1998.
Can: *Sacrilege: The Remixes*, Mute, 1997.
Charlatans UK: "Patrol," Beggars Banquet, 1994 • *Up to Our Hips*, Beggars Banquet/Atlantic, 1994 • *The Charlatans*, Beggars Banquet/Atlantic, 1995 • "Toothache," Beggars Banquet/Atlantic, 1995.
Cock Robin: *Cock Robin*, Columbia, 1985.
Hillage, Steve: *Fish Rising*, Blue Plate, 1975, 1991 • *Green*, Blue Plate, 1978, 1990 • *Live Herald*, Blue Plate, 1979, 1990 • *Open—Featuring Studio Herald*, Blue Plate, 1979, 1990 • *Rainbow Dome Musick*, Blue Plate, 1979, 1991 • *For to Next/And Not Or*, Blue Plate, 1983, 1990.
Hitchcock, Robyn: *Groovy Decay*, Albion, 1982 • *Gravy Deco*, Rhino, 1995 • *Uncorrected Personality Traits: The Robyn Hitchcock Collection*, Rhino, 1997.
It Bites: *Big Lad in the Windmill*, Geffen, 1986 • *Once Around the World*, Geffen, 1988 • *Eat Me in St. Louis*, Geffen, 1989.
Lockie, Ken: *The Impossible* (9 tracks), Virgin, 1981.
Orb, The: *The Orb's Adventures Beyond the Ultraworld*, Big Life/Mercury, 1991 • *Aubrey Mixes: The Ultraworld Excursions*, Caroline, 1992 • "Blue Room," Big Life/Mercury, 1992 • *U.F.Orb*, Big Life/Mercury, 1992.
Real Life: *Heartland*, Curb/MCA, 1983 • *Let's Fall in Love*, Curb, 1983 • "Send Me an Angel," Curb/MCA, 1983 • *Lifetime*, Curb, 1990.

Simple Minds: "League of Nations," Virgin, 1981 • *Sister Feelings Call*, Virgin, 1981 • *Sons and Fascination*, Virgin, 1981 • "The American," Virgin, 1981.
Sky Cries Mary: "Every Iceberg Is Afire" (remix), World Domination, 1994.
System 7: "Habibi," 10, 1991 • *System 7*, 10, 1991 • *777*, Caroline, 1992 • "Freedom Fighters," 10, 1992 • "Sinbad," Big Life, 1993 • *The Water Album*, Butterfly, 1994 • *Point Three: Fire and Water*, Astralwerks, 1995 • "Hangar 84," Butterfly/Big Life, 1996 • *The Power of Seven*, Butterfly, 1996 • *Golden Section*, Cleopatra, 1997 • "Rite of Spring," Butterfly/Big Life, 1997 • *System Express*, Cleopatra, 1997.
Taha, Rachid: "Indie," FFRR, 1994 • "Voilà Voilà," FFRR, 1994 • "Kelma," Mango, 1995, 1996 • *Ole Ole*, Island, 1996 • *Diwan*, Polydor, 1998.

Rupert Hine

Rupert Hine occupies a rarefied position in the pop-rock pantheon: he has enjoyed a profuse 25-year career as a producer of commercial and critical successes, and he has maintained a career of nearly 35 years as an acclaimed artist in his own right.

Few producers have worked with as wide a stylistic range of gold- and platinum-selling artists as Hine, including Chris DeBurgh (*The Getaway, Man on the Line*, No. 11 U.K.), The Fixx (*Shuttered Room, Reach the Beach*, No. 8, *Phantoms*, No. 19), Howard Jones (*Human's Lib, Dream into Action*, No. 10), Stevie Nicks (*The Other Side of the Mirror*, No. 10), Rush (*Presto*, No. 16, *Roll the Bones*, No. 3), Saga (*Worlds Apart*), Duncan Sheik (*Duncan Sheik*), and Tina Turner ("Better Be Good to Me," No. 5, *What's Love Got to Do With It?*, No. 17).

Hine has also produced milestone work by artists flying underneath the commercial radar: Kevin Ayers, Cafe Jacques (*Round the Back*), Camel (*I Can See Your House from Here*), Bob Geldof (*The Vegetarians of Love*), the Members, Milla, Underworld (*Underneath the Radar*), and of course, Hine himself (solo, as Thinkman, and as a member of Quantum Jump).

Rupert Hine was born in England in 1947 and was rocking in a "beat" band by the age of 14. He then shifted gears and became half of the "alternative folk" duo Rupert and David. The duo wrote songs, played in clubs, and, in 1965, walked into a publisher's office with guitars in hand, demoed "The Sound of Silence" live, and recorded it three weeks later for Decca. The single stayed well within the range of statistical probability

and didn't do much.

In the mid-'60s Hine pursued his interest in film and continued to write songs. By 1969 Hine was ready to try music again; by chance he happened across the name of an old friend on the back of a new record cover. The friend was Roger Glover (ex-Episode Six) and the band was Deep Purple. Hine contacted Glover through the record label; Glover liked the songs enough that he wanted to produce Hine's first album (*Pick Up a Bone*) on the band's own label, Purple.

By 1972, Deep Purple was one of the biggest bands on the planet; Glover called from Japan to tell Hine that he didn't have time to produce his next album, and that Hine should do it himself. Though not a commercial success, *Unfinished Picture* drew critical and music industry attention, and Hine began to get requests to produce other artists. Yvonne Elliman's *Food of Love* (which he also wrote songs for) in 1973 was his first outside production.

Hine produced some significant music in the '70s for original Genesis guitarist Anthony Phillips; Cafe Jacques ("Ain't No Love in the Heart of the City" is a soulful electro-pop gem); the Members; himself; and especially Kevin Ayers (ex-Soft Machine), whose *The Confessions of Dr. Dream* is a lost classic.

Dream, a spunky amalgam of pop and rock styles (recorded at Air in 1974) filtered through Ayers' avant-sensibility and sung in his startling bass, sounds remark-

ably modern even today. "Day by Day" opens the album funkily, with Hine on clavinet and a wailing backing trio featuring Doris Troy. "Didn't Feel Lonely Till I Thought of You" is one of the great rock workouts of the '70s. Ollie Halsall's (who happened to be recording with another band in the next studio) guitar solo sounds like it was "recorded on a separate piece of 1/4-inch tape, scrumbled up, thrown in the wastepaper basket, found several days later, straightened up, and reinserted," according to Hine. "He moved the whammy bar as fast as his pick was going—like some sort of St. Vitus dance in his right arm," to achieve a quavery, watery wonder of nature.

Ayers' then-girlfriend Nico (see John Cale entry) also appeared on the album, sharing vocals on the side-long title track. She agreed to appear only if the studio was "bedecked in flowers and a crate of champagne was brought in for her," recalls Hine, who also played ARP synthesizer throughout the album. This early keyboard wizardry was matched conceptually by Ayers' prescient take on technology: "It begins with a blessing / But ends with a curse / Making life easy / But making it worse" (from "It Begins with a Blessing," which included some "presampling sampling": Hine recorded an audio segment of American Indians whooping it up off the television, slowed it down, then sped it up for the track).

Hine came into his own as an artist (and producer) in the '80s, co-writing (with lyricist Jeannette Obstoj), co-producing (with Stephen Tayler), singing and playing most of the instruments on innovative, technology-driven albums *Immunity* and *The Wildest Wish to Fly* (with should-have-been hits "I Hang On to My Vertigo" and "No Yellow Heart"). Comparisons to *Scary Monsters*–era Bowie (see entry) would be obvious, except the recording of *Immunity*, in 1979, predates the release of *Monsters* by a year. *Wish* also prefigures the bright, punchy keyboard sound and pinched, processed vocals (by Cy Curnin) of the Fixx's breakthrough *Reach the Beach,* which Hine aptly describes as having "both feet in pop but [with] the bite and attack of rock," and "capturing the musical spirit of the '80s." Hine and the Fixx helped establish the commercial viability of post-punk new wave in the U.S. with the resounding "Stand or Fall" and "Red Skies," beguiling "Saved by Zero" (No. 20), propulsive "One Thing Leads to Another" (No. 4), and hypnotic "Secret Separation" (No. 19).

Hine achieved similar results with Howard Jones in the mid-'80s, moving the new wave bar even further into pop territory with the classics "What Is Love?," "Things Can Only Get Better" (No. 5), and "Life in One Day" (No. 19). He also helped move Tina Turner into a soulful, rocking '80s sound by producing and writing tracks (especially the cavernous "Better Be Good to Me") for the smash albums *Private Dancer, Break Every Rule,* and *Foreign Affair,* as well as the soundtrack to the *What's Love Got to Do With It?* film.

Hine feels the advent of the sampler and digital recording equipment in the late '70s and early '80s (which he helped pioneer on his solo albums) was a sea change that the industry is still absorbing and refining. "The sampler brought an explosion of realization that you could bring sounds from the real world (beyond musical instruments) and harness them in a musical way. It was seventh heaven to suddenly be able to do these things easily. Digital allowed you to multitrack—and move tracks around within a multitrack tape—without any generational loss or worry about noise."

However, as with most of the best producers, technology is only a tool for Hine. "The psychological aspects are as important as any technical attribute [a producer may have]. He should be alive and alert and interested in artists as people, and as communicators of intellectual and emotional ideas. If you can achieve that and keep your fix on those aspects—as opposed to the latest technology or fashions—then you are sourcing the song on the artists themselves and helping them flower and blossom." This Rupert Hine has been doing for over a quarter-century. —ERIC OLSEN

After the Fire: *Laser Love,* Epic, 1979 • "One Rule for You," Epic, 1979, 1981 (*England Rocks 1*).

Almond, Marc: *Jacky* (EP), Warner Bros., 1991.

Ayers, Kevin: *Confessions of Dr. Dream,* Island, 1974.

Cafe Jacques: "Ain't No Love in the Heart of the City," Epic, 1977, 1981 (*England Rocks 1*) • *Round the Back,* Epic, 1977 • *International,* Epic, 1978.

Camel: *I Can See Your House from Here,* Decca, 1979 • *Echoes: The Retrospective,* PolyGram, 1993.

Celtus: *Moonchild,* Soho Square/Sony, 1997.

De Burgh, Chris: "Don't Pay the Ferryman," A&M, 1983 • *The Getaway,* A&M, 1983 • *Man on the Line,* A&M, 1984 • *Power of Ten,* A&M, 1992.

Eight Seconds: *Almacantar,* Polydor, 1986.

Elliman, Yvonne: *Food of Love,* Purple, 1973 • *Best Of,* Polydor, 1997.

Fixx, The: *Shuttered Room,* MCA, 1982 • "One Thing Leads to Another," MCA, 1983 • *Reach the Beach,* MCA, 1983 • "Saved by Zero," MCA, 1983 • "The Sign of Fire," MCA, 1983 • "Are We Ourselves?," MCA, 1984 • "Less Cities, More Moving People," MCA, 1984 • *Phantoms,* MCA, 1984 • "Secret Separations," MCA, 1986 • *Walkabout,* MCA, 1986 • *One Thing Leads to Another: Greatest Hits,* MCA, 1989 • *Ink,* MCA, 1991.

Geldof, Bob: *Deep in the Heart of Nowhere,* Atlantic, 1986 • *The*

Vegetarians of Love, Atlantic, 1990 • *The Happy Club,* Polydor, 1993.

Greenslade, Dave: *Cactus Choir,* Warner Bros., 1976.

Hine, Rupert: *Unfinished Picture,* Purple, 1973 • *Immunity,* A&M, 1981 • *Waving Not Drowning,* A&M, 1982 • *Wildest Wish to Fly,* Island, 1983 • *Better Off Dead* soundtrack, A&M, 1991 • *The Deep End,* Permanent, 1994.

Jones, Howard: "What Is Love?," Elektra, 1983 • *Human's Lib,* Elektra, 1984 • *Dream into Action,* Elektra, 1985 • "Life in One Day," Elektra, 1985 • "Things Can Only Get Better," Elektra, 1985 • *Action Replay,* Elektra, 1986 • *The Best Of,* Elektra, 1993.

Jonesey: *Growing,* Dawn, 1973.

Les Negresses Vertes: *Zig Zague,* Virgin, 1995.

Little Heroes: *Watch the World,* Capitol, 1983.

Members, The: *At the 1980 Chelsea Night Club,* Caroline, 1979, 1991 • *The Choice Is Yours,* Virgin, 1980 • *Sound of the Suburbs: A Collection of the Members' Finest Moments,* Virgin, 1995.

Milla: *Divine Comedy* (6 tracks), SBK, 1994.

Nicks, Stevie: "Rooms on Fire," Modern, 1989 • *The Other Side of the Mirror,* Modern, 1989 • *Timespace: The Best Of,* Modern, 1991.

No Dice: *Two-Faced,* EMI/Capitol, 1979.

Noa: *Calling,* Geffen, 1996.

Nova: *Blink,* Arista, 1975.

Ongala, Remmy, and Orchestre Super Matimila: *Mambo,* Realworld/Caroline, 1992.

Phillips, Anthony: *Wise After the Event,* Arista, 1978 • *Sides,* Arista/Passport, 1979 • *Private Parts and Pieces,* Vol. 2, PVC, 1980.

Quantum Jump: *Quantum Jump,* Electric, 1976 • *Barracuda,* Electric, 1977.

Rebel Heels: *One by One by One,* Atlantic, 1988.

Rush: *Presto,* Atlantic, 1989 • *Chronicles,* Mercury, 1990 • *Roll the Bones,* Atlantic, 1991.

Saga: *Worlds Apart,* Portrait, 1982 • *Heads or Trails,* Portrait, 1983 • "On the Loose," Portrait, 1983.

Sagal, Katey: *Well,* Virgin, 1994.

Sheik, Duncan: *Duncan Sheik,* Atlantic, 1996 • "Barely Breathing," Atlantic, 1997.

Thanks to Gravity: *Start,* Capitol, 1998.

Thinkman: *Formula,* Island, 1986.

This Picture: *City of Sin,* Dedicated, 1994.

Thompson Twins: *Close to the Bone,* Arista, 1987 • "Get That Love," Arista, 1987 • *Best of (Greatest Mixes),* Arista, 1989 • *Greatest Hits,* Arista, 1996.

Turner, Tina: "Better Be Good to Me," Capitol, 1984 • *Private Dancer,* Capitol, 1984 • *Break Every Rule,* Capitol, 1986 • *Foreign Affair,* Capitol, 1989 • *What's Love Got to Do with It?* soundtrack, Capitol, 1993 • *Collected Recordings, Sixties to Nineties,* Capitol, 1994.

Underworld: "Underneath the Radar," Sire, 1988 •
Underneath the Radar, Sire, 1988.

Waterboys, The: *The Waterboys* (1 track), Chrysalis, 1983.

Wildlife: *Burning,* Chrysalis, 1980.

Holland-Dozier-Holland

(BRIAN HOLLAND, LAMONT DOZIER, EDWARD HOLLAND)

Brian Holland (born February 15, 1941), Lamont Dozier (born June 16, 1941), and Edward Holland (born October 30, 1939)—all from Detroit—were the most successful songwriter/producers of the '60s. Their run with Motown from 1961 to 1967 generated thirteen No. 1 hits for the Marvelettes ("Please Mr. Postman"), the Four Tops ("It's the Same Old Song," "Reach Out I'll Be There"), and most prolifically, the Supremes ("Where Did Our Love Go?," "Baby Love," "Come See About Me," "Stop! In the Name of Love," "Back In My Arms Again," "I Hear a Symphony," "You Can't Hurry Love," "You Keep Me Hangin' On," "Love Is Here and Now You're Gone," "The Happening").

The team's work, in conjunction (and competition) with that of Berry Gordy, Smokey Robinson, and Norman Whitfield (see entries) formed the backbone of Motown's "Golden Decade." In addition to the No. 1 hits, H-D-H wrote and produced dozens of other Top 20 hits for the aforementioned and other Motown artists, including Marvin Gaye, the Isley Brothers (see entry), Martha and the Vandellas ("I'm Ready for Love" is a personal favorite of Brian Holland), the Miracles, and Junior Walker and the All Stars. Holland, Dozier, and Holland were voted into the Rock and Roll Hall of Fame in 1990.

Brian Holland learned to play piano in church. "I would run up to the piano after church and start playing it," he says. Though never a particularly accomplished musician, he had a knack for melody that would become the foundation of the team's eventual success.

Both Brian and Edward (then called Eddie) were aspiring singers who recorded with Berry Gordy as early as 1958. Brian decided that singing wasn't for him, mostly because he was shy, and pursued songwriting and its implementational consequence, producing. With Robert Bateman, he co-wrote and co-produced

Motown's first No. 1, the Marvelettes' irresistible "Please Mr. Postman" in 1961. Eddie continued to pursue a recording career and hit the Top 30 in 1962 with "Jamie."

Lamont Dozier recorded (as "Lamont Anthony") in 1961 for Anna Records, owned by Berry's sister Gwen, and remained with the Motown family in relative obscurity for the next couple of years. There is some dispute as to the identity of the inaugural H-D-H team venture, but both Brian and Edward remember it to be "Forever." Brian recalls walking by the studio and hearing Dozier teasing out a melody on the piano. He recalls saying, "That's a pretty good song; let's see if we can finish it together." They did—with Edward contributing lyrics—and as produced by Brian for the Marvelettes, the song rose to No. 24 on the R&B chart in '63.

The team's first Top 40 hit was Martha and the Vandellas' "Come and Get These Memories" (No. 29), followed closely by their first smash (also with Martha), "Heat Wave" (No. 4). "Heat" is a swinging, hand-clapping sax number that speaks equally of revival tents, juke joints, and the Brill Building. A clever analogy between love and heat (in the "Fever" tradition) is belted by Martha Reeves (tied with Gladys Knight as Motown's most soulful woman) over a real R&B backing from Motown's house band, the Funk Brothers (see Berry Gordy entry); yet the feeling is never raw because of the brightness of the team's production. In fact, rhythmic drive coupled with bright, open, "friendly" production is the team's hallmark.

It was Brian who led in the studio because he could hear the records before they were recorded. Says Edward, "Brian has an exceptionally gifted ear. It was simple for him because he could hear the arrangements in his head. All he had to do was to convey that to the musicians. For others (like me) it's hit-and-miss and complicated. Other producers depend on the musicians to add flavor to the song, but Brian had it all in his head."

However, contrary to popular belief, H-D-H didn't enter the studio with complicated arrangements written out. The musicians were given a chord sheet and general direction, but they were encouraged to contribute ideas which the team either accepted or rejected. Also contrary to belief, "Motown didn't have a blueprint on how to produce records. They had the ability to allow us to go do what we needed to do with the product. We were allowed the freedom to work on things until we got them right," asserts Brian.

For H-D-H the process of writing flowed into the process of producing. If the process began with Brian, he would get a "feeling for the melody," he says. "I would let

Lamont and my brother know the kind of melody I was writing and see if they had an idea lyric-wise." Adds Edward, "I would make suggestions like 'Add two bars here, or four bars there.' Brian would ask me why, and then make adjustments once he was convinced I needed that to complete the idea lyrically. Originally, we would just write songs and then figure out who would sound best on them. But then as artists like the Supremes and the Four Tops became more successful, we would write for them. Often in the process of writing [for an artist] we would find out that the song didn't necessarily fit them, so we would give it to someone else."

While musicians were given artistic license, typically artists were not. Recalls Edward, "Once the song was done I would take the artists and teach them to sing the song. I would go over it and over it until I thought they understood the song, and then I would direct them in the studio. They would add their feelings. I still feel that Diana Ross has one of the most sensuous, sweet-sounding voices I've ever heard. Levi [Stubbs, of the Four Tops] has an exceptional voice. Marvin [Gaye] could hear something one time and pretty much comprehend what you wanted."

And it is the team's work with the Four Tops and the Supremes that best exemplifies their sound. The Tops (Stubbs, Obie Benson, Lawrence Payton, Duke Fakir) had 10 years of R&B vocal experience behind them when they signed with Motown in 1963. That R&B vocal harmony experience grounded them even as H-D-H took flight into their "classical period" of late 1966 to mid-1967 with "Reach Out, I'll Be There," "Standing in the Shadows of Love" (No. 6), "Bernadette" (No. 4), and "7 Rooms of Gloom" (No. 14). The Tops' earthy harmonies and Stubbs' stentorian pipes are never swamped by the melodies, the chording, or the tension and release (verse and chorus) model that H-D-H drew from sophisticated orchestral music for these songs, where archetypal black and archetypal white music reach an exquisite balance that reveals the power and beauty of both.

The Supremes' music was less grounded in the black tradition, and perhaps for that reason, they became the most successful of the Motown groups. Within the competitive Motown schema, once it became clear that the Supremes (and especially Diana Ross) were Berry Gordy's favorite, it behooved H-D-H to craft the most accessible possible sound for them in order to remain atop the pack. This they did by opening up a sound so wide that it was able to swallow America (and the world) whole.

The Supremes (Ross, Mary Wilson, Florence Ballard) were the first musical artists to truly transcend race.

Diana Ross's appeal as a woman was based upon transracial characteristics: style, grace, the figure and photo-friendliness of a model, and a transcendent eagerness to please men of every hue. Though never denying her blackness, Ross did not see race as her defining characteristic. Almost perversely, Ross demystified race for many Americans (especially whites) by proving that a black woman could display all of the offhand narcissism and giddy coyness of a Newport debutante.

H-D-H wrote and produced to this image, emphasizing Ross's sultry and sensuous vulnerability on songs like "Where Did Our Love Go?," "Baby Love," and "You Keep Me Hangin' On," gratifying men and women of all races with the notion that even the most perfect women are subject to heartache: even objects of desire, desire. All of this would have been of little consequence if not for the unyielding appeal of the songs. Is there a fan of popular music who can't sing the chorus of virtually every Supremes' No. 1? Who doesn't move to their pulsing, scintillating beats? Is there a more perfect production than "You Can't Hurry Love"? Just listen to the throbbing bass and tambourine intro, the snare and horn punctuations on the offbeat, and Ross's creamy, toothy vocal over a hopeful rhythm guitar.

Upon leaving Motown in 1968 over a royalty dispute, H-D-H formed the Invictus/Hot Wax labels where they hit again with Freda Payne ("Band of Gold," No. 3), Chairmen of the Board ("Give Me Just a Little More Time," No. 3) and the Honey Cone ("Want Ads," No. 1). Both Edward Holland and Lamont Dozier began singing again; Dozier hit the Top 30 twice in 1974 with "Trying to Hold On to My Woman" and "Fish Ain't Bitin'."

In April 1998, the Pullman Group signed a "finance securitization agreement" valued at about $30 million with H-D-H, backed by their future publishing rights. Their song catalog is valued at about $100 million.
—ERIC OLSEN

Chairmen of the Board: "Give Me Just A Little More Time," Invictus, 1970 • *Give Me Just a Little More Time,* Invictus, 1970 • "Pay to the Piper," Invictus, 1970.

Collins, Phil: "Two Hearts," Atlantic, 1988 (*Buster* soundtrack).

Dozier, Lamont: "Fish Ain't Bitin'," ABC, 1974 • *Out Here on My Own,* ABC, 1974 • "Trying to Hold on to My Woman," ABC, 1974 • *Black Bach,* ABC, 1975 • *Love and Beauty,* Invictus, 1975 • *Right There,* Warner Bros., 1976 • *Reddlin',* Warner Bros., 1977 • *Bittersweet,* Warner Bros., 1979 • *Inside Seduction,* Atlantic, 1991.

Eighth Day: *Best Of,* H-D-H, 1998 • "She's Not Just Another Woman," Invictus, 1971 • "You've Got to Crawl (Before

You Walk)," Invictus, 1971.

Elgins, The: *Darling Baby,* VIP, 1966 • "Heaven Must Have Sent You," VIP, 1966.

Fine Young Cannibals: *Finest,* MCA, 1996.

Four Tops: "Baby I Need Your Loving," Motown, 1964 • *Four Tops Second Album,* Motown, 1965 • "I Can't Help Myself (Sugar Pie, Honey Bunch)," Motown, 1965 • "It's the Same Old Song," Motown, 1965 • "Something About You," Motown, 1965 • *The Four Tops,* Motown, 1965 • *On Top,* Motown, 1966 • "Reach Out, I'll Be There," Motown, 1966 • "Standing in the Shadows of Love," Motown, 1966 • "7 Rooms of Gloom," Motown, 1967 • "Bernadette," Motown, 1967 • *Four Tops Live,* Motown, 1967 • *Greatest Hits,* Motown, 1967, 1987 • *Reach Out,* Motown, 1967, 1983 • "You Keep Running Away," Motown, 1967 • "Walk Away Renee," Motown, 1968 • *Anthology,* Motown, 1974, 1986 • *Indestructable,* Arista, 1988.

Franklin, Aretha: *Sweet Passion,* Atlantic, 1977.

Gaye, Marvin: *Can I Get a Witness?,* Tamla, 1963 • "Baby Don't You Do It," Tamla, 1964 • "How Sweet It Is to Be Loved By You," Tamla, 1964 • *How Sweet It Is,* Tamla, 1964 • "You're a Wonderful One," Tamla, 1964 • *Moods of Marvin Gaye,* Tamla, 1967 • "Your Unchanging Love," Tamla, 1967 • *Super Hits,* Tamla, 1970 • *Anthology,* Motown, 1974 • *Greatest Hits,* Motown, 1976, 1989 • *The Master: 1961–1984,* Motown, 1995.

Gibson, Debbie: *Anything Is Possible,* Atlantic, 1990 • *Smart Pack,* Atlantic, 1990.

Holland, Eddie: *Eddie Holland,* VIP/Motown, 1962 • "Leavin' Here," Motown, 1964.

Houston, Thelma: *Best Of,* Motown, 1991.

Isley Brothers: "This Old Heart of Mine," Tamla, 1966 • *This Old Heart of Mine,* Tamla, 1966 • *Greatest Hits and Rare Classics,* Motown, 1991 • *Rockin' Soul,* Vol. 1, Rhino, 1991 • *The Isley Brothers Story,* Vol. 1, Rhino, 1991.

Jackson 5: *Moving Violation,* Motown, 1975 • *Anthology,* Motown, 1976.

Jackson, Keisha: *Keisha,* Epic, 1991.

Jackson, Michael: *The Best Of,* Motown, 1975 • *Anthology,* Motown, 1976, 1989 • *One Day in Your Life,* Motown, 1981.

Jacobs, Lawrence-Hilton: *Lawrence-Hilton Jacobs,* ABC, 1978.

Joseph, Margie: *The Atlantic Sessions: The Best Of,* Ichiban/Soul Classics, 1994.

Martha and the Vandellas: "Come and Get These Memories," Gordy, 1963 • "Heat Wave," Gordy, 1963 • "Nowhere to Run," Gordy, 1965 • *Greatest Hits,* Motown, 1966 • "I'm Ready for Love," Gordy, 1966 • "Jimmy Mack," Gordy, 1967 • *Anthology,* Motown, 1974 • *Live Wire! The Singles, 1962–1972,* Motown, 1993.

Marvelettes, The: "Please Mr. Postman," Tamla, 1961 • *The Marvelous Marvelettes,* Tamla, 1963 • *The Marvelettes' Greatest Hits,* Tamla, 1966.

Miracles, The: "I Gotta Dance to Keep from Crying," Tamla, 1963 • *Doin' Mickey's Monkey,* Tamla, 1964 • *See also* Robinson, Smokey, and the Miracles.

Osmond, Donny: *Winning Combination,* Polydor, 1977.

Payne, Freda: "Band of Gold," Invictus, 1970 • "Bring the Boys Back Home," Invictus, 1970 • *Reaching Out,* Invictus, 1970.

Robinson, Smokey, and the Miracles: "(Come 'Round Here) I'm the One You Need," Tamla, 1966 • *Greatest Hits,* Vol. 2, Motown, 1968 • *Whatever Makes You Happy: More of the Best, 1961–1971,* Rhino, 1993 • *Thirty-Fifth Anniversary Box,* Motown, 1994.

Ross, Diana: *Diana: The Ultimate Collection,* Motown, 1993.

Ross, Diana, and the Supremes: *Diana Ross and the Supremes Greatest Hits,* Motown, 1967 • "In and Out of Love," Motown, 1967 • "Reflections," Motown, 1967 • "Forever Came Today," Motown, 1968 • *Reflections,* Motown, 1968, 1991 • *Diana Ross and the Supremes Greatest Hits,* Vol. 2, Motown, 1970, 1989 • *Anthology,* Motown, 1974, 1986 • *Diana Ross and the Supremes Greatest Hits* Vol. 1, Motown, 1986 • *The Best Of,* Motown, 1995 • *See also* the Supremes.

Staples, Mavis: *Mavis Staples,* Stax, 1969.

Supremes, The: "When the Lovelight Starts Shining Through His Eyes," Motown, 1963 • "Baby Love," Motown, 1964 • "Come See About Me," Motown, 1964 • "Where Did Our Love Go?," Motown, 1964 • *Where Did Our Love Go?,* Motown, 1964, 1989 • "Back in My Arms Again," Motown, 1965 • "I Hear a Symphony," Motown, 1965 • "Nothing But Heartaches," Motown, 1965 • "Stop! In the Name of Love," Motown, 1965 • *I Hear a Symphony,* Motown, 1966 • "Love Is Like an Itching in My Heart," Motown, 1966 • "My World Is Empty Without You," Motown, 1966 • *Supremes A-Go-Go,* Motown, 1966 • "You Can't Hurry Love," Motown, 1966 • "You Keep Me Hanging On," Motown, 1966 • "Love Is Here and Now You're Gone," Motown, 1967 • "The Happening," Motown, 1967 • *Reflections,* Motown, 1968 • *Greatest Hits and Rare Classics,* Motown, 1991.

Temptations, The: *Bare Back,* Atlantic, 1978 • *Emperors of Soul,* Motown, 1994 • *One By One: The Best of Their Solo Years,* Motown, 1996.

Walker, Junior, and the All Stars: *Shotgun,* Soul, 1965 • "(I'm a) Road Runner," Soul, 1966 • *Home Cookin',* Soul/Motown, 1969, 1994.

Wells, Mary: "You Lost the Sweetest Boy," Motown, 1963 • *Greatest Hits,* Motown, 1964 • "What's Easy for Two Is Hard for One," Motown, 1964.

Weston, Kim: *Greatest Hits and Rare Classics,* Motown, 1991.

Wonder, Stevie: *I Was Made to Love Her,* Tamla, 1967.

Winston Holness

(NINEY THE OBSERVER)

An accidentally severed thumb gave him the natural nickname "Niney" in Jamaica, and his early vocal group (which had a nice harmony hit called "Push Me in the Corner") was called the Observers. Producing variously as "Niney," "The Observer" (his studio band was known as the Observer All-Stars), and "Niney the Observer," Winston Holness began singing in the rocksteady era and producing in the early days of reggae, moving from classic cuts like Big Youth's "Dread in a Babylon" through a string of hits with Dennis Brown and others to bizarre later works with titles like *Freaks* and *Nuclear Jammin'*. His Jamaican records were, of course, released on the Observer label.

Niney first worked for producer Bunny Lee, later replacing Lee Perry at Joe Gibbs' studio when Perry went out on his own (see entries). Niney went independent in 1970. Some of his major productions include "Silver Words" by Ken Boothe, Delroy Wilson's fiery "Rascal Man," and his own judgment calls like "Blood and Fire" (voted Jamaican Song of the Year in 1971) and "Message to the Ungodly." Some of his big hits with Dennis Brown include "No More Will I Roam," "Westbound Train," "Cassandra," and "Wolf and Leopard." These and other early '70s 7-inch records helped define what we now call "roots" in Jamaican music.

He recorded at Randy's, Treasure Isle, Harry J's, Dynamic, Channel One (where he served as house producer in the '80s after being absent from the scene a while), and Joe Gibbs' studios in the main. He generally utilized the Soul Syndicate (which included "Fully" Fullwood on bass, Santa Davis on drums, Tony Chin and Chinna Smith on guitars, and Keith Sterling on keyboards). The strange combination of rivalry and complex interrelations inherent in the Kingston music scene made for some powerful and unusual records, like Max Romeo, Lee Perry, and Niney all singing on "When Jah Speak." Romeo scored for Niney with "The Coming of Jah" and "Rasta Band Wagon" in sparse productions typical of the producers' uncomplicated arrangements in the '70s. In those days Niney counted Bunny Lee, Clancy Eccles (see entry), and Perry among his friends.

Holness recorded Rastafarian singers—some producers would not—and some of his recordings blend the powerful punch of gut-grabbing reggae with an almost field-recording authenticity to the lyrics and vocals. Sang Hugh's "Rasta No Born Yah" and "Last Call

Fe Blackman" are only a few of his outstanding '70s productions. Records like these made his 45 releases worth seeking throughout reggae's "golden age."

An added incentive to buy Observer singles were the King Tubby dub B-sides. Niney's productions were already bass- and drum-heavy and Tubby's remixes trail you down echo-laden hallways past closing doors of vocals and guitars to the relentless throb at the end. The 1975 *Dubbing with the Observer* (reissued as half of a King Tubby's two-disc set) is currently the only other way to get some of these death-defying dubs. Some, like the mind-warping "Confusion in a Babylon" version are still too bold for any form but the Jamaican 7-inch single (though the A side made it to one of his anthologies). The controlled chaos of the track creates the feeling of the lyric's "mutiny on a sinking ship," anticipating the triple-time drumbeat of the much later jungle era. A similarly thick dub sound also backed DJs Alcapone, U Roy, Big Youth, and others (often over tracks first voiced by Dennis Brown), though these productions remain mainly on 7-inch.

Nuclear Jammin', produced by George Paulus in 1986, signaled an entirely different direction, one that the Observer thankfully didn't follow. A guitar-based, funkadelish hybrid kicks off the Chicago-recorded disc, which settles into a basement-groove reggae set featuring Niney as lead vocalist. It shows what might have happened if he'd let latent Lee Perry impulses control his soul, with cuts like "Pollution," "License to Kill," and "Every Pum Pum." These were his first vocals since the days of "Blood and Fire" and several searing Maxie, Niney, and Scratch cuts, and more than enough to last. At least, until the self-produced *Freaks* of 1992.

In later years a long-running deal with the Heartbeat label kept Niney's productions in the foreground as the compact disc radically altered the way reggae would be heard in North America. The label's commitment to reissues as well as new works kept Niney's classics on the racks and his new works in the eye. He produced a debut album for Peter Tosh's son Andrew and brought new talent like Baby Wayne forward. Niney was still producing artists like Jah Messengers and Ninja Kid, Dignitary Stylish, Wingy, Daddy Lizard, and Shark (as well as Dennis Brown, Sugar Minott, Frankie Paul, Yami Bolo, and others) in the early '90s. —CHUCK FOSTER

Baby Wayne: *Ram DJ*, Heartbeat, 1993.

Bolo, Yami: *He Who Knows It Feel It*, Heartbeat, 1991.

Brown, Dennis: *My Time*, Rohit, 1989 • *Just Dennis*, Trojan, 1975 • *Dennis Brown*, Observer, 1984, 1996 • *Money in My Pocket*, Trojan, 1981 • *Some Like It Hot*, Heartbeat, 1992 • *Cosmic Force*, Heartbeat, 1993 • *Open the Gate*, Heartbeat,

1995 • *Dennis*, Burning Sounds, 1996 • *Love & Hate: The Best of Dennis Brown* (3 tracks), VP, 1996.

Ethiopians, The: *Slave Call*, Heartbeat, 1977, 1992.

Heptones: *Better Days*, Rohit, 1978 • *King of My Own Town*, Jackal, c. 1985.

Isaacs, Gregory: *Dancing Floor*, Heartbeat, 1990 • *No Luck*, Lagoon, 1995.

Jah Messengers: *Reggae Time*, Heartbeat, 1993.

Little John: *Boombastic*, Heartbeat, 1990.

McGregor, Freddie: *Presenting Freddie McGregor*, Rhinouk, 1979 • *Freddie*, Heartbeat, 1980 • *Zion Chant*, Heartbeat, 1991.

Niney the Observer: *Freaks*, Heartbeat, 1992 • *Observer Attack Dub*, ROIR, 1994.

Observer All Stars and King Tubby's: *Dubbing with the Observer*, Attack, 1975.

Page One and the Observers: *Observation of Life Dub*, Carib Gems, (c. 1975.

Paul, Frankie: *Should I*, Heartbeat, 1991 • *Don Man*, Heartbeat, 1993.

Perry, Lee "Scratch": *Lord God Muzick*, Heartbeat, 1991.

Rose, Michael: *Michael Rose*, Heartbeat, 1993.

Third World: *Reggae Ambassadors: 20th Anniversary Collection*, Mercury, 1993.

Tosh, Andrew: *Original Man*, Attack, 1988.

COLLECTIONS

Legends of Reggae Music, Rohit, 1988.
Vintage Classics, Rohit, 1989.
Blood and Fire, 1971–1972, Trojan, 1988.
Bring the Couchie, Trojan, 1989.
Observation Station, Heartbeat, 1990.
Turbo Charge, Heartbeat, 1991.
Hard Works from the Observer All Stars, Heartbeat, 1992.
Dancehall Roughneck, Heartbeat, 1993.
Truth and Rights Observer Style, Heartbeat, 1994.

Joseph "Jo Jo" and Ernest Hookim

By the '70s the Jamaican recording business was undergoing tremendous change. Independents pushed forward with money from family businesses like television repair shops (Joe Gibbs; see entry), shoe stores (like the lovely Rosso label with its footwear icon), and some less savory sources. New labels and studios sprang up in and around Kingston. As the militant "rockers" style broke through, the place to be was Channel One.

Brothers Ernest and Jo Jo Hookim made their money rack-jobbing slot machines and jukeboxes before setting up their own recording studio in Kingston. Their first engineer was Syd Bucknor, moving in a trajectory from his own beginnings at Studio One to later English work for On U Sounds and others. When Bucknor left, Ernest himself manned the board and a whole new style was born.

With Ernest engineering and mixing, Jo Jo Hookim's productions defined the Channel One sound. Another brother, Kenneth, also did some producing. The house band was the Revolutionaries, the first professional teaming of Sly Dunbar and Robbie Shakespeare (see entry), whose drum-and-bass combination led the frontal assault of reggae. Ernest pushed Sly's drum far up in the mix, and it became *the* mix from that point on.

Channel One revolutionized the tempo of its time not in the least by updating original Studio One rhythms that led rock steady into reggae. Other producers, like GG's Alvin Ranglin, Phase One's Roy Francis, Blacka Morwell, Winston Riley, and Roy Cousins, used the studio to great effect, but from about 1974 through 1978 Jo Jo ruled. In the words of African Youth, everyone wanted to "Forward down a Channel One / Fe go sing my likkle song." And nearly everyone did.

"Right Time" by the Mighty Diamonds, "Ballistic Affair" with Leroy Smart, and Junior Byles' "Fade Away" were a few of the 45s that made Channel One number one by 1976. The Hookims helped return the horn section, so essential to ska but cast aside in the rock-steady and early reggae days, back into play as well. Besides the labels Hitbound, Channel One, and Well Charge in Jamaica, Hookim productions were released on Virgin, Cha Cha, Pressure Beat, Greensleeves, and Empire in the U.K., and United Artists, Shanachie, and Heartbeat in the U.S.

Top vocal groups like the Wailing Souls, the Jays, and Hell and Fire; DJs Ranking Joe, Ranking Trevor, Clint Eastwood, Lone Ranger, and Trinity; and singers like Ernest Wilson and John Holt all contributed to the Hookims' success on the 7-inch and 12-inch "disco single" formats they helped pioneer. Dub discs from the Revolutionaries helped define that genre, many mixed by Ernest ("the genius" according to the Diamonds). Theirs are still among the best dub albums ever released.

Whether cutting vocal duo Earth and Stone, DJ Dillinger, or the vital Revolutionaries rhythm tracks and dubs that underpinned them, Jo Jo and Ernest's openness to roots styles made for a progressive and impressive body of work. The best single CD retrospective of their work to date is *Hit Bound! The Revolutionary Sound of Channel One*. In the final days of the Hookims' reign at Channel One, Sly and Robbie packed up to tour with Peter Tosh and then Black Uhuru. A new house band, the Roots Radics, began to make their name as top studio outfit.

By the mid-'80s, as the digital era dawned, the brothers Hookim pulled the plug on their musical endeavors. Perhaps they understood the gamble of trying to compete with the myriad new studios popping up, calculated the odds, and decided to retire winners. Some of the most successful of the newcomers (like Penthouse and Exterminator) have succeeded by applying the Channel One formula of continually modernizing the classic rhythms for today's ear. —CHUCK FOSTER

Brown, Barry: *Far East*, Channel One, 1981.
Dillinger: "Bionic Dread/Eastman Skank," Mango, 1976 • *Bionic Dread*, Mango, 1976 • *CB 200*, Mango, 1976 • "Cokane in My Brain," Mango, 1977.
Earth and Stone: *Kool Roots*, Pressure Beat, 1979, 1996.
Eastwood, Clint: *Death in the Arena*, Cha Cha, c. 1978.
Heptones: *Good Life*, Greensleeves, 1979.
Jah Thomas: *Stop Yu Loafin'*, Greensleeves, 1978.
Lone Ranger: *M-16*, Hitbound, 1982.
Mighty Diamonds: *I Need a Roof*, JJ, 1976 • *Right Time*, Virgin, 1976 • *Stand Up to Your Judgement*, Channel One, 1978 • *Deeper Roots*, Virgin, 1979 • *Tell Me What's Wrong*, J&J, 1980 • *Go Seek Your Rights*, Virgin, 1990.
Ranking Joe: *Weakheart Fadeaway*, Shanachie, 1978.
Revolutionaries, The: *Revolutionary Sounds*, Well Charge/JA, 1976 • *Revolutionary Sounds*, Vol. 2, Well Charge/JA, 1976 • *Jonkanoo Dub*, Cha Cha, 1978 • *Reaction in Dub*, Cha Cha, 1978.
Roots Radics Band: *Seducer Dub Wise*, Hitbound, 1982.
Scorcher, Errol, and the Revolutionaries: *Rastafire: A Channel One Experience*, Unite Artists, 1978.
Smart, Leroy: "Ballistic Affair," Mango, 1976 • *Ballistic Affair*, Conflict, 1976.
Wailing Souls: *Best Of*, Empire, 1984.

COLLECTIONS
Vital Dub: Strictly Rockers, Well Charge/JA, 1976.
I Came I Saw I Conquered, Channel One, 1978.
Hit Bound! The Revolutionary Sound of Channel One, Heartbeat, 1989.

Trevor Horn

Trevor Horn, producer of hits by Seal and Yes, believes that chart success should be his goal whenever he enters the studio. "Anyone can make an unsuccessful record—why else would you bother to hire a producer other than to improve your chance to have a successful record?" Horn asks.

Horn (born July 15, 1949, in Durham, England) began his career as a songwriter and musician in the '70s, eventually hitting the American and British charts with the Buggles, a band who achieved nearly instantaneous fame with a track that Horn co-wrote, "Video Killed the Radio Star."

Horn's career, however, really took off in the early '80s after he entered the production realm: He supervised *90215* (No. 5) by Yes, the album with "Owner of a Lonely Heart" (No. 1) and "Changes"; *The Lexicon of Love* by ABC, the album featuring "The Look of Love" (No. 18) and "Poison Arrow"; and *Welcome to the Pleasuredome* by Frankie Goes to Hollywood, which included such hits as "Relax" (No. 10) "Two Tribes," and "The Power of Love."

The albums by Yes, ABC, and Frankie Goes to Hollywood are prime examples of Horn's interactive approach to record making. For instance, he adds drama with the stop-and-go introduction to "Owner of a Lonely Heart" and adds majestic strings on "The Look of Love."

Horn also plays keyboards, synthesizers, and bass on

some of the projects he produces, pointing out that what he contributes depends on the artist he is working with. "If you play too much on your [productions], you limit those records," Horn insists. "But having said that, there are occasions where I have, when everyone's gone, replaced the bass or added some backing vocals."

In the '90s Horn helped launch Seal's career, producing such hits as "Crazy" (No. 7), "Prayer for the Dying," and "Kiss from a Rose" (No. 1) from two albums that were released on Horn's ZTT label.

Horn says it was a "hard slog" to record "Prayer for the Dying," while "Kiss from a Rose" was envisaged as "sort of a medieval folk song." Also, Horn thought that "Crazy" did not initially sound like a hit song. "It sounded like an interesting idea, but then [Seal] was adamant that if he did the deal with us it had to be a hit single, so we just had to work on it until it was a hit."

Horn's other album productions or co-productions include Paul McCartney's *Flowers in the Dirt,* Rod Stewart's *A Spanner in the Works,* Simple Minds' *Street Fighting Years,* Mike Oldfield's *Tubular Bells II,* and Tina Turner's *Wildest Dreams.*

Horn tackles projects that are "a bit unusual" to keep things fresh. "I get bored fairly quickly with things, so I like to keep varying it," he explains. "I think it's a bit of an insult to an artist to show up and you try the same old tricks that you tried with the last artist. You have to get them excited because a good record only comes from people being excited."

In 1997 Horn reformed the Art of Noise to provide himself with an outlet for his songs. —BEN CROMER

ABC: *The Lexicon of Love,* Neutron, 1982 • "The Look of Love," Mercury, 1982 • *The Real Thing* (EP), Neutron, 1989 • *Absolutely ABC: The Best of ABC,* Mercury, 1990.

Act: *Laughter, Tears and Rage,* AVI, 1987.

Almond, Marc: *Jacky* (EP), Warner Bros., 1991.

Art of Noise: *Into Battle,* ZTT/Island, 1984.

Band Aid: "Do They Know It's Christmas?," Virgin/EMI, 1985 (*Now That's What I Call Music Xmas Album*).

Brennan, Marie: *Misty Eyed Adventures,* Mesa, 1995.

Buggles: *The Age of Plastic,* Island, 1980 • *Adventures in Modern Recording,* Carrere, 1981.

Cher: *It's a Man's World,* WEA, 1996.

Ferry, Bryan: "Dance with Life," Reprise, 1996 (*Phenomenon* soundtrack).

Frames DC: *Fitzcarraldo,* Elektra, 1996.

Frankie Goes to Hollywood: "Relax," ZTT/Island, 1983 • *Welcome to the Pleasuredome,* ZTT/Island, 1983 • "Bang," Arista, 1984 • "Two Tribes," ZTT/Island, 1984 • *Liverpool,* ZTT/Island, 1986 • *Bang . . . The Greatest Hits of,* Atlantic, 1994.

Godley and Creme: "Cry," Polydor, 1985 • *The History Mix, Vol. 1,* Polydor, 1985.

Horn, Trevor, and Hans Zimmer: "The Closing of the Year (Main Theme from *Toys*)," ZTT, 1992.

Japp, Philip: *Philip Japp,* A&M, 1983.

Jones, Grace: *Island Life,* Island, 1985 • *Slave to the Rhythm,* Manhattan/Island, 1985.

Jones, Tom: "If I Only Knew," Interscope, 1994 • *The Lead and How to Swing It,* Interscope, 1994.

Lewis, Donna, and Richard Marx: "At the Beginning," Atlantic, 1997.

MacGowan, Shane, and the Popes: *The Snake,* ZTT/WB, 1995.

Manilow, Barry: *I'd Really Love to See You Tonight,* Arista, 1997.

McCartney, Paul: *Flowers in the Dirt,* Capitol, 1989.

McLaren, Malcolm: "Buffalo Gals," Island, 1982 • *Duck Rock,* Island, 1983 • *Scratchin'* (EP), Charisma, 1984.

Oldfield, Mike: "Sentinel/Restructure," Warner Bros., 1992 • *Tattoo* (EP), Reprise, 1992 • *Tubular Bells II,* Reprise, 1992 • *Best Of,* Virgin, 1994.

Pet Shop Boys: "Left to My Own Devices," EMI America, 1988 • "Left to My Own Devices" (remix), EMI America, 1988 • "It's Alright," EMI, 1989 • *Discography: The Complete Singles Collection,* EMI America, 1991.

Propaganda: *Wishful Thinking,* ZTT/Island, 1985.

Reader, Eddi: "Nobody Lives Without Love," Atlantic, 1995 (*Batman Forever* soundtrack).

Reid, Terry: *The Driver* (5 tracks), Warner Bros., 1991.

Seal: "Crazy," ZTT/Sire/WB, 1991 • *Seal,* ZTT/Sire/WB, 1991 • "The Beginning," ZTT/Sire/WB, 1991 • "Newborn Friend," ZTT/Sire/WB, 1994 • *Seal (Second Album),* ZTT/Sire/WB, 1994 • "Kiss from a Rose," ZTT/Sire/WB, 1995.

Simple Minds: *Ballad of the Streets* (EP), A&M, 1989 • *Street Fighting Years,* A&M, 1989 • *Glittering Prize Simple Minds 1981–1992,* A&M, 1993.

Stewart, Rod: "Downtown Train," Warner Bros., 1989 • *Storyteller: The Complete Anthology,* Warner Bros., 1989 • *Downtown Train,* Warner Bros., 1990 • *Vagabond Heart,* Warner Bros., 1991 • "Your Song," Polydor, 1991 (*Two Rooms: Songs of Elton and Bernie Taupin*) • *If We Fall in Love Tonight,* Warner Bros., 1996.

Turner, Tina w/ Barry White, "In Your Wildest Dreams" (remix), Virgin, 1996 • *Wildest Dreams,* Virgin, 1996.

Yes: *90125,* Atlantic, 1983 • "It Can Happen," Atlantic, 1983 • "Owner of a Lonely Heart," Atco, 1983 • "Leave It," Atco, 1984 • "Owner of a Lonely Heart" (remix), Atco, 1984 • *Big Generator,* Atco, 1987 • "Owner of a Lonely Heart" (remix), American Gramaphone, 1991 • *Yesyears,* Atco, 1991.

Paul Hornsby

Paul Hornsby helped create and define the Southern rock sound of the '70s with such acts as the Marshall Tucker Band, Charlie Daniels Band, Wet Willie, and Grinder Switch.

Born in New Brockton, Alabama, on August 26, 1944, Hornsby's introduction to music came from his father, a fiddle player. Throughout his youth Hornsby followed his father from square dance to square dance, learning the whys and wherefores of country music.

After he discovered the electric guitar, Hornsby found the Ventures, and a world beyond country music opened up for him. R&B caught his attention in college, further broadening his palette. After spending 1966 on the road with a cover band, Hornsby (on keyboards) hooked up with Duane and Gregg Allman in 1967 to form the Hourglass. Before breaking up in 1970, the band released two (Hornsby concedes) forgettable albums, but did lay the foundation for a sinewy blues-rock sound that would come to fruition with the Allman Brothers Band.

After the Hourglass broke up, Duane moved to Muscle Shoals to start working on a solo album, and he asked Hornsby to come along to play on the demos. Hornsby became a fixture at Capricorn Studios and was eventually asked to help out with production. He first produced the Sundown (with future Allman Brothers Band and Sea Level keyboardist Chuck Leavell) in 1970, then he worked with Eric Quincy Tate.

Soon thereafter the Marshall Tucker Band (named after the owner of the rehearsal hall the band frequented in South Carolina) came through the doors. "I was ready to be a producer and we worked hard for a couple of months. By the time we were done with it I couldn't even hear it anymore," he says. "I didn't know if it was terrible or great or whatever. Within a month or two it was a hit record. Then it wasn't Paul Hornsby, keyboard player, it was Paul Hornsby, record producer. You get a hit album and all of a sudden it changes the hat you wear."

Hornsby's work with the Tucker Band was revolutionary in that it combined Toy Caldwell's fancy finger-picked lead guitar with Jerry Eubanks' jazzy flute and sax and Doug Gray's country-inflected vocals to create an elegant and sophisticated, yet earthy hybrid with great mass appeal. Six of Tucker's Hornsby-produced albums cracked the Top 40, with *Searchin' for a Rainbow* topping out at No. 15. Other highlights include the self-titled first album with "Can't You See," *A New Life,* and *Carolina Dreams* with "Heard It in a Love Song" (No. 14).

For five years Hornsby was one of the top producers in the South, achieving great success with the dope-and-chew, hippie country of Charlie Daniels (*Fire on the Mountain, Nightrider, Saddle Tramp*), including hit singles "Long Haired Country Boy" and "The South's Gonna Do It." Hornsby also did well with Southern rockers Grinder Switch and Wet Willie.

After 11 years in the business, and 7 years of constant studio work, Hornsby decided to retire in 1977 because he was tired and because music was changing ("Music changes more than bellbottoms and hemlines," according to Hornsby). It was a retirement that lasted until singer Randy Howard called in 1983 to ask if he could record at Muscadine, the small 8-track studio that Hornsby had built in Macon.

The album, which featured the controversial song "The All-American Redneck," brought Hornsby back to the roots of his production career where simplicity ruled. "It showed me that it's not the studio, it's the people and the music that make an album. This was cut on real substandard equipment in a bedroom and people liked it." —ERIC OLSEN AND DAVID JOHN FARINELLA

Caldwell, Toy: *Can't You See,* Pet Rock, 1998.

Cooder Browne: *Cooder Browne,* Lone Star, 1978.

Charlie Daniels Band: *Fire on the Mountain,* Kama Sutra, 1974 • "Long Haired Country Boy," Kama Sutra, 1975 • *Nightrider,* Kama Sutra, 1975 • "The South's Gonna Do It," Kama Sutra, 1975 • *Saddle Tramp,* Epic, 1976 • *High Lonesome,* Epic, 1977.

Daniels, Charlie: *Volunteer Jam,* Capricorn, 1976 • *Volunteer Jam 3 and 4,* Epic, 1978 • *Super Hits,* Columbia, 1994 • *Roots Remain,* Sony, 1996 • See also Charlie Daniels Band.

Grinder Switch: *Honest to Goodness,* Capricorn, 1974 • *Macon Tracks,* Capricorn, 1975 • *Pullin' Together,* Capricorn, 1976 • *Redwing,* Atco, 1977.

Heartwood: *Nothing Fancy,* GRC, 1975.

Howard, Randy: *The All-American Redneck,* Viva/WB, 1983.

Marshall Tucker Band: *Marshall Tucker Band,* Capricorn, 1973 • *A New Life,* Capricorn, 1974 • *Where We All Belong,* Capricorn, 1974 • "Fire on the Mountain," Capricorn, 1975 • *Searchin' for a Rainbow,* Capricorn, 1975 • *Long Hard Ride,* Capricorn, 1976 • *Carolina Dreams,* Capricorn, 1977 • "Heard It in a Love Song," Capricorn, 1977 • *Greatest Hits,* AJK, 1978, 1989 • *Together Forever,* Capricorn, 1978 • *The Best of the Marshall Tucker Band: The Capricorn Years,* Era, 1994.

Missouri: *Welcome Two Missouri,* Polydor, 1979.

Richards, Randy: *Randy Richards,* A&M, 1978.

Sundown: *Sundown,* Ampex, 1973.

Target: *Captured*, A&M, 1977.

Tate, Eric Quincy: *Drinking Man's Friend*, Capricorn, 1972.

Two Guns: *Balls Out*, Capricorn, 1977.

Waldorf, Marcia: *Memoranda*, Capricorn, 1975.

Wells, Kitty: *Forever Young*, Capricorn, 1974.

Wet Willie: *The Wetter the Better*, Capricorn, 1976 • *Greatest Hits*, Capricorn, 1977 • *Left Coast Live*, Capricorn, 1977.

Whitlock, Bobby: *Rock Your Sox Off*, Capricorn, 1976.

Dayton "Bones" Howe

Dayton "Bones" Howe (a particularly thin man) is one of the most important and prolific engineers in the history of West Coast recording, as well as the producer of monster hits for the Turtles ("It Ain't Me Babe," No. 8; "You Baby," No. 20), the Association ("Windy," No. 1; "Never My Love," No. 2; "Everything That Touches You," No. 10), and the Fifth Dimension ("Stoned Soul Picnic," No. 3; "Aquarius/Let the Sunshine In," No. 1; "Wedding Bell Blues," No. 1; "One Less Bell to Answer," No. 2), and Tom Waits' classic albums from the mid-'70s and early '80s.

Bones Howe was born in Minneapolis in 1933 and his earliest recollections are of playing 78s on his parents' floor-model Victrola (with hand crank and "steel and cactus needle"). When Howe was about 7, his father, a successful stock broker, moved the family to the sleepy resort town of Sarasota, Florida.

Howe became fascinated with radio both as a broadcast medium and as an electronic device; he taught himself to repair radios while he was still a child. Howe was in high school before he saw his first live band, and even though the Solid Six was a routine dance band, "playing stock arrangements of standards from the '40s," he was "blown away."

Howe graduated from high school in 1951 and taught himself to play drums with the goal of becoming a professional musician. Then the Korean war struck. " 'If you become a musician, you're going to get drafted and you're going to carry a rifle,' " Howe recalls his father saying. " 'So you should go to college and study communications and electronics.' " Howe did so at Georgia Tech in Atlanta, and within a few months he found a combo that needed a drummer. One thing led to another and during his last two years at Tech, Howe played six nights a week with a trio in a lounge and with a big band on weekends.

Howe became friendly with a lot of musicians who passed through town, including drummer Shelly Manne, who played with the Stan Kenton Band. Manne suggested that Howe get into recording because he was a musician who understood electronics. The recording engineers of the day were "old guys from radio and none of them [knew] what a rhythm section should sound like. None of them [had] played in a band. A light went off. I suddenly knew what I wanted to do," says Howe.

Howe graduated from Tech in 1956 with a bachelor of science in electronic engineering, put his drums in his '55 Chevy station wagon, and headed west with $200 in his pocket to be a recording engineer.

In a Hollywood club, Howe found a musician friend from Atlanta, who introduced him to a recording engineer named Val Valentin, who in turn invited Howe to drop by a session for Mel Tormé at the Radio Recorders studio. There Howe met chief engineer and studio partner Harry Bryan, who, though he believed Howe to be grotesquely overqualified for the job, hired him as an apprentice at $72 per week.

Howe was an eager apprentice and spent as much time as he could around the studio, helping to set up the equipment for sessions and soaking up information. Radio Recorders was a union shop and Howe's presence in the studio was strongly discouraged when he was off the clock. The union's irritation was multiplied when a year later Howe began mixing, condensing by 90 percent the traditional 10-year progression from apprentice to second engineer (then called "recordist") to (mixing) engineer.

A year later Howe became the jazz engineer at Radio Recorders when his friend Valentine left to go to Capitol. In 1961 Nesuhi Ertegun (see entry) came to L.A. to record Ornette Coleman. Howe engineered for Coleman, then got his first co-production credit with Ertegun on Red Mitchell and Harold Land's *Hear Ye* album.

Engineer Bill Putnam opened a studio on Sunset called United Recording in 1961, and Howe, looking for a change, joined him there. Howe was to be second engineer to Putnam on a Frank Sinatra album, "but Bill hit his head on the back of a mike boom and blacked out. I ended up engineering *Sinatra Swings* as a result," says Howe.

Howe engineered Jan and Dean records and met Lou Adler (see entry), who called Howe's 3-track work of the Everly Brothers' "Don't Ask Me to Be Friends," "the perfect mix," and recommended him to other producers. By the early '60s the three busiest engineers in L.A. were Al Schmitt (see entry), Eddie Brackett, and

Howe. Having run into each other and commiserated many times about their hard work and low pay, the trio decided to start an independent engineering company together. They wanted to be paid what musicians were being paid for sessions because they felt that "an engineer in the booth was contributing as much as a fiddle player," according to Howe.

Within three months, however, Schmitt had been hired to do A&R at RCA, Snuff Garrett (see entry) had hired Eddie Brackett to do all of his sessions at Liberty, and Howe was stuck up a tree. It was November 1962; Howe was 29 and knew "I didn't want somebody else dictating my life to me for the next 20 years. So I quit to become the first independent engineer. Putnam said, 'You can't do that, there aren't any independent engineers.' I said, 'There's one now.' The union tried to stop me, but gave in. None of the people who I thought would hire me did, and then when things looked bleakest, Lou Adler called me out of the clear blue sky and said 'I want you to engineer all of my records.' " Over the next few years Howe worked as an indie engineer with some of L.A.'s top producers including Adler, Terry Melcher, Joe Saraceno, and Snuff Garrett (see entries).

Ted Feigen, co-owner of the fledgling White Whale label, signed a new vocal group called the Crossfires and began looking for an up-and-coming (i.e. low-cost) producer to work with them. Herb Alpert suggested Howe. The band was renamed the Turtles, and their first release with Howe, a rocking version of Bob Dylan's "It Ain't Me Babe," was a hit in 1965. Hits "Let Me Be" and "You Baby" followed; Howe found a Gary Bonner–Alan Gordon song called "Happy Together" for the band, but they recorded it with producer Joe Wissert (see entry) and the relationship was over.

Over Christmas 1966, Howe was engineering a Grass Roots session for Adler when he decided he'd better go home to his wife and three kids. Adler was furious and didn't speak to him for months. As the year came to a close, Howe contemplated his future and decided that he would only take production work from then on.

Howe's work with the Association made them one of the top white American vocal groups of the '60s, although a few egos were bruised. The Association had hit with "Along Comes Mary" and "Cherish" before deciding to write their own material and unleashing "Pandora's Golden Heebie Jeebies" upon the world. Howe opined that the band needed great (i.e., outside) material, better musicians (than they were) in the studio, and an arranger. The band agreed to these tenets, but grumbled because, as Howe puts it, "There is a cer-

tain loss of ego when one has to tell a 16-year-old girl backstage, 'Well, I didn't really play drums on the record.' " Besides changing the band's recording practices, Howe's main contribution was finding Ruthann Friedman's "Windy" on a demo tape and changing the time signature from a 3/4 waltz to a 4/4 rock beat. "Windy" and "Never My Love" (written by the Addrisi brothers) are classics of what would now be called "soft rock."

Johnny Rivers (who owned the Soul City label) called Howe first to engineer and then to produce "the black Mamas and the Papas," the Fifth Dimension. Howe produced over a dozen Top 40 hits for the band between 1968 and 1972, the biggest being a cultural landmark, "Aquarius/Let the Sunshine In." Howe was still primarily known as an engineer until he cobbled together "Aquarius" (from the beginning of *Hair*) with the "Let the Sunshine In" line (from a song in the middle of the show called "The Flesh Failures") by means of a Hal Blaine drum break.

Now a hitmaker, Howe decided that he needed to produce a "significant artist" (one "who writes and performs his own material and has success with it," according to Geffen) to round out his portfolio. Geffen suggested Tom Waits. Howe's background in jazz and pop neatly prepared him for the atavistic beatnik Waits: a singer/songwriter who borrows nimbly from the noir side of various idioms (cool jazz, beat poetry, folk, Dixieland, cabaret) and funnels them through his mordant and ironic, yet romantic imagination, creating an oeuvre uniquely his own.

Howe recorded (mostly live to 2-track) Waits' standards like *Nighthawks at the Diner*, *Small Change* (with "Tom Traubert's Blues," "Step Right Up," "The Piano Has Been Drinking"), *Foreign Affairs* (with the Waits–Bette Midler duet "I Never Talk to Strangers"), and *Blue Valentine*. Eventually Waits too went his own way, because as Howe sees it, "Every relationship with an artist is a terminal relationship."

Bones Howe was the sound engineer for the historic *Monterey Pop* concert and film (which he has never seen) in 1967, and for the classic live *Elvis Christmas* TV special from 1968. He has been music supervisor for dozens of feature films, including *Serial Mom*, *The Prince of Tides*, *La Bamba*, and *Back to the Future*, and is still active in the business. —ERIC OLSEN

Alessi: *Alessi*, A&M, 1976 • "Oh Lori," A&M, 1976 • "Seabird," A&M, 1976.
Association, The: *Insight Out*, Warner Bros., 1967 • "Never My Love," Warner Bros., 1967 • "Windy," Warner Bros., 1967 • *Windy*, Warner Bros., 1967 • *Birthday Party*, Warner

Bros., 1968 • "Everything That Touches You," Warner Bros., 1968 • *Greatest Hits*, Warner Bros., 1968 • "Time for Livin'," Warner Bros., 1968 • "Dreamer," Elektra, 1981.

Carnival, The: *The Carnival*, Liberty/World Pacific, 1970.

Cunliffe, Bill: *Bill in Brazil*, Discovery, 1995.

Desmond, Andy: *Andy Desmond*, Ariola, 1978.

Dickson, Barbara: "Fallen Angel," Epic, 1978 • *Sweet Oasis*, Epic, 1978.

Eddy and the Showmen: *Squad Car: The Best of Eddie and the Showmen*, AVI, 1965.

Feldman, Victor: *Champagne Music for Cats Who Don't Drink*, VSOP, 1957, 1994.

Fifth Dimension: "Paper Cup," Soul City, 1967 • "Carpet Man," Soul City, 1968 • "Stoned Soul Picnic," Soul City, 1968 • *Stoned Soul Picnic*, Soul City, 1968 • "Sweet Blindness," Soul City, 1968 • *The Magic Garden*, Soul City, 1968 • "Aquarius/Let the Sunshine In," Soul City, 1969 • "California Soul," Soul City, 1969 • *The Age of Aquarius*, Soul City, 1969 • "Wedding Bell Blues," Soul City, 1969 • "Workin' on a Groovy Thing," Soul City, 1969 • "Blowing Away," Soul City, 1970 • "One Less Bell to Answer," Bell, 1970 • *Portrait*, Bell, 1970 • "Puppet Man," Bell, 1970 • "Save the Country," Bell, 1970 • "The Independence Medley," Bell, 1971 • *Live!* Bell, 1971 • "Love's Lines, Angles and Rhymes," Bell, 1971 • *Love's Lines, Angles and Rhymes*, Bell, 1971 • "Never My Love," Bell, 1971 • *Greatest Hits on Earth*, Arista, 1972, 1987 • "(Last Night) I Didn't Get to Sleep At All," Bell, 1972 • "If I Could Reach You," Bell, 1972 • *Individually and Collectively*, Bell, 1972 • "Together Let's Find Love," Bell, 1972 • "Living Together, Growing Together," Bell, 1973 • *Living Together, Growing Together*, Bell, 1973 • *Up Up and Away!* Arista, 1997.

Free Flight: *Soaring*, Palo Alto, 1983.

Garrett, Kelly: *Kelly*, RCA, 1975.

Jamal, Ahmad: *One*, 20th Century, 1978 • *Genetic Walk*, 20th Century, 1980 • *Intervals*, 20th Century, 1980.

Jazz at the Movies Band: *Film Noir*, Discovery, 1994 • *It's a Wonderful Life: Sax at the Movies*, Vol. 1, Discovery, 1995 • *One from the Heart: Sax at the Movies*, Vol. 2, Discovery, 1995.

Lewis, Jerry Lee: *Jerry Lee Lewis*, Elektra, 1979 • *Rockin' My Life Away: The Jerry Lee Lewis Collection*, Warner Bros., 1991 • *All Killer No Filler: The Anthology*, Rhino, 1993.

Lyme and Cybelle: "Follow Me," White Whale, 1966.

Marketts, The: "Out of Limits," Warner Bros., 1963.

Mendes, Sergio: *Love Music*, Bell, 1973.

Midler, Bette: *Broken Blossom*, Atlantic, 1977.

Mitchell, Red, and Harold Land: *Hear Ye!* Rhino, 1961, 1989.

Monkees, The: "A Man Without a Dream," Colgems, 1969 • *Instant Replay*, Colgems, 1969 • "Someday Man," Colgems, 1969 • *Listen to the Band*, Rhino, 1991.

Mull, Martin: *Near Perfect/Perfect*, Elektra, 1979.

Newton, Juice: *After the Dust Settles*, RCA, 1975.

w/ Silver Spur, *Juice Newton and Silver Spur*, RCA, 1975.

Nyro, Laura: *Stoned Soul Picnic: The Best of Laura Nyro*, Legacy, 1997.

Presley, Elvis: "If I Can Dream," RCA, 1968 • "Memories," RCA, 1968 • *Elvis's Gold Records*, Vol. 5, RCA, 1984 • *His Life and His Music*, Life and Times Music, 1995.

Price, Alan: *Lucky Day*, Jet, 1979 • *Rising Sun*, Jet, 1980.

Punch: *Punch*, A&M, 1971.

Rivers, Johnny: *Realization*, Imperial, 1968.

Routers, The: "Sting Ray," Warner Bros., 1962.

Sandpipers: *A Gift of Song*, A&M, 1971.

Shocked, Michelle: *Kind Hearted Woman*, Private, 1994, 1996.

Smokestack Lightning: *Off the Wall*, Bell, 1969.

Timberline: *The Great Timber Rush*, Epic, 1977 • *Timberline*, Epic, 1977.

Turtles, The: "It Ain't Me Babe," White Whale, 1965 • *It Ain't Me Babe*, White Whale, 1965 • "You Baby," White Whale, 1966 • *You Baby*, White Whale, 1966 • *Happy Together*, London/White Whale, 1967 • *Wooden Head*, White Whale, 1970 • *20 Greatest Hits*, Rhino, 1984.

Waits, Tom: *The Heart of Saturday Night*, Elektra, 1974, 1989 • *Nighthawks at the Diner*, Asylum, 1975 • *Small Change*, Asylum, 1976 • *Foreign Affairs*, Asylum, 1977 • *Blue Valentine*, Asylum, 1978 • *Heartattack and Vine*, Asylum, 1980 • *One from the Heart* soundtrack, Columbia, 1982.

Williams, Patrick: *Sinatraland*, Capitol, 1998.

Mike Howlett

After entering the business in the mid-'70s as bassist and drummer with the exotic and mutating prog-rock group Gong, Mike Howlett—one of the godfathers of modern rock—then collected three musicians, Andy Summers, Stewart Copeland, and Sting, to back him in a short-lived band called Strontium 90.

As the '70s became the '80s, Howlett helped midwife the new wave explosion when he produced essential albums by A Flock of Seagulls (*A Flock of Seagulls*, No. 10; *Listen*, No. 16), OMD (*Organisation*, No. 6 U.K.; *Architecture & Morality*, No. 6 U.K.), China Crisis (*Working with Fire and Steel*, No. 20 U.K.), Fischer-Z (*Word Salad*), Martha and the Muffins (*Metro Music, Trance and Dance*), Blancmange (*Happy Families*, with "Living on the Ceiling," No. 7 U.K.), Gang of Four (*Songs of the Free*), Joan Armatrading (*Secret Secrets*, No. 14 U.K.), and the Alarm (*Strength*, No. 18 U.K.), perfecting a neo-wall of sound that artfully blended electronic and organic instruments.

Born on the Fiji Islands ("I can claim that I'm the greatest Fijian record producer of all time," he says with a laugh), Howlett's family moved to Singapore when he was 8 and ended up in Australia a year later. Howlett learned music basics on a xylophone and ukulele before borrowing a guitar from a friend. He started his first band at the age of 12, and in 1968, before he had finished high school, he was playing bass for a cover band at the Whiskey A-Go-Go in Sydney.

In 1970 he won a trip to England with a soul-jazz band, the Affair, and joined Gong (see Steve Hillage entry) in 1973 for classic albums (*Angel's Egg, You, Shamal*), helping to transform them from spacey noodlers to forceful fusionists before leaving in 1976.

In August of that year Howlett and Virgin Records executive Carol Wilson went to hear a band called Last Exit, who were playing in a room above a pub in Newcastle, in the north of England. When Howlett walked in he was struck by the singer.

"There was Sting singing away and the rest of the band was a bunch of jazz rockers. It reminded me of Weather Report with Stevie Wonder [see entry] on vocals. Sting was doing the 'souly' singer thing at the time," he remembers.

After bumping into guitarist Andy Summers (ex–Kevin Ayers, ex–Eric Burdon, ex–Soft Machine) at a party in January 1977, Howlett began to piece together a live band to be called Strontium 90. "The drummer I had couldn't make it, so Sting said that he knew of another drummer, Stewart Copeland [ex–Curved Air]." Backing Howlett in Strontium 90 was the first time Sting, Summers, and Copeland played together. (Demos—including the original version of "Every Little Thing She Does Is Magic"—and live cuts from Strontium 90 were released as *Police Academy* in 1997.) Shortly after they became the Police.

Later that year Howlett got a call from Virgin, who wanted to release a live-and-rarities album from Gong. Howlett edited and mixed *Live, etc.,* and then a compilation album called *Short Circuits*. That album featured new music that bands like the Fall, the Buzzcocks, Joy Division, and Steel Pulse had recorded at the Electric Circus—a Manchester punk club—before it had closed. His involvement with those projects, as well as his relationship with Wilson, put him on the inside track to produce Martha and the Muffins ("Echo Beach") and OMD (Orchestral Manoeuvres in the Dark), including their stunning, propulsive techno-pop standard "Enola Gay" (No. 8 U.K.). OMD, like the early Human League, Pet Shop Boys (see

entry), and Depeche Mode, captured the fresh sonic rush of tuneful electronic music before it became trite.

Howlett's greatest and most successful productions are the first two albums by A Flock of Seagulls. Although singer/songwriter/keyboardist (and former hairdresser) Mike Score's unfortunate winged hairstyle (and the band's confused, silly image in general) muddied the issue of their greatness, the Seagulls and Howlett crafted a monolithic sound that beautifully melded Paul Reynold's phased, economic hard rock guitar (reminiscent of Brian May in early Queen or Bill Nelson in Be-Bop Deluxe) with Score's keyboard wash over Ali Score's simple-but-forceful drums on super tunes like "I Ran" (No. 9), "Space Age Love Song," "Telecommunication," and "Wishing" (No. 10 U.K.).

After a dramatically successful 10-year run with new wave, Howlett moved into hard rock with little success. "My managers thought I should go into rock 'n' roll and I went along with it," he says. "I didn't do it well and by the time I got back it was the early '90s. Then it was the rave scene and I should have gone right into that, but I didn't."

Instead he reunited his old bandmates in Gong. "I returned to the stage for the first time in 19 years in 1994 for a Gong reunion," explains Howlett. "From '78 onwards I may have played on a few tracks on an album here and there, but that was it. I'm excited about music again and I think my time might come around again."
—Eric Olsen and David John Farinella

A Flock of Seagulls: *A Flock of Seagulls,* Jive/Arista, 1981 • "I Ran," Jive/Arista, 1982 • *Listen,* Jive/Arista, 1983 • *Best Of,* Jive/Arista, 1987.

Alarm, The: *Strength,* IRS, 1985 • *Standards,* IRS, 1990.

Any Trouble: *Wheels in Motion,* Stiff, 1981.

Armatrading, Joan: *Secret Secrets,* A&M, 1985 • *Classics, Vol. 21,* A&M, 1989.

Berlin: *Love Life,* Geffen, 1984 • *Best Of, 1979–1988,* Geffen, 1988.

Blancmange: *Happy Families,* Decca/Island, 1982 • "Living on the Ceiling," London, 1982.

Broadberry, Jo, and the Standouts: *Jo Broadberry and the Standouts,* Revenge, 1983.

China Crisis: "Working with Fire and Steel," Virgin, 1983 • *Working with Fire and Steel* (EP), Virgin, 1983 • *Working with Fire and Steel and Possible Pop Songs,* Virgin, 1984 • *Collection,* Virgin, 1990.

Comsat Angels: *Land,* Jive/Arista, 1979 • *7 Day Weekend,* Jive/Arista, 1985.

Fischer-Z: "So Long," EMI America, 1980, 1983 (*Spinning Pups*) • *Word Salad,* United Artists, 1979 • *Going Deaf for a Living,* United Artists, 1980.

Gang of Four: *Songs of the Free*, Warner Bros., 1982 • "Producer," Warner Bros., 1983 (*Attack of the Killer B's*) • *A Brief History of the Twentieth Century*, Warner Bros., 1990.

Gong: *Live, etc.*, Virgin, 1977/1983.

Hunters and Collectors: *Hunters and Collectors*, Virgin, 1980.

La Union: *Tentacion*, WEA Latina, 1990.

Martha and the Muffins: *Metro Music*, Virgin, 1979 • *Trance and Dance*, Virgin, 1980 • *Far Away in Time*, Caroline, 1993.

OMD: *Organisation*, DinDisc, 1980 • *Architecture and Morality*, Virgin/Epic, 1981 • *OMD* (7 tracks), Virgin/Epic, 1981 • *Shame* (EP), Virgin, 1987 • *Best Of*, A&M, 1988.

Original Mirrors: *Heart Twango and Raw Beat*, Phonogram, 1981.

Penetration: *Moving Targets*, Blue Plate, 1978, 1990 • *Race Against Time*, Virgin, 1978.

Punishment of Luxury: *Laughing Academy*, United Artists, 1979.

Revillos: *Rev Up*, DinDisc, 1980.

Siren: *All Is Forgiven*, Mercury, 1989.

Sniff 'n' the Tears: *Love Action*, Chiswick, 1981 • *Best Of*, Chiswick, 1996.

Straight Eight: *Shuffle 'n' Cut*, Logo/RCA, 1980.

Strontium 90: *Police Academy*, Pangea, 1997.

Teardrop Explodes: *Kiliminjaro* (2 tracks), Mercury, 1980.

Thompson Twins: *In the Name of Love* (1 track), Hansa, 1981.

COLLECTIONS

Rhythms of Resistance: Music of Black Africa, Earthworks/Virgin, 1988.

Leon Huff

See KENNETH GAMBLE AND LEON HUFF

Chris Hughes

Chris Hughes has straddled two distinct musical worlds. He has produced (or co-produced) some of the best new wave ever recorded, including Adam and the Ants' *Kings of the Wild Frontier* (No. 1 U.K.), Tears For Fears' *The Hurting* (No. 1 U.K) and *Songs from the Big Chair* (No. 1 U.S., No 2 U.K.), Wang Chung's *Points on a Curve*, and the Polecats' great single "Make a Circuit with Me." In the other world, Hughes has walked with an older generation of rock dignitaries including Paul McCartney (see entry), Pete Townshend, and Robert Plant (see entry).

Hughes was born in 1954 and raised in London. He immersed himself in the usual British Invasion bands (Beatles, Stones) as well as classical orchestral music. In the late '70s he walked into Mercury A&R man David Bates's office in London looking for a record deal for the electronic music he composed in his small home studio by experimenting with analog tape, oscillators, and tone manipulation.

While waiting in the lobby for Bates, Hughes struck up a conversation with the owner of a small label (Do It) about their common aspirations and Hughes gave him a copy of his tape for a listen. While the tape was rejected by both executives, each was impressed with its production values and separately asked Hughes to work with some young bands.

Hughes' first project was a young band of punky new romantics called Adam and the Ants. After working on the raw demos that became *Dirk Wears White Sox*, Hughes and the Ants pursued a more melodic and heavily rhythmic path that became *Kings of the Wild Frontier* and *Prince Charming*.

Though he had been hired as producer, at Adam's request, Hughes joined the Ants as drummer. Under the name of "Merrick," Hughes (who had drummed since the age of 12) created the wild tribal beat that the Ants became known for. His tom-tom flailing and immediate production drove hits like "Ant Music" (No. 2 U.K.) and "Dog Eat Dog" (No. 4 U.K.). Both roles for Hughes ended when Ant decided to go solo in 1982.

Shortly thereafter David Bates phoned and asked Hughes if he would like to meet two young musicians from Bath, Roland Orzabal and Curt Smith, who had left the ska group Graduate to form Tears For Fears. According to Hughes the pair were reluctant to work with a producer because of an unpleasant earlier experience, but after a few meetings they set to work (with co-producer Ross Cullum) on "Mad World" (No. 3 U.K.).

"World" combines strange, syncopated percussion with moody synths and Smith's haunted vocals on killer lines like "I find it kind of funny / I find it kind of sad / The dreams in which I'm dying / Are the best I've ever had," to forge greatness. Other classics on *The Hurting* include the thumping alterna-soul of "Change" (No. 4 U.K.), and the sweeping synth-and-acoustic guitar of "Pale Shelter" (No. 5 U.K.).

Hughes helped push the band along, widening their emotional palette and encouraging songwriter Orzabal to sing more. The result was the five-times-platinum *Songs from the Big Chair.* "Everybody Wants to Rule the World" (No. 1) is one of the best singles of the last 20 years: the propulsive, circular beat and strong dual vocals from Smith and Orzabal carry a superior melody that is augmented by tinkling keyboard filigrees and great guitar work from Orzabal and Neil Taylor. "Head over Heels" (No. 3) and "Shout" also stand out.

"Shout" was one of the most challenging songs Hughes has ever worked on. "That song took us about three months to finish," he explains. "We'd keep putting it up on the mixer, but it didn't feel right." The song must have eventually felt right as it shot to No. 1.

While he continued to work with alterna-favorites like Wang Chung, Howard Jones, and the Polecats in the '80s; and Starclub, Definition of Sound, and Gene in the '90s, Hughes has also remixed Pete Townshend's "Let My Love Open the Door," produced Robert Plant's *Fate of Nations* album with the Tears For Fears-meets-Gin Blossoms single "29 Palms," and worked with Paul McCartney on the "Motor of Love" song from the *Flowers in the Dirt* album.

"It's quite extraordinary how gifted the guy is," Hughes says of McCartney. "Music just flows out of him, but there's no quality control," he says delineating the double-edged sword of genius. —ERIC OLSEN AND DAVID JOHN FARINELLA

Adam and the Ants: *Dirk Wears White Sox,* Do It/Epic, 1979, 1992 • "Ant Music," Epic, 1980 • "Dog Eat Dog," Epic, 1980, 1981 (*Exposed*) • "Killer in the Home," Epic, 1980, 1981 (*Exposed*) • *Kings of the Wild Frontier,* Epic, 1981 • *Prince Charming,* Epic, 1981 • *Antics in the Forbidden Zone,* Epic, 1990 • *Antmusic: The Very Best Of,* Arcade, 1994.

Ant, Adam: *B-Side Babies* (7 tracks), Legacy, 1994.

Associates, The: *Popera: The Singles Collection,* Sire/WB, 1990.

Definition of Sound: *Experience,* Fontana, 1996.

Gene: *Drawn to the Deep End,* Polydor, 1997.

Hughes, Chris: *Shift,* Point, 1994.

Jones, Howard: *Cross That Line,* Elektra, 1989 • "Everlasting Love," Elektra, 1989 • *The Prisoner* (EP), Atlantic, 1989 • *The Best Of,* Elektra, 1993.

McCartney, Paul: *Flowers in the Dirt,* Capitol, 1989.

Ocasek, Ric: "Emotion in Motion," Geffen, 1986 • *This Side of Paradise,* Geffen, 1986.

Plant, Robert: "29 Palms," Atlantic, 1993 • *Fate of Nations,* Atlantic, 1993.

Plastic Fantastic: "Fantastique No. 5," PFCD, 1996.

Polecats: "Make a Circuit with Me," Mercury, 1983 • *Make a Circuit with Me* (2 tracks), Mercury, 1983.

Propaganda: *1234,* Charisma, 1990.

Starclub: *Starclub,* Island, 1993.

Tears For Fears: "Pale Shelter," Mercury, 1983 • *The Hurting,* Mercury, 1983 • "Everybody Wants to Rule the World," Mercury, 1985 • "Head over Heels," Mercury, 1985 • "Shout," Mercury, 1985 • *Songs from the Big Chair,* Mercury, 1985 • "Mothers Talk," Mercury, 1986 • *Tears Fall Down (The Hits, 1982–1992),* Fontana, 1992 • *Saturnine Marshall and Lunatic,* PolyGram, 1996.

Townshend, Pete: *Coolwalkingsmoothtalkingstraightsmokingfirestoking: The Best Of,* Atlantic, 1996.

Vitamin Z: *Rites of Passage,* Geffen, 1985.

Wang Chung: "Dance Hall Days," Geffen, 1983 • *Points on the Curve,* Geffen, 1984 • *To Live and Die in L.A.* soundtrack, Geffen, 1985 • *Everybody Wang Chung Tonight: Greatest Hits,* Geffen, 1997.

Hugo and Luigi

Hugo (Peretti) and Luigi (Creatore) enjoyed an exceptional 30-year career from the '50s to the '70s as songwriters, producers, and label owners in pop, rock 'n' roll, and soul. At Mercury Records in the mid-'50s the pair produced the Gaylords ("The Little Shoemaker," No. 2) and Sarah Vaughan and had a series of hits with "Her Nibs" Georgia Gibbs, including the million-selling "Tweedle Dee" (No. 2) and "Dance with Me Henry (Wallflower)" (No. 1). In the late '50s they co-owned Roulette Records with the infamous Morris Levy and produced a bevy of hits for pop folksinger Jimmie Rodgers.

Then Hugo and Luigi, among the first independent producers, signed an unprecedented five-year, million-dollar deal with RCA in 1959, hitting with Della Reese's "Don't You Know" (No. 2), and the Isley Brothers (see entry), and co-writing/producing the Tokens' enormous "The Lion Sleeps Tonight" (No. 1)—a miraculous reworking of the Weavers' "Wimoweh," and the even older Zulu folk song "Mbube" (see Hank Medress entry). Most significantly, Hugo and Luigi then helped to invent soul music through a series of timeless classics with Sam Cooke. At RCA they also produced Perry Como ("Caterina"), Little Peggy March ("I Will Follow Him," No. 1), and Ray Peterson ("Tell Laura I Love Her," No. 7).

Hugo and Luigi co-wrote (with George Weiss) one of Elvis's most beloved hits, "Can't Help Falling in

Love." In the '70s they owned the Avco/Embassy label, writing and producing the Stylistics' "Let's Put it All Together" (No. 18) in 1974. They ended their run with a bang in 1975, producing Van McCoy's "The Hustle"—the first No. 1 of the disco era.

Hugo Peretti (born December 6, 1916) and Luigi Creatore (born December 21, 1920) were cousins. Peretti played trumpet and was working the Borseht Belt by his mid-teens. Later he played in Broadway pit bands and studied composition and arranging. Creatore's father had a symphonic band in Italy, which he brought to New York in 1902. Luigi was born and raised in midtown Manhattan's Hell's Kitchen. A brother and sister were concert pianists; another brother was a violinist. "I'm the only one who couldn't play a note and I'm the only one who made any money out of the music business," chuckles Creatore.

Creatore fought in World War II (he was at Pearl Harbor), and when he returned he tried to eke out a living as a writer. Hugo and Luigi reunited at Creatore's brother's wedding reception; Peretti's wife was an author of children's books, and Peretti asked his cousin if he would help her out with some ideas. This led to Hugo and Luigi collaborating on some children's songs for Mercury Records.

Mercury's president, Irving Green, asked if the pair would like to work on pop records, and their first hit was the Gaylords' "The Little Shoemaker" in 1954. They recorded the great Sarah Vaughan, including "Make Yourself Comfortable," "Whatever Lola Wants," "Mr. Wonderful," and "How Important Can It Be."

The pair also contributed to one of the most important commercial trends of the mid-'50s, the tidying-up of R&B songs for use by white artists for the white market. Depending on your point of view, this development (starting with the Crew-Cuts' version of the Chords' "Sh-boom" in 1954, and coming to painful fruition with Pat Boone whitewashing Fats Domino, Little Richard, and Big Joe Turner in 1955 and 1956) either helped smooth the way for the acceptance of rock 'n' roll and R&B by the white audience or was crass plundering of the R&B mine by white exploiters. It was doubtless both. Hugo and Luigi's contribution to this trend came in the person of Georgia Gibbs, a veteran big band and radio star, for whom they gentled LaVern Baker's "Tweedle Dee" and created a sanitized medley out of Hank Ballard's "Work with Me, Annie" and Etta James' "Roll with Me, Henry," now called "Dance with Me Henry (Wallflower)."

In 1957 Hugo and Luigi left Mercury to buy into Roulette Records (founded by George Goldner; see entry). The pair's biggest success at Roulette was the tuneful pop-folk of honey-throated Jimmie Rodgers, with whom they had a series of hits from 1957 to 1959, including "Honeycomb" (No. 1) and "Kisses Sweeter Than Wine" (No. 3); they also wrote hit songs "Oh-Oh, I'm Falling in Love Again" (No. 7) and "Secretly" (No. 3).

Hugo and Luigi took their "Hugo and Luigi Productions" to RCA Records in 1959. RCA had decided that they needed more youthful attractions like Elvis Presley. They approached Hugo and Luigi, who, being clearly in the driver's seat, asked for a salary and for the outrageous (for the time) producer's royalty of a penny an album. They also insisted upon producer's credit on all of their albums—another first. The deal generated more than $1 million over five years for the hit-making cousins.

The pair took a while to get going, and to adjust to RCA's straight-laced corporate atmosphere. They had an artistic breakthrough when they rejected their creamy-smooth past and recorded the Isley Brothers' raw, uproarious, call-and-response screamer, "Shout (Parts 1 and 2)," which only went to No. 47 on the pop chart at the time but established the pair's rock 'n' roll credentials and has sold over 1 million copies in the ensuing years.

Recalls Creatore, "We brought 'Shout' down to the review board at RCA and we played it. A guy sitting there said, 'I don't understand what they are saying.' I said, 'Well, the kids understand.' He said, 'But I don't understand this whole record, let's hear the other side.' So, we played the other side, which was a continuation. He said, 'I don't understand it.' I said, 'If you were 14 years old you would understand it.' "

With that success, Hugo and Luigi were able to lure Sam Cooke away from Keen Records (see Bob Keane and Bumps Blackwell entries) to RCA, and together they had 12 Top 20 hits, including indispensable classics "Chain Gang" (No. 2), "Cupid" (No. 17), "Twistin' the Night Away" (No. 9), "Bring It on Home to Me" (No. 13), and "Another Saturday Night" (No. 10). Their initial meeting at RCA in New York was a bit itchy—Cooke was used to working with a black producer and pretty much calling the shots—but when Cooke's voice cracked on the first run-through of a song, Creatore announced (according to author Daniel Wolff in his inspired Cooke bio, *You Send Me*), "Shit, they sent us the wrong guy," cracking everyone up and breaking the ice.

Attitude is everything according to Creatore: "Our career is based on somebody else's talent. The thing is to get it out of them, and to get it out of them you have to be friendly. You gotta show them you're on their side; your only purpose in life is to make a hit for them. We were good friends with Sam and he was a magical talent. For the most part, he would write songs and we would pick the ones to record."

Their first hit together was "Chain Gang," an oddly cheerful song given the topic, with grunting "ooh, aah" background vocals, spare electric guitar, the buttery soul that was Sam Cooke, and some odd percussion. After casting about the studio for an extended period of time, Cooke found the rhythmic oomph he was looking for, when, according to Wolff, one percussionist pounded on his leather stool seat and another beat the base of a mike stand with a piece of hollow metal, both in time with the grunter's ooh's and aah's.

"Cupid" is floating butterfly perfection with just the right orchestration (especially the French horn) from Hugo and Luigi, the sonic and psychic opposite of the equally great Southern grit of the bluesy "Bring It on Home to Me" (with Lou Rawls' earthy dueting).

After leaving RCA in 1964, the cousins and George Weiss wrote a musical about the Civil War called *Maggie Flynn*, starring Shirley Jones and Jack Cassidy; it lasted just 10 weeks on Broadway in 1968. They bought Avco/Embassy Records and had hits there with the Stylistics and Van McCoy, "but it wasn't enough to keep a label going," according to Creatore, and in 1979 they retired. Hugo and Luigi were also recording artists, with a hit album (*The Cascading Voices of the Hugo and Luigi Chorus*, No. 14) and a hit single ("Just Come Home"). Peretti died in 1986, after a lengthy illness.

Creatore sees his main talent as having been "a midwife—you don't make the baby, but you're there to get it out. We had a feeling for matching the material with an artist, a feeling for what the arrangement should be, and after that we stayed out of the artists' way other than to encourage them.

"It is also best to do all the work—the ideas, the feeling, the approach—before you get to the studio," says Creatore. "That's very important and people don't do that anymore. They go in and experiment in the studio. I think when you get into the studio it should be a happy occasion with everybody enjoying everything: 'Gee, that's great! Let's just try it once again with a little more of this.'

"I don't know how you make hits—with Hugo and me it just happened. There was a chemistry and it happened. There's not a school to go to become a producer. You can follow a producer around and see what a studio is like, but the rest is instinct. How do you get a feeling a song is a hit song? Before a hit is a hit I can't tell you how 'nothing' it seems—just another song. We thought 'The Lion Sleeps Tonight' was going to be a hit and the Tokens didn't. That time we were right. You do your best and sometimes it works." For Hugo and Luigi it worked many, many times. —ERIC OLSEN AND DAVID JOHN FARINELLA

Bowen, Jimmy: *Jimmy Bowen*, Roulette, 1957 • w/ Buddy Knox, *One Side Each*, Roulette, 1958 • *The Best Of*, Collectables, 1991 • w/ Buddy Knox, *The Complete Roulette Recordings*, Sequel, 1996.

Carmichael, Hoagy: *Hoagy Carmichael Songbook*, Bluebird/RCA, 1990.

Como, Perry: *For the Young At Heart*, RCA, 1961 • "You're Following Me," RCA, 1961 • "Caterina," RCA, 1962 • "(I Love You) Don't You Forget It," RCA, 1963 • *The Songs I Love*, RCA, 1963 • *Legendary Performer*, RCA, 1976 • *Yesterday and Today: A Celebration in Song*, RCA, 1993.

Cooke, Sam: "Chain Gang," RCA, 1960 • "Sad Mood," RCA, 1960 • "Cupid," RCA, 1961 • *Hits of the 50's*, RCA, 1961 • "That's It-I-Quit-I'm Moving On," RCA, 1961 • "Bring It on Home to Me," RCA, 1962 • "Having a Party," RCA, 1962 • "Nothing Can Change This Love," RCA, 1962 • *The Best of Sam Cooke*, RCA, 1962 • "Twistin' the Night Away," RCA, 1962 • *Twistin' the Night Away*, RCA, 1962 • "Another Saturday Night," RCA, 1963 • "Frankie and Johnny," RCA, 1963 • "Little Red Rooster," RCA, 1963 • *Mr. Soul*, RCA, 1963 • *Night Beat*, Abkco, 1963, 1995 • "Send Me Some Lovin'," RCA, 1963 • *Ain't That Good News*, RCA, 1964 • "Good News," RCA, 1964 • "Good Times," RCA, 1964 • "Tennessee Waltz," RCA, 1964 • "That Where It's At," RCA, 1964 • "A Change Is Gonna Come," RCA, 1965 • *Sam Cooke at the Copa*, RCA, 1965 • *Sam Cooke Live at the Harlem Square Club, 1963*, RCA, 1985 • *The Rhythm and the Blues*, RCA, 1995.

Cordell, Kim: *I Sing in a Pub*, Roulette, 1965.

Gary, John: *The Very Best Of*, RCA, 1997.

Gaylords, The: "The Little Shoemaker/Mecque, Mecque," Mercury, 1954.

Gibbs, Georgia: "Tweedle Dee," Mercury, 1954 • "Dance with Me Henry (Wallflower)," Mercury, 1955 • "I Want You to Be My Baby," Mercury, 1955 • "Sweet and Gentle," Mercury, 1955 • "Rock Right," Mercury, 1956 • *The Best of the Mercury Years*, Mercury, 1996.

Hugo and Luigi: "Just Come Home," RCA, 1959 • *When Good Fellows Get Together*, RCA, 1959 • *Let's Fall in Love*, RCA, 1963 • *The Cascading Voices of the Hugo and Luigi Chorus*, RCA, 1963.

Impacts, The: "Canadian Sunset," RCA, 1959.

Isley Brothers: "Shout (Part 2)," RCA, 1959 • *Rockin' Soul*, Vol. 1, Rhino, 1991 • *The Isley Brothers Story*, Vol. 1, Rhino, 1991 • *Shout: The RCA Sessions*, RCA, 1996.

Knox, Buddy: See Bowen, Jimmy.

March, Little Peggy: "I Will Follow Him," RCA, 1963 • *I Will Follow Him*, RCA, 1963 •

McCoy, Van, and the Soul City Symphony: *Disco Baby*, Avco,

1975 • "The Hustle," Avco, 1975 • *The Hustle and the Best Of,* H&L, 1976.

Mickey and Sylvia: *Love Is Strange,* Bear Family, 1990.

original cast: *Do Re Mi,* RCA, 1961, 1994 • *Little Me,* RCA, 1962 • *Maggie Flynn,* RCA, 1968.

Peterson, Ray: "Tell Laura I Love Her," RCA, 1960.

Reed, Vivian: *Brown Sugar,* H&L, 1976.

Reese, Della: "Don't You Know," RCA, 1959.

Rodgers, Jimmie: "Honeycomb," Roulette, 1957 • *Jimmie Rodgers,* Roulette, 1957 • "Kisses Sweeter Than Wine," Roulette, 1957 • "Are You Really Mine," Roulette, 1958 • "Bimbombey," Roulette, 1958 • "Make Me a Miracle," Roulette, 1958 • "Oh-Oh, I'm Falling in Love Again," Roulette, 1958 • "Secretly," Roulette, 1958 • "I'm Never Gonna Tell," Roulette, 1959.

Sedaka, Neil: *All-Time Greatest Hits,* Vols. 1–2, RCA, 1991.

Softones, The: *The Best Of,* Amherst, 1996.

Stylistics, The: "Let's Put It All Together," Avco, 1974 • *Let's Put It All Together,* Avco, 1974 • *All-Time Classics,* Amherst, 1976 • *Best Of,* Vol. 2, Amherst, 1976, 1985.

Tokens, The: "The Lion Sleeps Tonight," RCA, 1961 • *The Lion Sleeps Tonight,* RCA, 1962, 1994.

Steve "Silk" Hurley

Along with Marshall Jefferson and Frankie Knuckles (see entries), Steve "Silk" Hurley is considered one of house music's grand icons. And like Jefferson and Knuckles, Hurley has spanned the oftentimes limiting parameters of contemporary R&B music, moving freely from his club-dance roots into rhythm-based music that smartly incorporates elements of retro soul, contemporary hip-hip, and things that go pop.

Hurley's initiation into the music arena occurred when he formed the seminal house duo J.M. Silk in 1985. He and partner Keith Nunnally had three hits ("Music Is the Key," "I Can't Turn Around," "Shadows of Your Love") before they disbanded. Solo, Hurley had three No. 1 dance hits with "Jack Your Body," "Let the Music Take Control," and "Work It Out," which was also the title track of his debut album released in 1989.

Since then, his colorful career has spanned all four corners: DJing, remixing, producing, and songwriting. With each endeavor, Hurley has always demonstrated a knack for the catchy hook and memorable melody, two elements that work well on both radio and dance floors. Having attained much success with a roster of clients that includes Madonna, Janet Jackson, Crystal Waters,

Ten City, and Prince (see entry), Hurley has proved that he is not only a valuable asset but a musical force to be reckoned with.

If he has faced any obstacle over the years, it has been his insistence on not being pigeonholed. "I don't prefer any one particular genre of music over another. I just like good music," insists Hurley. "I don't want to only be thought of as an R&B producer or a dance music producer. For me, that's way too limiting. I am a producer who makes records. Period." But for a while, in the late '80s, Hurley felt as if he'd have to sacrifice one style of music for the other.

"You know, I came into the music industry via dance music and I somehow believed that I had to stay within that genre," says the Chicago native. "But then I came to the realization that there is nothing wrong with liking different styles of music and producing many styles of music."

Only after arriving at this conclusion did he have his first R&B hit with Chantay Savage's remake of the disco chestnut "I Will Survive." Although the song never quite made it to the top of the charts—it couldn't budge beyond the No. 2 position—it did manage to legitimize Hurley as an R&B producer. And while he has worked with such R&B artists as Boyz II Men, En Vogue, and Mint Condition, he continues to collaborate with dance floor divas like CeCe Peniston and former Sounds of Blackness frontwoman Ann Nesby. "That's where I got my start," he says, "I could never turn my back on the people who first supported me." —LARRY FLICK

Abdul, Paula: "Vibeology" (remix), Virgin, 1991.

Black Box: "I Don't Know Anybody Else," RCA, 1990 • "I Don't Know Anybody Else" (remix), RCA, 1990.

Blount, Tanya: *Natural Thing,* Polydor, 1994.

Clubland Featuring Zemya Hamilton, *Clubland,* Great Jones, 1992.

Dayne, Taylor: "I'll Wait" (remix), Arista, 1993.

D'Bora: *E.S.P.,* Smash, 1991.

Divinyls: "I Touch Myself" (remix), Virgin, 1991.

En Vogue: "Strange" (remix), Atlantic, 1990 • *Remix to Sing,* EastWest, 1991.

Gigolo Aunts: *Learn to Play Guitar,* Wicked Disc, 1997.

Hurley, Steven "Silk": *Work It Out Compilation,* Atlantic, 1989 • "Jack Your Body," London, 1992 • "Work It Out," Atlantic, 1992 • "The Word Is Love," Central Station, 1998.

Inner City: "Good Life" (remix), Virgin, 1988.

INXS: "Not Enough Time" (remix), Atlantic, 1992.

J.M. Silk: "I Can't Turn Around," RCA, 1992 • "Let the Music Play," RCA, 1992 • "Music Is the Key," D.J. International, 1992 • "Shadows of Your Love," D.J. International, 1992.

Jackson, Michael: "Jam" (remix), Epic, 1992 • "Remember the Time" (remix), Epic, 1992.

Jomanda: "Got a Love for You" (remix), Big Beat, 1991.

Love, Monie: *In a Word or 2*, Warner Bros., 1993.

M Doc: *Universal Poet*, Smash, 1991.

Malaika: *Sugar Time*, A&M, 1993.

Mellow Man Ace: "Mentirosa" (remix), Capitol, 1990.

Moore, Tina: *Tina Moore*, Street Life, 1995.

Nesby, Ann: "I'll Do Anything for You," Perspective, 1996 • *I'm Here for You*, Perspective, 1996 • "Hold On," Perspective, 1997.

New Order: "Fine Time" (remix), Qwest, 1988.

OMD: "Call My Name," Virgin, 1991.

Peniston, CeCe: *Finally*, A&M, 1992 • "Keep on Walkin'," A&M, 1992 • "We Got a Love Thang," A&M, 1992 • *Thought Ya Knew*, A&M, 1994 • *I'm Movin' On*, A&M, 1996.

Prince and the New Power Generation: "Gett Off" (remix), Paisley Park, 1991.

Principle, Jamie: "Baby Wants to Ride" (remix), FFRR, 1989 (*Silver on Black*) • *Love or Infatuation*, Smash, 1991 • "Baby Wants to Ride," London, 1992 • "You're All I've Waited For," Smash, 1992.

Pseudo Echo: "Funky Town" (remix), RCA, 1987.

Richie, Lionel: "Do It to Me" (remix), Motown, 1992.

Rush, Donell: *Comin' and Goin'*, RCA, 1993.

Savage, Chantay: *Here We Go*, RCA, 1993 • "Don't Let it Go to Your Head," RCA, 1994 • "I Will Survive," RCA, 1995.

Simply Red: "Something Got Me Started" (remix), EastWest, 1991.

Sims, Kym: "Too Blind to See It," Atco, 1992 • *Too Blind to See It*, Atco, 1992.

Vertical Hold: *Head First*, A&M, 1995.

Waters, Crystal: "Makin' Happy," Mercury, 1991.

Williams, Tene: *Tene Williams*, Pendulum, 1993.

Ice Cube

(O'SHEA JACKSON)

It would be difficult to select the one rapper who best exemplifies gangsta rap. A few choices come to mind, and all of them come from seminal rap group N.W.A (Niggaz With Attitude): Dr. Dre (see entry) or Eazy-E would be the first choice of some, but for many Ice Cube (born O'Shea Jackson, June 15, 1969, in Los Angeles) would be the selection.

When N.W.A released its first album in 1987, *N.W.A and the Posse*, then, a year later, the classic *Straight Outta Compton*, who could have guessed how far the Compton native would go in this rap game? Not that his talent wasn't evident even then, but by the time Cube left N.W.A and released his 1990 solo album, the classic-in-its-own-right *AmeriKKKa's Most Wanted* (No. 19), it was clear he would be here for the long run. The rap community has been better for it.

The brazen *AmeriKKKa's Most Wanted* set the pattern for future Cube recordings and productions: tough, forceful blasts of beats backing up his distinct, equally tough, and forceful delivery. He hasn't been able to match *AmeriKKKa's Most Wanted*, though he came close with 1991's *Death Certificate* (No. 2), which included "Steady Mobbin," "No Vaseline," "True to the Game," and "Black Korea." A year later, *The Predator* (No. 1), with "Wicked," "Check Yo Self," and "It Was a Good Day" (No. 15), was no joke; and even the lesser *Lethal Injection* from 1993, with "Bop Gun (One Nation)" and "What Can I Do?," was a respectable effort.

While continuing to provide himself with some of rap's best beats, Cube also lent some to others, like Yo Yo ("You Better Ask Somebody"), Da Lench Mob (*Guerillas in tha Mist* album), Mack 10 ("Take a Hit"), and Bootsy Collins and Bernie Worrell ("You Got Me Wide Open").

Cube is also central to Westside Connection, a rap trio filled out by Mack 10 and K-Dee. Though Westside Connection's 1996 album *Bow Down* was released while gangsta rap was on the commercial and critical downswing, it was unashamedly a gangsta rap album. The credits even read, "This album is dedicated to the hip hop nation. It's gangsta rap in it's [*sic*] highest form. A style invented on the West Coast. Your [*sic*] welcome."

Cube shared production on the album with others, including Bud'da, Binky, and Cedric Samson. The album includes the hit title track as well as "Gangstas Make the World Go Round," which flipped the script on the Stylistics' "People Make the World Go Round."

While keeping busy with rap, Cube has also won respect in recent years as an actor and director, appearing in films such as *Anaconda, Higher Learning, Boyz N the Hood*, and *Dangerous Ground*. —KEVIN JOHNSON

Da Lench Mob: *Guerillas in tha Mist*, Street Knowledge, 1992 • *Planet of Da Apes*, Priority, 1994, 1995.

Del Tha Funky Homosapien: *I Wish My Brother George Was Here*, Elektra, 1991, 1995.

Ice Cube: "AmeriKKKa's Most Wanted," Priority, 1990 • *AmeriKKKa's Most Wanted*, Priority, 1990 • *Kill at Will* (EP), Priority, 1990 • *Death Certicate*, Priority, 1991 • "How to Survive in South Central," Qwest/WB, 1991 (*Boyz N the Hood* soundtrack) • *The Predator*, Priority, 1992 • "Wicked,"

Priority, 1992 • "Check Yo Self," Priority, 1993 • "It Was a Good Day," Priority, 1993 • *Lethal Injection,* Priority, 1993 • *Bootlegs and B-Sides* (1 track), Priority, 1994 • "Bop Gun (One Nation)," Priority, 1994 • "You Know How We Do It," Priority, 1994 • *Featuring . . . Ice Cube,* Priority, 1997.

Jagwarr, Don: *Faded,* Priority, 1994.

Luke: *Uncle Luke,* Luther Campbell, 1996.

Mack 10: *Mack 10,* Priority, 1995 • *Based on a True Story,* Priority, 1997.

WC and the Maad Circle: *Curb Servin',* Payday/London, 1995.

Westside Connection: *Bow Down,* Priority, 1996 • "Gangstas Make the World Go Round," Lench Mob, 1997.

Yo Yo: *Make Way for the Motherload,* EastWest, 1991 • *Black Pearl,* EastWest, 1992 • *You Better Ask Somebody,* Atlantic, 1993.

COLLECTIONS

Friday soundtrack, Priority, 1995.

Jimmy Ienner

From his early days as a ghost singer to his production career as a hitmaker in the grand tradition (cloaked behind his Cheshire cat logo), Jimmy Ienner has preferred anonymity over fame. "I was reclusive—always have been, always will be. The joy for me was seeing it happen, not worrying about who knew I did it," he says.

Ienner's hits as a producer are all over the rock and pop-rock map, including the timeless power pop of the Raspberries ("Go All the Way," No. 5; "I Wanna Be with You," No. 16; "Let's Pretend"; and "Overnight Sensation," No. 18) and their erstwhile lead singer Eric Carmen ("All by Myself," No. 2; "Never Gonna Fall in Love," No. 11; "Make Me Lose Control," No. 3), the tough horn rock of Lighthouse ("One Fine Morning"), the underrated vocal virtuosity of Three Dog Night ("The Show Must Go On," No. 4; "Sure As I'm Sittin' Here," No. 16), the tartan teeny-pop of the Bay City Rollers ("I Only Want to Be with You," No. 12), and the heavy-cum-revivalist Grand Funk ("Some Kind of Wonderful," No. 3; "Bad Time," No. 4). As executive producer Ienner put together two of the most outrageously successful soundtracks of all time: the combined 15-times-platinum of *Dirty Dancing* and *More Dirty Dancing.*

Born in 1947, Ienner broke into the music world in his native New York early in life. By the time he was 16

he had ghost-sung on a number of hits (by the Drifters and others who must remain anonymous), worked in publishing, and even produced. His dislocating schedule sometimes took him directly from a three-point stance on the high school football field to a singer's stance at Brooklyn's Fox Theater. Though the pay was low, Ienner was content to work for knowledge in those early years.

The first time Ienner demonstrated that knowledge in the studio was during a session at Mirror Sound Studios for the Barons' "Pledge of a Fool" in 1962. "Everyone was 'yessing' producer Goddard Lieberson about a mix, but I told him I thought it stunk. Everybody else became sort of crazed, but he calmly asked why. I just told him what I thought." Ienner's intrepid honesty pushed him forward.

While Ienner had produced acts under pseudonyms (including Jay Francis), his first public album was with Canadian horn-rockers Lighthouse in 1970. Over his years in the business Ienner came to be of the opinion that his job as a behind-the-scenes man was to be as transparent as possible. "Someone once wrote, 'The most dominant style of Jimmy Ienner is not having his own style,' " he recalls approvingly.

Ienner's place in rock history is secure because of his work with the Raspberries—the British Invasion band from Cleveland who were too late for the '60s and too early for the Invasion revival of the late '70s. The Raspberries' unfashionability in their own time (1971 to 1974) stemmed from their goofy matching-suits image and unabashed songs about the joys and pains of young adulthood at a time when cynicism and irony were dominant themes in the news (Vietnam, Richard Nixon, Kent State) and rock 'n' roll (breakup of the Beatles, death at Altamont, glitter rock).

Eric Carmen sang with the purity of Paul McCartney (see entry); Wally Bryson played guitar like a combination of George Harrison and Pete Townshend; the songs (mostly by Carmen) alternately rocked and swooned in harmony; and it was all produced by Ienner with the power and delicacy of George Martin (see entry). Phil Spector (see entry) has nothing on Ienner's wall of sound on "Overnight Sensation (Hit Record)," the band's last hurrah.

Perhaps the band's greatest moment is the arpeggio-driven guitar rocker "I Wanna Be with You," which grabs the listener by the body and soul from the opening drum volley and holds on through the closing sax and guitar fade.

Ienner, as immune to fashion as the Raspberries, also took Grand Funk in a contrary direction. In preparation for the recording of "Some Kind of Wonderful" (originally by the Drifters), Ienner listened to the in-vogue big production sound of the time (1974) employed by artists as varied as Paul McCartney and Barry White. He decided that he would have to bring in the "states of New Jersey, New York, and Connecticut to make a bigger-sounding record." So he went in the opposite direction and made a record that has the raw immediacy of a demo. "That was a choice," he states firmly. "It wasn't chance. It caused impact because it was different."

After Ienner produced Eric Carmen's post-Raspberries solo album in 1975, he opted out of the production chair. "I stopped being one of the highest-paid producers in the world and became an executive because I got bored. I got bored with the fact that there weren't any more surprises and it was the same thing again and again," he explains.

While Ienner hasn't produced much since 1975 (he helped Carmen with "Make Me Lose Control" in 1988), he has been successfully involved in the business. He started his own label, Millennium (Meco, the Godz), in 1977. Ten years later his deft blend of vintage and vintage-sounding hits turned *Dirty Dancing* into a cultural phenomenon, one that has yet to run its lucrative course. He has done this and that since, maintaining his youthful outlook. "The future looks the same to me as it did when I was 11: it's what's coming and that makes it exciting." —ERIC OLSEN AND DAVID JOHN FARINELLA

Bay City Rollers: "Dedication," Arista, 1976 • *Dedication*, Arista, 1976 • "I Only Want to Be with You," Arista, 1976 • "Yesterday's Heroes," Arista, 1976 • *Greatest Hits*, Arista, 1977.

Blood, Sweat and Tears: *New City*, Columbia, 1975.

Carmen, Eric: "All By Myself," Arista, 1975 • *Eric Carmen*, Arista, 1976 • "Never Gonna Fall in Love Again," Arista, 1976 • "Make Me Lose Control," Arista, 1988 • *The Best Of*, Arista, 1988 • *Definitve Collection*, Arista, 1997.

Chambers Brothers: *Unbonded*, Avco, 1973.

Grand Funk: "Some Kind of Wonderful," Capitol, 1974 • *All the Girls in the World Beware*, Capitol, 1975 • "Bad Time," Capitol, 1975 • *Caught in the Act*, Capitol, 1975 • *Born to Die*, Capitol, 1976 • *Capitol Collector's Series*, Capitol, 1991.

Lighthouse: *Peacing It All Together*, RCA, 1970 • "One Fine Morning," Evolution, 1971 • *One Fine Morning*, Evolution, 1971 • "Take It Slow (Out in the Country)," Evolution, 1971 • *Thoughts of Movin' On*, Evolution, 1971 • "I Just Wanna Be Your Friend," Evolution, 1972 • "Sunny Days," Evolution, 1972 • *Sunny Days*, Evolution, 1972.

Medley, Bill: *Best Of*, Curb, 1990.

Murphy, J.F. and Salt: *The Last Illusion*, CBS, 1973 • *Urban Renewal (Murphy's Law)*, ABC, 1975.

Raspberries, The: "Go All the Way," Capitol, 1972 • "I Wanna Be with You," Capitol, 1972 • *Raspberries*, Capitol, 1972 • *Fresh*, Capitol, 1973 • "Let's Pretend," Capitol, 1973 • *Side 3*, Capitol, 1973 • "Overnight Sensation (Hit Record)," Capitol, 1974 • *Starting Over*, Capitol, 1974 • *Capitol Collectors Series*, Capitol, 1991 • *Power Pop*, Vols. 1–2, RPM, 1996.

Sha Na Na: *Sha Na Now*, Kama Sutra, 1975.

Three Dog Night: *Hard Labor*, ABC, 1974 • "Sure As I'm Sitting Here," Dunhill, 1974 • "The Show Must Go On," Dunhill, 1974 • *Comin' Down Your Way*, ABC, 1975 • *Joy to the World: Their Greatest Hits*, MCA, 1975 • *Celebrate: The Three Dog Night Story, 1965–75*, MCA, 1993.

COLLECTIONS

Dirty Dancing soundtrack, RCA, 1987.
More Dirty Dancing soundtrack, RCA, 1987.

Bruce Iglauer

A connoisseur of the blues, Bruce Iglauer launched Alligator Records in 1971 and has produced many of the albums his Chicago-based label is famous for—from the street-savvy Hendrix-derived power blues of Michael Hill to the traditional electric music of Iglauer's favorite son, Son Seals.

"One of the things I like about the blues is the broad dynamic variations and the buildups and bringdowns," says Iglauer, born in Ann Arbor, Michigan, on July 10, 1947. "I want musicians to play in the studio like they play in a club. I used to be a documentarian, and that [style] is usually great for somebody's first album, but you also have to help them grow as musicians and create studio situations that give them the tools to grow."

The first album Iglauer made with Osceola, Arkansas' Son Seals was a trio album. The second used a full horn section. Seals couldn't afford horns, let alone a horn arranger, so "I gave him the paints for his palette by hiring additional players," Iglauer says. "Even then, I had ideas about arrangements and grooves. I'm a fan, first of all. I have a pretty wide vocabulary in blues. I know a lot of songs, grooves, and chord changes, and I spend a great deal of time listening to this music live."

Now that his label issues about 12 albums a year, he can't produce them all himself. But he maintains a strong presence. "Not a single mix goes to record without my approval," says Iglauer, who also puts his stamp on song choices and engineers. "I'm definitely a control

'70s. "I was very taken with the first Paul Butterfield record," Iglauer says, "but I was already listening to records by Big Joe Williams, Bukka White, and Mississippi Fred McDowell." McDowell "was the guy who slapped me across the face," says Iglauer, who apprenticed with Bob Koester, the Chicagoan whose Delmark label was an early blues benchmark. Koester, and Arhoolie-owner Chris Strachwitz, are Iglauer's mentors.

Iglauer "barely" plays guitar and sings "significantly off-pitch," but he appreciates musicianship, especially when it comes from the heart. "By the time of my fifth album, Fenton Robinson's *Somebody Loan Me a Dime*, we were rehearsing five or six times before we went into the studio," he recalls. "One of the things I encourage artists to do is not fall back on their stock parts, to actually create a part which fits the individual song. I remember Mighty Joe Young, an excellent guitar player, struggling with the rhythm part on Robinson's 'I've Changed.' Joe was an excellent player, but the part didn't fall naturally under his fingers. In this case, Fenton created the part. Had we not rehearsed as extensively, Joe wouldn't have played it so well."

Perfectionism isn't the goal for Iglauer, however. "Passion is what I want on my records, above all, and I'll take all the rough edges and leave them on if the passion is there," he says. "Authenticity of emotion is the key. Isn't that what blues is supposed to be about? Aren't we supposed to believe all the words that come out of the singer's mouth? And isn't the instrumental supposed to tell the same story?"

Iglauer relies on engineers to translate what he envisions onto the DAT. "For the most part, I work in very good studios," he says. "I record on Neves and SSLs and bring in $6,000 Neumann mikes. I also like to make my records very ambient-sounding. I like people to hear musicians in a room and I like very much to close my eyes and see the band laid out before me."

Iglauer drives a Honda Civic and wears Reeboks (for casual) and cowboy boots (for dress). "It's never been about money for me." —CARLO WOLFF

freak," he says. "I will regularly send things back to be done over. I have heard at least a living room tape of every project."

He's not afraid to nick an idea he runs across in clubs. "If I hear a good idea, I'll steal it in a flash," he says. "I also feel as though blues cannot recycle. You can't make new blues records sound like old blues records. I encourage artists to experiment with, especially, more socially relevant and current lyrics. I don't want to hear any songs about mules, and the only cotton pickin' I allow in my songs is 'I went down to the store and picked a cotton shirt instead of one with cotton and polyester.' I want my artists to sing about things a current audience can relate to." He also wants people to dance to Alligator records.

"There's a difference between 'traditional' and made out of hardened concrete. Imagine if Muddy Waters had walked into a studio with Leonard Chess [see entry] and Leonard had said, 'Robert Johnson didn't play an electric guitar, so you can't either.'"

White, middle-class, and Jewish, Iglauer "grew up without worrying where the next meal was coming from," graduated with a B.A. in theater history from Lawrence College in Appleton, Wisconsin, and "never took a business course, never took a music course."

He came into the blues through folk music, unlike many of his peers, who got into classic American blues through its British variant, so fashionable in the '60s and

Arnold, Billy Boy: *Eldorado Cadillac*, Alligator, 1995.

Bell, Carey: *Deep Down*, Alligator, 1995 • *Good Luck Man*, Alligator, 1997 • *See also* Horton, Big Walter.

Big Twist and the Mellow Fellows: *Live from Chicago! Bigger Than Life!* Alligator, 1987.

Brooks, Lonnie: *Turn on the Night*, Alligator, 1990 • *Satisfaction Guaranteed*, Alligator, 1991 • *Deluxe Edition*, Alligator, 1997.

Buchanan, Roy: *When a Guitar Plays the Blues*, Alligator, 1985 • *Dancing on the Edge*, Alligator, 1986 • *Hot Wires*, Alligator, 1987.

Chenier, C.J.: *Too Much Fun*, Alligator, 1995 • *The Big Squeeze*, Alligator, 1996.

Collins, Albert: *Ice Pickin'*, Alligator, 1978 • *Frostbite*, Alligator, 1980 • *Frozen Alive!* Alligator, 1981 • *Don't Lose Your Cool*, Alligator, 1983 • *Live in Japan*, Alligator, 1984 • *Deluxe Edition*, Alligator, 1997.

Collins, Albert w/ Robert Cray and Johnny Copeland, *Showdown!* Alligator, 1985.

Copeland, Johnny: *See* Collins, Albert.

James Cotton Blues Band: *High Compression*, Alligator, 1984 • *Live from Chicago Mr. Superharp Himself,* Alligator, 1986 • *Harp Attack!* Alligator, 1990.

Cray, Robert: *See* Collins, Albert.

Ellis, Tinsley: *Trouble Time*, Alligator, 1992.

Guy, Buddy: *Stone Crazy!* Alligator, 1981.

Michael Hill's Blues Mob: *Bloodlines*, Alligator, 1994 • *Have Mercy*, Alligator, 1996.

Hole, Dave: *Ticket to Chicago*, Alligator, 1997.

Horton, Big Walter: *Big Walter Horton with Carey Bell,* Alligator, 1972, 1989.

Kinsey Report: *Edge of the City*, Alligator, 1987 • *Midnight Drive*, Alligator, 1989.

Lil' Ed and the Blues Imperials: *Roughhousin'*, Alligator, 1986 • *What You See Is What You Get*, Alligator, 1992.

Little Charlie and the Nightcats: *All the Way Crazy*, Alligator, 1987 • *The Big Break*, Alligator, 1989 • *Captured Live*, Alligator, 1991.

Mack, Lonnie: *Second Sight*, Alligator, 1987 • *Attack of the Killer V: Live*, Alligator, 1990.

Magic Slim and the Teardrops: *Raw Magic*, Alligator, 1983.

McClinton, Delbert: *Live from Austin*, Alligator, 1989.

Neal, Kenny: *Devil Child*, Alligator, 1989 • *Bayou Blood*, Alligator, 1992 • *Hoodoo Moon*, Alligator, 1994 • *Deluxe Edition*, Alligator, 1997.

Professor Longhair: *Crawfish Fiesta*, Alligator, 1980 • *Professor Longhair Anthology*, Rhino, 1993.

Rabson, Ann: *Music Makin' Mama*, Alligator, 1997.

Robinson, Fenton: *I Hear Some Blues Downstairs*, Alligator, 1977.

Saffire: *Hot Flash*, Alligator, 1991 • *Broadcasting*, Alligator, 1992 • *Old, New, Borrowed and Blue*, Alligator, 1994 • *Cleaning House*, Alligator, 1996 • *Live and Uppity*, Alligator, 1998.

Seals, Son: *Midnight Son*, Alligator, 1977 • *Live and Burning*, Alligator, 1978 • *Bad Axe*, Alligator, 1984 • *Living in the Danger Zone*, Alligator, 1991 • *Nothing But the Truth*, Alligator, 1994 • *Spontaneous Combustion*, Alligator, 1996.

Siegel Schwall Band: *Reunion Concert*, Alligator, 1988.

Taylor, Hound Dog w/ the Houserockers, *Beware of the Dog!* Alligator, 1976, 1991 • *Genuine Houserocking Music,* Alligator, 1982.

Taylor, Koko: *I Got What It Takes*, Alligator, 1975 • *Queen of the Blues*, Alligator, 1975 • *The Earthshaker*, Alligator, 1978 • *From the Heart of a Woman*, Alligator, 1981 • *An Audience With*, Alligator, 1987 • *Jump for Joy*, Alligator, 1990 • *Force of Nature*, Alligator, 1993.

Vaughn, Maurice John: *Generic Blues Album*, Alligator, 1986.

Webster, Katie: *Swamp Boogie Queen*, Alligator, 1988 • *Two Fisted Mama*, Alligator, 1990 • *No Foolin'*, Alligator, 1991.

Williamson, Sonny Boy: *Keep It to Ourselves*, Alligator, 1963, 1990.

Winter, Johnny: *Guitar Slinger*, Alligator, 1984 • *Serious Business*, Alligator, 1985 • *Third Degree*, Alligator, 1986.

COLLECTIONS

Living Chicago Blues, Vol. 1, Alligator, 1978, 1991: Carey Bell's Blues Harp Band, "Laundromat Blues" • Jimmy Johnson Blues Band, "Ain't That Just Like a Woman" • Left Hand Frank and His Blues Band, "Blues Won't Let Me Be" • Eddie Shaw and the Wolf Gang, "It's Alright."

Living Chicago Blues, Vol. 2, Alligator, 1978, 1991: Lonnie Brooks Blues Band, "Cold, Lonely Nights" • Magic Slim and the Teardrops, "Dirty Mother for You" • Pinetop Perkins, "Blues After Hours" • Johnny "Big Moose" Walker, "Cry, Cry Darling."

Living Chicago Blues, Vol. 3, Alligator, 1978, 1991: Lacy Gibson, "Crying for My Baby" • Lovie Lee and Carey Bell, "I Dare You" • A.C. Reed and the Sparkplugs, "Going to New York" • Scotty and the Rib Tips, "Big Leg Woman" • Sons of Blues, "Berlin Wall."

Living Chicago Blues, Vol. 4, Alligator, 1980, 1991: Big Leon Brook's Blues Harp Band, "Blues for a Real Man" • Andrew Brown, "I Got News for You" • Detroit Junior, "I Got Money" • Queen Sylvia Embry, "Blues This Morning" • Luther "Guitar Junior" Johnson, "Got to Have Money."

Genuine Houserockin' Music, Alligator, 1986: Lonnie Brooks, "Don't Take Advantage of Me" • Roy Buchanan, "Short Fuse" • Albert Collins, Robert Cray, and Johnny Copeland, "Blackjack" • James Cotton, "Ain't Doin' Too Bad" • James Cotton, Junior Wells, Carey Bell, and Billy Branch, "Down Home Blues" • Son Seals, "Goin' Home" • Hound Dog Taylor and the Houserockers, "Don't Blame Me" • Koko Taylor, "Come to Mama" • Johnny Winter, "Sound the Bell."

Genuine Houserockin' Music, Vol. 4, Alligator, 1989: Kinsey Report, "Midnight Drive" • Lil' Ed and the Blues Imperials, "Chicken, Gravy and Biscuits" • Little Charlie and the Nightcats, "Don't Do It" • Lonnie Mack, "Natural Disaster" • Delbert McClinton, "B Movie Boxcar Blues" • Koko Taylor, "Time Will Tell" • Katie Webster, "Two-Fisted Mama."

Jimmy Iovine

J immy Iovine is a legendary figure who produced or co-produced an exceptional array of rock and modern rock by Tom Petty (*Damn the Torpedoes*, No. 2; *Hard Promises*, No. 5; *Southern Accents*, No. 7), Stevie Nicks (*Bella Donna*, No. 1; *The Wild Heart*, No. 5; *Rock a Little*, No. 12), Bob Seger (*The Distance*, No. 5), Dire Straits (*Making Movies*, No. 19), U2 (*Under a Blood Red Sky, Rattle and Hum*, No. 1), Patti Smith (*Easter*, No. 20; *Dream of Life*), The Pretenders (*Get Close*), Graham Parker (*The Up Escalator*), and Lone Justice (*Lone Justice, Shelter*), among a multitude of others, between the late '70s and late '80s.

Since 1989 Iovine has co-owned (with Ted Field) the highly successful Interscope Records (and sublabels Nothing, Aftermath, and Trauma), with acts including Blackstreet, Bush, Dr. Dre, Nine Inch Nails, No Doubt, Smash Mouth, and the Wall Flowers.

Iovine was born in Brooklyn, New York, in 1953. He loved music, especially the rock of the Rolling Stones, Cream, Sly and the Family Stone, and Jimi Hendrix. Iovine played guitar in a band, "but I wasn't any good at all," he declares. Given his interest in music and the lack of employment prospects in other fields, Iovine felt fortunate to enter the recording industry in the early '70s when a cousin's friend introduced him to songwriter/producer Ellie Greenwich, who got him in the door at the Record Plant as a second engineer. The job was rough: Iovine had no electronics background, the hours were grueling, and having barely set foot out of Brooklyn before then, Iovine found Manhattan to be a strange world full of strange people. He spent his time "concentrating on doing the job and trying to figure out how to adapt culturally. They would throw you out if you made too many mistakes and I needed the job," he says.

Young, desperate, and dedicated, Iovine learned his trade quickly, engineering for John Lennon, then for Bruce Springsteen starting with *Born to Run* in '75. Iovine met Patti Smith when she was recording *Radio Ethiopia* at the Record Plant in 1976. They got along well and hung out together, and Smith asked Iovine to produce her next album—which turned out to be her commercial breakthrough, *Easter*. A solid, more rock-oriented affair than her punky first two albums, *Easter* rode to victory on the back of Smith's first hit single, "Because the Night" (No. 13).

The rousing anthem started as a demo written, recorded, and rejected by Springsteen for his *Darkness on the Edge of Town* album, which Iovine was engineering. Once Springsteen nixed the song from *Darkness*, Iovine asked Bruce if he could record it with Smith because he needed a single for her album, and he had "always found a woman singing from a man's point of view to be interesting," he says. Iovine's instinct was correct, as Smith's ballsy reading shot her into the mainstream and became the highest-charting Springsteen-penned single to that point.

Easter began a sensational 10-year run for Iovine (and his engineer Shelly Yakus) that included four great Tom Petty and the Heartbreakers albums, establishing them as *the* American rock 'n' roll band of the '80s. Not only did the albums all go Top 10, but Iovine (and co-producer Petty) turned Petty into a singles artist, scoring six Top 20 songs between 1979 and 1985, including "Don't Do Me Like That" (No. 10), "Refugee" (No. 15), "Don't Come Around Here No More" (No. 13), and with Stevie Nicks, whose *Bella Donna* album Iovine calls one of his favorites, "Stop Draggin' My Heart Around" (No. 3).

Iovine co-produced (with Mark Knopfler; see entry) the excellent Dire Straits album *Making Movies* with "Tunnel of Love" and the epic "Skateway." Iovine produced Lone Justice's self-titled cow-punk classic, featuring the mighty pipes of Maria McKee on her most appealing performances: Tom Petty and Mike Campbell's "Ways to Be Wicked" and her own "Sweet, Sweet Baby (I'm Falling)."

Iovine produced U2's classic live EP *Under a Blood Red Sky* in 1983, and then their double-album megawork *Rattle and Hum* in 1987. Though its reach exceeded its grasp, this collection of live and studio tracks contains one of the band's rockingest tunes, the Bo Diddley–rhythmed "Desire" (No. 3); the Memphis Horns–powered, Billie Holiday tribute, "Angel of Harlem" (No. 14); and the lovely, affecting "All I Want Is You" (No. 4 U.K.).

Having had a child and sensing that music was going to change, Iovine felt the icy breath of winter on his neck. By the time of *Hum*, "I felt like an athlete past his prime," sighs Iovine. "I felt that my best days as a producer were behind me, that there was no way a 20-year-old would want to work with me. I realized that I had to move on to something else to get back the feeling I had when I was a kid."

So he created Interscope. Did the feeling come back? "No, but close," he says. "There's no experience like making the records. You're in there with a bunch of people working together. There's a real bond that has nothing to do with business and only to do with emotion. When it's successful it's an incredible feeling."

How did he measure that success? "For me it was always hearing it on the radio. I'd say, 'Wow, I worked on that.' I fuckin' don't know why I was successful. I just know I brought an enthusiasm. I learned cooperation by working with people who were more talented than I am: Springsteen, Bono, John Lennon, Tom Petty. When I was a kid I gained a lot of respect for the process because I made some money and my life got better. I still have enormous respect for when someone comes in and makes a great record.

"The other side of it is instinct," he continues. "I have no idea how I know what I know about music. I went for feeling: the feeling I got when I first heard 'River Deep Mountain High,' or 'Sympathy for the Devil,' or 'I Want to Take You Higher.' Not the same sound, just the same feeling. With music it's either great or shitty. It's not that complicated."

At Interscope, Iovine functions as a meta-producer. "I love working with Teddy Riley, Dr. Dre, Trent Reznor [see entries]—people who are as true about what they are as some of the people I worked with when I was younger. I try to give them the independence that we fought for when I was in the studio: noninterference from the record company, yet support and belief at the same time. The label is a vehicle. My main job is to set the attitude of the place—a place where people can say 'this record company is not in my way.' Sometimes it's hard. Interscope is something I'm extremely proud of because it feels the way I pictured it would feel." —ERIC OLSEN

Breakfast Club: *Breakfast Club*, MCA, 1987 • "Right on Track," MCA, 1987.

Byron, D.L.: "You Can't Hurry Love," RSO, 1980 (*Times Square* soundtrack) • *This Day and Age*, Arista, 1980.

Chapman, Tracy: "House of the Rising Sun," Elektra, 1990 (*Rubaiyat: Elektra's 40th Anniversary*) • *Matters of the Heart*, Elektra, 1992.

Dire Straits: *Making Movies*, Warner Bros., 1980 • *Money for Nothing (Greatest Hits)*, Warner Bros., 1988.

Euthrymics: "Angel," Arista, 1989, 1992 • "Don't Ask Me Why," Arista, 1989 • *King and Queen of America* (EP), Arista, 1989 • *We Too Are One*, Arista, 1989 • *Greatest Hits*, Arista, 1991.

Face to Face: *Face to Face*, Epic, 1984.

Farner, Mark Band: *No Frills*, Atlantic, 1978.

Flame: *Queen of the Neighborhood*, RCA, 1977 • *Too Many Cooks*, RCA, 1978.

Fleischmann, Robert: *Perfect Stranger*, Arista, 1979.

Gene Loves Jezebel: *The House of Dolls*, Geffen, 1987 • "The Motion of Love," Geffen, 1987 • *The Motion of Love*, Geffen, 1987 • "Suspicion/Twenty Killer Hurts," Geffen, 1988.

Golden Earring: *Grab It for a Second*, MCA, 1978.

Hartman, Dan: "I Can Dream About You," MCA, 1984 • *Keep the Fire Burning* (3 tracks), Chaos, 1994.

Houston, Whitney: "Do You Hear What I Hear?," A&M, 1987 (*A Very Special Christmas*).

Jeff Healey Band: *See the Light*, Arista, 1988.

Jett, Joan w/ the Blackhearts, *Glorious Results of a Misspent Youth*, Blackheart/MCA, 1984 • *Flashback*, Blackheart, 1994.

Jones, Tom: *The Lead and How to Swing It*, Interscope, 1994.

King, B.B.: *King of the Blues*, Pickwick, 1995.

Lone Justice: *Lone Justice*, Geffen, 1985 • "Sweet, Sweet Baby (I'm Falling)," Geffen, 1985 • "Ways to Be Wicked," Geffen, 1985 • "Shelter," Geffen, 1986 • *Shelter*, Geffen, 1986.

Madonna: "Santa Baby," A&M, 1987 (*A Very Special Christmas*).

Meat Loaf: *Dead Ringer*, Epic, 1981.

Mother's Finest: *Live*, Epic, 1979 • *The Very Best of Mother's Finest: Not Your Mother's Funk*, Razor & Tie, 1997.

Motors, The: *Tenement Steps*, Virgin, 1980.

Moyet, Alison: *Raindancing*, Columbia, 1987.

Nicks, Stevie: *Bella Donna*, Modern, 1981 • "Edge of Seventeen," Modern, 1981 • w/ Don Henley, "Leather and Lace," Modern, 1981 • w/ Tom Petty and the Heart Breakers, "Stop Draggin' My Heart Around," Modern, 1981 • "After the Glitter Fades," Modern, 1982 • "If Anyone Falls," Modern, 1983 • "Stand Back," Modern, 1983 • *The Wild Heart*, Modern, 1983 • "Nightbird," Modern, 1984 • *Rock a Little*, Modern, 1985 • "Talk to Me," Modern, 1985 • "I Can't Wait," Modern, 1986 • w/ Tom Petty and the Heart Breakers, "Needles and Pins," MCA, 1986 • "Silent Night," A&M, 1987 (*A Very Special Christmas*) • *Timespace: The Best Of*, Modern, 1991.

Nile, Willie: *Golden Dawn*, Arista, 1981.

Paley Brothers: *Paley Brothers*, Sire, 1978.

Parker, Graham: *The Up Escalator*, Stiff/Arista, 1980 • *Passion Is No Ordinary Word: The Graham Parker Anthology*, Rhino, 1993.

Petty, Tom, and the Heartbreakers: *Damn the Torpedoes*, Backstreet, 1979 • "Refugee," Backstreet, 1980 • *Hard Promises*, Backstreet, 1981 • *Long After Dark*, Backstreet, 1982 • "You Got Lucky," Backstreet, 1982 • "Don't Come Around Here No More," MCA, 1985 • *Southern Accents*, MCA, 1985 • *Greatest Hits*, MCA, 1993 • *See also* Nicks, Stevie.

Pointer Sisters: "Santa Claus Is Coming to Town," A&M, 1987 (*A Very Special Christmas*).

Pretenders, The: "Don't Get Me Wrong," Real/Sire, 1986 • *Get Close*, Real/Sire, 1986 • "My Baby," Real/Sire, 1986 • "Have Yourself a Merry Little Christmas," A&M, 1987 (*A Very Special Christmas*) • *The Singles*, Sire, 1987.

Seger, Bob: *The Distance,* Capitol, 1982 • "Roll Me Away,"
Capitol, 1983.

Seger, Bob, and the Silver Bullet Band: "Shame on the
Moon," Capitol, 1982 • "Even Now," Capitol, 1983 • "The
Little Drummer Boy," A&M, 1987 (*A Very Special
Christmas*).

Simple Minds: "Alive and Kicking," Virgin/A&M, 1985 • *Once
Upon a Time,* Virgin/A&M, 1985 • "All the Things She
Said," Virgin/A&M, 1986 • "Sanctify Yourself,"
A&M/Virgin, 1986 • *Glittering Prize Simple Minds 1981–92,*
A&M, 1993.

Smith, Patti: "Because the Night," Arista, 1978 • *Easter,*
Arista, 1978 • *Dream of Life,* Arista, 1988 • "People Have
the Power," Arista, 1988 • *Masters,* Arista, 1996.

Springsteen, Bruce: "Santa Claus Is Coming to Town,"
Columbia, 1981.

Steinman, Jim: *Bad for Good,* Epic, 1981.

Stewart, Rod: *Storyteller: The Complete Anthology,* Warner
Bros., 1989.

Stewart, Sandy: *Catdancer,* Modern, 1984.

Thrashing Doves: *Bedrock Vice,* A&M, 1987.

U2: *Under a Blood Red Sky,* Island, 1983 • "Christmas (Baby
Please Come Home)," A&M, 1987 (*A Very Special
Christmas*) • "Angel of Harlem," Island, 1988 • "Desire,"
Island, 1988 • "Hallelujah Here She Comes," Island, 1988
• "Jesus Christ," Columbia, 1988 (*Folkways: A Tribute to
Woody Guthrie and Leadbelly*) • *Rattle and Hum,* Island, 1988
• "All I Want Is You," Island, 1989.

Zander, Robin: *Robin Zander,* Interscope, 1993, 1995.

Isley Brothers

Ernie Isley uses the image of a budding tree to
explain his view of the producer's mission. "The
producer should allow ideas to blossom and to recognize what's important," he explains. "A producer is
someone who has a feeling for and a trust in the project.
They allow it to be whatever it is going to be."

That's a lesson Ernie learned as a key part in one of
the most important musical families ever—the Isley
Brothers—who have moved fluidly through time and a
wide range of musical genres (including R&B, rock 'n'
roll, funk, psychedelic rock, and smooth urban soul) to
create an essential body of work.

Born and raised in Cincinnati, Ohio, brothers O'Kelly (December 25, 1937–March 31, 1986), Rudolph (born
April 1, 1939), Ronald (born May 21, 1941), and Vernon
(who died in a 1955 bicycle accident) Isley first began

performing as a gospel group in the early '50s. They
moved to the New York area in 1957 to record doo-wop
for Teenage Records.

Their first successful release, *Shout,* came out in
1959 and was produced by Hugo & Luigi (see entry).
That album featured the title track and "Twist and
Shout," both of which became rock 'n' roll party staples. After casting about in the mid-'60s (recording one
hit for Motown, "This Old Heart of Mine" in 1966), the
brothers returned with a vengeance in 1969, writing and
producing the Grammy-winning "It's Your Thing" (No.
2) for their own T-Neck Records.

The next version of the Isleys—as brothers Ernie
(guitar, drums), Marvin (bass, percussion), and brother-
in-law Chris Jasper (keyboards) joined up—took the
band into uncharted waters. In the early '70s, when
albums replaced singles as the basic unit of musical currency, black artists and producers like Norman Whitfield, George Clinton, Curtis Mayfield, Isaac Hayes,
Gamble and Huff (see entries) and the Isleys simultaneously elongated their music. The Isleys created a heavy,
funky bass and psychedelic guitar sound (from Ernie)
that became extremely popular with black and white
audiences alike.

The sound really came into its own with 1973's *3 +
3* album, which went to No. 8 and spawned the hit single "That Lady" (No. 6). *The Heat Is On,* their 1975
album, went all the way to No. 1, proving that the world
was ready for black rock from someone other than Jimi
Hendrix (who had toured with the Isleys in the mid-
'60s).

The band regularly hit the Top 10 throughout the
'70s (*Harvest for the World, Go for Your Guns, Showdown,
Go All the Way*) before Ernie, Marvin, and Jasper left to
form the trio Isley, Jasper, Isley in the '80s. The trio
reunited with Ronald and Rudolph under the Isley
Brothers rubric in 1991.

Where other musical families have fallen by the
wayside, the Isley Brothers have found a way to stay
strong for almost 50 years. Their success in performing,
business, writing, and production is unique—with hits
in five decades—and appears to be continuing into the
third millennium. —ERIC OLSEN AND DAVID JOHN
FARINELLA

Isley Brothers: "It's Your Thing," T-Neck, 1969 • *The Brothers:
Isley,* T-Neck, 1969 • *Get Into Something,* T-Neck, 1970 • *In
the Beginning,* T-Neck, 1970 • *Giving It Back,* T-Neck, 1971 •
"Love the One You're With," T-Neck, 1971 • *Brother,
Brother, Brother,* T-Neck, 1972 • *The Isleys Live,* T-Neck,
1972 • *3 + 3,* T-Neck, 1973 • "That Lady," T-Neck, 1973 •
"Fight the Power," T-Neck, 1975 • *The Heat Is On,* T-Neck,

1975 • *Harvest for the World*, T-Neck, 1976 • *Go for Your Guns*, T-Neck, 1977 • "The Pride," T-Neck, 1977 • *Showdown*, T-Neck, 1978 • "Take Me to the Next Phase," T-Neck, 1978 • *Timeless*, T-Neck, 1978 • "I Wanna Be with You," T-Neck, 1979 • *Winner Takes All*, T-Neck, 1979 • "Don't Say Goodnight (It's Time for Love)," T-Neck, 1980 • *Go All the Way*, T-Neck, 1980 • *Grand Slam*, T-Neck, 1981 • *Inside You*, Epic, 1981 • "Between the Sheets," T-Neck, 1983 • *Between the Sheets*, T-Neck, 1983 • *Greatest Hits*, Vol. 1, T-Neck, 1984 • *Masterpiece*, Warner Bros., 1985 • *T-Neck Years*, Vol. 1, *1969–1985*, Rhino, 1986 • *Smooth Sailin'*, Warner Bros., 1987 • *Spend the Night*, Warner Bros., 1988, 1989 • *Greatest Hits and Rare Classics*, Motown, 1991 • *The Isley Brothers Story*, Vol. 2, Rhino, 1991 • *Tracks of Life*, Warner Bros., 1992 • "I'm So Proud," Warner Bros., 1994 (*A Tribute to Curtis Mayfield*) • *Beautiful Ballads*, Legacy, 1995 • *Funky Family*, Legacy/Sony, 1995 • *Mission to Please*, Island, 1996 • "Tears," T-Neck, 1997.

Isley, Ernie: *High Wire*, Elektra, 1990.

Isley, Jasper, Isley: *Broadway's Closer to Sunset Blvd.*, CBS Associated, 1985 • "Caravan of Love," CBS Associated, 1985 • *Caravan of Love*, CBS Associated, 1985 • *Different Drummer*, Epic, 1987.

Pettus, Giorge: "I Wish," MCA, 1991 • *This Is Your Night*, MCA, 1991.

Winbush, Angela: *Sharp*, Mercury, 1985 • *It's the Real Thing*, Mercury, 1989 • *Angela Winbush*, Elektra, 1994 •

COLLECTIONS

Jackie Robinson Tribute: Stealing Home, Sony, 1997.

O'Shea Jackson

See ICE CUBE

Erik Jacobsen

For a man with a 30-year career in music, Erik Jacobsen has not worked with many artists or produced many albums. However, he has formed partnerships with a handful of artists, most notably the Lovin' Spoonful and Chris Isaak, that have enabled them to blossom fully. Jacobsen have also produced great music and big hits for Norman Greenbaum ("Spirit In the Sky,"

No. 3), the Sopwith Camel ("Hello, Hello"), and Tim Hardin.

"More than anything, helping someone put a song together is a big thrill for me," he says. "To pick and choose and inspire and put all of the good elements together. I like long-term projects with people, developing them instead of just going in for a production date."

Jacobsen was born in 1941 and grew up in Oak Park, Illinois, near Chicago. As a kid he was an avid blues fan and listened to WOPA, the legendary blues radio station, at night under the covers. He learned to play banjo at Oberlin College in Ohio and put together a folk-bluegrass band called the Knob Lick Upper 10,000. The band recorded two albums for Mercury Records in the early '60s (their A&R man was Quincy Jones; see entry), moving to New York in 1962. During a tour with the band in 1963 Jacobsen heard the Beatles for the first time and had a vision of the future.

Excited to carry out this vision, Jacobsen quit the Knob and found a musician who was willing to combine the rootsy feel and melodic sense of folk music with the drive of rock 'n' roll. That musician was singer/songwriter/jug-band veteran John Sebastian (Even Dozen Jug Band; the Mugwumps with future Mamas and Papas Cass Elliot and Denny Doherty). Over the next year, with the help of co-manager Bob Cavallo (see Rob Cavallo entry), Jacobsen and Sebastian pieced together the Lovin' Spoonful (Zal Yanovsky on lead guitar, Steve Boone on bass, Joe Butler on drums), whose first single "Do You Believe in Magic?" (No. 9) exemplified Jacobsen's hybrid vision.

Bob Dylan and the Byrds beat the Spoonful to the folk-rock punch by a few months and have received most of the accolades for developing the style, but the Spoonful had more hits than either between 1965 and 1967 (seven Top 10s) and is sadly overlooked in rock history. "Magic," with Sebastian's audacious electric autoharp, expressive voice, and frolicsome melody is a near-perfect single. Yanovsky and Sebastian's guitar interplay on "You Didn't Have to Be So Nice" is so memorable that it is still used in TV commercials. "Daydream" captured the (druggy) blue-sky euphoria and seemingly limitless possibilities of the mid-'60s. "Did You Ever Have to Make Up Your Mind?" in retrospect seems a sober reply to those limitless free love possibilities, and "Summer in the City" abruptly answered any questions regarding the Spoonful's ability to rock.

Tuneful all, and produced to last by Jacobsen, the Spoonful's singles stand tall, proudly waving at us across 30 years, albeit with a somewhat goofy grin. That grin dragged down many of the band's album cuts, and has diminished their status vis-à-vis their more "serious" peers, but certainly the band deserves a spot in the Rock and Roll Hall of Fame.

When the Spoonful moved to San Francisco, Jacobsen went along. There he hooked up with a band that combined a neo–Rudy Vallee vaudeville sound with psychedelia, the Sopwith Camel. That peculiar hybrid yielded one hit single ("Hello, Hello") from the band's first album and a lost-classic second album (*The Miraculous Hump Returns from the Moon*), with a brilliantly spacey and insinuating production from Jacobsen that is the equal of early Pink Floyd.

After working with Tim Hardin and Norman Greenbaum, Jacobsen took the rest of the '70s off because the music of the time left him cold. In 1981 Jacobsen met a young rockabilly singer with great promise named Chris Isaak.

Jacobsen nurtured Isaak through the '80s, resulting in 1989's brilliant *Heart Shaped World* (No. 7) with the hit single "Wicked Game" (No. 6): a sonorous and gauzy update on Roy Orbison featuring James Calvin Wilsey's dreamy, neo-surf guitar. Jacobsen's production moves like a fog of longing down a desolate strip of quarter-moon-lit beach and reverberates across a vast and uncaring sea.

Follow-ups *San Francisco Days* (with "Can't Do a Thing," "Two Hearts," and Neil Diamond's "Solitary Man") and *Forever Blue* (with "Somebody's Crying" and "Go Walking down There") move in similarly excellent, timeless circles where Elvis Presley, Roy Orbison, and Marty Robbins vie for dangerously beautiful women.

Baja Sessions (1996) finds Isaak south of the border, still blue, but holding up with the help of his friends and some great cover tunes, including "Only the Lonely," "South of the Border (down Mexico Way)," and "Yellow Bird." Also a successful actor, the handsome ex-boxer Isaak seemed to be at a crossroads in 1998, but with Jacobsen still at his side, at least we know whichever way he turns will sound good. —ERIC OLSEN AND DAVID JOHN FARINELLA

Blue Velvet Band: *Sweet Moments,* Warner Bros., 1969.
Elliot, Brian: *Brian Elliot,* Warner Bros., 1978.
Fifth Avenue Band: *Fifth Avenue Band,* Reprise, 1969.
Greenbaum, Norman: *Back Home Again,* Reprise, 1969 • "Spirit in the Sky," Reprise, 1970 • *Petaluma,* Reprise, 1973 • *The Best of: Spirit in the Sky,* Varese Sarabande, 1995.
Hardin, Tim: *Tim Hardin 4,* Verve, 1969 • *Reason to Believe,* Polydor, 1990 • *Hang on to a Dream,* Polydor, 1994.
Isaak, Chris: *Silvertone,* Warner Bros., 1985, 1990 • *Chris Isaak,* Warner Bros., 1987 • *Heart Shaped World,* Reprise, 1989 • "In the Heat of the Jungle," Reprise, 1989 (*Follow Our Tracks,* Vol. 2) • "Wicked Game," Reprise, 1990 • *San Francisco Days,* Reprise, 1993 • *Forever Blue,* Reprise, 1995 • "Graduation Day," Reprise, 1995 • *Baja Sessions,* Reprise, 1996 • "Dancin'," Reprise, 1996.
Lovin' Spoonful: *Do You Believe in Magic?* Kama Sutra, 1965 • "You Didn't Have to Be So Nice," Kama Sutra, 1965 • "Daydream," Kama Sutra, 1966 • *Daydreams,* Kama Sutra, 1966 • "Did You Ever Have to Make Up Your Mind?," Kama Sutra, 1966 • *Hums,* Kama Sutra, 1966 • "Nashville Cats," Kama Sutra, 1966 • "Rain on the Roof," Kama Sutra, 1966 • "Summer in the City," Kama Sutra, 1966 • "Darling Be Home Soon," Kama Sutra, 1967 • "Six O'Clock," Kama Sutra, 1967 • *The Best Of,* Kama Sutra, 1967 • *The Best Of,* Vol. 2, Kama Sutra, 1968 • *Anthology,* Rhino, 1990.
Nubin, Katie Bell: *Soul, Soul Searchin',* Verve, 1961.
Sebastian, John: *The Tarzana Kid,* Reprise, 1974.
Sopwith Camel: "Hello, Hello," Buddah, 1967 • *The Sopwith Camel,* Buddah, 1967 • *The Miraculous Hump Returns from the Moon,* Reprise, 1973 • *Hello Hello Again,* Sequel, 1990.
Stovall Sisters: *The Stovall Sisters,* Reprise, 1971.
Tazmanian Devils: *Tazmanian Devils,* Warner Bros., 1980.
Truckaway, William: *Breakaway,* Reprise, 1976.

Mick Jagger

See GLIMMER TWINS

Jah Shaka

England seems to freeze Jamaican musical styles in time, in much the way that Jamaican immigrants shiver in its colder northern climes. Twenty years after the possibilities of ska had been worked out and set aside in Kingston, the U.K. two-tone movement of the early '80s revived it, just as a whole new generation of New York and West Coast bands have done today. Rock-steady singers like Alton Ellis and Desmond Dekker were still welcome in England after JA turned to reggae. All this worked to international reggae's favor as dub, roots, and conscious vibes took hold in foreign soil and second-generation roots and dub producers like Mad Professor (see entry) and Jah Shaka inspired a movement that is still growing there today.

Jamaican-born Jah Shaka began his musical career as

a sound system operator in the time-honored tradition, albeit in his second home of south London. Though he did release solo albums as a vocalist (1983's *Revelation Songs* and 1988's *The Music Message* are two), Shaka is mainly revered for a lengthy series of dub albums called *Commandments of Dub*, which runs to a dozen volumes with separate titles like *Africa Drum Beats*, *Coronation Dub*, *Imperial Dub*, etc., issued from the early '80s through the early '90s. Like most of his work, they were released on his own label whose full title is Jah Shaka: King of the Zulu Tribe. His full catalog is now available in the U.S. on CD through Greensleeves.

In England Jah Shaka earned legendary status with a long-running series of sound system dances throughout the '70s. As popular for their atmospheric vibe as their deep roots sound, they functioned much like a Grateful Dead concert for reggae—a magical island of dance in vast placid surrounding environs. By the time he began releasing records in the early '80s, his name already had roots cachet in the U.K.

Besides producing dozens of artists like Junior Brown and Sgt. Pepper, and major '80s albums for U.K.-based singer Vivian Jones (the ethereal classic *Jah Works*) and roots daughter Sis Nya (*Jah Music*), both cut at Ravens Studios, he was responsible for the far-reaching dub remix release, *Jah Shaka Presents Dub Masters Volume One* (unfortunately there is no volume two), roots-pop collaboration *Jah Shaka Meets Aswad in Addis Ababa Studio*, and the visionary if strange *Dub Symphony*. Two collaborations with Mad Professor, *Jah Shaka Meets Mad Professor at Ariwa Sounds* and *New Decade of Dub*, combine their differing approaches to the same subject.

Jah Shaka also helped make a home for established roots artists from Jamaica in London. Though no slouch as a producer himself (having produced over 50 Twinkle Brothers albums), Twinkle Brother Norman Grant turned production over to Shaka for two excellent albums, *Rasta Surface* and *Right Way*. In 1992 Shaka cut an album at Remaximum for JA singer Willie Williams, *Natty with a Cause*, that began a new phase for both.

Shaka traveled to Jamaica in the early '90s to record an excellent comeback album for Max Romeo (possibly Shaka's best all-round production, *Far-I Captain of My Ship*) and the dub of same at JA's Music Works studio with the legendary Firehouse Crew backing. Using the same studio and lineup he recorded a follow-up for Williams (*See Me*), a career-reviving roots disc for Horace Andy, and *Glory to the King* for young Jamaican singer Icho Candy. He moved over to Leggo's studio for a follow-up with Max Romeo, *Our Rights*, in 1995. All were remixed and released as dub albums in a series titled *Jah Shaka Dub Salute* as well.

Whether producing vocal albums or remixing them to dub, Shaka's sound is clean, simple, spiritual, and digitally roots. He thus influenced a next generation of U.K. "digi" dub and roots bands that include the Disciples (long his own house band—they also recorded as the Jah Shaka All Stars), Dub Syndicate, and Alpha & Omega. In a way Shaka has carried the torch from early independent Jamaican producers (like the late Keith Hudson, who resettled and began producing in England before his untimely death in the '80s) to a now steady stream of '90s U.K. home studio and downtown roots productions. As one of his own vocal releases put it, "Jah Shaka is a warrior." —CHUCK FOSTER

Andy, Horace: *Horace Andy Meets Jah Shaka*, Jah Shaka, 1993.

Aswad: *Jah Shaka Meets Aswad in Addis Ababa Studio*, Jah Shaka, 1985.

Brown, Junior: *Fly Me Away Home*, Jah Shaka, c. 1985.

Candy, Icho: *Glory to the King*, Jah Shaka, 1993.

Disciples: *Disciples*, Jah Shaka, 1987 • *Addis Ababa Part 2*, Jah Shaka, 1992.

Dread and Fred: *Iron Works*, Jah Shaka, 1987 • *On High (Iron Works Part 2)*, Jah Shaka, 1991.

Fashimas: *In the Ghetto*, Jah Shaka, n.d.

Jah Shaka: *Revelation Songs*, Jah Shaka, 1983 • *Kings Music*, Jah Shaka, 1984 • *Message from Africa*, Jah Shaka, 1985 • *The Music Message*, Jah Shaka, 1988 • *My Prayer*, Jah Shaka, 1990.

Jones, Vivian: *Jah Works*, Jah Shaka, 1986.

Romeo, Max: *Far-I Captain of My Ship*, Jah Shaka, 1992.

Sis Nya: *Jah Music*, Jah Shaka, 1988.

Twinkle Brothers: *Right Way*, Jah Shaka, 1984 • *Rasta Surface*, Jah Shaka, 1991.

Williams, Willie: *Natty with a Cause*, Jah Shaka, 1992 • *See Me*, Jah Shaka, 1993.

COLLECTIONS

Commandments of Dub, Chapters 1–10, Jah Shaka, 1980–1991.
Brimstone and Fire, Jah Shaka, 1983.
Jah Shaka Meets Mad Professor at Ariwa Sounds, Ariwa, 1984.
Hits from the House of Jah Shaka, Jah Shaka, 1985.
Jah Shaka Presents: Dub Master, Vol. 1, Mango, 1989.
Jah Shaka Presents Dub Symphony, Mango, 1990.
Far-I Ship Dub, Greensleeves, 1992.
New Testaments of Dub, Part 1, Greensleeves, 1992.
Dub Salute, Vols. 1–5, Greensleeves, 1995.
New Decade of Dub, ARIWA, 1996.

Jimmy Jam and Terry Lewis

The long list of talent from Prince's (see entry) Minneapolis camp that surfaced in the '80s includes the Time, Sheila E., Jesse Johnson, Vanity 6, Apollonia 6, the Family, Wendy and Lisa, Madhouse, and a slew of others. But none proved as prolific or as enduring as songwriter/producers Jimmy Jam (James Harris III) and Terry Lewis, who have written and produced over 40 gold or platinum singles and albums. They have also won several Grammy Awards, ASCAP's Songwriters of the Year Award in 1988 and 1992, and ASCAP's Song of the Year Award for "On Bended Knee" in 1996.

The Minneapolis duo of Harris and Lewis (born 1946), started out as keyboardist and bassist, respectively, with the Time, arguably the best funk band of the '80s. They were fired by Prince after missing a Time gig because they were busy producing another act on the side. It proved to be the best thing that could have happened to them professionally, as they would go on to set the tone for much of '80s R&B.

It was Jam and Lewis who jump-started the once-stalled career of Janet Jackson with three multiplatinum albums (*Control, Janet Jackson's Rhythm Nation 1814* and *janet*—all No. 1). Together, they created a hit parade of singles for Jackson, including "Again" (No. 1), "That's the Way Love Goes" (No. 1), "What Have You Done for Me Lately?" (No. 4), "Love Will Never Do (Without You)" (No. 1), "Escapade" (No. 1), "Runaway" (No. 3), "Come Back to Me" (No. 2), and "Nasty" (No. 3), just to name a handful.

Jackson's brother Michael, probably seeing how much success Jam and Lewis brought to her, recruited them for "Scream" (No. 5), the lead single from *HIStory* featuring Janet on vocals (the clunky song wasn't among Jam and Lewis's best).

They gave the S.O.S. Band almost all of its hits with songs like "Just Be Good to Me," "The Finest," "Just the Way You Like It," and "Weekend Girl"; and surprised everyone when they gave English techno-funk band Human League the unexpected smash "Human" (No. 1).

They created their own version of Marvin Gaye and Tammi Terrell with Alexander O'Neal and Cherrelle, who had hits together ("Saturday Love" and "Never Knew Love Like This") and solos (Cherrelle's "I Didn't Mean to Turn You On" and "Everything I Miss at Home"; O'Neal's "Fake" and "Criticize"). It was Jam and Lewis who, during New Edition's hiatus convinced NE members Ricky Bell, Michael Bivins, and Ronnie DeVoe to form Bell Biv DeVoe.

The artists who've benefited from the Jam and Lewis golden touch could fill a book. Here's a sampling: Mrs. Terry Lewis, aka Karyn White ("Romantic," No. 1); Boyz II Men ("On Bended Knee," No. 1); George Michael ("Monkey," No. 1, and remix); Force MDs ("Tender Love," No. 10); and Ralph Tresvant ("Sensitivity," No. 4).

Jam and Lewis, who went on to form their own label, Perspective Records, in 1991, even scored in the gospel genre, producing hits for Sounds of Blackness like "Optimistic," "The Pressure," "Testify," and "Black Butterfly," as well as for Sounds of Blackness vocalist Ann Nesby on "This Weekend" and "Can I Get a Witness?"

Lately Jam and Lewis have started using samples—something they pointedly stayed away from for years. Sometimes the results have been brilliant: the sampling of Edie Brickell's "What I Am" for New Edition's "Something About You"; the Supremes' "Someday We'll Be Together" for Janet Jackson's "If"; the Stylistics' "You Are Everything" and James Brown's "The Payback" for Mary J. Blige's "Everything."

Though Jam and Lewis have jumped on a bandwagon that has caused them to lose some of their individuality, they remain the best R&B production duo since Kenny Gamble and Leon Huff (see entry). —KEVIN JOHNSON

All-4-One: *My Brother's Keeper,* Blitzz, 1997.

Alpert, Herb: "Diamonds," A&M, 1987 • *Keep Your Eye on Me,* A&M, 1987.

Austin, Patti: "The Heat of Heat," Qwest, 1985.

Blige, Mary J.: "Everything," MCA, 1997 • "I Can Love You/Love Is All We Need," MCA, 1997 • *Share My World,* MCA, 1997.

Boyz II Men: *II* (2 tracks), Motown, 1994 • "On Bended Knee," Motown, 1994 • *The Remix Collection* (1 track), Motown, 1995 • "4 Seasons of Loneliness," Motown, 1997 • *Evolution,* Motown, 1997.

Change: "It Burns Me Up/Lovely Lady," Atlantic, 1984.

Cherrelle: *Fragile,* Tabu, 1984 • "I Didn't Mean to Turn You On," Tabu, 1984 • "Artificial Heart," Tabu, 1985 • *High Priority,* Tabu, 1985 • "You Look Good to Me," Tabu, 1985 • "Everything I Miss at Home," Tabu, 1988 • "What More Can I Do for You?," Tabu, 1988 • *The Best Of,* Tabu, 1995.

Cherrelle and Alexander O'Neal: "Saturday Love," Tabu, 1986 • "Never Knew Love Like This," Tabu, 1988.

Color Me Badd: "Forever Love," Giant, 1992 • *Young, Gifted*

and Badd, Giant, 1992 • Time and Chance, Giant, 1993.

Day, Morris: *Daydreaming,* Warner Bros., 1988 • "Fishnet," Warner Bros., 1988.

Force M.D.'s: "Tender Love," Warner Bros., 1986.

4.0: *4.0,* A&M, 1997 • "Have a Little Mercy," Savvy / Perspective, 1997.

Gill, Johnny: *Johnny Gill,* Motown, 1990 • "Rub You the Right Way," Motown, 1990 • *Provocative,* Motown, 1993 • *Let's Get the Mood Right,* Motown, 1996 • *Favorites,* Motown, 1997 • "Maybe," Motown, 1997.

Grant, Angel: "Lil' Red Boat," Universal, 1998.

Human League: *Crash,* A&M, 1986 • "Human," A&M, 1986 • *Greatest Hits,* Virgin / A&M, 1988.

Jackson, Janet: *Control,* A&M, 1986 • "Nasty," A&M, 1986 • "What Have You Done for Me Lately?," A&M, 1986 • "When I Think of You," A&M, 1986 • "Control," A&M, 1987 • "Let's Wait Awhile," A&M, 1987 • *Janet Jackson's Rhythm Nation,* A&M, 1989 • "Miss You Much," A&M, 1989 • "Alright," A&M, 1990 • "Come Back to Me," A&M, 1990 • "Escapade," A&M, 1990 • "Rhythm Nation," A&M, 1990 • "Love Will Never Do (Without You)," A&M, 1991 • "Again," Virgin, 1993 • "If," Virgin, 1993 • *janet,* Virgin, 1993 • "That's the Way Love Goes," Virgin, 1993 • "Throb," Virgin, 1993 • "You Want This," Virgin, 1993 • "And On and On," Virgin, 1994 • "Any Time, Any Place," Virgin, 1994 • "Because of Love," Virgin, 1994 • *Design of a Decade* (4 tracks), A&M, 1995 • *Runaway,* A&M, 1995 • "What'll I Do?," Virgin, 1995 • "Got 'Til It's Gone," Virgin, 1997 • *The Velvet Rope,* Virgin, 1997 • "Together Again," Virgin, 1997 • "I Get Lonely," Virgin, 1998.

Jackson, Michael: *HIStory: Past, Present and Future, Part 1,* Epic, 1995 • *Blood on the Dancefloor: HIStory in the Mix,* MJJ, 1997.

Keith, Lisa: *Walkin' in the Sun,* Perspective, 1993.

Klymaxx: *Meeting in the Ladies Room* (1 track), MCA, 1984.

Knight, Gladys: *Just for You,* MCA, 1995.

LaBelle, Patti: *Gems,* MCA, 1994 • *Flame,* MCA, 1997 • "When You Talk About Love," MCA, 1997.

Lo-Key: *Where Dey At?* Perspective / A&M, 1992.

Lynn, Cheryl: "Encore," Columbia, 1984 • *Got to Be Real: The Best Of,* Columbia, 1996.

Michael, George: *Faith* (1 track), Columbia, 1988 • "Monkey," Columbia, 1988 • "Monkey" (remix), Columbia, 1988.

Mint Condition: *Meant to Be Mint,* Perspective, 1991 • *From the Mint Factory,* Perspective, 1993 • *Definition of a Band,* Perspective, 1996 • "What Kind of Man Would I Be?," Perspective, 1996.

Nesby, Ann: "I'll Do Anything for You," Perspective, 1996 • *I'm Here for You,* Perspective, 1996 • "Hold On," Perspective, 1997.

New Edition: "If It Isn't Love," MCA, 1988 • "Can You Stand

the Rain," MCA, 1989 • *Heart Break,* MCA, 1989 • *Greatest Hits,* Vol. 1, MCA, 1991 • *Home Again,* MCA, 1996 • *Solo Hits,* MCA, 1996 • "I'm Still in Love with You / You Don't Have to Worry," MCA, 1997 • "One More Day," MCA, 1997.

O'Neal, Alexander: *Alexander O'Neal,* Tabu, 1985 • "Criticize," Tabu, 1987 • "Fake," Tabu, 1987 • *My Gift to You,* Motown, 1988 • *Love Makes No Sense,* Tabu, 1993 • *The Best Of,* Tabu, 1995.

Raja-Nee: *Hot and Ready,* Perspective, 1994 • "Turn It Up," Perspective, 1994 • "Turn It Up" (remix), Perspective, 1994.

Ranks, Shabba: "Slow and Sexy," Epic, 1992 • *X-Tra Naked* (1 track), Epic, 1992.

Richie, Lionel: *Louder Than Words,* PolyGram, 1996.

S.O.S. Band: *Just the Way You Like It,* Tabu, 1984 • "Weekend Girl," Tabu, 1984 • "Borrowed Love," Tabu, 1986 • "Even When You Sleep," Tabu, 1986 • *Sands of Time,* Tabu, 1986 • "The Finest," Tabu, 1986 • *The Best Of,* Tabu, 1995.

Secada, Jon: *Secada,* SBK, 1997 • "Too Late, Too Soon," SBK, 1997.

Solo: "He's Not Good Enough," Perspective, 1995 • *New Classic Soul,* Perspective, 1995 • *Solo,* Perspective, 1995.

Sound of Blackness: *The Evolution of Gospel,* Perspective / A&M, 1991 • *The Night Before Christmas—A Musical Fantasy,* Perspective / A&M, 1992 • *Africa to America: The Journey of the Drum,* Perspective / A&M, 1994 • "Everything Is Gonna Be Alright," Perspective / A&M, 1994.

Stewart, Rod: *If We Fall in Love Tonight,* Warner Bros., 1996 • "When I Need You," Warner Bros., 1997.

Time, The: "Jerk Out," Reprise, 1990 • *Pandemonium,* Reprise, 1990.

Tresvant, Ralph: *Ralph Tresvant,* MCA, 1990 • "Sensitivity," MCA, 1991 • *It's Goin' Down,* MCA, 1994.

Vandross, Luther w/ Janet Jackson, "The Best Things in Life Are Free," Perspective, 1992 • "I Won't Let You Do That to Me," Epic, 1997 • *One Night with You: The Best of Love,* Vol. 2, Sony, 1997.

White, Barry: *The Icon Is Love,* A&M, 1994 • "Come On," A&M, 1995.

White, Karyn: *Ritual of Love,* Warner Bros., 1991 • "Romantic," Warner Bros., 1991 • *Hungah* (EP), Warner Bros., 1994 • *Make Him Do Right,* Warner Bros., 1994.

Williams, Vanessa: "Happiness," Mercury, 1997.

COLLECTIONS

Jackie Robinson Tribute: Stealing Home, Sony, 1997.

Randall Hage Jamail

Photo by Randall Jamail

While Randall Jamail (born 1957), owner of Houston-based Justice Records, had worked in nearly every musical genre including jazz, blues, country, rock, and punk in studios around the globe, he had never been concerned for his safety until he recorded a tribute album for Willie Nelson in 1996.

"A lot of people wanted to lynch me," he explains. "There's a writer in Houston who would just as soon see me crawl under a rock and die, and that feeling has spread like ebola to Austin and Dallas." Of course, when you drag the Lone Star State's favorite son through the sonic mud, you've got to expect a little negative feedback here and there.

Clearly not a "cover" album, the idea behind *Twisted Willie*, as Jamail explains it, was to take Nelson's music into a brand new realm. "It was our intention to have the artists interpret these songs as if they were a part of their own repertoire—as opposed to trying to tip their hats to Willie and do a country-esque sort of thing."

Listeners are treated to Johnny Cash (with Kim Thayil of Soundgarden, ex-Nirvana bassist Krist Novoselic, and Alice In Chains drummer Sean Kinney) transforming "Time of the Preacher," ex-Breeder Kelley Deal and Kris Kristofferson wreaking havoc on "Angel Flying Too Close to the Ground" (with an eerie sewing machine rhythm track from Deal), in addition to spirited renditions of other Nelson favorites by modern rockers and punks, including L7, Supersuckers, Reverend Horton Heat, Gas Huffer, and X.

"Ultimately—and this makes a lot of people cringe when they hear me say this—but I really feel ['Angel'] is one of the most successful tracks on the record. It is a total reinvention of the song," which was the point all along. "If a critic looks at this and is disturbed by it, then I consider that to be a compliment. I come from the school that thinks art should move the molecules a little bit. Also, for these kids to have done anything other than reinvent the song in a way that is consistent with the kind of music they make would have been a sham to Willie."

Jamail's first session for his new Justice Records was to have been with the world-class jazz vibraphonist Harry Sheppard in 1989, but Sheppard was not quite ready to record. Rather than scratching the studio time, Jamail grabbed a local singer by the name of Kellye

Gray and recorded *Standards in Gray* on the fly. The time was exciting because it pushed Jamail into the Houston jazz scene and introduced him to a number of legendary jazz musicians. "It was a great training ground," he says. "It led me to this whole world of jazz and I started producing some of the greatest jazz musicians in the world." Names like Herb Ellis, Ray Brown, and Ellis Marsalis started showing up on his gig sheets.

Jamail quickly built a reputation by recording his sessions live and with analog-only equipment. He put his stamp on 14 straight albums, but it wasn't until 1992's homeless benefit album *Strike a Deep Chord* (with Dr. John, Odetta, Johnny Copeland, and Ronnie Earl) that he feels he hit his stride. After the release of *Strike,* old friend Willie Nelson knocked on his door and the two recorded an album of standards that became Nelson's *Moonlight Becomes You.*

Just months later Jamail found himself in an altogether different situation with an altogether different personage. "In a weird serendipitous circumstance, I ended up at the Vatican with the Pope making his record." That record, performed by the Royal Philharmonic Orchestra with Gilbert Levine, was *The Papal Concert to Commemorate the Holocaust,* released in 1994.

All of these experiences have given Jamail a certain sense of confidence, which is infectious to the artists he works with. Before Jamail started to work on the sessions for Waylon Jennings' *Right for the Time,* the two sat down to talk about recording. "My comment to him was that he was still making great records, but the Waylon that I grew up with was so aggressive and his music was so raw that it was almost scary. In fact, there were only two guys who scared me at all when I was growing up (other than my dad). One of 'em was Waylon, and his records didn't scare me anymore."

Jennings remembers that meeting as well. "He said something to me about an album I'd done that had 'that edge.' He said that he'd like to see me get that again. I had missed it too, I knew it was gone." In addition to the material that Jamail selected, including a cover version of Simon and Garfunkel's "The Boxer," Jennings went back to rhythm guitar and playing on top of the beat. "The edge comes from playing on top of the beat. If you think on top of it, you can be on top."

It took some time, but Jamail convinced Jennings to record live in order to recapture even more energy. Jamail explains his philosophy: "It is that uncertainty of the live performance, the thing that happens when you respond to something that somebody else has just played, which makes you go in a direction that you would not have gone. It's that environment that creates 'that edge.' It's that thing that happens when an artist just about loses control and then has to find a way to get it back."

"It's a lot of fun is what it is," Jennings says now of recording live. "It gets you up on your toes." According to Jennings, it was the producer's attention that kept him on track. "You know, he was looking right down my throat—what I call walkin' in my sleep. He comes from a different angle, but somehow it works. Randall says that he isn't in the music business—he makes music. I like that. The other good thing about him is that he tells you what he thinks. When somebody can do that with me, I respect that," he says with a scary laugh. —DAVID JOHN FARINELLA

Benoit, Tab: *Nice and Warm*, Justice, 1992 • *What I Live For*, Justice, 1994 • *Standing on the Bank*, Justice, 1995.

Catney, Dave: *First Flight*, Justice, 1990 • *Jade Visions*, Justice, 1991 • *Reality Road*, Justice, 1994.

Dayton, Jesse: *Raisin' Cain*, Justice, 1995.

Ellis, Herb: *Roll Call*, Justice, 1991 • *Texas Swings*, Justice, 1992 • *Down-Home*, Justice, 1996.

Franks, Rebecca Coupe: *Suit of Armor*, Justice, 1991 • *All of a Sudden*, Justice, 1992.

Gray, Kellye: *Standards in Gray*, Justice, 1990.

Hellhole: *Hellhole*, Justice, 1994.

Jennings, Waylon: *Right for the Time*, Justice, 1996.

Karlsson, Stefan: *Room 292*, Justice, 1991 • *The Road Not Taken*, Justice, 1991.

Nelson, Willie: *Moonlight Becomes You*, Justice, 1993.

Royal Philharmonic Orchestra: *The Papal Concert to Commemorate the Holocaust*, Justice, 1994.

Ruffins, Kermit: *World on a String*, Justice, 1992 • *The Big Butter and Egg Man*, Justice, 1994.

Shaver, Billy Joe: *Highway of Life*, Justice, 1996.

Sheppard, Harry: *Viva Brazil*, Justice, 1990 • *This-a-Way That-*

a-Way, Justice, 1991 • *Points of View*, Justice, 1992.

Supersuckers: *Must've Been High*, Sub Pop, 1997.

Thrillcat: *(oneword)*, Justice, 1993 • *Green Thumb*, Justice, 1994.

Whittaker, Sebastian: *First Outing*, Justice, 1990 • w/ the Creators, *Searchin' for the Truth*, Justice, 1991 • w/ the Creators, *One for Bu!!* Justice, 1992.

Wonderland, Carolyn, and the Imperial Monkeys: *Bursting with Flavor*, Justice, 1997.

COLLECTIONS

Just Friends: A Gathering in Tribute to Emily Remler, Vols. 1–2, Justice, 1990, 1991.

Twisted Willie, Justice, 1996.

Lloyd James
(KING JAMMY, PRINCE JAMMY)

Born in the Waterhouse area of Kingston, Jammy built and repaired amplifiers and other electronic equipment before setting up his own sound system. After working in Canada for a few years, he returned to Jamaica as understudy to the great mix master and father of dub, King Tubby. Roots producer Yabby You loaned Jammy a rhythm track and he produced his first single (for Black Uhuru), released on his own Jammy's label. Jammy went on to produce their first album, *Love Crisis* (also released as *Black Sounds of Freedom*), and the influential concomitant dub LP.

Bunny Lee (see entry), a savvy producer who knew the business, took Jammy to England and helped him make connections. There, Jammy picked up a mixing board for his home studio that, modified over time, continues to pump out recordings today. In fact, as his studio grew over the years, it eventually pushed Jammy and his family out of their house.

Jammy worked with singers Half Pint, Echo Minott (with whom he got a big JA hit with the misogynist "What the Hell the Police Can Do"), Pad Anthony, and former Augustus Pablo–stable artists Hugh Mundell and Junior Reid.

A second trip to England brought a distribution deal with Greensleeves. On this, his own, and a variety of other labels he pumped out albums by Sugar Minott, Johnny Osbourne, and Frankie Paul as well as a series of dub albums—some in the "clash" style with other dub mixers, much as his revived sound system clashed (and continued to win) in local competitions.

It seems each era of Jamaican music has its kickoff record, and it was a Jammy production, "Under Me Sleng Teng" by Wayne Smith, that kicked off the "digital" or "computerized" era that has extended from the mid-'80s through the dancehall age. The song's structure is actually a slowed-down preset Casio rock rhythm, played by keyboardist Tony Asher. It immediately became the rage in Jamaica, ushering out the era of studio bands like the Aggrovators and Revolutionaries, and ushering in the less expensive if often less creative age of MIDI.

For Jammy and hundreds of other Jamaican producers, it made the voicing and mixing studio (based on the King Tubby model where rhythm tracks were brought in for vocals and transfer) competitive with established, more expensive studios able to record live drums and instruments. In fact, the big studios were going to have to change to compete with the independents now, as the entire island went "digital"—the same way ska, rock steady, reggae, dub, jungle, and ragga had consecutively come into play.

Alert to the possibilities and poised to take advantage of them, Jammy brought in Bobby "Digital" Dixon (see entry) as engineer, turning the day-to-day work over to him much as Tubby had to Jammy, Philip Smart, and Scientist. Next on board were Steely and Cleevie (see entry), who quickly became masters of the new style and ground out rhythms like so much sausage. When working for Tubby he had been known as Prince Jammy but later Jammy promoted himself from princehood to kingdom. The dancehall era also saw the rise of the DJ style and Jammy productions include early work from Shabba Ranks (then called Shabba Ranking) and England's Dominick.

By 1987 Jammy's productions ruled. Johnny Osbourne's "Budy Bye," Lieutenant Stitchie's grueling "Body Body," and Tenor Saw's "Pumpkin Belly" were a few big Jamaican hits that fueled the new approach and propelled the music from the roots sound of the '70s toward the raggamuffin dancehall feel of the '90s.

Perhaps because of his Waterhouse origins (his studio is right down the street from where he grew up) Jammy kept his door open to classic singers like Dennis Brown, John Holt, and Delroy Wilson, who often scored hits for him over these bare-bones demo-quality tracks. He also encouraged new talent like Dickie Ranking (later to become Snaggapuss), Cocoa Tea, and Super Cat. Jammy's anthologies, like the long-running *Super Stars Hit Parade* compilations, generally include a mix of experienced singers like Horace Andy, Linval Thompson, and Gregory Isaacs with the latest crop of singers and DJs.

The three-CD set *King Jammy: A Man & His Music* is a good sampling of his work from three decades. His productions form a natural link in the chain of styles reggae has traversed, and he's certainly one of Jamaica's most successful modern producers in terms of hits. Though the reggae community divides on the question of his major innovation—one 1986 Greensleeves album bears the warning "This album is computerized"—his place in its history is assured.

Jammy is still active today. His 1995 productions include Bounty Killer, Pinchers, Leroy Gibbons, and the late Garnett Silk's *Silky Mood*, with the hits "Lord Watch Over Our Shoulder" and "Fill Us Up with Your Mercy." Many of his protégés are at the top of the heap in the '90s as well: Bobby "Digital" Dixon and Steely and Clevie have gone on to their own productions, and even Jammy's son John John is making hits. Perhaps the time is right for a '90s revival of the "sleng teng" riddim—with some jungle modifications, of course. —CHUCK FOSTER

Anthony, Pad: *Nuff Niceness,* Jammy's/JA, 1985.
Bailey, Admiral: *Kill Them with It,* Live & Love, 1987 • *Think Me Did Done,* World Enterprises, 1987 • *Born Champion,* World Enterprises, 1989 • *Science Again,* Rohit, 1989.
Black Uhuru: *Love Crisis,* Third World, 1977 • *Black Sounds of Freedom,* Greensleeves, 1981 • *In Dub,* CSA, 1982 • *Love Dub,* Rohit, 1994.
Boothe, Ken: *Call Me,* Rohit, 1990
Bounty Killer: *No Argument,* Greensleeves, 1996.
Brown, Barry: *Prince Jammy Presents Barry Brown Showcase,* Jammy's/JA, 1980.
Brown, Dennis: *Slow Down,* Shanachie, 1985 • *History,* Live & Love, 1986 • *The Exit,* Trojan, 1986.
Campbell, Al: *Ain't Too Proud to Beg,* World Enterprises, 1990.
Clarke, Johnny: *Think About It,* Super Power, 1988.
Cocoa Tea: *The Marshall,* Jammy's, 1986 • *Come Again,* Super Power, 1987 • *I Am the Toughest,* Jammy's, 1992.
Cultural Roots: *Running Back to Me,* Mango, 1988.
Delgado, Junior: *Movin' down the Road,* World Enterprises, 1986.
Dominick: *Ready for Dominick,* World Enterprises, 1988.
Galaxy P: *Old Friends,* Charm, 1993.
Gibbons, Leroy: *Four Season Lover,* World Enterprises, 1998.
Half Pint: *Money Man Skank,* Jammy's, 1984 • *One In a Million,* Greensleeves, 1984 • *Pick Your Choice,* VP, 1993.
Holt, John: *Born Free,* World Enterprises, 1989 • *If I Were a Carpenter,* World Enterprises, 1989.
Isaacs, Gregory: *Come Along,* Live & Love, 1988 • *Heartbreaker,* Rohit, 1990.
Jammy's: *In Lion Style Dub,* Third World, 1977.
Jays, The: *Dance Dis Reggae,* Rohit, 1990.

Johnson, Anthony: *A Yah We Deh*, Jammy's, 1985.

Jolly Brothers: *Consciousness*, Liberty United, 1978.

King Kong: *Trouble Again*, Jammy's, 1986.

Lieutenant Stitchie: *Great Ambitions*, World Enterprises, 1987.

Melody, Courtney: *Bad Boy Reggae*, Rohit, 1990.

Minott, Echo: *What the Hell*, Jammy's, 1987.

Minott, Sugar: *Give the People*, Unite Artists, 1979 • *A Touch of Class*, Jammy's, 1990.

Mundell, Hugh: *Jah Fire*, Live & Love, 1980.

Murvin, Junior: *Apartheid*, Greensleeves, 1986.

Ninja Man: *Target Practice*, VP, 1991.

Nitty Gritty: *Turbo Charged*, Greensleeves, 1986.

Osbourne, Johnny: *Folly Ranking*, Positive Sounds, 1980 • *Reggae on Broadway*, Vista, 1983 • *Water Pumping*, Shanachie, 1983.

Palmer, Michael: *I'm So Attractive*, Jammy's, 1985.

Paul, Frankie: *Still Alive*, Jammy's, 1986 • *Sara*, Jammy's, 1987 • *Casanova*, Live & Love, 1988 • *Jammin'*, VP, 1991.

Phillips, Noel: *Youth Man Vibrations*, Arawak, 1981.

Pinchers (Delroy Thompson): *Bandolero*, Pow Wow, 1991 • *Got to Be Me*, World Enterprises, 1987.

Prince Jammy: *Kamikaze Dub*, Trojan, 1979, 1996 • *Strictly Dub*, Arawak, 1981 • *Destroys the Invaders*, Greensleeves, 1982 • *Computerized Dub*, Greensleeves, 1985 • *Dub War*, Vista, 1985.

Ranks, Shabba: *Star of the 90's*, Super Power, n.d.

Reid, Junior: *Big Timer*, VP, 1985.

Riley, Jimmy: *Give Love a Try*, World Enterprises, n.d.

Sanchez: *Here I Am*, VP, 1995 • *Brown Eye Girl*, VP, 1996.

Silk, Garnett: *Lord Watch Over Our Shoulders*, Greensleeves, 1995 • *Nothing Can Divide Us*, VP, 1995 • *Silky Mood*, VP, 1995.

Smart, Leroy: *Showcase*, Shuttle, 1985 • *We Rule Everytime*, Jammy's/JA, 1985.

Smith, Wayne: *Wicked Inna Dance Hall*, Rohit, 1990 • Youthman Skanking, Black Joy, 1982 • *Sleng Teng*, Greensleeves, 1986.

Stephens, Richie: *Sincerely*, VP, 1991.

Tibet, Admiral: *Come into the Light*, World Enterprises, 1987.

Tiger: *Bam Bam*, RAS, 1988 • *Love Affair*, Rohit, 1990 • *RAS Portraits*, RAS, 1997.

Travelers: *Black Black Minds*, Third World, 1977.

U Black: *Westbound Thing a Swing*, Third World, 1977.

Wales, Josey: *Cowboy Style*: Greensleeves, 1994.

COLLECTIONS

Bawling For Dancehall, Rohit, n.d.

Carolina My Darling, VP, 1994.

DJ Confrontation, Jammy's, 1987

Further East, Vols. 1–2, Live & Love, 1989.

Gilbert Is a Disaster, World Enterprise, 1988.

Jah Bless, VP, 1993.

Jammy's Chartbusters, Pow Wow, 1989

Killer Style, Jammy's, 1990

King Jammy: A Man and His Music 1: Roots and Harmony Style, RAS, 1991

King Jammy: A Man and His Music 2: Computer Style, RAS, 1991

King Jammy: A Man and His Music 3: Hits Style, RAS, 1991

Kutchie Meets the Penetentiary, Super Power, 1990

Prince Jammy Presents, Vols. 1–4, World Enterprise, 1986.

Super Star Hit Parade, Vols. 1–7, World Enterprise, n.d.

Sleng Teng Extravaganza, Melodie, 1985

Sleng Teng Extravaganza, Vol. 2, Jammy's, 1985

Sleng Teng, Jammy's, 1985

Super Star Hit Parade, Greensleeves, 1986

Ten to One, Jammy's, 1985

Top 10, Vols. 1–3, World Enterprises, 1989

Richard D. James

Richard James (aka Aphex Twin, AFX, Caustic Window, Polygon Window) is among the first generation of music makers to use the computer as a primary instrument, not just as a manipulation and editing tool. His genius spans various electronic music categories including the ambient, techno, hard-core, and trance subdivisions of house music, as well as his own brand of electro-noise experimentation. His *Selected Ambient Works Vol. II* (No. 11 U.K.) is a classic of the genre, as is his trance cum hard-core *Analogue Bubblebath* EP.

Richard James was born August 13, 1971, in the seaside town of Truro in southern England, and began his musical experimentation at the age of 10 with a modified piano and a tape machine. "When I was 10 it was just a game—same as playing with my cards, and it wasn't even my favorite game to start off with—just mucking around with tapes. I steadily got more and more into it; I got more satisfaction out of it, and got more and more obsessive about it. I probably peaked in obsession about a year ago and have remained at that level only because I couldn't be any more obsessed. I haven't got any more time."

James was 11 when he bought his first computer, which only had 1 kilobyte of memory. Every time he would play a different game, he would have to reprogram it into the hard drive. He became so good at memorizing the programs that he figured out how to program the computer itself. "I started writing my own software and games and such," he says. "I even wrote a music program; it didn't have any sound to it, but it won second place in a magazine software competition and I got 50 quid. I found this machine code that detuned the TV signal, and you get this really stupid noise out it. I did it on the keyboard and so I had like 10 notes, but they were just all fucked-up frequencies from the TV."

Rural living, though peaceful and picturesque, afforded James little in the way of sociocultural distractions (apart from getting into fights with his mates). Eventually an ad hoc dance culture began to evolve around him. "All my mates got into dance music around 1987 and wanted me to press out records of the electro music I was making so they could DJ with them. They made me do it, and I got addicted once I got into it. We used to organize really brilliant beach parties. It was pretty exciting times."

James is excited still; he describes a typical day's work. "There isn't any set method, I just approach it from whatever angle I'm thinking about. Today there wasn't much music. I am programming my own language based on randomness combined with human input. You give the computer all the rules from 10 [already completed] tracks and get the computer to jumble it all up at random. You get a really weird vibe from it because you are not traveling anywhere," he says.

"With most music you get the feeling you are moving through the track in time—even if you listen to it backwards, you still feel like you are moving forward. With this you don't feel like you are going anywhere. I don't think this stuff is really releasable because it just plays forever and it keeps changing all the time. As soon as you record it and listen back to that, then that's completely different." This is a profound philosophical issue. Can random sound be music? Can music exist divorced from time? James reveals deep insight in pointing out that when his (or any) random computer sequence is recorded, it is ontologically transformed: recording "pins down" randomness, neutralizing its power to surprise by giving it direction and order and fixing it in time.

"I love randomness and I don't know why. I guess I think of it like an artificial intelligence. Basically computers usually do things we expect them to do. With randomness you have no idea what it's going to do. With this program now it's a bit like making words: you put in syllables of words, and it comes up with new words. You knew what all the original syllables meant, but the 'words' it comes out with haven't been invented yet," he says.

Every day is different. "The other day I did a whole track in the nude, which is pretty good. I got out of the bath and was getting ready to get dressed and start doing a track, and just ended up sitting there for about seven hours with no clothes on. I just moved out on my own, so I can do things like that. It was pretty wicked."

Perhaps predictably, James' music veers between the very light and the very hard, with little in between. "I don't like middle ground at all. I am an extreme person. I like to get extremes from music. You can use the same [middle] sounds as everyone else, but I don't see the point in that."

Though still very young, James looks to the future. "I want to get some pretty mental things under my belt so I can look back when I'm old and say, 'Yeah, that was pretty mental.' I've had a pretty mental life already, but I want a more mental one. And to stay happy, which I've always managed to do. I want to do something where I get confused and don't understand, and then understand it." —ERIC OLSEN AND DAWN DARLING

AFX: ".942937 (Analogue Bubblebath 3)," Low Price Music, 1992, 1995 (*Best of Trance*) • *Analogue Bubblebath*, Vol. 2 (EP), Rabbit City, 1992 • "Analogue Bubblebath," TVT, 1994 • *Hangable Auto Bulb* (EP), Warp, 1995.

Aphex Twin: *Analogue Bubblebath* (EP), Mighty Force, 1991 • *Analogue Bubblebath III*, Rephlex, 1992, 1995 • "En Trange to Exit," BMG, 1992 (*Volume Four*) • *Xylem Tube* (EP), R&S, 1992 • *Digeridoo* (EP), R&S, 1993 • "On," Sire/WB, 1993 • *Selected Ambient Works 1985–92*, R&S, 1993 • *Analogue Bubblebath IV* (EP), TVT, 1994 • *Selected Ambient Works*, Vol. 2, Sire/WB, 1994 • *Words and Music*, Sire/WB, 1994 • *Classics*, R&S, 1995 • *Donkey Rhubarb* (EP), Warp, 1995 • *I Care Because You Do*, Sire, 1995 • *Ventolin* (EP), Warp/Sire, 1995 • *Ventolin (The Remixes)* (EP), Warp/Sire, 1995 • *Aphex Singles Collection*, WEA Japan, 1996 • *Girl/Boy* (EP), Warp, 1996 • *Richard D. James Album*, Warp/Sire, 1996 • *Come to Daddy* (EP), Sire, 1997.

Beatniks, The: "Another High Exit" (remix), VAP, 1994.

Beck: "The New Pollution" (remix), DGC, 1997.

Boa, Phillip, and the Voodoo Club: "Deep in Velvet" (remix), Motor, 1995.

Bryars, Gavin: *Raising the Titanic—The Aphex Twin Mixes* (EP), Point, 1995.

Caustic Window: *Joyrex J4* (EP), Rephlex, 1992 • *Joyrex J5* (EP), Rephlex, 1992 • "Mindstream" (remix), Mute, 1992 • *Joyrex J9* (EP), Rephlex, 1993.

Curve: "Falling Free" (remix), Anxious, 1993.

Gak: *Gak* (EP), Warp, 1994.

Glass, Phillip: "Heroes Symphony" (remix), Point, 1997.

Jesus Jones: "Zeros and Ones" (remix), Food, 1993.

Kinesthesia: "Empathy Box" (remix), Rephlex, 1996.

Meat Beat Manifesto: "Mindstream" (remix), Play It Again Sam, 1992.

Mescalinum United: "We Have Arrived" (remix), R&S, 1992.

Mike Flowers Pops: *The Freebase Connection: The Mike Flowers Pops Meets the Aphex Twin*, Lo, 1996.

Nav Katze: "Never Mind the Distortion" (remix), Victor, 1994.

Nine Inch Nails: "At the Heart of It All,"
Nothing/Interscope, 1995 • "The Beauty of Being
Numb," Nothing/Interscope, 1995.

Polygon Window: "Quoth," Wax Trax!/TVT, 1993 • *Surfing on Sine Waves*, Warp, 1993.

Powerpill: "Pac-Man," FFRR, 1992 (*Only for the Headstrong*, Vol. 2).

Seefeel: "Time to Find Me" (remix), Astralwerks, 1994.

Soft Ballet: "Twist and Turn" (remix), Alfa, 1993.

St. Etienne: "Hobart Paving" (remix), Heavenly, 1993 • *Casino Classics*, Heavenly, 1996.

John Jansen

In the late '80s, many panicky hairspray metal bands claimed to be trying to capture a classic Rolling Stones/Aerosmith sound. Cinderella, with the help of producer John Jansen, actually did so on their underrated third album, 1990's *Heartbreak Station*. Jansen produced many of the rawer, ballsier pop-metal bands at the end of the hairspray era, including Bang Tango, Faster Pussycat, Love/Hate, and Dirty Looks. In addition, Jansen's long career has been much more diverse than his metal reputation alone would suggest.

Jansen played guitar in bands in the '60s, but never liked playing live. He read about the job of producer in a magazine. "I called, wrote, and visited every recording studio in New York and when I got rejected by every one, I called them all again."

Living in Greenwich Village, he started to hang around Electric Lady Studio. "One day in 1969 I ran into Eddie Kramer [see entry] and he had just fired someone. He interviewed and hired me on the spot. Within six months, I was doing dates. My first session was Leon Russell. It was at 1 A.M. and Eddie didn't want to get out of bed after a Fillmore gig. My first producer job was [Jimi Hendrix's] *Rainbow Bridge*."

Two years later, Jansen moved to England, where Hendrix drummer Mitch Mitchell planned to build a studio. It never got built, but Jansen ran into Roger Daltry, who actually had a studio. "The Who had a studio called Ramport and I became chief engineer. I did Supertramp's *Crime of the Century*, Procol Harum, Joe Cocker, Nicky Hopkins."

After four years in England, he returned to New York and started to do some work at the Record Plant. "I got to know the people there and started to get work.

I was asked to engineer Alice Cooper. I was known as an engineer trying to get jobs as a producer. I was trying to hold out for production jobs."

He was introduced to Meatloaf songwriter Jim Steinman by Jimmy Iovine (see entry). They had just finished *Bat out of Hell* with Todd Rundgren (see entry) producing and had liked only one of his mixes. Iovine had mixed another track. They invited Jansen to try his hand and he ended up mixing three of the tracks, including the epic "Paradise by the Dashboard Light."

"They were these incredibly long songs that turned from guitar to organ to vocal. There was no computer mixing at that point, which it needed. It was labor-intensive and Jim was opinionated." Apparently, he got along with Steinman just fine, because he worked Steinman opuses for Bonnie Tyler, including the hit "Total Eclipse of the Heart," as well as Steinman's own *Bad for Good*.

In 1984, he did *New Sensations* with Lou Reed. "Lou Reed was great. He'd been making records live and wanted to try something new. His drummer was an architect and had to take exams during rehearsal, so we used a drum machine. On the record, the drummer plays over that. Lou played all the guitar. We used synthesizers, we brought in horns," and Jansen helped arrange as well. "I'm really proud of that record," he says.

Then his manager told him he needed to pick a specialty and stick with it. "I'd done a hard rock record with Britny Fox. That worked out well. I did Faster Pussycat and that did well too. I mixed the first Warrant record." So commercial metal found him. "I probably could've picked other kinds of music, but I enjoyed it."

Cinderella had done their first two albums in their hometown, Philadelphia. "They wanted outta Dodge," says Jansen. "We concocted a plan to go around the country, to do three songs at Woodstock, two songs in Philly because the bass player's wife was expecting a baby, and two songs in New Orleans. The logistics of moving the band, equipment, and tapes around was hell. In New Orleans, we flew in horns. Sometimes guys wouldn't work out and we'd have to get someone else. Time would be pressing and you'd have a dozen people in a hotel."

Despite all that, they ended up with a warm, relaxed, bluesy rock album that's got more of a sweaty club than an arena feel. "Love's Got Me Doin' Time" sounds like a track Aerosmith never quite managed to record and "Shelter Me" and "Sick for the Cure" revive the raucous R&B Stones sound of the early '70s.

Jansen did album after album in the late '80s and early '90s. Two of his last productions, Bang Tango's 1991 *Dance on Coals* and Love/Hate's 1992 *Wasted in America* actually bridged '80s commercial hard rock and

'90s alternative metal, and Jansen's work on them rejected most of the glossy, inflated production values of '80s hairspray metal.

But in 1992, his specialty turned around and bit him. "You could see on the horizon there was too much of it. It was hard to know which band was which anymore. I enjoyed a vacation when hard rock came to a halt. I was pretty burnt out after 25 years in the studio. It gave me a chance to explore other things—songwriting, multimedia, a couple of film gigs. I have a business doing Web sites. But I've missed it and I'm starting to look for new bands. I like it now because there are so many kinds of music. It's nice to hear U2 as well as the latest craze. I think it's healthy. I hope it stays that way."

Jansen says his production strengths include "my song sense, my engineering background, and my general organizational skills. When I hear a band and meet them, I imagine what their record will be like, then I figure out how to get from A to Z."

Surprisingly, he says he really enjoys mixing material other people have recorded. "When you're recording, you're thinking a lot about the mix at the end. There are no surprises. When you get someone else's stuff, it's new." —ANASTASIA PANTSIOS

Bad Romance: *Code of Honor,* Mercury, 1990.

Bang Tango: *Dancin' on the Coals,* Mechanic, 1991.

Bongos, The: *Beat Hotel,* RCA, 1985.

Britny Fox: *Britny Fox,* Columbia, 1988.

Cinderella: *Heartbreak Station,* Mercury, 1990 • *Once upon a . . . ,* Mercury, 1997.

Coast Road Drive: *Delicious and Refreshing,* Decca, 1979.

Cutting Crew: "(I Just) Died in Your Arms," Virgin, 1987.

DeVito, Karla: *Is This a Cool World or What?* Renaissance, 1981, 1996.

Dirty Looks: *Turn of the Screw,* Atlantic, 1989.

Faster Pussycat: *Wake Me When It's Over,* Elektra, 1989.

Good Rats: *Birth Comes to Us All,* Passport, 1978.

Heaven: *Knockin' on Heaven's Door,* Columbia, 1985.

Hendrix, Jimi: *Rainbow Bridge,* Reprise, 1971 • *Hendrix in the West,* Reprise, 1972 • *War Heroes,* Reprise, 1973 • *The Essential,* Reprise, 1978 • *First Rays of the New Rising Sun,* MCA, 1997 • *South Saturn Delta,* MCA, 1997.

Love/Hate: *Wasted in America,* Columbia, 1992.

McCullough, Henry: *Mind Your Own Business,* Dark Horse, 1975.

Miller, Frankie: *Dancing in the Rain,* Mercury, 1986.

Perkins, Carl: *Go Cat Go,* Dinosaur, 1996.

Reed, Lou: "I Love You, Suzanne," RCA, 1984 • "My Red Joystick," RCA, 1984 • *New Sensations,* RCA, 1984 • *Between Thought and Expression: The Lou Reed Anthology,* RCA, 1992.

States, The: *The States,* Chrysalis, 1979.

Streisand, Barbra: *Emotion* (1 track), Columbia, 1985.

T.S.O.L.: *Strange Love,* Enigma, 1990 • *Hell and Back Together 1984–90,* Restless, 1992.

Television: *Adventure,* Elektra, 1978.

Tyler, Bonnie: *Secret Dreams and Forbidden Fire,* Columbia, 1986.

Yipes!: *Yipes!* Millenium, 1979 • *A Bit Irrational,* Millenium, 1980.

J.J. Jeczalik

See ART OF NOISE

Marshall Jefferson

If Frankie Knuckles (see entry) is the godfather of house music, then Marshall Jefferson is its father. Credited with changing the very face of the beat-intense dance music—from its cheesy 808 drumbeat beginnings to a decidedly more emotional and soulful hybrid known as "deep house"—Jefferson is easily one of the most influential figures in house music.

With his 1986 platinum-selling single, "House Music Anthem (Move Your Body)," Jefferson gave the Chicago-based sound its first international hit. Additionally, the song introduced rolling piano swells, which to this day are an important component of many house tracks.

A dance music producer weaned on such '70s rock bands as Led Zeppelin, Black Sabbath, and Deep Purple, Jefferson has never been one to follow the rules when it comes to remixing, producing, and writing music. "Why should I follow someone else's lead?" queries Jefferson. "The music I make has always been a reflection of what I'm feeling at the time."

Indeed. Following the success of "House Music Anthem (Move Your Body)," Jefferson introduced "acid house" to the worldwide dance community via Phuture's "Acid Tracks." More popular in England and Europe than in his Chicago backyard, "acid house," complete with its zig-zagging caustic synth lines, quickly became the outmoded fashion of the day. (That's not to say that its influences are not felt today. The electronica dance artists of the late '90s keenly borrowed an idea or two from this aggressive sound.)

By 1988, Jefferson had collaborated with many artists, including Screamin' Rachel, Sleazy D, Lil' Louis, Steve "Silk" Hurley (see entry), and DJ Pierre. While there are many hits from this creative and nurturing period, its highlight is Marshall Jefferson presents the Truth's "Open Our Eyes," a deeply moving track that was the antithesis to acid house. It was also the song that ushered in the deep house movement.

Credited as the originator of deep house, Jefferson, over a three-year period, shifted house music from its early jackhammer leanings toward a more tasteful and sophisticated style, incorporating elements of retro R&B and spiritually soulful vocals. With deep house, Jefferson had found his signature sound. Working with such artists as Kim Mazelle, CeCe Rogers, and Vicky Martin, Jefferson not only launched the careers of many artists but fine-tuned a sound that has stood the test of time. Then, along came the Chicago trio Ten City, ushering in what would prove to be Jefferson's most impressive period. Combining the instrumental and vocal authenticity of a classic soul band with the verve of the underground club scene, the band, along with Jefferson, forever changed the course of dance music.

The most impressive thing about Jefferson—and what separates him from his peers—is his ability to write the classic song. Specializing in lyrics and melodies, Jefferson has always gone against the dance music trend of groove first and the rest will follow. For that, the club community can be grateful. —LARRY FLICK

Cabaret Voltaire: *Groovy, Laidback and Nasty,* EMI, 1990.
Chapter and Verse: "Thank You to Be Free" (remix), Virgin, 1992.
Dancing Flutes: "Do the Do," DJ International, 1989.
Dunn, Mike: "Everything Must Change," Desire, 1991.
Hall, Reggie: "Music," Final Vinyl/Big Life, 1992.
Idle and Wild: "Far Behind," Hott, 1994.
Jefferson, Marshall: Featuring Curtis McLean, "Step By Step," Freetown, 1995 • *Frankie Knuckles Presents Marshall Jefferson,* Trax, 1989 • "Move Your Body '90," Trax, 1990 • *Day of the Onion,* EFA, 1997.
Jungle Wonz (Marshall Jefferson): "Move Your Body," Trax, 1986 • "7 Ways," Trax, 1988 • "Time Marches On," A&M, 1988 (*House Hallucinates: Pump Up the World,* Vol. 1) • "The Jungle," Trax, 1989.
Mazelle, Kym: "I'm a Lover," Republic/Rough Trade, 1988 (*The Garage Sound of Deepest New York*).
Pasadenas, The: "Another Lover," Columbia, 1991 • "More Time for Love," Columbia, 1992.
Pet Shop Boys: "Being Boring" (remix), EMI, 1991.
Rogers, Richard: "Can't Stop Loving You," BCM, 1991.

Soul Family Sensation: "I Don't Even Know If I Should Call You Baby," One Little Indian, 1991.
Spirits: "Don't Bring Me Down," MCA, 1994.
System 7: "Sirenes" (remix), Cleopatra, 1997 • *System Express,* Cleopatra, 1997.
Ten City: "Devotion," Atlantic, 1987, 1989 • *Foundation,* Atlantic, 1989 • "That's the Way Love Is," Laserlight, 1989, 1993 (*Hip Hop House Party*) • "Whatever Makes You Happy," DMC, 1990, 1993 (*DMC CD Collection*).
Townsell, Lidell: "I'll Make You Dance," Hardcore, 1989 (*The Acid Trax Double Album #2*).
Truth, The: "Open Our Eyes" (remix), FFRR, 1989 (*Silver on Black*).
Umosia: "Unity," Urban, 1991 • "Love Don't Let Me Down," Other Side, 1992.
Watford, Michael, and Robert Owens: "Come Together," Recurrent, 1995 (*Club Classics '95*).

Dave Jerden

From the man who produced such classic alterna-rockers as *Nothing's Shocking* and *Ritual de lo Habitual* (No. 19) by Jane's Addiction, Alice in Chains' *Dirt* (No. 6), and Social Distortion's self-titled album comes this surprising quote: "There have been so many great producers, but I still listen to George Martin and Brian Wilson [see entries]," he says. "I bring a real pop sense to the party, but if you put me with a pop band it is terrible, it never works. But if you put me with a band like Jane's Addiction then it works, because it is something that I understand."

Jerden fell in love with the studio through the influence of his father. "He played bass, that's how I grew up. I never set out to be an engineer, but I did go to sessions with him and I would sit in the corner and watch everyone consult the engineer. He would be standing at a console with big knobs and I thought, 'Wow, that guy is Flash Gordon.'"

And Jerden was on his way. Jerden took his next step when a band he played with built a studio to record their own demos. "I was engineering, although I never really intended on being an engineer," he says. "I did it for a while and I was successful at it, but the bands I was working with would break up and form new bands and come back and ask me to [produce]. Then I kinda fell into it; I never intended to be a producer either. I like it a lot now, it's a great job. The best job on the planet.

"There are a lot of elements to it that are fun. You

are right at the front line cutting a record, you are right next to the music. I am in a new band every six to eight weeks, it keeps changing.

"I love music," he continues, "and I like musicians. They are my kind of people. I have a studio, so I like that aspect of it too. There are many facets to it, the technical, the creative, and the personal."

And that, in a nutshell, is why Jerden is successful: He has the engineering and musical background and his approach in the studio is decidedly personal. "When I work with a band it's a collaboration," he says. "It's not like it's my way or the highway. Everything on a record is something that we've all agreed upon." The collaborative spirit has run through Jerden's career, from his early days up through the Offspring's *Ixnay on the Hombre* album in 1997.

The challenge regarding the Offspring, in Jerden's eyes, was to follow up an album that had sold over 8 million copies (*Smash*). "When I met with Dexter Holland, the leader of the band, I said, 'I do many things when I make a record and one of them is to try and make you feel comfortable. I am aware that you sold a lot of records last time, so the idea this time around is to forget about that last record. I will do anything I can do to make you forget about that last record.'

"It was a good experience—my best records have always been good experiences with fun guys in the studio. You know the saying: 'My vibes, your vibes, everybody's vibes gets on tape.' If there is any tension or weirdness going on then it doesn't work, because it is a collaboration."

Jerden considers Jane's Perry Farrell to be the most important artist he has worked with. "Perry just came from a different place. Everyone else wanted to sound like Pat Benatar or Guns N' Roses, but he didn't care about any of that stuff. Actually, when I made the first record I got a call from Warner Bros. They said the record doesn't sound like anything out there and they were a little worried. I told that to Perry and he was happy."

The type of music that causes record label executives to scratch their heads is exactly what Jerden wants to produce. "I try to make it so people will get the music, understand what the band is doing. When people found out I was working with Jane's Addiction they told me that they were interested in the band, but they wondered what was there to do with a band like that. I said that conceptually I think of a band like them as MTV: 30-second sound bites and collages of imagery.

"They were young guys who were looking at a changing world, just like Jimi Hendrix was a guy who seemed to synthesize what was going on in the world and put it into sound," he says. "His sounds were perfect for the time, and Jane's Addiction were perfect for their time. They were just taking the collage of information that we get every day and putting it out in a poetic way. My contribution was to let everyone see the little nuances, instead of it just sounding like a jam."

Which brings him to the basic tenets of his recording philosophy: "Making an album is a privilege. It is also like theater in that you have the opportunity to captivate or bore someone for an hour. You are inviting yourself into someone's home and someone's brain. You should damn well entertain them. A lot of bands—even in live shows—think that they are too cool and if you don't get it then you are stupid. I don't buy that at all. I don't care what terms people put on 'pop music,' but it is pop music. I think the best producers have understood that. Years ago I thought that I was cool and I made terrible records," he finishes laughing. —DAVID JOHN FARINELLA

Alice in Chains: *Facelift,* Columbia, 1990 • "Sunshine," Columbia, 1990 • *Dirt,* Columbia, 1992.

Angelique: *Present,* Red Ant, 1998.

Anthrax: *Black Lodge* (EP), Elektra, 1993 • "Looking Down the Barrel of a Gun," Geffen, 1993 (*The Beavis and Butthead Experience*) • "Poison My Eyes," Columbia, 1993 (*Last Action Hero* soundtrack) • *Sound of White Noise,* Elektra, 1993 • "London," Fox, 1994 (*Airheads* soundtrack).

Armored Saint: *Symbol of Salvation,* Metal Blade, 1991.

Beat Farmers: *The Pursuit of Happiness,* Curb/MCA, 1987.

Biohazard: "Control," Warner Bros., 1996 • *Mata Leao,* Warner Bros., 1996.

Bullet Lavolta: *Swandive,* RCA, 1991.

Burning Sensations: *Burning Sensations,* Capitol, 1983.

Dig: *Wasteland,* Wasteland/Caroline, 1993 • "Curious George Blues," Fox, 1994 (*Airheads* soundtrack).

Ednaswap: *Wacko Magneto,* Island, 1997.

54.40: *Show Me,* Warner Bros., 1987.

Harrison, Jerry: *The Red and the Black,* Sire, 1981.

Indians, The: "Bed of Roses," RCA, 1993, 1994 (*Reality Bites* soundtrack) • *Indianism,* Polydor, 1993 • "Look Up to the Sky," Polydor, 1993.

Jane's Addiction: *Nothing's Shocking,* Warner Bros., 1988 • "Been Caught Stealing," Warner Bros., 1990 • *Ritual de lo Habitual,* Warner Bros., 1990 • "Stop," Warner Bros., 1990 • "Classic Girl," Warner Bros., 1991.

Knack, The: "My Sharona" (remix), RCA, 1994 (*Reality Bites* soundtrack).

Legal Weapon: *Life Sentence to Love,* MCA, 1988.

Love Spit Love: *Love Spit Love,* Imago, 1994 • "Am I Wrong?," Reprise, 1995 (*Angus* soundtrack).

Mary's Danish: *Experience* (1 track), Chameleon, 1990 • *Circa*, Morgan Creek, 1991.

Offspring, The: *Ixnay on the Hombre*, Columbia, 1997.

Orange 9mm: "Glistening," EastWest, 1994 • *Driver Not Included*, EastWest, 1995 • "Suspect," EastWest, 1995.

Poe: *Hello* (1 track), Modern/Atlantic, 1995 • "Trigger Happy Jack (Drive By a Go-Go)," Modern/Atlantic, 1995.

Public Image Limited (PIL): *That What Is Not*, Virgin, 1992.

Rattlebone: *Rattlebone* (EP), Hollywood, 1992.

Rust: *Bar Chord Ritual*, Atlantic, 1996.

Sacred Reich: *Independent*, Hollywood, 1993, 1995.

Social Distortion: *Social Distortion*, Epic, 1990 • *Somewhere Between Heaven and Hell*, Epic, 1992.

Spinal Tap: *Break Like the Wind*, MCA, 1992.

Stabbing Westward: *Darkest Days*, Columbia, 1998.

Sweet Water: *Superfriends*, EastWest, 1995.

What Is This: *Squeezed* (EP), San Andreas, 1984.

X: *Beyond and Back: The X Anthology*, Elektra, 1997.

Andy Johns

A ndy Johns' adaptable attitude and talent has generated a career that has spanned over 30 years as an engineer and producer of some of rock's most important music.

His older brother was a recording engineer and Andy hung around the studio as a kid. He became a tape operator in 1967 at Olympic Studios, which quickly led to engineering. "Back then, you didn't need to train for years. It wasn't as competitive. I got a lot of work straightaway." That work included four Led Zeppelin albums, four Rolling Stones albums, and three Ten Years After albums, as well as work with Jethro Tull, Blind Faith, Traffic, Joe Cocker, Humble Pie, Cat Stevens, Mott the Hoople, Free, and Rod Stewart.

His first production credit was on 1969's *A Head Rings Out* by Blodwyn Pig, a Tull offshoot, but he quickly returned to engineering. "I didn't know what I was doing then. I didn't have a clue."

He worked with the Rolling Stones from 1969 to 1973, engineering *Sticky Fingers*, *Exile on Main Street*, *Goat's Head Soup*, and *It's Only Rock & Roll*. "I learned patience. I learned to sift through take after take." He also learned that the song is the main thing. "They had no ego about who had written the original song or what the original concept was. They'd change it—it was whatever worked."

He also candidly admits that working with the Stones gave him "a bit of a drug problem. Working on *Exile* was really long, sitting around in the south of France waiting for the band to show up. There was always smack around. The boredom is why I started doing it. When I came back to start working, people weren't going to give me the responsibility of production, which was fine with me. I didn't feel ready."

With work slowing down in London, he moved to Los Angeles in 1975. It wasn't until 1980, however, that he dove into production and never looked back. In the '70s, he produced one significant project out of keeping with the rest of his work, Television's seminal 1977 *Marquee Moon*. "I got a phone call out of the blue from Tom Verlaine—he had been listening to *Goat's Head Soup*. I'd never met him. I flew to New York; I had no clue what the music was like or if we'd get on. My first impression was that they couldn't play and couldn't sing and the music was very bizarre. But after we finished mixing, we went to some rehearsal place and played it on these large speakers, and I was bowled over."

The early '80s were slow for him, but he says, "the back half of the '80s and early '90s were great." He transferred the skills he'd developed with classic British hard rock bands to the commercial hard rock bands rampant in the '80s, producing Joe Satriani, Van Halen, Ozzy Osbourne, House of Lords, Autograph, and Cinderella. He easily mastered the big, processed sound of the era, plumped out with keyboards taken from the commercial end of prog-rock and massed, choral-style vocals.

He cites Satriani's *The Extremist* as a favorite from that period. "I might mix it a little different now. It had that huge pompous echo and I've gone off that now. I liked the guitar parts and the instrumentation, which I had a large part in."

He notes the differences and similarities in production over the years: "In the late '60s and early '70s, you'd be working on three projects at the same time, three sessions a day with no days off. Each project was three or four weeks. You'd mount up a lot of credits. Now you're lucky if you do three a year. We didn't do preproduction then, hell no. But the music's still the same; the most important thing is to have great material. The people are the same; they still want to be rock stars and make money, and there's nothing wrong with that. At any one given time period, the same amount of people are getting it right and the same are not."

"We never had drum machines, synths and samples back then. If it all disappeared tomorrow I wouldn't miss it. One or two things I've heard sounded really fantastic. And now you can have as many tracks as you want, which is great if you don't abuse it. I've used it to my advantage and I've also abused it, loading on things. But you're still sitting behind a mixing board, in a lot of cases with the same speakers, and the mikes—well, people are seeking out the old mikes."

He cites his production strengths: "With arrangements, it's obvious to me when something isn't working and it's easy for me to figure out how to make it work. I think I have a firm grasp on how I want the thing to end up instead of vacillating all over the place. I think I have a strong grasp of groove and how to make it happen."

He has no favorite studio, specifying only that "the room where the instruments are has to sound good. The mixer is not important as long as it's not horrible and doesn't break down. The monitors have to be good. Tape machines can be analog or digital, I don't care. As years go by, I find that stuff is less and less important. I don't use drum machines or samplers. I get the sound from the room. If the sound isn't right, the guy's got the wrong gear—wrong guitar, wrong amps, wrong drums. I was doing a session with Bon Jovi and we were having a hard time getting a rhythm guitar sound. We tried all these different amps. I said, we've got to get this, we can't fix this in EQ. But we had this big old Neve equalizer and we put a lot of everything on it and it sounded great. It proved me wrong—another 'Johns is an idiot' night!"

His recent work includes sessions with Van Halen and Jason Bonham, an album with new Island act Wig, and work in Japan with a guitar rock band called Bees and a female artist, Zard.

"There's been ups and down," he says. "But I've had a lovely time. There's one or two things I'd change, but not much." —ANASTASIA PANTSIOS

Aldrich, Doug: *Highcentered,* Avalanche, 1996.

Autograph: *Loud and Clear,* RCA, 1987.

Axis: *Circus World,* RCA/Hologram, 1978.

Blodwyn Pig: *Ahead Rings Out,* A&M, 1969.

Bon Jovi: "Good Guys Don't Always Wear White," 550 Music/Epic, 1994 (*The Cowboy Way* soundtrack) • "Someday I'll Be Saturday Night," Mercury, 1995.

Broken Homes: *Wing and a Prayer,* MCA, 1990.

Bruce, Jack: *Out of the Storm,* RSO, 1974.

Cinderella: *Night Songs,* Mercury, 1986 • "Nobody's Fool," Mercury, 1986 • "Coming Home," Mercury, 1988 • "Don't Know What You Got (Till It's Gone)," Mercury, 1988 • *Long Cold Winter,* Mercury, 1988 • *Once upon a . . . ,* Mercury, 1997.

Detective: *Detective,* Swan Song, 1977.

DFK Band: *The Dudek, Finnigan, Kreuger Band,* CBS, 1980.

Dudek, Les: *Ghost Town Parade,* Columbia, 1978.

Free: *Highway,* A&M, 1970 • *Free Live,* A&M, 1971 • *Heartbreaker,* Island, 1973 • *Molten Gold: The Anthology,* Island, 1995.

House of Lords: *House of Lords,* RCA, 1988 • *Sahara,* RCA, 1990.

Hughes/Thrall: *Hughes/Thrall,* Epic, 1982, 1991.

Keys, Bobby: *Bobby Keys,* Warner Bros., 1972.

Kids: *Anvil Chorus,* Atco, 1975.

Killer Dwarfs: *Dirty Weapons,* Epic, 1990 • *Method to the Madness,* Epic, 1992.

Kossoff, Paul: *Koss,* DJM, 1977 • *Blue Blue Soul,* Music Club, 1997.

Loudness: *Hurricane Eyes,* Atco, 1987.

McAuley Schenker Group: *Perfect Timing,* Capitol, 1987.

Michael Schenker Group: *MSG,* Chrysalis, 1981.

Money, Eddie: *Where's the Party?* Columbia, 1983.

Moore, Gary: *Run for Cover,* 10, 1985.

Osbourne, Ozzy: *Just Say Ozzy,* Epic, 1990.

Price, Jim: *Sundego's Travelling Orchestra,* CBS, 1972.

Riggs: *Riggs,* Full Moon, 1982.

Satriani, Joe: *The Extremist,* Relativity, 1992 • *Time Machine,* Relativity, 1993.

Sky: *Don't Hold Back,* RCA, 1971 • *Sailor's Delight,* RCA, 1979.

Spanos, Danny: *Danny Spanos,* Windsong, 1980.

Stewart, Rod: *Foolish Behaviour,* Warner Bros., 1980 • *Storyteller: The Complete Anthology,* Warner Bros., 1989.

Stone Fury: *Burns Like a Star,* MCA, 1984 • *The Best Of,* MCA, 1988.

String Driven Thing: *Keep Yer Hand on It,* Charisma, 1975.

Tangier: *Four Winds,* Atco, 1989.

Television: *Marquee Moon,* Elektra, 1977 • "See No Evil," Arista, 1977, 1986 (*Rock at the Edge*).

Van Halen: *For Unlawful Carnal Knowledge,* Warner Bros., 1991 • *Van Halen Live: Right Here Right Now,* Warner Bros., 1993 • *Best Of,* Vol. 1, Warner Bros., 1996.

West, Bruce and Laing: *Why Dontcha,* CBS/Windfall, 1972 • *Whatever Turns You On,* RSO, 1973.

Whitlock, Bobby: *Bobby Whitlock,* Columbia, 1972 • *Raw Velvet* (1 track), Columbia, 1972.

Wig: *Wireland,* Island, 1997.

Wildside: *Under the Influence,* Capitol, 1992.

Wood, Ron: *1-2-3-4,* Columbia, 1981.

Wright, Gary: *Extraction,* A&M, 1970.

Glyn Johns

Few producers in the rock era can equal the accomplishments of Glyn Johns (born February 15, 1942, in Epsom, England), a producer and engineer who has collaborated with the Beatles, the Who, and the Rolling Stones, among many others.

Because he combines producing and engineering, Johns is able to exert control over more than one phase of the recording process. Moreover, he is a shrewd talent scout who has assembled bands and masterminded concept albums on more than one occasion.

Johns started as a studio engineer in the '60s for the Rolling Stones and the Beatles. He recorded the Beatles' impromptu concert on the roof of Apple Records that was captured in the film *Let It Be*. Moreover, he was responsible for engineering the Stones' essential concert album, *Get Yer Ya-Yas Out*.

As a producer, Johns has supervised a bevy of classic albums: *Who's Next* (No. 4) by the Who, *Desperado* by the Eagles, *Slowhand* (No. 2) by Eric Clapton, *Brave New World* by the Steve Miller Band, *Rock On* by Humble Pie, *The Ozark Mountain Daredevils*, and *Joan Armatrading* among them. "If You Want to Get to Heaven," a 1973 hit by the Ozark Mountain Daredevils; "Best of My Love," a No. 1 hit by the Eagles; and "Love and Affection," a 1976 hit by Joan Armatrading are prime examples of Johns' approach: He frames heartfelt vocals with sympathetic accompaniment without burdening the songs with superfluous augmentation.

Johns' instincts for good songs also led him to songwriter David Kennerley. Consequently, Johns masterminded two Kennerley-derived concept albums: *White Mansions* and *The Legend of Jesse James*. Moreover, Johns assembled Lazy Racer, an Anglo-American band that featured veteran session guitarist Tim Renwick and wistful singer Kelly Harland. Johns also produced the group's albums *Lazy Racer* and *Formula 2*, as well as Renwick's 1980 solo album, *Tim Renwick*.

Johns' work with the Who is also noteworthy. He engineered and co-produced the monumental *Who's Next*, the album featuring "Baba O'Reilly," "Bargain," "The Song Is Over," and "Won't Get Fooled Again" (No. 15). Johns, along with co-producer and one-time understudy Jon Astley (see entry), supervised the underrated *Who Are You* (No. 2) as well.

Johns' career, however, is not without controversy. For instance, he parted ways with the Eagles during the recording of *On the Border* (No. 17), convinced that the band should focus on the acoustic harmony of "Best of My Love" rather than the electric syncopation of "On the Border."

With Bill Szymczyk (see entry) at the helm, the Eagles soared to even greater heights with *Hotel California* while Johns took a different path by hooking up with Astley for Eric Clapton's *Slowhand* and *Backless* (No. 8). Johns also brought Joan Armatrading to critical acclaim with the albums *Joan Armatrading* and *Show Some Emotion*.

Although he has been less prolific in the '80s and '90s, Johns' gifts have not left him. His work with John Hiatt on *Slow Turning* and *Stolen Moments* earned him plaudits, as did his efforts on behalf of Belly for its 1995 album, *King*. —BEN CROMER

Armatrading, Joan: *Joan Armatrading*, A&M, 1976 • *Show Some Emotion*, A&M, 1977 • *To the Limit*, A&M, 1978 • *Steppin' Out*, A&M, 1979 • *Track Record*, A&M, 1983 • *Classics, Vol. 21*, A&M, 1989.

Belly: *King*, Sire/Reprise, 1995 • "Thief," Elektra, 1995 (*Tank Girl* soundtrack).

Benno, Marc: *Lost in Austin*, A&M, 1979.

Bernie Leadon, Michael Giorgiades Band: *Natural Progressions*, Asylum, 1977.

Brian Rogers Orchestra: *Plays the Melodies of Gallagher and Lyle*, A&M, 1977.

Brown, Danny Joe: *Danny Joe Brown and the Danny Joe Brown Band*, Epic, 1981.

Buckacre: *Morning Comes*, MCA, 1976.

Clapton, Eric: *The Rainbow Concert*, Polydor, 1973, 1995 • "Lay Down Sally," RSO, 1977 • *Slowhand*, RSO, 1977 • *Backless*, RSO, 1978 • "Promises," RSO, 1978 • "Wonderful Tonight," RSO, 1978 • *Crossroads*, Polydor, 1988 • *Crossroads 2: Live in the 70's*, Chronicles/Polydor, 1996.

Clash, The: *Combat Rock*, Epic, 1982.

Crosby, David: *Thousand Roads*, Atlantic, 1993.

Crosby, Stills, and Nash: *After the Storm*, Atlantic, 1994.

Davis, Tim: *Take Me As I Am*, Metro, 1972.

Denny, Sandy: *Who Knows Where the Time Goes*, Hannibal, 1986, 1991 • *The Best Of*, Island, 1987.

Dylan, Bob: *Real Live*, Columbia, 1985.

Eagles: "Take It Easy," Asylum, 1972 • *The Eagles*, Asylum, 1972 • "Witchy Woman," Asylum, 1972 • *Desperado*, Asylum, 1973 • "Peaceful Easy Feeling," Asylum, 1973 • *On the Border*, Asylum, 1974 • "Best of My Love," Asylum, 1975 • *Their Greatest Hits, 1971–1975*, Asylum, 1976.

Faces, The: *A Nod Is As Good As a Wink to a Blind Horse*, Warner Bros., 1971 • "Borstal Boys," Warner Bros., 1973 (*Appetizers*) • *Ooh La La*, Warner Bros., 1973 • "Stay with Me," Warner Bros., 1971.

Fairport Convention: *Rising for the Moon*, Island, 1971.

Fairweather-Low, Andy: *La Booga Rooga*, A&M, 1975 • *Be Bop 'n' Holla*, A&M, 1976.

Fame, Georgie: *Georgie Fame*, Island, 1974.

Family: *Family Entertainment*, Reprise, 1969.

Fools Gold: *Fools Gold*, Arista, 1976.

Fortunes, The: *The Very Best of: 1967–1973*, Taragon, 1995.

Gallagher and Lyle: *Gallagher and Lyle*, Capitol, 1972 • *Seeds*, A&M, 1973 • *Willie and the Lapdog*, A&M, 1973 • *The Last Cowboy*, A&M, 1974.

Green on Red: *This Time Around*, Off Beat, 1989, 1994.

Griffith, Nanci: *Storms*, MCA, 1989 • "It's a Hard Life Wherever You Go," Reprise, 1996 (*Party of Five* soundtrack).

Hiatt, John: *Slow Turning*, A&M, 1988 • *Stolen Moments*, A&M, 1990 • "The Rest of the Dream," A&M, 1990.

Holland, Jools, and the Millionaires: *Jools Holland and the Millionaires*, A&M/IRS, 1981.

Hopkins, Nicky, and Ry Cooder, Etc.: *Jamming with Edward*, RSR, 1972.

Humble Pie: *Humble Pie*, A&M, 1970 • *Rock On*, A&M, 1971 • *Classics, Vol. 14*, A&M, 1987.

Kossoff, Paul: *Blue Blue Soul*, Music Club, 1997.

Lambert and Nuttycombe: *At Home*, A&M, 1969.

Lane, Ronnie: *Anymore for Anymore*, GM, 1974.

Lazy Racer: *Lazy Racer*, A&M, 1979 • *Formula 2*, A&M, 1980.

Live Wire: *Live Wire*, A&M, 1979.

Local Boys: *Moments of Madness*, Island, 1983.

McGuinness Flint: *Happy Birthday Ruthy Baby*, Capitol, 1971 • *McGuinness Flint*, Capitol, 1971.

Midnight Oil: *Place Without a Postcard*, Columbia, 1981 • *20,000 Watt R.S.L.: Greatest Hits*, Columbia, 1997.

Nine Below Zero: *Don't Point Your Finger*, Capitol, 1981.

Nuttycombe, Craig: *It's Just a Life Time*, A&M, 1978.

Ozark Mountain Daredevils: *It'll Shine When it Shines*, A&M, 1974 • *The Ozark Mountain Daredevils*, A&M, 1974 • "Jackie Blue," A&M, 1975 • *The Best*, A&M, 1981.

Renwick, Tim: *Tim Renwick*, CBS, 1980.

Rolling Stones: *Get Yer Ya-Ya's Out*, London, 1970 • *Hot Rocks, 1964–1971*, London, 1972, 1995.

Ronstadt, Linda: *We Ran*, Elektra, 1998.

Satriani, Joe: *Satriani*, Relativity, 1995.

Scaggs, Boz: *Boz Scaggs and Band*, Columbia, 1971 • *Moments*, Columbia, 1971.

Steve Miller Band: *Children of the Future*, Capitol, 1968 • *Brave New World*, Capitol, 1969 • *Sailor*, Capitol, 1969 • *Your Saving Grace*, Capitol, 1970 • *The Best of Steve Miller, 1968–73*, Capitol, 1991.

Stewart, Rod: *Downtown Train*, Warner Bros., 1990.

subdudes, the: *Annunciation*, High Street, 1994.

Townshend, Pete: *Coolwalkingsmoothtalkingstraightsmokingfirestoking: The Best Of*, Atlantic, 1996.

Townshend, Peter, and Ronnie Lane: *Rough Mix*, Polydor, 1977.

Who, The: "Behind Blue Eyes," Decca, 1971 • *Who's Next*, Decca, 1971 • "Won't Get Fooled Again," Decca, 1971 • "Going Mobile," Decca, 1972 • *By Numbers*, MCA, 1975 • "Squeeze Box," MCA, 1975 • "Who Are You," MCA, 1978 • *Who Are You*, Polydor, 1978 • "Athena," Polydor, 1982 • *It's Hard*, Polydor, 1982 • *Who's Better, Who's Best—This Is the Very Best of the Who*, MCA, 1988 • *Thirty Years of Maximum R&B*, Polydor, 1995.

Wood, Ron, and Ronnie Lane: *Mahoney's Last Stand*, Atlantic, 1976.

COLLECTIONS

White Mansions, A&M, 1978.

The Legend of Jesse James, A&M, 1980.

Harry Johnson

See HARRY J

Wycliffe Johnson

See STEELY AND CLEVIE

Bob Johnston

Ask Bob Johnston who he's produced and he'll spend 20 minutes rattling names off the top of his head. Those names are among the most influential in the popular music of the last 35 years: Bob Dylan, Simon and Garfunkel, Johnny Cash, Carl Perkins, the Byrds, Willie Nelson, Jimmy Frazier. . . .

You've surely heard of the first six, but the last one? Here's a Bob Johnston story. "I produced a record with Jimmy Frazier called 'Droppin' Out of School' for the U.S. government," recalls Johnston, "and worked with Vice President Humphrey. The day the song was released, Frazier was driving about 100 mph in Detroit, all loaded, and went off a bridge," Johnston laughs.

Born May 14, 1932, in Fort Worth, Texas, Johnston comes from a musical family. His grandmother, Mamie Jo Adams, wrote "Till the Sands of the Deserts Grow Cold" and "When Irish Eyes Are Smiling," with George Sands. His mother, Diane Johnston, had a big hit with Gene Autry, "Sands of Texas"; her "Miles and Miles of Texas" became a hit for Asleep at the Wheel. His great uncle was a concert pianist; his great-grandfather, he claims, invented the railroad coupling.

Johnston plays guitar and contributed keyboard work to several Leonard Cohen albums, but he couldn't make it as a performing artist. "I can't play good enough, or I'd be playing now," Johnston says. He recorded for the Algonquin, Dot, and Mercury labels; his last single as an artist was "Flat Tire" in 1961 or 1962, produced by Clyde Otis. When Johnston went to Hollywood to perform the song on the *Wink Martindale Show* all hell broke loose. "You had to pantomime your record," recalls Johnston. "While I was singing, they were hollering, 'We want Ricky, we want Tommy,' it was either Ricky Nelson or Tommy Sands, I don't remember which. It was a joke—I was overweight, had two little boys, and I was trying to compete with Tommy Sands or Ricky Nelson."

He soon began focusing on writing demos. He was Columbia staff producer from 1965 to 1967, ran CBS in Nashville in 1967 and 1968, and quit in about 1969.

"I think they gave me $3,000 for producing *Highway 61 Revisited* [No. 3] and *Sounds of Silence*," Johnston says. "The next horror story was *Blonde on Blonde* [No. 9] and *Parsley, Sage, Rosemary and Thyme* [No. 4]. I think I got $4,000 or $5,000 for those. Then I went with a gentleman named John Eastman and he got me a percentage. From then on, I made my money."

His view of the record industry is jaundiced, his view of music warm. He joined CBS under Goddard Lieberson, "who swore he'd never relinquish control of CBS to a nonmusic man." But when Clive Davis took over the CBS presidency in 1966, things changed. "When they turned it over to him, it opened up the floodgates for attorneys and accountants who patted their feet out of time and whistled out of tune," Johnston opines.

Johnston was friends with John Hammond (see entry), the CBS Records A&R legend who brought Dylan and Springsteen to the label. "Hammond had more power than anybody because he and his wife played cards with [Columbia Broadcasting System founder] William Paley and Frank Stanton three times a week," Johnston says.

How did he learn to produce? "Off the top of my head," says Johnston. "I always tried to make [the sound] better and use new stuff and different ideas. You can listen to stuff I've done and it sounds just as good today on the radio as it did 30 years ago."

At one point, Johnston was mixing Cash, overdubbing Cohen, and recording Dylan. "I'm no different from anybody normal except I work awfully hard," Johnston says. "But I never considered it work. I knew what Dylan was doing: Dylan was changing the world. All these people were changing everything, making it a bigger place. People only think the '60s are gone, that the people in the '60s are gone, and that's not true. There's a thing I wrote. It says: "They were the children of the sun / And they came with a mighty rage / They are the children of the sun / And they've come to help everyone / They are your brothers and sisters, who have come to help set you free / These rock and rollers are the shock troops of the 21st century."

Johnston is talking to the American Association of Retired Persons (AARP) about forming a record company that splits profits with the artist. He thinks the state should subsidize artists. He also would like to see material from about 10 albums' worth of music he recorded with Waterboys head Mike Scott see the light of day.

"Most producers are so caught up in themselves, they think they are the ones who do everything," Johnston says. "I never believed that. I remember Dylan used to come to me and say, 'What do you think?' I'd look at him and say, 'What possible fucking difference could it make what anybody thinks?' He'd smile at me and walk off and come back a few minutes later and say, 'What do you think?' I'd say, 'Well, maybe if you had the drum or guitar stronger,' or maybe the drummer would say something. All I knew is, whatever he was putting down, I wanted to get. I had every engineer in the studio working, I had every mike turned on, I had him surrounded by microphones so when he jerked his head around, we wouldn't lose anything.

"I never claimed any responsibility for anything. I just always made sure that the sound was better than anybody else ever did, by experimenting all those years with making demos and using different engineers and different studios and nickel-and-dime equipment. So when I got to decent equipment, it was like something else.

"There's also the way I did placing and echoes. I went in the studio by myself and shut everything up and turned everything open," Johnston says. "The main thing I tried to do was when I walked out of the studio with a mix, you could turn the volume knob wide open and you could hear it and it was amazing. Most people mix by degrees, by the radio. They add so many highs and all, they forget about the actual product. I never tried to cut a hit. All I ever remember doing is getting the biggest, most powerful musical sound I could get so people could hear it all over the world." —CARLO WOLFF

Axton, Hoyt: *Less Than a Song,* A&M, 1973 • *Road Songs,* A&M, 1977.

Bell and Arc: *Bell and Arc,* Charisma, 1971.

Bell, Graham: *Graham Bell,* Charisma, 1972.

Byrds, The: *Dr. Byrds and Mr. Hyde,* Columbia, 1969 • *Greatest Hits,* Vol. 2, Columbia, 1972 • *Play Dylan,* CBS, 1980.

Carroll, Mickey: *Mickey Carroll,* RCA, 1976.

Cash, Johnny: "Folsom Prison Blues," Columbia, 1968 • *The Holy Land,* Columbia, 1968 • "A Boy Named Sue," Columbia, 1969 • "Daddy Sang Bass," Columbia, 1969 • *Johnny Cash at San Quentin,* Columbia, 1969 • "Sunday Morning Coming Down," Columbia, 1970 • "What Is Truth?," Columbia, 1970 • "Flesh and Blood," Columbia, 1971 • *Sunday Morning Coming Down,* Columbia, 1973 • *At Folsom Prison and San Quentin,* Columbia, 1975 • *Biggest Hits,* Columbia, 1987 • *The Essential Johnny Cash, 1955–1983,* Legacy, 1992 • "Folsom Prison Blues," A&M, 1995 (*Things to Do in Denver When You're Dead* soundtrack).

China: *China,* Epic, 1979.

Cliff, Jimmy: *Give Thanks,* Warner Bros., 1978.

Cohen, Leonard: *Songs from a Room,* Columbia, 1967 • *Songs of Love and Hate,* Columbia, 1971 • *Live Songs,* Columbia, 1973 • *The Best Of,* Columbia, 1975.

Dylan, Bob: *Highway 61 Revisited,* Columbia, 1965 • "Positively 4th Street," Columbia, 1965 • *Blonde on Blonde,* Columbia, 1966 • "I Want You," Columbia, 1966 • "Just Like Tom Thumb's Blues," Columbia, 1966 • "Rainy Day Women #12 & #35," Columbia, 1966 • "Sooner or Later (One of Us Must Know)," Columbia, 1966 • *John Wesley Harding,* Columbia, 1968 • "Lay Lady Lay," Columbia, 1969 • *Nashville Skyline,* Columbia, 1969 • *New Morning,* Columbia, 1970 • *Self Portrait,* Columbia, 1970 • *Dylan,* Columbia, 1973 • *Bootleg Series,* Columbia, 1991.

Ely, Joe: *Down on the Drag,* MCA, 1979 • *Time for Travellin': The Best of Joe Ely,* Vol. 2, Edsel, 1996.

Flatt and Scruggs: *Nashville Airplane,* Columbia, 1968.

Franklin, Aretha: *Jazz to Soul,* Columbia, 1992.

Gayden, Mac: *McGavlock Gayden,* EMI, 1973.

Hicks, Dan: *Original Recordings,* Epic, 1969.

Hicks, Dan, and His Hot Licks: *Dan Hicks and His Hot Licks,* Epic, 1969, 1995.

Hod and Marc: *Hod and Marc,* Bell, 1972.

Keith, Lisa: *Walkin' in the Sun,* Perspective, 1993.

Kershaw, Doug: *The Louisiana Man,* Warner Bros., 1978 • *The Best Of,* Warner Bros., 1989.

L.A. Jets: *The L.A. Jets,* RCA, 1976.

Lee, Alvin: *Rocket Fuel,* RSO, 1978.

Lindisfarne: *Fog on the Tyne,* Charisma/Elektra, 1971 • *Dingly Dell,* Charisma/Elektra, 1972.

Mayall, John: *Bottom Line,* DJM, 1979.

Moby Grape: *Truly Fine Citizen,* Columbia, 1970 • *Vintage: The Very Best Of,* Legacy, 1993.

Murphey, Michael: *Geronimo's Cadillac,* A&M, 1972 • *Cosmic Cowboy Souvenir,* EMI/A&M, 1973 • *Michael Murphey,* EMI/Epic, 1974 • *Blue Sky Night Thunder,* Epic, 1975 • *Swans Againsy the Sun,* Epic, 1975 • "Wildfire," Epic, 1975.

Nelson, Tracey: *Tracey Nelson,* Atlantic, 1974 • *Sweet Soul Music,* MCA, 1975.

Nelson, Willie: *Who'll Buy My Memories? The IRS Tapes,* Sony Special Products, 1992 • *A Classic and Unreleased Colection,* Rhino, 1995.

New Riders of the Purple Sage: *Oh What a Mighty Time,* Columbia, 1975 • *New Riders,* MCA, 1976 • *Who Are These Guys* MCA, 1977.

Noakes, Rab: *Rab Noakes,* A&M, 1972.

Orange Blossom Sound: *Orange Blossom Sound,* Epic, 1969.

Parsons, Gene: *The Kindling Collection,* Sierra, 1994.

Perkins, Carl: *Go Cat Go,* Dinosaur, 1996.

Robbins, Marty: "Ribbon of Darkness," Columbia, 1965 • "Tonight Carmen," Columbia, 1967 • "I Walk Alone," Columbia, 1968 • "My Woman, My Woman, My Wife," Columbia, 1970 • *All-Time Greatest Hits,* Legacy, 1972 • *A Lifetime of Song, 1951–1982,* Columbia, 1983 • *Biggest Hits,* Columbia, 1984 • *Super Hits,* Columbia, 1995 • *The Story of My Life: The Best of Marty Robbins, 1952–1965,* Legacy, 1996.

Scruggs, Earl Revue: *Anniversary Special,* Columbia, 1975 • *Super Jammin',* Columbia, 1984.

Seeger, Pete: *The World of Pete Seeger* (3 tracks), Columbia, 1973 • *Link in the Chain,* Columbia 1996.

Sharp, Dave: *Downtown America,* Dinosaur, 1996.

Shaver, Billy Joe: *When I Get My Wings,* Capricorn, 1976 • *Honky Tonk Hereos,* Bear Family, 1994 • *Restless Wind: The Legendary Billy Joe Shaver, 1973–1987,* Razor & Tie, 1995.

Simon and Garfunkel: "A Hazy Shade of Winter," Columbia, 1966 • "Homeward Bound," Columbia, 1966 • "I Am a Rock," Columbia, 1966 • *Parsley, Sage, Rosemary and Thyme,* Columbia, 1966 • *Sounds of Silence,* Columbia, 1966 • "At the Zoo," Columbia, 1967 • *Bookends,* Columbia, 1968 • *Collected Works,* Columbia, 1981, 1990.

Simon, Paul: *Paul Simon, 1964–1993,* Warner Bros., 1993.

Statler Brothers: *Flowers on the Wall: The Essential Statler Brothers,* Legacy/Columbia, 1996.

Toups, Wayne, and Zydecajun: *Blast from the Bayou,* Mercury, 1989.

Valente, Dino: *Dino Valente* (2 tracks), Epic, 1968.

Wainwright, Loudon, III: *Attempted Moustache,* Columbia, 1973.

Booker T. Jones

Memphis native Booker T. Jones believes the producer's role is to help the "artist realize his or her musical dreams." The namesake for Booker T. and the MGs, Jones was born on November 12, 1944, and became interested in music as a toddler when he received his first dime store drum.

At age 5 Jones taught himself chords on ukulele and piano, and by 9 he was also playing clarinet, followed by oboe, saxophone, flute, and brass. By age 14 he was sneaking into Memphis clubs, and two years later, after an introduction by his friend David Porter (see entry), he'd begun working sessions at Stax Records, mostly on keyboards.

In the early '60s, Booker T. Jones became synonymous with Booker T. and the MGs, (an acronym for "Memphis Group"), with Steve Cropper (see entry) on guitar, Al Jackson Jr. on drums, and on bass, first Lewis Steinberg, then Donald "Duck" Dunn. Not only did the band write and produce numerous hits for itself ("Green Onions," No. 3; "Hang 'Em High," No. 9; "Time Is Tight," No. 6) based upon Jones' cool organ and the subtly cooking rhythm section, it also played on records and on stage with Stax giants Otis Redding, Sam and Dave, Eddie Floyd, and Albert King. Jones produced William Bell, Judy Clay, the Astors, Carla Thomas, and Floyd for Stax in the '60s.

From 1962 to 1966, Jones also attended Indiana University in Bloomington, earning a bachelor of music degree. His senior recital was on trombone. In the '70s, Jones produced Willie Nelson's *Stardust* album, Bill Withers' *Just As I Am* album (with "Ain't No Sunshine," No. 3), and Rita Coolidge's "(Your Love has Lifted Me) Higher and Higher" (No. 2). He also played on albums by Ray Charles, Bobby Darin, Stephen Stills, and Barbra Streisand.

In 1992, Booker T. and the MGs were inducted into the Rock and Roll Hall of Fame. In 1993, the band backed Neil Young in U.S. and European tours. Jones lives in northern California with his wife and three children. Although he wouldn't be interviewed for this book, Jones answered some questions by fax. He said he brings his "own musical sense/style/arrangements" to production and makes sure to provide "continuity" and "good food" in the studio environment. He added he learned about melody, tempo, and emotion at Stax.

—CARLO WOLFF

Astors, The: "Daddy Didn't Tell Me," Stax, 1967.

Bell, William: "Eloise (Hang in There)," Stax, 1967 • "Everybody Loves a Winner," Stax, 1967 • "Everyday Will Be Like a Holiday," Stax, 1967 • "A Tribute to a King," Stax, 1968 • "I Forgot to Be Your Lover," Stax, 1969 • *Bound to Happen*, Pye, 1976 • *The Best Of*, Stax, 1991 • *A Little Something Extra*, Stax, 1992.

Bell, William, and Judy Clay: "Private Number," Stax, 1968.

Booker T. and the MGs: *Green Onions*, Stax, 1962 • *Soul Dressing*, Rhino, 1965, 1991 • *In the Christmas Spirit*, Rhino, 1966, 1991 • *And Now!* Rhino, 1966, 1992 • "Slim Jenkin's Place," Stax, 1967 • "Winter Snow," Stax, 1967 • *Doin' Our Thing*, Rhino, 1968, 1992 • "Soul Limbo," Stax, 1968 • *Soul Limbo*, Stax, 1968, 1991 • "Hang 'Em High," Stax, 1969 • *The Booker T. Set*, Stax, 1969 • "Time Is Tight," Stax, 1969 • *Uptight*, Stax, 1969, 1991 • *McLemore Avenue*, Stax, 1970, 1991 • *Melting Pot*, Stax, 1971, 1990 • *Universal Language*, Asylum, 1977 • *Groovin'*, Rhino, 1993 • *That's the Way It Should Be*, Columbia, 1994 • *The Very Best Of*, Rhino, 1994.

Clay, Judy: *Private Numbers*, Stax, 1974.

Coolidge, Rita: *Rita Coolidge*, A&M, 1971 • *Anytime Anywhere*, A&M, 1977 • "Higher and Higher," A&M, 1977 • *Love Me Again*, A&M, 1978 • *Satisfied*, A&M, 1979 • *Greatest Hits*, A&M, 1980.

Crowell, Rodney: *Street Language*, Columbia, 1986.

Five Blind Boys of Alabama: *Deep River*, Nonesuch, 1992.

Floyd, Eddie: "Big Bird," Stax, 1968 • *Chronicle: Greatest Hits*, Stax, 1979 • *California Girl/Down to Earth*, Stax, 1995.

Hinojosa, Tish: *Culture Swing*, Rounder, 1992 • *The Best of Sandia: Watermelon 1991–2*, Watermelon, 1997.

Jones, Booker T. w/ Priscilla Jones, *Booker T. and Priscilla*, A&M, 1971 • w/ Priscilla Jones, *Home Grown*, A&M, 1972 • *Try and Love Again*, A&M, 1979 • *The Best of You*, A&M, 1980 • *The Runaway*, MCA Master, 1989.

Jones, Priscilla Coolidge: *Flying*, Capricorn, 1979 • *See also* Jones, Booker T.

King, Albert, Steve Cropper, and Pop Staples: *Jammed Together*, Stax, 1969.

Klugh, Earl: *Magic in Your Eyes*, United Artists, 1979 • *Love Songs*, Capitol, 1981, 1996 • *The Best Of*, Vols. 1–2, Blue Note, 1991, 1992.

Memphis Horns: *High on Music*, RCA, 1976.

Nelson, Willie: "Blue Skies," Columbia, 1978 • "Georgia on My Mind," Columbia, 1978 • *Stardust*, Columbia, 1978 • "Pretty Paper," Columbia, 1979 • *Pretty Paper*, Columbia, 1979 • "White Christmas," Columbia, 1979 • *Greatest Hits and Some That Will Be*, Columbia, 1981 • *Without a Song*, Columbia, 1983 • *Super Hits*, Columbia, 1994 • *Pancho, Lefty, and Rudolph*, Sony, 1995 • *Super Hits*, Vol. 2, Columbia, 1995.

Swan, Billy: *You're OK, I'm OK*, A&M, 1978.

Thomas, Carla: *Gee Whiz: The Best Of*, Rhino, 1994.

Withers, Bill: *"Ain't No Sunshine,"* Sussex, 1971 • *Just As I Am,* Sussex, 1971 • *Lean on Me: The Best of Bill Withers,* Legacy, 1994.

Gareth Jones

Gareth Jones is one of the most important engineers and producers of British new wave in the '80s and '90s, producing or co-producing the techno-pop of Depeche Mode's *Some Great Reward* (No. 5 U.K.) and *Black Celebration* (No. 4 U.K.); Erasure's *Wild!* (No. 1 U.K.), *Erasure* (No. 14 U.K.), and *Cowboy;* the melodic neo-psychedelia of Wire's *The Ideal Copy* and *A Bell Is a Cup Until It Is Struck;* and the vibrant electronica of Sheep on Drugs' *From A to H and Back Again* and *Greatest Hits.*

Gareth Jones was born in the English countryside outside of London in 1954. He enjoyed classical and jazz music growing up, eschewing pop music until his midteens. Always interested in music and technology, Jones played piano, trumpet, and French horn and studied science in school. He also "mucked about with tape recorders" from an early age.

In college Jones realized that a living could be made combining music and technology, so he "wrote the usual kind of letter" to all the studios in England asking for an assistant's job. Receiving no replies, Jones decided he'd better get more experience in the general field and ended up as a junior trainee technical operator with BBC Radio in 1974.

Showing an aptitude for the job, Jones was promoted to junior studio manager—the radio equivalent of recording studio engineer. When told that he would not be directly involved with recording music for at least five more years, Jones wrote to the studios once again. This time he got a response from the owner of a small 8-track, Pathway, in London.

After working at both the BBC and Pathway for six months, Jones left the former to be a full-time recording engineer at the latter. Though at first he felt like he was "jumping off the deep end" at the studio—on his first session the drummer asked him to turn up the snare and he didn't know which drum that was ("Not the one that goes BOOM, the loud slappy one in the middle," quoth the drummer)—his work at Pathway was "excellent training because I had to deal with lots of quick projects with different bands and different kinds of music," he says. At Pathway, Jones' engineering projects

included Madness's first single, "The Prince" (1979), and John Foxx's first solo album after he left Ultravox, the minimalist electronic milestone *Metamatic* (1980).

Foxx then formed a collective with several other artists. Together they bought a warehouse that was converted into artists' studios, including a recording studio called the Garden. Jones helped create the starkly elegant studio and became staff engineer.

In 1983 Depeche Mode was looking for a place to record their third album; until then the group had worked at Blackwing Studios, owned by Eric Radcliffe (of Yazoo's *Upstairs at Eric's* fame). Jones was living in Brixton in south London at the time and listening to a lot of underground music and reggae. He had no interest in Depeche as they seemed to be a commercial synth-pop band. Depeche loved the Garden but didn't like the engineer they were working with, so Jones was brought in despite his negative predisposition. As these things often go, Jones, the band (Martin Gore, synths, songwriter; Dave Gahan, vocals; Andy Fletcher, synths; Alan Wilder, electronics), and their producer Daniel Miller (owner of Mute Records; see entry) got on famously and began an ongoing relationship that continues to this day.

The album recorded at the Garden, *Construction Time Again,* was a stylistic change for Depeche in that they wanted to move away from bouncy synth-pop into darker, moodier soundscapes, as on the classic anti-avarice single "Everything Counts" (No. 6 U.K.). Besides engineering the album, Jones contributed ideas such as recording the band's synths through amplifiers, affording a broader sonic reach through the use of distortion, and the like.

After the album was recorded at the Garden, it was mixed at Hansa Studios in Berlin, which at the time had the biggest SSL mixing board (56-channel) in the world. Jones felt his contributions merited inclusion in the production team, and he was given co-producer credit (with Miller and the band) for the next two Depeche albums—*Some Great Reward* and *Black Celebration*—which effectively began his production career.

Reward includes the clangorous single "Master and Servant" (No. 9 U.K.); the spooky, thought-provoking "Blasphemous Rumours" (No. 16 U.K.) and "Shake the Disease" (No. 18 U.K.); and the band's first U.S.-charting single "People Are People" (No. 13) (for which Jones did not receive production credit). *Celebration* features the great meditation on death "Fly on the Windscreen," as well as "Stripped" (No. 15 U.K.) and the peppy, paranoid "A Question of Time" (No. 17 U.K.).

Having met and fallen in love with Anete Humpe, lead singer of the German new wave–pop band Ideal, and delighted with the Hansa Studio, Jones moved to Berlin in 1983 and stayed until 1992. There Jones engineered and produced quite a few German bands, including Ideal and avant-noise band Einsturzende Neubauten.

In the late '80s Jones produced art-punk pioneers Wire and, over the course of two exceptional albums (*The Ideal Copy, A Bell Is a Cup Until It Is Struck*), aided in the band's transition from thrash minimalism to powerful, Gang of Four–type alterna-funk ("Ahead") and floral neo-psychedelia ("Kidney Bingos").

When the wall came down in 1989, Berlin changed from a cloistered enclave of the West embedded in the East to just another city and gradually lost its appeal for Jones, who returned to London in 1992.

Since then he has produced transplanted Australian Simon Bonney, the tasty jungle and electronica of Sheep on Drugs, and even reunited with old friends Depeche Mode to help mix and engineer tracks for *Ultra* (1997). He produced the instrumental soundtrack to the Australian film *To Have and to Hold* with Nick Cave in 1995. He has co-produced three albums for techno-poppers Erasure (Vince Clarke, Andy Bell), including the wildly successful *Wild!*, with the luxuriant "Blue Savannah" (No. 3 U.K.) and the anthemic "Star" (No. 11 U.K.).
—ERIC OLSEN

Bernhard, Sandra: "You Make Me Feel (Mighty Real)" (remix), 550 Music/Sony, 1994.

Bonney, Simon: *Forever,* Mute, 1992 • *Everyman,* Mute, 1995.

Can: *Sacriledge: The Remixes,* Mute, 1997.

Cave, Nick: w/ the Bad Seeds, "Weeping Song" (remix), Mute/Elektra, 1990 • w/ the Bad Seeds, "(I'll Love You) Till the End of the World," Warner Bros., 1991 (*Until the End of the World* soundtrack) • *To Have and to Hold* soundtrack, Mute Ionic, 1997.

Depeche Mode: "Blasphemous Rumours," Sire, 1984, 1991 • "Master and Servant," Sire, 1984 • *Some Great Reward,* Sire, 1984 • *Catching Up With,* Sire, 1985 • "Fly on the Windscreen" (remix), Sire, 1985, 1991 • "Shake the Disease," Sire, 1985, 1991 • *The Singles, 81–85,* Mute, 1985 • "A Question of Lust," Sire, 1986, 1991 • "A Question of Time," Sire, 1986, 1991 • *Black Celebration,* Sire, 1986, 1991 • "Stripped," Sire, 1986, 1991.

Einsturzende Neubauten: *Halber Mensch,* Thirsty Ear, 1985.

Erasure: "Blue Savannah," Sire, 1989 • "Drama" (remix), Sire, 1989 • *Wild!* Sire/Reprise, 1989 • "You Surround Me" (remix), American Gramaphone, 1989 • "Star," Atlantic, 1990 • *Pop! The First 20 Hits,* Sire, 1992 • "I Love Saturday," Mute, 1994 • *Erasure,* Mute/Elektra, 1995 • "Fingers and Thumbs (Cold Winter's Day)," Mute/Elektra, 1995 • "Stay with Me," Mute, 1995 • "Rock Me Gently," Conemy, 1996 • *Cowboy,* Maverick, 1997 • "Don't Say Your Love Is Killing Me," Mute, 1997 • "In My Arms," Maverick, 1997 • "Magic Moments," Mute/Maverick, 1997.

Galas, Diamanda: *Masque of the Red Death Trilogy,* Mute, 1993.

House of Love: *Spy in the House of Love,* Fontana, 1991.

Inspiral Carpets: *Life* (3 tracks), Mute/Elektra, 1990.

Nitzer Ebb: "Let Your Body Learn" (remix), Geffen, 1987.

Plan B: *Cyber Chords and Sushi Stories,* Imago, 1993 • "Life's a Beat," Imago, 1993.

Schmidt, Irmin: *Impossible Holidays,* Fine Line, 1996.

Sheep on Drugs: "15 Minutes of Fame," Smash, 1993 • *Greatest Hits,* Island, 1993 • "Track X," Smash, 1993 • "Cathode Ray," Smash, 1994 • *From A to H and Back Again,* Smash, 1994 • "Motorbike," Smash, 1994.

Tovey, Frank: *The Fad Gadget Singles,* Sire, 1987.

Tuxedomoon: *No Tears/Desire,* CramBoy, 1978, 1985 • *Suite en Sous-Sol—Time to Lose,* CBoy, 1987, 1997.

Wire: *The Ideal Copy,* Mute/Enigma, 1987 • *A Bell Is a Cup Until It Is Struck,* Mute/Enigma, 1988 • "The Drill" (remix), Mute, 1991 • *The A List: 1985–1990,* Mute, 1993.

Hugh Jones

Hugh Jones is a top English producer and engineer who has consistently brought out the best in a wide range of modern rock artists in the '80s and '90s, including Echo and the Bunnymen, Modern English, Icicle Works, Stan Ridgway, the Colourfield, Del Amitri, That Petrol Emotion, the Connells, Kitchens of Distinction, and the Bluetones. In particular, Jones produced three of the most important modern rock songs of the '80s: Modern English's "I Melt with You," Icicle Works' "Whisper to a Scream (Birds Fly)," and Ridgway's "The Big Heat."

Jones was born and raised in central London and was drawn to music early, playing guitar and piano and singing. The excitement of the Beatles led him to rock 'n' roll, but he also sang seriously, recording as a schoolboy with the Downside and Emmanuel School choirs for Benjamin Britten's *A Midsummer Night's Dream* opera.

Jones left school at 16 to pursue a life in the studio and got a job as an apprentice engineer at London's I.B.C. Studios. Jones' first solo engineering job was Chick Corea's *Light As a Feather* in 1972. Jones perfected his engineering skills recording orchestral pop at I.B.C. before taking a year off to cool his heels in a cottage in the country in 1977.

Remaining in the country, Jones took an engineering job with Rockfield Studios, which has been his favorite studio and his base of operations ever since. After engineering the Teardrop Explodes' (with Julian Cope) and Echo and the Bunnymen's first albums, Jones got his first production credit on the Bunnymen's second album, *Heaven Up Here* (No. 10 U.K.)—still one of his favorites. "They're attitude was 'We're really great, and even if we don't sell any records, we're still great,'" says Jones, who also played keyboards on the album. The Bunnymen's assumed greatness was yet to be proved (until their third album *Porcupine*), but Jones neatly balanced the guitar stylings of Will Sergeant with Ian McCulloch's dark evocative baritone and surrounded them with Peter de Freitas's crisp drums—especially on the title track and "No Dark Things."

In fact, great drum sound has been a Jones hallmark. In 1982 Jones produced a little-known band from Colchester's first album, *After the Snow*. Modern English would be just another nice little band if it weren't for the greatness of "I Melt with You," which opens with the vacuum-chamber rush of a guitar chord, followed immediately by a thunderous explosion of drums and bass that sent (especially American) revelers stomping across new wave dance floors in ecstasy for the rest of the '80s. The crushing drum backbeat propels the lower body, while a sweet tune playing off of the archetypal desire to stand outside of time in syncretizing love engages the emotions.

After "Melt" swept across America, the band was called to play before a writhing mass of tens of thousands in Daytona Beach for Spring Break '83, having never played a venue bigger than a pub. According to Jones, "When they played the first three bars of 'Melt,' the crowd erupted with recognition; it terrified the band so much they stopped playing and stared at each other," before recovering and finishing the song.

Though not the cultural icon that "Melt" became, Icicle Works' (a Liverpudlian trio led by singer/songwriter/multi-instrumentalist Ian McNabb) "Birds Fly" is an even better song, with even better drums. "Birds" begins with a lulling guitar arpeggio from McNabb that is soon chased away by octopus tom-tom pounding from drummer Chris Sharrock—a drumming that fills the air and echoes from the mountains to the sea. McNabb's guitar returns for the brilliant sing-along chorus and Jones whirls it all together into a seamless pop-rock masterpiece.

Jones arrived at the monstrous drum sound by chance. "Just experimenting, I put a little tape delay on the drums and found that the tempo of the delay was precisely the same tempo of the song, so that it was actually slapping [echoing] in rhythm with the song. It gave the whole thing 'that drive.'"

Leaving the comfort of his beloved Rockfield in 1985, Jones next sojourned to the dreaded Los Angeles to produce ex–Wall of Voodoo singer Stan Ridgway. Though the Ridgway album was more synthetic than his typical rock band sound, Jones again found an artist's center and helped the eccentric storyteller craft his most memorable melody and tuneful singing on "The Big Heat": a post-apocalyptic detective story highlighted by Bill Noland's electronic bass line, Ridgway's incongruous harmonica noodling, and some Eno-like (see entry) treated piano.

Jones' most important work of the '90s includes the lovely guitar-based alterna-pop of the Connells' *One Simple Word* (with "Stone Cold Yesterday"), the Cocteau Twins-meets-Ride guitar wash of Kitchens of Distinction's *Strange Free World* (with the majestic "Drive That Fast"), and the harder guitar slinging of the Stone Roses–like Bluetones on *Expecting to Fly*.
—ERIC OLSEN

Balaam and the Angel: *Greatest Story Ever Told,* Virgin, 1987.

Barone, Richard: *Clouds over Eden,* Mesa/Bluemoon, 1993.

Bauhaus: *Singles, 1981–1983* (1 track), Beggars Banquet, 1983 • "Spirit," Beggars Banquet, 1983.

Berry, Heidi: *Heidi Berry,* 4 A.D., 1993 • *Miracle,* 4 A.D., 1996.

Bluetones, The: *Expecting to Fly,* A&M, 1996 • "Slight Return," A&M, 1996.

Charlatans UK: *Between 10th and 11th* (1 track), Beggars Banquet, 1992 • "Subtitle," Beggars Banquet, 1992.

Clock DVA: *Advantage,* Polydor, 1983.

Colourfield, The: *Virgins and Philistines,* Chrysalis, 1985.

Connells, The: *One Simple Word,* TVT, 1990.

Damned, The: *Strawberries* (7 tracks), Bronze, 1982.

Del Amitri: *Del Amitri,* Chrysalis, 1985 • *Waking Hours,* A&M, 1990, 1995.

Died Pretty: *Doughboy Hollow,* Beggars Banquet, 1992 • *Trace,* Columbia, 1993 • *Caressing Swine (and Some History)* (EP), Columbia, 1994.

Dodgy: *Free Peace Sweet,* Mercury, 1997.

Dumptruck: *For the Country,* Big Time, 1987.

Echo and the Bunnymen: *Heaven Up Here,* Korova/Sire, 1981 • *Songs to Learn and Sing,* Korova/Sire, 1985, 1987.

Essential Logic: *Beat Rhythm News,* Rough Trade, 1979.

Family Cat: "Gone, So Long," Dedicated, 1994.

Glee Club: *Mine,* 4 A.D., 1994.

Hall, Terry: *The Collection: Terry Hall,* Chrysalis, 1993.

Icicle Works: *The Icicle Works,* Arista, 1984 • "Whisper to a Scream (Birds Fly)," Arista, 1984.

James: *Strip-Mine,* Sire, 1988.

Kitchens of Distinction: "Drive That Fast," A&M, 1990 •

"Gorgeous Love," A&M, 1990 • "Quick As Rainbows," A&M, 1990 • *Strange Free World,* A&M, 1990 • *The Death of Cool,* A&M, 1992.

Longpigs: *The Sun Is Often Out,* PolyGram, 1997.

Mary My Hope: *Suicide Kings,* Silvertone, 1989.

Modern English: "Melt with You," Sire, 1982 • *After the Snow,* Polydor/Sire, 1983 • *Ricochet Days,* Sire, 1984.

Monsoon: *Third Eye,* MSC, 1983.

Mothmen: *One Black Dot,* Do It, 1982.

Mutton Birds: *Envy of Angels,* Virgin, 1996.

Not Drowning, Waving: *Circus,* Reprise, 1993.

Pale Saints: *Flesh Balloon* (EP), 4 A.D., 1991 • *In Ribbons,* 4 A.D., 1992 • "Angel," 4 A.D., 1994 • *Slow Buildings,* 4 A.D., 1994.

Parachute Men: *Earth, Dogs and Eggshells,* Fire, 1990.

Ridgway, Stan: "Drive, She Said," Illegal, 1985 • *The Big Heat,* IRS Vintage, 1986, 1993.

Rubber Rodeo: *Scenic Views,* Eat/Mercury, 1984.

Saints, The: *All Fools' Day,* TVT, 1987.

Softies: *Nice and Nasty,* Charly, 1982.

Sound, The: *From the Lion's Mouth,* Korova, 1981.

Stump: *Fierce Pancake,* Chrysalis, 1988.

That Petrol Emotion: *Manic Pop Thrill,* Demon, 1986.

Ultra Vivid Scene: *Joy 1967–1990,* 4 A.D./Columbia, 1990.

Undertones, The: *Positive Touch,* Rykodisc, 1981, 1994.

Voice of the Beehive: *Let it Bee* (3 tracks), London, 1988 • *Honey Lingers* (2 tracks), London, 1991.

Mick Jones

Foreigner's Mick Jones looks upon record production as another weapon in his arsenal. Combining bursts of guitar with a wash of keyboards and synthesizers to frame Lou Gramm's dramatic vocals, Jones helped craft such Foreigner classics as "Feels Like the First Time" (No. 4), "Hot Blooded" (No. 3), "Double Vision" (No. 2), "Head Games" (No. 14), "Urgent" (No. 4), "Waiting for a Girl Like You" (No. 2), and "I Want to Know What Love Is," a ballad that reached No. 1 in 1985.

Jones has co-produced Foreigner's albums with Robert John "Mutt" Lange, Keith Olson, Roy Thomas Baker (see entries), the late Alex Sadkin, and others. "The people I've worked with have been engineers," Jones explains, adding that he enlists a co-producer primarily to manage the sound so he can concentrate on the musical direction.

Born in London on December 27, 1944, Jones paid his dues in the late '60s and early '70s playing guitar with Spooky Tooth, George Harrison, Leslie West, and French singer Johnny Hallyday. In fact, at one point following the demise of the sadly overlooked Spooky Tooth, Jones considering quitting music. "When Gary [Wright] left to do his solo album [*Dream Weaver*], I kind of felt stranded and spent that time [in the United States] with Leslie West," Jones recalls. "I wasn't even sure if I was cut out for this business. I was almost on the verge of going back to England and changing my life."

Yet Jones persevered. In 1976, he put together Foreigner, an Anglo-American band that was an immediate hit with audiences who embraced the band's moody, swaggering rock and synth–driven, soul-searching ballads. Ten years and numerous hits later, Jones followed his muse and tackled several production assignments, including Van Halen's *5150* and Billy Joel's *Storm Front* (both No. 1).

"People were saying, 'You've produced a lot of these Foreigner albums; you'd be great with other people,'" Jones explains. "I guess I really needed to prove something to myself: 'Is this just Foreigner or does my ability go further?'"

When Jones returned to Foreigner the hits came less frequently. Nevertheless, each album had its share of standouts, "Say You Will" (No. 6) and "I Don't Want to Live Without You" (No. 5) among them. Jones also found time to record a solo album, *Mick Jones.*

Jones and Gramm parted ways briefly in the early '90s, with Jones hiring singer Johnny Edwards for the disappointing *Unusual Heat.* Jones and Gramm reunited in 1994 for *Mr. Moonlight,* a fine effort produced by Jones with Gramm and Mike Stone (see entry) that included another exquisite Foreigner ballad, "Until the End of Time."

"There's nothing stronger than a great partnership because things that you don't realize yourself can be brought to your attention by the person you're working with," says Jones of his association with Gramm. "It's something we realize is very special. That doesn't happen very often in life." —BEN CROMER

Foreigner: "Cold As Ice," Atlantic, 1977 • *Foreigner,* Atlantic, 1977 • "Blue Morning, Blue Day," Atlantic, 1978 • *Double Vision,* Atlantic, 1978 • "Hot Blooded," Atlantic, 1978 • "Dirty White Boy," Atlantic, 1979 • "Head Games," Atlantic, 1979 • *Foreigner 4,* Atlantic, 1981 • "Urgent," Atlantic, 1981 • "Waiting for a Girl Like You," Atlantic, 1981 • *Records,* Atlantic, 1982 • *Agent Provocateur,* Atlantic, 1984 • "I Want to Know What Love Is," Atlantic, 1984 • "That Was Yesterday," Atlantic, 1985 • "Say You Will," Atlantic, 1987 • "I Don't Want to Live Without You,"

Atlantic, 1988 • *Inside Information,* Atlantic, 1988 • *Unusual Heat,* Atlantic, 1991 • *The Very Best . . . and Beyond,* Atlantic, 1992 • *Mr. Moonlight,* Priority, 1995.

Joel, Billy: *Storm Front,* Columbia, 1989 • "We Didn't Start the Fire," Columbia, 1989 • "And So It Goes," Columbia, 1990 • "I Go to Extremes," Columbia, 1990.

Jones, Mick : *Mick Jones,* Atlantic, 1989.

Spooky Tooth: *You Broke My Heart, So I Busted Your Jaw,* A&M, 1973 • *The Mirror,* Island, 1974.

Theatre of Hate: *Westworld,* Burning Rome, 1982.

Van Halen: *5150,* Warner Bros., 1986 • "Best of Both Worlds," Warner Bros., 1986 • "Dreams," Warner Bros., 1986 • "Why Can't This Be Love?," Warner Bros., 1986 • *Best Of,* Vol. 1, Warner Bros., 1996.

Quincy Jones

Even producers who are revered as among the greatest in the field—Phil Ramone, George Martin, Jerry Wexler, Arif Mardin, Tom Dowd [see entries]—hail Quincy Jones as unique in his achievement. Jones' most famous client, Michael Jackson, calls him "the king of all music." Among his distinctions are producing the top-selling record in history (Jackson's *Thriller*); winning the most Grammys of anyone outside of classical music; and a credit list that epitomizes popular music at its best: Ray Charles, Lionel Hampton, Count Basie, Sarah Vaughan, Dizzy Gillespie, Billy Eckstine, the Brothers Johnson, Lesley Gore, Aretha Franklin, Frank Sinatra, George Benson, Rufus and Chaka Khan, Patti Austin, Donna Summer, Paul McCartney (see entry), and Jackson, just to name a few.

Beyond the scope of his productions Quincy's persona itself serves as a paradigm for anyone wishing to make a mark on the entertainment world. In fact, the highest compliment that can be paid to a rising star like Babyface (see entry) is to be called a modern-day Quincy Jones.

And while many producers would trade a limb for Jones' studio career, the man's activities beyond recording are just as impressive. As a label executive, Jones presided over A&R at Mercury during that label's jazz heyday in the '50s and '60s; he later joined A&M, where he was also instrumental in talent acquisition; and, in 1980, Jones formed his own imprint, Qwest, under the auspices of Warner Bros. Records.

As a film-score composer, Jones was responsible for *In Cold Blood, The Out of Towners, The Color Purple,* and

his own *Listen Up: The Lives of Quincy Jones;* for TV Jones scored the ground-breaking miniseries *Roots* and wrote themes for *Sanford and Son, Bill Cosby Variety Series,* and *NBC Mystery Series;* as a publisher Jones created *Vibe* magazine, one of the most highly respected pop and urban music periodicals in the country. Furthermore, Jones executive-produced a raft of TV specials, including *An American Reunion* (covering Bill Clinton's first inauguration), *Nashville Salutes the Ryman,* and the series *Fresh Prince of Bel Air.* In short, Jones is an icon of American entertainment, a self-made entrepreneur whose power and influence cannot be overstated.

Born Quincy Delight Jones Jr. in Chicago on March 14, 1933, Jones was raised in Seattle, where he began his musical career in his teens playing in a group with Ray Charles. In 1950, Jones received a scholarship to the Berklee College of Music in Boston, where he attended classes during the day while playing in local strip clubs at night. The following year, he toured Europe with Hampton and Gillespie and decided to stay in Paris. There, Jones studied classical composition with pianist Nadia Boulanger, a former teacher of Stravinsky.

Returning to the U.S. in 1961, Jones was hired as vice president of A&R by Mercury; he was the first African American to hold that position with a major record label. He stayed with Mercury until 1968, producing, performing on, and arranging countless pop records by the likes of Gore, including her signature smash "It's My Party," "You Don't Own Me," and many others.

Featuring double-tracked vocals and full orchestral backup, those tracks leaped out of the radio in 1963, establishing Gore as an irresistible teen idol and Jones as a jazz- and classical-schooled producer with an uncanny ear for pop music.

For the next 20 years, Jones turned his attention to writing soundtracks and TV themes and recording numerous solo albums, of which *Sounds . . . and Stuff Like That, The Dude,* and *Back on the Block* all went platinum.

On his albums, Jones typically covers the entire musical spectrum, blending jazz, R&B, fusion, funk, rock, pop, and Latin music. On the songs with vocals, he has had the luxury of calling on his many friends in the business, including legends like Fitzgerald and Vaughan as well as contemporary stars ranging from Bobby McFerrin to Bono to Phil Collins. Although he sang as a kid, Jones decided he didn't want to sing on his solo records.

"As you start to work as an arranger for Ray Charles, Frank Sinatra, and Billy Eckstine, you don't kid yourself anymore," he says. "Tony Bennett, Aretha Franklin— give me a break. You're working with the greatest singers in the history of American music, and you're not out there trying to prove that you can sing, too. Next to Ray Charles, it's futility, man."

In 1984 Jones produced and arranged Sinatra's *L.A. Is My Lady,* featuring a big band, Las Vegas–style arrangement of "Mack the Knife." Many consider that work among the finest of Sinatra's long, illustrious career—one in which Jones' band (featuring the Brecker Brothers, Benson, Hampton, and others) and the Chairman of the Board shared a strong rapport.

"The better you know the artist as a person," Jones explains, "the easier it is to develop a musical sense." For Jackson's *Off the Wall,* for example, Jones and Jackson decided to showcase the young artist's maturity. The sentiment was it was time to grow up, "not to be a bubblegum singer anymore, to go out and feel everything you're supposed to feel at 21 years old," Jones recalls.

Although his career has been characterized by a Midas-like ability to turn music into gold, Jones says he never pays attention to the commercial potential of a project. He operates by "trusting the goose pimples," and he advises aspiring producers to "lead with your instincts and support them with your craft." —PAUL VERNA AND DANIEL LEVITIN

Austin, Patti: *Every Home Should Have One,* Qwest, 1981 • w/ James Ingram, "Baby Come to Me," Qwest, 1983 • *Patti Austin,* Qwest, 1983.

Benson, George: "Give Me the Night," Warner Bros., 1980 • *Give Me the Night,* Warner Bros., 1980 • *The George Benson Collection,* Warner Bros., 1981, 1988.

Brothers Johnson: "Get the Funk Out Ma Face," A&M, 1976 • "I'll Be Good to You," A&M, 1976 • *Look Out for #1,* A&M, 1976 • *Right on Time,* A&M, 1977 • "Strawberry Letter," A&M, 1977 • *Blam!* A&M, 1978, 1996 • *Light Up the Night,* A&M, 1980 • "Stomp!," A&M, 1980 • *Classics,* Vol. 11, A&M, 1987 • w/ L.T.D., *Brothers 'n' Love,* A&M, 1996.

Campbell, Tevin: *T.E.V.I.N.,* Warner Bros., 1991.

Charles, Ray: *Greatest Hits,* Vols. 1–2, DCC, 1987 • *The World of Ray Charles,* Garland, 1993 • *Genius and Soul: 50th Anniversary Collection,* Rhino, 1997.

Davis, Miles, and Quincy Jones: *Live at Montreux,* Warner Bros., 1993.

Duke, George: *Muir Woods Suite,* Warner Bros., 1996.

Eckstine, Billy: *Compact Jazz: Billy Eckstine,* Polydor, 1991.

Franklin, Aretha: *Aretha's Jazz,* Atlantic, 1972, 1984 • "Angel," Atlantic, 1973 • *Hey Now Hey, the Other Side of the Sky,* Atlantic, 1973 • "Master of Eyes," Atlantic, 1973 • *Ten Years of Gold,* Atlantic, 1976 • *30 Greatest Hits,* Atlantic, 1986 • *Queen of Soul: The Atlantic Recordings,* Rhino, 1992 • *The Very Best Of,* Vol. 2, Rhino, 1994.

Gillespie, Dizzy: *Compact Jazz: Dizzy Gillespie,* Verve, 1964, 1992.

Gore, Lesley: "It's My Party," Mercury, 1963 • "Judy's Turn to Cry," Mercury, 1963 • "She's a Fool," Mercury, 1963 • "I Don't Wanna Be a Loser," Mercury, 1964 • *Lesley Gore's Party,* Mercury, 1964 • "Maybe I Know," Mercury, 1964 • "That's the Way Boys Are," Mercury, 1964 • "You Don't Own Me," Mercury, 1964 • "Look of Love," Mercury, 1965 • "My Town, My Guy and Me," Mercury, 1965 • "Sunshine, Lollipops and Rainbows," Mercury, 1965 • *The Golden Hits of Lesley Gore,* Mercury, 1965, 1987 • *Love Me by Name,* A&M, 1975 • *It's My Party: The Mercury Years,* Mercury, 1996.

Horn, Shirley: *Loads of Love,* Verve, 1963, 1991.

Horne, Lena: *The Lady and Her Music: Live on Broadway,* Qwest, 1995.

Ingram, James: *It's Your Night,* Qwest, 1983 • w/ Michael McDonald, "Ya Mo B There," Qwest, 1984 • *The Power of Great Music: The Best Of,* Qwest/WB, 1991.

Jackson, Michael: w/ Diana Ross, "Ease on Down the Road," MCA, 1978 • "Don't Stop 'Till You Get Enough," Epic, 1979 • *Off the Wall,* Epic, 1979 • "Rock with You," Epic, 1979 • "Off the Wall," Epic, 1980 • "She's out of My Life," Epic, 1980 • w/ Paul McCartney, "The Girl Is Mine," Epic, 1982 • *Thriller,* Epic, 1982 • "Beat It," Epic, 1983 • "Billie Jean," Epic, 1983 • "Human Nature," Epic, 1983 • "P.Y.T.," Epic, 1983 • "Wanna Be Startin' Something," Epic, 1983 • "Thriller," Epic, 1984 • "Bad," Epic, 1987 • *Bad,* Epic, 1987 • w/ Siedah Garrett, "I Just Can't Stop Loving You," Epic, 1987 • "Another Part of Me," Epic, 1988 • "Dirty Diana," Epic, 1988 • "Man in the Mirror," Epic, 1988 • "The Way You Make Me Feel," Epic, 1988 • "Smooth Criminal," Epic, 1989 • *HIStory: Past, Present and Future, Part 1,* Epic, 1995.

Jones, Quincy: *Go West, Man,* Jasmine, 1957, 1988 • *This Is How I Feel About Jazz,* GRP, 1957, 1992 • *The Birth of a Band,* Vol. 1, Mercury, 1959 • *The Birth of a Band,* Vol. 2, Mercury, 1959, 1986 • *I Dig Dancers,* Mercury, 1961 • *Quintessence,* Impulse!, 1961, 1997 • *The Great Wide World of Quincy Jones Live!* Mercury, 1961, 1984 • *Bossa Nova,* Mercury, 1962, 1983 • *Plays Hip Hits,* Mercury, 1963 • *The Pawnbroker/The Deadly Affair,* Verve, 1965 • *Smackwater Jack,* Mobile Fidelity Sound Lab, 1971, 1991 • *The Hot Rock* soundtrack, Prophesy, 1972 • *Mode,* ABC, 1973 • *You've Got It, Bad Girl,* A&M, 1973 • *Body Heat,* A&M, 1974 • *Gula Matari,* A&M, 1974 • *Walking in Space,* A&M, 1974 • *Ironside,* Hamlet, 1975 • *Mellow Madness,* A&M, 1975 • *I Heard That!* A&M, 1976 • *We Had a Ball,* Sonic, 1976 • *Roots,* A&M, 1977 • *25th Anniversary Series,* Vol. 3, A&M, 1978 • *Sounds and Stuf Like That,* A&M, 1978 • "Stuff Like That," A&M, 1978 • *Superdisc,* A&M, 1979 • *Quincy and His Orchestra,* MFP, 1980 • "Ai No Corrida," A&M, 1981 •

"Just Once," A&M, 1981 • *The Dude*, A&M, 1981 • "One Hundred Ways," A&M, 1982 • *The Best*, A&M, 1982 • *Music Is My Life*, Hallmark, 1983 • *Take Five*, Happy Bird, 1983 • *This Is How I Feel*, Jasmine, 1984 • *Quincy Jones All Stars*, Esquire, 1986 • *The Quintessence*, Impulse/MCA, 1986 • *Classics*, Vol. 3, A&M, 1987 • *Love and Peace*, Street Life, 1988 • *Strike Up the Band*, Verve, 1988 • *The Best*, Vol. 2, Rebound, 1988, 1994 • *Compact Jazz*, Philips/PolyGram, 1989 • *Back on the Block*, Qwest, 1990 • "I'll Be Good to You," Qwest, 1990 • "The Secret Garden," Qwest, 1990 • *The Secret Garden (Sweet Seduction Suite)* (EP), Qwest, 1990 • w/ Tevin Campbell, "Tomorrow (A Better You, A Better Me)," Qwest, 1990 • "Setembro," Qwest/WB, 1991 (*Boyz N the Hood* soundtrack) • *Walk on the Wild Side*, Classic Jazz, 1994 • *Free and Easy, Live in Sweden, 1960*, Ancha, 1995 • *Pure Delight: The Essence of Quincy Jones*, Razor & Tie, 1995 • *Q's Jook Joint*, Qwest, 1995 • w/ Tamia, "You Put a Move on My Heart," Qwest, 1995 • *Greatest Hits*, A&M, 1996 • *Q live in Paris Circa 1960*, Qwest, 1996 • *Jazz 'Round Midnight*, PolyGram, 1997.

King, B.B.: *The Electric B.B.: His Best*, MCA, 1988 • *King of the Blues*, Pickwick, 1995.

Mandel, Johnny: *The Sandpiper*, Verve, 1965.

New Order: "Blue Monday 1988" (remix), Qwest, 1988.

Rufus: *Masterjam*, MCA, 1979.

Rufus and Chaka Khan: "Do You Love What You Feel?," MCA, 1980 • *The Very Best of Rufus and Chaka Khan*, MCA, 1996.

Sinatra, Frank: *L.A. Is My Lady*, Qwest, 1984.

Streisand, Barbra: *Till I Loved You*, Columbia, 1988.

Summer, Donna: *Donna Summer*, Casablanca/Mercury, 1982, 1994 • "Love Is in Control," Geffen, 1982 • "State of Independence," Geffen, 1982 • "The Woman in Me," Geffen, 1983 • *Anthology*, Casablanca/Mercury, 1993.

Tamia: *Tamia*, Qwest, 1998.

Thielemans, Toots: *Verve Jazz Masters 59*, PolyGram, 1996.

USA for Africa: "We Are the World," Columbia, 1985.

Vaughan, Sarah: *Sassy Swings the Tivoli*, Emarcy, 1963, 1987 • *Compact Jazz: Sarah Vaughan*, Verve, 1967, 1989 • *The Complete Sarah Vaughan on Mercury*, Vol. 4, Mercury, 1986 • *Walkman Jazz*, PolyGram, 1987 • w/ Quincy Jones, *Misty*, Mercury, 1990 • *The George Gershwin Songbook*, Vol. 2, Emarcy, 1990.

Washington, Dinah: *Compact Jazz: Dinah Sings the Blues*, Verve, 1961, 1989 • *First Issue: The Dinah Washington Story*, PolyGram, 1993.

West Coast All-Stars: "We're All in the Same Gang," Warner Bros., 1990.

Williams, Andy: *I Like Your Kind of Love: The Best of the Cadence Years*, Varese Sarabande, 1996.

Winans, The: *All Out*, Qwest, 1993.

COLLECTIONS

The Wiz, Motown, 1978.

Girl from Ipanema: The Antonio Carlos Jobim Songbook, Verve, 1996.

Wave: Jobim Songbook, Verve, 1996.

Blues in the Night: The Johnny Mercer Songbook, Verve, 1997.

Richard K. Jonckheere

See FRONT 242

David Kahne

Don't be surprised if David Kahne's name starts popping up on classical productions. Accustomed to working in a compact pop format, the California native would love to work on a larger, more leisurely scale. "I think about working with an orchestra," says the head of A&R at Reprise Records. "I think I have kind of an interesting combination of working on pop and rock and R&B stuff, and I think about scoring a film."

Not only was Kahne instrumental in shaping San Francisco new wave at the dawn of the '80s, he's continually seeking new ways to scramble genres and come up with intriguing sonics. Less influenced by producers than by specific records, Kahne cites Public Enemy's *Fear of a Black Planet*, the first Talking Heads album, XTC's *Black Sea*, and Sly and the Family Stone's album *Fresh*, with "Family Affair" on it, as inspirations. And Bartók's *Concerto for Orchestra*.

"Those are records that make me feel like getting up in the morning," Kahne says. "People think you're acting highbrow if you mention Bartók, but that piece makes you realize the infinitude of your task."

Born November 21, 1947, in Sacramento, California, Kahne is an Air Force brat. He entered music via the banjo, then learned to play piano, guitar, and bass. He studied bass and took a course in harmony at Cal State Sacramento. He worked in various bands in Texas and Sacramento and, in the mid-'70s, recorded for Capitol as part of Voudouris and Kahne.

At the end of the decade, "the artist thing fell apart like bad meat," and Kahne got into production on the ground floor, answering phones at Wally Heider's studio in San Francisco. "At night, I would listen to tapes and practice recording them," he says. "Then I started bringing bands in and demoing them in my spare time."

Among them was Pearl Harbour and the Explosions, a popabilly outfit from the Bay Area. Howie Klein put out their first single, "Drivin'," on the independent label 415 Records. When that became a regional hit, all the major labels that had turned it down originally came sniffing around Kahne again. He wound up going to Warner Bros. to produce the band's first album. "The only problem was, they made me recut stuff," he says. "Maybe the stuff I recorded in January wasn't real hi-fi, but it had this great spirit. I had to recut everything in September, and they [the band members] weren't friends anymore. It was ridiculous to recut those songs. From then on, I used demos whenever I could."

He wound up producing several key new wave bands for 415: Wire Train, Romeo Void, Rank and File, Translator. "Al Teller heard 'Everything That I'm Not' by Translator one morning, and loved it," says Kahne. Teller loved it even more when he learned it only cost $8,000 to produce—including Kahne's fee. That afternoon, when Teller heard Rank and File and discovered that Kahne had produced that too, Teller offered him a choice of jobs—with A&R Columbia or staff producer in L.A. Kahne took the Los Angeles job, but became eventually head of A&R at Columbia in 1992. The top position lasted until 1996, when he was fired. Among his numerous Columbia productions were several Fishbone records on Epic and the Bangles' *Different Light* (No. 2), which spawned the hit, "Walk Like an Egyptian" (No. 1).

His favorite productions are Romeo Void's *It's a Condition;* Greg Garing's *Alone,* an album on Paladin that ranks with the best of 1997; *Here's to the Ladies* by Tony Bennett; and *Truth and Soul* by Fishbone. Kahne says, "They seem like different expeditions to the top of different mountains. I think I got to the top on all four."

Regarding Garing's record, "Somebody said we should have called it 'Roy Orbital,' " Kahne says. Garing is a bluegrass player whose favorite band is Portishead, a moody, oddly jazzy British trip-hop band. "I made this looped-out bluegrass record," Kahne says of the Garing. "Technically, I made it kind of like a hip-hop record, but instead of making loops of the drums first, I made loops of his playing guitar, banjo, mandolin, and violin."

A thirtyish native of Erie, Pennsylvania, Garing played with Bill Monroe, so he's well-connected to old country styles. He also "sings great," says Kahne. "He's

got that swing ability in him. "I had never noticed how bluegrass and hip-hop use the same beat," he says. "They both imply 16th-note triplets really heavily, so when I put reggae beats and hip-hop beats underneath Garing, it was just like glue, it worked so well."

Another band he likes is Sugar Ray, whose hit 1997 album, *Floored,* he produced for Atlantic. The track "Fly" blends "hardcore guitar with hip-hop, and there's a rapper on it named Supercat," Kahne says. "It's just a combination of many elements that came together perfectly."

He enjoys working with Imogen Heap, "an amazing piano player and writer" whose album he produced for Almo. Kahne reworked several tracks Heap had recorded with former Eurythmic Dave Stewart (see entry). In her late teens, Heap is "100 percent musical, the way she listens. She can hear something once and do it back at you."

Besides being a fan of raw talent, Kahne also appreciates technology. "I record probably half my stuff on computer now," says Kahne, who's on his 18th computer. "I use a 32-track recorder, Mac-based. I like the SSL 9000 a lot. The program I use is called Logic Audio, which you can record on digitally. It's like recording onto a tape recorder, but when you bring the mikes in, you go to the audio interface on the computer rather than a tape machine. You've got separate tracks like on a regular analog machine, but once you're in the computer, you're digital, so you can do equalization and reverb and mixing and panning and level changes."

Besides a stunning library of samples, Kahne has stored several ballets on his Mac. One is based on *Peter Pan,* one on *The Hunchback of Notre Dame.* Another, *Vincristine,* was inspired by Jessica, Kahne's daughter, who died of cancer at age 6.

Vincristine is the generic name of the drug used to treat Jessica. The ballet is Kahne's way of grappling with his loss. In it, Vincristine is a goddess who can only tell the truth. "It's actually the name of the plant they make the drug from," Kahne says. "I figure cancer drugs are like the truth: If you don't get enough, they don't do you any good. If you get too much, they kill you."

—CARLO WOLFF

Archangel, Natalie: *Natalie Archangel,* Columbia, 1987.

Bangles: *All Over the Place,* Columbia, 1984 • "Hero Takes a Fall," Columbia, 1984 • *A Different Light,* Columbia, 1985 • "Manic Monday," Columbia, 1985 • "If She Knew What She Wants," Columbia, 1986 • "Walk Like An Egyptian," Columbia, 1986 • "Walking down Your Street," Columbia, 1987 • *Greatest Hits,* Columbia, 1990, 1995.

Bennett, Tony: *Steppin' Out,* Columbia, 1993 • *MTV Unplugged,* Columbia, 1994 • *Here's to the Ladies,* Columbia, 1995.

Collision: *Collision,* Chaos, 1992.

Colvin, Shawn: *Fat City,* Columbia, 1992 • *Cover Girl,* Columbia, 1994.

Dale, Dick: w/ the Del-Tones, *King of the Surf Guitar: The Best Of,* Rhino, 1989 • *Better Shred Than Dead: The Dick Dale Anthology,* Rhino, 1997.

Deacon Blue: *When the World Knows Your Name* (1 track), Columbia, 1989.

Fishbone: *Fishbone* (EP), Columbia, 1985 • *In Your Face,* Columbia, 1986 • *It's a Wonderful Life* (EP), Columbia, 1987 • *Truth and Soul,* Columbia, 1988 • "Sunless Saturday," Columbia, 1991 • *The Reality of My Surroundings,* Columbia, 1991 • *Fishbone 101: Nuttasaurusmeg Fossil Fuelin',* Sony, 1996.

Flourescein: *High Contrast Comedown,* No Name, 1997.

Garing, Greg: *Alone,* Paladin, 1997.

Heap, Imogen: *I Megaphone,* ALMO, 1998.

Hoffs, Susanna: "My Side of the Bed," Columbia, 1991 • *When You're a Boy,* Columbia, 1991.

Humans, The: *Happy Hour,* IRS, 1981.

Huxley, Parthenon: *Sunny Nights,* Columbia, 1988.

Kahn, Brenda: *Epiphany in Brooklyn,* Chaos/Columbia, 1992.

Kaukonen, Jorma: *Barbeque King,* RCA, 1980.

Lincoln: *Lincoln,* Slash, 1997.

Little Richard: "Rock Island Line," Columbia, 1988 (*Folkways: A Tribute to Woody Guthrie and Leadbelly*).

Love/Hate: *Blackout in the Red Room,* Columbia, 1990 • *Wasted in America,* Columbia, 1992.

Neville Brothers and Buddy Guy: "Born Under a Bad Sign," A&M, 1995 (*Things to Do in Denver When You're Dead* soundtrack).

Outfield, The: "My Paradise," Columbia, 1989 • "Voices of Babylon," Columbia, 1989 • *Voices of Babylon,* Columbia, 1989 • *Big Innings: The Best of the Outfield,* Sony, 1996.

Pearl Harbor and the Explosions: *Pearl Harbor and the Explosions,* Warner Bros., 1979, 1980.

Presidents of the U.S.A.: *Presidents of the United States,* Columbia, 1995.

Rank and File: *Sundown,* Slash, 1982 • "The Conductor Wore Black," Slash, 1983 (*Slash: The Early Sessions*).

Red Rockers: "Dead Heroes," Posh Boy, 1981 (*Rodney on the ROQ,* Vol. 2) • "China," 415/Columbia, 1983 • *Good as Gold,* 415/Columbia, 1983.

Romeo Void: *It's a Condition,* 415/Columbia, 1981 • "A Girl in Trouble (Is a Temporary Thing)," 415/Columbia, 1984 • *Instincts,* 415/Columbia, 1984 • *Warm in Your Coat,* Legacy, 1992.

Soul Coughing: *Irresistable Bliss* (9 tracks), Slash/WB, 1996 • "Super Bon Bon," Slash/WB, 1996 • "Soft Serve," Slash/WB, 1997.

Sublime: *Sublime,* MCA, 1996 • "Doin' Time," Gasoline Alley/MCA, 1997 • *What I Got* (EP), MCA, 1997.

Sugar Ray: *Floored,* Lava/Atlantic, 1997 • "Fly," Lava/Atlantic, 1997 • "RPM," Lava/Atlantic, 1997.

Sweet, Matthew: *Inside,* Columbia, 1986.

Tashan: "Love Is Forever," Chaos, 1993 • *For the Sake of Love,* Chaos, 1994.

Translator: *Heartbeats and Triggers,* 415/Columbia, 1982 • *No Time Like Now,* 415/Columbia, 1983 • *Everywhere That We Were: The Best Of,* Legacy, 1996.

Wire Train: *In a Chamber,* 415/Columbia, 1984 • *Last Perfect Thing: A Retrospective,* Legacy, 1996.

Gary Katz

G ary Katz produced the entire recorded output of Steely Dan, rated by audiophiles and production experts as among the highest-fidelity and best-produced records in the history of tape recording. His role in the production of these recordings was primarily organizational, inspirational, and logistical, leaving the musical decisions up to the principal members of the group, Walter Becker and Donald Fagen (see entry), and the recording and technical decisions to a team of the best engineers available, including Elliot Scheiner, Al Schmidt (see entries), and Roger Nichols.

Before Steely Dan was even a group, Katz was the A&R man who got Fagen and Becker their first job as songwriters for a publishing company. (Those song demos are available on several bootleg recordings, most prominently a two-CD set being sold by Catalyst Records without the band's permission.) When they had difficulty selling their songs to other artists, Katz suggested Becker and Fagen form a band of their own, and he got them their deal with ABC/Dunhill.

The work of the Katz-Becker-Fagen team is discussed in more detail under the entry in this volume for Becker and Fagen. Singly and in combination, Katz, Becker, and Fagen have continued to produce records, but most of the efforts have been relatively undistinguished. The most likely interpretation is that the trio brought a special chemistry to their records that could not be duplicated unless all the members were in place—not unlike the Beatles and George Martin.

However, Katz has had a role in some fine work by Dirk Hamilton, Laura Nyro, and the outrageous Root Boy Slim and His Sex Change Band, in addition to recent groove-oriented music by the Brand New Heavies and the Groove Collective. —DANIEL J. LEVITIN

Alarm, The: *Electric Folklore: Live,* IRS, 1989.

Brady, Paul: *Trick or Treat,* Fontana, 1991.

Cocker, Joe: *Civilized Man,* Capitol, 1984.

Eye to Eye: *Eye to Eye,* Automatic/Warner Bros., 1982 • *Shakespeare Stole My Baby,* Warner Bros., 1983.

Fagen, Donald: *The Nightfly,* Warner Bros., 1983 • "Century's End," Warner Bros., 1988.

Groove Collective: *Groove Collective,* Reprise, 1994 • "Nerd," Reprise, 1994 • "Whatchugot," Reprise, 1994.

Hamilton, Dirk: *You Can Sing on the Left,* ABC, 1976.

Harris, Hugh: *Words for Our Years,* Capitol, 1989.

House, James: *James House,* Atlantic, 1983.

Jordan, Marc: *Mannequin,* Warner Bros., 1978.

Kaye, Thomas Jefferson: *First Grade,* ABC, 1974 • *Thomas Jefferson Kaye,* ABC, 1976.

Lode: *Legs and Arms,* Geffen, 1996.

Love and Money: "Halleluiah Man," Mercury, 1989 • *Strange Kind of Love,* Fontana, 1989.

Mayfield, Curtis, and the Repercussions: "Let's Do It Again," Warner Bros., 1994 (*A Tribute to Curtis Mayfield*).

Nyro, Laura: *Walk the Dog and Light the Light,* Columbia, 1993 • *Stoned Soul Picnic: The Best of Laura Nyro,* Legacy, 1997.

Raw Stylus: "Believe in Me," Geffen, 1995 • *Pushing Against the Flow,* Geffen, 1995.

Repercussions, The: *Earth and Heaven,* Warner Bros., 1995.

Root Boy Slim and His Sex Change Band: *Root Boy Slim and His Sex Change Band,* Illegal/Warner Bros., 1978.

Ross, Diana: *Ross,* RCA, 1983 • *Greatest Hits: The RCA Years,* RCA, 1997.

Sanborn, David: "The Finer Things," Warner Bros., 1983 (*The King of Comedy* soundtrack).

Sanchez, Roger: *S-Man Classics: The Essential Sanchez Mixes,* Harmless, 1998.

Schlosser, Billy and Lisa: *Wake Up the Neighbors,* MCA, 1988.

Steely Dan: *You Gotta Walk It Like You Talk It (or You'll Lose That Beat)* soundtrack, Visa, 1971 • *Can't Buy a Thrill,* ABC, 1972 • "Do It Again," ABC, 1972 • *Countdown to Ecstasy,* ABC, 1973 • "Reeling in the Years," ABC, 1973 • *Pretzel Logic,* ABC, 1974 • "Rikki Don't Lose That Number," ABC, 1974 • "Black Friday," ABC, 1975 • *Katy Lied,* ABC, 1975 • *The Royal Scam,* ABC, 1976 • *Aja,* ABC, 1977 • "Deacon Blues," ABC, 1978 • "FM (No Static At All)," MCA, 1978 • "Josie," ABC, 1978 • "Peg," ABC, 1978 • *Gaucho,* MCA, 1980 • "Hey Nineteen," MCA, 1980 • "Time out of Mind," MCA, 1981 • *Gold,* MCA, 1982, 1991 • *A Decade of Steely Dan,* MCA, 1985, 1996 • *Citizen Steely Dan,* MCA, 1993.

Swinging Streaks: *Southside of the Sky,* Capricorn, 1993.

Vela, Rosie: *Zazu,* A&M, 1986.

Matthew King Kaufman

As owner and chief producer at Beserkley Records from the mid-'70s through the mid-'80s, Matthew King Kaufman created one of the coolest indie labels and helped create some of the finest power pop of all time. On a shoestring he produced or co-produced (with engineer Glen Kolotkin and Kenny Laguna; see entry) enduring albums by Earth Quake (*Rocking the World,* 8.5), Jonathan Richman—with and without the Modern Lovers—(*Jonathan Richman and the Modern Lovers, Rock and Roll with the Modern Lovers, Modern Lovers Live*), the Rubinoos (*The Rubinoos, Back to the Drawing Board*), and most popularly, Greg Kihn (*Greg Kihn Again, Rockihnroll, Kihnspiracy*). In addition, he co-produced and compiled one of rock's great collections, *Beserkley Chartbusters,* with hits by all of the above artists.

Born in 1946 and raised in Baltimore, Kaufman graduated from law school but never took the bar exam. Instead, he went to California to co-manage (with Allan Mason) the San Francisco rock band Earth Quake. Convinced they were to be the next Beatles, Kaufman helped the band get a two-record deal with A&M in 1970 and hung around the label picking up production tips from some of the greats, including Lou Adler and Glyn Johns (see entries).

After a few years Kaufman became frustrated with what he felt was A&M's ineptitude at marketing a hard rock band. "Earth Quake wasn't quite as good as another band on the label—Free—and A&M couldn't even break them. I told the band that A&M didn't understand them, and that we could do better on our own," he says.

There was one small problem: money. "I was watching TV late one night in 1973, and Reverend Ike came on and said, 'A guy drives by in a Cadillac and you can either love him or curse at him. If you curse at him, you're never going to get a Cadillac.' I loved it—this power of positive thinking line—and I wanted to encourage it, so I sent the man $10.

"A little later, I got back in the mail this cheap red cloth cut out with pinking shears, which was supposed to be a prayer cloth. The note with it said, 'Put this in your mailbox and money will show up.' I figured, 'What the hell' and put it in my mailbox.

"That night I was staring at Alcatraz and it turned

into the Beserkley Records logo. A line from a Gene McDaniels song—'I'm at the point of no return / And for me there'll be no turning back'—popped into my brain, and I knew I had to start my own label and call it 'Beserkley.' As it turned out, a snippet of an Earth Quake song had been used in the movie *The Getaway*. The snippet was vital because they used it to show that two different scenes were going on at the same time. The film's music director, Quincy Jones [see entry], hadn't cleared the rights with us. He sent me four or five times what this little snippet was worth just to shut me up. This check for $1,100 showed up three days after I put the prayer cloth in my mailbox. I had no idea that this money was on its way," he states.

The strangeness continued. "I cashed the check and took the money down to the track. By the end of that day I had $3,400, which covered the production budget for both Earth Quake's live album and *Chartbusters*. That's how we started."

From 1973 to 1975 Beserkley put out singles (assembled into *Chartbusters* in 1975). The first was Earth Quake's great dueling-guitar (Robbie Dunbar, Gary Phillips) version of the Easybeats' (see Vanda and Young entry) "Friday on My Mind"—for years a weekend kick-off staple at rock stations throughout the country. John Doukas's thick, powerful voice captures a feverish hedonism that was missing from both the original and David Bowie's (see entry) *Pinups* version.

Kaufman recalls, "96 percent of my production work was done before we entered the studio. I was with them in the rehearsal hall every day. Every part was worked out in advance. I didn't have the kind of budget to 'create' in the studio. But I never scrimped on the studio. We used CBS Studios on Folsom Street in San Francisco. The most important aspect of a studio is the microphones. CBS had great mike selection and all the effects you could need," he says.

All of that preparation allowed Kaufman to get the job done quickly. "I've never had a hit that wasn't a first take. The first take has the most feeling; after that you find yourself thinking about it rather than just doing it. The audience reacts to music on a very gut level: either they like it or they don't. That 'like' is formed from a lot of subconscious conclusions, and one of them is 'Is this person feeling it enough?'

"To record 'Roadrunner,' it took the 3 minutes and 35 seconds for the performance, about another 30 minutes to dump the background vocals on, and another 90 minutes to mix it," says proudly, referring to the classic Jonathan Richman single. The first version of "Roadrunner" (called "Roadrunner Once") had been produced by John Cale (see entry) for Warner Bros. in 1972,

but not released. (Beserkley subsequently licensed Cale's tapes and released them as the *The Modern Lovers* album in 1976.) Kaufman produced the second version ("Roadrunner Twice") and released the two versions together as a single in 1977, which reached an astonishing No. 11 in the U.K.

Kaufman's version of the song lacks the electric drive of the original, but it captures childlike wonder as well as anything ever recorded; Richman positively squirms with delight as the late-night open road stretches before him and the radio plays. His heart leaps out to fill all of the open space as stars wink in the black-ice sky.

"Jonathan was so prolific it was frightening," Kaufman says. "My problem with him was eliminating songs, not waiting for him to write good songs. My favorite session with Jonathan was 'Egyptian Reggae' (No. 5 U.K.). We came up with this idea of recording the whole song in the echo chamber in the bowels of the CBS studio. It smelled in there, but it was a great session. Glen Kolotkin is a great engineer—and he made it sound like a grown-up record."

Beserkley's purest pop came from the Rubinoos, a young Berkeley band. Jon Rubin's lead vocal on the band's cover of Tommy James and the Shondells' "I Think We're Alone Now," achieves an aching emotional vulnerability. The way he hangs on to the first line—"Children beha-a-ve"—simultaneously absorbs and mocks every humiliating parental slight ever directed at a teen. Besides "Alone," the first Rubinoos album is graced with excellent originals by guitarist/songwriter Tommy Dunbar (younger brother of Earth Quake's Robbie Dunbar), including the peppy "Leave My Heart Alone," the sprightly neo-soul of "Hard to Get," and the Raspberries-like rocker "Rock and Roll Is Dead."

Power-pop great "I Wanna Be Your Boyfriend" was the lead single from the band's second album, 1978's *Back to the Drawing Board*. Recalls Kaufman, " 'Boyfriend' [recorded in England] was played on the BBC more than any other record I had ever done, and just then all of these kids were buying Sex Pistols records and didn't want to hear boy-next-door rock. It was my biggest heartbreak. You miss by a day, you miss by a year, you miss," he philosophizes.

Kaufman didn't miss with Greg Kihn. Kihn, like Kaufman from Baltimore, moved to Berkeley in 1974 and sang backup on Earth Quake and Richman records before forming his own band. His second album, *Kihn Again*, contains a fine Byrds-ish version of Bruce Springsteen's "For You" and a stomping version of Buddy Holly's "Love's Made a Fool of You" (powered by lead guitarist Dave Carpenter).

Every subsequent Kihn album charted. *Rockihnroll* (1981) contains Kihn's breakthrough single, "The Breakup Song (They Don't Write 'Em)" (No. 15)—an exceptional midway point between Buddy Holly of the '50s and the Gin Blossoms of the '90s. Led by the relentless, clavinet-driven single "Jeopardy" (No. 2), *Kihnspiracy* shocked the world by reaching No. 15 in 1983.

Kaufman licensed the Beserkley catalog to Rhino in 1986 and took an extended siesta. The bear came out of hibernation in 1993 under the new name of "S.O.B." ("Son of Beserkley"), with records by the Uptones, Hobo, and Linda Brady. On the Fourth of July, 1998, S.O.B. transmogrified into Cyberphonics, with artists Stiff Richards and Engorged with Blood. Kaufman is married to veteran music journalist Jaan Uhelszki, a founding editor of *Creem* and the on-line music mag *Addicted to Noise.* —ERIC OLSEN

Earth Quake: *Why Don't You Try Me?*, A&M, 1972 • *Live*, Beserkley, 1975 • *Rocking the World*, Beserkley, 1975 • *8.5*, Beserkley, 1976 • *Leveled*, Beserkley, 1977 • *Two Years in a Padded Cell*, Beserkley, 1979.

Garcia, Jerry: *A Talk with Jerry Garcia*, S.O.B., 1996.

Hobo: *Hobo*, S.O.B., 1976, 1993.

Hyts: *Hyts*, Gold Mountain, 1989.

Kihn, Greg: *Greg Kihn*, Beserkley, 1976 • *Greg Kihn Again*, Beserkley, 1977 • *Next of Kihn*, Beserkley, 1978 • *With the Naked Eye*, Beserkley, 1979 • *Glass House Rock*, Beserkley, 1980 • *Rockihnroll*, Beserkley, 1981 • *Kihntinued*, Beserkley, 1982 • *Kihnspiracy*, Beserkley, 1983 • "Love Never Fails," Beserkley, 1983 • *Kihntagious*, Beserkley, 1984 • "Boys Won't Leave the Girls Alone," EMI America, 1985 • *Citizen Kihn*, EMI America, 1985 • "Lucky," EMI America, 1985 • "Love and Rock and Roll," EMI America, 1986 • *Kihnsolidation: The Best Of*, Rhino, 1989.

Greg Kihn Band: "The Breakup Song," Beserkley, 1981 • "Jeopardy," Beserkley, 1983.

Modern Lovers: *Live*, Beserkley, 1978.

Repulsa: *Repulsa*, S.O.B., 1994.

Richman, Jonathan, and the Modern Lovers: *Jonathan Richman and the Modern Lovers*, Beserkley, 1976 • *Rock and Roll with the Modern Lovers*, Beserkley, 1977 • *Back in Your Life*, Beserkley, 1979 • *Beserkley Years*, Rhino, 1987.

Rubinoos, The: "The Rubinoos," Beserkley, 1977 • *Back to the Drawing Board*, Beserkley, 1979 • *Garage Sale*, Big Deal, 1994.

Spitballs: *The Spitballs*, Beserkley, 1978.

Stiff Richards: *Stiff Richards*, S.O.B., 1996.

Tyla Gang: *Moonproof*, Beserkley, 1978.

Uptones, The: *Live*, S.O.B., 1995.

COLLECTIONS

Beserk Times, Beserkley, 1978.

Chartbusters: The Best of Beserkley, Beserkley/Rhino, 1975, 1986: Earth Quake, "Friday on My Mind," "Hit the Floor," "Madness," "Tall Order for a Short Guy," ˇ Greg Kihn, "All the Right Reasons," "Mood Mood Number," ˇ Jonathan Richman, "Government Center," "It Will Stand," "Roadrunner," "The New Teller" ˇ The Rubinoos, "I Think We're Alone Now," "I Wanna Be Your Boyfriend."

Lenny Kaye

Lenny Kaye is an inveterate New York scenester who has contributed significantly to rock 'n' roll history as a music critic and historian, musician, songwriter, and producer. Kaye is best known as the guitarist of the Patti Smith Group, one of the most important punk–new wave bands of the '70s. He has also produced or co-produced exceptional albums by Suzanne Vega (*Suzanne Vega*, No. 11 U.K.; *Solitude Standing*, No. 11), James (*Stutter*), Soul Asylum (*Hang Time*, with Ed Stasium; see entry), and Kristen Hersh (*Hips and Makers*, No. 7 U.K.) and compiled and annotated the classic '60s psychedelia collection *Nuggets*.

Born in New York and raised in New Brunswick, New Jersey, Kaye grew up with rock 'n' roll. In 1966 he cut a single under the pseudonym Link Cromwell for Hollywood Records (not the current Disney-owned label) called "Crazy Like a Fox" with the help of his uncle, who wrote the song. "It gave me a concrete validation of my identity. I had a single out there; it didn't do anything, but hey man, I was a rock guy. It gave me a sense that being part of the music wasn't some vague thing," he says.

He then started a garage band called the Zoo in New Brunswick. In the early '70s Kaye worked at Village Oldies in NYC and established his name as a writer and critic. In 1972 he put together one of the all-time best collections, *Nuggets*, wherein he assembled and discussed '60s garage-psychedelic classics by the Electric Prunes, the Standells, the Strangeloves, the Knickerbockers, the Seeds, and many others. His perceptive liner notes conclude with this paragraph:

"*Nuggets* has been designed primarily as a listening album; and whether you want to use it to remember that bittersweet moment when you first decided to let your hair grow/take up a picket sign/wonder what a deadly toke would feel like, or just welcome yourself into some surprisingly fine and memorable music, well, that's 'your trip.' I just hope you have as much fun letting it spin as I had putting it together."

His love and respect for the music is evident. Kaye wrote an article for *Jazz & Pop* magazine called "The Best of A Cappella" (anthologized in *The Penguin Book of Rock and Roll Writing*), which a young poet named Patti Smith read. She called to congratulate Kaye on the article, and shortly thereafter he began to back her poetry performances with a bit of *musique concrete* on guitar, beginning February 10, 1971, when he joined her at St. Mark's Church.

"Much to our surprise it began developing into a real musical concept as it went on," recalls Kaye. "By the mid-'70s it became an actual rock 'n' roll band [with Richard Sohl on piano, Ivan Kral on guitar and bass, and Jay Dee Daugherty on drums], which was surprising considering where we came from." They played regularly at legendary clubs like Max's Kansas City and CBGB, and became the artistic center of a scene that included the Ramones, Blondie, Television, and the Talking Heads.

The band's first album, *Horses* (produced by John Cale; see entry), a landmark fusion of poetry and rock 'n' roll, pushed them to the vanguard of the punk–new wave movement. Kaye played guitar and co-wrote songs with Smith on three more albums in the '70s (*Radio Ethiopia, Easter, Wave*), before Smith retired in 1980 to raise a family with her husband, ex-MC5 guitarist Fred "Sonic" Smith (who died in 1994). In 1996 Kaye played on, and co-produced (with Malcolm Burn; see entry) Smith's return album *Gone Again*.

In 1980 Kaye formed his own band, the Lenny Kaye Connection, and played around New York, recording one album in 1984. He also played with Jim Carroll and Eugene Chadborne. He continued writing for such publications as *Rolling Stone* and *Creem,* and got seriously into production in 1985 with New York neo-folkie Suzanne Vega's first album (co-produced with Steve Addabbo). Vega's light, clear voice gives artistic distance to her closely observed vignettes of city life, with echoes of performance artist Laurie Anderson and Laura Nyro. Kaye and Addabbo also produced Vega's commercial breakthrough, *Solitude Standing,* with the scintillating anti–child abuse standard "Luka" (No. 3), and the a cappella "Tom's Diner" (later remixed by D.N.A. with a hip-hop beat).

Kaye sees his various musical hats as a hedge against boredom. "When I get to the point where I'm not surprising myself anymore, I move to a parallel field," he says. "Sometimes you watch your star rise and fall, and

rather than get anxious about that, I look at it as a positive thing that moves you into different areas. You have to go through a lot of different things to grow.

"People always say to me, 'Do you find any conflict between being a writer and a musician?' When I'm writing a great paragraph, or watching an overdub make a song suddenly come to life in an unexpected way, or if I'm taking a really nice guitar solo that has a life of its own, I feel the same way. The burst of creative fire is the same sensation. I try not to divide these things. I think too often we compartmentalize life. The music business likes to have things compartmentalized for easier marketing," he says.

Kaye's approach to making an album very much reflects his career philosophy. "I like to have a lot of different styles within an album because that means an artist has a chance to move into whatever his next album will be, and it'll make sense. I don't believe in monochromatic records. I like to have a song with a little string quartet next to a piece of avant noise. Also, I've never been one for pure music; I like mongrel music where styles copulate with each other and form some weird child that sounds different. I have always liked that sense of possibility where you can put this weird element into something and all of a sudden everything spins."

Besides working with Smith again, Kaye is a contributing editor to the on-line rock magazine *Addicted to Noise.* In early 1998 Warner Books published *Waylon: An Autobiography,* co-authored by Waylon Jennings and Kaye. —ERIC OLSEN AND DAVID JOHN FARINELLA

Beautiful South: "Love Wars," Elektra, 1990 (*Rubaiyat: Elektra's 40th Anniversary*).

Berryhill, Cindy Lee: *Naked Movie Star,* Rhino, 1989.

D.N.A., featuring Suzanne Vega: "Tom's Diner" (remix), A&M, 1990.

Ginsberg, Allen: *The Ballad of the Skeletons* (EP), Mouth Almighty, 1996.

Hersh, Kristin: *Hips and Makers,* Reprise, 1994 • *Strings* (EP), 4 A.D., 1994.

Holcomb, Robin: *Robin Holcomb,* Elektra, 1990.

James: *Stutter,* Sire, 1986.

Kowanko, Chris: *Kowanko,* Morgan Creek, 1993.

Lenny Kaye Connection: *I've Got a Right,* Giorno Poetry Systems, 1984.

Malone, Michelle, and Drag the River: *Relentless,* Arista, 1990.

Shams: *Quilt,* Matador, 1992.

Smith, Patti: "Piss Factory," Mer, 1974 • *Gone Again,* Arista, 1996 • *Masters,* Arista, 1996.

Soul Asylum: *Hang Time,* A&M, 1988.

10,000 Maniacs: "These Days," Elektra, 1990 (*Rubaiyat: Elektra's 40th Anniversary*).

Vega, Suzanne: *Suzanne Vega*, A&M, 1985 • "Luka," A&M, 1987 • "Solitude Standing," A&M, 1987 • *Solitude Standing*, A&M, 1987 • "Tom's Diner," A&M, 1990.

Winter Hours: *Winter Hours*, Chrysalis, 1989.

COLLECTIONS

Elektrock, Elektra, 1985.

Nuggets: Original Artyfacts from the First Psychedelic Era, Sire, 1972, 1976.

Bob Keane

B ob Keane is an archetypal Southern California figure. His fascinating career in music extends over 60 years, from his days as a child prodigy jazz clarinetist in the '30s, to his ownership of Del-Fi Records (and subsidiaries Donna, Mustang, Bronco and Edsel) in the '50s and '60s, to Del-Fi's resurrection in the '90s. Keane has played, produced, or released great music from his own big band jazz to Sam Cooke, Ritchie Valens, and the Bobby Fuller Four.

In addition, Keane's famous open-door policy at Del-Fi helped fuel the SoCal surf music boom in the early '60s and inaugurate the careers of such future notables as Frank Zappa (see entry), David Gates (Bread), Leon Russell, Arthur Lee (Love), Glen Campbell, the Versatiles (Fifth Dimension), and Barry White.

Bob Keane was born Robert Kuhn in Manhattan Beach, California, on January 5, 1922, to a family that built homes along the coast from Palos Verdes to El Segundo. Keane began playing clarinet at age 7 and continued on the instrument when the family moved to Mexico City for three years. (His father was an engineer who was contracted to help build the Pan-American Highway.)

Back in L.A., Keane performed with the Los Angeles Philharmonic Orchestra at age 14. At 16, he started his own dance band; within the year Keane's band was hired as the opening act for a remote radio broadcast, and when the headliner canceled at the last minute, the band performed live over KFWB. The next day an MCA talent agent called Keane and offered to promote him as "The World's Youngest Band Leader," an offer he accepted. Seeking the best, Keane often snuck down to the Central District to play with black musicians like Nat "King" Cole and members of Duke Ellington's

band. Keane was offered a music scholarship to USC, but then World War II interrupted many a plan and Keane enlisted in the Air Force as an aviation cadet.

After the war Keane re-formed his band and became very popular up and down the West Coast. Keane recorded for Gene Norman's GNP label and even fronted Artie Shaw's band when the clarinet giant took a year off. By the '50s Keane was walking where the big shoes tread: hosting a TV variety show in L.A., conducting his 12-piece orchestra on NBC's *Hank McCune Show*, even dating a young Lana Turner. Keane took up the pseudonym "Keene" (changed to "Keane" around 1970) when the announcer on the McCune show mispronounced "Kuhn" as "Coon"—an epithet not to be hurled lightly in 1951.

But by the mid-'50s rock 'n' roll and R&B were replacing big band in the hearts of the young and Keane could smell a new wind blowing. In early 1957, one of his fans, John Siamas, from a wealthy family of Greek aircraft parts manufacturers, approached Keane about starting a company to record pop versions of Greek standards. Keane sensed that this concept was not necessarily the path to fortune and said so; at which point Siamas asked Keane if he knew any black musicians. He did, and thus began Keen Records.

The deal was that Keane would find and record talent, Siamas would put up the money, and they would split the profits evenly. Bumps Blackwell (see entry) had lost Little Richard to gospel and was now trying to return the favor by leading gospel singer Sam Cooke into pop. Specialty Records owner Art Rupe strongly disapproved of the move and released Cooke from his contract. Blackwell took Cooke to Keen, and in the summer of 1957 they released the smash hit "You Send Me."

But all Keane got out of the deal was the recording equipment Siamas had purchased for him. Keane sued but never got his half of the royalties because the agreement was oral. With the equipment from Keen and $2,500 from another investor, Keane started Del-Fi—named after the Greek oracle of inspiration, because, as his wife (a former comedienne) remarked, "You just got fucked by Greeks."

Del-Fi found success immediately with a recording of "Caravan" by pianist Henri Rose, which dominated the L.A. airwaves through the Christmas season. Warner Bros. was just starting a record division, and they purchased Rose's contract (and an album to be recorded by Keane) for $8,000; Keane bought out his partner and set sail alone.

Keane was having his new business cards made up when the salesman told him about a 15-year-old kid from Pacoima known as the "Little Richard of the San

Fernando Valley." His name was Ritchie Valenzuela. Keane went out to Pacoima that Saturday and watched the kid do a 15-minute set before a matinee at a movie theater. "He was up there with a little amplifier just banging away when I walked in and everyone was jumping up and down. He had complete control of the audience. Ritchie was like a young bull: humble yet very powerful. That's what I saw when I went in the movie theater," Keane says.

And not what he saw when he watched Lou Diamond Phillips portray Valens in *La Bamba* (1987). "He played Ritchie like a whiny mama's boy in that movie, which was about 25 percent accurate. But what the hell, it brought Ritchie back into the public's mind."

Keane and Valens (shortened at Keane's request) made a great team. Valens was full of energy, charisma, and ideas; the Spanish-speaking, veteran musician Keane was able to relate to Valens personally and culturally and shape his ideas into songs. Keane used his growing knowledge of the studio (the recording equipment was in his Silverlake home) to create "Donna" (No. 2) in his basement. Keane's innovation was to match the voice recording with a copy of itself milliseconds apart, thereby spreading and thickening the vocal sound across the listener's ears—the technique of "doubling" used to this day.

Valens' rockers were recorded at Hollywood's Gold Star studios with professional jazz and R&B musicians; the combination of Ritchie's raw vocals and wild reverbed guitar with the musicians' solid grooves made classics out of "Come On, Let's Go" and "La Bamba" (No. 22), and inspired generations of Mexican Americans (from Chan Romero to Los Lobos) to take up arms and rock out in a Latino mode.

Ritchie's death, with Buddy Holly and the Big Bopper in a plane crash in early 1959, devastated Keane personally and nearly killed the label. But he soldiered on, and his open-door policy generated over 500 singles of every stripe, including 17 Top 50 national hits by the likes of Chan Romero (the classic "Hippy, Hippy Shake"), Ron Holden ("Love You So," No. 7), Little Caesar and the Romans ("Those Oldies but Goodies," No. 9), Bobby Curtola ("Fortune Teller"), and teen actor Johnny Crawford ("Cindy's Birthday," No. 8; "Rumors," No. 12).

Says Keane, "If I heard something I liked, I'd either buy it from them if they'd already cut it or go into the studio and redo it or change it around. That's how I picked up David Gates and Leon Russell: they had just arrived from Oklahoma. Barry White walked in one day and Frank Zappa another with his doo-wop stuff. That's how we did it. If I liked it, I put it out."

But it was the surf and hot rod instrumentals by the likes of the Centurians ("Bullwinkle Part II"), the Lively Ones ("Surf Rider"), the Sentinels, the Impacts, Bruce Johnston's (later of the Beach Boys) Surfing Band, and the Darts (with lead guitarist Glen Campbell) that established Del-Fi as the indigenous L.A. label. The surf tunes, with their throbbing rhythm and supercharged picked electric guitar or sax leads, are party music galore and a pure recapitulation of the feelings generated by contact with the wet, the waves, and the wild of the sea. Hence, their timelessness.

Del-Fi had its own studio as part of its offices near Hollywood and Vine, and was technically ahead of its time from Keane's Valens innovations to "the first transistorized 8-track 300 Ampex deck in the city" in the mid-'60s. That's where the Bobby Fuller Four, Keane's last great discovery, recorded.

Fuller was a Buddy Holly fanatic from El Paso who came to Del-Fi in 1963 with some good material but no single that Keane could hear. Fuller came back over a year later with "Keep On Dancing," which Keane helped transform into "Let Her Dance" (with Keane himself tapping his way into percussive history on a Coke bottle), wherein they married the "La Bamba" beat to Fuller's (Hollyesque) West Texas tenor drawl and somehow made the hybrid work. Fuller's next hit was one of rock 'n' roll's greatest recordings, "I Fought the Law" (No. 9).

"Law" announces its arrival with a classic drum breakdown, followed by monumental hand claps and the best-recorded rhythm guitar (played by Fuller) of the '60s. Fuller's clean, clear vocals find the perfect balance between defiance and resignation on (Holly guitarist) Sonny Curtis's story of desperate action, retribution, and lost love. Unfortunately, the real world was again crueler than fiction: in July 1966 Fuller was found in his mother's car, covered in gasoline and blood and dead from asphyxiation. The case is unsolved.

This final tragedy was too much; combined with the change from a singles-based industry to a (much more expensive) album-based industry, it drove Keane out of the business. He got divorced, raised three sons (two of whom performed as the Keane Brothers, and at 12 and 13 had their own national TV show in the summer of 1977), and golfed.

La Bamba renewed interest in Valens, and *Pulp Fiction* (with "Bullwinkle" and "Surf Rider") in 1994 solidified interest in Del-Fi's surf classics. Now Keane has reissued most of his material on a series of excellent CDs, and Del-Fi is a sporty presence on the World Wide Web (www.delfi.com). Not bad for an old clarinetist. —ERIC OLSEN

Addrisi Brothers: "Cherrystone," Del-Fi, 1959 • *Cherrystone,* Del-Fi, 1997.

Ahbez, Eden: *Eden's Island: The Music of an Enchanted Isle,* Del-Fi, 1960, 1995.

Bobby Fuller Four: "I Fought the Law," Mustang, 1966 • "Let Her Dance," Mustang, 1966 • "Love's Made a Fool of You," Mustang, 1966 • *The Best Of,* Rhino, 1990 • *The Bobby Fuller Four,* Mustang/Del Fi, 1994 • *Shakedown! The Texas Tapes Revisited,* Del Fi, 1996.

Bright, Larry: *Shake That Thing,* Del-Fi, 1997.

Bruce Johnston Surfing Band: *Surfer's Pajama Party,* Del-Fi, 1994.

Centurians, The: *Bullwinkle Part II,* Del-Fi, 1964, 1995 • "Bullwinkle Part II," MCA, 1994 (*Pulp Fiction* soundtrack).

Crawford, Johnny: "Cindy's Birthday," Del-Fi, 1962 • "Rumors," Del-Fi, 1962 • "Your Nose Is Gonna Grow," Del-Fi, 1962 • "Proud," Del-Fi, 1963.

Curtola, Bobby: "Fortune Teller," Del-Fi, 1962.

Darts, The: *Hollywood Drag,* Del-Fi, 1964.

Defenders, The: *Drag Beat,* Del-Fi, 1964.

Deuce Coupes: *Hotrodder's Choice,* Del-Fi, 1963.

Holden, Ron: "Love You So," Donna, 1960 • *Love You So,* Del-Fi, 1994.

Impacts, The: *Wipe Out!* Del-Fi, 1994.

Keene, Bob: *Big Band Bash,* Americana, 1951 • *Bob Keene,* GNP, 1954 • *Stringin' Along,* Andex, 1957 • *Unforgettable Love Songs of the 50's,* Del-Fi, 1995.

Keene, Verrill: *An Afternoon Affair,* Del-Fi, 1967, 1996.

Little Caesar and the Romans: "Those Oldies but Goodies (Remind Me of You)," Del-Fi, 1961.

Lively Ones: *Great Surf Hits,* Del-Fi, 1963 • *Surf Drums,* Del-Fi, 1963 • *Surf Rider,* Del-Fi, 1963 • *This Is Surf City,* Del-Fi, 1963 • *Surfin' South of the Border,* Del-Fi, 1994 • *Hang Five! The Best Of,* Del-Fi, 1995.

Myers, Dave, and the Surftones: *Hangin' Twenty,* Del-Fi, 1963, 1994.

Romancers, The: *The Slauson Shuffle,* Del-Fi, 1995.

Romero, Chan: "Hippy, Hippy Shake," Del-Fi, 1959 • *Hippy, Hippy Shake,* Del-Fi, 1995.

Ronnie and Pomona Casuals: *Everybody Jerk,* Del-Fi, 1964, 1995.

Sentinals, The: *Big Surf,* Del-Fi, 1994.

Taylor, Felice: "I Feel Love Comin' On," Mustang, 1967 • "It May Be Winter Outside," Mustang, 1967.

Valens, Ritchie: "Come On, Let's Go," Del-Fi, 1958 • "Donna," Del-Fi, 1958 • "La Bamba," Del-Fi, 1958 • *The History of Ritchie Valens,* Rhino, 1981 • "La Bamba '87," Original Sound, 1987 • *The Ritchie Valens Story,* Rhino, 1993 • *Rockin' All Night: The Very Best Of,* Del-Fi, 1995.

COLLECTIONS

Del-Fi Record Hop, Del-Fi, 1960.

Big Surf Hits, Del-Fi, 1964.

Sun and Surf, Cars and Guitars, Del-Fi, 1994.

Hellbound Hotrods, Del-Fi, 1995.

Pulp Surfin', Donna, 1995.

Wild Surf! Del-Fi, 1996.

John Keane

Georgia native John Keane is a self-taught, thoughtful sound shaper. "I favor rootsier-type bands and I like organic sounds, as opposed to electronic, synthesized-type music," Keane says. "Most of the work I do is with bands or singer/songwriters, and I tend to favor sparse, uncluttered kinds of sounds without a lot of gimmicks. I focus on vocals and lyrics, especially." Born on January 21, 1959, in Athens, Georgia, Keane has always lived around there, has a wife and three kids, and likes to stay close to home. Besides, it's home to the University of Georgia, so it's an active community.

Born into a musical family, Keane is "mostly self-taught, just an inch at a time." His father plays guitar and sings and his mother plays piano. "Ever since I was about 12 or so, I had a tape recorder," he says. "I liked to

play into it and hear myself back. I've been playing guitar since I was 9 years old, and I always liked to fiddle around with tape recorders, especially overdubbing multiple parts together by bouncing from one recorder to another and playing along."

Keane's productions include recent Cowboy Junkies, early Indigo Girls, several tracks by R.E.M., and such undeservedly obscure bands and artists as Insane Jane and Grant McLennan. Insane Jane's *A Green Little Pill* was one of 1991's overlooked treasures. Former Go-Between McLennan wrought a small miracle in 1995 with *Horsebreaker Star*.

"When I moved into the house my studio is in now (John Keane Studios, owned by Keane Recording Ltd.), I started recording bands I was in and other people's bands," he says. "This was around 1981." He played in Phil and the Blanks and "various local thrown-together bands" and worked with T. Graham Brown, a hard, bluesy country singer based in Nashville. By 1985, when Phil and the Blanks broke up, he decided to get off the road, "play music as a hobby, and start recording."

A turning point came in 1984, when he started working with R.E.M., Athens' most famous band. That year, R.E.M., with local musician Brian Cook in tow, recorded a single for IRS at Keane's 8-track studio with Los Angeles's favorite cynical son, Warren Zevon.

"They recorded that single in about 15 minutes," Keane recalls. "They did the R.E.M. song 'Narrator,' along with the Easybeats' 'Going to Have a Good Time Tonight' on the B-side. It was the first time I'd worked with a band that had the status of R.E.M. They'd already made three or four albums, and that was the first vinyl I'd done that got released on a label of any kind." Keane took a course at the Recording Workshop in Chillicothe, Ohio, in 1985. Meanwhile, R.E.M. began to frequent his studio, recording B-sides and Christmas singles and "little ditties for movie scores and preproduction demos for their albums."

In 1986, Keane bought a 16-track console and started "making a lot of records, like the Indigo Girls' first LP, *Strange Fire*. That was another sort of turning point because it sold quite a few copies eventually. I also did Widespread Panic's debut, *Space Wrangler*. I still listen to that.

"I think my role is to help artists translate a band's vision onto tape and try to help them realize the sound they're hearing in their head," says Keane. "When an artist tells me a record is exactly the statement he or she wanted to make, I feel I've done my job, as opposed to putting my own stamp on it." He prefers being unobtrusive. He also doesn't like confrontation. "My manager, Greg Spotts, sends me tapes from time to time, and

if there are ones that I like, I'll give him a call, give him the go-ahead to make contact to see if the artist is interested in working with me," Keane says. "But there have been times I've turned down tapes, either because I didn't think the style of music was right for my production or I felt that maybe the band was okay but it had, like, a really weak drummer and I knew it would be a real uphill climb or I might be under pressure from the label to replace band members. I usually try to avoid that kind of situation." Keane also doesn't like to get between artists and their A&R representatives.

Keane cites the first 10,000 Maniacs album without Natalie Merchant. "I think it's really good," he says of the 1997 Geffen album. But near-simultaneous work with Widespread Panic complicated the situation. The reconstituted Maniacs didn't like some of the mixes, Michael Braugher redid some, and Geffen higher-ups still didn't hear a hit single, so the Maniacs eventually recorded a cover version of Roxy Music's "More Than This," in a mix by Chris Lord-Alge—who mixed the album a third time. The album became "real expensive," Keane says.

He gets most referrals from his manager; he also scours the local scene, leaving his card with bands he enjoys. He also attends South by Southwest every year, to "bounce around and try to see as many bands as I can. Last year, I met a guy there named Tom Freund, I thought he was really great, I'd love to make a record with him. He used to play in the Silos." He listens to Neil Young, the Allman Brothers, Tom Petty, the Wallflowers. He likes his production of Vic Chesnutt's *Is the Actor Happy?* and an Uncle Tupelo album he produced for Rockville in 1992.

Sometimes he mixes in Nashville, some five hours away. "In Atlanta, they're all hip-hop studios and they don't have equipment I like to use," says Keane, who uses a 2-inch, 24-track Otari MTR90 along with a Trident console; a lot of R.E.M.'s *Out of Time* was recorded at his studio. He also owns a Sony digital 8-track machine he can hook up, and "I'll rent a 48-track if I need one."

"I really love Athens because it's small enough where it doesn't take you very long to get anywhere," Keane says. "But it's big enough that there's a lot of stuff going on, a lot of bands to see. It's a really nice place to make a record. Bands like staying here. The climate's real nice, and they can get around on foot." —CARLO WOLFF

Bottle Rockets: *The Bottle Rockets,* East Side Digital, 1993.
Chesnutt, Vic: *Little,* Texas Hotel, 1990 • *Is the Actor Happy?,* Texas Hotel, 1995 • *About to Choke,* Capitol, 1996.
Chickasaw Mudd Puppies: *White Dirt,* PolyGram, 1990.

Cowboy Junkies: "Angel Mine," A&M, 1996 (*The Truth About Cats and Dogs* soundtrack) • *Lay It Down*, Geffen, 1996 • *Studio: Selected Studio Recordings, 1986–1995*, RCA, 1996.

Dime Store Prophets: *Fantastic Distraction*, SaraBellum, 1997.

Dudley, Anne: *Kavanagh QC: Original Music from the ITV Series*, Virgin, 1997.

Grapes: *Private Stock*, Intersound, 1995.

Indigo Girls: *Strange Fire*, Epic, 1987, 1989 • w/ Mike Stipe, "The Wonder Years," Atlantic, 1989 (*The Wonder Years: Music from the Emmy-Winning Show and Its Era*).

Insane Jane: *A Green Little Pill*, Sky, 1991.

Jenkins, Catfish: *Normaltown*, Kudzu, 1994.

Jody Grind: *One Man's Trash Is Another Man's Treasure*, Safety Net/DB, 1990.

Keen, Robert Earl: *Picnic (ECD)*, Arista, 1997.

Kilkenny Cats: *Hammer*, Texas Hotel, 1988.

Malone, Michelle: *New Experience*, Aluminum Jane/Sky, 1988, 1993.

McLennan, Grant: *Horsebreaker Star*, Beggars Banquet/Atlantic, 1995.

Musical Kings: "Cody Cody," Rhino, 1993 (*Conmemorativo: A Tribute to Gram Parsons*).

People Who Must: *The Road You Travel*, Creativeman, 1995.

Porn Orchard: *Urges and Angers*, C/Z, 1991.

R.E.M.: "I Walked with a Zombie," Sire/WB, 1990 (*Where the Pyramid Meets the Eye*).

Shadowcaste: *Set in Motion*, Barfly, 1994.

Snatches of Pink: *Send in the Clowns*, Dog Gone, 1987 • *Dead Men*, Dog Gone, 1989.

Stipe, Michael, and the Indigo Girls: "I'll Give You My Skin," RNA, 1991 (*Tame Yourself*).

10,000 Maniacs: *Love Among the Ruins*, Geffen, 1997.

Uncle Green: *15 Dryden*, New Vision/DB, 1988.

Uncle Tupelo: *March 16–20, 1992*, Rockville, 1992.

Vigilantes of Love: *Blister Soul*, Capricorn, 1995 • *V.O.L.*, Warner Bros., 1996.

Widespread Panic: *Space Wrangler*, Capricorn, 1988, 1992 • *Ain't Life Grand*, Capricorn, 1994 • *Bombs and Butterflies*, Capricorn, 1997 • *Light Fuse, Get Away*, Capricorn, 1998.

Orrin Keepnews

Orrin Keepnews (born March 2, 1923) is one of the most prolific producers in history. Although he has never actually counted, he has produced over 500 records in his 35-year career (more than one record every four weeks). He was the first to record legendary artists Bill Evans and Wes Montgomery and has figured promi-

INTERVIEW WITH ORRIN KEEPNEWS

Daniel J. Levitin: You said in your book that you've tried to maintain the attitude that it's the artist's album and not yours. But at the same time, it's your job to manage the recording session, so there's potential conflict there.

Orrin Keepnews: Yeah, but it's the kind of thing that tends to be more potential than actual. What you need to accomplish more than anything else is a very real working partnership between the artist and the producer, which means a recognition on both sides, sometimes implicit and sometimes explicit, that each has his areas of being the decision maker. I am never going to say to an artist: "That was the take, I'm not going to let you lift your horn on that tune again," but I'm not going to let somebody say to me, "Yeah, that was good enough, let's go on," if I don't believe it was. If you are able to establish a workable, creative relationship with the artist, you're going to come out pretty good or better. If you're not able to establish this, then neither of you belong in the studio.

DL: How do you relate to the technology of recording? How involved do you get with sounds, for instance?

OK: First of all, you have to realize that in my production work, I go back to 1-track: professionally, I'm a little older than stereo, so I've been through a lot of technological change, and I'm a passionate believer in using technology rather than letting technology use you.

DL: Could you give me an example?

OK: I think there are instances in which I will believe in the validity of overdubbing and layering, but I also believe that it can be drastically overused to undercut and do away with the spontaneity that's a very important part of jazz. A lot of that comes out now that so many people are recording live to 2-track again with digital, because multitrack digital still remains incredibly expensive. It gives me great pleasure to be able to tell a bass player, "No, you can't repair that part, it's there. Everybody else was playing great, you got a bad note or two, that's tough. We're going with this." Because a lot of musicians, particularly musicians who are playing instruments that can just be plugged in and taken direct, are aware of the fact that they don't really have a sound in the room—musicians get aware of these things very fast—so there are a lot of piano players, guitarists and bass players who for years have relied on being able to punch in and fix notes. And this sometimes has a very negative effect on performance. But on the whole, progress is a wonderful thing.

DL: There is a remarkable consistency of engineering in your albums in that the balances and the sounds are all very true. The drums always sound like drums, the piano like a piano . . . .

OK: I must confess at being a bit surprised about that. I know I've had a consistency of attitude; I didn't know I had a consistency of sound as well. I'm not denying it, I just didn't know it. I was doing an RCA reissue with a fabulous veteran engineer named Ray Hall recently, and he was trying to remember if he had ever done a session with me back in the old days, in the '50s. He was remembering one particular session which was a possibility, and he said, "All I remember about that session is that the producer wanted no echo." And I said, "If the producer wanted no echo, it must have been me." I have a feeling about natural sounds. If anything, I can be accused of being too dry. My philosophy of sound with jazz is that the sound is only a means to deliver the performance.

DL: You say in your book, *The View from Within*, that club owners are the last to know talent.

OK: Yes, although I might want to revise that and say that although they are the last, they may still be a little bit ahead of the critics. I've always been very suspicious of record reviewers and critics. As a producer I consider most reviewers my natural enemy. I'm aware that it's much more attention-getting to be negative; people remember bad reviews a hell of a lot more than they remember good reviews. And a good review is just saying an artist and the producer were effective, whereas in a bad review, [the reviewer] is saying 'I am more discerning and I am more clever than either the artist or the producer.'

DL: You are a big discoverer of talent . . . .

OK: I'm a pretty good developer of talent, I'm a pretty good accepter of recommendations for talent when it's in the early stages, but on principle, I don't know that anyone ever really discovers anybody.

DL: There are people who are known throughout the world as major forces in jazz, whom you are responsible for having brought to the world. My question is, do you find them yourself, or do they find you, as was the case when Cannonball ran into your office and said, "You have to go to Indianapolis and hear Wes Montgomery." When you first hear them, how do you know that they're going to be big? What do you listen for?

OK: I knew Cannonball and knew he was not the type to go running off at the mouth about anything. So I knew it was a very serious recommendation. I flew out to Indi-

anapolis and sat down at the bar where Wes was playing, and I would say that it took me between 14 and 20 seconds to realize that I was in the presence of something goddamned important. The first time I heard Thelonious Monk, I heard a test pressing of his first session for Blue Note, and I knew I was in the presence of something special.

DL: How?

OK: Invariably, it is someone with an individual voice, somebody who sounds like himself on that instrument. I would also say that it's someone whose obvious passion for what he's doing makes itself known to you; you just hear the music and you are hearing passion, you are hearing creativity, you are hearing the cry of an artist. So it seems like it's all happening instinctively and swiftly, like a flash of lightning, but what's actually happening is that your taste, your experience, your judgment, are all constantly operating within you and then something comes along that strikes you as being an embodiment of all these things together.

DL: Have you ever missed the boat on anybody who later became really big?

OK: I did pass on Coltrane at one point, although everyone else did at the time, too. I heard Coltrane in the Miles Davis Quintet of the mid-'50s, with Red Garland [piano], Paul Chambers [bass], and Philly Joe Jones [drums], and I heard what was really a rather ordinary, young bebop tenor player—which is exactly what everybody else was hearing at that time. I was really very busy listening to Miles for the first time, and listening to Philly for the first time, and that was about all I had room for.

DL: Was there anyone whom you heard and said "That's it!" but it didn't happen? Famous failures?

OK: There were a number of people I thought would be wonderful and they weren't, in the sense of their not becoming major stars. I still have not figured out why the very first person I ever recorded, Randy Weston, never got bigger. Now Randy Weston has been on the scene for upwards of 35 years, and he is recognized as a superior artist, but he's never been a star, he's never been famous to people outside the jazz world. And I never could understand why. I thought Randy had absolutely everything. There are really two steps to the discovery of genius. One is to hear it for the first time and to know it, and the other is to eventually have a significant amount of public and or critical agreement about your excitement.

—DANIEL J. LEVITIN

nently in the careers of Cannonball Adderley, Thelonious Monk, McCoy Tyner, Sonny Rollins, Stanley Clarke, and Flora Purim. He started three distinguished jazz labels: Riverside, Milestone, and Landmark.

While it is difficult to find a common sound throughout his work, it is easy to find a common vibe; Keepnews' genius is in his ability to capture jazz artists at their most comfortable, relaxed, and creative. In a medium that is primarily a live art form, Keepnews has managed to record some of the classic, definitive performances of the genre. Although it is difficult to single out highlights in Keepnews' long recording career, one particular session at the Village Vanguard in New York yielded two stunning CDs, the Bill Evans Trio's *Sunday at the Village Vanguard* and *Waltz for Debby*. The recordings capture Evans in an intimate setting, his improvisational skills at their peak. Monk's *Brilliant Corners* and *With John Coltrane* CDs are also must-haves, true classics in the jazz repertoire. These four albums are prototypes for what a generation of jazz artists have tried to achieve on tape.

—Daniel J. Levitin

Abercrombie, John, and John Scofield: *Solar*, Quicksilver, 1993, 1996.

Adderley, Cannonball: *Portrait of Cannonball*, Original Jazz Classics, 1958 • *Things Are Getting Better*, Original Jazz Classics, 1958 • *In San Francisco*, Original Jazz Classics, 1959 • w/ Bill Evans, *Know What I Mean?*, Original Jazz Classics, 1961, 1996 • *The Cannonball Adderly Quintet Plus*, Original Jazz Classics, 1961 • *Lovers . . .* , Fantasy, 1976 • *Best of the Capitol Years*, Blue Note , 1991 • *Jazz Profile*, Capitol, 1997 • *Greatest Hits*, Milestone, 1998.

Adderley, Nat: *Work Song*, Original Jazz Classics, 1960, 1989.

Baker, Chet: *In New York*, Original Jazz Classics, 1958, 1988 • *Plays the Best of Lerner and Loewe*, Original Jazz Classics, 1959, 1989 • *Chet Baker Introduces Johnny Pace*, Original Jazz Classics, 1959, 1990.

Barry Harris Quintet: *Preminado*, Original Jazz Classics, 1961, 1990.

Bill Evans Quintet: *Interplay*, DCC Jazz, 1962, 1996.

Bill Evans Trio: *Portrait in Jazz*, DCC Jazz, 1960, 1994 • *Explorations*, Original Jazz Classics, 1961 • *Sunday at the Village Vanguard*, Original Jazz Classics, 1961, 1987 • *Waltz for Debbie*, Original Jazz Classics, 1961, 1987 • *How My Heart Sings!*, Original Jazz Classics, 1962, 1989 • *Moonbeams*, Original Jazz Classics, 1962, 1990.

Blakey, Art: *Ugetsu*, Original Jazz Classics, 1963, 1989.

Blakey, Art, and the Jazz Messengers: *The Big Beat*, Blue Note, 1960, 1987 • *Caravan*, Original Jazz Classics, 1962 • *Kyoto*, Original Jazz Classics, 1964, 1990.

Bobby Timmons Trio: *In Person*, Original Jazz Classics, 1961, 1989.

Brooks, John Benson: *Alabama Concerto*, Original Jazz Classics, 1958, 1991.

Byrd, Charlie: Trio and Guests, *Byrd at the Gate*, Original Jazz Classics, 1963 • *Byrd Man*, Riverside/ABC, 1969 • *See also* Tjader, Cal.

Clay, James: *A Double Dose of Soul*, Original Jazz Classics, 1960, 1991.

Clifford Jordan Quartet: *Bearcat*, Original Jazz Classics, 1960, 1992.

Cox, Ida, and Coleman Hawkins: *Blues for Rampart Street*, Original Jazz Classics, 1961, 1991.

Davis, Eddie Lockjaw: *Afro-Jaws*, Original Jazz Classics, 1961, 1989.

DeJohnette, Jack: *The DeJohnette Complex*, Original Jazz Classics, 1968, 1991.

Dorham, Kenny: Quartet, *2 Horns/2 Rhythm*, Original Jazz Classics, 1957, 1990 • Septet, *Blue Spring*, Original Jazz Classics, 1959, 1990.

Drew, Kenny: Trio/Quartet/Quintet, *Trio/Quartet/Quintet*, Original Jazz Classics, n.d. • Trio, *Kenny Drew Trio*, Original Jazz Classics, 1956 • Quartet/Quintet, *This Is New*, Original Jazz Classics, 1957, 1990.

Edison, Harry Sweets, and Eddie Lockjaw Davis: *Jawbreakers*, Original Jazz Classics, 1962, 1990.

Evans, Bill: *New Jazz Conceptions*, Original Jazz Classics, 1956, 1988 • *The Solo Sessions*, Vols. 1–2, Milestone, 1963, 1989 • *The Bill Evans Album*, Columbia, 1971, 1996 • *The Complete Riverside Recordings (1956–1963)*, Riverside, 1987 • *Bill Evans: Secret Sessions*, Milestone, 1996 • *The Secret Sessions*, Milestone, 1997 • *See also* Bill Evans Quartet, Trio.

Feldman, Victor: *Merry Olde Soul*, Original Jazz Classics, 1961, 1989.

Friedman, Don: Trio, *A Day In the City*, Original Jazz Classics, 1961, 1991 • Trio, *Flashback*, Original Jazz Classics, 1963, 1997 • Quartet, *Dreams and . . .* , Riverside, 1964, 1998.

Golson, Benny: *The Other Side of Benny Golson*, Original Jazz Classics, 1958, 1990.

Gonsalves, Paul: *Gettin' Together*, Original Jazz Classics, 1961.

Goodman, Benny, and Jack Teagarden: *B.G. and Big Tea in NYC*, Decca Jazz, 1992.

Gordon, Dexter: *Blue Dex: Dexter Gordon Plays the Blues*, Prestige, 1973, 1996.

Gryce, Gigi, and the Jazz Lab Quintet: *Gigi Gryce and the Jazz Lab Quintet*, Original Jazz Classics, 1957, 1991.

Hampton, Lionel: *Midnight Sun*, Decca, 1947, 1993.

Hawkins, Coleman: *The Hawk Flies High*, Original Jazz Classics, 1957, 1987.

Hawkins, Webster, Carter: *Three Great Swing Saxophones*, Bluebird/RCA, 1989.

Heath Brothers: *Brothers and Others*, Antilles, 1991.

Heath, Jimmy: *New Picture*, Landmark, 1985, 1988 • *Nice People*, Original Jazz Classics, 1988.

Henderson, Joe: Sextet, *The Kicker,* Original Jazz Classics, 1967, 1990 • *The Milestone Years,* Milestone, 1994.

Henry, Ernie: *Last Chorus,* Riverside, 1957, 1998.

Herring, Vincent: *Dawnbird,* Landmark, 1993, 1994.

Hooker, John Lee: *That's My Story,* Original Blues Classics, 1960, 1991.

Hutcherson, Bobby: *Good Bait,* Landmark, 1984 • *Color Schemes,* Landmark, 1985, 1986 • *In the Vanguard,* Landmark, 1987 • *Landmarks, 1984–1986,* Landmark, 1991 • *Mirage,* Landmark, 1991.

Jackson, Milt: w/ Wes Montgomery, *Bags Meets Wes!,* DCC Jazz, 1962, 1996 • Milt Jackson Sextet, *Invitation,* Original Jazz Classics, 1963.

Johnny Griffin Orchestra: *The Big Soul Band,* Original Jazz Classics, 1960, 1990.

Jones, Philly Joe: Sextet, *Blues for Dracula,* Original Jazz Classics, 1958, 1991 • *Drums Around the World: Big Band Sounds,* Original Jazz Classics, 1959, 1992 • *Showcase,* Original Jazz Classics, 1960, 1990.

Jones, Sam: *The Soul Society,* Original Jazz Classics, 1960, 1992 • *Right Down Front: The Riverside Collection,* Riverside, 1988.

Kelly, Wynton: Trio and Sextet, *Kelly Blue,* Original Jazz Classics, 1958, 1989 • *Piano,* Original Jazz Classics, 1958, 1989.

Lateef, Yusef: *Every Village Has a Song,* Rhino, 1976, 1993 • *Anthology,* Rhino, 1994.

Lee Morgan Quintet: *Take Twelve,* Original Jazz Classics, 1962.

Lincoln, Abbey: *That's Him,* Original Jazz Classics, 1957, 1988 • *It's Magic,* Original Jazz Classics, 1958, 1990.

Miller, Mulgrew: *Keys to the City,* Landmark, 1985 • *The Countdown,* Landmark, 1989 • *Chapters 1 and 2,* 32 Jazz, 1998.

Mitchell, Blue: *Big 6,* Original Jazz Classics, 1958, 1991.

Monk, Thelonious: *Brilliant Corners,* Original Jazz Classics, 1956 • *The Unique Thelonious Monk,* Original Jazz Classics, 1956, 1987 • *Monk's Music,* Original Jazz Classics, 1957, 1987 • w/ Gerry Mulligan, *Mulligan Meets Monk,* Original Jazz Classics, 1957, 1988 • *Thelonious Himself,* Original Jazz Classics, 1957 • w/ John Coltrane, *Thelonious Monk with John Coltrane,* Original Jazz Classics, 1957, 1987 • Quartet, *Misterioso,* Original Jazz Classics, 1958, 1989 • Quartet, *Thelonious in Action,* Original Jazz Classics, 1958, 1988 • *5 by Monk by 5,* Original Jazz Classics, 1959, 1989 • *Alone in San Francisco,* Original Jazz Classics, 1959 • Quartet + Two, *At the Blackhawk,* Original Jazz Classics, 1960, 1988 • *In Italy,* Original Jazz Classics, 1961, 1990 • *Monk in France,* Original Jazz Classics, 1961, 1991 • *The Thelonious Monk Memorial Album,* Milestone, 1982, 1990 • *Thelonious Monk and the Jazz Giants,* Riverside, 1987 • *The Complete Riverside Recordings,* Riverside, 1988 • *Straight No Chaser* soundtrack, Columbia, 1989.

Montgomery, Buddy: *Ties of Love,* Landmark, 1987.

Montgomery, Wes: Trio, *Wes Montgomery Trio,* Original Jazz Classics, 1959, 1987 • *Movin' Along,* Original Jazz Classics, 1960 • *The Incredible Jazz Guitar of Wes Montgomery,* Original Jazz Classics, 1960, 1987 • *So Much Guitar!,* DCC Jazz, 1961, 1995 • *Full House,* Original Jazz Classics, 1962, 1987 • *Boss Guitar,* Original Jazz Classics, 1963, 1987 • *Fusion!,* Original Jazz Classics, 1963, 1989 • Trio, *Guitar On the Go,* Original Jazz Classics, 1963, 1990 • *Portrait of Wes,* Original Jazz Classics, 1963, 1990 • *The Artistry of Wes Montgomery,* Riverside, 1987 • *The Complete Riverside Recordings,* Riverside, 1990 • *Encores,* Vol. 2, *Blues 'n' Boogie,* Milestone, 1997 • See also Jackson, Milt.

Newman, David Fathead: *Back to Basics,* Milestone, 1977, 1991.

Purim, Flora: *500 Miles High,* Milestone, 1976.

Randy Weston Trio and Cecil Payne: *Jazz á la Bohemia,* Original Jazz Classics, 1956, 1990.

Riverside Reunion Band: *Mostly Monk,* Milestone, 1993 • *Hi-Fly,* Milestone, 1994.

Roach, Max: *Deeds, Not Words,* Original Jazz Classics, 1958, 1988.

Rollins, Sonny: *The Sound of Sonny,* Original Jazz Classics, 1957, 1991 • *Next Album,* Original Jazz Classics, 1972, 1988 • *The Cutting Edge,* Original Jazz Classics, 1974, 1990 • *Nucleus,* Original Jazz Classics, 1975, 1991 • *The Way I Feel,* Original Jazz Classics, 1976, 1991 • *Don't Stop the Carnival,* Milestone, 1978 • *Easy Living,* Milestone, 1978, 1996 • *The Essential Sonny Rollins on Riverside,* Riverside, 1987.

Rouse, Charlie: *Epistrophy,* 32 Jazz, 1988, 1997.

Soskin, Mark: *Rhythm Vision,* Prestige, 1980.

Taylor, Billy: *Uptown,* Original Jazz Classics, 1960, 1997.

Terry, Clark: *Duke with a Difference,* Original Jazz Classics, 1957, 1990 • Quartet, *In Orbit,* Original Jazz Classics, 1958, 1988.

Thielemans, Toots: *Man Bites Harmonica!,* Original Jazz Classics, 1958, 1989.

Tjader, Cal: w/ Charlie Byrd, *Tambu,* Fantasy, 1974, 1996.

Turner, Big Joe: *Every Day in the Week,* Decca/GRP, 1967.

Tyner, McCoy: *Sahara,* Original Jazz Classics, 1972, 1988 • *Song for My Lady,* Original Jazz Classics, 1973, 1988 • *Enlightenment,* Milestone, 1973, 1990 • *Song of the New World,* Original Jazz Classics, 1973, 1991 • *Fly with the Wind,* Original Jazz Classics, 1976 • *Supertrios,* Milestone, 1977 • *Together,* Fantasy, 1978, 1997.

Webster, Ben, and Joe Zawinul: *Soulmates,* Original Jazz Classics, 1963, 1991.

Whitfield, Weslia: *Lucky to Be Me,* Landmark, 1989, 1990 • *Beautiful Love,* Cabaret, 1993 • *Nice Work . . . If You Can Get It,* Landmark, 1995 • *Teach Me Tonight,* High Note, 1997 • *My Shining Hour,* Highnote, 1998.

Wilbur Ware Quintet: *The Chicago Sound,* Original Jazz Classics, 1957, 1989.

Zoot Sims Quintet: *Zoot!,* Original Jazz Classics, 1957, 1991.

R. Kelly

It's been an interesting trip to the top for Chicago's Robert Kelly, from his early days as frontman of R. Kelly and Public Announcement with "She's Got That Vibe" and "Honey Love" to the overheated R&B lothario of "Bump n' Grind" (No. 1) and "Sex Me" (No. 20). And there are the gospel overtones of "I Believe I Can Fly" and "Gotham City."

These are all self-produced hits. Meanwhile, Kelly has successfully joined the ranks of Kenneth "Babyface" Edmonds and Teddy Riley (see entries) as one of R&B's premier producers, creating hits for Toni Braxton ("I Don't Want To"), Aaliyah (*Age Ain't Nothin' But a Number*, No. 18), Changing Faces ("G.H.E.T.T.O.U.T."), the Isley Brothers ("Let's Lay Together"), Hi-Five ("Quality Time"), and the Winans ("Payday"). And it was Kelly who provided Michael Jackson with what was easily the best song on his *HIStory* epic: the tender, understated ballad "You Are Not Alone" (No. 1).

Kelly first flexed his production chops on the 1992 *Born into the '90s* album by R. Kelly and Public Announcement (which includes co-production from Mr. Lee and Wayne Williams). Its first single, "She's Got That Vibe," didn't seem to leave much room for a promising future, with its moldy new jack swing sound, though Kelly's voice easily broke through. Follow-up singles "Slow Dance" and "Hey Love" better reflect the style that would become known as Kelly's: slow, smooth, sexy beats, thick and creamy and doused with old-school funk.

The very next year, Kelly, still bearing his trademark beats, returned with *12 Play* (No. 2). Singles such as "Sex Me," "Bump n' Grind," and "Your Body's Callin' " (No. 13) and telling album cuts "Freak Dat Body" and "I Like the Crotch on You" firmly established Kelly as R&B's Freak of the Week.

The success of *12 Play* helped pave the way for other Kelly productions that would come that same year and the next, such as "Payday," "All You Ever Been Was Good," and "That Extra Mile" by the Winans; though his sound was more evident on his work with Changing Faces on songs like "Stroke You Up" (No. 3) and "Foolin' Around," Janet Jackson's "Any Time, Any Place" remix and on Aaliyah's *Age Ain't Nothin' But a Number* album, which included songs like "Back and Forth" (No. 5) and a remake of the Isley Brothers' "At Your Best (You Are Love)" (No. 6) and the title track. It was widely reported that Kelly married the then-underage Aaliyah, which brought on tons of bad press for the pair.

His sound wouldn't change much with 1995's *R. Kelly* (No. 1) album, and that was just fine, as evidenced by songs such as "I Can't Sleep Baby (If I)" (No. 5), "Down Low (Nobody Has to Know)" (No. 4), "Step in My Room," "Hump Bounce," and "Religious Love." (It's probably better to forget "You Remind Me of Something," No. 4.)

That album revealed the first real hint of a change in direction for Kelly. The song "Trade in My Life," featuring gospel music's Kirk Franklin and the Family, showed a more spiritual side. And in 1997, under the guiding hand of Franklin, Kelly became a born-again Christian. Ironically, after this revelation, one of the first songs heard from Kelly was the vulgar "Fucking You Tonight" from the Notorious B.I.G.'s 1997 album *Life After Death*. (Kelly sings the chorus, which includes the album's title, though the title and lyrics were later changed to "Lovin' You Tonight" for radio.)

The change, to say the least, is a remarkable one, considering some of Kelly's past exploits, such as dropping his pants onstage and creating music to make love by. Since becoming born-again, Kelly's music has taken a more inspirational turn, on songs like "I Believe I Can Fly" (No. 2; popular in black churches) from the *Space Jam* soundtrack (which won Grammy Awards for Best Male R&B Vocal Performance, Best R&B Song, and Best Song Written Specifically for a Motion Picture or for Television in 1996) and "Gotham City" (No. 9) from the *Batman and Robin* soundtrack. —KEVIN JOHNSON

Aaliyah: *Age Ain't Nothing But a Number,* Jive, 1994 • "At Your Best (You Are Love)," Jive, 1994 • "Back and Forth," Blackground/Jive, 1994.

Blige, Mary J.: *Share My World,* MCA, 1997.

Braxton, Toni: *Secrets* (1 track), LaFace, 1996 • "I Don't Want To," LaFace, 1997 • "I Love Me Some Him/I Don't Want To," LaFace, 1997.

Changing Faces: "Stroke You Up," Big Beat, 1994 • *Changing Faces,* Spoiled Rotten/Big Beat, 1995 • "Foolin' Around," Big Beat, 1995 • *All Day All Night,* Big Beat, 1997 • Featuring Jay-Z, "All of My Days," Big Beat, 1997 • "G.H.E.T.T.O.U.T.," Big Beat, 1997.

Ex Girlfriend: "You (the One for Me)," Reprise, 1994.

Gill, Johnny: *Let's Get the Mood Right,* Motown, 1996.

Hi-Five: *Keep It Goin' On,* Jive, 1992 • "Quality Time," Jive, 1993.

Isley Brothers: "Let's Lay Together," Island, 1996 • *Mission to Please,* Island, 1996.

Jackson, Janet: *Any Time, Any Place"* (remix), Virgin, 1993.

Jackson, Michael: *HIStory: Past, Present and Future Part 1,* Epic, 1995 • "You Are Not Alone," Epic, 1995 • *Blood on the Dancefloor: HIStory in the Mix,* MJJ, 1997.

Jones, Quincy: *Q's Jook Joint,* Qwest, 1995.

Kelly, R.: *12 Play,* Jive, 1993 • "Sex Me (Parts 1 and 2)," Jive, 1993 • "Bump and Grind," Jive, 1994 • "Summer Bunnies," Jive, 1994 • *Summer Bunnies* (EP), Jive, 1994 • "Your Body's Callin'," Jive, 1994 • *R. Kelly,* Jive, 1995 • "You Remind Me of Something," Jive, 1995 • w/ Ronald Isley, "Down Low," Jive, 1996 • "I Believe I Can Fly," Warner Sunset, 1996 (*Space Jam* soundtrack) • "I Can't Sleep," Jive, 1996 • "Gotham City," Warner Sunset, 1997 (*Batman and Robin* soundtrack).

Kelly, R., and Public Announcement: *Born into the 90's,* Jive,

1992 • "Honey Love," Jive, 1992 • "She's Got That Vibe," Jive, 1992 • "Slow Dance (Hey Mr. DJ)," Jive, 1992 • "Dedicated," Jive, 1993.

MC Lyte: *Bad As I Wanna B,* EastWest, 1996.

N Phase: *N Phase,* Maverick/Sire, 1994 • "Spend the Night," Maverick/Sire, 1994.

Ocean, Billy: *Time to Move On,* Jive, 1993.

Peaston, David: *Mixed Emotions,* MCA, 1991 • "String," MCA, 1991.

Price, Kelly: *Soul of a Woman,* Island Black, 1998.

Sparkle: *Sparkle,* Interscope, 1998.

Trin-I-Tee 5:7: *Trin-I-Tee 5:7,* Interscope, 1998.

Vandross, Luther: *One Night with You: The Best of Love,* Vol. 2, Sony, 1997 • "When You Call on Me," LV/Epic, 1997.

Williams, Vanessa: *Next,* Mercury, 1997.

Winans, The: *All Out,* Qwest, 1993 • "Pay Day," Qwest, 1993.

Jerry Kennedy

Since Jerry Kennedy entered the music business at 11, when he began recording for RCA, it has permeated his life. He has been an artist and songwriter and has produced Roger Miller, Johnny Rodriguez, the Statler Brothers, and Reba McEntire. Music is his life and his legacy. In addition to producing numerous hit records, Kennedy also produced three sons who followed him into the family business: Shelby, an executive at ASCAP in Nashville; Brian, a singer/songwriter who opened for Garth Brooks in 1997; and Gordon, a writer/artist/guitarist who co-wrote the Grammy-winning Eric Clapton hit, "Change the World."

"What else could I expect?" he says. "This is the stuff they grew up in." Kennedy's own entrance into music came early in Shreveport, Louisiana. "I was 9 years old when I started taking guitar lessons from Tillman Franks," he recalls. "When I was 10 or 11, the Tillman Franks Guitar Club had a radio show every Saturday morning playing country music. Tillman got me a recording contract when I was 11 and I did eight sides with RCA. . . . I was before Elvis in 1951 or 1952. Anyway, we did the RCA thing and I decided I didn't like being a singer—I'd rather pick. So I started trying to concentrate on guitar and going to school."

Kennedy spent his teenage years playing guitar. By the time he was 16, Franks had hired him to be a staff guitarist on the popular *Louisiana Hayride* radio show. When he wasn't performing on the *Hayride* or going to school, Kennedy could also be found on the road working with Franks and the legendary Johnny Horton.

He was introduced to production when his friend Shelby Singleton got a job in promotion for Mercury Records that eventually led to a gig as head of A&R at Mercury in Nashville. "He asked me to move up here with him," Kennedy says. "I didn't want to, but I was going to do it for a couple of months and try it. I came up here and haven't been back since—that was March 1961. Four weeks after we moved up here he asked me to go to work and be his assistant at Mercury. That was April 1, 1961, and I worked there until 1984." (Kennedy's tenure at Mercury was interrupted by a five-month stint at Epic in 1963, after which he returned to Mercury.)

Kennedy says his getting into production was "an accident" and being a producer really wasn't on his agenda when he moved to Nashville. "I preferred to be a picker," he says, "to stay on the other side of the glass. It's still my first love. All my idols are musicians."

However, a bad snowstorm kept Singleton from making a session and Kennedy had to fill in. "The first guy he asked me to produce, I think, was Rex Allen Sr. and I got a No. 1 record the first thing," he recalls. "I thought, 'Well, this isn't hard.'"

For Kennedy, finding hit songs has always been the most challenging aspect of producing. "I've always been most keenly aware of songs, and that's always been a real strong love, that pursuit of a song." He agrees with the Nashville Songwriters Association motto, "It all starts with a song," but Kennedy says producers around town knew its truth way before it was formalized.

"I used to listen to tons of songs and worked with many writers," he says. "I hope that today's producers take advantage of the many songwriters working Nashville. We had only a handful of publishers and producers to pick from."

At his production peak, Kennedy says, it wasn't unusual for him to have recording sessions scheduled for 10 A.M., 2, 6, and 10 P.M. "And then if you had to have something, you also had a session at 1 A.M.," he says. "I've done a few of those as a player. I would never do one as a producer because you were really tired if you had four sessions booked. You couldn't concentrate if you had four sessions booked. . . . There were 57 artists through here in 1962. There's no way you could do that today because of the technology. In those days when the producer walked into the studio, pickers were on the other side and the engineer sat down. When the red light went off, that was the record. There was no mixing, no anything. They just cut the tape, took it out into a little room, and mailed it off to be mastered. That was

the way we were doing them and it enabled us to cut a lot more product."

Even though technology has slowed the process, Kennedy likes the way it makes the records sound, "although I think there are some records from that time that I don't think will ever be able to be topped. Some magic dust fell and just got stuck. [On] the Patsy Cline stuff, Owen Bradley [see entry] nailed digital before digital. He cut the cleanest records I've ever heard. And some of the things Chet [Atkins; see entry] did with Jim Reeves and Don Gibson are so clean."

Though today's records may be sonically superior to most older records, Kennedy says that technology has changed the feel of the music. "When you bring people into the studio one at a time, it's just one of those prices you have to pay," he says. "They don't have the benefit of eye contact. With everything going down the way it was, some of that was so much magic it was unbelievable. I would love the feel we could get with everybody in the room. The player would feed off the artist just standing there doing it."

Kennedy says he's enjoyed the artists he's worked with and says there was never one who presented any problems. Jerry Lee Lewis had a reputation for being temperamental but, says Kennedy, "I loved working with this guy and we never had a cross word. I think he fought with everyone around me, but he and I got along great. He was something and still is."

Kennedy worked with Reba McEntire early in her career, during her stint on Mercury. "Reba is a trip," he says. "I spent so much time laughing . . . but she was absolutely one of the hardest-working artists I've ever seen. She would stand there and sing until her tonsils fell out and I challenged her with more. . . . I wanted to find something she couldn't do, but she could do everything I threw out there."

Kennedy says they used to play pranks on Johnny Rodriguez in the studio. "We used to pull some of the most unbelievable things. He was so naive," he says. "We did little things, like there was a button on the machine that would take things up exactly a half-tone, and he was one of the best I've ever seen at doing harmonies. He could just zero in on it and do his own harmony to what he had just done. So after we'd cut a record, we'd let the musicians take a break and he'd be the only one in the studio . . . and I'd hit that button. He'd sing a half-tone flat for the first two words. It only lasted two words. Then he came right up to it. That's how quick he was."

Roger Miller was another of Kennedy's favorite acts, and he says if it wasn't for his three sons, Miller's career might never have gotten off the ground. Miller wanted to move to Los Angeles and said the move would cost him $1,600. He wanted to get enough money from signing with Mercury to make the move. So Kennedy talked the label into the money, but they wanted Miller to cut 16 sides for which they'd pay him $100 apiece. Miller cut the songs, and Kennedy took them home to listen and pick the first single. However, he only had a small take-up reel on his machine at home and could only play the first six or seven songs. He did and picked a single from one of those.

A few days later he bought a bigger reel and began playing all the songs. "I was listening to the rest of it so I could sequence an album," he says. "When 'Dang Me' (No. 7; No. 1 country) came on, the kids came running into my office going wild. They were all little bitty guys—6, 4, and 2. I rewound it and kept playing it, and they would go crazy. So I called the president at Mercury and said I screwed up and needed to change the single. They said the record was pressed and ready to go. The president of the label called me the next day and said, 'I understand you want to redo this Roger Miller thing.' I said 'Yes, I have to. It's that important.'

"That's how close we came. If I hadn't picked up that reel. . . . The record was being mailed two days later, and once it went, what if nothing happened? In those days, everybody was a little nervous and fidgety. They were dropping artists after a record or two to get them out of here. 'Dang Me,' 'Chug-a-Lug' (No. 9; No. 3 country), and 'Do-Wacka-Do' were the three singles that came out of that $1,600 session."

There's still much that Kennedy would like to do. "I would like to cut a Top 10 record during the '90s," he says. "I did it in the '60s, the '70s, and the '80s. I don't know whether it will happen or not, but we'll give it a shot." —DEBORAH EVANS PRICE

Allen, Rex: "Don't Go Near the Indians," Mercury, 1962.
Bandy, Moe: "Till I'm Too Old to Die Young," Curb/MCA, 1987 • "You Haven't Heard the Last of Me," Curb/MCA, 1987 • "Americana," Curb, 1988 • "I Just Can't Say No to You," Curb, 1988 • No Regrets, Curb, 1988 • Many Mansions, Curb, 1989 • Greatest Hits, Curb, 1992.
Bare, Bobby: "Come Sundown," Mercury, 1970 • "How I Got to Memphis," Mercury, 1970 • "Please Don't Tell Me How the Story Ends," Mercury, 1971.
Boxcar Willie: Best Loved Favorites, Ranwood, 1989.
Bradshaw, Terry: "I'm So Lonesome I Could Cry," Mercury, 1976.
Burns, George: "I Wish I Was Eighteen Again," Mercury, 1980.
Carter, Anita: Ring of Fire, Bear Family, 1989.
Cramer, Floyd: The Piano Magic of, Ranwood, 1996.

Davis, Mac: Will Write Songs for Food, Columbia, 1994.
Drake, Pete: "Forever," Smash, 1964.
Drusky, Roy: w/ Priscilla Mitchell, "Yes, Mr. Peters," Mercury, 1965 • "If the Whole World Stopped Lovin'," Mercury, 1966 • "Rainbows and Roses," Mercury, 1966 • "The World Is Round," Mercury, 1966 • "Weakness in a Man," Mercury, 1967 • "Jody and the Kid," Mercury, 1968 • "My Grass Is Green," Mercury, 1969 • "Such a Fool," Mercury, 1969 • "Where the Blue and Lonely Go," Mercury, 1969 • "All My Hard Times," Mercury, 1970 • "I'll Make Amends," Mercury, 1970 • "Long Long Texas Road," Mercury, 1970 • "I Love the Way That You've Been Lovin' Me," Mercury, 1971 • "Red Red Wine," Mercury, 1971 • Songs of Love and Life, Mercury, 1995.
Dudley, Dave: The Best Of, Mercury, 1965 • "Truck Drivin' Son of a Gun," Mercury, 1965 • "What We're Fighting For," Mercury, 1965 • "Please Let Me Prove (My Love for You)," Mercury, 1968 • "There Ain't No Easy Run," Mercury, 1968 • "George (and the North Woods)," Mercury, 1969 • "The Pool Shark," Mercury, 1970.
Hall, Tom T.: "The Homecoming," Mercury, 1969 • "A Week in a Country Jail," Mercury, 1970 • I Witness Life, Mercury, 1970 • "Shoeshine Man," Mercury, 1970 • "The Year That Clayton Delaney Died," Mercury, 1971 • "(Old Dogs, Children and) Watermelon Wine," Mercury, 1972 • Greatest Hits, Vol. 1, PolyGram Country, 1972 • "Me and Jesus," Mercury, 1972 • "Ravishing Ruby," Mercury, 1973 • "Country Is," Mercury, 1974 • "I Care," Mercury, 1974 • "I Love," Mercury, 1974 • "That Song Is Driving Me Crazy," Mercury, 1974 • "Deal," Mercury, 1975 • Greatest Hits, Vol. 2, Mercury, 1975 • "I Like Beer," Mercury, 1975 • "Faster Horses (The Cowboy and the Poet)," Mercury, 1976 • "Your Man Loves You Honey," Mercury, 1977 • Song in a Seashell, Mercury, 1985 • Greatest Hits, Vol. 1 and 2, Mercury, 1993.
Harris, Stewart: Sing Me a Rainbow, Mercury, 1977.
Hee Haw Gospel Quartet: Best Of, Vols. 1–2, Ranwood, 1995/1996.
Jim and Jesse: Jim and Jesse: Bluegrass and More, Bear Family, 1993.
Lewis, Jerry Lee: The Greatest Live Show on Earth, Bear Family, 1964, 1991 • "Another Place, Another Time," Smash, 1968 • "She Still Comes Around (to Love What's Left of Me)," Smash, 1968 • What's Made Milwaukee Famous (Has Made a Loser out of "Me"), Smash, 1968 • Another Place, Another Time, Mercury, 1969 • "One Has My Name," Smash, 1969 • "She Even Woke Me Up to Say Goodbye," Smash, 1969 • "To Make Love Sweeter for You," Smash, 1969 • "Once More with Feeling," Smash, 1970 • "There Must Be More to Love Than This," Smash, 1970 • w/ Linda Gail, Together, Smash, 1970 • "Touching Home," Mercury, 1971 • "Chantilly Lace/Think About It Darlin'," Smash, 1972 •

Would You Take Another Chance on Me?/Me and Bobby "McGee," Smash, 1972 • "Let's Put It Back Together Again," Mercury, 1976 • "Middle Age Crazy," Mercury, 1977 • "Come On In," Mercury, 1978 • "I'll Find It Where I Can," Mercury, 1978 • Killer Country, Mercury, 1981, 1995 • Killer: The Mercury Years, Vol. 3, 1973–1977, PolyGram Country, 1989 • All Killer No Filler: The Anthology, Rhino, 1993.

Maines Brothers Band: "Everybody Needs Love on a Saturday Night," Mercury, 1985.

McDaniel, Mel: "Baby's Got Her Blue Jeans On," Capitol, 1985 • "Let It Roll (Let It Rock)," Capitol, 1985 • "Stand Up," Capitol, 1985 • "Stand on It," Capitol, 1986 • Greatest Hits, Capitol, 1987 • "Real Good Feel Good Song," Capitol, 1988 • Baby's Got Her Blue Jeans On, Branson, 1993.

McEntire, Reba: Reba McEntire, Mercury, 1977 • "Last Night, Every Night," Mercury, 1978 • Out of a Dream, Mercury, 1979 • "Runaway Heart," Mercury, 1979 • "Sweet Dreams," Mercury, 1979 • "(I Still Long to Hold You) Now and Then," Mercury, 1980 • "(You Lifted Me) Up to Heaven," Mercury, 1980 • Feel the Fire, Mercury, 1980 • "I Can See Forever in Your Eyes," Mercury, 1980 • Heart to Heart, Mercury, 1981 • "I Don't Think Love Ought to Be That Way," Mercury, 1981 • "Only You (and You Alone)," Mercury, 1981 • "Today All Over Again," Mercury, 1981 • "I'm Not That Lonely Yet," Mercury, 1982 • Unlimited, Mercury, 1982 • Behind the Scene, Mercury, 1983 • "Can't Even Get the Blues," Mercury, 1983 • "There Ain't No Future in This," Mercury, 1983 • "Why Do We Want (What We Know We Can't Have?)," Mercury, 1983 • "You're the First Time I've Thought About Leaving," Mercury, 1983 • Best Of, PolyGram Country, 1985 • Reba Nell McEntire, PolyGram Country, 1986, 1990 • Oklahoma Girl, Mercury, 1994.

Miller, Roger: "Chug-a-Lug," Smash, 1964 • "Dang Me," Smash, 1964 • "Do-Wacka-Do," Smash, 1964 • Roger and Out, Smash, 1964 • "Engine, Engine #9," Smash, 1965 • "England Swings," Smash, 1965 • Golden Hits, Smash, 1965 • "Kansas City Star," Smash, 1965 • "King of the Road," Smash, 1965 • "One Dyin' and A-Buryin'," Smash, 1965 • The Return of, Smash, 1965 • "Husbands and Wives," Smash, 1966 • Words and Music by Roger Miller, Smash, 1966 • "You Can't Roller Skate in a Buffalo Herd," Smash, 1966 • "Walkin' in the Sunshine," Smash, 1967 • "Little Green Apples," Smash, 1968 • "Me and Bobby McGee," Smash, 1969 • Best Of, Vol. 2, King of the Road, Mercury, 1992 • King of the Road, Epic, 1992.

Moran, Lester Roadhog: Alive at Johnny Mack Brown High School, Mercury, 1974 • w/ the Cadillac Cowboys, The Complete, Mercury, 1994.

Newbury, Mickey: Looks Like Rain, Mercury, 1969 • Live at Montezuma, Elektra, 1973.

Page, Patti: "Give Him Love," Mercury, 1971 • "Make Me

Your Kind of Woman," Mercury, 1971 • w/ Tom T. Hall, "Hello, We're Lonely," Mercury, 1972.

Rich, Charlie: "Mohair Sam," Smash, 1965 • The Complete Smash Sessions, Mercury, 1992 • Feel Like Going Home: The Essential, Legacy/Columbia, 1997.

Rodriguez, Johnny: "Pass Me By," Mercury, 1972 • "Ridin' My Thumb to Mexico," Mercury, 1973 • "You Always Come Back (to Hurting Me)," Mercury, 1973 • "Dance with Me (Just One More Time)," Mercury, 1974 • "Something," Mercury, 1974 • "That's the Way Love Goes," Mercury, 1974 • "We're Over," Mercury, 1974 • "I Just Can't Get Her Out of My Mind," Mercury, 1975 • "Just Get Up and Close the Door," Mercury, 1975 • "Love Put a Song in My Heart," Mercury, 1975 • Greatest Hits, Mercury, 1976 • "Hillbilly Heart," Mercury, 1976 • "I Couldn't Be Me Without You," Mercury, 1976 • "I Wonder If I Ever Said Goodbye," Mercury, 1976 • "Desperado," Mercury, 1977 • "We Believe in Happy Endings," Mercury, 1978 • You Can Say That Again, High Tone, 1996.

Russell, Johnny: "How Deep in Love I Am," Mercury, 1978.

Sahm, Doug: The Best of Doug Sahm, 1968–1975, Rhino, 1992.

Statler Brothers: "Flowers on the Wall," Mercury, 1965 • "Bed of Roses," Mercury, 1970 • Bed of Roses, Mercury, 1971 • "Do You Remember These?," Mercury, 1972 • Sing Country Symphonies in E Major, Mercury, 1972 • "The Class of '57," Mercury, 1972 • "I'll Go to My Grave Loving You," Mercury, 1975 • The Best of the Statler Brothers, Mercury, 1975 • "Thank God I've Got You," Mercury, 1976 • Country America Loves, Mercury, 1977 • "I Was There," Mercury, 1977 • "The Movies," Mercury, 1977 • "Do You Know You Are My Sunshine," Mercury, 1978 • Entertainers: On and Off the Record, Mercury, 1978 • Holy Bible: New Testament, Mercury, 1978 • Holy Bible: Old Testament, Mercury, 1978 • "The Official History on Shirley Jean Berrell," Mercury, 1978 • "Who Am I to Say?," Mercury, 1978 • "How to Be a Country Star," Mercury, 1979 • "Nothing As Original As You," Mercury, 1979 • "(I'll Even Love You) Better Than I Did Then," Mercury, 1980 • Best of Rides Again, Mercury, 1980 • Tenth Anniversary, Mercury, 1980 • The Best of the Statler Brothers, Vol. 2, Mercury, 1980 • "Charlotte's Web," Mercury, 1981 • "Don't Wait on Me," Mercury, 1981 • Years Ago, Mercury, 1981 • "You'll Be Back (Every Night in My Dreams)," Mercury, 1981 • "Whatever," Mercury, 1982 • "Guilty," Mercury, 1983 • "Oh Baby Mine (I Get So Lonely)," Mercury, 1983 • Today, Mercury, 1983 • "Atlanta Blue," Mercury, 1984 • Atlanta Blue, Mercury, 1984 • "Elizabeth," Mercury, 1984 • "One Takes the Blame," Mercury, 1984 • Christmas Present, Mercury, 1985 • "Hello Mary Lou," Mercury, 1985 • "My Only Love," Mercury, 1985 • Pardners in Rhyme, PolyGram Country, 1985 • "Sweeter and Sweeter," Mercury, 1985 • "Too Much on My Heart," Mercury, 1985 • "Count on Me," Mercury,

1986 • "Forever," Mercury, 1986 • *Radio Gospel Favorites,* Mercury, 1986 • "I'll Be the One," Mercury, 1987 • *Christmas Card,* PolyGram Country, 1988 • *Greatest Hits,* Mercury, 1988 • *Live and Sold Out,* PolyGram Country, 1989 • "More Than a Name on a Wall," Mercury, 1989 • *Music, Memories and You,* Mercury, 1990 • *All-American Country,* Mercury, 1991 • *Words and Music,* Mercury, 1992 • *Home,* Mercury, 1993 • *Today's Gospel Favorites,* Mercury, 1993 • *A 30th Anniversary Celebration,* Mercury Nashville, 1995 • *Innerview,* Mercury, 1997.

Vinton, Bobby: *Greatest Hits,* Curb, 1964 • *Timeless,* Curb, 1989 • *Mr. Lonely: Greatest Songs Today,* Curb, 1991.

Ward, Jacky: "Dance Her by Me (One More Time)," Mercury, 1975 • "I Never Said It Would Be Easy," Mercury, 1976 • "Fools Fall in Love," Mercury, 1977 • "Texas Angel," Mercury, 1977 • "A Lover's Question," Mercury, 1978 • "I Want to Be in Love," Mercury, 1978 • "Rhythm of the Rain," Mercury, 1978 • *The Best of Jacky Ward . . . Up 'Til Now,* Mercury, 1979 • "Wisdom of a Fool," Mercury, 1979 • "You're My Kind of Woman," Mercury, 1979 • "I'd Do Anything for You," Mercury, 1980 • *More Jacky Ward,* Mercury, 1980 • "Save Your Heart for Me," Mercury, 1980 • "That's the Way a Cowboy Rocks and Rolls," Mercury, 1980 • "Somethin' on the Radio," Mercury, 1981.

Whitman, Slim: *Best Loved Favorites,* Ranwood, 1991.

Wilson, Norro: "Do It to Someone You Love," Mercury, 1970.

Young, Faron: "I Just Came to Get My Baby," Mercury, 1968 • "Wine Me Up," Mercury, 1969 • "Your Time's Comin'," Mercury, 1969 • "Goin' Steady," Mercury, 1970 • "If I Ever Fall in Love (with a Honky Tonk Girl)," Mercury, 1970 • "Occasional Wife," Mercury, 1970 • "Leavin' and Sayin' Goodbye," Mercury, 1971 • "Step Aside," Mercury, 1971 • "It's Four in the Morning," Mercury, 1972 • "This Little Girl of Mine," Mercury, 1972 • "Just What I Had in Mind," Mercury, 1973 • "Some Kind of Woman," Mercury, 1974 • *The Hits,* Mercury Nashville, 1998.

Neil Kernon

Though Neil Kernon's career began in England in 1971 with some classic rock acts, he's one of the foremost proponents of modern computer technology in rock music.

He was introduced to guitar at age 7 by one of his accountant father's clients, classical guitarist John Williams, who would come over to the house with his guitar. He played in bands in his teens and then decided he wanted to do something musical after leaving school. A job at a publisher was unsatisfying. But producers Rodger Bain and Gus Dudgeon (see entries) had an office in the same building and suggested he apply for a job at Trident Recording. Starting there in 1971, he worked his way from tea boy to assistant engineer, working with artists like Elton John, David Bowie (see entry), the Rolling Stones, and Queen. Four years at Trident were followed by two years of engineering in France and working for Yes from 1976 to 1978, doing both live and studio engineering. By the late '70s, he was moving into production. "It was a logical step. People started to ask me to give my musical input. I found myself involved with songwriting, arrangement."

In 1980, he started working with Hall and Oates and did three albums for them at the peak of their commercial popularity. "I had great chemistry with them. They'd been doing disco records with David Foster [see entry] and Daryl said he wanted to do a new wave record." Instead, that association (Kernon is not credited as producer) produced sleek, creamy hits such as "Private Eyes" (No. 1), "Family Man," (No. 6), "Maneater" (No. 1), and "I Can't Go for That (No Can Do)" (No. 1).

In the '80s, Kernon found himself producing lots of commercial hard rock. The most notable releases were Dokken's 1985 *Under Lock and Key* and 1987 *Back for the Attack* (No. 13) and Queensryche's 1986 *Rage for Order.* The former was his biggest headache, the latter the proudest moment of his career. "I've done 200-odd records," he says, "and 99 out of 100, it's been great. The only two times it was a fiasco were the Dokken records. They had so many internal problems between Don [Dokken] and George [Lynch]. I don't know how they stayed together long enough for me to make one record, let alone two. I heard great songs but I found myself in the middle of a great feud."

Three months after finishing the Dokken album, he was in Seattle working with Queensryche. "It was exactly the opposite. It was a great positive experience for all of us. Any idea anyone had seemed to work. Every idea spawned another idea, which spawned another. We all wanted a high-tech heavy metal record that was cold-sounding. We all liked the idea of samples. I was getting into Macintosh computers. At that point sequencers were rudimentary. I'd get on-line and download sounds and load them into an emulator after racking up enormous phone bills. We planned it as we were recording. It was an effortless album to make."

A monumental-sounding album, *Rage for Order* creates the sense that each musician is surrounded by miles of pure, empty space, integrating samples seamlessly with thundering herds of guitars and Geoff Tate's bitingly theatrical vocals. It spawned a generation of inferior imitators.

Kernon returned to Dokken for more punishment with *Back for the Attack*. "I think I got the best performance of any Dokken record. At that point the relationship between George and Don was so strange. I'd schedule to work with George during the day and Don at night with an hour between them for George to escape." Those Dokken albums were the epitome of flashy power metal, buttressed by such commercial metal touches as multilayered vocal harmonies and thick, echo-rich arena sound. Kernon managed to forge a strong enough relationship with George Lynch to do Lynch Mob's *Wicked Sensation* album.

In the early '90s, Kernon moved from fluffy commercial metal bands like Britny Fox, Heaven's Edge, and Valentine to harder stuff like Flotsam and Jetsam and Skrew. He says, "The stuff I like is heavy stuff like Fear Factory, Machine Head, industrial stuff. One of the assistants on the Queensryche record was Dave Ogilvie [see entry], who was working on Skinny Puppy. I went to a Skinny Puppy show in Vancouver in 1986. It changed a lot for me. I loved the programming, the mechanical aspect of it. I liked stuff that demanded imagination when you listened to it. I started listening to more and more programmed stuff like Ministry's *Twitch* and *Land of Rape and Honey*. The first NIN record turned me right around. I got chills from it. I've done that kind of stuff in the last four years.

"I personally am happy that high-tech is being embraced. The speed computers are going is wonderful, the things you are able to do with music programs these days. Studiovision, Performer, the newer versions are pretty outrageous. The first thing I do in the morning is switch on my computer, clean my teeth, and put on coffee. Computing is integral to everything I do. I've been on e-mail for 14 years. Before the Internet I was on IMC, a music industry e-mail system. In studio, I've worked with SSL or Neve computerized boards. I do sequencing work with a Mac." Kernon also writes a column called "TechSonica" about all aspects of electronic music making for an on-line magazine called *Electronica Music* (www.electronicmusic.com).

Since the early '80s, the nomadic Kernon has moved from New York to Seattle to Phoenix to El Paso, working with young locals in each place. "I like to go and see bands wherever I'm living. I love to find stuff that's vital and different and special, instead of waiting for the label to find something and come to me. Eventually, I hope to get my own label.

"My greatest strength is in working as a catalyst, getting great performances from people, capturing a vibe. I don't spend ages with the drummer trying to get the perfect drum sound. I'm happy if we can get something that sounds great and the enthusiasm isn't beaten out of them."

In late 1997 Kernon took a big step toward achieving his dream when he became head of A&R at Chicago's Slipdisc Records. —ANASTASIA PANTSIOS

Anderson, Jon: *Animation,* Polydor, 1982.

Autograph: *Sign In Please,* RCA, 1984 • "Turn Up the Radio," RCA, 1984.

Aviator: *Aviator,* RCA, 1986.

Black Happy: *Peg Head,* Capricorn, 1993, 1995.

Bolton, Michael: *Everybody's Crazy,* Columbia, 1985.

Brand X: *Product,* Charisma, 1979 • *Do They Hurt?,* Charisma, 1980.

Britny Fox: *Boys in Heat,* Columbia, 1989.

Clay People: *Clay People,* Slipdisc, 1998.

Dokken: *Under Lock and Key,* Elektra, 1985 • "In My Dreams," Elektra, 1986 • *Back for the Attack,* Elektra, 1987 • "Burning Like a Flame," Elektra, 1987.

Flicks: *Go for the Effect,* Ariola, 1979.

Flotsam and Jetsam: *Cuatro,* MCA, 1992 • *Drift,* MCA, 1995.

FM: *Tough It Out,* Epic, 1988.

Heaven's Edge: *Heaven's Edge,* Columbia, 1990.

Helix: *Wild in the Streets,* Capitol, 1987.

Kansas: *Drastic Measures,* Epic, 1983.

Lynch Mob: *Wicked Sensation,* Elektra, 1990.

Nevermore: *Nevermore,* Ill Labels, 1995.

Nihil: *Drown,* Slipdisc, 1998.

Podunk: *Murlin's Dock,* Core, 1996.

Queensryche: *Rage for Order,* EMI America, 1986 • *Queensryche,* EMI America, 1983, 1989.

Rorschach Test: *Unclean,* Slipdisc, 1998.

Shy: *Excess All Areas,* RCA, 1987.

Skrew: *Shadow of Doubt,* Metal Blade, 1996.

Spys: *Spys,* WMI-America, 1982.

Streets: *First,* Atlantic, 1983.

Teeley, Tom: *Tales of Glamour and Distress,* A&M, 1984.

Townshend, Simon: *Moving Target,* Twenty One, 1985.

Valentine: *Valentine,* Giant, 1989.

XYZ: *Hungry,* Capitol, 1991.

David Kershenbaum

David Kershenbaum has been one of the more important figures in the American record business for the last 25 years, with involvement in over 40 gold and platinum records. He has produced or co-produced vital music by diverse artists, including Joan Baez (*Diamonds and Rust,* No. 11; *From Every Stage; Blowin' Away*), Tracy Chapman (the Grammy-winning *Tracy Chapman,* No. 1; *Crossroads,* No. 9), Joe Jackson (*Look Sharp,* No. 20; *I'm the Man,* No. 12 U.K.; *Night and Day,* No. 4), Graham Parker (*The Real Macaw*), Cat Stevens (*Izitso,* No. 7), B.W. Stevenson ("My Maria," No. 9), and Supertramp (*Brother, Where You Bound?* No. 21). As an executive with A&M, Kershenbaum brought Janet Jackson and Bryan Adams to the label. In 1990 he was a founding partner of the Morgan Creek Music Group, under the aegis of which he executive-produced the soundtracks to *The Last of the Mohicans* and *Robin Hood: Prince of Thieves* [which includes Bryan Adams' multiplatinum No. 1 single, "(Everything I Do), I Do For You"].

David Kershenbaum was born in Springfield, Missouri, and started listening to records at the age of 4 or 5. He taught himself to play guitar at the age of 6. Kershenbaum's interest in music was rivaled by his interest in technology: he borrowed his neighbor's Wollensack 2-track tape machine and recorded records, dropping in sound effects and announcements over the music.

As a preteen, Kershenbaum went on trips to Nashville with a friend of the family who was a music publisher and the producer of a national radio show broadcast from Springfield called *Country Music Jubilee* (hosted by Red Foley). Kershenbaum watched Chet Atkins (see entry) and other producers run sessions at RCA in Nashville, thinking that one day he would begin his career there. From his early teens on, Kershenbaum played in bands of various stripes. Attending Springfield's Dury College, Kershenbaum made friends with the son of the head of marketing for RCA and visited at his home in New York on breaks from school.

Out of school and facing the draft, Kershenbaum got a job with the Illinois National Guard through his cousin. Stationed in Peoria, Kershenbaum hooked up with a local advertising agency to write and perform jingles. He built a small recording studio for the agency and recorded local bands at night. Late in the spring of 1971 Kershenbaum went to L.A. for a week with some of his tapes, seeking a staff producer job with one of the major labels. RCA and Columbia were impressed enough with his work that they asked him to call back on the following Monday. Almost out of money, Kershenbaum stayed in town over the weekend; then the San Fernando earthquake of 1971 hit, caving in Columbia's ceiling and sending Kershenbaum to RCA by default.

RCA's headquarters were in New York, so Kershenbaum had to fly there to be officially hired. Maxing out his credit card, Kershenbaum made the trip only to find that the hiring executive had departed for a meeting in the Caribbean. At the end of his rope and about to give up, Kershenbaum saw his college friend's father at the end of a hallway, who then made the right calls and straightened everything out. Kershenbaum was hired to head RCA's new A&R office in Chicago.

On a scouting trip to Ohio 18 months later, Kershenbaum learned that the Chicago A&R office was being closed. He dashed back to the Windy City to plead his case to Ed Scanlon, the personnel man who had been brought in to shut the office down. Kershenbaum tracked down Scanlon at his hotel, went to his room, and poured his heart out for five minutes before the man informed him that although his name was, indeed, Ed Scanlon, he was a shoe wholesaler. Once he found the right Ed Scanlon and pleaded his case, Kershenbaum wasn't fired; instead he was sent to RCA's L.A. office.

In 1973 Kershenbaum signed and produced singer/songwriter B.W. Stevenson, who had a Top 10 hit with "My Maria" (No. 1 country for Brooks and Dunn in 1996) and a minor hit with "Shambala" (which Three Dog Night took to No. 3 the same year). A year later Kershenbaum struck out on his own as an independent producer. After "starving for about a year," he met an attorney who introduced him to Jerry Moss—the "M" of A&M—which led to a 14-year affiliation with the label.

The first major artist he worked with was Joan Baez. Kershenbaum helped the respected '60s folkie enter the pop world of the '70s with *Diamonds and Rust,* which produced two hit singles: her own title track and the Richard Betts–penned "Blue Sky." Kershenbaum assembled a great studio band for Baez featuring Larry Carlton, Dean Parks, Wilton Felder, Joe Sample, and Jim Gordon, who contributed to the thick but slick sound. After three more hit albums with Baez, Kershenbaum's next major accomplishment was the discovery and production of Joe Jackson.

Entranced by the new music coming out of England—especially Elvis Costello (see entry)—Kershenbaum went there as an independent scout for A&M in the summer of 1978. After dashing hither and yon throughout the summer, Kershenbaum was about to return home empty-handed when he got Jackson's tape on a Friday. Kershenbaum canceled his flight, listened repeatedly to the tape over the weekend, and signed Jackson on Monday.

Kershenbaum produced Jackson's classic first two albums, filled to the brim with lean, mean, tuneful, wavy rock 'n' roll. Jackson's remarkable vocal similarities to Costello somewhat overshadowed his great, keenly observed songs about relationships and society. *Look Sharp!* and *I'm the Man* have nary a stinker between them as the crack band of Gary Sanford (guitar), Dave Houghton (drums), Graham Maby (bass), and Jackson (keyboards) rock through "One More Time," "Got the Time," "I'm the Man," and great pop-ish singles "Is She Really Going Out With Him?" (No. 21) and "It's Different for Girls" (No. 5 U.K.). After a break, Kershenbaum and Jackson reunited in 1982 for *Night and Day:* Jackson's most popular album and a radical foray into sophisticated late-night cocktail jazz. "Steppin' Out" captures the cool excitement of urban nightlife, where one can "leave the TV and the radio behind" and abandon oneself to the communal siren call of the bright, colored lights. "Breaking Us in Two" (No. 18 U.K.) is a lovely, touching look at a doomed relationship.

In 1988 Kershenbaum produced Tracy Chapman's first solo album (recorded at Kershenbaum's own Powertrax studio in Hollywood), a remarkable statement by a young black woman in a contemporary folk setting. Kershenbaum's tasteful production polishes not to deflect but to focus attention on Chapman's powerful songs of yearning ("Fast Car," No. 6), social dysfunction ("Talkin' 'Bout a Revolution"), and love ("Baby Can I Hold You?," "For My Lover"). Kershenbaum describes Chapman as the kind of artist he "had been waiting for as a producer and listener," and one who gave him "chills from the raw emotion." They worked together again on a follow-up that was almost as good, *Crossroads.*

After two years with Morgan Creek in the early '90s, Kershenbaum is once again an independent producer, working with Kenny Loggins, the Williams Brothers, Joshua Kadison, and Billy Mann.

Kershenbaum sees the producer as someone who wears three hats, and he has tried them all. "In ascending order," he says, "those hats include: (1) the tap-dancing hat. Artists are suspicious of record company interference so you have to help them realize their dreams, while giving the record company the tools that they need to market the record so that there is some commercial realization at the end of the process. (2) The financial-responsibility hat, which is self-explanatory. And most important, (3) the emotional-coach hat. As a producer you may hear someone sing something that

melts your heart, but the minute the [record] light goes on, the artist freezes up. Or they do great but think that it isn't good enough, and then nothing is good enough. Or they beat themselves up. You have to figure out what makes them tick in order to get their gift out of them and onto tape. Without that gift, things can be technically perfect but devoid of feeling—and the feeling is what people react to most." —ERIC OLSEN

Any Trouble: *Any Trouble,* EMI America, 1983.
Axton, Hoyt: *Fearless,* A&M, 1976 • *Road Songs,* A&M, 1977.
Bade, Lisa: *Suspicion,* A&M, 1982.
Baez, Joan: "Blue Sky," A&M, 1975 • "Diamonds and Rust," A&M, 1975 • *Diamonds and Rust,* A&M, 1975 • *From Every Stage,* A&M, 1976 • *Gulf Winds,* A&M, 1976 • *Blowin' Away,* Portrait, 1977 • *The Best Of,* A&M, 1977 • *Classics,* Vol. 8, A&M, 1987 • *Rare, Live and Classic,* Vanguard, 1993 • *Greatest Hits,* A&M, 1996.
Boomerang: *Boomerang,* Atlantic, 1982.
Branigan, Laura: "Power of Love," Atlantic, 1987 • "Your Love," MCA, 1988 (*Salsa* soundtrack) • *The Best Of,* Atlantic, 1995.
Brooks, Elkie: *Shooting Star,* A&M, 1978.
Buck-O-Nine: *28 Teeth,* TVT, 1997.
Burns Sisters: *Endangered Species,* Columbia, 1989.
Cecilio and Kapono: *Elua,* Columbia, 1975, 1988.
Chapman, Tracy: "Baby Can I Hold You?," Elektra, 1988 • "Fast Car," Elektra, 1988 • "Talkin' 'Bout a Revolution," Elektra, 1988 • *Tracy Chapman,* Elektra, 1988 • "Crossroads," Elektra, 1989 • *Crossroads,* Elektra, 1989.
Coleman, Durrell: "Somebody Took My Love," Island, 1985.
Cox, John: *Sunny Day,* Questar Mission, 1997.
Crenshaw, Marshall: *Good Evening,* Warner Bros., 1989.
Curtis, Catie: *Truth from Lies,* Hear/Capitol, 1996.
Duran Duran: "Rio" (remix), Capitol, 1982.
Frampton, Peter: *Breaking All the Rules,* A&M, 1981 • *Shine On: A Collection,* A&M, 1992.
Gallagher and Lyle: *Breakaway,* A&M, 1976 • *Love on the Airwaves,* A&M, 1977.
Hall, Lani: *Double or Nothing,* A&M, 1979.
Havens, Richie: *The End of the Beginning,* A&M, 1976.
Hazard, Robert: *Wing of Fire,* RCA, 1984.
Hickman, Sara: "Hello, I Am Your Heart," Elektra, 1990 (*Rubaiyat: Elektra's 40th Anniversary*) • *Shortstop,* Elektra, 1990.
Hill, Kim: *The Fire Again,* Star Song, 1997.
Hues Corporation: *Love Corporation,* RCA, 1975 • *The Best Of,* RCA, 1977.
Jackson, Joe: *I'm the Man,* A&M, 1979 • "Is She Really Going Out with Him?," A&M, 1979 • *Look Sharp,* A&M, 1979 • *Night and Day,* A&M, 1982 • "Steppin' Out," A&M, 1982 • "Breaking Us in Two," A&M, 1983 • *Body and Soul,* A&M,

1984 • "Happy Ending," A&M, 1984 • "You Can't Get What You Want," A&M, 1984 • *Big World*, A&M, 1986 • *Live, 1980–1986*, A&M, 1988 • *Greatest Hits*, A&M, 1996.

Johnny and the Distractions: *Let It Rock*, A&M, 1982.

Kadison, Joshua: *Painted Desert*, SBK, 1993, 1995.

Knight, Jerry: *Jerry Knight*, A&M, 1980 • *Perfect Fit*, A&M, 1981.

Laws, Ronnie: *Mirror Town*, Columbia, 1986.

Loggins, Kenny: *Leap of Faith*, Columbia, 1991.

Mann, Billy: *Earthbound*, A&M, 1998.

Nelson, Loey: *Venus Kissed the Moon*, Warner Bros., 1989.

Origin, The: *The Origin*, Virgin, 1990.

Ozark Mountain Daredevils: *Don't Look Down*, A&M, 1977 • *The Best*, A&M, 1981.

Parker, Graham: *The Real Macaw*, Arista, 1983 • *Passion Is No Ordinary Word: The Graham Parker Anthology*, Rhino, 1993.

Peregrins: *Peregrins*, MCA Special Products, 1989.

R.A.F.: *R.A.F.*, A&M, 1980.

Reds, The: *The Reds*, A&M, 1979.

Schwarz, Stephen Michael: *Stephen Michael Schwarz*, RCA, 1974.

Shadowfax: *Folksongs for a Nuclear Village*, Capitol, 1987.

Show of Hands: *Show of Hands*, IRS, 1989.

Sterling: *City Kids*, A&M, 1979.

Stevens, Cat: *Izitso*, A&M, 1977 • *Footsteps in the Dark: Greatest Hits*, Vol. 2, A&M, 1984 • *Classics*, Vol. 24, A&M, 1987 • *Three*, Mobile Fidelity Sound Lab, 1996.

Stevenson, B.W.: *B.W. Stevenson*, RCA, 1972 • *Lead Free*, RCA, 1972 • *Calabasas*, RCA, 1973 • "My Maria," RCA, 1973 • *My Maria*, RCA, 1973 • *Pass This Way*, RCA, 1973 • "Shambala," RCA, 1973 • *The Best Of*, RCA, 1977.

Supertramp: *Brother Where You Bound?*, A&M, 1985 • "Cannonball," A&M, 1985.

Tarney-Spencer Band: *Three's a Crowd*, A&M, 1978 • *Run for Your Life*, A&M, 1979.

Vanwarmer, Randy: *The Things That You Dream*, Bearsville, 1983.

Williams Brothers: *The Williams Brothers*, Warner Bros., 1991 • "Can't Cry Hard Enough," Warner Bros., 1992.

Chris Kimsey

Veteran British producer and engineer Chris Kimsey takes a minimalist approach to the recording process. His production of Colin James and the Little Big Band is a case in point. "I think we cut it in about 10 days," Kimsey says proudly. "Mötley Crüe was in the next studio, and by the time we'd finished that album

they'd done one guitar solo. I heard later that they never used that solo anyway," he adds with a laugh. Although Kimsey has worked with such disparate acts as French pop icon Johnny Hallyday and Ireland's Chieftains, he is best known for his work with Peter Frampton, the Rolling Stones, and modern rock bands such as the Escape Club ("Wild, Wild West," No. 1), INXS (*Full Moon, Dirty Hearts*), Killing Joke (*Night Time*, No. 11 U.K.), Psychedelic Furs (*Midnight to Midnight*, No. 12 U.K.), and Soul Asylum (*Candy from a Stranger*). Kimsey has also worked with reggae legends Peter Tosh and Jimmy Cliff.

Kimsey engineered and co-produced the Stones' *Emotional Rescue* (No. 1), *Tattoo You* (No. 1), *Undercover* (No. 4), *Steel Wheels* (No. 3), and *Flashpoint* (No. 16). Indeed, Kimsey was an invaluable consultant to the Stones by helping select guitar sounds and by contributing ideas during writing sessions with Mick Jagger and Keith Richards. An example of his contributions to the Stones' canon is *Tattoo You*, a compilation of odds and ends from other sessions. "Mick and Keith weren't talking to each other and we had to get an album together," Kimsey recalls. "So I decided to go into the vaults." Kimsey points out that "Start Me Up" (No. 2) was originally recorded for *Some Girls*, while "Waiting on a Friend" (No. 13) dated from the *Goats Head Soup* period. "I'd just be left alone," Kimsey says with obvious glee. "They'd come in and say, 'Great, fantastic.' It was very easy to work with those guys."

Kimsey's initial contact with the Stones came about through his internship at Olympic Studios in London, one of the Stones' favorite recording locales. Kimsey joined Olympic in the late '60s as an assistant engineer, or "tea boy" in English parlance. That apprenticeship led Kimsey into engineering and co-producing album projects by Ten Years After, Spooky Tooth, Mott the Hoople, and Bad Company. Moreover, Kimsey worked with Peter Frampton on *Wind of Change, Frampton*, and *Frampton Comes Alive*, the largest-selling concert album in rock history. That landmark album was controversial in one respect: some charged that the audience's applause was boosted in the mix. "I remember a lot of people said, 'Oh, they've looped it and they've doubled it,' but we never did," Kimsey insists. "It was just a wonderful thing that we got on tape."

Moreover, *Frampton Comes Alive* was initially slated as a single disc. "[Frampton's manager] Dee Anthony said, 'Oh, we're only going to do a single album; no one wants a double album.' Then [A&M cofounder] Jerry Moss came down to the studio and heard the album and said, 'Where's the rest of it?' So we went back and mixed the other half," Kimsey adds with a chuckle.

With three decades in the industry, Kimsey has learned to lighten up. For instance, he used to be upset when an engineer was hired to remix his original mixes. Then, one day while driving in Los Angeles he heard "Miss You" on the radio and thought it was Bob Clearmountain's (see entry) remixed version without the saxophone solo. "I'm thinking, 'Bob is really good; this is fantastic,'" Kimsey muses. "Then all of a sudden the sax solo comes on. It was the best thing that could have happened to me." —BEN CROMER

Anderson Bruford Wakeman Howe: *Anderson Bruford Wakeman Howe*, Arista, 1989.

Cactus World News: *Urban Beaches*, MCA, 1986 • "Years Later," MCA, 1986.

Carillo: *Rings Around the Moon*, Atlantic, 1978.

Chieftains, The: *Long Black Veil*, RCA, 1995.

Cliff, Jimmy: *Special*, Columbia, 1982, 1989 • "Treat the Youths Right," Columbia, 1984 (*Rhythm Come Forward*) • *Super Hits*, Sony, 1997.

Cult, The: *Dreamtime*, Beggars Banquet, 1984 • *Resurrection Joe* (EP), Alex, 1991 • *High Octane Cult*, Warner Bros., 1996.

Dice: *The Dice*, Mercury, 1984.

Diesel Park West: *Shakespeare Alabama*, Food/EMI America, 1989.

Doc Holliday: *Doc Holliday*, Metro, 1973.

Duran Duran: *Liberty*, Capitol, 1990 • "Violence of Summer (Love's Taking Over)," Capitol, 1990.

Eat: *Epicure*, Fiction, 1993, 1994.

Escape Club: "Shake for the Sheik," Atlantic, 1988 • "Wild, Wild West," Atlantic, 1988 • *Wild, Wild West*, Atlantic, 1988 • "Walking Through Walls," Atlantic, 1989.

Fingerprintz: *Beat Noir*, Virgin/Stiff, 1981.

Fish: *Internal Exile*, Polydor, 1992.

Frampton, Peter: *Wind of Change*, A&M, 1972 • "I Can't Stand It No More," A&M, 1979 • *Where I Should Be*, A&M, 1979 • *Classics*, Vol. 12, A&M, 1989 • *Shine On: A Collection*, A&M, 1992 • *Greatest Hits*, A&M, 1996.

Gipsy Kings: *Compas*, Nonesuch, 1997.

Harrison, Mike: *Rainbow Rider*, Island, 1975.

INXS: *Full Moon, Dirty Hearts*, Atlantic, 1993.

James, Colin: w/ the Little Big Band, *Colin James and the Little Big Band*, Virgin, 1994 • *Bad Habits*, Elektra, 1995 • w/ the Little Big Band, "Surely (I Love You)," A&M, 1996 (*Kingpin* soundtrack).

James, Wendy: *Now Ain't the Time for Your Tears*, DGC, 1993.

Jett, Joan, and the Blackhearts: *Glorious Results of a Misspent Youth*, Blackheart/MCA, 1984.

Killing Joke: *Night Time*, Virgin EG, 1985 • "Eighties," Virgin America, 1986 • "Sanity," Virgin America, 1986 • *Brighter Than a Thousand Suns* (9 tracks), Virgin America, 1987 • *Laugh? I Nearly Bought One*, EG, 1992.

Kinky Machine: *Kinky Machine*, MCA, 1993.

Law, The: *The Law*, Atlantic, 1991.

London Symphony Orchestra: *Symphonic Music of the Rolling Stones*, RCA, 1994.

Marillion: "Kayleigh," Virgin/EMI, 1985 (*Now That's What I Call Music 5*) • *Misplaced Childhood*, Capitol, 1985 • *Brief Encounter* (EP), Capitol, 1986 • *Clutching at Straws*, Capitol, 1987 • *Six of One, Half-Dozen of the Other*, IRS, 1992.

Noiseworks: *Touch*, Columbia, 1988.

Novo Combo: *Novo Combo*, Polydor, 1981.

Piper: *Can't Wait*, A&M, 1977.

Psychedelic Furs: "Heartbreak Beat," Columbia, 1987 • *Midnight to Midnight*, Columbia, 1987 • *All of This and Nothing*, Columbia, 1988 • *B-Sides and Lost Grooves*, Legacy, 1994 • *Should God Forget: A Retrospective*, Columbia, 1997.

Reid, Terry: *Rogue Waves*, Capitol, 1979.

Rolling Stones: *Emotional Rescue*, Rolling Stones, 1980 • *Tattoo You*, Rolling Stones, 1981 • *Undercover*, Rolling Stones, 1983 • "Mixed Emotions," Rolling Stones, 1989 • "Rock and a Hard Place," Rolling Stones, 1989 • *Steel Wheels*, Rolling Stones, 1989 • "Almost Hear You Sigh," Rolling Stones, 1990 • *Flashpoint*, Rolling Stones, 1991 • "High Wire," Columbia, 1991.

Smith, Curt: *Soul on Board*, Mercury, 1993.

Soul Asylum: *Candy from a Stranger*, Columbia, 1998 • "Close," Columbia, 1998.

Squier, Billy: *Reach for the Sky: The Anthology*, Capitol, 1996.

Stainton, Chris: *Tundra*, Decca, 1976.

Strapps: *Secret Damage*, EMI, 1977.

Ten Years After: *Rock and Roll Music to the World*, Chrysalis/Columbia, 1972.

Tosh, Peter: "Johnny B. Goode," EMI, 1983 • *Mama Africa*, EMI, 1983 • *The Toughest*, Capitol, 1988 *The Best of Peter Tosh: Dread Don't Die*, EMI America, 1996.

Tracker: *Tracker*, Elektra, 1982.

Widowmaker: *Too Late to Cry*, Jet, 1977.

Williams, Jerry: *Gone*, Warner Bros., 1979.

Wyman, Bill: *Bill Wyman*, A&M, 1982.

John King

See DUST BROTHERS

Gary Klein

Gary Klein's career refutes conventional wisdom and proves that nice guys can finish first, even in the music business. A talented musician, songwriter, arranger, producer, and music-publishing innovator, Klein has been an industry stalwart for over 30 years. As a producer Klein has worked with some of the biggest names in the business, including Glen Campbell ("Southern Nights," No. 1; *Something 'Bout You Baby I Like; It's the World Gone Crazy*), Johnny Cash (*John R. Cash*), Judy Collins (*Hard Times for Lovers*), Mac Davis (*Stop and Smell the Roses,* No. 13; *Burnin' Thing*), Gladys Knight (*Miss Gladys Knight*), Liza Minnelli (*Live At the Winter Garden*), Dolly Parton (*Here You Come Again,* No. 20; *Heartbreaker; Dolly Dolly Dolly*), and Barbra Streisand (*Streisand Superman,* No. 3; *Songbird,* No. 12; *Wet,* No. 7).

Gary Klein was born on September 28, 1942, and grew up in Jamaica Estates, Queens. His father owned a children's retail clothing store. The family's next-door neighbor had a son who was a flautist with the Pittsburgh Symphony Orchestra; when Gary was 5, the flute player gave him a toy flute and gave him lessons whenever he could. He was Klein's first musical mentor.

About a year later, Klein discovered the inside of his parent's baby grand piano; he climbed inside and started plucking away at the strings and fiddling with the hammers. Eventually he climbed out and turned his attention to the keys, but Klein was always fascinated with the mechanisms behind the sounds. Blessed with a natural ear, Klein could soon plunk out on the piano virtually any melody he heard on record or the radio, providing entertainment for his parent's guests.

Next, the seemingly miraculous concept of tape recording overtook Klein's imagination. His parents succumbed to pressure and bought him a recorder when he was about 10; Klein immersed himself in recording, learning to create effects, mike placement, and other esoteric skills. Remarkably industrious and independent, Klein pursued his interest in piano—playing after school every day—and in how things work—tinkering with radios, recorders, and the like. He tested every tube when the family got a TV. He also wore out battery after battery listening to his Zenith transistor radio late into the night.

Though he never took piano lessons, Klein did take accordion for a time until he was dismissed for learning "unauthorized material" on his own. In Klein's next assault on the walls of Music, he rented instruments,

one at a time, from the local music store and learned to play a tune on each.

Though his friends tended to concentrate on one kind of music, Klein's taste was always eclectic: a trip to the record store might yield the gospel of Mahalia Jackson, the jazz of Miles Davis, and the orchestral music of the *Victory at Sea* soundtrack, as well as rock 'n' roll and country. Sonically sophisticated from an early age, Klein remembers when mono went to stereo. "It was revolutionary to have a spatial relationship between instruments—to hear where the horn section was—and I would listen and visualize where everyone sat," he says.

In his teens, Klein started to write songs with a friend of his older brother's, Hank Hoffman. Klein wrote melodies to Hoffman's lyrics, and eventually they got good enough to take the songs into New York to demonstrate them for publishers. They were signed to AME Publishers and had a hit in 1962 with "Bobby's Girl" (inspired by the birth of Klein's nephew Bobby) by Marcie Blane. Klein began to record demos for their songs—his first exposure to the recording studio ("Wow, look at all of those tape recorders!")—mastering the basics quickly.

Klein decided to go to school for music and chose the new C.W. Post campus of Long Island University. Though he had no formal training (save for a year of accordion lessons), the music faculty gave him credit for his desire and life experience and taught him the fundamentals from the ground up. Though he got a D in piano for "incorrect fingering," Klein graduated in 1964 with a solid foundation in composition, theory, and music history.

Before he graduated, Klein was going to school in the mornings and writing songs on his upright piano in his tiny Tin Pan Alley office in the afternoons. Hoffman had to quit songwriting to support his family, and Klein moved to Morris Levy's Big Seven Publishing. In 1966 Klein joined Koppelman-Rubin Associates as a writer/producer and went to L.A. for a year to open Koppelman-Rubin's West Coast office. He became fast friends with Tommy LiPuma and Al Schmitt (see entries) right away, and Klein's secretary ended up marrying LiPuma. Klein reveled in the camaraderie of the day: many producers and writers hung out at Martoni's in Hollywood and traded tips and gossip. Through Jack Nitzsche (see entry), Klein met the Buffalo Springfield, and even helped bail Neil Young out of jail after the "Sunset Strip riot" of late 1966.

Klein returned to New York. His first major production was Tim Hardin's only hit single, "Simple Song of Freedom," in 1969. He also produced Hardin's *Suite for Susan Moore and Damion* album, recorded entirely at

Hardin's Woodstock home. Klein ran mikes to every room of the house and the album was done on the fly. According to Klein, "Tim guaranteed that there would be music if I was ready to record at any time. Musicians were going to drop by. His son's bedroom was the control room. Tim would lay on his bed and start reading poetry into a mike with musicians playing behind him. Somehow it worked."

Klein followed Charles Koppelman to April/Blackwood Publishing in 1971 and Columbia Records in 1973. For Klein, most business has been personal. He produced the Mac Davis hit single "Stop and Smell the Roses" (No. 9) in 1974; by 1977 Davis's (former) wife Sarah was with Glen Campbell, whom she introduced to Klein. Klein produced Campbell, and when Campbell hooked up with Tanya Tucker in the early '80s, Klein produced her too. Campbell also led Klein to Roger Miller.

Klein hit his creative and commercial stride in the late '70s, producing Campbell, Dolly Parton, and Barbra Streisand. In the mid-'70s, Streisand's then-boyfriend Jon Peters was producing the album that turned out to be *ButterFly*. Columbia A&R chief Koppelman asked Klein to critique the work in progress. Klein determined that the album was most certainly not happening. Koppelman asked Klein to come with him to Streisand's ranch in Malibu to explain why.

When they arrived, Klein recalls, "Barbra asked me, with her long fingernail pointing at me, 'Who are you? What's your name? What do you do?' Barbra and Jon were on a bed listening to what had been recorded for the album on a huge sound system. Charles said, 'Gary is going to tell you what's going on,' and he played track one. I criticized it constructively, and did the same thing for each track, mentioning specifically the weaknesses of the players."

"I asked who was playing on the tracks," he continues, "and Peters said, 'Oh baby, they're the best in town.' Barbra asked who they were, and Peters didn't know anyone's name. Barbra said, 'Gary, continue,' and she started to trust me."

Klein ended up producing three of Streisand's best pop albums—*Streisand Superman, Songbird, Wet*—and the classic No. 1 singles "My Heart Belongs to Me" and (with Donna Summer) "No More Tears (Enough Is Enough)."

Klein recalls the "Tears" sessions. "There were too many divas for the room. They started off recording together, and then they recorded individually, trying to top each other. When we were almost finished, Barbra said, 'What do I need this for? I don't want to do it anymore.' I finally convinced her to finish by telling her

that this was the way to end the disco era on a high note."

Working with Streisand was rewarding but at times problematic. "She's the greatest singer I've ever heard, but she can be difficult. She knows what she wants and sometimes isn't very diplomatic about explaining it. Barbra also keeps an eye (and ear) on everything. She is always testing to make sure that you know what you are doing. Although she was afraid to let anyone take too much control away from her, I made the same deal with her that I made with all artists: 'I'll meet you halfway, I'll listen to you if you listen to me'—and she did."

Klein worked primarily with artists who didn't write their own songs, or who (like Dolly Parton) supplemented their own writing with outside material. "I spent most of my time, when I wasn't in the studio, trying to find songs. I would sit in my den with the phone turned off and the door closed and listen to tapes eight hours a day. I had a system where I put Velcro on each cassette and attached them to a huge Plexiglas wall, organized by when they came in and where they came from. I listened to them all."

Working on the *Superman* sessions with Streisand in L.A., Klein kept humming a tune that they weren't recording. That night he remembered that the tune was from a demo tape that was under his bed in New York. He called his wife Bonnie and asked her to overnight the tape to him in California. In that way, an unsolicited song ("Superman") by a then-unknown writer became the title track to a Streisand album.

Klein says that he most enjoyed working with Dolly Parton. "She's a very down-to-earth and sincere person. Once she likes you, that's it. She gave you responsibility and knew how to bring out the best in people: musicians, engineers, everyone. After we recorded 'Here You Come Again' (No. 3), I wanted Dolly's approval on the mix. She said, 'It's just my career in your hands—see ya.' Sometimes we would order a pitcher of margaritas and just chat. She is witty, sweet, funny, and smart. Don't be fooled by the twang."

Also on "Here You Come," Klein used a technique he discovered playing around inside the piano when he was 7 years old: he put masking tape across all of the piano strings, which gave them a muted, percussive, almost banjo-like quality. The pianist on the session, David Foster (see entry), was nonplussed but loved the sound when he heard it. When mixed with the regular piano, it gave the song an old-timey feel.

By 1987 Klein felt that music was changing away from him, and he was tired of living in the studio. His kids were growing up in New York and he was producing mostly in L.A., living a tiresome bicoastal existence.

So that year Klein reunited with his old friend Koppelman, who was starting the SBK company. SBK bought out the massive *CBS Songs* catalog and resold it to EMI at a considerable profit; Klein also went to EMI and developed the concept of "creative services" for music publishing.

His notion was that if the company's catalog was marketed to the professionals who license songs for film, TV, advertising, and the like, then EMI would get a bigger share of the pie. Besides creating EMI's ad campaign, Klein created "a set of professional tools to be given away to licensing professionals, by taking 90-second clips of our top income-earning songs (from the '20s through the '80s), and boxing them into a CD package with a discography booklet—over 1,000 songs in all."

The technique has been a tremendous marketing success and has been followed by other publishers. Staying on the cutting edge, Klein has now developed a professional licensing web site for EMI, with a lyric search engine, 45-second song clips, and online licensing at www.emimusicpub.com. —ERIC OLSEN

Brubeck, Darius: *Chaplin's Back,* Paramount, 1967.

Campbell, Glen: "Southern Nights," Capitol, 1977 • "Sunflower," Capitol, 1977 • *Southern Nights,* Capitol, 1978 • *Something 'Bout You Baby I Like,* Capitol, 1980 • *It's the World Gone Crazy,* Capitol, 1981 • *The Very Best Of,* Capitol, 1987 • *Gentle on My Mind: The Collection, 1962–1989,* Razor & Tie, 1997.

Cash, Johnny: *John R. Cash,* Columbia, 1974.

Collins, Judy: *Hard Times for Lovers,* Elektra, 1979 • *Forever: An Anthology,* Elektra, 1997.

Daniels, Charlie: *To John, Grease and the Wolfman,* Kama Sutra, 1972.

Davis, Mac: *Burning Thing,* Columbia, 1974 • "Stop and Smell the Roses," Columbia, 1974 • *Stop and Smell the Roses,* Columbia, 1974 • *Greatest Hits,* Columbia, 1979.

Dr. Buzzard and the Original Savannah Band: *Dr. Buzzard Goes to Washington,* Elektra, 1979.

Farina, Sandy: *All Alone in the Night,* MCA, 1980.

Gaffney, Henry: *Waiting for a Wind,* United Artists, 1978.

Hardin, Tim: *Tim Hardin 3: Live in Concert,* MGM, 1968 • "Simple Song of Freedom," Columbia, 1969 • *Suite for Susan Moore and Damion,* Columbia, 1969 • *Simple Songs,* Legacy, 1996.

Humperdinck, Engelbert: *Don't You Love Me Anymore?,* Epic, 1981 • *16 Most Requested Songs,* Columbia, 1996.

Ian, Janis: *Restless Eyes,* CBS, 1981.

Knight, Gladys: *Miss Gladys Knight,* Buddah, 1978 • *Blue Lights in the Basement,* RCA, 1996.

Ladd, Cheryl: *Cheryl Ladd,* Capitol, 1978 • "Think It Over,"

Capitol, 1978 • *Dance Forever,* Capitol, 1979.

Levine, Enid: *American Love,* Columbia, 1983.

Lewis, Gary: *Listen,* Liberty, 1968 • w/ the Playboys, *Gary Lewis and the Playboys,* Gold Rush, 1996.

Marshall Tucker Band: *Tuckerized,* Warner Bros., 1982.

Miller, Roger: *Making a Name for Myself,* 20th Century, 1979.

Mills, Stephanie: *Merciless,* Casablanca, 1983 • *The Best Of,* Mercury, 1995.

Minnelli, Liza: *Live At the Wintergarden,* Columbia, 1974.

Parton, Dolly: *Here You Come Again,* RCA, 1977 • "Baby I'm Burnin'," RCA, 1978 • *Dolly,* RCA, 1978 • "Heartbreaker," RCA, 1978 • *Heartbreaker,* RCA, 1978 • "Here You Come Again," RCA, 1978 • "It's All Wrong, But It's All Right/Two Doors Down," RCA, 1978 • "I Really Got the Feeling/Baby I'm Burning," RCA, 1979 • *Dolly Dolly Dolly,* RCA, 1980 • "Old Flames Can't Hold a Candle to You," RCA, 1980 • "Starting Over Again," RCA, 1980 • *Collectors Series,* RCA, 1985 • *Think About Love,* RCA, 1986 • *The Best There Is,* RCA, 1987 • *The RCA Years, 1967–1986,* RCA, 1993 • *The Essential Dolly Parton,* Vol. 2, RCA, 1997.

Plant and See: *Plant and See,* White Whale, 1968.

Sang, Samantha: *Emotion,* Private Stock, 1978.

Spector, Ronnie: *Unfinished Business,* Columbia, 1987.

Steinberg, David: *Booga, Booga,* Legacy, 1974, 1992.

Streisand, Barbra: "My Heart Belongs to Me," Columbia, 1977 • *Greatest Hits,* Vol. 2, Columbia, 1978, 1982 • "Love Theme from Eyes of Laura Mars," Columbia, 1978 • "Songbird," Columbia, 1978 • *Songbird,* Columbia, 1978 • *Streisand Superman,* Columbia, 1978 • *The Eyes of Laura Mars* (soundtrack), Columbia, 1978 • w/ Donna Summer, "No More Tears (Enough Is Enough)," Columbia, 1979 • *Wet,* Columbia, 1979 • "Kiss Me in the Rain," Columbia, 1980 • *Memories,* Columbia, 1982 • *Just for the Record,* Columbia, 1991.

Summer, Donna: *On the Radio,* Casablanca, 1979 • *The Summer Collection,* Mercury, 1985.

Thomas, B.J.: *Throwin' Rocks at the Moon,* Liberty, 1985.

Tucker, Tanya: *Should I Do It?,* MCA, 1981 • *The Best Of,* MCA, 1982 • *Collection,* MCA, 1992.

Wright Brothers: *Made in the USA,* Warner Bros., 1982.

COLLECTIONS

Annie (original cast), Sony, 1977, 1990.

KMFDM

See SASCHA KONIETZKO AND KMFDM

Mark Knopfler

Rock 'n' roll bands are rarely democracies. Mick and Keith (see Glimmer Twins entry) rule the Stones, Dave Gilmour is clearly in command of Pink Floyd, and Mark Knopfler decides the fate of Dire Straits. Indeed, Knopfler's importance to Dire Straits is without question: imagine Wings without McCartney or Traffic without Winwood.

Born August 12, 1949, in Glasgow, Scotland, Knopfler established himself as a masterful guitarist, singer, and composer with the band's first two albums: *Dire Straits*, the album with the essential "Sultans of Swing"; and *Communiqué*, an underrated classic that included the cryptic "Once upon a Time in the West."

By the time of the band's third album, *Making Movies* (No. 19), Knopfler had taken on production duties in tandem with Jimmy Iovine (see entry), resulting in a decidedly more mainstream sound, as evidenced by the kick-out-the-jams of "Solid Rock" and the sweeping drama of "Tunnel of Love."

Dire Straits' 1982 album, *Love over Gold* (No. 19), was a solo production by Knopfler that featured the elongated "Telegraph Road" and the mysterious "Private Investigations." Knopfler also produced the band's rare *Extended Play* disc, and *Twisting by the Pool*: a delightful slice of rock that displayed Knopfler's lighter side.

Knopfler also stepped out of his Dire Straits' persona to produce outside projects such as Bob Dylan's *Infidels* (No. 20) and Aztec Camera's *Knife*. Moreover, Knopfler's imprint was unmistakable on Tina Turner's recording of his song, "Private Dancer." In fact, Turner's version clearly followed Knopfler's demo, a track that would have fit nicely on *Love over Gold*.

In 1985, Knopfler produced Dire Straits' tour de force, *Brothers in Arms* (No. 1). Clearly one of Knopfler's crowning achievements, it catapulted the band to worldwide acclaim, resulting in such hits as the bouncy "Walk of Life" (No. 7) and the album's centerpiece, "Money for Nothing" (No. 1). "Money for Nothing" was inspired by a visit to an appliance store where Knopfler overheard a salesman's tirade against the excesses of MTV. Knopfler solidified the theme with guitar licks borrowed liberally from Z.Z. Top's Billy Gibbons and incorporated Sting's dulcet tones for the refrain, "I want my MTV," as the icing on the cake.

Knopfler began to explore new directions following *Brothers in Arms* that were purposely low-key: *Missing . . . Presumed Having a Good Time* was a bluegrass-folk hybrid credited to the Notting Hillbillies; *Neck and Neck* was a duet album with country music icon Chet Atkins (see entry); while *Local Hero, Cal, The Princess Bride*, and *Wag the Dog* were soundtrack projects that displayed Knopfler's organic approach to composing and producing.

In the '90s Knopfler continued to mix and match diverse projects such as Dire Straits' largely unheralded *On Every Street* (No. 12) and his superb 1996 solo album, *Golden Heart*, which included "Darling Pretty," a song also on the soundtrack to *Twister*.

A musical wanderer, Knopfler finally appears to have found a home by mixing the roots of rock from the United States with the roots of his homeland, Britain. It is a combination that he captures perfectly on *Golden Heart*. "It's all to do with the connections between black music and Celtic music," Knopfler told interviewer Ian Nicolson. "My idea of musical bliss is where the Delta meets the Tyne." —BEN CROMER

Atkins, Chet: w/ Mark Knopfler, *Neck and Neck*, Columbia, 1990.

Aztec Camera: *Knife*, Sire/Reprise, 1984.

Deville, Willy: *Miracle*, A&M, 1987.

Dire Straits: *Makin' Movies*, Warner Bros., 1980 • *Love over Gold*, Warner Bros., 1982 • *Twisting by the Pool* (EP), Warner Bros., 1983 • *Alchemy: Dire Straits Live*, Warner Bros., 1984 • *Brothers in Arms*, Warner Bros., 1985 • "Money for Nothing," Warner Bros., 1985 • "Walk of Life," Warner Bros., 1985 • "So Far Away," Warner Bros., 1986 • *Money for Nothing (Greatest Hits)*, Warner Bros., 1988 • *On Every Street*, Warner Bros., 1991 • *On the Night*, Warner Bros., 1993.

Dylan, Bob: *Infidels*, Columbia, 1983 • "Blind Willie McTell," Columbia, 1991 • *Bootleg Series*, Columbia, 1991 • *Greatest Hits*, Vol. 3, Columbia, 1995.

Jennings, Waylon: w/ Mark Knopfler, "Learning the Game," Decca, 1996 (*Not Fade Away [Remembering Buddy Holly]*).

Knopfler, Mark: *Local Hero* soundtrack, Warner Bros., 1983 • *Cal* soundtrack, Mercury, 1984 • *The Princess Bride* soundtrack, Warner Bros., 1987 • *Last Exit to Brooklyn* soundtrack, Warner Bros., 1989 • *Screenplaying*, Warner Alliance, 1993 • "Darling Pretty," Warner Bros., 1996 (*Twister* soundtrack) • *Golden Heart*, Warner Bros., 1996 • *Wag the Dog* soundtrack, PolyGram, 1998 • *See also* Atkins, Chet; Jennings, Waylon.

Newman, Randy: "It's Money That Matters," Reprise, 1988 • *Land of Dreams* (7 tracks), Reprise, 1988.

Notting Hillbillies: *Missing . . . Presumed Having a Good Time*, Warner Bros., 1990.

Turner, Tina: *Break Every Rule*, Capitol, 1986 • *Collected Recordings, Sixties to Nineties*, Capitol, 1994.

Frankie Knuckles

A s one of the pioneers of house music, Frankie Knuckles has played an integral role in elevating the industry stature of club DJs, as well as earning a reputation as one of the leading remixers and producers of the dance genre. Since he began gracing turntables in 1978, he has spun in countless venues around the world. But his heart still belongs to those spots where he first worked his groove spell: the famed Warehouse in Chicago and New York's legendary Paradise Garage, where he worked under the turntable guidance of the late, great Larry Levan.

He made his foray into remixing in 1981, when he revamped the disco classic "Let No Man Put Asunder" by First Choice on Salsoul Records. "It was way different back then," he says. "There was no such thing as going into the studio and cutting your own track. You had to make do with pre-existing tracks, which was tricky. But when it worked, it was magical."

From that record, Knuckles evolved into top-shelf remixer, adding his rich, R&B-leaning house sound to hundreds of records by artists that range from superstars like Janet Jackson and Toni Braxton to Alison Limerick and Adeva—with whom he would eventually form a brief studio partnership.

In fact, along the way, Knuckles has built a substantial sideline career as a recording artist. He issued two well-received albums on Virgin Records, *Beyond the Mix* and *Welcome to the Real World.*

"I love to do remix work, but I prefer to write and produce. There is a big difference between the two," he says, "even though remix work is postproduction work, and you're rewriting all those tracks and everything to existing songs."

To that end, Knuckles has recently taken on fewer remix projects, choosing only the tunes that "tickle my fancy," and focusing on establishing a distinctive voice as a songwriter. "It's a tough mountain to climb," he says. "But I've convinced myself that it cannot be much tougher than those I've already conquered. I'm feeling brave . . . and more creatively alive than ever." —LARRY FLICK

Braxton, Toni: "I Don't Want To" (remix), LaFace, 1997.
Cardwell, Joi: *Joi Cardwell,* Lightyear, 1997.
En Vogue: *Remix to Sing,* EastWest, 1991.
First Choice: "Let No Man Put Asunder" (remix), Salsoul, 1981.

Jackson, Janet: "Because of Love" (remix), Virgin, 1994.
Jefferson, Marshall: *Frankie Knuckles Presents Marshall Jefferson,* Trax, 1989.
Jonah, Julian: "It's a Jungle out There" (remix), Chrysalis, 1990.
Khan, Chaka: *Life Is a Dance (The Remix Project),* Warner Bros., 1989 • "Never Miss the Water," Reprise, 1996 • "Never Miss the Water" (remix), Reprise, 1996.
Knuckles, Frankie: w/ Satoshi Tomiie, "Tears," FFRR, 1989 (*Silver on Black*) • *Beyond the Mix,* Virgin, 1990 • "The Whistle Song," Virgin, 1991 • w/ Shelton Becton, "It's Hard Sometimes," Virgin, 1992 • "Love Can Change It," Virgin, 1996 • *Sessions,* Vol. 6, Ministry of Sound, 1997 • "You Got the Love," Trax, 1997 • w/ Jamie Principal, "Baby Wants to Ride," UCA, 1998.
Knuckles, Frankie, and Adeva: "Too Many Fish," Virgin, 1995 • *Welcome to the Real World,* Virgin, 1995 • "Whadda U Want (from Me)?," Virgin, 1995 • "Whadda U Want (from Me)?" (remix), Virgin, 1995.
New Edition: "Hit Me Off" (remix), MCA, 1996.
Ross, Diana: *Diana Extended: The Remixes,* Motown, 1994.
Rozalla: *Look No Further,* Epic, 1995.
Simpson, Ray: *Ray Simpson,* Virgin, 1992.
Stansfield, Lisa: "Never, Never Gonna Give You Up" (remix), Arista, 1998.
Tenaglia, Danny: *Color Me Danny,* Twisted America, 1997.
Truth: "Open Our Eyes" (remix), FFRR, 1989 (*Silver on Black*).
White, Karyn: *Hungah* (EP), Warner Bros., 1994.

COLLECTIONS
If You Love Dance, Epic, 1996.

Paul Q. Kolderie and Sean Slade

B oston-based record makers Paul Q. Kolderie and Sean Slade regard themselves as facilitators rather than producers. In fact, when asked to define their role in the studio, Kolderie cites the French word for producer: *réalisateur.*

"I thought that was a pretty good definition of what we do," observes Kolderie. "We like to work with a group and *realize* their songs—make a song, which might exist only as humming in the air, into something real, something people can buy and play on the radio. That's our job. We don't really look at it as if there's any particular way to do that." "We try to get a person to sound like they should be, and not impose some kind of engineering structure on them," adds Slade.

Even within a particular project, they try to approach each song independently. "That's a lot harder," says Slade, "but we've always been fans of that *White Album* approach, where each song has its own distinct atmosphere. Sometimes when I hear records my first criticism of them is that they sound like they were all recorded and mixed in one place at one time."

Employing their "do no harm" approach, Kolderie and Slade have turned out some of the most enduring albums of the '90s, including breakthroughs by Hole (*Live Through This*), Radiohead (*Pablo Honey*), Tracy Bonham (*The Burdens of Being Upright*), and the Mighty Mighty Bosstones (*Let's Face It, Question the Answers*), plus influential releases by Uncle Tupelo, Juliana Hatfield, Buffalo Tom, and the Lemonheads. Also, without Slade, Kolderie coproduced virtually all of Morphine's recordings.

Besides being one of the most highly regarded production duos in the industry, Kolderie and Slade are a regional power base onto themselves, operating mostly out of Fort Apache Studios in Cambridge—a facility they founded in an abandoned commercial laundry building in Roxbury, Massachusetts, and later sold.

Kolderie and Slade were so hot by 1994 that MCA Records signed the duo to a production deal that also included three other producer/engineers associated with Fort Apache: Gary Smith, Lou Giordano, and Tim O'Heir (see entries). Despite some critical success, the deal never produced commercial rewards and was eventually dissolved.

Kolderie, a native of Minneapolis, and Slade, who was born in Rockland County, New York, met in 1975 while students at Yale in New Haven, Connecticut. Both musicians, they played on some of the first punk-rock bands ever heard in that bastion of academia ("It was a comfortable, sort of middle-class rebellion," says Kolderie).

They graduated in the late '70s and "drifted up to Boston, where there was a really good music scene at the time," adds Kolderie. They set up a reel-to-reel 4-track in the attic they shared and essentially went into the studio business in the do-it-yourself style that prevailed at the time. Their little room was so popular, and Kolderie and Slade so proficient at recording local punk bands, that they decided to put their efforts into producing rather than performing. "By that time we had pretty much played in every bar in the Northeast," recalls Slade. "The whole romance of rock had started to wear off, but the fun of recording was still amazing.

So when we were forced to move out of that house we got together with this other guy across town and bought an 8-track, and that was the original Fort Apache." "It was a very rock 'n' roll studio," says Kolderie. "It was crude and ugly, just like the bands' practice spaces, so they felt very comfortable there."

In 1987, Kolderie and Slade opened a second, 24-track room in Cambridge to complement their original Roxbury studio, which had grown to 16 tracks. Soon, however, their Roxbury neighborhood was overrun by crack, forcing Kolderie and Slade to shut it down and consolidate the operation in Cambridge, where Fort Apache now resides. (A new, smaller room was added in 1994 a couple of blocks away in Cambridge to accommodate some of the local clientele that was shut out by the studio's growth from DIY shop to major facility.) "By that point, we did practically every gig in town," says Kolderie. "By being on top of the market like that, bands come to you and you get to work with the best bands. We got ourselves established early on, and we've been able to keep it going ever since."

Since both are equally capable of producing and engineering, Kolderie and Slade work in a tag-team format, where on any given track, one will be the de facto producer, the other the engineer. "That's the key," says Kolderie, "because even if you're a producer you've still got to hire an engineer. So because we both do that, we avoid hiring another person. That's why there's always room for two of us in that situation."

Diehard fans of vintage gear, Kolderie and Slade prefer Neve consoles to newer, more state-of-the-art boards. "We started going to other studios that had these old boards and we realized that they really are superior," says Kolderie. "I don't know why they don't apply those principles today. Technology marches on and it's marching resolutely backward. There's an emphasis on features and convenience over quality. It's like a car with all these fancy things, but when you open the hood it's got a real tiny engine in there and there's no power." —PAUL VERNA

Kolderie and Slade

Belly: "Are You Experienced?," Reprise, 1993 (*Stone Free: A Tribute to Jimi Hendrix*).

Blackfish: *Blackfish*, Epic, 1993.

Blake, Jamie: *Jamie Blake*, A&M, 1997.

Blameless: *The Signs Are All There*, China, 1996.

Bonham, Tracy: "Mother Mother," Island, 1996 • *The Burdens of Being Upright*, Island, 1996.

Buffalo Tom: *Let Me Come Over*, Beggars Banquet/RCA, 1992.

Clockhammer: *Klinefelter*, First Warning/RCA, 1991.

Collier, Gerald: *Gerald Collier*, Warner Bros., 1998.

Das Damen: *Mousetrap,* Twin/Tone, 1989.

Dink: *Blame It on Tito* (EP), Capitol, 1996 • "Numb," Capitol, 1996.

Dinosaur Jr.: *Fossils* (2 tracks), SST, 1991.

Echobelly: *On,* 550 Music, 1995.

Family Cat: *Magic Happens,* Arista, 1994 • "Wonderful Excuse," Dedicated, 1994.

Field Trip: *Ripe,* Slash, 1991.

Goo Goo Dolls: "Lazy Eye," Warner Sunset, 1997.

Hatfield, Juliana: *Only Everything,* Mammoth/Atlantic, 1995 • "Universal Heartbeat," Mammoth/Atlantic, 1995.

Hole: *Live Through This,* Geffen, 1994.

Lemonheads, The: *Lovey,* Atlantic, 1990 • *Favorite Spanish Dishes* (EP), Atlantic, 1991.

Lifter: *Melinda (Everything Was Beautiful and Nothing Hurt),* Interscope, 1996.

Linoleum: *Dissent,* DGC, 1997.

Mighty Mighty Bosstones: *Devil's Night Out,* Taang!, 1990 • *Let's Face It,* Big Rig, 1997 • "The Impression That I Get," Big Rig/Mercury, 1997.

Orangutang: "Bigger Chunk," Demigod, 1993 • *The Rewards of Cruelty,* Imago, 1993 • *Dead Sailor Acid Blues,* Imago, 1994.

Paw: "Surrender," A&M, 1994 (*S.F.W.* soundtrack).

Radiohead: *Pablo Honey,* Capitol/EMI, 1993 • *Anyone Can Play Guitar,* EMI, 1994 • "Creep," A&M, 1994 (*S.F.W.* soundtrack).

Radish: *Restraining Bolt,* Mercury, 1997.

Speedball Baby: *Cinema!* Fort Apache, 1996.

Stretch Princess: *Stretch Princess,* Wind Up, 1998.

Tackle Box: *Grand Hotel,* Rockville, 1994.

360's: *Illuminated,* Link/Hollywood, 1991.

Tripmaster Monkey: *Goodbye Race,* Sire/Reprise, 1994.

Uncle Tupelo: *No Depression,* Rockville, 1990 • *Still Feel Gone,* Rockville, 1991.

Upper Crust: *Let Them Eat Rock,* Upstart, 1995.

Wax: *13 Unlucky Numbers,* Interscope, 1995.

COLLECTIONS

This Is Fort Apache, Fort Apache/MCA, 1995.
Elmopalooza! Sony Wonder, 1998.

Paul Kolderie

Belly: "Broken," Warner Bros., 1996 (*Twister* soundtrack).

Big Dipper: *Craps,* Homestead, 1988.

Blood Oranges: *Corn River,* ESD, 1990.

Bullet Lavolta: *The Gift* (11 tracks), Taang!, 1989.

Come: *Gently, Down the Stream,* Matador, 1998.

Dethmuffen, Miles: *Clutter,* Rainbow Quartz, 1994.

Firehouse: *Flyin' the Flannel,* Columbia, 1991 • *Live Totem Pole* (EP), Columbia, 1992 • *Big Bottom Pow Wow,* Columbia, 1993.

Fuzzy: *Electric Juices,* Tag/Atlantic, 1996.

Gigolo Aunts: *Full-On Bloom* (EP), Alias, 1993 • *Flippin' Out,* RCA, 1994.

Jale: "Promise," Sub Pop, 1994.

Lemonheads, The: "Stove," Atlantic, 1991 (*A Matter of Degrees* soundtrack).

Mighty Mighty Bosstones: *More Noise and Other Disturbances,* Taang!, 1991 • "Where'd You Go?," Taang!, 1991 • *Question the Answers,* Mercury, 1994.

Morphine: *Good,* Rykodisc, 1992, 1994 • "Buena," Rykodisc, 1993 • *Cure for Pain* (9 tracks), Rykodisc, 1993 • "Cure for Pain," Rykodisc, 1993 • "Honey White," Rykodisc, 1995 • "Super Sex," Rykodisc, 1995 • *Yes,* Rykodisc, 1995 • *Like Swimming,* Dreamworks, 1997.

Pixies, The: *Death to the Pixies: 1987–1991,* Elektra, 1997.

Shatterproof: *Slip It Under the Door,* Fort Apache/MCA, 1995.

Throwing Muses: "Firepile," Sire/WB, 1992 (*Volume Four*) • *Red Heaven,* Sire/WB, 1992.

Vestrymen: *Ruby Ranch,* Vertebrae, 1993.

Sean Slade

Buffalo Tom: *Buffalo Tom,* Beggars Banquet, 1988, 1994 • *Birdbrain,* Beggars Banquet/RCA, 1990.

Cold Water Flat: *Cold Water Flat,* Fort Apache/MCA, 1995.

Green Magnet School: *Blood Music* (6 tracks), Sub Pop, 1992.

Hatfield, Juliana: *Forever Baby* (2 tracks, EP), Mammoth, 1992.

Sebadoh: *III,* Homestead, 1991.

360's: "Are You Experienced?," Hollywood, 1992 (*All the Young Dudes: The Link Records Anthology*) • *Supernatural,* Link/Hollywood, 1992.

Uncle Tupelo: "Won't Forget," Atlantic, 1991 (*A Matter of Degrees* soundtrack).

Vanilla Trainwreck: *Sofa Livin' Dreamazine,* Mammoth, 1991.

Volcano Suns: *Bumper Crop,* Homestead, 1987 • *Farced,* SST, 1988.

Leslie Kong

From the upstairs back room of Beverley's Record and Ice Cream Parlor (and stationery shop!) in Kingston, Jamaica, came some of early reggae's pivotal recordings. The first records by Bob Marley, Jimmy Cliff, John Holt, and Desmond Dekker—the last including the international smash "Israelites" (No. 9), which was the first reggae record most Americans ever heard, years before they knew what it was—were cut there by Leslie Kong. The Melodians, the Pioneers, and Toots and the Maytals also made some of their greatest music for Leslie Kong.

Kong's studio players included pianist Theophilus Beckford, bassist Lloyd Mason, hornmen Deadly Headley and Stanley Webbs, and Australian guitarist Dennis Cindry. Kong first recorded Cliff singing a jingle for the Ice Cream Parlor ("Dearest Beverley"), then got a monster hit with the ska song "Miss Jamaica." Dekker tells of having to push his way past Cliff and established ska master Derrick Morgan to be heard by Kong. Morgan bore the brunt of Prince Buster's (see entry) "Black Head Chinaman" for defecting to Kong from the Prince.

Some of Kong's major hits include "There's a Fire" by the Gaylads, Ken Boothe's "Now I Know" and "It's Gonna Take a Miracle," the Melodians' rasta-grooved "Rivers of Babylon" and "Rock It with Me" (the last two covered by Bony M and David Lindley, respectively), and scorching sides by the Maytals (including "She's My Scorcher" and "54-46 (That's My Number)." Many artists, including Boothe and Marley (who was actually completing a circuit since he started there) first fled to Kong after cutting their teeth at Studio One. Marley's first recordings, "Judge Not" and "One Cup of Coffee," were cut for Kong in Marley's teenage years. Dekker, who worked with him in a welding shop, brought him to Kong. After a lengthy stint with Coxsone Dodd (see entry), Marley and the Wailers returned to Kong and cut some excellent records released by Kong as *Best of the Wailers* and in later years under countless other titles. Marley and Cliff were to go on to international fame after signing with Chris Blackwell's (see entry) Island Records.

Another one of reggae's outstanding singers, John Holt, recorded first for Beverley's with Kong at the helm. "Forever I Will Stay" was recorded before Holt cut solo singles for Duke Reid (see entry) or Coxsone. As lead singer of the Paragons and in later solo recordings, he, too, sang some of reggae's outstanding work. Paul Simon (see entry) has been quoted as saying it was a Kong production, Jimmy Cliff's "Vietnam," played for him by Bob Dylan, that caused him to fly to Jamaica and book the same band for "Mother and Child Reunion." Kong's productions on the soundtrack to Perry Henzel's *The Harder They Come,* which starred Cliff, are among that seminal reggae album's outstanding cuts. They include the Maytals' "Pressure Drop" and "Sweet and Dandy" and Dekker's "007 (Shanty Town)."

Kong's production style was pure pop. Whether capturing the barely contained exuberance of the Pioneers' "Samfie Man," "Mother Ritty," and "Trouble Dey a Bush," the musical complexities of Bruce Ruffin's "Bit-

terness of Life," or Peter Tosh's original "Stop That Train," he delivered exciting tracks and clean vocals. "Freedom Street" by Ken Boothe, Dekker's "007 (Shanty Town)," and the Pioneers' "Long Shot (Kick de Bucket)" are the kind of recordings that helped build careers for the artists involved. You would not expect to see these artists and *not* hear them do these songs just as they sang them for Leslie Kong.

In addition, some of Kong's productions took on a life of their own in England, where cuts like Dekker's "It Mek" and the Maytals' "Monkey Man" were not only revered and played at punky reggae crossover dances but were reworked by U.K. bands as anthems of their own skinhead movement. Kong was also managing Desmond Dekker (who calls him "a very convincing guy" from a business standpoint) at the time of his death from heart failure in August 1971. In the late '80s, his son, calling himself I-Kong, issued an album featuring some of the original musicians, like Tommy McCook, Headley Bennett, and Winston Wright, from some of those great records produced by Leslie Kong.
—Chuck Foster

Cliff, Jimmy: *Two Worlds,* Beverley's, 1964 • *Jimmy Cliff,* Trojan, 1969 • "Vietnam/Come into My Life," A&M, 1969 • "Wonderful World, Beautiful People," A&M, 1970 • *Wonderful World, Beautiful People,* A&M, 1970 • *Reggae Legends/Jimmy Cliff* (6 tracks), Mango, 1984.

Dekker, Desmond: "007 (Shanty Town)," Beverley's, 1967 • *007 (Shanty Town),* Beverley's, 1967 • *Action,* Beverley's, 1968 • *Double Dekker,* Trojan, 1974, 1981 • *Original Reggae Hitsound,* Trojan, 1985 • *The Best of Desmond Dekker,* Rhino, 1992.

Dekker, Desmond, and the Aces: "Israelites," Uni, 1969 • *Israelites,* Uni, 1969 • "It Mek/Problems," Uni, 1969 • "You Can Get It If You Really Want," Uni, 1969.

Marley, Bob, and the Wailers: *Best Of,* Beverley's, 1970 • *Best Of,* URTI, 1981 • *Shakedown,* Ala, 1982 • *Soul Captives,* Ala, 1986 • *Early Years, 1969–1973,* Trojan, 1993.

Maytals, The: "54-46 (That's My Number)," Shelter, 1972.

Melodians, The: "Rivers of Babylon," Trojan, 1970 • *Sweet Sensation,* Mango, 1980.

Pioneers, The: *Long Shot,* Trojan, 1969 • *Battle of the Giants,* Trojan, 1970.

Toots and the Maytals: *Monkey Man,* Trojan, 1970 • "Pressure Drop," Trojan, 1970 • *Reggae Greats* (4 tracks), Mango, 1984 • *Don't Trouble,* Reggae Best, 1985 • *Reggae Collection,* Essex, 1985 • *Bla Bla Bla,* Esoldun, 1993.

COLLECTIONS

King Kong Compilation, Mango, 1981: Ken Boothe, "Freedom Street" • The Maytals, "Monkey Girl," "Monkey Man" •

The Melodians, "It's My Delight," "Sweet Sensation" • The Pioneers, "Long Shot Kick de Bucket" • Bruce Ruffin, "Bitterness of Life" • Delroy Wilson, "Gave You My Love."

The Best of Beverley's Records, or Masterpieces from the Works of Leslie Kong, Trojan, 1981: Ken Boothe, "It's Gonna Take a Miracle," "Now I Know" • The Gaylands, "There's a Fire" ˘ Bob Marley and the Wailers, "Cheer Up" "Soul Shakedown Party" • The Maytals, "She's My Scorcher" • The Melodians, "Rock It with Me" • Bruce Ruffin, "Dry Up Your Tears," "I'm the One" • Peter Tosh, "Soon Come."

Sascha Konietzko and KMFDM

S ascha Konietzko is founder, bassist, programmer, sometime vocalist, producer, and focal point for the German-American industrial group KMFDM (*Kleine Mitleid fur das Mehrheit:* "No Pity for the Majority"), perfecters of the metal guitar and electronic beats approach to industrial music. KMFDM has released classic albums *Money, Angst, Naive/Hell to Go, Nihil,* and *Xtort,* which feature some of industrial's best songs: "Virus," "Godlike," "Money," "Light," "A Drug Against War," "Sucks," and "Juke Joint Jezebel"—every one of which features razor-sharp guitars, hummable tunes, clever lyrics, and a danceable beat in the funky-to-brutal range.

Sascha Konietzko was born in 1961 and grew up in Hamburg, Germany. He chafed under a typically conservative father who didn't approve of his son's music ("What's all this fucking hippie-type, hash-consuming, nincompoop doodling noise?"), friends, hair ("hippie-to-be little girl"), or contemptuous attitude. Young Konietzko was torn between respect for his father's idiosyncratic pleasures (a professional hydrologist, Konietzko Sr. recorded tribal beats as a hobby while testing water along the Congo for the Belgian Royal Zoo) and rebellion against his father's autocratic ways.

Konietzko, a bassist, joined his first band when he was 11. His most pervasive early influences were glamrockers like T. Rex, Alice Cooper, Sweet, and Slade. In 1976, when punk rock was bubbling up in England and the U.S., Konietzko was in the first punk band in Hamburg. "It was definitely a very interesting time to make

music. Punk rock really opened my eyes in terms of 'you can just do it.' If there are enough people who think it's cool, then it's just cool. It doesn't need any education, just a fucking urge. That liberated me from all kinds of constraints that were put on me by my parents and society in general," he says. "Needless to say, everyone hated us: we were spitting beer, throwing raw meat and dead mice into the audience."

In the late '70s, another, even more radical musical form emerged: "industrial" music (with instrumentation that included power tools and metal objects beaten upon with implements of destruction) created by bands like Throbbing Gristle, SPK, and a little later, Berlin's Einsturzende Neubauten ("Collapsing New Buildings"). "Everything started to take shape, and I was really intrigued by the idea of a mix of industrial aggression with a more musical expression that was maybe going against the industrial ideal. I still liked glam-rock, and I liked the industrialists, too. I could pretend that I was a hard-liner and industrial noise was the coolest thing to listen to, but deep down, listening to metal vessels being smashed against each other continuously was not my idea of art. I've always felt there must be some sort of hybrid solution."

KMFDM was formed by Konietzko and German painter and performance artist Udo Sturm, on February 29, 1984, to perform for the opening of an exhibition of young European artists at the Grand Palais in Paris. The performance consisted of Konietzko on five bass guitars, run through five amplifiers placed "in strategically significant areas of the huge turn-of-the-century steel and glass construction"; Sturm on a "fragmented Arp 2600 synthesizer in feedback mode"; and "four Polish coal miners putting their tools of trade to work on the buildings," he recalls.

Back in Hamburg, Konietzko started another band called Missing Foundations with "audio-anarchist" Peter Missing, and, in conjunction with that band met percussionist/multi-instrumentalist En Esch. Konietzko, En Esch, and Englishman Raymond "Pig" Watts then began to record as KMFDM. The first KMFDM album, *What Do You Know, Deutschland?,* on the local Skysaw label, came out in 1986.

In 1987 the band met woodcut artist Brute, who has created their distinctive, brutish cover art ever since. In 1988 the band's next album, *Don't Blow Your Top,* was licensed by Chicago's industrial-leaning Wax Trax! label, thereby introducing the band to America. Konietzko was becoming a producer. "On [*Don't Blow Your Top*] I found myself taking on the role of coaching people into performances, saying, 'This was actually pretty good, but I think you can do it better, and don't scream so much.' The engineer was referring to me as 'producer,' and then I was like, 'Oh, so that's producing.'

The band's breakthrough came with the release of two singles, counted among industrial's greatest hits: "Virus" in 1989, and "Godlike" in 1990. "Virus" features an enormous guitar riff laid over a chunky hip-hop beat (evocative of the first Beastie Boys album), with distorted vocals comparing the contagiousness of society's ills with that of a virus, disseminated by the reckless pursuit of "more and faster." A slashing guitar line reminiscent of Slayer opens the medium-tempo chugger "Godlike": a tale of the seductive powers of fascism, keyed to the line, "Get on the right side / And you'll be godlike." Adventuresome dance floors from coast to coast succumbed to the band's (now transplanted to the U.S.) Teutonic powers.

KMFDM has mutated often around central figures Konietzko and En Esch. The *Xtort* version of the band features Gunter Schulz on guitars; Cheryl Wilson, Dorona Alberti, Nicole Blackman, Jennifer Ginsberg, and Chris Connelly on vocals; Ministry's William Rieflin on drums; and engineer/producer Chris Shepard, among others. "It's been a circle of people who find themselves again and again for recording. Everybody from the past always pops up in the future at some point, and it has become this organizational nightmare to keep it all together—to blend everybody's ideas into one product, one outcome. That's the most challenging part about it, and the most fascinating," says Konietzko.

The band's process of recording has become automated against time and space. "I live in Seattle, En Esch lives in New York, and Gunter—the guitarist—lives in British Columbia, so we have to send stuff around digitally," says Konietzko. "This just happened: I whipped out a bass-and-drum track and sent it to Gunter in Canada. He worked on it for a couple of weeks. I got the tape back, and instead of guitar, he did some weird sequencing stuff. I said, 'Wow, you were supposed to do guitar.' He said, 'Well I didn't feel like it, I felt like doing this other stuff.' Then I think, 'Okay, I guess this song isn't going to have a lot of guitar.' But I am coping with it. The material always comes back to me, so I guess I'm the focal point.

"I produce away when I get their material back: 'This is pretty cool. This we're going to turn into the verse. This is going to be the chorus.' Then we talk about vocal stuff, lyric ideas, concepts.

"Then it comes to the performance. 'Do I sing this? Does En Esch sing that? Do we sing it together, or is one the guest musicians going to be involved?' I have a small MIDI studio—a little basement-type situation. I use it pretty much for all the preproduction type of work, but then the real mixing and overdubbing happens at a big studio. You can figure that once an album is in stores, we are already working on the next one because it takes so fucking long," he concludes.

KMFDM have maintained their integrity and independence, staying with Wax Trax! (now owned by TVT) instead of signing with a major. They have built a fervent worldwide audience by touring and by the steady release of consistent, yet surprisingly varied material. 1995's *Nihil* even boasted a modern rock radio hit, the catchy "Juke Joint Jezebel." Each album has sold more than the one before, with *Xtort* topping the 200,000 mark—extraordinary for a genre band on an indie label.

Marvels Konietzko, "Our following has some really cultish dimensions that have been interesting and freaky at the same time. My phone number has to be one of the best-guarded secrets, but when I get a new one it pops out on the Internet in no time at all. En Esch is being shredded apart: we do a show—any show anywhere—and people frantically take pieces of his flesh and his garments as souvenirs.

"It seems almost like a disease: they learn about us and then there is this need to have everything that we have done—every time we have a new album, all our other albums kick in as well. There are probably hundreds of 'KMFDM' license plates and thousands of tattoos."

Konietzko ends with a little tale. "A little while ago I was in Chicago taking my wife's grandmother, who is in a wheelchair, down to the lake for a little walk. I am rolling her through the park and there is this wedding party somewhere in the bushes. They are taking pictures, and all of a sudden I hear my name and these people—the bride and groom and bridesmaids—are running to me. 'You're Sascha, can we take a picture with you?' In the meantime, Grandma is like, 'Who are those people? What do they want from you?' She knows what I do, but she doesn't hear so well and was baffled and flustered by these people chasing us around. And of course the people are like 'Oh, that's so nice of you taking Grandma to the lake.' " —ERIC OLSEN AND DAWN DARLING

Die Krupps: *Rings of Steel* (1 track), Cleopatra, 1995.

Excessive Force: "Blitzkrieg," TVT, 1993 • *Gentle Death*, TVT, 1993 • "Violent Peace," TVT, 1993.

KMFDM: *What Do You Know, Deutschland?*, Skysaw, 1986 • *UAIOE*, Wax Trax!, 1989 • *Virus* (EP), Wax Trax!, 1989 • "Godlike," Wax Trax!, 1990 • *Naive*, Wax Trax!, 1990 • "Split/Piggybank," Wax Trax!, 1991 • *Money*, Wax Trax!/TVT, 1992 • "Sucks," Wax Trax!/TVT, 1992 •

"Sucks" (remix), Wax Trax!/TVT, 1992 • *Angst,* Wax Trax!/TVT, 1993 • "Light" (remix), Wax Trax!/TVT, 1994 • *Naive/Hell to Go,* Wax Trax!/TVT, 1994 • "Juke Joint Jezebel," Wax Trax!/TVT, 1995 • *Nihil,* Wax Trax!/TVT, 1995 • *Rules* (EP), Wax Trax!/TVT, 1996 • "Son of a Gun," Wax Trax!/TVT, 1996 • "Son of a Gun" (remix), Wax Trax!/TVT, 1996 • *Xtort,* Wax Trax!/TVT, 1996.

Pet Shop Boys: "West End Girls" (remix), EMI, 1994.

White Zombie: "Black Sunshine" (remix), Geffen, 1992 • "Thunder Kiss '65" (remix), Geffen, 1992.

Al Kooper

Besides being the Hammond B-3 whiz who jump-started Dylan's biggest hit, "Like a Rolling Stone," Al Kooper is a jammer (on *Super Session,* with Stephen Stills and Michael Bloomfield; and on *Kooper Session,* with guitar master Shuggie Otis), a whammer (he's played with everybody from Dylan to Lynyrd Skynyrd to Thelonious Monster), and a writer of colorful prose. This loquacious Brooklyn native has written numerous columns for collectors' magazines, and his autobiography, *Backstage Passes and Backstabbing Bastards,* was published in 1998 by Billboard Books.

Born February 5, 1944, Alan Kooper began his professional career at age 13 by auditioning for the "So Tough" Casuals. According to the witty, short-form biography Kooper makes available to people who review his records, he had his "first real taste of pop music success during the nascent days of rock and roll as popular music" as a member of the Royal Teens, who had a Top 5 hit in 1958 with "Short Shorts" and a Top 30 hit a year later with "Believe Me."

"I was hanging around the fringes of the music business," this pop culture connoisseur says of the period immediately following the Teens' success. "I was playing sessions on guitar. People would hire me because their only alternative was to hire these jazz players to play this teenage music. These guys were smoking cigars, emulating what kids would play. So, they would hire me to get that 'dumb kid sound.' I assume that's why I was hired, because I really couldn't play anywhere near as well as these other guys."

According to the liner notes to *Al's Big Deal,* an anthology of Kooper material Columbia released in 1989, Kooper played on Gene Pitney's Musicor demos and wrote "This Diamond Ring" for Gary Lewis and the Playboys, a hit in 1965. In the early '60s, Kooper joined the Blues Project, yielding three albums of pioneering urban blues. Later that decade he played on Hendrix's *Electric Ladyland; The Who Sell Out;* and Dylan's *Highway 61 Revisited, Blonde and Blonde,* and *New Morning* albums and sparked the first (and best) Blood, Sweat and Tears album, *Child Is Father to the Man.*

Kooper left Blood, Sweat and Tears in 1968 to work for Columbia Records A&R, where he produced the Top 10 album *Super Session;* albums with Mike Bloomfield, Shuggie Otis, and jazzer Don Ellis; and his own solo debut, *I Stand Alone.* In addition to session work, he also scored films. He played organ, piano, and French horn on the Rolling Stones' "You Can't Always Get What You Want."

In 1972, Kooper moved to Atlanta, where he discovered Lynyrd Skynyrd and formed his own label, Sounds of the South, to put out their records. Kooper produced their first three albums, which included the massive hits "Sweet Home Alabama" (No. 8), "Saturday Night Special," and "Free Bird" (No. 19). In 1974, he sold Sounds of the South to MCA Records and moved to Los Angeles, where he also produced records by the Tubes, B.B. King, Nils Lofgren, and Rick Nelson. Kooper's production philosophy is "to fill in the gaps where the artist is deficient in getting his art across to the public. You never know what an artist's peaks and valleys are going to be, so it's best to have a well-rounded knowledge of songs, arranging, engineering, and psychology at your beck and call," he says.

"The best producers are the ones who have access to tools, and if the artist is well-rounded, you have to know when to step back and not be intrusive. There are two kinds of producers: ones who have something to prove, and ones who don't. I've been both and it's much better to be the latter."

The peripatetic Kooper lived in England in 1979, adding David Essex and Eddie and the Hot Rods to his production list. He also played on and arranged three tracks on George Harrison's *Somewhere in England* album, performing with remaining Beatles Harrison, Paul McCartney (see entry), and Ringo Starr on "All Those Years Ago," a No. 1 single in 1981.

Upon Kooper's return to the U.S. in 1980, he produced a record with country rocker Joe Ely, a native of his new home of Austin, Texas. He returned to Los Angeles the following year, toured with Dylan and the reunited Blues Project, and released *Championship Wrestling,* his first solo album in six years.

In his next job, as West Coast director of A&R for PolyGram Records, Kooper was instrumental in signing Richard Thompson. He also met film producer/director Michael Mann, who was riding high on the success of *Miami Vice*. Mann hired Kooper to score *Crime Story*. Not only did Kooper write original music for that TV series, he also produced some of the soundtrack for John Waters' *Cry Baby* film. In the latter part of the '80s, Kooper took a break from recording. During the '90s, he has toured with Joe Walsh, issued compilations of his own and the Blues Project, and worked with the Rock Bottom Remainders: a band of authors that includes Dave Marsh, Stephen King, Amy Tan, Matt Groening, and other literati.

He now records for independent label Musicmasters as head of the Rekooperators, featuring boyhood friend Harvey Brooks (an Electric Flagman) on bass and Jimmy Vivino on guitar. They have released three CDs: *Rekooperation*, *Soul of a Man*, and *Do What, Now?*
—CARLO WOLFF

Appaloosa: *Appaloosa*, Columbia 1969.

Bloomfield, Mike: w/ Al Kooper and Stephen Stills, *Super Session*, Columbia, 1967 • w/ Al Kooper, *The Live Adventures of Mike Bloomfield and Al Kooper*, Columbia, 1968 • *Don't Say That I Ain't Your Man*, Legacy, 1994.

Blues Project: *Reunion in Central Park*, MCA, 1973.

Chapman, Marshall: *Jaded Virgin*, Epic, 1978.

Devine, Sweet Linda: *Sweet Linda Devine*, Columbia, 1969.

Eddie and the Hot Rods: *Fish and Chips*, EMI, 1981.

Elijah: *Fanfares*, Sound of the South, 1973.

Essex, David: *Be-Bop the Future*, Mercury, 1981.

Four on the Floor: *Four on the Floor*, Casablanca, 1979.

Frankie and Johnny: *Sweetheart Sampler*, Warner Bros., 1973.

Green on Red: *Scapegoats*, Off Beat, 1991.

Henry, Freddy: *Get It Out in the Open*, Clouds, 1979.

Johnny Van Zandt Band: *No More Dirty Deals*, Polydor, 1980 • *Last of the Wild Ones*, Polydor, 1982.

Jones, Mose: *Get It Right*, MCA, 1973.

Judd, Phil: *The Swinger*, MCA, 1983.

King, B.B.: *King of the Blues: '89*, MCA, 1989.

Kooper, Al: *I Stand Alone*, Columbia, 1967 • *Kooper Session*, Columbia, 1969 • *Live Adventures*, Columbia, 1969 • *You Never Know Who Your Friends Are*, CBS, 1969 • *Easy Does It*, Columbia, 1970 • *A Possible Projection of the Future*, Columbia, 1971 • *New York City (You're a Woman)*, Columbia, 1971 • *The Landlord* soundtrack, United Artists, 1971 • *Naked Songs*, CBS, 1972 • *Possible Projection of Future*, Columbia, 1972 • *Al's Big Deal (Unclaimed Freight)*, Columbia, 1975, 1989 • *Act Like Nothing's Wrong*, United Artists, 1976 • *Four on the Floor*, Casablanca, 1979 • *Championship Wrestling*, Columbia, 1982 • *ReKooperation: A Nonverbal Scenic Selection*, Musicmasters, 1994 • *Soul of a Man: Live*, Musicmasters, 1996 • *See also* Bloomfield, Mike.

Lofgren, Nils: *Cry Tough* (5 tracks), A&M, 1976 • *The Best Of*, A&M, 1985.

Lynyrd Skynyrd: *Pronounced Leh-Nerd Skin-Nerd*, MCA, 1973, 1996 • "Free Bird," MCA, 1974 • *Second Helping*, MCA, 1974 • "Sweet Home Alabama," MCA, 1974 • *Nuthin' Fancy*, MCA, 1975 • "Saturday Night Special," MCA, 1975 • *Best of the Rest*, MCA, 1982 • *Legend*, MCA, 1987 • *Skynyrd's Innyrds: Their Greatest Hits*, MCA, 1989 • *Their Greatest Hits*, MCA, 1989 • *Lynyrd Skynyrd*, MCA, 1991.

Morse, Peter John: *On the Shoreline*, MCA, 1977.

Nelson, Rick: *Stay Young: The Epic Recordings*, Legacy, 1993.

Otis, Shuggie: *Shuggie Otis Plays the Blues*, Legacy, 1994.

Stills, Stephen: *See* Bloomfield, Mike.

Thelonius Monster: *Beautiful Mess* (1 track), Capitol, 1992.

Tubes, The: *The Tubes*, A&M, 1975 • *T.R.A.S.H. (Tubes Rarities and Smash Hits)*, A&M, 1981.

Vivino, Jimmy, and the Rekooperations: *Do What, Now?*, Musicmasters, 1997.

White, Lenny: *The Adventures of Astral Pirates*, Elektra, 1978.

Wilder, Webb: *Doo Dad*, Praxis/Zoo, 1991.

Danny Kortchmar

With every album that Danny Kortchmar produces, he thumbs his nose at the engineers who kept him from the console when he was starting out as a Los Angeles–based studio musician in the late '60s. "They never let you near the console," he says of his early days. "You got in there for three hours and it was like they were doing you a favor." So when Kortchmar got his first production gig, he was ecstatic. Since then, he's written, produced, and played with the likes of Don Henley, Freedy Johnston, James Taylor, and the Fabulous Thunderbirds.

In 1968, 18-year-old Kortchmar was playing guitar on Peter Asher (see entry) and Carole King album sessions. Although he wouldn't step behind the console for another 10 years, those early sessions planted the seeds of his production career.

"Peter Asher really wanted the musicians to think like producers," he explains. "He encouraged us to do that. We were all very competitive about coming up with ideas and good moves. Basically it was a very good training school—that and working with Carole King—for record production."

His first production credit was in 1979 for Louise Goffin, King's daughter. "I couldn't wait to get into it. Peter recommended me for the project and I felt really good about it. I used all my buddies and some guys that I'd always wanted to play with," he recalls. One of the

Photo by David Goggin ©1984

things he did that caused a bit of a commotion was to use young, largely unproven musicians on his sessions, like 19-year-old guitarist Steve Lukather, who worked on Goffin's debut.

Over the years, Kortchmar has worked hard not to be pigeonholed, though he admits he was heavily influenced by the Motown and Stax-Volt recordings of the '60s. "I grew up in the '60s and my gods were the guys who played on Motown records, the Stax-Volt bands, Curtis Mayfield's (see entry) guitar stylings, and Wilson Pickett doing 'I'm Gonna Cry.' If you listen to Ike and Tina Turner's 'I Think It's Gonna Work Out Fine,' the first four bars are the essence of coolness," he says.

His coproductions with Don Henley, Mike Campbell, and Greg Ladanyi (see entry) on the first three Don Henley albums constitute his most famous work. Kortchmar particularly favors such tunes as "Little Tin God," "I Will Not Go Quietly," "All She Wants to Do Is Dance" (No. 9), and "New York Minute." "That work is very close to me because I was contributing as a writer as well as a producer," he explains. "It's all connected: the playing and production. I can't see them as separate. Everything I know about music and all the experience I've had in music is what I bring to bear when I'm pro-

ducing. To be connected as a guitar player, I think, is very important to me."

As producer, Kortchmar aims to be as transparent as possible. "I try to capture their sound; I try to make the album sound like them, not me. I would say that I don't bring a sound with me, I bring technique and experience with me and maybe an aesthetic. My idea is to bring out what's there with whoever I'm working with. "You learn every time you go into the studio that there's new ways to solve problems," he adds. "To be in the studio is to improvise."

And adapt to technology. One thing Kortchmar has learned in his 20 years as producer is to welcome innovation. "Technology has helped everybody," he says. "These are all tools that get developed by people asking guys in the studio what they can do to make it easier, so they come up with these amazing things. There will come a point when the old technology, the classic gear like Neve and API consoles, will be considered an effect. Ultimately everything will end up on a hard disk, but it will go through these things in order to achieve the particular sonic warmth you want.

"At this point, every kid with a couple of A dats and a Mac has enough gear to make records that sound better than records that were made in the '70s," he says. "I think that's a good thing. I love the fact that it's been democratized; everybody has access to gear that sounds better than gear a lot of classic records were made on. It puts more music in the hands of the people."

A scan of Kortchmar's discography shows that he's worked on a wide variety of projects. Each has to affect him before he signs on, however. "I go after people whose stuff moves me," he says. "I don't have one thing that I stick to, because I'm interested in too many things, there's too much music going on that I like now," citing Garbage, Morphine, and DJ Shadow.

"I grew up listening to Coltrane, Muddy Waters, Marvin Gaye, Bill Monroe. These are people who will last forever," he says. "So I can't really get interested in something that I know is just a flash in the pan and that was started by the media, by MTV, and is just thrown away and replaced by the next cutting-edge thing. I've been around too long, I've seen disco come and go three or four times. It's like a revolving door."

Keep in mind that this issues from a man who appeared in the movie *Spinal Tap* as a member of the Thamesmen. "They called me, I think, because I had close enough to a Beatle haircut. I'm playing bass in the black and white documentary," he says. "It was the pinnacle of my career. That always impresses people, perhaps more than my actual musical background."

—DAVID JOHN FARINELLA

415

Bentall, Barney: *Barney Bentall and the Legendary Hearts,* Columbia, 1988.

Bon Jovi, Jon: "Blaze of Glory," Mercury, 1990 • "Miracle," Mercury, 1990.

Bourgeois, Brent: *Brent Bourgeois,* Charisma, 1990 • "Dare to Fall in Love," Charisma, 1990.

Cocker, Joe: *Night Calls,* Gold Rush, 1992, 1996 • *Long Voyage Home: The Silver Annivesay Collection,* A&M, 1995.

Fabulous Thunderbirds: *Roll of the Dice,* Private, 1995 • *High Water,* Highstreet, 1997.

Falcon, Billy: "Power Windows," Jambco, 1991 • *Pretty Blue World,* Jambco, 1991.

Ford, Robben, and the Blue Line: *Handful of Blues,* Blue Thumb, 1995.

Goffin, Louise: *Kid Blue,* Asylum, 1979 • *Louise Goffin,* Asylum, 1979.

Hall, Daryl, and John Oates: *Change of Season,* Arista, 1990 • "So Close," Arista, 1990.

Henley, Don: "Dirty Laundry," Asylum, 1982 • *I Can't Stand Still,* Asylum, 1982 • "All She Wants to Do Is Dance," Geffen, 1984 • *Building the Perfect Beast,* Geffen, 1984 • "The Boys of Summer," Geffen, 1984 • "Not Enough Love in the World," Geffen, 1985 • "Sunset Grill," Geffen, 1985 • *End of the Innocence,* Geffen, 1989 • "How Bad Do You Want It?," Geffen, 1990 • "New York Minute," Geffen, 1990 • "The Heart of the Matter," Geffen, 1990 • *Actual Miles: Henley's Greatest Hits,* Geffen, 1995.

Hoy, Johnny, and the Bluefish: *Trailing the Hootchy,* Tone Cool, 1995.

James, Colin: *Colin James,* Virgin, 1989.

Joel, Billy: "All About Soul," Columbia, 1993 • "The River of Dreams," Columbia, 1993 • *The River of Dreams,* Columbia, 1993 • "Lullabye (Goodnight, My Angel)," Columbia, 1994 • *Greatest Hits,* Vol. 3, Columbia, 1997.

Johnston, Freedy: *Never Home,* Elektra, 1997.

Kortchmar, Danny: *Kootch,* Warner Bros., 1973 • *Innuendo,* Asylum, 1980.

Lindley, David: *Mr. Dave,* WEA International, 1985.

Martin, Eric: "Information," Capitol, 1985.

Mr. Reality: *Mr. Reality,* Capitol, 1992.

Neville, Ivan: *If My Ancestors Could See Me Now,* Polydor, 1988 • "Falling Out of Love," Polydor, 1989 • "Not Just Another Girl," Polydor, 1989.

Nicks, Stevie: "Sometimes (It's a Bitch)," Modern, 1991 • *Timespace: The Best Of,* Modern, 1991.

Rebel Train: *Seeking Shelter,* EastWest, 1992.

Schmit, Timothy B.: *Tell Me the Truth,* MCA, 1983, 1990.

Sharkey, Feargal: *Wish,* Virgin, 1988.

Simon, Carly: *Letters Never Sent,* Arista, 1995.

Sister 7: *This the Trip,* Arista, 1997 • "Know What You Mean," Arista, 1998.

Slo Leak: *Slo Leak,* Pure, 1996.

Spin Doctors: *You've Got to Believe in Something,* Epic, 1996.

Spinal Tap: *Break Like the Wind,* MCA, 1992.

Stigers, Curtis: *Curtis Stigers,* Arista, 1991 • *Time Was,* Arista, 1991, 1995 • "Sleeping with the Lights On," Arista, 1992.

Taylor, James: *New Moon Shine,* Columbia, 1991.

Toto: *Kingdom of Desire,* Combat, 1993.

Venice: *Venice,* Modern, 1992.

Waite, John: "If Anybody Had a Heart," EMI-America, 1986 • *Essential,* Chrysalis, 1992.

Young, Neil: *Landing on Water,* Geffen, 1986 • *Lucky Thirteen,* Geffen, 1993.

Mark Stevan Kramer

As recording artist, musician (Shockabilly, Butthole Surfers, Bongwater, Ween, Half Japanese, various collaborations), producer (over 1,800 records), recording studio (Noise New York, Noise New Jersey, KnitNoise) and record label owner (Shimmy-Disc, Kokopop), "Kramer" (as he is mononymously known) has been a fixture on the New York–area indie and art-music scene for 20 years.

Mark Stevan Kramer was born November 30, 1958, and raised in the New York City area. As a child, he was a leading classical organist in New York State competitions, and seemed destined for a career in serious music.

He was also deeply interested in books and rock 'n' roll records. "When I read a novel I liked, I would read all of the other novels by the author. I did the same with music. I picked up the Rolling Stones and started listening to all of their stuff; when I came to *Their Satanic Majesties Request* I knew there was something very different about the way that record sounded. I looked at the record and there was a name on it: Glyn Johns [who engineered it; see entry]. For the Beatle records there was George Martin, and for the T. Rex albums there was Tony Visconti [see entries]. I started to realize that there were names [other than the artists] connected with these great records."

Kramer's path to keyboard glory was altered in high school when he failed to master the piano—a prerequisite for traditional music college admission. Kramer explains, "The organ uses a flat-fingered technique; the piano requires a hunched, crunched hand with curled fingers. The piano is a percussion instrument—you hammer the thing. People who study piano and then study organ have no trouble at all, but people who study organ and then piano have difficulty. That was the first failure I encountered in music and it drove me to marijuana and LSD in the mid-'70s."

Musically, Kramer turned his attention to avant garde composition. He was especially enamored of John Cage and LaMonte Young. "For all of my adolescence and early adulthood, I wanted to be the bespectacled and trim-bearded composer," he says. "It wasn't until I saw Philip Glass at the Peppermint Lounge—which was the loudest concert that I had ever seen—that I started getting back into amplitude, and through amplitude I came back into rock 'n' roll."

In the late '70s Kramer attended an alternative music school in Woodstock, New York (founded by Karl Berger and Ornette Coleman): the Creative Music Studio. Avant composer/sax player John Zorn and composer/guitarist Eugene Chadbourne taught there. While living in Woodstock, Kramer also met ex-Fug Ed Sanders. Kramer composed the music to Sanders' *The Karen Silkwood Cantata* and toured Europe on bass with a Fugs reunion in 1984. Kramer quit in the middle of the tour as a "reformed" Sanders had taken to apologizing onstage for the lyrics to classic Fugs' tunes such as "Coca Cola Douche," "I Feel Like Homemade Shit" and "Boobs a Lot": an affront Kramer could not countenance. Through Sanders, Kramer met Allen Ginsberg, with whom he occasionally studied poetry and meter.

In 1980 Kramer began to do live sound engineering for the Waitresses (see Chris Butler entry) and Sun Ra. Now playing bass, he joined a version of Gong that featured Daevid Allen (whom Kramer later produced), and future producers Bill Laswell, Fred Maher, and Michael Beinhorn (see entries). In 1982, Chadbourne invited Kramer to join a "country and western LSD band," called the Chadbournes, which soon mutated into Shockabilly.

"My first experience with producing was with Shockabilly in 1982," he says. "I had to hire myself to produce about 10 seconds before the session for *The Dawn of Shockabilly* EP began, because the guy who owned the equipment didn't even know how to put it together. My second production experience was the first full Shockabilly album, recorded in Greensboro, North Carolina, also in 1982.

"I got there just in time to see the owner of the studio wheeling a bunch of the equipment out, saying, 'I can leave this stuff here for about a week or so, but that's it, man, I'm shutting this fuckin' place down.' So he left me an 8-track machine and a few microphones and a mixer—the corner of which was on its side in a sink. That side of the board didn't work because it was in water. That severely limited me, but I'm also really proud of it.

"In 1984 we recorded Shockabilly's *Vietnam* album at Carla Bley's studio in Woodstock, Grog Kill, and that's when it dawned on me that the right way to do this would be to own my own recording studio," he says.

Kramer left Shockabilly to join the psychedelic punk provocateurs, Butthole Surfers, in 1985. "I thought the Butthole Surfers were going to be the biggest band in the world, but within six months I realized that the chances were greater that I would be killed in a car wreck. In those days, the designated driver for the Butthole Surfers was the one who had done the most LSD. The one who had done the most LSD had, naturally, done the least amount of drinking.

"The issue was forced when I got food poisoning on tour in the Midwest and flew home in a bag. I co-produced two albums with them—*Cream Corn* and *Rembrandt Pussy Horse*—but didn't play on them. No one played on them except Paul Leary. Gibby [Haynes] didn't even play, he just sang. Paul even played the drums," he reveals.

Another of Kramer's interests has been film. In 1983 he enrolled at the New School for Social Research's film department, but he soon dropped out when "the instructor got pissed off at me for using the 16 mm Bolex provided by the school for projects other than the school's," he says. He has studied film periodically at various New York schools ever since, and has studied theater at HB Studios and David Mamet's Atlantic Theater Company.

In 1987 Kramer became an entrepreneur and formed Shimmy-Disc Records to put out his own records and those of worthy others. Besides his solo and collaborative work (including Bongwater with singer/lyricist/actress Ann Magnuson; Captain Howdy with Penn Jillette of Penn and Teller; Milksop Holly with singer/songwriter Mara Flynn; partnerships with Jad Fair, Hugh Hopper, John S. Hall of King Missile, Daevid Allen of Gong, and many others), a menagerie of talent including B.A.L.L., Damon and Naomi, Dogbowl, Gwar, Lida Husik, Daniel Johnston, King Missile, and Uncle Wiggly have recorded for Shimmy-Disc—with virtually all of the records produced by Kramer. After a hiatus in the '90s, the label has been reanimated as a division of the Knitting Factory in Manhattan, which is also the home of his recording studio, KnitNoise.

Kramer's creative output has been impressive indeed: Bongwater put out perceptive and provocative records, most notably *The Power of Pussy*. His solo album *The Guilt Trip*, a triple-vinyl set, is deeply personal in its exploration of jagged human emotion—especially regret—awash in tuneful psychedelia.

As a producer, Kramer is responsible for important work by Butthole Surfers, Galaxie 500 (now mutated into Luna), and the aforementioned Shimmy-Disc artists. His biggest commercial production success has been Urge Overkill's hyperdramatic cover of Neil Diamond's "Girl, You'll Be a Woman Soon," featured prominently in the smash film *Pulp Fiction* and on its triple-platinum soundtrack.

Kramer recalls, "Urge Overkill came into the studio in late 1992 with two songs, but they needed another. We went to my CD collection and found this Neil Diamond compilation. They knew that song and said, 'This will be a ridiculous one to try.' They wanted to whip it off really quickly and then get out of the studio for a gig at Maxwell's in Hoboken that evening. But they mistakenly imbibed too much narcotic and passed out on the floor. That gave me the opportunity to overdub the toy piano, the grand piano, the final acoustic guitar track, and the tambourine and then mix the whole thing in about 15 minutes.

"I woke them up at 6 P.M., a half-hour late for their Maxwell's soundcheck, and said, 'Boys, this is your hit song. All people need do is hear it and you'll be famous.' They looked at me and turned white. They said, 'Kramer, if you think Urge Overkill is about hits, then we worked with the wrong producer.' "

Kramer's production philosophy allows for individuality rather than perfection. "The producer should help shape the music but not change it. A producer should allow accidents to occur. Shimmy-Disc has been built on irregularities and dissimilarities to other music. The more perfect you are, the more sane you sound and the more similar to other things. A lot of people have just turned away from [our music] because it's so full of holes, but so is life and so is the music that I love from my early days like the Rolling Stones.

"What I've always hated about someone like Babyface (see entry) is that there's never a note wrong. Despite the craft that he exhibits—and you have to admire that whether you like the music or not—it just sounds like it was all computers and there were no human beings involved."

Kramer closes with this unsettling admonition to those who would enter the music business: "Never forget what they did to you, but never let them know that you remember." —ERIC OLSEN

A.C. Temple: *Belinda Backwards,* Blast First, 1990.

A.T.S.: *Blood Drive,* Shimmy-Disc, 1994.

Alice Donut: *Revenge Fantasies of the Impotent,* Alternative

Tentacles, 1991 • "Halloween," Alternative Tentacles, 1992 (*Virus 100*) • *The Untidy Suicides of Your Degenerate Children,* Alternative Tentacles, 1992 • *Medication,* Alternative Tentacles, 1993.

Allen, Daevid: w/ Kramer, *Who's Afraid?,* Shimmy-Disc, 1992.

B.A.L.L.: *Period,* Shimmy-Disc, 1987 • *Bird,* Shimmy-Disc, 1988 • "Out of the Blue," Caroline, 1989 (*Bridge: A Tribute to Neil Young*) • *Trouble Doll,* Shimmy-Disc, 1989 • *Ball Four,* Shimmy-Disc, 1990.

Barnyard Slut: *Space Age Motel,* Dutch East, 1993.

Blueberry Spy: *Sing Sing,* Shimmy-Disc, 1995.

Bongos, Bass and Bob: *Never Mind the Sex Pistols,* 50 Skidillion Watts, 1988.

Bongwater: *Breaking No New Ground,* Shimmy-Disc, 1987 • *Double Bummer,* Shimmy-Disc, 1988 • "Mr. Soul," Caroline, 1989 (*Bridge: A Tribute to Neil Young*) • *Too Much Sleep,* Shimmy-Disc, 1989 • *The Power of Pussy,* Shimmy-Disc, 1990 • "You Don't Love Me Yet," Sire/WB, 1990 (*Where the Pyramid Meets the Eye*) • *The Big Sellout,* Shimmy-Disc, 1991 • *The Peel Sessions,* Dutch East, 1993.

Butthole Surfers: *Cream Corn from the Socket of Davis* (EP), Touch & Go, 1985 • *Rembrandt Pussy Horse,* Touch & Go, 1986.

Cable: *Whisper Firing Line,* Mushroom, 1996.

Captain Howdy: *Tattoo of Blood,* Shimmy-Disc, 1995 • *Money Feeds My Music Machine,* Knitting Factory, 1998.

Carney/Hild/Kramer: *Happiness Finally Came to Them,* Shimmy-Disc, 1987.

Chia Pet: "Hey Baby," Shimmy-Disc, 1993.

Damon and Naomi: *More Sad Hits,* Shimmy-Disc, 1992 • *The Wonderous World of Damon and Naomi,* Sub Pop, 1995.

Danielson Family: *Tell Another Joke on the Ol' Choppin' Block,* Tooth and Nail, 1997 • *Tri-Danielson,* Tooth and Nail, 1998.

Deep Jimi and the Zep Creams: *Funky Dinosaur,* EastWest, 1993.

Dogbowl: *Tit!* Shimmy-Disc, 1989 • *Cyclops Nuclear Submarine Captain,* Shimmy-Disc, 1991 • *Flan,* Shimmy-Disc, 1992 • w/ Kramer, *Hot Day in Waco,* Shimmy-Disc, 1993 • *Project Success,* Shimmy-Disc, 1993 • w/ Kramer, *Gunsmoke,* Shimmy-Disc, 1995.

Dopes: *Dawn of the Dopes,* WDOP, 1994.

Egomaniacs: *Egomaniacs,* Shimmy-Disc, 1993.

E-Trance: *E-Trance,* Shimmy-Disc, 1995.

Fair, Jad: w/ Kramer, *Roll Out the Barrel,* Shimmy-Disc, 1988.

False Front: *Criminal Kind,* Shimmy-Disc, 1993.

Fly Ashtray: *Tone Sensations of the Wonder Men,* Shimmy-Disc, 1994.

Frith, Fred: *The Technology of Tears,* SST, 1988.

Galaxie 500: *Today,* Rough Trade, 1987, 1991 • *Blue Thunder*

(EP), Rough Trade, 1989 • *On Fire*, Rough Trade, 1989 • *Galaxie 500*, Rykodisc, 1996.

Glen or Glenda: *Reasons in the Sun*, Knitting Factory, 1998.

Grenadine: *Goya*, Shimmy-Disc, 1992.

Gwar: *Hell-o!* Shimmy-Disc, 1988.

Half Japanese: *Music to Strip By*, 50 Skidillion Watts, 1987 • *The Band That Would Be King*, 50 Skidillion Watts, 1988 • *Greatest Hits*, Safe House, 1995.

Honeymoon Killers: *Sing Sing (1984–1994)*, Sympathy for the Record Industry, 1997.

Husik, Lida: *Bozo*, Shimmy-Disc, 1989 • *Your Bag*, Shimmy-Disc, 1992 • *The Return of Red Emma*, Shimmy-Disc, 1993.

I, Sharko: *I, Sharko*, Bomp, 1996.

Jehova's Waitresses: *Perfect Impossible*, Shimmy-Disc, 1994.

Jellyfish Kiss: *Plank*, Shimmy-Disc, 1990 • *Stormy Weather*, Shimmy-Disc, 1991.

Johnston, Daniel: *1990*, Shimmy-Disc, 1988 • *Artistic Vice*, Shimmy-Disc, 1990.

Jon Spencer Blues Explosion: *A Reverse Willie Horton*, Pubic Pop Can, 1992 • *The Jon Spencer Blues Explosion*, Caroline, 1992.

King Missile: *Fluting on the Hump*, Shimmy-Disc, 1987 • *They*, Shimmy-Disc, 1988 • *Mystical Shit*, Shimmy-Disc, 1990 • "Detachable Penis," Atlantic, 1992 • *Happy Hour*, Atlantic, 1992.

Kramer: w/ John Hall, *Real Men*, Shimmy-Disc, 1991 • "Insight," Alternative Tentacles, 1992 (*Virus 100*) • *The Guilt Trip*, Shimmy-Disc, 1993 • w/ Hugh Hopper, *A Remark Hugh Made*, Shimmy-Disc, 1994 • *The Secret of Comedy*, Shimmy-Disc, 1994 • *Music for Crying*, Creativeman, 1995 • w/ Hugh Hopper, *Huge*, Shimmy-Disc, 1997 • w/ David Hild, *Rubber Hair*, Shimmy-Disc, 1997 • *Let Me Explain Something to You About Art*, Tzadik, 1998 • *Songs from the Pink Death*, Knitting Factory, 1998 • *See also* Allen, Daevid; Carney/Hild/Kramer; Dogbowl; and Fair, Jad.

Laraaji: *Bring Forth*, Shimmy-Disc/Laraaji, 1987.

Lotion: *Lotion* (EP), KokoPop, 1992, 1993 • "Head," Shimmy-Disc, 1993 • *Tear* (EP), KokoPop, 1996.

Low: *I Could Live in Hope*, Vernon Yard, 1994 • *Long Division*, Vernon Yard, 1995 • *Transmission* (EP), Vernon Yard, 1996.

Morning Glories: "Chapter of Wills," KokoPop, 1993.

Nothing Painted Blue: *Power Trips Down Lovers Lane*, KokoPop, 1993.

Ovarian Trolley: *Crocodile Tears*, Shimmy-Disc, 1994.

Paleface: *Paleface*, Polydor, 1991 • *Raw*, Shimmy-Disc, 1995.

Pussy Galore: *Right Now*, Caroline, 1987.

Ralske, Kurt: "Tar, Iodine, Blood and Rust," Number Six, 1992 (*Guitarrorists*).

Raymond Listen: *Licorice Root Orchestra*, Shimmy-Disc, 1993.

Rein Sanction: *Broc's Cabin*, Sub Pop, 1991.

Semibeings: *Three Pawns Standing*, C/Z, 1996.

Sherman: *Transparent Extender*, Shimmy-Disc, 1993.

Shockabilly: *Colosseum*, Rough Trade, 1984 • *Earth vs. Shockabilly*, Rough Trade, 1984 • *The Ghost Of*, Shimmy-Disc, 1989 • *Live . . . Just Beautiful*, Shimmy-Disc, 1990 • *Vietnam and Heaven*, Shimmy-Disc, 1990.

Tadpoles: *Far Out*, Bakery, 1996.

Tucker, Maureen: *Life in Exile After Abdication*, 50 Skidillion Watts, 1989.

Uncle Wiggly: *There Was an Elk*, Shimmy-Disc, 1993 • *Across the Room and into Your Lap*, Shimmy-Disc, 1991.

Unrest: *Malcolm X Park*, Caroline, 1988.

Urge Overkill: *Stull* (EP), Touch & Go, 1992 • "Girl, You'll Be a Woman Soon," MCA, 1994 (*Pulp Fiction* soundtrack).

Velvet Cactus Society: *Velvet Cactus Society*, Shimmy-Disc, 1994.

White Zombie: *Pycho Head Blow Out!* Caroline, 1986.

Eddie Kramer

Eddie Kramer is associated with some of the most classic of classic rock bands. His name is inextricably linked with Jimi Hendrix, whose records he engineered during Hendrix's lifetime. He reassumed technical control over the material recently when the Hendrix family regained the rights to it. Along with co-producer John McDermott, he went back to the original 2-track masters and remastered them for release on CD. This followed years of confusing, haphazard releases in which Kramer had no involvement.

Kramer received music training in his native South Africa, studying classical piano and jazz. Moving to England at 19, he recorded jazz groups in a home studio before going to work for Pye Studios in 1964. He established the 2-track KPS Studios in 1965, which were bought out by Regency Sound in 1966. Kramer oversaw the construction of their new four-track studio. Later, he worked at Olympic Studio where he engineered for the Beatles, the Stones, the Small Faces, Traffic, and Hendrix.

In 1968, Kramer moved to the U.S. to work at Record Plant and Electric Lady Studios. He launched a relationship with Led Zeppelin, starting with their second album, and wound up engineering five albums in all. His producing career began in earnest following Hendrix's death. "There's a gray line between producing and engineering," he says. "I always wanted to be a producer."

Kramer's career always leaned toward heavier rock, though he has produced artists as diverse as Lena

Horne, classical guitarist John Williams, and the Kentucky Headhunters. "I've become known as that sort of producer, although classical is what I like to listen to. There's something very exciting about it if it's played well. I like all music. In the early '60s, jazz was my bread and butter. At Electric Ladyland I did everyone from Carly Simon to Voices of East Harlem. I'm not going to say I excel at any particular thing."

But he has worked many heavy bands, including Foghat, Ted Nugent and the Amboy Dukes, Twisted Sister, Alcatrazz, Raven, Loudness, Fastway, and Whitesnake. He established an ongoing relationship with Kiss, producing six albums as well as working on Ace Frehley's first solo album. "Kiss was a challenge because they couldn't play well when they started," recalls Kramer. "But the excitement was there. It was just a question of replacing inaccurate playing and making sure everything was in sync. I had the choice of two bands—Boston or Kiss. I heard the Boston demos and I told Tom Scholz I couldn't do anything with it, that he should just release it as it was."

Kramer was hired to record the original 1969 Woodstock Festival, which established one of his specialties: the live recording. He did live recordings for Kiss, Led Zeppelin, Hendrix, the Stones, and David Bowie (see entry). He also helped record (with Chris Kimsey; see entry) one of the most influential live albums of all time, *Frampton Comes Alive,* which launched the live-album craze.

Frampton had been known as a dynamic stage artist whose pedestrian studio albums never quite captured his charisma. Kramer carefully cleaned up and pieced together Frampton's live show to produce an album that conveyed the essence of Frampton the performer but maintained sufficient clarity to get Frampton the extensive radio airplay that had previously eluded him. "The most important thing is that the band understands that I'm there to record their performance. Whatever happens, I'm not going to get in their way. We can always go record another night. You make sure you have a good clear signal path, place mikes carefully, and make sure you have a good crew."

One of Kramer's recent productions was blues guitarist Buddy Guy's 1995 *Slippin' In.* Unbelievably, it was the first album he'd been associated with to win a Grammy. He cites it as one of his favorites. "That and Hendrix. I like the more blues-oriented stuff."

Kramer keeps his outlook fresh by generating outside projects, including co-authorship of a Hendrix biography with John McDermott called *Hendrix: Setting the Record Straight;* a photographic book of shots from his recording sessions; an instructional video on recording; the BBC documentary, *The Making of Electric Ladyland;* and a Hendrix tribute album called *Stone Free.* He also continues to produce when he finds a project that interests him. And he has served as a studio design consultant.

"A&R departments are populated by 20-year-olds who don't know much about the past or much about what I've done," he says. "You may not be the flavor of the week. I have to keep reinventing myself by not staying in one place too long. So I'm giving lectures, aligning myself with manufacturers, writing books, projects I invent myself. I've lectured at Berklee, Full Sail, GRT Institute. It's a constant challenge."

Kramer has seen many changes in recording in 30-plus years. "The one thing I say to kids is, 'Look at what we're doing.' Producers are sitting here with a 48-track digital SSL 9000, $100,000 worth of outboard gear, a Neumann 247. And we're using tube mikes, tube equalizers, tube limiters. They're picking out gear that's 50 years old. Why? Because it sounds better. It's ironic. It sounded better the way we used to do it. It's all in the name of technology. It may be quieter but does it sound better? No."

He adds, "A lot of the spontaneity has gone out of recording. There are so many options open to people. At the touch of a button you can create any sound you want. My worry is that songs are not that great. There's a proliferation of bands, an astounding amount of material being released. The public can't digest it. They're assaulted with a huge volume of information. Even in the studio, you're faced with so many choices. It becomes increasingly difficult to focus on songs. I think everyone agrees we're putting too much product out. It's a tough situation for the listening audience. That's why I like a lot of blues artists. They're the last bastions of sensibility."

Though Kramer engineered most of his earlier album productions, he's been bringing in outside engineers since the early '90s. This allows him to step back and focus on the music, acting as a mentor for the band. "I love to get involved with songs when they're being written, to help with the structure of the song. Maybe I'll tell them to slow a song down and all of a sudden it starts to come together. I have an extensive musical background I bring to bear. I make sure the album is finished in the preproduction phase. You know when you walk in the studio what you're going to play, but leave a little room for spontaneity. I like to get a band happy and confident and get great sounds for them. It should be a giggle and a laugh."

What attracts him to a new band is "guys who can play. I mean that as a generic term—it seems like girls are doing better than the guys. Some of the recordings I hear are really good. My 15-year-old daughter plays me these records and they're really great." —ANASTASIA PANTSIOS

Air Raid: *Air Raid,* 20th Century, 1981.

Alcatrazz: *Disturbing the Peace,* Capitol, 1985.

Amboy Dukes: *Marriage on the Rocks,* Polydor, 1969.

Angel: *On Earth As It Is in Heaven,* Casablanca, 1977 • *Anthology,* Mercury, 1992.

Anthrax: *Among the Living,* Island, 1987 • *I'm the Man* (EP), Island, 1987.

April Wine: *Live at El Mocambo,* Decca/Aquarius, 1977.

Blind Melon: "Out on the Tiles," Atlantic, 1995 (*Encomium: A Tribute to Led Zeppelin*).

Bolin, Tommy: *From the Archives,* Vol. 1, Rhino, 1996 • *From the Archives,* Vol. 2, Zebra, 1998.

Brownsville Station: *Brownsville Station,* Private Stock, 1977 • *Smoking in the Boy's Room: The Best Of,* Rhino, 1993.

Duke and the Drivers: *Cruisin',* ABC, 1975.

Fastway: *Fastway,* Columbia, 1983 • *All Fired Up,* Columbia, 1984.

Foghat: *Stone Blue,* Bearsville, 1978 • *Best Of,* Rhino, 1990 • *Best Of,* Vol. 2, Rhino, 1992.

Fotomaker: *Fotomaker,* Atlantic, 1978.

Frampton, Peter: *The Art of Control,* A&M, 1982.

Frehley, Ace: *Ace Frehley,* Casablanca, 1978 • "New York Groove," Casablanca, 1978 • *Frehley's Comet,* Megaforce, 1987 • *Trouble Walkin',* Megaforce, 1989 • *Loaded Deck,* Megaforce, 1998.

Guy, Buddy: "Red House," Reprise, 1993 (*Stone Free: A Tribute to Jimi Hendrix*) • *Slippin' In,* Silvertone, 1994 • *Live! The Real Deal,* Silvertone, 1996.

Havana Black: *Exiles in Mainstream,* Hollywood, 1991.

Hendrix, Jimi: *Cry of Love,* Polydor/Reprise, 1971 • *Rainbow Bridge,* Reprise, 1971 • *Hendrix in the West,* Reprise, 1972 • *War Heroes,* Reprise, 1973 • *The Essential,* Reprise, 1978 • *Ultimate Experience,* MCA, 1993 • *First Rays of the New Rising Sun,* MCA, 1997 • *South Saturn Delta,* MCA, 1997 • *BBC Sessions,* MCA, 1998.

Icon: *Night of the Crime,* Capitol, 1985.

Kings of the Sun: *Kings of the Sun,* RCA, 1988 • "Serpentine," RCA, 1988.

Kiss: *Kiss Alive,* Casablanca, 1975 • "Rock and Roll All Night (Live Version)," Casablanca, 1975 • "Hard Luck Woman," Casablanca, 1976 • *Rock and Roll Over,* Casablanca, 1976 • *Alive 2,* Casablanca, 1977 • "Calling Dr. Love," Casablanca, 1977 • *Love Gun,* Casablanca, 1977 • *Double Platinum,* Casablanca/Mercury, 1978 • *Smashes, Thrashes and Hits,* Mercury, 1988 • *Kiss Alive III,* Mercury, 1993.

Linhart, Buzzy: *Music,* Eleuthera, 1971.

Loudness: *Hurricane Eyes,* Atco, 1987.

Michael Stanley Band: *North Coast,* EMI America, 1981 • *Misery Loves Company: More of the Best, 1975–1983,* Razor & Tie, 1997.

Mott: *Shouting and Pointing,* Columbia, 1976.

Murphy, J.F., and Salt: *J.F. Murphy and Salt,* Elektra, 1971 • *Live,* Elektra, 1972.

Music: *Music,* Buddah, 1971.

NRBQ: *Scraps,* Kama Sutra, 1970 • *Workshop,* Kama Sutra, 1972 • *RC Cola and a Moon Pie,* Red Rooster/Rounder, 1986.

Perkins, Carl: *Go Cat Go,* Dinosaur, 1996.

Power Trio from Hell: *American Man,* Reprise, 1993.

Pretty Maids: *Future World,* Epic, 1987.

Randall, Elliott: *Randall's Island,* Polydor, 1973.

Raven: *The Pack Is Back,* Atlantic, 1986.

Restless, The: *The Restless,* Mercury, 1984.

Rodgers, Paul: *Now and Live,* Velvel, 1997.

Santana: *Viva!* Columbia, 1988.

Scream: *Let It Scream,* Hollywood, 1991.

Seal and Jeff Beck: "Manic Depression," Reprise, 1993 (*Stone Free: A Tribute to Jimi Hendrix*).

Sha Na Na: *Sha Na Na,* Kama Sutra, 1971.

Simms Brothers Band: *Attitude,* Elektra, 1980.

Simon, Carly: *Carly Simon,* Elektra, 1970 • "That's the Way I've Always Heard It's Should Be," Elektra, 1971 • *The Best Of,* Elektra, 1975.

Sir Lord Baltimore: *Sir Lord Baltimore,* Mercury, 1970, 1971, 1994.

Slash, Paul Rodgers, and Band of Gypsys: "I Don't Live Today," Reprise, 1993 (*Stone Free: A Tribute to Jimi Hendrix*).

Spin Doctors: "Spanish Castle Magic," Reprise, 1993 (*Stone Free: A Tribute to Jimi Hendrix*).

Spooky Tooth: *The Mirror,* Island, 1974.

Steeplechase: *Lady Bright,* Polydor, 1970.

Stories: *About Us* (4 tracks), Kama Sutra, 1973.

T.T. Quick: *Metal of Honor,* Megaforce, 1984, 1996.

Triumph: *Thunder Seven,* MCA, 1984 • "Follow Your Heart," MCA, 1985 • *Classics,* MCA, 1989.

Trower, Robin: *In the Line of Fire,* Atlantic, 1990.

Truth: *Truth,* Roulette, 1975.

Twisted Sister: *Under the Blade* (EP), Atlantic, 1985.

Waldman, Wendy: *Which Way to Main Street?,* Epic, 1982.

Zephyr: *Going Back to Colorado,* Warner Archives, 1971, 1994.

COLLECTIONS

In from the Storm: Jimi Hendrix Tribute, RCA, 1995.

Murray Krugman

See also SANDY PEARLMAN

Murray Krugman is a peripatetic music man who signed and co-produced (with Sandy Pearlman; see entry) Blue Öyster Cult, the Dictators, and Pavlov's Dog for Columbia in the '70s. He also co-produced (with Winter and Rick Derringer) the classic *Live/Johnny Winter And* album, and Mahavishnu Orchestra's (with John McLaughlin) monumental *Between Nothingness and Eternity*. After taking the '80s off from music, Krugman returned in the '90s as owner and producer of the Vermont-based acoustic music label Silverwolf, with artists including Caroline Aiken, Chris Chandler, Odetta, and Michael Veitch and live music from the Kerrville Folk Music Festival.

Murray Krugman was born April 8, 1948, in New York City. After graduating from Wesleyan College, he entered a Columbia Records training program and became a product manager in 1970. Krugman observed the recording process for a time, then co-produced the gold *Live/Johnny Winter And* album that successfully captured Winter's amalgam of blues riffs and rock 'n' roll energy for the first time.

Promoted to A&R, Krugman signed Blue Öyster Cult and co-produced, with their manager/lyricist, Sandy Pearlman, the band's first seven albums—albums that helped define metal, but whose intelligence and sonic scope far transcend today's rather cartoonish conception of the genre. The band's third album, *Secret Treaties*, beautifully fuses heaviness (especially Donald "Buck Dharma" Roeser) with tunefulness; the band's fifth and sixth albums, *Agents of Fortune* ("Don't Fear the Reaper," No. 12; "E.T.I.") and *Spectres* ("Godzilla," "Going Through the Motions," "I Love the Night") transcend metal and are among rock's best albums—period.

Krugman also signed the Dictators and Pavlov's Dog to Columbia and co-produced, again with Pearlman, their respective classic first albums. *The Dictators Go Girl Crazy* is a freakish blend of souped-up surf music, pseudofascist imagery, and self-conscious hedonism that helped put fun back into rock 'n' roll. Though not as fully realized, the second (*Manifest Destiny*) and third (*Bloodbrothers*) Dictators albums have great moments like the "fake live" "Search and Destroy" from *Destiny*, modeled after Aerosmith's "Train Kept a-Rollin.'"

Pavlov's Dog was another bizarre combination: a singer (David Surkamp) with an even higher and more quavery voice than Rush's Geddy Lee, meshed with a prog-rock group along the lines of McKendree Spring. A frightening concept, but *Pampered Menial* is blessed with great tunes ("Julia," "Natchez Trace") and multidimensional production.

In 1980 Krugman retired from the music biz to teach at an alternative school in Florida. In 1983 he returned to school to get his law degree; he practiced law from 1986 to 1989. In 1990 he built a nontoxic, nonpolluting home in Vermont, and in 1992 he started the Silverwolf label to record and release acoustic-based music ignored by other labels. —ERIC OLSEN

Aiken, Caroline: *Butler Field*, Silverwolf, 1997.

Blue Öyster Cult: *Blue Öyster Cult*, Columbia, 1971 • *Tyranny and Mutation*, Columbia, 1973 • *Secret Treaties*, Columbia, 1974 • *On Your Feet or on Your Knees*, Columbia, 1975 • *Agents of Fortune*, Columbia, 1976 • "Don't Fear the Reaper," Columbia, 1976 • *Spectres*, Columbia, 1977 • *Some Enchanted Evening*, Columbia, 1978 • *Workshop of the Telescopes*, Legacy, 1995.

Dictators: *Manifest Destiny*, Asylum, 1977 • *Blood Brothers*, Asylum, 1978 • *Go Girl Crazy*, Epic, 1975.

Mahavishnu Orchestra: *Between Nothingness and Eternity*, Columbia, 1973.

Pavlov's Dog: *Pampered Menial*, ABC, 1975 • *At the Sound of the Bell*, CBS, 1976.

Schwartz, Eddie: *Schwartz*, A&M Canada, 1978.

Stark Raving Chandler: *Generica*, Silverwolf, 1996.

Talas: *Talas*, Talas, 1979.

Veitch, Michael: *N.Y. Journal*, Silverwolf, 1998.

Winter, Johnny: *Live/Johnny Winter And*, Columbia, 1971.

COLLECTIONS

The Silverwolf Homeless Project, Silverwolf, 1994.
The 1995 Kerrville Highlights, Silverwolf, 1996.
The Women of Kerrville, Silverwolf, 1996.
The Kerrville 25th Anniversary, Silverwolf, 1997.

Eric Kupper

Eric Kupper was in the right place at the right time. A skilled musician with a fierce knowledge of dance music, Kupper got his start working as a keyboardist for a diverse handful of dance music producers and remixers. Since 1987, Kupper has worked his keyboard magic for such club luminaries as David Morales, Frankie Knuckles, Arthur Baker (see entries), Justin Strauss, Mark Kamins, and Richie Jones. When he's not being hired as a keyboard player for songs being remixed by others, he can usually be found remixing and producing—as well as playing keyboards—for artists. In 11 years, he has played on, remixed, and produced over 700 records.

In 1991, Kupper received his first major break as a producer. Frankie Knuckles was in the process of recording his debut album (for Virgin) and requested Kupper's production skills for one of the tracks. Together with Knuckles and John Poppo, Kupper co-produced—and penned—the now-classic No. 1 dance hit, "The Whistle Song," which went directly from the dance floor to the living room, thanks to its inclusion in a television commercial for Nestea iced tea.

Establishing himself as a songwriter who knows a thing or two about the melodic hook, Kupper has since collaborated with Billy Ray Martin, Crystal Waters, and RuPaul. Additionally, he has written and produced songs for Chanelle, Clubland, and Uncanny Alliance. In the remix department, Kupper's pop-injected productions have helped fuel the careers of Kate Bush ("Rubberband Girl"), Sheryl Crow ("All I Wanna Do"), and Robert Palmer ("You Are in My System").

Never one to take a breather, Kupper has, under the moniker K-Scope, released two full-length albums, both of which won international recognition for their coolly sophisticated underground grooves. His latest endeavor is the formation of Hysteria Records, an independent label that specializes in New York–style house music, both vocal and instrumental tracks. —LARRY FLICK

Abstract Truth: "Get Another Plan" (remix), Streetwave, 1996.

Bambaata, Afrika: *Don't Stop . . . Planet Rock* (remix, EP), Tommy Boy, 1992.

Bush, Kate: "Rubberband Girl" (remix), Columbia, 1993.

Chanelle: "Work That Body," Great Jones, 1994.

Clubland f/Zemya Hamilton: *Clubland f/Zemya Hamilton,* Great Jones/Island, 1992 • "Hypnotized," Great Jones/Island, 1992.

Coolbone: *Brass-Hop,* Hollywood, 1997 • "Nothin' but Strife," Hollywood, 1997.

Crow, Sheryl: "All I Wanna Do" (remix), A&M, 1994.

DJ Irene: *Underground Assault* (remix), Priority, 1998.

Dudley, Anne, and Jaz Coleman: "Ziggarats of Cinnamon," TVT, 1991.

808 State: "Oops" (remix), Tommy Boy/ZTT, 1991.

Information Society: *Peace and Love, Inc.,* Tommy Boy, 1992.

James, Jimmy: "Who Wants to Be Your Lover?" (remix), Interhit, 1997.

Knuckles, Frankie: *Beyond the Mix,* Virgin, 1990 • "The Whistle Song," Virgin, 1991.

K-Scope: *From the Deep,* IRS, 1995 • *K-Scope Project,* Tribal,

1995 • *K-Scope,* Vol. 2, Tribal, 1995 • w/ Eric Kupper, *Instant Music,* MCA, 1998.

Kupper/Campbell Project: "Never," Hysteria, 1996.

Marxman: *33 Revolutions per Minute* (1 track), A&M, 1993 • "All About Eve" (remix), A&M, 1993.

Material: "Eternal Drift" (remix), Axiom/Island, 1994.

Morgan, Jamie J.: *Shotgun,* Tabu, 1990.

P.M. Dawn: "The Ways of the Wind" (remix), Gee Street/Island, 1993 • *Jesus Wept,* Gee Street, 1995.

Palmer, Robert: "You Are in My System" (remix), Island, 1983.

Peniston, CeCe: "Finally," AM-PM, 1997.

RuPaul: "House of Love," Tommy Boy, 1992 • "Supermodel (You Better Work)," Tommy Boy, 1992 • *Back to My Roots* (EP), Tommy Boy, 1993 • *Supermodel of the World,* Tommy Boy, 1993 • *Foxy Lady,* Rhino/Atlantic, 1996 • "Snapshot," Rhino/Atlantic, 1996.

S' Express: "Nothing to Lose" (remix), Sire/WB, 1991.

Sybil: *Doin' It Now,* Next Plateau, 1993.

Uncanny Alliance: "Happy Day," A&M, 1994 • "Happy Day" (remix), A&M, 1994 • *The Groove Won't Bite,* A&M, 1994.

COLLECTIONS

This Is the Sound of Tribal U.K., IRS, 1994.

Works Eightball, K-Tel, 1998.

Greg Ladanyi

Crack mixer, engineer, and producer, Greg Ladanyi helped create some of the most popular and celebrated rock music of the '80s. As producer or coproducer, Ladanyi helped define a sophisticated but rootsy L.A. sound with such luminaries as Jackson Browne (*Hold Out,* No. 1; *Lawyers in Love,* No. 8), Don Henley (*I Can't Stand Still; Building the Perfect Beast,* No. 13), David Lindley (*El Rayo-X, Win This Record*), and Warren Zevon (*Bad Luck Streak in Dancing School,* No. 20; *Stand in the Fire; The Envoy*).

Ladanyi has also displayed a knack for working with international talent: co-producing Ireland's Clannad and the Church from New Zealand in the '80s and producing Latin American bands like Caifanes in the '90s. As mixer, Ladanyi has spun gold for the Jacksons, Asia, the Tubes, and Toto (whose *Toto IV* earned seven Grammys and sold over 3 million copies).

Born in 1953, Ladanyi has lived in Los Angeles since he was 2. As a teen, Ladanyi was a precocious entrepreneur, managing and booking bands and opening a series

Photo by David Goggin ©1994

of small recording studios around L.A. His first engineering job was for blues anarchist Captain Beefheart in the mid-'70s. Realizing his heart resided in the studio, Ladanyi then got an engineering job at a "real studio," the Sound Factory.

In the early '80s, Ladanyi opened the Complex recording studio with George Massenburg (see entry) and began producing in earnest. Jackson Browne's classic *Hold Out*—with standards "Boulevard" (featuring David Lindley's slashing hard rock guitar riff), "That Girl Could Sing," and "Hold On Hold Out"—achieves an edge and clarity missing from earlier Browne offerings, and was an astonishing production debut for Ladanyi. "I love it. I learned a lot about the values of making songs about things that matter. There are songs on that record that are very dear to me—that when I listen to them I remember exactly what happened to me on those days," he says.

Ladanyi also worked with Browne's exemplary guitarist and multi-instrumentalist, David Lindley. His *El Rayo-X* is a sparkling romp through various roots styles, including Tex-Mex (the title track), reggae ("She Took Off My Romeos"), zydeco ("Bye Bye Love"), New Orleans R&B ("Tu-ber-cu-lucas and the Sinus Blues"), and a stomping hard-rock demolition of "Mercury Blues."

Don Henley's *Building the Perfect Beast* came in 1984—an extremely appealing distillation of Henley's pop-rock sensibility minus the country influences of the Eagles. Singles "All She Wants to Do Is Dance" (No. 9)—propelled by a modern rock dance edge—and the

moody, thought-provoking "The Boys of Summer" (No. 5) remain Henley's finest solo moments.

Recalls Ladanyi on the process: "The main concern with Don was making sure that people heard 'Don Henley the solo artist,' not 'Don Henley the lead singer of the Eagles.' We changed everything about the way Don made records. We all agreed that Don was going to be a singer and not a drummer. Danny Kortchmar's (see entry) writing had a lot to do with that. So, with different rhythms and different guitar playing, the attack on Don's vocals became different from what he was doing with the Eagles."

Ladanyi sold his share of the Complex in the mid-'80s because he found himself spending more energy on the banalities of running a studio than on making records. In 1988 he co-produced (with the band and Waddy Wachtel) one of the finest modern rock moments of the decade, the Church's *Starfish*, an album of Beatlesque delicacy and melodicism ("Reptile," "Lost"), spiced with interludes of startling intensity ("Spark"). Surprise hit single "Under the Milky Way" (No. 24) brilliantly conveys ennui jolted by a sudden apprehension of the enormity of existence.

Besides technical excellence, the key to Ladanyi's success would appear to be his musical soul. "I think that music is a part of our lives that will always be an imaginative and creative link between generations. More and more now you see kids and adults listening to the same kind of music. Music is part of everybody's inner rhythm, inner souls, inner grooves. It lets you dream. It will always be a part of something in all of us." —ERIC OLSEN AND DAVID JOHN FARINELLA

Believers, The: *Extraordinary Life*, Savage, 1992.

Browne, Jackson: "Boulevard," Asylum, 1980 • *Hold Out*, Asylum, 1980 • "That Girl Could Sing," Asylum, 1980 • "Lawyers in Love," Asylum, 1983 • *Lawyers in Love*, Asylum, 1983 • "Tender Is the Night," Asylum, 1983.

Caifanes: *El Nervio Del Volcan*, RCA international, 1994 • *Historia*, RCA international, 1997.

Church, The: *Starfish*, Arista, 1988 • "Under the Milky Way," Arista, 1988.

Clannad: *Sirius*, RCA, 1988 • *Past Present*, RCA, 1989 • *Rogha: The Best of Clannad*, RCA, 1997.

Cruzados, The: *After Dark*, Arista, 1987.

Fleetwood Mac: "As Long As You Follow," Warner Bros., 1988 • *Greatest Hits*, Reprise, 1988 • *Behind the Mask*, Warner Bros., 1990 • "Save Me," Warner Bros., 1990.

Henley, Don: "Dirty Laundry," Asylum, 1982 • *I Can't Stand Still*, Asylum, 1982 • "All She Wants to Do Is Dance," Geffen, 1984 • *Building the Perfect Beast*, Geffen, 1984 • "The Boys of Summer," Geffen, 1984 • "Not Enough

Love in the World," Geffen, 1985 • "Sunset Grill," Geffen, 1985 • *Actual Miles: Henley's Greatest Hits,* Geffen, 1995.

Holster, David James: *Chinese Honeymoon,* CBS, 1979.

Jeff Healey Band: *See the Light,* Arista, 1988 • "Angel Eyes," Arista, 1989.

Kansas: *In the Spirit of Things,* MCA, 1988.

Lindley, David: *El Rayo-X,* Asylum, 1981 • *Win This Record,* Asylum, 1982 • *Mr. Dave,* WEA International, 1985.

Martin, Eric: *Eric Martin,* Capitol, 1985 • "Information," Capitol, 1985.

Newman, Troy: *Gypsy Moon,* EastWest, 1991 • "Love Gets Rough," EastWest, 1991 • *It's Like This,* Curb, 1995.

Parton, Dolly: "Straight Talk," Hollywood, 1992.

REO Speedwagon: *Building the Bridge,* Castle, 1996.

Shooting Star: *Silent Scream,* Virgin, 1985.

Snow, Phoebe: *Rock Away,* Mirage, 1981.

Stealin' Horses: *Stealin' Horses* (EP), Arista, 1988.

Toto: *IV,* Columbia, 1982.

Zevon, Warren: *Bad Luck Streak in Dancing School,* Asylum, 1980 • *Stand in the Fire,* Asylum, 1980 • *The Envoy,* Asylum, 1982 • *Quiet Normal Life: The Best Of,* Asylum, 1986 • *I'll Sleep When I'm Dead (An Anthology),* Rhino, 1996.

COLLECTIONS

Straight Talk soundtrack, Hollywood, 1992.

Puro Eskanol, Vol. 2, *Rice and Beans,* Aztlan, 1998.

Kenny Laguna

Kenny Laguna has been an important figure in rock music since the mid-'60s as musician, songwriter, arranger, producer, and artist manager. His most important productions include excellent work with the Beserkley label, Bow Wow Wow's classic new wave single "I Want Candy" (No. 9 U.K.), and co-production with Ritchie Cordell (see entry) and others of the Joan Jett catalog.

Kenny (now Ken) Laguna was born January 30, 1953, and grew up in Greenwich Village, New York. His first professional experience came at 13 playing keyboards behind the Shangri-Las, Regents, and others for high school dances sponsored by radio station WMCA. That year he also recorded his own single, "Do You Want to Know?" for Kama Sutra.

By 17 he was a veteran session man, having recorded (primarily on keyboards) with Tommy James and the Shondells ("Mony Mony," "I Think We're Alone Now"), Bob Diddley, Billy Joel, Barbra Streisand ("Stoney End"),

and the bubblegum factory of Kasenetz-Katz, including the Ohio Express ("Yummy Yummy," "Chewy Chewy"), 1910 Fruitgum Company ("Simon Says," "Indian Giver"), and Crazy Elephant ("Gimme Gimme Good Lovin' ").

Besides performing, Laguna also helped write and arrange songs (for which he received little credit), and like many another Tin Pan Alley veteran, learned his way around the studio by making demos. By the end of 1969 the bubblegum craze had run its course, so Laguna moved to L.A. to further his career. Instead he found mediocre music and lots of chemicals.

In 1972 he moved back to New York and nearly fell out of the music business altogether. "I went from being a big shot, flying all over the world for all these Ali fights, and now I can't pay the rent. I'm working for $60 a week, where before I wouldn't even get out of bed for $60. I think it cured me of the disease that Elvis and Tommy James had, though. It starts so young—where you're not who you are really—you're this guy on the radio," he sighs. Laguna next put in some time with Motown's office in England, working with Edwin Starr and meeting Pete Townshend of the Who. "All of a sudden I wasn't just a bubblegum guy, I was a bubblegum guy who was hanging out with the Who," he says with a laugh.

In 1973 Laguna came back to the States to tour and record one last time with Tommy James. While he was recording with James at Fantasy Studios in Berkeley, *San Francisco Chronicle* writer Joel Selvin introduced Laguna to Matthew King Kaufman (see entry), who had just started Beserkley Records. "Matthew was real interested in the techniques that were happening from New York—the whole Brill Building thing—because we had definite formulas that had been developed by Leiber and Stoller (see entry) about how you put percussion on the record, how you put the background vocals on, at what point they go on," and the like. Kaufman's group, Earth Quake, came in and played on the Tommy James album. "It was a good entrance into the modern world, so I started to assimilate myself."

In just five short years Laguna went from loading boxes on 12th Avenue to homes in England, New York, and California. For Beserkley, Laguna helped produce Greg Kihn, Jonathan Richman, Earth Quake, the Tyla Gang, and Spitballs. But Laguna's lasting fame is built upon his long-term relationship with Joan Jett. Laguna met Jett in 1979, shortly after the breakup of her band the Runaways; he has been her manager, co-writer, co-producer, and confidant ever since. Laguna and Jett, especially on the singles "I Love Rock 'n' Roll" (No. 1), "Crimson and Clover" (No. 7), "Do You Wanna Touch

Me?" (No. 20), and "I Hate Myself for Loving You" (No. 8) have achieved a smoking synthesis of pop tunefulness, hard rock riffs, and punk attitude.

Through it all, Laguna sees himself as a songwriter/arranger type of producer. "I find the engineering tasks laborious and more difficult than the natural thing, which is to create all the arrangements and then let it happen. I try to get all my basic tracks in the first three takes. If I can get a singer who can sing on the basic tracks, I do that as much as possible. I try to capture a certain energy and not strip it away by making things 'right.' Mistakes and imperfections are part of the magic." —ERIC OLSEN AND DAVID JOHN FARINELLA

Advertising: *Jingles,* EMI, 1978.

Bow Wow Wow: "Baby, Oh No," RCA, 1982 • "I Want Candy," RCA, 1982 • *I Want Candy* (4 tracks), RCA, 1982 • *The Last of the Mohicans* (EP), RCA, 1982.

Earth Quake: *Leveled,* Beserkley, 1977 • *Two Years in a Padded Cell,* Beserkley, 1979.

Evil Stig: *Evil Stig,* Warner Bros., 1995.

Gibbons, Steve: *Caught in the Act,* MCA, 1977.

James, Tommy: *In Touch,* Fantasy, 1976 • *The Solo Years (1970–1981),* Rhino, 1991.

Jett, Joan: "Dirty Deeds," Blackheart/Epic, 1990 • *Flashback,* Blackheart, 1994 • "Go Home," Blackheart/WB, 1994 • *Pure and Simple,* Blackheart/WB, 1994 • w/ Paul Westerberg, "Let's Do It," Elektra, 1995 (*Tank Girl* soundtrack).

Jett, Joan, and the Blackhearts: *Joan Jett,* Ariola, 1980 • "Bad Reputation," A&M, 1981 (*Urgh! A Music War*) • *Bad Reputation,* Boardwalk, 1981 • *I Love Rock 'n' Roll,* Boardwalk, 1981 • "Crimson and Clover," Boardwalk, 1982 • "Do You Wanna Touch Me?," Boardwalk, 1982 • "I Love Rock 'n' Roll," Boardwalk, 1982 • *Album,* MCA, 1983 • *Glorious Results of a Misspent Youth,* Blackheart/MCA, 1984 • "Good Music," Blackheart/Epic, 1986 • *Good Music,* Blackheart/Epic Associated, 1986 • "I Hate Myself for Loving You," Blackheart, 1988 • "Little Liar," Blackheart, 1988 • *Up Your Alley,* Epic Associated, 1988 • *The Hit List,* Epic, 1990 • *Notorious,* Blackheart/Epic Associated, 1991 • "Love Is All Around," Blackheart/WB, 1996 • "Real Wild Child (Wild One)," Royalty, 1997.

Kihn, Greg: *Next of Kihn,* Beserkley, 1978 • *With the Naked Eye,* Beserkley, 1979 • *Kihnsolidation: The Best Of,* Rhino, 1989.

Love, Darlene: *Paint Another Picture,* Columbia, 1990.

Metal Church: *Hanging in the Balance,* Blackheart, 1993.

Modern Lovers: *Live,* Beserkley, 1977.

Richman, Jonathan, and the Modern Lovers: *Back in Your Life,* Beserkley, 1979 • *Beserkley Years,* Rhino, 1987.

Spitballs: *The Spitballs,* Beserkley, 1978.

Tyla Gang: *Moonproof,* Beserkley, 1978.

Dennis Lambert

As a premier songwriter/producer for over 30 years, Dennis Lambert has scored huge hits in the pop, rock, R&B, and country fields (with songwriter/producer partner Brian Potter from 1969 to 1980) for artists including Glen Campbell ("Country Boy," No. 11), the Commodores ("Nightshift," No. 3), the Four Tops ("Keeper of the Castle," No. 10; "Ain't No Woman," No. 4), the Righteous Brothers ("Give It to the People," No. 20), Starship ("We Built This City," No. 1), and Tavares ("It Only Takes a Minute," No. 10).

As a producer Lambert has generated additional hits (Glen Campbell's "Rhinestone Cowboy," No. 1; Natalie Cole's "Pink Cadillac," No. 5; Kenny Loggins' "Nobody's Fool," No. 8; Player's "Baby Come Back," No. 1; the Righteous Brothers' "Rock and Roll Heaven," No. 3), and still more as a songwriter (Freddie and the Dreamers' "Do the Freddie"; Coven's "One Tin Soldier"; Hamilton, Joe Frank, and Reynolds' "Don't Pull Your Love"; the Grass Roots' "Two Divided by Love").

Dennis Lambert was born in New York City in 1948 and raised to be a child performer. His mother "was trying to get my brother or me to do something with what she perceived as our talents," says Lambert. "She had been a child actress and felt somewhat denied because her parents hadn't let her travel."

By the age of 8 Lambert was taking lessons in singing, elocution, and dance; and he met with an accompanist twice a week in an effort to build a variety act. For a time he performed on a syndicated TV show for kids, and when that ended he was told that it was time to take his act to nightclubs and hotels.

By age 12 Lambert had a recording contract, and for the next three years he recorded singles with various producers; though he didn't have a hit, he became fascinated with the recording process. By 15 Lambert realized that as an artist he would only be involved with making records a few weeks out of every six months. The studio and the people felt special to him and writing was a way to be involved with record making on a day-to-day basis.

Turned on by the "classic pop songwriting combined with youthful energy" of the Atlantic and Motown soul of the early '60s, Lambert began writing songs and producing demos on his own. His first production that sold was "The Girls with the Big Black Boots" for a group called the Paramounts in 1964. Quincy Jones (see entry), who was A&R chief at Mercury, bought the master, listened to more of the young writer/producer's work, and then hired Lambert to a staff A&R position. Lambert stayed with Mercury through mid-1966, assisting on an R&B hit, "I Dig You Baby," for Jerry Butler, and writing "Do the Freddie."

Lambert went to work for DCP, a record company owned by arranger/producer Don Costa (see entry) and songwriter Teddy Randazzo ("Going out of My Head," "Hurt So Bad"). This arrangement was short-lived as Lambert was drafted into the army in late 1966, and served until late 1968. After the army, Lambert rejoined Costa (who had moved to California), and brought with him a young Englishman named Brian Potter, whom he had met in England in 1965. Lambert and Potter began writing and producing together in 1969, and continued to do so through 1980 as one of the most successful teams of the '70s.

Also in 1969, the pair joined a new label, Talent Associates, where they signed Seals and Crofts and wrote "One Tin Soldier"—the lead track for the smash film *Billy Jack*. In 1971 they moved to ABC/Dunhill and wrote "Don't Pull Your Love" and "Two Divided by Love," and wrote and produced a series of hits for the Four Tops culminating in the excellent "Ain't No Woman." Invigorated by his writing and production success, Lambert made one last stab at a singing career, releasing a solo album (*Bags and Things*, produced by Steve Barri; see entry) in 1971. Though the album didn't sell, it was well received and a song from it, "Dream On," became a hit for both the Righteous Brothers and the Oak Ridge Boys.

In 1973 Lambert and Potter formed their own label, Haven (distributed by Capitol), and had a succession of hits with Tavares, Glen Campbell, and the Righteous Brothers. In 1978 the label folded and the pair produced the Hall and Oates–like "Baby Come Back" for Player, and Santana's *Inner Secrets* album. In 1980 Lambert and Potter worked on a musical together, then split.

After some time off, Lambert returned to music in 1982. He worked with Steve Barri at Motown, writing and producing for the Temptations, Dennis Edwards, and the Commodores (the elegiac "Nightshift"), among others. Lambert peaked again in the mid-'80s, executive-producing Starship's *Knee Deep in the Hoopla* (No. 7) with the No. 1 singles "Sara" and "We Built This City," and producing Natalie Cole's sly cover of Bruce Springsteen's "Pink Cadillac."

In the '90s Lambert has had continued success with the R&B quintet Riff ("My Heart Is Failing Me"), saxophonist Dave Koz's gold *Lucky Man* album, as well as songs written or produced for films like *The Santa Claus, The Karate Kid III, The Nutty Professor*, and many others.

Lambert is currently running his record label, Babylon, with releases from DJ Spanxx in 1997 and Dennis Edwards in 1998.

Throughout his career Lambert has brought his professionalism and deep melodies to every manner of contemporary music. "I have tried to keep myself interested by not locking into any one genre. You pay a price for that, though. Since I've never identified with one genre, I'm probably not first in anyone's mind for any given genre," he says. However, with 11 nominations and a Grammy ("Nightshift" won R&B Song of the Year), American Music Awards ("Rhinestone Cowboy"), and a boatload of BMI Songwriting awards, Dennis Lambert's talent transcends genre and stands the test of time.
—ERIC OLSEN

Beckett: *Beckett,* Curb, 1991.

Benson, George: *Twice the Love,* Warner Bros., 1988.

Campbell, Glen: "Rhinestone Cowboy," Capitol, 1975 • *Rhinestone Cowboy,* Capitol, 1975 • *Bloodline,* Capitol, 1976 • "Country Boy (You Got Your Feet in L.A.)," Capitol, 1976 • "Don't Pull Your Love—Then You Can Tell Me Goodbye (Medley)," Capitol, 1976 • *The Very Best Of,* Capitol, 1987 • *Essential,* Vol. 3, Capitol, 1995 • *Gentle on My Mind: The Collection, 1962–1989,* Razor & Tie, 1997.

Cole, Natalie: *Everlasting,* Manhattan/Elektra, 1987, 1991 • "I Live for Your Love," EMI/Manhattan, 1987 • "Pink Cadillac," EMI/Manhattan, 1988 • *Good to Be Back,* EMI, 1989.

Coming of Age: "Baby Be Still," Zoo, 1994.

Commodores, The: "Animal Instinct," Motown, 1985 • "Janet," Motown, 1985 • "Nightshift," Motown, 1985 • *Nightshift,* Motown, 1985 • "Goin' to the Bank," Polydor, 1986 • *United,* Polydor, 1986 • "Take It from Me," Polydor, 1987 • *The Ultimate Collection,* Motown, 1997.

Cordero, Louie: *Louie Cordero,* Trauma, 1996.

Cross, Christopher: *Window,* Priority, 1995.

DJ Spanxx: *Let's Go Party,* Babylon, 1997.

Edwards, Dennis: w/ Siedah Garrett, "Don't Look Any Further," Gordy, 1984 • *Don't Look Any Further,* Gordy, 1984 • "Amanda," Gordy, 1985 • "Coolin' Out," Gordy, 1985.

Five Star: "Whenever You're Ready," RCA, 1987.

Four Tops: "Ain't No Woman (Like the One I've Got)," Dunhill, 1973 • *Meeting of the Minds,* Dunhill, 1974 • *Shaft in Africa* soundtrack, Probe, 1974 • "Keeper of the Castle," Dunhill, 1972 • "Are You Man Enough?," Dunhill, 1973 • "Sweet Understanding Love," Dunhill, 1973 • "One Chain Don't Make No Prison," Dunhill, 1974 • *Greatest Hits (1972–1976),* MCA, 1982, 1987 • *Ain't No Woman (Like the One I Got),* MCA Special Products, 1987, 1994 • *Keepers of the Castle: Their Best, 1972–1978,* MCA, 1997.

Gooding, Cuba: *First Album,* Motown, 1978.

Grass Roots: *The Grass Roots,* Haven/Capitol, 1975 • *Anthology, 1965–1975,* MCA, 1991.

Hayward, Justin: *The View from the Hill,* CMC International, 1996.

Koz, Dave: *Lucky Man* (4 tracks), Capitol, 1993.

Little River Band: *World Wide Love,* Curb, 1991 • *Reminiscing,* CEMA, 1992.

Loggins, Kenny: *Back to Avalon,* Columbia, 1988 • "Nobody's Fool," Columbia, 1988.

Marley, Ziggy, and the Melody Makers: *The Time Has Come: The Best Of,* EMI America, 1988.

McCormick, Gayle: *Gayle McCormick,* Dunhill, 1971 • "It's a Cryin' Shame," Dunhill, 1971.

Medley, Bill: *Best Of,* Curb, 1990.

Moody Blues: "This Is the Moment," Polydor, 1995.

Morgan, Meli'sa: "Deeper Love," Capitol, 1987.

O'Jays, The: *Serious,* EMI America, 1989.

Original Caste: "One Tin Soldier," TA, 1969.

Player: "Baby Come Back," RSO, 1978 • *Danger Zone,* RSO, 1978 • *Player,* RSO, 1978 • "Prisoner of Your Love," RSO, 1978 • "This Time I'm in It for Love," RSO, 1978 • *Spies of Life,* RCA, 1981.

Redding, Gene: *Blood Brother,* Haven, 1974.

Riff: "Everytime My Heart Beats," SBK, 1991 • "If You're Serious," SBK, 1991 • "My Heart Is Failing Me," SBK, 1991 • *Riff,* SBK, 1991.

Righteous Brothers: "Dream On," Haven, 1974 • "Give It to the People," Haven, 1974 • *Give It to the People,* Capitol, 1974 • "Rock and Roll Heaven," Haven, 1974 • *The Sons of Mrs. Righteous,* Capitol, 1975 • *Anthology,* Rhino, 1989.

Robinson, Smokey: "Everything You Touch," Motown, 1990.

Rock Rose: *Rock Rose,* CBS, 1979.

Sands, Evie: *Estate of Mind,* Haven, 1974.

Santana: *Inner Secrets,* Columbia, 1978 • "One Chain Don't Make No Prison," Columbia, 1979 • "Stormy," Columbia, 1979.

Smith: *A Group Called Smith,* Dunhill, 1969.

Springfield, Dusty: *Cameo,* Philips/ABC, 1973 • *Anthology,* PolyGram, 1997.

Starship: *Knee Deep in the Hoopla,* Grunt, 1985 • "We Built This City," Grunt, 1985 • "Sara," Grunt, 1986 • *Starship's Greatest Hits: Ten Years of Change,* RCA, 1991.

Surface: *The Best of Surface: A Nice Time for Loving,* Columbia, 1991.

Tavares: *Check It Out,* Capitol, 1974 • "She's Gone," Capitol, 1974 • *Hard Core Poetry,* Capitol, 1975 • *In the City,* Capitol, 1975 • "It Only Takes a Minute," Capitol, 1975 • "Remember What I Told You to Forget/My Ship," Capitol, 1975 • *It Only Takes a Minute,* Capitol, 1997.

Temptations, The: "Love on My Mind Tonight," Motown, 1983 • *Surface Thrills,* Gordy, 1983 • *One By One: The Best of Their Solo Years,* Motown, 1996.

Warwick, Dionne: *Greatest Hits, 1979–1990,* Arista, 1989.

COLLECTIONS

Sing soundtrack, CBS, 1989.

Jon Landau

As critic, producer (Bruce Springsteen, the MC5, Jackson Browne), and manager, Jon Landau has been one of the most influential men in rock 'n' roll for over 30 years. As a brilliant young critic at *Crawdaddy* and *Rolling Stone* in the late '60s, Landau championed the Byrds, Rolling Stones, Otis Redding, Wilson Pickett, Sam and Dave, and Aretha Franklin and had the audacity to pan Jimi Hendrix, the Grateful Dead, and Cream. He soon became the most influential critic in the country. Landau parlayed that influence into a brief production career, then "discovered" Springsteen in the mid-'70s with the immortal line, "I have seen the future of rock and roll and his name is Bruce Springsteen."

Forsaking all others, Landau has managed and co-produced (on and off) Springsteen since the monumental *Born to Run* album, guiding all aspects of his career with very few missteps. In the mid-'90s Landau and partner Barbara Carr took Natalie Merchant and Shania Twain under their managerial wings, apparently to great effect.

Jon Landau was born in 1946 and grew up in the Boston suburb of Lexington. A music fanatic from an early age, Landau got his first guitar at 7 and found himself addicted to the rock 'n' roll of Chuck Berry and Little Richard by the time he was 10. He played in a number of folk and rock bands throughout high school and as a history major at Brandeis University. When his friend Don Law Jr. (see Don Law Sr. entry) arranged an audition for Landau's band, Jellyroll, with Columbia Records, Landau decided not to go through with it and dedicated himself to writing.

As Landau's writing matured, he became more interested in the business and technical sides of record making. Through his writing he met and became friends with actual record makers, including Capricorn Records' Phil Walden, Atlantic's Jerry Wexler (see entry), and Elektra's Jac Holzman.

It was Holzman and publicist Danny Fields who introduced Landau to the MC5, the anarchistic proto-punk-metal band from Detroit whose credo was "rock and roll, dope, and fucking in the streets." After the band was dropped by Elektra for political reasons (see Bruce Botnick entry), Landau began to get phone calls from the band's friends about finding them another record deal. Landau called Wexler, who told him he would sign the band to Atlantic if Landau would produce them.

"MC5's *Back in the USA* was the first album I produced," recalls Landau. "That was trial by fire. They lived in a commune by Ann Arbor and I went and lived with them. They were a terrific band and we spent four months making that album. It didn't do particularly well at the time [1970], but in the late '70s, at the beginning of punk, the album got slightly rediscovered and had some influence."

Landau helped hook up Boston's J. Geils Band with Atlantic, then produced two albums for James Taylor's brother—singer/songwriter Livingston—for Capricorn.

In 1973, having seen Bruce Springsteen perform, Landau wrote an essay for Boston's *Real Paper* that declared Springsteen to be rock's future. Not generally prone to critical hyperbole, Landau's declaration improved Springsteen's stock considerably. Springsteen was so moved that he called Landau, and they spoke for two hours. Among other things, they discussed the role of the producer in the recording process, according to Fred Goodman's book *The Mansion on the Hill,* of which Landau is a subject.

For his third album, Springsteen wanted to open up his sound and make a Phil Spector–type (see entry) record. The song "Born to Run" had been recorded by Springsteen and then-manager Mike Appel, but the rest of the album was proving problematic. Springsteen stayed in touch with Landau, seeking his input about songs and recording. Landau recommended New York's Record Plant (and engineer Jimmy Iovine; see entry) over the cheaper studios "Born to Run" was recorded at. Finally, Landau explains, he "kind of volunteered" to become a co-producer, and Springsteen "kind of asked." the result was *Born to Run* (No. 3), produced by Landau, Springsteen, and Appel.

Born to Run was the landmark where Springsteen's art matched the hype: a panoramic view of summer across the New York–New Jersey metro area, *Run* captures the raging energy at the nexus between adolescence and adulthood, the poignancy of dreams, and the magic of place.

Jackson Browne wanted to make a move similar to Springsteen's: from singer/songwriter to rock 'n' roller, and brought Landau in to produce *The Pretender,* Landau's second brilliant success in a row, with a clutch of classic songs including the title track, "The Fuse" and "Here Come Those Tears Again."

While litigation with Appel stalled Springsteen's career, Landau acted as unofficial adviser. When the suit was settled in 1977, Springsteen and Landau went to work on the next album, *Darkness on the Edge of Town* (No. 5). *Darkness* was Springsteen's adult/autumnal answer to the adolescent/summery *Born to Run.* The most telling moment is a line from "The Promised Land": "Mister, I ain't a boy, no, I'm a man / And I believe in the promised land."

While accepting the responsibility and limitations of adulthood, Springsteen clings to the notion of a land where, through steadfast faith, dreams can come true—not *will* come true, but can. The Promised Land—America at its best—consists of a well-lit field, some rules, and some officials to supervise those rules to make sure that an honest struggle can be made by all. While diminished from the open-ended dreams of *Born to Run,* the narrower vision of *Darkness* is compelling for its stubborn idealism in the face of realism. Landau's contributions were probably greatest on *Darkness,* where Springsteen defined himself as an adult artist after the hype and turmoil of *Born to Run.* Springsteen probably never needed him as much again.

Landau became Springsteen's manager as well as co-producer, and worked closely with Springsteen, Steve Van Zandt (see entry), and Chuck Plotkin (see entry) on subsequent albums *The River* (No. 1), *Born In the U.S.A.* (No. 1), *Live* (No. 1), *Tunnel of Love* (No. 1), *Human Touch* (No. 2), and *Lucky Town* (No. 3). While they have all contributed ideas regarding songs and arrangements, Springsteen has always been in the lead, according to Landau. The key to the team's success, Landau says, has been "just tuning in to Bruce and finding the right way to be supportive at the right time. It's hard for me to characterize it. It's not like it's a team of producers—it's three different people who are all co-producing Bruce and who are all relating directly to him."

Springsteen's intelligence and the march of time eventually led to him accepting more production responsibility. "I think with every artist—at least the ones who are really bright and interesting and brilliant like Bruce—as they make more records, they gradually master the studio. It's not like he's sitting there waiting for others to provide all this expertise, it is a form of interaction and feedback and support. And yeah, if you can come up with a fresh idea he's very open-minded, but he's also has such deep focus he knows where he's going all the time."

Landau looks back and sees how his love of music has driven each of his professional stops. "That certainly drove me into record production because it gave me a creative platform to contribute from. The writing was one way of expressing myself about music, but it really had its limitations because you're writing about some other people's music. When you're producer you really have a chance to participate in the creative process itself and to leave some footprints of your own on those records." —ERIC OLSEN AND DAVID JOHN FARINELLA

Browne, Jackson: *The Pretender,* Asylum, 1976 • "Here Come Those Tears Again," Asylum, 1977 • *The Next Voice You Hear: The Best of Jackson Browne,* Elektra/Asylum, 1997.

MC5: *Back in the USA,* Atlantic, 1970.

Springsteen, Bruce: *Born to Run,* Columbia, 1975 • *Darkness on the Edge of Town,* Columbia, 1978 • "Prove It All Night," Columbia, 1978 • "Fade Away," Columbia, 1980 • "Hungry Heart," Columbia, 1980 • *The River,* Columbia, 1980 • "Born in the U.S.A.," Columbia, 1984 • *Born in the U.S.A.,* Columbia, 1984 • "Cover Me," Columbia, 1984 • "Dancing in the Dark," Columbia, 1984 • "Pink Cadillac," Columbia, 1984 • "Glory Days," Columbia, 1985 • "I'm Goin' Down," Columbia, 1985 • "I'm on Fire," Columbia, 1985 • "My Hometown," Columbia, 1985 • w/ the E Street Band, *Live, 1975–1985,* Columbia, 1986 • "Merry Christmas Baby," Columbia, 1986 • w/ the E Street Band, "War," Columbia, 1986 • "Brilliant Disguise," Columbia, 1987 • "Tunnel of Love," Columbia, 1987 • *Tunnel of Love,* Columbia, 1987 • *Chimes of Freedom* (EP), Columbia, 1988 • "I Ain't Got No Home," Columbia, 1988 (*Folkways: A Tribute to Woody Guthrie and Leadbelly*) • "One Step Up," Columbia, 1988 • "Vigilante Man," Columbia, 1988 (*Folkways: A Tribute to Woody Guthrie and Leadbelly*) • "Viva Las Vegas," NME, 1990 (*The Last Temptation of Elvis*) • "57 Channels (and Nothin' On)," Columbia, 1992 • "Human Touch/Better Days," Columbia, 1992 • *Human Touch,* Columbia, 1992 • *Lucky Town,* Columbia, 1992 • *Greatest Hits,* Columbia, 1995 • "Secret Garden," Columbia, 1995 • *Plugged: In Concert,* Sony, 1997.

Taylor, Livingston: *Livingston Taylor,* Capricorn, 1970 • *Liv,* Capricorn, 1971 • *Echoes,* Capricorn, 1979.

Gary Langan

See ART OF NOISE

Robert John "Mutt" Lange

The reclusive and publicity-shy Mutt Lange is known for his arranging prowess and decided penchant for massive overdubbing. His doubled electric guitar sound (sometimes tripled, sometimes quadrupled) graces such prominent power-metal purveyors as Foreigner (*Foreigner 4,* No. 1), AC/DC (four albums including the 12-times-platinum *Back In Black*), and Def Leppard (also four albums, including *Hysteria,* No. 1, and *Pyromania,* No. 2).

With AC/DC, Lange helped to define not just a sound for '80s metal but a persona as well: the metal band as bad boys, teen ruffians with preadolescent humor (e.g., "Big Balls" and "The Jack") and a fuck-the-neighbors predilection for eardrum-bleeding volume levels. The songs "Back in Black," "You Shook Me All Night Long," and "Highway to Hell" are carefully crafted, near encyclopedic compendia of electric blues licks "borrowed" from a diverse collection of American bluesmen, yet they are played with such look-at-me bravado even the most conservative copyright counselor would probably look the other way. Although *Back in Black* is generally considered to be the band's best, the entire AC/DC-Lange discography is dominated by the one indispensable attribute of heavy metal that it is impossible to fake: the fire of raging hormonal adolescence. The recordings are not particularly clean (clean recordings are not necessarily incompatible with distorted guitars, as has been shown by Ted Templeman and Chris Thomas; see entries)—in fact, they are often disturbingly low-fi—but there is no question about the high energy they convey, which Lange cleverly captured.

Lange joined forces with the Cars during a critical period. Six years earlier the group had been in the forefront of the new wave movement, but sales were sagging. The Cars were in the midst of an identity crisis: the eighth-note bass lines and quirky synths that had seemed so alternative when the group first appeared were so heavily copied by 1984 that it rendered them ordinary. With Lange, the group reinvented itself as mainstream pop artists, scoring an astonishing five hit singles and U.S. sales of more than 3 million for *Heartbeat City* (No. 3). The heavily produced recording featured digitally sampled voices (a relatively new innovation and sound at the time) and multilayered digital synthesizers and samples, all varnished with a high-gloss (though not particularly hi-fi) sheen. Longtime fans of the Boston band lamented the lack of energy on *Heartbeat City*, but it is not clear with whom the fault lies. Lange had never been accused of sapping energy from AC/DC.

Between *Back in Black* and *Heartbeat City*, Lange recorded Def Leppard's *Pyromania*, establishing that band as one of the most popular metal groups of the '80s—with sales of 10 million. The follow-up took six years to make and sold 14 million. *Hysteria*, a densely layered magnum opus, had been painstakingly demoed by Lange part for part on a Portastudio, with Lange playing all the instruments and singing all the parts himself. "It was a great-sounding demo," recalls engineer David Thoener, one of several to work on the album, including Nigel Green and Neil Dorfsman. "It had all the guitar layering, the 30 voices in harmony and everything. Mutt wasn't there for all the recording because of prior commitments, and the plain fact that the record took six years. But we spoke on the phone while I was doing the sessions, and he told me, 'Just stay faithful to the demo. Just re-record everything professionally and you'll be okay.' " And okay it was. Although some critics have slagged Def Leppard's latter efforts as bubblegum metal (a term this reviewer finds contradictory), the band's records are marked by carefully orchestrated arrangements that convey both power and melodicism.

Lange also worked with a Nobel Peace Prize nominee. The Boomtown Rats brought Lange together with Bob Geldof, a neo-punk Irish peacenik whose band mixed traditional Irish themes with a Sex Pistols sensibility. The three albums they made together were all large successes in the U.K., but the group remained relatively unknown in the U.S. until Geldof spearheaded the famous (and much imitated) Live Aid concerts. The biggest American success was the frenetically tongue-in-cheek "I Don't Like Mondays," based on the true story of a San Diego teenager who explained a murderous rampage by simply reciting the phrase that was to become the title of the song. Geldof managed to get the song to market before the girl's trial, prompting her parents to file a lawsuit claiming adverse pretrial publicity.

After a few years out of the limelight, Lange reemerged in Nashville, producing country-pop singer Shania Twain (his wife). In 1997 Lange produced one of Bryan Adams' most recent comeback albums, the somewhat obscure *18 Till I Die*.

Thoener adds, "Mutt is a brilliant, brilliant man. Of all the producers I've worked with, he's the one I admire the most. He's a really terrific person. His philosophy is to be very low-key about the music business, not to do interviews. . . . He told me, 'Don't let anyone know what you think. If you don't do interviews, there's kind of a mystery about you. No one really knows what you think or why you think it.' " —DANIEL J. LEVITIN

AC/DC: *Highway to Hell,* Atlantic, 1979 • *Back in Black,* Atlantic, 1980 • "You Shook Me All Night Long," Atlantic, 1980 • "Back in Black," Atlantic, 1981 • *For Those About to Rock We Salute You,* Atlantic, 1981 • *Who Made Who,* Atlantic, 1986 • *Bonfire,* Elektra, 1997.

Adams, Bryan: "(Everything I Do) I Do It for You," A&M, 1991 • "Can't Stop This Thing We Started," A&M, 1991 • "There Will Never Be Another Tonight," A&M, 1991 • *Waking Up the Neighbours,* A&M, 1991 • "Do I Have to Say the Words?," A&M, 1992 • "Thought I'd Died and Gone to Heaven," A&M, 1992 • "Please Forgive Me," A&M, 1993 • *So Far, So Good,* A&M, 1993 • "Have You Really Ever Loved a Woman?," A&M, 1995 • *18 Till I Die,* A&M, 1996 • "Let's Make a Night to Remember," A&M, 1996 • "The Only Thing That Looks Good on Me Is You," A&M, 1996 • "I'll Always Be Right There," A&M, 1997.

Backstreet Boys: *The Backstreet Boys,* Jive/Zomba, 1997.

Bolton, Michael: "Said I Loved You . . . but I Lied," Columbia, 1993 • *The One Thing,* Columbia, 1993 • "Can I Touch You . . . There?," Columbia, 1995.

Boomtown Rats: *The Boomtown Rats,* Ensign, 1977 • *Tonic for the Troops,* Ensign, 1978 • "Keep It Up," Epic, 1979, 1981 (*Exposed*) • *The Fine Art of Surfacing,* Ensign, 1979 • "Looking After No. 1," Alex, 1977, 1991 [*Burning Ambitions (A History of Punk)*].

Broken Home: *Broken Home,* Sire, 1980.

Cars, The: "Drive," Elektra, 1984 • *Heartbeat City,* Elektra, 1984 • "Hello Again," Elektra, 1984 • "Magic," Elektra, 1984 • "Why Can't I Have You?," Elektra, 1984 • "You Might Think," Elektra, 1984 • *Greatest Hits,* Elektra, 1985 • *Just What I Needed: The Cars Anthology,* Rhino, 1995.

City Boy: *City Boy,* Vertigo/Mercury, 1976 • *Young Men Gone West,* Vertigo/Mercury, 1977 • *Book Early,* Vertigo/Mercury, 1978 • *Dinner at the Ritz,* Vertigo/Mercury, 1978 • *The Day the Earth Caught Fire,* Vertigo, 1979.

Clover: *Clover,* Mercury, 1977 • *Love on the Wire,* Vertigo, 1977.

Coyne, Kevin: *In Living Black and White,* Virgin, 1976.

Deaf School: *English Boys/Working Girls,* Warner Bros., 1970.

Def Leppard: *High 'n' Dry,* Vertigo/Mercury, 1981 • *Pyromania,* Vertigo/Mercury, 1982 • "Foolin'," Mercury, 1983 • "Photograph," Mercury, 1983 • "Rock of Ages," Mercury, 1983 • "Bringin' on the Heartbreak," Mercury, 1984 • "Animal," Mercury, 1987 • "Women," Mercury, 1987 • "Armageddon It," Mercury, 1988 • "Hysteria," Mercury, 1988 • *Hysteria,* Mercury, 1988 • "Love Bites," Mercury, 1988 • "Pour Some Sugar on Me," Mercury,

1988 • "Rocket," Mercury, 1988 • *Adrenalize*, Mercury, 1992.

Foreigner: *Foreigner 4*, Atlantic, 1981 • "Urgent," Atlantic, 1981 • "Waiting for a Girl Like You," Atlantic, 1981 • *Records*, Atlantic, 1982 • *The Very Best . . . and Beyond*, Atlantic, 1992.

Mallard: *In a Different Climate*, Virgin, 1977.

Michael Stanley Band: *Cabin Fever*, Arista, 1978 • *Misery Loves Company: More of the Best, 1975–1983*, Razor & Tie, 1997.

Motors, The: *Motors*, Virgin, 1977.

Ocean, Billy: "Loverboy," Jive/Arista, 1984 • "Get Outta My Dreams, Get Into My Car," Jive, 1988 • *Tear Down These Walls*, Jive, 1988 • *Greatest Hits*, Jive, 1989 • "License to Chill," Jive, 1989 • "I Sleep Much Better (in Someone Else's Bed)," Jive, 1990.

Outlaws: *Playing to Win*, Arista, 1978 • *Greatest Hits*, Arista, 1982 • *Best of the Outlaws: Green Grass and High Tides*, Arista, 1996.

Parker, Graham: *Passion Is No Ordinary Word: The Graham Parker Anthology*, Rhino, 1993.

Parker, Graham, and the Rumour: *Heat Treatment*, Mercury, 1976 • *The (Black) Pink Parker* (EP, 2 tracks), Mercury, 1977 • *The Parkerilla*, Mercury, 1978.

Records, The: *Shades in Bed*, Virgin, 1979 • *The Records* (3 tracks), Virgin, 1979 • *Smashes, Crashes and Near Misses*, Caroline, 1988, 1995.

Romeo's Daughter: "Don't Break My Heart," Jive, 1988 • *Romeo's Daughter*, Jive, 1988.

Rumour, The: *Max*, Vertigo/Mercury, 1977.

Savoy Brown: *Savage Return*, London, 1978 • *The Savoy Brown Collection*, Chronicles, 1993.

Supercharge: *Horizontal Refreshment*, Virgin, 1976 • *Body Rhythm*, Virgin, 1979.

Turner, Tina: *What's Love Got to Do with It?* soundtrack, Capitol, 1993 • "Why Must We Wait Until Tonight?," Virgin, 1993.

Twain, Shania: "(If You're Not in It for Love) I'm Outta Here," Mercury Nashville, 1995 • "Any Man of Mine," Mercury Nashville, 1995 • "The Woman in Me (Needs the Man in You)," Mercury, 1995 • *The Woman in Me*, Mercury, 1995 • "Whose Bed Have Your Boots Been Under?," Mercury, 1995 • "You Win My Love," Mercury Nashville, 1995 • "God Bless the Child," Mercury, 1996 • "Home Ain't Where the Heart Is (Anymore)," Mercury, 1996 • "No One Needs to Know," Mercury Nashville, 1996 • "Come On Over," Mercury, 1997 • *Come On Over*, Mercury, 1997 • "Don't Be Stupid, You Know I Love You," Mercury, 1997 • w/ Bryan White, "From This Moment On," Mercury, 1997 • "Honey I'm Home," Mercury, 1997 • "Love Gets Me Every Time," Mercury, 1997 • "Man! I Feel Like a Woman," Mercury, 1997 • "You're Still the One," Mercury Nashville, 1998.

Tycoon: *Tycoon*, Arista, 1978.

XTC: *White Music*, Virgin, 1978 • *Beeswax: Some B Sides, 1977–1982*, Virgin, 1982 • *Waxworks: Some Singles, 1977–1982*, DGC, 1984 • *Compact XTC: The Singles, 1978–1985*, Virgin, 1985.

Clive Langer and Alan Winstanley

The production team of Clive Langer and Alan Winstanley is among the most important and successful of British modern rock. Their hits span the '80s and '90s and virtually define the parameters of the genre. Best known for their career-long association with the London pop-ska band Madness (*One Step Beyond*, No. 2 U.K.; *Absolutely*, No. 2 U.K.; "House of Fun," No. 1 U.K.), the pair have also produced David Bowie ("Absolute Beginners," No. 2 U.K.; see entry), Bowie with Mick Jagger ("Dancing in the Streets," No. 1 U.K.), Bush (the five-times-platinum *Sixteen Stone*), Lloyd Cole (*Easy Pieces*, No. 5 U.K.), Elvis Costello (*Punch the Clock*, No. 3 U.K.; *Goodbye Cruel World*, No. 10 U.K.; see entry), Dexy's Midnight Runners (*Too-Rye-Ay*, No. 2 U.K.; "Come On Eileen," No. 1), Morrissey (*Kill Uncle*, No. 8 U.K.), They Might Be Giants ("Birdhouse in Your Soul," No. 6 U.K.), and many others.

Alan Winstanley was a London lad who, like so many others, was inspired by the Beatles to pick up a guitar. By 16 he was playing in bands, even recording with one for a French label. "When I was about 18 I realized that I wasn't going to be a great guitarist. I figured out that maybe production was a good thing to get into. Records by the Beatles, Motown, and Phil Spector [see entry] always sounded good to me and I put a lot of that down to production, as well as the songwriting.

"In 1970 I got a job at a tiny 4-track demo studio here in Fulham [London], TW Music. By the time I left in 1978 it was a 24-track studio. We did quite a lot of punk: Stranglers, Buzzcocks, Generation X. So that was my engineering background, though I would never class myself as a proper engineer," he says modestly. "I just sort of twiddled the knobs until it sounded good.

"Clive was in a band called Deaf School," Winstanley continues. "They came in and recorded their demos at TW, and that's how I met him. Then in 1978, I decided it was time to become a freelance producer, so I proclaimed to the world 'I am now a producer.' Luckily, I was asked to produce the fourth Stranglers [studio] album, *The Raven* (No. 4 U.K.), in the summer of 1979. I had already engineered the first three at TW studios. As I was mixing that record, I got a call from Clive saying that there was a band called Madness and would I help him produce their first album?"

North Londoner Clive Langer had an older brother who drew him into rock 'n' roll at a young age. The first single Langer bought was by the Shadows, and the first album he got was Bob Dylan's debut. At 9 he began taking flamenco guitar lessons from a friend's mother. By 11 he was in a band, the Blues. Langer remembers, "We played for the kids at the local Saturday morning pictures—it was pretty exciting. We wore blue polo necks and blue jeans. Very cool," he chuckles. "Then I went to secondary school, and I was fortunate that there were quite a few happening kids in that part of London. I was in a band there with Julien Temple [future writer and film director, with whom Langer later worked on the *Absolute Beginners* film soundtrack]. I went through what all kids went through in the late '60s: Hendrix, Cream, Doors, Crosby, Stills and Nash. Then I was obsessed by the whole Canterbury sound: Robert Wyatt, Caravan, Soft Machine," he says.

"I went to art college at Canterbury and one of tutors was Ian Dury. So I went to see Kilburn and the Highroads, Dury's first (and best) band. The next year I went to Liverpool, mainly because I was obsessed with John Lennon. The first day there I met a singer in this band called 'Deaf School,' " which he soon joined as guitarist and principal songwriter. "We rehearsed at an art college that had previously been a school for the deaf," he says—hence the band's name.

Langer also joined Brian Eno's (see entry) Portsmouth Symphonia. "It was a very arty thing. Everyone had to play an instrument that they didn't know, but you had to try. You couldn't just pick up an instrument and say 'I'm gonna join.' You had to have had a certain amount of experience at being bad at your instrument. I failed at the flute in grade 4 in school, so I played that," he adds cheerfully.

"On the first Deaf School I was listed as 'Cliff Hanger,' but I thought it was a bit silly so I changed it to 'Cliff Langer.' I was 'Cliff' for a long time to all the members of the band. The good thing was that I had to write. It taught me a lot about arrangements and listening to all different kinds of music. If the bridge of a song was from Kurt Weill, going into something like the Sex Pistols, we didn't mind. Whereas the music press seemed to mind a lot," he adds. "But we had a great time. We did three albums and the third album was produced by Mutt Lange [see entry]. I would sit around in the con-

trol room and I learned a lot from him. Then I got fed up with Deaf School—the whole punk thing was much more exciting—so we split up."

Langer then formed a group called Clive Langer and the Boxes, and recorded two albums in the late '70s. The Madness offer came in 1979. "I knew I wasn't up to it alone. Every time I had been at TW with Alan—as opposed to at TW with anyone else—the results were brilliant. So then my idea was to ask Alan to help out. I was comfortable working with him and he knew a lot more than I did about recording," he says.

Madness's cartoonish "nutty boy" image, cockney enunciation, and mutating neo-ska sound struck a deep chord in Britain, where they had 19 consecutive Top 20 hits between 1979 and 1985. Highlights include the manic ska propulsion of "One Step Beyond" (No. 7 U.K.), "Baggy Trousers" (No. 3 U.K.), and "Madness" (No. 16 U.K.); the carnivalesque "House of Fun" (No. 1 U.K.); and the double-time soca celebration "Wings of a Dove" (No. 2 U.K.). They also struck the Top 40 twice in the United States, with the irresistible nostalgia of "Our House" (No. 7), and the ska-orchestral hybrid "It Must Be Love."

When recorded in 1981, the strings on "It Must Be Love" (No. 4 U.K.) were a bold stroke. Recalls Langer, "We had the strings play pizzicato, 'plink, plink, plink,' which at that time required real musicians. It was quite an experiment and you took a lot of responsibility because you had to pay the bill. Now you can just use a sample." Winstanley adds, "A few years later Trevor Horn [see entry] told me that he nicked the pizzicato strings idea from us for the first ABC record—that was quite flattering really."

The duo's biggest international single thus far has been Dexy's Midnight Runners' "Come On Eileen": singer/songwriter Kevin "celtic soul brother" Rowland's tale of teen friendship turned to itchy lust. Langer says, "I didn't do much, I just sat there, but I think one of my contributions was to leave it alone. When something is really happening I don't mess with it, and that's a way of capturing it—though I didn't hear 'Eileen' as the hit. I liked the first single, 'Celtic Soul Brothers,' and it wasn't a hit. "I was really depressed, thinking, 'Oh God, how are we going to have a hit? This next single sounds like a nursery rhyme,' and of course that was its appeal. Alan was going, 'No, no, it's going to be a big hit,' and he was right."

Winstanley adds, "When I heard the demo, it didn't even have those lyrics. It was about James Brown, Van Morrison, and [Rowland]. But the melody got me. When I first heard it, I thought, 'This is going to be a hit record.' "

Unfortunately, Rowland couldn't stand the pressure of success. Langer says, "He was quite a self-destructive person; if he saw success he would want to go and mess with it. He didn't like the color of the cover of [the band's next album] *Don't Stand Me Down*. The label said it couldn't be changed—it would cost 10,000 pounds to change the cover of the album—and he went, 'Right, here's the check,' and he paid with a personal check to change the cover. It went from dark red P32 to P31. It was in him all along, fighting him all the time."

Not afraid of difficult personalities, Langer and Winstanley also worked with Elvis Costello for two albums—*Punch the Clock* and *Goodbye Cruel World*—in the mid-'80s. Though *Goodbye* is blessed with the charming "The Only Flame in Town," *Punch* is the better album. Consistently tuneful and smoothly soulful, *Punch* is Costello at his most relaxed and least fearful to please. "Everyday I Write the Book" boasts a beautifully turned melody, and a cheerful call-and-response chorus with backups Caron Wheeler (Soul II Soul) and Claudia Fontaine. Steve Nieve's keyboards tinkle along nicely, and as on the rest of the album, the TKO Horns provide spunky augmentation and counterpoint. The most powerful song on the album is the brooding, simmering "Shipbuilding" (co-written by Costello and Langer), featuring one of the last recorded performances from cool-jazz trumpeter Chet Baker.

Says Langer, "That was quite something. Chet Baker couldn't even get his head around the chord sequence—it wasn't jazz—it was a pop writer trying to write jazz. So Alan had to edit, like, five different solos with the whole band playing each time, the old traditional way. Chet was quite ill in lots of ways, but he was also quite amazing. He couldn't put that much into it, but what he had left, he put into it. Really amazing character."

Of the duo's work in the '90s, their productions of They Might Be Giants (the circuitous and beguiling "Birdhouse in Your Soul," the sublime remake of the Four Lads' "Istanbul") and Bush stand out. Rarely have differences in music making shone as starkly as between the first Bush album—Langer and Winstanley's *Sixteen Stone*—and Steve Albini's (see entry) production of the follow-up *Razorblade Suitcase*.

Stone takes a by-definition messy genre—grunge—and emphasizes the tunes within the roar, allowing power and melody to jointly reach out to the listener on songs like "Everything Zen," "Little Things," "Comedown," and "Machinehead." *Suitcase* is just a mess. "Bush's dream was to be a Nirvana/Pixies kind of band," says Langer. "We came along and we liked them and we did this album. It went massive and they went back to doing what they really wanted to do, but it was

like they were doing their demo-ish first album second, while we had done their commercial album. [Singer] Gavin Rossdale hadn't written [good] songs [for the second one], but no one was complaining because he had just sold 5 million records and they were all going 'Yes, yes, yes.'" —ERIC OLSEN AND DAWN DARLING

Langer and Winstanley

A House: "Everything I Am," Radioactive, 1995.

Adventures, The: *Trading Secrets with the Moon,* Elektra, 1989, 1990.

Aztec Camera: *Frestonia,* Reprise, 1995.

Black Velvet Band: *King of Myself* (6 tracks), Elektra, 1992.

Blur: "Chemical World" Food, 1993.

Bodysnatchers, The: "Easy Life," 2Tone/Chrysalis, 1981 (*Dance Craze* soundtrack).

Bowie, David: w/ Mick Jagger, "Dancing in the Streets," EMI America, 1985 • "Absolute Beginners," Virgin, 1986 • *Bowie: The Singles, 1969–1993,* Rykodisc, 1993.

Bright, Bette, and the Illuminations: *Rhythm Breaks the Ice,* Korova, 1981.

Bush: *Sixteen Stone,* Interscope, 1994 • "Bomb," Elektra, 1995 (*Tank Girl* soundtrack) • "Comedown," Interscope, 1995 • "Glycerine," Interscope, 1995 • "Little Things," Interscope, 1995 • "Machinehead," Interscope, 1995.

China Crisis: *Flaunt the Imperfection,* Virgin/WB, 1985 • *What Price Paradise,* Virgin/A&M, 1986 • *Collection,* Virgin, 1990.

Cole, Lloyd: w/ the Commotions, *Easy Pieces,* Geffen, 1985 • *Lost Weekend* (EP), Polydor, 1985 • *1984–1989,* Polydor, 1989.

Cope, Julian: *Floored Genius: The Best of Julian Cope and the Teardrop Explodes, 1979–1991,* Island, 1992.

Cornwell, Hugh: *Wolf* (2 tracks), Virgin, 1988.

Costello, Elvis: "The Only Flame in Town," Columbia, 1984 • *Best Of,* Columbia, 1985 • *Out of Our Idiot,* Demon, 1987.

Costello, Elvis, and the Attractions: "Everyday I Write the Book," Columbia, 1983 • *Punch the Clock,* Columbia, 1983 • *Goodbye Cruel World,* Columbia, 1984 • "I Wanna Be Loved," Columbia, 1984 • *Girls, Girls, Girls,* Columbia, 1989.

Darlahood: *Big Fine Thing,* Reprise, 1996 • "Grow Your Own," Reprise, 1996 • "Sister Dimentia," Reprise, 1997.

Days, Jeremy: *The Jeremy Days,* Polydor, 1990.

Dexy's Midnight Runners: "Jackie Wilson Said," Mercury, 1982 • "Let's Get This Straight from the Heart," Mercury, 1982 • "The Celtic Soul Brothers," Mercury, 1982, 1983 • *Too-Rye-Ay,* Mercury, 1982 • "Come On Eileen," Mercury, 1983 • *Don't Stand Me Down,* Mercury, 1985.

Drill Team: *Hope and Dream Explosion,* Reprise, 1997.

Fenster, Schnell: *The Sound of Trees,* Atlantic, 1990.

Finn, Tim: *Before and After,* Capitol, 1993 • "Hit the Ground Running," Capitol, 1993.

Haysi Fantayzee: "Shiny Shiny," EMI, 1983, 1993 (*Living in*

Oblivion: The 80s, Greatest Hits, Vol. 1).

Ho Hum: *Local,* Universal, 1996.

Hothouse Flowers: *People,* London, 1988 • *Home,* London, 1990.

Lovich, Lene: *Stateless . . . Plus,* Rhino, 1979, 1995.

Madness: "My Girl," Stiff, 1979 • *One Step Beyond,* Sire, 1979 • *Absolutely,* Sire, 1980 • "Baggy Trousers," Stiff, 1980 • "Embarrassment," Stiff, 1980 • *Work, Rest and Play* (EP), Stiff, 1980 • "Grey Day," Stiff, 1981 • "It Must Be Love," Virgin, 1981, 1989 • "Night Boat to Cairo," 2Tone/Chrysalis, 1981 (*Dance Craze* soundtrack) • "One Step Beyond," 2Tone/Chrysalis, 1981 (*Dance Craze* soundtrack) • "Razor Blade Alley," 2Tone/Chrysalis, 1981 (*Dance Craze* soundtrack) • "Return of the Los Palmas 7," Stiff, 1981 • *Seven,* Stiff, 1981 • "Shut Up," Stiff, 1981 • "Cardiac Arrest," Stiff, 1982 • *Complete Madness,* Virgin, 1982 • "Driving in My Car," A&M, 1982 (*Party Party* soundtrack) • "House of Fun," Stiff, 1982 • *Rise and Fall,* Stiff, 1982 • "Madness," 2Tone/Chrysalis, 1983 (*This Are Two Tone*) • *Madness,* Geffen, 1983 • "Our House," Geffen, 1983 • "The Sun and the Rain," Geffen, 1983 • "Tomorrow's (Just Another Day)," Stiff, 1983 • "Wings of a Dove," Stiff, 1983 • *Keep Moving,* Geffen, 1984 • "Michael Caine," Stiff, 1984 • "One Better Day," Stiff, 1984 • "Yesterday's Men," Virgin, 1984, 1988 • *Mad Not Mad,* Geffen, 1985 • "Uncle Sam," Virgin, 1985 • "Sweetest Girl," Virgin, 1986 • "Waiting for the Ghost Train," Virgin, 1986 • *Divine Madness,* Virgin, 1992 • *Total Madness: The Very Best Of,* Geffen, 1997.

Morrissey: "Ouija Board, Ouija Board," Sire/Reprise, 1989 • *Bona Drag* (5 tracks), Sire/Reprise, 1990 • "November Spawned a Monster," Sire/Reprise, 1990 • *Kill Uncle,* Sire/Reprise, 1991 • "Our Frank," Sire/Reprise, 1991 • "Sing Your Life," Sire/Reprise, 1991 • *World of Morrissey,* Sire, 1995.

Neville Brothers: *Uptown,* EMI America, 1987.

Nitecaps, The: *Go to the Line,* Sire, 1982.

Poi Dog Pondering: *Volo Volo* (6 tracks), Columbia, 1992.

Shift: *Get In,* Columbia, 1997 • "In Honor of Myself," Columbia, 1997 • "I Want to Be Rich," Columbia, 1998.

Style Council: "Have You Ever Had It Blue?," EMI America, 1986.

Symposium: *Symposium* (EP), Red Ant, 1998.

Teardrop Explodes: *Kilimanjaro* (3 tracks), Mercury, 1980 • *Piano* (2 tracks), Document, 1990.

They Might Be Giants: *Flood* (4 tracks), Elektra, 1990.

Wyatt, Robert: "Shipbuilding," Gramavision, 1981, 1986 • *Compilation,* Gramavision, 1991.

COLLECTIONS

Absolute Beginners soundtrack, EMI America, 1986.

Clive Langer

An Emotional Fish: *Junk Puppets,* Atlantic, 1993.

Langer, Clive: *I Want the Whole World,* Radar, 1978 • *Hope, Honour and Love,* Demon, 1988.

Madness: "The Prince," 2Tone, 1979.

Specials, The: "Concrete Jungle," 2Tone/Chrysalis, 1981 (*Dance Craze* soundtrack) • "Man At C & A," 2Tone/Chrysalis, 1981 (*Dance Craze* soundtrack) • "Nite Klub," 2Tone/Chrysalis, 1981 (*Dance Craze* soundtrack).

Teardrop Explodes: *Wilder,* Mercury, 1981.

Alan Winstanley

Burnel, J.J.: *Euroman Cometh,* United Artists, 1979.

Face Dance: *About Face,* Capitol, 1980.

Four Out of Five Doctors: *Four Out of Five Doctors,* Nemperor, 1980.

Langer, Clive, and the Boxes: *Splash,* F Beat, 1980.

Lovich, Lene: *Flex,* Stiff, 1979.

Original Mirrors: *Original Mirrors,* Mercury, 1980.

Rumour, The: *Purity of Essence,* Stiff, 1980.

Stranglers, The: "Don't Bring Harry," United Artists, 1979 • "Duchess," United Artists, 1979 • "Nuclear Device," United Artists, 1979 • *The Raven,* United Artists, 1979 • *IV,* A&M, 1980 • *Greatest Hits, 1977–1990,* Epic, 1990 • *About Time, When?,* 1995.

Sweet, Rachel: *Protect the Innocent,* Stiff, 1980 • *Fool Around: The Best Of,* Rhino, 1995.

Tenpole Tudor: *Eddie, Old Bob, Dick and Gary,* Stiff, 1981 • *Let the Four Winds Blow,* Stiff, 1981.

TV 21: *Thin Red Line,* Deram, 1981.

XTC: *Senses Working Overtime* (EP), Virgin, 1982 • *Dear God* (EP), Virgin, 1987.

Daniel Lanois

Music runs in his family, so it's no surprise native Québecois Daniel Lanois is a multi-instrumentalist. Born in Hull, Quebec, September 19, 1951, Lanois grew up with music all around. Not only did his father and grandfather play violin, his uncles sang.

"At that time, there was door-to-door canvassing, people looking for kids wanting to take up musical instruments," he recalls. "Conservatories would send out salespeople. They put me on slide guitar, which was quite common then," Lanois says. "Kids took that up, or accordion. And if you came from a family with more money, you took piano lessons."

At 15, Daniel Lanois began constructing a studio in

was directly through Brian Eno. I was working with him in Canada on the *On Land* record, and Eno got a call from Bono, wanting him to produce U2. Eno said, 'I don't want to produce right now, but there's this sort of whippersnapper here'—being myself—'who would love to do it.'" Eno and Lanois flew to London, and "Bono, a very compelling young man, essentially talked Brian into doing this and I did it with him." The record was 1984's *The Unforgettable Fire* (No. 12).

Lanois also wrote the score for Billy Bob Thornton's film *Sling Blade*. "I liked it because I was serving an existing piece of work," he says. "There it was, I had it on a screen; it was fun to be the last link in the chain. The whole thing was done in a month." He wrote the music in a former Mexican porno theater north of Los Angeles.

What he's best at is "creating an atmosphere, a vibe, that makes people feel like they should be doing something," he says. "I think it comes through commitment. I get people in a room and just by being so devoted and into what I do, it rubs off."

Lanois also produced the first album of new Dylan material in years, *Time out of Mind,* nabbing Dylan the Album of the Year Grammy for 1997. Lanois also produced Dylan's 1989 album *Oh Mercy.* For *Oh Mercy,* Dylan "showed up at the door and I had a whole setup ready to go: a chair for him, guitar sounds, an amazing vocal sound, and I'd made all the phone calls. All the musicians were ready to go. Why don't we say that preparation leads to good luck?"

On *Time,* "we surrounded ourselves with more people, more musicians, so it's a bigger sound and it's more rhythmic," Lanois says. "It's hard to describe it stylistically. There's one thing that has the feeling of an old dancehall in the late '50s, almost like a slow dance at the end of the prom." Lanois plays guitar on that track. Lanois thinks Dylan "was impressed with the level of commitment" Lanois expressed on *Oh Mercy.* "My wanting to work with him was obviously beyond fanship or adoration," he says. "It was obvious I had something to offer and I had done my work and I had something to give. You have to have something to give."

One album to which he gave more than he got was an embryonic work by Scott Walker (Noel Scott Engel), an Ohio native who became a star in England. Eno produced "several really great tracks" for Walker around 1985, the year after Walker released his last album. "I started a Scott Walker record, again with Brian Eno," Lanois recalls. "It was kind of my first lesson in learning how to blend with people and how to roll with the punches. It was all about psychology, not much about music. But I think Walker is great, and one day, those tracks might surface. "I get what I get, and from having

the family basement in Hamilton, Ontario, with his brother Bob. That little studio, Mastersound Recording, became really popular, Lanois says. "I took up the English language there and started recording local bands," says Lanois, a trace of French Canadian in his speech. "The word spread. We did hundreds of albums in that basement, including recordings with Rick James," a funkster-to-be from Buffalo who also was in a Toronto band with Neil Young called the Mynah Birds.

In 1979, his profile began to rise with the "Brian Eno connection," he says. Eno liked some tapes Lanois had worked on, called Lanois and traveled to Hamilton to collaborate on "some really beautiful music" by pianist/composer Harold Budd. Available in larger record stores, the Budd works can be found on the albums *On Land, Plateau of Mirror, The Pearl,* and *Apollo.*

"It's a body of work people don't hear because they're obscure records and people would rather talk about U2 and Peter Gabriel, whom I love," Lanois says. "But those other records never get a chance, and for me, they were the beginning of my experiments with sonics."

Word of mouth and a reputation for innovation get him work, Lanois suggests. "Peter Gabriel heard a Harold Budd record and wanted somebody to work on a soundtrack with him for a movie called *Birdy.* I was kind of the new kid on the block. The U2 connection made those records in the early '80s that were atmospheric, those tendencies stay with me. I still love some of those qualities, and though I'm constantly evolving, like anyone else involved with the arts, I'm not doing as many textures as I was five years ago. I only produce one or two records a year. I'm slow, I guess." And selective? "Let's use that word.

"I think great work is a combination of rough and ready captured performance—and then paying attention to details." —CARLO WOLFF

Blade, Brian: *Brian Blade Fellowship,* Blue Note, 1998.

Brook, Michael: w/ Brian Eno and Daniel Lanois, *Hybrid,* Editions E.G., 1990.

Coyote Shivers: *Coyote Shivers,* Mutiny, 1996.

Dylan, Bob: *Oh Mercy,* Columbia, 1989 • *Bootleg Series,* Columbia, 1991 • "Series of Dreams," Columbia, 1991 • *Greatest Hits,* Vol. 3, Columbia, 1995 • "Love Sick," Columbia, 1997 • *Time out of Mind,* Columbia, 1997.

Eno, Brian: *Apollo: Atmospheres and Soundtracks,* EG, 1983, 1986 • *Music for Film 3,* Opal/WB, 1988 • w/ Harold Budd, *The Pearl,* Editions E.G., 1984, 1990 • *Eno Box 1,* Virgin, 1994 • *See also* Brook, Michael.

Eno, Roger: *Voices,* EG, 1985.

Farafina: *Faso Denou,* Realworld/Caroline, 1993 • *See also* Hassell, Jon.

Gabriel, Peter: *Music from the Film Birdy,* Charisma, 1985 • "Big Time," Geffen, 1986 • "In Your Eyes," WTG, 1986 • "Sledgehammer," Geffen, 1986 • *So,* Geffen, 1986 • w/ Kate Bush, "Don't Give Up," Geffen, 1987 • *Shaking the Tree: 16 Golden Greats,* Geffen, 1990 • "Digging in the Dirt," Geffen, 1992 • "Kiss That Frog," Geffen, 1992 • "Steam," Geffen, 1992 • *Us,* Geffen, 1992 • "Blood of Eden," Virgin, 1993 • "Lovetown," Epic, 1993 (*Philadelphia* soundtrack).

Harris, Emmylou: *Wrecking Ball,* Elektra, 1995.

Hassell, Jon: *A.k.a. Darbari Java,* EG, 1983, 1990 • w/ Farafina, *Flash of the Spirit,* Intuition, 1993 • *Power Spot,* ECM, 1986, 1994.

Hothouse Flowers: *Home,* London, 1990.

Inqbator: *Hatched,* Pure, 1997.

Lanois, Daniel: "Sleeping in the Devil's Bed," Warner Bros., 1991 (*Until the End of the World* soundtrack) • *Acadie,* Warner Bros., 1993 • *For the Beauty of Wynona,* Warner Bros., 1993 • *Cool Water,* ITM, 1994 • *See also* Brook, Michael.

Luscious Jackson: *Fever In Fever Out,* Grand Royal, 1996 • "Naked Eye," Grand Royal, 1996.

Martha and the Muffins: *Far Away in Time,* Caroline, 1993.

Nelson, Willie: *Teatro,* Island, 1998.

Neville Brothers: "Sister Rosa," A&M, 1989 • *Yellow Moon,* A&M, 1989.

Oryema, Geoffrey: *Night to Night,* Caroline, 1997.

Parachute Club: *The Parachute Club,* Current, 1983.

Passengers: "Miss Sarajevo," Island, 1995.

Robertson, Robbie: *Robbie Robertson,* Geffen, 1987.

Sexsmith, Ron: *Ron Sexsmith* (1 track), Interscope, 1995.

Straw, Syd: *Surprise,* Virgin, 1989.

U2: "Pride (In the Name of Love)," Island, 1984 • "The Unforgettable Fire," Virgin/EMI, 1984, 1985 (*Now That's What I Call Music 5*) • *The Unforgettable Fire,* Island, 1984 • "Three Sunrises," Island, 1985 • *Wide Awake in America,* Island, 1985 • "I Still Haven't Found What I'm Looking For," Island, 1987 • "In God's Country," Island, 1987 • "Sweetest Thing," Island, 1987 • *The Joshua Tree,* Island, 1987 • "Where the Streets Have No Name," Island, 1987 • "With or Without You," Island, 1987 • *Achtung Baby,* Island, 1991 • "Mysterious Ways," Island, 1991 • "The Fly," Island, 1991 • "The Fly" (remix), Island, 1991 • "Until the End of the World," Warner Bros., 1991 (*Until the End of the World* soundtrack) • "Even Better Than the Real Thing," Island, 1992 • "One," Island, 1992 • "Who's Gonna Ride Your Wild Horses?," Island, 1992.

Weiland, Scott: *12 Bar Blues,* Atlantic, 1998.

COLLECTIONS

Angels in the Architecture, EG, 1987.

Sling Blade soundtrack, Island, 1996.

Songs of Jimmie Rodgers: A Tribute, Sony, 1997.

Bill Laswell

Master catalyst Bill Laswell has been pursuing the art of musical alchemy for nearly 20 years, melding disparate elements into a precious mix from his New York base. Although his reputation has tarnished a bit in recent years owing to some tin-eared excursions into ambient electronica, Laswell was one of the world's most fearless and fertile musical minds at his early '90s peak. He excelled in all manner of audio invention: from searching post-jazz hybrids to fierce fusions of rock and hip-hop; from priceless African field recordings to indescribable, out-of-this-world music. To Laswell, music really is a universal language, and he has no peer in bringing together great musicians from around the world for true cross-cultural communion. Voicing his credo, Laswell says, "Ultimately, musicians are not about instruments, and making records is not about equipment. It's about people. It's about ideas. It's about expression."

The Detroit native (born February 14, 1950) came up playing bass in funk bands and developing a great knowledge and love of all strains of black music. After moving to Manhattan in the '70s, he headed a loose collective of musicians and producers eventually known as Material. Diverse talents converged under the Material rubric, with African-American grooves the common currency. It seems incredible today, but an early Material record actually featured latter-day diva Whitney Houston intoning a soul ballad, with late free-jazz pioneer Archie Shepp blowing sax on the side. (A great rundown of this formative period is available on *Deconstruction: The Celluloid Years* on Restless.) Sundry Material outings and intriguing "new Africa" productions later, Laswell came to helm the 1982 sessions for Herbie Hancock's "Rock-It," producing one of the biggest instrumental hit singles ever.

In demand after that, Laswell began balancing big-name gigs alongside his more cutting-edge enthusiasms, with sessions for Mick Jagger's solo bow (*She's the Boss*, No. 13) coming on the heels of Afrika Bambaataa and John Lydon's underground club smash "World Destruction." And he also put his considerable bass-playing talents to use, including stints in the studio with Anton Fier's shifting art-pop ensemble the Golden Palominos and on the road with the heavy-metal jazz supergroup Last Exit (alongside guitarist Sonny Sharrock, drummer Ronald Shannon Jackson, and saxist Peter Brotzmann). In his quest for new sounds, Laswell helped provide comeback contexts for underappreciated artists like Sharrock, and he fielded dream teams for special projects. For the conceptual art-metal of Public Image Limited's *Album* (No. 14 U.K.), Laswell brought together former Cream stickman Ginger Baker, jazz drummer supreme Tony Williams, keyboardist/composer Ryuichi Sakamoto, Indian violin virtuoso L. Shankar, polyglot fretmeister Nicky Skopelitis, and lead guitar wizard Steve Vai. A glorious mix of talents, it entwined the intellectual and visceral in a way that has rarely been bettered.

Baker's 1986 album *Horses and Trees* was the start of something very special, with such players as Laswell, Skopelitis, Shankar, and P. Funk organ grinder Bernie Worrell concocting a sophisticated, spirit-infused brand of arcadian improv. The same players and raga-pastoral sensibility inflected much of Laswell's second solo set, *Hear No Evil* (although a hint of the Near Eastern desolation in Led Zeppelin's "Kashmir" appears on such heavy tracks as "Assassin"). Soon after came *Next to Nothing*, Skopelitis's solo debut and a fine slice of Ganges Delta blues in line with *Hear No Evil*. With *Seven Souls*, the classic Material album of 1989, Laswell was a pioneer in the spoken-word-with-music genre, laying dark recitations from William Burroughs atop the entrancing Indo-jazz of the period. (Long out of print, the album was reissued by Triloka in 1997 with four new remixes.)

Before the '80s were out, Laswell helmed Sakamoto's genre-bounding *Neo Geo* album, which accommodated everything from Debussyian solo piano and Asian folk songs to hyper Far East funk and lyrical ruminations from Iggy Pop. From there, Laswell indulged the fondness for biker metal he had shown on Motorhead's *Orgasmatron* with reductive, brute-force albums by Iggy Pop and the Ramones. But as the '90s dawned, his restless muse moved far afield. He began a series of African field recordings that are some of the finest of their kind, featuring Gnawan music of Marrakesh, Mandinka and Fulani music of Gambia, and the Master Musicians of Joujouka. It's all very potent stuff, superbly recorded in less-than-felicitous circumstances. But location is everything, Laswell says: "Some of these people have never been out of the area where they live. To put them on a plane to a place like New York, I'm positive that you wouldn't get the same music that they play at home."

The early '90s was Laswell's time, as he founded Axiom, an Island Records imprint devoted to his intrepid ways. The field recordings were Axiom projects, as was *The Dark Fire*, a gorgeous song cycle by Turkish oud genius Talip Ozkan; and *Soul Searcher*, a searing album of ragas by L. Shankar. But the pearls of the period were many. Sharrock's *Ask the Ages*—with John Coltrane drummer Elvin Jones, sax kingpin Pharoah Sanders, and young buck bassist Charnett Moffett—channeled the spirit of Coltrane with an intensity that makes it the late guitarist's most enduring testament. Another totem of the time was Jonas Hellborg's *The Word*, which saw the virtuoso acoustic bass guitarist joined by the Promethean Tony Williams on drums and the Soldier String Quartet. An indefinable album of indelible beauty, it's an apt example of Laswell's peerless musical matchmaking.

More great Axiom recordings continued apace in the decade's first half, including Skopelitis's *Ekstasis* (no doubt the album Carlos Santana wishes he would've made) and jazz composer/saxophonist Henry Threadgill's *Too Much Sugar for a Dime*, which was the start of a relationship that would extend to several exciting albums on Columbia. (The wonders of the first phase of Axiom are well-represented by two anthologies, *Illuminations* and *Manifestation*.) But as Laswell's prodigious output continued unabated, he began farming the overflow out to European labels like CMP and such dedicated indie imprints as Subharmonic and Strata. Some of the projects were promising, but a decline in quality was in evidence. The albums from Praxis—a trippy power trio with Laswell, drummer Brain, and oddball guitar phenom Buckethead—never realized their potential, and Laswell began churning out "ambient" music by the yard. *The Divination* series, the first such discs, were atmospheric and dubwise, but collaborations with the likes of Pete Namlook and Jonah Sharp of Spacetime Continuum were dead on arrival.

Around this time, Axiom's sales dipped, and Laswell's leash was reined in by Island's parent, Poly-Gram. Plus, a new "black rock" imprint on Rykodisc flopped immediately (owing more to the irredeemable lameness of the records than anything else). The empty exercises in electronica continued, too, with Laswell seemingly concerned less with making real music than flooding the shops with as much anonymous, pseudomystical product as possible. The Axiom "conceptual" sets begun around 1994 have been essays in mediocrity: *Axiom Ambient: Lost in the Translation* stripmined the Axiom catalog, fully living up to its subtitle; the widely heralded Axiom Funk was widely disappointing (the lovely contributions of late P. Funk guitarist Eddie Hazel excepted); and the pretentious *Altered Beats* DJ remix record was two hours of tedious knob twiddling. One of the picks of the latter-day Axiom litter is *Dreams of Freedom*, a superfluous yet appealing collection that overhauls classic Bob Marley songs in an ambient-dub fashion. (Even better is Laswell's Miles Davis exhumation project for Columbia, *Panthalassa*. With this set, Laswell merely clarifies the genius already in the grooves, revisiting the multitrack studio tapes of the trumpeter's electric era to fashion a highly compelling suite.)

Beyond any missteps over the years, great records have continued to dot Laswell's discography, giving listeners hope that he hasn't completely exhausted his talent. The last Material album, the all-star *Hallucination Engine,* is one of Laswell's finest pieces of record making, an out-and-out masterpiece that saw him using the studio to shape expansive studio improvisations after the fact—akin to Teo Macero's (see entry) contributions to Miles Davis's late '60s and early '70s material. Another African field recording, *The Trance of the Seven Colors,* summoned the primeval groove in a major way, with Pharoah Sanders playing alongside Gnawan griot Maleem Mahmoud Ghania. *Possession + African Dub: Off World One* from 1995 is by far Laswell's most effective ambient work yet, as it drags some nice performances from kora ace Foday Musa Suso and others through a deep, dark mix. Also, Threadgill's *Makin' a Move* and *Where's Your Cup?* are works of absolute inspiration, and

Laswell documents them with class. Finally, Laswell the bassist has shown that he can still kick out the jams, as he's done on several outré outings with avant-gardist John Zorn in *Painkiller;* and on *The Last Wave,* a ferocious free-jazz power-trio session as Arcana with British guitarist Derek Bailey and the late Tony Williams. And in one of his most powerhouse creations in years, Laswell played on and produced an all-star resuscitation of some of Williams' last sessions—the roiling Arcana set *Arc of the Testimony,* on Axiom. Despite his prodigal bent, Laswell is without a doubt one of the pivotal producers of the past two decades, exploding the possibilities for sonic cross-pollination and leaving behind some amazing records in the process. And you can bet that he has more to prove. In his new studio in West Orange, New Jersey (having recently moved from his longtime bunker in Greenpoint, Brooklyn), Laswell still molds and mutates music on a near daily basis. As he says, "There's no rest, and you're never done." —BRADLEY BAMBARGER

Aisha Kandisha's Jarring Effect: *Shabeesation*, Rykodisc, 1996.

Anderson, Laurie: *Mister Heartbreak* (3 tracks), Warner Bros., 1984.

Asana: *Asana*, Douglas, 1997.

Attar, Bachir: *The Next Dream*, CMP, 1993.

Automaton: *Dub Terror Exhaust*, Strata, 1994 • *Jihad*, Strata, 1994.

Axiom Funk: *Funkcronomicon*, Axiom, 1995.

Azonic: *Halo*, Strata, 1994.

Baker, Ginger: *Horses and Trees*, Celluloid, 1986, 1987 • *Middle Passage*, Axiom, 1990.

Bey, Hakim: *T.A.Z.*, Axiom, 1994.

Blind Idiot God: *Cyclotron*, Avant, 1993.

Bomb: *Hate Fed Love*, Sire, 1992.

Bootsy's Rubber Band: "Jungle Bass," 4th & B'Way, 1990.

Buckethead: *Day of the Robot*, Sub Meta, 1996 • *Colma*, CyberOctave, 1998.

Buddy Miles Express: *Hell and Back*, Rykodisc, 1994.

Bullen, Nicholas: *See* Laswell, Bill.

Chaos Face: *Doom Ride*, Subharmonic, 1994.

Clinton, George: *Hey Man . . . Smell My Finger*, Paisley Park, 1993.

Collins, Bootsy: *What's Bootsy Doin'?*, Columbia, 1988 • *Blasters of the Universe*, Rykodisc, 1995.

Cypher 7: *Decoder*, Strata, 1994.

Deadline: *Dissident*, Day Eight, 1991.

Death Cube K: *Disembodied*, Ion, 1997.

Dibango, Manu: *Afrijazzy*, Urban, 1987 • *Electric Africa*, Polydor, 1988 • *Bao Bao*, M.I.L., 1996.

Dieng, Ayib: *See* Lasell, Bill.

Divination: *Ambient Dub*, Vol. 1, Subharmonic, 1994 • *Ambient*

Dub, Vol. 2, *Dead Slow*, Subharmonic, 1994.

Ghania, Maleem Mahmoud: *The Trance of Seven Colors*, Axiom, 1994.

Golden Palominos: *The Golden Palominos*, OAO/Celluloid, 1983 • *A History (1982–1985)*, Restless, 1992 • *A History (1986–1989)*, Restless, 1993 • "Prison of the Rhythm" (remix), Restless, 1993 • "Heaven" (remix), Restless, 1994.

Hancock, Herbie: *Future Shock*, Columbia, 1983 • "Hardrock," Columbia, 1984 • *Sound-System*, Columbia, 1984 • *Perfect Machine*, Columbia, 1988 • w/ Foday Musa Suso, *Village Life*, Columbia, 1992.

Hardware: *Third Eye Open*, Rykodisc, 1994.

Hassan, Umar Bin: *Be Bop or Be Dead*, Axiom, 1993.

Hellborg, Jonas: *The Word*, Axiom, 1991.

Hendryx, Nona: *Nona*, RCA, 1983 • *The Art of Defense*, RCA, 1984 • "To the Bone," RCA, 1984.

Hosono, Haruomi: *N.D.E.*, Antilles, 1996.

Icehouse: *Full Circle*, Alex, 1994.

Inoue, Tetsu: See Laswell, Bill.

Jackson, Ronald Shannon: *Red Warrior*, Axiom, 1990, 1991 • *Taboo*, Venture, 1990.

Jagger, Mick: "Just Another Night," Columbia, 1985 • "Lucky in Love," Columbia, 1985 • *She's the Boss* (6 tracks), Columbia, 1985.

Kodo: *Ibuki*, TriStar, 1997.

Kunda, Toure: *Dance of the Leaves: Celluloid*, Restless, 1994.

Last Exit: *Iron Path*, Venture/Virgin, 1988.

Last Poets: *Oh My People*, Charly, 1984, 1996 • *Holy Terror*, Rykodisc, 1995 • *Time Has Come*, Mouth Almighty, 1997.

Laswell, Bill: *Basslines*, Charly, 1984, 1997 • *Hear No Evil*, Venture, 1988 • *Axiom Ambient: Lost in the Translation*, Axiom Ambient, 1994 • w/ Yosuke Yamashita, *Asian Games*, Verve, 1994 • w/ Tetsu Inoue, *Cymatic Scan*, Subharmonic, 1994 • w/ Nicholas Bullen, *Bass Terror*, Sub Rosa, 1995 • *Outer Dark*, Fax, 1995 • *Silent Recoil*, Low, 1995 • *Dark Massive*, Cleopatra, 1996 • *Oscillations*, Sub Rosa, 1996 • *Sacred System Chapter One: Book of Entrance*, ROIR, 1996 • w/ Tetsu Inoue and Atom Heart, *Second Nature*, Subharmonic, 1996 • *Ambience Dub*, Vols. 1–2, APC, 1997 • *City of Light*, Sub Rosa, 1997 • *Dub Meltdown*, Wordsound, 1997 • w/ Ayib Dieng, *Rhythmagick*, Subharmonic, 1997 • *Sacred System Chapter Two*, ROIR, 1997 • *Jazzonia*, Douglas, 1998 • w/ Sacred System, *Nagual Site*, RCA, 1998 • *Oscillations*, Vol. 2, Advanced Drum N Bass, Sub Rosa, 1998.

Laswell, Bill, and Mick Harris: *Equasions of Eternity*, Wordsound, 1996 • *Equasions of Eternity*, Vol. 2, Veve, Wordsound, 1998.

Laswell, Bill, and Pete Namlook: *Psychonavigation*, Subharmonic, 1994 • *Outland 2*, EFA, 1996 • *Psychonavigation 2*, EFA, 1996 • *Outland 3*, EFA, 1998.

Limbomaniacs: *Stinky Grooves*, In-Effect, 1990.

Mandingo: *New World Power*, Axiom, 1991.

Marley, Bob: *Dreams of Freedom: Ambient*, Island/Axiom/Tuff Gong, 1997.

Master Musicians of Jajouka: *Apocalypse Across the Sky*, Island, 1992.

Material: *Temporary Music*, Celluloid, 1981 • *Memory Serves*, Elektra Musician, 1982 • *One Down*, Elektra, 1982 • *Seven Souls*, Virgin, 1989 • *The Third Power*, Axiom, 1991 • "Desert Star," Restless, 1993 (*In Defense of Animals Benefit Compilation*) • "Eternal Drift," Axiom/Island, 1994 • "Eternal Drift" (remix), Axiom/Island, 1994 • *Hallucination Engine*, Axiom, 1994.

Mephiskapheles: *God Bless Satan*, Pass the Virgin, 1994, 1995.

Motorhead: *Orgasmatron*, Sinclair, 1990 • *All the Aces*, Castle, 1995 • *The Best of Motorhead*, Vol. 2, Roadrunner, 1995.

Nickelbag: *12 Hits and a Bump*, Iguana, 1996.

O.G. Funk: *Out of the Dark*, Rykodisc, 1994.

Ono, Yoko: *Starpeace*, Rykodisc, 1985, 1997 • *Ono Box*, Rykodisc, 1992.

Oyewole, Abiodun: *25 Years*, Rykodisc, 1996.

Ozkan, Talip: *The Dark Fire*, Axiom, 1992.

Parker, Maceo: *For All the King's Men*, 4th & B'Way, 1990.

Pop, Iggy: *Instinct*, A&M, 1988.

Possession: *African Dub: Off World One*, Sub Meta, 1996.

Praxis: *Transmutation (Mutatis Mutandis)*, Axiom, 1992 • *Metatron*, Subharmonic, 1994 • *Sacrifist*, Subharmonic, 1994.

Public Image Limited (PIL): *Public Image Ltd.*, Elektra, 1978, 1990 • *Album (Compact Disc)*, Elektra, 1986 • "Rise," Elektra, 1986 • *Greatest Hits So Far*, Atlantic, 1990.

Ramones: *Brain Drain*, Sire, 1989.

Sacred System: See Laswell, Bill.

Sakamoto, Ryuichi: *Neo Geo*, Epic, 1988.

Salas, Steve, and Colorcode: *Colorcode*, Island, 1990.

Samulnori: *Record of Changes*, CMP, 1988.

Sanders, Pharoah: *Message from Home*, Verve, 1996.

Schnabel, Julian: *Every Silver Lining Has a Cloud*, Island, 1995.

Scott-Heron, Gil: *Re-Ron*, Arista, 1984 • *The Best Of*, Arista, 1984.

Shaheen, Simon: *The Music of Mohamed Abdel Wahab*, Axiom, 1991 • *Turath: Masterworks of the Middle East*, CMP, 1992.

Shankar, Lakshminarayana: *Soul Searcher*, Axiom, 1992.

Sharrock, Sonny: *Guitar*, Enemy, 1986, 1994 • *Seize the Rainbow*, Enemy, 1987 • *Faith Moves*, CMP, 1989, 1992 • *Ask the Ages*, Axiom, 1992 • *Into Another Light*, Enemy, 1996.

Skopelitis, Nicky: *Next to Nothing*, Caroline, 1990 • *Ekstasis*, Axiom, 1993.

Slave Master: *Under the Six*, Rykodisc, 1994.

Sly and Robbie: *Rhythm Killers*, Island, 1987.

Sola: *Blues in the East*, Axiom, 1994 • w/ Liu and Wu Man, *China Collage*, Avant, 1996.

Somma One: *Hooked Light Rays*, Low, 1996.

Suso, Foday Musa: *New World Power*, Axiom, 1981, 1991 • *Jali Kunda: Griots of West Africa*, Ellipsis Arts, 1996 • *See also* Hancock, Herbie.

Swans: *The Burning World*, Uni, 1989.

Third Rail: *South Delta Space Age*, Antilles, 1995, 1997.

Threadgill, Henry: *Too Much Sugar for a Dime*, Axiom, 1993 • *Carry the Day*, Columbia, 1995 • *Makin' a Move*, Columbia, 1995 • w/ Make a Move, *Where's Your Cup?*, Columbia, 1997.

Time Zone: "World Destruction," Celluloid/Tommy Boy, 1984.

Ulmer, James Blood: *America: Do You Remember?*, Blue Note, 1987.

Vodu 155: *Vodu 155*, Mango, 1994.

White Zombie: *Make Them Die Slowly*, Caroline, 1989.

Wobble, Jah: *Heaven and Earth*, Island, 1995.

Worrell, Bernie: *Funk of Ages*, Rhino, 1991 • *Blacktronic Science*, Gramavision, 1993, 1994 • *The Other Side*, CMP, 1993.

Yamashita, Yosuke: *See* Laswell, Bill.

Yothu Yindi: *Freedom*, Mushroom/Hollywood, 1994.

Zillatron: *Lord of the Harvest*, Rykodisc, 1994.

COLLECTIONS

New Africa II, Celluloid, 1985.

Ancient Heart: Mandinka and Fulani Music of Gambia, Axiom, 1991.

Gnawa Music of Marrakesh: Night Spirit Masters, Axiom, 1991.

Bahia Black: Ritual Beating System, Axiom, 1992.

Manifestation: Axiom Collection II, Axiom, 1993.

Axion Dub: Mysteries of Creation, Axiom, 1996.

Time and Love: The Music of Laura Nyro, Astor Place, 1997.

Jali Kunda: Griots of West Africa and Beyond, Ellipsis Arts, 1997.

Reanimator: Black Market Science, Ion, 1998.

Latin Rascals

(ALBERT CABRERA AND TONY MORAN)

Tony Moran and Albert Cabrera, two struggling DJs, befriended each other in 1981 and formed the Latin Rascals. Their sole purpose: to create dance music. At a time when disco was fading into the background, Moran and Cabrera wanted to take what they had learned from their respective disco educations and parlay it into a full-time career. The only problem was that they didn't exactly know what they wanted, nor did they know how to go about getting it.

One thing for certain: WKTU/Disco 92 was the most popular radio station in New York at the time. Each weekday afternoon, the station would host the "lunch-time mix," a beat-mixed hour of nonstop club music. It was a religious experience for many, and Moran and Cabrera were determined to get at least one of their "bedroom edits" onto the show. With much perseverance, the duo got their wish and found themselves in great demand. Working around the clock, they would feverishly re-edit and splice songs to form a 20-minute mixed marathon. They soon became the darlings of the "lunch-time mix" and were contacted by industry veteran Arthur Baker (see entry), who offered them work at his Shakedown Studios. There, Moran and Cabrera began editing songs for some of pop world's major artists: Diana Ross, Bruce Springsteen, the Rolling Stones, Run-D.M.C., Madonna, Grace Jones, U2, and Duran Duran. Recalls Moran, "We created a whole new step in the record-making process. As the Latin Rascals, we became known for our editing work."

This step in the recording process became yet another expense for the artist. Was the process absolutely necessary? Apparently. Within two years, they received an offer by New York independent label, Fever Records, to produce and write a song for one of their acts, the Cover Girls. "Show Me" was the result, and not only did it become the Latin Rascals' first Top 40 gold record, but it ushered in the "freestyle" era of music, complete with its own roster of stars (Brenda K. Starr, Information Society, TKA, Safire, Nayobe), all of whom benefited from Moran and Cabrera.

The Latin Rascals were also artists, recording the massive club hits "Arabian Knights," "Bach to the Future," and a remake of "Don't Let Me Be Misunderstood." Productions for the Fat Boys ("The Twist," No. 16; "Wipe Out," No. 12) and the Cover Girls (Top 10 ballads "Wishing on a Star," "We Can't Go Wrong," "Promise Me") followed.

When the bottom dropped out of the freestyle music scene, Moran and Cabrera decided to end their business partnership. They discovered that the musical tides had changed. Separately, building on the foundations of house music, Moran and Cabrera eschew the strict underground house mentality many of their contemporaries favor, preferring to infuse their remixes and productions with hook-laden commercial appeal. Moran has collaborated with such pop superstars as Gloria Estefan, Celine Dion, Whitney Houston, Michael Jackson, Luther Vandross, Barry Manilow, and Jon Secada, while Cabrera has worked with C+C Music Factory, George Michael, Martha Wash, Nuyorican Soul, and George Benson. "It's funny," Moran once said, "the more success I get with the records I remix-produce, the more I'm willing to test what it is I can create. It's only based on success that you can begin to experiment. Until you reach that level, people only want what they know will work for them, as opposed to giving them what you think they should have." —LARRY FLICK

Latin Rascals

Bambaataa, Afrika: *Planet Rock: The Album,* Tommy Boy, 1986.
Beach Boys: *Still Cruisin',* Capitol, 1989.
Cover Girls: "Show Me," Fever, 1986 • "Because of You" (remix), Fever, 1987 • "Inside Outside," Fever, 1988 • "Promise Me," Fever, 1988 • *Show Me,* Fever, 1994 • *Greatest Hits,* Epic, 1998.
Coyote: *Muevete Bien,* Capitol Latin, 1994.
Fat Boys: *Crushin',* Tin Pan Apple/Polydor, 1987 • *Crushin'* (remix), Tin Pan Apple/Polydor, 1987 • "Wipeout," Tin Pan Apple/Polydor, 1987 • *Hard Again,* Tin Pan Apple/Polydor, 1988 • "Louie, Louie," Tin Pan Apple/Polydor, 1988 • "The Twist," Tin Pan Apple/Polydor, 1988 • *All Meat No Filler: The Best Of,* Rhino, 1997.
Ferry, Bryan: "Kiss and Tell" (remix), Reprise, 1987 • "The Right Stuff" (remix), Reprise, 1987.
Franklin, Aretha: "Freeway of Love" (remix), Arista, 1985.
La Flavour: "Mandolay," Seathru, 1979, 1987.
Latin Rascals: *Bach to the Future,* Tin Pan Apple, 1986 • *It Must Be You,* Tin Pan Apple, 1986 • *When She Goes,* Tin Pan Apple, 1989.
Melendez, Lisette: *True to Life* (6 tracks), Chaos, 1994.
Pet Shop Boys: "Opportunities" (remix), EMI America, 1986.
TKA: "One Way Love," Tommy Boy, 1986 • *Scars of Love,* Tommy Boy, 1987 • "Tears May Fall," Tommy Boy, 1988 • *Louder Than Love,* Tommy Boy, 1990 • *Greatest Hits,* Tommy Boy, 1992.
Zevon, Warren: "Leave My Monkey Alone" (remix), Virgin, 1987.

Albert Cabrera

Bass Brothas: *Bass Brothas Bring You Phat Bass,* Mic Mac, 1995.
Corina: "Summertime, Summertime," So So Def, 1997.
Space Bass: *Planet Bass,* Stealth, 1996.
Stingily, Byron: "Sing-a-Song," Nervous Dog, 1997.
Torres, Roberto: *Vallenatos a Mi Estilo,* Vol. 2, SAR, 1996.
Warp 9: *Phase Bass,* Intersound International, 1997.

COLLECTIONS

Bass Dreams, Solo Jam, 1995.
Bass Construction, Thump, 1995.
Bassrocker: Rock Tha Bass, Intersound International, 1996.
Bass Dates, Solo Jam, 1996.
Trip Hop Dance 2000, Intersound International, 1997.

Tony Moran

Concept of One: *Concept of One,* Cutting, 1993.
Cover Girls: "We Can't Go Wrong," Capitol, 1990 • "Funk Boutique," Epic, 1991 • *Here It Is,* Epic, 1992 • "Thank You," Epic, 1992 • "Wishing on a Star," Epic, 1992 • *Satisfy,* Quality, 1996 • "I Need Your Lovin'," Fever, 1997.
Cynthia: *Cynthia Remixes,* Mic Mac, 1995 • "Like A Star," Timber!/Tommy Boy, 1997.
Estefan, Gloria: "Corazon Prohibido," Epic, 1998 • "Heaven's What I Feel," Epic, 1998 • "Oye," Epic, 1998.
Houston, Whitney: "Step by Step" (remix), Arista, 1997.
Jackson, Janet: "Together Again" (remix), Virgin, 1997.
Jackson, Michael: *Blood on the Dance Floor: HIStory in the Mix,* MJJ/Sony, 1997.
K7: "Hi De Ho," Tommy Boy, 1994 • *Swing Batta Swing,* Tommy Boy, 1994.
Kenny G: "Havana" (remix), Arista, 1997.
Lamond, George: *It's Always You* (EP), Tommy Boy, 1994.
Lauper, Cyndi: "You Don't Know" (remix), Epic, 1996.
Manilow, Barry: "I'd Really Love to See You Tonight" (remix), Arista, 1997.
Nayobe: "Let's Party Tonight (We Can Dance, We Can Fly)," Sony/Latin, 1997.
Real McCoy: "One More Time," Arista, 1997.
Robin S.: *From Now On,* Atlantic, 1997.
Safire: *I Wasn't Born Yesterday,* Mercury, 1991.
Secada, Jon: *Secada,* SBK, 1997.
Selena: "A Boy Like That," RCA, 1996.
TKA: "You Are the One," Warner Bros., 1989.
Vandross, Luther: *One Night with You: The Best of Love,* Vol. 2, Sony, 1997 • *I Know,* Virgin, 1998.

Nick Launay

A studio prodigy of 19 when he remixed M's "Pop Muzik," Nick Launay has gone on to produce or co-produce crucial music of the modern rock era. Launay first specialized in early '80s British post-punk (Gang of Four, Killing Joke, Public Image Limited, the Slits), then worked with many of the biggest names in the history of Australian and New Zealand rock (Birthday Party, the Church, Tim Finn, INXS, Midnight Oil, Silverchair). In the '90s, Launay has scored with American acts such as Talking Heads, David Byrne, For Squirrels, the Posies, and most recently, Semisonic.

Launay was born in London in 1960, moved with his family to southern Spain when he was 9, and returned to England when he was 17. He quickly got a job at a studio, Tape One, where he learned to edit tape and master records onto vinyl.

In 1979 Launay created one of the first commercial 12-inch singles when he remixed and extended M's "Pop Muzik." Recalls Launay: "I basically did the thing after hours for fun. I edited between the instrumental version and the proper mix. I put lots of bits of tape backwards and made up other sections using edits and loops and stuff like that. Robin Scott, who was M, really loved [the extended version] and put it out. It got played on the radio almost as much as the original mix, which was good for my confidence."

That same year Launay began to work at the Town House studio, which was owned by Virgin Records; he learned from major producers such as Steve Lillywhite and Hugh Padgham (see entries) and worked on records by XTC, the Jam, Simple Minds, and Public Image. "I got on well with John Lydon [Public Image's leader, formerly Johnny Rotten of the Sex Pistols], so much so that he asked if I could mix a song; then he asked me to engineer and co-produce *The Flowers of Romance* [No. 20 U.K.]," says Launay.

Exposure from the Public Image album resulted in Launay producing the Gang of Four's *Another Day, Another Dollar* EP (with the punk-funk classic "To Hell with Poverty"), Killing Joke's *What's This For?* (with the punishing electro-punk standard "Follow the Leaders"), and the Slits' "Earthbeat" single. At the same time Launay was engineering Phil Collins' productions for John Martyn and Eric Clapton. "It was odd doing [conventional] music and the anarchistic kind of music at the same time," he says.

Then Launay made the Australian connection. The Boys Next Door had been formed in Melbourne in the mid-'70s, and had moved to London in the late '70s as the Birthday Party. Led by sex and horror–obsessed singer Nick Cave, the Party created a cacophonous din best exemplified by the Launay-produced "Release the Bats/Blast Off" single: a double dose of bowel-rattling rhythm, jabbing guitar noise, and Cave's unhinged caterwauling.

The Aussie connection made, Launay produced Midnight Oil's super *10, 9, 8, 7, 6, 5, 4, 3, 2, 1* at Town House in 1983. Their fifth album, but first released outside of Australia, *10* demonstrates Launay's ability to capture big-bang energy ("Read About It"), precise and subtle soundscapes ("Outside World"), and all of the above (the great "Power and the Passion").

Launay accompanied the band to Tokyo to record their next album, *Red Sails in the Sunset*, which demonstrates many of the same strengths as *10:* "Best of Both Worlds" rocks with near-punk vigor, "Shipyards of New Zealand" is eerie and spacious, and "Kosciusko" is a stomp through an angular but catchy melody. After an eight-year separation, Launay and the Oils reunited for perhaps the band's most tuneful album, 1993's *Earth and Sun and Moon.* Singles "My Country," "Outbreak of Love," and "Truganini" all boast ringing, mature melodies, thoughtful lyrics, and some of Peter Garrett's most natural singing.

Launay's greatest Aussie achievement is INXS's *The Swing.* Chock-full of modern rock radio hits (primarily written by keyboardist/guitarist Andrew Farriss and late singer Michael Hutchence), *The Swing* is the bridge between the band's experimental beginnings and their subsequent arena-filling success. "I Send a Message" is '80s alterna-funk at its finest; the title track rides in on a monster beat, joined by surprisingly jagged guitar and tough vocals from Hutchence; "Burn for You" is a chipper sing-along bolstered by a full background chorus. (The album's other hit, "Original Sin," was produced by Nile Rodgers; see entry.)

Although Launay came into production through the engineer's door, he apprehends music visually. "I see music as landscapes. The chorus will have a particular feeling to it that actually gives me a visual picture like a film. So then I say, 'Well it makes me feel like that, and certain instruments—like a mellotron or some sort of weird guitar sound with weird delays—gives me that feeling, so let's try that.' But I don't like using digital keyboards in place of band members, I like keeping it all very organic and flowing," he says.

Nick Launay now lives in Australia with his wife.
—Eric Olsen and David John Farinella

Armoury Show: "Castles in Spain," EMI America, 1985 • *Waiting for the Floods,* EMI America, 1985.

Automatic: *Transmitter,* Sony, 1997.

Big Pig: *Bonk,* A&M, 1988 • "Breakaway," A&M, 1988.

Birthday Party: "Release the Bats/Blast Off," 4 A.D., 1981.

Bishop, Stephen: *Bowling in Paris,* Atlantic, 1989.

Byrne, David: *Hanging Upside Down* (EP), Sire, 1992 • *Uh-Oh,* Luaka Bop/WB, 1992.

Church, The: *Seance,* Arista, 1983.

Finn, Tim: *Big Canoe,* Virgin, 1988.

For Squirrels: *Example,* 550 Music/Epic, 1995.

Gang of Four: *Another Day, Another Dollar* (EP), Warner Bros., 1982 • *A Brief History of the Twentieth Century,* Warner Bros., 1990.

Girls Against Boys: *Freak*on*ica,* Geffen, 1998.

INXS: *The Swing,* Atco, 1984.

Killing Joke: "Follow the Leaders," E.G., 1981 • *What's This For?,* Editions E.G., 1981, 1990.

Midnight Oil: *10, 9, 8, 7, 6, 5, 4, 3, 2, 1,* Columbia, 1983 •

"Power and the Passion," Columbia, 1983 • *Red Sails in the Sunset,* Columbia, 1985 • *Earth and Sun and Moon,* Columbia, 1993 • "My Country," Columbia, 1993 • "Outbreak of Love," Columbia, 1993 • "Truganini," Columbia, 1993.

Models: *Out of Sight Out of Mind,* Geffen, 1985.

Posies, The: *Amazing Disgrace,* DGC, 1996.

Public Image Limited: *The Flowers of Romance,* Warner Bros., 1981, 1989.

Semisonic: "Closing Time," MCA, 1998 • *Feeling Stangely Fine,* MCA, 1998.

silverchair: *Freak Show,* Epic, 1997.

Slits, The: "Earthbeat," Epic, 1981.

Spear of Destiny: *Grapes of Wrath,* Burning Rome, 1983.

Subrosa: *Never Bet the Devil Your Head,* 550 Music, 1997.

Talking Heads: *Popular Favorites: Sand in the Vasoline* (3 tracks), Sire, 1992.

Thompson, Marc Anthony: *Watts and Paris,* Reprise, 1989.

Don Law

D on Law stands astride the pillars of midcentury American music—having recorded arguably the single most important figure in blues history, Robert Johnson, in the '30s—Law then helped to found the Nashville music business by recording Lefty Frizzell, Flatt and Scruggs, Ray Price, Johnny Cash, Marty Robbins, Johnny Horton, Carl Smith, Jimmy Dean, and dozens of others in the '40s, '50s, and '60s for Columbia Records.

Born in London, England, in 1902, Law was well educated and sang with the London Choral Society. He began a series of picaresque wanderings in 1923 with a stay in Poland as a gun-toting cashier for a timber company, followed by a journey to New York to sell etchings in 1924. A friend invited Law to help work his ranch in Alabama, so he rode the range herding sheep, then turkeys. The ranch went bust and Law took the opportunity to pursue his deep fascination with the American cowboy. He ended up in Dallas as a bookkeeper for Brunswick Records. Gradually, Law moved into A&R, and when the American Record Corporation (ARC) bought Brunswick in 1931, he began working for a fellow Englishman similarly predisposed toward American roots music, Art Satherley, who would become his mentor.

Robert Johnson was born in 1911 in Hazelhurst, Mississippi, the illegitimate son of Julia Dodds and Noah Johnson. As a youth in Robinsonville, Mississippi, Johnson played a fair harmonica and a worse guitar with his brother Charles, Son House, and Willie Brown. A life of poverty and deprivation was made more bleak when Johnson's first wife died in childbirth. He was nineteen and she was sixteen.

For the next year Johnson wandered about the Delta. No one particularly missed him. He returned to Robinsonville on a Saturday night carrying his guitar the way an executioner carries an ax. The roadhouse doors swung in and Johnson walked purposefully to the stage as House, Brown, and the crowd filed outside for a break. Johnson began playing to his own echo in the empty room. Outside, the musicians and audience alike heard a noise so harsh and painful, yet so supple and thrilling, that 50 cigarettes made a collective hiss as they extinguished themselves in a dozen summer puddles. Everything was the same, yet everything was different about Johnson, and word quickly spread that he had "sold his soul to the devil to get to play like that," according to House in Greil Marcus's *Mystery Train.*

Word of Johnson's prowess spread as he traveled to St. Louis, Chicago, Detroit, and New York, catching every audience in his gaze and astounding them with his musicianship and power. A white music store owner named H.C. Speir passed on word about Johnson to Ernie Oertle, ARC's talent scout in the mid-South, and Oertle agreed to take Johnson to San Antonio to record with Don Law.

Law recorded Johnson's entire 29-song body of work direct to disc in a San Antonio hotel room in November 1936 and in a Dallas warehouse in June 1937. Though Johnson was 25 and 26 when he recorded, his smallish size and shy demeanor led Law to think he was a teenager. In fact, Johnson was so shy that he turned to face the wall when he recorded.

He wasn't as shy in public though; the night after his first session, Johnson was picked up on a vagrancy charge and worked over by the police, who also shattered his guitar. Law extricated him from the care of the constabulary and tucked him in his boardinghouse bed with the suggestion that he stay there until morning, leaving 45 cents for Johnson's breakfast. After returning to his dinner at the Gunter Hotel, Law got another call. This time it was Johnson, as Frank Driggs relates in the liner notes to *King of the Delta Blues Singers:*

"I'm lonesome."

"What do you mean you're lonesome," answered Law.

"I'm lonesome and there's a lady here. She wants 50 cents and I lacks a nickel." Women were Johnson's pleasure and his downfall; he was poisoned to death by a jealous husband at a roadhouse in 1938.

Johnson's greatness lies in his songwriting ("Cross Road Blues," "Come On in My Kitchen," "I Believe I'll Dust My Broom," "Sweet Home Chicago," "Love in Vain"); his haunted, high voice; and his complex walking bass and slide guitar style. He didn't merely accompany his voice with guitar, he played a sophisticated rhythmic counterpoint to his tales of hellhounds, meetings with the devil, and untrue women. In fact, Johnson held a dialogue with his guitar—an unresolved dialectic that reflected both the anguish and the exhilaration inherent in pursuing an unnamed satisfaction that was never to be his.

For Law, the blues and country-western were two sides of the same American coin. In 1938, he recorded "San Antonio Rose" (No. 15) with Bob Wills for Columbia. In 1942 he went to New York to record children's music. Then in 1945, Law returned to country music when he and Satherley divided the nation at El Paso, with Law responsible for sessions to the East.

Law took over the country department in 1953 when Satherley retired, becoming responsible for signing, recording, and promoting talent. Law moved to Nashville and was one of the first producers to work at Owen Bradley's (see entry) Quonset Hut—the first studio built on Music Row—thereby throwing Columbia's weight behind the burgeoning Nashville scene. In 1961, Law convinced Columbia to buy the Quonset Hut, turning it into Columbia Studio B. Law also helped found the Country Music Association.

In the '50s and early '60s Law recorded some of the greatest country music ever, finding in that music an emotional and melodic parallel to Robert Johnson: Carl Smith's plaintive "Darlin' Am I the One?,"; Lefty Frizzell's devastating "The Long Black Veil" (No. 6 country), an understated country gothic with murder, betrayal, and the ultimate sacrifice; Ray Price's agonized "Crazy Arms" (No. 1 country for 20 weeks) and "City Nights" (No. 1 country for 13 weeks). He helped bring country to a new audience with the No. 1 pop success of Johnny Horton's rousing "Battle of New Orleans" and Marty Robbins' "El Paso," with Robbins' smooth voice relating another tragic story of passion, murder, and flight over a Tex-Mex melody and poignant Spanish guitar.

Perhaps Law's finest country moment is the great Johnny Cash album I Walk the Line (1964), wherein he re-recorded six songs from his Sun days, including "I Walk the Line," "Hey Porter," "Wreck of the Old 97," "Big River," "Give My Love to Rose," and "Folsom Prison Blues." Unlike most re-recordings, these improve on the originals, Cash's voice having deepened and broadened with time. Law's production is fuller and more "western" than Sam Phillips' (see entry) original, more rockabilly versions, and the album functions as an updated greatest hits. Cash's line about killing a man in Reno "just to watch him die" is even more powerful this time around, and the damped-string electric guitar picking perfectly evokes the rhythm of the train that winds past the singer's cell, mocking his incarceration with its rolling freedom.

In the '60s Law was assisted by Frank Jones, who took over when Law semiretired in the mid-'60s, much as Law had taken over for his mentor Art Satherley years before. Don Law died in 1982 and, shockingly, has never been elected to the Country Music Hall of Fame. His son is the famous Boston concert promoter, Don Law Jr. —ERIC OLSEN

Cargill, Henson: "Skip a Rope," Monument, 1968.

Cash, Johnny: The Fabulous Johnny Cash, Columbia, 1958 • "Don't Take Your Guns to Town," Columbia, 1959 • Blood, Sweat and Tears, Legacy, 1963, 1994 • Ring of Fire (The Best of Johnny Cash), Columbia, 1963 • "I Walk the Line," Columbia, 1964 • I Walk the Line, Columbia, 1964 • w/ the Carter Family, Keep on the Sunny Side, Columbia Special Products, 1964 • Everybody Loves a Nut, Columbia, 1966 • Mean As Hell! Columbia, 1966 • Greatest Hits, Vol. 1, Columbia, 1967 • Biggest Hits, Columbia, 1987 • Come Along and Ride This Train, Bear Family, 1991 • The Essential Johnny Cash, 1955–1983, Legacy, 1992 • The Gospel Collection, Legacy, 1992 • Bitter Tears: Ballads of the American Indian, Legacy, 1994.

Collins Kids: Hop, Skip and Jump, Bear Family, 1991 • Rockin'est, Bear Family, 1998.

Collins, Tommy: Leonard, Bear Family, 1992.

Craddock, Crash: Boom Boom Baby, Bear Family, 1992.

Dean, Jimmy: "Big Bad John," Columbia, 1961 • Big Bad John and Other Fabulous Song and Tales, Columbia Special Products, 1961, 1993 • Greatest Hits, Columbia, 1966, 1998.

Dickens, Little Jimmy: I'm Little but I'm Loud: The Jimmy Dickens Collection, Razor & Tie, 1996 • Out Behind the Barn, Bear Family, 1998.

Ebsen, Buddy, and Irene Ryan: The Beverly Hillbillies, Legacy, 1993.

Emmons, Buddy: Amazing Steel Guitar: The Buddy Emmons Collection, Razor & Tie, 1997.

Everly Brothers: Classic, Bear Family, 1992 • Heartaches and Harmonies, Rhino, 1994.

Flatt and Scruggs: Foggy Mountain Jamboree, Columbia, 1957 • At Carnegie Hall, Columbia, 1963 • 1959–1963, Bear Family, 1992.

Garland, Hank: Jazz Winds from a New Direction, Collectors, 1960, 1993.

Gibson, Don: *The Fabulous Don Gibson*, Harmony, 1965 • *The Singer, the Songwriter*, Bear Family, 1991.

Hawkins, Hawkshaw: *Hawk, 1953–1961*, Bear Family, 1991.

Horton, Johnny: "The Battle of New Orleans," Columbia, 1959 • *Greatest Hits*, Columbia, 1960 • *The Spectacular*, Columbia, 1960 • *High on a Mountain, I Tell You What I See*, Bear Family, 1990 • *1956–1960*, Bear Family, 1991.

Jackson, Stonewall: *Greatest Hits*, Columbia, 1965.

Jim and Jesse: *Jim and Jesse: Bluegrass and More*, Bear Family, 1993.

Johnson, Robert: "Crossroad Blues," Columbia, 1990 • *The Complete Recordings*, Columbia, 1990.

King, Sid: *Gonna Shake This Shack Tonight*, Bear Family, 1991.

Miller, Frankie: *Sugar Coated Baby*, Bear Family, 1996.

Morgan, George: *Candy Kisses*, Bear Family, 1996 • "Almost," Columbia, 1952.

Murphy, Jimmy: *16 Tons of Rock and Roll*, Bear Family, 1989.

Perkins, Carl: *Whole Lotta Shakin'*, Columbia, 1958 • *Restless: The Columbia Years*, Legacy, 1992.

Piano Red: *The Doctor's In*, Bear Family, 1993.

Price, Ray: "Crazy Arms," Columbia, 1956 • "Heartaches By the Number," Columbia, 1959 • *Night Life*, Koch, 1963, 1996 • *Danny Boy*, Columbia, 1967 • "For the Good Times/Grazin' in Greener Pastures," Columbia, 1970 • "I Won't Mention It Again," Columbia, 1971 • "She's Got to Be a Saint," Columbia, 1972 • *San Antonio Rose*, Koch, 1973, 1996 • "You're the Best Thing That Ever Happened to Me," Columbia, 1973 • *Ray Price and the Cherokee Cowboys*, Bear Family, 1995.

Robbins, Marty: "I'll Go on Alone," Columbia, 1952 • "I Couldn't Keep from Crying," Columbia, 1953 • "Maybelline," Columbia, 1955 • "That's All Right," Columbia, 1955 • "I Can't Quit," Columbia, 1956 • "Singing the Blues," Columbia, 1956 • "Knee Deep in the Blues," Columbia, 1957 • "The Hanging Tree," Columbia, 1958 • "Big Iron," Columbia, 1959 • *Gunfighter Ballads and Trail Songs*, Columbia, 1959 • "Don't Worry," Columbia, 1960 • "El Paso," Columbia, 1960 • *More Gunfighter Ballads and Trail Songs*, Columbia, 1960 • *Hawaii's Calling Me*, Columbia, 1962 • "Ruby Ann," Columbia, 1962 • "Begging to You," Columbia, 1963 • "Smokin' Cigarettes and Drinkin' Coffee Blues," Columbia, 1963 • *Drifter*, Koch, 1964, 1997 • *All-Time Greatest Hits*, Legacy, 1972 • *A Lifetime of Song, 1951–1982*, CBS, 1983 • *Biggest Hits*, CBS, 1984 • *Country, 1951–1958*, Bear Family, 1991 • *Ruby Ann: Rockin' Rollin' Robbins*, Vol. 3, Bear Family, 1991 • *The Essential*, Legacy, 1994 • *Super Hits*, Columbia, 1995 • *The Story of My Life: The Best of Marty Robbins, 1951–1982*, Legacy, 1996 • *The Story of My Life: The Best of Marty Robbins, 1952–1965*, Legacy, 1996.

Sara and Maybelle Carter: *Sara and Maybelle: The Original Carters*, Koch, 1966.

Self, Ronnie: *Bop-a-Lena*, Bear Family, 1990.

Smith, Carl: *The Essential*, Legacy, 1991 • *Satisfaction Guaranteed*, Bear Family, 1996.

Stanley Brothers: *The Angels Are Singing*, Harmony, 1966 • *Flowers on the Wall: The Essential Statler Brothers*, Legacy/Columbia, 1996.

Wheeler, Onie: *Onie's Bop*, Bear Family, 1991.

COLLECTIONS

The Real Kansas City, Legacy/Columbia, 1939, 1996.

Ghosts of Mississippi soundtrack, Columbia, 1997.

Paul Leary

The irony isn't lost on Paul Leary that he may eventually be better known as a record producer than as co-founder and guitarist for those paragons of psychedelic stomp, the Butthole Surfers. "I may not know what I'm doing," he says, "but I don't let that stop me."

An audio autodidact from years of making homemade records with the Butthole Surfers, Leary also has achieved surprising success in more formal producing. He co-produced the Meat Puppets' first gold album, 1994's *Too High to Die*, and he was behind Austin, Texas, singer/songwriter savant Daniel Johnston's critically acclaimed *Fun*. In 1995 Leary added the Meat Puppets' *No Joke!* and the Supersuckers' *Sacrilicious Sounds* to his credits. The following year, he helmed Sublime's Top 20 eponymous smash, scoring his biggest hit to date.

With his modest, laid-back style, Leary seems more ideal sounding board and brew partner than conventional record producer. Emphasizing the overall good-time vibe of a session, the native Texan favors creative instinct over technical precision. And his self-professed fanaticism toward guitars and amps brings a player's sensibility to recording an album. "My role totally changes from record to record," Leary says, "but I'm basically a musician, and I just try to incorporate my vision of how things are supposed to sound with what other people want and are capable of."

Leary was a model match for the Meat Puppets, not only appreciating their stoner aesthetic but helping the band realize a more focused, forceful sound. But he resists credit, saying that working with the group was a dream come true. "I worshipped the Meat Puppets—I probably wouldn't have been in a band if it weren't for them," Leary says. "They're a blast to work with, too, and they know what they're doing. I think every guitar track was a first take."

As a veteran of unlikely recording situations, Leary isn't persnickety about his surroundings or gear. The homespun Johnston album—on which Leary arranged the songs and played various instruments, and engineered the tracks on ADAT—was "a true unplugged record," Leary says. "We had to unplug the meat freezer in his parents' garage to record the vocals."

With the Butthole Surfers, Leary helped concoct some of rock's most notorious albums on the fly. The band recorded 1987's *Locust Abortion Technician* in a house near Athens, Georgia, where the group was living at the time, tracking on an archaic Ampex 1-inch, 15-ips, 8-track tube tape machine. "We were doing bizarre, stupid things—like cutting tracks in the bathroom—because we didn't know any better," Leary says. "But lots of things come out better that way, believe it or not."

Contact with more experienced record makers has helped Leary refine his approach, though not so much from a technical or aesthetic standpoint as from a psychological one. From former Led Zeppelin bassist John Paul Jones—who produced the Butthole Surfers' 1994 *Independent Worm Saloon*—Leary learned that a producer who acts as "a captain at the helm" can serve a band well by helping it "shrug off all the politics and expectations and keep the record a work of art."

A conversation with producer Michael Beinhorn (see entry) provided some additional philosophical insight. "Talking with him, I realized that I hadn't gotten to the core of what it means to be producer," Leary recalls. "He asks the tough questions, like 'What does a musician really want from his music?' I never wanted to think about stuff like that, but now I see the worth in it."

The key thing his own experience has taught Leary about making records is that "you just never know what people are going to like. You do something you think is great, and people hate it. And you work on something and think you're struggling, and people end up loving it. That's still a mystery to me. It's like tossing bones."

—BRADLEY BAMBARGER

Bad Livers: *Delusions of Banjer*, Quaterstick, 1992 • "Dancing Days," Safe House, 1993 (*The Song Retains the Name, Volume II*).

Butthole Surfers: *Electriclarryland*, Capitol, 1996 • "The Lord Is a Monkey," Geffen, 1996 (*Beavis and Butt-head Do America* soundtrack).

Johnston, Daniel: *Fun*, Atlantic, 1994.

Leary, Paul: *The History of Dogs*, Rough Trade, 1991.

Meat Puppets: "Backwater," London, 1994 • *Too High to Die*, London, 1994 • *No Joke!* London, 1995.

Refreshments, The: *The Bottle and Fresh Horses*, Mercury, 1997.

Sublime: *Sublime*, MCA, 1996 • *Second Hand Smoke*, MCA, 1997 • *What I Got* (EP), MCA, 1997.

Supersuckers: "Born with a Tail," Sub Pop, 1995 • *Sacrilicious Sounds*, Sub Pop, 1995.

Toadies: "Paper Dress," Miramax/Hollywood, 1996 (*The Crow City of Angels* soundtrack).

John Leckie

"Vocals are important the way they sit in the mix," insists British producer/engineer John Leckie. "Sometimes I'll do a mix and someone says, 'Can you turn the vocal up?' And I'll say, 'No, you can't because the mix is built around that balance, and turning the vocal up throws the whole thing out of balance." Moreover, Leckie is quick to cite his favorite studio for recording vocals: EMI's Abbey Road Studios in London. Leckie calls Abbey Road one of the "figureheads of the British recording industry."

Leckie's fondness for Abbey Road is partly sentimental: He cut his teeth there during the '70s when he was an EMI staff engineer and producer. In fact, he got the job purely by happenstance. "I just wrote to all the studios in London," he says. "EMI replied and said, 'Start on Monday.' " Leckie's early assignments included John Lennon's *Plastic Ono Band*, George Harrison's *All Things Must Pass*, and Pink Floyd's *Meddle*, which Leckie calls "my first real engineering job." Leckie's other engineering credits include Paul McCartney's *Red Rose Speedway* and Mott the Hoople's *Mott*.

As a producer, Leckie hit his stride in the mid- to late '70s with a string of albums by Bill Nelson's Be-Bop Deluxe, including *Futurama*, *Sunburst Finish* (No. 17 U.K.), and *Modern Music* (No. 12 U.K.). Indeed, Leckie's work with Be-Bop Deluxe surely qualifies him for the Queen's honors list. Illustrating his penchant for the unexpected, Leckie positioned bold guitar leads alongside shimmering vocals to create a surreal effect on such classics as "Fair Exchange," "Sister Seagull," and "Ships in the Night."

After Leckie left EMI in 1978 to become an independent producer, he worked with Simple Minds, XTC, Magazine (the classic *Real Life*), Let's Active, the Stone Roses (the neo-'60s milestone *The Stone Roses*, with six

Top 40 hits in the U.K.) the Posies, Radiohead (*The Bends*, No. 6 U.K.), the Fall, Ride (*Carnival of Light*, No. 5 U.K.), the Verve, and Cast (*All Change*, No. 7 U.K.), among many others. That impressive collection of guitar-oriented modern rock bands underscores Leckie's preference for working with outfits that are "more inventive rather than conventional. I'm in a lucky position now where I can choose who I work with. As a producer I'm acting as a service to the band or to the artist," Leckie muses. "It's not like I'm a dictator saying 'This is the way it's going to be.' I work very much like a member of the band."

Ultimately, Leckie believes he has the best job in the world. "Every day you go in the studio and there is the opportunity to make magic," he marvels. "You might be booked in the studio for three weeks and by the time you get to the second week everyone's a little tired. I have to turn around to people and say, 'Hey, consider ourselves lucky to be doing this.' " —BEN CROMER

Adverts, The: *Crossing the Red Sea with the Adverts*, Bright, 1978.

After the Fire: *Laser Love*, Epic, 1979.

Ashkhabad: *City of Love*, Realworld/Caroline, 1993.

Be-Bop Deluxe: *Modern Music*, Harvest, 1976 • "Ships in the Night," Harvest, 1976 • *Sunburst Finish*, Harvest, 1976 • *Live in the Air Age*, Harvest, 1977 • *Drastic Plastic*, Harvest, 1978.

Cast: "Alright," Mother/Island, 1995 (*Mission: Impossible* soundtrack) • "Finetime," Polydor, 1995 • "Sandstorm," Polydor, 1995 • *All Change*, Polydor, 1996.

Cowboy Junkies: *Miles from Our Home*, Geffen, 1998.

Cuban Heels: *Cuban Heels*, Virgin, 1981.

Curve: "On the Wheel," American, 1995 (*The Doom Generation* soundtrack).

Doctors of Madness: *Figments of Emancipation*, Polydor, 1976 • *Doctors of Madness*, United Artists, 1978.

Doll, The: *Listen to the Silence*, Beggars Banquet, 1977.

Dukes of the Stratosphear: *Chips from the Chocolate Fireball (Anthology)*, Geffen, 1987 • *Psonic Psunspot*, Geffen, 1987 • "Vanishing Girl," Geffen, 1987.

Fall, The: *The Wonderful and Frightening World of the Fall*, Beggars Banquet/PVC, 1984 • "Spoilt Victorian Child," Beggars Banquet, 1985 (*One Pound Ninety-Nine*) • *This Nation's Saving Grace*, Beggars Banquet/PVC, 1985 • *Bend Sinister*, Beggars Banquet, 1986 • *The Domesday Pay-Off*, Big Time, 1987 • *458489 A Sides*, Beggars Banquet, 1990 • *458489 B Sides*, Beggars Banquet, 1990.

Felt: *Absolute Classic Masterpieces*, Futurist, 1992.

Gene Loves Jezebel: *Desire* (EP), Relativity, 1983 • *Immigrant*, Beggars Banquet, 1985 • "Worth Waiting For," Beggars Banquet, 1985 (*One Pound Ninety-Nine*).

Ginger: *Ginger* (EP), Nettwerk, 1994.

Grapes of Wrath: "I Am Here," Capitol, 1991 • *These Days*, Capitol, 1991.

Harper, Roy: *One of These Days in England*, Chrysalis, 1977 • *Bullinamingvase*, Harvest/Chrysalis, 1978.

Hitchcock, Robyn, and the Egyptians: *Respect*, A&M, 1993 • "The Yip Song," A&M, 1993 • *Greatest Hits*, A&M, 1996.

House of Freaks: *Tantilla*, Rhino, 1989.

Human League: *Travelogue*, Virgin, 1980.

Kula Shaker: *K*, Columbia, 1996 • *Summer Sun* (EP), Columbia, 1997.

Let's Active: *Every Dog Has His Day*, IRS, 1988.

Lilac Time: *And Love for All*, Fontana, 1990.

Lucy Show: *Mania*, Big Time, 1986 • "Land and Life," Big Time, 1987 (*Big Noise from Bigtime*).

Magazine: *Real Life*, Virgin, 1978 • *Rays and Hail*, Virgin, 1987 • *Scree (Rarities, 1978–1981)*, Blue Plate, 1991.

McGough, Roger: *A Summer with Monika*, Island, 1977.

Nelson, Bill: *Sound on Sound*, Harvest, 1979 • *Quit Dreaming and Get on the Beam*, Cocteau/Enigma, 1981, 1989 • *The Love That Whirls (Diary of a Thinking Heart)*, Cocteau/Enigma, 1982, 1989 • *Getting the Holy Ghost Across*, Portrait, 1986.

Owen, Mark: *Green Man*, RCA, 1996.

Partridge, Mr.: *Take Away*, Virgin, 1980.

Posies, The: *Dear 23*, DGC, 1990 • *Suddenly Mary* (EP), DGC, 1991.

Proof: *It's Safe*, Nemperor, 1980.

Radiohead: *My Iron Lung* (EP), EMI, 1994 • "Fake Plastic Trees," Capitol, 1995 (*Clueless* soundtrack) • *The Bends*, Capitol, 1995.

Ride: *Carnival of Light*, Sire/Reprise, 1994.

Silencers, The: *Dance to the Holy Man*, RCA, 1991.

Simple Minds: *Life in a Day*, Zoom, 1979 • *Real to Real Cacophony*, Zoom, 1979 • *Empires and Dance*, Arista, 1980.

Stone Roses: "Fool's Gold," Silvertone, 1989 • "She Bangs the Drum," Silvertone, 1989 • *The Stone Roses*, Silvertone, 1989 • "One Love/Something's Burning," Silvertone, 1990 • "I Wanna Be Adored," Silvertone, 1991 • "I Am the Resurrection," Silvertone, 1992 • *Turns to Stone*, Silvertone, 1992 • "Waterfall," Silvertone, 1992 • *The Complete*, Silvertone, 1995.

Thee Hypnotics: *Soul, Glitter and Sin*, Beggars Banquet/RCA, 1991.

Trash Can Sinatras: *Cake*, Go!, 1990.

Verve, The: *A Storm in Heaven*, Vernon Yard, 1993 • "Blue," Vernon Yard, 1993 • *No Come Down (B sides and Outtakes)*, Vernon Yard, 1993 • "Already There," American, 1995 (*The Doom Generation* soundtrack).

White, Andy: *Teenage*, Cooking Vinyl, 1997.

XTC: *3D* (EP), Virgin, 1978 • *Go 2*, Virgin, 1978 • *White Music*, Virgin, 1978 • *Beeswax: Some B Sides, 1977–1982*, Virgin,

1982 • *Waxworks: Some Singles, 1977–1982*, DGC, 1984 • *Compact XTC: The Singles, 1978–1985*, Virgin, 1985 • *Rag and Bone Buffet*, Geffen, 1990.

Bunny Lee

(EDWARD "STRIKER" LEE)

"**J**amaica's greatest producer" reads the not exactly humble credit on one of his discs, though the same title could be argued at different times for Byron Lee, Lee Perry, Coxsone Dodd, or Duke Reid (see entries). Bunny Lee's first work in the music business was for Reid, and his earliest productions came in the rock-steady era for the Caltone and WIRL labels. One thing the Duke must have schooled him in was using the best musicians. From a late '60s lineup that included stellar players like Gladdy Anderson on piano, Bobby Aitken on guitar, and a full horn complement, including "Dizzy" Johnny Moore, Vin Gordon, Val Bennett, and Lester Sterling, to his later work with the Aggrovators and others, Lee knew how to build a crisp track that held your interest.

Lee also got his hands on some of Jamaica's best vocal talent. Superbly gifted crooner Slim Smith and the amazingly soulful and wild Roy Shirley worked for him in the late '60s; distinctive roots singers Johnny Clarke and Cornell Campbell were regulars in the mid-'70s. His early productions include refined jazzy instrumentals, reggae covers of American soul hits, and startlingly original sounds like Stranger Cole's "Bangarang" and the Uniques' "Beatitude."

He produced Max Romeo's first album, an uneven mix of sufferer's tunes like "Rent Crisis" and "Two Faced People," and slackness (among the lowest: "I Woke Up in a Love Orgy" and "Pussy Watch Man"). He also scored a major underground hit in the U.K. with Romeo's naughty "Wet Dream" and the follow-up album. Val Bennett cut a version of the Dave Brubeck smash "Take Five" that made it a reggae standard, and his late '60s recording of Bob Marley and the Wailers' "Mr. Chatterbox" preceded their international fame.

But it was his '70s productions that helped define the militant rockers era with a sound that came to be called (because of his heavy-on-the-high-hat productions) "flying cymbals." His own labels—Lee's, Jackpot, and Justice—and the English Attack, Third World, and others, spewed out hundreds—possibly thousands—of 7-inch

singles not listed here. Though you wouldn't know it by what's available in the U.S. today, Bunny "Striker" Lee was one Jamaica's most prolific producers.

One good reason was his use of the legendary Osbourne "King Tubby" Ruddick, the electronic wizard and mixing engineer who single-handedly created dub (then handed it over to a series of hands-on trained students like Scientist, Phillip Smart, and Prince Jammy; see entry). Tubby mixed a seemingly endless number of 7-inch flip sides and dub versions for Lee and other producers, but a surprising number of the best King Tubby dubs, on albums or B-side 45s, are Bunny Lee productions. The combination of Ruddick's echo-laden track deconstruction and Lee's Aggro-active riddims—with ghostly wisps of vocals, relentless bass and drum, and isolated instruments swathed in echo and reverb and pulled in and out of the mix—are among reggae's finest moments. Though Tubby worked his magic with many producers, including Augustus Pablo, Lee Perry, and Niney the Observer (see entry), his work with Bunny Lee is what dub is all about. Similarly, singer John Holt, who made outstanding records with nearly every great Jamaican producer, had a giant early hit with Lee ("Stick by Me") and went on to record over a half-dozen albums with him. Besides his solo work, Slim Smith also cut many sides for Lee as lead singer of the Uniques (with Jimmy Riley and Lloyd Charmers backing).

In the '70s, now considered the golden age of reggae, Lee produced an impressive number of top Jamaican hits, kicking off with "Cherry Oh Baby" by Eric Donaldson and Delroy Wilson's "Better Must Come." "Cherry Oh" won the Jamaica Song Festival competition and was later covered by the Rolling Stones and the U.K.'s neo-reggae UB40. In addition, Lee had a knack for producing roots classics like Jah Frankie (Jones)'s sublime "Satta and Praise Jah" and an incredible succession of rockers-style "deep roots" singles for the distinctive vocalist Johnny Clarke.

"None Shall Escape the Judgment in This Time," written by Earl Zero, was Clarke's first record for Bunny Lee, for whom he cut the penetrating "Move Out of Babylon (Rastaman)," the cool but deadly "Cold I Up," and over 20 albums! Another singer who recorded profusely for Lee was Cornell Campbell, whose upper range suited Curtis Mayfield (see entry) covers or conscious originals like "Press Along Natty Dread." According to Clarke, Lee played his artists off against each other to get the best from each.

Bunny Lee's main studio band, the Aggrovators, featured the "best in a the business" like guitarist Chinna Smith and drummer Sly Dunbar, and they laid down some of the wickedest rhythms in reggae. It's said Sly and Robbie (Shakespeare; see Sly and Robbie entry) first worked together on an early Bunny Lee session. Lee returned to his instrumental roots with solo albums from regular session hornmen Tommy McCook and Bobby Ellis, featuring dub reggae backing (reusing the same tracks on which they'd underscored his singers).

Unlike many Jamaican producers, Striker didn't own his own studio until late in the game. Early recordings were done at Dynamic with Syd Bucknor on the board. By 1976, Sly and Robbie laid backing tracks for him at Channel One as the Revolutionaries. Voicing was usually done at Tubby's home mixing studio. In the early '80s, he also used Joe Gibbs' studio before finally setting up his own Striker Lee studio in Duhaney Park.

One kind of cool thing about Lee was he always seemed to keep a camera around. "Casual" shots (often Lee seems to be the only one posing) abound on back and sometimes even front cover photos—Campbell, Wilson, or Clarke with a girl or in front of a car (sometimes with a girl in front of a car); Lee with the engineers, singers, and hangers-on in the studio, lounging on a blanket in the yard or proudly posing with his family—a kind of visual recording that runs parallel to the records and provides an unusual documentation of those studio days. In the same way his recordings, mixing pop elements with hard rhythms, sweet singing, and deep-rooted unrest, preserve a Jamaica that, sadly, no longer exists.

In later years—the early '80s—the "riddim twins" cut Lee's tracks as Sly and Robbie before moving on to their own productions. Among the many artists he produced are DJs Dr. Alimantado, Big Joe, Dillinger, Clint Eastwood (not the movie star), I Roy, and Tapper (or Tappa) Zukie, who went on to become a well-known producer in his own right (see entry). Singers include Ken Boothe, Linval Thompson, and Jackie Edwards. He also cut albums with Don Carlos after that singer left Black Uhuru (prior to the recording of their first album) and before he returned to sing lead for the group again in the '90s.

"Striker" Lee also had a knack for bringing back artists who'd had hits in the past, often remaking their best-known songs in the constantly changing current style. At one point, it seemed, almost every major artist had redone their "Twenty Massive Hits" for Mr. Lee. Covering their own hits for Lee or other producers, these albums—like similar recordings done in the United States by Chuck Berry and Little Richard—may not be as satisfying as the originals, but they helped pay the rent and kept the artist in the public eye.

But Lee was not just a "do-over man." The soulful Delroy Wilson did great original work for him, as did

the incomparably edgy Leroy Smart (including his first album, with the generic Lee title "Super Star") and singer/songwriter Owen Grey. A decade after his first hits with Lee, Johnny Clarke cut a series of solid albums for him again, as did Cornell Campbell, despite the fact that his partings with artists were often notoriously rancorous. In recent years, Lee has limited his activity in the music business to licensing his productions to labels in France and Portugal. At present, a dubby instrumental album by the Aggrovators is his lone available stateside release. —CHUCK FOSTER

Aggrovators, The: *Aggrovators: Rasta Dub '76,* Attack, 1976 • *Aggrovators Meets the Revolutionaries at Channel One Studios,* Gorgon Records, 1977 • *Aggrovators Meets the Revolutionaries Part Two,* Micron, 1977 • *Aggrovators: Kaya Dub,* Attack, 1978 • *Aggrovators: Johnny in the Echo Chamber, Dubwise Selection, 1975–1976,* Attack, 1989 • "Aggrovators and King Tubby's: Dub Jackpot," Attack, 1990 • *Dub Justice,* Attack, 1990 • *Instrumental Reggae,* RAS, 1992 • "Black Unity," RAS, 1994 (*The Real Authentic Sampler 3*) • *See also* McCook, Tommy; Albums.

Alcapone, Dennis: *Guns Don't Argue,* Trojan, 1971 • *Investigator Rock,* Third World, 1977.

Andy, Horace: *Sings for You and I,* Clocktower, 1995 • *Twenty Incredible Hits,* Clocktower, n.d. • *See also* Collections.

Beenie Man: *All the Best,* JA, 1995.

Boothe, Ken: *Rock on Love,* JA, 1995.

Brown, Barry: *Superstar,* Bunny Lee, c. 1975 • *Showcase,* Third World, 1977 • *Step It Up Youthman,* Third World, 1979 • *The Best Of,* Culture Press, 1984 • *See also* Clarke, Johnny.

Campbell, Al: *Ain't That Loving You,* Jamaica Sound, 1989.

Campell, Cornell: *Ropin',* Third World, n.d. • *Cornell Campbell,* Trojan, 1973 • *Gorgon,* Angen, 1976 • *Yes I Will,* Micron, 1979 • *What's Happening to Me,* Joe Gibbs, 1982 • *Boxing,* Starflight, c. 1982 • *Fight Against Corruption,* Vista, 1983 • *The New Boss,* Lee's, 1984 • *20 Magnificent Hits,* Striker Lee, 1989 • *See also* Clarke, Johnny; Collections

Carlos, Don: *Pass Me the Lazer Beam,* Lagoon, 1983, 1995 • *Pure Gold,* Vista, 1983 • *Time Is the Master,* RAS, 1992 • *RAS Portraits,* RAS, 1997.

Clarke, Johnny: *Sings in Fine Style,* Clocktower, n.d. • *Lovers Rock Volume Five,* Third World, c. 1970 • *Enter Into His Gates With Praise,* Attack, 1974 • *Showcase,* Third World, c. 1975 • *Superstar,* Jackpot, c. 1975 • *Authorized Version,* Virgin, 1976 • *Rockers Time Now,* Virgin, 1976 • *Out of the Past,* World Enterprise, c. 1978 • *Sweet Conversation,* Third World, 1978 • *Wondering,* Imperial, 1978 • *Satisfaction,* Third World, 1979 • *I Man Come Again,* Black Music, 1982 • w/ Cornell Campbell, *Johnny Clarke Meets Cornell Campbell,* Vista, 1983 • *Reggae Party,* Vista, 1984 • *Sly and*

Robbie Present the Best of Johnny Clarke, Vista, 1985 • *20 Massive Hits,* Striker Lee/JA, 1985 • *Don't Trouble Trouble,* Attack, 1989 • *Authorized Rockers,* Virgin, 1991 • w/ Barry Brown, *Sings Roots and Culture,* Roots Records, 1992 • *Originally Mr.Clarke,* Clocktower, 1995 • *Roots Music,* JA, 1995 • *Rock With Me Baby,* JA, 1996.

Dillinger: *Dillinger Superstar,* Weed Beat, 1977 • *Top Ranking Dillinger,* Third World, 1978 • *Ranking Hard Core Dillinger,* Third World, 1978 • *3 Piece Suit,* Lagoon, 1993.

Donaldson, Eric: "Cherry Oh Baby," Trojan, 1971 • *Eric Donaldson,* Jaguar, 1971 • *Keep on Riding,* Dynamic, 1975.

Eastwood, Clint: *Jah Lights Shining,* Jamaica Sound, 1984 • *Step It Ina Zion!* Third World, n.d.

Edwards, Jackie: *Come to Me Softly,* Third World, 1979• *In Paradise,* Trojan, 1995 • *Escape,* JA, 1995.

Ellis, Bobby: *Bobby Ellis and the Professionals Meet the Revolutionaries,* Third World, 1977.

Ellis, Hortense: w/ Derrick Morgan, *Still in Love,* Conflict, n.d. • *The Queen of Rockers,* Imperial, n.d. • *Queen of Reggae Music,* JA, 1995.

Faith, George: *Bunny Lee Presents Soulful George Faith,* Hollywood, n.d.

Gray, Owen: *None of Jah-Jah's Children Shall Ever Suffer,* Imperial, n.d. • *Forward on the Scene,* Trojan, 1978 • *See also* Romeo, Max.

Heptones: "Give Me the Right," Micron, 1990 (*Reflections on Rock Steady*).

Holt, John: *Holt,* Dynamic, 1973 • *Still in Chains,* Dynamic/JA, 1973 • *Pledging My Love,* Striker Lee, 1975 • *Super Star,* Weed Beat, 1976 • *World of Love,* Weed Beat, 1977 • *Just a Country Boy,* Trojan, 1978 • *Here I Come Again,* Rohit, 1990 • *Treasure of Love,* Sonic Sounds, 1995.

I Roy: *Can't Conquer Rasta,* Justice, 1976 • *Crisis Time,* Virgin, 1976, 1998 • *Dread Baldhead,* Klik, 1976 • *Don't Check Me With No Lightweight Stuff,* Blood and Fire, 1997.

Jah Stich: *Original Ragga Muffin (1975–1977),* Blood and Fire, 1996 • *See also* Collections.

Jones, Jah Frankie: *Satta an Praise Jah,* Third World, 1977 • *Dance Cork,* World Enterprises, c. 1982.

Kelly, Pat: *Best of,* Vista Sounds, 1983.

Marley, Bob, and the Wailers: *Early Years, 1969–1973,* Trojan, 1993 • *See also* Collections.

McCook, Tommy: w/ the Aggrovators, *King Tubby Meets the Aggrovators at Dub Station,* Attack, 1975 • *Cookin',* Trojan, 1975 • *Super Star,* Weed Beat, 1977 • *Brass Rockers,* Striker Lee, 1994 • *Cookin' Shuffle,* JA, 1995.

Mighty Diamonds: "Jah Jah Bless the Dreadlocks," Sonic Sounds/JA, c. 1975 (*Striker Lee Presents: Oldies Keep Swinging*).

Miller, Count Prince: "Mule Train," Micron, 1990 (*Reflections on Rock Steady*).

Minott, Sugar: *The Leader of the Pack,* Black Roots, 1985.

Mittoo, Jackie: *Hot Blood,* Attack, 1977 • *Showcase Volume Three,* Jackie, 1998.

Pablo, Augustus: *In Roots Vibes,* Lagoon, 1997.

Paragons, The: *The Paragons Return,* Third World, 1979.

Ricks, Glen: *Hold On,* JA, 1995.

Romeo, Max: *Every Man Ought to Know,* Impact, 1970 • w/ Owen Gray, *Max Romeo Meets Owen Gray at King Tubby's Studio,* Culture Press, 1984 • *On the Beach,* Esoldun, 1992 • *Wet Dream,* Lagoon, 1993.

Scott, Ossie: *Super Sonic Sounds,* Sonic Sounds, 1994.

Sly and Robbie: *Meet King Tubby,* Lagoon, 1997 • *See also* Collections.

Smart, Leroy: *Live Up Roots Children,* Striker Lee, 1985 • *Super Star,* Third World, 1977.

Smith, Slim: *Early Days,* Clocktower, n.d. • *Very Best Of,* Pama, n.d. • *Just a Dream,* Clocktower, 1971 • "Everybody Needs Love," Sonic Sounds/JA, c. 1975 (*Striker Lee Presents: Oldies Keep Swinging*) • *Memorial,* Trojan, 1980 • w/ John Holt, *Classic Touch,* Third World, 1985 • *Rain from the Skies,* Trojan, 1992 • *Forever,* Rhino, 1995 • *This Feeling,* JA, 1995.

Smith, Slim, and the Uniques: *Best Of, 1967–1969,* Trojan, 1994 • *My Conversation,* Lagoon, 1994.

Trinity: *Big Big Man,* Lagoon, 1995.

U Brown: *Satta Dread,* Klik, 1977.

U Roy: *Rock With I,* RAS, 1992 • *Musical Vision,* Lagoon, 1993 • *Train to Zion,* Blood and Fire, 1997 • *See also* Albums.

Uniques, The: *Absolutely the Uniques,* Clocktower, 1969 • *Showcase,* Vol. 1, Third World, 1978.

Wayne, John: *Boogie Down,* Vista, 1983.

Wilson, Delroy: *Better Must Come,* Dynamic, 1971 • *Nice Times,* Jamaica Sound, c. 1975 • *Greatest Hits,* Jaguar/JA, 1976 • *True Believer in Love,* Carib Gems, 1977 • *Who Done It,* Third World, 1979 • *Living in the Footsteps,* Joe Gibbs FLA, 1981 • *Go Away Dream,* Black Music, 1982 • *Collection,* Striker Lee, 1985 • *My Special Lady,* World Enterprises, 1989 • "Can't Explain," Micron, 1990 (*Reflections on Rock Steady*) • *Money,* Clocktower, 1995.

Zukie, Tappa: *Peace in the Ghetto,* Virgin, 1976 • *Raggamuffun,* World Enterprises, 1986 • *See also* Collections.

COLLECTIONS

Dub War: Coxsone Vs. Quaker City, Imperial, n.d.

Golden Rockers, Clocktower, n.d.: w/ Horace Andy, "Don't Try to Use Me" ˘ Cornell Campbell, "Queen of the Minstrel" ˘ Pat Kelly, "Twelfth of Never" ˘ Lloyd and Devon, "Bum Ball" ˘ Dave Parker, "Girl of Dreams."

King Tubby and the Aggrovators: Dubbing in the Back Yard, Black Music, 1982.

King Tubby Studio Vs. Channel One Studio, Bumb, c. 1975

King Tubby: Majestic Dub, Star, n.d.

Lovers Rock, Vols. 1–2, 4–5, Cardinal, n.d.

Reggae Legends, Rohit, 1990.

Sly and Robbie: Master of Ceremony Dub, Imperial, c. 1982.

Songs for Jah: Reggae's Best, Lagoon, n.d.

Striker Lee Presents: Oldies Keep Swinging, Sonic Sounds/JA, c. 1975.

Best of Reggae Volume One, Micron, c. 1978: w/ Val Bennett, Val, "Take 5" ˇ Cornell Campbell, "The Minstrel" ˇ Bob Marley and the Wailers, "Mr. Chatterbox."

Dread Locks in Jamaica, Attack, c. 1978: w/ the Aggrovators, "Hold a Dub," "Killer Dub," "Roots Dub," "Star Dub," "Tradition Dub," "West Dub" ˇ Jah Stich, "The Killer" ˇ Little Joe, "Tradion Song" ˇ U Roy, "From Piller to Post," "Natty Hold the Candle" ˇ Tappa Zukie, "Jah Is I Guiding Star."

King Tubby and the Aggrovators: Shalom Dub, Klik, 1975.

King Tubby the Dubmaster Presents the Roots of Dub, Clocktower, 1975.

King Tubby the Dubmaster, Clocktower, c. 1975.

Strictly Rockers Ina Dread Land, Live & Love, 1976.

King Tubby the Dubmaster With the Waterhouse Posse, Vista, 1983.

Sly and Robbie: The Skatalites With Sly and Robbie and the Taxi Gang, Vista Sounds, 1983.

Sly and Robbie Meet King Tubby, Esoldun, 1984, 1991.

Dub War, Vol. 1, Vista, 1985.

Jumping With Mr. Lee, 1967–1968, Trojan, 1989.

King Tubby's Special, 1973–1976, Trojan, 1989.

Now This Is What I and I Call Version, Trojan, 1989.

Reflections on Rock Steady, Micron, 1990.

Dub Gone Crazy: The Evolution of Dub at King Tubby's, Blood and Fire, 1994.

If Deejay Was Your Trade, 1974–1977, Blood and Fire, 1995.

Straight to I Roy Head, Lagoon, 1995.

Bill Leeb and Rhys Fulber

(FRONT LINE ASSEMBLY)

Bill Leeb and ofttime partner Rhys Fulber have been remarkably consistent innovators with electronic music of every hue: from tribal ambient music in the guise of Delerium, to the traditional techno of Intermix, to the bone-crunching industrial of Front Line Assembly and Noise Unit, Leeb and Fulber have pushed barriers and created excellent music.

Bill Leeb was born in Vienna, Austria, and moved to Vancouver, Canada, when he was about 15. A violin and bass player, Leeb became interested in the electronic music of Kraftwerk and Tangerine Dream in the '70s. He also felt energized by the punk and new wave of the Sex Pistols, the Clash, Wire, XTC, Killing Joke, and early Human League. Leeb and his friends cEvin Key and Ogre (Kevin Ogilvie) formed Skinny Puppy (see David Ogilvie entry) as a loud electronic alternative to what they felt to be the insipid popular music of the early '80s. Leeb, under the pseudonym "Wilhelm Schroeder," played bass with Puppy (available on the *Brap* collection) until 1986, when he decided to go his own way. He formed Front Line Assembly with Michael Balch; synthman Rhys Fulber occasionally aided the duo.

They released cassette-only albums (now available as *Total Terror Part 1* and *Total Terror II*) and other albums in the late '80s. Front Line found its sound when Balch departed and Fulber joined the group for 1990's industrial classic *Caustic Grip*. *Grip* is a punishing, percolating miasma of body beats, keyboard lines, samples, and distorted vocals railing against a fascist future in the mode of Front 242 (see entry). Assembly uses machines to caution against mechanization and drive the body into a frenzy. *Grip* varies enough rhythmically and melodically—especially on "Iceolate" and the great "Provision" (one of industrial's greatest hits)—to avoid the sameness of much of the genre (a Leeb and Fulber hallmark in any style).

Tactical Neural Implant (1992) incorporates elements of techno ("Lifeline") and trance ("The Blade") into the industrial ("Final Impact," "Mindphaser") mix and has a less-punishing feel than *Grip*, but moves the body and chills the soul as effectively. Another standard. The same year the pair debuted their *Intermix* incarnation, a trance project of beauty and weight.

In 1994 Front Line took industrial aggression to its logical conclusion by adding balls-out metal guitar (by Devin Townsend and Don Harrison) to the electronic beats and synths on *Millennium*. Though less distinctive (echoes of Ministry, Nine Inch Nails, Skinny Puppy) than other of their work, the album stomps, roars, and grinds through standouts like the title track "Division of Mind," and "Sex Offender." The duo's Noise Unit album (*Strategy of Violence,* also from 1994) similarly crushes the spleen in an enjoyably vicious manner.

In 1995 Front Line switched to Metropolis Records and released *Hard Wired,* a varied and moody exercise in post-industrial electronic music, followed by the double CD *Live Wired* in 1996. Fulber was replaced by Chris Peterson in Front Line for *Flavour of the Weak:* more excellent post-industrial music peppered with touches of trip-hop, trance, and electronica. *Re-Wind* is a nice collection of the band's work on Metropolis.

Leeb began recording ambient music at home as early as 1989. "I have a keyboard setup at home; when I was in a late-night mood with nothing else to do, I'd paint soundscapes and make sound collages," he says. Those collages—with Fulber joining in—developed into several Delerium albums. In 1997 Leeb and Fulber created their most fully realized album (in any genre) to date, in the form of Delerium's *Karma*: a wondrous album sampling exotic cultures and the recesses of time. Reminiscent of but transcending the time-and-culture shifting of Dead Can Dance and Enigma, Delerium's tribal and chant symphonies are sublime, with sneaky verse-chorus-verse structure hidden inside. In fact, after exploring every manner of beat- and riff-driven music, Leeb and Fulber have taken to writing great songs. Aided by the voices and words of Sarah McLachlan (an elegant "Silence"), Kristy Thirsk (the gorgeous "Enchanted," "Wisdom," "Till the End of Time"), and the sampled voice of Dead Can Dance's Lisa Gerrard (the ethereal "Forgotten Worlds"), *Karma* delivers one soul-satisfying song after another.

Leeb and Fulber continue to deliver the goods as they roll through various permutations of electronic music; from the early pre-sampler days with primitive drum machines and analog synths, to the cutting-edge digital present, they have made music for the love of creating it. "We're like wild birds, we just fly around making music," says Leeb. —ERIC OLSEN

Cyberaktif: "Nothing Stays," Wax Trax!, 1990 • "Temper," Wax Trax!, 1990 • *Tenebrae Vision,* Wax Trax!, 1990.

Delerium: *Faces, Forms and Illusions,* Dossier, 1989 • *Morpheus,* Dossier, 1989 • *Syrophenikan,* Dossier, 1990 • *Euphoric,* Third Mind, 1991 • *Spiritual Archives,* Dossier, 1991 • *Stone Tower,* Dossier, 1991 • "Flowers Become Screens," Nettwerk, 1994 • "Incantation," Nettwerk, 1994 • *Semantic Spaces,* Nettwerk, 1994 • *Spheres,* Dossier, 1994 • *Spheres II,* Dossier, 1994 • *Karma,* Nettwerk, 1997.

Fear Factory: *Fear Is the Mindkiller* (EP, remix), Roadrunner, 1993.

Front Line Assembly: *Total Terror Part 1,* Cleopatra, 1986, 1993 • *The Initial Command,* Third Mind/KK, 1987 • *Total Terror II,* Cleopatra, 1987, 1994 • *Corroded Disorder,* Wax Trax!, 1988 • *Gashed Senses and Crossfire,* Wax Trax!, 1988 • *State of Mind,* Dossier/Cleopatra, 1988 • *Caustic Grip,* Wax Trax!, 1989 • "Digital Tension Dementia," Wax Trax!, 1989 • "Isolate," Wax Trax!, 1990 • "Provision," Wax Trax!, 1990 • "Virus," Wax Trax!, 1991 • *Tactical Neural Implant,* Third Mind, 1992 • "The Blade," Third Mind, 1992 • "Millenium," Roadrunner, 1994 • *Millenium,* Roadrunner, 1994 • "Circuitry," Metropolis, 1995 • *Hard Wired,* Metropolis, 1995 • "Surface Patterns," Roadrunner,

1995 • *Live Wired,* Metropolis, 1996 • "Plasticity," Metropolis, 1996 • *Colombian Necktie* (EP), Metropolis, 1997 • *Reclamation,* Roadrunner, 1997 • "Comatose," Metropolis, 1998 • w/ Bill Leeb, *Cryogenic Studios,* Cleopatra, 1998 • *Flavour of the Weak,* Metropolis, 1998 • *Re-Wind,* Metropolis, 1998.

Holophonia: *Psych-O-Range,* Cleopatra, 1997.

Intermix: *Intermix,* Third Mind, 1992 • *Phaze Two,* Third Mind, 1993 • *Ambient Intermix,* Instinct, 1994.

Noise Unit: *Grinding into Emptiness,* Wax Trax!, 1989 • *Resonance Frequency,* Dossier, 1990 • *Strategy of Violence,* Cleopatra, 1994 • *Decoder,* Dossier/Cleopatra, 1996 • *Drill,* Offbeat/Metropolis, 1997.

Penal Colony: *5 Man Job* (5 tracks), Cleopatra, 1995.

Synaesthesia: *Desideratum,* Hypnotic, 1995 • *Embody,* Cleopatra, 1995 • *Ephemeral,* Cleopatra, 1997.

Kyle Lehning

It's hard to believe now, but Kyle Lehning's first attempt to find employment in Nashville ended in disaster. It was 1971, he was fresh out of college, and no one was willing to take a chance on him. "I was sweeping out a recording studio for free, playing a bit on a few demos, and trying to get some kind of work somewhere. I couldn't get a job anywhere; I couldn't get a job as a second engineer or a janitor."

Instead, Lehning headed toward the unlikely outpost of Jackson, Mississippi. "There was a recording studio in

Jackson that needed a young, hungry engineer and I was both. So my wife, our 6-month-old baby, and I just packed up and took off. I was making $119 a week, I was thrilled. It was an amazingly serendipitous time for me to go down there, just pack up and go. It really was one of the most important moves that I ever made."

Lehning was only in Jackson for a few months before he came back to Nashville to work at Glaser Sound Studio, where he was an engineer for more than four years, working on projects by Waylon Jennings, Dr. Hook, Kenny Rogers, Jessi Colter, and many others. However, his work with author/songwriter/singer Shel Silverstein formed the basis for the producer he would soon become. "Up until the time I encountered him, I felt like a singer was an excuse for a bunch of musicians to get together, because instrumental music had always been important to me and I just didn't really get the singing part," he says. "Working with Shel, I paid attention to every syllable. He forced me to have an opinion about what was happening with a lyric. That was probably the biggest shift in becoming more competent as a music maker."

As he shifted into production work, Lehning began working with a number of pop acts, including Firefall and England Dan and John Ford Coley, for whom he produced a number of major hits, including "I'd Really Love to See You Tonight" (No. 2), "Nights Are Forever Without You" (No. 10), and "It's Sad to Belong."

His work with the duo in 1976 started a long association with Dan Seals (aka England Dan) that helped Lehning segue into country music. Together Seals and Lehning had a string of hit albums and singles, including "Bop" (No. 1 country), "They Rage On" (No. 5 country), "Addicted" (No. 1 country), and one of Lehning's favorite songs, "Everything That Glitters (Is Not Gold)" (No. 1 country). "I'm so proud of that song because it was one of those things that didn't have any of the trappings of hit records. It didn't fit any of the categories, it just had a heartfelt story honestly told instead of being full of big hooks," Lehning says. "As a producer, it was more framing a really neat story instead of just putting on the next effect and to try to keep those listeners glued to their radios and jumping out of their cars to buy the record."

When one listens to Lehning's work with Randy Travis, whom he has produced since Travis's first Warner Bros. album, the seminal Storms of Life, it's hard to believe that Lehning ever considered vocals anything other than paramount. "When I started making country records, the voice was everything," he says. "Everything else was secondary, and that wasn't an easy shift to make, but I learned. . . . With Randy, I knew he was as

interesting a singer as I'd ever heard or worked with, and that he was absolutely unshakably centered when it came to what he wanted to do, and that was all I knew."

What he couldn't have known was that he and Travis (and Keith Stegall [see entry] who produced two cuts on the multiplatinum Storms) were making country music history and ushering in the new country movement with Travis's traditionalist style. "When Storms was all done and mixed, Randy and I sat in the control room, just the two of us, listening back to the album, the whole thing from top to bottom. I looked over at him and said, 'You know, I think that's a real good record. Maybe if we sell 40,000 units, they'll let us make another one,' and he said, 'that would be good,' " he recalls with a sweet laugh. "And then Randy went to the Nashville Palace [restaurant] to fry catfish and I went out there to try to figure out what to do next."

Lehning's success with Travis, Seals, Ronnie Milsap, Baillie and the Boys, Cheryl Wheeler, and several other acts led to his being recruited to head Asylum Records in Nashville, where he is co-president. "I think it's very difficult for me to balance both jobs," he says. "I've been doing this for five years now and I'm still trying to learn a way to do it that gets the best out of me and I'm not sure I'm there yet. But, you know, the adventure of being part of a record company is worth the price I'm paying. It's easier to produce someone who's not on my label. I feel less responsible and therefore freer, less concerned with the results and more concerned with the moment, and I think that's the best way to make music."

Not that Lehning hasn't had success with artists on his own roster, most notably with superstar-in-the-making Bryan White, whom he produces with Billy Joe Walker Jr. White's biggest hit has been a beautiful, when-will-I-find-love ballad "Someone Else's Star" (No. 1 country). "I had heard the song, and [independently] Bryan had heard it," Lehning says. "We said, 'This is a beautiful song, we should try this,' before he was actually signed to the label. Billy Joe and I were in the studio with Bryan and we recorded it on an analog 24-track tape with Billy on guitar. That's the one that's on the record. We built the band around the performance."

That 24-track analog machine is one of Lehning's prize possessions. "I still record all my basic tracks on it," he says. "I try to do all the lead and background vocals in analog. I just interface with it better. It sounds more like the person I'm working with."

Lehning knows he's using analog in a primarily digital world. "I feel like a dinosaur, and I think the dinosaurs died because whoever was manufacturing dinosaur food decided there was something better out there, but the dinosaurs couldn't eat it," he jokes.

"Every time you turn around there's another analog tape company that's gone out of business."

For all his warmth and charm, Lehning says that when it comes to playing psychologist in the studio, he can be found lacking. "Frankly, I don't think I'm very good at that," he confesses. "There are some artists who I just would not work well with because they demand too much bolstering and I don't bolster well. I'm there because I believe in the artist, and I try not to be in the studio with the faint of heart. That's just not part of my makeup. I don't try to force things, I just try to keep the windows and the doors open so the good stuff will just flow through." —MELINDA NEWMAN

Baillie and the Boys: "Long Shot," RCA, 1988 • "(I Wish I Had a) Heart of Stone," RCA, 1989 • "I Can't Turn the Tide," RCA, 1989 • "She Deserves You," RCA, 1989 • "Fool Such As I," RCA, 1990 • *Lights of Home,* RCA, 1990 • "Perfect," RCA, 1990 • *The Best Of,* RCA, 1991 • "Treat Me Like a Stranger," RCA, 1991.

Bare, Bobby: *Sleeper Wherever,* CBS, 1979.

Barnett, Mandy: "A Simple I Love You," Asylum, 1996 • *Mandy Barnett,* Asylum, 1996 • "Maybe," Asylum, 1996 • "Now That's All Right with Me," Asylum, 1996.

Brother Phelps: "Any Way the Wind Blows," Asylum, 1995 • *Any Way the Wind Blows,* Asylum, 1995 • "Not So Different After All," Asylum, 1995.

Caldwell, Bobby: *August Moon,* Sindrome, 1991.

Davis, Stephanie: "It's All in the Heart," Asylum, 1993.

Day, Curtis: *Curtis Day,* Asylum, 1996.

England Dan and John Ford Coley: "I'd Really Like to See You Tonight," Big Tree, 1976 • "Nights Are Forever Without You," Big Tree, 1976 • *Nights Are Forever,* Big Tree, 1976 • *Dowdy Ferry Road,* Big Tree, 1977 • "Gone Too Far," Big Tree, 1977 • "It's Sad to Belong," Big Tree, 1977 • *Some Things Don't Come Easy,* Big Tree, 1978 • "We'll Never Have to Say Goodbye," Big Tree, 1978 • *Dr. Heckle and Mr. Jive,* Big Tree, 1979 • "Love Is the Answer," Big Tree, 1979.

Firefall: *Clouds Across the Sun,* Atlantic, 1979 • *Undertow,* Atlantic, 1979 • *Greatest Hits,* Rhino, 1992.

Hunley, Con: "Nobody Ever Gets Enough Love," Capitol, 1985 • "Blue Suede Shoes," Capitol, 1986.

Jones, George: *And Along Came Jones,* MCA, 1991 • *Friends in High Places,* Epic, 1991 • "You Couldn't Get the Picture," MCA, 1991 • "Honky Tonk Myself to Death," MCA, 1992 • "She Loved a Lot in Her Time," MCA, 1992.

McCoy, Neal: *Be Good at It,* Atlantic, 1997 • *Greatest Hits,* Atlantic Nashville, 1997 • "If You Can't Be Good (Be Good at It)," Atlantic, 1997 • "The Shake," Atlantic, 1997 • "Love Happens Like That," Atlantic, 1998 • "Party On," Atlantic, 1998.

McGee, Parker: *Parker McGee,* Big Tree, 1980.

Milsap, Ronnie: *Heart and Soul,* RCA, 1987 • w/ Kenny Rogers, "Make No Mistake, She's Mine," RCA, 1987 • "Snap Your Fingers," RCA, 1987 • "Where Do the Nights Go?," RCA, 1988 • *Greatest Hits,* Vol. 3, RCA, 1991.

Murray, Anne: "Slow Passin' Time," Capitol, 1988.

Nesler, Mark: *I'm Just That Way,* Asylum, 1998 • "Used to the Pain," Asylum, 1998.

Off Broadway U.S.A.: *Quick Turns,* Atlantic, 1980.

Osmond, Marie: w/ Dan Seals, "Meet Me in Montana," Capitol, 1985 • *The Best Of,* Curb, 1990 • *There's No Stopping Your Heart,* Curb, 1990.

Powers, Tom: *Love and Learn,* Big Tree, 1977.

Rogers, Kenny: *Greatest Hits,* EMI America, 1980 • *I Prefer the Moonlight,* RCA, 1987 • *Decade of Hits,* Warner Bros., 1997.

Seals, Dan: *Stones,* Atlantic, 1977 • *Harbinger,* Atlantic, 1980 • *Rebel Heart,* Liberty, 1982 • "My Baby's Got Good Timing," EMI, 1984 • "My Old Yellow Car," EMI, 1985 • "Bop," EMI America, 1986 • "Everything That Glitters (Is Not Gold)," EMI America, 1986 • *On the Front Line,* EMI America, 1986 • "I Will Be There," EMI America, 1987 • *The Best Of,* Liberty, 1987 • "Three Time Loser," EMI America, 1987 • "You Still Move Me," EMI America, 1987 • "Addicted," Capitol, 1988 • "One Friend," Capitol, 1988 • *Rage On,* Capitol Nashville, 1988 • "Big Wheels in the Moonlight," Capitol, 1989 • "They Rage On," Capitol, 1989 • "Bordertown," Capitol, 1990 • "Good Times," Capitol, 1990 • "Love on Arrival," Capitol, 1990 • *Early Dan Seals,* Liberty, 1991 • *Greatest Hits,* Capitol, 1991 • "Sweet Little Shoe," Warner Bros., 1991 • "Water Under the Bridge," Capitol, 1991 • "Mason Dixon Line," Warner Bros., 1992 • "When Love Comes Around the Bend," Warner Bros., 1992.

Stegall, Keith: "Whatever Turns You On," Epic, 1984 • "California," Epic, 1985 • *Keith Stegall,* Epic, 1985 • "Pretty Lady," Epic, 1985 • "I Think I'm in Love," Epic, 1986.

Thunder: *Headphones for Cows,* Atco, 1981 • *Thunder,* Atco, 1983.

Travis, Randy: "Diggin' Up Bones," Warner Bros., 1986 • "On the Other Hand," Warner Bros., 1986 • *Storms of Life,* Warner Bros., 1986 • *Always and Forever,* Warner Bros., 1987 • "Forever and Ever, Amen," Warner Bros., 1987 • "I Won't Need You Anymore (Always and Forever)," Warner Bros., 1987 • *Old 8 x 10,* Warner Bros., 1987 • "Promises," Warner Bros., 1987 • "Honky Tonk Moon," Warner Bros., 1988 • "I Told You So," Warner Bros., 1988 • "Too Gone Too Long," Warner Bros., 1988 • "Written in Stone," Warner Bros., 1988 • *An Old Time Christmas,* Warner Bros., 1989 • "Deeper Than the Holler," Warner Bros., 1989 • "Is It Still Over?," Warner Bros., 1989 • *No Holdin' Back,* Warner Bros., 1989, 1995 • *Old Time Christmas,* Warner Bros., 1989 • "Hard Rock Bottom of Your Heart,"

Warner Bros., 1990 • "He Walked on Water," Warner Bros., 1990 • *Heroes and Friends,* Warner Bros., 1990 • w/ George Jones, "A Few Ole Country Boys," Warner Bros., 1991 • "Forever Together," Warner Bros., 1991 • "Heroes and Friends," Warner Bros., 1991 • *High Lonesome,* Warner Bros., 1991 • "Point of Light," Warner Bros., 1991 • "Better Class of Losers," Warner Bros., 1992 • *Greatest Hits, Vols. 1–2,* Warner Bros., 1992 • "I'd Surrender All," Warner Bros., 1992 • "If I Didn't Have You," Warner Bros., 1992 • "An Old Pair of Shoes," Warner Bros., 1993 • "Before You Kill Us All," Warner Bros., 1994 • *This Is Me,* Warner Bros., 1994 • "Whisper My Name," Warner Bros., 1994 • "The Box," Warner Bros., 1995 • "This Is Me," Warner Bros., 1995 • "Are We in Trouble Now," Warner Bros., 1996 • *Full Circle,* Warner Bros., 1996 • "Would I," Warner Bros., 1996 • "Price to Pay," Warner Bros., 1997 • *Greatest #1 Hits,* Warner Bros., 1998.

Wheeler, Cheryl: *Circles and Arrows,* Philo, 1990, 1995 • *Driving Home,* Philo, 1993.

White, Bryan: *Bryan White,* Asylum, 1994 • "Eugene You Genius," Asylum, 1994 • "Look at Me Now," Asylum, 1995 • "Rebecca Lynn," Asylum, 1995 • "Someone Else's Star," Asylum, 1995 • *Between Now and Forever,* Asylum, 1996 • "I'm Not Supposed to Love You Anymore," Asylum, 1996 • "So Much for Pretending," Asylum, 1996 • "Love Is the Right Place," Asylum, 1997 • "One Small Miracle," Asylum, 1997 • *Right Place,* Asylum, 1997 • "Sittin' on Go," Asylum, 1997 • "That's Another Song," Asylum, 1997 • "Tree of Hearts," Asylum, 1998.

Wilson Brothers: *Another Night,* Atlantic, 1980.

Wynette, Tammy: *Best Loved Hits,* Epic, 1990 • w/ Randy Travis, "We're Strangers Again," Epic, 1991 • *Tears of Fire: The 25th Anniversary Collection,* Epic, 1992.

COLLECTIONS
Traveller soundtrack, Asylum, 1997.

Jerry Leiber and Mike Stoller

Producing is a young man's game, says Jerry Leiber. As the lyricist half of Leiber and Stoller, he and Mike Stoller formulated the three-minute (or two-minute) single that defined early rock 'n' roll. Brilliant songwriters—one could say their method and lucidity prefigured Lennon and McCartney—they were not the total businessmen the record industry has come to demand.

Leiber and Stoller wrote such indelible '50s, '60s, and '70s hits as "Hound Dog" (cut by Big Mama Thornton, popularized by Elvis Presley); the Coasters' "Down in Mexico," "Searchin' " (No. 3), and "Young Blood" (No. 8); the Clovers' "Love Potion #9"; Ben E. King's "Spanish Harlem" (No. 10); LaVern Baker's "Saved"; Peggy Lee's "Is That All There Is?" (No. 11); and Stealers Wheel's "Stuck in the Middle with You" (No. 6).

In the '90s, their key production is the original cast album of *Smokey Joe's Cafe,* a wildly successful revue showcasing their greatest hits. Co-produced with Atlantic Records executive Arif Mardin, the soundtrack of *Smokey Joe's Cafe* has become an international hit and helped revive their profile as songwriters, says Stoller.

"Jerry writes stories and they are visual," he says. "I write music, I collaborate. In our early stuff, it was just sort of spontaneous: a word, a note, a note, a word, a phrase, a tune, a chord, you know. We sat together, or I sat at the piano, and Jerry paced around the room. Jerry writes lyrics, I write music, and we edit each other, of course. We've been working together for 47 years now, but we always did that."

Stoller was born March 13, 1933, in Queens, New York. Leiber was born April 25, 1933, in Baltimore. They came together in Los Angeles in 1950, when Modern Records chief Lester Sill "introduced us to the cottage industry of small labels," Leiber says. It was the heyday of the independents, which were introducing vernacular styles to American pop. Art Rupe's Specialty label had Little Richard; Eddie and Leo Bihari were recording Charles Brown and Amos Milburn on Aladdin; and Sid Nathan had King. It was at King that Leiber got his first taste of the record business, working as a packing clerk on Pico Boulevard and learning tricks of the trade from Nathan's right-hand man, King A&R chief Ralph Bass (see entry).

By the time they were 20, Leiber and Stoller had placed tunes with Jimmy Witherspoon, Little Esther Phillips, Brown, Milburn, Little Willie Littlefield (the first man to sing Leiber and Stoller's classic 12-bar blues, "Kansas City"), and Ray Charles.

Their production of "Hound Dog" caught the ear of Atlantic Records, which in 1955 signed them to the first independent production deal. Their tenure with Atlantic ended in 1961, following a dispute over $18,000 Atlantic was discovered to owe them. While they got their $18,000, Leiber and Stoller lost their artists to the label—and watched as their erstwhile protégé, Phil Spector (see entry) took over their stable.

In the meantime, they did quite well with Presley,

who recorded more than 20 songs by the pair, including "Love Me," "Loving You," "Jailhouse Rock" (Stoller is sure the same man engineered Big Mama Thornton's "Hound Dog" and "Jailhouse Rock"), "Treat Me Nice," and "Trouble."

In the early '60s, they released records under their own labels, Daisy and Tiger. These stiffed. It wasn't until 1964, when they founded the legendary Red Bird label with George Goldner (see entry) that they struck gold on their own. They scored hits with the Dixie Cups ("Chapel of Love," co-produced with Ellie Greenwich and Jeff Barry; see entry), the Jelly Beans ("I Wanna Love Him So Bad," produced by Jeff Barry and Ellie Greenwich), and the Shangri-Las ("Leader of the Pack," produced by Jeff Barry and Shadow Morton; see entry). They also ran into trouble when they discovered that Goldner, the founder of such earlier labels as Roulette, Gee, Rama, and Gone, was siphoning off records and funds to support his gambling habit.

An attempt to merge Red Bird and Atlantic not only failed, it led to increasing friction between Atlantic principals Ahmet Ertegun and Jerry Wexler (see entries), according to the detailed, dramatic book *Atlantic and the Godfathers of Rock and Roll,* by Justine Picardie and Dorothy Wade.

"We were Red Bird, and we brought Goldner in," says Leiber. "We were about to go out of business. We had $18,000 in the bank. Me and Mike sat down and Mike said we better fold." They had 13 masters, too, masters they didn't know how to market. "We never learned the record business," Leiber says. "All we learned to do was make records. We didn't know how to press, distribute, or promote them."

So the two went for a drink in midtown Manhattan and ran into Old Town label founder Hymie Weiss, sitting at a table with Goldner. Weiss was blowing cigar smoke into Goldner's face and calling him a schmuck for losing control of various labels to Morris "Moishe" Levy. Word is Levy loaned Goldner gambling money and, when Goldner welshed on it, took over Goldner's labels.

When Weiss went to the bathroom, Leiber offered Goldner a promotion job. When Weiss returned, he asked what they were doing. "George says, 'We're making a deal,' " Leiber recalls. "Hymie starts laughing. George says, 'Hymie, can I have your cigar a minute?' Hymie says, 'You don't smoke.' George says, 'I do as of now.' He took the cigar out of Hymie's hand and Hymie said, 'Come on, George, don't be a schmuck.' George blew the smoke in Hymie's face and said, 'We'll see who's the schmuck now.' "

Sire chief-to-be Seymour Stein joined Goldner in the promotion of these Leiber and Stoller records, and the Red Bird run was great—but it only lasted a year. Failed negotiations with Atlantic and Goldner's George Goldner Enterprises—in effect, a parallel Red Bird whose profits accrued only to Goldner—scuttled the Red Bird enterprise. "We had this marvelous streak of hits," Leiber says. "In fact, Atlantic called us because they had gone kind of soft and they wanted to merge with us and sell to Warner Bros. We had two meetings with them; one ended up in a sort of funny bad way." Leiber suspects negotiations fell through because of Lee Eastman, an attorney who usually disliked Goldner. In this case, he became bedfellows with Goldner and, Leiber suggests, subverted the talks because he thought there would be no demand for his legal work in such a merged company.

Nevertheless, Leiber and Stoller continued to notch hits throughout the decade by such artists as Jay and the Americans, Brook Benton, Leslie Uggams, and the Exciters. In 1969, they produced Peggy Lee's recording of their "Is That All There Is?," a dramatic torch song that signaled their new, more theatrical direction.

"In terms of what we experienced, production was selection of the songs, casting of the singer with the song and casting musicians as well," says Leiber. "Sometimes, you didn't have to cast them because they were in a band, like Johnny Otis [see entry] had a band (that's Otis's band backing Big Mama Thornton on the original "Hound Dog"). When we got into more sophisticated productions, we'd hand-pick the orchestra," Leiber says. "When we got with the Coasters, it was small, but it had to be letter-perfect in terms of being able to play a certain way."

The production style varied, says Stoller. "First of all, I would think about the groups that we worked with—the Robins first, then the Coasters, the Drifters, and so on. The most important time, in a way, was the weeks of rehearsal before the recording session. With the Coasters, I would sit at the piano and work with them on setting background harmonies. Jerry would work with the lead singers, we would outline the general concept, and the ideas for the arrangement would come. I would write out the charts and I played piano on the sessions."

Despite such meticulousness, spontaneity would occasionally win. "One of the last sessions we did in Los Angeles, on 'Searchin' and 'Young Blood,' we spent most of the time on 'Young Blood' and other songs, and had about five minutes to go," Stoller says. One background singer wasn't available, so Obadiah Jesse, who was known as Young Jessie, was quickly pressed into service. Union rules limited recording to four sides in three hours, so they created "Searchin' " in a "mad dash," and it became one of the Coasters' biggest hits.

"When we started recording, it was just a short time after they'd finished cutting on wax. We started in the studio in 1950 or 1951 on mono tape. It was bouncing tape to tape and intercutting and doing all kinds of things to make it more of a plastic art," Stoller says. "If we had a great refrain, sometimes we'd duplicate it and make sure every time it came up it was just as hot as the other time by recording it onto another piece of tape and splicing it back in. We'd sometimes cut an 'S' off a word if we could keep the rhythm from jumping. When you remove a piece of tape from something, there's a possibility the rhythm will jump forward. So we'd have to find the right places to do it and jump back in."

In 1957, they began to record the Coasters at Atlantic Studios in New York, cutting tracks on an 8-track machine with engineer Tom Dowd (see entry). Stoller recalls the machine as an Ampex using inch-wide tape. "We used it as mono in the sense that we went for the performance, everybody playing at the same time. It had not reached the stage where a bass player was brought in and recorded a whole tune, then they added a drummer, then a guitar. What it enabled us to do was to fix up the vocal performance by having some empty tracks. Or, if we needed one line enunciated better, or if the harmony went off in one spot, we could punch it back in."

He and Leiber have recorded on 32 tracks, "and we've certainly done it digital," Stoller says. "As a producer, those tracks give you extra room for your really major elements, which on a song are the vocals. "Ultimately, the best stuff is when you get a real performance from beginning to end, like the go-for-broke performances we used to do on mono. If somebody flubbed in the middle, that was pretty much the end of the recording of the tune. If there are a lot of elements of salvation in multitrack, it loses spontaneity. In effect, it's a different animal. A recording is a recording and a live performance is a live performance."

"There were things we devised, like a percussion grouping called the Leiber Stoller Bag," Leiber says. "It was a combination of four or five Brazilian drums with skins, drums of different sizes that were played by hand or with big sticks. This was a variation of a samba, called a baion. It had an incredibly infectious beat"— Leiber goes "dunk da dunk da dunk"—"and on top, a triangle playing 16th notes, then a string bass on the bottom." Not only did this "bag" figure heavily in Leiber and Stoller records, it also caught the fancy of Leiber protégé Burt Bacharach (see entry). Bacharach, Leiber says, "made pretty much of a great career in utilizing it in almost every record he made with Dionne Warwick."

Dionne Warwick, with Dee Dee Warwick and Cissy Houston, began as backup for the Drifters.

"Our earliest influences were great blues singers and boogie-woogie piano players," Stoller says, citing Albert Ammons, Pete Johnson, Meade Lux Lewis, Jimmy Witherspoon, Charles Brown, Roy Brown, and Amos Milburn. He also cites Maxwell Davis, the house producer for Aladdin Records, who also worked for Federal.

"We're out of the mainstream of pop, rock 'n' roll productions," Leiber says. "I think that's really essentially for young guys. It's a very high-energy output field, and it has to do with the producer connecting with the audience and the music. I don't want to sound like a fuddy-duddy, but when we were making all those hits, we were the market. "When we started, there were a lot of old A&R men at the studios. They'd say, 'Do you think the kids will like this?' We'd say, 'What do you mean, the kids? We *are* the kids.' " —CARLO WOLFF

Brooks, Elkie: *Two Days Away,* A&M, 1976.

Brown, Ruth: *Miss Rhythm (Greatest Hits and More),* Atlantic, 1959, 1990 • *Rockin' in Rhythm: The Best of Ruth* (1 track), Rhino, 1996.

Butler, Jerry: *Need to Belong,* Vee-Jay, 1964.

Clovers, The: *The Very Best of the Clovers,* Rhino, 1998.

Coasters, The: "Searchin'," Atco, 1957 • *The Coasters,* Atco, 1957 • "Young Blood," Atco, 1957 • "Yakety Yak," Atco, 1958 • "Along Came Jones," Atco, 1959 • "Charlie Brown," Atco, 1959 • "I'm a Hog for You," Atco, 1959 • "Poison Ivy," Atco, 1959 • "That Is Rock and Roll," Atco, 1959 • *One by One,* Atco, 1960 • "Run Red Run," Atco, 1960 • "Little Egypt," Atco, 1961 • *On Broadway,* King, 1963 • *Young Blood,* Atlantic, 1982 • *The Ultimate Coasters,* Warner Bros., 1988 • *Greatest Hits,* Rhino, 1989 • *50 Coastin' Classics,* Rhino, 1992 • *The Very Best Of,* Rhino, 1994.

Dillard, Varetta: *Got You on My Mind,* Vol. 1, Bear Family, 1989 • *Lovin' Bird,* Vol. 2, Bear Family, 1989.

Dino and Sembello: *Dino and Sembello,* A&M, 1974.

Dixie Cups: "Chapel of Love," Red Bird, 1964 • *Chapel of Love,* Red Bird, 1964.

Drifters, The: "Fools Fall in Love," Atlantic, 1957 • "There Goes My Baby," Atlantic, 1959 • "Save the Last Dance for Me," Atlantic, 1960 • "This Magic Moment," Atlantic, 1960 • "Up on the Roof," Atlantic, 1962 • "On Broadway," Atlantic, 1963 • *The Drifter's Golden Hits,* Atlantic, 1966 • *Rockin' and Driftin': The Box Set,* Rhino, 1996.

Exciters, The: *Tell Him,* United Artists, 1962.

Flash Cadillac: *No Face Like Chrome,* Epic, 1974 • *Rock 'n' Roll Forever,* Epic, 1975.

Hunt, Tommy: *Biggest Man,* Kent, 1997.

Jackson, Chuck: *The Very Best of Chuck Jackson, 1961–1967,* Varese Sarabande, 1997.

Jay and the Americans: *She Cried,* United Artists, 1962 • *Come a Little Bit Closer,* Gold Rush, 1996.

Johnson, Marv: *You Got What It Takes,* EMI Legends, 1992.

King Curtis: *Instant Groove,* Edsel, 1969.

King, Ben E.: "Spanish Harlem," Atco, 1960 • *Spanish Harlem,* Atco, 1961 • "Stand by Me," Atco, 1961, 1986 • *Anthology,* Atlantic, 1993 • *The Very Best of Ben E. King,* Rhino, 1998.

Lee, Peggy: "Is That All There Is?," Capitol, 1969 • *Mirrors,* A&M, 1975.

Leiber, Jerry: *Scooby Doo,* Kapp, 1959.

Leiber-Stoller Big Band: *Yakety Yak,* Atlantic, 1961.

Mickey and Sylvia: *Love Is Strange,* Bear Family, 1990.

Minnelli, Liza: *Gently,* Angel, 1996.

Presley, Elvis: *King Creole,* RCA, 1958.

Procol Harum: *Procol's Ninth,* Chrysalis, 1975 • *The Chrysalis Years, 1973–1977,* Chrysalis, 1989.

Rafferty, Gerry: *Clowns to the Left, Jokers to the Right,* Raven, 1997.

Robins, The: "Smokey Joe's Cafe," Atlantic, 1955, 1985 (*Atlantic Rhythm and Blues, 1952–1955*).

Rossi, Steve: *Try to Remember,* Red Bird, 1965.

Shangri-Las: *Bulldog,* Red Bird, 1965.

Spector, Phil: *Back to Mono, 1958–1969,* Abkco, 1991.

Stealers Wheel: *Ferguslie Park,* A&M, 1973 • *Stealers Wheel,* A&M, 1973 • "Stuck in the Middle with You," A&M, 1973 • "Star," A&M, 1974.

Tolliver, Joan: *Joan Tolliver,* Kapp, 1964.

Turner, Big Joe: *Big, Bad and Blue: The Big Joe Turner Anthology,* Rhino, 1994.

Turner, Sammy: *Lavender Blue Moods,* Big Top, 1959.

Uggams, Leslie: *What's an Uggams?,* Atlantic, 1968.

Wheeler, Billy Ed: *A New Bag of Songs,* Kapp, 1962.

Walker, T-Bone: *Very Rare,* Warner Bros., 1973.

COLLECTIONS

The Brill Building Sound: Singers and Songwriters Who Rocked the 60's, Era, 1993.

Smokey Joe's Cafe: The Songs of Leiber and Stoller (original cast), Atlantic Theater, 1995.

Songbook, Alex, 1995.

Craig Leon

Craig Leon was a visionary New York A&R man and producer in the '70s who discovered and recorded punk–new wave icons the Ramones (*Ramones*), Suicide (*Suicide*), Blondie ("X Offender"), Richard Hell and the Voidoids (*Blank Generation* EP), Willie Alexander and the Boom Boom Band (self-titled debut, *Meanwhile . . . Back in the States*), and Moon Martin (*Shots from a Cold Nightmare, Escape from Domination*), among many others. Leon also co-produced (with Kim King) one of the earliest documentations of New York's new music scene, *Live at CBGB's,* with classic performances from Mink DeVille, Tuff Darts (with Robert Gordon), and the Shirts.

In the early '80s Leon produced the Bangles (self-titled EP), the Beat Farmers (*Van Go*), Rodney Crowell (*But What Will the Neighbors Think?*), and the Sir Douglas Quintet (*Border Wave*), before moving to England in the mid-'80s to produce Doctor and the Medics (*Laughing at the Pieces*), the Pogues (*Red Roses for Me*), the Go-Betweens (*Tallulah*), Flesh for Lulu (*Big Fun City*), and many others.

Leon—who is also a composer and instrumental artist (with and without his wife, "electronic folk artist" Cassell Webb)—has kept going strong in the '90s, producing Jesus Jones (*Liquidizer*), the Fall (*Extricate; Shift-Work,* No. 17 U.K.; *Code: Selfish*), the Chills (*Sunburnt*), Eugenius (*Mary Queen of Scots*), and the much-anticipated Blondie reunion album.

Craig Leon was born July 1, 1952, in Miami, Florida. He endured 12 years of instruction in piano, composition, theory, harmony, and musicology. His first musical memory is of listening repeatedly to an Angel recording of Beethoven's *6th Symphony* on his portable phonograph. Later in Leon's childhood, late-night rock 'n' roll and blues radio helped fill sleepless nights with dreams and visions. The first record Leon bought was Howlin' Wolf's "Smokestack Lightning," which sounded to him

like a horror story (another of his childhood enthusiasms—maybe that's why he didn't sleep).

As a teen, Leon played in a succession of unknown bands and did some session work as a keyboardist. Eventually he built his own demo studio with the help of his friend, the late producer and engineer Alex Sadkin (Bob Marley, Thompson Twins), and recorded local bands (Southern Steel, in the early '70s, was his first production).

Producer Richard Gottehrer (see entry) brought the Climax Blues Band in to Leon's studio to do preproduction for their *Sense of Direction* (1974) album. Gottehrer liked Leon's studio and arranging skills so much that he persuaded Leon to sell his share of the studio and move to New York to work for Gottehrer's (and co-owner Seymour Stein's) Sire Records, where Leon quickly became an A&R man.

As a very junior A&R man ("I didn't know if I was supposed to empty the trash cans or not"), Leon was suddenly thrust into the role of producer when Gottehrer abruptly left Sire in the middle of recording an album for the Canadian band Chilliwack in 1975. *Rockerbox* became Leon's first nationally released production.

Though only 22, Leon says he felt very comfortable in the studio, and that he was "doing something that I should do. I wasn't quite engineering yet, but I was really fascinated with the different sonic textures you could get through processing and the like. It was all very new back then: if you had a digital delay, a couple of compressors, and two echo plates you were very lucky."

Working for Sire, Leon became involved with the percolating New York underground music scene. One summer night in 1975 Leon went to CBGB looking for Patti Smith (see John Cale, Jimmy Iovine, Lenny Kaye entries), who was already signed to Arista. Owner Hilly Kristal suggested that Leon come back later that week to see a show with two bands named Talking Heads and the Ramones. "I went to that show and there were literally four people in the audience besides me, but the bands were phenomenal.

"With the Ramones, I scouted them and then I had to develop them. A lot of people didn't even think they could make a record. There were weeks of preproduction on a very basic level: like when the songs started and when they ended. Their early sets were one long song until they ran out of steam or fought. You could see it as a performance art–type thing, where you had a concise 17-minute capsule of everything you ever knew about rock 'n' roll. Or you could see it as 22 little songs. They had a very serious concept of what they wanted to do, but then we had to get the execution up to the point of actually being able to do it. It was the original drummer, Tommy ["Ramone" Erdelyi], who had the concept of what they should sound like, and what they should look like," says Leon.

"After we worked out all of that stuff, we did the album very quickly in the studio. The studio, Plaza Sound, was great. Some early Blondie and Talking Heads stuff was recorded there too. It was the old NBC Symphony Orchestra rehearsal hall, and it had been turned into a studio. With the Ramones we had these three big rehearsal halls and we put their Marshall amps in separate rooms so they wouldn't bleed. I remember the bass player [Dee Dee "Ramone" Colvin] and the guitar player [Johnny "Ramone" Cummings] standing in the hallway with their amps in separate rooms, and the drums in a booth way at the back of this immense studio. You could crank it up and still get isolation, which is why it sounds big and dry at the same time."

The Ramones' first album is a roaring minimalist icon, and is considered by many to be the first real American punk record. Layers and layers of accumulated bloat and sheen were stripped away to reveal the basic energy, drive, and primitive melodicism of rock 'n' roll. The Ramones' sound was blazing early '60s surf music played through the overdriven distortion of Blue Cheer and Black Sabbath. Yet, according to Leon, the Ramones saw themselves as a pop band. "In our naiveté, we thought they were going to be bigger than the Beatles. They had even named themselves after Paul McCartney's [see entry] early stage name, 'Paul Ramone.'" In retrospect, it is almost miraculous that an album as radical as the first Ramones record—on a label, Sire, that was a small indie at the time [1976]—charted at all [it reached No. 111].

"The whole New York music thing was seen as an extension of the art scene, so we thought we were doing something cultural. It might have been pretentious, but what the hell, we were having fun. We really thought we were doing something groundbreaking and new. A lot of that is missing today, although I still try to find artists like that to work with," he says.

If the first Ramones album is the most important record Leon has made, the first album by the aggro-electronic duo Suicide (Alan Vega on vocals, Martin Rev on keyboards and percussion) is probably second. Recalls Leon, "They were one of the first bands I saw in New York. I figured any band that could drive the jaded crowd out of Max's Kansas City must be doing something right. They were doing James Brown in this bizarre electronic way, with whips and chains directed at the audience. They saw it as an art experiment. Alan is a painter as well. I was fascinated by the German minimalist group Can at the time, and I was into the echoed vocals of dub that I had learned through working with Bob Marley and Lee Perry [see entry] on the Martha Velez record, so we applied those things to the production.

"We had about an hour of preproduction before we did the record at Ultima Studios," he continues. "I think the guy who financed the record paid off the janitor to leave the door open for us, and we recorded it over the weekend. A lot of that went down live to tape, and then was manipulated in the mix." The album is remarkably varied for just a keyboard player and a singer. Leon and Rev get a real percussive thump out on "Ghost Rider" and "Rocket U.S.A." "Cheree" is a throbbing, beautiful love song. "Johnny" cops an old-time rock 'n' roll riff and makes it swing electronically. Vega alternately coos and shrieks his way through the epic "Frankie Teardrop."

Suicide might be the single most influential album that never charted anywhere for any length of time. It is certainly the progenitor of both the techno-pop of Human League, Depeche Mode, and Erasure and the jagged avant noise of the "no wave" bands like the Contortions, Teenage Jesus and the Jerks, and eventually, Sonic Youth.

Leon then moved in a radically different musical direction, but a direction not so different regarding recording techniques. He produced country singer Rodney Crowell's (see entry) second album. "That was one of my favorites. He had the Hot Band, which was essentially Elvis's band at the time: Tony Brown [see entry], Emory Gordy Jr., Albert Lee. It was essentially a 'live in the studio' record, like a lot of the punk records. He wanted a very edgy, hard, and dry sound compared to what he had been doing. His first album was very lush. It was one of the first really credible things I did that wasn't New York punk," he says.

"On a 'live' recording like that you have to do it until you get it right, until it sounds like a 'record,' but you have to know when it's gone over the limit and is starting to get stale. Then you have to stop it and start it all over again. The Sir Douglas Quintet reunion was done like that. They brought in all of their original equipment from the '60s to Electric Lady and recorded 40 songs live in three days," Leon notes. "The opposite of that is the modern pop or techno stuff that is constructed. You have a bunch of different parts in a computer and you move them around until it sounds right. My own stuff, or my wife's, are constructed from a score," he says.

Leon moved to L.A. in the early '80s, and after a few years, he was tired of it. "There was still an indie scene [in England], and I came over just to see what was happening. I talked to a few different record people about

artists and a bunch of interesting projects came through in just one day. One of those was for my wife, who was in a bunch of Texas psychedelic bands in the '60s. One thing led to another and we just ended up staying. We're very happy here because we get a bit of an outlet for our own music, which is harder to find in the States. Also, things are much faster here. I love working with really fresh, new bands that are just getting their ideas together and need someone to coordinate them. It's a really fulfilling role for me to help them along." —ERIC OLSEN

Adult Net: *Honey Tangle*, Fontana, 1989.

Alexander, Willie: *Meanwhile . . . Back in the States*, MCA, 1978 • w/ the Boom Boom Band, *Willie Alexander and the Boom Boom Band*, MCA, 1978 • *Willie Loco Boom Boom Ga Ga, 1975–1991*, Northeastern, 1992.

Angel and the Reruns: "Why Do Good Girls Like Bad Boys?," IRS, 1984 (*Bachelor Party* soundtrack).

Angel Corpus Christi: *White Courtesy Phone*, ALMO Sounds, 1995.

Bangles: *Bangles* (EP), Faulty Products, 1982.

Beat Farmers: "Riverside," Curb/MCA, 1986 (*Rad* soundtrack) • *Van Go*, Curb, 1991.

Blondie: "X Offender/In the Sun," Private Stock, 1976.

Burns, Lisa: *Lisa Burns*, MCA, 1978.

Chilliwack: *Rockerbox*, Sire, 1975.

Chills, The: *Sunburnt*, Flying Nun, 1996.

City Lights: *Silent Dancing*, Sire, 1975.

Cobalt 60: *Elemental*, Edel America, 1996.

Crowell, Rodney: *But What Will the Neighbors Think?*, Warner Bros., 1980 • *The Rodney Crowell Collection*, Warner Bros., 1989.

Demons: *Demons*, Mercury, 1977.

Doctor and the Medics: *Laughing at the Pieces*, IRS, 1986 • "Spirit in the Sky," IRS, 1986 • *I Keep Thinking It's Thursday*, IRS, 1987.

Eugenius: "Blue Above the Rooftops," Atlantic, 1994 • *Mary Queen of Scots*, Atlantic, 1994.

Fall, The: *Extricate*, Cog Sinister/Fontana, 1990 • *Shift-Work*, Cog Sinister/Fontana, 1991 • "Arid Al's Dream," Cog Sinister, 1992 (*Volume Four*) • *Code: Selfish*, Cog Sinister/Fontana, 1992.

Fibonaccis: *Best Of: Repressed*, Restless, 1992.

Flesh for Lulu: *Big City Fun*, Statik/Caroline, 1985 • *Blue Sisters Swing* (EP), Statik, 1985.

45 Grave: "Insurance from God," Enigma, 1983, 1985 (*The Enigma Variations*) • *Sleep in Safety*, Enigma, 1983 • *A Tale of Strange Phenomena*, Enigma, 1984.

Go-Betweens, The: *Tallulah*, Beggars Banquet, 1987.

Hell, Richard, and the Voidoids: *Blank Generation* (EP), Stiff, 1976.

Jesus Jones: *Liquidizer,* Food/SBK, 1990.

Junior Cottonmouth: *Bespoke,* Atlantic, 1997.

Killjoys, The: *Starry,* Mushroom, 1994.

Kind, The: *Pain and Pleasure,* ThreeSixty, 1983.

LaMarca: *LaMarca,* Scotti Brothers, 1986.

Leon, Craig: *Nommos,* Takoma, 1982.

LeRoi Brothers: *Forget About the Danger . . . Think About the Fun,* Columbia, 1984.

Levellers, The: "Far from Home," China, 1991.

Martin, Moon: *Shots from a Cold Nightmare,* Capitol, 1978 • *Escape from Domination,* Capitol, 1979.

New Fast Automatic Daffodils: *Bong,* Mute, 1992 • *Body Exit Mind,* Mute/Elektra, 1993.

Owen, Mark: *Green Man,* RCA, 1996.

Pierce, Jeffrey Lee: *Wildweed,* Statik, 1985.

Pogues, The: *Red Roses for Me,* Stiff, 1984.

Primitives, The: *Lovely* (3 tracks), RCA, 1988.

Ramones: *Ramones,* Sire, 1976 • *Ramones Mania,* Sire, 1989 • *All the Stuff and More,* Vol. 1, Sire, 1990.

Records, The: *Crashes,* Virgin, 1980 • *Smashes, Crashes and Near Misses,* Caroline, 1988, 1995.

Ruff, Garfeel: *Garfeel Ruff,* Capitol, 1979.

Sir Douglas Quintet: *Border Wave,* Chrysalis, 1981 • *Live Texas Tornado,* Takoma, 1998.

Suicide: "Cheree," TVT, 1977, 1991 (*The Groups of Wrath*) • "I Remember," TVT, 1977, 1991 (*The Groups of Wrath*) • *Suicide,* Red Star, 1977 • *Suicide,* Restless, 1990.

Thought, The: *The Thought,* MCA, 1985.

Twilley, Dwight: *Twilley,* Arista, 1979.

Velez, Martha: *Escape from Babylon,* Sire, 1976.

Webb, Cassell: *Thief of Sadness,* Venture, 1988 • *Llano,* Venture, 1989 • *Songs of a Stranger,* Venture, 1989 • *House of Dreams,* Offbeat, 1993.

Weirdos: *Weird World, 1977–1981* (1 track), Frontier, 1991.

Zmed, Adrian: "Little Demon," IRS, 1984 (*Bachelor Party* soundtrack).

COLLECTIONS

Live at CBGB's (Home of Underground Rock), Atlantic, 1976.

Patrick Leonard

An expert keyboard man, Patrick Leonard is also an exceptional songwriter/producer who has collaborated on some of Madonna's most beloved hits ("Live to Tell," No. 1; "Where's the Party?"; "La Isla Bonita," No. 4; "Who's That Girl?," No. 1; "Cherish," No. 2; "Like a Prayer," No. 1; "I'll Remember," No. 2) in addition to Bryan Ferry's great *Bete Noir* (No. 9 U.K.). He has also written and produced for Bryan Adams (*MTV Unplugged*), Hiroshima (the gold *Another Place*), Rod Stewart (*Vagabond Heart,* No. 10; *Unplugged . . . and Seated,* No. 2; *If We Fall in Love Tonight*), Roger Waters (*Amused to Death,* No. 8 U.K.), and Peter Cetera ("One Good Woman," No. 4). As an artist, Leonard has assembled and led the bands Toy Matinee and Third Matinee and released a solo album (*Rivers*).

Patrick Leonard was born in Crystal Falls on the Upper Peninsula of Michigan in 1957 and grew up in the suburbs of Chicago. Leonard, whose father was a musician, started playing piano at a very young age. By 17 he was good enough to quit high school and hit the road with a succession of show bands. By 1977 Leonard was in a band, Trillion, that recorded an album for Epic. Another band, Software, released a jazz album for an MCA subsidiary in 1981.

Leonard moved to L.A. and made his living playing sessions through the mid-'80s. In 1984 he played keyboards and did programming for the Jacksons on their Victory Tour. Around this time, he had some of his songs covered by Stephanie Mills. He was then hired as music director for Madonna's first big tour in 1985, and while on the road, he collaborated with her on several songs that ended up on the *True Blue* (No. 1) album, including the thoughtful ballad "Live to Tell," the effervescent dance number "Where's the Party?" (inexplicably never released as a single), and the beguiling Latin fantasy "La Isla Bonita." Leonard also contributed as co-writer and co-producer to 1989's monster *Like a Prayer* (No. 1) album, including the anthemic title track and the ebullient "Cherish." Madonna-Leonard work from the '90s includes "Hanky Panky" (No. 10), "I'll Remember," and four songs on the recent *Ray of Light* album.

Leonard feels his creative success with Madonna is just one of those vagaries of nature. "I think it boils down to chemistry. It really just has to do with my chord changes, melodic and rhythmic stuff, and vibe; and her lyrics, melodies, and vibe. The two of us make this soup that really seems to work every time. I don't think there's anything more to it than that. Look at any team of people that have had an impact, and they're never as good on their own. I've had the experience of working with both David Gilmour and Roger Waters, and I can see that the chemistry between the two of them *was* Pink Floyd."

Following his ongoing work with Madonna, Leonard's second most important collaboration has been with Bryan Ferry on his moody, squirming *Bete Noir* album. Leonard used his expertise with electronic instruments to help create a seething, rhythmic stew of romance and intrigue (Leonard co-wrote five of the tracks and co-produced the entire album with Ferry). The single "Kiss and Tell" finds a supple groove and a clean melody for a tale of romantic bartering. "Zamba" floats on a strange syncopation to reveal a sharp autumnal image of loss. "The Right Stuff" packs a loping punch, and the title track closes the album with a gypsy flourish.

Though the album is great, Leonard isn't satisfied with it. "I don't think that record was fully realized. Bryan was going through management changes and things were dragging a bit. We just had to finish it, and we did. We probably used machines a little too much because of the way we were working.

"There are some good qualities to that record," he continues. "I learned a lot of interesting things—bizarre things I would have never tried—like taking trumpet solos that were done for one song, sampling them and taking a piece, flipping it backwards, dropping it down a fifth and putting it in a different song. Now that is stuff that everybody eats for breakfast, but in 1987 it wasn't. Now you can just do it with ProTools."

Leonard lives in Colorado with his wife and sees his task for the future as making music for "an audience I think is being ignored: i.e., grown-ups." —ERIC OLSEN AND DAVID JOHN FARINELLA

Adams, Bryan: "Back to You," A&M, 1997 • *MTV Unplugged*, A&M, 1997.

Cetera, Peter: "Best of Times," Full Moon/WB, 1988 • "One Good Woman," Full Moon/WB, 1988 • *One More Story*, Full Moon/WB, 1988.

DeLory, Donna: *Donna DeLory*, MCA, 1992, 1993.

Dream Academy: *Remembrance Days* (1 track), Reprise, 1987.

Ferry, Bryan: *Bete Noire*, Reprise, 1987 • "Kiss and Tell," Reprise, 1987 • "The Right Stuff," Reprise, 1987 • "Limbo," Reprise, 1988.

Fleetwood Mac: "Heart of Stone," Warner Bros., 1992.

Fox, Kim: "Sweetest Revenge," Dreamworks, 1998.

Hiroshima: *Another Place*, Epic, 1985.

Kamen, Nick: *Us* (1 track), Sire, 1988.

lang, k.d.: "Love Affair," Warner Bros., 1996 (*Twister* soundtrack).

Lennon, Julian: *Mr. Jordan*, Atlantic, 1989.

Leonard, Patrick: *Rivers*, Warner Bros., 1997.

Loggins, Kenny: *Back to Avalon*, Columbia, 1988.

Madonna: "Live to Tell," Sire, 1986 • "Open Your Heart," Sire, 1986 • *True Blue*, Sire, 1986 • "La Isla Bonita," Sire, 1987 • "Where's the Party?," Sire, 1987 • "Who's That Girl?," Sire, 1987 • *You Can Dance*, Sire, 1987 • "Cherish," Sire, 1989 • "Like a Prayer," Sire, 1989 • *Like a Prayer*, Sire, 1989 • "Oh Father," Sire, 1989 • "Hanky Panky," Sire, 1990 • *I'm*

Breathless, Sire, 1990 • *Royal Box*, Sire, 1990 • *The Immaculate Collection*, Sire, 1990 • "I'll Remember," Maverick/Sire/WB, 1994 • *Something to Remember*, Maverick, 1995 • *Ray of Light* (4 tracks), Warner Bros., 1998.

Phillips, Chynna: *Naked and Sacred*, EMI, 1995.

Scaggs, Boz: "Cool Running," Columbia, 1988.

Schascle: *Haunted by Real Life*, Reprise, 1991.

Stewart, Rod: "Broken Arrow," Warner Bros., 1991 • *Vagabond Heart*, Warner Bros., 1991 • "Have I Told You Lately," Warner Bros., 1993 • "Reason to Believe," Warner Bros., 1993 • *Unplugged . . . and Seated*, Warner Bros., 1993 • "Having a Party," Warner Bros., 1994 • "People Get Ready," Warner Bros., 1994 (*A Tribute to Curtis Mayfield*) • *If We Fall in Love Tonight*, Warner Bros., 1996.

Third Matinee: *Meanwhile*, Reprise, 1994.

Waters, Roger: *Amused to Death*, Columbia, 1992.

Watley, Jody: *Jody Watley*, MCA, 1987 • "Most of All," MCA, 1988 • *You Wanna Dance With Me?* (remix), MCA, 1990 • Greatest Hits, MCA, 1996.

COLLECTIONS
Sing soundtrack, CBS, 1989.

Gerald Levert

Gerald Levert was born into music. The son of Eddie Levert, a member of soul trio the O'Jays, who have been making classic vocal music for 40 years, Levert started playing drums and piano at home with his father and younger brother, Sean. Before he was in his teens, he was fooling around with tape recorders in the family basement, doing overdubs of his own voice, teaching himself whatever he could. "I knew what a producer did: He brought it all together. I knew I wanted to have control over big string sections, horn sections," he says. His father urged him to focus on songwriting in addition to performing, so he would always have a source of income. As urban music in the '80s focused more and more on songwriter/producers, it was good advice.

While still in his teens, he hooked up with Marc Gordon. The two clicked as a songwriting team and formed the group Levert, featuring Gordon and the two Levert brothers. They released their debut album in 1985.

Gerald Levert (born July 13, 1966, in Cleveland) recalls: "That was actually my first production job. We did it at home and gave it to Atlantic. They said, 'You're not ready to produce yet.' I was mad, I was ready to kill someone. They had other producers come in on the first album. So we took the money we made from touring and we went out to Los Angeles and worked with Craig Cooper, a very good arranger. We spent all our money to prove we could do as good as or better than the producers on our first album."

With their 1986 R&B hit "(Pop Pop Pop Pop) Goes My Mind" and support from Atlantic's Sylvia Rhone, the Levert-Gordon songwriting team became red-hot. "[Rhone] loved the work I did—that's what gave me my breakthrough. The first outside group I did was Troop. Then Miki Howard, Stephanie Mills, James Ingram. The more our group grew, the more people asked to work with us," Levert says.

Levert formed Trevel Productions, based in their hometown of Cleveland, and Levert brought artists there to record. They also discovered, signed, and produced hometown artists such as Men at Large and the Rude Boys.

When Gerald Levert launched his solo career in search of a sound that differed from the group's, he started writing and producing with Edwin "Tony" Nicholas, a member of the Levert touring band. That partnership persists to this day. The success of Levert's solo albums led to still other work, including Regina Belle, Freddie Jackson, Silk, the New Edition reunion album, and Barry White's 1995 comeback hit, "Practice What You Preach" (No. 18).

After Levert released its final album in 1997, Gerald Levert formed his own label, Global Soul, distributed through BMG. His first signing was the O'Jays, the act he once said he'd most like to work with. Now he says his dream is to work with Stevie Wonder (see entry; "We've talked, but so far we've missed each other") and Michael Jackson ("I'd give him a killer R&B sound. He needs another 'Who's Loving You?' ")

Though his basic sound is traditional R&B, with emphasis on romantic ballads, the ambitious and tireless Levert has always tried to incorporate new musical ideas. Like many of his contemporaries, he has listened to rap and cherry-picked a few ideas to spice up his sound. Levert likes to record at his On the Way Studio in Cleveland and mix at Sigma Sound in Philadelphia. "I like the feel and have a great rapport with the people there," he says. The team he relies on includes partner Nicholas, engineers Ron Shaffer and Mike Tarsia, and guitarist Randy Bowland. "They know the vibe I want on each song. Being a producer is about having a team around you who know what the record is about, what you are feeling," Levert says. "They help me make it happen."

Equipment isn't important to him. "I'm more of a feel person. My partner Tony is into equipment, modules, keyboard effects. The average person listening to the radio doesn't know what I used. I've never taken the time to understand it." Nicholas does much of the keyboard and programming work on their productions, although Levert also handles some, and they favor live string and horn players for the lush, traditional soul sound.

Levert's specialty is background vocal arrangements, which he says people call the earmark of his sound. "I didn't understand it for a while. People would say to me, 'That's one of your songs,' and I'd say, 'How did you know?' "

His strength, he feels, is his ability to work with vocalists. "When I cut a vocal on an artist, I understand, because I'm a singer. I cut a reference track but I won't let them listen to it and get used to it; I only let them hear it a little bit. I want them to put out their own flavor."

He writes and produces songs with an ear toward performance. "I try to make sure the song builds and has a big ending. I like a song with a climax; it has to go somewhere. It's good to watch the person perform. When they do the song, I want them to be able to perform it. With Patti [LaBelle] or my dad, I know what they would do with the song." —ANASTASIA PANTSIOS

Belle, Regina: "Love T.K.O.," Columbia, 1995.

Clark, Rhonda: *Rhonda Clark,* Tabu, 1992.

Drama: *Open Invitation,* Perspective, 1994 • "See Me," Perspective, 1994.

Gill, Johnny: *See* Levert, Gerald.

Howard, Miki: w/ Gerald Levert, That's What Love Is, Atlantic, 1988 • "Crazy," Atlantic, 1988 • *Miki Howard,* Atlantic, 1989.

Ingram, James: "I Wanna Come Back," Warner Bros., 1989 • *It's Real,* Warner Bros., 1989.

Jackson, Freddie: *Private Party,* Street Life, 1995 • "Rub Up Against You," Street Life, 1995.

Jackson, Millie: "Something You Can Feel," Jive, 1988 • *The Tide Is Turning,* Jive, 1988.

Joe: *All That I Am,* Jive, 1997.

LaBelle, Patti: *Flame,* MCA, 1997 • "Shoe Was on the Other Foot," MCA, 1997.

Levert: "I'm Still," Tempre, 1985 • "Let's Go Out Tonight," Atlantic, 1986 • *The Big Throwdown,* Atlantic, 1987 • "Addicted to You," Atco, 1988 • *Just Coolin',* Atlantic, 1988 • "My Forever Love," Atlantic, 1988 • "Pull Over," Atlantic, 1988 • "Sweet Sensation," Atlantic, 1988 • "Gotta Get the Money," Atlantic, 1989 • featuring Heavy D, *Just Coolin',* Atlantic, 1989 • "All Season," Atlantic, 1990 • "Rope a Dope Style," Atlantic, 1990 • *Rope a Dope Style,*

Atlantic, 1990 • "Baby I'm Ready," Atlantic, 1991 • "Give a Little Love," Atlantic, 1991 • "abc-123," Atlantic, 1993 • *For Real Tho'*, Atlantic, 1993 • "Good 'Ol Days," Atlantic, 1993 • "Like Water," Atlantic, 1997 • "Sorry Is," Atlantic, 1997 • *The Whole Scenario*, Atlantic, 1997 • "True Dat," Atlantic, 1997.

Levert, Gerald: *Private Line*, EastWest, 1991 • "Can You Handle It?," EastWest, 1992 • "Answering Service," EastWest, 1994 • "Can't Help Myself," EastWest, 1994 • *Groove On*, EastWest, 1995 • "How Many Times?," EastWest, 1995 • w/ Keith Sweat and Johnny Gill, *Levert Sweat Gill*, Elektra, 1997 • *Love and Consequences*, EastWest, 1998.

Levert, Gerald, and Eddie Levert Sr.: "Baby Hold on to Me," EastWest, 1992 • "Already Missing You," EastWest, 1995 • *Father and Son*, EastWest, 1995 • "Wind Beneath My Wings," EastWest, 1996.

Levert, Sean: "Put Your Body Where Your Mouth Is," Atlantic, 1995 • "Same One," Atlantic, 1995.

Little, J.: "The Hump Is On," Atlantic, 1995.

McBride, Geoff: "No Sweeter Love," Arista, 1990.

Men at Large: *Men at Large*, EastWest, 1992 • "Use Me," EastWest, 1992 • "You Me," EastWest, 1992 • "So Alone," EastWest, 1993 • "Um Um Good," EastWest, 1993 • "Would You Like to Dance (with Me)?," EastWest, 1993 • "Holiday," EastWest, 1995 • "Let's Talk About It," EastWest, 1995.

Mills, Stephanie: *Home*, MCA, 1989.

New Edition: *Home Again*, MCA, 1996.

O'Jays, The: "Out of My Mind," EMI, 1989 • *Serious*, EMI America, 1989 • *Heartbreaker*, EMI America, 1993 • "Somebody Else Will," EMI, 1993 • *Love You to Tears*, Volcano, 1997 • "What's Stopping You?," Global Soul, 1997.

One of the Girls: "Do Da What," EastWest, 1993 • *One of the Girls*, EastWest, 1993.

Pendergrass, Teddy: *A Little More Magic*, Elektra, 1993 • "Voodoo," Elektra, 1993.

Rice, Gene: *Gene Rice*, RCA, 1993.

Rude Boys: "Come On Let's Do This," Atlantic, 1990 • *Rude Awakening*, Atlantic, 1990 • "Go Ahead and Cry," Atlantic, 1992 • "My Kinda Girl," Atlantic, 1992 • *Rude House*, Atlantic, 1992.

Silk: *Silk* (1 track), Elektra, 1995.

Solo: *4 Brothas and a Bass*, A&M, 1998.

Special Generation: *Butterflies*, Bust It, 1992.

Subway: *Good Times*, Biv 10/Motown, 1995 • "This Lil' Game We Play," Biv 10/Motown, 1995.

Sweat, Keith: See Levert, Gerald.

Troop: "Mamacita," Atlantic, 1988 • *Troop*, Atlantic, 1988 • "That's My Attitude," Atlantic, 1990 • *Attitude*, Atlantic, 1991.

Washington, Keith: "Believe That," Qwest, 1993 • *You Make It Easy*, Qwest, 1993 • "Trippin," Qwest, 1994.

White, Barry: "Practice What You Preach," A&M, 1994 • *The Icon Is Love*, A&M, 1994 • "There It Is," A&M, 1995.

Wilde, Eugene: "Ain't Nobody's Business," Magnolia/MCA, 1989.

Williams, Christopher: *Adventures in Paradise*, Geffen, 1989 • "One Girl," Geffen, 1990.

Winans, The: *All Out*, Qwest, 1993.

COLLECTIONS

12 Soulful Nights of Christmas, Part 1, So So Def, 1996.

Stewart Levine

A career producer, arranger, and musician with successes over 30-plus years, Stewart Levine has specialized in long-term relationships with artists across the popular music spectrum. Levine began as a jazz and world music producer and label owner (Chisa) in partnership with expatriate South African trumpeter/activist Hugh Masekela (*Hugh Masekela Is Alive and Well at the Whiskey; The Promise of a Future*, No. 17; "Grazing In the Grass," No. 1) in the mid-'60s, then hooked up with the (Jazz) Crusaders (the gold *Southern Comfort, One, The Second Crusade*) for a long run in the '70s.

After a break, he returned to recording with Minnie Riperton (*Adventures in Paradise*, No. 18) in 1975, then moved into a Southern jazz-rock groove with Dixie Dregs (*Freefall*), the Marshall Tucker Band (the gold *Together Forever, Running Like the Wind, Tenth*), and the Allman Brothers Band side project, Sea Level (*Sea Level, Cats on the Coast*).

Levine produced a series of albums for blues legend B.B. King (*Midnight Believer, Take It Home*) in the late '70s and early '80s, before notching his biggest commercial hit with Joe Cocker and Jennifer Warnes' "Up Where We Belong" (No. 1) in 1982, the Academy Award–winning sandpaper-and-honey ballad from *An Officer and a Gentleman*.

Levine produced Womack and Womack's profound debut (*Love Wars*) in 1984, then moved to England to work with a series of soulful new wave acts, including Boy George (*Sold*); Curiosity Killed the Cat (*Keep Your Distance*, No. 1 U.K.); Hothouse Flowers (*Songs from the Rain*, No. 7 U.K.); and most successfully, Manchester's Simply Red (*Picture Book*, No. 16; "Holding Back the Years," No.

1; *A New Flame,* No. 1 U.K.; "If You Don't Know Me by Now," No. 1; *Stars,* No. 1 U.K.; *Life,* No. 1 U.K.).

Stewart Levine was born and raised in the Bronx and took up the clarinet at age 7. Inspired by neighbor Stan Getz, Levine switched to the sax at 12 and was playing professionally by 14. The jazz-loving teen prodigy attended the New York High School For Music and Art and went on the road with the dance bands of Billy May, Buddy Morrow, and Stan Kenton, from whom he picked up the gist of arranging.

After high school Levine majored in theory at the Manhattan School of Music from 1960 to 1964, where Hugh Masekela was a classmate. Masekela was born in 1939 in Witbank, South Africa, and played trumpet with South African dance bands as a teenager. An outspoken opponent of apartheid, he studied at London's Guildhall School of Music before coming to the Manhattan School on a scholarship from Harry Belafonte.

Levine and Masekela joined forces to create the Chisa record label to introduce a deeply grooved and tuneful hybrid of African and jazz music to America. *The Emancipation of Hugh Masekela* began the partnership in 1966. "We were trying to create a consciousness for South African and third world music," says Levine.

Their partnership peaked artistically and commercially in 1968 with the release of *The Promise of a Future,* a hugely successful album that featured "Grazing in the Grass": a strutting *mbaqanga* (a blend of traditional Zulu and black American pop music) that was both familiar and exotic. Levine and Masekela worked together on and off through the mid-'80s in a variety of jazz, traditional African, and dance-pop styles.

Levine helped develop the lazy, funky, percolating rhythms now called "rare groove" with the Crusaders on over a dozen albums throughout the '70s. Led by pianist Joe Sample, tenor saxman Wilton Felder, and drummer Stix Hooper, the Crusaders were formed as the Swingsters in Houston in 1954. They moved to L.A. and became the Jazz Crusaders in 1960. By the time Levine came along in 1970, the group had gelled into an R&B-jazz monster. Perhaps their finest albums are *One* from 1972 and *The Second Crusade* from 1973, which show off the band's sound at its most distinctive.

After Chisa was folded into Tommy LiPuma's (see entry) Blue Note label in 1973, Levine became an independent producer. He put together a music festival called *When We Were Kings* around an Ali-Foreman fight to create higher consciousness about African music.

In the late '70s Levine moved away from R&B with some fine jazzy Southern rock for Macon's Capricorn label, including the excellent *Cats on the Coast* album by Sea Level (with Allman Brothers Band members Chuck Leavell on keyboards, Jai Johanny Johanson on congas, Lamar Williams on bass), and a string of albums for the later Marshall Tucker Band.

Encouraged by English response to the Womack and Womack album, Levine moved there in 1984 and "reinvented" himself as a soul-leaning new wave producer. Curiosity Killed the Cat's *Keep Your Distance* was a huge hit in the mode of Level 42 or Johnny Hates Jazz, with a particularly insistent hit single in "Misfit." "One Tongue" (from *Songs from the Rain*) by Ireland's Hothouse Flowers has a lovely Waterboys-like feel.

But Levine found his best Anglo-soul outlet in Simply Red. Singer/songwriter Mick "Red" Hucknall wails in a combustible tenor like the offspring of Aretha Franklin and Van Morrison. The band's debut, *Picture Book,* is particularly strong: their cover of "Money's Too Tight (to Mention)" is ruefully funny over a strong groove, and Hucknall's own "Holding Back the Years" is an enduring ballad. Red's cover of Harold Melvin and the Blue Notes' "If You Don't Know Me by Now" does justice to the deeply soulful original. The band's '90s work has been much more successful in Europe than the U.S.: *Stars* charted weakly in the U.S., but sold around 9 million copies worldwide and spawned five hit singles in the U.K. *Life* fared similarly.

Levine is now back in the U.S., keeping a low profile, playing his sax again and enjoying his new family. "I'm sort of reacquainting myself with the reasons why I became a musician," he says. In August 1997 Levine helped produce (and conducted the orchestra for) the smashing *Songs and Visions* concert at London's Wembley Stadium. With a lineup of Rod Stewart, Jon Bon Jovi, Chaka Khan, Steve Winwood, Robert Palmer, Toni Braxton, k.d. lang, Seal, and Mary J. Blige, the show was a "celebration of the classic songs of the last 40 years, with each year introduced by archive video footage depicting familiar events," according to a press release.

For Levine, the most constant aspect of production has been the learning. "Every time I've entered a studio, I've never walked out without learning something. There's something new that always comes up: the relationship of instruments, the essence of a groove, some sort of magic about electronics, some way to coax a performance out of someone. There are so many things that can happen in the studio in a day, that if you're awake and alive and caring, you must learn." Levine has learned well and applied that knowledge to make superb music for a very long time. —ERIC OLSEN AND DAVID JOHN FARINELLA

Adams, Arthur: *Love My Lady,* A&M, 1979.
Adams, Oleta: *Evolution,* Fontana, 1993.

Alpert, Herb, and Hugh Masekela: *Herb Alpert and Hugh Masekela,* A&M, 1978.

Anderson, Jon: *In the City of Angels,* Columbia, 1988.

Benson, George: *Love Remembers,* Warner Bros., 1993.

Berg, Matraca: *The Speed of Grace,* RCA, 1993.

Blancmange: *Believe You Me,* Sire/London, 1985.

Boy George: *Sold,* Virgin, 1987 • w/ Culture Club, *At Worst . . . The Best of Boy George and Culture Club,* ERG, 1993.

Capaldi, Jim: *One Man Mission,* Atlantic, 1984.

Cocker, Joe: w/ Jennifer Warnes, "Up Where We Belong," Island, 1982 • *Civilized Man* (5 tracks), Capitol, 1984 • *Best Of,* Capitol, 1993 • *Long Voyage Home: The Silver Anniversay Collection,* A&M, 1995.

Crawford, Hank: *Heart and Soul,* Rhino, 1992.

Crawford, Randy: *Everything Must Change,* Warner Bros., 1976.

Crusaders, The: *Pass the Plate,* Chisa, 1971 • *One,* ABC, 1972 • *Hollywood,* Motown, 1973, 1994 • *The Second Crusade,* Blue Thumb, 1973 • *Unsung Heroes,* ABC, 1973 • *Scratch,* ABC, 1974 • *Southern Comfort,* ABC, 1974 • *Chain Reaction,* Blue Thumb, 1975 • *Those Southern Nights,* ABC, 1976 • *Free as the Wind,* ABC, 1977 • *Life in the Modern World,* MCA, 1988 • *At Their Best,* Motown, 1992 • *Way Back Home,* Blue Thumb, 1996 • *Priceless Jazz,* GRP, 1998.

Curiosity Killed the Cat: *Keep Your Distance* (6 tracks), Mercury, 1987 • "Misfit," Mercury, 1987.

Dixie Dregs: *Freefall,* Capricorn, 1976.

Dore, Charlie: *Listen,* Chrysalis, 1981.

Dozier, Lamont: *Reddlin',* Warner Bros., 1977.

Dr. John: *Goin' Back to New Orleans,* Warner Bros., 1992.

Ella Mental: *Ella Mental,* Warner Bros., 1989.

Everyday People: *You Wash, I'll Dry,* SBK, 1990.

Gangsters of Love: *Gangsters of Love,* Capitol, 1973.

Hart, Robert: *Cries and Whispers,* Atlantic, 1989.

Hayes, Bonnie: *Bonnie Hayes,* Chrysalis, 1987.

Hothouse Flowers: "An Emotional Time," London, 1993 • "Isn't It Amazing," London, 1993 • "One Tongue," London, 1993 • *Songs from the Rain,* London, 1993.

Jazz Crusaders: *Old Socks, New Shoes . . . New Socks, Old Shoes,* Chisa, 1970.

Jiva: *Jiva,* Dark Horse, 1975.

King, B.B.: *Midnight Believer,* ABC, 1978 • *Take It Home,* MCA, 1979 • *There Must Be a Better World Somewhere,* MCA, 1981 • *Love Me Tender,* MCA, 1982 • *There Is Always One More Time,* MCA, 1991 • "Woman's Got Soul," Warner Bros., 1994 (*A Tribute to Curtis Mayfield*) • *King of the Blues,* Pickwick, 1995.

LaBelle, Patti: *Be Yourself,* MCA, 1989 • "If You Asked Me To," MCA, 1989 • *Greatest Hits,* MCA, 1996.

Lewis, Huey: "Once Upon a Time in New York City," Disney, 1988 (*Oliver and Company* soundtrack) • "Little Bitty Pretty One," Elektra, 1995.

Lewis, Huey, and the News: "(She's) Some Kind of Wonderful," Elektra, 1994 • "But It's Alright," Elektra, 1994 • *Four Chords and Several Years Ago,* Elektra, 1994.

Lins, Ivan: *Love Dance,* Reprise, 1988 • *Awa Yio,* Reprise, 1991.

Marshall Tucker Band: "Dream Lover," Capricorn, 1978 • *Together Forever,* Capricorn, 1978 • "Last of the Singing Cowboys," Warner Bros., 1979 • *Running Like the Wind,* Warner Bros., 1979 • "It Takes Time," Warner Bros., 1980 • *Tenth,* Warner Bros., 1980 • *The Best Of: The Capricorn Years,* Era, 1994.

Masekela, Hugh: *The Emancipation of Hugh Masekela,* Chisa, 1966 • *Hugh Masekela Is Alive and Well at the Whiskey,* Uni, 1967 • *Hugh Masekela's Latest,* Uni, 1967 • "Grazing in the Grass," Uni, 1968 • *The Promise of a Future,* One Way, 1968, 1993 • *Masekela,* Uni, 1969 • *Reconstruction,* Mo Jazz, 1970, 1994 • *Hugh Masekela and the Union of South Africa,* Mo Jazz, 1971, 1994 • *Home Is Where the Music Is,* Blue Thumb, 1972 • *I Am Not Afraid,* Blue Thumb, 1974 • *The Boy's Doin' It,* Casablanca, 1975 • *Melody Maker,* Casablanca, 1976 • *Techno-Bush,* Jive, 1984 • *Waiting for the Rain,* Jive, 1985 • *See also* Alpert, Herb.

Mbulu, Letta: *Letta,* A&M, 1978.

McKone, Vivienne: *Vivienne McKone,* London, 1993.

Moon: *Too Close for Comfort,* Epic, 1976.

Oz, William: *William Oz,* Capitol, 1979.

Rare Earth: *Back to Earth,* Motown, 1975 • *Greatest Hits and Rare Classics,* Motown, 1991.

Richie, Lionel: *Back to Front,* Motown, 1992 • "Do It to Me," Motown, 1992 • *Truly: The Love Songs,* Motown, 1997.

Riperton, Minnie: *Adventures in Paradise,* Epic, 1975.

Russell, Brenda: *Love Life,* A&M, 1981.

Sample, Joe: w/ Soul Committee, *Did You Feel That?,* Warner Bros., 1994 • *The Best of Joe Sample,* Warner Bros., 1998.

Scaggs, Boz: "Heart of Mine," Columbia, 1988 • *Other Roads,* Columbia, 1988.

Sea Level: *Cats on the Coast,* Capricorn, 1977 • *Sea Level,* Capricorn, 1977 • "That's Your Secret," Capricorn, 1977 • *The Best Of,* Polydor, 1977 • *On the Edge,* Capricorn, 1978.

Simply Red: "Holding Back the Years," Elektra, 1985 • "Money's Too Tight (to Mention)," Elektra, 1985 • *Picture Book,* Elektra, 1985 • "A New Flame," Elektra, 1989 • *A New Flame,* Elektra, 1989 • "If You Don't Know Me by Now," Elektra, 1989 • "It's Only Love," Elektra, 1989 • "You've Got It," Elektra, 1989 • "Something Got Me Started," EastWest, 1991 • "Stars," EastWest, 1991 • *Stars,* EastWest, 1991 • "For Your Babies," EastWest, 1992 • *Montreux* (EP), EastWest, 1992 • "Thrill Me," EastWest, 1992 • "Your Mirror," EastWest, 1992 • "Fairground," EastWest, 1995 • *Life,* EastWest, 1995 • "Remembering the First Time," EastWest, 1995 • *Greatest Hits,* EastWest, 1996.

Sly and the Family Stone: *Ain't But the One Way,* Warner Bros., 1983.

Stigers, Curtis: *Time Was,* Arista, 1991, 1995.

Untouchables, The: *Wild Child* (9 tracks), Stiff/MCA, 1985 • *Dance Party* (1 track), Stiff/MCA, 1986.

Womack and Womack: *Love Wars,* Elektra, 1984.

COLLECTIONS

Casey's Shadow soundtrack, CBS, 1978.

License to Kill soundtrack, MCA, 1995.

Terry Lewis

See JIMMY JAM AND TERRY LEWIS

Henry Lewy

Henry Lewy (born in Magdeburg, Germany, in 1926), is regarded as one of the top recording engineers of the '60s and '70s. He also played an important role in producing key recordings by Joni Mitchell, Neil Young, Stephen Bishop, Leonard Cohen, and others. A kindly, gentle presence in the studio, Lewy had the ability to cultivate a mood and set his artists at ease.

Lewy came to the U.S. in 1940 at the age of 14, fleeing the Nazis. He worked as a radio announcer for many years in San Diego, Los Angeles, and Las Vegas. "I got tired of radio announcing, so I started going to class to become an engineer. I got a job at Liberty Recorders and I was an engineer there for a while. United/Western bought them and I engineered recordings there for many years," he says.

At Liberty, Lewy lent his luster to music by the likes of Sergio Mendes ("Fool on the Hill"), Jimmy Webb (*Letters*), Boyce and Hart (see entry; "I Wonder What She's Doing Tonite"), the Supremes, and Phil Ochs.

In 1967, when Herb Alpert opened up A&M studios, he hired Lewy as a staff engineer; he remained there until 1977. Lewy eased from engineering into production in the late '60s, culminating is his work on seven stellar Joni Mitchell albums in the '70s, including *Ladies of the Canyon, Blue* (No. 15), *For the Roses* (No. 11), *Court and Spark* (No. 2), *the Hissing of Summer Lawns* (No. 4), and *Hejira* (No. 13). (There is no production credit on most of these albums, and Lewy's title ranges from

"engineer," to "engineer and advise," to the somewhat whimsical "sound and guidance." Co-production credit is generally now given to Lewy and Mitchell.) *Court and Spark* is among the finest engineering jobs of the '70s.

Lewy also worked on Neil Young's *Harvest* (No. 1), considered by many to be Young's finest album. *Harvest,* along with Lewy-produced LPs by the Flying Burrito Brothers, David Blue, and the Dillards, set the standard for the California country-rock sound that the Eagles would cash in on.

Lewy also worked on another audiophile favorite. Although his participation in 1983's *Famous Blue Raincoat* by Jennifer Warnes is obliquely credited (he is acknowledged only as the recording's "guardian angel"), there is little doubt that his technical guidance helped to establish its reputation as one of the best recordings in history—a CD often used for demonstration purposes in high-end audio stores.

"On the albums I produced, I got completely involved in the production," Lewy recalls. "I was a French horn player, but I never did arrangements myself—I hired the arrangers, booked the players. And I followed through on all the details of getting the album done—the mastering, cover art, you name it. Now I'm retired. I haven't done any music in years. I enjoy sitting in Pacific Palisades looking at the ocean." —DANIEL J. LEVITIN

Armatrading, Joan: *How Cruel* (EP), A&M, 1979.

Axton, Hoyt: *Southbound,* A&M, 1975.

Baez, Joan: *Where Are You Now, My Son?,* A&M, 1973 • *Here's to Life,* A&M, 1974 • *The Best Of,* A&M, 1977 • *Classics, Vol. 8,* A&M, 1987 • *Rare, Live and Classic,* Vanguard, 1993 • *Greatest Hits,* A&M, 1996.

Batteaux: *Batteaux,* CBS, 1973.

Bishop, Stephen: *Careless,* ABC, 1976 • "On and On," ABC, 1977 • *On and On: Best Of,* MCA, 1994.

Blue, David: *Stories,* Asylum, 1971.

Braden, John: *John Braden,* A&M, 1968.

Cohen, Leonard: *Recent Songs,* Columbia, 1979.

Dillards, The: *The Fantastic Expedition of Dillard and Clark,* Edsel, 1969, 1990.

Elliot, Richard: *Initial Approach,* Blue Note, 1984, 1991.

Flying Burrito Brothers: *The Gilded Palace of Sin,* A&M, 1969 • *Burrito Deluxe,* A&M, 1970 • *Farther Along: The Best Of,* A&M, 1988.

Honk: *Honk,* Epic, 1974.

Kittyhawk: *Race for the Oasis,* EMI America, 1981.

Kunkel, Leah: *I Run with Trouble,* CBS, 1980.

Long Ryders: *10-5-60* (EP), PVC, 1983 • *Native Sons,* Frontier, 1984.

Magnusson, Jakob: *Special Treatment,* Warner Bros., 1979.

Mitchell, Joni: "Big Yellow Taxi," Reprise, 1970 • *Ladies of the Canyon*, Reprise, 1970 • *Blue*, Reprise, 1971 • *For the Roses*, Asylum, 1972 • "You Turn Me On, I'm a Radio," Asylum, 1972 • *Court and Spark*, Asylum, 1974 • "Free Man in Paris," Asylum, 1974 • "Help Me," Asylum, 1974 • *The Hissing of Summer Lawns*, Asylum, 1975 • *Shadows and Light*, Elektra, 1980, 1988.

Morrison, Van: *The Common One*, Mercury, 1980.

Parsons, Gram: *Warm Evenings, Pale Mornings, Bottled Blues*, Raven, 1992, 1997.

Paxton Brothers: *The Paxton Brothers*, ABC, 1975.

Riperton, Minnie: *Minnie*, Capitol, 1979.

Sea Train: *Sea Train*, A&M, 1969.

Sill, Judee: *Judee Sill*, Asylum, 1972 • *Heart Food*, Asylum, 1973.

Spheeris, Jimmy: *The Dragon Is Dancing*, CBS, 1975.

Sainte-Marie, Buffy: *Sweet America*, ABC, 1976.

Timber: *Part of What You Hear*, Kapp, 1970.

Young, Neil: *Harvest*, Reprise, 1972.

Steve Lillywhite

Whether it's anthems like "Sunday Bloody Sunday" from U2, post-punk raveups like "Yeah Yeah Yeah Yeah Yeah" by the Pogues, poppy new wave from the Thompson Twins and XTC, slamming hard rock from the Rolling Stones, jazzy alterna-pop from the Dave Matthews Band, or confessional modern rock from Morrissey, Steve Lillywhite has been one of England's most important producers for over 20 years.

Lillywhite was born in 1955, and at 17 became a tea boy at PolyGram's studio. He graduated to engineer, and followed a common route into production when his demo for Ultravox was snapped up by Island Records in 1977. He produced the band's classic self-titled debut with Brian Eno (see entry) and was offered a staff producer position with Island.

Lillywhite became a new wave whirlwind, churning out essential music by Eddie and the Hot Rods (with Ed Hollis, the smoking rabble-rouser "Do Anything You Wanna Do," No. 9 U.K.), Siouxsie & the Banshees (*The Scream*, No. 12 U.K.), and XTC (*Drums and Wires*) before the end of the '70s.

With the arrival of the '80s, Lillywhite stepped up with the third *Peter Gabriel* (No. 1 U.K.) album; five tracks on the Psychedelic Furs' self-titled debut (No. 18 U.K.); their second album, *Talk Talk Talk*, with the original "Pretty in Pink"; and most importantly, a group of very young men from Dublin, U2.

Lillywhite's sparkling, radiant sound jumps from the grooves from the first note of U2's spectacular debut, *Boy*, as "I Will Follow" rides on Larry Mullen's drums and the Edge's angular guitar into history. While neither *Boy* nor its follow-up, *October*, tore up the charts at the time (though both are now platinum), *War* (No. 12) with "Sunday Bloody Sunday," "New Year's Day" (No. 10 U.K.), and "Two Hearts Beat As One" turned U2 into a worldwide phenomenon in 1984.

Another band Lillywhite effectively nurtured was Big Country, whose tartan "In a Big Country" (No. 17) and "Fields of Fire" (No. 10 U.K.) from *The Crossing* (No. 18) became '80s staples. If Lillywhite's work with U2 and Big Country emphasized rock guitar, his work the Thompson Twins (*In the Name of Love*) showed an affinity for synth-pop.

In the middle of the decade, Lillywhite oversaw Simple Minds' best album, *Sparkle in the Rain* (No. 1 U.K.), with "Waterfront" (No. 13 U.K.), "Up on the Catwalk" and "Book of Brilliant Things." He also helped move the Rolling Stones into a tough, almost metallic sound with *Dirty Work* (No. 4, co-produced with Jagger and Richards; see Glimmer Twins entry) in 1986. "Harlem Shuffle" (No. 5) was the band's biggest hit in five years, and "One Hit (to the Body)" just rocks.

In the late '80s Lillywhite worked with punkish Celtic neo-traditionalists the Pogues, producing the exceptional *If I Should Fall from Grace with God*, with the headlong title track, and the band's biggest hit, "Fairytale of New York" (No. 2 U.K.), now a modern rock Christmas standard featuring an affecting duet between the band's snaggletoothed lead singer, Shane MacGowan, and Lillywhite's wife Kirsty MacColl.

Lillywhite also hooked up with modern rock icons Talking Heads for their last album, the Afro-Caribbean–influenced *Naked* (No. 19), and for Head singer/guitarist/songwriter David Byrne's solo album *Rei Momo*.

The '90s has seen continued excellence from Lillywhite in the form of the La's brilliant neo-British Invasion debut, *The La's* (with "There She Goes," No. 13 U.K.), three energetic Morrissey albums (*Vauxhall and I*, No. 1 U.K.; *Southpaw Grammar*, No. 4 U.K.; *Maladjusted*), and some lovely music from Kirsty MacColl (*Kite*, *Electric Landlady*). In addition, he has produced the hugely popular American rhythm-and-jamming Dave Matthews Band (quadruple-platinum *Under the Table and Dreaming*; *Crash*, No. 2; *Before These Crowded Streets*) and executive-produced the AIDS benefit album *Red Hot + Blue*. —DAVID JOHN FARINELLA AND ERIC OLSEN

Armatrading, Joan: *Walk Under Ladders*, A&M, 1981 • *The*

Key, A&M, 1983 • *Track Record,* A&M, 1983 • *Classics, Vol. 21,* A&M, 1989.

Big Country: "Fields of Fire," Mercury/Sire, 1983 • "In a Big Country," Mercury/Sire, 1983 • *The Crossing,* Mercury/Sire, 1983 • *Steeltown,* Mercury, 1984 • "Where the Rose Is Sown," Mercury, 1984 • "Wonderland," Mercury, 1984 • *Wonderland* (EP), Mercury, 1984.

Brains: *Brains,* Mercury, 1980 • *Electronic Eden,* Mercury, 1981.

Buzzards: *Jellied Eels to Record Deals,* Chrysalis, 1979.

Byrne, David: *Rei Momo,* Luaka Bop/Sire, 1989.

Crenshaw, Marshall: *Field Day,* Warner Bros., 1983.

Crossfire Choir: *Crossfire Choir,* Passport, 1986.

Dave Matthews Band: *Under the Table and Dreaming,* RCA, 1994 • *Crash,* RCA, 1996 • *Before These Crowded Streets,* RCA, 1998 • "Don't Drink the Water," RCA, 1998.

Eddie and the Hot Rods: *Life on the Line,* Island, 1977 • *End of the Beginning: The Best Of,* Island, 1995.

Engine Alley: *Engine Alley,* Mother, 1994.

Foxton, Bruce: *Touch Sensitive,* Arista, 1984.

Frida: *Shine,* Epic, 1984.

Gabriel, Peter: *Peter Gabriel,* Mercury, 1980 • *Shaking the Tree: 16 Golden Greats,* Geffen, 1990.

Happy Mondays: "Hallelujah," *Elektra, 1989* (The MacColl Mix).

Harry, Debbie, Iggy Pop, and Thompson Twins: "Well, Did You Evah!," Chrysalis, 1990.

La's, The: "I Can't Sleep," Go!/London, 1990 • *The La's,* Go!/London, 1990 • "There She Goes," Go!/London, 1990.

MacColl, Kirsty: "A New England," Stiff, 1985 • *Kite,* Charisma, 1990 • *Electric Landlady,* Charisma, 1991 • "Walking down Madison," Charisma, 1991 • *Titanic Days,* IRS, 1993 • *Galore,* Virgin, 1995.

Members, The: *At the 1980 Chelsea Night Club,* Caroline, 1979, 1991 • *The Members at the Chelsea Nightclub,* Virgin, 1979 • *Sound of the Suburbs: A Collection of the Members' Finest Moments,* Virgin, 1995.

Morrissey: "Boxers," Parlophone, 1994 • "Hold on to Your Friends," Parlophone, 1994 • "Now My Heart Is Full," Sire/Reprise, 1994 • "Sunny," Parlophone, 1994 • "The More You Ignore Me, the Closer I Get," Sire/Reprise, 1994 • *Vauxhall and I,* Sire/Reprise, 1994 • *Southpaw Grammar,* Sire/Reprise, 1995 • *World of Morrissey,* Sire, 1995 • "Alma Matters," Mercury, 1997 • *Maladjusted,* Mercury, 1997.

O'Connor, Sinead: "Success Has Made a Failure of Our Home," Capitol, 1992.

Penetration: *Coming Up for Air,* Virgin, 1979.

Phish: *Billy Breathes,* Elektra, 1996.

Pogues, The: "Fairytale of New York," Island, 1987 • *If I Should Fall from Grace,* Island, 1988 • *Peace and Love,* Island, 1989 • "Yeah Yeah Yeah Yeah Yeah," A&M, 1988, 1989

(*Lost Angels* soundtrack) • *Yeah, Yeah, Yeah, Yeah, Yeah* (EP), Island, 1990 • *Essential Pogues,* Island, 1991.

Pretenders, The: *Get Close,* Real/Sire, 1986 • "Roomful of Mirrors," Sire, 1986.

Psychedelic Furs: *The Psychedelic Furs* (5 tracks), Columbia, 1980 • *Talk Talk Talk,* Columbia, 1981 • *All of This and Nothing,* Columbia, 1988 • *Should God Forget: A Retrospective,* Columbia, 1997.

Robinson, Tom: "Can't Keep Away," IRS, 1980, 1981 (*IRS Greatest Hits,* Vols. 2–3).

Rods, The: "Do Anything You Wanna Do," Island, 1977.

Rolling Stones, The: *Dirty Work,* Rolling Stones, 1986 • "Harlem Shuffle," Rolling Stones, 1986 • "One Hit (to the Body)," Rolling Stones, 1986.

Sector 27: *Sector 27,* Fontana/IRS, 1980.

Simple Minds: *Sparkle in the Rain,* Virgin/A&M, 1983 • *Glittering Prize Simple Minds, 1981–1992,* A&M, 1993.

Siouxsie & the Banshees: "Hong Kong Garden," Polydor, 1978 • *The Scream,* Polydor, 1978 • *Once Upon a Time/The Singles,* Polydor, 1981.

Snips: *Video King,* Jet, 1978.

Steel Pulse: *Handsworth Revolution,* Mango, 1978 • *Reggae Greats* (1 track), Mango, 1984.

Talking Heads: *Naked,* Sire, 1988 • "Nothing but Flowers," Sire, 1988 • "Sax and Violins," Warner Bros., 1991 (*Until the End of the World* soundtrack) • *Popular Favorites: Sand in the Vasoline,* Sire, 1992.

Thompson Twins: "In the Name of Love," Arista, 1982 • *In the Name of Love,* Arista, 1982 • *Set,* Tee, 1982 • *Best Of,* Arista, 1989 • *Big Trash,* Red Eye, 1989 • *Greatest Hits,* Arista, 1996.

Thunders, Johnny: *So Alone,* Sire, 1978, 1992.

Toyah: *The Chageling,* Safari, 1982.

Travis: *Good Feeling,* Independiente, 1997.

U2: *Boy,* Island, 1980 • "Gloria," Island, 1981 • *War,* Island, 1981 • "New Year's Day," Island, 1983 • "Sunday Bloody Sunday," Island, 1983 • "Two Hearts Beat As One," Island, 1983 • *The Joshua Tree,* Island, 1987 • "Where the Streets Have No Name," Island, 1987 • "With or Without You," Island, 1987 • *Achtung Baby,* Island, 1991 • "Mysterious Ways" (remix), Island, 1991 • "Even Better Than the Real Thing," Island, 1992.

Ultravox: *Ultravox!,* Island, 1977.

Urban Verbs: *Early Damage,* Warner Bros., 1981.

World Party: *Bang,* Ensign/Chrysalis, 1993.

XTC: *White Music,* Virgin, 1978 • *Drums and Wires,* Virgin, 1979 • "Life Begins at the Hop," Virgin, 1979 • "Making Plans for Nigel," Virgin, 1979 • *Black Sea,* Virgin, 1980 • "Generals and Majors," Virgin, 1980 • "Take This Town," RSO, 1980 (*Times Square* soundtrack) • "Towers of London," Virgin, 1980 • *Beeswax: Some B Sides, 1977–1982,* Virgin, 1982 • *Waxworks: Some Singles, 1977–1982,* DGC,

1984 • *Compact XTC: The Singles, 1978–1985*, Virgin, 1985 • *Dear God* (EP), Virgin, 1987 • *Rag and Bone Buffet* (3 tracks), Geffen, 1990.

Lawrence Lindo

See JACK RUBY

Alfred Lion

Alfred Lion founded Blue Note Records at the start of 1939, and it could be said he is as important to jazz as Ahmet Ertegun (see entry) is to R&B. Born on April 21, 1908, Lion became interested in jazz early on. In 1925, Lion noticed a concert poster for Sam Wooding's orchestra near his favorite ice skating arena in his native Berlin. According to the official history of Blue Note Records, he went in to the show out of sheer curiosity.

With little success, he began to scour Berlin for recordings of this unique American black music, but there were few records and no sources of information about jazz. In 1930, while working for an import-export firm, he made a business trip to the United States, where he was able to absorb considerable knowledge on the subject; he also purchased more than 300 records. In 1938, after eight years of travel for his firm, he finally settled in the U.S. in order to escape the right-wing Nazi domination of his homeland and to be close to the source of his passion, jazz.

On December 23, 1938, he attended John Hammond's (see entry) celebrated *Spirituals to Swing* concert at Carnegie Hall, featuring boogie-woogie piano masters Albert Ammons and Meade Lux Lewis. On January 6, 1939, he took Ammons and Lewis to a New York studio to make some private recordings. Instinctively, he provided their favorite beverages and food and created an atmosphere of respect, appreciation, and warmth that brought out the best in these men. They took turns at the piano, recording four solos each before relinquishing the bench to the other man. The long session ended with two stunning duets. Blue Note Records was finally a reality.

That May, the label's first brochure carried a mission statement Lion would rarely deviate from. It read: "Blue Note Records are designed simply to serve the uncompromising expressions of hot jazz or swing, in general. Any particular style of playing which represents an authentic way of musical feeling is genuine expression. By virtue of its significance in place, time and circumstance, it possesses its own tradition, artistic standards and audience that keeps it alive. Hot jazz, therefore, is expression and communication, a musical and social manifestation, and Blue Note Records is concerned with identifying its impulse, not its sensational and commercial adornments."

Lion's next session, on April 17, 1939, was an all-star quintet, the Port of Harlem Jazzmen. In order to capture the intimacy and vitality of the music, he called the session for 4:30 in the morning, when the artists had finished their club dates. Night sessions were almost unheard of at this time. Two months later, he did another Port of Harlem date, adding Sidney Bechet, who would have a major role in the label's growth during the next 14 years.

By the end of 1941, Lion's childhood friend Francis Wolff had caught the last boat out of Germany bound for the United States. He found employment at a photographic studio and joined forces with Lion at night to continue Blue Note. Lion and Wolff—if Lion enabled the sound, Wolff developed the look—ran Blue Note until it was sold.

Because of World War II, Lion largely suspended operations in 1942, securing distribution through Milt Gabler's (see entry) Commodore Records. But he and Wolff resumed in 1943. Toward the end of that year, they moved Blue Note to 767 Lexington Avenue, which remained the label's home until 1957. As big bands died an economic death, many fine swing soloists began to organize swingtets (usually three horns and four rhythm), affordable formats for small clubs and independent jazz labels. Blue Note began documenting this genre in mid-1944. The first date was by the magnificent, underrated tenor saxophonist Ike Quebec, and it bore another jazz classic, "Blue Harlem." After four more exceptional dates with Quebec, and other dates with Tiny Grimes, John Hardee, Jimmy Hamilton, and Benny Morton, Blue Note halted new recordings in September 1946. Except for two sessions with Babs Gonzales in the spring of 1947, the hiatus lasted 12 months.

Jazz was changing again, and Lion and Wolff could no longer resist the modern bebop movement. Quebec had become a close friend and adviser to both of them. Just as he had ushered in their swingtet phase, he would also bring them into modern jazz. He introduced them to Bud Powell, Thelonious Monk, Tadd Dameron, and others and coaxed them into beginning to document the new music. Soon they were recording Dameron, Fats Navarro, and Bud Powell and giving Monk, Art Blakey, and James Moody, among others, their first dates as leaders.

They also gave Horace Silver his best shot and, during the '50s and '60s, recorded all the lions of jazz, both old (like Quebec) and young (Sonny Rollins recorded some incredible Blue Note dates, as did Jimmy Smith). While Blue Note always enjoyed strong sales with Jimmy Smith, Horace Silver, and others, Donald Byrd's *A New Perspective*, a unique 1963 album for jazz group and wordless choir, began crossing over to more general audiences. The next year, the label released two albums that notched lengthy stays on the pop charts: Lee Morgan's *The Sidewinder* and Horace Silver's *Song for My Father*.

In addition to continuing its hard bop tradition with Morgan, Hank Mobley, Silver, and Blakey and with younger men like Herbie Hancock, Wayne Shorter, Bobby Hutcherson, Grant Green, Freddie Hubbard, and Joe Henderson, the label also moved into the avant garde. Lion and Wolff's first such project was Jackie McLean's 1963 group with Grachan Moncur, Bobby Hutcherson, and Tony Williams, all of whom would soon be recording their own albums as well.

The label was sold to Liberty in 1966, and, after Wolff died in 1971, Blue Note began to lose its vitality. Even though Lion kept his hand in at the label after the sale, his presence there diminished with time. A guest of honor at the label's relaunch by EMI in 1985, Lion visited Japan in 1986 and died on February 2, 1987 near San Diego.

Michael Cuscuna (see entry), a noted producer in his own right, and Charlie Lourie, who also founded Mosaic Records, helped revive Blue Note in the mid-'80s. Cuscuna wrote the official history of Blue Note, on which this bio is based. He considers Lion a role model. "I was always fascinated with Blue Note," says Cuscuna. "I couldn't have defined it at the time, but their records just had a higher quality. I realized later that much of the way Alfred Lion worked was similar to the way I started to work with jazz, which is that rehearsals are essential, and before rehearsals, planning sessions with the artist are critical. If you don't have a concept and goal going in, no matter how simple the record, it's going to hurt, because too much will be left to trial and error. Everything you do in a recording studio dissipates energy, so the more focused you can be, the better off you are. The way Alfred used to work, he would do planning sessions with the artist to talk about sidemen and he would encourage musicians to create new music that was really well-arranged, not just jam session stuff;

he would pay for rehearsals, and then in most cases at the studio stage, he would be able to get musicians who had tackled this difficult material to get off a good take in two or three takes."

The idea was to capture the freshness of creativity and improvisation. "What he was always concerned with, too, was how it felt," Cuscuna says of Lion. "He was working off the intellect and the gut, and the musicians knew when it was the take because they could look through the glass and see Alfred and [label co-owner] Francis Wolff doing a little dance in [engineer] Rudy Van Gelder's control room." —CARLO WOLFF

Adderley, Cannonball: *Somethin' Else*, Mobile Fidelity Sound Lab, 1958, 1992 • *Jazz Profile*, Capitol, 1997.

Ammons, Albert: w/ Meade Lux Lewis, *The First Day*, Blue Note, 1939, 1992.

Blakey, Art: *A Night at Birdland*, Vols. 1–3, Blue Note, 1954, 1987 • *Moanin'*, Blue Note, 1958, 1987 • *Buhaina's Delight*, Blue Note, 1962, 1992 • *Three Blind Mice*, Vol. 2, Blue Note, 1962 • *Freedom Rider*, Blue Note, 1963 • *Free for All*, Blue Note, 1987 • *Best Of*, Blue Note, 1989 • *Orgy in Rhythm*, Vols. 1–2, Capitol, 1997 • *See also* Moody, James.

Blakey, Art, and the Jazz Messengers: *At the Cafe Bohemia*, Vol. 1, Blue Note, 1955 • *At the Cafe Bohemia*, Vol. 2, Blue Note, 1955, 1987 • *At the Jazz Corner of the World*, Blue Note, 1959, 1994 • *The Big Beat*, Blue Note, 1960, 1987 • *Mosaic*, Blue Note, 1961, 1987 • *Night in Tunisia*, Blue Note, 1963, 1989 • *The History of the Jazz Messengers*, Blue Note, 1992 • *Jazz Profile*, Capitol, 1997.

Brooks, Tina: *True Blue*, Blue Note, 1960, 1994.

Brown, Clifford: *Memorial Album*, Blue Note, 1953, 1989 • *Complete Blue Note/Pacific Jazz*, Pacific Jazz, 1954, 1995 • *The Best of Clifford Brown*, Blue Note, 1998.

Burrell, Kenny: *The Best Of*, Blue Note, 1957, 1995 • *At the Five Spot*, Blue Note, 1959 • *Blue Lights*, Vol. 1, Blue Note, 1959, 1989.

Byrd, Donald: *Fuego*, Blue Note, 1960, 1987 • *Byrd in Flight*, Blue Note, 1960, 1996 • *Donald Byrd at the Half Note Cafe*, Blue Note, 1960, 1997 • *Free Form*, Blue Note, 1961, 1989 • *Mustang!*, Blue Note, 1966 • *Blackjack*, Blue Note, 1967 • *A New Perspective*, Blue Note, 1988 • *Blue Break Beats*, Blue Note, 1998.

Chambers, Paul: *Whims of Chambers*, Blue Note, 1956 • *Paul Chambers Quintet*, Blue Note, 1957, 1996 • *Bass on Top*, Blue Note, 1959.

Cherry, Don: *Symphony for Improvisers*, Blue Note, 1966, 1994.

Clark, Sonny: *Cool Struttin'*, Blue Note, 1958 • *Dial 'S' for Sonny*, Blue Note, 1959, 1997 • *Leapin' and Lopin'*, Blue Note, 1961.

Coleman, Ornette: *The Best of Ornette Coleman*, Blue Note, 1998.

Coles, Johnny: *Little Johnny C,* Blue Note, 1963, 1996.

Coltrane, John: *Blue Train,* Blue Note, 1957, 1997 • *Art of John Coltrane,* Blue Note, 1992.

Corea, Chick: *The Best Of,* Blue Note, 1993.

Davis, Miles: *Volume 2,* Blue Note, 1953, 1989 • *Volume 1,* Blue Note, 1954, 1988 • *The Best Of,* Blue Note, 1958, 1992 • *Ballads and Blues,* Blue Note, 1958, 1996 • *The Blue Note and Capitol Recordings,* Capitol, 1993 • *Jazz Profile,* Blue Note, 1998.

Davis, Walter Jr.: *Davis Cup,* Blue Note, 1995.

Dolphy, Eric: *Out to Lunch,* Blue Note, 1964, 1987.

Donaldson, Lou: *Blues Walk,* Blue Note, 1959, 1987 • *Sunny Side Up,* Blue Note, 1960, 1995 • *Gravy Train,* Blue Note, 1961 • *Alligator Boogaloo,* Blue Note, 1967, 1987 • *The Best Of,* Vol. 1, *1957–1967,* Blue Note, 1993 • *Blue Break Beats,* Blue Note, 1998.

Dorham, Kenny: *Afro-Cuban,* Blue Note, 1955 • *Whistle Stop,* Blue Note, 1961 • *Round About Midnight at the Cafe Bohemia,* Blue Note, 1995 • *The Best Of: The Blue Note Years,* Blue Note, 1996.

Freddie Redd Quartet: *The Connection,* Blue Note, 1960, 1994.

Gilmore, John: *Blowing in from Chicago,* Blue Note, 1957.

Gonzales, Babs: *Weird Lullaby,* Blue Note, 1992, 1997.

Gordon, Dexter: *Dexter Calling,* Blue Note, 1961 • *A Swingin' Affair,* Blue Note, 1962 • *Go!,* Blue Note, 1962, 1987 • *Gettin' Around,* Blue Note, 1965, 1987 • *The Complete Blue Note 60's Sessions,* Blue Note, 1965, 1996 • *Ballads,* Blue Note, 1991 • *Jazz Profile,* Blue Note, 1998.

Green, Bennie: *Soul Stirrin',* Blue Note, 1959.

Green, Grant: *Grant Stand,* Blue Note, 1961, 1987 • *Green Street,* Blue Note, 1961 • *Feelin' the Spirit,* Blue Note, 1962, 1987 • *Born to Be Blue,* Blue Note, 1962, 1989 • *Complete Quartets with Sonny Clark,* Blue Note, 1962, 1997 • *Idle Moments,* Blue Note, 1963, 1988 • *Solid,* Blue Note, 1964, 1979 • *I Want to Hold Your Hand,* Blue Note, 1965 • *Matador,* Blue Note, 1965, 1990 • *Street of Dreams,* Blue Note, 1967 • *The Best Of,* Vol. 1, Blue Note, 1993 • *Sunday Mornin',* Blue Note, 1996 • *Jazz Profile,* Blue Note, 1997.

Greene, Dodo: *My Hour of Need,* Blue Note, 1962.

Griffin, Johnny: *A Blowing Session,* Blue Note, 1957 • *The Congregation,* Blue Note, 1957, 1994.

Hancock, Herbie: *Takin' Off,* Blue Note, 1962, 1987 • *Inventions and Dimensions,* Blue Note, 1963, 1989 • *Empyrean Isles,* Blue Note, 1964, 1985 • *Best of the Blue Note Years,* Blue Note, 1988 • *Cantaloupe Island,* Blue Note, 1994 • *Jazz Profile,* Capitol, 1997.

Henderson, Joe: *Page One,* Blue Note, 1963, 1988 • *Inner Urge,* Blue Note, 1964, 1989 • *In 'n Out,* Blue Note, 1964, 1994 • *Mode for Joe,* Blue Note, 1966, 1988 • *The Blue Note Years,* Blue Note, 1993 • *Ballads and Blues,* Capitol, 1997.

Hill, Andrew: *Black Fire,* Blue Note, 1963, 1995 • *Judgement!,* Blue Note, 1964, 1994 • *Smoke Stack,* Blue Note, 1964 • *Point of Departure,* Blue Note, 1989.

Hipp, Jutta: w/ Zoot Sims, *Jutta Hipp with Zoot Sims,* Blue Note, 1956.

Hope, Elmo: *Trio and Quintet,* Blue Note, 1957.

Horace Silver Quintet: w/ J.J. Johnson, *Cape Verdean Blues,* Blue Note, 1965, 1989.

Horace Silver Quintet and Trio: *Blowin' the Blues Away,* Blue Note, 1959, 1987.

Horace Silver Trio: *Spotlight on Drums,* Blue Note, 1952, 1989.

Hubbard, Freddie: *Goin' Up,* Blue Note, 1960 • *Ready for Freddie,* Blue Note, 1961, 1995 • *Hub-Tones,* Blue Note, 1962, 1989 • *Here to Stay,* Blue Note, 1962, 1996 • *Breaking Point,* Blue Note, 1964, 1991 • *The Best Of,* Columbia, 1973, 1990 • *Hub Cap,* Blue Note, 1995 • *Ballads,* Capitol, 1997 • *Jazz Profile,* Blue Note, 1997.

Hutcherson, Bobby: *Components,* Blue Note, 1965, 1994 • *Happenings,* Blue Note, 1966, 1996 • *Stick Up!,* Blue Note, 1966.

Jackson, Milt: *Milt Jackson,* Blue Note, 1952, 1989.

Johnson, J.J.: *Eminent J.J. Johnson,* Vols. 1–2, Blue Note, 1953/1955, 1989.

Jones, Elvin: *Poly-Currents,* Blue Note, 1969, 1997.

Jordan, Clifford: w/ John Gilmore, *Blowing in from Chicago,* Blue Note, 1957, 1994 • *Cliff Craft,* Blue Note, 1959, 1997.

Jordan, Duke: *Flight to Jordan,* Blue Note, 1960, 1987.

Jordan, Sheila: *Portrait of Sheila,* Blue Note, 1962, 1989.

Kelly, Wynton: *Piano Interpretations,* Blue Note, 1951, 1991.

La Roca, Pete: *Basra,* Blue Note, 1965, 1995.

Lateef, Yusef: *Every Vilage Has a Song,* Rhino, 1976, 1993 • *Anthology,* Rhino, 1994.

Lewis, Meade Lux: *The First Day,* Blue Note, 1939, 1992 • *See also* Ammons, Albert.

McCann, Les: *Relationships: The Les McCann Anthology,* Rhino, 1993.

McLean, Jackie: *New Soil,* Blue Note, 1959, 1989 • *Swing, Swang, Swung,* Blue Note, 1959, 1997 • *Bluesnik,* Blue Note, 1961, 1989 • *Let Freedom Ring,* Blue Note, 1962, 1987 • *Destination Out,* Blue Note, 1964 • *Right Now,* Blue Note, 1965, 1991 • *New and Old Gospel,* Blue Note, 1967, 1996 • *Jackie's Bag,* Blue Note, 1995.

Mobley, Hank: *Hank Mobley and His All Stars,* Blue Note, 1957 • *Peckin' Time,* Blue Note, 1958, 1988 • *Soul Station,* Blue Note, 1960, 1987 • *Workout,* Blue Note, 1961, 1988 • *Roll Call,* Blue Note, 1961, 1997 • *Another Workout,* Blue Note, 1962, 1997 • *No Room for Squares,* Blue Note, 1963, 1989 • *A Caddy for Daddy,* Blue Note, 1965, 1990 • *A Slice of the Top,* Blue Note, 1966, 1979 • *The Best Of: The Blue Note Years,* Blue Note, 1996.

Moncur, Grachan III: *Some Other Stuff,* Blue Note, 1964.

Monk, Thelonious: *Genius of Modern Music,* Vols. 1–2, Blue

Note, 1947/1952, 1989 • *Best of the Blue Note Years,* Blue Note, 1991 • *Jazz Profile,* Blue Note, 1998.

Monterose, J.R.: *J.R. Monterose,* Blue Note, 1956, 1994.

Moody, James: w/ Art Blakey, *New Sounds,* Blue Note, 1948, 1991.

Morgan, Lee: *Candy,* Blue Note, 1959, 1987 • *Leeway,* Blue Note, 1960, 1995 • *The Sidewinder,* Blue Note, 1963, 1989 • *Tom Cat,* Blue Note, 1964, 1990 • *Dippin',* Blue Note, 1965 • *The Gigolo,* Blue Note, 1965, 1989 • *The Procrastinator,* Blue Note, 1967, 1995 • *Rajah,* Blue Note, 1985, 1996 • *Best Of,* Blue Note, 1988 • *Jazz Profile,* Capitol, 1997 • *Blue Break Beats,* Blue Note, 1998.

Parlan, Horace: *Us Three,* Blue Note, 1960, 1997 • *Happy Frame of Mind,* Blue Note, 1995.

Patton, John: *Let 'Em Roll,* Blue Note, 1965, 1993 • *Blue John,* Blue Note, 1986, 1995.

Pearson, Duke: *Sweet Honey Bee,* Blue Note, 1966, 1993.

Powell, Bud: *The Amazing,* Blue Note, 1951, 1989 • *The Amazing,* Vol. 2, Blue Note, 1953, 1989 • *The Scene Changes,* Blue Note, 1958 • *Best Of,* Blue Note, 1989 • *Jazz Profile,* Vol. 8, Capitol, 1997.

Quebec, Ike: *Heavy Soul,* Blue Note, 1961 • *Blue and Sentimental,* Blue Note, 1961, 1995 • *The Art of Ike Quebec,* Blue Note, 1962, 1992 • *Soul Samba,* Blue Note, 1962, 1996 • *Easy Living,* Blue Note, 1995 • *Ballads,* Blue Note, 1997.

Red, Sonny: *Out of the Blue,* Blue Note, 1960.

Rollins, Sonny: *Volume 1,* Blue Note, 1956, 1984 • *Volume 2,* Blue Note, 1957, 1985 • *Night at the Village Vanguard,* Vols. 1–2, Blue Note, 1957, 1987 • *Newk's Time,* Blue Note, 1959, 1990 • *Best Of,* Blue Note, 1989 • *Jazz Profile,* Blue Note, 1998.

Shaw, Woody: *Dark Journey,* 32 Jazz, 1997.

Shorter, Wayne: *JuJu,* Blue Note, 1964 • *Night Dreamer,* Blue Note, 1964, 1987 • *Et Cetera,* Blue Note, 1965, 1981 • *The Soothsayer,* Blue Note, 1965, 1990 • *Adam's Apple,* Blue Note, 1966, 1987 • *The All Seeing Eye,* Blue Note, 1966, 1994 • *Speak No Evil,* Blue Note, 1965 • *Best Of,* Blue Note, 1988 • *Jazz Profile,* Blue Note, 1997.

Silver, Horace: *Horace Silver Trio,* Blue Note, 1953, 1989 • *Further Explorations By the Horace Silver Quintet,* Blue Note, 1959, 1997 • *Horace-Scope,* Blue Note, 1960, 1990 • *Tokyo Blues,* Blue Note, 1962 • *Silver's Serenade,* Blue Note, 1963 • *Song for My Father,* Blue Note, 1964, 1989 • *The Jody Grind,* Blue Note, 1966, 1991 • *Horace Silver and the Jazz Messengers,* Blue Note, 1987 • *Best Of,* Blue Note, 1988 • *The Best Of,* Vol. 2, Blue Note, 1989 • *Jazz Profile,* Blue Note, 1997 • *See also* Horace Silver Quintet, Trio.

Sims, Zoot: *See* Hipp, Jutta.

Smith, Jimmy: *A New Star, A New Sound: Jimmy Smith at the Organ,* Vol. 1, Blue Note, 1956, 1997 • *Incredible Jimmy Smith at Club Baby Grand,* Vols. 1–2, Blue Note, 1956 • *Jimmy Smith at the Organ,* Vol. 3, Blue Note, 1956 • *House*

Party, Blue Note, 1957, 1996 • *Plays Pretty for You,* Blue Note, 1957 • *Cool Blues,* Blue Note, 1958, 1990 • *Home Cookin',* Blue Note, 1959, 1984 • *The Sermon,* Blue Note, 1960, 1987 • *Crazy Baby!,* Blue Note, 1960, 1989 • *Midnight Special,* Blue Note, 1960, 1989 • *Open House/Plain Talk,* Blue Note, 1960, 1992 • *Back at the Chicken Shack,* Blue Note, 1962, 1987 • *Prayer Meetin',* Blue Note, 1963, 1988 • *I'm Movin' On,* Blue Note, 1967, 1995 • *The Best Of,* Blue Note, 1987 • *Jazz Profile,* Blue Note, 1997.

Three Sounds: *Bottoms Up,* Blue Note, 1959 • *Here We Come,* Blue Note, 1961 • *Babe's Blues,* Blue Note, 1962, 1988 • *Black Orchid,* Blue Note, 1963 • *Introducing the Three Sounds,* Blue Note, 1987 • *Best Of,* Blue Note, 1993 • *See also* Turrentine, Stanley.

Turrentine, Stanley: w/ the Three Sounds, *Blue Hour,* Blue Note, 1960, 1995 • *Look Out,* Blue Note, 1960, 1987 • *Z.T.'s Blues,* Blue Note, 1961, 1988 • *Comin' Your Way,* Blue Note, 1961 • *Up at Minton's,* Blue Note, 1961, 1994 • *Jubilee Shout,* Blue Note, 1962, 1988 • *That's Where It's At,* Blue Note, 1962, 1988 • *Never Let Me Go,* Blue Note, 1963, 1992 • *Joyride,* Blue Note, 1965, 1987 • *Spoiler,* Blue Note, 1966 • *Easy Walker,* Blue Note, 1969, 1997 • *The Best Of,* Blue Note, 1989 • *Ballads,* Blue Note, 1993.

Tyner, McCoy: *The Real McCoy,* Blue Note, 1967 • *The Best Of: The Blue Note Years,* Blue Note, 1996 • *Jazz Profile,* Blue Note, 1997.

Willette, Baby Face: *Face to Face,* Blue Note, 1961 • *Stop and Listen,* Blue Note, 1961, 1994.

Williams, Tony: *Spring,* Blue Note, 1965, 1987.

Young, Larry: *Unity,* Blue Note, 1965, 1986 • *The Art of Larry Young,* Blue Note, 1992.

Tommy LiPuma

Tommy LiPuma produces five, maybe six, albums a year. Not surprisingly, all are either on GRP or Impulse!, the jazz labels he runs. While he began work as a barber, he soon gravitated to music, ascending from stock boy to his current position as president of GRP and Impulse! Records.

"I love all kinds of music," says LiPuma. "I can't say I'm into rap when I go home. I don't sit down and listen to the Notorious B.I.G. or the Butthole Surfers. At the same time, I am into some pop things. I think the Smashing Pumpkins are great."

Born in Cleveland July 5, 1936, LiPuma began listening to the radio early. "When I was 10, I ventured upon a rhythm 'n' blues station—it was WJMO-AM—and

that was it. I started discovering everybody from the Nat Cole Trio and Louis Jordan to Ruth Brown. Then, when I was 16 or 17, I discovered jazz. Stan Getz was the first person I heard. But once I heard Getz—I was a saxophone player—I discovered the guys: Lester Young, Ben Webster, and Coleman Hawkins. There were so many goddamn great saxophone players back then: Zoot Sims, Richie Kamuca, I could name 50 of them. Unlike today."

LiPuma played saxophone in a band in Cleveland with Nick DeCaro, an arranger who moved to the West Coast in the mid-'60s to help LiPuma put together early successes on A&M, Herb Alpert and Jerry Moss's label. His first job in the record industry was working promotion in 1960 for M.S. Distributors in Cleveland. Soon, he was working for Liberty Records, first in the Los Angeles promotion department, then in the New York publishing department. In New York, he plugged songs and supervised demos for Randy Newman, Jackie DeShannon, and Leon Russell. He produced his first single in 1965: "Lipstick Traces," a regional hit for Cleveland soulmen the O'Jays.

In 1966, LiPuma became the first staff producer for then-new label A&M. His first gold record was the Sandpipers' "Guantanamera." He also scored big with a couple of "silly records" by Claudine Longet, a cute French girl who hit with *Claudine* (No. 11) and *The Look of Love* in 1967. His chief collaborator on the Sandpipers and Longet discs was DeCaro, his Cleveland buddy.

Although he has produced some albums he's not happy with (including albums by B.W. Stevenson and Stephen Bishop), his perceived failures are far outweighed by those he considers successes: all the records he's produced for George Benson; records he made with Michael Franks, Claus Ogerman, Natalie Cole, Barbra Streisand (LiPuma produced her 1973 No. 1 platinum seller, *The Way We Were*), and Dave Mason's gold *Alone Together.*

LiPuma became senior vice president of A&R at Elektra Records in 1990, working with such artists as David Sanborn and Anita Baker. He has earned 30 Grammy nominations, produced 18 gold and platinum albums and has sold an estimated 45 million discs. His productions include George Benson's "On Broadway" (No. 7); Natalie Cole's *Unforgettable with Love* (No. 1) album, co-produced with David Foster and Andre Fischer (see entries); and Michael Franks' single, "Popsicle Toes." He won Grammys for his work with George Benson, Jennifer Holiday, Bob James and David Sanborn, Miles Davis, Dr. John, and Rickie Lee Jones, and Natalie Cole.

He became president of GRP and Impulse! Records in 1995. He doesn't care what the musical genre is as long as the material is good—and accessible. "It's not like I consciously go for the accessibility," he says, "though there are times certain elements occur to me. It has more to do with bouncing off of me. I consider myself the ears of the person out there. I don't consider myself on a different plane from John Q., and if someone's bothering me, I assume it's going to bother him."

He says he's been told he was responsible for the advent of so-called smooth jazz, because of the fusion (and lighter) albums he produced in the '70s and early '80s. "Obviously, it's a compliment to hear that," he says, "but it's not like I've consciously tried to do that. I love all types of music, and what I want to do more than anything else is present the act in the best manner that it can be represented."

To come up with models for LiPuma, a producer who also runs a label (make that labels), one must go back to Leonard and Phil Chess of Chess Records, and brothers Ahmet and Nesuhi Ertegun, who, with Jerry Wexler, ran Atlantic Records (see entries).

Is there synergy between the administrative and the creative roles? "I can't say there's anything applicable of one to the other, other than the fact you're in a position to be able to make decisions," LiPuma says. "The positive aspects of it are that you're able to make the decisions and pick the priorities and not do a record that you have no control over. This is my first experience at being president and having to deal with 25 different acts. At times, it's very, very invigorating, at times it's overwhelming."

In regard to his production sound, LiPuma cites such influences as Quincy Jones and Creed Taylor (see entries). "Quincy, early on, from the stuff he was doing on EmArcy," says LiPuma. "Dinah Washington, Sarah Vaughan. I'd have to say that a big influence was Creed Taylor, in the way his mind worked. He was probably the daddy of having acts that were strictly jazz do pop things," such as the albums guitarist Wes Montgomery recorded for Taylor's influential label, CTI. Taylor also worked with organist Jimmy Smith and Brazilian singer/composer Antonio Carlos Jobim and helped turn jazz guitarist George Benson into a pop commodity equally known for his vocals.

Even before he began to recognize such contemporaries, LiPuma started to recognize his predecessors, like Milt Gabler (see entry), the Commodore Records honcho who produced Billie Holiday for that label, and John Hammond (see entry), the visionary Columbia Records executive.

"Milt Gabler went from Louis Armstrong and Louis Jordan and Billie Holiday to Buddy Holly," LiPuma says. "Then you had somebody like John Hammond, who went from Benny Goodman and some of the later Billie Holiday records to Bob Dylan and Bruce Springsteen. That was the whole deal to me: They liked music. it didn't matter whether it was jazz or rock 'n' roll or whatever. Is it good? is the criterion."

He would like to produce Tony Bennett. "He's just the consummate vocalist," LiPuma says. "I've got to go back to 'Because of You' with this guy. I was probably 10 or 12, and I've been listening to him ever since. Here he is, still doing it. He's wonderful."

LiPuma doesn't play sax anymore, but he's thought about it. "I have a close friend, Stewart Levine [see entry], who produced Simply Red and Boy George and all the Crusaders records," LiPuma says. "He's a saxophone player and he really got back into it. He's playing his ass off. I told him I didn't know whether I have the fortitude to get my chops back. The one thing I miss is, it's a great way to express yourself.

"There's something really organic about playing a saxophone," says LiPuma. "You can bend notes, you can growl. Obviously, at the end of a production project, you feel a certain sense of satisfaction, but it isn't as immediate or personal." —CARLO WOLFF

Austin, Patti: *Getting Away with Murder*, Qwest, 1985 • "Honey for the Bees," Qwest, 1985.

Aztec Camera: *Love*, Sire, 1987.

Baker, Anita: *Rhythm of Love* (4 tracks), Elektra, 1994.

Benson, George: *Breezin'*, Warner Bros., 1976 • "This Masquerade," Warner Bros., 1976 • *In Flight*, Warner

Bros., 1977 • "On Broadway," Warner Bros., 1978 • *Weekend in L.A.*, Warner Bros., 1978 • *Livin' Inside Your Love*, Warner Bros., 1979 • "Love Ballad," Warner Bros., 1979 • *The George Benson Collection*, Warner Bros., 1981, 1988 • w/ Earl Klugh, *Collaboration*, Warner Bros., 1987 • *While the City Sleeps . . .* , Warner Bros., 1986 • *Twice the Love*, Warner Bros., 1988 • *Tenderly*, Warner Bros., 1989 • *That's Right*, GRP, 1996.

Bishop, Stephen: *Red Cab to Manhattan*, Warner Bros., 1980 • *On and On: Best Of*, MCA, 1994.

Blades, Ruben: "Hopes on Hold," Elektra, 1988 • *Nothing but the Truth*, Elektra, 1988.

Brecker, Michael: *See* Ogerman, Claus.

Bryson, Peabo: "Love Always Finds a Way," Elektra, 1985 • *Take No Prisoners*, Elektra, 1985.

Claus Ogerman Orchestra: *Gate of Dreams*, Warner Bros., 1977.

Cole, Natalie: *Unforgettable with Love*, Elektra, 1991 • "Take a Look," Elektra, 1993 • *Take a Look*, Elektra, 1993 • *Holly and Ivy*, Elektra, 1994.

Crawford, Randy: *Secret Combination*, Warner Bros., 1981 • *Windsong*, Warner Bros., 1982 • *Nightline*, Warner Bros., 1983.

Davis, Miles: *Tutu*, Warner Bros., 1986 • *Amandla*, Warner Bros., 1989.

De Caro, Nick: *Italian Graffiti*, Blue Thumb, 1974.

Deodato: *Love Island*, Warner Bros., 1978.

Doves, The: *Affinity*, Elektra, 1991.

Dr. John: *City Lights*, A&M, 1978 • *Tango Palace*, A&M, 1979 • *In a Sentimental Mood*, Warner Bros., 1989 • *Mos' Scocious: The Dr, John Anthology*, Rhino, 1993 • *Afterglow*, Blue Thumb, 1995.

Evans, Bill: *You Must Believe in Spring*, Warner Bros., 1981, 1988.

Everything But The Girl: "Driving," Blanco y Negro, 1990 • *Driving* (EP), Blanco y Negro, 1990 • *The Language of Life*, Atlantic, 1990 • *Best Of*, Blanco y Negro, 1996.

Larsen-Feiten Band: *Full Moon*, Warner Bros., 1972, 1982.

Franks, Michael: *The Art of Tea*, Warner Bros., 1975 • "Popsicle Toes," Reprise, 1976 • *Sleeping Gypsy*, Warner Bros., 1977 • *Burchfield Nines*, Warner Bros., 1978, 1988 • *One Bad Habit*, Warner Bros., 1980 • *Blue Pacific*, Reprise, 1990 • *The Best of Michael Franks: A Backward Glance*, Warner Bros., 1998.

Gilberto, Joao: *Amoroso/Brasil*, Warner Archives, 1977, 1993.

Grusin, Dave: *Two for the Road: The Music of Henry Mancini*, GRP, 1997.

Harrison, Donald: *Noveau Swing*, Impulse!, 1997.

Hewett, Howard: *Allegiance*, Elektra, 1992.

Hicks, Dan: *Where's the Money?*, Blue Thumb, 1971 • *Striking It Rich*, Blue Thumb, 1972 • *Last Train to Hicksville*, Blue Thumb, 1973 • *It Happened One Bite*, Warner Bros., 1978.

Holliday, Jennifer: *Best Of,* Geffen, 1996.

Hollywood Beyond: *If,* Warner Bros., 1987.

Humphrey, Paul: *American, Wake Up,* Blue Thumb, 1974.

James, Bob: w/ David Sanborn, *Double Vision,* Warner Bros., 1986.

Jarreau, Al: *Glow,* Warner Bros., 1976 • *Live in Europe,* Warner Bros., 1977 • *Look to the Rainbow: Live in Europe,* Warner Bros., 1977 • *In London,* Warner Bros., 1985 • *Best Of,* Warner Bros., 1996 • *Live in London,* Warner Bros., 1984.

Klugh, Earl: *The Best of Earl Klugh,* Warner Bros., 1998 • *See also* Benson, George.

Krall, Diana: *Only Trust Your Heart,* GRP, 1995 • *All for You (A Dedication to the Nat King Cole Trio),* Impulse!, 1996 • *Love Scenes,* Impulse!/GRP, 1997.

Larsen, Neil: *Jungle Fever,* A&M, 1978 • *High Gear,* A&M, 1979.

Larsen-Feiten Band: *The Larsen-Feiten Band,* Warner Bros., 1980.

Longet, Claudine: *Claudine,* A&M, 1967 • *The Look of Love,* A&M, 1967.

Mark Almond Band: *The Best Of,* Rhino, 1973, 1991 • *Other People's Rooms,* A&M, 1975.

Mason, Dave: *Alone Together,* Blue Thumb, 1970 • *Headkeeper,* Blue Thumb, 1972 • *Dave Mason Is Alive,* Blue Thumb, 1973 • *The Very Best Of,* MCA, 1978.

Montez, Chris: "Call Me," A&M, 1966.

Newman, David "Fathead": *House of David Newman: Fathead Anthology,* Rhino, 1993.

Newman, Randy: *Land of Dreams* (4 tracks), Reprise, 1988.

Nicholls, Roger: *A Small Circle of Friends,* A&M, 1967.

Ogerman, Claus: w/ Michael Brecker, *Cityscape,* Warner Bros., 1982 • *Featuring Randy Brecker,* GRP, 1991 • *See also* Claus Ogerman Orchestra.

O'Jays, The: "Lipstick Traces," Imperial, 1965.

Perez, Danilo: *PanaMonk,* Impulse!, 1996.

Peterson, Ricky: *Nightwatch,* Warner Bros., 1990.

Reed, Eric: *Musicale,* GRP, 1996 • *Pure Imagination,* Impulse!, 1998.

Ruff, Michael: *Once in a Lifetime,* Warner Bros., 1984.

Russell, Brenda: *Two Eyes,* Warner Bros., 1983.

Salinas, Luis: *Salinas,* GRP, 1997.

Sample, Joe: *Spellbound,* Warner Bros., 1989 • *Ashes to Ashes,* Warner Bros., 1990 • *Invitation,* Warner Bros., 1993 • *The Best Of,* Warner Bros., 1998.

Sanborn, David: *Love Songs,* Warner Bros., 1988 • *Pearls,* Elektra, 1995 • *See also* James, Bob.

Sandpipers, The: "Guantanamera," A&M, 1966 • *Greatest Hits,* A&M, 1970.

Scott, Jimmy: *All the Way,* Sire, 1992.

Seawind: *Light the Light,* A&M, 1979.

Sinatra, Frank: *Duets,* Capitol, 1993.

Southwind: *Ready to Ride,* Blue Thumb, 1970 • *What a Place to Land,* Blue Thumb, 1973.

Steele, Jevetta: *Here It Is,* Columbia, 1993.

Stevenson, B.W.: *We Be Sailing,* Warner Bros., 1975.

Streisand, Barbra: *The Way We Were,* Columbia, 1974 • *Greatest Hits,* Vol. 2, Columbia, 1978, 1982 • *The Mirror Has Two Faces* soundtrack, Columbia, 1996.

Stuff: *Stuff,* Warner Bros., 1977 • *Right Stuff,* Warner Bros., 1996.

Szabo, Gabor: *High Contrast,* Blue Thumb, 1970.

Tyner, McCoy: *What the World Needs Now: The Music,* GRP, 1997.

Upchurch, Phil: *Lovin' Feeling,* Blue Thumb, 1971 • *Darkness Darkness,* Blue Thumb, 1982.

Whitfield, Mark: *The Marksman,* Warner Bros., 1990.

Yellowjackets: *Yellowjackets,* Warner Bros., 1981 • *Mirage à Trois,* Warner Bros., 1983 • *Samurai Samba,* Warner Bros., 1985.

Young, Steve: *Rock, Salt and Nails,* Edsel, 1969, 1994.

COLLECTIONS

Casino Lights, Warner Bros., 1989.

Glengarry Glen Ross soundtrack, Elektra, 1992.

Scott Litt

According to Scott Litt, recognizing when the vibe isn't right at a session is one of the most important components of a record producer's talents. Litt believes that the man behind the console should be ready to apply "different things for different people. You should always do things according to the situation at hand. Seeing how different people create and what they need is a big part of it." He is quick to add "it's not worth making enemies unless you're really right. And you gotta know when you're really right and push for something. You gotta choose your points. It's more like a democracy. Unless an artist is looking to you to help with things, like arranging, etc."

Scott Litt has applied this philosophy to his work with a celebrated combo that hails from Athens, Georgia. He has done his thing with R.E.M., beginning with their *Document* (No. 10) album in 1987, and it is probably with their music that many people associate the man. But there is much more.

He was born in New York City in 1954 and experienced his first spiritual connection to music through AM radio around 1965. After youthful fascinations with a small reel-to-reel tape recorder "with a little silver microphone" and jamming with friends on a Farfisa organ, he went on to major in math in college in Colorado. A class in audio engineering ("math and engineering seemed similar," says he) led to a job at an 8-track studio specializing in radio voice-overs and commercial production.

Litt made his way back to the Big Apple in 1978 and sought work as an engineer. "I didn't have a clue. I picked up the phone book and began to go down the studio headings in the Yellow Pages alphabetically." No one answered at "AAA Recorders" but upon ringing up the second listing he landed a gig at an uptown facility called A-1 Sound Studio, which was owned and operated by Atlantic Records co-founder Herb Abramson. It was there that Litt sampled the tail end of the old school, seat-of-the-pants era of recording in NYC. "He had really eccentric gear like an old MCI console that he got from the Atlantic settlement. The faders worked in the opposite direction—pull them toward you and things got louder instead of going down. Nothing was aligned properly. Thread up anything on the tape machine and see if it records it!"

Clientele included old-timers like Butterbeans and Suzie, itinerant disco guys off the street, a blind singer with his dog—and Patti Smith! "People paid in cash and the engineers would split up the money at the end of the sessions because we wouldn't get paid otherwise! It was hilarious and great."

Following a few months at A-1, Litt scored a job at the legendary Power Station, where he worked as a staff engineer/producer between 1978 and 1983. He rubbed elbows daily with the likes of Bob Clearmountain (see entry), Neil Dorfman, and James Farber. "People like Chic, Bruce Springsteen, Diana Ross, David Bowie [see entry] would kind of bump into each other in the lobby and talk. It was a really creative time and an amazing time to learn."

His first production forays were joint efforts with Lance Quinn on albums by Sylvain Sylvain and Robert Gordon (both for RCA). After he mixed most of the dB's first album, *Stands for Decibels,* the group enlisted Litt to produce their second LP, *Repercussion,* in the summer of 1981. "We couldn't afford to do it at the Power Station because we didn't have the budget, so I took a leave of absence and we did it at Rampart Studio in England. That was my first furious, full-on production on my own."

Litt made his first big chart splash with "Walking on Sunshine" (No. 9, co-produced with Pat Collier; see entry) by Katrina and the Waves in 1985. "I took a track that was kind of a demo and we added horns and drums in one night. We started at 3 in the afternoon and by 8 A.M. the next morning it had turned into this awesome track. That was a real highlight."

Following the success of "Sunshine," Litt left the Power Station for the world of freelancing, which consisted mostly of engineering and mixing gigs in the United States, Canada, and England. "Those couple of years after you leave the studio and then get your own thing going, it's a tough little transition."

The split proved to be a wise move. R.E.M. dug Litt's work with the dB's and contacted him to cut "Romance," a song for an Alan Rudolph film *Made in Heaven.* "The track didn't come out particularly well but for the two days we worked we had a good time, so they asked me to produce their next album, which was *Document.* With that album it was basically like being another member. Throw in an idea once in a while, if it gets shot down that's totally cool. And try to have the perspective of everybody, you know, working with a group."

Litt and R.E.M. went on together to create a catalog of diverse discs. On *Out of Time* (No. 1) they consciously went for orchestration. On *Green* (No. 12) they were trying to push the boundaries of the sounds they could achieve. A darker, more intimate feel surfaced on *Automatic for the People* (No. 2). *Monster* (No. 1) was "always meant to be loud. They were going to go on tour. We all knew it. It seemed like the thing to do. That was cut like in a rehearsal. We brought tape machines around all over the place. That was a roughshod kind of a record."

This penchant for variety recalls the aforementioned credo of "different things for different people." Many times retaining the charm of the original demo is just what the doctor ordered. "Particularly when it's a first record with a band. Indigo Girls is one that affected me in that way. It's like, don't screw it up, do what emotionally got you in the first place. Let them do that and also have some fun and experience the studio."

Nirvana's *MTV Unplugged in New York* (No. 1) album was finished after Kurt Cobain's death. "On an emotional level and a physical level, on many levels, it was a very hard thing to do and put together. I feel great about it."

Some of Scott Litt's favorite works among his own productions are also some of the lesser-known. One example is *So Much Water So Close to Home* by Paul Kelly and the Messengers. Another is That Petrol Emotion's *Chemicrazy,* an album he refers to as an "awesome, awesome record. They taught me a lot."

Litt's production experience has led him to new ventures in songwriting and the birth of a new record label, Outpost. But despite all his success, going with the right "vibe" remains the crux of the Scott Litt raison d'être. "You've got to go with your instincts. Then, if it doesn't work, well, at least you've got your shot. But making a record that you don't feel good about, and then if it doesn't do well, it's like you've never found ground zero. You never found if it was your music or just the way that the music was produced. There's nothing worse than hating the experience of creating a record and not having fun in the studio because it's a great place to be and it's a great haven. And it's a great thing to instill in people that it can be fun. And creating that atmosphere is important." —DENNIS DIKEN

Beat Rodeo: *Home in the Heart of the Beat,* IRS, 1986.
Catherine Wheel: "The Nude," Fontana/Mercury, 1994.
Days of the New: *Days of the New,* Outpost, 1997 • "Touch, Peel, and Stand," Outpost, 1997.
dB's, The: *Repercussion,* Albion, 1982.
Gordon, Robert: *Are You Gonna Be the One?,* RCA, 1981 • *Too Fast to Live, Too Young to Die,* RCA, 1982 • *Robert Gordon Is Red Hot,* Bear Family, 1989.
Heyden: *The Closer I Get,* Outpost, 1998.
Indigo Girls: "Closer to Fine," Epic, 1989 • *Indigo Girls,* Epic, 1989 • *Nomads Indians Saints,* Epic, 1990 • *Live: Back on the Bus, Y'all,* Epic, 1991.
Juliana Hatfield 3: *Become What You Are,* Mammoth/Atlantic, 1993 • "Spin the Bottle," RCA, 1993, 1994 (*Reality Bites* soundtrack).
Katrina and the Waves: *Katrina and the Waves,* Capitol, 1985 • "Que Te Quiero," Capitol, 1985 • "Walking on Sunshine," Capitol, 1985 • "Is That It?," Capitol, 1986 • *Waves,* Capitol, 1986.
Kelly, Paul, and the Messengers: *Gossip,* A&M, 1987 • *So Much Water So Close to Home,* A&M, 1989.
Nirvana: *MTV Unplugged in New York,* DGC, 1994.
Pylon: *Chain* (1 track), Sky, 1990.
R.E.M.: *Document,* IRS, 1987 • "Romance," Asylum, 1987 (*Made in Heaven* soundtrack) • "The One I Love," IRS, 1987 • *Eponymous,* IRS, 1988 • *Green,* Warner Bros., 1988 • "It's the End of the World As We Know It," IRS, 1988 • "Stand," Warner Bros., 1988 • "Pop Song 89," Warner Bros., 1989 • "First We Take Manhattan," Atlantic, 1991 (*I'm Your Fan*) • "Fretless," Warner Bros., 1991 (*Until the End of the World* soundtrack) • "Losing My Religion," Warner Bros., 1991 • *Out of Time,* Warner Bros., 1991 • "Radio Song," Warner Bros., 1991 • "Shiny Happy People," Warner Bros., 1991 • *Automatic for the People,* Warner Bros., 1992 • "Drive," Warner Bros., 1992 • "Everybody Hurts," Warner Bros., 1993 • "It's a Free World Baby," Warner Bros., 1993 (*Coneheads* soundtrack) • "Man on the Moon," Warner Bros., 1993 • w/ Natalie Merchant, "Photograph," Rykodisc, 1993 (*Born to Choose*) • "Bang and Blame," Warner Bros., 1994 • "Find the River," Warner Bros., 1994 • *Monster,* Warner Bros., 1994 • "What's the Frequency Kenneth?," Warner Bros., 1994 • *Songs That Are Live* (EP), Warner Bros., 1995 • "Strange

Currencies," Warner Bros., 1995 • "Bittersweet Me," Warner Bros., 1996 • "Electrolite," Warner Bros., 1996 • *New Adventures in Hi-Fi,* Warner Bros., 1996 • w/ William S. Burroughs, "Star Me Kitten," Warner Bros., 1996 (*Songs in the Key of X*).
Reckless Sleepers: *Wake Up to the Big Boss Sounds,* IRS, 1988.
Replacements, The: *All Shook Down,* Sire/Reprise, 1990 • *Don't Sell or Buy, It's Crap,* Sire/Reprise, 1991 • *All for Nothing/Nothing for All,* Warner Bros., 1997.
Shear, Jules: *Horse of a Different Color: The Jules Shear Collection,* Razor & Tie, 1995.
Smith, Patti: *Dream of Life,* Arista, 1988 • *Masters,* Arista, 1996.
Stamey, Chris: *It's a Wonderful Life,* DB, 1983 • *It's Alright* (2 tracks), A&M, 1987.
Sweet, Matthew: *Inside,* Columbia, 1986.
That Petrol Emotion: *Chemicrazy,* Virgin, 1990.
Westerberg, Paul: "Dyslexic Heart," Epic Soundtrax, 1992 (*Singles* soundtrack).
Woodentops: *Wooden Foot Cops on the Highway,* Columbia, 1988.

Warne Livesey

Warne Livesey is an English producer, engineer, musician, and songwriter who has been involved with some of the more successful and interesting modern rock albums of the '80s and '90s. In the '80s Livesey produced or co-produced Midnight Oil's platinum *Diesel and Dust* (No. 21) and gold *Blue Sky Mining* (No. 20), The The's *Infected* (No. 14 U.K.) and *Mind Bomb* (No. 4 U.K.), Deacon Blues' *When the World Knows Your Name* (No. 1 U.K.), and Scraping Foetus off the Wheel's *Hole* and *Nail.* In the '90s he guided Jesus Jones' *Perverse* (No. 6 U.K.), All About Eve's *Touched by Jesus* (No. 17 U.K.), the House of Love's *Babe Rainbow,* and Prick's self-titled first album.

Londoner Warne Livesey played bass with a number of bands in school, but his sense of sonic perfection prohibited him from fully enjoying the experience. "I felt that certain elements of the way music should sound could never be attained live, and that frustrated me," he explains. So Livesey took to the studio and worked at a number of smaller London studios, "doing very low level production work for very small labels."

On one of those small productions Livesey met David Lord (producer of Peter Gabriel, Icehouse), who encouraged and mentored him. By the early '80s

Livesey was ready for his first major production, the vicious proto-industrial noise of Jim Thirwell's (aka Foetus, Scraping Foetus off the Wheel, Foetus Inc., Foetus Interruptus, etc.) *Hole*. "That album was absolutely invaluable in terms of developing what I do. I was in a situation with someone who was essentially not a musician—who can't really play any instrument—but who absolutely insisted on playing everything on the record (in studios that were very cheap and had no equipment), and whose ideas were absolutely enormous. I had to figure out how to get the absolute best out of very limited ability and very limited equipment," he says.

While it was painstaking, Livesey's work with Thirwell utilized both his musical and engineering experience: a duality that has served him well ever since. "I tend to get involved with both sides of recording: with the arrangement side in terms of developing parts, improving upon them, or even inventing parts when they are needed; and, at the same time, controlling the sound aspects. For me the two things go hand-in-hand. You can't have a great sound without having the right parts at the right time. A wrong part in the arrangement is never going to sound any good, no matter how well you record it."

During the sessions for The The's *Infected* album, Livesey spent time as producer, engineer, arranger, and musician (bass, organ, background vocals). Livesey became so involved with the musical side of the process that he and singer/songwriter/instrumentalist Matt Johnson sometimes switched roles. "That's an interesting way of doing things. I would sit at the keyboards and pull up sounds and create parts and he would produce me. Then we would switch around and he would pick up a guitar. The boundary between artist and producer was completely eroded." Livesey also contributed music and production work to four tracks on The The's great *Mind Bomb* album, including the moody hit single "The Beat(en) Generation" (No. 18 U.K.).

Livesey's greatest commercial success to date has come with Australian political rockers Midnight Oil. Livesey helped bring out the tunefulness inherent in band's energetic sound, crafting a worldwide hit out of "Beds Are Burning" (No. 17), the band's heartfelt plea on behalf of Australian aborigines found on the *Diesel and Dust* album. Other album highlights include the inertial "Dreamworld" and the quietly urgent "The Dead Heart." Though a lesser statement than *Diesel*, *Blue Sky Mining* continued the band's momentum and also hit big.

In the '90s Livesey has drifted toward bands that combine electronic beats with organic instrumentation to create cutting-edge hybrids. Livesey produced Jesus Jones' smash *Perverse* with swirling hits "The Devil You Know" (No. 10 U.K.) and "The Right Decision." He co-produced (with Trent Reznor; see entry) the first Prick album, which combines elements of industrial, goth, and pop into a dynamic, enveloping near-masterpiece, exemplified by the single "Animal."

In a retro mode, Livesey also produced the underappreciated *Babe Rainbow* by '60s revivalists the House of Love. He co-wrote two songs on the album with band leader Guy Chadwick, including the compelling, Spencer Davis-esque "You Don't Understand."

Though Livesey has worked thus far with various permutations of modern rock, he doesn't want to be compartmentalized. "My taste is eclectic enough to work with pretty much any style. I love classical, jazz, extreme industrial, dance music. As long as it's interesting and inventive and trying in some way to push the boundaries a bit, then it holds my interest." —ERIC OLSEN AND DAVID JOHN FARINELLA

All About Eve: *Touched by Jesus*, Vertigo, 1991.

Big Dish: *Satellites*, EastWest, 1991.

Cope, Julian: *Saint Julian*, Island, 1987 • *Floored Genius: The Best of Julian Cope and the Teardrop Explodes, 1979–1991*, Island, 1992.

Cracknell, Sarah: *Lipslide*, Gut, 1997.

Deacon Blue: *When the World Knows Your Name*, Columbia, 1989.

Higsons, The: *Music to Watch Girls By*, Two Tone, 1984.

House of Love: *Babe Rainbow*, Fontana/Mercury, 1992.

Icehouse: *Measure for Measure*, Chrysalis, 1986.

Jesus Jones: *Perverse*, Food/EMI, 1993 • "The Devil You Know," Food/EMI, 1993 • "The Right Decision," Food/EMI, 1993.

Matthew Good Band: *Underdogs*, Darktown, 1997.

Midnight Oil: "Beds Are Burning," Columbia, 1987 • *Diesel and Dust*, Columbia, 1987 • "The Dead Heart," Columbia, 1988 • "Blue Sky Mine," Columbia, 1990 • *Blue Sky Mining*, Columbia, 1990 • *20,000 Watt R.S.L.: Greatest Hits*, Columbia, 1997.

Prick: *Prick* (6 tracks), Nothing/Interscope, 1995.

Scraping Foetus off the Wheel: *Hole*, Thirsty Ear, 1984, 1995 • *Nail*, Thirsty Ear, 1985, 1995.

Suddenly Tammy!: *We Get There When We Do*, Warner Bros., 1995.

The The: "Infected," Epic, 1986 • *Infected*, Epic, 1986 • *Mind Bomb* (4 tracks), Epic, 1989 • "The Beat(en) Generation," Epic, 1989.

Whipping Boy: *Heartworm*, Columbia, 1996.

Young, Paul: *Other Voices*, Columbia, 1990 • *From Time to Time: The Singles Collection*, Columbia, 1991.

Lords of Acid

See PRAGA KHAN AND THE LORDS OF ACID

Chris Lowe

See PET SHOP BOYS

Nick Lowe

British singer/songwriter/bassist/producer Nick Lowe has a keen understanding of pop music. Indeed, the unassuming Lowe crafts "pure pop for now people," as he puts it.

Born March 24, 1949, in Suffolk, Lowe's career began in the '60s with Brinsley Schwarz, a pub-rock band that included keyboardist Bob Andrews and guitarist Schwarz, later luminaries with Graham Parker and the Rumour. In fact, Lowe's work with Brinsley Schwarz sowed the seeds for his later pop explorations: "(What's So Funny 'Bout) Peace, Love and Understanding?," featured on the band's 1974 swan song, *New Favourites*, was a buoyant paean to the Summer of Love that was recut by Elvis Costello (see entry) in 1978 with Lowe at the helm.

In 1975, Lowe hooked up with Jake Riviera's Stiff label, churning out morsels of pop such as "So It Goes," "Heart of the City," "I Love the Sound of Breaking Glass" (No. 7 U.K.), and "Little Hitler," singles that were captured on the British release, *The Jesus of Cool*, retitled *Pure Pop for Now People* in the U.S.

Lowe was also collaborating regularly with singer/guitarist/producer Dave Edmunds (see entry), turning out such tracks as "Here Comes the Weekend," "I Knew the Bride (When She Used to Rock and Roll)," and "What Did I Do Last Night?," which featured the band Rockpile put together by Edmunds and Lowe.

Lowe became a veritable hit factory with his production of albums by Elvis Costello and Graham Parker. A case in point: Parker's *Stick to Me* (No. 19 U.K.) album. Lowe was recruited after Parker had nearly abandoned the project; the result was one of Parker's best efforts. On the title track, Lowe supports Parker's sneering vocal with pounding drums, backstreet horns, and Brinsley Schwarz's blazing guitar leads.

Lowe's early solo work reached its zenith with the 1979 release, *Labour of Lust*. That masterwork included his lone American hit, "Cruel to Be Kind" (No. 12), featuring masterful drumming by Terry Williams; Mickey Jupp's naughty rocker, "Switchboard Susan," featuring a nifty guitar solo from Billy Bremner; and "Cracking Up," with Edmunds' churning guitar echoing Lowe's moody vocal. In 1980 Rockpile released its lone album as a group, *Seconds of Pleasure*, a disappointing effort compared with the highs reached by the band when supporting Edmunds' and Lowe's solo efforts. Lowe, however, did turn in one classic: "When I Write the Book."

Lowe's '80s albums included *The Abominable Showman*, featuring such highlights as "We Want Action" and "Time Wounds All Heels"; *Nick Lowe and His Cowboy Outfit*, which included Jupp's "You'll Never Get Me Up in One of Those"; and *The Rose of England*, a masterpiece on a par with his classic *Labour of Lust*, including John Hiatt's "She Don't Love Nobody" and the boastful "Seven Nights to Rock."

In the '90s, Lowe cut back his outside production to concentrate on solo work. Consequently, *The Impossible Bird*, *Party of One*, and *Live! On the Battlefield* reflect Lowe's slightly lower profile. In addition to Rockpile, Lowe was part of the band, Little Village. He also produced albums by his one-time wife, Carlene Carter, and by ex-Ace frontman Paul Carrack. —BEN CROMER

Carrack, Paul: *Suburban Voodoo*, Epic, 1982, 1995 • *The Carrack Collection*, Chrysalis, 1988.

Carter, Carlene: *Blue Nun*, F-Beat/WB, 1977, 1981 • *Musical Shapes*, F-Beat, 1980 • *Hindsight 20/20*, Warner Bros., 1996.

Cash, Johnny: *The Essential Johnny Cash, 1955–1983*, Legacy, 1992.

Costello, Elvis: "Alison," Stiff, 1977 • "Less Than Zero," Stiff, 1977 • *My Aim Is True*, Stiff/CBS, 1977 • "(What's So Funny 'Bout) Peace, Love and Understanding?," Columbia, 1978 • *This Year's Model*, Columbia, 1978 • "Oliver's Army," Columbia, 1979 • *Elvis Costello*, Columbia, 1980 • *Taking Liberties*, Columbia, 1980 • *Ten Bloody Mary's and Ten How's Your Fathers*, Demon, 1980, 1995 • *Trust*, F-Beat/CBS, 1981 • *Best Of*, Columbia, 1985 • *Out of Our Idiot*, Demon, 1987 • *2 1/2 Years*, Rykodisc, 1993.

Costello, Elvis, and the Attractions: *Armed Forces*, Columbia, 1979 • *Get Happy*, Columbia, 1980 • *Girls, Girls, Girls*, Columbia, 1989 • *Blood and Chocolate*, Columbia, 1986.

Cliff, Jimmy: w/ Elvis Costello and the Attractions, "Seven-Day Weekend," Columbia, 1986 (*Club Paradise* soundtrack).

Damned, The: *Damned, Damned, Damned,* Stiff, 1977 • *Music for Pleasure,* Stiff, 1977 • *Best Of* (2 tracks), DAM 1, 1981 • *The Light at the End of the Tunnel,* MCA, 1988.

Dr. Feelgood: *Be Seeing You,* United Artists, 1977 • *A Case of the Shakes,* United Artists/Stiff, 1980.

Edmunds, Dave: *Subtle As a Flying Mallet,* RCA, 1975 • *Track on Wax 4,* Swan Song, 1978 • *Repeat When Necessary,* Swan Song, 1979 • *Twangin',* Swan Song, 1981 • *The Dave Edmunds Anthology (1968–1990),* Rhino, 1993.

Fabulous Thunderbirds: *T-Bird Rhythm,* Chrysalis, 1982 • *The Essential Fabulous Thunderbirds Collection,* Chrysalis, 1991.

Hiatt, John: *Riding with the King* (5 tracks), Geffen, 1983 • *Living a Little, Laughing a Little,* Raven, 1996.

Impossible Birds: See Lowe, Nick.

Jupp, Mickey: *Juppanese* (side 1), Stiff, 1978.

Katydids: *Katydids,* Reprise, 1990.

Lowe, Nick: *Buy 1* (EP), Stiff, 1976 • "So It Goes," Stiff, 1976 • *Jesus of Cool (Pure Pop for Now People),* Radar/CBS, 1978 • *Pure Pop for Now People (Jesus of Cool),* Columbia, 1978 • "Cruel to Be Kind," Columbia, 1979 • *Labour of Lust,* Columbia, 1979 • *Nick the Knife,* Columbia, 1982 • *The Abominable Showman,* Columbia, 1983 • "Half a Boy and Half a Man," Columbia, 1984 • *Nick Lowe and His Cowboy Outfit,* Columbia, 1984 • *The Rose of England,* Columbia, 1985 • *Pinker and Prouder Than Previous,* Columbia, 1988, 1990 • *Basher: The Best Of,* Columbia, 1989 • *The Wilderness Years,* Demon, 1991 • *Boxed,* Demon, 1994 • w/ the Impossible Birds, *The Impossible Bird,* Upstart, 1994 • *Live! On the Battlefield* (EP), Upstart, 1995 • *Dig My Mood,* Demon, 1998 • "You Inspire Me," Demon, 1998.

Mavericks, The: "True Love Ways," Decca, 1996 (*Not Fade Away [Remembering Buddy Holly]*).

Men They Couln't Hang: *Night of 1,000 Candles,* Diablo, 1985, 1997.

Moonlighters: *Rush Hour,* Demon, 1983.

Parker, Graham: *Passion Is No Ordinary Word: The Graham Parker Anthology,* Rhino, 1993.

Parker, Graham, and the Rumour: *Heat Treatment* (1 track), Mercury, 1976 • *Howlin' Wind,* Mercury, 1976 • *Stick to Me,* Mercury, 1977 • *The (Black) Pink Parker* (EP, 2 tracks), Mercury, 1977.

Pretenders, The: "Stop Your Sobbing," Real/Sire, 1979 • *The Pretenders* (1 track), Real/Sire, 1979 • *The Singles,* Sire, 1987.

Rain: *A Taste Of . . . ,* Columbia, 1992.

Rockpile: *Seconds of Pleasure,* Columbia, 1980.

Wreckless Eric: *Wreckless Eric,* Stiff, 1978 • *Big Smash* (1 track), Stiff, 1980.

Jeff Lynne

In 1968 Jeff Lynne was recording at Advision Studios in London when a friend asked if he wanted to attend a Beatles recording session at EMI's Abbey Road Studios. Lynne jumped at the chance to watch the Beatles at work on the *White Album,* never envisaging that someday he would produce recordings by Britain's pop icons.

More than 25 years later, Lynne's ultimate fantasy was fulfilled when he molded two of John Lennon's demos, "Free As a Bird" (No. 6) and "Real Love" (No. 11), into completed tracks for the Beatles' *Anthology* (No. 1). "It was the biggest thrill and the most scary thing at the same time," says Lynne. "The greatest part for me was the banter in the studio: Just them reminiscing and talking, and including me [in the conversation]."

Lynne's enthusiasm never waned, despite the technical deficiencies of Lennon's demos. "The voice on 'Free As a Bird' wasn't very loud on the original, with just the piano, and obviously the EQ was a bit peculiar because it was recorded on a Walkman or something," Lynne explains. "I'd be thrilled to bits when we'd get something good down and it would suddenly start to come together."

Lynne has always viewed production as an extension of songwriting and performing. Born December 30, 1947, in Birmingham, England, Lynne became interested in production in the late '60s when he helped record two albums by his band, Idle Race. Lynne's production expertise grew during his stint with Roy Wood in the Move, resulting in the classic "California Man/Do Ya" (No. 7 U.K.) single.

Lynne and Wood then hatched the Electric Light Orchestra before Wood jumped ship to form another band, Wizard. "It was a bit of a shambles," says Lynne of the embryonic ELO. "Roy left after about six months, so I just took it on and tried to make it into what we'd imagined it would have been (had Wood remained). Early ELO tracks such as "Roll Over Beethoven" (No. 6 U.K.) and "Showdown" (No. 12 U.K.) were experiments that ultimately led to Lynne's production trademark: layers of guitars, keyboards, and vocals that created a mosaic of sound. "I'd think bigger was better," Lynne says of his days in ELO. "Instead of one piano, I'd have six pianos. I'd fill every hole between every bass drum-beat with something else and then I'd want to keep doing more backing vocals, which drove engineers mad."

Lynne hit his stride with *Eldorado* (No. 16), *Face the Music* (No. 8), *A New World Record* (No. 5), *Out of the Blue* (No. 4), and *Discovery* (No. 5): albums that featured tight, melodic pop rock such as "Can't Get It out of My Head" (No. 9), "Fire on High," "So Fine," "Livin' Thing" (No. 13), "Telephone Line" (No. 7), "Sweet Talkin' Woman" (No. 17), and "Last Train to London."

Lynne says that ELO's songs were completed in stages, with the backing tracks often finished before he wrote the lyrics. "That forced me to do the words," Lynne says. "So nobody ever knew the tunes except me."

Although largely unheralded, ELO's later albums, such as *Time* (No. 16), *Secret Messages* (No. 4 U.K.), and *Balance of Power* (No. 9 U.K.), did include some gems: "Twilight," "Rock 'n' Roll Is King" (No. 19), and "Calling America" (No. 18 U.K.). By then, however, Lynne was ready for something new. "I had a call from George Harrison via Dave Edmunds, who said, 'Oh, George said he'd like for you to work with him,' " says Lynne of Harrison's 1987 album, *Cloud Nine* (No. 8).

Lynne and Harrison followed that project with the Traveling Wilburys, an ad hoc assemblage that also included Tom Petty, Bob Dylan, and Roy Orbison. Organized on a whim, the band's first song, "Handle with Care," was originally intended as a bonus track for the European release of a Harrison maxi-single. "It came out so good that [Warner Bros. executive] Mo Ostin said, 'You can't use this as a throwaway; you might as well use it for your group because you're all playing on it,' " Lynne recalls.

In the late '80s and early '90s Lynne recorded a second Wilburys album; completed a solo project, *Armchair Theatre,* that demonstrated his deft pop touch on "Lift Me Up" and "Every Little Thing"; and produced solo discs by Petty and Orbison that yielded Petty's "I Won't Back Down" (No. 12) and Orbison's "You Got It" (No. 9), hits with major contributions by Lynne. "If I write the song I usually end up producing it," Lynne explains. "The two go hand-in-hand to me because when you nurse the song into being you should look after it."

A perfectionist, Lynne admits that he is "obsessive about certain things. I don't really use reverb at all; I like things dry." A convert to digital, Lynne's views changed during a conversation with the Police's Stewart Copeland. "I said to him, 'It's only naughts [zeros] and ones—how can that be music?' He said, 'Well, what are those funny little squiggly things on the tape? Only iron bits of oxide.' I thought, 'Actually, he's right.' "

Lynne prefers analog recording for drums and bass, pointing out that "you can distort analog" to achieve an effect. "I haven't discovered a way to do that on digital."

When Lynne is not working on an album at home in Los Angeles, he can usually be found in another studio. Yet, wherever Lynne is recording, the studio is his home. "I love making records. There's nothing else I'd rather do and I have great fun doing it." —Ben Cromer

Beatles, The: *Anthology 1,* Apple/Capitol, 1995 • "Free As a Bird," Apple/Capitol, 1995 • *Anthology 2,* Apple/Capitol, 1996 • *Real Love* (EP), Apple/Capitol, 1996.

Cocker, Joe: *Night Calls,* Gold Rush, 1992, 1996 • *Best Of,* Capitol, 1993.

Eddy, Duane: *Twang Thang: Anthology,* Rhino, 1993.

Edmunds, Dave: *Information,* Columbia, 1983, 1991 • "Slipping Away," Columbia, 1983 • *Riff Raff,* Columbia, 1984 • *The Dave Edmunds Anthology (1968–1990),* Rhino, 1993.

Electric Light Orchestra: *No Answer,* Jet/Epic, 1972 • *ELO II,* Jet/Epic, 1973 • *On the Third Day,* Jet/Epic, 1973 • "Roll Over Beethoven," United Artists, 1973 • "Showdown," United Artists, 1973 • *Eldorado,* Jet/Epic, 1974 • "Ma Ma Ma Belle," United Artists, 1974 • "Can't Get It out of My Head," United Artists, 1975 • "Evil Woman," United Artists, 1975 • *Face the Music,* Jet/Epic, 1975 • *A New World Record,* Jet/Epic, 1976 • "Livin' Thing," United Artists, 1976 • *Olé,* Jet/Epic, 1976 • "Strange Magic," United Artists, 1976 • "Do Ya," United Artists, 1977 • *Out of the Blue,* Jet/Epic, 1977 • "Rockaria," United Artists, 1977 • "Telephone Line," United Artists, 1977 • "Turn to Stone," Jet, 1977 • "Mr. Blue Sky," Jet, 1978 • "Sweet Talkin' Woman," Jet, 1978 • "Confusion," Jet, 1979 • *Discovery,* Jet/Epic, 1979 • "Don't Bring Me Down," Jet, 1979 • *Greatest Hits,* Jet, 1979 • "Shine a Little Love," Jet, 1979 • "The Diary of Horace Wimp," United Artists, 1979 • "All Over the World," MCA, 1980 • "Don't Walk Away," Jet, 1980 • "I'm Alive," MCA, 1980 • "Last Train to London," Jet, 1980 • "Xanadu," MCA, 1980 • *Xanadu* soundtrack, MCA, 1980 • "Hold on Tight," Jet, 1981 • "Ticket to the Moon," Jet, 1981 • *Time,* Jet/Epic, 1981 • "Twilight," Jet, 1981 • "Rock 'n' Roll Is King," Jet, 1983 • "Secret Messages," Jet, 1983 • *Secret Messages,* CBS Associated, 1983 • *Balance of Power,* CBS Associated, 1986 • "Calling America," CBS, 1986 • *Afterglow,* Epic, 1990 • *Part Two,* Scotti Brothers, 1991 • *Strange Music: The Best Of,* Legacy/Epic, 1995.

Harrison, George: *Cloud Nine,* Dark Horse, 1987 • "Got My Mind Set on You," Dark Horse, 1987 • "When We Was Fab," Dark Horse, 1988 • *Best of Dark Horse, 1976–1989,* Dark Horse, 1989.

Jones, Tom: *The Lead and How to Swing It,* Interscope, 1994.

Lynne, Jeff: *Armchair Theater,* Reprise, 1990.

McCartney, Paul: *Flaming Pie,* Capitol, 1997 • "The World Tonight," Capitol, 1997.

Move, The: *Looking On,* Capitol, 1971 • "California Man/Do Ya," Capitol, 1972 • *Split Ends,* United Artists, 1972 • *The Collection,* Castle, 1986 • *Message from the Country: The Jeff Lynne Years, 1968–1973,* EMI, 1989 • *Great Move! The Best Of,* EMI Legends, 1994.

Newman, Randy: *Land of Dreams* (1 track), Reprise, 1988.

Newton-John, Olivia: *Olivia,* Festival, 1972, 1992 • *Olivia's Greatest Hits,* Vol. 2, MCA, 1982.

Orbison, Roy: *Mystery Girl* (3 tracks), Virgin, 1989 • "You Got It," Virgin, 1989 • "I Drove All Night," MCA, 1991 • *Nintendo White Knuckle Scorin',* MCA, 1991 • *King of Hearts,* Virgin, 1992 • *The Very Best Of,* Virgin, 1997.

Petty, Tom: "Free Falling," MCA, 1989 • *Full Moon Fever,* MCA, 1989 • "I Won't Back Down," MCA, 1989 • "Runnin' Down a Dream," MCA, 1989 • "A Face in the Crowd," MCA, 1990.

Petty, Tom, and the Heartbreakers: "Into the Great Wide Open," Gone Gator/MCA, 1991 • *Into the Great Wide Open,* Gone Gator/MCA, 1991 • "Learning to Fly," Gone Gator/MCA, 1991 • *Greatest Hits,* MCA, 1993.

Raye, Julianna: *Something Peculiar,* Reprise, 1992.

Shannon, Del: *Rock On,* MCA, 1991.

Shrieve, Michael: *Stiletto,* Atlantic, 1989 • *The Big Picture,* Atlantic, 1989.

Starr, Ringo: *Time Takes Time,* Private, 1992 • "Weight of the World," Private, 1992.

Traveling Wilburys: "Handle with Care," Wilbury/WB, 1988 • *The Traveling Wilburys,* Wilbury/WB, 1988 • "End of the Line," Wilbury/WB, 1989 • *Vol. 3,* Wilbury/WB, 1990.

Wilson, Brian: *Brian Wilson,* Sire/Reprise, 1988.

Wood, Roy: *You Can Dance the Rock 'n' Roll: The Roy Wood Years, 1971–1973,* Harvest/EMI, 1989.

Tim Mac

Tim Mac's production career grew out of a specific musical milieu, the flourishing Minneapolis scene of the mid- to late '80s. Although Minneapolis never enjoyed the explosive breakout that Seattle did, it has produced an array of indie and major-label acts in the last decade.

The self-taught Mac opened his first studio, Six Feet Under, in the basement of a rundown old house he was living in. Since he knew many of the area's punk bands (he played in one, Halo of Flies) and his rates were cheap, he acquired many clients, both local and underground bands from elsewhere doing the van circuit. For $40, he'd turn out four songs in four hours—tracks that

frequently ended up on the 7-inch discs that fueled the pre-Nirvana underground scene. (He even recorded a very young Green Day.)

Much of his work was for Amphetamine Reptile. Founded by Halo of Flies' Tom Hazelmyer, the label specialized in a dense, abrupt form of heavy underground rock. By the early '90s, AmRep was doing full-length CDs, most of which were recorded at Mac's place. When bands like Helmet and Unsane reached the majors in the wake of *Nevermind,* their sound became influential on '90s metal.

After five years, Mac closed his studio to do stints as a live soundman with Helmet and a Minneapolis band he'd recorded who were newly signed to Reprise, Babes in Toyland. Mac assisted on the recording of Babes in Toyland's 1992 Reprise debut *Fontanelle,* produced by Sonic Youth's Lee Ranaldo. Although, like the band, he maligns the book's truthfulness, he's the pretension-puncturing voice of reality in the studio scenes in Neal Karlen's 1994 book, *Babes in Toyland: The Making and Selling of a Rock Band.* Mac does, however, own up to the attitudes he expressed there.

Mac is a Minneapolis version of Chicago's Steve Albini (see entry), without the elaborate system of rationalizations to justify major-label work in light of his punk-cred pronouncements. Though Mac is largely skeptical of the major-label system (largely based on his observations with Babes), he has no problem with big budgets and quality studio gear as long as the integrity of the performance is maintained. What makes punk, he says, is people playing off one another to create music they believe in.

He believes his ability to work quickly, stay out of the way, and make a band feel at ease are his strengths. "I like bands to not even be aware that I am there," he says. "Nothing should distract from their performance." Naturally, he prefers to record as live as possible and, because of his background, doesn't find bare-bones gear a hindrance. "The idea of recording is to capture a band. If they are more interested in exploring every studio possibility, they're not really a band."

When he returned to Minneapolis from the road in 1992, Mac supervised construction of his own custom studio in AmRep's building, graduating to 16-track ("still Tascam stuff, though"). In his four years there, he recorded many of the aggressive bands on the AmRep roster such as Cows, Today Is the Day, Chokebore, Hammerhead, Love 666, Janitor Joe, Supernova, and many others. The rapport he'd developed with Babes in Toyland led to his being tapped to produce the band's sophomore Reprise effort, 1995's *Nemesisters.* More uneven but rawer and more dynamic, it more accurately captures the essence of this manic, unpredictable punk band.

In 1996, he recorded the Cows' careening *Whorn,* graduating from the 1-inch Tascam to an Ampex 2-inch 16- track. He also recorded Lollipop's AmRep debut, which he proudly notes is "totally 100 percent live." Though the sound, led by buzzing dust-storm guitars, lacks glossy radio friendliness, it's a swirl of distinctive parts that interact dynamically. Mac severed his connection with AmRep in late 1996 to go freelance. In 1997, he traveled to Chicago to produce Gaunt's Warner Bros. debut, and to California for Supernova's second album. His years spent wringing decent sounds out of minimal equipment gave him an ability to adapt to different environments quickly. He's also adept at producing a recording that sounds rough while maintaining the integrity of the individual instruments. —ANASTASIA PANTSIOS

A 10 O'Clock Scholar: *Quitest,* Grass, 1996.

Babes in Toyland: *Painkillers* (EP), Reprise, 1993 • "Calling Occupants of Interplanetary Craft," A&M, 1994 (*If I Were a Carpenter*) • *Nemesisters,* Reprise, 1995 • "We Are Family," Reprise, 1995.

Balloon Guy: *Soundbull,* Generator, 1995.

Chokebore: *Motionless,* Amphetamine Reptile, 1993.

Cows: *Peacetika,* Amphetamine Reptile, 1991 • *Old Gold (1989–1991),* Amphetamine Reptile, 1996 • *Whorn,* Amphetamine Reptile, 1996.

Dumpster Juice: *That Not So Fresh Feeling,* Spanish Fly, 1993 • *Who Died in Here?,* Spanish Fly, 1996.

Finn, Mickey: *Mickey Finn,* Bomb, 1996.

Gaunt: *Yeah, Me Too,* Amphetamine Reptile, 1995 • *Bricks and Blackouts,* Warner Bros., 1998.

Guzzard: *Get a Witness,* Amphetamine Reptile, 1993 • *Quick, Fast, in a Hurry,* Amphetamine Reptile, 1995.

Halo of Flies: *Music for Insect Minds,* Amphetamine Reptile, 1991.

Hammerhead: *Evil Twin* (2 tracks), Amphetamine Reptile, 1993 • *Into the Vortex,* Amphetamine Reptile, 1994.

Janitor Joe: *Big Metal Birds,* Amphetamine Reptile, 1993.

Love 666: *Please Kill Yourself So I Can Rock,* Amphetamine Reptile, 1996.

Mother's Day: *If I Only Had a Brain,* ABomb, 1993.

90 Pound Wuss: *Where the Meager Die of Self Interest,* Tooth&Nail, 1997.

Rocket Fuel Is the Key: *Consider It Contempt,* Thirsty Ear, 1996.

Shiv: *Flayed and Ashamed,* Thirsty Ear, 1996.

Smut: *Secret Center,* Spanish Fly, 1996.

Steeplejack: *Kitchen Radio,* Dejadisc, 1996.

Straw Dogs: *John Perkins John Perkins,* SMA, 1995.

Superball 63: *Loadstar,* Big Money, 1993.

Supernova: *Supernova,* Amphetamine Reptile, 1998.

Today Is the Day: *Supernova,* Amphetamine Reptile, 1994.

Teo Macero

Asking Teo Macero for a production discography exasperates him. "Oh, Christ," he says, "I've produced thousands of records. I did spoken word with Goddard Lieberson; we did multiple sets—*Hamlet, The Subject Was Roses.* I have banjo records up the elbow. I did most of the jazz while I was at Columbia. I had 25 artists at one time." Lieberson was president of Columbia Records in the '50s, when he stacked the company's catalog with musicals and jazz. Succeeding Lieberson in 1966: Clive Davis, who brought the company into the rock era.

These days, Macero—who knows how to hold a grudge—is writing all kinds of music. He has largely retired from record production, a field he figured in heavily from the mid-'50s to the early '80s. His latest charges: Trumpeter Wallace Roney, for Warner Bros.; pianist Geri Allen, for Blue Note; and, as one of three producers, former Living Colour guitarist Vernon Reid, on the tough *Mistaken Identity,* a 1996 Epic/550 release.

From 1957 to 1975, as a staff producer for Columbia Records, Macero produced most of the key Miles Davis records. He continued producing Davis until 1983. He wrote arrangements for Lionel Hampton, Charlie Byrd, and Andre Kostelanetz—Kostelanetz alone was making five albums a year at the time—while at Columbia. He quit in 1975 because he and label chief Davis did not get along. "They wanted me out," says Macero. "Goddard Lieberson was in charge of the whole company; I did a lot of work for him, and toward the end, I reported to him because Clive and I didn't get along. I mailed my expense accounts to Lieberson, and I told him, 'When you go, they'll come after me within six months.'

"He died, and about six months later, I got a call where they offered me a contract" in lieu of firing. Macero signed a two-year pact, then quit. He says Columbia vaults still contain 10 or 11 albums' worth of unreleased Miles Davis material he produced. (Clive Davis, by the way, resigned in 1975, following a controversy over use of company funds; he now heads Arista Records.)

Since the mid-'70s, Macero has been producing records and writing music. "I sort of laid low, got a little disillusioned," Macero says. "For 20 years with the company, I was treated pretty shabby."

Macero admits that toward the end of his tenure, he might have "been a little difficult" to deal with. But, he says, "I fought for Miles a number of times and saved his ass from being thrown off the label."

He also says he rescued *The Graduate,* the 1968 blockbuster that made Dustin Hoffman a star. "I was doing Brubeck that morning, got a call from an executive vice president asking me to see a movie that afternoon," Macero recalls. The honcho told Macero other producers had failed to tie together a soundtrack—which the company needed within three days. Macero viewed the movie, "used my brain, worked with the engineer, and came up with a record," he says. "We sold 8 million records. I made a lot of money."

But when Macero asked Davis for a bonus, Davis said, "I don't think you deserve it. Anybody could have done it," Macero recalls. Macero took the $1,500 Davis offered him; meanwhile, neither Paul Simon (see entry) nor Art Garfunkel ever thanked him for putting the soundtrack together (it gave them their second No. 1 single, "Mrs. Robinson") and didn't give him a complimentary ticket to their legendary 1991 Central Park concert. Macero's still miffed.

Born October 30, 1925, in Glens Falls, New York, Macero used to listen to big bands that came through, and learned to play saxophone; he has recorded several ultramodern jazz albums of his own, for the Prestige, Columbia, Debut, and Palo Alto labels. He won platinum and gold record awards for producing records by Davis, Basie, and Ellington. He had hits with Ramsey Lewis, Davis, Kostelanetz, Broadway shows. "There must be 20, 25 gold records in my attic," he says.

The Long Island resident says he's written "100 ballets at least, Jesus Christ, and all kinds of chamber works, and for large orchestras. From time to time, I conduct an orchestra, play with an orchestra."

The first recording Macero made was in 1949, as a student at the Juilliard School of Music. *Explorations* was experimental; it included overdubs, which was radical for the time. It was released in 1950. Macero graduated from Juilliard in 1953. "I'd play a part, put it on a machine, put on another part, play against that, and add that," Macero recalls. "The trouble with the acetates is they kept getting slower and slower. Still, it swings its ass off."

Macero played sax on Mingus's epochal "Pithecanthropus Erectus," produced by Ahmet Ertegun. "Those squeaks and squawks and all that shit are me," he says. "I never got credit."

In the early '50s, Macero was playing in a group with avant garde clarinetist John LaPorta, another artist who recorded for Debut. "We were doing a lot of freaky stuff," he says. At Juilliard, a Macero piece was performed. It used 12 tones and odd bar signatures and featured a percussion ensemble and a brass ensemble on stage, 12 saxophones in the mezzanine, 2 tubas and 4 trombones in a far balcony, five conductors and a singer. "Each one conducted their part of the score, and I conducted them, and it won a prize of $1,500," Macero says. "It was like the beginning of stereo. It was quadraphonic. I have a record of it, but it's only monaural. They said when you sat in the audience, the music was coming through the floor like a mushroom, like an atomic bomb. They talk today about Third Stream and all that horseshit; if you listen to that stuff, it's like baby music compared to some of the other stuff because it doesn't really use the elements of classical music."

To be a producer, "attend a rehearsal and listen to the music before you make a record," Macero advises. "With Miles, I listened to the music on the telephone. Then you go to rehearsals, listen to the bands, see what they're doing. Usually, the bands are already set, you go into the studio, work with an engineer, and make the record, or CD, whatever you want to call it. After that, you listen to it, evaluate it, and take out all the crap."

Is that easy? "It is for me," Macero says. "I've been doing it since, for chrissake, my first record date was 1950, *Explorations,* I did it for [bassist Charles] Mingus's label, Debut. I paid for it myself. Everybody takes credit for the Third Stream. Gunther Schuller comes along, thinks he discovered it. We get no credit for it: me, Mingus, [vibraharpist] Teddy Charles."

"A lot of contemporary records sound awful," he says. "There's no echo, no high end, no excitement. They don't use the right techniques to make it right. A certain kind of echo I've used, I had three or four machines made at CBS, reverb machines or switchers that would switch channels. I understand they're not going to try to remix any of the old records after this box set [Macero is talking about a six-CD deluxe set of Miles Davis–Gil Evans recordings Columbia issued in 1996]. They're just going to use the original masters I made. That tells you something, whatever that is."

Macero says Columbia plans to put out everything Davis recorded there. "I don't know the exact order, or when," he says. "There are a lot of records I did that I'm not going to tell them about, how they were made or what the takes are. *In a Silent Way,* they're never going to be able to figure out. There were a lot of tapes involved, we cut it down, and I used the same material over and over again. If they're smart enough to figure it out, that's great.

"I'm not difficult," Macero says. "My head is always

into music. I'm totally committed to the artist. Totally. I don't listen to anybody in the studio except the artist, and maybe the engineer. After so many years, you do get a little crusty.

"If you try to tell the artist, he won't listen to you," he says. "Miles would leave it up to me to make all the fucking decisions. People today, they want to be the producer, the writer, they want to do everything. I'm saying, Jesus Christ, then do it yourself. Save yourself some money." —CARLO WOLFF

Allen, Geri: *Eyes . . . in the Back of Your Head,* Blue Note, 1997 • See also Geri Allen Trio.

Allison, Mose: *I Love the Life I Live,* Columbia, 1960 • *Allison Wonderland,* Rhino, 1994.

Auracle: *Glider,* Chrysalis, 1978.

Azzolina, Jay: *Never Too Late,* Antilles, 1988.

Barbieri, Gato: *Gato . . . para Los Amigos,* Dr. Jazz, 1984.

Basie, Count: *See* Ellington, Duke.

Bellson, Louie, and the All-Star Orchestra: *Duke Ellington: Black, Brown & Beige,* Musicmasters, 1994.

Bennett, Tony: *Something,* Columbia, 1970 • *40 Years: The Artistry of Tony Bennett,* Sony, 1991, 1997.

Blake, Michael: *Kingdom of Champa,* Intuition, 1997.

Brubeck, Dave: *Gone with the Wind,* Columbia, 1959 • *Time Out,* Columbia, 1959 • *The Real Ambassadors,* Legacy, 1962, 1994 • *At Carnegie Hall,* TriStar, 1963, 1995 • *Angel Eyes,* Columbia, 1965 • *Jazz Impressions of New York,* Columbia, 1965, 1990 • *Anything Goes: The Music of Cole Porter,* Columbia, 1966, 1991 • *Time In,* Columbia, 1966 • *West Side Story,* Columbia, 1966 • *Jazz Collection,* Columbia, 1970, 1989 • *Great Concerts: Amsterdam, Copenhagen,* Columbia, 1988 • *Time Signatures: A Career Retrospective,* Columbia, 1992.

Byrd, Charlie: *Brazilian Byrd,* Legacy, 1965, 1994 • *Let It Be,* Columbia, 1970.

Clancy Brothers: *Christmas,* Legacy, 1969, 1993.

Coryell, Larry: *L'Oiseau de Feu (Firebird)/Petrouchka,* Philips, 1984.

Davis, Miles: *Jazz at the Plaza,* Vol. 1, Columbia, 1958 • *Milestones,* Columbia, 1958 • *Porgy and Bess,* Columbia, 1958 • *Kind of Blue,* Columbia, 1959 • *Sketches of Spain,* Columbia, 1960 • *Live Miles: More Music from the Legendary,* Columbia, 1961, 1987 • *Some Day My Prince Will Come,* Columbia, 1961 • *Quiet Nights,* Columbia, 1962 • *Seven Steps to Heaven,* Columbia, 1963 • *Four & More,* Columbia, 1964 • *My Funny Valentine: Miles in Concert,* Columbia, 1964 • *My Funny Valentine + Four & More: The Complete,* Legacy, 1964, 1992 • *Cookin' at the Plugged Nickel,* Columbia, 1965, 1987 • *'58 Session,* Legacy, 1965, 1994 • *ESP,* Columbia, 1965 • *Miles Smiles,* Columbia, 1966 • *Nefertiti,* Columbia, 1967 • *Sorcerer,* Columbia, 1967 • *Filles*

De Kilamanjaro, Columbia, 1968 • *Miles in the Sky,* Columbia, 1968 • *In a Silent Way,* Columbia, 1969 • *A Tribute to Jack Johnson,* Columbia, 1970 • *Bitches Brew,* Columbia, 1970 • *Live Evil,* TriStar, 1971, 1994 • *On the Corner,* Columbia, 1972 • *In Concert,* Sony, 1973, 1997 • *Big Fun,* TriStar, 1974, 1994 • *Agharta,* Columbia, 1975 • *Pangaea,* Columbia, 1975 • *Water Babies,* Columbia, 1976 • *The Man with the Horn,* Columbia, 1981 • *Live at the Plugged Nickel 1965,* Columbia, 1982 • *We Want Miles,* Columbia, 1982 • *Star People,* Columbia, 1983 • *Ballads,* Columbia, 1988 • *Miles and Coltrane,* Columbia, 1988 • *Live at Newport, 1958 and 1963,* Legacy, 1994 • *Highlights from the Plugged Nickle,* Columbia, 1995 • *The Complete Live Live at the Plugged Nickel,* Columbia, 1995 • w/ Gil Evans, *The Complete Columbia Studio Recordings,* Columbia, 1996 • w/ Gil Evans, *Best Of,* Legacy, 1997 • *Greatest Hits,* Legacy, 1997 • *Miles Davis at Carnegie Hall: Complete,* Legacy/Columbia, 1998.

Die Elefanten: *Immer Alle Immer Mich,* Tropical, 1992.

Ellington, Duke: *Blues in Orbit,* Columbia, 1960 • w/ Count Basie, *First Time! the Count Meets the Duke,* Columbia, 1961 • *Hommage á Duke,* TriStar, 1996.

Evans, Gil: *See* Miles Davis.

Farlow, Tal: *Trilogy,* Inner City, 1981.

Ferguson, Maynard: *Chameleon,* Columbia, 1974 • *The Best Of,* Columbia, 1982.

Fitzgerald, Ella: *Newport Jazz Festival, Live,* Legacy, 1973, 1995.

Flanagan, Tommy: *Trinity,* Inner City, 1980.

Gas Mask: *Gas Mask,* Tonsil, 1970.

Geri Allen Trio: *Twenty One,* Blue Note, 1994.

Getz, Stan: *The Best of Two Worlds,* Columbia, 1975, 1991 • *The Lyrical Stan Getz,* Columbia, 1988.

Hammond, John Jr.: *Little Big Man,* Columbia, 1971.

Hampton, Lionel: *Mostly Ballads,* Musicmasters, 1989, 1992.

Horn, Paul: *The Altitude of the Sun,* TM, 1975, 1989.

Johnson, J.J.: *Trombone Master,* Columbia, 1960 • *J.J. Inc.,* Columbia, 1961, 1997.

Klugh, Earl, and Hiroki Miyano: *Hotel California/Super Guitar Duo,* Verve, 1983.

Konitz, Lee: *Round and Round,* Musicmasters, 1988, 1995.

Kostelanetz, Andre, and His Orchestra: *Plays Broadway's Greatest Hits,* Columbia, 1977 • *Carmen Without Words,* CBS, 1990.

Lambert, Hendricks and Ross: *The Hottest New Group in Jazz,* Columbia, 1959, 1996 • *Twisted: The Best Of,* Rhino, 1992.

Lewis, Ramsey: *Sun Goddess,* Columbia, 1981.

Loren Schoenberg Jazz Orchestra: *Time Waits for No One,* Musicmasters, 1987.

Lounge Lizards: *The Lounge Lizards,* EG, 1981 • *Live from the Drunken Boat,* Europa, 1983.

Macero, Teo: *What's New,* Columbia, 1956 • *With the Prestige*

Jazz Quartet, Prestige, 1957, 1992 • *Swinging Guys and Dolls*, Musical Heritage, 1959 • *Time + 7*, Finnadar, 1965 • *Impressions of Charles Mingus*, Palo Alto, 1983 • *Acoustical Suspension*, Doctor Jazz, 1984 • *Fusion*, Europa, 1985 • *The Best Of*, Stash, 1990.

Makem, Tommy, and the Clancy Brothers: *In Person at Carnegie Hall/In Concert/Luck of the Irish*, Columbia, 1997.

McRae, Carmen: *Sings Lover Man and Other Billie Holiday Classics*, Sony, 1997.

Miller, Glen: *The Miller Sound Lives Forever*, Laserlight, 1997.

Mingus, Charles: *Mingus Ah Um*, Columbia, 1959 • *Nostalgia in Times Square*, Columbia, 1959, 1979 • *Shoes of the Fisherman's Wife*, Columbia, 1959, 1988 • *The Complete 1959 CBS Charles Mingus Sessions*, Mosaic, 1959 • *Mingus Dynasty*, Columbia, 1960 • *Let My Children Hear Music*, Columbia, 1971 • *Charles Mingus and Friends in Concert*, Columbia, 1972 • *Thirteen Pictures: The Charles Mingus Anthology*, Rhino, 1993.

Monk, Thelonious: *Round Midnight*, TriStar, 1957, 1996 • *Monk's Dream*, Columbia, 1962 • *Criss-Cross*, Columbia, 1963 • *Big Band and Quartet in Concert*, Legacy, 1964, 1994 • *It's Monk's Time*, Columbia, 1964 • *Solo Monk*, Columbia, 1965 • *Straight, No Chaser*, Columbia, 1966 • *Monk Underground*, Columbia, 1968 • *Monks Blues*, Columbia, 1968 • *The Composer*, Columbia, 1968 • *Underground*, Columbia, 1968 • *Live at the Jazz Workshop 1964*, Columbia, 1982 • *Monk*, Pausea, 1983 • *Tokyo Concert*, Columbia, 1984 • *Live at the It Club: Complete*, Legacy/Columbia, 1998 • *Monk Alone: The Complete Columbia Solo Studio Recordings, 1962–1968*, Legacy/Columbia, 1998.

Mulligan, Gerry: *What Is There to Say?*, Columbia, 1960, 1994.

Murad, Jerry, and His Harmonicats: *Greatest Hits*, Columbia, 1990.

Olatunji, Babatunde: *Drums of Passion*, CBS, 1959.

Orchestra U.S.A.: *Jazz Journey*, Columbia, 1963.

Palmer, Robert: *Don't Explain*, EMI, 1990 • "Mercy Mercy Me (The Ecology)," EMI, 1991 • *Ridin' High*, EMI, 1992 • *Honey*, EMI, 1994.

Reid, Vernon, and Masque: *Mistaken Identity*, 550 Music, 1996.

Roney, Wallace: *Misterios*, Warner Bros., 1994 • *The Wallace Roney Quintet*, Warner Bros., 1996.

Rushing, Jimmy: *Mr. Five by Five*, Columbia, 1980.

Scott, Bobby: *For Sentimental Reasons*, Musicmasters, 1989.

Whitmore, James: *Will Rogers' U.S.A.*, Columbia, 1971.

COLLECTIONS

Irma La Douce (original cast), Sony Classical, 1960.

The Girl Who Came to Supper (original cast), Sony Classical, 1963.

Anyone Can Whistle (original cast), CBS, 1964.

The Graduate soundtrack, Columbia, 1968.

Over Here! (original cast), Sony Broadway, 1974, 1992.

New Brew: Jazz Interpretations of Andrew Lloyd Webber, Unity, 1987.

Gavin MacKillop

Though still a young man, Gavin MacKillop has been one of the leading producers of melodic modern rock for nearly 15 years, with several classic albums to his credit: The Church's profound *Priest = Aura*, General Public's bubbly *All the Rage* (No. 26), Mae Moore's voluptuous *Bohemia*, Straightjacket Fits' criminally overlooked *Melt*, and Toad the Wet Sprocket's platinum alterna-folk-rock standards *Fear* and *Dulcinea*. In addition, he produced the Rembrandts' infectious "I'll Be There for You" (No. 17), the theme from TV's *Friends*. MacKillop, a complete studio man, engineers and mixes all of his productions.

A native of Glasgow, Scotland, Gavin MacKillop was born in 1962. His parents exposed him to classical music and encouraged him to study piano and sing in the choir, but his older sister exposed him to the titillating pleasures of rock 'n' roll, dangling records by David Bowie (see entry), Mott the Hoople, and the Faces before his tender ears. She even took him to his first concert—Bowie—when he was 12. In high school MacKillop became interested in the dynamics of sound and began dabbling with electronic equipment while he continued to play the piano. He attended the University of Britain, but left for London in 1978 before he finished school.

In London, punk was all the rage and MacKillop thrilled to the energy of the Clash, Sex Pistols, and the like. He ran live sound for lesser bands and hung out in the studio when some of the bands recorded. Feeling at home in the studio, MacKillop wrote away to area studios looking for work. He got a job as a runner for Virgin's Townhouse Studio. Although he was only 19, he was already old for an entry-level position: The studios tended to hire kids right out of school, in part so they wouldn't have to pay them.

MacKillop trained under some great producers, including Hugh Padgham, Steve Lillywhite (see entries), Peter and Greg Walsh. His big break came when General Public (led by Dave Wakeling and Ranking Roger, ex of the English Beat) had some problems with their producer Colin Fairley (Elvis Costello, Nick Lowe), and called upon MacKillop to bridge the gap.

The result was *All the Rage,* an album that didn't even chart in the U.K but was a huge modern rock radio hit in the United States. Bolstered by Wakeling's smoky vocals, one great ("Tenderness") and three very good songs ("Never You Done That," "Hot Your Cool," "General Public") in a bright, ska-influenced pop-rock mode, *Rage* stayed on the U.S. charts for almost a year in 1984. For all of the album's success, MacKillop modestly defers credit: "I didn't have a clue what I was doing, or at least I certainly didn't think so. I was only 21, and had assisted for only a couple of years." In 1985 MacKillop decided to go freelance because his contract with Townhouse/Virgin was too restrictive. His first independent project took him to Australia to work with Hunters and Collectors, and his production of *Human Frailty* brought the quirky band closer to the mainstream. He returned to London and worked with Shriekback (the radically sedate *Big Night Music),* Howard Devoto's Luxuria, Thrashing Doves, and Red Lorry Yellow Lorry before the acid house wave swept Britain at the turn of the decade and grated against his organic sensibilities.

MacKillop was invited to speak before a producers and engineers group in the U.S. and discovered that much of his work had been popular here—especially with college radio—and a lightbulb lit suggesting that the States might be a better location for his career. After recording Straightjacket Fits' swirling, jangling *Melt* (one of MacKillop's favorites) in New Zealand and Australia in 1990, he produced Toni Child's second album in New York.

MacKillop's next major break came when he hooked up with Santa Barbara's Toad the Wet Sprocket in 1991. "They auditioned a bunch of producers for their third album. I did a day's preproduction rehearsal with them—where they played a couple of songs and we threw some ideas around—and they picked me to do that record. We went to Reno, Nevada, and locked ourselves away for the winter, and they kind of discovered how the studio can be both your friend and your enemy. Although we all loved the record, there were a couple of spots where we thought we'd gone too far," confides MacKillop.

Perhaps. Though classified an "alternative" band (often a catchall category of last resort), Toad is really a '90s update of the folk and country rock of the Byrds or the Eagles (Glen Phillip's vocals recall Glenn Frey); MacKillop's full, bold production finds this connection by dispensing with the undertone of self-conscious irony that typifies "alternative" music. Perhaps this

absence is the true alternative. Regardless, *Fear* made the band ubiquitous on rock, light rock, and adult radio with such staples as "Walk on the Ocean" (No. 18), "All I Want" (No. 15), and "I Will Not Take These Things for Granted," and the album stands firm.

The band's next album, *Dulcinea,* was something of a reaction against the lushness of *Fear.* "After a year of touring, Toad was looking for a much more live-sounding record. They wanted to minimize the overdubs and to make sure that every part was essential to the song. On *Fear* they were experimenting with organs and string quartets and such, but on *Dulcinea* it was getting back to the core of the four-piece band," he says. The result is a cleaner, tighter, but not necessarily better, record. Though blessed with excellent songs: "Fly from Heaven," "Something's Always Wrong," and "Fall Down," the album doesn't hang together quite as well as *Fear.*

1992 was a particularly fine year for MacKillop as he produced the Church's excellent, languid *Priest = Aura,* and coproduced (with the Church's lead singer Steve Kilbey) Canadian singer Mae Moore's beautiful and penetrating *Bohemia. Priest* is the Church's second best album (following *Starfish*), as Kilbey wanders through a series of darkly insistent melodies highlighted by "Aura," "Ripple," and the timeless "Feel," which lopes elegantly on a denatured hip-hop beat.

Bohemia plays something like a distaff Church album: nobly strummed or picked guitars pushing haunting melodies (all written by Moore) from the depths of an unseen well. Moore's vocals are reminiscent of Suzanne Vega or Margo Timmins' (of the Cowboy Junkies) chilly beauty. Highlights abound, but "Arrow," the title track, and the gorgeous "Ophelia" rise above.

A common thread through MacKillop's work is his sensitivity to voice. "I love working on vocals. I've worked with producers over the years who dread doing vocals, which to me is odd. I've also worked with people who don't even have a sketch vocal when they're doing recording. I can't work at all without a vocal. Even if the lyrics aren't finished, which is often the case, I have to have that melody to work around.

"When I hear a song I tend to get an aural picture of it. I view music as being very three-dimensional: it's very tall and wide and deep, and it goes back. I'm always proud of a mix if I can see inside it. And I'm not doing drugs either." Whether you can see it or not, much of MacKillop's work is an intense pleasure to hear. —ERIC OLSEN AND DAWN DARLING

Athenaeum: *Radiance,* Atlantic, 1998 • "What I Didn't Know," Atlantic, 1998.

Barenaked Ladies: "Brian Wilson," Reprise, 1997.

Charthogs, The: *The Charthogs,* Normal, 1993 • *Do Your Mind?,* Third Stone, 1994.

Childs, Toni: *House of Hope,* A&M, 1991.

Chills, The: *Soft Bomb,* Warner Bros., 1992.

Church, The: "Feel," Arista, 1992 • *Priest = Aura,* Arista, 1992.

Cry Charity: *Peace Love Humiliation,* Morgan Creek, 1992.

Ferrick, Melissa: *Massive Blur,* Atlantic, 1993.

General Public: *All the Rage,* IRS, 1984 • "Hot Your Cool," IRS, 1984 • "Never You Done That," IRS, 1984 • "Tenderness," IRS, 1984 • *Hand to Mouth,* IRS Vintage, 1986.

Goo Goo Dolls: *Superstar Car Wash,* Metal Blade/WB, 1993.

Hunters and Collectors: *Human Frailty,* IRS, 1986 • "Is There Anybody in There?," IRS, 1986, 1991 (*IRS Greatest Hips,* Vol. 4, *The Remixes*).

Low and Sweet Orchestra: *Goodbye to All That,* Interscope, 1996.

Luxuria: *Unanswerable Lust,* Beggars Banquet, 1986.

Moore, Mae: *Bohemia,* Epic, 1992 • *Dragonfly,* TriStar, 1995.

Red Lorry Yellow Lorry: *Blow,* Beggars Banquet, 1989.

Rembrandts, The: "I'll Be There for You," EastWest, 1995.

Shriekback: *Big Night Music,* Island, 1986 • "Gunning for the Buddah," Island, 1987.

Straitjacket Fits: *Melt,* Arista, 1990 • *Missing from Melt,* Arista, 1991.

Sugarspoon: *Sugarspoon,* MCA, 1996.

Thrashing Doves: *Trouble in the Home,* A&M, 1989.

Tin Tin (Stephen Duffy): "Kiss Me" (remix), 10, 1984.

Toad the Wet Sprocket: "All I Want," Columbia, 1991 • *Fear,* Columbia, 1991 • "Walk on the Ocean," Columbia, 1991 • *Five Live* (EP), Columbia, 1992 • *Dulcinea,* Columbia, 1994 • "Fall Down," Columbia, 1994 • "Something's Always Wrong," Columbia, 1994 • "Good Intentions," Reprise, 1995 (*Friends* soundtrack) • *In Light Syrup,* Columbia, 1995 • *Coil* (CD-extra), Columbia, 1997.

Water: *Nipple,* MCA, 1995.

Wilde, Danny, and the Rembrandts: *Spin This!,* Elektra, 1998.

Mad Professor

(NEIL FRASER)

Born in Guyana, Neil "Mad Professor" Fraser resembles many Jamaican producers of a generation earlier in having come to music from a background in electronics. "First I was an electronic technician," he says. "I was always playing with wires and electronics. Then I went to England and I got even more into the music side. I thought I'd like to build a studio so I got myself some equipment, a solder iron, and I started from 2-track stereo. My first machine was an Akai and I built an echo and a reverb as well. Then I went on to Teac 4-track. My first dub album, some of the tracks were actually recorded on 4-track, then later it was dubbed up to 16." Most of his work has been issued on his own Ariwa (Yoruba for "communication") label in England; much of it has been reissued in the U.S. by RAS.

The name "Mad Professor," he explains, "came around like three different times in my career. When I was a kid I was inside most of the time with wires and radio sets while everyone was calling me trying to get me to play football and cricket. I wouldn't come, and some of the other guys would start to say 'Well, he's a mad professor.'

"Then it came again going to school in England, the same thing happened—I wouldn't really partake in English school business. I was always fiddlin' with various electrical things. Then when I started the studio now it was like it was unheard of to record in your sitting room in London, so away from what everyone was doing that many people said, 'Oh, you're mad, it wouldn't work.' So that's how I got my name."

From "very basic" beginnings—"The studio wasn't properly soundproofed, you could hear the buses from outside, the dogs barking"—Fraser slowly built up one of the most respected reggae studios in the U.K. "We've been 24-track from 1984," he says. By around 1987 it was "mainly a commercial studio" where he mixed the work of others, often uncredited. "We had to make anything and everything work because there was no money to do any better." These days the studio, which has relocated and upgraded several times, is so state-of-the-art even Mad Professor admits he "kinda gets lost in the technical, in the computer side. Right now," he sighs, "I think we've got more outputs than inputs for our desk." Recently he debuted the new Are We Crazy studio, an Ariwa offspring, as well.

Fraser's successes have occurred in the arena of lovers rock, a romantic style of reggae that served as "British soul" on the U.K. charts, with artists such as Susan Cadogan, Kofi, and Sandra Cross, as well as roots (with superior works for singers Earl Sixteen, Horace Andy, and DJ founding father U Roy) and dub, where he's helped return reggae to traditional values while extending the frontier and opening the field for a new generation of visionary practitioners. He put together a stable of artists and musicians, like Black Steel and Robotiks, and has given many new artists ("on the first rung of success," as he says) a start.

He recorded a long-running series of discs with U.K. DJ (or MC, as they're styled there) Macka B, whose humor and wit add a new dimension to the genre. Popular toaster Pato Banton was first captured and then recaptured by his sound. In addition, he produced some great later albums for established artists like Johnny Clarke, and sometime-producer, always-artist Lee "Scratch" Perry (see entry). The work these artists did for him in the '80s and '90s rivals the quality of their own classic Jamaican recordings.

Engineering and mixing his own productions (for his own label) and playing live shows both with tape decks and effects and full bands as well as DJs and singers ("I like a varied diet," he explains), he's one of the few producers with a string of albums released in his own name who doesn't do vocals. "When I sing, it rains," he smiles, the glint in his eye telling you where he got his name. Told this might be a good thing, he allows, "I guess if you need rain then it's good." Still, he says, "I try to stay on that side of the desk." He occasionally does talking intros to his own dubs "when I'm high enough."

Some of his most popular productions have been his own series of dub releases, stripping down the basic tracks he used for vocals and remixing them into dense, spacy, electronic, throbbing soul food for the adventurous.

Mad Professor often mixes it up with other producers, splitting albums with the Jah Shaka (see entry) and Dub Judah, producing other producers or giving his mix to others' productions, as with albums by U.K.'s Black Roots or roots singer Bob Andy. He's also taken on some crossover projects, like U.K.'s Ruts, Japan's Havana Exotica, and Germany's Puls Der Zeit. "I do some odd things," he admits. His experimental edge doesn't stop there—the 1994 dub release *It's a Mad Mad Mad Mad Professor* boasts it is "recorded in Dubarama" and sounds like it. On the latest volume of his new series *Black Liberation Dub* (which follows his lengthy *Dub Me Crazy* series) he samples the voice of Louis Farrakhan, who began his own career as a calypso singer.

Like a namesake from a Hammer horror film loosely based on a Universal monster, Mad Professor has taken Jamaican roots music and dub to heart and transformed it into something at once maniacal and comforting. His "clash" LPs with other producers resemble those end-of-the-film grapples with the Wolfman, Frankenstein, and other mutations, and even though they all crash through the floor in flames, by the end we know they'll be back in the lab intact or, even better, slightly altered, in a sequel. In a musical field that sometimes takes itself too seriously, Neil Fraser punctuates the air with laughter, masking his serious intent to hijack the universe and alter its musical course.

Perhaps the greatest hallmark of a Mad Professor production is that, despite the ultramodern overtones, the underpinning is roots reggae. "It's roots that really attracted me to reggae," he explains. "Whilst I always like very good productions, like the Philly productions, good arrangement stuff, I also like a lot of roots. So I thought for me to really carry on the reggae, I'd like to continue with some good roots. If anything, make roots—but with quality." —CHUCK FOSTER

Andy, Horace: *Life Is for Living,* RAS, 1995 • *Roots and Branches,* Ariwa, 1997.

Anti-Social Workers and Mad Professor: *Punky Reggae Party,* Ariwa, 1983.

Banton, Pato, and Mad Professor: *Mad Professor Captures Pato Banton,* RAS, 1990 • *Mad Professor Recaptures Pato Banton,* RAS, 1990.

Benjamin, Tony, and the Sane Inmates: *Reggae Rebel,* Ariwa, 1983.

Black Steel: *Jungle Warrior,* Ariwa, 1988.

Clarke, Johnny: *Yard Style,* Ariwa, 1983 • *Give Thanks,* Ariwa, 1985.

Cross, Sandra: *Comet in the Sky,* Ariwa, 1988 • *Country Life,* RAS, 1992 • *Foundation of Love,* Ariwa, 1992 • *This Is Sandra Cross,* RAS, 1992.

Culture, Peter: *Facing the Fight,* Ariwa, 1984.

Elektro-Robotik Dub Orchestra: *Strictly Automatik,* Ariwa, 1994.

Irie, Nolan: *Work So Hard,* Ariwa, 1993.

Irie, Tippa: *Rebel on the Roots Corner,* RAS, 1994.

Jah Shaka and Mad Professor: *Jah Shaka Meets Mad Professor at Ariwa Sounds,* RAS, 1984 • *New Decade of Dub,* Ariwa, 1996.

Kofi: *Black with Sugar,* RAS, 1989, 1990 • *Wishing Well,* Ariwa, 1992.

Lodge, J.C.: *Love for All Seasons,* RAS, 1996 • *RAS Portraits,* RAS, 1997.

Macka B: *Sign of the Times,* RAS, 1986 • *Buppie Culture,* RAS, 1990 • *Looks Are Deceiving,* RAS, 1990 • *Natural Suntan,* RAS, 1990 • *We've Had Enough,* RAS, 1990 • *Peace Cup,* RAS, 1991 • *Roots Ragga,* RAS, 1993 • *Discrimination,* RAS, 1994 • *Here Comes Trouble,* Ariwa, 1994 • *Hold onto Your Culture,* RAS, 1995 • *Suspicious,* Ariwa, 1998.

Mad Professor: *Black Roots, Dub Factor: The Mad Professor Mixes,* Nubian, n.d. • *Dub Me Crazy,* RAS, 1982 • *Dub Me Crazy, the Second Chapter: Beyond the Realms of Dub,* Ariwa, 1982 • *Dub Me Crazy Pt. 3: The African Connection,* Ariwa, 1983 • *Dub Me Crazy 4: Escape to the Asylum Dub,* RAS, 1983, 1990 • *Dub Me Crazy 6: Schizophrenic Dub,* Ariwa, 1986 • *Dub Me Crazy 5: Who Knows the Secret of the Master Tape?,* RAS, 1987 • *Dub Me Crazy 7: The Adventures of a Dub Sampler,* Ariwa, 1987 • *Stepping in Dub-Wise Country,* Ariwa,

1987 • *Dub Me Crazy 8: Experiments of the Aural Kind*, Ariwa,
1988 • *Dub Me Crazy 9: Science and the Witchdoctor*, RAS,
1989 • *A Feast of Yellow Dub*, RAS, 1990 • *Dub Me Crazy 10:
Psychedelic Dub*, RAS, 1990 • *Dub Me Crazy 11: Hi-jacked to
Jamaica*, RAS, 1991 • *Dub Me Crazy 12: Dub Maniacs on the
Rampage*, Ariwa, 1992 • *True Born African Dub*, RAS, 1992 •
The Lost Scrolls of Moses, RAS, 1993 • *Black Liberation Dub*,
RAS, 1994 • *It's a Mad, Mad, Mad, Mad Professor*, RAS, 1994
• *Anti-Racist Dub Broadcast*, RAS, 1995 • *Black Liberation
Dub Chapter 2: Anti-Racist Dub Broadcast*, RAS, 1995 • *In a
Rub a Dub Style*, Blue Moon, 1995 • *The African Connection*,
Ariwa, 1995 • *Beyond the Realms of Dub*, Ariwa, 1996 • *Black
Liberation Chapter 3: Evolution of Dub*, RAS, 1996 • *Caribbean
Taste of Technology*, Ariwa, 1996 • *Dub Take the Voodoo out of
Reggae*, Ariwa, 1997 • *Dub You Crazy with Love*, Ariwa, 1997
• *RAS Portraits*, RAS, 1997 • *Under the Spell of Dub*, Ariwa,
1998 • *See also* Anti-Social Workers; Banton, Pato; Jah
Shaka; Perry, Lee.

Massive Attack: "Sly" (remix), Circa, 1994 • "Risingson"
(remix), Virgin, 1997.

Mother Nature: *A Breath of Fresh Air*, Ariwa, 1984.

Perry, Lee "Scratch": *Who Put the Voodoo 'Pon Reggae?*, RAS,
1996.

Perry, Lee "Scratch," and the Mad Professor: *Dub Take the
Voodoo Out of Reggae*, RAS, 1990 • *Mystic Warrior Dub*,
RAS, 1990 • *Black Ark Experryments*, RAS, 1995 •
Experryments at the Grass Roots of Dub, RAS, 1995 • *Super
Ape Inna Jungle*, RAS, 1995.

Princess Sharifa: *Heritage*, Ariwa, 1993.

Puls Der Zeit and the Mad Professor: *At Checkpoint Charlie*,
Danceteria/ROIR, 1989.

Ranking Ann: *Something Fishy Going On*, Ariwa, 1983 • *A Slice
of English Toast*, RAS, 1991.

Robotiks: *Man and Machine*, Ariwa, 1985 • *My Computer's
Acting Strange*, Ariwa, 1986.

Sargeant Peper: *Judgement Day*, Ariwa, 1983.

Sister Audrey: *Populate*, Ariwa, 1991.

Sixteen, Earl: *Babylon Walls*, RAS, 1992.

Smith, Kendell: *Time Running Out*, Ariwa, 1988.

Soul Coughing: "Sugar Free Jazz" (remix), Slash/WB, 1995.

Taugenixe: *Reggae Ron*, Ariwa, 1983.

U Roy: *True Born African*, Ariwa/RAS, 1991 • *Smile a While*,
Ariwa/RAS, 1993 • *Babylon Kingdom Must Fall*, RAS, 1996.

Wild Bunch: *The Wild Bunch*, Ariwa, 1984.

Yabby You: *Yabby You Meets Mad Professor and Black Steel at
Ariwa Studio*, RAS, 1993.

COLLECTIONS

*Dub Judah/Mad Professor: In Captivity Dub Chronicles Dub Factor
3*, Nubian, 1995.

The Ariwa Possee, Ariwa, 1983.

This Is Lovers Reggae 2, RAS, 1992.

This Is Lovers Reggae 3, RAS, 1993.

Jah Shaka Meets Mad Professor at Ariwa Sounds, Ariwa, 1984.

Roots Daughters, RAS, 1988.

Bob Andy's Dub Book As Revealed to Mad Professor, Ariwa, 1989.

Ariwa Hits '89, Ariwa, 1989.

Roots Daughters, Vol. 2, Ariwa, 1990.

This Is Lovers Reggae, Ariwa/RAS, 1991: Brown Sugar, "Hello
Stranger" • Sandra Cross, "So in Love" • Marie Dawn,
"What Is This?" • Intense, "You Are the One" • Kofi, "I'm
So Proud" • John McLean, "We Both Belong" • John
McLean and Kofi, "Things May Come" • Robotiks and
Fenton Smith, "Blood Is Thicker Than Water" • Royal
Blood, "Slippin Away" • Leroy Simmons, "I've Got to
Know" • Paulette Tajah, "Lonely."

The Ariwa Twelfth Anniversary Album, Ariwa, 1992.

Rupununi Safari, Steaming Jungle: The Jungle Dub Experience 2,
RAS, 1995.

Mazaruni! The Jungle Dub Experience, RAS, 1995.

Reanimator: Black Market Science, Ion, 1998.

Brent Maher

Brent Maher remembers the day he experienced an
epiphany in his career. It was around 1978, and
Maher was producing Dave Loggins in Nashville.
Keyboardist Randy Goodrum stayed after a session to
play Maher his love-gone-wrong "Bluer Than Blue,"
which Maher subsequently coproduced as a huge pop
hit for Michael Johnson.

"It was a complete awakening," Maher says. "The
song just devastated me, and all of a sudden I realized
I'd been making records starting from the wrong
premise. It's like a little lightbulb went off and emotion
shot through this boy and it woke me up, like, 'Brent,
great records aren't made from hip chord changes. Hit
records are made from emotions.' And I didn't get that
until that point. I wasn't really centered on what I feel
now is what a producer has to have a grip on, which is
you have to have a song sense and you have to be emotionally moved by what you're doing, not just impressed
by how good somebody is."

Born in 1946, Maher settled in Nashville after getting out of the Air Force in the late '60s, landing a job
at Foster Recording where engineer Bill Porter became
his mentor. "My only aspiration was to be a really good
engineer," recalls Maher. "The word 'producer,' I probably didn't even know how to spell it, let alone what the
guy did."

Maher relocated to Las Vegas when Porter asked him to help out at United Recording there. "It was an unbelievable learning experience," says Maher, "because that was the time when all the Motown acts—Diana Ross, Gladys Knight—and later R&B acts like Ike and Tina Turner, started working Las Vegas. It was the turnover from Jerry Vale and all those guys, it was another generation. They were there for two or three weeks and most of them were always behind on albums. They'd be in Vegas so they would come in and either finish records or start them. Literally, one day I was recording Guy Lombardo and the next day I'd be working with Sly Stone [see entry]."

Maher was slowly making the transition from engineer to producer when he got a break from Ike and Tina Turner, for whom he had engineered two albums. At his wife's suggestion, he played the duo two songs he'd written, "Work on Me," and "Love Come Down." The pair decided to record both. While Maher recalls little friction between the couple at the time, years later when he saw *What's Love Got to Do with It?*, a movie based on Tina Turner's life, he understood much more. "I saw the movie and it made me sick to my stomach," he says, "because a lot of things I didn't get [in Vegas], I got then."

Maher continued to work at United even after Porter had left the studio, at least, that is, until fate intervened. "Some rather unsavory people got involved in the studio and Bill got aced out," Maher says. "I was stuck there and one day I went to work to make some tape copies, and the place had burned down."

Maher returned to Nashville, engineering and producing pop acts. He resisted producing country acts until Dottie West came calling. "I'd engineered some country records, but never produced one," he says. "I went over to Dottie's house and fell in love with her. We did a whole album without one acoustic guitar on it. It was pretty progressive stuff at the time."

West also marked Maher's return to songwriting. He co-wrote "Lesson in Leaving," which became one of West's biggest hits. But it was with the Judds that Maher experienced his greatest production and songwriting success. In the early '80s, Maher's daughter was in a Nashville area hospital recovering from a serious car accident. One of her nurses, Naomi Judd, was an aspiring singer who sang with her daughter, Wynonna. "After Diana was let out of the hospital, Naomi gave me a tape that she and Wy had done, literally, in their own living room," recalls Maher. "I'm not proud to say this, but it took me two or three weeks before I stuck that tape in my car player. My wife was so mad because Naomi took such good care of my daughter. My wife

told me not to come home until I heard that tape. I finally played it and by the time I got to work, I was so excited that I called Naomi and said I wanted to come over and talk."

Together, Maher and the Judds made history. Maher, who runs his own publishing company, Moraine Music Group, and co-owns Creative Workshop Recording Studios, produced all 10 Judds albums, which have sold more than 16 million copies. He also wrote a few of the pair's biggest hits, including "Born to Be Blue" (No. 5 country) and "Girls Night Out," "Rockin' with the Rhythm of the Rain," and the 1983 Academy of Country Music Song of the Year "Why Not Me" (all No. 1 country).

Maher says they had no idea they were creating musical history. "We just wanted to make great music," he says. "We were in a time when country music had gotten real pop, everyone was trying to cut crossover records, and we were pretty scaled down. We just went in fearless. I felt like we had the whole world on our side."

Although the spats between mother and daughter were well-known, Maher says he never had a problem with them. "Oddly enough, we never had one struggle in the studio. Now that sounds nuts, but that was the common ground. There were a few times doing vocals where we'd have an emotional moment, and where we'd just sit there and talk about what was going on, but it was never something between those two; it would be some outside scene going on. They both wear their hearts on their sleeves. You can hurt Wynonna real easy and you can hurt Naomi real easy, but in the studio, we always just got in there and rocked out."

Maher split with the Judds after Naomi retired because of illness and Wynonna decided to work with Tony Brown (see entry) on her solo records. However, he and Wynonna reunited in 1997 for her solo album *The Other Side*. "Everything we're doing just seems hip, cool, and fresh," says an enthusiastic Maher. "As much as I loved Wy [before] and knew I was dealing with one of the premier singers, I have another whole level of respect for her talent. The songs we go after now are different than they were with [the Judds] because you don't have to wonder if there are duet possibilities or is it a song she can sing with her mother right next to her."

Although he's had success producing male artists, Maher seems to strike a special chord with women. Among those he's produced are Kathy Mattea, Shelby Lynne, Michelle Wright, and Sylvia. He admits he has no idea why he works so well with the ladies, but it could be the sense of confidence he gives them. "I don't know why that is," he says. "I only know that when I'm in the studio with someone, it's someone I totally believe in. I'm thrilled to be with them, I'm lucky to be in the same room with them." —MELINDA NEWMAN

Campbell, Stacy Dean: "Baby Don't You Know," Columbia, 1992 • *Lonesome Wins Again*, Columbia, 1992 • "Poor Man's Rose," Columbia, 1992 • "Rosalee," Columbia, 1992.

Darin, Bobby: *As Long As I'm Singing: The Bobby Darin Collection*, Rhino, 1995.

Great Plains: "A Picture of You," Columbia, 1991 • *Great Plains*, Columbia, 1991 • "Faster Gun," Columbia, 1992 • "Iola," Columbia, 1992 • "Dancin' with the Wind," Magnatone, 1996 • "Healin' Hands," Magnatone, 1996 • *Homeland*, Magnatone, 1996.

Hutton, Sylvia: *Anthology*, Renaissance, 1997.

Johnson, Michael: "Bluer Than Blue," EMI America, 1978 • *The Michael Johnson Album*, EMI America, 1978 • *Dialogue*, EMI America, 1979 • "This Night Won't Last Forever," EMI America, 1979 • *You Can Call Me Blue*, EMI America, 1980 • "Gotta Learn to Love Without You," RCA, 1986 • *Wings*, RCA, 1986 • "Crying Shame," RCA, 1987 • "Give Me Wings," RCA, 1987 • "Ponies," RCA, 1987 • "The Moon Is Still over Her Shoulder," RCA, 1987 • "I Will Whisper Your Name," RCA, 1988 • "That's That," RCA, 1988 • *That's That*, RCA, 1989 • *Michael Johnson*, Atlantic Nashville, 1992.

Judds, The: "Mama He's Crazy," RCA, 1984 • *The Judds: Wynonna and Naomi*, Curb/RCA, 1984 • "Why Not Me?," RCA, 1984 • *Why Not Me?*, Curb/RCA, 1984 • "Girls Night Out," RCA, 1985 • "Have Mercy," RCA, 1985 • "Love Is Alive," RCA, 1985 • *Rockin' with the Rhythm*, Curb/RCA, 1985 • "Grandpa (Tell Me 'bout the Good Old Days)," RCA, 1986 • "Rockin' with the Rhythm of the Rain," RCA, 1986 • *Christmas Time with the Judds*, Curb/RCA, 1987 • "Cry Myself to Sleep," RCA, 1987 • *Heartland*, Curb/RCA, 1987 • "I Know Where I'm Going," RCA, 1987 • "Maybe Your Baby's Got the Blues," RCA, 1987 • *Greatest Hits*, Curb/RCA, 1988 • "Turn It Loose," RCA, 1988 • "Change of Heart," RCA, 1989 • "Let Me Tell You About Love," RCA, 1989 • *River of Time*, Curb/RCA, 1989 • "Young Love," RCA, 1989 • "Guardian Angels," Curb, 1990 • *Love Can Build a Bridge*, Curb/RCA, 1990 • "One Man Woman," Curb, 1990 • *Greatest Hits*, Vol. 2, Curb/RCA, 1991 • "John Deere Tractor," Curb, 1991 • *The Judds Collection, 1983–1990*, RCA, 1992 • *Collector's Series*, RCA, 1993 • *Talk About Love*, RCA, 1993 • *This Country's Rockin'*, RCA, 1993 • *Girl's Night Out: The Essential Collection Of*, RCA, 1994 • *Live Studio Sessions*, RCA, 1994 • "Silver Bells," RCA, 1997.

Loggins, Dave: *One Way Ticket to Paradise*, Epic, 1977 • *David Loggins*, Epic, 1979.

Lynne, Shelby: "Feelin' Kind of Lonely Tonight," Morgan Creek, 1993 • *Temptation*, Morgan Creek, 1993 • "Another Chance at Love," Magnatone, 1994 • *Restless*, Magnatone, 1995 • "Slow Me Down," Magnatone, 1995.

Mattea, Kathy: "Lonesome Standard Time," Mercury, 1992 • *Lonesome Standard Time*, Mercury, 1992 • *Good News*, Mercury, 1993 • "Listen to the Radio," Mercury, 1993 • "Standing Knee Deep in a River (Dying of Thirst)," Mercury, 1993.

McCready, Rich: "Hangin' On," Magnatone, 1996 • *Rich McCready*, Magnatone, 1996 • "Thinkin' Strait," Magnatone, 1996.

Medley, Bill: *Sweet Thunder*, Liberty, 1981.

Perkins, Carl: *Born to Rock*, Liberty, 1990.

Rogers, Kenny: *We've Got Tonight*, Razor & Tie, 1983, 1994 • *I Prefer the Moonlight*, RCA, 1987 • *The Gift*, Magnatone, 1996 • *The Greatest Christmas of Them All*, Magnatone, 1996 • *Across My Heart*, Magnatone, 1997.

Sylvia: "Cry Just a Little," RCA, 1985 • "Fallin' in Love," RCA, 1985 • *One Step Closer*, RCA, 1985 • "Nuthin' Ventured Nuthin' Gained," RCA, 1986.

West, Dottie: "A Lesson in Leavin'," United Artists, 1980 • "Are You Happy Baby?," Liberty, 1981 • "What Are We Doin' in Love?," Liberty, 1981 • *Wild West*, Liberty, 1981.

Wynonna: "Come Some Other Rainy Day," Curb, 1997 • *The Other Side*, Curb/Universal, 1997 • "When Love Starts Talkin'," Curb, 1997 • "Always Will," Curb, 1998.

Fred Maher

A precocious and extraordinary talent, drummer Fred Maher was performing and recording with Material by the age of 16. He played with Lou Reed's band in the mid-'80s before joining arty transatlantic dance-poppers Scritti Politti as drummer, programmer, and co-producer. Having set off in a techno-pop direction, Maher then completed that journey, producing Information Society's gold debut album in 1988. He has since both played on and produced superior modern rock albums by Lou Reed, Matthew Sweet, Lloyd Cole, Luna, Katell Keineg, Eve's Plum, Sexpod, and 10,000 Maniacs.

Fred Maher was born December 3, 1962, and raised on the Upper West Side of Manhattan. The son of a writer, Maher was interested in music and art, playing drums and drawing from an early age. As a child he loved the eclecticism of Top 40 radio, and then switched his allegiance to heavier music; as a drummer he was enthralled with the mighty sticks of Led Zeppelin's John Bonham. Maher failed the entrance test for the New York High School of Music and Art as a drummer, so he attended the school of Art and Design.

In regular jam sessions held by students of the various arts high schools, Maher met keyboardist and future producer Michael Beinhorn (see entry). Beinhorn introduced Maher to the trippy art-rock of Gong, Henry Cow, Eno (see entry), Roxy Music, and their ilk.

Beinhorn and Maher met bassist Bill Laswell (see entry) and they all played in Daevid Allen's New York version of Gong, then formed Material in 1979. The exceptionally influential band (and breeding ground of producers) played an acerbic form of improvisational dub funk that occasionally veered into straighter dance matter ("Bustin' Out" with Nona Hendryx). Material recorded in Martin Bisi's (see entry) Brooklyn loft studio and developed an easy familiarity with the process through experimentation. "We were definitely into the studio-as-instrument thing," says Maher. "I suppose that's why we all became producers."

Maher met legendary New York guitarist Robert Quine (Voidoids, Lou Reed) through a Material offshoot band called Deadline. Another branch of the Material family was Massacre, a vicious speed-metal trio with Laswell, Maher, and Henry Cow guitarist Fred Frith. Maher left Material in 1981—burnt out on the music scene at 18—and became a bike messenger. He then enrolled in architecture school at Cooper Union in the East Village.

Along the way Maher had met David Gamson through a girlfriend, who had said, "You ought to meet this guy David, he's into all of that crap you listen to." Gamson, who was a music composition major at Sarah Lawrence, asked Maher to play on a school project, an electronic cover of "Sugar, Sugar" that was eventually licensed to the Rough Trade label. In a peculiar twist of fate, the test pressing of Gamson's next Rough Trade single was mixed up in the mail with a test pressing of the first Scritti Politti album. Both Gamson and Scritti leader Green Gartside then called the label to say, "You sent me the wrong record, but what you sent me is kind of cool."

While Maher was at Cooper Union, Robert Quine asked him to join a new Lou Reed band; Maher played drums on 1983's *Legendary Hearts* and 1984's *New Sensations* (Reed scheduled the recording of the latter around Maher's Christmas break from Cooper Union). Then Gamson's mother called Maher to tell him that Gamson had joined Scritti Politti; that Gamson and Gartside were coming to New York to record; and would he, Maher, like to join them? Goodbye Cooper Union.

Other than three songs produced by Arif Mardin (see entry), the three Scrittis co-produced *Cupid and Psyche 85* (No. 5 U.K.) themselves—a year-long project that Maher considers his "master's degree in studio technology." The album is a classic of melodic, jittery dance pop, centered around Gartside's wispy vocals and oblique, allusive lyrics. The group-produced hits, "The Word Girl" (No. 6 U.K.) and "Perfect Way" (No. 11), are perky technological marvels—the former in a pop-reggae mode, the latter a blizzard of cut-up beats, centrifugal keyboard runs, and a vocal conjuring the image of an English Michael Jackson (interestingly, Maher worked on Marlon Jackson's only solo album, *Baby Tonight,* in 1987).

Maher also performed on, but didn't do production work for, the second Scritti album, *Provision,* in 1988. Maher didn't have time to co-produce the second Scritti album because he was producing the Information Society. Though Maher was a drummer, he was equally fascinated with studio technology. Instead of feeling threatened by his first exposure to a Linn drum machine, he "thought it was the greatest thing ever. I loved the perfection of it, but of course I grew tired of that machine perfection over the next few years," he says.

Most of his "drum" work with Scritti was in fact drum programming. So he was ready when the all-electronic Information Society called. A techno-pop breakthrough, *Information Society* added a heavier thump to poppy dance tunes than had been done by similar bands like Erasure. The huge single "What's on Your Mind" (No. 3), which sounds like a cross between Noel and Duran Duran, dominated the dance floors and the airwaves. Another single, "Walking Away" (No. 9) did nearly as well.

Suddenly Maher was a red-hot techno-pop producer. Surely he was destined to ride the crest of this breaking wave to fortune and glory. Instead Maher went no-tech and returned to Lou Reed, drumming on and co-producing *New York,* the rock iconoclast's most acclaimed (and best-selling) album of the decade. Reed had been hesitant to work with a producer who "hadn't done anything with any fucking guitars," but Maher convinced him to give it a one-day trial in the studio.

In one day they recorded and mixed "Romeo Had Juliette," the lead track from the album. Though Maher rented a state-of-the-art Simmons drum machine for the record, he never used it. As Reed's liner notes for the album say, "You can't beat two guitars, bass, drums." Maher got a guitar recording tip from producer David Allen (with whom he co-produced Matthew Sweet's *Earth*): put a microphone inside the back of the amplifier, as well as one in front of it, to get added depth when they are mixed together.

Maher's two most important albums of the '90s both came in 1991. Lloyd Cole is a Scottish modern rock singer/songwriter in the manner of Robyn Hitchcock or John Wesley Harding who has not been appropriately appreciated in the U.S.; his 1984 album *Rattlesnakes* (with his band the Commotions) is one of the decade's best. Cole moved to New York in 1990 and Maher co-produced his fine self-titled solo debut (No. 11 U.K.) in 1990, but *Don't Get Weird on Me Babe* is even better. Maher put his guitar-recording skills to good use on the jangling Byrdsian songs, especially "Tell Your Sister," "She's a Girl and I'm a Man" and "Pay for It." What a band! Cole and Robert Quine on guitars, Maher on drums, Matthew Sweet on bass and backing vocals. The album displays extraordinary range—percussion-and-accordion Latin pop on "Man Enough," moody orchestral numbers "There for Her" and "Margo's Waltz," Eagles-like (except for the Scottish brogue) country rock on "Weeping Wine"—and superior songwriting throughout.

Much of the same crew recorded Matthew Sweet's gold *Girlfriend* (both albums were largely recorded at New York's Axis Studios): Maher co-producing and playing drums, Quine and Cole (in addition to Television's Richard Lloyd) on guitars, Sweet on bass. Sweet shows as much range as Cole, with the whole operation skewed a few notches harder. Throughout, Sweet's songwriting and singing shine along with Maher's sensitive production. The title track is one of the great rockers of the '90s: Quine's searing leads burn through the intro and the breaks, and Sweet's ballsy tenor conveys determination and vulnerability as he tries to persuade a young woman that she should be his girlfriend.
—ERIC OLSEN

Breeders, The: "Divine Hammer," 4 A.D./Elektra, 1993.
Cartier, Daniel: *Avenue A,* Rocket, 1997.
Ceberano, Kate: *Globe,* Elektra, 1994.
Cole, Lloyd: *Lloyd Cole,* Gold Rush, 1990, 1996 • "Chelsea Hotel," Atlantic, 1991 (*I'm Your Fan*) • *Don't Get Weird on Me Babe,* Capitol, 1991.
Doro: *Love Me in Black,* WEA Germany, 1998.
Eve's Plum: *Cherry Alive,* 550 Music/Epic, 1995.
Gouds Thumb: *Gouds Thumb,* Critique, 1996.
Information Society: "Lay All Your Love on Me," Tommy Boy, 1988 • "Walking Away," Tommy Boy, 1988 • "What's on Your Mind (Pure Energy)," Tommy Boy, 1988 • *Information Society,* Tommy Boy, 1988 • "Repetition," Tommy Boy, 1989 • "Think," Tommy Boy, 1990 • "How Long," Tommy Boy, 1991 • *Hack,* Tommy Boy, 1991 • *Don't Be Afraid,* Cleopatra, 1997.
Keineg, Katell: *O Seasons O Castles,* Elektra, 1994.
Lord, Mary Lou: *Got No Shadow,* Work, 1998.
Luna: *Lunapark,* Elektra, 1992 • *Slide* (EP), Elektra, 1993.
Paige, Kevin: "Don't Shut Me Out," Chrysalis, 1989 • *Kevin Paige,* Chrysalis, 1989.
Quine, Robert, and Fred Maher: *Basic,* EG, 1984.
Reed, Lou: *New York,* Sire, 1989.
Rhatigan, Suzanne: *To Hell with Love,* Imago, 1992.
Scritti Politti: *Cupid and Psyche 85* (6 tracks), Warner Bros., 1985.
Sexpod: *Goddess Blues,* Slab/CMC, 1997.
Sweet, Matthew: *Earth,* A&M, 1989, 1993 • "Girlfriend," Zoo, 1990 • *Girlfriend,* Zoo, 1991.
10,000 Maniacs: "More Than This," Geffen, 1997 • "Rainy Day," Geffen, 1997 • *Love Among the Ruins,* Geffen, 1997.
T-42: *Intruder* (5 tracks), Columbia, 1992.
Trip Shakespeare: *Across the Universe,* A&M, 1990.
Ultra Vivid Scene: *Rev,* Columbia, 1992.
VAST: *Visual Audio Sensory Theater,* Elektra, 1998.

David Malloy

For David Malloy, becoming a record producer was a natural: it was the family business. "My dad was in the business, so I grew up in the business," he says of his father, Jim, whose credits as producer and engineer span Henry Mancini, Elvis Presley, and Chet Atkins (see entry). "I started writing songs when I was 15 and started in the studio as a gopher when I was about 18."

Born in Fort Dodge, Iowa, Malloy moved to Los Angeles with his family when he was 18 months old. "I just kind of knew from an early age that I was going to be a record producer, and when the time came I was just going to do it, and do it well," he says.

At 13, his family moved to Nashville, but Malloy admits country music wasn't originally his thing. "I grew up in the generation of the Beatles and the Stones and was influenced by a lot of beach music because of my early childhood in L.A.—Jan and Dean, the Beach Boys, and that kind of stuff," he relates. "I really didn't start to hear country music until I was 18 and started working in the studios here in Nashville. The reason for the huge success I had with Eddie Rabbitt was because of my pop and rock influences bleeding into my newfound country influences—which helped create that sound."

Rabbitt was Malloy's first real project as a producer. He had worked in his father's studio and for Jack

Clement (see entry), spending time experimenting whenever he could. He also worked for Ray Stevens for a while; after leaving Stevens' employ, he and his father started a publishing company.

One of the younger Malloy's first discoveries was a young songwriter from New Jersey named Eddie Rabbitt. "Rabbitt was doing his own harmonies," Malloy recalls of those early work tapes, "and he had this unique sound going between his voice and doing his own harmonies. I really loved the sound I was hearing because I'd never heard anything like it before."

Malloy helped Rabbitt land a deal with Elektra Records and a string of hits followed: "I Love a Rainy Night" (No. 1), "Drivin' My Life Away" (No. 5), "I Don't Know Where to Start" (No. 2 country), and "Suspicions" (No. 1 country). Malloy worked with Rabbitt for 13 years. "I really wouldn't do another project," he says of that time period. "I would engineer and stuff, but I didn't really want to work with anybody but Eddie. We had a special sound working and I didn't want to share that sound with anybody else."

Eventually Malloy did branch out. He produced the Kenny Rogers hit "Love Will Turn You Around" (No. 1 country) for the movie *Six Pack;* Dolly Parton's *Real Love* album; and Rosanne Cash's Grammy-winning *Rhythm and Romance* album, which included the hit single "I Don't Know Why You Don't Want Me" (No. 1).

In an effort to broaden his reach, Malloy moved back to Los Angeles to pursue non-country projects, but didn't have much success in that marketplace. "I just got tired of country music and the Nashville scene and wanted a break in the pop and rock thing because I always felt I had it in my head to do it," he comments. "I went out there and got songs cut as a writer [by Roy Orbison, Greg Allman, and Fleetwood Mac]. . . . But I didn't realize how well-known I was as a country producer until I went to L.A. and tried to get some other work."

After Malloy moved back to Nashville, he co-produced Daryle Singletary's debut for Giant Records and is credited with helping Mindy McCready land her deal at RCA. He also produced her sophomore effort, *If I Don't Stay the Night.*

Malloy says he enjoys finding and developing new talent as well as working with established acts. "Working with a new artist, I feel I'm more like a diamond cutter and I have a diamond in the rough," he says. "I have to trim all the garbage away to get down to the essence of what the diamond is. If it's an artist who's already big, I try to ask myself, 'What does this person mean to the public? How does the public perceive this person and what can I do to enhance that vision? What kind of

record can I do to make this record bigger and make them bigger than life?'

"I don't have a set style of production," he says. "I feel I'm a chameleon. I become the artist in my head, and when I make the record I'm trying to be as much them as they are instead of making them come to me and inserting them into me. I think that's why my records sound different from artist to artist."

Malloy says he's always wanted to take risks as a producer and give audiences something unique. "I was always trying to change things up, always trying to stay a step ahead of everybody," he says. "I don't know if I was trying to stay a step ahead as much as I was exploring or reaching for something, which is unusual because country isn't known to be a format where you explore and reach.

"I just go for what I feel in my heart is right. I think music is sold from the heart. It has to reach into something deeper. People have to feel like they can't wait to hear it on the radio. I don't think I ever made a record where I didn't scare the heck out of the promotion staff." —DEBORAH EVANS PRICE

Badfinger: *Airwaves,* Elektra, 1979 • *The Best Of,* Vol. 2, Rhino, 1990.

Brannen, John: *Mystery Street,* Apache, 1988 • *John Brannen,* Mercury, 1993.

Brooks, Karen, and Randy Sharp: *That's Another Story,* PolyGram Country, 1992.

Burnette, Billy: "Nothin' to Do (And All Night to Do It)," Warner Bros., 1992.

Cash, Rosanne: "I Don't Know Why You Don't Want Me," Columbia, 1985 • *Rhythm and Romance,* Columbia, 1985 • "Second to No One," Columbia, 1986 • *Hits, 1979–1989,* Columbia, 1989 • *Super Hits,* Columbia, 1998.

Comeaux, Amie: *Moving Out,* Polydor, 1994.

Creed: *Creed,* Elektra, 1978.

Crowell, Rodney: *The Rodney Crowell Collection,* Warner Bros., 1989.

McCready, Mindy: "Guys Do It All the Time," BNA, 1996 • "Ten Thousand Angels," BNA, 1996 • *Ten Thousand Angels,* BNA, 1996 • "A Girl's Gotta Do (What A Girl's Gotta Do)," BNA, 1997 • *If I Don't Stay the Night (ECD),* BNA, 1997 • "What If I Do," BNA, 1997 • Featuring Richie McDonald, "Maybe He'll Notice Her Now," BNA, 1997 • "The Other Side," BNA, 1998 • "You'll Never Know," BNA, 1998.

McEntire, Reba: *What If It's You,* MCA Nashville, 1997 • *If You See Him,* MCA, 1998.

Parton, Dolly: "Don't Call It Love," RCA, 1985 • w/ Kenny Rogers, "Real Love," RCA, 1985 • *Real Love,* RCA, 1985 • "Think About Love," RCA, 1986 • *Think About Love,* RCA,

1986 • "'Tie Our Love (in a Double Knot)," RCA, 1986 • *The Best There Is*, RCA, 1987.

Parton, Stella: *Love Ya,* Elektra, 1979.

Pirates of the Mississippi: *Paradise,* Giant, 1995.

Rabbitt, Eddie: "Drinkin' My Baby (Off My Mind)," Elektra, 1976 • *Rocky Mountain Music,* Elektra, 1976 • "I Just Want to Love You," Elektra, 1978 • *Rabbitt,* Elektra, 1978 • "You Don't Love Me Anymore," Elektra, 1978 • *Loveline,* Elektra, 1979 • "Suspicions," Elektra, 1979 • "Drivin' My Life Away," Elektra, 1980 • "Gone Too Far," Elektra, 1980 • "I Love a Rainy Night," Elektra, 1980 • *Horizon,* Elektra, 1981 • "Step by Step," Elektra, 1981 • "I Don't Know Where to Start," Elektra, 1982 • "Someone Could Lose a Heart Tonight," Elektra, 1982 • *Step by Step,* Mercury, 1982 • w/ Crystal Gayle, "You and I," Elektra, 1982 • *All Time Greatest Hits,* Warner Bros., 1983 • *Radio Romance,* Mercury, 1983 • *The Best Of/Greatest Hits,* Vol 2, Warner Bros., 1983 • "You Can't Run from Love," Warner Bros., 1983 • *#1's,* Warner Bros., 1985 • *Greatest Country Hits,* Curb, 1991.

Roberts, Bruce: *Cool Fool,* Elektra, 1980.

Rogers, Kenny: "Love Will Turn You Around," Liberty, 1982 • *20 Greatest Hits,* Liberty, 1983 • *See also* Parton, Dolly.

Sharp, Randy: *See* Brooks, Karen.

Singletary, Daryle: *Daryle Singletary,* Giant, 1995 • "I Let Her Lie," Giant, 1995 • "I'm Living up to Her Low Expectations," Giant, 1995 • *All Because of You,* Giant, 1996 • "Too Much Fun," Giant, 1996 • "Workin' It Out," Giant, 1996 • "Amen Kind of Love," Reprise, 1997 • "Even the Wind," Giant, 1997 • "The Used to Be's," Giant, 1997.

Smith, Sammi: *Mixed Emotions,* Elektra, 1977.

Souther, John David: *Home By Dawn,* Warner Bros., 1984.

Tucker, Tanya: *Changes,* Arista, 1982.

Earle Mankey

An L.A. legend, Earle Mankey has been an integral part of the power pop, new wave, punk, and indie rock scene there for almost 30 years as guitarist for Sparks, solo artist, engineer for the Beach Boys, and producer for definitive L.A. artists from the '70s (the Runaways, the Pop, 20/20, Weirdos), '80s (Walter Egan, the Three O'Clock, the Long Ryders, Concrete Blonde, the Droogs), and '90s (the Leaving Trains, Possum Dixon, Lazy Cowgirls, Cockeyed Ghost). Most of Mankey's productions have been recorded at his own studio, Earle's Psychedelic Shack, in suburban Thousand Oaks.

Earle Mankey was born March 8, 1947, in Washington, Pennsylvania, and moved with his family to suburban Los Angeles around 1960. Shortly thereafter, Mankey's father bought a Sony 2-track tape recorder, and the younger Mankey's fate was sealed. He got deeply into recording (usually bands with which he played guitar), experimenting with sounds and overdubbing maniacally. This process led to an interest in electronic engineering, in which Mankey earned a degree from UCLA.

While at UCLA, Mankey met an eccentric pair of brothers, Ron and Russell Mael, and with Mankey's brother Jim on bass, they formed Halfnelson. The band's bizarre art pop was captured on its self-titled debut in 1972, produced by Todd Rundgren (see entry), which bore some resemblance to England's Roxy Music—if only for strangeness. The record was met with slack-jawed incomprehension; shortly thereafter the band changed its name to Sparks and released a second album, *A Woofer in Tweeter's Clothing.* Russell's freakish vibrato falsetto (occasionally varied with a startlingly deep, gargly bass), Ron's Charlie Chaplin-meets-Hitler look, and the band's ornate mini-operettas with titles like "Whippings and Apologies" and "Here Comes Bob" again failed to find an audience. The Maels then broke up the band, moved to England, and started over again (see Muff Winwood entry), enjoying a long and frequently brilliant career, which has continued into the '90s in a variety of art rock and new wave styles.

After the two albums with Sparks, Mankey got a job as recording engineer and manager of the Beach Boys' Brother studio in Santa Monica. Brain Wilson (see entry) was in his ultra-weird period at the time (mid-'70s), but the band managed to generate *15 Big Ones, Love You, Light Album,* and *Keepin' the Summer Alive* with Mankey engineering. Mankey was most impressed that, despite Wilson's mental debilitation, he could make snap judgments regarding songs and arrangements that were often dead on.

As studio manager, Mankey could bring bands to the studio to record in his off time; New York's Mumps—Lance Loud's fusion of punk and pop—was Mankey's first production in 1975. Mankey met idiosyncratic producer Kim Fowley in 1976 and worked with him on various projects for Helen Reddy (*Ear Candy*), power-poppers the Quick, and prototypical all-girl punk-pop band, the Runaways. *Queens of Noise* features blonde singer/actress Cherie Currie, future rock queen Joan Jett on guitar and vocals, and future metal star Lita Ford on bass. "California Paradise" is Currie's rocking best, and "I Love Playin' with Fire" sounds just like a Joan Jett song, complete with her patented feral scream.

In 1979 Mankey produced one of the decade's best

albums with the debut of 20/20, a power-pop classic. All the usual suspects are there in the band's melodies, harmonies, and alternately ringing and slamming guitars (Beatles, Byrds, Raspberries, Who), but there is plenty of new wave energy (and synth work), which makes the record contemporary and, in fact, timeless. The album opening, "The Sky Is Falling," is pure Mankey: weird keyboard noodling and UFO buzzings, followed by the crack and crashing of the sky.

With no time to clear the debris, the oft-anthologized "Yellow Pills" explodes with sparkling clarity and psychedelic power. Stomping power chords, burbling synth, and the phased singing of guitarists Steve Allen, Chris Silagyi, and bassist Ron Flynt contribute to the masterpiece. A new world seems to be revolving into view as Allen sings, "Everybody feels like they were / Just made by the Creator, / So come take a walk down my street / With your head up by the phone lines." In the bridge the singer admits that the elevation may be artificially induced by his "yellow pills," but at that time no consequences were in sight.

Mankey did his part in creating the magic, heaping delayed vocals over the throbbing, sparkling mix. "By the break [just before the third verse] we had 40 or 50 vocal delays that built to a climax—and then released into nothingness," he recalls fondly. Amazingly, the rest of the album continues nearly at the quality level of "Pills," especially the remainder of side 1: "Cheri," "Out of Time," "Tell Me Why," and "Tonight We Fly."

In the early '80s Mankey helped usher stars of L.A.'s "paisley underground" to record with the brilliant Syd Barrett/Move/Beatles-inspired poppy psychedelia of the Three O'Clock's *Baroque Hoedown* EP and *Sixteen Tambourines* album. Mankey helped develop another trend in 1983 with the Long Ryder's tuneful, neo-Byrdsian roots rock, but returned to true greatness in 1986 with the debut of Concrete Blonde, a punky new wave trio featuring singer/bassist Johnette Napolitano and Earle's brother Jim on guitar.

While the group later evolved into a moody pop band under the guidance of Chris Tsangarides (see entry), on the debut, Jim's driving, insinuating guitar and Napolitano's evocative Chrissie Hynde–like alto rock with liberated passion. Every song on side 1 is memorable: the loping shuffle of "True," psychobilly drive of "Your Haunted Head," extended menace of "Dance Along the Edge," and the bittersweet farewell of "Song for Kim" stick in the mind long after the record is over, but it is "Still in Hollywood" that is the career maker.

On the guitar thrasher "Hollywood," Napolitano's voice ranges from near-conversational storytelling in the verses to a raging howl for the choruses. The band compresses into one song the hope, glamour, squalor, and resignation that has made the "City of Dreams" a bipolar magnet—equally attracting and repelling—for 100 years. Tough, funny, and compassionate, Napolitano sings in the voice of someone who had been struggling to make it in Hollywood's rock 'n' roll quagmire for nearly 10 years when she wrote the song in 1985. With this song she made it.

In the '90s, Mankey, who is married with two teenage children, has continued to record almost daily (he just loves "to twiddle those knobs"). He has now recorded hundreds of bands at his Earle's Psychedelic Shack recording studio, helping to bring a musical legitimacy to inexperienced bands and roughing up overly slick bands. Besides technical ability, Mankey has the gift of taste.

Perhaps his most notable '90s recording is Possum Dixon's Interscope debut. Mankey brings out the best in this energetic L.A. angst-rock band, especially on the excellent "Watch the Girl Destroy Me," wherein singer/songwriter/bassist Robert Zabrecky muses upon his Hamlet-like powerlessness to alter the action of the title.

Mankey loves his job but thinks that bands should have a little more fun. "Bands should lighten up and add some silliness to their records. Young guitar bands are some of the most conservative people on earth. You have to be accomplished enough musically to play in the groove and interact with each other to form a single musical idea, but after you get those musical parts interacting, then give me a surprise." —ERIC OLSEN

Alternating Boxes: "Dogtown," Polydor, 1984.

Apache Dancers: *War Stories*, IRS, 1990.

Brown, Arthur: *Requiem*, Remote, 1982.

Cockeyed Ghost: *Keep Yourself Amused*, Big Deal, 1996 • *Neverest*, Big Deal, 1997.

Concrete Blonde: *Concrete Blonde*, IRS, 1986 • *Recollection: The Best of Concrete Blonde*, IRS, 1996.

Department of Crooks: *Plan 9 from Las Vegas*, Ichiban, 1997.

Dickies, The: *Great Dictations (The Definitive Dickies Collection)*, A&M, 1989.

Dream 6: *Dream 6*, Happy Hermit, 1983.

Droogs, The: *Stone Cold World*, PVC, 1984, 1987 • *Kingdom Day*, PVC, 1987.

Egan, Walter: *The Last Stroll*, Columbia, 1981.

Elevators, The: *Frontline*, Arista, 1980.

Hoffman, Kristian: *I Don't Love My Guru Anymore*, Eggbert, 1993, 1994 • *Earthquake Weather*, Eggbert, 1997.

Last, The: *Gin and Inuendo*, SST, 1996.

Lazy Cowgirls: *Ragged Soul*, Crypt, 1995.

Leaving Trains: *Transportational D. Vices,* SST, 1989 • *Sleeping Underwater Survivors,* SST, 1990 • *Drowned and Dragged* (EP), SST, 1995.

Long Ryders: *10-5-60* (EP), PVC, 1983.

Lucky: *Live a Little,* Temple Bar, 1995.

Mankey, Earle: *Earle Mankey* (EP), Select, 1981 • *Earle Mankey,* Frigidisk, 1981, 1998 • *Real World* (EP), Happy Hermit, 1985.

Mumps, The: *Fatal Charm: A Brief History of a Brief History,* Eggbert, 1994.

Nine, Mark: *This Island Earth,* Underworld, 1994.

Paley Brothers: *The Paley Brothers,* Sire, 1978.

Permanent Green Light: *Against Nature,* Rockville, 1993 • "The Goddess Bunny," Flipside, 1995 (*R.A.F.R.: Flipside Compilation*).

Pop, The: *Go,* Arista, 1979.

Possum Dixon: *Possum Dixon,* Interscope, 1993.

Purple Bosco: *Deeper,* IRS, 1995.

Quick, The: *Mondo Deco,* Mercury, 1976.

Reddy, Helen: *Ear Candy,* Capitol, 1977 • "You're My World," Capitol, 1977 • *I Am Woman: The Essential Helen Reddy Collection,* Razor & Tie, 1998.

Runaways, The: *Queens of Noise,* Mercury, 1977 • *The Best Of,* Mercury, 1987.

Sacrilicious: *When You Wish upon a Dead Star,* Frontier, 1995.

Skunks, The: *The Skunks,* Republic, 1982.

Solipsistics, The: *Whatever Makes You Happy,* Frigidisk, 1997 • *Wish in One Hand,* Frigidisk, 1997.

Sparks: *In the Swing,* Spectrum, 1993.

Stool Pigeons: *Gerry Cross the Mersey: British Inversion,* Vol. 2, Sympathy For the Record Industry, 1997.

Tearaways: *Ground's the Limit,* Pinch Hit, 1997.

Three O'Clock: *Baroque Hoedown,* Frontier, 1982 • *Sixteen Tambourines,* Frontier, 1983 • *Baroque Hoedown/Sixteen Tambourines,* Frontier, 1993.

20/20: *20/20,* Epic, 1979 • *20/20/Look Out!,* Oglio, 1979, 1995.

Weirdos: *Weird World 1977–1981* (2 tracks), Frontier, 1991.

Arif Mardin

The list of records Arif Mardin has produced since he began at Atlantic Records more than 30 years ago occupies nearly five pages, and it's nowhere near comprehensive. It reads like a history of pop and rock, particularly the soul-inflected variety. First, as an assistant to Atlantic co-owner Nesuhi Ertegun (see entry), the Turkish-born aristocrat was involved in pop rock. His first production for the label, in 1966, was the Young Rascals, which he crafted with the Rascals and engineer Tom Dowd (see entry).

Among those who have benefited from Mardin's astute, painterly hand are trumpeter Freddie Hubbard; saxophonists Charles Lloyd and King Curtis; singers Aretha Franklin, Cher, Dusty Springfield, Laura Nyro, and Chaka Khan; and such groups as Hall and Oates, the Average White Band, the Bee Gees, and the Modern Jazz Quartet.

In December 1996, Mardin extended his deep-seated relationship with Atlantic by signing a new, long-term pact to continue as the label's senior vice president. The six-time Grammy Award winner joined the label in 1963.

Born March 15, 1932, in Istanbul, Mardin graduated from Istanbul University and studied at the London School of Economics. In 1957, he married his wife, Latife. The following year, instead of going into his father's gas station chain business, Mardin became the first recipient of the Quincy Jones Scholarship at the Berklee College of Music in Boston. After graduation, he taught at Berklee for a year; eventually, he was made a trustee of the school and awarded an honorary doctorate.

Prior to his first semester at Berklee, however, he made some key connections that would stand him in particularly good stead. He attended the Lenox School in Massachusetts' Berkshire Mountains, studying with such notable jazz and Third Stream figures as Gunther

Photo by Julie Mardin

Schuller, George Russell, John Lewis, and Max Roach. A composition Mardin wrote for Lenox faculty so impressed Atlantic co-owner Ertegun that after Mardin's Berklee tenure, Ertegun hired him as an assistant and archivist at Atlantic Records.

He soon became production manager at the label and was named a vice president in 1969. He was obviously a quick study; his first project, the Rascals' "Good Lovin'," went to No. 1. It was recorded to 8-track; the background vocals were done separately from Felix Cavaliere's lead. Music was beginning to flex technological muscles. "In 1963 or 1964, the artist would choose the song, then go into a small office and work with the arranger," Mardin recalls. "The following day, an orchestra—two guitars, Fender bass, piano, maybe a Wurlitzer, a drummer, 10 to 12 strings and a few woodwinds—would come together. The vocalist would be in a separate booth. The record would be made right there, no overdubs. Tom Dowd would mix it to a mono 1/4-inch tape, with the correct balance. He would also record it to 8-track."

The aim of the process was purity, Mardin says. But that could be restricting, and as technology progressed, constraints were loosened. One day, when Ray Charles was recording "Believe to My Soul," Charles didn't like the way some female backup vocalists sounded. So Dowd told Charles four tracks were free to record on, and "Charles filled those in himself," Mardin says. "He sang the girls' parts."

In 1969, Mardin released the first of his two solo albums, *Glass Onion* (*Journey,* a less thematic work, followed several years later). *Glass Onion* included Mardin's jazzy arrangement of the Rascals' 1967 hit, "How Can I Be Sure?"; the Mardin version ultimately became a lounge hit in London dance clubs—in 1996.

In the '70s, after creating a monster funk aggregation in the Scottish group Average White Band, his greatest achievement was producing the Bee Gees. With the brothers Gibb, Mardin scored worldwide hits in the melodic disco of "Jive Talkin' " (No. 1), "Nights on Broadway" (No. 7), and "Fanny (Be Tender with My Love)" (No. 12). Mardin says he didn't realize the Bee Gees were breaking ground; he also didn't sense how big they'd be. But he and the Bee Gees worked hard during that era, particularly on *Main Course* (No. 14), their 1975 breakthrough. Barry, Robin, and Maurice Gibb listened to a lot of rhythm 'n' blues before making that album. "I really enjoyed those sessions," Mardin says, adding he especially relished Barry Gibb's falsetto. "I always like vocalists to hurt up here," he jokes, pointing to his throat.

Since the Bee Gees' heyday ended at the dawn of the '80s, Mardin has notched major successes with Chaka Khan ("I Feel for You," No. 3) and Scritti Politti, whose *Cupid and Psyche '85* was one of the most interesting blends of funk and disco of that decade (Mardin produced three tracks on it).

Although he doesn't produce many full albums, he produces numerous tracks and singles. He keeps current by listening to the radio when he's in Los Angeles, ordering the latest discs and studying them at home. He also studies videos. In addition, he writes modern classical music and enjoys early 20th-century work in that genre, above all the music of Alban Berg and Arnold Schoenberg.

Mardin's latest full album production is Linda Eder's *Only Love.* But he also has recently cut tracks on Regina Carter, Bebe Winans, Bette Midler, Eric Martin, Patti LaBelle, Carly Simon, Anita Baker, Dr. John, and, of course, the Bee Gees.

"I like layers in music that give you the feeling of distance," Mardin says. "I like having things going on in the background. You have something to define the farthest point, then things that are nearer." Mardin's own albums have remarkable depth of field.

If Mardin enjoys the freedom technology can give, he also views it as a double-edged sword. "I think that over the years, engineers and producers have been deferring their judgment until later," he says. "It goes back to the end of the period when the end product was achieved in the studio. Technology became so huge. Too many choices are available. When I'm recording, I usually commit to sounds right there.

"I like to take advantage of technology, but I don't want to be a slave to it." —Carlo Wolff

Allison, Mose: *Allison Wonderland,* Rhino, 1994 • *Best Of,* Sequel, 1995 • *The Sage of Tippo,* 32Jazz, 1998.

Allman, Duane: *Anthology,* Capricorn, 1972 • *Anthology II,* Capricorn, 1974.

Art Farmer Quartet: *Live at the Half Note,* Rhino, 1964, 1989.

Average White Band: *Average White Band,* Atlantic, 1974 • "Cut the Cake," Atlantic, 1975 • *Cut the Cake,* Atlantic, 1975 • "If I Ever Lose This Heaven," Atlantic, 1975 • "Pick Up the Pieces," Atlantic, 1975 • "School Boy Crush," Atlantic, 1975 • "Queen of My Soul," Atlantic, 1976 • w/ Ben E. King, *Benny and Us,* Atlantic, 1977 • *Person to Person,* Atlantic, 1977 • *Soul Searching,* Atlantic, 1977 • *The Atlantic Family Live at Montreux,* Atlantic, 1978 • *Warmer Communications,* RCA/Atlantic, 1978 • *Pickin' Up the Pieces: Best of, 1974–1980,* Rhino, 1992.

Baker, Anita: "You Belong to Me," Elektra, 1990 (*Rubaiyat: Elektra's 40th Anniversary*) • *Rhythm of Love* (1 track), Elektra, 1994.

Barron, Kenny: See Owens, Jimmy

Bee Gees: *Mr. Natural,* Rolling Stones, 1974 • "Jive Talkin',"

Joseph, Margie: *Margie Joseph,* Atlantic, 1973 • *Sweet Surrender,* Atlantic, 1974 • *Margie,* Atlantic, 1975 • *Feeling My Way,* Atlantic, 1976 • *The Atlantic Sessions: The Best Of,* Ichiban/Soul Classics, 1994.

Junior: "Somebody," London, 1984 • *Best Of,* Mercury, 1995.

Khan, Chaka: *Chaka,* Warner Bros., 1978 • "I'm Every Woman," Warner Bros., 1978 • *Naughty,* Warner Bros., 1980 • "What Cha' Gonna Do for Me," Warner Bros., 1981 • *What Cha' Gonna Do for Me,* Warner Bros., 1981 • *Chaka Khan,* Warner Bros., 1982 • "I Feel for You," Warner Bros., 1984 • *I Feel for You,* Warner Bros., 1984 • "Own the Night," MCA, 1985 • "This Is My Night," Warner Bros., 1985 • "Through the Fire," Warner Bros., 1985 • *Destiny,* Warner Bros., 1986 • "Love of a Lifetime," Warner Bros., 1986 • "Tight Fit," Warner Bros., 1986 • "Earth to Mickey," Warner Bros., 1987 • *Life Is a Dance (The Remix Project),* Warner Bros., 1989 • *The Woman I Am,* Warner Bros., 1992 • *Epiphany: The Best of Chaka Khan,* Vol. 2, Reprise, 1996 • "Never Miss the Water," Reprise, 1996 • "Papillon," Reprise, 1996 • "Your Love Is All I Know," Reprise, 1997.

King Curtis: *Instant Groove,* Edsel, 1968 • *Sweet Soul,* Atlantic, 1968 • *Live At Fillmore West,* Atlantic, 1971.

King, Ben E.: *Anthology,* Atlantic, 1993 • *See also* Average White Band.

LaBelle, Patti: *Flame,* MCA, 1997.

Liner: *Liner,* Atlantic, 1979.

Lloyd, Charles: *Dream Weaver,* Atlantic, 1966 • *At His Best,* JCI, 1987.

Lulu: *Melody Fair,* Atco, 1970 • *From Crayons to Pefume: The Best of Lulu,* Rhino, 1994.

Mama's Pride: *Mama's Pride,* Atlantic, 1976.

Manchester, Melissa: *Hey Ricky,* Arista, 1982 • "You Should Hear How She Talks About You," Arista, 1982 • *Emergency,* Arista, 1983 • *Greatest Hits,* Arista, 1983 • *If My Heart Had Wings,* Atlantic, 1995 • *The Essence Of,* Arista, 1997.

Manhattan Transfer: *The Very Best Of,* Rhino, 1994 • *Tonin',* Atlantic, 1995.

Mann, Herbie: *Push Push,* Embryo, 1971 • *Evolution of Mann: The Herbie Mann Anthology,* Rhino, 1994.

Mardin, Arif: *Glass Onion,* Atlantic, 1969 • *Journey,* Atlantic, 1975.

Midler, Bette: *Bette Midler,* Atlantic, 1973, 1995 • *Thighs and Whispers,* Atlantic, 1979, 1995 • "Wind Beneath My Wings," Atlantic, 1989 • "From a Distance," Atlantic, 1990 • *Some People's Lives,* Atlantic, 1990 • "Every Road Leads Back to You," Atlantic, 1991 • *For the Boys* soundtrack, Atlantic, 1991 • "Night and Day," Atlantic, 1991 • *Experience the Divine: Bette Midler's Greatest Hits,* Atlantic, 1993 • *Bette of Roses,* Atlantic, 1995.

Mizelle, Cindy: *Cindy Mizelle,* Atlantic, 1994.

Modern Jazz Quartet: *Plastic Dreams,* Atlantic, 1972 • and Friends, *A 40th Anniversary Celebration,* Atlantic Jazz, 1994 • *Celebration,* Atlantic, 1994.

Najee: *Just an Illusion,* EMI America, 1992 • "All I Ever Ask," EMI America, 1993.

Nelson, Willie: *Shotgun Willie,* Atlantic, 1973 • *The Troublemaker,* Columbia, 1976 • *Greatest Hits and Some That Will Be,* Columbia, 1981 • "Uncloudy Day," Columbia, 1981 • *A Classic and Unreleased Colection,* Rhino, 1995.

Nyro, Laura: *Christmas and the Beads of Sweat,* Columbia, 1970 • *Stoned Soul Picnic: The Best Of,* Legacy, 1997.

O'Keefe, Danny: "Good Time Charlie's Got the Blues," Signpost, 1972 • *O'Keefe,* Signpost, 1972 • *Breezy Stories,* Atlantic, 1973.

Oliphant, Grassella: *The Grass Is Greener,* Atlantic, 1968.

Owens, Jimmy: w/ Kenny Barron, *You Had Better Listen,* Atlantic, 1968.

Page, Tommy: *Tommy Page,* Sire, 1988 • "A Shoulder to Cry On," Sire, 1989 • *Paintings in My Mind,* Sire, 1989 • "When I Dream of You," Sire, 1990.

Ponty, Jean-Luc: *Mystical Adventures,* Atlantic, 1982, 1992.

Pratt, Andy: *Resolution: The Andy Pratt Collection,* Razor & Tie, 1976, 1996 • *Shiver in the Night,* Nemperor, 1977.

Prine, John: *John Prine,* Atlantic, 1971 • *Diamonds in the Rough,* Atlantic, 1972 • *Sweet Revenge,* Atlantic, 1974 • *Great Days: The John Prine Anthology,* Rhino, 1993.

Queen: *Hot Space,* Elektra, 1982.

Rankin, Kenny: *After the Roses,* Atlantic, 1980, 1990.

Rascals, The: "I Ain't Gonna Eat Out My Heart Anymore," Atlantic, 1965 • *I've Been Lonely Too Long,* Atlantic, 1967 • "People Got to Be Free," Atlantic, 1968 • *The Very Best Of,* Rhino, 1993.

Sahm, Doug: *Doug Sahm and Band,* Atlantic, 1973 • *The Best of Doug Sahm, 1968–1975,* Rhino, 1992.

Sayer, Leo: *World Radio,* Warner Bros., 1982 • *Have You Ever Been in Love?,* Warner Bros., 1983 • *All the Best,* Gold Rush, 1996 • *The Show Must Go On: Anthology,* Rhino, 1996.

Scritti Politti: "Wood Bees (Pray Like Aretha Franklin)," Warner Bros., 1984 • *Cupid and Psyche '85* (3 tracks), Warner Bros., 1985.

Simon, Carly: *Boys in the Trees,* Elektra, 1978 • "You Belong to Me," Elektra, 1978 • *Spy,* Elektra, 1979 • *Film Noir,* Arista, 1997.

Sir Douglas Band: *Texas Tornado,* Atlantic, 1973.

Springfield, Dusty: *Dusty in Memphis,* Atlantic, 1968, 1981 • "Son of a Preacher Man," Atlantic, 1969 • *Anthology,* PolyGram, 1997 • *The Very Best of Dusty Springfield,* Mercury Chronicles, 1998.

Starr, Ringo: *Ringo's Rotogravure,* Polydor/Atlantic, 1973 • *Ringo the 4th,* Polydor/Atlantic, 1977 • *Starr Struck: Best Of,* Vol. 2, Rhino, 1989.

Stitt, Sonny: *Stitt Plays Bird,* Atlantic, 1963.

Streisand, Barbra: *Higher Ground,* Columbia, 1997 • "If I Could," Columbia, 1998.

Waller, Robert James: *The Ballads of Madison County,* Atlantic, 1993.

Warwick, Dionne: *Sings Cole Porter,* Arista, 1990.

Whirling Dervishes: *Music of the Whirling Dervishes,* Atlantic, 1993.

White, Tony Joe: *The Train I'm On,* Atlantic, 1972.

Winans, BeBe: *BeBe Winans,* Atlantic, 1997.

Winans, BeBe and CeCe: "If Anything Ever Happened to You," Capitol, 1994 • "Love of My Life," Capitol, 1995 • *Relationships,* Capitol, 1995 • *Greatest Hits,* Sparrow, 1996.

Worth, Irene: *Her Infinite Variety: Irene Worth As the Women of Shakespeare,* Sony Classical, 1993.

Young Rascals: "Good Lovin'," Atlantic, 1966.

COLLECTIONS

Labyrinth soundtrack, Atlantic, 1986.

Singers, Atlantic Jazz, 1987.

Beaches soundtrack, Atlantic, 1988.

Saxophones, Vol. 2, Atlantic Jazz/Rhino, 1988.

Gypsy (original cast), Atlantic, 1993.

Jackie Robinson Tribute: Stealing Home, Sony, 1997.

Smokey Joe's Cafe: The Songs of Leiber and Stoller (original cast), Atlantic Theater, 1995.

Family Thing (original soundtrack), Edeltone, 1996.

Hunchback of Notre Dame (original soundtrack), Disney, 1996.

Rent (original Broadway cast), Dreamworks SKG, 1996.

Marley Marl

(MARLON WILLIAMS)

Long before Sean "Puffy" Combs, DJ Premier or Jermaine Dupri (see entries), there was New York's Marley Marl, one of rap's earliest superproducers. From the mid-'80s to the very early '90s, Marley Marl, much like Combs or Dupri, presided over a slew of artists for whom he supplied the beats. Marl did the job at Warner Bros.–distributed Cold Chillin' Records, home to Roxanne Shante, Big Daddy Kane, Biz Markie, M.C. Shan, and Kool G Rap. Some cuts include "Raw" by Big Daddy Kane and "Go On Girl" by Shante.

Marl (born Marlon Williams September 30, 1962, in Queens, New York) was a radio DJ before he became one of the innovators of sampling as a producer. Marl was responsible for many of LL Cool J's better '90s records, including the stellar *Mama Said Knock You Out*

(No. 16) album, as well as songs like "Funkadelic Relic," "Stand by Your Man" and "Straight from Queens."

Marl was also a part of the lauded production team that worked on TLC's 1992 *Oooooooohhh . . . on the TLC Tip* (No. 14) album, contributing the songs "Das Da Way We Like 'Em," and "This Is How It Should Be Done."

Though Cold Chillin' no longer employs him, Marl carries on. He's the main force behind Lords of the Underground, for example, producing songs such as "Tic Toc" and *Keepers of the Funk.* —KEVIN JOHNSON

Abdul, Paula: "Straight Up" (remix), Virgin, 1988.

Alkaholiks, Tha: "Hip Hop Drunkies," RCA, 1997 • *Likwidation,* RCA, 1997.

Bell Biv DeVoe: *WBBD-Bootcity!* (remix album), MCA, 1991.

Biz Markie: "Make the Music with Your Mouth," Prism, 1986 • *Biz's Baddest Beats,* Cold Chillin', 1987, 1995 • *Goin' Off,* Cold Chillin', 1988, 1995 • "Vapors," Cold Chillin', 1988.

Capone-N-Noriega: *War Report,* Penalty, 1997.

Cooly Live: *Livewire,* RCA, 1992.

Craig G: *The Kingpin,* Atlantic, 1989.

Da Youngsta's: *The Aftermath,* EastWest, 1993 • "Hip Hop Ride," EastWest, 1994 • *No Mercy,* Atlantic, 1994.

De'1: *16 with a Bullet,* Reprise, 1993 • *Day One,* Reprise, 1993.

En Vogue: *Remix to Sing,* EastWest, 1991.

Fat Boys: "Crushin' " (remix), Tin Pan Apple/Polydor, 1987.

Fat Joe: *Don Cartegena,* Atlantic, 1998.

Heavy D and the Boyz: *Living Large,* MCA, 1987 • *Big Tyme,* MCA, 1989 • "Gyrlz, They Love Me," Uptown, 1990 • *Peaceful Journey,* Uptown/MCA, 1991 • *Nuttin' but Love,* Uptown, 1994.

Intelligent Hoodlum: *Tragedy: Saga of a Hoodlum,* A&M, 1993.

Kane, Big Daddy: "Ain't No Half-Steppin'," Cold Chillin'/WB, 1988 • *Long Live the Kane,* Cold Chillin'/WB, 1988 • "Raw," Warner Bros., 1988 (*Colors* soundtrack) • "I'll Take You There," Cold Chillin'/WB, 1989 • *It's a Big Daddy Thing* (1 track), Cold Chillin'/Reprise, 1989.

Khan, Chaka: *Life Is a Dance (The Remix Project),* Warner Bros., 1989.

King Tee: *Tha Triflin' Album,* Capitol, 1993.

Kool G Rap: "Butcher Shop," Warner Bros., 1988 (*Colors* soundtrack).

Kool G Rap and DJ Polo: *Road to the Riches,* Cold Chillin', 1989, 1995 • *Killer Kuts,* Cold Chillin', 1996 • *Rated XXX,* Cold Chillin', 1996.

KRS-One vs. M.C. Shan: *The Battle for Rap Supremecy,* Cold Chillin', 1996.

L.L. Cool J: "Around the Way Girl," Def Jam/Columbia, 1990 • *Mama Said Knock You Out,* Def Jam/Columbia, 1990 • "The Boomin' System," Def Jam/Columbia, 1990 • "6 Minutes of Pleasure," Def Jam/Columbia, 1991 •

"Mama Said Knock You Out," Def Jam/Columbia, 1991 • *14 Shots to the Dome* (7 tracks), Def Jam, 1993 • "Back Seat (of My Jeep)/Pink Cookies in a Plastic Bag," Def Jam/Columbia, 1993 • "Stand by Your Man," Def Jam/Columbia, 1993 • *All World*, Def Jam, 1996.

Lords of the Underground: "Funky Child," Pendulum, 1993 • *Here Come the Lords*, Pendulum/Elektra, 1993 • *Keepers of the Funk*, Pendulum, 1994 • "Tic Toc," Pendulum, 1994.

Love, Monie: "Full Term Love," Giant, 1992 • *In a Word or 2*, Warner Bros., 1993.

M.C. Shan: *Down by Law*, Cold Chillin', 1987, 1995 • w/ T.J. Swan, "Left Me Lonely," Cold Chillin', 1987 • "A Mind Is a Terrible Thing to Waste," Warner Bros., 1988 (*Colors* soundtrack) • *Born to Be Wild*, Cold Chillin', 1988.

Marley Marl: *The Queensbridge Sessions*, Tuff City, 1996.

Master Ace: "Me and the Biz," Cold Chillin', 1990 • *Take a Look Around*, Cold Chillin', 1990.

MC Lyte: *Eyes on This*, First Priority, 1989.

Mic Geronimo: *Vendetta*, Blunt, 1997.

Real Live: *The Turnaround: A Long Awaited Drama*, Big Beat, 1996.

Shante, Roxanne: "Bite This," Pop Art, 1985 • "Queen of Rocks," Pop Art, 1985 • "Go on Girl," Warner Bros., 1988 (*Colors* soundtrack) • *Bad Sister*, Cold Chillin', 1989 • *Greatest Hits*, Cold Chillin', 1995.

TLC: *Oooooohhh . . . on the TLC Tip*, LaFace, 1992.

World Renown: *World Renown*, Warner Bros., 1995.

COLLECTIONS

In Control, Vols. 1–2, Cold Chillin', 1988 and 1991.

Christopher Martin

See DJ PREMIER AND GURU

George Martin

Sir George Martin is a popular music icon who helped define the role of the modern record producer. Knighted in 1996, Martin's contributions to the Beatles canon are so indelible that he is often called the "fifth Beatle." He has also produced big hits and important records by a constellation of stars including America, Jeff Beck, Cheap Trick, Stan Getz, the Little River Band, Paul McCartney (see entry), Kenny Rogers, UFO, and Ultravox, as well as his own orchestral music.

Born January 3, 1926, in London, Martin was trained in classical music at the Guildhall School of Music. Martin began his career in 1950 as assistant to the head of A&R at EMI's Parlophone Records. There, he produced classical discs and comedy recordings such as *Peter Sellers and the Goon Show*. "It was a fascinating time because things were changing so quickly," Martin recalls. "I was very lucky to be there at that time because being in the midst of changes, I was not only part of them, I was actually urging them along, too."

With recording technology in its infancy, Martin and his technicians had to improvise to accurately reproduce the sound of a live performance. Therefore, he experimented with microphone techniques such as binaural and stereo pairs. "They had lovely ambience," Martin says of his early EMI recordings, many of which have been reissued on compact disc. "They say, 'We've got a record that doesn't bear your name, but we're sure you had something to do with it.' They tell me what it is, and I say, 'Yes, I made that record in 1952,' or whenever it was."

By 1955, Martin was head of Parlophone, the weak stepchild in the EMI empire. Parlophone's fortunes, however, changed dramatically in 1962 when Martin found the Beatles. Martin's musical acumen and mannered creativity perfectly complemented the Beatles' elfin innocence and madcap muses. In fact, it is hard to imagine how the Beatles could have blossomed under another producer.

Martin's early Beatles classics such as "Love Me Do" (No. 1), "P.S. I Love You" (No. 10), "Please, Please Me" (No. 3), "From Me to You" (No. 1 U.K.), "Thank You Girl," and "She Loves You" (No. 1) burst with youthful exuberance. Recorded in 2-track mono, Martin heightened the effect with such flourishes as hand claps, syncopated percussion, and brassy harmonica. "In those days, pop records were not issued in stereo," Martin explains. "After the Beatles were established we realized we had to make special stereo mixes. But stereo mixes, even in 1964, were still considered unimportant; and in fact, the Beatles would attend the mono mixes, but they'd leave it to [engineer] Geoff Emerick [see entry] and me to do the stereos."

In 1964, Martin and the Beatles began to move beyond the traditional pop music boundaries. For instance, a feedback-induced guitar riff opens "I Feel Fine" (No. 1), while "Eight Days a Week" (No. 1) begins with a faded-in guitar line. By 1965, Martin and the Beatles had honed their formula to a fine art, resulting in such perfect pop songs as "Ticket to Ride" (No. 1), "I

Need You," "You're Going to Lose That Girl," and "Help!" (No. 1). Moreover, the band's studio experimentation took on even greater importance. For example, "Norwegian Wood" incorporated a sitar for a Far Eastern feel, while "You've Got to Hide Your Love Away" was Lennon's take on Bob Dylan.

By the time Martin and the Beatles made *Revolver* (No. 1) in 1966, there was no turning back. The Beatles stopped touring that August to concentrate on studio work, presaging the band's most creative period. Consequently, Martin was given more time in the studio to satisfy the Beatles' every whim. For example, he manufactured nautical sounds for the whimsical "Yellow Submarine" (No. 2) and scored a string quartet for the plaintive "Eleanor Rigby" (No. 11).

In late 1966, Martin and the Beatles reached a creative apogee: "Penny Lane" (No. 1) and "Strawberry Fields Forever" (No. 8), possibly the Beatles' finest single, followed by the album, *Sgt. Pepper's Lonely Hearts Club Band* (No. 1).

Martin's efforts, however, were aided by a new tool: 4-track recording. "I tended to put the bass and drums together on one track and the guitars together on another track and keep two tracks for voices so that one track would be lead vocal and the second track would be backing vocals plus guitar solos or whatever," Martin recalls.

"By putting my available sound on two tracks, I could mix the two together at a later stage, getting much more compression and hardness. When we wanted anything more complicated, either you compressed more onto one track to begin with, or you went from a 4-track to another 4-track, which is what we did mainly on *Pepper*."

With two 4-track machines giving him 8-track capability, Martin crafted a musical kaleidoscope that stands alone as a monument to creativity. For instance, to evoke a circus atmosphere in "Being for the Benefit of Mr. Kite," Martin had to satisfy Lennon's desire to "smell the sawdust." "I wondered how we'd actually get a steam organ playing the sounds," Martin muses. "You couldn't, so we just sort of faked it on various organs at different speeds, with me playing one and John playing another."

"I got Geoff Emerick to cut them up into 15-inch pieces of roughly a second each," Martin adds. "I said, 'Throw them up in the air, pick them up again, and stick them back together.' That made a kind of mélange of sound that when you played it you didn't hear a Sousa march anymore but you did hear a cacophony of steam organ sounds. And it worked."

The 1968 double album, *The Beatles* (No. 1), aka *The White Album*, was a clear departure from *Pepper*, with a stark, scaled-down feel. Each of the Beatles also worked separately with Martin in the studio. Even so, the album yielded such memorable songs as "While My Guitar Gently Weeps," "Mother Nature's Son," "Birthday," "Martha My Dear," and "Helter Skelter."

Martin and the Beatles suffered a temporary falling-out in early 1969, a rift that began with the ill-fated *Let It Be* project. Originally titled *Get Back*, Paul McCartney's idea for a documentary of the Beatles in the studio, without overdubs or studio wizardry, began with good intentions but quickly evolved into an unfocused mess. The shelved session tapes, featuring an acoustic gem, "Two of Us," and the back-to-the-future reprise of an early Beatles song, "The One After 909," were later turned over to Phil Spector (see entry) to resurrect into an album, *Let It Be*, released in 1970. Before that would happen, however, the Beatles had reunited with Martin at their old stomping ground, EMI's Abbey Road Studios, to make one last statement: *Abbey Road* (No. 1), released in 1969.

Abbey Road was a mature work that showed just how far the Beatles and Martin had progressed. "Come Together" (No. 1), "Something" (No. 3), "Octopus' Garden," and "Here Comes the Sun" led to a delightful

EMI'S ABBEY ROAD STUDIOS

EMI's Abbey Road Studios in London is arguably the most famous recording studio in the world. A hothouse of creativity, Abbey Road is where producer George Martin captured nearly all of the Beatles' albums: *Please Please Me* (1963) through *Abbey Road* (1969). Yet, the list of classic albums recorded at Abbey Road does not stop with the Beatles: Pink Floyd's *Dark Side of the Moon*; Al Stewart's *Year of the Cat*; Be-Bop Deluxe's *Sunburst Finish*; and a major part of the Zombies' *Odyssey and Oracle* are others.

Abbey Road, besides being home to Martin, was the breeding ground for Alan Parsons, John Leckie, Geoff Emerick, Chris Thomas, and Ken Scott (see entries). Parsons, appointed by EMI in 1997 to head Abbey Road Studios following the retirement of Ken Townsend, has been a devotee of Abbey Road since his first job with EMI in the late '60s. "There's a tremendous history in the place," Parsons muses. "More hit records have been made there than in any other studio on earth. There's a great feeling of being a part of history when you work there."

Curiously, Abbey Road did not become the studio's official name until after it was immortalized by the Beatles album. In an interview with Brian Southall for the book *Abbey Road*, Paul McCartney says the band decided to name the album after the studio as an homage to the band's recording home. "It is Abbey Road and for everyone who didn't know the name of the studio, that would imply something kind of mystical—a Monastery Avenue sorta thing," McCartney told Southall.

As for Parsons, returning to Abbey Road as director of studio operations is a special homecoming, even though he never really stopped working at the studio as a freelance producer. "There's just this sort of unwritten rule that once you go to Abbey Road, you always come back." —BEN CROMER

suite that included "Because," "You Never Give Me Your Money," "Golden Slumbers," and "The End."

The Beatles' breakup in 1970 gave Martin the freedom to produce other acts, resulting in albums by Seatrain, America, Jeff Beck, Gary Brooker, Jimmy Webb, UFO, Cheap Trick, and Ultravox. Martin's work with America was particularly fruitful, resulting in such delightful songs as "Tin Man" (No. 4), "Hold Me Tight," and "Sister Golden Hair" (No. 1). Martin also was able to capture Beck's extraordinary talent on *Blow by Blow* (No. 4), the guitarist's most successful album as a solo artist. Moreover, Martin continued to work on projects with Paul McCartney, including the soundtrack to *Live and Let Die*.

Although Martin was one of the prime reasons for the Beatles' recording success, he says EMI did not pay him accordingly. Consequently, he left EMI in 1965 to form Associated Independent Recordings (AIR) with John Burgess (see entry) and Ron Richards from EMI and Peter Sullivan from Decca Records. "EMI was run by a lot of gentlemen on the main board who had no concept at all about what recording was about and they paid their staff remarkably badly, including me," Martin says. "By the time 1962 came along I was still making less than £3,000 [$5,000] a year."

In 1969, Martin and company invested in a companion venture: AIR Studios. The success of AIR London led to expansion to the West Indies with AIR Montserrat, a studio and resort that was destroyed by Hurricane Hugo in 1989. Martin also built a new AIR London in 1992.

The dean of pop-rock producers, Martin is an audio Picasso who paints "aural pictures," as he puts it. "I always think in terms of seeing my sounds.

"Music is the most important thing of all," Martin surmises, adding that he uses technology as a means to an end. "I think if you can do service to music through your techniques, through your technology, then that's what your aim should be."

Action: *The Ultimate Action,* Edsel, 1980.
Aerosmith: "Come Together," Columbia, 1978 • *Greatest Hits,* Columbia, 1980 • *Pandora's Box,* Columbia, 1991.
America: *Holiday,* Warner Bros., 1974 • "Tin Man," Warner Bros., 1974 • "Daisy Jane," Warner Bros., 1975 • *Hearts,* Warner Bros., 1975 • *History,* Warner Bros., 1975 • "Lonely People," Warner Bros., 1975 • "Sister Golden Hair," Warner Bros., 1975 • *Hideaway,* Warner Bros., 1976 • "Today's the Day," Warner Bros., 1976 • *Harbor,* Warner Bros., 1977 • *Live,* Warner Bros., 1977 • *Silent Letter,* Capitol, 1979.
American Flyer: *American Flyer,* United Artists, 1976.
Beatles, The: *Please Please Me,* Parlophone, 1963 • *With the Beatles,* Parlophone, 1963 • "A Hard Day's Night," Capitol, 1964 • *A Hard Day's Night,* Capitol, 1964 • "Ain't She Sweet," Atco, 1964 • "And I Love Her," Capitol, 1964 • *Beatles for Sale,* Parlophone, 1964 • "Can't Buy Me Love," Capitol, 1964 • "Do You Wanna Know a Secret," Vee-Jay, 1964 • "I Feel Fine," Capitol, 1964 • "I Saw Her Standing There," Capitol, 1964 • "I Want to Hold Your Hand," Capitol, 1964 • "I'll Cry Instead," Capitol, 1964 • *Introducing the Beatles,* Vee-Jay, 1964 • "Love Me Do," Capitol, 1964 • "Matchbox," Capitol, 1964 • *Meet the Beatles!,* Capitol, 1964 • w/ Tony Sheridan, "My Bonnie," MGM, 1964 • "P.S. I Love You," Tollie, 1964 • "Please Please Me," Vee-Jay, 1964 • "She Loves You," Swan, 1964 •

"She's a Woman," Capitol, 1964 • "Slow Down," Capitol, 1964 • *Something New,* Capitol, 1964 • "Thank You Girl," Vee-Jay, 1964 • *The Beatles' Second Album,* Capitol, 1964 • "Twist and Shout," Tollie, 1964 • *Beatles '65,* Capitol, 1965 • *Beatles VI,* Capitol, 1965 • "Daytripper," Capitol, 1965 • "Eight Days a Week," Capitol, 1965 • "Help," Capitol, 1965 • *Help!,* Capitol, 1965 • "I Don't Want to Spoil the Party," Capitol, 1965 • "I'm Down," Capitol, 1965 • "Ticket to Ride," Capitol, 1965 • "Yesterday," Capitol, 1965 • *A Collection of Oldies,* Parlophone, 1966 • "Eleanor Rigby," Capitol, 1966 • "Nowhere Man," Capitol, 1966 • "Paperback Writer," Capitol, 1966 • "Rain," Capitol, 1966 • *Revolver,* Capitol, 1966 • *Rubber Soul,* Capitol, 1966 • "We Can Work It Out," Capitol, 1966 • "Yellow Submarine," Capitol, 1966 • *Yesterday and Today,* Capitol, 1966 • "All You Need Is Love," Capitol, 1967 • "Baby You're a Rich Man," Capitol, 1967 • "Hello Goodbye," Capitol, 1967 • "Penny Lane," Capitol, 1967 • *Sgt. Pepper's Lonely Hearts Club Band,* Capitol, 1967 • "Strawberry Fields Forever," Capitol, 1967 • "Hey Jude," Capitol, 1968 • "Lady Madonna," Capitol, 1968 • *Magical Mystery Tour,* Capitol, 1968 • "Revolution," Apple, 1968 • *The Beatles (White Album),* Apple, 1968 • *Yellow Submarine,* Apple, 1968 • *Abbey Road,* Apple, 1969 • "Come Together/Something," Apple, 1969 • "Don't Let Me Down," Apple, 1969 • "Get Back," Apple, 1969 • "The Ballad of John and Yoko," Apple, 1969 • "Let It Be," Apple, 1970 • *Let It Be,* Apple, 1970 • *1962–1966,* Parlophone/Capitol, 1973 • *1967–1970,* Capitol, 1973, 1993 • "Got to Get You into My Life," Capitol, 1976 • *Rock and Roll Music,* Parlophone/Capitol, 1976, 1980 • *Live at the Hollywood Bowl,* Capitol, 1977 • *Love Songs,* Parlophone/Capitol, 1977 • *The Beatles Collection,* Capitol, 1978 • *Rarities,* Parlophone/Capitol, 1980 • *Rock and Roll Music,* Vol. 2, Capitol, 1980 • *20 Greatest Hits,* Parlophone/Capitol, 1982 • *Reel Music,* Parlophone/Capitol, 1982 • "The Beatles' Movie Medley," Capitol, 1982 • "Twist and Shout," Capitol, 1986 • *Past Masters,* Vols. 1–2, Parlophone, 1988 • *The Beatles Box Set,* Capitol, 1992 • *Anthology 1,* Apple/Capitol, 1995 • *Anthology 2,* Apple/Capitol, 1996 • *Anthology 3,* Capitol, 1996 • *Real Love* (EP), Apple/Capitol, 1996.

Beck, Jeff: *Blow by Blow,* Epic, 1975 • *Wired,* Epic, 1976 • *Beckology,* Legacy/Epic, 1991, 1995.

Black, Cilla: *Cilla,* Parlophone, 1965 • *Sher-oo!,* Parlophone, 1968 • *Surround Yourself with Cilla Black,* Parlophone, 1969 • *Sweet Inspiration,* Parlophone, 1970 • *Images,* Parlophone, 1971 • *Day by Day,* Parlophone, 1973.

Black, Don: *Songbook,* Play It Again, 1995.

Brooker, Gary: *No More Fear of Flying,* Chrysalis, 1979.

Carreras, Jose: *Sings Andrew Lloyd Webber,* Teldec, 1990 • *Hollywood Golden Classics,* Atlantic, 1991.

Cheap Trick: *All Shook Up,* Epic, 1980 • *Sex America Cheap Trick,* Sony, 1996.

David and Jonathan: "Michelle," Capitol, 1966 • *The Very Best Of,* See for Miles, 1997.

Dion, Celine: *Let's Talk About Love,* 550 Music, 1997.

Edward's Hand: *Stranded,* RCA, 1970.

Flanders and Swann: *Complete,* Capitol, 1994.

Gerry and the Pacemakers: *The Best of Gerry and the Pacemakers: The Definitive Collection,* Collectables, 1991, 1995 • *Gerry Cross the Mersey: All the Hits Of,* Razor & Tie, 1995.

Getz, Stan: *Dynasty,* Verve, 1971, 1991 • *The Artistry of Stan Getz,* Vol. 2, Verve, 1992 • *Verve Jazz Masters #8: Stan Getz,* Verve, 1994.

Gibb, Robin: "Oh Darlin'," RSO, 1978.

George Martin Orchestra: *Off the Beatle Track,* Parlophone, 1964 • *The Beatles Girls,* United Artists, 1966.

Harrison, George: *The Best Of,* Capitol, 1976.

John, Elton: "Candle in the Wind/The Way You Look Tonight," Rocket, 1997.

King's Singers: *This Is the King's Singers,* Angel, 1987.

Kramer, Billy J., and the Dakotas: *Listen to Billy J. Kramer,* Parlophone, 1963 • *Billy Boy,* Parlophone, 1965 • *The Best Of,* EMI, 1991.

Laine, Cleo: *Born on a Friday,* RCA, 1976, 1993.

Lennon, John: *Imagine* soundtrack, Capitol, 1988.

Little River Band: *Time Exposure,* Capitol, 1981 • *Reminiscing,* CEMA, 1992 • "Take It Easy on Me," Capitol, 1981 • "The Night Owls," Capitol, 1981.

Mahavishnu Orchestra: *Apocalypse,* Legacy, 1974, 1990.

Martin, George, and Wings: *Live and Let Die* soundtrack, United Artists, 1973 • *See also* George Martin Orchestra.

McCartney, Paul: w/ Stevie Wonder, "Ebony and Ivory," Columbia, 1982 • "Take It Away," Columbia, 1982 • *Tug of War,* Columbia, 1982 • *Pipes of Peace,* Parlophone/CBS, 1983 • w/ Michael Jackson, "Say, Say, Say," Columbia, 1983 • *Give My Regards to Broad Street,* Columbia, 1984 • "No More Lonely Nights," Columbia, 1984 • *All the Best,* Capitol, 1987 • *Flaming Pie,* Capitol, 1997.

Paul Winter Consort: *Icarus,* Epic, 1972.

Perkins, Carl: *Go Cat Go,* Dinosaur, 1996.

Preston, Billy: *The Best Of,* A&M, 1988.

Rogers, Kenny: *Greatest Hits,* EMI America, 1980 • *The Heart of the Matter,* RCA, 1985 • "Morning Desire," RCA, 1986 • "Tomb of the Unknown Love," RCA, 1986 • *Decade of Hits,* Warner Bros., 1997.

Seatrain: *Marblehead Messenger,* One Way, 1971, 1993 • *Seatrain,* Capitol, 1971.

Sedaka, Neil: *A Song,* Elektra, 1977.

Stackridge: *Do the Stanley,* MCA, 1973 • *Extravaganza,* Sire, 1974 • *Man in the Bowler Hat,* MCA, 1974 • *Pinafore Days,* Sire, 1974.

Starr, Ringo: *Sentimental Journey,* Apple, 1970.

Temperance Seven: *Direct from the Balls Pond Rio,* Parlophone, 1962.

Temperance Seven: *Family Album,* Parlophone, 1964.

UFO: *No Place to Run,* Chrysalis, 1980 • *The Best and the Rest,* Chrysalis, 1988.

Ultravox: *Quartet,* Chrysalis, 1983 • *Collection,* Chrysalis, 1984.

Ure, Midge, and Ultravox: *If I Was: The Very Best Of,* Chrysalis, 1993.

Webb, Jimmy: *El Mirage,* Atlantic, 1977 • *Archive,* WEA, 1993.

Wings: "Live and Let Die," Apple, 1973 • *Wings Greatest Hits,* Capitol, 1978, 1986.

Wonder, Stevie: *Song Review: A Greatest Hits Collection,* Motown, 1996.

COLLECTIONS

That Was the Week That Was, Parlophone, 1964.

Sgt. Pepper soundtrack, A&M/RSO, 1978.

James Bond: Best of 30th Anniversary Collection, Capitol, 1992.

Tommy (original Broadway cast), RCA, 1993.

The Glory of Gershwin, Mercury, 1994.

Harry Maslin

Producer, engineer, and studio owner, Harry Maslin has been an important figure on both the East and West Coasts for 25 years. As a producer or co-producer, Maslin's hits have ranged from the flyweight pop of Air Supply ("Every Woman in the World," No. 5; "The One That You Love," No. 1; "Even the Nights Are Better," No. 5) and the Bay City Rollers ("You Made Me Believe in Magic," No. 10; "The Way I Feel Tonight"), to David Bowie's (see entry) exquisite soul period (*Young Americans,* No. 9; "Fame," No. 1; *Station to Station,* No. 3; "Golden Years," No. 10). A torchy hit with Melissa Manchester ("Don't Cry Out Loud," No. 10), and Hot Tuna's excellent statement in Americana-metal (*Hoppkorv*) are further evidence of Maslin's broad reach.

Born in Philadelphia in 1949, Maslin played sax and guitar and dabbled in electronics as a youth. By the late '60s he was running live sound for such legends as Jimi Hendrix, Janis Joplin, and Cream at Philly's Electric Factory nightclub. He veered into band management, and in that capacity took Woody's Truck Stop into the studio to do some demo work. Maslin stepped in to correct some bad mixes and impressed one and all with the results.

Finding the studio more interesting than management, Maslin went to work at New York's Regent Sound Studios for two years in the early '70s and then moved to the Hit Factory. He became chief engineer there and worked with James Taylor, Carly Simon, Dionne Warwick, and many others. Maslin experienced his "first taste of production" when he finished up a Bonnie Raitt album (*Streetlights*) in 1974 after original producer Jerry Ragovoy left for personal reasons.

Maslin went to the Record Plant that same year and engineered a number of R&B sessions. Meanwhile, in a move away from glam rock to what he called "plastic soul," David Bowie had recorded the swinging "Young Americans," with producer Tony Visconti (see entry) and a new band featuring Willy Weeks on bass, Luther Vandross on background vocals, and David Sanborn on sax at Philadelphia's Sigma Sound (made famous by Gamble and Huff; see entry) in the fall of 1974. Bowie and Visconti had also recorded "Win," "Right," "Somebody up There Likes Me" and the great "Fascination" (co-written by Vandross) at Sigma, but then Bowie went back on tour and Visconti returned to London. The tapes were sent to the Record Plant to be mixed by Maslin.

Bowie had a falling-out with his management company, MainMan, over the direction of his new music and his drug use, among other things, and the album was put on hold. Then in November, recalls Maslin, "I was home one day with my then-girlfriend and a couple of friends and we had had a couple of glasses of wine. I get a call on the phone and it's David Bowie. He says, 'Look, you gotta do me a favor. You have to get me some time at Record Plant because I want to finish my album so I can get home by Christmas, and it's getting late.'

"I said, 'No problem, let me see what I can do.' He said, 'You gotta do one other thing for me—you gotta produce the rest of the album.' I took the phone away from my ear like I was hallucinating, then put it back and said, 'Ah, I think I can do that.' I hung up the phone and told my friends and they all thought I was full of shit."

Maslin helped Bowie produce "Across the Universe" and the funky classic "Fame"—with John Lennon playing and singing along—and ended up with co-production credit for every song on the album except "Young Americans."

Pleased with their work together, Bowie then asked Maslin to co-produce his next album—his highest-charting in the U.S.—*Station to Station.* Recorded at Cherokee Studios in Hollywood with Bowie in character as the icy, arch-European Thin White Duke, *Station* is a strange but ultimately successful amalgam of Bowie's *Young American* soul stylings and muscular rock jamming (led by lead guitarist Earl Slick).

The title track is a 10-minute medley of mechanical beats and soul-rock riffing that somehow combines Kraftwerk and early Bruce Springsteen. "Golden Years" is great, tuneful, uptempo soul and was the only song on the album to be recorded quickly and easily. "TVC15" is strange—even for Bowie—with lyrics inspired by his starring role in the science fiction film classic *The Man Who Fell to Earth,* Roy Bittan's jaunty whorehouse piano, martial dance beats, and a mesmerizing refrain. "Stay" rocks to the dual guitars of Carlos Alomar and Earl Slick and Dennis Davis's syncopated drumming. With Bowie wired on coke, working vampire's hours, writing and rewriting songs in the studio, *Station* was very difficult to make and made Maslin's reputation as a producer.

On a roll, Maslin produced another great West Coast album (recorded and mixed at Wally Heider Studios in San Francisco) in 1976: Hot Tuna's *Hoppkorv.* On the album, the group, led by Jefferson Airplane alums Jorma Kaukonen on guitar and Jack Casady on bass, is the farthest they ever got from their country blues beginnings, but the commingling of Kaukonen's fingerpicked acoustic guitar with his own overdriven electric guitar and Casady's fuzz bass achieves glorious results on "Watch the North Wind Rise," "It's So Easy," and "Bowlegged Woman, Knock Kneed Man."

After the Tuna album, Maslin decided to move to California. "In New York I had a reputation as an engineer/producer, but in California I had the reputation as a producer. So I wanted to see what I could do out there," he says.

Maslin became involved with Clive Davis's Arista Records and the Bay City Rollers in 1977. "That's about as far away from my taste musically as I might want to go, but on the other hand I saw it as a real fun opportunity. At the time the hype around them was like the Beatles: they had hordes of people following them and the press was going nuts. I didn't care that it might not be a great career move; in any case, we did two albums together."

Staying with Arista, Maslin next hooked up with Australian MOR stalwarts, Air Supply. The group's chirpy vocals and bland romantic musings yielded a remarkable series of hits. Maslin was responsible for four of the group's No. 5 hits and a No. 1 in the early '80s. He used his Air Supply money to create Image Recording Studios in 1983.

Since then Maslin has run the studio (Madonna, Tammy Wynette, Guns N' Roses, Tina Turner, and Fleetwood Mac have recorded there) and engineered quite a bit, including work for Michael Jackson's *HISto-ry* album. —Eric Olsen and David John Farinella

Air Supply: "Every Woman in the World," Arista, 1980 • *Lost in Love,* Arista, 1980 • "Here I Am," Arista, 1981 • "Sweet Dreams," Arista, 1981 • "The One That You Love," Arista, 1981 • *The One That You Love,* Arista, 1981 • "Even the Nights Are Better," Arista, 1982 • *Now and Forever,* Arista, 1982 • *Greatest Hits,* Arista, 1983 • *The Earth Is . . . ,* Giant, 1991.

Bay City Rollers: *Greatest Hits,* Arista, 1977 • *It's a Game,* Arista, 1977 • "The Way I Feel Tonight," Arista, 1977 • "You Made Me Believe in Magic," Arista, 1977 • *Strangers in the Wind,* Arista, 1978.

Bowie, David: "Fame," RCA, 1975 • "Young Americans," RCA, 1975 • *Young Americans,* RCA, 1975 • "Golden Years," RCA, 1976 • *Station to Station,* RCA, 1976 • *Changesbowie,* Rykodisc, 1984, 1990 • "Fame 90," Rykodisc, 1990 • *Bowie: The Singles, 1969–1993,* Rykodisc, 1993.

Carmen, Eric: *Tonight Your Mine,* Arista, 1980 • *The Best Of,* Arista, 1988.

Hollywood Stars: *The Hollywood Stars,* Arista, 1977.

Hot Tuna: *Hoppkorv,* Grunt, 1976.

Manchester, Melissa: "Don't Cry Out Loud," Arista, 1978 • *Don't Cry Out Loud,* Arista, 1978 • *Greatest Hits,* Arista, 1983 • *Essence Of,* Arista, 1997.

Michael Stanley Band: *Greatest Hints,* Capitol, 1979 • *Misery Loves Company: More of the Best, 1975–1983,* Razor & Tie, 1997.

Nervous Eaters: *Nervous Eaters,* Arista, 1980.

Patton, Robbie: *No Problem,* Atlantic, 1984.

Sesto, Camilo: *Camilo,* Elektra, 1983.

Slick, Earl: *The Earl Slick Band,* Arista, 1976.

Striker: *Striker,* Arista, 1978.

George Massenburg

For a man whose name begins with a G, George Massenburg has an uncanny dislike for the G words most often used to describe him: "genius," "guru," "great," "golden ears," "Grammy winner." He once went as far as screaming: "I hate gurus. I shit gurus!" at this writer, who made the mistake of employing that word in a 24-point headline about him.

Despite easily meeting the criteria for all those appellations, Massenburg steadfastly refuses to let his triumphs go to his head. Instead, he maintains a level of

automation through his proprietary George Massenburg Labs (GML) system; building the first parametric equalizer (and thereby coining the term); fervently supporting and constructively criticizing digital sound; and looking beyond the knobs and faders to see music in its purest form.

"I would like to see the musical moment protected and revealed," he says. "Producing to me is not necessarily defining the music. Sometimes it's identifying it." He adds that a producer is "a person who's willing to be blamed for the commercial failure of a record and also willing to have the artist take all of the credit for the success of a record; a person who does so for the love of the process, and for that rare thrill of the musical moment that connects."

Inspired by his mentor, Peter Asher (see entry), and by such other renowned producers as George Martin (see entry), Nat Hiken (who created, wrote, and produced the *Phil Silvers Show*), Phil Ramone (see entry), David Anderle (see entry) and British actor, director, and practicing physician Jonathan Miller, Massenburg never imposes his sonic agenda on a project, preferring instead to approach each record "as if learning everything all over again."

Like many technological innovators who are also music producers—most notably Ramone—Massenburg regards technology as a means to a creative end. "What technology is supposed to do," says Massenburg, "is be capable and proficient and then go into the background. It's not supposed to call attention to itself. The best technology doesn't."

Asked to describe the ideal recording studio, Massenburg spares no details: "My ideal recording situation is one that I haven't quite built yet," he explains. "Digital, so as to be consistent with everything else in the future, but with all of the joy, comfort, and listening safety of analog; practical, intuitive, friendly, cross-compatible integrated user interfaces; extraordinary precision, response, and resolution (minimum 192 kHz sample rate, 24 linear monotonic bits, distributed clocks with 0.5 ps jitter throughout), and storage capacity; next-generation, real-space, multichannel ambience generators; modern military reliability; and, oh, fine baroque acoustics and décor; a live room with diffusion, *diffusion*, DIFFUSION; DC-supplied lighting, of course, plus lizard, alligator, and M&M lights."

Massenburg's choice of a digital studio is based not on a sonic preference but on his conviction that digital is the technology of the future and must be nurtured and improved. "As we get into digital, we figure we missed something; it should sound a lot better than this," he observes. "I'm fond of saying I'm not in digi-

humility that borders on self-deprecation and makes for some fascinating conversation.

Asked if he regards himself primarily as a producer, an engineer, an equipment designer, or a pioneer in the field of console automation, Massenburg replies, "I consider myself mainly a pain in the ass. That's what I specialize in."

On the other hand, Massenburg is just as capable of unleashing verbal fusillades at his colleagues. In fact, he says he knew he wanted to become a record producer when he realized that he could "do as well as, if not better than, many of the so-called record producers." He adds, "There are guys who make you want to go home and swallow poison. I come in contact with many producers who are deeply stupid and deeply unintuitive. If genius were to land with a thud in front of them, they'd piss on it."

Among his many distinctions, the terminally opinionated and diversely talented Massenburg is known for producing and/or engineering such titles as Little Feat's *Feats Don't Fail Me Now*, Valerie Carter's *Just a Stone's Throw Away*, 10,000 Maniacs' *In My Tribe*, Linda Ronstadt's *Cry Like a Rainstorm, Howl Like the Wind*, and Lyle Lovett's *Joshua Judges Ruth*; designing and building a line of universally acclaimed mixers, equalizers, compressors, preamplifiers, and converters; pioneering console

tal because it sounds good. I'm in digital because there's a lot of work to be done to make it sound better."

A native of Macon, Georgia, Massenburg's earliest musical memories are of listening to AM radio pouring out raw, sexually charged R&B by such pioneers as the Coasters, Howlin' Wolf, and Wilson Pickett. The Massenburg family eventually settled in Baltimore, where George lived down the street from another audio innovator, Deane Jensen. The two dabbled together on various projects, including a ham radio set, no doubt laying the groundwork for a lifelong fascination with audio. Massenburg studied bassoon and trombone for years, playing in his school marching band. But when he realized where the women were, he switched to electric bass.

He attended Johns Hopkins University for two years but, admittedly a poor student, he dropped out. "When I went to school, I didn't learn anything," he says. "My biggest adversaries were my professors. I had to learn on my own."

Accordingly, Massenburg started his first recording studio in Baltimore in the early '70s and built the first parametric equalizer, a unit that would establish him as a first-rate equipment designer. The young audio enthusiast moved to Paris in 1973 and worked for the now-defunct Europa Sonar studios and then for Barclay Records.

"Americans were loathed in Paris in the '70s," he recalls. "But it was healthy to have my values rejected. Americans should get around the world and be despised a little." While Massenburg was in Paris, his Baltimore studio had attracted the attention of Little Feat. In the summer of 1974, Massenburg returned to Paris from a trip on the French island of Corsica to find his mailbox stuffed with telegrams from Little Feat's A&R rep at Warner Bros., Clyde Bakkemo. Each telegram was successively more urgent, leading up to one that offered Massenburg a free flight to Baltimore to record Little Feat's *Feats Don't Fail Me Now* in 1974. Massenburg took the job and has since amassed a discography that has earned him a secure place among the world's A list producers. But just don't call him a guru. —PAUL VERNA

Carter, Valerie: *Just a Stone's Throw Away*, Columbia, 1977.
Flim and the BB's: *New Pants*, Warner Bros., 1990.
Harris, Emmylou: *Portraits*, Warner Bros., 1996 • *See also* Trio.
Little Feat: *Hoy-Hoy*, Warner Bros., 1981, 1990 • "Hate to Lose Your Lovin'," Warner Bros., 1988 • *Let It Roll*, Warner Bros., 1988 • *Shake Me Up*, Morgan Creek, 1991.

Lovett, Lyle: "Friend of the Devil," Arista, 1991 (*Deadicated*) • *Joshua Judges Ruth*, Curb/MCA, 1992.
Neville, Aaron: "Everybody Plays the Fool," A&M, 1991 • *Warm Your Heart*, A&M, 1991 • *To Make Me Who I Am*, A&M, 1997.
Parton, Dolly: *See* Trio.
Raitt, Bonnie: *Nine Lives*, Warner Bros., 1986 • *The Bonnie Raitt Collection*, Warner Bros., 1990.
Ronstadt, Linda: *Mas Canciones*, Elektra, 1991 • *Frenesi*, Asylum, 1992 • *Winter Light*, Asylum, 1994 • *Feels Like Home*, Asylum, 1995 • "Walk On," Elektra, 1995 • *Dedicated to the One I Love*, Elektra, 1996 • *We Ran*, Elektra, 1998 • *See also* Trio.
Simon, Carly: "Coming Around Again," Arista, 1986 • *Coming Around Again*, Arista, 1987.
Taylor, James: *Classic Songs Live*, Columbia, 1993.
Toto: "Pamela," Columbia, 1988 • *The Seventh One*, Columbia, 1988 • *Past to Present, 1977–1990*, Columbia, 1990.
Trio (Dolly Parton, Linda Ronstadt, Emmylou Harris): "Telling Me Lies," Warner Bros., 1987 • "To Know Him Is to Love Him," Warner Bros., 1987 • *Trio*, Warner Bros., 1987 • "Wildflowers," Warner Bros., 1988.
Webb, Jimmy: *Suspending Disbelief*, Elektra, 1993.
Wiedlin, Jane: "Blue Kiss" (remix), IRS, 1985, 1991 (*IRS Greatest Hips*, Vol. 4, *The Remixes*) • "Blue Kiss," IRS, 1985 • *Jane Wiedlin*, IRS, 1985 • *Very Best Of*, EMI, 1993.

Sylvia Massy

One of rock's rare female producers, Sylvia Massy describes herself as "wild and crass," an adventurous person with a preference for harder, edgier rock and young, fresh bands. She'll try anything, including shooting and smashing a piano during a Tool session and recording a guitar being thrown off a cliff for Machines of Loving Grace's *Gilt*.

She was introduced to recording technology by her high school band teacher. In the '80s, she played with bands in San Francisco and always found herself playing the producer's role. "I've always felt comfortable in a studio setting," she says. She found an entry-level position at a Northern California studio where she worked with artists like Mojo Nixon, the Adolescents, and Exodus. She produced an indie record with the Sea Hags, who signed to Chrysalis, "and then ran off to L.A. to record their major-label debut. I realized if I wanted to produce I would have to move to L.A."

Soon after arriving in L.A., she landed at Lion Share

Studios where she found herself assisting Phil Ramone (see entry) on a Barbra Streisand album. She moved to Larrabee Sound, where she assisted on Prince (see entry), Seal, Paula Abdul, Aerosmith, Julio Iglesias, Johnny Cash, and Jacksons sessions while recording friends' bands on her off time.

Some friends she'd worked with at Tower Records when she first came to town had a band called Green Jelly, known for its crude novelty songs and colorful show, which landed a record deal. At the same time, Green Jelly's drummer's other band, Tool, got signed, and Massy launched her career by producing both bands' debuts.

"We recorded at the same time in the same studio with the same drummer and same drummer set—but it was so different. The Green Jelly sessions were filled with toys, lights, decorations. For Tool, the lights were low. There was a pentagram on the wall. The equipment was very specific with Tool. We used Randall heads for a very compressed, gritty sound and old Les Paul guitars. With Green Jelly, it was all whatever."

"All you need is one record on the charts and you've got enough momentum to keep you going for a while," she says. So, as Tool's 1992 EP *Opiate,* and 1993 full-length platinum debut *Undertow,* garnered favorable attention for their bleakly aggressive music, Massy found steady work among a glut of new bands including Old Hickory, Stomp Box, Greta, and Econoline Crush.

She worked on the solo album by Flea (of the Red Hot Chili Peppers) and the recording of the Tibetan Relief Concert in New York in June 1997, which featured the likes of Sonic Youth, Radiohead, Rancid, Beastie Boys, the Wallflowers, Alanis Morrisette, Blur, and Bjork.

Though she leans toward heavier rock, her productions have been diverse in tone and attitude, from the slapdash mix of thrashy guitars and samples on Green Jelly's 1993 *Cereal Killer* soundtrack to the purposeful, heavy guitar rock of Skunk Anansie's 1995 *Paranoid and Sunburnt.* The latter slides from in-your-face aggression to stripped-down, emptied-out segments filled mainly by vocalist Skin's snarling defensiveness. Tool's *Undertow* also deftly blends brooding, minimalist passages with dense guitar, bass, and drum explosions that fill up the whole track. Massy's 1996 Love and Rockets' track, "Sweet Lover Hangover," features both acoustic and electric guitars under gauzy layers of keyboards.

Currently, she's assembling her own facility in the B room at her favorite studio, Sound City. "With home studios so easy to come by, more artists are doing recording at home," she says. "Producers are brought in more for organization and editing and arranging. I'm trying to anticipate that by setting up my own studio where I can work for months at a time and develop young acts. I hope to get it finished in the next two years. When I'm not working, the studio will continue to generate income."

Though woman producers are a rarity, she says, "I haven't had any heartbreaking instances of being passed over for a job. Sometimes I'll go into the studio and the studio manager will ask if I'm the manager's assistant; they won't expect me to be the producer. Susan Rogers was kind of my mentor; she was the only woman I knew in the industry for the longest time. I got a chance to assist her at Larrabee Sound. It was a big deal for me as a woman in the industry. But the older I get, I realize it's very hard for a woman in any field to concentrate on anything this hard. I want to have a family, and I feel at one point I'm going to have to call it quits before my time is up—which, for me, is very sad." —ANASTASIA PANTSIOS

Babes in Toyland: "Say What You Want," A&M, 1994 (*S.F.W.* soundtrack).

Econoline Crush: *The Devil You Know,* Restless, 1998.

Green Jelly: *Cereal Killer* soundtrack, Zoo, 1993 • "Three Little Pigs," Zoo, 1993.

Greta: *No Biting,* Mercury, 1993 • "Jesus Crux," Stardog/Mercury, 1994.

Love and Rockets: *Sweet F.A.,* American, 1996 • "Sweet Lover Hangover," Beggars Banquet/American, 1996.

Machines of Loving Grace: *Gilt,* Mammoth, 1995.

Old Hickory: *Other Eras . . . Such As Witchcraft,* A&M, 1997.

Red Hot Chili Peppers: "Love Rollercoaster," Geffen, 1996 (*Beavis and Butt-head Do America* soundtrack).

Skunk Anansie: *Paranoid and Sunburnt,* One Little Indian, 1995 • "Weak," Mother/Island, 1995 (*Mission: Impossible* soundtrack).

Spade Ghetto Destruction: *Spade Ghetto Destruction,* Volcano, 1994.

Stikkitty: *In This Age Without Heroes,* Chrysalis, 1993.

Stomp Box: *Stress,* Columbia, 1994.

Tool: *Opiate* (EP), Zoo, 1992 • "Sober," Zoo, 1993 • *Undertow,* Zoo, 1993.

COLLECTIONS

Tibetan Freedom Concert, Grand Royal/Capitol, 1997.

Masters At Work

("LITTLE" LOUIE VEGA AND KENNY "DOPE" GONZALEZ)

Since joining forces, "Little" Louie Vega and Kenny "Dope" Gonzalez have set the standard for remixing by reconstructing records for the likes of Bjork, Deeelite, Debbie Gibson, Queen Latifah, and many others. As Masters At Work, they've developed a knack for sending records that seemed to have little club potential (Tito Puente, the Neville Brothers, St. Etienne) to the top of the dance charts. Original MAW productions, including the Bucketheads, Barbara Tucker, the Braxtons, and the Nuyorican Soul album project (featuring Tito Puente, Eddie Palmieri, Roy Ayers, George Benson, India, and Jocelyn Brown), have established them as premier producers. With the formation of MAW Records, Masters At Work set out to further develop themselves as a production force while exposing the fresh talent of other producers and artists.

While Kenny and Louie both started out as DJs, the roads they traveled were quite different. Louie seemed destined for a career in music from birth. His father, Louie Vega Sr., is an accomplished jazz and Latin sax player, and his uncle, Hector LaVoe, was a famed salsa singer. While still in his teens, Louie started spinning at the Devil's Nest, Heartthrob, and Studio 54. By the time he started doing production work, he had worked in nearly every club in New York and had reached near-legendary status as a DJ in the dance community.

Kenny "Dope," meanwhile, was doing mobile DJ work with his crew, who called themselves the Masters At Work. While dropping hip-hop at neighborhood parties, he decided he could create beats and tracks at least as well as the people on the records he was spinning, and so created Dope Wax, his own label. After several underground hits on his own, he started doing tracks for other New York indies, including Strictly Rhythm, Cutting, Nervous, and Big Beat.

By the time mutual friend Todd Terry (to whom Kenny lent the name Masters At Work for the 1988 release, "Alright, Alright"; see entry) introduced him to "Little" Louie, he had built a reputation as one of the best beatmen in town, well-versed in hip-hop, dancehall, and house.

With a unique presence as DJs, remixers, and producers, Masters At Work continue to use their blend of hip-hop, house, jazz, and Latin roots to create unique musical experiences that defy boundaries and conventional limitations. —LARRY FLICK

Masters at Work

Bel Canto: "Rumor," Lava, 1996.

BG, Prince of Rap: "Take Control of the Party" (remix), Columbia, 1991.

Bjork: "Violently Happy" (remix), Elektra, 1994.

Brown, Jocelyn: "It's Alright I Feel It," Talkin' Loud, 1997.

Bucketheads: *All in My Mind*, Henry Street/ Atlantic, 1995 • "Got Myself Together," Henry Street/Big Beat, 1995 • "The Bomb (These Sounds Fall into My Mind)," Henry Street/Positiva, 1995 • *The Dungeon Tapes*, Positiva, 1995.

Deeee Lite: "Runaway" (remix), Elektra, 1992.

Incognito: *Remixed*, Verve, 1996.

Ken-Lou: "Gimme Groove/The Bounce," Strictly Rhythm, 1995 • *The Bounce*, MAW, 1995 • "Thru the Skies," MAW, 1997.

King, Diana: "Stir It Up" (remix), Chaos, 1994.

Limerick, Alison: *Club Classics* (remix, 1 track), BMG, 1996.

Louvette: *Crazy in Love*, Private I/Mercury, 1998.

Marshall, Carla: "Class and Credential" (remix), Chaos, 1994.

Masters At Work: "Blood Vibes/Jump on It," Cutting, 1993 • "Give It to Me," Cutting, 1993 • *Masterworks*, Cutting, 1995 • w/ Dave Seaman, *Mixmag Live, Vol. 10*, Mixmag, 1995 • *Sessions 5*, Ministry of Sound, 1995 • *Masterworks: Essential Kenlou House*, MAW, 1997 • *MAW Sampler*, MAW, 1997 • "To Be in Love," MAW, 1997.

Masters At Work, featuring India: "I Can't Get No Sleep," Cutting, 1994 • "When You Touch Me," Cutting, 1994 • *I Can't Get No Sleep '95*", Cutting, 1995.

MK, featuring Alana: "Love Changes" (remix), Charisma, 1993.

Nuyorican Soul: "You Can Do It (Baby)," GRP, 1996 • "It's Alright, I Feel It," GRP, 1997 • *Nuyorican Soul*, GRP, 1997 • featuring India, "Runaway," GRP, 1997.

Stingily, Byron: "Flying High," Nervous Dog, 1997.

Terry, Todd, Kenny Gonzalez, and Louie Vega: *Todd, Louie and Kenny*, Strictly Rhythm, 1994.

Tha Grope 1: *Mission Complete*, Solo, 1996.

200 Sheep: "The Hard Times March," The Label, 1995.

Vandross, Luther: *I Know*, Virgin, 1998.

Watley, Jody: *Flower*, Atlantic, 1998.

Williams, Freedom: *Freedom*, Columbia, 1993.

Winans, BeBe: "Thank You," Atlantic, 1998 • *BeBe Winans*, Atlantic, 1997

Kenny Dope Gonzalez

DJ Skribble/Anthony Acid: *MDMA*, Vol. 1, Warlock, 1998.

Dope, Kenny: *Boomin' in Ya Jeep*, Freeze, 1993 • *Pushin' Dope* (EP), TNT, 1994 • "Supa Cat," Big Beat, 1994 • "Jam the Mace," Tu Chicks, 1997 • *Bucketbootleg* (EP), Henry St., 1998.

Funky Poets: *True to Life*, 550 Music, 1993.

Gonzalez, Kenny : *Dope on Plastic 3*, React, 1996.

Lighter Shade of Brown: *Layin' in the Cut,* Mercury, 1994.

Supercat: *The Good, the Bad, the Ugly, and the Crazy,* Columbia, 1994

Little Louie Vega

Brothers Like Outlaw: *The Oneness of II Minds in Unison,* Gee Street, 1992.

Cover Girls: "Because of You," Fever, 1987 • *We Can't Go Wrong,* Capitol, 1989 • *Show Me,* Fever, 1994 • "I Am Woman," Fever/Warlock, 1996.

Double J: *Hitman,* 4th & B'Way, 1991.

Eighth Wonder: "Cross My Heart" (remix), WTG, 1988.

Fiorillo, Elisa: "You Don't Know" (remix), Chrysalis, 1987.

Gibson, Debbie: "Only in My Dreams" (remix), Atlantic, 1986 • "Out of the Blue" (remix), Atlantic, 1987.

Groove Collective: "Whatchugot" (remix), Reprise, 1994.

India: *Llego la India,* Sony Discos, 1996.

Information Society: "What's on Your Mind (Pure Energy)" (remix), Tommy Boy, 1988.

Latin Rascals: *When She Goes* (1 track), Tin Pan Apple, 1989.

Lil' Louis: "French Kiss," Epic, 1989 • *From the Mind of Lil' Louis,* Epic, 1989.

Lil' Louis and the World: *Journey with the Lonely,* Epic, 1992 • "Saved My Life," Epic, 1992.

Little Louie and Marc Anthony: *When the Night Is Over,* Atlantic, 1991.

Masta Ace Incorporated: *Sittin' On Chrome,* Delicious Vinyl, 1995 • "The I.N.C. Ride," Delicious Vinyl, 1995.

Melendez, Lisette: "Goody Goody" (remix), Chaos, 1994.

Nice 'N Smooth: *Ain't a Damn Thing Changed,* Ral, 1991 • "Old to the New," Chaos, 1994 • *Jewel of the Nile,* Ral/Island, 1995.

Nocera: "Let's Go" (remix), Sleeping Bag, 1987.

Noel: "Silent Morning" (remix), 4th & B'Way, 1987 • "Like a Child," 4th & B'Way, 1988 • *Noel,* 4th & B'Way, 1988.

Queen Latifah: "Come into My House" (remix), Tommy Boy, 1990 • *Nature of a Sista,* Tommy Boy, 1991.

Russo, Pam: "It Works for Me," 4th & B'Way/Island, 1988.

Stingily, Byron: "Sing-a-Song," Nervous Dog, 1997.

Tucker, Barbara: "Beautiful People," Strictly Rhythm, 1994 • "Stay Together," Strictly Rhythm, 1995.

Vega, Little Louie: *Live at the Underground Network,* Strictly Rhythm, 1993 • *Strictly Rhythm Mix,* Vol. 2, Strictly Rhythm, 1994 • "Clap Your Hands," Boot Leg, 1997.

Curtis Mayfield

Curtis Mayfield is one of most respected and beloved figures in American music over the last 40 years. As songwriter, singer, guitar player, producer, and label owner, Mayfield helped define a smooth but earthy soul music in the '60s and '70s that came to be known as the "Sound of Chicago." A figure analogous to Smokey Robinson (see entry) in Detroit, Mayfield's greatest contribution is writing, singing, and later producing for his own group, the Impressions, creating an indispensable body of melodic, deeply spiritual music, with emotions ranging from the reverential to the joyous. Concurrent with his Impressions work, Mayfield wrote and produced for some of Chicago's finest, including ex-Impression Jerry Butler ("Find Another Girl"), Gene Chandler ("Nothing Can Stop Me"), Walter Jackson, and, most successfully, Major Lance ("The Monkey Time," No. 8; "Um Um Um Um Um Um," No. 5).

Mayfield was born June 3, 1942, to a peripatetic family that eventually alighted in the Cabrini-Green projects on Chicago's North Side. Three of Mayfield's cousins were in the Northern Jubilee Gospel Singers (as was Jerry Butler), and he was harmonizing with them by the age of 7. Given a guitar by a family member, Mayfield developed his own tuning and, inspired by his mother's love of poetry, he was writing songs by his early teens.

Mayfield had a group called the Alphatones, but Butler invited the 15-year-old to join a new group called the Impressions. The group wrote a song called "For Your Precious Love," and with Butler's resolute baritone in the lead, found themselves with a No. 11 hit in 1958. A year later Butler was gone and the group went into limbo, but Mayfield continued to tour with and write for Butler ("He Will Break Your Heart"). With the money earned, Mayfield took the Impressions to New York to record a song of his called "Gypsy Woman"—a mysterious and strangely touching doo-wop-meets-flamenco love song replete with Mayfield's sly guitar accents and clicking Spanish percussion. While there is no producer credited, surely it was Mayfield's hand that crafted this No. 20 hit.

In 1962 the brothers Brooks (Richard and Arthur) left; the Impressions were now a trio consisting of Mayfield, Fred Cash, and Sam Gooden. With Jerry Pate producing, arranging, and bringing a new emphasis to horns and rhythm, Mayfield and the Impressions entered their golden period with the glorious gospel and rumba "It's Alright" (No. 4), highlighted by Mayfield's soaring falsetto and clipped rhythm guitar.

The group followed with the classic ballad "I'm So Proud" (No. 14); besides being a lovely evocation of personal devotion, it also began Mayfield's subtle but unyielding affirmation of black pride in the midst of the civil rights movement. "Keep On Pushing" (No. 10) continued the group's predilection for waltz time and, much more importantly, sang in high sanctified harmony of the need to "reach that higher goal" of social equality. Mayfield's melodicism and delicacy prevented the Impressions from being labeled militant, but the people knew.

"People Get Ready" (No. 14) is Mayfield's most enduring song, a transcendent gospel melody exhorting people to prepare for the train to salvation on one level, and to freedom in a newly reconfigured America (the Civil Rights Act had just passed) on another level—faith being the only ticket needed for either passage.

A man with an entrepreneurial bent, Mayfield started two labels in 1966: Mayfield (the Fascinations), and Windy C (the Five Stairsteps). In 1968 he began his enduring Curtom label ("Cur" from Curtis, "tom" from partner Eddie Thomas), signing the Five Stairsteps and the Impressions, for whom Mayfield then took over production. "Fool for You," "This Is My Country" and "Choice of Colors" round out the great Mayfield Impressions collection.

After 16 Top 40 hits with the Impressions, Mayfield went solo in 1970, eventually releasing 15 charting albums, including 3 golds: *Curtis* (No. 19), *Back to the World* (No. 16), and his masterpiece, *Superfly* (No. 1). Upon going solo, Mayfield's first hits were "(Don't Worry) If There's a Hell Below We're All Going to Go," and the great "Move On Up" (No. 12 U.K.) from *Curtis*. "Move" found Mayfield moving into a faster, harder, driving percussion-and-horn arrangement; the extended album jam kept him on the cutting edge of the new groove and orchestral black music with Gamble and Huff, Norman Whitfield, and Isaac Hayes (see entries) that eventually mutated variously into disco and what is now called acid jazz.

Mayfield's solo career reached its apogee with *Superfly* in 1972—a soundtrack to a black action flick—much as Isaac Hayes' career had peaked the year before with the soundtrack to *Shaft*. Mayfield composed the entire original score, which superbly accents the excitement and pathos in a story of a drug dealer out for one last big score. Mayfield finds a pusher's swaggering midtempo funk groove to define the tone of the soundtrack, which is blessed with four great songs: "Freddie's Dead" (No. 4) strikes a perfect balance between sympa-

thy and contempt, with orchestral highs matching thumping bass lows and Mayfield's quavery, delicate voice refusing to look away. "Superfly" (No. 8) is Latin-tinged street-funk reminiscent of War—again seeing both sides of a complex character. "Give Me Your Love" (a hit single when covered by Barbara Mason with Mayfield producing the following year) is sensuous, insistent proto-disco. "Pusherman" revels in the seductive power of one who possesses forbidden fruit, and should have been another smash single.

Mayfield later successfully scored the films *Claudine* (with Gladys Knight and the Pips' "On and On," No. 5), *A Piece of the Action,* and *Short Eyes* (in which he appeared). In the '70s he also wrote and produced for Aretha Franklin ("Something He Can Feel") and the Staple Singers ("Let's Do It Again," No. 1). Mayfield analyzes the producer's job and required skills: "It's very important to have trust from the artist you're producing so that your ideas lock in with their ideas and abilities (and the musicians') to get the best for everyone. Of course, locking all of that in *is* the producing," he says.

"I believe my skills are God-given. I've never had any lessons other than in house and church and singing with a group in harmony. As a producer I know what I want in my mind before it's done. It's almost like an architect who can look at a piece of property and know where the house goes."

After a number of reunion tours with the Impressions and Jerry Butler, and a vibrant career as a solo artist, writer, and producer, Mayfield was injured in a tragic freak accident on August 1990 as he performed at an outdoor concert in Brooklyn, New York. High winds dislodged a lighting rig, causing it to collapse on him, damaging his spine and leaving him paralyzed from the chest down.

A successful tribute album, *All Men Are Brothers: A Tribute to Curtis Mayfield,* featuring Whitney Houston, Elton John, the Isley Brothers (see entry), Aretha Franklin, Eric Clapton, and B.B. King, was released in 1994. In 1996 Mayfield made a tremendously courageous comeback—with the help of some of today's top producers, including Daryl Simmons and Narada Michael Walden (see entries)—in the form of the excellent *New World Order* album.

Mayfield was inducted into the Rock and Roll Hall of Fame with the Impressions in 1991 and as a solo artist in 1999. He received the BMI Lifetime Achievement Award in 1994. *People Get Ready: The Curtis Mayfield Story* (heavy on the solo career, a little light on the Impressions, no outside productions) is an admirable career retrospective. Mayfield lives with his family in Atlanta. —Eric Olsen and David John Farinella

Butler, Billy, and the Chanters: "I Can't Work No Longer," Okeh, 1965.

Butler, Jerry: "Find Another Girl," Vee-Jay, 1961 • "I'm Telling You," Vee-Jay, 1961.

Clifford, Linda: *If My Friends Could See Me Now,* Charly, 1978, 1995 • *Here's My Love,* RSO, 1981.

Fascinations, The: "Girls Are Out to Get You," Mayfield, 1967 • *Out to Getcha,* Sequel, 1997.

Five Stairsteps: "Come Back," Windy C, 1966 • "World of Fantasy," Windy C, 1966 • "You Waited Too Long," Windy C, 1966 • "Ooh Baby Baby," Windy C, 1967 • *The Five Stairsteps,* Windy C, 1967.

Five Stairsteps and Cubie: "Don't Change Your Love," Curtom, 1968 • "Stay Close to Me," Curtom, 1968 • "We Must Be in Love," Curtom, 1969 • *Love's Happening,* Curtom, 1969.

Franklin, Aretha: "Jump," Atlantic, 1976 • "Something He Can Feel," Atlantic, 1976 • *Sparkle* soundtrack, Atlantic, 1976 • *Ten Years of Gold,* Atlantic, 1976 • "Look into Your Heart," Atlantic, 1977 • *Almighty Fire,* Atlantic, 1978 • *Queen of Soul: The Atlantic Recordings,* Rhino, 1992 • *The Very Best Of,* Vol. 2, Rhino, 1994 • *Love Songs,* Atlantic, 1997.

Impressions, The: "Gypsy Woman," ABC-Paramount, 1961 • *Greatest Hits,* MCA, 1965, 1982 • "Fool for You," Curtom, 1968 • "This Is My Country," Curtom, 1968 • *This Is My Country,* Curtom/Buddah, 1968 • "Choice of Colors," Curtom, 1969 • *Check Out Your Mind,* Curtom, 1969 • *The Young Mods' Forgotten Story,* Curtom/Buddah, 1969 • "Check Out Your Mind," Curtom, 1970 • "Love Me," Curtom, 1971 • *Times Have Changed,* Curtom, 1971 • *Check Out Your Mind/Times Have Changed,* Sequel, 1972, 1996 • *The Very Best of the Impressions,* Rhino, 1997.

Jackson, Walter: "It's All Over," Okeh, 1964 • *It's All Over,* Okeh, 1964 • *Welcome Home,* Okeh, 1965 • *Walter Jackson's Greatest Hits,* Okeh/Epic, 1987 • *The Best of Walter Jackson: Welcome Home, The Okeh Years,* Legacy, 1996.

Knight, Gladys: *Blue Lights in the Basement,* RCA, 1996.

Knight, Gladys, and the Pips: "On and On," Buddah, 1974 • *Claudine* soundtrack, Buddah, 1974 • *The Best of Gladys Knight and the Pips,* Right Stuff, 1998.

Lance, Major: "Hey Little Girl," Okeh, 1963 • "The Monkey Time," Okeh, 1963 • *The Monkey Time,* Okeh, 1963 • "Rhythm," Okeh, 1964 • *The Best of Major Lance,* Okeh, 1964 • "The Matador," Okeh, 1964 • "Um Um Um Um Um Um," Okeh, 1964 • *Major's Greatest Hits,* Okeh, 1965.

Mason, Barbara: "Give Me Your Love," Buddah, 1973 • *Give Me Your Love,* Buddah, 1973 • *The Very Best of Barbara Mason,* Sequel, 1996.

Mayfield, Curtis: *Curtis,* Curtom, 1970 • *Curtis/Live,* Curtom, 1971 • "(Don't Worry) If There's a Hell Below We're All Going to Go" Curtom, 1971 • "Get Down," Curtom, 1971 • "Move On Up," Curtom, 1971 • *Roots,* Curtom, 1971 • "Beautiful Brother of Mine," Curtom, 1972 • "Freddie's Dead," Curtom, 1972 • "Pusherman," Sire/WB, 1972, 1991 (*Pimps, Players and Private Eyes*) • "Superfly," Curtom, 1972 • *Superfly,* Curtom, 1972 • "We Got to Have Peace," Curtom, 1972 • *Back to the World,* Curtom, 1973 • "Can't Say Nothin'," Curtom, 1973 • *Curtis in Chicago,* Curtom/Buddah, 1973 • "Future Shock," Curtom, 1973 • "If I Were Only a Child Again," Curtom, 1973 • *Got to Find a Way,* Curtom/Buddah, 1974 • "Kung Fu," Curtom, 1974 • "Mother's Son," Curtom, 1974 • "Sweet Exorcist," Curtom, 1974 • *Sweet Exorcist,* Curtom, 1974 • "So in Love," Curtom, 1975 • *There's No Place Like America Today,* Curtom/WB, 1975 • *Give, Get, Take and Have,* Curtom/WB, 1976 • "Only You Babe," Curtom, 1976 • "Party Night," Curtom, 1976 • "Do Do Wap Is Strong in Here," Curtom, 1977 • *Never Say You Can't Survive,* Curtom/WB, 1977 • *Short Eyes,* Curtom/WB, 1977 • "Show Me Love," Curtom, 1977 • *Do It All Night,* Curtom/WB, 1978 • "You Are, You Are," Curtom, 1978 • w/ Linda Clifford, "Between You Baby and Me," Curtom, 1979 • *Heartbeat,* Curtom/RSO, 1979 • *Love Me, Love Me Now,* Curtom/RSO, 1980 • w/ Linda Clifford, "Love's Sweet Sensation," Curtom/RSO, 1980 • *Something to Believe In,* Curtom/RSO, 1980 • w/ Linda Clifford, *The Right Combination,* Curtom/RSO, 1980 • "Tripping Out," Curtom/RSO, 1980 • *Love Is the Place,* Boardwalk, 1981 • "She Don't Let Nobody (but Me)," Boardwalk, 1981 • *Honesty,* Boardwalk, 1982 • "Baby It's You," CRC, 1985 • *We Come in Peace with a Message of Love,* CRC/Ichiban, 1985 • *Take It to the Streets,* CRC/Ichiban, 1990 • *The Anthology, 1961–1977,* MCA, 1992 • "New World Order," Warner Bros., 1996 • *New World Order,* Warner Bros., 1996 • *People Get Ready: The Curtis Mayfield Anthology,* Rhino, 1996.

Scott, Freddie: *Cry to Me: The Best of Freddie Scott,* Sony, 1998.

Staple Singers: "Let's Do It Again," Curtom, 1975 • *Let's Do It Again,* Curtom, 1975 • "New Orleans," Curtom, 1976 • *Pass It On,* Warner Bros., 1976.

COLLECTIONS

Chess Rhythm and Roll, MCA, 1994.

Curtis Mayfield's Chicago Soul, Legacy, 1995.

Get on the Bus: Music from and Inspired by the Motion Picture, Interscope, 1996.

Chess Soul: A Decade of Chicago's Finest, MCA, 1997.

Jackie Robinson Tribute: Stealing Home, Sony, 1997.

Paul McCartney

If McCartney had only been known for the production of his first solo album (*McCartney*, No. 1), he would stand among the ranks of the great producers. The album broke barriers for recording quality and exerted an enormous influence on a generation of musicians by demonstrating what could be done at home on a 4-track with one person playing all the instruments. Stevie Wonder, Mitchell Froom, David Kahne (see entries), and Sting are among those heavily influenced by the album. The sonics and production still sound fresh today, with deeply warm bass guitar tones, double-tracking, and myriad echo and delay effects. In addition, McCartney has produced or co-produced his entire post-Beatles catalog, a set that contains remarkable consistency of sound spanning a 30-year period.

McCartney (born June 18, 1942, in Liverpool) got his first production credit in 1968, for the No. 2 hit "Those Were the Days" by the Apple label artist Mary Hopkin. In 1969, McCartney wrote the tune "Come and Get It" for Apple artists Badfinger and arranged the song for the group note for note.

McCartney's production style is characterized by his ability to come up with countless instrumental hooks and "ear candy" in his songs; when McCartney is at his best, the listener can keep picking out parts never before heard, even after hundreds of listenings.

McCartney's second solo album, *Ram* (No. 2), featured improved sonics over his first effort, with expert engineering by Phil Ramone, production assistance from James William Guercio (see entries), and performances by the Los Angeles Philharmonic. More so than on any other McCartney or Wings album, *Ram* has the ear candy that made him famous: "Long Haired Lady" and "Uncle Albert/Admiral Halsey" (No. 1) are songs that never sound the same way twice.

One of the ways that *Ram* was given its uncanny Beatles-like sound had to do with Paul's bass guitar coming through with the deep, resonant quality that made the bottom end on *Abbey Road* so distinctive. "I remember how we recorded that bass sound!" recalls Phil Ramone. "We called down to the front desk at the studio and had them round up all the Pultecs they could get their hands on and every EQ in the place; we also got this UREI parametric equalizer. We just rolled up the bass on everything we could, as much as we could get on disc. [We knew] that the bass would be heard on radio."

There are moments on several McCartney-produced albums in which he captures the Beatles sound and vibe better than anyone (for example, "Dear Boy," "Bluebird," and the Lennon-inspired "Let Me Roll It"). One of McCartney's famous aspirations in the Beatles was to authentically reproduce the sound and composition style of a '30s show tune. Attempts included "Your Mother Should Know" and "Honey Pie," but on 1975's "You Gave Me the Answer" (from the album *Venus and Mars*, No. 1) McCartney captured it perfectly and has not tried again since.

In 1984, McCartney collaborated with George Martin (see entry) to produce *Give My Regards to Broad Street*, which included re-recordings of McCartney's Beatles songs. For new renditions of "Good Day Sunshine" and "Eleanor Rigby," McCartney and Martin went back to the original Beatles master tapes and transferred the horn and string parts to multitrack, where McCartney overdubbed new vocals and occasional instrumental accompaniment.

Other production highlights include the 1977 album *Thrillington*, on which McCartney arranged, produced, and conducted a nightclub-style instrumental version of the entire *Ram* album under the pseudonym Percy Thrillington. The single "Country Dreamer" (available as a bonus track on the British and U.S. versions of the CD *Red Rose Speedway*, No. 1) forms the final part of an ode to the country trilogy begun with "Mother Nature's Son" (the Beatles' *White Album*), and "Heart of the Country" (*Ram*).

On *Band on the Run* (No. 1), McCartney experimented with the type of theme development and composition style he had employed on side 2 of the Beatles' *Abbey Road*: themes from the songs "Band on the Run" (No. 1), "Jet" (No. 7), "Mrs. Vanderbilt," and "Picasso's Last Words" are brought together in a finale at the end of the album.

The big thing McCartney lost when he left the Beatles (and began producing himself) was the objectivity and "sounding board" that he had in the other Beatles and in George Martin. As a result, although his best-quality material is as good as his Beatles output, the minimum is considerably lower and as such, so is the mean (average) of his solo output. In Joan Goodman's *Playboy* interview, she asked McCartney how he judges the good material from the bad, and McCartney replied that he ran it by Linda and the kids. So Paul went from using George Martin and three of the best musicians in the world to advise him to his wife and children.

As McCartney admitted to interviewer Steve Grant: "I know I've lost my edge. . . . I do need a kind of outside injection, stimulation, and it's not there anymore.

And remember, the edge came from all the Beatles. If Ringo or George didn't like anything—it was out. My stuff has gotten more poppy without that outside stimulus."

Perhaps it is this change in work habits that accounts for the wide quality range in the McCartney solo catalog. Each album he has produced has at least one or two gems, and some of them many, many more. The frustration is in having to wade through the tunes that might have been better left off, such as "Cook of the House" from *Wings at the Speed of Sound* (No. 1), or "Only Love Remains" from *Press to Play*.

Then there is the problem of a seemingly endless string of cloying throwaway ditties such as "Listen to What the Man Said" and "Silly Love Songs" (both No. 1), for which we can only blame ourselves. If it weren't for their annoying and overwhelming popularity, Sir Paul might get the message that these are not an acceptable use of his prodigious songwriting talents. —DANIEL J. LEVITIN

Badfinger: *Magic Christian Music,* Apple, 1970, 1991 • *Best Of,* Capitol, 1995.

Beatles, The: *Anthology 1,* Apple/Capitol, 1995 • *Anthology 2,* Apple/Capitol, 1996 • *Real Love* (EP), Apple/Capitol, 1996.

Eddy, Duane: *Twang Thang: Anthology,* Rhino, 1993.

Hopkin, Mary: "Those Were the Days," Apple, 1968 • "Goodbye," Apple, 1969 • *Postcard,* Apple, 1969 • *Those Were the Days* (4 tracks), Apple, 1972.

McCartney, Paul: *McCartney,* Apple, 1970 • "Another Day," Apple, 1971 • "Coming Up," Columbia, 1980 • *McCartney 2,* Parlophone/CBS, 1980 • "Spies Like Us," Capitol, 1985 • "Wonderful Christmastime," Virgin/EMI, 1985 (*Now That's What I Call Music Xmas Album*) • *Press to Play,* Capitol, 1986 • "Press," Capitol, 1986 • "Stranglehold," Capitol, 1986 • *All the Best,* Capitol, 1987 • *Back in the USSR,* Capitol, 1988, 1991 • *Flowers in the Dirt,* Capitol, 1989 • "This One," Capitol, 1989 • "Birthday," Capitol, 1990 • "Figure of Eight," Capitol, 1990 • "It's Now or Never," NME, 1990 (*The Last Temptation of Elvis*) • *Tripping the Live Fantastic,* Capitol, 1990 • *Unplugged,* Capitol, 1991 • "Hope of Deliverance," Capitol, 1993 • *Paul Is Live,* Capitol, 1993 • *Flaming Pie,* Capitol, 1997 • "The World Tonight," Capitol, 1997.

McCartney, Paul and Linda: *Ram,* Apple, 1971 • "Uncle Albert/Admiral Halsey," Apple, 1971.

McCartney, Paul, and Wings: *Band on the Run,* Apple, 1973 • "Helen Wheels," Apple, 1973 • "My Love," Apple, 1973 • *Red Rose Speedway,* Apple, 1973 • "Band on the Run," Capitol, 1974 • "Jet," Apple, 1974 • "Listen to What the Man Said," Capitol, 1975.

McGear, Mike: *McGear,* Warner Bros., 1974.

Perkins, Carl: *Go Cat Go,* Dinosaur, 1996.

Starr, Ringo: *Stop and Smell the Roses* (3 tracks), RCA/Boardwalk, 1981 • *Starr Struck: Best Of,* Vol. 2, Rhino, 1989.

Thrillington, Percy: *Thrillington,* Capitol, 1977.

Wings: "Hi Hi Hi," Apple, 1972 • *Venus and Mars,* Capitol, 1975 • "Venus and Mars Rock Show," Capitol, 1975 • "Let 'Em In," Capitol, 1976 • "Silly Love Songs," Capitol, 1976 • *Wings at the Speed of Sound,* Capitol, 1976 • *Wings over America,* Capitol, 1976 • "Maybe I'm Amazed," Capitol, 1977 • *London Town,* Capitol, 1978 • *Wings Greatest Hits,* Capitol, 1978, 1986 • "With a Little Luck," Capitol, 1978 • *Back to the Egg,* Columbia, 1979 • "Getting Closer," Columbia, 1979 • "Goodnight Tonight," Columbia, 1979 • *See also* McCartney, Paul, and Wings.

COLLECTIONS

For Our Children, Disney, 1991.

Buzz McCoy and Groovie Mann

(MARSTON DALEY AND FRANK NARDIELLO)

A flaming disco ball of unknown origin slammed into a drive-in theater showing *Christian Zombie Vampire,* fusing unspeakable screen characters, molten squares of glass, guzzling revelers, backseat gropers, and the shrieking theater sound system into an alloy known as My Life With the Thrill Kill Kult.

Buzz McCoy (aka Marston Daley) and Groovie Mann (aka Frank Nardiello) are the creative forces behind this bizarre union of disco-industrial music, sleazy omnisexuality, and B-movie horror. Inadvertently created and self-produced, Thrill Kill have released a slew of dance club hits since 1988 with such expressive titles as "Kooler Than Jesus," "Devil Bunnies," "The Days of Swine and Roses," "Cuz It's Hot," "Waiting for Mommie," "The International Sin Set," "Leathersex," "Sex on Wheels," "Blue Buddha," "Glamour Is a Rocky Road," and greatest of all, "A Daisy Chain 4 Satan." Their back-to-back albums *Confessions of a Knife* and *Sexplosion!* stand with the best that either the disco or industrial genres have produced.

Buzz McCoy grew up in a small town in Massachusetts in the '60s and '70s and moved to Boston after high school. As the baby of the family, he spent much of his childhood alone, listening to an inherited record collection that ranged from Aerosmith to Donna Summer to Frank Sinatra to Motown. While living in Boston, Buzz played bass in a punk band called Zero Zero that received some airplay on college radio, but after a brief stint in San Francisco, Zero Zero petered out. His return to Boston truncated by lack of success and boredom, Buzz joined some friends in Chicago in the mid-'80s. Through these friends, Buzz met Groovie Mann, and the pair ended up living across the street from one another. Through the twin conveniences of proximity and unemployment, Buzz and Groovie indulged their mutual taste for bad horror films. Submersion in the genre convinced the pair that they could create cinema no worse than what they were watching. Their premise of a runaway taking up with a satanic cult generated the title *My Life With the Thrill Kill Kult*. With a killer title and delusions of sleazy glory, Buzz and Groovie began to take action upon their vision, perfecting their fake blood recipe, setting things on fire in the basement, and filming scenes. Inspired by the results, they resolved to score their evolving creation. Both had vaguely musical backgrounds, and by slapping together this and that with drum machines, synthesizers, and a febrile imagination, they made Thrill Kill a musical entity as well as a film title. Through the grapevine, Chicago's industrial-gothic Wax Trax! label (Ministry, Revolting Cocks, Front 242, Meat Beat Manifesto) became intrigued by the pair's film music.

Wax Trax! encouraged Buzz and Groovie to shape these sounds into songs, and their first releases were 1988 singles "First Cut," "Shock of Point Six," and "Resisting the Spirit." The songs were undistinguished, but promising enough that Buzz and Groovie were sent to Belgium to record with a friend who had a real studio, Luc Van Acker (Revolting Cocks). They wrote and recorded their first album, *I See Good Spirits and I See Bad Spirits,* in less than two weeks, mixed it in less than a week, and returned to the States not as B-movie auteurs but as legitimate recording artists.

Flush with excitement, Buzz and Groovie were struck with a revelation. "We were like, 'Hey, we're a band now. Maybe we should go on tour. That would be cool.' I always wanted to go on tour when I was little." Buzz and Groovie began seeking bandmates from among friends and acquaintances, cast members of their movie, and suitably tawdry strangers found in bars: adding keyboardist Thomas "Buck Ryder" Locklear, dancer/singer Jacky Blacque, and a mutating pack of scantily clad women known as the Bomb Gang Girlz. Buzz and Groovie essentially transplanted the attitude and accoutrements of their *Thrill Kill* film onto the stage, creating a writhing performance project and its accompanying throbbing soundtrack. *Spirits* is still a bit fuzzy and unfocused, but on *Kooler Than Jesus* the troupe finds the right admixture of socioreligious commentary and caustic, bouncing beats. The band casts aspersions on both sides of the God-Satan dichotomy, finding absurdity in either absolute, and tries on symbols for fit, like a semiotic Madonna.

Thrill Kill hit greatness with 1990's *Confessions of a Knife*. Whereas their first two albums were collections of songs, *Knife* holds up as a unit—a genuinely frightening examination of compulsion in its many forms: drugs, mental illness, sex, murder, and hints of retribution ("Do You Fear the Inferno Express?"). The album opens with the original mix of "A Daisy Chain 4 Satan," a pulsating beat and a recurring descending bass line set the mood for samples of a young woman confiding, "I live for drugs . . . I get drugs free . . . I freaked out very, very badly—I freaked out on acid. . . ."

The woman's inert proclamations are interrupted by one of the most bloodcurdling screams on record: a tortured, buzzing Tarzan wail of aggressive misery. Groovie's distorted, stressed lead vocal bears the weight of the world as he descends into the quivering miasma that is his own brain. "Here I will dream, why? / Give me a drink / I need to think, now / I've gotta wreck my sinking brain." References to mysterious "black boots," defiant eruptions like "Go forever loaded," and the confessional "It's too bad I need time to sleep / Forget my problems before I wake / Then it's TIME TO GO ON," convey an empathy with a struggling soul that is as strangely touching as it is disturbing. Incredibly, the 12-inch remix (by Buzz and Paul Barker of Ministry) of "Daisy Chain" is even more powerful, with the drumbeat doubled and the bass pumped up.

Other album highlights include "The Days of Swine and Roses," with its chanted "Christian zombie vampire" refrain and gnarly bass line; "Waiting for Mommie," with its Chic-like rhythm track and demands from "Mommie" to "Get your hard ass over here"; and a remix of "Kooler Than Jesus."

Sexplosion! is equally successful, trading the gothic horrors of *Knife* for the jet-setting Euro-sleaze feel of a soft-porn Matt Helm movie. "The International Sin Set" sums up the "film's" ambitions: heavy on glamour, illicit tanglings, queasy pseudo-brass squawking, and a jumping disco beat. "Leathersex" forthrightly sings the praises of leather to beef up one's sex life, set to another disco groove. "Sex on Wheels" is Thrill Kill's best-known song, with a driving guitar line reminiscent of "Walk This Way," surrounded by screeching tires, a rumbling bass, and a literal notion of auto-erotica. Subsequent albums include the trance-techno of *13 Above the Night,* the lavish horns and wheels of *Hit and Run Holiday,* and the rather lackluster *A Crime for All Seasons.*

Buzz is humble about his abilities and accomplishments: "Everything I've learned has been trial and error. I don't know anything about engineering or sonics. If I started putting the latest sound from the latest outboard gear in my music, it would set [the music] in a certain time frame. I think the way our music sits now, it's more haphazard and timeless." —ERIC OLSEN AND DAWN DARLING

Death Ride 69: *Screaming down the Gravity Well,* Fifth Column, 1996.

My Life With the Thrill Kill Kult: *I See Good Spirits and I See Bad Spirits,* Wax Trax!, 1988 • *My Life With the Thrill Kill Kult* (EP), Wax Trax!, 1988 • "A Daisy Chain 4 Satan/Cuz It's Hot," Wax Trax!, 1990 • *Confessions of a Knife,* Wax Trax!, 1990 • *Kooler Than Jesus,* Wax Trax!, 1990 • "Leathersex," Wax Trax!, 1991 (*Volume One*) • "Sex on Wheels," Wax Trax!, 1991 • *Sexplosion!,* Wax Trax!, 1991 • "Her Sassy Kiss," Warner Bros., 1992 (*Cool World* soundtrack) • "Sex on Wheelz" (remix), Warner Bros., 1992 (*Cool World* soundtrack) • *13 Above the Night,* Interscope, 1993 • "Blue Buddha," Interscope, 1993 • "Final Blindness," Interscope, 1993 • "After the Flesh," Interscope/Atlantic, 1994 (*The Crow* soundtrack) • *Hit and Run Holiday,* Interscope, 1995 • *A Crime for All Seasons,* Red Ant, 1997 • "Sexy Sucker," Red Ant, 1997.

Thomas McElroy

See DENZIL FOSTER AND THOMAS McELROY

Andy McKaie

While Andy McKaie has had many different jobs over the course of his career in the music business, including rock critic and publicist, it's in his role as reissue producer that he feels most fulfilled. Not only does he get a chance to hear tremendous amounts of great music, he gets to reintroduce that music to the public. "The ultimate enjoyment I've had in the business so far," he says from his offices at MCA Records, "is to learn all I can about an artist and then apply that to making a package that people enjoy—that sounds good, reads good, feels good. When I listen to [a good package], I go 'Yeah.' That really gives me a buzz." As vice president of catalog development and A&R for Universal's Music Special Markets, McKaie has created packages or reissues for artists as varied as B.B. King, Lynyrd Skynyrd, Elton John, Jody Watley, the Mamas and the Papas, and the entire Chess Records catalog.

After sketching out a release schedule, McKaie has been known to search the vast MCA vaults in Los Angeles for the original 2-track stereo masters. "I used to spend a lot of time looking for tapes," he recalls. "I'm not a member of the union, but there's a forklift you can use to get to our tapes. I got into trouble for using it. I was going so often I couldn't always have somebody take me, so I learned how to use the forklift. I would go up and down to find the tapes that I wanted. I did hand searches constantly. Now I'm down to doing hand searches every couple of months because I've already found the masters."

As soon as he finds them he sticks yellow Post-It notes on the boxes so everyone knows where to find them. He also uses those Post-Its to advise the project engineers on sonic things to watch out for as well as track listings and any other information he can think of to add. "I don't want to complicate things," he explains. "The more information I can provide, the easier their job is."

While McKaie has no formal engineering or musical background, over the years he's trained his ears to hear what is working and what is not. He admits, "I'm very lucky because I have some really good engineers at my disposal. I used to spend a ton of time in the studio, but because all of the engineers have been working with me for a long time now, they are used to me. They know what I want to hear for the most part, and many times they've dealt with the artist over and over again, obviously, because we release the same artist quite often. So, it's a lot smoother than it used to be. In the bad ol' days, on a package that included 45 tracks on a double CD, there were times when I would have to go in and personally sit down at the board and remix 36 to 38 of them. But, the good times now, there are times when I do not have to go there at all."

Instead, he concentrates on creating collections and box sets. He's been heading up MCA's reissue and collection program since 1986, and over the years he's learned what makes a project successful. Each year he works with a variety of musical genres and eras and a blend of superstars, stars, and the wrongfully forgotten to create packages. "I try to create series, as well as themes, that work," he explains. "I try to take advantage of circumstances—such as our recent Mamas and the Papas collection."

In 1998, the seminal California folk band was inducted into the Rock and Roll Hall of Fame, and Cass Elliot's daughter did a number of press dates to publicize the facts behind her mother's death. "Suddenly it provided a lot of interest, so we remastered the first album and created a new *Greatest Hits* album. Everything sounds so much better—it looks better, feels better."

Sometimes a project is done for the mere reason it's important to do. "You have to do other things that do not necessarily look like they are going to be front-of-the-burner kinds of projects. When we first started the Cass Elliot project she hadn't been selling any records and the Mamas and the Papas' sales had dropped off rather considerably. But we did it—we did it because I thought it was the right thing to do." McKaie has also championed re-releases by Les Paul (his Decca recordings between 1936 and 1947; see entry), Billie Holiday (*The Complete Decca Recordings,* which garnered him a Reissue Coproducer of the Year Grammy), and B.B. King (who had been stuck in record store bargain bins till McKaie came along). Perhaps McKaie's most important contribution has been his stewardship of the Chess Records reissue and collection campaign. Many classic recordings by Muddy Waters, Howlin' Wolf, Chuck Berry, Sonny Boy Williamson, and dozens of others are now available for the first time in years.

McKaie—who was born in Flushing, New York, in 1946 and moved to Los Angeles in 1981—has received critical acclaim (including Reissue of the Year awards from *Rolling Stone, The Village Voice,* and *CD Review*) and won two Grammy Awards (as Reissue Producer of the Year for *Chuck Berry: The Chess Box,* and the aforementioned Holiday release). More than accolades and sales, though, for McKaie it's the diversity of his work and its reception that matters. "It's the music and the results. I got a letter from a guy about Bing's records and he was thrilled to pieces. That is the result that counts.

"I try to keep it diverse. I don't get bored and I've learned a lot about music. I consider myself a nonmusician, though I can find middle C and a few other things," he says with a laugh. "I consider myself a professional listener. At first it was a little scary approaching new things as a nonmusician, but it's been fun and challenging." —DAVID JOHN FARINELLA

COMPILATIONS

Almanac Singers: *Complete General Recordings,* MCA, 1996.

Alice Cooper: *Prince of Darkness,* MCA, 1989.

Andrews Sisters: *Greatest Hits: The 60th Anniversary Collection,* MCA, 1998 • *See also* Crosby, Bing.

Apaka, Alfred: *The Best Of,* Vol. 2, MCA, 1987 • *The Best Of,* Vol. 1, MCA, 1989 • *Best of the Decca Years: The Singer,* MCA, 1989 • *Best of the Decca Years,* Vol. 2, MCA, 1990.

Berlin, Irving: *The 100th Anniversary Collection,* MCA, 1988.

Berry, Chuck: *Chuck Berry: The Chess Box,* Chess/MCA, 1988 • *His Best,* Vols. 1–2, Chess/MCA, 1997.

Bishop, Stephen: *On and On: Best Of,* MCA, 1994.

Bland, Bobby Blue: *Turn on Your Love Light: The Duke Recordings,* Vol. 2, MCA, 1964.

Brady Bunch: *It's a Sunshine Day: The Best Of,* MCA, 1993.

Commander Cody: *Too Much Fun: Best Of,* MCA, 1990.

Crosby, Bing: *Bing! His Legendary Years, 1931–1957,* MCA, 1989 • *Bing Crosby and the Andrews Sisters: Their Complete Recordings Together,* MCA, 1996 • *Top 'O the Morning: His Irish Collection,* MCA, 1996.

Dells, The: *Oh What a Night! The Great Ballads,* MCA, 1998.

Del-Vikings, The: *Come Go with Me: The Best Of,* Hip-O, 1997.

Diamond, Neil: *Glory Road: 1968–1972,* MCA, 1992, 1995.

Diddley, Bo: *The Chess Box,* Chess/MCA, 1990 • *His Best,* Chess/MCA, 1993.

Dramatics, The: *Be My Girl: Their Greatest Love Songs,* Hip-O, 1998.

Earle, Steve: *Ain't Ever Satisfied: The Steve Earle Collection,* Hip-O, 1996.

El Chicano: *Viva El Chicano! Their Very Best,* MCA, 1976.

Elliot, Mama Cass: *Dream a Little Dream: The Cass Elliot Collection,* MCA, 1997.

Fisher, Eddie: *The Very Best Of,* MCA, 1968.

Flamingos, The: *Complete Chess Masters Plus,* MCA, 1997.

Four Tops: *Keepers of the Castle: Their Best, 1972–1978,* MCA, 1997.

Fulson, Lowell: *The Complete Chess Masters,* Chess/MCA, 1997.

Grass Roots: *Greatest Hits,* Vols. 1–2, MCA, 1987 • *All Time Greatest Hits,* MCA, 1996.

Guy, Buddy: *The Complete Chess Studio Sessions,* Chess/MCA, 1992 • *Buddy's Blues,* MCA, 1997.

Henry, Clarence Frogman: *Ain't Got No Home,* Chess, 1994.

Herman, Woody: *Best of the Decca Years, 1939–1944,* Decca/MCA, 1988.

Holiday, Billie: *The Complete Decca Recordings,* Decca, 1950, 1991.

Holly, Buddy: *Greatest Hits,* MCA, 1996.

Hooker, John Lee: *The Best of, 1965–1974,* MCA, 1992 • *His Best Chess Sides,* MCA, 1997 • *The Complete '50s Chess Recordings,* Chess/MCA, 1998.

Howlin' Wolf: *Ain't Gonna Be Your Dog,* Chess/MCA, 1994 • *His Best,* Chess/MCA, 1997.

Impressions, The: *Greatest Hits,* MCA, 1965, 1982.

James, Etta: *Her Best,* Chess/MCA, 1997.

John, Elton: *Greatest Hits, 1976–1986,* MCA, 1992.

Jordan, Louis: *Five Guys Named Moe,* Decca, 1946, 1992 • *Five Guys Named Moe: Original Decca Recordings,* Vol. 2, Decca, 1952, 1992.

King, B.B.: *How Blue Can You Get? Classic Live, 1964–1994,* MCA, 1996.

Kinks, The: *Lost and Found, 1986–1989,* MCA, 1991.

LaBelle, Patti: *Greatest Hits,* MCA, 1996.

Lee, Brenda: *The Brenda Lee Anthology,* Vol. 1, *1956–1961,* MCA, 1991 • *The Brenda Lee Anthology,* Vol. 2: *1962–1980,* MCA, 1991.

Lee, Peggy: *Black Coffee,* MCA, 1956, 1994 • *The Best of the Decca Years,* MCA, 1997.

Lewis, Ramsey: *Greatest Hits,* MCA, 1973.

Little Milton: *Welcome to the Club,* MCA, 1994.

Little Walter: *Confessin' the Blues,* Chess/MCA, 1976, 1996 • *Essential,* MCA, 1993 • *His Best,* MCA, 1997.

Lynyrd Skynyrd: w/ Ron O'Brien, *Lynyrd Skynyrd,* MCA, 1991.

Mamas and the Papas: *Greatest Hits,* MCA, 1998.

McGuire Sisters: *Greatest Hits,* MCA, 1989.

Mills Brothers: *All Time Greatest Hits,* MCA, 1997.

Mills, Stephanie: *Greatest Hits,* MCA, 1996.

Moonglows, The: *Blue Velvet: The Ultimate Collection,* Chess, 1993 • *Their Greatest Hits,* MCA, 1997.

Nelson, Ricky: *The Best of, 1964–1975,* MCA, 1990.

New Edition: *Solo Hits,* MCA, 1996.

Night Ranger: *Greatest Hits,* Camel, 1989.

One Way: *The Best of, Featuring Al Hudson and Alicia Myers,* MCA, 1996.

Parker, Junior: *Junior's Blues/The Duke Recordings,* Vol. 1, MCA, 1992.

Poco: *Crazy Loving: The Best of Poco, 1975–1982,* MCA, 1989.

Pointer Sisters: *Yes We Can: The Best of the Blue Thumb Recordings,* Hip-O, 1997.

Ready for the World: *Oh Sheila! RFTW's Greatest Hits,* MCA, 1993.

Riperton, Minnie: *The Best of Her Chess Years,* Chess/MCA, 1997.

Rogers, Jimmy: *Complete Chess Recordings,* Chess/MCA, 1997.

Rufus and Chaka Khan: *The Very Best of Rufus and Chaka Khan,* MCA, 1996.

Steppenwolf: *Born to Be Wild: A Retrospective, 1966–1990,* MCA, 1991.

Thomas, Irma: *Something Good: Muscle Shoals,* Chess, 1990.

Thornton, Big Mama: *Hound Dog: The Peacock Recordings,* MCA, 1992.

Tiffany: *Greatest Hits,* Hip-O, 1996.

Turner, Ike and Tina: *Bold Soul Sister: The Best of the Blue Thumb Recordings,* Hip-O, 1997.

Watley, Jody: *Greatest Hits,* MCA, 1996.

Waters, Muddy: *The Chess Box,* Chess, 1989 • *One More Mile,* Chess/MCA, 1994 • *His Best, 1947–1955,* Chess/MCA, 1997 • *His Best, 1956–1964,* Chess/MCA, 1997.

Williams, Roger: *The Artists Choice,* MCA, 1992.

Williamson, Sonny Boy: *His Best,* Chess/MCA, 1997.

Wishbone Ash: *The Best of Wishbone Ash,* MCA, 1997.

Womack, Bobby: *Only Survivor: The MCA Years,* MCA, 1996.

Wright, O.V.: *The Soul of O.V. Wright,* MCA, 1992 • *Blues Volume 6: 50's Rarities,* MCA, 1991.

VARIOUS ARTISTS

Porgy and Bess (original cast), MCA, 1940, 1992 • *High Spirits* (original cast), MCA, 1964., 1996 • *The Best of Duke: Peacock Blues,* MCA, 1992 • *Rock Around the Clock: The Decca Rock and Roll Collection,* Decca, 1994 • *Stardust: The Classic Decca Hits and Standards Collection,* Decca, 1994 • *Chess Rhythm and Roll,* MCA, 1994 • *Car Wash* soundtrack, MCA, 1996 • *'80's Hits Back,* Hip-O, 1996 • *'80's Hits Back,* Vol. 3, Hip-O, 1996 • *ABC's of Soul,* Vols. 1–3, Hip-O, 1996 • *Mission Accomplished: Themes for Spies,* Hip-O, 1996 • *Soulful Grooves,* Vols. 1–2, Hip-O, 1996 • *Soulful Ladies of the 80's,* Hip-O, 1996 • *Glory of Love: Sweet and Soulful Love Songs,* Hip-O, 1996 • *Thinking About You: A Collection of Modern Love Songs,* Hip-O, 1996 • *Merry Soulful Christmas,* MCA, 1996 • *Quiet Storms Two,* MCA, 1996 • *Chess Blues Classics: 1947–1956,* Chess/MCA, 1997 • *Chess Blues Classics: 1957–1967,* Chess/MCA, 1997 • *Glory of Love: 50's Sweet and Soulful Love Songs,* Hip-O, 1997 • *Glory of Love: 70's Sweet and Soulful Love Songs,* Hip-O, 1997 • *Glory of Love: 80's Sweet and Soulful Love Songs,* Hip-O, 1997 • *Synth Me Up: 14 Classic Electronic Hits,* Hip-O, 1997 • *Aristocrat of the Blues: 50th Anniversary Collection,* MCA, 1997 • *Chess Blues Piano Greats,* MCA, 1997 • *Chess Blues-Rock Songbook,* .MCA, 1997 • *Chess Soul: A Decade of Chicago's Finest,* MCA, 1997 • *Chess Blues Guitar: Two Decades of Killer Fretwork, 1949–1969,* Chess/MCA, 1998 • *Rock She Said: On the Pop Side,* Hip-O, 1998 • *Rock She Said: Guitars and Attitudes,* Hip-O, 1998 • *Life's Highway,* Hip-O, 1998 • *The King's Record Collection,* Vols. 1–2, Hip-O, 1998 • *Cover You: A Tribute to the Rolling Stones,* Hip-O, 1998 • *Bluegrass Essentials.,* MCA, 1998.

REISSUES

Armstrong, Louie: *What a Wonderful World,* MCA, 1968, 1988.

Diddley, Bo, with Chuck Berry: *Two Great Guitars,* Chess, 1964, 1993.

Hooker, John Lee: *Live at the Cafe Au Go Go (and Soledad Prison),* MCA, 1966, 1996 • *Urban Blues,* Beat Goes On, 1967, 1994.

James, Etta: *Come a Little Closer,* MCA, 1974, 1996 • *Essential,* MCA, 1993.

King, B.B.: *Live at the Regal,* BGO, 1965, 1995.

McGhee, Brownie, and Sonny Terry: *A Long Way from Home,* MCA, 1969, 1998.

Rotary Connection: *Rotary Connection,* MCA, 1968, 1996.

Rush, Otis, with Albert King: *Door to Door,* Chess, 1970, 1994.

Schifrin, Lalo: *Music from Mission Impossible,* Hip-O, 1967, 1996.

Stitt, Sonny: *Sonny Stitt,* MCA, 1958, 1994.

Waters, Muddy: *Muddy Brass and the Blues,* Chess/MCA, 1967, 1993 • *Electric Mud,* MCA, 1968, 1996 • *Live,* Chess/MCA, 1971, 1977.

Meat Beat Manifesto

See JACK DANGERS

Huey P. Meaux

Huey P. Meaux doesn't give interviews. It's hard when you're in prison. Meaux—whose productions were synonymous with Gulf Coast rock in the '60s and '70s—is in a federal penitentiary in Huntsville, Texas, charged with child pornography, having sex with minors, and cocaine possession. Houston police arrested Meaux in January 1996, when a search of his Sugar Hill Recording Studios uncovered drugs and child pornography. Helping bust Meaux was his adopted son, Ben, and Shannon McDowell Brasher, who, as Shannon McDowell, was abused by Meaux.

The key document on Meaux, who was born on March 10, 1929, is Joe Nick Patoski's article, "Sex, Drugs and Rock & Roll," published in *Texas Monthly* in May 1996. In it, Patoski, a senior editor at the magazine and a former rock promoter (his most colorful client might have been Joe "King" Carrasco and the Crowns, a cheesy Tex-Mex outfit of the '80s), describes his disillusionment at discovering Meaux was as much pervert as producer.

I tried to reach Meaux in the summer of 1997 by fax-ing his lawyer a list of questions limited to his production style. In mid-July that year, Meaux took umbrage at my exclusively music-oriented questions and forbade me to print anything about the charges that landed him in the pen. Around Christmas, however, Meaux wrote me again, wishing me and the co-editors of this book happy holidays.

The information contained in this bio is based on Patoski's article. Searching the Web yields some Meaux data, but it's mainly about records the "crazy Cajun" produced, such as albums by Freddy Fender, Jerry Lee Lewis, and the Sir Douglas Quintet. His productions are vivid, have a lot of high end, and sound organic. His aim was presence; he made great use of echo and his records sound great on AM radio.

Meaux grew up outside of Kaplan, Louisiana, near Lafayette. At age 12, his family moved to Winnie, Texas, where his father, accordionist Stanislaus Meaux, fronted a band featuring a teenaged Huey as drummer. At that time, his buddies on the set included George Jones, pianist Moon Mullican, and disc jockey J.P. Richardson, aka the Big Bopper.

In 1959, Meaux produced his first hit, "Breaking Up Is Hard to Do," by Jivin' Gene Bourgeois. Such swamp-pop hits as Barbara Lynn's soulful "You'll Lose a Good Thing" (No. 8), and Big Sambo's "The Rains Came" followed. Eventually, Meaux would own many labels and the Sugar Hill studios and manage artists.

Meaux soon shifted operations to Houston, where he became known for his good ear and promotional talents. "The song makes the singer and the producer," Meaux told Patoski. "Promotion makes all of it."

His master stroke was fashioning a Tex-Mex rock band from San Antonio after British Mods and dubbing it the Sir Douglas Quintet. Fronted by the charismatic Doug Sahm, the Quintet hit No. 13 with "She's About a Mover" in 1965. Meaux scored a hit with the earliest all-Mexican band to chart, Sunny and the Sunliners performing Little Willie John's "Talk to Me" (No. 11) in 1963. He also hit with B.J. Thomas and the Triumphs' version of Hank Williams' "I'm So Lonesome I Could Cry" (No. 8) in '66.

But there were misses as well: Meaux couldn't score with brothers Johnny and Edgar Winter and claimed he never got credit for his "discovery" of ZZ Top. Meaux also was known for taking advantage of writers and singers. No one ever questioned his showmanship or talent for palaver.

Meaux scored his biggest hit with Fender's "Before the Next Teardrop Falls," No. 1 in early 1975. The two found kinship in their prison experience: Fender had done Louisiana time in Angola for marijuana possession, while Meaux spent three years in prison in the late '60s for conspiracy to violate the Mann Act (shades of Chuck Berry). Fender's second assault on the charts, a remake of his 1959 regional smash "Wasted Days and Wasted Nights," reached No. 8. Both tunes scored by recycling swamp-pop melodies as modern country by replacing horn charts with steel guitars and female choruses.

By the mid-'80s, the bloom was off the Meaux and Fender roses. After he survived a 1981 bout with throat cancer, Meaux scored his last major production hit with Rockin' Sidney Simien's 1985 "(Don't Mess with) My Toot-Toot" and effectively withdrew from the production scene to focus on music publishing. He sold Sugar Hill in 1986 but continued to lease offices there.

In November 1994, Meaux narrowly escaped death in a car accident, even as the troubles with his adopted son, Ben, worsened. In September 1995, after an incident in which Ben pulled a knife on him, Meaux sent Ben to an Outward Bound wilderness training camp in Utah. Before he went, a girl who remains unidentified told Ben about Huey's cocaine use and the functions of his hidden back office. It was there, in the recording studio, that Meaux had brought many young girls to pose for videos and photos in exchange for coke, liquor, jewelry, and money.

In January 1996, Shannon McDowell Brasher went to the Houston police and exposed Meaux's party room. The thousands of pictures of nude children were enough to convict Meaux of possession of child pornography, a third-degree felony carrying a 2- to 10-year sentence. If Meaux is proved to have traded photographs across state lines, the charges could escalate to a federal offense carrying a maximum penalty of 20 years. As it is, his multiple felony convictions will keep him in jail for at least 15 years.

Meaux also faces a $10 million civil suit from Shannon Brasher, who alleges that Meaux began molesting her when she was 9 years old and that the abuse continued for 16 years, until 1995. —CARLO WOLFF

Barry, Joe: *Joe Barry,* ABC, 1977.
Big Sambo: "The Rains Came," Eric, 1962.
Cates Gang: *Wanted,* Metro, 1970.
Fender, Freddy: *Are You Ready for Freddy?,* ABC, 1975 • "Before the Next Teardrop Falls," Dot, 1975 • *Before the Next Teardrop Falls,* ABC, 1975, 1994 • w/ the Sir Douglas Quintet, *Reunion of the Cosmic Brothers,* Crazy Cajun, 1975 • "Secret Love," Dot, 1975 • "Wasted Days and Wasted Nights," Dot, 1975 • *If You're Ever in Texas,* Dot, 1976 • *Rockin' Country,* ABC, 1976 • "You'll Lose a Good Thing," ABC/Dot, 1976 • *Swamp Gold,* ABC, 1978 • *Tex Mex,* ABC, 1979 • *The Texas Balladeer,* Starflite, 1979 • *Together*

We Drifted Apart, Starflite, 1980 • *The Best Of,* MCA Nashville, 1996.
Friedman, Kinky: *Lasso from El Paso,* Epic, 1976.
Gilley, Mickey: *Mickey Gilley,* Crazy Cajun, 1974.
Hawkins, Screamin' Jay: *Screamin' Jay Hawkins,* Philips, 1970.
Hombres: "Let It Out," Verve, 1967.
Jivin' Gene: "Breaking Up Is Hard to Do," Mercury, 1959.
Lewis, Jerry Lee: *Killer: The Mercury Years,* Vol. 3, 1973–1977, PolyGram Country, 1989 • *All Killer No Filler: The Anthology,* Rhino, 1993.
Lynn, Barbara: "You'll Lose a Good Thing," Jamie, 1962 • *Promises,* Bear Family, 1997.
McLain, Floyd: "Sweet Dreams," MSL, 1966.
McLain, Tommy: *Backwoods Adventure,* Starflite, 1979.
Rockin' Sidney: "My Toot Toot," Epic, 1985.
Sahm, Doug: *Live,* Bear Tracks, 1989 • *Best of, 1968–1975,* Rhino, 1992.
Sir Douglas and the Texas Tornados: *Texas Rock for Country Rollers,* ABC, 1976.
Sir Douglas Quintet: "She's About a Mover," Tribe, 1965 • *Together After Five,* Smash, 1970 • *The Return of Doug Saldana,* Philips, 1971 • *See also* Fender, Freddy.
Sunny and the Sunliners: "Talk to Me," Tear Drop, 1962.
Talbert, Wayne: *Houston Nickle Bag,* Mercury, 1970.
The Good, the Bad, and the Ugly: *The Good, the Bad, and the Ugly,* Mercury, 1970.
Thomas, B.J.: w/ the Triumphs, "I'm So Lonesome I Could Cry," Scepter, 1966 • *Greatest Hits,* Scepter, 1969 • *Greatest Hits,* Rhino, 1991.
Walker, T-Bone: *Legendary T-Bone Walker,* Brunswick, 1967.
Williams Jr., Hank: *Living Proof: The MGM Recordings, 1963–1975,* Mercury, 1992.
Winter, Johnny: *Ease My Pain,* Sundazed, 1996 • *Livin' in the Blues,* Sundazed, 1997.

Hank Medress

Hank Medress, though less well known than many of his peers, has had an extraordinary 40-year career in the music business, with a hand in 30 Top 40 hits. Medress was a member of the vocal group the Tokens ("The Lion Sleeps Tonight"), but the Tokens were not only a singing group; they were also an extremely successful production team, with hits for the Chiffons, Randy and the Rainbows ("Denise," No. 10), the Happenings, and Robert John ("The Lion Sleeps Tonight," No. 3), from the early '60s through the early '70s.

Medress then struck out on his own and, mostly in partnership with Dave Appell, had more hits with Tony Orlando and Dawn, Frankie Valli ("Our Day Will Come," No. 11), Dan Hill (with Vonda Shepard, "Can't We Try," No. 6), and Buster Poindexter, as well as fine albums for Melissa Manchester, Pousette-Dart Band, and many others. Today, Medress runs the new Bottom Line record label.

Hank Medress was born on November 19, 1938, in Brooklyn. From the beginning Medress had two loves: music and basketball. Music won. In 1955, Medress and Neil Sedaka formed a quartet at Lincoln High School called the Linc-Tones. Lead singer Jay Siegel joined the group in 1956; in 1958, Sedaka left to pursue a solo career and that group petered out.

The following year the Margo brothers—Mitch and Phil—began rehearsing with Medress. In 1960, Medress and the Margos wrote "Tonight I Fell in Love" and brought Siegel in to sing lead for them. The foursome worked up four songs, including "Tonight" and "Wimoweh," a Weavers hit from the early '50s that was based on an old Zulu chant about a slumbering lion. Medress, determined to make it this time, met a woman on the subway, struck up a conversation, and convinced her to invest in a four-song, self-produced recording session for the group, now called the Tokens.

Medress hawked the masters on Tin Pan Alley and sold "Tonight" to Warwick Records, where it was released and quickly rose to No. 15. Soon after, the group left for RCA over a royalty dispute with Warwick. RCA producers Hugo Peretti and Luigi Creatore (see entry) loved "Wimoweh" but decided that the song needed English lyrics, which the producers (and partner George Weiss) then derived from the original Zulu chant. With Siegel's soaring falsetto lead, "The Lion Sleeps Tonight"—a doo-wop rendering of an African folk song by four whites from Brooklyn—rocketed to No. 1 in late 1961, and has sold about 6 million copies to date. The Tokens continued as a recording entity into the '70s, but they would never again have a Top 20 hit as performers.

Though the Tokens recorded for RCA, Capitol Records called in 1962 and offered them a production deal (as "Bright Tunes") with an office and a budget of $12,000 (which would cover about six two-sided singles). "We used that budget up in about a week and a half," says Medress, "but we also made a publishing deal that allowed us to use the Capitol studios to make demos free of charge." One day young songwriter Ronnie Mack (who died of cancer shortly thereafter) came into the Tokens' office with a demo he had recorded with upper Manhattan schoolmates the Chiffons (Judy

Craig, Barbara Lee, Patricia Bennett, Sylvia Peterson). "When we heard those girls sing the beginning of 'He's So Fine' ["doo-lang doo-lang doo-lang doo-lang"], I looked at the guys and said, 'Oh my God,' " because he knew he had one of the great songs of the girl group era in front of him.

"So here we are without money, but we could use the Capitol studio for demos, so we recorded 'He's So Fine' as a demo," recalls Medress. Besides producing, the Tokens also played the backing instruments on the recording (Mitch Margo on piano, Phil Margo on drums, Medress on bass, Siegel on guitar). Incredibly, Capitol passed on the record, so the team brought it to Doug Morris (future president of Atlantic) at Laurie Records. "They literally locked the door and wouldn't let us out," says Medress.

After that No. 1, the producers and the Chiffons followed up with Carole King and Gerry Goffin's "One Fine Day." The team liked the demo King brought over so much that they erased the vocals and recorded the Chiffons over the original backing: great driving piano line, sprightly beat, motivating rhythm guitar and bass. With the Chiffons' yearning vocals on top, the team had another smash (No. 5). The producers and the Chiffons clicked with two more Top 40s ("A Love So Fine," "I Have a Boyfriend") and a No. 10—the Motowny "Sweet Talkin' Guy"—making them one of the more successful girl groups of the era.

Ever ambitious, the young producers established their own label in 1964, B.T. (from "Bright Tunes") Puppy. Besides producing and releasing Tokens records—the most successful of which was "I Hear Trumpets Blow" (No. 30)—the team also produced the Happenings for the label and had four Top 15s with them, including "See You in September" and "I Got Rhythm" (both No. 3). The Tokens also wrote, sang, and produced successful commercials for Clairol, Pan Am, and Ban and recorded as backup singers with many other artists, including Bob Dylan, Connie Francis, and Del Shannon.

"We were like a factory in the '60s," says Medress. "There was a time when we had six records on the charts as producers, and we continued to record and perform. But toward the end of the '60s it became clear to me that we didn't have that hunger to be a great performing group anymore. I realized that production was where I wanted to concentrate my energies," he says.

Former Cameo artist (the Applejacks), songwriter ("Bristol Stomp," "The Wah Watusi"), and producer Dave Appell joined the team when they took on the Dawn project in 1970. The Tokens had performed live shows with Tony Orlando (who was then a solo artist) in the early '60s, and Medress had stayed in touch with him through the years. When the producers recorded the song "Candida" with Dawn, they decided that they loved the song but not the singer (who shall remain nameless).

Orlando was by then a manager at April-Blackwood Music Publishing, and almost daily, Medress implored Orlando to help him find the right singer. Finally, Medress asked Orlando to sing it himself. Orlando politely turned him down, saying that he had a "real job" and a family—and besides, his wife would kill him. Finally Orlando agreed to do the recording on the condition that his identity remain a secret. To everyone's astonishment, the bright, Latin-inflected pop song (in the manner of the Drifters' "Under the Boardwalk") became a million-seller, reaching No. 3. The similar follow-up, "Knock Three Times," did even better, reaching No. 1. There was no hiding now.

To fight the bogus groups hitting the road as "Dawn," Orlando had to come clean, hit the road, or hang it up. Besides his job, another obstacle for Orlando was that he had gained a lot of weight since his teen-idol days. Orlando made the commitment, lost the weight, and with Telma Hopkins and Joyce Vincent, became the "real" Dawn. The trio eventually racked up 13 Top 40 hits and hosted a successful TV show in the mid-'70s.

Medress and Appell, splitting with the Tokens, took over the production of the group—which became "Dawn, Featuring Tony Orlando"—in time for the next No. 1, the classic (if corny) coming-home-from-prison pop song, 1973's "Tie a Yellow Ribbon Round the Old Oak Tree." The group had become "Tony Orlando and Dawn" by the time of their final No. 1, "He Don't Love You (Like I Love You)," co-written by Curtis Mayfield (see entry) in 1975.

Medress and Appell produced Pierce Arrow and the Pousette-Dart Band during a country rock period in the late '70s; then Appell (several years Medress's senior) retired. In the '80s Medress worked on projects for the Nylons, Phoebe Snow, and the Weathergirls and had a big hit with Dan Hill and Vonda Shepard. His best effort, however, was producing David Johansen's turn (in the guise of "Buster Poindexter") to jump blues and big-band music 10 years ahead of the '90s swing revival. The 1987 album *Buster Poindexter* explodes with swinging nightlife energy, and the single "Hot, Hot, Hot" has become a standard.

In the '90s Medress spent some time in Canada with SBK and served three years as president of EMI Music Publishing ("my corporate sell-out"). He is now head-ing legendary New York nightclub the Bottom Line's new record label, the purpose of which is to release live recordings from the club's vaults, starting with Harry Chapin in 1998. —ERIC OLSEN

Chapin, Harry: *Bottom Line Encore Collection,* Bottom Line, 1998.

Chiffons, The: "A Love So Fine," Laurie, 1963 • "He's So Fine," Laurie, 1963 • "I Have a Boyfriend," Laurie, 1963 • "One Fine Day," Laurie, 1963 • *One Fine Day,* CEMA Special, 1963, 1996 • "Nobody Knows What's Goin' On," Laurie, 1965 • "Out of This World," Laurie, 1966 • "Sweet Talkin' Guy," Laurie, 1966 • *Sweet Talkin' Guy,* Laurie, 1966.

Davis, Mac: *Greatest Hits,* Columbia, 1979.

Dawn: "Candida," Bell, 1970 • *Candida,* Razor & Tie, 1970, 1996 • "Knock Three Times," Bell, 1970 • "I Play and Sing," Bell, 1971 • "Summer Sand," Bell, 1971 • *See also* Orlando, Tony, and Dawn.

Four Pennies: "When the Boy's Happy (the Girl's Happy Too)," Rust, 1963.

Group With No Name: *Moon over Brooklyn,* Casablanca, 1976

Happenings, The: "Go Away Little Girl," B.T. Puppy, 1966 • "Goodnight My Love," B.T. Puppy, 1966 • "See You in September," B.T. Puppy, 1966 • *The Happenings,* B.T. Puppy, 1966 • w/ the Tokens, *Back to Back,* B.T. Puppy, 1967 • "I Got Rhythm," B.T. Puppy, 1967 • "My Mammy," B.T. Puppy, 1967 • *Psycle,* B.T. Puppy, 1967 • "Breaking Up Is Hard to Do," B.T. Puppy, 1968 • "Music, Music, Music," B.T. Puppy, 1968 • *The Happenings' Golden Hits,* B.T. Puppy, 1968 • *The Best Of,* Sequel, 1995.

Hill, Dan: w/ Vonda Shepard, "Can't We Try," Columbia, 1987 • *Dan Hill,* Columbia, 1987 • "Never Thought (That I Could Love)," Columbia, 1987.

Johansen, David: *From Pumps to Pompadour: The David Johansen Story,* Rhino, 1995.

John, Robert: "The Lion Sleeps Tonight," Atlantic, 1971.

Manchester, Melissa: *Bright Eyes,* Bell, 1974 • *Essence Of,* Arista, 1997.

Newton-John, Olivia: *The Rumour,* MCA, 1988, 1993.

Nylons, The: *Rockapella,* Windham Hill, 1989 • *The Best Of,* Windham Hill, 1993 • *Perfect Fit,* Windham Hill, 1997.

Orlando, Tony: *I Got Rhythm,* Casablanca, 1979 • *The Casablanca Years,* Casablanca/Mercury, 1996.

Orlando, Tony, and Dawn: "What Are You Doing Sunday," Bell, 1971 • "Tie a Yellow Ribbon Round the Old Oak Tree," Bell, 1973 • "Who's in the Strawberry Patch with Sally," Bell, 1973 • "Look into My Eyes Pretty Woman," Bell, 1974 • "Steppin' Out (Gonna Boogie Tonight)," Bell, 1974 • "He Don't Love You (Like I Love You)," Elektra, 1975 • "Mornin' Beautiful," Elektra, 1975 • "You're All I Need to Get By," Elektra, 1975 • "Cupid," Elektra, 1976 •

To Be with You, Elektra, 1976 • *The Best Of,* Rhino, 1994.

Pierce Arrow: *Pierce Arrow,* Columbia, 1977 • *Pity the Rich,* Columbia, 1978.

Poindexter, Buster: *Buster Poindexter,* RCA, 1987 • "Hot, Hot, Hot," RCA, 1987 • *Buster Goes Berserk,* RCA, 1989.

Pousette-Dart Band: *3,* Capitol, 1978.

Randy and the Rainbows: "Denise," Rust, 1963.

Snow, Phoebe: *Something Real,* Elektra, 1989.

Tokens, The: "Tonight I Fell in Love," Warwick, 1961 • "He's in Town," B.T. Puppy, 1963 • "I Hear Trumpets Blow," B.T. Puppy, 1966 • *I Hear Trumpets Blow,* B.T. Puppy, 1966 • "It's a Happening World," Warner Bros., 1967 • "Portrait of My Love," Warner Bros., 1967 • "She Let's Her Hair Down (Early in the Morning)," Buddah, 1969 • "Don't Worry Baby," Buddah, 1970 • *Both Sides Now,* Buddah, 1971 • *See also* The Happenings.

Valli, Frankie: "Our Day Will Come," Private Stock, 1975 • *Our Day Will Come,* Private Stock, 1975.

Weather Girls: "Well-a-Wiggy," Columbia, 1985.

Joe Meek

If Joe Meek is one of the more curious figures in British pop history, he's also one of the most significant. Though he remains best known to Americans for his two transatlantic smashes, the Tornadoes' eerily majestic, 12-million-selling 1962 instrumental "Telstar" (the first British rock record to top both U.S. and U.K. charts), and the Honeycombs' 1964 hit "Have I the Right?" (No. 5), Meek was far more influential than his U.S. chart history would indicate.

In addition to being England's first independent producer, Meek was a resourceful, ultraprolific sonic trailblazer who churned out innumerable sides (many of which he wrote) in a wide array of styles. Many of these were made in a tiny, cluttered studio in his London apartment, where the eccentric auteur recorded flamboyantly individual music on relatively crude and largely self-built equipment, experimenting with multitracking, bizarre sound effects, and liberal (and, at the time, radical) use of echo, distortion, and compression.

Though his quirky approach flew in the face of the conventions of the ultraconservative pre-Beatles British recording industry, Meek's offbeat methods yielded 45 Top 50 hits in the U.K. between 1960 and 1966 (during which time he produced no less than 250 singles). While a substantial portion of his prodigious output was hack work, Meek's most memorable productions resonate

with a distinctive combination of sonic adventurism and heartfelt strangeness that's earned him a dedicated cult following that's stronger than ever three decades after his self-inflicted death.

Despite being tone-deaf and unable to play an instrument or carry a tune (as his surviving song demos attest), Meek—born Robert George Meek on April 5, 1929, in the country town of Newent in Gloucestershire—showed an aptitude for sound and electronics early in life. Moving to London in 1953, he got a job with straitlaced IBC Studios, where he broke with tradition by experimenting with microphone placement, isolating individual instruments for better reproduction, and even tinkering with distortion. The unusually prominent drum sound of the Humphrey Lyttleton Band's 1956 "Bad Penny Blues" helped make that Meek-produced disc the first jazz record to make the British Top 20.

But Meek's violent temper—and his paranoia that his co-workers were spying on him in order to steal his recording "secrets"—led him to leave IBC in 1957. He was subsequently hired by jazz producer Denis Preston to design and run the state-of-the-art Lansdowne Studios. The royalties from the Meek composition "Put a Ring on Her Finger" (a U.S. hit for Les Paul and Mary Ford and a U.K. B-side for Tommy Steele) enabled him to build a roster of artists whom he'd had the foresight to sign directly to himself.

He brought that stable with him when, in January 1960, he became a partner in a new independent label, Triumph. Flying in the face of industry wisdom, Triumph scored a string of Meek-produced hits before financial and distribution problems put it out of business. Meek struck out on his own—with financial support from one Major Banks, who had previously backed Triumph—and launched RGM Sound, based in a small three-story apartment-studio above a North London leathergoods shop.

Clem Cattini, the Tornadoes' drummer and subsequently one of England's top session players, described the scene at RGM: "If people could have seen the equipment, they'd never have believed it. You'd walk up the stairs to a scruffy studio, with egg boxes and bits of carpet stuck on the walls. Singers went in the loo to get the echo. The control room was a death trap and bits of the ceiling once fell down on top of my drums. Every so often you'd have to stop recording if a heavy lorry drove past."

Cattini also notes Meek's hair-trigger obstinacy, which was likely to be engaged whenever anyone disagreed with him. "He had a very violent temper," he recalls. "He was never wrong. That was one of his downfalls. One day, I picked up the phone at the studio and it was Phil Spector [see entry]. Joe picked up the phone and shouted, 'You pinched all my sounds. Fuck off!' "

From RGM, Meek churned out a startlingly diverse array of material, which was then licensed to a variety of labels. The best of these boast an eerie majesty that distinguished them from anything else in British popular music of the time—for example, actor John Leyton's spooky epic "Johnny Remember Me," which became a No. 1 hit, Meek's first, for six weeks in the summer of 1961. Meek's output often reflected such obsessions as outer space, horror films, and spiritualism (he often claimed to receive songwriting help from the spirit world, including the late Buddy Holly) and used a variety of economical sound effects (the prominent beat in "Have I the Right?" was achieved by having the band stomp in time on the staircase in Meek's hallway).

Meek's oddball artist stable included Holly-style rocker Mike Berry, macabre loon Screaming Lord Sutch, and West Indian bodybuilder Ricky Wayne, as well as various house bands, including the Tornadoes (whose bleach-blonde bassist Heinz was eventually groomed by Meek for a solo career), the Saints, the Outlaws, and the Flee-Rakkers, along with numerous handsome (if dubiously talented) young male protégés.

Though Meek's stock-in-trade was pop singles, his most elaborate opus was his 1960 "stereo fantasy" LP *I Hear a New World,* credited to the Blue Men.

The album (not released in complete form until 1991) is a fanciful vision of extraterrestrial life that featured a veritable catalog of Meek's bag of sonic tricks, including sped-up and reversed instruments and voices, along with "running water, bubbles blown through drinking straws, half-filled milk bottles being banged with spoons, the teeth of a comb drawn across the serrated edge of an ashtray, electrical circuits being shorted together, the bog being flushed."

By 1965, Meek's homespun empire had begun to crumble. The British beat-group boom (led by the Beatles, whom Meek, ironically, had turned down) had made Meek's style seem old hat, and a November 1963 bust for "persistently importuning for an immoral purpose" had a devastating effect on the producer. So did a series of lawsuits and financial disputes with his artists, as well as a serious run-in with the British tax authorities.

Additionally, Meek's homosexuality made him a target for persecution; at one point police attempted, without success, to implicate him in a grisly, much-publicized murder case. All of these factors helped contribute to Meek's volatile, ever-increasing paranoia.

On February 3, 1967—the eighth anniversary of the death of Meek's beloved Buddy Holly—Meek shot his landlady, Violet Shenton, to death and then killed himself. —SCOTT SCHINDER

Berry, Mike: "Don't You Think It's Time?," HMV, 1962 • *A Tribute to Buddy Holly* (EP), HMV, 1963.

Blue Men: *See* Meek, Joe.

Broonzy, Big Bill: *1955 London Sessions,* Sequel, 1994.

Cox, Michael: "Angela Jones," Triumph, 1960.

Duncan, Johnny: *Last Train to San Fernando,* Bear Family, 1996.

Ford, Emile, and the Checkmates: *Why You Want to Make Those Eyes at Me?,* Pye, 1959.

Fortune, Lance: "Be Mine," Pye, 1959.

Heinz: "Just Like Eddie," Decca, 1963.

Honeycombs, The: "Have I the Right?," Interphon, 1964 • *Here Are the Honeycombs,* Vee-Jay, 1964.

Leyton, John: "Johnny Remember Me," Top Rank, 1961 • "Wild Wind," Top Rank, 1961.

Lyttleton, Humphrey: *Best of Hump, 1949–1956,* Parlophone, 1972.

Meek, Joe: w/ the Blue Men, *I Hear a New World,* RPM, 1991 • *Work in Progress: The Triumph Sessions,* RPM, 1994 • *304 Holloway Road,* Castle, 1996 • *Joe Meek's Fabulous Flee-Rakkers,* See for Miles, 1997 • *The Musical Adventures Of,* Musicrama, 1997.

Tornadoes, The: "Telstar," London, 1962 • *Telstar* (EP), Decca, 1962 • *The Sounds Of* (EP), Decca, 1962 • "Globetrotter," Decca, 1963 • *More Sounds from the Tornados* (EP), Decca, 1963 • *Tornado Rock* (EP), Decca, 1963 • *The Original Sixties Hits,* Music Club, 1994 • *The Very Best Of,* Music Club, 1997.

COLLECTIONS

The Joe Meek Story, Decca, 1977.

The Joe Meek Story, Vol. 1, Line, 1991.

The Joe Meek Story, Vol. 2, *The Pye Years,* Sequel, 1991.

The Joe Meek Story, Vol. 3, *The Complete Houston Wells,* Sequel, 1994.

The Joe Meek Story, Vol 4, *The Best of Michael Cox,* Sequel, 1994.

It's Hard to Believe It: The Amazing World of Joe Meek, Razor & Tie, 1995.

Let's Go! Joe Meek's Girls, RPM, 1996.

Early Years, RPM, 1997.

Terry Melcher

Singer, songwriter, and music publisher Terry Melcher was one of the most important West Coast rock 'n' roll producers of the '60s. Melcher first hit big with the Rip Chords ("Hey Little Cobra," No. 4) in 1964; then, as staff producer at Columbia, he worked with the Byrds as they helped create folk and country rock on some of the era's most important albums: *Mr. Tambourine Man* (1965, No. 6), *Turn! Turn! Turn!* (1966, No. 17), *Ballad of Easy Rider* (1969), and *(Untitled)* (1970). In addition, Melcher produced Paul Revere and the Raiders, generating eight Top 30 hits. After a hiatus from the studio, Melcher returned in the mid-'80s to write and produce for the Beach Boys, culminating in the No. 1 hit "Kokomo" in 1988, over 23 years after his first No. 1 single, the Byrds' "Mr. Tambourine Man."

Melcher was born in February 1942 to an 18-year-old Doris Day and her first husband, trombone player Al Jorden. The couple separated soon after Terry's birth, and Day resumed her singing career, which drew her to Hollywood by 1948. Terry took the name of Day's third (of four) husbands, agent/producer Marty Melcher, who died in 1968.

A singer from childhood, Melcher made his first recording in 1961 when he borrowed a combined $300 from a college friend and Jack Nitzsche (see entry) and made a demo at Gold Star Studios (home of Phil Spector's recordings; see entry). Melcher took his Ricky Nelson–sounding demo to Columbia, where they were impressed enough to invite him into their producer-trainee program in New York.

After he went through the program he returned to L.A., where he made his first deal: signing up future Beach Boy Bruce Johnston. As Bruce and Terry they hit the mid-charts with, per Melcher, the "half-assed surf" song "Summer Means Fun" in the summer of 1964.

In the same musical vein, when songwriters Phil Stewart and Ernie Bringas brought some songs into his family's publishing company, Melcher signed them to a recording deal at Columbia, calling them the Rip Chords. After a couple of mid-charters, Melcher had his first smash when he and Johnston, backing Stewart and Bringas on vocals (joined by ace drummer Hal Blaine and Glen Campbell on guitar), recorded "Hey Little Cobra"—an at least three-quarter-assed hot rod number. Melcher and Johnston then wrote, played all of the instruments on, and sang backing for one of Pat Boone's last charting records, "Beach Girl."

In the fall of 1964, a group called the Jet Set, featuring guitarist/singer Jim (later Roger) McGuinn on electric 12-string guitar, bassist Chris Hillman, guitarist/singer Gene Clark, drummer Michael Clarke, and singer/guitarist David Crosby, entered World Pacific studio to record a demo of an unreleased Bob Dylan song called "Mr. Tambourine Man." The demo got them a deal with Columbia in late 1964, and Melcher was assigned to produce them. Melcher smoothed the arrangement away from the band's march beat, informed the band that while McGuinn, Crosby, and Clark would be singing, only McGuinn was going to play on the (now) Byrds' first single.

Says Melcher, "I thought the only guy in the band who could play well enough to record was McGuinn, so I used all the normal guys I used for the sessions: Blaine, Leon Russell [keyboards], Larry Knechtel [bass], Jerry Cole [rhythm guitar]. Basically, I took the bass-drum groove from 'Don't Worry Baby' and put 'Tambourine Man' over it, and just had McGuinn weave his Rickenbacker 12-string through the whole thing. I put him on [i.e., overdubbed] about four times, so it just jangled forever."

That endless jangling and the group's thrilling harmonies essentially created folk rock. The Byrds' harmonies and Melcher's 12-string-over-surf production set a standard that the Beatles—and Brian Wilson (see entry) himself—would soon be emulating. Although the Byrds had two No. 1s in "Tambourine" and "Turn! Turn! Turn!," and three other standards in "All I Really Wanna Do," "The Bells of Rhymney," and "I'll Feel a Whole Lot Better," they turned away from Melcher after their first two albums. In his excellent *The Nearest Faraway Place: Brian Wilson, the Beach Boys, and the Southern California Experience,* author and *Billboard* publisher Timothy White quotes McGuinn as conceding Melcher's production contributions: Melcher brought "that creamy California sound that he superimposed on the rough-edged folk-rock sound that we were doing, and I think . . . it gave a luster to it that it wouldn't have had."

After four years, Melcher and the Byrds reconciled in 1969 for *Ballad of Easy Rider,* by which time the Byrds had pioneered country rock. By *Ballad,* McGuinn was the only original Byrd remaining and the three-and-four-part harmony of the early sound had largely been replaced by solo vocal leads from McGuinn, bassist John York, and tasty country-rocking lead guitarist Clarence White. The title track is a bluegrassy McGuinn great. "Jesus Is Just Alright" is the original gospel-rock recording of an arrangement the Doobie Brothers had a hit with three years later.

(Untitled) is better still. A double-album set, record 1

is a live recording of spiky, rock arrangements of Byrds standards, including "Lover of the Bayou," "Mr. Tambourine Man," and 16 freaky minutes of "Eight Miles High." The studio disc contains some great country-rock moments: McGuinn's "All the Things," "Take a Whiff (on Me)," and especially his poignant sagebrush ode to a wild horse, "Chestnut Mare."

Paul Revere and the Raiders are (conceding an excellent counter-case from Three Dog Night; see Richie Podolor entry), the most unappreciated rock band of the '60s and early '70s. Coming out of Seattle in the early '60s with a Standells and Seeds rawness, the band's gimmicky colonial garb has no doubt blinded some to the qualities of its tough, tuneful rock 'n' roll. In just three years, 1965 to 1967, Melcher and the Raiders kicked out four Top 10 albums.

Mark Lindsay's ballsy vocals, Revere's organ, and Jim Valley's wailing lead guitar drove through stomping hits like "Steppin' Out"; the Kinks-like "Just Like Me" (No. 11); the first anti-drug hit, "Kicks" (No. 4); "Hungry" (No. 6); Lindsay and Melcher's (with some beachy harmonies) "Good Thing" (No. 4);and "Him or Me—What's It Gonna Be?" (No. 5).

In 1967 Melcher became the Beatles' subpublisher for the U.S., Canada, and Japan, and primarily attended to such duties through the '70s. Melcher's Equinox production company signed a deal with his hero Brian Wilson in the mid-'70s that came to naught. Also in the '70s, Melcher recorded two solo albums, including one with backing vocals from Doris Day.

On a bizarre side note, Melcher's affiliation with the Beatles and the Beach Boys apparently led aspiring songwriter Charles Manson to approach him about a recording contract in 1968. Melcher declined, and in 1969 he moved to England. His former home on Cielo Drive was where Manson's minions murdered Sharon Tate and four others on August 9, 1969.

In the late '70s and early '80s Melcher concentrated on real estate until Mike Love and Bruce Johnston asked him to help them find some new Beach Boys material. In 1985 Melcher and Love co-wrote "Getcha Back," which entered the Top 30, and in 1986 Melcher produced a new charting version of "California Dreamin' " for the band.

Throughout the '80s, the Beach Boys had placed several songs in films (*The Big Chill, Lethal Weapon 2, Troop Beverly Hills, Soul Man*); in 1987 the amassed brain trust of Melcher, Love, ex-Papa John Phillips, and Scott McKenzie (of "San Francisco" fame) decided to try to write a song for the film *Cocktail*, derived from the scene where the Tom Cruise character moves from New York to Jamaica. Recalls Melcher, "We went into it to see if anyone could write a major hit for the band besides Brian. I figured a lot of their hits had been travelogs like 'Surfin' USA' and 'California Girls.'

"John Phillips had this idea about a kind of blues song about some place the band would go before they broke up. We changed all the words and chords around and I wrote the chorus. As far as the feel goes, I always loved Jimmy Buffett records, so I got a steel drummer; Van Dyke Parks played the accordion, Ry Cooder played the guitar and the slide, and Jim Keltner was the drummer, going for a 'Margaritaville' kind of thing [see Norbert Putnam entry].

"I just layered it until it all started to shimmer. What really made it was the out-of-tune accordion: it glued everything together, especially with the steel drum. Then we left the falsettos out of the harmonies rather than having somebody copy Brian."

The song shot to No. 1 and led the *Still Cruisin'* album to gold. Today Melcher is Doris Day's manager and they are neighbors in Carmel, California. —ERIC OLSEN AND DAVID JOHN FARINELLA

Beach Boys: "Califoria Dreamin'," Capitol, 1986 • "Rock 'n' Roll to the Rescue," Capitol, 1986 • "Kokomo," Elektra, 1988 (*Cocktail* soundtrack) • "Still Cruisin'," Capitol, 1989 • *Still Cruisin'*, Capitol, 1989 • *Summer in Paradise*, Brother, 1992 • *Good Vibrations: Thirty Years of the Beach Boys*, Capitol, 1993.

Boone, Pat: "Beach Girl/Little Honda," Dot, 1964 • *More Greatest Hits*, Varese Sarabande, 1994.

Bruce and Terry: "Summer Means Fun," Columbia, 1964 • *The Best of Bruce and Terry*, Sundazed, 1966, 1998.

Byrds, The: "All I Really Wanna Do," Columbia, 1965 • "Feel a Whole Lot Better," Columbia, 1965 • *Mr. Tambourine Man*, Columbia, 1965 • "Mr. Tambourine Man," Columbia, 1965 • "Turn! Turn! Turn!," Columbia, 1965 • "It Won't Be Wrong," Columbia, 1966 • "Set You Free This Time," Columbia, 1966 • *Turn! Turn! Turn!*, Columbia, 1966 • *Greatest Hits*, Columbia, 1967 • "Ballad of Easy Rider," Columbia, 1969 • *Ballad of Easy Rider*, Columbia, 1969 • *(Untitled)*, Columbia, 1970 • "Jesus Is Just Alright," Columbia, 1970 • *Byrdmaniax*, Columbia, 1971 • *Greatest Hits*, Vol. 2, Columbia, 1972, 1989 • *Play Dylan*, CBS, 1980.

Catalinas, The: *Fun Fun Fun*, Epic, 1964.

Day, Doris: *Move Over Darling*, Bear Family, 1997.

Freeway: *Freeway*, Decca, 1979.

Gentle Soul: *Gentle Soul*, Epic, 1968.

Hot Doggers: *Surfin' U.S.A.*, Epic, 1963.

Johnston, Bruce: *Surfin' Round the World*, Sundazed, 1963, 1997.

Melcher, Terry: *Terry Melcher*, Reprise, 1974 • *Royal Flush*, RCA, 1976.

Parsons, Gene: *The Kindling Collection,* Sierra, 1994.

Revere, Paul, and the Raiders: *Here They Come,* Columbia, 1965 • "Just Like Me," Columbia, 1965 • "Steppin' Out," Columbia, 1965 • "Good Thing," Columbia, 1966 • "Hungry," Columbia, 1966 • *Just Like Us,* Columbia, 1966 • "Kicks," Columbia, 1966 • *Midnight Ride,* Columbia, 1966 • "The Great Airplane Strike," Columbia, 1966 • *A Christmas Present—and Past,* Columbia, 1967 • "Him or Me—What's It Gonna Be?," Columbia, 1967 • w/ Mark Lindsay, "I Had a Dream," Columbia, 1967 • "Peace of Mind," Columbia, 1967 • *Revolution!,* Sundazed, 1967, 1996 • *Spirit of '67,* Columbia, 1967 • "Ups and Downs," Columbia, 1967 • *All-Time Greatest Hits* (12 tracks), Columbia, 1972 • *The Legend of Paul Revere,* Legacy, 1990 • *The Essential Ride, 1963–1967,* Legacy, 1995.

Rip Chords: "Gone," Columbia, 1963 • "Here I Stand," Columbia, 1963 • "Hey Little Cobra," Columbia, 1963 • *Hey Little Cobra and Other Hot Rod Hits,* Columbia, 1964 • "Three Window Coupe," Columbia, 1964 • *Three Window Coupe,* Sundazed, 1964, 1996.

Rising Sons: *Rising Sons, Featuring Taj Mahal and Ry Cooder,* Legacy, 1992.

Daniel Miller

Daniel Miller is the most influential figure in the history of techno-pop. As artist (the Normal, Silicon Teens), founder and owner of Mute Records (and sublabels Blast First, NovaMute, the Grey Area), and producer (Depeche Mode, Yazoo, Fad Gadget), Miller has had a hand in many of the genre's finest moments.

Miller was born on February 14, 1951, in London and was attracted to the wild rock 'n' roll of Elvis Presley and Chuck Berry from a very early age. When he was 12 he got deeply into the Beatles, only to be disillusioned by what he felt to be their sellout record, "She Loves You." He gravitated toward the R&B-based rock of the Stones, the Who, and the Kinks, which in turn led him to the blues of John Mayall and John Lee Hooker.

Miller took up the guitar at around 12, and later the sax, but considers himself "a hopeless musician." In the early '70s he was turned on to the electronic music of German groups like Kraftwerk, Tangerine Dream, Neu, Faust, Amon Duul, Can, and the like, affectionately known as "Krautrock." Miller loved the possibilities for fresh sounds that electronics afforded, as well as the opportunities for nonmusicians. As punk unfolded in the mid-'70s, he even anticipated that the synthesizer would become its central instrument (which certainly became true of industrial and new wave, if not of punk itself).

Beginning to experiment with electronic music in punk's anarchic spirit, Miller bought a microphone and used it to treat his sax with effects, wresting tortured tones that God never intended from the unsuspecting instrument.

Meanwhile, in the real world, Miller attended film school and worked as a film editor. He kept up with new music as a club DJ from 1974 to 1976 and purchased a synthesizer when they became cheaper in the late '70s. On a summer trip to Greece, he read the car crash–sex novel *Crash* and was captivated by its premise that crashes are the final extension of pornography, as flesh and machine violently unite. He even wrote a screenplay based on the book, but when that went nowhere, he turned his attentions to creating a song that would evoke the imagery and tone of the book, "Warm Leatherette."

Released as the first single on his own Mute Records in 1978, "Leatherette" struck a postmodern chord and sold a remarkable 40,000 copies in the U.K. A rapid, thin electronic beat, synth braps, and a rising, falling two-note vamp support Miller's detached monotone recitation of an accident and its aftermath, culminating with the lines, "A tear of petrol is in your eye, / The handbrake penetrates your thigh, / Quick! let's make love / Before you die." The inorganic minimalism of the backing and Miller's dry tone drain the flesh and blood from the scene, leaving an icy erotic frisson.

After the unexpected success of the single, Miller signed Fad Gadget to Mute and entered a "real" studio, engineer Eric Radcliffe's Blackwing in London, for the first time. Miller felt self-conscious producing Gadget; he had never worked in front of anyone before. Perhaps in response, he created a phantom band, Silicon Teens, and recorded a burbling all-electronic album of classic rock 'n' roll songs, including "Memphis, Tennessee," "You Really Got Me," and "Judy in Disguise," aptly called *Music for Parties,* essentially wrapping up his career as an artist in 1980.

Keyboardists Vince Clarke and Andrew Fletcher had formed a new romantic band in the Basildon area of London in 1976 called No Romance in China, which evolved into Composition of Sound by 1979 when guitarist/keyboardist Martin Gore joined. The addition of singer David Gahan in 1980 completed the lineup, and the group's name was changed to Depeche Mode ("fast fashion" in French).

The group's key move was to forsake all nonelectronic instruments; around the clubs of London they gained a large following, attracted by their snappy dance beats and Clarke's insistent, memorable melodies. Miller saw Depeche live and signed them to Mute.

Their first single was "Dreaming of Me," whose proudly artificial opening beat and two-note "Close Encounters" synth beacon signaled the creation of techno-pop. The song's jaunty, mid-tempo tune is conveyed by Gahan's earnest Ringo-meets-Eno vocals and a plinking keyboard line, supported by whizzing synth washes and cheerful harmonies. A near-giddy cheerfulness underpins the whole affair. "Dreaming" reached the middle of the U.K. charts in spring 1981, followed almost immediately by a second single.

"New Life" jumps out of the box much more quickly, rushing at the listener with the urgency—cleverly augmented by a circumambulatory synth line—of "Complicating, circulating, new life," generating an image of greenish plasma coursing through incipient veins. "Life" shot to No. 11 in the U.K., the first of a remarkable 24 consecutive Top 30 hits in the U.K. for the band.

The third single, "Just Can't Get Enough" (No. 8 U.K.), was an even bigger hit, breaking the band in the U.S., where the song received ubiquitous airplay on modern rock stations like L.A.'s KROQ. An irresistible, bubbling synth line bounces in, joined by a synth bass, offset by an almost ska-like fricative on the upbeat, as Gahan sings Clarke's most enduring melody. A sunny classic.

On the strength of the three singles and a general melodic consistency, the album *Speak and Spell* hit No. 10 in the U.K. and charted in the U.S. Miller was suddenly a hit producer and Mute was the home of a new genre.

Then suddenly Clarke left Depeche to form Yazoo with singer Alison Moyet. The first Yazoo album, *Upstairs at Eric's* (as in Radcliffe) is another techno-pop landmark, showcasing Clarke's melodies and Moyet's dramatic, statuesque alto. Yazoo rose to No. 2 U.K. by mid-1982, with three more great singles, seemingly indicating that that Clarke had taken Depeche Mode's future with him.

Produced by Miller, Radcliffe, and Clarke, *Eric's* is highlighted by the brilliant synth ballad "Only You" (No. 2) and two dance classics: the throbbing "Don't Go" (No. 3 U.K.)—with Moyet wailing soul diva-style—and the shimmering, squirming "Situation." Yazoo would do one more album together, the self-produced *You and Me Both*, before Moyet went solo and Clarke formed Erasure with the Moyet soundalike Andy Bell.

In spite of general assumptions as to its imminent demise, Depeche carried on with Gore taking over the writing duties and Alan Wilder replacing Clarke on synths. Despite three more hit singles, *A Broken Frame* (No. 8) feels like a place-keeping effort, with Gore feeling around for his own voice, yet not wanting to stray too far from Clarke's successful sound.

Gore found that voice on two sensational singles in 1983, "Get the Balance Right" (No. 13 U.K.) and "Everything Counts" (No. 6 U.K.). "Balance" has a deeper, richer sound than earlier Depeche—much less rinky-tinky—and a darker tone and theme: pondering one's responsibility to the world and acknowledging that all actions have consequences. This change was akin to Bruce Springsteen's move from the adolescent summer of *Born to Run* to the young adult autumn of *Darkness on the Edge of Town*.

"Everything Counts" weaves sonically within a carnivalesque setting between the queasy dark of the funhouse and the cotton-candy light of the carousel, while the lyrics question the ethics of materialism. Albums *Construction Time Again* (No. 6 U.K.) and *Some Great Reward* (No. 5 U.K., with Gareth Jones added to the production crew; see entry) continued the shift toward introspection and deeper, darker music. "People Are People" (No. 13) reached an industrial-like clanging murkiness, making the fact that it was the band's first U.S. pop hit all the more noteworthy.

Miller is extremely proud of his work with the band. "We were all learning at the same time, and there was a really steep learning curve. Eric [engineer Radcliffe] helped us to become more creative with samplers and synthesizers. We felt that we were pretty much on the cutting edge of electronic music at the time. We were making records that sounded really different, and that, combined with very strong songs and great live performances, was very exciting."

While this was unfolding, Miller became more and more absorbed in running his label. What started as a vehicle for his own electronic noodlings became one of the most successful indie labels in the U.K. with a roster that has included—in addition to the aforementioned acts—Nick Cave and the Bad Seeds, Cabaret Voltaire, Einsturzende Neubauten, Inspiral Carpets, Moby, Nitzer Ebb, Renegade Soundwave, Sonic Youth, Throbbing Gristle, Wire, and many others. By the time of Depeche's *Black Celebration* (No. 4 U.K.) in 1986, Miller was a label owner trying to find the time to produce.

"*Black Celebration* wasn't an easy record to make," says Miller. "At the end of it we all said, 'I think we should get somebody else to produce.' I remember when the sessions for *Music for the Masses* (No. 10 U.K.) started with Dave Bascombe [see entry]; I went down to the studio to see how it was going on the first day, and when I left the studio I felt elated that I was no longer responsible for making the record." —ERIC OLSEN AND DAVID JOHN FARINELLA

Can: *Sacrilege: The Remixes,* Mute, 1997.

Depeche Mode: "Dreaming of Me," Sire, 1981, 1991 • "Just Can't Get Enough," Sire, 1981, 1991 • "New Life," Sire, 1981, 1991 • *Speak and Spell,* Sire, 1981 • *A Broken Frame,* Sire, 1982 • "Leave in Silence," Sire, 1982, 1991 • "See You," Sire, 1982, 1991 • "The Meaning of Love," Sire, 1982, 1991 • *Construction Time Again,* Sire, 1983 • "Everything Counts," Sire, 1983 • "Get the Balance Right," Sire, 1983, 1991 • "Love in Itself," Sire, 1983, 1991 • "Blasphemous Rumours," Sire, 1984, 1991 • "Master and Servant," Sire, 1984 • "People Are People," Sire, 1984 • *People Are People,* Sire, 1984 • *Some Great Reward,* Sire, 1984 • *Catching Up With,* Sire, 1985 • "Fly on the Windscreen," Sire, 1985, 1991 • "It's Called a Heart," Sire, 1985, 1991 • "Shake the Disease," Sire, 1985, 1991 • *The Singles, '81–'85,* Mute, 1985 • "A Question of Lust," Sire, 1986, 1991 • "A Question of Time," Sire, 1986, 1991 • *Black Celebration,* Sire, 1986, 1991 • "Stripped," Sire, 1986, 1991 • *Music for the Masses,* Sire, 1987 • "Never Let Me Down Again," Sire, 1987.

Erasure: "Victim of Love" (remix), Mute/Sire, 1987 • "Star" (remix), Atlantic, 1990 • "Breath of Life" (remix), Sire/Reprise, 1992.

House of Love: *Spy in the House of Love,* Fontana, 1991.

I Start Counting: *Catalogue,* Mute, 1991 • "Still Smiling," Mute, 1991.

Khan, Chaka: *Life Is a Dance (The Remix Project),* Warner Bros., 1989.

Moyet, Alison: *Singles,* Columbia, 1995.

Nitzer Ebb: "Let Your Body Learn" (remix), Geffen, 1987 • "Lightning Man" (remix), Geffen, 1990.

Normal, The: "Warm Leatherette/T.V.O.D.," Mute, 1978, 1997.

Pere Ubu: *Cloudland* (1 track), Fontana, 1989.

Recoil: "Faith Healer" (remix), Sire/Reprise, 1992.

Rental, Robert, and the Normal: *Live at the West Runton Pavillion,* Rough Trade, 1981.

Silicon Teens: *Music for Parties,* Mute/Sire, 1980.

Tovey, Frank: *Snakes and Ladders,* Sire, 1986 • *The Fad Gadget Singles,* Sire, 1987.

Wire: *The A List: 1985–1990,* Mute, 1993.

Yazoo: "Don't Go," Mute/Sire, 1982 • "Only You," Mute/Sire, 1982 • "Situation," Mute/Sire, 1982 • *Upstairs at Eric's,* Mute/Sire, 1982 • "Nobody's Diary," Mute, 1996.

COLLECTIONS

Homage to Neu, Cleopatra, 1998.

Jimmy Miller

Jimmy Miller represented the cinema verité style of record production that reached its zenith in the late '60s and early '70s: Set up the microphones and capture a performance.

Miller, producer of classic albums by Traffic, Blind Faith, Spooky Tooth, and the Rolling Stones, was an American who achieved his greatest fame in Britain. He emigrated in 1966 just in time to see the English reaction to the psychedelia and pop experimentation that blossomed in San Francisco. Miller's first successes came in 1966 and 1967 with two classic singles by the Spencer Davis Group, the British blue-eyed soul band fronted by child prodigy Steve Winwood: "Gimme Some Lovin' " (No. 7) and "I'm a Man" (No. 10).

When Winwood bolted the band to form Traffic, Miller followed Winwood's muse, capturing the essence of the flower-power era with such tracks as "Dear Mr. Fantasy," "Forty Thousand Headmen," "Pearly Queen," and Dave Mason's "Feelin' Alright."

In 1968 Miller was tapped by the Rolling Stones to produce the single "Jumpin' Jack Flash" (No. 3), a magnificent song that rejuvenated the Stones after the debacle of *Their Satanic Majesties Request.* Miller followed that single with an equally fine album, *Beggars Banquet* (No. 5). Featuring Mick Jagger's spirited "Sympathy for the Devil" and the leering "Stray Cat Blues," the album was the harbinger of even greater things to come.

Between 1969 and 1973, with Miller along for the ride as producer, the Stones released a series of albums that defined rock 'n' roll at the time: *Let It Bleed* (No. 3), *Get Yer Ya-Yas Out* (No. 6), *Sticky Fingers* (No. 1), and *Exile on Main Street* (No. 1).

Miller's exact role in spawning such tracks as "Gimme Shelter," "Midnight Rambler," Brown Sugar" (No. 1), "Tumbling Dice" (No. 7), "Can't You Hear Me Knocking?," "Happy," and "Wild Horses" is unclear. In any case, Miller's bohemian spirit likely contributed to a relaxed feel in the studio, a key element of the Stones' modus operandi.

Miller's other productions during this era include Blind Faith's lone album, *Blind Faith* (No. 1); Spooky Tooth's moody *Spooky Two,* and Delaney and Bonnie and Friends' magic bus ride around Britain, *On Tour with Eric Clapton.*

Miller's fortunes rose and fell, much like a shooting star, when rock 'n' roll grew into an industry, leaving Miller, the quintessential free spirit, high and dry. Yet in the '80s and '90s he was involved with vital music from Motorhead, the Plasmatics, Johnny Thunders, the Wedding Present, and Primal Scream. Miller died in October 1994. He was 52. —BEN CROMER

Beck, Jeff: *Beckology*, Legacy/Epic, 1991, 1995.

Blind Faith: *Blind Faith*, Atlantic, 1969.

Capaldi, Jim: *The Contender* (1 track), Polydor, 1978.

Clapton, Eric: *Crossroads*, Polydor, 1988.

Delaney and Bonnie: *On Tour with Eric Clapton*, Atlantic, 1970 • *The Best Of*, Rhino, 1972, 1990.

Dripping Lips: *Ready to Crack?*, Alive, 1998.

Falcon, Billy: *Falcon Around*, MCA, 1980.

Family: *Music in a Doll's House*, See for Miles, 1968.

Gibbons, Steve: *Short Stories*, Wizard, 1971.

Ginger Baker's Air Force: *Ginger Baker's Air Force*, Polydor, 1970.

Kracker: *Kracker Brand*, RSR, 1973.

Motorhead: *Bomber*, Castle, 1979, 1996 • *Overkill*, Bronze, 1979 • *All the Aces*, Castle, 1995 • *The Best of Motorhead*, Vol. 2, Roadrunner, 1995.

Move, The: *The Best Of*, A&M, 1974.

Ocean Colour Scene: *Ocean Colour Scene*, Fontana, 1992.

Plasmatics: *New Hope for the Wretched*, Stiff, 1980.

Price, Jim: *Kids Nowadays Ain't Got No Shame*, A&M, 1971.

Primal Scream: "Movin' On Up," Sire/WB, 1991 • *Screamadelica* (2 tracks), Sire/WB, 1991.

Rolling Stones, The: *Beggars Banquet*, Decca/London, 1968 • "Jumpin' Jack Flash," London, 1968 • "Street Fightin' Man," London, 1968 • "Honky Tonk Woman," London, 1969 • *Let It Bleed*, Decca/London, 1969 • *Through the Past, Darkly (Big Hits Vol. 2)*, Abkco, 1969 • "You Can't Always Get What You Want," London, 1969 • "Brown Sugar," Rolling Stones, 1971 • *Sticky Fingers*, Rolling Stones, 1971 • "Wild Horses," Rolling Stones, 1971 • *Exile on Main Street*, Rolling Stones, 1972 • "Happy," Rolling Stones, 1972 • *Hot Rocks, 1964–1971*, London, 1972, 1995 • *More Hot Rocks (Big Hits and Fazed Cookies)*, Abkco, 1972 • "Tumbling Dice," Rolling Stones, 1972 • "Angie," Rolling Stones, 1973 • *Goat's Head Soup*, Rolling Stones, 1973 • "Doo Doo Doo Doo Doo (Heartbreaker)," Rolling Stones, 1974 • *Made in the Shade*, Columbia, 1975 • *Metamorphosis*, Decca/ABK, 1975 • *Singles Collection: The London Years*, Abkco, 1989 • *The Rolling Stones Rock and Roll Circus*, Abkco, 1996.

Savage Rose: *Refugee*, RCA, 1972.

Sky: *Don't Hold Back*, RCA, 1971 • *Sailor's Delight*, RCA, 1979.

Spencer Davis Group: "Gimme Some Lovin'," United Artists, 1966, 1970 (*Progressive Heavies*) • "I'm a Man," United Artists, 1967, 1970 (*Progressive Heavies*) • *Gimme Some Lovin'*, CEMA, 1967, 1992 • *Best of the Spencer Davis Group*, Gold Rush, 1996.

Spooky Tooth: *It's All About*, Island, 1968 • *Spooky Two*, Island, 1969 • *Tobacco Road*, A&M, 1971 • *The Best Of*, Island, 1976.

Thunders, Johnny: *In Cold Blood*, Castle, 1983, 1997 • *Too Much Junkie Business*, ROIR, 1983 • *Diary of a Lover*, PVC, 1984.

Traffic: *Mr. Fantasy*, Island/United Artists, 1967 • *Traffic*, Island/United Artists, 1968 • *Last Exit*, Island/United Artists, 1969 • "Dear Mr. Fantasy," United Artists, 1970 (*Progressive Heavies*) • "Feelin' Alright," United Artists, 1970 (*Progressive Heavies*) • "Forty Thousand Headmen," United Artists, 1970 (*Progressive Heavies*).

Trapeze: *Hold On*, Aura/Paid, 1979.

Uriah Heep: *A Time of Revelation*, Castle, 1996.

Wedding Present: *Hit Parade 2*, First Warning, 1993.

Whitlock, Bobby: *Bobby Whitlock* (1 track), Columbia, 1972 • *Raw Velvet*, Columbia, 1972.

Winwood, Steve: *Finer Things*, Island, 1995.

COLLECTIONS

Boston Gets Stoned, Botown, 1993.

Marcus Miller

Marcus Miller is an incredibly diverse musician who views that very quality as both curse and opportunity. "My greatest gift and my worst problem is the same: diversity," says Miller, who has worked with artists as varied as Miles Davis, Luther Vandross, Boz Scaggs, and E.U. (the Washington, D.C., go-go band that hit big with "Da' Butt" from Spike Lee's *School Daze* film).

While best known as a bass player—Miller was a seminal figure in the Miles Davis band of the early '80s—he also is a producer. Miller has lent his talents behind the board not only to Davis but also to David Sanborn, Vandross, the Temptations, and Lonnie Liston Smith. He also produces his own albums and has a studio in his home.

Born June 14, 1959, in Brooklyn, Miller grew up in Jamaica, Queens. He attended the High School of Music and Art, where his classmates included drummers Kenny Washington and Omar Hakim. Miller started his musical career on clarinet at age 10 but picked up the bass three years later. "I didn't switch," says Miller, "I just added bass because I wanted to play in the dance bands in my neighborhood and the clarinet wasn't cutting it."

After high school, he decided to focus on bass because he saw more opportunity there, but he continued to play clarinet while at Queens College in the mid-'70s. In 1977, he began playing bass on commercial sessions; his first major outing was on *Big City,* a record drummer Lenny White released on the Atlantic subsidiary, Nemperor.

By his early twenties, Miller was a professional, working on fusion records, jazz records, even disco. Among discs he's contributed to are ones by Donald Fagen, Tom Browne, David Liebman, Tom Scott, the Crusaders, Michael Urbaniak, and Lisa Fischer. "As a session guy I was doing a lot of fusion, a lot of R&B, some disco," he recalls. "Eventually, I got into the house band on *Saturday Night Live*; it was 1979 or 1980, Eddie Murphy's first year." He met Sanborn in that band; he also met Vandross around that time. On the weekends, he'd work in Roberta Flack's group.

"Eventually, Miles called me, based on hearing my name around New York City," Miller says. The year was 1981. Working with Davis freed Miller up considerably. Not only did he perform on such later Columbia records by Davis as *Man with the Horn, We Want Miles,* and *Star People* (among Davis's most "pop" productions); Miller also produced two Davis albums for Warner Bros.: *Tutu* and *Amandla.*

While he was doing well professionally before joining Davis, Miller didn't feel he was expressing himself completely. "I didn't feel like I was playing toward my strength," he says. "Working with Miles gave me so much freedom as a composer."

Before he produced the two Warner Bros. albums for Davis, he produced his own Warner Bros. discs: *Suddenly* in 1981, and *Marcus Miller* in 1983. By the time he was ready to do a third, the company had changed, so he left. Since leaving Warner, Miller has released three solo albums: *Tales, The Sun Don't Lie,* and a live disc. All these discs are on PRA (GRP rereleased the last), a label Miller formed to release his work. PRA also manages Miller, Sanborn, and keyboardist Joe Sample.

Although he's played all kinds of music, his firmest grounding remains jazz, says Miller. "To me, jazz started out as the hippest music ever created, and when it was in its heyday, it represented what was going on in the street. At a certain point in the '40s, jazz was the voice of black America, the music people danced to, partied to, and listened to for inspiration."

But rock 'n' roll came along, shouldering jazz aside. A genre based on rhythm supplanted one based on melody, Miller says. "Now, jazz has a hard time, so mainstream listeners have had a hard time," he says. "When my mother listened to jazz, it wasn't a stretch. She knew all the songs because she was hearing them on the radio, so she could really appreciate the different treatments jazz offered them. You didn't have to go to school to learn the rules."

Rock separated jazz from the mainstream, and the jazz musician has had a hard time reconnecting; fusion, in the '70s, made a strong attempt in the hands of such musicians as Chick Corea, Herbie Hancock, and John McLaughlin. But when lesser musicians capitalized on fusion's most prominent facets—volume and technique—the music was diluted. "I came up in that fusion era, and I've been trying to find new ways to connect jazz to pop music and keep that same original spirit," Miller says. "I still get excited by new rhythms I hear in the street, in the same way Miles and Bird did. In the beginning, people were dancing to bebop—until the intellectual side grew and overpowered it."

He likes to keep his music immediate, his productions vivid. "In the '80s," he says, "technology played a bigger part. Not only did I write music on computer, a lot of the drums were computer-generated. Now I use computers more as a tool: to write the songs, in preproduction, and to store information. I use them in postproduction to splice takes together, maybe tune up a vocal if it needs help.

"I've been playing bass and producing and doing movies (among his soundtracks: *The Great White Hype, The 6th Man, Bebe's Kids,* and *Siesta*) and writing songs," Miller says. "I've been pretty spread out. That's basically the way I work best: I like to have a lot of things going on. The downside is, my development in each area is probably slower than it would be if I concentrated on one," he adds. "If it looks like I'm pretty low-profile on the producer tip, it's because for the past couple of years, I've been out on the road with my band, developing my solo career. Before that, people hadn't seen me play the bass in years because I was producing. I'm just trying to find that balance." —CARLO WOLFF

Cactus Brothers: *The Cactus Brothers,* Capitol, 1993.
Cole, Natalie: *Everlasting,* Manhattan/Elektra, 1987, 1991 • "When I Fall in Love," EMI, 1988.
Crusaders, The: *Healing the Wounds,* GRP, 1991.
Davis, Miles: *Tutu,* Warner Bros., 1986 • *Siesta,* Warner Bros., 1987 • *Amandla,* Warner Bros., 1989.
E.U.: "Da' Butt," Manhattan/EMI, 1988 (*School Daze* soundtrack) • *Livin' Large* (1 track), Virgin, 1989.
Faithfull, Marianne: *Faithfull: A Collection of Her Best Recordings,* Island, 1994.
Flack, Roberta: "Oasis," Atlantic, 1988 • *Softly with These Songs: The Best Of,* Atlantic, 1993.
France: *France,* WEA, 1996.
Hollywood Beyond: *If,* Warner Bros., 1987.
Jamaica Boys: "(It's That) Lovin' Feeling," Warner Bros.,

1987 • "Spend Some Time With Me," Warner Bros., 1988 • *J-Boys*, Reprise, 1989 • "Pick Up the Phone," Reprise, 1990 • "Shake It Up!," Reprise, 1990.

Jarreau, Al: *Tenderness*, Reprise, 1994.

Jordan, Stanley: *Cornucopia*, Blue Note, 1990.

Khan, Chaka: "I Want," Warner Bros., 1992 • *The Woman I Am*, Warner Bros., 1992.

Miller, Marcus: *Suddenly*, Warner Bros., 1981 • "Lovin' You," Warner Bros., 1983 • *Marcus Miller*, Warner Bros., 1983 • *The Sun Don't Lie*, PRA, 1993 • *Tales*, PRA, 1995 • *Live and More*, GRP, 1998.

Najee: *Just an Illusion*, EMI America, 1992.

Sanborn, David: *Backstreet*, Warner Bros., 1983 • *Straight to the Heart*, Warner Bros., 1984 • "Love and Happiness," Warner Bros., 1985 • *Change of Heart*, Warner Bros., 1987 • "Chicago Song," Warner Bros., 1987 • *Close-Up*, Reprise, 1988 • *Love Songs*, Warner Bros., 1988 • "Slam," Reprise, 1988 • *Another Hand*, Elektra, 1991 • *Upfront*, Elektra, 1992 • "Got to Give It Up," Elektra, 1994 • *Hearsay*, Elektra, 1994 • *The Best Of*, Warner Bros., 1994.

Shorter, Wayne: *High Life*, Verve, 1995.

Smith, Lonnie Liston: *Dreams of Tomorrow*, Doctor Jazz, 1979, 1983.

Temptations, The: "Do You Really Love Your Baby?," Gordy, 1985 • *Emperors of Soul*, Motown, 1994.

Vandross, Luther: *Busy Body*, Epic, 1983 • "It's Over Now," Epic, 1985 • *The Night I Fell in Love* (3 tracks), Epic, 1985 • " 'Til My Baby Comes Home," Epic, 1985 • *Give Me the Reason*, Epic, 1986 • "Stop to Love," Epic, 1986 • "I Really Didn't Mean It," Epic, 1987 • "So Amazing," Epic, 1987 • w/ Gregory Hines, "There's Nothing Better Than Love," Epic, 1987 • "Any Love," Epic, 1988 • *Any Love*, Epic, 1988 • "She Won't Talk to Me," Epic, 1988 • "Here and Now," Epic, 1989 • *The Best of Luther Vandross: The Best of Love*, Epic, 1989 • "Treat You Right," Epic, 1990 • "Don't Want to Be a Fool," Epic, 1991 • "Power of Love," Epic, 1991 • *Power of Love*, Epic, 1991 • "Sometimes It's Only Love," Epic, 1992 • "The Rush," Epic, 1992 • "Heaven Knows," LV/Epic, 1993 • "Little Miracles (Happen Everyday)," LV/Epic, 1993 • "Never Let Me Go," LV/Epic, 1993 • *Never Let Me Go*, Epic, 1993 • *Your Secret Love*, Epic, 1996 • "I Can Make It Better," LV/Epic, 1997 • *One Night With You: The Best of Love*, Vol. 2, Sony, 1997 • *I Know*, Virgin, 1998.

Washington Jr., Grover: "Summer Nights," Columbia, 1987 • *Strawberry Moon*, Columbia, 1990.

Wright, Bernard: "Who Do You Love?," EMI, 1985.

COLLECTIONS

For Our Children Too, Rhino, 1996.

Mitch Miller

Mitch Miller is a classically trained oboist who became an arranger, conductor, producer, and one of the most popular recording artists of the '50s and '60s. As musical director and producer at Mercury and then at Columbia, he nurtured and produced Tony Bennett, Rosemary Clooney, Frankie Laine, Johnny Mathis, Guy Mitchell, Johnny Ray, Marty Robbins, Frank Sinatra, and countless others.

Miller was born July 4, 1911, in Rochester, New York, and played piano from age 6, oboe from age 12. After graduating from the Eastman School of Music, he played with orchestras in the Rochester area and then became a soloist with the CBS Symphony from 1936 to 1947.

In the late '40s he headed Mercury Records' popular music department, where his biggest success came with Frankie Laine, including "That Lucky Old Sun," "Mule Train," and "The Cry of the Wild Goose" (all No. 1). He switched to Columbia in 1950, where he led the country crossover revolution, having popular artists such as Tony Bennett ("Cold, Cold Heart," No. 1), Rosemary Clooney ("Half As Much," No. 1), Guy Mitchell ("Singing the Blues," No. 1), Jo Stafford ("Jambalaya," No. 3), and Joan Weber ("Let Me Go Lover," No. 1) record rearranged country songs. He also returned the favor by leading country singer Marty Robbins into the pop market ("A White Sport Coat and a Pink Carnation," No. 2).

Starting in 1950 Miller began recording with his own orchestra and singers, hitting No. 1 with "The Yellow Rose of Texas" single, and with albums *Sing Along with Mitch*, *Christmas Sing Along with Mitch*, and *Holiday Sing Along with Mitch*. He also hosted the popular *Sing Along with Mitch* TV show from 1961 to 1964.

Miller's antipathy to rock 'n' roll is legendary (he refused to sign Buddy Holly to Columbia), feeling it to be "unmusical." He is unapologetic to this day—dismissing even the Beatles' music as cobbled together in the studio—and still feisty as ever. Dennis Diken and Paul Verna conducted the following interview (pages 538–539).

Bennett, Tony: "Because of You," Columbia, 1951 • "Cold, Cold Heart," Columbia, 1951 • "Rags to Riches," Columbia, 1953 • w/ Count Basie, *In Person!*, Master Sound/Legacy, 1959, 1994 • *40 Years: The Artistry of Tony Bennett*, Columbia, 1991, 1997.

Dennis Diken: You've said that producers in the '40s and '50s were a different breed from today's producers. How so?

Mitch Miller: Well, in the '40s and '50s they had to be a

different breed because when you were through with the record, there was nothing you could do with it. It had to go right to the plant because there was no editing. It was direct to disc. If you wanted to change one thing, you had to do the whole side over again. So you weren't able to save some great performances that you only needed maybe four bars of. You had to know how to balance. There was no such thing as a remix. You had to know how to talk to the engineer. You had to have a good engineer. You had to have musicians who could play on the first day because many times that was it. You had to have arrangers who'd knew what they were doing like Percy Faith and Paul Weston and Ray Conniff. The artists came in prepared. The standard was four 10-inch sides per session, so we'd do four 3 1/2-minute songs in three hours.

And so the producers, like Jack Kapp, he could go do Louis Armstrong or Guy Lombardo or Ella Fitzgerald. Paul Weston could do it. Percy Faith could do it. Actually, I could do it, because we knew what we were talking about. It wasn't, "Let's see what we'll do tomorrow while we listen tonight," because it was impossible to do, therefore the people who made the product had to know every angle in the business, and that's why some of these records that we made sound better than the CDs today, because you had perspective, you have everything on them. And the engineering is just fantastic. We had no limiters in those days.

DD: How much preparation did you do before a session? Did you rehearse with the artists?

MM: Sometimes, but not always. I had only people who could take directions. I didn't have any cripples. I mean, Jerry Wexler [see entry] could take groups who couldn't perform. He'd work with them for a month or two on three sides and get it absolutely sensational. I couldn't do it. First place, I didn't have the patience, and second place, I had too many artists to take care of. And so, the artists started with the way they were chosen because if you look at it now, the only people who have long lives, 40 or 50 years later, were on Columbia and I chose them: Rosie Clooney, Vic Damone, Johnny Mathis, Tony Bennett, Frankie Laine if he were singing to me, Percy Faith if he were alive, Erroll Garner, the Four Lads, Johnnie Ray, Jo Stafford. I just inherited [Jo] from Capitol—her manager brought her over—but she never, never had a hit record till she came to Columbia. Then she had "Jambalaya," "You Belong to Me." She had one after the other.

DD: Those artists, did you scout them yourself?

MM: Oh, sure. Somebody would tell me about them, I'd listen to them, and I could tell in three minutes whether I wanted to record them. There was Lena Horne. All the artists on Colum-

bia have lasted; they all had their trademarks. Nobody has to tell you who they are. Two bars, you know who they are.

If you listen to Vic Damone, when I first started recording Vic Damone he was a Frank Sinatra clone, and you can't blame him. There were [many] guys imitating the king, but they had qualities that they weren't bringing out. But you'll notice that every hit record that Vic Damone had simply does not sound like Frank Sinatra. Those are the things that the producer has to do at the moment when it's happening, or else it's gone. Now they have a thousand chances.

Back then when you were in a studio and the musicians were in there and you knew that that was it, there was an interaction that went on. You couldn't explain it; you only knew when it wasn't there. Now these multiple tracks where many people don't even see each other, meet each other, you know it's not there. Every note is there, it's homogenized, carpenterized, and structured. Nobody's risking anything.

Paul Verna: And they're deferring all the decisions till later instead of making them on the spot.

MM: They're not smart enough to make them on the spot! They're deferring, they don't know what to do. They say, "We'll listen and come back tomorrow."

PV: It's ironic that you say that, because you were a pioneer in overdubbing and using acetates or tapes to create something that wasn't immediate or wasn't live.

MM: Yes, but I didn't whip it to death. I used it as a tool. You must remember, all these things if used as a tool are one thing, if used as a crutch are totally maddening.

PV: Are there any records that are layered and overdubbed that you do like?

MM: Well, I don't listen that much because, you see, all these people are manufactured. This is no condemnation or criticism of, for instance, Whitney Houston. You know she's a great singer, but you know everything she does is planned. It's laid out there. When I recorded Mahalia Jackson, here she was with her grapes and a piano player playing the piano or organ in the studio all alone and the short hairs would stand up on your back because every time she'd sing a song, it was different. Or Duke Ellington, when he was creating something right in the studio. His way of arranging was, he would hardly ever write anything out. He would say, 'Try this, try that,' and boom, you had a piece. He was fabulous.

PV: What do you think of the CD as a medium?

MM: Anything that brings a listener into the process, that makes them experience what's going on to a greater degree, is a plus.

DD: Were there any records that came out after the '50s, talking about a multitrack recording, that excited you in any way because it was multitracked?

MM: Les Paul [see entry]. But Les would be the first to tell you I was the first to do multitrack.

DD: What were your impressions of the impact of tape when it was first introduced.

MM: My first impression was that it was a fabulous tool. No matter what it was, a symphony, jazz, or whatever, if you had a performance that had a big hunk of a great interpretation on it and you couldn't use it because something happened technically—the microphone could have made a noise or the balance wasn't right later in the piece—you could save it and go from there on. See, that's using it as a tool. You do that right at the moment. When you're through that night or that afternoon, you could send it to a factory. Whereas now, they worry each other. I call it music onanism.

The ones who make the most money on all these albums are the people in the editing rooms. They're there for years! Try this, try that. And then at the end you play what they had before and what they have after and there's hardly any difference anyway. I've been in studios where they have four, five mikes on the drum set. What's going on? The ear doesn't listen that way. Then they have to put it on the track, then they have to try this, then they have to sweeten it, then they have to add a voice. They'll try anything, and at the end, an album that should have cost maybe with today's prices, $75,000 or $100,000, ends up costing $2 million, most of which went to the editing room, and you'll find on nine tenths of these albums, most of these musicians never met each other.

DD: How many mikes did you put on the drums?

MM: Just one above, and then you didn't open it unless you needed it. It was there in case you needed it.

DD: If you heard an artist today that you really dug, would you want to go into the studio and produce your way? Would you still have that desire to do that?

MM: Yes, but that's a big "if," because how many record companies would do it, how many record companies would back you? It's a whole different thing now. It's a joke. There's a hall, 20 vice presidents, what the fuck do they do? I mean, what is it to make a record? This one's in charge of this, this one's in charge of that, then suddenly they realize. . . . A lot of them are being fired now.

DD: What do you think of the producer/engineer school?

MM: I'll judge a producer only who went in and got it. That's a producer.

DD: What about a producer that would cut a music track complete and then overdub the vocalist?

MM: Wrong! Why should it be artificial? See, they don't have anyone who can make a decision, boom, like that. It's like Michael Jordan with basketball. He makes the basket or he doesn't. And they want 20 chances to make the basket . . . .

PV: Looking back, is there anybody you didn't get to work with that you would have liked to work with?

MM: Oh, sure. Somebody like Ella [Fitzgerald]. Just to capture her, not to tell her what to do. I did tell Norman [Granz, Verve Records founder and producer; see entry] what to tell her. And you'll notice, if you play the Rodgers and Hart album, I said, 'Norman, tell her to sing exactly the way she does, but to sing the song to a special person in her life when she's in the studio.' That's all.

DD: What did you think of the Beatles when they first hit?

MM: See, I only look at quality, and . . . when you listen closely, you hear the edits, the different tempos. They couldn't even keep a tempo.

DD: The Columbia studio on 30th Street that was in operation during the '50s and early '60s was built in an old church. I've noticed on Columbia records from that studio that there was a unique reverb sound. You could identify a Columbia record by the reverb sound.

MM: Yes, [it was] natural. But it was very tough. You had to know your business to work in there because you made that reverb work for you.

DD: Was that a chamber?

MM: No, sometimes a touch of chamber, but it was the room. We had curtains where if we wanted certain areas to be less reverbant we'd pull the curtains. No rock 'n' roll groups wanted to use that studio because balance means nothing to them in the studio. They're each in their little enclosure, so there's no leakage—and even then it's all dry so they add the reverb later on.

DD: Did you have plate reverb there as well?

MM: No. The first reverb I worked with was Bob Fine at Mercury Records. I came to Bob and I said to him, 'Bob, all the records I've ever heard, the voice sounds like it's coming through a hunk of cotton. There's no halo around it. You've gotta put a halo around the voice.' He was a genius, so the first thing he did—this was at the old Reeves Studio, in the Beaux Arts building—he put a loudspeaker in the toilet, put a mike there, and he took the signal from the studio, then just cracked the mike in the toilet and put them together. It came out on the record, but nobody knew how it was done. This is those early Mercury records.

PV: What is a typical workweek for you now? Do you play, do you arrange, do you produce?

MM: I don't produce any records because I can't work that way. What I do is mostly the conducting. The Boston Pops, all of the major symphony orchestras, the London Symphony. You see, I brought the same ideas that I use in classical music to pop music. All it is, is striving for excellence.

—DENNIS DIKEN AND PAUL VERNA

Boyd, Jimmy: "I Saw Mommy Kissing Santa Claus," Columbia, 1952.

Clooney, Rosemary: "Beautiful Brown Eyes," Columbia, 1951 • "Come On-a My House," Columbia, 1951 • "Half As Much," Columbia, 1952 • w/ Marlene Dietrich, "Too Old to Cut the Mustard," Columbia, 1952.

Day, Doris: "A Guy Is a Guy," Columbia, 1952 • "Secret Love,' Columbia, 1953 • "Whatever Will Be, Will Be (Que Sera, Sera)," Columbia, 1953.

Dietrich, Marlene: *The Cosmopolitan Marlene Dietrich*, Legacy, 1993, 1997.

Four Lads, The: "Moments to Remember," Columbia, 1955 • "No, Not Much," Columbia, 1956 • "Standing on the Corner," Columbia,1956.

Laine, Frankie: "Mule Train," Mercury, 1949 • "That Lucky Old Sun," Mercury, 1949 • "Cry of the Wild Goose," Mercury, 1950 • "Jezebel," Columbia, 1951 • "Rose, Rose, I Love You," Columbia, 1951 • "Blowing Wild," Columbia, 1953 • "I Believe," Columbia, 1953 • "I'm Just a Poor Bachelor," Columbia, 1953 • *On the Trail,* Bear Family, 1990 • *The Frankie Laine Collection: The Mercury Years,* Mercury, 1991 • *On the Trail Again,* Bear Family, 1992.

Mathis, Johnny: *Johnny's Greatest Hits,* Columbia, 1958 • *Good Night, Dear Lord,* Columbia, 1959, 1994 • *Heavenly,* Columbia, 1959 • *Open Fire, Two Guitars,* Columbia, 1959, 1995 • *Love Songs,* Columbia, 1988 • *Music of Johnny Mathis: A Personal Collection,* Legacy/Columbia, 1995 • *The Ultimate Hits Collection,* Columbia, 1998.

Miller, Mitch: *Mitch Miller,* Columbia, 1952.

Miller, Mitch, and His Orchestra and Chorus: "Tzena, Tzena, Tzena," Columbia, 1950 • "Meet Mister Callaghan," Columbia, 1952 • "Napoleon," Columbia, 1954 • "The Yellow Rose of Texas," Columbia, 1955 • "Lisbon Antigua (in Old Lisbon)," Columbia, 1956 • "Theme Song (from 'Song for a Summer Night')," Columbia, 1956 • "March from the River Kwai and Colonel Bogey," Columbia, 1958 • "The Children's Marching Song (Nick Nack Paddy Whack)," Columbia, 1959.

Miller, Mitch, and the Gang: *Christmas Sing Along with Mitch,* Columbia, 1958 • *More Sing Along with Mitch,* Columbia, 1958 • *Sing Along with Mitch,* Columbia, 1958 • *Folk Songs Sing Along with Mitch,* Columbia, 1959 • *Party Sing Along with Mitch,* Columbia, 1959 • *Still More Sing Along with Mitch,* Columbia, 1959 • *Fireside Sing Along with Mitch,* Columbia, 1960 • *March Along with Mitch,* Columbia, 1960 • *Memories Sing Along with Mitch,* Columbia, 1960 • *Saturday Night Sing Along with Mitch,* Columbia, 1960 • *Sentimental Sing Along with Mitch,* Columbia, 1960 • *Happy Times! Sing Along with Mitch,* Columbia, 1961 • *Holiday Sing Along with Mitch,* Columbia, 1961 • *Mitch's Greatest Hits,* Columbia, 1961 • *TV Sing Along with Mitch,* Columbia, 1961 • *Your Request Sing Along with Mitch,* Columbia, 1961 • *Family Sing Along with Mitch,* Columbia, 1962 • *Rhythm Sing Along with Mitch,* Columbia, 1962 • *Peace Sing-Along,* Atlantic, 1970 • *34 All Time Great Sing Along Selections,* Columbia, 1988 • *16 Most Requested Songs,* Legacy, 1989 • *Favorite Irish Sing-Alongs,* Legacy, 1992.

Mitchell, Guy: "My Heart Cries for You," Columbia, 1950 • "My Truly, Truly Fair," Columbia, 1951 • "Singing the Blues," Columbia, 1956 • "Knee Deep in the Blues," Columbia, 1957 • "Heartaches by the Number," Columbia, 1959 • *Heartaches by the Number,* Bear Family, 1970.

Page, Patti: "Money, Marbles and Chalk," Mercury, 1949.

Patti Page Quartet: "With My Eyes Wide Open I'm Dreaming," Mercury, 1949.

Ray, Johnnie "Cry," Okeh, 1951 • *Cry,* Intercontinental, 1990, 1996 • "Just Walking in the Rain," Columbia, 1956.

Robbins, Marty: "A White Sport Coat and a Pink Carnation," Columbia, 1957 • "She Was Only Seventeen," Columbia, 1957 • "The Story of My Life," Columbia, 1957 • *A Lifetime of Song, 1951–1982,* CBS, 1983 • *Country, 1951–1958,* Bear Family, 1991 • *Ruby Ann: Rockin' Rollin' Robbins, Vol. 3,* Bear Family, 1991 • *The Story of My Life: The Best of Marty Robbins, 1952–1965,* Legacy, 1996.

Sinatra, Frank: "American Beauty Rose," Columbia, 1950 • "Goodnight Irene," Columbia, 1950 • w/ Dagmar, "Mama Will Bark," Columbia, 1951 • "Bim Bam Baby," Columbia, 1952.

Stafford, Jo: "Jambalaya," Columbia, 1952.

Weber, Joan: "Let Me Go Lover," Columbia, 1954.

COLLECTIONS

Blue Skies: The Irving Berlin Songbook, Verve, 1996.

Willie Mitchell

Willie Mitchell talks like he produces: smoothly, mysteriously. "I look for getting the best we can," says the veteran Memphis producer, who steered Hi Records through 15 glory years in the '60s and '70s. "How do I do that? I talk to the people, tell them what I feel, see how they feel and how we can get the best out of them. It's communication."

Best known for his work with Al Green, Mitchell (born March 1, 1928, in Ashland, Mississippi) began producing at the dawn of the '60s, working with such instrumentalists and groups as Ace Cannon and the Bill Black Combo. He also plays trumpet and keyboards— "If I have to play on a session, I play"—and progressed from producing instrumentals to working with such vocalists as O.V. Wright, Ann Peebles, and, finally, Green. He also produced an album, on Duke, for Bobby "Blue" Bland in the mid-'60s.

"It wasn't a vision thing," Mitchell says of his productions. "I'm looking to get the best music out of musicians to come through the radio that people can feel. Feeling is my biggest aspect." Rhythm, too, is important, "so when you sing, you got to be rhythmic, you got to sing with a real rhythm feel."

Syl Johnson, who, like Green, recorded "Take Me to the River," certainly sang with a rhythmic feel: check out "Back for a Taste of Your Love" or "I Want to Take You Home (to See Mama)." So did Peebles, using melisma to trace a painfully persuasive emotional portrait on her biggest hit, "I Can't Stand the Rain." And, of course, there was Green, a sanctified soulman who delivered such classics as "Call Me (Come Back Home)" (No. 10), "I'm Still in Love with You" (No. 10), and the ineffable "Love and Happiness." "It was wonderful working with Al Green," Mitchell says. "I got him as a young kid. We worked together, wrote songs together, made things happen."

During the '60s, Hi Records shared musicians with Stax/Volt, the other Memphis powerhouse. "I did a lot of stuff with Stax," says Mitchell. "We were, like, partners in music. There was no competition. Stax basically had my rhythm section—Al Jackson Jr. and all those people. We did what we had to do."

Mitchell says he learned a lot about producing from Onzie Horn, a Memphis legend who played keyboards and xylophone and studied with Billy Strayhorn and Quincy Jones (see entry). It was Horn who helped Isaac Hayes (see entry) "put together" Shaft, Mitchell says.

"I wasn't influenced," Mitchell says. "I just heard music in my head, went into the studio and tried to put it down." He grew up in Memphis to the music of Count Basie, Duke Ellington, Lionel Hampton, Dinah Washington.

"I use different chords from what a lot of people use," Mitchell says. "What I hear, I get musicians to accomplish. It's challenging, but I try to use the best musicians, and they understand what I'm trying to accomplish. We go for sounds. If I hear something I want to hear, we'll work on it. "I use Memphis musicians because I know what they're going to do and I know how it's going to come out," Mitchell says. "I'm very comfortable here."

An independent producer since 1980, Mitchell works out of Royal Studios in Memphis, where he laid down his most famous tracks. He recently produced sessions for Tom Jones and loaned the Willie Mitchell Horns to *Come on Home,* a blues tribute album by Boz Scaggs. He

also produced an album by bluesman Jimmy King.

He doesn't rely on technology, Mitchell says. "I come from the hip: real organ, real piano, real saxophones, real guitar. Synthesizers? Maybe a line or something, but nothing dominant. I believe in real music."

Any favorites? "When I do a record, I don't look back on it," Mitchell says. "I don't cry over spilt milk. I have had records that didn't happen. I had a bunch of records that did happen. I never look back. I don't think about it. A record be on your head so long. When a record's over, it's over."

Did he sense how many of the records he produced would be classics? "You can feel it, man, you can feel a good record," Mitchell says. "Records are good or bad, one of the two." —CARLO WOLFF

Barraclough, Elizabeth: *Hi,* Bearsville, 1979.

Bassett, Johnny: *Cadillac Blues,* Cannonball, 1998.

Bland, Bobby "Blue": *Ain't Nothing You Can Do,* Duke, 1964.

Bryant, Don: *Doing the Mustang,* Hi, 1991.

Butterfield, Paul: *North South,* Bearsville, 1980.

Clay, Otis: "Trying to Live My Life Without You," Hi, 1972 • *That's How It Is,* Hi, 1991 • *You Are My Life,* Hi, 1995 • *The Best of the Hi Years,* Capitol, 1996 • *This Time Around,* Bullseye Blues, 1998 • See also Clayton, Willie.

Clayton, Willie: w/ Otis Clay, *Chicago Soul Greats,* Hi, 1995.

Doss, Kenny: *Movin' on a Feelin',* Bearsville, 1980.

Green, Al: *Green Is Blues,* Hi, 1970 • "I Can't Get Next to You," Hi, 1970 • *Al Green Gets Next to You,* Hi, 1971 • *Let's Stay Together,* Hi, 1971 • "Tired of Being Alone," Hi, 1971 • "I'm Still in Love with You," Hi, 1972 • *I'm Still in Love with You,* Hi, 1972 • "Let's Stay Together," Hi, 1972 • "Look What You Done for Me," Hi, 1972 • "You Ought to Be with Me," Hi, 1972 • "Call Me (Come Back Home)," Hi, 1973 • *Call Me,* Hi, 1973 • "Here I Am (Come and Take Me)," Hi, 1973 • *Explores Your Mind,* Hi, 1974 • "Livin' for You," Hi, 1974 • *Livin' for You,* Hi, 1974 • "Sha-La-La (Makes Me Happy)," Hi, 1974 • "Full of Fire," Hi, 1975 • *Full of Fire,* Hi, 1975 • *Greatest Hits,* the Right Stuff/Capitol, 1975, 1995 • *Is Love,* Hi, 1975 • "L-O-V-E (Love)," Hi, 1975 • *Have a Good Time,* Hi, 1976 • "Love and Happiness," Hi, 1977 • *He Is the Light,* PSM, 1985, 1995 • *Love Ritual: Rare and Unreleased (1968–1976),* MCA, 1989 • *Greatest Hits,* Vol. 2, Motown, 1992 • *Anthology,* the Right Stuff, 1997.

Johnson, Syl: *Back for a Taste of Your Love,* Hi, 1973 • *Music to My Ears,* Hi, 1994 • *The A-Sides,* Hi, 1994 • *The Best of the Hi Years,* Capitol, 1996.

King, Little Jimmy, and the King James Version Band: *Soldier for the Blues,* Bullseye Blues, 1997.

McCracklin, Jimmy: *High on the Blues,* Stax, 1971.

Mitchell, Willie: *Ooh Baby You Turn Me On/Live at the Royal,*

Hi, 1967, 1993 • *Soul Serenade,* Hi, 1968 • *Solid Soul/On Top,* Hi, 1969, 1994 • *Listen Dance,* Bearsville, 1971, 1981 • *The Best Of,* Hi, 1972.

Orito: *Soul Joint,* Vertex, 1995.

Peebles, Anne: "Part Time Love," Hi, 1970 • *Part Time Love,* Hi, 1971 • *Straight from the Heart,* Hi, 1972 • "I Can't Stand the Rain," Hi, 1973 • *I Can't Stand the Rain,* Hi, 1974 • *Tellin' It,* Hi, 1976 • *If This Is Heaven,* Hi, 1978 • *The Handwriting Is on the Wall,* Hi, 1979 • *Lookin' for a Lovin',* Hi, 1990 • *The Best of the Hi Years,* Capitol, 1996 • *U.S. R&B Chart Hits,* Hi, 1996.

Rush, Otis: *Any Place I'm Going,* House of Blues, 1998.

Shannon, Preston: *Midnight in Memphis,* Bulleye Blues, 1996.

Staples, Pops: *Peace to the Neighborhood,* Pointblank, 1992.

Winchester, Jesse: *Talk Memphis,* Bearsville, 1981.

Wright, Marva: *Marvalous,* Mardi Gras, 1995.

Wright, O.V.: *Memory Blues,* MCA, 1968 • *Bottom Line,* Hi, 1978 • *Into Something I Can't Shake Loose,* Hi, 1978 • *We're Still Together,* Hi, 1979 • *That's How Strong My Love Is,* Hi, 1991 • *The Soul of O.V. Wright,* MCA, 1992.

Young Fresh Fellows: *Doc Sharpie Is a Bad Man* (2 tracks), Frontier, 1992.

COLLECTIONS

History of Hi Records R&B, Vol. 1, *The Beginning,* Hi, 1988.

The Minit Records Story, EMI, 1995.

Hi Times: The Hi R&B Years, the Right Stuff, 1995.

Sex and Soul, Vol. 2, EMI, 1996.

Fonce Mizell

See THE CORPORATION

Chips Moman

F ew producers in modern music have left their stamp on more landmark musical projects than Chips Moman. From playing guitar on sessions at Sun Records, to starting the legendary Stax label, to being one of the creative forces in country's '70s outlaw movement, Moman's production prowess has been critical.

A native of LaGrange, Georgia, Moman was born in 1936 and moved to Memphis at 14. "When I was about 15 or 16, I was hired by a guy named Warren Smith at Sun Records to play guitar," he recalls. "Later on, I went with Johnny and Dorsey Burnette to California, where I started playing sessions." He also began to be involved in production.

Upon returning to Memphis in 1960, Moman and his friend Jim Stewart started Satellite Records. "We had to change the name to Stax because someone had the Satellite label," Moman says. "Carla Thomas was one of the first artists we signed, then the Marquees, William Bell, and Rufus Thomas." The label operated out of an old theater Moman ran across.

He stayed at Stax until 1963, then built American Studios across town in north Memphis. Wilson Pickett, the Boxtops, and Joe Tex were among the artists who recorded for Moman's American Group Productions. Moman and co-producer Tommy Cogbill produced such Neil Diamond hits as "Sweet Caroline," "Holly Holy" (uncredited), and "Brother Love's Traveling Salvation Show." Moman also produced Paul Revere and the Raiders.

"I had Sandy Posey [known for] 'Born a Woman,' and 'Single Girl' " (both No. 12), Moman says. "She was a secretary there at the studio. Out of that studio we had over 100 hit records in two years. A lot of them I produced, a lot of them I was just involved in the production. . . . I did so many people I can't recall."

Moman says he never thought what they were doing would have lasting impact. "We were just having fun," he says. "We were just enjoying the music. Mainly, the Stax sound, to me, was the horns. There weren't a lot of people using horns in those days. We always used a lot of horns on those things, and the rhythm section was really important, too. We didn't use a whole lot of echo on stuff. The players had a tremendous amount to do with it, guys like Wayne Jackson, Andrew Love, Gilbert Caples, Floyd Newman."

Around 1972, Moman moved to Nashville. "I was thinking about retiring," Moman says. "All my friends were there [in Nashville], all the musicians I'd been working with had gone to Nashville when I closed down. So I went to Nashville and next thing I knew I was making records again. One of the first things I did was 'Hey Won't You Play Another Somebody Done Somebody Wrong Song' (No. 1). I did the early records on B.J. Thomas—'Hooked on a Feeling' (No. 5) and 'The Eyes of a New York Woman'—in Memphis, before I came to Nashville."

Moman won a Grammy for "Hey Won't You" and soon became as influential in the Nashville scene as he had been in Memphis. He was an integral figure in country music's outlaw movement in the '70s. He and

Bobby Emmons co-wrote "Luckenbach, Texas (Back to the Basics of Love)," a No. 1 hit for Waylon Jennings for six weeks in 1977. That helped initiate a new era in the country genre. Moman produced "Luckenbach" and "Mamas Don't Let Your Babies Grow Up to Be Cowboys" (No. 1 country), and such tunes fueled the outlaw movement that helped bring a new demographic to country music.

Moman has a very laid-back approach to producing. "I just go in the studio and try to have good songs and I try to have a good time," he says. "Having a good time is the only way it works for me. . . . You can be way too serious about music. Music's not to be serious about—it's to enjoy. I'm a good audience," he says. "A lot of singers who've worked with me have said that looking through the glass at me would determine whether they were up or down."

Moman says he would often work with more than one artist during a day. "Sometimes I would be doing two at once," he says. "I was recording Roy Hamilton and Elvis at the same time. I was doing Elvis at night and Roy during the day. In 1969 I did 'Suspicious Minds,' 'Kentucky Rain,' and 'In the Ghetto,' those records. With Elvis, there was no problem with him hitting. All he needed was a song."

Moman recorded two albums with Presley and went on to record many other landmark albums, such as Willie Nelson's *Always on My Mind* and *City of New Orleans,* and both Highwaymen albums, featuring Nelson, Jennings, Kris Kristofferson, and Johnny Cash. Another big multi-artist Moman production was the Class of '55 album on Mercury that reunited Sun legends Jerry Lee Lewis, Carl Perkins, Johnny Cash, and Roy Orbison. "I put that together. It was a very difficult project to do," Moman recalls. "I only had three days to do that with four artists. I wish I could do that album again and have more time. For one thing, I'd switch some of the songs around and change which artist sang this song and which artist sang that song. I never did think I had that right."

During most of his career, Moman operated as an independent producer, with the exception of 1973, when he served as chief of Warner Bros. Nashville. "I hated it. I tried it, but there was not any music to it," he says. "I'd go to California and sit in an office and read contracts. We'd just talk about the deals. . . . We never listened to the music."

He also tried his hand at starting record labels, but none measured up to Stax. In the late '60s he started Entrance, a CBS Records–distributed label. During the '70s he operated as an independent, working on numerous CBS projects. Then in 1982, he started Triad with partners Phil Walden and Buddy Killen. The venture was short-lived because, Moman says, they "had different ideas" on how to run the business.

Though many producers say they can tell immediately when a song is going to be a hit, Moman admits that picking a hit is tricky business. "A lot of times I could tell [when something was going to be a hit] and a lot of times I thought I had a hit but didn't," he says. "No one knows for sure. My theory is if I like it, other people will like it. I just do what I love and try to enjoy the session instead of trying to be clever."

In 1995, Moman produced Rivers Rutherford for Giant Records, but the label dropped him before the project was released. After that, Moman decided to return to Georgia, play golf, and enjoy life. "I'm not through yet," he says. "I'm just taking time off. I'll be back and go back into production. I'm still writing. A songwriter is what I originally wanted to be." —DEBORAH EVANS PRICE

Alaimo, Steve: *Anthology,* Hot Productions, 1997.

Allman Brothers Band: *Dreams,* Polydor, 1989.

Backalley Bandits: *The Backalley Bandits,* London, n.d.

Bell, William: "You Don't Miss Your Water," Stax, 1962 • "Somebody Mentioned Your Name," Stax, 1963.

Box Tops: *Dimensions,* Bell, 1968 • *The Ultimate Box Tops,* Warner Special Products, 1987 • *The Best of the Box Tops: Soul Deep,* Arista, 1996 • "Sweet Cream Ladies, Forward March," Mala, 1968 • "Soul Deep," Mala, 1969.

Burke, Solomon: *Home in Your Heart: Best Of,* (2 tracks), Rhino, 1992 • *The Very Best Of,* Rhino, 1998.

Burnette, Billy: *Billy Burnette,* Polydor, 1972, 1979 • *Between Friends,* Polydor, 1979.

Cash, Johnny, and Waylon Jennings: "Even Cowgirls Get the Blues," Columbia, 1986 • *Heroes,* Razor & Tie, 1986, 1995.

Clark, Petula: *In Memphis,* Warner Bros., 1970 • *Blue Lady: The Nashville Sessions,* Varese Vintage, 1995.

Class of '55: *Memphis Rock and Roll Homecoming,* America/Smash, 1986.

Colter, Jessi: *Rock and Roll Lullabye,* Triad, 1984.

Cymarron: "Rings," Entrance, 1971.

Davis, Paul: *A Little Bit of Paul Davis,* Bang, 1974.

Diamond, Neil: "Brother Love's Traveling Salvation Show," Uni, 1969 • *Sweet Caroline,* MCA, 1969 • *And the Singer Sings His Songs,* MCA, 1976 • *Glory Road: 1968–1972,* MCA, 1992, 1995 • *In My Lifetime,* Sony, 1996.

Earl Scruggs Revue: *Bold and New,* CBS, 1978.

Gatlin Brothers: *Biggest Hits,* Columbia, 1988.

Gentrys, The: *Keep on Dancin',* MGM, 1965 • *Time,* MGM, 1966.

Haggard, Merle: w/ Willie Nelson, "Pancho and Lefty," Epic,

1983 • w/ Willie Nelson, *Pancho and Lefty,* Epic, 1983 • *His Epic Hits: First Eleven . . . To Be Continued,* Epic, 1984 • *Down Every Road,* Capitol, 1996.

Highwaymen: "Desperados Waiting for a Train," Columbia, 1985 • "Highwayman," Columbia, 1985 • *Highwayman,* Columbia, 1985 • *Highwayman II,* Columbia, 1990 • "Silver Stallion," Columbia, 1990.

Jennings, Waylon: "Luckenbach, Texas (Back to the Basics of Love)," RCA, 1977 • *Ol' Waylon,* RCA, 1977 • "The Wurlitzer Prize / Lookin' for a Feeling," RCA, 1977 • *Greatest Hits,* RCA, 1979 • *Black on Black,* RCA, 1982 • *Are You Sure Hank Done It This Way,* RCA, 1992 • *Only Daddy That'll Walk the Line: The RCA Years,* RCA, 1993 • *The Essential,* RCA, 1996 • *See also* Cash, Johnny.

Jennings, Waylon, and Willie Nelson: "I Can Get Off on You," RCA, 1978 • "Mamas, Don't Let Your Babies Grow Up to Be Cowboys," RCA, 1978 • *Waylon and Willie,* RCA, 1978 • "Just to Satisfy You," RCA, 1982 • *Waylon and Willie 2,* RCA, 1982 • *Take It to the Limit,* CBS, 1983 • *Double Barrel Country: The Legends of Country Music,* Madacy, 1998.

Kershaw, Doug: *Douglas James Kershaw,* Warner Bros., 1973.

Kristofferson, Kris: *Repossessed,* Mercury, 1986 • "They Killed Him," Mercury, 1987 • *Singer / Songwriter,* Momument / Sony, 1991.

Nelson, Willie: *Sweet Memories,* RCA, 1979, 1994 • "Always on My Mind," Columbia, 1982 • *Always on My Mind,* Columbia, 1982 • *Take It to the Limit,* Columbia, 1983 • *City of New Orleans,* Columbia, 1984 • "City of New Orleans," Columbia, 1984 • "Partners After All," Columbia, 1986 • "Heart of Gold," Columbia, 1987 • w/ Julio Iglesias, "Spanish Eyes," Columbia, 1988 • *What a Wonderful World,* Columbia, 1988 • "Twilight Time," Columbia, 1989 • *Super Hits,* Columbia, 1994 • *Super Hits, Vol. 2,* Columbia, 1995 • *See also* Jennings, Waylon, and Willie Nelson.

Orbison, Roy: *King of Hearts,* Virgin, 1992.

Perkins, Carl: "Birth of Rock and Roll," America / Smash, 1986.

Phillips, Esther: *The Best of, 1962–1970,* Rhino, 1997.

Posey, Sandy: "Born A Woman," MGM, 1966 • "Single Girl," MGM, 1966 • *Single Girl,* MGM, 1966 • "I Take It Back," MGM, 1967 • *I Take It Back,* MGM, 1967 • "What a Woman in Love Won't Do," MGM, 1967 • *Looking At You,* MGM, 1968 • *The Best Of,* Collectables, 1995.

Presley, Elvis: *From Elvis in Memphis,* RCA, 1969 • "Suspicious Minds," RCA, 1969 • *The Memphis Record,* RCA, 1969 • *Back in Memphis,* RCA, 1970, 1992 • *Elvis Gospel, 1957–1971,* RCA, 1989 • *Heart and Soul,* RCA, 1995.

Revere, Paul, and the Raiders: *Going to Memphis,* Columbia, 1968.

Roe, Tommy: *Full Bloom,* Monument, 1978.

Royal, Billy Joe: *Billy Joe Royal,* Polydor, 1980.

Rush, Merilee: "Angel of the Morning," Bell, 1968.

Stewart, Gary: *Cactus and Rose,* RCA, 1980 • *Essential,* RCA, 1997.

Thomas, B.J.: *Raindrops Keep Falling on My Head,* Scepter, 1969 • *Everybody's Out of Town,* Scepter, 1970 • "I Just Can't Help Believing," Scepter, 1970 • *Most of All,* Scepter, 1971 • "(Hey Won't You Play) Another Somebody Done Somebody Wrong Song," ABC, 1975 • *Help Me Make It to My Rocking Chair,* ABC, 1975 • *Reunion,* ABC, 1975 • *Everybody Loves a Rain Song,* MCA, 1978 • *The Very Best of B.J. Thomas,* Varese, 1997 • "Hooked on A Feeling," Sceptor, 1968 • *Greatest Hits,* Rhino, 1990, 1991.

Thomas, Carla: *Hidden Gems,* Stax, 1992.

Van Zandt, Townes: *Flyin' Shoes,* Tomato, 1978.

Warwick, Dionne: "You've Lost That Loving Feeling," Scepter, 1969.

Weinstein and Strodl: *Cook Me Up Your Taste,* Capitol, 1969.

Womack, Bobby: "(I Wanna) Make Love to You," MCA, 1986 • *Womagic,* MCA, 1986 • *Midnight Mover,* Capitol, 1993 • *Only Survivor: The MCA Years,* MCA, 1996.

Wynette, Tammy: *Biggest Hits,* Epic, 1983 • *Best Loved Hits,* Epic, 1990 • *Tears of Fire: The 25th Anniversary Collection,* Epic, 1992.

COLLECTIONS

The Minit Records Story, EMI, 1995.

Vincent Montana Jr.

The multifaceted Vince Montana Jr. is known as a composer, arranger, conductor, musician (he is a renowned vibraharpist), and producer for such groundbreaking disco acts as the Salsoul Orchestra and MFSB. Montana was also responsible, along with Leon Huff and Kenny Gamble (see entry), for creating and nurturing what would later be referred to as "The Sound of Philadelphia." A man of many soulful moods, Montana has proven himself one of the industry's hardest-working professionals, consistently adhering to a strict work ethic that values creativity, originality, and above all, quality.

Born February 12, 1928, and raised in south Philadelphia, Montana has been plying his musical wares since the early '50s, when he worked in various jazz clubs as a backup musician for such artists as Charlie "Bird" Parker and Sarah Vaughan. Desiring a change of pace, Montana moved to Las Vegas, where he played with many show bands. But a few years later, he returned to

Philadelphia to play sessions for Cameo Parkway and Chancellor Records, recording with the likes of Chubby Checker, Frankie Avalon, Fabian, and Bobby Rydell. Shortly thereafter, he became a member of the Mike Douglas Television Show Band.

After a year with Douglas, Montana left to become a major figure in the nascent Philly Sound. He assumed various roles in working with the likes of Eddie Kendricks, Billy Paul, Harold Melvin and the Blue Notes, Blue Magic, the Trammps, the O'Jays, the Spinners, and Lou Rawls. While this work produced over 50 gold and platinum albums, Montana is still widely recognized as the guiding light behind the Salsoul Orchestra, the disco era's most successful 42-piece unit. This could explain why, in 1996, he was tapped by producers "Little" Louie Vega and Kenny "Dope" Gonzalez (see entry) to participate in the Nuyorican Soul project.

It was always Montana's vision to create an orchestra that could recast the Big Band sound within a discotheque environment. But his musical creation would be a fusion of sorts, combining plush string arrangements with zesty salsa rhythms and percolating Afro-Cuban beats. "We could not use the word 'salsa' along with the word 'soul'; it just didn't sound right," he says. "So we abbreviated the word 'salsa,' combined it with soul,' and the Salsoul Orchestra was conceived."

In addition to gold album sales and numerous hit singles (most notably, "The Salsoul Hustle"; "Tangerine," No. 18; "Runaway"; and "Magic Bird of Fire"), the orchestra garnered a multitude of awards from various organizations—Disco Band of the Year, Top Instrumental Orchestra of the Year, Top Disco Orchestra of the Year—and Montana was dubbed Outstanding Producer of the Year.

Vince Montana Jr. may not realize it, but the nine albums he recorded with the Salsoul Orchestra completely altered the shape of the disco movement.

—LARRY FLICK

Charo and the Salsoul Orchestra: *Cuchi-Cuchi,* Salsoul, 1977.
Fania All Stars: *Crossover,* Columbia, 1979.
Fat Larry's Band: *Feel It,* Hot Productions, 1977, 1994.
Gilberto, Astrud: *Girl from Ipanema,* Prime Cuts, 1997.
Incognito: *Remixed,* Verve, 1996.
MFSB: *Love Is the Message* (1 track), Philadelphia International, 1973.
Montana: *A Dance Fantasy,* Atlantic, 1978.
Montana Orchestra: *Merry Christmas/Happy New Year's,* MJS, 1981.
Salsoul Orchestra: "The Salsoul Hustle," Salsoul, 1975 • *The Salsoul Orchestra,* Salsoul, 1975 • *Christmas Jollies,* Salsoul, 1976, 1996 • "Nice 'n' Nasty," Salsoul, 1976 • *Nice 'n' Nasty,*

Salsoul, 1976 • "Tangerine," Salsoul, 1976 • "Magic Bird of Fire," Salsoul, 1977 • *Greatest Disco Hits/Music for Non-Stop Dancing,* Salsoul, 1978 • *Up the Yellow Brick Road,* Salsoul, 1978 • *Christmas Jollies II,* Salsoul, 1981 • "Christmas Jollies," Salsoul, 1983 • *Magic Journey,* Salsoul, 1994 • *Anthology,* Salsoul/Capitol, 1996.

COLLECTIONS
The Original Salsoul Classics: 20th Anniversary, Salsoul, 1992.
12-Inch Gold Master Series, Vol. 1, Salsoul, 1994.
Philly Sound (1966–1976) Kenny Gamble and Leon Huff, Legacy, 1997.

Bob Montgomery

Whether it was a newcomer or an established act in need of a career boost, Bob Montgomery has long been known as a producer who could get the job done. His credits include Marty Robbins, Eddy Arnold, Lobo, B.J. Thomas, Janie Frickie, and Vern Gosdin.

Born May 12, 1937, in Lampasas, near Lubbock, Texas, Montgomery began his music career as an artist and songwriter. While in his teens, he performed in a

duo with his best friend, Buddy Holly. In the early '60s, he moved to Nashville to develop his craft as a songwriter and found phenomenal success. His song "Misty Blue" has been recorded over 300 times by artists as diverse as Dorothy Moore, Wilma Burgess, and Eddy Arnold. He penned the Patsy Cline hit "Back in Baby's Arms" and several cuts for his pal Holly, including "Love's Made a Fool of You," "Wishing Well" and "Heartbeat." On an international scale, he's had songs cut by Cliff Richard, Herman's Hermits, and Englebert Humperdinck.

Montgomery proved no less successful as a producer. "Songwriting and publishing were a natural bridge to producing," Montgomery says, citing a Mel Tillis song titled "Stateside" as his entrée to the field. "I learned I knew nothing about producing at the time, but the record was Top 20."

During his tenure with United Artists Records in the mid-'60s, he produced Del Reeves, Johnny Darrell, Bobby Lewis, and Bobby Goldsboro's multimillion-selling single, "Honey." He and Goldsboro left the label to form the House of Gold publishing company in 1970. One of Nashville's most successful publishing operations, House of Gold was responsible for such hits as "Love in the First Degree," "Behind Closed Doors," and "Wind Beneath My Wings" and launched the careers of such Music Row successes as Arista Nashville president Tim DuBois, managers Johnny Slate and Johnny Morrison, and Blackhawk members Van Stephenson and Dave Robbins.

After selling House of Gold in the early '80s, Montgomery formed a joint venture company with Warner Bros. Music, Writers House Music, which he developed before moving on to Tree Publishing. When Tree sold to Sony in 1989, he joined Sony Music as head of A&R and initiated a joint publishing venture, Miss Dot Music. Among the hits he produced while at Sony were Vern Gosdin's "Chiseled in Stone" (No. 6 country); Marty Robbins' "Some Memories Just Won't Die" (No. 10 country); and the Joe Diffie hits "Home" (No. 1 country), "If You Want Me To" (No. 2 country), and "Ships That Don't Come In" (No. 5 country).

Montgomery says finding a great song, then wringing the emotion out of it, are key to making hit records. "Making sure the songs are right and guiding the project to a final product that is of superior quality" is a priority, according to Montgomery. "I try to get a performance from the artist. Sometimes that performance may not be technically perfect, but it has the feeling. That is the most important thing. . . . The challenge is being the diplomat who can tell the artist no and still achieve the desired result and the reward is when that happens."

He finds technology useful, but often overused, at "the expense of realism and feeling." Montgomery is running a new publishing company with his wife, Cathy, traveling extensively, and "working on my tan."
—DEBORAH EVANS PRICE

Arnold, Eddy: *Somebody Loves You*, RCA, 1979 • *Essential*, RCA, 1996.

Bailey, Razzy: *If Love Had a Face*, RCA, 1979 • "Loving Up a Storm," RCA, 1980 • *Razzy Bailey*, RCA, 1980 • "Friends/Anywhere There's A Jukebox," RCA, 1981 • "I Keep Coming Back/True Life County Music," RCA, 1981 • *Midnight Hauler/Scratch My Back (and Whisper in My Ear)*, RCA, 1981 • *Feelin' Right*, RCA, 1982 • "She Left Love All Over Me," RCA, 1982.

Ballard, Roger: "Two Steps in the Right Direction," Atlantic, 1993.

Carpenter, Mary Chapin, and Kevin Montgomery: "Wishing," Decca, 1996 (*Not Fade Away [Remembering Buddy Holly]*).

Crawford, Randy: *Miss Randy Crawford*, Warner Bros., 1977.

Crickets, The: *Bubblegum, Bop, Ballads and Boogies*, Philips, 1973 • *Remnants*, Mercury, 1973 • *Long Way from Lubbock*, Philips, 1974.

Dale, Kenny: *Only Love Can Break a Heart*, Capitol, 1979.

Darrell, Johnny: "Ruby, Don't Take Your Love to Town," United Artists, 1967.

Diffie, Joe: *A Thousand Winding Roads*, Epic, 1990 • "Home," Epic, 1990 • "If You Want Me To," Epic, 1990 • "If the Devil Danced (in Empty Pockets)," Epic, 1991 • "Is It Cold in Here?," Epic, 1991 • "New Way (to Light Up an Old Flame)," Epic, 1991 • "Next Thing Smokin'," Epic, 1992 • *Regular Joe*, Epic, 1992 • "Ships That Don't Come In," Epic, 1992 • "Startin' Over Blues," Epic, 1992 • "Honky Tonk Attitude," Epic, 1993 • *Honky Tonk Attitude*, Epic, 1993 • "John Deere Green," Epic, 1993 • "Prop Me Up Beside the Jukebox (If I Die)," Epic, 1993.

Dixiana: *Dixiana*, Epic, 1992 • "That's What I'm Working on Tonight," Epic, 1992 • "Waitin' for the Deal to Go Down," Epic, 1992.

Foster, Lloyd David: "I Can Feel the Fire Goin' Out," Columbia, 1985 • "I'm Gonna Love You Right out of the Blues," Columbia, 1985.

Frickie, Janie (Fricke): "It Ain't Easy Bein' Easy," Columbia, 1982 • *It Ain't Easy*, Columbia, 1982 • "He's a Heartache (Looing for a Place to Happen)," Columbia, 1983 • *Love Lies*, Columbia, 1983 • "Tell Me a Lie," Columbia, 1983 • "Let's Stop Talkin' About It," Columbia, 1984 • "Your Heart's Not in It," Columbia, 1984 • "She's Single Again," Columbia, 1985 • "Somebody Else's Fire," Columbia, 1985 • "The First Word in Memory Is Me," Columbia, 1985 • *Very Best Of*, Columbia, 1985, 1991 • "Easy to

Please," Columbia, 1986.

Goldsboro, Bobby: *California Wine,* United Artists, 1972 • "Autumn of My Life," United Artists, 1968 • "Honey," United Artists, 1968 • "Muddy Mississippi Line," United Artists, 1969 • *Today,* United Artists, 1969 • "Watching Scotty Grow," United Artists, 1970 • *Come Back Home,* United Artists, 1971 • *We Gotta Start Lovin',* United Artists, 1971 • *Summer (the First Time),* United Artists, 1973 • *The Best Of,* Collectables, 1996.

Gosdin, Vern: *Chiseled in Stone,* Columbia, 1987 • *Alone,* Columbia, 1988 • "Chisled in Stone," Columbia, 1988 • "Set 'Em Up Joe," Columbia, 1988 • "I'm Still Crazy," Columbia, 1989 • "That Just About Does It," Columbia, 1989 • *10 Years of Hits Newly Recorded,* Columbia, 1990 • "Is It Raining at Your House?," Columbia, 1990 • "Right in the Wrong Direction," Columbia, 1990 • "Tanqueray," Columbia, 1990 • "This Ain't My First Rodeo," Columbia, 1990 • "A Month of Sundays," Columbia, 1991 • "I Knew My Day Would Come," Columbia, 1991 • *Out of My Heart,* Columbia, 1991 • "The Garden," Columbia, 1991 • *Super Hits,* Columbia, 1993.

Gray, Mark: "Diamond in the Dust," Columbia, 1984 • *Magic,* Columbia, 1984 • "Smooth Sailing (Rock in the Road)," Columbia, 1985.

Haggard, Merle: "Amber Waves of Grain," Epic, 1985 • *Amber Waves of Grain,* Epic, 1985 • "Out Among the Stars," Epic, 1986.

Jennings, Waylon: *The Eagle,* Epic, 1990 • "Where Corn Don't Grow," Epic, 1990 • "Wrong," Epic, 1990 • w/ Willie Nelson, "If I Can't Find a Clean Shirt," Epic, 1991 • "What Bothers Me Most," Epic, 1991.

Lewis, Bobby: "Love Me and Make It All Better," United Artists, 1967.

Lobo: *Lobo,* MCA, 1979 • "Where Were You When I Was Falling in Love?," MCA, 1979 • *Greatest Hits,* Curb, 1990.

Lynne, Shelby: *Sunrise,* Epic, 1976, 1989 • "I'll Lie Myself to Sleep," Epic, 1990 • "Things Are Tough All Over," Epic, 1990 • *Tough All Over,* Epic, 1990 • "What About the Love We Made," Epic, 1991.

Morris, Gary: *Why Lady Why,* Warner Bros., 1983, 1987 • *Greatest Hits,* Vol. 2, Warner Bros., 1990.

Palmer, Keith: "Don't Throw Me in the Briarpatch," Epic, 1991 • *Keith Palmer,* Epic, 1991 • "Forgotten but Not Gone," Epic, 1992.

Reeves, Del: "A Dime at a Time," United Artists, 1967 • "Good Time Charlies," United Artists, 1968.

Rivers, Johnny: *Road,* Atlantic, 1974.

Robbins, Marty: "Some Memories Just Won't Die," Columbia, 1982 • *A Lifetime of Song, 1951–1982,* CBS, 1983 • *Super Hits,* Columbia, 1995.

Roberts, Austin: "Rocky," Private Stock, 1975 • *Rocky,* Private Stock, 1975.

Ryles, John Wesley: *Let the Night Begin,* MCA, 1979.

Sheppard, T.G.: "Don't Say It with Diamonds (Say It with Love)," Columbia, 1988.

Stevens, Ray: *Don't Laugh Now,* RCA, 1982 • *Collector's Series,* RCA, 1992.

Stevenson, B.W: *Lost Feeling,* Warner Bros., 1977.

Thomas, B.J: *Shining,* Cleveland Int./Epic, 1984 • "The Girl Most Likely To," Cleveland Int./Epic, 1985.

Tillis, Mel: "Stateside," Kapp, 1966.

Whitman, Slim: *Angeline,* Epic, 1984.

Wynette, Tammy: "Let's Call It a Day Today," Epic, 1990 • "What Goes with Blue," Epic, 1991 • *Tears of Fire: The 25th Anniversary Collection,* Epic, 1992.

David Morales

As a club DJ, remixer, and producer, David Morales has climbed to the highest point of clubland. He is heralded as one of the key figures in bringing house music to the forefront of pop and has been honing his unique blend of pop melody, soul rhythm, and tribal percussion since 1987.

"From as far back as I can remember, I always responded to the groove of a record first," he says. "When you heard cars zooming by, it was the beat that people remembered. It was the percussion that the kids who were playing stickball would stop and shake their body to. I wanted to make music that would make people stop everything and shake their ass."

In 1989, Morales—who was born August 21, 1961, in Brooklyn—did more than that, presiding over the turntable decks at the Red Zone, a Manhattan nightclub he rapidly developed into one of the prime taste-making music spots in the U.S. The raw, aggressive way he blended tracks on his turntables soon came to be known as "the Morales Red Zone mix" in inner circles.

"The key to those tracks was the live percussion," he recalls. "Everyone else at the time was building tracks from samples, which was wack. I think the real motion of a record can only come from a human being breaking it down with congas, shakers, and whatever else he can grab. And then you wrap that shit with a thick bass line and some sweet keyboards and you have a phat track that people could jam to."

Along the way, Morales has lent his sound to countless artists, spanning the dance music underground and pop superstars. It's probably easier to cite the acts he has not worked with, given a discography that includes several Mariah Carey hits—most notably "Dream Lover," which landed him a Grammy nomination in 1996—as well as singles with Madonna, Michael Jackson, Luther Vandross, Gloria Estefan, Whitney Houston, Seal, Janet Jackson, and Toni Braxton.

"I think the defining moment of my career was when I was in the studio with Mariah and she wasn't singing exactly the way I envisioned her voice working with the groove," he says. "I had to stop the track and tell this woman, who is one of the great singers in pop music, to stop and sing it differently. It was scary at first, but she respected my vision and perspective. From there, I never had any fear."

By 1991, Morales was ready for the next level and started recording his own album of original material. Working with a variety of musicians and singers under the group name the Bad Yard Club, he completed *The Program* for Mercury Records in 1993. That set gave way to several worldwide club hits, including the now-classic single "In De Ghetto," featuring vocals by Crystal Waters of "Gypsy Woman" pop-dance fame.

All the while, Morales has continued to spin, frequently guesting on MTV's *The Grind* and such renowned venues as Ministry of Sound in the U.K. He is also helming his independent label, Definity Records, which will be devoted to his first love: "the hardcore house sound that has made me who and what I am today. My wish is to grow and reach the highest possible plateau in music, but to never lose touch with the street." —LARRY FLICK

Ace of Base: "Living in Danger" (remix), Arista, 1994.
Adevax: "It Should Have Been Me," Smack/Capitol, 1991.
Adventures of Stevie V: "Dirty Cash (Money Talks)," Mercury, 1990 • "Jealousy," Mercury, 1990.
Baka Boys: *Quick Mix,* Thump, 1995.
Bjork: "Big Time Sensuality" (remix), Elektra, 1994 • "Hyperballad/Enjoy" (remix), One Little Indian, 1997.
Brand New Heavies: "Dream on Dreamer" (remix), Delicious Vinyl, 1992.
Braxton, Toni: "You're Makin' Me High" (remix), Arista, 1996.
Carey, Mariah: *Daydream,* Columbia, 1995 • *Butterfly,* Columbia, 1997 • "Butterfly," Columbia, 1997 • "My All," Columbia, 1998.
Cerrone: *Best,* Pure, 1995.
Chimes, The: "1-2-3" (remix), Columbia, 1989.
Cox, Deborah: "Who Do U Love," Arista, 1996.
Criminal Element Orchestra: *Locked Up,* WTG, 1989.
Davis, Carlene: *Carlene Davis,* Gee Street, 1992.
Georgio: "Bedrock" (remix), Motown, 1987.
Incognito: *Remixed,* Verve, 1996.
Inner Circle: "Sweat (A La La La La Long)" (remix), Big

Beat/Atlantic, 1993 • "Bad Boys" (remix), Big Beat/Atlantic, 1994.
Jackson, Janet: "Throb" (remix), Virgin, 1993 • "Because of Love" (remix), Virgin, 1994.
Jamiroquai: "Cosmic Girl" (remix), Work, 1996.
Khan, Chaka: *Life Is a Dance (The Remix Project),* Warner Bros., 1989.
Knuckles, Frankie: *Beyond the Mix,* Virgin, 1990.
Lazy, Doug: "H.O.U.S.E." (remix), Atlantic, 1990.
Londonbeat: "I've Been Thinking About You" (remix), Radioactive, 1991.
Madonna: "Deeper and Deeper" (remix), Maverick/Sire/WB, 1992.
Maxi Priest: *Fe Real,* Charisma, 1992 • "Groovin' in the Midnight," Virgin, 1992 • *Man with the Fun,* Virgin, 1996.
Maxi Priest and Shaggy: "That Girl" (remix), Virgin, 1996.
Miles, Robert: "One and One" (remix), Arista, 1996.
Morales, David, and the Bad Yard Club: *The Program,* Mercury, 1993 • "Gimme Love (Eenie Meenie Miny Mo)," Mercury, 1994 • "In De Ghetto," Mercury, 1994 • "The Program," Mercury, 1994.
Morgan, Jamie J.: *Shotgun,* Tabu, 1990.
Peniston, CeCe: "Finally" (remix), Tommy Boy, 1991, 1992 (*MTV Party to Go,* Vol. 3) • *Finally,* A&M, 1992 • "Hit by Love" (remix), A&M, 1994 • *Thought Ya Knew,* A&M, 1994 • *Before I Lay (You Drive Me Crazy) (EP),* A&M, 1996.
Pet Shop Boys: "Jealousy" (remix), Parlophone, 1991 • "Where the Streets Have No Name (I Can't Take My Eyes off of You)" (remix), EMI, 1991 • "So Hard" (remix), EMI, 1994 • *Disco 2,* EMI, 1995.
Pride in Politix: "Hold On," EastWest, 1991.
Ranks, Shabba: "Mr. Loverman" (remix), Tommy Boy, 1991, 1993 (*MTV Party to Go,* Vol. 3) • *X-Tra Naked* (1 track), Epic, 1992.
Robin S.: "I Want to Thank You" (remix), Atlantic, 1993 • *Show Me Love* (1 track), Atlantic, 1993.
Ross, Diana: *Diana Extended: The Remixes,* Motown, 1994.
Safire: *I Wasn't Born Yesterday,* Mercury, 1991.
Spice Girls: "Who Do You Think You Are?," Virgin, 1997.
Technotronic: "Get Up! (Before the Night Is Over)" (remix), SBK, 1990 • *Trip on This (The Remixes),* Capitol, 1990.
Ten City: *No House Big Enough,* EastWest, 1992.
Turner, Tina: "Goldeneye" (remix), Virgin, 1995.
U2: "Lemon" (remix), Island, 1993 • "Stay (Faraway So Close)" (remix), Island, 1993 • "Discotheque" (remix), Island, 1997.
Vandross, Luther: *One Night with You: The Best of Love,* Vol. 2, Sony, 1997.
Vega, Little Louie: *Strictly Rhythm Mix,* Vol. 2, Strictly Rhythm, 1994.
Watley, Jody: *Affairs of the Heart,* MCA, 1991 • *Intimacy,* MCA, 1993 • *Greatest Hits,* MCA, 1996.

Ministry of Sound Presents the Sessions, Vol. 7, Ministry of Sound, 1997.

Tony Moran

See LATIN RASCALS

Jonathan More

See COLDCUT

Giorgio Moroder

Italian-born (April 26, 1940, in Oristel) composer and producer Giorgio Moroder is the pioneer of hi-NRG dance. His innovative use of synthesizers, married with sequencers, in the late '70s not only placed him in the stratosphere of dance music history; it also earned him a well-deserved reputation as one of the great pop experimentalists.

The track that started it all was 1977's "I Feel Love" (No. 6) by Donna Summer. "I had several hits in Europe before meeting Donna," he says. "Some with German acts, some Italian, some French. . . . I also had hits myself and a huge hit with a group from England called Chicory Tip and the song 'Son of My Father,' which then became a big hit here. That was all danceable music but not disco. Ironically, 'I Feel Love' was my first real attempt at the genre."

More platinum came from the Moroder-Summer combination, as well as musical scores for films like *Midnight Express* (1978), *Foxes* (1979), *American Gigolo* (1980), *Flashdance* (1982), *Neverending Story* (1984), and the German release *Forever Dancing* (1992). Hit singles for Moroder during his 20-year career include Sparks' "Beat the Clock" (No. 10 U.K.); Japan's "Life In Tokyo"; Blondie's "Call Me" (No. 1); Irene Cara's "Flashdance . . . What a Feeling" (No. 1; it also won the 1983 Oscar for Best Song from a Movie); his collaboration with the

Human League's Philip Oakey, "Together in Electric Dreams" (No. 3 U.K., followed by a full album, *Chrome*); a collaboration with Kajagoogoo's lead singer Limahl, "The Never Ending Story" (No. 17); and Melissa Manchester's "Thief of Hearts."

Along the way, Moroder also began to cultivate a career as a recording artist in his own right. He won acclaim for his work on the soundtrack to *Midnight Express* in 1978, scoring a pop and dance hit with a single from that album, "Chase." One of the rarest Moroder albums is his 1981 album, $E = MC^2$.

"That was very costly, it was the first album in which 90 percent was recorded live to a 2-track digital machine," he says. "At that time there was only one machine that could do it, [owned by] some guy from Utah. We had problems. The software was called 'Microcomposer,' and we had several piano players; some players are inside the piano, some on top. We had four or five piano players playing live, the drummer live; the melodies were recorded, and I sang live to the tracks. It was a little bit of a mess. The cost was something like $15,000 per day—enormous. I'm not Billy Idol or Led Zeppelin, I got nervous because of the new technology, certain things weren't happening the way I wanted them to. It was around 1981, I think—the first time digital technology was being used to record music."

In 1997, Moroder again rose to pop and club prominence, thanks to the U.S. release of "Carry On," a collaboration with Donna Summer that garnered a Grammy nomination as Best Dance Recording. The single was released in the States on the Priority-distributed Interhit Records. Although he's pleased with the recognition, he finds the new dance music scene a little baffling at times. "It's not like it was when disco was just around and that's it, one style," he says. "It's a bit of a problem, especially in the way that everyone is trying to push their own style. It's not exactly healthy."

Currently living in Beverly Hills, Moroder is writing material for two musical theater projects. The first is an adaptation of work from the hit film *Flashdance.* The other is a project that will initially be performed in Germany. —LARRY FLICK

Angel: *Sinful,* Casablanca, 1979 • *Anthology,* Mercury, 1992.

Berlin: *Love Life,* Geffen, 1984 • *Count Three and Pray,* Geffen, 1986 • "Take My Breath Away," Columbia, 1986 • *Best Of, 1979–1988,* Geffen, 1988.

Big Trouble: "Crazy World," Epic, 1987.

Blondie: "Call Me," Chrysalis, 1980 • *Best Of,* Chrysalis, 1981.

Bowie, David: *Bowie: The Singles, 1969–1993,* Rykodisc, 1993 • "Cat People (Putting Out Fire)," RCA, 1982.

Brooklyn Dreams: *Music, Harmony and Rhythm: The Casablanca Years,* Casablanca, 1996.

Cara, Irene: "Flashdance . . . What a Feeling," Casablanca, 1983 • *What a Feelin',* Geffen, 1983 • "Why Me?," Geffen/Network, 1983 • "Breakdance," Network/Geffen, 1984.

DeBarge: *Rhythm of the Night,* Motown, 1985 • *Greatest Hits,* Motown, 1986.

Giorgio: *Knights in White Satin,* Oasis, 1976 • *From Here to Eternity,* GTO, 1977 • w/ Chris, *Love's in You, Love's in Me,* GTO, 1978.

Hagar, Sammy: "Winner Takes It All," Columbia, 1987.

Hagen, Nina: *Fearless,* Epic, 1983 • *14 Friendly Abductions: The Best Of,* Legacy/Columbia, 1996.

Harry, Debbie: "Rush Rush," Chrysalis, 1983 • *Once More into the Bleach,* Chrysalis, 1989.

Heaven 17: "Designing Heaven," Eternal, 1996.

Ian, Janis: *Night Rains* (2 tracks), CBS, 1979.

Jackson, Janet: *Dream Street,* A&M, 1984.

Japan: "Life in Tokyo," Ariola, 1979 • *Assemblage,* Virgin, 1981 • *The Singles,* Alex, 1996.

John, Elton: *Duets,* MCA, 1993 • w/ RuPaul, "Don't Go Breakin' My Heart," MCA, 1994.

Kajagoogoo/Limahl: *Too Shy: The Singles and More,* Gold Rush, 1996.

Kane, Madleen: *Don't Want to Lose You,* Chalet, 1981 • *12 Inches and More,* TSR, 1994.

Kelly, Roberta: *Zodiac Lady,* Oasis, 1977 • *Gettin' the Spirit,* Casablanca, 1978.

Lane, Suzi: *Ooh La La,* Elektra, 1979.

Limahl: "The Never Ending Story," EMI, 1984, 1993 (*Living in Oblivion: The '80s Greatest Hits,* Vol. 2) • *See also* Kajagoogoo/Limahl.

Loggins, Kenny: "Danger Zone," Columbia, 1986 • "Meet Me Half Way," Columbia, 1987 • *Back to Avalon,* Columbia, 1988 • *Greatest Hits,* Columbia, 1997 • *Yesterday, Today and Tomorrow: The Greatest Hits,* Columbia, 1997.

Manchester, Melissa: "Thief of Hearts," Casablanca, 1984.

Medley, Bill: *Best Of,* Curb, 1990.

Moroder, Giorgio: *Music from 'Battlestar Galactica',* Casablanca, 1978 • "Chase," Casablanca, 1979 • *E = MC²,* Casablanca, 1979 • *Magic Movie Hits,* PolyGram International, 1998 • *See also* Oakey, Philip, and Giorgio Moroder.

Munich Machine: *Whiter Shade of Pale,* Casablanca, 1978 • *Body Shine,* Casablanca, 1979.

Newton-John, Olivia: *Olivia,* Festival, 1992 • *Back to Basics: The Essential Collection, 1971–1992,* Geffen, 1992 • "I Need Love," Geffen, 1992.

Oakey, Philip, and Giorgio Moroder: "Together in Electric Dreams," A&M, 1984 • *Chrome,* A&M, 1985.

Sigue Sigue Sputnik: *Flaunt It,* Manhattan/EMI, 1986 • "Love Missile F1-11," EMI, 1986, 1993 (*Living in Oblivion: The '80s Greatest Hits,* Vol. 2).

Sparks: *Number 1 in Heaven,* Virgin/Elektra, 1978 • "Beat the Clock," Virgin, 1979 • *Terminal Jive,* Virgin, 1980.

Summer, Donna: *A Love Trilogy,* GTO/Oasis, 1975 • "Love to Love You Baby," Oasis, 1975 • *Four Seasons of Love,* GTO/Casablanca, 1976 • "I Feel Love," Casablanca, 1977 • *I Remember Yesterday,* GTO/Casablanca, 1977 • *Once Upon a Time,* Casablanca, 1977 • "I Love You," Casablanca, 1978 • "Last Dance," Casablanca, 1978 • *Live and More,* Casablanca, 1978 • "MacArthur Park," Casablanca, 1978 • "Bad Girls," Casablanca, 1979 • *Bad Girls,* Casablanca, 1979 • "Dim All the Lights," Casablanca, 1979 • w/ Brooklyn Dreams, "Heaven Knows," Casablanca, 1979 • "Hot Stuff," Casablanca, 1979 • On the Radio Greatest Hits, I & II, Casablanca, 1979 • w/ Barbra Streisand, "No More Tears (Enough Is Enough)," Columbia, 1979 • "Cold Love," Geffen, 1980 • "On the Radio," Casablanca, 1980 • "The Wanderer," Geffen, 1980 • *The Wanderer,* Geffen, 1980 • "Walk Away," Casablanca, 1980 • *The Summer Collection,* Mercury, 1985 • *The Dance Collection,* Casablanca, 1987 • *Anthology,* Casablanca/Mercury, 1993 • *Melody of Love (EP),* Casablanca, 1994 • *I'm a Rainbow,* Casablanca/Mercury, 1996 • w/ Giorgio Moroder, "Carry On," Interhit, 1997.

Sylvers, The: *Disco Fever,* Casablanca, 1979.

Three Degrees: *New Dimension,* Ariola, 1978 • *3-D,* Ariola, 1980.

COLLECTIONS

Midnight Express, soundtrack, Casablanca, 1978 • *American Gigolo,* soundtrack, Polydor, 1980 • *Foxes,* soundtrack, Casablanca, 1980 • *Cat People,* soundtrack, Backstreet/MCA, 1982 • *Flashdance,* soundtrack, Casablanca, 1983 • *Superman 3,* soundtrack, Warner Brothers, 1983 • *Metropolis* soundtrack, Atlantic, 1984 • *The Never Ending Story* soundtrack, Gold Rush, 1984, 1996.

George "Shadow" Morton

If ever there was a story made for a Frank Capra film, it's George "Shadow" Morton's. We fade in on a young George Morton hitchhiking his way back into New York City on a snowy morning in 1964. When nobody picks him up he calls an old friend, who asks him how much money he has in his pockets. Our young hero finds 70 cents, and his friend says, "You've got enough for six cups of coffee and an emergency phone call. I'll see you in a few minutes."

After his friend picked him up, the two talked about an old friend, Ellie Greenwich, who had just struck it big in Manhattan as a songwriter. The next day, with nothing to do, Morton dialed information, got Greenwich's phone number at Red Bird Records, and made a date to meet her the next day.

"So, with my last dollar hidden in my shoe, I hitched into New York with my best clothes on. She was very very polite—very nice, very courteous." As Morton explains it, as he stood up to leave, Greenwich's partner Jeff Barry (see entry) turned from the piano and asked him what he did for a living. "I said, 'Just about nothing. I'm like you, I write songs.' That was my slap at him." Instead of backing down, Barry asked Morton to bring a song in the following Tuesday, and Morton agreed.

He got back home, called a friend in Long Island and asked him if he could rent his 1-track studio; he called another friend and asked him to bring a piano-bass-guitar-drums quartet to the studio on Sunday; and then he found an all-girl singing group, who eventually became the Shangri-Las. None of his friends would believe he had any songs, nor did they believe he could pull this off, but come Sunday they were all ready for him.

"The ironic part of the story is, between my con and all the help I was getting, I was pumped up. I was so thrilled with myself that I was driving down the road on Sunday afternoon, and it dawned on me that I did not have a song." So he pulled over to the side of the road, wrote down the lyrics, and walked into the studio like he owned the place. They knocked the song out and Morton was ready for his Tuesday appointment.

When the date rolled around he played the 7 1/2-minute song for Greenwich and Barry once. Barry picked it up, asked if he could play it for somebody else, and then walked out the door. "I was talking to Ellie and when it got awkward I said, 'Ellie, I'm going to leave. This guy takes my record, he's gone 10, 15 minutes, and I get the feeling I'm getting set up for a joke.'

She said, 'You're not.' I said, 'How do you know?' She said, 'You don't know? You've got a hit.' "

A few minutes later another guy opened the door waving the record over his head asking if Morton had written and produced it. He said yes to the writing, yes to the producing, and they guy offered him $250 a week and an office with his name on the door. Oh, and he was going to release the record in a couple of weeks. The song, "Remember (Walkin' in the Sand)," went to No. 5 in 1964 and launched the careers of the Shangri-Las and George Morton.

The inspiration for that song was the inspiration for every project he worked on for the next 12 years. "I didn't really have any," he says with a laugh. "I guess I was just in a goddamn panic to write a song. We could get all spiritual about it, but I didn't have a lot of time to think about the type of song I wanted to write, it just came out that way."

The same thing happened with "Leader of the Pack" (No. 1). Morton was sitting around his office one day when Jerry Leiber (see entry) knocked on the door and asked him if he had any ideas for a new Shangri-Las song. Morton, who was feeling rich and had been thinking about buying a motorcycle, suggested a song about a girl who meets and falls in love with a biker.

Leiber looked at him like he was crazy and said that no DJ in the world would play a song about a Hell's Angel. But, just for good measure, he asked if he had a title for the song and Morton shot back, "Yeah, 'Leader of the Pack.' "

Nobody was too keen on the song idea, so Morton went behind everybody's back and booked studio time in Hempstead, Long Island. "My wife woke me up and asked me if I had booked studio time," he remembers. "I said I had and she said they were all down at the studio waiting for me. I got up and asked her to bring a piece of paper and a pencil to the shower with a bottle of champagne. She couldn't find a pencil so I grabbed one of my kids' crayons and a piece of cardboard and I wrote 'Leader of the Pack' right there. I went into the studio and cut the track and then sent it to the office."

He thought that was the end of it and went off for a mild three-day party. One morning about 4 A.M. someone from the record label found him and informed him that he had another hit. "So, that's the way it was and it went like that for 12 to 14 years. It was a hell of a time."

That post–"Leader of the Pack" soirée was not the only three-day disappearing act Morton pulled during his stint working with Red Bird. Greenwich has said that she and Barry gave Morton the nickname "Shadow" because no one ever seemed to know where he was, and he would never show up for appointments.

Luck followed Morton again when Shelly Finkle dragged him to see a cover band called the Pigeons. Although he was impressed with their musicianship, he wasn't interested in working with a cover band. Finkle was outside trying to convince him to work with the band when Morton heard something strange coming from inside the club. He walked back into the club and saw Mark Stein playing the piano. Morton asked him what he was doing, and when Stein said he was rehearsing, Morton asked, "You learn a song by getting a 45 record and playing it at 33? He said, 'If I play it slow I can write down all of the chords quicker.' I said, 'From now on that's the way you're going to play all of your songs. You have just found your style.' They changed their name from the Pigeons to Vanilla Fudge."

Soon thereafter Morton took them into the studio for the first time to record their 1967 self-titled debut. They recorded three other albums together, and in 1998 they were talking about working together again. Their psychedelic cover of "You Keep Me Hangin' On," a No. 6 hit in 1967, was their highest-charting song.

In 1974 Morton worked with the New York Dolls, a band that stretched him beyond his past experience. He was recording the Dolls classic *Too Much, Too Soon* at night and an 11-piece all-female band during the day. "That was a challenge on me. It was a hell of a time. I was trying to prove to myself and the rest of the world that I could do it. The New York Dolls album was an absolute ball, I had a great time cutting them. They showed more raw, stripped-down talent and pure energy," he recalls.

There were other challenges. "I had to lean people against the wall so they would not fall down. I have spent a lot of time in my life with people in the studio helping them out. I start with information, move into suggesting, then I move into prayer, and then I move into threatening them with their lives. I've thrown chairs through windows in order to make a point. This was a time when it was getting hairy, but I was dealing with four off-the-wall crazy guys who just let it all hang out. I thought it was a great fun album."

Having fun seems to be the key for the kid who was raised in the suburban Long Island town of Hicksville. After 20 or so years in the music business this kid from Hicksville was reading a profile of another Hicksville kid, Billy Joel, in *Rolling Stone* magazine. The interviewer asked Joel to comment on Morton, and Joel declined, saying he would not say anything about Morton until he was paid the $67 Morton owed him. Morton called him up and said, "Billy, what's with the $67? He said, 'I was the piano player on 'Remember (Walkin' in the Sand).'" I said, 'You were that skinny 14-year-old? ' He said, 'That was me and I never got paid.' " Roll credits as Morton hands Joel the $67, with interest. —DAVID JOHN FARINELLA

Blues Project: *Anthology,* PolyGram, 1997.

Haystack Balboa: *Haystack Balboa,* Polydor, 1970.

Ian, Janis: *Janis Ian,* MGM, 1967 • "Society's Child," Verve, 1967 • *Society's Child,* MGM, 1967 • *For All the Seasons of Your Mind,* Verve, 1968 • *The Secret Life of J. Eddie Fink,* Verve, 1968 • *Society's Child: The Verve Recordings,* Polydor, 1995.

Johansen, David: *From Pumps to Pompadour: The David Johansen Story,* Rhino, 1995.

Mott the Hoople: "Keep a Knockin'," Atlantic, 1974 • "Midnight Lady," Atlantic, 1974 • *Rock and Roll Queen,* Atlantic, 1974.

New York Dolls: "Human Being," TVT, 1974, 1991 (*The Groups of Wrath*) • "Stranded in the Jungle," TVT, 1974, 1991 (*The Groups of Wrath*) • *Too Much Too Soon,* Mercury, 1974 • *Rock and Roll,* Mercury, 1994.

Pacheco, Tom: *Great American Heartland,* RCA, 1976 • *The Outsider,* RCA, 1976.

Shangri-Las, The: "Give Him a Great Big Kiss," Red Bird, 1964 • "Leader of the Pack," Red Bird, 1964 • "Give Us Your Blessings," Red Bird, 1965 • "I Can Never Go Home Anymore," Red Bird, 1965 • *Leader of the Pack,* Red Bird, 1965 • "Long Live Our Love," Red Bird, 1966.

Uncle Chapin: *Uncle Chapin,* Polydor, 1992.

Vanilla Fudge: *Vanilla Fudge,* Atlantic, 1967 • *Renaissance,* Atlantic, 1968 • *The Beat Goes On,* Atlantic, 1968 • "You Keep Me Hangin' On," Atco, 1968 • *Psychedelic Sundae: The Best Of,* Rhino, 1993.

COLLECTIONS

The Brill Building Sound: Singers and Songwriters Who Rocked the 60's, Era, 1993.

Mickie Most

Mickie Most is an enigma. While his success as a producer is undeniable, he has engendered controversy on more than one occasion. Born June 20, 1938, in Aldershot, England, Most began his career in the early '60s as a performer signed to Decca Records in London; none of his singles reached the U.K. Top 40.

When his singing career stalled, Most entered the production realm, scoring an immediate hit with one of the finest singles in rock history: "House of the Rising Sun" (No. 1) by the Animals. Most's production approach was to simply capture the band's raw emotion on this and other Animals' hits such as "We Gotta Get Out of This Place" (No. 13), "Don't Let Me Be Misunderstood" (No. 15), and "It's My Life."

In 1965, Most added Manchester's Herman's Hermits and flower child Donovan [Leitch] to his stable. Herman's Hermits' "Listen People" (No. 3) and "No Milk Today," both written by Graham Gouldman, captured teen angst with a Mersey beat feel, while Donovan's "Sunshine Superman" (No. 1), with lead guitar by session man Jimmy Page (see entry), and the hypnotic "Season of the Witch" incorporated Eastern mysticism into a pop format.

Most also produced Lulu's soaring ballad, "To Sir with Love" (No. 1) and the Nashville Teens' magnificent rocker, "Tobacco Road" (No. 14). Yet, Most did not have a universal Midas touch. A case in point: Most's production of the Yardbirds, the legendary band that included, at one time or another, three of rock's greatest axemen: Eric Clapton, Jeff Beck, and Jimmy Page.

In 1967, Page was trying to keep the band together, hoping to move the group toward heavier rock while retaining its blues core. Most, however, wanted to generate hit singles by bringing in outside material that the band felt was unsuitable. The result was disastrous. Most took the complex, creative Yardbirds and put them in a straitjacket with such tracks as "Little Games" and "Ha Ha Said the Clown." None of the Most-produced Yardbirds tracks were hits.

Page, on the other hand, begged Most to let him produce the B-sides of the Yardbirds' singles. As a result, Page crafted superb blues rock such as "Drinking Muddy Water" and the mind-expanding "Think About It," the band's final statement before Page formed Led Zeppelin.

Most also produced Jeff Beck's early solo efforts, including the searing masterwork, *Truth* (No. 15). Beck, however, rebelled when Most suggested he record "Love Is Blue," playing his guitar out of tune on the session. Today, the track sounds like a parody.

Another controversy concerns "Beck's Bolero," a B-side that turned up on the *Truth* album, which includes Beck and Page on guitars and John Paul Jones on bass. Simon Napier-Bell, producer of the Yardbirds when Beck and Page were in the lineup, told interviewer Jim Green in *Trouser Press* that he and Beck, not Most, produced the song. "Mickie Most put his name on it later," says Napier-Bell. "He took over producing the Yardbirds, and Jeff wanted that track as a B-side for 'Hi Ho Silver Lining.' I let him have it and he put his name on it. Talk about being naive; I just said, 'What the hell, I don't need it.' "

In the '70s, Most built a mobile studio, RAK, and formed a record label with the same name. His chart success continued with hits by Hot Chocolate, CCS, Mud, and Suzi Quatro. (He also produced snazzy, riff-heavy albums by underrated British session guitarist Chris Spedding on the label.) Moreover, he produced the 1991 hit by Kim Wilde, "Kids in America." Since then, RAK and Most have been largely inactive. —BEN CROMER

Animals, The: "House of the Rising Sun," MGM, 1964 • "I'm Crying," MGM, 1964 • *The Animals*, Colgems/MGM, 1964 • *The Animals on Tour*, MGM, 1964 • *Animal Tracks*, Colgems/MGM, 1965 • "Bring It on Home to Me," MGM, 1965 • "Don't Let Me Be Misunderstood," MGM, 1965 • "It's My Life," MGM, 1965 • "We Gotta Get Out of This Place," MGM, 1965 • *The Best of the Animals*, Abkco, 1966, 1987 • *The Complete Animals*, EMI, 1990.

Beck, Jeff: *Truth*, Columbia, 1968 • *Beck-Ola*, Columbia, 1969 • *Beckology*, Legacy/Epic, 1991, 1995.

Black, Don: *Songbook*, Play It Again, 1995.

Browne, Duncan: *Duncan Browne*, Rak, 1973.

CCS: *CCS*, Rak, 1972 • *The Best Band in the Land*, Rak, 1973.

Donovan: "Mellow Yellow," Epic, 1966 • "Sunshine Superman," Epic, 1966 • "Epistle to Dippy," Epic, 1967 • *Mellow Yellow*, Pye/Epic, 1967 • *Sunshine Superman*, Pye/Epic, 1967 • "There Is a Mountain," Epic, 1967 • "Wear Your Love Like Heaven," Epic, 1967 • *Barabajagal*, Epic, 1968 • *Gift from a Flower to a Garden*, Pye/Epic, 1968 • "Hurdy Gurdy Man," Epic, 1968 • *Hurdy Gurdy Man*, Epic, 1968 • "Jennifer Juniper," Epic, 1968 • "Lalena," Epic, 1968 • "Atlantis," Epic, 1969 • w/ Jeff Beck Group, "Goo Goo Barabajagal," Epic, 1969 • *Greatest Hits*, Epic, 1969 • "To Susan on the West Coast Waiting," Epic, 1969 • *Cosmic Wheels*, Epic, 1972 • *Donovan*, Rak, 1977 • *Troubador: The Definitive Collection, 1964–1976*, Legacy, 1992.

Felix, Julie: *Clotho's Web*, Rak, 1972.

Heavy Metal Kids: *Kitsch*, Rak, 1977.

Herman's Hermits: "I'm into Something Good," MGM, 1964 • *Introducing Herman's Hermits*, Colgems/MGM, 1964 • "Can't You Hear My Heartbeat?," MGM, 1965 • *Herman's Hermits*, Colgems/MGM, 1965 • "I'm Henry VIII, I Am," MGM, 1965 • "Just a Little Bit Better," MGM, 1965 • "Mrs. Brown You've Got a Lovely Daughter," MGM, 1965 • "Silhouettes," MGM, 1965 • "Wonderful World," MGM, 1965 • "A Must to Avoid," MGM, 1966 • *Both Sides of Herman's Hermits*, Colgems/MGM, 1966 • "Dandy," MGM, 1966 • "East West," MGM, 1966 • *Hold On* soundtrack, MGM, 1966 • "Leaning on a Lamp Post," MGM, 1966 • "Listen People," MGM, 1966 • "This Door Swings Both Ways," MGM, 1966 • *Blaze*, MGM, 1967 • "Don't Go Out in the Rain (You're Gonna Melt)," MGM, 1967 • "Museum," MGM, 1967 • "No Milk Today," MGM, 1967 • "There's A Kind Of A Hush," MGM, 1967 • *There's a Kind of a Hush*, Colgems/MGM, 1967 • "I Can Take or Leave Your Loving," MGM, 1968 • *Mrs. Brown You've Got a Lovely Daughter*, Colgems/MGM, 1968 • *Their Greatest Hits*, Abkco, 1973.

Hopkin, Mary: *Those Were the Days* (5 tracks), Apple, 1972.

Hot Chocolate: *Cicero Park*, Rak, 1974 • "Disco Queen," Big Tree, 1975 • "Emma," Big Tree, 1975 • *Hot Chocolate*, Rak,

1975 • "You Sexy Thing," Big Tree, 1975 • *Man to Man,*
Rak, 1976 • "So You Win Again," Big Tree, 1977 • "Every
1's a Winner," Infinity, 1978 • *Everyone's a Winner,*
Rak/Infinity, 1978 • *Going Through the Motions,*
RAK/Infinity, 1979 • *Class,* RAK, 1980 • *Mystery,*
RAK/EMI, 1982 • *Love Shot,* Rak, 1983.

Lee, Brenda: *Top Teen Hits,* Decca, 1965 • *Anthology,* Vols. 1–2,
1956–1980, MCA, 1991.

Lulu: *Something to Shout About,* Decca, 1965 • *Lulu Loves to
Love Lulu,* Columbia, 1967 • *"To Sir with Love,"* Epic,
1967 • *Lulu's Album,* Columbia, 1969 • *From Crayons to
Pefume: The Best Of Lulu,* Rhino, 1994.

Nashville Teens: *Tobacco Road,* One Way, 1964, 1997.

New World: *Believe in Magic,* RAK, 1973.

Quatro, Suzi: *Aggro-Phobia,* RAK 1977.

Racey: *Smash and Grab,* RAK, 1979.

Reid, Terry: *Bang, Bang . . . You're Terry Reid,* Epic, 1969 • *Move
Over for Terry Reid,* Epic, 1969 • *Terry Reid,* Epic, 1969.

Spedding, Chris: *Chris Spedding,* RAK, 1976 • *I'm Not Like
Everybody Else,* RAK, 1980 • *Ready! Spedding! Go!,* EMI, 1984.

Stewart, Rod: *Storyteller: The Complete Anthology,* Warner
Brothers, 1989.

Tee: *Totally,* Motown, 1995.

Wilde, Kim: "Kids in America," EMI, 1981, 1991.

Yardbirds, The: *Little Games Sessions and More,* Gold Rush,
1967, 1996.

COLLECTIONS

RAK's Greatest Hits, EMI, 1991: The Animals, "House of the
Rising Sun," 1964 • Jeff Beck, "Hi Ho Silver Lining," 1967
• Duncan Browne, "Journey," 1972 • CCS, "Whole Lotta
Love," 1970 • Adrian Gurvitz, "Classic," 1982 • Jeff Beck
Group and Rod Stewart, "I've Been Drinking," 1973 •
Kenny, "The Bump," 1974 • Mud, "Tiger Feet," 1974 •
Nashville Teens, "Tobacco Road," 1964 • New World,
"Tom Tom Turnaround," 1971 • Peter Noone, "Oh You
Pretty Thing," 1971 • Cozy Powell, "Dance with the
Devil," 1973 • Suzi Quatro, "Can the Can," 1973 • Racey,
"Lay Your Love on Me," 1978 • Chris Spedding, "Motor
Bikin'," 1975.

Bob Mould

Bob Mould grew up in the small upstate New York
town of Malone. He began "knowing what music
was about" at 5. The year was 1966. The music was
the Beatles, the Hollies, the Byrds, Dave Clark Five, the
Who.

The reason Mould was so hip to pop so young is
because the people who sold cigarettes to his dad's grocery store also stocked jukeboxes. So when they inserted
new singles into those garish old machines, his dad
would buy the old records for a penny apiece. Mould still
has 90 percent of those 45s. They were his schooling.

Since then, Mould has become known for his assault
guitar, his highly personal lyricism, and a unique melodicism. Leader of Hüsker Dü, then leader of Sugar,
Mould has also been on his own off and on during the
'90s. His latest production project is Verbow, a Chicago
band that released its debut album on Sony 550 in 1997.

"As far as what makes a song move, what makes a
song speak to people, it's just in there, it's not something I studied," he says. "It was hours and hours of listening to music, during all of my childhood. I have no
formal musical training. I can't even read guitar tabla-
ture. But by the time I was 9, I was able to sit down and
write songs on a keyboard because I knew how things
were supposed to go.

"I have a pretty good idea, when I hear a song,
whether it's working. It's more or less because of being
a fan. I guess that was my criterion for becoming a producer."

When he was 9, he pretended he had a music studio
in his bedroom. He would use tape guns to punch out
labels saying "Recording Studio, Stay Out, Four and
Eight Track Recordings Made Here." "It wasn't serious,
but I thought it was at the time," Mould says. "Through
that, I developed my own notation that I still use, as far
as making notes for myself. I can't do charts for other
people. If I was hearing a part [in my head], I'd just
either play it for them or hum it."

During the '80s, he produced "a lot of stuff," he says.
Is there a Mould sound? "I think I can get a pretty decent
guitar sound out of just about anybody," he says. "I
think I know how to arrange vocals pretty well. I know
when and when not to use percussion."

Being a producer "is a big job," says Mould, who
returned to New York in August 1997 after a few years
laying back in Austin. "It involves so much more than
knowledge of a console and of notes on a sheet of
paper. It's about being a referee, an authority figure, a
therapist, it's about being a baby-sitter at times. It's
about building people's egos up, being able to question
people in a productive way."

Technology? Not that interested. "I use automated
consoles for mixing records just to make things move a
little quicker. I don't know anything about MIDI, so I
don't know much about rigging that stuff up. I don't go
for keyboard-oriented stuff, as a rule. As for the dreaded
click track, it depends on the song and the drummer.

"I don't do 24-track edits; either you get it or you don't," he adds. "I want it to be a continuous, original track. I'll overdub the hell on things, but I want the rhythm tracks top-to-bottom natural. I don't know if people can tell the difference, but I think I can. I don't mind layering, I don't mind punching in to get a word or two fixed, but I'm more organic. I like things to be natural."

He doesn't like to rewrite others' songs, but he'll question a part in a song; if the writer can justify it, Mould will let it stay. "Most times, in the things I've produced, the songs are fine as they are," he says. "I wouldn't be getting involved otherwise. It's more like I want to provoke the writer in the sense of making them really think about the song."

Mould would like to produce guitarist Richard Thompson (a major influence), but "he's pretty stuck with Mitchell Froom" (see entry). He'd also like to produce Frank Black—and My Bloody Valentine. As for the latter, "I'd like to produce them just so we could get another record out," he laughs.

He says he's sought out for production work "every week, it seems, and maybe once every two or three years I'll hear something. My ratio of what I get called on to what I do is probably 1 in about 200. I just don't hear it in a lot of stuff."

Much of the music he's asked to produce sounds finished to him, he says: "It sounds like the people who are making the work have such a strong idea of it, they don't need me. Whereas if I hear newer artists who obviously have a gift for writing but may be a little lost at the delivery stage, I feel I can do my job." —CARLO WOLFF

Hüsker Dü: *Land Speed Record,* New Alliance, 1981 • *Everything Falls Apart,* Reflex, 1982 • *Metal Circus,* Reflex/SST, 1983 • *Zen Arcade,* SST, 1984 • *Flip Your Wig,* SST, 1985 • *New Day Rising,* SST, 1985 • *Candy Apple Grey,* Warner Brothers, 1986 • *Eight Miles High/Makes No Sense (EP),* SST, 1986 • *Warehouse: Songs and Stories,* Warner Brothers, 1987.
Magnapop: *Hot Boxing,* Priority, 1994.
Mould, Bob: *Workbook,* Virgin, 1989 • *Black Sheets of Rain,* Virgin, 1990 • "Can't Fight It," Arista, 1993 (*No Alternative*) • *Bob Mould,* Rykodisc, 1996 • *Egoverride (EP),* Rykodisc, 1996 • *Last Dog and Pony Show,* Rykodisc, 1998.
Soul Asylum: *Say What You Will,* Twin/Tone, 1984 • *Made to Be Broken,* Twin/Tone, 1986 • *Time's Incinerator,* Twin/Tone, 1987.
Sugar: *A Good Idea* (EP), Rykodisc, 1992 • "Changes," Rykodisc, 1992 • *Copper Blue,* Rykodisc, 1992 • *Helpless* (EP), Rykodisc, 1992 • "If I Can't Change Your Mind,"

Rykodisc, 1992 • *If I Can't Change Your Mind* (EP), Rykodisc, 1992 • *Beaster,* Rykodisc, 1993 • "Running Out of Time," Rykodisc, 1993 (*Born to Choose*) • "Believe What You're Saying," Rykodisc, 1994 • *File Under Easy Listening,* Rykodisc, 1994 • "Gee Angel," Rykodisc, 1994 • "Your Favorite Thing," Rykodisc, 1994 • *Besides,* Rykodisc, 1995.
Verbow: *Chronicles,* 550 Music, 1997.
Zulus: *Down on the Floor,* Slash, 1988.

M People

M People is known for soulful dance music laden with hooks. By combining '60s soul, '70s disco, and '90s dance beats (they've eschewed the alternative '80s), Heather Small (born January 20, 1965, in London), Mike Pickering (born 1958 in Manchester), and Paul Heard (born October 5, 1960, in London) have shaped and nurtured a sound that is undeniably pop dance, yet all their own. "As far as I'm concerned there are only two categories of music: music I like and music I don't like," says founding member Pickering. With M People, it is obvious what he likes.

M People has released four albums: *Bizarre Fruit, Elegant Slumming, Northern Soul* (released only in England), and *Fresco.* Each demonstrates a knack for creating music that is sophisticated, funky, and authentic. In fact, the critically acclaimed, multimillion-selling *Slumming* spawned numerous U.K. pop hits and No. 1 worldwide dance hits, including "How Can I Love You More?," "One Night in Heaven," and "Excited." It also won England's coveted Mercury Music Prize for 1994's Best Album of the Year (beating out Blur, Shara Nelson, Paul Weller, and the Prodigy).

M People harks back to the mid-'80s, when Pickering was a well-respected DJ working Manchester's legendary Hacienda nightclub, where he regularly treated the clubgoers to American house music. At the same time, he was the A&R contact for Factory Records, signing such bands as James and Happy Mondays. He also played sax for the label's seminal dance act, Quando Quango, and did remixes for New Order.

When he left Factory for the fledgling Deconstruction Records, Pickering, in addition to handling A&R, formed his own band, T-Coy, one of the first U.K. house outfits. Raised on Motown, Stax, and Philly International, Pickering began writing, but realized he needed a partner with richer musical training who could turn his ideas into songs. Paul Heard was that man. Classically trained, Heard was the bassist for U.K. groups Working Week, Strawberry Switchblade, and Orange Juice.

By 1991, the seeds for M People had been planted. Today, the band is an international success. "Our music is there to inspire some hope and to pay respect to the power of soul." And what is soul? "Any music that you feel and that you deliver with emotion." With a vision so pure, simple, and surprisingly fresh, M People is a quintessential '90s pop group and production unit.
—LARRY FLICK

A Certain Ratio: "Mello" (remix), Rob's, 1992.

ABC: "One Better World" (remix), Neutron, 1989 • "The Real Thing" (remix), Neutron, 1989.

Annette: "Dream 17," Deconstruction, 1988 • "Dream 17" (remix), Deconstruction, 1988.

Denver, Karl: "Wimoweh," Factory/London, 1989, 1997 (*Different Colours, Different Shades: The Factory, Story Part 2*).

Electronic: "Getting Away with It" (remix), Warner Brothers, 1990.

Inspiral Carpets: "Two Worlds Collide" (remix), Mute, 1992.

M People: "How Can I Love You More?," Deconstruction, 1991 • "Colour My Life," Deconstruction, 1992 • "Someday," Deconstruction, 1992 • "Don't Look Any Further," Deconstruction, 1993 • "Padlock," Epic, 1993 • *Elegant Slumming,* Epic, 1994 • "Elegantly American," Deconstruction, 1994 • "Excited," Epic, 1994 • "Moving On Up," Epic, 1994 • "One Night in Heaven," Epic, 1994 • "Open Your Heart," Epic, 1994 • "Renaissance," Deconstruction, 1994 • "Sight for Sore Eyes," Deconstruction, 1994 • *Bizarre Fruit,* Epic, 1995 • *Bizarre Fruit,* Vol. 2, Deconstruction, 1995 • "Itchycoo Park," Deconstruction, 1995 • "Kahlua, Music for Your Mouth," Deconstruction, 1995 • "Love Rendezvous," Deconstruction, 1995 • *Northern Soul,* Deconstruction, 1995 • "Search for the Hero," Epic, 1995 • "Fantasy Island," BMG, 1997 • *Fresco,* Deconstruction, 1997 • "Angel Street," BMG, 1998.

Minogue, Kylie: "Time Will Pass You By," Deconstruction, 1994.

New Order: "World in Motion" (remix), Qwest/WB, 1990.

Revenge: "Pineapple Face," Atlantic, 1990.

Sanchez, Roger: *S-Man Classics: The Essential Sanchez Mixes,* Harmless, 1998.

James Mtume

James Mtume is an R&B songwriter, composer, and Grammy Award–winning producer. He is also a skilled musician who, in the early '70s, migrated from his hometown of Philadelphia to New York to share the stage with such jazz legends as Sonny Rollins, Joe Henderson, and Freddie Hubbard. While playing with Hubbard, Mtume came to the attention of Miles Davis, who requested that he join his group as a percussionist.

Joining Davis's group in 1971, Mtume spent five years recording and touring with the inimitable trumpeter. Says Mtume, "Those were my Ph.D. years. What greater college could I have gone to?" True, but it should also be noted that he spent his undergraduate years with his father, Jimmy Heath, a great jazz saxophonist.

During these "Ph.D. years," Mtume was also an in-demand session player, recording with Larry Coryell (*Aspects*), Tiger McCoy (*Asante*), Lonnie Liston Smith (*Astral Traveling*), Rollins (*Nucleus*), and Roberta Flack (*Blue Lights in the Basement*). A year after Mtume left Davis's camp, he joined Flack's band, where he befriended guitarist Reggie Lucas. Within one year, Lucas and Mtume had formed a songwriting and production partnership that yielded numerous gold and platinum records, including the classic Roberta Flack–Donny Hathaway duet, "The Closer I Get to You"; Stephanie Mills' "Never Knew Love Like This Before" (No. 6), "Sweet Sensation," and "What Cha Gonna Do with My Lovin' "; and the stellar *You Know How to Love Me* by the late Phyllis Hyman.

Accumulating hit after hit for other artists was fine, but ultimately, Mtume decided that the energy he was putting into the careers of others could be better channeled into a band of his own. Thus, Mtume was born. Under that name, Mtume, Lucas, vocalist Tawatha Agee, keyboardist Phil Fields, and bassist Ray Johnson, recorded seven albums between 1978 and 1985. Although Mtume's success was checkered at best, the quintet did score two major hits. In 1983, they had a No. 1 R&B hit with the incredibly sexy "Juicy Fruit" and, a year later, reached No. 2 with "You, Me and He," a song oozing with sensuality.

By the time the group disbanded in the mid-'80s, Mtume's perspective on the history and development of black music and the important issues of musical integrity became obvious: He slowly and quietly put a halt to his contemporary R&B music productions. "I refused to do music I didn't believe in, and I preferred to leave gracefully with my integrity intact," he says. But his creativity and passion for discovering and mentoring were not silenced for long.

"I began to realize that black music was being reduced to a collection of hit records in the absence of hit careers," says Mtume. "I discovered that upcoming artists were completely unaware of the history of the pioneers they were emulating; some had never even worked with live musicians." A mentor was needed and he stepped in. A successful record producer again—witness Mary J. Blige's "(You Make Me Feel Like) A Natural Woman"—Mtume has further established himself as a multifaceted musical talent, applying his tasteful urban touch to domestic and foreign films, commercial jingles, and most recently, television, where he was the music director for the Fox TV drama, *New York Undercover*. —LARRY FLICK

Ayers, Roy: "Slip 'n Slide," Columbia, 1985 • "Hot," Columbia, 1986 • "Programmed for Love," Columbia, 1986.

Blige, Mary J.: "(You Make Me Feel Like) A Natural Woman," Uptown/MCA, 1995 • *Share My World*, Uptown/MCA, 1997.

Comsat Angels: *7 Day Weekend*, Jive/Arista, 1985.

Freeze Factor: *Chill*, Epic, 1989.

Hailey, K-Ci: "If You Think You're Lonely Now," Mercury, 1995.

Heath Brothers: *Expressions of Life*, Columbia, 1981.

Hyman, Phyllis: *You Know How to Love Me*, Arista, 1980 • *Under Her Spell: Phyllis Hyman's Greatest Hits*, Arista, 1989 • *The Legacy Of*, Arista, 1996.

K-Ci and Jo-Jo: *Love Always*, MCA, 1997 • *See also* Hailey, K-Ci.

Levert: *Bloodline*, Atlantic, 1986 • "Fascination," Atlantic, 1987.

Mills, Stephanie: "What Cha Gonna Do with My Lovin'," Twentieth Century, 1979 • *What Cha Gonna Do with My Lovin'*, Twentieth Century, 1979 • "Never Knew Love Like This Before," Twentieth Century, 1980 • "Sweet Sensation," Twentieth Century, 1980 • *In My Life: Greatest Hits*, Casablanca, 1985, 1990 • *The Best Of*, Mercury, 1995.

Mtume: *Kiss This World Goodbye*, Epic, 1978 • *In Search of the Rainbow Seekers*, Epic, 1980 • "Juicy Fruit," Epic, 1983 • *Juicy Fruit*, Epic, 1983, 1989 • "C.O.D. (I'll Deliver)," Epic, 1984 • "You, Me and He," Epic, 1984 • *You, Me and He*, Epic, 1984 • *Native Son* soundtrack, MCA, 1985 • "Breathless," Epic, 1986 • "P.O.P. (Pursuits of Pleasure) Generation," Epic, 1986 • *Theater of the Mind*, Epic, 1986 • "Body and Soul," Epic, 1987.

Native: "Love Ain't No Holiday," Jamaica, 1984.

Nu Romance Crew: "Tonight," EMI, 1987.

Spinners: *Can't Shake This Feelin'*, Atlantic, 1981.

Tawatha: "Are You Serious?," Epic, 1987 • "Did I Dream You?," Epic, 1987 • "Thigh Ride," Epic, 1987.

Tease: "I Can't Stand the Rain," Epic, 1988.

COLLECTIONS

Get On the Bus: Music from and Inspired by the Motion Picture, Interscope, 1996.

Mr. Colson

See DOUG OLSON

Kurt Munkacsi

Working with composer Philip Glass and music director Michael Riesman, Kurt Munkacsi has helped blur the boundaries in contemporary music for well over a quarter of a century. Munkacsi's Glass works have wedded the techniques of classical composition and pop production, achieving commercial success with avant-garde aspirations. Together, Munkacsi and Glass have also produced '80s new wavers Polyrock and the Waitresses (see Chris Butler entry).

From the Euphorbia Productions/Looking Glass Studios complex in downtown Manhattan, Munkacsi and Riesman have rehearsed, recorded, and produced dozens of finished albums from Glass's compositions and supervised scores of related projects. The Euphorbia team employs an expansive aesthetic, using the latest technology and overdubbing strategies to free its sessions from the strictures of traditional classical recording. "Whereas most classical music is captured as a sonic photograph, we've always set out to make recordings for the medium," Munkacsi says. "Rather than just document performances, we aim to create soundscapes—listening experiences meant to be heard on loudspeakers."

Munkacsi and Glass began making records together in the early '70s, breeding the nascent Euphorbia approach on such monolithic minimalist recordings as *Music in 12 Parts*, originally released on Glass's Chatham Square label. Recording exclusively for CBS in the '80s, the Glass-Munkacsi-Riesman troika applied itself to the full spectrum of music making—from the intimate (*Glassworks, Solo Piano*) to the epic (the grand opera trilogy *Einstein on the Beach, Satyagraha*, and *Akhnaten*). In 1997, Sony Classical released a three-disc retrospective of Glass's CBS years to coincide with his 60th birthday, with the sequencing and editing supervised by Munkacsi.

For much of the '90s, Euphorbia has had two creative outlets: Nonesuch and Point Music, Glass's joint-venture label with the Philips Music Group. Nonesuch releases projects bearing the Glass name, including such landmarks as the soundtrack to the film *Powaqqatsi*, a definitive rendition of *Einstein on the Beach*, and the multimedia opera *La Belle et la Bête (Beauty and the Beast)*. Nonesuch also issued a new three-disc recording of *Music in 12 Parts* as well as such overlooked beauties as Glass's score to *The Secret Agent*. The label released a 10-disc boxed set in 1998 that included new recordings.

For Point, the Euphorbia team mostly executive-produces albums by outside artists, such as composer Gavin Bryars' moving ambient collage *The Sinking of the Titanic* and the predictably popular but surprisingly effective *Symphonic Pink Floyd* (arranged by Jaz Coleman, the classically trained frontman of influential heavy rockers Killing Joke). Point is also the imprint for Glass's more crossover-type projects, such as his hit *Low* and *Heroes* symphonies based on the themes of David Bowie and Brian Eno (see entries) and the lovely incidental music he improvised with African kora virtuoso and composer Foday Musa Suso for a revival of Jean Genet's *The Screens*.

Even with a work as ostensibly traditional as 1993's *Low Symphony*—recorded with conductor Dennis Russell Davies and the Brooklyn Philharmonic Orchestra—Munkacsi and Riesman used their customary technique of doubling organic sounds with synthesizers. By blending synthesized tones with real strings and woodwinds, they were able to create "an instrument that doesn't exist in nature," Munkacsi says. "We can make it sound larger than life, which is what we're always after."

A different kind of textural fusion was produced on 1988's *Powaqqatsi*, which mingled non-Western music with Glass's already Eastern-leaning compositional style. Various instrumentalists and singers from around the world contributed to the project, in addition to a larger, more orchestral version of the intimate, revolving group of musicians in the Glass Ensemble. According to Munkacsi, differences in intonation and the challenges of reading Glass's intricate notation made getting appropriate contributions from the various international musicians difficult. To overcome that, the Euphorbia crew sampled the exotic instruments and then used

multitrack digital editing and computer sequencing to tailor the performances and integrate them into the blend of acoustic instruments.

The recording of *Powaqqatsi* marked a milestone for Euphorbia: the use of digital technology to invent new solutions to musical problems. "That album was the most advanced thing we had done so far," Munkacsi says. "With 105 discrete tracks, the music became a fluid process. It was our first step into nonlinear recording, using digital sound files instead of analog tape. We could go from point A to point C, bypassing point B."

Such technical fluency has since become a Euphorbia hallmark, making possible such complex creations as *La Belle et la Bête*. Glass's opera, based on the film by Jean Cocteau, demanded all of the Euphorbia team's expertise and then some. It started out simply enough, with Glass composing new music for the film, equipped with just a VCR and his piano. But the production eventually became intensely complicated because of the "synchronization nightmare," Munkacsi says. To create the proper effect, the vocalists had to time their singing to perfectly match the movements of the original film actors on the accompanying screen. Everything from the difficult job of casting and rehearsing the singers to designing the elaborate MIDI web of controllers and synthesizers made it a "highly experimental piece," Munkacsi says. "We made the process up as we went along."

Even though he composes in the time-honored tradition in a multimedia age, Glass has been able to issue a quantity of work that perhaps even Bach would have found substantial. And that's a testimony to Munkacsi and Euphorbia's efficacy. "If you came to my house, the only equipment you would find is a piano and an electric pencil sharpener," Glass says. "But I'm the only composer I know who has this much backup, and that's what has enabled me to be so productive." —BRADLEY BAMBARGER

Galas, Diamanda: *Plague Mass*, Mute, 1991.
Glass, Philip: *Music in Similar Motion and Music in Fifths*, Chatham Square, 1973 • *Music in 12 Parts*, Virgin, 1974, 1990 • *North Star*, Virgin, 1977 • *Dance Pieces*, CBS Masterworks, 1982, 1987 • *Solo Music*, Shandar, 1978 • *Glassworks*, CBS, 1982 • *Koyaanisqatsi* soundtrack, Island, 1983 • *The Photographer*, CBS, 1983 • w/ Kronos Quartet, *Mishima: A Life in Four Chapters* soundtrack, Nonesuch, 1985 • *Satyagraha*, Atlantic, 1985 • "Freezing," Portrait, 1986 • *Songs from Liquid Days*, Portrait, 1986 • *Akhnaten*, Atlantic, 1987 • *Powaqqatsi* soundtrack, Nonesuch/Elektra, 1988 • *The Thin Blue Line*, Atlantic, 1988 • *1,000 Airplanes on the Roof*, Venture/Atlantic, 1989 • *Solo Piano*, Columbia, 1989 • *Songs from the Trilogy*,

Columbia, 1989 • w/ Philip Glass, *Shankar/Glass Project,* Private, 1990 • w/ Philip Glass, *Passages,* Private, 1991 • w/ Foday Musa Suso, *Music From The Screens,* Point Music, 1992 • *Low Symphony,* Point Music, 1993 • *Anima Mundi* soundtrack, Nonesuch, 1994 • *Two Pages . . . ,* Elektra, 1994 • *Heroes Symphony,* Point Music, 1997 • *Kundun,* Point Music, 1997 • *The Secret Agent,* Nonesuch, 1997 • See also Philip Glass Ensemble.

Hwong, Lucia: *House of Sleeping Beauties,* Private, 1985 • *Secret Luminescence,* Private, 1987.

Indoor Life: *Sunshine Superman,* Elektra, 1986.

Philip Glass Ensemble: *Einstein on the Beach,* Nonesuch, 1976, 1993 • *Hydrogen Jukebox,* Nonesuch, 1993.

Polyrock: *Polyrock,* RCA, 1980 • "Changing Hearts," RCA, 1981 (*Blits*) • "Love Song," RCA, 1981 (*Blits*).

S'Express: "Music Lover" (remix), Rhythm King/Capitol, 1989.

Shankar, Ravi: *Inside the Kremlin,* Private, 1989 • *In Celebration,* Angel, 1995 • See also Glass, Philip.

Waitresses, The: "I Know What Boys Like," Polydor, 1980 • *Wasn't Tomorrow Wonderful,* Polydor, 1980 • "Wasn't Tomorrow Wonderful," Polydor, 1980 • *The Best of The Waitresses,* Polydor, 1990.

COLLECTIONS

Patty Hearst: Her Own Story soundtrack, Nonesuch, 1988.

Hugh Murphy

"The voice is the most important thing," insisted producer Hugh Murphy. "It's all a bunch of chords and people making noise and when you put the voice on all of a sudden it comes into focus, like a Polaroid."

Murphy's unassuming manner masked his keen sensibility for the art of recording. Best known for his long collaboration with Gerry Rafferty, Murphy co-produced Rafferty's hits "Baker Street" (No. 2), "Right down the Line" (No. 12), "Get It Right Next Time," and "Days Gone Down (Still Got the Light in Your Eyes)" (No. 17).

Born August 4, 1946, in London, Murphy began his career in the mid-'60s as a demo producer for Shel Talmy's (see entry) Orbit Music. Murphy's maiden voyage as a producer was the 1967 album by Sweet Thursday, a band that included Nicky Hopkins and Jon Mark. The Murphy-Rafferty partnership began in 1970 when Murphy, then a staff producer at Transatlantic Records, was assigned to produce Rafferty's *Can I Have My Money Back?*

When Rafferty signed with A&M Records to launch Stealers Wheel, Murphy struck out on his own, producing albums by Lindisfarne's Alan Hull and the folk-rock group Jack the Lad. After Stealers Wheel folded, Rafferty invited Murphy to co-produce *City to City* (No. 1), which included "Baker Street," a poignant song about big-city disillusionment that had an irresistible saxophone hook (by Raphael Ravenscroft) cradling the melody.

"I tried [the melody line] on a guitar and that didn't work and tried it with voices and that didn't work," Murphy explained. "Then one day I was listening to a Joni Mitchell record and there was a sax playing and it really sounded great, so I thought, 'Sax, of course—a street sound.'" Despite the song's quality, Murphy and Rafferty had to beg the record company to release "Baker Street" as a single. "They actually said it was too good for the public," Murphy said incredulously. "Right down the Line," another tour de force from *City,* grabbed listeners with a spooky electric guitar line, underscored by syncopated wood blocks. "We nicked the percussion feel from the Roland rhythm box," Murphy admitted. "It was done to a beguine or something on the Roland, so we just nicked that and got someone to play it."

Rafferty's next album, *Night Owl,* included "Days Gone Down (Still Got the Light in Your Eyes)" and "Get It Right Next Time," examples of how Murphy's production embraced Rafferty's voice with a tasteful mosa-

Photo by Ben Cromer © 1995

ic of keyboards, guitars, and synthesizers. The duo produced one more album, *Snakes and Ladders,* before taking a sabbatical.

During the separation, Murphy contributed lyrics to Van Morrison's *Beautiful Vision* album and produced projects by Bonnie Tyler, Linda Thompson, and Ringo Starr. Rafferty and Murphy reunited for *North and South,* a marriage of Celtic folk with pop rock that featured the bittersweet ballad "Hearts Run Dry." Murphy's '90s production credits include Rafferty's *On a Wing and a Prayer* and *Over My Head,* as well as folk-country-rock guitarist Jerry Donahue's *Neck of the Wood.*

In an industry characterized by egos as large as the Grand Canyon, Murphy's modest, offhand approach was endearing. Once, when asked to describe how he handles a mix, Murphy pointed to a knob on the control board and says, "Just wiggle it about until you think it sounds right."

Hugh Murphy died of cancer in October of 1998.
—BEN CROMER

Betjeman, Sir John: *Late Flowering Love,* Charisma, 1974.
Brady, Paul: *Hard Station,* Polydor/WEA, 1982 • *Songs and Crazy Dreams,* Fontana, 1992.
Cartwright, Dave: *Masquerade,* DJM, 1979.
Digance, Richard: *Live at the Queen Elizabeth Hall,* Chrysalis, 1978.
Donahue, Jerry: *Neck of the Wood,* Cross Three, 1994.
Gracious: *Gracious,* Capitol, 1970 • *This Is,* Philips, 1972.
Harrold, Melanie: *Melanie,* DJM, 1979.
Heron, Mike: *Mike Heron,* Casablanca, 1979.
Jack the Lad: *Jack the Lad,* Charisma, 1974 • *The Old Straight Track,* Charisma, 1974 • *It's Jack,* Asylum, 1975.
Jackson, Ray: *In the Night,* Mercury, 1980.
Kid Gloves: *Kid Gloves,* Buddah, 1972.
Kilburn and the High Roads: *Handsome,* Pye, 1975.
Lindisfarne: *Chocs Away,* UK, 1975.
Mark Almond Band: *Mark Almond Band,* Line, 1971, 1996 • *The Best Of,* Blue Thumb, 1973 • *The News,* Mercury, 1979 • *The Best Of,* Rhino, 1991.
Rafferty, Gerry: *Can I Have My Money Back?,* Track/Blue Thumb, 1971 • *Gerry Rafferty* (1 track), Transatlantic/Visa, 1974, 1978 • "Baker Street," United Artists, 1978 • *City to City,* United Artists, 1978 • "Home and Dry," United Artists, 1978 • "Right down The Line," United Artists, 1978 • "Days Gone Down (Still Got the Light in Your Eyes)," United Artists, 1979 • "Get It Right Next Time," United Artists, 1979 • *Night Owl,* United Artists, 1979 • *Snakes and Ladders,* United Artists, 1980 • *North and South,* Avalanche, 1987, 1995 • *Right down the Line: The Best of Gerry Rafferty,* Gold Rush, 1989, 1996 • *On a Wing and a Prayer,* Avalanche, 1992 • *Over My Head,* Avalanche, 1994 •

Clowns to the Left, Jokers to the Right, Raven, 1997.
Ravenscroft, Raphael: *Her Father Didn't Like Me Anyway,* Portrait, 1979.
Shearson, Gary: *Dingo,* Charisma, 1974.
Starr, Ringo: *Scouse the Mouse,* Polydor, 1977.
Stray: *Stray,* Track, 1970 • *Suicide,* Track, 1971.
Styvers, Laurie: *Spilt Milk,* Warner Brothers, 1972.
Sweet Thursday: *Sweet Thursday,* Epic, 1967, 1973.
Thompson, Linda: *One Clear Moment,* Warner Brothers, 1978 • *Dreams Fly Away,* Rykodisc, 1996.
Thompson, Richard: *Watching the Dark: The History of Richard Thompson,* Hannibal, 1993.
Tyler, Bonnie: *Goodbye to the Island,* RCA, 1981.

Jeff Murphy

Since Jeff Murphy began producing records in the early '70s, he has come to value rawness over perfection. Immediacy has at least as much of a place in rock 'n' roll as studio refinement, says Murphy. His key vehicle: Shoes, one of the great (and least-heard) American power-pop bands.

Murphy plays guitar and sings; his brother, John, plays bass; their friend, Gary Klebe, plays guitar. Together with various drummers, the Murphy brothers and Klebe have released numerous records as Shoes. After three Shoes releases on Elektra—*Present Tense,* co-produced with Mike Stone (see entry); *Tongue Twister,* co-produced with Richard Dashut (see entry); and *Boomerang* —Shoes has released three more of its own full-length albums—and records by its friends—on its own label, Black Vinyl Records, and its affiliate, Broken Records. Shoes headquarters is in Zion, north of Chicago.

Murphy has also produced several bands for major labels, including the first Material Issue album, *International Pop Overthrow,* on Mercury, in 1991. He calls that effort "really a great record of rawness."

Born December 3, 1954, in Berwyn, a southern Chicago suburb, Murphy is a self-taught musician who has always stayed close to home. He and his brother have been music nuts since they were kids. Murphy began producing in 1973, working on such early Shoes albums as *One In Versailles, Heads or Tails,* and *Bazooka.*

"I just really love the whole recording process," he says. "When I was a kid, they had those little bitty, 3-inch reel-to-reel machines. Walgreen's is where I saw the one I really wanted. My folks got it for me for Christmas one year, and I recorded everything."

He recorded sound bites from such TV shows as *Wild, Wild West, The Patty Duke Show,* and *The Munsters.* "Even now, if I see a rerun of an old show on Nickelodeon, I'll call John and laugh," he says. "There were certain bites we'd play to death."

Seeing the Beatles on *Ed Sullivan* in 1964 transformed Murphy. "I was just impressed by the fact that they swept everything," he says. "Their performance was the talk, and they became a fun phenomenon to be involved in. My father had left the family about a year prior to that, so the Beatles gave my brother and me a great distraction."

According to the account of early Shoes days in *As Is,* a mail order–only compilation of rarities and B-sides Shoes issued on Black Vinyl in 1997, the key records influencing the band were Grin's *1 + 1; Something/Anything,* by Todd Rundgren; *#1 Record* and *Radio City,* by Big Star; and *Sincerely,* by the Dwight Twilley Band.

While brother John collected pop memorabilia of the day—"He'd know to take a magazine and stick it in the closet, saying this will be worth money someday," Murphy says—Jeff was deep into the mystery of recording. Not only did he subscribe to audio and stereo magazines as a teenager, he bought an old reel-to-reel recorder that had sound on sound and echo. He would create "weird little recordings" with John and Gary. Jeff also worked at Radio Shack after school. In 1973, this savvy consumer bought his first four-channel tape machine, a Tascam 3340. Shoes recorded its earliest material—*Heads or Tails, One in Versailles, Bazooka,* even *Black Vinyl Shoes*—on the Tascam.

By mid-1975, Murphy had moved into his own place, equipping it with a mixer, echo units, and compressors he bought with money he earned working in a factory as a printer.

In January 1979, the big time came knocking, first in the form of Sire chief Seymour Stein, then by way of Elektra vice president Kenny Buttice. Stein met the group several times, indicating he'd sign Shoes once he returned from a meeting abroad. But while Stein was in France, Buttice called "and made us this absolutely great deal," Murphy says.

Shoes signed with Elektra as a production company, giving this fledgling band control over who it worked with and what songs it did. "That's really the fun of the record industry," Murphy says. "The phone can ring and just change your life." Despite the deal, Elektra management soon changed; the label fired its college department and failed to pump money into videos. Meanwhile, R.E.M. was emerging from the college scene into the mainstream and MTV was just beginning to gain clout.

Shoes did four videos from *Present Tense,* MTV put them into rotation, but Elektra didn't support the band. Meanwhile, Shoes (under Gary Klebe's name) had produced Spooner, a Madison, Wisconsin, band featuring future Garbage brain Butch Vig (see entry). Spooner invited Shoes to Madison to join Spooner at a show; a video was made of that, but Elektra blocked it even though MTV wanted it, Murphy says.

"Just as we were finishing the third record, people were getting fired from Elektra, and you could see the writing on the wall," says Murphy. "There was too much infighting, things weren't getting done. A couple of weeks after we delivered the tapes, the company was basically shut down by Warner Bros. They fired most of the staff, dropped most of the bands, moved to New York, and restarted with a different staff and different bands." Elektra did not, of course, drop such groups as the Cars, the Eagles, or Queen.

"We went independent again," Murphy says. "We went back to putting out our own records." The contract with Elektra stipulated it had to buy out what was left of the term, "so we took the money and started our own studio."

"When you record something, you're capturing a mood," he says. Murphy is melodically oriented, "a sucker for ear candy." And if the drums sound good, chances are the whole record does.

Early on, drumming was a problem. "Drums can be tricky," says Murphy, "and that's where a lot of the power of a track lies. In early Shoes recordings, we were so much in pursuit of what we saw as the ideal drum sound that we missed the emotion."

Now Murphy focuses on feeling rather than finish. "The presentation is important, but maybe the perfect presentation is low-fi for that particular mood. It's the same way that very often visually, something shot documentary-style, with a handheld camera or on cheap 8-millimeter film, better captures an intimacy and a mood than something perfectly filmed on videotape, which is a much more accurate medium."

On *Either Way,* a record he released in 1997 under the Nerk Twins name (the other Nerk is Herb Eimerman), the feeling was natural. "We just reacted," Murphy says. "We didn't write things much before we started. We just kind of came together in the studio. It was an effort to get back to [the atmosphere of] early Shoes, which was very uninhibited. Then, if we happened to have something laying around the studio, a saxophone, say, we would use it. That's the fun of doing music. We were the judges of what was good and bad, and we would do what we felt was right," he says of the early Shoes period. "I think our instincts are our best ally.

We're not very good musicians, but we have very good musical instincts." —CARLO WOLFF

Bad Examples: *Bad Examples,* Waterdog, 1993 • *Meat: The Bad Examples,* Waterdog, 1994.

Day One: *Hallowed Ground,* Black Vinyl, 1993.

Eimerman, Herb: *From Your Window,* Black Vinyl, 1992.

Fun with Atoms: *Northern Distortion,* Black Vinyl, 1996.

Insanity Wave: *Do the Worm,* Spin Art, 1998.

Kibler, Dan: *Haunted,* Big Deal, 1996 • *Capsule,* Big Deal, 1998.

Material Issue: "Diane," Mercury, 1991 • *International Pop Overthrow,* Mercury, 1991 • "Valerie Loves Me," Mercury, 1991 • *Destination Universe,* Mercury, 1992 • "What Girls Want," Mercury, 1992 • *Telecommando Americano,* Rykodisc, 1997.

Material Issue and Liz Phair: "The Banana Splits Song," MCA, 1995 (*Saturday Morning Cartoon's Greatest Hits*).

Nerk Twins: *Either Way,* Broken, 1997.

Shoes: *Heads or Tails* (EP), self released, 1975 • *Bazooka,* self released, 1976 • *One in Versailles,* self released, 1976 • *Black Vinyl Shoes,* Black Vinyl, 1977, 1994 • *Present Tense,* Elektra, 1979 • "Too Late," Elektra, 1979 • *Tongue Twister,* Elektra, 1981 • *Boomerang,* Elektra, 1982 • *Shoes' Best,* Black Vinyl, 1987 • *Shoes on Ice,* Black Vinyl, 1990 • *Propeller,* Black Vinyl, 1995 • "Tore a Hole," Black Vinyl, 1995 • *As Is,* Black Vinyl, 1996 • *Fret Buzz,* Black Vinyl, 1996.

Squares, The: *Answer,* Squares, 1990.

Frank Nardiello

See BUZZ McCOY and GROOVIE MANN

Christopher Neil

Christopher Neil, writing in *Making Music* (edited by George Martin; see entry), believes producers must rely on their instincts to guide them when crafting songs. "In the end, it all comes down to instinct," writes Neil. "You get a gut feeling when an arrangement is right."

Best known for his work with Mike and the Mechanics and Sheena Easton, Neil began his career as a singer and actor with the *Jesus Christ Superstar* troupe. In the '70s, Neil recorded several singles with Paul Nicholas for Mickie Most's RAK Records before launching his production career with Nicholas's 1977 solo hit, "Heaven on the Seventh Floor" (No. 6).

In 1981 Neil and Easton, the Scottish lass who was a relative unknown before she signed with EMI Records, struck immediate gold with "Morning Train (Nine to Five)" (No. 1), a song that Neil molded from a rough demo into a hit single. "As with many demos, the structure was incorrect," Neil recalls in *Making Music.* "They'd started with the bridge, which was all wrong. But there was a great hook."

Neil's other hits for Easton include "Modern Girl" (No. 18), "You Could Have Been with Me" (No. 15), and the sublime "For Your Eyes Only" (No. 4), the theme song for the James Bond film. Neil also produced Gerry Rafferty's overlooked gem, *Sleepwalking,* during this period.

Genesis's guitarist Mike Rutherford, looking for a producer for his busman's holiday, Mike and the Mechanics, selected Neil to produce the band's debut album, resulting in such hits as "All I Need Is a Miracle" (No. 5) and "Silent Running" (No. 6). Neil also produced the band's biggest hit, "The Living Years" (No. 1), as well as the excellent solo album by Mechanics singer Paul Carrack, *One Good Reason.*

Neil's commercial sensibilities are his greatest asset, resulting in well-crafted pop rock that ultimately focuses attention on tight performances of good, kook-laden songs. —BEN CROMER

A-ha: *East of the Sun, West of the Moon,* Warner Bros., 1991.

Brown, Andy: *Good Advice,* EMI, 1972.

Carrack, Paul: "Don't Shed a Tear," Chrysalis, 1987 • *One Good Reason,* Chrysalis, 1987 • "Button off My Shirt," Chrysalis, 1988 • "One Good Reason," Chrysalis, 1988 • *The Carrack Collection,* Chrysalis, 1988 • "When You Walk in the Room," Chrysalis, 1988.

Cher: *It's a Man's World,* Reprise, 1996.

Chorale: *Chorale,* Arista, 1979.

Dion, Celine: *Unison,* Epic, 1990 • "(If There Was) Any Other Way," Epic, 1991 • "Where Does My Heart Beat Now?," Epic, 1991 • *The Color of My Love,* 550 Music, 1993 • "Think Twice," 550 Music, 1994.

Dollar: *Shooting Stars,* Carrere, 1979.

Easton, Sheena: "For Your Eyes Only," Liberty, 1981 • "Modern Girl," EMI America, 1981 • "Morning Train (Nine to Five)," EMI America, 1981 • *Sheena Easton,* EMI America, 1981 • "You Could Have Been with Me," EMI America, 1981 • *You Could Have Been with Me,* EMI, 1981 • *Madness, Money and Music,* EMI, 1982 • "When He Shines," EMI America, 1982 • *The World of Sheena Easton:*

The Singles Collection, EMI America, 1993.

Essex, David: *Imperial Wizard,* Mercury, 1979.

Hain, Marshall: *Dancing in the City,* Harvest/Capitol, 1978 • *Free Ride,* Harvest/Capitol, 1978.

Kenny, Gerard: *Made It in the Rain,* RCA, 1979 • *Living on Music,* RCA, 1980.

Marillion: *Holidays in Eden,* IRS, 1992 • *Six of One, Half-Dozen of the Other,* IRS, 1992.

Marvin, Hank: *All Alone with Friends,* Polydor, 1983.

Mike and the Mechanics: "All I Need Is a Miracle," Atlantic, 1985 • *Mike + the Mechanics,* Atlantic, 1985 • "Silent Running (on Dangerous Ground)," Atlantic, 1985 • "Taken In," Atlantic, 1986 • "Nobody's Perfect," Atlantic, 1988 • "The Living Years," Atlantic, 1988 • *The Living Years,* Atlantic, 1988 • "Seeing Is Believing," Atlantic, 1989 • "Word of Mouth," Atlantic, 1991 • *Word of Mouth,* Atlantic, 1991.

Moody Blues: *Keys of the Kingdom,* Polydor, 1991 • "Say It with Love," Polydor, 1991.

Nicholas, Paul: "Heaven on the Seventh Floor," RSO , 1977 • *Paul Nicholas,* RSO, 1977.

Other Ones: "Holiday," Virgin, 1987 • *The Other Ones,* Virgin, 1987 • "We Are What We Are," Virgin, 1987.

Rafferty, Gerry: *Sleepwalking,* United Artists, 1982 • *Right down the Line: The Best Of,* Gold Rush, 1989, 1996 • *Clowns to the Left, Jokers to the Right,* Raven, 1997.

Sayer, Leo: *Have You Ever Been in Love?,* Warner Bros., 1983 • *The Show Must Go On: Anthology,* Rhino, 1996.

Stevens, Shakin': *The Bop Won't Stop,* Epic, 1983.

Tyler, Bonnie: *Free Spirit,* Atlantic, 1996.

Waterman, Dennis: *Dennis Watterman,* EMI, 1980.

Wavelength: *Hurry Home,* Ariola, 1982.

Wax UK: *Magnetic Heaven/American English,* Renaissance, 1997.

Williams, Geoffrey: *Heroes, Spies and Gypsies,* Atlantic, 1988.

Ken Nelson

Nashville is known as the home of country music, but aficionados know California's Bakersfield sound is also important. Ken Nelson was one of the architects of that distinctive style, producing more than 170 acts in his 35 years at Capitol Records, including Buck Owens, Tex Ritter, Bobby Bare, Roy Acuff, Roy Rogers and Dale Evans, and Merle Haggard.

Born January 19, 1911, in Caledonia, Minnesota, Nelson grew up in Chicago, where he got his start in the music business. He credits the legendary Lee Gillette

with introducing him to record production. "I got into it through Lee," Nelson recalls. "He was one of the greatest producers who ever lived. He produced Nat 'King' Cole, Guy Lombardo, Tennessee Ernie Ford, and Kay Starr. It goes on and on."

He and Gillette began their music careers singing in the Campus Kids, a successful trio that performed on the *Fibber McGee and Molly* radio show. Nelson got in on the ground floor of FM radio when he returned from the service. In the '40s, executives from a new label, Capitol, asked Gillette to initiate a transcription service focusing on "hillbilly western" music. Nelson and Gillette stayed in touch.

In the late '40s, Capitol, facing a strike by the musicians union, tried to record as much music as possible. When a scheduling conflict prevented Gillette from recording a session in New York, Gillette asked Nelson to stand in. That was his first production job. "It was difficult because the singer was drunk," Nelson recalls. "It turned out okay; he wasn't so drunk he couldn't sing."

In the record company's panic to record everything possible before a strike, it tapped Nelson to record numerous Chicago acts. "So I went ahead and did them," he says. "My first hit record was 'Buttons and Bows' (No. 5) with the Dinning Sisters."

Ultimately, Gillette hired Nelson, who moved to California to work for Capitol. "At that time, record companies weren't giving records to radio stations," Nelson says. "Stations had to buy their records and transcriptions [the precursors of LPs] were rented to the stations. We provided programs and literature. We had to pro-

vide so many selections a month. I came to California and took over that department. Capitol inadvertently put transcriptions out of business because they realized they could sell more records by giving radio stations records. So they did, and when they did that, other companies started giving records away as promotions."

When Capitol decided to put Gillette in their pop division, Nelson took over as head of the country department. He spent 35 busy and rewarding years at the label. He went to Capitol in 1948, took over the country division in 1950, and remained at the label until he retired from his post as vice president of the country division at age 65.

A favorite is Buck Owens. "Buck Owens is, I think, one of the greatest guys," Nelson says. "We are still great friends. He started out playing guitar for Tommy Collins. Tommy, Buck, and I took a trip to Nashville because Tommy was going to play in the Grand Ole Opry. Buck kept bugging me that he wanted to sing. . . . One day we were in the studio and had finished a session and I said 'Okay, go in and let me hear you sing.' He sang about 16 bars and I said 'Okay, that's enough." It was good enough for me to know the guy had something. So I signed him."

Nelson and Owens cut such classics as "I've Got a Tiger by the Tail" and "Together Again" (both No. 1 country). "Buck had a tremendous sense of musicianship, and he had a tremendous sense of picking the right songs and writing his own songs. Everything he did was tops."

Haggard, another key Nelson act, almost didn't sign with Capitol; Nelson had to overcome Haggard's loyalty to another label to get him. Nelson says his admiration for Haggard's talent created unique challenges as a producer. "The only difficult part was that I was enthralled with his singing," says Nelson. "Sometimes I'd be listening to his singing instead of what was going on. He was very easy to record, and Buck was, too. I never had any problem with any artist."

Nelson's work with Owens and Haggard helped shape the Bakersfield sound, but Nelson declines credit. "No, it was the musicians who created the sound," he says. "In those days we used to record four numbers in three hours; today, of course, they don't do that and I think it's wrong. On so many records, they make the background, then the singer adds his voice to it. I don't see how they can get the feel that way. They lose the emotional impact, in my opinion."

Nelson says he doesn't know what makes a successful producer. "All I know is that you sign an artist for what the artist can do, not for what you can do. The artist either has it or not. The only thing you can do is recognize the ability of the artist and to see the artist gives the most emotional performance he can during the session."

Two who got away were Kitty Wells and Willie Nelson. Nelson couldn't see "girls selling," so he passed on signing Wells to Capitol. Willie Nelson was signed to Victor at the time and wasn't selling there. Ken figured he would be a stiff at Capitol, too.

At the time of this interview, Nelson was a vibrant 86-year-old with a busy social life that included golf games with his grandson and visits with other family and friends.

Any regrets? "What's to regret? the only thing I regret is that I didn't make more hit records. I guess I made a few, but I didn't really make them. The artists did." —DEBORAH EVANS PRICE

Brown, Hylo: *Hylo Brown and the Timberliners,* Bear Family, 1992.

Burton, James: w/ Ralph Mooney, *Corn Pickin' and Slick Slidin,* See for Miles, 1968, 1993.

Carman, Jenks Tex: *Hillbilly Hula,* Bear Family, 1991.

Collins, Tommy: *Leonard,* Bear Family, 1992.

Dinning Sisters: "Buttons and Bows," Capitol, 1948.

Farmer Boys: *Flash, Crash and Thunder,* Bear Family, 1991.

Freberg, Stan: *Capitol Collectors Series,* Capitol, 1990 • *Presents the United States of America, Parts 1 and 2,* Rhino, 1996.

Haggard, Merle: *Greatest Hits,* MCA, 1982 • *Merle Haggard's Greatest Hits,* MCA, 1982 • *His Greatest and His Best,* MCA, 1985 • *Capitol Collectors Series,* Capitol, 1990 • *More of the Best,* Rhino, 1990 • *Untamed Hawk,* Bear Family, 1995 • *Down Every Road,* Capitol, 1996 • *Vintage Collection Series,* Capitol, 1996.

Haggard, Merle, and the Strangers: "Mama Tried," Capitol, 1968 • "Sing Me Back Home," Capitol, 1968 • "Swinging Doors," Capitol, 1968 • "The Legend of Bonnie and Clyde," Capitol, 1968 • "Hungry Eyes," Capitol, 1969 • "Okie from Muskogee," Capitol, 1969 • *Same Train, a Different Time . . . Songs of Jimmie Rodgers,* Koch, 1969, 1995 • "Workin' Man Blues," Capitol, 1969 • "The Fightin' Side of Me," Capitol, 1970 • *The Fightin' Side of Me,* Capitol, 1970 • "Daddy Frank (The Guitar Man)," Capitol, 1971 • "Grandma Harp/Turnin' Off a Memory," Capitol, 1972 • *The Best of the Best Of,* Capitol, 1972 • "If We Make It Through December," Capitol, 1973 • "Things Aren't Funny Anymore," Capitol, 1974 • "Kentucky Gambler," Capitol, 1975 • "Cherokee Maiden/What Have You Got Planned Tonight Diana?," Capitol, 1976 • "The Roots of My Raising," Capitol, 1976 • *The Land of Many Churches,* Razor & Tie, 1991, 1997.

Husky, Ferlin: "Gone," Capitol, 1956 • "Wings of a Dove," Capitol, 1960 • *The Heart and Soul Of,* Capitol, 1963 • *Ferlin*

Huskey, Dot/MCA, 1982 • *Vintage,* Capitol, 1996.

Jackson, Wanda: *Right or Wrong,* Bear Family, 1992 • *Vintage Collections,* Capitol, 1996.

James, Sonny: *Greatest Hits,* Curb/Capitol, 1986 • *Greatest Hits,* Columbia, 1992.

Jim and Jesse: *Jim and Jesse, 1952–1955,* Bear Family, 1992.

Louvin Brothers, The: *Tragic Songs of Life,* Capitol, 1956 • *A Tribute to the Delmore Brothers,* Capitol, 1960 • *Satan Is Real,* Capitol, 1960 • *Christmas with the Louvin Brothers,* Razor & Tie, 1997.

Maddox, Rose: *Sings Bluegrass,* Capitol Nashville, 1962, 1996.

Mooney, Ralph: *See* James Burton.

Morse, Ella Mae: *Barrelhouse, Boogie and Blues,* Bear Family, 1997.

Owens, Buck: "Under Your Spell Again," Capitol, 1959 • "Act Naturally," Capitol, 1960 • *Buck Owens,* Sundazed, 1961, 1995 • *You're for Me,* Sundazed, 1962, 1995 • "Love's Gonna Live Here," Capitol, 1963 • *On the Bandstand,* Sundazed, 1963, 1995 • "I've Got a Tiger by the Tail," Capitol, 1964 • "Together Again," Capitol, 1964 • *Christmas with Buck Owens,* Capitol, 1965, 1990 • *All-Time Greatest Hits,* Vol. 1, Capitol, 1990 • *Collection, 1959–1990,* Rhino, 1992.

Owens, Buck, and His Buckaroos: *I Don't Care,* Capitol, 1964 • *Together Again/My Heart Skips a Beat,* Capitol, 1964 • *Before You Go/No One but You,* Sundazed, 1965, 1995 • *I've Got a Tiger by the Tail,* Capitol, 1965 • *The Instrumental Hits,* Sundazed, 1965, 1995 • *Open Up Your Heart,* Sundazed, 1966, 1995 • *Roll Out the Red Carpet,* Capitol, 1966 • "How Long Will My Baby Be Gone?," Capitol, 1968 • "Johnny B. Goode," Capitol, 1969 • "Tall Dark Stranger," Capitol, 1969 • "Who's Gonna Mow Your Grass?," Capitol, 1969 • "Made in Japan," Capitol, 1972 • *Live at Carnegie Hall,* CMF, 1988 • *In Japan,* Sundazed, 1997.

Ritter, Tex: *High Noon,* Bear Family, 1992.

Shepard, Jean: *The Melody Ranch Girl,* Bear Family, 1996.

Starr, Kay: *Capitol Collectors Series,* Capitol, 1991.

Thompson, Hank: *At the Golden Nugget,* Capitol, 1961 • *Vintage,* Capitol, 1996.

Travis, Merle: *Walkin' the Strings,* Capitol, 1960.

Vincent, Gene: "Be-Bop-A-Lula," Capitol, 1956.

Vincent, Gene, and His Blue Caps: *The Bop That Just Won't Stop,* Capitol, 1956 • "Woman Love," Capitol, 1956 • *The Capitol Collectors Series,* Capitol, 1990 • *The Screaming End: The Best Of,* Razor & Tie, 1997.

Wakely, Jimmy: *Vintage Collections Series,* Capitol, 1996.

West, Speedy, and Jimmy Bryant: *Flamin' Guitars,* Bear Family, 1997.

Williams, Tex: *Vintage Collection Series,* Capitol, 1996.

Work, Jimmy: *Making Believe,* Bear Family, 1993.

Young, Faron: *The Classic Years, 1952–1962,* Bear Family, 1992.

Ron Nevison

"Y ou always have to go for a performance," insists Ron Nevison. "Passion and impact is what I try to bring to something." Nevison's diverse résumé includes Heart, Starship, John Waite, the Babys, UFO, Meat Loaf, Melissa Manchester, and Ozzy Osbourne.

And while many veteran acts have often reached new audiences under his tutelage, Nevison resists being branded as the rescuer of performers in search of chart salvation. "In the case of a group like the Babys, they'd only done one album before I got hold of them," Nevison argues. "And UFO had done several albums before I did *Lights Out.* I just looked at it as the next step in their career."

For Meat Loaf's *Welcome to the Neighborhood* (No. 17), Nevison crafted an album that acknowledged the artist's multiplatinum history by incorporating Meat Loaf's trademarks: strong lyrics that convey drama and liberal use of acoustic piano and electric guitar. "If you listen back to the stuff that [producer/songwriter] Jim Steinman did with him, you'll see the same threads," Nevison explains, noting he's a Steinman fan.

Nevison engineers approximately 90 percent of the projects he produces, employing outside engineers when necessary. He even had two studios going simultaneously for the Meat Loaf album. "I was engineering in one and running back and forth with another engineer doing other work," he recalls.

To simplify mixing, Nevison incorporates studio effects when cutting the basic tracks; he also keeps the basic tracks to a manageable number. "There's not six tracks of vocals where I want the first verse here and the second verse there," he says. "It's hard enough to mix an album: You can get sidetracked by all these other things."

Initially a singer, the Philadelphia native gravitated toward engineering and production as a way to combine his childhood passions for music and electronics. His career took off in the late '60s and early '70s, when he started mixing concerts by Traffic, Derek and the Dominoes, and the Jefferson Airplane. Subsequently, Nevison relocated to England to find work as a studio engineer; however, he soon found himself in business with Pete Townshend building remote studios. That partnership built the infamous Ronnie Lane Mobile used by Led Zeppelin, Bad Company, and the Who. Nevison also engineered many of these recordings, including Bad Company's explosive debut, *Bad Company*, and Zeppelin's *Physical Graffiti*.

Nevison migrated to Los Angeles in 1975, starting a roller-coaster string of hits: "Jane" (No. 14) and "Find Your Way Back" by Starship; "High on You" (No. 8) by Survivor; "I'd Lie for You (And That's the Truth)" (No. 13) by Meat Loaf; "Isn't It Time" (No. 13) by the Babys; "Alone" (No. 1) and "Never" (No. 4) by Heart; and "We Just Disagree" (No. 12) by Dave Mason.

Indeed, Nevison's studio date book is nearly always full. However, even a producer with his success record occasionally sings the blues when the phone stops ringing. "A lot of times I get jobs because somebody else couldn't make it or somebody else turned it down, just like I'll turn something down and somebody else will get that," he says. "You start working on something and somebody else calls you up and you can't do it; then it's 'Why didn't you call me a month ago?'" —BEN CROMER

Alexis: *Alexis,* MCA, 1977.

Babys, The: *Broken Heart,* Chrysalis, 1977 • "Isn't It Time," Chrysalis , 1977 • "Every Time I Think of You," Chrysalis, 1979 • *Head First,* Chrysalis, 1979 • *On the Edge,* Chrysalis, 1980 • *Anthology,* Gold Rush, 1981, 1996.

Bad English: *Backlash,* Epic, 1991 • "Straight to Your heart," Epic, 1991.

Call, Alex: *Alex Call,* Arista, 1983.

Candlebox: *Happy Pills,* Warner Bros., 1998.

Chicago: *Chicago 19,* Reprise, 1988 • "I Don't Wanna Live Without Your Love," Reprise, 1988 • "Look Away," Reprise, 1988 • *Greatest Hits, 1982–1989,* Full Moon/Reprise, 1989 • "You're Not Alone," Reprise, 1989 • "Chasin' the Wind," Reprise, 1991 • *XXI,* Reprise, 1991 • *Heart of Chicago,* Vol. 2, *1967–1998,* Warner Bros., 1998.

Chilli Willi and the Red Hot Peppers: *Bongos over Balham,* B&C, 1974.

Cocker, Joe: *Cocker,* Capitol, 1986.

Damn Yankees: "Coming of Age," Warner Bros., 1990 • *Damn Yankees,* Warner Bros., 1990 • "High Enough," Warner Bros., 1990 • "Come Again," Warner Bros., 1991 • *Don't Tread,* Warner Bros., 1992 • "Where You Goin' Now," Warner Bros., 1992 • "Silence Is Broken," Warner Bros., 1993.

Europe: *Out of This World,* Epic, 1988 • "Superstitious," Epic, 1988 • *1982–1992,* Epic, 1993 • *Super Hits,* Legacy/Epic, 1998.

Finnigan, Mike: *Black and White,* CBS, 1978.

Firehouse: *3,* Epic, 1995 • "I Live My Life for You," Epic, 1995.

Flo and Eddie: *Moving Targets,* Mondo, 1976 • *Best Of,* Rhino, 1987.

Foghat: *Road Cases,* Plum, 1998.

Grand Funk Railroad: *Bosnia,* Capitol, 1997.

Heart: *Heart,* Capitol, 1985 • "Never," Capitol, 1985 • "These Dreams," Capitol, 1985 • "What About Love?" Capitol, 1985 • "If Looks Could Kill," Capitol, 1986 • "Nothin' At All," Capitol, 1986 • "Alone," Capitol, 1987 • *Bad Animals,* Capitol/EMI, 1987 • "There's the Girl," Capitol, 1987 • "Who Will You Run To?," Capitol, 1987 • "I Want You So Bad," Capitol, 1988 • *Greatest Hits,* Capitol, 1997 • *These Dreams: Heart's Greatest Hits,* Capitol, 1997.

Jamison, Jim: w/ Survivor, *Collection,* Scotti Brothers, 1994.

Jefferson Airplane: *Jefferson Airplane,* Epic, 1989.

Jefferson Starship: *Freedom at Point Zero,* Grunt, 1979 • "Jane," Grunt, 1979 • "Find Your Way Back," Grunt, 1981 • *Modern Times,* Grunt, 1981 • "No Way Out," Grunt, 1984 • *Nuclear Furniture,* Grunt, 1984 • *At Their Best,* RCA, 1993 • *See also* Starship.

Johansen, David: *Live It Up,* Blue Sky, 1982 • *From Pumps to Pompadour: The David Johansen Story,* Rhino, 1995.

Kiss: "Crazy Crazy Nights," Mercury, 1987 • *Crazy Nights,* Mercury, 1987 • "Reason to Live," Mercury, 1988.

Manchester, Melissa: *Tribute,* Mika, 1989 • *If My Heart Had Wings,* Atlantic, 1995.

Mason, Dave: *Flowing Free Forever,* Columbia, 1977 • *Let It Flow,* Columbia, 1977 • "We Just Disagree," Columbia, 1977 • *Mariposo De Oro,* Columbia, 1978 • *Long Lost Friend: The Best Of,* Legacy/Columbia, 1995.

Meat Loaf: "I'd Lie for You (and That's the Truth)," MCA, 1996 • "Not a Dry Eye in the House," MCA, 1996 • *Welcome to the Neighborhood,* MCA, 1996.

Michael Schenker Group: *Michael Schenker Group,* Chrysalis, 1981 • *Essential,* Chrysalis, 1992.

Money, Eddie: *Playing for Keeps,* Columbia, 1980 • *Super Hits,* Columbia, 1997.

Neil, Vince: *Exposed,* Warner Bros., 1993.

Never the Bride: *Never the Bride,* Atlantic, 1995.

Night Ranger: *Neverland,* Legacy, 1997.

Osbourne, Ozzy: "Shot in the Dark," CBS Associated, 1986 • *The Ultimate Sin,* Epic, 1986, 1995 • *The Ozzman Cometh: Greatest Hits,* Epic, 1997.

Shooting Star: *Silent Scream,* Virgin, 1985.

Slick, Grace: *Software,* RCA, 1984.

Smith, Rex: *Camouflage,* CBS, 1983.

Starship: *Starship's Greatest Hits: Ten Years of Change,* RCA, 1991.

Survivor: "High on You," Scotti Brothers, 1984 • "I Can't Hold Back," Scotti Brothers, 1984 • *Vital Signs,* Scotti Brothers, 1984 • "First Night," Scotti Brothers, 1985 • "The Search Is Over," Scotti Brothers, 1985 • "Is This Love?," Scotti Brothers, 1986 • *When Seconds Count,* Scotti Brothers, 1986, 1992 • "How Much Love," Scotti Brothers, 1987 • "Man Against the World," Scotti Brothers, 1987 • *See also* Jamison, Jim.

Thin Lizzy: *Night Life,* Vertigo/Mercury, 1974 • *Dedication: The Very Best of Thin Lizzy,* Mercury, 1991.

This Picture: *City of Sin,* Dedicated, 1994 • "Hands on My Soul," Dedicated, 1994.

UFO: *Lights Out,* Chrysalis, 1977 • *Obsession,* Chrysalis, 1978 • *Strangers in the Night,* Chrysalis, 1979 • *Essential,* Chrysalis, 1992.

Waite, John: *Essential,* Chrysalis, 1992.

Werner, David: *Imagination Quota,* RCA, 1975.

Wetton, John: *Battle Lines,* Avalanche, 1994.

Wilson, Ann: "The Best Man in the World," Capitol, 1986.

Wolf and Wolf: *Wolf and Wolf,* Morroco, 1984.

COLLECTIONS

Reading Festival 1973, Gaff Masters, 1973.

Queens Logic, Epic, 1990.

Bryan "Chuck" New

Bryan "Chuck" New has been an expert and affable asset as engineer, mixer, and remixer to several milestone recordings by Def Leppard, the Cars, Massive Attack, Billy Ocean, the Sugarcubes, and Whodini. As producer New guided some of the '80s, most successful rap and R&B, including Neneh Cherry, D.J. Jazzy Jeff & the Fresh Prince, and Kool Moe Dee. In the '90s he has gravitated to modern rock, producing goth-pop superstars the Cure, as well as Pop Will Eat Itself and Dub War.

Bryan New was born October 17, 1961, and grew up in Buckhurst Hill, a small village in northern England. When he played guitar in typical schoolboy rock bands, London seemed a world away. Playing music came to seem an unpromising career choice, and New got into a recording studio trainee program, ending up at Manfred Mann's south London studio, the Workhouse.

He moved to Battery Studios—owned by Jive Records—in 1982 and almost immediately began assistant-engineering for Mutt Lange's (see entry) production of Def Leppard's *Pyromania.* "It was a real eye opener. I don't know if you know anything about Mutt Lange—he's particularly finicky and he's right to be so for his style of production—but I'd never been through anything like that before: Mutt slaving over a guitar part for days, rather than hours. Before that it was just a process of getting a song on tape; it didn't occur to me that you could control all those elements and make something totally different out of it," says New.

And that wasn't the only thing Lange changed. "Mutt has a penchant for giving people nicknames. In the course of the year or more that I worked on *Pyromania,* he gave me 20 or 30 nicknames and Chuck was the one that stuck. He thought I looked like a Chuck." With Lange, New also worked on records for the Cars and Bryan Adams. New went from assistant to engineer at Battery, recording the hugely successful Billy Ocean album *Suddenly* and mixing for *Love Zone* and *Tear Down These Walls.*

Many people don't know that a lot of great American hip-hop was recorded in London at Battery, through the Jive connection. New engineered for Whodini in the mid-'80s, and again had his eyes opened. "I barely knew what sampling was, and we did a lot of that with Whodini. Rap had been kind of slow to catch on in England."

By 1987 New was ready to produce, and in one remarkable year he co-produced the platinum *How Ya Like Me Now* by Kool Moe Dee, and the triple-platinum *He's the D.J., I'm the Rapper* (No. 4) by D.J. Jazzy Jeff & the Fresh Prince (Will Smith). Moe Dee's accessible but deeply funky title track is a hip-hop classic with piercing synth stabs, James Brown samples, and Moe's no-nonsense boast-rap. "Wild Wild West," a hugely thumping tale of Moe's manly preference for hands over guns in urban conflict, is another hip-hop standard.

Jazzy Jeff and the Fresh Prince's singles "Nightmare on My Street" (No. 15) and the great teen lament "Parents Just Don't Understand" (No. 12) demonstrated Will Smith's sizable charisma nearly 10 years before he became a major movie star. The duo's middle-class attitudes and values helped break rap with the middle-class white audience.

In 1990 New became involved with the peculiar genius that is Robert Smith of the Cure when he rearranged two tracks ("Pictures of You" and "The Caterpillar") for the Cure's *Mixed Up* (No. 14) remix album. He also mixed the band's smoking version of the Doors' "Hello, I Love You" for Elektra's 40th Anniversary *Rubaiyat* album. Then in 1993 New actually co-produced the band with Smith, helping to create a swirling, psychedelic trance version of Jimi Hendrix's "Purple Haze," the best track on the gold *Stone Free: A Tribute to Jimi Hendrix* album.

New and Smith then co-produced the Cure's exemplary live album *Show,* recorded during the Wish tour in Detroit, and its auxiliary EP, *Sideshow.* Another live album of older material from the tour was recorded in, and entitled, *Paris.* The atmosphere on all is a gothy haze, but the playing is sharp and Smith's mood is light. New's virtuous mix carries it all from the concert hall to your lap—the only thing missing is the line to the bathroom.

Lately New has been entering the studio to produce new bands like the thunderous funk metal of Dub War. From having been involved primarily with the technical side of production through engineering, mixing, remixing, and the cut-and-paste of hip-hop, New is entering a new phase. "When I started I was just happy to be doing it and to finish the record. Now I'm appreciating the way an artist is feeling. In the dance and remix side of things, the artist's role can be almost secondary, so you don't get to appreciate them as much as you maybe should. It's taken me quite a long time to understand the way people are in the studio and how they react to situations and emotions," he says.

"I'm trying to work on that side of it right now: making sure the environment is right for the artist and taking care of things technically that they, as musicians, may not know. I'm trying to make the whole recording process as smooth as possible for them without interfering with what they are trying to do."

Examples?

"For Dub War I went in with the idea of recording a song at a time, rather than cutting all the basic tracks at once, and then having the drummer being bored while all of the other parts are being added on; it made the band more interested in the whole album and fueled a number of different ideas." —ERIC OLSEN AND DAVID JOHN FARINELLA

Blood Brothers: *Honey and Blood,* Jive, 1988.
Boogie Down Productions: "I'm Still #1" (remix), Jive, 1988.
Butler, Jonathan: *Introducing,* Jive, 1987.
Cherry, Neneh: *Raw Like Sushi* (1 track), Virgin, 1989.
Cranes: "Jewel" (remix), Dedicated/RCA, 1993.
Cure, The: *Mixed Up* (2 tracks), Fiction/Elektra, 1990 • "Friday I'm in Love" (remix), Fiction, 1992 • "Burn," Interscope/Atlantic, 1993, 1994 (*The Crow* soundtrack) • *Paris,* Elektra, 1993 • "Purple Haze," Reprise, 1993 (*Stone Free: A Tribute to Jimi Hendrix*) • *Show,* Elektra, 1993 • *Sideshow* (EP), Elektra, 1993.
D.J. Jazzy Jeff & the Fresh Prince: "Nightmare on My Street," Jive, 1988 • "Brand New Funk," Jive, 1988 • *He's the D.J., I'm the Rapper,* Jive, 1988 • "Parents Just Don't Understand," Jive, 1988.
Dub War: *Pain,* Earache, 1997.
Jaz: "Hawaiian Sophie," EMI, 1989.
Kingmaker: *Celebrated Working Man* (EP), Sacred H., 1991.
Kool Moe Dee: *I'm Kool Moe Dee,* Jive, 1986 • *Best,* Jive, 1987 • "How You Like Me Now," Jive, 1987 • *How Ya Like Me Now,* Jive, 1987 • "No Respect," Jive, 1987 • "No Respect" (remix), Jive, 1987 • "Wild Wild West," Jive, 1988 • "Wild Wild West" (remix), Jive, 1988 • "I Go to Work" (remix), Jive, 1989 • *Greatest Hits,* Jive, 1993.

Pop Will Eat Itself: *Amalgamation* (EP), Nothing/Interscope, 1994 • *Dos Dedos Mis Amigos,* Nothing/Interscope, 1994 • "Everythings Cool," Nothing/Interscope, 1994 • "Ich Bin Ein Auslander," Nothing/Interscope, 1994 • "R.S.V.P.," Nothing/Interscope, 1994.
Raheem: "Self Preservation," A&M, 1989 (*Lost Angels* soundtrack).
Roman Holliday: "Motor Mania" (remix), Jive, 1983.
Sugarcubes: *It's-It,* Elektra, 1992.

Ted Niceley

Intensity of product and sensitivity of process: that uncommon combination has marked such pace-setting Ted Niceley productions as Girls Against Boys' *Venus Luxure No. 1 Baby* and Shudder to Think's *Pony Express Record,* examples of state-of-the-art alt-rock. By never sacrificing psychology to methodology, he has been able to make the most of varying musical scenarios.

"It's easy when recording to obliterate everything that's unique and good about a band," Niceley says. "A lot of the musicians I work with will say, 'I want that sound you got on *Venus Lux,* or give me that *Pony Express* thing.' But, you know, I didn't record the drums with Girls Against Boys any differently than I did with Shudder to Think. The band is the sound, and performance is everything."

A journeyman musician before his days behind the board, Niceley was a close observer of the Washington, D.C., hardcore scene of the early '90s who eventually made a name for himself producing early classics by D.C. straightedge heroes Fugazi. Not only did he produce Fugazi's *13 Songs* and *Repeater,* and subsequent Girls Against Boys and Shudder to Think records; his production palette also includes albums as diverse as Jawbox's *For Your Own Special Sweetheart* and Tripping Daisy's modern rock hit *I Am an Elastic Firecracker.* He also produced a set of platinum discs by French rockers Noir Desir and tracks by alt-popsters Cinnamon.

"What I always try to impart to music is an intense feeling, whether it's on the mellow end or something really heavy," Niceley says. "Bringing out the elements of the band that are being overlooked, maximizing the sounds and feelings that are already in a piece of music but may be hidden—that's what I do."

Niceley's ability to accentuate the positive made his most influential associations long-term. After the touchstone *Venus Luxure No. 1 Baby* of 1993, he produced Girls

Against Boys' *Cruise Yourself* and *House of GvsB*, completing a trio of discs on the Chicago Touch & Go label that helped garner the band acres of well-deserved indie cred before it landed a deal with Geffen.

In shepherding 1994's *Pony Express Record*, Niceley helped Shudder to Think fashion a classic essay in post-punk art rock, its dissonant drama, audacious harmonic reach, and daring rhythmic complexity requiring painstaking technical and emotional care (with a nod to the glorious mix by Andy Wallace, who helped bring out all the crunch and detail; see entry).

Niceley went on to produce the debut album by Shudder guitarist Nathan Larson's all-star side band Mind Science of the Mind, which was nearly as impressive as *Pony Express Record* in its depth, spirit, and sonic allure. Niceley was also on hand for Shudder's second album for Epic, the trim, tuneful, and woefully under-appreciated *50,000 B.C.* In its more mellifluous way, the album was even more searching than *Pony Express Record*, abandoning dark prog-rock for an idiosyncratic rapprochement with classic rock 'n' roll.

Larson points out that Shudder to Think's metallic glam and Girls Against Boys' industrial-strength sex rock are "poles apart sonically," which helps show that Niceley doesn't have an aesthetic program as much as organizational genius. "On *Pony Express Record* and, especially, *50,000 B.C.*, he made us address each and every part of a song and why it was there," Larson adds.

Indeed, for Niceley, record making is more ear than gear (although he has sworn by his sampler-equipped Eventide Harmonizer), and he has only one true technical credo: Always have the red light on. He says, "Musicians always say, 'You weren't recording that, were you?' And I always reply, 'Hell, yes, I was, and you'll be glad I did.' "

Since he came of age in the '60s, Niceley says his auditory apparatus benefited from the example of several generations of music: from the British Invasion and psychedelia to Aerosmith and Cheap Trick, from punk rock and new wave to Nirvana and the alternative revolution. "I'm a big believer in sound as reference," he says. "Sounds set me off, inspires me. More than anything, the radio of the '60s and '70s—where you could hear some classic R&B tune back-to-back with T. Rex or Led Zeppelin—was a big influence on me. Whenever I hear something cool, I always say, 'I can hear that on the radio.' —BRADLEY BAMBARGER

Buck Pets: *To the Quick*, Restless, 1993.
Cinnamon: *The Courier*, Island, 1997.
Dead Milkmen: *Soul Rotation*, Hollywood, 1992.
Frente: *Shape*, Mammoth, 1996.

Fugazi: *13 Songs* (7 tracks), Dischord, 1989 • *Repeater*, Dischord, 1990 • *In on the Kill Taker*, Dischord, 1993.
Girls Against Boys: "Bullet Proof Cupid," Touch & Go, 1993 (*Suburbia* soundtrack) • *Cruise Yourself*, Touch & Go, 1994 • *Venus Luxure No. 1 Baby*, Touch & Go, 1993 • *Disco 666*, Touch & Go, 1996 • *House of GvsB*, Touch & Go, 1996 • "Superfire," Touch & Go, 1996.
High Back Chairs: *Curiosity and Relief*, Dischord, 1992.
Jawbox: *For Your Own Special Sweetheart*, Atlantic, 1994 • *Savory + 3* (EP), Atlantic, 1994.
Keene, Tommy: *Places That Are Gone* (EP), Dolphin, 1984 • *The Real Underground*, Alias, 1993.
Mind Science of the Mind: *Mind Science of the Mind*, Epic, 1996.
Monsterland: *Destroy What You Love*, Seed, 1993 • *At One with Time*, Seed, 1994.
Noir Desir: *666667 Club*, Polydor, 1996.
Ruth Ruth: *Laughing Gallery*, Ventrue/American, 1995 • "Uptight," Ventrue/American, 1996.
Shudder to Think: "Hit Liquor," Dischord, 1992 • "Animal Wild," Thirsty Ear/Chaos/Columbia, 1993 (*Sweet Relief*) • *Pony Express Record*, Epic, 1994 • *50,000 B.C.*, Epic, 1997 • "Red House," Epic, 1997.
Stanford Prison Experiment: *The Gato Hunch*, World Domination, 1995.
Trampoline: *Dormer*, Spin Art, 1993.
Trippin' Daisy: *I Am an Elastic Firecracker*, Island, 1995.

Joe and Phil Nicolo
(BUTCHER BROTHERS)

Twins Joe and Phil Nicolo, aka the Butcher Brothers, have exec-produced, produced, mixed, and engineered an astonishing array of music over the last 20 years. They are owners of Philadelphia's Studio 4, and Joe is president and co-owner of the wildly successful Columbia imprint Ruffhouse. Between the two of them (separately or as the Butcher Brothers), they have produced the rap of Boo-Yaa T.R.I.B.E., Cash Money, the Goats, Hard Corps, Kris Kross, the Psycho Realm, Schoolly D, and Urban Dance Squad; the rock, modern rock, and metal of Anthrax, Big Chief, Dandelion, Dishwalla, Fig Dish, Life of Agony, Mighty Mighty Bosstones, Skypark, and Urge Overkill; and the everything

INTERVIEW WITH JOE AND PHIL NICOLO

Eric Olsen: Do you approach things differently when you're doing a hip-hop versus a mainstream versus a hard-rock record?

Joe Nicolo: From a preproduction standpoint there's a little bit different mindset. With a band you're probably going over arrangements, and with a hip-hop thing you're going more through parts, loops, samples. But the overall process is basically the same. You want something to grab your attention—something has to change your life as you know it, so to speak, and then you want to capture whatever that essence is on tape.

Phil Nicolo: And try to get it in a real flowing, emotional way. Whether it's a vocal performance or a musical performance, capturing that on tape and creating an atmosphere. . . . I don't know if you can tell, but we like to have fun. It's like coming over to Joe and Phil's house with state-of-the-art incredible equipment, in a really cool environment where you can feel relaxed and kick ass and create music.

It's worked. The very first record we did in the new place was Dishwalla, and it did great. "Counting Blue Cars" (No. 15) was on the charts for, like, a year. These guys had never made a record, but they came in and they felt really good and they played and J.R. [Richards] sang and it just translated into the record.

EO: How do you work together?

JN: It depends on the act and what's happening on any given day. Phil has great technical ability in mixing a record from a sonic standpoint—he gets great sounds. I have a shorter attention span and I usually gotta run in and out of the room a lot. I'm more trying to figure out what wacky thing can we do in the overall principal of the song and Phil's getting the incredible drum sounds. But it varies.

PN: It does. There will be times when Joe will come in with his sampler. I can barely put a sample into the damn thing, but he plays it like an instrument. He brings it in, and all of a sudden you've got this industrial loop going on underneath that changes the whole texture of the music. I think it's really cool that two heads are better than one and

we get along great. So, I'll bring it to step 1, and then Joe will bring it to step 2, and I'll bring it to step 3. We sort of magnify each other's talents. In every case, the stuff that we work on together is the best stuff that we've done.

EO: What are your most important records?

JN: For me two records come to mind: Schoolly D's *Saturday Night,* because we didn't know what we were doing and we were establishing an aesthetic at the time that seems to still hold up today.

After that the next thing would have to be Cypress Hill, because at that moment nothing sounded like Cypress Hill to me. I was a 35-year-old white guy from the suburbs, but this shit was slamming. I loved it. When it came out it made a statement that no other rapper at that point had made.

Most recently it would have to be the Fugees. And being nominated for a Record and Song of the Year Grammy with Billy Joel ["River of Dreams," No. 3, co-produced with Danny Kortchmar; see entry] was a personal accomplishment.

PN: I think the things we often feel strongest about are the things that go the furthest. The early Hooters stuff was monumental because it was the first real record I worked on with Rick Chertoff. Kris Kross—it was so weird about the song "Jump"—I didn't think it would do anything. Also, I love the Wailing Souls and Dishwalla stuff.

EO: Has anything changed over time?

JN: Thank God it's as exciting as ever. Working with someone like Billy Joel, I still get goose bumps. I'm watching Billy Joel playing different parts and he's asking me my opinion on them! It is still exciting to hear the music develop, and at the end of the night feel pumped about it. As long as I still get that charge I'm still going to have fun doing it, and we're still going to put out 120 percent. So, in a lot of respects it hasn't changed: it's still that excitement of watching the creative process happen and feeling so lucky to be a part of it. —ERIC OLSEN AND DAVID JOHN FARINELLA

---

else of Goat, James Hall, Hamell on Trial, Billy Joel, Taj Mahal, and Wailing Souls!

The brothers Nicolo were born August 21, 1955, in Wayne, Pennsylvania, outside of Philadelphia. By the age of 7 they were fascinated with music (Beatles, Motown) and with the process of recording. As teens they built their own recording studio in their parents' attic, and friends, neighbors, and countrymen kept them busy recording. They attended Temple University and built another studio there, followed by yet another

studio with partner Dave Johnson called Half Track when they graduated Temple in 1977.

The brothers built Studio 4 downtown in 1980, where many of Philly's finest musicians recorded—often with producer Rick Chertoff (see entry)—including the Hooters, Tommy Conway and the Young Rumblers, Robert Hazard, as well as D.J. Jazzy Jeff & the Fresh Prince.

Joe became "Joe the Butcher" around 1982 when editing tape for the late producer Ray Monahan, who said: "You need a nickname. The way you chop up tape, let's call you 'Joe the Butcher.' " Joe said, "Perfect, because my father literally was 'Joe the butcher.' " In fact, since Studio 4 moved to suburban Conshohocken in 1994, it has been located across the street from what was Joe Sr.'s butcher shop for 35 years.

Joe and Schoolly D manager Chris Schwartz started Ruffhouse Records in 1986 to capitalize on the wealth of rap talent from the Philly area. In the late '80s Joe produced, engineered, or mixed (for other labels) Schoolly, the 7A3, Steady B, Blackmale, Roxanne Shante, and many others, establishing his rap rep. After foundering under an onerous distribution deal with Enigma in 1987 and 1988, Ruffhouse came to fruition when distribution was switched to Columbia. The label's first release was Cheba's "The Piper" in 1990, and their first hit was Tim Dog's "Fuck Compton" (with Joe mixing), which topped the rap charts in 1991 and fueled the east-west rap wars.

The label came into its own with the release of the first Cypress Hill album, a double-platinum slice of THC-soaked L.A. Latino rap, exec-produced and mixed by Joe. Ruffhouse's biggest hit came in 1992 when a pair of Atlanta 12-year-olds under the wing of Jermaine Dupri (see entry) released the quadruple-platinum No. 1 hit *Totally Krossed Out* (with Joe and Phil engineering and mixing, and Joe exec-producing). The label's other cash cow, both a commercial and critical success, has been the Fugees, whose album *The Score* went quadruple-platinum in 1996; solo releases from Fugees Wyclef Jean, Lauryn Hill, and Pras have all succeeded as well.

Butcher Brothers

Anthrax: *Stomp 442*, Elektra, 1995.
Dog Eat Dog: *Play Games*, Roadrunner, 1996.
Getaway Cruiser: *Getaway Cruiser*, 550 Music, 1998.
Hamell on Trial: *The Chord Is Mightier Than the Sword*, Mercury, 1997.
Kris Kross: "I Missed the Bus," Ruffhouse/Columbia, 1992.
Mighty Mighty Bosstones: *Question the Answers*, Mercury, 1994.
Pretenders and Kool Keith: "My City Was Gone" (remix), Dreamworks, 1998 (*Small Soldiers* soundtrack).
Skypark: *Am I Pretty?*, Word, 1998.
Urge Overkill: "Positive Bleeding," Geffen, 1993 • *Saturation*, Geffen, 1993 • "Sister Havana," Geffen, 1993 • "Take a Walk," Arista, 1993 (*No Alternative*) • *Exit the Dragon*, Geffen, 1995.

Joe Nicolo

Bad Mutha Goose and the Brothers Grimm: *Bad Mutha Goose and the Brothers Grimm* (EP), Alpha International, 1991.

Boo-Yaa T.R.I.B.E.: *New Funky Nation*, 4th & B'Way, 1990.
Cash Money and Marvelous: *Where's the Party At?*, Sleeping Bag, 1988.
Cheba: "The Piper," Ruffhouse, 1990.
Electric Love Muffin: *Rassafranna*, Fever/Restless, 1989.
Goats, The: *Tricks of the Shade*, Ruffhouse/Columbia, 1992 • "?Do the Digs Dug?" (remix), Ruffhouse/Columbia, 1993 • *No Goats No Glory*, Ruffhouse/Columbia, 1994 • "Rumblefish," Ruffhouse/Columbia, 1994.
Hard Corps: *Def Before Dishonor*, Interscope, 1991.
Joel, Billy: "The River of Dreams," Columbia, 1993 • *The River of Dreams*, Columbia, 1993 • *Complete Hits Collection, 1974–1997*, Columbia, 1997 • *Greatest Hits*, Vol. 3, Columbia, 1997.
Kris Kross: *The Best of Kris Kross Remixed '92*, Ruffhouse, 1992, 1996 • *Totally Krossed Out*, Ruffhouse/Columbia, 1992 • "Warm It Up" (remix), Ruffhouse/Columbia, 1992 • *Da Bomb*, Ruffhouse/Columbia, 1993 • "It's a Shame," Ruffhouse/Columbia, 1993.
Kubota, Toshi: "Just the Two of Us" (remix), Columbia, 1995.
Larr, Larry: *Da Wizzard of Odds*, Ruffhouse, 1991.
Mahal, Taj: *Like Never Before*, Private, 1991.
Martin, Keith: "Moment in Time" (remix), Ruffhouse/Columbia, 1995.
Max and Sam: "Young Man Rumble," Ruffhouse/Columbia, 1994.
Mellow Man Ace: "Mentirosa" (remix), Capitol, 1990.
Psycho Realm: *The Psycho Realm*, Ruffhouse/Columbia, 1997.
Redhead Kingpin: "Pump It Hottie" (remix), Virgin America, 1989.
Schoolly D: *Saturday Night! The Album*, Jive, 1987.
7A3, The: *Coolin' in Cali'*, Geffen, 1988 • "Party Time!" (remix), Geffen, 1988 • "Drums of Steel," Avenue/Rhino, 1989, 1992 (*Rap Declares War*).
Silk Tymes Leather: *It Ain't Where Ya From . . . It's Where Ya At*, Geffen, 1990 • "New Jack Thang," Geffen, 1990.
Skatemaster Tate: *Do the Skate*, 4th & B'Way, 1991.
Spearhead: *Home*, Capitol, 1994 • "People in tha Middle," Capitol, 1994.
Tashan: "Love Is Forever" (remix), Chaos, 1993.
This Picture: "Heart of Another Man," Dedicated, 1994.
Trip 66: *Trip 66*, Sony, 1996.

COLLECTIONS
Zebrahead soundtrack, Ruffhouse, 1992.

Phil Nicolo

Big Chief: *Platinum Jive*, Capitol, 1994.
Dandelion: *Dyslexicon*, Ruffhouse/Columbia, 1995.
Dishwalla: *Pet Your Friends*, A&M, 1995 • "Counting Blue Cars," A&M, 1996.

Fig Dish: *When Shove Goes Back to Push*, A&M, 1997.

Goat: *Great Life*, Ruffhouse/Columbia, 1998.

Hall, James: *Pleasure Club*, Geffen, 1996.

Life of Agony: *Soul Searching Sun*, Roadrunner, 1997.

Urban Dance Squad: *Persona Non Grata*, Virgin, 1994.

Wailing Souls: *All Over the World* (1 track), Chaos, 1992 • "Shark Attack" (remix), Chaos, 1993.

Niney the Observer

See WINSTON HOLNESS

Jack Nitzsche

Composer, arranger, songwriter, and producer, Jack Nitzsche has enjoyed a diverse musical career that spans four decades, much of it in the musical background. From his arrangements and performances for classic Phil Spector (see entry) recordings to his produc-

tion work with Neil Young and Graham Parker, to his 45 film scores (including the Oscar-winning song "Up Where We Belong" from *An Officer and a Gentleman*), Jack Nitzsche is a monumental force whose achievements are relatively unknown, outside of an appreciative musical community.

Born in Chicago in 1937, Nitzsche was raised on a farm in the tiny Michigan town of Newaygo, about 40 miles north of Grand Rapids. "It means 'fishbone in your throat' in Native American," says Nitzsche in a scratchy drawl. "It was miserable. I couldn't wait to get out of there. White kids beat me up for being German," Nitzsche says of his World War II childhood.

His parents had left Germany and removed an "e" from the spelling of their name (perhaps in an effort to distance themselves from their ancestor, the famed philosopher Friedrich Nietzsche, some of whose ideas were expropriated by the Nazis). Growing up, Nitzsche was a prize pupil at the piano; he also studied clarinet and later saxophone.

Already deeply immersed in the new music of rock 'n' roll, Nitzsche would listen to local radio and make a list of the songs played and check off the ones he thought would become hits (most often he found he was right). After he graduated from nearby Howard City High School in 1955, he immediately moved to Muskegon, Michigan, where he worked at a steel foundry during the day and played tenor saxophone at night with a local band.

In his spare time the future film scorer studied orchestration through a correspondence course offered by the Westlake School out of Los Angeles. He stayed in Miskeegan "long enough to make enough money to get to L.A.," where he finished his studies at Westlake.

In Hollywood in the early '60s he was taken under the wing of Sonny Bono, who taught him a great deal about the music business. One of his early gigs in Hollywood in 1962 was on the set of Elvis Presley's movie *Girls, Girls, Girls*. Nitzsche "performed" on a false piano in the band featured in the movie backing up the King.

Nitzsche rose among the ranks of studio musicians of the day, and it wasn't long before he was working exclusively for Phil Spector as a member of the legendary "wrecking crew" (a moniker that Nitzsche insists was invented by drummer Hal Blaine much after the fact). Nitzsche performed on "just about any instrument you can think of" throughout the prodigious run of hits under Spector's supervision.

Unknown to many, Jack Nitzsche was responsible for the arrangements that defined Spector's trademark "Wall of Sound." While Nitzsche tires of the fact that Spector took credit for this, he still speaks highly of the

Photo by Ben Cromer © 1987

producer and their relationship. "We were a good team," says Nitzsche, "I understood what he wanted. I liked records the way he did. He was a producer who knew what he wanted to hear and he got it. It just got too nuts."

Arranging for Spector proved to be great training for his promotion to producer. "Most of my life as an arranger I was already producing," says Nitzsche. "Most of what a producer does now, that was always the function of the arranger back then." Many of Nitzsche's first productions were for Jackie DeShannon. She and Nitzsche had a stormy three-year affair during which they wrote many songs together, including the hit single "Needles and Pins," recorded by the Searchers in 1964 and Tom Petty and Stevie Nicks in 1986. Although co-writing credit is attributed to Sonny Bono, Nitzsche explains that "Sonny was having a rough time then. He was going through his first divorce." Jack Nitzsche also had a minor hit of his own with "Lonely Surfer" in 1963.

Throughout the late '60s and early '70s Nitzsche produced Jackie DeShannon, Crazy Horse, Buffalo Springfield, and Neil Young. "We've been friends for so many years off and on . . . we've been enemies too," says Nitzsche of his sometimes stormy relationship with Young.

Neil Young's *Harvest* (No. 1) had four producers, including Young, Elliot Mazer, Henry Lewy (see entry), and Nitzsche. Nitzsche played piano on the sessions (as he would on several of Neil Young's records) and also produced the songs "A Man Needs a Maid" and "There's a World." He also created the lush string arrangements that accompany those songs. "When I listen back to 'A Man Needs a Maid' now, I'm embarrassed," reflects Nitzsche on his over-the-top, yet splendid arrangement. "There's too much going on. Even at the time I had trouble with it. But Neil loved it and he asked Bob Dylan what he thought, and he liked it. So Neil went with it."

Nitzsche also co-produced Neil Young's self-titled debut album, produced *Life,* and created the string arrangement for the cut "Such a Woman" on Young's *Harvest* sequel, *Harvest Moon* (No. 16).

Nitzsche's work with Graham Parker resulted in Parker's epochal record *Squeezing Out Sparks.* "I didn't know who he was when they hired me," says Nitzsche of the two-week recording session, "and I don't think he knew me. But that worked to our advantage. It turned out to be a great record." For the powerful ballad "You Can't Be Too Strong," Nitzsche suggested that Graham Parker abandon his plans for a full-blown arrangement of the song and instead perform it on electric piano and guitar only. The song, which deftly deals with the sub-ject of abortion, was performed so movingly that it left everyone in the studio shell-shocked: "After it was laid down, he was so emotionally moved . . . everyone was, no one could work anymore that evening," says Nitzsche of the experience.

Jack Nitzsche has composed scores for some 45 films, including *One Flew Over the Cuckoo's Nest, An Officer and a Gentleman, 9 1/2 Weeks, Starman, Mermaids, Razor's Edge, Blue Sky, The Exorcist,* and Dennis Hopper's *The Hot Spot,* a gratifying experience that featured the performances of Miles Davis, Taj Mahal, and John Lee Hooker.

Having worked primarily in film for the last 15 years, Nitzsche has been itching to produce albums again. "It's such a hermit's life," he says of the film-scoring profession. Despite a recent bout of ill health, he speaks excitedly of several upcoming album projects planned with Neil Young, Willy DeVille, Marianne Faithful, and an anthology of his own work that includes over 30 songs.

Nitzsche acknowledges that he has never been one for self-promotion and that could partially explain why his work has often been overlooked in some circles. But given the enormous output, it's safe to consider that Jack Nitzsche has not had a lot of time for self-reflection either. "When I look at a list of all the things I've done," he observes, "it really does blow my mind. I really did a lot of stuff and nobody knows it." —JACK ARKY

Buffalo Springfield: *Again,* Atco, 1967 • *Buffalo Springfield* (1 track), Atco, 1973.

Christie, Lou: *Enlightnin'ment: The Best Of,* Rhino, 1991.

Crazy Horse: *Crazy Horse,* Reprise, 1971.

Day, Doris: *Move Over Darling,* Bear Family, 1997.

DeShannon, Jackie: *Me About You,* Liberty, 1968.

Germs, The: "Going Down, Lion's Share," Sony/WB, 1979.

Gordon, Alan: *Alley and the Soul Sneakers,* Capitol, 1978.

Hiatt, John: *Living a Little, Laughing a Little,* Raven, 1996.

Jagger, Mick: "Memo to Turner," Warner Bros., 1970.

Lind, Bob: *The Best of Bob Lind: You Might Have Heard My Footsteps,* EMI, 1993.

Mamas and the Papas: *Creeque Alley,* MCA, 1991, 1995.

Mink De Ville: *Cabretta,* Capitol, 1977 • *Return to Magenta,* Capitol, 1978 • *Coup de Grace,* Atlantic, 1981.

Nagle, Ron: *Bad Rice,* Warner Bros., 1970.

Nelson, Rick: *Playing to Win,* Capitol, 1981.

Neville Brothers: *The Neville Brothers,* Capitol, 1979 • *Treacherous: A History of the Neville Brothers,* Rhino, 1988, 1995 • *The Very Best Of,* Rhino, 1997.

Nitzsche, Jack: *Performance* soundtrack (original score), Warner Bros., 1970, 1990 • *Dance to the Hits of the Beatles,* Reprise, 1964 • *Choppin' 66,* Reprise, 1966 • *One Flew over the Cuckoo's Nest* soundtrack, Fantasy, 1975.

Parker, Graham: w/ the Rumour, "Saturday Night Is Dead," Arista, 1979, 1986 (*Rock at the Edge*) • w/ the Rumour, *Squeezing Out Sparks,* Arista, 1979 • *Passion Is No Ordinary Word: The Graham Parker Anthology,* Rhino, 1993.

Pepper, Art: *Jazz Profile,* Blue Note, 1997.

Phillips, Michelle: *Victim of Romance,* A&M, 1977.

Rolling Stones, The: *Singles Collection: The London Years,* Abkco, 1989.

Sainte-Marie, Buffy: *She Used to Wanna Be a Ballerina,* Vanguard, 1971.

Sumner: *Sumner,* Asylum, 1980.

Twilley, Dwight: *The Great Lost Twilley Album,* Shelter, 1993 • *XXI,* The Right Stuff, 1996.

Young, Neil: *Neil Young,* Reprise, 1968 • *Harvest,* Reprise, 1972 • w/ Crazy Horse, *Life,* Geffen, 1987.

COLLECTIONS

Performance soundtrack, Warner Bros., 1970, 1990.

Blue Collar soundtrack, MCA, 1978.

Cruisin' soundtrack, CBS, 1980.

The Hot Spot soundtrack, Antilles, 1990.

Jim Ed Norman

One of the contemporary Nashville scene's most prolific producers, Jim Ed Norman also played a key role in the development of the West Coast country-rock sound of the '70s.

Born October 16, 1948, in Fort Edwards, Florida, he first surfaced playing keyboards in the little-known outfit Felicity, which played the Texarkana circuit during the mid-'60s and issued their lone single, "Hurtin'," in 1967. The group, which also included future Eagles frontman Don Henley on drums, evolved into Shiloh in 1969, soon relocating to the Los Angeles area, where they helped pioneer country rock with their self-titled 1970 debut LP. Shiloh disbanded, and a few years later Norman resurfaced as an arranger and pianist on Eagles albums, including 1974's *On the Border* and its follow-up, *One of These Nights.* He also worked with Linda Ronstadt and Country Joe MacDonald.

Norman's production career began during the late '70s with Jennifer Warnes' 1977 hit "Right Time of the Night" (No. 6) and albums from the New Riders of the Purple Sage, the Coon Elder Band, and Rains and Harris. In 1979, he teamed with Anne Murray for her LP *New Kind of Feeling,* followed two years later by her quadruple-platinum *Christmas Wishes.*

Material for Glenn Frey, Mickey Gilley, Jennifer Warnes, Michael Martin Murphey, and Johnny Lee followed during the first half of the '80s. In 1986 Norman began a lengthy collaboration with Hank Williams Jr. and co-producer Barry Beckett (see entry) that yielded a series of hit LPs, including *Montana Cafe; Born to Boogie; Wild Streak; Lone Wolf;* and *Pure Hank,* with No. 1 country hit singles "Mind Your Own Business" and "Born to Boogie."

Norman's concurrent success with performers ranging from Kenny Rogers, to Beth Nielsen Chapman, to Kathie Lee Gifford led to his appointment as president of Warner/Reprise's Nashville offices in 1989.

While some producers embrace Nashville's traditions by subscribing to the hackneyed Nashville sound, Norman eschews the formulaic, insisting on capturing the essence of the artist. This sensitivity to performers has earned Norman a number of admirers, including fellow producer Scott Hendricks (see entry), who worked as an engineer for Norman. Hendricks recalls one defining moment under Norman's tutelage when Norman honored a commitment made to a singer by a record label, knowing the woman would never be a star.

"It was painfully obvious that this girl did not deserve a recording contract," Hendricks recalls. "Jim Ed turned to me and said, 'I know what you're thinking: Why are we wasting our time on something that is not going to make it? I'll tell you why we're doing it: This is possibly one of the highlights of this girl's life and we owe it to her to make this experience the best it can be.'"
—BEN CROMER

Anderson, John: "Down in Tennessee," Warner Bros., 1985 • "It's All Over Now," Warner Bros., 1985 • "Countrified," Warner Bros., 1986 • "Honky Tonk Crowd," Warner Bros., 1986 • "You Can't Keep a Good Memory Down," Warner Bros., 1986 • "What's So Different About You?," Warner Bros., 1987 • *Greatest Hits,* Vol. 2, Warner Bros., 1990.

Bandana: *Bandana,* Warner Bros., 1985 • "It's Just Another Heartache," Warner Bros., 1985 • "Lovin' Up a Storm," Warner Bros., 1985.

C.Y. Walkin' Band: *Love the Way It Feels,* Parachute, 1979.

Chapman, Beth Nielsen: *Beth Nielsen Chapman,* Reprise, 1990 • *You Hold the Key,* Reprise, 1993 • *Sand and Water,* Warner Bros., 1997.

Cochran, Anita: *Back to You,* Warner Bros., 1997 • "Daddy Can You See Me?," Warner Bros., 1997 • w/ Steve Wariner, *What If I Said,* Warner Bros., 1997 • "Will You Be Here?," Warner Bros., 1998.

Coon Elder Band: *The Coon Elder Band,* Mercury, 1977.

Cummings, Chris: "The Kind of Heart That Breaks," Warner Bros., 1997 • *Chris Cummings,* Warner Bros., 1998.

DeShannon, Jackie: *You're the Only Dancer,* Amherst, 1977.

Dunn, Holly: *Milestones: Greatest Hits,* Warner Bros., 1991.

Foremen, The: "Ain't No Liberal," Reprise, 1995 • *Folk Heroes,* Reprise, 1995 • *What's Left,* Reprise, 1996.

Forester Sisters: *A Christmas Card,* Warner Bros., 1987, 1992 • *Greatest Hits,* Warner Bros., 1989 • *Sunday Meetin',* Warner Bros., 1993 • *Greatest Gospel Hits,* Warner Bros., 1997.

Frey, Glenn: *No Fun Aloud,* Asylum, 1982 • "The One You Love," Asylum, 1982.

Frickie, Jane (Fricke): *Sleeping with Your Memory,* Columbia, 1981 • "Don't Worry 'Bout Me Baby," Columbia, 1982 • *Greatest Hits,* Columbia, 1989, 1992.

Frizzell, David: w/ Shelly West, "Do Me Right," Viva/WB, 1985.

Gayle, Crystal: "Cry," Warner Bros., 1986 • "Nobody Should Have to Love Like This," Warner Bros., 1987 • "Only Love Can Save Me Now," Warner Bros., 1987 • "Straight to the Heart," Warner Bros., 1987 • "Nobody's Angel," Warner Bros., 1988 • *Mountain Christmas,* Intersound, 1996.

Gayle, Crystal, and Gary Morris: "Makin' Up for Lost Time," Warner Bros., 1986 • "Another World," Warner Bros., 1987 • "All of This and More," Warner Bros., 1988.

Gibbs, Terri: *Old Friends,* Warner Bros., 1985 • "Rockin' in a Brand New Cradle," Warner Bros., 1985 • "Someone Must Be Missing You Tonight," Warner Bros., 1985.

Gifford, Kathy Lee: *It's Christmas Time,* Warner Bros., 1993 • *Sentimental,* Warner Bros., 1993.

Gilley, Mickey: "Stand by Me," Full Moon, 1980 • *That's All That Matters,* Epic, 1980 • "True Love Ways," Epic, 1980 • *You Don't Know Me,* Epic, 1980 • *A Headache Tomorrow (Or a Headache Tonight),* Epic, 1981 • "Lonely Nights," Epic, 1982 • *Put Your Dreams Away,* Epic, 1982 • *Fool for Your Love,* Epic, 1983 • "Talk to Me," Epic, 1983 • *You've Really Got a Hold on Me,* Epic, 1983 • *Ten Years of Hits,* Epic, 1987 • *Biggest Hits,* Epic, 1989.

Griffith, Glenda: *Glenda Griffith,* Ariola, 1977.

Hammond, Albert: *Your World and My World,* CBS, 1981.

Harris, Emmylou: *Duets,* Reprise, 1990.

Hinojosa, Tish: *Destiny's Gate,* Warner Bros., 1994 • *Dreaming from the Labyrinth,* Warner Bros., 1996 • *Sonar del Laberinto,* Warner Bros., 1997.

Jeffries, Herb: *The Bronze Buckaroo (Rides Again),* Warner Western, 1995.

Lee, Brenda: *Brenda Lee Christmas,* Warner Bros., 1991.

Lee, Johnny: "I Can Tell by the Way You Dance," Warner Bros., 1980 (*Coast to Coast* soundtrack) • *Lookin' for Love,* Asylum, 1980 • "One in a Million," Asylum, 1980 • "Pickin' Up Strangers," Warner Bros., 1980 (*Coast to Coast* soundtrack) • *Bet Your Heart on Me,* Full Moon, 1981 • *Sounds Like Love,* Full Moon, 1982 • *Greatest Hits,* Full Moon, 1983, 1990.

McAnally, Mac: "Back Where I Come From," Warner Bros., 1990 • "Down the Road," Warner Bros., 1990.

Morris, Gary: *Faded Blue,* Warner Bros., 1984 • "Baby Bye Bye," Warner Bros., 1985 • "I'll Never Stop Loving You," Warner Bros., 1985 • "Lasso the Moon," Warner Bros., 1985 • "100% Chance of Love," Warner Bros., 1986 • "Anything Goes," Warner Bros., 1986 • *Hits,* Warner Bros., 1987 • *Greatest Hits,* Vol. 2, Warner Bros., 1990 • *See also* Gayle, Crystal, and Gary Morris.

Murphey, Michael Martin: *Michael Martin Murphey,* EMI/America, 1982 • "What's Forever For," Liberty, 1982 • *The Best Of,* Liberty, 1984, 1995 • "Carolina in the Pines," EMI, 1985 • "What She Wants," EMI, 1985 • "Fiddlin' Man," Warner Bros., 1986 • "Rollin' Nowhere," Warner Bros., 1986 • "Tonight We Ride," Warner Bros., 1986 • w/ Holly Dunn, "A Face in the Crowd," Warner Bros., 1987 • "A Long Line of Love," Warner Bros., 1987 • "I'm Gonna Miss You, Girl," Warner Bros., 1987 • w/ Ryan Murphey, "Talkin' to the Wrong Man," Warner Bros., 1988 • *Land of Enchantment,* Warner Bros., 1989 • "Never Given' Up on Love," Warner Bros., 1989 • *Sagebrush Symphony,* Warner/Westerm, 1995 • *Horse Legends,* Warner Bros., 1997.

Murray, Anne: "You Needed Me," Capitol, 1978 • "Broken Hearted Me," Capitol, 1979 • "I Just Fall in Love," Capitol, 1979 • *I'll Always Love You,* Capitol, 1979 • *New Kind of Feeling,* Capitol, 1979, 1995 • "Shadows in the Moonlight," Capitol, 1979 • *A Country Collection,* Capitol, 1980 • "Could I Have This Dance?," Capitol, 1980 • *Somebody's Waiting,* Capitol, 1980 • "Blessed Are the Believers," Capitol, 1981 • *Christmas Wishes,* Liberty, 1981 • "A Little Good News," Capitol, 1983 • *A Little Good News,* Capitol, 1983 • "Just Another Woman in Love," Capitol, 1984 • w/ Dave Loggins, "Nobody Loves Me Like You Do," Capitol, 1984 • "I Don't Think I'm Ready for You," Capitol, 1985 • "Time Don't Run Out on Me," Capitol, 1985 • *Greatest Hits,* Liberty, 1989 • *Greatest Hits,* Vol. 2, Liberty, 1989 • w/ Kenny Rogers, "If I Ever Fall in Love Again," Capitol, 1989 • *The Best of the Season,* EMI, 1994.

New Riders of the Purple Sage: *Marin County Line,* MCA, 1978.

O'Connor, Mark: w/ Steve Wariner, "Now It Belongs to You," Warner Bros., 1991 • "Restless," Warner Bros., 1991 • *The New Nashville Cats,* Warner Bros., 1991 • *Heroes,* Warner Bros., 1993 • "The Devil Comes Back to Georgia," Warner Bros., 1993.

Osmond Brothers: *One Way Rider,* Curb/WB, 1984 • "Any Time," Warner Bros., 1985.

Pinkard and Bowden: *Live in Front of a Bunch of Dickheads,* Warner Bros., 1989.

Rains and Harris: *Rains and Harris,* RCA, 1977.

Rogers, Kenny: "When You Put Your Heart in It," Reprise,

1988 • *Christmas in America,* Reprise, 1989 • "Planet Texas," Reprise, 1989 • *Something Inside So Strong,* Reprise, 1989 • "The Vows Go Unbroken (Always True to You)," Reprise, 1989 • w/ Dolly Parton, "Love Is Strange," Reprise, 1990 • *20 Great Years,* Reprise, 1991 • *Back Home Again,* Warner Bros., 1991 • "If You Want to Find Love," Reprise, 1991 • "Lay My Body Down," Reprise, 1991 • *Decade of Hits,* Warner Bros., 1997.

Shannon, Del: "In My Arms Again," Warner Bros., 1985.

Shaw, Victoria: "Tears Dry," Reprise, 1994 • "Forgiveness," Reprise, 1995 • *In Full View,* Reprise, 1995 • "Don't Move," Reprise, 1997 • *Victoria Shaw,* Warner Bros., 1997.

Sheppard, T.G.: "Coast to Coast," Warner Bros., 1980 (*Coast to Coast* soundtrack) • *Slow Burn,* Curb/WB, 1984 • "One Owner Heart," Warner Bros., 1985 • "You're Going Out of My Mind," Warner Bros., 1985 • *All-Time Greatest Hits,* Warner Bros., 1991.

Southern Pacific: "Someone's Gonna Love Me Tonight," Warner Bros., 1985 • *Southern Pacific,* Warner Bros., 1985 • "Thing About You," Warner Bros., 1985 • "A Girl Like Emmylou," Warner Bros., 1986 • "Killbilly Hill," Warner Bros., 1986 • "Perfect Stranger," Warner Bros., 1986 • "Reno Bound," Warner Bros., 1986 • "Don't Let Go of My Heart," Warner Bros., 1987 • "Midnight Highway," Warner Bros., 1988 • "New Shade of Blue," Warner Bros., 1988 • "Any Way the Wind Blows," Warner Bros., 1989 • "I Go to Pieces," Warner Bros., 1990 • "Reckless Heart," Warner Bros., 1990 • *Greatest Hits,* Warner Bros., 1991.

Thomas, B.J.: *I Believe,* Warner Resound, 1997.

Warnes, Jennifer: *Jennifer Warnes,* Arista, 1977 • "Right Time of the Night," Arista, 1977 • *The Best Of,* Arista, 1982.

West, Shelly: "Don't Make Me Wait on the Moon," Viva/WB, 1985 • *Don't Make Me Wait on the Moon,* Viva/WB, 1985 • "Now There's You," Viva/WB, 1985 • *See also* Frizzell, David.

Williams, Hank Jr.: "Country State of Mind," Curb/WB, 1986 • *Live,* Curb/WB, 1986 • "Mind Your Own Business," Warner Bros., 1986 • *Montana Cafe,* Curb/WB, 1986 • "Born to Boogie," Warner Bros., 1987 • *Born to Boogie,* Warner Bros., 1987 • "Heaven Can't Be Found," Curb/WB, 1987 • "When Something Is Good (Why Does It Change)," Curb/WB, 1987 • "If the South Woulda Won," Curb/WB, 1988 • *Wild Streak,* Warner Bros. , 1988 • "Young Country," Curb/WB, 1988 • "Finders Are Keepers," Curb/WB, 1989 • *Greatest Hits,* Vol. 3, Curb/WB, 1989 • "There's a Tear in My Beer," Curb/WB, 1989 • "Ain't Nobody's Business," Curb/WB, 1990 • *America (The Way I See It),* Curb/WB, 1990 • "Good Friends, Good Whiskey, Good Lovin'," Curb/WB, 1990 • "I Mean I Love You," Curb/WB, 1990 • *Lone Wolf,* Curb/WB, 1990 • "Man to Man," Curb/WB, 1990 • *Pure Hank,* Warner Bros. , 1990 • "Angels Are Hard to Find," Curb/WB, 1991 • "If It Will It Will," Curb/WB, 1991 • *The Bocephus Box: Hank Williams Jr. Collection, '79–'92,* Capricorn, 1992.

COLLECTIONS

Snoopy (original cast), DRG, 1976.
Skynyrd Friends, MCA, 1995.
Childrens Christmas Favorites, Warner Bros., 1996.
Christmas Carols for Children, Warner Bros., 1996.
Na Mele O Paniolo (Hawaiian Cowboy Songs), Warner Bros., 1997.

Gil Norton

Even though Gil Norton had been making his living as a producer since he was 19, it wasn't until he was sitting down with Black Francis (now Frank Black) of the Pixies and going over the songs for the (now gold) *Doolittle* album that he learned one of the most important lessons of his production career. As Francis was playing him the songs on an acoustic guitar he had an eerie feeling that they just weren't long enough. He kept prodding Francis to repeat things, find a chorus, or rebuild the track altogether. After a long, fruitless conversation, Norton was beginning to wonder how he was going to make an entire album out of 90-second songs.

"We went through this whole conversation, as far as the length of all these songs, and after it all he took me down to a record store in Boston. He got Buddy Holly's *Greatest Hits* out and said, 'Look at the times on all of those.' They were all like, 1 minute, 50 seconds, 1 minute, 40 seconds; 2 minutes, 10 seconds was an epic. So, you couldn't really argue," he says with a laugh. "That was the whole conversation. I learned a lot from that and over a period of time working with him. It's always nice working with a band over part of their career and watching them grow."

Although he's nurtured several alt-rock bands, including Foo Fighters, Catherine Wheel, Echo and the Bunnymen, Belly, and James, he laughs off the notion that he's an Alternative Producer God. "This alternative thing has been a bit weird for me," he says. "I've never got my head around it. I can see it's not mainstream as such. I mean, yeah there's always been those sorts of bands, and those sorts of attitudes that I like, trying to do something different. I didn't really set out to do any of that, I must admit. I started off with groups like China Crisis and OMD. I've done a lot of different types of music. I just like bands with guitars more than synth-pop bands." Among the more conventional rock bands he's produced are Seven Day Diary and the Meices. He's even worked with the melodic bands Counting Crows and Del Amitri.

Norton became interested in production when he was studying music in college. He got a summer job at a Liverpool studio, quickly graduating from gofer to engineer to producer. "I really didn't know what a producer did," he says. "It was more that the bands couldn't tune the drum kit, so you'd tune the kit and kind of give them advice when they'd go wrong. Then you get a credit for producing as well. Most of it was because I just had to get the session finished and the only way was to say, 'Okay, this is the way we've got to do this.' So I sort of drifted into it."

His engineering background serves him well. "I'm a producer, tape operator," he explains. "That's what I do now. I do lots of my own drop-ins, especially if I'm working the guitar parts out. I'd much rather get everyone out of the control room and just leave me with the guitarist in there."

Among his production tenets: All bands are different and preproduction is revealing. "Most of the production is done in the rehearsal room—where it's cheap, for starters. For lots of reasons it's where you organize your arrangements. Once you've got your arrangements organized and the band knows what it's supposed to be doing, it makes life in the studio a lot easier."

He uses technology but doesn't fetishize it: during the recording of Counting Crows' *Recovering the Satellites*, Norton and engineer J. Bradley Cook used Digidesign's ProTools as well as a handful of valve compressors and tube microphones. "They're all just tools to me," he says. "They're all just things you use for various things. If they get in the way, you don't use them, and if they're a help, you do use them."

Production "should be a fun, creative process in the studio where people learn and develop," Norton says. "You're trying to capture what's in the songwriter's imagination, really." —DAVID JOHN FARINELLA

Age of Electric: *Make a Pest a Pet,* Universal, 1996.
Auto De Fe: *Tatitum,* Spartan, 1985.
Belly: "Feed the Tree," Sire/Reprise, 1993 • *Star* (4 tracks), Sire/Reprise, 1993.
Blink: *A Map of the Universe,* Lime, 1995.
Blue Aeroplanes: *Swagger,* Ensign/Chrysalis, 1990 • *World View Blue,* Ensign/Chrysalis, 1990.
Catherine Wheel: *Chrome,* Mercury, 1993 • *Happy Days,* Fontana/Mercury, 1995 • *Like Cats and Dogs,* Fontana/Mercury, 1996.
Counting Crows: *Recovering the Satellites,* Geffen, 1996.

Del Amitri: *Waking Hours,* A&M, 1990, 1995 • "Always the Last to Know," A&M, 1992 • *Change Everything,* A&M, 1992.
Echo and the Bunnymen: "The Killing Moon," Korova/Sire, 1983 • *Ocean Rain,* Korova/Sire, 1984 • "Seven Seas," Korova/Sire, 1984 • *Echo and the Bunnymen* (1 track), Sire, 1987.
Fatima Mansions: *Lost in the Former West,* Kitchenware, 1995.
Foo Fighters: *The Colour and the Shape,* Roswell, 1997.
Heart Throbs: *Cleopatra Grip,* Elektra, 1990.
Hurrah: *Tell God I'm Here,* Kitchenware/Arista, 1987.
James: *James,* Fontana, 1990 • "Sit Down," Fontana, 1991.
Longpigs: "On and On," Mother/Island, 1995 (*Mission: Impossible* soundtrack) • *The Sun Is Often Out,* PolyGram, 1997.
McCulloch, Ian: "Proud to Fall" (remix), Sire/Reprise, 1989.
Meices, The: *Dirty Bird,* London, 1996.
Pale Saints: *The Comforts of Madness,* 4 A.D., 1990.
Pere Ubu: "Worlds in Collision," Fontana, 1991 • *Worlds in Collision,* Fontana, 1991.
Pixies, The: *Doolittle,* 4 A.D./Elektra, 1989 • *Bossa Nova,* 4 A.D./Elektra, 1990 • "I Can't Forget," Atlantic, 1991 (*I'm Your Fan*) • *Trompe le Monde,* 4 A.D./Elektra, 1991 • "Alec Eiffel," 4 A.D./Elektra, 1992 • *Death to the Pixies: 1987–1991 ,* Elektra, 1997.
Roachford: *Permanent Shade of Blue,* Epic, 1995.
Seven Day Diary: *Skin and Blister,* Warner Bros., 1995.
Terrorvision: *Regular Urban Survivors,* EMI, 1996.
Throwing Muses: *Throwing Muses,* 4 A.D., 1986 • *The Fat Skier* (EP), 4 A.D./Sire, 1988.
Tribe: *Abort,* Slash, 1991.
Triffids, The: *Born Sandy Devotional,* Hot/Rough Trade, 1986 • *Calenture,* Island, 1987.

Brendan O'Brien

Brendan O'Brien's current day gig has been a source of curiosity since he was around 9. Not an aspiration, mind you, just a curiosity. "I was always reading who produced records and wondering what the hell that meant," he says with a Southern drawl. He found out when he entered the studio with his own bands, "When we were making demos for my band, I was always the guy who was the engineer, miserable with pressure. I was always in the middle of it and I slowly did more engineering."

For O'Brien, the switch from musician to engineer to producer stems from his initial fascination with music. "I have always wanted to play music and I've always played the guitar, and now I get to play with different artists," he says.

Imagine jamming with Pearl Jam, Stone Temple Pilots, Neil Young, or even Rage Against The Machine. Nevertheless, an afternoon jam with Mike McCready and Stone Gossard doesn't replace the passion he brings to the producer's chair. "This is something that I have always wanted to do," he explains. "I have always wanted to be the guy who helps get records together. I've always appreciated that as a kid, just as much as I liked guitar players."

O'Brien began as an engineer in Atlanta. "I engineered some records early on that [bands] liked and then they would hire me to produce," he explains. "Then they found out I was a musician. There's an understanding there that seems to be very helpful to me and the artist."

O'Brien's first production credit, on Atlanta's Coolies, whetted his appetite for the craft. "Even when I engineered—and I was happy being an engineer—there was a time when I wanted to be in the producer's seat. It probably made some of the producers that I worked with a little bit crazy. I understand that more now than I did then, and I appreciate it more now than I did then, but that is what I wanted. And once you start calling yourself a producer, many times other producers don't want to hire you as an engineer, so there is really no turning back."

He jumped headlong into Atlanta's music scene and began working with a number of local bands, including Uncle Green, for DB Records. The first Uncle Green record he produced, You, was released in 1989. After a 1991 Uncle Green follow-up, O'Brien's career broke wide open. The vehicle? Core (No. 3), the 1992 Stone Temple Pilots six-times-platinum disc. In 1993, he worked with perhaps modern rock's biggest band, Pearl Jam, on Vs., followed by Vitalogy, No Code (all No. 1), and the new Yield.

O'Brien has built a reputation for recording deep, lush albums. Many late '90s bands and fellow producers regularly cite him as an inspiration. He doesn't get it. "I don't really know how to respond to that," he says. "I think that each record I approach differently. If you compare each record—say, a Pete Droge record versus a Stone Temple Pilots record, or a Pearl Jam record versus a Michael Penn record—they are very different-sounding records.

"Honestly there is no real method to it. When we made the records, I set the band up and went from there. I tend not to make them from machines, I tend to make them with musicians playing them. I feature vocals prominently and I like to hear loud guitars. I guess in that way there is something that goes on there. But as far as having a sound? Maybe the ones that sell a lot have a sound."

He likes hip-hop and loves to listen to "machine-based" records like Nine Inch Nails, but he'd rather leave the mystery of machines to producers such as Dallas Austin and the Dust Brothers (see entries).

So it's no surprise that O'Brien is more comfortable with analog technology than digital. That's fitting, since his inspiration remains '60s analog records, like the Beatles'. He also loves the Beach Boys and Led Zeppelin. "I have never had a career plan," he says. "I just take things as they come and I make decisions as they go along."

Although he's proud to have worked with Neil Young and Bob Dylan and happy with his productions, O'Brien is still striving for more. To insure proud moments to come, he recently launched 57 Records, a custom Epic subsidiary based in Atlanta (a highlight of the roster is Pete Droge, whose 1998 album Spacey and Shakin' O'Brien produced). "I didn't want to get into a situation where I was making records that I thought were the way that I wanted to make them, and then didn't have a say in what happened to them or how they even got finished," he says. "I was able to get to the point where I was able to get control of that or have a say in that. But who knows what the future will bring?"
—DAVID JOHN FARINELLA

Baird, Dan: "I Love You Period," American, 1992 • *Love Songs for the Hearing Impaired*, Def American, 1992 • *Buffalo Nickel*, American, 1996.

Boston, Anne Richmond: *The Big House of Time*, DB, 1990.

Coolies, The: *Doug (A Rock Opera)*, DB, 1988.

Droge, Pete: w/ the Sinners, *Necktie Second*, American, 1994 • w/ the Sinners, *Find a Door*, American, 1996 • *Spacey and Shakin'*, 57 Records/Epic, 1998.

Dylan, Bob: *Greatest Hits*, Vol. 3, Columbia, 1995.

Georgia Satellites: "Hippy Hippy Shake," Elektra, 1988 (*Cocktail* soundtrack) • *Buffalo Nickel*, American, 1996.

Jackyl: *Jackyl*, Geffen, 1992.

King's X: *Dogman*, Atlantic, 1994 • *The Best of King's X*, Atlantic, 1997.

Law, Johnny: *Johnny Law*, Metal Blade, 1991.

Pearl Jam: "Crazy Mary," Thirsty Ear/Chaos/Columbia, 1993 (*Sweet Relief*) • *Vs.*, Epic, 1993 • "Tremor Christ/Spin the Black Circle," Epic, 1994 • *Vitalogy*, Epic, 1994 • "I Got Id/Long Road," Epic, 1995 • "Daughter/Yellow Ledbetter," Epic, 1996 • *No Code*, Epic, 1996 • "Who You Are," Epic, 1996 • "Given to Fly," Epic, 1998 • "Wishlist," Epic, 1998 • *Yield*, Epic, 1998.

Penn, Michael: *Resigned*, 57 Records, 1997.

Rage Against The Machine: "Bulls on Parade," Epic, 1996 • *Evil Empire,* Epic, 1996.

Raging Slab: *Dynamite Monster Boogie Concert,* Def American, 1993.

Right As Rain: *Undertown,* DB, 1988 • *Stop, Look and Listen,* DB, 1991.

Shaver, Billy Joe: *Unshaven: The Live Album,* Volcano/Zoo, 1995.

Soundgarden: *Alive in the Superunknown,* A&M, 1995.

Stone Temple Pilots: *Core,* Atlantic, 1992 • "Plush," Atlantic, 1992 • "Big Empty," Interscope/Atlantic, 1993, 1994 (*The Crow* soundtrack) • "Interstate Love Song," Atlantic, 1994 • *Purple,* Atlantic, 1994 • "Vasoline," Atlantic, 1994 • "Dancing Days," Atlantic, 1995 (*Encomium; A Tribute to Led Zeppelin*) • *Tiny Music . . . Songs from the Vatican,* Atlantic, 1996 • "Trippin' on a Hole in a Paper Heart," Atlantic, 1996 • "Art School Girl," Atlantic, 1997 • "Tumble in the Rough," Atlantic, 1997.

Sweet, Matthew: *100% Fun,* Zoo, 1995 • *Blue Sky on Mars,* Zoo, 1997.

3 Lb. Thrill: *Vulture,* 57 Records, 1995.

Tony Rich Project: "Like a Woman" (remix), LaFace, 1996.

Uncle Green: *You,* DB, 1989 • *What an Experiment His Head Was,* DB, 1991 • *Book of Bad Thoughts,* Atlantic, 1992.

Westerberg, Paul: "Stain Yer Blood," Reprise, 1995 (*Friends* soundtrack) • *Eventually,* Reprise, 1996.

Young, Neil: "Downtown," Reprise, 1995 • *Mirror Ball,* Reprise, 1995 • "Throw Your Hatred Down," Reprise, 1995.

Ric Ocasek

If you had to make a list of the producers who know about writing big-time pop hooks, it would include Ric Ocasek, creator of such great songs as "My Best Friend's Girl," "You Might Think," and "Shake It Up" for his group, the Cars. Who would have better pushed Nada Surf's "Popular," or Romeo Void's "Never Say Never" from concept to reality?

The key to his success? Producing bands that don't need much work. "I don't think that you should pick a band to produce that you think needs to be changed around to become something else," Ocasek says. "I am sure there are producers with egos that like to change the band into their own thing, but I don't feel that's right. You choose a band to produce because they are already good. It is not hard to produce a band that is already great. I think that is why I like to do first albums,

because if [the band] has already created a new sound, then why try to redo it? The reason you think they are great in the first place is what they sound like; you just want to make sure that they sound like that when they are done with the record."

What Ocasek (born March 23, 1949, in Baltimore) brings is perspective. "I'm sort of the outside ear," he says. "Sometimes the songs that get the people the deals should be the songs on the record, the way they are without even having them produced. I always check the demo to make sure that what we are doing is better than the demo."

Nada Surf's Matthew Caws says Ocasek practiced what he preached on the band's 1996 release, *High/Low.* Caws admired Ocasek's work with Weezer and "because he had done Bad Brains, Suicidal Tendencies, and Romeo Void. He's so versatile. Also, he is a songwriter. I was excited because he would know how to protect the hooks. Overproduction can really destroy the song."

Ocasek's production talent began to come clear in the early '80s in his work with Peter Dayton, Suicide (with Alan Vega and Martin Rev), and his own 1982 solo debut, *Beatitude.* "I always loved the technology of the studio and, of course, the music part," he says. "It's fun to be a part of someone's creative output and to make sure that bands get what they want on tape and are not afraid of technology. I think I was sympathetic, being an artist myself, to some of these other bands."

He recalls being bewildered during the recording of the Cars' eponymous debut in 1978, which was produced by Roy Thomas Baker (see entry). But he learned fast. And one of the key lessons he learned was that keeping a band's unique sound is critical. "I think one of the first things that bands have to know is that they can say no to a producer and they *should* be able to say no," he says. That is a lesson he learned the hard way while the Cars were working on their most successful album, *Heartbeat City,* with producer Robert John "Mutt" Lange (see entry). "I think we originally went to him because we knew his reputation as a heavy metal producer," Ocasek recalls. "We wanted to get a bigger guitar sound, but we also knew that he was heavy-handed. We didn't fully realize how heavy," he says with a laugh.

"It turned out to be more of a keyboard-oriented record and the guitars were not too important to Mutt. He was going through a keyboard phase. Mutt was a great producer and way more meticulous than one should be. However, one can't disregard his success with the productions he does, no matter how long they take."

Heartbeat City took too long for Ocasek, however. He got tired of Lange's poring over details, tweaking ad infinitum. "We had a little problem with time and whether we felt that the performances were already there, which they were many times and many hours and days before he thought so," he says.

Caws notes Ocasek works fast. Nada Surf's record was recorded in 11 days and mixed in 6, "and he tricked me into doing all the vocals. I am a pretty insecure singer, so after we would do a song he would say, 'Hey, why don't you go out and throw down a scratch vocal? We'll do the other ones later.' Then a few days later I asked about doing vocals and he said they were done. They didn't all hold that way, but a set of vocals on the album are first-take shots." Not only is Ocasek quiet and unobtrusive, he's on the money, says Caws. "He had an infuriating habit of always being right—right away," Caws says. "Like we would do three takes of a song and he would say, 'It's number two.'"

"I want [the band] to feel comfortable and think they are working with another artist and songwriter, not a technician," Ocasek says. "I think I understand the politics of people in bands and how they get along with each other and how much attention each person in a band might need to feel confident that they are not being left out."

Although he has recorded all over the world, including in his own studio, which he sold in the late '80s, he likes to do some recording in the basement of his home. Not only does he use the 24-track studio to write and record his own demos, he offers bands lower rates. He has recorded several Alan Vega albums there and laid down some vocal tracks for Weezer's double-platinum eponymous debut (No. 16).

Ocasek likes the warmth of analog tape, though he's dipped into digital. "The technology is faster and you can do more tricks," he explains. "But I would never mix to digital; it's good to start with the warmth."

For all his production prowess, the song remains the bottom line. "Being in a studio a lot might be good for me to know the technology," he says. "But songs have to sung with one guitar or one keyboard before they can really be embellished. They kind of have to sit on their own." —DAVID JOHN FARINELLA

Bad Brains: *Rock for Light*, Abst/PVC, 1983 • *God of Love*, Maverick/WB, 1995.

Bad Religion: *The Gray Race*, Atlantic, 1996.

Black 47: *Black 47* (EP), SBK, 1992 • *Fire of Freedom*, SBK, 1992.

Buell, Bebe: *Covers Girls* (EP), Rhino, 1981.

Cars, The: "Coming up You," Elektra, 1987 • *Door to Door*, Elektra, 1987 • "Strap Me In," Elektra, 1987 • "You Are the Girl," Elektra, 1987 • *Just What I Needed: The Cars Anthology*, Rhino, 1995.

Cole, Lloyd, and the Commotions: *Rattlesnakes* (remix, 3 tracks), Geffen, 1984.

D Generation: *No Lunch*, Columbia, 1996.

Dayton, Peter: *Love at First Sight*, Shoo Bop, 1981.

Hole: "Gold Dust Woman," Miramax/Hollywood, 1996 (*The Crow: City of Angels* soundtrack).

Johnny Bravo: *Then Again, Maybe I Won't*, Arista, 1996.

Nada Surf: *High/Low*, Elektra, 1996.

Ocasek, Ric: *Beatitude*, Geffen, 1982 • "Steal the Night," Warner Bros., 1982, 1983 (*The King of Comedy* soundtrack) • "Emotion in Motion," Geffen, 1986 • *This Side of Paradise*, Geffen, 1986 • "True to You," Geffen, 1986 • *Fireball Zone*, Reprise, 1991 • *Quick Change World*, Reprise, 1993 • "Hang on Tight," Columbia, 1997 • *Troubilizing*, Columbia, 1997.

Peste: *Peste*, Matador, 1996.

Rev, Martin: *See* Vega, Alan.

Romeo Void: "Never Say Never," 415/Columbia, 1982 • *Warm in Your Coat*, Legacy, 1992.

Suicide: *A Way of Life*, Wax Trax!, 1989 • *Suicide*, Restless, 1990 • *Why Be Blue*, Enemy, 1992.

Vega, Alan: w/ Martin Rev, *Alan Vega and Martin Rev*, Ze, 1980 • *Saturn Drive*, Ze, 1983.

Weezer: "Undone: The Sweater Song," DGC, 1994 • *Weezer*, DGC, 1994.

Eddy Offord

Eddy Offord has had an exceptional career as engineer and producer spanning the late '60s to today—with major commercial and critical hits strewn throughout—revolving around the seemingly incongruous geographical dipoles of London and Atlanta. Offord was the most important and successful recorder of progressive rock in the '70s, co-producing (with the band) all of Yes's great albums and engineering Emerson, Lake and Palmer's best (*Emerson, Lake and Palmer, Pictures at an Exhibition, Trilogy*).

Then, after falling in love with America on tour with Yes, Offord relocated to Atlanta, turned a musical 180, and had AOR hits with Art in America, Blackfoot, (Dixie) Dregs, Platinum Blonde (*Alien Shores*, five-times-platinum in Canada), and Billy Squier. After a break, Offord returned to prominence in the '90s with a Yes reunion album, soprano Americana from Valerie Carter, rocking blues from Tinsley Ellis, the My Bloody Valentine-meets-Mazzy Star noise-pop of Medicine, and most important, 311's punky hard-grooving first two albums, including the roiling ska-funk classic "Do You Right."

Eddy Offord was born and raised in London and took an abiding interest in rock 'n' roll for the first time in the early '60s, when he heard the surfish English instrumental group the Shadows, picked up a guitar, and tried to copy the licks. He was a fan of the Beatles, the Stones, the Who, and Cream, and played in bands of his own throughout school.

In the summer of 1967, in his late teens, Offord was looking for a job when he saw an ad for a trainee sound engineer in the paper. He went to the studio, Advision, and "as soon as I heard the music coming out of those big speakers, I was blown away. There was no turning back for me," he says.

He started as tea boy, then quickly became second engineer. There were nights when he'd wrap up a session, kick the band out, have his own band (Dizzy Heights) dash in, set up, and he'd spend the rest of the evening in the control room simultaneously playing guitar and mixing.

Less than a year after entering the studio Offord made his name as an engineer when he recorded Julie Driscoll, Brain Auger, and the Trinity's No. 5 U.K. hit "This Wheel's on Fire" in 1968. That same year he worked on the first album by Idle Race, a group that included a young guitar player named Jeff Lynne (see entry). Offord's next break came when he engineered the second album by an arty fusion-folk-classical rock band named Yes in 1970 and hit it off so well with the members that they asked him to co-produce their next album with them, 1971's *The Yes Album* (No. 5 U.K.).

Since Yes has been around so long, mutated into so many different versions, offshoots and factions, and put out its share of self-important aimless dreck, it is easy to forget what a bracing, fresh triumph *The Yes Album* was. "Yours Is No Disgrace" opens with crisp staccato riffs from guitarist Steve Howe, bassist Chris Squire, and drummer Bill Bruford, then continues with tricky interplay between the above and keyboardist Tony Kaye. What could have turned to mush in less capable hands stays separated, clean, and precise without ever growing cold in Offord's. Offord's production spotlights the individual virtuosity of the players and their remarkable interplay without ever sacrificing the beauty of the melodies or losing the feel of a song.

While Jon Anderson's lyrics have always smacked of free-associative cosmic gibberish, his piping, overgrown-choirboy voice can be appreciated for its pure tonality. Pundits tend to overemphasize the importance of lyrics because the words are often the easiest aspect of a song to latch onto, but unless the lyrics are particularly acute, poignant, or inane, to paraphrase Robert Christgau, most songs have lyrics because they don't want to be instrumentals.

So while I have no idea what "Yours Is No Disgrace" is actually about, it sounds damn good. Howe particularly shines. "Starship Trooper" carries on in a similar, but more expansive, less frantic mode, and provided the name for a movie 20 years later. Howe doesn't so much bedazzle here as impress with the tastefulness of his chord deconstructions, finger-picked acoustic interludes, and the grandeur of the song's long three-chord coda (subtitled "Wurm").

The brilliant, pristine medley "Your Move/All Good People" is probably the band's high-water mark. A bright, shining melody, keening harmonies, briskly strummed acoustic guitar and pipe accompaniment, and advice that actually makes sense ("Don't surround yourself with yourself") add up to pure listening pleasure. The second half of the medley returns to lyrical opacity ("I've seen all good people turn their heads each day"), but it's a rousing good ride nonetheless.

The next album, *Fragile* (No. 4), replaced Kaye with Rick Wakeman on keyboards and took further steps into symphonic structure and sci-fi imagery, including the first of many trippy Roger Dean album covers. The 10 1/2 minute "Heart of the Sunrise" boasts dramatic simultaneous band workups, much fine playing, and Anderson's ever-pleasing voice. "Long Distance Runaround" has a charming fugue-like intro, and "The Fish" is almost funky, in Yes's hyper-Anglo, angular manner. *Fragile* also has "Roundabout" (No. 13), a churning maelstrom of instrumental and vocal prowess that would be worthy of Mahavishnu Orchestra or Weather Report at their most frantic if it weren't for the pop perfection of the tune. But otherwise, less-distinctive melodies and fraying cohesion drop *Fragile* a step below *The Yes Album*.

On *Close to the Edge* (No. 3) from 1972, the band's grand(iose) ambitions were equaled by its execution and the quality of its material for the last time. All of side 1 is taken up with the four-part title track with references to "seasoned witches," "colonies of the sky," returning periodically to the anticipatory image of "close to the edge." What lies beyond the edge is unclear—something about the healing of the human race by benevolent space beings. But somehow it all holds together with energetic instrumental passages—this time focusing on Rick Wakeman's dancing fingers on a variety of keyboards—interspersed with dreamy soft moments, culminating in Anderson's fervent yin-yang observation, "I get up, I get down," followed by the sound of a rain forest full of birds taking flight. A sonic triumph for Offord, including the innovative use of multitracked a cappella choral stabs, which Roy Thomas Baker (see entry) and Queen would become famous for a few years later. Side 2 is dominated by the stunning beauty of "And You and I," where all of the band's strengths coalesce into another four-course meal, this one satisfying on all levels.

Offord recalls the time. "It was a blast; it was wonderful. In the early '70s making records was such an experimental kind of a trip, because we only had four tracks. It was a real adventure. I think today it's a little easier and a bit old hat," he says.

"So many people had ideas and wanted things to go in certain directions. They weren't fighting with one another, but almost. I think one of my biggest things was to try to approach it logically like a referee, so that everyone felt like they had a say in the process."

Yes asked Offord to go on the road with them to reproduce the sonic discoveries they had made in the studio, so he mixed down a lot of vocal parts and sound effects onto 1/4-inch tape, which he manipulated like a DJ from two Revox tape machines during their live shows. Offord became so much a part of band's sound that they pictured him on the back cover of *Close to the Edge*.

Offord built his own portable studio while working with Yes and recorded ex–E Street Band keyboardist David Sancious, Andy Pratt, and Levon Helm's RSO All-stars on it in Woodstock, New York, and elsewhere. Then he moved to Atlanta and transferred his system into an old theater that he bought and renovated for the purpose of recording. Now Offord lives and works out of Los Angeles, a man whose successes span four different decades over 30 years and show no sign of abating.

—ERIC OLSEN AND DAVID JOHN FARINELLA

Aaron, Jay: *Inside Out*, Warner Bros., 1990.
Apostles, The: *The Apostles*, Victory, 1992.
Art in America: *Art in America*, Pavillion, 1983, 1996.
Baker Gurvitz Army: *Hearts on Fire*, Mountain, 1976.
Blackfoot: *Vertical Smiles*, Atco, 1984.
Blackjack: *World's Apart*, Polydor, 1980.
Brown, Nappy, and the Heartfixers: *Tore Up*, Alligator, 1984.
Carter, Valerie: *The Way It Is*, Countdown, 1996.
Dixie Dregs: *Divided We Stand: Best of the Dixie Dregs*, Grand Slamm, 1989.
Dregs: *Industry Standard*, Arista, 1982.
Ellis, Tinsley: *Cool on It*, Alligator, 1991 • *Storm Warning*, Alligator, 1994.
Helm, Levon, and the RCO Allstars: *Levon Helm and the RCO Allstars*, Edsel, 1977, 1996.
Howe, Steve: *Beginnings*, Atlantic, 1975.
Idle Race: *Birthday Party*, Liberty, 1968.

Jo Jo: *JoJo Jojo*, Ariola, 1988.
Lindisfarne: *Happy Daze*, Warner Bros., 1974.
Medicine: *Her Highness*, American, 1995.
Pallas: *Arrival Alive*, Cool King, 1983, 1991 • *The Sentinel*, Harvest, 1984.
Platinum Blonde: *Alien Shores*, Epic, 1985 • "Somebody Somewhere," Epic, 1986.
Pratt, Andy: *Motives*, Nemperor, 1979.
Reid, Terry: *River* (2 tracks), Atlantic, 1973.
Rozetta: *Where's My Hero?*, 20th Century, 1980.
Sancious, David : *Just As I Thought*, Arista, 1980.
Sancious, David, and Tone: *True Stories*, Arista, 1978.
Squier, Billy: *Tale of the Tape*, Capitol, 1980.
311: "Do You Right," Capricorn, 1993 • *Music*, Capricorn, 1993 • *Grassroots*, Capricorn, 1994.
Wet Willie: *Wet Willie*, Capricorn, 1971, 1998 • *Wet Willie II*, Capricorn, 1972, 1998 • *Greatest Hits*, Capricorn, 1977.
Yes: *Fragile*, Atlantic, 1971 • *The Yes Album*, Atlantic, 1971 • "Your Move," Atlantic, 1971 • "America," Atlantic, 1972 • "And You and I," Atlantic, 1972 • *Close to the Edge*, Atlantic, 1972 • "Roundabout," Atlantic, 1972 • *Tales from the Topographic Oceans*, Atlantic, 1973 • *Yessongs*, Atlantic, 1973 • *Relayer*, Atlantic, 1974 • *Drama*, Atlantic, 1980 • *Classic Yes*, Atlantic, 1981 • "I've Seen All Good People" (live), Atlantic, 1981 • "Roundabout" (live), Atlantic, 1981 • *Union*, Arista, 1991 • *Yesyears*, Atco, 1991.
Ziggurat: *Melodic Scandal*, Robox, 1982.

Dave Ogilvie

D ave "Rave" Ogilvie has become one of the most important producer/engineer/mixers of the industrial-metal hybrid, working with Skinny Puppy, Nine Inch Nails, Ministry, Marilyn Manson, Hilt, Drown, Rob Halford's Two, and others. He has also produced more melodic alterna-rock by the likes of 54.40, Caterwaul, Low Pop Suicide, and the Water Walk.

Born in Montreal in 1960, Dave Ogilvie was an intense music fan who spent hours mining through records in search of the auditory mother lode. In his midteens, Ogilvie was particularly impressed with Pink Floyd, whose dense, layered productions offered fertile ground for exploration. A lover of great pop tunes, he was also drawn to the more brooding, ominous side of music.

On a course to take over his father's business, Ogilvie was supposed to study business in college, but found that his attention was drawn again to music. He took some music courses, got involved with a local studio, and became fascinated with the technical aspects of recorded music.

Ogilvie hooked up with an engineer named Lindsay Kidd who was moving to Vancouver to work with the burgeoning scene there, centered around mainstream '80s rockers Loverboy, Bryan Adams, and the like. Though musically not his cup of meat, Ogilvie learned the basics of sound engineering from producer Bruce Fairbairn (see entry), who took him under his wing.

After engineering for a few years, Ogilvie was recording edgy Vancouver band 54.40 as they fired a series of producers, finally asking Ogilvie to take over. He produced *Set the Fire* in 1984, as well as their self-titled follow-up in 1986 and *Fight for Love* in 1989.

"I loved it. It was a real personal thing, like being part of the family. I wasn't a musician, but the studio was a way to be with the musicians. Vancouver worked out great because there were so many people there recording—Little Mountain studios had Bob Rock [see entry] and Bruce Fairbairn and they were doing Aerosmith, Mötley Crüe, Bon Jovi," he says.

"After a while I got into the opposite side of it, working with really underground music and stuff that people really didn't accept at that time. Everybody was looking at me like I was crazy: 'How could you be listening to the Skinny Puppy stuff?' I didn't want to work on factory rock records. I was doing records that were done in a month for no money. I couldn't have been happier when machines came along to help you make music, but I think that scared a lot of people for years."

Skinny Puppy came into being when percussionist/synth player cEVIN Key left pop-electronic band Images in Vogue, and joined with vocalist Nivek Ogre (Kevin Ogilvie) in order to pursue the more sinister side of electronic music, with nods to Throbbing Gristle, Joy Division, and Cabaret Voltaire. Horror film samples and imagery, Ogre's harsh, distorted vocals, and determined electrobeats set the tone.

Keyboardist/bassist Bill Leeb (see entry) added to the harsh, distorted sound, and Dave Ogilvie began to help them record. The band's earliest work, from 1981 to 1985, can now be found on the *Back and Forth* and *Brap* reissues. Puppy's first full-length album was 1985's *Bites,* highlighted by the headlong dance floor staple "Assimilate," a relatively melodic, sprightly number, with Ogre's patented death rattle vocals being the main nod to industrial darkness.

In 1986 Leeb left to found Front Line Assembly, replaced by Dwayne Goettel, and a more varied sound emerged on *Mind: The Perpetual Intercourse.* The extended single release of "Dig It" from the album is the band at its most compelling: a syncopated, clanging, hip-hop beat drives a spasmodic shiver through the dancer's body, as stabbing guitar blasts punctuate the downbeat, while poltergeists of heavy machinery shockingly thrum then disappear and Ogre snarls the percussive refrain, "Dig it, dig it."

The extended single version of "Addiction," originally from *Cleanse, Fold and Manipulate* is another great, complete with lurching, jerking beat, high keyboard drone, and more grim vocals. In 1989 Puppy partnered with Chicago metal-industrial pioneer Al Jourgensen of Ministry to create *Rabies.* Jourgensen and Ogre trade wrenching vocals, augmented by Jourgensen's stun guitar and a deeper, thicker production. "Tin Omen" is a metal-industrial classic, evoking the horrors of violence at home and abroad with a special emphasis on the death of innocence that was the Kent State massacre. Puppy's attack on violence through violent music and imagery can be seen either as hypocritical or homeopathic, depending upon where your ox gets gored.

Around this time Ogilvie moved to Chicago and participated in the thriving industrial scene revolving around Ministry and Wax Trax! Records. He engineered for Ministry's milestone *A Mind Is a Terrible Thing to Taste* album and ran live sound for the Ministry offshoot, Revolting Cocks.

Ogilvie returned to Skinny Puppy for the relentless, aptly named *Too Dark Park,* an audio *Silent Spring* portraying environmental apocalypse. By 1992's *Last Rights,* the band was running on uninspired vapors, and 1996's comeback, *The Process,* incorporated more melodic sounds and actual unprocessed singing into the mix; highlights are tunes like "Death" that adhere to the punishment-and-distortion model. Puppy's excellence is best sampled from the *12" Anthology,* a collection of dance remixes that covers all of the band's most distinctive material, including "Dig It," "Addiction," "Assimilate," and "Testure" (an antivivisection screed originally found on *Vivisect VI*).

Of Ogilvie's lighter work, although Caterwaul's name sounds like still more cacophonous punishment, their sound is actually located some point on a continuum between Siouxsie & the Banshees and Concrete Blonde. Singer Betsy Martin is a woman of many voices, but on the compelling *Portent Hue* she comes off best on the naturalism of "Small Things in Heaven," and the Siouxsie-like canyon leaps of "Manna and Quail." The *Water Walk's (thingamajig)* is the very soul of the intelligent, melodic, tasteful music that is now called adult alternative, especially the memorable "Never Leaving Eden Again."

In the late '90s Ogilvie went to work with Nine Inch Nail's Trent Reznor (see entry), doing remixes for NIN and David Bowie (see entry) and co-producing Marilyn Manson's scabrous industrial shock-rock opus *Antichrist Superstar*. Though Manson's self-serving, gratuitously "shocking" ditties are adolescent in most of the worst senses of the word, the sound Ogilvie and Reznor achieve is always powerful, occasionally exciting ("1996"), and even catchy ("The Beautiful People").

—ERIC OLSEN AND DAVID JOHN FARINELLA

Bowie, David: "Heart's Filthy Lesson" (remix), Virgin, 1995 • "I'm Afraid of Americans" (remix), Virgin, 1997.

Caterwaul: *Portent Hue,* IRS, 1990.

Contagion: "Turn of the Screw" (remix), World Domination, 1992.

Dead Surf Kiss: *Narcotic Nevada,* Oceana, 1985, 1991.

Die Krupps: "Enter Sandman" (remix), Hollywood, 1993 • "One" (remix), Hollywood, 1993.

Dink: *Dink* (1 track), Capitol, 1994.

Drown: *Hold on to the Hollow,* Elektra, 1994.

54.40: *Set the Fire,* MO=DA=MU, 1984 • *54.40,* Reprise/WB, 1986 • "Baby Ran," Reprise, 1986 • *Fight for Love,* Reprise, 1989.

hHead: *Jerk,* Capitol, 1995.

Hilt: *Orange Pony,* Nettwerk America, 1988 • *Call the Ambulance Before I Hurt Myself,* Nettwerk, 1990 • *Journey to the Center of the Bowl,* Nettwerk, 1991.

Killing Joke: "Democracy" (remix), Zoo, 1995.

Low Pop Suicide: *On the Cross of Commerce* (2 tracks), World Domination/Capitol, 1993.

Malhavoc: *Get Down,* Cargo, 1994.

Marilyn Manson: *Antichrist Superstar* (14 tracks), Nothing/Interscope, 1996.

Mötley Crüe: "Hooligan's Holiday" (remix), Elektra, 1994.

Mystery Machine: *Glazed,* Nettwerk, 1992.

Nine Inch Nails: "Reptile" (remix), Nothing/Interscope, 1994.

Psyclone Rangers: *Feel Nice,* World Domination, 1993, 1994.

Rigor Mortis: *Rigor Mortis,* Capitol, 1989.

Skinny Puppy: *Remission* (EP), Nettwerk, 1984 • *Bites,* Nettwerk, 1985 • *Mind: The Perpetual Intercourse,* Gold Rush, 1986, 1996 • *Cleanse, Fold and Manipulate,* Nettwerk/Capitol, 1987 • *Vivisect VI,* Nettwerk/Capitol, 1988 • *Rabies,* Nettwerk/Capitol, 1989 • *12"Anthology,* Nettwerk/Capitol, 1990 • *Too Dark Park,* Nettwerk/Capitol, 1990 • *ain't it dead yet?,* Nettwerk, 1991 • "Inquisition," Nettwerk/Capitol, 1992 • *Last Rites,* Nettwerk/Capitol, 1992 • "Ode to Groovy," Restless, 1993 (*In Defense of Animals Benefit Compilation*) • *Brap,* Nettwerk, 1996 • "Cult," American, 1996 (*Suburbia* soundtrack) • *The Process,* American, 1996.

SNFU: *The One Voted Most Likely to Succeed,* Epitaph, 1995.

Tear Garden: *Tired Eyes,* Nettwerk, 1986 • *Slowly Burning,* Nettwerk, 1987 • *The Last Man to Fly,* Nettwerk, 1992.

Thought Industry: *Songs for Insects,* Metal Blade, 1992.

24 Gone: *The Spin,* Oceana/Onslot, 1990.

Water Walk: *(thingamajig),* Nettwerk/IRS, 1990.

Tim O'Heir

One of the real troopers of the indie rock trenches, engineer/producer Tim O'Heir spent nearly 10 years working out of the Boston area's legendary Fort Apache Studios recording hundreds of demos, singles, and albums. He has produced or co-produced classics for Bob Evans, Come, Crumb, Folk Implosion, Fuzzy, Hot Rod, Possum Dixon, Sebadoh, Six Finger Satellite, and Superdrag. Revered for a raging guitar sound, O'Heir also has a feel for the more melodic side of alt-rock.

Tim O'Heir was born in 1963 and grew up in the working-class Boston suburb of Lowell. By junior high he loved attitudinal rock 'n' roll bands like the Rolling Stones and started taking guitar lessons. A high schooler in 1977, O'Heir saw the Sex Pistols on TV and threw himself into the punk–new wave rebellion: the aggression, realism, and individualism of the movement seemed an antidote to the generic arena rock he heard on the radio.

O'Heir attended Boston's Massachusetts College of Art as a multimedia major and became fascinated with the interaction of film, video, and music. He also found "plenty of people to play my kind of music" and formed a band, Production Club, with Wally Gagell (who later co-produced tracks for the *Kids* soundtrack with O'Heir). Realizing that his primary interest was in the audio side of the equation, O'Heir created a home studio in a loft with a 4-track recorder and a six-channel mixer, and started recording local band demos and small film projects.

O'Heir then got an internship at a video postproduction facility, which led to a job as an audio assistant. He was fired for being a "wiseass punk rocker," but then landed a similar job at Polymedia, a swank 16-track audio studio dealing primarily with commercials. After about a year O'Heir became the studio's chief engineer; to compensate for his low pay, O'Heir was given the opportunity to use the studio after hours and on weekends. He produced fine demos for several local bands for next to nothing, then suddenly the bands stopped coming.

When he called, the bands told O'Heir that they were now going to Fort Apache, an 8-track studio in the depressed Roxbury section of Boston operated by Gary Smith, Sean Slade, and Paul Kolderie (see entries). O'Heir was fed up with jingles and voice-overs—though these had given him an excellent background in recording every manner of instrument and musical style—and wanted to record rock bands for real; so he called Fort Apache looking for a job. His timing was good, as the studio was in the process of moving from Roxbury to Cambridge and looking to pick up more business.

For four years beginning in 1987, O'Heir worked a construction or restaurant job by day, then, often without time to shower or change, recorded indie bands at Fort Apache by night. By 1992 his colleagues had graduated to national and major-label artists, so O'Heir was left to record virtually all of the local and indie acts for the studio. He likens this period of 16-hour-a-day recording work to an addiction. "If you're not there, you feel you are missing something because there is something new to learn every day. It's a philosophy class, a technical class, a music appreciation class all in one, and it becomes an obsession," he says. "It also became a blur. People come up to me in clubs and talk to me for half an hour about a session we did together in 1993, and I have no recollection of it," he confides.

Eventually the credits piled up and O'Heir broke out of the local music ghetto, recording in Los Angeles and elsewhere. O'Heir sequenced Sebadoh's (led by former Dinosaur Jr. member Lou Barlow) album *Bubble & Scrape* in 1993, then produced their *Bakesale* in 1994. More coherent, less noisy, and vastly better recorded than their previous efforts, O'Heir's clean-but-not-sterile production allows Barlow's and Jason Lowenstein's songwriting to come to the fore, and gained O'Heir much respect and attention.

O'Heir (co-producing) and Barlow gained even more attention through the surprise-hit soundtrack to the film *Kids*, for which they recorded eight songs under the names Folk Implosion (Barlow and John Davis) and Deluxx Folk Implosion (Barlow, Davis, Bob Fay, and Mark Perretta). Ranging from the punk tantrum "Daddy Never Understood" to the trip-hop of "Nothing Gonna Stop," "Simean Groove," "Natural One" and "Wet Stuff," to the mysterioso instrumentals "Jenny's Theme" and "Crash," Barlow demonstrates a Neil Young–like talent level and similar ability to genre-hop with impunity.

The Neil Young comparison became even more apt when Sebadoh returned in 1996 with *Harmacy*, a superi-

or collection of folky and mildly grungy love songs of stark emotional honesty that actually cracked the album charts and elevated Barlow to the artistic and commercial top of the indie rock heap. —ERIC OLSEN

Alloy: *Paper Thin Front,* Engine, 1994.

Battershell: *Sunshine in Popopia,* NG, 1997.

Bob Evans: *The Bradley Suite,* Skene, 1995.

Boy Wonder: *Wonder Wear,* Roadrunner, 1997.

Cold Water Flat: *Listen,* Sonic Bubblegum, 1993 • *Cold Water Flat,* Fort Apache/MCA, 1995.

Come: *Eleven: Eleven,* Matador, 1992.

Cordelia's Dad: *Cordelia's Dad,* Omnium, 1990, 1996.

Crumb: *Romance Is a Slowdance,* Qwest, 1996.

Deluxx Folk Implosion: "Daddy Never Understood," London, 1995.

Dirt Merchants: *Scarified,* Sony, 1996.

Elevator Drops: *People Mover,* Time Bomb, 1997.

Engine 88: *Snowman,* Caroline, 1997.

Fat Tuesday: *Everybody's Got One,* Red Decibel, 1993 • "High and Low," Columbia, 1994.

Folk Implosion: "Crash," London, 1995 • "Jenny's Theme," London, 1995 • "Natural One," London, 1995 • "Nothing Gonna Stop," London, 1995 • "Raise the Bells," London, 1995 • "Simean Groove," London, 1995 • "Wet Stuff," London, 1995.

Fuzzy: "Flashlight," Seed, 1994 • *Fuzzy,* Seed, 1994 • "Lemon Rind," Seed, 1995 • *Electric Juices,* Tag/Atlantic, 1996.

Glazed Baby: *Karmic Debt,* Red Decibel, 1994.

Gren: *Camp Grenada,* IRS, 1995.

Hank: *Are You Insane?,* Blackheart, 1995.

Hot Rod: *SpeedDangerDeath,* Caroline, 1993.

Moving Targets: *Take This Ride,* Taang!, 1993.

New Radiant Storm King: *August Revival,* Grass, 1996.

Only Living Witness: *Prone Mortal Form,* Century, 1993 • *Innocents,* Century, 1996.

Possum Dixon: *Star Maps,* Interscope, 1996.

Red Bliss: *Gateway to Joy,* Axis, 1991 • *Fishkill,* Axis, 1992.

Red Tomato: "Cars," Shimmy-Disc, 1993.

Scrawl: *Nature Film,* Elektra, 1998.

Sebadoh: *Bakesale ,* Sub Pop, 1994 • "Skull" (remix), Sub Pop, 1994 • *Harmacy,* Sub Pop, 1996.

Six Finger Satellite: *Six Finger Satellite* (EP), Sub Pop, 1991.

SK-70: *Nananoxynol-9* (EP), Sonic Bubblegum, 1995.

Slapshot: *Sudden Death Overtime,* Taang!, 1990 • *Blast Furnace,* We Bite America, 1993, 1995.

Smackmellon: *Smackmellon* (EP), Cherrydisc, 1994 • *Blue Hour,* Relativity, 1995.

Smashing Orange: *The Glass Bead Game,* Chameleon, 1993.

Spore: *Fear God/She's So Heavy* (EP), Taang!, 1993 • *She Knows Better,* Taang!, 1993 • *Giant,* Taang!, 1994.

Supahead: *Caulk,* Too Damn Hype, 1994.

Superdrag: *Regretfully Yours*, Elektra, 1996 • "Sucked Out,"
   Elektra, 1996.
Tulips: *Buxom* (1 track), Ear, 1992.
Upper Crust: *Let Them Eat Rock*, Upstart, 1995.

COLLECTIONS
This Is Fort Apache, Fort Apache/MCA, 1995.

Milton Okun

Milt Okun—musician, singer, teacher, conductor, arranger, publishing executive, author—was the most successful popularizer of folk music in the '60s and '70s, arranging and producing for the Chad Mitchell Trio, Peter, Paul and Mary, and John Denver, among many others. Okun's productions for Denver yielded ten gold and four platinum albums, as well as ten Top 20 hits, of which four reached No. 1 ("Sunshine on My Shoulders," "Annie's Song," "Thank God I'm a Country Boy," "I'm Sorry"). In the '80s Okun helped expose the talents of opera singer Plácido Domingo to a popular audience. In addition, Okun's music publishing company, Cherry Lane (run for years by Okun's sister-in-law, Jean Vinegar), is one of the more successful players in the field.

Milt Okun was born December 23, 1923, in Brooklyn. He was something of a prodigy as a pianist, starting to play at age 4. Okun was on course to be a concert pianist until he contracted a kidney disease, nephritis, at 16, prior to the advent of antibiotics. Okun couldn't play piano for the two years of his recuperative period. When he returned to playing he found—to his great dismay—that he had lost the "naturalness and spontaneity that you need to be a major pianist," and he decided to pursue a career as a music teacher.

Okun graduated from New York University with a degree in music education in 1949 and got his master's from the Oberlin Conservatory of Music in 1951, thereafter becoming an NYC junior high music teacher. While he was teaching in the early and mid-'50s, Okun, a lover of folk music, also recorded nine albums of traditional folk songs as a singer/guitarist for the Stinson, Riverside, and Warwick labels. His subspecialty was playing folk songs with symphony orchestras; he wrote the orchestra arrangements himself and played a number of concerts with orchestras across the country.

Okun's friend Robert DeCormier was Harry Belafonte's conductor; in 1957 DeCormier hired Okun to play piano for a Belafonte summer tour. After the tour Okun accepted a full-time job with Belafonte, first as pianist and then as background singer. Belafonte then organized a 12-man vocal group called the Belafonte Folk Singers, of which Okun became a member; the group toured with Belafonte and recorded three albums of their own for RCA between 1958 and 1961.

In 1958 DeCormier quit and Okun became Belafonte's conductor and arranger. Okun believes that Belafonte's late '50s albums weren't as successful as his mid-'50s classics because producer Bob Bollard didn't have an ear for the right take. "It was a lesson to me that a marvelous singer with the best arrangements in the world could be destroyed by an unfeeling producer," he says.

While he was working for Belafonte, Okun was hired to do arrangements for folk records by artists such as Leon Bibb, Esther Ofarim, Paul Robeson, and Martha Schlamme, mostly for the Vanguard label. Okun then came upon the Chad Mitchell Trio, recently arrived in New York from Washington state and playing at Greenwich Village's Blue Angel club. Okun brought the trio songs and arranged and co-produced their first album for Colpix in 1960. In the liner notes to Varese Sarabande's *The Chad Mitchell Trio Collection*, member Mike Kobluk says Okun was "responsible for any success we had. He was the leveling influence, the coach, the referee, and the person with the musical taste who helped to develop ours." Okun then helped the trio get a deal with Kapp Records through Belafonte's production company and arranged and produced subsequent albums through the mid-'60s; these included their hits "Lizzie Borden," "The Marvelous Toy," and "The John Birch Society."

At the end of 1960, Okun's contract with Belafonte ran out and it was not renewed—he knows not why. Though he was disappointed at the time, Okun calls this "the best thing that ever happened to me," because he was forced to leave the Belafonte umbrella and go out on his own. (Okun had a measure of poetic justice: Irving Burgie, aka Lord Burgess, wrote most of Belafonte's biggest hits, including "Day-O," "Jamaica Farewell," "Come Back Liza," "Kingston Market," and "Angelina." When his publishing contract with Belafonte's company ran out in the '80s, Okun's Cherry Lane offered Burgie a deal that has increased his annual income five-fold. As a result of Burgie's success, Belafonte even brought his own publishing to Cherry Lane for a time.)

Soon after Okun left Belafonte, manager/producer Albert Grossman hired him to arrange for and "direct" (today Okun would be called the producer and Grossman the executive producer) his new folk trio, Peter (Yarrow), Paul (Stookey) and Mary (Travers). "I desperately tried to avoid it because they were terrible when they came to me," Okun confides. "Mary sang flat, and the two guys didn't much like her. I asked three different arrangers to take them over from me, but each one said they were hopeless. I thought they were hopeless too. I worked with them for about nine months and they finally got seven or eight songs down.

"Their first show was at Gerde's Folk City in Manhattan. Maynard Solomon—the head of Vanguard Records and an old friend—sat down next to me and just started laughing at these kids because they really sounded awful; I didn't even admit that I had done the arrangements, but the audience just loved them. They cheered and cheered. The next day I told Al, 'Those guys have got to shave their beards and Mary has got to get a decent dress,' and he just smiled at me. He knew better than I what was happening."

If they were so bad, why was anyone interested?

"There were four folk groups happening at the time and they were all clean-cut: the Kingston Trio, the Brothers Four (for whom Okun was musical director), the Chad Mitchell Trio, and the Limeliters. Al thought there was room for a beatnik-type group, and he was right. Peter and Paul were very solid guitar players—that was the foundation of their sound. Although they were slow to learn songs, once they had them down they did them perfectly, which they do to this day. Also, while their voices weren't musically great, they were distinctive and very appealing."

Regardless of the trio's steep learning curve, the combination of Grossman's savvy, Okun's musical acumen, and their own magical vocal blend led their debut album, *Peter, Paul and Mary*, to No. 1 for seven weeks in 1962, selling 2 million copies and spinning off classics like "Lemon Tree," "500 Miles," "If I Had a Hammer," and the protest song "Cruel War." With Grossman producing, Okun arranging and directing, and a sincere commitment to social justice, PP&M became the most popular folk group of the '60s, recording songs that have come to define a generation, including Yarrow's "Puff (The Magic Dragon)" and Bob Dylan's "Blowin' in the Wind" and "Don't Think Twice, It's All Right." By 1967 Okun was co-producing the trio with Grossman, and they generated more greats in "I Dig Rock and Roll Music" (No. 9), "Too Much of Nothing," and the group's only No. 1 single, John Denver's "Leaving on a Jet Plane" in 1969.

Meanwhile, when Chad Mitchell went solo in 1965, he was replaced in the renamed Mitchell Trio by a young singer/songwriter from New Mexico named John Deutschendorf, who continued with the group until it broke up in 1968 (Okun produced the group's later

records on Mercury). Okun suggested that Deutschendorf change his name to "Denver" and go solo.

Fortunately, Okun was able to secure a four-album deal from RCA, because it was Denver's fourth album, *Poems, Prayers and Promises* (No. 15), led by the singalong classic "Take Me Home Country Roads" (No. 2), that finally hit in 1971. (Although "Sunshine on My Shoulders" was included on *Poems,* it wasn't released as a single until 1974.) *Poems,* 1972's *Rocky Mountain High* (No. 4), and 1974's *Back Home Again* (No. 1; his most solid studio album, with the No. 5 title track, "Annie's Song," "Sweet Surrender," No. 13, and "Thank God I'm a Country Boy") form the unshakable foundation of Denver's enormous folk and country-pop career, a career that was often maligned in the cynical '70s because of the singer's sunny disposition and earnest environmentalism. But talent will out: since Denver's untimely death in an experimental airplane accident in late 1997, people have begun to remember what he was (a great entertainer and singer/songwriter of high quality), not what he wasn't (an innovator or challenger of the status quo).

Okun gives an example of Denver's integrity: when Denver's first publishing deal with Cherry Lane expired in the mid-'70s—at the peak of his commercial success—he chose to renew with Cherry Lane under the same terms as his original deal rather than to exercise his clout and demand a more favorable deal or go elsewhere.

In the '80s Okun's conservatory-trained sensibilities found their greatest expression in a series of records with the great Spanish-born Mexican operatic tenor Plácido Domingo (one of the "Three Tenors"). Their first album together, *Perhaps Love* (No. 18), went platinum and is representative of their formula: provide a lush orchestral bed over which Domingo's resonant instrument floats through a collection of newish pop songs ("Annie's Song," "Perhaps Love" with John Denver, "Time After Time") and standards ("American Hymn," "Yesterday," "To Love"). —Eric Olsen

Carreras, Jose, Plácido Domingo, and Luciano Pavarotti: *Christmas Favorites from the World's Favorite Tenors,* Sony Classical, 1995.

Carter, Anita: *Ring of Fire,* Bear Family, 1989.

Chad Mitchell Trio: *The Chad Mitchell Trio Arrives,* Colpix, 1960 • *The Best of the Chad Mitchell Trio: The Mercury Years,* Chronicles/Mercury, 1998.

Denver, John: *Rhymes and Reasons,* RCA, 1969 • *Take Me to Tomorrow,* RCA, 1970 • *Whose Garden Was This,* RCA, 1970 • *Aerie,* RCA, 1971 • "Friends with You," RCA, 1971 • *Poems, Prayers and Promises,* RCA, 1971 • "Take Me Home, Country Roads," RCA, 1971 • "Everyday," RCA, 1972 • "Goodbye Again," RCA, 1972 • *Rocky Mountain High,*

RCA, 1972 • "Farewell Andromeda (Welcome to My Morning)," RCA, 1973 • *Farewell Andromeda*, RCA, 1973 • *Greatest Hits*, RCA, 1973 • "I'd Rather Be a Cowboy," RCA, 1973 • "Please, Daddy," RCA, 1973 • "Rocky Mountain High," RCA, 1973 • *Take Me Home Country Roads and Other Hits*, RCA, 1973 • "Annie's Song," RCA, 1974 • "Back Home Again," RCA, 1974 • *Back Home Again*, RCA, 1974 • *Beginnings, with the Mitchell Trio*, Mercury, 1974 • *Denver Gift Box*, RCA, 1974 • *John Denver's Greatest Hits*, RCA, 1974 • "Sunshine on My Shoulders," RCA, 1974 • *An Evening with John Denver*, RCA, 1975 • "Calypso/I'm Sorry," RCA, 1975 • "Christmas for Cowboys," RCA, 1975 • "Fly Away," RCA, 1975 • *Rocky Mountain Christmas*, RCA, 1975 • "Sweet Surrender," RCA, 1975 • "Thank God I'm a Country Boy," RCA, 1975 • *Windsong*, RCA, 1975 • "Baby, You Look Good to Me Tonight," RCA, 1976 • *I Want to Live*, RCA, 1976 • "It Makes Me Giggle," RCA, 1976 • "Like a Sad Song," RCA, 1976 • "Looking for Space," RCA, 1976 • *Spirit*, RCA, 1976, 1998 • *Greatest Hits*, Vol. 2, RCA, 1977 • w/ the Muppets, *John Denver and the Muppets: A Christmas Together*, Laserlight, 1977, 1996 • "How Can I Leave You Again," RCA, 1977 • "My Sweet Lady," RCA, 1977 • "I Want to Live," RCA, 1978 • "It Amazes Me," RCA, 1978 • *John Denver*, RCA, 1979, 1998 • "Autograph," RCA, 1980 • *Autograph*, RCA, 1980 • "Dancing with the Mountains," RCA, 1980 • w/ Sylvie Vartan, "Love Again," RCA, 1984 • *Greatest Hits*, Vol. 3, RCA, 1985 • *Reflections: Songs of Love and Life*, RCA, 1996 • *The Rocky Mountain Collection*, RCA, 1996 • *Country Roads Collection*, RCA, 1997 • *Forever, John*, RCA, 1998 • *Greatest Country Hits*, RCA, 1998.

Domingo, Plácido: *Christmas With*, CBS, 1981 • *Perhaps Love*, CBS, 1981 • w/ John Denver, "Perhaps Love," Columbia, 1982 • *My Life for a Song*, CBS, 1983 • *Always in My Heart*, CBS, 1984 • *Save Your Nights for Me*, CBS Masterworks, 1985 • *A Love Until the End of Time*, CBS Masterworks, 1987 • *Entre Dos Mundos*, Sony Masterworks, 1992 • "Virgen Lava Penales," Disney, 1994 (*Navidad en Las Americas*).

Fat City: *Welcome to Fat City*, Paramount, 1972.

Highwaymen, The: *Michael Row the Boat Ashore: The Best Of*, EMI America, 1992.

Irish Rovers: *On the Shores of Americay*, MCA, 1971.

Liberty: *Liberty*, Windsong, 1978.

Miller, Roger: *Off the Wall*, Windsong, 1977.

Mitchell Trio: *That's the Way It's Gonna Be*, Mercury, 1965 • *Violets of Dawn*, Mercury, 1965 • *Alive!*, Mercury, 1967.

Nyro, Laura: *The First Songs*, Columbia, 1966, 1973 • *Stoned Soul Picnic: The Best of Laura Nyro*, Legacy, 1997.

Paxton, Tom: *The Marvellous Toy and Other Gallimaufry*, Flying Fish, 1984 • *Goin' to the Zoo*, Rounder, 1997 • *I've Got a Yo-Yo*, Rounder, 1997.

Peter, Paul and Mary: *Album 1700*, Warner Bros., 1967 • "I Dig Rock and Roll Music," Warner Bros., 1967 • "Too Much of Nothing," Warner Bros., 1967 • *Late Again*, Warner Bros., 1968 • "Leaving on a Jet Plane," Warner Bros., 1969 • *Peter, Paul and Mommy*, Warner Bros., 1969, 1990 • *10 Years Together: The Best Of*, Warner Bros., 1970.

Shaw Brothers: *Follow Me*, RCA, 1974.

Smotherland, Michael: *Michael Smotherland*, Windsong, 1977.

Starland Vocal Band: "Afternoon Delight," Windsong, 1976 • "California Day," Windsong, 1976 • *Starland Vocal Band*, Windsong, 1976 • "Hail! Hail! Rock and Roll," Windsong, 1977 • *Rear View Mirror*, Windsong, 1977 • *Late Night Radio*, Windsong, 1978.

Travers, Mary: "Follow Me," Warner Bros., 1971 • *Mary*, Warner Bros., 1971 • *Morning Glory*, Warner Bros., 1972 • *All My Choices*, Warner Bros., 1973.

Yarrow, Peter: "Don't Ever Take Away My Freedom," Warner Bros., 1972 • *Peter*, Warner Bros., 1972.

Andrew Loog Oldham

Andrew Loog Oldham is a fascinating figure integral to the development of rock 'n' roll in the '60s; he managed, molded, and produced the Rolling Stones from a scruffy R&B cover outfit in 1963 into the second most important group in rock history by the time he parted ways with them in 1967. While he was guiding the Stones, Oldham also discovered, produced, and managed the lovely and fragile Marianne Faithfull ("As Tears Go By," No. 9 U.K.) and headed one of Britain's most important independent labels, Immediate, which from 1965 to its closing in 1970 boasted hits by the Small Faces, the Nice, Chris Farlowe, P.P. Arnold, Fleetwood Mac, Humble Pie, and Amen Corner. Subsequently, Oldham moved to the U.S. and became an independent producer (Donovan, Humble Pie, Jimmy Cliff, Bobby Womack) before meeting a Colombian movie star and gravitating with her to Bogota, where he has lived since the early '80s.

Andrew Loog Oldham was born in London in 1944, the son of an English woman and an U.S. Air Force officer killed that year in a bombing mission over Germany. Oldham fancied himself a star in the making from early childhood; by age 11 he was already familiar with the streets of Soho, where he hung out at coffee shops and talked about music. Buddy Holly, Elvis Presley, Eddie Cochran, and Johnny Otis particularly caught his ear through the '50s.

"America's gift to England was music. Lyrics and rhythm became our escape and our hope. We had no idea what a 'boardwalk' or a 'Spanish Harlem' was, but they provided food for the imagination and helped us realize that we didn't all have to get a regular job," he says.

Oldham left Wellingborough College at 16 and sauntered into the boutique of fashion designer Mary Quant requesting work. "When I left school I went into fashion because in England at that time fashion *was* pop. Before there was music there was clothes and image," he says. Though he neither sang nor played an instrument, Oldham figured his quickest path to stardom was as a pop singer, a path he pursued with no particular success under names including "Sandy Beach" and "Chancery Lane" while he worked for Quant.

When it became clear that a pop singer's life was not to be his, Oldham repaired to the French Riviera where he, with the help of a young heiress and two journalists, concocted a bizarre kidnapping scheme wherein the ill-gotten booty was to be raised not through ransom but from selling the story of the kidnapping to the London *Daily Express.* Unfortunately for the plotters, the girl's father obtained an injunction against publication of the story in any English newspaper, thereby thwarting the scheme.

Returning to London, Oldham turned to a slightly more reputable occupation, public relations, to seek his fame and fortune. He promoted English pop singer Mark Wynter for a time, then in early 1962, he promoted American producer Phil Spector (see entry) on a visit to England. Oldham was in awe of Spector for being the first producer to become at least as famous as the artists he produced. Spector left Oldham with the admonition (should he ever become a producer) to never record at a record company's own studio, but to pay for the sessions elsewhere and then lease the tapes to the record company, thereby retaining control of the recording process and, potentially, more money.

In early 1963 Oldham was hired by Beatles manager Brian Epstein to promote the Beatles and Gerry and the Pacemakers. After promoting "Please Please Me" for the Beatles and "How Do You Do It?" for Gerry, Oldham was working on the Fab Four's "From Me to You" when destiny intervened. "A journalist I was pitching, Peter Jones of the *Record Mirror,* sent me off to see the Stones at the Crawdaddy Club in Richmond, probably to get me off his back. I saw them April 23, 1963, and then I knew what I had been training for. The main

thing they had was passion, which has served them to this day," Oldham says.

At the time the Rollin' Stones (named for the Muddy Waters song; Oldham added the "g")—Brian Jones and Keith Richards on guitars, Mick Jagger on vocals and harmonica, Bill Wyman on bass, Charlie Watts on drums, and Ian Stewart on piano—were a ragged R&B cover band, but their run at the Crawdaddy had generated much attention, and with the Beatles on their way up, no one wanted to miss the next big thing.

The Stones took to Oldham's youth, confidence, and vision and allowed themselves to be talked out of a verbal management agreement they had with Crawdaddy owner Giorgio Gomelsky, who was in Switzerland attending his father's funeral at the time. Oldham's first act as manager was to demote the shambling Stewart (the "6th Stone," Stewart recorded with the band until his death in 1985) from the band's live act for not keeping with Oldham's image of a lean-and-mean Stones.

"I took the Stones to Dick Rowe at Decca, and I knew he would sign them because he had turned down the Beatles. He had a great track record in the '50s, including Billy Fury, and he should be remembered not as the guy who turned down the Beatles but as the guy who signed the Rolling Stones," says Oldham emphatically.

"In England at that time you had four record companies that controlled everything: EMI, Decca, Philips, and Pye," he continues. "The 9-to-5 mentality of the record companies would not have served the Rolling Stones. What I saw in the club, which had to be brought as much as possible onto record, could not have been done with shirts and ties, so I became a record producer to protect my vision of their image: there are always opposites and I saw the Rolling Stones as the anti-Beatles. I didn't have to be technically proficient. I didn't play an instrument, wasn't an engineer or a technician, but I had a vision," he says.

"I had no idea what I was doing in the studio the first time. I had £40 to spend, at £5 or £6 an hour. I was looking at the clock and it was 5:55 P.M.—time was nearly up. We had recorded three songs, so I said 'Right, that's it.' The engineer said, 'What about mixing?' (we were working on 4-track), and I said, 'What's that?' He explained it to me; I said, 'You do it and I'll pick it up in the morning.' A year and a half later I was an expert and wouldn't let anybody else touch anything," he says.

In June of 1963 the Stones' first single, a cover of Chuck Berry's "Come On" was released and went to No. 21 in the U.K. The follow-up in November was a cover of the dreaded Beatles' "I Wanna Be Your Man," which did even better, rising to No. 12 U.K. By February of 1964, they reached the U.K. Top 10 with Buddy Holly's "Not Fade Away," which also cracked the Top 50 in the U.S.

"Once we got going, we had to keep coming up with a new single every six weeks. We did a couple of singles, an EP [*The Rolling Stones*], then an album [*England's Newest Hitmakers: The Rolling Stones*, No. 1 U.K., No. 11 U.S]. One of the keys to production is to pick the right environment for the act to function in. For an example, after the first (largely disastrous) American tour in 1964, as a reward for being pros, I took the Stones to Chess to record at the home of their idols," Oldham says.

While he was both the Stones' manager and producer, Oldham's greatest contribution to the group was "making them write. The Stones weren't writing yet, and I realized that for them to keep pumping out the singles, they had to come up with their own material. A group that can't write is like a pilot flying without a parachute. 'Tell Me (You're Coming Back),' from the first album, was the first song Mick and Keith wrote that the group recorded. It was a great beginning; once they mastered writing singles, there was a period from 1965 to 1967 where we couldn't go wrong. We would cut four or five tracks a day. There were no prisoners: if a song wasn't happening after 20 minutes, next case," he says emphatically.

"From 1964 to 1967 we only recorded in America: 80 percent at RCA in Hollywood. There's something to be said for stepping out into sunshine on the Sunset Strip for a break rather than into the drizzling rain of West Hampstead. Environment counts, and the Stones were about—even when they were writing—American music. English music was not about something as honest and personal as 'Stand by Me.' Because of their passion for it, the Stones were able to embody American music rather than just play it," he says.

"Ironically," Oldham continues, "even though we were playing American music and recording there, it took us longer to get big in America because image wasn't an issue we could use. The mainstream press didn't care that much yet about pop culture. It wasn't until after Monterey and Woodstock that the American press realized that this thing wasn't going to go away and return to Frank Sinatra, Mantovani, and all things comfortable. Also the fallout from the Vietnam war helped reinforce the seriousness of the counterculture," he observes acutely.

Oldham's enduring legacy is the amazing music the Stones and he generated during the two years between the squirmingly lascivious "Satisfaction" (No. 1 U.S. and U.K.)—one of the greatest rock songs ever—released in

May of 1965, and the hit-filled *Flowers* compilation (No. 3), released in July of 1967. In between were the incredibly self-aware narcissism of "Get Off of My Cloud" (No. 1 U.S. and U.K.); the chamber music gentility and vulnerability of "As Tears Go By" (No. 6); the bemused urban modernity of "19th Nervous Breakdown" (No. 2); and the Stones' first timeless album, *Aftermath* (No. 1 U.S. and U.K.), with the simultaneously mocking and empathetic drug song "Mother's Little Helper" (No. 8), the incredibly groovy and misogynistic "Under My Thumb" and "Out of Time," the lovely "Lady Jane," and the exotic "Paint It Black" (No. 1 U.S. and U.K.).

Inevitably, the relationship between Oldham and the Stones changed over the years. "Money and fame can interfere with everything. There's nothing like the first run, but having that first run right away can spoil you. After a while I couldn't pick up the phone and say 'Hey Brian' or 'Hey Mick' because someone would ask 'Who's calling?'

"We got a little too big for our britches in England, and even me—a press agent—didn't realize that 'Mick Jagger' is spelled just the same way when the press is bringing you down as when it is building you up. Then came the drug busts. Basically I let them down because I panicked and left England. I didn't stand by them. That was basically the end because I didn't put my balls on the table for them," Oldham admits.

"Another thing—and this is the downside of my infatuation with the Phil Spector persona—a manager shouldn't get too much space in the media. It will backfire. In addition, I don't think that what I brought to the table would have been relevant after Led Zeppelin came along, and it changed to albums and stadiums from singles and concert halls. Also, I might not have lived through it. That's when it all became serious: the money, the drugs, the whole thing."

Now Oldham lives in Bogota with his wife and teenage son, periodically producing bands like Argentina's Ratones Paranoicos. "I'm very happy: I've never had to get a regular job. I've been taken into different cultures, been given great educations and great energy to live with, and I survived the rock 'n' roll lifestyle."
—ERIC OLSEN

Andrew Oldham Orchestra: *Plays Maggie May*, Decca, 1964 • *East Meets West*, Parrot, 1965.

Arnold, P.P.: *The First Lady of Immediate* (2 tracks), Immediate, 1967 • *Kafunta*, Immediate, 1968.

Browne, Duncan: *Give Me Take You*, Immediate, 1968.

Cliff, Jimmy: *In Concert: The Best of Jimmy Cliff*, Reprise, 1976.

Compania Ilimitada: "Siloe," CBS International, 1986 • *Cronica Bajo El Sol* (1 track), CBS International, 1993.

Dick and Dee Dee: *The Best of Dick and Dee Dee* (1 track), Varese Sarabande, 1995.

Donovan: *Essence to Essence,* Epic, 1973 • *Troubador: The Definitive Collection, 1964–1976,* Legacy, 1992.

Faithfull, Marianne: "As Tears Go By," London, 1964 • *Marianne Faithfull,* London, 1965 • *Is This What I Get for Loving You?,"* Decca, 1967 • *Greatest Hits,* Abkco, 1969, 1987 • *Faithfull: A Collection of Her Best Recordings,* Island, 1994.

Humble Pie: *Street Rats,* A&M, 1975.

Mardones, Benny: *Thank God for Girls,* Private Stock, 1978.

Oxa, Anna: *Anna Oxa,* RCA, 1979.

Ratones Paranoicos: *Hecho En Memphis,* Sony International, 1993.

Rolling Stones, The: "Come On," London, 1963 • *12 x 5,* Decca/London, 1964 • "I Wanna Be Your Man," London, 1964 • "It's All Over Now," London, 1964 • "Little Red Rooster," London, 1964 • "Not Fade Away," London, 1964 • "Tell Me (You're Coming Back)," London, 1964 • *The Rolling Stones,* Decca/London, 1964 • "Time Is on My Side," London, 1964 • "(I Can't Get No) Satisfaction," London, 1965 • *December's Children,* London, 1965 • "Get Off of My Cloud," London, 1965 • "Heart of Stone," London, 1965 • *Now,* London, 1965 • *Out of Our Heads,* Decca/London, 1965 • "The Last Time," London, 1965 • *The Rolling Stones No. 2,* Decca/London, 1965 • "19th Nervous Breakdown," London, 1966 • *Aftermath,* Decca/London, 1966 • "As Tears Go By," London, 1966 • *Big Hits/High Tide and Green Grass,* Abkco, 1966 • *Got Live If You Want It,* London, 1966 • "Have You Seen Your Mother, Baby, Standing In the Shadow?," London, 1966 • "Lady Jane," London, 1966 • "Mother's Little Helper," London, 1966 • "Paint It Black," London, 1966 • *Between the Buttons,* Decca/London, 1967 • "Dandelion," London, 1967 • *Flowers,* Decca/London, 1967 • "Let's Spend the Night Together," London, 1967 • "Ruby Tuesday," London, 1967 • "We Love You," London, 1967 • *Through the Past, Darkly (Big Hits, Vol. 2),* Abkco, 1969 • *Hot Rocks 1964–1971,* London, 1972, 1995 • *More Hot Rocks (Big Hits and Fazed Cookies),* Abkco, 1972 • *Metamorphosis,* Decca/ABK, 1975 • *Singles Collection: The London Years,* Abkco, 1989.

Shannon, Del: *. . . And the Music Plays On,* Sunset, 1978 • *The Liberty Years,* EMI Legends, 1991.

Sunday Funnies: *Benediction,* Rare Earth, 1972 • *Sunday Funnies,* Rare Earth, 1981.

Twice As Much: *That's All,* Immediate, 1968.

Werewolves: *Ship of Fools,* RCA, 1978 • *Werewolves,* RCA, 1978.

Womack, Bobby: w/ Patti Labelle, "It Takes a Lot of Strength to Say Goodbye," Beverly Glen, 1984 • *The Poet 2,* Beverly Glen, 1984.

Keith Olsen

Keith Olsen is one of the most prolific and successful rock producers of the '80s and '90s, accumulating an impressive roster of platinum-sellers that includes Pat Benatar, Fleetwood Mac, Foreigner, the Grateful Dead, Ozzy Osbourne, Scorpions, Rick Springfield, and Whitesnake.

Olsen, tongue slightly in cheek, says that about 70 of the 85 million albums in circulation bearing his name were recorded at his own studio, Goodnight L.A., a former radiator shop Olsen and studio designer George Augsberger took over and remade in 1978. Not only was Olsen tired of chasing down someone else's studio, he didn't like shifting studios, wasting time and losing money in the process. "I thought we could get the best equipment around, put it in a room, charge a reasonable rate to my own artists and everything would be fine," he says.

Goodnight L.A., which went public in the '90s, is stocked with the latest—and the best vintage—technology. It boasts a Trident DI-AN board, Sony 3324s, outboard gear such as a Publison DHM 89 B2, Neve stereo limiters and compressors, Lexicon's 102 digital delay, a handful of Yamaha reverbs, and an Eventide H949 harmonizer. Although he jumped on the digital bandwagon early, Olsen doesn't believe in exclusivity. "It's all con-

jecture," he says of the analog versus digital question. "You can make digital sound real good, you can make analog sound real good. A lot of it depends on the source. If it's a great song played really well, it could be recorded on a minicassette recorder and sound good."

The most important thing a producer does is helping the artist. "Getting the artist's creativity on tape in a way that works for the market you're going after" is key, Olsen says. It's not about punching a clock, it's about communication, he suggests. Critical to that is keeping it simple. "If a 5-piece band sounds like a 25-piece band, something's wrong with the picture," he says. "You have a lot of ghosts. What I mean is what happens when you go out live? You've got to be able to recreate what you've done in the studio live. I think a band like Green Day showed it best. They're doing pop music, that's all. It's punk-pop music because of the green hair? No, it's pop music played real honest, real in your face."

The work Olsen did in the '80s with Whitesnake, Starship, Sammy Hagar, Scorpions, Ozzy Osbourne, Rick Springfield—hair bands, pop metal, and arena rock—was "great for the time," he says, "but now things are different. I think it's a misconception that somebody who did that stuff in the '80s can't do anything new today—that anything they touch today is going to sound like an old hair band."

So in the mid-'90s, Olsen began to work with some lesser-known bands, even unsigned bands like San Francisco–based Ted 302. "The Ted stuff does not sound old, it's not a power-ballad band from the '80s or the early '90s. It sounds today and that's what I like," he says.

Working with an established band is "more rewarding to the pocket book," if and when that band sells 8 to 10 million CDs. But dealing with a new, hungry band is more creatively rewarding. "They're not worried about topping their last record because there was no last record," Olsen says. "The pressure's not as great; in fact, sometimes it's a much more creative environment because you're working on the first one where you're setting the direction of the sound." —DAVID JOHN FARINELLA

Airborne: *Airborne,* Columbia, 1979.
Babys, The: *On the Edge,* Chrysalis, 1980 • *Union Jacks,* Chrysalis, 1980 • *Anthology,* Gold Rush, 1981, 1996 • *Fame and Fortune,* Atlantic, 1986.
Bad Company: "This Love," Atlantic, 1986.
Baker, Richard, and the Score Group: *Richard Baker and the Score Group,* Kore Group, 1993.
Ballard, Russ: *At the Third Stroke,* Epic, 1978.
Barclay, Nickey: *Diamonds in A Junkyard,* Arista/America, 1976.
Benatar, Pat: *Crimes of Passion,* Chrysalis, 1980 • "Hit Me with Your Best Shot," Chrysalis, 1980 • "Fire and Ice," Chrysalis, 1981 • *Precious Time,* Chrysalis, 1981 • "Treat Me Right," Chrysalis, 1981 • *Best Shots,* Chrysalis, 1989 • *All Fired Up,* Chrysalis, 1995 • *16 Classic Performances,* EMI, 1996.
Buckingham Nicks: *Buckingham Nicks,* Polydor, 1973.
Cado Belle: *Cado Belle,* Anchor, 1976.
Cain, Tane: *Tane Cain,* RCA, 1982.
Carnes, Kim: *Cafe Racers,* EMI America, 1983.
Dinner, Michael: *Tom Thumb the Dreamer,* Fantasy, 1976.
Emerson, Lake and Palmer: *In the Hot Seat,* Victory, 1994.
Emmanuel: *Grandes Exitos,* Sony International, 1996.
Fleetwood Mac: *Fleetwood Mac,* Reprise, 1975 • "Over My Head," Reprise, 1975 • "Rhiannon (Will You Ever Win?)," Warner/Reprise, 1976 • "Say You Love Me," Reprise, 1976 • *Greatest Hits,* Reprise, 1988.
Fools Gold: *Mr. Lucky,* CBS, 1977.
Foreigner: "Blue Morning, Blue Day," Atlantic, 1978 • "Double Vision," Atlantic, 1978 • *Double Vision,* Atlantic, 1978 • "Hot Blooded," Atlantic, 1978 • *Records,* Atlantic, 1982 • *The Very Best . . . and Beyond,* Atlantic, 1992.
Geronimo Black: *Geronimo Black,* Uni, 1972.
Grateful Dead: *Terrapin Station,* Arista, 1977 • *The Arista Years,* Arista, 1996.
Hagar, Sammy: *Standing Hampton,* Geffen, 1981 • *Three Lock Box,* Geffen, 1982 • "Your Love Is Driving Me Crazy," Geffen, 1982 • *Unboxed,* Geffen, 1994.
Heart: *Passion Works,* Epic, 1983.
I-Ten: *Taking a Cold Look,* Epic, 1983.
James Gang: *Passin' Thru,* ABC, 1972.
Kingdom Come: *Kingdom Come,* Polydor, 1987 • *In Your Face,* Polydor, 1989.
Lake, Greg: *From the Beginning: Retrospective,* Rhino, 1997.
Lynch Mob: *Lynch Mob,* Elektra, 1992.
Millenium: *Begin,* CBS, 1970.
Money, Eddie: "Heaven in the Back Seat," Columbia, 1991 • "I'll Get By," Columbia, 1991 • *Right Here,* Columbia, 1991.
Mr. Big: *Lean into It,* Atlantic, 1991.
Nelson, Rick: *Stay Young: The Epic Recordings,* Legacy, 1993.
Night Ranger: *Man in Motion,* MCA, 1988.
Osbourne, Ozzy: *No Rest for the Wicked,* Epic, 1989 • *The Ozzman Cometh: Greatest Hits,* Epic, 1997.
Preview: *Preview,* Geffen, 1983.
Reno, Mike, and Ann Wilson: "Almost Paradise . . . Love Theme from Footloose," Columbia, 1984.
REO Speedwagon: "Here with Me," Epic, 1988.
Riopelle, Jerry: *Take a Chance,* ABC, 1975.
Saga: *Wildest Dreams,* Atlantic, 1987.
Santana: *Marathon,* Columbia, 1979 • "Winning," Columbia, 1981 • *Zeebop* (3 tracks), Columbia, 1981 • *Viva!* Columbia, 1988.
Santana, Carlos: *Blues for Salvador,* Columbia, 1987.

Scorpions: *Crazy World,* Mercury, 1990 • "Send Me an Angel," Mercury, 1991 • "Wind of Change," Mercury, 1991 • *Pure Instinct,* Atlantic, 1996 • *Deadly Sting: The Mercury Years,* Mercury, 1997.

Sheila: *Little Darlin',* Carrere, 1981.

Slocum, Jamie: *Somewhere Under Heaven,* CPI/Curb, 1996.

Song: *Album,* MGM/Verve, 1967.

Sons of Champlin: *A Circle Filled with Love,* Ariola, 1976.

Southgang: *Group Therapy,* Charisma, 1992.

Springfield, Rick: "I've Done Everything for You," RCA, 1981 • "Jessie's Girl," RCA, 1981 • *Working Class Dog,* RCA, 1981 • "Don't Talk to Strangers," RCA, 1982 • *Success Hasn't Spoiled Me Yet,* RCA, 1983, 1995 • "Rock of Life," RCA, 1988 • *Greatest Hits,* RCA, 1989.

Starship: "It's Not Over ('Til It's Over)," Grunt, 1987 • *No Protection,* RCA, 1987 • *Starship's Greatest Hits: Ten Years of Change,* RCA, 1991.

Sun Sawed in 1/2: *Fizzy Lift,* Not Lame, 1997.

.38 Special: "Like No Other Night," A&M, 1986 • "Somebody Like You," A&M, 1986 • *Strength in Numbers,* A&M, 1986 • *Flashback: The Best Of,* A&M, 1987.

Troiano, Dominic: *Dom,* Mercury, 1972 • *Tricky,* Mercury, 1973.

Waite, John: *Essential,* Chrysalis, 1992.

Walsh, Joe: *The Confessor,* Warner Bros., 1985 • *Greatest Hits: Little Did He Know,* MCA, 1997.

Weir, Bob: *Heaven Help the Fool,* Arista, 1978.

Whitesnake: "Here I Go Again," Geffen, 1987 • "Is This Love," Geffen, 1987 • *Whitesnake,* Geffen, 1987 • "Give Me All Your Love," Geffen, 1988 • "Fool for Your Loving," Geffen, 1989 • *Slip of the Tongue,* Geffen, 1989 • "The Deeper the Love," Geffen, 1989 • "Now You're Gone," Geffen, 1990 • *Greatest Hits,* DGC, 1994.

Doug Olson

(MR. COLSON)

Doug Olson won't name the band he played in that recorded at Smart Studios 10 or 11 years ago. "It was just a local band, best left buried," he says. But Olson, who's better known as Mr. Colson, will admit that that initial foray into the Appleton, Wisconsin, facility owned by producer and Garbage head Butch Vig (see entry) led to work as a producer for Colson himself.

Now, Olson is known for his producing such hard rock and power-pop bands as Sons of Elvis, Walt Mink, and Paw. He has also made a name for himself as a mixer and engineer. Often, it's hard for him to draw the lines, which is fine with him. "A lot of what I do as an engineer is the same as what I would do as a producer, depending on the person I'm working with," he says. "But as a producer, the ultimate responsibility is yours, so the weight is on your shoulders. If it sucks, it's more your fault. And if it's great, you get more credit."

Born September 30, 1964, in Madison, Olson began studying piano at age 5, took up guitar seven years later, and played in bands from ages 15 to 25. "In the course of playing in bands, the studio thing just sort of grew," he says. "The next thing I knew, I was making records."

After making numerous demos of punk bands, Olson's first official production was *Honey Bubble,* by the Tar Babies, on Southern California punkcore label SST. Not only was that 1989 effort his production baptism, it also led to the Mr. Colson moniker. On that record, his name was mistakenly listed as Doug Colson. "Here it comes out, and my name's wrong," Olson says. "I think it was Butch who really started it. I think we were working on a Young Fresh Fellows record, and Butch or somebody in that band started giving me a hard time: 'Mr. Colson, Mr. Colson' every time I came in in the morning." He began taking production credit as Mr. Colson on that Young Fresh Fellows album. "I thought, actually, that's kind of fun."

Olson didn't listen to records for production values until he became a producer himself. "A couple of records that really sort of hit me over the head with sound were *Scary Monsters* by David Bowie [see entry], *London Calling* by the Clash, most of the Beatles stuff," he says. "The Beatles were good. The problem with the Beatles is people imitate them and make things that sound 'Beatlesque,' which can be kind of a trap. You can get all kinds of musical inspiration from them without actually copying them."

If inspiration is one watchword for Olson, another is immediacy. "I've leaned more toward fairly aggressive rock stuff," he says, "though I like things to have sort of a human element. I like to make things sound tight, but I don't like to overdo it. The more a band is able to project some kind of identity or uniqueness, the better. I'd rather something have a little character and not be quite perfect.

"A lot of records nowadays are so polished and perfected," he says. "Technology is inert to me. You can do whatever you want with it, but it's so easy to go in there with your computer and make everyone hit the bull's eye on every single note. There are records where you can hear that they did that, and they sound impressive on first listen. But I don't think those records are ones you're going to keep listening to."

His most successful productions—in a commercial sense—are *Dragline*, a record Paw released on A&M in 1991, and an album by the Watchmen, a Canadian group. The Watchmen album, *In the Trees*, never came out in the U.S., but went platinum in Canada.

Among his favorite recent productions is *Colossus*, the fourth album by Walt Mink. Released on the independent Deep Elm label and recorded in an old thermometer factory in Brooklyn, this lean, nervy disc cost $3,000 to $4,000 to produce. "It doesn't sound like it," he says. "It sounds a little more expensive than that." Indeed: not only was this Walt Mink's most diverse record, its textural variety eloquently reflects the diversity of its song stylings.

"You got to wear a lot of different hats as a producer," Colson says. "At the beginning, a lot of the action is in rehearsal, making sure the songs flow, that the cool parts are repeated if they need to be, a little fine-tuning. Some bands are really good at arranging songs, like Walt Mink." (The group broke up in 1997.)

Such records don't need a lot of tinkering, Colson suggests. "On other records, we've gone in and done some serious changes," he says. "But even when we do, I go in from the standpoint of 'Let's try some different versions of this.' I don't want to, like, threaten somebody with me coming in and changing everything they do. Even if I catalyze something, I still want things to originate from the band, because they won't be true to the band otherwise." —CARLO WOLFF

Barking Tribe: *Serpent Go Home*, Rykodisc, 1991.

Cherubs: *Icing*, Trance Syndicate, 1992.

Dead Hot Workshop: *River Otis* (2 tracks), Seed, 1994.

Dwarves, The: *Thank Heaven for Little Girls*, Sub Pop, 1991 • "Underworld," Sub Pop, 1993.

Fretblanket: *Junkfuel*, Atlas, 1994.

Hall, Ed: *Gloryhole*, Trance, 1991.

Paw: *Dragline*, A&M, 1993.

Puller: *Closer Than You Think*, Tooth and Nail, 1998.

Sons of Elvis: *Glodean*, Priority, 1995.

Spring Heeled Jack USA: *Songs from Suburbia*, Ignition, 1998.

Sprinkler: *More Boy, Less Friend*, Sub Pop, 1992.

Tar Babies: *Honey Bubble*, SST, 1989 • *Death Trip*, Sonic Noise, 1992.

13 Engines: *Conquistador*, Nettwerk, 1995.

Tumbleweed: *Weedseed*, Seed, 1992 • *Sundial*, Seed, 1993.

Vanilla Trainwreck: *Sounding to Try Like You*, Mammoth, 1992 • *Mordecai*, Mammoth, 1994.

Walt Mink: *Miss Happiness*, Caroline, 1992 • *Colossus*, Deep Elm, 1997.

Watchmen, The: *In the Trees*, Uni Canada, 1994 • *Waiting for a Brand New Day*, Uni Canada, 1996.

Michael Omartian

Michael Omartian believes producers get better results in the studio if they approach recording as a way to bring out the essence of an artist. "I don't go in and say, 'Okay, here's the deal: I'll do everything and you just sing the song.' I rely heavily on the passion and the instincts of an artist. To me, that is the recipe for a hit song," Omartian says.

Omartian, a veteran pop and contemporary Christian music producer with a résumé that includes Amy Grant, Rod Stewart, and Christopher Cross, adds that a record producer is similar to a movie producer because both must secure a strong supporting cast. "You're there to help cast the players," he says. "Guys like Quincy Jones [see entry] really work like a film producer because they put combinations of people together."

Although he worked in Los Angeles for many years, Omartian moved to Nashville for a "fresh start," as he puts it. "There was a certain honesty about the way the music was cut in Nashville," he adds. "I come from a strong playing background in the '70s that went very much into the MIDI domain in the '80s, but I got tired of siting in front of a computer doing computer music. It was refreshing to come here and see everyone playing live. "It started with the Amy Grant project, *Heart in Motion* (No. 10)," Omartian says. "Either people from Nashville were going to L.A. to work with me or I was going to Nashville to do background vocals or whatever."

Grant's quadruple-platinum album yielded such hits as "I Will Remember You" (No. 20) and "That's What Love Is For" (No. 7), a song cowritten by Omartian. He also supervised Peter Cetera's duet with Grant, "The Next Time I Fall" (No. 1), as well as Cetera's 1986 single, "Glory of Love" (No. 1). "There was tremendous resistance in the past between Nashville's country and L.A.'s pop, but it seems like some of these barriers are starting to fall," he says.

Omartian believes in tackling projects from conception to final mix. Consequently, he is adamantly opposed to a common industry practice of hiring several producers for an album, then handing over the project to a different producer for the mix. "You end up with a hodgepodge and a disjointed mess on a record," he insists. "You want to go down with the record knowing you did the whole record, or you want to have a great ride."

Born November 26, 1945, in Evanston, Illinois, Omartian made his mark as a session keyboard player and arranger in the '70s, including three stellar albums for Steely Dan: *Pretzel Logic, Katy Lied,* and *Aja.* "The whole thing was about economy," Omartian explains. "Working with them probably had a whole lot more to do with what molded me as someone who tries not to put too much into something. I learned to pull back and find out what's important. Those guys were masters of that."

In 1978 he joined Warner Bros. as a nonexclusive producer, charting with such hits as Rod Stewart's "Infatuation" (No. 6) and "Some Guys Have All the Luck" (No. 10), as well as Christopher Cross's "Sailing" (No. 1) and "Ride Like the Wind" (No. 2). Omartian recommended that Warner Bros. sign Cross to a contract. "Chris had been submitting tapes to Warner Bros. for a long time," Omartian recalls. "I remember [Warner executives] Lenny [Waronker; see entry] or Russ [Titelman; see entry] saying, 'We just got another tape from this Christopher Cross guy.' So they put the thing on and either 'Sailing' or 'Ride Like the Wind' came on and everyone just sat there. I'm looking around going, 'What's the matter with these people? Why aren't they hearing this? This is fantastic.' They were 4-track demos that were pretty unsophisticated but you could tell he had something."

During his seven years with Warner Bros., Omartian also kept busy doing sessions for Ricki Lee Jones, Al Jarreau, Eric Clapton, and Michael Jackson. In 1985, he went independent, landing jobs with such pop and Christian artists as Kathy Troccoli, Gary Chapman, and Steve Camp. Omartian has also recorded several solo albums and participated in *The Players,* the instrumental disc that earned a Dove award. "I've always had a heart for this music because I'm a Christian myself," says Omartian, adding that his joy comes from crafting good songs. "That's where the joy comes in, with the song," Omartian surmises. "It makes it even better when you end up producing your own song because you have so much invested in it that it becomes part of your soul."
—Ben Cromer

Ashton, Susan: *A Distant Call,* Sparrow, 1996.

Bishop, Stephen: *Bowling in Paris,* Atlantic, 1989.

Bolton, Michael: "How Am I Supposed to Live Without You?," Columbia, 1989 • *Soul Provider,* Columbia, 1995.

Bounce the Ocean: *Bounce the Ocean,* Private, 1991.

Camp, Steve: *Taking Heaven by Storm,* Warner Alliance, 1993 • *Mercy in the Wilderness,* Warner Alliance, 1994.

Campbell, Tevin: *T.E.V.I.N.,* Warner Bros., 1991.

Carman: *The Standard,* Sparrow, 1993.

Carter, Raymone: *Raymone Carter,* Reprise, 1991 • "The Way You Love Me," Reprise, 1991.

Cetera, Peter: "Big Mistake," Warner Bros., 1986 • "Glory of Love," Full Moon, 1986 • *Solitude/Solitaire,* Full Moon, 1986 • *You're the Inspiration: A Collection,* River North, 1997.

Cetera, Peter and Amy Grant: "The Next Time I Fall," Full Moon, 1986.

Chapman, Gary: *The Light Inside,* Reunion, 1993 • *Shelter,* Reunion, 1996.

Chater, Kerri: *Part Time Love,* Warner Bros., 1978.

Cher: *I'd Rather Believe in You,* Warner Bros., 1976.

Crackin': *Crackin',* Polydor, 1975 • *Special Touch,* Warner Bros., 1978.

Cross, Christopher: *Christopher Cross,* Warner Bros., 1979 • "Never Be the Same," Warner Bros., 1980 • "Ride Like the Wind," Warner Bros., 1980 • "Sailing," Warner Bros., 1980 • "Arthur's Theme (Best That You Can Do)," Warner Bros., 1981 • "Say You'll Be Mine," Warner Bros., 1981 • "All Right," Warner Bros., 1983 • *Another Page,* Warner Bros., 1983 • "No Time for Talk," Warner Bros., 1983 • *Think of Laura',* Warner Bros., 1983 • "Charm the Snake," Warner Bros., 1985 • *Every Turn of the World,* Warner Bros., 1985 • *Back of My Mind,* Warner Bros., 1988.

Darling, Helen: *Helen Darling,* Decca, 1995 • "Jenny Come Back," Decca, 1995.

Dion: *Streetheart,* Warner Bros., 1976.

First Call: *Human Song,* Epic, 1992 • *La Razon de Cantar,* Myrrh, 1994.

4Him: *Ride,* Verity, 1994, 1997 • *The Message,* Verity, 1997 • *Obvious,* Benson, 1998.

Furay, Richie Band: *I've Got a Reason,* Asylum, 1976.

Gaines, Billy and Sarah: *Come on Back,* Warner Bros., 1996.

Grant, Amy: *Heart in Motion,* A&M, 1991 • "That's What Love Is For," A&M, 1991 • "I Will Remember You," A&M, 1992 • *House of Love,* A&M, 1994 • "Big Yellow Taxi," A&M, 1995.

Gruska, Jay: *Which One of Us Is Me?,* Warner Bros., 1984.

Howell, Kurt: *Kurt Howell,* Reprise, 1992.

Imperials, The: *Priority,* Word, 1981.

Jackson, Jermaine: *Jermaine Jackson,* Arista, 1984 • "Tell Me I'm Not Dreaming (Too Good to Be True)," Arista, 1984 • "(Closest Thing to) Perfect," Arista, 1985 • "Do You Remember Me?," Arista, 1986 • "I Think It's Love," Arista, 1986 • *Precious Moments,* Arista, 1986 • "Words into Action," Arista, 1986.

Jacksons, The: *2300 Jackson Street,* Epic, 1989.

Johnston, Tom: *Still Feels Good,* Warner Bros., 1981.

Kim, Andy: "Rock Me Gently," Capitol, 1974.

Kreuger, Jim: *Sweet Salvation,* CBS, 1978.

Loggins, Kenny: *Vox Humana,* Columbia, 1985.

Manilow, Barry: *Summer of '78,* Arista, 1996.

Maxus: *Maxus,* Warner Bros., 1981.

O'Day, Alan: "Undercover Angel," Pacific, 1977.

Mark Opitz

A leading figure in the Australian rock 'n' roll industry for the last 20 years, Mark Opitz has produced classics of Aussie hard rock and new wave for the Angels, Jimmy Barnes and Cold Chisel, Divinyls, Hoodoo Gurus, and INXS. In addition, Opitz has produced British and American bands of note, including Flesh for Lulu, the Ocean Blue, and Steelheart. Opitz co-owned one of Australia's finest studios, Rhinoceros, from the early '80s until it was closed in the mid-'90s, and he recently helped reorganize one of Australia's leading record labels, Mushroom, with an eye toward multimedia.

Mark Opitz was born in 1952 in Brisbane, Australia. He saw his first concert at age 12 and it was a whopper: the Beatles. Opitz was practicing soccer goal kicks at the park when his brother came running: " 'Hurry, go home and change. We're going to see the Beatles.' I couldn't even believe that they were in the country, let alone that I was going to see them," he says. "Tickets were $2, marked down from $3.25 because the show wasn't sold out, and there were four other acts." Two years later he was blown away by the Yardbirds with Jimmy Page (see entry) on lead guitar; he also saw the Rolling Stones three times in the space of a few years.

Opitz took up the bass and decided in high school that he was going to be either a record producer or a film director. After school, Opitz left Brisbane to go to work for the Australian Broadcasting Corporation in Sydney, where he trained in various aspects of television production before landing in the audio department. While playing in blues bands on the side, Opitz became an audio engineer for the ABC, specializing in telecasts of the Sydney Opera and a wide variety of music-related shows.

Opitz decided to actively pursue a record production career in 1975, so he made a list of all of the recording studios in Sydney, rated by desirability. Résumé and references in hand, Opitz walked in the door of the first studio on his list, EMI, to find that they had just sacked a technician in the tape-dubbing room. Opitz was grossly overqualified for the job, but he was in door.

He quickly graduated to the next step in the process, mastering. Besides mastering EMI product, the facility also did work for many other Australian labels, and Opitz got to know label managers and A&R people. After a year of mastering Opitz was offered the position of label manager for Capitol Records in Australia, which was great, but more of a marketing and administrative position than a creative one. The general manager of EMI, Steven Shrimpton (who later became manager for Paul McCartney; see entry), then installed Opitz as a staff producer at EMI, ruffling many a skipped-over feather in the process.

Opitz had been working with many an unknown band on weekends, practicing his recording techniques and developing sounds. One of those bands sold an Opitz-produced demo to another label and, thinking they were doing him a big favor, gave Opitz production credit. This, of course, violated his deal with EMI and Opitz was forced to resign.

Fortunately, Harry Vanda and George Young (see entry)—for whom Opitz had done mastering work—heard of his plight and offered him a production job with their company. Opitz became their engineer, working on hit releases by AC/DC, John Paul Young, Rose Tattoo, and Vanda and Young's own Flash and the Pan.

Soon Vanda and Young turned over a hard rock band they had found, the Angels, to their protégé Opitz. After a year of seeking a special sound for the band, Opitz finally found the right combination of settings and karma and created a chunky, slashing hard guitar sound that is emulated to this day (Guns N' Roses have cited the Angels/Opitz guitar sound as an important influence).

That sound conquered Australia: The Angels' *Face to Face* (Opitz's first official production credit)—with the classic rocker "Marseilles"—went five-times-platinum (platinum in Australia is 35,000 copies) in 1978, and did reasonably well when released in the United States (under the band name "Angel City") in 1980. Opitz and the Angels' next album together, *No Exit,* did nearly as well.

Opitz continued his multiplatinum roll with Cold Chisel's *East* in 1980. A sweaty pub-rock band led by singer Jimmy Barnes, Chisel is probably the most popular band of all time in Australia (bigger than AC/DC, INXS, Midnight Oil, etc.), and though they didn't export as successfully as some of their compatriots to North America and Europe, Chisel, with Opitz as their producer, dominated the Australian charts throughout the first half of the '80s. Opitz feels Chisel to be "as uniquely Australian as Vegemite," and their blue-collar concerns perhaps weren't exotic or extreme enough for the foreign markets. The band is at their best on *Swingshift,* a live album with grit jammed into the grooves and supercharged with band-audience rapport.

In the midst of this extraordinary success, Opitz accepted an A&R position with WEA Australia. He signed the Divinyls, a new wave–power-pop duet led by

singer Christina Amphlett and guitarist Mark McEntee. Opitz emphasized the band's rawer, harder side on *Desperate,* as opposed to the poppy sound that eventually caught on when the duo hooked up with first Mike Chapman, then David Tickle (see entries) later in their career.

Opitz also helped bring INXS to WEA Australia (Atco in America) and produced their first great album, *Shabooh Shoobah,* in 1982, which went gold in the U.S. and made them stars. *Shabooh* is the most new wavy of the band's albums, and is many a long-term fan's favorite. Michael Hutchence's vocals are more malleable and less strident than they were to become, and though the songwriting isn't as consistent as on some later albums (*Kick, Welcome to Wherever You Are*), *Shabooh* contains three of the group's very best songs, the swooping hookfest "The One Thing," the halting Aussie-ska of "Black and White," and the majestic keyboard and treated-guitar wave classic "Don't Change."

After five years, Opitz reunited with INXS in 1987 and paired them with Jimmy Barnes on two songs for *The Lost Boys* soundtrack, the rollicking retro-rocker "Good Times" (written by Vanda and Young, who gave Opitz the thumbs-up on this version), and "Laying Down the Law."

Opitz produced three more INXS albums in the early '90s; by then Hutchence and the Farriss brothers' band (Tim, guitar; Andrew, keyboards and guitar; Jon, drums) was one of the biggest in the world. *Live Baby Live* functions as an adequate greatest hits collection, but cavernous echo, overloud audience noise, and uninspired performances contribute to a sense of detachment that is overcome only on "The One Thing" and "Suicide Blonde."

Vastly better is *Welcome to Wherever You Are* (No. 16), a varied and subtle masterpiece with surprising touches: Near Eastern tonalities on "Questions"; industrial-style distorted vocals on "Heaven Sent"; a nod to U2-style electro-pop on "Communication"; the funky "Taste It"; and the insinuating single "Not Enough Time." "Baby Don't Cry" is a rousing '60s-style pop-rock singalong, and "Beautiful Girl" (pleasantly reminiscent of the Stones' "Waiting On a Friend") is among the group's simplest, loveliest songs. Opitz's deft production expertly fits the mood of each song with the appropriate technology and arrangement.

Full Moon, Dirty Hearts is similar but not quite as much. "The Gift" and "Time" display a nice feel for electro-industrial dance styles, and "Please (You Got That . . .)" features vocals from the great Ray Charles (check out the killer house remix by E-Smoove not included on the album), but nothing else stands out. Unfortunately,

Welcome will be the group's last great album, as Michael Hutchence committed suicide in late 1997.

Of Opitz's Australian productions, the Hoodoo Gurus' *Blow Your Cool* stands out as a fine slab of power pop, especially the double-time stompers "Where Nowhere Is" and "Party Machine." Opitz also produced British goth-rockers Flesh for Lulu's underappreciated *Plastic Fantastic* with a pleasing crunch; and co-produced (with John Porter; see entry) Ocean Blue's excellent debut, featuring the modern-rock radio standard "Between Something and Nothing"—a slice of early '80s A Flock of Seagulls–style new wave miraculously transported to 1989. In the '90s Opitz traveled about Europe working with various artists before returning to Australia to work with Mushroom Records. —ERIC OLSEN

Angels (Angel City): *Face to Face*, Epic, 1978, 1980 • *No Exit*, Albert, 1979 • *Out of the Blue* (EP), Albert, 1979.

Australian Crawl: *Semantics*, EMI, 1984.

Barnes, Jimmy: *Bodyswerve*, Mushroom, 1984 • *For the Working-Class Man*, Mushroom, 1985 • *Jimmy Barnes*, Geffen, 1986 • *Freight Train Heart*, Geffen, 1988 • *See also* INXS.

Clapton, Richard: *Great Escape*, WEA Australia, 1982 • *Solidarity*, Mushroom, 1984, 1991.

Cold Chisel: *East*, Elektra, 1980 • *Swingshift*, WEA Australia, 1981 • *Circus Animals*, Elektra, 1982 • *The Barking Spiders Live 1983*, WEA Australia, 1984 • *Teenage Love*, Alex, 1995.

Deckchairs Overboard: "Walking in the Dark," Regular, 1984 • *Deckchairs Overboard*, Regular, 1985.

Divinyls: *Desperate*, Chrysalis, 1983 • *What a Life*, Chrysalis, 1985 • *Essential Divinyls*, Chrysalis, 1991.

Eurogliders: *This Island* (1 track), Columbia, 1984 • *This Island/Absolutely*, Renaissance, 1984, 1996.

Flesh for Lulu: *Plastic Fantastic*, Capitol, 1989.

Ghost of an American Airman: *Life Under Giants*, Hollywood, 1992.

Hitmen, The: *The Hitmen*, WEA Australia, 1981.

Hoodoo Gurus: *Blow Your Cool*, Elektra, 1987 • *Electric Soup: The Singles Collection*, RCA, 1992 • *Gorilla Buscuit: B-Sides and Rarities*, RCA, 1993.

Hunters and Collectors: *Juggernaut*, Mushroom, 1998.

Inqbator: *Hatched*, Pure, 1997.

INXS: *Shabooh Shoobah*, Atco, 1982 • "The One Thing," Atco, 1983 • w/ Jimmy Barnes, "Good Times," Atlantic, 1987 • w/ Jimmy Barnes, "Laying Down the Law," Atlantic, 1987 • *Live Baby Live*, Atlantic, 1991 • "Not Enough Time," Atlantic, 1992 • *Welcome to Wherever You Are*, Atlantic, 1992 • "Beautiful Girl," Atlantic, 1993 • *Full Moon, Dirty Hearts*, Atlantic, 1993 • "Please (You Got That . . .)," Atlantic, 1993 • "The Gift," Atlantic, 1993.

Kelly, Paul: *Words and Music*, Vanguard, 1998.

Mental As Anything: "Apocalypso," Regular, 1984 • *Cyclone Raymond*, Columbia, 1989.

Models, The: "Out of Mind out of Sight," Geffen, 1986 • *Out of Mind out of Sight*, Geffen, 1985 • *Media*, Mushroom, 1987.

1927: *1927*, EastWest Australia, 1992.

Noiseworks: *Noiseworks*, Columbia, 1987.

Ocean Blue: "Between Something and Nothing," Reprise, 1989 (*Follow Our Tracks*, Vol. 2) • *The Ocean Blue*, Sire, 1989.

Party Boys: *Live at Several 21st Birthday Parties*, Oz, 1983.

Red House: *The Red House*, SBK, 1990.

Reels, The: *The Reels*, Polydor, 1979.

Roxus: *Nightstreet*, Savage, 1992.

Steelheart: *Steelheart*, MCA, 1990 • "I'll Never Let You Go," MCA, 1991 • "She's Gone (Lady)," MCA, 1991.

Venetians, The: *Amazing World*, Chrysalis, 1987 • "So Much for Love," Chrysalis, 1987.

Johnny Otis

I t's around noon one summer day when Johnny Otis gets on the phone to respond to a writer seeking to sum up Otis's work in less than a book. Otis doesn't stay on the phone long. Not only does he have his Sebastopol, California, farm to run (he grows apple

trees and sells organic apple juice), he has a band to manage and records to push. Records that are quite far from the mainstream.

Otis recently released *Johnny Otis R&B Dance Party* on his own J&T label. He also produced *Spirit of the Black Territory Bands* for the folk label Arhoolie. He's working on "a goofy thing called Booger and the Boomerangs, an Australian rap guy," he says. "He's really comic." Booger's album will probably be released on Otis's label.

Otis also continues to play, mostly piano, a little vibes. He's been doing that for well over 50 years, pumping African-American music as hard as he can into the U.S. mainstream. It's not an easy task. But Otis, also a sculptor and painter, is uniquely qualified: He turned black at an early age.

As a kid, he couldn't understand why a black friend wasn't admitted to the Boy Scouts. He also balked when a school counselor suggested he not hang out with his black friends. Otis's father was the grocer in the black community in Berkeley, where he grew up. All his friends and playmates were black.

"I didn't know I was white," Otis says. "I got immersed in the culture, in people's homes, and they in mine. This culture tells us blacks have to go that way and whites this way. They do the same thing to Jewish people, Asians, and Hispanics. I don't know when we're going to cure ourselves of racism. It's all wrapped up in being brutal toward gays and toward women.

"Just because you see a cancer doesn't mean you know how to cure it," he adds. "It grows out of this predatory capitalism we live in, where less than 10 percent of the population owns and controls about 80 percent of the wealth. The rest of us are left scrambling."

Johnny Veliotes was born December 28, 1921, in Vallejo, California. His skin is white, his sensibility colorblind. His Saturday morning radio show over Pacifica Network FM powerhouse KPFA draws the biggest listening audience in Northern California, he says. "A lot of that has to do with me trying to keep the flame alive with gospel, early rock 'n' roll, rhythm 'n' blues," Otis says. "It's not me. It's that music. You love it. It reflects the heart of the African-American community at a nicer time."

Whether he thought those times were nicer while he lived them is another story. His affinity for African-American music, however, is undeniable. Not only did he make rhythm 'n' blues history by writing and performing the 1958 hit, "Willie and the Hand Jive." He also wrote "Every Beat of My Heart" (originally recorded in 1952 by the Royals on the Federal label, it was a 1961 hit for Gladys Knight and the Pips, on Vee-Jay);

Etta James' "The Wallflower (aka "Roll with Me, Henry"), a hit on Modern in 1954; and led the orchestra that backed the doomed Johnny Ace on "Pledging My Love," a 1954 hit on Duke. He also wrote the Fiestas' "So Fine," a hit in 1959.

Otis himself had a hit in the '40s with "Harlem Nocturne" and performed with or wrote for everybody from Jimmy Rushing to Ivy Anderson to Sugarcane Harris to Roy Milton to the Premieres to his son, Shuggie, an exceptional guitarist in his own right.

Otis was not only in on the beginning of rhythm 'n' blues—he helped define it. His career straddles swing, the big band era, and rhythm 'n' blues. He recorded, either as a solo artist, an orchestra leader, or a sideman, for Capitol, Epic, Mercury, Columbia, Aladdin, Excelsior, Federal, Dig, Ultra, Modern, Mexie, Laff, and Eldo, among other labels.

"I've always been involved in black music," he says, "African-American artistry. You know, the artistry's gone out of the music. There are good production values and singers, but I beg to be excused; if rap is all there is, one tune after another after another for 10 years, it's more than regression, it's a stonewall. Not that some of it isn't nice."

Why is rap so popular? "I can take a guess," says Otis. "I think television had a lot to do with it. Jimi Hendrix told me—I knew him as a blues player—he said, 'Well, man, I got tired of not eating three meals a day, so I went to England and got me a couple of white boys, and now I'm making money.' He did make millions. Young black stars saw that and started in that direction. The funny thing is, black artists have become a parody of a parody of themselves, chasing that buck."

It's been years since Otis recorded for a major label. "They don't want me," he says. "They need somebody who believes new music is great. I don't. I think it sucks. Our audience is white yuppies and baby boomers, and we play every weekend here in Santa Rosa, and we go on the road. I'm lucky. I have a strong band and great singers. Otherwise, it wouldn't mean shit."

As for technology, it has always played a great part in record production. Without it, Otis points out sagely, there would be no records, only "guys on stage, or women, shouting with a megaphone." In his home studio, he has "24 tracks, ADATs and DATs and all that stuff, and a computer that runs it," he says. "I don't get the same power and depth as when I use my 16-track early Ampex machine, especially with bass and drums. Analog is different than digital; I don't know why, but I notice when I use a 24-track machine I lose a lot. When I use a 16-track—maybe it's because the tracks are bigger—I have that power and warmth.

"I'm talking all this profound shit, and I haven't had a hit record in 155 years," Otis says, laughing. "You go in the studio or go on the bandstand, you got to do what you do and what you love. You can try to be contemporary and commercial, but if you don't like it, it's not going to happen, is it?"

Johnny Otis was inducted into the Rock and Roll Hall of Fame in 1994. —CARLO WOLFF

Harris, Sugarcane: *Sugarcane Harris,* Epic, 1970.

Otis, Johnny: *Rock and Roll Hit Parade,* Vol. 1, Dig, 1957 • *The Johnny Otis Show,* Capitol, 1958 • *Cold Shot,* Sonet, 1969 • *Cuttin' Up,* Epic, 1970 • *The Original Johnny Otis Show,* Vols. 1–2, Savoy, 1970 • *Live at Monterey,* Epic, 1971 • *Formidable,* Ember, 1972 • *Pioneers of Rock,* Starline, 1973 • *Bulldog, Bullfrog,* 1975 • *Rock 'n' Roll History,* Capitol, 1979 • *The New Johnny Otis Show,* Sonet/Alligator, 1981 • *Rock 'n' Roll Revue,* Charly, 1982 • *The Capitol Years,* Capitol, 1989 • *Creepin' with the Cats: The Legendary Dig Masters,* Ace, 1991 • *Let's Live It Up,* Charly, 1991 • *Spirit of the Black Territory Bands,* Arhoolie, 1992 • *Otisology,* Kent, 1995 • *Johnny Otis R&B Dance Party,* J&T, 1997 • *The Greatest Johnny Otis Show,* Ace, 1998.

Otis, Shuggie: *Here Comes,* Epic, 1970 • *Freedom Flight,* Epic, 1971 • *Shuggie Otis Plays the Blues,* Legacy, 1994.

Turner, Big Joe: *Great Rhythm and Blues,* Vol. 4, Blues Spectrum, 1993.

Hugh Padgham

By happening upon a novel and exciting snare drum sound during the tracking of Peter Gabriel's third album, and later parlaying that sound into a hit-making blueprint for the likes of Phil Collins, Genesis, the Police, Sting, and Melissa Etheridge, British producer/engineer Hugh Padgham did more to influence the sound of popular music than any other producer in the '80s.

Exemplified by such groundbreaking tracks as Gabriel's "Intruder," Collins' "In the Air Tonight" (No. 19), and Frida's "I Know There's Something Going On" (No. 13), the Padgham sound consists of a loud, heavily reverberated snare drum, abruptly cut off by a noise gate. It's no coincidence that Collins—the drummer on all three of the above tracks—enjoyed his commercial peak during the early to mid-'80s with records produced by Padgham.

Beyond the success of the handful of artists

Padgham was producing at the time—and his own stratospheric rise from little-known engineer to superstar producer—the trademark drum sound infiltrated the music world via MIDI, synthesizers, and drum machines. It seemed that every record by every artist of that period—from new wave provocateurs Missing Persons to King of Pop Michael Jackson, from hair band Bon Jovi to folkie-turned-world-music-trailblazer Paul Simon—featured some form of the gated snare drum many referred to as "the Phil Collins sound." And most of the "drums" at the time emanated from machines whose presets evoked that Padgham-inspired effect.

Although Padgham humbly admits to being "flattered" that the world picked up on his sonic coinage, he downplays his role in the innovation. "At the time I didn't think I'd invented anything. It was at the end of the new wave era, and everybody was rebelling against the very dead '70s thing where everything was trapped to death."

Indeed, Gabriel, Collins, and Padgham mentor Steve Lillywhite (see entry)—who produced the Gabriel LP in question—deserve at least as much credit as Padgham for putting such a novel sound on a record. However, Padgham was talented enough to make it his calling card for the better part of a decade, and astute enough to move beyond "the drum thing" when it threatened to pigeonhole him as a one-trick pony. He acknowledges a backlash against that sound and says he is appalled at some of his own mid-'80s productions—even such widely acclaimed records as the Police's *Synchronicity*

Photo by H. Hashimoto

(No. 1): "I can't even listen to it because the snare is so loud," says Padgham

Although he still uses thunderous drum sounds, notably on Melissa Etheridge's 1995 release *Your Little Secret* (No. 6), Padgham also likes to go to the opposite extreme. "Sometimes I get bored with that big drum sound and I do it the other way," he says. "There's a song on Sting's *Mercury Falling* (No. 5) album, 'Lithium Sunset,' which has the driest drum sound you could possibly have."

While the popularity of some of Padgham's biggest clients—Sting, Collins, Genesis, and Etheridge—has faded somewhat in recent years, Padgham has continued to actively seek and produce cutting-edge talent. For instance, he discovered Sheryl Crow, secured her a record deal, and produced her debut album—only to see it shelved in favor of *Tuesday Night Music Club,* which he did not produce. But the experience empowered Padgham to nurture the careers of other up-and-coming artists, including blues-rocker Beth Hart and jazzy pop singer/songwriter/pianist Kami Lyle. In the meantime, Padgham has also worked with such established stars as the Bee Gees, traditional Celtic–new age sensations Clannad, and mainstays Collins, Etheridge, and Sting.

Trained as an engineer, Padgham does not pretend to be a songwriter, musician, arranger, or sound sculptor and views his function as "an invisible catalyst" for the artist. "When I make a record, I'm there to enhance, advise, and make the best out of the songs that the artist has written, because, distinct from other producers who are also very talented writers, like David Foster and Babyface [see entries], I've come up from the engineering side," says Padgham. "I understand music, I've learned piano and guitar, but I've never been a big writer and I don't purport to go into the studio with an artist and change their songs."

Padgham takes a no-nonsense approach to record making—a quality that no doubt contributed to the chemistry he shares with Etheridge. "One of the things about being a producer is being diplomatic and being able to coax the artists into producing the best performances at the right time," he explains. "With Melissa you don't have to do that. When she says, 'Okay, I'm going to sing this song now,' you don't have to do anything except be there to capture it, and occasionally hint on this aspect or that aspect. There's none of this, 'Oh, I can't sing now because the moon's not in the right house.' She's the kind of girl who'll eat lunch and then say, 'I want to sing now.'"

If Padgham understands a straightforward work ethic, it's probably because he rose through the ranks the hard way. He started as a teenager playing bass in bands and quickly figured out that he was not destined to be a brilliant musician. Concurrent with that realization came another epiphany when he stumbled on a photo of a recording studio in a magazine: "I saw this picture of a studio and said, 'This is unbelievable,'" recalls Padgham. "It was probably an 8-track board or something, but we're talking 1970 here, and I went, 'Wow, that's what I want to do.'" It wasn't long before Padgham would get his first taste of a real studio thanks to a friend who had a homegrown but impressive facility: "the perfect marriage of music and technology," as he puts it.

Possessed with unflappable determination and a healthy measure of cockiness, Padgham wrote to every studio in the London area hoping to get a job. He eventually landed a gig as a tape operator—or "tea boy," as studio gofers are called in Britain—at the then-hip, long-defunct Advision Studios, assisting producer Eddy Offord (see entry) on Yes and Emerson, Lake and Palmer sessions. From there Padgham moved to nearby Landsowne Studios, where he worked on records by Uriah Heep and a raft of avant-garde and traditional jazz artists, assisted on jingles and covers of Top 20 chart hits, and eventually earned the trust of his boss. "I learned by assisting on millions of different things and eventually started engineering," Padgham says. "On those records, everything was done at once in a studio that wasn't very big, so you really had to have your act together. But I started getting frustrated at not being able to do the work I wanted to do, the rock stuff."

Padgham would get his wish in 1978, when he successfully applied for an engineering post at Townhouse Studios, Virgin Records' new facility in London. Already famous for operating the Manor outside of London—which was inaugurated with Mike Oldfield's *Tubular Bells* extravaganza—Virgin was in the process of building a studio empire that would also include Olympic Studios in London.

By then Padgham had amassed a wealth of technical and logistical expertise, and not only did he get the staff engineering job at Townhouse, he also helped build it. To this day, the studio retains his stamp. Among the records he cut there in the famous stone studio known informally as "the drum room" were XTC's *Black Sea* and *Drums and Wires,* both with Lillywhite producing, and *English Settlement* (No. 5 U.K.) on his own; Gabriel's third, also with Lillywhite; Collins' *Face Value* (No. 7), *Hello, I Must Be Going* (No. 8), and *No Jacket Required* (No. 1); Frida's "Something's Going On"; and Howard Jones' "No One Is to Blame" (No. 4), also featuring Collins on drums.

Despite his success at the Townhouse, in 1980, Padgham went independent. He remembers it as an exciting period, but a "worrying" one as well. "Going freelance was great because I got paid more in a week than I got in a year working for Virgin Records, but I was always worrying about what was going to happen the next week," he recalls.

Although Padgham says he still worries a bit, his anxiety level is much lower than it used to be, and he finds himself able to enjoy other things in life besides record making. "I try to have a little bit of life in between records, because at one point it was literally back-to-back records and I would be booked up for 18 months sometimes," says Padgham. "And it got frightening: if one record ran over a little it would run into the next; then it was like a freakout period."

Allowing time between projects has afforded Padgham the luxury of indulging in his hobbies, which include car racing, airplane flying, software development, and gardening. Padgham and his manager, Dennis Muirhead, have also launched a music publishing company they hope will dovetail with Padgham's production.

Ever the pragmatist, Padgham refuses to let himself get complacent and lives by the credo that "you're only as good as your last record." Accordingly, he attacks every project as if it's his "first and last," marching to whatever drum beat his client happens to play. And of course, making that drum sound larger than life. —PAUL VERNA

Ant, Adam: "Puss 'n Boots," Epic, 1983 • *Strip,* Epic, 1983.

Bee Gees: *Still Waters,* Polydor, 1997 • "Still Waters Run Deep," Polydor, 1997.

Beth Hart Band: *Immortal,* Lava, 1996.

Bishop, Stephen: *Bowling in Paris,* Atlantic, 1989 • *On and On: Best Of,* MCA, 1994.

Bland, Bobby: *You've Got Me Loving You,* MCA, 1990.

Bowie, David: "Blue Jean," EMI America, 1984 • *Changesbowie,* Rykodisc, 1984, 1990 • "Tonight," EMI America, 1984 • *Tonight,* EMI America, 1984 • *Bowie: The Singles, 1969–1993,* Rykodisc, 1993.

Call, The: *The Call,* Mercury, 1982 • *The Walls Came Down: The Very Best of the Mercury Years,* Mercury, 1991.

Clannad: *Lore,* Atlantic, 1996.

Collins, Phil: *Face Value,* Atlantic, 1981 • *Hello, I Must Be Going,* Atlantic, 1982 • "Don't Lose My Number," Atlantic, 1985 • *No Jacket Required,* Atlantic, 1985 • "One More Night," Atlantic, 1985 • w/ Marilyn Martin, "Separate Lives," Atlantic, 1985 • "Sussudio," Atlantic, 1985 • "Take Me Home," Atlantic, 1986 • *12"rs,* Atlantic, 1988 • *. . . But Seriously,* Atlantic, 1989 • "Another Day in Paradise," Atlantic, 1989 • "Do You Remember?," Atlantic, 1990 • "I Wish It Would Rain Down," Atlantic,

1990 • "Something Happened on the Way to Heaven," Atlantic, 1990 • "Burn Down the Mission," Polydor, 1991 (*Two Rooms: Songs of Elton and Bernie Taupin*) • "Dance into the Light," Atlantic, 1996 • *Dance into the Light,* Atlantic, 1996 • "It's in Your Eyes," Atlantic, 1997.

Dream Academy: *Remembrance Days,* Reprise, 1987.

Etheridge, Melissa: "Come to My Window," Island, 1993 • *Yes I Am,* Island, 1993 • "I'm the Only One," Island, 1994 • "Like the Way I Do/If I Wanted To," Island, 1995 • *Your Little Secret,* Island, 1995 • "Nowhere to Go," Island, 1996.

Fixx, The: *React,* MCA, 1987 • "Red Skies," MCA, 1987 • "Stand or Fall," MCA, 1987 • *One Thing Leads to Another: Greatest Hits,* MCA, 1989.

Fordham, Julia: *Porcelain,* Virgin, 1989, 1990 • *Swept,* Virgin, 1991.

Frida: *Something's Going On,* Atlantic, 1982 • "I Know There's Something's Going On," Atlantic, 1983.

Genesis: *Abacab,* Atlantic, 1981 • "No Reply At All," Atlantic, 1981 • "Abacab," Atlantic, 1982 • *Genesis,* Atlantic, 1983 • "That's All," Atlantic, 1983 • "In Too Deep," Atlantic, 1986 • "Invisible Touch," Atlantic, 1986 • *Invisible Touch,* Atlantic, 1986 • "Land of Confusion," Atlantic, 1986 • "Throwing It All Away," Atlantic, 1986 • "Tonight, Tonight, Tonight," Atlantic, 1986 • *Turn It on Again: The Best of 1981–1983,* Vertigo, 1991.

Hall and Oates: *Rock and Soul Live: The Video,* RCA, 1984.

Hoffner, Helen: *Wild About Nothing,* Magnet/East West, 1992.

Human League: *Hysteria,* A&M, 1984 • "The Lebanon," A&M, 1984 • *Greatest Hits,* Virgin/A&M, 1988.

Jones, Howard: *Action Replay,* Elektra, 1986 • "No One Is to Blame," Elektra, 1986 • *One to One,* Elektra, 1986 • *The Best Of,* Elektra, 1993.

Lyle, Kami: *Blue Cinderella,* MCA, 1997.

McCartney, Paul: "Spies Like Us," Capitol, 1985 • *Press to Play,* Capitol, 1986 • "Press," Capitol, 1986 • "Stranglehold," Capitol, 1986.

Mummy Calls: "Beauty Has Her Way," Atlantic, 1987 (*The Lost Boys* soundtrack).

Pilgrim, Billy: *Billy Pilgrim,* Atlantic, 1994.

Police, The: "Every Little Thing She Does Is Magic," A&M, 1981 • *Ghost in the Machine,* A&M, 1981 • "Every Breath You Take," A&M, 1983 • *Synchronicity,* A&M, 1983 • "Synchronicity II," A&M, 1983 • *Message in a Box,* A&M, 1993 • "Wrapped Around Your Finger," A&M, 1983 • *See also* Sting.

Shocked, Michelle: *Arkansas Traveler,* Mercury, 1992.

Split Enz: "Six Months in a Leaky Boat," A&M, 1982 • *Time and Tide,* A&M, 1982 • *Conflicting Emotions,* A&M, 1983 • *Enz of an Era,* Mushroom, 1983 • *Collection 1973–1984,* Concept, 1986 • *History Never Repeats: The Best Of,* A&M, 1987 • *Best Of,* Chrysalis, 1994.

Sting: "All This Time," A&M, 1991 • "Come Down in Time," Polydor, 1991 (*Two Rooms: Songs of Elton and Bernie Taupin*) • *The Soul Cages,* A&M, 1991 • "Fields of Gold," A&M, 1993 • "If I Ever Lose My Faith in You," A&M, 1993 • *Ten Summoner's Tales,* A&M, 1993 • "When We Dance," A&M, 1994 • "I'm So Happy I Can't Stop Crying," A&M, 1996 • "Let Your Soul Be Your Pilot," A&M, 1996 • *Mercury Falling,* A&M, 1996 • "The Bed's Too Big Without You," A&M, 1996 (*The Truth About Cats and Dogs* soundtrack) • "You Still Touch Me," A&M, 1996 • w/ the Police, *The Very Best Of,* A&M, 1997.

Tin Machine: "One Shot," Victory, 1991 • *Tin Machine II,* Victory, 1991.

Waitresses, The: "Bruiseology," Polydor, 1983 • *Bruiseology,* Polydor, 1983 • *The Best of the Waitresses,* Polydor, 1990.

XTC: "Ball and Chain," Epic, 1982 • *Beeswax: Some B Sides, 1977–1982,* Virgin, 1982 • *English Settlement,* Epic, 1982 • "Senses Working Overtime," Epic, 1982 • *Senses Working Overtime* (EP), Virgin, 1982 • *Compact XTC: The Singles, 1978–1985,* Virgin, 1985 • *Rag and Bone Buffet* (5 tracks), Geffen, 1990.

Yearwood, Trisha: *Hearts in Armor* (1 track), MCA, 1992 • "Walkaway Joe," MCA International, 1994.

Young, Paul: *Between Two Fires,* Columbia, 1986 • "Some People," Columbia, 1986 • "Why Does a Man Have to Be So Strong," Columbia, 1987 • *From Time to Time: The Singles Collection,* Columbia, 1991.

COLLECTIONS

When the Wind Blows soundtrack, Virgin, 1987.

Jimmy Page and Robert Plant

Jimmy Page (born January 9, 1944, in Heston, England) was a member of the English supergroup the Yardbirds, and had done frequent session work on guitar (Donovan, the Who, the Kinks, Them, Joe Cocker) before forming Led Zeppelin, one of the most successful bands in rock history, with sales of 50 million in the U.S. alone. Together with vocalist Robert Plant (born August 20, 1948, in Bromwich, England), an accounting dropout from Cambridge University, he produced the entire Led Zeppelin catalog.

Led Zeppelin (No. 10) was recorded in less than a week and set the formula for all the albums to follow: hard, metallic, blues riff–based songs with lyrics leaning heavily on the occult and Anglo-Saxon myth, combined with beautiful acoustic interludes, such as "Black Mountain Side." Dripping with sexuality, the albums completely pulverize any distinction between the intellectual and the animal, the masculine and the feminine, the gentle and the monstrously barbarous.

For the first four albums, the band recorded the basic tracks live in the studio, creating a ton of vibe on the recordings, with lots of bleed-through and murky sonics. Beginning with *Houses of the Holy* (No. 1), the band used a more traditional layering approach, which allowed John Bonham's drum sound to become more clearly prominent. Indeed, *Houses* contains some of the best drum sounds of the time, highlighted on "The Bridge" and "D'yer Mak'er" (No. 20).

Page's guitar playing is technically sloppy—he was the least technically proficient musician in the group—but he wrote those parts, among the most memorable and imitated in rock. His solos are carefully crafted. The solo in "Stairway to Heaven," for example, was pieced together from three or four separate takes; careful listeners can hear the "punch-ins," where one take gives way to another.

"Jimmy Page may not have been technically perfect," notes Alex Van Halen. "There were times when his fingers sounded like they were stuck together, but who cares?" It is a testimony to their arranging genius that Page and Plant could squeeze such novelty out of so many stolen blues riffs.

Plant's vocal style, also among the most imitated (by bands such as Whitesnake, Jane's Addiction, and Van Halen) was most remarkable for his confused, triumphant anger and the overt sexuality of his voice. He typically sounds as though he is on the verge of an orgasmic frenzy, leading to widespread (though unconfirmed) speculation that he sang many of the takes with a raging hard-on. At his best he is untouchable, at his worst he sounds neutered (from *Presence,* No. 1, on).

Zeppelin released nine albums in 10 years, and all were at least double-platinum. *Led Zeppelin IV* (No. 2) stayed on the charts for 259 weeks and sold 16 million copies, buoyed by the most overplayed song in history, "Stairway to Heaven" (which was never actually released as a single). Following the breakup of the band, which resulted from drummer John Bonham's accidental death in 1980, Page formed and produced albums for the Firm, a tired, formulaic effort. In his 1994 reunion with Plant, *No Quarter* (No. 4), they rearranged traditional Led Zeppelin material in imaginative ways. Their 1998 follow-up, *Walking into Clarksdale,* is a tough return to their Celtic and quasi-oriental roots.

Before reuniting with Page, Plant had a largely successful solo career, highlighted by *Pictures at Eleven* (No. 5) and *Now and Zen* (No. 6). —DANIEL J. LEVITIN

JIMMY PAGE

Coverdale/Page: *Coverdale/Page,* Geffen, 1993.

Firm, The: "Radioactive," Atlantic, 1985 • "Satisfaction Guaranteed," Atlantic, 1985 • *The Firm,* Atlantic, 1985 • *Mean Business,* Atlantic, 1986.

Led Zeppelin: *Led Zeppelin,* Atlantic, 1969 • *Led Zeppelin II,* Atlantic, 1969 • "Whole Lotta Love," Atlantic, 1969 • "Immigrant Song," Atlantic, 1970 • *Led Zeppelin III,* Atlantic, 1970 • "Black Dog," Atlantic, 1971 • *Zoso,* Atlantic, 1971 • "Rock and Roll," Atlantic, 1972 • "D'yer Mak'er," Atlantic, 1973 • *Houses of the Holy,* Atlantic, 1973 • *Physical Graffiti,* Swan Song, 1975 • *Presence,* Swan Song, 1976 • *Soundtrack from the Film the Song Remains the Same,* Swan Song, 1976 • *In Through the Out Door,* Swan Song, 1979 • *Coda,* Swan Song, 1982, 1994 • *Led Zeppelin Box Set,* Atlantic, 1990 • *Remasters,* Atlantic, 1992 • *Led Zeppelin Box Set II,* Atlantic, 1993 • *The Complete Studio Recordings,* Atlantic, 1993 • *The BBC Session,* Atlantic, 1997.

Lord Sutch: *Lord Sutch and Heavy Friends,* Cotillion, 1970.

Mayall, John: *London Blues, 1964–1969,* Deram, 1992.

Page, Jimmy: *Death Wish II* soundtrack, Swan Song, 1982 • *Outrider,* Geffen, 1988.

JIMMY PAGE AND ROBERT PLANT

Page, Jimmy, and Robert Plant: *No Quarter: Jimmy Page and Robert Plant Unledded,* Atlantic, 1994 • *Walking Into Clarksdale,* Atlantic, 1998.

ROBERT PLANT

Amos, Tori: "Down by the Seaside," Atlantic, 1995 (*Encomium: A Tribute to Led Zeppelin*).

Plant, Robert: *Pictures at Eleven,* Swan Song, 1982 • "Big Log," Es Paranza, 1983 • *Principle of Moments,* Es Paranza, 1983 • "Little by Little," Es Paranza, 1985 • *Shaken 'N' Stirred,* Es Paranza, 1985 • *Now and Zen,* Es Paranza, 1988 • "Ship of Fools," Es Paranza, 1988 • "Tall Cool One," Es Paranza, 1988 • "Hurting Kind (I've Got My Eyes on You)," Es Paranza, 1990 • "Let's Have a Party," NME, 1990 (*The Last Temptation of Elvis*) • *Manic Nirvana,* Es Paranza, 1990 • "29 Palms," Atlantic, 1993 • *Fate of Nations,* Atlantic, 1993.

Tim Palmer

Tim Palmer has produced or co-produced an exceptional range of modern rock groups and music since the mid-'80s, including An Emotional Fish ("Celebrate"), the Mighty Lemon Drops, the Mission (*God's Own Medicine,* No. 14 U.K., *Carved in Sand,* No. 7 U.K.), Robert Plant, Tears For Fears (*Elemental,* No. 5 U.K., *Raoul and the Kings of Spain*), Texas (*Southside,* No. 3 U.K.), David Bowie's (see entry) Tin Machine (*Tin Machine,* No. 3 U.K), and Wire Train. Palmer is also a top-shelf mixer, working with Concrete Blonde, the Cure, Cutting Crew, Duran Duran, James, Mother Love Bone, and Pearl Jam, and recently Sepultura and Reel Big Fish.

Tim Palmer was born in 1962 in the north of England, near Scotland, and moved with his family to London when he was about 10. He became a devotee of punk as a teen, playing bass and guitar and singing in various unruly outfits. "We weren't that good, and that's probably why I decided to go to the other side of the glass," he says.

Palmer visited producer Phil Wainman's Utopia studio with his father, and a few weeks later got called to be a tea boy. "I think I've been in a studio ever since. I feel that way anyway, because I've worked pretty consistently." Palmer did the usual schlepping and observing, then moved up to assistant engineer.

In 1983 he worked as an assistant on the *Local Hero* soundtrack for producer/performer Mark Knopfler (see

entry) and engineer Neil Dorfsman. At this point Palmer realized he would have trouble keeping his mouth shut during sessions. "They were doing guitar takes and I'd say, 'That was great, you should keep that one.' I remember them looking around. On the second day Mark and Neil took me aside and said, 'We respect that you're really into the project and you're keen, but do you think you could not contribute so much?' I was gutted."

Then the keen young Palmer became Colin Thurston's (see entry) assistant on the first Kajagoogoo album. Thurston and co-producer Nick Rhodes (from Duran Duran) only wanted to work until early evening, so they'd let Palmer carry on after that. When it came time to do B-sides and some album cuts, Palmer got to produce them; the band and label were pleased and Palmer got a co-production credit and a gold album for his wall.

Pleased to be producing, Palmer also felt that he was being herded pretty far down the primrose synth-pop path, and he really wanted to make some red-blooded rock. He got his wish when an engineering job for certified rocker Robert Plant eventually turned into a co-production credit: 1985's gold *Shaken 'N' Stirred* (No. 20).

"I had to lie a little bit, because through the '80s it had been all drum machines. At Utopia, bands would come in with their sequencers and their drum machines and that was it. So I had only recorded a proper drum kit maybe twice, but I didn't tell that to Robert because I didn't want to lose the gig," Palmer says. The situation was daunting for Palmer because he was leaving Utopia for the first time, didn't know how to record drums, and at that point had never even owned a Led Zeppelin record. "When I was in school I was listening to the Clash; all the boring people who did extra homework were listening to ELO and Zeppelin."

Palmer and Plant didn't have many common reference points, "so Robert brought me all the Led Zeppelin records and said, 'Here, check out my old band and see if you like them,'" which he did. After the hit *Shaken*, Plant and Palmer worked together on the even bigger *Now and Zen* (No. 6) in 1988.

After *Shaken*, Palmer became known for his guitar sound and he worked with various six-string slinging bands, including the Mission's top-selling goth-pop, and the Mighty Lemon Drops. On the Drops' great *World Without End*, Palmer found a perfect synthesis of his earlier pop work and his new big-guitar sound. "Inside Out" is one of the great modern rock songs of the '80s, invoking the charm and tunefulness of the guitar-driven '60s, with the drum punch (which Palmer had evidently figured out by then) of the late '80s. With echoes of the Bunnymen, the Lemon Drops carve out a rocking good niche with "One By One," "Hear Me Call," and "Hollow Inside."

For Palmer, 1987 was a very good year; in addition to his great work with the Lemon Drops, he guided San Francisco's Wire Train to their own resounding power pop on *Ten Women*. While Train's jangling guitar rock originates from an L.A. Byrdsian source, the Drops' stems from the British Invasion; but the bands are hard-strumming cousins from the evidence of "She Comes On," "She's a Very Pretty Thing," and especially "Certainly No One" from *Ten Women*.

Since then Palmer has achieved tremendous success with Texas, Tears For Fears, Tin Machine, and a variety of young modern rock bands. Palmer brings the whole package to the job of production. "If I work with a band, I'm trying to help them achieve a certain goal. I hear the tapes, I like what they're doing, and I think, 'Yes, I can make that better, I can help them achieve that.' Because I've been an engineer, and also because I'm a musician of sorts, I fill in the gaps where their weaknesses are," he says.

"A lot of time it's a case of getting the atmosphere right more than anything else. Let's face it, if they sing well and play well, then if the EQ is slightly off, you can do something later. It's getting it out of them that's important, and by making them feel comfortable and making them feel that you're the man for the job, they're more likely to achieve success.

"The producer is there to help the band realize their vision," he continues, "but at the same time, to be the ears of the record-buying public. You're there to say, 'Look, you're in the band, you've played the song 50 times. I'm coming in fresh. I want to enjoy the song, but here's why I'm not enjoying it and why other people may not.'"

Two extremes in the way Palmer works would be with Tears For Fears and Tin Machine. With Tears For Fears, Palmer was in essence a band member, playing guitar, percussion, and other instruments along with founder/singer/songwriter Roland Orzabal and his co-writer Alan Griffiths. With Tin Machine, it was four cranky veteran virtuosi (Bowie, Reeves Gabrels on guitar, Hunt Sales on drums, Tony Sales on bass) who just wanted to rip, so Palmer rolled tape and got the hell out of the way.

Palmer also got to play on the single most successful record he has been involved with, Pearl Jam's epochal *Ten*, which he mixed. On "Oceans" Palmer is credited with playing "pepper shaker and fire extinguisher." "I was hitting the extinguisher with a couple of sticks and shaking a pepper shaker because we couldn't wait for a percussion box to come from London. I went to the kitchen and tried a couple of different condiments until I found one that sounded good."

Ironically, just prior to *Ten*, Palmer's career had reached a low point when he had been told by a major-label A&R geek in L.A. that he didn't have "the sensibility to mix an American rock band." He mixed Pearl Jam—as American as rock bands get—"as instinctively and creatively as possible," and the 10 million people who have bought *Ten* think he did pretty well. —ERIC OLSEN AND DAVID JOHN FARINELLA

An Emotional Fish: *An Emotional Fish*, Atlantic, 1990 • "Celebrate," Atlantic, 1990.

Burning Tree: *Burning Tree*, Epic, 1990.

Fretblanket: *Junkfuel*, Atlas, 1994.

Gene Loves Jezebel: "Jealous," Geffen, 1990 • *Kiss of Life*, Geffen, 1990 • *From the Mouths of Babes*, AV, 1995.

Gigantic: *Disenchanted*, Columbia, 1996.

Gods Child: *Aluminum*, Qwest/WB, 1996.

House of Love: *House of Love* (2 tracks), Creation/Fontana, 1988 • "Shine On," Fontana, 1990 • *A Spy in the House of Love* (1 track), Fontana, 1991.

Kajagoogoo: *White Feathers*, One Way, 1983, 1994 • "Hang on Now" (remix), EMI America, 1983 • w/ Limahl, *Too Shy: The Singles and More*, EMI, 1993.

Kinky Machine: *Kinky Machine*, MCA, 1993.

Legal Reins: *Please, the Pleasure*, Arista, 1989.

Limahl: *Don't Suppose*, EMI, 1984 • "Only for Love," EMI, 1985 • *See also* Kajagoogoo.

Mighty Lemon Drops: *World Without End*, Sire/Reprise, 1988 • *Laughter* (2 tracks), Sire/Reprise, 1989.

Mission, The: "Garden of Delight," Chapter 22, 1986 • *God's Own Medicine*, Mercury, 1986 • "Stay with Me," Mercury, 1986 • "Wasteland," Mercury, 1986 • "Severina," Mercury, 1987 • "Butterfly on a Wheel," Mercury, 1990 • *Carved in Sand*, Mercury, 1990 • "Deliverance," Mercury, 1990 • *Grains of Sand*, Mercury, 1990 • "Into the Blue," Mercury, 1990.

Ned's Atomic Dustbin: "All I Ask of Myself Is That I Hold Together," Furtive/Work, 1995 • *Brainbloodvolume*, Furtive/Work, 1995 • "Stuck," Furtive/Work, 1995.

Neverland: *Neverland*, Interscope, 1991.

Ocean Colour Scene: *Ocean Colour Scene*, Fontana, 1992.

Plant, Robert: "Little By Little," Es Paranza , 1985 • *Shaken 'n' Stirred*, Esparanza/Atlantic, 1985 • *Now and Zen*, Atlantic, 1988 • "Ship of Fools," Es Paranza , 1988 • "Tall Cool One," Es Paranza , 1988.

Silverjet: *Pull Me Up . . . Drag Me Down*, Virgin, 1997.

Sponge: *Wax Ecstatic*, Epic, 1996.

Superdeluxe: *Via Satellite*, Revolution, 1997.

Tears For Fears: *Tears Roll Down (The Hits, 1982–1992)*, Fontana, 1992 • "Break It Down Again," Mercury, 1993 •

Elemental, Mercury, 1993 • *Raoul and the Kings of Spain*, Epic, 1995.

Texas: "I Don't Want a Lover," Mercury, 1989 • *Southside*, Mercury, 1989 • "In My Heart," Mercury, 1991 • *Mother's Heaven*, Mercury, 1991 • "Alone with You," Mercury, 1992.

Tin Machine: *Tin Machine*, EMI, 1989 • *Tin Machine II*, Victory, 1991.

Wire Train: "Diving," Columbia, 1987 • "She Comes," Columbia, 1987 • *Ten Women*, 415/Columbia, 1987 • *Last Perfect Thing: A Retrospective*, Legacy, 1996.

Thom Panunzio

Thom Panunzio worked his way up through the ranks to become a great engineer at New York's fabled Record Plant in the '70s, participating in classic albums by John Lennon, Bruce Springsteen, and Patti Smith. Then, while continuing to engineer and mix (U2, Bob Dylan, Aerosmith, Marshall Crenshaw), Panunzio began producing and co-producing in the early '80s, putting together an exceptional rock 'n' roll, punk–new wave, and jazz career with Agent Orange, Alice Cooper, the Beat Farmers, Black Sabbath, Deep Purple, Del Lords, the Jeff Healey Band, Joan Jett, Dave Koz, Mink DeVille, Elliott Murphy, Stevie Nicks, Iggy Pop, Reverend Horton Heat, and Link Wray. He has also specialized in recording live shows for the likes of Springsteen (Panunzio recently helped Springsteen put together his *Tracks* box set), U2, and countless others.

Thom Panunzio was born in the northern New Jersey town of River Edge (20 minutes from Manhattan), and was a guitar-and-cars man from childhood. His favorite band was the Beatles, but his favorite guitarist was Keith Richards (see entry). He played guitar in many rock units, including the Lost, thereby funding his education at Fairleigh Dickinson University as a music major and even recording a few singles. It was in primitive studios recording demos and little-heard singles that Panunzio became fascinated with the world on the other side of the glass. Unlike many other producer/musicians, Panunzio does not feel a conflict between producing and playing.

"Playing and recording are the same to me. One of the bands I was in was recording a demo in the early '70s, and the way the guy worked the knobs—controlling the level of each instrument—it seemed like he was actually creating the song for which we had just laid down the parts. The producer/engineer was like the greatest musician of the group. I still play the equipment in the studio like an instrument," he says.

Panunzio decided to pursue a career in knob-twirling magic in 1974 (one year short of college graduation) and set up an interview at Manhattan's famed Record Plant through a friend who was a receptionist there. "They didn't really hire me at first; I just never left after the interview. There's always something you can do for people in a recording studio, so I started doing errands and favors for all these great guys: Jimmy Iovine, Jack Douglas, Bob Ezrin [see entries], Shelly Yakus," he says.

"After I had been showing up every day for a couple of weeks, they decided to hire me. Normally you'd start as a runner; then you'd work in the tape library; then, if you didn't lose too many tapes, they'd let you learn how to make tape copies. They let me skip the first two jobs, and I started running the tape copy room—I guess because I'd shown that I was responsible. The tape copy room was actually a pretty intense job—you had to make copies of what all five studios had recorded that day. If you could survive that, then you'd become an assistant engineer," he says.

"One day I got a knock on the door and it was Roy Secala, one of the owners of the studio and John Lennon's engineer. He said, 'Thom, come with me,' and the next thing I knew I was in the middle of a John Lennon session. Jimmy Iovine was the assistant and he wasn't there, so they needed someone to fill in for him. You have to understand, the Beatles changed my life and here I was working with John Lennon, my favorite Beatle. I was in awe. I had never worked on a session before. I had no idea what the protocol was. I knew where the tapes were kept and that was about it.

"The rock 'n' roll gods blessed me; John was fantastic. He was one of the biggest stars in the world, I was a green kid, and he took the time to teach me everything I needed to know to function in the studio: how to set the mikes up, how to run the recorder ('Don't go that far back on the tape; we're working on the chorus, you only go back to a little before the chorus'). He explained all of this to me very calmly. Jimmy didn't have the time or the patience to tell me how to do things—he just wanted them done. No one works harder than he does, and he expects you to work just as hard.

"I managed to survive. Jimmy gradually took over as the engineer for John because Roy was busy running the studio, and I became Jimmy's assistant. We did *Walls and Bridges* (1974), and *Rock and Roll* (1975)," says Panunzio.

"After working with John, we went immediately into the studio with Bruce and started *Born to Run* [see Jon Landau entry], which took a whole year. That session was very different: Springsteen wasn't established yet like John Lennon was. Bruce was going to make a record that turned everybody's head if it killed him. It almost killed us too, working 16 hours a day, 7 days a week," he says with a chuckle.

"Like Jimmy, Bruce expected you to work as hard as he did. It actually felt good to work that hard: I felt appreciated, and we were making a great record. A lot of times you don't know how a record is really going because you are so caught up in the day-to-day details. One day Bruce was doing the vocals to 'Thunder Road' and it took a while because he was changing the lyrics as he went. I had a copy of the lyrics so I would know where we were on the tape, and I was following along. All of a sudden I got shivers up my back and I knew we were really doing something special, making history. He was singing about growing up in Jersey; he was singing about me! Until Bruce, there was no one special from Jersey," Panunzio says.

Panunzio was assistant producer to Todd Rundgren (see entry) on Patti Smith's *Wave* in 1979, but his first real production credit came in 1980 on legendary rock 'n' roll guitarist Link Wray's *Live from El Paradiso* (co-produced with Richard Gottehrer; see entry), recorded live in Amsterdam. "I've gone camping in better vans than the one we recorded that record from. It was also one of the loudest concerts I've ever been to—they handed out ear plugs at the door," he says.

Panunzio's production credits from the '80s include important records by Paul Butterfield, Gene Loves Jezebel, the Graces, the Jeff Healey Band, Joan Jett, Mink DeVille, Elliott Murphy, and Iggy Pop. But he really came into his own as a producer in the '90s working with a variety of punk and alt-rock bands, pop-rock diva Stevie Nicks, and continuing with rocker Joan Jett (see Kenny Laguna entry).

Real Live Sound, by veteran Orange County punk-surf rockers Agent Orange, is a killer live album; I.C.U's *Defy* rocks satisfyingly in the manner of an unhinged Joan Jett; Casey Scott updates Patti Smith's '70s poet-rocker model on the excellent and unfortunately ignored *Creep City*; and Panunzio's best '90s work is the ripsnorting psychobilly of the Reverend Horton Heat on the high-test *It's Martini Time.* Panunzio also produced Black Sabbath's highly successful double-CD live *Reunion* album, released in late 1998.

Panunzio also now runs his own production company, Eye Out. The company's first release was young thrash trio Puzzle Gut's debut in 1997. "As far as who I work with, a band either excites me or it doesn't. If it does, then I can perhaps add something and help them achieve their vision. It's really important to see a band live; in the studio you are trying to recreate the spirit of what they do live. After you see them and get to know them, you listen to any demos or records they may have already done. Next you go into preproduction—you go to their rehearsals and help pick out the good songs. Then you go through the arrangements and add to them or, sometimes, take away from them. Then you record and mix."

A memory grounds Panunzio and helps keep him focused. "The first time I picked up a guitar, I felt something special; my whole career has just been a continuation of that, looking for that feeling," he says with a smile. —ERIC OLSEN

Agent Orange: *Real Live Sound,* Restless, 1991.

Alice Cooper: *Classiks,* Epic, 1995 • *A Fistful of Alice,* Guardian, 1997.

Beat Farmers: *Poor and Famous,* Curb, 1989, 1991.

Black Sabbath: *Reunion* (15 tracks), Epic, 1998.

Butterfield, Paul: *The Legendary Paul Butterfield Rides Again,* Amherst, 1986.

Cell Mates: *Between Two Fires,* Scotti Bros., 1992.

Circus of Power: *Magic and Madness,* Columbia, 1993.

Deep Purple: *The Battle Rages On,* Giant, 1993.

Del Lords: *Lovers Who Wander,* Enigma, 1990.

Gene Loves Jezebel: *The Motion of Love,* Geffen, 1987.

Graces, The: *Perfect View* (2 tracks), A&M, 1989.

Heat, Reverend Horton: *It's Martini Time,* Interscope, 1996.

I.C.U.: *Defy,* Radical, 1993.

Inspector 7: *The Infamous . . . ,* Radical, 1997.

Jeff Healey Band: *See the Light* (1 track), Arista, 1988 • *Cover to Cover,* Arista, 1995.

Jett, Joan: *Flashback,* Blackheart, 1994 • "Go Home," Blackheart/WB, 1994 • *Pure and Simple,* Blackheart/WB, 1994.

Jett, Joan and the Blackhearts: *Glorious Results of a Misspent Youth,* Blackheart/MCA, 1984 • "Good Music," Blackheart/Epic, 1986 • *Good Music,* Blackheart/Epic Associated, 1986 • *Notorious* (9 tracks), Blackheart/Epic Associated, 1991 • *Fit to Be Tied: Great Hits By,* Blackheart/Mercury, 1997.

Jones, Tom: *The Lead and How to Swing It,* Interscope, 1994 • w/ Tori Amos, "I Wanna Get Back with You," Interscope, 1995.

Koz, Dave: *Off the Beaten Path,* Capitol, 1996 • *December Makes Me Feel This Way,* Capitol, 1997 • "That's the Way I Feel About You," Capitol, 1997.

Massey, Will T.: *Will T. Massey,* MCA, 1991.

Mink DeVille: *Coup de Grace* (1 track), Atlantic, 1981.

Mother's Finest: *Black Radio Won't Play This Record,* Scotti Brothers, 1992.

Murphy, Elliott: *Affairs,* Courtisane, 1981 • *Going Through Something: The Best Of,* Dejadisc, 1996.

Nicks, Stevie: "Maybe Love Will Change Your Mind," Modern, 1994 • *Street Angel,* Modern, 1994.

Nile, Willie: *Golden Dawn,* Arista, 1981.

Nuclear Valdez: *I Am I,* Epic, 1989.

Pop, Iggy: *Party,* Arista, 1981.

Puzzle Gut: *Puzzle Gut,* Interscope, 1997.

Revolver: *Calle Mayor,* WEA Latina, 1997.

Scott, Casey: *Creep City,* Signal/Capitol, 1993.

Smith, Patti: *Wave,* Arista, 1979 • *Masters,* Arista, 1996.

Soul Asylum: "Black Gold/Never Really Been" (live), Columbia, 1993.

Uninvited, The: *The Uninvited,* Atlantic, 1998.

Wray, Link: *Live At El Paradiso,* Instant, 1980.

COLLECTIONS

The Ozz-Fest Live, Red Ant, 1997.

Felix Pappalardi

F elix Pappalardi was a talented arranger, producer, bassist, and singer best known for his association with Mountain—a band that combined two forceful personalities in Pappalardi and guitarist/singer Leslie West—and for his production of Cream.

Born December 30, 1939, in the Bronx, Pappalardi's early successes included producing the Youngbloods hit "Get Together" (No. 5) and arranging and producing Cream's classic "Sunshine of Your Love" (No. 5), "White Room" (No. 6), and "Crossroads." He also produced West's band, the Vagrants (an ill-timed version of "Respect" that came out weeks before Aretha's), then produced West's 1969 solo effort, *Mountain.* That led to the formation of the band Mountain, resulting in such tracks as "Mississippi Queen," "The Animal Trainer and the Toad," "Never in My Life," "Nantucket Sleighride," and "Theme from an Imaginary Western."

"When Felix started working for me, it was like a dream come true," West told Richard Skelley in *Goldmine* magazine. Adds Mountain drummer Corky Laing: "Leslie certainly was the soul of Mountain, and still is, by way of his voice and guitar playing. But in terms of thrust and commercial value—yeah, they used Felix as the market value."

Pappalardi also was involved in Mountain's business affairs as co-owner of the label and publishing company Windfall Records with Mountain manager Bud Praeger.

When Mountain ran its course, Pappalardi continued his involvement with Windfall Records and later released an excellent solo album for A&M Records.

On April 17, 1983, Pappalardi was murdered by his wife and songwriting partner, Gail Collins. —BEN CROMER

Back Door: *8th Street Nites,* Warner Bros., 1973.

Bedlam: *Bedlam,* Chrysalis, 1973.

Bo Grumpus: *Before the War,* Atco, 1968.

Bruce, Jack: *Songs for a Tailor,* Polydor, 1969 • *Willpower: A 20-Year Retrospective,* Atco, 1989.

Clapton, Eric: *Crossroads,* Polydor, 1988.

Cream: *Disraeli Gears,* Polydor, 1967 • "Sunshine of Your Love," Atco, 1968 • *Wheels of Fire,* Atco, 1968 • "White Room," Atco, 1968 • "Badge," Atco, 1969 • "Crossroads," Atco, 1969 • *Goodbye,* Atco, 1969 • *Live Cream, Volume 1,* Polydor, 1970, 1983 • *Live Cream, Volume 2,* Atco, 1972 • *Strange Brew: The Very Best of Cream,* Polydor, 1983 • *Those Were the Days,* Polydor, 1987.

Dead Boys: *We Have Come for Your Children,* Sire, 1978.

Flock, The: *Inside Out,* Mercury, 1975.

Hot Tuna: *Double Dose,* Grunt, 1978.

Jolliver, Arkansaw: *Home,* Bell, 1969.

Kensington Market: *Avenue Road,* Warner Bros., 1968 • *Aardvark,* Warner Bros., 1969.

Mountain: *Climbing,* Windfall, 1970 • "Mississippi Queen," Windfall, 1970 • *Mountain,* Windfall, 1970 • *Flowers of Evil,* Windfall, 1971 • *Nantucket Sleighride,* Island/Windfall, 1971 • "The Animal Trainer and the Toad," Windfall, 1971 • *Live,* Island/Windfall, 1972 • *The Road Goes On Forever,* Windfall, 1972 • *Avalanche,* Epic, 1974 • *Twin Peaks,* CBS, 1976 • *Go for Your Life,* Scotti Bros., 1985 • *Over the Top,* Legacy/Columbia, 1995.

Natural Gas: *Natural Gas,* Private Stock, 1976.

Pappalardi, Felix: w/ Creation, *Felix Pappalardi and Creation,* A&M, 1976 • *Don't Worry Mum,* A&M, 1979.

Rea, David: *By the Grace of God,* CBS, 1971.

Sierra: *Sierra,* Mercury, 1977.

Vagrants, The: "Respect," Atco, 1967.

West, Leslie: *Mountain,* Columbia, 1969, 1996 • *Blood of the Sun: 1969–1975,* Raven, 1996.

Young, Jesse Colin: *Love on the Wing,* Warner Bros., 1977 • *Greatest Hits,* Award, 1998.

Youngbloods, The: "Get Together," RCA, 1969 • *Get Together,* RCA, 1969.

Alan Parsons

In 1967, Alan Parsons was working for EMI Records at its suburban Hayes, Middlesex facility, a far cry from EMI's Abbey Road Studios in London, home studio of the Beatles. When Parsons (born December 20, 1949) heard the Beatles' *Sgt. Pepper,* he decided to cast his fate to the wind and apply for a post at Abbey Road. "There was no better place to learn than at Abbey Road," says the British producer/engineer, who also leads the Alan Parsons Project. "There was an enormous variety of different kinds of music, so everybody got a good grounding in all areas. I would be working with what would have been referred to then as a heavy underground band one day and the next day I'd be working with Otto Klemperer and a classical session."

Parsons was an assistant engineer on the Beatles' *Let It Be* and *Abbey Road.* In fact, he was involved with the *Let It Be* sessions on the roof of the Apple building on Savile Row, which turned out to be the Beatles' final concert. That led to work as an engineer for such EMI acts as the Hollies and Pink Floyd, including the latter's monumental *Dark Side of the Moon.* "I hadn't actually been an engineer for very long when *Dark Side of the Moon* came out," Parsons recalls, acknowledging the project as a major boost to his career. "We'd have leads running all around the building and tape machines in the corridors outside the control rooms. It was quite a complex arrangement."

Parsons, who earned a Grammy Award for his engineering work on *Dark Side,* was initially a bit fuzzy regarding the album's concept. "I remember Roger [Waters] telling me what it was toward the end of the album," says Parsons. "In fact, I was one of the people that had to go and answer questions for possible use of dialogue [as one of the mad voices]. I was one of the voices that might have been used on the album, but I wasn't."

Parsons also engineered songs on Paul McCartney's *Red Rose Speedway,* as well as hits by the Hollies, including "He Ain't Heavy, He's My Brother" and "The Air That I Breathe." Moreover, Parsons' engineering experience enabled him to move with ease into production in the mid-'70s, supervising albums by Cockney Rebel, John Miles, Pilot, and Al Stewart.

"Production took a turn in the '70s to become a more technical job, and even more so in the '80s, as MIDI and synthesizers and drum machines became an important part of a lot of recording," Parsons explains.

"So a lot of producers by default became engineers because they had to work with computers and machines so much."

Stewart's *Year of the Cat* (No. 5) and *Time Passages* (No. 10), as well as Miles' sadly overlooked *Rebel*, aptly demonstrate Parsons' prodigious abilities: He crafted sonic landscapes characterized by strong vocals and a delicately balanced mosaic of guitars, bass, drums, and keyboards, sometimes embossed by an orchestra.

When Parsons formed the Alan Parsons Project in 1975, he recruited Eric Woolfson and Andrew Powell to bring cohesion to a loose-knit organization of singers and musicians such as Miles, Allan Clarke, Colin Blunstone, Steve Harley, Ian Bairnson, and Stuart Elliot. The first Project album, the Edgar Allan Poe–based *Tales of Mystery and Imagination*, was a tour de force that spawned such songs as "The Raven" and "(The System of) Doctor Tarr and Professor Feather." That was followed by the equally fine *I Robot* (No. 9), a concept album that pitted man against computer. It boasted such songs as "I Wouldn't Want to Be Like You" and "Some Other Time."

Although Parsons was still on the EMI payroll during the early Project years, he eventually struck out on his own. In the '80s his Project albums included *The Turn of a Friendly Card* (No. 13), *Eye in the Sky* (No. 7), *Ammonia Avenue* (No. 15) and *Stereotomy*. Parsons also produced the musical *Freudiana*, which was staged in Vienna.

In the '90s, Parsons produced orchestral sessions for *The Symphonic Music of Yes* and released an excellent concert recording from his 1994 European tour, *The Very Best—Live*. In 1996, he released *On Air*, a concept album about the human will to fly that included a CD-ROM.

In 1997, Parsons was named vice president of EMI Studios Group in London, the organization that oversees Abbey Road Studios. —BEN CROMER

Alan Parsons Project: "(The System of) Doctor Tarr and Professor Feather," 20th Century, 1976 • *Tales of Mystery and Imagination*, 20th Century, 1976 • *I Robot*, Arista, 1977 • "I Wouldn't Want to Be Like You," Arista, 1977 • *Pyramid*, Arista, 1978 • "Damned If I Do," Arista, 1979 • *Eve*, Arista, 1979 • *The Turn of a Friendly Card*, Arista, 1980 • "Games People Play," Arista, 1981 • "Time," Arista, 1981 • "Eye in the Sky," Arista, 1982 • *Eye in the Sky*, Arista, 1982 • *The Best Of*, Arista, 1983 • *Ammonia Avenue*, Arista, 1984 • "Don't Answer Me," Arista, 1984 • "Prime Time," Arista, 1984 • *Vulture Culture*, Arista, 1984 • "Days Are Numbers (The Traveller)," Arista, 1985 • "Let's Talk About Me," Arista, 1985 • *Stereotomy*, Arista, 1985 • *Gaudi*,

Arista, 1987 • *The Best Of,* Vol. 2, Arista, 1987 • *The Instrumental Works Of,* Arista, 1988 • *Box Set,* Alex, 1993 • *Try Anything Once,* Arista, 1993 • *Very Best—Live,* RCA, 1995 • *On Air,* River North, 1996 • *Definitive Collection,* Arista, 1997.

Ambrosia: *Somewhere I've Never Travelled,* 20th Century, 1976.

Cockney Rebel: "Mr. Soft," EMI, 1974 • *The Psychomodo,* EMI, 1974.

Ford, Dean: *Dean Ford,* EMI, 1975.

Harley, Steve, and Cockney Rebel: "Make Me Smile (Come Up and See Me)," EMI, 1975 • "Mr. Raffles (Man It Was Mean)," EMI, 1975 • *The Best Years of Our Lives,* EMI, 1975 • *A Closer Look,* EMI, 1976.

Hollies, The: *Crazy Steal,* Epic, 1978.

Keats: *Keats,* Renaissance, 1984, 1996.

Miles, John: "High Fly," London, 1976 • "Music," London, 1976 • *Rebel,* Decca/London, 1976 • *More Miles Per Hour,* Decca/Arista, 1979 • *Sympathy,* Decca/Arista, 1980.

Parsons, Alan: "Blown by the Wind," River North, 1997.

Pilot: *From the Album of the Same Name,* EMI, 1974 • "Magic," EMI, 1975 • *Second Flight,* EMI, 1975 • *Two's a Crowd,* Arista, 1977.

Stewart, Al: *Modern Times,* CBS, 1975 • *Year of the Cat,* Janus, 1976 • "Year of the Cat," Janus, 1977 • "Time Passages," Arista, 1978 • *Time Passages,* Arista, 1978 • "Song on the Radio," Arista, 1979 • *Best Of,* Arista, 1981.

Tin Drum: *Real World,* Bai, 1996.

Yes: w/ London Philharmonic Orchestra, *Symphonic Music of Yes,* RCA, 1993.

Zak, Lenny: *Lenny Zak,* A&M, 1979.

COLLECTIONS

Freudiana, American Gramaphone, 1990.

Les Paul

Dear Mrs. Polfus,

Your boy, Lester, will never learn music, so save your money. Please don't send him for any more piano lessons. —*A note from Les Paul's piano teacher.*

Although the list of contributions that Les Paul (born Lester Polfus, June 9, 1915, in Waukesha, Wisconsin) has made to the recording industry is staggering, he maintains that his inventions and discoveries are nothing spectacular. "Someone would have figured this all out; there's too many heads out there in the world," he says from his New Jersey home. "I just happened to be the first one. I could have been the last one."

Does he ever wonder what recording would be like if he hadn't discovered how to do such things as multi-track recording, overdubbing, building a solid body electric guitar (the ever-popular Les Paul), and adding echo, delay, and reverb to tracks? "Yeah, I think of it and I thank God for being given the opportunity to do it," he says. "I never think of it as anything ingenious or unusual, other than the fact that it was there and no one thought of it. It wasn't anything more than punching a hole in a piano roll or putting your finger on the grid of the tube [of a radio] to get the speaker to jump. I'm happy that it's out there and I'm glad that I'm recognized for it. It ain't going to mean anything when I'm gone, it don't mean anything when I'm here, other than the fact that I'm very pleased."

Of course, if it wasn't for his mother's love of music, her player piano, Victrola, telephone, and weak bladder, none of this would have come to fruition. "It all seemed to come together with me in the living room at my mother's house. She had just gotten a player piano and you had to pump it," says Paul. "So she asked if I would run home from school and pump that piano for her because she had a weak bladder." He did, and by watching the piano play and monitoring the Victrola nearby, he discerned their different pitches and how they worked.

While that piqued his auditory curiosity, her 1928 purchase of a console radio put the 13-year-old Paul into overdrive. "The curiosity was: What in the world would happen if I disconnected the speaker and put a phonograph pickup there? This is back in the day when you had a needle that you screwed in and a magnet and a coil that moved the needle. I put it in the same place the speaker was and turned up the volume gradually on the radio until I felt the needle moving," he recalls.

He remembers yelling at his mother, who sat by watching her son play with her radio. He then had to find an input, so he touched the grid of the tube on the radio. "It made noise and I thought, 'Man, that sounds to me like some sort of input.' I knew it was the beginning. I took the mouthpiece of the telephone and talked into it and got it to come out of the radio."

Those early explorations and discoveries flavored the way Paul looked at every aspect of the recording business. He has played barn dances, worked on the Fred Waring radio show, and performed with Bing Crosby, Judy Garland, and the Andrews Sisters; he has recorded hundreds of sides for a variety of artists, most importantly his own recordings with Mary Ford. The breadth and depth of his experience help, he says. "It's

not absolutely necessary, but it's a great advantage. If you can be an engineer and a musician, those two are very complementary."

In the early '30s, Paul straddled country and jazz. But some five years into the business, he had to choose between the two. "In the morning, I was hillbilly and at night I was playing jazz with Roy Eldridge, Coleman Hawkins, Nat Cole, Art Tatum," he recalls. He opted for jazz, although he found it difficult to leave the $1,000 he was earning weekly playing country.

In 1931, he entered the recording studio for the first time, working on numerous transcriptions. Three years later, he recorded under the name of "Rhubarb Red," discovering the art of balancing instrumentals and vocals and working with a gravity-feed recording machine he now calls barbaric. In 1937, he formed the Les Paul Trio and moved to New York.

Little by little, he says, these experiences piled up, so when he moved to California and started working with several Hollywood stars in his garage studio, he was an accomplished musician and engineer. Although he contributed to hundreds of albums, the key ones he admits to producing are the ones he did with his wife, Mary Ford, along with Joe Bushkin's 1968 *Play It Again, Joe*.

At his home studio, Paul worked with Crosby, Gene Austin, the Andrews Sisters, André Previn, Kate Kaiser, and Jenny Sims. "They all recorded in my garage and I was a producer on all those dates," he says. "I just automatically told them things. I guess I engineered and produced them, but I didn't know that at the time; it was just part of my life."

Paul is still enthralled by studios and enjoys checking out the latest technology. But essentially, the work remains the same. "We make the mikes better and cheaper," he says. "The guitar is the same thing, refined. I don't care if it's analog or digital, it's the same thing, only better. You know, way back in the beginning, my prediction was, it will never be right until no parts are moving."

Expanding on a theory he unveiled at an engineering society meeting in 1954, Paul says, "As long as you have something spinning, it's wrong. It has got to be done when it's put on a chip and you put it in your pocket."

Although he's interested in current music, he wonders where the "beautiful songs are being written." He suggests that "tomorrow's music" is evolving, but he doesn't know what shape it will take. Through the years, Paul has been offered business opportunities he's declined because he wants, above all, to play guitar. One of those offerings came from Bing Crosby, who in the early '40s told Paul he'd build him a studio which, if it thrived, would expand into a Les Paul House of Sound chain. "As we were driving I said, 'You know, Bing, I don't think I'd want to do that,' Paul recalls. " 'If I do, then I won't be playing my guitar, and that's what I love to do.' "

Paul still makes music every Monday night in New York. "It's the greatest therapy in the world. I feel sorry for the guy who retires when he's 55," he says. "You know, I can't do what I used to do when I was 20 or 30. With the arthritis I got, Christ, I got no fingers. But what I got, I play. A knuckle here, a knuckle there. You forget about the arthritis and everything else when you're playing." —DAVID JOHN FARINELLA

Bushkin, Joe: *The Road to Oslo/Play It Again, Joe,* DRG, 1968, 1985.

Paul, Les: w/ the Andrews Sisters, "Rumors Are Flying," Decca, 1946 • "Lover/Brazil," Capitol, 1948 • "What Is This Thing Called Love?," Capitol, 1948 • "Goofus," Capitol, 1950 • "Little Rock Getaway," Capitol, 1950 • "Nola," Capitol, 1950 • "Jazz Me Blues," Capitol, 1951 • "Jingle Bells," Capitol, 1951 • "Josephine," Capitol, 1951 • "Carioca," Capitol, 1952 • "Lady of Spain," Capitol, 1952 • "Meet Mister Callaghan," Capitol, 1952 • "Sleep," Capitol, 1953 • "The Kangaroo," Capitol, 1953 • "Mandolino," Capitol, 1954 • *Les Paul Now,* London, 1968 • *The Guitar Artistry Of,* One Way, 1971 • *Les Paul Story Vols 1 and 2,* Capitol, 1974 • *The World Is Still Waiting for Sunrise,* Capitol, 1974 • *Multi trackin',* London, 1979 • *Les Paul: The Legend and the Legacy,* Capitol, 1991 • *The Complete Decca Trios (1936–1947),* MCA, 1997 •

Paul, Les, and Mary Ford: *Hawaiian Paradise,* Decca, 1949 • *New Sounds,,* Vol. 1, Capitol, 1950 • "Tennessee Waltz," Capitol, 1950 • "How High the Moon," Capitol, 1951 • "I Wish I Had Never Seen Sunshine," Capitol, 1951 • "Just One More Chance," Capitol, 1951 • "Mockin' Bird Hill," Capitol, 1951 • *New Sounds,,* Vol. 2, Capitol, 1951 • "The World Is Waiting for the Sunrise," Capitol, 1951 • "Whispering," Capitol, 1951 • *Bye Bye Blues,* Capitol, 1952 • *Galloping Guitars,* Decca, 1952 • "I'm Confessin (That I Love You)," Capitol, 1952 • "In the Good Old Summertime/Smoke Rings," Capitol, 1952 • "My Baby's Coming Home/Bye Bye Blues," Capitol, 1952 • "Take Me in Your Arms and Hold Me," Capitol, 1952 • "Tiger Rag," Capitol, 1952 • "Don'cha Hear Them Bells," Capitol, 1953 • "I'm Sitting on Top of the World," Capitol, 1953 • "Vaya con Dios/Johnny (Is the Boy for Me)," Capitol, 1953 • "I Really Don't Want to Know," Capitol, 1954 • "I'm a Fool to Care," Capitol, 1954 • "Whither Thou Goest," Capitol, 1954 • "Amukiriki (The Lord Willing)," Capitol, 1955 • "Hummingbird," Capitol, 1955 • *Les and Mary,* Capitol, 1955, 1970 • *The Hitmakers,* Capitol, 1955 • "Cinco Robles (Five Oaks)," Capitol, 1957 • *Time to Dream,* Capitol, 1957,

1971 • "Put a Ring on My Finger," Columbia, 1958 • *Lover's Luau,* CBS, 1959 • *The Hits of Les and Mary,* Capitol, 1960 • "Jura (I Swear I Love You)," Columbia, 1961 • *Bouquet of Roses,* CBS, 1962 • *Warm and Wonderful,* CBS, 1962 • *Swingin' South,* CBS, 1963 • *The Fabulous Les Paul and Mary Ford,* Harmony/Columbia, 1965 • *16 Most Requested Songs,* Columbia, 1996 • *Love Songs by Les Paul and Mary Ford,* Ranwood, 1997 • *A Class Act,* Columbia, 1998 • *Bye Bye Blues/A Time to Dream,* See for Miles, 1998 • *Hummingbird/How High the Moon,* Touch of Class, 1998.

Brian Paulson

Brian Paulson (not to be confused with new age composer Brian E. Paulson) has become one of the most important producer/engineers of indie rock over the last 15 years. He has made something of a subspecialty out of the alterna-country twang rock of Uncle Tupelo, the Jayhawks, (ex-Replacement) Slim Dunlop, Son Volt, Soul Asylum, Wilco, and Kelly Willis; but he has also produced (or "recorded" in indie credit terminology) the neo-'20s jazz of Squirrel Nut Zippers, the voracious genre-munching of Beck, and a host of post-punk and art-noise bands, including Archers of Loaf, Babes in Toyland, Flour, the Jesus Lizard, Killdozer, Lazy, Slint, the Spinanes, Superchunk, Tsunami, and Unrest.

Brian Paulson was born in 1961 and grew up in northern Minnesota, the land of Paul Bunyan and Babe, the Blue Ox. He played guitar in some noisy bands and ended up mixing live sound for Minneapolis demigods Husker Du (see Bob Mould entry) and the Replacements. His first productions were for indie bands that had no money, so his live-sounding recording aesthetic evolved out of necessity.

Paulson moved to Chicago in the late '80s and worked with indie maestro Steve Albini (see entry) for a time, including co-producing the textured noise of Slint's 1991 *Spiderland* album, still his favorite. "I'm probably most pleased with that one because the music and sonics were unique for the time. The band was prepared and everything just fell into place. I can't imagine that one being any different. There are little things I would love to go back and fix up, but then it wouldn't be what it is. That record had a tremendous influence as well."

By 1993 Paulson's name was all over the place: on records by Minneapolis punk women Babes in Toyland,

Chapel Hill's pop-punkers Superchunk, and post-punk duo the Spinanes; on B-sides ("By the Way" and "Everybody Loves a Winner") for Soul Asylum's huge "Runaway Train" single, on the twisted guitar pop of Unrest's *Perfect Teeth,* and most importantly, on Uncle Tupelo's *Anodyne.*

Dueling singer/songwriters Jay Farrar and Jeff Tweedy brought a post-post-modern sensibility—"been there, done that, felt superior to it (life, society, emotion, musical forms), rejected the superiority, and went back to do it again"—to traditional country rock instrumentation (acoustic and electric guitars, fiddle, mandolin, bass, and drums), and that combination came to define a new genre variously called Americana, No Depression (after Uncle Tupelo's first album), or, more broadly, alternative country.

Anodyne is full of heartfelt, poignant roots numbers (Tweedy's "Acuff-Rose," "New Madrid," and "No Sense in Lovin' "; Farrar's "Slate," "Anodyne," "Fifteen Keys," "High Water"), interspersed with spirited rockers (Tweedy's "The Long Cut," "We've Been Had"; Farrar's "Chickamauga") to form a deeply rooted, topsoil-smelling whole. Paulson's production is clean, warm, and full enough to push the songs forward, but spare enough to never call attention to itself.

For Paulson it was a nice change of pace. "It was like 'Well, this is a refreshing break from the grinding Midwestern guitars that I've been dealing with for the past 10 years.' " It turned into more.

In a development as momentous in some circles as Lennon and McCartney bidding each other an acrimonious adieu, Farrar and Tweedy split in 1994: Farrar to form Son Volt and Tweedy to carry on with the remnants of Tupelo, now called Wilco. In a tribute to Paulson's personality and talents, he continued to record with both.

Son Volt's *Trace* takes Farrar even further back into America's past, where the Scotch-Irish folk tradition crosses the Atlantic and takes root in Appalachia before it branches off into bluegrass, Nashville country, Western swing, rockabilly, and modern commercial country. *Trace* crosses much of the territory covered by Neil Young or the Band. "Windfall" is pure mournful midtempo bluegrass, with Dave Boquist's sawing fiddle, swerving lap steel guitar, and Farrar's wavering-voiced but earnest benediction: "May the wind take your troubles away." "Live Free" is rocking electric two-step. "Tear Stained Eye" is classic Big Sky shuffle. "Route" rocks with a grunge-like intensity, as does "Drown." As Paulson sees it, "*Trace* is Jay Farrar at his most focused and defined. Basically he refined his art and pretty much nailed it on that record." *Straightaways* (1997) is more of the consistently satisfying same.

Wilco's *A.M.* also came out in 1995. It leans more to the rock side of roots rock, with Tweedy's voice reminiscent of the Replacements' Paul Westerberg. In fact, the excellent "I Must Be High" sounds like Westerberg singing lead on what would be a good Lemonheads song. Ringing good electric guitars chopping through a rootsy Replacements/Stones underbrush elevate "Casino Queen," "Box Full of Letters," and "Blue Eyed Soul." "That's Not the Issue" is a rolling banjo bluegrass workout, and "Should've Been in Love" is just a great country rock tune that would have done the early Eagles proud. Though slightly less distinctive than Son Volt, Wilco stands tall. In this case, the breakup of a productive partnership yielded not disaster but double the fine music.

In 1996 Paulson had his biggest commercial hit when he made the unlikely move into the Squirrel Nut Zippers' maniacally faithful representation of '20s jazz. Somehow, that very monomaniacism rendered the band cutting-edge modern rock; *Hot* actually cracked the Top 30 in 1997, the first real commercial showing of the current swing revival. The album's standout is singer/guitarist Tom Maxwell's fiendishly expressive reworking of an old calypso song, "Hell," which became a modern-rock radio staple wherein fire-and-brimstone cautions against the hubris of materialism achieve a truly frightening Bosch-like physicality. Great horn line too.

The band's success caught everyone—Paulson included—off guard. "I never would have guessed it. It seems like the Zippers were the perfect thing when MTV decided to throw out the guitars, before they could plug in electronica: 'Oh, here's something kind of fun.' I like that record a lot. It's not as good as it could have been, but what do you expect for a week of recording? That was crazy fun. I always try to find something new, something different, something that's going to keep me excited." —ERIC OLSEN AND DAVID JOHN FARINELLA

A Minor Forest: *Inindependence,* Thrill Jockey, 1998.

Archers of Loaf: *All the Nation's Airports,* Elektra, 1996 • *White Trash Heroes,* Alias, 1998.

Arcwelder: *Pull,* Touch & Go, 1993 • *Xerxes,* Touch & Go, 1994.

Babes in Toyland: *Painkiller,* Warner Bros., 1993.

Barking Tribe: *Serpent Go Home,* Rykodisc, 1991.

Beck: *Odelay* (1 track), DGC, 1996.

Carpetbaggers, The: *Nowhere to Go but Down,* Twin/Tone, 1994.

Coctails: *Long Sound,* Carrot Top, 1995.

Cows: *Taint Pluribus Taint Unum,* Treehouse, 1987.

Dollface: *Corvette Summer,* Crackpot, 1994.

Dunlap, Slim: *The Old New Me,* Medium Cool, 1993.

Flour: *Fourth and Final,* Touch & Go, 1994.

Gastr Del Sol: *The Serpentine Similar,* Teen Beat, 1993 •
Crookt, Crackt, or Fly, Drag City, 1994.

Gaunt: *Bricks and Blackouts,* Warner Bros., 1998.

Golden Smog: *Weird Tales,* Rykodisc, 1998.

Janitor Joe: *Lucky,* Amphetamine Reptile, 1994.

Jayhawks, The: *Sound of Lies,* American, 1997 • "Think
About It," American, 1997.

Jesus Lizard: *Show,* Giant, 1994.

Karl Hendricks Trio: *For a While, It Was Funny,* Merge, 1996.

Killdozer: *Uncompromising War on Art Under the Dictatorship of
the Proletariat/Burl,* Touch & Go, 1994.

Lazy: *Some Assembly Required,* Roadrunner, 1994.

Polvo: *This Eclipse* (EP), Merge, 1995.

Seam: *The Pace Is Glacial,* Touch & Go, 1998.

Slint: "Good Morning Captain," London, 1991, 1995 (*Kids*
soundtrack) • *Spiderland,* Touch & Go, 1991.

Son Volt: *Trace,* Warner Bros., 1995 • *Straightaways,* Warner
Bros., 1997 • *Switchback* (EP), Warner Bros., 1997.

Soul Asylum: "By the Way/Everybody Loves a Winner,"
Columbia, 1993.

Spinanes, The: *Manos,* Sub Pop, 1993.

Squirrel Nut Zippers: *The Inevitable,* Mammoth, 1995 •
"Hell," Mammoth, 1996 • *Hot,* Mammoth, 1996.

Superchunk: *Foolish,* Merge, 1993 • "The First Part," Merge,
1994.

Tripmaster Monkey: *Practice Changes,* Elektra, 1996.

Tsunami: *The Heart's Tremolo,* Simple Machines, 1994.

Uncle Tupelo: *Anodyne,* Sire/Reprise, 1993 • "Effigy," Arista,
1993 (*No Alternative*) • *The Long Cut* (EP), Sire/Reprise,
1993.

Unrest: *Perfect Teeth,* Teen Beat/4 A.D., 1993.

Wedding Present: *Hit Parade 2,* First Warning, 1993.

Wilco: *A.M.,* Sire, 1995.

Willis, Kelly: "Fading Fast," A&M, 1996 (*Boys* soundtrack) •
Fading Fast (EP), A&M/Crystal Clear Sound, 1996.

Charlie Peacock

F rom writing and producing his own records to
working with acts such as Out of the Grey, Margaret Becker, and Sarah Masen, Charlie Peacock has
established a reputation as a musical maverick. His writing and recording experience includes recording as a
mainstream act on Island Records during his early days

and winning Christian Music Producer of the Year three
years running.

Peacock (born Charles William Ashworth) grew up
north of Sacramento, the son of a music teacher who
nurtured his appreciation of music and his talent. "He
was a proud dad," Peacock says. "He never dreamed I
could have this kind of success because we came from a
small town. He would have been happy if I was just a
music teacher. But I've always been very risk-oriented.
In the music business you have to be."

Peacock began taking risks in the business in 1983,
when he landed his first record deal and produced his
own debut. "As a result, I was working with some people and they said, 'You did a good job, why don't you
produce this other record?' and that was a 77's record
called *All Fall Down.*"

Peacock recorded five albums on the West Coast for
Exit/Island and, later, for Jamz before relocating to
Nashville in 1989. "Sacramento is not a music town. If
you're an artist, you can live pretty much anywhere if
you have a record deal, but if you're going to be a producer or a session musician, you'd better get to a music
town. I came out here to cut some vocals on Margaret
Becker and fell in love with the place."

In Nashville, Peacock quickly became one of the
most successful producers in contemporary Christian
music (CCM). He has worked with a wide range of
artists, including Becker, Cheri Keaggy, Out of the Grey
husband and wife Scott and Christine Dente, Tony Vincent, Scott Krippayne, Say-So, Bob Carlisle, Avalon,

Michelle Tumes, Eric Champion, and Brent Bourgeois. His work in the CCM industry earned him the Gospel Music Association's Dove Award for Producer of the Year three years running: 1995, 1996, and 1997.

He fondly recalls producing the Out of the Grey debut, where he deployed experimental arrangements. He also considers Becker's *Soul* album a sonic breakthrough. He enjoyed producing his own *Strangelanguage* and *Everything That's on My Mind*. "If you are going to produce a lot of different types of music, you have to really love music and have a knowledge of several genres," Peacock says. "And I think that's where I fit in. I can play lots of different kinds of music and I appreciate lots of different kinds of music."

Peacock says that as a producer, it's as important to know when to hold back as it is to give direction. "I've always been one of those people where if someone is unsure and not knowing what to do next, I'll have 15 ideas and I'll present one of them," he says. "I think that's one part of being a producer, but as you get older, you learn to hold the ideas back to see what an artist has to say, to be a gap-filler who can be an encourager."

He thinks he learned about organization and direction from his band teacher father. "I used to watch him and even took some classes from him," Peacock recalls. Peacock says he tries to help artists craft what they think their album should be. "It's not right to think of another artist's album as your place to get all your ideas out," he says. "The best producers aren't dictators. If you listen to a record I produced, it's not just full of my choices but the artist's choices, maybe even the record company's choices."

He also likes a positive attitude. "I really love to work with an artist who doesn't think the world owes them anything," he says. "Those are my favorite artists to work with, who are real humble, who recognize all their talents are a gift."

In addition to performing and producing, Peacock is a songwriter who views his producing as an extension of his writing. Technological advances help, he says. "I believe that different technologies have an ideology of their own in the same way that a hammer does in many ways. There's an old saying: 'To a man with a hammer, everything looks like a nail.' To a man with a sampler, everything looks like a sample. It's just another tool, and your ideas have to be greater than your tools. It should be that your ideas are so profound and good and interesting and compelling that you need tools to carry them off rather than just buying tools and technology and saying, 'Well, what kind of interesting thing can I do with this?'"

In 1995, Peacock took his aspirations to another level when he launched his own record company, Re:Think. The label's first release was a sampler, *Oh Point Oh: The Re:Think Collection*. During the summer of 1996, the label also released Peacock's *Strangelanguage* album, as well as the debut disc by Sarah Masen, a 1997 Dove nominee for Best New Artist. After developing the label into a formidable force in the industry, Peacock sold the venture to EMI in June 1997, but he remains president and retains all creative control in signings and A&R.

"I feel like I'm just starting to get this thing of music," Peacock says. "I feel like my best music—my best productions and my best songs—are ahead of me. I want to continually get better at what I do."

—Deborah Evans Price

Avalon: *Avalon,* Chordant, 1997 • *A Maze of Grace,* Sparrow, 1998.

Becker, Margaret: *Simple House,* Sparrow, 1991, 1993 • *Steps of Faith, 1987–1991,* Sparrow, 1992 • *Immigrant's Daughter,* Sparrow, 1993 • *Soul,* Sparrow/Capitol, 1993 • *Grace,* Sparrow, 1995.

Bevill, Lisa: *All Because of You,* Sparrow, 1994.

Bourgeois, Brent: *Come Join the Living World,* Reunion, 1995.

Carlisle, Bob: *Bob Carlisle,* Sparrow, 1993 • *Collection,* Sparrow, 1997.

Ebo, Vince: *Love Is the Better Way,* Warner Bros., 1992.

Jimmy A: *Entertaining Angels,* Sparrow, 1991.

Keaggy, Cheri: *Child of the Father,* Sparrow, 1994 • *My Faith Will Stay,* Sparrow, 1996.

Masen, Sarah: *Sarah Masen* (extended CD), Chordant, 1996 • *Carry Us Through,* Capitol, 1998.

Out of the Grey: *Diamond Days,* Sparrow, 1994 • *Gravity,* Sparrow, 1995.

Peacock, Charlie: *Lie Down in the Grass,* Exit, 1984 • *West Coast Diaries,* Vols. 1–3, Sparrow, 1987–1988 • *Love Life,* Sparrow, 1991, 1993 • *Everything That's on My Mind,* Sparrow, 1995 • *In the Light: The Very Best Of,* Re:Think, 1996 • *Strangelanguage* (extended CD), Re:Think, 1996.

77's, The: *All Fall Down,* Exit, 1984.

Switchfoot: *Legend of Chin,* Chordant, 1997.

Tumes, Michelle: *Listen,* Sparrow, 1998.

Vincent, Tony: *Tony Vincent,* Star Song, 1995.

COLLECTIONS

Our Christmas, Word/Epic, 1990.

COMPILATIONS

Coram Deo: Under the Gaze of God, Sparrow, 1992.
Coram Deo: En La Presencia de Dios, Sparrow, 1993.
Coram Deo II: People of Praise, Sparrow, 1994.
Oh Point Oh: The Re:Think Collection, Re:Think, 1996.

Sandy Pearlman

See also MURRAY KRUGMAN

A former Woodrow Wilson Fellow in the history of ideas, Sandy Pearlman is the Hunter Thompson of rock: a gonzo producer of searing intellect and vast vision. Pearlman, born in Far Rockaway, New York, has made important contributions in a number of different areas of rock as songwriter, producer, critic, manager, recording studio owner, and label executive. His management clients have included a who's who of influential artists in their respective genres, including Romeo Void (one of the first new wave bands), Black Sabbath, Aldo Nova, and the Dictators. In the '80s, he pioneered the mega-tour stadium format of several bands traveling together, sharing promotional, production, and travel costs—a format that persists today with Lollapalooza, Lilith, and related tour packages.

His most prominent influence has manifested itself through his long association with Blue Öyster Cult, and their collective role as progenitors of the genre now known as heavy metal. In fact, it was Pearlman who first coined the term "heavy metal" for music in his 1968 review of the Byrds' *Artificial Energy* in *Crawdaddy* magazine. Steppenwolf picked up the phrase ("heavy metal thunder") in "Born to Be Wild" eight months later.

Around the same time, as a student at the State University of New York at Stony Brook, he saw a campus group named the Soft White Underbelly, told them they were great, and named them Blue Öyster Cult, making them the first band to use an umlaut: the now all-too-omnipresent Germanic infusion. Pearlman managed and produced BOC throughout most of their career, and wrote the lyrics to most of their songs, virtually defining the mythic/gothic/occult lyricism that is still a heavy metal mainstay. With BOC, Pearlman co-produced (with Murray Krugman; see entry) one of the great songs in rock, "(Don't Fear) the Reaper" (No. 12)—the first teen love–suicide pact song in a genre now full of them. Other BOC standout tracks are the hilarious "Godzilla" and the epic "Astronomy." Latter-day BOC albums are alternately tedious and stunningly brilliant.

Pearlman co-produced (with Krugman) other landmarks: the first American punk record (and arguably the first punk record anywhere), *The Dictators Go Girl Crazy,* in 1975, and the first gothic rock record, *Pampered Menial* by Pavlov's Dog, also in 1975. In 1984 he produced the first L.A. paisley underground record, Dream Syndicate's *Medicine Show.* He produced the Clash's *Give 'Em Enough*

Rope, a record that has earned such bipolar reviews that critics say it is either far and away the best album ever made by the English group or its absolute nadir.

Pearlman has owned his own recording studios for two decades, veritable confection shops of the latest and most exotic outboard equipment on the planet. He was one of the first owners of the Publison reverb and keeps his room stocked with an eclectic balance of old tube gear and API console modules and the newest solid state or hybrid signal processors. —DANIEL J. LEVITIN

Blue Öyster Cult: *Blue Oyster Cult,* Columbia, 1972 • *Tyranny and Mutation,* Columbia, 1973 • *Secret Treaties,* Columbia, 1974 • *On Your Feet or on Your Knees,* Columbia, 1975 • *Agents of Fortune,* Columbia, 1976 • "Don't Fear the Reaper," Columbia, 1976 • *Spectres,* Columbia, 1977 • *Some Enchanted Evening,* Columbia, 1978 • *Extraterrestrial Live,* Columbia, 1982, 1990 • *Club Ninja,* Columbia, 1986 • *Imaginos,* Columbia, 1988 • *Bad Channels,* Moonstone, 1992 • *Workshop of the Telescopes,* Legacy, 1995.

Clash, The: "English Civil War," Epic, 1979 • *Give 'Em Enough Rope,* Epic, 1979 • "Tommy Gun," Epic, 1979 • *Story of the Clash,* Vol. 1, Epic, 1988 • *The Singles,* TriStar, 1996.

Dictators, The: *Manifest Destiny,* Asylum, 1977 • "Search and Destroy," Asylum, 1977 • *Blood Brothers,* Asylum, 1978 • *The Dictators Go Girl Crazy,* Epic, 1975.

Dream Syndicate: *Medicine Show,* A&M, 1984 • *Tell Me When It's Over: The Best Of,* Rhino, 1992.

Pavlov's Dog: *Pampered Menial,* ABC, 1975 • *At the Sound of the Bell,* CBS, 1976.

Shakin' Street: *Shakin' Street,* CBS, 1980.

Dan Penn

A lthough Dan Penn hasn't produced many records, the ones he has done define not only Southern soul, but blue-eyed soul. They were the first few hits by the Box Tops, the legendary and short-lived band led by reluctant pop icon Alex Chilton. In the twilight of 1967 and the spring of 1968, such Penn-produced Box Tops smashes as "The Letter" (No. 1), "Neon Rainbow," and "Cry Like a Baby" (No. 2) staved off at least some of the second British Invasion even as they defined a new kind of all-American music.

Born November 16, 1941, in Vernon, Alabama, Penn (whose real name is Daniel Pennington) lives in Nashville, where he's building a studio in his basement. He made some good money in his glory days. For some reason he says he's a songwriter more than a producer; among his tunes are "The Dark End of the Street" (immortalized by troubled Memphis soul figure James Carr), "Do Right Woman, Do Right Man" (Aretha Franklin), and "I'm Your Puppet," a smash for James and Bobby Purify.

Penn's chief collaborators have been Chips Moman of Memphis's legendary American Recording Studios (see entry) and Spooner Oldham. Spoon and Penn still tour occasionally, Penn playing acoustic guitar and Spooner on keyboards. A 1991 acoustic gig got Penn a recording contract that resulted in his only available domestic solo album, 1994's beautiful *Do Right Man,* on Sire Records. *Nobody's Fool,* his 1973 solo album, became an instant collector's item; it's now available only as an import.

"I made up my mind a long time ago I wanted to be a songwriter," he says. "I quit gigging around 1965, and I didn't play a true gig again until I went to the Bottom Line in 1991. I got offered a deal to do a record there, so three years later I did the record, so now I've got this little semi-artist thing going again. I enjoy that." Penn and Oldham will "go anywhere," Penn says, noting the pair played the Chicago Blues Festival in early June 1997. Any tapes of those gigs? No, says Penn. "I'm not into flaws," he says. "Not my own, anyway."

To Penn, production means responsibility. "I feel when you say who's produced a record, you say who's responsible for it. I carry that all the way to the material, you know, whether you wrote it or not. If you got the wrong songs—or if you cut the right songs wrong—the responsibility is yours."

Penn is outfitting his basement studio with a drum booth, a piano, a Hammond B3, a vocal booth, an old MCI 600, a 16-track Ampex 2-inch recorder and four D88s, and Tascam digital 8-track units. It will have 16 tracks analog, 32 tracks digital. He'll use it primarily for himself, he says, but he will rent it out.

Besides the Box Tops, Penn produced a Ronnie Milsap record "before he went country" in the early '70s and, in 1995, an album by a singer/pianist from Mobile, Alabama, named Hal Newman. The Newman record was never released.

What continues to be released is Box Tops material. In spring 1997, Arista released *Soul Deep,* a Box Tops compilation that starts with "The Letter," a very brief hit written by Wayne Carson Thompson. Produced by Penn, it was the top single in the country in the fall of 1967. It was produced at American Recording Studios, where Moman had hired Penn to write and produce.

While the Box Tops story is old news to Penn, he still tells it with zest. "I wanted to produce my own record," he says. "I was young and I had written hits and

engineered a hit, so that's why I came to Memphis. I thought I could get a chance to produce at American. I wasn't getting that much encouragement at Fame to produce." Penn was a staffer for owner Rick Hall (see entry) at Fame Studios in Muscle Shoals, Alabama.

"I went to Memphis and started hanging with Chips Moman. We were co-producing, so to speak. I got tired of him producing and me sitting over in a chair going, 'Uh huh.' After about six months of that, I said, 'Look, man, I'm going to stop producing records with you because you're doing the production and I'm just hanging out. I want to cut a record myself. I don't know why, but that's the only thing that's going to make me happy. I got to get my licks in.'

"He says, 'Okay, Penn,' [then] brought this little band in, with Roy Mack, the manager." The singer in this band was not to Penn's liking, however. "He was making kind of a spectacle of himself," so Penn told Mack to bring him another one. A week later, the band reappeared, with Alex Chilton as the singer. "So I gave him a tape that had 'The Letter' on it, and they went off and did it," Penn says. "They came back about two weeks later, we went in and cut it. I put some strings and horns on it, and late at night, we put a jet plane on the end and mixed it down. I didn't know it was going to be that big. I thought it was a pretty good record. It's a pretty good record even today."

After "The Letter" sold 4 million copies, he was under great pressure to come up with a follow-up. "That was my high point as a producer then," he says of that epochal single. "But the very high point was 'Cry Like a Baby,' because 'The Letter' was a fluke until I cut 'Cry.' Then it wasn't a fluke anymore. 'Cry Like a Baby,' in my mind, made me a producer. If you just cut one record and that's all you ever cut, I'd still be walking around going, 'What?' Because there's no verification you know what you're doing. I had to struggle; 'Neon Rainbow' was the second [Box Tops] record, did a half million, nowhere near what 'The Letter' did. That's a failure in the music business. Bell Records wanted another 'Letter.' I said, 'Uh uh, I don't do sequels.' "

After the lesser sales of "Neon Rainbow," Penn began to doubt himself, to second-guess. After "Rainbow," Wayne Carson Thompson's well had run dry. "It was time to cut again, and I couldn't buy a hit," Penn recalls. He set up another Box Tops session, but there were no songs. "So it hit me: 'You're going to have to write the song.' Producing ain't nothing, but writing, you're back against the wall."

So Penn told Spooner Oldham about the jam he was in and they decided to write a song together. "We stayed together for a night and a day, and nothing's happening," Penn says. "We were doing everything to try to make it happen. We tore up paper, threw it in the can, wrote down ideas. The middle of the afternoon of the second day, nothing had happened. We're tired and worn to a frazzle. So we went across the street to have breakfast, at 2 or 3 in the morning.

"We're sitting there all dejected and feeling really bad because we'd failed to do what we had said we could do," Penn continues. "Spooner just put his head over on the table and said, 'I could just cry like a baby.' It just froze me. I said, 'What'd you say, Spooner?' He said, 'I could cry like a baby.' I said, 'Spooner, that's it.'"

They left the booth, "paid some money, said 'keep the change,'" went back across the street to American. "By the time we got to the door, we already had the melody and the first two lines," Penn says. "That was without instruments, just slapping the leg. Suddenly, we were wide awake. I said, 'You run for the organ, I'll run for the machines.' We turned on the lights and the machines, got the mike up, put a roll of 1/4-inch tape on, and we wrote the song while I rolled the tape. Just changed our world completely."

That morning, at 10, the Box Tops cut "Cry Like a Baby," which sold more than a million. "That was my high point," says Penn, "because I say I'm a songwriter first. That entailed everything. It entailed proving I could cut a second record. After I cut that record, I never wondered, was I a record producer?" —CARLO WOLFF

Alaimo, Steve: *Anthology*, Hot Productions, 1997.
Backalley Bandits: *The Backalley Bandits*, London, 1978.
Box Tops: "Neon Rainbow," Mala, 1967 • "The Letter," Mala, 1967 • "Choo Choo Train," Mala, 1968 • "Cry Like a Baby," Mala, 1968 • *Cry Like a Baby*, Bell, 1968 • "I Met Her in Church," Mala, 1968 • *Non Stop*, Bell, 1968 • *The Letter/Neon Rainbow*, Bell, 1968 • *The Ultimate Box Tops*, Warner Special Products, 1987 • *The Best of the Box Tops: Soul Deep*, Arista, 1996.
Burke, Solomon: *Home in Your Heart: Best Of* (2 tracks), Rhino, 1992.
Milsap, Ronnie: *Ronnie Milsap*, Warner Bros., 1971.
Penn, Dan: *Nobody's Fool*, Repertoire, 1973, 1997 • *Do Right Man*, Sire, 1994.
Phillips, Esther: *The Best of 1962–1970*, Rhino, 1997.
Thomas, Irma: *Safe with Me*, Paula, 1981.

Hugo Peretti

See HUGO AND LUIGI

Lee "Scratch" Perry

("THE UPSETTER")

Tomes could not contain the myth, much less the facts, when it comes to the Upsetter, Lee "Scratch" Perry (aka Pipeckck Jackxon). Perhaps Jamaica's most unusual producer, Perry (born 1936 in St. Mary's) began his career like many others, working for Coxsone Dodd (see entry). He rose through the ranks from engineer to arranger to work for Prince Buster, Clancy Eccles, Sonia Pottinger, and Joe Gibbs (see entries) before establishing the Upsetter label with his own productions in 1968. By the end of the 1960s, he was gaining attention with a spate of instrumental releases by a handpicked band dubbed the Upsetters.

Part of Perry's fame came from combining what was undoubtedly the hottest backing band in Jamaica (including the bass-and-drum combination of Aston and Carlton Barrett, the inspiration for the team of Sly and Robbie; see entry) with the hottest vocal group of the day, then known as the Wailers.

Bob Marley, Peter Tosh, and Bunny Livingston had Jamaican hits before Perry, but they moved to the head of the class with Scratch. As their music became more rebellious, this mighty combination of singers, players, and producer forged a sound that laid the foundation for reggae's international acceptance.

The Upsetter's earliest work includes uncredited productions for Coxsone and others. Though technically an engineer, he served as arranger, producer, co-producer, and artist. The name "Scratch" came from one of his early vocals for Dodd, "Chicken Scratch." His other names were earned or picked up along the way.

If ever there was a Jamaican producer who pushed the ever-widening but still proverbial envelope, it was Perry, often brilliant, sometimes mad, eternally fascinating. In 1969, he had a continental hit with "Return of Django," the first in a long line of spaghetti-western theme instrumentals. That year, Perry produced four mainly instrumental Upsetter albums issued in England—*The Upsetter, Return of Django, Clint Eastwood*, and *Many Moods of the Upsetter* (reissued as the two-volume *Best of the Upsetter*).

The following year saw two more Upsetter albums (*Scratch and the Upsetters Again* and *Eastwood Rides Again*). The 1970 Upsetters also served as backing band on two vocal albums produced by Perry: *Prisoner of Love*, which featured soul shouter Dave Barker (half of the duo Dave and Ansel Collins); and the record that changed the face of reggae, *Soul Rebels,* by Bob Marley and the Wailers.

Scratch first worked with the Wailers at Studio One. Though there are really only two albums' worth of Perry-produced Wailers material (and a couple of tracks Marley recorded with Perry years later), the tracks have been endlessly reshuffled and repackaged to create a discographer's nightmare. Early Trojan albums *Rasta Revolution* and *African Herbsman* cover the ground fairly well. A scarce dub of half the tracks (*Soul Rebels Pt. 2*) is not exactly duplicated on the double-album release *Soul Revolution 1 and 2* from the same label. Excluding the dub mixes, the double album *Bob Marley: The Lee Perry Sessions* gathers them all.

In the early '70s, Perry issued over 100 singles in England—and even more in Jamaica—refining his sound from instrumentals to a dub-rooted backing for vocal groups, DJs, and singers (himself included). A long-running series of U.K.-issue artist/producer anthologies took its name (*Tighten Up*) from one of these classic tunes. Perry pumped out his own anthologies (like *Battle Axe*), helped inspire the U.K. lover-rock movement with Susan Cadogan's *Hurt So Good,* and began his early experiments with dub (*Rhythm Shower, Blackboard Jungle Dub*) with the help of mix maestro and fellow musical saboteur King Tubby. He was also the first to record the great U Roy, with "Earth's Rightful Ruler."

In the mid-'70s, Perry set up his own 4-track Black Ark studio and produced a string of incomparable albums for Island records, among them Max Romeo's *War in a Babylon.* With Perry, Romeo made the transition from exploited child singer of semipornographic ditties to Rastafarian prophet with a poetic edge. Perry's own *Super Ape* sets broke new ground for dub, mixing sound effects, echo, and snatches of vocal with ever-advancing power. Perry was moving beyond even Tubby with a dub sound that became instantly identifiable. His sound became increasingly intoxicating, underwater, dense, and masked—and finally began to fray at the edges.

Before this happened he created some of the finest Jamaican recordings ever, including outstanding roots music from singers like Leo Graham, Watty Burnett, the Gatherers, and the Silvertones. Studded throughout the vast number of obscure singles on Justice League, Upsetter, Black Ark, and just plain blank 7-inch singles are gems like "Conscious Man" by the Jolly Brothers, "Think So" by the Meditations, and Mahailia Saunders' "On the Tip of My Tongue." Perry also recorded DJs such as Jah Lion (Jah Lloyd's name when he worked with Scratch) and Prince Jazzbo, who went on to his own production career in the '80s and '90s. Perry's work with sensitive singer Junior Byles alone should earn him a lifetime achievement award for capturing some essence of the human soul on cuts like "Beat Down Babylon," "Place Called Africa," and the deeply moving "Long Way."

The Upsetter's own fame overrode that of many of his artists; as happened with only a handful of other producers, Perry's name, not that of his singers, insured record sales. His solo vocals, on the album *Roast Fish, Collie Weed and Cornbread,* was nonstop and over the top, whether he sang about "Big Neck Police," his "Favorite Dish," or the need to "Throw Some Water in (Your Radiator)." Other great Perry vocals from this time include the dark "Dreadlocks in Moonlight," the marvelous anticlerical "Baffling Smoke Signal" and the vicious "White Belly Rat."

In 1977 Mango released falsetto wonder Junior Murvin's *Police and Thieves.* The title song was to become a punk anthem when covered in the U.K. by the Clash. Like that disc, George Faith's *To Be a Lover* and *Party Time* by the Heptones featured a richly textured mesh of slow hard reggae played by seasoned players like Boris Gardiner, Keith Sterling, and Winston Wright, overlaid with more guitars than you've ever heard in reggae, phase-shifted and flanged to infinity. Faith (soul singer Earl George's nom de Perry) was additionally swathed in the backing vocals of the Meditations and the Mighty Diamonds.

All the best elements of a vocal trio are brought out on the Heptones disc, though the sound is unconventional by any standard. Like the Wailers, the Heptones did a lengthy spell with Coxsone Dodd, but in Perry's hands developed a more militant sound. Group members Barry Llewelyn and Leroy Sibbles both provide excellent tunes. Still, Perry's own "Sufferer's Time" is one of the standout tracks.

"He's amazing," says Heptones lead singer Leroy Sibbles of Perry. "He's one hell of a guy, for real. We did that album *Party Time* for Island records—during all that time the guy, before we were ready for voicing or whatever, would take us to the beach in the morning. I was born in Kingston, Jamaica, and I didn't know there was this place where you have this cave and there's fresh water just a walk away from the beach. He showed us all that and it was like another Christopher Columbus. He call it 'Jah Pool.' 'Let's go have a dip in Jah Pool and bless our spirit before we record.' That's the Upsetter."

Perry's 4-track studio had one of reggae's most distinctive sounds. He also decorated it—walls, door, and windows—in much the same collage-like manner as he did his tracks. Scratch's backyard studio became a personal statement as well as a destination for international artists looking to share in the Perry magic. The air began to thicken.

The free rein of creativity at Black Ark included predigital sampling from nonmusical sources like crying babies and seemingly disconnected snatches of televised or animal sounds, as Perry's behavior became increasingly erratic. After so many years of challenging the accepted, Scratch began to make people damn nervous. The eventual cult classic *Heart of the Congos* was refused by Island, and Perry's public falling-out with Chris Blackwell (see entry; who amazingly never sued him when he issued a 12-inch with the chorus, "Chris Blackwell Is a Vampire"), though not that different from similar severances from Coxsone Dodd or Joe Gibbs, helped end the Black Ark chapter.

Perry defaced and set fire to the studio, cementing his reputation for madness. After the destruction of Black Ark, Perry began a new career as an unpredictable, dadaist word machine, dispensing bizarre interviews and irregular, yet often brilliant, works. In his new persona, he seldom produced any but his own records and often left production of those to others. His lyrics—sometimes scat-babyish punundrums concerned with matters equal part fecal and financial—continued to fascinate a growing cult throughout the '80s and '90s, and his brilliant early productions now fetch among the highest prices in reggae's rapidly rising collectible singles market. Two issues of *The Upsetter* magazine with a thorough discography of singles and albums up to 1970, and a Lee Perry special from Grand Royal with a lengthy biography, timeline, recent interview, and photographs of the remains of Black Ark, attest to his continuing drawing power. So does an anthology Island released in 1997.

In recent years, Perry completed his mythological circuit, marrying a Swiss heiress and retiring, it is said, to a chalet from which he occasionally emerges for interviews, recording with kindred souls like Adrian Sherwood (see entry), even a reunion LP with Coxsone Dodd called *The Upsetter and the Beat.* He's done a series of excellent albums and dub releases with Mad Professor (see entry), who says working with Perry "was like you didn't know what to expect 'cause so many people said so many things. I found Scratch very together, and up to now, he's still very together. For instance, we'd be doing a song and he'd record 13 different vocal tracks. Then later he'd say, 'Okay, let's copy them off,' and he would remember which track had which vocal. Incredible! And you know, when you hear him sing, you can hear, like, the voice of Bob. You can hear that very close Bob Marley connection."

Perry uses his craziness like a shield to ward off intruders while his imagination bubbles. The blithe "I Am a Madman," from 1986's *Battle of Armageddon,* shows he never lost his sense of humor in this regard. A brilliant album for Island/Mango here (i.e., 1990's *From the Secret Laboratory*), a burst of scatological foolishness there, interviews with very little basis in what passes for reality, and reissues galore have helped keep a mystical glow around this enigmatic creative force, who helped turn Jamaican music on its head, then headed for the hills. And to everyone's amazement, Perry recently showed up in California for two well-received live gigs, and is working with the Beastie Boys. —CHUCK FOSTER

Barker, Dave, and the Upsetters: *Prisoner of Love,* Trojan, 1970, 1995.

Brotherhood: "African Freedom," Seven Leaves, 1993 (*Heart of the Ark,* Vol. 2).

Byles, Junior: *Beat Down Babylon,* Dynamic, 1972 • w/ Omar Perry, "The Thanks We Get," Heartbeat, 1985 (*Lee Perry and the Upsetters: Some of the Best*) • *Beat Down Babylon: The Upsetter Years,* Trojan, 1987 • "Long Way," Trojan, 1991 (*Out of Many the Upsetter*) • "Place Called Africa," Trojan, 1991 (*Out of Many the Upsetter*) • *Curly Locks: Best of Junior Byles and the Upsetters,* Heartbeat, 1996.

Cadogan, Susan: *Hurt So Good,* Trojan, 1975, 1995.

Clash, The: *The Clash* (1 track), Epic, 1977 • *Story of the Clash,* Vol. 1, Epic, 1988 • *The Singles,* TriStar, 1996.

Congos, The: *Heart of the Congos,* VP/Blood and Fire, 1977, 1996 • "At the Feast," Trojan, 1990 (*Build the Ark*).

Dub Syndicate: *Research and Development,* On-U-Sound, 1996.

Faith, George: *To Be a Lover,* Mango, 1977.

Graham, Leo: "Voodooism," Pressure Sounds, 1996 (*Lee Perry: Voodooism*).

Heptones, The: "Sufferer's Time/Sufferer's Dub," Island, 1976 • *Party Time,* Mango, 1977.

Heywood, Winston: "Long Long Time," Trojan, 1990 (*Build the Ark*).

Inspirations: "Tighten Up," Trojan, 1994 (*People Funny Boy—Early Recordings*).

Isaacs, David: "Place in the Sun," Trojan, 1994 (*People Funny Boy—Early Recordings*).

Jah Lion: *Colombia Colly,* Mango, 1976 • "Police and Soldier," Mango, 1976 • "Wisdom," Mango/Island, 1982 (*Countryman* soundtrack).

Jolly Brothers: "Cool Down," Seven Leaves, 1993 (*Heart of the Ark,* Vol. 2) • *Conscious Man,* Roots, 1992.

Lee and Jimmy: "Rasta Train," Pressure Sounds, 1996 (*Lee Perry: Voodooism*).

Lewis, Aurelia Aura: *Full Experience,* Blue Moon, 1976.

Marley, Bob, and the Wailers: "Duppy Conquerer," Shelter, 1970 • *Soul Rebels,* Trojan, 1970 • *Bob Marley: The Lee Perry*

Sessions, Konexion, 1973 • *African Herbsman,* Trojan, 1974 • *Rasta Revolution,* Trojan, 1974 • *Soul Revolution 1 and 2,* Trojan, 1988 • *Early Years: 1969–1973,* Trojan, 1993.

Murvin, Junior: "Police and Thieves," Mango, 1977 • *Police and Thieves,* Mango, 1977 • "Tedious," Mango, 1977.

Mystic Eyes: "Forward with Love," Seven Leaves, 1982 (*Heart of the Ark*).

Nicholson, Henrick: "Brotherly Love," Seven Leaves, 1993. (*Heart of the Ark,* Vol. 2).

Perry, Lee: *The Upsetter,* Trojan, 1969 • *Africa's Blood,* Trojan, 1972 • "Dreadlocks in Moonlight," Mango / Island, 1976, 1982 (*Countryman* soundtrack) • "Roast Fish and Corn Bread," Island, 1976 • w/ Kalo Kawongolo and Seke Molenga, *From the Heart of the Congo,* Runnetherlands, 1977 • *Roast Fish, Collie Weed and Cornbread,* Lion of Judah / JA, 1978 • *Revolution Dub,* Anachron, 1979 • *Scratch on the Wire,* Island, 1979 • *The Return of Pipeckck Jackxon,* Black Star Liner, 1980 • w/ the Majestics, *Mystic Miracle Star,* Heartbeat, 1982 • *The Upsetters Chapter One,* Clocktower, 1982 • *Megaton Dub,* Seven Leaves, 1983 • *Megaton Dub 2,* Seven Leaves, 1983 • *Best of One and Two,* Pama, 1984 • *History Mystery Prophesy,* Mango, 1984 • w/ the Silvertones, "Finger Mash," Heartbeat, 1985 (*Lee Perry and the Upsetters: Some of the Best*) • "People Funny Boy," Heartbeat, 1985 (*Lee Perry and the Upsetters: Some of the Best*) • *Time Boom X De Devil Dead,* On-U-Sound, 1987 • *Give Me Power,* Trojan, 1988 • *Meets Bullwackies in Satan's Dub,* ROIR, 1988 • *Satan Kicked the Bucket,* Rohit, 1988, 1990 • *Scratch Attack!,* Clocktower, 1988 • *Excaliburman,* Seven leaves, 1989 • w/ Mad Professor, *Mystic Warrior,* RAS, 1989 • *Open the Gate,* Trojan, 1989 • *From the Secret Laboratory,* Mango, 1990 • *Message from Yard,* Rohit, 1990 • *Public Jestering,* Attack, 1990 • "White Belly Rat," Trojan, 1990 (*Build the Ark*) • *Lord God Muzick,* Heartbeat, 1991 • *Soundzs from the Hot Line,* Heartbeat, 1992 • "You Crummy," Trojan, 1994 (*People Funny Boy—Early Recordings*) • *The Quest,* Abraham, 1995 • *Upsetter in Dub,* Heartbeat, 1997 • *Archive,* Rialto, 1998 • *Dry Acid,* Trojan, 1998 • w/ Mad Professor, *Live at Maritime Hall,* Maritime Hall, 1998.

Perry, Lee, and the Upsetters: *Scratch and the Upsetters Again,* Trojan, 1970, 1995 • *Blackboard Jungle Dub,* Clocktower, 1973 • *Kung Fu Meets the Dragon,* Justice League, 1975, 1995 • *Cloak and Dagger,* Black Art, 1979 • *Some of the Best,* Heartbeat, 1985 • *Upsetter Box Set,* Trojan, 1985 • *Battle of Armageddon,* Trojan, 1986 • *All the Hits,* Rohit, 1989, 1994 • *Build the Ark,* Trojan, 1990 • "Kentucky Skank," Trojan, 1991 (*Out of Many the Upsetter*).

Prince Jazzbo: *Ital Corner,* Clocktower, 1980 • "Croaking Lizard," Mango, 1985 (*Lee Perry: Reggae Greats*).

Prodigal: "4 and 20 Dread Locks," Seven Leaves, 1982 (*Heart of the Ark*).

Righteous: "Them Don't Know Love," Seven Leaves, 1993 (*Heart of the Ark,* Vol. 2).

Romeo, Max, and the Upsetters: *Transition,* Rohit, 1975, 1990 • "One Step Forward," Island, 1976 • "War in a Babylon," Island, 1976 • *War in a Babylon,* Mango, 1976.

Rowe, Keith: "Groovy Situation," Mango, 1985 (*Lee Perry: Reggae Greats*).

Scott, Bunny: "I've Never Had It So Good," Seven Leaves, 1982 (*Heart of the Ark*).

Sibbles, Leroy: "Rasta-Fari," Seven Leaves, 1982 (*Heart of the Ark*).

Silvertones, The: *Silver Bullets,* Trojan, 1973, 1996.

Sixteen, Earl: "Freedom," Seven Leaves, 1993 (*Heart of the Ark,* Vol. 2) • *Phoenix of Peace,* Seven Leaves, 1993.

Smith, Slim: "What a Situation," Trojan, 1994 (*People Funny Boy—Early Recordings*).

Tosh, Peter: *Honorary Citizen,* Legacy, 1997.

Twin Roots: "Jah Say Love," Seven Leaves, 1993 (*Heart of the Ark,* Vol. 2).

U Roy: "Stick Together," Trojan, 1991 (*Out of Many the Upsetter*).

Upsetters, The: *Return of Django,* Trojan, 1969, 1995 • *Eastwood Rides Again,* Trojan, 1970, 1995 • *Rhythm Shower,* Upsetters, 1973 • *Super Ape,* Mango, 1976 • "Three in One," Island, 1976 • *Return of the Super Ape,* Upsetters, 1977 • *Double Seven,* Trojan, 1995.

Wailers, The: "Trenchtown Rock," Island, 1971.

Watty and Tony: "Rise and Shine," Pressure Sounds, 1996 (*Lee Perry: Voodooism*).

Zap Pow: "River Stone (Version)," Pressure Sounds, 1996 (*Lee Perry: Voodooism*) • "River," Pressure Sounds, 1996 (*Lee Perry: Voodooism*).

COLLECTIONS

Battle Axe, Trojan, 1972, 1995.

Scratch and Company Chapter One: The Upsetters, Clocktower, c. 1976.

Africa's Blood, Trojan, 1980, 1995.

The Upsetter Collection, Trojan, 1981.

Give Me Power, 1970–1973, Trojan, 1988.

Magnetic Mirror Master Mix, Anachron, 1989.

Open the Gate, Trojan, 1989.

Version Like Rain, 1972–1978, Trojan, 1989.

Public Jestering, Attack, 1990.

Larks from the Ark: 18 Crucial Tracks from Lee Perry, Artist and Producer, Nektar Masters, 1995.

Words of My Mouth: The Producer Series, Trojan, 1996.

Richard Perry

I n the '70s and '80s, Richard Perry combined the glamour of Hollywood with the attitude of London and Los Angeles to produce chart successes by Ringo Starr, Harry Nilsson, Leo Sayer, Carly Simon, Art Garfunkel, and the Pointer Sisters, among many others.

Born June 18, 1942, in Brooklyn, Perry's prolific career as a hitmaker began in 1968 with Tiny Tim's back-to-the-future hippie paean, "Tip-Toe Thru' the Tulips with Me" (No. 17). Even then, Perry's pop eclecticism was immediately evident when the dapper producer took on projects by Ella Fitzgerald, Fats Domino, Theodore Bikel, Johnny Mathis, and Barbra Streisand, including Streisand's 1970 hit "Stoney End" (No. 6).

Perry's production of *Nilsson Schmilsson* (No. 3) in 1971 was characteristically dramatic, generating such hits as "Without You" (No. 1), a sterling ballad by Badfinger's Pete Ham and Tom Evans; "Coconut" (No. 8), a bouncy slice of fun; and "Jump into the Fire," a churning rocker that showed Nilsson at his most energetic.

Perry's production of Carly Simon's 1972 album *No Secrets* (No. 1) resulted in the revealing "You're So Vain" (No. 1), a song with harmonies by Mick Jagger that was reportedly about actor Warren Beatty.

Perry's profile increased exponentially when he supervised Ringo Starr's 1973 album, *Ringo* (No. 2), which included such hits as "Photograph" (No. 1), "Oh My My" (No. 5), and "You're Sixteen" (No. 1). The ex-Beatle's album garnered heavy publicity because it included guest appearances by Starr's three erstwhile colleagues: John Lennon, Paul McCartney (see entry), and George Harrison. Perry basked in the resultant glow, enabling him to sew up album projects with Art Garfunkel and Andy Williams. Indeed, Perry used his London connections to secure contributions by Harrison and pianist Nicky Hopkins on Williams' *Solitaire* album, giving the veteran crooner a semblance of credibility with the blue jean generation.

Perry's reputation was temporarily marred in 1974 with his production of Martha Reeves' vastly overbudget *Martha Reeves*, a critical and commercial flop. But he rebounded with such hits as Ringo Starr's "No No Song" (No. 3); Burton Cummings' "Stand Tall" (No. 10); and Leo Sayer's "You Make Me Feel Like Dancing" (No. 1), "When I Need You" (No. 1), and "How Much Love" (No. 17).

Perry formed Planet Records in 1979, signing such acts as the Pointer Sisters and Night, a band featuring former Manfred Mann's Earth Band singer Chris Thompson. The Pointer Sisters gave the label its greatest success, scoring a string of 13 Top 40 hits beginning with 1978's "Fire" (No. 2)—a song written by Bruce Springsteen—through "Slow Hand" (No. 2), "I'm So Excited" (No. 9), "Jump (for My Love)" (No. 3), and culminating with "Goldmine" in 1986.

Perry was mostly inactive in the '90s, resurfacing in 1995 to produce the Temptations' *For Lovers Only.* —BEN CROMER

Anders and Poncia: *The Anders and Poncia Album,* Warner Bros., 1969.

Bikel, Theodore: *A New Day,* Elektra, 1969.

Bones, The: *Bones,* Signpost, 1972.

Branigan, Laura: *Laura Branigan,* Atlantic, 1990 • "Moonlight on Water," Atlantic, 1990.

Bryson, Peabo: *Through the Fire,* Columbia, 1994.

Captain Beefheart: *Safe As Milk,* Buddah, 1967, 1970.

Charles, Ray: *My World,* Warner Bros., 1993 • *Genius and Soul: 50th Anniversary Collection,* Rhino, 1997.

Cummings, Burton: *Burton Cummings,* Portrait, 1976 • *My Own Way to Rock,* Portrait, 1977 • "Stand Tall," Portrait, 1978 • *The Burton Cummings Collection,* Rhino, 1994.

DeBarge: "Rhythm of the Night," Gordy, 1985 • *Rhythm of the Night,* Motown, 1985 • *Greatest Hits,* Motown, 1986 • *The Ultimate Collection,* Motown, 1997.

Diamond, Neil: *Primitive,* Columbia, 1984.

Domino, Fats: *Fats Is Back,* Reprise, 1968.

Fanny: *Fanny,* Reprise, 1970 • *Charity Ball,* Reprise, 1971 • *Fanny Hill,* Reprise, 1972.

Fitzgerald, Ella: *Ella,* Reprise, 1969 • *Ella: Things Ain't What They Used to Be (and You'd Better Believe It),* Reprise, 1989.

4 P.M.: *Jackin' Boots,* Reprise, 1991.

Full Swing: *Good Times Are Back,* Planet, 1982.

Garfunkel, Art: *Breakaway,* Columbia, 1975 • "I Only Have Eyes for You," Columbia, 1975 • *Garfunkel: Best Of,* Columbia, 1990.

Hart, Corey: *Attitude and Virtue,* Warner Bros., 1992.

Holy Mackerel: *Holy Mackerel,* Reprise, 1968.

Iglesias, Julio: w/ Diana Ross, "All of You," Columbia, 1984 • *1100 Bel Air Place* (3 tracks), Columbia, 1984 • w/ Willie Nelson, "To All the Girls I've Loved Before," Columbia, 1984.

Jones, Tom: *The Lead and How to Swing It,* Interscope, 1994 • w/ Tori Amos, "I Wanna Get Back with You," Interscope, 1995.

King, Marva: *Feels Right,* Planet, 1981.

LaBelle, Patti: "Oh People," MCA, 1986 • *Greatest Hits,* MCA, 1996.

Manchester, Melissa: *Greatest Hits,* Arista, 1983 • *Essence Of,* Arista, 1997.

Manhattan Transfer: *Coming Out,* Atlantic, 1976 • *Bop Doo Wopp,* Atlantic, 1984 • *Anthology: Down in Birdland,* Rhino, 1992.

Mathis, Johnny: *You've Got a Friend,* Columbia, 1971 • *Music of Johnny Mathis: A Personal Collection,* Legacy/Columbia, 1995.

Medley, Bill: *Right Hee and Now,* Planet, 1982.

Night: "Hot Summer Nights," Planet, 1979 • *Night,* Planet, 1979.

Nilsson, Harry: *Nilsson Schmilsson,* RCA, 1971 • "Without You," RCA, 1971 • "Coconut," RCA, 1972 • "Jump into the Fire," RCA, 1972 • *Son of Schmilsson,* RCA, 1972 • *Songwriter,* RCA, 1972 • "Spaceman," RCA, 1972 • *Son of Dracula* soundtrack, RCA, 1974 • *All Time Greatest Hits,* RCA, 1978.

Osborne, Jeffrey: "You Should Be Mine (The Woo Woo Song)," A&M, 1986.

Phillinganes, Greg: *Pulse,* Planet, 1984.

Pointer Sisters: *Energy,* Planet, 1978 • "Fire," Planet, 1979 • "Happiness," Planet, 1979 • *Priority,* Planet, 1979 • "He's So Shy," Planet, 1980 • *Special Things,* Planet, 1980 • *Black and White,* Planet, 1981 • "Slow Hand," Planet, 1981 • *So Excited,* Planet, 1981 • "American Music," Planet, 1982 • *Greatest Hits,* RCA, 1982, 1989 • "Should I Do It?," Planet, 1982 • *Break Out,* Planet, 1983 • "Automatic," Planet, 1984 • "I'm So Excited," Planet, 1984 • "Jump (for My Love)," Planet, 1984 • "Neutron Dance," MCA, 1984 (*Beverly Hills Cop* soundtrack) • "Baby Come and Get It," Planet, 1985 • *Contact,* Planet, 1985 • "Dare Me," RCA, 1985 • "Freedom," RCA, 1985 • "Goldmine," RCA, 1986 • "Twist My Arm," RCA, 1986 • "All I Know Is the Way I Feel," RCA, 1987 • *Sweet and Soulful,* RCA, 1987 • *The Best of 1978–1981,* RCA, 1993.

Pointer, June: *Baby Sister,* Planet, 1983.

Puckett, Gary: *The Gary Puckett Album,* Columbia, 1971 • *Looking Glass,* Legacy, 1992.

Reeves, Martha: *Martha Reeves,* MCA, 1974.

Ross, Diana: *Baby It's Me,* Motown, 1977 • "Gettin' Ready for Love," Motown, 1977 • *Anthology,* Motown, 1986, 1995.

Saad, Sue, and the Next: *Sue Saad and the Next,* Planet, 1980.

Saffan, Mark: *Mark Saffan and the Keepers,* Planet, 1981.

Sayer, Leo: *Endless Flight,* Warner Bros., 1976 • "Easy to Love," Warner Bros., 1977 • "How Much Love," Warner Bros., 1977 • "Thunder in My Heart," Warner Bros., 1977 • *Thunder in My Heart,* Warner Bros., 1977 • "When I Need You," Warner Bros., 1977 • "You Make Me Feel Like Dancing," Warner Bros., 1977 • *Leo Sayer,* Warner Bros., 1978 • *All the Best,* Gold Rush, 1996 • *The Show Must Go On: Anthology,* Rhino, 1996.

Shepard, Vonda: *The Radical Light,* Reprise, 1992.

Simon, Carly: *No Secrets,* Elektra, 1973 • "The Right Thing to Do," Elektra, 1973 • "You're So Vain," Elektra, 1973 • "Haven't Got Time for the Pain," Elektra, 1974 • *Hot Cakes,* Elektra, 1974 • w/ James Taylor, "Mockingbird," Elektra, 1974 • "Attitude Dancing," Elektra, 1975 • *Playing Possum,* Elektra, 1975 • *The Best Of,* Elektra, 1975 • "Nobody Does It Better," Elektra, 1977 • *Coming Around Again,* Arista, 1987.

Starr, Ringo: "Photograph," Apple, 1973 • *Ringo,* Apple, 1973 • *Goodnight Vienna,* Apple, 1974 • "Oh My My," Apple, 1974 • "You're Sixteen," Apple, 1974 • "It's All Down to Goodnight Vienna/Oo-Wee," Apple, 1975 • "No No Song/Snookeroo," Apple, 1975 • "Only You," Apple, 1975 • *Blast from Your Past,* Gold Rush, 1976, 1996.

Stewart, Rod: "The Motown Song," Warner Bros., 1991 • *Vagabond Heart,* Warner Bros., 1991.

Streisand, Barbra: *Stoney End,* Columbia, 1970 • "Stoney End," Columbia, 1970 • *Barbra Joan Streisand,* Columbia, 1971 • *Live at the Forum,* Columbia, 1972 • *Greatest Hits,* Vol. 2, Columbia, 1978, 1982 • *Emotion* (1 track), Columbia, 1984 • "Emotion," Columbia, 1985 • *Just for the Record,* Columbia, 1991.

Summer, Donna: *All Systems Go,* DGC, 1987 • "Dinner with Gershwin," DGC, 1987.

Temptations, The: *For Lovers Only,* Motown, 1995.

Thompson, Chris, and Night: "If You Remember Me," Planet, 1979.

Tiny Tim: *God Bless Tiny Tim,* Reprise, 1968 • *Second Album,* Reprise, 1968 • "Tip-Toe Thru' the Tulips with Me," Reprise, 1968 • *For All My Little Friends,* Reprise, 1969.

Travis, Randy: "It's Just a Matter of Time," Warner Bros., 1989 • *No Holdin' Back,* Warner Bros., 1989, 1995 • *Greatest Hits,* Vol. 2, Warner Bros., 1992 • *Greatest #1 Hits,* Warner Bros., 1998.

Turner, Tina: *Collected Recordings, Sixties to Nineties,* Capitol, 1994.

Van Eaton, Lon and Derek: *Who Do You Out Do,* A&M, 1975.

Williams, Andy: *Solitaire,* Columbia, 1973.

COLLECTIONS

The Spy Who Loved Me (original soundtrack), Gold Rush, 1977, 1996.

Champ (original soundtrack), Planet, 1979.

James Bond: Best of 30th Anniversary Collection, Capitol, 1992.

For Our Children Too, Rhino, 1996.

Pet Shop Boys

(CHRIS LOWE AND NEIL TENNANT)

Oh, the Pet Shop Boys. At once, their music is detached yet totally connected; decidedly witty yet melancholic; incredibly intellectual yet ultra-hip. Vocalist Neil Tennant (born July 10, 1954, in Gosforth, Tyne and Wear, England) and keyboardist Chris Lowe (born October 4, 1959, in Blackpool, Lancashire), the Londoners who are the Boys, have, since their inception in 1986, been making a fierce brand of melodic, synth-driven post-disco dance music. In so doing, they have also rewritten the rules on what it means to be a pop band. And since the duo is a highly respected production entity, the same could be said about what they've done to the role of the producer.

A chance meeting in an electronics store brought together Tennant, a Polytechnic of North London graduate who majored in history and later took a job as a pop journalist at *Smash Hits,* and Lowe, who studied architecture at Liverpool University. After discovering a mutual love of dance music, they began collaborating on song ideas.

But first they needed a name. So, in typical droll manner, they named themselves after some friends who happened to work in a pet shop. "We thought it sounded like an English rap group," says Tennant. With the arrival of their first single, "West End Girls" (No. 1), the Pet Shop Boys were a pop success. While they had definitely arrived, sitting nicely atop the pop chart, many still considered them a one-hit wonder. Not so.

In 1989, with three albums (*Please,* No. 7; *Actually,* No. 2 U.K.; and *Introspective,* No. 2 U.K.) and one EP (*Disco*) to their credit, the Pet Shop Boys collaborated with Liza Minnelli (and producer/remixer Julian Mendelsohn) on her album, *Results* (No. 6 U.K.). Polished in a glitzy Broadway manner, *Results* surprised many with a clever choice of cover material (Stephen Sondheim's "Losing My Mind; Tanita Tikaram's "Twist in My Sobriety"; Yvonne Elliman's "Love Pains") and Tennant-Lowe originals, including the wry "Rent," which was a hit for the Pet Shop Boys one year earlier. Yes, the production may have been a tad dramatic and excessive, but it fit Minnelli like a form-fitting Halston gown from her Studio 54 days.

Belying their fondness for divas, the Pet Shop Boys connected with another singer who hadn't had a hit in years—Dusty Springfield. Requesting her vocal presence on their "What Have I Done to Deserve This?" (No. 2), the Pet Shop Boys found in her a melodramatic determination. In 1990, they produced half of her album, *Reputation* (No. 18 U.K.). "She's very much a pop singer and her voice instinctively goes very well with our music," explains Tennant. "She looks at making records like climbing a mountain. You have to grind yourself up. It's going to be quite a long journey. . . . " That said, Tina Turner's album, *Wildest Dreams,* contains a song, "Confidential," written and co-produced by the Boys.

Behavior (No. 2 U.K.), the fifth Pet Shop Boys album, was co-produced by Harold Faltermeyer, chosen because the Boys wanted to use old analog synthesizers. This album found the duo leaving their platform shoes behind; the disco ball had been taken down and stored for possible future use. In their place were classical nuances, soundtracky moments, and major bits of bold songwriting. "So Hard" (No. 4 U.K.), "How Can You Expect to Be Taken Seriously?" and "Jealousy" (No. 10 U.K.) dealt with infidelity, pop stars, and jealousy, respectively. In retrospect, says Tennant, "The album was more reflective and more musical-sounding, and it probably didn't have irritatingly crass ideas in it, like our songs often do."

In 1991, the Pet Shop Boys launched their own record label, Spaghetti, with the single "Heaven Must Have Sent You Back to Me" by Cicero. A year later, the label released the soundtrack to the film *The Crying Game,* which featured several Pet Shop Boys productions, including the title track (No. 15), sung by Boy George.

As with *Behavior,* the Pet Shop Boys' next few albums maintained a biting and revelatory mood. There was one major difference, though: the swirling disco ball had been put back into motion. *Very* (No. 1 U.K.), co-produced by Stephen Hague (see entry), is so titled because, as Tennant testifies, "It is very Pet Shop Boys. It's very up, it's very high energy, it's very romantic, it's very sad, it's very pop, it's very danceable, and some of it is very funny."

Midway through the decade, they did their first ever remix of another artist's record—"Girls and Boys," by Blur. "We did it because we thought it would be fun," says Lowe. "And also, because we thought it could be more of a dance track." By 1996, the Pet Shop Boys had released their twelfth album, *Bilingual,* and just as their first album (released 10 years earlier) stretched pop music's boundaries, so too did this one. Such fine purveyors of pop music, those Pet Shop Boys. —LARRY FLICK

Blur: "Girls and Boys" (remix), SBK, 1994.
Bowie, David: "Hallo Spaceboy," RCA, 1996.

Boy George: "The Crying Game," SBK/EMI, 1993 (*The Crying Game* soundtrack).

Boy George and Culture Club: *At Worst . . . The Best of Boy George and Culture Club,* ERG, 1993.

Cicero and Sylvia Mason-James: "Live for Today," SBK/EMI, 1993 (*The Crying Game* soundtrack).

Electronic: "Getting Away with It," Factory/London, 1989, 1997 (*Too Young to Know, Too Wild to Care: The Factory Story, Part 1*) • "Disappointed," Warner Bros., 1992 (*Cool World* soundtrack) • *For You* (EP), Parlophone, 1996.

Minnelli, Liza: *Results,* Epic, 1989.

Pet Shop Boys: *Disco,* EMI America, 1986 • "In the Night," EMI America, 1986 • "Paninaro," EMI America, 1986 • "Paninaro" (remix), EMI America, 1986 • "A New Life," Manhattan/EMI, 1987 • *Actually,* Manhattan/EMI, 1987 • "You Know Where You Went Wrong," EMI America, 1987 • "Always on My Mind," Manhattan/EMI, 1988 • "Do I Have To?," Manhattan/EMI, 1988 • "Domino Dancing," Manhattan/EMI, 1988 • "Heart," EMI America, 1988 • *Introspective,* EMI America, 1988 • "Being Boring," EMI, 1990 • "So Hard," EMI, 1990 • "Bet She's Not Your Girlfriend," EMI, 1991 • *Discography: The Complete Singles Collection,* EMI America, 1991 • "DJ Culture," EMI, 1991 • "How Can You Expect to Be Taken Seriously?," EMI, 1991 • "I Want a Dog," EMI, 1991 • "Jealousy," EMI, 1991 • "Miserablism," EMI, 1991 • "Music for Boys," EMI, 1991 • "Overture to 'Performance'," EMI, 1991 • "Was It Worth It?," EMI, 1991 • "Was It Worth It?" (remix), EMI, 1991 • "Where the Streets Have No Name (I Can't Take My Eyes Off of You)," EMI, 1991 • "Go West," EMI, 1993 • *Relentless* (EP), Parlophone, 1993 • *Very,* EMI, 1993 • "Absolutely Fabulous," EMI, 1994 • "Can You Forgive Her?," EMI, 1994 • "I Wouldn't Normally Do This Kind of Thing," EMI, 1994 • "Liberation," EMI, 1994 • "We All Feel Better in the Dark," EMI, 1994 • "Yesterday When I Was Mad," EMI, 1994 • *Alternative,* EMI America, 1995 • *Disco 2,* EMI, 1995 • *Bilingual,* Atlantic, 1996 • "Se a Vida E," Parlophone, 1996 • "Somewhere," Parlophone, 1997 • *Essential Pet Shop Boys,* EMI, 1998 • "Red Letter Day," Atlantic, 1998.

Springfield, Dusty: *Reputation* (5 tracks), Parlophone/Casablanca, 1990 • *Anthology,* PolyGram, 1997.

Tenaglia, Danny: *Color Me Danny,* Twisted America, 1997.

Thompson, Carroll: "Let the Music Play," SBK/EMI, 1993 (*The Crying Game* soundtrack).

Turner, Tina: *Wildest Dreams,* Virgin, 1996.

Norman Petty

orman Petty, the producer of Buddy Holly's trailblazing efforts of the '50s, was a pioneer of music production. Petty owned the studio in Clovis, New Mexico, that Holly and his band, the Crickets, stumbled upon after Holly was rudely bounced out of Nashville following disastrous sessions with Owen Bradley (see entry) at Bradley's Barn. In retrospect, heading out of area code 615 was the best thing that ever happened to Holly—and to Petty as well.

Born in Clovis in 1927, Petty was a music impresario who dabbled in music, songwriting, arranging, producing, and managing. In fact, he simultaneously managed Holly's career while serving as his producer. The Holly-Petty combination was magical, beginning with a song Holly had cut in Nashville that was deemed a disaster by Music City USA: "That'll Be the Day" (No. 1). Based on a line John Wayne uttered in *The Searchers*, the song was a massive success in Petty's hands because he was able to capture Holly's attitude: a brash but playful persona bubbling with youthful enthusiasm.

Petty also allowed Holly to record at will, giving his prized client the freedom to experiment in the studio. The result was a stream of hits in 1957 and 1958: "Not Fade Away," "Rave On," "Heartbeat," "It's So Easy," "Peggy Sue" (No. 3), and "Words of Love," among them.

"Words of Love" was especially notable because Petty employed overdubbing techniques for the first time, allowing Holly to record both lead and harmony vocals as well as lead and rhythm guitars. "Well, All Right" was another tour de force: this mature effort showed Holly at his peak, with jangling acoustic guitars and syncopated percussion supporting a tender-but-tough vocal.

After Holly's untimely death in a plane crash in February 1959, Petty continued to mine previously unreleased material for new Holly releases. Probably the best Holly track Petty reworked was "Crying, Waiting, Hoping," a demo recorded shortly before Holly's death that harkened back to his early efforts with Petty in Clovis.

Petty produced other hits outside of his work with Holly, including a No. 1 single for Jimmy Gilmer and the Fireballs in 1963: "Sugar Shack." Petty's name, however, will be forever linked to the legacy of Charles Hardin "Buddy" Holly.

Petty died in Holly's hometown of Lubbock, Texas in 1984. —BEN CROMER

Baby: *Baby,* Mercury, 1975.

Beast: *Beast,* Evolution, 1970.

Fireballs, The: *The Fireballs,* Sundazed, 1960, 1996 •
"Torquay," Top Rank, 1959 • "Bulldog," Top Rank, 1960 •
"Quite a Party," Warwick, 1961 • "Daisy Petal Pickin',"
Dot, 1964 • "Bottle of Wine," Atco, 1968 • *Bottle of Wine,*
Stateside, 1968 • *Come On, React,* Atco, 1969 • *Gunshot,*
Sundazed, 1996.

Gilmer, Jimmy, and the Fireballs: "Sugar Shack," Dot, 1963 •
Sugar Shack: The Best Of, Varese Vintage, 1996.

Hester, Carolyn: *At Town Hall,* Bear Family, 1965, 1990.

Holly, Buddy: "Peggy Sue," Coral, 1957 • *Buddy Holly,* Coral,
1958, 1968 • "Rave On," Coral, 1958 • *That'll Be the Day,*
Decca, 1958 • *Reminiscing,* Coral, 1963 • *Buddy Holly*
Collection, MCA, 1993 • *Greatest Hits,* MCA, 1996.

Holly, Buddy, and the Crickets: "I'm Looking for Someone
to Love," Brunswick, 1957 • "Oh, Boy!," Brunswick, 1957
• "That'll Be the Day," Brunswick, 1957 • *The Chirping*
Crickets, Brunswick, 1957 • "Early in the Morning," Coral,
1958 • "Maybe Baby," Brunswick, 1958 • "Think It Over,"
Brunswick, 1958 • "Well, All Right," Coral, 1958 • "It
Doesn't Matter Anymore," Coral, 1959 • *The Buddy Holly*
Story, Coral, 1959 • *The Buddy Holly Story,* Vol 2, Coral,
1960 • *Showcase,* Coral, 1964 • *The Original Voices of*
Crickets, Magnum, 1996.

Knox, Buddy: "Party Doll," Roulette, 1957.

Noland, Terry: *Hypnotized,* Bear Family, 1990.

Norman Petty Trio: *Corsage,* VIK, 1957 • *Moondreams,*
Columbia, 1959 • *Petty for Your Thoughts,* Top Rank, 1960.

Orbison, Roy: *The Very Best Of,* Virgin, 1996.

COLLECTIONS

Rock Around the Clock: The Decca Rock and Roll Collection,
Decca, 1994.

Sam Phillips

S am Phillips is not only a record producer, he's also a
cultural revolutionary. "He started a revolution of
hope," says his son, Knox, and the numerous artists
whose sound he helped birth in the '50s readily agree.
As founder of Sun Records, Phillips gave voice to rock
'n' roll by nurturing talent that wasn't considered bankable by mainstream record companies. "I am very
proud of the things I've done and they way I've done
them," Phillips says. "But that absolutely doesn't mean
I've done it all right."

Born January 5, 1923, in Florence, Alabama, Phillips

got his start in radio in the '40s. "I was lucky to get a
break," says Phillips, who lives in Memphis. "I wasn't a
great announcer, but apparently I could convey something." After garnering experience in his native state, he
relocated to Tennessee and worked for a while at a station in Nashville before settling in Memphis at WRAC.
"I got to work with the big bands here, which we fed to
the networks," he says of working with Tommy and
Jimmy Dorsey and Glenn Miller on shows broadcast
from the Peabody Hotel.

"I had no idea when I was working at the little stations that I would ever see a band, let alone be actually
mixing the sound of a 14- or 15-piece band. "I think that
I was born to be a person that could hear music real
well," Phillips says. "I was a member of a band in high
school and I formed a little 13- or 14-piece small band
out of a 72-piece marching band. I never really cared for
music as a profession because I didn't think I was all that
great."

Despite his early love for music, Phillips originally
aimed to be a criminal defense attorney. "Somehow or
the other, fate just worked it out for me to ultimately
get to do something that I have wound up loving and
appreciating," he says. "Looking back it was probably
the best job that any person could ever have. As hard as
it was, and as many hours as it required, it was also an
absolute joy to do because deep down in my soul I had
an affinity for music and people—especially people who
didn't have the opportunity to express themselves, but
did have the ability. . . ."

The first artists he produced were mostly poor and
black. "They didn't have the opportunity in many ways to
get somebody to listen to them," he says. "I was always
very honest and dealt straight with my artists about what
I heard. . . . I could read people. I knew how difficult it
was to do an audition when you've never seen a studio—
and many of them had not even seen a microphone.

"To be a good producer, you shouldn't miss much of
the potential of the person. Keep in mind that I dealt
with people who had not had any opportunity and that
was the beauty part of it. I just felt like there was a fantastic ocean of untapped talent sitting there, not ready
to be molded, but ready to be cut loose. The worst thing
you can do is overproduce. That's what is happening
today so much. I'm not criticizing. I'm just saying that
that is the one disease that has no place in a studio today
or then."

Phillips began producing acts in his off hours, when
he wasn't working at the radio station. Even before
starting Sun Records in 1950, Phillips was gaining a reputation producing acts for the RPM and Autumn labels.
His early work included B.B. King, Roscoe Gordon, Ike

Turner, and the great Howlin' Wolf. Phillips recorded what many consider the first rock 'n' roll record, "Rocket 88," with Jackie Brenston fronting Ike Turner's Kings of Rhythm, which Phillips licensed to Chess.

"The Rocket 88 Oldsmobile had come out and that's what every person wanted," he recalls. "Ike was playing the piano. It was his band, the Kings of Rhythm, with Ike as lead vocals; later, he started playing guitar and bass. He was a very good musician, but he really could not sing. I said, 'Ike, do you have anybody else in the band [who can sing]? I like the feel of the band a lot, but I haven't found anything vocally that I can do anything with right now.' He said 'Oh, yeah—Jackie.' "

They made the record with Brenston on lead vocals. That made it special—that, and some bad equipment, says Phillips. The police stopped the band on its way to Memphis because the car was too full, but after checking with Phillips, they let the band continue traveling. A little farther up the road, however, the guitar amplifier fell out of the car, bursting the cone. Phillips stuffed a roll of brown paper into the amplifier and got a "rubbing sound" on the session.

Coaxing unique sounds and moving performances became Phillips's trademarks as a producer. During his years at Sun, he produced legendary records by Elvis Presley, Jerry Lee Lewis, Johnny Cash, Roy Orbison, Charlie Rich, and numerous other acts as rock 'n' roll became a dominant force in popular music.

Did Phillips have any idea that Sun would have the impact on music and popular culture that it did? "No, I did not, and I would be absolutely untruthful if I said I did," he admits. "I just knew that there was music in these people and that they had fun.

"There was something about Elvis that was Elvis," Phillips muses. "He just had it. When this guy was entertaining you from that stage, he gave every emotion that was ever possible. Every song he sang hit the audience no matter what song he sang."

Most rock historians consider Elvis's Sun sides, including "Mystery Train," "That's All Right," "Good Rockin' Tonight," and "Blue Moon of Kentucky"—later assembled into the *The Sun Sessions*—as the moment when the rock 'n' roll revolution (as opposed to isolated rock 'n' roll songs) truly began. Many also consider *The Sun Sessions* to be the greatest rock 'n' roll album of all time, with the moment of historical forces colliding as Elvis blended black R&B with white country to create the most important musical alloy of the 20th century.

And all Phillips did was get out of his artists' way. "If my musicians got uptight, my big statement was always, 'If you make a mistake of any sort, I don't care what it is, I want a big one. Don't you hold back to keep from making a mistake,' " he says. " 'You'll kill the feel of the whole damn thing.' "

When time came for Presley to move on, Phillips sold his contract to RCA Records for $35,000. "I sold all the stuff I had on Elvis, all the tapes, everything," he says. "Steve Sholes wanted me to go to work for RCA, but I told him there was no way I could contribute on a major label." Phillips is not a corporate type.

In addition to his Memphis operation, Phillips opened a studio in Nashville in the early '60s. It was run by his protégé, Billy Sherrill (see entry), who went on to become one of Nashville's most successful producers. After he sold that in 1963 or 1964, he can't recall which, he sold Sun in 1969. The buyer was Shelby Singleton.

Phillips sold the studios because he realized he couldn't compete with major labels offering artists he'd nurtured guarantees he couldn't match. "I wish that our system had been a little more forgiving to us smaller people financially, but that's not the way we operate in this democracy," he says. "They had every right to do that. I was smart enough not to stay in there and fight them. Before I threw away money trying to compete with them and lost everything I worked so long and hard to make, [I decided] I will not do it. If I can't do it right, I won't do it at all."

Phillips owns five radio stations and some publishing interests. With the exception of contributing his production skills to a John Prine album his son Knox was working on in 1997, he hasn't produced in years. He finds it hard to release control, he suggests. "I didn't trust anybody at merchandising," he says. "I drove an average of 60,000 to 70,000 miles a year for about seven years during the [Sun heyday]. You get to a point where if you create something, [you're reluctant] to turn it over to somebody; you lose control of what should have been done with that record."

Changes in technology also concern him. He values creativity above all, considers excessive overdubbing the bane of modern recording, and doesn't want to work in the new milieu. "I've just done well and enjoyed life and I'm thankful for it," Phillips says. "Most of all, I'm really thankful for having had the opportunity to play a part in music that has changed the world for the better."
—DEBORAH EVANS PRICE

Adams, Billy: "Betty and Dupree/Got My Mojo Workin'," Sun, 1964 • "Reconsider Baby/Ruby Jane," Sun, 1964 • w/ Jesse Carter, "Trouble in Mind/Lookin' for Mary Ann," Sun, 1964 • "Open the Door Richard/Rock Me Baby," Sun, 1966.

Alton and Jimmy: "Have Faith in My Love/No More Cryin' the Blues," Sun, 1959.

Anderson, Brother James: *I'm Gonna Move in the Room with the Lord/I'm Tired, My Soul Needs Resting,* Sun, 1967.

Anthony, Rayburn: "Alice Blue Gown/St. Louis Blues," Sun, 1959 • "Who's Gonna Shoe Your Pretty Little Feet/There's No Tomorrow," Sun, 1960 • "How Well I Know/Big Dream," Sun, 1962.

Blackwell, Otis: "Breathless," Sun, 1958.

Blake, Tommy: w/ the Rhythm Rebels, "Lordy Hoody/Flat Foot," Sun, 1957 • "Sweetie Pie/I Dig You Baby," Sun, 1958.

Bradford, Walter: "Dreary Nights/Nuthin' But the Blues," Sun, 1952.

Brenston, Jackie: "Rocket 88," Chess, 1951.

Brooks, Dusty, and His Tones: "Heaven or Fire/Tears and Wine," Sun, 1953.

Bruce, Edwin: "Rock Boppin Baby/More Than Yesterday," Sun, 1957 • "Sweet Woman/Part of My Life," Sun, 1958.

Burgess, Sonny: "Red-Headed Woman/We Wanna Boogie," Sun, 1956 • *Ain't Got a Thing/Restless,* Sun, 1957 • "My Bucket's Got a Hole in It/Sweet Misery," Sun, 1957 • "Itchy/Thunderbird," Sun, 1958 • *Classic Recordings, 1956–1959,* Bear Family, 1989 • *We Wanna Boogie,* Rounder, 1990 • *Hittin' That Jug! The Best of Sonny Burgess,* AVI, 1995.

Cagle, Wade, and the Escorts: "Groovey Train/Highland Rock," Sun, 1961.

Cash, Johnny: "Cry! Cry! Cry!/Hey! Porter," Sun, 1955 • "So Doggone Lonesome/Folsom Prison Blues," Sun, 1955 • "Train of Love/There You Go," Sun, 1956 • "Don't Make Me Go/Next in Line," Sun, 1957 • "Thanks a Lot/Luther Played the Boogie," Sun, 1959 • "You Tell Me/Goodbye Little Darlin'," Sun, 1959 • *Up Through the Years, 1955–1957,* Bear Family, 1986 • *The Essential Johnny Cash, 1955–1983,* Legacy, 1992.

Cash, Johnny, and the Tennessee Two: "Get Rhythm/I Walk the Line," Sun, 1956 • "Ballad of a Teenage Queen/Big River," Sun, 1957 • "Home of the Blues/Give My Love a Rose," Sun, 1957 • "Guess Things Happen That Way/Come in Stranger," Sun, 1958 • "I Just Thought You'd Like to Know/It's Just About Time," Sun, 1958 • "The Ways of a Woman in Love/You're the Nearest Thing to Heaven," Sun, 1958 • "Katy Too/I Forgot to Remember to Forget," Sun, 1959 • "Straight As in Love/I Love You Because," Sun, 1959 • "Oh, Lonesome Me/Life Goes On," Sun, 1960 • "Port of Lonely Hearts/Mean-Eyed Cat," Sun, 1960 • "The Story of Broken Heart/Down the Street to 301," Sun, 1960 • "Sugartime/My Treasure," Sun, 1961 • "Blue Train/Born to Lose," Sun, 1962 • "Wide Open Road/Belshazar," Sun, 1964.

Chaffin, Ernie: "Feelin Low/Lonesome for My Baby," Sun, 1957 • "I'm Lonesome/Laughin' and Jokin," Sun, 1957 •

"(Nothing Can Change) My Love for You/Born to Lose," Sun, 1958 • "Don't Ever Leave Me/Miracle of You," Sun, 1959.

Chapel, Jean: "Welcome to the Club/I Won't Be Rockin' Tonight," Sun, 1956.

Clement, Jack: "Ten Years/Your Lover Boy," Sun, 1958 • "The Black Haired Man/Wrong," Sun, 1958.

Climates, The: "No You for Me/Breakin' Up Again," Sun, 1967.

Cotton, James: "Cotton Crop Blues/Hold Me in Your Hands," Sun, 1954 • "My Baby/Straighten Up Baby," Sun, 1954 • *See also* Little Milton.

Crane, Sherry: "Willie, Willie/Winnie the Parakeet," Sun, 1959.

Cunnningham, Buddy: "Right or Wrong/Why Do I Cry?," Sun, 1954.

DeBerry, Jimmy: "Take a Little Chance/Time Has Made a Change," Sun, 1953.

Doctor Ross: "Come Back Baby/Chicago Breakdown," Sun, 1953 • "The Boogie Disease/Jukebox Boogie," Sun, 1954.

Dorman, Harold: "I'll Stick by You/There They Go," Sun, 1961 • "Uncle Jonah's Place/Just One Step," Sun, 1961 • "In the Beginning/Wait 'Til Saturday Night," Sun, 1962.

Earls, Jack, and the Jimbos: "Slow Down/A Fool for Loving You," Sun, 1956.

Emerson, Billy "The Kid": "I'm Not Going Home/The Woodchuck," Sun, 1954 • "No Teasing Around/If Lovin' Is Believing," Sun, 1954 • "Move Baby, Love/When It Rains It Pours," Sun, 1955 • "Red Hot/No Greater Love," Sun, 1955 • "Little Fine Healthy Thing/Something for Nothing," Sun, 1956.

Feathers, Charlie: "Defrost Your Heart/Wedding Gown of White," Sun, 1955.

Five Tinos: "Don't Do That/Sittin' by the Window," Sun, 1955.

Four Upsetters: "Surfin' Calliope/Wabash Cannonball," Sun, 1963 • "Midnight Soiree/Crazy Arms," Sun, 1962.

Garth, Gay, and Handy Jackson: "Got My Application Baby/Trouble (Will Bring You Down)," Sun, 1953.

Gene Lowery Singers: *See* Johnson, Bill; Lewis, Jerry Lee; Richy, Paul; Roberts, Lance; Sheridan, Bobby; Strength, Bill; Wilson, Sonny.

Gordon, Roscoe: "Booted," Chess, 1951 • "Just Love Me Baby/Weeping Blues," Sun, 1955 • "The Chicken (Dance with Love)/Love for You, Baby," Sun, 1955 • "Cheese and Crackers/Shoobie Oobie," Sun, 1956 • "Sally Jo/Torro," Sun, 1958.

Gorgeous Bill: "Carleen/Too Late to Right Wrong," Sun, 1965.

Grayzell, Rudy: "Judy/I Think I Love You," Sun, 1958.

Gunter, Hardrock: "Gonna Dance All Night/Fallen Angel," Sun, 1954.

Haggett, Jimmy: "No More/They Call Our Love a Sin," Sun, 1955.

Harmonica Frank: "The Great Medical Menagerist/Rockin' Chair Daddy," Sun, 1954.

Harris, Ray: *Where'd You Stay the Night?/Come on Little Mama,* Sun, 1956 • "Greenback Dollar, Watch and Chain/Foolish Heart," Sun, 1957.

Hill, Raymond: "Bourbon Street Jump/The Snuggle," Sun, 1954.

Honeycut, Glenn: "I'll Be Around/I'll Wait Forever," Sun, 1957.

Hosea, Don: "Since I Met You/U Huh Unh," Sun, 1961.

Hot Shot Love: "Wolf Call Boogie/Harmonica Jam," Sun, 1954.

Houston, David: "Sherry's Lips/Miss Brown," Sun, 1966.

Howlin' Wolf: "Moaning at Midnight/How Many More Years," Chess, 1951 • *Cadillac Daddy: Memphis Recordings,* Rounder, 1989 • *Memphis Days: Definitive Edition,,* Vol. 1, Bear Family, 1989.

Hunt, D.A.: "Lonesome Ol' Jail/Greyhound Blues," Sun, 1953.

Hunter, John: "Boogie for Me Baby," 4 Star, 1950.

Isle, Jimmy: "I've Been Waiting/Diamond Ring," Sun, 1958 • "Time Will Tell/Without a Love," Sun, 1959 • "What a Life/Together," Sun, 1959.

Jay II, Ira: "You Don't Love Me/More Than Anything," Sun, 1960.

Jean, Bobbie: "Cheaters Never Win/You Burned the Bridges," Sun, 1960.

Jesters, The: "Cadillac Man/My Babe," Sun, 1966.

Jimmy and Walter: "Easy/Before Long," Sun, 1953.

Johnson, Bill: w/ the Gene Lowery Singers, "Bobaloo/Bad Times Ahead," Sun, 1960.

Jones Brothers: "Look to Jesus/Every Night," Sun, 1955.

King, B.B.: "She's Dynamite," RPM, 1951.

Klein, George: "U.T. Party Part I/U.T. Party Part II," Sun, 1961.

Lee, Dickey, and the Collegiates: "Memories Never Grow Old/Good Lovin'," Sun, 1957 • "Fool, Fool, Fool/Dreamy Night," Sun, 1958.

Lewis, Jerry Lee: "Crazy Arms/End of the Road," Sun, 1956 • "Great Balls of Fire/You Win Again," Sun, 1957 • "It'll Be Me/Whole Lot of Shakin' Going On," Sun, 1957 • "Whole Lotta Shakin' Goin' On," Sun, 1957 • "Break Up/I'll Make It All Up to You," Sun, 1958 • "Down the Line/Breathless," Sun, 1958 • "High School Confidential/Fools Like Me," Sun, 1958 • "It Hurt Me So/I'll Sail My Ship Alone," Sun, 1958 • "The Return of Jerry Lee/Lewis Boogie," Sun, 1958 • "Let's Talk About Us/The Ballad of Billy Jo," Sun, 1959 • "Little Queenie/I Could Never Be Ashamed of You," Sun, 1959 • "Lovin Up a Storm/Big Blon' Baby," Sun, 1959 • "John Henry/Hang Up My Rock and Roll Shoes," Sun, 1960 • w/ the Gene Lowery Singers, "Old Black Joe/Baby Baby Bye Bye," Sun, 1960 • "When I Get Paid/Love's Made a Fool of Me," Sun, 1960 • "Bonnie B./Money," Sun, 1961 • "Cold Cold Heart/It Won't Happen with Me," Sun, 1961 • "Save the Last Dance for Me/As Long As I Live," Sun, 1961 • "What'd I Say?/Livin' Lovin Wreck," Sun, 1961 • "I've Been Twistin'/Ramblin Rose," Sun, 1962 • "Sweet Little Sixteen/How's My Ex Treating You," Sun, 1962 • "Good Golly Miss Molly/I Can't Trust Me (in Your Arms)," Sun, 1963 • *Classic,* Bear Family, 1989 • *All Killer No Filler: The Anthology,* Rhino, 1993.

Lewis, Jerry Lee: w/ Linda Gail Lewis, "Teenage Letter/Season of My Heart," Sun, 1963 • "Carry Me Back to Old Virginia/I Know What It Means," Sun, 1965 • *The Sun Story,* Vol. 5, Sun, 1977 • *Up Through the Years, 1958–1963,* Bear Family, 1988 • *Rare tracks,* Rhino, 1989 • *Great Balls of Fire,* Sun, 1997.

Lewis, Linda Gail: "Nothin' Shakin (But the Leaves on the Trees/Sittin and Thinking," Sun, 1963 • *See also* Lewis, Jerry Lee.

Lewis, Sammy, and Willie Johnson Combo: "I Feel So Worried/So Long Baby Goodbye," Sun, 1955.

Little Junior's Blue Flames: "Feelin Good/Fussin' and Fightin' (Blues)," Sun, 1953 • "Mystery Train/Love My Baby," Sun, 1953.

Little Milton: "Beggin' My Baby/Somebody Told Me," Sun, 1953 • "If You Love Me/Alone and Blue," Sun, 1954 • "Homesick for My Baby/Lookin' for My Baby," Sun, 1955 • w/ James Cotton, *Mystery Train,* Rounder, 1990 • *The Sun Masters,* Rounder, 1990.

Load of Mischief: "Back in My Arms Again/I'm a Lover," Sun, 1968.

London, Johnny: "Drivin' Slow/Flat Tire," Sun, 1952.

Louis, Joe Hill: "We All Gotta Go Sometime/She May Be Yours (But She Comes to Me Sometimes)," Sun, 1953 • *The Be-Bop Boy with Walter Horton and Mose Vinson,* Bear Family, 1992.

Marainey, Big Memphis: "Call Me Anything But Call Me/Baby No! No!," Sun, 1953.

McGill, Jerry, and the Topcoats: "I Wanna Make Sweet Love/Lovestruck," Sun, 1959.

Mercer, Will: "You're Just My Kind/The Ballad of St. Marks," Sun, 1959.

Miller Sisters: "Ten Cats Down/Finders Keepers," Sun, 1956 • "There's No Right Way to Do Me Wrong/You Can Tell Me," Sun, 1956.

Nix, Willie: "Baker Shop Boogie/Seems Like a Million," Sun, 1953.

Orbison, Roy: *You're My Baby/Rockhouse,* Sun, 1956 • "Chicken Hearted/I Like Love," Sun, 1957 • "Sweet and Easy to Love/Devil Doll," Sun, 1957 • *For the Lonely: A*

Roy Orbison Anthology, Rhino, 1988 • "Ooby Dooby/Go! Go! Go!," Sun, 1956.

Owen, Mack: "Walkin' and Talkin'/Somebody Just Like You," Sun, 1960.

Parchman, Kenneth: *Love Crazy Baby/I Feel Like Rockin'*, Sun, 1956.

Pendarvis, Tracy: "A Thousand Guitars/Is It Too Late?," Sun, 1960 • "Southbound Line/Is It Me?," Sun, 1960 • "Belle of the Suwanee/Eternally," Sun, 1961.

Penner, Dick: "Your Honey Love/Cindy Lou," Sun, 1957.

Perkins, Carl: "Blue Suede Shoes/Honey, Don't!," Sun, 1955 • "Let the Jukebox Keep on Playing/Gone! Gone! Gone!," Sun, 1955 • "Sure to Fall/Tennessee," Sun, 1955 • "Boppin' the Blues/All Mama's Children," Sun, 1956 • "Honey Don't," Sun, 1956 • "I'm Sorry I'm Not Sorry/Dixie Fried," Sun, 1956 • "Forever Yours/That's Right," Sun, 1957 • "Glad All Over/Lend Me Your Comb," Sun, 1957 • "Matchbox/Your True Love," Sun, 1957 • *Original Sun Greatest Hits*, Rhino, 1987 • *Honky Tonk Gal*, Rounder, 1989.

Peterson, Earl: "Boogie Blues/In the Dark," Sun, 1954.

Pitman, Barbara: "I Need a Man/No Matter Who's to Blame," Sun, 1956.

Poindexter, Doug: "No, She Cares No More for Me/My Kind of Carryin' On," Sun, 1954.

Powers, Johnny: "With Your Love with Your Kiss/Be Mine, All Mine," Sun, 1959.

Presley, Elvis: "Blue Moon of Kentucky," Sun, 1954 • "Good Rockin' Tonight," Sun, 1954 • "I Don't Care If the Sun Don't Shine," Sun, 1954 • "That's Alright Mama," Sun, 1954 • "Baby Let's Play House," Sun, 1955 • "I Forgot to Remember to Forget," Sun, 1955 • "I'm Left, You're Right, She's Gone," Sun, 1955 • "Milkcow Blues Boogie," Sun, 1955 • "Mystery Train," Sun, 1955 • "You're a Heartbreaker," Sun, 1955 • "Blue Moon," Sun, 1956 • "I Love You Because," Sun, 1956 • "I'll Never Let You Go," Sun, 1956 • "Just Becuase," Sun, 1956 • "Trying to Get You," Sun, 1956 • *The Sun Sessions*, Sun/RCA, 1976 • *The Complete Sun Sessions*, RCA, 1987.

Priesman, Magel: "I Feel So Blue/Memories of You," Sun, 1958.

Prisonaires, The: "A Prisoner's Prayer/I Know," Sun, 1953 • "Baby Please/Just Walkin' in the Rain," Sun, 1953 • "My God Is Real/Softly and Tenderly," Sun, 1953 • "There Is Love in You/What'll You Do Next," Sun, 1954.

Randy and the Radiants: "My Way of Thinking/Truth from My Eyes," Sun, 1965 • "Peel-a-Boo/Mountain High," Sun, 1965.

Rhodes, Slim: "Don't Believe/Uncertain Love," Sun, 1955 • "The House of Sin/Are You Ashamed of Me?," Sun, 1955 • "Gonna Romp and Stomp/Bad Girl," Sun, 1956 • "Take and Give/Do What I Do," Sun, 1956.

Rhythm Rockers: "Fiddle Bop/Jukebox Help Me Find My Baby," Sun, 1956.

Rich, Charlie: "Lonely Weekends," Philips International, 1960 • *Lonely Weekends: Best of the Sun Years*, AVI, 1996 • *Feel Like Going Home: The Essential*, Legacy/Columbia, 1997.

Richardson, Rudi: "Fools Hall of Fame/Why Should I Cry?," Sun, 1957.

Richy, Paul: w/ the Gene Lowery Singers, "The Legend of the Big Steeple/Broken Hearted Willie," Sun, 1960.

Riley, Billy Lee, and His Little Green Men: "Trouble Bound/Rock with Me Baby," Sun, 1956 • "Flying Saucer Rock and Roll/I Want You Baby," Sun, 1957 • "Red Hot/Pearly Lee," Sun, 1957 • "Baby, Please Don't Go/Woulnd't You Know," Sun, 1958 • "No Name Girl/Down by the Riverside," Sun, 1959 • "One More Time/Got the Water Boilin Baby," Sun, 1959 • *Classic Recordings, 1956–1960*, Bear Family, 1990.

Ripley Cotton Choppers: "Blues Waltz/Silver Bells," Sun, 1953.

Roberts, Lance: w/ the Gene Lowery Singers, "The Good Guy Always Wins/The Time Is Right," Sun, 1960.

Rockin' Stockings: "Yulesville USA/Rockin' Old Lang Syne," Sun, 1960.

Rossini, Tony: "I Gotta Know (Where I Stand)/Is It Too Late?," Sun, 1960 • "Well I Ask Ya/Darlene," Sun, 1961 • *(Meet Me) After School/Just Around the Corner*, Sun, 1962 • "Nobody/Moved to Kansas City," Sun, 1964.

Rossini, Tony, and the Chippers: "You Make It Sound So Easy/New Girl in Town," Sun, 1962.

Self, Mack: "Every Day/Easy to Love," Sun, 1957.

Seratt, Howard: "Troublesome Waters/I Must Be Saved," Sun, 1954.

Sheridan, Bobby: w/ the Gene Lowery Singers, "Sad News/Red Man," Sun, 1960.

Simmons, Gene: "Drinkin Wine/I Done Told You," Sun, 1958.

Sisk, Shirley: "I Forgot to Remember to Forget/Other Side," Sun, 1961.

Smith, Ray: "So Young/Right Behind You Baby," Sun, 1958 • "Why, Why, Why/You Made a Hit," Sun, 1958 • "Sail Away/Rockin Bandit," Sun, 1959 • "Travelin Salesman/I Won't Miss You ('til You Go)," Sun, 1961 • "Candy Doll/Hey, Boss Man," Sun, 1962.

Smith, Warren: "Black Jack David/Ubangi Stomp," Sun, 1956 • "Rock and Roll Ruby/I'd Rather Be Safe Than Sorry," Sun, 1956 • "Got Love It You Want It/I Fell in Love," Sun, 1957 • "So Long I'm Gone/Miss Froggie," Sun, 1957 • "Goodbye Mr. Love/Sweet Sweet Girl," Sun, 1959 • *The Classic Recordings, 1956–1959*, Bear Family, 1992.

Smokey Joe: "The Signifying Money/Listen to Me Baby," Sun, 1964.

Snow, Eddie: "Ain't That Right/Bring Your Love Back Home to Me," Sun, 1955.

Stinit, Dane: "Don't Knock What You Don't Understand/Always on the Go," Sun, 1966 • "That Muddy Ole River (Near Memphis Tennessee)"/"Sweet Country Girl," Sun, 1967.

Strength, Bill: w/ the Gene Lowery Singers, "Senorita/Guess I'd Better Go," Sun, 1960.

Sun Rays: "Love Is a Stranger/The Lonely Hours," Sun, 1958.

Taylor, Vernon: "Breeze/Today Is a Blue Day," Sun, 1958 • "Sweet and Easy to Love/Mystery Train," Sun, 1959.

Teenangels, The: "Ain't Gonna Let You (Break My Heart)/Tell Me My Love," Sun, 1963.

Thomas, Jr., Rufus: "Bear Cat (The Answer to "Hound Dog")/Walkin in the Rain," Sun, 1953 • "Tiger Man (King of the Jungle)/Save That Money," Sun, 1953.

Turner, Ike, and the Kings of Rhythm: *Kings of Rhythm,* Flyright, 1981.

Wade and Dick: "Bop, Bop Baby/Don't Need Your Lovin' Baby," Sun, 1957.

Wheeler, Onie: "Jump Right Out of This Jukebox/Tell 'Em Off," Sun, 1959.

Williams, Jimmy: "Please Don't Cry over Me/That Depends on You," Sun, 1957.

Wilson, Sonny: w/ Gene Lowery Singers, "The Great Pretender/I'm Gonna Take a Walk," Sun, 1960.

Wimberly, Maggie Sue: "Daydreams Come True/How Long," Sun, 1955.

Wood, Anita: "I'll Wait Forever/I Can't Show How I Feel," Sun, 1961.

Wood, Bobby: "Human Emotions/Everybody's Searchin," Sun, 1961.

Yates, Bill: w/ His T-Birds, "Don't Step on My Dog/Stop Wait Listen," Sun, 1964 • "Big Big World/I Dropped My M&M's," Sun, 1966.

Yelvington, Malcolm: w/ the Star Rhythm Boys, "Drinkin' Wine Spo-Dee-O-Dee/Just Rollin Along," Sun, 1954 • "Rockin' with My Baby/It's Me Baby," Sun, 1956.

COLLECTIONS

Blue Flames: Best of the Sun Years, Rhino, 1990.
Memphis Ramble: Sun Country Collection, Vol. 1, Rhino, 1990.

Robert Plant

See JIMMY PAGE AND ROBERT PLANT

Chuck Plotkin

Scholar, musician, label executive, and confidant to superstars, Chuck Plotkin has quietly created an enormously important body of work over the last 25 years. He produced and helped to launch the careers of singer/songwriters Wendy Waldman and Karla Bonoff in the early '70s. As head of A&R for David Geffen's Asylum label in the mid-'70s he had artistic and commercial success with Andrew Gold and, particularly, Orleans. Plotkin began his most important and enduring affiliation—with Bruce Springsteen—in the late '70s when he came to the rescue during the mixing of *Darkness on the Edge of Town;* he has co-produced every Springsteen album since, including the recent *Tracks* compilation. Plotkin has also produced exceptional music for Bob Dylan, Dan Bern, Bette Midler, Tommy Tutone, and Dwight Twilley.

Charles Plotkin was born in the mid-'40s and raised in the Beverlywood and Westwood areas of Los Angeles. There were all kinds of music in the house: his father had been a musician, but young Chuck's favorites were rock 'n' roll, folk, and R&B. Plotkin played guitar, bass, keyboard, drums, and banjo in various ensembles at University High, and then at Claremont College in Pomona. In college, Plotkin played in a jug band that exists to this day.

After graduating from Claremont with a degree in philosophy and literature, Plotkin attended and completed law school at USC. Part of Plotkin's law school curriculum included providing counseling through the USC Law Center, and soon musician friends—and friends of friends—were coming in seeking advice on music business-related matters.

"Through that I realized that there were a lot of dishonest creeps who didn't like artists in the record business." Plotkin also came to the realization that he was not a great musician, singer, or songwriter, and that he would "rather help someone make a great record than make mediocre music of my own. It wasn't a sour compromise, but a glorious revelation that I could make a living in music helping people instead of being a lawyer or a businessman."

Toward the end of his second year of law school, Plotkin was in a restaurant in Venice when the waitress came up to him and said, "Normally I sing when I'm through waiting on people, but since you're the only one here, I won't sing if you don't want me to." He encouraged her to sing. "She knocked me out. She did some old blues stuff, some songs we had done in the jug band, and then some songs I didn't know, which it turned out she had written. Her name was Wendy Waldman," Plotkin says.

"One night, after about the third or fourth time I had seen her, we started talking after the show and became friends. I told her she should be doing something more than singing for people eating dinner. We put a band together called Bryndle: Wendy Waldman, Andrew Gold, Kenny Edwards [from Stone Poneys], and Karla Bonoff. All acoustic. We added a drummer at some point. That was my first thing: helping Wendy get a band together, then helping the band get the music together, then trying to get a record deal," he says.

"I graduated from law school and I didn't take the bar," he continues. "I figured I had a few months before the band would break up, and I really wanted to see if I could make it at this business. We did a showcase at the Troubadour and got a deal with A&M; they wouldn't let me produce the first record because I hadn't produced anything yet. During the recording the producer was weak: he would say, 'Great!,' but I knew it wasn't working.

"The company didn't like the record. I said, 'I know what went wrong—let me fix it. Give me one weekend in a studio, let me choose the songs, and let me do them the way I want to do them.' We worked our butts off, rehearsed a lot for a few weeks, went into the studio and cut eight new songs on a Saturday and mixed them on Sunday. A&M loved it, but Lou Adler [see entry] also loved it and said he wanted to produce them. I said, 'Don't make the same mistake again! The reason you want to go ahead is the work I did in two days.' But they wouldn't listen. Lou cut some stuff with them and it was all right, but it was never released.

"As far as being a producer, I just bought a hat and wrote 'Producer' on it. I became fanatically engaged in the process. After the A&M experience, I wanted to do my own thing and then turn it into a label. If they liked it, great; if not, fine. I built a studio in Hollywood, called Clover, with a friend from law school who had a little bit of money. We built the board, the faders, everything from scratch. We had enough customers for it to pay for itself right from the beginning. Unfortunately by then the band had broken up: too many writers," he says.

With the luxury of his own studio, Plotkin set about to record Wendy Waldman's first solo album in 1973. "We cut Wendy's debut solo album in that little studio for $7,000 (plus studio costs) over a period of about six months. I went to Warner Bros. with it and they said, 'We don't know how we are going to market this, but we'll put it out—it's brilliant.' That was my production

debut. We got great press, including Stephen Holden's lead review in *Rolling Stone* calling it the 'debut of the year.' He heard everything that we were trying to do. We didn't sell many records though, maybe 5,000 copies.

"Next I did a record for David Geffen's Asylum label with Steve Ferguson—a great talent, but he didn't fit any of the boxes and slipped through the cracks. I feel deeply responsible for helping the artist find a way to connect with the right audience, and in that case it didn't happen. I've had many sleepless nights wondering if there was something more I could have done to help a record get its fair shot in the world. That doesn't necessarily have to do with sales: Wendy's only sold 5,000, but it communicated deeply with a certain audience and launched her career," he says.

"Then I did a Rod Taylor record. Though none of these sold much, Geffen told me, 'None of the things you have come up with haven't interested me. You have impeccable taste.' We talked over a period of months, and then he hired me to run A&R for Asylum," says Plotkin.

Plotkin had his first commercial success at Asylum. He produced the timeless pop of Andrew Gold's first solo album in 1975, an album blessed with Gold's sweet but never cloying voice and sharp, tuneful songwriting. It was Plotkin's first foray into the album charts (albeit the lower end), but that same year he penetrated deep into the album and singles charts with Orleans, a plucky folk-rock group from New York led by singer/guitarist/songwriter John Hall.

"Orleans had made two records already for ABC, and those hadn't been successful. I saw the band live and couldn't believe they were being dropped. I got a hold of the first two records (the second one wasn't even going to be released) to see what had gone wrong. Everything was almost, but not quite, right: the songs, vocals, tempos, arrangements. If each is 90 percent right, and you start multiplying .9 by .9 by .9, pretty soon you end up down in the 70 percent range, and that doesn't cut it. 'Dance with Me' had been recorded for the second record, but the tempo was wrong and it didn't have much vitality. We rearranged it and recut it, and when it hit [No. 6] I was so relieved. Finally something worked in the real world. It meant that I probably knew what I was doing. It also gave me some credibility in the industry and people didn't think David was so crazy for hiring me.

"I met Jon Landau [see entry] when he came out to California to produce a Jackson Browne album for Asylum in 1976; I helped him some with the record and we became friends. I got a call from him in early 1978. He was working with Bruce Springsteen on *Darkness,* and they were having some problems with the mixing, which was more from exhaustion than anything else; they had been working on it for 18 months. He said the sound was veering between 'dull' and 'shrill,' and would I come by and give it a listen. I said, 'Sure.' I was in New York on Asylum business and I went into the studio a couple of nights after work, and with my fresh ears, I was able to help them mix the album. The chemistry between us was really good. I left Asylum to finish this record with Bruce and I haven't regretted it for a minute," he states emphatically.

"After that Bruce helped me get an independent production deal with Columbia in the early '80s. I did Tommy Tutone and Bob Dylan there in 1981," he says. Plotkin produced the catchy new wave of *Tommy Tutone 2* (No. 20), featuring the smash "867-5309/Jenny" (No. 4) and Bob Dylan's *Shot of Love.* Included on *Shot* is the powerful and moving "Every Grain of Sand."

"Early in the process I realized things were going to be different," says Plotkin. "Bob doesn't like to use headphones—one of the reasons the record sounds like it does is that there were live monitors out in the studio. I realized that I couldn't speak over the monitors, so I figured I'd go out there, get on a tambourine or a conga drum and just be out there. We weren't doing takes, I just ran the tape the whole time," he says.

"On 'Every Grain of Sand,' Bob sat down at the piano and started to play. I didn't know if he was going to sing, but there was no microphone at the piano. I grabbed a mike out of a stand, leaned out in front of him, and held the mike while he sang. That was the take we used.

"All you're ever really doing as producer is being a kind of midwife. You have to do different amounts and different kinds of things for different artists at different times. Sometimes you do what looks like a good deal, and sometimes you do nothing—just be a witness or hold a mike.

"The producer's contribution varies so much: there were days on [Springsteen's] *The Ghost of Tom Joad* (No. 11) when all I would do is play [Plotkin is credited with keyboards on "Youngstown"]. Other times there were serious discussions about what songs fit into what the album is essentially about. Part of what you bring to a project is the enthusiasm of a fan. That's why I don't work on anything that I don't really love," he says.

"With a Bruce record, we take a week or two in the middle of a production and just listen to what we have done so far: switch from being the artist to being a listener, from cooking to eating. It's important to get out of the micro and get a macro view. It's good to blow out

some real hard work in an almost orgiastic frenzy and then just stop for a while and listen.

"The *Tom Joad* record is extraordinary. [Academy Award winner] 'Streets of Philadelphia' (No. 9) and 'Secret Garden' are something too. Bruce is still doing stunning things after 25 years. With Bruce now, the power doesn't come from noise, it comes from the density of the writing, the characters, the stories. His songs are like a collection of short stories, with the music being part of the story. He has found his voice again, and I'm proud to be a part of it," he concludes. —Eric Olsen

Alexander, Karen: *Isn't It Always Love,* Asylum, 1975.

Allan, Laura: *Laura Allan,* Elektra, 1978.

Bern, Dan: *Dan Bern,* Work, 1993, 1997 • *Dog Boy Van* (EP), Work, 1997.

Chapin, Harry: *Living Room Suite,* Elektra, 1978 • *The Gold Medal Collection,* Elektra, 1988.

Dylan, Bob: *Shot of Love,* Columbia, 1981 • *Bootleg Series,* Columbia, 1991 • *Greatest Hits,* Vol. 3, Columbia, 1995.

Ferguson, Steve: *Steve Ferguson,* Asylum, 1973.

Floating House Band: *Floating House Band,* Takoma, 1972.

Gold, Andrew: *Andrew Gold,* Asylum, 1975 • "That's Why I Love You," Asylum, 1975 • *Thank You for Being a Friend: The Best Of,* Rhino, 1997.

Hall, John: *John Hall,* Asylum, 1978.

Idle Tears: *Idle Tears,* MCA, 1986.

Jelly: *A True Story,* Asylum, 1979.

Lawrence, Doc: *Doc Lawrence,* Chameleon, 1992.

Midler, Bette: "Favorite Waste of Time," Atlantic, 1983 • *No Frills,* Atlantic, 1983 • "Beast of Burden," Atlantic, 1984 • *Experience the Divine—Bette Midler's Greatest Hits,* Atlantic, 1993.

Olsson, Kai: *Once in a While,* EMI, 1975.

Orleans: "Dance with Me," Asylum, 1975 • "Let There Be Music," Asylum, 1975 • *Let There Be Music,* Asylum, 1975 • "Still the One," Asylum, 1976 • *Waking and Dreaming,* Asylum, 1976 • "Reach," Asylum, 1977 • *Still the One,* Elektra, 1990.

Scialfa, Patti: *Rumble Doll,* Columbia, 1993.

Shakers: *Yankee Reggae,* Asylum, 1976.

Sonia Dada: *My Secret Life,* Capricorn, 1998.

Springsteen, Bruce: "Fade Away," Columbia, 1980 • "Hungry Heart," Columbia, 1980 • *The River,* Columbia, 1980 • *Nebraska,* Columbia, 1982 • "Born in the U.S.A.," Columbia, 1984 • *Born in the U.S.A.,* Columbia, 1984 • "Cover Me," Columbia, 1984 • "Dancing In the Dark," Columbia, 1984 • "Pink Cadillac," Columbia, 1984 • "Glory Days," Columbia, 1985 • "I'm Goin' Down," Columbia, 1985 • "I'm On Fire," Columbia, 1985 • "My Hometown," Columbia, 1985 • w/ the E Street Band, *Live 1975–1985,* Columbia, 1986 • "Merry Christmas Baby,"

Columbia, 1986 • w/ the E Street Band, "War," Columbia, 1986 • "Brilliant Disguise," Columbia, 1987 • "Fire," Columbia, 1987 • "Tunnel of Love," Columbia, 1987 • *Tunnel of Love,* Columbia, 1987 • *Chimes of Freedom* (EP), Columbia, 1988 • "I Ain't Got No Home," Columbia, 1988 (*Folkways: A Tribute to Woody Guthrie and Leadbelly*) • "One Step Up," Columbia, 1988 • "Vigilante Man," Columbia, 1988 (*Folkways: A Tribute to Woody Guthrie and Leadbelly*) • "Viva Las Vegas," NME, 1990 (*The Last Temptation of Elvis*) • "57 Channels (and Nothin' On)," Columbia, 1992 • *Human Touch,* Columbia, 1992 • "Human Touch/Better Days," Columbia, 1992 • *Lucky Town,* Columbia, 1992 • "Streets of Philadelphia," Epic, 1993 (*Philadelphia* soundtrack) • *Greatest Hits,* Columbia, 1995 • "Secret Garden," Columbia, 1995 • *The Ghost of Tom Joad,* Columbia, 1995 • *Tracks,* Columbia, 1998.

Taylor, Rod: *Rod Taylor,* Asylum, 1973.

Tommy Tutone: *Tommy Tutone 2,* Columbia, 1981 • "867-5309/Jenny," Columbia, 1982.

Twilley, Dwight: *Scuba Diver* (2 tracks), EMI America, 1982 • *The Great Lost Twilley Album* (1 track), Shelter, 1993 • *XXI,* The Right Stuff, 1996.

Waldman, Wendy: *Love Has Got Me,* Warner Bros., 1973 • *Gypsy Symphony,* Warner Bros., 1974 • *Love Is the Only Goal: The Best of Wendy Waldman,* Warner Archives, 1996.

COLLECTIONS

The Wizard of Oz In Concert: Dreams Come True, Rhino, 1996.

Richard Podolor

It could be argued that Richard Podolor has spent his entire life in the studio. While other kids his age were playing baseball and chasing girls, he was soldering together consoles and playing piano and guitar (he studied classical guitar with Vicente Gomez). From his early career as an L.A. session guitarist, recording artist, and studio owner (American Recording Company, established with his parents Mike and Ethel in 1958), through his stint in the army, where he gave over 400 classical guitar concerts, to his production work with Three Dog Night, Steppenwolf, Iron Butterfly, the Souther Hillman Furay Band, Phil Seymour, 20/20, and Gwen Mars, Podolor has had a remarkably long and successful career in the music industry.

That said, in Podolor's eyes, there is barely a rule book to follow. "The rule book is just partially existent

and you gotta go out on a limb every so often," he says. "The only guarantee is that if you play it safe you'll never get anywhere. That is a guarantee. Everything I've ever done in this business has always been going out on a limb, taking a chance, doing something everybody else says absolutely don't do. You have to sit there and make up your own mind. Any time you try something new, you're going to get opposition. Unfortunately, that's the name of the game."

In addition to his classical studies, Podolor played guitar in country bands, and at 16 (in 1957) he played on his first hit record, Bonnie Guitar's "Dark Moon." At 17 he played on Ned Miller's "From a Jack to a King," which went Top 10 country when it was re-released in 1962. As a session man and engineer at American, Podolor worked on such smash hits as "Teen Beat" and "Let There Be Drums" by Sandy Nelson, "Alley Oop" by the Hollywood Argyles, and "Cherry Pie" by Skip and Flip. Not content to just be a sideman, under the nom de plume "Richie Allen," Podolor released a string of successful surf albums in the early '60s, including the hit single "Stranger from Durango."

Throughout the '60s Podolor found himself in the studio either as an engineer or as a musician with such acts as the Electric Prunes, Paul Williams, the Grateful Dead, the Turtles, Donovan, and the Monkees. He got his first official producer's work at the dawn of the '70s working with Steppenwolf and Three Dog Night. He struck gold with 12 Top 20 Three Dog Night hits, including No. 1's "Mama Told Me Not to Come," "Joy to the World," and "Black and White"; and Top 5's "An Old Fashioned Love Song," "Never Been to Spain," and "Shambala." Podolor's work with the band makes up the core of their vastly underappreciated canon.

Around the same time as he was working with Steppenwolf and Three Dog Night, Podolor kept busy with albums by Blues Image (including the classic single "Ride Captain Ride," No. 4), Iron Butterfly, the Dillards, and a solo album by Steppenwolf's lead singer John Kay. *Billboard* recognized his production success in 1970, ranking him the No. 4 producer in the country. In 1974 Podolor produced a gold album for the Souther Hillman Furay Band, and in the early '80s he recorded two of power pop's finest albums: Phil Seymour's first solo album (with the great "Precious to Me"), and 20/20's second album, *Look Out!*

As Podolor explains, his success has not been a fluke. "I enjoy what I do, I enjoy music and I love hit records. I always had an affinity for recording hit records," he says. "The four-minute package does something to your emotions, so I'm always in search of something that does something musically." Then again, he jokes, if he knew what made a hit record, "I'd have it in the computer by the morning and you could buy it on a floppy."

The truth of the matter is quite simple, he insists. "In all honesty, I just grew up with it. First of all, it's something I can't wait to hear again and I'm not bored with it. I get very moved about music. The particular notes put together in a certain way will actually affect a person emotionally, especially me. Ironically, what I like a great part of an audience likes, a commercial audience. And it's never changed over the years I've been making records."

While he has had tremendous success once the music is out, it hasn't always been that simple in the studio. "It was stressful to cut certain albums with certain projects," he explains. "As an engineer I did one of the Grateful Dead albums, and everything was so slow and laid back and there was very little charisma involved in the whole project. Then you do a Three Dog Night album and you got three lead singers—each one has a different vocal style—and you're sharing the backup band. One moment it's absolutely insane and the next moment you're discussing a fishing trip."

Just as there is no rule book, in Podolor's past there has not been much consistency as far as session vibe. "I've done so many albums, each one has its own experience," he says. "But when they say, 'no pain no gain,' I really believe it. When things get comfortable, when everything does fall into place, I kind of get a little nervous, a little skeptical, because it's almost too easy and I know it should not be that easy. Sometimes I'll even make it hard, I'll create some kind of an obstacle.

"I always try to put 10 percent misery into all my work," he continues with a laugh, "90 percent is fine, I'll go by the book, I'll do whatever I learn, but I'll always try to put something a little fresh in that's an obstacle. If you get around it you created something new in order to do so. That's kind of a little bit of, I guess, a policy."

Along with his lifelong friend and engineer Bill Cooper, Podolor has kept American Recording Company and his production career humming along. Through trial and error, success and failure, he's learned some very important lessons. As an example he points to some of his earliest sessions where he'd walk in with strict ideas about the song, the guitar riffs, and the sound. "I never worked off chemistry in the beginning," he says. "I found out years later that my best work was when I just played the guitar. I played on a lot of those records, but I never even want the credit for it, because the best is to sit back, get a perspective, and get the best out of the band. I always try to take whatever's given to me, the tools in any band and any project, and try to get the best out of them. Some of the finest records, if I

ever did any that good, were not made with necessarily great musicians. Usually on the contrary, it's just the way they interplay and the simplicity." —DAVID JOHN FARINELLA

Alcatrazz: *Dangerous Games*, Capitol, 1986.

Alice Cooper: *Special Forces*, Warner Bros., 1981.

Allen, Richie: "Stranger from Durango," Imperial, 1960 • *Stranger from Durango*, Imperial, 1962 • *Surfer's Slide*, Imperial, 1963 • *The Rising Surf*, Imperial, 1963.

Appice, Carmine: *Carmine Appice*, Pasha/WEA, 1981 • *Rockers*, Pasha/WEA, 1981.

Black Oak Arkansas: *Ain't Life Grand*, Atco, 1975 • "Strong Enough to Be Gentle," MCA, 1975 • *X-Rated*, MCA, 1975 • *Best Of*, Atco, 1977 • *Hot and Nasty: The Best Of*, Rhino, 1993.

Blues Image: *Open*, Atco, 1970 • *Red White and Blues Image*, Atco, 1970 • "Ride Captain Ride," Atco, 1970.

Burnette, Billy: "Try Me," MCA, 1986 • *Try Me*, MCA, 1986.

Cameron, Jeff: *Out of the Blue*, Sonic Atmospheres, 1991.

Dillards, The: *Roots and Branches*, Anthem, 1972.

Glass Family: *Electric Band*, Warner Bros., 1967.

Gwen Mars: *Magnosheen*, Hollywood, 1995.

Head East: *Gettin' Lucky*, A&M, 1977.

Iron Butterfly: "Easy Rider (Let the Wind Pay the Way)," Atco, 1970 • *Live*, Atco, 1970 • *Metamorphosis*, Atco, 1971 • *Light and Heavy: The Best Of*, Rhino, 1993.

Jellyroll: *Jellyroll*, MCA, 1970.

Kay, John: *My Sporting Life*, ABC/Dunhill, 1973.

Kay, John, and Steppenwolf: *Wolftracks*, Allegiance, 1983.

Rowan Brothers: *The Rowans*, Asylum, 1975.

Rubicon: *American Dreams*, 20th Century, 1980.

S.S. Fools: *S.S. Fools*, CBS, 1976.

Seymour, Phil: *Phil Seymour*, Boardwalk, 1980 • "Precious to Me," Boardwalk, 1981 • *Phil Seymour 2*, Boardwalk, 1982 • *Precious to Me*, The Right Stuff, 1996.

Souther Hillman Furay Band: "Fallin' in Love," Asylum, 1974 • *The Souther Hillman Furay Band*, Asylum, 1974.

Steppenwolf: "Screaming Night Hog," Dunhill, 1970 • *Steppenwolf Seven*, MCA, 1970, 1989 • "Who Needs Ya," Dunhill, 1970 • "For Ladies Only," Dunhill, 1971 • *For Ladies Only*, Dunhill, 1971 • "Ride with Me," Dunhill, 1971 • "Snow Blind Friend," Dunhill, 1971 • *Rest in Peace, 1967–1972*, Dunhill, 1972 • *Steppenwolf Gold: Their Greatest Hits*, Dunhill, 1972 • *Born to Be Wild: A Retrospective*, MCA, 1991.

Three Dog Night: *Captured Live at the Forum*, State/Dunhill, 1970 • *It Ain't Easy*, Dunhill, 1970 • "Mama Told Me (Not to Come)," Dunhill, 1970 • *Naturally*, Dunhill, 1970 • "One Man Band," Dunhill, 1970 • "Out in the Country," Dunhill, 1970 • "An Old Fashioned Love Song," Dunhill, 1971 • *Harmony*, Dunhill, 1971 • "Joy to the World,"

Dunhill, 1971 • "Liar," Dunhill, 1971 • "Black and White," Dunhill, 1972 • "Never Been to Spain," Dunhill, 1972 • "Pieces of April," Dunhill, 1972 • *Seven Separate Fools,* Dunhill, 1972 • "The Family of Man," Dunhill, 1972 • *Around the World with Three Dog Night,* Dunhill, 1973 • *Cyan,* Probe/Dunhill, 1973 • "Let Me Serenade You," Dunhill, 1973 • "Shambala," Dunhill, 1973 • *Joy to the World: Their Greatest Hits,* MCA, 1975 • *It's a Jungle,* Passport, 1983 • *Celebrate: The Three Dog Night Story, 1965–1975,* MCA, 1993.

20/20: *Look Out!,* Portrait, 1981.

Twilley, Dwight: *XXI,* The Right Stuff, 1996.

Bob Porter

A name sure to come up in connection with soul jazz is that of Bob Porter, producer extraordinaire, writer, radioman, film consultant, and discographer. Since 1968, Porter, a New Jersey resident who retains his Boston accent, has produced more than 150 albums, largely for Prestige, but also for such labels as Milestone, Savoy, Atlantic, and Westbound. The brand of jazz with which Porter is most associated is accessible jazz leavened by funk or, in his words, "jazz instrumentalists playing a funky beat."

Born on June 20, 1940, in Wellesley, Massachusetts, Porter has been a record collector since his teens—and he got into music far earlier. "I was always into records," he recalls. "I remember getting a Woody Herman 10-inch LP—it was *Live at Carnegie Hall*—on my 11th birthday. That was my first record. At the time, I didn't try to categorize anything. I just bought what I liked, and I liked everything from white swing bands to R&B vocal groups. But I'm a jazz guy first."

Porter's productions, whether of big-toned tenorman Gene Ammons, organist Johnny "Hammond" Smith, or vocalist Etta Jones, resonate with warmth, focus on the beat, and champion the groove. Small wonder Porter's favorite musician was Ammons, a Chicago sax master who died in 1974. "He was simply a guy who knew how to take command of the audience," Porter says. "He had a presence that was unbelievable, and he had a naturally soulful sound, a big sound. He could play at a variety of tempos. He was a great ballad player, but he had these funky blues lines he'd come up with all the time."

Since 1968, when he joined Prestige Records as a producer, Porter has helmed recordings by the likes of Illinois Jacquet, Charles Earland, Houston Person, and David Newman. He joined Prestige when its recording director was Don Schlitten. Schlitten was interested in his own roster of modern jazz artists. Porter's job was to build Prestige's soul-jazz roster, focusing on the more accessible aspects of the genre. "I knew the idiom reasonably well," he says. "I'd always been a fan of the McDuffs, [Richard] 'Groove' Holmes, the Jimmy Smiths, the Grant Greens, Arnett Cobb, Jacquet, all those guys. That's still my favorite music today. It's got a soul of its own."

His biggest hit, he says, was the Prestige album *Black Talk,* a late 1969 Prestige date by organist Charles Earland. It's one of the earliest, and most successful, examples of a jazz combo integrating rock repertoire into soul jazz and made it onto *Billboard*'s Soul LP charts, as did Ammons' *The Boss Is Back,* another Porter production. "At the time, there was no jazz chart and no R&B chart," he says. "Everything was on soul albums, and that's where a lot of my stuff hit. Jazz and blues and R&B are black music," he says. "I don't care who plays it, I still refer to it as black music. I use the terms interchangeably sometimes."

Porter says he was greatly influenced by Esmond Edwards, a Prestige producer especially adept at tune selection, configuring rhythm sections and getting the maximum out of a small combo. Edwards went on to similar work at Chess, Verve, and Columbia. "He was the guy who had the greatest impact on me because his records were coming out when I was thinking about getting into music as a career," Porter says. "There were other guys, like Bob Weinstock—not so much as a producer but as a guy who had the record business figured out—and Norman Granz [see entry]. I'm also a great admirer of Creed Taylor [see entry]."

He calls Weinstock a mentor who taught him about the relationship between radio and records, schooled him in trends and the vagaries of distribution. Granz, says Porter, "always had the best musicians. It seemed that in the '50s, Clef, Norgran, and Verve were the best jazz labels; the *Jazz at the Philharmonic* records were very exciting."

Taylor, meanwhile, effectively introduced fashion to jazz records, bedding instrumentalists in a singer's setting that boasted great arrangements, strings, brass, even full orchestras, Porter says. Taylor's work for Verve, A&M, CTI, and Kudu "had the best sound, the best cover art, and a very classy approach," he says. "He made the best bossa nova records. Nobody else was close."

Porter left Prestige in 1971 for Westbound Records, where he worked in 1972 and 1973. Since 1974, he has been a freelance producer. He was primarily at Savoy Records from 1975 to 1980, primarily at Atlantic Records from 1986 to 1991. He has produced 96 reissue titles for Savoy, 106 reissue titles for Atlantic, and another 50-plus for other labels. "I've got to go to a label and sell it on the artist," he says. "A few times, a label has come to me. But generally speaking, I have to sell the label on the artist first. Then I've got to make the deal. Then I've got to make the record. That's essentially what a freelance producer does in this day and age."

The advantage of being a staff producer is access to publicity, promotion, and sales people—"the kinds of people who routinely come up with creative ideas," Porter says. "If you're a freelancer, you have to get a pass before they let you upstairs."

What helps Porter make records is the stability of the people he works with. He uses either Bernard Purdie or Idris Muhammad on drums, for example, and relies on Rudy Van Gelder for engineering. "I let Rudy worry about the sound decisions," says Porter. "I try to stay out of his way. He knows what to do."

He also wants one of his preferred drummers for a soul-jazz date, as he has since 1970. "Both Purdie and Muhammad are fortunate in that Van Gelder gets their drum sound," he says. "The microphone loves those guys. It just seems to pick up their nuances. There are people who seem to record especially well, as opposed to necessarily being the greatest players in the world. It's more a function in pop music, in the sense that certain musicians and rhythm sections get hot for a period of time," Porter says. "But those two drummers work in a variety of different circumstances. Those are the two key guys."

Porter suggests that his role is to nurture a session, not command it. "I am not a director in the sense that a movie director moves people through their paces," he says. "If I do my job well, I have done most of it before we go into the studio: pick a band and at least have a focus. A lot of times, we'd go into the studio with no paper [written charts] whatsoever, and that's still true today. I'm not opposed to somebody coming in with some chord changes written out; that would be nice, in fact. But a lot of my sessions have been without anything written out, and I tend to use a lot of the same guys. They're accustomed to the drill, they know how to make music under these circumstances."

Besides his production work, Porter writes about jazz. He has contributed to *Cashbox, Down Beat, Jazz Journal International,* and *Jazz Times,* and his liner notes for *The Complete Charlie Parker* on Savoy won a Grammy Award in 1979. Not only has he written about jazz, he has also written about R&B and doo-wop. He also is a member of the International Association of Jazz Record Collectors, the National Academy of Recording Arts and Sciences, the Blues Foundation, and the Duke Ellington Jazz Society. From 1987 to 1992, he was affiliated with the Rock and Roll Hall of Fame.

Porter also hosts a syndicated blues show, *Portraits in Blue,* broadcast over 30 National Public Radio stations. He is a consultant to Music Choice, a digital music channel available through select cable television systems and via DirecTV.

"I don't make records for the pot smokers in the corner," he says. "I make records for people to groove to. It's functional music. Soul jazz, at one point, was the preferred social music of black adults because of its utility. You could just sit there and dig it, or have it functioning through your body while you were carrying on a conversation. You can't listen to bebop like that. You have to pay attention."

Clearly, album production isn't his only gig, however. "I work as much as I want to work, but I've not been full-time anything for many years," Porter says. "I'm a record dealer, I'm a radio personality in both local and national markets, I program the blues channel for Music Choice. I do lots of different things. That has worked for me." —CARLO WOLFF

Adams, Pepper: *Urban Dreams,* Palo Alto, 1981.

Allison, Mose: *Best Of,* Sequel, 1995.

Ammons, Gene: *Brother Jug,* Prestige, 1969 • *Legends of Acid Jazz,* Prestige, 1970, 1997 • *Night Lights,* Prestige, 1970 • *The Black Cat,* Prestige, 1970 • *The Boss Is Back!,* Prestige, 1970 • w/ Sonny Stitt, *As You Talk That Talk!,* Prestige, 1971 • *My Way,* Prestige, 1971.

Argo, Judy: *True Love Ways,* Sterling, 1994.

Breakstone, Joshua, with Tommy Flanagan and Jim Knepper: *Evening Star,* Contemporary, 1987, 1992.

Bryant, Rusty: *Legends of Acid Jazz,* Prestige, 1969, 1996 • *Night Train Now!,* Prestige, 1969 • *Returns,* Prestige, 1969 • *Soul Liberation,* Prestige, 1970 • *Fire Eater,* Prestige, 1971 • *Wild Fire,* Prestige, 1971 • *Until It's Time for You to Go,* Prestige, 1974.

Butler, Billy: *This Is,* Prestige, 1968 • *Guitar Soul,* Prestige, 1969 • *Yesterday, Today and Tomorrow,* Prestige, 1970 • *Night Life,* Prestige, 1971.

Chandler, Gary: *Outlook,* Eastbound, 1972.

Cobb, Arnette: *Live at Sandy's!* Vols. 1–2, Muse, 1978 • *Keep on Pushin',* Bee Hive, 1984.

Crawford, Hank: *Indigo Blue,* Milestone, 1983, 1991 • *Midnight Ramble,* Milestone, 1983 • *Down on the Deuce,* Original Jazz Classics, 1984, 1997 • *Roadhouse Symphony,* Milestone, 1985 • *Mr. Chips,* Milestone, 1987 • *Night Beat,* Milestone, 1989 • *Groove Master,* Milestone, 1990 • *Portrait,*

Milestone, 1991 • *Heart and Soul*, Rhino, 1992 • *South-Central*, Milestone, 1993 • *Tight*, Milestone, 1996 • *After Dark*, Milestone, 1998.

Crawford, Hank and Jimmy McGriff: *Soul Survivors*, Milestone, 1986 • *Steppin' Up*, Milestone, 1987 • *On the Blue Side*, Milestone, 1990 • *Road Tested*, Milestone, 1997.

Criss, Sonny: *Criss Craft*, Muse, 1975, 1992 • *Out of Nowhere*, 32 Records, 1976, 1997.

Dickenson, Vic: *Quintet*, Storyville, 1976.

Donaldson, Lou: *Play the Right Thing*, Milestone, 1991 • *Birdseed*, Milestone, 1992 • *Caracas*, Milestone, 1994.

Earland, Charles: *Front Burner*, Milestone, 1988, 1992 • *Black Talk*, Prestige, 1969 • *Black Drops*, Prestige, 1970 • *Living Black!*, Prestige, 1970, 1997 • *Soul Story*, Prestige, 1971 • *Third Degree Burn*, Milestone, 1989.

Easley, Bill: *First Call*, Milestone, 1991.

Ellis, Pee Wee: *Home in the Country*, Savoy, 1977.

Ford, Ricky: *Flying Colors*, Muse, 1980 • *Tenor of the Times*, Muse, 1981 • *Interpretations*, Muse, 1982.

Frazier, Ceasar: *Hail Ceasar!*, Eastbound, 1972 • *75*, 20th Century/Westbound, 1973.

Funk Inc.: *Chicken Lickin'*, Prestige, 1972 • *Urban Renewal*, Prestige, 1996.

Hardman, Bill: *Politely*, Muse, 1981.

Holmes, Richard Groove: *That Healin' Feelin'*, Prestige, 1968 • *Good Vibrations*, Muse, 1977 • *Shippin' Out*, Muse, 1977.

Humes, Helen: *Helen Humes and the Muse All-Stars*, Muse, 1979 • *Helen*, Muse, 1980.

Jackson, Willis: *Gator's Groove*, Prestige, 1968 • *Swivel Hips*, Prestige, 1968 • *Gatorade*, Prestige, 1971 • *Bar Wars*, 32 Records, 1977, 1997 • *Nothing Butt*, Muse, 1980.

Jacquet, Illinois, and His Big Band: *Jacquet's Got It*, Atlantic, 1988.

Jefferson, Eddie: *Godfather of Vocalese*, Muse, 1976, 1990.

Jones, Boogaloo Joe: *My Fire*, Prestige, 1968 • *Boogaloo Joe*, Prestige, 1969 • *Legends of Acid Jazz*, Prestige, 1969, 1996 • *No Way!*, Prestige, 1970 • *Right On Brother!*, Prestige, 1970 • *What It Is*, Prestige, 1971.

Jones, Etta: *75*, 20th Century, 1975.

Jones, Sam: *Something in Common*, Muse, 1977.

Katz, Dick: *In High Profile*, Bee Hive, 1984.

Kiener, Barry: *Live at Strathallen*, Strathallen, 1982.

Kynard, Charles: *Professor Soul*, Prestige, 1968 • *Reelin' with the Feelin'*, BGP, 1969, 1995 • *Soul Brotherhood*, Prestige, 1969 • *Afro-Disiac*, Prestige, 1970 • *Wa-Tu-Wa-Zui*, Prestige, 1971.

Levy, Ron: *Zim, Zam, Zoom: Acid Blues on B-3*, Bullseye Blues, 1996.

Mabern, Harold: *Rakin' and Scrapin'*, Prestige, 1969 • *Workin' and Wailin'*, Prestige, 1969 • *Greasy Kid Stuff*, Prestige, 1970.

Mance, Junior: *Truckin' and Trakin'*, Bee Hive, 1984.

Martino, Pat: *Desperado*, Prestige, 1970, 1992.

Mason, Bill: *Gettin' Off*, Eastbound, 1972.

Mauro, Turk: *Heavyweight*, Phoenix Jazz, 1980.

McGriff, Jimmy: *City Lights*, Jam, 1981 • *Movin' Upside the Blues*, Jam, 1981 • *The Countdown*, Milestone, 1983, 1991 • *Skywalk*, Milestone, 1984 • *State of the Art*, Milestone, 1985 • *The Starting Five*, Milestone, 1986 • *Blue to the Bone*, Milestone, 1988 • *The Dream Team*, Milestone, 1997.

Muhammad, Idris: *Black Rhythm Revolution!*, Prestige, 1970 • *Legends of Acid Jazz*, Prestige, 1970, 1996 • *Peace and Rhythm*, Prestige, 1971.

Newman, David Fathead: *Fire! Live at the Village Vanguard*, Rhino, 1989.

19th Hole: *Smilin'*, Eastbound, 1972.

Patterson, Don: *Brothers Four*, Prestige, 1969 • *Donnybrook*, Prestige, 1969 • *Oh Happy Day*, Prestige, 1969 • *Tune Up*, Prestige, 1969.

Person, Houston: *Goodness!*, Original Jazz Classics, 1969, 1995 • *Soul Dance*, Prestige, 1969 • *Legends of Acid Jazz*, Prestige, 1970, 1996 • *Person to Person*, Prestige, 1970 • *Truth*, Prestige, 1970 • *Houston Express*, Prestige, 1971 • *Houston Person*, Eastbound, 1973 • *Island Episode*, Prestige, 1973, 1997.

Phillips, Sonny: *Legends of Acid Jazz*, Prestige, 1969, 1997 • *Sure 'Nuff*, Prestige, 1969 • *Black Magic*, Prestige, 1970 • *Black on Black*, Prestige, 1970.

Ponder, Jimmy: *Down Here on the Ground*, Milestone, 1984 • *So Many Stars*, Milestone, 1985.

Prysock, Arthur: *A Rockin' Good Way*, Milestone, 1985 • *This Guy's in Love with You*, Milestone, 1986, 1991 • *Today's Love Songs, Tomorrow's Blues*, Milestone, 1988.

Pucho and the Latin Soul Brothers: *Jungle Fire*, Prestige, 1970.

Purdie, Bernard: *Legends of Acid Jazz*, Prestige, 1971, 1996 • *Purdie Good!*, Prestige, 1971 • *Shaft*, Prestige, 1971.

Rodney, Red: *The Red Tornado*, Muse, 1975 • *Home Free*, Muse, 1977 • *The Three R's*, Muse, 1979 • *Alive in New York*, Muse, 1980 • *Hi Jinx at the Vanguard*, Muse, 1980 • *Live at the Village Vanguard*, Muse, 1980 • *Night and Day*, Muse, 1981.

Roomful of Blues: See Vinson, Eddie Cleanhead.

Smith, Johnny Hammond: *Black Feeling!*, Prestige, 1969 • *Legends of Acid Jazz*, Prestige, 1969, 1996 • *Soul Talk*, Prestige, 1969 • *Here It 'Tis*, Prestige, 1970 • *What's Goin' On?*, Prestige, 1971.

Snafu: *All Funked Up*, Capitol, 1975.

Sparks, Melvin: *Legends of Acid Jazz*, Prestige, 1970, 1996 • *Sparks!*, Prestige, 1970 • *Spark Plug*, Prestige, 1971 • *The Texas Twister*, Eastbound, 1973.

Spencer, Leon: *Legends of Acid Jazz*, Prestige, 1970, 1997 • *Sneak Preview*, Prestige, 1970 • *Louisiana Slim*, Prestige, 1971.

Stitt, Sonny: *Soul Electricity*, Prestige, 1968 • *Night Letter*, Prestige, 1969 • *Black Vibrations*, Prestige, 1971 • *Legends of*

Acid Jazz, Prestige, 1971, 1997 • *Turn It On,* Prestige, 1971 • *My Buddy,* Muse, 1975 • *Sonny's Back,* Muse, 1980 • *In Style,* Muse, 1981 • *Last Stitt Sessions,* Vols. 1–2, Muse, 1982 • *See also* Ammons, Gene.

Sullivan, Ira: *Does It All,* Muse, 1981.

Tate, Buddy: *Hard Blowin',* Muse, 1978 • *Live at Sandy's,* Muse, 1978.

Tate, Grady: *TNT,* Milestone, 1991 • *Body and Soul,* Milestone, 1993.

Turner, Big Joe: *Blues Train,* Muse, 1983 • *Big, Bad and Blue: The Big Joe Turner Anthology,* Rhino, 1994.

Vinson, Eddie Cleanhead: *The Clean Machine,* Muse, 1977 • *Hold It Right There,* Muse, 1978 • *Live at Sandy's,* Muse, 1978 • w/ Roomful of Blues, *Eddie Cleanhead Vinson and Roomful of Blues,* Muse, 1982.

White, Carla: *Mood Swings,* Milestone, 1988, 1992.

Williams, Joe: *That Holiday Feeling,* Verve, 1990.

COLLECTIONS

Atlantic Rock and Roll, Atlantic, 1991.

COMPILATIONS

Brown, Ruth: *Miss Rhythm, Greatest Hits And More,* Rhino, 1989.

Drifters, The: *1959–1965 All-Time Greatest Hits and More,* Atlantic, 1988.

Horne, Lena: *Stormy Weather: The Legendary Lena (1941–1958),* RCA Bluebird, 1990.

Oscar Peterson Trio: *Jazz at the Philharmonic,* Verve, 1953.

Parker, Charlie: *Yardbird Suite: The Ultimate Collection,* Rhino, 1997.

Turner, Big Joe: *Big Joe Turner's Greatest Hits,* Atlantic Jazz, 1958, 1989.

VARIOUS ARTISTS

Gentle Duke, Prestige, 1997.
Modern Jazz Piano, Savoy, 1946, 1956.

REISSUES

Ammons, Gene: *The Gene Ammons Story: The 78 Era,* Prestige, 1955, 1992.

Burrell, Kenny: *Monday Stroll,* Savoy Jazz, 1957, 1994.

Byrd, Charlie: *Midnight Guitar,* Savoy Jazz, 1957, 1994.

Clarke, Kenny: *Kenny Clarke Meets the Detroit Jazzmen,* Savoy Jazz, 1956, 1994.

Cohn, Al: *The Progressive Al Cohn,* Savoy Jazz, 1953, 1996.

Eckstine, Billy: *Everything I Have Is Yours,* Verve, 1965, 1991.

Ellington, Duke: *Recollections of the Big Band Era,* Atlantic, 1963, 1989.

Ervin, Booker: *Down in the Dumps,* Savoy Jazz, 1961, 1994.

Jackson, Milt: *Plenty, Plenty Soul,* Atlantic, 1957, 1992.

Parker, Charlie: *Bird at the Hi-Hat,* Blue Note, 1954, 1993.

Raeburn, Boyd: w/ David Allyn, *Jewells,* Savoy Jazz, 1949, 1996.

Ravens, The: *The Greatest Group of Them All,* Savoy Jazz, 1978, 1995.

7th Avenue Stompers: *Fidgety Feet,* Savoy Jazz, 1958, 1994.

Singer, Hal: *Rent Party,* Savoy Jazz, 1956, 1996.

Turner, Big Joe: *Have No Fear, Big Joe Turner Is Here,* Savoy Jazz, 1947, 1995.

Vaughan, Sarah, and Lester Young: *One Night Stand: Town Hall Concert 1947,* Capitol, 1947, 1997.

Wayne, Chuck, Brew Moore, Zoot Sims: *Tasty Pudding,* Savoy Jazz, 1953, 1994.

David Porter

Not only is David Porter one of the few composers in history to have records in the national charts in four consecutive decades, he is active in publishing and production, owns several businesses at the Memphis International Airport, and is working with several acts on the MCA Records roster. And some of his songwriting is paying off real, real big.

The ninth of 12 children, Porter was born November 21, 1941, in Memphis. He started singing at age 8, in Rose Hill Baptist Church on Virginia Avenue. Another member of his church choir was Maurice White (see entry), who would go on to create Earth, Wind and Fire.

Porter's first record was "Farewell," released on the Golden Eagle label in Memphis. He learned about production at Savory Records and Hi Records, according to his official biography.

It was at Stax Records that he came into his own, however—more as a producer than a performer. (He would record three solo records, all instant collector's items; the first was *Gritty, Groovy and Gettin' It,* on Enterprise.) His greatest vehicle was Sam and Dave, his greatest collaborator Isaac Hayes (see entry). It is impossible to consider Stax without considering David Porter. Whether his profile has ever been high enough remains in question.

"I was the first staff writer for Stax Records," says Porter. "I actually was there when it was called Satellite Records, in 1961 or 1962; my memory for dates is not excellent." Chips Moman (see entry) was working there, before he left to found American Recording Studios. With Moman gone, Steve Cropper (see entry) came on board; he and Porter were the staff. All the other musicians were on contract, like bassist Lewis

Steinberg and drummer Al Jackson Jr. After Booker T. And the MGs scored with "Green Onions" in 1962, Porter paid his dues by touring with the band and singing vocals on college dates across the country.

In 1963 or 1964, Porter became a full-time songwriter at Stax (the name is a contraction of the last names of the owners, brother and sister Jim Stewart and Estelle Axton). He soon began collaborating with Cropper.

"When you write your material and take it into the studio, for all intents and purposes you're producing the product, because everyone has to follow your lead," Porter says. "I was naive and didn't realize what producing was. It is putting structure and formation to a completed piece of product, starting with the material that's created from the writer, then developing the relationship between the written material and the artist and making the marriage work through completion."

In 1966, he began a run with Isaac Hayes, primarily producing Sam Moore and Dave Prater. The hits came fast and hard: "You Got Me Hummin'," "When Something Is Wrong with My Baby," "You Don't Know Like I Know," "Soul Man" (No. 2), "Hold On, I'm Coming," "I Thank You" (No. 9). The string lasted until 1969, when Stax began to capsize under the weight of corporate problems and cultural strain.

"Every time I went into the studio, I tried to bring some personality that's unique to me," says Porter. "When I was young, we were trying to do that. Isaac Hayes and I had a very successful run; you could feel the Hayes-Porter, Porter-Hayes personality in the work, even though each song had its own individuality that made it commercial."

The earthiness and power of the lyric, combined with a unique energy, made their productions successful, Porter says. "Stax Records had a laid-back vibration but that laid-back spirit always had energy to it. And me, it didn't allow you very much time to just lay down. 'Hold On, I'm Comin' is an example of that. 'Soul Man' is an example of that. The melodies are strong, yet there's meat in what the message is about. That was the Hayes-Porter signature."

Atlantic partner Jerry Wexler (see entry) brought Sam and Dave to Hayes and Porter in Memphis. "Porter and Hayes were to the '60s what Leiber and Stoller [see entry] were to the '50s—poets with precisely the right punch," Wexler has said.

"We put Hayes and Porter into Sam and Dave," Porter says. "Those performers you hear are structured performances by Isaac and me. We taught the songs, we taught the peaks in the songs, established who would sing line by line. We set ad libs into songs. Sam and Dave would stand in front of the mike. I would stand on the other side of the mike, directing them. That was how we recorded Sam and Dave."

In 1970, the Porter-Hayes partnership ended; Hayes had notched a tremendous hit album in *Hot Buttered Soul* and was working it on the road. "It made sense for him to go out and make all that money, and I was in the studio," Porter says.

Among the works Porter produced, wrote, or performed on are ones by the Emotions, the Rance Allen Group, the Soul Children, Otis Redding, Shirley Brown, and Johnnie Taylor. He also produced Lou Rawls and James and Bobby Purify. Porter says all the tunes by Sam and Dave were produced by Hayes and him.

"There were statements put on records that the record was produced by 'staff,' " says Porter. "Several of the records Isaac and I produced had that, by order of Jim Stewart." That robbed the pair of credits. "I'm not a fortune teller, but as I look back on that, it appears to me he [Stewart] was not interested in giving us too much notoriety or publicity as producers, because it would get to other people, who would then try to outbid him and take us away.

"A producer has to be a psychiatrist, a psychologist, a motivator, a preacher," says Porter. "It's getting all the creative juices working with people you're working with, so you can motivate them to make some contribution. If you contract a bass player for a session and give that musician a particular line to play, he's not a great session musician if he doesn't bring some kind of personal interpretation to the line. And if the personal interpretation complements the song, you use it. That makes you the producer. You should know what works and what doesn't work to complement the idea."

While Porter never was a major solo artist in his own right, he's clearly proud of what he's done. And he's benefiting from it in unexpected ways. Just before Stax closed in 1975, Porter produced an album for the Emotions on the label that included a tune called "Blind Alley," by no means a hit. In the past 20 years, however, "Blind Alley" has been sampled by the likes of LL Cool J and Bell Biv DeVoe and figures prominently in the songs "Rump Shaker" (by Wreckx-N-Effect) and, above all, Mariah Carey's "Dream Lover."

Because Porter owns a third of the song as a writer, each time it's sampled he gets a royalty. "That was a production that ended up a flop at the time because of all the crises at Stax," Porter says, "but the song was on an L.L. album that went double-platinum, Bell Biv DeVoe went gold, 'Rump Shaker,' I think went double-platinum, and Mariah sold 14 million. How do you think that makes me feel? I feel real good." —Carlo Wolff

Bar-Kays: "Give Everybody Some," Volt, 1967 • "Soul Finger," Volt, 1967 • *Soul Finger,* Volt, 1967.

Bell, William: *The Best Of,* Stax, 1991 • *Little Something Extra,* Stax, 1992.

Clay, Judy: *Private Numbers,* Stax, 1974.

Edwards, John: *Life, Love and Living,* Cotillion, 1976.

Emotions, The: *Chronicle: Greatest Hits,* Stax, 1991.

Estelle, Myrna S.: *Sweet Inspiations,* Stax, 1973.

Hayes, Isaac: *The Best Of,* Vol. 1, Stax, 1986.

Jackson, Chuck, and Maxine Brown: "Hold On, I'm Coming," Stax, 1967.

Jean and the Darlings: "How Can You Mistreat the One You Love?," Stax, 1967.

John, Mable: "You're Good Thing Is About to End," Stax, 1966 • *Stay Out of the Kitchen,* Stax, 1968, 1993.

King, Albert: w/ Steve Cropper and Pop Staples, *Jammed Together,* Stax, 1969.

Porter, David: *Gritty, Groovy and Gettin' It,* Enterprise, 1970 • *Into a Real Thing,* Enterprise, 1971 • *Victim of the Joke?,* Stax, 1971, 1995.

Purify, James, and Bobby: "I Take What I Want," Bell, 1967.

Redding, Otis: *Remember Me,* Stax, 1992 • *Otis! The Definitive Otis Redding,* Rhino, 1993.

Sam and Dave: *Double Dynamite,* Stax, 1966 • "Hold On, I'm Comin'," Stax, 1966 • *Hold On, I'm Comin',* Stax, 1966 • "Said I Wasn't Gonna Tell Nobody," Stax, 1966 • "You Don't Know Like I Know," Stax, 1966 • "You Got Me Hummin'," Stax, 1966 • "Soothe Me," Stax, 1967 • "Soul Man," Stax, 1967 • *Soul Men,* Stax, 1967 • "When Something Is Wrong with My Baby," Stax, 1967 • "I Thank You," Stax, 1968 • *I Thank You,* Stax, 1968 • "Wrap It Up," Stax, 1968 • *Sweat and Soul Anthology,* Vol. 2, Rhino, 1993 • *Sweat and Soul Anthology,* Rhino, 1993 • *The Very Best Of,* Rhino, 1995.

Soul Children: *Soul Children,* Stax, 1969 • "The Sweeter He Is," Stax, 1969 • *Chronicle,* Stax, 1979 • *Hold On, I'm Comin',* Stax, 1997.

Taylor, Johnnie: "I Had a Dream," Stax, 1966 • "I've Got to Love Somebody's Baby," Stax, 1966.

Thomas, Carla: "How Do You Quit?," Stax, 1965 • "B-A-B-Y," Stax, 1966 • "Let Me Be Good to You," Stax, 1966 • *Hidden Gems,* Stax, 1992 • *Gee Whiz: The Best Of,* Rhino, 1994.

Vera, Billy, and Judy Clay: *Storybook Children/Greatest Love,* Soul Classics, 1995.

John Porter

John Porter's production career has veered fascinatingly between the cool of modern rock and the heat of the blues. A guitar player and bassist, Englishman Porter became infatuated with the blues as a teen, then careened wildly in the direction of avant-garde art rock when he joined Roxy Music in the early '70s—a dichotomy that has defined his musical life ever since. His most important modern rock productions include Bryan Ferry, the Smiths, Billy Bragg, the Alarm, School of Fish, and Velocity Girl. While continuing his modern rock work in the '90s, Porter—now transplanted to Los Angeles—has returned to his first love, the blues, with productions for Buddy Guy (including his sensational, Grammy-winning *Damn Right, I've Got the Blues*), Keb' Mo', B.B. King, Taj Mahal, John Mayall, Otis Rush, and Chris Thomas (not the producer of the same name).

John Porter was born in 1947 and grew up in Leeds, in the north of England. He enjoyed classical music as a child, especially "strident" pieces like "The Ride of the Valkyries," but then he heard Little Richard sing "Lucille" on a radio request program when he was 10. "I went ape-shit. That really changed my life. I knew that was what I liked, and I haven't changed much, actually. I still like kind of the same things," says Porter.

"When I was 13 another very seminal thing happened. My friend next door had an older sister, and her boyfriend was a record rep. He gave her the records that he didn't like, then she'd pass on the ones that she didn't like to her younger brother, and now and again he'd pass on to me the ones he didn't like. So I would get the dregs of the dregs of the dregs. Amongst them there was a DJ copy of Freddie King doing 'Hideaway,' with 'I Love the Woman' on the B-side. The same day he gave me James Brown doing 'This Old Heart.'

"Those two records just completely destroyed me," he continues, "because they had a special voice. I was just crazy about the Freddie King one, but I wasn't sure if he was playing a guitar or a violin because I had never heard that kind of sustain and vibrato before, and it just knocked me sideways. I wanted to make that noise—still do, really.

"So I kept going on and on and on about a guitar, and I got a Russian guitar that cost £4 for Christmas that year. I started to try to play like Freddie King. I got totally hooked on the blues, which in England at that time was very difficult, there wasn't much around. But I joined record libraries and read *Down Beat* and everything I could to find out about it.

"Subsequently, I got a paper route and I found out about this place called Randy's Record Shop in Tennessee. I got their lists and saved up my paper route money and every three or four weeks I'd send off and get some albums: a lot of which were on the Crown label because they were cheap. You never knew what you were going to get—I just had to order them and hope for the best. There were great B.B. King records and some that weren't so good.

"Then I joined a band as a guitar player just playing any old rubbish, boogie-woogie and stuff. I played in other bands, and got to back up some of the American blues singers when they came over to England. This was very unfortunate for them, but it was great for me.

"I went to Newcastle University in 1965 because it seemed like there was a great music scene: it had the first all-night club in England, and a university band called the Gasboard. I joined that band, and we did Bobby Bland, Freddie King, B.B. King, and stuff like that. We had a horn section—which was pretty rare—and Bryan Ferry was in the band, although at the time we didn't think he could sing. We gigged around and were pretty popular in northern England," says Porter.

For a brief time in the early '70s Porter played guitar on sessions in L.A., but he had to sell his guitar and return to England when he couldn't get a green card or join the musicians union.

Porter had worked with Ferry in various configurations since college, and he accepted an invitation to join Roxy Music in 1973. Porter played on the classic *For Your Pleasure* (No. 4 U.K.) album (see Brian Eno entry), but refused to be photographed with the group for the album because he didn't wish to be seen "dressing like a pansy," and besides, he didn't really like the music.

Pleasure did extremely well, and Ferry, itching to try his hand at a solo effort, asked Porter to help him produce it. Porter hired some musicians he knew, including members of the Average White Band, Roxy drummer Paul Thompson, and future Roxyite Eddie Jobson. *These Foolish Things* (No. 5 U.K.) would establish Ferry's pattern of recording idiosyncratic versions of standard tunes ("A Hard Rain's a-Gonna Fall," No. 4 U.K., "The Tracks of My Tears," the title track) for his '70s solo albums, while keeping his original material for Roxy Music. Porter played on three more Ferry albums before a dispute arose regarding credits and they parted ways.

For the remainder of the '70s Porter played sessions for Island, and in various bands, including Everyone, with producer-to-be Bob Sargeant (see entry). He gigged with Eric Clapton and the Faces' Ronnie Lane

and traveled to Hong Kong and Morocco. At the dawn of the '80s Porter went to New York to record with a band called the Blood Poets, but that effort disintegrated amid a flurry of egos and drugs. He returned to London broke, skinny, and despondent.

Fate intervened on his behalf one evening in a West End club owned by John Mayall's son. "I bumped into this lady at the bar, she was sitting there and I thought, 'She is really beautiful.' So I asked her to buy me a drink and we've been together ever since." After she became pregnant, they decided to get married and she laid down the law about their future. At her insistence he create a résumé of his qualifications, with which he then blanketed every music-related company in London.

Three days later the BBC called and asked Porter to come in the following Monday as a contract producer for live broadcasts. He worked there about a year and a half and produced around 300 bands, opening his eyes to a whole new world of music.

One of the bands he worked with was a cluster of sensitive young rockers called the Smiths. Jeff Travis, of the now-defunct Rough Trade label, called Porter one day and asked him to fix up the sound on the album the Smiths had just recorded. Although the Smiths weren't black, and they sure weren't funky, he decided to give it a go anyway; with an infusion of cash from Sire Records, Porter added lots of overdubs and essentially re-produced *The Smiths* (No. 2 U.K.) in 1984. Ten years after the first Ferry album, Porter was once again the somewhat reluctant producer of a hugely successful, sweepingly romantic, ultra-European alt-rock act.

Characterized by the alternately driving and delicate guitars of Johnny Marr and the exhibitory emotional self-flagellation of singer/lyricist (Stephen) Morrissey, *The Smiths* struck a chord with moody youths everywhere. The single "What Difference Does It Make?" (No. 12 U.K.) is a great, rocking struggle between faith and nihilism (that John Porter, in spite of himself, could no doubt relate to).

An odd collection of live BBC tracks with three different producers (including Porter), and studio recordings with Porter, *Hatful of Hollow* (No. 7 U.K.) is even more powerful than the band's debut. "How Soon Is Now?" is a long, trance-inducing, locomotive-rhythmed rock number with sensational dueling guitars from Marr and Porter, and a controlled but heartbreaking emotional outpouring from Morrissey ("You stand on your own, / And you leave on your own, / And you go home, and you cry, / And you want to die"). "Please Please Please Let Me Get What I Want" is a delicate, spare, contained cry of hope—hope that is not too loud as to call attention to itself.

After two more great singles—"Panic" (No. 11 U.K.) and "Ask" (No. 14 U.K.) in 1986—Porter and the band parted ways. Morrissey's heart-, soul-, and spleen-on-his-sleeve emotional honesty has been the source of much comment and merriment over the years, but his sincerity and artistic integrity are worthy of respect. "Whether or not you agree with it, he means it," says Porter. "I was having a growing process at the time and I realized you didn't have to go to the Southside of Chicago, or down to New Orleans to find people who are soulful—it comes out in very many ways." Porter also enjoyed a great working relationship with Marr—"How Soon Is Now?" is an amazing tapestry of guitar textures—and would like to work with him again someday.

In the '90s Porter has found the perfect balance of soul-satisfying blues work with some of his heroes, including Buddy Guy, Taj Mahal, B.B. King, and Otis Rush; and fresh modern rock, including the first School of Fish album with buzzing, fuzzy guitars and high, clear vocals in a tasty neo-psychedelic stew.

What does Porter get out of his job? "My biggest buzz has always been, and will always be, to get a bunch of great musicians together in a room and just listen to them play. Producers get to do that." —ERIC OLSEN AND DAWN DARLING

Ainley, Charlie: *Too Much Is Not Enough,* Nemperor, 1978.
Alarm, The: *Eye of the Hurricane,* IRS, 1987 • "Rain in the Summertime," IRS, 1987 • "Presence of Love," IRS, 1988 • *Standards,* IRS, 1990.
Blasters, The: *At Home,* Private, 1996.
Bragg, Billy: *Talking with the Taxman About Poetry,* Elektra, 1986.
Chameleons, The: *Radio 1 Evening Show,* Dutch East, 1993.
Circle C: *Circle C,* DGC, 1991.
Crash Vegas: *Stone,* London, 1993.
Drivin' n' Cryin': *Wrapped in Sky,* Geffen, 1995.
Eye and I: *Eye and I,* Epic, 1992.
Ferry, Bryan: "A Hard Rain's a-Gonna Fall," Atco, 1973 • *These Foolish Things,* Atco, 1973 • *See also* Roxy Music.
Gillespie, Dana: *Ain't Gonna Play No Second Fiddle,* RCA, 1974.
Go-Go's, The: "Good Girl," IRS, 1995 • *Return to the Valley of the Go-Go's,* IRS, 1995.
Guy, Buddy: *Damn Right, I've Got the Blues,* Silvertone, 1991 • *Feels Like Rain,* Silvertone, 1993 • "She's a Superstar," A&M, 1995 (*Things to Do in Denver When You're Dead* soundtrack).
Haworth, Bryn: *Let the Days Go By,* Island, 1974.
Keb' Mo': *A Little Mo',* Okeh/Epic, 1994 • *Keb' Mo',* Okeh/Epic, 1994 • *Just Like You,* Okeh/Epic, 1996.
Killing Joke: *Fire Dances,* EG, 1983.
King, B.B.: *Deuces Wild,* MCA, 1997.
Mahal, Taj: *Dancing the Blues,* Private, 1993 • *Phantom Blues,* Private, 1996 • *Senor Blues,* Private, 1997.

Mayall, John: *Blues for the Lost Days,* Silvertone, 1997.
Miracle Legion: *Drenched,* Morgan Creek, 1992.
Moe: *No Doy,* 550 Music, 1996.
Muldaur, Maria: *Meet Me at Midnight,* Black Top, 1994.
Ocean Blue: *The Ocean Blue,* Sire, 1989.
Reed, Jimmy: "Take Out Some Insurance on Me Baby," A&M, 1995 (*Things to Do in Denver When You're Dead* soundtrack).
Roxy Music: w/ Bryan Ferry, *Street Life: 20 Greatest Hits,* EG, 1986.
Rush, Otis: *Ain't Enough Comin' In,* This Way Up, 1994 • *This Way Up,* This Way Up, 1994.
School of Fish: *Live in L.A.* (EP), Capitol, 1991 • *School of Fish,* Capitol, 1991 • "Three Strange Days," Capitol, 1991 • "Wrong," Capitol, 1991.
Smiths, The: *Hatful of Hollow* (6 tracks), Rough Trade/Sire, 1984 • "Heaven Knows I'm Miserable Now," Rough Trade/Sire, 1984 • "How Soon Is Now?," Rough Trade/Sire, 1984 • *The Smiths,* Rough Trade/Sire, 1984 • "What Difference Does It Make?," Rough Trade/Sire, 1984 • "William, It Was Really Nothing," Rough Trade/Sire, 1984 • "Ask," Rough Trade/Sire, 1986 • "Panic," Rough Trade/Sire, 1986 • *The World Won't Listen* (3 tracks), Rough Trade, 1986 • *Louder Than Bombs* (12 tracks), Rough Trade/Sire, 1987 • "Sweet and Tender Hooligan," Reprise, 1987, 1995 • *Best,* Vols. 1–2, Sire, 1992 • *Singles,* Reprise, 1995.
Something Happens: *Bedlam a Go Go,* Charisma, 1992.
Terrell: *Beautiful Side of Madness,* Point Blank, 1996.
Thomas, Chris: *21st Century Blues,* Private, 1995.
Tribe: *Sleeper,* Slash, 1993.
Velocity Girl: *Simpatico,* Sub Pop, 1994 • *Sorry Again* (EP), Sub Pop, 1994.
Wild Colonials: *This Can't Be Life,* DGC, 1996.

COLLECTIONS
A Smile Like Yours soundtrack, Elektra, 1997.
Rock and Roll Doctor (A Tribute to Lowell George), CMC International, 1998.

Sonia Pottinger

The indigenous record scene that sprang up in Kingston, Jamaica, in the early '60s was dominated by men, and to a great degree it still is. Women producers were unheard of in Jamaica before Sonia Pottinger, and a more successful one has yet to arrive.

Sonia Eloise Pottinger was a one-woman liberation movement. She was the leading Jamaican female producer in the rock-steady era, to which she made significant contributions. In the early reggae period she did major work with Errol Dunkley, Culture, Marcia Griffiths, and others. She owned her own record shop, pressing plant, and publishing company and produced, manufactured, and distributed her own records. After the death of Duke Reid (see entry) she licensed his catalog and reissued his product as well as her own.

The shop (like a related early label) was called Tip-Top; it was located on Orange Street not far from Prince Buster's (see entry) store. "My husband had a hardware store," she explains, "Hardware and Cycle we called it. We had bought this place, 103 Orange Street. And I was determined.

"He was rough," she says of her ex-husband. "I don't know if he didn't want me in the same business with him, but he would speak out of turn and I just didn't like it. So I saved some money and opened a restaurant down Orange Street, a little below him. There was a bakery higher up the road that I used to take cakes from. They had a cake named 'Tip-Top,' so I called it 'Tip-Top Restaurant and Record Store.'"

In Jamaica you get used to seeing combination dry cleaners or restaurants and record stores—nearly every second or third shop you enter has some records for sale. "The record store was on the other side of the restaurant," she explains. "I ran the restaurant and it did very well. But after a while I wasn't getting enough time with my children and I just kept the record store."

Estranged from her husband, with three children, Pottinger had to make a living. "By profession I was an accountant and a typist. But it would not be enough to take care of three children and make them live in the lifestyle I would like them to. Things began to get bad with us, it wasn't working out, I wasn't happy, the children were nervous. I made up my mind. My ex-husband—he's dead now—used to go in the studio and make some song. And so I went to the studio one day after I saved up some money, and I did quite a number of tunes."

The first release, Joe White and Chuck's R&B-country–flavored "Every Night," was cut at Federal and was a big Jamaican hit. Later she recorded in Duke Reid's Treasure Isle studio with Errol Brown at the board and the likes of Sly and Robbie's (see entry) Revolutionaries providing the rhythms. Other studios include Wirl, Dynamics, Channel One, Lee Perry's (see entry) Black Ark, and Aquarius. She released singles, 12-inches, and albums on her own Gayfeet, High Note, and Sky Note labels.

In rock-steady days, she produced singers and vocal groups like the Valentines (guitarist Tony Chin's first group with his brother, before joining Soul Syndicate— he currently plays with the American reggae band Big Mountain). The Conquerors, the Gaylads, and Justin Hinds and the Dominoes are among many others. A few of her big rock-steady hits were "The Whip" by the Ethiopians, Stranger and Patsy's "Down by the Trainline," "Little Nut Tree" by the Melodians, and Ken Boothe's "Say You." And, as Errol Dunkley later sang on one of her productions, she liked to do things "a little way different."

Pottinger's label became a haven for songwriter Bob Andy and for some of reggae's leading ladies, such as Patsy (Millicent Todd), Lorna Bennett, and later members of Bob Marley's I-Threes, backup singers Judy Mowatt and Marcia Griffiths. Early reggae hits include "I Shall Sing" and "Emergency Call" from Mowatt (who first recorded for Pottinger under the name of Julian), Griffiths' "Stepping Out of Babylon" and "Dreamland" and the sublime "Struggling," from the lesser-known Sharon Black. Pottinger herself sang background now and then as well.

A producer's job, she says, is "to correct, to blend your talent with theirs. Sometimes an artist comes to you and he just has a song. You have to go to the piano with him and rehearse and hear what it sounds like, correct it grammatically; at least that is what I do. Then lay the rhythm track. Sometimes when you go home you listen and hear where the horns should be and that sort of thing. You go back to the studio with a horn section and you say, 'I would like so and so, what do you think of so and so?'"

This interactive method defines her style of production. "We worked with a togetherness," she says. "Everybody had an input, from the artist who comes with the tune to the musicians who are going to bang it out to the total finishing of the music and the mixing with an engineer afterward. You sit down quietly and you arrange and mix and drop out and put in—from total togetherness, a blend of everybody's thought."

Her "everyday people" approach often brought out a side of a singer or group other producers never saw. Jackie Edwards' "Get Up" is one of his most inspired singles, and roots cuts like Well Pleased and Satisfied's "Chat Chat," "Chatty Chatty Mouth" by the Mellolads, and the relaxed urgency of "(I Ain't Got) No Time to Lose" by Earth and Stone all found great popularity as 45s, standing with the artists' best work. She produced an early instrumental album for the Hippy Boys, whose drum-and-bass core powered Lee Perry's later Upsetters and Bob Marley's Wailers.

She also cut four albums by the prolific reggae group Culture, which include some of their hardest singles, like "This Train" and "Natty Never Get Weary." Two "foreign" greatest hits packages draw from these recordings as well. She took the group from their bitter breakup with Joe Gibbs (see entry) to a worldwide touring schedule they still maintain today.

In keeping with her Christian beliefs, she formed a gospel label called Glory. For a woman in Kingston's notoriously misogynist record industry to do so much was amazing. "I just lived my humble way," she says. "I never interfered; I had to keep a low profile because I didn't want them to feel I'm getting big. I thought in my lifetime that being the only woman in the industry they would have been gentler and kinder to me. But they were not." Since her position didn't give her an advantage, she stepped out of the mold in sound as well as sex. "I liked to dress up my music, sweeten it," she says of the lone violin that starkly outlines some Justin Hinds vocals on *From Jamaica with Reggae*. "I wanted it to have a different flavor." When Culture blasted across the waters with *International Herb*, it was the same, almost folksy, feel of the music that helped bring home the militant themes.

"Some of the producers just did it for the money, while some of us got totally involved," Pottinger says. "I take an interest in those times, even for the appearance of the artist. When I arranged for Culture to play in England I personally sent down to the store, got samples of fabric to make them suits. I saw up to their very outfit to go. With the older artists like Marcia Griffiths," she says, "If they're going on a show, I like to see what they're going to be wearing."

A series of dub albums, all mixed by Errol Brown (who originally worked for Reid but blossomed as part of the High Note team), as well as hundreds of B-side versions on singles, are among the '70s' sturdiest dubs. Never satisfied to imitate, Pottinger always kept the musical standard high and aimed for the ear of the common people. She is retired but not inactive. "I'm into flowers, I'm into ceramics, I do gymnastics and all that sort of thing," she says. In recent years, the American Heartbeat label has assembled a series of compilations, both vocal and dub, from her vaults. —CHUCK FOSTER

Andy, Bob: *Lots of Love and I*, Sky Note, 1978.
Culture: *Harder Than the Rest*, Virgin, 1978 • *Cumbolo*, Shanachie, 1979, 1989 • *International Herb*, Virgin, 1979 • *Trod On*, Heartbeat, 1979, 1993 • *See also* Albums.
Dowe, Brent: *Build Me Up*, Trojan, 1974.
Dunkley, Errol: *Darling Oh!*, Trojan, 1972, 1991.

Griffiths, Marcia: *Naturally*, High Note, 1978 • *Steppin'*, Sky Note, 1979.
Hippy Boys: *Reggae with the Hippy Boys*, High Note, n.d..
Melodians, The: *Pre-Meditation*, Sky Note, 1986.
Well Pleased and Satisfied: "Sweetie Come from America," Columbia, 1976, 1986 (*Club Paradise* soundtrack).

COLLECTIONS

Old Hits of the Past, High Note, c. 1975: Julian, "I Shall Sing" • Stranger and the Angels, "Let the Power Fall."
Time to Remember, High Note, c. 1975: Judy Mowatt, "Cry to Me" "I Love You," "I'm Alone," "Too Good for Me" • Patsy, "Hanging On" • Saints, "Brown Eyes" • Joe White and Chuck, "Every Nite."
Dub Expression, High Note, c. 1978.
Medley Dub, High Note, c. 1978.
Culture Dub, High Note, 1978.
Culture in Dub, Sky Note, 1978.
Hottest Hits from the Vaults of Treasure Island, Front Line/Virgin, 1979: Alton and the Flames, "Cry Tough" • Phillis Dillon, "Right Track" • Dobby Dobson, "Loving Pauper" • The Jamaicans, "Things You Say You Love" • The Melodians, "Come On Little Girl" • The Paragons, "The Tide Is High" • The Sensations, "I'll Never Fall in Love," "Those Guys" • Silver Tones, "Midnight Hour" • Vic Taylor, "Heartaches" • The Techniques, "Queen Majesty" • Three Tops, "It's Raining."
Put on Your Best Dress: Sonia Pottinger's Rocksteady, 1967–1968, Attack, 1990: Stranger Cole and Patsy, "Tell It to Me" • The Conquerors, "What a Agony," "Won't You Come Home" • Monty Morris, Monty, "Play It Cool," "Put on Your Best Dress" • Patsy, w/ the Count Ossie Band, "Pata Pata Rock Seady" • The Valentines, "All in One," "Blam Blam Fever."
Musical Feast, Heartbeat, 1991: Ken Boothe, "Lady with the Starlight," "Say You" • Stranger Cole and Patsy, "Down by the Trainline" • Errol Dunkley, "You'll Never Know" • Gaylads, "ABC Rocksteady," "It's Hard to Confess" • The Melodians, "Little Nut Tree," "Swing and Dine" • Delano Stewart, "Stay a Little Bit Longer," "That's Life" • Teddy and the Conquerors, "Home Bound" • Victors, "Easy Squeeze."
Culture in Dub: 15 Dub Shots, Heartbeat, 1994.
Dub Over Dub: 27 Track Dub Extravaganza, Heartbeat, 1996.
Reggae Songbirds: 17 Great Tracks from High Note, Heartbeat, 1996: Lorna Bennett, "It's My House" • Sharon Black, "Struggling" • Marcia Griffiths, "Hurting Inside," "Stepping out of Babylon," "Sweet Brown Sugar" • Lillian Williams, "Why Did You Use Me?"
Reggae Train: More Great Hits from the High Note Label, Heartbeat, 1996: Culture, "This Train" • Earth and Stone, "No Time to Lose" • Marcia Griffiths, "Dreamland" • Hell

and Fire, "Love and Harmony" • Justin Hinds and the Dominoes, "Wipe Your Weeping Eyes" • Reggae George, "Fig Root" • Well Pleased and Satisfied, "Chat Chat."

Praga Khan and the Lords of Acid

Belgian Praga Khan (born Maurice Engelen), German-born Jade 4 U (Nikkie Van Lierop) and Oliver Adams have produced a blizzard of exceptional electronic dance music (new beat in the late '80s, acid house in the early '90s, various permutations of techno in the mid- and late '90s) under a phone book's worth of appellations, including Channel X, Digital Orgasm, the Immortals, MNO (for "Maurice Nikkie Oliver"), Tattoo of Pain, and, most popularly, Lords of Acid, whose "I Sit on Acid" is arguably the best-known acid-techno song of all time.

Without ever sacrificing a ruthless beat, the trio (collectively, singly, and in combination with others) have managed to infuse personality, melody, verve, and sometimes real menace into typically mechanistic and depersonalized genres. As an example of the trio's domination, they are responsible for 4 of the 11 songs on the best-selling *Rave 'Til Dawn*—a compilation that was an attempt to summarize the entire rave movement through 1992. They have also placed tracks on the gold *Sliver*, and the platinum *Mortal Kombat* soundtracks.

Maurice Engelen was born January 7, 1959, into a prominent Belgian family, and he grew up a rock fanatic. The first album he bought was Alice Cooper's *Billion Dollar Babies* in 1973. He loved "shocking live shows" and would rush to see Cooper, the Tubes, or Plasmatics when they came to Belgium. When he was 17, Engelen, a guitarist and keyboardist, formed the shock-rock band Booty and the Boot Fuckers, which was popular with the kids, less so with the parents.

Engelen also came under the sway of the electronic music of Eno (see entry), Kraftwerk, Tangerine Dream, and Amon Duul; and dark beat bands like Joy Division, Cabaret Voltaire, and Throbbing Gristle. Engelen formed the Antler Subway record label with a partner in 1982 to release proto-industrial body music by bands like A Split Second.

By the mid-'80s Engelen was also DJ and proprietor of the wildly successful Happy House nightclub in Aarschot, Belgium, where he booked many of the same acts that he released on his label, in addition to other top alternative and dance acts. He also became a tour promoter and managed two of Belgium's most popular groups of the time: Won Ton Ton (who released the album *Home* in 1989, produced by Richard Gottehrer; see entry), and 2 Belgians.

Engelen began to augment his club DJing with a drum machine and keyboards. One night in 1987, he was playing an A Split Second record in his club when he had the sudden impulse to slow it down from 45 rpm to 33 rpm; this seemed to draw even greater attention to the beat and deepen the bass. The crowd went bananas and new beat was born.

With Chris Inger, who had a small home studio, Engelen started to make new beat records of his own in 1987 under various names (101, the Musical Reporters, Save Sex, etc.), and releasing them on Antler Subway. The pair's very first single, "Blow Job," became a smash and caused immediate scandal: the producer who programmed the song on trans-European Sky TV was fired immediately after its broadcast.

With a heavy mid-tempo beat, deep bass, and flashes of industrial harshness and samples, new beat became the rage of Europe, with Antler Subway as its base. Engelen compiled and Antler released the first new beat compilation, *This Is New Beat*, which sold 60,000 copies in the first month of release in tiny Belgium alone.

While he was making records with Inger, Engelen met alluring singer Van Lierop when she sang backup on one of his records. They began to kick ideas around and she joined the merry band of hitmakers. Together the threesome created Lords of Acid in 1989, and made the transition from new beat to acid.

Their first single, "I Sit on Acid"—slightly faster and somewhat harder than new beat, with cheerfully psychedelic beeps and boops, a haunted house keyboard line, and Van Lierop's orgasmic vocals (consisting mostly of squeals and the repeated line, "Sit on your face, I wanna sit on your face")—came to define the genre. Still among the most requested electro-dance songs on dance floors around the globe, the song also introduced the band to the U.S.

Oliver Adams, a young studio wizard, then came along and joined the Lords production team, replacing Inger. They recorded the classic album *Lust* in 1991, which helped define techno (again a bit faster and heavier than its predecessor), as "I Sit" had defined acid, and earlier work had helped define new beat. Perhaps the finest single-artist techno album of the first half of the '90s, *Lust* sold over 450,000 copies in the U.S. alone on the strength of its sex, drugs, and frenzied-dancing credo. That, and no less than five dance floor classics— "I Sit," "Take Control," "Let's Get High," "The Most Wonderful Girl," and, best of all, "Rough Sex," a hilarious though disturbing declaration of Engelen's preference for "pure sex, deep sex, hot sex, rough sex" over "bright moons, winking stars, red wine" or "love letters"—delivered over a truly lubricious, whooping, and buzzing techno track.

The group's second album, *Voodoo-U,* takes techno to its logical conclusion, variously adding industrial-metallic guitar, hard-core, jungle, breakbeat, and ragga into the gloriously hedonistic mix.

Engelen discusses his modus operandi. "This is how I work with Lords of Acid: First of all, I need to be in the mood. Sometimes it takes me two years to start writing a Lords of Acid album because it is very erotic and blah, blah, blah. I have to be in a sexual mood. I think about an orgasm or whatever, and I put the idea into music. Oliver is a technician but also a musician—he knows what I am talking about right away, we work real well together. We do a lot of different lines and rhythms, and then we go on the computer and skip this, skip that, and what's left—that's what we use, music-wise.

"Then Nikkie comes in, and she is a very sexy girl. I tell her the ideas for the songs, and then we start to interact, and we write the lyrics together. It works very, very well like that. We've done it hundreds of times like that and it always works. For example, for the latest album [*Our Little Secret*], I told her, 'This song is about pussy. So let's think about it from a funny angle—people think it's a pussy cat, but it can be another kind of pussy too.'

"The first album was very techno. The second album was very hard-core, very industrial. The third one is a combination of the two—the midway point between techno and hard core. You have still the humor, but you also have very sexy songs. It's the best of both worlds," Engelen says.

Engelen's creativity keeps him young. "I don't feel any older than 25. I keep looking forward. I see friends from when I was 22, and they're still talking about things that happened then. To them it's like a big thing, but to me there's big things happening every day. I enjoy every day when I go to work so I am a happy guy. To me it would be like a nightmare to have a regular job at a factory or something.

"Sometimes when I go to bed, I get upset because I have to wait another six hours until I can go back to the studio. I'm a very creative guy—when I am mixing a record, I am already thinking about the next project. It would kill me to work under one name because each is

a different aspect of my personality. But it causes problems too: Praga Khan's 'Injected with a Poison' and Digital Orgasm [Engelen and Van Lierop's diva-house outlet] hit at about the same time in England [1993]. You go on *Top of the Pops* one week as Praga Khan, and two weeks later as Digital Orgasm. The record companies were pissed off, but I think it's funny," he laughs.

For more information on the trio's various projects, check out their outstanding official website at http://lordsofacid.pragakhan.com. —ERIC OLSEN

Praga Khan and Lords of Acid

Adams, Oliver: "Free the World" (remix), Antler Subway/Caroline, 1991 (*Techno Mancer*).

Alice in Chains: "Again" (remix), Columbia, 1996.

Angel Ice: "Je N'Aime Que Toi," Beat Box, 1991.

Channel X: "A Million Colours," Antler Subway/Caroline, 1991 (*Techno Mancer*) • "Groove to Move," Antler Subway/Caroline, 1991 (*Techno Mancer*) • "Rave the Rhythm," Beat Box, 1991.

Code Red: "Dreamer Dream," SBK, 1992 (*Rave 'Til Dawn*).

Digital Orgasm: "Running out of Time" (remix), Antler Subway/Caroline, 1991 (*Techno Mancer*) • "Startouchers," Antler Subway/Caroline, 1991 (*Techno Mancer*) • "Running out of Time," Whte Lbls, 1992 • *Do It,* American, 1993, 1997 • "Guilty of Love," American, 1993 • "Guilty of Love" (remix), Antler Subway/Whte Lbls, 1993.

G.T.O.: "Elevation" (remix), React, 1992.

Gravity Kills: *Manipulated (remixes),* TVT, 1997.

Groove Reactor: "Magick," Antler Subway/Caroline, 1991 (*Techno Mancer*).

Immortals, The: *Mortal Kombat: The Album,* Vernon Yard, 1994.

Inner Light: "Phantasia," Mental Radio, 1990.

Jade 4 U: "Messenger of Love," Antler Subway/Caroline, 1991 (*Techno Mancer*).

Jarre, Jean Michel: "Chronologie" (remix), Dreyfus/Polydor, 1993.

Lords of Acid: "I Sit on Acid," Wing, 1990 • "Let's Get High," Caroline, 1991 • *Lust,* Caroline, 1991 • "Take Control," Caroline, 1991 • "Hey Ho," Antler Subway, 1992 • "I Must Improve My Bust," Caroline, 1992 • "I Must Improve My Bust" (remix), Caroline, 1992 • "Rough Sex," Caroline, 1992 • "Rough Sex" (remix), Caroline, 1992 • "The Crab Louse," American, 1994 • *Voodoo-U,* American, 1994 • "Do What You Wanna Do," Whte Lbls, 1995 • *Our Little Secret,* Antler Subway, 1997 • "Rubber Doll," Antler Subway, 1997 • "Pussy," Antler Subway, 1998.

Musical Reporters: "Blow Job," Antler Subway, 1987.

101: "Rock to the Beat," Antler Subway, 1988.

Praga Khan: "Bula Bula," Antler Subway, 1988 • "Rock to the

Beat," Antler Subway, 1988 • "Rave Alarm," Beat Box, 1991 • "Free Your Body," Beat Box, 1992 • "Injected with a Poison," SBK, 1992 (*Rave 'Til Dawn*) • *A Spoonful of Miracles,* RCA, 1993 • "I Feel Good," Proft, 1993 • "Phantasia Forever," Mental Radio, 1993 • "Rave Alert," Antler Subway/Caroline, 1993 • "Begin to Move," Mental Radio, 1994 • "Gun Buck," Logic, 1995 • *Conquers Your Love,* Never, 1996 • "Jazz Trippin'," Never, 1997 • "Love Me Baby," Never, 1997 • "Injected with a Poison '98," Never, 1998 • *Pragamatic,* Never, 1998.

Pride and Passion: "Feel the Need in Me," Antler Subway, 1987.

Save Sex: "I Don't Do a Thing," Antler Subway, 1987.

Science Lab: "Flesh and Blood," Mental Radio, 1990.

Shakti: *Demonic Forces* (EP), Antler Subway, 1987.

Tattoo of Pain: *Vengeance Is Mine,* Antler Subway, 1996.

Time Zone: "The World of God," Mental Radio, 1991.

White Zombie: "Electric Head Pt. 1" (remix), Geffen, 1996.

Oliver Adams

Atomizer 2: "Liberty and Freedom" (remix), Antler Subway/Caroline, 1991 (*Techno Mancer*).

Channel X: *Tuned In . . . Turned On,* Never, 1997.

L.A. Style: *L.A. Style* (1 track), Arista, 1993.

Parametric: "Where Is God," Antler Subway/Caroline, 1991 (*Techno Mancer*).

Pink Stanly Ford: "A New Style Baby" (remix), Antler Subway/Caroline, 1991 (*Techno Mancer*).

Ultra Shock: "Sound of E," Logic, 1995.

Bill Price

An expert in the technical aspects of production, Bill Price is best known for his work on albums by the Sex Pistols and the Clash. Price, who began work as an engineer for Decca Records in 1962, has also produced albums by Jesus and Mary Chain, the Waterboys, and, most recently, Fluffy. An unabashed novice when he entered the field, Price scored with his first production effort, and he has been honing his craft ever since. Fluffy's *Black Eye,* which Price recorded, mixed, and produced at Metropolis Studios, his favorite London venue, is pure, exhilarating punk circa 1997.

"I've been basically working as an engineer for over 30 years," says Price, who lives in the western part of England, near Bristol. "At various stages, I've worked as a producer. Sometimes, I'm the contractor being paid for the work; sometimes, it's just falling into that chair.

Some well-known things I've officially been credited with producing include *Never Mind the Bollocks* (No. 1 U.K.) by the Sex Pistols, and the Clash's *Sandinista!* (No. 19 U.K.)"

The *Bollocks* disc, released to huge controversy in 1977, credits Price and his old friend, Chris Thomas (see entry), as producers. "*Bollocks* was a very interesting situation," Price says. "I did a lot of album tracks with the band; my friend, Chris Thomas, did some singles with them, including singles sessions, and an album was put together from those tracks. It got a little confusing, because the production company that was organizing it was trying not to pay anybody," he continues. "That is how we got a very strange credit; all the tracks on the album were produced by Chris or me." While he won't say it, the spanner in the works was punk impresario Malcolm McLaren.

"Chris and I got that credit on that album so we could sort it out ourselves, the complication being that certain songs Chris had done a version on, certain songs I had done a version on. The management kept changing running orders and playing with different versions. It was almost as if they were trying to convince me that all the tracks were going to be done by Chris and trying to convince Chris all the tracks would be done by me."

Price mastered the album "about three times in different running orders and versions, and the final mastering was done at the 11th hour." No such problems attended his engineering of *London Calling* (produced by Guy Stevens), and *Sandinista!,* arguably the high points in the Clash's career. "The Clash were a wonderful band to work with," Price says. "The enthusiasm of Joe Strummer and the prowess of Mick Jones—the combination was quite magical. That was the nearest I've ever gotten to working with a Lennon and McCartney [see entry], so to speak. They were a very sweet pair of guys."

Recently, Price produced *Black Eye,* Fluffy's debut album; he also "did a little mixing" for the American version of the Charlatans' latest album. "The American music business is a lot less fashion-conscious than the English music business, and Americans tend to hold onto things they love dearly a bit longer," he says. "So things that might be considered passé in Europe are still very popular in America. The term 'rock dinosaur' doesn't really mean a lot in America, does it? A rock dinosaur that would be reviled in Europe would be revered in the United States."

It's not about cultural turnover, it's about sentimentality, Price suggests. "In Europe, the pop culture is something of the moment, and laughing at the pop culture of yesterday is a very European attitude, whereas in America, it's something to be celebrated," he says.

The dominance of dance rock in England has "tended to make traditional rock sounds appear very hackneyed, where very European dance sounds, in America, are a little bit frightening, sort of unknown territory. People feel a little safer with the traditional rock sound."

He cites electronica darlings Prodigy for market savvy. Prodigy, a band he likes, has refashioned its cutting-edge dance beat to a harder rap beat. "I guess they've done this because they feel that would be more user-friendly to the American market," Price says.

While Price still produces, he doesn't work constantly. He has paid his dues. During the '60s, he engineered such singers and bands as Tom Jones, Eric Clapton, the Moody Blues, Engelbert Humperdinck, and John Mayall. In 1970, George Martin (see entry) hired him to join the team designing and constructing AIR Studios in London. Appointed chief engineer at AIR, Price worked there with Mott the Hoople, Stevie Wonder (see entry), Pink Floyd, Stan Getz, and Paul McCartney. In the mid-'70s, AIR became part of the Chrysalis group of companies, and Price moved to Wessex to redesign and re-equip the studios there. He was appointed studio manager and chief engineer. That also is where he formed his friendship with producer Chris Thomas. Price engineered Thomas's productions of Elton John, the Who's Pete Townshend, and the Pretenders.

"I'm a knob twiddler," Price says. "I'm the style of producer who hopefully gets the best out of a band who really want to work on their own. Quite often, I've worked with bands I felt needed the sort of producer who would write the song for them and maybe hire the rhythm section to play it. But I'm not that sort of producer; nowadays, I wouldn't do the gig in the first place."

While he uses psychology to nurture a band, he also uses technology. "These days, I always work on 24-track, 48-track, or 72-track analog," he says. "I did quite a lot of work on digital multitrack, and I had quite a few problems come up." Tracks would drop off and become irretrievable, leading to numerous phone calls and additional expense. "I soon made a discovery that I really hated anything that had been recorded and mixed digitally," he says. "It didn't seem to sound as good to me as analog. In the course of several projects, I was finding that if I recorded something digital on multitrack, I had to mix it analog; or, if I wanted to mix something digital, it would be fine as long as I recorded it multitrack analog. If something hadn't been through the analog domain, I found I couldn't get the punch, the loudness in the sound."

When he began in the business, the engineer recorded the album, and the producer, "as such, was called the A&R man," Price says. "What he did was hire the artist and find the repertoire. Now the term 'A&R man' applies to a position in a record company, and that position in record making grew to be known as a record producer."

What Price and his colleagues in Repro, the British producer and engineer lobby, want is a new designation, perhaps "sound director," Price says. Copyright issues surrounding the agglomeration of multimedia and the new forms of music distribution such as the Internet and satellite TV are prompting new definitions, he suggests. It's a long way from 1962, when the Decca Record Company hired Price "as a young whippersnapper to make tea." "My first bit of engineering was a record called 'Tell Me When' by the Applejacks," recalls Price. "I was assisting on the session and the star engineer overindulged himself at the pub and was unable to attend. The A&R person was quite distraught and didn't know whether to abandon the session or not. I convinced him I was capable of finishing it, and he said 'fair enough.' "

Fortunately, the indisposed engineer had set up the session effectively for the A side; all there was left to do was produce the other side. "By sheer fluke, when the A side and the B-side got played to the A&R meeting at Decca Records," Price says, "the head of A&R preferred the B-side. It went to No. 1." —CARLO WOLFF

Big Audio Dynamite: *Megatop Phoenix,* Columbia, 1989 • *Greatest Hits,* Columbia, 1995.

Clash, The: "I Fought the Law," Epic, 1979 • *The Clash* (1 track), Epic, 1979 • *Black Market Clash* (3 tracks), Epic, 1980 • *Sandinista!,* Epic, 1980 • "The Call-Up," Epic, 1980 • "Hitsville U.K.," Epic, 1981 • *Story of the Clash,* Vol. 1, Epic, 1988 • *The Singles,* TriStar, 1996.

Doll by Doll: *Remember,* Automatic, 1979.

Fluffy: *5 Live* (EP), the Enclave, 1996 • *Black Eye,* the Enclave, 1996.

Jesus and Mary Chain: "April Skies," Blanco y Negro/WB, 1987 • *Darklands* (6 tracks), Blanco y Negro/WB, 1987 • "Happy When It Rains," Blanco y Negro/WB, 1987.

Kinsey Report: *Powerhouse,* Charisma, 1991.

My Little Funhouse: *Standunder,* Geffen, 1992.

Racing Cars: *Downtown Tonight,* Chrysalis, 1976.

RPLA: *Metal Queen Hijack,* Giant, 1994.

Sex Pistols: "God Save the Queen," Virgin, 1977 • "Holidays in the Sun," Virgin, 1977 • *Never Mind the Bollocks,* Virgin/WB, 1977 • "Pretty Vacant," Virgin, 1977.

Stradlin, Izzy: *117 Degrees,* Geffen, 1998.

Waterboys, The: *Dream Harder,* Geffen, 1993 • *Glastonbury Song* (EP), Geffen, 1993 • "The Return of Pan," Geffen, 1993.

Prince

The Minneapolis sound of the early '80s was a spirited blend of funk, disco, synth-pop, R&B, soul, and rock played by a multiracial, gender-blending group of musicians under the tutelage of the child prodigy Prince (self-renamed in the '90s with an unpronounceable hieroglyph, followed by "The Artist Formerly Known as Prince," then simply "The Artist" in rapid succession). Though obviously inspired by Sly and the Family Stone (see entry), Prince found his voice in the apparent duality of sex and God, rather than through Sly's peace, love, and drugs.

Prince channeled a fair amount of his quirky mystique into the careers of a collage of protégés: the Time ("Jungle Love," No. 20; "The Bird"), Vanity 6 ("Nasty Girl"), Apollonia 6 ("Sex Shooter"), Sheila E ("The Glamorous Life," No. 6; "A Love Bizarre," No. 11), and Sheena Easton ("Sugar Walls," No. 9) as well as members of his own bands the Revolution (Wendy and Lisa) and the New Power Generation. For a period of time in the mid-'80s, Prince and his clan challenged Michael Jackson and Madonna for supremacy over the pop world.

Prince has made his mark with over 50 pop and R&B chart appearances, including five No. 1 singles ("When Doves Cry," "Kiss," "Let's Go Crazy," "Batdance," "Cream"), five singles in the Top 5 ("Most Beautiful Girl in the World," "Sign 'O' the Times," "Raspberry Beret," "U Got the Look," "Purple Rain"), three No. 1 albums (*Purple Rain, Around the World in a Day, Batman*), in addition to the hugely successful film *Purple Rain.*

On June 7, 1958, in Minneapolis, Prince Rogers Nelson graced the world with his royal presence. The young Prince (named after his father's jazz combo, the Prince Rogers Trio) was deeply affected by his parent's marital strife and subsequent family instability. After graduating from Central High School on his 18th birthday, Prince continued with his job at Moon Sound Studio, where mentor Chris Moon instructed him in production and Prince helped Moon write songs in a 50-50 split.

After the pair had no luck securing a deal, Moon contacted local ad man Owen Husney, who agreed to manage Prince, provided him with a small allowance and his first synth, and advised him to drop his last name. Husney's past relationship with Warner Bros. vice president Russ Thyret would prove pivotal to Prince's signing. Husney's belief in Prince's talent was so strong that he insisted the young star be allowed to produce, write, and play all instruments on his albums with Warner Bros. After passing a "studio test" with producers Gary Katz, Russ Titelman, and Ted Templeman (see entries), Prince signed a six-figure contract—one of the largest ever for a new artist.

Prince's debut album, *For You,* sold 150,000 copies and received a modicum of critical praise. "Soft and Wet/So Blue," the first single from *For You,* sold 350,000 copies and reached No. 12 on the R&B chart. Prince's third album, *Dirty Mind,* basically another one-man show, started to make inroads with the pop audience, but didn't have a strong single and was a step back commercially from his second album, *Prince.* "When You Were Mine" is the surprise of the album—a punchy, melodic new wave tune that could have come from the Police (and they would have been happy to have it). *Dirty Mind* is the artistic bridge between the Prince of the past and Prince of the future.

Prince began to gain a reputation as a highly charismatic, if over-the-top, performer: he stalked the stage in bikini briefs and high-heeled boots, simulating sex with his guitar and various band members. This behavior raised eyebrows and inspired his next album title, *Controversy,* a bright synth-pop splashed with black dance rhythms. Prince's natural voice replaced much of the falsetto of previous albums. The title track is classic Prince; it deals with the sexual, social, and racial closed-mindedness of the time with gospel intensity.

Released in October of 1981, *Controversy* was created during a prolific time in Prince's career. In between *Mind* and *Controversy,* he put together a great funk group, the Time, which featured future production stars Jimmy "Jam" Harris on keyboards and Terry Lewis (see entry) on bass; Cynthia Johnson, the original lead singer, who left to sing with Lipps, Inc. of "Funkytown" fame; guitarist Jesse Johnson, who went on to a solo career; and lead singer Morris Day, who sparred with Prince in the film *Purple Rain* and had a solo hit with "Fishnet." Though filled with raw talent, most of the magical moments on the Time's first three albums were generated by Prince.

1999 (No. 9) is Prince's masterpiece. The double-LP format gave him more space to stretch out, and he finally connected with the pop audience. Chock-full of hits, the album's best includes the apocalyptic "1999" (No. 12), with its chunky guitar riffs, anthemic melody, and jubilant vocal. "Little Red Corvette" (No. 6), a musical comparison between the feminine mystique and a muscle car, succeeds on every level, with the elegant tension of the verses answered by the flowing organs, pounding drums, orgasmic guitar, and vocal ejaculations of Prince on the choruses. Prince's frenzy shifts into overdrive on the effervescent "Delirious" (No. 8), and the funky, upbeat "Let's Pretend We're Married" is a manifestation of Prince's Seventh Day Adventist upbringing: true carnal pleasure can only be achieved through guilt-free association, leading to self-deception.

Prince sold out numerous shows across the country on the *1999* tour (with Vanity 6 and the Time as supporting acts) and received *Rolling Stone*'s Artist of the Year award for 1982 and Musician of the Year at the Black Music Awards. While on tour, Prince jottted down ideas in a "purple journal" he kept with him at all times. In that journal were the seeds of *Purple Rain*. With a multitude of individuals financing the project, the script was fleshed out and Prince was cast as the lead. Real Minneapolis scenesters (including the Time and Apollonia 6) formed much of the supporting cast. The semiautobiographical plot tells of the struggles, rivalries, and mercurial rise to fame of the "Kid" and the scene around him. The *Purple Rain* soundtrack spent 24 weeks at No. 1 on the pop charts and turned Prince into a superstar. The proceeds also allowed him to build Paisley Park, the full-service recording studio and office complex near Minneapolis that serves as his headquarters.

The classic single "When Doves Cry" is daringly sparse compared to previous work, with beautifully crafted Beethovian synth lines and Hendrix-style guitar punctuating a forthright beat and soulful tune. "Let's Go Crazy," which cemented Prince's rock 'n' roll reputation, is as euphoric and maniacal as the title implies. The title track, an echoey and bombastic pop ballad, was clearly overproduced but rode all the way to No. 2 on the success of the film and the soundtrack.

Prince has never again achieved this level of across-the-board success, but he has many other outstanding moments in his (too?) prolific career. *Around the World in a Day* was the follow-up to *Rain* and Prince's attempt to take the eclecticism of *Rain* even further afield. The Beatlesque album produced a couple of hits, including the charming "Raspberry Beret," but generated mixed reviews.

In 1986 Prince pursued another movie, *Under the Cherry Moon*, which attempted to elevate petulance to the level of artistic ideal. It flopped, but the soundtrack, *Parade*, yielded the jittery funk of "Kiss." Spooky and erotic, "Kiss" was originally written for Mazarati, a side project of Prince's bass player Mark Brown. Prince scribbled some lyrics down, came up with the tune on acoustic guitar, sang it into a tape recorder, and told Mazarati to come up with the rest. After the band worked up an arrangement and played it for Prince, he repossessed the tune. Prince giveth and Prince taketh away.

The inspiration for 1987's near-classic *Sign 'O' the Times* (No. 6) dates back to Sly Stone's dark and brooding *There's a Riot Goin' On*. Ghetto uprisings, deteriorating race relations, and AIDS caused Prince to augment his sex-and-God ethos. The title track warns and confides. "Housequake" jams to an edgy hip-hop beat, and "I Could Never Take the Place of Your Man" (No. 10) is a brilliant pick-up line delivered in one of Prince's most infectious pop-rock melodies.

It has grown harder to separate the wheat from the chaff since *Sign*. The hard funk of "Alphabet Street" (No. 8) and "Gett Off" and the lovely neo-soul of "The Most Beautiful Girl in the World" are Prince's most pleasing songs of the late '80s and '90s. In the '90s, music has taken a back seat to the infamous name change and Prince's battles with his former label, Warner Bros. —Dawn Darling and Eric Olsen

Abdul, Paula: *Spellbound*, Captive, 1991.

Apollonia 6: *Apollonia 6*, Warner Bros., 1984 • "Sex Shooter," Warner Bros., 1984.

Campbell, Tevin: "Round and Round," Paisley Park/WB, 1990 • *T.E.V.I.N.*, Warner Bros., 1991 • *I'm Ready*, Qwest, 1993 • "The Halls of Desire," Qwest, 1993.

Chavez, Ingrid: *May 19, 1992*, Paisley Park/WB, 1991.

Clinton, George: *Hey Man . . . Smell My Finger*, Paisley Park, 1993.

Cymone, Andre: "Dance Electric," Columbia, 1985.

Easton, Sheena: "Sugar Walls," EMI America, 1985 • *Lover in Me*, MCA, 1988 • *The World Of: The Singles Collection*, Capitol, 1993 • See also Prince.

Electra, Carmen: "Go Go Dancer," Paisley Park/WB, 1992.

Ellis, T.C.: *True Confessions* (4 tracks), Paisley Park/WB, 1991.

Khan, Chaka: *C.K.*, Warner Bros., 1988.

LaBelle, Patti: *Be Yourself*, MCA, 1989 • "Yo Mister," MCA, 1989.

Lane, Lois: "Qualified," Polydor, 1992.

Louie Louie: "Dance unto the Rhythm," Hardback/WB, 1993.

Love, Monie: "Born 2 Breed," Chrysalis, 1993 • "In a Word or 2," Chrysalis, 1993 • *In a Word or 2*, Warner Bros., 1993.

Madonna: *Like a Prayer*, Sire, 1989.

Martika: "Love . . . Thy Will Be Done," Columbia, 1991 • *Martika's Kitchen*, Columbia, 1991.

Mayte: "The Most Beautiful Boy in the World," NPG, 1994.

New Power Generation: *New Power Soul*, NPG, 1998.

Prince: "Controversy," Warner Bros., 1979 • "I Wanna Be Your Lover," Warner Bros., 1979 • *Prince*, Warner Bros., 1979 • *Dirty Mind*, Warner Bros., 1980 • *Controversy*, Warner Bros., 1981 • "Alphabet St.," Paisley Park, 1988 • "Alphabet St." (remix), Paisley Park, 1988 • *Black Album*, Erotic City/WB, 1988, 1994 • *Lovesexy*, Paisley Park, 1988

• "Batdance," Warner Bros., 1989 • *Batman: Music from the Motion Picture,* Warner Bros., 1989 • "Feel U Up," Warner Bros., 1989 • "Partyman," Warner Bros., 1989 • "Partyman" (remix), Warner Bros., 1989 • *The Scandalous Sex Suite* (EP), Warner Bros., 1989 • "New Power Generation," Paisley Park, 1990 • "Thieves in the Temple," Paisley Park, 1990 • "Nothing Compares ,", Paisley Park, 1993 • "Pink Cashmere," Paisley Park, 1993 • *The Hits 1,* Paisley Park, 1993 • *The Hits 2,* Paisley Park, 1993 • *The Hits/The B Sides,* Paisley Park, 1993 • *The Beautiful Experience* (EP), Bellmark, 1994 • "Purple Medley," Warner Bros., 1995 • *Emancipation,* NPG, 1996 • *Crystal Ball,* NPG, 1998 • *For You,* Warner Bros., 1978 • "Soft and Wet," Warner Bros., 1978 • "1999," Warner Bros., 1982 • *1999,* Warner Bros., 1982 • "D.M.S.R.," Warner Bros., 1982 • "Delirious," Warner Bros., 1983 • "Little Red Corvette," Warner Bros., 1983 • "Hot Thing," Paisley Park, 1987 • "Housequake," Paisley Park, 1987 • "Housequake" (remix), Paisley Park, 1987 • "I Could Never Take the Place of Your Man," Paisley Park, 1987 • "If I Was Your Girlfriend," Paisley Park, 1987 • "Sign 'O' the Times," Paisley Park, 1987 • *Sign 'O' the Times,* Paisley Park, 1987 • "U Got the Look," Paisley Park, 1987 • "U Got the Look" (remix), Paisley Park, 1987 • "I Wish U Heaven," Paisley Park, 1988 • "Scandalous!," Warner Bros., 1989 • w/ Sheena Easton, "The Arms of Orion," Warner Bros., 1989 • *Graffiti Bridge* soundtrack, Paisley Park/WB, 1990 • *Come,* Warner Bros., 1994 • "Letitgo," Warner Bros., 1994 • "Space," Warner Bros., 1994 • "The Most Beautiful Girl in the World," NPG/Bellmark, 1994 • *Chaos and Disorder,* Warner Bros., 1996 • *Girl 6* soundtrack, Warner Bros., 1996.

Prince and the New Power Generation: "Cream," Paisley Park, 1991 • "Diamonds and Pearls," Paisley Park, 1991 • *Diamonds and Pearls,* Paisley Park, 1991 • "Gangster Glam," Paisley Park, 1991 • "Gett Off," Paisley Park, 1991 • "Insatiable," Paisley Park, 1991 • *[Prince symbol],* Paisley Park, 1992 • "7," Paisley Park, 1992 • "Money Don't Matter 2 Night," Paisley Park, 1992 • "My Name Is Prince," Paisley Park, 1992 • "Sexy MF," Paisley Park, 1992 • "The Morning Papers," Paisley Park, 1993 • "Eye Hate U," NPG/Warner Bros., 1995 • *The Gold Experience,* NPG/Warner Bros., 1995 • "Girl 6," Warner Bros., 1996 • "Gold," NPG, 1996.

Prince and the Revolution: "17 Days . . . ," Warner Bros., 1984 • "Erotic City," Warner Bros., 1984 • "I Would Die 4 U," Warner Bros., 1984 • "Let's Go Crazy," Warner Bros., 1984 • "Let's Go Crazy" (remix), Warner Bros., 1984 • "Purple Rain," Warner Bros., 1984 • *Purple Rain,* Warner Bros., 1984 • "When Doves Cry," Warner Bros., 1984 • "America," Paisley Park, 1985 • *Around the World in a Day,* Paisley Park, 1985 • "Pop Life," Paisley Park, 1985 •

"Raspberry Beret," Paisley Park, 1985 • "Take Me with U," Warner Bros., 1985 • "Anotherloverholenyohead," Paisley Park, 1986 • "Kiss," Paisley Park, 1986 • "Kiss" (remix), Paisley Park, 1986 • "Mountains," Paisley Park, 1986 • *Parade,* Paisley Park, 1986.

Sevelle, Taja: "Love Is Contagious," Paisley Park, 1987 • *Taja Sevelle,* Paisley Park, 1987.

Sheila E.: "The Belle of St. Mark," Paisley Park, 1984 • "The Glamorous Life," Paisley Park, 1984 • *The Glamorous Life,* Paisley Park, 1984 • "A Love Bizarre," Paisley Park, 1985 • *Romance 1600,* Paisley Park, 1985.

Staples, Mavis: "Melody Cool," Paisley Park/WB, 1990 • "Time Waits for No One," Paisley Park/WB, 1990 • *The Voice,* NPG, 1995.

Steele, Jevetta: *Here It Is,* Columbia, 1993.

Time, The: *The Time,* Warner Bros., 1982 • *What Time Is It?,* Warner Bros., 1982 • "Grace," Warner Bros., 1983 (*Attack of the Killer B's*) • "Ice Cream Castles," Warner Bros., 1984 • *Ice Cream Castles,* Warner Bros., 1984 • "Jungle Love," Warner Bros., 1984 • "The Bird," Warner Bros., 1985.

Vanity 6: "Nasty Girl," Warner Bros., 1982 • *Vanity 6,* Warner Bros., 1982.

Prince Be (ATTREL CORDES) and P.M. Dawn

T he discovery of the sound that made Prince Be (born May 15, 1970) and his band, P.M. Dawn, popular can be attributed to happenstance. He says he had no idea his love of harmony and melody would bring him into the studio to work with acts such as the Bee Gees, Elton John, and Jody Watley. But the work he and his brother and partner, J.C. (Jarett Cordes) "the Eternal," were doing on their debut prefigured that.

He recalls they were working with a 24-track machine when they realized they were only using eight of those tracks. "There's gotta be something we can do with those," Prince Be recalls thinking. "The engineer said we could track something two and three times and that sounded cool, so we thought it would sound better after a hundred times," he says. In the end, they simplified, however, reducing the mix to only "seven layers per note in the harmony."

Prince Be grew up in Jersey City, New Jersey, during the '70s, on a steady diet of the Beach Boys, Paul Revere, the Beatles, Sly and the Family Stone, and Kool and the Gang. During his club-spinner days he discovered the underground hip-hop scene, Zeppelin, and Hendrix. He has made this hodgepodge of influences the basis of a successful career as a producer and musician.

Perhaps the band's first No. 1 hit, "Set Adrift on Memory Bliss" from their debut album, *Of the Heart, of the Soul and of the Cross: The Utopian Experience,* proves the point best. Prince Be was only 21 when that album was released. "The first couple of albums, I was doing raps," he recalls. "Then I moved into R&B and ballads. The people sort of like that, and that was the category." P.M. Dawn is now out to make soft-spoken rap records and ballads: "Then we tried to delve into everything. Now I don't know what we're going to try and do. I think we're going to make some shit up, we're going to attempt to make up a new genre."

Although he had always been fascinated by music, it wasn't until he worked on P.M. Dawn's 1991 debut that he became interested in producing. "As an artist I was always saying, 'Hey, could you hook this up for me this way?' Then I started asking a lot of questions. I made friends with an engineer and he schooled me on pretty much everything I use nowadays. He taught me everything and then I started getting into programming," he explains. "When it came down to a sound or a song, I always had good ideas. I just didn't know how to execute them."

He brings a laptop computer and a Kurzweil K2500 keyboard to each session. He may also bring a Tascam DA-88s, for ease of use. He says he thinks people use him for melodies and vocals, especially the ethereal kind, in which he specializes.

Working with the Bee Gees and Elton John impressed him. "It was weird, because I've listened to Elton John my whole life. I met him, it was cool, and then it was just a vibe," he says. "The Bee Gees, though, I've worshipped my entire life. I had to get off the head trip that this was the fucking Bee Gees," he says. "We were in there working and Barry [Gibb] was, like, 'I want more input from Be.' Everything I heard has the Bee Gees sound and it was like fucking God to me anyway. I was pretty happy with the old shit. They were like, 'I want some really different-sounding stuff.' I tried to produce it like the Bee Gees and it turned out pretty good." The song was "Still Waters Run Deep." He would like to produce a hip-hop album. He would also like to produce Cyndi Lauper.

"What I wanted to do from the get-go was make records," he says. "When I was young I used to worship records. I just wanted to make a contribution. I didn't necessarily want to be remembered, but I wanted to be the guy to tell music: 'Go that way.' It's cool, man. Not a lot of people understand what contributions we've made to music. Which is cool for me, because I like to stay on the low anyway." —DAVID JOHN FARINELLA

Ambersunshower: "Running Song," Gee Street, 1997 • *Walter T. Smith,* Gee Street, 1997.

Backstreet Boys: *The Backstreet Boys,* Jive/Zomba, 1997.

Bee Gees: *Still Waters,* Polydor, 1997 • "Still Waters Run Deep," Polydor, 1997.

Boy George and Culture Club: *At Worst . . . The Best of Boy George and Culture Club,* ERG, 1993.

Bryant, Dana: *Wishing from the Top,* Warner Bros., 1996.

Emosia: *Lover's Paradise,* Warlock, 1995.

Franklin, Aretha: *Greatest Hits, 1980–1994,* Arista, 1994.

Gravity Kills: "Enough" (remix), TVT, 1996 • *Manipulated* (remixes), TVT, 1997.

John, Elton: *Duets,* MCA, 1993 • *Of the Heart, of the Soul and of the Cross: The Utopian Experience,* Gee Street, 1991 • "Set Adrift on Memory Bliss," Gee Street, 1991.

P.M. Dawn: "Set Adrift on Memory Bliss" (remix), Tommy Boy, 1991, 1992 (*MTV Party to Go,* Vol. 2) • "I'd Die Without You," Gee Street, 1992 • "Paper Doll," Gee Street, 1992 • "Looking Through Patient Eyes," Gee Street, 1993 • *The Bliss Album,* Gee Street, 1993 • "The Ways of the Wind," Gee Street/Island, 1993 • "The Ways of the Wind" (remix), Gee Street/Island, 1993 • "You Got Me Floatin'," Reprise, 1993 (*Stone Free: A Tribute to Jimi Hendrix*) • "Downtown Venus," Gee Street, 1995 • *Jesus Wept,* Gee Street, 1995 • "Sometimes I Miss You So Much (Dedicated to the Christ Consciousness)," Gee Street, 1995 • "If You Never Say Goodbye," Warner Bros., 1996 (*Songs in the Key of X*) • *Vibrations of Love and Anger and the Ponderance of Life and Existence,* Gee Street/island, 1996 • "X-Files Theme," Warner Bros., 1996 (*Songs in the Key of X*).

Prince Be: Featuring Ky-mani, "Gotta Be . . . Movin' On Up," Gee Street, 1998.

Simply Red: "Stars" (remix), EastWest, 1991.

Prince Buster
(CECIL CAMPBELL)

Cecil "Bustamente" Campbell—named after a popular Jamaican prime minister—was born May 28, 1938, and became known to the world as "Prince Buster." He began his show business career as a prizefighter. He sang live at Tilly Blackman's Glass Bucket Club and served a stint as sound system bouncer for Coxsone Dodd (see entry) before setting up his own sound, opening a record store on Orange Street in Kingston, and cutting his first record in 1959 at the 1-track recording facilities of the Jamaica Broadcast Company.

The record, "Oh Carolina" by the Folkes Brothers, is considered by many the opening salvo of reggae. Its combination of acoustic ska without horns and the Nyahbingi rhythm of Count Ossie's Rastafarian drummers made it an immediate sound system hit, though it was far too unorthodox to achieve radio airplay at the time.

Using the West Indies Studios on Bell Road in Kingston, Buster poured out a truly astounding number of 45s in a wide variety of ska, rock-steady, and early reggae styles. When Buster began making records, his only competition was Duke Reid's (see entry) Treasure Isle and C.S. Dodd's Studio One.

He recorded Eric "Monty" Morris, Owen Grey, Millie Small, and many others. Buster cut some of the most exciting early 45s by Toots and the Maytals, like "Pain in My Belly," "Little Flea," and "Dog War" aka "Broadway Jungle," a delightful and chaotic recording that includes animal noises, a band that won't quit, insane harmonies, and the wailing, full-throttle power of Toots Hibbert's magnificent vocal.

But unlike Reid or Dodd, Buster's biggest artist was himself. Many Jamaicans felt that he was not in the same league as a vocalist with the likes of Jackie Opel or Slim Smith, but it was exactly this "everyman" delivery that warmed the hearts of his fans. He was affectionately known as "the Voice of the People" (the name of his sound system and one of his early labels). In truth some of his '60s records, like "Judge Dread," point toward the DJs and dub poets who came much later. His "Ten Commandments" scored not only in Jamaica and England but actually was released (with a follow-up album) by RCA in the United States.

While many of Buster's productions were what we would today call "conscious" (like "Ethiopia," "African Blood," or "Three More Rivers to Cross"), he was also one of the pioneers of "slackness" (suggestive lyrics), which came to dominate the later dancehall era. His avowed affiliation with Islam (the crescent moon and star motif adorns his record label from the early days) and political awareness (he and Peter Tosh were both arrested protesting South Africa's apartheid in the early '60s) didn't keep him from cutting tunes like "Big Five" or "Bald Head Pum Pum."

Buster toured England where he became and remains a major ska figure. Cuts like "Al Capone" helped spark the original skinhead movement. Buster first appeared on *Ready Steady Go* in 1964 and did a brief American tour in 1967.

Buster was one of the few (Coxsone was another) who realized the value of the back catalog and continued to reissue classic tracks as often as new recordings in the early '70s. In Buster's case his altered flip sides, lack of dates, and label similarities have proven the bane and delight of collectors, who can seldom be certain which combination was original—unlike most reggae singles, Buster combined songs instead of dubbing up the B side—and are continually surprised to find previously unknown songs on the backs of otherwise well-known cuts.

Buster ceased recording and began concentrating on reissues by the mid-'70s. He compiled a three-record set called *Original Golden Oldies*. One volume contains his own hits, like "Time Longer Than Rope," "Black Head Chinaman," and "Madness" (which the U.K. Two-Tone group covered and took its name from); another has various artists, like Monty Morris, the Folkes Brothers, and Buster; and the third is a collection of his work with Toots and the Maytals.

The English Skank label released a series of collections called *The Blue Beat Years* (reissuing albums originally released on that English label) in the '80s as well. In the early '90s the Jamaican-born New Yorker DJ Shaggy had a massive hit with a new version of "Oh Carolina," Buster's first production, sparking a new interest in this essential figure from the early days of ska.

A marvelous retrospective two-CD set of Buster's works was issued in Japan in the early '90s. The first volume of a recent two-volume Rhino set features many of Buster's great productions. Keith Scott, who compiled the tracks for the Rhino set, says Buster has just finished building a new studio in Miami and will soon begin reissuing his catalog on CD. —CHUCK FOSTER

Bunny and Skitter: "Chubby," Rhino, 1996 (*Roots of Reggae, Vol. 1, Ska*).

Buster: "Ain't That Saying a Lot," RCA, 1967.

Folkes Brothers: "Oh Carolina," Mango, 1993 (*Story of Jamaican Music*).

Holt, John: *Greatest Hits*, Prince Buster/Melodisc, 1972, 1984.

Morris, Monty: "Black Head Chinaman," Prince Buster, c. 1974 (*Prince Buster Record Shack Presents Original Golden Oldies*, Vol. 2) • "Humpty Dumpty," Prince Buster, c. 1974 (*Prince Buster Record Shack Presents Original Golden Oldies*, Vol. 2).

Prince and Princess Buster: "Ten Commandments from Woman to Man/Ain't That Saying a Lot," RCA, 1967.

Prince Buster: *Fabulous Greatest Hits,* Melodisc, 1967, 1980 • *Live on Tour,* Skank, 1967, 1988 • *She Was a Rough Rider,* Skank, 1968, 1988 • *Big Five,* Melodisc, 1972, 1988 • *Ten Commandments,* RCA, 1967 • *Judge Dread,* Prince Buster, 1967 • *Ten Commandments/Don't Make Me Cry,"* Philips, 1967 • Wreck a Pum Pum, Blue Beat, 1968 • "Hard Man Fe Dead," Mango, 1993 (*Story of Jamaican Music*) • *The Prophet,* Esoldun, 1994.

Prince Buster and His All Stars: *King of Ska,* Quattro, 1992.

Prince Buster and the Ska Busters: "That Lucky Old Sun/Don't Make Me Cry," Atlantic, 1967.

Prince Buster's All Stars: "Judge Dread," Rhino, 1996 (*Roots of Reggae,,* Vol. 2, *Rock Steady*) • "Madness," Rhino, 1996 (*Roots of Reggae,,* Vol. 1, *Ska*) • "Ten Commandments (From Man to Woman)," Rhino, 1996 (*Roots of Reggae,* Vol. 1, *Ska*).

Princess Buster and Her Jamaicans: "Ten Commandments from Woman to Man," King, 1967.

Toots and the Maytals: *Prince Buster Record Shack Presents Original Golden Oldies,* Vol. 3, Prince Buster, 1967.

White, Joy: *Sentimental Reasons,* Germain, 1979.

COLLECTIONS

Prince Buster Record Shack Presents Original Golden Oldies, Vols. 1–2, Prince Buster, c. 1974.

Jack Joseph Puig

Jack Joseph Puig has just finished mixing "I Don't Wanna Be in Your Life" by Atlantic recording artist Athenaeum (for producer Gavin MacKillop; see entry) and he's emotionally spent. "I said, 'This song is a heartland song, one of those songs that everybody can relate to. When I mixed it, I pictured this girl and she just got in a fight with her boyfriend and they broke up. It's 3 o'clock in the morning, she's in her little Honda Accord with the little high school tassel in the window, and she's getting a Coke at 7-Eleven. This song comes on the radio and she says, "Fuck that guy, this is my anthem." She cranks it up and that's how she relates to that song and that's what it means to her.'"

That anecdote illustrates Puig's approach to mixing and producing, from the Black Crowes to Jellyfish to Tonic: show heart. In Puig's eyes, a producer's job is to interpret songcraft to a band, then help the band realize the song to its fullest. "The highest compliment I aspire to—and when I don't get it I feel as if I failed—is when a record is being played back, an artist says, 'That's what

I was hearing in my head. How did you do that?' That's when I know I nailed it," Puig says. "The coolest drum sound—and I'm a person that has a reputation for great sound—doesn't mean anything next to the song coming out of the speakers." Emotional satisfaction is what's key.

He earned his reputation for big, clean sound playing bass in various Los Angeles bands and making several demos. He started as an engineer and evolved into a producer, although he still mixes often for the likes of Seven Mary Three, John Hiatt, Semisonic, and the aforementioned Athenaeum. "I think producer, period, is a dying breed," Puig says. "The engineer/producer is coming to the forefront only because it's one less person between the music and the speakers."

As an engineer, he has worked with the producers who most influenced his view of the music business: Bill Schnee (who generally gets the credit for coming up with the American bass drum sound), Glyn Johns (J.J.P. did nine albums with him; see entry), and Arif Mardin (see entry). "Glyn is the first engineer/producer in the lineage," Puig says. "He's kind of the Yoda figure to me, at least a Jedi knight, if not Obi-Wan Kenobi. I learned about how raw it should be, and pelvic energy, from Glyn. With Arif, I learned about the psychology and chemistry of production; I learned about song structure and the vocal owning the record, the whole concept of framing the artist with instrumentation and the volume of the instruments. With Bill, I just learned about all the details."

Working with those three laid the foundation for Puig's own career. "My dream has been to merge the '60s, '70s, and '80s and create something in the '90s or 2000s to blend 'em all," he says. While that trio showed him the way, Paul Rothchild's (see entry) work with Janis Joplin also made a tremendous impact.

"The most important thing to me, without a doubt, is that the song comes out of the speaker emotionally, however you gotta get there. One thing I will always admire is Paul Rothchild's work on 'Mercedes Benz.' The reason that happened is they couldn't find an arrangement that worked." Rothchild and the band had tried everything, from acoustic guitar to piano to shaker. Ultimately, Joplin's naked vocal worked.

"The producer is the rarest breed, because the producer has to be everything that an artist is, and in his own right, he's an artist himself, except he can't act the same way," he explains. "He can't throw tantrums, he has to [suppress] his own artistic feelings for the sake of what the artist thinks. He has to jump in and be the artist when the artist can't, and jump out when he's not supposed to be the artist. In a sense, when you're a producer you are a chemist, a dentist, and a psychiatrist."

The chemist puts everything together (players, song sequence, keys of songs, ambience). The psychiatrist takes care of the band's mental health by encouraging its members, perhaps even "acting a little miffed if the vocal isn't *angst* enough." The psychiatrist also deals with the record company, the engineer, the support system. As the dentist, "you're yanking performances out or you're putting a little Novocain and numbing something when it hurts. You're constantly motivating."

Puig knew it was time for him to jump into the producer's chair when he heard the first demos from Jellyfish. His producing debut was their first album, *Bellybutton;* Puig considers that and its follow-up, *Spilt Milk,* two of the best he's ever worked on. After that shiny pop, he jumped to the Grays and the Black Crowes. "I just love commercial music," he says. "I think jazz is very self-indulgent, it's not for the listener. I like music that's for the listener, because I'm a listener. I grew up listening to the radio and to records; I still buy 10 to 15 CDs a week. I have no interest in making a country record, jazz record, or R&B record, but I love anything in commercial pop rock. The Black Crowes are unlike Jellyfish, but it's another arm of that realm. If you're focused on just wanting to bring the song out and frame the artist properly, it doesn't matter if it's the Black Crowes or Soundgarden."

Puig's studio setup is quite elaborate. "I can't do things they did in the '60s, '70s, and '80s without the things they used then," he says. "You can't take a dbx 160x and make it sound like a classic tube compressor that was used on Ringo Starr or John Bonham. I have six of the Beatles' EMI modules, because if I want the 'Taxman' guitar sound, I'm only going to get it with them."

Although Puig's room at Ocean Way Studios in Los Angeles is stocked with assorted pedals, modules, and equipment, he doesn't force them on a band for a certain Puig sound. "I want the uniqueness of what they do," he explains. "The only time I would interject something is if I think it would be a neat color. I always have my stuff set up in the studio and I let [the band] discover it. They're just tools they use. When you work with very talented people, what you want is what they do. That's what makes the record unique, their concept of their music and the way they play together. You want to be out of the picture, you want to pull out what they're about. I've always been a behind-the-scenes person and I've always loved that. When people think the band I'm working with is great, I'm happy." —DAVID JOHN FARINELLA

Black Crowes: *Amorica,* American, 1994 • "Better When You're Not Alone," American, 1996 • "Blackberry,"

American, 1996 • "Good Friday," American, 1996 • "One Mirror Too Many," American, 1996 • *Three Snakes and One Charm,* American, 1996.

Dimestore Hoods: *Dimestore Hoods,* MCA, 1996.

Fabulon: *All Girls Are Pretty,* Chrysalis, 1993.

Fischer, John: *Dark Horse,* Myrrh, 1982.

Grays, The: *Ro Sham Bo,* Epic, 1994 • "Very Best Years," Epic, 1994.

Hodgson, Roger: *Hai Hai,* A&M, 1987.

Hoffs, Susanna: "All I Want," London, 1996 • *Susanna Hoffs,* London, 1996.

Jellyfish: *Bellybutton,* Charisma, 1990 • "I Wanna Stay Home," Charisma, 1990 • "Joining a Fan Club," Charisma, 1993 • *Spilt Milk,* Charisma, 1993 • "He's My Best Friend," Epic Soundtrax, 1994 (*Threesome* soundtrack).

Lincoln: *Lincoln,* Slash, 1997.

Shift: "I Want to Be Rich" (remix), Columbia, 1998.

Taff, Russ: *Medals,* Myrrh, 1985 • *Russ Taff,* Myrrh/A&M, 1987 • *We Will Stand: Yesterday and Today,* Word/Epic, 1994.

Tonic: *Lemon Parade,* Polydor, 1996.

Verve Pipe: "The Freshmen," RCA, 1997.

COLLECTIONS

Legacy: A Tribute to Fleetwood Mac's Rumours, Lava/Atlantic, 1998.

Norbert Putnam

Norbert Putnam was an ace session bassman in Muscle Shoals and Nashville in the '60s before he became one of the most important and successful producers of folk and country rock in the '70s and early '80s with Joan Baez, Jimmy Buffett, Dan Fogelberg, John Hiatt, New Riders of the Purple Sage, Pousette-Dart Band, Jesse Winchester, and many others, in addition to being a studio owner and music publisher. Putnam has also produced gospel and contemporary Christian music for Shirley Caesar, Michael Card, the Oak Ridge Boys, and Leon Patillo.

Norbert Putnam grew up in Muscle Shoals, Alabama. There was an acoustic stand-up bass in the house as Putnam's father had played with bluegrass bands as a young man. When Putnam was 15, a school friend wanted to start a band to play the Elvis Presley, Johnny Cash, Carl Perkins rockabilly coming out of Sam Phillips's (see entry) Sun Records in Memphis, "and you have to be the bass player because you have one," his friend insisted logically. At that point Putnam had "never touched the thing." His father taught him how to tune it but said, "I don't want you making a lot of noise in the house."

Two or three years later, Putnam was playing electric bass in the best band in Muscle Shoals, an R&B, rock 'n' roll outfit called Dan Penn (see entry) and the Pallbearers; they traveled in a '56 Cadillac hearse, playing the college circuit (University of Alabama, Ole Miss, Auburn) on the weekends. The Pallbearers (Putnam, David Briggs—not the L.A. producer of the same name—on keyboards, Jerry Carrigan on drums) backed a Muscle Shoals bellhop/singer named Arthur Alexander on a demo for producer Rick Hall (see entry) in 1962. The recording, "You Better Move On," was licensed by Dot and became a Top 30 hit.

The Pallbearers, college students by then, dropped out of school to become the house rhythm section at Hall's Fame Studios. For the next few years the Pallbearers backed hits for the Tams, Tommy Roe, and others, helping to create the Muscle Shoals sound—a hybrid of southern R&B and rock 'n' roll—before moving to Nashville in 1965.

For the next several years the trio played hundreds of Nashville sessions for artists as diverse as Henry Mancini, Al Hirt, Tony Joe White, Roy Orbison, Joan Baez, Ray Stevens, the Monkees, Manhattan Transfer, J.J. Cale, and Elvis Presley (*I'm 10,000 Years Old, Elvis Country, You'll Never Walk Alone, Love Letters from Elvis,* and *Elvis Sings the Wonderful World of Christmas*). Around 1970 Putnam became friends with a janitor at CBS named Kris Kristofferson; Putnam's trio backed him on demos and within a year Kristofferson was one of Nashville's most celebrated songwriters.

Putnam then heard from Joan Baez, who wanted to move into a more contemporary sound—with Kristofferson producing—blending the best rock and country players in Nashville, to be assembled by Putnam and recorded at his and Briggs' new studio, Quadrophonic. Putnam booked the musicians and showed up 15 minutes before the first session was scheduled to begin. Kristofferson looked troubled, disoriented, perhaps even inebriated. "I'm not producing the record," he told Putnam. "All of these knobs and buttons and lights just confuse me—you produce it."

Over the next five days in mid-1971, Baez, Putnam, and Nashville's best recorded 24 songs—a double-album set—with Putnam producing and playing bass and Baez recording her vocals and guitar parts live in the studio with the band. Only background choruses were dubbed in later. Stopping by the studio over those five days were songwriters Mickey Newbury, Jerry Jeff Walker, and a young man covering the session for *Billboard,* Jimmy Buffett.

When it came time to record the refrain to "The Night They Drove Old Dixie Down" (No. 3), Putnam thought it would be cool to assemble a large chorus to give the song a concert sing-along feel; so he gathered the musicians, hangers-on, and visitors (15 in all) into a motley choir and recorded them on the now-familiar refrain. "That was the magic moment in the song," says Putnam. Not only was "Dixie" Baez's biggest hit, but the album, *Blessed Are,* went gold and climbed to No. 11. Putnam was suddenly Nashville's folk-rock producer.

While Putnam was producing the Baez sessions, legendary executive Clive Davis advised him that his success as a session man—with a player's emphasis on musical precision—would have little bearing on his success as a producer. Davis said to him, "We don't sell music, we sell emotion. If you can bring me a record that gives me chill bumps, we can sell it." Putnam thought this was hooey until he went to overdub some vocal lines with Baez because they were slightly off-pitch. Baez redid the lines, but they didn't feel right, so they left in the originals. "That album went platinum and I haven't received a letter yet complaining that Joanie's vocals were sharp or flat. That record convinced me that Clive had a point," he says. "Jimmy Buffett—who was the most off-pitch of all, but who was a great communicator—later convinced me Clive was right."

Over the next several years Putnam produced folk-rock milestones for Eric Andersen, David Buskin, Dan Fogelberg (including his first and best album, *Home Free,* and the double-platinum *Nether Lands* and *Phoenix*), Steve Goodman, Ian Matthews, and Buffy Sainte-Marie (including her only Top 40 single, "Mister Can't You See," from the *Moonshot* album). Over the same time Putnam helped create the "hippie country" genre with albums for Flying Burrito Brothers, New Riders of the Purple Sage (the exceptional and mythic *The Adventures of Panama Red,* which went gold), and Jesse Winchester.

But Putnam made his greatest impact when he reconnected with the pitch-challenged former journalist Jimmy Buffett for a series of gold and platinum albums in the late '70s and early '80s. In 1976 Buffett and Putnam went down to Miami to hang out on Buffett's sailboat, and in the process they created a new subgenre (and later a movement, the "Parrotheads") by blending elements of calypso, mariachi, country, and rock 'n' roll into a beach-strolling hybrid Putnam calls "Caribbean rock."

Their first album together, *Changes in Latitudes, Changes in Attitudes* (No. 12), is still the quintessential Buffett album, containing his only Top 10 hit, the classic of tropical dissipation and wavering self-deception,

"Margaritaville" (No. 8). "Margaritaville" represents Buffett at his most appealing and insightful. The song's story takes place in Mexico, always a refuge for Americans at odds with the American Dream—a dream hung on the twin hooks of individual opportunity and individual responsibility. Some people need to escape the responsibility hook for a while to facilitate soul exploration or just to decompress. Where would you rather be? Basking in the perpetual summer of a snow-white *playa* sipping margaritas and chuckling at the tourists, or huddled around a short-circuiting space heater in a Buffalo hovel? Fictional characters, including Fred C. Dobbs, Augie March, and Buffett's semiautobiographical persona, have chosen the Mexican alternative.

"Margaritaville"'s Caribbean-mariachi-country melody is cheerful yet reflective, its lilt tempered with an aftertaste of regret. The song's power lies in its acknowledgment that the life of dissipation must be the shadow against which real life shines, not the screen that real life is shown upon. Responsibility can be an awesome weight, but ultimately we must accept responsibility for what it is: the internal demand to live up to our own values. Clearly, the character's lifestyle here doesn't coincide with his values. Rather than living a life of ease, he is living a life of intense internal conflict—a life he can only perpetuate with liberal applications of alcohol. Buffett doesn't even want to face up to the fact that he is drinking alcohol, which he disguises with mixes and rituals—rituals that are wearing thin.

The great turning point comes when Buffett's character accepts the possibility that he bears culpability for his actions. ("Some people claim that there's a woman to blame, / Now I think, hell, it could be my fault"). This reckoning requires such an effort that Buffett needs an instrumental break to contemplate it, where we are again reminded by the music's languid splendor how pleasant this dissipation can be and why an army of weekend sailors, beach bums, and dissipaters have retreated into Buffett's world for over 25 years. But it was under Putnam's watch that the archetype was perfected and found its finest expression. —ERIC OLSEN

Addrisi Brothers: *We've Got to Get It On Again*, CBS, 1972 • *Addrisi Brothers*, Buddah, 1977 • "Slow Dancin' Don't Turn Me On," Buddah, 1977.

Andersen, Eric: *Blue River*, CBS, 1972 • *Best Songs*, Arista, 1977 • *Stages: The Lost Album*, Legacy, 1991.

Baez, Joan: *Blessed Are*, Vanguard, 1971 • "Let It Be," Vanguard, 1971 • "The Night They Drove Old Dixie Down," Vanguard, 1971 • *Come from the Shadows*, A&M, 1972 • "In the Quiet Morning," A&M, 1972 • *Hits . . . Greatest and Otherwise*, Vanguard, 1973 • *Where Are You*

Now, My Son?, A&M, 1973 • *The Joan Baez Country Music Album*, Vanguard, 1979 • *Classics*, Vol. 8, A&M, 1987 • *Rare, Live and Classic*, Vanguard, 1993 • *Greatest Hits*, A&M, 1996.

Brewer and Shipley: *Welcome to Riddle Bridge*, Capitol, 1975.

Buffett, Jimmy: "Changes in Latitudes, Changes in Attitudes," ABC, 1977 • *Changes in Latitudes, Changes in Attitudes*, ABC, 1977 • "Margaritaville," ABC, 1977 • "Cheeseburger in Paradise," ABC, 1978 • "Livingston Saturday Night," ABC, 1978 • "Manana," ABC, 1978 • *Son of a Son of a Sailor*, ABC, 1978 • *You Had to Be There*, MCA, 1978 • "Fins," MCA, 1979 • "Volcano," MCA, 1979 • *Volcano*, MCA, 1979 • *Coconut Telegraph*, MCA, 1980 • "Survive," MCA, 1980 • "It's My Job," MCA, 1981 • *Somewhere over China*, MCA, 1981 • *Songs You Know by Heart*, MCA, 1985 • *Boats, Beaches, Bars and Ballads*, MCA, 1992.

Buskin, David: *David Buskin*, CBS, 1972.

Caesar, Shirley: *Christmasing*, Word/Epic, 1986, 1991.

Card, Michael: *Present Reality*, Sparrow, 1981 • *Scandalon*, Sparrow, 1993.

Chase, Carol: *The Chase Is On*, Casablanca, 1980.

Donovan: *7-Tease*, Epic, 1974 • *Troubador: The Definitive Collection, 1964–1976*, Legacy, 1992.

Flying Burrito Brothers: *Flying Again*, CBS, 1975.

Fogelberg, Dan: *Home Free*, Columbia, 1972 • *Nether Lands*, Epic, 1977 • "Longer," Epic, 1979 • *Phoenix*, Epic, 1979 • "Heart Hotels," Epic, 1980 • *Portrait: The Music of Dan Fogelberg, 1972–1997*, Sony, 1997.

Ghent, Tom: *Yankee's Rebel Son*, MCA, 1972.

Goodman, Steve: *Steve Goodman*, Buddah, 1971 • *No Big Surprise: Anthology*, Red Pajamas, 1994.

Hall, Jimmy: *Touch You*, Epic, 1980 • *Cadillac Tracks*, Epic, 1982.

Hiatt, John: *Warming Up to the Ice Age*, Geffen, 1985 • *Living a Little, Laughing a Little*, Raven, 1996.

Horn, Jim: *Neon Nights*, Warner Bros., 1988.

Kerr, Richard: *Richard Kerr*, Epic, 1976.

Knetchel, Larry: *Mountain Moods*, Capitol, 1979, 1990.

Kristofferson, Kris: *To the Bone*, Monument, 1981.

Matthews, Ian: *Go for Broke*, Columbia, 1976.

New Riders of the Purple Sage: *The Adventures of Panama Red*, Columbia, 1973 • *The Best Of*, Columbia, 1976.

Newbury, Mickey: *After All These Years*, Mercury, 1981.

Nitty Gritty Dirt Band: *Let's Go*, Liberty, 1983 • *20 Years of Dirt*, Warner Bros., 1988.

Oak Ridge Boys: *Light*, Heartwarming, 1972.

Parsons, Gene: *The Kindling Collection*, Sierra, 1994.

Patillo, Leon: *Brand New*, Sparrow, 1987.

Pousette-Dart Band: *Pousette-Dart Band*, Capitol, 1976 • *Amnesia*, Capitol, 1977 • *Never Enough*, Capitol, 1979.

Sainte-Marie, Buffy: "He's an Indian Rider in the Rodeo," Vanguard, 1972 • "Mister Can't You See," Vanguard, 1972

• *Moonshot,* Vanguard, 1972 • *Quiet Places,* Vanguard, 1973 • *Buffy,* Vanguard, 1974 • *Native North American Child* (3 tracks), Vanguard, 1974 • *Changing Woman,* MCA, 1975.

Shurtleff, Jerry: *State Farm,* A&M, 1972.

Splinter: *Two Man Band,* Dark Horse, 1977.

Toby Beau: *More Than a Love Song,* RCA, 1979.

Winchester, Jesse: *A Touch on the Rainy Side,* Bearsville, 1978.

Phil Ramone

Most of the great producers of the pop era have been specialists of one sort or another: Quincy Jones a master arranger, Ahmet Ertegun an entrepreneur and a song man, John Hammond a talent scout, and Babyface the epitome of the '90s variety writer/producer (see entries).

Phil Ramone, by contrast, has been more things to more people than any other producer of his stature. A consummate music man, Ramone brings to his craft formal training as a player (he was a prodigious violinist who gave a command performance for Queen Elizabeth when he was 10); a recording engineer; a technology innovator; a keen listener who is considered a

member of the sanctified "golden ears" population; a multimedia wizard whose accomplishments in film, TV, and theater rival his record production résumé; and a compassionate, avuncular figure who makes even the most insecure performers feel that, as long as Phil's in the house, everything is cool.

Ramone rose through the ranks of the industry the old-fashioned way: by slogging it out for years as an engineer before earning the right to be called a producer. But unlike many producers who arrived at the job through engineering, Ramone takes a broad, holistic approach to his work. On any given day in the studio, he might rearrange a song, write a string score, coach a vocalist, reconfigure a rhythm part, mitigate a political feud, zone in on an irritating EQ frequency, test a new piece of equipment, berate an engineer for not keeping pace with him, reminisce about accidentally hanging up on President John Kennedy prior to a White House event, and warm the hearts of the studio staff by being equally attentive to everyone, from the owner to the security guard.

At a recent industry function honoring Ramone, sounds and images spoke louder than words. As slides portrayed him working with the likes of Frank Sinatra, Barbra Streisand, Billy Joel, Paul Simon (see entry), Quincy Jones, Paul McCartney (see entry), André Previn, John Barry, Peter, Paul and Mary, Gloria Estefan, Julian Lennon, Sinéad O'Connor, and Judy Collins, the sound system filled the room with an aural collage of songs he produced and engineered.

The audience heard lines like "I love you just the way you are," "Still crazy after all these years," "Tangled up in blue," "Everybody's talkin' at me," "It's my party and I'll cry if I want to," "You can get anything you want at Alice's Restaurant," and "Raindrops keep falling on my head." As his wife, Karen Ramone (formerly Karen Kamon of *Flashdance* fame), sums it up, "All of us have lived our lives humming these songs in the shower."

Ramone's reputation as a great producer would have been sealed if he had made only a fraction of the records that he did. The fact that he made volumes upon volumes worth of seminal albums makes him that much larger a figure in American popular music.

His standing is further enhanced by his accomplishments outside of the recording studio, which are staggering. A film lover, Ramone has indulged in his passion for the visual medium by producing music for some of the most memorable soundtracks of our times, including *Midnight Cowboy, A Star Is Born, Yentl,* and *Flashdance.* Similarly, Ramone has worked as an audio designer for theater, with credits ranging from *Hair* to *Liza with a 'Z'* to *Promises Promises.* He has also produced the cast albums of *Passion, Starlight Express, Pippin,* and *Little Shop of Horrors,* among others.

For television, Ramone has supervised music for Grammy and Academy Awards telecasts, the Jimmy Carter inaugural concert special, Paul Simon and Simon and Garfunkel programs, the Emmy-winning TV version of *Liza with a 'Z', The Jim Henson Hour,* and other programs.

Ramone is also one of the most technically advanced producers in the business. His name comes up alongside such consummate engineers as Bob Ludwig, Doug Sax, George Massenburg (see entry), Bernie Grundman, Allen Sides, Roger Nichols, and Bob Clearmountain (see entry). Notably, he is the only one among them who has distinguished himself more for production than engineering. The most eloquent sign of Ramone's role as a technology maven is a plaque at Sony headquarters in Tokyo honoring the first CD ever pressed. The title? Billy Joel's *The Stranger* (No. 2), which Ramone produced.

Born in South Africa in 1940 and raised in New York, Ramone was headed for a life in classical music when he enrolled at Juilliard as a teenager. However, he found the formal training at Juilliard constrictive and started dabbling in jazz and recording. He took a job as an engineer at New York's famed A&R studio in the late '50s, inspired by such contemporaries as Tom Dowd, Al Schmitt (see entries), and Bill Schwartau.

"It's a bit of a lost art, the studio system," he says, referring to A&R, Muscle Shoals, Motown, and other self-contained hit-making studios. "What was developed in the '60s, that kind of team effort, created incredible relationships. What became a dream band was usually four guys who were not only studio guys but didn't want to do jingles. They wanted to make records."

After years of engineering such indelible tracks as Jobim and Astrud Gilberto's "The Girl from Ipanema" and Lesley Gore's "It's My Party," Ramone got his first production credit in 1969, when film music composer/producer John Barry insisted Ramone be duly recognized for his contribution to the *Midnight Cowboy* soundtrack.

Ramone proceeded to produce Simon, Phoebe Snow, Bob Dylan, Peter, Paul and Mary, and others from the late '60s through the early '70s. He worked at a furious pace, often juggling three projects at A&R. He recalls one instance in which he was working with Simon, Joel, and Chicago at the same time. "It was crazy, totally nuts," he says. "You could plan your life as well as you could, but sometimes somebody would cancel a booking. It would look like May and June would be clear because Billy was supposed to be on the road and Paul would say, 'I'm definitely not working this sum-

mer, we'll work more toward the fall.' But then Paul would come up with an idea and start to do something. Now he's on a roll, and when he's on a roll he's going to stay. And the collision was fun but it was crazy."

Although he was firmly established by the mid-'70s, it was Billy Joel's 1977 blockbuster, *The Stranger,* that catapulted Ramone to international recognition as a total producer. (It was no accident that Ramone was shown with the members of Joel's band in the back cover photo on *The Stranger.*) "The pressure on *The Stranger* was intense," recalls Ramone. "Everybody at the label loved Billy and was determined that he should have a hit record, but he'd been there five, six years and nothing big had happened, as it had for Bruce Springsteen and other people."

As if his staggering accomplishments across the spectrum of popular entertainment weren't enough, Ramone—who, based on the amount of work he put in, earned the right to an early retirement—decided in his mid-50s to take on the challenge of running a start-up record label, N2K Encoded Music. Founded by GRP Records entrepreneurs David Grusin and Larry Rosen, N2K struggled to make a dent in the marketplace, and at press time, the label had been downsized. Nevertheless, Ramone produced and executive-produced a raft of records in a short time, including titles by Swamp Boogie Queen, Kyle Davis, and Arturo Sandoval.

Like many label-affiliated producers, Ramone has the latitude to take on outside projects. Accordingly, he has worked in recent years on projects by Johnny Mathis, the Brian Setzer Orchestra, Patricia Kaas, Michael Crawford, Raul Di Blasio, Barry Manilow, Peter, Paul and Mary, and Japanese artist Shinji, as well as the cast recording for *Company.*

In the '90s, Ramone has not shown the Midas Touch he had in the '70s and '80s. However, his work during this decade bears important distinctions. For one, he co-produced Frank Sinatra's 1993 *Duets* (No. 2) release, which turned out to be the late crooner's best-selling album ever (at triple-platinum) and a comeback story that filtered over to Sinatra compadres like Tony Bennett.

Duets was also a technologically ground-breaking project, since it was the first album of its caliber to be recorded using fiber optic hookups between remote studios. Thus, many of Sinatra's duets partners—who on that release included Charles Aznavour, Gloria Estefan, Aretha Franklin, Bono, Liza Minnelli, and Streisand—were not present in the studio with him while recording their parts.

The Ramone-produced *Duets II* (No. 9), like so many sequels, did not capture the imagination of the public to the extent that its predecessor had. Nevertheless, it was certified platinum, and it featured a panoply of stars across a wide musical spectrum, from Antonio Carlos Jobim to Stevie Wonder (see entry), Willie Nelson, Linda Ronstadt, and Frank Sinatra Jr.

Ramone says the Sinatra sessions hinged on making the veteran singer comfortable. Because Sinatra had not sung in a recording studio in 10 years, he felt uneasy wearing headphones and being isolated from the orchestra. Accordingly, Ramone built a platform for Sinatra to stand on in the main recording space and gave him a hand-held, wireless microphone. "There's something sterile about the light and the big microphone hanging and the big circumstance," says Ramone. "That's why Sinatra was uncomfortable. He likes to sit and he likes to stand next to the stool. I'll do anything [to make a singer comfortable]. If you sing lying down I'll be there."

Another of Ramone's recent distinctions is his little-known pioneering role in the swing revival. As early as 1995—long before Royal Crown Revue and the Squirrel Nut Zippers attained mainstream success—Ramone was hanging out at such Los Angeles haunts as the Viper Room, scouting for talent and checking out the scene. That year, Ramone produced the Setzer Orchestra's underrated *Guitar Slinger,* which prefigured by more than two years Setzer's crossover success with "Jump Jive an' Wail." "It's amazing that they found this kind of interest—the chartreuse look with the pink and the bright colors, the '50s," says Ramone of the present-day swing artists. "Growing up in that period, to me it was like the '56 Chevy was something you looked at in the window and said, 'Oh, boy, someday.'"

Ironically for someone who does most of his work in world-class studios, Ramone has been one of the prime movers of the personal studio revolution of the '90s. He relishes his Tascam DA-88 and Yamaha 02R–based workshop, which lives in a converted horse barn on his property in Bedford, New York. In fact, Ramone road-tested the 02R at Capitol Studios in Los Angeles in a session with an unsigned artist he was working with at the time. Footage from the session was used in a Yamaha promotional video for the ground-breaking product. "There's a lot more interest in how you make the record and a lot of nicer tools to work on your demos," says Ramone. "And, as in motion pictures, the demo may be the one you never beat. When you're making a demo, it could turn out to be a record."

Although Ramone enjoys a hit as much as the next person, he is not as motivated by chart success as he is by the record-making process itself. "The pureness of the joy of being in the studio and having something grow, there's no treat like it," he says. "When it's suc-cessful and it reaches an audience, you're on a good roll. But you cannot come off it just because something went down. There are too many circumstances that you have no control over."

An optimist and a workaholic by nature, Ramone is as restless and positive about the future as he was when he started out. "I'm thrilled that I'm still active in doing what I want to do," he says. "We're kind of like athletes. There's a point at which you're either athletically fit or you're out, and nobody wants to be around making bad records. I certainly don't." —PAUL VERNA

Allman, Duane: *Anthology II,* Capricorn, 1974.

Bacharach, Burt: "I'll Never Fall in Love Again," A&M, 1969 • *Make It Easy on Yourself,* A&M, 1969 • *Burt Bacharach,* A&M, 1971 • *Living Together,* A&M, 1973 • *Greatest Hits,* A&M, 1974 • *Futures,* A&M, 1977.

Barry, John: *Midnight Cowboy* soundtrack, EMI America, 1969, 1989.

Bennett, Tony: *Tony Bennett on Holiday,* Columbia, 1997.

Branigan, Laura: *Over My Heart,* Atlantic, 1993 • *The Best Of,* Atlantic, 1995.

Brian Setzer Orchestra: *Guitar Slinger,* Interscope, 1996 • "Honky Tonk," Interscope, 1996 (*MOM: Music for Our Mother Ocean*) • *The Dirty Boogie,* Interscope, 1998.

Brigati: *Lost in the Wilderness,* Elektra, 1976.

Briley, Martin: *Dangerous Moments,* Mercury, 1985.

Carpenter, Karen: *Karen Carpenter,* A&M, 1996.

Carpenters, The: *Lovelines,* A&M, 1989.

Cassidy, David: *David Cassidy,* Enigma, 1986.

Chicago: "Alive Again," Columbia, 1978 • *Hot Streets,* Columbia, 1978 • "No Tell Lover," Columbia, 1978 • "Street Player," Columbia, 1979 • *XIII,* Columbia, 1979 • *Greatest Hits,* Vol. 2, Columbia, 1981 • *If You Leave Me Now,* Columbia, 1982 • *Heart of Chicago,* Vol. 2, *1967–1998,* Warner Bros., 1998.

Cole, Natalie: *Stardust,* Elektra, 1996.

Crosby, David: *Thousand Roads,* Atlantic, 1993.

Di Blasio, Raul: *Latino: Piano de America,* Ariola Int., 1995.

Elliot, Mama Cass: *Dream a Little Dream: The Cass Elliot Collection,* MCA, 1997.

Estefan, Gloria: *Christmas Through Your Eyes,* Epic, 1993.

Everything But the Girl: *Best Of,* Blanco Y Negro, 1996.

Franklin, Aretha: *A Rose Is Still a Rose,* Arista, 1998.

Garfunkel, Art: *Breakaway,* Columbia, 1975 • *Watermark,* Columbia, 1977 • w/ James Taylor and Paul Simon, "Wonderful World," Columbia, 1978 • *Garfunkel: Best Of,* Columbia, 1990.

Get Wet: *Get Wet,* Boardwalk, 1981.

Grusin, Dave: *Dave Grusin Presents West Side Story,* N2K, 1997.

Heatwave: *Hot Property,* Epic, 1979 • *The Best of Heatwave: Always and Forever,* Legacy, 1996.

(Evergreen)," Columbia, 1976 • w/ Kris Kristofferson, *A Star Is Born*, Columbia, 1977 • *Greatest Hits*, Vol. 2, Columbia, 1978 • *Memories*, Columbia, 1982 • *Yentl* soundtrack, Columbia, 1983 • "Till I Loved You," Columbia, 1988 • *Till I Loved You*, Columbia, 1988 • *A Collection: Greatest Hits and More*, Columbia, 1989 • *Just for the Record*, Columbia, 1991.

Swamp Boogie Queen: *Ill Gotten Booty*, N2K, 1998.

Thielemans, Toots: *Verve Jazz Masters 59*, PolyGram, 1996.

Titus, Libby: *Libby Titus*, CBS, 1977.

Toto La Momposina Sus Tambores: *La Candela Viva*, Realworld/Caroline, 1993.

U2: "Stay (Faraway So Close)," Island, 1993.

Williams, Patrick: *10th Avenue*, Soundwings, 1987.

COLLECTIONS

Casino Royale soundtrack, Varese Sarabande, 1968, 1990.

You Are What You Eat soundtrack, CBS, 1968.

Pippen (original Broadway cast), Motown, 1972.

Magic Show (original soundtrack), Bell, 1974.

Chicago (original cast), Arista, 1975.

Reds soundtrack, Warner Bros., 1981.

Flashdance soundtrack, Casablanca, 1983.

The Little Shop of Horrors (original cast), CBS, 1983.

Music and Songs from Starlight Express, MCA, 1987.

James Bond: Best of 30th Anniversary Collection, Capitol, 1992.

Passion (original Broadway cast), Angel, 1994.

EFX (original cast), Atlantic Theater, 1995.

Company, (1995 Broadway Cast) Angel, 1996.

Big (original cast), Universal, 1996.

A Funny Thing Happened on the Way to the Forum, (1996 Broadway cast)Angel, 1996.

Legacy: A Tribute to Fleetwood Mac's Rumours, Lava/Atlantic, 1998.

Endless Miles: A Tribute to Miles Davis, N2K, 1998.

Antonio "L.A." Reid

Although best-known for his work with Kenny "Babyface" Edmonds (see entry), Reid has put his own indelible stamp on "smooth" R&B. It's a sound built on the Motown stylings of his youth. While the Motown influence is clear, another is less expected. "I actually liked Steely Dan a lot, the way that they mixed their records and some of their instrumentation," Reid says from LaFace Records' Los Angeles offices. "I think that is where the 'smoothness' of our music comes from, but I was influenced by a lot of

things. I was a big fan of John Bonham of Led Zeppelin and the drum sound they had back then. It's kind of funny that a lot of rap stars these days don't know they are sampling Led Zeppelin, but they have been sampled and resampled so much that [the rappers] don't know where it comes from."

Reid, born June 7, 1957, first played the drums at 8 or 9, and by 14, he was working in clubs around his Cincinnati hometown. He evolved into a writer with Midnight Star; a collaboration with Edmonds sealed his songwriting fate. "While we were in the studio together, we hit it off as friends," Reid remembers. "It kinda went from there." Eventually Edmonds joined Reid's band, the Deele, and the two started writing and producing together.

While his production discography reads like a who's who of smooth R&B, it wasn't a genre he was aiming to conquer or inspire. "We focused on songs and artists," he says. "We never said we were going to do a certain type of music. The only thing we focused on was that we would be honest about music and honest about songs and about the potential of an artist."

That arrangement led the two to form LaFace Records in Atlanta in 1989, home to such multiplatinum acts as Toni Braxton (who has sued the label) and TLC. And while Edmonds has built up an impressive array of writing and producing credits, Reid is the backbone of the label. "All I do is LaFace," he says. "I work at LaFace, I run it every day and night, from every point. I sleep, eat, and drink LaFace Records."

Although he and Edmonds are rarely in the studio together anymore, they executive-produce nearly every record on their label. They live in different cities, too. "We really work well together this way," Reid says. "I am more of an executive producer now, and I spend a lot of my time with young producers and writers, and collect music that way. Obviously, 'Face' still goes to the studio every night and day, but at the end of a given period we come together and compare notes and see what we have."

It was as part of the production team that Reid executed one of his best projects, he suggests. "The thing that is probably most dear to me, the one that sticks out the most, is Bobby Brown. "There was a real chemistry there. Whenever he came into the studio he really made the songs come to life." The key product was *Don't Be Cruel* (No. 1), Brown's 1989 album. It yielded such hits as the title track (No. 8), "Roni" (No. 3), and "Every Little Step" (No. 3).

One reason that session was so commercially successful was that by then, Reid (who was married for a time to singer Pebbles) had become comfortable in the studio. "By 1988, we sort of felt like we had it down and knew our way around the studio," he says. "I won't say that it was easy, but we knew what we were looking for out of a particular performance or performer."

"Honesty to the music" and surrounding himself with young talent explain his longevity, he says. And he'll keep working. "I'll rest when I'm dead," Reid says.
—David John Farinella

Abdul, Paula: *Forever Your Girl*, Virgin, 1988 • "Knocked Out," Virgin, 1988 • *Shut Up and Dance: Dance Mixes*, Virgin, 1990.

After 7: *After 7*, Virgin, 1989 • "Heat of the Moment," Virgin, 1989 • "Can't Stop," Virgin, 1990 • "Ready or Not," Virgin, 1990 • *Very Best Of*, Virgin, 1997.

Az Yet: *Az Yet*, LaFace, 1996.

Babyface: "It's No Crime," Solar, 1989 • *Lovers*, Columbia, 1989 • *Tender Lover*, Solar/Epic, 1989 • "My Kinda Girl," Solar, 1990 • "Tender Lover," Solar, 1990 • "Whip Appeal," Solar, 1990 • *A Closer Look*, Epic, 1991 • featuring Toni Braxton, "Give U My Heart," Epic, 1992 • "For the Cool in You," Epic, 1993 • *For the Cool in You*, Epic, 1993 • "Never Keeping Secrets," Epic, 1993 • "And Our Feelings," Epic, 1994 • "When Can I See You?," Epic, 1994 • *When Can I See You Again?* (EP), Epic, 1995 • "Every Time I Close My Eyes," Epic, 1996.

Bell Biv DeVoe: *Hootie Mack*, MCA, 1993 • "Something in Your Eyes," MCA, 1993.

Boys, The: "Dial My Heart," Motown, 1988 • *Messages from the Boys*, Motown, 1988 • "Lucky Charm," Motown, 1989.

Boyz II Men: "End of the Road," Biv 10, 1992 •

Cooleyhighharmony (Spanish), Motown, 1993 • *II* (1 track), Motown, 1994.

Braxton, Toni: "Love Shoulda Brought You Home," LaFace, 1992 • "Another Sad Love Song," LaFace, 1993 • "Breathe Again," LaFace, 1994 • *Toni Braxton*, LaFace, 1994 • "You Mean the World to Me," LaFace, 1994 • *Secrets* (1 track), LaFace, 1996.

Brown, Bobby: "Don't Be Cruel," MCA, 1988 • *Don't Be Cruel*, MCA, 1989 • "Every Little Step," MCA, 1989 • "On Our Own," MCA, 1989 • "Rock Wit' Cha," MCA, 1989 • "Roni," MCA, 1989 • *Dance . . . Ya Know It!*, Motown, 1990 • *Bobby* (3 tracks), MCA, 1992 • "Good Enough," MCA, 1992 • "Humpin' Around," MCA, 1992 • *Remixes in the Key of B*, MCA, 1993.

Dame, Damian: *Damian Dame*, LaFace, 1991 • "Exclusivity," LaFace, 1991 • "Right Down to It," LaFace, 1991.

Davis, Mary: *Separate Ways*, Tabu, 1989.

Deele, The: *Material Thangz*, Solar, 1985 • *Eyes of a Stranger*, Solar, 1988 • "Two Occasions," Solar, 1988.

Easton, Sheena: *The Lover in Me*, MCA, 1988 • "The Lover in Me," MCA, 1989.

Franklin, Aretha: *Greatest Hits, 1980–1994*, Arista, 1994 • "Honey," Arista, 1994.

Gill, Johnny: "Fairweather Friend," Motown, 1990 • *Johnny Gill*, Motown, 1990 • "My, My, My," Motown, 1990 • *Provocative*, Motown, 1993 • *Favorites*, Motown, 1997.

Goodie Mob: *Soul Food*, LaFace, 1995.

Houston, Whitney: "I'm Your Baby Tonight," Arista, 1990 • *I'm Your Baby Tonight*, Arista, 1990 • "Miracle," Arista, 1991 • "My Name Is Not Susan," Arista, 1991 • "I'm Every Woman," Arista, 1992 (*The Bodyguard* soundtrack).

Jackson, Jermaine: *You Said*, LaFace, 1991 • "I Dream I Dream," LaFace, 1992.

Jacksons, The: *2300 Jackson Street*, Epic, 1989 • "Nothin (That Compares 2 U)," Epic, 1989.

John, Elton, and the Sounds of Blackness: "Amen," Warner Bros., 1994 (*A Tribute to Curtis Mayfield*).

Jones, Donnell: *My Heart*, LaFace, 1996.

Mac Band, featuring the McCampbell Brothers: "Roses are Red," MCA, 1988 • "Stuck," MCA, 1988.

New Edition: *Solo Hits*, MCA, 1996.

Outkast: *ATLiens*, LaFace, 1996 • "Jazzy Belle," LaFace, 1997.

Pebbles: *Pebbles* (1 track), MCA, 1987 • "Girlfriend," MCA, 1988 • "Girlfriend" (remix), MCA, 1988 • *Always*, MCA, 1990 • "Giving You the Benefit," MCA, 1990 • "Love Makes Things Happen," MCA, 1990 • w/ Salt-N-Pepa, "Backyard," MCA, 1991.

Salter, Sam: "After 12, Before 6," LaFace, 1997 • *It's on Tonight*, LaFace, 1997.

Society of Soul: *Brainchild*, LaFace, 1995.

The Tony Rich Project: *Words*, LaFace, 1995.

TLC: "Baby-Baby-Baby," LaFace, 1992 • *Oooooooohhh . . . on the*

TLC Tip, LaFace, 1992 • *CrazySexyCool*, LaFace/Arista, 1995.

Usher: *My Way*, LaFace, 1997.

Whispers, The: *Just Gets Better with Time*, Solar, 1987 • "Rock Steady," Solar, 1987.

White, Karyn: *Karyn White*, Warner Bros., 1988 • "The Way You Love Me," Warner Bros., 1988 • "Love Saw It," Warner Bros., 1989 • "Secret Rendezvous," Warner Bros., 1989 • "Superwoman," Warner Bros., 1989 • *Make Him Do Right*, Warner Bros., 1994.

Duke Reid

Arguably the most influential sound system operator of the early '60s, ex-policeman Duke Reid used profits from his and his wife's Treasure Isle Liquor Store (converting the upstairs back room to one of the island's early recording studios) to become one of the first and finest Jamaican record producers. He showcased American R&B on his Treasure Isle Time radio show, often traveling to the United States in search of new records, and his earliest productions like "Duke's Cookies" (1959) and "Joker" (Duke Reid All Stars) drew heavily on this sound. Reid's no-nonsense approach to production (ably aided by engineer Byron Smith), as well as his flamboyant image as a neo-western badman, helped build his outsized reputation.

"He used to wear two guns and a Winchester 73 across his shoulder and a big cowboy-lookin' hat," says singer John Holt. "He have a box downstairs in the store so he could hear exactly what's going on upstairs in the studio. So if anything is goin' that he doesn't really appreciate, then he would come upstairs and fire a lot of blank shots." Holt's appreciation for the Duke, despite such theatrics, is apparent.

Holt, who recorded solo and as lead singer of the Paragons for Reid (including "The Tide Is High," later a big hit for Blondie in an almost note-for-note copy of Reid's arrangement), says of Reid: "He is a type of man who really help Jamaican music to get where it is right now. He's a good man, because he used to record actually everybody that come in—never refuse a talent—and he was the sort of man who encourage you as a youth to do good things with whatever you're earning now so you could be a man when you get much bigger. And he used to pay you for your work." This last quality alone set him apart from many of his peers.

Reid's early ska hits included Don Drummond's "Eastern Standard Time" (Drummond was named best trombonist in a 1965 Playboy jazz poll), Tommy McCook and the Skatalites' explosive "Nuclear Weapon," and Stranger Cole's "Rough and Tough." His in-house band boasted jazz-trained guitarist Ernest Ranglin and Skatalites Drummond, McCook, and others. Reid waxed some of the last of the Jamaican swing "big bands" of the '40s and '50s that led into the ska revolution, like Drumbago's Orchestra. Sadly, most went unrecorded.

Reid was also responsible for bringing major American acts like Fats Domino to Jamaica to perform. His sound system, Trojan (from which the major English reggae label took its name), was the one to beat—often, it's said, for muscle as well as music. Reid and other producers enlarged the practice of selling their 45s, originally cut as dub plates for their own sound system, to the public. This was the beginning of the Jamaican record industry.

By 1967 rock steady, a slower-paced style that moved the singer to the fore, emerged with the Duke as one of its main proponents. Alton Ellis and the Flames, Phyllis Dillon, Shenley Duffus, the young Freddy McKay, and dozens of vocal groups like the Silvertones, the Maytals, the Jamaicans, and Justin Hinds and the Dominoes ruled the dance as recorded by Reid. Among the Duke's greatest records are "Willow Tree" by Alton Ellis, John Holt's evanescent "Ali Baba," and early recordings by the Techniques, featuring the unique voice of the late Slim Smith. As the sound began to change again, evolving into what we now call reggae, Reid began another musical revolution when he recorded DJ U Roy toasting over a series of earlier Paragons hits in 1970.

Though the DJ was a regular feature of the sound systems, with chatters like Count Matchuki and Prince Pompadou haranguing the crowd over instrumentals or dub plates, U Roy's records began a revolution that extends in a straight line to dancehall DJs Shabba Ranks and Buju Banton. Within months U Roy held four of the top five Jamaican chart positions—something no singer had ever done—all Reid productions. Voiced over existing Reid rock-steady rhythms, these innovative recordings created a new style that would inspire American rap. Reid recorded other DJs over older hits as the market for the new sound expanded.

After his death in 1974, Reid's catalog was taken over by Sonia Pottinger (see entry), who continued to reissue his classics in Jamaica on albums like the three-volume *Hottest Hits*, *Rock Steady Beat*, and *Duke Reid's Golden Hits*. Many of his best records were also pressed in England on the Trojan label on collections like *Gems from*

Treasure Isle and Baba Boom. Several excellent anthologies like Treasure Chest and More Hottest Hits from Treasure Isle are now available on CD from the Heartbeat label. —CHUCK FOSTER

Alcapone, Dennis, and Lizzy: Soul to Soul: DJ's Choice, Trojan, 1973.

Dillon, Phyllis: One Life to Live, Treasure Isle, 1968, 1996.

Drummond, Don: Greatest Hits, Treasure Isle, 1989.

Ellis, Alton: Mr. Soul of Jamaica, Treasure Isle, c. 1968 • Cry Tough, Heartbeat, 1993.

Hinds, Justin: w/ the Dominoes, Early Recordings, Esoldun/ROIR, 1991.

Holt, John: Like a Bolt, Treasure Isle, c. 1967.

Maytones, The: Keep the Fire Burning, Burning Sounds, 1973.

McCook, Tommy: Tommy McCook, Attack, 1974.

Paragons, The: The Original Paragons, Treasure Isle/Sky Note, n.d. • On the Beach, Treasure Isle, 1968.

Roy, Hugh: "Flashing My Whip," Shelter, n.d.

Skatalites, The: Skatalites Plus, Treasure Isle, 1966 • Foundation Ska, Heartbeat, 1996.

Techniques, The: Run Come Celebrate, Heartbeat, 1993.

U Roy: Version Galore, Virgin Frontline, 1971, 1978 • U Roy, Attack, 1974 • With Words of Wisdom, Virgin Frontline, 1979.

COLLECTIONS

Run Rhythm Run: Rock Steady and Reggae Instrumentals, Heartbeat, 1996.

Here Comes the Duke, Treasure Isle, n.d.: Joya Landis, "Kansas City" • Ken Parker, "True, True, True."

Rock Steady Beat, Treasure Isle, c. 1968.

Treasure Isle Hottest Hits, Vols. 1–3, Treasure Isle, c. 1979.

Music Is My Occupation: Instrumentals, 1962–1965, Trojan, 1965.

Original Ska Explosion, Carib Gems, 1962.

Soul of Jamaica, Trojan, 1968.

Duke Reid's Golden Hits, Treasure Isle, 1969: Justin Hinds, w/ the Dominoes, "Here I Stand" • The Paragons, "Only a Smile."

Birth of Ska, Trojan, 1972.

Hottest Hits, Treasure Isle, 1979: The Melodians, "Come On Little Girl" • The Paragons, "The Tide Is High" • The Sensations, "Those Guys" • The Techniques, "Queen Majesty."

Hottest Hits, Vol. 2, Treasure Isle, 1979: Alton Ellis, "Girl I've Got Date" • Freddie McKay, "Love Is a Treasure."

Hottest Hits, Vol. 3, Treasure Isle, 1979: Justin Hinds, "Sinners" • John Holt, "Ali Baba" • John Holt, "Stealing Stealing."

Gems from Treasure Isle, Trojan, 1982: Alton Ellis, "Rock Steady" • The Techniques, "You Don't Care" • Three Tops, "It's Raining" • U Roy, "Flashing My Whip."

Ba-Ba-Boom Time, 1967–1968, Trojan, 1988: The Gladiators,

"Sweet Soul Music" • The Tennors, "Weather Report" • The Termites, "Love Up Kiss Up" • Three Tops, "Do It Right."

Duke Reid's Rock Steady, 1967–1968, Trojan, 1989: The Silvertones, "Slow and Easy" • Lyn Tait, "Spanish Eyes."

Dance Crasher: Ska to Rock Steady, Trojan, 1988: Baba Brooks and Band, "Independence Ska," 1965 • Stranger Cole, "Rough and Tough," 1962 • Don Drummond, "Garden of Love," 1964; "Let George Do It," 1964 • Alton Ellis and the Flames, "Dance Crasher," 1965 • The Skatalites, "Latin Goes Ska," 1964; "Street Corner," 1965.

Shufflin' on Bond Street: Jamaican R&B and Ska Instrumentals, 1959–1966, Trojan, 1989.

Cultural Things, Esoldun, 1991: The Conquerors, "Lonely Strret" • The Tennors, "Hopeful Village."

Skatalites and Friends: Hog in a Cocoa, 1962–1968, Esoldun, 1991.

Tribute to the Skatalites, 1962–1968, Esoldun, 1991.

Top Rock Steady, Esoldun, 1992.

Version Affair, Vol. 2, Esoldun, 1992.

Duke Reid's Treasure Chest, Heartbeat, 1992: Duke Reid Group, "Soul Style" • The Ethiopians, "Mother's Tender Care" • The Royals, "We Are in the Mood" • The Silvertones, "Midnight Hour" • U Roy, "Everybody's Bawling."

Midnight Confession: Duke Reid's Greatest Rocksteady Moods, Esoldun, 1993.

Treasure Isle Dub, Vols. 1–2, Esoldun, 1993.

More Hottest Hits from Treasure Isle, Heartbeat, 1994.

Run Rhythm Run: Rock Steady and Reggae Instrumental from Treasure Isle, Heartbeat, 1996.

Allen Reynolds

Allen Reynolds' single greatest career achievement may be producing Garth Brooks, the top-selling solo album artist in U.S. history, but to suggest that this is his only musical contribution would be a mistake. Others with whom he has made great music are Don Williams, Crystal Gayle, Emmylou Harris, Kathy Mattea, and Hal Ketchum (with co-producer Jim Rooney). Reynolds is considered a bit of an iconoclast in Nashville; he doesn't glad-hand or schmooze, and he prefers art to commerce. He also doesn't mince words.

Reynolds has a long history in music. Born August 18, 1938, in North Little Rock, Arkansas, Reynolds worked as a bank branch manager by day in Memphis while pursuing his musical career as a songwriter and producer at night. Perhaps his most notable musical contribution during that period is the Vogues' "Five

O'Clock World," which was written about his frustrations in the workplace. He eventually opened a production and publishing company in Memphis with a partner. He relocated to Nashville in the early '70s at the behest of producer Jack Clement (see entry), whom Reynolds had known for years in Memphis.

"Jack was not my mentor, not in the sense that he deliberately tried to teach me," Reynolds says. "But he liked me and thought I had talent. He allowed me to watch him work from time to time, and he was kind enough to answer some of my questions, always truthfully. He's a deeply talented and thoroughly honest man, still one of my best friends."

Reynolds also learned from Don Williams, whom Reynolds produced early in his career as a producer in Nashville. "One of the most powerful things I learned [from Don] was that the microphone is like an ear placed that close to a singer's mouth that you didn't have to project or 'let them have it in the balcony,' that you could convey powerful emotions and achieve subtle nuance without raising your voice or trying too hard," Reynolds says. "It was a perfect illustration that in making records, less is usually more. Working with Don also furthered my confidence in the power of songs to define careers."

And if there's one thing Reynolds has done, it's to find or produce songs that have become artists' signature songs, such as "The Dance" and "Friends in Low Places" (both No. 1 country) for Garth Brooks, and "Where've You Been?" (No. 10 country) for Kathy Mattea. "I always know how much I like something," says Reynolds. "I loved 'The Dance,' 'Friends in Low Places,' and 'Where've You Been?' When you feel that way, you offer them proudly to the public and you'll usually be gratified with the response. I have always had a high regard for the audience and I play up to them, never down. If there's anything about me that is uncommon, it is this attitude. Most people in this business are more cynical than I am, especially people who market records at the label and also to people at radio. In fairness, however, I have to mention that Kathy's label surprised us by coming to us and asking if they could release 'Where've You Been?' as a single. I'm still surprised by that. I had to strongly request to Capitol Records to release 'The Dance' as a single because they wanted to move on to a new album. 'Friends in Low Places' had everyone's support."

Like many Nashville producers, Reynolds has a stake in a publishing company. He owns 25 percent of Forerunner/Foreshadow Songs, but he insists on having no involvement in the day-to-day running of the firm, to avoid conflict of interest. "For producers or artists to be writers and have publishing companies is an invitation to corruption," he says. "It can be an incentive to rationalize lowering your standards and being unreceptive to outside songs that are possibly better than in-house stuff. I've seen this kind of thinking since first being around the business. Many years ago, when I was working with Don Williams, it occurred to me that in a business where so many games were played with material, my competitive advantage was going to be that I never closed my doors to a song. I never have."

And often, songs he wrote have fit the bill. Artists who have cut his material include Waylon Jennings, Mickey Gilley, Don Williams, Emmylou Harris, Juice Newton, George Jones, Johnny Cash, and Hank Williams Jr. He wrote a number of hits for Crystal Gayle (whom he also produced), including one of the biggest of her career, "Ready for the Times to Get Better" (No. 1).

Reynolds works out of Clement's old studio, Jack's Tracks, which Reynolds purchased years ago. "Owning my own studio makes scheduling a breeze and allows me to have a constant set of reference points. Another advantage is privacy," he says. "I'm not in the studio business, however; I don't rent it out to the general public. That way, it's always available to me. I might also add that I've never made a profit on the studio itself, but having it has probably helped me have greater success as a producer, and that's where I've made a profit."

Although careful to keep his studio full of equipment that makes his artists sound the best they can, he says technology can never be considered anything other than a means to make better records. "Technology has changed and improved a lot . . . but entertainment is what it's all about and we all need to be careful not to let technology distract us," he says. "People don't buy records because they like their technology. . . . Try to keep technology as inconspicuous as possible. Try to be very entertaining. If you bore people and never surprise them, they simply won't come, won't buy, won't care."

One artist with whom Reynolds is aligned who clearly doesn't bore people is Brooks. The two have worked together on every Brooks album since his self-titled debut came out in 1989. At 13 million, Brooks's 1990 album, *No Fences,* is the top-selling country album in history. In second place is Brooks's 1991 album, *Ropin' the Wind,* at 11 million. As impressed as Reynolds is with Brooks as an artist, his true respect for him is as a man. "His understanding of what he does has always impressed me, whether it is writing a song, singing, putting on a stage show, visiting with the fans, managing his career, imagining the future," Reynolds says.

"He also seems to embrace without complaint or cynicism the things that are required of a famous recording artist. Almost all the artists I've known like having hits, success, money, fame; but many have real trouble with the realities of celebrity and the responsibilities of a career. I've never seen this with Garth. . . . Our collaboration proceeds much as it always has: an honest, open dialogue, respect and friendship. I've learned a lot from working with Garth and I'm still learning." —MELINDA NEWMAN

Asleep at the Wheel: *Tribute to the Music of Bob Wills and the Texas Playboys,* Liberty, 1993 • *Still Swingin',* Liberty, 1994.

Brooks, Garth: *Garth Brooks,* Liberty, 1989 • "If Tomorrow Never Comes," Capitol, 1989 • "Much Too Young (to Feel This Old)," Capitol, 1989 • "Friends in Low Places," Capitol, 1990 • *No Fences,* Liberty, 1990 • "Not Counting You," Capitol, 1990 • "The Dance," Capitol, 1990 • "Unanswered Prayers," Capitol, 1990 • "Rodeo," Capitol, 1991 • *Ropin' the Wind,* Capitol Nashville, 1991 • "Shameless," Capitol, 1991 • "The Thunder Rolls," Capitol, 1991 • "Two of a Kind, Workin' on a Full House," Capitol, 1991 • "What She's Doing Now," Liberty, 1991 • "Against the Grain," Liberty, 1992 • *Beyond the Season,* Capitol Nashville, 1992 • "Papa Loved Mama," Liberty, 1992 • "Somewhere Other Than the Night," Liberty, 1992 • *The Chase,* Liberty, 1992 • "The Old Man's Back in Town," Liberty, 1992 • "The River," Liberty, 1992 • "We Shall Be Free," Liberty, 1992 • "Ain't Going Down ('Til the Sun Comes Up)," Liberty, 1993 • "American Honky-Tonk Bar Association," Liberty, 1993 • "Dixie Chicken," Liberty, 1993 • *In Pieces,* Liberty, 1993 • "Learning to Live Again," Liberty, 1993 • "That Summer," Liberty, 1993 • "Callin' Baton Rouge," Liberty, 1994 • "Hard Luck Woman," Mercury, 1994 (*Kiss My Ass: Classic Kiss Regrooved*) • "One Night a Day," Liberty, 1994 • "Standing Outside the Fire," Liberty, 1994 • "The Red Strokes," Capitol Nashville, 1994 • "White Christmas," Liberty, 1994 • *Fresh Horses,* Capitol, 1995 • "It's Midnight Cinderella," Capitol, 1995 • "Rollin'," Capitol, 1995 • "She's Every Woman," Capitol Nashville, 1995 • "That Ol' Wind," Capitol, 1995 • "The Fever," Liberty, 1995 • *The Hits,* Liberty, 1995 • "The Old Stuff," Capitol, 1995 • "The Beaches of Cheyenne," Capitol Nashville, 1996 • "The Change," Capitol, 1996 • "A Friend to Me," Capitol, 1997 • "Belleau Wood," Capitol, 1997 • *Cowboy Cadillac,* Capitol, 1997 • "Do What You Gotta Do," Capitol, 1997 • "How You Ever Gonna Know," Capitol, 1997 • "I Don't Have to Wonder," Capitol, 1997 • "Long Neck Bottle," Capitol Nashville, 1997 • "Santa Looked a Lot Like Daddy," Capitol, 1997 • *Sevens,* Capitol Nashville, 1997 • "She's Gonna Make It," Capitol, 1997 • "Take the Keys to

My Heart," Capitol, 1997 • "Two Pina Coladas," Capitol, 1997 • "You Move Me," Capitol, 1997 • *Limited Series,* Capitol, 1998 • "Something with a Ring to It," Capitol, 1998 • "Uptown Down-Home Good Ol' Boy," Capitol, 1998.

Cactus Brothers: *The Cactus Brothers,* Capitol, 1993.

Gayle, Crystal: "I'll Get Over You," United Artists, 1976 • "Don't It Make My Brown Eyes Blue," United Artists, 1977 • *We Must Believe in Magic,* United Artists, 1977 • "You Never Miss a Real Good Thing (Till He Says Goodbye)," United Artists, 1977 • "Ready for the Times to Get Better," United Artists, 1978 • "Talking in Your Sleep," United Artists, 1978 • *Classic Crystal,* Liberty, 1979, 1994 • "Half the Way," Columbia, 1979 • *Miss the Mississippi,* Liberty, 1979, 1991 • *We Should Be Together,* United Artists, 1979 • "Why Have You Left the One You Left Me For?," United Artists, 1979 • *Favorites,* Liberty, 1980 • "If You Ever Change Your Mind," Columbia, 1980 • "It's Like We Never Said Goodbye," Columbia, 1980 • *These Days,* Liberty, 1980, 1992 • *Hollywood, Tennessee,* Liberty, 1981 • "Too Many Lovers," Columbia, 1981 • "Our Love Is on the Faultline," Warner Bros., 1983 • "Never Ending Song of Love," Capitol, 1990 • *Super Hits,* Columbia, 1998.

Harris, Emmylou: *Brand New Dance,* Reprise, 1990 • "Wheels of Love," Reprise, 1991 • *At the Ryman,* Reprise, 1992 • *Cowgirl's Prayer,* Asylum, 1993 • "High Powered Love," Asylum, 1993 • *Songs of the West,* Warner Bros., 1994 • "Thanks to You," Asylum, 1994 • *Portraits,* Warner Bros., 1996.

Ketchum, Hal: "Past the Point of Rescue," Curb, 1991 • *Past the Point of Rescue,* Curb, 1991 • "Small Town Saturday Night," Curb, 1991 • "Five O'Clock World," Curb, 1992 • "I Know Where Love Lives," Curb, 1992 • "Sure Love," Curb, 1992 • *Sure Love,* Curb, 1992 • "Hearts Are Gonna Roll," Curb, 1993 • "Mama Knows the Highway," Curb, 1993 • "Someplace Far Away (Careful What You're Dreaming)," Curb, 1993 • "(Tonight We Just Might) Fall in Love Again," Curb, 1994 • *Every Little Word,* Curb, 1994 • "That's What I Get (for Losin' You)," Curb, 1994 • "Every Little Word," Curb, 1995 • "Stay Forever," Curb, 1995 • "Veil of Tears," Curb, 1995 • *The Hits,* MGC/Curb, 1996.

LeDoux, Chris: "Whatcha Gonna Do with a Cowboy," Liberty, 1992 • *Whatcha Gonna Do with a Cowboy,* Liberty, 1992 • *American Cowboy,* Liberty, 1994 • *Best Of,* Liberty, 1994.

Lovett, Ruby: *Ruby Lovett,* Curb/MCA, 1997.

Mattea, Kathy: *From My Heart,* Mercury, 1985 • "He Won't Give In," Mercury, 1985 • "Heart of the Country," Mercury, 1985 • "It's Your Reputation Talkin'," Mercury, 1985 • *Walk the Way the Wind Blows,* Mercury, 1986 • "Train of Memories," Mercury, 1987 • *Untasted Honey,*

Mercury, 1987 • "You're the Power," Mercury, 1987 • "Eighteen Wheels and a Dozen Roses," Mercury, 1988 • "Goin' Gone," Mercury, 1988 • "Life As We Knew It," Mercury, 1988 • "Untold Stories," Mercury, 1988 • "Burnin' Old Memories," Mercury, 1989 • "Come from the Heart," Mercury, 1989 • "Where've You Been?," Mercury, 1989 • *Willow in the Wind,* Mercury, 1989 • *A Collection of Hits,* Mercury, 1990 • "A Few Good Things Remain," Mercury, 1990 • w/ Tim O'Brien, "The Battle Hymn of Love," Mercury, 1990 • "Time Passes By," Mercury, 1991 • *Time Passes By,* Mercury, 1991 • "Whole Lotta Holes," Mercury, 1991 • "Asking Us to Dance," Mercury, 1992 • *Good News,* Mercury, 1993.

Memphis Boys: *The Memphis Boys,* Vanguard, 1990.

Springer, Roger: "The Right One Left," MCA, 1992.

Williams, Don: *Greatest Hits,* Vol. 1, MCA, 1975 • "It's Who You Love," RCA, 1992 • "Too Much Love," RCA, 1992 • *I've Got a Winner in You,* MCA Special Products, 1995 • *The Best Of,* RCA, 1995 • *Volumes 1 and 2,* Edsel, 1997.

Yearwood, Trisha: w/ Garth Brooks, "In Another's Eyes," MCA, 1997 • *Songbook: A Collection of Hits,* MCA Nashville, 1997 • *Where Your Road Leads,* MCA, 1998.

Trent Reznor

Trent Reznor is a producer, composer, artist, and business conglomerate of one. As an artist, Reznor is the main (and sometimes only) member of the industrial rock group, Nine Inch Nails. Although Reznor has worked with other producers—John Fryer, Adrian Sherwood (see entries), Flood, Keith LeBlanc—he has taken the lead role on all Nine Inch Nails releases: the double-platinum *Pretty Hate Machine* with singles "Head Like a Hole" and "Down in It"; the *Broken* EP (No. 7), which won a Grammy for Best Metal Album in 1992; and *The Downward Spiral* (No. 2), with hit singles "Closer" and "March of the Pigs."

For Reznor's label, Nothing, he has co-produced shock-rock band Marilyn Manson's *Portrait of an American Family, Smells Like Children,* and *Antichrist Superstar,* with the hit single "The Beautiful People." He also produced tracks for art rocker Prick's self-titled 1995 release. In addition, Reznor has produced and compiled successful and eclectic soundtracks for Oliver Stone's *Natural Born Killers* (No. 19), and David Lynch's *Lost Highway.*

Trent Reznor, born May 16, 1966, conjures a panoply of images: champion in heroic leather, mud-smeared Dionysiac, grim masochist, hollow-eyed nihilist. In the flesh, however, the slight and seemingly delicate Reznor is generally regarded as thoughtful, affable, and articulate. Reznor trained in classical piano from the age of 5, and his prodigious talents were encouraged by the grandparents who raised him in the rural town of Mercer, Pennsylvania, when his parents divorced. Mercer's reverence for athletic prowess over creative achievement may have dually spurred Reznor's ambition and alienation.

Reznor majored in computer engineering at Allegheny College briefly before he packed up and moved to Cleveland, Ohio. Reznor played with several bands, including Exotic Birds, but it wasn't until he went solo and was forced to develop his own material that his talent came through.

Nine Inch Nails consisted of one member, Trent Reznor, on its brilliant 1989 debut, *Pretty Hate Machine.* Though crude when compared with his later efforts, *Pretty Hate Machine* is perhaps still Reznor's most satisfying work. The album's synths, samples, drum loops, and guitar convey a heady brew of self-hatred, unrequited love, defiance, spiritual despair, and not-so-hidden idealism. The anthemic "Head Like a Hole," an industrial dance song, is heavily electronic, with primitive drum loops and an urgent synth line in the verse, yielding to pummeling guitar in the chorus. "Down in It" is a hot funk-synth number that balances the chill of "Head." "Something I Can Never Have" has elegantly orchestrated keyboards, weaving natural and unnatural sounds with Reznor's half-sung, half-spoken vocal. "Something" shows Reznor at his best: composing vulnerability into painful, bittersweet insight.

It would be almost four years before Reznor released 1992's *Broken* EP. The delay was due in part to Reznor's infamous battle with the label TVT over artistic control. Bailed out financially by Interscope label owner Jimmy Iovine (see entry), Reznor was set up with his own label, Nothing, and given complete autonomy.

Broken (co-produced with Flood), a contract-settler between TVT and Nothing, is an aural assault, at times unlistenable, and guaranteed to give even the most rabid NIN fan a piercing headache. Reznor, clearly angered and resentful on "Happiness Is Slavery" (no hidden message there), lets loose with an arsenal of caustic beats, raging metal guitars, and distorted, hysterical vocals. "Gave Up" is a little tamer, with an insistent but not punishing beat, but still riding on pessimistic waves of disgust. The highlight is "Wish," where the rushing pace and wall of guitars can't hide a real melody.

Reznor, free at last, wore his artistic freedom on his

sleeve while creating the masterful concept album *The Downward Spiral*. A cache of lyrical and musical depth, Reznor continued to explore the deepest, darkest corners of his mind while expanding his sonic horizons exponentially.

Reznor explained the process behind *Downward* to Alan Di Pernal in *Guitar World*: "I wanted it to be a departure from *Broken* [which was] a real hard-sounding record that was just one big blast of anger. . . . I didn't want to box Nine Inch Nails into a corner, where everything would be faster and harder than the last record—where every song had to say, 'Look how tough we are.' I don't think that's really me. . . . On this record, I was more concerned with mood, texture, restraint, and subtlety, rather than getting punched in the face 400 times. . . . The big overview was of somebody who systematically throws away every aspect of his life and what's around him—from personal relationships to religion. This person is giving up to a certain degree, but also finding some peace by getting rid of things that were bogging him down."

Downward's disparate songs range from the murky and sparse "Piggy" to the aggressive, stalking percussion of "March of the Pigs," with grinding guitar noise broken by a lilting piano interlude where Reznor asks, "Doesn't it make you feel better?" The vulgar ("I want to fuck you like an animal, I want to feel you from the inside"), pulsing single "Closer" shows Reznor has a little disco left in him that sets his animal urges to boogying. *Downward* (co-produced with Flood) demonstrates Reznor's instrumental mastery on the poignant "A Warm Place"; oddly cradled between the sarcasm of "Big Man with a Gun"'s metallic rock and the halting noise experiment "Eraser," "A Warm Place" seems simultaneously otherworldly and innerworldly as the solitary heart of an unborn throbs in its fluid home—where all is still well and innocent.

Reznor has used Nothing as a platform to sign and produce bands, most notably Marilyn Manson and Prick. Manson is a crass, malignant wart, and at worst is a cheap imitator of theatrical rock (think Kiss, Alice Cooper); at best Manson conjures uncomfortable moments of scabrous truth, as on "Get Your Gunn," a ripping cover of Patti Smith's "Rock and Roll Nigger," and on "The Beautiful People." —Dawn Darling

Bowie, David: "I'm Afraid of Americans" (remix), Virgin, 1997 • "The Heart's Filthy Lesson" (remix), Virgin, 1995.
Butthole Surfers: "Who Was in My Room Last Night?" (remix), Capitol, 1993.
Curve: "Missing Link" (remix), Charisma, 1992.
KMFDM: "Light" (remix), Wax Trax!/TVT, 1994.

Machines of Loving Grace: "Burn Like Brilliant Trash" (remix), Mammoth, 1992.
Marilyn Manson: "Get Your Gunn," A&M, 1994 (*S.F.W.* soundtrack) • *Portrait of an American Family*, Nothing/Interscope, 1994 • *Smells Like Children*, Nothing/Interscope, 1995 • *Antichrist Superstar* (14 tracks), Nothing/Interscope, 1996.
Megadeth: "Symphony of Destruction" (remix), Capitol, 1992.
Nine Inch Nails: "Burn," Nothing/Interscope, 1994 (*Natural Born Killers* soundtrack) • "Closer," Nothing/Interscope, 1994 • "Dead Souls," Interscope/Atlantic, 1994 (*The Crow* soundtrack) • "Down in It," TVT, 1989 • "Down in It" (remix), TVT, 1989 • "Happiness in Slavery," A&M, 1994 (*Woodstock 94*) • "Head Like a Hole," TVT, 1989 • "Head Like a Hole" (remix), TVT, 1989 • "Hurt," Nothing/Interscope, 1994 • "Hurt" (remix), Nothing/Interscope, 1995 • "March of the Pigs," Nothing/Interscope, 1994 • "Sin," TVT, 1989 • "Terrible Lie," TVT, 1989 • "Terrible Lie" (remix), TVT, 1989 • "The Perfect Drug," Nothing, 1997 • "Wish," Nothing/Interscope, 1994 • *Broken* (EP), Nothing/Interscope, 1992 • *Pretty Hate Machine*, TVT, 1989 • *The Downward Spiral*, Nothing/Interscope, 1994.
Prick: *Prick* (4 tracks), Nothing/Interscope, 1995.

COLLECTIONS

Natural Born Killers soundtrack, Nothing/Interscope, 1994.
Lost Highway soundtrack, Nothing/Interscope, 1997.

Deke Richards

See THE CORPORATION

Keith Richards

See GLIMMER TWINS

Colin Richardson

Colin Richardson is one of the newer stars of heavy music production, although he has been engineering since the late '70s. He started after leaving school in Manchester, England, at age 16. "I dived in three weeks before I left school, rang up a bunch of studios, and got a job. I was always a fan of music," he recalls. "In school, I was the kid who carried all the cool metal albums around in his schoolbag—Deep Purple, Black Sabbath, Led Zeppelin. Originally, I just wanted to be an engineer."

He worked in a couple of different studios in Manchester (on projects by bands like Happy Mondays and Echo and the Bunnymen) and later in Yorkshire, where he is now based. "I ended up working at a studio in Driffield, where I live now," he says. "Then another studio in Driffield called Slaughterhouse was looking for an engineer. I ended up there for four years. It burned down in November 1990."

That fire was the catalyst for Richardson's production career. He had engineered several projects at Slaughterhouse for British heavy music label Earache. They liked his work and suggested he produce their bands on a freelance basis. "I'd worked with Napalm Death. Nobody else really knew how to handle all that aggression. They said it was the first time they'd come across someone who was really into it."

His first project was Fudge Tunnel's *Hate Songs in E Minor.* "It took two weeks to record, five days to mix, a typical Earache budget at the time. But they liked what I did, and other people started seeing my name on the backs of jackets."

Not everyone was impressed. His first job in the U.S. in 1991 took him to Tampa's Morrisound Studio, ground zero for death-metal production. Unbeknown to Richardson, this particular band had wanted Morrisound's Scott Burns (see entry) to produce, and gave the easygoing Richardson a difficult time. "They thought I was some alternative guy from England. When I met them, I got blank stares. Every suggestion I made was shouted down by the band. The engineer was saying awful things about me behind my back. At the end of the album, the drummer shouted, 'See you, asshole. Get back to England.' That was probably the worst session of my life. From that I learned how to handle a situation. I looked back afterwards and thought I should've said this or that. But the next thing I did in the States was Brutal Truth and they were angels."

In fact, with bands like Napalm Death, Fudge Tunnel, Bolt Thrower, and Carcass under his belt, Richardson had learned a lot about working with dark, extreme music, coming up with a sound that, although crowded and dense, maintains a full dynamic range and lets the guitars blaze through. "I've always tried to make the guitars louder and in-your-face. My strength is working with speed music and keeping things dry and upfront," he says. "It's kind of a clinical music. There are two ways of recording it: you can do everything but the vocals live or you can build it up. You can lose a certain amount of excitement doing that, but if the band is inexperienced, I will do it. There's no right or wrong way. I listen to the band and decide which to use."

In slightly over half a decade, Richardson has several significant projects under his belt, including two albums with Los Angeles techno-metalists Fear Factory and two with Machine Head, one of the '90's hottest young groove–thrash metal bands. Both are on Roadrunner, a label he's worked for extensively. "I was working on Brutal Truth and Monte Conner [from Roadrunner] was friends with the singer. He knew I was in town, so he gave me a call. He said, 'I've got a project that I think is really good for you.' It was Fear Factory." Their unique sound, combining death metal and industrial-style sampling, won them raves for their 1992 debut, *Soul of a New Machine.*

Richardson met his wife, Lora, while working on *Soul;* she was Fear Factory's manager. However, she split with them before the recording of the second album, *Demanufacture,* creating tension. "The lead singer perceived bad blood between Lora and him. He couldn't get to her, so he took it off on me. There was also second-album pressure and he couldn't handle it. But the album turned out well."

He also recently mixed an album for Overkill, who was looking for a '90s edge to its classic '80s thrash sound. "I'm flexible studiowise," he says. "I had a good time at Bearsville in Woodstock. I enjoyed Larabee in L.A., although I don't particularly like L.A. The staff can make a studio a lot of the time. Gear is gear. The X factor is the band and the band's equipment. The playing area is important, especially a good drum room. I prefer studios in the middle of nowhere to ones in the city. I'd rather the band is comfortable in the studio than that it looks like a hospital and the band feels like they can't put their feet up on the gear."

Looking ahead, he says, "It's easy to become typecast in what I'm doing. The few times I've tried to venture into other roles, they said 'He's fine for extreme bands, but he wouldn't be right for this.' I think I'd like to stay in the aggressive field, but I don't get off on death metal anymore. That style of singing—the cookie monster vocals—was cool in its day. When I hear it now, I cringe. I'd like to do a band like Tool." —ANASTASIA PANTSIOS

Blackstar: *Barbed Wire Soul*, Prosthetic, 1998.

Bolt Thrower: *War Master*, Earache, 1991, 1995 • *The IVth Crusade*, Earache, 1996.

Brutal Truth: *Extreme Conditions Demand Extreme Responses*, Earache, 1992 • *Perpetual Conversion*, Relativity, 1992 • *Need to Control*, Earache, 1994.

Carcass: *Symphonies of Sickness*, Earache, 1990 • *Necroticism: Descanting the Insalubrious*, Earache, 1992 • *Heartwork*, Earache, 1994, 1996 • *Wake Up and Smell the Carcass*, Earache, 1996.

Dearly Beheaded: *Temptation*, Fierce, 1996.

Disincarnate: *Dreams of a Carrion Kind*, Roadrunner, 1993.

Exploited, The: *Beat the Bastards*, Triple X, 1996.

Extreme Noise Terror: *Damage 381*, Earache, 1997.

Fear Factory: *Soul of a New Machine*, Roadrunner, 1992 • *Fear Is the Mindkiller* (EP), Roadrunner, 1993 • *Demanufacture*, Roadrunner, 1995 • *Remanufacture*, Roadrunner, 1997.

Fetish 69: *Anti-Body*, Relapse, 1994.

Fudge Tunnel: *Hate Songs in E Minor*, Earache/Relativity, 1991.

Gorefest: *Mindloss*, Pavement, 1991, 1996 • *False*, Nuclear Blast, 1992.

In the Nursery: *Koda*, ITN, 1988, 1996.

Machine Head: *Burn My Eyes*, Roadrunner, 1994 • *The More Things Change . . .* , Roadrunner, 1997.

Mercyless: *Coloured Funeral*, Century Media, 1993.

Napalm Death: *Death by Manipulation*, Earache, 1991 • *Utopia Banished*, Earache, 1992 • *Diatribes*, Earache, 1996 • *Breed to Breathe*, Earache, 1997 • *Inside the Torn Apart*, Earache, 1997.

O.W.P.: *Silver or Lead*, Roadrunner, 1993.

Scat Opera: *About Time*, Metal Blade, 1991.

Sinister: *Diabolical Summoning*, Nuclear Blast, 1993.

Garth Richardson

(GGGARTH)

Garth Richardson, known professionally as GGGarth because of his stutter, grew up in Toronto, hanging around the studio watching his producer father, Jack Richardson (see entry) work with artists like Bob Seger, Alice Cooper, and Rush. He always knew he'd follow in his dad's footsteps and was doing demos for local bands while in his teens as well as engineering albums such as Alice Cooper's *Constrictor*.

Young Richardson's career took off after he engineered the Red Hot Chili Peppers' 1989 *Mother's Milk* album. It caught the ear of the members of the political rap-metal band Rage Against The Machine, who asked him to produce their 1993 debut. Although he says he doesn't want to be typecast, he's worked successfully with many bands whose music is on the rageful, assaultive end of heavy music. He has a special knack for working with adventurous indie bands with strong underground reputations who've just reached major-label level. He has taken them when they're in danger of being accused by their fans of selling out and helped them maintain their sonic integrity.

Some old fans may miss the turgidness of the bands' old, low-budget records. But Richardson can balance power and clarity and find a wide range of tonal colorations in heavy music, capturing powerful drumming under biting guitars. He helmed L7's *Hungry for Stink*, the Jesus Lizard's major-label debut *Shot*, Sick of It All's *Built to Last*, Surgery's *Shimmer*, and all of the Melvins' work on Atlantic. What interests him is "records that aren't pop, not radio-friendly records. I like young, street-attitude bands, not somebody trying to be like what's already in the Top 10."

Richardson is proud to have won Canada's Juno Award for Producer of the Year for his work with the Melvins and Jesus Lizard, beating out Bryan Adams, Bruce Fairbairn (see entry), and David Foster (see entry). "It shows people have an appreciation for underground," he says.

He likes to set up an interactive studio environment. "I've adapted a system of setting up a PA the way they play so that the drummer can hear himself. I use multiple guitar amps so that the guitar player can hear his sound. And I try to not have glass between me and the singer. When you're dealing with someone's thoughts, it's hard to always have to use a talkback button. At first they get scared because they've never done it that way before. Then they get into it."

As for the producer's role, "Think of me as a camp counselor," he says. "I try to make them feel comfortable. I try to make them feel like they are not in the studio. My role is to help the band make the record they've always wanted to make."

He doesn't like to work with bands that use drugs in the studio. "I try to screen more now, ask around. I've had friends go through that whole mess and I don't like it."

Although he enjoys working in different studios and getting different sounds, Sound City in Van Nuys, California, is his favorite. "It's where I did Rage, Melvins. It's got an old '70s vibe, with brown carpet on the wall and an old Neve console. It's a nonthreatening place. People don't get scared because it's too clean and neat."

Eventually, Richardson would like to teach or do film work. "I definitely wouldn't want to work for a label," he says. "They only understand how to make money; they don't understand how to make records. It's weird to have someone from the label come in and tell the singer he doesn't understand the lyrics, when the singer is living with six friends because he has no money and this guy has a big car and an expense account."
—ANASTASIA PANTSIOS

Boo-Yah T.R.I.B.E.: "Rumors of a Dead Man," Hollywood, 1993.

Brilliant Orange: *Love and Evolution,* Oceana/Onslot, 1990.

Catherine Wheel: *Adam and Eve,* Mercury, 1997.

Dashboard Prophets: *Burning Out the Inside,* No Name, 1996.

Dead Brain Cells: *Universe,* Combat, 1989.

Jesus Lizard: *Shot,* Capitol/EMI, 1996.

L7: "Can I Run?," Slash, 1994 • *Hungry for Stink,* Slash, 1994.

Man Will Surrender: *Man Will Surrender,* Revolution, 1997.

Melvins: *Houdini,* Atlantic, 1993 • *Stoner Witch,* Atlantic, 1994 • *Stag,* Atlantic, 1996.

Mötley Crüe: *Motley Crue,* Elektra, 1994.

Parade of Losers: *P.O.L.,* Giant, 1995.

Pleasure Thieves: "My Favorite Drug/It's Too Late," Hollywood, 1991.

Rage Against The Machine: *Rage Against The Machine,* Epic Associated, 1992 • "Freedom," Epic Associated, 1994.

Sick of It All: "Jungle," Elektra, 1996 • *Built to Last,* Elektra, 1997.

Skunk Anansie: *Stoosh,* Epic, 1997.

Surgery: *Shimmer,* Amphetamine Reptile, 1994.

Sword: *Sweet Dreams,* Roadrunner, 1988.

Testament: *Low,* Atlantic, 1994 • *Signs of Chaos: The Best of Testament,* Mayhem, 1997.

Ugly Kid Joe: *Menace to Sobriety,* Mercury, 1995.

Urge, The: *Master of Styles,* Immortal, 1998.

Voodoo Glow Skulls: *Firme,* Epitaph, 1995.

Jack Richardson

Jack Richardson is a collaborative producer, not an autocratic one. "One of the things I try not to do is impose too much of a personal stamp," he says. "I'm interested in getting the best of the qualities indigenous to the group. I really don't want people to say, 'That's a Jack Richardson record.' I work on the basic of a fairly democratic relationship. We discuss everything, and eventually I make a decision on the direction. But it will be based on the input from the group. It's the group's music."

Not that Richardson hasn't worked with strong-minded individuals. Take Bob Seger, the Detroit rocker for whom Richardson produced "Night Moves," a No. 4 hit in early 1977. "We set it all up," Richardson says of those sessions. Richardson was supposed to go to Detroit to cut some tracks on Seger, but that never worked out, so Seger and his group flew to Richardson's Nimbus 9 Productions in Toronto, where they cut a few unreleased tracks, including a take on the Supremes' "My World Is Empty Without You" and the funky original, "Long, Long Gone."

The sessions weren't yielding a hit. Then one day Richardson walked by as Seger was noodling around on the piano. Richardson heard a potential hit in Seger's playing, so he and some Seger musicians, along with three female singers, put the tune together. "When it was finished—and this is the story you won't hear—we sent it to Punch Andrews, Bob's manager in Detroit, and got a call back saying it wasn't the way he'd have done it." Richardson told Andrews he should have produced the track. Meanwhile, Richardson was pretty tight with Canadian powers at Seger's label, Capitol, and invited them to hear the tracks. Turns out John Carter, then Capitol's director of A&R, had heard only two of the tunes Seger's group had cut at Nimbus 9; he hadn't heard "Night Moves." Carter dug the tune, Richardson suggested a few edits, and forgot about it. Next thing he knew, he was in New York producing the Brecker Brothers for Arista and opened up *Billboard* to discover "Night Moves" was No. 98 with a bullet. "I think, to a great degree, it was a big factor in the re-emergence of Seger as a major artist," Richardson says of the track.

Another artist-in-transition Richardson worked with was the group Poco. Richardson produced that band's *A Good Feelin' to Know, Crazy Eyes* (the elegiac 1973 album many consider the group's best), and *Seven.* "I was approached by Poco's manager at the time," Richardson recalls. "This was, I guess, 1970. I went out to Boulder, spent three or four days with them, liked what I heard, and said yes." The band stayed intact for the first two albums; Richie Furay left after *Crazy Eyes* to join Souther Hillman Furay, and after *Seven,* Timothy Schmitt left for the Eagles. Poco never really recovered.

While Richardson may be best known for mainstream rock 'n' roll—besides Seger, he produced the Guess Who from the time they started in 1968 until their breakup in 1975, Michael Bolotin (now Michael

Bolton), Alice Cooper, and Starz—he also prides himself on contributing to the audiophile canon.

Not only was Richardson head of Nimbus 9 from its 1968 launch to its 1980 demise, he also founded and headed a subsidiary, Umbrella Records. The Umbrella recordings are all direct-to-disc, which Richardson loves "because of the great fidelity." He and Doug Sax, of Hollywood's Mastering Lab, are pioneers in the process. "The basic premise is, we were eliminating a lot of the stages recordings were going through at the time," he says. "Recording direct to disc means you bypass multi-track taping, mixdown to 1/4-inch tape, then down to stereo 1/4-inch; it eliminates the tape formats, so the performance had to take place completely for each side. When you're cutting a lacquer, you can't stop and start again," Richardson says. "It's full-blown stereo."

According to the cover notes on *Rough Trade Live,* an Umbrella recording from 1974, "The reason direct-to-disc recording is so difficult and so rarely done is largely the complex task it imposes on the disc-cutting engineer. The direct-to-disc process prevents the use of a computer built into the cutting lathe and, instead, forces the cutting engineer to make the many delicate adjustments to the lathe during the recording that would have been handled, ordinarily, by the computer."

"We had a console we had modified considerably at our studio," Richardson says. "We took all the transformers out, those big pieces of metal that in a lot of cases influence the sound so when you wind up with your final product, it may not be as true as when they're not involved. Whenever you put an electric signal through iron, there's resistance, and whenever you provide resistance through any process, there's a coloring, if not a loss," Richardson says. "The purest transfer of sound is a piece of wire, and once you start introducing elements to that piece of wire before its final stage, you're introducing elements that will color or transform that signal."

Richardson comes to his perfectionism organically. Born in Toronto on July 23, 1929, he plays bass and cello and has performed everything from country to jazz to big band. He began playing professionally in 1946, joined the musicians union the following year, and worked in various Canadian bands. In the early '50s, he was part of a club act with singer Billy O'Connor; Richardson and O'Connor wound up doing several television shows on the emerging CBC network. They also did radio shows for various sponsors. But in 1957, Richardson decided the music business "was a little unstable" and went into advertising.

In 1960, he joined McCann-Erickson and eventually came to handle all Coca-Cola radio and television advertising in Canada. In 1967, his Nimbus 9 Productions signed the Guess Who as its first recording artist, and the following year, he built his studio. There, Richardson took on Bob Ezrin (see entry) as an apprentice producer, signed singer Bonnie Dobson and the group Copper Penny, and ultimately took on Jack Douglas (see entry) as an engineer. (Douglas went on to produce Aerosmith and Yoko Ono.)

Among his favorite productions are the Guess Who's *American Woman* (No. 9) and *Share the Land* (No. 14) albums; Max Webster's *Universal Juveniles* (featuring Rush on the track "Battle Scar"); and *Wasn't That a Party?,* a hit for the (Irish) Rovers.

If Richardson has slowed down in production, he remains active as an academic, teaching audio engineering and production at Fanshawe College in London, about 110 miles west of Toronto.

Oh, yes. There's one more key Richardson production: his son, Garth (see entry). Not only did GGGarth win a prestigious Juno award as best producer of 1996 for the Rage Against The Machine debut, he has produced albums by the Catherine Wheel, Jesus Lizard, the Melvins, and Sick of It All. And not only is Garth more active than his father, "he's making more money that I did, too," says Jack Richardson. —CARLO WOLFF

Alice Cooper: "Eighteen," Warner Bros., 1971 • *Love It to Death,* Warner Bros., 1971 • *Muscle of Love,* Warner Bros., 1973 • "Teenage Lament '74," Warner Bros., 1973 • *Greatest Hits,* Warner Bros., 1974, 1988.

Allman Brothers Band: *Dreams,* Polydor, 1989.

Badfinger: *Say No More,* Radio, 1981.

Barnaby Bye: *Touch,* Atlantic, 1974.

Bear, Richard T.: *Bear,* RCA, 1979 • *Red Hot And Blue,* RCA, 1979.

Beck, Joe: *Watch the Time,* Polydor, 1977.

Betts, Dickey: *Atlanta's Burning Down,* Arista, 1978.

Bolotin, Michael: *The Early Years,* RCA, 1991 • *The Artistry of Michael Bolotin,* RCA, 1993.

Bolton, Michael: See Bolotin, Michael.

Brecker Brothers: *Don't Stop the Music,* Arista, 1977 • *The Brecker Brothers Collection,* Vol. 1, Jive, 1981.

Clayton-Thomas, David: *Clayton,* ABC, 1978.

Creach, Papa John: *The Cat and the Fiddle,* DJM, 1977.

Guess Who: *Canned Wheat,* RCA, 1969 • "Laughing," RCA, 1969 • "These Eyes," RCA, 1969 • "Undun," RCA, 1969 • *Wheatfield Soul,* RCA, 1969 • "American Woman," RCA, 1970 • "Hand Me Down World," RCA, 1970 • "No Sugar Tonight," RCA, 1970 • "No Time," RCA, 1970 • "Share the Land," RCA, 1970 • *Share the Land,* RCA, 1970 • "Albert Flasher," RCA, 1971 • "Rain Dance," RCA, 1971 • *So Long, Bannatyne,* RCA, 1971 • *The Best Of,* RCA, 1971 •

Live at the Paramount, RCA, 1972 • *Rockin*, RCA, 1972 •
#10, RCA, 1973 • "Clap for the Wolfman," RCA, 1974 •
"Dancin' Fool," RCA, 1974 • *Flavours*, RCA, 1974 • *Road
Food*, RCA, 1974 • "Star Baby," RCA, 1974 • *Power in the
Music*, RCA, 1975 • *The Way They Were*, RCA, 1976 • *The
Best Of: Live*, Compleat, 1986 • *Track Record: The Guess
Who Collection*, RCA, 1988 • *These Eyes*, BMG Special, 1997
• *Ultimate Collection*, RCA, 1997.

Gypsy: *Unlock the Gate*, RCA, 1973.

Hope: *Hope*, A&M, 1973.

Manowar: *Hail to England*, MFN, 1984 • *Sign of the Hammer*,
Grand Slamm, 1985.

Max Webster: *Universal Juveniles*, Mercury, 1980.

McBride, Bob: *Here to Sing*, MCA, 1978.

Moonlighters, The: *The Moonlighters*, Amherst, 1977.

Moxy: *Under the Light*, Polydor, 1978.

Noah: *Noah*, RCA, 1970.

Poco: *A Good Feelin' to Know*, Epic, 1972 • *Crazy Eyes*, Epic,
1973 • *Seven*, Epic, 1974 • *The Very Best Of*, Epic, 1975 • *The
Forgotten Trail (1969–1974)*, Epic, 1990.

Rovers, The: "Wasn't That a Party?," Cleveland International,
1981 • *Wasn't That a Party?*, Cleveland International, 1981
• *Pain in My Past*, Cleveland International, 1982.

Seger, Bob: "Night Moves," Capitol, 1976 • *Night Moves* (1
track), Capitol, 1976.

Starz: *Coliseum Rock*, Capitol, 1978.

Stormin' Norman and Suzy: *Ocean of Love*, Polydor, 1978.

Straight Lines: *Straight Lines*, Epic, 1980.

Tomlinson, Malcolm: *Comin' Outta Nowhere*, A&M, 1977.

Tornader: *Hit It Again*, Polydor, 1977.

Tufano and Giammarese: *The Tufano and Giammarese Band*,
Ode, 1974 • *Other Side*, Ode, 1976.

White Wolf: *Standing Alone*, RCA, 1984.

Wilderness Road: *Wilderness Road*, CBS, 1972 • *Universal
Juveniles*, Mercury, 1980.

Teddy Riley

R&B music owes a lot to producer Teddy Riley. During the late '80s, when rap was taking over from R&B, Riley came along and saved the day. The initial rescue came through a string of productions in 1987 and 1988, including Johnny Kemp's "Just Got Paid" (No. 10), Keith Sweat's "I Want Her" (No. 5), and "Groove Me" by Riley's own group, Guy. These bright, bouncy songs were breaths of fresh air.

In a stroke of genius Riley (born October 8, 1967, in Harlem) mixed contemporary hip-hop–styled beats with soulful singing to create a simple formula that struck a chord within the music industry. He was even able to fend off a challenge from yet another sound coming up in R&B: British soul, exemplified by Nellee Hooper and Soul II Soul. (Riley would eventually do a remix of Soul II Soul's "Keep On Movin'.")

Riley is in demand for production and remixing. Bobby Brown and Michael Jackson have likely benefited the most. For Brown, Riley helped craft "Get Away" (No. 14) and "Two Can Play That Game." Jackson used Riley on "Remember the Time," (No. 3), "Jam," "In the Closet" (No. 6), "She Drives Me Wild," and "Why You Wanna Trip on Me?," from his underrated *Dangerous* (No. 1) album.

Heavy D & the Boyz got hits out of Riley's "Now That We Found Love" (No. 11) and "Is It Good to You?," while Today scored with "Him or Me," "Take It Off," and "Style." But even Riley couldn't revive New Kids on the Block, who resurfaced in 1994 under the not-so-clever new moniker NKOTB and a handful of Riley songs, "You Got the Flavor," "Girls," and "Never Let You Go."

Guy's eponymous 1987 debut remains the quintessential new jack swing album. The tunes "Groove Me" and "Teddy's Jam" (which inspired "Teddy's Jam 2" on Guy's 1992 follow-up, *The Future*, No. 16) made it a hit. But Guy soon split, over the proverbial musical differences, reuniting briefly in 1996 for "Tell Me What You Like," from the *New York Undercover* soundtrack. Two other former Guys, Damion and Aaron Hall, recorded poorly received solo albums.

Riley, meanwhile, forges ahead, forming new groups and continuing to produce others, like Men of Vizion's album *Personal*, the "My Love" remix for Mary J. Blige, the "Stay" remix for Eternal, "All This Love" for Patti LaBelle, the "Just Another Day" remix for Queen Latifah, "90's Girl" by Blackgirl, "Rump Shaker" (No. 2) by Wreckx-N-Effect, and Hi-Five's "I Like the Way (The Kissing Game)" (No. 1).

But Riley has stayed most visible with Blackstreet, his post-Guy group, which debuted in 1994 with a self-titled album that included hits "Before I Let You Go" (No. 7), "Joy," and "Booti Call." Its even more successful follow-up, 1997's *Another Level*, contained the hits "No Diggity" (featuring Dr. Dre), "Fix," and "Don't Leave Me." —KEVIN JOHNSON

Al B., Sure!: *In Effect Mode*, Warner Bros., 1988.

Big Bub: *Timeless*, Uptown/Universal, 1997.

Blackstreet: "Before I Let You Go," Interscope, 1994 •
Blackstreet, Interscope, 1994 • "Booti Call," Interscope,
1994 • "Tonight's the Night," Interscope, 1995 • *Another
Level*, Interscope, 1996 • with special guests Ol' Dirty

Bastard & Slash, "Fix," Interscope, 1997 • featuring Dr. Dre, "No Diggity," Interscope, 1997 • "(Money Can't) Buy Me Love," Interscope, 1997.

Blige, Mary J.: "My Love" (remix), Uptown/MCA, 1993 • *What's the 411? The Remixes,* Uptown/MCA, 1993.

Blondie: "Rapture" (remix), Chrysalis, 1988.

Brown, Bobby: *Bobby* (7 tracks), MCA, 1992 • "Get Away," MCA, 1993 • *Remixes in the Key of B,* MCA, 1993 • "That's the Way Love Is," MCA, 1993.

Brown, Foxy: *Ill Na Na,* Violator/Def Jam, 1996.

Butler, Jonathan: *More Than Friends,* Jive, 1988.

Child, Jane: "Don't Wanna Fall in Love" (remix), Warner Bros., 1989.

Deja: *Made to Be Together,* Virgin, 1989.

DJ Jazzy Jeff and the Fresh Prince: *Code Red,* Jive, 1993 • "I'm Looking for the One (to Be with Me)," Jive, 1993.

Dogg, Nate: *G-Funk Classics,,* Vol. 1, Death Row, 1997.

Eternal: "Stay" (remix), EMI, 1994.

Father: "69," Uptown/MCA, 1993 • *Sex Is Law,* Uptown/MCA, 1993.

Guy: "Groove Me," Uptown/MCA, 1988 • *Guy,* Uptown/MCA, 1988 • "Teddy's Jam," Uptown/MCA, 1988 • "I Like," Uptown/MCA, 1989 • featuring Teddy Riley, "My Fantasy," Motown, 1989 • "I Wanna Get with U," Uptown/MCA, 1990 • *The Future,* Uptown/MCA, 1990 • "Let's Chill," Uptown/MCA, 1991.

Hammer: *The Funky Headhunter,* Giant, 1994.

Heavy D and the Boyz: *Living Large,* MCA, 1987 • *Big Tyme,* MCA, 1989 • "We Got Our Own Thang," MCA, 1989 • "Is It Good to You?," Uptown, 1991 • "Now That We Found Love," Uptown, 1991 • "Now That We Found Love" (remix), Tommy Boy, 1991, 1992 (*MTV Party to Go,* Vol. 2) • *Peaceful Journey,* Uptown, 1991 • *Nuttin' But Love,* Uptown, 1994.

Hicks, Taral: *This Time,* Motown, 1997.

Hi-Five: *Hi-Five,* Jive, 1990 • "I Like the Way (The Kissing Game)," Jive, 1991.

Houston, Whitney: "Step by Step" (remix), Arista, 1997.

Ingram, James: "It's Real" (remix), Warner Bros., 1989.

Jackson, Janet: "I Get Lonely," Virgin, 1998.

Jackson, Michael: *Dangerous,* Epic, 1991 • "In the Closet," Epic, 1992 • "Jam," Epic, 1992 • "Remember the Time," Epic, 1992 • *HIStory: Past, Present and Future, Part 1,* Epic, 1995 • "Blood on the Dance Floor," Epic, 1997 • *Blood on the Dancefloor: HIStory in the Mix,* MJJ, 1997.

Jacksons, The: *2300 Jackson Street,* Epic, 1989.

Jay-Z: *In My Lifetime,* Def Jam, 1997 • featuring Blackstreet, "The City Is Mine," Def Jam, 1998.

Jones, Glenn: *All for You,* Jive, 1990 • *The Best of Glenn Jones,* Jive, 1992.

Jones, Tom: *The Lead and How to Swing It,* Interscope, 1994.

Kane, Big Daddy: *It's a Big Daddy Thing* (1 track), Cold Chillin'/Reprise, 1989.

Kemp, Johnny: "Just Got Paid," Columbia, 1988 • *Secrets of Flying,* Columbia, 1988.

Kool Moe Dee: *I'm Kool Moe Dee,* Jive, 1986 • *Best,* Jive, 1987 • "Go See the Doctor," Jive, 1987 • "How You Like Me Now," Jive, 1987 • *How Ya Like Me Now,* Jive, 1987 • "No Respect," Jive, 1987 • "Wild Wild West," Jive, 1988 • "I Go to Work," Jive, 1989 • *Knowledge Is King,* Jive, 1989 • "They Want Money," Jive, 1989 • *Funke Funke Wisdom,* Jive, 1991 • *Greatest Hits,* Jive, 1993.

LaBelle, Patti: "All This Love," MCA, 1994 • *Gems,* MCA, 1994.

Lord Tariq and Peter Gunz: *Make It Reign,* Codeine/Columbia, 1998.

Men of Vizion: "House Keeper," MJJ, 1996 • *Personal,* MJJ, 1996.

NKOTB: *Face the Music,* Columbia, 1994.

Nutta Butta: featuring Teddy Riley and Anonymous, "Freak Out," Lil' Man, 1998.

Positive K: "Black Cinderella," PosK, 1997 • *Straight to the Moon,* Island, 1997.

Pure Soul: "I Want You Back," Step Sun, 1995 • *Pure Soul* (2 tracks), Step Sun, 1995.

Queen Latifah: "Just Another Day" (remix), Motown, 1993.

Queen Pen: featuring Teddy Riley, "Man Behind the Music," Lil' Man/Interscope, 1997 • *My Melody,* Lil' Man/Interscope, 1997 • featuring Eric Williams, "All My Love," Lil' Man/Interscope, 1998 • featuring Teddy Riley, Nutta Butta, Markell & Jesse, "Party Ain't a Party," Lil' Man/Interscope, 1998.

Rampage: *Scout's Honor . . . By Way of Blood,* Elektra, 1997 • "We Getz Down," Elektra, 1997.

Redhead Kingpin: "Pump It Hottie" (remix), Virgin America, 1989.

Riley, Teddy: *The Harlem Sessions,* Ol' Skool, 1996.

Soul II Soul: "Keep on Movin' " (remix), Virgin, 1989.

Starpoint: *Have You Got What It Takes?,* Elektra, 1990.

Sweat, Keith: "I Want Her," Vintertainment, 1988 • *I'll Give All My Love to You,* Vintertainment, 1990.

SWV: *Remixes,* RCA, 1995.

Tha Truth: featuring Keith Murray, "Makin Moves," Priority, 1997.

Today: "Him Or Me," Motown, 1988 • *Today,* Motown, 1988.

Winans, The: *Return,* Qwest, 1990.

Wreckx-N-Effect: *Wreckx-N-Effect,* Motown, 1989 • *Hard or Smooth,* MCA, 1992 • "Rump Shaker," MCA, 1992 • "Rump Shaker" (remix), MCA, 1992 • "Knock-N-Boots," MCA, 1993 • *Rap's New Generation,* MCA, 1996.

COLLECTIONS

Get on the Bus: Music from and Inspired by the Motion Picture, Interscope, 1996.

John A. Rivers

Producer/engineer John A. Rivers has helped create some of England's best music over the last 20 years, engineering for the Specials (and offshoots the Special A.K.A. and Fun Boy Three) and producing profound music with Dead Can Dance, Love and Rockets (and solo efforts from Daniel Ash and David J), Xymox, and Ultramarine. He has also produced fine records throughout the modern rock spectrum for Close Lobsters, Dr. Robert, Felt, the Jazz Butcher, Ocean Colour Scene, Slipstream, Swell Maps, and Yatsura. In addition, Rivers is a classically trained pianist and contemporary classical composer in his own right.

John A. Rivers (not to be confused with the American rock singer Johnny Rivers or the American rap producer John Rivers) was born in Folkestone, England, on a date that shall remain unidentified ("This is showbiz," he says). Rivers started playing piano at 4 and got into electronics at 10, building his first tape recorder at 13. He left school early and went on the road as a professional musician for several years. "When I settled down, the music and electronics came together and I built my first studio," he says.

Rivers' first success as a producer came with artnoise band Swell Maps (led by brothers Nikki Sudden and Epic Soundtracks) in 1979. He engineered for ska greats the Specials and their offshoots, Special A.K.A. and Fun Boy Three in the early '80s, and then made his greatest mark with productions for Love and Rockets and Dead Can Dance.

When the seminal gothic-punk band Bauhaus split in 1983, lead singer Peter Murphy headed off for a solo career, while guitarist Daniel Ash, drummer Kevin Haskins, and bassist David J formed Love and Rockets. Rivers began a run of albums of great sonic depth and drama with Love and Rockets' debut, *Seventh Dream of a Teenage Heaven,* recorded at his own Woodbine Studio in 1985.

The songs are structurally simple, with an emphasis on repeated guitar, bass, and drum figures built up layer by layer into a dronelike series of tuneful tidal waves washing over the listener. This approach builds to near-overwhelming intensity on the classic "The Dog End of the Day," as Ash and J's deadpan multitracked vocals create a spooky disembodied chorus that seems to arise out of Haskins' determined tom-tom and bass drum pounding. "Haunted When the Minutes Drag" builds to a similar end over an electronic beat spiced with jolting boinks and metallic hisses. "Saudade" is a beautiful acoustic guitar piece from Ash reverbed out across a quivering purple landscape, accented with echoed percussive strikes that seem to originate from miles away. Rivers' lush keyboard washes enfold the scene in gossamer. The title track creates more moody mystery as Ash and J trade hit-and-run vocal lines from around sonic corners over Ash's fuzzed and extended guitar attacks and an ominous syncopated beat. Rivers' enormous production never strays from grandeur into the grandiose—a tour de force.

The following year's *Express,* though not possessed of the same overall impact as *Seventh,* has even better individual songs. "Kundalini Express" shows off Ash's great hard rock riffing ability as Ash and J trade choo-choo/karma metaphors in their lowest registers. Rivers favors body blows over reverb on this one. "All in My Mind" should have been the band's first smash single, blessed with a great sing-along tune and bouncy beat over acres of hard-strummed acoustic guitars and fuzzy electric riffing. "Ball of Confusion" is a psychedelic, hard-grooving update of the Temptations' classic. Dopey title notwithstanding, "Yin and Yang the Flower Pot Man" is another milestone. Rivers employs some of his wave-of-sound multitracking techniques as the band ratchets up the tempo to a triple-time Bo Diddley beat, which it miraculously maintains for 6 minutes of knuckle-flaying strumming and ritualistic drum-thumping. The album's momentum is disrupted by an unnecessary "acoustic version" of "All in My Mind" (it was pretty acoustic in the first place), but closes strongly with "An American Dream."

Also in the mid-'80s, Rivers began to make indelible music with Dead Can Dance, a rotating phalanx of players around singer/songwriters Brendan Perry and Lisa Gerrard incorporating medieval, gothic, Eastern European, Middle Eastern, and various other ancient and sacred musical influences into songs and tone poems with mythic titles like "The Host of Seraphim," "Song of Sophia," and "De Profundis."

While in description all of this screams of pretension, in practice these disparate elements are bound together into a captivating—and at times awe-inspiring—sonic composite of much greater breadth and devotion than similarly inspired new age piffle. Dead Can Dance honors both the spiritual and aesthetic aspects of these musics. Rivers' luxuriant production creates distinct atmospheres for each piece, and the albums he worked on—*Spleen and Ideal, Within the Realm of a Dying Sun, The Serpent's Egg*—are the group's most profound and affecting.

Of his work in the '90s, Rivers is particularly proud of his work with Ocean Colour Scene, a neo-'60s band championed by Oasis and Paul Weller, who are a sensation in England but haven't caught on in the U.S. yet. "You guys should check them out," says Rivers. "I think you'd like them. [Singer] Simon Fowler is brilliant; he's the only person I've ever seen get a spontaneous standing ovation in a recording studio."

Also of note in the '90s is Rivers' work on Ultramarine's exquisite *United Kingdoms:* a witty, affable collection of swingy, breezy, semi-ambient instrumentals (and two superb vocal numbers—the U.K. hit single "Kingdom," and "Happy Land"—both sung with winning nonchalance by former Soft Machine legend Robert Wyatt) played on organic instruments (violin, clarinet, flute, sax, trumpet, accordion) in combination with percolating electronic percussion and keyboard work from writer/leaders Ian Cooper and Paul Hammond.

Among the U.K.'s finest engineers, Rivers has mixed feelings about contemporary technology. "I love to be able to edit digitally; I can do things I would never be able to do with tape. I master all my records directly onto hard disk and compile the albums here [at Woodbine], so while an album is in progress, I can burn a sample CD and get a real feel for what the record is going to sound like. But I don't like the way that technology tries to impose itself on studios. A lot of it is unnecessary. Besides, they don't put enough knobs on modern equipment—it's all buttons and keys. It's a real shame because I love to twist knobs," Rivers chuckles.

"I still record on 24-track analog [as opposed to digital] because I like the sound of it," he continues. "There are some potential problems with analog-to-digital conversion that I would rather avoid, but the main problem is that if you record in digital you don't get tape compression. Tape is wonderful because you exchange nasty irks and little peaks for compression, which gives a little burst of bright distortion in exchange for the peak. This makes it sound just as loud, but electrically it can be half the voltage, which means you can make your records louder. Even people who record on digital multitrack like to put the finished mix through, say, half-inch analog tape just to get compression involved. I suspect someone will invent a tape compression simulator some day, but no one has yet."

Hmm. But even if you are not an engineer, your ears will tell you that John A. Rivers knows how to make great records. —ERIC OLSEN

Ash, Daniel: *Coming Down,* RCA, 1990 • "This Love," RCA, 1990 • *Foolish Thing Desire,* Columbia, 1992 • "Get out of Control," Columbia, 1992.

Bubblemen, The: "The Bubblemen Are Coming/Bubblemen Rap," Beggars Banquet, 1986.

Clan of Xymox: *Hidden Faces,* Tes, 1997.

Close Lobsters: *Foxheads Stalk This Land,* Enigma, 1988.

Darkside, The: *All That Noise,* Beggars Banquet, 1991.

David J: "I'll Be Your Chauffeur," RCA, 1990 • *Songs from Another Season,* RCA, 1990.

Dead Can Dance: *Spleen and Ideal,* 4 A.D., 1985 • *Within the Realm of a Dying Sun,* 4 A.D., 1987 • *The Serpent's Egg* (4 tracks), 4 A.D., 1988 • *A Passage in Time,* Rykodisc, 1991.

Dr. Phibes and the Wax Equations: "Sugarblast," 50 Seal Street, 1991 (*Volume One*).

Dr. Robert: *Realms of Gold,* Pure, 1997.

Dylans, The: *Godlike* (EP, 3 tracks), Beggars Banquet, 1991.

Eider, Max: *Best Kisser in the World,* Big Time, 1987 • "Quiet Lives," Big Time, 1987 (*Big Noise from Bigtime*).

Eyeless in Gaza: *Photographs As Memories,* Cherry Red, 1980 • *Caught in Flux,* Cherry Red, 1981 • *Drumming the Beating Heart,* Cherry Red, 1982 • *Rust Red September,* Cherry Red, 1983.

Felt: *Crumbling the Antiseptic Beauty,* Cherry Red, 1982 • *The Splendour of Fear,* Cherry Red, 1983 • *Absolute Classic Masterpieces,* Futurist, 1992.

Jacobites: w/ Nikki Sudden, *Jacobites,* Mammoth, 1984, 1994.

Jazz Butcher: *A Scandal in Bohemia,* Glass, 1984 • *Sex and Travel,* Glass, 1985 • *Distressed Gentlefolk,* Big Time, 1986.

Love and Rockets: "Haunted When the Minutes Drag," Beggars Banquet, 1985 (*One Pound Ninety-Nine*) • "If There's a Heaven Above," Beggars Banquet, 1985 • *Seventh Dream of Teenage Heaven,* Beggars Banquet, 1985 • *Express,* Big Time, 1986.

Lukie D: *The Place to Be,* Anansi, 1997.

Manifesto: *Manifesto,* EastWest, 1993.

Mexico 70: *The Dust Has Come to Stay,* Big Pop, 1994 • "Wonderful Lie," Big Pop, 1994.

Ocean Colour Scene: *B-Sides: Seasides and Freerides* (4 tracks), MCA, 1997.

Pastels, The: *Up for a Bit with the Pastels,* Velvel, 1987, 1997 • *Truckload of Trouble* (2 tracks), Seed, 1993.

Quays, Ronan: *The Ebbing Wings of Wisdom,* De Nova Dacapo, 1996.

Slipstream: *Be Groovy or Leave,* Che, 1997.

Sudden, Nikki: *Back to the Coast,* Gasatanka, 1990 • *See also* Jacobites.

Swell Maps: *A Trip to Marineville,* Rough Trade, 1979 • *Jane from Occupied Europe,* Rough Trade, 1980 • *Whatever Happens Next . . . ,* Rough Trade, 1981 • *Collision Time Revisited,* Mute, 1989.

These Immortal Souls: *I'm Never Gonna Die Again,* Mute, 1992.

Ultramarine: "Kingdom," Blanco Y Negro, 1993 • *United Kingdoms,* Sire/Giant, 1993.

Urusei Yatsura: *Kewpies Like Watermelon* (EP), Che/Sire, 1996 • *We Are Yatsura,* Primary, 1996.

Xymox: "Shame," Wing/Mercury, 1989 • *Twist of Shadows*, Wing/Mercury, 1989.

COLLECTIONS

Little Indian, Big City (original soundtrack), Hollywood, 1996.

Smokey Robinson

Smokey Robinson is second in importance only to Berry Gordy (see entry) in the development of Motown Records, the most important and successful American musical force of the '60s and early '70s. As a singer with the Miracles (42 pop chart hits) and then as a solo act (24 pop chart hits), Smokey has been the best interpreter of his own classic songs of love and loss. As a songwriter/producer he has been instrumental in the careers of Mary Wells, the Temptations, Marvin Gaye, the Marvelettes, and the Supremes, helping to create a sound undeniably black in origin but transcendently human in execution.

William "Smokey" Robinson was born in Detroit on February 19, 1940, and by age 6 he had written and performed his first song in a school play, *Uncle Remus*. He sang in the obligatory church choir and listened to all kinds of music, but he especially favored smooth jazz stylist Sarah Vaughan and vocal groups like Detroit's Nolan Strong and the Diablos. At Northern High School, Robinson and his friends (Pete Moore, Ronnie White, Bobby Rogers, and later, Claudette Rogers, who would become his wife) formed their own vocal group, called the Matadors, in 1954.

The Matadors auditioned for Jackie Wilson's manager in the summer of 1957, just after Robinson's graduation from high school. They failed the audition "miserably," as Smokey told author Gerri Hershey in her excellent survey of soul music, *Nowhere to Run:* "We were slinking out of there like dogs when this guy . . . introduced himself as Berry Gordy, and he wanted to know where we got this little song we did, 'My Mamma Done Told Me.' "

Robinson had written it, and he had about a hundred others in a notebook. Gordy helped Robinson cultivate his honeyed falsetto and his songwriting. Robinson had a knack for rhyming, but Gordy emphasized continuity: think of songs as stories. He also suggested a name change to the Miracles. The Miracles' first single was Gordy's response to the Silhouettes' "Get a Job,"

presciently titled "Got a Job." Licensed to George Goldner's (see entry) End Records, it was released on February 19, 1958, the 18th birthday of both Robinson and Bobby Rogers.

Although the song reached No. 1 R&B, Gordy's royalty check was for $3.19. Gordy had written hits for Jackie Wilson, Marv Johnson, and Barrett Strong but had seen very little cash for his efforts. This last insult enabled Robinson to talk Gordy into forming Tamla Records, and their first release was the Miracles' "Way over There" in 1959. It was Smokey's first solo production, and although it wasn't a national hit, it did sell out its run of 60,000 copies. Tamla's next release was Gordy's production of the Miracles on Smokey's tune "Shop Around," and the bouncy Mama-knows tune shot to No. 2 pop. Motown and the Miracles were on their way.

Smokey has a special relationship with his own songs, and his high tenor soothes and soars through the classic Miracles repertoire. After the peppy adolescent pop of "Shop," "You Really Got a Hold on Me" (No. 8) in 1963 began a string of increasingly sophisticated songs that led Bob Dylan to call Smokey "the world's greatest living poet."

"Hold" was inspired by Sam Cooke, and the churchy piano and call and response are gospel, where agony and ecstasy vie for the singer's soul. Smokey has a Zen-like gift (which complements his vaguely Asian looks) for balancing seeming contradictions: "I don't like you, but I love you," and "you do me wrong, my love is strong" in "Hold"; "I've got sunshine on a cloudy day," from "My Girl"; the titles and imagery of "Choosy Beggar," "My Smile Is Just a Frown (Turned Upside Down)" and "The Tears of a Clown."

Robinson's next classic was "Oooh Baby Baby" (No. 16) with an atavistic, echoey doo-wop feel. Smokey's gossamer vocal and shimmering strings suspend time at the moment just before emotion breaks, as he builds a case that repeatedly yields to an unarticulated call to reconciliation, "oooh baby baby."

"The Tracks of My Tears" (No. 16) treads similar thematic ground. A beautiful, regret-tinged guitar figure opens into a strong backbeat and the Miracles' light "doo doo doo"s. The singer's character is more confident here than on "Oooh Baby Baby," as he states his case against the appearance of happiness.

"Going to a Go-Go" (No. 11) reminded the world that Robinson could rock as the Miracles accompany him down a swinging little street that leads to the happening. Percussion percolates and piano rollicks through a brassy arrangement that celebrates life and the beat.

"More Love" returned to smooth Smokey-land, where his lilting falsetto can convey devotion as well as regret. A great James Jamerson bass burbles out of a field of lush strings as Smokey's wordless "hmm" conveys peace and sweet desire. "More," with its ever-expanding vista of love, is the mirror-image of "Hold," where desire is debilitating and confining. Having learned from experience, Robinson's "I Second That Emotion" (No. 4) cautiously threaded between his previous extremes of emotion and makes a case for love contingent upon doing it right, in which case he "seconds that emotion."

"The Tears of a Clown" (No. 1) recapitulated the happy veneer theme and consolidated everything Smokey had learned about production, using piccolo highs and saxophone lows to create a festive circus feel that is chased by a rocking beat and Robinson's most powerful vocal. He seems to find heretofore untapped reserves of air. Smokey's words are sorrowful, but he seems simultaneously elated to have found the right images to convey that pain.

Robinson left the Miracles in 1972 and moved from Detroit to L.A., following the migration of the Motown offices. "Quiet Storm" is sophisticated adult pop with a jazzy arrangement, and for better or worse, gave name to a genre. "Cruisin' " (No. 4) updates the Miracles sound and is sly, soulful pop.

Robinson was appointed vice president of Motown in 1961, and he took his company responsibilities seriously. As Berry Gordy once remarked, "He's the most unselfish artist I've ever met. Not only does he write hits for himself, but [for] everyone else." Some of his best work with others includes Mary Wells' sultry "Two Lovers" (No. 7), a tale of a good lover and his evil twin, who turn out to be the same person in a classic Smokey twist. Her "My Guy" reached No. 1 on the strength of a gently rocking beat, Wells' self-assured vocal and another great Smokey melody.

Robinson put the Temptations on the map with the smash "My Girl" (No. 1), which is much more than the gender reverse of "My Guy." The intro is instantly recognizable genius: the three-note bass line repeated, the ascending guitar line that feels like home, the swanky finger snaps, the drum break. Then David Ruffin enters with his greatest vocal—a gospel-tinged reverie of private sunshine, warmth, and honeyed music, hovering above a cushion of Temptin' harmonies where "Under the Boardwalk" meets "I Only Have Eyes for You."

Robinson ended his run with the Temptations with the aggressive, even menacing "Get Ready." Chattering sax, a charging beat, and Eddie Kendricks's falsetto soaring through a great chorus give his lover fair warning that wildness awaits her.

Forty years after he and Berry Gordy began the Motown revolution, Smokey is still a viable recording artist in the '90s. He was inducted into the Rock and Roll Hall of Fame in 1987 and won the Grammys' Living Legend Award in 1989. —ERIC OLSEN

Contours, The: *Do You Love Me*, Motown, 1962, 1988 • "Can You Do It," Gordy, 1964 • "First I Look at the Purse," Gordy, 1965 • "The Day She Needed Me," Gordy, 1965.

Four Tops: *Reach Out*, Motown, 1967, 1983 • *Anthology*, Motown, 1974, 1986.

Gaye, Marvin: "Ain't That Peculiar," Tamla, 1965 • "I'll Be Doggone," Tamla, 1965 • "One More Heartache," Tamla, 1966 • "Take This Heart of Mine," Tamla, 1966 • *Moods of Marvin Gaye*, Tamla, 1967 • *Super Hits*, Tamla, 1970 • *Anthology*, Motown, 1974 • *The Master (1961–1984)*, Motown, 1995.

Holloway, Brenda: "When I'm Gone," Tamla, 1965.

Isley Brothers: *Greatest Hits and Rare Classics*, Motown, 1991.

Marvelettes, The: *The Marvelous Marvelettes*, Tamla, 1963 • "Don't Mess with Bill," Tamla, 1966 • *The Marvelettes' Greatest Hits*, Tamla, 1966 • "You're the One," Tamla, 1966 • "The Hunter Gets Captured by the Game," Tamla, 1967 • *The Marvelettes*, Tamla, 1967 • "Here I Am Baby," Tamla, 1968 • "My Baby Must Be a Magician," Tamla, 1968 • *Sophisticated Soul*, Tamla, 1968.

Miracles, The: "Way over There," Tamla, 1959, 1962 • "Shop Around," Tamla, 1960 • *Hi! We're the Miracles*, Tamla, 1961 • *Cookin' with the Miracles*, Tamla, 1962 • "I'll Try Something New," Tamla, 1962 • *I'll Try Something New*, Tamla, 1962 • *Shop Around*, Tamla, 1962 • "You've Really Got a Hold on Me," Tamla, 1962 • "A Love She Can Count On," Tamla, 1963 • *Christmas with the Miracles*, Tamla, 1963 • *The Fabulous Miracles*, Tamla, 1963 • *Doin' Mickey's Monkey*, Tamla, 1964 • *From the Beginning*, Tamla, 1964 • "I Like It Like That," Tamla, 1964 • *I Like It Like That*, Tamla, 1964 • "That's What Love Is Made Of," Tamla, 1964 • *The Mircales on Stage*, Tamla, 1964 • *Away We Go-Go*, Tamla, 1965 • *Going to a Go-Go*, Tamla, 1965 • *Miracles from the Beginning*, Tamla, 1965 • "My Girl Has Gone," Tamla, 1965 • "Oooh Baby Baby," Tamla, 1965 • "The Tracks of My Tears," Tamla, 1965 • "Choosey Beggar," Tamla, 1966 • "Going to a Go-Go," Tamla, 1966 • "I Second That Emotion," Tamla, 1967 • "The Love I Saw in You Was Just a Mirage," Tamla, 1967.

Moments, The: "Sexy Mama," Stang, 1974.

Rare Earth: *Greatest Hits and Rare Classics*, Motown, 1991.

Robinson, Smokey: *Smokey*, Tamla, 1973 • *Pure Smokey*, Tamla, 1974 • "Baby That's Backatcha," Tamla, 1975 •

"Quiet Storm," Tamla, 1975 • *Quiet Storm,* Tamla, 1975 • *Smokey's Family Robinson,* Tamla, 1976 • *Big Time,* Tamla, 1977 • *Deep in My Soul,* Tamla, 1977 • *Love Breeze,* Tamla, 1978 • *Smokey's World,* Tamla, 1978 • *Smokin',* Tamla, 1978 • "Cruisin'," Tamla, 1979 • *Where There's Smoke . . . ,* Tamla, 1979 • *Warm Thoughts,* Tamla, 1980 • *Touch the Sky,* Tamla, 1983 • *Essar,* Motown, 1984 • *Smoke Signals,* Motown, 1986 • *Blame It on Love . . . ,* Motown, 1990 • *Love, Smokey,* Motown, 1990 • "Double Good Everything," SBK, 1991 • *Double Good Everything,* SBK, 1991 • "I Love Your Face," SBK, 1992 • "Rewind," SBK, 1992 • *Ultimate Collection,* Motown, 1997.

Robinson, Smokey, and the Miracles: "More Love," Tamla, 1967 • "Special Occasion," Tamla, 1967 • "The Love I Saw in You Was Just a Mirage," Tamla, 1967 • *The Tears of a Clown,* Tamla, 1967 • "Baby, Baby, Don't Cry," Tamla, 1968 • *Greatest Hits,* Vol. 2, Motown, 1968 • "If You Can Wait," Tamla, 1968 • *Special Occasion,* Tamla, 1968 • "Yester Love," Tamla, 1968 • "Abraham, Martin and John," Tamla, 1969 • "Doggone Right," Tamla, 1969 • "Point It Out," Tamla, 1969 • *Time Out,* Tamla, 1969 • *Four in Blue,* Tamla, 1970 • "The Tears of a Clown," Tamla, 1970 • "I Don't Blame You at All," Tamla, 1971 • "Satisfaction," Tamla, 1971 • *What Love Has Joined Together,* Tamla, 1971 • *Whatever Makes You Happy: More of the Best, 1961–1971,* Rhino, 1993 • *Thirty-Fifth Anniversary Box,* Motown, 1994 • *Anthology: The Best Of,* Motown, 1995.

Ross, Diana, and the Supremes: *Anthology,* Motown, 1974, 1986 • *The Best Of,* Motown, 1995.

Supremes, The: "The Composer," Motown, 1969 • "Floy Joy," Motown, 1971 • *Let the Sun Shine In,* Motown, 1969 • *Greatest Hits and Rare Classics,* Motown, 1991 • *See also* Ross, Diana, and the Supremes.

Taylor, Bobby, and the Vancouvers: *Bobby Taylor and the Vancouvers,* Motown, 1968, 1994.

Temptations, The: "I Want a Love I Can See," Gordy, 1963 • "I'll Be in Trouble," Gordy, 1964 • *Meet the Temptations,* Motown, 1964 • "The Way You Do the Things You Do," Gordy, 1964 • "Don't Look Back," Gordy, 1965 • "It's Growing," Gordy, 1965 • "My Baby," Gordy, 1965 • "My Girl," Gordy, 1965 • "Since I Lost My Baby," Gordy, 1965 • *The Temptin' Temptations,* Gordy, 1965 • *The Temptations Sing Smokey,* Motown, 1965 • "You've Got to Earn It," Gordy, 1965 • "Get Ready," Gordy, 1966 • *Gettin' Ready,* Gordy, 1966 • *Greatest Hits,* Vol. 1, Motown, 1966 • *Anthology,* Motown, 1973 • *All the Million Sellers,* Rhino, 1981 • *Reunion,* Motown, 1982 • *Emperors of Soul,* Motown, 1994.

Warwick, Dionne: *Reservations for Two,* Arista, 1986.

Wells, Mary: "The One Who Really Loves You," Motown, 1962 • *The One Who Really Loves You,* Motown, 1962 • "Two Lovers," Motown, 1962 • "You Beat Me to the Punch," Motown, 1962 • "Laughing Boy," Motown, 1963 • *Two Lovers,* Motown, 1963 • "Your Old Stand By," Motown, 1963 • *Greatest Hits,* Motown, 1964 • "My Guy," Motown, 1964 • *My Guy,* Motown, 1964 • "What's Easy for Two Is Hard for One," Motown, 1964.

Weston, Kim: *Greatest Hits and Rare Classics,* Motown, 1991.

Sylvia Robinson

It wasn't enough for Sylvia Robinson to make music history as half of Mickey and Sylvia and, later, simply as Sylvia. During her stint as half of McHouston "Mickey" Baker and Sylvia, Robinson (born March 6, 1936, in New York City) scored with the 1957 hit "Love Is Strange" and resurfaced in 1973 to perform and co-produce "Pillow Talk" (No. 3). But Robinson wasn't done. In fact, she'd only just begun. With her husband, Joe, Robinson created Sugarhill Records in Englewood, New Jersey, the independent label that single-handedly made rap a viable genre.

At Sugarhill, the Robinsons created a home for rap, scoring the first Hot 100 rap hit with "Rapper's Delight" by the Sugarhill Gang in 1979. "Rapper's Delight" is infectious, bouncy, and positive (though it sounds simplistic by today's standards). And it paved the way for use of samples in rap music, borrowing liberally from Chic's "Good Times" (prompting litigation by Chic). Three years later, Sugarhill Records released what's considered the first piece of socially conscious rap: *The Message,* by Grandmaster Flash and the Furious Five. Besides the indelible title track, that landmark album contained "Scorpio" and "It's Nasty."

For the next several years, Sugarhill Records would maintain a grip on rap music, with follow-ups from the Sugarhill Gang and Grandmaster Flash as well as rap songs by Sequence, West Street Mob, Treacherous Three, and Crash Crew. Though the label fell apart in the late '80s, its legacy is indisputable. The beats from "The Message," for example, were resurrected by Sean "Puffy" Combs (see entry) for his No. 1 "Can't Nobody Hold Me Down" (recorded under the name Puff Daddy) and for Ice Cube's "Check Yo Self." And in early 1997, Rhino Records released a five-CD box set, *The Sugarhill Records Story,* which includes "The Message ('97 Dungeon Mix)." —KEVIN JOHNSON

Furious Five: featuring Cowboy Melle Mel and Scorpio, "Step Off," Sugar Hill, 1984.

Grandmaster and Melle Mel: "White Lines (Don't Do It)," Sugar Hill, 1983.

Grandmaster Flash: *Message from Beat Street: The Best Of,* Rhino, 1994 • *Adventures of Grandmaster Flash: More of the Best,* Rhino, 1996.

Grandmaster Flash and the Furious Five: "The Adventures of Grandmaster Flash on the Wheels of Steel," Sugar Hill, 1981 • "The Message," Sugar Hill, 1982 • *The Message,* Sugar Hill, 1982.

Grandmaster Melle Mel and the Furious Five: "Beatstreet Breakdown," Atlantic, 1984.

Moments, The: "Love on a Two-Way Street," Stang, 1970.

Shirley (And Company): "Shame Shame Shame," Vibration, 1975.

Sugarhill Gang: "Rapper's Delight," Sugar Hill, 1979 • *Sugarhill Gang,* Sugar Hill, 1979 • *The Best Of,* Rhino, 1996.

Sylvia: "Pillow Talk," Vibration, 1973 • *Pillow Talk: The Sensuous Sounds of Sylvia,* Rhino, 1996.

Turner, Ike, and Tina Turner: *Proud Mary: The Best Of,* EMI America, 1975, 1991.

Turner, Tina: *Collected Recordings, Sixties to Nineties,* Capitol, 1994.

Whatnauts, The: *The Definitive Collection,* Deep Beats, 1997.

Wilson, Charlie: *You Turn My Life Around,* MCA, 1992.

COLLECTIONS

The Sugar Hill Story, Vol. 2 Sugar Hill, 1989.
The Sugar Hill Records Story, Rhino, 1997.

William Robinson

See SMOKEY ROBINSON

Bob Rock

Bob Rock's credit sheet isn't supposed to have the words "produced by" anywhere near his name. Featured performer, yes. Producer, no. "When I started working at a studio I was supposed to be a rock 'n' roll star, but it didn't turn out that way," he explains. "I ended up getting a job as an assistant engineer at Little Mountain, a studio up in Vancouver. Through that, it basically opened up the world of recording. I was kinda interested in it, like any musician, but I decided

that I should get into it." He engineered albums at Little Mountain for Canadian producer Bruce Fairbairn (see entry). "As that went along, I was drawn to the production end," Rock says. "For a lot of different reasons the engineering thing was not quite enough of a creative outlet for me. I gained a lot of knowledge from working with other producers and Bruce Fairbairn, but I wanted to put it into my own application."

Rock is overly modest regarding his musicianly success: he was the guitarist for the Payolas, an excellent early '80s new wave band that peaked on the Mick Ronson–produced (see entry) *No Stranger to Danger* in 1982, with the classic single "Eyes of a Stranger." Next, Rock and fellow Payola Paul Hyde formed the duo Rock and Hyde and put out the successful *Under the Volcano* album in 1987.

But his true destiny lay in recording others. Rock's engineering influences are more English than American. "Being in Vancouver, the engineers I learned from were English. There was a different approach there. I tended to look to some of those records in the '70s, then a little more American influence later on," he says, citing Steely Dan's *Aja*.

Because of his engineering background, his production approach is "to try and help artists achieve what they want to achieve artistically," Rock says. "I also try to make a contemporary record. "I try to make bands I work with, like Veruca Salt, as comfortable as possible. There are guys who are purely vibe guys and there are guys who are really technical. I'm sure that everyone has their own distinct style."

Photo by Scotty Baxter

Some say there is a Bob Rock sound. Rock doesn't hear it that clearly. "I think part of my sound comes from the fact that I did engineer and mix, but I think the Cult record sounds a lot different than Metallica, and from the successful Bon Jovi records that I have done, to Cher to Veruca Salt. I tend to magnify the strongest things in a band. I wouldn't say my things sound small. The records that stick out are the ones that seem to sound so good on the radio, so I always try and make those things count."

Rock's detractors claim he's molded a band to his own expectations. They particularly cite Metallica's 1991 eponymous release and its 1996 *Load* (both No. 1). But Rock says he embraces change even though diehard fans don't. "Bands change and want to move on," he says. "I think diehard fans will always be upset that they are not doing *Kill 'Em All* and *Master of Puppets* and all that stuff. Before I did the black album [the self-titled release], I thought they were the world's best-kept secret, and to go from 2.5 million to 14 million copies sold—I look at that as a positive thing."

Working with a younger, less established band like Veruca Salt is challenging and exciting as well. "It was great to open their eyes to a lot of things and do my job," Rock says. "In the future, I hope to work with a lot more younger bands. The established bands bring a different challenge—you need to help them continue what they are doing on their level of success. It's great to have that open palette to do whatever you want with to help a band make an album. It's great to do one and then another." —David John Farinella

Blue Murder: *Blue Murder,* Geffen, 1989.

Bon Jovi: "Bed of Roses," Jambco, 1992 • *Keep the Faith,* Jambco, 1992 • "I'll Sleep When I'm Dead," Jambco, 1993 • "In These Arms," Jambco, 1993 • "Keep the Faith," Jambco, 1993.

Cher: *Love Hurts* (2 tracks), Geffen, 1991 • "Save Up All Your Tears," Geffen, 1991.

Cult, The: "Edie (Ciao Baby)," Sire/Reprise, 1989 • "Fire Woman," Sire/Reprise, 1989 • *Sonic Temple,* Sire/Reprise, 1989 • *The Cult,* Sire/Reprise, 1994 • *High Octane Cult,* Warner Bros., 1996.

Electric Boys: *Funk-o-Metal Carpet Ride,* Atco, 1990.

James, Colin: *Colin James,* Virgin, 1989.

Kingdom Come: *Kingdom Come,* Polydor, 1987 • "Get It On," Polydor, 1988.

Little Caesar: "Chain of Fools," DGC, 1990 • *Little Caesar,* DGC, 1990 • "In Your Arms," DGC, 1991.

Loverboy: *Big Ones,* Columbia, 1989 • "Too Hot," Columbia, 1989.

Metallica: "Enter Sandman," Elektra, 1991 • *Metallica,*

Elektra, 1991 • "The Unforgiven," Elektra, 1991 • "Sad but True," Elektra, 1992 • "Wherever I May Roam," Elektra, 1992 • "Hero of the Day," Elektra, 1996 • *Load,* Elektra, 1996 • "Until It Sleeps," Elektra, 1996 • "King Nothing," Elektra, 1997 • *Re-Load,* Elektra, 1997 • "The Memory Remains," Elektra, 1997 • "The Unforgiven II," Elektra, 1998.

Mötley Crüe: "Dr. Feelgood," Elektra, 1989 • *Dr. Feelgood,* Elektra, 1989 • "Kickstart My Heart," Elektra, 1989 • "Don't Go Away Mad (Just Go Away)," Elektra, 1990 • "Same Ol' Situation (S.O.S.)," Elektra, 1990 • "Without You," Elektra, 1990 • *Decade of Decadence,* Elektra, 1991 • "Primal Scream," Elektra, 1991 • "Hooligan's Holiday," Elektra, 1994 • *Motley Crue,* Elektra, 1994.

Payolas: *Introducing Payolas* (EP), IRS, 1980 • "Jukebox," IRS, 1980, 1981 (*IRS Greatest Hits,* Vols. 2–3).

Rock and Hyde: "Dirty Water," Capitol, 1987 • *Under the Volcano,* Capitol, 1987.

Roth, David Lee: *A Little Ain't Enough,* Warner Bros., 1990.

Skid Row: *Subhuman Race,* Atlantic, 1995.

Subhumans: *Pissed Off with Good Reason,* Essential Noise, 1996.

Veruca Salt: *Eight Arms to Hold You,* Outpost, 1997 • "Volcano Girls," Outpost, 1997.

Nile Rodgers and Bernard Edwards

The disco era of the '70s is memorable partly because of the creative duo of Nile Rodgers and Bernard Edwards. Working with a variety of pop, rock, and soul singers, they changed the musical landscape with their signature: incisive, bass-heavy rhythms. And although the disco movement was faltering by the early '80s, the duo continued to have an influence.

Guitarist Rodgers (born September 19, 1952, in New York) and bassist Edwards (born October 31, 1952, in Greenville, Connecticut) met in 1972 as members of the Big Apple Band, which backed New York City on the hit, "I'm Doin' Fine Now." Later, with Walter Murphy at the helm, they scored a 1977 No. 1 pop and dance hit with "A Fifth of Beethoven." When disco's pulsating beats went worldwide, the Big Apple Band changed its name to Chic. It also changed its sound. Chic became synonymous with lush beats, sophisticated rhythms, and soulful vocals.

With their first single, the million-selling "Dance, Dance, Dance (Yowsah, Yowsah, Yowsah)" (No. 6) Chic became an overnight sensation. Suddenly, their sound was heard in every discotheque, and the hits kept coming: "Le Freak" (No. 1) and "I Want Your Love" (No. 7) in 1978, "Good Times" (No. 1) in 1979. Because of their production and songwriting savvy, other artists began lining up for their services. As a production unit, the duo found themselves face-to-face with Sister Sledge ("We Are Family," No. 2, and "He's the Greatest Dancer," No. 9), Diana Ross ("I'm Coming Out," No. 5, and "Upside Down," No. 1), and Debbie Harry ("Backfired" and "The Jam Was Moving"). Throughout, they continued recording as Chic, but as disco's light began to dim, the group's popularity dwindled. Still, their imprint would be felt for years to come. Both Queen and the Sugarhill Gang used the sinewy bass line from "Good Times" for their respective hits, "Another One Bites the Dust" and "Rapper's Delight." After nine studio albums and four greatest hits collections, the band called it quits in 1992.

By 1985, Rodgers and Edwards were individual producers. Their clients included David Bowie, Madonna, Mick Jagger, Duran Duran, the B-52's, and INXS. Rodgers became a popular and much sought after producer who, to this day, remains busy. Edwards, too, kept a hectic production schedule, working with such artists as Rod Stewart, Missing Persons, Nona Hendryx, Robert Palmer, and Power Station. He died of pneumonia in 1996 at age 43. —LARRY FLICK

Nile Rodgers and Bernard Edwards

Chic: *C'Est Chic,* Atlantic, 1978 • *Chic,* Atlantic, 1978 • "Dance, Dance, Dance (Yowsa, Yowsa, Yowsa)," Atlantic, 1978 • "Everybody Dance," Atlantic, 1978 • "Le Freak," Atlantic, 1978 • "Good Times," Atlantic, 1979 • "I Want Your Love," Atlantic, 1979 • "My Forbidden Lover," Atlantic, 1979 • *Risque,* Atlantic, 1979 • "Real People," Atlantic, 1980 • *Real People,* Atlantic, 1980 • "Rebels Are We," Atlantic, 1980 • *Chic Chic,* Atlantic, 1981 • *Take It Off,* Atlantic, 1981 • *Tongue in Chic,* Atlantic, 1982 • *Believer,* Atlantic, 1983 • "Jack Le Freak," Atlantic, 1987 • *Dance, Dance, Dance: The Best of Chic,* Atlantic, 1991 • *Best of Chic,* Vol. 2, Rhino, 1992 • "Chic Mystique," Warner Bros., 1992 • *Chic-ism,* Warner Bros., 1992 • *Everybody Dance,* Rhino, 1995.

Duran Duran: "A View to a Kill," Capitol, 1985 • *Decade,* Capitol, 1989.

Harry, Debbie: *Koo-Koo,* Chrysalis, 1981 • "The Jam Was Moving," EMI, 1981, 1993 (*Living in Oblivion: The 80s Greatest Hits,* Vol. 2) • "Backfired," Chrysalis, 1988 • *Once More into the Bleach,* Chrysalis, 1989.

Ross, Diana: *Diana,* Motown, 1980 • "I'm Coming Out,"

Motown, 1980 • "Upside Down," Motown, 1980 • *Swept Away,* RCA, 1984 • *Anthology,* Motown, 1986, 1995 • *Diana: The Ultimate Collection,* Motown, 1993 • *Diana Extended: The Remixes,* Motown, 1994.

Sheila B and Devotion: *Sheila B and Devotion,* Carrere, 1980.

Sister Sledge: "He's the Greatest Dancer," Cotillion, 1979 • *We Are Family,* Cotillion, 1979 • "We Are Family," Cotillion, 1979 • *Love Somebody Today,* Cotillion, 1980 • *Best of Sister Sledge (1973–1985),* Rhino, 1992.

COLLECTIONS
Soup for One soundtrack, Mirage/WEA, 1982.

Nile Rodgers

All-4-One: *On and On,* Blitzz, 1998.

Anderson, Laurie: *Home of the Brave* (1 track), Warner Bros., 1986.

Asbury Jukes: *See* Southside Johnny.

Ashford and Simpson: w/ Maya Angelou, *Been Found,* Ichiban, 1996.

B-52's, The: *Cosmic Thing* (6 tracks), Reprise, 1989 • "Roam," Reprise, 1990 • *Good Stuff,* Reprise, 1992 • "Revolution Earth," Reprise, 1992 • *Time Capsule: Greatest Hits,* Warner Bros., 1998.

Bailey, Philip: *Inside Out,* Columbia, 1986.

Beavis and Butt-head: "Come to Butt-head," Geffen, 1993.

Beck, Jeff: *Flash,* Epic, 1985, 1995 • *Beckology,* Legacy/Epic, 1991, 1995.

Bowie, David: "China Girl," EMI America, 1983 • *Let's Dance,* RCA, 1983 • "Let's Dance/Cat People," EMI America, 1983 • "Modern Love," EMI America, 1983 • *Changesbowie,* Rykodisc, 1984, 1990 • "Real Cool World," Warner Bros., 1992 (*Cool World* soundtrack) • *Black Tie White Noise,* Savage/BMG, 1993 • *Bowie: The Singles, 1969–1993,* Rykodisc, 1993 • "Jump They Say," Savage/BMG, 1993 • "Miracle Goodnight," Savage/BMG, 1993 • "Little Wonder" (remix), Virgin, 1997.

Carnes, Kim: "Invitation to Dance," EMI, 1985.

Clapton, Eric: "Stone Free," Reprise, 1993 (*Stone Free: A Tribute to Jimi Hendrix*) • "You Must Believe Me," Warner Bros., 1994 (*A Tribute to Curtis Mayfield*).

Cole, Samantha: *Samantha Cole,* Uptown/Universal, 1997 • *Without You* (EP), Uptown/Universal, 1997.

Dan Reed Network: *Slam,* Mercury, 1989 • *The Heat* (1 track), Mercury, 1991.

Duran Duran: *Arena,* Capitol, 1984 • "The Wild Boys," Capitol, 1984 • "Notorious," Capitol, 1986 • "Skin Trade," Capitol, 1986 • "Meet El Presidente," Capitol, 1987 • *Notorious,* Capitol, 1987 • *Decade,* Capitol, 1989.

Easton, Sheena: "Do It for Love," EMI, 1985 • *The World of Sheena Easton: The Singles Collection,* EMI America, 1993.

Ferry, Bryan: "Help Me," EG/WB, 1986.

Gregory, Michael: *Station X,* Island, 1983.

INXS: "Original Sin," Atco, 1984 • *The Swing,* Atco, 1984.

Jagger, Mick: *She's the Boss* (3 tracks), Columbia, 1985.

Jarreau, Al: *L Is for Lover,* Warner Bros., 1986 • "Moonlighting (Theme)," MCA, 1987 • *Best Of,* Warner Bros., 1996.

Jones, Grace: "I'm Not Perfect (But I'm Perfect for You)," Manhattan, 1986 • *Inside Story,* Manhattan, 1986.

Madonna: "Dress You Up," Sire, 1984 • "Like a Virgin," Sire, 1984 • "Angel," Sire, 1985 • "Into the Groove," Sire, 1985 • "Into the Groove" (remix), Sire, 1985 • *Like a Virgin,* Sire, 1985 • "Material Girl," Sire, 1985 • "Over and Over," Sire, 1987 • *You Can Dance,* Sire, 1987 • *Royal Box,* Sire, 1990 • *The Immaculate Collection,* Sire, 1990 • "Love Don't Live Here Anymore," Maverick, 1996.

Max, Christopher: "Serious Kinda Girl," EMI, 1989.

Murphy, Eddie: *So Happy,* CBS, 1989.

Ocasek, Ric: *Fireball Zone,* Reprise, 1991.

Rodgers, Nile: *Adventures in the Land of the Good Groove,* Mirage, 1983 • *B-Movie Matinee,* Warner Bros., 1985 • "Let's Go Out Tonight," Warner Bros., 1985.

Roth, David Lee: *Your Filthy Little Mouth,* Reprise, 1994.

Sanchez, Marta: *Azabache,* Mercury, 1997 • "Moja Mi Corazon," Mercury, 1997.

Sister Sledge: "Frankie," Virgin/EMI, 1985 (*Now That's What I Call Music 5*).

Southside Johnny: *Trash It Up,* Mirage, 1983 • w/ the , *All I Want Is Everything: The Best of (1979–1991),* Rhino, 1993.

Stray Cats: *Runaway Boys: A Retrospective, 1981–1992,* Capitol, 1997.

System, The: "Coming to America," Atco, 1988.

Thompson Twins: *Here's to Future Days,* Arista, 1985 • "Lay Your Hands on Me," Arista, 1985 • "King for a Day," Arista, 1986 • *Best Of,* Arista, 1989 • *Greatest Hits,* Arista, 1996.

Vaughan Brothers: *Family Style,* Epic Associated, 1990.

Vaughan, Jimmie: "Six Strings Down," Epic, 1994 • *Strange Pleasure,* Epic, 1994 • *Out There,* Epic, 1998.

Wet Wet Wet: *Part One,* London, 1994.

Young, Paul: *Other Voices,* Columbia, 1990.

Bernard Edwards

ABC: *Alphabet City,* Mercury, 1987 • "When Smokey Sings," Mercury, 1987 • *Absolutely ABC: The Best of ABC,* Mercury, 1990.

Cocker, Joe: *Cocker,* Capitol, 1986.

Distance, The: *Under the One Sky,* Reprise, 1989.

Edwards, Bernard: *Glad to Be Here,* WEA, 1983.

Hendryx, Nona: *The Heat,* RCA, 1985.

Hollywood Beyond: *If,* Warner Bros., 1987.

Hugh, Grayson: *Road to Freedom,* MCA, 1992.

Hunter, Ian, with Mick Ronson: *Y U I Orta,* Mercury, 1989.

Jacksons, The: "Time Out for the Burglar," MCA, 1987.

Missing Persons: *Color in Your Life,* Capitol, 1986 • *The Best Of,* Capitol, 1987.

Palmer, Robert: "Discipline of Love," Island, 1985 • *Riptide,* Island, 1985 • "Addicted to Love," Island, 1986 • "Hyperactive," Island, 1986 • "I Didn't Mean to Turn You On," Island, 1986.

Party, The: *Free,* Hollywood, 1992.

Platinum Blonde: *Contact,* Epic, 1987.

Power Station: *The Power Station,* Gold Rush, 1985, 1996 • "Communication," Capitol, 1985 • "Get It On (Bang a Gong)," Virgin/EMI, 1985 (*Now That's What I Call Music 5*) • "Some Like It Hot," Capitol, 1985 • *Living in Fear,* Guardian/Angel, 1997 • "She Can Rock It," Guardian, 1997.

Ross, Diana: *Endless Love,* Mercury, 1981 • "Telephone," Label?, 1985.

Starpoint: "Tough Act to Follow," Elektra, 1989.

Stewart, Rod: "Forever Young," Warner Bros., 1988 • "Lost in You," Warner Bros., 1988 • *Out of Order,* Warner Bros., 1988 • "Crazy About Her," Warner Bros., 1989 • "My Heart Can't Tell You No," Warner Bros., 1989 • *Storyteller: The Complete Anthology,* Warner Bros., 1989 • *Downtown Train,* Warner Bros., 1990 • "This Old Heart of Mine," Warner Bros., 1990 • *Vagabond Heart,* Warner Bros., 1991 • *A Spanner in the Works,* Warner Bros., 1995 • *If We Fall in Love Tonight,* Warner Bros., 1996.

Triplets, The: *Break the Silence,* Elektra (EP), 1986.

Watley, Jody: "Don't You Want Me," MCA, 1987 • *Jody Watley,* MCA, 1987 • *You Wanna Dance with Me?* (remix), MCA, 1990 • *Greatest Hits,* MCA, 1996.

Mick Ronson

Mick Ronson was one of the great guitar players of the '70s, helping to transform David Bowie (see entry) from "oddity" to superstar, then contributing mightily as sideman, arranger, and producer to the careers of Lou Reed, Mott the Hoople, Ian Hunter, David Johansen, Bob Dylan, Roger McGuinn, the Payolas, and Morrissey, among many others. A shy but charismatic figure, Ronson also maintained an interesting, if sporadic, solo career.

Mick Ronson was born in 1947 and grew up in Hull in the north of England. As a child Ronson played violin, recorder, harmonium, and guitar. Outwardly reserved, Ronson practiced guitar-hero poses in the privacy of his own room as he slashed out Jeff Beck riffs. Many a young guitarist would likewise emulate him in the '70s. Ronson played with local groups Voice and Wanted before hooking up the Rats, yet another Anglo R&B group in the tradition of Pretty Things, Them, the early Rolling Stones, and the Yardbirds. The young guitarist made his recording debut behind British folk singer Michael Chapman on the 1969 album *Fully Qualified Survivor*. After a few singles and a tour of France with the Rats, a disillusioned Ronson returned to Hull and the quiet life of a gardener.

But horticulture lost out to music when Ronson was summoned to London in 1970 to work with David Bowie on the follow-up to his first hit single, "Space Oddity." Bowie and bassist/producer Tony Visconti (see entry) were assembling a hard rock band to blow away Bowie's frouffy, flower power image. With the addition of ex-Rat Woody Woodmansey on drums, *The Man Who Sold the World* lineup was complete.

Man rocks with an authority that startles even today. While the material is uneven and Visconti's production is somewhat pinched, *Man* is Bowie's first classic album. Ronson's guitar propels the opus "Width of a Circle"; he riffs viciously like Jimmy Page (see entry) and solos on the twang bar with a Jeff Beck–like intensity. "All the Madmen" is one of the most successful examples of Bowie's career-long fascination with the Outsider. The title track is driven by Ronson's melodic lines and a spunky Latin beat.

After *Man*, Bowie returned to songwriting and Ronson returned to Hull, where he recorded a single, "The Fourth Hour of My Sleep," under the name Ronno. When Bowie was through writing *Hunky Dory* (*Hunky Dory* through *Pinups* were produced by Bowie and Ken Scott; see entries), Ronson, Woodmansey, and another ex-Rat, bassist Trevor Bolder, answered the call to London. This time Ronson acted as band leader and arranger as his electric guitar flash was subsumed within a delicate mix of piano, strings, and acoustic guitar. Ronson helped bring Bowie's melodic gifts to the fore with brilliant arrangements of Bowie's career theme "Changes," the lush "Life on Mars," the wistful and affecting "Kooks," and Bowie's evocation of spiritual impotence, "Quicksand." Ronson's bowel-shaking electric guitar returns to give "Queen Bitch" the edge it demands, giving a foretaste of the glory that was to be the Spiders from Mars.

Bowie's next album, *The Rise and Fall of Ziggy Stardust and the Spiders from Mars* (No. 5 U.K.), defined an era as completely as "Rock Around the Clock," Elvis's *Sun Sessions,* or the Beatles' first album. Bowie and the Spiders created a compelling, dangerous, and mythic world of glittering cosmic androgyny powered by rock 'n' roll. The greatness of the Spiders band emboldened Bowie

to envision himself as a superstar, although he hadn't come close to attaining that status in real life yet. Bowie's risk was backed up by the music on the album, which is the most consistent, tuneful, and least self-indulgent of his career. *Ziggy* is also Ronson's greatest musical moment as he played guitars and keyboards and co-arranged the album with Bowie.

"Soul Love" is a perfect example of the contrast that Ronson seemed to be able to bring out in Bowie's music. The "baby" background vocals that Ronson and Bowie share have an otherworldly lightness, while Bowie's soul sax swings gently, and Ronson's fuzzy Les Paul gooses the song with heaviness at the right moments. "Lady Stardust" introduces the Ziggy character in all of his decadent glory with makeup, long black hair, and "animal grace," as Ronson's piano and Bowie's longing vocals lend the song an elegiac flavor. Ronson's guitar line on the title track is a study in melodic economy. "Suffragette City" rocks with Ronson's pounding piano and driving Les Paul. The stomping chorus and the immortal line "Wham Bam Thank You Ma'am" contribute to make it Bowie and Ronson's most memorable song.

The year 1972 was an astonishing time for Bowie and Ronson as *Ziggy* was released and they worked together to resurrect the careers of both Lou Reed (*Transformer*) and Mott the Hoople (*All the Young Dudes*). *Transformer* was Lou Reed's comeback after the collapse of the Velvet Underground and the disappointment of his first solo album. While coy and fey in parts, *Transformer* sounds like a Spiders album, with Ronson handling lead guitar, piano, and recorder as well the string and bass arrangements. The album emphasizes Reed's humor and melodic gift and made him accessible to the teeming masses for the first (and, for many, the last) time. "Walk on the Wild Side" (No. 16), Reed's only hit single, is a sly and sultry classic. Herbie Flower's acoustic bass and the "colored girls" ' "doot da doot" background vocals are deft touches that jerk the song out of time and leave it next to an eternal street lamp somewhere in New York City. "Satellite of Love" is Reed's most beautiful solo moment. Ronson's lovely piano line, and his and Bowie's background vocals, are unmistakable and perfect.

Ronson and Bowie achieved similar results for Mott the Hoople with *All the Young Dudes*. Mott had been a journeyman hard rock English band with moments of inspiration ("Rock and Roll Queen," "Thunderbuck Ram") but no sustained momentum. Bowie and Ronson moved the band's image slightly in the glam direction, sharpened the songwriting ("One of the Boys," "Ready for Love"), and brought in killer outside material (Lou Reed's "Sweet Jane" and Bowie's own "All the Young Dudes"). "All the Young Dudes" (No. 3 U.K.) was Mott's biggest hit single and put the band on the map. The band did well with *Ziggy*-style arrangements highlighting Mick Ralph's clean but powerful guitars; Verden Allen's organ; and the contrast between Ralph's high, thin vocals and Ian Hunter's grainy bellow.

Ronson and the Spiders continued with Bowie for two more albums, *Aladdin Sane* and *Pinups* (both No. 1 U.K.). *Sane* yielded two more classics, "Panic in Detroit" and "The Jean Genie," as well as Ronson's hardest guitar on record, the crunching and squealing "Cracked Actor." *Pinups* is a collection of cover songs that was received with mixed enthusiasm, and this response, coupled with Bowie's natural restlessness, led to the breakup of the band. Neither Bowie nor Ronson was ever again to find as symbiotic or successful a partnership.

After the breakup of the Spiders, Mick Ronson went solo and released the Bowie-like *Slaughter on Tenth Avenue* (No. 9 U.K.) in 1974—the highlight of which was a searing guitar instrumental version of the title track—followed the next year by the less self-conscious *Play Don't Worry*. *Play* is the more successful of the two, featuring ripping takes of "Girl Can't Help It," "White Light/White Heat," and Ronson's own "Billy Porter." Ronson's lead vocals are competent but not distinctive, and he never felt at home alone in the spotlight.

Ronson then briefly joined Mott the Hoople, playing on the song "Saturday Gigs." When Mott broke up, Ronson hooked up with Ian Hunter in a partnership that filled a void for both: Ronson missed a lead figure like Bowie, and Hunter missed guitarist Mick Ralphs, who had left Mott to form Bad Company (a band whose commercial success and longevity is as inexplicable as it is depressing) with singer Paul Rodgers (ex of Free).

Ronson played on and produced several Hunter albums, including his exceptional first album ("Once Bitten, Twice Shy," No. 14 U.K.; "I Get So Excited"), featuring Mick's best guitar work away from Bowie, and *You're Never Alone with a Schizophrenic,* with the hits "Cleveland Rocks" (now the theme of *The Drew Carey Show*) and "Ships" (later covered by Barry Manilow).

Mick joined Bob Dylan's *Rolling Thunder Revue* tour in 1975. He appeared on the *Hard Rain* live album and also in Dylan's four-hour improvised film of the tour, *Renaldo and Clara*. Another Rolling Thunder player, former Byrd Roger McGuinn, asked Ronson to produce and play on his *Cardiff Rose* album. Other Mick Ronson productions include albums by the Iron City Houserockers, David Johansen, the Payolas, Rich Kids, Ellen Foley, and Morrissey's best album *Your Arsenal* (No. 4

U.K.). "Ronno" died of liver cancer in 1993 at age 46.
—Eric Olsen

Dal Bello, Lisa: *Who Man for Says,* Capitol, 1984.

Dead Fingers Talk: *Storm the Reality Studios,* Pye, 1978.

Fatal Flowers: *Johnny B Is Back,* Atlantic, 1988 • *Pleasure Ground,* Atlantic, 1989.

Foley, Ellen: *Night Out,* Epic, 1979 • "We Belong to the Night," Epic, 1979, 1981 (*Exposed*).

Gillespie, Dana: *Weren't Born a Man* (2 tracks), RCA, 1973.

Hunter, Ian: *Ian Hunter,* CBS, 1975 • "Once Bitten, Twice Shy," CBS, 1975 • *You're Never Alone with a Schizophrenic,* Chrysalis, 1979 • *Welcome to the Club,* Chrysalis, 1980 • *Short Back and Sides,* Chrysalis, 1981 • *Shades of Ian Hunter,* Chrysalis, 1988.

Iron City Houserockers: *Have a Good Time (but Get Out Alive),* MCA, 1980 • *Pumping Iron and Sweating Steel: The Best Of,* Rhino, 1992.

Johansen, David: *In Style,* Blue Sky, 1979 • *From Pumps to Pompadour: The David Johansen Story,* Rhino, 1995.

Jones, David Lynn: *Hard Times on Easy Street,* Mercury, 1987 • "High Ridin' Heroes," Mercury, 1988.

Los Illegals: *Internal Exile,* A&M, 1983.

Lulu: "The Man Who Sold the World/Watch That Man," Chelsea, 1973 • *From Crayons to Perfume: The Best of Lulu,* Rhino, 1994.

McGuinn, Roger: *Cardiff Rose,* Columbia, 1976 • *Born to Rock and Roll,* Columbia, 1991.

Morrissey: "Tomorrow," Sire/Reprise, 1992 • "We Hate It When Our Friends Become Successful," Sire/Reprise, 1992 • *Your Arsenal,* Sire/Reprise, 1992 • "You're the One for Me Fatty," Sire/Reprise, 1992 • *World of Morrissey,* Sire, 1995.

Payolas, The: *No Stranger to Danger,* A&M, 1982 • *Hammer on a Drum,* A&M, 1983.

Reed, Lou: *Transformer,* RCA, 1972 • "Walk on the Wild Side," RCA, 1973 • *Walk on th Wild Side: The Best Of,* RCA, 1977 • *Between Thought and Expression: The Lou Reed Anthology,* RCA, 1992.

Rich Kids: *Ghosts of Princes in Towers,* EMI, 1978.

Ronson, Mick: *Slaughter on Tenth Avenue,* RCA, 1974 • *Play Don't Worry,* RCA, 1975 • *Heaven and Hull,* Epic, 1994 • *Only After Dark,* Golden Years, 1995.

Sargeant, Bob: *First Starring Role* (3 tracks), RCA, 1974.

Sexgang, Andi: *Arco Valley,* Jungle, 1989.

Thomas, Ian: *Riders on Dark Horses,* Mercury, 1984.

Urgent: "Running Back," EMI, 1985.

Paul Rothchild

Paul Rothchild was one of the great musical revolutionaries of the '60s. First, he helped to record the folk revival of the early '60s, including such artists as the Charles River Valley Boys, Geoff Muldaur, and Tom Rush. Then, as staff producer for Elektra Records, he helped bash down the barrier between acoustic and electric music with the Paul Butterfield Blues Band. He then reached the highest artistic and commercial heights—producing '60s archetypes Love, the Doors, and Janis Joplin. The '70s were fertile as well; Rothchild produced important work by an eclectic bunch, including the Everly Brothers, Elliott Murphy, Bonnie Raitt, John Sebastian, Freddie Hubbard, Outlaws, and Bette Midler's version of the Joplin mythos, *The Rose* (No. 12).

Paul Rothchild was born April 18, 1935, in Brooklyn to an opera singer and a British businessman and grew up in Greenwich Village. By 1961, Rothchild was a salesman for a record distributor in Cambridge, Massachusetts. A fan of classical and jazz, Rothchild was strolling around Harvard Square one evening in 1962 when he dropped into a coffeehouse, Club 47. A bluegrass band was playing that night, the Charles River Valley Boys, and Rothchild walked out of the club a convert. Upon learning that the band had no records out, he offered to record them himself. When Rothchild discovered that there were no recording studios in Boston, he and a technician friend obtained permission to record in a Harvard University library on Sundays. Rothchild printed 1,000 copies of the Boys' first record; they sold out rapidly, so he recorded other Club 47 folkies. Soon, in addition to local artists like Boston University co-ed Joan Baez, the Cambridge scene was drawing national acts like Theodore Bikel and Sonny Terry and Brownie McGhee—the folk revival was on.

Rothchild's entrepreneurial success came to the attention of Bob Weinstock of Prestige Records in New York, who hired Rothchild to be his folk department for $135 per week. Over the next six months, Rothchild recorded 13 albums with talent such as Tom Rush and Geoff Muldaur. This success was in turn noticed by another folk buff, Jac Holzman of Elektra Records, who hired Rothchild in 1964 with the freedom to sign any folk artist who could sell 5,000 or more albums.

Rothchild heard about a group in Chicago that was combining the grit of the blues with the excitement of electric music, the Paul Butterfield Blues Band. On a visit to Chicago, Rothchild was blown away by the band. At the end of a long night's club crawl through Chicago with Butterfield, he also found a guitarist who "tore [his] mind apart," Rothchild told Joe Smith in *Off the Record*. Michael Bloomfield had turned down Butterfield's offer to join his group innumerable times, but when Rothchild and Bloomfield sat down together and did "a half hour of intense intellectual Jew at each other," Bloomfield agreed to join the band.

After two false starts (a studio session and a live session—the studio session was released in 1995 on Rhino as *The Long Lost Elektra Paul Butterfield Tapes*), Elektra put out *The Paul Butterfield Blues Band,* one of the great blues albums of the '60s, featuring Butterfield on harmonica and vocals; Bloomfield and Elvin Bishop on guitars; and Jerome Arnold and Sam Lay, veterans of Howlin' Wolf's band, on bass and drums respectively.

Rothchild and Holzman got the band included in the 1965 Newport Folk Festival, a first for an electric band at the pristine acoustic festival. Musicologist Alan Lomax introduced the band with a diatribe against electric music, after which Butterfield's (as well as Dylan's and Peter, Paul and Mary's) manager, Albert Grossman, punched Lomax in the nose. Impressed, Bob Dylan picked the Butterfield band to back him up for his first-ever electric set the next day.

Rothchild was the only member of the festival management who had ever recorded electric music, so he was asked to run the sound for Dylan's set. As the band struck up the opening to "Maggie's Farm" on electric instruments, "it seemed like everybody on my left wanted Dylan to get off the stage, and everybody on my right wanted him to stay. . . . Here comes Pete Seeger with an ax wanting to cut the power cables. It was the turning point. The old guard realized the world was changing."

By 1965 Johnny Rivers and the Byrds had put Hollywood's Sunset Strip and clubs like the Whisky A-Go-Go and Ciro's on the map. Keyboardist Ray Manzarek and singer/songwriter Jim Morrison had met in film school at UCLA and had decided to form a band together. In the best '60s tradition, guitarist Robby Krieger and drummer John Densmore were in Manzarek's meditation class, and when they all got together, it clicked.

Rothchild saw the band live at the Whisky in July 1966 and was astonished—so much so that he wanted to create a studio album that was an "aural documentary" of their live set. Manzarek's inventive organ dominated the live sound, complemented well by Krieger's blues riffs, jazzy runs, and Spanish finger picking on guitar and Densmore's fluid, interpretive drumming. Morrison was the focal point, his commanding baritone grabbing the ear while his erratic antics and arresting good looks captured the eye. Rothchild's most enduring achievement is capturing that sound in the studio.

Rothchild's first sessions at Sunset Sound for *The Doors* (No. 2) went well—the band was well prepared by a year's worth of nightly gigs—and several songs were recorded in only two or three takes. But that was not to last. According to Jerry Hopkins in *No One Here Gets Out Alive,* at the recording session of "The End," Morrison was inebriated, laying on the floor in the corner of the Sunset Sound studio near the drums, softly mumbling the words to his Oedipal nightmare: "Fuck the mother, kill the father, fuck the mother, kill the father, fuck the mother, kill the father. . . ." As Rothchild tried to capture his attention, Morrison picked up a television set and threw it toward the control room.

Rothchild ended the session and sent Morrison off with a girlfriend. As the young woman drove down Sunset, Morrison suddenly opened the car door and bolted down the street on foot. He dashed to the studio, scaled the gate, penetrated an outer and an inner door, then panting, peeled off his clothes. Feeling heat all around him, Morrison did the sensible thing—he yanked a fire extinguisher from the wall and doused the studio. Alerted by the woman, Rothchild returned to the studio and persuaded the naked, dripping, foamy Morrison to leave and left word with the owner to charge the damage to Elektra. The next day the studio was spotless and they got "The End," one of the most dramatic moments on record, in two takes.

The Doors is a great and enduring album, wherein Morrison explores the dark side with the seriousness of an artist over a deep and appealing sonic palette laid down by the band and Rothchild. While Morrison the person can be viewed as a pretentious, self-destructive clown who drank himself to death by age 27, Morrison the artist was one of best singers, lyricists, and performers in rock history.

"Break On Through" bounds in on the momentum of Densmore's irresistible double-time bossa nova cymbal ride, Manzarek's charging organ bass, and Krieger's tough unison guitar. Rothchild's production is timelessly immediate and alive, and Morrison delivers his sermon with a bodhisattva's certainty. "You know the day destroys the night, / Night divides the day, / Try to run, Try to hide, / Break on through to the other side." Morrison captures the good-and-evil, light-and-dark dichotomy with an eerie economy. There are no rookie jitters here: The Doors arrived whole and complete.

"Light My Fire," a Robby Krieger composition and the band's signature tune, stretches out on great Manzarek and Krieger solos but returns home on ballsy Morrison vocals and an insistent melody. The song shot

to No. 1 and remains a radio staple. Rothchild's production and Bruce Botnick's (see entry) engineering isolate the instruments from the vocals, creating a classic, clean, but live sound.

The Doors' next album, *Strange Days* (No. 3), was nearly as good as the first, but Morrison's personal demons and the band's dearth of material limited the next two albums, *Waiting for the Sun* (No. 1) and *The Soft Parade* (No. 6—with horns!) to a few great songs, "Hello, I Love You" (No. 1), "Five to One," "Touch Me" (No. 3).

Morrison Hotel (No. 4) was a return to form, with Morrison and the band's toughest singing and playing on the great alcoholic's hymn "Roadhouse Blues," the nasty "Peace Frog," and the elegiac "Waiting for the Sun."

By 1970, Rothchild had recorded Janis Joplin's career-topping swan song, *Pearl* (No. 1), an album he described in James Riordan's *Break On Through* as "a labor of total love by the most loving and dedicated musicians I'd ever worked with. . . . That music was full of heart, the way it's supposed to be." *Pearl* said it all with "Move Over," "Cry Baby," "Get It While You Can," and a phenomenal "Me and Bobby McGee" (No. 1). Almost miraculously, "McGee" contains both Joplin's most tender and frenzied moments. The meticulous but understanding Rothchild had finally run out of patience with the living psychodrama that was Jim Morrison, so he passed on the production reins to engineer Botnick and the band for *L.A. Woman.* With Joplin and Morrison both soon to die, an era was over.

The Doors albums combined sell more than 1 million copies per year to this day, and Rothchild's elegant yet gutsy production is a vital part of that enduring success. The band has called him "the fifth Door." Paul Rothchild died in 1995 after a five-year bout with lung cancer. His son Dan is a member of Tonic and produced Better Than Ezra's hit "Good." —Eric Olsen

Ars Nova: *Ars Nova,* Elektra, 1968.

Ashton, Mark: *Modern Pilgrims,* RCA, 1988.

Bloomfield, Mike: *Don't Say That I Ain't Your Man,* Legacy, 1994.

Blues Project: *Anthology,* PolyGram, 1997.

Buckley, Tim: *Tim Buckley,* Elektra, 1966.

Butterfield Blues Band: *The Original Lost Elektra Sessions,* Rhino, 1964, 1995 • *Sometimes I Just Feel Like Smilin',* Elektra, 1971.

Charles River Valley Boys: *The Charles River Valley Boys,* Prestige/Folklore, 1962 • *Beatle Country,* Rounder, 1966, 1995.

Clear Light: *Clear Light,* Elektra, 1967.

Cottonwood South: *Cottonwood South,* CBS, 1974.

Crosby, Stills, Nash and Young: *Crosby, Stills, Nash and Young*, Atlantic, 1991.

Doors, The: "Light My Fire," Elektra, 1967 • "Love Me Two Times," Elektra, 1967 • "People Are Strange," Elektra, 1967 • *Strange Days*, Elektra, 1967 • *The Doors*, Elektra, 1967 • "Hello, I Love You," Elektra, 1968 • "The Unknown Soldier," Elektra, 1968 • *Waiting for the Sun*, Elektra, 1968 • "Runnin' Blue," Elektra, 1969 • *Soft Parade*, Elektra, 1969 • "Tell All the People," Elektra, 1969 • "Touch Me," Elektra, 1969 • *Absolutely Live*, Elektra, 1970 • *Morrison Hotel*, Elektra, 1970 • "Roadhouse Blues," Elektra, 1970 • "You Make Me Real," Elektra, 1970 • *American Prayer*, Elektra, 1978, 1995 • *Alive She Cried*, Elektra, 1983 • "Gloria," Elektra, 1983 • *The Best Of*, Elektra, 1985, 1991 • *Live at the Hollywood Bowl*, Elektra, 1987 • *In Concert*, Elektra, 1991 • *The Doors* soundtrack, Elektra, 1991 • *The Doors Box Set*, Elektra, 1997.

Everly Brothers: *Stories We Could Tell*, RCA, 1972 • *Heartaches and Harmonies*, Rhino, 1994.

Fast Fontaine: *Fast Fontaine*, EMI America, 1981.

Fuller, Jesse: *Favorites*, Prestige, 1965.

Funky Kings: *The Funky Kings*, Arista, 1976.

Goodthunder: *Goodthunder*, Elektra, 1972.

Hill, Joel Scott, Johnny Barbata, and Chris Ethridge: *L.A. Getaway*, Atco, 1971.

Hubbard, Freddie: *High Energy*, CBS, 1974.

Jazz at the Movies Band: *Body Heat*, Discovery, 1993.

Joplin, Janis: "Cry Baby," Columbia, 1971 • "Get It While You Can," Columbia, 1971 • "Me and Bobby McGee," Columbia, 1971 • *Pearl*, Columbia, 1971 • *Janis* soundtrack, Columbia, 1972 • *Greatest Hits*, Columbia, 1973, 1995 • *Janis*, Legacy, 1993.

Koerner, Ray and Glover: *The Return of Koerner, Ray and Glover*, Elektra, 1965.

Love: "7 and 7 Is," Elektra, 1967 • *Da Capo*, Elektra, 1967 • *Love Story: 1966–1972*, Rhino/Elektra, 1995.

Martino, Pat: *Joyous Lake*, Warner Bros., 1976.

Midler, Bette: *The Rose*, Atlantic, 1979 • "The Rose," Atlantic, 1980 • "When a Man Loves a Woman," Atlantic, 1980 • *Experience the Divine: Bette Midler's Greatest Hits*, Atlantic, 1993.

Mitchell, Joni: *Clouds*, Reprise, 1969.

Murphy, Elliott: *Lost Generation*, RCA, 1975.

Neil, Fred: *A Little Bit of Rain*, Elektra, 1965 • *Bleeker and MacDougal*, Elektra, 1965.

Noonan, Steve: *Steve Noonan*, Elektra, 1968.

Ochs, Phil: *All the News That's Fit to Sing*, Elektra, 1964 • *I Ain't Marching Anymore*, Elektra, 1965 • *Farewells and Fantasies Collection*, Rhino, 1997.

Outlaws: *Outlaws*, Arista, 1975 • "There Goes Another Love Song," Arista, 1975 • "Breaker-Breaker," Arista, 1976 • *Lady in Waiting*, Arista, 1976 • *Greatest Hits*, Arista, 1982 • *Best of the Outlaws: Green Grass and High Tides*, Arista, 1996.

Paul Butterfield Blues Band: *The Paul Butterfield Blues Band*, Elektra, 1965 • *East West*, Elektra, 1966 • *Golden Butter: The Best Of*, Elektra, 1972.

Raitt, Bonnie: *Home Plate*, Warner Bros., 1975 • "Runaway," Warner Bros., 1977 • *Sweet Forgiveness*, Warner Bros., 1977 • *The Bonnie Raitt Collection*, Warner Bros., 1990.

Rhinoceros: *Rhinoceros*, Elektra, 1968.

Rush, Tom: *Got a Mind to Ramble*, Prestige, 1963 • *Tom Rush*, Elektra, 1965 • *Classic Rush*, Elektra, 1970.

Sebastian, John: *John B. Sebastian*, Reprise, 1970 • "She's a Lady," Reprise, 1970 • *Cheapo Cheapo Productions Presents Real Live John Sebastian*, Reprise, 1971 • *The Four of Us*, Reprise, 1971 • *The Tarzana Kid*, Reprise, 1974.

Shear, Jules: *Horse of a Different Color (1976–1989)*, Razor & Tie, 1994.

Spoelstra, Mark: *State of Mind*, Elektra, 1966.

Van Ronk, Dave: *Let No One Deceive You*, Flying Fish, 1992.

Tom Rothrock and Rob Schnapf

After spending the mid-'80s working as coffee caddies at the Record Plant in Los Angeles, Tom Rothrock and Rob Schnapf have spent the '90s pushing faders, twisting knobs, and reversing gates, learning that in record production nothing works twice.

The pair have worked with an interesting array of modern rockers, including Beck, Dog Society, Toadies, Wool, and current troubadour-of-the-month Elliott Smith (featured on the *Good Will Hunting* soundtrack). They have also produced Poison and Stevie Nicks.

They learned how valuable tag-team producing can be on the *Mic City Sons* album for punkers Heatmiser. "I just got real tired and went back to the hotel," Rothrock says. "Rob stayed on 'til 4 A.M. and they just got an amazing vocal." They've also used the team approach on mixing sessions for the D Generation's *No Lunch* album with much success. If one becomes frustrated, the other can solve the problem, they suggest.

This team began at the Micro Plant, above the Record Plant. They would pile all their gear in a room, call bands they knew, and start recording around midnight. Shortly thereafter, the duo built the Pleasure Dome studios in Van Nuys. "We had to make the nut every month," comments Rothrock. "I'd be stuck in there a week or two a month engineering or producing something just to make the rent money." So, when the decided to move up and build "a bigger dome" they decided to go all out.

The Shop, open since the early '90s, is distant from the Los Angeles hustle and bustle. Located in Arcadia, in Humboldt County, the studio sits on Rothrock's family property. "The barn was laying there and was falling down. It was either have the fire department torch this thing or put a lot of work back into it," Rothrock says. "Rob and I are both fans of old everything, whether it's furniture or cars, so 90 percent of what the signal passes through was built between 1945 and 1975. As Rob always says, it's state-of-the-art '70s." They've also amassed an oddball collection of tube gear from the '40s and '50s. The Shop is their sanctuary.

Rothrock explains, "Whatever you had patched up last is still sitting there. We've left mixes up for a month and gone from Los Angeles to New York, and then the company will say, 'Can you turn up the vocal a little bit?' and we'll go back up and it'll still be laying there. The sonic philosophy is to wring everything out of the instrument and the room and the hands that are playing it," Rothrock says. "What you hear should be as much of the actual event happening in the room as we can bring to wherever you are listening. We are trying to pull you into where we were at the time it happened."

They don't want to "overthink" the process and believe the performance is critical. "It starts and ends with the song," Rothrock says. "Also, staying out of the way and having enough vision to know not to have a heavy-handed influence, so it stays true to the artist."

"It's definitely finding the strengths of the artist and accentuating them," Schnapf adds. That vision persuaded them to form the Bongload label, occasional home to Beck and launching pad for such bands as Further and Wool. The two now split their time between Bongload and major labels. "They're rewarding in different ways," says Schnapf. "Sometimes, when you do too much of the Bongload thing, it's really nice to do a major-label thing, because you make the record and hand it off." Adds Rothrock, "On the other hand, sometimes it's nice to see it all the way through." —DAVID JOHN FARINELLA

Rothrock and Schnapf

Beck: *Mellow Gold,* DGC, 1994 • *Odelay* (1 track), DGC, 1996 • "Feather in Your Cap," Geffen, 1997 (*Suburbia* soundtrack).
Burnside, R.L.: *Mr. Wizard,* Epitaph, 1997.
Dog Society: *Test Your Own Eyes,* EastWest, 1993.

Fu Manchu: *Daredevil,* Bongload, 1995.
Gooch, Agnes: *Blind,* Revolution, 1997.
Heatmiser: *Mic City Sons,* Caroline, 1996.
Lord, Mary Lou: *Got No Shadow,* Work, 1998.
Lutefisk: *Deliver from Porcelain: Theme and Variations,* Bongload, 1995 • *Burn in Hell, Fuckers,* Bongload, 1997.
Muzza Chunka: *Fishy Pants,* Rowdy, 1993.
My Head: *Endless Bummer,* Capitol, 1996.
Nicks, Stevie: "Love's a Hard Game," Modern, 1991.
Poison: *Swallow This Live,* Capitol, 1991.
Pop Defect: *Punch Drunk,* Flipside, 1992.
Quinine: *Regrets Only,* Bongload, 1995.
Smith, Elliott: *Either/Or,* Kill Rock Stars, 1997 • *XO,* Bongload, 1998.
Toadies: "Possum Kingdom," Interscope, 1994 • *Rubberneck,* Interscope, 1994.
Vitamade: *Everything You Need,* Bongload, 1995.
Wool: *Box Set,* London, 1994.

Tom Rothrock

Beck: "Loser," DGC, 1993.
Wool: *Budspawn,* London, 1992.

Tom Rowlands

See CHEMICAL BROTHERS

Rick Rubin

Rick Rubin has produced rap, heavy metal, rock, and country. He has been called everything from "the next Phil Spector" (see entry) to "Satan's Record Producer." All he wants to do is make good records.

Born Frederick Jay Rubin on Long Island, New York, in 1963, Rubin began his career in his New York University dorm room by producing rap act T. La Rock and Jazzy Jay. Their "It's Yours" sold 90,000 locally—and caught the ear of New York party promoter Russell Simmons.

Rubin and Simmons launched the Def Jam label in 1984, releasing LL Cool J's first single, "I Need a Beat." Rubin sold the smash 12-inch from his dorm room, but that didn't last as Def Jam became the most successful new label of the '80s, with a roster of talent including

LL, Public Enemy, Slick, 3rd Bass, Beastie Boys, and Slayer.

Rubin's 1986 production of the Beasties' *License to Ill* (No. 1) brought rap and hard rock together into a 5 million–selling party—a party that also included his co-production of Run-D.M.C.'s killer *Raising Hell* (No. 3) that same year. When Rubin wanted to release *Reign in Blood,* Slayer's speed–death-metal opus, Def Jam distributor Columbia refused; Rubin and Simmons broke up, and Rubin relocated to Los Angeles to found Def American (later American Recordings). With Def American, Rubin branched out into a wide variety of musical genres, including metal, hardcore rap, Southern roots rock (the Black Crowes), and heavy, heavy metal (Danzig). He also produced records by bands that weren't signed to him, including the Cult's flower-metal classic *Electric,* Red Hot Chili Peppers' commercial breakthrough *Blood Sugar Sex Magik* (No. 3), Tom Petty's *Wildflowers* (No. 8), and Mick Jagger's *Wandering Spirit* (No. 11).

"I like doing different kinds of stuff and I always have," says Rubin. "As soon as I started making rock records after making rap records, I was unanimously told: 'You're a rap producer and you shouldn't be making heavy metal records.' Then it was: 'You shouldn't be making rock records, because you make heavy metal records.' I've been labeled a lot of things over the years and I just try to make records I like."

His early likes include albums by AC/DC, Kiss, the Plasmatics, the Ramones, the Beatles, James Brown, and Trouble Funk. The more theatrical rock bands of the late '70s and early '80s particularly turned his head. "At the time . . . that was a really exciting thing that was going on in music, and I think there will always be that irreverent, theatrical element to some rock 'n' roll," he says.

Since he is not an engineer (and doesn't want to be), his focus is the concept behind the album "and knowing what I want to hear and working with people to help me achieve that," he says. "I have a fair idea of what I do, but I don't know what a lot of other producers do," he says. "I just do whatever I hear and do my best. Sometimes it turns out okay and sometimes not. But, I'm pretty happy with the records that I've made. I don't really listen back to them all that often, but usually we're finished when enough work has gone into it and I'm feeling comfortable."

He has no particular philosophy of production, but "I think most of the sessions I do are song-oriented," Rubin says. "Like in the case of Johnny Cash, he'll write some songs, he'll look for songs and send them to me, and I'll look for songs and send them to him. We'll exchange and spend a good deal of time in preproduction, figuring out what the songs should be. With the

Chili Peppers, they'll write a volume of material and then we'll go through it and work on the arrangements and the structure and figure out if any of them can be improved or which ones should be left out. With rap records, it's a completely different process," he continues. "That's more of a producer-driven format where it would be my responsibility to actually come up with the tracks. Working on something I haven't worked on before is usually really exciting."

He's not in awe of career artists like Petty or Jagger: "I think I'm more concerned with consistency in the attitude of the performer than in making records that sound like their other records." And he doesn't think he has a particular sound. "Some producers have a sound regardless of who they work with that's kind of interpreted that way," Rubin says. "I think my records do have a sound, but I don't think it's the sound that takes away from what an artist does. I think there's a thread that runs through my records, but it's not my sound. I think [the thread] is usually a very personal, pure, kind of stripped-down, in-your-face version of whatever the artist does." He cites Cash's *Unchained* and Petty's *Wildflowers* as meeting those standards.

Rubin doesn't play favorites. "There are good ones in different directions that don't really compete with each other. They are more their own things. I think *Blood Sugar Sex Magik* is a really great record. I couldn't put any of those records up against each other to say which is more definitive of the records I've made. I think they are all definitive. It's fun working on new things, working on new songs," Rubin says. "It's always exciting when you are in the studio and you hear a great take of something. When you hear an idea in your head and you don't know where it comes from, and then you try it and it sounds good, it's always like a magical experience." —DAVID JOHN FARINELLA

AC/DC: "Big Gun," Columbia, 1993 (*Last Action Hero* soundtrack) • *Ballbreaker,* EastWest, 1995 • "Hard As a Rock," EastWest, 1995.

Aerosmith: "Rocking Pneumonia and the Boogie Woogie Flu," Def Jam, 1987 (*Less Than Zero* soundtrack).

Bangles: "Hazy Shade of Winter," Def Jam, 1987 • *Greatest Hits,* Columbia, 1990, 1995.

Beastie Boys: "(You Gotta) Fight for Your Right (to Party)," Def Jam, 1986 • "Hold It, Now Hit It," Def Jam, 1986 • "It's the New Style," Def Jam, 1986 • *Licensed to Ill,* Columbia, 1986 • "Paul Revere," Def Jam, 1986 • "Brass Monkey," Def Jam, 1987 • "She's Crafty," Columbia, 1987 • "Slow Ride," Avenue/Rhino, 1992 (*Rap Declares War*).

Cash, Johnny: *American Recordings,* American, 1994 • *Unchained,* American, 1996.

Clay, Andrew Dice: *Andrew Dice Clay,* American, 1989 • *Dice Rules,* Reprise, 1991 • *40 Too Long,* American, 1992 • *The Day the Laughter Died: Part II,* American, 1993.

Cult, The: *Electric,* Sire, 1987 • "Wild Flower," Sire, 1987 • "The Witch," Warner Bros., 1992 (*Cool World* soundtrack) • *High Octane Cult,* Warner Bros., 1996.

Digital Orgasm: "Guilty of Love" (remix), Antler Subway/Whte Lbls, 1993.

Danzig: *Danzig,* Def American, 1988 • *Thrall/Demonsweatlive,* Def American, 1993 • *4,* American, 1994 • "Mother," American, 1994.

Danzig II: *Lucifuge,* American, 1990.

Danzig, Glen, and the Power and Fury Orchestra: "You and Me (Less Than Zero)," Def Jam, 1987 (*Less Than Zero* soundtrack).

Donovan: *Sutras,* American, 1996.

Flipper: *American Grafishy,* Def American, 1992.

Four Horsemen: *Nobody Said It Was Easy,* American, 1991.

Jagger, Mick: *Wandering Spirit,* Atlantic, 1992 • "Sweet Thing," Atlantic, 1993.

Jett, Joan: *Flashback,* Blackheart, 1994.

Jett, Joan, and the Blackhearts: "She's Lost You," Def Jam, 1987 (*Less Than Zero* soundtrack).

Krush Groove All Stars: "Krush Groovin'," Warner Bros., 1985.

L.L. Cool J: "I Need a Beat," Def Jam, 1984 • "I Can't Live Without My Radio," Def Jam, 1985 • *Radio,* Def Jam, 1985 • "Rock the Bells," Def Jam, 1985 • "You'll Rock," Def Jam, 1986 • "Going Back to Cali," Def Jam, 1988 • *Walking with a Panther,* Def Jam, 1989 • *All World,* Def Jam, 1996 • w/ Flea, Dave Navarro, and Chad Smith, "I Make My Own Rules," Warner Bros., 1997 (*Howard Stern's Private Parts*).

Masters of Reality: *Masters of Reality,* Delicious Vinyl, 1988.

Nine Inch Nails: "Piggy" (remix), Nothing/Interscope, 1995.

Orbison, Roy: "Life Fades Away," Def Jam, 1987 (*Less Than Zero* soundtrack).

Original Concept: "Can You Feel It?," Def Jam, 1986.

Osbourne, Ozzy, with Type O Negative: "Pictures of Matchstick Men," Warner Bros., 1997 (*Howard Stern's Private Parts*).

Petty, Tom: *Wildflowers,* Warner Bros., 1994 • "You Don't Know How It Feels," Warner Bros., 1994 • "It's Good to Be King," Warner Bros., 1995.

Petty, Tom, and the Heartbreakers: *Greatest Hits,* MCA, 1993 • "Mary Jane's Last Dance," MCA, 1994 • *She's the One* soundtrack, Warner Bros., 1996 • "Walls," Warner Bros., 1996.

Poison: "Rock and Roll All Nite," Def Jam, 1987 (*Less Than Zero* soundtrack).

Public Enemy: "Bring the Noise," Def Jam, 1987 (*Less Than Zero* soundtrack).

Red Devils: *King King,* American, 1992.

Red Hot Chili Peppers: *Blood Sugar Sex Magik,* Warner Bros., 1991 • "Give It Away," Warner Bros., 1991 • "Sikamikanico," Reprise, 1992 (*Wayne's World* soundtrack) • "Under the Bridge," Warner Bros., 1992 • "Search and Destroy," Geffen, 1993 (*The Beavis and Butt-head Experience*) • "Soul to Squeeze," Warner Bros., 1993 (*Coneheads* soundtrack) • "Blood Sugar Sex Magik," A&M, 1994 (*Woodstock 94*) • "My Friends," Warner Bros., 1995 • *One Hot Minute,* Warner Bros., 1995 • "Melancholy Mechanics," Warner Bros., 1996 (*Twister* soundtrack) • *Under the Covers: Essential Red Hot Chili Peppers,* EMI, 1998.

Run-D.M.C.: "My Adidas," Profile, 1986 • *Raising Hell,* Profile, 1986 • "Walk This Way," Profile, 1986 • "You Be Illin'," Profile, 1986 • "Christmas in Hollis," A&M, 1987 (*A Very Special Christmas*) • "It's Tricky," Profile, 1987 • "Mary, Mary," Profile, 1988 • *Together Forever: Greatest Hits, 1983–1991,* Profile, 1991.

Sir Mix-a-Lot: *Mack Daddy,* Def American, 1991 • "Baby Got Back," Tommy Boy, 1992, 1993 (*MTV Party to Go,* Vol. 3) • "Jump on It," Rhyme Cartel/American, 1996.

Slayer: *Reign in Blood,* Def Jam, 1986 • "In-a-Gadda-Da-Vida," Def Jam, 1987 (*Less Than Zero* soundtrack) • *South of Heaven,* American, 1988 • *Seasons in the Abyss,* Def American, 1990 • *Live: Decade of Aggression,* American, 1991 • *Diabolus in Musica,* American/Columbia, 1998.

System of a Down: *System of a Down,* Sony, 1998.

Trouble: *Trouble,* American, 1990 • *Manic Frustration,* American, 1992.

David Rubinson

L ike contemporary Jim Dickinson (see entry), who studied stage at Baylor University in Texas, David Rubinson has a background in theater. Not only was the Brooklyn native a stage carpenter and lighting technician at Queens College in New York; his first production was Marc Blitzstein's *The Cradle Will Rock,* with Leonard Bernstein as musical director. The year was 1963.

Rubinson is now largely retired from the record business, and back to the theater. His primary gig is managing Marcel Marceau, the legendary French mime. Rubinson splits his time between San Francisco, Paris, and New York, managing Marceau and such record producer/players as Narada Michael Walden (see entry) and Ryuichi Sakamoto.

Rubinson was born on August 7, 1942. His father was a draughtsman for New York City, and his mother

taught first grade. Rubinson joined the musicians union when he was 15. From 1964 to 1969, he was a staff producer for Columbia Records, where he shepherded the careers of such artists as Moby Grape, Taj Mahal, and the Chambers Brothers. His productions straddle rock and jazz, covering artists as disparate as Bobby Womack, the Joy of Cooking's Terry Garthwaite, Santana, Herbie Hancock, and the Pointer Sisters.

Rubinson left New York for San Francisco in 1969. From 1969 to 1971, he and Bill Graham were partners in the Fillmore Corp. Rubinson left to form David Rubinson and Friends and Adamsdad Management. In 1976, Rubinson built the Automatt, the first fully automated recording studio in San Francisco. From 1981 to 1984, as its president and chief executive officer, Rubinson represented producers, artists, studio representatives, and engineers who felt they were being unfairly taxed by the state of California. His efforts led to new legislation.

In 1982, he suffered a heart attack, prompting coronary artery bypass graft surgery; the following year, he retired from record production. In 1985, he closed the Automatt, where his productions included the bulk of Herbie Hancock's most popular records (including *Secrets, Monster,* and *V.S.O.P.,* a quintet album featuring drummer Tony Williams, trumpeter Freddie Hubbard, saxophonist Wayne Shorter, and bassist Ron Carter).

Although the rail-thin, stylishly dressed Rubinson doesn't miss the stress of his record producing days, he looks back on them with some nostalgia. "Being a producer then was like being the director of a film," he says, "sometimes writing tunes, picking and arranging the songs. "I learned on my feet," says Rubinson, who

apprenticed under Columbia Records chief Goddard Lieberson. "I learned in the demo studios of New York."

At Columbia, he learned to record by producing Broadway and off-Broadway musicals. That meant "you had to read a score and record everything at one time," he says. It was vocals in the middle, orchestra on the sides, recording real time. "Everything was leaking into everything else. I listened and watched and did."

The first acts he signed were Tim "Hey, Joe" Rose (who now works in finance in New York City, Rubinson says) and the Chambers Brothers. Next was Taj Mahal. Mahal, the great blues and roots performer whose real name is Henry Frederickson, now lives in Hawaii and records for Private Music. As "company hippie," Rubinson also signed Moby Grape (at that time, Columbia was still making albums by Percy Faith and Ray Conniff, Rubinson notes wryly).

He speaks particularly proudly of the Chambers Brothers, who were performing old blues and Isley Brothers (see entry) material when Rubinson decided to contemporize them. "They were writing their own songs, contemporary, angry folk songs with electric guitars," he recalls. He overdubbed psychedelic electronic effects on "Time Has Come Today," but when it was first released, in 1966, it stiffed.

"What was on it was strange: electronic harpsichord, backward stuff, cowbells," he says. Within a year of initial release, the Chambers Brothers had begun to jam on the tune in performance at New York's Electric Circus. The jam was so inspired, Rubinson begged Columbia for an opportunity to record a whole album. Columbia okayed a $12,000 budget, and Rubinson and the Brothers cut the record in three days, updating "Time" with effects by Rubinson himself. The snazzed-up, extended version of "Time Has Come Today" (No. 11) hit the same time free-form FM radio was starting, so it became a big radio hit in 1967, first in San Francisco and later, nationwide. Although AM radio edited it way down, it eventually became a commercial smash.

"With pop, you have a specific audience in mind," Rubinson says. "You're making art for commerce. When you're producing jazz, you're producing the expression of the art of the moment, and the market is not a consideration. "It's much purer; jazz is about spontaneity. As Wayne Shorter said, composition is just improvisation slowed down."

Rubinson is proud to have crafted records that made a difference, including Herbie Hancock's *Headhunters* (No. 13), a 1973 masterpiece that effortlessly jumbled rock, jazz, and funk. He says he puts "lots of foot," or bass, into his productions. "I don't think of myself as one of the major producers," Rubinson says, noting he quit the field "because it was contributing to my health not being optimal." —CARLO WOLFF

Aum: *Resurrection*, Fillmore, 1969.

Barbieri, Gato: *Tropico*, A&M, 1978 • *Fire and Passion*, A&M, 1988.

Burns, Jack, and Avery Schreiber: *In One Head and Out the Other*, CBS, 1970.

Chambers Brothers: *The Time Has Come*, Columbia, 1967 • "Time Has Come Today," Columbia, 1968 • *Love, Peace and Happiness*, Columbia, 1969 • "Wake Up," Columbia, 1969 • "Love, Peace and Happiness," Columbia, 1970 • *Greatest Hits*, Columbia, 1971 • *Right Move*, Avco, 1975.

Corea, Chick, and Herbie Hancock: *Chick Corea and Herbie Hancock*, Polydor, 1979 • *See also* Hancock, Herbie.

Elvin Bishop Group: *The Elvin Bishop Group*, Fillmore, 1969 • *Feel It*, Fillmore, 1970.

Garthwaite, Terry: *Terry*, Arista, 1975.

Hammer, Jan: *Hammer*, San Francisco Sound, 1971.

Hancock, Herbie: *Mwandishi*, Warner Bros., 1971 • *Head Hunters*, Columbia, 1973 • "Chameleon," Columbia, 1974 • *Thrust*, Columbia, 1974 • *Death Wish* soundtrack, Columbia, 1975 • *Man-Child*, Columbia, 1975 • *Secrets*, Columbia, 1976 • *An Evening with Herbie Hancock and Chick Corea*, Columbia, 1978 • *Sunlight*, Columbia, 1978 • *Feets Don't Fail Me Now*, Columbia, 1979 • *Greatest Hits*, Columbia, 1980, 1990 • *Monster*, Columbia, 1980 • *Mr. Hands*, Columbia, 1980 • *Magic Windows*, Columbia, 1981 • *Quartet*, Columbia, 1982 • *Mwandishi: The Complete Warner Bros. Recordings*, Warner Archives, 1995.

Hansen, Randy: *Randy Hansen*, Capitol, 1980.

Headhunters: *Survival of the Fittest*, Arista, 1975 • *Straight from the Gate*, Arista, 1977.

Heartsfield: *Foolish Pleasures*, Mercury, 1975 • *Collector's Item*, CBS, 1977.

Hoodoo Rhythm Devils: *The Barbecue of De Ville*, Blue Thumb, 1972 • *What the Kids Want*, Blue Thumb, 1972.

Labelle: *Chameleon*, Epic, 1976.

LaBelle, Patti: *Patti LaBelle*, Epic, 1977 • *Tasty*, Epic, 1978 • *You Are My Friend: Ballads*, Sony, 1997.

Lamb: *Sign of Change*, Fillmore, 1970 • *Cross Between*, Warner Bros., 1971.

Mahal, Taj: *Taj Mahal*, Columbia, 1967 • *The Natch'll Blues*, Columbia, 1968 • *Giant Step*, Columbia, 1969 • *The Real Thing*, Columbia, 1971 • *Happy to Be Just Like I Am*, Columbia, 1972 • *The Taj Mahal Anthology*, Columbia, 1977 • *Taj's Blues*, Legacy, 1992.

Malo: *Dos*, Warner Bros., 1972 • *Malo*, Warner Bros., 1972 • "Suavecito," Warner Bros., 1972 • *Evolution*, Warner Bros., 1973.

Meters, The: *Funkify Your Life*, Rhino, 1995.

Moby Grape: *Moby Grape*, San Francisco Sound, 1967, 1994 • "Omaha," Columbia, 1967 • *Grape Jam*, San Francisco Sound, 1968, 1994 • *Wow*, San Francisco Sound, 1968, 1994 • *'69*, Columbia, 1969 • *20 Granite Creek*, Columbia, 1971 • *Moby Grape '83*, San Francisco Sound, 1983 • *Vintage: The Very Best Of*, Legacy, 1993.

Monk, Thelonius: *Round Midnight*, TriStar, 1957, 1996.

Peter, Paul and Mary: *Reunion*, Warner Bros., 1978.

Petrucciani, Michael, Jim Hall, and Wayne Shorter: *Power of Three*, Blue Note, 1986.

Pointer Sisters: "Yes We Can Can," Blue Thumb, 1973 • "Fairytale," ABC/Blue Thumb, 1974 • *That's a Plenty*, Blue Thumb, 1974 • *The Pointer Sisters Live at the Opera House*, ABC/Blue Thumb, 1974 • "How Long (Betcha' Got a Chick on the Side)," ABC/Blue Thumb, 1975 • *Steppin'*, ABC/Blue Thumb, 1975 • *Having a Party*, ABC/Blue Thumb, 1977 • *Retrospect the Best Of*, MCA, 1981 • *Yes We Can: The Best of the Blue Thumb Recordings*, Hip-O, 1997.

Quintet, The: *V.S.O.P.*, Columbia, 1977.

Santamaria, Mongo: *Greatest Hits*, Columbia, 1983.

Santana: *Amigos*, Columbia, 1976 • *Festival*, Columbia, 1976 • "Let It Shine," Columbia, 1976 • *Moonflower*, Columbia, 1977 • *Viva!*, Columbia, 1988 • *Live at the Fillmore '68*, Legacy, 1997 • *The Best of Santana*, Columbia, 1998.

Santana, Carlos: *The Swing of Delight*, Columbia, 1980.

Shine, John: *Music for a Rainy Day*, Columbia, 1975.

Snow, Phoebe: *It Looks Like Snow*, Columbia, 1976 • "Shakey Ground," Columbia, 1976 • *The Best Of*, Columbia, 1982.

Victoria: *Secrets of the Bloom*, Atlantic, 1971 • *Victoria*, San Francisco, 1971.

Vitous, Miroslav: *Magical Sheperd*, Warner Bros., 1976.

Womack, Bobby: *Safety Zone*, United Artists, 1975 • *Midnight Mover*, Capitol, 1993 • *Soul of Bobby Womack*, Capitol, 1996.

COLLECTIONS

Apocalypse Now soundtrack, Elektra, 1979.
Jazz at the Opera House, CBS, 1983.

Jack Ruby
(LAWRENCE LINDO)

Jack Ruby can be seen briefly in the British documentary *Roots, Rock Reggae*, screening vocalists and material while sitting in his Jamaican studio yard. Despite the nervousness of some of the singers auditioning, the languid and laid-back feel of the scene also characterizes Ruby's roots production style. His studio band, the Black Disciples, included drummer "Horse-mouth" Wallace (star of another reggae movie, *Rockers*), bassist Robbie Shakespeare (see Sly and Robbie entry), and usually, Tony Chin on rhythm guitar. On later recordings, Sly and Robbie led the band, generally joined by Third World's Steven "Cat" Coore.

In the mid-'70s, Ruby recorded at Randy's, Harry J (see entry), Federal, Channel One, and Joe Gibbs' (see entry) studios. Within a few years he had his own studio in Ocho Rios, which may explain his ability to attract "country" (a Jamaican term that equates to "folksy" in the U.S.) harmonizers, in an ambiance in high contrast to the dog-eat-dog pace of the "city" studios. Even in those later days, however, like nearly every other Jamaican producer of his day, he still mixed his tapes at King Tubby's studio in Kingston.

Ruby issued his product in Jamaica on his own Fox and Wolf labels. He produced several "first wave" reggae classics issued in the mid-'70s by Island records, including Burning Spear's groundbreaking *Man in the Hills* and *Marcus Garvey* albums. Though Burning Spear had recorded extensively for Coxsone, these were the albums that broke the then-trio (Rupert Willington, Delroy Hines, and lead singer Winston Rodney—who in later years assumed the name as a solo singer), internationally. Ruby also produced the crucial dub version of *Marcus Garvey*, titled *Garvey's Ghost*. Though this was his lone dub album, versions on those Fox and Wolf 45s show they weren't his only work in this field.

Justin Hinds and the Dominoes' two Island albums, *Jezebel* and *Just in Time*, were Ruby productions as well. The much-anthologized "Carry Go Bring Come" from *Jezebel* (remaking in the reggae style their early ska hit for Duke Reid; see entry) was even issued by Island as a U.S. single. Though most of the singer's recording was done under his real name "Hinds," it was altered to "Hines" for these two discs.

In 1980, the New York Clappers label re-released *Crucial Records Presents Jack Ruby Hi-Fi*, an anthology that included tracks by the Revealers and Earth Last Messengers. The latter contribute "Hypocrites," the kind of conscious tune Jack Ruby brought out of his artists. A live cassette issued by the same label in 1982, *Jack Ruby Hi-Power*, is a rare document of his sound system in action.

Jack Ruby also appeared in the U.K. Channel 4 TV series *Reggae: Deep Roots Music*. An excellent interview with him, clearly outlining his orientation to roots and culture, is reproduced in the tie-in book of the same title (Proteus Books, London, 1982). His plea for an end to gunplay rings out after all these years and the violent deaths of artists like Prince Far I, Peter Tosh, and the great King Tubby himself.

After a spell of inactivity Ruby produced the first two albums for the group Foundation, *Flames* and *Heart Feel It,* at the end of the '80s. In this same period he also cut an album for the reformed Earth Messengers (*Ivory Towers*) and two for Jamaican singer Donovan. All five were issued in the U.S. on Mango. From this same circle of singers (members of all three groups worked interchangeably over the years) came Link 'n' Chain, whose *New Day* was Ruby's last production before his untimely death.

Says Errol "Keith" Douglas, lead singer of the group Foundation, "Most people love the rhythm section more than the lyrics. You have people who listen to the lyrics more. The two of them go along, but the lyrics are the main thing still, you know? Jack Ruby is a man that typical upon the lyrics: No matter what rhythm go on, him always want to have good lyrics—conscious vibration. With Jack Ruby, you have to have something positive. Something you know will live on. Is a man cool still. Not a man operate like some brethren. Mostly him can joke and steady yourself. Not rushing towards it. A man really nice to work with. Some men dem money a go Mafia bread. But with Jack Ruby, just relax back yourself and study life." —CHUCK FOSTER

Burning Spear: *Harder Than the Best,* Mango, 1976, 1991 • *Marcus Garvey,* Mango, 1975 • *Garvey's Ghost,* Mango, 1976 • *Man in the Hills,* Island, 1976.

Donovan: *World Power,* Mango, 1988 • *Banzani!,* Mango, 1989.

Earth Messengers: *Ivory Towers,* Mango, 1989.

Foundation: *Flames,* Mango, 1988 • *Heart Feel It,* Mango, 1989.

Hines, Justin, and the Dominoes: "Carry Go Bring Come / Jezebel," Island, 1976 • *Jezebel,* Mango, 1976 • *Just in Time,* Mango, 1978.

Link 'N' Chain: *New Day,* RAS, 1990, 1991.

COLLECTIONS

Crucial Records Presents Jack Ruby, Clappers, 1980: Ken Boothe, "Peace Time" • Earth Last Messengers, "Hypocrites" • Jah Coller, "Jah Coller Speaks his Mind" • Lennox Miller, "Better Must Come" • The Revealers, "Jail House Free."

Jack Ruby Hi-Power, Clappers, 1982.

Jack Ruby Presents Black Foundation, Heartbeat, 1995.

Todd Rundgren

Since he first picked up a guitar, Todd Rundgren has put his indelible stamp on a wide swath of excellent music. Rundgren has been the driving force behind the bands Nazz, Runt ("We Gotta Get You a Woman," No. 20) and Utopia (*Adventures In Utopia*). In between, he has maintained an ongoing solo career highlighted by the timeless albums *Something/Anything?* and *A Wizard, a True Star* and singles "I Saw the Light" (No. 16), "Hello, It's Me" (No. 5), and "Can We Still Be Friends?"

Rundgren's production career spans 30 years and includes all of his own releases and a multitude of others, including Badfinger ("Baby Blue," No. 14), the Band (*Stage Fright*, No. 5), Grand Funk (*We're an American Band*, No. 2; *Shinin' On*, No. 5), Meat Loaf (12-times-platinum *Bat out of Hell*), New York Dolls (their seminal self-titled debut), Psychedelic Furs (*Forever Now*, with "Love My Way"), the Patti Smith Group (*Wave*), and XTC (*Skylarking*).

In the '80s and '90s Rundgren has pioneered interactive software and Internet music distribution, testing and pushing the boundaries of pop culture. Musicians, fans, and critics agree Rundgren has not stood still since the first Nazz release in 1968.

Born June 22, 1948, in Upper Darby, Pennsylvania, Rundgren was in locally popular Woody's Truck Stop in high school before gaining a larger reputation in 1968 with the Nazz. Their version of "Hello, It's Me" was a minor national hit. In mid-1969 Rundgren left the band to work as a solo artist and band leader under the name of Runt (with Hunt and Tony Sales, sons of Soupy), and as a staff producer at Albert Grossman's Bearsville Records. Hitting with the bouncy, wistful single "We Gotta Get You a Woman," Runt released two albums before Rundgren went officially solo with the classic *Something/Anything?* in 1972, a mostly one-man operation that overflows with wit, melody, and charm. Synthesizing Philly soul with British invasion rock, the double album features "I Saw the Light," "Couldn't I Just Tell You," "It Wouldn't Have Made Any Difference," "Black Maria," and the hit version of "Hello, It's Me."

By then Rundgren had produced American Dream, Ian and Sylvia, the Butterfield Blues Band, Jericho, and James Cotton, but he came to prominence with the release of Badfinger's *Straight Up*, which he co-produced with George Harrison.

In 1973 Rundgren released his second great album in a row, *A Wizard, a True Star*, wherein he used the studio as an instrument, seamlessly running together side 1 under the rubric of "International Feel"—again with melodies galore, including a touching, radiant version of "Never Never Land." Side 2 offers Rundgren originals "Sometimes I Don't Know What to Feel," "Just One Victory," and a cool soul medley.

Rundgren's next album, *Todd*, was a step down in consistency (a recurring theme), but still has "A Dream Goes on Forever," and "Sons of 1984." Rundgren's solo albums have been spotty affairs ever since, with his live *Back to the Bars*, and *The Hermit of Mink Hollow* (with "Can We Still Be Friends?," "All the Children Sing," and the clever "Onomatopoeia") as pleasant exceptions.

Rundgren also formed the band Utopia with Roger Powell on keyboards, Kasim Sulton on bass, and Willie Wilcox on drums. *Adventures in Utopia* and *Oops! Wrong Planet* are the highlights of several albums that typically have functioned as an outlet for Rundgren's more esoteric progressive rock leanings.

Of Rundgren's outside productions, the highlights are many over a large catalog. The most notable include Grand Funk's move from boogie sludge to crisp, tuneful rock 'n' roll on *We're an American Band*, with its kick-ass title track (No. 1) and "Walk Like a Man" (No. 19); and the follow-up *Shinin' On* with the No. 1 remake of "The Loco-Motion" (and an army of overdubbed vocals). Rundgren's taste and sense of proportion is perhaps most starkly apparent in the contrast between his production of Meat Loaf's neo-Spectorian extravaganza *Bat out of Hell* (which emphasizes the humor and drama inherent in the Wall of Sound), without ever yielding to the bombast-for-bombast's-sake so evident in the multiproducer sequel *Bat out of Hell II: Back to Hell*.

Also of top importance is the New York Dolls' proto-punk first album, where men in drag never sounded so tough as on "Personality Crisis," "Looking for a Kiss," "Frankenstein," and every other song on this crucial classic. The Psychedelic Furs' *Forever Now* exhibits Rundgren's ability to take a band with promise and adjust the lens so that everything comes into focus and stands proudly in relief. A fine selection of Rundgren's outside productions are collected on Rhino's *Todd Rundgren: An Elpee's Worth of Productions*.

An excellent engineer, mixer, and life-long technology buff, Rundgren helped develop interactive music software that enables the listener to vary the music in his TR-I projects. More recently, he has helped pioneer the Web as a direct source of music, bypassing the industry delivery apparatus entirely. Refer to his Web site at www.tr-i.com for more information. Rundgren has worked in video (his "Time Heals" was the second video ever shown on MTV) and radio. —DAVID JOHN FARINELLA AND ERIC OLSEN

American Dream: *The American Dream*, Ampex, 1969.

Badfinger: *Straight Up*, Apple, 1971 • "Baby Blue," Apple, 1972 • *Ass*, Apple, 1973 • *Best Of*, Capitol, 1995.

Band, The: *Stage Fright*, Capitol, 1970.

Bourgeois Tagg: "I Don't Mind at All," Island, 1987 • *Yoyo*, Island, 1987.

Butterfield Blues Band: *Live*, Elektra, 1970 • *Sometimes I Just Feel Like Smilin'*, Elektra, 1971.

Cassidy, Shaun: *Wasp*, Warner Bros., 1980 • *Greatest Hits*, Curb/Capitol, 1993.

Cavaliere, Felix: *Felix Cavaliere*, Bearsville, 1974.

Cheap Trick: *Next Position Please*, Epic, 1983 • *Sex America Cheap Trick*, Sony, 1996.

Derringer, Rick: *Guitars and Women*, Blue Sky, 1979 • *Rock and Roll Hootchie Koo: The Best Of*, Sony, 1996.

Fanny: "All Mine," Warner Bros., 1973 (*Appetizers*) • *Mother's Pride*, Reprise, 1973.

Farner, Mark: *Mark Farner*, Atlantic, 1978.

Grand Funk: "Walk Like a Man," Capitol, 1973 • "We're an American Band," Capitol, 1973 • *We're an American Band*, Capitol, 1973 • "Shinin' On," Capitol, 1974 • *Shinin' On*, Capitol, 1974 • "The Loco-Motion," Capitol, 1974 • *Capitol Collector's Series*, Capitol, 1991.

Halfnelson: *Halfnelson*, Bearsville, 1971.

Hall and Oates: *War Babies*, Atlantic, 1974 • *Atlantic Collection*, Rhino, 1996.

Hello People: *The Handsome Devils*, ABC, 1974 • *Bricks*, ABC, 1975.

Hillage, Steve: *L*, Virgin, 1976.

Hunter: *Dreams of Ordinary Men*, Polydor, 1987.

Ian and Sylvia: *Great Speckled Bird*, Ampex, 1970.

James Cotton Blues Band: *Takin' Care of Business*, Capitol, 1970.

Jericho: *Jericho*, Ampex, 1971.

Johansen, David: *From Pumps to Pompadour: The David Johansen Story*, Rhino, 1995.

Joplin, Janis: *Janis*, Legacy, 1993.

Klingman, Moogy: *Mark Moogy Klingman*, Capitol, 1972.

Linhart, Buzzy: *Buzzy Linhart*, Kama Sutra, 1972.

Lords of the New Church: *Killer Lords* (1 track), IRS, 1986 • *Live for Today* (EP), Virgin, 1986.

Meat Loaf: *Bat out of Hell*, Cleveland International/Epic, 1977 • "Paradise by the Dashboard Light," Epic, 1978 • "Two Out of Three Ain't Bad," Epic, 1978 • "You Took the Words Right out of My Mouth," Epic, 1979.

Nazz, The: "Hello, It's Me," SGC, 1968 • *The Nazz*, SGC, 1968 • *Nazz Nazz*, SGC, 1969 • *Nazz 3*, SGC, 1970.

New England: *Walking Wild*, Elektra, 1981.

New York Dolls: *The New York Dolls*, Mercury, 1973 • *Rock and Roll*, Mercury, 1994.

Paul Butterfield Blues Band: *Golden Butter: The Best Of*, Elektra, 1972.

Psychedelic Furs: *Forever Now*, Columbia, 1982 • *All of This and Nothing*, Columbia, 1988 • *B-Sides and Lost Grooves*, Legacy, 1994 • *Should God Forget: A Retrospective*, Columbia, 1997.

Pursuit of Happiness: *Love Junk*, Chrysalis, 1988 • *One Sided Story*, Chrysalis, 1990.

Roadmaster: *Roadmaster*, Village, 1978.

Rubinoos, The: *Party of Two*, Warner Bros., 1983.

Rundgren, Todd: "I Saw the Light," Bearsville, 1972 • *Something/Anything?*, Bearsville, 1972 • *A Wizard, a True Star*, Bearsville, 1973 • "Hello It's Me," Bearsville, 1973 • "Is It My Name?," Warner Bros., 1973 (*Appetizers*) • *Todd*, Bearsville, 1974 • *Todd Rundgren's Utopia*, Bearsville, 1974 • *Initiation*, Bearsville, 1975 • *Faithful*, Bearsville, 1976 • "Good Vibrations," Bearsville, 1976 • *Back to the Bars*, Bearsville, 1978 • "Can We Still Be Friends?," Bearsville, 1978 • *Hermit of Mink Hollow*, Bearsville, 1978 • *Healing*, Bearsville, 1981 • *The Tortured Artist Effect*, Bearsville, 1982 • *A Cappella*, Rhino, 1985, 1988 • *Anthology (1968–1985)*, Rhino, 1989 • *Nearly Human*, Warner Bros., 1989 • *2nd Wind*, Warner Bros., 1991 • *The Individualist*, ION, 1995 • *The Very Best Of*, Rhino, 1997 • *With a Twist*, Guardian, 1997 • "Day Job," Forward/Rhino, 1993 • *No World Order*, Forward/Rhino, 1993 • *No World Order Lite*, Forward/Rhino, 1994.

Runt: *Runt*, Bearsville, 1970 • "We Gotta Get You a Woman," Ampex, 1970 • *The Ballad of Todd Rundgren*, Bearsville, 1971.

Shaffer, Paul: *The World's Most Dangerous Party*, SBK, 1993.

Shear, Jules: *Watch Dog*, EMI America, 1983 • *Jules*, EMI America, 1984 • *Horse of a Different Color (1976–1989)*, Razor & Tie, 1994.

Smith, Patti: *Wave*, Arista, 1979 • *Masters*, Arista, 1996.

Sobule, Jill: *Things Here Are Different*, MCA, 1990.

Sparks: *Profile: Ultimate Collection*, Rhino, 1991.

Steinman, Jim: *Bad for Good*, Epic, 1981.

System 7: *Golden Section*, Cleopatra, 1997.

Takano, Hiroshi: *Cue*, Toshiba, 1990 • *Awakening*, Toshiba, 1992.

Tom Robinson Band: *TRB 2*, EMI, 1979.

Tubes, The: *Remote Control*, A&M, 1979 • *T.R.A.S.H. (Tubes Rarities and Smash Hits)*, A&M, 1981 • *Love Bomb*, Capitol, 1985 • "Piece by Piece," Capitol, 1985.

Utopia: *Another Live*, Bearsville, 1975 • *Oops, Wrong Planet*, Bearsville, 1977 • *Ra*, Bearsville, 1977 • *Adventures in Utopia*, Bearsville, 1980 • *Deface the Music*, Bearsville, 1980 • "Set Me Free," Bearsville, 1980 • *Swing to the Right*, Bearsville, 1982 • *Oblivion*, Passport/WB, 1983.

What Is This: "I'll Be Around," MCA, 1985 • *What Is This,* MCA, 1985.

Winchester, Jesse: *3rd Down, 110 to Go,* Bearsville, 1972.

XTC: *Skylarking,* Geffen, 1986 • "Dear God," Geffen, 1987 • *Dear God* (EP), Virgin, 1987 • *Rag and Bone Buffet* (2 tracks), Geffen, 1990.

Zerra: *Zerra 1,* Mercury, 1984.

COLLECTIONS

Todd Rundgren: An Elpee's Worth of Productions, Rhino, 1992.

Carl Ryder

See BOMB SQUAD

Leo Sacks

L eo Sacks has become one of the most conscientious and prolific reissue and compilation producers in the business. Specializing in '70s soul through Sony's Rhythm and Soul and EMI's Heart of Soul series, Sacks has lovingly researched and crafted packages for the O'Jays, the Isley Brothers (see entry), Harold Melvin and the Blue Notes, Labelle, Bobby Womack, Ike and Tina Turner, Natalie Cole, Freddie Jackson, Earth, Wind and Fire, Tavares, Lou Rawls, Aretha Franklin, MFSB, Marvin Gaye, and dozens more. He has helped draw attention to lesser-known figures such as Bunny Sigler, Z.Z. Hill, D.J. Rogers, Marlena Shaw, Walter Jackson, and Enchantment. And he has assembled numerous multiple-artist collections based upon such themes as a tribute to Jackie Robinson, love and lust, Chicago soul (centered around Curtis Mayfield; see entry), and Philadelphia soul (centered around Philadelphia International Records, Gamble and Huff's label; see entry). Sacks' passion for music is not sequestered in the past: he has also produced and co-produced original '90s records for the late, great New Orleans gospel and soul singer Raymond Myles, New York alterna-rockers Astro Chicken, and Iron City Houserockers leader Joe Grushecky.

Leo Sacks was born in 1957, the son of a psychologist and a medical copywriter, and grew up in a large building filled with a gaggle of therapists and analysts on the west side of Manhattan. Radio, and in particular Top 40 giant WABC, was a constant companion. The first song that imposed itself upon his young consciousness was the Four Tops' "Reach Out I'll Be There" in 1966. "I can still recall the moment when the intensity of Levi Stubbs' voice struck me—I can reach out and touch it," he says. Shortly thereafter his father gave him his first two albums: *Meet the Beatles* and Herb Alpert and the Tijuana Brass's *Whipped Cream and Other Delights.* "From those I got hooks, horns, and harmonies," he states.

Sacks' parents always emphasized literacy and education; his mother encouraged him to read the *New York Times* and circle the words he didn't understand when he was a young child. He also made the connection between music and the printed word at an early age. "I was always enthralled with rock criticism. Mike Jahn was the rock critic at the *Times* in the late '60s and I always read him, picking up the lingo."

One of Sacks' father's patients was a floor manager at the Fillmore East; he gave young Sacks tickets to a Friday night late show featuring Derek and the Dominos in 1971 (the lad fell asleep before the end of the show). Later Sacks saw the Fillmore's last show, with Laura Nyro, and he remembers someone suggesting that they go home and listen to her records after the concert. "This great connection was made for me between seeing an artist live and going home to celebrate them with a tangible piece of their soul: a record," he says.

By 14 Sacks was writing record reviews for his high school newspaper; he reviewed a Chicago–Bruce Springsteen show at Madison Square Garden "using all of these buzzwords I had picked up from reading reviews," he says. "The first line was, 'Chicago brought their solid musical professionalism to a sold-out Madison Square Garden last week exhibiting a tour de force' blah, blah, blah. I wrote it in longhand the next morning, pecked it out on a typewriter, and then slipped it under the door at the *Village Voice.* They ended up printing it! I got a $65 check and it was the easiest money I ever made."

Sacks went to City College of New York after high school and continued to review shows and records in abundance. Richard Goldstein, an editor at the *Voice,* was his creative writing teacher at CCNY. After Sacks wrote a piece on the culture of concerts for the class, Goldstein contacted an editor friend at *Rolling Stone,* who printed the story there.

By 19 Sacks was writing for the industry trade magazine *Cash Box.* The more he wrote, the more Sacks delved into the history of the music he loved—especially blues, R&B, and soul—using his interviews with musicians to investigate their roots and influences. In an interview with Allman Brothers Band keyboardist Chuck Leavell, Sacks learned about Otis Spann. Sacks traced Spann's work back to the Muddy Waters band of the '50s, which led to an exploration of electric Chicago blues in general. Sacks traded disco promos for '60s Stax albums with another *Cash Box* writer, and from there dove into the Memphis soul world. He constructed a forest of musical trees in his mind, connecting roots and branches with trunks and dancing on piles of leaves.

In 1980 Sacks went to *Billboard,* where he stayed until 1984 first as a reporter, then as East Coast radio editor. He was the first at the publication to write about such notables as Anita Baker, Jimmy Jam and Terry Lewis (see entry), and Marshall Crenshaw.

Fulfilling a dream to be a hard-news journalist, Sacks worked at the city desk of the *New York Post* from 1984 to 1986, while his musical expression found an outlet in regular freelance pieces for such publications as the *Village Voice, Musician, People* magazine, the *L.A. Times,* and the *San Francisco Chronicle.* He moved into television in 1986 as a news writer for the New York bureau of CNN, where he was part of an Emmy-winning team that covered the *Challenger* disaster. He wrote copy for local New York television news and *CBS Morning News* in 1987, and then moved to CBS radio as a news editor until the end of 1988. After six months off to recover from all of this frenetic activity, Sacks returned to television as a field producer for Visnews (now Reuters TV) in mid-1989, where he later covered U.N. developments during the Gulf War.

The following year, 1990, was a year of sea change for Sacks: on the music-writing front, he placed profiles of LaVern Baker and Wilson Pickett in the official Rock and Roll Hall of Fame induction booklet; even more importantly, he was invited by PolyGram reissue and compiler chief Harry Weinger to check out the company's tape vaults—a near-religious experience for Sacks, who was "awe-struck."

Sacks assisted his mentor Weinger on a James Brown collection (*Messing with the Blues*) and decided he liked "making music more than writing about music," following the lead of such influential music journalists turned record men as John Hammond, Jerry Wexler, and Jon Landau (see entries). After compiling collections of Jerry Butler, Bobby Womack, Brass Construction, Bar-Kays, and others for PolyGram, Sacks met Sony's Tony Martell, who had helped build Epic into a soul powerhouse in the '70s. Martell asked Sacks to help him reintroduce this legacy through the Rhythm and Soul series.

Since his first release for Rhythm and Soul, the Isley Brothers' *Beautiful Ballads* in 1994, Sacks has produced over four dozen soul collections or reissues for Sony, in addition to another two dozen releases for the EMI Heart of Soul series. *Ballads* was an auspicious beginning for Sacks as the album actually found its way onto the charts, an extremely unusual occurrence for a non-soundtrack collection. The Isleys have been one of Sacks' favorite subjects; he has reissued much of their classic soul and rock '70s catalog, and compiled an exquisite three-CD career-overview box set.

Sacks' finest collection, and one of the finest packages ever assembled, is *The Philly Sound: Kenny Gamble, Leon Huff and the Story of Brotherly Love (1966–1976).* A marvel of scholarship, sociocultural awareness, musical acuity, sonic care, and sumptuous design, the three-CD package is a model and exemplar of what such things can and should be.

The foundation of this achievement is, of course, the music: virtually all of Gamble and Huff's historic hits (many arranged by Bobby Martin or Thom Bell; see entry) with the Intruders, Jerry Butler, Wilson Pickett, Billy Paul, Harold Melvin and the Blue Notes, O'Jays, MFSB, and many others are included, in addition to important Philadelphia International label hits by other artists and producers. With engineer Tom Ruff, Sacks has mastered these tracks with great care to preserve the warmth of the original vinyl, while taking advantage of the clarity and brightness of digital.

To augment the music, Sacks created a 70-page full-color booklet with action photos that is alone worth the price of admission. Besides detailed track-by-track information on studio personnel, musicians, and charting, there is an introduction from poet Nikki Giovanni; tributes from interested parties, including Gamble, Huff, Bell, Michael Jackson, Quincy Jones (see entry), Curtis Mayfield, and Isaac Hayes (see entries), among others; mini-bios on every artist in the package; and a dozen essays by august scribes on topics from Gamble and Huff's place in the history of race relations to thorough discussions of the musicians, arrangers, and janitors who helped create the sound of Philadelphia. The booklet is so abundant that perhaps the CDs accompany it, rather than vice versa.

Sacks' original productions include the fine guitar-driven, poppy alt-rock of the now-defunct Astro Chicken, the rootsy rock of Joe Grushecky, and most importantly, the glorious gospel and soul of New Orleans icon Raymond Myles—a former public school music teacher and regular at the annual New Orleans Jazz and Heritage Festival who was murdered in New Orleans in October of 1998 in an apparent robbery. Sacks not only produced *A Taste of Heaven* in 1995, but put it out on his own Honey Darling label. It, along with two demos

Sacks recently produced with Myles' singers and band under the name of Church Street, will be central to the inspirational singer's legacy. Sacks is now working with New York singer/songwriter Michael Miller. —ERIC OLSEN

Astro Chicken: *Disposable,* Honey Darling, 1996 • *Sugar Water* (2 tracks), Meaningful, 1998.

Grushecky, Joe, and the Houserockers: *End of the Century,* Razor & Tie, 1992.

Knight, Gladys, and the Pips: *Live at the Roxy (1980),* Legacy/Epic, 1998.

Myles, Raymond: *A Taste of Heaven,* Honey Darling, 1995.

COMPILATIONS

A Taste of Honey: *Beauty and the Boogie,* Heart of Soul/EMI, 1997.

Ashford and Simpson: *Count Your Blessings: The Gospel According to Ashford and Simpson,* Heart of Soul/EMI, 1996.

Bar-Kays, The: *The Best of the Bar-Kays,* Mercury, 1993.

Davis, Tyrone: *In the Mood: The Best of Tyrone Davis,* Legacy/Columbia, 1996.

Earth, Wind and Fire: *Elements of Love: The Ballads,* Legacy/Columbia, 1996 • *Greatest Hits,* Legacy/Columbia, 1998.

Emotions, The: *Best of My Love: The Best of the Emotions,* Legacy/Columbia, 1996.

Enchantment: *If You're Ready: The Best of Enchantment,* Heart of Soul/EMI, 1996.

Franklin, Aretha: *The Early Years,* Legacy/Columbia, 1997.

Heatwave: *Always and Forever: The Best of Heatwave,* Legacy/Epic, 1996.

Hill, Z.Z.: *This Time They Told the Truth: The Columbia Years,* Legacy/Columbia, 1997.

Hyman, Phyllis: *The Legacy of Phyllis Hyman,* Arista Masters, 1996.

Intruders, The: *Cowboys to Girls: The Best of the Intruders,* Legacy/Epic, 1995.

Iron City Houserockers: *Pumping Iron, Sweating Steel: Best of the Iron City Houserockers,* Rhino, 1992 • *Beautiful Ballads,* Legacy/Epic, 1994 • *Funky Family,* Legacy/Epic, 1995.

Jackson, Freddie: *For Old Times' Sake: The Freddie Jackson Story,* Heart of Soul/EMI, 1996.

Jackson, Walter: *The Best of Walter Jackson: Welcome Home, the Okeh Years,* Legacy, 1996.

LaBelle, Patti: *You Are My Friend: The Love Album,* Legacy/Epic, 1997.

Lynn, Cheryl: *Got to Be Real: The Best of Cheryl Lynn,* Legacy/Columbia, 1996.

Manhattans, The: *Kiss and Say Goodbye: The Best of the Manhattans,* Legacy/Columbia, 1995.

Marie, Teena: *Lovergirl: The Teena Marie Story,* Legacy/Epic, 1997.

Melvin, Harold, and the Blue Notes: *If You Don't Know Me By Now: The Best Of,* Legacy/Epic, 1995 • *Blue Notes and Ballads,* Legacy/Epic, 1997 • *Blue Notes and Ballads,* Legacy/Epic Associated, 1998.

MFSB: *Love Is the Message: The Best of MSFB,* Legacy/Epic, 1995.

Moore, Melba: *A Little Bit Moore: The Magic of Melba Moore,* Heart of Soul/EMI, 1997.

O'Jays, The: *Love Train: The Best of the O'Jays,* Legacy/Epic, 1994 • *Give the People What They Want,* Legacy/Epic, 1995 • *Let Me Make Love to You,* Legacy/Epic, 1995 • *In Bed with the O'Jays: Their Greatest Love Songs,* Heart of Soul/EMI, 1996.

Peaches and Herb: *Love Is Strange: The Best of Peaches and Herb,* Legacy/Epic, 1996.

Persuasions, The: *Man, Oh Man: The Power of the Persuasions,* Heart of Soul/EMI, 1997.

Rawls, Lou: *Love Is a Hurtin' Thing: The Silk and Soul of Lou Rawls,* Heart of Soul/EMI, 1997.

Rene and Angela: *Come My Way: The Best of Rene and Angela,* Heart of Soul/EMI, 1996.

Rogers, D.J.: *Message Man: The Columbia Years,* Legacy/Columbia, 1998.

Sigler, Bunny: *Sweeter Than the Berry: The Best of Bunny Sigler,* Legacy/Epic, 1996.

Spinners: *One of a Kind Love Affair (The Anthology),* Atlantic, 1991.

Tavares: *It Only Takes a Minute: A Lifetime with Tavares,* Heart of Soul/EMI, 1997.

Taylor, Johnny: *Rated X-tradinaire: The Best of Johnny Taylor,* Legacy/Columbia, 1996.

T-Connection: *Everything's Still Cool: The Best of T-Connection,* Heart of Soul/EMI, 1997.

The Three Degrees: *When Will I See You Again: The Best of the Three Degrees,* Legacy/Epic, 1996.

Williams, Deniece: *Gonna Take a Miracle:The Best of Deniece Williams,* Legacy/Columbia, 1996.

Womack, Bobby: *Midnight Mover: The Bobby Womack Story,* EMI, 1993 • *Stop on By: The Soul of Bobby Womack,* Heart of Soul/EMI, 1996 • *At Home in Muscle Shoals,* Legacy/Columbia, 1997.

VARIOUS ARTISTS

Blood, Sweat and Beers, Risky Business, 1993.

Rubber Souled, Risky Business, 1993.

Soul of Viet Nam, Risky Business, 1993.

Lost Soul, Legacy/Epic, 1994.

Am I Black Enough for You, Legacy/Epic, 1995.

Curtis Mayfield's Chicago Soul, Legacy/Epic, 1995.

From Philly with Love, Legacy/Epic, 1995.

Legacy's Rhythm and Soul Revue, Legacy/Epic, 1995.

Sex and Soul, Vols. 1–2, Heart of Soul/EMI, 1996.

The Soul of Seduction, Legacy, 1996.

Sex and Soul, Vol. 3, Heart of Soul/EMI, 1997.

The Philly Sound: Kenny Gamble, Leon Huff and the Story of Brotherly Love (1966–1976), Legacy, 1997.

Jackie Robinson Tribute: Stealing Home, Sony, 1997.

REISSUES

Gaye, Marvin: Midnight Love and the Sexual Healing Sessions, Legacy/Columbia, 1998.

Isley Brothers: The Brothers Isley, Legacy/Epic Associated, 1969, 1997 • Get into Something, Legacy/Epic Associated, 1970, 1997 • Givin' It Back, Legacy/Epic Associated, 1971, 1997 • Brother, Brother, Brother, Legacy/Epic Associated, 1972, 1997.

Labelle: Phoenix, Epic, 1975, 1998.

Turner, Ike and Tina: What You Hear Is What You Get: Live at Carnegie Hall, Heart of Soul/EMI, 1971, 1996.

Wild Magnolias: Wild Magnolias, Polydor, 1993 • They Call Us Wild, Polydor, 1994.

Withers, Bill: Live at Carnegie Hall, Legacy/Columbia, 1973, 1997.

Eric "Vietnam" Sadler

See BOMB SQUAD

Ron Saint Germain

R on Saint Germain has been one of the top American mixers for over 20 years, working on albums for U2, Kraftwerk, Killing Joke, Tool, Soundgarden, Ben E. King, Ornette Coleman, McCoy Tyner, Dexter Gordon, Charles Earland, and (posthumously) Jimi Hendrix. Saint Germain also helped lead the dance remix craze in the early '80s and has been an important producer since the late '80s, specializing in modern rock bands like Bad Brains, Sonic Youth, Living Colour, 311, Dillon Fence, and Luxx, as well as producing alterna-country renegade Steve Earle, metallurgists Bonham

and Princess Pang, and jazzers Paquito D'Rivera and Bill Frisell.

Ron Saint Germain was born in Frankfurt, Germany, the third of four children in an U.S. Air Force family (he has been a pilot himself for 20 years). His younger sister was "made in Japan"; the family also touched down in Okinawa, Washington state, Nebraska, Wisconsin, upstate New York, and Virginia, where Ron graduated from high school in the mid-'60s.

Saint Germain's first musical memory is of baby-sitters bringing Elvis Presley records to his house in the '50s. The two constants in Saint Germain's peripatetic childhood were his close-knit family and music on the radio. Saint Germain bought his first drum kit for $99 at Sears as a high schooler in Virginia, and within two weeks he was in a band. He picked up the guitar at the same time so he would have something to practice at night when it was too late to play the drums.

Saint Germain graduated from Virginia Commonwealth University in 1970 with a degree in theater and film and a minor in music. He then moved to New York, where he starred in a Broadway production of *Hair*. Over the next few years, Saint Germain appeared in four movies, a soap opera, and many commercials before deciding to forsake acting for music.

Returning to Virginia, Saint Germain hooked up with some old college buddies and formed a band that gained a fair amount of regional attention. Through contacts from his theater days, Saint Germain finagled some time after hours at Manhattan's Select Sound studio, where his band repaired to record demos. This was Saint Germain's first experience in a studio, but he felt "immediately attracted to the board," which reminded him of the aircraft control panels of his childhood. The engineer running the session was having trouble getting the right sound for the band, so Saint Germain started tweaking dials and pushing faders, and suddenly the sound came together.

He dragged the demo around from label to label, and while he didn't get a deal, he did get favorable comments on the sound of the demo. The band broke up, and Saint Germain repeated the process with a few other bands before economics dictated a different tack; the studio seemed like the place to go. Saint Germain looked on the back of his favorite records and made a list of the studios where they were made, starting with New York's Record Plant.

Saint Germain called the Record Plant, made an appointment, and was hired on the spot as an engineer trainee in December of 1972. As he walked into the studio proper from the business office, Saint Germain literally bumped into John Lennon. Saint Germain took "meeting a Beatle on my first day to be a good omen," although he was fired about three weeks later. Saint Germain moved to Media Sound, where he stayed for four years learning the engineering trade with such future notables as Bob Clearmountain and Michael Barbiero (see entries).

In 1976 Saint Germain became an independent engineer, and in the early '80s he became a prime remixer, punching up album tracks for single release and doing extended dance remixes—then becoming the rage—for dozens of artists across the pop, rock, R&B, and new wave spectrums, including A Flock of Seagulls, Arcadia, Ashford and Simpson, Cock Robin, the Cult, the Cure, Terence Trent D'Arby, Aretha Franklin, Dan Hartman, Mick Jagger (see "Glimmer Twins" entry), Kraftwerk, Diana Ross, and Peter Wolf.

After about five years of remix work, Saint Germain longed to get into album production and mixing; he began refusing remixes in 1986 and was mostly out of it by 1987. His first important production was an extremely influential album with black punk, reggae, metal legends Bad Brains in 1986 (*I Against I*). He followed that with two more albums with the band (*Quickness* and *The Youth Are Getting Restless*) in 1989 and 1990, and their ripping performance (with Henry Rollins) of MC5's "Kick Out the Jams" for the *Pump Up the Volume* soundtrack.

The year 1990 was huge for Saint Germain; in addition to the Bad Brains work, he co-produced Sonic Youth's best, most accessible, and first commercially successful album, *Goo*. On *Goo*, the Youths' art noise meets song structure and the result is galvanizing. "Dirty Boots" is hypnotic, rocking, and even danceable. "Cool Thing" features Kim Gordon's beguiling deadpan vocal and some observations from Chuck D. over a noisy guitar war between Thurston Moore and Lee Renaldo.

Saint Germain worked with another great black rock band in 1991, Living Colour. He produced two tracks for the *Biscuits* EP, including their smoldering rendition of James Brown's "Talkin' Loud and Sayin' Nothing," highlighted by Vernon Reid's riffing guitar and Corey Glover's soulful vocal. In 1993 Saint Germain got to do a whole album with the band, their excellent swan song *Stain*, which is blessed with the moody Seal-like alterna-soul of "Nothingness" and a frightening, clanging study in alienation, "Auslander." That year Saint Germain also handled Colour's loving tribute to Jimi Hendrix, "Crosstown Traffic," for the *Stone Free: A Tribute to Jimi Hendrix* album.

Saint Germain's single greatest production is the grooving punk-funk of Omaha's 311. Their self-titled gold album from 1995 (No. 12) stayed on the charts most of that year, brilliantly juggling hip-hop and ska rhythms from drummer Chad Sexton and bassist P. Nut, harmony vocals from Nicholas Hexum and Count Sa, and swanky, stanky, fuzzy guitar from Tim Mahoney and Hexum. "Down," "All Mixed Up," and "Purpose" are genre classics and became modern rock radio staples.

After 25 years of recording, Saint Germain knows what he wants to accomplish as a producer. "I want to help a band find their sound sonically and emotionally. First, I have to forge a personal relationship with them to find out what their songs mean. I'm very big on lyrics—I want a lyric sheet from the demo stage on so I can know what the band is about.

"Then we go to preproduction," he continues, "and that's when their ideas and my ideas come out. We have to be completely open to each other. If I make a suggestion, it may not end up on the record but it may inspire the band to come up with another idea that we all like better. Musicians tend to overplay—a lot of times music gets in the way of the song—so I often suggest that they cut back. By the time we go into the studio we should have a flight plan so that we can all feel comfortable and confident.

"For the recording, I like to have the band play together [as opposed to in sections] to get more of a live performance feel. I have found that if it isn't in the basic track, you're not going to get it with overdubs. Overdubs should enhance a performance, not be a substitute for it. I try hard to inspire the band to a great performance—to show them that I am excited by their music—and get that on tape.

"Production is like photography of sound: there are situations where the photographer manipulates everything including the subject, background, light, and color. The producer has analogous tools of manipulation—especially today with all of the technology—but the most impactful photography *and* sound recording comes from capturing a real moment to the best of your technical ability. The key is to be ready when that moment happens because it may never happen again," he says. —ERIC OLSEN

A Flock of Seagulls: "Space Age Love Song" (remix), Jive, 1982 • "Wishing (If I Had a Photograph of You)" (remix), Jive, 1983.

Ant, Adam: "Apollo 9" (remix), Epic, 1985.

Arcadia: "Election Day" (remix), Capitol, 1985.

Ashford and Simpson: "Solid" (remix), Capitol, 1984.

Bad Brains: *I Against I*, SST, 1986 • *Quickness*, Caroline, 1989 • w/ Henry Rollins, "Kick Out the Jams," MCA, 1990 (*Pump Up the Volume* soundtrack) • *The Youth Are Getting Restless*, Caroline, 1990.

Bonham: *Mad Hatter* (4 tracks), WTG, 1992.

Buck Pets: *The Buckpets,* Island, 1989.

Cock Robin: "When Your Heart Is Weak" (remix), Columbia, 1985.

Cult, The: "Wild Flower" (remix), Sire, 1987.

Cure, The: "Hot Hot Hot" (remix), Elektra, 1987 • *Mixed Up* (1 track), Fiction/Elektra, 1990.

D'Arby, Terence Trent: "Wishing Well" (remix), Columbia, 1987.

Dillon Fence: *Daylight* (EP), Mammoth, 1992 • *Rosemary,* Mammoth, 1992.

D'Rivera, Paquito: *Manhattan Burn,* Columbia, 1986 • *Celebration,* Columbia, 1987.

Earle, Steve, and the Dukes: *Shut Up and Die Like an Aviator,* MCA, 1991.

Franklin, Aretha: "Jimmy Lee" (remix), Arista, 1986.

Frisell, Bill, and Vernon Reid: *Smash and Scatteration,* Rykodisc, 1989.

Gene Loves Jezebel: "Jealous" (remix), Geffen, 1990.

Hammer, Jan: "Miami Vice Theme" (remix), MCA, 1985.

Hartman, Dan: "I Can Dream About You" (remix), MCA, 1984.

Holliday, Jennifer: "I Rest My Case" (remix), Geffen, 1985.

Jagger, Mick: "Just Another Night" (remix), Columbia, 1985 • "Lucky in Love" (remix), Columbia, 1985.

Jones, Keziah: *African Space Craft,* Delabel France, 1995.

Kashmir: *Cruzential,* Sony Denmark, 1996.

Kraftwerk: "Musique Non Stop" (remix), Warner Bros., 1986 • "The Telephone Call" (remix), Warner Bros., 1986.

Living Colour: *Biscuits* (EP), Epic, 1991 • "Auslander," Epic, 1993 • "Crosstown Traffic," Reprise, 1993 (*Stone Free: A Tribute to Jimi Hendrix*) • "Nothingness," Epic, 1993 • "Nothingness" (remix), Epic, 1993 • *Stain,* Epic, 1993 • *Pride,* Epic, 1995 • *Super Hits,* Legacy, 1998.

Luxx: *Luxx,* Push, 1998.

Motherland: *Peace 4 Me,* Epic, 1994.

Osborne, Jeffrey: "Plane Love" (remix), A&M, 1983.

Osborne, Jeffrey: "The Borderlines" (remix), A&M, 1984.

Princess Pang: *Princess Pang,* Metal Blade, 1988.

Revenge: "Pineapple Face" (remix), Atlantic, 1990.

Ross, Diana: "Chain Reaction" (remix), RCA, 1985 • "Eaten Alive" (remix), RCA, 1985.

Rule 62: *Rule 62,* Maverick, 1997.

Sonic Youth: *Goo,* DGC, 1990 • "Titanium Expose," MCA, 1990 (*Pump Up the Volume* soundtrack) • *Dirty Boots + 5* (EP), DGC, 1991.

Super Junky Monkey: *Parasitic People,* TriStar, 1996.

311: *311,* Capricorn, 1995.

Wolf, Peter: "I Need You Tonight" (remix), EMI America, 1984 • "Lights Out" (remix), EMI America, 1984.

Paul Samwell-Smith

Born May 8, 1943, in Richmond, Surrey, just outside London, Samwell-Smith excelled as the bassist of the Yardbirds, etching his expressive playing on such classics as "Heart Full of Soul," "I'm a Man," and "The Train Kept-a Rollin'."

Simon Napier-Bell hired Samwell-Smith to co-produce the Yardbirds' classic 1966 album *The Yardbirds,* released in the United States under the title *Over Under Sideways Down.* Napier-Bell, speaking to Jim Green in *Trouser Press* magazine, points out that he had little experience in the studio, so he relied heavily on Samwell-Smith: "I hired the best studio and engineers, and I had Paul Samwell-Smith too." *The Yardbirds* was a tour de force, featuring Jeff Beck's sitar-like workout on "Over Under Sideways Down" (No. 13) alongside the explosive "What Do You Want" and "Lost Women."

In 1969, three years after he left the Yardbirds to concentrate on production, Samwell-Smith produced the debut album by Renaissance, a band formed by ex-Yardbirds Keith Relf and Jim McCarty that juxtaposed classical musings with rock improvisation. Relf and McCarty jumped ship after the band's second album, assigning the rights to the name Renaissance to others. Relf died in 1976 of electrocution while playing guitar at his home in England.

Meanwhile, Samwell-Smith began a long association with Cat Stevens, producing a string of hits in the early '70s: "Peace Train" (No. 7), "Moon Shadow," "Wild World" (No. 11), "Where Do the Children Play," "Morning Has Broken" (No. 6), and "Oh Very Young" (No. 10). Stevens and Samwell-Smith briefly parted company in the mid-'70s, with the duo reuniting in 1974 for Stevens' album *Buddah and the Chocolate Box,* and again in 1979 for his *Back to Earth.*

Samwell-Smith also produced Carly Simon's 1971 album *Anticipation,* which cemented his reputation as a producer sympathetic to the nascent singer/songwriter movement. He has worked at intervals with Simon into the '90s.

In 1983, Samwell-Smith joined forces with fellow Yardbirds Jim McCarty and Chris Dreja for the 25th anniversary of London's fabled Marquee Club. Adding assorted vocalists and guitarists, the group recorded two albums under the unlikely moniker Box of Frogs.

Samwell-Smith, never one for self-promotion, maintains a low profile, resurfacing on occasion to lend his prodigious talents to such projects as Jethro Tull's underrated 1982 album, *The Broadsword and the Beast* (No. 19), and Beverly Craven's wistful 1990 debut album, *Beverly Craven*. —BEN CROMER

All About Eve: *Scarlet and Other Stories,* Mercury, 1989.

Amazing Blondel: *Evensong,* Edsel, 1970, 1996 • *Fantasia Lindum,* Edsel, 1971, 1996.

Beck, Jeff: *Beckology,* Legacy/Epic, 1991, 1995.

Box of Frogs: *Box of Frogs/Strange Land,* Renaissance, 1984, 1996.

Chapman, Beth Nielsen: *You Hold the Key,* Reprise, 1993.

Cohn, Marc: *Burning the Daze,* Atlantic, 1998.

Craven, Beverly: *Beverly Craven,* Epic, 1991 • *Love Scenes,* Epic, 1994.

DeBurgh, Chris: *At the End of a Perfect Day,* A&M, 1977.

Germino, Mark: *London Town and Barnyard Remedies,* RCA, 1986.

Hamill, Claire: *October,* Island, 1973.

Head, Murray: *Say It Ain't So,* Island, 1975 • *How Many Ways,* MLC, 1981.

Illusion: *Illusion,* Island, 1978.

Jethro Tull: *The Broadsword And the Beast,* Chrysalis, 1982 • *Anniversary Collection: The Best Of,* Chrysalis, 1993.

Renaissance: *Renaissance,* Renaissance, 1969, 1996.

Roche, Terry, and Maggie Roche: *Seductive Reasoning,* Columbia, 1975.

Simon, Carly: *"Anticipation,"* Elektra, 1971 • *Anticipation,* Elektra, 1971 • *"Legend in Your Own Time,"* Elektra, 1972 • *The Best Of,* Elektra, 1975 • *Spoiled Girl,* Epic, 1983 • *Coming Around Again,* Arista, 1987 • *"Give Me All Night,"* Arista, 1987 • *Have You Seen Me Lately?,* Arista, 1990 • *Letters Never Sent,* Arista, 1995.

Stevens, Cat: *Mona Bone Jakon,* A&M, 1970 • *Tea for the Tillerman,* A&M, 1970 • *"Moon Shadow,"* A&M, 1971 • *"Peace Train,"* A&M, 1971 • *Teaser And the Firecat,* A&M, 1971 • *"Wild World,"* A&M, 1971 • *Catch Bull at Four,* A&M, 1972 • *"Morning Has Broken,"* A&M, 1972 • *"Sitting,"* A&M, 1972 • *Buddha And the Chocolate Box,* A&M, 1974 • *"Oh Very Young,"* A&M, 1974 • *Greatest Hits,* A&M, 1975 • *Back to Earth,* A&M, 1978 • *"Bad Brakes,"* A&M, 1979 • *Footsteps in the Dark: Greatest Hits, Vol. 2,* A&M, 1984 • *Classics, Vol. 24,* A&M, 1987 • *Three,* Mobil Fidelity Soundlab, 1996.

Yardbirds, The: *"Over Under Sideways Down,"* Epic, 1966 • *Over Under Sideways Down,* Columbia/Epic, 1966 • *Roger the Engineer,* Edsel, 1966, 1986 • *Little Games,* EMI America, 1967, 1996 • *Little Games Sessions and More,* Gold Rush, 1967, 1996.

Roger "S" Sanchez

Roger Sanchez (born June 1, 1967) has always operated in advance of his dance music colleagues. From the beginning of his career, he has consistently strived to redefine the boundaries of the house music underground, starting in 1990 under the rubric of Underground Solution with "Luv Dancin'." That single proved that the texture of a thick bass line and a simple melody could rise above the confines of a small venue into mainstream consciousness and onto crossover radio airwaves. The track was eventually re-recorded with singer Jasmine, further expanding its already ardent international audience—and providing a glimpse into Sanchez's creative grasp. "I'll never forget hearing that record played in a club for the first time," Sanchez says. "Watching people react to it was a revelation. I knew this record was different from other music I'd worked on. It would take me on an exciting and educational trip that money could never buy."

Part of his odyssey included a lengthy stint at the top of the major-label remix heap, adding his jazzy touch to countless club acts. One of those records, would, once again, change the course of career travel for Sanchez: "Take Me Back to Love Again" by Kathy Sledge, the record that has arguably defined his career as a remixer. "That was one of the first records that I really got to show people that I could handle something with real depth," he says of a song he transformed from sultry rhythm 'n' blues to a full-throttle, gospel-spiced mover. "It wasn't only a case of recutting the keyboards and beat. We went back into the studio with Kathy and she resang the song. It was chemical, man. We connected and really respected one another—and that brought out the best we had to offer."

Along the way, Sanchez further developed his image in clubland with a brief foray into independent label ownership and management. In 1995, he formed Narcotic Records, an outlet that earned a solid reputation for its cutting-edge releases by Sanchez, among others.

What explains Sanchez's tenure in dance music is an ongoing passion for stepping behind the turntables. "To me, spinning records can almost be as creative as producing and remixing," he says. "A great DJ can just take a record and give it an entirely new sound or vibe, just with the way he deals with the beats or a chord progression." Sanchez still spins regularly, serving longtime disciples of his hallowed Ego Trip traveling parties, which were the talk of New York and Europe during the late '80s and early '90s.

"DJing was part of what drew me into music," says the Queens, New York, native who divided his early twenties between seasoning his musical aptitude and studying architecture at the Pratt Institute. "For a while I tried to do both. But what can I say—music was what touched me more deeply. I had to give it a shot."

—LARRY FLICK

Basia: "Drunk on Love" (remix), Epic, 1994.

Brotherhood of Soul: "I'll Be Right There," Narcotic, 1995.

Cheeks, Judy: *Respect,* Critique, 1996.

DJ Keoki: *Transatlantic Move,* Moonshine, 1996.

El Mariachi: "Cuba," Strictly Rhythm, 1996.

Gordon, Lonnie: *Bad Mood,* Gold Rush, 1994, 1996.

Ilegales: "Sueno Contigo (Dreaming of You)," Ariola, 1997.

Incognito: "Everyday" (remix), Talkin' Loud, 1995 • "I Hear Your Name" (remix), Talkin' Loud, 1995 • *Remixed,* Verve, 1996.

Jackson, Michael: "Dangerous" (remix), Epic, 1992 • "Jam" (remix), Epic, 1992 • *Blood on the Dancefloor: HIStory in the Mix,* MJJ/Sony, 1997.

John, Elton: "Don't Go Breaking My Heart" (remix), MCA, 1994.

M People: "Movin' on Up" (remix), Epic, 1994.

Orchestra 7: featuring Kathee, *Liquid Paradise,* Soho Latino, 1992 • *Love Is the Message,* CBS international, 1992.

Police, The: "Voices Inside My Head" (remix), A&M, 1993.

Rockers Uptown: "Magnificent," Tribal, 1991.

Ross, Diana: "I Will Survive" (remix), Motown, 1995.

Sanchez, Roger "S": *Illegal* (EP), TNT, 1994 • w/ DJ Pierre, *Mixmag Live! Vol. 16: Americana,* Mixmag, 1995 • *Roger S. Megamix,* Freeze, 1995 • "Deep," Narcotic, 1997 • *United DJ's of America,* Vol. 8, DMC America, 1997 • *S-Man Classics: The Essential Sanchez Mixes,* Harmless, 1998.

Shinas, Sofia: *Sofia Shinas,* Warner Bros., 1992.

Sledge, Kathy: "Take Me Back to Love Again" (remix), Epic, 1992 • "Another Star," Narcotic, 1995.

Ten City: "Goin' Up in Smoke" (remix), Columbia, 1994.

Underground Solution: "Luv Dancin'," Strictly Rhythm, 1990, 1995.

Watford, Michael: *Michael Watford,* EastWest, 1994.

White, Barry: "Love Is the Icon" (remix), A&M, 1994.

Ya Kid K: "Let This Housebeat Drop" (remix), SBK, 1992.

COLLECTIONS

Roger Sanchez Presents Hard Times: The Album, Narcotic/Hard Times, 1995.

Roger S. Presents Strictly for the Underground, Strictly Rhythm, 1995.

Johnny Sandlin

Johnny Sandlin's earliest musical memory is listening to the kitchen window radio when he was a little kid in his native Decatur, Alabama. He can't remember not liking music. "I'd sing in the car until you shut me up," recalls Sandlin, who's produced the Allman Brothers, Bonnie Bramlett, Widespread Panic, Elvin Bishop, and Johnny Jenkins. "I always wanted to play an instrument."

Born April 16, 1945, Sandlin took up trumpet early, but asthma interfered, so he switched to piano. He hated the lessons, and when he saw Elvis Presley on *The Ed Sullivan Show* in 1954, "it was all over"—he had to have a guitar. "When I was 11, I begged and pleaded and cried, everything I could to talk my folks into getting me a guitar. They came across, with a Kay: tough strings, the action was real hard."

But Sandlin practiced, and at age 13, joined his first band, the Rainbows, which also included Norman Owens, aka Butch Owens, a bass player Jerry Lee Lewis shot (not fatally, fortunately).

Eventually, Sandlin learned drums, which he still plays. "Rick Hall [see entry] started using me on sessions over at Fame when I was about 17. There, I met Jerry Carrigan, an incredible drummer who went on to play with Elvis; pianist David Briggs; and bassist Norbert Putnam [see entry]." Hall had cut a hit with Arthur Alexander ("You Better Move On," 1961), and Sandlin played on some Jimmy Hughes and Tommy Roe records.

"Back then, it wasn't like now, where everybody in the world's got a guitar," Sandlin says. "I had a nice guitar and amp, so one of the attractions for hiring me was, Rick would be playing electric guitar and say, 'Hey, John, we might need acoustic guitar.' Then, that acoustic guitar doesn't sound that good. What about a six-string bass? Rick finally said, 'Hey, John, why don't you come up here and help me listen to this one?' " Such questions were the way Hall got Sandlin to figure out what went into a session. "I learned a lot then I didn't even realize," Sandlin says. "These guys I was playing with were my heroes."

He started producing with Eddie Hinton, a Southern guitarist of erratic reputation and extraordinary musicality who died in 1995. Hinton was the singer in the Five Minutes, a band also featuring Sandlin, bassist Mabron McKinney, and keyboardist/rhythm guitarist player Paul Hornsby (see entry). "We kept a cutout of Colonel Sanders on stage," says Sandlin. "He was the fifth Minute."

Sandlin, who cites Hinton as his major influence on

producing, is working on Hinton's last material, adding bass and drums to 2-track demos made in 1994 and earlier. The tunes, 14 in all, may be released on Capricorn, Sandlin says.

Sandlin cut an instrumental version of Johnny Otis's (see entry) "Willie and the Hand Jive" on Hinton in 1968. Backed by a rendition of Canned Heat's "Goin' up the Country," it was sold to Atlantic, which put out promotional copies but never an official release.

Sandlin knew Rick Hall and Quin Ivy (who'd produced Percy Sledge) and he'd "started an album on Duane" with Capricorn Records founder Phil Walden. In 1966 and 1967, Sandlin was playing drums in the Hourglass, with Duane and Gregg Allman and Paul Hornsby. When Bill McEwen saw the Hourglass, the Nitty Gritty Dirt Band honcho flipped out, advising the band to move to California and become rock stars.

The graft didn't take. Hourglass released "two pretty mediocre albums" on Liberty, then moved back home in 1968. Sandlin took some of the money he'd earned out west to cut tracks at Fame, including a B.B. King medley featuring Duane Allman. The tape, which convinced Hall to hire Duane Allman, led to Allman's playing lead on Wilson Pickett's "Hey Jude," Allman's breakthrough as a session player.

Sandlin has had some ups and plenty of downs. "The best band I've ever heard was the Aquarium Rescue Unit, "he says, referring to the successor to the Hampton Grease Band, an avant-garde rock band of the '70s. The Aquarium leader is Col. Bruce Hampton, who also lent his moniker to the earlier incarnation.

He is also enthused about a record he cut on Oteil Burbridge, the Aquarium Rescue Unit bassist. "It's jazz, it's great music by great musicians," Sandlin says. He also enjoyed producing Gregg Allman's *Laid Back* (No. 13) and *Ton Ton Macoute,* Johnny Jenkins' great 1970 Capricorn debut. (Sandlin also produced Jenkins' more conventional, equally accomplished 1996 "comeback," *Blessed Blues,* on Capricorn.)

He's had failures, too. One that hurt was the time he was offered a chance to produce Bob Seger "right before he took off"—and turned it down. "I was busy at the time, and I passed," Sandlin says. Producing the troubled husband-and-wife team of Gregg Allman and Cher was also difficult. "They were just too diverse in their musical backgrounds," Sandlin says diplomatically.

"In music, the main thing I look for is something I believe," Sandlin says. "I want to believe in the artist, what they're doing and their purpose. The reason they're doing it is because they have to, it's what they're supposed to be doing. It's not a contrived thing. I got to do something from the heart.

"Col. Bruce Hampton and I were talking, and I subscribe to his theory: we don't choose to do this, it chooses us," Sandlin says. In his "earth biography," Hampton says he's from Atlanta, but Sandlin believes otherwise. "Sun Ra was from Saturn, Bruce is from Jupiter," he says.

On a more terrestrial level, Sandlin still listens to productions by Quincy Jones (see entry). He likes what Babyface (see entry) is doing these days, too. "I think he makes the best-sounding records of everybody," Sandlin says. "Take the Clapton single, 'If I Could Change the World.' It's so open, you can hear every instrument. I don't care if you play it on a TV speaker or studio monitors. Everything is so clear, has tone to it, and depth. I'd like to take some lessons from him."

Since 1984, Sandlin has owned and operated Duck Tape Music Production and Publishing in Decatur, where he operates a 32-track studio. Besides the Allman Brothers, his production credits include Alex Taylor, Doug Kershaw, Microwave Dave and the Nukes, former Temptation Eddie Kendricks, the Rockets, and Wet Willie. He won platinum awards for producing, mixing, and mastering several Allman Brothers records, including the classic *Brothers and Sisters* (No. 1) with "Ramblin' Man" (No. 2), and has recorded well over 120 artists.
—CARLO WOLFF

Allman Brothers Band: *Brothers and Sisters,* Capricorn, 1973 • "Jessica," Capricorn, 1973 • "Ramblin' Man," Capricorn, 1973 • "Louisiana Lou and Three Card Monty John," Capricorn, 1975 • "Nevertheless," Capricorn, 1975 • *The Road Goes On Forever,* Polydor, 1975 • *Win, Lose or Draw,* Capricorn, 1975 • *Dreams,* Polydor, 1989.

Allman, Duane: *Anthology,* Capricorn, 1972 • *Anthology II,* Capricorn, 1974.

Allman, Gregg: *Laid Back,* Polydor, 1973 • "Midnight Rider," Capricorn, 1973 • *The Greg Allman Tour,* Capricorn, 1974 • *One More Try: An Anthology,* PolyGram, 1997.

Allman, Gregg, and Cher: *Allman and Woman,* Warner Bros., 1977.

Betts, Richard: *Highway Call,* Capricorn, 1974.

Bishop, Elvin: *Let It Flow,* Capricorn, 1974 • "Travelin' Shoes," Capricorn, 1974 • *Juke Joint Jump,* Capricorn, 1975 • "Sure Feels Good," Capricorn, 1975 • *Sure Feels Good: The Best Of,* Polydor, 1992.

Blue Miracle: *Blue Miracle,* Autonomous, 1994.

Bramlett, Bonnie: *It's Time,* Capricorn, 1974 • *Ladie's Choice,* Capricorn, 1976.

Burbridge, Oteil: *Love of a Lifetime,* Nile, 1997.

Cowboy: *Reach for the Sky,* Capricorn, 1971 • *5'll Getcha Ten,* Capricorn, 1972 • *Boyer and Talton,* Capricorn, 1974 • *Why Quit When You're Losing,* Capricorn, 1975 • *The Best of Cowboy: A Different Time,* Polydor, 1993.

Hall, Jimmy: *Rendezvous with the Blues,* Capricorn, 1996.

Hampton, Col. Bruce, and the Aquarium Rescue Unit: *Col. Bruce Hampton and the Aquarium Rescue Unit,* Capricorn, 1992 • *Mirrors of Embarrassment,* Capricorn, 1993.

Hydra: *Land of Money,* Capricorn, 1975.

Jenkins, Johnny: *Ton Ton Macoute,* Capricorn, 1970 • *Blessed Blues,* Capricorn, 1996.

Jupiter Coyote: *Cemeteries and Junkyards,* Autonomous, 1991, 1993 • *Wade,* Autonomous, 1993 • *Lucky Day,* Autonomous, 1995.

Karloff, Billy, and the Extremes: *Let Your Fingers Do the Talking,* Warner Bros., 1981.

Kendricks, Eddie: *Love Keys,* Atlantic, 1981.

Kershaw, Doug: *The Best Of,* Warner Bros., 1989.

Kingfish: *Trident,* Jet, 1978.

Laing, Corky: *Makin' It on the Street,* Elektra, 1977.

Look, The: *We're Gonna Rock,* Plastic, 1981.

McClinton, Delbert: *Second Wind,* Mercury, 1978, 1993 • *Keeper of the Flame,* Capricorn, 1979.

Melting Pot: *Burn, Cauldron, Bubble,* Ampex, 1970.

Microwave Dave and the Nukes: *Goodnight Dear,* Blues Works, 1996.

Mull, Martin: *Normal,* Capricorn, 1974 • *Mulling It Over: Musical Oeuvre View,* Razor & Tie, 1998.

Outlaws, The: *In the Eye of the Storm,* Arista, 1979.

Rockets, The: "Can't Sleep," RSO, 1979 • "Oh Well," RSO, 1979 • *Rockets,* RSO, 1979 • *Turn Up the Radio,* RSO, 1979 • "Desire," RSO, 1980 • *No Ballads,* RSO, 1980.

Taylor, Alex: *Alex Taylor with Friends and Neighbours,* Capricorn, 1971 • *Dinnertime,* Capricorn, 1972.

Tim Weisberg Band: *The Tim Weisberg Band,* United Artists, 1977 • *Rotations,* United Artists, 1978.

Wells, Kitty: *Forever Young,* Capricorn, 1974.

Wet Willie: "Airport," Warner Bros., 1973 (*Appetizers*) • *Drippin' Wet/Live,* Capricorn, 1973 • *Greatest Hits,* Capricorn, 1977.

White Witch: *White Witch,* Capricorn, 1973.

Widespread Panic: *Space Wrangler* (1 track), Capricorn, 1988, 1992 • *Widespread Panic,* Capricorn, 1991 • *Everyday,* Capricorn, 1993.

Joe Saraceno

As songwriter, producer, and performer, Joe Saraceno was responsible for some of the best rock and surf instrumentals of the '60s, hitting with the Marketts ("Surfer's Stomp"; "Out of Limits," No. 3; "Batman Theme," No. 17), the Routers ("Let's Go," No. 19), the T-Bones ("No Matter What Shape Your Stomach's In," No. 3), and the great Ventures (*The Ventures A-Go-Go,* No. 16; "Hawaii Five-O," No. 4; *Hawaii Five-O,* No. 11).

Joe Saraceno was born May 16, 1937, in Utica, New York. He graduated from St. Lawrence University with a degree in business administration and psychology in 1958. A singer and a "very poor saxophone player," Saraceno had no visions of a career in showbiz, but seeking warmth, he moved to Los Angeles in the summer of 1958 and got a job as an auditor with an insurance company.

At the famous Schwab's Drugstore in Hollywood Saraceno ran into a friend from college who introduced him to a singer, Tony Savonne. On a lark, Saraceno and Savonne wrote a song together. They demoed the song and sent it to local labels ABC Paramount, Dore, and Era.

Two weeks later Era called the pair in, and to their amazement, signed them as artists. The single, "The Freeze," became a national hit, reaching No. 33 in mid-1958. "Tony and Joe" appeared on *American Bandstand* in Philadelphia, then went on tour, which Saraceno hated. For the *Bandstand* appearance, Saraceno had to call in sick for Thursday and Friday to his auditor's job. Sure enough, his boss watched *Bandstand* that weekend and Saraceno was fired on Monday. So showbiz it was to be.

Saraceno wrangled some financing and started to make records. He hit immediately, co-producing Russ Regan's Christmas novelty hit "The Happy Reindeer" (recorded under the name "Dancer, Prancer and Nervous"), which went to No. 34 in late 1959. The first record Saraceno produced solo was former Rock 'n' Roll Trio member Dorsey Burnette's "(There Was a) Tall Oak Tree," another hit that reached No. 23 in early 1960. After charting modestly with an instrumental, Sir Chauncey's "Beautiful Obsession," Saraceno had participated in four national hits in about a year and a half.

After a brief stint with a company owned by Fred Astaire, Saraceno went to work for Regan's fledgling Candix Records, where he signed a group called the Pendletones (after the Pendleton shirt favored by surfers) in 1961 on the basis of their song "Surfin'." Regan and Saraceno suggested a new name for the band, the Beach Boys. Lacking adequate financing to adequately distribute "Surfin'" (which snuck up to No. 75 nonetheless), Saraceno gave the boys their release, and they moved on to Capitol and history.

In the meantime, Saraceno and partner Mike Gordon wrote and produced the first surf-themed song to crack the Top 40, "Surfer's Stomp," which made it to No. 31 in early 1962 for a studio band, the Marketts. Saraceno says, "I was in a beach bar and everyone was doing a dance I'd never seen before. One of the girls said it was called the 'surfer stomp,' so we wrote a song with that pattern in mind. I got [guitarist] Tommy Tedesco, [saxophonist] Plas Johnson, [drummer] Ed Hall and some other guys together, and we made the record."

Later in 1962, Saraceno and Gordon made an even bigger instrumental hit with the Routers' "Let's Go," whose clap-clap, clap-clap-clap beat is now ubiquitous as a cheer at high schools and colleges. In late 1963 Saraceno and the Marketts made it into the Top 5 with a surfy version of the theme song from the *Outer Limits* TV show. A threatened lawsuit forced a title change to "Out of Limits," but didn't slow down the record.

After all of these instrumental hits, Dolton Records brought Saraceno in to work with the Ventures—the top rock instrumental group of all time. The Seattle natives (Nokie Edwards on lead guitar, Don Wilson on rhythm guitar, Bob Bogle on bass, Mel Taylor on drums) had had a series of hit singles but wanted to improve their album sales. Saraceno emphasized thematic albums, with hits of the day done in the clean but rocking Ventures style, interspersed with originals. The method worked, *The Ventures A-Go-Go, Where the Action Is, Go with the Ventures!, Wild Things!,* and the classic *Hawaii Five-O* all were at least Top 40 albums.

Hawaii Five-O went gold in 1969, and Saraceno's masterful production of the title track made it the band's biggest single and greatest song since "Walk—Don't Run" in 1960. "Five-O" rolls in on a wave of portentous drums; Edwards' guitar and a horn section then carry the compelling, dramatic melody through some ripping maneuvers before triumphantly stepping ashore in the white foam conclusion.

Besides racking up millions in domestic sales, Saraceno's 21 studio albums with the Ventures have sold millions more overseas, especially in Japan, where the band members are demigods. It is inconceivable that this band is still not in the Rock and Roll Hall of Fame.

Apart from his Ventures work, Saraceno was a staff producer for Liberty for several years, from 1965 into the early '70s. In 1965 he thought he heard a hit song in an Alka Seltzer TV commercial jingle. He obtained permission from the company to elongate the jingle to song length and then, in a brilliant marketing ploy, sent out packets of Alka-Seltzer along with promo copies of the record (recorded by another studio-concocted band, the T-Bones) to radio stations with the note: "Please play this record; if you don't like it, throw the Alka-Seltzers into water and drink heartily." The record went Top 5.

In the '80s and '90s Saraceno has done very well with his songwriting and publishing catalogs, placing many of his songs in feature films and TV programs. —ERIC OLSEN

Burnette, Dorsey: "(There Was a) Tall Oak Tree," Era, 1960.
Dancer, Prancer, and Nervous: "The Happy Reindeer," Capitol, 1959.
Denny, Martin: *Hawaii Tattoo,* Liberty, 1964.
Fire and Rain: *Fire and Rain,* Mercury, 1973 • *Living Together,* 20th Century, 1975.
Frost, Thomas and Richard: *Thomas and Richard Frost,* UNI, 1972.
Gentlehood: *Gentlehood,* CBS, 1973.
Marketts, The: "Balboa Blue," Liberty, 1962 • "Surfer's Stomp," Liberty, 1962 • *Surfer's Stomp,* Liberty, 1962 • "Out of Limits," Warner Bros., 1963 • *The Marketts Take to Wheels,* Warner Bros., 1963 • *Out of Limits ,* Sundazed, 1964, 1996 • "Vanishing Point," Warner Bros., 1964 • "Batman Theme," Warner Bros., 1966 • *Batman Theme,* Warner Bros., 1966.
McDaniels, Gene: *Best of Gene McDaniels: A Hundred Pounds of Clay,* Collectables, 1995.
O'Jays, The: "Lipstick Traces," Imperial, 1965.
Routers, The: "Let's Go," Warner Bros., 1962 • "Sting Ray," Warner Bros., 1962 • *Let's Go with the Routers,* Warner Bros., 1963.
Sir Chauncey: "Beautiful Obsession," Warner Bros., 1960.
Sunshine Company: "Back on the Street Again," Imperial, 1967 • *Happy Is the Sunshine Company,* Imperial, 1967 • *Sunshine and Shadows,* Imperial, 1968 • *The Sunshine Company,* Imperial, 1968.
T-Bones, The: "No Matter What Shape Your Stomach's In," Liberty, 1965 • *No Matter What Shape Your Stomach's In,* Liberty, 1965 • "Sippin' 'n Chippin'," Liberty, 1966.
Tony and Joe: "The Freeze," Era, 1958.
Turso, Ronnie: *I Played the Clown,* Calliope, 1977.
Ventures, The: *The Fabulous Ventures/The Ventures A-Go-Go,* One Way, 1964, 1997 • *Play Guitar with the Ventures* Vol. 2, Dolton, 1965 • *The Ventures A-Go-Go,* Liberty, 1965 • *The Ventures Christmas Album,* Razor & Tie, 1965, 1996 • *Batman/TV Themes,* See for Miles, 1966, 1997 • *Go with the Ventures!,* Dolton, 1966 • *Guitar Freakout,* Dolton, 1966 • *Guitar Freakout/Wild Things!,* One Way, 1966, 1997 • *Play Guitar with the Ventures,* Vols. 3–4, Dolton, 1966 • *Play Guitar with the Ventures,* Vols. 3–4, See for Miles, 1966, 1997 • "Secret Agent Man," Dolton, 1966 • *Where the Action Is,* Dolton, 1966 • *Wild Things!,* Dolton, 1966 • *$1,000,000 Weekend,* Liberty, 1967 • *Play Guitar with the Ventures Vol. 7,* Liberty, 1967 • *Super Psychedelics,* Liberty, 1967 • *Flights of Fantasy,* Liberty, 1968 • *Flights of Fantasy/Underground Fire,* One Way, 1968, 1996 • *The Horse,* Liberty, 1968 • *Underground Fire,* Liberty, 1968 • "Hawaii Five-O," Liberty, 1969 • *Hawaii Five-O,* Liberty, 1969 • "Theme from 'A Summer Place,' " Liberty, 1969 • *Only Hits!,* United Artists, 1973 • *The Jim Croce Songbook,* United Artists, 1974 • *The Ventures Play the Carpenters,*

United Artists, 1974 • *NASA 25th Anniversary Commemorative Album*, Award Masters, 1984 • *Walk, Don't Run: The Best Of*, EMI America, 1990 • *Tele-Ventures: The Ventures Perform the Great TV Themes*, EMI, 1996.

Bob Sargeant

B
ob Sargeant, after a 10-year career as a musician and a brief solo career, became one of the most successful producers of the early British new wave era, helming classics for the English Beat, Haircut 100, and dozens of great John Peel BBC radio sessions. He also produced excellent records for the Damned, the Ruts, Monochrome Set, the Woodentops, and XTC and had a series of pop smashes with Breathe in the late '80s.

Bob Sargeant was born in Newcastle, in northern England. At 14 he bought an electric guitar and started rocking: John Lennon was his hero and biggest musical influence. A friend also got an electric guitar, and the pair hooked up with a drummer (the butcher's son) and a bass player to play Beatles and Stones rock 'n' roll around town.

R&B bands like Them and Newcastle's Animals were all the rage by 1965, so Sargeant decided to buy a Vox Continental organ to join in on the sound. He joined Newcastle's Junco Partners in 1966, a mod-R&B band that also backed American blues artists when they came through town, most notably Freddie King and Howlin' Wolf. The band went psychedelic in 1969 and recorded an album in 1970, by which time Sargeant was the singer.

Sargeant moved to London to join a folky band, Everyone, headed by Andy Roberts (with John Porter; see entry). When that band ended in 1971, Sargeant joined Mick Abrahams' (ex of Jethro Tull) band on keyboards. In 1972 and 1973, Sargeant worked on his own material, and in 1974, he recorded his solo album, *First Starring Role*, which he co-produced with Mick Ronson (see entry) and Dave Mackay. From Ronson, Sargeant picked up the idea of adding textures (strings, horns, etc.) to standard rock 'n' roll instrumentation—by then he had realized that he liked the studio a lot better than live work. Sargeant is pleased with the album musically (though he hates the glammy cover), but it didn't sell enough to earn his advance back for the label, so he became "one of the great unrecouped" and was dropped.

Sargeant did some London session work, and then

punk arrived in the mid-'70s. He helped drummer Rat Scabies and his band the White Cats (soon Join the Damned) make some demos, which were well received. A copy of the band's demo was sent to the BBC's legendary John Peel, who used it on his radio show in 1977.

Sargeant called Peel and asked if there were any openings for producers for the "live" (recorded earlier that day) music portion of his show. There were, and Sargeant produced for Peel for over two years, including performances by Buzzcocks, Gang of Four, Madness, Gary Numan, the Police, the Undertones, and Manchester's the Beat (called the "English Beat" in the U.S.), among dozens of others.

The experience was fantastic, says Sargeant. "I had a new band in every day to do four songs, and I had 10 hours to record and mix those songs for broadcast that night. It really taught me discipline and helped me learn the planning and logistics side of production. Another great benefit was that a number of bands asked me to produce their next single for them," he says.

Sargeant produced a number of these singles for indie labels, including "Rebellious Jukebox" for the Damned, and then he produced the Beat's first single, a tightly rocking ska version of Smokey Robinson's (see entry) "Tears of a Clown" (No. 6 U.K.), which shot up the charts in late 1979. An exceptional record, "Tears" features Dave Wakeling's great dusky vocal, exceptionally crisp drumming from Everett Morton, and authentic sax work from 50-year-old Jamaican, Saxa.

In mid-1980, Sargeant and the band recorded the outstanding *I Just Can't Stop It* (No. 3 U.K.), which is (along with the Specials' first album) one of the two best albums of the British ska revival of the late '70s and early '80s, and one of the greatest albums of the '80s, period. Mixing killer covers ("Tears" and a deeply soulful version of Andy Williams' "Can't Get Used to Losing You," No. 3 U.K.) with first-rate originals ("Hands Off . . . She's Mine," No. 9 U.K.; "Mirror in the Bathroom," No. 4 U.K, an amazingly acute analysis of narcissism; the ambiguous "Twist and Crawl"), the album yielded four hit singles and created a sensation. Perhaps a bit rushed, the band's second album, *Wha-ppen?* (No. 3 U.K.), slowed down the tempo and didn't live up to the standards of the first, but was another huge U.K. hit in 1981.

Through the Beat's British label, Arista, Sargeant was handed Haircut 100 in 1982, "one of a half-dozen London-based, rich Thatcherite, club boy" neo-soul bands (ABC, Spandau Ballet, Level 42, etc.) of the time. Though the shortest-lived of the lot (only one album before singer/songwriter Nick Heyward went solo), Haircut made the biggest splash and generated the single best album of the milieu, *Pelican West* (No. 2 U.K.)— an extremely tuneful, breezy amalgam of calypso and Latin rhythms, cool jazz stylings, and cotton candy pop soul. The album was also a hit (No. 31) in the U.S., and the singles "Love Plus One" and "Favorite Shirts (Boy Meets Girl)" became staples of American modern rock radio.

The Beat's third album, *Special Beat Service,* was a return to greatness and also a hit in the U.S.; Sargeant had produced four smash albums and over a dozen hit singles in only two years. *Special* returns to quicker tempos than *Wha'ppen?,* though is less ska and more modern pop rock than *I Just Can't Stop It.* Wakeling's singing and the band's (including Andy Cox on guitar and David Steele on bass, who went on to form Fine Young Cannibals) writing are better than ever on "I Confess," "Sugar and Stress", "Ackee 1-2-3," and the great "Save It for Later."

Sargeant produced the semi-acoustic, rootsy new wave of the Woodentops' fine *Giant* album in 1986, then came across Breathe, a suburban London pop group led by singer/songwriter David Glasper. Their first album, *All That Jazz,* stalled on the charts, and then "Hands to Heaven" was released in the U.S. Ironically, the pleading love song was perceived as having a religious theme in Salt Lake City and gradually swept across the Bible belts of the Midwest and the South to become a No. 2 hit in the U.S. A similar '80s-style big ballad, "How Can I Fall" (No. 3), did almost as well, and the slick up-tempo shuffle "Don't Tell Me Lies" went to No. 10. The album went gold, and a second, *Peace of Mind,* yielded two more Top 40 hits, but then Glasper went into semi-retirement in Thailand, where he now has a wife and child.

In the '90s Sargeant has had tremendous success in Scandinavia with artists such as Grethe Svensen and has returned to his roots, helping to develop young British rock bands through his Regimental Music company.
—Eric Olsen

Adventures, The: *The Adventures,* Chrysalis, 1985.

Any Trouble: *Where Are All the Nice Girls?,* Compass, 1980, 1997.

Breathe: *All That Jazz,* A&M, 1987 • "Hands to Heaven," A&M, 1987 • "How Can I Fall," A&M, 1987 • "Don't Tell Me Lies," A&M, 1989 • featuring David Glasper, "Does She Love That Man?," A&M, 1990 • *Peace of Mind,* A&M, 1990 • "Say a Prayer," A&M, 1990.

Buzzards: *Jellied Eels to Record Deals* (1 track), Chrysalis, 1979.

Buzzcocks: *The Peel Sessions* (3 tracks), Strange Fruit, 1989.

Carpettes: *Frustration Paradise,* Beggars Banquet, 1979.

Damned, The: *Phantasmagoria,* MCA, 1985 • *The Light at the End of the Tunnel,* MCA, 1988.

English Beat: "Ranking Full Stop," 2Tone/Chrysalis, 1979, 1983 (*This Are Two Tone*) • "Tears of a Clown," 2Tone/Chrysalis, 1979, 1983 (*This Are Two Tone*) • "Best Friend," Sire, 1980 • "Hands Off . . . She's Mine," Sire, 1980 • *I Just Can't Stop It,* Sire, 1980 • "Mirror in the Bathroom," Sire, 1980 • "Too Nice to Talk To," Sire, 1980 • "Big Shot," 2Tone/Chrysalis, 1981 (*Dance Craze* soundtrack) • "Doors of Your Heart," Sire, 1981 • "Drowning," Sire, 1981 • "Mirror in the Bathroom" (live), 2Tone/Chrysalis, 1981 (*Dance Craze* soundtrack) • "Ranking Full Stop" (live), 2Tone/Chrysalis, 1981 (*Dance Craze* soundtrack) • *Wha'ppen?,* Sire, 1981 • "I Confess," IRS, 1982 • "Jeanette," IRS, 1982 • "Save It for Later," IRS, 1982, 1983 • *Special Beat Service,* IRS, 1982 • "Can't Get Used to Losing You" (remix), IRS, 1983 • *What Is Beat,* IRS, 1983.

Fall, The: *Live at the Witch Trials,* San Francisco/IRS, 1979 • "Rebellious Jukebox," IRS, 1979, 1981 (*IRS Greatest Hits,* Vols. 2–3).

Friends Again: *Trapped and Unwrapped,* Phonogram, 1984.

Gang of Four: *The Peel Sessions,* Dutch East, 1990.

Haircut 100: "Love Plus One," EMI, 1982, 1993 (*Living in Oblivion: The 80s Greatest Hits,* Vol. 2) • *Pelican West,* Arista, 1982.

Hall, Terry: *The Collection: Terry Hall,* Chrysalis, 1993.

Lotus Eaters: *No Sense of Sin,* Arista, 1984.

Madness: *The Peel Sessions,* Dutch East, 1988.

Monochrome Set: *Strange Boutique,* Arista, 1980 • *Colour Transmission,* Virgin, 1987 • *Tomorrow May Be Too Long: The Best Of,* Caroline, 1995.

Monroes, The: *Face Another Day,* Parlophone, 1985.

Numan, Gary: *The Peel Sessions,* Strange Fruit, 1989.

Q-Tips: *Q-Tips,* DinDisc, 1980.

Ruts, The: *The Crack,* Virgin, 1979, 1994.

Sargeant, Bob : *First Starring Role,* RCA, 1974.

Svensen, Grethe: *Loves of a Woman* (4 tracks), BMG Norway, 1993 • *Your Beauty,* BMG Norway, 1995.

Terry, Blair, and Anouchka: *Ultra Modern Nursey Rhymes,* Chrysalis, 1989.

Transmitters: *Twenty Four Hours,* Ebony, 1978.

Undertones, The: *The Peel Sessions,* Strange Fruit, 1986.

V.I.P.'s, The: *Beat Crazy!,* Tangerine, 1997.

Wire: *The Peel Sessions,* Dutch East, 1989.

Woodentops, The: *Giant,* Rough Trade/Columbia, 1986.

XTC: "Great Fire," Virgin, 1983 • *Mummer* (1 track), Virgin, 1983 • *Compact XTC: The Singles, 1978–1985,* Virgin, 1985.

Elliot Scheiner

lliot Scheiner started his career as an assistant engineer at A&R Studios in 1967, working under Phil Ramone (see entry). "He taught me just about everything there was to know back then. The first room I worked in had a 3-track broadcast console, with two limiters and two equalizers, and that was it. If the sound wasn't bright enough, you moved the mike; if you wanted an effect, you moved the mike. You had to rely on mike placement for everything."

Striking out on his own in 1973, Scheiner has the dubious distinction of being the first engineer in New York to go freelance, though he continued to work at A&R for a time, on commission instead of straight salary (a radical concept at the time). His first major engineering assignment was Van Morrison's classic *Moondance* album, which also signaled the beginning of Scheiner's production career. "We were getting ready to mix," he recalls. "It was around Christmastime, and Van said, 'I'm not gonna be here, I'm going home to Woodstock to be with my family, so why don't you mix it and just send it to me?' So the drummer [Gary Malabar] and I ended up mixing it by ourselves and we sent it up to him, and that was it. He didn't change anything, he loved it. So when the next album came around (*His Band and Street Choir*), I was supposed to co-produce with Van, though in the end there was some bad blood between us, so I ended up with a 'production coordinator' credit instead."

But it was Scheiner's work on Felix Cavaliere's *Destiny* that proved to be an even more significant springboard. The album may not have been a commercial success, but it became a personal favorite of two up-and-coming artists named Walter Becker and Donald Fagen (see entry). Within a short time, Scheiner was ensconced in Davelin Studios in Los Angeles, doing the tracking for Steely Dan's *The Royal Scam*—his first significant gig outside of New York City. Scheiner went on to engineer both *Aja* and *Gaucho* (winning Grammys for both), as well as Fagen's first solo effort, *Nightfly*.

Although he would go on to produce and engineer for many major artists (including Billy Joel, Glenn Frey, Jimmy Buffett, Toto, Bruce Hornsby, Natalie Cole, Jennifer Warnes, Barbra Streisand, Dave Grusin, and Pavarotti), Scheiner's career took a new turn when he was asked by the Eagles to engineer their 1994 MTV special, subsequently released as the best-selling *Hell Freezes Over* (No. 1) album. This led to work on other MTV specials, including Fleetwood Mac's 1997 regrouping, *The Dance,* and that of another revived artist of the '70s, John Fogerty (see entry).

Scheiner is currently heavily involved in surround sound, having completed 5.1 remixes of Steely Dan, Eagles, Fleetwood Mac, and Bonnie Raitt material. Along with legendary engineers Ed Cherney and Al Schmitt (see entry), Scheiner is also involved with the launch of a new record label that plans to issue all of its releases both in stereo and surround sound. "It's going to be a small jazz label—just something for us to have fun with, to help develop artists that haven't had a chance."

Only once has Scheiner ever done a production without doing the engineering as well. "The engineer I used was great, but when it got down to mixing, I couldn't let it go. I probably should have, I should have let the guy who recorded it mix it. I didn't, and consequently I did a bad job, so it was a bad experience for me."

"I love engineering, though. That's where I started, and I love that art form. It would be hard for me to put it down. I'm probably going to end up hiring somebody to do certain stuff for me, like vocal overdubs or guitar overdubs; I don't have to sit behind the console for that stuff. But for tracking and for mixing, I feel like I need to be there, I need to be a part of it." —HOWARD MASSEY

America: *Human Nature,* Oxygen, 1998.

Ashford and Simpson: *Solid,* MCI, 1984, 1995.

Buffett, Jimmy: *Off to See the Lizard,* MCA, 1989 • *Feeding Frenzy,* MCA, 1990 • *Boats, Beaches, Bars and Ballads,* MCA, 1992.

Cranberries, The: "Dreams," A&M, 1994 (*Woodstock 94*).

Eagles, The: *Hell Freezes Over,* Geffen, 1994 • "The Girl from Yesterday," Geffen, 1994.

Exile: *Shelter from the Night,* Epic, 1987 • "Feel Like Foolin' Around," Epic, 1988 • "I Can't Get Close Enough," Epic, 1988 • "It's You Again," Epic, 1988 • "Just One Kiss," Epic, 1988 • *Super Hits,* Epic, 1993.

Fleetwood Mac: "Landslide," Reprise, 1997 • "Silver Springs," Reprise, 1997 • *The Dance,* Reprise, 1997.

Fogerty, John: *Premonition,* Warner Bros., 1998.

Frey, Glenn: *Soul Searchin',* MCA, 1988 • "True Love," MCA, 1988 • "Livin' Right," MCA, 1989 • "Part of Me, Part of You," MCA, 1991 • "I've Got Mine," MCA, 1992 • *Strange Weather,* MCA, 1992 • *Live,* MCA, 1993.

Hornsby, Bruce, and the Range: "Mandolin Rain," RCA, 1986 • "The Way It Is," RCA, 1986 • *The Way It Is,* RCA, 1986 • "Every Little Kiss," RCA, 1987.

New York Rock and Soul Revue: *Live at the Beacon,* Giant, 1991.

P.M.: *P.M.,* Warner Bros., 1988.

Rodgers, Paul: "The Hunter," A&M, 1994 (*Woodstock 94*).
Swamp Boogie Queen: *Ill Gotten Booty*, N2K, 1998.
Toto: *Tambu*, Legacy, 1996.
Warnes, Jennifer: *The Hunter*, Private, 1992.

COLLECTIONS
Working soundtrack, Columbia, 1978.

Al Schmitt

One of the most important recordists of this half-century, Al Schmitt has won seven Grammys for engineering pop, jazz, and rock over a still-vibrant 50-year career that has seen recording technology go from mono direct-to-disc to today's megatrack digital effusion. Known for his magical microphone selection and placement, Schmitt has also produced important music and great records across the musical spectrum for David Benoit, George Benson, Jackson Browne, Sam Cooke, Duane Eddy, Hot Tuna, Al Jarreau, Jefferson Airplane, Hugo Montenegro, Diane Schuur, and Neil Young.

Brooklyn-native Al Schmitt is literally a child of the studio: his uncle owned the first independent recording studio in New York City, Harry Schmitt's Recording, on West 46th Street. Starting at the age of 6 in the late '30s, young Al spent much of his free time observing the proceedings, cleaning patch cords, getting piano tips from Art Tatum, and meeting such notables as Bing Crosby, Orson Welles, and the Andrews Sisters.

Watching even big bands being recorded with only one microphone, Schmitt absorbed the niceties of mike balance at a time when it meant everything to the sound quality of a record. "They would move everybody around until they got the balance right, and then they made everybody take their shoes off because you could hear them stomping their feet. I would look out and see that some of the guys had holes in their socks," Schmitt recalls with a chuckle.

Schmitt served in the navy for a couple of years in the late '40s; after he got out in 1950, his uncle arranged for him to apprentice at a small New York studio called Apex Recording, where Schmitt's mentor was the great Tom Dowd (see entry). Three months into his training—"when I was qualified, maybe, to do a voice-and-piano demo"—Schmitt was waiting at the studio on a Saturday for a "Mr. Mercer" to show up to record a demo. "The elevator doors opened up and all of these musicians started coming out. I thought, 'Oh, my God, something's wrong here.' I couldn't reach Tommy and I couldn't reach my boss. This was no demo: it was the Duke Ellington Orchestra in to record for Mercer Records [owned by Duke's son Mercer and Leonard Feather].

"So I had to do it—it was my first date," Schmitt continues. "The nice thing about it was that I didn't have a lot of time to think. Duke Ellington couldn't play piano for the recording because he was signed to Columbia at the time, but he sat next to me and calmed me; Billy Strayhorn played piano," he says.

Schmitt stayed at Apex for two years, then followed Dowd to Coastal Recording Studios, where they did dates for the Atlantic, Prestige, and Sittin' In With labels. In the late '50s Schmitt moved to Los Angeles to work at Radio Recorders, where he became friends with Bones Howe (see entry); together they engineered Henry Mancini's Grammy-winning *The Music From Peter Gunn* for RCA in 1958. Schmitt engineered numerous sessions for Mancini and others for RCA; when RCA opened its own studio at Sunset and Vine, Schmitt was the first engineer hired. He engineered many of Hugo and Luigi's (see entry) productions of Sam Cooke and won his first engineering Grammy for Mancini's *Hatari!* (featuring "Baby Elephant Walk") in 1962. In 1963 Schmitt became a staff producer at RCA.

"Producers would call me to engineer dates, and these guys would come in and they would be on the phone the whole time talking to their bookies or whoever. Or they wouldn't show up at all. Or they would come in for one song and then leave—we would do the next song and it would be the hit. So I said, 'Wait a minute, I'm doing all of this work and these guys are getting all of the money and all of the glory for it.' So I started doing production work at RCA in 1963," he says.

"In those days you were given a roster of maybe 8 or 10 artists to produce, and you did two or three albums a year with each. I was in the studio constantly." While at RCA, Schmitt took over production of Sam Cooke ("always a joy to work with, really special") after Hugo and Luigi's contract expired, and produced his last hit, the wild "Shake" (No. 7) in late 1964. He produced the surf band the Astronauts and co-produced (with Lee Hazlewood) twangy guitar great Duane Eddy. In the mid-'60s he produced Eddie Fisher's final stabs at the charts and Hugo Montenegro's hugely successful film and TV music albums, and in 1967 he took over production of one of San Francisco's most important rock exports, the Jefferson Airplane.

The Airplane are perhaps *the* archetypal Summer of

Love band: with the motto "Jefferson Airplane loves you," trippy "feed-your-head" lyrics, a communal Haight-Ashbury lifestyle, and a musical style cobbled together from folk rock (singer Marty Balin, guitarist/singer Paul Kantner), blues, and roots rock (legendary guitarist Jorma Kaukonen and bassist Jack Casady, who went on to form Hot Tuna), all doused liberally with psychedelics. When provocative, strident former fashion model Grace Slick replaced a pregnant Signe Anderson on female lead vocals in late 1966, the group's classic lineup was complete.

Schmitt produced four albums for the Airplane, starting with their third, 1967's *After Bathing at Baxter's* (No. 17). *Crown of Creation* (No. 6) followed in 1968. The exceptional live album *Bless Its Pointed Little Head* (No. 17) came in 1969, as did the group's last great album, *Volunteers* (No. 13).

Balin and Kantner's title track for *Volunteers* is the band's best rocker ever; Kantner's "We Can Be Together" is a last, wistful rallying cry for the disappearing ideals of the '60s; Slick's "Hey Frederick" begins quietly before building into an eight-minute jam highlighted by Kaukonen's guitar rampage; and the Airplane's fine version of "Wooden Ships" is more organic and evocative than CSN's.

Schmitt took the Airplane's craziness in stride. "That was my first experience with doing complicated multi-track recording, with songs taking a week to record instead of a few hours. On top of that, the band was bringing motorcycles and a tank of nitrous oxide into the studio. It was a little bit frustrating because I was used to people being prepared, on time, and in the right frame of mind, but I also learned an awful lot from them about spontaneity," he says. "We would start at 8 P.M. and go all night. I'd go home, get a few hours' sleep, and then go back to the studio to record Eddie Fisher in the morning.

"One night I got a call from Jack at 8, and he asked if we were working that night. I said, 'Yes, right now.' He said, 'We'll be right down.' He was calling from San Francisco. We started at 11," Schmitt laughs.

Schmitt became an independent producer in 1967. "My salary at RCA was $17,500, plus I could earn up to $5,000 more in bonuses for the year if my records did well. That was it. There was no point structure. The producer was on a salary. The companies were making an awful lot of money in those days. Nowadays, a top producer can get 5 points [percent] on a record; back then, the artist was getting that. Producers make a lot more money now. On the other hand, money can be a drawback: records cost hundreds of thousands of dollars to make these days, which puts a lot of pressure on everyone, and most of the labels are run by accountants, not creative people," he says.

While Schmitt was producing in the '60s, he couldn't engineer the same project because of union restrictions. He returned to engineering in the '70s and became a Grammy machine, picking up the engineering award for George Benson's *Breezin'* in 1976 ("of the eight songs on the album, six were recorded on the first take"); Steely Dan's *Aja* (considered by many to be one of the best-engineered albums ever) in 1977, and "FM (No Static At All)" in 1978.

In the '70s Schmitt produced the great first Hot Tuna album (the punch was spiked with LSD at the club where the record was recorded, and everyone got dosed), co-produced two classic platinum Jackson Browne albums—*For Everyman* (with "Take It Easy" and "Redneck Friend") and *Late for the Sky* (No. 14, with "Fountain of Sorrow" and "For a Dancer")—in addition to a series of albums with Al Jarreau: *We Got By, Glow, Look to the Rainbow: Live in Europe* (Schmitt's favorite Jarreau), and *All Fly Home*. He also co-produced (with Young and David Briggs; see entry) Neil Young's quirky *On the Beach* (No. 16).

Schmitt struck Grammy treasure again in 1982 for engineering *Toto IV* (an album that sounded great but said very little), and he primarily concentrated on engineering throughout the decade, working with heavy hitters of every uniform: Michael Franks, Larry Carlton, Kenny Rogers, Kenny G, George Benson, Ruben Blades, Dr. John, and on and on.

In the '90s, forever young and busier than ever, Schmitt has balanced engineering with production. He has engineered for Frank Sinatra, Bob James, Shirley Horn, Michael Bolton, Diana Ross, Milt Jackson, Barbra Streisand, Diana Krall, Jon Secada, Carly Simon, Celine Dion, and Brandy and picked up two more Grammys: for Natalie Cole's *Unforgettable* in 1991 and Quincy Jones' (see entry) *Q's Jook Joint* in 1996. He has also produced for Joe Sample, Diane Schuur, and Tony Darren.

Unlike others who pine for the past, Schmitt embraces modern technology. "All of this technology allows you to go back in and tune a vocal, or punch in a part, or rearrange things after the fact, and makes the recording process more creative than it used to be." Schmitt was elected into the Engineers Hall of Fame in 1997; he has now produced, engineered, or mixed over 150 gold and platinum albums. His place in history is secure. —ERIC OLSEN

Astronauts: "Baja," RCA Victor, 1963 • *Surfin' with the Astronauts*, RCA Victor, 1963 • *Competition Coupe*, RCA Victor, 1964 • *Rarities*, Bear Family, 1991.

Benoit, David: *American Landscape,* GRP, 1997.

Benson, George: w/ the Count Basie Orchestra, *Big Boss Band,* Warner Bros., 1990.

Browne, Jackson: *For Everyman,* Asylum, 1973 • *Late for the Sky,* Asylum, 1974 • *The Next Voice You Hear: The Best of Jackson Browne,* Elektra/Asylum, 1997.

Cooke, Sam: *Sam Cooke at the Copa,* Abkco, 1964, 1987 • "Shake," RCA, 1965 • *Sam Cooke's Night Beat,* Abkco, 1995.

Darren, Tony: *Sun Song,* Telarc, 1998.

Dr. John: "No More Mr. Nice Guy," Sony Wonder, 1994 (*Swan Princess* soundtrack).

Eddy, Duane: *Twangy Guitar, Silky Strings/Water Skiing,* One Way, 1962, 1998 • *Twangin' the Golden Hits/Twangin' Country Songs,* One Way, 1963, 1998 • *The Best of Duane Eddy/Lonely Guitar,* One Way, 1964, 1998.

Feliciano, Jose: *Light My Fire,* Prism, 1992, 1997.

Fisher, Eddie: "Games That Lovers Play," RCA, 1966 • *Games That Lovers Play,* RCA, 1966 • "People Like You," RCA, 1967 • *People Like You,* RCA, 1967.

Go Go's: *Swim with the Go Go's,* RCA, 1964.

Horn, Paul: *Dream Machine,* Tomato, 1978.

Hot Tuna: *Hot Tuna,* RCA, 1970.

Jarreau, Al: *We Got By,* Warner Bros., 1975 • *Glow,* Warner Bros., 1976 • *Look to the Rainbow: Live in Europe,* Warner Bros., 1977 • *All Fly Home,* Warner Bros., 1978 • *Best Of,* Warner Bros., 1996.

Jefferson Airplane: *After Bathing at Baxter's,* RCA, 1967 • "Ballad of You and Me and Pooneil," RCA, 1967 • "Watch Her Ride," RCA, 1967 • "Crown of Creation," RCA, 1968 • *Crown of Creation,* RCA, 1968 • "Greasy Heart," RCA, 1968 • *Bless Its Pointed Little Head,* RCA, 1969 • "Volunteers," RCA, 1970 • *Volunteers,* RCA, 1970 • and offshoots, *Flight Log (1966–1976)* (7 tracks), Grunt, 1977 • *The Best Of,* RCA, 1980 • *White Rabbit and Other Hits,* RCA, 1990 • *Jefferson Airplane Loves You,* RCA, 1992.

Montenegro, Hugo: *Original Music from the Man from U.N.C.L.E,* Razor & Tie, 1966, 1997 • *Music from "A Fistful of Dollars," "For a Few Dollars More," and "The Good, the Bad and the Ugly,"* RCA, 1968, 1995 • *The Good, the Bad and the Ugly,* RCA, 1992.

Red Eye: *Red Eye,* Pentagram, 1971.

Red Wilder Blue: *Red Wilder Blue,* Pentagram, 1972.

Sample, Joe: *Old Places Old Faces,* Warner Bros., 1996 • *The Best of Joe Sample,* Warner Bros., 1998.

Schuur, Diane: *Love Walked In,* GRP, 1996 • *Blues for Schuur,* GRP, 1997.

Spirit: *Farther Along,* Mercury, 1976.

T.I.M.E.: *Smooth Ball,* Liberty, 1969.

Traylor, Jack, and Steelwind: *Child of Nature,* Grunt, 1971.

Turnquist Remedy: *Turnquist Remedy,* Pentagram, 1970.

Young, Neil: *On the Beach,* Reprise, 1974.

Rob Schnapf

See TOM ROTHROCK AND ROB SCHNAPF

Ken Scott

Ken Scott, who began his career in the mid-'60s at EMI's Abbey Road Studios in London, still calls the Beatles his biggest influence. "They were always into experimentation," says Scott, who worked with the band during the *White Album* period. "They didn't care how something worked, they were interested in what it did and what you could get out of it. And that's always been my whole thing."

A London native who later engineered and produced projects for David Bowie (see entry), Elton John, and Supertramp, Scott says "Yer Blues," a track from the *White Album,* is an example of the Beatles' singular approach. "We were messing around with some vocals on one of George's tracks and trying ridiculous things and I turned to [John] Lennon and said, 'The way you guys are recording, you'll want to record next door next.' He just looked at me and once we'd finished doing the vocal he said, 'Okay, now let's do "Yer Blues,"' and I want to record it next door.' I thought, 'What have I let myself in for?'"

The *White Album,* Scott adds, also demonstrated the Beatles' newfound independence. Longtime Beatles producer George Martin (see entry) was out of town for many of the sessions, leaving assistant Chris Thomas (see entry) in charge. Moreover, the band was working individually with Thomas, Scott, Geoff Emerick (see entry), and Ken Townsend on many of the tracks, requiring a number of hands to capture it all. "We really let it rip the last night of doing the *White Album* because it had to be finished," Scott recalls. "George [Martin] was leaving to come over to the States and he had to bring the tapes with him. I remember being in Studio Two mixing; George was downstairs in Number One [studio] with John listening to some of the mixes of John's stuff; Paul [McCartney; see entry] was probably in Number Three with Ken doing something; we were just using all of them."

In search of greener pastures at the end of 1968, Scott joined an independent studio, Trident. He soon became enamored of Trident's innovative approach to recording and its laid-back atmosphere, a stark contrast to EMI's clinical surroundings. "The first time I'd heard of Trident was with the Beatles working on 'Hey Jude,' " Scott says. "They had wanted to move from 4-track to 8-track, and Trident was the first independent studio in England to have 8-track, so they just booked some time to see what it was like. I went down to Trident the last day to hear the mix of 'Hey Jude' and was absolutely blown away."

Scott is also proud of his contributions to Jeff Beck's 1968 classic *Truth,* even though he says Mickie Most (see entry) should not have received sole production credit for the project. "[Most] turned up for the mixes, but it was Peter Grant who went on to Led Zeppelin fame [as manager] who was there for all the recording sessions," Scott says.

During his Trident years, Scott worked with producer Gus Dudgeon (see entry) on a string of albums by Elton John, including *Madman Across the Water, Honky Chateau,* and *Don't Shoot Me (I'm Only the Piano Player).* Scott says what impressed him most about John was his prolific writing ability. "Bernie [Taupin] used to go up early every night to his room at the beginning of the whole project and he'd just sit there and write," Scott remembers. "He'd bring down what he'd written the next morning and give it to Elton, who would go through the songs and try to work things out on the piano. [John] literally wrote 'Rocket Man' in 10 minutes; it was astounding."

Scott's first production, in tandem with David Bowie, was Bowie's *Hunky Dory* album. That led to projects with Procol Harum, Lindisfarne, Happy the Man, Stanley Clarke, Billy Cobham, and Supertramp, including that band's 1975 tour de force, *Crime of the Century* (No. 4 U.K.), one of the finest albums of the '70s. That project received so much praise that Scott had difficulty following up. "It was a problem for me at that time because I thought I'd achieved perfection," Scott explains. "Nothing seemed to match up with that. We had to at least try and equal or do better on *Crisis? What Crisis?* (No. 20 U.K.) For me there are a couple of tracks that are better than anything on *Crime,* but as an overall album it didn't flow as well."

Scott then moved to the States and hooked up with such acts as Devo, the Dixie Dregs, and the Tubes. Although the Tubes were more successful after they signed with Capitol Records, Scott claims the band's essence was lost when the label brought in other musicians to replace everyone but Fee Waybill. "They had their biggest hit on Capitol—but it wasn't the Tubes," Scott insists. "To me, a producer's job is to bring out the best in the band in the way they want to be brought out. I don't quite understand the mentality of 'Let's sign a band and then completely change them.' " —Ben Cromer

Batteau, David: *Happy in Hollywood,* A&M, 1976.

Beck, Jeff: *There and Back,* Epic, 1980 • *Beckology,* Legacy/Epic, 1991, 1995.

Bowie, David: "Changes," RCA, 1972 • *Hunky Dory,* RCA, 1972 • "Star Man/Suffragette City," RCA, 1972 • "The Jean Genie," RCA, 1972 • *Ziggy Stardust and the Spiders from Mars,* RCA, 1972 • *Aladdin Sane,* RCA, 1973 • "Drive-In Saturday," RCA, 1973 • "Life on Mars," RCA, 1973 • *Pinups,* RCA, 1973 • "Sorrow," RCA, 1973 • *Changesbowie,* Rykodisc, 1984, 1990 • *Bowie: The Singles 1969–1993,* Rykodisc, 1993.

Clarke, Stanley: *Journey to Love,* Nemperor, 1975 • *School Days,* Nemperor, 1976.

Cobham, Billy: *Crosswinds,* Atlantic, 1974 • *Total Eclipse,* Atlantic, 1974 • *Shabazz,* Atlantic, 1975.

Dada: "Dizz Knee Land," IRS, 1992 • *Puzzle,* IRS, 1992.

Devo: *Duty Now for the Future,* Warner Bros., 1979 • *Greatest Hits,* Warner Bros., 1990 • *Greatest Misses,* Warner Bros., 1990.

Dixie Dregs: *What If,* Capricorn, 1978 • *Night of Living Dregs,* Capricorn, 1979.

Esperanto: *Esperanto Rock Orchestra,* A&M, 1973.

Gamma: *Gamma 1,* Elektra, 1979.

Happy the Man: *Crafty Hands,* Arista, 1978.

Harrison, Don: *Not Far from Free,* Mercury, 1977.

Kansas: "Play the Game Tonight," Kirshner, 1982 • *Vinyl Confessions,* Kirshner, 1982.

Level 42: "Hot Water," Polydor, 1986 • *World Machine,* Polydor, 1986 • *The Remix Collection,* Connoisseur, 1996.

Mahavishnu Orchestra: *Visions of the Emerald Beyond,* Columbia, 1975.

Michalski and Oosterveen: *M&O,* CBS, 1979.

Missing Persons: "Destination Unknown," EMI, 1982, 1993 (*Living in Oblivion: The 80s Greatest Hits,* Vol. 2) • *Missing Persons* (EP), Capitol, 1982 • *Spring Session M,* Capitol, 1982 • "Words," Capitol, 1982 • "Walking in L.A.," Capitol, 1983 • "Windows," Capitol, 1983 • *The Best Of,* Capitol, 1987.

Moore, Tim: *High Contact,* Asylum, 1979.

Pilot: *Pilot,* RCA, 1972.

Rads: *Life's a Gamble,* EMI, 1985.

Rubber Rodeo: *Heartbreak Highway,* Mercury, 1986.

Sheriff, Jamie: *No Heroes,* Polydor, 1980.

Supertramp: *Crime of the Century,* A&M, 1974 • "Dreamer," A&M, 1974 • "Bloody Well Right," A&M, 1975 • *Crisis, What Crisis?,* A&M, 1975.

3-D: *3-D,* Polydor, 1980.

Tubes, The: *Young And Rich,* A&M, 1976 • *T.R.A.S.H. (Tubes Rarities and Smash Hits),* A&M, 1981.

White Heart: *Inside,* Curb, 1995.

Erick Sermon

Who could have predicted where "You Gots to Chill" would lead? That EPMD classic, from the rap duo's 1988 debut album *Strictly Business,* was the first shot from producer-rapper Erick Sermon (born November 25, 1968, in Bayshore, New York), and the hip-hop community should be thankful it wasn't the last.

"You Gots to Chill," co-produced by Sermon and his partner Parrish Smith (EPMD stands for "Erick and Parrish Making Dollars"), would become the trademark of the group, of Sermon solo, and even of Sermon's outside productions.

A thick, old-school funk beat—Zapp's "More Bounce to the Ounce," to be exact—anchored "You Gots to Chill," which was also marked by the duo's deadpan delivery. The duo stuck to that blueprint through several follow-up albums, including *Unfinished Business, Business as Usual,* and *Business Never Personal* (No. 14) and hit singles such as "Crossover," "Head Banger," and "Rampage."

That blueprint would also carry over into Sermon's work without Smith. An unexplained dispute between the two led to the break-up of EPMD after the 1992 release of *Business Never Personal.* The two didn't reunite for five years.

Sermon didn't suffer that much in the interim, however, either as a rapper or as a producer. He went on to run his own Def Squad crew of acts, including successful rappers such as Keith Murray, Redman, and K Solo. Sermon worked some of that old EMPD magic on each of these acts, especially Redman and Murray.

Redman has had three successful Sermon-produced albums: *Whut? Thee Album, Dare Iz a Darkside* (No. 13), and *Muddy Waters.* Songs that helped establish him include "Blow Your Mind," "How High?," "Whateva Man," and "Time 4 Sum Aksion." "Get Lifted" and "Rhyme," from the albums *The Most Beautifullest Thing in the World* and *Enigma,* made a name for Murray.

Stepping outside of Def Squad, Sermon scored a slam dunk for basketball star Shaquille O'Neal with "I'm Outstanding." And in 1996, Sermon dove into R&B, producing SWV's "On & On," and most of the songs on Alphonso Hunter's *Blacka Da Berry.*

In 1997, to the surprise of nearly everyone in rap, EPMD reunited for the *Back to Business* album, including the single, "The Joint." —KEVIN JOHNSON

Baka Boys: *Quick Mix,* Thump, 1995.

Blackstreet: *Blackstreet,* Interscope, 1994 • "Booti Call," Interscope, 1994.

Boss: *Born Gangstaz* (2 tracks), DJ West/Chaos, 1993.

Bounty Killer: *My Xperience,* VP, 1996.

Clinton, George: "If Anybody Gets Funked Up (It's Gonna Be You)," 550 Music/Epic, 1996 • *The Awesome Power of a Fully Operational Mothership,* 550 Music/Epic, 1996.

Def Squad: *El Niño,* Def Jam, 1998 • "Full Cooperation," Def Jam, 1998.

Dr. Dre and Ed Lover: "It's Going Down," Relativity, 1995.

EPMD: *Strictly Business,* Priority, 1988 • "You Gots to Chill," Fresh, 1988 • *Unfinished Business,* Priority, 1989 • *Business as Usual,* Def Jam, 1991 • "Gold Digger," Def Jam, 1991 • featuring LL Cool J, "Rampage," Def Jam, 1991 • *Business Never Personal,* RAL/Chaos, 1992 • "Crossover," Def Jam, 1992 • "Head Banger," Def Jam, 1993 • *Back in Business,* Def Jam, 1997 • "Richter Scale," Def Jam, 1997 • "The Joint," Def Jam, 1997.

Heavy D and the Boyz: *Nuttin' but Love,* Uptown, 1994.

Hollister, Dave: "Weekend," Dreamworks, 1998.

Hunter, Alfonzo: *Blacka Da Berry,* Def Squad, 1996 • "Just the Way (Playas Play)," Def Squad, 1996 • "Weekend Thang," Def Squad, 1997.

Illegal: *The Illegal,* Rowdy, 1993 • *The Untold Truth* (2 tracks), Rowdy, 1993 • "We Getz Busy," Rowdy, 1993.

Jamal: "Keep It Real," Rowdy, 1996.

Jodeci: "Feenin' " (remix), Uptown/MCA, 1994.

K Solo: *Time's Up,* Atlantic, 1992.

Kapeon: "No Jurisdiction," Penalty, 1995.

LL Cool J: featuring Method Man, Redman, DMX, Canibus, and Master P, "4, 3, 2 ,1," Def Jam, 1997 • *Phenomenon,* Def Jam, 1997.

MC Breed: *To da Beat Ch'all,* Wrap, 1996.

Murray, Keith: "The Most Beautifullest Thing in This World," Jive, 1994 • *The Most Beautifullest Thing in This World,* Jive, 1994 • "Get Lifted," Jive, 1995 • *Enigma,* Jive, 1996 • "The Rhyme," Jive, 1996.

O'Neal, Shaquille: *Shaq Diesel* (3 tracks), Jive, 1993 • "I'm Outstanding," Jive, 1994 • *Shaq Fu: Da Return,* Jive, 1995 • *The Best Of,* Jive, 1996.

Redman: "Blow Your Mind," Def Jam, 1992 • *Whut? Thee Album* (11 tracks), RAL, 1992 • "Time 4 Sum Aksion," Def Jam, 1993 • "Tonight's Da Night," Def Jam, 1993 • *Dare Iz a Darkside* (3 tracks), RAL, 1994 • "Can't Wait," Def Jam, 1995 • w/ Method Man, "How High," Def Jam, 1995 • *Muddy Waters,* Def Jam, 1996 • "Pick It Up," Def Jam, 1997 • "Whateva Man," Def Jam/Mercury, 1997.

Run-D.M.C.: *Down with the King* (1 track), Profile, 1993.

Sermon, Erick: *No Pressure,* Def Jam/Chaos, 1993 • "Stay Real," Def Jam/Chaos, 1993 • "Bomdigi," Def Jam/Chaos, 1995 • *Bomdigi* (EP), Def Jam/Chaos, 1995 •

Double or Nothing, Def Jam/Chaos, 1995 • "Welcome," Def Jam, 1996 • w/ Keith Murray and Redman, "Rapper's Delight," Priority, 1997.

Shadz of Lingo: *A View to a Kill,* Limp, 1994.

Super Cat: "Girlstown," Columbia, 1995 • *The Struggle Continues,* Columbia, 1995.

SWV: *New Beginning,* RCA, 1996.

Tha Truth: *Makin' Moves . . . Everyday,* Priority, 1997.

COLLECTIONS

Insomnia: The Erick Sermon Compilation, Interscope, 1996.

Robert Shakespeare

See SLY AND ROBBIE

Harold Shedd

As a producer, Harold Shedd has been responsible for launching some of country music's most unusual and enduring acts. He produced 13 albums on country supergroup Alabama and introduced K.T. Oslin and Shania Twain to country audiences. During his career on Nashville's Music Row, he's worked with Dobie Gray, Glen Campbell, Roger Miller, Mel Tillis, and Toby Keith.

The Bremen, Georgia, native played in a band as a youth, then switched to radio, working his way up from on-air personality to the owner of stations in three Southern cities. In 1972, he sold his radio stations and moved to Nashville. "I left radio to come here and was mainly doing radio and TV commercials, writing, producing, and selling jingles," he recalls. "I built a recording studio and produced jingles and it evolved into record production. The main difference," he says, "is that a great song is about four minutes, and in a jingle you try to be informative and creative in 30 to 60 seconds. In a song you try to do that same thing, but it's more relating experiences in songs than jingles. A great jingle is really a mini hit. That was always my approach to it."

Shedd began his career as a record producer in the late '70s, working with acts on MDJ, an independent label that launched Wildcountry, the Myrtle Beach, South Carolina, bar band that ultimately evolved into Alabama. "We had an album done and put out a couple of singles off it," Shedd recalls. "[There was] a song called 'I Wanna Come Over' that was originally on Limbo International records. MDJ bought it and re-released it on MDJ. It went to No. 32 in *Billboard*. Then we released 'My Home's in Alabama.' It was an interesting time because originally the song was over eight minutes long and we edited it and got it to five minutes, released it, and it went to No. 17." These were country hits.

Then RCA picked up the group and the rest is history. "The first RCA release was 'Tennessee River' in 1980, and it went to No. 1 and we had 21 in succession after that," Shedd says. "It was kind of a fairy-tale story because when we made the deal on the first Alabama album, I think they paid me $25,000 for that album and it sold over 2 million."

To what does Shedd attribute Alabama's success? "They were the first group in country music, other than Bob Wills and the Texas Playboys, that played and wrote their own music," he says. "They had some great songs and everybody was dedicated to the cause."

Shedd continued to work with Alabama until 1988,

when the Academy of Country Music named them Group of the Decade. He then assumed a post as vice president of A&R for Mercury Records Nashville. The first act he signed was the Kentucky Headhunters. He was also responsible for signing Billy Ray Cyrus, David Daniel, Sammy Kershaw, Shania Twain, and Toby Keith. He became president of the label in 1993 and reactivated the Polydor label (which was eventually taken over by A&M).

Shedd resigned his post at Mercury in mid-1996, citing "creative differences" and saying "sometimes it's time to move on." He admits to being somewhat frustrated by changes in the industry. "The toughest part for me was the fact that music, first of all, is an emotional experience. It's not like selling cars," he says. "And it's got to the point where it's consulted and researched to death. It's killing the business as we knew it."

But Shedd isn't giving up. At press time, he and former Mercury Nashville vice president Paul Lucks were planning to launch their own label, and he was looking at talent as far away as Spain and Australia to fill its roster. Shedd also plans to develop a pilot for a new sitcom. He also continues to own and operate the Music Mill, a studio and publishing complex that has become one of Music Row's most popular facilities since he opened it in 1982.

Shedd says he's enjoyed working with the artists he's been associated with and has learned a lot along the way. "The guy I learned the most from in the studio was Glen Campbell," he relates. "He's just so musical and so spontaneous and creative that you have to pay attention to keep up. Roger Miller was the same way. He was just a genius when it came to writing and performing.

"Randy Owen [of Alabama] is one of the really great singers. The thing that made him different and unique is that he never came back to re-sing anything. When the day ended, Randy's vocals were done. Now singers have to come back and sing for two or three weeks."

Shedd enjoys working with different personalities. "To get the peak performance out of an artist, you have to be on the same channel, and be able to communicate and understand what they are trying to achieve," he says. "You have to make an artist comfortable and have an environment in which they can be creative and do their best." —DEBORAH EVANS PRICE

Alabama: "My Home's in Alabama," MDJ, 1980 • *My Home's in Alabama*, RCA, 1980 • "Tennessee River," RCA, 1980 • "Why Lady Why," RCA, 1980 • "Feel So Right," RCA, 1981 • *Feels So Right*, RCA, 1981 • "Love in the First Degree," RCA, 1981 • "Old Flame," RCA, 1981 • "Close Enough to Perfect," RCA, 1982 • "Mountain Music," RCA, 1982 • *Mountain Music*, RCA, 1982 • "Take Me Down," RCA, 1982 • "Dixieland Delight," RCA, 1983 • "Lady Down on Love," RCA, 1983 • "The Closer You Get," RCA, 1983 • *The Closer You Get*, RCA, 1983 • "If You're Gonna Play in Texas (You Gotta Have a Fiddle in the Band)," RCA, 1984 • "Roll on (Eighteen Wheeler)," RCA, 1984 • *Roll On*, RCA, 1984 • "When We Make Love," RCA, 1984 • *Alabama Christmas*, RCA, 1985, 1992 • "(There's a) Fire in the Night," RCA, 1985 • "40 Hour Week (For a Livin')," RCA, 1985 • *40 Hour Week*, RCA, 1985 • "Can't Keep a Good Man Down," RCA, 1985 • "There's No Way," RCA, 1985 • *Greatest Hits*, RCA, 1986 • "She and I," RCA, 1986 • *The Touch*, RCA, 1986 • "Touch Me When We're Dancing," RCA, 1986 • *Just Us*, RCA, 1987 • "Tar Top," RCA, 1987 • "You've Got the Touch," RCA, 1987 • "Face to Face," RCA, 1988 • "Fallin' Again," RCA, 1988 • *Live*, RCA, 1988 • *Greatest Hits*, Vol. 2, RCA, 1991 • *Gonna Have a Party . . . Live*, RCA, 1993 • *In the Beginning*, RCA, 1994 • "Angels Among Us," RCA, 1995 • *Super Hits*, RCA, 1996 • *Super Hits*, Vol. 2, RCA, 1998.

Alexander, Daniele: *First Move*, Mercury, 1989 • "Where Did the Moon Go Wrong," Mercury, 1989 • w/ Butch Baker, "It Wasn't You, It Wasn't Me," Mercury, 1990 • *I Dream in Color*, Mercury, 1991.

Baker, Butch: "Party People," Mercury, 1988 • *We Will*, Mercury, 1989.

Brody, Lane: "He Burns Me Up," EMI, 1985 • *Lane Brody*, EMI, 1985.

Campbell, Glen: "A Lady Like You," Atlantic, 1984 • *Letter to Home*, Atlantic, 1984 • "(Love Always) Letter to Home," Atlantic, 1985 • "Call Home," Atlantic, 1986 • "Cowpoke," Atlantic, 1986 • *Gentle on My Mind: The Collection, 1962–1989*, Razor & Tie, 1997.

Chance, Jeff: "Hopelessly Falling," Curb, 1988 • *Picture on the Wall*, Mercury, 1991 • *Walk Softly on the Bridges*, Mercury, 1992.

Comeaux, Amie: *Moving Out*, A&M Nashville, 1994 • "Who's She to You," A&M Nashville, 1994.

Corbin/Hanner: "Concrete Cowboy," Mercury, 1991 • "I Will Stand by You," Mercury, 1992 • "Just Another Hill," Mercury, 1992 • *Just Another Hill*, Mercury, 1992 "Any Road," Mercury, 1993.

Daniel, Davis: *Davis Daniel*, Polydor, 1994 • "I Miss Her Missing Me," Mercury, 1994 • "William and Mary," Polydor, 1994 • "Tyler," A&M Nashville, 1995 • *I Know a Place*, A&M, 1996.

Gray, Dobie: *From Where I Stand*, Capitol, 1986 • "That's One to Grow On," Capitol, 1986 • "The Dark Side of Town," Capitol, 1986.

Gregory, Clinton: *Clinton Gregory*, A&M Nashville, 1995 • "You Didn't Miss a Thing," A&M Nashville, 1995.

Hurley, Libby: "Don't Get Me Started," Epic, 1987 • "You Just Watch Me," Epic, 1988.

Keith, Toby: "A Little Less Talk and a Lot More Action," Mercury, 1993 • "He Ain't Worth Missing," Mercury, 1993 • "Should've Been a Cowboy," Mercury, 1993 • *Toby Keith*, Mercury, 1993 • *Boomtown*, Polydor, 1994 • "Upstairs Downtown," A&M Nashville, 1994 • "Who's That Man," Polydor, 1994 • "Wish I Didn't Know Now," Mercury, 1994 • "Big Ol' Truck," A&M Nashville, 1995 • *Christmas to Christmas*, Polydor Nashville, 1995 • "Santa I'm Right Here," Mercury, 1995.

Knight, Jeff: *Easy Street*, Mercury, 1992 • *They've Been Talkin' About Me*, Mercury, 1992.

Mandrell, Louise: "Do I Have to Say Goodbye," RCA, 1987 • *The Best Of*, BNA, 1994.

McEntire, Reba: *My Kind of Country*, MCA, 1984 • "How Blue," MCA, 1985 • "Somebody Should Leave," MCA, 1985 • *Greatest Hits*, MCA, 1987.

Normaltown Flyers: *The Normaltown Flyers*, Mercury, 1991 • *Country Boy's Dream*, Mercury, 1992.

Oslin, K.T.: "80's Ladies," RCA, 1987 • *80's Ladies*, RCA, 1987 • "Do Ya," RCA, 1987 • "I'll Always Come Back," RCA, 1988 • *This Woman*, RCA, 1988 • "Didn't Expect It to Go Down This Way," RCA, 1989 • "Hold Me," RCA, 1989 • *Love in a Small Town*, RCA, 1990 • *Greatest Hits: Songs from an Aging Sex Bomb*, RCA, 1993 • *New Way Home*, RCA, 1993.

Reeves, Ronna: *Only the Heart*, Mercury, 1991 • "The More I Learn (The Less I Understand About Love)," Mercury, 1992 • *The More I Learn*, Mercury, 1992 • "We Can Hold Our Own," Mercury, 1992 • "What If You're Wrong," Mercury, 1992 • "He's My Weakness," Mercury, 1993 • "Never Let Him See Me Cry," Mercury, 1993 • *What Comes Naturally*, Mercury, 1993.

Tillis, Mel: w/ Glen Campbell, "Slow Nights," MCA, 1984 • "California Road," RCA, 1985 • "You Done Me Wrong," RCA, 1985 • "You'll Come Back (You Always Do)," Mercury, 1988.

Twain, Shania: "Dance with the One That Brought You," Mercury, 1993 • *Shania Twain*, Mercury, 1993 • "What Made You Say That," Mercury, 1993.

Twister Alley: "Nothing in Common But Love," Mercury, 1993 • *Twister Alley*, Mercury, 1993 • "Young Love," Mercury, 1994.

Wildcountry: "I Wanna Come Over," MJD, 1979.

Williams, Becky: *Becky Williams*, Mercury, 1994.

Wright, Chely: "He's a Good Ole Boy," A&M Nashville, 1994 • "'Till I Was Loved by You," A&M Nashville, 1994 • *Woman in the Moon*, A&M Nashville, 1994 • "Listenin' to the Radio," A&M Nashville, 1995 • "Sea of Cowboy Hats," A&M Nashville, 1995 • *Right in the Middle of It*, A&M Nashville, 1996.

Billy Sherrill

Many country fans would call George Jones' hit, "He Stopped Loving Her Today" (No. 1 country) the greatest country song ever recorded. They have producer Billy Sherrill to thank for that and other hits, such as David Houston's "Almost Persuaded," Charlie Rich's "Behind Closed Doors," Ray Charles and Willie Nelson's "Seven Spanish Angels," and Tammy Wynette's "Stand by Your Man" and "D-I-V-O-R-C-E" (all No. 1).

Sherrill was born November 5, 1936, in Phil Campbell, Alabama, about 30 miles south of Muscle Shoals. He got his start in the music business performing in a rock 'n' roll group called the Fairlanes with Rick Hall (see entry), who also went on to become a successful producer. "We had no hits," says Sherrill of the Fairlanes. "We were lucky to make $75 a week. We didn't even have a contract."

He moved to Nashville in the early '60s and worked at a little studio. "Sam Phillips [see entry] bought it and everybody left," he recalls. "I stayed and started working for Sam and started making my own little records. I'd play all the instruments and Sam gave me the run of the studio. [It was] Sam Phillips Recording Studio. I never did do the Memphis thing. His big operation was in Memphis, the Sun Records thing. I came along in a whole different division over here. I was kind of like the manager, the engineer, the janitor, and everything else. There was only one guy working and that was me."

Phillips became Sherrill's mentor. "I learned everything from Sam," Sherrill says. "He taught me more than any person. He taught me what was important, what wasn't important. I loved him. And when you were around him, time stood still. Sam Phillips—once they made him, they broke the mold. He told me not to be a perfectionist," Sherrill recalls. "If there's a little distortion on the record, so what? Nobody will ever hear it. Don't worry about 10,000, 12,000 cycles because a radio station rolls off at four and nobody can hear it but dogs. If it doesn't sound good on a little $2 kitchen radio, don't hype it up and turn your speakers up and just all kinds of things like that. He's the best."

Against Phillips's advice, Sherrill took a job with Epic Records, following Jerry Kennedy's (see entry) return from there to resume working with his friend Shelby Singleton at the Smash and Mercury labels. "I called Sam and told him I was going to Epic Records. He said, 'Billy boy, it's a bad mistake.' He said 'You've got a good job here with old Sam forever, but once you get there, they'll cut your throat in seconds. All them New York guys up there aren't like us.' I said, 'Well, I'll have to give it a shot.' And that's the way I got started. I was at Epic a long time, 15 years or so.

"Then Bob Johnston [see entry], who was A&R for Columbia, quit and they asked me to do both, and I said, 'Why not?' So I did them both for a while and it was fun. Then it ceased being fun. So I quit." His contract expired and he burned out.

Musical talent doesn't count in being a producer, Sherrill says, "just an ear for what you think [people will like]. In fact, I think having musical talent is a detriment. If you can play or sing, that doesn't mean anything, even though I think the greatest country producer in the world was Owen Bradley [see entry], and he's a good musician. I think the ability to figure out if anybody is going to buy this [is important]. If it knocks all the musicians out in the studio, then you might as well throw it away because nobody is going to buy it. It's figuring out what's commercial."

Sherrill honed that talent to a fine art. He's the man responsible for bringing Tammy Wynette to the attention of the world. "She came in and sang me a song, and I said, 'Hey, that's pretty good, but I don't think the song is that strong.' It was like I just broke her heart. I told her I wasn't jiving her and that I really loved the way she sang, but I didn't have any songs for her."

The next day Sherrill tried to pick up a record called "Apartment #9" by a male artist on an independent label. When they couldn't reach an agreement, Sherrill decided to cut the song on Wynette. "I called her and asked her if she wanted to make a session the next morning. She said, 'Don't kid me. I'm not in the mood.' I said, 'Be at my office tomorrow morning. I found a song.' We made 'Apartment #9' and that was it."

Sherrill always had a knack for choosing hit singles—even when his artists didn't agree. "George Richey [Wynette's husband] said she cried when they told her we were going to release 'Another Lonely Song' because I made her say 'damn' in the record, and it broke her heart," says Sherrill. "She thought she was going to lose all her fans. I called her and told her she was out of her mind, and I wouldn't do anything to hurt her career, and she got over it. I told her she couldn't say 'darn' because it wouldn't rhyme with 'am.' So we did it and it worked out for the best."

Sherrill also says George Jones didn't think "He Stopped Loving Her Today" would be a hit. "He said, 'Ain't nobody gonna buy that morbid S.O.B.," recalls Sherrill. "I said, 'Well nobody may buy it, but it's your next single."

Sherrill preferred to work one artist at a time. "Larry Butler was a good friend of mine and he did four, five, or six at one time," Sherrill says. "He was doing Bobby Goldsboro and Kenny Rogers and stuff. That way you can't get a reading on things. I have to get it over with and done and wrap it up and look around and say who's next."

Sherrill chose to give the artists he worked with room to be creative. When it came to producing Jones, Sherrill says, "I turned it on and let it go. You can't push a rope. It's like trying to push a piece of spaghetti or something. You have to give George his space and let him do his thing."

A key to making hit records is great songs. "I had a lot of good buddies that wrote a lot of good songs at Tree Music and Combine," Sherrill says. "I was very lucky to find good songs. And I had a bunch of good co-writers, so if we couldn't find them we'd write them. . . . I'd call ol' Glenn Sutton and say, 'We have to do something; I have a session tomorrow and I have no songs.' So he'd come over and we'd write.

"We wrote a whole bunch of hits. All night long we'd spend writing. One morning I told my wife, Charlene, 'We wrote a song last night called "Almost Persuaded,"' and she said, 'Isn't that an old hymn?' I said, 'Yeah' but after I sang it to her, she said, 'You have to be kidding.' I said, 'I don't care. It's going to be David Houston's next single.' And it went to No. 1 for weeks. You never know. They said don't cut a waltz or anything over 2 minutes 30 seconds, and make sure the punch line is at the top right quick. And we broke all the rules. The punch line was 3 minutes into the song and it was a slow waltz. You never know what people will like."

Sherrill is effectively retired. "I don't know a thing about Music Row anymore," he says. "My office is here, but most of the time, I'm in Florida or on my boat. . . . I don't think it would be much fun anymore. I have a feeling it's not the same as it was 10 years ago."

He admits part of his disillusionment came because of his disagreement with CBS executives over his work with Shelby Lynne—as an independent producer. "She's the best singer I ever took into a studio," he says. "Whoever was up there [at the label] didn't like what I did with Shelby. So nothing ever happened and that was the straw that broke the camel's back." Sherrill says he gets called frequently to produce, but doesn't plan to unless something extraordinary comes along. —DEBORAH EVANS PRICE

Bishop, Joni: "Heart Out of Control," Columbia, 1987.
Cash, Johnny: *The Baron,* Columbia, 1981 • "The Chicken in Black," Columbia, 1984 • *Biggest Hits,* Columbia, 1987.

Charles, Ray: *Friendship,* Columbia, 1984 • w/ B.J. Thomas, "Rock and Roll Shoes," Columbia, 1984 • w/ George Jones, "We Didn't See a Thing," Columbia, 1984 • w/ Mickey Gilley, "It Ain't Gonna Worry My Mind," Columbia, 1985 • w/ Willie Nelson, "Seven Spanish Angels," Columbia, 1985 • w/ Hank Williams Jr., "Two Old Cats Like Us," Columbia, 1985 • "Dixie Moon," Columbia, 1986 • "The Pages of My Mind," Columbia, 1986 • *Genius and Soul: 50th Anniversary Collection,* Rhino, 1997 • and Friends, *Super Hits,* Columbia, 1998.

Coe, David Allan: *Greatest Hits,* Columbia, 1978 • *Human Emotions,* Columbia, 1978 • *Spectrum VII,* Columbia, 1979 • *Compass Point,* Columbia, 1980 • *I've Got Something to Say,* Columbia, 1980 • *Encore,* Columbia, 1981 • *Invictus (Means Unconquered),* Columbia, 1981 • *Tenessee Whiskey,* Columbia, 1981 • *D.A.C.,* Columbia, 1982 • *Rough Rider,* Columbia, 1982 • *Castles in the Sand,* Columbia, 1983 • *Hello in There,* Columbia, 1983 • "It's Great to Be Single Again," Columbia, 1984 • *Just Divorced,* Columbia, 1984 • "Mona Lisa Lost Her Smile," Columbia, 1984 • "Ride 'Em Cowboy," Kat Family, 1984 • "Don't Cry Darlin'," Columbia, 1985 • "I'm Gonna Hurt Her on the Radio," Columbia, 1985 • "She Used to Love Me a Lot," Columbia, 1985 • "A Country Boy (Who Rolled the Rock Away)," Columbia, 1986 • w/ Willie Nelson, "I've Already Cheated on You," Columbia, 1986 • "Need a Little Time Off for Bad Behavior," Columbia, 1987 • "Tanya Montana," Columbia, 1987 • *Super Hits,* Columbia, 1993 • *Super Hits,* Vol. 2, Columbia, 1996.

Costello, Elvis: *Almost Blue,* F-Beat/CBS, 1981 • *Best Of,* Columbia, 1985.

Dalton, Lacy J.: "Crazy Blue Eyes," Columbia, 1979 • "Hard Times," Columbia, 1980 • *Hard Times,* Columbia, 1980 • "Hillbilly Girl with the Blues," Columbia, 1980 • *Lacy J. Dalton,* Columbia, 1980 • "Losing Kind of Love," Columbia, 1980 • "Tennessee Waltz," Columbia, 1980 • "Everybody Makes Mistakes/Wild Turkey," Columbia, 1981 • "Takin' It Easy," Columbia, 1981 • *Takin' It Easy,* Columbia, 1981 • "Whisper," Columbia, 1981 • "16th Avenue," Columbia, 1982 • *16th Avenue,* Columbia, 1982 • "Slow Down," Columbia, 1982 • "Dream Baby (How Long Must I Dream)," Columbia, 1983 • *Dream Baby,* Columbia, 1983 • *Greatest Hits,* Columbia, 1983 • "Windin' Down," Columbia, 1983.

Duncan, Johnny: "Baby's Smile, Woman's Kiss," Columbia, 1971 • "One Night of Love," Columbia, 1971 • "There's Something About a Lady," Columbia, 1971 • "Fools," Columbia, 1972 • "Sweet Country Woman," Columbia, 1973 • "Talkin' with My Lady," Columbia, 1973 • "Stranger," Columbia, 1976 • *The Best of Johnny Duncan,* Columbia, 1976 • "Thinkin' of a Rendezvous," Columbia, 1976 • "A Song in the Night," Columbia, 1977 • *Come a*

Little Bit Closer, Columbia, 1977 • "It Couldn't Have Been Any Better," Columbia, 1977 • "Hello Mexico (And Adios Baby to You)," Columbia, 1978 • *Johnny Duncan's Greatest Hits,* Columbia, 1978 • "She Can Put Her Shoes Under My Bed (Anytime)," Columbia, 1978 • *The Best Is Yet to Come,* Columbia, 1978 • *See You When the Sun Goes Down,* Columbia, 1979 • "Slow Dancing," Columbia, 1979 • *Straight from Texas,* Columbia, 1979 • "The Lady in the Blue Mercedes," Columbia, 1979 • "Acapulco," Columbia, 1980 • "I'm Gonna Love You Tonight (In My Dreams)," Columbia, 1980 • *In My Dreams,* Columbia, 1980 • "Play Another Slow Song," Columbia, 1980 • "All Night Long," Columbia, 1981.

Duncan, Johnny, and Janie Frickie: "Come a Little Bit Closer," Columbia, 1977 • "He's out of My Life," Columbia, 1980 • *Nice 'n' Easy,* Columbia, 1980 • "Jo and the Cowboy," Columbia, 1975.

Fairchild, Barbara: *This Is Me,* Columbia, 1978.

Frickie, Janie: "What're You Doing Tonight," Columbia, 1977 • "Baby It's You," Columbia, 1978 • "Playin' Hard to Get," Columbia, 1978 • "Please Help Me I'm Falling" (In Love with You)," Columbia, 1978 • *Singer of Songs,* Columbia, 1978 • "But Love Me," Columbia, 1979 • "I'll Love Away Your Troubles for Awhile," Columbia, 1979 • "Let's Try Again," Columbia, 1979 • *Love Notes,* Columbia, 1979 • *From the Heart,* Columbia, 1980 • "Pass Me by (If You're Only Passing Through)," Columbia, 1980 • *Greatest Hits,* Columbia, 1989, 1992 • *See also* Duncan, Johnny, and Janie Frickie.

Goldberg, Barry: *Blowing My Mind,* Epic, 1966.

Griffith, Andy: *Somebody Bigger Than You and I,* Columbia, 1996.

Haggard, Merle: w/ George Jones, *A Taste of Yesterday's Wine,* Epic, 1982 • w/ George Jones, "Yesterday's Wine," Epic, 1982 • *His Epic Hits: First Eleven . . . To Be Continued,* Epic, 1984 • "Almost Persuaded," Epic, 1987 • *Greatest Hits of the 80's,* Epic, 1990 • *Super Hits,* Epic, 1993.

Harris, Emmylou: *Duets,* Reprise, 1990.

Houston, David: "Mountain of Love," Epic, 1963 • "Chickashay/Passing Through," Epic, 1964 • *David Houston,* Epic, 1964 • "Love Looks Good on You," Epic, 1964 • "One If for Him, Two If for Me," Epic, 1964 • "Livin' in a House Full of Love," Epic, 1965 • "Sweet, Sweet Judy," Epic, 1965 • "A Loser's Cathedral/Where Would I Go? (But to Her)," Epic, 1966 • "Almost Persuaded," Epic, 1966 • *Almost Persuaded,* Epic, 1966 • w/ Tammy Wynette, "My Elusive Dreams," Epic, 1967 • *My Elusive Dreams,* Epic, 1967 • "With One Exception," Epic, 1967 • "You Mean the World to Me," Epic, 1967 • "Already It's Heaven," Epic, 1968 • "Have a Little Faith," Epic, 1968 • w/ Tammy Wynette, "It's All Over," Epic, 1968 • "Where Love Used to Live," Epic, 1968 • "Baby,

Baby (I Know You're a Lady)," Epic, 1969 • *David,* Epic, 1969 • "I'm Down to My Last 'I Love You,' " Epic, 1969 • "My Woman's Good to Me," Epic, 1969 • w/ Barbara Mandrell, "After Closing Time," Epic, 1970 • *Baby, Baby,* Epic, 1970 • "Wonders of the Wine," Epic, 1970 • *Wonders of the Wine,* Epic, 1970 • *American Originals,* Columbia, 1989.

Jim and Jesse: *Berry Pickin',* Epic, 1969 • *Jim and Jesse: Bluegrass and More,* Bear Family, 1993.

Jones, George: "A Picture of Me Without You," Epic, 1972 • *A Picture of Me Without You,* Epic, 1972 • *George Jones,* Epic, 1972 • "Loving You Could Never Be Better," Epic, 1972 • "We Can Make It," Epic, 1972 • "Nothing Ever Hurt Me Half As Bad (As Losing You)," Epic, 1973 • *Nothing Ever Hurt Me Half As Bad (As Losing You), Epic, 1973* • *"Once You've Had the Best," Epic, 1973* • *"What My Woman Can't Do," Epic, 1973* • In a Gospel Way, Epic, 1974, 1997 • "The Door," Epic, 1974 • "The Grand Tour," Epic, 1974 • *The Grand Tour,* Epic, 1974 • "Memories of Us," Epic, 1975 • *Memories of Us,* Epic, 1975 • "These Days (I Barely Get By)," Epic, 1975 • *Alone Again,* Epic, 1976 • "Her Name Is . . . ," Epic, 1976 • "The Battle," Epic, 1976 • *The Battle,* Epic, 1976 • "You Always Look Your Best (Here in My Arms)," Epic, 1976 • *I Wanna Sing,* Epic, 1977 • "If I Could Put Them All Together (I'd Have You)," Epic, 1977 • "Old King Kong," Epic, 1977 • "Bartender's Blues," Epic, 1978 • *Bartender's Blues,* Epic, 1978 • "I'll Just Take It Out in Love," Epic, 1978 • *My Very Special Guests,* Epic, 1979 • "Someday My Day Will Come," Epic, 1979 • "He Stopped Loving Her Today," Epic, 1980 • *I Am What I Am,* Epic, 1980 • "If Drinkin' Don't Kill Me (Her Memory Will)," Epic, 1980 • "I'm Not Ready Yet," Epic, 1980 • *Encore,* Epic, 1981 • *I'm Still the Same Old Me,* Epic, 1981 • "Same Old Me," Epic, 1981 • "Still Doin' Time," Epic, 1981 • *Anniversary: Ten Years of Hits,* Epic, 1982 • *All-Time Greatest Hits,* Vol. 1, Epic, 1983 • "I Always Get Lucky with You," Epic, 1983 • *Jones Country,* Epic, 1983 • "Shine on (Shine All Your Love on Me)," Epic, 1983 • *Shine On,* Epic, 1983 • "Tennessee Whiskey," Epic, 1983 • *By Request,* Columbia, 1984 • *Ladies Choice,* Epic, 1984 • "She's My Rock," Epic, 1984 • *Who's Gonna Fill Their Shoes,* Epic, 1984 • "You've Still Got a Place in My Heart," Epic, 1984 • *You've Still Got a Place in My Heart,* Epic, 1984 • w/ Brenda Lee, "Hallelujah, I Love You So," Epic, 1985 • w/ Lacy J. Dalton, "Size Seven Round (Made of Gold)," Epic, 1985 • "The One I Loved Back Then (The Corvette Song)," Epic, 1985 • "Who's Gonna Fill Their Shoes," Epic, 1985 • "Somebody Wants Me out of the Way," Epic, 1986 • *Wine Colored Roses,* Epic, 1986 • "I Turn to You," Epic, 1987 • "The Right Left Hand," Epic, 1987 • *Too Wild Too Long,* Epic, 1987 • "Wine Colored Roses," Epic, 1987 • w/ Shelby Lynne, "If I Could Bottle This Up," Epic, 1988 •

"I'm a Survivor," Epic, 1988 • *One Woman Man,* Epic, 1988 • "The Bird," Epic, 1988 • "The Old Man No One Loves," Epic, 1988 • *First Time Live,* Epic, 1989 • "I'm a One Woman Man," Epic, 1989 • "Radio Lover," Epic, 1989 • "The King Is Gone (So Are You)," Epic, 1989 • "Writing on the Wall," Epic, 1989 • *Greatest Hits,* Epic, 1990 • *Hallelujah Weekend,* Columbia, 1990 • *Super Hits,* Epic, 1990 • *Friends in High Places,* Epic, 1991 • *Greatest Hits,* Vol. 2, Epic, 1992 • *Super Hits,* Vol. 2, Epic, 1993 • *The Spirit of Country: The Essential George Jones,* Legacy, 1994 • *Songs I Wanta Sing,* Sony Special, 1995 • See also Haggard, Merle.

Jones, George, and Johnny Paycheck: "Mabelline," Epic, 1978 • "You Can Have Her," Epic, 1979 • *Double Trouble,* Epic, 1980 • "When You're Ugly Like Us (You Just Naturally Got to Be Cool)," Epic, 1980 • "You Better Move On," Epic, 1981.

Jones, George, and Tammy Wynette: "Take Me," Epic, 1971 • *We Go Together,* Epic, 1971 • *Me And the First Lady,* Epic, 1972 • "Old Fashioned Singing," Epic, 1972 • "The Ceremony," Epic, 1972 • *We Love to Sing About Jesus,* Epic, 1972 • "Let's Build a World Together," Epic, 1973 • *Let's Build a World Together,* Epic, 1973 • "We're Gonna Hold On," Epic, 1973 • *We're Gonna Hold On,* Epic, 1973 • w/ Tina Jones, *George, Tammy and Tina,* Epic, 1974 • "(We're Not) the Jet Set," Epic, 1974 • "We Loved It Away," Epic, 1974 • "God's Gonna Get'cha (For That)," Epic, 1975 • "Golden Ring," Epic, 1976 • *Golden Ring,* Epic, 1976 • "Near You," Epic, 1976 • *Greatest Hits,* Epic, 1977 • "Southern California," Epic, 1977 • "A Pair of Old Sneakers," Epic, 1980 • *Together Again,* Epic, 1980 • "Two Story House," Epic, 1980 • *Greatest Hits,* Vol. 2, Epic, 1992 • *Super Hits,* Epic, 1995.

Lewis, Jerry Lee: *Classic,* Bear Family, 1989.

Lynne, Shelby: *Sunrise,* Epic, 1976, 1989 • "Little Bits and Pieces," Epic, 1989.

Mandrell, Barbara: "Playing Around with Love," Columbia, 1970 • *Super Hits,* Columbia, 1971, 1997.

Moore, Scotty: *The Guitar That Changed the World,* CBS, 1964.

Nabors, Jim: *Help Me Make It Through the Night,* Columbia, 1971.

Nelson, Willie: *Super Hits,* Vol. 2, Columbia, 1995.

Paycheck, Johnny: "She's All I Got," Epic, 1971 • "Someone to Give My Love To," Epic, 1972 • "Loving You Beats All I've Ever Seen," Epic, 1975 • "I'm the Only Hell (Mama Ever Raised)," Epic, 1977 • "Slide Off Your Satin Sheets," Epic, 1977 • *Armed and Crazy,* Epic, 1978 • "Friend, Lover, Wife," Epic, 1978 • "Georgia in a Jug / Me and the IRS," Epic, 1978 • *Greatest Hits,* Vol. 2, Epic, 1978 • "Take This Job and Shove It," Epic, 1978 • "Drinkin' and Drivin'," Epic, 1979 • *Everybody's Got a Family, Meet Mine,* Epic, 1979 • "The Outlaw's Prayer," Epic, 1979 • "Fifteen Beers," Epic, 1980 • "In a Memory of a Memory," Epic, 1980 •

New York Town, Epic, 1980 • *Mr. Hag Told My Story,* Epic, 1981 • *Biggest Hits,* Epic, 1987 • *Double Trouble,* Razor & Tie, 1996 • *She's All I Got,* Koch, 1998 • *See also* Jones, George, and Johnny Paycheck.

Peaches and Herb: *The Best Of: Love Is Strange,* Legacy/Epic, 1996.

Posey, Sandy: *Why Don't We Go Somewhere and Love,* Columbia, 1972.

Remains, The: *The Remains* (5 tracks), Spoonfed, 1966, 1978.

Rich, Charlie: *Set Me Free,* Koch, 1968, 1994 • *The Fabulous Charlie Rich,* Koch, 1968, 1994 • "Life's Little Ups and Downs," Epic, 1969 • "July 12, 1939," Epic, 1970 • "Nice 'n' Easy," Epic, 1970 • "A Part of Your Life," Epic, 1971 • *Boss Man,* Koch, 1971, 1994 • *Behind Closed Doors,* Columbia, 1972 • "I Take It on Home," Epic, 1972 • *The Best Of,* Epic, 1972 • "Behind Closed Doors," Epic, 1973 • "The Most Beautiful Girl," Epic, 1973 • "A Very Special Love Song," Epic, 1974 • "I Love My Friend," Epic, 1974 • *The Silver Fox,* Epic, 1974 • *Very Special Love Songs,* Epic, 1974 • "All Over Me," Epic, 1975 • "Every Time You Touch Me (I Get High)," Epic, 1975 • *Every Time You Touch Me (I Get High),* Epic, 1975 • "My Elusive Dreams," Epic, 1975 • "America, the Beautiful," Epic, 1976 • "Road Song," Epic, 1976 • Silver Linings, Epic, 1976 • "Since I Fell for You," Epic, 1976 • "Easy Look," Epic, 1977 • "Rollin' with the Flow," Epic, 1977 • *Rollin' with the Flow,* Epic, 1977 • "Beautiful Woman," Epic, 1978 • w/ Janie Frickie, "On My Knees," Epic, 1978 • *Super Hits,* Epic, 1995 • *Feel Like Going Home: The Essential,* Legacy/Columbia, 1997.

Robbins, Marty: "Among My Souvenirs," Columbia, 1976 • "El Paso City," Columbia, 1976 • *El Paso City,* Columbia, 1976 • "Return to Me," Columbia, 1977 • *All Around Cowboy,* Columbia, 1979 • *The Performer,* Columbia, 1979 • *A Lifetime of Song 1951–1982,* CBS, 1983 • *Biggest Hits,* CBS, 1984 • *Super Hits,* Columbia, 1995.

Rodriguez, Johnny: "Down on the Rio Grande," Epic, 1979 • "Fools for Each Other," Epic, 1979 • *Rodriguez,* Epic, 1979 • "What'll I Tell Virginia," Epic, 1979 • "Love, Look at Us Now," Epic, 1980 • "North of the Border," Epic, 1980 • *Through My Eyes,* Epic, 1980 • *After the Rain,* Epic, 1981 • *Super Hits,* Epic, 1995.

Sherrill, Billy: *Classical Country,* Epic, 1967.

Stampley, Joe: *I Don't Lie,* Epic, 1979.

Tucker, Tanya: "Delta Dawn," Columbia, 1972 • "Love's the Answer/The Jamestown Ferry," Columbia, 1972 • "Blood Red and Goin' Down," Columbia, 1973 • "What's Your Mama's Name," Columbia, 1973 • "The Man That Turned My Mama On," Columbia, 1974 • "Would You Lay with Me (in a Field of Stone)?," Columbia, 1974 • *Would You Lay with Me (in a Field of Stone)?,* Columbia, 1974 • *Greatest Hits,* Columbia, 1975 • "I Believe the South Is Gonna Rise Again," Columbia, 1975 • *The Sound of*

Tanya Tucker, Columbia, 1975 • *Super Hits,* Columbia, 1998.

Vinton, Bobby: *More of Bobby Vinton's Greatest Hits,* Epic, 1966 • "Please Love Me Forever," Epic, 1967 • "I Love How You Love Me," Epic, 1968.

Watson, Gene: "Everybody Needs a Hero," Epic, 1987 • "Honky Tonk Crazy," Epic, 1987.

Williams, Andy: *You Lay So Easy on My Mind,* Columbia, 1974.

Williams, Hank Jr.: *Greatest Hits,* Vol. 2, Warner Bros., 1985, 1990 • *The Bocephus Box: Hank Williams Jr. Collection '79–'92,* Capricorn, 1992.

Wynette, Tammy: "I Don't Wanna Play House," Epic, 1967 • "Your Good Girl's Gonna Go Bad," Epic, 1967 • *Your Good Girl's Gonna Go Bad,* Legacy, 1967, 1995 • "D-I-V-O-R-C-E," Epic, 1968 • *D-I-V-O-R-C-E,* Koch, 1968, 1997 • "Stand by Your Man," Epic, 1968 • "Take Me to Your World," Epic, 1968 • "I'll See Him Through," Epic, 1969 • *Inspiration,* Epic, 1969 • "Singing My Song," Epic, 1969 • *Stand by Your Man,* Epic, 1969 • "The Ways to Love a Man," Epic, 1969 • "He Loves Me All the Way," Epic, 1970 • "Run, Woman, Run," Epic, 1970 • *Tammy's Touch,* Epic, 1970 • *The First lady,* Epic, 1970 • *The Ways to Love a Man,* Epic, 1970 • "The Wonders You Perform," Epic, 1970 • "Good Lovin' (Makes It Right)," Epic, 1971 • "We Sure Can Love Each Other," Epic, 1971 • *We Sure Can Love Each Other,* Epic, 1971 • "Bedtime Story," Epic, 1972 • *Bedtime Story,* Epic, 1972 • "My Man (Understands)," Epic, 1972 • *My Man,* Epic, 1972 • "Reach Out Your hand," Epic, 1972 • "Kids Say the Darndest Things," Epic, 1973 • " 'Til I Get It Right," Epic, 1973 • "(You Make Me Want to Be) a Mother," Epic, 1974 • "Another Lonely Song," Epic, 1974 • *Another Lonely Song,* Epic, 1974 • "Woman to Woman," Epic, 1974 • "I Still Believe in Fairy Tales," Epic, 1975 • *I Still Believe in Fairy Tales,* Epic, 1975 • *Woman to Woman,* Epic, 1975 • *Christmas with Tammy,* Epic, 1976 • " 'Til I Can Make It on My Own," Epic, 1976 • *'Til I Can Make It on My Own,* Epic, 1976 • "You and Me," Epic, 1976 • *You And Me,* Epic, 1976 • "Let's Get Together (One Last Time)," Epic, 1977 • *Let's Get Together,* Epic, 1977 • "One of a Kind," Epic, 1977 • *One of a Kind,* Epic, 1977 • "I'd Like to See Jesus (on the Midnight Special)," Epic, 1978 • "Womanhood," Epic, 1978 • *Womanhood,* Epic, 1978 • *Just Tammy,* Epic, 1979 • "No One Else in the World," Epic, 1979 • "They Call It Making Love," Epic, 1979 • "He Was There When I Needed You," Epic, 1980 • *Only Lonely Sometimes,* Epic, 1980 • "Starting Over," Epic, 1980 • *Biggest Hits,* Epic, 1983 • "Alive and Well," Epic, 1986 • *Anniversary: 20 Years of Hits,* Epic, 1987 • *Greatest Hits,* Epic, 1989 • *Best Loved Hits,* Epic, 1990 • *Tears of Fire: The 25th Anniversary Collection,* Epic, 1992 • *Super Hits,* Epic, 1996 • *See also* Jones, George, and Tammy Wynette.

Adrian Sherwood

A drian Sherwood has been a revolutionary force for over 20 years on the beat music scene where reggae, dub, industrial, and world music come together to form a groovy, thumping whole. Infatuated with reggae and dub from an early age, Sherwood was a London club DJ in his early teens. By his early 20s, Sherwood had owned three labels: Caribgems, Hitrun, and the legendary On-U-Sound, which continues to this day.

For On-U—which began as a loose live performance group in 1979—Sherwood has produced and performed with a rotating cast under various guises, including African Head Charge, Creation Rebel, Dub Syndicate, New Age Steppers, Mark Stewart and Maffia, and most famously, Tackhead. He has produced other reggae and dub artists, including the great Lee "Scratch" Perry (see entry), Prince Far I, Bim Sherman, Singers and Players, and Little Annie.

Sherwood has also produced or co-produced seminal industrial and electronic music by Ministry, Cabaret Voltaire, Skinny Puppy, KMFDM, and Nine Inch Nails; as well as punk and post-punk by the Slits, the Fall, and the Pogues' Shane MacGowan. In addition, Sherwood has been one of the premier remixers of the last 15 years, reworking Blur, Depeche Mode, Einsturzende Neubauten, Living Colour, Shriekback, Simply Red, and dozens of others to great effect.

Adrian Sherwood was born on the outskirts of London in 1958. By the tender age of 11, he was lurking about the door of a reggae club to hear the music. Within two years he was DJing at the club for teenage reggae parties. Sherwood attributes his proclivity for black music to growing up in a multiracial community. "I think England's unique in that we have a very, very healthy cross-fertilization of musical cultures in London. I have mates who are Indian, Chinese, Japanese, African, Jamaican—everybody's in London and everyone does tend to mix up a lot here."

After high school, Sherwood and a Jamaican friend started buying Jamaican reggae records and reselling them in the north of England, where such things were scarce. Within a year they were doing well enough to start their own label, Caribgems, which released reggae albums by Black Uhuru, Trinity, Dillinger, and others in the U.K. (now re-released by Sherwood under his Pressure imprint).

"I loved reggae first, but then dub became the thing. We used to smoke loads of weed and sit around, and the dub records were great: all the funny noises and everything. While you are lying on your back, with a very nice spliff and a huge bassline running over your chest, it's fucking great," he affirms.

Sherwood next started Hitrun, which released his own band, a dub collective called Creation Rebel, and records by Prince Far I. Although Sherwood plays "some bass," he considers the mixing board his main instrument, appropriate for his transformation from DJ to producer.

"I bullshit my way along, really," he says. "I had enough money to run a session, so I ran a session. I paid the musicians, told the bass player what to play. I made a kind of dub album—for, like, 300 U.S. dollars [re-released as Creation Rebel's *Historic Moments*]—and it sold a lot more than the stuff we had licensed from Jamaica because I made it for people like myself, who wanted it a bit spacier.

"I thought, this is easy. You get together some good players, you get the whole system together. If you pay for the musicians and studio time and you run a session, then you're the producer. Then by playing more and more I got more proficient and more confident, and as the years went by people started paying me good amounts of money to help them make their records."

The On-U-Sound label was started in 1980 and released the New Age Steppers (members of Creation Rebel, the Slits, Public Image), African Head Charge, Mothmen (which eventually became Simply Red's rhythm section), and others.

Around 1984 Sherwood met drummer Keith Leblanc, bassist Doug Wimbish (later of Living Colour), and guitarist Skip McDonald (the trio had been the house band at Sugar Hill Records; see Sylvia Robinson entry) at the *New Music Seminar* in New York, and together they became Tackhead. Performing and recording on their own (*Friendly As a Hand Grenade*), and with white "toaster" (Jamaican for "rapper") Gary Clail, Tackhead put on extravaganzas in the mid-'80s with live and recorded music, "all twisted and dubbed live through the PA mixing desk while maybe three rhythms, sound effects and chants play[ed] simultaneously" (per the liner notes to 1987's *Tackhead Tape Time*), with Clail—an ex-scaffolder and second-hand cortina salesman—expressing himself rhythmically through a megaphone. *Tape Time* is a trippy dub, industrial, hip-hop classic riding on crunchy, spiky beats, liberally spiced with spoken word samples, big guitar riffs, and Clail's vaguely leftist raps.

For 1991's *The Emotional Hooligan,* most of the On-U stable (Dub Syndicate, Bim Sherman, Style Scott, Big Youth, Strange Parcel, etc.) joined Sherwood, Clail, and Tackhead for an extraordinarily tuneful, affecting plea for social justice and ethical living. Rather than the jittery, clever, sonic collage of *Tape, Hooligan* returns to Sherwood's reggae-dub past for loping, elongated grooves and thick, echoey production. "Food, Clothes and Shelter" boasts great harmony reggae singing stating the deceptively obvious: all humans need food, clothes, and shelter. The Billy Bragg of dub, Clail gently exhorts us to live better on the title track, "Magic Penny" (with a child charmingly singing a nursery rhyme about the rewards of giving), and "Human Nature."

Sherwood has also greatly affected the course of industrial music. After veering toward harder beats and the liberal use of sampling in his own music in the mid-'80s, Sherwood midwifed Ministry's transformation from poppy techno-weenies into the dark, edgy industrialists they are known and feared-as today, on 1985's *Twitch.* While that album didn't take the band all the way into *The Land of Rape and Honey* (as would occur when bassist Paul Barker joined, and founder/singer Al Jourgensen added metallic electric guitar to the electronic-based mix), it was Sherwood who transformed Jourgensen's faux-English pop singing into distorted, whispery menace, raised the electronic beats in the mix to a mechanistic assault, and brought in a heavy quotient of noise for percussive and atmospheric effect.

In 1987 Sherwood produced the rubbery, jagged industrio-funk of Cabaret Voltaire's *Code,* with the dance floor thumpers "Don't Argue" and "Here to Go." That same year he produced and remixed Skinny Puppy's syncopated, undulating "Deep Down Trauma Hounds," and in 1988 he co-produced and co-mixed KMFDM's (see Sasha Konietzko entry) clangorous *Don't Blow Your Top,* including the dub-industrial tour de force "King Kong Dub Rubber Mix." Sherwood completed his '80s industrial campaign by co-producing and remixing (with Keith Leblanc) Nine Inch Nails' (see Trent Reznor entry) hip-hop, industrial masterpiece "Down in It" from the seminal *Pretty Hate Machine.* Sherwood also remixed a sensational, churning version of "Sin" from the album.

In the '90s Sherwood has run his labels (On-U, Pres-

sure); played and produced with Tackhead, Clail, Dub Syndicate, and other configurations; co-produced the Fall, Shane MacGowan, Bim Sherman; and tackled a wide range of remixes. He is particularly pleased with the musical state of affairs in England today. "It's very much like the punk-rock time really, a time of energy and optimism. None of the record companies know what to sign, there's loads of good underground, a good club scene going again, and people believe the music is theirs. The drum and bass and jungle stuff, it's got nothing to do with any other country; it's our thing, which I think is great." —ERIC OLSEN AND DAWN DARLING

African Head Charge: *My Life in a Hole in the Ground,* On-U-Sound, 1981, 1991 • *Environmental Studies,* On-U/EFA, 1982, 1998 • *Drastic Season,* On-U-Sound, 1983, 1990 • *Songs of Praise,* On-U-Sound, 1991 • *In Pursuit of Shashamane Land,* Restless, 1994 • "Touchi," Restless, 1994.

Audio Active: *Apollo Choco,* On-U-Sound, 1997.

Blur: *Bustin' and Dronin',* Food, 1998.

Cabaret Voltaire: "Don't Argue," Parlophone/EMI, 1986 • *Code,* Manhattan/EMI, 1987 • "Here to Go," Manhattan/EMI, 1987.

Clail, Gary: w/ Tackhead, *Tackhead Tape Time,* Nettwerk/Capitol, 1987 • w/ On-U Sound System, *End of the Century Party,* On-U-Sound, 1989 • w/ On-U Sound System, *The Emotional Hooligan,* RCA, 1991 • *Keep the Faith,* Yelen, 1996.

Creation Rebel: *Historic Moments,* Vols. 1–2, On-U-Sound, 1994/1995.

Depeche Mode: "Master and Servant" (remix), Mute, 1984 • "People Are People" (remix), Mute, 1984 • "Useless" (remix), Mute, 1997.

Dub Syndicate: *The Pounding System,* On-U-Sound, 1982, 1988 • *One Way System,* ROIR, 1983, 1987 • *Tunes from the Missing Channel,* On-U-Sound, 1985 • *Strike the Balance,* On-U-Sound, 1990 • "Ravi Shankar," On-U-Sound, 1992 (*Volume Four*) • *Echomania,* On-U-Sound, 1993 • *Stoned Immaculate,* On-U-Sound, 1994 • *Ital Breakfast,* On-U-Sound, 1996 • *Research and Development,* On-U-Sound, 1996.

Einsturzende Neubauten: "Yu Gung" (remix), Some Bizarre, 1985.

Fall, The: *Slates* (EP), Rough Trade, 1981 • *Extricate,* Cog Sinister/Fontana, 1990.

I Start Counting: "Still Smiling" (remix), Mute, 1991.

Jalal: *On the One,* on the One, 1996.

KMFDM: *Don't Blow Your Top,* Wax Trax!, 1988 • "Rip the System," Wax Trax!, 1989.

Leblanc, Keith: *Major Malfunction,* World, 1986 • *Stranger Than Fiction,* Nettwerk/Enigma, 1989.

Little Annie: "Everything and More," On-U-Sound, 1992

(*Volume Four*) • *Short, Sweet and Dread*, On-U-Sound, 1992.

Little Axe: *The Wolf That House Built*, Sony, 1995 • *Slow Fuse*, Wired, 1996.

Living Colour: "Auslander" (remix), Epic, 1993 • "Sunshine of Your Love" (remix), Epic, 1994.

MacGowan, Shane, and the Popes: *Crock of Gold*, ZTT, 1997.

Ministry: "Over the Shoulder," Sire/WB, 1985 • *Twitch*, Sire/WB, 1986 • *Box* (3 tracks), Sire/WB, 1993.

New Age Steppers: *New Age Steppers*, On-U-Sound/Statik, 1980, 1982 • *Action Battlefield*, On-U-Sound/Statik, 1981 • *Foundation Steppers*, On-U-Sound, 1983.

Nine Inch Nails: "Down in It," TVT, 1989 • "Down in It" (remix), TVT, 1989 • *Pretty Hate Machine* (1 track), TVT, 1989 • "Sin" (remix), TVT, 1990 • "Happiness in Slavery" (remix), TVT/Interscope, 1992.

On-U-Sound: *See* Clail, Gary.

Pal Judy: *Pal Judy*, ROIR, 1982, 1990.

Perry, Lee "Scratch": *Time Boom X De Devil Dead*, On-U Sound, 1987 • *From the Secret Laboratory*, Mango, 1990.

Primal Scream, Irvine Welsh, and On-U-Sound: "The Big Man and Scream Team Meet the Harmony Army Uptown," Creation, 1996.

Prince Far I: w/ the Arabs, *Cry Tuff Dub Encounter, Chapter 1*, ROIR, 1978 • *Message from the King*, Frontline/Virgin, 1979 • w/ the Arabs, *Cry Tuff Dub Encounter, Chapter 3*, Daddy Kool, 1980.

Revolutionary Dub Warriors: *State of Evolution*, On-U-Sound, 1996.

Sherman, Bim: *Across the Red Sea*, On-U-Sound, 1982, 1998 • *Miracle*, Mantra, 1997.

Shriekback: "Hand on My Heart" (remix), Arista, 1984.

Simply Red: "Holding Back the Years" (remix), Elektra, 1985.

Singers and Players: *War of Words*, On-U-Sound, 1981, 1998 • *Revenge of the Underdog*, On-U-Sound, 1982, 1997 • *Staggering Heights*, On-U-Sound, 1983, 1993 • *Leaps and Bounds*, On-U-Sound, 1984 • *Vacuum Pumping*, On-U-Sound, 1988.

Skinny Puppy: *Mind: The Perpetual Intercourse*, Gold Rush, 1986, 1996 • *12" Anthology*, Nettwerk/Capitol, 1990.

Slits, The: "Man Next Door," Y/Rough Trade, 1980.

Spearhead: "People in tha Middle" (remix), Capitol, 1994.

Stewart, Mark: w/ the Maffia, *Learning to Cope with Cowardice*, On-U-Sound, 1983, 1991 • *Metatron*, Restless, 1990 • *Control Data*, Mute, 1996.

Strange Parcels: "Disconnection," Restless, 1994.

Tackhead: *Friendly As a Hand Grenade*, TVT, 1989 • *See also* Clail, Gary.

Wolfgang Press: "Christianity" (remix), American, 1995 (*The Doom Generation* soundtrack).

COLLECTIONS

Pay It All Back, Vol. 5, On-U-Sound, 1995.

Axion Dub: Mysteries of Creation, Axiom, 1996.
In Dub Daze, Cleopatra, 1996.
Dubitamin, EFA, 1996.

Hank and Keith Shocklee

See BOMB SQUAD

Daryl Simmons

In the beginning, it was enough for producer/songwriter Daryl Simmons to be just a silent partner, and that's exactly what he was—and still is, at least technically speaking, since Silent Partner is the name of his production company. Simmons worked diligently behind the scenes with Babyface and L.A. Reid (see entries) during much of their heyday, maintaining a much lower profile than his partners. For a while, at least, it was okay with Simmons. "It was cool to me," says Simmons. "I got to work on projects with them,

and I was writing for them and making good music along with them."

Simmons shares many of his earliest production credits with Reid and Babyface, including superhits like Bobby Brown's "Humpin' Around" (No. 3), Boyz II Men's "End of the Road" (No. 1), and Toni Braxton's "Breathe Again" (No. 3) and "Love Shoulda Brought You Home." Despite having a presence on many high-profile hits, says Simmons, "I had my own life. I wasn't a famous guy. No one knew my face. That was kind of cool to me—the best job to have. I learned a lot."

While working with Reid and Babyface, Simmons says he was mainly interested in songwriting, but they pushed him into production. "They were getting overloaded and told me I needed to do some of these projects: to get in on Karyn White, the Boyz, and Bobby Brown. I got pushed into them," says Simmons, who worked as a sideman for the Deele, Babyface and Reid's '80s R&B band. Simmons' relationship with Babyface goes back to the late '70s, when they were members of the Indianapolis band Manchild.

His first production job was the Boyz' "Dial My Heart" in 1988, but he didn't receive credit for it. By this time, Simmons had picked up much in the way of business and musical sense from his partners. They taught him to "make sure the lyrics are very strong, the melodies are very strong, the track is doing what it should be doing—not too much—and to know when to add certain things and when to take certain things out."

Armed with this knowledge, Simmons was ready for his first flight sans the dynamic duo: Ralph Tresvant's "Stone Cold Gentleman" in 1991, which featured a rap from Brown. "That was very scary. I was used to having the same partners, but this time I was responsible from beginning to end," although he worked on the song with a new occasional partner, producer Kayo. Together, Simmons and Kayo have produced "Baby I'm for Real" and "Can He Love You Like This" for After 7, and "Just My Luck" by Alyson Williams, among many others.

After Babyface and Reid stopped producing together in the mid-'90s, Simmons decided it was time to start his own Silent Partner Productions company. His productions bear a strong resemblance to those of Babyface: if you didn't know any better, you'd have thought that was Babyface's hand on Xscape's "Do You Want To," Monica's "Why I Love You So Much," or Dru Hill's "In My Bed," all produced by Simmons. And frankly, artists have sought out Simmons' talent when Babyface wasn't available, but they still wanted the Babyface sound. "I always say I don't have a sound, but I learned so much from Face that my style is a part of his style," opines Simmons, whose R&B-pop sound is unmistak-able with its butter-smooth beats and instantly recognizable hooks.

Simmons is sorry he'll never have the opportunity to apply this sound to the great Marvin Gaye. "He was the dream person I always wanted to work with," Simmons says. Of course, he could still produce a remake of a Gaye song with another artist, but Simmons says he will never do that. "That's something sacred to me. It should be left untouched. He's the person who got me into the whole vocal thing—all the harmonies—and brought my ear closer to paying attention to the background and things that make records special."

Though Simmons enjoys working with veterans, he gets a special thrill from producing newcomers like Dru Hill, Deborah Cox, and Aaliyah. "The new artists are so young and hungry. They have so much spirit. I love seeing them start with nothing and then watching them develop if they have the success. I get pleasure out of being a part of that."

One new act that hasn't caught on, A Few Good Men, has been Simmons' biggest disappointment. He, Babyface, and Dallas Austin (see entry) all worked on the R&B group's album *Take a Dip*, which would seem to insure its success. But the album never clicked with the public. "It didn't happen and I don't know why. It's one of those things—one of those mysteries of the business. It's not in the cards for everybody," he cautions.

Simmons probably surprised a few people when he took on country singer Wynonna for the song "Making My Way (Any Way That I Can)" for *The Associate* soundtrack. Until then he had only worked with R&B and pop artists. "That was a great experience. We hit it off and became friends. I'd love to do more things with country artists," says Simmons. "I wanted it to sound like one of her records. I didn't want to change her."

Simmons has reached the kind of peaks other producers can only dream about, including a Grammy for "End of the Road," which is his favorite production. "It's one of those records you can hear on the radio and still get goose bumps from the feeling of the performance. There was so much feeling. I remember how it happened: I flew to Philly and only had so many hours to get the vocals. Wanya's [Morris] voice was gone. I felt sorry for him because he had to sing it, but he did."

Simmons believes there are more peaks in front of him. "I'd like to think there's something else out there for me—something really good." —KEVIN JOHNSON

A Few Good Men: *Take a Dip*, LaFace, 1995 • "Have I Never," LaFace, 1996.

Aaliyah: *One in a Million* (1 track), Blackground Enterprises, 1996.

Abdul, Paula: *Head over Heels* (1 track), Virgin, 1995.

After 7: "Baby I'm for Real/Natural High," Virgin, 1992 • *Takin' My Time,* Virgin, 1992 • "Can He Love You Like This?," Virgin, 1993 • "Truly Something Special," Virgin, 1993 • *Very Best Of,* Virgin, 1997.

Babyface: featuring Toni Braxton, "Give U My Heart," Epic, 1992 • "For the Cool in You," Epic, 1993 • *For the Cool in You,* Epic, 1993 • "Never Keeping Secrets," Epic, 1993 • "And Our Feelings," Epic, 1994 • "When Can I See You?," Epic, 1994 • *When Can I See You Again?* (EP), Epic, 1995 • "Every Time I Close My Eyes," Epic, 1996.

Barrio Boyzz: *How We Roll,* Capitol, 1995.

Bell Biv DeVoe: *Hootie Mack,* MCA, 1993 • "Something in Your Eyes," MCA, 1993.

Boyz II Men: "End of the Road," Biv 10, 1992.

Braxton, Toni: "Love Shoulda Brought You Home," 1992 • "Another Sad Love Song," LaFace, 1993 • *Toni Braxton,* LaFace, 1993 • "Breathe Again," LaFace, 1994 • "You Mean the World to Me," LaFace, 1994.

Braxtons, The: *So Many Ways,* Atlantic, 1996.

Brown, Bobby: *Bobby* (3 tracks), MCA, 1992 • "Good Enough," MCA, 1992 • "Humpin' Around," MCA, 1992 • *Remixes in the Key of B,* MCA, 1993.

Campbell, Tevin: "Can We Talk?," Qwest, 1993 • *I'm Ready,* Qwest, 1993 • "Always in My Heart," Qwest, 1994 • "I'm Ready," Qwest, 1994.

Carey, Mariah: *Music Box,* Columbia, 1993 • "Never Forget You/Without You," Columbia, 1994.

Cox, Deborah: *Vol. 2,* Arista, 1998.

Downing, Will: "All About You," Mercury, 1997 • *Invitation Only,* Mercury, 1997.

For Real: *Free,* Rowdy, 1996 • "The Saddest Song I Ever Heard," Rowdy, 1997.

Franklin, Aretha: *Greatest Hits 1980–1994,* Arista, 1994 • "Honey," Arista, 1994 • "Willing to Forgive," Arista, 1994 • *A Rose Is Still a Rose,* Arista, 1998.

Gill, Johnny: *Provocative,* Motown, 1993 • *Favorites,* Motown, 1997.

Hill, Dru: *Dru Hill,* Island, 1996 • "In My Bed," Island, 1997 • "Never Make a Promise," Island, 1997 • "We're Not Making Love No More," LaFace, 1997.

Jackson, Jermaine: *You Said,* LaFace, 1991.

Mayfield, Curtis: *New World Order,* Warner Bros., 1996 • "No One Knows About a Good Thing," Warner Bros., 1997.

Monica: *Miss Thang,* Rowdy, 1995 • "Why I Love You So Much/Ain't Nobody," Rowdy, 1996 • *The Boy Is Mine,* Arista, 1998.

New Edition: *Solo Hits,* MCA, 1996.

Pebbles: *Always,* MCA, 1990.

Powell, Jesse: *Jesse Powell,* MCA, 1996.

Shanice: *21 Ways to Grow,* Motown, 1994.

SWV: *New Beginning,* RCA, 1996.

Tamia: *Tamia,* Qwest, 1998.

TLC: "Baby-Baby-Baby," LaFace, 1992.

Tresvant, Ralph: *Ralph Tresvant,* MCA, 1990 • "Stone Cold Gentleman," MCA, 1991.

White, Karyn: *Make Him Do Right,* Warner Bros., 1994.

Williams, Alyson: *Alyson Williams,* Columbia, 1991 • "Just My Luck," Columbia, 1992.

Winans, CeCe: *Everlasting Love,* PMG/Atlantic, 1998.

Wynonna: "Makin' My Way (Any Way That I Can)," Motown Soundtracks, 1996 (*The Associate* soundtrack).

Xscape: *Feels So Good* (EP), So So Def/Columbia, 1995 • *Off the Hook,* So So Def/Columbia, 1995 • "Do You Want To/Can't Hang," So So Def, 1996 • *Traces of My Lipstick,* So So Def/Columbia, 1998.

COLLECTIONS

Fame L.A., Mercury, 1998.

John Simon

John Simon—keyboardist, songwriter, arranger, multi-instrumentalist, recording artist—has spent 35 exceptional years making music. He was one of the most important American producers of the last half of the '60s, producing and arranging indispensable albums by Simon and Garfunkel, Blood, Sweat and Tears, Leonard Cohen, Big Brother and the Holding Company (with Janis Joplin), and the Band. Simon has also played with Eric Clapton, Dave Mason, Taj Mahal, Bob Dylan, Joni Mitchell, Howlin' Wolf, and countless others.

John Simon was born August 11, 1941, in Norwalk, Connecticut. A lifelong "compulsive musician," Simon was taught violin and piano from the age of 4 by his father, a country doctor. He gravitated toward the piano because it was "easier for a little kid to play than the violin," he says. Simon didn't become good enough at the piano to be a serious classical player because he preferred "playing baseball to practicing," but he found that it came naturally to him. He is blessed with perfect pitch and he can sight-read "flies off the wall. If music is a language, I speak music," he says matter-of-factly.

Simon played jazz in various bands and combos in high school and in college (at Princeton), taking one band to the finals in the first Georgetown Intercollegiate Jazz Festival. After interviewing with various headhunters who came to Princeton seeking fresh meat, Simon was offered two jobs upon his graduation in 1963: jingle writer with a major New York ad agency and producer trainee at Columbia Records. Both paid $85 per week. He accepted the latter.

"I knew music, but Columbia taught me about the record business," Simon says. "I went to the factory to see how little wafers of vinyl were pressed by a waffle iron–like machine into records. I went with the salesmen to radio stations to see how little pieces of green paper with dead presidents on them were turned into airplay. I went to the art department and the liner notes department and spent a lot of time with the engineers learning to splice tape, place microphones, use equalizers, compressors, limiters, echo, reverb, and everything else they could think of about recording," he says.

"While I was training, I also was assisting Columbia's president, the legendary Goddard Lieberson, on original cast albums of Broadway shows. He was a composer as well as a label president and knew and loved music, unlike today where the presidents are all accountants and lawyers. Anyway, we would do so much planning that we would record the album on a Sunday (when the show was dark), and the record would be in the stores by Tuesday," he says.

Ken Glancy took over the Columbia stable of producers—then called the A&R department—and moved Simon into the pop department, which included jazz and rock 'n' roll. He began assisting producers with lower-profile artists like jazzers Charles Lloyd and Joe Mooney and polka king Frankie Yankovic.

"One day a guy came into my office saying he was 'Brian Epstein's [the Beatles' manager] American associate,' and he had a tape by an unnamed band from Lehigh University doing a song co-written by Paul Simon and Bruce Woodley (of the Seekers) called 'Red Rubber Ball.' Everyone else had turned it down, but I thought the tape was pretty good, so I screwed up my courage and asked the boss for $3,000 to make a demo," says Simon.

That bouncy, clean demo became a No. 2 hit in the summer of 1966 for the Cyrkle (named by John Lennon) and was followed two months later by a similar hit, "Turn-Down Day" (No. 16). John Simon was a hit producer.

Having made a hit for a third party with a Paul Simon song, John Simon then worked with the real thing, producing Simon (see entry) and Garfunkel's hit "Fakin' It" in the summer of 1967. John Simon's *Sgt. Pepper* meets "Good Vibrations" mini-opera arrangement is the key to the record, which opens with an eerie high-pitched drone hovering above a syncopated percussion-and-handclap beat, casting an immediate air of apprehension.

The opening quickly gives way to a slippery blues-rock acoustic guitar riff that underpins the body of the song, Paul Simon's meditation on the dissonance between a projected external veneer and contradictory internal reality. The effort to hold up this veneer—a veneer that hides falsehood in relationships, social discourse, and finally even personal identity—wears at the song's character, as conveyed with spiderweb delicacy and strength by Simon and Garfunkel's interweaving high-and-higher tenors.

As the duo sing the tale, John Simon flashes now-you-hear-it, now-you-don't backing prestidigitations behind them, including choral, horn, string, and his own organ flourishes. The opening percussion bit reappears to underscore the choruses and other select dramatic moments, and the entire song structure disappears momentarily near the end to interject a moment—complete with sound effects—from the character's previous life as a tailor in Victorian England! Somehow, the Simons and Garfunkel pull off this ontological treatise as a great pop-rock song.

For the remainder of the '60s and into the early '70s, John Simon seemed to capture the spirit of the age: he produced and arranged Blood, Sweat and Tears' first album, *Child Is Father to the Man*, one of horn rock's finest moments, with Al Kooper (see entry) providing bluesy vocals and organ on indelible tunes, including "I Love You More Than You'll Ever Know" and "I Can't Quit Her." Simon produced Leonard Cohen's classic gold debut, *Songs of Leonard Cohen*, including some of the basso poet's best-loved and most profound songs: "Suzanne," "Sisters of Mercy," "So Long, Marianne" and "Hey, That's No Way to Say Goodbye."

Walking on air, Simon went from Cohen into another epochal moment, Big Brother and the Holding Company's *Cheap Thrills*, No. 1 for eight weeks on the strength of Janis Joplin's most rocking performances: "Ball and Chain," "Summertime," and the soul-wrenching "Piece of My Heart" (No. 12).

Then, while helping Peter Yarrow (of Peter, Paul and Mary; see Milt Okun entry) edit his rockumentary *You Are What You Eat*, Simon met members of Bob Dylan's backup band and repaired with them to their communal home in Saugerties, New York, to help them put together the demos that would become the Band's *Music from Big Pink*. Perhaps the greatest album of what is now called "Americana," *Big Pink* was recorded by four Canadians (Robbie Robertson on guitar, Rick Danko on bass, and Richard Manuel and Garth Hudson on keyboards), an Arkansan (Levon Helm on drums), and a Yankee (Simon). Like the finest folk music, the album yields fresh dividends 30 years after its release, yet is unquestionably rock 'n' roll in its attitude, instrumentation, and sonics. Simon not only produced but helped arrange and played on *Big Pink* and the platinum follow-up, *The Band* (No. 9), which was recorded in a converted pool hall in Los Angeles.

Big Pink is a sublime mixture of the traditional (the spooky murder and loyalty-unto-death ballad "Long Black Veil") and the neotraditional (Dylan's "This Wheel's on Fire" and "I Shall Be Released," Robertson's "The Weight"). For *The Band*, Robertson took over writing duties and responded spectacularly with "The Night They Drove Old Dixie Down," "Up on Cripple Creek," "Rag Mama Rag," "Look Out Cleveland" and "The Unfaithful Servant." If *Big Pink* isn't the greatest Americana album, then *The Band* is.

Simon's relationship with the Band continued in the '70s as he co-produced *Stage Fright* (No. 5) with Todd Rundgren (see entry) and co-produced (with Robertson and Rob Fraboni; see entry), conducted, and arranged the Band's farewell concert and film *The Last Waltz* (No. 16) in 1978. Simon reunited with a Robertson-less Band when he co-produced their *Jericho* in 1993.

Simon spent much of the '70s playing live and on record with greats Eric Clapton, Taj Mahal, Joni Mitchell, Bob Dylan, and Howlin' Wolf and (encouraged by Paul Simon) recording his own solo albums *John Simon's Album* and *Journey*. While they are perhaps not up to his '60s standards, he also produced notable records for jazz great Gil Evans, new wave–leaning troubadour Steve Forbert, silky jazz-pop vocalist Michael Franks, bluegrasser John Hartford, eccentric singer/songwriter Hirth Martinez, and hornman David Sanborn.

In the '80s Simon composed classical music, wrote musicals, and performed a nightclub act with his wife, actress C.C. Loveheart. In the '90s Simon has returned to recording himself (*Out on the Street, Harmony Farm*) and others (A.C. Croce, Emmylou Harris, Pierce Turner), bringing an organic '60s aesthetic (minimal overdubs, no drum machines, no click tracks) to the '90s.
—Eric Olsen

Band, The: *Music from Big Pink*, Capitol, 1968 • "The Weight," Capitol, 1968 • *The Band*, Capitol, 1969 • "Up on Cripple Creek," Capitol, 1969 • "Rag Mama Rag," Capitol, 1970 • *Stage Fright*, Capitol, 1970 • *The Last Waltz*, Warner Bros., 1978 • *Jericho*, Pyramid, 1993 • *Across the Great Divide*, Capitol, 1994.

Barraclough, Elizabeth: *Elizabeth Barraclough*, Bearsville, 1978.

Beth, Karen: *New Moon Rising*, Buddah, 1975.

Big Brother and the Holding Company: *Cheap Thrills*, Columbia, 1968 • "Piece of My Heart," Columbia, 1968.

Blood, Sweat and Tears: *Child Is Father to the Man*, Columbia, 1970 • *Greatest Hits*, Columbia, 1972.

Charles, Bobby: *Bobby Charles*, Bearsville, 1972.

Cohen, Leonard: *The Songs of Leonard Cohen*, Columbia, 1968 • *The Best Of*, Columbia, 1975.

Croce, A.J.: *A.J. Croce*, Private, 1993.

Cyrkle: "Please Don't Ever Leave Me," Columbia, 1966 • *Red Rubber Ball*, Columbia, 1966 • "Red Rubber Ball," Columbia, 1966 • "Turn-Down Day," Columbia, 1966 • "I Wish You Could Be Here," Columbia, 1967 • *Neon*, Columbia, 1967.

Ducks: *The Ducks*, Just Sun, 1973.

Electric Flag: *American Music Band*, Columbia, 1969 • *Best Of*, Columbia, 1971 • *Old Glory: The Best Of*, Legacy, 1995.

Elliot, Mama Cass: "California Earthquake," Dunhill, 1968 • *Dream a Little Dream*, Dunhill, 1968 • *Dream a Little Dream: The Cass Elliot Collection*, MCA, 1997.

Evans, Gil: *Where Flamingos Fly*, A&M, 1971 • *Priestess*, Antilles, 1983.

Faro, Rachel: *Refugees*, RCA, 1974.

Faryar, Cyrus: *Islands*, Elektra, 1973.

Forbert, Steve: *Jackrabbit Slim*, Nemperor, 1979 • "Romeo's Tune," Nemperor, 1979 • *Best of Steve Forbert: What Kinda Guy?*, Legacy, 1993.

Franks, Michael: *Tiger in the Rain*, Warner Bros., 1977.

Galdston and Thom: *American Gypsies*, Warner Bros., 1972.

Harris, Emmylou: *Duets*, Reprise, 1990.

Hartford, John: *Morning Bugle*, Warner Bros., 1972.

Jackie and Roy: *Forever*, Musicmasters, 1995.

John Simon Trio/Doug Patterson: *Legacy*, Muse, 1996.

Joplin, Janis: *Farewell Song* (4 tracks), Columbia, 1982 • *Janis*, Legacy, 1993.

Kips Bay Ceili Band: *Digging In*, Green Linnet, 1993.

Kooper, Al: *Act Like Nothing's Wrong*, United Artists, 1982.

Lagrene, Birelli: *15*, Antilles, 1982.

Lightfoot, Gordon: *Did She Mention My Name?*, United Artists, 1968.

Lomax, Jackie: *Three*, Warner Bros., 1972.

Mamas and the Papas: *Creeque Alley*, MCA, 1991, 1995.

Martinez, Hirth: *Hirth from Earth*, Warner Bros., 1972 • *Big Bright Street*, Warner Bros., 1977.

Matrix: *Tale of the Whale*, Warner Bros., 1979.

Sanborn, David: *Heart to Heart*, Warner Bros., 1978 • *The Best Of*, Warner Bros., 1994.

Sapo: *Sapo*, Bell, 1974.

Scott, Bobby: *From Eden to Canaan*, Columbia, 1977.

Seals and Crofts: *Seals and Crofts 1&2*, Warner Bros., 1969, 1974 • *Down Home*, Bell, 1970.

Simon and Garfunkel: "Fakin' it," Columbia, 1967 • *Bookends* (4 tracks), Columbia, 1968 • *Old Friends* (3 tracks), Columbia, 1997.

Simon, John: *John Simon's Album*, Warner Bros., 1969 •

Journey, Warner Bros., 1972 • *Out on the Street,* Vanguard, 1992 • *Harmony Farm,* Pioneer, 1995.

Staton Brothers: *The Staton Brothers,* Epic, 1972.

Turner, Pierce: *Now Is Heaven,* Green Linnet, 1993.

COLLECTIONS

You Are What You Eat soundtrack, CBS, 1968.

The Best Little Whorehouse in Texas soundtrack, MCA, 1978.

Beautiful Thing soundtrack, MCA, 1996.

Paul Simon

Paul Simon is one of an elite club of artists that includes Stevie Wonder, Paul McCartney, Prince, Richard Carpenter, Brian Wilson, and John Fogerty (see entries): all of these artists have successfully produced themselves. Simon's production style is marked by sonic clarity, imaginative arrangements, and the integration of world music with mainstream popular music. As half of Simon and Garfunkel, and their principal musical arranger and sometime producer, Paul Simon oversaw the creative activity of one of the most successful duos in pop music history.

Simon has embraced both musical and technical innovations throughout his career. In 1966, *Sounds of Silence* (produced by Bob Johnston and Tom Wilson; see entries) was the first album to be recorded with eight simultaneous tracks, accomplished by synchronizing two 4-track machines to one another. By contrast, the

Beatles recorded *Sgt. Pepper* the following year with only four simultaneous tracks (they increased the available tracks by bouncing down between two 4-track machines). Similarly, "The Boxer" (No. 7, with Art Garfunkel and Roy Halee; see entry), recorded in 1969, was the first commercial 16-track recording, accomplished by synchronizing two 8-track machines.

Through his use of Latin American polyrhythms and other third world influences, Simon presaged the world beat movement by over 20 years. His 1970 "El Condor Pasa" (No. 18), based on a Peruvian folk melody, featured Latin American musicians Los Incas. The following year Simon recorded the Latin-inflected "Me and Julio down by the Schoolyard" with Roy Halee and traveled to Jamaica to record "Mother and Child Reunion" (No. 4) with members of Toots and the Maytals. In 1986 he was the first mainstream pop artist to incorporate traditional African rhythms with *Graceland* (No. 3), an album primarily recorded in South Africa.

Simon, born October 13, 1941, in Newark, New Jersey, began his recording career at 15 as a musician and singer on demos for a variety of songwriters, including sessions with Burt Bacharach (see entry). Typically, Simon sang a number of vocal parts, including background doo-wop–style harmonies, and played guitar and bass. Carole King on drums and keyboards was a frequent collaborator on these early demo sessions.

While still in their teens, Simon and classmate Art Garfunkel recorded an album under the name of Tom and Jerry. A few years later they were signed to Columbia Records. "In the early days of Simon and Garfunkel," Simon explains, "the record label had assigned us producers because that's how things were done. But really, between Roy Halee, who was the engineer, and Artie and me, we knew how to make records. I had already been making records since I was 15, and Halee and Garfunkel both had training in classical music."

Bookends (No. 1) in 1968 was the first recording on which Simon received a production credit. It also signaled his new maturity as a songwriter and producer. The album is resplendent with ear candy, sounds and aural images that enhance Simon's molecular melodicism. "Fakin' It" (produced by John Simon; see entry), in particular, showcases high production techniques we now take for granted because they've been imitated so often: organ parts and vocals flying in and out, echoed claps supporting the snare drum, strings and background vocals doubling each other, a string quartet in the third chorus punctuated with trumpet and trombone hits. The multiple vocal and guitar layerings of "Mrs. Robinson" (No. 1, with Garfunkel and Halee) and "A Hazy Shade of Winter" (produced by Johnston) created new and exciting sonic textures, a distinctive sound that listeners and radio craved.

The Halee-Simon team were geniuses with echoes and reverbs. Beginning with *Bookends* and continuing through *Bridge over Troubled Water,* they introduced some of the most musical and tasteful echoes ever committed to tape. *Bridge over Troubled Water* took two years to make; it sold 5 million U.S. copies and was the No. 1 U.S. album for 10 weeks in a row.

Part of Simon's production expertise was knowing when to sing and when to give the vocals to Art Garfunkel. "I never had a particular feel for [singing] that song," Simon says regarding the title track, although he performed it often in concert after the duo broke up. The song was perfect for Garfunkel's angelic tenor, and Simon gave it a dramatic presentation: the song begins with solo grand piano, followed by a gradual buildup and the addition of instruments until it reaches a crescendo with full strings—and an enormous cannon-like snare drum recorded in an echo chamber—to augment its already ethereal sound. "Cecelia" (No. 4) was built on top of a demo tape recorded at Simon's house, with Garfunkel and him clapping the rhythm track on a piano bench. "The Boxer" featured a snare drum recorded in an elevator shaft, a bass harmonica, and massively layered vocal parts that create the illusion of an entire chorus of Simons and Garfunkels. "Baby Driver" was rendered with double-tracked baritone saxophone.

Paul Simon (No. 4), the artist's first solo album, was primarily a showcase for the songs, a respite from the heavy (and at times compulsively detail-oriented) production of *Bridge.* One highlight is the enchanting Simon–Stephane Grappelli instrumental collaboration, "Hobo's Blues."

With the release of his second solo album, *There Goes Rhymin' Simon* (No. 2), Simon was back to not just recording records, but producing them, in a release whose influence is still felt today. *Rhymin'* (with Halee and Phil Ramone; see entry) was one of the first commercially released vinyl albums to be produced in a quadraphonic version (the additional two channels were encoded on the disc and could be reproduced at home using quadraphonic amplifiers and decoders). Working with engineers Jerry Masters and Phil Ramone and session players drawn from the Muscle Shoals Rhythm Section, Simon created an album that still sounds fresh. The snare drum and vocal echoes on "Kodachrome" (No. 2) are beautifully balanced, chamber-created sounds that must have required hours of exacting microphone and speaker adjustments. Continuing his quest to integrate a variety of musical styles, Simon employed the Dixie Hummingbirds to sing mel-

lifluous background vocals on the gospel-inspired "Tenderness."

"Something So Right" provided the road map for how '70s singer/songwriters would approach the rock ballad. "Was a Sunny Day" married calypso and reggae to rock five years before the Police. "St. Judy's Comet" was a lilting, shuffling lullaby that John Lennon paid tribute to in 1980's "Beautiful Boy."

The production of *Still Crazy After All These Years* (No. 1, with Ramone) was also high-quality and high-gloss (and was also released in a quadraphonic vinyl version). Decidedly more mainstream than *Rhymin' Simon,* it netted Simon a Grammy for Album of the Year and yielded the No. 1 single "50 Ways to Leave Your Lover," as well as three other hit singles, "Gone at Last," "My Little Town" (No. 9, a duet with Garfunkel), and the title cut.

Graceland also won Simon a Grammy for Album of the Year. One of the most surprising, rewarding, and enjoyable albums ever, it is also on many scholarly lists of best-produced albums of all time, alongside *Sgt. Pepper* and Pink Floyd's *Dark Side of the Moon. Graceland* combined traditional African rhythms, harmonies, and musicians with Simon's perspicacious lyrics and melodies. The production itself was an engineer's nightmare: African instruments recorded live with little or no separation, multiple triggered inputs, songs that were created out of jam sessions and edited together via 24-track tape. Halee rose to the occasion.

The Rhythm of the Saints (No. 4) used a similar approach to composition: Simon essentially jammed with a group of musicians, and from those sessions edited tape until he had the basic tracks for a dozen songs. He added lyrics and melodies and the overdubs of traditional instruments and vocals later. The album experienced disappointing sales compared to *Graceland* (2 million versus 5 million). Simon's theory is that the public found it hard to embrace because there was no drum kit on the entire record. Other speculations are that the vocals were merely mixed too softly or the timing of the release was off.

In 1994, Simon produced *Picture Perfect Morning* for his wife, Edie Brickell. One of his most prominent productions for another artist, the album has the expected high production and sheen and shows a tasteful regard for the role of production in framing the songs, not overshadowing them. It is very much Brickell's album, not Simon's; the producer creates a gentle, supportive frame for her easy, flowing songs and expressive, unlabored vocals.

Simon's latest production is 1997's *The Capeman,* his first attempt at a Broadway musical. Despite high musi-

cal values (and lyrics by Nobel Prize–winning poet Derek Walcott), the album stiffed and the musical failed.
—DANIEL J. LEVITIN

Baez, Joan: *Speaking of Dreams*, Guardian/Angel, 1989, 1996.
Brickell, Edie: "Good Times," Geffen, 1994 • *Picture Perfect Morning*, Geffen, 1994.
Frank, Jackson C.: *Blues Run the Game*, Mooncrest, 1965, 1996.
Garfunkel, Art: *Breakaway*, Columbia, 1975.
Ladysmith Black Mambazo: *Shaka Zulu*, Warner Bros., 1987 • *Journey of Dreams*, Warner Bros., 1988.
Nelson, Willie: "Graceland," Columbia, 1993.
Perkins, Carl: *Go Cat Go*, Dinosaur, 1996.
Roche, Terry, and Maggie Roche: *Seductive Reasoning*, Columbia, 1975.
Simon and Garfunkel: *Bookends*, Columbia, 1968 • "Mrs. Robinson," Columbia, 1968 • "The Boxer," Columbia, 1969 • "Bridge over Troubled Water," Columbia, 1970 • *Bridge over Troubled Water*, Columbia, 1970 • "Cecelia," Columbia, 1970 • "El Condor Pasa," Columbia, 1970 • "America," Columbia, 1972 • "For Emily, Wherever I May Find Her," Columbia, 1972 • "My Little Town," Columbia, 1975 • *Collected Works*, Columbia, 1981, 1990 • *The Concert in Central Park*, Warner Bros., 1982, 1988 • "Wake Up Little Susie," Warner Bros., 1982 • *Old Friends*, Columbia, 1997.
Simon, Paul: "Duncan," Columbia, 1972 • "Me and Julio down by the Schoolyard," Columbia, 1972 • "Mother And Child Reunion," Columbia, 1972 • *Paul Simon*, Columbia, 1972 • "American Tune," Columbia, 1973 • "Kodachrome," Columbia, 1973 • "Loves Me Like a Rock," Columbia, 1973 • "Something So Right," Columbia, 1973 • *There Goes Rhymin' Simon*, Columbia, 1973 • w/ Phoebe Snow, "Gone at Last," Columbia, 1975 • "Still Crazy After All These Years," Warner Bros., 1975 • *Still Crazy After All These Years*, Warner Bros., 1975 • "50 Ways to Leave Your Lover," Columbia, 1976 • "Slip Slidin' Away," Columbia, 1977 • "One Trick Pony," Warner Bros., 1980 • *One Trick Pony* soundtrack, Warner Bros., 1980 • "Allergies," Warner Bros., 1983 • *Hearts and Bones*, Warner Bros., 1983 • *Graceland*, Warner Bros., 1985 • "You Can Call Me Al," Warner Bros., 1985 • "Graceland," Warner Bros., 1986 • "The Boy in the Bubble," Warner Bros., 1987 • *Negotiations and Love Songs (1971–1986)*, Warner Bros., 1988 • "The Obvious Child," Warner Bros., 1990 • *The Rhythm of the Saints*, Warner Bros., 1990 • *Paul Simon's Concert in the Park*, Warner Bros., 1991 • *Paul Simon, 1964–1993*, Warner Bros., 1993 • "Bernadette," Warner Bros., 1997 • *Songs from the Capeman*, Warner Bros., 1997.
Titus, Libby: *Libby Titus*, CBS, 1977.

Ed Simons

See CHEMICAL BROTHERS

Mike Simpson

See DUST BROTHERS

David Sinclair

See TAPPA "TAPPER" ZUKIE

Sean Slade

See PAUL Q. KOLDERIE and SEAN SLADE

Sly and Robbie
(LOWELL DUNBAR AND ROBERT SHAKESPEARE)

As reggae's best-known rhythm section, Sly and Robbie backed the best in the business: Peter Tosh, Black Uhuru, and Ini Kamoze are but a few of the touring acts whose live presence was made all the more formidable by their distinctive drum and bass interaction. They backed—in their case you could almost say fronted—hundreds of other Jamaican artists on thousands of sessions as well, cutting tracks for nearly all the major reggae producers before becoming producers themselves. They have produced and played for major nonreggae acts like Bob Dylan and Grace Jones as well.

Lowell "Sly" Dunbar (born May 10, 1952) played drums for Skin Flesh and Bones, one of the hottest studio bands of the early '70s, and his drumming was a good part of what made their soul-groove sound on records by artists from Al Brown to Merlene Webber. Robert "Robbie" Shakespeare (born September 27, 1953) started playing bass in the strong, simple mode of his early hero, Wailers bassist Aston "Familyman" Barrett, but slowly developed his own decorative style. The two first joined forces in the Aggrovators, for producer Bunny Lee (see entry), in Joe Gibbs' (see entry) Professionals, and in other amorphous studio bands (in which the players often changed but the name stayed the same); they shortly cemented their partnership as the bass-and-drum combination for the Revolutionaries. Together they formed an unbeatable musical combination that transformed reggae.

The Revolutionaries were the house band for Channel One and defined the militant rockers style that swept Kingston in the mid-'70s. Working for producers Alvin Ranglin, Jo Jo Hookim (see entry), Bunny Lee, and a host of others, Sly and Robbie were on the cutting edge of the development of the reggae sound and responsible for many of its changes. Revolutionaries dubs and rhythm tracks backed so many artists in this period it would be easier to list records Sly and Robbie *didn't* play on than ones they did. They soon became the most in-demand session players on the island.

Under the name Word Sound and Power, they were the driving force behind Peter Tosh after he left the Wailers, touring extensively while still jobbing out as Jamaica's hottest session team. Tosh's 1978 album *Bush Doctor* co-credits production to Word Sound and Power, while the following year's *Mystic Man* gives production credit to Tosh and Robert Shakespeare. Sly and Robbie played behind Bunny Wailer at one point too. The "Ryddim Twins," as they were also known, were soon in demand as producers as well, often cutting albums for artists they had previously played for under the aegis of Bunny Lee and others.

After backing a trio of vocalists called Black Uhuru on their first Prince Jammy–produced (see entry) album, Sly and Robbie went on to produce a series of records for the group that brought international acclaim, a major production deal with Island Records and a relentless touring schedule. Through a series of finely crafted albums that modernized the once-basic reggae rhythm, Sly and Robbie forged a new sound, eventually becoming such an integral part of the band that they appeared on album covers as a five-piece. This period included two of Black Uhuru and reggae's finest albums, *Sinsemilla* and *Red*.

During this time Sly and Robbie set up their own Taxi label in Jamaica, issuing product internationally

under that name through a series of distribution deals. After Uhuru, they went on to a series of their own Taxi tours, bringing classic artists like Marcia Griffiths and new talent like Ini Kamoze into major rock arenas. The band often included guitarist Mikey Chung and, like their recordings, nearly always included Robbie Lyn on keyboards as well. Sly's constant experimenting—always modifying rhythms—as well as the duo's exposure to new sounds and equipment while traveling, led to innovations in reggae like syndrums. Sly's machine-like playing style and futuristic sounds opened the door to the digital age and changed the face of Jamaican music forever.

Roots productions include Gregory Isaacs's classics "Soon Forward" and "Slave Driver," Horace Andy's "Zion Gate," and Sugar Minott's "Herbman Hustling." In the lovers style, their work with Dennis Brown reigns supreme. They also produced an album for U.K. lovers stylist Maxi Priest. Concurrent with their own productions they backed Sugar Minott for George Phang, Gregory Isaacs for Gussie Clarke (see entry), Michael Prophet for Delroy Wright, Jackie Mittoo for Bunny Lee, and many more. It almost seemed at one point that if Sly and Robbie didn't at least play on it, it wasn't reggae. They are among the only Jamaican producers ever accredited with "name above the title": the tag "Sly and Robbie present" is used on many of their own productions and others they played on.

As artists they also released albums produced by others, like *The Summit,* an early Fattis Burrell (see entry) production; 1985's *Language Barrier,* produced by Bill Laswell (see entry); *Material* (featuring guest stars like Herbie Hancock, Bob Dylan, and Doug E. Fresh) and the follow-up, *Rhythm Killers,* also produced by Laswell and Material. In 1989, KRS-One produced them for the Island album *Silent Assassin*.

In the early '90s, Taxi scored again with Chaka Demus and Pliers and a tune called "Murder She Wrote," cut over a revamped and updated rhythm based on Toots and the Maytals' "Bam Bam." They went on to record dozens of dancehall artists, like Flourgon, Lady Ann, and Jigsy King. They also released *Sly and Robbie Remember Precious Times,* on which the rhythm-section-turned-producers sing. Still, their major hits cut a swath through early roots to raggamuffin dancehall; Sly and Robbie perfectly exemplify the secret that dancehall and reggae are one and the same. They must be the only rhythm team that's backed both Peter Tosh and Yellowman.

Both Dunbar and Shakespeare still do session work alone and together for other producers, but they've maintained their edge as Jamaica's leading production team. In a universe where rhythm is king, Sly and Robbie have probably been responsible for more of the rhythmic variations that make up reggae than anyone else. Like American session drummer Hal Blaine, when someone wants to remake a classic reggae rhythm, there's a good chance they can play it best since they played it the first time too. —CHUCK FOSTER

Beenie Man: featuring Chevelle Franklyn, "Dancehall Queen," Island Jamaica, 1997 • *Many Moods of Moses,* VP, 1997.

Black Uhuru: *Black Uhuru,* Virgin, 1979 • *Showcase,* D-Roy, 1979 • *Sensimilla,* Mango, 1980 • *Red,* Mango, 1981 • "Sponji Reggae/Push Push," Mango, 1981 • *Chill Out,* Island, 1982 • *Anthem,* Island, 1983 • *Guess Who's Coming to Dinner,* Heartbeat, 1983 • *The Dub Factor,* Mango, 1983 • *Reggae Greats,* Mango, 1984 • *Brutal Dub,* RAS, 1986 • "Somebody's Watching You," Mango, 1989 (*Jammin'*).

Bounty Killer: *My Xperience,* VP, 1996.

Brown, Dennis: "Sitting and Watching," Mango/Island, 1982 (*Countryman* soundtrack) • *Brown Sugar,* RAS, 1988 • *Love & Hate: The Best of Dennis Brown* (5 tracks), VP, 1996.

Cliff, Jimmy: "(Your Love Keeps Liftin') Higher and Higher," Interscope/Atlantic, 1994.

Culture: *Culture at Work,* Shanachie, 1986.

Curiosity Killed the Cat: *Keep Your Distance* (6 tracks), Mercury, 1987.

Cutty Ranks: "Hustle, Hustle," Profile, 1994 (*Dancehall Style,* Vol. 4).

Demus, Chaka, and Pliers: "I Wanna Be Your Man," Mango, 1993 • "Murder She Wrote," Mango, 1993.

Dunbar, Sly: *Sly, Wicked and Slick,* Front Line, 1977 • *Sly-Go-Ville,* Mango, 1982 • *See also* Collections.

Guthrie, Gwen: "Padlock," Garage, 1985 • "Peanut Butter," Garage, 1985.

Half Pint: *Victory,* RAS, 1986 • *See also* Collections.

Isaacs, Gregory: *Sly and Robbie Present Gregory Isaacs,* RAS, 1988 • *Cool Ruler: Soon Forward-Selection* (1 track), Frontline, 1990.

Jones, Grace: *Nightclubbing,* Island, 1980 • *Warm Leatherette,* Island, 1980 • *Livin' My Life,* Island, 1982.

Kamoze, Ini: *Ini Kamoze,* Island, 1984 • *Statement,* Island, 1984 • "Trouble You a Trouble Me," Mango, 1984 (*Reggae Greats: Strictly for Rockers*) • *Pirate,* Mango, 1986 • *Here Comes the Hotstepper,* Columbia, 1995 • *See also* Collections.

Lady Saw: *Passion,* VP, 1997.

Mad Cobra: *Hard to Wet, Easy to Dry* (9 tracks), Columbia, 1992.

Maxi Priest: "Wild World," Virgin, 1987 • *Maxi Priest,* Virgin, 1988 • "Some Guys Have All the Luck," Virgin America, 1989 (*Slaves of New York* soundtrack) • *Bonfide,* Charisma,

1990 • "Close to You," Charisma, 1990 • *Fe Real,* Charisma, 1992 • "Groovin' in the Midnight," Virgin, 1992 • *Man with the Fun,* Virgin, 1996.

Minott, Sugar: "Rub-a-Dub Sound," Mango, 1984 (*Reggae Greats: Strictly for Rockers*) • *Sugar and Spice,* RAS, 1990 • "Herbsman Hustling," Tommy Boy, 1994 (*Big Blunts: 12 Smokin' Reggae Hits*) • *RAS Portraits,* RAS, 1997 • *The Best Of,* VP, 1998.

Morales, David, and Bad Yard Club: *The Program,* Mercury, 1993.

New Order: "Ruined in a Day" (remix), Qwest/WB, 1993.

Papa San: *Rough Cut,* Pow Wow, 1992 • *See also* Collections.

Rebel, Tony: "My Way or the Highway," Chaos, 1994.

Red, Danny: "Rolling Stone Girl," Sony, 1995.

Riley, Jimmy: *Rydim Driven,* Mango, 1981 • *See also* Albums.

Salter, Sam: *It's on Tonight,* LaFace, 1997.

Shaggy: *Midnite Lover,* Virgin, 1997.

Sly and Robbie: *Gambler's Choice,* Taxi, 1980 • *Sixties Seventies + Eighties = Taxi,* Mango, 1981 • *Reggae Greats: A Dub Experience,* Mango, 1984 • *Remember Precious Times,* RAS, 1992 • *Mambo Taxi,* VP, 1997 • *Friends,* EastWest, 1998.

Spanner Banner: "Chill," Island Jamaica, 1995 • *Chill,* Island Jamaica, 1995.

Taxi Gang with Sly and Robbie: *Electro-Reggae,* Mango, 1986 • *The Sting,* Moving Target/Celluloid, 1986.

Thompson, Linval: *Starlight,* Mango, 1988.

Toots and the Maytals: *Reggae Greats* (2 tracks), Mango, 1984.

Tosh, Peter: *Bush Doctor,* Rolling Stones, 1978 • *The Toughest,* Capitol, 1988 • *The Best of Peter Tosh: Dread Don't Die,* EMI America, 1996 • *Honorary Citizen,* Legacy, 1997.

Yellowman: *Girls Them Pet,* Taxi, 1986 • *Rambo,* Moving Target, 1986.

COLLECTIONS

Sound of Taxi, Taxi, n.d.

Taxi Production Presents the Sounds of the 80's, Taxi, n.d.

Sound of Sound, Pow Wow, n.d.

Sly and Robbie Present: Taxi, Taxi, 1981: Viceroys, "Heart Made of Stone" • Wailing Souls, "Old Broom," "Sweet Sugar Plum."

Crucial Reggae, Taxi, 1984: Sly Dunbar, "Unmetered Taxi" • Mighty Diamonds, "Pass the Kouchie" • The Rolands, "Johnny Dollar."

Taxi Gang, Taxi, 1984.

Taxi Wax, Taxi, 1984.

Sound of Taxi, Vol. 2, Taxi, 1986.

Taxi Connection: Live in London, Taxi, 1986.

Taxi Fare, Taxi, 1987.

Sly and Robbie Present: DJ Riot, Mango, 1990: Daddy Lizard, "One Burner" • Flourgon, "Minimum Wages" • Red Dragon, "Wine and Go Down" • Tiger, "Raggamuffin" • Trinity, "Judgement Day."

Two Rhythms Clash, RAS, 1990: Half Pint, "Cost of Living" •
Tappa Zukie, "Legal."

Sound of the Nineties, Taxi, 1990.

Taxi X-mas, RAS, 1991.

Sly and Robbie Present: The Punishers, Mango, 1993: Charlie
Chaplin, "Sweet Janice" • Jigsy King, "Any Way You Deh"
• Lady Ann, "Worries" • Luciano, "Feel Like Paradise" •
Roundhead, "Pressure You Hate."

Ragga 'Pon Top, Pow Wow, 1993: Baby Wayne, "Move with the
Crowd" • Papa San, "Little Crook."

Sly and Robbie Present: The Speeding Taxi, Sonic Sounds, 1993:
Horace Andy, "Zion Gate" • Ken Boothe, "Show and
Tell" • Ini Kamoze, "Call the Police" • Carlton Livingston,
"Tricksters" • Jimmy Riley, "My Woman's Love."

Keith Haring: A Retrospective, the Music of His Era, Logic, 1997.

Don Smith

Even though Don Smith looks to the masters for
inspiration—Glyn Johns, George Martin, and Phil
Spector (see entries)—he prefers to allow a song to
do the work for him. "You should try to let the song tell
you what to do instead of me telling you what to do,"
he says. "Usually, I try to get the band to open up their
minds a little bit and leave their brains outside and let
the song tell us what to do. If it's a good song, it will tell
us and come out great. I think if you try to force some
stuff on it, it's going to make a song worse."

Smith has guided younger bands, like Star 69, Jackopierce, and Cravin' Melon, and experienced artists,
such as Cracker and John Hiatt. The first time Smith
entered the studio was as a guitarist in a Dallas band. He
quickly discovered his true role was as producer, not
musician. After working as an engineer in Dallas, he ran
his own studio for a while, then moved to Los Angeles.

He first worked with War, then Blood, Sweat and
Tears. Finally, Keith Olsen (see entry) called on Smith to
help him complete Olsen's Goodnight L.A. Studios.
"While I was there he asked me to work with Jimmy
Iovine (see entry) on Stevie Nicks's first album," Smith
remembers. "I worked on that for about three to four
weeks of overdubs. Then Jimmy asked me to mix the
record and I co-mixed it with Shelley Yackus. Then I
started doing stuff with Jimmy, and he introduced me to
Tom Petty and we did 'Stop Dragging My Heart
Around.' " That led to work on albums for the Pointer
Sisters, Jeffrey Osborne, and Bette Midler; Smith also
remixed U2's 1984 album, *Under a Blood Red Sky.*

Smith considers digital technology "vanilla" and
prefers old Neves, APIs, or Fairchilds. He likes "the color
of the old equipment," he says. The units "have a sound
to 'em. Most of the digital stuff I don't like the sound of;
the guitars sound like they got razor blades all of a sudden. There's no warmth or character."

He would love to return to the '60s and '70s. "There
was a lot of bullshit back then, too, but the songs were
good and they had a different sound. Now [music] all
reminds me of American cars, they all look the same."

He tries to give a song staying power. "I don't try to
do a Phil Spector thing," he says. "I try to let the band
be the band as much as possible. When it sounds the
least produced, I think it sounds the best. I just try to let
the music take care of itself." —DAVID JOHN FARINELLA

Bash and Pop: *Friday Night Is Killing Me,* Sire/Reprise, 1993.

Call, The: *Into the Woods,* Elektra, 1987 • *The Best of the Call,*
Warner Bros., 1997.

Camper Van Beethoven: *Virgin Years,* Virgin, 1994.

Cracker: *Cracker,* Virgin, 1992 • *Kerosene Hat,* Virgin, 1993 •
"Low," Virgin, 1994 • *Gentleman's Blues,* Virgin, 1998.

Cravin' Melon: *Red Clay Harvest,* Mercury, 1997.

Davis, Jimmy, and Junction: "Kick the Wall," QMI, 1987 •
Kick the Wall, QMI, 1988.

Deadeye Dick: *Whirl,* Ichiban, 1995.

Dramarama: *Vinyl,* Chameleon, 1991 • *The Best of
Dramarama: 18 Big Ones,* Rhino, 1996.

Fabulous Thunderbirds: *Hot Stuff: The Greatest Hits,* Epic
Associated, 1992.

54.40: *Dear, Dear,* Sony Canada, 1992 • *Smilin' Buddha Cabaret,*
TriStar, 1994.

Five Easy Pieces: *Five Easy Pieces,* MCA, 1998.

From Good Homes: *Open Up the Sky,* RCA, 1995.

Germano, Lisa: "You Make Me Want to Wear Dresses"
(remix), Capitol, 1993.

Hiatt, John: *Walk On,* Capitol, 1995.

Himmelman, Peter: *Flown This Acid World,* Epic, 1992.

Hollowbodies, The: *Viva la Dregs,* Polydor, 1998.

Jackopierce: *The Finest Hour,* A&M, 1996 • *Decade, 1988–1998,*
Crystal Clear Sound, 1998.

Love, G., and Special Sauce: *Coast to Coast Motel,* Okeh/Epic,
1995.

Meices, The: *Dirty Bird* (1 track), London, 1996.

Perfect: *When Squirrels Play Chicken* (EP), Restless, 1996.

Rebel Train: *Seeking Shelter,* EastWest, 1992.

Rembrandts, The: *The Rembrandts,* Atco, 1990 • *LP,* EastWest,
1995.

Richards, Keith: *Live at the Hollywood Palladium,* Virgin, 1991.

Rutledge, James: *Hooray for Good Times,* Capitol, n.d.

Star 69: *Eating February,* Radioactive, 1997 • "I'm Insane,"
Radioactive, 1997.

Too Many Cooks: *Decadence,* Start, 1995.

Tragically Hip: *Up to Here,* MCA, 1989 • *Road Apples,* MCA, 1991.

Wire Train: *Wire Train,* MCA, 1990.

Gary Smith

An impresario of the Boston indie rock scene of the late '80s and '90s centered around the Fort Apache Studios, Smith has produced fundamental records by the Blake Babies, the Chills, the Connells, the Feelies, Juliana Hatfield, the Pixies, and Pylon, as well as producing and managing Throwing Muses and ex-Muse/ex-Breeder/ex-Belly singer/songwriter Tanya Donelly.

Gary Smith was born in 1958 in Newport, Rhode Island, and spent many a summer day sneaking under fences to attend the Newport Jazz and Folk festivals, from which he learned that music can be as much a lifestyle as an art. Newport was full of preppies with trust funds, and Smith, the son of schoolteachers and humanitarians, soon developed the sense that the "way wealth worked in the world" was, in fact, "fucked." He also played guitar in bands, wrote songs, and took an interest in recording, fiddling with tape recorders from an early age.

Smith earned a B.A. in philosophy from Colby College ("an uptight sub–Ivy League school in rural Maine"), where he also helped build the school's 4-track recording studio with a music professor named Adrian Lowe, who had been a pioneer in the field of electronic music. Smith worked at the studio through his sophomore year, took a year off to play in a band, then returned to school. Smith's college years corresponded with the punk revolution, and the raw vitality and social egalitarianism of the Clash, Gang of Four, and their peers reached deep into his heart, especially against "the gold-leaf background" of Colby.

Smith graduated, then studied architecture for a year at the Sorbonne in Paris. Having decided to give music another go, he moved to Boston and formed Lifeboat, an early '80s pop-leaning alt-rock band that released an album on Dolphin. In an effort to promote the local indie rock scene, Smith helped put together a compilation in 1983 called *Boston Pops,* which sold reasonably well in the area. Smith co-produced the Blaros' contribution to the collection and enjoyed the experience.

Smith then became aware of an interesting all-woman band from Newport called Throwing Muses, and got them added to some live dates with Lifeboat. After a show in Providence, the band's manager asked Smith to produce some demos for the Muses. Smith—a huge fan by then—agreed, and they recorded a demo tape in 1984 that garnered a boatload of favorable press. The Muses—led by singer/songwriter/guitarists Kristin Hersh and (her stepsister) Tanya Donelly—developed an extremely influential and accomplished version of noise pop, years ahead of similar bands like Britain's My Bloody Valentine and Lush.

Similarly drawn by the bipoles of pop melodies and fulminating noise were the Pixies, whom Smith saw opening for the Muses at Boston's Rat Club in early 1987. Smith, astonished, went backstage and introduced himself to singer/songwriter/guitarist Black Francis (born Charles Thompson, now recording as "Frank Black"), guitarist Joey Santiago, bassist/singer Kim Deal (later of the Breeders), and drummer David Lovering.

Smith had recently thrown in with Paul Kolderie and Sean Slade's (see entry) 8-track Fort Apache studio collective (which also included producer/engineers Lou Giordano and Tim O'Heir; see entries) and offered to record the Pixies there. In March, Smith and the Pixies recorded 18 songs in three days. The demo was passed around, and Ivo Watts, head of England's arty 4 A.D. label (who had recently signed Throwing Muses), signed the Pixies and released eight of the songs as *Come On Pilgrim.*

The Pixies, with their myriad contradictory impulses—stream-of-consciousness lyrics, alternately mumbled and shrieked; surf-influenced melodies, harmonies, and guitar stylings; jarring atonality and diaphanous delicacy, often displayed within the same song—penetrated deep into the alt-rock culture and became an archetype.

Lifeboat had run aground in early 1987 after recording tracks with Mitch Easter (see entry) that are "still in the can somewhere," but Smith still considered himself primarily a "band guy," albeit without portfolio. When the Pixies took off, the production work flooded in for both Smith and Fort Apache. By the end of 1987, the studio had relocated to Cambridge from the blighted Roxbury area of Boston, and had been upgraded to a 16-track. With the move, Smith and partner Joe Harvard became primary owners of Fort Apache, and Smith was no longer just another "band guy."

Through the early '90s Smith produced what he terms "high-cred, low-sales" records for out-of-town bands, in addition to continued work with Throwing Muses and local faves Blake Babies (led by Juliana Hatfield). "Eventually I got sick and tired of parasitic managers and the way that record companies were treating the fans and the bands, so I called up Juliana Hatfield (who had just left Blake Babies) and Tanya Donelly (who had just left Throwing Muses) and asked if I could take care of their careers, which is basically what I have been doing since 1992."

Smith is far too dismissive of his production accomplishments, though he does modestly allow that his best were, perhaps, recorded with a "gracious realism." Several of Smith's productions reside at the very pinnacle of the organic alt-pop records of the time. The pure Kiwi-meets-Brian Wilson pop of New Zealand's Chills lives up to the title of the first song on *Submarine Bells*: "Heavenly Pop Hit." Martin Phillipps's slightly raggedy vocals keep things from getting too slick on an album that tastes like a burbling mountain spring.

Pylon (from Athens, Georgia) evokes early R.E.M. tonalities and instrumentation supporting a remarkable female singer—Vanessa Briscoe Hay—who sounds like a cross between the Divinyls' Christina Amphlett and Skyhooks' Graeme Strachan. *Chain* charges ahead with rhythmic intensity through great tune after great tune, including "Look Alive," "Catch," "This/That," and on and on. With appropriate promotion they could have been a contender.

New Jersey's Feelies—led by the dueling guitars of Glenn Mercer and Bill Million—is another alt-rock legend that deserves vastly wider recognition (though the Chills', Pylon's, and Feelies' relative obscurity coincides with Smith's view that great artists must toil outside of the mainstream or be corrupted by it). *Time for a Witness* navigates in a nether-world of intense compression, somewhere between punk aggression and alt-rock introversion, sounding something like Television performing mid-'60s electric Bob Dylan. The first three songs—the title track, "Waiting," and "Sooner or Later"—are classics from an extraordinary album.

It is easy to see why Smith chose to work with Hatfield and Donelly, two talented and attractive singer/songwriters with impeccable indie rock credentials and baby doll voices. Smith first produced Hatfield's trio, Blake Babies, including their great *Sunburn* album, on which Hatfield sings beguiling guitar-pop tunes to hapless boyfriends that range from venomous ("I'm Not Your Mother," "Star") to wistful ("I'll Take Anything," "Kiss and Make Up"). Hatfield's solo debut *Hey Babe* is similar, if slightly more mainstream. Featuring sometime-boyfriend Evan Dando of the Lemonheads on guitars and background vocals, there is much jangly strumming on catchy songs, including "Everybody Loves Me but You" "I See You," "Forever Baby," and "Ugly."

Through the '80s Throwing Muses albums were largely dominated by Kristin Hersh; Tanya Donelly

stepped briefly into the spotlight with her "Dragonhead" and "Angel" songs from 1989's *Hunkpapa;* but by 1991's *The Real Ramona,* Donelly's "Not Too Soon" and "Honeychain" were the most interesting songs on the Muses' album. She briefly joined Kim Deal's Breeders in 1991 after leaving the Muses, then formed her own band, Belly, in 1992. Belly's two excellent albums—the gold *Star* (co-produced by Gil Norton; see entry), and *King* (produced by Glyn Johns; see entry)—were both hits, and the single "Feed the Tree" was a modern rock radio smash.

Smith returned to production work for Donelly's solo debut, *Lovesongs for Underdogs,* in 1997. Smith has had, at best, modest success thus far with releases (Cold Water Flat, Shatterproof, Speedball Baby) on his own Fort Apache imprint (distributed by MCA), discovering in the process that it is difficult to be the record label and the artist's friend at the same time—a source of pain for a man with a Wobbly soul. Yet Smith forges on, having chosen the celebratory arena of rock 'n' roll over a dour life of placard carrying, a man of integrity in a faithless world. —ERIC OLSEN

Blake Babies: *Earwig,* Mammoth, 1989, 1991 • *Sunburn,* Mammoth, 1990 • *Rosy Jack World* (1 track), Mammoth, 1991 • *Innocence and Experience,* Mammoth, 1993.
Blaros, The: "Heartbreak Hospital," self-released, 1983 (*Boston Pops*).
Bragg, Billy: "Accident Waiting to Happen" (Red Star mix), Elektra, 1991 • "You Woke Up My Neighborhood," Elektra, 1991.
Chills, The: *Submarine Bells,* Slash/WB, 1990.
Connells, The: *Fun and Games,* TVT, 1989.
Donelly, Tanya: *Lovesongs for Underdogs,* Warner Bros., 1997.
Feelies, The: "Invitation," A&M, 1991 • *Time for a Witness,* A&M, 1991.
Hatfield, Juliana: *Forever Baby* (EP, 3 tracks), Mammoth, 1992 • *Hey Babe,* Mammoth, 1992 • *I See You* (EP, 2 tracks), Mammoth, 1992.
Pixies, The: *Come on Pilgrim,* 4 A.D./Elektra, 1987, 1992 • *Death to the Pixies: 1987–1991*, Elektra, 1997.
Pylon: *Chain,* Sky, 1990.
Scrawl: *Smallmouth,* Rough Trade, 1990.
10,000 Maniacs: *Candy Everybody Wants* (EP), Elektra, 1993.
Throwing Muses: *House Tornado,* 4 A.D./Sire, 1987 • *Hunkpapa,* Sire, 1989 • "Matter of Degrees," Atlantic, 1991 (*A Matter of Degrees* soundtrack).
Walkabouts, The: *Scavenger,* Sub Pop, 1991 • "Where the Deep Water Goes," Sub Pop, 1991.

COLLECTIONS
This Is Fort Apache, Fort Apache/MCA, 1995.

Harry Smith

Harry Smith is one of the truly singular figures of 20th-century American culture: a brilliant polymath who made major contributions to sound recording, record collecting, independent film making and animation, the visual arts, hermetic philosophy, and what might be termed "outsider anthropology."

His 1952 *Anthology of American Folk Music,* released on Moe Asch's Folkways Records, is arguably the single most significant and influential collection of such material ever assembled. It deeply affected both the folk music revival and the maturation of rock 'n' roll. Re-released on compact disc to wide acclaim (and two Grammy Awards) in 1997 by Smithsonian Folkways, the *Anthology* continues to serve as a uniquely profound, yet wildly entertaining introduction to some of America's greatest musical traditions, and has helped to spark critical interest in a figure whose full career remains obscure. Smith's artistic works—many of which have disappeared—have yet to be revealed to a popular audience.

Born in Portland, Oregon, on May 29, 1923, Harry Everett Smith spent his formative years in the Pacific Northwest. The only child of theosophically inclined parents, he began serious study of and interaction with the region's aboriginal tribes at a young age. As a teenager, Smith gained local notoriety (and a color photograph in a national magazine) through his precocious efforts as an amateur anthropologist; he collected sacred artifacts, studied tribal languages, and recorded ceremonial songs on a disc recorder (the present whereabouts of these recordings and artifacts is unknown).

Matriculating at the University of Washington as an anthropology student, he was poised for an academic career when a fateful trip to Berkeley brought him into contact with a new type of bohemian culture—as well as *Cannabis sativa*—and suggested a different future.

Smith soon moved to Berkeley, where he began creating groundbreaking abstract films and paintings (many explicitly correlated to the developing bebop of Dizzy Gillespie, Charlie Parker, and Thelonious Monk) and pursuing the esoteric studies that would serve as the thematic basis for much of his subsequent work, including the *Anthology*. Smith was strongly involved with San Francisco's nascent Art in Cinema movement and showed his films, with live improvised jazz accompaniment, at jazz clubs and the now-defunct San Francisco Museum of Art. He also created several exuberant abstract murals for the walls of the legendary nightspot Jimbo's Bop City in the Fillmore district.

Throughout this period Smith was also amassing the legendary collection of rare recordings that would later be distilled into the *Anthology* and making contacts in the folk and jazz worlds. (He later claimed that he had first experienced peyote during a visit to a California motor court run by the semiretired Sara Carter.) The full extent of Smith's personal involvements (and possible collaborations) with such legendary musicians as Monk, Parker, and Gillespie remains to be brought to light.

In late 1951, Smith moved to New York; his patron was Baroness Hilla Rebay, of Solomon Guggenheim's Museum of Non-Objective Painting. She admired Smith's abstract paintings and films. The *Anthology of American Folk Music* was completed and released the following year, after which Smith sold his record collection to the New York Public Library and Moe Asch. At this time Smith also began a significant association with the legendary Lionel Ziprin, designing eccentric greeting cards for Ziprin's Inkweed Arts company and undertaking a massive recording project involving Ziprin's grandfather, Rabbi Naftali Zvi Margolies Abulafia. This project, which resulted in a 15-record set of kabalistic song, has never seen commercial release.

Smith's next major known recording venture occasioned an extended 1964 visit to Anadarko, Oklahoma, where he made the recordings released as *The Kiowa Peyote Meeting* in the Ethnic Folkways Library series in 1973 (as well as the wonderful psychedelic travelog film No. 14, *Late Superimpositions*). Although the project seemed to be in jeopardy when Smith was thrown in jail on the night of his arrival, this experience introduced him to the finest peyote singers he had met and gave him a new understanding of this extremely spiritual music. Though Smith believed the Kiowa recordings marked an evolutionary advance beyond the methods of the *Anthology*, they have to date only reached a limited audience.

Spring 1965 saw Smith recording and co-producing the first record by essential '60s miscreants the Fugs. *The Village Fugs* was released later that year on Folkways Records and marked a pioneering incursion by bohemian literati into the exploding rock scene, alternating settings of Blake and Swinburne with "Peace, Pot, and Pussy"—maddened anthems such as "Slum Goddess" and "I Couldn't Get High."

Another project combining literary and musical interests was the early '70s recording of songs performed by longtime friend Allen Ginsberg, released as *First Blues: Rags, Ballads, and Harmonium Songs* on Folkways in 1981.

Smith's later recordings made use of advances in portable equipment technology, and increasingly focused on the ineffable sonic properties of environments. A massive series, the anthropologically titled *Materials for the Study of the Religion and Culture of the Lower East Side*, included spoken-word, documentary, and ambient sound recordings. Many tapes were also made during Smith's tenure as "shaman-in-residence" (1988–1991) at Boulder's Naropa Institute.

Smith's death at the Chelsea Hotel on November 27, 1991, initiated a period of archiving, research, and restoration that has brought his work to new and wider audiences. The unprecedented praise earned by the reissue of the *Anthology* has opened the door to the wider range of Smith's accomplishments, which remain to be discovered and preserved. —PHILIP SMITH

Fugs, The: *The Village Fugs/The Fugs First Album,* Fantasy, 1965, 1994 • *The Fugs Second Album,* Fantasy, 1966, 1994.

Ginsberg, Allen: *First Blues: Rags, Ballads and Harmonium Songs,* Folkways, 1981.

COLLECTIONS

Anthology of American Folk Music, Vols. 1–3, Smithsonian/Folkways, 1952, 1997.

The Kiowa Peyote Meeting, Ethnic Folkways Library, 1973.

Phil Spector

Perhaps it should have occurred to someone that Phil Spector (born December 26, 1940, in the Bronx, New York) had a bit of Midas in him when the first song he ever wrote and produced, "To Know Him Is to Love Him" (No. 1) by his band, The Teddy Bears, sold over 1 million copies. His investment? Some studio time (at Hollywood's Gold Star) and $40. It was 1958 and a 17-year-old Spector had just launched a career that would take him from the highest of highs in the early '60s, to the lows of the late '60s, and the shadows by the early '70s.

Spector's career began in 1957 (his family had moved to Los Angeles in the early '50s) as a member of the Sleepwalkers with future Beach Boy Bruce Johnston, future producer Kim Fowley, and drummer Sandy Nelson. By 1958 he was a producer. By the time he was 23, writer Tom Wolfe had dubbed him the "First Tycoon of Teen." By the time he was 34, he had twice been declared DOA after two car accidents three months

apart—and survived. He is the most referred-to name in this book, and his Wall of Sound is either held up as a paradigm to aspire to or reviled as egomaniacal bombast.

Spector's legend is notorious, his influence profound, his credit list rightfully admired. Perhaps his career is best summed up by a quote attributed to him circa 1973: "I really believed in what was going on and I did try to change the music—I did try to change it and it was a painful experience, it was hard, basically, because there were not many people to do it with, there was not much help. It really rested on my ability to do things with my music and sounds. I don't know if I was consciously trying to change it, but musically I was definitely trying to do what I really felt was right."

What was right to Spector's ears apparently was right to a lot of other people's as well. Immediately after leaving Atlantic Records, where he was named head of A&R at age 20, Spector began to develop his Wall of Sound. Some of the musicians he used to produce that sound included drummer Hal Blaine, guitarist Larry Knechtel, bassist Carol Kaye, saxophonist Steve Douglas, and percussionist Sonny Bono. That sound, which some say he "borrowed" from Jerry Leiber and Mike Stoller (see entry), "sweetened" a track with larger-than-life strings, vocals, and percussion instruments. The goal—from finding or writing the song, to hiring the musicians, to recording the song—was to make the song as far out and overwhelming as possible.

After the Teddy Bears and Atlantic, Spector worked with a number of producers, including Lee Hazlewood, Lester Sill, and Leiber and Stoller. In 1962, Spector took his show on the road and launched the Philles label, scoring over 20 hit records by such artists as the Crystals, Darlene Love, Bobb B. Soxx and the Blue Jeans, the Ronettes, and the Righteous Brothers. After his success in 1958, Spector's next No. 1 came in 1962, with the Crystals' "He's a Rebel." With classic Spector subterfuge, the Crystals didn't really sing, either on that top hit or on the No. 11 "He's Sure the Boy I Love," because of touring conflicts; instead, it was the Blossoms with Darlene Love on lead who recorded them. The actual Crystals (Barbara Alston, LaLa Brooks, Dee Dee Kennibrew, Mary Thomas, and Patricia Wright) scored four other Top 20 hits for Spector, including "There's No Other (Like My Baby)" which went to No. 20, "Uptown" (No. 13), "Da Doo Ron Ron (When He Walked Me Home)" (No. 3), and "Then He Kissed Me" (No. 6).

Other artists Spector nurtured to Top 20 stardom include Ray Peterson ("Corinna Corinna," No. 9), the Paris Sisters ("I Love How You Love Me," No. 5), Curtis

Lee ("Pretty Little Angel Eyes," No. 7), and his song-writing compatriot on several projects, Gene Pitney ("Town Without Pity," No. 3). Spector also produced perhaps the best rock 'n' roll Christmas album of all time, *A Christmas Gift for You* (No. 6; later rereleased as *Phil Spector's Christmas Record*), with timeless performances from Darlene Love, the Ronettes, Bob B. Soxx and the Blue Jeans, and the Crystals.

Spector has said that he views his work as "impressionistic sound productions," and virtually all of those impressionistic '60s hits were recorded at Gold Star—first on a 3-track, then a 4-track—all in mono, with engineer Larry Levine. The Wall of Sound came from the studio's echo chambers and the platoons of musicians that Spector recorded together—without isolation—in a small room with a high ceiling.

And while he and the acts on the Philles roster were rolling down the gold brick road, the wheels suddenly came off of the wagon in 1966. Spector's (literally) largest production to date, Ike and Tina Turner's "River Deep, Mountain High" was a commercial flop in the U.S., reaching only No. 88 (but in the U.K. it soared to No. 3). The hypersensitive Spector closed his label and, for all intents and purposes, stopped producing.

He came out of his self-imposed exile for a series of records in the '70s, including the Beatles' swan song *Let It Be* (No. 1), which he pieced together from live tracks. He also added a monstrous orchestral backing to Paul McCartney's (see entry) "The Long and Winding Road" (No. 1). Keeping to former Beatles, Spector lent his texture to George Harrison's finest, *All Things Must Pass* (No. 1), and worked with John Lennon on the classics *Plastic Ono Band* (No. 6) and *Imagine* (No. 1).

In retrospect, Leonard Cohen's *Death of a Ladies' Man* from 1977 is pricelessly charming. Spector wrote the music—in a classic late '50s, early '60s pop style—for Cohen's languid tales of torn romance, and Cohen responded with his best singing. Listening to it today, it's great to hear Cohen outside of his usual spare settings.

Spector also produced the Ramones epic *End of the Century*—their best-selling studio album—and in keeping with the Spector tradition, one that fans of the band either love or hate. The album made explicit the connection between early '60s pop rock and the punk band's psyche, and it holds up as both a Ramones and a Spector classic: Spector's idiosyncrasies never overwhelm the roar of "Chinese Rock" or "Rock 'n' Roll High School," and the Spectorish "Do You Remember Rock 'n' Roll Radio?" rollicks with just the right retro touches. The band's remake of the Ronette's "Baby I Love You" is as touching as it is fun.

Spector has remained in seclusion for most of the last 20 years. In a 1998 legal development, the Ronettes (Phil's ex-wife Ronnie, now Greenfield; Estelle Bennett; Nedra Talley Ross) won the right to sue Spector for $12 million in back royalties, claiming they haven't been paid any since 1963. Darlene Love won a back-royalty judgment against Spector in 1997. —DAVID JOHN FARINELLA AND ERIC OLSEN

Alley Cats: "Puddin n' Tain," Philles, 1963.

Beatles, The: "The Long and Winding Road/For You Blue," Apple, 1970 • *1967–1970,* Capitol, 1973, 1993 • *Let It Be,* Apple, 1970.

Bob B. Soxx and the Blue Jeans: "Not Too Young to Get Married," Philles, 1963 • "Why Do Lovers Break Each Other's Hearts?," Philles, 1963 • "Zip-a-Dee-Doo-Dah," Philles, 1963 • *Zip-a-Dee-Dee-Dah,* Philles, 1963.

Bruce, Lenny: *The Law, the Language and Lenny Bruce,* Spector/Warner, 1975.

Charles, Sonny, and the Checkmates Ltd.: "Black Pearl," A&M, 1969 • "Love Is All I Have to Give," A&M, 1969 • "Proud Mary," A&M, 1969.

Checkmates Ltd.: *Love Is all We Have to Give,* A&M, 1969.

Cher and Harry Nilsson: "A Love Like Yours," Warner Spector, 1975.

Clapton, Eric: *Crossroads,* Polydor, 1988.

Cohen, Leonard: *Death of a Ladies' Man,* Columbia, 1977.

Crystals, The: "He's a Rebel," Philles, 1962 • *He's a Rebel,* Philles, 1962 • "There's No Other (Like My Baby)," Philles, 1962 • *Twist Uptown,* Philles, 1962 • "Uptown," Philles, 1962 • "Da Doo Ron Ron," Philles, 1963 • "He's Sure the Boy I Love," Philles, 1963 • *The Crystals Sing the Greatest Hits,* Philles, 1963 • "Then He Kissed Me," Philles, 1963 • *The Best Of,* Abkco, 1992.

Dion: *Born to Be with You,* Phil Spector International, 1975.

Francis, Connie: "Second Hand Love," MGM, 1962.

Harrison, George: *Living in the Material World,* Capitol, 1973, 1992 • "Isn't It a Pity," Apple, 1970 • "My Sweet Lord," Apple, 1970 • *All Things Must Pass,* Apple, 1971 • "Bangla-Desh," Apple, 1971 • "Deep Blue," Apple, 1971 • "What Is Life," Apple, 1971 • *The Concert for Bangla Desh,* Apple, 1972 • *Extra Texture,* Apple, 1975 • *The Best Of,* Capitol, 1976.

Jay and the Americans: *Come a Little Bit Closer,* Gold Rush, 1996.

Kessell, Barney: *Slow Burn,* Phil Spector International, 1965.

King, Ben E.: "Spanish Harlem," Atco, 1960.

Lee, Curtis: "Pretty Little Angel Eyes," Dunes, 1961 • "Under the Moon of Love," Dunes, 1961.

Lennon, John: w/ Yoko Ono, *Wedding Album,* Rykodisc, 1969, 1997 • "Instant Karma," Apple, 1970 • *Plastic Ono Band,* Apple, 1970 • w/ Yoko and the Plastic Ono Band, "Happy

Xmas (War Is Over)," Apple, 1971 • "Imagine," Apple, 1971 • *Imagine,* Apple, 1971 • "Jealous Guy," Capitol, 1971 • "Mother," Apple, 1971 • "Power to the People," Apple, 1971 • *Some Time in New York City,* Apple, 1972 • "Woman Is the Nigger of the World," Apple, 1972 • *Rock 'n' Roll* (4 tracks), Apple, 1974 • *Menlove Ave.,* Capitol, 1986 • *Imagine* soundtrack, Capitol, 1988 • *Shaved Fish,* Parlophone, 1988 • *John Lennon Collection,* Capitol, 1990 • *Lennon,* Capitol, 1991 • *Lennon Legend: The Very Best of John Lennon,* Apple, 1997.

Love, Darlene: "(Today I Met) the Boy I'm Gonna Marry," Philles, 1963 • "A Fine Fine Boy," Philles, 1963 • "Christmas (Baby Please Come Home," Philles, 1963 • "Wait 'Til My Bobby Gets Home," Philles, 1963 • *The Best Of,* Abkco, 1992.

Mason, Bobbie Jo: "Ringo I Love You," Annette, 1964.

Nilsson, Harry, and Cher: "A Love Like Yours," Warner Spector, 1975.

Ono, Yoko: *Season of Glass,* Geffen, 1981 • *Ono Box,* Rykodisc, 1992 • *See also* Lennon, John.

Paris Sisters: "Be My Boy," Gregmark, 1961 • "I Love How You Love Me," Gregmark, 1961 • "He Knows I Love Him Too Much," Gregmark, 1962.

Peterson, Ray: "Corinna, Corinna," Dunes, 1961 • "I Could Have Loved You So Well," Dunes, 1962.

Pitney, Gene: "Every Breath I Take," Musicor, 1961.

Ramones: *End of the Century,* Sire, 1980 • *Ramones Mania,* Sire, 1988.

Righteous Brothers: *Greatest Hits,* Philles, 1964 • "Hung on You," Philles, 1965 • "Just Once in my Life," Philles, 1965 • *Just Once in My Life,* Philles, 1965 • "Unchained Melody," Philles, 1965 • "You've Lost That Lovin' Feeling," Philles, 1965 • *Back to Back,* Philles, 1966 • "Ebb Tide," Philles, 1966 • *Anthology 1962–1974,* Rhino, 1989 • "Unchained Melody," Verve, 1990 • *Unchained Melody—Very Best Of,* Polydor, 1991.

Ronettes, The: "Be My Baby," Philles, 1963 • "(The Best Part of) Breakin' Up," Philles, 1964 • "Baby I Love You," Philles, 1964 • "Do I Love You?," Philles, 1964 • *Presenting the Fabulous Ronettes,* Philles, 1964 • "Walking in the Rain," Philles, 1964 • "Born to Be Together," Philles, 1965 • "Is This What I Get for Loving You?," Philles, 1965 • *The Best Of,* Abkco, 1992.

Ross, Diana, and the Supremes: *The Best Of,* Motown, 1995.

Spector, Phil: *Back to Mono, 1958–1969,* Abkco, 1991.

Spector, Ronnie: "Try Some, Buy Some," Apple, 1971.

Teddy Bears: "To Know Him Is to Love Him," Dore, 1958 • "I Don't Know You Anymore," Imperial, 1959 • "Oh Why," Imperial, 1959 • *The Teddy Bears Sing,* Imperial, 1959.

Turner, Ike, and Tina Turner: "River Deep, Mountain High," Philles, 1966 • *River Deep, Mountain High,* Philles, 1966.

Turner, Tina: *Collected Recordings, Sixties to Nineties,* Capitol, 1994.

COLLECTIONS

Phil Spector's Christmas Album, Pavillion, 1963, 1981.

Phil Spector's Greatest Hits, Warner/Spector, 1977.

Early Productions, 1958–1961, Rhino, 1983.

Twist and Shout, WEA, 1989.

Back to Mono, 1958–1969, Abkco, 1991.

The Brill Building Sound: Singers and Songwriters Who Rocked the 60's, Era, 1993.

Spot

Spot produced the cream of red-blooded American punk in the late '70s and early '80s—in particular bands affiliated with the archetypal SoCal indie label SST (and its affiliate New Alliance), including Black Flag, Descendants, Hüsker Dü, Meat Puppets, and Minutemen. With the punk movement grown stale by the mid-'80s, Spot followed his own eccentric muse to Austin, Texas, where he has carved out a career as a multi-instrumentalist performing traditional Celtic music blended with Zappa-and-Zorn art noise.

Spot was born Glen Lockett in the Crenshaw area of Los Angeles in the early '50s. His musical taste was formed by the eclecticism of AM Top 40 radio from the late '50s through the mid-'60s. "I listened to everything. We would sing Marvin Gaye, the Beatles, and Roger Miller in the schoolyard. The first record I ever bought was 'Washington Square' by the Village Stompers in 1963. I got my first guitar for Christmas in 1963, a Silvertone acoustic. I worked on guitar for a while, then started playing the drums, and ended up in my first band with some classmates in the eighth grade," he recalls.

"I didn't study much in school because I knew I wanted to do music. After I had to return my rented drums, I went back to guitar and learned to play, mostly from the radio and records. The psychedelic era came in and I really liked that. It was new and really good music to listen to when you were depressed. I didn't have that much of a social life—'the music was my only friend,' to paraphrase the Doors—so naturally when you hear something like that you think, 'Oh my God, someone knows what I'm going through,' " he sighs.

"It was real problematic to put together a band that would do anything other than covers in those days. I was always trying to put something together to do my own stuff, but I never really had that chance in the '60s and '70s. I ended up being one of these bums out in the street in Hollywood playing music for change so I could eat. For a certain part of my life I was more or less homeless. When I had a place to live, I would sit in my house all day and play and write.

"I figured if I could record some stuff, that would be great. I bought an old Sony tape deck and some microphones and recorded myself and other things: I would hang the mike out the window and record the neighbors' door opening and shutting without their knowing about it and weird stuff like that. Then I got a Teac 4-track. I had a dream about having some kind of studio," he says.

"In 1975 I was hanging out in Hermosa Beach because I was a foosball fanatic and there were about five places to play there. You could come down from L.A. and just dominate the tables. I was absolutely homeless and I met these folks who were building a recording studio on the corner of Hermosa and Pier called Media Art. I just walked in off of the street one day and thought, 'I should get involved with this.' I helped them build the studio and they let me live there.

"One thing leads to another and I became the staff engineer at the studio as the owners gradually lost interest. We had a dirt-cheap lease so we could offer really great rates. The equipment was basic analog 8-track (which we later upgraded to 16- and eventually 24-track; our 8-track had recorded Jimi Hendrix, the 16 was later sold to Eddie Van Halen) and it was great for rock 'n' roll, but mostly we got really awful light-rock or disco. Under those circumstances, any music with some guts or creativity—hard rock, metal, jazz—was a breath of fresh air. The jazz was fun: they would get their levels and go for it: no overdubbing and messing around. I hated tuning the drums for hours to get them to sound like an Elton John record for some of these light-rock sessions," he says. Spot also wrote reviews and features for the local entertainment weekly, *Easy Reader,* and was a professional photographer specializing in skateboarding and rollerskating.

By 1978 Spot (named after a softball incident) was producing demos after hours on spec. Spot's reign of punk terror began when he produced a band of "neighborhood goons" called Black Flag. "By then I was really into rollerskating and skateboarding on the Strand—if I wasn't in the studio I was skating—and I met those guys in the alleyways of Hermosa; they lived near the local skate shop Wild Wheels. I persuaded Black Flag to come in Media Art to record; we did a live session in October 1979 that is some the best stuff they have ever done," he says. Five tracks were released as part of *Everything Went Black* in 1982.

Black Flag at the time was Greg Ginn on guitar (he formed SST to put out Black Flag records), Chuck Dukowski on bass, Robo on drums, and Keith Morris (later of Circle Jerks) on vocals. Whether those tracks are the band's finest is debatable among reasonable people, but they do rock awfully hard. Somewhere between Black Sabbath and the Ramones, Flag attacks short (nothing over 2:07), brutish tunes with titles like "Revenge," "Depression," and "Wasted" with animalistic intensity and admirable economy. Ginn's guitar slashes and burns, Robo's drums keep the vehicle between the lines, and Morris's vocals rant against various social and personal evils.

The band's first nonsingle release was the *Jealous Again* EP in 1980. Chavo Pederast (Ron Reyes) had replaced Morris on vocals. Slightly tighter but similar to the "live" tracks, Flag was finally among the recorded living. Media Art was shut down in 1981, so Spot and the band went to Hollywood's Unicorn Studios to record their masterpiece, *Damaged.* A second guitarist/vocalist, Dez Cadena, was added to the lineup, and bellowing hulk Henry Rollins was brought in to sing lead. Loaded with punk classics like "Rise Above," "Gimmie, Gimmie, Gimmie," and a new version of "Depression," *Damaged* also displays a sense of humor regarding the band's suburban heritage on "Six Pack" and "TV Party." The twin guitar attack and group vocals give the songs added depth without degenerating into clutter.

Litigation with SST's distributor Unicorn prevented the release of new material by Flag until 1984, and the time off from recording afforded Ginn time to concentrate of the development of SST. His virtually flawless taste and personal integrity accounts for the fact that much of the best punk of the era bears the SST (or new Alliance) logo, and Spot was the label's key producer until the mid-'80s.

From San Pedro came the uncategorizable trio Minutemen (named dually for the brevity of their songs and their watchful gaze upon society): D. Boon on guitars and lead vocals, Mike Watt on bass, and George Hurley on drums made music that pulled elements from punk, funk, and jazz and assembled them into brief, stabbing vignettes on the Spot EP (co-produced with Ginn) *Paranoid Time* in 1980, *The Punch Line* in 1981, the great *What Makes a Man Start Fires?* in 1982, and *Buzz or Howl Under the Influence of Heat* in 1983.

Meat Puppets were (and still are) another eccentric trio: this one from Arizona, featuring brothers Curt and Cris Kirkwood on shared vocals, guitar, and bass, respectively, and Derrick Bostrom on drums. *Meat Puppets* from 1981 is serviceable thrashy punk, but *Meat Puppets II* from 1983 finds the band creating an affecting brand of Southwestern music that sounds like Roger McGuinn high on peyote, fronting the Replacements in the desert on great cowpunk songs, including "The Whistling Song," "New Gods," "Lost," "Lake of Fire" (later covered by Nirvana), and "Split Myself in Two." *Up on the Sun* finds the band more relaxed with their Southwestern vision; the title track is a spacious desert delicacy with Curt's always pitch-challenged vocals wavering pleasantly in and out of focus. "Swimming Ground," with beautifully picked and phased guitar from Curt, is a watery wonder.

Ginn found Minneapolis natives Hüsker Dü playing to a near-empty club in Chicago. Still another trio—this one led by Bob Mould (see entry) on guitar and vocals and Grant Hart on drums and vocals—Husker Du is best discussed under Mould's separate entry, but Spot helped guide the band through its early sloppy-thrashy records to its status as the most melodic of punk bands by the mid-'80s. Particularly noteworthy during Spot's run is the band's ripping cover of the Byrds' "8 Miles High" (released on a single) and the *Zen Arcade* album, both from 1984.

In comparison to the often-bizarre noises emanating from the aforementioned SST talent, the Descendants were a virtually conventional punk band, writing short, playful, tight numbers from the perspective of the eternally bemused adolescent. Singer Milo Aukerman, drummer Bill Stevenson, and a revolving crew of guitarists and bassists put out several smoking albums and EPs in the '80s, including the Spot-produced *Fat* EP (with "My Dad Sucks," "I Like Food," and the eight-second "Weinerschnitzel") and *Milo Goes to College* ("Suburban Home," "Bikeage," the defiant "I'm Not a Loser").

"Once the punk stuff started, I was pumped up," says Spot. "No one had any money, but we had opportunities and we took advantage of them. My philosophy was to get the band in, make them feel good in the room, then roll the tape and let them play. I wanted to get them when they were inspired and not afraid of the process. I started to lose interest when bands decided that since R.E.M. was popular, it was time for them to be popular too; they stopped being what they were and started laboring over things, trying to get a certain 'sound.' I still worked, but the romance was over.

"I got out of L.A., moved to Austin in 1986, and started playing again. I got into playing traditional Irish music because it had always been a dream of mine to be some kind of fiddler, and in Austin there were numerous opportunites to play traditional music. I love 'tune sessions' with just a bunch of people sitting around playing tunes. When it really gets going, there's nothing like it. I try to keep things raw and rough. I play solo and

with bands, live, and I record for my own No Auditions label," he says. "It's what I love." —ERIC OLSEN

Angry Samoans: *Inside My Brain* (EP), PVC, 1981, 1987.

Bad Mutha Goose: *Rev It Up,* Fable, 1988.

Big Boys: *Fun Fun Fun* (EP), Moment, 1982 • *Lullabies Help the Brain Grow,* Moment, 1982 • *No Matter How Long the Line Is at the Cafeteria, There's Always a Seat!,* Enigma, 1984 • *Wreck Collection,* Unseen Hand, 1988, 1989 • *The Fat Elvis,* Touch & Go, 1993 • *The Skinny Elvis,* Touch & Go, 1993.

Black Flag: *Jealous Again* (EP), SST, 1980 • "No Values," Posh Boy, 1980 (*Rodney on the ROQ,* Vol. 1) • *Damaged,* SST, 1981 • "Rise Above," Posh Boy, 1981 (*Rodney on the ROQ,* Vol. 2) • *Everything Went Black* (20 tracks), SST, 1982 • *Six Pack* (EP), SST, 1982, 1990 • *First Four Years,* SST, 1983 • "I've Heard It Before," SST, 1983 (*The Blasting Concept*) • "Jealous Again," SST, 1983 (*The Blasting Concept*) • *Family Man,* SST, 1984 • *My War,* SST, 1984 • *Slip It In,* SST, 1984 • "TV Party," San Andreas, 1984 (*Repo Man* soundtrack) • "Louie Louie," SST, 1990 (*Duck and Cover*).

Cavemen, The: *. . . Yeah,* Midnight, 1986.

Cerebros Exprimidos: *Demencia,* Grita, 1996.

Crucifucks: *The Crucifucks,* Alternative Tentacles, 1985 • *Thy Will Be Done,* Alternative Tentacles, 1992.

Crust: *Crust/The Sacred Heart of Crust,* Trance Syndicate, 1991.

D.C. 3: *This Is the Dream,* SST, 1985.

Descendants: *Fat* (EP), New Alliance, 1981 • *Milo Goes to College,* New Alliance, 1982 • *Two Things at Once,* SST, 1985, 1987 • *Bonus Fat* (EP), SST, 1990 • *Somery* (9 tracks), SST, 1991.

Dicks, The: *Kill from the Heart,* SST, 1983 • *1980–1986,* Alternative Tentacles, 1997.

Hall, Ed: *Gloryhole* (1 track), Trance, 1991.

Hand of Glory: *Far from Kith and Kin,* Skyclad, 1990.

Happi Family: *Lucky,* 50 Skidillion Watts, 1990.

Hickoids: *Waltz a Crossdress Texas,* Toxic Shock, 1989.

Hüsker Dü: *Everything Falls Apart,* Rhino, 1982 • *Metal Circus* (EP), Reflex/SST, 1983 • "Real World," SST, 1983 (*The Blasting Concept* • "Eight Miles High," SST, 1984, 1990 (*Duck and Cover*) • *Zen Arcade,* SST, 1984 • *New Day Rising,* SST, 1985.

Kamikaze Refrigerators: *Happy Thoughts,* Unseen Hand, 1987.

Meat Puppets: *Meat Puppets,* SST, 1982 • *Meat Puppets II,* SST, 1983 • "Tumblin' Tumbleweeds," SST, 1983 (*The Blasting Concept*) • *Up on the Sun,* SST, 1985 • *No Strings Attached* (11 tracks), SST, 1990.

Miller, Ed: *Border Background,* Folk Legacy, 1989.

Minutemen: *Paranoid Time* (EP), SST, 1980 • *Post-Mersh,* Vol. 1, *The Punchline/What Makes a Man Start Fires?,* SST, 1981, 1987 • "Search," Posh Boy, 1981 (*Rodney on the ROQ,* Vol. 2) • *The Punchline* (EP), SST, 1981 • *What Makes a Man Start Fires?,* SST, 1982 • "Boiling," SST, 1983 (*The Blasting*

Concept) • *Buzz or Howl Under the Influence of Heat*, SST, 1983, 1991 • "Games," SST, 1983 *(The Blasting Concept)* • *Post-Mersh*, Vol. 2, *Buzz or Howl Under the Influence of Heat/Project Mersh*, SST, 1983, 1987.

Misfits: *Earth A.D./Wolfsblood*, Plan 9, 1983 • *Collection II*, Caroline, 1995.

Necros: *Conquest for Death*, Touch & Go, 1983.

Nigheist: "Walking Down the Street," Thermidor, 1982 • *Understanding Basic Economics*, Thermidor, 1984.

Nip Drivers: *Kill Whitey*, New Alliance, 1983.

Offenders, The: *Endless Struggle*, Rabid Cat, 1985.

Overkill: "Hell's Getting Hotter," SST, 1983 *(The Blasting Concept)* • *Triumph of the Will*, SST, 1983.

Phantom Tollbooth: *Power Toy*, Homestead, 1988.

Plebs: *A Collection of Question Marks*, New Alliance, 1982.

Plimsouls, The: *Zero Hour* (EP), Beat, 1980.

Poison 13: *Poison 13*, Wrestler, 1985 • *Wine Is Red, Poison Is Blue*, Sub Pop, 1994.

Raszebrea: *Cheap Happiness or Lofty Suffering*, Unseen Hand, 1985.

Rhythm Pigs: *Choke on This*, C/Z, 1986.

Saccharine Trust: *Paganicons*, SST, 1981 • "A Human Certainty," SST, 1983 *(The Blasting Concept)* • *Surviving You, Always*, SST, 1984.

Saint Vitus: *Saint Vitus*, SST, 1984 • *Hallow's Victim*, SST, 1985 • *The Walking Dead*, SST, 1985 • *Heavier Than Thou*, SST, 1991.

Secret Hate: *Vegetables Dancing*, New Alliance, 1983.

Slovenly: *Thinking of Empire*, SST, 1986.

Spot: *Artless Entanglements*, No Auditions, 1987 • *Picking Up Where I Left Off*, No Auditions, 1987 • *On the Mountain*, No Auditions, 1992 • "Yo! Marry Me," No Auditions, 1992 • *Removals . . . Others Isms* (EP), No Auditions, 1996 • *Unhalfbaking*, Upland, 1999.

Spot Removal: "Paper!/St. Anne's Reel," No Auditions, 1993.

Stains: "Get Revenge," SST, 1983 *(The Blasting Concept)* • *The Stains*, SST, 1983.

Subhumans: *No Wishes No Prayers*, SST, 1983.

Sugar Shack: *Charmer*, Fistpuppet, 1992.

Tail Gators: *Swamp Rock*, Wrestler, 1985.

Tar Babies: *Fried Milk*, SST, 1987.

Texas Instruments: *Texas Instruments*, Rabid Cat, 1987 • *Sun Tunnels*, Dr. Dream, 1988 • *Crammed into Infinity*, Dr. Dream, 1990.

UXA: *Illusions of Grandeur*, Posh Boy, 1981.

Van Helsdingen, Rene: *After the Third Window*, Munich, 1980.

Vogue: "Sahara/Shattered Peace," Aret, 1983.

COLLECTIONS

Cracks in the Sidewalk (EP), SST, 1980, 1988.

Chunks, SST, 1981, 1988.

Ed Stasium

Give a quick scan of just a partial listing of Ed Stasium's production and engineering discography and you will see that the company is nothing to sneeze at: the Ramones, Living Colour, the Smithereens, Joan Jett and the Blackhearts, Hoodoo Gurus, Soul Asylum, Marshall Crenshaw, the Jeff Healey Band, the Long Ryders, Fetchin' Bones, Julian Cope, the Dickies. A closer look reveals that Stasium seems to attract mostly guitar-oriented rock bands. Is this arrangement coincidental or by choice?

"Actually, nothing in my career has been by choice. I just happened to be somewhere at the right time and it just sort of developed and became its own little animal. I just love to record. I just love to make records. That was my destiny somehow, since I was a kid," says Stasium.

He sees himself as "a catalyst, a collaborator, helping the artist to realize his vision. I try to become another member of the band for that period of time we're together in the studio. I'm not a songwriter. I work with people who write their own songs, but I do help with arrangements. The song is always the most important thing. As soon as I hear the demos, I have a vision of the arrangement and where it's going to go."

The path of Stasium's destiny is marked by a series of milestones and colorful happenstance. Young Stasium became wise to the existence of records throughout the '50s via Martin Bloch's *Make-Believe Ballroom* radio program and his parents' pre–rock 'n' roll pop disc collection.

At a 1961 New Year's Eve party, Stasium was transfixed by his first sighting of a working reel-to-reel tape recorder. "I heard the music playing and I didn't see a record player. I saw the reels turning and after a while, I put two and two together." When he heard his voice on tape for the first time that night, "that was it. Oh my God. Oh my God. That was a startling revelation for me." A succession of obsessions with Stasium's own personal tape machines followed.

Like a lot of boys of the '60s, Stasium played guitar and bass in a series of bands. "I was the guy with my 1965 Strat in one hand and a Lafayette tape recorder in the other." One fine aggregation called Brandywine signed a production deal with Ritchie Havens' Stormy Forest concern, and Stasium found himself in his first "real" session (at New York City's Media Sound Studio) with a real engineer (Bob Margouleff) and producer at the helm. The band subsequently cut an album in 1971 for Decca affiliate Brunswick.

Typically, Brandywine fell apart amidst arguments and small claims court settlements after their album went nowhere fast. "Certified lead," says Ed. He, his girlfriend, and their crying 6-month-old son were inhabiting Stasium's parents' basement when one fine day Stasium found himself in Bamberger's department store in Plainfield at a sale on bicycles. The destitute Stasium purchased bicycles, two for $110. A bargain, for sure. "I bought them with the last money that I had in this world. I have no idea why!"

But in fact, it was destiny. The next day, pedaling around Greenbrook with his girlfriend, they ran into Mike Bonagura, an ex-bandmate of Stasium's (and later a successful songwriter in his own right), who informed Stasium that, "Hey, my father's friend Tony Camillo is building a recording studio in his basement in Somerville. His partner, Tony Bongiovi, is an engineer, and he said that if I start a band, we can record down there and put out a record!"

The next day, the two chaps visited the digs, where a shell of a studio was still in the dust-covered, console-on-the-floor, nails-and-hammer phase. "It was a mess." Over the course of the next year, as Stasium collected unemployment and played swim clubs, he assisted in the construction of the room and, in doing so, learned the makings of a state-of-the-art recording facility from the ground up. In the summer of 1972, Tony Bongiovi, who was also working at Media Sound in NYC, brought Stasium to witness a session with Kool and the Gang. "I had the worst case of hiccups in my life that day."

After a satisfactory basic track was waxed, Bongiovi turned to Stasium and said, "Eddie, you record the vocals, I'm going out for a sandwich. This was a Top 10 recording act! The singer said, 'Let's try one on another track,' and I'm there 'homina, homina, homina, homina.' I had no idea what I was doing! I somehow sensed how to work the patchbay, do overdubs and punch-ins on the spot. It was totally sink or swim. I'm nervous as hell, but I'm not showing it, of course. Tony ended up coming back two-and-a-half hours later. I did it! That one day at Media Sound passed me through my freshman year of engineering and producing school."

In September 1975, Stasium was ready for a change. He had grown weary of the routine production methodology at Venture and had become enamored with the current standard of British production, particularly the "Trident sound." He attended the Audio Engineering Society show in New York and brought home a copy of *DB* magazine, which had a help wanted ad: Le Studio at Morin Heights in Montreal was seeking an engineer to work with a Trident A Series console. "I called the number in the ad the moment that I saw it. I flew up to Canada the next day, interviewed with Yale Brandeis and André Perry, and was hired on the spot. Perry was the guy who did the remote hotel room recording of Plastic Ono Band's "Give Peace a Chance" during John and Yoko's famous honeymoon "bed-in" for peace. He was Montreal's *enfant terrible*, the big recording dude up there."

Far ahead of its time, Morin Heights was a "fabulous, fabulous studio out in the woods on a hill. They had the Trident console, a Studer machine, all this great outboard gear. Anything that was new, André would get. I remember one winter night, sitting looking out the big window overlooking the lake, being so thrilled that tears came to my eyes."

From November 1975 through August 1976, Stasium took his recording schooling to the next level in Canada, cutting slews of French-Canadian projects. It was there that he worked with the man who produced Queen, just as "Bohemian Rhapsody" was making a big splash. "If there was anybody who influenced me profoundly with recording and production concepts, it was Roy Thomas Baker [see entry]. I remember his jovial presence fondly. He was always having fun, always doing something ridiculous, like recording a fire extinguisher with a 414, just to see what it sounds like. Nuts. The guy's absolutely out of his bean."

Until this time, Stasium had only worked within the padded-drum, dead-sounding, drastically isolated world of '70s recording technique. Baker opened Stasium's eyes and ears to room sound. "He would try all of these wacky things, like mikeing things 20 feet away, mikeing the back of guitar amps, pointing mikes away from the drums to get a room sound and putting it on the overhead tracks. Everything clicked for me. Why didn't I think of all this?!" —DENNIS DIKEN

Alda Reserve: *Love Goes On,* Sire, 1979.

Baby Animals: *Shaved and Dangerous,* Imago, 1993, 1996.

Big F: *Is,* Chrysalis, 1993 • *Patience Peregrine* (EP), FFF, 1993.

Biohazard: *State of the World Address,* Warner Bros., 1994.

Burning Rome: *Burning Rome,* A&M, 1982.

Cavedogs, The: *Joyrides for Shut-Ins,* Enigma, 1990 • *Tayter Country,* Restless, 1990 • *Six Tender Moments* (1 track), Capitol, 1991.

Collision: *Coarse,* Chaos, 1995.

Cope, Julian: *Julian Cope* (EP, 1 track), Island, 1986 • "World Shut Your Mouth," Island, 1986, 1987 (*Island Sampler #1*) • *Saint Julian,* Island, 1987 • *Floored Genius: The Best of Julian Cope and the Teardrop Explodes, 1979–1991,* Island, 1992.

Crenshaw, Marshall: *Collection*, MCA, 1991 • *Life's Too Short*, Paradox/MCA, 1991.

Crossfire Choir: *Back to the Wall*, track, 1988.

Dickies, The: *Stukas over Disneyland* (4 tracks), Restless, 1983.

Dogstar: *Our Little Visionary*, Freeworld, 1997.

Face to Face: *Confrontation*, Epic, 1985, 1986.

Fetchin Bones: "Slaves," RNA, 1991 (*Tame Yourself*) • *Monster*, Capitol, 1989.

Five Eight: *Gasolina*, Velvel, 1997.

Heat, Reverend Horton: *Space Heater*, Interscope, 1998.

Heretix: *Gods and Gangsters*, Island, 1990.

Hoodoo Gurus: *Crank*, Zoo, 1994 • "The Right Time," Praxis/Zoo, 1994.

Jeff Healey Band: *Hell to Pay*, Arista, 1990.

Jett, Joan: "Go Home," Blackheart/WB, 1994 • *Pure and Simple*, Blackheart/WB, 1994.

Junkyard: *Sixes, Sevens and Nines*, Geffen, 1991.

Kilgore: *Search for Reason*, Warner Bros., 1998.

Living Colour: *Vivid*, Epic, 1988 • "Cult of Personality," Epic, 1989 • "Open Letter (to a Landlord)," Epic, 1989 • "Elvis Is Dead," Epic, 1990 • "Solace of You," Epic, 1990 • *Times Up*, Epic, 1990 • *Biscuits* (EP), Epic, 1991 • *Pride*, Epic, 1995 • *Super Hits*, Legacy, 1998.

Long Ryders: *Two Fisted Tales*, Island, 1987.

Love Nut: *Baltimucho*, Big Deal, 1998.

Miracle Legion: *Out to Play* (EP), Morgan Creek, 1992.

Motorhead: *The Best of Motorhead*, Vol. 2, Roadrunner, 1995.

Pursuit of Happiness: *The Downward Road*, Mercury, 1993.

Ramones, The: "I Wanna Be Sedated," RSO, 1978, 1980 (*Times Square* soundtrack) • *Road to Ruin*, Sire, 1978 • *It's Alive*, Sire, 1979, 1995 • *Too Tough to Die*, Sire/WB, 1984 • *Ramones Mania*, Sire, 1989 • *All the Stuff and More*, Vol. 2, Sire, 1991 • *Mondo Bizarro*, Radioactive, 1992.

Rattlers, The: *Rattled*, Bacchus, 1985, 1997.

Sighs, The: *What Goes On*, Charisma, 1992.

Smithereens, The: *11*, Enigma, 1989 • "A Girl Like You," Enigma, 1989 • "Blues Before and After," Enigma, 1990 • *Blow Up*, Capitol, 1991 • *Attack Of*, Capitol, 1995.

Something Happens: *Stuck Together with God's Glue*, Charisma, 1990.

Soul Asylum: *Hang Time*, A&M, 1988.

Tea Party: *The Edges of Twilight*, Chrysalis, 1995.

Translator: *Translator*, 415/Columbia, 1985 • *Evening of the Harvest*, 415/Columbia, 1986 • *Everywhere That We Were: The Best Of*, Legacy, 1996.

22 Jacks: *Overserved*, Label?, 1998.

COLLECTIONS

Rock 'n' Roll High School soundtrack, Sire, 1979.

Steely and Clevie

(WYCLIFFE JOHNSON AND CLEVELAND BROWNE)

In Jamaica, nearly everyone in the record industry wants to produce. Countless independent labels have been formed by engineers, singers, DJs, and instrumentalists. Horn players, guitarists, and even percussionists have their own labels and produce. Sly and Robbie (see entry) paved the way for the "rhythm section" producers, and Sly's own trajectory, from riveting machine-like drummer to the island's first full-scale deployment of programmed drums, opened the door for '90s digital rhythm masters Wycliffe "Steely" Johnson and Cleveland "Clevie" Browne.

Cleveland Browne came from a musical background; two of his brothers, Danny and Dalton, are separately established rhythm builders in their own right and longtime members of the Bloodfire Posse. Steely played keyboards for the Roots Radics in their dancehall days. Though they played "real" drums and keyboards, both were excited by the new possibilities of programming and sequencing that many of their contemporaries abhorred.

When Prince Jammy (see entry) recognized the potential for digital technology in the Jamaican recording industry around 1986, he installed Steely and Clevie as his "studio group." With Bobby "Digital" Dixon (see entry) on the board and Steely and Clevie building the tracks, Prince Jammy became king. The rhythmic duo played for Jammy on hits by Dennis Brown, Cocoa Tea, and dozens of others.

But like Jammy himself after serving an apprenticeship to the great King Tubby, Steely and Clevie, who also cut tracks for Digital and many other producers in the dancehall era, from old-timers like Winston Riley and Gussie Clarke (see entry) to newcomers such as Mr. Doo, began producing their own records in the late '80s. Recording mainly at Mixing Lab and Music Works, they reaped the benefits of the digital age they helped to usher in. Their label, Steely and Clevie, was distributed in the U.S. by VP.

The keyboard bass became the new lead sound, replacing bass, and the duo pumped out singles by DJs Flourgon, Nardo, Shabba Ranks, and Johnny P and singers Johnny Osbourne, Tony Tuff, and Admiral Tibet. A major album for singer Freddie McGregor (who co-produces with Clevie's brother Dalton and for whom Clevie played keyboards before cleaving to Steely), and a big hit for DJ Tiger ("Windscreen") added to their reputation. Numerous anthologies, including *Soundboy Clash* on Profile, are among their best and most representative work as producers and players.

The pair were also the first to record an album with the ethereal vocalist Garnett Silk, though it wasn't issued until he'd gone on to record and release albums for other producers. The young conscious singer's tragic death in the mid-'90s seemed to sound a wake-up call in dancehall and signaled a return to the roots themes of the '70s for singers and DJs alike. The ability to spot talent and a willingness to record up-and-coming artists are among the keys to their success.

In 1992 Steely and Clevie produced an album for the Heartbeat label called *Steely and Clevie Play Studio One Vintage* in which they regrouped many original artists on hits they had had for Coxsone Dodd (see entry) in the '70s. A 12-inch remix of "You Don't Love Me (No, No, No)" by Dawn Penn caught hold, and gave them a monster U.S. hit as well. The lead-in sample ("Wake the town and tell the people") from DJ U Roy has since become one of the most used sound bites in the business.

Though the crush of "new independents" in the mid-'90s brought names like Mafia and Fluxy to the fore, Steely and Clevie continue to pound out rhythms with the likes of J.C. Lodge, Aswad and Maxi Priest, Foxy Brown, Henkel Irie, Daddy Blue, and Little Twitch. —CHUCK FOSTER

Heavy D and the Boyz: *Blue Funk,* Uptown/MCA, 1992.
Mad Cobra: *Hard to Wet, Easy to Dry* (1 track), Columbia, 1992.
McGregor, Freddie: *Now,* VP, 1991.
Ocean, Billy: *Time to Move On,* Jive, 1993.
Paul Frankie: *Steely and Clevie Present F.P. the Veteran,* VP, 1991.
Penn, Dawn: *No, No, No* (5 tracks), Big Beat, 1994 • *See also* Collections.
Ranks, Shabba: *As Raw As Ever* (2 tracks), Epic, 1991 • *X-Tra Naked* (3 tracks), Epic, 1992 • *A Mi Shabba,* Epic, 1995 • *See also* Collections.
Silk, Garnett: *Love Is the Answer,* VP, 1994.
Steely and Clevie: *Before the Time,* Steely and Clevie, 1996 • *High Gear,* VP, 1997 • *See also* Collections.
Stitchie, Lt.: *The Governor,* Atlantic, 1989 • *Rude Boy,* Atlantic, 1993.
Supercat: *The Good, the Bad, the Ugly, and the Crazy,* Columbia, 1994.
Tiger: "Cool Me Down," Chaos, 1993 (*Cool Runnings* soundtrack) • *Claws of the Cat* (4 tracks), Chaos, 1993.

COLLECTIONS

At the Top, Black Solidarity, 1988.
Bursting Out, Steely and Clevie/VP, 1988.
Can't Do the Work, Steely and Clevie/VP, 1988: Daddy Blue,

"Inna the Business Long" • Daddy Lizard, "Fight over Request" • Henkel Irie, "Jamaican Girl," Johnny P., "Can't Wash and Cook" • Little Twitch, "Watch Your Friends Them" • Nardo Ranks, "She Nah Tell Me No" • Shabba Ranks, "Can't Do the Work" • Untouchable Chris, "You Nuh Woman Yet."

Frighten Friday, Steely and Clevie/VP, 1989: Dirtsman, "Borrow Man," "Style Brand New" • Flourgon, "Stand Up One Side and Rock" • Johnny P., "Nasty Man" • Queen Paula, "Move Up" • Singing Melody, "One in a Million People" • Steely and Clevie, "Market Sound" • Tuffest, "Frighten Friday," "How You So Fat."

Limousine, Steely and Clevie/VP, 1989: Foxy Brown, "Baby Can I Hold You?," Sugar Minott, "Are You Ready?," Admiral Tibet, "Devil Pickney" • Tony Tuff, "Fling It."

More Poco, VP, 1990: Capleton, "Granny" • Cutty Ranks, "Retreat" • Nardo Ranks, "Cemetary" • Steely and Clevie, "More Poco."

Steely and Clevie Present Soundboy Clash, Profile, 1991: Bionic Steve, "How Dem a Go Manage" • Captain Barkey, "Do the Poco" • Cocoa Tea, "Unfaithful to I" • Daddy Lilly, "Get Up and Come" • General Degree and Major Bones, "Reggae Rub-a-Dub Rock" • Red Rose, "Sunshine."

Steely and Clevie Play Studio One Vintage, Heartbeat, 1992: The Cables, "Be a Man" • The Clarendonians, "He Who Laugh Last" • Alton Ellis, "Ain't That Loving You" • Dawn Penn, "You Don't Love Me (No, No, No)" • Leroy Sibbles, "Fatty Fatty" • The Silvertones, "Smile."

Keith Stegall

Keith Stegall remembers the first time he was in a recording studio, long before he began working with such country stars as Alan Jackson, John Anderson, and Terri Clark. "I was 9 years old and I had an uncle who was a producer in Texas. We would visit him on weekends, and while my parents were talking and having coffee, I would be in the studio playing around with every instrument or playing with the tape machine and listening to stuff. It was like being in a big toy box. Certain things happen to you that set the course for you, and that was definitely one of the things that set me in motion to become a record producer."

Stegall, born November 1, 1954, in Wichita Falls, Texas, grew up in Louisiana. His father sang and played steel guitar with Johnny Horton. He graduated with a degree in religion from Centenary College in Shreveport, Louisiana, and attended graduate school at the

University of Denver before pursuing his musical career. Stegall moved to Nashville in 1979, where he became a staff writer for CBS Songs. He then became a performer and is now also vice president of A&R for Mercury Records Nashville.

His talents as a producer are matched by his songwriting abilities, and he's written a number of hits for various artists, including Al Jarreau's "We're in This Love Together," Clay Walker's "If I Could Make a Living," and Travis Tritt's "Between an Old Memory and Me." Nevertheless, Stegall seldom pitches his own material to the acts he works with. "It's very tough for me," he says. "I have a hard time pitching songs [to artists I'm producing] because I think that system has been so abused here in Nashville, and that bothers me."

Stegall also recognizes talent. He produced a live album on Randy Travis that helped him get his record deal. (He also produced two cuts on Travis's groundbreaking 1986 Warner Bros. debut, *Storms of Life,* but since he was in the middle of cutting his own album, Stegall left the rest to Kyle Lehning; see entry.) He produced the demos that got Jackson his deal and convinced Terri Clark to hold off on a record deal until he could work with her.

"There's a mutual respect and a mutual trust that goes on between him and me," Stegall says of his work with Jackson. "He knows that I can get inside his head and know where he wants to go and that I'm never going to compromise his music. I'll bring him songs that I think will be career songs, not things that will just get him on the radio."

With Stegall guiding, Jackson has sold more than 20 million albums. *Don't Rock the Jukebox* and *A Lot About Livin' (and a Little 'Bout Love)* won Album of the Year honors from the Academy of Country Music in 1991 and 1992, respectively. "Chattahoochee" (No. 1 country) was named the Country Music Association's Single of the Year for 1993.

Most of the artists Stegall has produced—Jackson, Sammy Kershaw, John Anderson—know what they want, which suits Stegall just fine. "I can deal with an artist who's bullheaded and knows what he wants to do," he says. "It's harder to define that when you have somebody who's not sure. I'd rather not make records with people who don't have a sure sense of who they are."

Stegall has been working with engineer John Kelton for more than a decade. "I'll do a lot of overdub engineering, especially with some artists who feel uncomfortable having a lot of people around," he says, "but I have found it is so much easier for me when it gets down to the mix stage of things to leave and come back with fresh ears. I can get myself into a corner if I start second-guessing myself because I'm not an engineer by trade. I prefer to track simultaneously analog and digital so that I can borrow from both of those formats," he says. "I really prefer to leave instruments like the drums, bass, and fiddle in analog and acoustic guitars and piano in digital. I'm still very much a fan of older microphones, Neumann microphones. There's a bunch of vintage gear out there that you can't beat."

Stegall has learned never to stop rolling tape; with studio musicians, he usually has a usable tape by the second pass. "Usually my second take is the one that's on the record because the musicians aren't thinking too much yet," he says. "Vocals are probably the most arduous process for me in making a record. I'm very much a believer in comping vocals because if you stop and start them in the middle of the track, it messes with their focus. With Alan, I let him sing a track four times and get four performances and then pick the best lines out of each performance.

"I tell every artist that I work with when we start the project, 'This is not my record, it's your record. This records need to be what you're hearing in your head. You communicate to me what you're hearing and let's try to get it on tape.' All I'm trying to do is be an architect of what they're imagining."

In 1996 Stegall released his own latest album, *Passages,* to much acclaim. —MELINDA NEWMAN

Anderson, John: "Small Town," Mercury, 1997 • "Somebody Slap Me," Mercury, 1997 • "Takin' the Country Back," Mercury, 1998 • *Takin' the Country Back,* Mercury, 1997.

Austin, Bryan: *Bryan Austin,* Patriot, 1994 • "Radio Active," Patriot, 1994.

Byrd, Tracy: "That's the Thing About a Memory," MCA, 1992 • *Tracy Byrd,* MCA, 1993 • "Why Don't That Telephone Ring?," MCA, 1993.

Clark, Terri: *Terri Clark,* Mercury, 1985 • "Better Things to Do," Mercury, 1995 • "When Boy Meets Girl," Mercury, 1995 • "If I Were You," Mercury, 1996 • *Just the Same,* Mercury, 1996 • "Poor, Poor Pitiful Me," Mercury, 1996 • "Emotional Girl," Mercury, 1997 • "Just the Same," Mercury, 1997 • *How I Feel,* Mercury, 1998 • "Now That I Found You," Mercury, 1998.

Coty, Neal: *Chance and Circumstance,* Mercury, 1997.

Cyrus, Billy Ray: "It's All the Same to Me," Mercury, 1997 • *The Best of Billy Ray Cyrus: Cover to Cover,* Mercury, 1997 • "Time for Letting Go," Mercury, 1998.

Dennis, Wesley: "Don't Make Me Feel at Home," Mercury Nashville, 1995 • "I Don't Know (but I've Been Told)," Mercury Nashville, 1995 • *Wesley Dennis,* Mercury Nashville, 1995 • "Who's Counting," Mercury Nashville, 1995.

Jackson, Alan: "Blue Blooded Woman," Arista, 1989 •

"Chasin' the Neon Rainbow," Arista, 1990 • "Here in the Real World," Arista, 1990 • *Here in the Real World,* Arista, 1990 • "Wanted," Arista, 1990 • "Don't Rock the Jukebox," Arista, 1991 • *Don't Rock the Jukebox,* Arista, 1991 • "I'd Love You All Over Again," Arista, 1991 • "Someday," Arista, 1991 • *A Lot About Livin' (and a Little 'Bout Love),* Arista, 1992 • "Dallas," Arista, 1992 • "Love's Got a Hold on You," Arista, 1992 • "Midnight in Montgomery," Arista, 1992 • "She's Got the Rhythm (and I Got the Blues)," Arista, 1992 • "Chattahoochee," Arista, 1993 • "Honky Tonk Christmas," Arista, 1993 • Honky Tonk Christmas, Arista, 1993 • "Mercury Blues," Arista, 1993 • "Tequila Sunrise," Giant, 1993 (*Common Thread: The Songs of the Eagles*) • "Tonight I Climbed the Wall," Arista, 1993 • "Tropical Depression," Arista, 1993 • "(Who Says) You Can't Have It All," Arista, 1994 • "Gone Country," Arista, 1994 • "Livin' on Love," Arista, 1994 • "Summertime Blues," Arista, 1994 • *Who I Am,* Arista, 1994 • *Greatest Hits Collection,* Arista, 1995 • "I Don't Even Know Your Name," Arista, 1995 • "Song for the Life," Arista, 1995 • "Tall, Tall Trees," Arista, 1995 • *Everything I Love,* Arista Nashville, 1996 • "Home," Arista, 1996 • "I'll Try," Arista, 1996 • "Little Bitty," Arista, 1996 • "Rudolph the Red-Nosed Reindeer," Arista, 1996 • "A Holly Jolly Christmas," Arista, 1997 • "A House with No Curtains," Arista, 1997 • "Between the Devil and Me," Arista, 1997 • "Everything I Love," Arista, 1997 • "There Goes," Arista, 1997 • "Who's Cheatin' Who," Arista, 1997 • "I'll Go on Loving You," Arista Nashville, 1998.

Kershaw, Sammy: "Meant to Be," Mercury, 1996 • "Politics, Religion and Her," Mercury, 1996 • *Politics, Religion and Her,* Mercury Nashville, 1996 • "Fit to Be Tied," Mercury, 1997 • *Labor of Love,* Mercury, 1997 • "Love of My Life," Mercury, 1997 • "Honky Tonk America," Mercury, 1998 • "Matches," Mercury, 1998.

Mason, Brent: *Hot Wired,* Mercury, 1997.

Neville, Aaron: *Tattooed Heart,* A&M, 1995.

Shenandoah: "Hey Mister (I Need This Job)," RCA, 1992 • *Leavin's Been a Long Time Comin,* RCA, 1992 • *Long Time Comin',* RCA, 1992 • "Rock My Baby," RCA, 1992.

Stegall, Keith: "1969," Mercury, 1996 • "Fifty Fifty," Mercury, 1996 • *Passages,* Mercury, 1996.

Tobin, Karen: *Carolina Smokey Moon,* Atlantic Nashville, 1991.

Travis, Randy: "On the Other Hand," Warner Bros., 1986 • *Storms of Life,* Warner Bros., 1986 • *Greatest Hits,* Vol. 1, Warner Bros., 1992 • *Greatest #1 Hits,* Warner Bros., 1998.

Turner Nichols: "Moonlight Drive-In," BNA, 1993 • "She Loves to Hear Me Rock," BNA, 1993 • *Turner Nichols,* BNA, 1993.

Wills, Mark: "High Low and in Between," Mercury, 1996 • "Jacob's Ladder," Mercury, 1996 • *Mark Wills,* Mercury, 1996 • "Places I've Never Been," Mercury, 1997 • *Wish You Were Here,* Mercury Nashville, 1998.

David A. Stewart

C reative whirlwind Dave Stewart (not to be confused with the keyboard player of the same name usually affiliated with Barbara Gaskin)—songwriter, guitarist, keyboardist, video creator, film and television producer-director, photographer, label owner—was the musical and production force behind the Eurythmics, his platinum '80s new wave–pop-rock duo with Annie Lennox.

Besides producing all but the first Eurythmics album, Stewart has guided Alisha's Attic, Jon Bon Jovi, Candy Dulfer, Bob Dylan, Aretha Franklin, Bob Geldof, Russian rocker Boris Grebenshikov, Daryl Hall, Imogen Heap, Mick Jagger, Londonbeat, Neville Brothers, Tom Petty and the Heartbreakers, the Ramones, and Feargal Sharkey to much excellent music.

Post-Eurythmics, Stewart has done music for film, recorded with Dave Stewart and the Spiritual Cowboys, and lately joined the digital revolution, releasing his 1998 solo album, *Sly Fi,* through his Web site (*www.davestewart.com*), which features many other cybergoodies as well.

David A. Stewart was born September 9, 1952, in Sunderland, England. Dave's brother, four years his senior, introduced him to American artists like bluesmen Mississippi John Hurt, Robert Johnson (Stewart produced the award-winning film *Deep Blues*—an investigation of the history and legacy of Delta Blues music—as a tribute to these influences), and Bob Dylan.

Stewart was a fine athlete in his childhood, but a knee injury channeled his energies into music. He picked up the guitar and was writing songs by his midteens. After attending a show by folkies Amazing Blondel when he was 15, Stewart became so enamored of the group that he traveled with them for a time, occasionally sitting in on guitar. At 17 Stewart went to London and signed a publishing contract with Chris Blackwell's (see entry) Island Music. Later Stewart formed an acoustic four-piece called Longdancer that had two records on Elton John's Rocket label in 1973 and 1974.

In the summer of 1976 Stewart met Annie Lennox, an alluring former Royal Academy of Music student who was waitressing at a London restaurant, and they became musical and romantic partners. The pair joined with singer/songwriter/guitarist Pete Coombes to form the Catch in 1977, which by 1979 had evolved into the Tourists. The Tourists put out three semi-psychedelic power-pop albums, including the excellent *Reality*

Effect, highlighted by Lennox's spirited vocals on an inspired cover of the Dusty Springfield hit "I Only Want to Be with You" (No. 4 U.K.), Coombes' rousing "So Good to Be Back Home Again" (No. 6 U.K.), and Stewart's production debut on Coombes' "The Loneliest Man in the World."

The Tourists went their separate ways in 1980, and Stewart and Lennox became Eurythmics. They recorded their first album, *In the Garden,* in Germany with Conny Plank producing and members of D.A.F. and Can guesting. "Conny untaught me everything I had learned about studios and made me look at them a different way. He helped me get over the myth that the studio is a scary place, and that everything has to be in control—I like things out of control. The previous producers and engineers I had worked with thought that if you record things perfectly onto tape, that makes a record, whereas my idea is that you create as much chaos as you possibly can, and try to capture some of the magic that comes flying out," Stewart says.

"I started recording on my own in my bedroom on a 4-track, and then I moved up to 8-track and a Soundcraft mixing desk, which Adam Williams helped me learn to run. I quickly got into making sounds and recording them without worrying about whether they were right or wrong. It just seemed natural to record with Annie: the two of us were obsessed with each other to the point of folie à deux, and often it was just the two of us recording alone," he says.

Though the pair's romantic relationship was over by the time of the second Eurythmics album, 1983's breakthrough *Sweet Dreams (Are Made of This)* (No. 3 U.K.), their amazing musical relationship (co-writing virtually all of the Eurythmics' songs together) lasted until the end of the decade, generating seven smash albums (30 million albums sold worldwide), over 20 U.K. charting singles, and ten U.S. Top 40 singles.

Sweet Dreams features the synth-pop classic title track (No. 1), and the jittery, dreamy "Love Is a Stranger" (No. 6 U.K.); these and virtually all subsequent hits took advantage of the burgeoning video revolution with dramatic clips scripted by Stewart displaying Lennox in a series of indelible roles ranging from male gigolo to bouncing-bodiced gothic heroine (neatly symbolizing her equally broad range of vocal styles: icy Julie Andrews clean soprano to toasty gutbucket soul).

Late 1983 saw the release of the exceptional *Touch* album, No. 1 in the U.K. and platinum in the U.S. The most endearing of the duo's albums, *Touch* has grand moody techno-pop in the form of "Here Comes the Rain Again" (No. 4) and the touchingly vulnerable "Who's That Girl?" (No. 3 U.K.), and the ebullient calyp-so-inflected brilliance of "Right by Your Side" (No. 10 U.K.).

The duo plunged furthest into electronic terrain with the soundtrack to *1984,* which treats Lennox's vocals as just another instrument in the tapestry save for "Sexcrime (1984)" (No. 4 U.K)—one of techno-pop's greatest hits—and the jazzy, Everything But the Girl–like "For the Love of Big Brother."

For 1985's *Be Yourself Tonight* (No. 3 U.K., platinum in the U.S.), Stewart kicked aside his synth (save for the lovely "There Must Be an Angel," No. 1 U.K.), picked up a guitar, and started bashing. "Would I Lie to You?" (No. 5) rocks on Stewart's power chords, Lennox's ballsy soul-rock singing, and a punchy horn section. The '60s soul connection is made explicit in Lennox's duet with Aretha Franklin, "Sisters Are Doin' It for Themselves" (No. 9 U.K.). The bluesy "It's Alright (Baby's Coming Back)" (No. 12 U.K.) is equally soulful.

By 1985 Stewart had also made a name for himself as an outside writer/producer: producing the Ramones' "Howling at the Moon (Sha La-La)" single; co-writing and co-producing three tracks for Tom Petty and the Heartbreakers' *Southern Accents* (No. 7), including the psychedelic hit single (with Stewart on a boingy sitar) "Don't Come Around Here No More" (No. 13); writing tracks for and producing Feargal Sharkey's (former lead singer of the Undertones) solo debut (No. 7 U.K.), including the No. 1 U.K. hit "A Good Heart"; and producing tracks for Aretha Franklin's *Who's Zooming Who* (No. 13) album.

If anything, Stewart was even busier in 1986: generating another Eurythmics album, *Revenge* (No. 3 U.K.); co-writing songs for and co-producing Daryl Hall's *Three Hearts in the Happy Ending Machine,* including the hooky hit "Dreamtime" (No. 5); co-writing and co-producing (with Hall and Jagger; see entry) Mick Jagger's title track to the film *Ruthless People* (the following year Stewart co-produced Jagger's *Primitive Cool*). Stewart also fulfilled a dream by co-producing and playing on Bob Dylan's *Knocked Out Loaded* album.

Stewart married singer Siobhan Fahey (Bananarama, Shakespear's Sister) in 1987, the same year that Eurythmics' *Savage* (No. 7 U.K.), something of a return to techno-pop, was released. After receiving a flood of interesting demos from aspiring artists over the years, Stewart formed Anxious Records in 1988 to help some of that music see the light of day. The label's best-known artists thus far have been Londonbeat and Curve.

Stewart is now dividing his restless attention equally between music, photography, film, and his new Web-only TV show, *Sly-Fi TV* (available at the aforementioned Web address), episodes of which have featured Bob Dylan, Bono, Deepak Chopra, and director Robert Altman. "I'm interested in really creative things all day long, and I always want to be with everybody forever now," says Stewart, explaining his fecund and multifarious career in a single pregnant sentence. —ERIC OLSEN

Alisha's Attic: *Alisha Rules the World,* Mercury, 1997.

An Emotional Fish: *Junk Puppets,* Atlantic, 1993.

Bon Jovi, Jon: *Destination Anywhere,* Mercury, 1997.

Campbell, Dirk Mont: *Music from a Round Tower,* East Side Digital, 1997.

Dulfer, Candy: *Saxuality,* Arista, 1992 • *The Best Of,* N2K, 1998.

Dylan, Bob: *Knocked Out Loaded,* Columbia, 1986.

Eurythmics: "Love Is a Stranger," RCA, 1983 • "Right by Your Side," RCA, 1983 • "Sweet Dreams (Are Made of This)," RCA, 1983 • *Sweet Dreams (Are Made of This)* (10 tracks), RCA, 1983 • *Touch,* RCA, 1983 • "Who's That Girl?," RCA, 1983, 1984 • *1984 (For the Love of Big Brother),* RCA, 1984 • "Here Comes the Rain Again," RCA, 1984 • "Sexcrime (1984)," RCA, 1984 • *Be Yourself Tonight,* RCA, 1985 • "Julia," RCA, 1985 • w/ Aretha Franklin, "Sisters Are Doin' It for Themselves," RCA, 1985 • "There Must Be an Angel (Playing with My Heart)," RCA, 1985 • "Would I Lie to You?," RCA, 1985 • "It's Alright (Baby's Coming Back)," RCA, 1986 • "Missionary Man," RCA, 1986 • *Revenge,* RCA, 1986 • "The Miracle of Love," RCA, 1986 • "Thorn in My Side," RCA, 1986 • "When Tomorrow Comes," RCA, 1986 • "Beethoven (I Love to Listen To)," RCA, 1987 • "I Need a Man," RCA, 1987 • *Savage,* RCA, 1987 • "Shame," RCA, 1987 • "You Have Placed a Chill In My Heart," RCA, 1988 • "Don't Ask Me Why," Arista, 1989 • *King and Queen of America* (EP), Arista, 1989 • "Revival," Arista, 1989 • *We Too Are One,* Arista, 1989 • "Angel," Arista, 1990 • *Greatest Hits,* Arista, 1991 • *Live, 1983–1989,* Arista, 1993.

Franklin, Aretha: *Who's Zooming Who,* Arista, 1985.

Geldof, Bob: *Deep In the Heart of Nowhere,* Atlantic, 1986.

Grebenshikov, Boris: *Radio Silence,* Columbia, 1988.

Hall, Daryl: "Dreamtime," RCA, 1986 • "Foolish Pride," RCA, 1986 • *Three Hearts In the Happy Ending Machine,* RCA, 1986 • "Someone Like You," RCA, 1987.

Hall, Terry: *The Collection: Terry Hall,* Chrysalis, 1993.

Heap, Imogen: *I Megaphone,* ALMO, 1998.

Jagger, Mick: "Ruthless People," Epic, 1986 • "Let's Work," Columbia, 1987 • *Primitive Cool,* Columbia, 1987 • "Throwaway," Columbia, 1987.

Lennox, Annie, and Al Green: "Put a Little Love In Your Heart," A&M, 1988.

Londonbeat: *In the Blood,* Radioactive, 1991.

Neville Brothers: *Brother's Keeper,* A&M, 1990.

Petty, Tom, and the Heartbreakers: "Don't Come Around Here No More," MCA, 1985 • "Make It Better (Forget About Me)," MCA, 1985 • *Southern Accents,* MCA, 1985 • *Greatest Hits,* MCA, 1993.

Ramones: "Howling at the Moon (Sha La-La)," Sire/WB, 1984 • *Too Tough to Die* (1 track), Sire/WB, 1984.

Sharkey, Feargal: "A Good Heart," A&M, 1985 • *Feargal Sharkey,* A&M, 1985 • "You Little Thief," A&M, 1985 • "Someone to Somebody," A&M, 1986.

Stewart, Dave: introducing Candy Dulfer, "Lily Was Here," Arista, 1991 • *Greetings from the Gutter,* EastWest, 1995 • *Sly Fi,* Digital Artists, 1998.

Stewart, Dave, and the Spiritual Cowboys: *Dave Stewart and the Spiritual Cowboys,* Arista, 1990 • *Lily Was Here* soundtrack, Anxious, 1990 • *Honest,* Arista, 1991.

Texas: *White on Blonde* (1 track), Mercury, 1997.

Tourists, The: *Reality Effect* (1 track), Logo/Epic, 1979 • "The Loneliest Man in the World," Logo, 1979 • *Should Have Been Greatest Hits,* Legacy, 1984, 1990.

Williams Brothers: *The Williams Brothers,* Warner Bros., 1991.

Wilsons, The: *The Wilsons,* Mercury, 1997.

COLLECTIONS

The Ref (original soundtrack), Imago, 1994.

Sylvester Stewart

See SLY STONE

Mike Stoller

See JERRY LEIBER AND MIKE STOLLER

Mike Stone

Englishman Mike Stone—a top engineer in the '70s—was the king of the multiplatinum rock producers in the '80s. His productions and co-productions generated platinum-plus albums for April Wine, Asia, Journey, Queen, Ratt, and Whitesnake, with over 40 million copies sold in the U.S. alone. For good measure, Stone also helped generate 12 Top 20 singles with those same artists. Stone has also produced important new wave, punk, and metal for GBH, Helix, Shoes, and Y&T.

Mike Stone was born and raised in Berkshire, in south-central England. "Music is all I ever wanted to do. I loved American music: the Doors, Love, Paul Butterfield, and lots of blues bands. When I was 14 I went up to London with my sister every week, and I would hang out down at the Marquis and other clubs. I saw the Who, Yes, the Nice, Rory Gallagher, Fleetwood Mac, John Mayall, loads of great bands," says Stone.

"I played guitar, trombone, and piano, but I wasn't any good at any of them. I also loved the technical aspects of recording music, so I worked on that too. I started trying to get into studios three years before I finished school.

"When I finished school I became an accountant, but that only lasted six months. I got fired because I wouldn't get my hair cut. Then I went to work in a seat belt factory until I got an interview with April-Blackwood music publishing in Soho. I met a guy in the lobby, Graham Dee, who was a producer, and he had Parkinson's disease. He was having trouble dialing the phone, so I asked if I could help. He said 'No!' When we walked out, he asked me what I was doing at April-Blackwood, and I told him that I was trying to get into music—like I'd been trying to do for years," he sighs, the memory still vivid.

Stone asked Dee if he needed a lift. Dee accepted and directed Stone to drive to Trident—one of the top studios in London—where Dee introduced Stone as his best friend to the managing director. This was a Thursday—Stone started on Monday. It was 1970 and Stone was 18.

Stone was a tea boy for nine months; the first person he made tea for was George Harrison, who was at Trident to make *All Things Must Pass,* with Phil Spector producing and Ken Scott engineering (see entries). Elton John and Genesis also recorded there, and it was with Genesis that Stone got his first assistant engineering credit. His first engineering credit came on the classic debut Queen album, produced by Roy Thomas Baker (see entry) and John Anthony.

Stone became chief engineer at Trident, recording and mixing for Lou Reed, America, Joe Walsh, Al Stewart, Ace, and Strawbs, among many others. His first major production job came when he co-produced Queen's *News of the World* (No. 3) with the band in 1977. *News* was a return to fine rocking form for the band after the success of gimmicky, campy pop confections like "Bohemian Rhapsody," "You're My Best Friend," and "Somebody to Love." The medley of "We Will

Rock You" into "We Are the Champions" (No. 4) features a great Freddie Mercury vocal and is a sports event staple worldwide; "Sheer Heart Attack" and "Fight from the Inside" rock like the band means it on the strength of Brian May's guitar and Roger Taylor's vocals and drums.

Stone engineered all of the Kiss solo albums in 1978 and then returned to production with what may be his finest album, Shoes' (see Jeff Murphy entry) *Present Tense,* in 1979. Neither platinum nor even gold, *Tense,* co-produced with the band, is one of the greatest power-pop albums, with nary a hole in a collection of tuneful, ringing classics, including "Tomorrow Night," "Too Late," "Your Very Eyes" and "In My Arms Again." The excellent production is contained but deep, with no distractions from the superb singing, playing, and songwriting.

In 1981 Stone finally arrived: In January *The Nature of the Beast,* by Canadian melodic hard-rockers April Wine, went platinum. In February Journey's live *Captured* (No. 9), a reasonable recapitulation of the band's career to that point, did double-platinum business.

Then in August, Journey's studio album *Escape* (No. 1) was unleashed on the world. With Steve Perry's impressive, even soulful, operatically trained high tenor cutting through the very definition of '80s arena rock and power ballads, people robotically marched to their record stores and bought an inconceivable 9 million copies of an album that is basically just pretty good. If somewhat grandiloquently produced by Stone and Kevin Elson, the album is better than many and certainly no worse than hundreds like it, but for some reason it became a must-have. "Don't Stop Believin'" (No. 9) has a good beat and a catchy tune. "Who's Crying Now" (No. 4) is a nice ballad. The title track rocks convincingly—if somewhat stiffly in a prog-rock manner—on the strength of Santana veteran Neal Schon's guitar, as does "Dead or Alive." I suppose the clincher for many was the truly pretty ballad "Open Arms" (No. 2), but still, 9 million?

With the floodgates open, no mortal was going to stem the tide. While Journey was a real rock band with an honorable history, Asia was a studio-construct of prog-rock superstars (Geoffrey Downes on keyboards and Steve Howe on guitar, both ex of Yes; Carl Palmer on drums, ex-ELP; John Wetton on bass and lead vocals, ex of King Crimson, Roxy Music, and many another arty band). Had the members brought with them the best of their respective former units, miracles might have been wrought. However, with production slipping across the line into the clearly bombastic—multidubbed cascading background vocals supporting Wetton's manly, straining baritone on essentially meaningless lyrics, all riding on a cushion of cheesy '80s electronic keyboard nonsense, Palmer's beat-challenged drums, and canyons-worth of echo—miracles were not achieved. It would be difficult to ascertain what need the sales of 4 million copies of *Asia* (No. 1) met in 1982. The even-less distinctive *Alpha* (No. 6) sold another million in 1983.

Journey, looking positively gritty in comparison with Asia, came back in 1983 for another 5 million with *Frontiers,* another pretty good album with inexplicable sales figures, until you realize that about half the people who bought *Escape* gave the follow-up a try.

To be fair, in the midst of all of this platinum pomposity Stone produced the careening, vicious punk of GBH in 1981, the bluesy guitar rock of Gary Moore in 1985, and the California alterna-country of the Textones and the rousing good-time metal of Helix in 1987. But the man has always had a way with melodic hard rock, and that brings us to Whitesnake.

By 1987 Stone had learned that by backing off from the lush, multidubbed background vocals a bit, pumping the guitar a smidge, and draining the reverb/echo off the lead vocal a tad (except in the "freaky" parts), you could still get the sales without alienating your core hard-rock crowd. Besides, Whitesnake, led by former Deep Purple singer David Coverdale, rocked way harder than either Journey or Asia, and still did ballads for the girls. *Whitesnake* (No. 2) sold 8 million albums and wrapped up Stone's remarkable '80s—wrapped it up except for the nine tracks that he placed on Journey's *Greatest Hits,* which has sold 8 million copies since its release in 1988.

With homes in three different countries—England, Ireland, Portugal—that he spent a total of six months in over the mad '80s, Stone has settled down a bit in the '90s. He is working with adventuresome bands like One Way System, Broken Bones, and Manchester's Ten. He's working on this and that (like transferring live concerts from Dutch TV onto DVD) and not worrying about where his next meal is coming from. But if he ever does have that concern again, there's always melodic hard rock. —ERIC OLSEN

April Wine: "Just Between You and Me," Capitol, 1981 • "Sign of the Gypsy Queen," Capitol, 1981 • *The Nature of the Beast,* Capitol, 1981 • "Enough Is Enough," Capitol, 1982 • *Power Play,* Capitol, 1982 • *Animal Grace,* Capitol, 1984 • "This Could Be the Right One," Capitol, 1984.

Asia: *Asia,* Geffen, 1982 • "Heat of the Moment," Geffen, 1982 • "Only Time Will Tell," Geffen, 1982 • *Alpha,* Geffen, 1983 • "Don't Cry," Geffen, 1983 • "The Smile Has Left Your Eyes," Geffen, 1983 • *Astra,* Geffen, 1985 • "Go," Geffen, 1985 • *Then and Now,* Geffen, 1990.

Barnes, Jimmy: "Driving Wheels," Geffen, 1988 • *Freight Train Heart,* Geffen, 1988 • "Too Much Ain't Enough," Geffen, 1988.

Boot: *Boot,* Agape, 1972.

Broken Bones: *Complete Singles,* Cleopatra, 1996.

Charlie: *Fantasy Girls,* Polydor, 1976.

Delaney, Sean: *Highway,* Casablanca, 1979.

Discharge: *Why,* Clay, 1981 • *Hear Nothing, See Nothing, Say Nothing,* Clay, 1982.

Easy Street: *Under the Glass,* Capricorn, 1977.

Foreigner: *Mr. Moonlight,* Priority, 1995.

GBH: "City Baby Attacked by Rats," Alex, 1981, 1991 (*Burning Ambitions [A History of Punk]*) • *Leather, Bristles, Studs and Acne* (EP), Clay, 1981.

Helix: *Wild in the Streets,* Capitol, 1987.

Journey: *Captured,* Columbia, 1981, 1996 • "Don't Stop Believin'," Columbia, 1981 • *Escape,* Columbia, 1981 • "Who's Crying Now," Columbia, 1981 • "Open Arms," Columbia, 1982 • "Still They Ride," Columbia, 1982 • "After the Fall," Columbia, 1983 • "Faithfully," Columbia, 1983 • *Frontiers,* Columbia, 1983 • "Send Her My Love," Columbia, 1983 • "Sepatate Ways (Worlds Apart)," Columbia, 1983 • "Only the Young," Geffen, 1985 • *Greatest Hits,* Columbia, 1988, 1996 • "When You Love a Woman/Message of Love," Columbia, 1996.

Moore, Gary: *Run for Cover,* Ten, 1985.

New England: *New England,* Infinity, 1979 • *Explorer Suite,* Elektra, 1980.

One Way System: *Forgotten Generation,* Cleopatra, 1996.

Queen: *News of The World,* Elektra, 1977 • "We Are the Champions," Elektra, 1977 • "We Will Rock You," Elektra, 1977 • "It's Late," Elektra, 1978 • "Spread Your Wings," Elektra, 1978.

Ratt: *Reach for the Sky,* Atlantic, 1988.

Romantics, The: *Strictly Personal,* Nemperor, 1981.

Schon, Neal, and Jan Hammer: *Here to Stay,* Columbia, 1982.

Shaw, Tommy: "Girls with Guns," A&M, 1984 • *Girls with Guns,* Absolute, 1984, 1996 • "Lonely School," A&M, 1984.

Shoes: *Present Tense,* Elektra, 1979 • "Too Late," Elektra, 1979 • *Shoes' Best,* Black Vinyl, 1987.

Simms Brothers Band: *The Simms Brothers Band,* Elektra/Atlantic, 1979.

Textones, The: *Cedar Creek,* Enigma, 1987.

Whitesnake: "Is This Love," Geffen, 1987 • "Still of the Night," Geffen, 1987 • *Whitesnake,* Geffen, 1987 • "Give Me All Your Love," Geffen, 1988 • *Greatest Hits,* DGC, 1994.

Y&T: *Ten,* Geffen, 1990.

Sly Stone

(SYLVESTER STEWART)

Sly Stone, born Sylvester Stewart on March, 15, 1944, in Dallas, Texas, personifies a music legend's fall from grace. The late '60s and early '70s was a time of highest hope and deepest betrayal in America: The nation seemed open to the possibilities of peace, love, and understanding; yet war, hatred, and fear refused to be conquered, and the truest believers became victims of their own disillusionment. Stone lived the drama to the fullest, making some of the most buoyant and thoughtful music of the era and transforming black and white music; yet he collapsed under the weight of his ideals as the promise gave way to realities he couldn't bear and the drugs turned on him.

Sly's career in music began early, as the prodigy recorded a gospel song at age 4. The Stewarts moved to the working-class suburb of Vallejo, California, in 1953 and Sly continued to blossom. He mastered guitar and drums, among many instruments, and played in several high school bands, where he met sax player Jerry Martini and trumpeter Cynthia Robinson. After Stone took courses from Vallejo Junior College in music theory, he met pioneering radio DJ Tom Donahue in 1964, who asked Sly to record and produce for his Autumn Records.

Stone's vision already cut across musical and racial barriers. He produced the Mojo Men (at one time called Sly and the Mojo Men), the Vejtables, the Beau Brummels, Grace Slick and the Great Society, and Bobby Freeman as well as recording some singles of his own. Freeman's "Swim" is jumping rock 'n' roll, carrying on the noble dance theme tradition of the twist and the watusi. The Brummels had a notable run of three Top 40 hits in 1965 in a pleasant British Invasion-style of pop rock. "Laugh Laugh" (No. 15), with its mournful harmonica, jiggling tambourines and jangling guitars, is the standout.

Seeking the spotlight, of sorts, for himself, Stone went to broadcast school and began DJing at the newly established black music station, KSOL, in 1966. Sly was energetic and innovative, rumbling witticisms and street slang and expanding the black music format to include the Beatles, Bob Dylan, and Lord Buckley. In the back of Sly's mind, a germ was planted that these disparate musical styles could live together in a single group.

Sly's germ blossomed into his colorful, freaky, musical creation, Sly and the Family Stone. Sly wrote the songs, created the arrangements, and handled the pro-

duction but allowed each member to express his or her individual identity. The Family's mixture of blacks and whites, men and women, blended brother Freddie Stewart on electric guitar, sister Rose on electric piano, along with Robinson, Martini, and Martini's cousin Gregg Errico (the two white guys) on drums. The outside recruit was bass player Larry Graham (later of Graham Central Station), solid founder of street funk bass playing. His percussive popping and thumping bass sound put the thunk into funk before Bootsy Collins took up the technique.

With the elements in place, the first single by Sly and the Family Stone, "I Ain't Got Nobody/I Can't Turn You Loose," had enough energy to interest Epic Records, but their first LP, 1967's A Whole New Thing, never caught on or up with the feel and excitement of their live shows. It wasn't until their next LP, Dance to the Music, that the band began to catch fire. The title song was a perfect representation of the live Family sound: a vibrant amalgam of positivity, fuzz bass, doo-wop, rock guitar and horns (alternately blasting the melody and commenting upon it with elegant filigrees) in the context of a traditional R&B revue. Only a few months later, Motown's Norman Whitfield (see entry) was taking the Temptations into Sly land with "Cloud Nine."

The summer of 1969 found Sly and the Family Stone rising to the heights of popularity and critical acclaim on the wings of their phenomenal LP Stand! (No. 13). The album gave birth to the band's first No. 1 hit, "Everyday People," a song that defined the band's social ideals in the way that "Dance" defined its musical thoughts. "People" displays a calm rationality that is driven home by the steady beat and repeated piano figure. Sly reasons about the dignity of the individual in the face of mindless categorization. The charm of the nursery rhyme refrain cuts through centuries of cultural bias and reminds us of the simple truth that "we got to live together," or die separately. Also on the album are the racially ambidextrous "Don't Call Me Nigger, Whitey" and the anthemic, orgasmic "I Want to Take You Higher."

That same summer, Sly and the Family Stone stormed the stage at Woodstock in rainbow get-ups, flashing sequins and electricity, and came away superstars. If the attendees weren't already high enough, many feel that when Sly cried out "I Want to Take You Higher" at the end of the band's set, the festival, and an era, reached its frenzied peak.

The band capitalized on this momentum with Greatest Hits (No. 2) in 1970, which featured three recent singles as well as work from earlier albums. The vocal trading of "Everybody Is a Star" created a familial atmosphere that touched people in the ghetto, in Haight-Ashbury, and on Mainstreet, U.S.A. The 45 flip side offered the booty-womping funk of "Thank You (Falettinme Be Mice Elf Agin)." Together they reached No. 1.

If James Brown is the father of funk, then Sly is the multi-culti ambassador who brought it to all the people. Chanted unison vocals, Freddie's whiplash guitar, and, most of all, Larry Graham's gut-wrenching bass propel "Thank You" into the realm of the sublime. The languid slow-jam, "Hot Fun in the Summertime" (No. 2) brought a refreshing tonic of much-needed innocence to the era of Vietnam.

Unfortunately, Sly took his obsession with "highness" literally (note the frequency of the word "high" in titles and lyrics), and came to confuse the easy high of drugs with the more difficult, more satisfying highs of music, love, and the simple joy of existence. With the drugs came increasing paranoia and self-absorption that were expressed first and best on 1971's *There's a Riot Goin' On*. *Riot* lacks the spunk and positivity of his previous work, but Sly's incredible talent still shines through the murk. Drummer Greg Errico left during the production, disillusioned with Sly's own disillusionment and unreliability. Sly further damaged the family feel by playing most of the instruments on the album and isolating himself from the other band members in a cocaine cocoon.

Ironically, *Riot* was the band's only No. 1 album. The most impressive track is the quietly funky, disturbing "Family Affair" (No. 1). "Affair" chronicles the divergent paths of two sons—one good, one bad, but both good to Mom "because blood is thicker than the mud." Perhaps these two characters represent Sly's own internal dichotomy. The soulful bass burbles along quietly, Graham's happy thump but a memory. Freddie's guitar is transmogrified into moody wah-wah bleeps. "(You Caught Me) Smilin' " is twisted jazzy soul that finds Sly nearly blowing out his microphone with vocal outbursts. The bizarre "Spaced Cowboy" is an entertaining blend of clip-clop beats, funk bass, and Sly's delirious yodeling, and "Thank You for Talkin' to Me Africa" regresses the urban funk of the original "Thank You" into a languid tour of the heart of darkness. "Runnin' Away" displays a classic simple melody in the "Everyday People" vein, played by Cynthia on her noble red trumpet and sung by sister Rose (shadowed by Sly's subterranean double) on such painfully self-aware lines as, "The deeper in debt, the harder you bet." It was the last great Family Stone song.

After *There's A Riot Goin' On*, Larry Graham left the band to pursue other interests, but also to escape Sly. Thereafter, Sly's music took a backseat to multiple drug

and weapons violations. With his almost unlimited talent, he squeezed out two more hits: the ironic "If You Want Me to Stay" (No. 12) and the self-instructive "Time for Livin'." Though Sly has attempted several comebacks, he has never recaptured the public's attention. The spirit of the Family Stone lives in the blatant imitation of Prince; the funk of George Clinton; the psychedelic soul of Isaac Hayes, Curtis Mayfield, and Norman Whitfield (see entries); and the jazzy, rocking soul of Earth, Wind and Fire, Kool and the Gang, and War. —DAWN DARLING AND ERIC OLSEN

Beau Brummels: *Introducing,* Sundazed, 1965, 1994 • "Just a Little," Autumn, 1965 • "Laugh Laugh," Autumn, 1965 • *Volume 2,* Autumn, 1965 • "You Tell Me Why," Autumn, 1965 • *You Tell Me Why/Don't Talk to Strangers,* Sundazed, 1965, 1994 • *The Best of the Beau Brummels,* Rhino, 1987 • *Autumn of Their Years,* Big Beat, 1994 • *San Francisco Sessions,* Sundazed, 1996.

Freeman, Bobby: "C'mon and Swim," Autumn, 1964.

Funkadelic: *The Electric Spanking of War Babies,* Warner Bros., 1981.

Jefferson Airplane: *Jefferson Airplane Loves You,* RCA, 1992.

Little Sister: "You're the One—Part 1," Stone Flower, 1970 • "Somebody's Watching You," Stone Flower, 1971.

Mojo Men: *Sly Stone and the Mojo Men,* WPC, 1993.

Sly and the Family Stone: "I Ain't Got Nobody," Loadstone, 1966 • *A Whole New Thing,* Epic, 1967 • "Dance to the Music," Epic, 1968 • *Dance to the Music,* Epic, 1968 • "Everyday People," Epic, 1968 • *Life,* Epic, 1968 • "Hot Fun in the Summertime," Epic, 1969 • "Sing a Simple Song," Epic, 1969 • "Stand!," Epic, 1969 • *Stand!,* Epic, 1969 • "Everybody Is a Star," Epic, 1970 • *Greatest Hits,* Epic, 1970 • "I Want to Take You Higher," Epic, 1970 • "Thank You (Falettinme Be Mice Elf Agin)," Epic, 1970 • "Family Affair," Epic, 1971 • *There's a Riot Goin' On,* Epic, 1971 • "Runnin' Away," Epic, 1972 • *Fresh,* Legacy, 1973, 1991 • "If You Want Me to Stay," Epic, 1973 • "Time for Livin'," Epic, 1974 • *Back on the Right Track,* Warner Bros., 1979 • *Anthology,* Epic, 1981.

Stewart, Sly: "Buttermilk Pt. 1," Autumn, 1964 • "I Just Learned How to Swim," Autumn, 1964 • "Temptation Walk Pt. 1," Autumn, 1965.

Stone, Sly: *Small Talk,* Epic, 1974 • *High Energy,* Epic, 1975 • *High on You,* Epic, 1975 • *Heard You Missed Me, Well I'm Back,* Epic, 1976 • *Ain't but the One Way,* Warner Bros., 1983 • *Slyest Freshest Funkiest Rarest,* Magicalmystery, 1995.

COLLECTIONS

Precious Stone: In the Studio with Sly Stone, 1963–1965, Ace, 1994.

Dance with Me: The Autumn Teen Sound, Rhino, 1994.

Jackie Robinson Tribute: Stealing Home, Sony, 1997.

Stephen Street

After spending a number of years attempting to make it as a musician, Stephen Street saw that it was better to give than to receive. He went from playing in bands to guiding them to their own unique sound and vision, first as an assistant engineer, then as an engineer, and finally, as a producer in studios around London. His first job was at Island Records' basement studio, The Fallout Shelter. "I was the only assistant at the studio for a while, so my training was pretty intense," he says. "I was also lucky that the engineers I worked with there were very talented and were quite prepared to let me get some hands-on experience. I wasn't just making tea."

Inspired by the fresh sound of engineer/producers Steve Lillywhite, Martin Hannett (see entries), and Martin Rushent, Street first put his stamp on the Mighty Lemon Drops' *Happy Head* in 1986. He engineered the Smiths' *The Queen Is Dead* in 1985 and then produced their enigmatic "Girlfriend in a Coma" (No. 13 U.K.) in 1987; that relationship carried through to singer Morrissey's first solo album in 1988, *Viva Hate* (No. 2 U.K.), for which Street played guitar and bass, wrote all of the music to Morrissey's lyrics, and served as producer. The partnership continued through four Top 10 U.K. hits representing Morrissey's most tuneful work, ending with "Interesting Drug" (No. 9 U.K.) in 1989. "Everyday Is Like Sunday" (No. 9 U.K.) is a brilliant evocation of desolation as represented by a gray seaside town in the off-season, and is Morrissey's finest solo moment.

Apart from his writing partnership, Street feels that "it's a producer's job to help translate an artist's musical ideas into a professional-sounding recording. . . . I see an analogy between a record producer and a film director in that both work with the artist to help present their talent to the public in the best possible way. The studio has a labyrinth of possibilities, with all the sonic effects and treatments available, and it's my responsibility to guide any act I work with through that labyrinth. I also have to focus on capturing the best possible performance of a song and make sure the 'sound' around it is right and sympathetic to the song.

"I like to think of recordings I've made as having taken an audio snapshot of the artist at that particular time in their career," he continues. "I certainly do not feel I should impose a sound on an act. It should be their talent that is being showcased, not mine."

Street has had a hand in some of the finest modern rock moments of the '90s. He has produced most of the Blur hits, including the great neo-Invasion tune "There's No Other Way" (No. 8 U.K.), the clever Brit-pop classic "Girls and Boys" (No. 5 U.K.), "Country House" (No. 1 U.K.), and "The Universal" (No. 5 U.K.). Street also produced the exceptionally successful first two albums by Ireland's Cranberries: the 4 million–selling *Everybody Else Is Doing it, So Why Can't We?* (No. 1 U.K.), and the 5 million–selling *No Need to Argue* (No. 6). Besides keenly spotlighting Dolores O'Riordan's lilting vocals, Street's productions for the band have ranged from the dreamy "Linger" (No. 8), through the lush "Dreams," to the stately big-guitar sound (from Noel O'Riordan) of "Zombie" (No. 14 U.K.).

Street has had a particular knack for working with new-wavey female singers, with highlights including the Darling Buds' underappreciated "Crystal Clear," Danielle Dax's great trip-hop cover of the Beatles' "Tomorrow Never Knows," as well as tracks for Pretenders and Sleeper.

"I'm known for working with alternative guitar pop bands quite early in their careers," he explains, "and I like the fact that I've been involved with them before they made it big. It makes you feel you've been instrumental in helping them get there. I would say I would like to work with the next big thing that is currently unknown, rehearsing somewhere and beginning to attract interest from some A&R people. Mind you, if the Eels were interested in doing something, I would be delighted." Although he's already worked with his two favorite bands, the Smiths and Blur, he's sorry he couldn't have produced R.E.M. before they attained commercial success.

Technology is complex but accessible, suggests Street, adding he hews to no single production method. "Amateur musicians know a fair bit about the creative and technical possibilities of modern technology, thanks to home recording studios and the plethora of magazines dealing with electronic equipment," he says. "I have carefully tried to purchase equipment that helps to speed up the process. The Otari Radar is a perfect example; it helps me achieve the backing tracks I want so much quicker than having to edit 24-track tape."

His production philosophy? Leave well enough alone and don't get in the way. "If it ain't broke, don't fix it," he says. —DAVID JOHN FARINELLA AND ERIC OLSEN

Blur: *Leisure* (7 tracks), SBK, 1991 • "There's No Other Way," SBK, 1991 • "Bang," SBK, 1992 • "For Tomorrow," SBK,

1993 • *Moden Life Is Rubbish,* SBK, 1993 • "Young and Lovely," Food, 1993 • "Girls and Boys," Food/SBK/ERG, 1994 • *Parklife,* SBK, 1994 • "Country House," Virgin America, 1995 • "Stereotypes," Food, 1995 • *The Great Escape,* Virgin America, 1995 • "The Universal," Virgin America, 1995 • "Charmless Man," Food, 1996 • "Beetlebum," Virgin, 1997 • *Blur,* Virgin, 1997 • *Bustin' and Dronin',* Food, 1998.

Bradford: *Shouting Quietly,* Sire, 1990.

Catatonia: *Way Beyond Blue,* Blanco y Negro, 1996.

Cole, Lloyd: *Love Story,* Rykodisc, 1995.

Cranberries, The: *Everybody Else Is Doing it, So Why Can't We?,* Island, 1993 • "Linger," Island, 1993 • "(They Long to Be) Close to You," A&M, 1994 (*If I Were a Carpenter*) • *No Need to Argue,* Island, 1994 • "Zombie," Island, 1994 • "Dreams," Mother/Island, 1995 (*Mission: Impossible* soundtrack) • "Ridiculous Thoughts," Phantom, 1995.

Darling Buds: *Crawdaddy* (9 tracks), Columbia, 1990 • "Crystal Clear," Columbia, 1990 • *Erotica Plays* (EP), Epic, 1991 • *Erotica,* Chaos, 1992.

Dax, Danielle: *Blast the Human Flower,* Sire/WB, 1990 • "Tomorrow Never Knows," Sire/WB, 1990.

Durutti Column: "Love No More," Factory/London, 1989, 1997 (*Different Colours, Different Shades: The Factory Story, Part 2*) • *Sex and Death,* FFRR, 1995.

Dylans, The: *The Dylans,* Beggars Banquet/RCA, 1991.

Echobelly: "Close But . . . ," Rhythm King, 1995.

Fat Lady Sings: *The Fat Lady Sings,* Atlantic, 1993.

Intastella: *What You Gonna Do,* Planet 3, 1995.

Kingmaker: *The Best Possible Taste,* Chrysalis, 1995.

Mighty Lemon Drops: *Happy Head,* Sire, 1986.

Morrissey: "Everyday Is Like Sunday," Sire, 1988 • "Suedehead," Sire, 1988 • *Viva Hate,* Sire/Reprise, 1988 • "Interesting Drug," Sire, 1989 (*Follow Our Tracks,* Vol. 2) • "The Last of the Famous International Playboys," Sire, 1989 • *Bona Drag* (6 tracks), Sire, 1990.

Pretenders, The: "Bold As Love," Reprise, 1993 (*Stone Free: A Tribute to Jimi Hendrix*) • "977," Warner Bros., 1994 • *Last of the Independents* (4 tracks), Sire/WB, 1994 • "Angel of the Morning," Reprise, 1995 (*Friends* soundtrack) • *Isle of View,* Warner Bros., 1995.

Psychedelic Furs: "All That Money Wants," CBS, 1988 • *World Outside,* Columbia, 1991 • *B-Sides and Lost Grooves,* Legacy, 1994 • *Should God Forget: A Retrospective,* Columbia, 1997.

Real People: *The Real People* (3 tracks), Relativity, 1991.

Shaw, Sandi: *Sandi Shaw* (8 tracks), Rough Trade, 1988.

Sleeper: "Atomic," Capitol, 1996 (*Trainspotting* soundtrack) • "Nice Guy Eddie," Arista, 1996 • *The It Girl,* Arista, 1996.

Smiths, The: "Girlfriend in a Coma," Sire, 1987 • "I Started Something I Couldn't Finish," Sire, 1987 • "Last Night I Dreamt That Somebody Loved Me," Sire, 1987 • *Louder Than Bombs* (2 tracks), Rough Trade/Sire, 1987 • *Strangeways, Here We Come,* Sire, 1987 • *Best,* Vols. 1–2, Sire, 1992 • *Singles,* Reprise, 1995.

Thousand Yard Stare: *Hands On,* Polydor, 1992.

Triffids, The: *The Black Swan,* Island, 1988.

James Stroud

James Stroud is one of the busiest producers in Nashville; he's helmed platinum or multiplatinum records for some of Music City's heaviest hitters, including Clint Black, Tim McGraw, John Anderson, Tracy Lawrence, Lorrie Morgan, and Clay Walker. *Billboard* named him Top Country Producer in 1990, 1994, and 1995. "I'm a very busy producer and I've been, at times, scolded about that," he admits. "If I could do one act and be happy with it, I would, but I enjoy working with these people so much and being with the musicians, it's hard for me to say no."

Stroud began as a session drummer, most notably as part of the famed Muscle Shoals rhythm section with Barry Beckett (see entry). He worked on albums by Paul Simon (see entry), Bob Seger, the Pointer Sisters, Gladys Knight, and others. In so doing, he learned about song structure.

The Shreveport, Louisiana, native settled in Nashville after his tenure in Muscle Shoals, eventually segueing from studio player to producer. His breakthrough came in 1976, when he produced R&B singer Dorothy Moore's multiformat smash, "Misty Blue" (No. 3). He also began producing country artists like Charlie Daniels, the Bellamy Brothers, and Eddie Rabbitt. For much of the '80s, Stroud ran an independent publishing company, The Writer's Group, which he eventually sold to EMI. He became a staff producer at MCA/Universal and, later, Capitol Nashville. In the early '90s, he came to run his own label as head of Giant Records' Nashville division. In 1997, he became head of Dreamworks' Nashville office. He also co-owns publishing company Hamstein Cumberland Music Group.

"It's very tough to run a label and if you don't have the right staff around you, you're just going to fail," he says. "The one thing I do want to do in the future is slow down and not do as much production and learn the administrative side because it's so interesting, and I think I can do it pretty well."

Meanwhile, he has continued to make his mark as a producer of one hit album after another. His first great country success came with superstar Clint Black, whom he has produced since Black's 3 million–selling 1989 debut, *Killin' Time*. His work with Black embodies criteria Stroud considers universal. "First of all, I have to see the artist perform, because that is really what you're trying to do—you're trying to get what the artist does on stage on tape," he says. "Clint's a perfect example. I wanted to be a producer known for making the artist's music, so I wanted to have an artist where I could use the artist's band in the studio [as opposed to Nashville studio musicians, the norm]. I went to see Clint in a little club outside of Houston and I thought if we could make this band a recording band, it would be great."

They rehearsed during the day and performed at night, working up a repertoire bound to be popular: "Killin' Time" and "Better Man" (both No. 1 country) were played before a club before they were recorded. "So what we did was spend time in the club during the day working up the music and then at night, we'd play it for the people and if they responded in a positive way, we'd use those songs. 'Killin' Time,' 'Better Man,' all those songs were played in front of a club full of people before they were ever recorded."

Stroud values every minute he can spend with an act before taping. "I'm totally against how fast records are made in Nashville. I'm one of them, but I'm totally against it," he says. "I love preproduction. I like to be around the artist and get some kind of relationship with him or her and then go make the record. It's hard to do, but if you're professional enough and you're good enough, you can pull it off."

Working with a new artist presents a special challenge. "You're molding an artist's career through his music, so what you have to do is create a history. You have to make sure that what you're doing is something the artist will want to do for 10 years and not make the mistake of making a type of music that's not him. If the artist doesn't have a strong identity, then you have to step in and be the identifier. What's tough on a producer is to figure out what the strong points are on an artist and then enhance those points in a minute amount of time."

Stroud learned that lesson from his mentor, Jimmy Bowen (see entry). Stroud worked under Bowen at both MCA and Capitol. "He gives tough love," Stroud says of Bowen. "The one thing that he did teach me was whatever you do, do not make a producer's record, make the artist's record."

Schooled in pop and rhythm 'n' blues, Stroud occasionally returns to his roots, such as when he produced a song by Melissa Etheridge for the 1995 *Boys on the Side* soundtrack. However, his heart is in country. "Every once in a while I want to produce something else," he

admits. "I came from an R&B and rock 'n' roll background and I like to tough on that every once in a while, but I have learned a great respect for country music. There is a way to do country music that is as good as any music that is done, and there's a purity of it and an emotion to it, and if you can capture that, there's nothing better." —MELINDA NEWMAN

Akins, Rhett: "More Than Everything," Decca, 1997 • "Better Than It Used to Be," Decca, 1998 • *What Livin's All About*, Decca, 1998.

Allen, Deborah: *All That I Am*, Giant, 1994 • "Break These Chains," Giant, 1994.

Anderson, John: "Let Go of the Stone," BNA, 1992 • "Seminole Wind," BNA, 1992 • *Seminole Wind*, BNA, 1992 • "Straight Tequila Night," BNA, 1992 • "When It Comes to You," BNA, 1992 • "I Fell in the Water," BNA, 1993 • "I've Got It Made," BNA, 1993 • "Money in the Bank," BNA, 1993 • *Solid Ground*, BNA, 1993 • "Bend It Until It Breaks," BNA, 1994 • *Christmas Time*, BNA, 1994 • *Country Till I Die*, BNA, 1994 • "I Wish I Could Have Been There," BNA, 1994 • "Mississippi Moon," BNA, 1995 • "Paradise," BNA, 1995 • *Swingin'*, BNA, 1995 • *Greatest Hits*, BNA, 1996 • "Long Hard Lesson Learned," BNA, 1996 • *Paradise*, BNA, 1996 • *Super Hits*, BNA, 1998.

Bellamy Brothers: "Rebels Without a Clue," Curb, 1988 • "Big Love," Curb, 1989 • *Greatest Hits*, Vol. 3, MCA, 1989.

Black, Clint: "Better Man," RCA, 1989 • "Killin' Time," RCA, 1989 • *Killin' Time*, RCA, 1989 • "Nobody's Home," RCA, 1989 • "Nothing's News," RCA, 1989 • "Walkin' Away," RCA, 1989 • *Put Yourself in My Shoes*, RCA, 1990 • "Put Yourself in My Shoes," RCA, 1990 • "Loving Blind," RCA, 1991 • "One More Payment," RCA, 1991 • "Where Are You Now," RCA, 1991 • "Burn One Down," RCA, 1992 • *The Hard Way*, RCA, 1992 • "This Nightlife," RCA, 1992 • "We Tell Ourselves," RCA, 1992 • "A Bad Goodbye," RCA, 1993 • *Clint Black*, RCA, 1993 • "Desperado," Giant, 1993 (*Common Thread: The Songs of the Eagles*) • "No Time to Kill," RCA, 1993 • *No Time to Kill*, RCA, 1993 • "State of Mind," RCA, 1993 • "When My Ship Comes In," RCA, 1993 • "A Good Run of Bad Luck," RCA, 1994 • "Half the Man," RCA, 1994 • *One Emotion*, RCA, 1994 • "Tuckered Out," RCA, 1994 • "Untanglin' My Mind," RCA, 1994 • "Life Gets Away," RCA, 1995 • *Looking for Christmas*, RCA, 1995 • "One Emotion," RCA, 1995 • "Summer's Comin'," RCA, 1995 • "'Til Santa's Gone (Milk and Cookies)," RCA, 1995 • "Wherever You Go," RCA, 1995 • *Greatest Hits*, RCA, 1996 • "Like the Rain," RCA, 1996 • "The Kid," RCA, 1996 • "Half Way Up," RCA, 1997 • "Nothin' but the Taillights," RCA, 1997 • *Nothin' but the Taillights*, RCA, 1997 • "Something That We Do," RCA, 1997 • "The Shoes You're Wearing," RCA, 1998.

Black, Clint, and Martina McBride: "Still Holding On," RCA, 1997.

Carson, Jeff: "Santa Got Lost in Texas," Curb, 1995.

Carter, Carlene: "Something Already Gone," Atlantic, 1994 • "Hurricane," Giant, 1995 • *Little Acts of Treason*, Giant, 1995 • "Love Like This," Giant, 1995 • *Hindsight 20/20*, Warner Bros., 1996.

Charlie Daniels Band: *Homesick Heroes*, Epic, 1988 • *Simple Man*, Epic, 1989 • "A Few More Rednecks," Epic, 1990 • "Mister DJ," Epic, 1990 • *See also* Daniels, Charlie.

Collie, Mark: *Tennessee Plates*, Giant, 1995 • "Three Words, Two Hearts, One Night," Giant, 1995.

Collins, Jim: "The Next Step," Arista, 1997 • "My First, Last, One and Only," Arista Nashville, 1998 • *The Next Step*, Arista Nashville, 1998.

Dalton, Lacy J.: "Hard Luck Ace," Universal, 1989 • *Survivor*, Universal, 1989 • "The Heart," Universal, 1989 • "Black Coffee," Capitol, 1990 • *Best Of*, Liberty, 1993.

Daniels, Charlie: "Boogie Woogie Fiddle Country Blues," Epic, 1988 • "Cowboy Hat in Dallas," Epic, 1989 • "Simple Man," Epic, 1989 • "Honky Tonk Life," Epic, 1991 • "Little Folks," Epic, 1991 • *Renegade*, Epic, 1991 • *Super Hits*, Columbia, 1994 • *Roots Remain*, Sony, 1996 • *See also* Charlie Daniels Band.

Diamond, Neil: *Tennessee Moon*, Columbia, 1996.

Ellis, Darryl, and Don Ellis: "Goodbye Highway," Epic, 1992 • "No Sir," Epic, 1992 • *No Sir*, Epic, 1992 • "Something Moving in Me," Epic, 1992.

England, Ty: "Irresistible You," RCA, 1996 • *Two Ways to Fall*, RCA, 1996.

Etheridge, Melissa: "I Take You with Me," Arista, 1995 (*Boys on the Side* soundtrack).

Falcon, Billy: *Letters from a Paper Ship*, Mercury, 1994.

Flamingo, Hank: *Hank Flamingo*, Giant, 1994.

Forester Sisters: "You Again," Warner Bros., 1987 • *Greatest Hits*, Warner Bros., 1989 • "Love Will," Warner Bros., 1989.

Goldens, The: "Put Us Together Again," Epic, 1988.

Greenwood, Lee: *If Only for One Night*, MCA, 1989.

Haggard, Marty: "Trains Make Me Lonesome," MTM, 1988.

Haggard, Merle: "In My Next Life," Curb, 1994 • *Merle Haggard 1994*, Curb, 1994.

Hutchens, The: "Knock, Knock," Atlantic Nashville, 1995 • *Knock, Knock*, Atlantic Nashville, 1995.

J.J. White: "Heart Break Train," Curb, 1991 • *Janice and Jayne*, Curb, 1991 • "The Crush," Curb, 1991 • "Jezebel Kane," Curb, 1992 • "One Like That," Curb, 1992.

Keith, Toby: *Dream Walkin'*, Mercury, 1997 • "We Were in Love," Mercury, 1997 • "Double Wide Paradise," Mercury, 1998 • "Dream Walkin'," Mercury, 1998.

Keith, Toby: w/ Sting, "I'm So Happy I Can't Stop Crying," Mercury, 1997.

King Floyd: *Choice Cuts*, Waldoxy, 1994.

Knoblock, Fred: "Why Not Me," Scotti Brothers, 1980 • *Why Not Me*, Scotti Brothers, 1980.

Lawrence, Tracy: "Sticks and Stones," Atlantic, 1991 • "Runnin' Behind," Atlantic, 1992 • "Somebody Paints the Wall," Atlantic, 1992 • *Sticks and Stones*, Atlantic, 1992 • "Today's Lonely Fool," Atlantic, 1992 • "Alibis," Atlantic, 1993 • *Alibis*, Atlantic, 1993 • "Can't Break It to My Heart," Atlantic, 1993 • "My Second Home," Atlantic, 1993 • *I See It Now*, Atlantic, 1994 • "If the Good Die Young," Atlantic, 1994 • "If the World Had a Front Porch," Atlantic, 1995.

Lee, Robin: *Heart on a Chain*, Atlantic, 1991 • "Nothin' but You," Atlantic, 1991.

Little Texas: "Some Guys Have All the Love," Warner Bros., 1991 • "First Time for Everything," Warner Bros., 1992 • *First Time for Everything*, Warner Bros., 1992 • "What Were You Thinkin'," Warner Bros., 1992 • "You and Forever and Me," Warner Bros., 1992 • *Big Time*, Warner Bros., 1993 • "God Blessed Texas," Warner Bros., 1993 • "I'd Rather Miss You," Warner Bros., 1993 • "What Might Have Been," Warner Bros., 1993 • "My Love," Warner Bros., 1994 • "Stop on a Dime," Warner Bros., 1994 • *Greatest Hits*, Warner Bros., 1995 • "Bad for Us," Warner Bros., 1997 • *Little Texas*, Warner Bros., 1997 • "The Call," Warner Bros., 1997.

Lynne, Shelby: "Don't Cross Your Heart," Epic, 1991 • w/ Les Taylor, "The Very First Lasting Love," Epic, 1991.

Malchak, Tim: *Different Circles*, Universal, 1989 • "If You Had a Heart," Universal, 1989.

Mandrell, Barbara: *No Nonsense*, Liberty, 1990 • *The Best Of*, Liberty, 1992.

McBride, Martina: *Evolution*, RCA, 1997.

McCoy, Neal: "There Ain't Nothin' I Don't Like About You," Atlantic Nashville, 1992 • "Where Forever Begins," Atlantic Nashville, 1992 • *Where Forever Begins*, Atlantic Nashville, 1992 • "Now I Pray for Rain," Atlantic Nashville, 1993 • *Greatest Hits*, Atlantic Nashville, 1997.

McGraw, Tim: *Tim McGraw*, Curb, 1993 • "Don't Take the Girl," Curb, 1994 • "Down on the Farm," Curb, 1994 • "Indian Outlaw," Curb, 1994 • "Not a Moment Too Soon," MCA, 1994 • *Not a Moment Too Soon*, Curb, 1994 • *All I Want*, Curb, 1995 • *An Hour with Tim McGraw*, Curb, 1995 • "Can't Really Be Gone," Curb, 1995 • "I Like It, I Love It," Curb, 1995 • "Refried Dreams," Curb, 1995 • "All I Want Is a Life," Curb, 1996 • "Maybe We Should Sleep on It," Curb, 1996 • "She Never Let's It Go to Her Heart," Curb, 1996 • "Everywhere," Curb, 1997 • *Everywhere*, Curb, 1997 • "Just to See You Smile," Curb, 1998 • "One of These Days," Curb, 1998 • "You Turn Me On," Curb, 1998.

McGraw, Tim, with Faith Hill: "It's Your Love," Curb, 1997 • "One Night at a Time," MCA, 1997.

McMillan, Terry: *Somebody's Comin'*, Giant, 1997.

Mensy, Tim: "This Ol' Heart," Giant, 1992 • *This Ol' Heart*, Giant, 1992.

Mitchell, McKinley: *Complete Malaco Collection*, Waldoxy, 1992.

Moore, Dorothy: "Misty Blue," Malaco, 1976.

Morgan, Lorrie: "Back in Your Arms Again," BNA, 1995 • *Greatest Hits*, BNA, 1995 • "I Didn't Know My Own Strength," BNA, 1995 • *Greater Need*, BNA, 1996 • "I Just Might Be," BNA, 1996 • "Standing Tall," BNA, 1996 • "Go Away," BNA, 1997 • "Good As I Was to You," BNA, 1997 • "One of Those Nights Tonight," BNA, 1997 • *Shakin Things Up*, BNA, 1997 • "I'm Not That Easy to Forget," BNA, 1998 • *Super Hits*, BNA, 1998.

Morgan, Lorrie: w/ Jon Randall, "By My Side," BNA, 1996.

Neville Brothers: *Mitakuye Oyasin Oyasin: All My Relations*, A&M, 1996.

Norwood, Daron: "Cowboys Don't Cry," Giant, 1994 • *Daron Norwood*, Giant, 1994 • "If I Ever Love Again," Giant, 1994 • "If It Wasn't for Her I Wouldn't Have You," Giant, 1994.

Olsson, Nigel: *Changing Tides*, Bang, 1980.

Orrall and Wright: "She Loves Me Like She Means It," Giant, 1994.

Osmond, Marie: "Like a Hurricane," Curb, 1989 • *The Best Of*, Curb, 1990 • *25 Hits Special Collection*, Curb, 1995.

Overstreet, Paul: "Love Helps Those," MTM, 1988 • "All the Fun," RCA, 1989 • "Sowin' Love," RCA, 1989 • *Sowin' Love*, RCA, 1989 • "Richest Man on Earth," RCA, 1990 • "Seein' My Father in Me," RCA, 1990 • *Best Of*, RCA, 1994.

Pirates of the Mississippi: "Honky Tonk Blues," Capitol, 1990 • "Feed Jake," Capitol, 1991 • *Pirates of the Mississippi*, Capitol, 1991 • "Speak of the Devil," Capitol, 1991 • *Best Of*, Liberty, 1994 • *Paradise*, Giant, 1995.

Rabbitt, Eddie: *Ten Years of Greatest Hits*, Liberty, 1990.

Regina Regina: "More Than I Wanted to Know," Giant, 1997 • *Regina Regina*, Giant, 1997.

Robbins, Dennis: "Home Sweet Home," Giant, 1992 • *Man with a Plan*, Giant, 1992 • "My Side of Town," Giant, 1992 • *Born Ready*, Giant, 1994 • "Mona Lisa on Cruise Control," Giant, 1994.

Rogers, Kenny: *If Only My Heart Had a Voice*, Giant, 1993.

Scott, Marilyn: *Dreams of Tomorrow*, Atco, 1979.

Singletary, Daryle: *Daryle Singletary*, Giant, 1995 • "I Let Her Lie," Giant, 1995 • "I'm Living Up to Her Low Expectations," Giant, 1995 • *All Because of You*, Giant, 1996 • "Too Much Fun," Giant, 1996 • "Workin' It Out," Giant, 1996 • "Amen Kind of Love," Reprise, 1997 • "Even the Wind," Reprise, 1997 • "The Used to Be's," Giant, 1997.

S-K-O (Schuyler, Knoblock and Overstreet): "You Can't Stop Love," MTM, 1986 • "American Me," MTM, 1987 • "Baby's Got a New Baby," MTM, 1987 • "No Easy Horses," MTM, 1987 • "This Old House," MTM, 1987 •

"Givers and Takers," MTM, 1988.

Sonnier, Jo-El: *Tears of Joy*, Liberty, 1991.

Stone, Doug: "I Never Knew Love," Epic, 1993 • *More Love*, Epic, 1993 • "Addicted to a Dollar," Epic, 1994 • *Greatest Hits,*, Vol. 1, Epic, 1994 • "Little Houses," Epic, 1994 • "More Love," Epic, 1994 • "Born in the Dark," Columbia, 1995 • "Faith in Me, Faith in You," Columbia, 1995 • *Faith in Me, Faith in You*, Columbia, 1995 • "Sometimes I Forget," Columbia, 1996 • *Super Hits*, Columbia, 1997.

Taylor, Les: *Blue Kentucky Wind*, Epic, 1991 • "I've Gotta Mind to Go Crazy," Epic, 1991.

Tillman, Robert Duke: *Thinking of You*, Ace, 1992.

Toliver, Tony: *Tony Toliver*, Curb, 1991, 1992 • *Half Saint Half Sinner*, Rising Tide, 1996.

Travis, Randy: "Out of My Bones," Dreamworks, 1998 • "The Hole," Dreamworks, 1998 • *You and You Alone*, Dreamworks, 1998.

Tritt, Travis: "Take It Easy," Warner Bros., 1994.

Vance, Vince, and the Valiants: "All I Want for Christmas Is You," Waldoxy, 1995.

Vincent, Rhonda: *Written in the Stars*, Giant, 1993 • *Trouble Free*, Giant, 1996.

Walker, Clay: "Live Until I Die," Giant, 1993 • "What's It to You?," Giant, 1993 • "Dreaming with My Eyes Open," Giant, 1994 • "If I Could Make a Living," Giant, 1994 • *If I Could Make a Living*, Giant, 1994 • "Where Do I Fit in the Picture?," Giant, 1994 • "White Palace," Giant, 1994 • *Clay Walker*, Giant, 1995 • "Hypnotize the Moon," Giant, 1995 • *Hypnotize the Moon*, Giant, 1995 • "My Heart Will Never Know," Giant, 1995 • "Only on Days That End in 'Y'," Giant, 1995 • "This Woman and This Man," Giant, 1995 • "Who Needs You Baby," Giant, 1995 • "Bury the Shovel," Giant, 1996 • "One, Two I Love You," Giant, 1997 • "Rumor Has It," Giant, 1997 • *Rumor Has It*, Giant, 1997 • "Then What," Giant, 1997 • "Watch This," Giant, 1997 • *Greatest Hits*, Giant, 1998 • "Ordinary People," Giant, 1998.

Ward, Chris: "Fall Reaching," Giant, 1996 • *One Step Beyond*, Giant, 1996.

Whittaker, Roger: *You Deserve the Best*, Capitol, 1990.

Wild Rose: "Breakin' New Ground," Universal, 1989 • "Go Down Swingin'," Capitol, 1990 • *Straight and Narrow*, Liberty, 1990.

Williams, Hank Jr.: *Maverick*, Curb/Capricorn, 1991 • "Come On over to the Country," Curb/Capricorn, 1992 • "Hotel Whiskey," Curb/Capricorn, 1992 • *The Bocephus Box: Hank Williams Jr. Collection, '79–'92*, Capricorn, 1992 • "Everything Comes Down to Money and Love," Curb/Capricorn, 1993 • *Out of Left Field*, Curb/Capricorn, 1993.

Williams, Christopher: "If You Say," Giant, 1995 • *Not a Perfect Man*, Giant, 1995.

Wright, Curtis: *Curtis Wright,* Liberty, 1992 • "Hometown Radio," Liberty, 1992 • "If I Could Stop Lovin' You," Liberty, 1993.

Zaca Creek: *Broken Heartland,* Giant, 1993.

COLLECTIONS

Songs of Jimmie Rodgers: A Tribute, Sony, 1997.

DeVante Swing

In the beginning, DeVante Swing (born Donald DeGrate Jr.) was simply one-fourth of Jodeci, one of the most successful R&B pop vocal bands of the '90s. Swing, his brother Dalvin, and other brothers K-Ci and JoJo Hailey, have delivered a more soulful, funkier, and lustier alternative to Boyz II Men, with hits such as "Freak'n You" (No. 14), "Lately" (No. 4), "Cry for You" (No. 15), "What About Us?," "Feenin'," and "Love U 4 Life."

Swing's production talent surfaced in 1991 with Jodeci's 3 million–selling debut, *Forever My Lady* (No. 18). It included not only the title track hit but also "Stay," "Come and Talk to Me" (No. 11), and "I'm Still Waiting" (some early hits were co-produced with Al B. Sure!). Swing extended his streak with 1993's *Diary of a Mad Band* (No. 3) and 1995's *The Show, the After-Party, the Hotel* (No. 2).

He became in demand for outside work, producing Montell Jordan's "What's On Tonight," Mary J. Blige and K-Ci Hailey's "I Don't Want to Do Anything," Changing Faces' "Keep It Right There," Horace Brown's "You Need a Man," Christopher Williams' "All I See," CeCe Peniston's "I See Love," and songs for Al B. Sure!, Usher, and Jeff Redd. He also produced himself on "Gin & Juice," which appeared on the *Dangerous Minds* soundtrack.

Swing also has produced some tracks for Death Row, including 2Pac's "No More Pain" and H-Town's "Part-Time Lover," and Jodeci with Tha Dogg Pound's "Come Up to My Room" from the *Murder Was the Case* soundtrack. —KEVIN JOHNSON

Blige, Mary J.: *What's the 411?* (1 track), Uptown/MCA, 1992 • w/ K-Ci Hailey, "I Don't Want to Do Anything," Uptown/MCA, 1993 • *What's the 411? The Remixes,* Uptown/MCA, 1993.

Brown, Horace: *Horace Brown,* Motown, 1996.

Changing Faces: *Changing Faces,* Spoiled Rotten/Big Beat, 1995 • "Keep It Right There," Spoiled Rotten/Big Beat, 1995.

Cooper, Michael: *Get Closer,* Reprise, 1992.

H-Town: w/ Al B. Sure!, "Part Time Lover," Death Row/Interscope, 1994 (*Above the Rim* soundtrack).

Jodeci: "Come and Talk to Me" (remix), Tommy Boy, 1991, 1993 (*MTV Party to Go,* Vol. 3) • "Forever My Lady," Uptown, 1991 • *Forever My Lady,* Uptown/MCA, 1991 • "Gotta Love," Uptown, 1991 • "Come and Talk to Me," Uptown, 1992 • "Stay," Uptown, 1992 • "Cry for You," Uptown, 1993 • *Diary of a Mad Band,* Uptown, 1993 • "Lately," Uptown, 1993 • "Let's Go Through the Motions," Uptown, 1993 • "I'm Still Waiting," Uptown/MCA, 1994 • "What About Us?," Uptown, 1994 • "Freak'n You," Uptown, 1995 • "Love U 4 Life," Uptown, 1995 • *The Show, the After-Party, the Hotel,* Uptown/MCA, 1995 • "Get on Up," MCA, 1996.

Jodeci with Tha Dogg Pound: "Come Up to My Room," Death Row, 1994 (*Murder Was the Case* soundtrack).

Jordan, Montell: *More to Tell,* Def Jam, 1996 • "What's on Tonight," Mercury, 1997.

K-Ci and Jo-Jo: *Love Always,* MCA, 1997.

Peniston, CeCe: *Finally,* A&M, 1992.

Redd, Jeff: *Quiet Storm,* Uptown, 1990.

Rezell, B: "Blowed Away," Death Row/Interscope, 1994 (*Above the Rim* soundtrack).

Sista: *4 All the Sistas Around da World,* Elektra, 1994 • "Brand New," Elektra, 1994.

Sure!, Al B.: *Private Times and the Whole 9!,* Warner Bros., 1990 • "Had Enuf?," Warner Bros., 1992 • *Sexy Versus,* Warner Bros., 1992.

Swing, DeVante: "Gin & Juice," MCA, 1995 (*Dangerous Minds* soundtrack).

Thompson, Tony: *Sexsational,* Giant, 1995.

2Pac: *All Eyez on Me* (1 track), Death Row, 1996.

Usher: "Can U Get Wit It," LaFace, 1994 • *Usher* (1 track), LaFace, 1994.

Williams, Christopher: *Changes,* Uptown/MCA, 1992.

Bill Szymczyk

Born February 13, 1943, in Muskegon, Michigan, Bill Szymczyk got his first taste of sonics in the navy working sonar. When he mustered out in February 1964, he enrolled in the New York Institute of Technology for television courses, but never attended. He also worked part-time at Dick Charles Recording Service, a Seventh Avenue studio where all the Screen

Left to right: David Speizo, Bill Szymczyk, Michael Stanley.
Photo by Henry Diltz

Gems demos were being cut; the Screen Gems roster included Gerry Goffin and Carole King, Neil Sedaka and Diamond, Howard Greenfield: "A hell of a stable," Szymczyk says.

Szymczyk realized then that the record business was what he wanted. Hands-on experience was the only route available in those days, when studios contained two mono recorders. "It was really a good training ground because you had to get your shit together on your basic track: drums, bass, and guitar," Szymczyk says. "This is pre-Dolby, pre-everything. You had to be good, so by the time your 10th or 12th generation (of tape) came on with the lead vocal, you could still hear the basic track."

In 1965, Szymczyk moved to Regent Sound, a 4-track master studio that didn't do demos. "They would do 35-piece dates, big union dates, Quincy Jones [see entry] conducting 30 pieces, everybody live at one time," he recalls. "You'd have to do three or four cuts in three hours. That really got your chops together, too."

From 1965 to 1967, Szymczyk worked for numerous producers, including R&B specialists Jerry Ragovoy (Lorraine Ellison, Howard Tate) and Van McCoy (the Shirelles, the Drifters, "The Hustle"). "I'd do the white folkies during the day and the R&B stuff at night," he recalls. He worked on records by Eric Andersen, Tom Rush, Phil Ochs, some Joni Mitchell demos, and Jim and Jean. He also worked on records by Ellison, Tate, and Erma Franklin, engineering for Ragovoy at the latter's Hit Factory. He became Ragovoy's chief engineer.

"At this time, I was a freelance engineer and doing quite well," he says. "I was doing 100 hours a week and making almost a grand a week, which was big bucks in

those days." It was 1968; Szymczyk was also dabbling in producing. "Nobody had hired me to do it for real yet," he says, "so I'd find a band or an artist and make records with them at 2 in the morning, after hours."

His first album production was Harvey Brooks, former Electric Flag bassist. It was called *How to Play Electric Bass*, on Elektra. The year was 1967. The following year, Szymczyk's break came with Otis Smith, head of sales for ABC/Paramount Records in New York. Heavily into A&R, Smith would hire two or three producers to cut acts at the Hit Factory, where Szymczyk engineered.

When Bob Thiele (see entry) quit ABC/Paramount, Smith asked Szymczyk if he'd like to fill the position and be a producer—for $300 a week. Despite the cut in income, Szymczyk took the job "because I wanted to produce. I wanted to wear both hats. You engineer, you sit there and do what the producer tells you to do. In producing, you're the boss. I figured I knew what the hell I was doing."

He did enough to produce *Time Changes,* by Ford Theater, a Boston band. Next up: B.B. King. Szymczyk saw B.B. was on the ABC/Paramount roster and asked to produce him. The attitude was, whites should produce whites, "let them black guys do the blues," Szymczyk was told. But Szymczyk said he wanted to awaken kids to the blues and thought he could cross B.B. over. "I sat down with B in a hotel room in New York for about an hour and told him I wanted to put some newer, younger, more modern musicians around him instead of the same basic, tired licks," Szymczyk recalls.

"It took a bit of talking, but he acquiesced, said, 'Let's do half of it my way, half of it your way.' " Released on ABC subsidiary Bluesway in early 1969, *Live and Well* didn't crack the pop charts wide open (it peaked at No. 56). But *Completely Well,* its sequel, reached No. 38 a few months later, spawning "The Thrill Is Gone," B.B. King's highest-charting pop single (No. 15). "That was my first big hit record," Szymczyk says. "It felt good to have a vision, be able to do it and have it work."

ABC also wanted him to sign a rock band. A fan of the Who, the Beatles, and Clapton, Szymczyk wanted "to do one of those types, too." So he contacted an old friend, Dick Korn, who was tending bar at Otto's Grotto in the old Statler Building in Cleveland. Otto's Grotto was a favorite haunt of underground rockers of the day. Szymczyk ended up traveling to Cleveland, hanging out at the Grotto, and being knocked out by the James Gang and their guitarist singer Joe Walsh. "In the course of a six-month period, I signed two bands out of there," Szymczyk says. "One was the James Gang; the other was Silk, which had Michael Stanley on it. Due to my success with B, the powers-that-be in New York said, 'Go ahead.' I was rocking."

Yer' Album, the James Gang's debut, was released in 1969. The album got the Gang on the map; opening for the Who on tour also helped. *James Gang Rides Again,* released in 1970, did better, peaking at No. 20, their highest chart position. The original Gang was exhausted by 1973, when Walsh went solo.

At the end of 1969, the New York division of ABC was shut down, 80 people were fired, and only 2 survived: Szymczyk and Otis Smith. "When we woke up in the '70s," Szymczyk says, "we were working for Jay Lasker at ABC/Dunhill." Szymczyk worked for ABC/Dunhill for 13 months. On February 9, 1971, he was thrown out of bed at 6 in the morning by the North Ridge earthquake, a 6.5 monster. "Eight days later, I was living in Denver, and I was an independent producer."

Szymczyk spent most of 1971 securing financing for the independent label Tumbleweed, which released albums by Dewey Terry, Rudy Romero, and Michael Stanley. That same year, he hooked up with the J. Geils Band; he produced six of their albums on Atlantic, between *The Morning After* and *Live! Blow Your Face Out.* The biggest Geils hit was "Give It to Me," which reached No. 30 in 1973 (in 1981, post-Szymczyk, the band hit No. 1 with "Centerfold"). At the same time, he was producing Joe Walsh for ABC, crafting *Barnstorm* and *The Smoker You Drink, The Player You Get* (No. 6). As an independent, he was "doing way better than doing it for the corporate structure."

Szymczyk went totally independent in 1972, and two years later, Walsh joined the Eagles, who wanted to rock out more. Then the Eagles hired Szymczyk in 1972, and shortly were cutting "Already Gone" and "James Dean." Between 1971 and 1975, Szymczyk produced the Eagles' *On the Border* (No. 17, with Glyn Johns; see entry), *One of These Nights, Hotel California, The Long Run* (all No. 1), and *The Eagles Live* (No. 6). In 1975 alone, he produced the Michael Stanley Band's *You Break It, You Bought It;* REO Speedwagon's *This Time We Mean It;* Elvin Bishop's *Struttin' My Stuff* (No. 18); as well as the Eagles and J. Geils.

Szymczyk was living in Colorado, working in Los Angeles, San Francisco, or New York with the Geils band, and devoting nearly full time to the Eagles—something had to give. He moved to Miami, becoming an in-house producer at Criteria Studios; Ron and Howard Albert (see entry) were the house engineers, their primary clients were Atlantic honchos Tom Dowd and Jerry Wexler (see entries).

In the early to mid-'70s, Szymczyk also produced Rick Derringer's *All American Boy;* albums by Jo Jo Gunne and top Gunne Jay Ferguson; Wishbone Ash; and the Fabulous Rhinestones. In 1976, he built his own studio, Bayshore Recording, in Miami's Coconut Grove, cutting an album by the Outlaws and some tracks for Bob Seger's *Against the Wind* (No. 1). He also signed a production deal with Elektra/Asylum, yielding *Plantation Harbor* by former Barnstorm drummer Joe Vitale and *Alive Alone* by Jefferson Starship and Elvin Bishop throat Mickey Thomas. In 1981 he produced the Who's *Face Dances* (No. 4). Finally, in 1983 or 1984, he can't remember exactly, Szymczyk dropped out.

The Eagles had broken up, his first marriage was breaking up, he had to shut down his studio. "I'd had it," he says. "I was toast." He spent the rest of that decade effectively in retreat. "Between mailbox money and the settlement from getting out of the studio, it was time to just do nothing for a while," says Szymczyk, adding he used to drink, smoke, and do drugs—but no more. "You don't do all those Eagles albums without joining in," he says. "Those wonderful '70s. I'm sure glad I went through them. I'm even happier I survived them."

In 1987, he remarried, and in 1990, moved to Little Switzerland, North Carolina, to live in a cabin he'd bought from Criteria Studios owner Herb Emerman. He has built a studio at home. In 1991, he recorded Walsh's *Songs for a Dying Planet* for the Pyramid label. It was Szymczyk's first production in four years.

Szymczyk has produced albums on numerous technological levels, from mono to 48-track digital. "It's all basically the same," he says, "it's just a different medium to store your information. The quality now is obviously much better than it was with two mono machines and 15 generations, but even now, my favorite way of recording is a 24-track analog machine with Dolby SR. That's what I have in my basement.

"I'm sort of back, I'm half back," he says. "It's really tough for me now, because the type of music I do is not being made, it's not being sold, it's not being played—or listened to—except on oldies stations. That would be your Eagles, your Who, your basic AOR staples of the '70s and '80s. There's no such thing as album rock anymore. That's what I do the best, and the genre that's the closest right now is what's coming out of Nashville, so I've been spending quite a lot of time there trying to crack that town. It's hard; they've got a nice little closed shop and they're not nuts about carpetbaggers, and it's all real formulaic there. Very, very cut-and-paste."

He hopes there are no signatures to a Szymczyk production. "To me, the job of the producer is to get the artist's ideas and brains on tape and CD and out there," he says. "It isn't necessarily what I'm about, but what he or she is about." —CARLO WOLFF

Bishop, Elvin: "Struttin' My Stuff," Capricorn, 1975 • *Struttin' My Stuff*, Capricorn, 1975 • "Fooled Around and Fell in Love," Capricorn, 1976 • *Hometown Boy Makes Good*, Capricorn, 1976 • "Spend Some Time," Capricorn, 1976.

Bold: *Bold*, ABC, 1969.

Brooks, Harvey: *How to Play Electric Bass*, Elektra, 1967.

Collins, Albert: *There's Gotta Be a Change*, Tumbleweed, 1972.

Derringer, Rick: *All American Boy*, Blue Sky, 1973 • "Rock and Roll, Hoochie Koo," Blue Sky, 1973 • "Teenage Love Affair," Blue Sky, 1973 • *Rock and Roll Hootchie Koo: The Best Of*, Sony, 1996.

Doherty, Denny: *Watcha Gonna Do*, Dunhill, 1970.

Eagles, The: "Already Gone," Asylum, 1974 • "James Dean," Asylum, 1974 • *On the Border*, Asylum, 1974 • "Lyin' Eyes," Asylum, 1975 • "One of These Nights," Asylum, 1975 • *One of These Nights*, Asylum, 1975 • "Take It to the Limit," Asylum, 1975 • *Their Greatest Hits, 1971–1975*, Asylum, 1976 • "Hotel California," Asylum, 1977 • *Hotel California*, Asylum, 1977 • "Life in the Fast Lane," Asylum, 1977 • "New Kid in Town," Asylum, 1977 • "Please Come Home for Christmas," Asylum, 1978 • "Heartache Tonight," Asylum, 1979 • "The Long Run," Asylum, 1979 • *The Long Run*, Asylum, 1979 • "I Can't Tell You Why," Asylum, 1980 • *The Eagles Live*, Asylum, 1980 • "Seven Bridges Road," Asylum, 1981 • *Greatest Hits*, Vol. 2, Asylum, 1982.

Fabulous Rhinestones: *Freewheelin'*, Just Sun, 1973.

Ferguson, Jay: *All Alone in the End Zone*, Asylum, 1976 • "Thunder Island," Asylum, 1977 • *Thunder Island*, Asylum, 1977 • *Real Life Ain't This Way*, Asylum, 1979.

Ford Theatre: *Time Changes*, Probe, 1968.

Holien, Danny: *Danny Holien*, Tumbleweed, 1971.

Hooker, John Lee: *Endless Boogie*, MCA, 1971, 1991 • *The Best Of, 1965–1974*, MCA, 1992.

J. Geils Band: "Lookin' for a Love," Atlantic, 1971 • *The Morning After*, Atlantic, 1971 • *Bloodshot*, Atlantic, 1973 • "Give It to Me," Atlantic, 1973 • *Ladies Invited*, Atlantic, 1973 • "Make Up Your Mind," Atlantic, 1973 • "Must of Got Lost," Atlantic, 1974 • *Nightmares and Other Tales from the Vinyl Jungle*, Atlantic, 1974, 1990 • *Hotline*, Atlantic, 1975 • *Blow Your Face Out*, Atlantic, 1976 • *The J. Geils Band Anthology: Houseparty*, Rhino, 1993 • *Houseparty*, Rhino, 1993.

James Gang: "Funk #49," ABC, 1969 • *Rides Again*, ABC, 1969 • *Yer' Album*, ABC, 1969 • "Midnight Man," ABC, 1970 • *Thirds*, ABC, 1970 • "Walk Away," ABC, 1970 • *Live in Concert*, ABC, 1971.

Jo Jo Gunne: *Bite Down Hard*, Asylum, 1972 • *Jumpin' the Gunne*, Asylum, 1973.

Kimmel, Tom: *5 to 1*, Mercury, 1987 • "That's Freedom," Mercury, 1987.

King, B.B.: *Completely Well*, ABC, 1969, 1998 • "Get Off My Back Woman," Bluesway, 1969 • *Live And Well*, Bluesway,

1969 • "The Thrill Is Gone," Bluesway, 1969 • "Ask Me No Questions," ABC, 1970 • "Chains and Things," ABC, 1970 • "Hummingbird," ABC, 1970 • *Indianola Mississippi Seeds*, ABC, 1970 • *Live at Cook County Jail*, ABC, 1970, 1998 • "So Excited," BluesWay, 1970 • *The Best of B.B. King* (4 tracks), MCA, 1980 • *How Blue Can You Get? Classic Live, 1964–1994*, MCA, 1996.

Kooper, Al: *Championship Wrestling*, Columbia, 1982.

Mamas and the Papas: *Creque Alley*, MCA, 1991, 1995.

McCabe, Pete: *The Man Who Ate the Plant*, Tumbleweed, 1973.

Michael Stanley Band: *You Break It, You Bought It*, Epic, 1975 • *Ladies' Choice*, Epic, 1976 • *Stagepass*, Epic, 1977 • *Misery Loves Company: More of the Best, 1975–1983*, Razor & Tie, 1997.

Outlaws: "Hurry Sundown," Arista, 1977 • *Hurry Sundown*, Arista, 1977 • *Greatest Hits*, Arista, 1982 • *Best of the Outlaws: Green Grass and High Tides*, Arista, 1996.

REO Speedwagon: *This Time We Mean It*, Epic, 1975.

Sanders, Pharoah: "Astral Traveling," Impulse!, 1970, 1988 (*The Impulse! Collection*, Vol. 1) • *Thembi*, Impulse!, 1971 • *Priceless Jazz Collection*, Impulse!, 1997.

Santana: *Shango*, Columbia, 1982.

Seger, Bob, and the Silver Bullet Band: "Against the Wind," Capitol, 1980 • *Against the Wind*, Capitol, 1980.

Silk: *Smooth As Raw Silk*, TW, 1969.

Stanley, Michael: *Michael Stanley*, Tumbleweed, 1972 • *Friends and Legends*, MCA, 1973 • See also Michael Stanley Band.

Terry, Dewey: *Chief*, Tumbleweed, 1972.

Thomas, Mickey: *Alive Alone*, Elektra, 1981.

Vitale, Joe: *Plantation Harbor*, Asylum, 1981.

Walsh, Joe: *Barnstorm*, ABC, 1972 • "Meadows," ABC, 1973 • "Rocky Mountain Way," ABC, 1973 • *The Smoker You Drink, The Player You Get*, ABC, 1973 • *So What?* (1 track), ABC, 1974 • *But Seriously Folks*, Asylum, 1978 • "Life's Been Good," Asylum, 1978 • "Space Age Whiz Kid," Full Moon, 1983 • *You Bought It . . . You Name It*, Full Moon, 1983 • *Songs for a Dying Planet*, Epic, 1992 • *Greatest Hits: Little Did He Know*, MCA, 1997.

Who, The: "Don't Let Go the Coat," Warner Bros., 1981 • *Face Dances*, Polydor, 1981 • "You Better You Bet," Warner Bros., 1981 • *Who's Better, Who's Best—This Is the Very Best of the Who*, MCA, 1988 • *The Who: Thirty Years of Maximum R&B*, Polydor, 1995.

Wishbone Ash: *There's the Rub*, MCA, 1974 • *Time Was: The Wishbone Ash Collection*, MCA, 1993.

COLLECTIONS

Zachariah soundtrack, Probe, 1971.

Ghosts of Mississippi soundtrack, Columbia, 1997.

Shel Talmy

"**I** 've always maintained that a lousy band with a good song will have a hit, but the reverse isn't true," says Shel Talmy, the legendary producer of the Kinks and the Who. "We've all known absolutely wonderful performing bands who couldn't get arrested because they had no material."

Indeed, Talmy's reputation was earned by paying close attention to the quality of song and arrangement. "Most bands are too subjectively involved with their material to be able to see how it goes together at the beginning, the middle, and the end," he explains. "I've always felt that one of my functions was to put the material into the proper order."

For evidence of Talmy's collaborative powers, one need look only to his work with the Kinks' Ray Davies. "Ray was extremely prolific. He used to go and write a dozen songs overnight and come in and play them, and I'd say, 'Yeah, this one is definite; that one, go back and write some more,' " Talmy recalls. "I heard about four bars of 'Sunny Afternoon' and said, 'That is going to be a No. 1 record.' " It hit No. 1 U.K. in 1966.

Talmy disdains the notion that hits can be written in the studio, preferring to begin sessions with completed songs. "I like to be about 90 percent sure of what we're going to come out with, leaving the last 10 percent for something spontaneous."

The Chicago native moved to Los Angeles to attend UCLA, graduated, and got his start as an engineer at Conway Studios in Los Angeles. He worked with Capitol's Nik Venet (see entry). In 1962 he took off for England for what was intended to be a summer holiday; he ended up in London, working as an independent producer for Dick Rowe at Decca Records.

"Fortunately he was very pro-American," Talmy says of Rowe, adding that his arrangement with Decca allowed him to freelance for other labels. "I think I was the first independent producer in London."

Talmy quickly demonstrated a keen eye for talent. In addition to finding the Kinks and the Who, he groomed David Bowie (see entry) for stardom. "He was about 17 when I found him," Talmy muses, pointing out that his work with Bowie, such as the 1966 disc "Can't Help Thinking About Me" was ahead of its time.

Talmy severed his relationship with Decca when the label passed on the Kinks, prompting Talmy to get the band a deal with Pye Records. The chemistry between Talmy and the Kinks was immediate, leading to such classics as "You Really Got Me" (No. 1 U.K.), "All Day and All of the Night" (No. 2 U.K.), "Tired of Waiting for You" (No. 1 U.K.), and "Sunny Afternoon."

Talmy experimented with feedback and mikeing techniques, allowing him to capture Dave Davies' aggressive lead guitar work and the up-front drumming of Bobby Graham, a session player sitting in for the Kinks' Mick Avory. "When I got to London everybody was mikeing drums with about 4 or 5 mikes, so I started doing it with 12 mikes and everybody said, 'You're mad. You'll never get the sound because they'll conflict.' About six months later everybody was doing the same thing.' "

Talmy points out that his early Kinks recordings were in mono because a Pye executive refused to advance funds for studio time. "He decided, after I brought the band into Pye, that he was going to charge me for the sessions. I said, 'Fine, I'll do them in mono because it's cheaper.' That lasted until 'You Really Got Me'; he decided that he wasn't going to charge me and we could do them in stereo."

Yet Talmy's efforts to craft good recordings were often hindered when mastering engineers at Reprise Records, the Kinks' American label, got hold of the tapes sent over from England. Consequently, records such as "You Really Got Me" and "Tired of Waiting" were mastered in reprocessed stereo, with gratuitous reverb added by the American engineers. "I started supervising the mastering in England, but then they sent the tapes over to the U.S. and they would remaster it. There was no control over it," Talmy laments.

His production of the early singles by the Who was equally bold, resulting in such hits as "I Can't Explain" (No. 8 U.K.), "Anyway, Anyhow, Anywhere" (No. 10 U.K.), and "My Generation" (No. 2 U.K.). Talmy's relationship with the band ended prematurely because of what he characterizes as a power play with the band's management. "I never made anything but hits with them," he recalls. "Then one day I got a letter from [manager] Kit Lambert and the band saying, 'Your services are no longer required.' "

Even so, Talmy continued to rack up such hits as Manfred Mann's "The Mighty Quinn" (No. 1 U.K.) and Chad and Jeremy's "A Summer Song" (No. 7). In the late '60s, he hooked up with the British folk band Pentangle and produced albums by ace session pianist Nicky Hopkins and the Welsh band Amen Corner.

Talmy's transition to the punk era was rocky. "When punk hit I said, 'It's time for me to go back home,' " Talmy adds with a laugh. "I did a single with the Damned just to see if I hated it as much as I did." With the exception of one-offs such as the Sorrows'

1980 album, *Love Too Late,* Talmy left studio work to concentrate on his publishing and computer ventures. "I thought, 'This is it; I'm retired.' Then I got bored out of my mind and got back into it."

Talmy began to meet with A&R staffers at record labels to announce his return; however, he soon realized there was a generation gap. "With very few exceptions most of the A&R people today have never produced a record and have barely been inside a studio," he says, adding wryly, "The first step was to convince people that I really hadn't died several years ago." —BEN CROMER

Amen Corner: *The Return of the Magnificent 7,* Immediate, 1971.

Bachelors, The: "I Wouldn't Trade You for the World," London, 1964.

Berman, Shelly: *Live Again!,* Chuckle, 1995.

Blues Project: *Lazarus,* Capitol, 1974 • *Anthology,* PolyGram, 1997.

Bowie, David: w/ the Lower Third, "Can't Help Thinking About Me," Warner Bros., 1966 • *Images 1966–67,* London, 1973 • *Early On (1964–1966),* Rhino, 1991.

Chad and Jeremy: "A Summer Song," World Artists, 1964 • "Willow Weep for Me," World Artists, 1964 • "Yesterday's Gone," World Artists, 1964 • *Yesterday's Gone,* World Artists, 1964.

Coven, The: *Blood on the Snow,* Buddah, 1974.

Creation, The: "Making Time/Try and Stop Me," Planet, 1966 • "Painter Man/Biff Bang Pow," Planet, 1966 • *Creation '66–67,* Charisma, 1973 • *How Does It Feel to Feel?,* Edsel, 1982 • *Our Music Is Red with Purple Flashes,* Diablo, 1998.

Damned, The: *Music for Pleasure,* Stiff, 1977.

Davies, Dave: "Death of a Clown," Pye, 1967.

Easybeats, The: "Friday on My Mind," United Artists, 1967 • *Friday on My Mind,* Fan Club, 1967, 1985 • *Good Friday,* United Artists, 1967.

Ecotour: *Weekend Guru,* Chameleon, 1990.

Fumble: *Poetry in Lotion,* RCA, 1974.

Fuzztones, The: *Come Out Fighting Genghis Smith,* CBS, 1967 • *In Heat,* Beggars Banquet/RCA, 1989.

Harper, Roy: *Folkjokeopus,* Science Friction, 1968, 1995.

Hopkins, Nicky: *The Revolutionary Piano Of,* Columbia, 1966, 1995.

Interpreters: *Back in the U.S.S.A.,* Volcano, 1997.

Jamison, Jim: *When Love Comes Down,* Scotti Brothers, 1991 • w/ Survivor, *Collection,* Scotti Brothers, 1993 • w/ Survivor, *Collection,* Vol. 2, Scotti Brothers, 1994.

Jansch, Bert: *Birthday Blues,* Reprise, 1969.

Jon and the Niteriders: *Splashback* (EP), Bomp, 1982.

Jones, David: *See* Bowie, David.

Kinks, The: "All Day and All of the Night," Reprise, 1964 • *The Kinks,* Pye, 1964 • "You Really Got Me," Reprise, 1964 • *Kinda Kinks,* Pye, 1965 • *Kinks Size/Kinkdom,* Rhino, 1965 • "Set Me Free," Reprise, 1965 • "Till the End of the Day," Reprise, 1965 • "Tired of Waiting for You," Reprise, 1965 • *You Really Got Me,* Reprise, 1965 • "Dedicated Follower of Fashion," Reprise, 1966 • *Face to Face,* Pye/Reprise, 1966 • *Kinks Kontroversy,* Pye, 1966 • "Sunny Afternoon," Reprise, 1966 • *Live at Kelvin Hall,* Reprise, 1967, 1990 • "Waterloo Sunset," Reprise, 1967 • *Something Else by the Kinks,* Reprise, 1968 • *The Kinks Kronicles,* Reprise, 1972 • *The Great Lost Kinks Album,* Reprise, 1973 • *The Kinks Greatest Hits,* Rhino, 1989 • *You Really Got Me/Kinda Kinks,* Mobile Fidelity, 1996.

Kristine: *I'm a Song* (5 tracks), Power Exchange, 1976.

Little, Rich: *Unclear and President Danger,* Orchard Lane, 1994.

Manfred Mann: "Just Like a Woman/I Wanna Be Right," Fontana, 1966 • "Semi-Detached Suburban Mr. James/Morning After the Party," Fontana, 1966 • *As Is,* Fontana, 1967 • "Ha! Ha! Said the Clown/Feeling So Good," Fontana, 1967 • "Sweet Pea/One Way," Fontana, 1967 • "My Name Is Jack," Fontana, 1968 • "The Mighty Quinn (Quinn the Eskimo)/By Request Edwin Garvey," Mercury, 1968.

Mick Cox Band: *Mick Cox Band,* Capitol, 1973.

Nancy Boy: "Deep Sleep Motel," Sire, 1996 • *Nancy Boy,* Sire, 1996.

Pentangle: *Basket of Light,* Transatlantic/Reprise, 1969 • *Sweet Child,* Transatlantic/Reprise, 1969 • "Light Flight/Cold Mountain," Transatlantic/Reprise, 1970 • *History Book* (4 tracks), Transatlantic/Reprise, 1972.

Rumplestiltskin: *Rumplestiltskin,* Bell, 1970.

Seanor and Koss: *Seanor and Koss,* Reprise, 1972.

Sorrows, The: "Christabelle," Epic, 1981 (*Exposed*) • *Love Too Late,* Pavilion, 1981.

Spreadeagle: *The Piece of Paper,* Charisma, 1972.

String Driven Thing: *String Driven Thing,* Charisma, 1972 • *The Machine That Cried,* Charisma, 1972.

Survivor, The: *See* Jamison, Jim.

White, Chris: *Mouth Music,* Charisma, 1976.

Who, The: "Anyway Anyhow Anywhere/Daddy Rolling Stone," Decca, 1965 • "I Can't Explain/Bald Headed Woman," Decca, 1965 • "My Generation," Decca, 1965 • *My Generation,* Brunswick, 1965 • "Substitute," Decca, 1966 • *Meaty Beaty Big and Bouncy,* Decca, 1971 • *Who's Better, Who's Best—This Is the Very Best of the Who,* MCA, 1988 • *The Who: Thirty Years of Maximum R&B,* Polydor, 1995.

Creed Taylor

reed Taylor is a hands-on producer with enough aesthetic savvy and business sense to know when to be hands-off. As head of the CTI label, Taylor helped shape what came to be known as crossover music, expanding the jazz base of guitarists George Benson and Wes Montgomery, saxophonists Stan Getz and Grover Washington Jr., and arranger Eumir Deodato to the pop field.

Taylor founded Impulse!, CTI, and Kudu; headed Verve; and produced everyone from John Coltrane to Esther Phillips. He lives in New York, where he and son John run CTI. Among Taylor's productions are an album by trombonists J.J. Johnson and Kai Winding; Bethlehem albums by thrush Chris Connor in 1955 and 1956 (one 10-inch, "Lullabys of Birdland," sold 150,000 copies); ABC Paramount productions of Lambert, Hendricks and Ross's *Sing a Song of Basie* and Ray Charles' *Genius + Soul = Jazz* (No. 4); Gil Evans' great *Out of the Cool*; Stan Getz's *Jazz Samba* (No. 1); the 1962 Verve album that put bossa nova on the map with "Desafinado" (No. 15); the Grammy Award–winning *Getz/Gilberto* (No. 2), a 1963 Verve album pairing Getz with Brazilian singer/guitarist Joao Gilberto and yielding the smash "Girl from Ipanema" (No. 5, with Gilberto's wife Astrud on vocal); Bill Evans' *Conversations with Myself;* Wes Montgomery's *California Dreamin';* Freddie Hubbard's *Red Clay;* and hit CTI records by Hubert Laws, Grover Washington Jr., Esther Phillips, Bob James, George Benson, and Deodato.

Born May 13, 1929, in White Gate, Virginia, Taylor grew up listening to bluegrass and gospel. "I was literally inundated with bluegrass," Taylor says, but his favorite source of music was Symphony Sid, live from Birdland, over WABC-AM, New York.

In 1950, Taylor recalls dropping in to 52nd Street clubs to hear idols Charlie Parker, Dizzy Gillespie, and Miles Davis. "It was like a dream," he says. Taylor attended Duke University, where he earned a bachelor's degree in psychology and led a band called the Five Dukes, playing in resorts in Virginia and South Carolina.

How did he become a producer? "I prepared myself, not knowing exactly what I was going to do, by listening to every record I could get my hands on, including all the stuff that was coming out on Blue Note, Prestige, and Dial," he says. In 1954, Taylor became head of Bethlehem Records, and two years later he joined ABC Paramount, where he started the Impulse! label. In 1962,

after Norman Granz (see entry) had sold the Verve label to MGM, Taylor became head of Verve (where he produced *Movin' Wes,* Wes Montgomery's first crossover effort, in 1964). In 1967, he moved to A&M, where he produced Antonio Carlos Jobim, Montgomery, and old friend Quincy Jones (see entry).

In 1970, Taylor founded CTI, using Bob James, Don Sebesky, and Eumir Deodato as arrangers. It was on that label that he launched or greatly furthered the careers of Hubert Laws, Stanley Turrentine, and Esther Phillips, not to mention George Benson, a jazz guitarist whose pop vocals brought him disdain from the purist jazz community.

Taylor's "biggest contribution was to make substantive modern jazz palatable to a wide audience," says Mark Gridley, a jazz academician who wrote *Jazz Styles* and contributed to the *New Grove Dictionary of Jazz.* "He was a packager, and he took control of the sound. Not only did he do that with existing bands like Getz's; in the late '50s and early '60s, he produced some of the best sessions by Getz, Johnny Hodges, and Oliver Nelson."

Working with his favorite engineer, Rudy Van Gelder, Taylor crafted sonically plush, visually enticing albums employing tasteful echo. "What he did that was so innovative was get the sound real slick," Gridley says. "When he got the A&M and CTI thing going, he would get existing giants like Herbie Hancock, Ron Carter, Freddie Hubbard, and Milt Jackson to do stuff that had a groove. He would get this sound—it's partly the choice of settings on the recording console, it's partly reverb, it's partly echo—with a balance so you can hear all the instruments very well, and a high level of polish. Sebesky and James would make it really slick, with backgrounds that would keep a nice groove. When Herbie or Freddie made their own records, there was always a little too much for the average listener to handle. Taylor would produce records that were very uncluttered in the solos."

"When companies were converting analog recordings to digital in the early days of the CD years, they took 2-track masters that were originally sequenced and mixed for vinyl," says Taylor, who favors digital recording. "Vinyl had special acoustic needs, in that the closer the song got to the center of the LP, the smaller the audio spectrum became to fit the music." He recommends using multitracks to mix down to digital 2-track, noting "the latitude of the audio spectrum on the new CD mix has no sonic limitations."

While Taylor popularized jazz, he doesn't consider his efforts precursors of smooth, or NAC, jazz. "Take the evolution of George Benson," he says. "When he hasn't crossed over into pop, he has had only one place to go for several years: smooth jazz, the NAC format. Even Stan Getz would have slid into that category. I would look for ways to frame a player in what I believed to be a broader, more appealing background or context in which he could perform and still sound like himself," Taylor says. "I didn't necessarily love putting big string sections behind Wes Montgomery, but I knew that Montgomery sounded like no other guitar player before or since, except his clones, and that he would remain Wes Montgomery no matter what kind of perfume I might sprinkle behind his recordings."

Taylor says he could listen to Montgomery practice scales all night, but he put Montgomery into a context that would get him radio airplay and make people listen. He asked Montgomery to change rhythm sections, arguing that greater commercial success would allow Montgomery to reach a larger audience. In fact, on A&M, Montgomery attained not only fame but financial comfort far greater than what he enjoyed playing the "unadulterated jazz" purists love about his early Riverside recordings. Unfortunately, a fatal heart attack ended Montgomery's career in early 1968. He was 43.

Taylor was most productive in the '70s, scoring hit after hit with albums on CTI. These lavishly produced, glossily packaged discs regularly boasted eye-catching covers by Pete Turner, state-of-the-art, accessible arrangements, and pristine production.

While the advent of the compact disc gave CTI a few good years as it converted its catalog to the digital format, it wasn't as active as it should have been, Taylor admits. In the '90s, Taylor has produced albums by bassist Charles Fambrough, guitarist Larry Coryell, and Rhythmstick, an all-star band that included trumpeters Dizzy Gillespie and Art Farmer, percussionists Airto and Tito Puente, guitarists John Scofield and Robben Ford, and saxophonists Phil Woods and Bob Berg. He has a contract with Japanese Polydor and, besides albums, has been producing high-definition, hour-long jazz films. —CARLO WOLFF

Ammons, Gene: *Boss Tenors: Straight Ahead from Chicago 1961,* Verve, 1961, 1992.

Austin, Patti: *Live at the Bottom Line,* CTI, 1978, 1984 • *Body Language,* CTI, 1980 • *The Best of Patti Austin* (10 tracks), Epic, 1994.

Baker, Chet: w/ Gerry Mulligan, *Carnegie Hall Concert,* Columbia, 1974, 1994 • *She Was Too Good to Me,* Columbia, 1974, 1987.

Barretto, Ray: *La Cuna,* Columbia, 1979, 1995.

Beck, Joe: *Beck,* Kudu, 1975 • w/ David Sanborn, *Beck and Sanborn,* Columbia, 1975, 1991.

Benson, George: *Shape of Things to Come,* A&M, 1969, 1998 • *Tell It Like It Is,* A&M, 1969, 1998 • *The Other Side of Abbey Road,* A&M, 1970, 1998 • *Bad Benson,* CTI/CBS, 1974 • *In Concert Carnegie Hall,* CTI/CBS, 1975 • w/ Joe Farrell, *Benson and Farrell,* Columbia, 1976, 1991 • *Good King Bad,* Columbia, 1976, 1991 • *Space,* CTI, 1978 • *The George Benson Collection,* Warner Bros., 1981, 1988 • *The Best,* Rebound, 1981, 1994 • *Best Of,* CTI/CBS, 1989 • *White Rabbit,* CTI/CBS, 1995 • *I Got a Woman and Some Blues,* A&M, 1998.

Bill Evans Trio: *Trio '64,* Verve, 1963 • *Trio '65,* Verve, 1965, 1993 • *With Symphony Orchestra,* Verve, 1965.

Byrd, Charlie: *See* Getz, Stan.

Burrell, Kenny: *For Charlie Christian and Benny Goodman,* Verve, 1967, 1990 • *God Bless the Child,* CTI/CBS, 1971, 1987 • *Verve Jazz Masters 45,* Verve, 1995 • *Guitar Forms,* Verve, 1997.

Carter, Ron: *Blues Farm,* CTI, 1973 • *Spanish Blue,* Columbia, 1975, 1991.

Charles, Ray: *Genius + Soul = Jazz,* Impulse!, 1961 • *Greatest Hits,* Vols. 1–2, DCC, 1987 • *The World of Ray Charles,* Garland, 1993 • *Genius and Soul: 50th Anniversary Collection,* Rhino, 1997.

Chroma: *Music on the Edge,* CTI, 1991.

Coltrane, John: *Africa Brass Sessions,* Vols. 1–2, Impulse!, 1961 • *Retrospective: Impulse,* GRP, 1967.

Connor, Chris: *Cocktails and Dusk,* Bethlehem, 1955 • "Lullabys of Birdland," Bethlehem, 1956 • *Sings Lullabys of Birdland,* Bethlehem, 1956.

Coryell, Larry: *Live from Bahia,* CTI, 1992 • *Fallen Angel,* CTI, 1993 • *I'll Be Over You,* CTI, 1994.

Crawford, Hank: *Heart and Soul,* Rhino, 1958, 1992.

CTI Allstars: *California Concert: The Hollywood Palladium,* CTI/CBS, 1971.

Deodato: *Prelude,* CTI, 1972 • "Also Sprach Zarathustra (2001)," CTI, 1973 • *Deodato 2,* CTI, 1973 • *In Concert (Felt Forum),* CTI/CBS, 1977, 1989.

Desmond, Paul: *Skylark,* Columbia, 1973 • *Pure Desmond,* Columbia, 1974, 1995 • *The Best Of,* Columbia, 1975, 1990.

DJ Uncle Al: *Liberty City,* On Top, 1996.

Dorham, Kenny, and the Jazz Prophets: *Kenny Dorham and the Jazz Prophets,* Chess, 1998.

Ellington, Duke: *Hommage a Duke,* TriStar, 1996.

Evans, Bill: *Compact Jazz,* Verve, 1962, 1987 • *Empathy/A Simple Matter of Conviction,* Verve, 1962, 1991 • *Conversations with Myself,* Verve, 1963, 1992 • w/ Jim Hall, *Intermodulation,* Verve, 1966 • *Best of Live on Verve,* Verve, 1997 • *The Complete Bill Evans on Verve,* Verve, 1997 • *See also* Bill Evans Trio; Getz, Stan.

Evans, Gil: "Where Flamingos Fly," Impulse!, 1961, 1988 (*The Impulse! Collection,* Vol. 1) • *The Individualism of Gil Evans,* Verve, 1988 • *Out of the Cool,* Impulse!, 1962, 1996.

Fambrough, Charles: *The Proper Angle,* Mesa/Bluemoon,

1991 • *The Charmer,* CTI, 1992 • *Blues at Bradley's,* CTI, 1993.

Farmer, Art: w/ Jim Hall, *Big Blues,* CTI/CBS, 1979, 1989 • *The Best Of,* Legacy, 1990.

Farrell, Joe: *Moon Germs,* Columbia, 1972 • *Outback,* CTI, 1979 • *See also* Benson, George; Joe Farrell Quartet.

Flow: *Flow,* CTI, 1970.

Gary McFarland Orchestra: *How to Succeed in Business Without Really Trying,* Verve, 1995.

Getz, Stan: *Big Band Bossa Nova,* Verve, 1962 • w/ Charlie Byrd, "Desafinado," Verve, 1962 • *Focus,* Verve, 1962, 1997 • w/ Charlie Byrd, *Jazz Samba,* Verve, 1962 • w/ Joao Gilberto, *Getz/Gilberto,* Verve, 1963 • w/ Luiz Bonfa, *Jazz Samba Encore!,* Verve, 1963 • w/ Joao Gilberto, *Getz/Gilberto 2,* Verve, 1964, 1993 • w/ Bill Evans, *Stan Getz and Bill Evans,* Verve, 1964 • w/ Joao Gilberto and Astrud Gilberto, "The Girl from Ipanema," Verve, 1964 • *With Laurindo Almeida,* Verve, 1966 • *Sweet Rain,* Verve, 1967, 1983 • *Voices,* Verve, 1967 • *Compact Jazz: Getz and Friends,* Verve, 1991 • *The Artistry of Stan Getz,,* Vols. 1–2, Verve, 1991/1992 • *Nobody Else But Me,* Verve, 1994 • *Verve Jazz Masters #8: Stan Getz,* Verve, 1994 • *Bossa Nova: Verve Jazz Masters 53,* Verve, 1996 • *Life in Jazz: A Musical Biography,* Verve, 1996 • *Jazz 'Round Midnight,* Verve, 1998.

Gilberto, Astrud: *Look at the Rainbow,* Verve, 1966, 1991 • *A Certain Smile, a Certain Sadness,* Verve, 1966, 1998 • *Beach Samba,* Verve, 1967, 1993 • *With Stanley Turrentine,* CTI/CBS, 1990 • *Jazz 'Round Midnight,* Verve, 1996 • *See also* Getz, Stan.

Green, Grant, and Donald Byrd: *His Majesty Funk/Up with Donald Byrd,* Verve, 1995.

Green, Urbie: *The Fox,* CTI, 1976.

Hall, Jim: *Concierto,* Columbia, 1975, 1991 • *Youkali,* CTI, 1992 • *See also* Evans, Bill; Farmer, Art.

Harrison, Donald: *The Power of Cool,* CTI, 1994.

Hawkins, Coleman, and Roy Eldridge, Johnny Hodges: *Hawkins! Eldridge! Hodges! Alive!,* Verve, 1962, 1992.

Holdsworth, Allan: *Velvet Darkness,* Columbia, 1977, 1990.

Hubbard, Freddie: *Red Clay,* CTI/CBS, 1970, 1991 • *Sky Dive,* Columbia, 1972, 1991 • *Straight Life,* CTI, 1970 • *First Light,* CTI/CBS, 1972 • *The Best Of,* Columbia, 1973, 1990 • w/ Stanley Turrentine, *In Concert,* Vols. 1–2, CTI/CBS Associated, 1974.

Jackson, Milt: *Olinga,* CTI/CBS, 1974 • *Sunflower,* CTI/CBS, 1974 • *See also* Turrentine, Stanley.

James, Bob: *One,* CTI, 1975 • *Two,* CTI, 1975 • *Three,* CTI, 1976 • *Four,* CTI, 1977.

Jarrett, Keith: *Foundations,* Rhino/Atlantic, 1968.

Jobim, Antonio Carlos: *The Composer of 'Desafinado,' Plays,* Verve, 1963 • *Wave,* A&M, 1968, 1989 • *Stone Flower,* Legacy, 1971, 1990 • *Jazz 'Round Midnight,* Verve, 1998.

Joe Farrell Quartet: *Joe Farrell Quartet,* CTI/CBS, 1970.

Johnson, J.J., and Kai Winding: *Jay and Kai,* Savoy, 1954 • *The Great Kai and J.J.,* Impulse!, 1960, 1997.

Jones, Quincy: *This Is How I Feel About Jazz,* GRP, 1957, 1992 • *The Pawnbroker/The Deadly Affair,* Verve, 1965 • "Bridge over Troubled Water," A&M, 1970 • *Gula Matari,* A&M, 1974 • *Walking in Space,* A&M, 1974 • *I Heard That!,* A&M, 1976 • *The Best,* A&M, 1982 • *Classics,* Vol. 3, A&M, 1987 • *Greatest Hits,* A&M, 1996.

Kelly, Wynton: *Smokin' at the Half Note,* Verve, 1965.

Kirk, Rahsaan Roland: *Rip, Rig and Panic/Now Please Don't You Cry, Beautiful Edith,* Emarcy, 1967, 1992.

Konitz, Lee: *Motion,* Verve, 1961, 1998.

Lambert, Hendricks and Ross: *Sing a Song of Basie,* GRP, 1958, 1972 • *Twisted: The Best Of,* Rhino, 1992.

Laws, Hubert: *Afro Classic,* Columbia, 1970 • *Crying Song,* CTI/CBS, 1970, 1991 • *Morning Star,* CTI, 1972 • *Carnegie Hall,* CTI, 1973 • *The Rite of Spring,* CTI/CBS, 1973 • *In the Beginning,* CTI, 1974 • *The Best Of,* Columbia, 1975, 1990 • *The San Francisco Concert,* CTI/CBS, 1977.

Montgomery, Wes: *Movin' Wes,* Verve, 1964, 1997 • *Goin' out of My Head,* DCC, 1965, 1993 • *Bumpin',* Verve, 1965, 1997 • *California Dreaming,* Verve, 1966 • *Plays the Blues,* Verve, 1966, 1992 • *Silver Collection,* Verve, 1966, 1992 • *Tequila,* Verve, 1966 • *A Day in the Life,* A&M, 1967, 1989 • *Greatest Hits,* A&M, 1967, 1996 • "Windy," A&M, 1967 • *Classics,* Vol. 22: Wes Montgomery, A&M, 1968 • *Down Here on the Ground,* A&M, 1968, 1998 • "Georgia on My Mind," A&M, 1968 • *Road Song,* A&M, 1968, 1989 • *The Final Years,* A&M, 1968 • *Compact Jazz,* Verve, 1987, 1992 • *Impressions: The Verve Jazz Sides,* Verve, 1995 • *Talkin' Verve: The Roots of Acid Jazz,* Verve, 1996 • *Ultimate Wes Montgomery,* Verve, 1998 • *See also* Smith, Jimmy.

Moriera, Airto: *The Best Of,* Legacy, 1994.

Mulligan, Gerry: *See* Baker, Chet.

Nelson, Oliver: *Blues and the Abstract Truth,* Impulse!, 1961, 1995 • "Stolen Moments," Impulse!, 1961, 1988 (*The Impulse! Collection,* Vol. 1)

O'Connell, Bill: *Lost Voices,* CTI, 1993.

O'Day, Anita: *All the Sad Young Men,* Verve, 1961, 1998.

Oscar Pettiford Orchestra: *Deep Passion,* Impulse!, 1957.

Phillips, Esther: "What a Difference a Day Makes," Kudu, 1975 • *What a Difference a Day Makes,* Columbia, 1975.

Prysock, Arthur, and Count Basie: *Arthur Prysock and Count Basie,* Verve, 1965, 1991.

Rhythmstick: *Rhythmstick,* Castle, 1990, 1996.

Rosenthal, Ted: *Calling You,* CTI, 1992.

Sanborn, David: *See* Beck, Joe.

Sebesky, Don: *The Rape of El Morro,* CTI, 1975.

Simone, Nina: *Baltimore,* Legacy, 1978, 1995.

Smith, Jimmy: *Bashin': The Unpredictable Jimmy Smith,* Verve, 1962, 1997 • *Any Number Can Win,* Verve, 1963, 1998 • *Christmas Cookin',* Verve, 1964, 1992 • *The Cat,* Verve,

1964, 1998 • *Organ Grinder Swing*, Verve, 1965, 1991 • w/
Wes Montgomery, *Further Adventures of Jimmy and Wes*,
Verve, 1966, 1993 • *Hootchie Kootchie Man*, Verve, 1966 •
w/ Wes Montgomery, *Dynamic Duo*, Verve, 1967, 1991 •
The Best Of, Verve, 1967 • *Plays the Blues*, Verve, 1968 • *Jazz
'Round Midnight*, Verve, 1994 • *Talkin' Verve: The Roots of
Acid Jazz*, Verve, 1996 • *Got My Mojo Workin'*, Verve, 1997.

Smith, Johnny Hammond: *Breakout*, Kudu, 1971 • *Wild
Horses Rock Steady*, Kudu, 1971 • *Higher Ground*, Columbia,
1974.

Soul Flutes: *Trust in Me*, A&M, 1968.

Swallow, Steve: *1961*, ECM, 1961.

Taylor, Billy: *My Fair Lady Loves Jazz*, Paramount, 1957.

Thigpen, Ed: *Out of the Storm*, Verve, 1966, 1998.

Thompson, Lucky: *Tricotism*, Impulse!, 1993.

Three Sounds: *Blue Genes*, Verve, 1963 • *Beautiful Friendship*,
Limelight, 1965.

Thus Spokez: *Acid Jazz*, CTI, 1996.

Tjader, Cal: w/ Eddie Palmieri, *El Sonido Nuevo*, Verve, 1966,
1993 • *Compact Jazz*, Verve, 1989, 1992 • *Jazz 'Round
Midnight*, Verve, 1996 • *Talkin' Verve: The Roots of Acid
Jazz*, Verve, 1996 • *Several Shades of Jade/Breeze from the
East*, PolyGram, 1997.

Turrentine, Stanley: *Sugar*, CTI, 1970, 1994 • w/ Milt
Jackson, *Cherry*, CTI/CBS, 1972, 1988 • *Don't Mess with
Mr. T*, Columbia, 1973 • *The Best Of*, Legacy, 1990 • *See also*
Hubbard, Freddie.

Upchurch, Phil, and Tennyson Stephens: *Phi
Upchurch/Tennyson Stephens*, Kudu, 1975.

Wanderley, Walter: *Cheganca*, Verve, 1966 • *Samba Swing!*,
Scamp, 1996 • *Rain Forest*, Verve, 1998.

Washington, Grover Jr.: *All the King's Horses*, Motown, 1972,
1992 • *Inner City Blues*, Mo Jazz, 1972, 1995 • *Soul Box*,
Vols. 1–2, Motown, 1973, 1991/1992 • *Feels So Good*,
Kudu, 1975 • *Mister Magic*, Mo Jazz, 1975, 1995 • *A Secret
Place*, CTI/Motown, 1976 • *Live at the Bijou*, Motown,
1978, 1992 • *Anthology*, Motown, 1981 • *Greatest
Performances*, Motown, 1983, 1991 • *The Best Of*, Motown,
1996.

Watts, Ernie, and Gilberto Gil: *Afoxe*, CTI, 1992.

Wilkins, Jack: *Mexico*, CTI, 1984, 1992.

Winding, Kai: *The in Instrumentals*, Verve, 1965 • *See also*
Johnson, J.J.

COLLECTIONS

Girl from Ipanema: The Jobim Songbook, Verve, 1996.

Ted Templeman

Warner Bros. executive and staff producer Ted
Templeman has had a long-running relationship
with the Doobie Brothers and Van Halen, and
has produced some of the most highly regarded albums
by Van Morrison, Little Feat, and Nicolette Larson.

Templeman (born October 24, 1944, in Santa Cruz,
California) began as one of the five vocalists in San
Francisco–based, hippie-era Harper's Bizarre, best-
known for their 1967 hit with Paul Simon's (see entry)
"59th Street Bridge Song (Feelin' Groovy)." Produced
by Lenny Waronker (Templeman's future boss at
Warners; see entry), it captured the flower power innocence of the day with its airy harmonies and Summer of
Love acoustic guitars.

When the group disbanded, Waronker convinced
Templeman to get into production. Templeman's
"school" was Frank Sinatra recording sessions.
Waronker hired him to write an arrangement for a
Nancy Sinatra album, and Templeman started to play
drums and sing on recording sessions to learn more
about the studio process. In 1971, on the basis of a

INTERVIEW WITH ALEX VAN HALEN

Daniel Levitin: How do you and Ted get your drum sounds?

Alex Van Halen: Well, the first thing is to get the drums to sound the way I want them from where I'm sitting. They have to sound right before you put up mikes, a lot of people don't realize that. It's also important to bring the drums to the recording studio a good 12 hours before the session, and to make sure the temperature and humidity in the recording room don't change between load-in and recording. This way the drums can get acclimated to the studio environment, and they're more likely to hold their tuning. I think a drum should resonate freely, not be taped up or damped; and it should have both of its heads on. If you discover a ring in the drum while you're recording, that means either it wasn't tuned properly or the heads aren't right; I don't think you should go in with duct tape and tissue paper to reduce the ring.

DL: How do you tune the drums? Do you tune them to resonate with the key of the song you're doing?

AVH: No. Buddy Rich used to say you don't tune the drum, you tension the drum. A shell resonates at a specific tone and each drum is different—it depends on what wood it's made out of, how many ply it is. . . . As you tighten the head the drum sings. If you go beyond that, it sounds like a piece of popcorn, if you go below, it sounds like a thud. Once you find the sweet spot, that's it, that's where you want to be. Sometimes you hit a resonant frequency. It causes a sympathetic ring in the other drums, and if that happens, you can usually tune the drum just a little higher or lower and still be in the sweet spot. Of course, this only counts if the mikes are far away enough from the head. So, no, I don't tune to the song.

DL: What about mikeing?

AVH: In the early '70s, bands like Led Zeppelin and Cream—Bonham and Baker—wouldn't let anybody near the drum kit with a mike—I know this 'cause I've talked to them. They always had to be recorded from a distance and then the drummer would accommodate. But then a funny thing happened and engineers wanted to be able to pan things and isolate them. Of course, if you put a mike a 1/4-inch from a drum head you're not going to get a drum sound, you're going to get a small, plastic "poof." So they developed these ambience boxes, but they don't sound anything like a real room to me, even the best of them. The distance of the mikes, the phasing, all these things aren't properly represented in the box. The close mikeing makes things simple for in-house engineers—it didn't really matter who the drummer or the band was.

On *Van Halen* [engineer] Don Landee asked me to take the front heads off the kick drums, and I said, "What's the matter with you, the drums are supposed to have two heads!" But he knew a lot more about recording than I did, so I accommodated him and his style of working at that point.

I kept hammering Don, and I said, drums make sound omnidirectionally, and I understand it's difficult to capture, but you gotta put the mikes back a little bit. Of course, when you do that you get a problem with phase cancellation and you have to work on it, and the drummer has a responsibility to keep the levels right between the cymbals and the kick and the other drums. The point of close mikeing was to expedite the recording process, and I guess some fools don't think drums are as important as drummers do. It's funny because the drums are the only acoustic instrument on our records—you change the drums and it changes the whole sound of the record. So now we record the drums from a distance.

Now, on the toms and kick we typically use Sennheiser 421s up close, and a shotgun for the snare. And then room mikes, of course. On the kick there's a mike inside, one on the front head and one about 5 feet away. We don't use all the mikes in the mixes. We don't layer the songs, we all play together on the rhythm tracks—it's always a crap shoot—so it's better to have some of these extra mikes on tape.

DL: How does the band approach arranging?

AVH: What makes the four of us different from most bands is that the rhythm section is not the bass and the drums, it is the guitar and the drums. I play with the guitar, and with what Ed is doing rhythmically—if you notice on all the records, it is really the drums and guitar that create the turbulence, the movement. Mike [Anthony, bassist] just carries the bottom, down there, providing the subsonic qualities.

Because Ed's guitar is very fat, and what Ed plays is very intricate, there's a lot of stuff to play off of. Sometimes I accent with it, sometimes against it. The rhythm that Ed does in two beats I may stretch out to two measures. And interestingly enough, he's also very rhythmically attuned—you know, he used to be a drummer and I used to be a guitarist until we switched. The way he fits in is as a third percussive element. Everything's more intertwined, in a Bach fugue kind of way. —Daniel J. Levitin

demo tape, Templeman convinced Warner Bros. to sign the Doobie Brothers. In 1971, he co-produced the Doobie Brothers debut with Waronker; he and Van Morrison then co-produced gold album *Tupelo Honey*.

From Morrison, Templeman learned the importance of spontaneity in the studio, and of getting the first take—a technique he has used with great success with many of the artists he works with. "My concept of a good producer," Templeman said in a 1980 *Record World* interview, "is if you listen to Van Halen or Montrose or the Doobies or Little Feat, you can't really tell who produced them. I think that's the mark of a good producer. It's just an album, and you recognize the artist, you don't hear the producer—you don't say, 'That's a Ted Templeman sound' or something. I try to make sure my trip isn't on their record."

Indeed, Templeman's forte is his invisibility. The aformentioned artists, as well as Aerosmith, Cheap Trick, and Eric Clapton, have a strong, distinctive sound of their own, which they know Templeman won't attempt to overshadow. Templeman produced all of the Doobies' '70s and early '80s albums, including 1978's triple-platinum *Minute by Minute*, which won the group four Grammys, including Record of the Year for "What a Fool Believes" (No. 1; on which Templeman also played drums). All Doobie records under Templeman's stewardship went gold, most were platinum, and *Minute by Minute* stayed at No. 1 on the charts for five consecutive weeks—and on the Top 200 for a year and a half. The Doobie Brothers were one of the most successful bands of the '70s.

Templeman's collaboration with Van Halen helped usher in the modern era of heavy metal and hard rock. Prior to 1978, Led Zeppelin was held to be the metal archetype, with their blues-based approach to electric music and Robert Plant's (see Jimmy Page and Robert Plant entry) overtly sexual vocal delivery. "Led Zeppelin was actually bad for rock and roll," explains Reprise Records president and rock historian Howie Klein, "because everybody wanted to sound like them. It got to the point that every new band had to reference Led Zeppelin."

The 1978 Van Halen debut established a sound that was completely different, an aural assault that was harder, rawer, and at the same time technically more astute than anything before. Van Halen paved the way for speed metal and successors such as Metallica, Queensryche, Dokken, Slayer, and other bands who would have otherwise been tethered to Zep's legacy.

Templeman, like any producer, has had some misses, such as 1985's *Behind the Sun*, in which a disoriented-sounding Clapton wanders through an album of poorly recorded, vibeless tracks. And one of Cheap Trick's many "comeback" albums, 1994's *Woke Up with a Monster* (with Bruce Fairbairn; see entry), seems to just miss the mark with mediocre songs, albeit excellent recording and performances. Templeman is an A&R executive with Warner Bros. —DANIEL J. LEVITIN

Aerosmith: *Done with Mirrors*, Geffen, 1985.

Beau Brummels: *The Beau Brummels*, Warner Bros., 1975.

BulletBoys: *BulletBoys*, Warner Bros., 1988 • "For the Love of Money," Warner Bros., 1989 • "Smooth Up," Warner Bros., 1989 • "Rock Candy," Reprise, 1992 (*Wayne's World* soundtrack) • *Za-Za*, Warner Bros., 1993.

Cale, John: *Seducing Down the Door*, Rhino, 1995.

Captain Beefheart: *The Spotlight Kid*, Reprise, 1971 • *Captain Beefheart and the Magic Band*, Reprise, 1972 • *Clear Spot*, Reprise, 1972.

Carrera: *Carrera*, Warner Bros., 1983.

Carrere, Tia: "Ballroom Blitz," Reprise, 1992 (*Wayne's World* soundtrack) • "Why You Wanna Break My Heart?," Reprise, 1992 (*Wayne's World* soundtrack).

Cheap Trick: *Woke Up with a Monster*, Warner Bros., 1994.

Clapton, Eric: *Behind the Sun*, Duck/WB, 1985 • "Forever Man," Duck/WB, 1985 • "See What Love Can Do," Duck/WB, 1985 • "Loving Your Lovin'," Reprise, 1992 (*Wayne's World* soundtrack).

Doobie Brothers: *The Doobie Brothers*, Warner Bros., 1971 • "Listen to the Music," Warner Bros., 1972 • *Toulouse Street*, Warner Bros., 1972 • "China Grove," Warner Bros., 1973 • "Dark Eyed Cajun Woman," Warner Bros., 1973 (*Appetizers*) • "Jesus Is Just Alright," Warner Bros., 1973 • "Long Train Running," Warner Bros., 1973 • *The Captain and Me*, Warner Bros., 1973 • "Another Park, Another Saturday," Warner Bros., 1974 • "Eyes of Silver," Warner Bros., 1974 • *What Were Once Vices Are Now Habits*, Warner Bros., 1974 • *Black Water*, Warner Bros., 1975 • *Stampede*, Warner Bros., 1975 • "Sweet Maxine," Warner Bros., 1975 • "Take Me in Your Arms (Rock Me)," Warner Bros., 1975 • *Best Of*, Warner Bros., 1976 • "'Takin' It to the Streets," Warner Bros., 1976 • *Takin' It to the Streets*, Warner Bros., 1976 • "Wheels of Fortune," Warner Bros., 1976 • "Echoes of Love," Warner Bros., 1977 • "It Keeps You Runnin'," Warner Bros., 1977 • "Little Darlin' (I Need You)," Warner Bros., 1977 • *Livin' on the Fault Line*, Warner Bros., 1977 • "Dependin' on You," Warner Bros., 1979 • "Minute by Minute," Warner Bros., 1979 • *Minute by Minute*, Warner Bros., 1979 • "What a Fool Believes," Warner Bros., 1979 • "One Step Closer," Warner Bros., 1980 • *One Step Closer*, Warner Bros., 1980 • "Real Love," Warner Bros., 1980 • *Best Of*, Vol. 2, Warner Bros., 1981 • "Keep This Train A-Rollin'," Warner Bros., 1981 • "Here to Love You," Warner Bros., 1982 • *Farewell Tour*, Warner

Bros., 1983 • "You Belong to Me," Warner Bros., 1983 • *Listen to the Music,* Warner Bros., 1993.

Ellison, Lorraine: "Many Rivers to Cross," Warner Bros., 1973 (*Appetizers*) • *Lorraine Ellison,* Warner Bros., 1974.

Hagar, Sammy: *VOA,* DGC, 1984, 1986 • *Unboxed,* Geffen, 1994.

Honeymoon Suite: "Love Changes Everything," Warner Bros., 1988 • *Racing After Midnight,* Warner Bros., 1988.

Johnston, Tom: *Everything You've Heard Is True,* Warner Bros., 1979.

Larson, Nicolette: "Lotta Love," Warner Bros., 1978 • *Nicolette Larson,* Warner Bros., 1978 • *In the Nick of Time,* Warner Bros., 1979 • *Radioland,* Warner Bros., 1980 • *All Dressed Up and No Place to Go,* Warner Bros., 1982.

Little Feat: *Sailin' Shoes,* Warner Bros., 1972 • *Time Loves a Hero,* Warner Bros., 1977 • *Hoy-Hoy,* Warner Bros., 1981, 1990.

McDonald, Michael: "I Gotta Try," Warner Bros., 1982 • "I Keep Forgettin'," Warner Bros., 1982 • *If That's What It Takes,* Warner Bros., 1982 • "No Lookin' Back," Warner Bros., 1985 • *No Lookin' Back,* Warner Bros., 1985 • *Take It to Heart,* Reprise, 1990 • "All We Got," Reprise, 1991.

Montrose: *Montrose,* Warner Bros., 1973 • *Paper Money,* Warner Bros., 1975.

Morrison, Van: "Tupelo Honey," Warner Bros., 1971 • *Tupelo Honey,* Warner Bros., 1971 • "Wild Night," Warner Bros., 1971 • "Jackie Wilson Said (I'm in Heaven When You Smile)," Warner Bros., 1972 • "Redwood Tree," Warner Bros., 1972 • *Saint Dominic's Preview,* Warner Bros., 1972 • *It's Too Late to Stop Now,* Warner Bros., 1974, 1987 • *The Best of Van Morrison,* Mercury, 1990.

Roth, David Lee: "California Girls," Warner Bros., 1984 • *Crazy from the Heat,* Warner Bros., 1985 • *Just a Gigolo / I Ain't Got Nobody,* Warner Bros., 1985 • *Eat 'Em and Smile,* Warner Bros., 1986 • "Goin' Crazy!," Warner Bros., 1986 • *Sonrisa Salvaje,* Warner Bros., 1986 • "That's Life," Warner Bros., 1986 • "Yankee Rose," Warner Bros., 1986.

Royal Crown Revue: *Mugzy's Move,* Warner Bros., 1996 • *The Contender,* Warner Bros., 1998.

Simon, Carly: *Another Passenger,* Elektra, 1976.

Van Halen: "Jamie's Crying," Warner Bros., 1978 • "Runnin' with the Devil," Warner Bros., 1978 • *Van Halen,* Warner Bros., 1978 • "You Really Got Me," Warner Bros., 1978 • "Beautiful Girls," Warner Bros., 1979 • "Dance the Night Away," Warner Bros., 1979 • *Van Halen 2,* Warner Bros., 1979 • "And the Cradle Will Rock," Warner Bros., 1980 • *Women and Children First,* Warner Bros., 1980 • *Fair Warning,* Warner Bros., 1981 • "(Oh) Pretty Woman," Warner Bros., 1982 • "Dancing in the Street," Warner Bros., 1982 • *Diver Down,* Warner Bros., 1982 • *1984,* Warner Bros., 1983 • "Hot for Teacher," Warner Bros., 1984 • "I'll Wait," Warner Bros., 1984 • "Jump," Warner Bros., 1984 • "Panama," Warner Bros., 1984 • *For Unlawful Carnal Knowledge,* Warner Bros., 1991 • "Top of the World," Warner Bros., 1991 • "Right Now," Warner Bros., 1992 • *Best of,* Vol. 1, Warner Bros., 1996.

Danny Tenaglia

Indulging in a sound as hard-edged as it is soulful, Danny Tenaglia has created a niche for himself in dance music's ever-fickle world of hip producers and trendy remixers. Since his debut recording in 1988—"Waiting for a Call" by Deepstate—Tenaglia has kept busy, honing his songwriting, production, and remixing skills. He has remixed and produced well over 200 songs, released two albums, and beat-mixed numerous compilations.

His discography includes superstars Madonna ("Human Nature"), Janet Jackson ("Pleasure Principle"), Michael Jackson ("Thriller"), and Crystal Waters ("100% Pure Love"); as well as such club luminaries as Joi Cardwell ("Soul to Bare"), Grace ("Not Over Yet"), Vanessa Daou ("Two to Tango"), Cerrone ("Supernature"), and Daphne ("Change"). In 1995, Tribal America Records released the debut long-player from Tenaglia, *Hard and Soul.* The album spawned four worldwide club hits: "Bottom Heavy," "Look Ahead," "Oh No," and "$ (That's What I Want)." With this album, Tenaglia not only joined the ever-growing list of remixers/producers turned artists; he solidified his reputation as a man who was serious about his craft. This was followed by *Tourism* in 1998.

While Tenaglia's albums usually merge deep underground beats with emotional rhythms and soulful musings, his one-off 12-inch singles, for a variety of independent labels and under a variety of monikers, have always journeyed down a more experimental and quirky path; Soulboy's "Harmonica Track" (from *Color Me Danny*) is an example.

With a style, verve, and quality all his own, no wonder the Pet Shop Boys (see entry) requested Tenaglia's def production skills for their last album, *Bilingual.* "It was truly an overwhelming experience working with them," said Tenaglia, shortly after his involvement with the pop-dance duo. "You know, I always appreciated them for having a finger on the pulse of club culture, and then to actually work with them. It was a dream come true." When all was said and done, Tenaglia co-produced "Before" and "Saturday Night Forever," both on the album, and "The Boy Who Couldn't Keep His Clothes On," the B-side to the single "Red Letter Day."

Like many dance music remixers/producers, Tenaglia received his musical training as a DJ. Although he created a name for himself in the Manhattan club scene, the native New Yorker left home, with his records, for Miami in 1985.

"I was the house DJ at Cheers. At the time, it was the only club in Miami staying open until 7 A.M. on weekends. I remember introducing the people to all the New York garage stuff and early Chicago house music. I was living for those sounds," he recalls. Apparently tired of the fun and sun, Tenaglia returned home five years later to DJ and create music with feeling. —LARRY FLICK

Cardwell, Joi: "Soul to Bare" (remix), Eight Ball, 1997.

Cerrone: "Supernature" (remix), Pure, 1995.

Daou, Vanessa: "Two to Tango," MCA, 1996.

Daphne: "Change," Maxi, 1994.

Deepstate: "Waiting for a Call," Atlantic, 1988.

East 17: *Steam*, London, 1995.

Funky Green Dogs: *Get Fired Up*, MCA, 1996.

Grace: "Not Over Yet" (remix), Perfecto/Kinetic/Reprise, 1996.

Jackson, Janet: "Pleasure Principle" (remix), A&M, 1995.

Jackson, Michael: "Thriller" (remix), Epic, 1995.

Madonna: "Human Nature" (remix), Maverick/Sire, 1995.

O'Hearn, Patrick: *Black Delilah*, Private, 1990.

Pet Shop Boys: "Before," Atlantic, 1996 • "Red Letter Day," Atlantic, 1997 • *Bilingual* (2 tracks), Atlantic, 1996.

Rapination and Kym Mazelle: "Love Me the Right Way '96" (remix), Logic, 1996.

Right Said Fred: "Don't Talk Just Kiss" (remix), Charisma, 1992 • "I'm Too Sexy" (remix), Charisma, 1992.

Tenaglia, Danny: featuring Roxy, "$ (That's What I Want)," Tribal, 1995 • *Bottom Heavy* (EP), Tribal, 1995 • *Hard and Soul*, Tribal/IRS, 1995 • featuring Carole Sylvan, *Look Ahead* (EP), Tribal, 1995 • *Maxi Records: Maximum Dance Floor Capacity*, Maxi, 1995 • *Gag Me with a Tune*, MCA, 1996 • "Oh No," MCA, 1996 • *Color Me Danny*, Twisted America, 1997 • "Elements," Frontline, 1997 • w/ Celeda, "Music Is the Answer," MCA, 1998 • *Tourism*, MCA, 1998.

Urohauz: "Hauz Mix," Profile, 1989 • "Intru-mental Mix," Profile, 1989 • "Tekno-mental Mix," Profile, 1989.

Waters, Crystal: "100% Pure Love" (remix), Mercury, 1994.

Neil Tennant

See PET SHOP BOYS

Todd Terry

Todd Terry (born April 18, 1967) has been steeped in dance music since he started listening to European dance records as a Brooklyn teenager. Already devoted to his turntables as DJ, he heard something different in those tracks, and he "went for the difference."

"I never got a break in New York," he says. "But England happened right away, so I catered to it." By 1994, Terry had hit big in England and Europe, and his reputation was growing in the U.S. In addition to DJ appearances, Terry was cutting the first of his now-classic underground house tracks. "Bango (To the Batmobile)," "Sume Sigh Say," and "I'll Take You to Love"—released under monikers such as the Todd Terry Project, House of Gypsies, and Naked Music NYC—are considered essential DJ listening.

In 1995, the Ministry of Sound's eponymous U.K. label released *A Day in the Life*, a collection of Terry's hot dancefloor tracks. In 1996, he created the "Todd Terry Presents . . ." platform, setting up a context in which to work with favorite singers and performers. The first single release, "Keep On Jumpin'," (on Logic Records), featured a vocal workout from divas Martha Wash and Jocelyn Brown, together for the first time. The song became a No. 1 club track in the U.S. and a dozen other countries.

All the while, Terry continued to break new ground as a producer/remixer. From Snap to Annie Lennox to Bjork, Terry's mixes bridge the ground between club cool and commercial accessibility. In 1995, his remix for Everything But The Girl's "Missing" (No. 2) became a worldwide smash, giving the British duo their first hit. In 1996, he rode the charts with mixes for Garbage ("Stupid Girl"), the Cardigans ("Love Fool"), Everything But The Girl ("Wrong"), among others. He also produced a Robin S. track ("Givin' U All That I Got") for the multiplatinum *Space Jam* soundtrack. His most recent work includes mixes for 10,000 Maniacs ("More Than This"), Jamiroquai ("Alright"), the Cardigans ("Been It"), and the Lightning Seeds ("You Showed Me"), as well as his own artist album for Logic Records,

Ready for a New Day, which features the vocals of Wash, Brown, and disco legend Shannon.

Terry works round the clock and delights in the "inexhaustible challenge" of production and remixing. "I've also learned from watching others that the world keeps on spinning and the music changes faster than light," he says. "You either keep moving and stay plugged in or forever fall out of the race." —LARRY FLICK

Babble: "Love Has No Name" (remix), Reprise, 1996.
Bjork: "Hyperballad/Enjoy" (remixes), One Little Indian, 1997.
Blakeley, Peter: "I've Been Lonely" (remix), Giant, 1993.
Boden, Brigid: "Oh, How I Cry," A&M, 1996.
Cardigans, The: "Been It" (remix), Mercury, 1997 • "Lovefool" (remix), Mercury, 1996.
Co Ro: *Co Ro,* Alliance, 1991, 1996.
Cover Girls: "I Need Your Lovin' " (remix), Fever, 1997.
Crawford, Randy: "Forget Me Nots" (remix), Bluemoon/Atlantic, 1996.
Cynthia: "Like a Star" (remix), Timber!/Tommy Boy, 1997.
Digital Orgasm: "Running Out of Time" (remix), Whte Lbls, 1992.
Dr. Alban: *Look Who's Talking,* Logic, 1995.
Everything But The Girl: "Missing" (remix), Atlantic, 1994 • "Wrong" (remix), Atlantic, 1996 • *Best Of,* Blanco y Negro, 1996.
Fresh, Doug E.: *Play,* Gee Street, 1995.
Full Intention: "America (I Love America)" (remix), Big Beat, 1996.
Garbage: "Stupid Girl" (remix), ALMO, 1996.
Giggles: "Love Letter," Cutting, 1987 • *He Loves Me . . . He Loves Me Not,* Cutting, 1992.
Goats, The: "?Do the Digs Dug?" (remix), Ruff House/Columbia, 1993.
Dope, Kenny: *Boomin' in Ya Jeep,* Freeze, 1993.
Gordon, Lonnie: *Bad Mood,* Gold Rush, 1993, 1996.
House of Gypsies: "Another Worry," Freeze, 1995 • "Feel the Rhythm," Loudhouse, 1997 • "Sume Sigh Say," Freeze, 1994.
Jamiroquai: "Alright" (remix), Work, 1997.
Kenny G: "Havana" (remix), Arista, 1997.
Lennox, Annie: "Little Bird" (remix), Arista, 1993.
Lightning Seeds: *You Showed Me* (remix), Epic, 1997.
Louvette: *Crazy in Love,* Private I/Mercury, 1998.
Luke: *Uncle Luke,* Luther Campbell, 1996.
Naked Music NYC: "I'll Take You to Love," XL/Ore, 1996.
Nerissa: *In the Rain,* Select, 1993.
Richie Rich Meets the Jungle Brothers: "I'll House You," PWL America, 1991 (*Best of 90's Dance Music,* Vol. 1, *Hip-House Jam*)

Robin S.: "Givin' U All That I Got," Atlantic, 1996 (*Space Jam* soundtrack) • *From Now On,* Atlantic, 1997.
Royal House: "Party People," Idlers/Warlock, 1988 • *Can You Party?,* Idlers/Warlock, 1988 • *Come Over Here, Baby,* Idlers/Warlock, 1990.
Sham and the Professor: "The Light's Gone Out (in My Backyard)," Priority, 1995.
Shamen, The: "Phorever People" (remix), Epic, 1992.
Snap!: "Rhythm Is a Dancer" (remix), Arista, 1992.
Sugarcubes: *It's-It,* Elektra, 1992.
Technotronic: *Trip on This (The Remixes),* Capitol, 1990.
10,000 Maniacs: "More Than This" (remix), Geffen, 1997.
Todd Terry Project: "Bango (to the Batmobile)," Fresh, 1987 • "Weekend," Warlock, 1998 • *See also* Terry, Todd.
Terry, Todd: *Sound Design,* TNT, 1992 • *Unreleased Projects,* Vols. 3–4, Freeze, 1993 • *Black Jack* (EP), TNT, 1994 • w/ Kenny Gonzalez and Louie Vega, *Todd, Louie and Kenny,* Strictly Rhythm, 1994 • *Unreleased Projects,* Vols. 5–6, Freeze, 1994 • *A Day in the Life,* Ministry of Sound, 1995 • *A Night in the Life of Todd Terry: Live at Hard Times,* Hard Times, 1995 • *Sax* (EP), TNT, 1995 • *Sound Design,* Vol. 2, Freeze, 1995 • *Unreleased Projects,* Vol. 7, Freeze, 1995 • *Weekend 95,* Ore, 1995 • *Sax,* Freeze, 1996 • *Back from the Dead* (EP), Hard Times, 1997 • *Clouds* (EP), in House, 1997 • *Final EP* (EP), Hard Times, 1997 • featuring Shannon, "It's Over Love," Logic, 1997 • w/ Martha Wash, "Something's Going On," Logic, 1997 • *The Raid EP* (EP), in House, 1997 • *Todd Terry Presents Ready for a New Day,* Logic, 1997.
3T: "Tease Me," Columbia, 1996.
Ultra Nate: "y" (remix), Warner Bros., 1993.
Wash, Martha: *Martha Wash,* RCA, 1993 • w/ Jocelyn Brown, "Keep on Jumpin'," Logic, 1996 • *The Collection,* Logic, 1997.

COLLECTIONS

Rave-Ology, Vols. 2–3, Freeze, 1993.
Keith Haring, a Retrospective: The Music of His Era, Logic, 1997.

Marty Thau

Marty Thau is first and foremost a visionary. After spending most of the '60s as one of the top promo men in the record business (with stops at the Cameo/Parkway and Buddah labels), Thau forsook a cushy position with a mainstream production company in 1972 to manage the rebirth of rock 'n' roll in the form of the New York Dolls, whom he guided until 1975.

Having entered New York's underground rock demi-monde with the Dolls in the early '70s, Thau was integral to the scene's development as a spawning ground of punk–new wave stars by the late '70s. His good will and energy directly aided the careers of the Ramones, Blondie, and Richard Hell, and he produced Suicide, (Boston's) the Real Kids, the Fleshtones, and others for his own Red Star label. Thau has now revived Red Star, rereleasing his most crucial music (including the compilation *Songs of the Naked City*) and pursuing new talent with the adventuresome attitude of his '70s classics.

Marty Thau was born December 7, 1938, in the Bronx, and loved music from the beginning, including the well-crafted songsmanship of Irving Berlin, Cole Porter, and the like from his parents' generation, the gutty R&B of the early '50s (Sam "The Man" Taylor, "Screamin' " Jay Hawkins), and the rock 'n' roll explosion of the mid-'50s, especially Elvis Presley. Thau's cousin and friend Elaine was one of the first presidents of the Jerry Lee Lewis Fan Club.

After high school, Thau attended New York University and graduated with a degree in communication arts. He then served a stint in the army and, upon his release in 1963, got a job as an advertising trainee at *Billboard* magazine. Through *Billboard* he met and became friends with ex-teen star Tony Orlando (who had had two hits in 1961; see Hank Medress entry). He also got reacquainted with his cousin Elaine, who called him up after seeing his name in the magazine. The trio became close and spent a good deal of time together; eventually, Elaine and Tony got married.

By 1964 Orlando had spent three years trying unsuccessfully to resurrect his career; he asked Thau to manage him, suggesting that Thau would do no worse than the $90 per week that he was making at *Billboard*. Thau agreed, but although he lined up sessions for Orlando with both Burt Bacharach and Bert Berns (see entries), neither produced a hit. Thau was married by then, and with Orlando's career stalled out, it was time to get a real job.

While Thau had been managing Orlando, another friend, Neil Bogart, had become a promotions man, first for MGM and then Cameo/Parkway in 1965. Bogart invited Thau to join him as a radio promotions man at Cameo—the "real job" Thau had been looking for. For a year Thau traveled the country five days a week handing out records and pressing the flesh under every broadcast antenna he could find. He helped place 28 records on the charts that year, including a national No. 1, Question Mark and the Mysterians' "96 Tears."

In early 1967 Thau went to a new label, Buddah, as vice president of promotion, where he enjoyed great success promoting a series of smash hits for bubblegum legends 1910 Fruitgum Co. and Ohio Express, as well as hits for the Brooklyn Bridge ("The Worst That Could Happen"), Edwin Hawkins Singers ("Oh Happy Day"), Isley Brothers ("It's Your Thing"; see entry), and Lemon Pipers ("Green Tambourine").

By 1970 Thau was burned out on the promotion circus and became a partner in an independent record production company, Inherit Productions, with producer Lewis Merenstein. In Thau's two years there, the company released classic albums by Van Morrison (*Astral Weeks, Moondance*), John Cale (*Vintage Violence;* see entry), and Mike Bloomfield with Barry Goldberg (*Two Jews' Blues*).

Restless again by early 1972, Thau left Inherit to become head of A&R for Paramount Records. Less than six months later he wandered into a New York Dolls show (singer David Johansen, guitarists Sylvain Sylvain and Johnny Thunders, bassist Arthur Kane, drummer Billy Murcia) at New York's Mercer Arts Center and saw a group that resurrected the outrageousness, fun, and sheer exuberance that had been missing from rock 'n' roll since the heyday of Elvis, Little Richard, and Jerry Lee Lewis. The Dolls' urban street kid attitude, gender-parodying costumes, party ethic, and ripping tunes (drawn from such disparate influences as early '60s girl groups, harmonica blues, Southern soul, novelty songs, '50s rock 'n' roll—all of it revved up for the '70s) stunned Thau out of his complacency and inspired him to champion their (ultimately lost) cause. He left Paramount to become their manager.

If one feels compelled to identify the first '70s punk band, the Dolls are a logical choice: they were the first to overtly reject the slickness and bloat of '70s corporate rock, the first to find a compelling voice to express that rejection, and the first band to unite the amorphous New York underground rock scene since the Velvet Underground (the arty, somber Velvets were more art-noise minimalists than a punk band) in the late '60s.

Thau's experience with the Dolls was both satisfying and heartbreaking. He produced the band's first real demos (which were released as *Lipstick Killers* by ROIR in 1981) and raised their profile exponentially; yet, in his first tour of England with the band, drummer Billy Murcia died in a drug-related accident (he was replaced by Jerry Nolan). Already perceived by the mainstream media and the record industry as evil, drug-addicted transvestites (they were enthusiastic heterosexuals according to Thau), Murcia's death hardened those attitudes toward the band in addition to whipping their fans into an even greater frenzy.

In the face of strident industry antipathy, Thau finally got the band signed to Mercury in late 1972. The Dolls wanted Phil Spector (see entry), but Todd Rundgren (see entry) ended up producing their archetypal first album, which was released in early 1973 to mostly rave reviews (although some critics felt that Rundgren had overly tamed their sound). The album sold around 100,000 copies, which Thau viewed as an excellent start but the label viewed as disappointing, given the band's notoriety. When the second album (*Too Much Too Soon*), produced by Shadow Morton (see entry), fared about the same, Mercury dumped the band. By 1975 Thau (and his financial backers, Leber and Krebs) had had enough.

"I thought all along that it was just a matter of time before they broke through because I saw it happen in certain locales—like Cleveland—where they would go back and play and allow the fans to adjust to them. Eventually the band imploded: you can only go so far with five people, two of whom are drug addicts, and one is an alcoholic [Thunders and Nolan have subsequently died]. I implored them to get it together and work hard and write new material, but it just didn't happen," he says.

A call from Jerry Nolan in late 1975 revived Thau's sagging spirits. Nolan told him of the scene growing up around the notorious Bowery club CBGB, with exciting bands like the Ramones, Patti Smith, Television, Blondie, and Richard Hell playing there. Thau developed an immediate rapport with the Ramones, who wanted him to manage them; but after his Dolls experience, Thau was loathe to trod that path again. He instead produced their first demos (available on the *Songs of the Naked City* collection): the roaring "Judy Is a Punk," and the sweet "I Wanna Be Your Boyfriend," which together proved that the band could be successfully recorded and got them signed to Sire (where their classic first album was produced by Craig Leon; see entry).

Thau and Richard Gottehrer (see entry) hooked up in 1976 to start a production company, Instant Records, and signed Blondie, Richard Hell, and Robert Gordon. Leon and Gottehrer (with Thau sitting in and contributing ideas) produced Blondie's first single, "X Offender," which Thau then licensed to Private Stock.

Thau, always on the move, opted out of Instant and started his own Red Star label in late 1976. He signed and produced Boston's punky Real Kids, and then signed and co-produced (with Leon) his most important record: Suicide's startling debut in 1977. "As a producer my greatest credential is the Suicide record. They were such a creative and original entity, carving out new turf. I think that recording really stands up," he says.

Formed in 1970 by sculptor/singer Alan Vega and avant-jazz keyboardist Martin Rev, the duo's bizarre confrontational shows—leatherman Vega pounding the stage and walls with a heavy chain, Rev extorting sounds both vicious and otherworldly from his early synth—sought to disrupt rather than entertain. Light-years ahead of their time, Suicide was in essence a synth-pop duo (with a serious punk attitude) 10 years before the phrase was even coined. After sitting out a few years, Suicide returned to the scene in 1976 still confrontational (they caused riots in Europe), but musically much more mature and varied.

The album consists of seven timeless songs flawlessly recorded. "Ghost Rider," "Rocket U.S.A.," and "Johnny" offer Vega's whispery baritone echoing urgently over Rev's throbbing synth landscape. "Cheree" is a stunningly beautiful synth tapestry, evocative of the Velvets' "Sunday Morning"; "Frankie Teardrop" is a horrific 10-minute biography of the title character.

Thau also co-produced an exceptional solo album by Martin Rev, *Clouds of Glory*; recorded in 1981 and 1984, released in 1985, *Clouds* is a fascinating electronic workout replete with space, ambient, trance, and other techno elements, again wondrously ahead of its time.
—Eric Olsen

Dirty Angels: "Rock and Roll Love Letter," Sire, 1975.
Fleshtones: *Blast Off*, ROIR, 1982, 1990 • *Fleshtones*, Red Star, 1982, 1996.
New York Dolls: *Lipstick Killers (Mercer Street Sessions)*, ROIR, 1981, 1994 • *Live in Concert Paris '74*, Red Star, 1998.
Ramones: "I Wanna Be Your Boyfriend," TVT, 1975, 1991 (*The Groups of Wrath*) • "Judy Is a Punk," TVT, 1975, 1991 (*The Groups of Wrath*).
Real Kids: *The Real Kids*, Red Star, 1977.
Rev, Martin: *Clouds of Glory*, New Rose, 1985.
Suicide: "Cheree," TVT, 1977, 1991 (*The Groups of Wrath*) • "I Remember," TVT, 1977, 1991 (*The Groups of Wrath*) • *Suicide (Red Star)*, Red Star, 1977 • *Suicide (Restless)*, Restless, 1977, 1990 • *Zero Hour*, Red Star, 1997.

COLLECTIONS
Songs of the Naked City, Red Star, 1997.

Bob Thiele

B ob Thiele was one of the most versatile producers of all time. His production work may bear the mark of an impresario and enthusiast rather than that of a technician or expert musician. Thiele's productions include records by John Coltrane and Buddy

Holly; the McGuire Sisters; his wife, Teresa Brewer ("Ricochet," No. 2; "Jilted," No. 6); Steve Lawrence and Jack Kerouac; and Louis Armstrong, Otis Spann, and Duke Ellington.

Born in Sheepshead Bay, Brooklyn, on July 27, 1922, to a well-off family, Thiele early on became enthralled by glamour in athletics, on screen, and in music. As a teenager in Forest Hills, Queens, he began to listen to jazz by such luminaries of the time as Art Hodes and Chick Webb. He also began to develop an entrepreneurial bent, promoting himself into his own radio show at age 14. During a stint as DJ at WBYN, a Brooklyn station with studios in midtown Manhattan, he talked about and played jazz records. His show caught the ear of brothers Nesuhi and Ahmet Ertegun (see entry), who later founded Atlantic Records. His shows also plunged him into café society and the jazz ferment of the time.

In 1938, Thiele launched his first label, Signature Records, recording Yank Lawson and His Orchestra and the Chicago Rhythm Kings, featuring pianist Hodes and trumpeter Marty Marsala. That same year, he founded *Jazz*, the first magazine devoted to that musical form. In *Jazz*, Thiele published some of the more notable writers of the time, including Charles Edward Smith and Frederic Ramsey Jr.

"The first record I ever set out to make was four piano solo sides by Joe Sullivan," Thiele told Joe Smith in *Off the Record*, Smith's 1988 "oral history" of music. "I booked the studio, I booked Joe, and then I didn't have enough money. Mind you, I was about 16 years old. I couldn't pay for anything. So I never showed up, and we never made the records, and Joe never recorded, and that was the end of that.

"But I had drive. I had to record people, anybody, or just be in the record business. I had to record unknown players, just find players that I felt were great and put them on records, and then put the records out." Signature went out of business in 1948, but only after Thiele had recorded some of the better swing-era musicians, such as saxophonists Coleman Hawkins and Lester Young and pianists Earl Hines and Erroll Garner.

In 1952, he joined Decca Records, taking over its subsidiary, Coral, two years later. At Coral, he recorded work by artists as diverse as Buddy Holly, the McGuire Sisters, and Steve Lawrence. With comedian Steve Allen as his partner, Thiele founded the Hanover-Signature label in 1959, which released an album of Kerouac reading his poetry to jazz. In 1961, he encouraged trumpeter Louis Armstrong to record Duke Ellington songs with Ellington himself at the piano. The resulting Roulette recording was hailed as a rejuvenation for both trumpeter and keyboardist.

That same year, Thiele joined ABC Records, where he shortly became responsible for some key recordings on its fabled subsidiary, Impulse! At Impulse!, which Creed Taylor (see entry) founded, Thiele made mainstream jazz recordings by Ellington and Hawkins; avant-garde records such as Archie Shepp's *Fire Music;* and such Coltrane linchpins as *A Love Supreme, Ballads,* and the seminal *Live at the Village Vanguard.*

"As I recall it," Thiele recounts in *What a Wonderful World,* his 1995 autobiography, "Coltrane was at first extremely withdrawn and reticent to talk about anything; our friendship began during those nights we recorded. Sometimes these things happen. I've grown up with musicians [Thiele played clarinet and occasionally recorded a big band under his own name]. . . . In this instance, as the music progressed and Trane became comfortable with the surroundings and results, his natural warmth and friendliness surfaced, and we hit it off."

The music Coltrane and his quartet played during those three nights in 1961 was not only epochal but startling. It was to Thiele's credit (and the quick thinking of the fastidious, brilliant engineer Rudy Van Gelder) that it was recorded; in 1997, the *Vanguard Sessions* were released in their entirety in a four-CD set.

In 1969, Thiele founded the Flying Dutchman label (for jazz) and its sister imprint Blues Time (for blues). It was on Dutchman that Thiele recorded guitarist Larry Coryell, saxophonist Gato Barbieri, and *The Revolution Will Not Be Televised,* Gil Scott-Heron's brilliant hip-hop precursor.

In 1972, Thiele married Teresa Brewer, using his position as record mogul to record her in numerous settings for his Doctor Jazz label. And when the film *Good Morning, Vietnam* was released in 1987, it made a big seller of a Louis Armstrong track Thiele had written with George David Weiss some 20 years earlier. That track, "What a Wonderful World," became the title of Thiele's autobiography. Clearly a man who ached to stay ahead of the trend, Thiele was gregarious and sociable; he also liked his liquor. While he continued to produce into the '80s, his '60s and '70s recordings guarantee him a place in the producer pantheon. Thiele died of kidney failure on January 30, 1996. —CARLO WOLFF

Armstrong, Louis: w/ Duke Ellington, *Together for the First Time,* Mobile Fidelity Sound Lab, 1961, 1988 • w/ Duke Ellington, *Complete Sessions,* Roulette, 1961, 1990 • *What a Wonderful World,* Decca Jazz, 1968, 1996 • *Stardust,* Portrait, 1988 • "Wonderful World," A&M, 1988 • *All Time Greatest Hits,* MCA, 1994.

Art Blakey Quartet: *A Jazz Message,* Impulse!, 1963, 1986.

Asmussen, Svend: *June Night,* Decca Jazz, 1983.

Ayler, Albert: *Albert Ayler in Greenwich Village,* Impulse!, 1967, 1989 • *Cry,* Impulse!, 1967, 1992.

Barbieri, Gato: *Gato,* Flying Dutchman, 1971 • *Legend of Gato Barbieri,* Flying Dutchman, 1973.

Basie, Count: "What'cha Talkin'?," Impulse!, 1962, 1988 (*The Impulse! Collection,* Vol. 1) • *Count Basie and the Kansas City 7,* Impulse!, 1962, 1996 • *See also* Brewer, Teresa.

Berlin, Irving: *The 100th Anniversary Collection,* MCA, 1988.

Blakey, Art: "Alamode," Impulse!, 1961, 1988 (*The Impulse! Collection,* Vol. 1) • *The Jazz Messengers,* Columbia, 1997 • *See also* Art Blakey Quartet.

Blythe, Arthur: *Lenox Avenue Breakdown,* Columbia, 1979 • *In the Tradition,* Columbia, 1980.

Braff, Ruby: *Very Sinatra,* Red Baron, 1981.

Brewer, Teresa: "Ricochet," Coral, 1953 • "Jilted," Coral, 1954 • w/ Count Basie, *Songs of Bessie Smith,* Signature, 1973 • *16 Most Requested Songs,* Columbia, 1977, 1991 • *American Music Box,* Vol. 1, *Songs of Irving Berlin,* Doctor Jazz, 1983 • *I Dig Big Band Singers,* Doctor Jazz, 1983 • *Live at Carnegie Hall and Montreaux,* Doctor Jazz, 1983 • *Teenage Dance Party,* Bear Family, 1989 • *The Best Of,* MCA, 1989 • w/ Mercer Ellington, *Cotton Connection,* Doctor Jazz, 1990 • and Friends, *Memories of Louis,* Red Baron, 1991 • *Softly I Swing,* Red Baron, 1991 • *See also* Ellington, Duke; Hackett, Bobby.

Brown, Michael: *Alarums and Excursions,* Impulse!, 1962.

Burnette, Johnny, and, the Rock 'n' Roll Trio: *Tear It Up* (3 tracks), Solid Smoke, 1956, 1978 • *Rockabilly Boogie,* Bear Family, 1989.

Carter, Benny: "Cotton Tail," Impulse!, 1961, 1988 (*The*

Impulse! Collection, Vol. 1) • and His Orchestra, *Further Definitions,* Impulse!, 1961.

Cherry, Don: *Human Music,* Flying Dutchman, 1969.

Cocker, Joe: *Across from Midnight,* Capitol, 1997.

Coleman Hawkins Quartet: *Today and Now,* Impulse!, 1963, 1996.

Coltrane, John: w/ Johnny Hartman, "Lush Life," Impulse!, 1962, 1988 (*The Impulse! Collection,* Vol. 1) • "What's New," Impulse!, 1962, 1988 (*The Impulse! Collection,* Vol. 1) • *Live at the Village Vanguard,* Impulse!, 1962, 1990 • w/ Johnny Hartman, *John Coltrane and Johnny Hartman,* Impulse!, 1963, 1995 • *Impressions,* Impulse!, 1963, 1987 • *Live at Birdland,* Impulse!, 1963, 1992 • *Newport '63,* Impulse!, 1963 • *Coltrane Live at Birdland,* Impulse!, 1964, 1989 • *Om,* Impulse!, 1965, 1989 • *First Meditations,* GRP, 1965, 1992 • *New Thing at Newport,* Impulse!, 1965, 1992 • *The Major Works of John Coltrane,* Impulse!, 1965, 1992 • *Dear Old Stockholm,* Impulse!, 1965, 1993 • *A Love Supreme,* Impulse!, 1965, 1995 • *Sun Ship,* Impulse!, 1965, 1995 • *Living Space,* Impulse!, 1965, 1998 • *Meditations,* Impulse!, 1966, 1996 • *Live at the Village Vanguard Again!,* Impulse!, 1966, 1997 • *Expression,* Impulse!, 1967, 1993 • *Retrospective: Impulse,* GRP, 1967 • *Stellar Regions,* Impulse!, 1967, 1995 • *The Gentle Side of John Coltrane,* Impulse!, 1975, 1991 • *To the Beat of a Different Drummer,* Impulse!, 1981 • *Transition,* Impulse!, 1993 • *More John Coltrane,* GRP, 1998 • *See also* Ellington, Duke; John Coltrane Quartet.

Coryell, Larry: *Barefoot Boy,* Flying Dutchman, 1971 • *Fairyland,* Mega, 1971.

Davis, Richard: *See* Jones, Elvin.

David Murray Quartet: *Black and Black,* Red Baron, 1992 • *Special Quartet,* DIW/Columbia, 1992.

Eden's Children: *Eden's Children,* ABC, 1968.

Ellington, Duke: *Hot Summer Dance,* Red Baron, 1960, 1991 • w/ John Coltrane, *Duke Ellington and John Coltrane,* Impulse!, 1962, 1995 • w/ Coleman Hawkins, *Duke Ellington Meets Coleman Hawkins,* Impulse!, 1962, 1995 • w/ Coleman Hawkins, "Mood Indigo," Impulse!, 1962, 1988 (*The Impulse! Collection,* Vol. 1) • *Priceless Jazz,* GRP, 1962, 1998 • w/ Teresa Brewer, *It Don't Mean a Thing If It Ain't Got That Swing,* Columbia, 1991 • *See also* Armstrong, Louis.

Ellington, Mercer: *See* Brewer, Teresa

Garner, Erroll: *Classic Pianos,* Doctor Jazz, 1944.

Gillespie, Dizzy: *Swing Low, Sweet Cadillac,* Impulse!, 1967, 1996.

Grappelli, Stephane: *My Other Love,* Columbia, 1991.

Hackett, Bobby, and Teresa Brewer: *What a Wonderful World,* Columbia, 1973.

Hamilton, Chico: *Man from Two Worlds,* Impulse!, 1963, 1993 • *The Dealer,* Impulse!, 1967.

Hampton, Lionel: *You Better Know It!!!,* Impulse!, 1965, 1994.

Hartman, Johnny: *I Just Dropped By to Say Hello,* Impulse!, 1963, 1995 • *Priceless Jazz Collection,* GRP, 1964, 1997 • *The Voice That Is,* Impulse!, 1965, 1994 • *Unforgettable,* Impulse!, 1966, 1995 • *See also* Coltrane, John.

Hawkins, Coleman: w/ Lester Young, *Classic Tenors,* Signature/CBS, 1943, 1989 • w/ Lester Young and Ben Webster, *The Big Three,* Doctor Jazz, 1946, 1990 • *Desafinado: Bossa Nova and Jazz Samba,* Impulse!, 1962, 1997 • *Wrapped Tight,* GRP, 1965, 1991 • *Coleman Hawkins in the '50s: Body and Soul Revisited,* Decca Jazz, 1993 • *See also* Coleman Hawkins Quartet; Ellington, Duke.

Hicks, John: w/ Cecil McBee and Elvin Jones, *Power Trio,* Jive/Novus, 1991 • *Crazy for You,* Red Baron, 1992 • *Friends Old and New,* Novus, 1992 • *Lover Man: A Tribute to Billie Holiday,* Red Baron, 1993.

Hines, Earl: *Spontaneous Explorations,* Contact, 1964 • *Reunion in Brussels,* Red Baron, 1965, 1992 • *Here Comes Earl "Fatha" Hines,* Red Baron, 1993.

Hodges, Johnny: *Everybody Knows Johnny Hodges,* GRP, 1965, 1992.

Holly, Buddy: *Buddy Holly,* Coral, 1958, 1968 • "Rave On," Coral, 1958 • *Greatest Hits,* MCA, 1996.

Hooker, John Lee: *Live at the Cafe Au Go Go (and Soledad Prison),* MCA, 1966, 1996 • *Simply the Truth,* One Way, 1969 • *The Best of John Lee Hooker, 1965–1974,* MCA, 1992.

Hubbard, Freddie: *The Artistry of Freddie Hubbard,* GRP, 1962, 1996 • *The Body and the Soul,* Impulse!, 1963, 1996.

Jackson, Milt: *Statements,* GRP, 1964, 1993.

Jamal, Ahmad: *Tranquility,* Impulse!, 1968.

John Coltrane Quartet: *Ballads,* Impulse!, 1962, 1995 • *Coltrane,* Impulse!, 1962 • *Crescent,* Impulse!, 1964, 1996 • *The John Coltrane Quartet Plays,* Impulse!, 1965, 1997.

Johnson, J.J.: *Proof Positive,* Impulse!, 1964, 1993.

Jones, Elvin: *Illumination!,* Impulse!, 1963, 1998 • *Dear John C.,* Impulse!, 1965, 1993 • w/ Richard Davis, *Heavy Sounds,* Impulse!, 1968, 1989 • *See also* Hicks, John.

Jones, Quincy: *The Quintessence,* MCA Jazz, 1961, 1986 • "Quintessence," Impulse!, 1961, 1988 (*The Impulse! Collection,* Vol. 1).

Kerouac, Jack: *Poetry for the Beat Generation,* Hanover-Signature, 1959.

King, B.B.: *Lucille,* MCA, 1968, 1992 • *Back in the Alley,* MCA, 1973 • *King of the Blues,* MCA, 1992.

Laine, Frankie: *The Very Best of (ABC Years),* Taragon, 1996.

Lateef, Yusef: *Live at Pep's,* Impulse!, 1964, 1993 • *Every Village Has a Song,* Rhino, 1976, 1993.

Lawrence, Steve: "The Banana Boat Song," Coral, 1956 • "Party Doll," Coral, 1957 • *Here's Steve Lawrence,* Coral, 1958.

Lawson, Yank: *That's a Plenty,* Signature/CBS, 1943, 1993.

Mann, Herbie: *When Lights Are Low,* Portrait, 1957, 1988.

Manne, Shelly: *Shelly Manne and His Friends,* Doctor Jazz,
1944, 1990 • *2-3-4,* Impulse!, 1962, 1994 • *Shelly Manne and Co.,* Flying Dutchman, 1967.

Marcus, Steve: *Smile,* Red Baron, 1993.

McBee, Cecil: *See* Hicks, John.

McCoy Tyner Trio: *Reaching Forth,* Impulse!, 1962, 1998.

McGuire Sisters: "Christmas Alphabet," Coral, 1954 • "Goodnight, Sweetheart, Goodnight," Coral, 1954 • "Muskrat Ramble," Coral, 1954 • "Sincerely," Coral, 1954 • "He," Coral, 1955 • "It May Sound Silly," Coral, 1955 • "Something's Gotta Give," Coral, 1955 • "Ev'ry Day of My Life," Coral, 1956 • "Picnic," Coral, 1956 • "Sugartime," Coral, 1957 • "May You Always," Coral, 1958 • *Greatest Hits,* MCA, 1989.

McKenna, Dave: *This Is the Moment,* Portrait, 1958, 1988.

Memphis Minnie: *I Ain't No Bad Gal,* Portrait, 1941, 1988.

Mingus, Charles: *Mingus Plays Piano,* Mobile Fidelity Sound Lab, 1963, 1990 • *Mingus Mingus Mingus Mingus Mingus,* Impulse!, 1963, 1995 • *The Black Saint and the Sinner Lady,* Impulse!, 1963, 1995 • *Priceless Jazz,* GRP, 1963, 1997 • *Thirteen Pictures: The Charles Mingus Anthology,* Rhino, 1993.

Murray, David: *Ming's Samba,* Portrait, 1989 • *MX,* Red Baron, 1992 • *Jazzasaurus Rex,* Red Baron, 1993 • *Saxmen,* Red Baron, 1994 • *See also* David Murray Quartet.

Nelson, Oliver: *More Blues and Abstract Truth,* Impulse!, 1964, 1997 • *Sound Pieces,* Impulse!, 1966, 1991 • *Skull Session,* Flying Dutchman, 1975.

Noland, Terry: *Hypnotized,* Bear Family, 1990.

O'Day, Anita: *Hi Ho Trailus Boot Whip,* Flying Dutchman, 1947 • *I Told Ya I Love Ya: Now Get Out,* Columbia, 1991.

Phil Woods Quartet: *Warm Woods,* Portrait, 1957, 1988.

Phillips, Flip: *Melody from the Sky,* Doctor Jazz, 1949.

Plaster Casters Blues Band: *The Plaster Casters Blues Band,* Bluestime, 1969.

Ray Bryant Trio: *Now's the Time,* Doctor Jazz, 1959, 1986.

Revolutionary Blues Band: *The Revolutionary Blues Band,* Coral, 1969.

Roach, Max: *It's Time,* Impulse!, 1962, 1996.

Rollins, Sonny: "Hold 'Em Joe," Impulse!, 1965, 1988 (*The Impulse! Collection,* Vol. 1) • *On Impulse!,* Impulse!, 1965 • *Alfie,* Impulse!, 1966, 1997 • *East Broadway Rundown,* Impulse!, 1967, 1995 • *There Will Never Be Another You,* Impulse!, 1978.

Roy Haynes Quartet: *Out of the Afternoon,* Impulse!, 1962, 1996.

Ryerson, Ali: *I'll Be Back,* Red Baron, 1993.

Salvation: *Gypsy Carnival Caravan,* ABC, 1968.

Sanders, Pharoah: *Tauhid,* Impulse!, 1966, 1993 • *Karma,* Impulse!, 1969, 1995 • *Oh Lord, Let Me Do No Wrong,* Doctor Jazz, 1987 • *Priceless Jazz Collection,* Impulse!, 1997.

Scott, Shirley: *Queen of the Organ,* Impulse!, 1965, 1993 • *Roll 'Em,* Impulse!, 1966, 1995.

Scott-Heron, Gil: *New Black Poet,* Flying Dutchman, 1970 •

Pieces of a Man, Flying Dutchman, 1971, 1995 • *Free Will,* Flying Dutchman, 1972, 1995 • *Small Talk at 125th and Lenox,* Flying Dutchman, 1972, 1995 • *The Revolution Will Not Be Televised,* RCA Bluebird, 1975, 1988 • *The Best Of,* Arista, 1984.

Sears, Big Al: *Sear-iously,* Bear Family, 1992.

Shaw, Artie: *Free for All,* Four Star, 1988.

Shepp, Archie: *Four for Trane,* Impulse!, 1964, 1997 • *Fire Music,* Impulse!, 1965, 1995 • *On This Night,* Impulse!, 1965, 1995 • *Live in San Francisco,* Impulse!, 1966, 1998 • *Mama Too Tight,* Impulse!, 1966.

Smith, Lonnie Liston: *Watercolors,* Jive/Novus, 1970, 1992 • *Golden Dreams,* Bluebird, 1973, 1992 • *Astral Traveling,* Flying Dutchman, 1974 • *Expansions,* Flying Dutchman, 1974, 1995 • *Visions of a New World,* Flying Dutchman, 1975, 1995 • *Renaissance,* RCA, 1976 • *The Best Of,* RCA, 1978 • *Rejuvenation,* Doctor Jazz, 1985 • *Make Someone Happy,* Doctor Jazz, 1989 • *Cosmic Funk,* Flying Dutchman, 1995.

Spann, Otis: *Blues Are Where It's At,* Beat Goes On, 1967, 1996 • *The Bottom of the Blues,* Beat Goes On, 1968, 1996 • w/ T-Bone Walker, Eddie Vinson, and Joe Turner, *Blue Rocks,* Flying Dutchman, 1973 • *Down to Earth: The Bluesway Recordings,* MCA, 1995.

Stitt, Sonny: *Salt and Pepper,* Impulse!, 1963, 1997.

Stone, Jesse: *Jesse Stone Alias Charles Calhoun,* Bear Family, 1996.

Strayhorn, Billy: *Lush Life,* Red Baron, 1965, 1992.

Szabo, Gabor: *The Sorcerer,* Impulse!, 1967, 1990.

Terry, Clark: *What a Wonderful World: For Lou,* Red Baron, 1993.

Thomas, Leon: *Full Circle,* Flying Dutchman, 1973.

Turner, Big Joe: *Singing the Blues,* Mobile Fidelity Sound Lab, 1967, 1990 • w/ T-Bone Walker, *Bosses of the Blues,* RCA Bluebird, 1972, 1989 • *Roll 'Em,* Bluesway, 1973 • *See also* Spann, Otis.

Turrentine, Stanley: w/ Shirley Scott, *Let It Go,* Impulse!, 1966, 1992.

Tyner, McCoy: *Today and Tomorrow,* Impulse!, 1963, 1992 • *Nights of Ballads and Blues,* Impulse!, 1963, 1997 • *McCoy Tyner Plays Ellington,* Impulse!, 1964, 1997 • *44th Street Suite,* Red Baron, 1991 • *Priceless Jazz Collection,* GRP, 1998 • *See also* McCoy Tyner Trio.

Vinson, Eddie "Cleanhead": *Cherry Red,* Bluesway, 1967 • *See also* Spann, Otis.

Walker, T-Bone: *Dirty Mistreater,* MCA, 1968 • *Funky Town,* Beat Goes On, 1969 • *See also* Spann, Otis.

Webster, Ben: *See You at the Fair,* Impulse!, 1964, 1993 • *See also* Hawkins, Coleman.

Williams, Billy: "I'm Gonna Sit Right Down and Write Myself a Letter," Coral, 1957.

Young, Lester: *See* Hawkins, Coleman.

COLLECTIONS

Feel Good with the Good Music of Doctor Jazz, Vol. 1, Doctor Jazz, 1987.

Chris Thomas

When Chris Thomas was a student at London's Royal Academy of Music in the early '60s, one of his classmates was an unassuming pianist named Reg Dwight. In the late '60s, when he was working as a production assistant for George Martin (see entry), Thomas renewed his acquaintance with Dwight, who was then a struggling session player using the stage name Elton John, playing on tracks such as the Hollies' "He Ain't Heavy, He's My Brother."

John's reputation has long since been cemented; one factor that has contributed to his longevity is the quality of his recordings, specifically the production imprint of Chris Thomas. In fact, Thomas's steady hand is clearly evident on such hits as "Simple Life," "The One" (No.

9), "Club at the End of the Street," "The Last Song," and "You Can Make History (Young Again)." Thomas's diverse portfolio also includes the Pretenders, INXS, Paul McCartney (see entry), Pete Townshend, Roxy Music, and Pink Floyd.

Born January 13, 1947, in London, Thomas characterizes his work as "filling in the colors of a picture." And Thomas paints on a broad canvas. Characteristically, his musical portraits are a glorious kaleidoscope of sounds: jutting guitars and syncopated drums fleshed out by creative use of horns, keyboards, and synthesizers underpinning strong vocals. Moreover, Thomas's tracks have an open, airy feel that leave plenty of room for improvisation. "What I normally do is build something; mix as you're going along," Thomas explains, citing two cases where rough mixes became final mixes: the Pretenders' "Tattooed Love Boys" and Elton John's "Blue Avenue." Thomas constructs a mix by taking the "best bits" from several takes and melding them into a seamless whole. "You've got to balance it very carefully," he cautions. "With vocals, you may have to listen to each phrase a dozen times to come up with a master vocal; one phrase might begin strongly but collapse at the end."

Thomas approaches each session with the enthusiasm of a songwriter recording a demo. "It's a bit of a childlike attitude," he admits. "It's easy to get inspired by great songs." Given his background at the Royal Academy of Music, it is not surprisingly that Thomas sees the producer's role as facilitating the creative process by capturing the best performance. "My job is to help writers get their song realized in recorded form—even if it means shutting up and saying nothing."

At the Academy, Thomas played the violin and piano. He considers himself a master of neither. "I'm technically atrocious," he admits. After his musical studies, he played bass guitar in a local band before choosing the lower profile of record production.

Joining George Martin's AIR Productions in 1968, Thomas immediately assisted Martin with AIR's top client: the Beatles. It was quite a start for the 21-year-old apprentice. "I was scared stiff," Thomas recalls. "At one point I overheard John [Lennon] complaining to someone, 'He's not really doin' his stuff' and thought he was talking about me." Luckily, Lennon was not referring to Thomas; in fact, Lennon insisted that Thomas receive credit for his contributions to The Beatles (commonly called the White Album): Thomas played harpsichord on "Piggies" and scored the horns on "Savoy Truffle."

Thomas's first solo production was the 1969 debut by the Climax Blues Band, with "A Stranger in Your Town." In the '70s, Thomas expanded his portfolio to include Procol Harum, Bryan Ferry, Roxy Music, Badfinger, John Cale (see entry), and the Sex Pistols. He also had a hand in one of the most successful albums in history: Pink Floyd's The Dark Side of the Moon. The group wanted an outside opinion, so they asked Thomas to supervise the mix.

Concurrently, Thomas began experimenting with different recording techniques. "I was working on using echo and making things sound big," he explains. Thomas's versatility, enabling him to move from the melodic sentimentality of Badfinger to the vaudevillian excess of Roxy Music, gave him the moxie to tackle the debut album by the Sex Pistols. Yet, in spite of the Sex Pistols' notorious public image, Thomas found the group easy to work with. "I heard the demo and thought they had the potential to be a great rock band. Their attitude [in the studio] was great: it was all down to Paul [Cook] and Steve [Jones]."

Thomas's work with the Pretenders brought more accolades: "Brass in Pocket" (No. 14), "I Go to Sleep" (No. 7 U.K.), "Message of Love" (No. 11 U.K.) and "Back on the Chain Gang" (No. 5) were compact, energetic creations that oozed with excitement. Thomas also reunited with Paul McCartney for the final Wings album, Back to the Egg (No. 8), one of few instances where McCartney had used an outside producer.

In 1980 Thomas began a fruitful partnership with Pete Townshend that yielded three superb albums: Empty Glass, All the Best Cowboys Have Chinese Eyes (No. 5), and White City. Townshend offered Thomas the producer's role with the Who, but Thomas declined, citing a "division of loyalty" if he produced both acts.

Thomas's work with INXS again proved his Midas touch: X (No. 5) was the band's best effort, highlighted by songs such as "Lately" and "Bitter Tears." Thomas calls INXS "brilliant," but management problems created a less-than-perfect atmosphere in the studio. "X was not an easy record to make," he admits.

Elton John's chart resurgence in the '80s and '90s was due in part to Thomas's presence; in fact, "Sacrifice," earned John his first British No. 1 single as a solo performer. "The demo for 'Sacrifice' was so good," Thomas recalls. "I wanted to give it a really nice rhythm underneath, that sexy element. Elton's songs are written as a song: I hardly ever have to alter the construction," Thomas marvels, adding that "Elton can knock off a classic song in 15 minutes."

Thomas claims he usually can't spot hit singles; however, on two occasions he did predict success: Roxy Music's "Love Is the Drug" (No. 2 U.K.) and the Pretenders' "Brass in Pocket," which Thomas remembers with particular fondness. "Chrissie [Hynde] said 'that song goes on the album over my dead body,'" Thomas adds with a laugh. —BEN CROMER

Abrahams, Mick: *At Last,* Chrysalis, 1972.

Adams, Bryan, Rod Stewart, and Sting: "All for Love," A&M, 1994.

Badfinger: *Ass,* Apple, 1973 • *Badfinger,* Warner Bros., 1973 • *Wish You Were Here,* Warner Bros., 1974 • *The Best Of,* Vol. 2, Rhino, 1990 • *Best Of,* Capitol, 1995.

Cale, John: "Paris 1919," Warner Bros., 1973 (*Appetizers*) • *Paris 1919,* Reprise, 1973 • *Seducing Down the Door,* Rhino, 1995.

Christopher Milk: *Some People Will Drink Anything,* Reprise, 1972.

Climax Blues Band: *Climax Chicago Blues Band,* Sire, 1969 • *A Lot of Bottle,* Sire, 1970 • *The Climax Blues Band Plays On,* Sire, 1970 • *Tightly Knit,* Sire, 1970.

Detroit, Marcella: w/ Elton John, "Ain't Nothing Like the Real Thing," London, 1994 • *Jewel,* London, 1994.

Ferry, Bryan: *Let's Stick Together,* Atlantic, 1976 • *See also* Roxy Music.

Human League: "(Keep Feeling) Fascination" (remix), A&M, 1983 • *Hysteria,* A&M, 1984 • "The Lebanon," A&M, 1984 • *Greatest Hits,* Virgin/A&M, 1988.

INXS: "Listen Like Thieves," Atlantic, 1985 • *Listen Like Thieves,* Atlantic, 1985 • "This Time," Atlantic, 1985 • "What You Need," Atlantic, 1985 • "Devil Inside," Atlantic, 1987 • *Kick,* Atlantic, 1987 • "Need You Tonight," Atlantic, 1987 • "Never Tear Us Apart," Atlantic, 1988 • "New Sensation," Atlantic, 1988 • "Disappear," Atlantic, 1990 • "Suicide Blonde," Atlantic, 1990 • *X,* Atlantic, 1990 • "Bitter Tears," Atlantic, 1991.

John, Elton: "Chloe," Geffen, 1981 • "Nobody Wins," Geffen, 1981 • *The Fox,* Rocket, 1981 • "Blue Eyes," Geffen, 1982 • "Empty Garden (Hey Hey Johnny)," Geffen, 1982 • *Jump Up,* Rocket, 1982 • "I Guess That's Why They Call It the Blues," Geffen, 1983 • "I'm Still Standing," Geffen, 1983 • "Kiss the Bride," Geffen, 1983 • *Too Low for Zero,* Rocket/Geffen, 1983 • *Breaking Hearts,* Rocket/Geffen, 1984 • "Sad Songs (Say So Much)," Geffen, 1984 • "Who Wears These Shoes," Geffen, 1984 • "In Neon," Geffen, 1985 • *Greatest Hits,* Vol. 3, *1979–1987,* MCA, 1987 • "A Word in Spanish," MCA, 1988 • "I Don't Wanna Go On with You Like That," MCA, 1988 • *Reg Strikes Back,* MCA, 1988 • "Healing Hands," MCA, 1989 • *Sleeping with the Past,* MCA, 1989 • "Club at the End of the Street," MCA, 1990 • "Sacrifice," MCA, 1990 • *Greatest Hits, 1976–1986,* MCA, 1992 • "The Last Song," MCA, 1992 • "The One," MCA, 1992 • *The One,* MCA, 1992 • *Duets,* MCA, 1993 • "Simple Life," MCA, 1993 • "Can You Feel the Love Tonight," Hollywood, 1994 • "Circle of Life," Hollywood,

1994 • *Love Songs,* MCA, 1996 • "You Can Make History (Young Again)," MCA, 1996 • "Candle in the Wind/The Way You Look Tonight," Rocket, 1997 • *The Big Picture,* Rocket, 1997 • "Recover Your Soul," Rocket, 1998.

Kokomo: "I Can Understand It," Epic, 1975, 1981 (*England Rocks 3*) • *Kokomo,* CBS, 1975.

Krazy Kat: *China Seas,* Mountain, 1977.

Miller, Frankie: *Full House,* Chrysalis, 1977 • *The Very Best Of,* Chrysalis, 1993.

Miss World: *Miss World,* Atlantic, 1992.

Nirvana: *Dedicated to Markos Three,* Pye, 1970.

Pretenders: *Pretenders,* Real/Sire, 1979 • "Brass in Pocket," Sire, 1980 • "Talk of the Town," RSO, 1980 (*Times Square* soundtrack) • *Pretenders 2,* Real/Sire, 1981 • "Back on the Chain Gang," Warner Bros., 1982, 1983 (*The King of Comedy* soundtrack) • "My City Was Gone," Sire, 1982 • "2000 Miles," Real, 1983 • "In the Sticks," Warner Bros., 1983 (*Attack of the Killer B's*) • "Middle of the Road," Sire, 1983 • *Learning to Crawl,* Real/Sire, 1984 • *The Singles,* Sire, 1987 • *Last of the Independents* (1 track), Sire/WB, 1994.

Procol Harum: *Home,* RZ/A&M, 1970 • *Broken Barricades,* Chrysalis, 1971 • "Conquistador," A&M, 1972 • *Live in Concert with the Edmonton Symphony Orchestra,* Chrysalis, 1972 • *Grand Hotel,* Chrysalis, 1973 • "Toujours l'Amour," Warner Bros., 1973 (*Appetizers*) • *Exotic Birds and Fruit,* Chrysalis, 1974 • *Classics, Vol. 17,* A&M, 1987 • *The Chrysalis Years, 1973–1977,* Chrysalis, 1989.

Pulp: *Different Class,* Island, 1995 • "I Spy," Mother/Island, 1995 (*Mission: Impossible* soundtrack) • "Held the Aged," Island, 1997.

Quiver: *Gone in the Morning,* Warner Bros., 1972.

Rambow, Philip: *Jungle Law,* EMI, 1981.

Rice, Tim: *Collection: Stage and Screen Classics,* Rhino, 1996.

Roxy Music: *For Your Pleasure* (5 tracks), Atco, 1973 • *Stranded,* Atco, 1973 • *Siren,* Atco, 1975 • *Viva,* Atco, 1976 • w/ Bryan Ferry, *Street Life: 20 Greatest Hits,* EG, 1986.

Sadistic Mika Band: *Sadistic Mika Band,* Harvest, 1974 • *Hot! Menu,* Harvest, 1975.

Sex Pistols: "God Save the Queen," Virgin, 1977 • "Holidays in the Sun," Virgin, 1977 • *Never Mind the Bollocks,* Virgin/WB, 1977 • "Pretty Vacant," Virgin, 1977 • *Filthy Lucre Live,* Virgin, 1996.

Shakespear's Sister: *Hormonally Yours* (1 track), London, 1992 • "Stay," London, 1992.

Spedding, Chris: *Hurt,* Rak, 1977 • *Guitar Graffiti,* Rak, 1978 • *Ready! Spedding! Go!,* EMI, 1984.

Stewart, Dave, and the Spiritual Cowboys: *Dave Stewart and the Spiritual Cowboys,* Arista, 1990.

Stewart, Rod: *If We Fall in Love Tonight,* Warner Bros., 1996.

Thrashing Doves: *Bedrock Vice,* A&M, 1987.

Tom Robinson Band: *Power in the Darkness,* EMI, 1978.

Townshend, Pete: *Empty Glass,* Atco, 1980 • "Let My Love

Open the Door," Atco, 1980 • *All the Best Cowboys Have Chinese Eyes,* Atco, 1982 • "Face the Face," Atco, 1985 • *White City,* Atco, 1985.

Wings: *Back to the Egg,* Columbia, 1979 • "Getting Closer," Columbia, 1979.

COLLECTIONS

Concerts for the People of Kampuchea, Atlantic, 1981.
The Lion King soundtrack, Walt Disney, 1994.

Keith Thomas

Many people in the music industry think Nashville only produces country and contemporary Christian music. Producer Keith Thomas is correcting that perception. The Grammy Award–winning producer has worked with Vanessa Williams, Whitney Houston, Luther Vandross, Peabo Bryson, Amy Grant, Expose, BeBe and CeCe Winans, and Selena. His credits include co-writing and producing Grant's hit "Baby Baby" (No. 1) and producing Williams' "Save the Best for Last" (No. 1) and "Colors of the Wind" (No. 4) from *Pocahontas.* He produced "Wannagirl," a hit for Jeremy Jordan, and "Hearts Don't Think (They Feel)!" for Natural Selection.

"I love to take the artist and design a sound for them," Thomas says. "To me, what a producer does is look at an artist and see what he can do to bring out the best in that artist. . . . My job is to enhance what the artist is trying to accomplish, to really understand what they're about and try to give them a bigger platform to do what they're doing. When I first started out, trying to establish myself, it was more about people hearing my licks and what I could do. I guess that's part of growing. I really now to try to make each record unique to the artist I'm working on. And I think that's working."

A native of Conyers, Georgia, Thomas developed a love for music at an early age. At 9, he was playing in his father's band. By college, he was writing songs and performing with a gospel act called the Sharrett Brothers. In 1979, he moved to Nashville and became the first staff writer at Ronnie Milsap's publishing company, Milsap Music. Milsap recorded some of his tunes and Thomas used the time as a training ground, writing songs, producing demos, and experimenting in the studio.

The following year he signed with Word Music and launched a career as an artist, recording two jazz albums for the label. During his six years with Word he worked with Christian artists such as the Imperials, Kenny Marks, the Gaither Vocal Band, First Call, and Carman. He started his own publishing and production company, Yellow Elephant Music, and produced BeBe and CeCe Winans' debut album in 1987. The album won CeCe a Grammy for Best Soul Gospel Performance, and also served to elevate Thomas's visibility as a producer. The calls started pouring in.

He began working with Vanessa Williams, producing such hits as "The Sweetest Days" (No. 18) and "Colors of the Wind." His list of credits continued to build and featured a diversity of work, ranging from Selena's "I Could Fall in Love," to the 1995 Pepsi "Choice of a New Generation" jingle, to Amy Grant and Vince Gill's "House of Love."

Thomas is a staff producer with Sony Music in New York. His agreement allows him to continue to produce Grant, Williams, and one outside act a year. Thomas enjoys working with diverse artists in different genres and says being a producer is somewhat like being an actor. "It's like acting in that you assume the character," he relates. "I feel like I have a lot to offer in different styles of music."

Thomas says he tries to create an environment that is conducive to creativity when working with an artist. "I try to make the artist feel comfortable," Thomas says. "Sometimes I'll ask them to think of a certain thing while they're singing that would make them sing totally different, and they are impressed with themselves after they hear it. When we're doing vocals, I'm constantly trying to create a visual setting in their minds for a certain line or certain verse—more or less playacting."

In 1992, Thomas bought the Bennett House, the Franklin, Tennessee, studio he'd worked at on and off for years. The 1875 building has two studios: Thomas's private workplace and one for rent. The Bennett House is also home to Thomas Hogue Casselman (THC) Entertainment, a company Thomas founded with marketing executive Don Casselman and composer/producer Joe Hogue. THC specializes in creating music for films, television, and advertising projects.

"I feel I am an artist in a sense," Thomas says. "I think that's why I get so attached to the stuff I work on." —Deborah Evans Price

Belle, Regina: *Reachin' Back* (4 tracks), Columbia, 1995.
Bolton, Michael: *This Is the Time: The Christmas Album,* Columbia, 1996 • *All That Matters,* Columbia, 1997.
Bonoff, Karla: "Standing Right Next to Me," MCA, 1994.
Bryson, Peabo: *Through the Fire,* Columbia, 1994.

Carman: *Live . . . Radically Saved,* Sparrow, 1988 • *Comin' On Strong,* Word, 1992 • *Absolute Best,* Sparrow, 1993 • *Addicted to Jesus,* Sparrow, 1993 • *Revival in the Land,* Sparrow, 1993.

Expose: *Greatest Hits* (2 tracks), Arista, 1995.

First Call: *La Razon de Cantar,* Myrrh, 1994.

Grant, Amy: "Baby Baby," A&M, 1991 • *Heart in Motion,* A&M, 1991 • "Good for Me," A&M, 1992 • w/ Vince Gill, "House of Love," A&M, 1994 • *House of Love,* A&M, 1994 • "Lucky One," A&M, 1994 • *Behind the Eyes,* Myrrh/A&M, 1997 • "Takes a Little Time," A&M, 1997 • "Like I Love You," A&M, 1998.

Imperials, The: *One More Song for You,* Word, 1982.

Ingram, James: *Always You,* Warner Bros., 1993.

Jackson, Rebbie: *Yours Faithfully,* MJJ, 1998.

Johnson, Puff: *Miracle,* Columbia, 1996.

Jordan, Jeremy: *Try My Love,* Giant, 1993 • "Wannagirl," Giant, 1993.

Lorenz, Trey: *Trey Lorenz,* Epic, 1992.

McKnight, Brian: *Anytime,* Mercury, 1997.

Natural Selection: "Hearts Don't Think (They Feel)!," EastWest, 1991.

Perry, Phil: *Pure Pleasure,* GRP, 1994.

Selena: *Dreaming of You,* EMI Latin, 1995.

Tamia: "Make Tonight Beautiful," Virgin, 1997 (*Speed 2: Cruise Control*).

Thomas, Keith: *Instrumental Appetite,* Word, 1983 • *Kaleidoscope,* Word, 1987.

Troccoli, Kathy: *Kathy Troccoli,* RCA, 1994 • "Tell Me Where It Hurts," RCA, 1994.

Vandross, Luther: *One Night with You: The Best of Love,* Vol. 2, Sony, 1997.

Williams, Vanessa: *The Comfort Zone,* Wing, 1991 • "Just for Tonight," Wing, 1992 • "Save the Best for Last," Wing, 1992 • "The Sweetest Days," Wing, 1994 • "Colors of the Wind," Disney, 1995 (*Pocahontas* soundtrack) • *The Sweetest Days,* Wing/Mercury, 1995 • *Next,* Mercury, 1997 • w/ Chayanne, "Refugio de Amor," Epic, 1998.

Winans, BeBe and CeCe: *BeBe and CeCe Winans,* Sparrow, 1987 • "I.O.U. Me," Capitol, 1987 • "Heaven," Capitol, 1988 • *Heaven,* Sparrow, 1988 • "Celebrate New Life," Capitol, 1989 • "Lost Without You," Sparrow, 1989 • *Different Lifestyles,* Capitol, 1991 • "Depend on You," Capitol, 1992 • w/ Mavis Staples, "I'll Take You There," Capitol, 1992 • "It's O.K.," Capitol, 1992 • *Greatest Hits,* Sparrow, 1996.

COLLECTIONS

Our Christmas, Word/Epic, 1990.

Steve Thompson

See MICHAEL BARBIERO AND STEVE THOMPSON

Mike Thorne

Mike Thorne—keyboardist, scholar, journalist, record executive, studio owner, multimedia entrepreneur, composer—is one of the most important and successful producers of punk, post-punk, techno-pop and new wave over the last 20 years. His productions include the amazing verité document of the mid-'70s London punk scene, *The Roxy London W.C.2 (Jan.–Apr. '77),* and albums by Wire, Soft Machine, the Shirts, John Cale (see entry), Soft Cell, Nina Hagen, Bronski Beat, Roger Daltrey, Communards, Sir Michael Tippett, Laurie Anderson, China Crisis, Hilly Kristal, Peter Murphy, Blur, and Information Society, among many others.

Mike Thorne was born in Sunderland, in the north of England, in 1948. Thorne began formal classical piano lessons at the age of 10, which he continued for eight years. Gradually Thorne came to appreciate the music over which he was laboring, and by his midteens he was enthusiastically playing difficult 20th-century composers such as Schoenberg and Messiaen. While he was a committed musician, Thorne also excelled scholastically and received his B.A. from Oxford in physics in 1969.

Thorne maintains that when he left for Oxford he "barely knew the names of the Beatles," but while he was there he became a pop fan, discovering "all of this fun music, especially the harder stuff: Stones, Doors, anything with a bit of muscle. I like music to be confrontational, intense. My interest has been about 50-50 classical and pop ever since. I've always liked music left of center. It's a double-edged sword: most of the time it will disappear because the record companies don't put their marketing weight behind it, but the other side is that if something left of center goes, it goes all the way, like 'Tainted Love.' "

While in college Thorne made party tapes and set up the sound systems to play them on—a hardware and software man. When he returned home after Oxford, Thorne decided to "do it right" and built a mobile DJ system and light show from scratch, which he then took down to London and operated as "Heavy Henry" ("heavy" for the music, hard rock and soul; "henry" for an electrical unit of inductance)—"15 guineas, extra after 2 A.M."—which he operated three nights a week from 1969 until 1973.

In 1970 Thorne got a job as tea boy, then as assistant engineer, at De Lane Lea Music, "a tough, dirty rock 'n' roll studio in London," where he worked on sessions for Fleetwood Mac and Deep Purple. Thorne left the studio in 1971, then joined *Hi-Fi News and Record Review* in 1972, where he wrote classical and pop record reviews. At the same time Thorne studied music composition with noted composer Buxton Orr at the Guildhall School of Music and Drama. From 1974 to 1976 Thorne was editor of *Studio Sound,* which he helped develop from a hobbyist U.K. publication into a professional magazine with worldwide distribution.

Feeling that he would rather do it than write about it, Thorne decided to pursue an A&R position and was hired by EMI in March 1976. Among his charges were the Sex Pistols and Kate Bush. "I didn't know how I was supposed to behave. Instead of hanging around with other A&R people, I was bumping around the streets seeing all this fun new stuff, this energetic music—punk—which is really just pop music with a little bit of a point and a lot of edge. It was still a small scene: you'd go to the Roxy and the Marquee in London, or to CBGB and Max's Kansas City in New York and you'd hear about everything that was going on."

In the course of his travels several bands asked Thorne to produce them. "I said no because making a record deals with people's personal intensities (or at least the records I care to make) and is not like processing canned peas. That was too much responsibility. But I looked around and said, 'I can do it better than most of these Herberts.' Off I went." Indeed. In 1977 alone Thorne produced five albums, including the first documentation of the London punk scene, the great *Roxy London W.C.2 (Jan.–Apr. '77)* live compilation. The raw, unapologetic awfulness of it all is bracing: the bands can barely play, but they have something to say and they say it with boundless energy and certitude.

Also in 1977 Thorne produced a (French) gold record for the "French Rolling Stones," Telephone, and Wire's great, angular, dissonant, abrupt first album *Pink Flag.* Thorne's relationship with Wire (Colin Newman, vocals and guitar; Bruce Gilbert, guitar and synth; Graham Lewis, bass; Robert Gotobed, drums) stemmed directly from the Roxy recordings and he was the first to take them into the studio. "When we went in the first day [for *Pink Flag*] I took a jar of home-grown just so they could settle into the studio. I didn't want them to

get precious and to put the pressure on the first day. Everybody got completely ripped and the studio fear was gone after that," he says. The band played all of the album's 21 songs live in the studio.

With the success of his productions, Thorne became staff producer at EMI in addition to his A&R duties. In 1978 and 1979 Thorne produced two more Wire albums, *Chairs Missing* and *154,* which he played keyboards on as well. He also played live with the band, which was difficult: "They played things twice as fast live, and I am no way a virtuoso," he chuckles. By *154* in 1979 Wire had evolved musically (or had become bored with punk minimalism) and were adding a languid, melodic element to the mix (that sound became predominant when the band reunited after five years in the mid-'80s, especially on *A Bell Is a Cup . . . Until It Is Struck*). "There was an incredible step up in their playing capabilities when we went into *154,*" Thorne said in a 1996 interview with Kevin Eden. "When Wire [had] played the songs in the studio it was generally getting the cheese-grater guitars and jangly bashy noises right, so if you take out all of that it leaves a big gap, which has to be filled. And it was filled very creatively. We experimented with the whole studio," he said. "I still think it's an exceptional album and it still amazes me . . . just how unique it sounds," he said.

After *154* Thorne left EMI and moved to New York to become an independent producer, working predominantly out of the Media Sound studio. Thorne purchased one of the first Synclaviers (the computer synthesizer built in Vermont by the New England Digital Company—after NED's crash in 1992, Thorne was a director of the new Synclavier Company for a time), which he has used on many a production. In 1980 he produced albums for former Wire leader Colin Newman, John Cale, and Soft Machine, but in 1981 he hit the commercial jackpot with techno-pop's biggest hit ever, Soft Cell's "Tainted Love" (No. 1 U.K., U.S. Hot 100 for almost a year) from their *Non-Stop Erotic Cabaret* (No. 5 U.K.) album.

"Tainted Love" (originally an obscure soul single from the '60s by Gloria Jones) finds a perfect blend of electronic chill from synthman David Ball and vocal heat from singer Marc Almond. Ball's haunted-house synth melody line and plinking synth "anh anh" on the one beat of each measure provide a spooky, watery pool in which the flamboyant Almond emotively splashes about, decrying the "tainted love" of the title. "Taint" conjures a particularly livid brand of putrefaction, implying the uncomfortable truth that love doesn't just evaporate, but lingers in an increasingly fetid, yet still alluring state. It is ironic that the song hit just before the world became aware of a by-product of literally tainted love, AIDS. Even better than the album and single version is the 12" medley with "Where Did Our Love Go?," a poignant coda that finds Almond pleading for release in an ever-diminishing voice from the exquisite torture of his predicament.

Thorne produced four more Top 10 U.K. singles and two Top 10 U.K. albums for the duo, though none connected quite like the archetypal "Tainted Love." Thorne worked with Nina Hagen, the The, and Hilly Kristal (owner of CBGB) in 1982 and 1983 before hitting again in a big way with another techno-pop unit—this one a trio—Bronski Beat (Jimmy Somerville on vocals, Steve Bronski and Larry Steinbachek on keyboards) achieved an extremely rare feat on the classic Thorne-produced album *The Age of Consent* (No. 4 U.K.): an overtly political gay manifesto that is never shrill, accusatory, or intentionally off-putting (other than perhaps "Need a Man Blues"), but is instead warm, emotionally inclusive, and musically amazing.

Lyricist Jimmy Somerville emphasizes not the "otherness" of gays, but the emotional needs of all kinds of outcasts on originals "Smalltown Boy" (No. 3 U.K.), "Why?"(No. 6 U.K.), a smoky version of the Gershwin's "It Ain't Necessarily So" (No. 16 U.K.), and a remake of Donna Summer's disco classic "I Feel Love" (with Marc Almond; No. 3 U.K.). Thorne's production is supple yet tough and Somerville's falsetto is a force of nature. Since then, Thorne has produced the great poppy new wave of Aimee Mann's 'Til Tuesday ("Voices Carry," No. 8), Somerville's Communards (the great "Disenchanted"; "Don't Leave Me This Way," No. 1 U.K.; "So Cold the Night," No. 8 U.K.), Roger Daltrey, Siouxsie & the Banshees, China Crisis, Laurie Anderson, Blur, Peter Murphy, and Information Society. Thorne also built his own studio, the Stereo Society, which has evolved since its inception in 1986 into what Thorne calls "one of the most powerful music rooms in the world." A man whose life has been steeped in technology, Thorne has strong opinions on the subject: "Technology is a good servant but a bad master. Technology should be at the service of the person, not the other way round. Too much music is driven by technology and the process: the fingers do the walking, not the soul. But if we control technology, we find new means of expression, new ways of waking people up. That funny area where you sense something new but know we have to build on some cultural past, is, for me, the best hangout. Technology is developing increasingly quickly. It's always a balance of terror between what's possible and what we actually do with it," says Thorne. "Because technology gives us many new things to learn and assimilate, we can easily slip behind and sound dated unless we lean on instinct at least as much as the User Manual. There are so many new possibilities coming at us that it's hard to sit and think quietly in a corner: so much noise can drive us catatonic. And let's not forget those analog computers from Gibson and Steinway."

Thorne is now embarking upon a new technological venture—four CDs released through a new Web site (www.stereosociety.com) and the Stereo Society: his own first album done in an edgy electronic manner, but featuring the Uptown Horns as a central part of the sound (integral vocalists include Kit Hain, Sarah Jane Morris, and Lene Lovich); a Hilly Kristal album called *Mad Mordechai*; an album by Philadelphia synth-and-guitar duo the Reds (for which Thorne is the electronic rhythm section) called *Cry Tomorrow;* and an album by the "oddly compelling microtonal composer and bassoon virtuoso" from Brooklyn, Johnny Reinhard. Thorne is also writing *Music in the Machine,* a book touching upon his many enthusiasms, which will also be available through the deep, ambitious Web site.

—ERIC OLSEN

Albania: "Could This Be Love?," Stiff, 1982.

Almond, Marc: "Adorned and Explored," Mercury, 1995 • "The Idol," Mercury, 1995.

Anderson, Laurie: *Strange Angels,* Warner Bros., 1989.

Berlin Blondes: *Berlin Blondes,* EMI, 1980.

Betty: *Hello Betty,* Betty Rules, 1991 • *Kiss My Sticky* (EP), Betty Rules, 1994.

Blur: *Leisure* (3 tracks), SBK, 1991.

B-Movie: "Remembrance Day," Some Bizarre/Sire, 1982.

Bronski Beat: "It Ain't Necessarily So," London/MCA, 1984 • "Smalltown Boy," London/MCA, 1984 • *The Age of Consent,* London/MCA, 1984, 1997 • "Why?" London/MCA, 1984 • *Hundreds and Thousands,* London/MCA, 1985, 1997 • w/ Marc Almond, "I Feel Love," London/MCA, 1985.

Cale, John: *Honi Soit,* A&M, 1981.

Carmel: *The Drum is Everything,* London, 1984 • *Everybody's Got a Little Soul,* London, 1987.

China Crisis: *Diary of a Hollow Horse,* Virgin/A&M, 1989 • *Collection,* Virgin, 1990.

Communards: "You Are My World," London, 1985 • *Communards,* London/MCA, 1986 • "Disenchanted," London, 1986 • "Don't Leave Me This Way," London/MCA, 1986 • "So Cold the Night," London, 1986 • "You Are My World '87," London, 1987 • "There's More to Love," London, 1988.

Daltrey, Roger: *Parting Should Be Painless,* Atlantic, 1984 • "Walking in My Sleep," Atlantic, 1984 • *Martyrs and Madmen: The Best of Roger Daltrey,* Rhino, 1997.

Furniture: *Food, Sex and Paranoia,* Arista, 1989.

Gryphon: *Treason,* Harvest, 1977.

Hagen, Nina: *Nunsex Monkrock,* CBS, 1982 • *14 Friendly Abductions: The Best Of,* Legacy/Columbia, 1996.

Hain, Kit: *Spirits Walking Out,* Mercury, 1981 • *Looking for You,* Mercury, 1982 • *School for Spies,* Mercury, 1983.

Holly and the Italians: *Holly and the Italians,* Virgin, 1982.

Hollywood Beyond: *If,* Warner Bros., 1987.

Human Sexual Response: *In a Roman Mood,* DFOTM/Passport, 1981.

Information Society: "Going, Going, Gone," Tommy Boy, 1992 • "Peace and Love, Inc.," Tommy Boy, 1992 • *Peace and Love, Inc.,* Tommy Boy, 1992.

Kean, Sherry: *Mixed Emotions,* Capitol, 1983 • *People Talk,* Capitol, 1984.

Metro: *New Love,* EMI, 1979.

Murphy, Peter: *Holy Smoke,* RCA, 1992 • "The Sweetest Drop," RCA, 1992.

Newman, Colin: *A–Z,* Beggars Banquet, 1980.

Reds, The: *Shake Appeal,* Sire Canada, 1984.

Rich Kids: "Rich Kids," EMI, 1977.

Rockats: *Make That Move* (EP), RCA, 1983.

Shirts, The: *The Shirts,* Harvest/Capitol, 1978 • *Street Light Shine,* Harvest/Captol, 1979.

Siouxsie & the Banshees: "Song from the Edge of the World," Wonderland/Polydor, 1987.

Soft Cell: "Bedsitter," Some Bizarre, 1981 • *Non-Stop Erotic Cabaret,* Some Bizarre/ Sire, 1981, 1996 • "Tainted Love/Where Did Our Love Go?," Some Bizarre, 1981 • "It's a Mug's Game," Amnesia, 1982 • *Non-Stop Ecstatic Dancing* (EP), Some Bizarre/Sire, 1982 • "Say Hello, Wave Goodbye," Some Bizarre, 1982 • "Tainted Love," Sire, 1982 • "Torch," Some Bizarre, 1982 • "What," Some Bizarre/Sire, 1982 • "Where the Heart Is," Some Bizarre, 1982 • "Loving You, Hating Me," Some Bizarre/Sire, 1983 • "Numbers," Some Bizarre/Sire, 1983 • *Soul Inside* (EP, 2 tracks), Some Bizarre/Sire, 1983 • *The Art of Falling Apart,* Some Bizarre/Sire, 1983 • *The Singles, 1981–1985,* Some Bizarre/Sire, 1986.

Soft Machine: *Alive and Well in Paris,* Harvest, 1978 • *Land of Cockayne,* EMI, 1981.

Somerville, Jimmy: *The Singles Collection, 1984–1990,* London, 1990.

Strangelove: "Time for the Rest of Your Life," Food, 1994 • *Time for the Rest of Your Life,* Food, 1994.

Telephone: *Telephone,* Marconi, 1977.

'Til Tuesday: "Looking over My Shoulder," Epic, 1985 • "Voices Carry," Epic, 1985 • *Voices Carry,* Epic, 1985 • *Coming Up Close: A Retrospective,* Sony, 1996.

Urban Verbs: *The Urban Verbs,* Warner Bros., 1980.

Wire: "1.2.X.U.," Alex, 1977, 1991 (*Burning Ambitions [A History of Punk]*) • Pink Flag, Harvest, 1977 • *Chairs Missing,* Harvest, 1978 • *154,* Harvest/WB, 1979 • *On Returning (1977–1979),* Restless Retro, 1989.

COLLECTIONS

The Roxy London W.C.2 [Jan.–Apr. '77]), EMI, 1977: the Adverts, "Bored Teenagers" • the Buzzcocks, "Breakdown," "Love Battery" • Eater, "15," "Don't Need It" • Johnny Moped, "Hard Loving Man" • Slaughter and the Dogs, "Boston Babies," "Runaway" • the Unwanted, "Freedom" • Wire, "1.2.X.U.," "Lowdown" • X-Ray Spex, "Oh Bondage! Up Yours!"

Colin Thurston

After engineering classics for Iggy Pop and David Bowie (see entry) in the '70s, Colin Thurston became a first-rank producer in the early '80s with British new wave landmarks from Duran Duran, Talk Talk, Kajagoogoo, Bow Wow Wow, Howard Jones, Magazine, and Human League.

Colin Thurston was born in 1947 to British parents residing in Singapore. He learned to play guitar, played in bands, and became an advertising jingle writer. Thurston's father told him that he wouldn't get anywhere writing jingles in Singapore and that he should relocate to England, which he did in 1972.

Resuming his jingle career in England, Thurston began to put in studio time supervising the recording of his jingles. "I watched a guy sitting at the console doing this magic: he would turn something and the whole sound would change. I thought, 'This is cool—I want to do this.'"

Thurston continued to write jingles, but when a friend told him of an engineer position opening at a small 8-track studio, he jumped at the opportunity; the current engineer was leaving and had to find a replacement before he could go. Thurston went to the studio to meet with the engineer and felt overwhelmed by the equipment. Though Thurston feigned familiarity with it, the engineer was not fooled and said, "You don't know anything about this, do you?" Thurston admitted as much, but the engineer was leaving the next day for Holland and was stuck with Thurston, of whom the engineer then inquired, "Can you learn fast?" The pair spent the whole night going over the equipment and putting a label on each piece as to its function.

After Thurston's all-nighter, a reggae band came in for the morning's first session. Thurston was able to get some sounds the band liked, and instantly, he was an engineer. He moved from studio to studio, working his way up the food chain from 8-track to 16-track to 48-track; along the way he engineered for some early Billy Ocean hits.

Thurston met producer Tony Visconti (see entry) and helped Visconti put together his Good Earth Studios. He also met one of Visconti's most notable clients, David Bowie, who asked Thurston to engineer for his and Mick Ronson's (see entry) co-production of Iggy Pop's *Lust for Life* album, which was recorded at Hansa Studios in Berlin in 1977. Thurston also engineered one of the better-recorded albums of the '70s, Bowie's *Heroes*.

Thurston's first production was Magazine's (led by former Buzzcock Howard DeVoto) *Secondhand Daylight* in 1979, followed by the Human League's *Reproduction* the same year. Thurston also produced Human League's influential single, "I Don't Depend on You" (recorded under the band name "The Men").

One night in 1980, Thurston, plagued by jet lag from a trip to the U.S., was dragged out by his manager to hear a band called Duran Duran (named after a character in the film *Barbarella*). The band's first song, "Girls on Film," snapped Thurston out of his lethargy, and by the end of the night he was itching to produce them. The band was so well rehearsed that when they and Thurston went into the studio for four days to record two songs for a single, they ended up recording five songs, and were well on their way to completing the classic *Duran Duran* (No. 3 U.K.) album. Influenced equally by disco, techno-pop, and hard-rocking Spiders from Mars–period Bowie, Duran Duran created inventive music with great rhythmic drive (generated by thumping bassist John Taylor and drummer Roger Taylor—no relation), searing Mick Ronson–like guitar (from Andy Taylor—no relation either), new wavy textures (from keyboardist Nick Rhodes), and distinctive vocals (from Simon Le Bon).

Side 1 of *Duran Duran* is about as exciting and consistent as new wave gets: a long, moody electro-dance intro leads into "Planet Earth" (No. 12 U.K.), with Rhodes' synth swooping, hissing, and voicing a convincing "sax" solo over a supple Chic-like groove from the rhythm section. "Girls on Film" (No. 5 U.K.), besides being a great song, is the most convincing piece of funk from English white boys on record. After a fashion-camera sound effect intro, a precise but huge-sounding syncopated drum groove rolls in accompanied by spine-snapping bass, quivery synth washes, and Le Bon's lyric about the vicious glamour of supermodeling (three of the Duranies later married fashion models). "Is There

Anyone out There?" keys on Taylor's punchy guitar and another fine melody, and "Careless Memories" charges through on an ominous techno beat and Le Bon's toughest singing.

The band's second album, *Rio* (No. 2 U.K.), recorded shortly after the debut, is another superbly produced new wave gem. *Rio* displays a wide sonic palette: the familiar rocking alterna-disco of the title track (No. 14), "Hungry Like the Wolf" (No. 3), "My Own Way" (No. 14 U.K.), and "Hold Back the Rain"; a jazz-and-jangle sound of slippery fretless bass and guitar arpeggios on "Lonely in Your Nightmare"; angular Gang of Four–type punk-funk muscle on "New Religion"; and a lush, engulfing wall-of-synths cushion on the alterna-ballad "Save a Prayer" (No. 2 U.K.).

Together, the first two Duran Duran albums sold over 3 million copies in the U.S. alone, verified that a band could be dancey and ballsy at the same time, and solidified the commercial appeal of new wave at a critical juncture in the music's development. In addition, the Duranies helped establish the power of music video (and its primary outlet MTV) as a marketing tool through a series of enormously popular clips featuring the fashionable, photogenic band. Duran Duran moved on to other producers after *Rio*, and while they have had some bright moments since, they have never again put together an album that could hold the jockstrap of *Duran Duran* or *Rio*—a testament to Thurston's production acumen.

Still in 1982, Thurston produced Talk Talk's first album, *The Party's Over*, featuring another thumping alterna-disco anthem, the conveniently named "Talk Talk." Thurston then veered in the direction of pure blue-eyed Brit soul for Kajagoogoo's *White Feathers* (No. 5 U.K.) album, which includes their frothy white-chocolate classic "Too Shy" (No. 1 U.K.). "Shy" was scheduled to be the B-side of another single until Thurston plucked it from the jaws of obscurity and set it on the path to No. 1. Thurston also produced alterna-pop singer/songwriter Howard Jones' first hit, "New Song" (No. 27), in 1984.

In the late '80s and '90s, Thurston produced and engineered successful German albums for Camouflage, Zette, Sally Oldfield, 6 Was 9, and Thomas Barquee, as well as Canadian albums for Alta Moda and Neo A4. Along the way Thurston has picked up a couple of truths for recording artists: If you want to convey happiness through a song, smile when you sing. And in order to up the energy level of any recording session, play to a live audience, even if that audience is in your head. —Eric Olsen

Books: *Expertise,* Logo, 1980.

Bow Wow Wow: *I Want Candy* (2 tracks), RCA, 1981 • *See Jungle! See Jungle!,* One Way, 1981, 1997 • *Girl Bites Dog,* EMI, 1993 • *The Best of Bow Wow Wow,* RCA, 1996.

Camouflage: "Heaven (I Want You)," Atlantic, 1991 • *Meanwhile,* Atlantic, 1991 • "This Day," Atlantic, 1991.

Carpettes: *Fight Amongst Yourselves,* Beggars Banquet, 1980.

Duran Duran: "Careless Memories," EMI, 1981 • *Duran Duran,* Harvest, 1981 • "Girls on Film," Harvest, 1981 • "My Own Way," EMI, 1981 • "Planet Earth," Harvest, 1981 • *Carnival* (EP), Capitol, 1982 • "Hungry Like the Wolf," Capitol, 1982 • "Rio," Capitol, 1982 • *Rio,* Harvest, 1982 • "Save a Prayer," Capitol, 1985 • *Decade,* Capitol, 1989.

Flip: *Flip,* Private, 1985.

Human League: *Reproduction,* Virgin, 1979.

Interview: *Big Oceans,* Virgin, 1979.

Japp, Philip: *Philip Japp,* A&M, 1983.

Jones, Howard: *Human's Lib* (1 track), EMI, 1984 • "New Song," EMI, 1984 • *The Best Of,* Elektra, 1993.

Kaja: *Extra Play,* EMI America, 1985 • "Turn Your Back on Me," EMI America, 1985.

Kajagoogoo: "Hang on Now," EMI America, 1983 • "Too Shy," EMI, 1983, 1993 (*Living in Oblivion: The 80s Greatest Hits,* Vol. 1) • *White Feathers,* One Way, 1983, 1994 • *Islands,* EMI, 1984.

Kajagoogoo/Limahl: *Too Shy—The Singles and More,* Gold Rush, 1996.

Kissing the Pink: *Naked,* Atlantic, 1983.

Landscape: "European Man," RCA, 1981 (*Blits*).

Loz Netto: *Bzar,* 21 Records, 1982 • *Loz Netto,* 21 Records, 1983.

Magazine: *Secondhand Daylight,* Virgin, 1979 • *Rays and Hail,* Virgin, 1987 • *Scree (Rarities, 1978–1981),* Blue Plate, 1991.

Men, The: "I Don't Depend on You," Virgin, 1979.

Moon, Eve: *Eve Moon,* Capitol, 1981.

Numan, Gary: *The Fury,* Numa, 1985.

Only Ones: *Baby's Got a Gun,* CBS, 1980.

Our Daughter's Wedding: *Digital Cowboy* (EP), EMI America, 1981.

Ross, Alan: *Are You Free This Saturday,* Ebony, 1977.

Secret Affair: *Business As Usual* (2 tracks), I-Spy, 1982.

Talk Talk: "Talk Talk," EMI, 1982, 1993 (*Living in Oblivion: The 80s Greatest Hits,* Vol. 1) • *The Party's Over,* EMI/EMI-America, 1982 • *The Very Best Of,* EMI, 1990.

David Tickle

Ranging far and wide geographically and stylistically through '80s and '90s new wave, pop, and rock, David Tickle has engineered or mixed for such diverse stars as (Americans) Blondie, Jackson Browne, Prince (see entry) and (the U.K.'s) Genesis, Police, Rod Stewart, and U2. He has also produced or co-produced for (Americans) Belinda Carlisle, 4 Non Blondes, Wire Train, (Australian/New Zealanders) Divinyls, Split Enz, Swingers, (Canadians) Gowan, Platinum Blonde, Red Rider, (the U.K.'s) Adam Ant, Joan Armatrading, Joe Cocker, and the Vapors.

Englishman David Tickle's ambition from the age of 7 was to be a film director. At 14 in 1974, he decided that record production was his calling and chose engineering as "the quickest way into it." At 17 Tickle got his foot in the door in a studio in Manchester, and within three months he was engineering. He produced some demos for a band and went down to London to play them for various record companies, including Ringo Starr's Ringo Records. Starr was building a new studio at the time and liked Tickle enough to make him chief engineer when Startling Studio was finished.

In 1978 Tickle found an impressive band of New Zealanders and Australians residing in England and took them into the studio to make a demo. The band recorded two songs with Tickle, then returned to Australia. Meanwhile, Tickle saw an ad in the British musicians' publication *Music Week* that read: "Best engineer in England required. Money no object. Inquire at this phone number."

Tickle, brimming with confidence, called, then met with the man who had placed the ad, producer/songwriter Mike Chapman (see entry). Chapman was starting Dreamland Records and looking for a producer trainee. Tickle's first project with Chapman was to help mix Blondie's classic *Parallel Lines* in early 1978. (Dreamland subsequently put out records in the early '80s by Lita Ford, Suzi Quatro, Michael DesBarres, and others.)

Next Tickle accompanied Chapman to Kentucky, where Chapman instructed him in the dark arts of songwriting and arranging as Chapman wrote and produced the No. 1 hit "Kiss You All Over" for American pop-rockers (soon to be country stars) Exile. "Mike was a tremendous teacher," says Tickle.

By 1979 Chapman was ready to launch Dreamland. Although Chapman was interested in signing Split Enz—the band Tickle had demoed the year before—he decided not to because, according to Tickle, Chapman wanted to keep Tickle as his assistant and not send him off to produce on his own. Tickle became angry and left, stopping by his attorney's office in New York on the way back to England from Kentucky. There, Tickle found out that the demo he had cut the year before for Split Enz—"I See Red," a smoking power-pop stomper—had been released as a single and was a Top 10 hit in Australia.

Two weeks later, Tickle was in Australia producing his first album, Split Enz' poppy new wave great, *True Colours*. Split Enz—led by the brothers Tim and Neil Finn (later of Crowded House)—had gone from an extravagantly eccentric performance-art troupe (prone to vertiginous, multihued coifs) in the early '70s to a relatively straight new wave unit by 1979. Neil's "I Got You" (No. 12 U.K.)—a hypnotic neo-'60s classic—prefigures his accessible Crowded House sound, as does his "Missing Person." Tim's incurably twisted pop is the more difficult, but ultimately more endearing and enduring: "Shark Attack"—with hilariously cheesy synth churning-water sounds from Eddie Rayner—is similar in energy and sensibility to his "I See Red." "I Hope I Never" finds Tim in his upper register on a beautiful, dramatic piano-and-strings ballad.

Waiata, the follow-up, is almost as fine. Tim's "Hard Act to Follow" combines his trademark melodic gymnastics with the breakneck speed of "Red" to yield the band's best up-tempo song. His "I Don't Wanna Dance" and "Clumsy" also stand out, as do Neil's "History Never Repeats" and "One Step Ahead."

Tickle was still only 21 when *Waiata* came out and he found American record companies reluctant to entrust such a young man with production responsibilities, so he worked in Australia (Swingers), England (Department S, the Vapors), and Canada (Gowan, Platinum Blonde, Red Rider) into the mid-'80s.

Tickle made his American debut in 1984 when he was hired by Prince to mix singles from *Purple Rain,* one of the key albums of the '80s. Prince called Tickle "the sixth member of the Revolution," and Tickle mixed tracks for *Around the World in a Day* and *Parade,* as well as doing the sound design for the *Purple Rain* tour and studio design for Prince's Paisley Park facility. Though Tickle did not receive promised co-production credits, he was at least well paid for his efforts.

Tickle did another superstar session for which he didn't receive a production credit: he "recorded and mixed" two songs—"God Part 2" and "All I Want Is You"—for U2's *Rattle and Hum* (produced by Jimmy Iovine; see entry) in 1987. "U2 were looking for the next evolution of their sound. For 'God Part 2' they came in

to L.A.'s Ocean Way Studios two hours a day for four days, and jammed around a single theme. No one wore headphones or concerned themselves with the recording process, they just jammed with each other and a drum machine. I captured all of this material, spent another three or four days sifting through it, and extracted three minutes of it for the final song. They used the studio—the medium—as a writing tool for the first time. They also learned to play against drum loops and drum machines, and they used that a lot on their next album, *Achtung Baby.*"

Tickle had a surprise smash with Divinyls' self-titled album (No. 15) in 1990. The duo of singer Christina Amphlett and guitarist Mark McEntee had made previous attempts to break into the American market (see Mark Opitz entry), but it took Tickle's tight-but-resonant production and the monster single "I Touch Myself" (No. 4)—a sly bit of new wave autoerotica—to push the band into the U.S. gold.

Pulling another rabbit out of his hat, Tickle turned an unknown San Francisco band, 4 Non Blondes, into a platinum act when he produced their 1993 album *Bigger, Better, Faster, More!* (No. 13). The three-woman, one-man, rootsy alterna-rock band led by singer/songwriter Linda Perry (reminiscent of Concrete Blonde's Johnette Napolitano), astonished the business with their showing, especially the single "What's Up" (No. 14), a brilliantly catchy (if philosophically vague) meditation on the meaning of life at 25.

Tickle had to join the magician's union after his third trick of the decade: guiding Adam Ant into a third musical incarnation (punk, new romantic, adult alternative crooner) at a time when Ant had been written off as not only dead but decomposed. Recorded with a fine band, including Ant mainstay Marco Pirroni and Morrissey band member Boz Boorer on guitars, *Wonderful* turns down the energy and volume to reveal a thoughtful, mature man with a knack for a gentle tune. The title track reached into the Top 25 in the U.K., the Top 40 in the U.S., and became a modern rock and adult alternative radio smash here.

Besides running his own 32-track digital recording studio in Calabasas, California, Tickle has returned his attention to his first love, film, and is writing screenplays. For Tickle, music and film are synergistic tools toward a greater calling. "My focus as a 21st-century man is to bring enlightenment to the masses through the use of multimedia, always under the guise of entertainment," he says. This enlightenment will come through the sharing of "feelings and emotions," because "feelings and emotions are the closest thing to spirit." —Eric Olsen

Ant, Adam: "Wonderful," Capitol, 1995 • *Wonderful*, Capitol, 1995.

Armatrading, Joan: *What's Inside*, RCA, 1995.

Bentall, Barney, and the Legendary Hearts: *Barney Bentall and the Legendary Hearts*, Columbia, 1988.

Carlisle, Belinda: *A Woman and a Man*, ARK 21, 1997.

Childs, Toni: "Don't Walk Away," A&M, 1988 • *Union*, A&M, 1988.

Cocker, Joe: "Sorry Seems to Be the Hardest Word," Polydor, 1991 (*Two Rooms: Songs of Elton and Bernie Taupin*) • *Night Calls*, Gold Rush, 1992, 1996 • *Best Of*, Capitol, 1993 • *Long Voyage Home: The Silver Anniversay Collection*, A&M, 1995.

Department S: *Is Vik There*, Stiff, 1981.

Divinyls: *Divinyls*, Virgin, 1990 • "I Touch Myself," Virgin, 1990.

4 Non Blondes: *Bigger, Better, Faster, More!*, Interscope, 1992 • "What's Up," Interscope, 1993.

Gowan: *Strange Animal*, Columbia, 1985 • *Great Dirty World*, Columbia, 1987.

Hanoi Rocks: *Two Steps from the Move*, Epic, 1984.

Johnson, Eric: *Tones*, Capitol, 1986.

Platinum Blonde: *Standing in the Dark*, Epic, 1983.

Red Rider: *Neruda*, Capitol, 1983 • *Breaking Curfew*, Capitol, 1984.

Shaking Family: *Dreaming in Detail*, Elektra, 1990.

Shipley, Ellen: *Breaking Through the Ice Age*, RCA, 1980.

Spence, Judson: *Judson Spence*, Atlantic, 1988 • "Yeah, Yeah, Yeah," Atlantic, 1988.

Split Enz: *Frenzy*, A&M, 1979, 1982 • "I See Red," Mushroom, 1979 • "I Got You," A&M, 1980 • *True Colours*, A&M, 1980 • *Waiata*, A&M, 1981 • *Enz of an Era*, Mushroom, 1983 • *Collection, 1973–1984*, Concept, 1986 • *History Never Repeats: The Best Of*, A&M, 1987 • *Best Of*, Chrysalis, 1994 • *Spellbound*, Mushroom, 1997.

Swingers: *Practical Jokers*, Mushroom, 1981 • *Counting the Beat*, Backstreet, 1982 • "Starstruck," Mushroom, 1982.

Trudell, John: *AKA Grafitti Man*, Rykodisc, 1992.

Vapors, The: *Magnets*, United Artists, 1981.

Wire Train: *Wire Train*, MCA, 1990.

COLLECTIONS

Legend soundtrack, MCA, 1986.

Three O'Clock High soundtrack, Atlantic, 1987.

Wharton Tiers

New York engineer/producer/drummer/guitarist Wharton Tiers has been at the heart of the East Coast experimental and indie rock scene for over 15 years. Since his Fun City recording studio opened in 1982, Tiers has recorded over 100 albums, producing adventuresome milestones of guitar-based noise and thunder by Sonic Youth, Glenn Branca, Dinosaur Jr., Surgery, Unsane, Helmet, and Quicksand, in addition to the warped pop of Unrest.

Wharton Tiers was born in Philadelphia in 1953 and had an early fascination with tape recorders—his father sold them. A drummer in his childhood, Tiers played in high school rock bands, then attended Villanova University. Upon graduation with a degree in English in 1976, he moved to New York and played drums and percussion with performance artist Laurie Anderson, a band called Theoretical Girls (with guitarist/composer Glenn Branca), and many others.

Tiers started Fun City studio primarily to record his own music, but to defray some of the cost, he opened up for business. His first client was Sonic Youth in 1983. In this early version of Sonic Youth, guitarists Thurston Moore and Lee Renaldo strangled dissonant cries from their oddly tuned instruments while bassist Kim Gordon and drummer Bob Bert held down some semblance of a beat; Moore or Gordon periodically chanted and sang. The combined EP *Confusion Is Sex* and *Kill Yr. Idols* display this activity to arresting effect; while always seeming on the verge of centrifugal derangement, some element in the mix—now Gordon's maniacal rhythmic chant, now the drums, now frantic guitar chording—always holds it together.

Tiers has worked with Sonic Youth on and off ever since; he and Don Fleming (see entry) and the band recently co-produced their 1998 release *A Thousand Leaves*. "It's fun working with people now and again over time because you get a real sense of how far they have come artistically and how they have progressed as musicians," says Tiers. While hardly less experimental, Sonic Youth is certainly smoother than it was 15 years ago.

Tiers' next major accomplishment came in the form of the exceptionally influential proto-grunge of Dinosaur Jr. J Mascis's wah-wahed and fuzzed guitar assault on fairly straightforward rock songs returned the guitar hero to a position of underground coolness; his laconic, pitch-challenged vocals could turn even an AOR cliché like Peter Frampton's "Show Me the Way" into something hip. *Fossils,* released in 1991, assembles the band's singles from 1985 through 1988. Tiers' productions in the collection include "Show Me the Way" and two other songs from *You're Living All Over Me,* in addition to the band's astonishing rendition of the Cure's "Just Like Heaven." Dino's version begins with surprising fidelity to the goth-gloom classic original, but as the band hits the refrain, an anvil chorus shouts in metallic unison while Mascis's guitar pounds out barbed-wire power chords, startling poor Robert Smith out of his mascara. The ending is no less shocking and abrupt.

Tiers met wholesome-looking guitarist Page Hamilton playing with Glenn Branca, but there is nothing wholesome about the music of Helmet: a precision-tooled aural assault of shouted and barked vocals, massively powerful guitar ripped from the very bowels of Hamilton's amplifier, and stop-start rhythms meant to dislocate and disturb. The band breaks periodically from the abrupt stops and, through the repetition of sledge-hammer riffs, builds momentum to a fever pitch before breaking down again. All of this requires exceptional musicianship and is perversely addicting.

Strap It On from 1990 established the parameters of the band's attack, but the gold *Meantime* from 1992 took them to another quantum level of precision, sonic clarity, and power; it ranks with Nirvana's *Nevermind* among the greatest *hard* rock albums of the decade. "Unsung," which cautions against the easy way out of suicide, builds to such an unbearable level of intensity that I threw up the first time I heard it. This is a good thing.

For Tiers 1992 was a smokin' good year as he also produced tracks for Cop Shoot Cop's great industrial-noise core album *Consumer Revolt,* Branca's *Symphony #2,* and Biohazard's *Urban Discipline,* among others.

Tiers composes and writes in many different styles, including solo piano, synth-based instrumentals, opera, and symphonic works. The Wharton Tiers Ensemble, a unit featuring multiple guitar players (Paul Johnson, Dave Roby, John Tanzer, R.B. Korbet, and Tiers), released an album of instrumentals, *Brighter Than Life,* in 1996. "Sheet Metal Workers" is a roiling rocker that nicely evokes the aural behavior of the title characters. "Heat Seeker" has a tom-tom-pounding neo-surf feel, while "Lasmo" is a killer noise-rock jam. —ERIC OLSEN

Beme Seed: *Purify,* Number Six, 1992.
Biohazard: *Urban Discipline,* Roadrunner, 1992.
Branca, Glenn: *Symphony #6 (Devil Choirs at the Gates of Heaven),* Atavistic, 1989, 1993 • *Symphony #2 (The Peak of the Sacred),* Atavistic, 1992 • *Symphony #8 and #10 (The Mystery),* Atavistic, 1994.
Can: *Sacrilege: The Remixes,* Mute, 1997.

Combine: *The History of American Rock and Roll,* Caroline, 1996.
Cop Shoot Cop: *Consumer Revolt* (2 tracks), Big Cat, 1992.
Das Damen: *Jupiter Eye,* SST, 1987 • *Triskaidekaphobe,* SST, 1988.
Dentists, The: *Deep Six,* EastWest, 1995.
Dinosaur Jr.: *You're Living All Over Me,* SST, 1987 • *Fossils* (4 tracks), SST, 1991.
Dustdevils: *Struggling, Electric and Chemical,* Matador, 1990.
Eggs: *Bruiser,* Teen Beat, 1992.
Helmet: *Strap It On,* Amphetamine Reptile, 1990 • *Meantime,* Interscope, 1992 • "Distracted," Rykodisc, 1993 (*Born to Choose*).
Honeymoon Killers: *Sing Sing (1984–1994),* Sympathy for the Record Industry, 1997.
Jenifer Convertible: *Wanna Drag,* Beloved, 1997.
Juicy: *Olive Juicy,* Slow River, 1996.
Lunachicks: *Babysitters on Acid,* Blast First, 1990.
Of Cabbages and Kings: *Basic Pain, Basic Pleasure,* Triple X, 1990 • *Never Too Late,* Triple X, 1991 • *Hunter's Moon,* Triple X, 1992.
Quicksand: *Manic Compression,* Island, 1995.
Rust: *Rust* (EP), Atlantic, 1994.
Sonic Youth: *Confusion Is Sex/Kill Yr. Idols,* DGC, 1983, 1995 • "Bee-Bee's Song," Geffen, 1997 (*Suburbia* soundtrack) • "Sunday," Geffen, 1997 (*Suburbia* soundtrack) • "Tabla in Suburbia," Geffen, 1997 (*Suburbia* soundtrack) • *A Thousand Leaves,* DGC, 1998.
Surgery: *Nationwide,* Amphetamine Reptile, 1990.
Tiers, Wharton: *Brighter Than Life,* Atavistic, 1996.
Tulips: *Buxom* (2 tracks), Ear, 1992.
Unrest: *Isabel Bishop* (EP), 4 A.D., 1993 • *Fuck Pussy Galore and All Her Friends,* Matador, 1994.
Unsane: *Unsane,* Matador, 1991.
Upsidedown Cross: *Evilution,* Taang!, 1993.
Velvet Monkeys: *Rake,* Rough Trade, 1990.

Russ Titelman

Russ Titelman is known for the broad range of artists he has worked with, including Steve Winwood, Randy Newman, James Taylor, Eric Clapton, George Benson, Paul Simon (see entry), Ladysmith Black Mambazo, Rufus, Rickie Lee Jones, and Ry Cooder.

Titelman (born August 16, 1944, in Los Angeles) began as a guitarist and singer on demos and records for Phil Spector (see entry), including releases with the Spectors Three and the Paris Sisters. In the early '60s,

are utterly transparent; the producer's contributions are so well woven into the songs and performances it is impossible to single out a list of devices or gimmicks that characterize their work.

Titelman's philosophy is driven by a desire to capture each artist's unique musicality. "The most important thing a producer can do," he says, "is to get the personality of the artist on tape." To accomplish this, Titelman assumes different roles for different artists. For Steve Winwood's *Back in the High Life* (No. 3), the pair spent a week of 10-hour days in heavy preproduction, editing tape, trying out ideas, and putting the songs together. Conversely, Randy Newman would typically enter a project with the whole album written and arranged beforehand.

With the huge and unexpected success of Eric Clapton's *Unplugged* (No. 1) Titelman (perhaps unwittingly) ushered in an entire era of *MTV Unplugged* albums.
—Daniel J. Levitin

Titelman was a staff writer for Don Kirshner, working with the likes of Gerry Goffin and Carole King. In 1965 he played guitar for the *Shindig* television show, and then worked as a session guitarist. While working together on the film *Performance*, he and Jack Nitzsche (see entry) wrote "Gone Dead Train," which was sung and conducted by Randy Newman. Newman, Cooder, Lowell George, and Titelman played the music for the movie, and thus began Titelman's long associations with these artists. Titelman's first production was the debut album for Lowell George's band Little Feat in '70, whom he had brought to Warner Bros. Shortly after, he was hired as an A&R executive there, a position that he held until 1997.

Titelman's co-productions with Lenny Waronker (see entry) for Ry Cooder (*Paradise and Lunch*) and James Taylor (*Gorilla*, No. 6; *In the Pocket*, No. 16) best exemplify his unique contributions. It is maddeningly difficult to get background vocals to sound big without crowding out the lead vocal and lead instruments. Jeff Lynne (see entry), for example, resorts to giving them a narrow-band EQ to squeeze them in. But one trademark of the Titelman-Waronker style is that a lot of music is packed into the mix without crowding. Part of this is engineering, but most of it is arrangement, giving parts space to breathe. These three albums are textbook examples of how to do it right—and make it sound easy. The production techniques they use on the albums

Allman Brothers Band: *Dreams*, Polydor, 1989.

Allman, Gregg: *Playin' Up a Storm*, Capricorn, 1977 • *One More Try: An Anthology*, PolyGram, 1997.

Austin, Patti: *Getting Away with Murder*, Qwest, 1985 • "Getting Away with Murder," Qwest, 1986.

Bee Gees: "Alone," Polydor, 1997 • *Still Waters*, Polydor, 1997.

Benson, George: "20/20," Warner Bros., 1984 • *20/20*, Warner Bros., 1985 • "I Just Wanna Hang Around You," Warner Bros., 1985 • "New Day," Warner Bros., 1985.

Clapton, Eric: *Journeyman*, Reprise, 1989 • "Bad Love," Duck/Reprise, 1990 • *24 Nights: Live from Albert Hall*, Reprise, 1991 • "Layla," Duck/Reprise, 1992 • *Rush* soundtrack, Warner Bros., 1992 • "Tears in Heaven," Duck/Reprise, 1992 • *Unplugged*, Duck/Reprise, 1992 • *From the Cradle*, Duck/Reprise, 1994.

Cole, Jude: *Jude Cole*, Reprise, 1987.

Cooder, Ry: *Chicken Skin Music*, Reprise, 1976, 1988 • *Paradise and Lunch*, Reprise, 1974.

Crackin': *The Making of a Dream*, Warner Bros., 1977.

Credibility Gap: *A Great Gift Idea*, Reprise, 1973.

Dean, James: *James Dean: Original Soundtrack Excerpts*, Warner Bros., 1975.

Dion: *Suite for Late Summer*, Warner Bros., 1972.

Graham Central Station: *Graham Central Station*, Ol' Skool, 1974, 1996 • *The Best Of*, Vol. 1, Warner Bros., 1996.

Harrison, George: *George Harrison*, Dark Horse, 1979 • *Best of Dark Horse, 1976–1989*, Dark Horse, 1989.

Jones, Rickie Lee: "Chuck E's in Love," Warner Bros., 1979 • *Rickie Lee Jones*, Warner Bros., 1979 • *Pirates*, Warner Bros., 1981 • *Naked Songs Live and Acoustic*, Reprise, 1995.

Khan, Chaka: "(Krush Groove) Can't Stop the Street," Warner Bros., 1985 • "Tight Fit," Warner Bros., 1986 •

C.K., Warner Bros., 1988 • "It's My Party," Warner Bros., 1988 • "Baby Me," Warner Bros., 1989 • *Life Is a Dance (The Remix Project),* Warner Bros., 1989 • *Epiphany: The Best of Chaka Khan,* Vol. 2, Reprise, 1996 • *See also* Rufus and Chaka Khan.

LaBounty, Bill: *Bill LaBounty,* Warner Bros., 1981.

Ladysmith Black Mambazo: *Journey of Dreams,* Warner Bros., 1988.

Lightfoot, Gordon: *Dream Street Rosie,* Warner Bros., 1980 • *Gord's Gold,* Vol. 2, Warner Bros., 1988.

Little Feat: *Hoy-Hoy,* Warner Bros., 1981, 1990 • *Little Feat,* Warner Bros., 1970.

Loveinreverse: "Blueprint for a Possible Song," Reprise, 1996 • "I Inject You," Reprise, 1996 • "I Was Here," Reprise, 1996 • *I Was Dog,* Reprise, 1996 • "I'm a Contradiction," Reprise, 1996.

Makeba, Miriam: *Sangoma,* Warner Bros., 1988.

McDonald, Michael: *Blink of an Eye,* Reprise, 1993.

McVie, Christine: *Christine McVie,* Warner Bros., 1984 • "Get a Hold on Me," Warner Bros., 1984.

Mike and the Mechanics: *Word of Mouth,* Atlantic, 1991.

Mitchell, Adam: *Redhead in Trouble,* Warner Bros., 1979.

Muldaur, Jenni: *Jenni Muldaur,* Reprise, 1992.

Nascimento, Milton: *Angelus,* Warner Bros., 1994 • *Nascimento,* Warner Bros., 1997.

Newman, Randy: *Live,* Reprise, 1971 • *Sail Away,* Reprise, 1972 • *Good Old Boys,* Warner Bros., 1974 • *Little Criminals,* Warner Bros., 1977 • "Short People," Warner Bros., 1977 • *Born Again,* Warner Bros., 1979 • *Ragtime,* Elektra, 1981 • *Trouble in Paradise,* Warner Bros., 1983.

Parsons, Gene: *Kindling,* Warner Bros., 1974 • *The Kindling Collection,* Sierra, 1994.

Rufus and Chaka Khan: "Ain't Nobody," Warner Bros., 1983 • *Live-Stompin' at the Savoy,* Warner Bros., 1983 • "Ain't Nobody," Polydor, 1984 (*Breakin'* soundtrack).

Sanborn, David: *Straight from the Heart,* Warner Bros., 1984.

Sargent, Laurie: "Without Letting Go," Reprise, 1996 (*Party of Five* soundtrack) • *Heads and Tales,* Reprise, 1997.

Simon, Paul: "Allergies," Warner Bros., 1983 • *Hearts and Bones,* Warner Bros., 1983 • *Negotiations and Love Songs (1971–1986),* Warner Bros., 1988 • *Paul Simon, 1964–1993,* Warner Bros., 1993.

Snow, Phoebe: *Something Real,* Elektra, 1989.

Taylor, James: *Greatest Hits,* Warner Bros., 1976, 1988 • *Gorilla,* Warner Bros., 1975 • "How Sweet It Is (to Be Loved by You)," Warner Bros., 1975 • *In the Pocket,* Warner Bros., 1976.

Waits, Tom: "Rainbow Sleeve," Warner Bros., 1980, 1983 (*The King of Comedy* soundtrack).

Walden, Narada Michael: *Ecstasy's Dance: The Best Of,* Rhino, 1996.

Wilson, Brian: *Brian Wilson,* Sire/Reprise, 1988.

Winwood, Steve: "Back in the High Life," Island, 1986 • *Back in the High Life Again,* Island, 1986 • "Freedom Overspill," Island, 1986 • "Higher Love," Island, 1986 • *Chronicles,* Island, 1987 • "The Finer Things," Island, 1987 • *Finer Things,* Island, 1995.

Womack and Womack: *Transformation to the House of Zekkariyas,* Warner Bros., 1993.

COLLECTIONS

The Brill Building Sound: Singers and Songwriters Who Rocked the 60's, Era, 1993.

Allen Toussaint

Allen Toussaint, an exceptional pianist and arranger in the '50s, was the most important producer and songwriter of New Orleans R&B and rock 'n' roll of the '60s. He produced and wrote classic, gently funky rhythm numbers and timeless ballads for Lee Dorsey, Barbara George, Clarence "Frogman" Henry, Jesse Hill, Ernie K-Doe, Chris Kenner, the Meters, Aaron Neville, the Showmen, Benny Spellman, and Irma Thomas.

Toussaint, along with partner Marshall Sehorn, built the Sea-Saint recording studios in the '70s—Paul Simon and Paul McCartney (see entries) both recorded there—and continued to produce excellent records for Chocolate Milk, Dr. John, Albert King, Labelle, the Wild Tchoupitoulas (aka the Meters and the Neville Brothers), himself, and many others.

In the '90s Toussaint formed a new label, NYNO, to produce and release indigenous New Orleans music (including his own first album in nearly 20 years), and in 1998 he was elected to the Rock and Roll Hall of Fame. In addition to those he has produced, Toussaint has written songs covered by Herb Alpert and the Tijuana Brass, Glen Campbell ("Southern Nights"), Al Hirt, Little Feat, Robert Palmer, the Pointer Sisters ("Yes We Can Can"), Bonnie Raitt, Rolling Stones, Boz Scaggs, and countless others.

Allen Toussaint was born January 14, 1938, in the Gert Town neighborhood of New Orleans. "It was the piano itself that prompted me to take up music. When I was a small child my Aunt Ethlyn sent an upright piano to our house for my sister, and when I touched the keys I was delighted. My sister started taking lessons, and when I would pick out little melodies, she would tell me what notes they were," says Toussaint in his soothing Crescent City tones.

"I loved the piano and played every day, learning to play by ear listening to records and the radio. The piano players I loved best were Professor Longhair, Lloyd Glenn, Albert Ammons, and Ray Charles. I listened to boogie-woogie, hillbilly, and my mother loved classical so I heard a lot of that. Our piano was out of tune by a half-tone, so I learned Grieg's *Piano Concerto in A minor*, in B flat," he chuckles.

When he was 13, Toussaint joined a neighborhood band called the Flamingos (not the doo-wop group of the same name) and began to play at dances and socials. A few years later the Flamingos were playing in "joints . . . maybe places we shouldn't have been playing," he says. He was also arranging for the band—pulling horn parts off records—and writing. By 17 Toussaint was playing sessions for Smiley Lewis at Cosimo Matassa's legendary J&M Studio (see Bumps Blackwell entry), and playing the Dew Drop Inn with Earl King.

Fats Domino's producer Dave Bartholomew (see entry) heard Toussaint at the Dew Drop and asked him to play a "Domino-like" piano part for a Domino session that the Fatman himself would not be attending. Domino dubbed the vocals to "I Want You to Know" sometime later, and it became a hit in late 1957. After that, Toussaint says, "people considered me someone to be reckoned with."

After Toussaint was hired by an RCA producer to accompany several auditioning artists, the producer realized that Toussaint was the real talent. He recorded *The Wild Sound of New Orleans* (under the name "Al Tousan") in just two days in 1958, and although the album didn't sell, one song from it, "Java," became an enormous hit for Al Hirt a few years later.

When Joe Banashak started his Minit label in early 1960, Toussaint was again hired to accompany an open audition. In one amazing night Minit signed Jessie Hill, Benny Spellman, Irma Thomas, and Aaron Neville to join Ernie K-Doe on the fledgling label's roster. Toussaint, at 22, became the creative force behind the label: arranging, producing, playing on, and writing a staggering number of regional and national hits from 1960 until he was drafted into the army in 1963.

Toussaint's collective of singers backed each other, and his band (Chuck Badie on bass, James Black on drums, Roy Montrell on guitar, Nat Perrilliat and Clarence Ford on saxes, along with Toussaint on piano and various other hornmen) laid down a consistent, syncopated groove that struck a balance between big-city slick and down-home grit.

Toussaint's first hit at Minit was Jesse Hill's outlandish "Ooh-Poo-Pah-Doo," a shout-type, call-and-response R&B rocker that followed a butt-wiggling groove to No. 28. In 1961 there was an explosion of Toussaint creativity: Clarence "Frogman" Henry delivered an open-arms pop vocal over Toussaint's brassy big band–style arrangement on "But I Do" (No. 4), followed a couple months later by the similar "You Always Hurt the One You Love" (No. 12), with Toussaint measuring out the triplets on the piano.

Ernie K-Doe (Kador) helped arrange the Toussaint-penned "Mother-in-Law" into a hook-happy smash hung on Benny Spellman's bass vocal ("mo-other-in-law") lead-in to each verse line, a swinging mid-tempo Big Easy beat, clever domestic-complaint lyrics, and a jaunty little Professor Longhair/Fats Domino piano solo from Toussaint. Not only was the song K-Doe's, Toussaint's, and Minit's first chart-topper; it was the first No. 1 *ever* to be recorded in New Orleans (neither Fats Domino nor Little Richard ever had a No. 1).

Still in 1961, Toussaint hit the Top 10 three more times with Chris Kenner's R&B standard "I Like It Like That" (No. 2), Barbara George's soulful "I Know (You Don't Love Me No More)" (No. 3), and the great Lee Dorsey's first national hit, "Ya Ya" (No. 7)—a snappy nonsense tune reminiscent of Huey "Piano" Smith's "Don't You Just Know It."

Dorsey became Toussaint's most prolific hitmaker; his classic R&B voice a perfect vehicle for some of Toussaint's best songwriting: the rocking, guitar-based "Ride Your Pony"; the bluesy "Get Out of My Life Woman"; the genuine Southern soul of "Holy Cow"; the brilliant, syncopated "Working in a Coal Mine" (No. 8), where the black-collar complaint of the lyrics is subverted by Dorsey's cheerful reading and the remarkable bass hammer-and-chisel rhythm; and Dorsey's final hit, 1969's spare, aptly titled "Everything I Do Gonh Be Funky."

When the draft ended Toussaint's run in 1963, he formed a band at Fort Hood, Texas, that first recorded his "Whipped Cream" (the title track of a Tijuana Brass No. 1 album, and later the theme song of the *Dating Game*).

Toussaint remembers his Minit days fondly. As he told authors Grace Lichtenstein and Laura Dankner in their excellent *Musical Gumbo: The Music of New Orleans*: "It was the real thing. . . . When we were recording, sometimes we'd make a 'human fade'—we would just play softer and softer. We didn't have any overdubbing. When one guy took a solo, the other guys would stand up and snap their fingers and dance around the studio. We were having a wonderful time."

When Toussaint returned to the Big Easy in 1965 he began another roll: in addition to the Dorsey hits, he produced Aaron Neville's quavery, melismatic classic,

"Tell It Like It Is" (No. 2) and soul diva Betty Harris's "Nearer to You." His new house band—known in the '50s as the Hawketts—was Art Neville on keyboards, Ziggy Modeliste on drums, George Porter on bass, and Leo Nocentelli on guitar, regrouped in 1968 as the Meters. New Orleans' answer to Memphis's Booker T. and the MGs (see Booker T. Jones and Steve Cropper entries)—another versatile, mixed-race funk unit—the Meters had a series of great instrumental albums in the late '60s and early '70s, with hits including "Sophisticated Cissy," "Cissy Strut," "Ease Back" and "Chicken Strut," that worked a Big Easy elegance into a funky backbeat, with Neville's organ and Nocentelli's guitar picking up the vague, chord-based melodies.

In the '70s Toussaint produced several excellent albums under his own name, as well as Meters-backed greats for Dr. John (*In the Right Place,* with "Right Place Wrong Time," No. 9), Labelle (*Nightbirds,* No. 7, with "Lady Marmalade," No. 1), and the Meters-Nevilles combine, the Wild Tchoupitoulas, whose lone album is a celebratory Mardi Gras classic.

Toussaint formed NYNO Records in the mid-'90s to give New Orleans music a national outlet. In his founding open letter, Toussaint displays a keen sense for what makes New Orleans music special: "In New Orleans, the music isn't just in the clubs or on the dance floor, it's in everything. You can feel it in the street, see it in the buildings and taste it in the food. The syncopation and the strut of the second line brass bands; the frenzied intensity of the Mardi Gras Indian chants; and the driving rhythms of blues, jazz and R&B are as essential to this city as eating and sleeping." Allen Toussaint has been as essential to the music of New Orleans, as the music has been to the city. —ERIC OLSEN

Andrews, James: *Satchmo of the Ghetto,* NYNO, 1998.
Badger: "A Dream of You," Epic, 1974, 1981 (*England Rocks 3*) • *White Lady and Badger,* CBS, 1974.
Bryant, Browning: *Browning Bryant,* Warner Bros., 1974.
Castenell, Amadee: *Amadee,* NYNO, 1996.
Chocolate Milk: "Action Speaks Louder Than Words," RCA, 1975 • *Action Speaks Louder Than Words,* RCA, 1975 • *Chocolate Milk,* RCA, 1976 • *Comin',* RCA, 1976 • *We're All in This Together,* RCA, 1976 • *Milky Way,* RCA, 1979 • *Ice Cold Funk: The Greatest Grooves of Chocolate Milk,* Razor & Tie, 1998.
Cocker, Joe: *Luxury You Can Afford,* Asylum, 1978 • *Long Voyage Home: The Silver Anniversary Collection,* A&M, 1995.
Cool Riddims: *Pledge to My People,* NYNO, 1998.
Costello, Elvis: *Out of Our Idiot,* Demon, 1987.
Darling, Grace: *Imaginary Lover,* NYNO, 1997.
Dorsey, Lee: "Ya Ya," Fury, 1961 • "Do-Re-Mi," Fury, 1962 •

"Ride Your Pony," Amy, 1965 • "Get Out of My Life Woman," Amy, 1966 • "Holy Cow," Amy, 1966 • *The New Lee Dorsey,* Amy, 1966 • "Working in the Coal Mine," Amy, 1966 • *Go-Go Girl',* Amy, 1967 • "Everything I Do Gonh Be Funky," Amy, 1969 • *Yes We Can,* Polydor, 1970 • *Yes We Can . . . and Then Some,* Polydor, 1970, 1993 • *Night People,* ABC, 1978 • *Gonh Be Funky,* Charly, 1980.
Dr. John: *In the Right Place,* Atco, 1973 • "Right Place Wrong Time," Atco, 1973 • "Such a Night," Atco, 1973 • "(Everybody Wanna Get Rich) Rite Away," Atco, 1974 • *Desitively Bonnaroo,* Atco, 1974 • *Mos' Scocious: The Dr. John Anthology,* Rhino, 1993.
Gale, Eric: *Touch of Silk,* CBS, 1980.
George, Barbara: "I Know (You Don't Love Me No More)," AFO, 1961 • "You Talk About Love," AFO, 1962.
Hamilton, Larry: *Larry Hamilton,* NYNO, 1997.
Harris, Betty: "Nearer to You," Sansu, 1967.
Henry, Clarence "Frogman": "But I Do," Argo, 1961 • "Lonely Street," Argo, 1961 • "You Always Hurt the One You Love," Argo, 1961.
High Cotton: *High Cotton,* Island, 1975.
Hill, Jesse: "Ooh-Poo-Pah-Do (Part Two)," Minit, 1960 • "Whip It on Me," Minit, 1960.
Hill, Z.Z.: *Keep On Lovin' You,* United Artists, 1975.
James Montgomery Band: *The James Montgomery Band,* Island, 1976.
James, Etta: *Changes,* T-Electric, 1980.
Johnson, Wallace: *Whoever's Thrilling You,* NYNO, 1996.
K-Doe, Ernie : "I Cried My Last Tear," Minit, 1961 • "Mother-in-Law," Minit, 1961 • "Te-Ta-Te-Ta-Ta," Minit, 1961 • *Mother-in-Law,* Minit, 1962.
Kenner, Chris: "I Like It Like That," Instant, 1961 • "Land of 1,000 Dances," Instant, 1963.
King Biscuit Boy: *King Biscuit Boy,* Epic, 1974.
King, Albert: *New Orleans Heat,* Tomato, 1979.
Labelle: *Nightbirds,* Epic, 1974 • "Lady Marmalade," Epic, 1975 • *Phoenix,* Epic, 1975.
LaBelle, Patti: *Released,* Epic, 1980 • *Greatest Hits,* MCA, 1996 • *You Are My Friend: Ballads,* Sony, 1997.
Lefevre, Mylon: *Rock and Roll Resurrection,* Mercury, 1979.
Lewis, Ramsey: *Routes* (side 2), CBS, 1980.
Mayall, John: *Notice to Appear,* ABC, 1976.
Meters, The: "Cissy Strut," Josie, 1969 • "Ease Back," Josie, 1969 • "Look-Ka Py Py," Josie, 1969 • "Sophisticated Cissy," Josie, 1969 • *The Meters,* Josie, 1969 • "Chicken Strut," Josie, 1970 • "Hand Clapping Song," Josie, 1970 • *Look-Ka Py Py,* Rounder, 1970, 1990 • *Struttin',* Josie, 1970 • *Cabbage Alley,* Reprise, 1972 • *Cissy Strut,* Island, 1974 • *Rejuvenation,* Reprise, 1974 • *Fire on the Bayou,* Reprise, 1975 • *Trick Bag,* Reprise, 1976 • *Good Old Funky Music,* Rounder, 1990.
Miller, Frankie: *High Life,* Chrysalis, 1974.

Morgan, Oliver: *I'm Home,* NYNO, 1998.

Myles, Raymond, and The Rams: *Heaven Is the Place,* NYNO, 1997.

Neville Brothers: *Treacherous: A History of the Neville Brothers,* Rhino, 1988, 1995 • *Treacherous Too: A History of the Neville Brothers,* Vol. 2, *1955–1987,* Rhino, 1991 • *The Very Best Of,* Rhino, 1997.

Neville, Aaron: "Over You," Minit, 1960 • "Tell It Like It Is," Parlo, 1966 • "She Took You for a Ride," Parlo, 1967 • *The Classic Aaron Neville: My Greatest Gift,* Rounder, 1990.

New Birth Brass Band: *D-Boy,* NYNO, 1997.

Roden, Jess: *Jess Roden,* Island, 1974.

Showmen, The: "It Will Stand," Minit, 1961.

Spellman, Benny: "Lipstick Traces," Minit, 1962.

Thomas, Irma: "It's Raining," Minit, 1962 • "Ruler of My Heart," Minit, 1962.

Toussaint, Allen: as Al Tousan, *The Wild Sound of New Orleans,* RCA, 1958 • *From a Whisper to a Scream,* Scepter, 1970 • *Toussaint,* DJM, 1970 • *Life, Love and Faith,* Warner Bros., 1972 • *Southern Nights,* Warner Bros., 1975 • *The Allen Toussaint Collection,* Reprise, 1991 • *Connected,* NYNO, 1996 • *New Orleans Christmas,* NYNO, 1997.

Wild Tchoupitoulas: "Hey Hey (Indians Comin')," Antilles, 1976, 1987 (*The Big Easy* soundtrack) • *The Wild Tchoupitoulas,* Mango, 1976.

COLLECTIONS

The New Orleans Hit Story: 20 Years of Big Easy Hits, 1950–1970, Charly, 1993.

Rock and Roll Doctor (A Tribute to Lowell George), CMC International, 1998.

Roger Troutman

Producer/songwriter/singer Roger Troutman put a heavy responsibility on the record producer. Born November 29, 1951, in Hamilton, Ohio, Troutman was known for his influential funk band Zapp, for his solo career under the name of "Roger," and for his trademark, almost patented, voice box effect. He said the producer "is responsible for making sure the writers write, the singers sing, the clappers clap, the editors edit, the engineers engineer, the record companies record, and the legal departments legal."

The producer is "like the lawyer in a trial," Troutman continued. "He's gotta take all the information and try to present it to the jury so they can judge, make a choice about it. And they try to make this one say more

and this one say not so much. Whoever I'm working with, I try to get them to do things the best they know how."

From childhood, Troutman readied himself to be a producer. He remembered tinkering and fumbling around with the most intricate parts of his tape recorder. As he grew older, Troutman played in bands with his brothers, especially the great cover band Roger and the Human Body, which played "anywhere and everywhere" during the mid- to late '70s. During this time, he met folks like George Clinton (see entry) and Bootsy Collins, who introduced him to the recording scene, specifically people at Warner Bros.

Troutman and his brothers Larry, Terry, and Lester eventually formed Zapp ("Zapp" is Terry's nickname). Troutman learned that groups are supposed to have producers, and that role was thrust upon him. "I had a knack," he said. "Warner Bros. had a funk guru in me with a Darth Vader sound [the voice box] and a George Clinton feeling. I was forced to produce myself because of how unorthodox I was," said Troutman, who admired producers such as Gamble and Huff, Jerry Wexler, Arif Mardin, and Norman Whitfield (see entries). He didn't feel the younger producers had proved themselves yet.

Troutman and Zapp scored big right out of the box in 1980 with the release of its self-titled debut album (No. 19). That album included Zapp's first hit, the still slammin' "More Bounce to the Ounce," and was Troutman's first official production (with Bootsy Collins). " 'More Bounce' " established me as some sort of funky space cadet or something," he said.

With this first album, Troutman had already established a sound that would mark his career. His synthesized beats are known for their thick, hard feel and usually call for immediate action on the dance floor. He described the sound he created simply as "the black experience [much like] the projects and chitlins." But identifying him even more strongly was the voice box, which actually isn't as electronic as one might think. "It's a plastic tube connected to a keyboard. That's the essence of it. On stage I hide it inside of a concoction to mask the unsightly parts," said Troutman, who brought two to each live performance in case one failed him. During his career, he went through "about a million" of these contraptions.

Troutman created the voice box long before there was a Zapp, while he and his brothers were still working as the Human Body. He and his brothers thought the box would provide variety, since they didn't have a female vocalist. The popularity of the first *Star Wars* film and the Darth Vader character helped popularize the device, he said. This box, coupled with his beats, carried him a long way.

Throughout the '80s Zapp, with Troutman usually in the driver's seat, released a series of albums: *Zapp II, Zapp III, The New Zapp IV U* and *Zapp V,* and songs from these albums, like "I Can Make You Dance," "Dance Floor," "Doo Wa Ditty (Blow Tha Thing)," and "So Ruff, So Tuff," became funk standards. A parallel solo career as Roger kicked off one year after the first Zapp album; highlights include *The Many Facets of Roger, The Saga Continues,* and *Unlimited!* His biggest single hit has been "I Want to Be Your Man" (No. 3).

Troutman and Zapp's influence is heavily felt among today's younger crop of R&B music makers, who sought him out through the family-owned Roger Tee Enterprises. In 1996, Troutman and his voice box were featured on the Grammy-nominated "California Love" by rappers 2Pac and Dr. Dre (see entry). The same year, he produced a song for newcomer Eric Benet and "Scandalous" for the Click.

Troutman's classics routinely pop up in movies ("More Bounce to the Ounce" throughout John Singleton's *Boyz N the Hood*), and Troutman scored the Martin Lawrence comedy *A Thin Line Between Love and Hate,* which included the Troutman-produced title track by H-Town. "I always wanted to do that," he said of scoring the film. He especially enjoyed watching scenes from the film one by one in the recording studio, an activity he'd always dreamed about.

Other career highlights included working with Curtis Mayfield (see entry) on his 1996 *New World Order* album, helping to establish the career of Shirley Murdock by writing and producing for her ("As We Lay"), and his remake of "I Heard It Through the Grapevine." "That just took the industry by surprise. All the executives, the jocks, everybody slammed on the brakes when they heard that. I was going down the freeway, heard the song, and pulled over. That thing just floored me: the guitars, the baritone sax matching the bass—we threw everything but the kitchen sink into that song."

Working with Dr. Dre and 2Pac was another highlight. "They wanted to make a song without samples. We built the song from the ground up. Dre wouldn't have wanted to do that if all the other rappers hadn't been sampling my music." Troutman said, "I'm most proud of black America accepting me as part of the black experience—young people, old people, and rappers." Tragically, Troutman was shot to death outside his Dayton recording studio in April of '99, apparently the victim of a murder-suicide at the hand of his brother, Harry, who was found dead nearby.—KEVIN JOHNSON

Benet, Eric: *True to Myself* (! track), Warner Bros., 1996.
Click, The: *Game Related* (1 track), Sick Wid' It, 1995 • "Scandalous," Sick Wid' It, 1996.
H-Town: "A Thin Line Between Love and Hate," Jac-Mac, 1996.
Human Body: *Cosmic Roundup,* Elektra, 1985.
Lynch: "Magic Spell," Capitol, 1989.
MC Blvd: *I Remember You Homie,* ITP, 1997.
Murdock, Shirley: "No More," Elektra, 1986 • "As We Lay," Elektra, 1987 • "Be Free," Elektra, 1987 • "Go On Without You," Elektra, 1987 • *Shirley Murdock!,* Elektra, 1987 • *A Woman's Point of View,* Elektra, 1988 • "Husband," Elektra, 1988 • "You Brought Me Sunshine," Elektra, 1990 (*Rubaiyat: Elektra's 40th Anniversary*) • "In Your Eyes," Elektra, 1991 • "Stay with Me Tonight," Elektra, 1991 • "Let There Be Love!," Elektra, 1992.
Phajja: *Seize the Moment,* Warner Bros., 1997.
Roger: "I Heard It Through the Grapevine," Warner Bros., 1981 • *The Many Facets of Roger,* Warner Bros., 1981 • "Bucket of Blood," Warner Bros., 1984 • "In the Mix," Warner Bros., 1984 • *The Saga Continues,* Warner Bros., 1984 • "Girl, Cut It Out," Warner Bros., 1985 • "I Want to Be Your Man," Reprise, 1987 • *Unlimited,* Reprise, 1987 • "(Everybody) Get Up," Reprise, 1991 • "Take Me Back," Reprise, 1992 • *See also* Zapp and Roger.
Zapp: "More Bounce to the Ounce," Warner Bros., 1980 • *Zapp,* Warner Bros., 1980 • "Dance Floor (Part 1)," Warner Bros., 1982 • *Zapp II,* Warner Bros., 1982 • "I Can Make You Dance," Warner Bros., 1983 • *Zapp III,* Warner Bros., 1983 • "It Doesn't Really Matter," Warner Bros., 1985 • *The New Zapp IV U,* Warner Bros., 1985 • "Computer Love," Warner Bros., 1986 • "Itchin' for a Twitchin'," Warner Bros., 1986 • "Ooh Baby Baby," Reprise, 1989 • "Ooh Baby Baby" (remix), Reprise, 1989 • *Zapp V,* Reprise, 1989 • *All the Greatest Hits,* Reprise, 1993 • "I Want to Be Your Man," Reprise, 1993 • *Compilation: Greatest Hits Vol. 2 and More,* Warner Bros., 1996.
Zapp and Roger: "Mega Medley," Reprise, 1993 • "Slow and Easy," Reprise, 1993 • featuring Shirley Murdock and Charlie Wilson, "Computer Love," Reprise, 1994 • "Living for the City," Reprise, 1996.

Chris Tsangarides

Though Chris Tsangarides's name is associated with the '80s new wave of British heavy metal (NWOBHM), he has made a concerted and successful attempt to avoid being pigeonholed. A majority of his past projects are metal, including a diverse group

He rates that band as one of his favorites. "Phil Lynott was more than a musician. In fact, a musician would be the last thing I'd say he was. He was more of a poet. The way he could phrase lyrics was superb. His style of writing was great."

In 1976, Tsangarides found himself working with the band that influenced most subsequent power metal: Judas Priest. He was assistant engineer on their 1976 *Sad Wings of Destiny*. "The engineer got sick and I took over. We kept in touch over the years." In the late '80s, they heard a song he'd produced on MTV, and when they learned who it was, they called him to do 1990's *Painkiller*.

Soon after Tsangarides produced that first album with Moore, NWOBHM was in full swing. Tsangarides felt right at home producing the high-voltage riffing of bands like Anvil, Helloween, Loudness, Killer Dwarves, Anthem, Rock Goddess, Sledgehammer, and even the poppier metal of glamsters Tigertailz. Admittedly, some of the music was strictly utilitarian, but he was able to produce a whole palette of fiery, frontal guitar sounds, underpinned by big, ballsy-sounding rhythm sections. In fact, he has developed his own special microphone technique, Vortex, for recording guitars. "It's very loud and gives the guitar a big sound to put on records."

Though metal was his bread and butter in the '80s, Tsangarides also produced Stiv Bators' post–Dead Boys band, Lords of the New Church; Tom Jones; porn pinup Samantha Fox ("She could not sing. Every single note she recorded had to be put in tune"); and one of his favorites, Los Angeles alternative rockers, Concrete Blonde.

"I have never asked to produce anyone," says Tsangarides. "They always ask for me to produce them. That way you have respect straightaway before you walk into the studio. Concrete Blonde called me because they liked Thin Lizzy. They saw my name on the back of an album cover. They turned up in England. Immigration called and said, 'We have this band here.' They never even called. They had recorded the tracks in their house; they brought the tape over and asked me to mix. That was *Free*. I went on to do *Bloodletting*, which I think is their best album, and *Walking in London*.

"I pride myself that I've never done a corporate rock band," he says. "Anything that has a bit of credibility is what I'm into—if there's a bit of humor or a message and the artists truly believes what they are doing. Miles Copeland came into the studio when we were doing *Bloodletting* and asked, 'What's the single?' [Vocalist] Johnette [Napolitano] stormed out of the studio and left the building."

of quality acts like Judas Priest, Helloween, Bruce Dickinson, Girlschool, Tygers of Pan Tang, Ozzy Osbourne, Black Sabbath, King Diamond, and Exodus. But his production, engineering, and mixing discography is also studded with respected nonmetal acts, like Joan Armatrading, Concrete Blonde, Jan Hammer, Sisters of Mercy, the Tragically Hip, Depeche Mode, and Billy Ocean.

"I've been fortunate enough to have opportunities to work not exclusively in one field of music. But you have to have a break to do something," he points out. "It's a two-edged sword. You do get typecast. But it's better to be known for something than nothing." And Tsangarides's affinity for blitzkrieg power metal is undeniable.

His interest in playing trumpet in his school's brass band waned after he saw Jimi Hendrix performing "Purple Haze" on TV. "I was smitten. I started a band." Although he went to business college, a friend who was working at a studio as an engineer extolled the job and suggested he try it. Soon he was working at Morgan Studios in London. That was in 1975. "Black Sabbath, Yes, Judas Priest all worked there. I eventually became an engineer. I didn't want to be a producer when I started. I fell into it by default. I started working on an album with a chap named Gary Moore, and he asked me to produce (1979's *Back on the Streets*). Damned if I didn't have a hit. I went on to do Thin Lizzy."

His production style has become more relaxed over the years. "In the '80s, things were ridiculously overdone. I was doing things a billion times trying to get it perfect. I learned you have to move on. Things started sounding fresher. The secret is, when technology comes in, use it to your advantage, don't let it use you. When any toy came in in the '80s, you'd use it on everything."

"I use both digital and analog. If I do an album that's basically synth-based, I will use analog recording. It warms it up. The distortion is nicer to my ear. It can become too perfect, a bit unfeeling."

He likes to set up the whole band in the studio and record everyone. "I'll keep the drums; the bass and guitar are to guide the drummer. So drummer plays with band, not with click track. Then I'll put the bass and guitar on. I don't want it to be anal. If people are comfortable with the environment and the people around them, they will give the best performance."

"I don't like the dictator style of producer. I tell a band, 'We're going to get *your* sound.' I've had guitar players say, 'Can you make me sound like Gary Moore or Eddie Van Halen?' I had a situation where the singer took two weeks to get a vocal sound and that was in the headset, not the mikes. He finally blurted out, 'I'm as good as Ian Gillian or Rob Halford.' He thought I was comparing him to every other singer I'd worked with."

Word of mouth and contacts provide Tsangarides with a steady stream of projects. His 1992 production, *Fully Completely,* for Canadian superstars Tragically Hip led to more projects in Canada. He recently did another album with Gary Moore and recorded a concerto called *Millennium* with guitar pyrotechnician Yngwie Malmsteen, the Prague Symphony, and a 140-voice choir, with Yoel Levi conducting. He's also a composer of film and commercial music and has his own band, Pro-Z-ak, that plays dance music with drum samples and heavy guitars. —ANASTASIA PANTSIOS

Anthem: *Bound to Break,* King, 1986 • *Show Carries On,* King, 1987 • *Gypsy Ways,* King, 1988 • *Hunting Time,* King, 1989 • *Domestic Booty,* King, 1991.
Anvil: *Metal on Metal,* Attic, 1982 • *Forged in Fire,* Attic, 1983.
Armatrading, Joan: "Rosie," A&M, 1979.
Baron Rojo: *Baron Al Rojo Vivo,* Zafiera Disc, 1984.
Black Sabbath: *The Eternal Idol,* Warner Bros., 1987.
Borich: *Angels Hand,* Mushroom, 1979.
Broon: *Broon,* Harvest Germany, 1994.
Child: *Total Recall,* Hansa, 1979.
Comsat Angels: *7 Day Weekend,* Jive/Arista, 1985 • "Believe It," Jive, 1985 • "New Hearts and Hand," Jive, 1985.
Concrete Blonde: *Free,* IRS, 1989 • *Bloodletting,* IRS, 1990 • "Joey," IRS, 1990 • "I Want You," MCA, 1991 (*Point Break*

soundtrack) • "Ghost of a Texas Ladies' Man," IRS, 1992 • *Walking in London,* IRS, 1992 • *Recollection: The Best of Concrete Blonde,* IRS, 1996.
Dickinson, Bruce: *Tattooed Millionaire,* Columbia, 1990.
ELO II: *One Night,* CMC International, 1997.
Exodus: *Force of Habit,* Capitol, 1992.
Fortnox: *Fortnox,* Epic, 1982.
Fox, Samantha: *I Wanna Have Some Fun,* Jive, 1988.
Gillan, Ian: *Toolbox,* EastWest, 1991.
Girl: *Sheer Greed,* Jet, 1980.
Helloween: *Pink Bubbles Go Ape,* EMI, 1991.
Jones, Tom: *Live @ Moment* (video), Zomba/Jive, 1989.
Jubiaba: *Jubiaba,* MCA, 1978.
Judas Priest: *Painkiller,* Columbia, 1990 • *Metal Works '73–'93,* Columbia, 1993.
Killer Dwarfs: *The Killer Dwarfs,* Attic, 1983.
Killing Joke: "A Southern Sky," EG, 1986 • *Brighter Than a Thousand Suns* (1 track), Virgin America, 1987.
King Diamond: *Conspiracy,* Roadracer, 1989 • *Dangerous Meeting,* Roadrunner, 1992.
Lords of the New Church: *Method to Our Madness,* IRS, 1984 • *Killer Lords* (3 tracks), IRS, 1986.
Loudness: *Heavy Metal Hippys,* Warner Bros., 1994.
Lynott, Phil: *Solo in Soho,* Warner Bros., 1980.
Magnum: *Marauder,* Jet, 1980.
Malmsteen, Yngwie: *Magnum Opus,* Music for Nations, 1995 • *Inspiration,* Music for Nations, 1996 • *Facing the Animal,* Mercury, 1998.
Money: *First Investment,* Gull, 1979.
Moore, Gary: *Dirty Fingers,* Roadrunner, 1980, 1984 • *Back on the Streets,* MCA, 1979 • *Live at the Marquee,* Castle, 1987.
Mountain: *Over the Top,* Legacy/Columbia, 1995.
Osbourne, Ozzy: *The Ultimate Sin,* CBS Associated, 1986.
Rock Goddess: *Hell Hath No Fury,* A&M, 1983.
Slave Raider: *What Do You Know About Rock 'n Roll?,* Jive, 1989.
Sledgehammer: *Blood on Their Hands,* Illuminated, 1984.
Spider: *Rough Justice,* A&M, 1984.
Thin Lizzy: "Hollywood," Warner Bros., 1982 • *Renegade,* Warner Bros., 1982 • "Cold Sweat," Warner Bros., 1983 • *Life,* Vertigo, 1983 • *Thunder and Lightning,* Warner Bros., 1983.
Tigertailz: *Berzerk,* MFN, 1990.
Tragically Hip: *Fully Completely,* MCA, 1992.
Tygers of Pan Tang: *Wild Cat,* MCA, 1980 • *Spellbound,* MCA, 1981.
Y&T: *Mean Streak,* A&M, 1983 • *The Best of Y&T, 1981–1985,* A&M, 1990.

COLLECTIONS

Nativity in Black: Tribute to Black Sabbath, Sony, 1994.

Bjorn Ulvaeus

See BENNY ANDERSSON AND BJORN ULVAEUS

Conrad Uno

"I like to drink coffee, I like to go to baseball games, I like to play golf—and I like to record really fun bands. But you could do that with a couple of microphones and an analog tape deck. My needs are minimal. If I really need to get into anything more technical than that, I can take it to someone who knows what they're doing. I don't dislike all the new technology in any way, I think it's fantastic that they're figuring out all kinds of new ways to do stuff. I just don't care about it."

That sums up the production philosophy of one Conrad Uno, who came by his singular moniker by means that, at his request, shall remain under wraps. What is known is that many of the artists that have worked with him regard Uno as a "number one" type of a guy. One can check this claim with the Young Fresh Fellows, Mudhoney, the Fastbacks, Supersuckers, or even the Presidents of the United States of America. The late cult hero Jimmy Silva made his best recordings with Uno.

Uno makes his home in Seattle, Washington. It is

there, in the basement of his home, that his Egg Studio resides. The centerpiece of the control room is the Custom Spectrasonics console (with custom-built Audiotronics faders) that originally called the Stax Studio B home in the mid- to late '60s. His tape machine is the Tascam MSR-165. The offices of his PopLlama record company are within walking distance of Egg. Can you say laid-back?

"For what I do, the way I like to do it is to kind of encourage creativity and spontaneity and the idea that I'm sort of a catalyst, a helper. Making it happen for people who are actually doing it is the way I envision my role in the studio. So many other things are involved, of course, but that's probably what I feel I can do that's the most important.

"I don't like to belabor stuff, I don't like to overwork stuff. I work fast. The only time when things can slow down on you is in rearranging in the studio when you're actually cutting the tracks. I like to encourage people to experiment—try things, and listen to them, and move on, and cut it. I'm a studio owner and it's a little studio and it's kind of my own little world. I'm not real big on preproduction.

"I produce on the fly, and that does create an aspect of a style or a sound, but only if that's there for the band. I guess a key element in it is working with bands that enjoy that or can appreciate that. I just don't have the patience or the desire to create things that are painstakingly developed and processed and pushed and pulled and made into a final perfect gem. I much prefer a totally sort of opposite way of doing it and you end up with a gem depending on how you look at things."

To this day, Mr. Uno dislikes the "P" word and considers himself a producer "by default." He started at age 15 by doing home recordings of "quirky, weird stuff" on various tape decks; eventually, under the name Pink Chunk he released a version of "Louie, Louie" that "garnered a lot of attention in "really weird circles" (it was once Lester Bangs' pick hit of the week). Conrad went on to play bass in a number of bands, mostly with avant-garde leanings, and found himself in the possession of assorted PA and other musical gear when the groups split up. He bought an 8-track machine in order to record the local bands he dug that he thought no one else would ever get into. "I always think in terms of realizing that the people next door might be geniuses, and maybe not just some weirdos that live on the street. You can't just discount them because they live in your neighborhood. At least it's an interesting way to look at people.

"My setup wasn't really a studio, but it was being called a studio. Scott McCaughey and Chuck Carroll of Young Fresh Fellows came to me and asked if I would help them record their first album *Fabulous Sound of the Pacific Northwest* [in 1984]. Although I had a certain amount of experience in areas that would help me with recording it, I was very ill-equipped to do so. We did it fast and it was really fun. Basically, they said I was the producer—while we were doing it and when we were done—and put my name on the album as a producer, and called me certain other names. And that's why I'm a producer.

"Really, my whole style of doing things hasn't changed since that first album. My ability and my theory of what it is I'm doing has had to adjust a little bit and my experience has grown, but the basic idea is intact.

"For me, when producing is actually a happening thing—when I'm enjoying it—is when I feel like I'm in the band. There is nothing like playing music when it's happening, when it really feels good and you're doing it for the right reasons and it's fun. Production could never compare to that. But the closest thing is when you actually are feeling like you're a member of a band and your ideas seem to be in sync with what's going on and it's all working and it's just about as fun, in a way."

The Young Fresh Fellows were among the few bands Uno purposely cites in his experience as having "the guts to be so damn loose and have so much fun and be free about it and to allow me to say, 'That is in the can, I know there's four mistakes in it and it's really funky, but once we do this and this, it's gonna be so great.' Another band that trusts Conrad implicitly is proto-grungers Mudhoney. "They're like the Young Fresh Fellows' little brothers." Their 1991 album *Every Good Boy Deserves Fudge* was cut on Uno's 8-track machine.

Uno believes in taping the rehearsal in the studio. "If you miss the first take, it's gonna be the best one ever. Even better, if the band doesn't know you're cutting it, of course."

The recent success of the Presidents of the United States of America has made the name Conrad Uno more recognizable to the musically minded masses of the '90s. Their double-platinum debut album (No. 6) was produced by "Connie" at Egg. "The Presidents, an amazing band, happened to be at the right place at the right time. They're very similar to the Fellows in their attitudes and in their overall ability to just make you have a good time because you're their friend. The Fellows were always a little out of sync with the rest of the world. The Presidents seem to have a more clear connection to the time and place they are in."

Conrad Uno, the talented yet reluctant record producer, sums up his tiny PopLlama label, and in so doing, capsulizes his lot in life. "My record company is small and is not in the habit of creating demand. It's in the habit of creating music and then hoping people like it, which isn't a very aggressive sales thing. That's just kind of the way it's always been."

As any self-respecting studio owner and operator will confirm, coffee is a commodity consumed by colleagues constantly. Band members, engineers, gobo schleppers, producers, visiting A&R geeks—everyone's entitled to their fix of fresh, piping hot java. This knowledge is not lost on the king of Egg Studios. How does he take his cup o' joe? He adds milk "almost always," but stresses that "I'll go through periods where if it's really well-brewed, I'll drink it black." Conrad Uno concludes that "every once in a while in the studio, if it's been sitting there too long, it requires sugar. Sugar and a lot of whitener." —DENNIS DIKEN

Bratmobile: "Kiss and Ride," Homestead, 1992 • *Pottymouth*, Kill Rock Stars, 1993.

Capping Day: *Post No Bills*, Pop Llama, 1990.

Derelicts, The: *Don't Wanna Live*, Sub Pop, 1991.

Dharma Bums: *Haywire: Out Through the Indoor*, Frontier, 1989.

Fall-Outs, The: *The Fall-Outs*, Super Electro, 1995.

Fastbacks, The: *The Question Is No* (5 tracks), Sub Pop, 1992.

Flipp: *Flipp*, Hollywood, 1997.

Gilmore, Jimmie Dale: *See* Mudhoney.

Groovy Ghoulies: *Born in the Basement*, Lookout, 1996 • *World Contact Day*, Lookout, 1996.

La Donnas: *Shady Lane*, Scooch Pooch, 1996.

Love Battery: *Between the Eyes*, Sub Pop, 1992 • *Dayglo*, Sub Pop, 1992.

Makers, The: *Hunger*, Estrus, 1997.

Minus 5 of Scott McCaughey: *My Chartreuse Opinion*, Hollywood, 1997.

Monkeywrench, The: *Clean As a Broke-Dick Dog*, Sub Pop, 1992.

Muddy Frankenstein: *Dance with Evil*, Rock Boss International, 1997.

Mudhoney: *Every Good Boy Deserves Fudge*, Sub Pop, 1991 • *Let It Slide* (EP), Sub Pop, 1991 • "Overblown," Epic Soundtrax, 1992 (*Singles* soundtrack) • *Piece of Cake*, Reprise, 1992 • "Make It Now," Ruff House/Columbia, 1994 (*Brainscan* soundtrack) • w/ Jimmie Dale Gilmore, *Mudhoney/Jimmie Dale Gilmore* (EP), Sub Pop, 1994.

Picketts, The: *Paper Doll*, Pop Llama, 1992 • *The Wicked Picketts*, Rounder, 1995.

Posies, The: *Success*, Pop Llama, 1998.

Presidents of the U.S.A.: "Lump," Columbia, 1995 • *The Presidents of the U.S.A.*, Columbia, 1995 • "Peaches," Columbia, 1996 • *Pure Frosting*, Columbia, 1998.

Shame Idols: *I Got Time*, Frontier, 1995 • *Rocket Cat*, Frontier, 1997.

Sicko: *You Can Feel the Love in This Room*, Empty, 1994.

Silva, Jimmy, and the Goats: *Heidi/Remnants of the Empty Shell*, East Side Digital, 1991.

Smugglers, The: *In the Hall of Fame*, PopLlama, 1993.

Squirrels, The: *What Gives?*, Pop Llama, 1990 • *Harsh Toke of Reality*, PopLlama, 1994.

Stumpy Joe: *One Way Rocket to Kicksville*, Pop Llama, 1991.

Supersuckers: *La Mano Cornuda*, Sub Pop, 1994.

Symon-Asher: *Three Color Sun*, Miramar, 1995.

Young Fresh Fellows: *The Fabulous Sounds of the Pacific Northwest*, Pop Llama, 1984 • *Topsy Turvy*, Pop Llama, 1985 • *The Men Who Loved Music*, Frontier, 1987 • *Totally Lost*, Frontier, 1988 • *This One's for the Ladies*, Frontier, 1989 • *Doc Sharpie Is a Bad Man* (1 track), Frontier, 1992 • *It's Low Beat Time!*, Frontier, 1992.

Zeke: *Flat Tracker*, Scooch Pooch, 1996.

Steven Van Zandt

Steven Van Zandt is an important artist (Little Steven and the Disciples of Soul), songwriter, and political activist (the anti-apartheid project "Sun City"); he was also guitarist and de facto leader of Bruce Springsteen's E Street Band, as well as co-producer of Springsteen's great albums *The River* and *Born in the U.S.A.* (both No. 1), which between them have sold almost 20 million copies. Van Zandt has also written songs for and produced Southside Johnny and the Asbury Jukes, Ronnie Spector, Gary "U.S." Bonds, Lords of the New Church, Lone Justice, Darlene Love, and Meatloaf.

Steven Van Zandt was born November 22, 1950, in Boston, but grew up in South Jersey. "The first record I remember buying was Little Anthony and the Imperials' 'Tears on My Pillow.' My emotional involvement increased a bit when I was 11 or 12 with 'Twist and Shout' by the Isley Brothers, 'Pretty Little Angel Eyes' by Curtis Lee, and 'Sherry' by the Four Seasons. I didn't have too many records, but I was passionate about the ones I had. I had to rebuy 'Twist and Shout' and 'Sherry' because I wore them out," writes Van Zandt in his manifesto, which can be found on his Web site at www.littlesteven.com.

"I had my first epiphany some time during the 77th playing of 'Pretty Little Angel Eyes.' It was an overwhelming, deeply spiritual, exciting yet calming warm flood of emotion that I didn't understand but I knew connected me in some permanent way to music. It was either an epiphany or puberty kicking in—I'll never know—but it was intense. . . .

"I had my second epiphany . . . on June 13, 1964. The Rolling Stones played the Hollywood Palace show on T.V. and that was it for me. They may have been from another planet like the Beatles but somehow they were accessible—and relatable. They were ugly, aloof, sloppy, crazy, casual, confident, and totally out of place. They were perfect. It even made sense to me that Dean Martin, who I was and am a big fan of, made fun of them and put them down. I had no problem then and have no trouble now reconciling these two contradictory species that co-exist in me."

The very next night Van Zandt went to his first rock show at a Sea Bright beach club and saw the Mods, one of the big local bands. "In my mind the Mods were the living embodiment of the Stones fantasy I had just seen on T.V. The timely juxtaposition was awesome. Here were local guys actually doing it. . . . My attraction for bands was essentially two things. First, the camaraderie, the family, the gang, the team, the group of friends hanging out together appealed to me. Secondly, it allowed those with a limited amount of talent but a lot of determination, such as myself, to participate. . . .

"In 1965 Bob Dylan took the folk and blues traditions, and the integral consciousness of existing reality, and went electric. His profound impact and influence on the Beatles—the archetypal pop band, the Rolling Stones—the archetypal rock band, and with the road paved by the Byrds—the archetypal sound of the new consciousness, changed everything forever. The release of Dylan's 'Like a Rolling Stone' was, at least symbolically if not literally, the birth of the art form of rock. . . .

"Rock music is a lifestyle. It is art. It is cynicism. It is singers who are great singers who do not have great voices. It is totally dependent on live performance. It has lyrics that are personally expressive and deeply emotional. . . . It demands attention. It is usually written or co-written by the singer. It is judged by its influence, credibility, and respect. It is bands. The classic rock artist's image is dour, serious, frustrated, confused, controversial, political, spiritual, isolated, and a threat to society's status quo."

Van Zandt set about to make real his vision of rock. He was friends with Bruce Springsteen, playing in Springsteen's Steel Mill in 1969–1970 and the Bruce Springsteen Band in 1971. When Springsteen was signed to Columbia in 1972, Van Zandt went his own way and joined with another local singer, Southside Johnny Lyons, to form a '60s-style, horn-driven rock-and-soul band: Southside Johnny and the Asbury Jukes.

The band stumbled upon a club in Asbury Park, the Stone Pony, that was about to close, and persuaded the owner to let them do their thing: sweaty covers of '50s and '60s soul, blues, and R&B classics, interspersed with atavistic originals provided by Van Zandt and Springsteen. "The Stone Pony didn't close; in fact, it expanded. Between Bruce's thing and our thing, it became a scene all of a sudden. Then Bruce asked me to join his band for a seven-week tour in 1975—I ended up staying seven years."

Southside and the Jukes finally got a record contract in 1976; although Van Zandt was no longer in the band, he had written many of the band's songs and arranged most of the others, so he was the logical choice to produce the band's first album, *I Don't Want to Go Home.*

"Production is made up of four things: composition, arrangement, performance, sound," he says. "I had been a performer for quite a while. I was always an arranger. I had been writing a little bit, but the sound was something I had to learn about. It took a while. Having grown up in the '60s, I didn't think '70s music sounded very good: everything was close-miked and stale and dead, without the live excitement of the '60s records. I wanted to bring things back to what I grew up with. I have basically tried to do that ever since: natural, organic, as live as possible."

Van Zandt succeeded wildly. *I Don't Want to Go Home* is one of the great albums of the '70s. Lyons' voice is an amazing, soulful instrument that inhabits great song after great song: Van Zandt wrote the tuneful, swinging, horns-and-strings title track and the hilarious, jaunty, funky duet between Lyons and the great Lee Dorsey (see Allen Toussaint entry), "How Come You Treat Me So Bad?" Springsteen contributed the simmering, understated "The Fever," generating Lyons' most passionate, nuanced performance, and "You Mean So Much to Me"—another great duet—this one with ex-Ronette Ronnie Spector (see Phil Spector entry). The inspired covers include Solomon Burke's "Got to Get You off My Mind," and an amazing version of Sam and Dave's "Broke Down Piece of Man," featuring Lyons trading lines with an inspired Van Zandt.

While he played with the E Street Band, Van Zandt also wrote for and produced the very fine second and third Southside albums: *This Time It's for Real* and *Hearts of Stone.* Critiques Van Zandt: "They were all very different, and all very differently flawed. I would learn one thing and screw up another. The first one was based on the live show, and my rhythm guitar was a big part of that sound. I basically eliminated it from the record because I wasn't really in the band anymore, but I took out one of the main elements of the sound and I've regretted that ever since."

Throughout the '70s Van Zandt, one of Springsteen's oldest friends, became a more and more integral part of the E Street Band's live show and Springsteen's recordings. He arranged the horns for "Tenth Avenue Freeze-Out" on *Born to Run* in 1975. He played guitar, and was given "production assistance" credit for 1978's *Darkness on the Edge of Town,* but Van Zandt came to the fore as player and co-producer (with Springsteen, Jon Landau, and Chuck Plotkin) on 1980's *The River.*

A phenomenal two-record set that confirmed Springsteen's greatness as an artist and proved the E Street Band (Springsteen on vocals and guitar, Van Zandt on harmony vocals and guitar, Clarence Clemons on sax, Danny Federici on organ, Garry Tallent on bass, Max Weinberg on drums, Roy Bittan on piano) to be one of the finest rock 'n' roll units of all time, *The River* has the scope and particularity of a great novel and just plain rocks.

Side 2 of the original vinyl is not only one of the great rock album sides, it in fact recapitulates important developments in the history of rock 'n' roll. On "Hungry Heart" Van Zandt finds the holy grail of the perfect drum sound: Mighty Max Weinberg's (who is now band-leader for *Late Night With Conan O'Brien*) snare thwaps like a slap in the face as Springsteen gleefully sings in his upper register one of his strangest songs: a song that exults in the sheer exuberance of following one's heart, regardless of consequences. Amoral exuberance is what the original rock 'n' roll explosion was all about.

"Out in the Street" is in the classic tradition of work-hard-for-the-man, party-harder-for-yourself of songs from "Rip It Up" to "Working for the Weekend." "Crush on You" continues the amoral exuberance with humor and style: while his voice nearly blows out his mike, Springsteen's roaming eye and gyrating pelvis celebrate the instant, almost impersonal, rush of a crush. Springsteen's exuberant spirit is frustrated on "You Can Look (But You Better Not Touch)," as delights from women to lamps are dangled in front of him—all just out of reach—invoking such anthems to frustration as "Summertime Blues" and "(I Can't Get No) Satisfaction." The ambivalence of longing is beautifully, touchingly addressed on the rolling ballad "I Wanna Marry You." In the course of the side, Springsteen has gone from generalized lust and jean-splitting energy to a specific longing for one woman—a young, single, working mother of two. Two amazing couplets stand out as the singer confesses his firmly grounded, sober love: "To say I'll make your dreams come true would be wrong / But maybe darlin' I could help them along," and, "There's something happy and there's something sad / 'Bout wanting somebody oh so bad."

Finally, the heedless exuberance of the original rock 'n' roll revolution is turned on its head as consequences—as awesome and inexorable as death—raise their ugly heads on the lovely, dreadful "The River." A young man from the symbolic and literal darkness of a valley escapes to frolic in verdant fields and swim in a cleansing, soothing river with his girlfriend, who becomes pregnant as a result. The price paid for their brief glimpses of freedom is the bondage of marriage and a construction job for the singer on his 19th birthday. There are few things sadder than youth's vision of limitless possibilities narrowed to grim responsibility—"Now I just act like I don't remember / Mary acts like she don't care"—a responsibility that laughs at the very exuberance that rock 'n' roll celebrates—"Is a dream a lie if it don't come true / Or is it something worse?" Springsteen doesn't have the answer, but he has found a disturbing and profound question.

Van Zandt co-wrote and co-produced (with Springsteen) Gary "U.S." Bonds' remarkable comeback albums *Dedication* (including the hit single "This Little Girl," No. 11) in 1981, and *On the Line* (with "Out of Work") in 1982. He formed Little Steven and the Disciples of Soul and released the splendid *Men Without Women* in 1982, *Voice of America* in 1984, *Freedom No Compromise* in 1987, and *Revolution* in 1989 (he regrets producing himself—"I have no patience and have basically put out demos"—but as always, he's too hard on himself). As a result of his travels and "political awakening," Van Zandt assembled, wrote, and produced (with Arthur Baker; see entry) the exceptionally successful anti-apartheid anthem "Sun City" in 1985.

After 30 years in music, this man of conscience and action is trying something new: beginning January of 1999 he could be seen acting the role of Silvio Dante in HBO's acclaimed dramatic series, *The Sopranos,* about a present-day New Jersey Mafia family. —ERIC OLSEN

Arc Angels: *Arc Angels,* DGC, 1992.
Artists United Against Apartheid: "Sun City," Manhattan, 1985 • *Sun City,* Manhattan, 1985.
Bonds, Gary "U.S.": *Dedication,* EMI America, 1981 • "Jole Blon," EMI America, 1981 • "This Little Girl," EMI America, 1981 • *On the Line,* EMI America, 1982 • "Out of Work," EMI America, 1982 • "Standing in the Line of Fire," Phoenix, 1985 • *The Best Of,* EMI America, 1996.
Demolition 23: *Demolition 23,* Renegade Nation/PolyGram, 1993.
Fashek, Majek: *Spirit of Love,* Interscope, 1991.
Little Steven: "Out of the Darkness," EMI America, 1984 • *Voice of America,* EMI America, 1984 • "Vote!," EMI America, 1984 • *Freedom No Compromise,* Manhattan, 1987 • *Revolution,* RCA, 1989 • "The Time of Your Life," MLA, 1995 (*Nine Months* soundtrack).
Little Steven and the Disciples of Soul: "Forever," EMI America, 1982 • *Men Without Women,* EMI America, 1982.
Lone Justice: "Shelter," Geffen, 1986 • *Shelter,* Geffen, 1986.
Lords of the New Church: *Killer Lords* (2 tracks), IRS, 1986.
Love, Darlene: "All Alone on Christmas," Fox/Arista, 1992 (*Home Alone 2* soundtrack).
Meat Loaf: "Amnesty Is Granted," MCA, 1995 • *Welcome to the Neighborhood,* MCA, 1996.
Priviero, Massimo: *Nessuna Resa Mai,* WEA Italy, 1990.
Southside Johnny and the Asbury Jukes: "I Don't Want to Go Home," Epic, 1976 • *I Don't Wanna Go Home,* Epic, 1976 • *This Time It's for Real,* Epic, 1977 • *Hearts of Stone,* Epic, 1978 • *Havin' a Party with Southside Johnny,* Epic, 1979 • *Better Days,* Impact, 1991 • *All I Want Is Everything: The Best of (1979–1991),* Rhino, 1993.
Spector, Ronnie: "Say Goodbye to Hollywood," Epic, 1977.
Springsteen, Bruce: "Fade Away," Columbia, 1980 • "Hungry Heart," Columbia, 1980 • *The River,* Columbia, 1980 • "Born in the U.S.A.," Columbia, 1984 • *Born in the U.S.A.,* Columbia, 1984 • "Cover Me," Columbia, 1984 • "Dancing in the Dark," Columbia, 1984 • "Pink Cadillac," Columbia, 1984 • "Glory Days," Columbia, 1985 • "I'm Goin' Down," Columbia, 1985 • "I'm on Fire," Columbia, 1985 • "My Hometown," Columbia, 1985 • *Greatest Hits,* Columbia, 1995 • *Tracks,* Columbia, 1998.

Harry Vanda and George Young

There's every likelihood that Harry Vanda (born March 22, 1947, in the Hague, Netherlands) and George Young (born November 6, 1947, in Glasgow, Scotland) would be little known outside of their chosen home of Australia, doing exactly what they are doing today—producing native bands and having an occasional hit—had not one Australia band they were close to gotten lucky. Vanda and Young were fortunate not only to have several international hits with various pop bands but also to work with, and be instrumental in shaping the sound of, one of the most influential heavy metal bands of all time: AC/DC.

Vanda and Young immigrated to Australia from Holland and Scotland, respectively, when they were very young and played in numerous local bands before striking gold with the Easybeats, who scored a worldwide hit with "Friday on My Mind" in 1967. The group moved to England to be more in the center of things, but Vanda and Young returned to Australia when it broke up in 1970. They began working as a production and songwriting team for Albert Productions, an off-shoot of Australia's J. Albert Publishing. They produced many young artists; an album of their own, under the name Marcus Hook Roll Band; and an album for former Easybeats vocalist Stevie Wright, which produced the Australian hit "Evie" in 1974.

In 1973, George Young's kid brothers, Malcolm and Angus, assembled an unfashionably gritty, stripped-down heavy bar band they dubbed AC/DC. The junior Youngs benefited from Vanda and Young's experience in the business as well as in the studio. Vanda and Young cut AC/DC's first single, which was a hit in parts of Australia, in 1973 and then worked with the band to help them make the transition from cover band to original act on their 1975 debut *High Voltage*. They went on to produce AC/DC's next five albums, 1976's *TNT* and *Dirty Deeds Done Dirt Cheap*, 1977's *Let There Be Rock* (No. 17 U.K.), 1978's *Powerage*, and the live *If You Want Blood, You've Got It* (No. 13 U.K.). The latter three all went platinum.

They helped the band convert raw ideas to songs that featured simple, yet inexorably catchy, melodies over riff-oriented, churning guitar grooves. In 1978, Atlantic, the band's American label, decided that the band's sound lacked the slickness needed to compete on the radio with bands like Boston and Styx and tapped Robert John "Mutt" Lange (see entry) to produce 1979's *Highway to Hell*. That album did indeed break AC/DC as an international supergroup. However, the music was merely a continuation of the band's distinctive sound, somewhat polished up. What is significant (and influential) about AC/DC was, in part, thanks to their original producers.

Vanda and Young went on to work with other Australian metal bands, such as Rose Tattoo. They also did more pop-oriented projects, including John Paul Young's 1978 international hit "Love Is in the Air" (No. 7). They also recorded themselves under the name Flash and the Pan, releasing several albums in the late '70s and early '80s, including a Top 10 U.K. hit, "Waiting for a Train."

In 1988 Vanda and Young co-produced (with Lange) AC/DC's *Blow Up Your Video* (No. 12). They continue to produce and write songs, working almost exclusively with acts unknown outside of Australia and New Zealand. —ANASTASIA PANTSIOS

AC/DC: *Jailbreak* (EP), Atlantic, 1974, 1994 • *Dirty Deeds Done Dirt Cheap*, Atlantic, 1976 • *High Voltage*, Atlantic, 1975, 1976 • *Let There Be Rock*, Atlantic, 1977 • "Gone Shootin'," Geffen, 1978, 1996 (*Beavis and Butt-head Do America*

soundtrack) • *If You Want Blood, You've Got It* Atlantic, 1978 • *Powerage*, Atlantic, 1978 • *Who Made Who*, Atlantic, 1986 • *Blow Up Your Video*, Atco, 1988 • *Bonfire*, Elektra, 1997.

Cheetah: *Rock and Roll Women*, Epic, 1981.

Easybeats, The: *Falling Off the Edge of the World*, United Artists, 1968 • *Friends*, Polydor, 1970.

Flash and the Pan: "And the Band Played on (Down Among the Dead Men)," Ensign/Epic, 1978 • *Flash and the Pan*, Epic, 1979 • "Hey, St. Peter," Epic, 1979 • *Lights in the Night*, Epic, 1980 • *Headlines*, Epic, 1982 • *Pan-O-Rama*, Epic, 1983 • "Waiting for a Train," Easy Beat, 1983 • *Collection*, Epic, 1994.

Haffy's Whiskey Sour: "Shot in the Head/Bye Bye Bluebird," Deram, 1971.

Marcus Hook Roll Band: *The Marcus Hook Roll Band*, Capitol, 1973.

Paintbox: "Get Ready for Love/Can I Get to Know You?," Youngblood, 1971.

Rose Tattoo: *Assault and Battery*, Carrere/Mirage, 1981 • *Rock 'n' Roll Outlaws*, Carrere/Mirage, 1981 • *Scarred for Life*, Carrere, 1982.

Saints, The: *Prodigal Son* (1 track), TVT, 1990.

Vanda, Harry, and George Young: *Early Morning Wake-Up Call*, Epic, 1985 • *Night in France*, Epic, 1988.

Wright, Stevie: *Hard Road*, Polydor, 1974 • *Black Eyed Bruiser*, Albert, 1975.

Young, John Paul: "Love Is in the Air," Scotti Brothers, 1978 • *Love Is in the Air*, Ariola/Scotti Brothers, 1978 • *Heaven Sent*, Ariola/Midsong, 1980.

VARIOUS ARTISTS
Strictly Ballroom soundtrack, CBS, 1992.

Junior Vasquez

Junior Vasquez (born Donald Mattern, August 24, 1946, in Philadelphia, Pennsylvania) is a unique dance music producer, capable of making a night-club a vehicle to carry revelers off on intense, joyful journeys. He pushes people's buttons, forces them to feel a variety of emotions and always leaves them grinning. For a taste of the magic, try *Junior Vasquez Live*, a collection that testifies to his strength as DJ and as one of the leading producers of dance music in the world.

He now attracts a degree of attention unusual for clubland. His distinctive, often tribalistic grooves have graced the music of such superstars as Madonna, Cher, and Janet Jackson. He's recently added a few notches to his renegade belt by branching out from the dance floor to the guitar-driven realm of John Mellencamp, spicing up the veteran rocker's recent work with a genre-bending rhythm-pop sensibility. And if that's not enough, he is honing his natural ear for classic pop melodies by writing songs with a fairly broad range of artists, spanning established acts like Cyndi Lauper and appealing newcomers like Wild Orchid.

At the core of all of this activity, however, is Vasquez's first love—weaving tunes behind turntables. It's the point from which he conjures most magic. It's also apparently where he is happiest. He particularly enjoys Arena, the New York City club where he spins every Saturday night. "There's nothing more addicting or totally empowering than bringing people together through music," he says. "I think I'd die if I didn't have a place to DJ. It's so deeply a part of who I am."

Vasquez's rise to fame began eight years ago when he opened a club in Manhattan called Bassline. His vision was a strictly after-hours underground club; the gutted warehouse later became the legendary Sound Factory. Vasquez proved that the flex of a finger can add dimension to a record, and the way he strings songs together can send partyers on an energetic, cathartic journey.

"There's an indescribable emotion that comes from being in the midst of a great song, whether it's yours or someone else's," he says. "But of course, there's nothing greater than being the creator, the man who is weaving the groove. That's when you feel most powerful—and most magical." —LARRY FLICK

Barlow, Gary: *Open Road,* Arista, 1997.
Bertei, Adele: "Zami Girl" (remix), Imago, 1994.
Bowie, David: "Little Wonder" (remix), Virgin, 1997.
Campbell, Tevin: "Round and Round" (remix), Paisley Park/WB, 1990.
Cher: "One by One" (remix), Reprise, 1996.
Church, The: "Feel" (remix), Arista, 1992.
Connie and Junior: "Lift Me Up," Eightball, 1997.
DJ Skribble/Anthony Acid: *MDMA,* Vol. 1, Warlock, 1998.
Dolce and Gabbana: "Music" (remix), Popular, 1996.
Ellis, T.C.: *True Confessions* (1 track), Paisley Park/WB, 1991.
Funky Green Dogs: "Fired Up" (remix), MCA, 1997.
Gibson, Debbie: *Deborah,* Espiritu, 1997 • "Only Words," Jellybean, 1997.
Houston, Whitney: "I Wanna Dance with Somebody (Who Loves Me)" (remix), Arista, 1995, 1996 • *Why Does It Hurt So Bad?* (remix), Arista, 1996 • "Step by Step" (remix), Arista, 1997.
Jones, Tom: "She's a Lady," MCA, 1995.
Jose and Luis: "Do It to the Rhythm," Sire, 1993 (*New Faces*) •

"Queen's English," Sire, 1993 (*New Faces*) • "You Want to Touch Me," Sire, 1993 (*New Faces*).
lang, k.d.: "You're O.K" (remix), Warner Bros., 1996.
Lauper, Cyndi: *Hat Full of Stars,* Portrait, 1993 • "Come on Home," Epic Dance, 1995 • "Come on Home" (remix), Epic Dance, 1995 • "You Don't Know" (remix), Epic, 1996.
Lazonby, Peter: "Wave Speech" (remix), Pagoda, 1996.
Le Click: "Call Me" (remix), Logic, 1997.
Lisa Lisa: *LL 77,* Pendulum, 1994 • "When I Fell in Love," Pendulum, 1994.
Madonna: "Causing a Commotion" (remix), Sire, 1987.
Mellencamp, John: *Mr. Happy Go Lucky,* Mercury, 1996.
Mullen, Larry Jr.: "Theme from Mission Impossible," Mother, 1996.
Parton, Dolly: "Peace Train" (remix), Flipit, 1996.
Peniston, CeCe: "Hit by Love" (remix), A&M, 1994.
Pet Shop Boys: "Yesterday When I Was Mad" (remix), EMI, 1994 • *Disco 2,* EMI, 1995.
Prince: "Hot Thing" (remix), Paisley Park, 1987.
Qkumba Zoo: "Child (Inside)" (remix), Arista, 1996.
Quest, J.: *The Quest Is On,* Mercury, 1995.
Race: featuring Who's Dat Girl?, "Fantasy," Scorch/Warlock, 1997.
Robinson, Vicki Sue: "House of Joy," Pagoda, 1997.
S., Robin: "I Want to Thank You," Atlantic, 1993 • *Show Me Love* (1 track), Atlantic, 1993.
Siouxsie & the Banshees: "Fear (of the Unknown)" (remix), Geffen, 1991.
Sound of Blackness: "Everything Is Gonna Be Alright" (remix), Perspective/A&M, 1994 • "Children of the World," Lightyear, 1996.
Spice Girls: "2 Become 1" (remix), Virgin, 1997 • "Say You'll Be There" (remix), Virgin, 1997.
Stansfield, Lisa: *#1 Remixes* (remix), Arista, 1998.
Technotronic: *Trip on This (The Remixes),* Capitol, 1990.
Vasquez, Junior: "Get Your Hands off My Man," Tribal America, 1994 • *Nervaas* (EP), Tribal America, 1994 • *Best of Junior Vasquez: Just Like a Queen,* Hot, 1995 • "Reap (What You Sow)," MCA, 1995 • "If Madonna Calls," Groovilicious, 1996 • "I Am Thin and Gorgeous," Pagoda, 1997 • *Junior Vasquez Live,* Vol. 1, Drive Archive, 1997 • "Come Together," Drive Archive, 1998 • *Junior Vasquez Live,* Vol. 2, Pagoda, 1998.
Wild Orchid: "Talk to Me," RCA, 1997.
Yello: "Tied Up" (remix), Mercury, 1988.

COLLECTIONS

If You Love Dance, Epic, 1996.
Keith Haring: A Retrospective: The Music of His Era, Logic, 1997.
Works Eightball, K-Tel, 1998.

"Little" Louie Vega

See MASTERS AT WORK

Nik Venet

N ikolas Kostantinos Venetoulis made no bones
about his attitude. "I don't make records for
unconscious people," said the veteran producer in
an interview in the summer of 1997. "After going to a
concert or buying a CD of one of my artists, you should
have more information than before, you should be
more enlightened. I still get an average of 200 e-mails a
month from people who tell me their lives were altered
by Fred Neil, John Stewart, or Dory Previn. I don't think
there are many other people, unless we're talking about
Jesus Christ or L. Ron Hubbard, who have altered that
many lives. And I'm not looking to alter lives. I'm looking to perpetuate an art form." Inveterate smoker Venetoulis, better known as Nik Venet, died January 2, 1998,
of Burkitt's lymphoma.

A fan of Nat "King" Cole producer Lee Gillette and
of John Hammond (see entry), Venet, the legendary

Columbia Records A&R man who produced Billie Hol-
iday and Bob Dylan and signed Bruce Springsteen,
shaped the records and careers of Glen Campbell, Linda
Ronstadt, Jim Croce, Lou Rawls, the Beach Boys, Bobby
Darin, Dory Previn, Carl Reiner and Mel Brooks, Orson
Welles, and Lord Buckley.

In 1997, Venet produced records by California
singers Sarah Kim Wilde and Harriet Schock for his new
label, Evening Star. He also taught songwriting and production and was a trustee of the National Academy of
Recording Arts and Sciences (NARAS).

Born December 3, 1936, in Baltimore, Venet started
producing when he was about 15. The earliest sessions
involved young Nik and some friends making Dixieland
music in a studio. "We had no idea what we were doing,
but a group of friends decided we'd make a Dixieland
record," he recalls. "So we rounded up everybody with
an instrument, I put them in a room and everybody
said, 'What are we going to play?' I said, 'The World Is
Waiting for the Sunrise,' and that was my first command as a producer."

In his late teens, on a visit to Shreveport, Venet got
together with guitarist Jimmy Burton (as James Burton,
he was one of Elvis's main men), "a kid named Waylan
Humphries, a kid named Lewis on drums, and Dale
Hawkins on vocals. Dale Hawkins had a song called
'Susie-Q.' We went into a radio station at midnight
when they closed down and put various people in different rooms; the drummer was out in the bathroom,
and someplace in there we stuck Dale; I was in the engineer's booth. We were using a Roberts mono tape
recorder and recorded 'Susie-Q.' It was everybody's production. There were no such words as producer then;
there were no credits on records."

This merry band drove a 7 1/2 inch tape of the
Hawkins song to Chicago in a 1949 Cadillac. Leonard
Chess bought the record, added echo, pressed a 45 and
a 78, and Hawkins became a star for a year. By the end
of the decade, Venet had made it to Los Angeles, securing a job at World Pacific Records, an influential (and
long-defunct) jazz label owned by Richard Bock. There,
Venet helped on records by the likes of jazz orchestra
leader Gerald Wilson and trumpeter Chet Baker. He
also produced records by Lord Buckley, a brilliant repro-
bate whose jazzy, irreverent humor defined hip and convinced Venet to record Carl Reiner and Mel Brooks as
the 2000 Year Old Man when Venet got to Capitol at the
dawn of the '60s. It also was at World Pacific that Venet
met Ravi Shankar. The great Hindu sitarist "gave me
my world view of music," Venet says. Venet also
claimed to have introduced the notorious Kim Fowley
to the record business.

Venet's first million-seller at Capitol was "When I Fall in Love," by the Lettermen. It was 1961, the last year for 78s—and so early in the pop era that the 78 rpm version of the single bears the listing "fox trot."

Singularity in an artist appeals to Venet. So do careers. Venet says he brought Linda Ronstadt out, giving her prominence in the Stone Poneys, a Los Angeles group whose "Different Drum" reached No. 13 in December 1967. Venet was offered "It Must Be Him" for Ronstadt to record but turned it down, considering it retrograde and demeaning to women. "I wanted a song with an attitude and point of view that created a career," Venet said. " 'Different Drum' made a career only because it was a girl singing 'You may not be pretty' to a guy. The song that made it big that year had the lyric, 'My God, if it's not him, I will surely die.' I turned that song flat down, told the writer it was a piece of shit. The guy said it was going to be a big hit, but I wasn't talking about sales, I was talking about quality." Vikki Carr's "It Must Be Him" reached No. 3 at the end of September 1967.

"It's not what you do in the studio, it's what you don't do," he said. "Everything should be to the point where the artist is free to express an emotional feeling without anything interrupting the flow, like the producer saying, 'Let's try it this way.' It should come from the lyric and the attitude of the artist, which has been worked on before you go into the studio. Making a CD is the last thing a singer/songwriter should do. Today, everybody says, 'I'm making a CD.' Let me hear the songs."

Venet can only take the artist as far as he or she can go. "I can't refine any more than the artist really is," said Venet. "I take the artist to exactly where they are, and not any further. That's why I like doing two, three, or four albums on an artist before they become internationally known. It's a kind of grooming. It's also a matter of distillation. Hemingway said, when someone asked him how he got those wonderful small paragraphs, that it's real easy: 'You write and you write and you write, and after a couple of dozen years, you get all the shit out of your system.' "

Any production he's particularly proud of? Fred Neil's *Sessions*, released on Capitol in 1968. It's long and—criminally—out of print. "I love Fred Neil's stuff," Venet said. "Fred Neil's *Sessions* was the most honest album I'd made. Up until that time, you'd only had non-lyric, jazz records that were spontaneous. Working with Fred, letting the tapes roll with two machines and three engineers so you wouldn't have to stop for anything and continuing to record as the artist found his mood and let it run, letting it go the way he interpreted it that night."

Not only is *Sessions* one of the great works-in-progress in recorded music; it showcases a singer/guitarist at the height of his powers (Neil, who wrote the classics "Everybody's Talking," "The Other Side of This Life," and "The Dolphins," is a reclusive Floridian who hasn't released a record since 1971) and at his lowest voice. This record, which was mixed as it was recorded, is remarkably deep. "It's not what I did at the session," Venet says, "it's what I did before and what I didn't do. I did not let anything interfere with the artist's free flow, and none of those musicians were told what to play or how to play. They all worked off Neil's lyric and mood. For an analogy, I'll tell you to close your eyes, relax and fall backwards, and I'll catch you. That's absolute trust."
—CARLO WOLFF

Beach Boys: "Surfin'," Capitol, 1962 • "Ten Little Indians," Capitol, 1962 • "409," Capitol, 1962 • "Surfin' Safari," Capitol, 1962 • *Surfin' Safari*, Capitol, 1962 • "Shut Down," Capitol, 1963 • "Surfin' U.S.A.," Capitol, 1963 • *Surfin' USA*, Capitol, 1963 • *Close-Up*, Capitol, 1969 • *Made in the U.S.A.*, Capitol, 1986 • *Good Vibrations: Thirty Years of the Beach Boys*, Capitol, 1993.

Buckley, Lord: *The Way Out Humor of Lord Buckley*, World Pacific, 1959 • *Buckley's World*, World Pacific, 1968.

Buddies, The: *Go Go with the Buddies*, Wing, 1965 • *The Buddies and the Compacts*, Wing, 1965.

Campbell, Glen: *Big Bluegrass Special*, Capitol Nashville, 1962, 1996 • *Too Late to Worry, Too Blue to Cry*, Capitol, 1963 • *By the Time I Get to Phoenix*, Capitol Nashville, 1967, 1996 • *Essential*, Vol. 3, Capitol, 1995 • *Gentle on My Mind: The Collection, 1962–1989*, Razor & Tie, 1997.

Cashman and West: *AM FM Blues: Their Very Best*, Razor & Tie, 1993.

Croce, Jim: *Bombs Over Puerto Rico*, Bear Family, 1996.

Dalton, Karen: *It's So Hard to Tell Who's Gonna Love You the Best*, Koch, 1969, 1997.

Darin, Bobby: *18 Yellow Roses*, Capitol, 1963 • *You're the Reason I'm Living*, Capitol, 1963 • *From Hello Dolly to Goodbye Charlie*, Capitol, 1964 • *Capitol Collectors Series*, Capitol, 1989 • *As Long As I'm Singing: The Bobby Darin Collection*, Rhino, 1995.

Four Preps: *Capitol Collectors Series*, Capitol, 1989.

Gerdes, George: *Obituary*, United Artists, 1971 • *Son of Obituary*, United Artists, 1972.

Haskell, Jimmie: *Sunset Surf*, Capitol, 1963.

Hearts and Flowers: *Now Is the Time for Hearts and Flowers*, Capitol, 1967 • *Of Horses, Kids and Forgotten Women*, Capitol, 1968.

Hedge and Donna: *All the Friendly Colours*, Capitol, 1969.

Hondells, The: *Go Little Honda*, Mercury, 1964 • *The Hondells*, Mercury, 1964 • *Greatest Hits*, Curb, 1996.

King Curtis: *Soul Serenade,* Capitol, 1964 • *Blow Man, Blow!,* Bear Family, 1965, 1993.

Leaves, The: *All the Good That's Happening,* One Way, 1967, 1994.

Lettermen, The: "When I Fall in Love," Capitol, 1961 • *All Time Greatest Hits,* Capitol, 1974 • *Capitol Collectors Series,* Capitol, 1992.

Lothar and the Hand People: *Space Hymn,* Capitol, 1969.

Mad River: *Mad River,* Capitol, 1969 • *Paradise Bar and Grill,* Capitol, 1994.

Maffitt-Davies: *The Rise and Fall of Honesty,* Capitol, 1969.

Matthews, Ian: *Hit and Run,* Columbia, 1977.

McCann, Les: *Relationships: The Les McCann Anthology,* Rhino, 1993.

Neil, Fred: *Everybody's Talkin',* Capitol, 1966 • *Fred Neil,* Capitol, 1967 • *Sessions,* Capitol, 1968 • *The Very Best Of,* See for Miles, 1986.

Payne, Dinsmore: *Dinsmore Payne,* United Artists, 1973.

Previn, Dory: *On My Way to Where,* United Artists, 1970 • *Mythical Kings and Iguanas,* United Artists, 1971 • *Reflections in a Mud Puddle,* United Artists, 1971 • *Mary C. Brown and the Hollywood Sign,* United Artists, 1972 • *Live at Carnegie Hall,* United Artists, 1973 • *Dory Previn,* Warner Bros., 1974.

Rawls, Lou: w/ Les McCann, *Stormy Monday,* Blue Note, 1962, 1990 • *The Best from Lou Rawls,* Capitol, 1968 • *The Legendary Lou Rawls,* Blue Note, 1992 • *Love Is a Hurtin' Thing: The Silk and Soul of Lou Rawls,* EMI America, 1997.

Reiner, Carl, and Mel Brooks: *The Complete 2000 Year Old Man,* Rhino, 1994.

Riley, Billy Lee: *Harmonica Beatlemania,* Mercury, 1964.

Roman, Murray: *Busted,* United Artists, 1972.

Ronstadt, Linda: *Different Drum,* Capitol, 1974 • *Greatest Hits,* Vol. 1, Asylum, 1976.

Schock, Harriett: *Rosebud,* Evening Star, 1997.

Scott, Jack: *Classic Scott,* Bear Family, 1994.

Sellers, Maxine: *Life Is Short, But It Is Wide,* Capitol, 1975.

Serendipity Singers: *Don't Let the Rain Come Down: The Best Of,* Chronicles/Mercury, 1998.

Stewart, John: *California Bloodlines,* Capitol, 1969 • *Phoenix Concerts Live,* RCA, 1974 • *Cannons in the Rain/Wingless Angels,* Bear Family, 1975 • *Wingless Angels,* RCA, 1975 • *California Bloodlines/Willard,* Bear Family, 1989 • *The Complete Phoenix Concerts,* Bear Family, 1990.

Stone Poneys: "Different Drum," Capitol, 1967 • *Different Drum,* Capitol, 1967 • *The Stone Poneys,* United Artists, 1972.

Taylor, Allan: *American Album,* United Artists, 1973.

Thomas, Guthrie: *Guthrie Thomas 1,* Capitol, 1975.

Vettes, The: *Rev-Up,* MGM, 1963.

Waldman, Wendy: *Wendy Waldman,* Warner Bros., 1975 • *Love Is the Only Goal: The Best Of,* Warner Archives, 1996.

Walker, Sammy: *Sammy Walker,* Warner Bros., 1976 • *Blue Ridge Mountain Skyline,* Warner Bros., 1977.

Welles, Orson: *The Begatting of the President,* Mediarts, 1970.

Wilde, Sarah Kim: *Embers,* Evening Star, 1997.

COLLECTIONS
Salvation soundtrack, Angel, 1969.

The Brill Building Sound: Singers and Songwriters Who Rocked the 60's, Era, 1993.

Mike Vernon

A s a mainstay at Decca Records in London during the heyday of the British blues boom, Mike Vernon was responsible for producing classic albums by John Mayall's Bluesbreakers, Savoy Brown, and Ten Years After. Moreover, as head of Blue Horizon Records, Vernon molded Fleetwood Mac, then led by guitar whiz kid Peter Green, into an international attraction. Indeed, Vernon's prodigious talents helped fuel the worldwide popularity of British blues-rock in the '60s and '70s.

Born in Harrow, Middlesex, England, on November 20, 1944, Vernon started Blue Horizon as a fanzine label even before he joined Decca Records in London in 1962 after an intense lobbying effort. Three years later, Vernon produced the classic album by John Mayall with Eric Clapton: *Bluesbreakers.* "It went to No. 1 on the *Melody Maker* album chart and the irony is that nobody at Decca apart from myself, engineer Gus Dudgeon (see entry), and a few other people who were into the music knew who John Mayall or Eric Clapton was," Vernon muses.

Vernon points out that Clapton's novel guitar playing also required a different recording approach. "Eric set up this big Marshall amp and Gus looked at it and said, 'My God, how am I going to record that?' We found that the best way was to put microphones at a distance and get the space of the room, something that had been done 15 or 20 years before at CBS Studios and at Atlantic Studios."

"When we started with the Bluesbreakers it was 4-track," Vernon adds. "We had to lay bass, drums, organ, and a rhythm guitar first and put the [guitar] solos on another track. We had to do the vocal and the horn section on another track. If we ran out of tracks we dumped it across to a second 4-track, mixing that down to stereo, giving us two more tracks."

The success of the Mayall-Clapton album led to a series of seminal Vernon-produced albums featuring British guitar heroes: Mayall's *A Hard Road* with Peter Green and *Crusade* with Mick Taylor; Savoy Brown's *Blue Matter,* featuring Kim Simmonds; and Ten Years After's self-titled debut, featuring Alvin Lee. In 1967, Vernon launched Blue Horizon, even though he was still a Decca staff producer, with one act: Peter Green's Fleetwood Mac.

"We had cut three or four songs as demos and I went to Decca and played them the tracks," Vernon recalls. "But Decca refused to let me put them out on the Blue Horizon label. They said, 'You can have it on Decca with a Blue Horizon credit but we can't let you have your own label.' I went to CBS [now Sony] and they leapt at the chance. When Decca found out that I had a Fleetwood Mac record coming out that I'd produced on Blue Horizon and distributed by CBS, I was very politely told to leave."

Vernon's understanding of the blues idiom enabled him to capture the essence of Green's powerful, evocative songs, such as "I Loved Another Woman," "Rollin' Man," "A Fool No More," "Man of the World" (No. 2 U.K.), "Albatross" (No. 1 U.K.), and Green's best-known track, "Black Magic Woman."

"To make a commercial, radio-friendly blues record back then was extremely difficult," Vernon says. "Peter came up with the intro for 'Black Magic Woman' that was like a godsend, because the instant you heard it, you knew what it was: it was indelibly printed in your brain. Coupled with a great groove and a wonderful guitar solo, it was destined to be a hit."

Vernon points out that Fleetwood Mac's success gave him the freedom to develop other acts. "CBS said, 'Look, there's the door, it's wide open; do what you want, as long as it doesn't cost us an arm and a leg. We don't care as long as you're selling records.' So we went off and recorded Johnny Shines and Sunnyland Slim and Otis Spann. I was in the studio consistently for something like four years recording blues stuff, but very little of it didn't sell."

After Fleetwood Mac departed Blue Horizon for Warner Bros., Vernon hooked up with the Dutch band, Focus, for a string of successful albums for Sire Records in the '70s: *Moving Waves* (No. 8), *At the Rainbow,* and *Focus III* (No. 6 U.K.). Vernon also produced tracks for Freddy King's *Burglar* album.

In the '80s, Vernon found another act: Level 42, a jazzy pop-funk unit that charted in Britain and the U.S. Returning to the blues in the '90s, Vernon started two labels: Indigo and Code Blue. Code Blue album productions include Bo Diddley's *A Man Amongst Men,* with

contributions from Rolling Stones guitarists Keith Richards (see Glimmer Twins entry) and Ron Wood; John Primer's *The Real Deal;* and Eric Bibb's *Me to You.* In 1996 Vernon compiled a boxed set of highlights from his famed Blue Horizon label.

Vernon's legacy is not all blues-related. In fact, he produced Bloodstone's hit, "Natural High" (No. 10). "I may be the only white British record producer to produce an all-black American soul act in America," says Vernon. —BEN CROMER

Artwoods, The: *The Artwoods,* Spark, 1966.

Bacon Fat: *Grease One for Me,* Blue Horizon, 1970.

Bennett, Duster: *Smiling Like I'm Happy,* Blue Horizon, 1968 • *Bright Lights,* Blue Horizon, 1969 • *12 DB's,* Blue Horizon, 1970.

Bibb, Eric: *Me to You,* Code Blue, 1998.

Bloodstone: "Natural High," London, 1973 • *Unreal,* London, 1974 • *Do You Wanna Do a Thing?,* London, 1976 • *The Very Best of Bloodstone,* Rhino, 1997.

Blues 'N Trouble: *Hat Trick,* Blue Horizon, 1987.

Bowie, David: *David Bowie,* Deram, 1967, 1989 • *Images,* Deram, 1967.

Boyd, Eddie: *Eddie Boyd and His Blues Band,* Decca, 1967 • *7936 South Rhodes,* Epic, 1968.

Bridges, Eugene Hideaway: *Born to Be Blue,* Blueside, 1998.

Butler, George "Wild Child": *These Mean Old Blues,* Bullseye Blues, 1991 • *Stranger,* Bullseye Blues, 1994.

Chicken Shack: *40 Blue Fingers Freshly Packed and Ready to Serve,* Blue Horizon, 1968 • *O.K. Ken,* Blue Horizon, 1968 • *The 100 Ton Chicken,* Blue Horizon, 1969 • *Accept,* Blue Horizon, 1970.

Clapton, Eric: *Crossroads,* Polydor, 1988.

Climax Blues Band: *Gold Plated,* Sire, 1976.

Diddley, Bo: *A Man Amongst Men,* Code Blue/Atlantic, 1996.

Diversions: *Soul Survivors,* Polydor, 1977.

Dr. Feelgood: *Let It Roll,* United Artists, 1979.

Dupree, Champion Jack: *When You Feel the Feeling You Was Feeling,* Blue Horizon, 1968 • *Champion Jack Dupree and Mickey Baker,* Sire, 1969.

Edwards, David Honeyboy: *Delta Bluesman,* Earwig, 1992.

Ellis: *Why Not,* Epic, 1973.

Fleetwood Mac: "Albatross," Epic, 1968 • "Black Magic Woman," Epic, 1968 • *Fleetwood Mac,* Blue Horizon, 1968 • *Mr. Wonderful,* Blue Horizon, 1968 • "Need Your Love So Bad," Epic, 1968 • *English Rose,* Blue Horizon, 1969 • "Man of the World," Immediate, 1969 • *Black Magic Woman,* Epic, 1971 • *Greatest Hits,* CBS, 1971 • *Fleetwood Mac in Chicago 1969,* Blue Horizon/Sire, 1975.

Focus: *Moving Waves,* Blue Horizon/Sire, 1971, 1973 • *Focus 3,* Polydor/Sire, 1972 • "Sylvia," Polydor/Sire, 1972 • *At the Rainbow,* Polydor/Sire, 1973 • "Hocus Pocus," Sire,

1973 • *Hamburger Concerto,* Polydor/Atco, 1974 • *Focus,* Polydor/Sire, 1975 • *Ship of Memories,* Sire, 1977 • *Hocus Pocus: The Best of Focus,* EMI, 1994.

Ford, Robben: *Discovering the Blues,* Rhino, 1997.

Foster Brothers: *On the Line,* Rocket, 1977.

Hayward, Rick: *Rick Hayward,* Blue Horizon, 1971.

Hoax, The: *Sound Like This,* Code Blue, 1995.

Jellybread: *First Slice,* Blue Horizon, 1969.

Johnny and the Roccos: *Bop a Dee Bop a Doo,* Big Beat, 1997.

Jupp, Mickey: *Some People Can't Dance,* A&M, 1982.

Kane, Candye: *Swango,* Sire, 1998.

King, Freddie: *Burglar,* PolyGram, 1974 • *Larger Than Life,* RSO, 1975.

Kothari, Chim: *Sound of Sitar,* Deram, 1966.

Level 42: *Level 42,* Polydor, 1981 • "Love Games," Polydor, 1981 • "Starchild," Polydor, 1981 • "Turn It On," Polydor, 1981 • "Are You Hearing (What I Hear)," Polydor, 1982 • "The Chinese Way," Polydor, 1982 • *The Pursuit of Accidents,* Polydor, 1982 • "Weave Your Spell," Polydor, 1982 • *The Remix Collection,* Connoisseur, 1996.

Lightnin' Slim: *London Gumbo,* Blue Horizon, 1972.

Mayall, John: w/ Eric Clapton, *Bluesbreakers,* Decca/London, 1966 • *A Hard Road,* Decca/London, 1967 • *Crusade,* Decca/London, 1967 • *Raw Blues,* Deram, 1967 • *The Blues Alone,* Mobile Fidelity, 1967, 1996 • *Bare Wires,* Decca/London, 1968 • *Blues from Laurel Canyon,* Decca/London, 1968 • *Diary of a Band,* Vols. 1–2, Decca, 1968 • *Looking Back,* Decca/London, 1969 • *Thru' the Years,* Decca, 1971 • *London Blues 1964–1969,* Deram, 1992 • *As it All Began: The Best of John Mayall and the Bluesbreakers, 1964–1968,* Deram, 1998.

McCray, Larry: *Delta Hurricane,* Virgin, 1993.

Mick Clarke Band: *Steel and Fire,* Burnside, 1989.

Olympic Runners: *Out in Front,* London, 1975 • *Hot to Trot,* Chipping Norton, 1977 • *Keepin' It Up,* RCA, 1978 • *Puttin' It on You,* Polydor, 1978 • *Dancealot,* Polydor, 1979 • *Out of the Ground,* RCA, 1979.

Owens, Jay: *The Blues Soul of Jay Owens,* Indigo, 1994.

Perfect, Christine: *Christine Perfect,* Blue Horizon, 1970.

Primer, John: *The Real Deal,* Code Blue, 1996.

Roachford: *Roachford* (6 tracks), Epic, 1988.

Robertson, Sherman: *I'm the Man,* Code Blue, 1994 • *Here and Now,* Code Blue, 1996.

Savoy Brown: *Shake Down,* Decca, 1967 • *Getting to the Point,* Decca/Parrot, 1968 • *A Step Further,* Parrot, 1969 • *Blue Matter,* Decca/Parrot, 1969 • *The Savoy Brown Collection,* Chronicles, 1993.

Sharpe, Rocky, and the Replays: *Rock It to Mars,* Chiswick, 1980 • *Come On Let's Go,* Chiswick, 1981 • *Rama Lama,* Chiswick, 1981 • *Shout Shout,* Chiswick, 1981 • *Stop Please Stop,* Polydor, 1983.

Shines, Johnny: *Last Night's Dream,* Warner Bros., 1968.

Smith, Gordon: *Long Overdue,* Blue Horizon, 1968.

Spann, Otis: *Biggest Thing Since Colossus,* Rewind/Columbia, 1969, 1995.

Starr, Edwin: *Edwin Starr,* GTO, 1977.

Stewart, Rod: *Storyteller: The Complete Anthology,* Warner Bros., 1989.

Sunnyland Slim: *Midnight Jump,* Blue Horizon, 1969.

Ten Years After: *Ten Years After,* Deram, 1967 • *Stonehenge,* Deram, 1968 • *Undead,* Deram, 1968 • *Alvin Lee and Company,* Deram, 1972.

Topham, Top: *Ascension Heights,* Blue Horizon, 1970.

Velez, Martha: *Hypnotized,* Polydor, 1972.

Vernon, Mike: *Bring It Back Home,* Blue Horizon, 1971 • *Moments of Madness,* Sire, 1973.

Wilson, U.P.: w/ Paul Orta and the Kingpins, *Attack of the Atomic Guitar,* Red Lightnin', 1993.

Witherspoon, Jimmy: w/ Robben Ford, *Live,* LAX, 1977 • *Blues, the Whole Blues and Nothing but the Blues,* Indigo, 1992 • *Love Is a Five Letter Word,* Avenue Jazz, 1998.

Youlden, Chris: *Second Sight,* Ruff, 1995.

Butch Vig

While Butch Vig is modest about his role in the success of Nirvana's seven-times-platinum *Nevermind* (No. 1)—arguably the most influential album of the '90s—his knack for balancing noise and melody no doubt contributed to the record's greatness. "At the time, given the kind of records I was making, and having a pop sensibility, it seemed like the chemistry was really perfect for me to start working with Nirvana," says Vig. "They were an amazing band, extremely powerful, and [late Nirvana frontman] Kurt [Cobain] wrote amazing songs that were just so hooky. I was somehow able to capture that, to get the punk passion down, but also get really good, strong performances out of them and keep all the key elements of the songs really, really focused. It wasn't like I invented anything new."

Since *Nevermind,* Vig has produced albums for Smashing Pumpkins, Soul Asylum, Freedy Johnston, L7, and Sonic Youth and played drums for and produced his own band, Garbage. Although much of his recent work has been highly crafted and melodic, Vig (born in Viroqua, Wisconsin, in 1957) likes to keep his roots in the punk-rock underground of his adopted hometown: Madison, Wisconsin. "There is a certain energy you get from the quicker records that you do," he says from Smart Studios in Madison, his headquarters since 1984.

"A lot of the punk bands didn't necessarily pay attention to the performance; they were more interested in just getting the right vibe down or getting a lot of passion and intensity on tape. I love that, and I love noise as much as I love melody. I think that is still the combination I have brought to a lot of the records that I have done, even the Garbage records. There are a lot of weird mistakes and noisy things that we will leave on the tracks, or things we deliberately try to find or create to screw things up a bit or give them some character.

"The trick is to find the balance between making something work, making a part of a performance really tight, and keeping the energy and the vibe to it and the feeling to it—kind of walking that line between making it perfect and making it fucked up." Or, as one writer put it, Vig can find the pop gleam buried in the noisy muck.

After taking four semesters of electronic music at the University of Wisconsin, learning how to process a wide variety of sounds and scoring films for other students, Vig had a good feel for how to transmit a mood sonically.

When Vig, Steve Marker, and Doug "Duke" Erikson—his partners in Smart Studios and Garbage—remix a song the original is stripped down and rebuilt. "It is really scary every time I start a remix," says Vig. "I have no idea what I want to do. I put the track up and start tinkering with it, processing the sound and try to take it somewhere new and still try to retain the integrity or the sensibility of the artist, so even though you take it in a new direction it still sounds like U2 or Beck.

"I grew up listening to pop music and Top 40 and I love all kinds of music," Vig says. "The Beatles, Tijuana Brass, Frank Sinatra, and country music. Even though Smart Studios started doing a lot of independent underground stuff in the mid-'80s, bands I was in always wrote pop stuff that was very melodic and hooky. After a lot of work as a rock producer, when I got the chance to pick and choose [pop projects], I jumped at it."

He works with artists who have a clear idea of what they want. "I get involved with artists in terms of arrangement and songs, and trying to get the right kind of performances out of them, but I really like it when they have a clear sense of what they want to do."

It's also important to Vig, on a practical level, to build trust between the artist and producer. "A lot of that has to do with me breaking out some beers and making the artist feel comfortable and not afraid to try things and trust you if you say, 'I think that you can do this better,' or, 'You should try this on the outro.' I'm trying to get their guard down to a certain extent, because working with someone on a record can be intensely personal.

"I have to remember that it's not my record," he says. "With Garbage it is, but even there I'm just part of that band. I think that for a while, in the '70s and even into the '80s, people looked to the producer as a god. Some of the producers, to a certain extent, wanted that reputation. A lot of the stuff that I do is pretty easygoing. I can be pretty intense when it comes to the work ethic or trying to push an artist in a certain direction, but I also try to make it as easy as possible for them."

—DAVID JOHN FARINELLA

Chainsaw Kittens: *Flipped Out in Singapore*, Mammoth, 1992.
Cosmic Pychos: *Blokes You Can Trust*, Amphetamine Reptile, 1991.
Depeche Mode: "In Your Room" (remix), Sire/Reprise, 1993.
Die Kreutzen: *Century Days*, Touch & Go, 1988 • *Gone Away*, Touch & Go, 1989 • *Cement*, Touch & Go, 1991.
Drain: *Pick Up Heaven* (1 track), Trance Syndicate, 1992.
Fire Town: *In the Heart of Heart Country*, Atlantic, 1987.
Fluid, The: *Glue* (EP), Sub Pop, 1990.
Garbage: *Garbage,* ALMO, 1995 • "Subhuman," Feedback, 1995 • "Vow," ALMO, 1995 • "#1 Crush," Capitol, 1996 (*William Shakespeare's Romeo and Juliet* soundtrack) • "Milk," ALMO, 1996 • "Only Happy When It Rains," ALMO, 1996 • "Stupid Girl," ALMO, 1996 • "Queer," ALMO, 1997 • "Push It," ALMO, 1998 • *Version 2.0,* ALMO, 1998.
Helmet: "Milktoast," Interscope/Atlantic, 1994 (*The Crow* soundtrack) • w/ David Yow, "Custard Pie," Atlantic, 1995 (*Encomium: A Tribute to Led Zeppelin*).
Johnston, Freedy: "Bad Reputation," Elektra, 1994 • *This Perfect World*, Elektra, 1994 • "This Perfect World," A&M, 1994, 1996 (*Kingpin* soundtrack).
Killdozer: *Intellectuals Are the Shoeshine Boys of the Ruling Elite/Snakeboy*, Touch & Go, 1985, 1989 • *12-Point Buck,* Touch & Go, 1988 • *12-Point Buck/Little Baby Buntin'*, Touch & Go, 1989 • *For Ladies Only,* Touch & Go, 1990 • *Uncompromising War on Art Under the Dictatorship of the Proletariat/Burl,* Touch & Go, 1994.
L7: *Bricks Are Heavy*, Slash, 1992 • "Let's Lynch the Landlord," Alternative Tentacles, 1992 (*Virus 100*).
Laughing Hyenas: *Life of Crime,* Touch & Go, 1990.
Les Thugs: "Moon over Marin," Alternative Tentacles, 1992 (*Virus 100*).
Nirvana: "Come As You Are," DGC, 1992 • *Incesticide* (1 track), DGC, 1992 • "Lithium," DGC, 1992 • *Nevermind,* DGC, 1992 • "Smells Like Teen Spirit," DGC, 1992 • *Singles,* Alex, 1996.
Overwhelming Colorfast: *Overwhelming Colorfast,* Relativity, 1992.

Rousers, The: *In Without Knocking,* Boat, 1986.

Smashing Pumpkins: "Tristessa," Sub Pop, 1990 • "Cherub Rock," Hut, 1991 • *Gish,* Caroline, 1991 • *Lull,* Caroline, 1991 • "Drown," Epic Soundtrax, 1992 (*Singles* soundtrack) • *Siamese Dream,* Virgin, 1993 • "Today," Virgin, 1993 • *Pisces Iscariot* (8 tracks), Virgin, 1994.

Sonic Youth: *Dirty,* DGC, 1992 • "Sugar Kane," DGC, 1993 • "Bull in the Heather," DGC, 1994 • *Experimental Jet Set and No Star,* DGC, 1994.

Soul Asylum: *Let Your Dim Light Shine,* Columbia, 1995 • "Misery," Columbia, 1995 • "Promises Broken," Columbia, 1996.

Spooner: *Wildest Dreams,* Boat, 1988 • *The Fugitive Dance,* Dali/Chameleon, 1990.

Tad: *8-Way Santa,* Sub Pop, 1991.

U2: "Staring at the Sun/North and South of the River," Island, 1997.

Unrest: *Fuck Pussy Galore and All Her Friends,* Matador, 1994.

Urge Overkill: *Americruiser,* Touch & Go, 1990.

Young Fresh Fellows: *Electric Bird Digest,* Frontier, 1991 • *Doc Sharpie Is a Bad Man* (4 tracks), Frontier, 1992.

Tony Visconti

Two recent, high-profile covers of David Bowie (see entry) songs illustrate the degree to which Tony Visconti's production sensibility has influenced a generation of musicians: Nirvana's "The Man Who Sold the World" and the Wallflowers' "Heroes." More than mere interpretations of two of Bowie's most inspired compositions, these recordings are tributes to Visconti's skills as a writer, arranger, orchestrator, and producer—from the ascending bass line of "The Man Who Sold the World" (which Visconti wrote and played) to Robert Fripp's wailing, sustained electric guitar lines in "Heroes," which the Wallflowers copied to a T.

Visconti gets a kick out of knowing that two of the hottest bands of the '90s have so favorably responded to work he did nearly a quarter-century ago. In fact, having produced such "iconic" recordings is his biggest source of professional pride. "The most gratifying experience of my career has been producing a recording that has become a classic and iconic, such as [T. Rex's] 'Get It On (Bang a Gong)' (No. 1 U.K.) and 'Heroes,' and knowing it at the time," says Visconti.

There is no shortage of such groundbreaking productions in his résumé. Although he will forever be identified with Bowie and T. Rex—the majority of whose work he produced—Visconti also lent his expertise to seminal albums by Thin Lizzy, Iggy Pop, Badfinger, Strawbs, Gentle Giant, the Alarm, the Stranglers, Adam Ant, Rick Wakeman, Boomtown Rats, Sparks, the Moody Blues, and others.

"My mission is to make the artist's dreams come true," he says. "I only work with artists who have a strong, radical vision. As a former recording artist, I know how hard it was to translate dreams onto tape without an ally."

Born in Brooklyn on April 24, 1944, Visconti got into record production by accident. He and his first wife, Siegrid, had a songwriting partnership that landed them a deal with the New York–based Howard Richmond Organization. Although the Viscontis never made it as a writing team (except for a moderately successful parody called "Long Hair"), Tony's demos were so good that Richmond offered the young musician a job as house record producer. "One day I got called into my publisher's office and he said, 'I love your demos, but I don't like your songs,'" Visconti told *Billboard* in a 1995 interview. "I was very depressed, but the next minute he said, 'But I would like you to be the house record producer. I'm starting a label, and I think you're the guy to do it.'"

Coincidentally, the Richmond studio was in the same Columbus Circle building as Atlantic Records'

Photo by May Pang

famed facility, where Ahmet Ertegun, Jerry Wexler, Arif Mardin, and Tom Dowd (see entries) were making history with the likes of Aretha Franklin and King Curtis—both of whom a young Visconti was lucky enough to observe in session.

Visconti's big break occurred when the late British producer Denny Cordell (see entry), who was fresh from cutting Procol Harum's "A Whiter Shade of Pale," wandered into the Richmond office and introduced himself. When Visconti revealed that he was the company's staff producer, Cordell said, "Well, you're my American cousin, because I'm the house record producer for this very same company in London," according to Visconti's recollection.

Cordell invited Visconti to serve a stint as his assistant in London. Although Visconti did not plan on staying more than six months, he wound up spending 19 years in the U.K. and carving out a career as one of the top record makers of his time. Cordell entrusted Visconti not only with engineering and mixing duties (of which Joe Cocker's *With a Little Help from My Friends*, the Move's *Shazam*, and Procol Harum's *Shine On Brightly* stand out), but also with the operation of in-house studio and the scouting of talent. In the latter category, Visconti's first discovery was none other than Marc Bolan.

"I went into a club called U.F.O. and I heard Marc Bolan's voice drifting up the stairwell," he recalled in the *Billboard* interview. "It was that lovely, quivering, bluesy voice that he had. There were 300 kids around the stage, silent, and I had never seen 300 kids silent before. It was like a religious experience, and I was sucked in. I finally went up to the front of the stage and I looked at this beautiful little guy with this strange voice, and I thought, 'This guy is a star!' "

Bolan and his partner in the group they called Tyrannosaurus Rex, Steve Peregrine Took, auditioned for Cordell at the offices of Essex Music, Richmond's London affiliate. Although Cordell agreed to sign the act, he made it clear to Visconti that he viewed Bolan's band as a token underground act and accordingly offered only £400 to make the first LP (which was oddly titled *My People Were Fair and Had Sky in Their Hair, But Now They're Content to Wear Stars on Their Brow*). Although the aforementioned album did not blow down record store doors, it was enough of a critical success to attract other cult artists to Visconti, notably David Bowie.

Introduced by Essex head David Platz, Bowie and Visconti became fast friends and partners in one of the most dynamic and successful artist-producer relationships in the history of the business. The first fruit of their collaboration was Bowie's breakthrough album,

Space Oddity (with the exception of the title track, which was done by Gus Dudgeon; see entry). The record catapulted both their careers and led to a 10-year association marked by a string of seminal records, including *The Man Who Sold the World, David Live* (No. 8), *Young Americans* (No. 9, with Bowie and Harry Maslin; see entry), *Low* (No. 11, remainder with Bowie), *Heroes* (No. 3 U.K.), *Stage* (No. 5 U.K.), *Lodger* (No. 4 U.K.), and *Scary Monsters* (No. 1 U.K.). Visconti and Bowie also collaborated (as co-producers) on another rock 'n' roll classic: Iggy Pop's *The Idiot*.

Clearly, the young record maker from America had found a home on the other side of the Atlantic. In 1971, he married Mary Hopkin, a protégé of Paul McCartney (see entry) who had scored with the folk hit "Those Were the Days." The year they were married, Visconti produced the album *Earth Song, Ocean Song* by his new wife.

Visconti remembers the '70s as a heady time when he would ride his motorcycle around Europe and find offbeat venues to make records. He worked with Bowie in Berlin, Bolan and T. Rex in France, and others in whatever country happened to offer a less onerous tax situation than Britain.

The fact that Visconti's reputation was made on British rock music is an irony considering that he was born in Brooklyn to an Italian family and started out playing traditional Italian and Latin songs in the Catskills. Among the other artists whose art he elevated during the decade of excess were Badfinger, Strawbs, Gentle Giant, Carmen, Marsha Hunt, Osibisa, Gasworks, Ralph McTell, Tom Paxton, Wings (for whom he orchestrated the epochal *Band on the Run* album), Sparks, Argent, Thin Lizzy, and others.

The albums that attained the most commercial success are not necessarily the ones Visconti remembers most fondly. "I remember the incredible hard work and integrity it took to make the first two Gentle Giant albums," he recalls. "I've had many such experiences in my career and that is the exactly why I became a record producer."

The end of the '70s signaled the close of an era for Visconti. His two biggest clients were out of the picture: Bolan had died in a car crash on September 16, 1977, and Bowie had a falling out with Visconti following the *Scary Monsters* project, which was released in 1980. Furthermore, his marriage to Hopkin ended. Forced to expand his horizons beyond the icons he nurtured to worldwide success, Visconti embraced new wave, post-punk, and experimental rock projects, managing somehow to keep a foot planted in the mainstream. He worked with the Radiators, the Stranglers, Hazel

O'Connor, John Hiatt, the Boomtown Rats, Elaine Paige, Difford and Tilbrook, Adam Ant, the Moody Blues, Les Rita Mitsouko, U2, and the Alarm.

Although his '80s records did not transcend to the degree that his work with Bowie, T. Rex, Badfinger, Sparks, and Thin Lizzy did, Visconti remained an adventurous, uncompromising producer. By 1989, he was ready for another wholesale change in life and career. That year, he married a woman he affectionately describes as his second "Beatle babe": May Pang, who is best known for her liaison with John Lennon in the early '70s. Concurrently with his third wedding, Visconti decided to move back to the U.S., resettling in the New York area with Pang and starting a new family. (He has a son and a daughter from his marriage to Hopkin.)

Since then, Visconti has operated out of a home studio equipped with state-of-the-art digital recording and MIDI equipment, as well as vintage microphones, guitars, and basses he acquired over the years. Although he continues to work in commercial facilities, Visconti's studio has allowed him maximum flexibility and inspiration on a variety of projects throughout the '90s, including albums by the Dwellers, the Seahorses, an unreleased record by Los Angeles–based singer/songwriter Christian Lane (as well as orchestration for Deborah Gibson and engineering for Annie Haslam's Renaissance). At press time, Visconti was working on projects by Gibson, D-Generation, and Luscious Jackson.

Visconti also co-wrote an independently released album by New York singer/songwriter Alex Forbes. Although the record did not achieve commercial success, it reawakened the producer's long-dormant interest in songwriting—a discipline he hopes to continue exploring in the coming years, along with his thriving work as an orchestrator and arranger.

In addition, Visconti has used his apartment as a headquarters for his side work teaching the Alexander technique—a system of body alignment designed to improve posture, respiration, circulation, and overall functioning. Perhaps signaling yet another chapter in his career, Visconti recently reunited with Bowie following 18 years apart. They worked together on Bowie's contributions to a *Rugrats* project and a John Lennon tribute album, for which Bowie recorded "Mother." They also discussed the possibility of working on an entire album together, although Visconti admits those conversations are in early stages.

As he reflects on his more than three decades as a producer, arranger, writer, and musician, Visconti offers the following advice to neophytes: "The music business lures people who think they can make it rich quickly with a hit record. Occasionally that happens, but to survive and prosper in the recording industry you must be certain of possessing great talent and you must get as much training as you can afford in music and technology." He adds, "When I started, the industry was using 4-track as a standard medium. With today's multiformats and digital technology, I pity the novice just starting out. You have a lot to learn—in a hurry!"

Visconti also has an excellent Web site that functions as an autobiography and newsletter as to his activities at www.tonyvisconti.com. —PAUL VERNA

Adam and the Ants: *Antics in the Forbidden Zone*, Epic, 1990 • *Antmusic: The Very Best Of*, Arcade, 1994.

Afraid of Mice: *Afraid of Mice*, Charisma, 1981.

Alarm, The: *Change*, IRS, 1989 • "Sold Me Down the River," IRS, 1989 • *Standards*, IRS, 1990.

Altered Images: *Bite*, Portrait/Epic, 1983 • *I Could Be Happy: The Best Of*, Epic, 1997.

Anderson, Jon: *Animation*, Atlantic, 1982.

Ant, Adam: "Vive Le Rock," Epic, 1985 • *Vive Le Rock*, Epic, 1985 • *B-Side Babies* (4 tracks), Legacy, 1994.

Argent: *Counterpoints*, RCA, 1975.

Badfinger: *Magic Christian Music* (5 tracks), Apple, 1970, 1991 • *Best Of*, Capitol, 1995.

Bolan, Marc, and T. Rex: *Zinc Alloy and the Modern Hidden Riders of Tomorrow*, Chronicles, 1974, 1997.

Boomtown Rats: *Mondo Bongo*, Mercury/CBS, 1980 • "The Elephants Graveyard," Epic, 1981 (*Exposed*) • *The Boomtown Rats* (EP), Columbia, 1982 • *V Deep*, Mercury/CBS, 1982.

Bowie, David: *Space Oddity*, RCA, 1969, 1972 • *The Man Who Sold the World*, RCA, 1970 • *David Live*, RCA, 1974 • "Knock on Wood," RCA, 1974 • "Young Americans," RCA, 1974 • *Young Americans*, RCA, 1975 • "Heroes," RCA, 1977 • *Heroes*, RCA, 1977 • *Low*, RCA, 1977 • "Sound and Vision," RCA, 1977 • "Beauty and the Beast," RCA, 1978 • *Stage*, RCA, 1978 • "Boys Keep Swinging," RCA, 1979 • "D.J.," RCA, 1979 • *Lodger*, RCA, 1979 • "Alabama Song," RCA, 1980 • "Ashes to Ashes," RCA, 1980 • "Fashion," RCA, 1980 • *Scary Monsters*, RCA, 1980 • "Scary Monsters (and Super Creeps)," RCA, 1981 • "Up the Hill Backwards," RCA, 1981 • *Bertolt Brecht's Baal*, RCA, 1982 • *Ziggy Stardust Live*, RCA, 1983 • *Changesbowie*, Rykodisc, 1984, 1990 • "Sound and Vision" (remix), Tommy Boy, 1991 • *Bowie: The Singles, 1969–1993*, Rykodisc, 1993.

Caravan: *Better by Far*, Arista, 1977.

Carmen: *Fandangos in Space*, RZ/Dunhill, 1973 • *Dancing on a Cold Wind*, RZ, 1974.

Difford and Tilbrook: *Difford and Tilbrook*, A&M, 1984 • "Love's Crashing Waves," A&M, 1984.

Dirty Tricks: *Hit and Run,* Polydor, 1976 • *Night Man,* Polydor, 1977.

Dwellers, The: *Whatever Makes You Happy,* EMI, 1995.

Electric Angels: *Electric Angels,* Atlantic, 1990.

Eno, Brian: *Eno Box 1,* Virgin, 1994.

Gasworks: *Gasworks,* Regal, 1972.

Gentle Giant: *Gentle Giant,* Vertigo, 1971 • *Acquiring the Taste,* Vertigo, 1972.

Gibbons, Steve: *Down in the Bunker,* Polydor, 1978 • *Street Parade,* RCA, 1980.

Griff, Zaine: *Ashes and Diamonds,* Automatic/Warner Bros., 1980.

Haysi Fantayzee: *Battle Hymns for Children* (2 tracks), Regard, 1983.

Hiatt, John: *All of a Sudden,* Geffen, 1982 • "Take Time to Know Her," Warner Bros., 1983 (*Attack of the Killer B's*) • *Living a Little, Laughing a Little,* Raven, 1996.

Hopkin, Mary: *Earth Song, Ocean Song,* Apple, 1971 • *Those Were the Days* (1 track), Apple, 1972.

Hunt, Marsha: *Woman Child,* Track, 1971.

Juniors Eyes: *Juniors Eyes,* A&M, 1969.

Legend: *Legend,* Vertigo, 1970.

Les Rita Mitsouko: *The No Comprendo,* Virgin France, 1989 • "Tongue Dance," Virgin America, 1989 (*Slaves of New York* soundtrack) • *Re,* Virgin France, 1990 • *Marc and Robert,* Alex, 1992.

McTell, Ralph: *Not Till Tomorrow,* Reprise, 1972 • *Easy,* Reprise, 1973.

Modern Romance: *Trick of the Light,* WEA, 1983.

Moody Blues: "The Other Side of Life," Polydor, 1986 • *The Other Side of Life,* Polydor, 1986, 1989 • "Your Wildest Dreams," Polydor, 1986 • "I Know You're Out There Somewhere," Polydor, 1988 • *Sur la Mer,* Polydor, 1988 • *Greatest Hits,* Threshold/Polydor, 1989 • *Keys of the Kingdom,* Polydor, 1991 • "Say It with Love," Polydor, 1991.

Mouskouri, Nana: *Nana in English,* Verve, 1988.

Move, The: *Movements: 30th Anniversary Anthology,* West Side, 1997.

O'Connor, Hazel: *Breaking Glass,* A&M, 1980 • *Cover Plus,* Albion, 1981.

Omaha Sherriff: *Come Hell or High Water,* RCA, 1977.

Osibisa: *Osibisa,* MCA, 1971 • *Woyaya,* MCA, 1972.

Paige, Elaine: *Stages,* K-Tel, 1983 • *Encore,* Atlantic Theater, 1996.

Paxton, Tom: *Peace Will Come,* Reprise, 1972 • *New Songs for Old Friends,* Reprise, 1973.

Pleasure Bombs: *Days of Heaven,* Atco, 1991.

Polecats: *Make a Circuit with Me* (1 track), Mercury, 1983.

Pop, Iggy: *The Idiot,* RCA, 1977.

Radiators, The: *Ghost Town,* Chiswick, 1978.

Ross, Alan: *Are You Free This Saturday?,* Ebony, 1977.

Seahorses, The: *Do It Yourself,* Geffen, 1997.

Sparks: *Indiscreet,* Island, 1975 • *Profile: Ultimate Collection,* Rhino, 1991 • *In the Swing,* Spectrum, 1993.

Stranglers, The: *La Folie,* Liberty, 1981.

Strawbs: *Dragonfly,* A&M, 1970 • *Just a Selection of Antiques and Curios,* A&M, 1970 • *From the Witchwood,* A&M, 1971 • *Grave New World,* A&M, 1972 • *A Choice Selection of Strawbs,* A&M, 1993.

Surprise Sisters: *The Surprise Sisters,* Good Earth, 1976.

T. Rex: "Ride a White Swan," Blue Thumb, 1970 • *T. Rex,* Fly/Reprise, 1970 • *Electric Warrior,* Fly/Reprise, 1971 • "Hot Love," Reprise, 1971 • "Jeepster," Fly/EMI, 1971 • "Bang a Gong (Get It On)," Reprise, 1972 • *Bolan Boogie,* Fly, 1972 • "Children of the Revolution," EMI, 1972 • "Metal Guru," EMI, 1972 • "Solid Gold Easty Action," EMI, 1972 • "Telegram Sam," Reprise, 1972 • *The Slider,* EMI/Reprise, 1972 • "20th Century Boy," EMI, 1973 • "Born to Boogie," Warner Bros., 1973 (*Appetizers*) • *Tanx,* Chronicles, 1973, 1997 • "The Groover," EMI, 1973 • "Truck On (Tyke)," EMI, 1973 • "Light of Love," EMI, 1974 • "Teenage Dream," EMI, 1974 • *Bolan's Zip Gun,* Chronicles, 1975, 1997 • "New York City," EMI, 1975 • *Futuristic Dragon,* Chronicles, 1976, 1997 • "I Love to Boogie," EMI, 1976 • "London Boys," EMI, 1976 • *Dandy in the Underworld,* Chronicles, 1977, 1997 • *Marc (Words and Music),* Pye, 1978 • *T. Rex in Concert,* Marc, 1981 • *Great Hits 1972–1977: The A-Sides,* Chronicles, 1994, 1997 • *Great Hits 1972–1977: The B-Sides,* Chronicles, 1994, 1997 • *Light of Love,* Chronicles, 1997 • *Messing with the Mystic,* Chronicles, 1997 • *See also* Tyrannosaurus Rex *and* Bolan, Marc, *and* T. Rex.

Thin Lizzy: *Bad Reputation,* Vertigo/Mercury, 1977 • "Dancing in the Moonlight," Vertigo/Mercury, 1977 • *Live and Dangerous,* Vertigo/WB, 1978 • "Rosalie/Cowboy's Song" (live medley), Vertigo/WB, 1978 • *Black Rose (A Rock Legend),* Vertigo/WB, 1979 • "Do Anything You Want To," Vertigo/WB, 1979 • "Waiting for An Alibi," Vertigo/WB, 1979 • *Life,* Vertigo, 1983 • *Dedication: The Very Best of Thin Lizzy,* Mercury, 1991.

Tyrannosaurus Rex: *My People Were Fair and Had Sky in Their Hair . . . but Now They're Content to Wear Stars on Their Brows,* RZ, 1968 • "One Inch Rock," RZ, 1968 • *Prophets, Seers and Sages, the Angels of the Ages,* RZ, 1968 • *Unicorn,* RZ/Blue Thumb, 1969 • *A Beard of Stars,* RZ/Blue Thumb, 1970 • *See also* T. Rex.

U2: *Wide Awake in America,* Island, 1985.

Visconti, Tony: *Breaking Glass* soundtrack, Spectrum, 1995.

Wakeman, Rick: *Rhapsodies,* A&M, 1979 • *Voyage: The Very Best Of,* A&M, 1997.

COLLECTIONS

Brace Yourself! A Tribute to Otis Blackwell, Shanachie, 1994.

Michael Wagener

A s a teenager in Germany, Michael Wagener played with an early version of power-metal band Accept. Later, he worked for a company in Hamburg that built and imported recording equipment. It had a small studio and Wagener started to engineer sessions for local bands, quickly realizing he'd found his niche.

On a trip to the U.S. in 1979, he met vocalist Don Dokken, who suggested that he could get more work in the States. For several years, Wagener made frequent trips to the U.S., doing mainly demos and indie releases. He worked extensively with the well-regarded metal band Dokken, producing their 1979 indie release, their 1983 Elektra debut *Breaking the Chains,* and their 1985 platinum *Under Lock and Key* (Wagener's first big record, co-produced with Neil Kernon; see entry). "We kept [George Lynch and Don Dokken] apart," he recalls. "[Kernon] would be doing guitars in Hollywood and I'd

Photo by Wolf Hoffman

be doing vocals in Redondo Beach. Jeff and Mick would go between. To this day I don't know why they don't get along. Why do countries go to war?"

Wagener only partly produced the band's 1995 comeback album, *Dysfunctional,* because of the length of time it took and his commitment to other projects. "I wasn't there for recording the guitar parts, which I regretted later," says Wagener. "I got back to do the remix and wasn't happy. There was just too much grief and fighting."

Wagener moved to Los Angeles permanently in 1984 when asked to do a single for punk darlings X, beginning a period of staggering output, most of it metal-related. Between 1984 and 1992, Wagener produced or mixed records by a pantheon of '80s metal stars, including his old band Accept, Great White, Raven, Stryper, Poison, Metallica, Alice Cooper, W.A.S.P., Keel, White Lion, Megadeth, Krokus, Flotsam and Jetsam, Overkill, Skid Row, Extreme, Saigon Kick, Mötley Crüe, Ozzy Osbourne, and Warrant. "I pretty much worked with everyone I would have liked to—except Van Halen. I did a lot of guitar-based bands and I played guitar myself. [Eddie Van Halen] is the greatest living guitarist."

He did turn down two projects that turned out to be hot: Soundgarden and Guns N' Roses. Of the former he says, "I thought it wasn't up my alley and I couldn't add much to the record. It was definitely a mistake." As for GN'R, "I'm totally against drugs. I said, I don't want to deal with that. Financially, that probably hurt me quite a bit. But it was the right decision."

Wagener cites Roy Thomas Baker and "Mutt" Lange (see entries) as his biggest influences, which is clear in his lavish, classically '80s style of production—densely layered vocals, masses of guitars, and cavernous sound—although Wagener added his own brawny metallic edge. Skid Row's self-titled 1988 debut (No. 6) was probably the best realization of his style, with catchy, melodramatic melodies heightened by massive production. The sweeping, well-shaped thundering and shouting of "Youth Gone Wild" has never been surpassed.

Wagener's output slowed in the mid-'90s, as business and production styles changed. "The business got smaller in terms of the size of record production. It went more in terms of garage production. You never got the money anymore to spend time to get a decent record. You had to compromise and I don't like to do that. I removed myself."

In August 1996, he moved to Nashville, where he built his own studio, Wire World. "People go into expensive studios under a time pressure. That's part of the reason I built my studio. If we go over two or three weeks, there's no pressure. For art, it's positive," he says. "I got a reputation for being an expensive producer. It wasn't me, it was the studios."

He prefers a consistent studio environment, saying "every studio has little flaws, little good things. As long as you know the situation, you can deal with it." And he's completely sold on digital. "I started using digital early, in 1981, in Germany. I was fascinated by the clearness and the way the drums came back very powerful. I like the storage medium to be neutral. If I want distortion, I insert it. If you want analog sound, a bit of tube gear gives you the sound before you put it on tape, warms it up. I never leave the digital domain anymore."

He describes his production philosophy: "The band is the bible of what they want to do. If it's completely out of line with what I want to do, then I shouldn't be doing the project. I try to keep them on track for their direction. I think being able to keep atmosphere in the studio at a positive level is one of the most important things."

Though Wagener continues to work with a lot of metal-oriented music, including his friends from Skid Row and Accept, he's recently done adult contemporary and pop projects and says, "If it's good music I wouldn't shy away from anything. My heart is in rock music. I grew up with Deep Purple and Accept. [But I like] the Wallflowers, No Doubt. It's different music but it's quality." —Anastasia Pantsios

Accept: *Restless and Wild*, Portrait, 1983 • *Predator*, Sweat Shop, 1997.

Alice Cooper: *Constrictor*, MCA, 1986 • *Raise Your Fist and Yell*, MCA, 1987 • *Prince of Darkness*, MCA, 1989.

Bonfire: *Fireworks*, RCA, 1987 • *Point Blank*, RCA, 1989.

Brighton Rock: *Young, Wild and Free*, Atco, 1986.

Dokken: *Breaking the Chains*, Elektra, 1983 • *Dokken*, Elektra, 1983 • *Under Lock and Key*, Elektra, 1985 • *"In My Dreams,"* Elektra, 1986 • *Back on the Streets*, Elektra, 1989 • *Dysfunctional*, Columbia, 1995.

Extreme: *Pornograffitti*, A&M, 1990 • "More Than Words," A&M, 1991.

Faithful Breath: *Gold 'n Glory*, Mausoleum, 1984.

45 Grave: *Sleep in Safety*, Enigma, 1983 • *A Tale of Strange Phenomena*, Enigma, 1984 • "Partytime," Enigma, 1984 • "Partytime" (remix), Enigma, 1984 (*The Return of the Living Dead* soundtrack).

Freak of Nature: *Gathering of Freaks*, Music for Nations, 1992.

Great White: *Great White*, EMI America, 1984.

Keel: *Keel*, MCA, 1987.

Malice: *In the Beginning*, Atlantic, 1985.

Osbourne, Ozzy: *Live and Loud* (video), Epic Video, 1993.

Outrage: *Live Until Deaf*, EastWest Japan, 1995.

Raven: *All for One*, Neat, 1983.

Raven: *Stay Hard*, Atlantic, 1985.

Roberts, Kane: *Kane Roberts*, MCA, 1987.

Saigon Kick: *Saigon Kick*, Third Stone, 1991.

Savage Grace: *Master of Disguise*, Important, 1984.

Shire: *Shire*, Enigma, 1983.

Skid Row: "18 and Life," Atlantic, 1989 • "I Remember You," Atlantic, 1989 • "Makin' a Mess," Atlantic, 1989 • *Skid Row*, Atlantic, 1989 • "Youth Gone Wild," Atlantic, 1989 • *Slave to the Grind*, Atlantic, 1991 • "Wasted Time," Atlantic, 1992.

Streetfighter: *Shoot You Down!*, Venus, 1984.

Stryper: *Soldiers Under Command*, Enigma, 1985 • *Can't Stop the Rock: The Stryper Collection, 1984–1991*, Hollywood, 1991.

T.T. Quick: *Metal of Honor*, Megaforce, 1984, 1996.

Testament: *Live at the Fillmore*, Megaforce, 1995 • *Signs of Chaos: The Best of Testament*, Mayhem, 1997.

Warrant: *Dog Eat Dog*, Roadrunner, 1992 • *Best Of*, Legacy, 1996.

White Lion: "Tell Me," Atlantic, 1988 • "Wait," Atlantic, 1988 • "When the Children Cry," Atlantic, 1988 • *Big Game*, Atlantic, 1989 • "Little Fighter," Atlantic, 1989 • *Pride*, Atlantic, 1989 • "Radar Love," Atlantic, 1989 • *Best Of*, Atlantic, 1992.

X: *Ain't Love Grand*, Elektra, 1985 • "Burning House of Love," Elektra, 1985 • *Beyond and Back: The X Anthology*, Elektra, 1997.

Narada Michael Walden

Narada Michael Walden (born April 23, 1952, in Kalamazoo, Michigan), a singer, songwriter, drummer, studio owner, and producer, played in John McLaughlin's Mahavishnu Orchestra from 1974 to 1976, and with Jeff Beck in 1975. After moving to the Bay Area in the late '70s, Walden began producing records at David Rubinson's (see entry) Automatt Studios, working with artists such as Stacy Lattisaw, Angela Bofill, and Patti Austin and perfecting a smooth, high-gloss R&B sound that was to make him one of the most sought-after producers of the '80s and '90s.

In 1985, he worked on demo tapes with a then-unknown Tori Amos, although the direction they were

his records, Walden added his own distinctive and ebullient drumming and keyboards to the tracks.

Walden subsequently worked on projects with Clarence Clemons and Jackson Browne (the hit "You're a Friend of Mine," No. 18), Barbra Streisand, Eddie Murphy, Kenny G, Starship, Elton John and Kiki Dee ("True Love"), George Benson, and Al Jarreau.

Walden has continued to produce and record his own solo albums, beginning with his 1976 debut, a fusion album that expanded on the sounds he had perfected with Mahavishnu Orchestra. As fusion waned, Walden moved into more traditional pursuits, performing more pop-oriented songs and singing them. Four of his solo releases have made the *Billboard* album charts: *Awakening, The Dance of Life, Victory,* and *Confidence.*

Walden's Tarpan Studios, in the Marin County foothills, has become one of the premier private facilities in the world. Throughout Walden's career, the immensely talented engineer David Frazier has manned the boards, contributing to Walden's famous vocal sound and polished mixes. —DANIEL J. LEVITIN

taking failed to bear fruit. (Those who have heard the tracks compare them to early Madonna, with sped-up and double-tracked vocals.)

In 1986, Clive Davis asked Walden to produce a new Arista Records artist, Whitney Houston. Walden and his stable of writers contributed the songs, Walden produced, and the resulting debut was one of the most successful in history, with U.S. sales in excess of 10 million and a stunning three No. 1 hits: "How Will I Know," "Greatest Love of All," and "Saving All My Love for You." The album stayed at No. 1 for 14 weeks and on the *Billboard* album charts for over three years. While Whitney Houston was still on the charts, the team released her second release, the Walden-produced *Whitney,* which yielded four top hits: "Didn't We Almost Have It All," "I Wanna Dance with Somebody (Who Loves Me)," "So Emotional," and "Where Do Broken Hearts Go?" The album sold over 6 million units in the U.S., was No. 1 for 11 weeks, and stayed on the *Billboard* charts for 85 weeks.

In July 1985, Arista released the Walden-produced comeback album for Aretha Franklin, *Who's Zoomin' Who?* (No. 13), featuring two smashes co-written by Walden, the title track (No. 7) and the No. 3 hit "Freeway of Love." With funkier grooves and mesmerizingly catchy rhythms, *Zoomin'* was a tour de force of production technique, harkening back to the glory days of Motown and Atlantic soul records, but with a stamp indelibly and deliciously Walden's own. As on many of

Austin, Patti: *Patti Austin,* Qwest, 1984.

Belle, Regina: "Baby Come to Me," Columbia, 1989 • *Stay with Me,* Columbia, 1989 • *Passion,* Columbia, 1993.

Benson, George: "Kisses in the Moonlight," Warner Bros., 1986 • "Shiver," Warner Bros., 1986 • *While the City Sleeps . . . ,* Warner Bros., 1986.

Bofill, Angela: "Too Tough," Arista, 1982 • *Best Of,* Arista, 1986.

Campbell, Tevin: *T.E.V.I.N.,* Qwest, 1991 • "Tell Me What You Want Me to Do," Qwest, 1991 • *I'm Ready,* Qwest, 1993 • "Don't Say Goodbye Girl," Qwest, 1994 • "Keep on Pushin'," Warner Bros., 1994 (*A Tribute to Curtis Mayfield*).

Carey, Mariah: *Mariah Carey,* Columbia, 1990 • "Vision of Love," Columbia, 1990 • "I Don't Wanna Cry," Columbia, 1991.

Cherrelle: "Never in My Life," Tabu, 1991 • "Still in Love with You," Tabu, 1992.

Clemons, Clarence: *Hero,* Columbia, 1985 • w/ Jackson Browne, "You're a Friend of Mine," Columbia, 1985 • *A Night with Mr. C,* Columbia, 1989.

Cole, Natalie: *Good to Be Back,* EMI, 1989 • w/ Freddie Jackson, "I Do," EMI, 1989.

Color Me Badd: *Now and Forever,* Giant, 1996 • "The Earth, the Sun, the Rain," Giant, 1996.

Dayne, Taylor: *Soul Dancing,* Arista, 1992 • *Send Me a Lover,* Arista, 1993.

Dorsey, Marc: "People Make the World Go Round," 40 Acres and a Mule, 1994 (*Crooklyn* soundtrack).

Easton, Sheena: "So Far So Good," EMI, 1986 • *The World of Sheena Easton: The Singles Collection,* EMI America, 1993.

Fischer, Lisa: "How Can I Ease the Pain?," Elektra, 1991 • "Save Me," Elektra, 1991 • *So Intense,* Elektra, 1991.

Four Tops: *Indestructable,* Arista, 1988.

Franklin, Aretha: "Freeway of Love," Arista, 1985 • "Who's Zooming Who?," Arista, 1985 • *Who's Zoomin' Who?,* Arista, 1985 • "Another Night," Arista, 1986 • *Aretha,* Arista, 1986 • "Jimmy Lee," Arista, 1986 • "If You Need My Love Tonight," Arista, 1987 • w/ George Michael, "I Knew You Were Waiting for Me," Arista, 1987 • "Rock-a-Lott," Arista, 1987 • w/ Elton John, "Through the Storm," Arista, 1989 • "Everyday People," Arista, 1991 • *What You See Is What You Sweat,* Arista, 1991 • *A Rose Is Still a Rose,* Arista, 1998.

Germaine, Nikita: *Sweet As it Comes,* Motown, 1993.

Green, Al: "Your Heart's in Good Hands," MCA, 1995.

Hancock, Herbie: *Lite Me Up,* Columbia, 1982.

Hewett, Howard: *Allegiance,* Elektra, 1992 • "Save Your Sex for Me," Elektra, 1992.

Hicks, D'Atra: *D'Atra Hicks,* Capitol, 1989 • "Sweet Talk," Capitol, 1989 • "You Make Me Want to Give It Up," Capitol, 1989.

Hicks, Taral: *This Time,* Motown, 1997.

Houston, Whitney: "How Will I Know," Arista, 1986 • *Whitney Houston,* Arista, 1986 • "I Wanna Dance with Somebody (Who Loves Me)," Arista, 1987 • "So Emotional," Arista, 1987 • *Whitney,* Arista, 1987 • "One Moment in Time," Arista, 1988 • "Where Do Broken Hearts Go?," Arista, 1988 • *I'm Your Baby Tonight,* Arista, 1990 • "All the Man That I Need," Arista, 1991 • "I Belong to You," Arista, 1991 • "I'm Every Woman," Arista, 1992 (*The Bodyguard* soundtrack) • "I'm Every Woman" (remix), Arista, 1992 • "Look into Your Heart," Warner Bros., 1994 (*A Tribute to Curtis Mayfield*).

Hyman, Phyllis: *The Legacy Of,* Arista, 1996.

Illenberger, Ralf: *Circle,* Narada/Atlantic, 1988.

Jarreau, Al: "Blue Angel," Reprise, 1992 • *Heaven and Earth,* Reprise, 1992 • "It's Not Hard to Love You," Reprise, 1992 • *Best Of,* Warner Bros., 1996.

John, Elton: *Duets,* MCA, 1993 • w/ Kiki Dee, "True Love," MCA, 1993.

Johnson, Puff: "Forever More," Work/Columbia, 1996 • *Miracle,* Work/Columbia, 1996.

Kenny G: "Songbird," Arista, 1987.

Knight, Gladys: "License to Kill," MCA, 1989 (*License to Kill* soundtrack).

Lattisaw, Stacy: *Sixteen,* Cotillion, 1983, 1990 • w/ Johnny Gill, *Perfect Combination,* Cotillion, 1984, 1990.

Luba: *Between Earth and Sky,* Capitol, 1990.

Mayfield, Curtis: *New World Order,* Warner Bros., 1996 • "Back to the Living Again," Warner Bros., 1997.

Milira: *Back Again!!!,* Apollo/Motown, 1992 • "One Man Woman," Apollo/Motown, 1992.

Murphy, Eddie: "Put Your Mouth on Me," Columbia, 1989 • *So Happy,* Columbia, 1989 • "Till the Money's Gone," Columbia, 1989.

NKOTB: *Face the Music,* Columbia, 1994.

Nova: *Vimana,* Arista, 1976 • *Wings of Love,* Arista, 1977.

O'Jays, The: "Emotionally Yours," EMI America, 1991 • *Emotionally Yours,* EMI America, 1991.

Paris, Mica: "I Wanna Hold On to You," Island, 1993 • *Whisper a Prayer,* Island, 1993.

Pendergrass, Teddy: *Truly Blessed,* Elektra, 1991.

Pointer Sisters: "Be There," MCA, 1987.

Rawls, Lou: *It's Supposed to Be Fun,* Blue Note, 1990.

Richie, Lionel: *Dancing on the Ceiling,* Motown, 1986.

Ross, Diana: "Take Me Higher," Motown, 1995 • *Take Me Higher,* Motown, 1995 • "If You're Not Gonna Love Me Right," Motown, 1996 • "Voice of the Heart," Motown, 1996.

Russell, Brenda: "Stop Running Away," A&M, 1990 • *Greatest Hits,* A&M, 1992, 1994.

Shanice: "I Love Your Smile," Motown, 1991 • *Inner Child,* Motown, 1991 • "I'm Cryin'," Motown, 1992 • "Lovin' You," Motown, 1992 • "Silent Prayer," Motown, 1992.

Sister Sledge: *Love Somebody Today,* Cotillion, 1980 • *All American Girls,* Cotillion, 1981 • *Best of Sister Sledge (1973–1985),* Rhino, 1992.

Starship: "Nothing's Gonna Stop Us Now," Grunt, 1987 • *No Protection,* RCA, 1987 • *Starship's Greatest Hits: Ten Years of Change,* RCA, 1991.

Stewart, Jermaine: "Jody," Arista, 1986 • "We Don't Have to Take Our Clothes Off," Arista, 1986.

Streisand, Barbra: *A Collection: Greatest Hits and More,* Columbia, 1989.

Taylor, James, and Regina Belle: "All I Want Is Forever," Epic, 1989.

Walden, Narada Michael: *I Cry, I Smile,* Atlantic, 1978 • *Awakening,* Atlantic, 1979 • *The Dance of Life,* Atlantic, 1979 • *Victory,* Atlantic, 1980 • *Confidence,* Atlantic, 1982 • *Looking at You, Looking at Me,* Atlantic, 1983 • w/ Patti Austin, "Gimme, Gimme, Gimme," Warner Bros., 1985 • "The Nature of Things," Warner Bros., 1985 • *The Nature of Things,* Warner Bros., 1985 • "Divine Emotions," Reprise, 1988 • "Wild Thing," Reprise, 1988 • "If There's a Hell Below, We're All Going to Go," Warner Bros., 1994 (*A Tribute to Curtis Mayfield*) • *Ecstasy's Dance: The Best Of,* Rhino, 1996.

Warwick, Dionne: *Friends,* Arista, 1985.

Winwood, Steve: *Junction Seven,* Virgin, 1997.

COLLECTIONS

James Bond: Best of 30th Anniversary Collection, Capitol, 1992.

The Associate soundtrack, Motown Soundtracks, 1996.

Andy Wallace

The diverse career of mixmaster Andy Wallace is marked by his involvement with artists who are influential, critically acclaimed, or on the cusp of commercial success. Though recent years have seen him handle production on Bad Religion's major-label debut *Stranger Than Fiction*, Jeff Buckley's *Grace*, Sepultura's *Chaos A.D.* album, and White Zombie's platinum breakthrough, *La Sexorcisto: Devil Music Vol. 1*, he is still in demand as a mixer; his recent projects in that capacity include silverchair's *Freakshow*, Cracker's *The Golden Age*, Rancid's *And Out Come the Wolves*, Helmet's *Betty*, both Rage Against the Machine albums, Ben Folds Five's *Whatever and Ever Amen*, and Rush's *Test for Echo*.

After playing guitar and bass and singing in bands in the late '60s and early '70s, New Yorker Wallace headed to Los Angeles, where he opened a studio called Hit West in 1974. As head engineer he also produced records, mainly by unknown artists. In 1979, he moved back to New York and began to do dance club remixes with producers like Shep Pettibone and Arthur Baker (see entry). "The scene in New York was more the kind of music I wanted to do," he says. "The Los Angeles scene was very post-Eagles. I heard things coming out of New York like 'Planet Rock,' and the aggressiveness of it was familiar to me. I started bringing rock elements into club records. Now it's standard, but in the early '80s, dance music was all synth-based. I was interested in bringing the styles together."

As the remix craze caught on in the '80s, Wallace was called by many artists to do club remixes, including Iggy Pop, Bruce Springsteen, New Model Army, Prince (see entry) and N.W.A. Hooking up with Def Jam mogul Rick Rubin (see entry) opened doors for Wallace. Rubin involved him with two landmark albums: Run-D.M.C.'s *Raising Hell*, which coupled the band with Aerosmith on the latter's "Walk This Way" to blast a hole in the wall between rap and metal, and the Cult's 1987 album *Electric*, perhaps the first alternative-style metal record.

"It was a good meeting of minds," he says of the latter. "I was into making dry, in-your-face records, big and punchy with not a lot of reverb. When Rick hooked up with the Cult, their previous albums were layered with a lot of reverb. They wanted to get away from that."

He continued to work with Rubin, engineering and mixing Slayer's groundbreaking albums *Reign in Blood*, *Seasons in the Abyss*, and *South of Heaven*. "*Reign in Blood* was the first album I did that was that hard. We went in with the aim of plowing over Metallica. Rick called and said, 'Are you interested?' and I said, 'Well, it's something I haven't done before.' But as harsh as *Reign in Blood* is, it's a musical record, not just a noise record."

His success at capturing heavy sounds led to a long relationship with Brazilian thrashers Sepultura. He mixed several albums for them and produced 1993's *Chaos A.D.* and 1997's *Blood-Rooted*.

Wallace is particularly proud of Buckley's *Grace*. "I've probably gotten more attention from that album than White Zombie, which sold more but didn't have the same impact in the industry." He was preparing to produce Buckley's second album at the time of the singer's untimely death in 1998. *Grace* "wasn't an easy album to make," he says. "Jeff was going through a high degree of development as an artist. Preproduction was a lot of work. The songs had no arrangements. The recording process involved such a variety of styles and textures, from the lightest acoustic guitar to overdriven guitar through a Marshall amp. There was more experimentation than on a lot of records, an exciting use of chords and melodies, yet they don't have an esoteric vibe. I feel we totally accomplished what we wanted to do."

In fact, *Grace* wonderfully showcases Buckley's apparently limitless vocal range. Wallace describes his strengths as "working with an artist on the music, refining riffs, coordinating bass and drum parts. I sing, so I can work with singers well and get a good performance out of them. I can gain their confidence because I make sure they understand I'm not bullshitting them. If I don't get something they're doing, I'll say, 'I don't understand why you want to do this.' I will listen to them. It's their record. I try to find ways to make what they want to do work.

"Having a vision of how sounds blend together gives me an ability to get things down on tape in a good way. A big part of production is sorting out a lot of stuff that shouldn't be on the record, helping the artist lose stuff that's in their way."

Wallace particularly likes working in Daniel Lanois's (see entry) New Orleans studio Kingsway, where he recorded with Blind Melon. "It's a mansion, basically, not a proper studio. There are limitations all over the place, like no built-in wiring; we had to run cable everywhere. But I find it challenging to work in an environment with limitations. If you had the world's most thorough, complete, and adaptable recording studio and no budget limitations, you might have trouble defining when you were done.

"Certain things I absolutely need. I need the equipment to be dependable. I'm less likely to be forgiving of that kind of thing than of a leak in the roof. As far as gear is concerned, I'm not a techno-crazed person. The room doesn't have to have the ultimate outboard gear. I've worked with live players, I've worked with just machines and sequencers and I've combined the two," he says. "I don't find it at all threatening." —ANASTASIA PANTSIOS

Alice Cooper: *The Last Temptation,* Epic, 1994 • *Classiks,* Epic, 1995.

Bad Religion: "Stranger Than Fiction," S.F.T.R.I., 1994 • *Stranger Than Fiction,* Atlantic, 1994.

Blind Melon: "Soup," A&M, 1994 (*Woodstock 94*) • *Soup,* Capitol/EMI, 1995 • *Nico,* Capitol/EMI, 1996.

Buckley, Jeff: *Grace,* Columbia, 1994.

Cola: *Whatnot,* Interscope, 1997.

Faith No More: *King for a Day/Fool for a Lifetime,* Slash/Reprise, 1995 • *Ricochet* (EP), Slash/Reprise, 1995.

Front 242: "Religion" (remix), Epic, 1993.

Front, The: *The Front,* Columbia, 1989.

Moore, John: *Distortion,* Polydor, 1991.

Ned's Atomic Dustbin: *Are You Normal?,* Chaos/Columbia, 1992 • "Not Sleeping Around," Chaos/Columbia, 1992.

Nirvana: *Lithium* (EP), DGC, 1992 • *Singles,* Alex, 1996.

Poorboys, The: *Pardon Me,* Hollywood, 1992.

Radio Active Cats: *Radio Active Cats,* Warner Bros., 1991.

Rollins Band: "Low Self Opinion," Imago, 1992 • *The End of Silence,* Imago, 1992.

Sepultura: *Chaos A.D.,* Roadrunner, 1993 • *Blood-Rooted,* Roadrunner, 1997.

Slayer: *Reign in Blood,* Def Jam, 1985 • *Seasons in the Abyss,* Def American, 1990.

White Zombie: "Black Sunshine," Geffen, 1992 • *La Sexorcisto: Devil Music Vol. 1,* Geffen, 1992 • "Thunder Kiss '65," Geffen, 1992 • "Thunder Kiss '65" (remix), Ruff House/Columbia, 1994 (*Brainscan* soundtrack).

Yeofi: *Necessary Madness,* Atlantic, 1996.

COLLECTIONS

Nativity in Black: Tribute to Black Sabbath, Sony, 1994.

Masters of the Banjo, Arhoolie, 1994.

Matt Wallace

Since the late '80s, Matt Wallace has been one of the heroes of modern rock, producing records that balance profitability with artistic integrity. In a survey of unsigned bands, more artists said they hoped someday to work with Wallace than any other producer (second on the list was Mitchell Froom; see entry). Wallace is especially sensitive to an artist's sound and image, and has never been accused of causing a group to "sell out" or of making them sound too commercial.

Wallace (born January 10, 1960, in Tulsa, Oklahoma) cut his teeth producing demo tapes and independent LPs for new wave bands in the San Francisco Bay Area in the early '80s. Wallace would often work 20-hour days. It was not atypical for him to work several sessions a day for different bands at different studios. As an engineer, he was admired for his speed and ability to capture the energy of a band with minimal setup, and in the first take.

Shortly after the success of Faith No More's indie debut *We Care A Lot,* Wallace moved to Los Angeles, where he continued to produce that group's efforts, including 1987's *Introduce Yourself* (co-produced with Steve Berlin; see entry), with a remake of "We Care a Lot," and the million-selling album *The Real Thing* (No. 11), with the heavily rotated MTV hit "Epic" (No. 9).

In 1989 Wallace produced the Replacements' classic *Don't Tell a Soul,* with their only charting single, "I'll Be You." He subsequently worked with their ex-singer Paul Westerberg on his solo album *14 Songs* in 1993. Also in 1993, Wallace was making records of complexity and polish: John Hiatt's *Perfectly Good Guitar* and School of Fish's *Human Cannonball.*

At the same time, Wallace kept his reputation with the alternative camp by producing several tracks on *If I Were a Carpenter* (the 1994 tribute to the Carpenters that he conceived with journalist David Konjoyan). Wallace produced cuts by 4 Non Blondes, Sheryl Crow, Dishwalla, Matthew Sweet, and Redd Kross. —DANIEL J. LEVITIN

4 Non Blondes: "Bless the Beasts and the Children," A&M, 1994 (*If I Were a Carpenter*).

Chagall Guevara: *Chagall Guevara,* MCA, 1991.

Crow, Sheryl: "Solitaire," A&M, 1994 (*If I Were a Carpenter*).

Deftones: "Teething," Miramax/Hollywood, 1996 (*The Crow City of Angels* soundtrack).

Dimestore Hoods: *Dimestore Hoods,* MCA, 1996.

Dishwalla: "It's Going to Take Some Time," A&M, 1994 (*If I Were a Carpenter*).

Dog's Eye View: *Daisy,* Columbia, 1997 • "Homecoming Parade," Columbia, 1997.

Enormous: *Busman's Holiday,* A&M, 1996 • "Sweet Is," A&M, 1997.

Faith No More: *We Care a Lot,* Mordam, 1985 • *Introduce Yourself,* Slash, 1987 • "Epic," Reprise, 1989 (*Follow Our Tracks,* Vol. 2) • *The Real Thing,* Slash/Reprise, 1989 • "Falling to Pieces," Slash, 1990 • *Angel Dust,* Slash/Reprise, 1992 • "Easy," Slash, 1993.

Hiatt, John: *Perfectly Good Guitar,* A&M, 1993 • *Hiatt Comes Alive at Budokan,* A&M, 1994 • *The Best of John Hiatt,* Capitol, 1998.

Hoffs, Susanna: *Susanna Hoffs,* Mercury, 1996.

Howlin' Maggie: *Honeysuckle Strange,* Columbia, 1996.

Kreviazuk, Chantal: "Surrounded," Columbia, 1997 • *Under These Rocks and Stones,* Columbia, 1997.

Lock Up: *Something Bitchin' This Way Comes,* Manifesto, 1990, 1997.

Red Five: *Flash,* Interscope, 1996.

Redd Kross: "Yesterday Once More," A&M, 1994 (*If I Were a Carpenter*).

Replacements, The: *Don't Tell a Soul,* Sire/Reprise, 1989 • "I'll Be You," Sire/Reprise, 1989 • *All for Nothing/Nothing for All,* Warner Bros., 1997.

Rogers, Kimm: *Two Sides,* Island, 1992.

Royal Jelly: *Royal Jelly,* Island, 1994.

Satchel: *Family,* Sony, 1996.

School of Fish: *Human Cannonball,* Capitol, 1993.

Sons of Freedom: *Sons of Freedom,* Slash, 1988.

Spent Poets: *The Spent Poets,* Geffen, 1992.

Sweet, Matthew: "Let Me Be the One," A&M, 1994 (*If I Were a Carpenter*).

Tiny Buddy: *Ginormous,* Fish of Death, 1995.

Toad the Wet Sprocket: *Pale,* Columbia, 1990.

Toll, The: *Sticks & Stones & Broken Bones,* DGC, 1991.

Train: *Train,* TriStar, 1998.

Weapon of Choice: *Nutmeg Phantasy,* Loosegroove, 1998.

Westerberg, Paul: *14 Songs,* Sire/Reprise, 1993 • "Knockin' on Mine," Sire/Reprise, 1993 • "Sunshine," Reprise, 1995 (*Friends* soundtrack).

Wildflowers, The: *Tales Like These,* Slash, 1990.

Lenny Waronker

L enny Waronker's father, Si Waronker, was a violinist in the 20th Century Fox Orchestra, working with award-winning conductor Alfred Newman (Randy Newman's uncle). Young Lenny (born October 3, 1941) spent his early years on the soundstage watching his father play. He graduated from the University of Southern California, worked for Metric Music Publishers, and later as a publicist at his father's record company, Liberty. He was hired as an A&R executive at Warner Brothers in 1966; he eventually became label president, a position he held until 1996. His avuncular presence in the studio, both for artists he has produced and the scores of additional artists under his A&R tutelage (George Har-

rison; John Fogerty, Lindsey Buckingham, and Brian Wilson, see entries) has given warmth and confidence to hundreds of recordings. Few producers have had the consistent high quality and breadth of repertoire: there is not one album on his discography that was not either a commercial or critical success, and most were both.

Among many highlights are Ry Cooder's debut album and *Paradise and Lunch* (with Russ Titelman; see entry), in which the guitarist presented his own versions of classic roots and blues songs, delivered in an engagingly quirky voice. If the ultimate measure of a producer is the ability to capture great performances on tape, Waronker is easily among the greatest. The Waronker-produced recordings of Cooder's "Police Dog Blues" and "Ditty Wah Ditty" and Maria Muldaur's "Midnight at the Oasis" (No. 6) capture some of the finest moments on record. According to Waronker, "Midnight" was a sonic movie, a soundtrack for a film he and the artists only imagined, a technique he often employs in "painting with sound," as he refers to his work.

One trademark of Waronker's productions is his ability to capture a sound and vibe and make the music as if the musicians had been playing together for years. This is most evident on two James Taylor records, which exude a deep and warm sincerity: *Gorilla* (No. 6) and *In the Pocket* (No. 16), both with Titelman.

"I work with creative people, and more often than not it was their creativity that made me look good," Waronker says. "And when you're dealing with lots of

people and they're bouncing off each other, if you give them a chance to be who they are, then you have a better chance than not of coming up with something interesting and creative.

"Russ [Titelman] and I had a real feeling for James Taylor, as I think he had for us. And if that got onto the record, that's great. In the case of Cooder and [Randy] Newman it is sort of like family—people we've both spent a long time with. Those were far from being casual records. Though there was lots of laughing and lots of joking and trying to keep the environment as light as possible, it was a fairly intense scene." —DANIEL J. LEVITIN

Allman Brothers Band: *Dreams,* Polydor, 1989.
Allman, Gregg: *Playin' Up a Storm,* Capricorn, 1977 • *One More Try: An Anthology,* Polydor, 1997.
Beau Brummels: *Triangle,* Warner Bros., 1967 • *Bradley's Barn,* Warner Bros., 1968 • *The Beau Brummels,* Warner Bros., 1975.
Clapton, Eric: *Behind the Sun,* Duck/WB, 1985 • "Forever Man," Duck/WB, 1985 • "See What Love Can Do," Duck/WB, 1985 • "Loving Your Lovin'," Reprise, 1992 (*Wayne's World* soundtrack).
Cooder, Ry: *Ry Cooder,* Reprise, 1970 • *Boomer's Story,* Reprise, 1972 • *Into the Purple Valley,* Reprise, 1972 • *Paradise and Lunch,* Reprise, 1974.
Doobie Brothers: *The Doobie Brothers,* Warner Bros., 1971.
Everly Brothers: *Roots,* Warner Bros., 1968 • *Home Again,* RCA, 1985 • *Heartaches and Harmonies,* Rhino, 1994.
Guthrie, Arlo: *Running down the Road,* Rising Son, 1969, 1991 • *Washington County,* Rising Son, 1970, 1991 • *Hobo's Lullaby,* Reprise, 1972 • "The City of New Orleans," Reprise, 1972 • "Lovesick Blues," Warner Bros., 1973 (*Appetizers*) • *The Last of the Brooklyn Cowboys,* Reprise, 1973 • *Arlo Guthrie,* Reprise, 1974 • *Amigo,* Reprise, 1975 • *All Over the World,* Rising Son, 1991 • *25th Anniversary Edition,* Rising Son, 1994.
Harper's Bizarre: *Anything Goes,* Warner Bros., 1967 • *Feelin' Groovy,* Warner Bros., 1967 • "The 59th Street Bridge Song," Warner Bros., 1967 • *The Secret Life of Harper's Bizarre,* Warner Bros., 1968 • *Four,* Warner Bros., 1969.
Hawn, Goldie: *Goldie,* Warner Bros., 1972.
Jones, Rickie Lee: "Chuck E's in Love," Warner Bros., 1979 • *Rickie Lee Jones,* Warner Bros., 1979 • *Pirates,* Warner Bros., 1981.
Lightfoot, Gordon: "If You Could Read My Mind," Reprise, 1970 • *If You Could Read My Mind,* Reprise, 1970 • *Don Quixote,* Warner Archives, 1972, 1994 • "Carefree Highway," Reprise, 1974 • "Sundown," Reprise, 1974 • *Sundown,* Reprise, 1974 • *Cold on the Shoulder,* Reprise, 1975 • *Gord's Gold,* Reprise, 1975 • *Summertime Dream,* Reprise, 1976 • "The Wreck of the Edmund Fitzgerald,"

Warner Bros., 1976 • *Endless Wire,* Reprise, 1978 • *Dream Street Rosie,* Warner Bros., 1980 • *Gord's Gold,* Vol. 2, Warner Bros., 1988.
McDonald, Michael: "I Gotta Try," Warner Bros., 1982 • "I Keep Forgettin'," Warner Bros., 1982 • *If That's What It Takes,* Warner Bros., 1982.
Muldaur, Maria: "I'm a Woman," Reprise, 1974 • *Maria Muldaur,* Reprise, 1974 • "Midnight at the Oasis," Reprise, 1974 • *Waitress in a Donut Shop,* Reprise, 1974 • *Sweet Harmony,* Reprise, 1976.
Newman, Randy: *Randy Newman,* Reprise, 1968 • *12 Songs,* Reprise, 1970 • *Live,* Reprise, 1971 • *Sail Away,* Reprise, 1972 • *Good Old Boys,* Warner Bros., 1974 • *Little Criminals,* Warner Bros., 1977 • "Short People," Warner Bros., 1977 • *Born Again,* Warner Bros., 1979 • *Ragtime,* Elektra, 1981 • *Trouble in Paradise,* Warner Bros., 1983 • *The Natural* soundtrack, Atlantic, 1984, 1989.
Parks, Van Dyke: *Song Cycle,* Warner Bros., 1968.
Simon, Paul: *Paul Simon, 1964–1993,* Warner Bros., 1993.
Stewart, Rod: *Vagabond Heart,* Warner Bros., 1991 • *If We Fall in Love Tonight,* Warner Bros., 1996.
Taylor, James: *Gorilla,* Warner Bros., 1975 • "How Sweet It Is (To Be Loved by You)," Warner Bros., 1975 • *Greatest Hits,* Warner Bros., 1976, 1988 • *In the Pocket,* Warner Bros., 1976.
Waits, Tom: "Rainbow Sleeve," Warner Bros., 1980, 1983 (*The King of Comedy* soundtrack).
Wilson, Brian: *Brian Wilson,* Sire/Reprise, 1988.

Don Was

U nlike many producers who succeed in only one genre, Don Was has produced hits for artists of virtually every musical stripe: from pop, rock, and alternative to country, jazz, and Latin.

Don Was (born Donald Fagenson on September 13, 1952) told *Billboard,* in a 1997 special issue dedicated to him, that he attributes that ability to his formative years in Detroit in the '60s and '70s, where, in addition to learning how to produce records, he was a working musician. "I was playing five nights a week," he says. "It was the nature of the gigs to be playing with Hungarian gypsies one day and then a heavy metal band the next day. It was an amazing experience that I think really permeated all the subsequent records I've made."

He also began making quirky funk-rock records with partner David Was (born David Weiss) under the moniker Was (Not Was). "There was a street in Detroit

Photo by David Goggin ©1998

ly is. You kind of have to learn how to draw the information out, but when I get stumped, I'll play a Brian Wilson record and I'll find the way out of a problem I might have."

Was' first official production credit was the debut single from Was (Not Was) on Ze Records in 1981, followed by the group's debut album on Island Records. "If you listen to that first Was (Not Was) album, that's an album made by guys who had no idea what they were doing whatsoever, and that's the charm of the record," Was says. "I'd love to be able to get back to that."

Those early Was (Not Was) projects drew not only critical acclaim but adoration from a number of British acts, such as Helen Terry, Brother Beyond, Marilyn and Floy Joy, all of whom had Was-produced albums in the early '80s. "What happened was that Was (Not Was) got this following in England, especially for being these white funksters. And all these English acts actually sought me out. They flew over here on their own bread," Was recalls. "They wanted to come to Detroit, get the Motown tour, work with real soul musicians. It was a soul Disneyland."

Early on, Was learned the key to being a good producer. "Listening's the whole thing," he says. "That's the thing about producing records. Listen to what the artist really wants to do, listen to them when they're talking, listen to them when they sing the song, listen to what the song's about, listen to what the record company needs. Just shut up and listen for a minute, man, and things fall into place pretty easily."

Was was clearly listening during the mid- to late '80s, when he started to come into his own as a producer. Among the artists he worked with were Carly Simon, k.d. lang, and Roy Orbison, the B-52's and, of course, Bonnie Raitt. His production of lang and Orbison's "Crying" was his first project to win a Grammy, for Best Country Duet, in 1988, but it was his work on Raitt's No. 1 *Nick of Time,* which won four Grammys in 1989, including Album of the Year, that catapulted him into the rank of superstar producer. "I'm proud of *Nick of Time,* and it's certainly a highlight of my life," says Was, "but I actually think *Luck of the Draw* (No. 2) is a much better record."

Was has worked with an astonishing array of acts, including Iggy Pop, Bob Seger, Jewel, Michael McDonald, Bob Dylan, Elton John, Neil Diamond, Paula Abdul, Jackson Browne, Willie Nelson, Waylon Jennings, Travis Tritt, and the Rolling Stones.

"The people who have influenced me greatly, in the last few years anyway, are Willie Nelson, Keith Richards [see "Glimmer Twins" entry], and Bob Dylan," says Was. "They are three guys who are completely feel-ori-

called Woodward Avenue," he remembers. "It was like a cruising street, but you'd also drag race, but essentially, you'd cruise up and down Woodward and try to pick up girls. After a night of failure, which was most nights, David and I used to go back to my place where we had a little 2-track recorder and we'd vent our frustrations by playing songs and recording them. So we got into rock 'n' roll because we couldn't get the girls. It's kind of tragic, isn't it?"

Several more experienced hands were willing to give Was support. "There were people who provided opportunities for me to stumble and make mistakes and I'm grateful for that," he says. "Jack Tann and John Lewis were two guys who had a studio in Detroit and they just gave me free run of it. Detroit was weird, there wasn't a lot of music business. There wasn't a Phil Spector [see entry] down the street, there wasn't a way to take a master class. The Motown door was closed to me, and by then, the late '70s, they were really closed. What these guys allowed me to do was try to figure it out by myself."

Many of Was' greatest teachers lived nowhere near Detroit. "If you listen to records, it's all there for me," he says. "For me, Brian Wilson or Burt Bacharach [see entries] are people who made amazing lessons, who if you just listened to them, you were going to learn. Really, everything you need to know is in *Pet Sounds,* it real-

ented and aren't analytical about stuff. They're just dealing with the emotional level of the music and how it feels. "I approach every moment with a beginner's mind. I was kind of panicked before we started the Stones records, and Keith said, 'Just remember, when we get to the studio, improvise, adapt, and overcome.' And I thought, 'Wow, what a load of shit,' but in fact, he was completely right. . . . If I'd gone in with a program or something planned ahead of time with a guy like that, who's strictly a feel musician, I would have just had to discard it anyway, and it would have been more trouble to discard it than just make up a new one on the spot. That's really how I try to approach it as a musician and as a producer, and it's probably the best way to go through life in general, is just feel your way through."

His work on the Stones' *Voodoo Lounge* (No. 2), Raitt's *Longing in Their Hearts* (No. 1) and *Rhythm, Country and Blues*, a melding of country and R&B artists, led to Was winning the coveted Producer of the Year trophy at the 1995 Grammy Awards.

Was has produced material for movie soundtracks for years, but he has now taken his passion for movies to another level. His 1995 documentary on Brian Wilson, *I Just Wasn't Made for These TImes*, won the Golden Gate Award at the 1995 San Francisco Film Festival and was also nominated for a Cable Ace Award. He also directed a short film for the enhanced CD version of his latest project, Orquestra Was, in addition to starting his own movie production company.

However, he stresses that he's not about to give up producing albums or making his own music. "I really feel like I'm just starting to make some decent records and just starting to be a human being, man. I'm embarrassed at what I was 20 years ago, and how ignorant I was. I'm just now starting to see a glimmer of truth," he says, before adding, with a laugh, "but I'm sure that's just an illusion."

He actually enters the studio every day with a healthy dose of fear. "There isn't a day when I'm driving to the studio that I don't think, 'What if it doesn't work?' " he says. "I've had days where my back hurts, but I've never had days where I've just stood in the studio and shrugged my shoulders and said, 'I can't figure out anything to do.' " —MELINDA NEWMAN

Abdul, Paula: *Spellbound,* Virgin, 1991.

Atkinson, Sweet Pea: *Don't Walk Away,* Ze, 1982.

B-52's, The: "Channel Z," Reprise, 1989 (*Follow Our Tracks,* Vol. 2) • *Cosmic Thing* (4 tracks), Reprise, 1989 • "Love Shack," Reprise, 1989 • "Good Stuff," Reprise, 1992 • *Good Stuff,* Reprise, 1992 • "Is That You Mo-Dean?," Reprise, 1992 • "(Meet) the Flintstones," MCA, 1994 (*The*

Flintstones soundtrack) • *Time Capsule: Greatest Hits,* Warner Bros., 1998.

Brother Beyond: *I Should Have Lied,* EMI, 1983.

Browne, Jackson: *I'm Alive,* Elektra, 1993.

Cavaliere, Felix: *Dreams in Motion,* MCA, 1994.

Clegg, Johnny: "These Days," Capitol, 1993 • *In My African Dream,* Rhythm Safari, 1994.

Cocker, Joe: *Organic,* 550 Music, 1996.

Crenshaw, Marshall: *Lesson #1,* Warner Bros., 1983.

Cristina: *Sleep It Off,* Mercury, 1984.

Crosby, David: *Thousand Roads,* Atlantic, 1993.

Dead Milkmen: "Smokin Banana Peels" (remix), Enigma, 1989.

Diamond, Neil: *Lovescape,* Columbia, 1991 • *In My Lifetime,* Sony, 1996.

Dulli, Greg, Dave Pirner, Thurston Moore, Don Fleming, etc.: *Backbeat* soundtrack, Virgin, 1994.

Dylan, Bob: "Handy Dandy," Columbia, 1990 • *Under the Red Sky,* Columbia, 1990 • *Greatest Hits,* Vol. 3, Columbia, 1995 • *MTV Unplugged,* Columbia, 1995.

Faithfull, Marianne: *Faithfull: A Collection of Her Best Recordings,* Island, 1994 • "Ghost Dance," Island, 1994.

Floy Joy: *Into the Hot,* Virgin, 1983 • *Weak in the Presence of Beauty,* Virgin, 1983.

Frey, Glenn: "Part of Me, Part of You," MCA, 1991 • *Strange Weather,* MCA, 1992.

Gold, Andrew: *Thank You for Being a Friend: The Best of Andrew Gold,* Rhino, 1997.

Haza, Ofra: *Kirya 1992,* EastWest, 1992.

Highwaymen, The (Johnny Cash, Willie Nelson, Kris Kristofferson, Waylon Jennings): *The Road Goes On Forever,* Liberty, 1995.

Jaguares: *El Equilibrio de los Jaguares,* RCA International, 1996.

Jennings, Waylon: *Waymore's Blues (Part II),* RCA, 1994 • *The Essential,* RCA, 1996.

Jewel: "Have a Little Faith in Me," Reprise, 1996 (*Phenomenon* soundtrack).

John, Elton: *To Be Continued . . .* (4 tracks), MCA, 1990 • "You Gotta Love Someone," MCA, 1990 • *Duets,* MCA, 1993 • w/ Bonnie Raitt, "Love Letter Straight from the Heart," MCA, 1994.

Khaled, Cheb: *Khaled,* Cohiba, 1992 • "Cheeba," Mango, 1993 • *N'ssi N'ssi,* Mango, 1993, 1995 • *Serbi Serbi,* Cohiba, 1994 • *Sahra,* Barclay, 1997.

King, B.B.: *King of the Blues,* MCA, 1992.

Knack, The: *Serious Fun,* Charisma, 1991 • *Retrospective: The Best of the Knack,* Capitol, 1992.

Kristofferson, Kris: *A Moment of Forever,* Justice, 1995.

lang, k.d., and Roy Orbison: "Crying," Virgin, 1988 (*Hiding Out* soundtrack).

Lasley, David: *Raindance,* EMI, 1983.

Lovett, Lyle: "You Can't Resist It," Curb/MCA, 1991 (*Switch* soundtrack) • w/ Randy Newman, "You Got a Friend in

Me," Touchstone, 1995 (*Toy Story* soundtrack).

McClinton, Delbert: *Never Been Rocked Enough,* Curb/MCA, 1992 • *Delbert McClinton,* Curb/Capitol, 1993.

McDonald, Michael: "Take It to Heart," Reprise, 1990 • *Take It to Heart,* Reprise, 1990.

Mommyheads: *Mommyheads,* Geffen, 1997.

Nelson, Willie: "Blue Hawaii," Epic Soundtrax, 1992 (*Honeymoon in Vegas* soundtrack) • *Across the Borderline,* Columbia, 1993.

Neville, Aaron: w/ Tricia Yearwood, "I Fall to Pieces," MCA, 1994 • w/ Robbie Robertson, "Crazy Love," Reprise, 1996 (*Phenomenon* soundtrack).

Newman, Randy: "Make Up Your Mind," Warner Bros., 1994 (*The Paper* soundtrack) • *Randy Newman's Faust,* Reprise, 1995.

Nicks, Stevie: "Won't Somebody Stand by Me?," Arista, 1994 (*Boys on the Side* soundtrack).

1,000 Points of Light: "Read My Lips," Polydor, 1992.

Orbison, Roy: *King of Hearts,* Virgin, 1992 • *The Very Best Of,* Virgin, 1997.

Orquestra Was: *Forever's a Long, Long Time,* Verve Forecast, 1997.

Pop, Iggy: *Brick by Brick,* Virgin, 1990 • "Livin' on the Edge of the Night," Virgin, 1990 (*Black Rain* soundtrack) • w/ Kate Pierson, "Candy," Virgin, 1990.

Raitt, Bonnie: "Have a Heart," Capitol, 1990 • *Nick of Time,* Capitol, 1990 • *Luck of the Draw,* Capitol, 1991 • "Something to Talk About," Capitol, 1991 • "I Can't Make You Love Me," Capitol, 1992 • "Nick of Time," Capitol, 1992 • "Not the Only One," Capitol, 1992 • *Longing in Their Hearts,* Capitol, 1994 • "Love Sneakin' Up on You," Capitol, 1994 • "You," Capitol, 1994 • *Road Tested,* Capitol, 1995 • w/ Bryan Adams, "Rock Steady," Capitol, 1995 • "You Got It," Arista, 1995 (*Boys on the Side* soundtrack).

Rolling Stones, The: "Rock and a Hard Place" (remix), Columbia, 1989 • "Love Is Strong," Virgin, 1994 • "Out of Tears," Virgin, 1994 • *Voodoo Lounge,* Virgin, 1994 • *Stripped,* Virgin, 1995 • *Bridges to Babylon,* Virgin, 1997.

Sambora, Richie: *Undiscovered Soul,* Mercury, 1998.

Seger, Bob, and the Silver Bullet Band: *The Fire Inside,* Capitol, 1991 • "The Real Love," Capitol, 1991.

Shear, Jules: "When Love Surges," EMI America, 1983.

Shepard, Vonda: *The Radical Light,* Reprise, 1992.

Shocked, Michelle: *Arkansas Traveler,* Mercury, 1992 • "Come a Long Way," Mercury, 1992.

Shrieve, Michael: *Stiletto,* Atlantic, 1989 • *The Big Picture,* Atlantic, 1989.

Simon, Carly: *Spoiled Girl,* Epic, 1983 • "Come Back Home," Epic, 1985.

Starr, Ringo: *Time Takes Time,* Private, 1992 • "Weight of the World," Private, 1992.

Stuart, Marty: *Marty Party Hit Pack,* MCA, 1995.

Terry, Helen: *Blue Notes,* Virgin, 1983.

Tritt, Travis: "More Than You'll Ever Know," Warner Bros., 1996 • *The Restless Kind,* Warner Bros., 1996 • featuring Lari White, "Helping Me Get Over You," Warner Bros., 1997 • "She's Going Home with Me," Warner Bros., 1997 • "Still in Love with You," Warner Bros., 1997 • "Where Corn Don't Grow," Warner Bros., 1997.

Twitty, Conway: *The Conway Twitty Collection,* MCA, 1994.

Untouchables, The: "Freak in the Street" (remix), Stiff/MCA, 1986.

Voice of the Beehive: *Honey Lingers* (1 track), London, 1991.

Was (Not Was): *Was (Not Was),* Ze/Island, 1981 • "Wheel Me Out/Hello Operator," Ze, 1981 • *Born to Laugh at Tornadoes,* Ze/Geffen, 1983 • "Spy in the House of Love," Chrysalis, 1988 • "Walk the Dinosaur," Chrysalis, 1988 • *What Up, Dog?,* Chrysalis, 1988 • "Anything Can Happen," Chrysalis, 1989 • *Are You Okay?,* Chrysalis, 1990 • "How the Heart Behaves," Chrysalis, 1990 • "Papa Was a Rolling Stone," Chrysalis, 1990 • *Hello Dad . . . I'm in Jail,* Phonogram, 1992.

Wasserman, Rob: *Trios,* GRP, 1994.

White, Lari: *Best Of,* RCA, 1997.

Willis, Kelly: "Heaven's Just a Sin Away," MCA, 1993 • *Kelly Willis,* MCA, 1993 • "Whatever Way the Wind Blows," MCA, 1993.

Wilson, Brian: *I Just Wasn't Made for These Times* (video), MCA, 1995.

Young, Paul: *The Crossing,* Sony UK, 1993.

COLLECTIONS

Earth Girls Are Easy soundtrack, Vestron, 1989.

For Our Children, Disney, 1991.

Rhythm, Country and Blues, MCA, 1994.

It's Now or Never: The Tribute to Elvis, Mercury, 1994.

Songs of Jimmie Rodgers: A Tribute, Sony, 1997.

Tom Werman

Tom Werman is bitter about the music business. He says he can't get a job in it these days, though he produced albums that together sold more than 40 million units. His clients include Ted Nugent, Cheap Trick, Blue Öyster Cult, Mother's Finest, Molly Hatchet, and the Producers—at Epic, the company Werman worked for from 1970 to 1982. They also include West Coast hair metal icons like Mötley Crüe and Dokken, whom Werman produced at Elektra, where he went to work in 1982.

As soon as he got there, Joe Smith, who hired him, was kicked upstairs and replaced by Bob Krasnow, "who really didn't let me do my job," he says. Nevertheless, Krasnow contracted Werman to produce two records a year for two years at Elektra. Now, he says, he can't get work, so he's decided to open a sandwich shop that bakes its own bread in Los Angeles, where he lives.

"The work stopped dead as soon as Seattle came," says Werman, who was born in Boston on March 2, 1945. "As soon as hair bands were deemed stupid and old, I was deemed stupid and old," he says. "That's the way A&R thinks. I'm through with music," says Werman, who produced the demos for Cheap Trick's latest "comeback" and is miffed that Trick, whose most successful work he shaped, didn't choose him for their whole album.

"I'm very disappointed that I have to leave the field, but I can't make a living in it. I love music, it's my number one passion, and I'd love to work with it. I didn't network myself well enough so I'd get a cushy job—or any job."

Werman had many good years, however; he's been trading stocks, gets "meager royalties," and says he's a good investor, which is not surprising, considering his business background. What's remarkable about him is his blend of business acumen and musical taste. His best records—Cheap Trick's gold *In Color*, platinum *Heaven Tonight*, and *Dream Police* (No. 6)—are brawny power pop, delivered with drive and efficiency.

Werman grew up in Boston and, after earning a master's degree in business administration from Columbia University, wrote CBS seeking work. "I knew CBS was the biggest, most legitimate marketing organization, and that they would pay attention to my M.B.A.,"

Werman says. "I finally got to Clive Davis, who was then president of CBS Records. He said, 'We don't have any jobs at Columbia, but we need an assistant to the director of A&R at Epic.' So he sent me out to see if I knew anything."

Turns out Werman did. Not only had he played guitar in a Boston band called the Walkers in the mid-'60s—"We turned down an audition with Brian Epstein because of the draft," he claims—he'd played such New York clubs as the Metropole and Delmonico's, where he'd gotten to know B-list socialite Baby Jane Holzer and met Jimi Hendrix. Werman sat in with Hendrix at Ondine's, playing rhythm guitar.

In 1970, two months after he joined Epic, he signed REO Speedwagon. Shortly after, he went to work for Don Ellis, a veteran record man whom Werman calls a fine administrator, but "a little too old for what I wanted. I wanted Epic to get into rock 'n' roll, and they were in pop. They had no rock 'n' roll except for the Dave Clark Five, and Jeff Beck was just starting to make records by himself. In quick succession, I tried to sign Rush, whom I had free and clear; they were turned down because they wanted $75,000 for two albums. Then I tried to sign Kiss, because I had signed the band Kiss came from, Wicked Lester, a big pop band with lots of harmonies. Gene Simmons and Paul Stanley sang in that band."

Wicked Lester broke up, but Stanley (real name: Stan Eisen), Simmons (real name: Gene Klein) and Peter Criss auditioned for Epic as a three-piece. "They had a beautiful show, and they ended by throwing a bucket of silver confetti on us," Werman recalls. "We walked out and Don said, 'What the fuck was that?' That was the end of Kiss [at Epic]. This must have been 1972."

After he failed with Rush and Kiss, he tried to sign Lynyrd Skynyrd; when he brought Ellis to Macon, Georgia, to catch its show, Ellis's response was great band, no songs. Werman then tried to sign Manhattan Transfer to Columbia, to no avail. Finally, Ellis left Epic and was replaced by Steve Popovich, who eventually founded Cleveland International. Popovich asked Werman whom he wanted to sign; Werman said Ted Nugent. He got the okay and went on to produce Nugent's key early records. This was in 1975. "The first Ted Nugent record I did was platinum, so all of a sudden I was a brilliant young producer," says Werman.

In short order, he signed Cheap Trick and Molly Hatchet; he produced Trick's second album, *In Color*, because the band's first producer, Jack Douglas (see entry), was busy with Aerosmith. "I started producing everything I signed," says Werman, who claims to have been instrumental in signing Boston to Epic. "Five Ted

Nugents, three Cheap Tricks, five Molly Hatchets, two Mother's Finest, and two Producers, in a very short span of time. I moved to the West Coast because I liked working out there. I never did an album in New York."

In 1982, he left Epic to become vice president of A&R at Elektra, where in short order he produced Mötley Crüe's *Shout at the Devil* (No. 17) and Dokken's *Tooth and Nail* (with Roy Thomas Baker; see entry). Shortly thereafter, he found himself an independent producer, however. He produced the Crüe through the mid-'80s, lent his talents to such lesser metal lights as Poison and Kix, and went out—at least for now—on a high metal note with Lita Ford's *Dangerous Curves,* Pariah's *To Mock a Killingbird,* and Hash's eponymous Elektra debut.

"A good producer does virtually everything," Werman says. "A good producer is a good talent scout. You pick the best songs with the band, arrange them, rehearse them, get a budget together, get the right kind of studio for each phase of the record, hire the right engineer, then get down to every little decision, like what kind of beat is on the bass drum, what kind of mikes to use, what kind of heads to put on the drums, how you're going to record the basic tracks, what order you overdub in, how to get the best performance."

Any signature to Werman productions? "Rhythm," he says. "There are two things I like to do. I like to reinforce rhythms. I did all my own percussion." He overdubbed all percussion except conga on his productions, he says. "I like to do that, and I'm really good at backing vocals. I also like continuing suspended notes. I like a pedal tone, one note going continuously through a verse or a chorus, played on different instruments, with different textures, peaking in and out. A good example would be [Cheap Trick's] 'Surrender,' which didn't have a keyboard in it until I introduced the keyboard, which I stole from 'Baba O'Riley.' The Who were my inspiration. The Beatles, the Stones, and the Who were what I wanted to incorporate in my records. That's why I was so good with Cheap Trick, because they wanted to be the Beatles and I wanted them to be the Who."

—CARLO WOLFF

Babylon A.D.: *Babylon A.D.,* Arista, 1989 • *Nothing Sacred,* Arista, 1992.

Beck, Jeff, and Jan Hammer: *Live with the Jan Hammer Group,* Epic, 1977.

Blue Öyster Cult: "In Thee," Columbia, 1979 • *Mirrors,* Columbia, 1979 • *Workshop of the Telescopes* (1 track), Legacy, 1995.

Boy Meets Girl: *Boy Meets Girl,* A&M, 1985 • "Oh Girl," A&M, 1985.

Brownsville: *Air Special,* CBS, 1978.

B'zz, The: *Get Up,* Epic, 1983.

Cheap Trick: *In Color,* Epic, 1977 • *Heaven Tonight,* Epic, 1978 • "Surrender," Epic, 1978 • "Dream Police," Epic, 1979 • *Dream Police,* Epic, 1979 • "Voices," Epic, 1979 • *Sex America Cheap Trick,* Sony, 1996.

Dokken: *Tooth and Nail,* Elektra, 1984 • "Alone Again," Elektra, 1985.

Ford, Lita: *Dangerous Curves,* RCA, 1991 • "Shot of Poison," RCA, 1991 • *Greatest Hits,* RCA, 1993.

Glass Tiger: *Best of Glass Tiger: Air Time,* ERG, 1993.

Graveyard Train: *The Graveyard Train,* Geffen, 1993.

Hash: *Hash,* Elektra, 1993.

Hawks, The: *The Hawks,* CBS, 1981.

Jason and the Scorchers: *Still Standing,* EMI America, 1986.

Junkyard: *Junkyard,* Geffen, 1989.

Kix: *Blow My Fuse,* Atlantic, 1988 • "Don't Close Your Eyes," Atlantic, 1989 • *Hot Wire,* EastWest, 1991.

Krokus: *Change of Address,* Arista, 1986 • "School's Out," Arista, 1986 • *Staye Awake All Night: The Best Of,* Arista, 1989.

L.A. Guns: *Cocked and Loaded,* PolyGram, 1989.

Love/Hate: *Blackout in the Red Room,* Columbia, 1990.

Molly Hatchet: *Molly Hatchet,* Epic, 1978 • *Flirtin' with Disaster,* Epic, 1979 • *Beatin' the Odds,* Epic, 1980 • *Take No Prisoners,* Epic, 1981 • *No Guts, No Glory,* Epic, 1983 • *Greatest Hits,* Epic, 1985 • *Super Hits,* Legacy/Epic, 1998.

Mother's Finest: *Mother's Finest,* Epic, 1976 • *Another Mother Further,* Epic, 1977.

Mötley Crüe: *Shout at the Devil,* Elektra, 1983 • "Home Sweet Home," Elektra, 1985, 1991 • "Smokin' in the Boys Room," Elektra, 1985 • *Theater of Pain,* Elektra, 1985 • "Girls Girls Girls," Elektra, 1987 • *Girls Girls Girls,* Elektra, 1987 • "You're All I Need," Elektra, 1987 • *Decade of Decadence,* Elektra, 1991.

Myrick, Gary, and the Figures: *Gary Myrick and the Figures,* Epic, 1980.

Nugent, Ted: *Ted Nugent,* Epic, 1975 • *Free for All,* Epic, 1976 • "Cat Scratch Fever," Epic, 1977 • *Cat Scratch Fever,* Epic, 1977 • *Double Live Gonzo,* Epic, 1978 • *Weekend Warrior,* Epic, 1978 • *State of Shock,* Epic, 1979 • *Great Gonzo: The Best of Ted Nugent,* Epic, 1981 • *If You Can't Lick 'Em . . . Lick 'Em,* Atlantic, 1988 • *Super Hits,* Legacy/Epic, 1998.

Off Broadway U.S.A.: *On,* Atlantic, 1980.

Pariah: *To Mock a Killingbird,* Geffen, 1993.

Poison: "Every Rose Has Its Thorn," Enigma/Capitol, 1988 • "Fallen Angel," Enigma/Capitol, 1988 • "Nothn' But a Good Time," Enigma, 1988 • *Open Up and Say Ahhh,* Enigma/Capitol, 1988 • "Your Mama Don't Dance," Enigma/Capitol, 1988 • *Greatest Hits, 1986–1996,* Capitol, 1996.

Producers, The: *The Producers,* Portrait, 1981 • *You Make the Heat,* Portrait, 1982.

Roby, Falk and Bod: *Kentucky Gambler,* CBS, 1973.

Steelheart: *Tangled in Reins,* MCA, 1992.

Stranger: *Stranger,* Sony Special Products, 1982, 1992.

Stryper: *Against the Law,* Enigma, 1990 • *Can't Stop the Rock: The Stryper Collection, 1984–1991,* Hollywood, 1991.

Tearaways: *Ground's the Limit,* Pinch Hit, 1997.

Trout, Jake, and the Flounders: *I Love to Play,* Capitol, 1998.

Twisted Sister: "I Wanna Rock," Atlantic, 1984 • *Stay Hungry,* Atlantic, 1984 • "We're Not Gonna Take It," Atlantic, 1984.

Jerry Wexler

J
erry Wexler, equally proud of being able to motivate and not knowing how to run a mixing board, believes there are three kinds of record producers. "The first is the documentarian," says the former Atlantic Records executive. "That would be Alan Lomax, recording in the field. That's also Leonard Chess [see entry], who would go to a bar in Chicago and find Muddy Waters. Then he would replicate in the studio what Muddy Waters did the night before in the bar.

"The second way—and Phil Spector [see entry] is a genius at this—is where he's a songwriter, musician, engineer-type person, a combination thereof, who creates the record out of his own sensibility, where the artist is only one element in the whole creation.

"The third kind there's no name for, but I call the function serving the artist," says Wexler. "That's me, Ahmet [Ertegun; see entry], George Avakian, John Hammond [see entry], Bob Thiele [see entry], so many of us. We're all record fans, blues and jazz fans, record collectors. I call us guys who are in on a pass. Who the

Wexler with Aretha Franklin. Photo by Jim Marshall.

fuck do we think we are that we could go in a studio and dominate? There was hubris. Under what other notion could we imagine we could go into the studio and assemble a record? We couldn't read a music chart, we couldn't play an instrument, and we couldn't run a board."

Wexler was born January 10, 1917, in New York City. His father was a Talmudic scholar turned window cleaner. Wexler was exposed to music by his mother, who loved to play the piano. "Her fervor and intent far exceeded her talent," he says. She played Schumann and Liszt; Wexler, meanwhile, listened to black music on the radio.

As a teenager, Wexler held odd jobs such as garment packer and movie usher. This street kid from Washington Heights also worked as a writer for *Billboard* (where he got the name of one chart changed from "Race" to "Rhythm & Blues Records") and published several pieces of fiction before joining Atlantic Records in 1952 as executive vice president. He abandoned writing for two reasons: he's a perfectionist and he wanted to make money.

The first session Wexler worked on was for LaVern Baker's "Soul on Fire/How Can You Leave a Man?" He wrote the tunes with Ahmet Ertegun and the unsung Jesse Stone, Atlantic's chief arranger. "I probably behaved myself and kept my mouth shut," he recalls. "We had these great sidemen. I was in terror of all these great musicians."

During the '50s, Wexler learned more about producing, shed some of his fears regarding musicians, and helped Atlantic become a powerhouse. But he didn't come into his own as a producer until the '60s, when he saw how records were made in Muscle Shoals, Alabama, and Memphis. Not only did he cut records at Fame and Muscle Shoals Sound studios, he viewed record making in the South as more organic and spontaneous than its more sophisticated, less vital New York counterpart.

At Atlantic, Wexler had worked with arrangers and spent much time on preproduction. "Once you were committed to an arranger on paper," he says, "you were carried along with the flow of the arrangement.

"We made great records with the Drifters, Joe Turner, Clyde McPhatter, Chuck Willis, with great arrangers like Jesse Stone, Ray Ellis, and Howard Biggs (the last was the original arranger for the Ravens, a doo-wop group)," Wexler says. "But from 1961 on, entropy started to set in. We were starting to run dry because our arrangers were pretty much written out and the musicians were repeating themselves. When I went to Stax in Memphis to arrange for Atlantic's distribution of Stax and Volt, I was rejuvenated." The rejuvenation came in the form of Wilson Pickett, a soul shouter from

Prattsville, Alabama, whose "It's Too Late" became a hit—a bigger one for Solomon Burke than for Pickett, much to the latter's chagrin—in 1963.

Between 1965 and 1967, first at Stax, then at Fame, Wexler and Pickett cut such monster hits as "Land of 1,000 Dances" (No. 6), "Mustang Sally," "Everybody Needs Somebody to Love" (all with Rick Hall; see entry), "In the Midnight Hour," and "Funky Broadway" (No. 8).

In 1967, Atlantic was sold to Warner Bros. and Wexler moved to Florida and semiretirement. He officially left Atlantic in 1975, the year Stax folded for good. Besides Pickett, Wexler produced the seminal Aretha Franklin records on Atlantic, as well as Dusty Springfield's classic 1969 disc, *Dusty in Memphis* (with Tom Dowd and Arif Mardin; see entries). In the '70s, he produced or co-produced records by Franklin, Sam and Dave, Delaney and Bonnie, Ronnie Hawkins, Dr. John, Willie Nelson, Maggie Bell, Allen Toussaint (see entry), Etta James, Jose Feliciano, and Bob Dylan. In the '80s, Wexler produced albums by McGuinn-Hillman, Dylan, Billy Vera, and Carlos Santana.

One album he produced in the early '80s that never made it out was by Linda Ronstadt. Wexler invited Ronstadt and her then-beau, California Gov. Jerry Brown, to his house in East Hampton and played her records by Lee Wiley, Mildred Bailey, and Billie Holiday. Ronstadt swooned, telling him she, too, wanted to cut a sophisticated jazz record.

So Wexler assembled reedmen Al Cohn and Ira Sullivan, bassist George Mraz, trumpeter Walter Bolden, pianist Tommy Flanagan, and guitarist Tal Farlow. Unfortunately, Wexler recalls, "Ronstadt wouldn't sing. She didn't want to sing. Dusty Springfield did the same thing when we did *Dusty in Memphis*. I like to have the singer there, interacting with the musicians, because the interplay between singer and rhythm section can yield a much more empathetic track than dropping the singer in later.

"The way I work is, I have the rhythm section play the track into shape, but not finished. At that point, I bring the singer in and start to tweak. Now the drummer will have new ideas—especially the drummer. There will be different endings and turnarounds."

Everything was in place for Ronstadt when she got to Village Recorders in Los Angeles. "It was just myself and a local engineer," Wexler recalls. "She put the vocals down, but she didn't like the end product and finally said, 'I'm not putting the record out.' This idea was the nucleus of the records she made with Nelson Riddle. Linda Ronstadt needed the comfort, the cushion, of those strings and horns."

Springfield, by contrast, reveled in the stark, minimalist arrangements Wexler crafted for *Dusty in Memphis*. Unlike Ronstadt, she immersed herself in the project. "When a singer is overdubbing," says Wexler, "she always wants to hear more, get a lot in the track. This results in a weakened output on the part of the singer, though they don't realize it. So my fight is always to feed them the bare minimum; this makes them push. Now they're out there, projecting. Otherwise, they float in a sea of Jell-O.

"Dusty wouldn't buy it, wouldn't let me lower the feed. She kept saying, 'More, more, more,' until I did something I never dreamed I would do. We maxed out on the microphones, had it so loud I couldn't put a phone to my ear, it would have blown my eardrum. She kept saying to me, 'Give me more, I can still hear myself.' So Dusty Springfield did all of these fabulous vocals, phoning it in from memory, in a sense. She never heard what she did. It's an absolute paradox."

When Wexler brought Bob Dylan to Muscle Shoals to record the *Slow Train Coming* album (No. 3 in 1982), Dylan wanted "to be in the middle of a band, not off in a booth," so Wexler brought the band into the center of the studio, without isolation booths or baffling, "like it was a jam session."

"As they began playing," he says, "I had the engineer record them on 1/4-inch tape. When they hit a groove, I'd separate them and put everybody back into isolation or baffling. Then I'd play the tape they'd just recorded back through their phones and they would play to it. When they hit a groove, playing now, we'd stop the tape, count off, and record. That day, we made four perfect tracks."

Like Ertegun, Wexler believes in the voice. While rhythm and arrangements are key to the classic Atlantic canon, the voice makes the tunes memorable. "Voices," Wexler muses, citing Franklin, Ray Charles, Ben E. King, and Ruth Brown. "It seems strange to have to stress that. But nobody ever seems to talk about having great singers. Everything was always about personality, good instrumentation. We always looked for bel canto. Contrast that with Phil Spector. Remember, I said Phil Spector was a genius. But think of his roster and conjure up some names that would equate with my list."

Among the great singers Wexler produced was Etta James. Not only did he craft her 1978 Warner Bros. album *Deep in the Night*; he produced *The Right Time*, her 1992 album for Elektra. "I was very unhappy with the result," says Wexler. "I brought in Hank Crawford to do horns, which was a real reach, because nobody thinks of doing Hank Crawford with an R&B record anymore. I thought we had a masterpiece, but Etta James insisted on bringing in a synthesizer to double the horn lines. It was her misguided notion that this would somehow catapult her into the '90s."

In a war of wills, the artist always wins. "I represent a record company, to bring them a finished product," Wexler says. "But at the same time, my notion is, I'm there to serve this person. Every artist's next album is the fulcrum of their career from that point on. To me, it's just another project. Think about the artist's insecurities, ego, precarious position in today's music, no matter how big they are. There are no more automatics in next albums. It's the nature of the business."

Wexler has little praise for current music. "Quality is relevant in classical music and jazz, and, I think, in the blues," he says. "But pop, by definition, is selected by, aimed at, and validated by the common denominator, which is American taste. You know what Mencken said: 'Nobody ever went broke betting against the American mentality.'"

Since the James album, Wexler has split his time between his homes in East Hampton and Sarasota. Does he get any calls to produce? "How many people want to hire an 80-year-old man to perpetrate rock 'n' roll?" —CARLO WOLFF

Allman, Duane: *Anthology*, Capricorn, 1972 • *Anthology II*, Capricorn, 1974.

Baker, LaVern: "Soul on Fire," Atlantic, 1953, 1985 • *Jim Dandy Got Married'*, Atlantic, 1957 • "I Cried a Tear," Atlantic, 1958 • *Soul on Fire: The Best of LaVern Baker*, Rhino, 1991.

Barton, Lou Ann: *Old Enough*, Asylum, 1982.

Bassett, Steve: *Bassett, Steve*, CBS, 1984.

Bell, Maggie: *Queen of the Night*, Polydor/Atlantic, 1974.

Blakeley, Ronnie: *Welcome*, Warner Bros., 1975.

Bridgewater, Dee Dee: *Dee Dee Bridgewater*, Atlantic, 1976.

Brown, Ruth: *Miss Rhythm (Greatest Hits and More)*, Atlantic, 1959, 1990 • *Rockin' in Rhythm: The Best of Ruth* (10 tracks), Rhino, 1996.

Burke, Solomon: "Just Out of Reach (of My Two Open Arms)," Atlantic, 1961 • "Got to Get You Off My Mind," Atlantic, 1965 • *King of Rock and Soul*, Atlantic, 1966 • *Home in Your Heart: Best of Solomon Burke*, Rhino, 1992 • *The Definition of Soul*, Point Blank, 1997 • *The Very Best of Solomon Burke*, Rhino, 1998.

Carnes, Kim: *Sailin'*, A&M, 1976.

Carter, Betty: *Round Midnight*, Atco, 1963, 1992.

Charles, Ray: *The Great*, Atlantic, 1956 • *The Genius Of*, Rhino, 1959, 1990 • "(Night Time Is) the Right Time," Atlantic, 1959 • "I Believe to My Soul," Atlantic, 1959 • "What'd I Say," Atlantic, 1959 • *The Best Of*, Rhino, 1970, 1988 • "Come Rain or Come Shine," Warner Bros., 1983

(*The King of Comedy* soundtrack) • w/ Milt Jackson, *Soul Brothers/Soul Meeting*, Atlantic, 1989 • *The Birth of Soul— The Complete Atlantic R&B*, Rhino, 1991 • *Blues and Jazz*, Rhino, 1994 • *The Best of Ray Charles: The Atlantic Years*, Rhino, 1994 • *Genius and Soul: 50th Anniversary Collection*, Rhino, 1997.

Cher: *3614 Jackson Highway*, Atlantic, 1969.

Chords, The: "Sh-Boom," Cat, 1954 • "One Mint Julep," Atlantic, 1952 • "Blue Velvet," Atlantic, 1955 • *Down in the Alley: The Best of the Clovers*, Atlantic/Rhino, 1991 • *The Very Best of the Clovers*, Rhino, 1998.

Connor, Chris: *Sings the George Gershwin Almanac of Song*, Atlantic, 1957, 1989.

Crawford, Hank: *Heart and Soul*, Rhino, 1992.

Crewe, Bob: *Motivation*, Elektra, 1977.

Darin, Bobby: *That's All*, Atco, 1959 • *Ultimate Bobby Darin*, Warner Bros., 1988 • *Splish Splash*, Atco, 1991 • *As Long As I'm Singing: The Bobby Darin Collection*, Rhino, 1995.

Davis, Eddie "Lockjaw": *That's All*, FD Music, 1986.

Delaney and Bonnie: *To Delaney from Bonnie*, Atco, 1970 • *The Best Of*, Rhino, 1972, 1990.

DeShannon, Jackie: *Jackie*, Atlantic, 1972.

Dire Straits: *Communique*, Warner Bros., 1979 • *Money for Nothing (Greatest Hits)*, Warner Bros., 1988.

Dixon, Floyd: *Marshall Texas Is My Home*, Specialty, 1958.

Donovan: *Lady of the Stars*, Allegiance, 1983.

Dr. John: *Gumbo*, Atco, 1972 • *Mos' Scocious: The Dr. John Anthology*, Rhino, 1993.

Drew, Kenny Jr.: *Kenny Drew Jr.*, Antilles, 1992 • *Look Inside*, Antilles, 1993.

Drifters, The: "Money Honey," Atlantic, 1953 • "White Christmas," Atlantic, 1955 • *Take You Where the Music's Playing*, Atlantic, 1965 • *Rockin' and Driftin': The Box Set*, Rhino, 1996.

Dupree, Champion Jack: *Blues from the Gutter*, Atlantic, 1958.

Dylan, Bob: *Slow Train Coming*, Columbia, 1979 • *Saved*, Columbia, 1980 • *Bootleg Series*, Columbia, 1991 • *Greatest Hits, Vol. 3*, Columbia, 1995.

Electric Flag: *The Band Kept Playing*, Atlantic, 1974.

Farr, Gary: *Addressed to the Censors of Love*, Atco, 1973.

Feliciano, Jose: *Sweet Soul Music*, Private Stock, 1976.

Finnigan, Mike: *Mike Finnigan*, Warner Bros., 1976.

Franklin, Aretha: "(You Make Me Feel Like) a Natural Woman," Atlantic, 1967 • *Aretha Arrives*, Atlantic, 1967 • "Baby I Love You," Atlantic, 1967 • "Chain of Fools," Atlantic, 1967 • "Do Right Woman, Do Right Man," Atlantic, 1967 • "I Never Loved a Man (The Way I Love You)," Atlantic, 1967 • *I Never Loved a Man the Way I Love You*, Atlantic, 1967 • "Respect," Atlantic, 1967 • *(Sweet Sweet Baby) Since You've Been Gone*, Atlantic, 1968 • "Ain't No Way," Atlantic, 1968 • *Aretha in Paris*, Rhino, 1968, 1995 • *Aretha Now*, Atlantic, 1968 • *Lady Soul*, Atlantic,

1968 • *Live at Paris Olympia,* Atlantic, 1968 • "See Saw," Atlantic, 1968 • "The House That Jack Built," Atlantic, 1968 • "Think," Atlantic, 1968 • "Share Your Love with Me," Atlantic, 1969 • *Soul '69,* Atlantic, 1969 • "Don't Play That Song," Atlantic, 1970 • *Spirit in the Dark,* Atlantic, 1970 • *This Girl's in Love with You,* Atlantic, 1970 • "Brand New Me," Atlantic, 1971 • *Live at Fillmore West,* Atlantic, 1971 • "Oh Me Oh My (I'm a Fool for You Baby)," Atlantic, 1971 • "Rock Steady," Atlantic, 1971 • *Amazing Grace,* Atlantic, 1972 • *Aretha's Jazz,* Atlantic, 1972, 1984 • *Young, Gifted and Black,* Atlantic, 1972 • "I'm in Love," Atlantic, 1974 • *Let Me in Your Life,* Rhino/Atlantic, 1974, 1995 • *With Everything I Feel in Me,* Atlantic, 1974 • "Without Love," Atlantic, 1974 • *You,* Atlantic, 1975 • *Ten Years of Gold,* Atlantic, 1976 • *30 Greatest Hits,* Atlantic, 1986 • *Queen of Soul: The Atlantic Recordings,* Rhino, 1992 • *The Very Best Of,* Vols. 1–2, Rhino, 1994 • *Love Songs,* Atlantic, 1997 • *Aretha's Blues,* Rhino, 1998.

Fritts, Donnie: *Prone to Learn,* Atlantic, 1974.

Goldberg, Barry: *Barry Goldberg,* Atlantic, 1974.

Guitar Slim: *Atco Sessions,* Atlantic, 1988.

Hathaway, Donny: *Donny Hathaway,* Atlantic, 1971 • *Live,* Atlantic, 1972 • *Extension of a Man,* Atlantic, 1973 • *In Performance,* Atlantic, 1980.

Hawkins, Ronnie: *The Hawk,* Atlantic, 1971.

James, Etta: *Deep in the Night,* Warner Bros., 1978 • *The Right Time,* Elektra, 1992.

King Curtis: *Instant Groove,* Edsel, 1968 • *That Lovin' Feelin',* Atlantic, 1966 • *Plays the Great Memphis Hits,* Atlantic, 1967 • *Everybody's Talkin',* Atco, 1972.

King, Ben E.: "Don't Play That Song (You Lied)," Atco, 1962 • *Anthology,* Atlantic, 1993.

Lulu: *Melody Fair,* Atco, 1970 • *From Crayons to Perfume: The Best of Lulu,* Rhino, 1994.

McGuinn Hillman: *McGuinn Hillman,* Capitol, 1980.

McGuinn, Clark and Hillman: *Return Flight,* Edsel, 1992.

McPhatter, Clyde: *Deep Sea Ball: Best Of,* Atlantic, 1991.

Nelson, Willie: *Phases and Stages,* Atlantic, 1974 • *A Classic and Unreleased Collection,* Rhino, 1995.

Newman, David "Fathead": *House of David Newman: Fathead Anthology,* Rhino, 1993.

Orlando, Tony: *Tony Orlando,* Elektra, 1978.

Pickett, Wilson: "In the Midnight Hour," Atlantic, 1965 • "Land of 1,000 Dances," Atlantic, 1966 • "Mustang Sally," Atlantic, 1966 • *The Exciting Wilson Pickett,* Atlantic, 1966 • "Everybody Needs Somebody to Love," Atlantic, 1967 • "Funky Broadway," Atlantic, 1967 • "I Found a Love," Atlantic, 1967 • "Sugar, Sugar," Atlantic, 1970 • *Man and a Half: The Best Of,* Atlantic, 1992.

Professor Longhair: *'Fess Anthology,* Rhino, 1993 • *Professor Longhair Anthology,* Rhino, 1993.

Radner, Gilda: *Live from New York,* Warner Bros., 1979.

Sahm, Doug: *Doug Sahm and Band,* Atlantic, 1973 • *Texas Tornado,* Atlantic, 1974 • *Best Of, 1968–1975,* Rhino, 1992.

Sam and Dave: *Sweat and Soul Anthology,* Vol. 2, Rhino, 1993.

Sanford Townsend Band: *Sanford Townsend Band,* Warner Bros., 1976 • "Smoke from a Distant Fire," Warner Bros., 1977.

Santana: *Havana Moon,* Columbia, 1983.

Sir Douglas Band: *Texas Tornado,* Atlantic, 1973.

Springfield, Dusty: *Dusty in Memphis,* Atlantic, 1968, 1981 • "Son of a Preacher Man," MCA, 1969 • *Anthology,* PolyGram, 1997 • *The Very Best Of,* Mercury Chronicles, 1998.

Staple Singers: *Unlock Your Mind,* Warner Bros., 1978.

Staples, Mavis: *Oh, What a Feeling,* Warner Bros., 1979.

Stone, Jesse: *Jesse Stone Alias Charles Calhoun,* Bear Family, 1996.

Sullivan, Ira: *Horizons,* Discovery, 1983.

Tate, Eric Quincy: *Eric Quincy Tate,* Cotillion, 1971.

Toussaint, Allen: *Motion,* Reprise, 1978 • *The Allen Toussaint Collection,* Reprise, 1991.

Turner, Big Joe: *The Boss of the Blues,* Atlantic, 1956 • *Big Joe Turner's Greatest Hits,* Atlantic Jazz, 1958, 1989 • *Rhythm and Blues Years,* Atlantic, 1959 • *Big, Bad and Blue: The Big Joe Turner Anthology,* Rhino, 1994.

Vera, Billy, and Judy Clay: *The Best of Billy Vera and the Beaters* (2 tracks), Rhino, 1986 • *Storybook Children/Greatest Love,* Soul Classics, 1995.

Walker, T-Bone: *T-Bone Blues,* Atlantic Jazz, 1960, 1989.

White, Tony Joe: *The Train I'm On,* Atlantic, 1972 • *The Best Of,* Warner Bros., 1973.

Wishbone Ash: *Locked In,* MCA, 1976.

COLLECTIONS

The Wiz (original soundtrack), MCA, 1978.

Atlantic Rhythm and Blues, 1952–1955, Atlantic, 1985: LaVerne Baker, "Tomorrow Night," 1954, "Tweedlee Dee," 1954, "Play It Fair," 1955 • The Cardinals, "The Door Is Still Open," 1955 • Ray Charles, "Mess Around," 1953, "Greenbacks," 1954, "I Got a Woman," 1954, "A Fool for You," 1955, "This Little Girl of Mine," 1955 • Clyde McPhatter and the Drifters, "Money Honey," 1953, "Such a Night," Atlantic, 1953, "Honey Love," 1954, "White Christmas," Atlantic, 1954, "Watcha Gonna Do?," 1955 • Professor Longhair, "Tipitina," 1954 • Big Joe Turner, "Shake, Rattle and Roll," 1954, "Flip, Flop and Fly," 1955.

Atlantic Rhythm and Blues, 1955–1958, Atlantic, 1985: LaVerne Baker, "Jim Dandy," 1956 • Ray Charles, "Drown in My Own Tears," 1956, "Hallelujah, I Love Her So," 1956, "Lonely Avenue," 1956 • The Chords, "Devil or Angel," 1956, "Love, Love, Love," 1956 • The Cookies, "In Paradise," 1956 • The Drifters, "Fools Fall in Love," 1956 • Ivory Joe Hunter, "Since I Met You Baby," 1956, "Empty

Arms," 1957 • Clyde McPhatter, "Treasure of Love," 1956, "Without Love (There Is Nothing)," 1956, "A Lover's Question," 1958 • Big Joe Turner, "Corrine Corrina," 1956, "Midnight Special Train," 1956, "The Chicken and the Hawk," 1956 • Chuck Willis, "It's Too Late," 1956, "Betty and Dupree," 1957, "C.C. Rider," 1957, "Hang Up My Rock and Roll Shoes," 1958, "What Am I Livin' For?," 1958.

Atlantic Honkers, Atlantic, 1986: Arnett Cobb, "Mr. Pogo," 1954, "Night," 1954, "Flying Home Mambo," 1955, "Light Like That," 1955 • King Curtis, "Long Tall Sally," 1965, "Memphis Soul Stew," 1967 • Jesse Stone, "Barrel House," 1955, "Hey Tiger," 1955, "Night Life," 1955.

Mainstream, Atlantic Jazz, 1987.

Family Thing (original soundtrack), Edeltone, 1996.

Jackie Robinson Tribute: Stealing Home, Sony, 1997.

Maurice White

Maurice White is the leader/singer/songwriter/drummer/producer for Earth, Wind and Fire, the most successful soul-funk group of the '70s, and one of the most important black bands of all time, with 7 Grammys, over 30 charting singles (seven Top 10s), and 20 charting albums (seven more Top 10s) from the '70s into the '90s. White has stirred EWF's joyous blend of gospel, funk, jazz, rock, disco, and African music into a soulful, thumping nectar that he describes as "my love, my heart." White, a house drummer for Chess in the '60s, has also written and produced soul, jazz, and AC hits for Atlantic Starr, El DeBarge, the Emotions, Jennifer Holliday, Ramsey Lewis, Barbra Streisand, Deniece Williams, and himself.

Maurice Williams was born one of nine children December 19, 1941, in Memphis, and raised by his grandmother while his father attended medical school in Chicago. White listened to R&B, blues, jazz, and early rock 'n' roll throughout his childhood, and sang gospel in church, at home, and with a quartet, the Rosehill Jubilettes. Styling themselves after Sam Cooke's Soul Stirrers, the Jubilettes traveled throughout the South performing at churches.

At 12, White saw a marching band strut through the streets of Memphis and became fixed on the power of the drum. He went home, broke a broom in half, and started rat-a-tat-tatting on any available surface. In junior high White became friends with multi-instrumentalist Booker T. Jones (see entry) and they played together in various jazz ensembles. As a high school student, White played in a hot R&B band, the Mad Lads, and after graduation he joined his parents in Chicago.

White was a premed student at Crane (now Malcolm X) Junior College when he passed the band room and felt inexorably drawn to the drum seat; he switched his major to music. In 1962 White got a call to play for a Betty Everett Vee-Jay session, the session that yielded the classic "You're No Good." Now White was a real professional musician. He played on sets for Jerry Butler, the Impressions, John Lee Hooker, Jackie Wilson, and others. Then his friend Louis Satterfield pointed him in the direction of the legendary Chess Records.

White became house drummer at Chess from 1962 to 1967, playing on hundreds of soul, blues, and jazz records for Little Milton, Etta James, Billy Stewart, Willie Dixon (see entry), Howlin' Wolf, Sonny Boy Williamson, and Ramsey Lewis. "I was in there every day from noon until 6 P.M., then I'd go to school at the Chicago Conservatory of Music from 7 P.M. until 10 P.M., then I'd go play at a club," says White.

White feels that his background as a drummer was the perfect training for his future as bandleader and producer. "The drummer has to learn everyone else's part as well as his own. He has to think in terms of how everything fits together," he says.

White replaced drummer Red Holt in the Ramsey Lewis Trio in 1967, and went on tour with him for most of the next two years, becoming a seasoned veteran of the road as well as the studio. White and keyboard players Wade Flemons and Don Whitehead formed a trio in 1969 called the Salty Peppers and recorded a single for their own Hummit Records called "La La Time," which was picked up by Capitol. The trio headed to Los Angeles to pursue a deal and, with the addition of White's younger brother Verdine on bass, a guitarist, horn section, and Sherry White sharing lead vocals, changed their name to Earth, Wind and Fire—a name derived from the elements of White's astrological chart. White's ambitious goal for the band was to master the "four principles of music: composition, musicianship, production, and performance."

The 10-man band played around L.A. until they were signed to Warner Bros. by Joe Smith, and assigned Joe Wissert (see entry) as producer. That group recorded two albums, *Earth, Wind and Fire* and *The Need of Love,* which were only moderate sellers and yielded no pop hits.

On tour in Denver, White found singer/drummer Philip Bailey when Bailey's pop band, Friends and Love, opened for EWF in 1971. When the original EWF broke up in 1972 under the strain of limited success, the White brothers formed a new band, recruiting Bailey to sing and percuss. The band hooked up with crack manager Bob Cavallo (see Rob Cavallo entry) and then signed to Columbia. They released two more albums with Wissert producing, *Last Days and Time* and *Head to the Sky,* the latter of which was the band's first hit, cracking the Top 30.

Everything began to come together when White joined Wissert in the production duties for *Open Our Eyes* (No. 15) in 1974, but a whole new universe opened up when White took over primary production duties (assisted by arranger Charles Stepney) for good on *That's the Way of the World* (No. 1) in 1975. A mature, confident classic of exceptional tunes, thrilling gospel harmonies, and sophisticated horns, anchored by a cutthroat-funky rhythm section, *World* was originally envisioned as a movie soundtrack. "Happy Feelin' " features White's African thumb piano, the kalimba (also the name of his production company); "Reasons" is a silky soul ballad standard; "Shining Star" (No. 1) is a deeply grooved funk workout with White and Bailey trading lines, ending with a timeless a cappella sing-along that leaps out of the speakers; the title track is another standard, a jazzy, mid-tempo jam keyed to a distant trombone line (by White's old Chicago friend Louis Satterfield) and White and Bailey's octaved dual lead.

The rest of the '70s brought nothing but multiplatinum for the band, whose wildly costumed, lighted, and staged live shows (eventually featuring special effects by magician Doug Henning) became legendary. *Gratitude* (No. 1) is a rousing double-live album that includes two more great studio numbers: "Can't Hide Love," and the bouncy dance floor filler "Sing a Song" (No. 5).

In 1977 EWF released its best overall album, *All 'n All* (No. 3), showcasing White's newfound interest in Brazilian rhythms and an overt move into metaphysical lyrics. A magical blend of Latin jazz and soul, *All* is highlighted by the great "Fantasy" with Bailey's impossibly soaring falsetto and White's funky versifying on "Serpentine Fire" (No. 13), but there are no bumps on this superhighway—even the instrumental interludes stick in the brain and heart.

A *Best Of* (No. 6) album in 1978 sold over 4 million copies and included two new singles: an uptown soul version of the Beatles' "Got to Get You into My Life" (No. 9) and the band's disco perennial, "September" (No. 8). The following year EWF, in cahoots with the female trio the Emotions, grabbed disco by the balls with another great, "Boogie Wonderland" (No. 6), which derived from the *I Am* (No. 3) album. "After the Love Is Gone" (No. 2), another exemplary and moving ballad, ended the decade in high style.

White fielded his own label, ARC, through Columbia in the late '70s and early '80s, which released albums by the Emotions, Deniece Williams, and EWF. EWF went on hiatus from 1983 until 1987, during which time White released a moderately successful solo album and produced for other artists. His most successful outside productions include the Emotions' "Best of My Love" (No. 1); Ramsey Lewis's (with EWF) "Sun Goddess"; albums for Jennifer Holliday (*Feel My Soul*) and Deniece Williams (*This Is Niecy*); and three tracks for Barbra Streisand's platinum *Emotion* (No. 19).

White has recently completed upgrading Kalimba into a state-of-the-art recording studio, which combined with Kalimba Records and the Kalimba International production company, comprise his Magnet Vision company, located in Santa Monica, California. The finest single reflection of White's spectacular career with EWF is the Legacy box set *The Eternal Dance,* a must-have for the discriminating. —ERIC OLSEN

Atlantic Starr: "Armed and Dangerous," Manhattan, 1986 • *All in the Name of Love,* Manhattan, 1987.

Carter, Valerie: *Just a Stone's Throw Away,* Columbia, 1977.

DeBarge, El: "Another Chance," Warner Bros., 1992 • *In the Storm,* Warner Bros., 1992 • "You Know What I Like," Warner Bros., 1992.

Earth, Wind and Fire: "Devotion," Columbia, 1974 • "Mighty Mighty," Columbia, 1974 • *Open Our Eyes,* Columbia, 1974 • "Shining Star," Columbia, 1975 • "That's the Way of the World," Columbia, 1975 • *That's the Way of the World,* Columbia, 1975 • "Can't Hide Love," Columbia, 1976 • "Getaway," Columbia, 1976 • *Gratitude,* Columbia, 1976 • "Saturday Night," Columbia, 1976 • "Sing a Song," Columbia, 1976 • *Spirit,* Columbia, 1976 • *All 'n All,* Columbia, 1977 • "Fantasy," Columbia, 1977 • "Serpentine Fire," Columbia, 1977 • *Best Of,* Vol. 1, ARC/Columbia, 1978 • "Got to Get You into My Life," Columbia, 1978 • *I Am,* ARC/Columbia, 1978 • "After The Love Has Gone," ARC/Columbia, 1979 • w/ the Emotions, "Boogie Wonderland," ARC/Columbia, 1979 • "In the Stone," Columbia, 1979 • "September," ARC/Columbia, 1979 • *Faces,* ARC/Columbia, 1980 • "Let Me Talk," Columbia, 1980 • "And Love Goes On," Columbia, 1981 • "Let's Groove," ARC/Columbia, 1981 • *Raise!,* ARC/Columbia, 1981 • *Powerlight,* Columbia, 1982 • "Wanna Be with You," ARC/Columbia, 1982 • *Electric Universe,* Columbia, 1983 • "Fall in Love with Me," Columbia, 1983 • "Magnetic," Columbia, 1983 • "System of Survival," Columbia, 1987 • "Thinking of You," Columbia, 1987 • *Touch the World,* Columbia, 1987 • *Best Of,* Vol. 2, Columbia, 1988 • "Evil Roy," Columbia, 1988 • "You and I," Columbia, 1988 • "For the Love of You,"

Columbia, 1990 • *Heritage,* Columbia, 1990 • *Eternal Dance,* Columbia, 1992 • *Millennium,* Reprise, 1993 • "Spend the Night," Reprise, 1993 • "Sunday Morning," Reprise, 1993 • "Two Hearts," Reprise, 1994 • *Elements of Love: The Ballads,* Columbia, 1996 • *Greatest Hits Live— Tokyo, Japan,* Pyramid/Rhino, 1996 • *In the Name of Love,* Pyramid/Rhino, 1997 • "Revolution," Pyramid/Rhino, 1997.

Emotions, The: "Flowers," Columbia, 1976 • *Flowers,* Columbia, 1976 • "I Don't Wanna Lose Your Love," Columbia, 1976 • "Best of My Love," Columbia, 1977 • "Don't Ask My Neighbors," Columbia, 1977 • *Rejoice,* Columbia, 1977, 1990 • *Best of My Love: The Best Of,* Legacy, 1996.

Holliday, Jennifer: *Feel My Soul,* Geffen, 1983 • "I Am Love," Geffen, 1983 • *Best Of,* Geffen, 1996.

Ingram, James: *Always You,* Warner Bros., 1993.

Lewis, Ramsey: *Sun Goddess* (2 tracks), Columbia, 1974, 1987 • w/ Earth, Wind and Fire, "Hot Dawgit," Columbia, 1975 • w/ Earth, Wind and Fire, "Sun Goddess," Columbia, 1975 • *Salongo,* Columbia, 1976 • *Sky Islands,* GRP, 1993.

Ravel, Freddie: *Sol to Soul,* PolyGram, 1996.

Steele, Jevetta: *Here It Is,* Columbia, 1993.

Streisand, Barbra: *Emotion* (3 tracks), Columbia, 1984.

Urban Knights: *Urban Knights,* GRP, 1995 • *Urban Knights 2,* GRP, 1997.

Weathers, Barbara: *Barbara Weathers,* Reprise, 1990 • "My Only Love," Reprise, 1990.

White, Maurice: "I Need You," Columbia, 1985 • *Maurice White,* Columbia, 1985 • "Lady Is Love," Columbia, 1986.

Williams, Deniece: "Free," Columbia, 1976 • *This Is Niecy,* Columbia, 1976.

COLLECTIONS

Get On the Bus: Music from and Inspired by the Motion Picture, Interscope, 1996.

Norman Whitfield

"The whole thing at the company was about competition, and competition breeds giants."
—NORMAN WHITFIELD

Norman Whitfield stands as the most adventure-some and funky of the giant Motown songwriter/producers (Holland-Dozier-Holland, Smokey Robinson, Berry Gordy himself; see entries). His greatest work—"I Heard It Through the Grapevine," "War,"

and seven years of hits with the Temptations—ranks among the finest pop music of the last 50 years.

Norman Whitfield was born in Harlem in 1943 where he developed twin interests in music and billiards. Whitfield's family fortuitously ended up in Detroit when his father's car broke down on the way back to New York from an aunt's funeral in California.

By age 18, Whitfield had already written and produced local hits for the Distants and the Synetics. The persistent, observant youth could be found loitering about the Motown office, "always staring at something," Berry Gordy told Nelson George in *Where Did Our Love Go?* Tall, thin, and quiet, Whitfield somewhat creepily watched for a year before he was hired in 1962 by Gordy at $15 per week to listen to demos and rate them for future release as part of Motown's mysterious Quality Control department. Following two long years of rating and waiting, Whitfield finally wrote and produced his first songs for Motown, the Velvelettes' "Needle in a Haystack" and the Marvelettes' "Too Many Fish in the Sea."

The mild success of these songs led to a call up to the majors, the Temptations. The temptin' Temptations, the group with "five lead singers" (David Ruffin, who was replaced by Dennis Edwards in 1968, Eddie Kendricks, Paul Williams, Otis Williams, and Melvin Franklin), became *the* male vocal group of the '60s and the early '70s. Mellifluous harmonies, dynamic dance steps, and killer material provided primarily by Smokey Robinson and Norman Whitfield (with co-writers Eddie Holland and Barrett Strong) yielded 43 Top 10 hits over 25 years.

After recording a series of unsuccessful singles with Motown beginning in 1962, the Temptations hooked up with Smokey Robinson for their first smash, "The Way You Do the Things You Do," in 1964. Whitfield's first attempt was "Girl (Why You Wanna Make Me Blue)," which climbed to No. 26 on the pop chart, disappointing by Motown standards. Whitfield had to again step aside for the next eighteen months as Smokey Robinson cranked out hit after hit for the group, including their signature tune, "My Girl." After Smokey's "Get Ready" stalled at No. 29 in 1966, Whitfield was brought back in to take another swing.

Whitfield came into his own with the classic "Ain't Too Proud to Beg" (No. 13). Benny Benjamin's crisp drum intro commands the listener's attention as David Ruffin's abject first line is wrenched from his soul: "I know you want to leave me, but I refuse to let you go." The song bounces along jauntily behind the fabulous Funk Brothers, the Motown house band, with the Temptations twirling and gesturing as Ruffin pleads for his relationship, and perhaps for his life. His friends lend concerned support on the chorus, but Ruffin's regret-strained voice tells us that he is ultimately alone—so, so alone. This is on the other side of the universe from the satisfied pop of "My Girl."

"Beauty Is Only Skin Deep" (No. 3), and the passionate "(I Know) I'm Losing You" (No. 8) and "I Wish It Would Rain" (No. 4), also featured Ruffin on lead as the hits continued. Firmly established as the Temptations' writer/producer, Whitfield kept up the Motown tradition of cross-pollination when he and Barrett Strong wrote "I Heard It Through the Grapevine," which sold 2.5 million copies and reached No. 2 for Gladys Knight and the Pips in 1967. Whitfield let the group contribute its smoking up-tempo vocal arrangement, featuring Knight's churchy soul-belt call and the Pips' empathetic, indignant response. Whitfield also produced the Knight hits "Friendship Train" (No. 17) and "The Nitty Gritty" (No. 19).

In one remarkable week in October 1968, Motown released both Marvin Gaye's "I Heard It Through the Grapevine" and the Temptations' "Cloud Nine" (No. 6). Gaye's "Grapevine," which had been in the can for over a year, sat atop the pop chart for seven weeks. Critic Dave Marsh selected it as the best single of all time in his *Heart of Rock and Soul,* and *Mojo* magazine selected it No. 5 in its 1997 review of the all-time greatest singles.

Gaye's version embodies all of the insinuation and intrigue inherent in the lyrics. The recording opens with a tambourine strike redolent of gypsy campfires, closely stalked by a hushed piano figure; a furtive high-hat pulse joins in as the tambourine shudders a sibilant warning. A guitar doubles the piano, a muted trumpet rears it head, and Marvin Gaye's magical instrument wordlessly crescendos into the opening line, "Oooh, I bet you're wondrin' how I knew."

With the beat made explicit and strings swirling about, commenting, embellishing, Whitfield's arrangement matches Gaye's thrilling vocal line for line as he sways through the stages of grief from suspicion to anger to hopeful denial to stunned acceptance. Had Whitfield written and produced nothing else, he would still belong in this book.

In the mid- to late '60s Sly Stone (see entry) psychedelicized black music by combining peace, love, and social conscience with gospel melodies, funky beats, and rock 'n' roll. Whitfield wanted to follow him onto the new vibe with the Temptations. When David Ruffin, always suspect as a team player, blew off a 1968 live performance, he was fired and replaced by ex-Contour Dennis Edwards, whose gut-bucket shout was perfect for Whitfield's trip into uncharted waters. Whitfield began to write and use the studio differently as his hair sprouted into a militant afro, and the old Funk Brothers house band began to break up.

Uriel Jones replaced the ailing Benny Benjamin on drums. Bob Babbitt replaced James Jamerson on bass, while Dennis Coffey and Wah-Wah Watson came in on guitar. Jones tells Nelson George that "Cloud Nine" began "as a beat on the cymbal. . . . He'd have you sit and play that two or three minutes by itself, and he'd tell you to add a certain beat on the foot. Actually, what he's doing is just listening to see what he wants to add to it. . . . A lot of times we'd just sit and play and just rap on the tune until somebody just opens up and does something. We'd have as many as 12 or 13 guys in there just grooving on the rhythm."

"Cloud Nine" experiments with structure, rough social commentary, and vocal trade-offs in the context of a lyric that accepts, or at least sympathizes with, drug use. Many were stunned. The adrenaline rush, the funk, the freaky instrumentation, and the social realism that Whitfield and the Temptations strung out on "Cloud Nine," "Psychedelic Shack" (No. 7), "Ball of Confusion (That's What the World Is Today)" (No. 3), and especially "Papa Was a Rolling Stone" (No. 1) directly influenced Isaac Hayes, Curtis Mayfield, Gamble and Huff (see entries), Barry White, among many others, and eventually led to the extended grooves and shameless hedonism of disco.

Gradually Whitfield's experimentation with the Temptations yielded diminishing returns, and he turned his attention elsewhere. In 1970 he produced the uncompromising "War" (No. 1) for the leather-lunged Edwin Starr, and in 1971 he worked more paranoid magic with the Undisputed Truth's "Smiling Faces Sometimes" (No. 3).

In 1976, he left Motown and formed his own label, Whitfield, and scored the gold soundtrack for the movie *Car Wash* (No. 14), performed by his new group, Rose Royce. Royce, with lead singer Gwen Dickey, also hit with "I Wanna Get Next to You" (No. 10) and "Love Don't Live Here Anymore," which Madonna took to No. 1 almost 20 years later.

Norman Whitfield (along with Barrett Strong) has been honored with the National Academy of Songwriters' Lifetime Achievement Award, but he still awaits induction into the Rock and Roll Hall of Fame, an honor that is long overdue. —ERIC OLSEN

Fair, Yvonne: *The Bitch Is Black,* Motown, 1975.

Four Tops: *Anthology,* Motown, 1974, 1986.

Gaye, Marvin: "I Heard It Through the Grapevine," Tamla, 1968 • *I Heard It Through the Grapevine,* Motown, 1968,

1985 • *In the Groove,* Tamla, 1968 • *M.P.G.,* Tamla, 1969 • "That's the Way Love Is," Tamla, 1969 • *That's the Way Love Is,* Tamla, 1969 • "Too Busy Thinking About My Baby," Tamla, 1969 • "How Can I Forget," Tamla, 1970 • *Super Hits,* Tamla, 1970 • "The End of Our Road," Tamla, 1970 • *Anthology,* Motown, 1974 • *Greatest Hits,* Motown, 1976, 1989 • *The Norman Whitfield Sessions,* Motown, 1994 • *The Master: 1961–1984,* Motown, 1995.

Hutch, Willie: *In Tune,* Whitfield, 1979.

Isley Brothers: *Greatest Hits and Rare Classics,* Motown, 1991.

Jesse Gang: "Back Up," Geffen, 1987.

Knight, Gladys, and the Pips: "Everybody Needs Love," Soul, 1967 • *Everybody Needs Love,* Soul, 1967 • "I Heard It Through the Grapevine," Soul, 1967 • *Feelin' Bluesy,* Soul, 1968 • "I Wish It Would Rain," Soul, 1968 • "It Should Have Been Me," Soul, 1968 • "The End of Our Road," Soul, 1968 • "Friendship Train," Soul, 1969 • "The Nitty Gritty," Soul, 1969 • *Nitty Gritty,* Soul, 1969 • "You Need Love Like I Do (Don't You)," Soul, 1970 • *All the Greatest Hits,* Motown, 1972 • *Anthology,* Motown, 1974 • *Silk 'n Soul,* Motown, 1978.

Martha and the Vandellas: *Live Wire! The Singles, 1962–1972,* Motown, 1993.

Marvelettes, The: *The Marvelous Marvelettes,* Tamla, 1963 • "Too Many Fish in the Sea," Motown, 1964 • *The Marvelettes' Greatest Hits,* Tamla, 1966.

Pointer Sisters: *Yes We Can: The Best of the Blue Thumb Recordings,* Hip-O, 1997.

Rare Earth: "(I Know) I'm Losing You," Rare Earth, 1970 • *Ecology,* Rare Earth, 1970 • *Ma,* Motown, 1973, 1994 • *Greatest Hits and Rare Classics,* Motown, 1991.

Robinson, Smokey, and the Miracles: *Whatever Makes You Happy: More of the Best, 1961–1971,* Rhino, 1993.

Rose Royce: *Greatest Hits,* Warner Bros., 1976 • "Car Wash," MCA, 1977 • "Do Your Dance—Part 1," Whitfield, 1977 • "I Wanna Get Next to You," MCA, 1977 • *In Full Bloom,* Ol' Skool, 1977, 1996 • *Strikes Again,* Whitfield, 1978 • "Love Don't Live Here Anymore," Whitfield, 1979 • *Rainbow Connection,* Whitfield, 1979.

Ross, Diana, and the Supremes: *Anthology,* Motown, 1974, 1986.

Ruffin, Jimmy: "Don't You Miss Me a Little Bit Baby," Motown, 1967 • "Gonna Give Her All the Love I Got," Motown, 1967 • *Ruff 'n' Ready,* Motown, 1967.

Starr, Edwin: "War," Gordy, 1969 • "Stop the War Now," Gordy, 1970 • *War and Peace,* Gordy, 1970 • "Funky Music Sho Nuff Turns Me On," Gordy, 1971 • *Involved,* Gordy, 1971 • *Motown Superstar Series,* Vol. 3, Motown, 1980.

Temptations, The: "Girl (Why You Wanna Make Me Blue)," Gordy, 1964 • *The Temptin' Temptations,* Gordy, 1965 • "(I Know) I'm Losing You," Gordy, 1966 • "Ain't Too Proud to Beg," Gordy, 1966 • "Beauty Is Only Skin Deep," Gordy, 1966 • *Gettin' Ready,* Gordy, 1966 • *Greatest Hits,* Vol. 1, Motown, 1966 • "Loneliness Made Me Realize It's You That I Need," Gordy, 1967 • *With a Lot o' Soul,* Gordy, 1967 • "You're My Everything," Gordy, 1967 • "Cloud Nine," Gordy, 1968 • "I Could Never Love Another (After Loving You)," Gordy, 1968 • "I Wish It Would Rain," Gordy, 1968 • "Please Return Your Love to Me," Gordy, 1968 • *Wish It Would Rain,* Gordy, 1968 • *Cloud Nine,* Gordy, 1969 • "Don't Let the Joneses Get You Down," Gordy, 1969 • "I Can't Get Next to You," Gordy, 1969 • w/ Diana Ross and the Supremes, "I'll Try Something New," Motown, 1969 • *Puzzle People,* Gordy, 1969 • "Runaway Child, Running Wild," Gordy, 1969 • "Ball of Confusion (That's What the World Is Today)," Gordy, 1970 • *Greatest Hits,* Vol. 2, Motown, 1970 • "Psychedelic Shack," Gordy, 1970 • *Psychedelic Shack,* Gordy, 1970, 1989 • "Ungena Za Ulimwengu (Unite the World)," Gordy, 1970 • "It's Summer," Gordy, 1971 • "Just My Imagination," Gordy, 1971 • *Solid Rock,* Gordy, 1971 • "Superstar (Remember How You Got Where You Are)," Gordy, 1971 • *The Sky's the Limit,* Gordy, 1971 • *All Directions,* Gordy, 1972 • "Papa Was a Rolling Stone," Gordy, 1972 • "Take a Look Around," Gordy, 1972 • *1990,* Gordy, 1973 • *Anthology,* Motown, 1973 • "Hey Girl (I Like Your Style)," Gordy, 1973 • "Masterpiece," Gordy, 1973 • *Masterpiece,* Gordy, 1973, 1989 • "The Plastic Man," Gordy, 1973 • "Let Your Hair Down," Gordy, 1974 • *All the Million Sellers,* Motown, 1981 • "Miss Busy Body (Get Your Body Busy)," Gordy, 1983 • "Sail Away," Gordy, 1984 • *Hum Along and Dance: More of the Best, 1963–1974,* Rhino, 1993 • *Emperors of Soul,* Motown, 1994.

Turner, Spyder: *Music Web,* Warner Bros., 1978.

Undisputed Truth: *Face to Face with the Truth,* Gordy, 1971 • "Smiling Faces Sometimes," Gordy, 1971 • *Undisputed Truth,* Gordy, 1971 • "You Make Your Own Heaven and Hell Right Here on Earth," Gordy, 1971 • *The Best Of,* Motown, 1991.

Velvelettes, The: "Needle in a Haystack," Motown, 1964 • "He Was Really Saying Something," Motown, 1965.

Weston, Kim: *Greatest Hits and Rare Classics,* Motown, 1991.

COLLECTIONS

Car Wash soundtrack, MCA, 1976, 1996.

Marlon Williams

See MARLEY MARL

Brian Wilson

"I believe that music is God's voice," Brian Wilson has stated, and his admirers might well agree that Wilson's best work is as close to heaven as popular music can get. One of the few pop geniuses, Wilson is a visionary and recording pioneer whose use of the studio as an instrument helped usher in a new era of sonic experimentation in the late 1960s. As the mastermind of the Beach Boys' wildly successful early sound—and as architect of such groundbreaking albums as the classic *Pet Sounds* (No. 10) and the legendary unreleased magnum opus *Smile*—Wilson employed innovative recording techniques to produce accessible, emotionally resonant music. Since *Smile* became one of pop history's most tantalizing what-ifs, the productivity of the once-prolific Wilson has been inconsistent because of his well-publicized battles with drugs and mental illness, but his vintage work continues to inspire new generations of adherents.

Born June 20, 1942, in the Los Angeles suburb of Hawthorne, Wilson emerged as a musical prodigy early in life despite being virtually deaf in his right ear since childhood. Inspired by the Four Freshmen, he spent time harmonizing with younger brothers (and future Beach Boys) Carl and Dennis, developing the blueprint for the group's intricate vocal blend, which spotlighted Brian's soaring falsettos.

Wilson found further inspiration in Phil Spector's (see entry) Wall of Sound production style. As he later explained, "I learned how to conceive of the framework of a song, to think in terms of production, rather than songwriting, when I really got familiar with Spector's work. I started to see the point of making records. You design the experience to be a record rather than just a song."

The Beach Boys—initially managed by the Wilsons' domineering and often abusive father Murry, himself a frustrated songwriter—scored a national hit with their first single, "Surfin'" in 1963, while Brian and his brothers were still in high school. Although Capitol A&R man Nik Venet (see entry) is credited as producer on the quintet's first two LPs, Brian was actually allowed to run the band's recording sessions long before receiving his first official production credit—at the time, an unheard-of degree of artistic control.

Once officially designated as producer, Wilson had the clout to move the band from Capitol's in-house studios to Western Recording in Hollywood, also working occasionally at Gold Star, where Spector had recorded many of his classics.

Under Brian's direction, the Beach Boys had 16 U.S. Top 40 hits from 1962 to 1965. On the nine studio albums they recorded during that period, Wilson—assisted by engineer Chuck Britz—balanced commercial savvy and a rapidly evolving sense of experimentation that was reflected in often unconventional songwriting, inventive vocal and instrumental arrangements, and painstakingly detailed recording methods. Because of his partial deafness, and his preference for controlling all aspects of the listening experience, Wilson has always preferred mono to stereo; in the '60s, when Capitol released both mono and stereo mixes of the band's albums, Brian generally handled the mono mix, while Britz oversaw the stereo version.

After a nervous breakdown led Wilson to retire from touring in December 1964, he was able to focus his creative energies on studio work, and this newfound freedom was reflected in the quantum leap of the Beach Boys' next album, *Today!* (No. 4). Cutting backing tracks with the cream of L.A.'s session players (many of whom had worked with Spector), Wilson produced music that was both musically challenging and lyrically mature.

Beginning early in his career, Wilson also lent his production skills to other artists, including the Honeys, a female vocal trio that included Wilson's wife Marilyn Rovell, and frequent Beach Boys session guitarist (and

Photo by David Goggin ©1995

Brian's temporary touring replacement) Glen Campbell, whose 1965 single "Guess I'm Dumb" is one of Wilson's most evocative productions.

Wilson's finest moment, as both artist and producer, was the Beach Boys' 1966 tour de force, *Pet Sounds*. The album was Wilson's most ambitious production to date, and he outdid himself, using near-orchestral dynamics, unexpected chord structures, unconventional vocal arrangements, and unlikely combinations of instruments (including bass harmonica, French horn, harpsichord, Theremin, oboe, vibes, sleigh bells, empty beverage bottles, and various combinations of horns and strings).

Often beginning a session with nothing more than a chord pattern, Wilson would work with the musicians to build the songs' arrangements from scratch. By this point, an observant journalist had pointed out that Wilson worked more like a modern Mozart than a rock musician.

The production triumph of *Pet Sounds* was all the more remarkable considering Wilson was still working with relatively primitive equipment. The album's instrumental tracks were recorded on either 3- or 4-track, after which Wilson would mix a mono instrumental track onto one channel of an 8-track machine (still a novelty at the time), leaving seven tracks for the complex vocals. On a handful of songs, Wilson even duplicated the group's multipart harmonies on his own, overdubbing all of the vocals himself.

Though it fared relatively poorly by the Beach Boys' lofty sales standards, *Pet Sounds* was an instant classic and is generally credited as establishing the idea of the rock album as legitimate art. The Beatles acknowledged it as a major influence on *Sgt. Pepper's Lonely Hearts Club Band,* and it's Paul McCartney's (see entry) all-time favorite album.

At the same time as the *Pet Sounds* sessions, Wilson spent the then-astronomical sum of $16,000 making what many consider his masterpiece, "Good Vibrations" (No. 1). Recorded in six studios over six months, this multipart "pocket symphony" included distinct movements and numerous tempo changes. In his most experimental production to date, Wilson recorded numerous musical fragments incorporating variations on the song's melodic themes and different combinations of instruments, which he miraculously assembled into a cohesive whole that was both a breakthrough technical achievement and a timeless pop classic.

"Good Vibrations" became a million-selling smash, but the euphoria evaporated when the even more elaborate *Smile* album—an epically ambitious work incorporating even more complex compositional and production elements than Wilson, or anyone, had yet attempted—ran aground. Apparently because of a combination of Brian's increasingly fragile mental state, his bandmates' lack of confidence in the project, and disputes between the Beach Boys and Capitol Records, the album was shelved prior to its completion. But the finished tracks that have emerged since, on subsequent Beach Boys albums and the 1993 box set *Good Vibrations: Thirty Years of the Beach Boys,* as well as on numerous bootlegs, indicate that *Smile* would have been a formidable achievement indeed.

After *Smile* derailed his creative momentum, Wilson retreated to an increasingly peripheral role in the group. Though he would not produce another full Beach Boys album until the much-hyped 1976 misfire *15 Big Ones* (No. 8), Wilson's scattered contributions to the band's late '60s and early '70s albums demonstrated that he was still capable of delivering memorable music and brilliant production when the mood struck him. He finally released a long-promised solo album in 1988, and was the subject of a 1994 film documentary, *I Just Wasn't Made for These Times,* directed by fan and fellow musician/producer Don Was (see entry). He released *Imagination,* a sumptuous solo album with several new versions of old Beach Boys songs, in 1998. —SCOTT SCHINDER

American Spring: *American Spring,* United Artists, 1972.

Beach Boys: "Be True to Your School," Capitol, 1963 • "In My Room," Capitol, 1963 • "Little Deuce Coupe," Capitol, 1963 • *Little Deuce Coupe,* Capitol, 1963 • "Surfer Girl," Capitol, 1963 • *Surfer Girl,* Capitol, 1963 • *All Summer Long,* Capitol, 1964 • *Beach Boys Concert,* Capitol, 1964 • *Christmas Album,* Capitol, 1964 • "Dance, Dance Dance," Capitol, 1964 • "Don't Worry Baby," Capitol, 1964 • "Fun, Fun, Fun," Capitol, 1964 • "I Get Around," Capitol, 1964 • *Shut Down Vol 2,* Capitol, 1964 • "Wendy," Capitol, 1964 • "When I Grow Up (To Be a Man)," Capitol, 1964 • *Beach Boys Party,* Capitol, 1965 • "California Girls," Capitol, 1965 • "Do You Wanna Dance?," Capitol, 1965 • "Help Me Rhonda," Capitol, 1965 • "Kiss Me Baby," Capitol, 1965 • *Summer Days Summer Nights,* Capitol, 1965 • "The Little Girl I Once Knew," Capitol, 1965 • *Today!,* Capitol, 1965 • "Barbara Ann," Capitol, 1966 • "God Only Knows," Capitol, 1966 • "Good Vibrations," Capitol, 1966 • *Pet Sounds,* Capitol, 1966 • "Sloop John B," Capitol, 1966 • "Wouldn't It Be Nice," Capitol, 1966 • *Beach Boys Deluxe Set,* Capitol, 1967 • "Heroes and Villains," Brother, 1967 • "Wild Honey," Capitol, 1967 • *Wild Honey,* Capitol, 1967, 1981 • *Best of the Beach Boys,* Vol. 3, Capitol, 1968 • "Darlin'," Capitol, 1968 • "Do It Again," Capitol, 1968 • *Friends,* Capitol, 1968, 1981 • *Smiley Smile,* Capitol, 1968 • *Stack-o-Tracks,* Capitol, 1968 • *20/20,* Capitol, 1969 • *Close-Up,* Capitol,

1969 • "I Can Hear Music," Capitol, 1969 • *Sunflower,*
Reprise, 1970 • *Do You Wanna Dance?,* MFP, 1971 • *Surf's*
Up, Caribou/Reprise, 1971 • *Carl and the Passions—So*
Tough/Pet Sounds, Brother/Reprise, 1972 • *Girls,* Capitol,
1972 • *So Tough,* Brother, 1972 • *Holland,* Caribou/Reprise,
1973 • *Endless Summer,* Capitol, 1974 • *Spirit of America,*
Capitol, 1975, 1987 • *Wow! Great Concert!,* Pickwick, 1975 •
15 Big Ones, Reprise, 1976 • *"Its O.K.,"* Brother, 1976 •
"Rock and Roll Music," Capitol, 1976 • *Love You,* Reprise,
1978 • *M.I.U. Album,* Reprise, 1978 • "Good Timin',"
Brother, 1979 • *Girls on the Beach,* Capitol, 1980 • *Sunshine*
Dream, Capitol, 1982 • *Rarities,* Capitol, 1983 • "Little
Saint Nick," Virgin/EMI, 1985 (*Now That's What I Call*
Music Xmas Album) • *Made in the U.S.A.,* Capitol, 1986 •
Still Cruisin', Capitol, 1989 • *Good Vibrations: Thirty Years of*
the Beach Boys, Capitol, 1993 • w/ Lorrie Morgan, "Don't
Worry Baby," River North, 1996 • w/ James House,
"Little Deuce Coupe," River North, 1996 • w/ Doug
Supernaw, "Long Tall Texan," River North, 1996 • *Stars*
and Stripes, Vol. 1, A&M, 1996 • *Perfect Harmony,* EMI,
1997 • *The Pet Sounds Sessions: A 30th Anniversary Collection,*
Capitol, 1997.

Campbell, Glen: "Guess I'm Dumb," Capitol, 1965 •
Essential, Vol. 3, Capitol, 1995.

Hondells, The: "Little Honda," Mercury, 1964 • *Greatest Hits,*
Curb, 1996.

Three Dog Night: *Celebrate: The Three Dog Night Story,*
1965–1975, MCA, 1993.

Wilson, Brian: "Caroline No," Capitol, 1966 • *Brian Wilson,*
Sire/Reprise, 1988 • "Goodnight Irene," Columbia, 1988
(*Folkways: A Tribute to Woody Guthrie and Leadbelly*) • *I Just*
Wasn't Made for These Times (video), MCA, 1995 •
Imagination, Giant, 1998.

Wilsons, The: *The Wilsons,* Mercury, 1997.

COLLECTIONS

For Our Children, Disney, 1991.

The Brill Building Sound: Singers and Songwriters Who Rocked the
60's, Era, 1993.

Norro Wilson

N orro Wilson is one of a handful of current producers in Nashville whose career has straddled
several decades, trends, and musical sea changes.
Wilson began producing in the early '70s, scoring with
such artists as Joe Stampley, Buck Owens, and Charley
Pride. He survived country's "Urban Cowboy" phase,

helming albums by acts like Mickey Gilley, Reba McEntire, and John Anderson.

After a career slump in the late '80s, he bounced
back, producing well-received records by such acts as
Sammy Kershaw, the legendary George Jones, and hot
newcomer Mindy McCready (with co-producer David
Malloy; see entry).

Production started out as a second career for Wilson
(born April 4, 1938, in Scottsville, Kentucky), a writer of
hit songs by the likes of the late Charlie Rich ("The
Most Beautiful Girl") and George Jones ("The Grand
Tour"). In 1996, the prolific Wilson was inducted into
the Nashville Songwriters Hall of Fame.

In addition to being a songwriter, he worked at Al
Gallico Publishing in Nashville in the '60s, before
becoming head of A&R at Warner Bros. in Nashville.
When his production career took off, he still kept a hand
in publishing as CEO of Merit Music, until that company was sold.

Wilson says he can't believe the arrogance of people
trying to advise him on how to make records today. "I
think a lot of these people who have attitudes wouldn't
even have a job if it weren't for the songwriter," he says.
"You've got all these people who come from someplace—I have no idea where they come from—but
they've never written a song, they've never produced a
record, they've never done any of it; yet, they seem to
know all of it. I get very confused over that."

Wilson says that even though he still loves producing, in the late '90s the task is more frustrating than ever.
"Today, in our marketplace, I almost think producers
are the low guy on the totem pole. We're all treated
with committees. . . . It's like hiring a guy to build your
house and then getting a bunch of neighbors to
approve. We've always picked out the songs because of
what we do. I mean I think I'm better than the average
guy because I've got 40 songwriter awards.

"I've never felt, in general, that artists hear the best
songs for themselves," he says. "Many times, they will
choose a song that doesn't fit them at all. It may be a hit
song, but it doesn't fit the artist. What we do as producers is spend our daily life thinking about a song fitting an artist. The act goes out on the road and works
and entertains and a whole bunch of other stuff. They
don't lock into that particular mode the way we do. It
isn't just the damn quarterback who's responsible for all
that, and if you're not going to believe in your coach,
what's the point?"

Wilson thinks Nashville's emphasis on females with
flat stomachs and men who look great in Wranglers has
taken us away from the basics—great voices singing
great songs. In part, he blames the technology that

makes it possible to comp and tune vocals. "A lot of these artists who roll into town with their cute little jeans and their little black hats and the women with their cute little rears, they come in looking great," he says. "They're good marketing, and if they can sing half a lick, then all of a sudden we make stars out of them. I can tell you right now, Eddy Arnold did not go into a session unprepared. Today, when you have to comp it and tune a whole damn song, line after line, I'm not sure they shouldn't have stayed home and pumped gas."

For the last several years, Wilson has produced many albums with partner Buddy Cannon. Their relationship started when former Mercury Nashville president Harold Shedd (see entry) asked them to produce the first of several successful albums by Sammy Kershaw. "It's just been a thrill," says Wilson of working with Cannon. "I call him Bat Ears. He's real picky with pitch and everything."

Wilson is busy, working with Mindy McCready, Kenny Chesney, newcomers Shannon Brown and Chad Brock—and George Jones. "With George, you just wait for him to say, 'It's time for me to leave and go get on my tractor,' " jokes Wilson. "Hopefully you can get an hour and a half out of him before he wants to leave. With him, it's [creating] a comfort zone. Radio isn't worth a damn to him. They don't ever play him so we don't give a flip, we just cut the best stuff and it just turns out so good because he ends up doing songs that he loves. And when he loves them, baby, he will wear you out."

Wilson knows that wisdom and experience are not always valued in an industry obsessed with youth. However, he adds, he's not ready for a rocking chair yet. "It excites me to death to be working with these young artists. I respect the fact that it's a very young business, [but] I've always said that I'd like to be the country Jerry Wexler [see entry]. I'm still fighting to do this as long as they'll let me. I'd like to kind of be like Richard Petty, back here bumping those young guys, saying, 'Don't forget, I'm back here, pal. Don't cop an attitude too quick because the old man's back here watching.' " — MELINDA NEWMAN

Allen, Rex Jr.: *Brand New,* Warner Bros., 1978 • *Oklahoma Rose,* Warner Bros., 1980 • w/ Rex Allen Sr., *Singing Cowboys,* Warner Western, 1995.

Anderson, John: *John Anderson,* Warner Bros., 1980 • *Two,* Warner Bros., 1981.

Asleep at the Wheel: *Asleep at the Wheel,* CBS, 1974 • *The Swingin' Best Of,* Epic, 1992.

Bailey, Razzy: *The Midnight Hour,* RCA, 1984.

Brock, Chad: *Chad Brock,* Reprise, 1998 • "Evangeline," Reprise, 1998.

Chesney, Kenny: "A Chance," BNA, 1997 • *I Will Stand,* BNA, 1997 • "She's Got It All," BNA, 1997 • "I Will Stand," BNA, 1998 • "That's Why I'm Here," BNA, 1998.

Evans, Sara: "Cryin' Game," RCA, 1998.

Francis, Connie: *Souvenirs,* PolyGram, 1996.

Frickie, Janie (Fricke): "Always Have, Always Will," Columbia, 1986.

Gattis, Keith: *Keith Gattis,* RCA, 1996 • "Titanic," RCA, 1997.

Gilley, Mickey: "Your Memory Ain't What It Used to Be," Epic, 1985 • "You've Got Something on Your Mind," Epic, 1985 • "Doo-Wah Days," Epic, 1986 • *Back to Basics,* Epic, 1986.

Gilley, Mickey, and Charly McClain: *Surround Me with Love,* Epic, 1981.

Hunley, Con: *I Don't Want to Lose You,* Warner Bros., 1980 • "What Am I Gonna Do About You?," Capitol, 1985.

Jones, George: "High Tech Redneck," MCA, 1993 • *High Tech Redneck,* MCA, 1993 • w/ Sammy Kershaw, "Never Bit a Bullet Like This," MCA, 1994 • "Honky Tonk Song," MCA, 1996 • *I Lived to Tell It All,* MCA, 1996 • *It Don't Get Any Better Than This,* MCA, 1998.

Jones, George, and Tammy Wynette: "One," MCA, 1995.

Kershaw, Doug: *Ragin' Cajun,* Warner Bros., 1976.

Kershaw, Sammy: "Cadillac Style," Mercury, 1991 • *Don't Go Near the Water,* Mercury, 1991 • "Anywhere but Here," Mercury, 1992 • "Don't Go Near the Water," Mercury, 1992 • "Yard Sale," Mercury, 1992 • "Haunted Heart," Mercury, 1993 • *Haunted Heart,* Mercury, 1993 • "Queen of My Double Wide Trailer," Mercury, 1993 • "She Don't Know She's Beautiful," Mercury, 1993 • "Christmas Time's a Comin'," Mercury, 1994 • *Christmas Time's a Comin',* Mercury, 1994 • *Feelin' Good Train,* Mercury, 1994 • "Fire and Rain," Mercury Nashville, 1994 (*Red Hot and Country*) • "I Can't Reach Her Anymore," Mercury, 1994 • "National Working Woman's Holiday," Mercury, 1994 • "Southbound," Mercury, 1994 • "Third Rate Romance," Mercury, 1994 • "If You're Gonna Walk, I'm Gonna Crawl," Mercury, 1995 • *The Hits, Chapter 1,* Mercury, 1995 • "Your Tattoo," Mercury, 1995 • *Politics, Religion and Her,* Mercury Nashville, 1996.

McClain, Charly: *Biggest Hits,* Epic, 1985 • "Radio Heart," Epic, 1985 • *10-Year Anniversary,* Epic, 1987.

McClain, Charly, and Wayne Massey: "With Just One Look in Your Eyes," Epic, 1985 • "You Are My Music, You Are My Song," Epic, 1985.

McCready, Mindy: "Guys Do It All the Time," BNA, 1996 • "Ten Thousand Angels," BNA, 1996 • *Ten Thousand Angels,* BNA, 1996 • "A Girl's Gotta Do (What a Girl's Gotta Do)," BNA, 1997 • featuring Richie McDonald, "Maybe He'll Notice Her Now," BNA, 1997.

McEntire, Reba: *Just a Little Love,* MCA, 1984 • *Greatest Hits,* MCA, 1987.

Owens, Buck: *Buck Owens,* Warner Bros., 1976 • *Our Old Mansion,* Warner Bros., 1977 • *Collection, 1959–1990,* Rhino, 1992.

Price, Ray: *Sometimes a Rose,* Columbia, 1992.

Pride, Charley: *Greatest Hits,* Vol. 2, RCA, 1972 • "Never Been So Loved (In All My Life)," RCA, 1981 • *Charley Pride Live,* RCA, 1982 • "Mountain of Love," RCA, 1982 • "You're So Good When You're Bad," RCA, 1982 • "Night Games," RCA, 1983 • "Why Baby Why," RCA, 1983 • "Missin' Mississippi," RCA, 1984 • *Night Games,* RCA, 1993.

Smith, Margo: "Don't Break the Heart That Loves You," Warner Bros., 1978 • *Don't Break the Heart That Loves You,* Warner Bros., 1978 • "It Only Hurts for a Little While," Warner Bros., 1978 • *A Woman,* Warner Bros., 1979 • *Just Margo,* Warner Bros., 1979.

Stampley, Joe: "Soul Song," Dot, 1973 • "Roll on Big Mama," Epic, 1975 • "All These Things," ABC/Dot, 1976 • *The Best Of,* Varese Sarabande, 1995.

Twain, Shania: "Dance with the One That Brought You," Mercury, 1993 • *Shania Twain,* Mercury, 1993 • "What Made You Say That?," Mercury, 1993.

Wariner, Steve: *Midnight Fire,* RCA, 1983 • "Don't Give Up on Love," RCA, 1984.

Whitley, Keith: "Turn Me to Love," RCA, 1984 • *Essential,* RCA, 1996.

Wynette, Tammy: *Tears of Fire: The 25th Anniversary Collection,* Epic, 1992 • *See also* Jones, George.

COLLECTIONS

Skynyrd Friends, MCA, 1995.

Thom Wilson

Thom Wilson (not to be confused with the late Tom Wilson) has had five distinct careers in music: SoCal engineer-in-training working on pop records by the likes of Seals and Crofts in the '70s; full-on punk-rock producer extraordinaire with the Adolescents, T.S.O.L., the Dead Kennedys, the Vandals, and the like in the early '80s; engineer for high-end pop productions, including Madonna and the *Flashdance* soundtrack in the mid-'80s; top TV soundman for MTV specials and network series, including *Roseanne, A Different World,* and *Grace Under Fire* in the late '80s; and in the '90s, a return to punk production with Iggy Pop, the Joykiller, and most notably, the Offspring, whose 1994 album

Smash (No. 4) has sold over 5 million copies in the U.S., making it the best-selling independent record ever.

Thom Wilson was born November 16, 1951, in San Diego, and grew up there. He played guitar in high school and listened to Janis Joplin, Quicksilver Messenger Service, Sons of Champlin, early Steve Miller Band, and other bluesy, rootsy West Coast artists in his teens. Although he had no particular background in electronics, Wilson got involved with some friends in a live sound company ("the equipment was barbaric by today's standards") in the early '70s and picked up some knowledge of basic acoustics.

One of Wilson's partners had access to a trust fund, and this partner had the notion to move to L.A. and become a player in the sound biz. He and Wilson moved to L.A. in 1973, finding a third partner who wanted to build a recording studio, which Mr. Trust Fund then financed and Wilson helped build in North Hollywood. Though Wilson had never set foot in a recording studio before then, by the time the 24-track Davlen (later Larrabee North) Studio was completed in 1974, he was something of an expert in studio design and construction.

Wilson worked as an assistant engineer at Davlen, where he was tutored by crack engineers Bill Schnee and Eric Prestidge, who emphasized the importance of sonic quality regardless of musical genre. After three years at Davlen, Wilson hopped around a bit, stopping at Richard Perry's (see entry) Studio 55 for a time before settling at Seals and Crofts' Dawnbreaker studio as an engineer in 1977. There he worked with legendary engineer/producer Roy Halee (see entry) on a Rufus album, and "learned about marrying the roles of engineer and producer." Through various pop projects, Wilson was also exposed to a technique he did not want to employ when he became a producer: overdub endlessly until the original performance is morphed out of existence.

In 1980 a call came that would permanently alter Wilson's career: he was asked to engineer the first Stiv Bators (former lead singer of the Dead Boys) album, *Disconnected,* for Greg Shaw's Bomp Records. "It was a rudderless ship, and having a big mouth, I started donating my opinions. Stiv appreciated it, and I ended up co-producing the record with him," Wilson says.

On the Bators, as on virtually every other album he has engineered or produced, Wilson used a drum-recording technique that he picked up from Bill Schnee, who had picked it up from Glyn Johns (see entry). Roughly, the technique uses "two large diaphragm condenser microphones, one placed directly over the center of the drum, and the other placed on a different vertical plane behind the floor tom facing across the drum. You get an acoustical phase situation that translates beautifully to drums," Wilson says. He then keys the rest of the instruments to that drum sound.

Lisa Fancher, who also worked at Bomp Records, was starting her own label, Frontier. She liked Bators' record, so she asked Wilson to work on Frontier's first record, the debut of Orange County punks the Adolescents. Although Wilson was brought in as engineer, he again expressed himself freely over the three-day recording process and ended up as producer. The album has all of the energy and drive of hard-core punk, but Wilson's clear, clean production brings out the musicality of such classics as "Amoeba," and a lot of people sat up and took notice.

Wilson next engineered and produced two punk notables in the same weekend: a China White EP and T.S.O.L.'s debut *Dance with Me*. Suddenly, Wilson was among the West Coast punk producers (with Geza X and Spot; see entries). The Dead Kennedys heard *Dance with Me* and asked Wilson up to San Francisco to produce their *In God We Trust, Inc.* EP in 1981 and *Plastic Surgery Disasters* album in 1982.

Continuing his roll, Wilson produced (another) classic Orange County punk band's first album, the Vandals' *Peace Through Vandalism*, also in 1982 (still around —in altered form—today, the Vandals' satirical punk remains potent). *Peace* contains the mock spaghetti western thrasher "Urban Struggle," which parodies the mutability of culture fashion as the singer pledges undying allegiance to the cowboy way, before confessing at the end of the song that he "couldn't make it as a punker."

In 1984 the Vandals and Wilson did to hip-hop what they had done to cowboy music, with the great "Lady Killer" from *When in Rome Do As the Vandals*. "Killer" rips to a hyper-revved funk beat, with singer Stevo scratching on the turntables and spewing a tongue-knotting mélange of ghettoistic non sequiturs relating to a bar called Lady Killer.

For T.S.O.L's *Beneath the Shadows*, the band switched from hard-core punk to a much more melodically varied kind of creepy goth-punk, with Greg Kuehn's moody keyboards joining Ron Emory's guitar in Wilson's superb mix. Singer Jack Delauge (last name now "Grisham," leader of the Joykiller) rails against the night on "Soft Focus," "Send My Thoughts," and "The Other Side"—a great album.

By the end of 1984 the punk rose had lost its bloom and the scene wilted, but Wilson sees his first five years in punk as a golden age. "These young people were just getting out of the educational system and looking at the political atmosphere around them. They expressed a lack of confidence in a future for themselves and dealt with the emotional baggage that comes with that. They made some authentic and great music. I helped out some with musical issues, but I never got involved with the lyrics—I felt that was sacred territory. My goal was simply to make punk rock listenable without watering down the message," he says.

With punk not happening, Wilson began to work with producer/artist Michael Sembello as an engineer; Wilson engineered Sembello's "Maniac" for the *Flashdance* soundtrack, which was exec-produced by Phil Ramone (see entry). Through Ramone, Wilson engineered Madonna's "Crazy for You" for the *Vision Quest* soundtrack in 1983 (which wasn't released until 1985).

In 1987 Wilson was asked to be the music producer for Fox's *The Joan Rivers Show*. When that ended, other shows called and he became a leading TV sound engineer, working on four *MTV Awards* shows (featuring performances by the Rolling Stones, Metallica, Queensryche, Prince, Mariah Carey, Pearl Jam, Red Hot Chili Peppers, and Neil Young), and network series *Roseanne*, *A Different World*, and *Grace Under Fire*. He enjoyed the discipline of the work (he stayed in TV until 1994), but felt a certain alienation in coming from the recording studio, where sound was everything, to television, where sound was "usually less important than the food."

On a summer break from television in 1989, Wilson got a call from Brian Holland, lead singer of yet another Orange County punk group, the Offspring. Huge fans of Wilson's records with T.S.O.L., the Vandals, and the Adolescents, Holland had spent several months tracking Wilson down in an effort to get him to produce the Offspring's first album. Wilson, flattered, complied. *The Offspring* was recorded over about a month at a "little semi-pro studio down in Anaheim," and it showed promise. *Ignition* was recorded three years later for Epitaph and it was better still, but when *Smash* was recorded in 1994, all hell broke loose.

Smash focuses all of the Offspring's strengths—Noodles' ripping punk guitar, Holland's pleasantly straining high-end vocals, an airtight rhythm section of Ron Welty on drums and Greg K on bass, excellent songwriting combining the topical with a sense of humor ("Come Out and Play," "Self Esteem")—into one of the '90's best punk packages. With Green Day's *Dookie* (see Rob Cavallo entry) selling an astonishing 9 million copies, 1994 was the year of the punk.

The commercial success of punkish bands like Jane's Addiction, Red Hot Chili Peppers, and Nirvana in the late '80s and early '90s had acclimated listeners' ears to punk tempos, and when both Green Day and the Offspring put together well-written, performed, and produced collections that felt authentic to the concerns of ever-anxious youth (and their nostalgic older brothers and sisters), the cash registers sang. Ironically, neither the music, the themes, or Wilson's production techniques had changed all that much from his deeply underground punk days of the early '80s.

Wilson, a 20-year overnight success when *Smash* shocked the world in 1994, now lives and works out of Santa Cruz, California, where he has built a home studio. —ERIC OLSEN

Adolescents, The: *The Adolescents,* Epitaph, 1981, 1997.

Agnew, Rikk: *All By Myself,* Frontier, 1982.

Bators, Stiv: *Disconnected,* Bomp, 1980 • "Too Much to Dream," Bomp, 1980 • *The Church and the New Creatures,* Lolita, 1983.

Bouncing Souls: *Maniacal Laughter,* B.Y.O, 1996.

China White: *Danger Zone* (EP), Frontier, 1981.

Choir Invisible: *Choir Invisible,* Frontier, 1981.

Christian Death: *Only Theatre of Pain,* Future, 1982, 1997.

Cody, Phil: *The Sons of Intemperance Offering,* Interscope, 1996.

D.I.: *Ancient Artifacts,* Triple X, 1989.

D.O.A.: *Bloodied but Unbowed/War on 45,* Restless, 1992.

Dead Kennedys: *In God We Trust, Inc.* (EP), Alternative Tentacles, 1981 • *Plastic Surgery Disasters,* Alternative Tentacles, 1982 • *Give Me Convenience or Give Me Death,* Alternative Tentacles, 1987.

Face to Face: *Big Choice,* Victory/A&M, 1995 • "Debt," Victory/A&M, 1995.

Jon and the Niteriders: *Live at the Whiskey,* Bomp, 1981.

Joykiller, The: *The Joykiller,* Epitaph, 1995 • *Static,* Epitaph, 1996 • *Three,* Epitaph, 1997.

Legal Weapon: *Death of Innocence,* Triple X, 1991.

Offspring, The: *The Offspring,* Nitro, 1989, 1995 • "Take It Like a Man," FS, 1990, (*The Big One*) • *Ignition,* Epitaph, 1992 • "Come Out and Play," Epitaph, 1994 • "Self Esteem," Epitaph, 1994 • *Smash,* Epitaph, 1994 • "Smash It Up," Atlantic, 1995 (*Batman Forever* soundtrack).

Pop, Iggy: "I Wanna Be Your Dog," Miramax/Hollywood, 1996 (*The Crow: City of Angels* soundtrack) • *Naughty Little Doggie,* Virgin, 1996.

Red Wedding: *Up and Down the Aisle* (EP), Bernis, 1982.

Slush: *North Hollywood,* Discovery, 1997.

Storm and Her Dirty Mouth: *Storm and Her Dirty Mouth,* Popmafia, 1998.

T.S.O.L.: "Dance with Me," Oglio, 1981, 1995 (*Punk University,* Vol. 2) • *Dance with Me,* Frontier, 1981 • *Weathered Statues,* Alternative Tentacles, 1997 • *Beneath the Shadows,* Alternative Tentacles, 1982.

Vandals, The: *Peace Through Vandalism,* Restless, 1982, 1989 • "Urban Struggle," Oglio, 1982, 1994 (*The Obscurity File*) •

Peace Through Vandalism/When in Rome Do As the Vandals, Time Bomb, 1982, 1995 • *When in Rome Do As the Vandals,* National Trust, 1984 • *Slippery When Ill,* Restless, 1989.

Youth Brigade: *Sound and Fury,* BYO, 1983.

Tom Wilson

D o you know this man? He was president of the Young Republican Club and graduated *cum laude* from Harvard in 1954. He founded the jazz label Transition the following year and began producing jazz radio programs in 1958. He was jazz A&R director for Savoy Records and executive assistant to the director of the New York State Commission for Human Rights at the same time. He became a producer for Columbia and then MGM in the '60s, where he worked with Bob Dylan, Simon and Garfunkel, and the Animals. He discovered, signed, and produced the Mothers of Invention, Blues Project, Hugh Masekela, and the Velvet Underground. He was an African American.

Thomas Blanchard Wilson Jr.—Tom Wilson—is one of the forgotten greats of the music business. Wilson was born in 1931 and grew up in Waco, Texas, where he attended Moore High School. Wilson was invited to Harvard where he became involved with the Harvard New Jazz Society and radio station WHRB. He later credited all of his success in the music business to the radio station.

Following his work with Savoy and brief stints with United Artists and Audio Fidelity, Wilson was hired as staff producer at Columbia in 1963. Wilson's most significant contributions to Columbia were his three and a half albums with Bob Dylan. Wilson replaced the credited producer, John Hammond (see entry), for the final *Freewheelin'* session in April, 1963 in response to Albert Grossman's (Dylan's new manager) attempt to get Dylan out of his Columbia contract on a technicality. The young protest singer could hardly reject the young black man brought in to produce him. Four songs on the album, "Girl from the North Country" (one of Dylan's best love songs), "Masters of War" (an unsparing antiwar song), "Talkin' World War III Blues," and "Bob Dylan's Dream" were recorded by Wilson and the solo Dylan.

Dylan's next album was *The Times They Are a-Changin'* (No. 20), another classic recorded solo. Wilson's main input was to roll the tape and nod sagely, but the proof is in the pudding: Wilson pointed Dylan in the direction he needed to be pointed and got out of the way. The results include the title track (one of Dylan's most beloved songs), the relentless murder-suicide tale "The Ballad of Hollis Brown," and another exquisite downer, "The Lonesome Death of Hattie Carroll." The album cemented Dylan's position as the most important young American recording artist and made him a star.

Another Side of Bob Dylan, Dylan solo still, includes more classics, "It Ain't Me Babe," "Mr. Tambourine Man," "All I Really Want to Do," and "My Back Pages." Wilson consciously entered into the folk-rock arena when he dubbed a band backing onto an old recording of Dylan doing "House of the Rising Sun." The result was not released, but the seed was planted and Dylan's next album, *Bringing It All Back Home* (No. 6) was half-acoustic, half-electric. The folk spell was broken (see Paul Rothchild entry). Wilson helped ease the nervous Dylan's transition into an ensemble player, according to Clinton Heylin in *Bob Dylan: The Recording Sessions.*

Dylan's next, *Highway 61 Revisited* (No. 3), was his first all-electric album, and the first song recorded was one of his greatest, "Like a Rolling Stone" (No. 2). Wilson brought his friend Al Kooper (see entry) to watch a Bob Dylan session and play a little guitar alongside Mike Bloomfield. Kooper ended up inventing the hypnotic organ sound that dominates the song in a happy accident that both Dylan and Wilson allowed to occur.

The Kooper-Bloomfield meeting led to the *Super Sessions* album and a band called the Blues Project, which Wilson produced after his move to MGM. Apparently, Dylan and Wilson had an undocumented falling-out of some kind, for "Rolling Stone" was their final song together and Bob Johnston (see entry) took over for the rest of *Highway.*

Wilson also recorded Simon and Garfunkel's first album, *Wednesday Morning 3 A.M.* The acoustic album wasn't selling until a Boston DJ started playing "The Sounds of Silence." Paul Simon (see entry) was in Europe and Art Garfunkel had gone back to school when Wilson added a rhythm section behind the track and released it as a single. Intrusive maybe, but Wilson's ears were dead on as the single shot to No. 1 and kick-started the career of the most important duo of the '60s. Then Wilson left for MGM/Verve.

David Anderle (see entry) was a young talent scout for MGM/Verve in Los Angeles in 1965. Frank Zappa (see entry) and the Mothers performed a heady mixture of psychedelic blues rock, twisted doo-wop, art noise, social commentary, and potty humor in a zone where irony twisted back on itself in an endless loop of inscrutable intentions. Anderle saw the Mothers at the

Red Velvet club and was smitten. He was having a hard time getting anyone at the label to take Zappa seriously when Wilson was hired as head of East Coast A&R. Anderle coaxed Wilson out from New York to see the band, and to Anderle's amazement, Wilson "got them" right away and the band was signed, launching the careers of both Zappa and Anderle.

Zappa has declared his allegiance to Wilson. "Tom Wilson was a great guy. He had vision, you know? And he really stood by us. . . . I remember the first thing that we recorded was 'Any Way the Wind Blows,' and that was okay. Then we did 'Who Are the Brain Police?' and I saw him through the glass and he was on the phone immediately to New York going, 'I don't know!' Trying to break it to 'em easy, I guess."

"I don't know" or not, Wilson allowed the Mothers' project to grow from a single into an album, and then from an album into an extravaganza that cost $21,000 at a time when the average rock album ran $5,000. Wilson funded a 22-piece orchestra. The editing was nightmarish. According to Zappa, "Wilson was sticking his neck out. He laid his job on the line by producing the album."

After *Freak Out!* sold surprisingly well, Wilson went even further into the unknown with Zappa on *Absolutely Free,* which dispensed with token pop songs entirely in favor of jazzy meanderings, pseudo-operatic singing, and exposition upon Zappa's recurrent themes of cheese, shoes, the government, and his abstemious attitude toward mind-altering substances.

While working on *Free,* Wilson was simultaneously supervising the Velvet Underground's first album, an album that reveled in the sensory-based hedonism that the puritanical Zappa railed against. Both "art" bands—the garish Mothers and the somber Velvets—shared a surface freakiness that masked the underlying gulf between them. The fact that both bands performed in Andy Warhol's Exploding Plastic Inevitable at the Trip in Los Angeles is one of Warhol's greatest ironies. It is not known how Wilson felt about this juxtaposition, but it is clear that his mind was large enough to encompass both points of view; perhaps the bands were even the personifications of his own internal contradictions.

The Velvet Underground (name borrowed from an S&M novel) was formed in 1964 when singer/guitarist/songwriter Lou Reed (Louis Firbank) and Welsh multi-instrumentalist John Cale (see entry) met and decided to form a rock band (eventually with Sterling Morrison on bass and Maureen Tucker on percussion), drawing on their interest in R&B, the free-form jazz of Albert Ayler and Ornette Coleman, and the classical avant-garde of John Cage and La Monte Young. They sought not just to entertain but to challenge: to prove that rock 'n' roll could be dangerous again. They came under the wing of Andy Warhol (who brought in Austrian actress/model/chanteuse Nico) and became fixtures on the Village bohemian art scene.

Tom Wilson had seen the Velvets in the Village in 1965 and wanted to work with them. He told them of his impending move to MGM/Verve and suggested they wait, because according to bassist Sterling Morrison in Heylin's *From the Velvets to the Voidoids,* Wilson swore that "at Verve we could do anything we wanted. And he was right." *The Velvet Underground and Nico* was produced with money from a shoe salesman by the band under the vague supervision of Andy Warhol. When MGM signed the Velvets, they were given 10 hours at an L.A. studio to rerecord four songs with Wilson—not coincidentally, the four most important songs on one of the most important rock albums ever recorded.

"Waiting for the Man," with a breezy rock groove, follows a Reed character into the black section of town where he deferentially explains to one and all that he isn't there for the women, but for his "man," his drug dealer. Reed is almost giddy with self-contempt as his need for drugs drags his social status below that of ghetto dwellers. That defiant self-contempt defines the Velvets' status as the first postmodern band and the progenitor of the entire punk–new wave movement.

"Heroin" takes the external adventure of obtaining drugs into the internal realm and captures the seduction of addiction with a power, beauty, and grace that make it all the more frightening. "Venus in Furs" captures both the power of the drone (that was so essential to the Velvets' live sound) and harnesses its ability to convey an ennui of almost black-hole density. "All Tomorrow's Parties" is Nico's finest moment (Wilson also produced her beguiling first solo album). Wilson and the band construct a towering aural monument to ephemeral glamour with the pulse of dread, Cale's supportive rolling piano, and Reed's destabilizing frantic guitar.

As with Zappa's second, Wilson followed the Velvets faithfully into the void for their follow-up, *White Light/White Heat,* a cacophonous, relentless assault on the ears and good taste. If Wilson had ever been beholden to the hit-making machinery at Columbia, between Zappa and the Velvets, surely, he was its slave no more, as he unleashed idiosyncratic assaults upon middle-American values from both coasts.

According to all sources, Wilson was tall (about 6 feet, 4 inches), thin, handsome, intelligent, witty, and charismatic. He was also intensely driven into a bewildering array of endeavors, including production, music publishing, management, wine, women and song. He was one of the founding owners, with Chris Stone and Gary Kellgren (Wilson's engineer), of the legendary Record Plant recording studio in New York.

It would appear that Wilson has not been embraced by the black community as a pioneer. Despite his position on the New York Civil Rights Commission, "he lived his life unapologetically as a human being, not as a black man," according to his friend Wally "Famous" Amos, the cookie magnate and former William Morris agent.

Coral Browning, a girlfriend from Wilson's time in London in the early '70s, agrees. "Tom felt let down by blacks. He felt that after the civil rights successes of the '50s and '60s, blacks should stop complaining and get on with it. He felt they caused many of their own problems by carrying such large chips on their shoulders." Perhaps it was the Young Republican in him.

Wilson was forceful, independent, and "took shit from no one," according to Amos, who relates a story of waiting with Wilson for a cab in New York in the late '60s. The cabby slowed down, then saw the black men waiting and took off. Wilson shouted after the man in his Texas drawl, "I'm smarter than you, better-looking than you, and I can buy and sell you. So get the hell out of here."

After an amazing, but brief, 47 years, Tom Wilson died of a heart attack at his Los Angeles home in 1978.
—Eric Olsen

Animals, The: *Animalization,* MGM, 1966.

Bagatelle: *11 PM Saturday,* ABC, 1966.

Barron, Bill: *The Tenor Stylings Of,* Savoy, 1961, 1993.

Beacon Street Union: *The Eyes of the Beacon Street Union/The Clown Died in Marvin Gardens,* See for Miles, 1968, 1998.

Bird, Tony: *Tony Bird,* Columbia, 1976.

Blues Project: *Projections,* MGM, 1966 • *Anthology,* PolyGram, 1997.

Booker Little 4: *Booker Little 4 and Max Roach,* Blue Note, 1958, 1992.

Burdon, Eric, and the Animals: "Don't Bring Me Down," MGM, 1966 • "Help Me Girl," MGM, 1966 • "Inside-Looking Out," MGM, 1966 • "See See Rider," MGM, 1966 • "Monterey," MGM, 1967 • "San Franciscan Nights," MGM, 1967 • "When I Was Young," MGM, 1967 • *Winds of Change,* MGM, 1967 • *Eric Is Here,* MGM, 1968 • "Sky Pilot," MGM, 1968 • *The Twain Shall Meet,* MGM, 1968 • *The Best Of, 1966–1968,* Polydor, 1991.

Central Nervous System: *I Could Have Danced All Night,* Music Factory, 1968.

Coltrane, John: *Coltrane Time,* Blue Note, 1959, 1991 • *Art of John Coltrane,* Blue Note, 1992.

Country Joe and the Fish: *C.J. Fish,* Vanguard, 1970 • *The Collected,* Vanguard, 1987.

Dion: *Bronx Blues: The Columbia Recordings*, Columbia, 1991 • *The Road I'm On*, Legacy, 1997.

Dylan, Bob: *The Freewheelin'*, Columbia, 1963 • *Another Side Of*, Columbia, 1964 • *The Times They Are a-Changin'*, Columbia, 1964 • *Bringing It All Back Home*, Columbia, 1965 • *Highway 61 Revisited*, Columbia, 1965 • "Like a Rolling Stone," Columbia, 1965 • *Bootleg Series*, Columbia, 1991.

Ervin, Booker: *Cookin'*, Savoy, 1960, 1993 • *Down in the Dumps*, Savoy Jazz, 1961, 1994.

Fear Itself: *Fear Itself*, Dot, 1969.

Francis, Connie: *Souvenirs*, PolyGram, 1996.

Fraternity of Man: *The Fraternity of Man*, ABC, 1966 • *Get It On*, Dot, 1967.

Garfunkel, Art: *Up 'Til Now*, Columbia, 1993.

Harris, Eddie: *Cool Sax, Warm Heart*, Columbia, 1964.

Harumi: *Harumi*, Verve, 1968.

Jim and Jean: *Changes*, Verve, 1966.

Last Ritual: *Last Ritual*, Capitol, 1969.

Long, Barbara: *The Voice of Barbara Long: Soul*, Savoy, 1961.

Masekela, Hugh: *The Lasting Impression of Ooga Booga*, Verve, 1965, 1996.

Mothers of Invention: *Freak Out*, MGM, 1966.

Nico: *Chelsea Girl*, MGM, 1971.

Perry Robinson 4: *Funk Dumpling*, Savoy, 1962, 1995.

Professor Longhair: *Live on the Queen Mary*, One Way, 1975, 1993.

Rae, Johnny: *Opus de Jazz*, Vol. 2, Savoy, 1961, 1992.

Road: *Road*, Natural Resource, 1972.

Scott-Heron, Gil: *The Best Of*, Arista, 1984.

Seeger, Pete: *Story Songs*, Columbia, 1961 • *I Can See a New Day*, Columbia, 1964 • *God Bless the Grass*, Columbia, 1966 • *Strangers and Cousins*, Columbia, 1969 • *The World of Pete Seeger*, Columbia, 1973 • *Link in the Chain*, Sony, 1996.

Simon and Garfunkel: *Wednesday Morning 3 A.M.*, Columbia, 1965 • "The Sounds of Silence," Columbia, 1966 • *Sounds of Silence*, Columbia, 1966 • *Collected Works*, Columbia, 1981, 1990 • *Old Friends*, Columbia, 1997.

Simon, Paul: *Paul Simon, 1964–1993*, Warner Bros., 1993.

Smith, Louis: *Here Comes Louis Smith*, Blue Note, 1957.

Soft Machine: *Soft Machine*, One Way, 1968.

Sun Ra: *Sound of Joy*, Delmark, 1957, 1991 • *The Futuristic Sounds Of*, Savoy, 1961.

Taylor, Cecil: *Jazz Advance*, Transition/Blue Note, 1955, 1991 • *Love for Sale*, Blue Note, 1959, 1998.

Three Dog Night: *Celebrate: The Three Dog Night Story, 1965–1975*, MCA, 1993.

Two Friends: *Two Friends*, Natural Resources, 1972.

Velvet Underground: *The Velvet Underground and Nico*, MGM, 1967 • *White Light/White Heat*, MGM, 1968 • *The Best Of*, Verve, 1989 • *Peel Slowly and See*, Polydor, 1995.

Zappa, Frank, and the Mothers of Invention: *Absolutely Free*, Barking Pumpkin/Rykodisc, 1967, 1988.

Alan Winstanley

See CLIVE LANGER AND ALAN WINSTANLEY

Muff Winwood

Muff Winwood has been a fixture in the British music business for over 35 years as musician, producer, and record company executive. With Muff on bass, and his future-superstar younger brother Steve on keyboards and wildly soulful vocals, Birmingham's Spencer Davis Group rose to the top of the British beat-group heap in 1965 and 1966. Soon after, Steve left to form Traffic and Muff went into A&R. Muff Winwood's production career is limited to the '70s, but in that decade he guided exceptional albums by Kevin Ayers, Dire Straits, and Sparks, in addition to important records by Russ Ballard, the Fabulous Poodles, Patto, and Sutherland Brothers and Quiver.

Muff (Mervyn) Winwood was born into a musical family in Birmingham, June 12, 1943. "My brother was amazing; he could just play any instrument when he was a tiny little child. It was really weird. I would look at him and say, 'How can I compete?' I finally gave up on playing [in 1967] because I didn't want to feel second to him, though I'm incredibly proud of him," Winwood says.

"Anyway, we started in our father's band doing weddings and bar mitzvahs in the mid-'50s. Steve was a small child in short pants. Then I formed a New Orleans–style jazz band; I played banjo and guitar and Steve played honky-tonk piano.

"When Steve was about 13 [1961], he was listening to Ray Charles and his voice started to change. He just started singing in this great R&B voice, and he's had it ever since. A local folksinger named Spencer Davis came and sang with our jazz band. We realized we all liked R&B and blues, so we formed a band with Steve singing like Ray Charles and Spencer singing like Leadbelly. Pretty soon we were filling the clubs in Birmingham, and Chris Blackwell [see entry] came along and became our manager and got us a record deal. We had two big hits, 'Gimme Some Lovin'' and 'I'm a Man,' and then we split up," says Winwood.

Steve left the Spencer Davis Group in 1967 to form Traffic, and Muff accepted an invitation to join Chris Blackwell's new Island Records in A&R. Though the label started with a bang by signing Traffic, it was only a five-man operation, and Winwood's ostensible A&R position also included promotion, tour booking, and stuffing records into boxes.

Winwood brought the jazz- and blues-influenced rock band Patto—led by the legendary guitarist Ollie Halsall (see Rupert Hine entry) and singer Mike Patto—to the label in 1970, but Blackwell "didn't hear them at all," says Winwood. "I really loved them (it turned out that Blackwell's commercial considerations were correct because they didn't happen) so, probably as a favor, he said, 'You could produce them if you think you know how it should work, and then we'll see what happens.' I did that, and when the record was finished he still didn't like them, so we licensed the record to Vertigo. The second was also on Vertigo, and then Blackwell finally put the third album out on Island," Winwood recalls.

In the United States, the first two albums by L.A. band Sparks (from 1972 and early 1973) had failed to generate much more than embarrassed silence. The Mael brothers—Ron and Russell—then broke up the original band (which featured Earle Mankey; see entry) and moved to England in mid-1973, where at least the press had been kind. Sparks was reformed in late 1973 with Adrian Fisher on guitar, Martin Gordon on bass, and Dinky Diamond on drums, in addition to Ron's varied keyboards and Russell's mock-operatic vocals. The new band kicked with greater rhythmic intensity, and the Mael brothers' songwriting found its voice in a hard-charging art-pop: a bizarre alliance of Roxy Music, Richard Wagner, and the Chipmunks.

"In 1973 it happened with Blackwell again," remembers Winwood. "I brought in Sparks—who were at the very forefront of synthesizer-based rock music—and Blackwell didn't hear them either. They were so weird that Los Angeles hadn't been able to handle them, and they had had to come to London. Blackwell said exactly the same thing about me cutting a few tracks and then seeing what happens. We cut 'This Town Ain't Big Enough for the Both of Us' (No. 2 U.K.)—and there was no denying that this cut was going to be a smash—so Blackwell put it out on Island. The album, *Kimono My House* (No. 4 U.K.), did very well, so we did another one, *Propaganda* (No. 9), which was also a hit," he says.

"This Town Ain't Big Enough for the Both of Us" follows Russell over a busy roller-coaster melody conveying a series of Walter Mitty scenes involving stampeding zoo animals, aerial combat, cannibals, and the terrors of pursuing women. Dynamically alternating between orchestral keyboard accompaniment and kick-ass rock, "This Town" is one of the great singles of the '70s.

Kimono is a garden of freakish delights: "Amateur Hour" (No. 7 U.K.) marches to a double-time beat, as Russell's comparatively naturalistic singing recommends practice as the remedy for sexual naiveté. "Thank God It's Not Christmas" is an impassioned rocker that pursues the recurring theme of awkwardness between the sexes, as does "Hasta Mañana, Monsieur" and "Equator." Fisher's guitar rocks throughout the album and the tough arrangements balance Russell's tendency toward the twee.

Propaganda was a worthy follow-up to *Kimono,* with similar themes and virtues. "Never Turn Your Back on Mother Earth" (No. 13 U.K.) is an elegant Spectorish pop song cautioning the listener that Mother Nature can be a bitch. "Something for the Girl with Everything" (No. 17 U.K.) is favorably reminiscent of "This Town" without being derivative. "Achoo" is the album's best and most thought-provoking song, using the sneeze as metaphor for everything from a romantic brush-off to the voice of the downtrodden, culminating in an astonishing multitracked chorus of "achoos."

Blackwell then asked Winwood to manage the Island studios, which in essence gave him his own studio from which to produce. Winwood's next major accomplishment was on the opposite end of the vocal spectrum from Sparks: idiosyncratic former Soft Machine basso Kevin Ayers' *Yes We Have No Mananas* in 1977. Though not quite up to the rarefied level of Ayers' *Bananamour* or *The Confessions of Dr. Dream, Mananas* has more great fretwork from Ollie Halsall and excellent songs, including originals "Everyone Knows the Song," "Help Me," and "Blue," in addition to a jazzy version of "Falling in Love Again."

Never a slave to fashion, a year later, in the midst of the punk explosion in England, Winwood found a band of neotraditionalists in Dire Straits who had more in common with Fats Domino, Bob Dylan, and even the Grateful Dead than they than they did with their iconoclastic contemporaries. Singer/songwriter Mark Knopfler's (see entry) brilliant guitar work is a clean-picking country- and bluegrass-derived rock style in the manner of Elvis Presley sideman James Burton or an intensified Jerry Garcia.

"I had done some album—I think it was the Sutherland Brothers—that they really loved, and though Vertigo got to them before Island did, they asked me if I'd produce the record," says Winwood. "It wasn't a difficult album to produce, just a case of helping the band to understand the art of how things work in the studio and making sure that their live freshness came across on the record," he says. One of the best albums of the '70s, *Dire Straits* (No. 2) boasts a sound warm and clear in equal parts from engineer Rhett Davies (see entry), which perfectly frames "Sultans of Swing" (No. 4), "Down to the Waterline," "Water of Love," and "Lions"—most set to some version of a swinging New Orleans–Caribbean beat. Winwood's only regret was that he—a man who had worked with his own brother, and had produced the Sutherland Brothers and the Mael brothers of Sparks—couldn't keep the Knopfler brothers together. Rhythm guitarist David left the band right after *Dire Straits* was recorded.

Winwood accepted a position as head of A&R for CBS U.K. (now Sony) and retired from production around 1980. "I fancied doing A&R rather than sitting night after night after night in the studio," he says. Winwood has been an A&R executive ever since, signing Terence Trent D'Arby, Sade, Psychedelic Furs, Wham!, the The, Paul Young, Bonnie Tyler, Prefab Sprout, Des'ree, and Jamiroquai. —ERIC OLSEN

After the Fire: *Laser Love,* Epic, 1979.

Ayers, Kevin: *Yes We have No Manañas,* Harvest, 1976.

Ballard, Russ: "Winning," Epic, 1976, 1981 (*England Rocks 1*) • *Winning,* Epic, 1976.

Dire Straits: *Dire Straits,* Warner Bros., 1978 • "Sultans of Swing," Warner Bros., 1978 • *Money for Nothing (Greatest Hits),* Warner Bros., 1988.

Fabulous Poodles: "Mirror Star," Epic, 1978, 1981 (*England Rocks 1*) • *Mirror Stars,* Epic, 1978 • *Think Pink,* Blue/Epic, 1979 • *His Master's Choice,* Sequel, 1995.

Goodhand-Tait, Philip: *Teach an Old Dog New Tricks,* Chrysalis, 1977.

Milk 'n' Cookies: *Milk 'n' Cookies,* Island, 1975.

Mott the Hoople: *Rock and Rol Queen,* Atlantic, 1974.

Noel Redding Band: *Clonakilty Cowboys,* RCA, 1975.

Patto: *Patto,* Vertigo, 1970 • *Hold Your Fire,* Vertigo, 1971 • *Roll 'Em, Smoke 'Em, Put Another Line Out,* Island, 1972.

Sparks: "Amateur Hour," Island, 1974 • *Kimono My House,* Island, 1974 • "Never Turn Your Back on Mother Earth," Island, 1974 • *Propaganda,* Island, 1974 • "This Town Ain't Big Enough for the Both of Us," Island, 1974 • "Something for the Girl with Everything," Island, 1975 • *Profile: Ultimate Collection,* Rhino, 1991 • *In the Swing,* Spectrum, 1993.

Sutherland Brothers Band: *The Sutherland Brothers Band,* Island, 1970.

Sutherland Brothers and Quiver: "(I Don't Want to Love You but) You've Got Me Anyway," Epic, 1972, 1981 (*England Rocks 3*) • *Lifeboat,* Island, 1972 • *Dream Kid,* Island, 1973 • *Beat of the Street,* Island, 1974.

Joe Wissert

Joe Wissert received his studio training as a teenager working at Philadelphia's Cameo/Parkway label in the early '60s, before he became an exceptionally successful producer of pop rock, folk rock, R&B, pop, and white soul working with the Turtles, Lovin' Spoonful, Gordon Lightfoot, Earth, Wind and Fire, Helen Reddy, Boz Scaggs, J. Geils Band, and many others from the late '60s into the '80s.

Joe Wissert was born in Philadelphia. As a teen in the late '50s he placed third in a dance contest on *American Bandstand*. He expressed his fascination with records to Dick Clark, who put him in touch with a record label, Cameo/Parkway, where Wissert then worked while still in high school. A nonmusician, Wissert learned the basics of recording from the likes of songwriter/producers Thom Bell, Kenny Gamble, Leon Huff (see entries), Dave Appell, and Kal Mann, moving up from gofer to second engineer to engineer on records for the Orlons, Dovells, and many other rock 'n' roll, pop, and R&B artists in the early '60s.

After a stay in New York in the mid-'60s working mostly with R&B artists, Wissert moved to L.A. He supervised a minor hit for the Righteous Brothers, "Melancholy Music Man," for the Koppelman-Rubin production company (who got the credit) in early 1967, but his first official production was the equivalent of hitting a home run in his first major league at bat. The Turtles—an L.A. pop-rock harmony group led by Howard Kaylan and Mark Volman (Flo and Eddie)—had had a few hits with producer Bones Howe (see entry), but with Wissert and the great "Happy Together," they went right to No. 1 in 1967. Wissert, recording on 8-track at Sunset Studios, with Bruce Botnick (see entry) engineering, got Kaylan's lead vocal in one take.

Garry Bonner and Alan Gordon, who wrote "Happy Together," also wrote the rocking "She'd Rather Be with Me" (No. 3), and the subdued "You Know What I Mean" (No. 12) and "She's My Girl" (No. 14) for Wissert and the Turtles, all in 1967. Concluding that banner year, Wissert produced the Lovin' Spoonful's last Top 40 hit, "She Is Still a Mystery."

Wissert became a staff producer with Warner Bros. in 1970 and moved into folky singer/songwriter terrain to co-produce (with Lenny Waronker; see entry) Gordon Lightfoot's *If You Could Read My Mind* (No. 12) album, including the Canadian troubadour's haunting title track (No. 5), one of the highlights of the genre.

Wissert also produced Lightfoot's next, the excellent *Summer Side of Life* in 1971.

Also in 1971, Wissert began a long-term relationship with a new R&B group, Earth, Wind and Fire. Led by drummer/singer Maurice White (see entry), EWF was an experimental jazzy unit that hadn't totally found its legs when Wissert started working with them for Warner Bros. The first album, *Earth, Wind and Fire,* barely charted, although it featured some interesting music in the almost-psychedelic "Fan the Fire" and the ballad "Love Is Life." *The Need of Love* fared slightly better, cracking the Top 100, as did the third album (and first for Columbia) *Last Days and Time,* which featured sassy and brassy "Time Is on Your Side" and a stunning kalimba performance from White on "Power."

On the gold *Head to the Sky* the familiar EWF soul blend began to come together. Philip Bailey delivers a Curtis Mayfield–like (see entry) falsetto lead on the classic ballad "Keep Your Head to the Sky," and "Evil" jams to a Santana-like Latin beat. The platinum *Open Our Eyes* (No. 15)—co-produced with White (who subsequently took over production of the group) and Charles Stepney—was Wissert's final and best work with the band. The Top 30 single "Mighty Mighty" is a righteous funk number, "Feelin' Blue" is an expressive light samba, and the title track is a fine jazzy gospel ballad.

While EWF was Wissert's R&B outlet in the first half of the '70s, transplanted Australian Helen Reddy was his pop voice. Wissert's work with Reddy was in the "auteur" model of production (pick the songs, have them arranged, assemble the musicians, bring in the singer), and after starting auspiciously with the gold *Free and Easy* (No. 8) album and a No. 1 single—the twisted love story "Angie Baby"—in late 1974, Wissert and Reddy notched four more Top 40 singles ("Emotion," "Bluebird," "Somewhere in the Night," No. 19, "I Can't Hear You No More"), a Top 10 ("Ain't No Way to Treat a Lady"), and two more gold albums (*No Way to Treat a Lady,* No. 11; *Music, Music,* No. 16) in a run through the mid-'70s.

As Wissert's work with Reddy ended, he began work on one of the best albums of the '70s—and the most important of his career—Box Scaggs' five-times-platinum *Silk Degrees* (No. 2). Produced by Wissert and arranged by keyboardist David Paich, *Degrees* is the very apex of cool blue-eyed soul, and stayed on the charts for 115 weeks, from early 1976 into 1978.

The band—a collection of the highest-end studio musicians including Paich, Jeff Porcaro on drums, David Hungate on bass, Fred Tackett and Louie Shelton on guitars—would become Toto a couple of years later. The songs, mostly by Scaggs and Paich, are all first-rate, but the album, released in early 1976, didn't hit right away. The first single, the sprightly "It's Over" straggled to No. 38 in May. The album's most memorable song, "Lowdown"—with Hungate's serious funk bass line, Paich's flutey synth melody, and Scaggs' sly vocal—languished for weeks after its summer release until it was picked up by an urban station in Philadelphia and then by a rock station in Cleveland. With the squeeze coming from both urban and rock stations, Top 40 finally picked it up and the record rode to No. 3 in August. "Lido Shuffle" (No. 11) also hit, but other songs on the album are good enough to have been hit singles: "We're All Alone" is an exquisite ballad (Scaggs' original is superior to Rita Coolidge's No. 7 version), and "Georgia" is exemplary uptown horn soul.

Scaggs, Wissert, and Porcaro returned for 1977's *Down Two, Then Left,* but Paich had left by then to form Toto. The difference is clear, especially in the songwriting (several songs were co-written by Scaggs and Michael Omartian; see entry), which yielded no Top 40 singles, though the fine "Hard Times" and "Hollywood" came close. The album is good, not great, and went platinum largely on the coattails of *Silk Degrees.*

Wissert closed out the '70s with a rocking J. Geils album—the gold *Sanctuary* highlighted by the hit single "One Last Kiss"—and an interesting new wave album from the Sinceros. He produced Dave Mason's last charting album, the cleverly titled *Old Crest of a New Wave,* in 1980 before taking a break from the studio for the first time in almost 20 years. Wissert moved to Australia in 1985 and stayed until 1992, producing two albums for the popular Aussie group GangGajang. He is now back in L.A. working with baby bands, including one led by singer/songwriter Holly Montgomery, and enjoying life. —ERIC OLSEN

DeShannon, Jackie: *Me About You,* Imperial, 1968.

Earth, Wind and Fire: *Earth, Wind and Fire,* Warner Bros., 1971 • "Love Is Life," Warner Bros., 1971 • "I Think About Lovin' You," Warner Bros., 1972 • *Last Days and Time,* Columbia, 1972 • *The Need of Love,* Warner Bros., 1972 • "Evil," Columbia, 1973 • *Head to the Sky,* Columbia, 1973 • "Keep Your Head to the Sky," Columbia, 1973 • "Devotion," Columbia, 1974 • "Mighty Mighty," Columbia, 1974 • *Open Our Eyes,* Columbia, 1974 • *Gratitude,* Columbia, 1976 • *Best Of,* Vol. 2, Columbia, 1988 • *Eternal Dance,* Columbia, 1992 • *Elements of Love: The Ballads,* Columbia, 1996.

Flo and Eddie: *Illegal, Immoral and Fattening,* CBS, 1975 • *Best Of,* Rhino, 1987.

Friedman, Ruthann: *Constant Companion,* Warner Bros., 1970.

GangGajang: *GangGajang*, Mercury Australia, 1985 • *True to the Tone*, Alex, 1990, 1992.

Head, Murray: *Nigel Lived*, Columbia, 1972.

Heaters: *Energy Transfer*, CBS, 1980.

Ian, Janis: *Janis Ian*, Columbia, 1978.

J. Geils Band: "One Last Kiss," EMI America, 1978 • *Sanctuary*, EMI America, 1978 • "Take It Back," EMI America, 1979 • *The J. Geils Band Anthology: Houseparty*, Rhino, 1993.

Jans, Tom: *Dark Blonde*, Columbia, 1976.

Jay and the Americans: *Come a Little Bit Closer*, Gold Rush, 1996.

Lane, Robin, and the Chartbusters: *Robin Lane and the Chartbusters*, Warner Bros., 1980.

Lightfoot, Gordon: "If You Could Read My Mind," Reprise, 1970 • *If You Could Read My Mind*, Reprise, 1970 • "Summer Side of Life," Warner Bros., 1971 • *Summer Side of Life*, Warner Bros., 1971 • "Talking in Your Sleep," Warner Bros., 1971 • *Gord's Gold*, Reprise, 1975.

Lovin' Spoonful: "She Is Still a Mystery," Kama Sutra, 1967 • *Everything Playing*, Kama Sutra, 1968 • "Money," Kama Sutra, 1968 • *Anthology*, Rhino, 1990.

Mason, Dave: *Old Crest on a New Wave*, Columbia, 1980 • "Save Me," Columbia, 1980 • *Long Lost Friend: The Best Of*, Legacy/Columbia, 1995.

Reddy, Helen: "Angie Baby," Capitol, 1974 • *Free and Easy*, Capitol, 1974 • "Ain't No Way to Treat a Lady," Capitol, 1975 • "Bluebird," Capitol, 1975 • "Emotion," Capitol, 1975 • *Greatest Hits and More*, Capitol, 1975 • *No Way to Treat a Lady*, Capitol, 1975 • "Somewhere in the Night," Capitol, 1975 • "I Can't Hear You No More/Music Is My Life," Capitol, 1976 • *Music, Music*, Capitol, 1976 • *Imagination*, MCA, 1983 • *I Am Woman: The Essential Helen Reddy Collection*, Razor & Tie, 1998.

Righteous Brothers: *Anthology*, Rhino, 1989.

Savage Grace: *Savage Grace*, Reprise, 1970.

Scaggs, Boz: "It's Over," Columbia, 1976 • "Lowdown," Columbia, 1976 • *Silk Degrees*, Columbia, 1976 • "What Can I Say," Columbia, 1976 • *Down Two, Then Left*, Columbia, 1977 • "Hard Times," Columbia, 1977 • "Lido Shuffle," Columbia, 1977 • "Hollywood," Columbia, 1978 • *Hits!*, Columbia, 1980.

Sinceros: *The Sound of Sunbathing*, Columbia, 1979.

Small Wonder: *Small Wonder*, Columbia, 1976 • *Growin'*, Columbia, 1977.

Turtles, The: "Happy Together," White Whale, 1967 • *Happy Together*, London/White Whale, 1967 • "She'd Rather Be with Me," White Whale, 1967 • "She's My Girl," White Whale, 1967 • "You Know What I Mean," White Whale, 1967 • *More Golden Hits*, White Whale, 1970.

COLLECTIONS

Tango, Tellus, 1997.

Stevie Wonder

When Saginaw, Michigan, native Steveland Morris (born May 13, 1950) was signed to Motown Records at age 12, Berry Gordy (see entry) dubbed him "Little Stevie Wonder." He was not only one of the first artists to be given creative control over his records (beginning in 1969); he was also one of the first to produce himself, along with Brian Wilson, Paul Simon, and John Fogerty (see entries).

An accomplished multi-instrumentalist, Wonder could easily have parlayed his talents into a career as a session drummer, keyboardist, harmonica player, or vocalist. But his soaring compositional skill and ability to create records with ear-friendly hooks and harmonic depth have made him one of the major artistic forces of the last 40 years.

As a producer, Wonder has exerted an enormous influence. Beginning with 1972's *Music of My Mind*, and on his collaborations with synthesizer pioneers Bob Margouleff and Malcolm Cecil, Wonder has emphasized seamlessly layered arrangements and a painter's attention to minute details in the stereo mix: repeated listenings to Wonder's mixes reveal previously hidden parts and tonal colors. Wonder and his team use the stereo mix as another instrument, not just to blend or separate sounds but to create intricate soundscapes; they have consistently pushed the recording envelope, creating some of the cleanest and most natural productions in recording history.

Wonder's forte as a producer is arranging. While packed with musical ideas, his arrangements never seem crowded and the groove is never buried. His distinctive horn parts are Motown-meets-Ellington: prime examples are on the No. 1 hits "You Are the Sunshine of My Life" (horns are only on the single version, not the album track); "I Wish," and "Sir Duke." Most of all, Wonder sets a vibe, a studio presentation so vivid his fans feel personally connected to him through his recordings. A key factor is his supple voice, which exudes a warm and joyous familiarity.

His 1971 *Where I'm Coming From*, the first album on which Wonder got production credit, was fundamentally transitional; no one could have anticipated the breakthroughs that were to follow. *Music of My Mind* and *Talking Book* (No. 3) were records in the truest sense, each a carefully sequenced album of material that flowed gracefully from track to track, deftly balancing tempos, keys, instrumentation, and mood. On the No.

INTERVIEW WITH STEVIE WONDER

Daniel J. Levitin: Starting with *Talking Book* your recordings started to sound a lot better. How did this change in recording quality come about?

Stevie Wonder: The two people who started with me in the beginning of all this, from when I did *Music of My Mind,* were Bob Margouleff and Malcolm Cecil. And they were very innovative in their thinking. They had their own album out [Tonto's Talking Headband], working with the Moog synthesizer and the Arp and all that kind of stuff. What they were really doing was making colors and creating pictures—sound pictures—if only for the fact they were working with a synthesizer at that time. And being from England influenced Malcolm; the English had another way of thinking about engineering: "image-ineering." You know, they would have the drums on one side and the voices on the other side, and their concept of stereo was just discrete channels of different things. Malcolm would say, "Well, listen, let's have the drums like, facing the drummer." And I said, "No, let's have it like I'm sitting at the drums . . . "

DL: Yes! With the high hat on the left and the toms sweeping around . . .

SW: So it's like the listener is actually a part of it, like they're sitting behind the drums. We would go back and forth and talk about different ideas of creating song pictures, and that's really how it began. So it was the talents of these incredible engineers, Bob and Malcolm, and then later, Gary Olazabal and John Fishback, with *Songs in the Key of Life.*

DL: I'm interested in your process of building songs up. In a lot of cases you're playing all the instruments yourself; did that come from your making demos by yourself and then realizing that the demo was good enough to release, or did you just say, "Hey, I'm just going to do it all because I can play the part I want and make it sound the way I want"?

SW: It is a combination of both. I started out [making records] with other producers, and they did the best they could with lots of songs. But once I got into producing, I realized that my songs didn't have the rawness I wanted.

DL: When you sit down to record a new song and you're playing all the instruments, do you hear all the parts in your head before you do the drum track, or does it build up gradually? How does all this come together?

SW: Sometimes I start with a sequence of the song and use that as a base; I can play the drums or whatever over the sequence. But for the most part, once I start playing, I usually know what I want and I mess around and do it a couple different ways until it feels it's in the pocket of that song.

DL: So you record just the drum track by itself? With all the fills and everything before you record anything else?

SW: I played the drums first on "Superstition." On "Higher Ground" I played the clavinet first.

DL: And then you added the drums to the clavinet?

SW: Yes.

SW: With "Superstition," I started the drums first. And I was just humming the melody and stuff.

DL: So you had it all in your head, like Mozart, right? You had the whole song in your head and you're just playing it out. You knew where every fill needed to go.

SW: Right. And if you're hearing it in your own head, you get very excited, and [sings "Superstition" and drum fills] you hear all the different beats, all the breaks and stuff that you do. So I was thinking about the beat and I was thinking about Stax, you know, the drums and everything, and the groove. Sometimes I would rush a little bit, but it's all part of the whole feel.

DL: I'd like to talk about your horn arrangements. In "You Are the Sunshine of My Life," the version on the album doesn't have any horns, but the single version does. Did you record horns for the album and decide not to use them later?

SW: After, after . . .

DL: Did the record company come to you and say, "Hey, Steve baby, we're going to release this as a single, we need to goose it up somehow," or . . .

SW: I just thought of doing it. It's funny. After [*Talking Book*] came out, I wanted to put horns on it—I thought it would be great because there were some spaces in there that needed something—[sings]—and it kind of worked well, like a pocket you know, like a hand in a glove. You have the voices in there, in the background [sings background vocal part]—so again, it was kind of being an architect, building that building, being an artist, and creating the sculpture.

DL: With *Conversation Peace* you used drum machine tracks . . .

SW: Actually, we had a combination of drum machine and live drums. But let me ask you a question: You know you can sequence, but you can also put a drum sound in a computer and you can have it without the quantization. What do you think about that?

DL: You mean, you sequence the part but you turn off the quantization . . .

SW: Right.

DL: And you let it drift.

SW: Right. You let it do whatever.

DL: Well the thing that I don't like about that is that you don't get the subtle changes in sound that I would hear when you're physically hitting a snare drum. Each time the stick hits the skin, it's going to hit it with a little different velocity and a little different pressure, so you have this wealth of sound coming off the . . .

SW: Go ahead.

DL: Well, coming off the instrument itself, the snare drum, the kick, the cymbal, whatever it is, there's this human variability, you could call it error, you can call it mistakes . . .

SW: Let me ask you this though, because, I mean, this is a great discussion because obviously people have been saying to me for years, "Look, Stevie, do it all like you did it before. Play all the stuff, don't sequence anything." But actually you can't do things the same way because people are tied into a time clock kind of thing.

DL: What do you mean?

SW: Well, I mean people nowadays want to hear a precise rhythm. So, for instance, with *Songs in the Key of Life,* I used a click track. On a certain level, I would have to use some kind of time reference because it gets sloppy if you don't.

DL: There are two things the machines are doing. One is, they're making the time more precise; rigid, some would say. The other is, they're getting rid of the variability in the tones you get from the drums unless you can somehow get like a hundred different snare samples . . .

SW: Collect all the samples, right. And obviously they're writing software everyday to do more and more of this kind of stuff, so it is possible. But there is a great challenge in playing this stuff. You really have to have engineers who have the patience and are willing to get that live drum sound the way you want to get it. Because, you know—[laughs]—all you have to do is go to a library of different samples and say, "Hey, that's exactly what I want."

DL: What did you do in the old days?

SW: You know, I wouldn't wait. [laughs] Basically, I think what happens is when the technology is there, you use it, right? So you have to make sure the people you're working with are all the way in tune with what you want to do. If they want to take the time to really do it, you can feed off each other with that. When I do a sequence at home I bring it into the studio and it's all there, and I have gotten comfortable with the way it sounds. Sometimes, once I've brought it in, the engineers will say, "Why don't you do this live?" or whatever. Often, then, we will sample me playing a drum, and substitute that sample into the sequence.

DL: You're saying it feels like a waste of time to you and the engineers to take all the time to get a live drum sound and to get it locked in with the click track, when all you have to do is turn on a box.

SW: I think that what is happening with me lots of times and with the finest of engineers is, I might want to do something at 9 at night which gets me maybe finishing at 5 or 6 or 7 in the morning. Some people just don't want to do that anymore; they get tired, or they've got families. So you've got to get a new crew of people in at 7 and you've gotta get, you know, you gotta stay with the whole thing. 'Cause, I mean, I'm just as excited about music as I was when I was 18. —DANIEL J. LEVITIN

---

1 hit "Superstition," originally written for guitarist Jeff Beck, Wonder layers three parts, coaxing the sounds of a distorted wah-wah guitar from his battery of keyboards, resplendent with guitar-like articulation and tones. "You Are the Sunshine of My Life" was an instant jazz standard, one of a handful of songs from the rock-pop era likely to be played at weddings and jazz clubs alongside such compositions as "Yesterday," "My Funny Valentine," "Misty," and "Close to You."

Innervisions (No. 4 in 1973), which many consider his peak, is a textbook case of tasteful and innovative production. The aural collage, "Living for the City" (No. 8), evokes the sights and smells of a rural Mississippian's trip to Manhattan and its tragic consequences. It is Wonder's unique gift that he can tell poignant, thought-provoking stories in a completely un-self-conscious way, and with an insistent backbeat.

The two No. 1 albums, 1975's *Fulfillingness' First Finale* and 1976's two-record *Songs in the Key of Life,* complete the trilogy begun with *Innervisions.* All three earned Grammy Awards for Album of the Year. Indeed, 1977's Album of the Year Grammy winners Fleetwood Mac quipped in their acceptance speech, "We'd like to thank Stevie Wonder . . . for not releasing an album this year." While all of Wonder's albums are experimental, these three are especially packed with artistic creativity, evoking the Beatles from 1965 to 1969 or John Fogerty from 1968 to 1971.

Songs in the Key of Life may best represent Wonder's breadth as an artist and producer; it is his personal favorite. Crisper than the dark-sounding *Fulfillingness',* the album covers an enormous musical terrain—spiritual, fusion instrumental, old Motown, pop, ska, ballad, rock, R&B, and genres that are Wonder's own, exemplified by the uncategorizable and powerful "Village Ghettoland" and "Pasttime Paradise."

In 1979, Wonder released *Journey Through the Secret Life of Plants* (No. 4), a meandering and lugubrious two-record set designed as a film soundtrack. Wonder's analog to George Harrison's *Wonderwall Music,* this was a release even diehard fans had trouble getting their heads around.

In Square Circle (No. 5 in 1985) was one of the first all-digital recordings of an American-made pop album. Unfortunately, its first-rate material was marred by harsh engineering and brittle tones. And 1995 found Wonder experimenting with digital sampling and sequencing on *Conversation Peace* (No. 16), a collection of excellent material that sold only marginally. "I'm New" featured innovative vocal harmonies and recording techniques with the group Take Six. That same year, Wonder released a two-CD set of live performances, *Natural Wonder,* featuring rearrangements of many Wonder staples. In late 1996, Motown released a two-CD set of greatest hits spanning the artist's 35-year career, *Stevie Wonder Song Review,* along with some new and previously unreleased tracks.

More than most other self-producers, Wonder has produced a number of outside projects over the years, most notably Minnie Riperton's "Lovin' You" (No. 1), Spinners' "It's a Shame" (No. 14), Jermaine Jackson's "Let's Get Serious" (No. 9), as well as albums by his then-wife Syreeta Wright, Third World, and Whitney Houston.
—Daniel J. Levitin

Collins, Tyler: *Girls Night Out,* RCA, 1989.

Hampton, Lionel: *For the Love of Music,* Mojazz, 1995.

Harrell, Grady: *Come Play with Me,* RCA, 1989.

Houston, Whitney: *I'm Your Baby Tonight,* Arista, 1990 • w/ Stevie Wonder, "We Didn't Know," Arista, 1992.

Iglesias, Julio: *Non Stop,* Columbia, 1988.

Jackson 5: *Anthology,* Motown, 1977.

Jackson, Jermaine: "Let's Get Serious," Motown, 1980 • *Let's Get Serious,* Motown, 1980 • "You're Supposed to Keep Your Love for Me," Motown, 1980 • *Greatest Hits and Rare Classics,* Motown, 1991.

John, Elton: *Duets,* MCA, 1993.

John, Keith: "I Can Only Be Me," Manhattan/EMI, 1988 (*School Daze* soundtrack).

Murphy, Eddie: *How Could It Be?,* Columbia, 1985.

Riperton, Minnie: *Perfect Angel,* Epic, 1974 • "Lovin' You," Epic, 1975.

Robinson, Smokey: *Warm Thoughts* (1 track), Tamla, 1980.

Ross, Diana: w/ the Supremes, *Anthology,* Motown, 1974, 1986 • *The Force Behind the Power* (3 tracks), Motown, 1991.

Spinners: "It's a Shame," V.I.P., 1970 • *Best Of,* Atlantic, 1978 • *One of a Kind Love Affair,* Rhino, 1991.

Supremes, The: *Greatest Hits and Rare Classics,* Motown, 1991 • *See also* Ross, Diana.

Syreeta: *Syreeta,* MoWest, 1972 • *Stevie Wonder Presents Syreeta,* Motown, 1974 • "Harmour Love," Motown, 1975

• *One to One,* Motown, 1975.

Take 6: *Join the Band,* Reprise, 1994.

Third World: "Try Jah Love," Columbia, 1984 (*Rhythm Come Forward*) • *You've Got the Power,* CBS, 1989 • *Best Of,* Legacy, 1993 • *Reggae Ambassadors: 20th Anniversary Collection,* Mercury, 1993.

Warwick, Dionne: *Friends,* Arista, 1985.

Williams Brothers, The: *Still Standing,* Blackberry, 1997.

Wonder, Stevie: *Eivets Rednow,* MoJazz, 1968, 1995 • "Signed, Sealed, Delivered, I'm Yours," Tamla, 1970 • *Signed Sealed and Delivered,* Tamla, 1970 • "If You Really Love Me," Tamla, 1971 • "We Can Work It Out," Tamla, 1971 • *Where I'm Coming From,* Tamla, 1971 • *Greatest Hits,* Vol. 2, Motown, 1972, 1991 • *Music of My Mind,* Tamla, 1972 • "Superstition," Tamla, 1972 • "Superwoman (Where Were You When I Needed You)," Tamla, 1972 • *Talking Book,* Tamla, 1972 • "Higher Ground," Tamla, 1973 • *Innervisions,* Tamla, 1973 • "Living for the City," Tamla, 1973 • "You Are the Sunshine of My Life," Tamla, 1973 • "Boogie on Reggae Woman," Tamla, 1974 • "Don't You Worry 'Bout a Thing," Tamla, 1974 • *Fulfillingness' First Finale,* Tamla, 1974 • "You Haven't Done Nothin'," Tamla, 1974 • *Songs in the Key of Life,* Tamla, 1976 • "Another Star," Tamla, 1977 • "As," Tamla, 1977 • "I Wish," Tamla, 1977 • "Sir Duke," Tamla, 1977 • *Journey Through the Secret Life of Plants,* Tamla, 1979 • "Send One Your Love," Tamla, 1979 • *Hotter Than July,* Tamla, 1980 • "I Ain't Gonna Stand for It," Tamla, 1980 • "Master Blaster (Jammin')," Tamla, 1980 • "Do I Do," Tamla, 1982 • *Original Musiquarium l,* Tamla, 1982 • "That Girl," Tamla, 1982 • "I Just Called to Say I Love You," Motown, 1984 • "Love Light in Flight," Motown, 1984 • *The Woman in Red,* Motown, 1984 • "Go Home," Tamla, 1985 • *In Square Circle,* Tamla, 1985 • "Overjoyed," Tamla, 1985 • "Part-Time Lover," Tamla, 1985 • "Land of La-La," Tamla, 1986 • *Characters,* Motown, 1987 • "Skeletons," Motown, 1987 • w/ Michael Jackson, "Get It," Motown, 1988 • "My Eyes Don't Cry," Motown, 1988 • "You Will Know," Motown, 1988 • "With Each Beat of My Heart," Motown, 1989 • "Keep Our Love Alive," Motown, 1990 • "Fun Day," Motown, 1991 • "Gotta Have You," Motown, 1991 • "I'm the One Who Loves You," Warner Bros., 1994 (*A Tribute to Curtis Mayfield*) • *Conversation Peace,* Motown, 1995 • "For Your Love," Motown, 1995 • *Natural Wonder,* Motown, 1995 • "Tomorrow Robins Will Sing," Motown, 1995 • "Treat Myself," Motown, 1995 • *Song Review: A Greatest Hits Collection,* Motown, 1996.

COLLECTIONS

Jungle Fever soundtrack, Motown, 1991.

Get on the Bus: Music from and Inspired by the Motion Picture, Interscope, 1996.

Brad Wood

Brad Wood, part owner and on-site producer/engineer of Chicago's Idful Music, has worked on over 400 records. Wood's big break came in 1993 with the debut of angst-rocker Liz Phair. That album, *Exile in Guyville,* was a distaff musical response to the Rolling Stones' *Exile on Main Street,* and moved Wood to the head of the Chicago indie rock class. Coming off the wild acclaim (*Spin* magazine's Album of the Year) and exposure generated by that album, Wood produced Phair's next album, *Whip-Smart* (which cracked the Top 30), fellow Chicagoans Veruca Salt on their *American Thighs,* and crucial albums by Jale (*Dreamcake, So Wound*), Ben Lee (*Grandpaw Would, Something to Remember Me By*), Red Red Meat (*Jimmywine Majestic, Bunny Gets Paid*), Seam (*The Problem with Me*), Sunnyday Real Estate (*Diary*), That Dog (*Retreat from the Sun*), and his own band—the jazzy Shrimp Boat (*Cavale, Duende, Speckly*). In 1998 Wood broke through to the majors with co-productions of the Smashing Pumpkins' *Adore,* Liz Phair's *Whitechocolatespaceegg,* and Whale's *All Disco Dance Must End in Broken Bones.*

Brad Wood and Cheap Trick share the hometown of Rockford, Illinois. Born February 15, 1964, Wood's musical training began in the third grade on the saxophone, and he was something of a "wunderkind, a little prodigy," playing jazz all the way through college, where he was a sax major.

Wood made the big move to Chicago in 1987. In 1988 he and college friend Brian Deck began building Idful Music, a name taken in jest from a philosophy professor's proclivity for Freudian musical references. Studying recording techniques at Northern Illinois University in classes with titles like "The Acoustical Physics of Sound," Wood and Deck used the smarts they gained to create a studio grounded in sound acoustical concepts.

"We wanted to build a big live room that had a lot of reverberance—long reverb times," says Wood. "We wanted to have big ambient drum sounds without using digital reverb. It has to do with aesthetic: How does the space sound? How do you like spending your time there? In a place where no one is happy, you can't make good music."

It was Wood's frustration with recording experiences in high school bands that led him to his own studio. He explains, "I can't stand to have [music] coming out sounding like shit, and that was really the main reason I started. I couldn't stand the status quo. I wanted my records to sound like the Clash's *London Calling,* or a Sex Pistols record, or Pere Ubu for that matter. I didn't want it to sound anything like Emerson, Lake and Palmer." The young studio owners first made use of Idful for their own recording purposes: Wood joined Shrimp Boat in 1989, and Deck is the drummer for Red Red Meat. Eventually they had to open their doors to the public for financial reasons.

Wood's role as producer varies based on the needs of the artist he's working with. "Sometimes I am just a recordist: 'Please make it sound like we sound.' That happens a lot and it's harder than people would imagine. Then there are times when a band will say, 'We have 16 songs, but can only put 12 on the record,' and I might give my opinion on what songs are my favorites. And there are times when people just have ideas, and that's much more involved."

Wood believes Phair's *Exile in Guyville* is his crowning achievement. *Exile* is a sardonic journey through smartly crafted melodies and expletives, chronicling a female-centric view of relationships. Wood says Phair's album fell in the production middle ground: she came to him with songs, but he helped with all the arrangements. "Most of those songs, I played drums, bass, keyboards, so I had a pretty big hand in the arrangement."

Exile is full of great songs: "6' 1" is a brisk percussive guitar rock number with Wood on percussion, bass and backing vocals. The sparse "Glory" features Phair on guitar and vocals and Wood on organ. Wood makes excellent use of Phair's rough, whispery vocals as they sweep back and forth in an echoey aural landscape. The radio-friendly "Never Said" clearly rocks, as Wood once again displays his prowess on drums and bass, and studio-mate Casey Rice plays an impressive lead guitar.

Regardless of his input, Wood doesn't claim any creative credit for the album. When accused of humility, he's quick to erase such notions. "It's not humble at all, it's knowing your fucking place. As far as I'm concerned with Liz, it's her name on the record, her face on the cover, and she has to deal with the press. I came up with all kinds of cool parts—but they're just parts, and parts are parts."

In with the women, Wood's next major production was the female-fronted Veruca Salt's *American Thighs. Thighs* is thick as malted milk and went gold on the tiny Minty Fresh label despite generating accusations of an uncomfortable similarity to the Breeders. "Seether," an in-your-face rocker that was ubiquitous on modern rock radio in 1994, is heavy on chunky riffs pleasantly complemented by cherubic harmonies from singer/guitar players Nina Gordon and Louis Post, as Wood captures a live-in-the-studio excitement. "Forsythia" has an engaging bass line and a quirky melody, again taking advantage of the pleasing vocals. "Victrola" is adrenaline-charged rock.

Clearly a producer/engineer on the rise, Wood brings out the uniqueness of the performers he works with and captures the heart of a performance. Wood's musicianship, trained ear, and technical ability allow him to deliver these gifts. To the aspiring masses, Wood offers this advice: "Don't feed the suits, don't fuck the talent," and "try not to use too much digital reverb on your drums, because it doesn't sound good and it will date your music in a way that you might not be happy about." —DAWN DARLING

Best Kissers in the World: "Come On Come On Come On," MCA, 1996 • "Willie Nelson," MCA, 1996.

Boom Hank: *Nuisance,* Pravda, 1993.

Chia Pet: *Meha,* Johann's Face, 1993.

Eleventh Dream Day: *Two Sweeties* (EP), City Slang Records, 1992 • *Ursa Major,* Atavistic, 1994.

Far: *Tin Cans with Strings to You,* Immortal, 1996.

Freakwater: *Dancing Underwater,* Thrill Jockey, 1991 • *Feels Like the 3rd Time,* Thrill Jockey, 1993 • *Old Paint,* Thrill Jockey, 1995.

God and Texas: *Criminal Element,* Restless, 1993 • *Double Shot,* Restless, 1994.

Hardvark: *Memory Barge,* DGC, 1995.

Hum: *Electra 2000,* Martians Go Home, 1993, 1997.

Jale: *Dreamcake,* Sub Pop, 1994 • *So Wound,* Sub Pop, 1996.

King Kong: *Funny Farm,* Drag City, 1993.

Lee, Ben: *Grandpaw Would,* Grand Royal, 1995 • *Something to Remember Me By,* Grand Royal, 1997.

Loud Lucy: *Breathe,* DGC, 1995.

Menthol: *Menthol,* Capitol, 1995.

Mysteries of Life: *Come Clean,* RCA, 1998.

Noise Addict: *Meet the Real You,* Grand Royal, 1996.

Number One Cup: *Kim Chee Is Cabbage,* Flydaddy, 1996 • *Wrecked by Lions,* Flydaddy, 1997.

Phair, Liz: *Exile in Guyville,* Matador, 1993 • "Supernova," Matador, 1994 • *Whip-Smart,* Matador, 1994 • *Whitechocolatespaceegg,* Capitol, 1998.

Placebo: *Placebo,* Caroline, 1996.

Red Red Meat: "Flank," Sub Pop, 1993 • *Jimmywine Majestic,* Sub Pop, 1993 • *Bunny Gets Paid,* Sub Pop, 1995.

Seam: *Kernal* (EP), Touch & Go, 1993 • *The Problem with Me,* Touch & Go, 1993 • *Are You Driving Me Crazy?,* Touch & Go, 1995.

Sheik, Duncan: "Reasons for Living" (remix), Atlantic, 1997.

Shrimp Boat: *Speckly,* Specimen Products, 1989 • *Duende,* Bar None, 1991 • *Cavale,* Bar None, 1993.

Smashing Pumpkins: *Adore,* Virgin, 1998.

Spinanes, The: *Strand,* Sub Pop, 1996.

Squash Blossom: "She," Mother Jones, 1995 (*You Are What You Shoot*).

Sunny Day Real Estate: *Diary,* Sub Pop, 1993 • "8," Atlantic, 1995 (*Batman Forever* soundtrack) • *Sunny Day Real Estate,* Sub Pop, 1995.

Tar: *Roundhouse,* Amphetamine Reptile, 1990 • *Clincher,* Touch & Go, 1993.

That Dog: *Retreat from the Sun,* DGC, 1997.

Tortoise: *Tortoise,* Thrill Jockey, 1994.

Trenchmouth: *Trenchmouth Versus the Light of the Sun,* Skene/Atlantic, 1995 • *Construction of New Action,* Vol. 1, Skene, 1996.

Uptighty: "If There's a Heaven Above," Mother Jones, 1995 (*You Are What You Shoot*).

Veruca Salt: *American Thighs,* Minty Fresh, 1994.

Whale: *All Disco Dance Must End in Broken Bones,* Virgin, 1998.

Toby Wright

Toby Wright's father, a jazz musician, started his son on flute and clarinet as a kid, but Wright's interest in making a living in music didn't ignite until he was out of school. He took a four-year program at the New York Institute of Audio Research while working in maintenance at Electric Lady Studios. "The maintenance chief was always complaining about the engineers who couldn't fix anything," Wright recalls. "I didn't want to be yelled at."

He moved to Los Angeles, first working in maintenance at Cherokee Studio and later building One on One in the mid-'80s, where he was an engineer. "The first 15 or 16 albums recorded there all went platinum: Heart's *Bad Animals,* Dokken's *Tooth and Nail,* two Mötley Crüe albums."

Wright was heavily influenced by his work there with Ron Nevison (see entry). "I learned a lot of things to do and not to do from him. I learned that the song is the most important thing and without the song you don't have anything. I also learned how not to treat people. He was a bit of a tyrant and did a lot of yelling. One day he was yelling at Ann Wilson and he made her cry. He didn't get the best performance out of her that day."

His first production opportunity came after an assistant engineering stint on Metallica's 1988 *And Justice for All.* He was asked to do their track, "Stone Cold Crazy," for Elektra's 40th-anniversary record *Rubaiyat.* The track won a heavy metal Grammy.

After a few obscure production assignments out of the country, he was approached by Columbia's Nick Terzo to mix an 8-track live recording of Alice in Chains. Although it never saw official release, Wright and the band clicked, and he was asked to do their 1994 *Jar of Flies* EP, which debuted at No. 1 and sold over 4 million copies. "It was recorded and mixed in 10 days," Wright says. "Everything was written, recorded, and produced on the spot. I don't know if we could ever repeat that. My philosophy was whatever happened, happened. I've done all their recording from that day on. I'm kind of proud of that fact."

Jar of Flies was acoustic and more minimal than their previous work, although it had the band's trademark languorous, detuned drawl of a sound. On the band's 1995 self-titled album, Wright continued to strip down the layers of guitars that the band had used early on. "A few tracks took the older approach, but we found at the end that it didn't sound as defined," he says.

Wright co-produced Slayer's 1994 *Divine Intervention* (No. 8); he says an attempt to update them by introducing them to loops failed. "They'd go, that's really killer. But in the end, they said 'Fuck it, let's just make a Slayer record.' " They did.

He co-produced a Kiss album in late 1995 that was shelved when the band decided to do their reunion tour. It's on the bootleg market as *Carnival of Souls: The Final Sessions* (and was released by Mercury under that name in 1997). "Gene and Paul came to me with a bunch of songs. I was a Kiss fan since I was a kid; being in the room with them scared the shit out of me. I said, 'You know what? These are good songs. I can lend my ear to their sound.' If it gets released, it'll be acclaimed as one of their best records. The old stuff was bubblegum by comparison."

Wright worked with T Bone Burnett (see entry) on the Wallflowers' 1996 hit, *Bringing Down the Horse,* and with Peter Collins (see entry) on Queensryche's *Here in the Now Frontier.* He says, "I'd drop the production end of my life to work with a talented producer on an engineering level to absorb different approaches."

His association with the famously troubled band, Alice in Chains, continued in 1998 with the Jerry Cantrell solo album, *Boggy Depot.* "I kind of specialize in working with problem children," Wright says. "I love those guys as musicians and I don't judge them outside the studio. So the drummer drinks too much and throws shit. I say, put him in the studio and I'll deal with it. It's always a drama. That's what attracts me to them: I think I can help them. [Lead singer] Layne [Staley] is a sweet and endearing person. To see someone like that with such a big problem makes me want to help.

"It took seven months to make the last AiC record. Eventually they came to the studio. When we did *MTV Unplugged* (No. 3), Jerry was sick as a dog. Five minutes before they went on stage he was barfing his brains out. And that was a live record—not one overdub."

Wright's easygoing nature extends to his choice of studios. "Anywhere will work as long as the band is comfortable and the sound is accurate in the room. Monitors are the most important thing. If you can hear correctly, you can record a brilliant record.

"All technology is just a tool," he says. "You have to find the applicable tool that works in that particular situation. My production philosophy is to make sure the songs are all there and get out of the way." —ANASTASIA PANTSIOS

Alice in Chains: "What the Hell Have I," Columbia, 1993 • *Alice in Chains,* Columbia, 1995 • *Unplugged,* Columbia, 1996.

Cantrell, Jerry: *Boggy Depot,* Columbia, 1998.

Fishbone: *Fishbone 101: Nuttasaurusmeg Fossil Fuelin',* Sony, 1996.

Gillis, Brad: *Gilrock Ranch,* Guitar, 1993.

Kiss: *Carnival of Souls: The Final Sessions,* Mercury, 1997.

Metallica: "Stone Cold Crazy," Elektra, 1990 (*Rubaiyat: Elektra's 40th Anniversary*).

Nixons, The: *The Nixons,* MCA, 1997.

Primus: *Rhinoplasty* (ECD), Interscope, 1998.

Slayer: *Divine Intervention,* American, 1994.

Soul Asylum: "Can't Even Tell," Columbia, 1994.

Whitley, Chris: *Terra Incognita,* Sony, 1997.

Frank Zappa

At some time during his incredibly prolific and polymath life as guitarist, songwriter, composer, conductor, satirist, producer, free speech activist, and all-around social gadfly, Frank Zappa said: "Without deviation [from the norm], 'progress' is not possible. In order for one to deviate successfully, one has to have at least a passing acquaintance with whatever norm one expects to deviate from."

Throughout his career Zappa not only mastered musical genres as varied as jazz, modern classical, rock, doo-wop, R&B, and pop; he created whole new subsets of music as a solo artist and in various configurations of the Mothers of Invention. And if his goal hadn't been to deviate from the norm, music would have been cheated

Photo by Steve Shapiro

of one of the richest bodies of work of the last 30 years, highlighted by popular favorites such as the gold *Overnite Sensation* and *Apostrophe* (No. 10), *One Size Fits All, Sheik Yerbouti,* and the extremely soulful *Hot Rats,* with Captain Beefheart, Jean-Luc Ponty, and Sugar Cane Harris; but also by the difficult and challenging *Orchestral Favorites, London Symphony Orchestra,* Vols. 1–2, and *The Yellow Shark,* as performed by the Ensemble Modern. Beginning with the third Mothers album, *We're Only in It for the Money,* Zappa produced dozens of albums of his own music and still found time to produce artists as varied as Captain Beefheart, Lenny Bruce, Wild Man Fischer, the GTO's, and Grand Funk.

Frank Zappa was born December 21, 1940, in Baltimore, Maryland, but his family eventually settled down in the semidesert of Southern California in 1950. His first interest in music was R&B, and throughout the early '60s Zappa played with a number of club R&B bands with names like the Masters and the Soul Giants. After scoring a low-budget film in 1963, he purchased the Pal Recording Studio in Cucamonga from Paul Buff, who had built his own recording console and a 5-track, 1/2-inch tape recorder. Zappa changed the name to Studio Z and started what he called "the beginning of a life of obsessive overdubbage—nonstop 12 hours a day."

While working in Studio Z and continuing to play guitar in local bands, Zappa was befriended by the singer Don Van Vliet, who eventually morphed into Captain Beefheart. Zappa and Van Vliet recorded songs such as "Metal Man Has Won His Wings," "Cheryl's Canon," and a cover of Little Richard's "Slippin' and Slidin' " under the name the Soots. Zappa took the tracks to Dot Records' Milt Rogers, who stated flatly, "We can't release these—the guitar is distorted." Though the Soots didn't make it into the mainstream, Zappa and Beefheart stayed in touch, and when Beefheart had the opportunity to record *Trout Mask Replica* in 1969 he turned to Zappa.

The original idea behind recording the album, Zappa admits in his autobiography (*The Real Frank Zappa Book*) was to do it as "an anthropological field recording" in Beefheart's house in the San Fernando Valley of California. Along with engineer Dick Kunc, a Shure 8-channel mixer mounted in a briefcase, and a Uher portable tape recorder, they set to record Captain Beefheart and His Magic Band's seminal release. They got a couple of songs into the sessions at the house when Van Vliet changed his mind on the sessions and wanted to move it to a proper studio in Glendale.

Of course, before, during, and after his outside production work Zappa was consumed with his own band, the Mothers of Invention. From their debut, *Freak Out!* (produced by Tom Wilson; see entry), to his final solo releases, Zappa kept an active role in all parts of the recording process. What's interesting to note is that Zappa was an artist/producer who had the ability and talent to move from old-school recording dates where compressors and equalizers were stunning technological advances to his use of the Synclavier to compose orchestral works in the later days of his career.

Producer/engineer Joe Chiccarelli (see entry) credits Zappa with changing his thinking about recording. "I went from the standard hi-fi model of getting everything to sound good to pushing the limits in search of the unique. Good sound quality wasn't enough for Zappa. He wanted his recordings to have character, to jump up and surprise you. He always had a vision of the way he wanted things, and he would go to any lengths musically, lyrically, or with recording techniques to achieve that vision. Zappa opened my eyes and twisted me." Chiccarelli learned to experiment on such Zappa discs as *Baby Snakes, Joe's Garage, Live in New York,* and *Shut Up and Play Your Guitar.*

From his experimentation within the studio and the live setting it seems clear that Zappa was comfortable with technology and used it to his creative advantage whenever possible. In fact, without much fanfare,

Zappa's work with the London Symphony Orchestra was an engineering feat. From altering microphone assignments to designing virtual isolation booths in the orchestra to using a Lexicon 224-X digital reverb processor during the mixing process, Zappa took what was destined to be a recording disaster and made it a masterpiece.

In addition to his work with the Mothers (and the various incarnations thereof), Zappa produced a number of albums destined to deviate from the norm. Whether it was the warped-girl-group GTO's, or savant naif Wild Man Fischer, or his early mentoring of Alice Cooper, Zappa attempted to push the artists into uncharted territory.

Though his outside production list is relatively slight, it can be argued that Zappa's effect on modern music (a term he seemingly despised) came via his work as an artist. While *Freak Out!* introduced the world to Zappa's vision, he was never content to stay rooted in one musical genre for very long. Throughout his life Zappa remained true to the notion that music is a gift, and it was his responsibility as an artist to manifest that gift wherever the muse led him. Zappa, who eschewed drugs and alcohol, but who was a lifelong smoker, died of prostate cancer on December 4, 1993. He is survived by his wife, Gail, and four children, including the guitarist Dweezil and actress Moon Unit (who performed vocals on Zappa's only Top 40 hit, "Valley Girl"). Zappa was inducted into the Rock and Roll Hall of Fame in 1995.

Virtually all of Zappa's music has been digitally remastered for CD and is available through Rykodisc or the official Zappa Family Trust Web site at www.zappa.com. —DAVID JOHN FARINELLA AND ERIC OLSEN

Bruce, Lenny: *The Berkeley Concert*, Bizarre, 1968.
Captain Beefheart: *Trout Mask Replica*, Straight, 1969.
Ensemble Modern: *The Yellow Shark*, Rykodisc, 1993, 1995.
Fischer, Wild Man: *An Evening with Wild Man Fischer*, Bizarre, 1968.
George, Lowell, and the Factory: *Lightning-Rod Man*, Rhino, 1993.
Grand Funk Railroad: *Good Singing Good Playing*, MCA, 1976.
GTO's, The: *Permanent Damage*, Straight, 1969.
Hollywood Persuaders: *Drums a Go-Go*, Original Sound, 1965.
London Symphony Orchestra: *Zappa*, Vols. 1–2, Rykodisc, 1983, 1995.
Mothers: *Grand Wazoo*, Bizarre, 1972 • *Just Another Band from L.A.*, Bizarre, 1972 • *Over-nite Sensation*, Discreet, 1973.
Mothers of Invention: *Cruising With Ruben and the Jets*, Rykodisc, 1968, 1995 • *We're Only in It for the Money*, Rykodisc, 1968, 1995 • *Uncle Meat*, Rykodisc, 1969, 1995 •

Burnt Weeny Sandwich, Rykodisc, 1970, 1995 • *Weasels Ripped My Flesh*, Rykodisc, 1970, 1995 • *Fillmore East—June 1971*, Rykodisc, 1971, 1995 • *200 Motels*, Rykodisc, 1971, 1997 • *Freaks and Motherfu@#$%^*, Foo-Eee, 1991 • *The Ark*, Foo-Eee, 1991 • *'Tis the Season to Be Jelly*, Foo-Eee, 1991 • *Unmitigated Audacity*, Foo-Eee, 1991.
Ruben and the Jets: *For Real*, Mercury, 1973 • *Con Safos*, Edsel, 1995.
Shankar, L.: *Touch Me There*, Zappa, 1979.
Simmons, Jeff: *Lucille Has Messed Up My Mind*, Straight, 1969.
Zappa, Dweezil: *Havin' a Bad Day*, Barking Pumpkin, 1984.
Zappa, Frank: *Lumpy Gravy*, Verve, 1968, 1995 • *Hot Rats*, Rykodisc, 1969, 1995 • *Chunga's Revenge*, Rykodisc, 1970, 1995 • *Waka Jawaka*, Rykodisc, 1972, 1995 • *'(Apostrophe)*, Rykodisc, 1974, 1995 • *"Don't Eat the Yellow Snow,"* Rykodisc, 1974, 1995 • w/ Captain Beefheart, *Bongo Fury*, Rykodisc, 1975, 1995 • *Zoot Allures*, Rykodisc, 1976, 1995 • *Zappa in New York*, Rykodisc, 1977, 1995 • *Studio Tan*, Rykodisc, 1978, 1995 • *"Dancin' Fool,"* Zappa, 1979, 1995 • *Joe's Garage, Acts 1, 2, & 3*, Zappa, 1979, 1995 • *Orchestral Favorites*, Rykodisc, 1979, 1995 • *Sheik Yerbouti*, Zappa, 1979, 1995 • *Sleep Dirt*, Rykodisc, 1979, 1995 • *Tinsel Town Rebellion*, Rykodisc, 1981, 1995 • *You Are What You Is*, Rykodisc, 1981, 1995 • *Baby Snakes*, Rykodisc, 1982, 1995 • *Shut Up 'n Play Yer Guitar*, Rykodisc, 1982, 1995 • *Ship Arriving Too Late to Save a Drowning Witch*, Rykodisc, 1982, 1995 • *"Valley Girl,"* Barking Pumpkin, 1982, 1995 • *The Man from Utopia*, Rykodisc, 1983, 1995 • *Boulez Conducts Zappa: The Perfect Stranger*, Rykodisc, 1984, 1995 • *Them or Us*, Rykodisc, 1984, 1995 • *Thing-Fish*, Rykodisc, 1984, 1995 • *Francesco Zappa*, Rykodisc, 1984, 1995 • *Frank Zappa Meets the Mothers of Prevention*, Rykodisc, 1985, 1995 • *Does Humor Belong in Music?*, Rykodisc, 1986, 1995 • *Jazz from Hell*, Rykodisc, 1986, 1995 • *Guitar*, Rykodisc, 1988, 1995 • *You Can't Do That on Stage*, Vols. 1–3, Rykodisc, 1988/1989, 1995 • *Broadway the Hard Way*, Rykodisc, 1989, 1995 • *Make a Jazz Noise Here*, Rykodisc, 1991, 1995 • *The Best Band You Never Heard in Your Life*, Rykodisc, 1991, 1995 • *You Can't Do That on Stage*, Vols. 4–6, Rykodisc, 1991/1992, 1995 • *Civilization Phase III*, Barking Pumpkin, 1994, 1995 • *Any Way the Wind Blows*, Foo-Eee, 1991, 1995 • *As An Am*, Foo-Eee, 1991, 1995 • *Beat the Boots*, Foo-Eee, 1991, 1995 • *Piquantique*, Foo-Eee, 1991, 1995 • *Saarbrucken 1979*, Foo-Eee, 1991, 1995 • *Strictly Commercial: The Best of Frank Zappa*, Rykodisc, 1995 • *Läther*, Rykodisc, 1996 • *The Lost Episodes*, Rykodisc, 1996 • *Have I Offended Someone?*, Rykodisc, 1997 • *Strictly Genteel: A Classical Introduction*, Rykodisc, 1997.
Zappa, Frank, and the Mothers of Invention: *Roxy and Elsewhere*, Discreet, 1974 • *One Size Fits All*, Discreet, 1975 • *Playground Psychotics*, Rykodisc, 1992, 1995 • *Ahead of Their Time*, Rykodisc, 1993, 1995.

Joe Zawinul

Creativity and control seem synonymous for Joe Zawinul, a protean keyboardist who made his early mark with Dinah Washington, Cannonball Adderley, and Miles Davis. His most famous gig was as co-head of Weather Report, which he founded with saxophonist Wayne Shorter in 1970. The definitive jazz-rock band, Weather Report melded memorable melodies to freewheeling improvisation in the 17 albums it released from 1971 to 1986. In the past decade, Zawinul has led such groups as Weather Update and Zawinul Syndicate, producing and recording under those names and his own. He also has produced records by Malian string instrumentalist Salif Keita and Hindu percussionist Trilok Gurtu—like Zawinul himself, musicians whose jazz is both worldly and otherworldly. Among his most recent forays are a classical work, *Stories of the Danube,* and *My People,* a world music work.

Born in Vienna on July 7, 1932, Zawinul took up music at age 5, beginning with the accordion. He later turned to piano, studying it at the Vienna Conservatory. He left Austria for the United States in 1959, studying at Berklee College of Music in Boston for a mere week before hitting the road in Maynard Ferguson's band. He worked with Ferguson, then Washington, joining Adderley's band in 1961. He performed and recorded with the great saxophonist throughout the decade, writing "Mercy, Mercy, Mercy" during that tenure.

Although he played on Miles Davis's seminal *Bitches Brew,* he decided to ally with Shorter rather than be a Davis sideman (Davis named another 1969 work, *In a Silent Way,* after a Zawinul tune). Zawinul's Weather Report years garnered numerous awards for both best keyboardist and best band. If Zawinul is egotistic, he has good reason.

"For me, production means to be more or less responsible for the entire product, regardless of who writes music on it," Zawinul says. "Wayne is a great, great composer, but often, I edited his work. I never changed it, because it was written very wonderfully, and we never changed any of my work, either. But his compositions were often very stretched, like a tree with many branches."

What Zawinul likes about the Weather Report years is "we always did what we wanted to do. We didn't make any compromises in order to sell records." He tried to bring form to Weather Report, he suggests. "Maybe that's the best way to describe the music Wayne had written in those days," Zawinul says. "Wonderful motifs, wonderful bass lines, but sometimes it drifted away. I think the job of a producer is to be an artistic director, someone setting up things. I think I was always good in setting up people to do certain things, playing-wise."

For Zawinul, production is intimately bound up with the act of creation, which is essentially improvisatory. But improvisations must be framed by purpose and discipline to have an effect, he implies. "Certain people have a quality to lead other people, and some don't," Zawinul says. "Wayne will follow, but he doesn't hold your hand; he's totally walking on his own, he has his own creative process. When we used to mix records, I'd take Wayne's part by itself—it was a melody standing on its own—and play mine on its own. The creative process is happening because of both. So, going back to production, it is to have the oversight, the concept of formulating an album. For me, music is nothing. For me, music is only what it means to others. What it does to people is very, very important."

One of Zawinul's key vehicles of communication is the synthesizer. Not only can he coax unworldly, oddly human sounds from it, the sense of color and tonality he conveys through it distinguishes his productions. Zawinul calls his music difficult but instinctive. It takes talented musicians to play it, he says.

Highly rhythmic and multitextured, Zawinul's records, whether group or solo, are world music in the truest sense. That's why he's using Richard Bona, a bassist from Cameroon, Venezuelan singer Thania Sanchez, Ivory Coast kalimba master Paco Sery, and Brooklyn guitarist Gary Paulson in his band. "I don't want to play tomorrow what I played last week," he says. "I'm lucky to have the gift, and I'm very lucky to have the people around me, to play this music I play. To play this music, I need very keen people."

Technology is just another element in his work. To him, such distinctions as organic and synthetic don't seem to matter. "Technology is a tool," Zawinul says. "An instrument doesn't play by itself; unless a master plays it, it sounds like a piece of shit. People have a totally wrong concept because they use synthesizers as a novelty. Some producers turn a couple of knobs and feel like they know how to use it. I use it because I play it like

I play all my other acoustic instruments: I'm finding a sound I really can play in my heart. "I talk to the instrument. I love it. But I started out playing accordion, which is the first synthesizer. You have different stops, you have different sounds."

So musically voracious is Zawinul that he invented an instrument he calls the "pepe." "It looks like a weapon, it is very small," he says. "It is long—from your neck down to about your hipbone—and a hand wide. It has buttons like on a button accordion, and a double-reed mouthpiece like an oboe. There are microphones in there and it is breath-controlled." He owns the only example of these "saxophone-sounding" instruments, he says.

What makes a record a good production is quality and continuity. "You put on the first tune on a CD, you should not have to pick it up," Zawinul says. "That, to me, is a good production. Storytelling is the whole purpose. Instead of words, you say it with tones. Tones have many languages. And storytelling is what we always do." —CARLO WOLFF

Gurtu, Trilok: *Crazy Saints*, CMP, 1993.

Keita, Salif: *Amen*, Mango, 1991 • *The Mansa of Mali: A Retrospective*, Mango, 1995.

Weather Report: *Weather Report*, Columbia, 1971 • *I Sing the Body Electric*, Columbia, 1972 • *Sweetnighter*, Columbia, 1973 • *Mysterious Traveler*, Columbia, 1974 • *Tale Spinnin'*, Legacy, 1975, 1994 • *Black Market*, Columbia, 1976 • *Heavy Weather*, Columbia, 1977 • *Mr. Gone*, Columbia, 1978 • *8:30*, Legacy, 1979, 1994 • *Night Passage*, Columbia, 1980 • *Domino Theory*, Columbia, 1984 • *This Is This!*, Columbia, 1985, 1991.

Zawinul, Joe: *Money in the Pocket*, Atco, 1966 • *Dialects*, Columbia, 1986 • *Immigrants*, Columbia, 1988, 1991 • w/ Zawinul Syndicate, *Black Water*, TriStar, 1989, 1996 • *My People*, Escapade, 1992, 1996 • w/ Zawinul Syndicate, *Lost Tribes*, Columbia, 1992 • *Stories of the Danube*, PolyGram, 1996 • w/ Zawinul Syndicate, *World Tour*, Zebra, 1998.

Richie Zito

Considering all the records he worked on before 1986's "Take Me Home Tonight" (No. 4), it's surprising that Richie Zito considers that one his breakthrough moment. For the 13 years previous to the Eddie Money single, Zito worked with Elton John, Giorgio Moroder (see entry), Berlin, and the Motels, to name only a few. "I always look to that as the beginning of my production career, because before that I was still trying to find my footing as a record producer," he says.

Zito moved to Los Angeles from New York in 1973 to find his fortune as a session guitar player. "I just kinda scuffled around," he explains. "Then little by little I started to build a session clientele. During the '70s I toured with a variety of people, and by the late '70s I had a pretty good little list of people who I worked for as a guitar player. In 1980 I joined Elton John's band and I made three albums as a member of his band and did one world tour. I always flirted with production, I was always looking for the way to make the segue from musician to producer. One of the clients I had was Giorgio Moroder, who was pretty well known, obviously, for kinda inventing disco and Donna Summers and all that stuff."

During what he calls the "flashdance era," Zito gave up all of his other commitments and threw his guitar picks in with Moroder. He worked exclusively as a musician and arranger on a wide variety of soundtrack projects, "I would do vocals, oversee some of the mixes," Zito says. "He was really great in giving me the opportunity to sort of practice being a record producer with his career and his credibility on the line. I didn't want to let down his belief and trust."

So he worked hard and one of his first nonsound-track co-production credits was Berlin's tune "No More Words," a hit in 1984. From there he worked with the Motels and Toni Basil, and on the aforementioned Eddie Money sessions. One of the things that helped him all along was his guitar ability. When asked whether or not he plays on the sessions he produces, he answers with a laugh: "Yes, I love to play. Once a musician, always a musician. If I work with bands that have stellar guitar players, I might strum an acoustic part or do a keyboard overdub. When I did Cheap Trick, I did a lot of keyboard stuff because there was no keyboard player in the band, and I had a really talented synthesizer programmer with me. On Eddie Money's record I played quite a bit, but I did a Bad English record with Neal Schon on guitar and Jonathan Cain as the keyboard player and I didn't touch an instrument, not even a tambourine."

His musical background also gives him the ability to walk the walk, as it were. "If you are a musician, you actually speak the language, and therefore I have always felt lucky that I didn't have to say, 'Hey listen, can you try something a little more blue, or something that feels a little more abstract or oblique?' I can actually say, 'Play a C chord.' Or I can say, 'I have an idea for a part,' and grab and instrument and actually display my idea. It has been very helpful because when they see what I mean, then they grab a guitar or a keyboard, put their spin on it, and make it their own." It also levels the playing field between producer and artist, he thinks. "They can't bulldoze you to the same extent. It cuts through a lot and it gets things more direct."

Of course, there are those successful producers who are not musicians first and Zito gives them equal praise. "It's just part of what I bring to the table. I think that a record producer, in the truest sense of the word, has a multifaceted role: part psychologist, part arranger, part instigator of performances, and part sounding board. You can have a lot of those qualities and make great records, but I do think that being a musician does give you a leg up on the guys who aren't."

Just as he was attracted to good songs with good singers when he was working as a session cat, Zito has continued that theme into his production career. "I think that producers tend to be attracted to the same kinds of things," he says. "I've seen guys who are solo-oriented, guys who are singer-oriented, and guys who are musician-oriented. They tend to say yes to the same kinds of things in the same way that actors and directors say yes to the same kinds of movies. Bruce Willis generally doesn't go from action movies to Shakespeare," he says. "I think that people tend to do their best work when it is something close to their heart and soul.

"A real good singer and a real good song have always attracted me: any artist who displays an ability to write and sing believably. As a kid I was a guitar player, and I was always at the mercy—I don't mean that negatively, but rather positively—of a good singer."

While his career has spent a lot of time at the top of the charts and he's received plenty of accolades, Zito's name stays in the middle of a controversy that just won't die. Ten years after the release of the platinum *Lap of Luxury* (No. 16), the members of Cheap Trick are still complaining about Zito's production. "Oh, they hate my guts," Zito says. "I have myriad emotions when I read those things, but the one emotion that seems to stick the most firm—you know emotions tend to be fleeting sometimes—is that I am really proud of that record, and it's too bad that they're not. Sure I wish I was there to do 'I Want You to Want Me,' but I wasn't. Let's put it this way, I wasn't alone in the decision-making process, but I will be happy to take all the blame just as much as I would be happy to take all the credit.

"So, based on that scenario, when left to my own devices I made decisions based on what I thought they needed at the time. It yielded a fairly successful album and a very successful single ["The Flame," No. 1], and success is a double-edged sword. They've experienced three things in their life: success on their terms, success not on their terms, and a lack of success both on their terms and not on their terms. If that is a bitter pill to swallow, then that's a bitter pill to swallow. I would do it all over again," he adds. "They liked me better after the *Busted* album, and that wasn't as good. I'll take less of the credit for that."

What album does he want to be remembered for? "It *used* to be *Lap of Luxury*," he answers with a chuckle. "I think when the producer does the job right, it is the artist who is remembered. I think that the very nature of what we do is a subordinate role. The real job of a producer is to help artists realize their dream—realizing one's vision can get confusing. When [producers] are doing our best work, we are helping clear away some of the confusion. I grew up listening to the radio and records, and I'm thankful that I've had the chance to be part of it. That's all I care about." —DAVID JOHN FARINELLA

Animotion: "I Engineer," Casablanca, 1986 • "I Want You," Casablanca, 1986 • *Strange Behavior,* Casablanca, 1986 • *Obsession: The Best Of,* Mercury, 1996.

Bad English: *Bad English,* Epic, 1989 • "Forget Me Not," Epic, 1989 • "When I See You Smile," Epic, 1989 • "Heaven Is a 4 Letter Word," Epic, 1990 • "Possession," Epic, 1990 • "Price of Love," Epic, 1990.

Basil, Toni: *Toni Basil,* Virgin, 1984 • *The Best Of: Mickey and Other Love Songs,* Razor & Tie, 1994.

Berlin: *Love Life,* Geffen, 1984 • "No More Words," Geffen, 1984 • *Best Of, 1979–1988,* Geffen, 1988.

Cappello, Tim: "I Still Believe," Atlantic, 1987 (*The Lost Boys* soundtrack).

Cheap Trick: "Don't Be Cruel," Epic, 1988 • "Ghost Town," Epic, 1988 • *Lap of Luxury,* Epic, 1988 • "The Flame," Epic, 1988 • "Never Had a Lot to Lose," Epic, 1989 • *Busted,* Epic, 1990 • "Can't Stop Falling into Love," Epic, 1990 • "Wherever Would I Be," Epic, 1990 • *Sex America Cheap Trick,* Epic, 1996.

Cher: "Save Up All Your Tears," Geffen, 1991.

Cocker, Joe: *Cocker,* Capitol, 1986 • *Best Of,* Capitol, 1993 • *Long Voyage Home: The Silver Anniversay Collection,* A&M, 1995.

Cult, The: *Ceremony,* Sire, 1991 • *High Octane Cult,* Warner Bros., 1996.

Davis, Martha: "Don't Tell Me the Time," Capitol, 1987 • *Policy,* Capitol, 1987.

Dukes: *The Dukes,* Warner Bros., 1979.

Heart: "All I Wanna Do Is Make Love to You," Capitol, 1990 • *Brigade,* Capitol, 1990 • "I Didn't Want to Need You," Capitol, 1990 • "Stranded," Capitol, 1990 • "Secret," Capitol, 1991 • *Greatest Hits,* Capitol, 1997 • *These Dreams: Heart's Greatest Hits,* Capitol, 1997.

Heavy Bones: *Heavy Bones,* Reprise, 1991.

Kinison, Sam: *Leader of the Banned,* Warner Bros., 1990.

Kotzen, Richie: *Mother Head's Family Reunion,* Geffen, 1994.

Life by Night: *Life by Night,* EMI America, 1985.

Loggins, Kenny: *Back to Avalon,* Columbia, 1988 • "Tell Her," Columbia, 1989.

Martin, Eric: *I'm Only Fooling Myself,* Capitol, 1986.

Money, Eddie: *Can't Hold Back,* Columbia, 1986 • "I Wanna Go Back," Columbia, 1986 • "Take Me Home Tonight," Columbia, 1986 • "Endless Nights," Columbia, 1987 • "We Should Be Sleeping," Columbia, 1987 • *Nothing to Lose,* Columbia, 1988 • "Walk on Water," Columbia, 1988 • *Greatest Hits: The Sound of Money,* Columbia, 1989 • "Let Me In," Columbia, 1989 • "The Love in Your Eyes," Columbia, 1989 • w/ Ronnie Spector, "Everybody Loves Christmas," CMC International, 1997 • "If We Ever Get Out of This Place," CMC International, 1997 • *Super Hits,* Columbia, 1997.

Motels, The: "Shame," Capitol, 1985 • "Shock," Capitol, 1985 • *Shock,* Capitol, 1985.

Neville Brothers: *Uptown,* EMI America, 1987 • *Treacherous Too: A History of the Neville Brothers,* Vol. 2, *1955–1987,* Rhino, 1991 • *The Very Best Of,* Rhino, 1997.

New Frontier: *New Frontier,* Mika/Polydor, 1988.

O'Bannion, John: *John O'Bannion,* Elektra, 1981.

Poison: *Native Tongue,* Capitol, 1993 • *Greatest Hits, 1986–1996,* Capitol, 1996.

Red 7: *When the Sun Goes Down,* MCA, 1987.

Rolie, Greg: *Gringo,* Columbia, n.d.

White Lion: *Mane Attraction,* Atlantic, 1991 • *Best Of,* Atlantic, 1992.

Wilson, Ann, and Robin Zander: "Surrender to Me," Capitol, 1988 (*Tequila Sunrise* soundtrack).

Tappa "Tapper" Zukie

(DAVID SINCLAIR)

David "Tappa Zukie" Sinclair, though born in Jamaica in 1955, made his first record in the JA DJ style, "Jump and Twist" (Ethnic, 1973) in England for producer Larry Lawrence under the name "King Tapper." That year also saw the release of "Message to Pork Eaters" (as "Topper Zukie," on the Jungle label) and several singles produced by Bunny Lee (see entry). During his lengthy performance career he also recorded for producers Lord Koos, Yabby You, and Prince Jammy (see entry).

His first album, *Man Ah Warrior* (Klik, 1975) produced by Clem Bushay, was reissued to a wider audience on Patti Smith's Mer label in 1977. The cover was also a striking early work by photographer Robert Mapplethorpe. Along with Zukie's performance at Rainbow '78, this disc had significant impact on the punk movement.

By the next LP, *M.P.L.A.,* Tappa was back home in Kingston, producing himself and others for his own labels Stars, New Star, and Tappa. He had a major hit in JA and in England with the self-produced "Oh Lord" in 1978. Recording in the '70s at Channel One with the Revolutionaries, Tappa displayed a special flair for producing "natural" roots singers like Ras (or Prince) Allah, Ronnie Davis, and Errol Dunkley, as well as fellow DJ's Big Youth and U Roy. His production of Horace Andy on "Natty Dread A What She Want" was a U.K. dancehall favorite. Among his outstanding contributions are his own *Tappa Zukie International* LP with choice cuts "What About the Half," "Pontious Pilot," and "Down and Touch," Junior Ross and the Spears' apocalyptic *Babylon Fall,* and roots trio Knowledge's debut *Hail Dread,* issued in the U.S. on A&M.

Nearly 20 years after most of these records, Zukie

hit the top again with Beres Hammond's *Putting Up Resistance*. Hammond was working on another album in New York at the time but Tappa's relentless persistence whenever he returned to Jamaica resulted in one of the singer's finest albums. Hammond refers to Sinclair as "a friend [who] won't let go" and was "always in my skin" to record.

"He is a good producer," says this emotive singer whose own work spans nearly three decades. "Unorthodox or whatever one wants to call it but he gets the right sound." An album of songs on this rhythm was issued by RAS as *Massive Resistance,* with contributions from Yasus Afari and others. All these later recordings were recorded at Leggo Studios and Mixing Lab, but with the essential musical lineup—Sly, Robbie (see entry), and Chinna Smith—the same.

Tappa's early 7-inch hits, "Pick Up the Rockers" (Klik, U.K., 1975) and the slightly later "Quarter Pound of Ichens" (Godfather), are jarring, breathless, and raw heart-of-the-ghetto tracks that make today's rap sound like uptown posing, and his recent slightly unnerving digital productions manage to retain this surreal, inflammatory edge. His work in the '80s and '90s with '70s Jamaican hitmakers like Cornell Campbell and Max Romeo helped revitalize their careers. He cut albums with the Mighty Diamonds, Dennis Brown, and Gregory Isaacs, and two crucial dub albums as well.

In the late '80s and early '90s Tappa Zukie regrouped his forces and began issuing some of the wickedest 45s Jamaica had heard in some time, crucial roots music with a new sound backing. His new productions from this period can be compared only to those of former Black Uhuru singer Junior Reid whose JR label was also zeroing in on a modern, metallic, and uncompromising sound.

One by one he cornered classic and upcoming singers and DJs, consistently giving them back some of their best contemporary work. Artists produced in this period include Brigadier Jerry, Frankie Paul, and Junior Reid himself.

Not satisfied merely to write, DJ, produce, and own his own label, Tappa now has his own pressing plant and distributes from his present location on Eastwood Park Road in Kingston. —CHUCK FOSTER

Bolo, Yami: *Cool and Easy,* RAS, 1994 • *Born Again,* RAS, 1996.
Brown, Dennis: *Death Before Dishonor,* Tappa, 1989.
Campbell, Cornell: *Follow Instructions,* Mobiliser, 1983 • *Press Along Natty,* Tappa/JA, c. 1991.
Hammond, Beres: *Putting Up Resistance,* RAS, 1992, 1996.
Heptones, The: *Pressure,* RAS, 1995.
Isaacs, Gregory: *The Unforgettable,* Rohit, 1989.

Knowledge: *Hail Dread,* A&M, 1978.
Mighty Diamonds: *Leaders of Black Country,* Tappa, 1985.
Minott, Sugar: *RAS Portraits,* RAS, 1997.
Paul, Frankie: *Hard Work,* RAS, 1994.
Prince Allah: *Heaven Is My Roof,* Tappa, 1976.
Ras Allah: *Heaven Is My Roof,* Stars, 1976.
Romeo, Max: *Cross or the Gun,* Tappa, c. 1992.
Ross, Junior, and the Spears: *Babylon Fall,* Stars, 1976.
Thomas, Ruddy: *The Very Best,* Tappa, 1983.
Zukie, Tappa: *Tappa Zukie in Dub,* Blood and Fire, 1975, 1995 • *M.P.L.A.,* Virgin Frontline, 1976, 1978 • *Escape from Hell,* Stars, 1977 • *Man from Bosrah,* Stars, 1977 • *Living in the Ghetto,* Stars, 1978 • *Tappa Zukie International,* New Star, 1978 • *Tapper Roots,* Virgin, 1978 • *Blackman,* Stars/JA, 1979 • *Earth Running,* Tappa, 1983 • *People Are You Ready,* Stars, 1983 • *Raggamuffin,* World Enterprises, 1986 • *From the Archives,* RAS, 1995 • *Deep Roots,* RAS, 1996.

COLLECTIONS

Roots Man Connection, Stars, c. 1978.
X-Rated Dancehall, Tappa, c. 1991.
Dance Hall Jam, Tappa, c. 1992.
Gun Shop, Tappa, c. 1992.
No Name on the Bullet, Tappa, c. 1992.
Best of the Best, Vol. 1, RAS, 1993: Yami Bolo, "Be Still Babylon" • Brigadier Jerry, "Bangarang" • Dennis Brown, "Death Before Dishonor" • Half Pint, "Cosmopolitan Girl" • Beres Hammond, "Putting Up Resistance" • Beres Hammond and U Roy, "Resistance" • Gregory Isaacs, "One Man Against the World" • J.C. Lodge, "Between the Sheets" • Sugar Minott, "Sprinter Stayer" • Frankie Paul, "Keep the Faith" • Junior Reid, "Love Is the Answer" • Michael Rose, "Centenary."
Massive Resistance, RAS, 1994: Yasus Afari, "The Revolution" • Yami Bolo, "Dominion" • Brigadier Jerry, "Keep It Up" • Half Pint, "The System" • Sugar Minott, "Center of Attraction" • Jack Radics, "Assistance" • Cutty Ranks, "Hypocritical System" • Leroy Smart, "Poor Man Struggle."
Old Time D.J. Comeback . . . Again!, RAS, 1994: Dennis Alcapone, "Teacher Teacher" • Big Youth, "Back in Time" • Brigadier Jerry, "Raggamuffin" • Dillinger, "Cocaine" • I Roy, "A Fi Talk" • Jah Micky, "It's of the Pass" • Jah Stitch, "How Long" • Massive Dread, "Action" • Prince Jazzbo, "So the West Was Won" • Rankin Joe, "Kings Time" • Scotty, "Information" • Trinity, "Trinity Is My Name" • U Brown, "Bits of Paper" • U Roy and J.C. Lodge, "Satisfy My Soul" • Tappa Zukie, "Judge I Oh Lord."

Glossary

acoustics. The science of sound. In recording and live-sound applications, the word is used to describe the sonic characteristics of a room.

Adat. A modular, digital, multitrack recording system using VHS videotape; developed by Alesis Corp. in the early '90s. *See also* **DA-88.**

analog. Adjective that describes a recording system that reproduces sound by creating an "analogous" electronic signal, i.e., a replica of a sound wave.

A&R. Acronym for "artist & repertoire." The department at a record company responsible for talent acquisition and recording projects.

assistant engineer. The person who assists the producer and engineer in a recording session; also called second engineer.

bouncing. transferring audio from one track or group of tracks to another.

comp. Abbreviation for composite; assembling a recording of a performance, usually a vocal take, by taking the best sections of different performances and editing them together.

compressor. A studio processing device that evens out a recorded signal, trimming the peaks in loud passages and raising the apparent volume of softer passages. *See also* **limiter.**

console. *See* **mixer.**

control room. The space in a recording studio in which the producer, engineer, and assistant monitor the session.

DA-88. A modular, digital, multitrack recording system that uses Hi-8 videotape; developed by Tascam Corp. in the early '90s. *See also* **Adat.**

DAT. Acronym for digital audio tape—a cassette-like medium that stores digital audio on magnetic tape. A popular mixing and mastering format in the '90s.

desk. *See* **mixer.**

DIY. Acronym for "do it yourself." In music recording, the term refers to the late '70s, early '80s punk and post-punk eras, when groups would record, mix, and release music on their own grassroots labels.

digital. A recording system that creates a numerical representation of a sound wave by taking samples of the sound thousands of times per second.

digital editing. *See* **editing.**

editing. Deleting a portion of a recording by physically cutting the tape (tape editing) or removing part of a sound file in a computer (digital editing).

engineer. An audio professional in charge of the technical aspects of a recording session.

EQ. *See* **equalizer.**

equalizer. A processing device that alters a sound wave on a frequency-specific basis.

5.1-channel. A system of recording in which five speakers are placed around the center of a control room or listening environment in the following configuration: left, center, and right speakers in front of the listener; left and right speakers in the rear. The .1 refers to the subwoofer, which reproduces low bass frequencies and typically sits on the floor in the center-front area of the listening environment.

gofer. In North American lingo, the lowest-ranking employee of a recording studio; the counterpart of the British "tea boy."

ISDN. Integrated services digital network, a system that allows high-quality transmission of audio, video, and other digital data over fiber optic lines.

limiter. A type of compressor that prevents a signal from exceeding a predetermined level.

master. A tape, disc, or digital file that embodies the

final product of a recording, mixing, or mastering session.

mastering. The last creative step in the recording process. Mastering usually takes place in a mastering studio, where a stereo or multichannel mix is tweaked according to the specifications of the artist, producer, or engineer.

microphone (mike). An electro-acoustic device that reproduces an electronic representation of a waveform.

MIDI. Musical instruments digital interface. A language developed by the Roland Corp. that allows digital devices like synthesizers, drum machines, tape recorders, mixers, and effects processors to control one another.

mixer. A device used to create a stereo or multichannel master from several synchronous sound sources; also called a console or, more commonly in Britain, a desk.

monitor. Synonym for speaker in recording studio lingo.

multichannel. A medium that delivers sound through more than two speakers. *See also* **5.1-channel, surround-sound.**

multitrack recorder. A device that records multiple channels of time-synchronized audio on a tape or other medium, thereby allowing the user to "build" music by layering sounds on top of one another.

nearfield. In studio lingo, an adjective used to describe small speakers placed near the engineer's seat, as opposed to main speakers, usually mounted in the wall that divides the control room from the record-ing space. The use of nearfield monitors has increased dramatically in the '90s.

overdubbing. Recording additional tracks onto master reels.

preproduction. The process of preparing to make a master recording. Preproduction can take days, weeks, or months and can encompass everything from writing, rehearsing, and arranging to recording demos.

producer. The person who oversees the creative, technical, and financial aspects of a recording session.

project studio. A small, workshop-like environment—often in the home of a musician, producer, or engineer—used for aspects of a recording project that do not require the services of larger, professional studios.

speaker. A device that converts electric energy into acoustic energy.

second engineer. *See* **assistant engineer.**

stereo. Abbreviation of "stereophonic." A recording and playback system that delivers two discrete channels of sound over two separate speakers.

surround-sound. Catchall term for multichannel mediums.

tape editing. *See* **editing.**

tape-op. Abbreviation for tape operator; chiefly British term used to describe a recording assistant or gofer.

tea boy. Informal term used in Britain to describe the lowest-ranking employee in the recording-studio hierarchy.

Timeline

1877: Thomas Edison invents the phonograph.

1904: Columbia introduces the first flat record playable on both sides.

1940s: Les Paul, Sidney Bechet, Mitch Miller, Bill Putnam, and other recording pioneers develop multitracking.

1948: RCA Victor introduces the 45 rpm vinyl single and Columbia introduces the 33⅓ rpm long-play, formats which were to dominate the industry until the early 1990s.

1948: Tape is first used on recording sessions.

Early 1960s: The audiocassette is introduced as a consumer recording medium.

Early 1960s: Producer Phil Spector conceives the "Wall of Sound," a studio recording technique that yields a big, rich sound exemplified in such hits as the Ronettes' "Be My Baby."

June 1, 1967: The Beatles album *Sgt. Pepper's Lonely Hearts Club Band,* arguably their peak and a record held up as a milestone of creative studio recording, is released in the U.K.

1960s–1970s: The track capacity of major recording studios increases from 4 to 8 to 16 to 24.

Late 1970s: Oxford, U.K.–based console manufacturer Solid State Logic (SSL) sells its first console to the London studio Townhouse, where it is used to record and mix hits by XTC, Phil Collins, Peter Gabriel, and others.

1982: Sony and Phillips introduce the compact disc (CD), a digital audio format delivered on a 5-inch disc read by an optical laser.

1984: Roland, Yamaha, and Sequential Circuits introduce musical instrument digital interface (MIDI), a digital protocol that allows synthesizers, drum machines, effects processors, tape recorders, and other electronics devices to control one another.

1980s: The sampler—a digital device that records and plays short snippets of sound—gains prominence as a recording tool, especially among hip-hop artists.

Late 1980s: Sony and Studer introduce 48-track digital reel recorders, which quickly become the state of the art in high-end studios.

1990s: The CD overtakes the LP and cassette as the leading consumer sound carrier.

1991: Tascam and Alesis introduce the DA-88 and Adat, respectively. Both are 8-track, tape-based digital recorders that can be daisy-chained together to form multitrack systems of virtually unlimited capacity.

1993: The Frank Sinatra *Duets* album is recorded by musicians in different cities linked together in real time via the use of integrated services digital network (ISDN) lines.

1995: Yamaha unveils the 02R digital recording console, a small, inexpensive, automated digital mixer designed to interface with the DA-88, Adat, and other digital multitracks.

1996: A group of consumer electronics manufacturers, film studios, and software developers introduce the digital video disk (DVD)—a format that would later be rechristened digital versatile disk to denote its audio and multimedia capacities.

1999: Music companies, consumer electronics manufacturers, and software companies develop a standard for DVD audio.

Index

$24.95 USA

THE ENCYCLOPEDIA OF
Record Producers

**INCLUDES INCISIVE ESSAYS ON
500 OF THE MOST INFLUENTIAL
RECORD PRODUCERS IN HISTORY:**
- Their lives and times
- The artists and music they produced
- How they worked
OVER 35,000 DISCOGRAPHIC ENTRIES

ABOUT THE AUTHORS:
ERIC OLSEN has written for numerous
publications including *Playboy, Option,*
Billboard's *Airplay Monitor,* and
Alternative Press, and is co-author
of *Networking in the Music Industry.*
He lives in Aurora, Ohio.

PAUL VERNA, Pro Audio/Technology
Editor and Reviews Editor at *Billboard*
magazine in New York City, is also
a freelance producer/engineer who
operates a New York–based mobile
recording studio, Vernacular Sound.

Clevelander CARLO WOLFF, a well-
known music reviewer, is a regular
contributor to *The Boston Globe,* the
Cleveland Plain Dealer, Goldmine,
DISCoveries, and *Jazz.*

Cover design by Bob Fillie,
Graphiti Design, Inc.

BILLBOARD BOOKS
An imprint of
Watson-Guptill Publications
1515 Broadway
New York, NY 10036

"One of the truly indispensable reference books on the annals of the music industry. . . . There's only one place where Jerry Wexler, Brian Wilson, George Martin, Glyn Johns, Berry Gordy Jr., Arif Mardin, Russ Titelman, Rick Rubin, Babyface Edmonds, Mitchell Froom and Niney The Observer have ever come together to do a mental mixdown on the art of record production over the last century, and that's in the journalistic control room created in the pages of *The Encyclopedia of Record Producers.*"

TIMOTHY WHITE, Editor in Chief of *Billboard*

"A landmark publication. . . . Messrs. Olsen, Verna and Wolff have compiled the ultimate guide to the sonic archi-tects, alchemists and just plain old artisans who've helmed the great waxings of rock, soul, blues, jazz, country, metal, indie, and about any other genre or sub-genre you might care to cite. The mini-bios are spot-on, the discographies indispensable, the omissions almost nonexistent."

BARNEY HOSKYNS, U.S. editor of *MOJO* magazine

"A formidable tour-de-force,. . . with the most current information about both the leading lights and the under-appreciated geniuses in the field of record production. Everything you always wanted to know about record producers but didn't know who to ask is here."

JAAN UHELSZKI, *Rolling Stone Online*

"An immensely satisfying book. It goes immediately onto my perrmanent reference shelf."

BEN EDMONDS, former editor of *Creem* magazine

"This exceptionally well-researched and far-ranging book shines a long overdue spotlight on the often unsung heroes of recorded music."

IRA ROBBINS, editor of *The Trouser Press Guide to '90s Rock*

"One-stop shopping for music producers."

BRIAN WILLIAMS, NBC News Anchor